To the Student:

A Study Guide is available through your bookstore. The purpose of the Study Guide is to assist you in studying and reviewing the text material and provide you with a means of self-testing. The Study Guide provides a chapter review, study exercises, true-false and multiple choice questions. These may be used both in your initial study of the chapter material and in your subsequent review. If the Study Guide is not in stock in your bookstore, ask the bookstore manager to order a copy for you.

FEDERAL TAXATION

2006 EDITION

❖ General Editors ❖

James W. Pratt, D.B.A., CPA
William N. Kulsrud, Ph.D., CPA

❖ Contributing Authors ❖

Gregory A. Carnes, Ph.D., CPA
Northern Illinois University

Edward J. Schnee, Ph.D., CPA
University of Alabama

Marguerite R. Hutton, Ph.D., CPA
Western Washington University

Steven C. Thompson, Ph.D., CPA
Texas State University

Robert W. Jamison, Ph.D., CPA
Indiana University

John C. Tripp, Ph.D., CPA
University of Denver

Michael A. O'Dell, Ph.D., CPA
Arizona State University

Michael J. Tucker, J.D., Ph.D., CPA
Quinnipiac College

Nathan Oestreich, Ph.D., CPA
San Diego State University

James L. Wittenbach, D.B.A., CPA
University of Notre Dame

James W. Pratt, D.B.A., CPA
University of Houston

William N. Kulsrud, Ph.D., CPA
Indiana University

THOMSON

Australia · Canada · Mexico · Singapore · Spain · United Kingdom · United States

Federal Taxation
2006 Edition

General Editors

James W. Pratt, D.B.A, C.P.A
William N. Kulsrud, Ph.D., C.P.A.

Executive Editor:
Michael Stranz

Custom Product Developer:
Greg Albert

Marketing Coordinators:
Lindsay Annett and Sara Mercurio

Production/Manufacturing Supervisor:
Donna M. Brown

Senior Project Coordinator:
K.A. Espy

Pre-Media Services Supervisor:
Dan Plofchan

Senior Prepress Specialist:
Kim Fry

Cover Design:
Candice Swan

Cover Image:
© Getty

Compositor:
Cadmus

Printer:
Westgroup,
Eagan, MN

Peer review, class testing, and accuracy are primarily the responsibility of the author(s).

For permission to use material from this text or product, contact us by:
Tel (800) 730-2214
Fax (800) 730 2215
www.thomsonrights.com

Federal Taxation / Pratt & Kulsrud – 2006 Edition
p. 1592
ISBN 0-759-35175-9

PREFACE

INTRODUCTION TO THOMSON AND THE PRATT & KULSRUD TAXATION SERIES

Thomson is pleased to announce the integration of the Pratt & Kulsrud Taxation Series into its offerings. Thomson is committed to delivering this highly respected series in the familiar reader-friendly format it is known for with additional enhancements to make this series the best value for your students. In addition to revisions and updates to reflect the new tax laws, we've created a website, added TurboTax® and additional resources for instructors.

For over 20 years, the Pratt & Kulsrud Taxation Series has provided the type of tax text that has earned the respect of educators, students, and professionals alike. The tax series grew out of Jim Pratt's belief that there should be a comprehensive textbook that combined the most relevant topics related to the taxation of both individuals and businesses. This comprehensive text, *Federal Taxation*, was the first of its kind. It quickly became one of the leading books in both the academic and professional continuing education markets after its 1984 debut. From there, demand for coverage of additional topics related to individuals and businesses, led to the creation of two separate texts, *Individual Taxation* and *Corporate, Partnership, Estate and Gift Taxation*.

The hallmark of this series' success has been its readability—its ability to interest and motivate with exceptionally clear explanations and examples of the tax law. It has consistently held to the principle that the key to learning taxation is grasping the underlying purpose for each and every rule. For this reason, the authors and editors have made a concerted effort to provide the background, both a conceptual and historical foundation, which they feel is essential to understanding.

WELCOME TO 2006 EDITION

This text is designed for use by undergraduate or graduate accounting, business, or law students in their study of Federal taxation. The numerous examples and computational illustrations used to explain the more complex rules concerning the Federal income taxation of individuals, corporations, partnerships, estates, and trusts should also make this text suitable for use in a self-study program.

The primary emphasis of this text is the Federal income taxation of individuals (17 chapters). In addition, abbreviated coverage of the other basic areas of taxation is also provided. Three chapters are devoted to the income taxation of regular corporations and shareholders—from formation to liquidation; and one chapter each is provided for partnerships and S corporations. Federal estate and gift taxation is discussed in one chapter; and two additional chapters contain the related topics of the income taxation of estates, trusts, and beneficiaries and the major aspects of family tax planning. Our goal is covering all these topics in a single volume is to give instructors maximum flexibility in the design of their own courses. It is neither our intention nor our belief that all this material should be covered in a traditional three-hour, one-semester course.

The 2006 Edition has been revised to reflect the two major changes in the tax law in 2004: The American Jobs Creation Act of 2004 and The Working Families Tax Relief Act of 2004. The 2006 Edition has also been revised to reflect significant judicial and administrative developments during the past year. As we go to press with this edition, there are various tax proposals being considered in Congress that may lead to significant and immediate changes in the tax law. Should any of these proposals become enacted during the year, we will continue our long-standing policy of preparing an update supplement for current users of the text. Tax updates, new tax forms, and inflation adjustments are also posted on a regular basis to our web site at **www.pktax.thomson.com**.

In addition to the standard discussion questions and computational problems contained at the end of every chapter of this text, several chapters contain comprehensive tax return problems and cumulative problems that require an understanding of material presented in earlier chapters and completion of some tax forms. Also, Appendix D contains two comprehensive tax return problems for individual taxpayers. These problems require completion of some of the most common tax forms and are ideal for course projects. Each of these problems requires approximately 6 to 10 hours for completion. These tax return problems are intended to supplement other end-of-chapter problems by requiring students to relate tax rules to actual tax return compliance procedures.

ENHANCED SUPPORT FOR INSTRUCTORS

NEW! www.pktax.thomson.com
A valuable resource to view tax forms, the latest tax updates, access instructor materials and more.

Solutions Manual
Contains solutions to the discussion questions and computational problems at the end of each chapter. These solutions are referenced to specific pages and examples from the text, and where appropriate, to supporting statutory or administrative authorities.

Instructor's Guide
Contains solutions to the tax research problems, tax return problems (including the two comprehensive tax return problems contained in Appendix D), and a test bank containing over 1000 objective questions (true-false and multiple choice), with answers referenced to specific pages and examples in the text.

NEW! IRCD (Instructor Resource CD)
Contains all instructor resources and includes ExamView Thomson's testing software and Word files for maximum flexibility.

FEATURES

Chapter Lecture Outlines
Contains summaries of key points in each chapter and are available on the IRCD.

Learning Objectives
At the beginning of each chapter, a summary of key points that students should have an understanding of after reading the chapter.

Problem Materials
Available at the end of each chapter and contain Discussion Questions and Multiple Choice Problems that highlight topics discussed in the chapter.

You Make the Call
Hypothetical situations requiring reasoning and judgment.

Check Your Knowledge
Unusual cases that challenge the students' understanding of tax law.

NEW!
This highly rated and best-selling tax software comes free with the *Federal Taxation*, 2006 Edition. **TurboTax® Basic** guides you step-by-step through individual returns on IRS-approved forms. TurboTax® **Business** offers help and advice on corporations, S corporations, partnerships of up to 100 partners, and LLCs as well as estates and trusts. **TurboTax® Business** covers corporation, partnership, and fiduciary income taxes and gives your students practical, hands-on experience. Related questions have been added throughout the text, enabling students to take advantage of the tax preparation software.

ADDITIONAL OFFERINGS FROM THE PRATT & KULSRUD TAXATION SERIES

The series includes new editions of:

***Individual Taxation*, 2006 Edition** ISBN 0759351821 – The numerous examples and computational illustrations used to explain the more complex rules concerning the Federal income taxation of individuals makes this text suitable for first course in Federal taxation undergraduate or graduate accounting, business, or law students.

***Corporate, Partnership, Estate and Gift Taxation*, 2006 Edition**, ISBN 0759351864 – The text emphasizes those areas of taxation generally accepted as essential to the education of those pursuing careers in taxation or tax-related fields and is intended for advanced topics in Federal taxation undergraduate or graduate accounting, business, or law students.

ABOUT THE AUTHORS

James W. Pratt

James W. (Jim) Pratt is the PricewaterhouseCoopers Professor of Accountancy & Taxation at the University of Houston's C. T. Bauer College of Business and Director of its Master of Accountancy program. Jim joined the faculty in 1972 after receiving his doctorate degree from the University of Southern California. He has published articles in leading professional journals such as the *Journal of Accountancy, Journal of Taxation, Journal of Corporate Taxation, Journal of Partnership Taxation*, and *The Tax Adviser*. In addition to his contributions as an author and editor, he has received several awards for outstanding teaching. He has also taught in continuing professional education programs for over thirty years and has served as a tax training consultant for several national and local accounting firms.

William N. Kulsrud

William N. (Bill) Kulsrud is an Associate Professor of Accounting at the Kelley School of Business of Indiana University-Indianapolis/Bloomington and Chair of the Master of Professional Accountancy program. Bill joined the faculty in 1979 after receiving his Ph.D. from the University of Texas. He has published numerous articles, appearing in leading professional journals such as the *Journal of Taxation, Journal of Corporate Taxation, The Tax Adviser, Taxation for Accountants* and *Taxes–The Tax Magazine*. He has also served as an editorial adviser to the Tax Adviser, Journal of Accountancy, and Journal of the American Taxation Association. In addition to his contributions as an author and editor, he has received many awards for outstanding teaching. In 1990 he was named Accounting Educator of the Year by the Indiana C.P.A. Society. He has also taught hundreds of professional education programs for national and local accounting firms and developed materials used in their continuing education programs. He is currently the co-coordinator of the National Tax Education Program sponsored by the AICPA and the University of Illinois. In addition, he now serves on the prestigious AICPA Individual Taxation Technical Resource Panel.

ACKNOWLEDGEMENTS

Professional and technical services received from Jan Tiefel.

Reviewers and accuracy checks: Teresa Stephenson, University of Kentucky; Ray Krasniewski, The Ohio State University; Lindsey Schiesser, Deloitte and Touche; George Spaeth, KPMG; Barbara Stayton, Brown Wheeldon Tafoya & Barrett PC; Kenda Beery, Indiana University-Purdue University Indianapolis.

TO THE STUDENTS

A Study Guide (ISBN 0759351791) to accompany the text is available through your bookstore. The purpose of the Study Guide is to assist you in studying and reviewing the text material and provide you with a means of self-testing. The Study Guide provides a chapter review, study exercises, true-false and multiple-choice questions. These may be used both in your initial study of the chapter material and in your subsequent review.

Contents in Brief

Part VI
EMPLOYEE COMPENSATION AND RETIREMENT PLANS

Part VII
CORPORATE TAXATION

Part VIII
FLOW-THROUGH ENTITIES

Part IX
FAMILY TAX PLANNING

APPENDICES AND INDEX

Contents

Chapter 3 TAXABLE ENTITIES, TAX FORMULA, INTRODUCTION TO PROPERTY TRANSACTIONS

Chapter 4 PERSONAL AND DEPENDENCY EXEMPTIONS; FILING STATUS; DETERMINATION OF TAX FOR AN INDIVIDUAL; FILING REQUIREMENTS

Part II
GROSS INCOME

Chapter 5   GROSS INCOME

Chapter 6   GROSS INCOME: INCLUSIONS AND EXCLUSIONS

Part III
DEDUCTIONS AND LOSSES

Chapter 7   OVERVIEW OF DEDUCTIONS AND LOSSES

Chapter 8   EMPLOYEE BUSINESS EXPENSES

Chapter 9   CAPITAL RECOVERY: DEPRECIATION, AMORTIZATION, AND DEPLETION

Chapter 10   CERTAIN BUSINESS DEDUCTIONS AND LOSSES

Chapter 11 ITEMIZED DEDUCTIONS

Chapter 12 DEDUCTIONS FOR CERTAIN INVESTMENT EXPENSES AND LOSSES

Part IV
ALTERNATIVE MINIMUM TAX AND TAX CREDITS

Chapter 13 THE ALTERNATIVE MINIMUM TAX AND TAX CREDITS

Part V
PROPERTY TRANSACTIONS

Chapter 14 PROPERTY TRANSACTIONS: BASIS DETERMINATION AND RECOGNITION OF GAIN OR LOSS

Chapter 15 NONTAXABLE EXCHANGES

Chapter 16 PROPERTY TRANSACTIONS: CAPITAL GAINS AND LOSSES

Chapter 17 PROPERTY TRANSACTIONS: DISPOSITIONS OF TRADE OR BUSINESS PROPERTY

Part VI
EMPLOYEE COMPENSATION AND RETIREMENT PLANS

Chapter 18 EMPLOYEE COMPENSATION AND RETIREMENT PLANS

Part VII
CORPORATE TAXATION

Chapter 19 CORPORATIONS: FORMATION AND OPERATION

Chapter 20 CORPORATE DISTRIBUTIONS, REDEMPTIONS AND LIQUIDATIONS

Chapter 21 TAXATION OF CORPORATE ACCUMULATIONS

Part VIII
FLOW-THROUGH ENTITIES

Chapter 22 TAXATION OF PARTNERSHIPS AND PARTNERS

Chapter 23 S CORPORATIONS

Part IX
FAMILY TAX PLANNING

Chapter 24 THE FEDERAL TRANSFER TAXES

Chapter 25 INCOME TAXATION OF ESTATES AND TRUSTS

Chapter 26 FAMILY TAX PLANNING

APPENDICES AND INDEX

Part I

INTRODUCTION TO
THE FEDERAL TAX SYSTEM

❖ Contents ❖

1-18 *Tax Rate Schedules and Rate Concepts.* An examination of the tax rate schedules for single taxpayers (see the inside cover of the text) indicates that the tax is a "given dollar amount" plus a percentage of taxable income exceeding a particular level.

   a. Explain how the "given dollar amounts" are determined.

   b. Assuming the taxpayer has a taxable income of $50,000 and is single, what is his tax liability for 2005?

   c. Same facts as (b). What is the taxpayer's marginal tax rate?

   d. Same facts as (b). What is the taxpayer's average tax rate?

   e. Assuming the taxpayer has tax-exempt interest income from municipal bonds of $30,000, what is the taxpayer's effective tax rate?

1-19 *Tax Equity.* Taxpayer R has a taxable income of $20,000. Similarly, S has a taxable income of $20,000. Each taxpayer pays a tax of $1,000 on his income.

   a. Discuss whether the tax imposed is equitable. Include in your discussion comments concerning horizontal and vertical equity.

   b. Assume S has a taxable income of $40,000 and pays a tax of $2,000 on his income. Discuss whether the tax imposed is equitable in light of this new information.

1-20 *Tax Fairness.* R and S both own homes in Houston. Both have an appraised value of $200,000 and, consequently, both R and S pay $5,000 in real property taxes. Explain why such a tax may be considered fair by some and unfair by others.

1-21 *Understanding Tax Rate Concepts.* Indicate whether the following statements are true or false and, if false, explain why.

   a. Tax-exempt income would cause the taxpayer's average tax rate to increase.

   b. Tax-exempt income would cause the taxpayer's marginal tax rate to decrease.

   c. Tax-exempt income would cause the taxpayer's effective tax rate to decrease.

1-22 *Understanding Tax Rate Concepts.* Indicate whether the following statements are true or false and, if false, explain why.

   a. From a technical point of view, sales taxes are progressive.

   b. From a popular point of view, sales taxes are regressive.

   c. From a popular point of view, sales taxes are proportional.

   d. From a technical point of view, there are no regressive taxes in the United States.

1-23 *Think Tax.* From a tax perspective, a transaction that may make sense for one taxpayer may be complete nonsense for another. Consider two married taxpayers, H and W who earn $500,000 per year and L and M who earn $20,000 per year. Both plan on buying interest-paying bonds with a face value of $1,000, either State of Indiana bonds paying 6% tax-exempt interest or AT&T bonds paying eight percent taxable interest. Assume the bonds are in all other respects equivalent (e.g., price, risk, etc.). Show (with calculations) why it would make perfect sense for H and W to buy the Indiana bonds but it would be foolish for L and M to buy the Indiana bonds.

1-24 *Identifying Tax Expenditures.* Indicate whether the following would be considered a tax expenditure.

   a. Tax deduction allowed for payment of gasoline purchased by a taxicab driver who owns and operates his own taxicab business.

   b. Deduction for charitable contributions made by individual taxpayers.

   c. Postponement of taxation of income earned on an individual's savings in an Individual Retirement Account until such income is distributed.

   d. Straight-line depreciation of an office building used in a trade or business.

   e. Tax credit for purchase of electric automobile.

   f. Deduction for interest paid on a home mortgage.

1-25   *Advantages and Disadvantages of Tax Expenditures.* Indicate whether the following would be considered an advantage or disadvantage of a tax expenditure.

  a.   Administrative costs less than other forms of government financial assistance
  b.   Beneficiaries easily identified
  c.   Only those entitled to financial assistance receive it
  d.   Costs and budgetary effects readily assessed
  e.   Benefits (e.g., from deductions) rise and fall without direct approval from the government
  f.   Less palatable to beneficiaries
  g.   Effect on tax system

1-26   *Taxable Gifts.* M made the following cash gifts during 2005:

To her son	$50,000
To her daughter	50,000
To her niece.	10,000

  a.   If M is unmarried, what is the amount of taxable gifts she has made in 2004?
  b.   If M is married and her husband agrees to split gifts with her, what is the total amount of taxable gifts made by M and her husband for 2005?

1-27   *Taxable Estate.* R dies in 2005. R made taxable gifts during his lifetime in 1987, 1988, 1990, 1994, and 1996 but paid no Federal transfer taxes due to the unified transfer tax credit in effect in those years. What effect will these taxable gifts have on determining the following:

  a.   R's Federal taxable estate?
  b.   The rates imposed on the Federal taxable estate?

1-28   *Estate Tax Computation.* T died in a car accident on January 4, 2005. He owned the following property on his date of death:

Cash	$ 75,000
Stocks and bonds	700,000
Residence	430,000
Interest in partnership	350,000
Miscellaneous personal property	25,000

Upon T's death, he owed $80,000 on the mortgage on his residence. T also owned a life insurance policy. The policy was term life insurance which paid $200,000 to his mother upon his death. Its value immediately before his death was $0. T had all of the incidents of ownership with regard to the policy.

During his life, T had made only one gift. He gave a diamond ring worth $30,000 (it was an old family heirloom) to his daughter in 1995. No gift taxes were paid on the gift due to the annual exclusion (gift-splitting was elected) and the unified transfer tax credit in effect for that year. The ring was worth $50 000 on his date of death.

T's will contained the following provisions:

  a.   To my wife I leave all of the stocks and bonds.
  b.   To my alma mater, State University, I leave $50,000 to establish a chair for a tax professor in the Department of Accounting in the School of Business.
  c.   The residue of my estate is to go to my daughter.

Compute T's estate tax before any credits other than the Federal estate tax credit.

1-29   *Inheritance Taxes.* This year Bob died, leaving $500,000 to his heirs. His state of residence imposes an inheritance tax. Indicate whether the following statements are true or false and, if false, explain why. Consider using the Internet to find information on how the inheritance tax laws of your state operate.

    a. The amount of the inheritance tax is $0 since Bob's estate does not exceed the 2005 taxable threshold of $1,500,000.

    b. Assume Bob is single. The amount of inheritance tax due from Bob's estate, like the Federal estate tax, is the same regardless of whom he names as the beneficiaries.

    c. Assume Bob is married. The amount of inheritance tax due from Bob's estate—like the Federal estate tax—is zero if he leaves the entire amount to his surviving spouse or children.

    d. Any inheritance tax paid by Bob's estate may be used to reduce any Federal estate tax his estate owes.

1-30 *Excess FICA Taxes.* During 2005 E earned $70,000 of wages from employer X and $30,000 of wages from employer Y. Both employers withheld and paid the appropriate amount of FICA taxes on E's wages.

    a. What is the amount of excess taxes paid by E for 2005?

    b. Would it make any difference in the amount of E's refund or credit of the excess of FICA taxes if he was a full-time employee of each employer for different periods of the year, as opposed to a full-time employee of X and a part-time employee of Y for the entire year?

1-31 *Self-Employment Tax.* During 2005 H had earnings from self-employment of $50,000 and wages of $78,000 from employer X. Employer X withheld and paid the appropriate amount of FICA taxes on H's wages. Compute H's self-employment tax liability for 2005. What is the amount of H's income tax deduction for the self-employment taxes paid?

1-32 *Tax Awareness.* Assume that you are currently employed by Corporation X in state A. Without your solicitation, Corporation Y offers you a 20 percent higher salary if you will relocate to state B and become its employee. What tax factors should you consider in making a decision as to the offer?

Chapter 2

TAX PRACTICE AND RESEARCH

LEARNING OBJECTIVES

Upon completion of this chapter you will be able to:

- Describe the basic features of tax practice: compliance, planning, litigation, and research

- Identify typical career paths in taxation

- Understand the rules of conduct that must be followed by those who perform tax services

- Appreciate the role of ethics in tax practice and the responsibilities of tax practitioners

- Explain the key penalties that influence positions taken on tax returns

- Describe the process in which Federal tax law is enacted and subsequently modified or evaluated by the judiciary

- Interpret citations to various statutory, administrative, and judicial sources of the tax law

- Identify the source of various administrative and judicial tax authorities

- Locate most statutory, administrative, and judicial authorities

- Evaluate the relative strength of various tax authorities

- Understand the importance of communicating the results of tax research

CHAPTER OUTLINE

INTRODUCTION

Before jumping into the rules and regulations that must be applied to determine the taxpayer's tax liability, one should have at least an appreciation of the basic nature of tax practice and how to go about finding answers to tax questions. This chapter lays the necessary foundation by first exploring exactly what it is that tax professionals do and the rules of conduct that they must observe while doing it. The chapter concludes by identifying the various sources of tax law and how they may be accessed and used to solve a particular tax question.

TAX PRACTICE IN GENERAL

There are essentially four aspects of tax practice: compliance, planning, litigation, and research. Although these may be thought of as discrete areas, as a practical matter, tax professionals are normally involved in all four.

Tax Compliance. The area of tax compliance generally encompasses all of the activities necessary to meet the statutory requirements of the tax law. This largely involves the preparation of the millions of tax returns that must be filed by individuals and other organizations each year. Interestingly, the reliance of individuals on professional return preparation is rather a recent phenomenon. There was a time when most individuals prepared their own returns and H & R Block was unheard of. However, the ever-increasing complexity of the tax law has made professional assistance almost a necessity and in fact created a tax preparation industry. It is currently estimated that 5 out of every 10 taxpayers seek the services of a professional tax preparer every year. Tax preparation services are typically performed by Certified Public Accountants (CPAs), attorneys, enrolled agents (individuals who have passed a two-day examination given by the IRS), and commercial tax return preparation services. But there are no special requirements that must be met to become a tax return preparer. Consequently, anyone willing to try his or her hand at mastering the tax law—as well as any shysters who think there is a buck to be made—can hang out a shingle. In fact, the advent of personal computers and sophisticated yet user-friendly software have made tax preparation easier for everyone, including those who want to get into the tax preparation business. Note, however, that only CPAs, attorneys, and enrolled agents are authorized to practice before the IRS and are therefore able to represent taxpayers beyond the initial audit (e.g., at the Appellate level).

As might be imagined, the day-to-day tasks of those working in the tax compliance area typically surround preparation of a tax return. They collect the appropriate information from the taxpayer and then analyze and evaluate such data for use in preparing the required tax return or other tax filing. But tax compliance goes far beyond merely placing numbers in boxes. In many cases, completion of the return requires tax research to determine the appropriate treatment of a particular item. Preparation of a return may also uncover tax planning opportunities that can be shared with the client to obtain future savings. In addition, tax compliance involves representation of the taxpayer before the IRS during audits and appeals.

Tax Planning. Perhaps the most rewarding part of tax practice is tax planning and the sense of satisfaction one gets from helping clients minimize their tax liability. As explained in the previous chapter, tax planning is simply the process of arranging one's financial affairs in light of their potential tax consequences. Unlike the weather, taxpayers often have some degree of control over their tax liability, and it is the job of the tax adviser to help the taxpayer whenever possible. A great deal of tax planning is simply an outgrowth of the tax compliance process. Well-trained tax professionals often recognize a situation where a little planning could have brought a more favorable result. In these so-called *closed fact* situations, it is typically too late to do anything until the opportunity once again presents itself, typically the next year. On the other hand, taxpayers about to embark on a transaction—an *open fact* situation—may engage a tax adviser to determine the tax consequences and how to structure the transaction to obtain the most beneficial outcome.

Tax Litigation. As might be expected, taxpayers and the IRS do not always agree on the tax treatment of a particular item. Many disputes and controversies are settled during an appeals process within the IRS itself. Others, however, are ultimately resolved in a court of law. Tax litigation is a very specialized but often lucrative area of tax practice. In most cases, tax litigation is conducted only by licensed attorneys. However, accountants and others, including the taxpayer himself, can represent the taxpayer in certain situations. In addition, accountants often assist legal counsel and provide litigation support.

Tax Research. Most practitioners believe that tax research is the most interesting part of tax practice. Tax research is simply the process of obtaining information and synthesizing it to answer a particular tax question. Regardless of the area of tax practice—compliance, planning, or litigation—tax research plays an important part.

Tax research generally involves identifying tax issues, finding relevant information on the issues, and assessing the pertinent authority to arrive at a conclusion. Unfortunately, the law is not so straightforward that the answer to any tax question is readily available. Consequently, being able to do the research is an important skill for anyone involved in tax. For example, a decorator that works out of her home may want to know whether the cost of maintaining a home office can be deducted in computing taxable income. It may seem that a common problem like this could be easily resolved, but it is often much more difficult than might be imagined. To answer this question, the tax adviser may be required to sift through mounds of information—rules, regulations, IRS pronouncements, and court cases—in order to determine the proper treatment. Even if an answer seems apparent, the dynamic nature of the tax law often requires the practitioner to constantly update his or her research to ensure that it is current and has not been changed by some recent development.

TAXATION AS A PROFESSIONAL CAREER

The need for tax advisory services has grown almost exponentially in recent years. The growth is not surprising given the growth in the tax law. Over the past 35 years, there have been tax law changes virtually every year. During this time Congress has turned to the tax system again and again to attack not only the country's economic ills but its social problems as well. The end result is a tax law, both Federal and state, that is forever changing and quite complex. Consequently, individuals and organizations have increasingly needed to call upon tax specialists to help them cope with the law. These demands on the tax profession have created tremendous opportunities for those interested in careers in taxation.

The tax specialists of today wear a number of hats. They act as tax consultants as well as business advisers. They help individuals and business owners with tax compliance, keep them informed of changes in the tax law, and assist them in personal financial planning. Tax advisers not only consult on Federal and state income tax matters; they also prepare sales, payroll, and franchise tax returns. Industry and government also employ tax specialists who are involved in planning and compliance. Here are some examples of activities in which the tax specialist might be involved:

- A husband and wife want to transfer their business to their children. Should they sell the business to the kids or would they be better off just giving it to them? A tax specialist can compare the income tax consequences of a sale to that of a gift or bequest and help design the best plan in light of the couple's wishes.

- A taxpayer wants to sell her corporation. Should she sell the stock or cause the corporation to sell its assets? A tax specialist can explain the tax and nontax factors affecting the decision.

- An individual and his son are forming a new business. Should it be operated as a corporation, an S corporation, a partnership, or a limited liability company? A tax specialist can help with the analysis.

- A corporation is planning on opening operations in a foreign country. A tax specialist can help reorganize the company to help minimize U.S. and foreign taxes.

- A corporation is considering the establishment of a retirement plan. A tax adviser who specializes in employee benefits can provide information regarding the tax considerations.

- A taxpayer is seeking a divorce. A tax specialist can explain the tax consequences.

- A corporation and its subsidiaries are thinking about filing a consolidated tax return. The tax specialist can assist the taxpayer in filing such a return, preparing estimated tax payments, or reviewing a corporation's tax returns.

- The IRS wants to deny the taxpayer a deduction for meals and entertainment. The tax specialist might represent an individual during the IRS examination or present oral and written arguments before an IRS appeals conference and (if qualified) before the U.S. Tax Court.

In these and similar matters, the tax specialist is often an important member of the client's professional advisory team and works with other high-caliber individuals to minimize client costs. For example, if a business owner is seeking estate planning advice, the team typically includes the individual's attorney, accountant, life insurance agent, and tax adviser.

Thousands of men and women enjoy successful careers in taxation. They are highly respected as professionals and are well compensated for their work. Those in tax rarely find their jobs boring or dull. Tax work, particularly once one has paid one's dues and built a firm foundation, is interesting and challenging. Moreover, working in a tax department along with other professionals with like interests can be a vastly rewarding personal experience. Tax professionals also serve the public good by raising the standard of tax practice and administration and by working with other groups to improve the tax system.

RULES OF TAX PRACTICE: RESPONSIBILITIES AND ETHICS

Over the past several years there has been a great deal of attention focused on ethics in business. The world of taxation has not escaped this attention. Unethical behavior of taxpayers and tax preparers has always been a serious concern of the tax system, primarily because of its reliance on voluntary compliance.

Anyone who has ever filed an income tax return recognizes the potential for bilking the system. It is as easy as underreporting income or overstating deductions. What is perhaps more important is that it can be done with so little risk. The current audit rate is so low—approximately 1 percent—that many dishonest taxpayers think they can exploit the system with little chance that they will ever get caught. That the tax system is such an easy mark was underscored recently in testimony given before the House Ways and Means Oversight Subcommittee by two practitioners convicted of tax fraud for illegal refund schemes. In his testimony, Barry Becht, a 36-year-old former tax return preparer, explained that, before he was convicted and sent to Federal prison, he had "helped" his clients reduce their tax liabilities by over $750,000 simply by overstating their deductions. Surprisingly, Becht did not share in his client's windfalls. Allegedly his only purpose was to build up his practice! The other convicted felon, Frazier Todd, reported that he had gained more than $500,000 in only two years using electronic filing schemes. Shortly after college and with the help of a few courses on computers, accounting, and business, Todd had set up a tax-preparation service near public housing in Atlanta. There he was able to strike deals with low-income taxpayers who allowed him to use their names and social security numbers to falsify wage statements (W-2 forms). He then proceeded to file returns electronically, which enabled him to obtain a refund before the IRS discovered that the returns were phony. Unfortunately, the stories of Becht and Todd are just two illustrations of how easy it is to abuse the system. Near the close of 1993, the IRS estimated that the "tax gap," the amount of unpaid taxes (income, payroll, and excise) due to cheating and fraud, was over $150 billion annually.

The problems of tax fraud do not go unnoticed, however. To safeguard the system, encourage compliance, and promote ethical behavior, the government has adopted a number of mechanisms. Among these is an intricate set of penalties that can be applied to both taxpayers and tax return preparers. These penalties cover a variety of violations, such as failure to file and pay taxes on a timely basis, negligence in preparing the tax return, and outright fraud. While the penalties are usually monetary in nature, criminal penalties—such as the jail sentences given to Mr. Becht and Mr. Todd—may result if the taxpayer goes beyond these civil offenses and purposefully attempts to evade tax. The failure-to-file and failure-to-pay penalties—penalties that typically result not because taxpayers are trying to deceive the government but simply because they are late in filing and paying their taxes— are discussed in Chapter 4. The focus in this chapter is on the responsibilities of taxpayers and tax return preparers in filing returns and the major penalties that may be imposed with respect to positions taken on returns.

TAXPAYER PENALTIES

In a 1985 IRS survey, one out of every five people reported that they cheated on their tax return. In the same survey, 41 percent said they believed that their fellow taxpayers also cheated. Similarly, Professor Peggy Hite found in a 1993 survey of Indiana residents that 40 percent of the individuals asked indicated that they definitely would not voluntarily report prize income, such as money won in a lottery or similar contests and sweepstakes.[1] Another 30 percent were somewhat wishy-washy in their answers, suggesting that, depending on the circumstances, they also would not report the income. But anyone thinking about cheating should recognize that it can be quite expensive. The IRS has over 140 penalties in its arsenal that it could apply. In their simplest form, these penalties provide that as long as taxpayers do not cheat and make a good faith effort to determine their tax liability, they have no reason to worry. But in reality the ethical problems created by the tax system for taxpayers and tax preparers can be difficult to resolve. Unfortunately, the law rarely provides clear-cut answers, leaving taxpayers wondering what they should do.

As an illustration, consider two taxpayers, both with bad backs, who bought $5,000 hot tubs on the hope that they might have some therapeutic value. Can the taxpayers deduct their costs as a medical expense? Even if they researched the question every day of the week for a month, the answer may not be clear. Should the fact that the answer is not clear preclude them from deducting their expenses? Some taxpayers might be inclined to simply abandon the issue, pay the tax and never worry about it again. But others might believe that there is some support for their position and want to take the deduction. So assume in this case taxpayer A deducts the expense and taxpayer B deducts not only the cost of the tub but, banking on the audit lottery, also deducts the entire cost of the house on the grounds that it serves as a rehabilitation facility. What happens if both returns are audited and the agent rejects the deductions of both taxpayers? Obviously the system of punishment should fit the crime. And this is what Congress has attempted to do by creating a penalty system that fairly treats taxpayers who in good faith believe that their position has validity but at the same time discourages taxpayers from taking frivolous positions, hoping that the audit lottery will never pick their number.

As the penalty discussion below will reveal, the tax law has its own way of dealing with taxpayers who stray too far from the correct position. While the system is complex, it is somewhat analogous to the way a mother treats her teenage son who is apt to stay out beyond his 12 o'clock curfew. If the son is a few minutes late, there will probably be no penalty if he has a reasonable explanation. On the other hand, if he gets home two hours late, the penalty will probably be severe unless he called to say he would be late. But if he never called, punishment is a virtual certainty unless his story is truly believable and backed by witnesses. And, of course, if her son lies, he will be grounded forever. Although the rules for breaking curfew are not completely analogous to those for taxpayers that take erroneous positions on returns, the comparison may be useful. If a taxpayer takes an incorrect position with respect to a *small* amount, there will be no penalty as long as there is a *reasonable basis* for the position. On the other hand, if the tax dollars involved are *substantial*, a penalty is normally imposed unless the taxpayer has *substantial authority* for the position or, alternatively, has disclosed the position and has a reasonable basis for it. Of course, if the taxpayer commits blatant fraud, the penalties could be quite harsh. These ethical standards for taxpayers are embedded in two types of penalties: accuracy-related penalties and penalties for fraud.

---

[1]   "Nearly 1 in 3 Would Cheat on Taxes," *The Indianapolis Star*, April 7, 1994, B1.

ACCURACY-RELATED PENALTIES

What happens if a waiter simply fails to report all of his tips? What if a 70-year-old grandmother fails to file her return believing that senior citizens do not have to pay tax? And what if the taxpayer deducts the cost of his daughter's wedding as business entertainment? As might be expected, the IRS does not treat such transgressions lightly. If the taxpayer's behavior can be characterized as negligent, a penalty in addition to the regular tax may be imposed. In 1989 Congress consolidated several existing penalties relating to negligence into a so-called accuracy-related penalty. The accuracy-related penalty is generally 20 percent of the portion of the tax underpayment. The principal accuracy-related penalties include[2]

- ▸ Negligence or disregard of rules and regulations
- ▸ Substantial understatement of income tax
- ▸ Substantial valuation misstatement.

Note that these penalties do not stack on top of each other. The IRS must pick which one it wants to assess.

Negligence Penalty (Insubstantial). The negligence penalty, as an accuracy-related penalty, is 20 percent of the portion of the tax underpayment that is attributable to negligence or disregard of the rules and regulations.[3] For example, assume a taxpayer forgets to report $1,000 that he received for consulting during the year. If the taxpayer is in the 28 percent tax bracket, the underpayment is $280 and the penalty would be $56 (20% × $280). Note that when the day of reckoning comes, the taxpayer will be required to pay the underpayment, interest on the underpayment from the original due date, and the penalty, if any. The taxpayer may also owe interest on the penalty. Interest on the penalty generally starts to run when the taxpayer has been notified of the penalty, usually sometime after the audit. Under § 6601(e)(2)(B) interest must be paid on the failure-to-file penalty, accuracy-related penalties, and the fraud penalty.

Negligence is generally defined as any failure to do what a reasonable and ordinarily prudent person would do under the circumstances. To avoid the negligence penalty, the taxpayer must make a reasonable attempt to comply with the law. The negligence penalty is usually imposed when the taxpayer fails to report income or claims large amounts of unsubstantiated expenses. For example, a waitress who fails to report her cash tips would probably get hit with the penalty, as would the businessperson who claims thousands of dollars of business entertainment expenses with little or no substantiation—a specific requirement for travel and entertainment expenses. A taxpayer is automatically considered negligent and liable for the 20 percent penalty if he or she fails to report any type of income for which there is an information return filed by the party paying the income (e.g., Form 1099). In other situations, determination of whether the penalty should be imposed is in the hands of the auditor. It is important to note, however, that taxpayers who intentionally attempt to deceive the government are normally not subject to the negligence penalty but rather the more severe fraud penalty discussed below.

For most taxpayers, the most important aspect of the negligence penalty concerns its relationship to positions taken on returns.

Example 1. This year D graduated with a marketing degree from the University of Arkansas and immediately took a job with a publishing company as a sales representative. The company did not provide her with an office, so she worked out of her

---

[2]   § 6662.

[3]   § 6662(c).

home. After talking with her boss at work, she found out that he deducted his home office expenses as business expenses on his return. Knowing little about tax, she followed her boss's lead and deducted $3,000 of expenses related to her home office. Two years later D's return was audited and the agent informed her that he planned to deny her deduction for the home office expenses. Assuming the agent is correct, another issue is raised: should the negligence penalty apply since D has taken an incorrect position on the return?

Prior to 1994 the taxpayer could avoid the negligence penalty as long as the position was not frivolous and it was disclosed on the return. But that approach apparently inspired taxpayers to play the audit lottery. For example, aggressive taxpayers might take a questionable deduction, disclose it, then hope that they would never be audited. Even if they got caught, there was little risk since disclosure protected them against a negligence penalty in every situation except where the position was frivolous or patently improper. In other words, as long as the position was nonfrivolous—that is, the taxpayer had some basis on which to argue the disclosed position (e.g., a merely arguable or merely colorable claim)—the negligence penalty could be avoided.[4] Believing that the ethical standard set by this rule was far too low, the Revenue Reconciliation Act of 1993 changed the rules. Under the new approach, taxpayers are forced to be far more cautious about the positions they take on their returns.

A negligence penalty can be assessed unless the taxpayer has a *reasonable basis* for the position taken on the return regardless of whether it is disclosed on the return.[5] What the new approach means to taxpayers is that in situations where the potential tax understatement is insubstantial they can ethically take a position that is contrary to the rules and regulations without fear of the negligence penalty as long as the position has a reasonable basis. Of course, the critical issue here is what constitutes a reasonable basis.

Although any definition of a "reasonable basis" would be subject to debate, the regulations do provide some guidance. According to the regulations, the reasonable basis standard is met if the return position is "arguable, but fairly unlikely to prevail in court."[6] Practitioners generally interpret this to mean that a position has a reasonable basis if it has at least a 20 percent chance of succeeding (without regard to the possibility that it might not be discovered at all). Apparently, this represents a slight increase in the level of support required by the nonfrivolous standard for disclosed positions under prior law. In the final analysis, however, the standard leaves a great deal to be desired. The regulations do provide one additional insight that may be useful: the "too good to be true" rule. This rule indicates that the reasonable basis standard is not met if the taxpayer fails to make a reasonable attempt to determine the correctness of a position that seems too good to be true.

Substantial Understatement Penalty. The substantial understatement penalty, like its sibling, the negligence penalty, is an accuracy-related penalty that is 20 percent of the portion of the underpayment of tax due to any substantial understatement of income tax.[7] The understatement is considered substantial if it exceeds the larger of (1) 10 percent of the correct tax or (2) $5,000.

---

[4]   Reg. §§ 1.6662-3(b)(3) and 1.6694-2(c)(2).

[5]   See Predmore, "New Reasonable Basis Standard for Return Disclosure Likely to Be Troublesome," *Journal of Taxation* (January, 1994), p. 25, which indicates that, until the regulations are modified, "disclosure of a not frivolous position should suffice to avoid the negligence penalty." Discussions with other practitioners suggest that nonfrivolous positions probably can no longer be protected through disclosure.

[6]   § 6662(d).

[7]   § 6662(d). For tax years beginning after October 22, 2004, the Jobs Act modifies the definition of "substantial" for corporate taxpayers for purposes of the accuracy-related penalty for substantial understatements. Now a corporate taxpayer has a substantial understatement if the amount of the understatement exceeds the lesser of (1) 10% of the tax required to be shown on the return for the tax year (or, if greater, $10,000), or (2) $10 million.

The major difference between the substantial understatement penalty and the negligence penalty concerns the level of authority required to avoid penalty for an erroneous *undisclosed* position. In effect, Congress is telling taxpayers that if the risky position they are taking involves a substantial amount of tax and they are *unwilling to disclose* the position, the degree of support they must have is greater than simply a reasonable basis. The substantial understatement penalty applies to undisclosed positions unless the taxpayer has *substantial authority* for the position. It is unclear what the substantial authority requirement calls for, but it seems clear that it is somewhat more stringent than the 1 in 3 test of the realistic possibility of success standard discussed below but less demanding than the more-likely-than-not requirement, a more than 50 percent chance, related to certain positions taken with respect to certain tax shelter investments. For purposes of the substantial authority analysis, only materials published by Congress, the IRS, and the courts are relevant. Conclusions suggested by tax professionals in treatises, legal periodicals (which provide the basis of many arguments), or the like are not to be considered.[8]

The degree of support necessary to avoid the substantial understatement penalty drops down a notch if the taxpayer is willing to disclose the position. The substantial understatement penalty can be avoided if the taxpayer makes *adequate disclosure* and has a *reasonable* basis for his position. What constitutes adequate disclosure is many times clearer than what constitutes a reasonable basis. Disclosure is considered adequate if the position is explained on a special form intended just for this purpose, Form 8275 or 8275-R, or on the return in accordance with rules issued by the IRS each year.[9] In effect, when the tax dollars involved are material, taxpayers must meet a much higher standard—substantial authority—than is normally applied unless they are willing to disclose the position.

Substantial Valuation Misstatement. The tax law often requires taxpayers and tax return preparers to provide valuations for certain items. For example, taxpayers are generally entitled to a deduction for the fair market value of property given to qualified charitable organizations. What happens if a taxpayer in the 30 percent bracket gives a work of art that he says is worth $6,000 when its value is really closer to $2,000? The answer is that he has saved $1,200 ($4,000 × 30%) if he wins the audit lottery. But if the IRS does catch him, the taxpayer may face an accuracy-related penalty for substantial valuation misstatement. A 20 percent penalty is imposed on the underpayment of tax attributable to the misstatement.[10] The taxpayer avoids the penalty, however, if the misstatement does not exceed 200 percent of the correct value or if the amount of tax underpayment attributable to the misstatement is less than $5,000 ($10,000 for corporations). Thus the taxpayer above, who overstated the correct value by 300 percent, would still escape the valuation penalty since the amount of tax attributable to the misstatement, $1,200, is less than the $5,000 threshold. However, the taxpayer could still be subject to the negligence or the substantial understatement penalties.

Summary of Penalties for Inaccurate Returns. There is a great deal of confusion over penalties concerning erroneous positions on tax returns and what one can do to avoid them. Nevertheless, Exhibit 2-1 summarizes the three accuracy-related penalties discussed above and what defenses are available to the taxpayer. After a great deal of studying, it may become clear that the likelihood of a penalty depends on three factors: the amount of the potential understatement, whether the taxpayer has disclosed the

---

8   Reg. § 1.6692-4(d)(3)(iii).

9   Reg. § 1.6694-2(c)(3).

10   § 6662(e).

position adequately, and the level of support that there is for the position. As a rule, if the tax dollars are not significant, a reasonable basis protects the taxpayer from penalty. On the other hand, if the tax dollars are substantial, the taxpayer is protected only if there is substantial authority or if there is disclosure with reasonable basis. Exhibit 2-2 summarizes the various standards of compliance and ranks them according to their level of certainty. Note that in all cases the taxpayer can avoid the penalties by showing that there was *reasonable cause* for the position taken or that he or she acted in *good faith*. Obviously, these are both purely subjective determinations based on the individual facts and circumstances.

EXHIBIT 2-1
The 20 Percent Penalty for Inaccurate Returns and Defenses: § 6662

1. Negligence (insubstantial)
   ▶ Defined: Reasonable attempt to comply with the tax laws
   ▶ Defenses:
     — Reasonable basis (disclosure is unnecessary)
     — Exercise of reasonable care in preparing tax return
     — Reasonable cause and good faith

2. Substantial understatement
   ▶ Defined: Understatement greater than 10% of tax or $5,000, whichever is larger
   ▶ Defenses:
     — Understatement does not exceed threshold
     — Disclosure with reasonable basis
     — No disclosure with substantial authority
     — Reasonable cause and good faith

3. Substantial valuation misstatement
   ▶ Defined: Misstatement more than 200% of correct valuation
   ▶ Defenses:
     — Misstatement does not exceed threshold
     — Amount of underpayment of tax is less than $5,000
     — Reasonable cause and good faith

EXHIBIT 2-2
Standards of Compliance Required to Avoid Penalties

1. Frivolous position
   ▶ Defined: Patently improper
     — No protection for frivolous positions

2. Not frivolous position
   ▶ Defined: Not patently improper, merely arguable
     — Pre-1994: Protection against negligence with disclosure
     — Post-1993: Apparently no protection

3. Reasonable basis
   ▶ Defined: Arguable but fairly unlikely to prevail in court
     — Protects against insubstantial negligence
     — Protects against substantial understatement if position disclosed

4. Realistic possibility of success
   ▶ Defined: More than one in three chances for success
     — Protects against insubstantial negligence without disclosure
     — Protects against substantial negligence with disclosure

5. Substantial authority
   ▶ Defined: Supporting authorities are substantial (Congress, IRS, or court cases)
     — Protects against insubstantial and substantial negligence without disclosure (except tax shelter item)

6. More-likely-than-not
   ▶ Defined: Greater than 50 percent chance of succeeding
     — Protects against insubstantial and substantial negligence without disclosure including tax shelter items

7. Reasonable cause and good faith
   ▶ Defined: Facts and circumstances determination
     — Protects normally against all penalties

FRAUD

When the taxpayer attempts to defraud the government, the tax law imposes a minimum penalty equal to 75 percent of the amount of underpayment attributable to the fraud.[11] *In addition*, the taxpayer may also be subject to the criminal penalties for fraud. Criminal penalties can be as high as $100,000 ($500,000 for corporate taxpayers) and imprisonment for up to five years. Despite these penalties, taxpayers by the thousands are willing to play the audit lottery, including some rich and famous tax felons:[12]

▶ Leona Helmsley, New York hotel magnate, who will forever be remembered for her offhand comment to her housekeeper, "we don't pay taxes; only the little people pay taxes." Helmsley, convicted in 1992 for deducting millions of dollars of personal expenses, including renovations to her personal residence, was fined more than $7 million and sentenced to four years in prison (served 18 months).

---

[11] § 6663.

[12] See in part "Famous Faces from IRS Hall of Shame," *Sacramento Bee*, March 29, 1994. Metro Final Scene, D3.

- Pete Rose, baseball player and all-time leader in hits (4,256). Rose failed to report income from memorabilia shows and gambling and served five months in prison.

- Spiro Agnew, vice-president during the Nixon era. Agnew, who failed to report income from bribes, was fined $10,000 and had a three-year suspended sentence.

- Chuck Berry, famous rock'n'roll star of Johnny B. Goode fame. Berry underreported his income by $110,000 in 1979 and served four months in prison.

- Aldo Gucci, famous designer. Gucci pleaded guilty to $7 million of tax fraud in 1989 and was sentenced to one year in jail and fined $30,000.

- Al Capone, racketeer and mobster. Capone, convicted of tax evasion in 1931, was fined $50,000 and served eight years of a ten-year sentence, then retired to his Miami estate.

- Willie Nelson, country and western singing star. Nelson ran up his tax bill to over $32 million. He served no time in prison, but part of the bill was paid from part of his ranch, which was seized by the IRS.

Civil fraud has not been clearly defined, but it requires more than simply negligent acts or omissions by the taxpayer. There is a fine line between fraud and negligence (to which a lesser penalty applies, as explained above). Fraud does not occur by accident. It is a willful and deliberate attempt to evade tax. For example, consider a taxpayer who is entitled to a deduction of $19,000. What penalty applies if he transposed the digits and claimed a deduction of $91,000? Fraud occurs only if it can be shown that the taxpayer knew that the amounts reported on the return were false. In this regard, the IRS must prove this to be true by a "preponderance of evidence." Thus for the transposition error above, the fraud penalty can be upheld if the IRS can carry its burden of proof and show that the taxpayer intentionally transposed the numbers. Lacking this, the negligence or substantial understatement penalty would probably be assessed. Note that before the *criminal* fraud penalty can be imposed, the IRS must show that the taxpayer intentionally tried to evade tax "beyond a shadow of any reasonable doubt." All of those in the "hall of shame" above found that this is not an impossible task. As a practical matter, the penalty imposed—negligence, civil, or criminal fraud—depends on the severity of the offense and the ability of the IRS to carry the burden of proof.

> **Example 2.** Dr. Bradford Calloway paid his children, all of whom were under 12 years of age, $11,000 for performing various tasks relating to his business. The kids did such chores as mail sorting, trash collecting, and answering the telephone. Although expenses incurred in carrying on a business such as these are normally deductible, the IRS did not believe that children that age could perform work worth that much money for any business. The Tax Court agreed with the IRS, and the judge added a fraud penalty, explaining that "We find it inherently incredible that Calloway, an intelligent and educated professional man, would pay a total of $11,138.56 for such services, performed by small children on a part-time basis, or that he could seriously believe that such payments represented reasonable and deductible compensation for services rendered in his medical practice ... particularly in the face of his accountant's contrary advice."[13]

TAX PREPARER PENALTIES

Understanding the penalty structure becomes doubly hard when a tax preparer is involved. What are the responsibilities of tax preparers when the client is unscrupulous

---

[13] A. J. Cook, *A. J.'s Tax Court* (St. Luke's Press, 1987), p. 96.

or simply wants to take an aggressive position? As a practical matter, it is not the totally dishonest taxpayer that presents difficulties for tax return preparers. Most practitioners can easily walk away from such engagements. The more perplexing and more common problems concern situations where the client wants the preparer to take an aggressive position on issues for which the answer is unclear. Similarly, taxpayers may want to pursue a particular position because they view the law as arbitrary or capricious or they are not receptive to the preparer's response. These situations often present an ethical dilemma for the preparer. What side should the practitioner take? Should the preparer sign the return if he or she disagrees with the taxpayer? First, it needs to be emphasized that the tax practitioner is being paid to be an advocate for the client, not an independent third party hired to provide an unbiased or neutral opinion. It is the job of the tax expert to explain the relevant considerations and possible consequences, including positions that may be contrary to the law but which may be defensible. That done, it is not the right of the practitioner to impose his or her own set of moral values on the client. The final decision is to be made by the client after reviewing the alternatives provided. If the practitioner believes that the client's actions violate his or her personal code of ethics, the practitioner should withdraw from the engagement.

Beyond the basic preparer-client relationship, there are a number of other forces at work that affect whether the preparer signs the return containing a risky position. First, even if an answer to a particular question does exist, the costs of uncovering it probably cannot be recovered from the client. Second, given the small percentage of tax returns that are audited, there is only a slight chance that either the taxpayer or preparer will ever come face to face with the IRS. Third, preparers, like most people, want to please their customers and find it hard to just say no. When these dynamics are present, they make it relatively easy for practitioners to resolve an issue in favor of the client, notwithstanding the lack of reasonable support for the position. This is particularly true when the practitioner knows that the unprincipled competitor down the street will do whatever the client wants and at a cheaper price. On the other hand, the practitioner's sense of public duty, concern about his or her personal and professional reputation, and possible legal liability may cause him or her to be something less than an advocate for the client. As might be expected, the practitioner's proper role in these situations is not clearly defined. There are, however, in addition to the preparer's own personal code of ethics, some guidelines that a preparer generally must follow in carrying on a tax practice.

Individuals who prepare tax returns are subject to a variety of rules regulating their professional conduct. The rules governing tax practice are contained in Treasury Circular Number 230 and various provisions of the Internal Revenue Code. In addition, CPAs and attorneys engaged in tax practice must also follow the rules of conduct imposed by their professional organizations: the American Institute of Certified Public Accountants (AICPA) and the American Bar Association (ABA). The general rules of conduct prescribed by the AICPA for all CPAs concern a variety of matters such as independence, integrity, objectivity, advertising, contingent fees, and responsibilities of the accountant when undertaking an engagement—but none of these are directly related to tax practice. Acknowledging that individuals engaged in tax practice have ethical concerns beyond those covered in the general rules of conduct, the AICPA has developed Statements on Standards for Tax Services (SSTSs). These statements, currently eight in number, provide additional guidelines for professional conduct of CPAs in tax practice. Similarly, the ABA Standing Committee on Ethics and Professional Responsibility has also issued certain opinions regarding an attorney's conduct when practicing before the IRS.

Tax Return Positions. As might be imagined, the rules and applicable penalties concerning practitioner conduct as set forth by Circular 230, the Internal Revenue Code, the AICPA, and the ABA deserve a chapter devoted solely to these topics. In essence, however, the most important penalty for those preparing returns is that contained in § 6694(a) of the Internal Revenue Code. Section 6694(a) provides that a $250 penalty is imposed on the preparer of a tax return if any part of an understatement of the liability on a return is due to an *undisclosed* position for which there was not a *realistic possibility* of success. Note that the penalty applies to any paid preparer regardless of whether the person is a CPA, enrolled agent, friend, or relative. If the preparer is compensated, the penalty could apply.[14] This standard is met "if a reasonable and well informed analysis by a person knowledgeable in the tax law would lead such a person to conclude that the position has approximately a one in three, or greater, likelihood of being sustained on its merits."[15] The AICPA's Statements on Standards for Tax Services also adopt this standard in *SSTS No. 1*, which states that a member of the AICPA should not recommend to a taxpayer a position (or prepare or sign a return that contains a position) with respect to the tax treatment of any item on a return unless the CPA has a good faith belief that the position has a realistic possibility of success. The ABA and Circular 230 also embrace the realistic possibility standard. A violation of this standard under Circular 230 can result in disbarment from practice before the IRS, but only if the violation is willful, reckless, or the result of gross incompetence.

At first glance, it would appear that the size of penalty imposed by the IRS, $250, is so small that it would do little to dissuade preparers from taking whatever position a client wishes. The ramifications of a violation under Circular 230 also seem more academic than real since disbarment occurs only if the violation was willful or reckless. What may not be apparent, however, is the significance of this standard *and* its violation should a disgruntled client end up suing the preparer for malpractice. In a civil action against a preparer, the courts, both judges and juries, typically rely on expert testimony to assess whether the preparer should be held liable. In such case, it is not too hard to imagine a judge or jury believing that the preparer was negligent once an expert has explained that the preparer has already been penalized under § 6694(a). Even if the preparer is ultimately exonerated, the costs to defend such action could be substantial. Moreover, failing to observe such a standard could ultimately cost the practitioner the loss of his or her professional license to practice as a CPA or attorney. In short, it is not the size of the penalty that the practitioner fears but the other consequences that the penalty may trigger.

> **Example 3.** T, a CPA, has prepared the tax return for D&G Home Products for the past 15 years. It is normally a week-long job and worth well over $10,000 to T's practice. He also does the monthly preparation of financial statements worth another $20,000 per year. This year G spent more than $100,000 on a Super Bowl excursion for its customers. In preparing the return, D&G insists that it should be able to deduct all of the expenses, but T has some reservations. T understands there have been some recent changes in the law in this area but does not have time to adequately research the issue, and, even if he did, he doubts whether he could charge for the time spent. He also knows that this is a lucrative engagement and he wants to continue the relationship with the client. Finally, T recognizes that it is highly unlikely that the return will ever be audited. Consequently, T decides to sign the return and worry about it only if a problem arises. But what happens if the return is audited, the position is overturned, and a preparer penalty is assessed on the grounds that the return contained an undisclosed position that did not have a realistic possibility of success? While the penalty would be monetarily small, the real concern is the effect of the reversal on the client. D&G may have a short memory once it is forced to pay the tax, interest, and perhaps a substantial

---

14   See § 7701(a)(36) for a definition of preparer.

15   Reg. § 1.6694-2(b).

understatement penalty and interest on the penalty. It may not remember conversations with T and his admonitions. In the end, the corporation may feel that it was misled and sue T for malpractice and hundreds of thousands of dollars. In such a proceeding, D&G may have the upper hand since it has been determined by a court of law that the position was unrealistic under that standards of § 6694(a) and T has therefore failed to meet his ethical responsibilities as established for tax practitioners in the AICPA's Statements on Standards for Tax Service.

The decision that all practitioners ultimately face with every return they prepare is whether they can in good faith sign the tax return as preparer. The key factor in making this decision is whether the position advanced on the return has a realistic possibility of success. In fact, Circular 230 states specifically that a practitioner *may not sign a return unless the realistic possibility standard is met or adequate disclosure exists.*

It should be emphasized that a preparer can breathe much more easily if the taxpayer is willing to adequately disclose the position. SSTS No. 1 sets the ethical standard, allowing the preparer to prepare and sign the return provided the position is not frivolous and it is appropriately disclosed. Similarly, the preparer penalty of § 6694(a) does not apply to disclosed positions. In many cases, however, the taxpayer does not want to disclose the position, therefore returning the preparer to the original dilemma—determining whether there is a realistic possibility that the position will be upheld. Note that, even if there is a disclosure, the *taxpayer* can still be liable for negligence penalties unless there is a *reasonable basis* for the taxpayer's treatment of the disclosed item. Thus, even though preparers can absolve themselves from liability as long as the position is nonfrivolous and there is disclosure, the taxpayer is subject to a higher standard.

> **Example 4.** This year P&P, a large public accounting firm, prepared the return for T Corporation, a valued *Fortune* 500 client. The return contained a somewhat risky position involving a material amount of tax. Assuming the position has a realistic possibility of being upheld, P&P can sign the return without fear of penalty regardless of whether the position is disclosed. However, if the position is rejected, the taxpayer could very well be subject to the substantial understatement penalty unless there is substantial authority for the position or the taxpayer discloses and has a reasonable basis for the position. Thus, if there is no disclosure, if the return is audited, and if it is determined that the realistic possibility standard is satisfied but the substantial authority test is not, P&P is off the hook but T must pay a 20 percent penalty. These differing results place the preparer and taxpayer in a conflict that can be avoided only if the preparer carefully communicates the distinction. Even then the client might be miffed and find another preparer.

In addition to the $250 penalty for preparing a return that contains an undisclosed position for which there is not a realistic possibility of success, the tax law provides a number of other penalties to encourage ethical conduct by preparers. For example, a penalty of $1,000 per return is imposed where the preparer willfully attempts to understate the liability of the taxpayer or where the preparer understates the taxpayer's liability by reckless or intentional disregard of the rules or regulations.[16] The law also contains a number of criminal penalties for preparers with fines of up to $10,000 and imprisonment for up to three years.[17]

---

[16] § 6694(b).

[17] See §§ 7206, 7207, and 7216.

Other Guidelines for CPAs. As suggested above, the Statements on Standards for Tax Services provide a number of other guidelines for members of the AICPA who are tax practitioners. There are currently eight statements. *SSTS No. 1*, regarding tax positions, was covered at length above. The remaining statements generally fall into one of two categories: (1) return preparation issues (SSTS Numbers 2, 3, and 4) and (2) issues that arise after a return is filed (SSTS Numbers 5, 6, and 7). Some of these statements are summarized below.

- *SSTS No. 2: Answers to Questions on the Return.* When there are questions on a return that have not been answered, the CPA should make a reasonable effort to obtain appropriate answers from the taxpayer and provide the answers to the questions on the return. The significance of the question in terms of the information's effect on taxable income or loss and tax liability may be considered in determining whether the answer to a question may be omitted. However, omission of an answer is not justified simply because the answer may prove to be disadvantageous to the taxpayer.

- *SSTS No. 3: Certain Procedural Aspects of Preparing Returns.* In preparing or signing a return, a CPA may, without verification, rely in good faith on information furnished by the taxpayer or a third party. However, the CPA cannot ignore the implications of information furnished, and should make reasonable inquiries if the information appears to be incorrect, incomplete, or inconsistent either by itself or on the basis of other facts known to the CPA. When preparing the current return, the CPA should make use of returns from prior years wherever feasible. If the tax law or regulations impose conditions with respect to the tax treatment of an item (e.g., substantiating documentation), the CPA should make appropriate inquiries to determine if the conditions are met. In addition, when preparing a return, the CPA should consider relevant information known to the CPA from the tax return of another taxpayer, but should also consider any legal limitations relating to confidentiality.

- *SSTS No. 4: Use of Estimates.* Unless it is prohibited by the Internal Revenue Code or other tax rule, a CPA may prepare returns involving the use of the taxpayer's estimates, if under the circumstances, exact data cannot be obtained in a practical manner. When estimates are used, they should be presented in such a manner as to avoid the implication of greater accuracy than that which exists. The CPA should be satisfied that estimated amounts are reasonable under the circumstances.

- *SSTS No. 6: Knowledge of Error (Return Preparation).* A CPA should advise the taxpayer promptly upon learning of an error in a previously filed return, or upon learning of a taxpayer's failure to file a required return. The advice of the CPA may be oral, and should include a recommendation of the measures to be taken. The CPA is not obliged to inform the IRS and may not do so without the permission of the taxpayer, except where required by law. If the CPA is requested to prepare the current year's return and the taxpayer has not taken appropriate steps to correct an error on a prior year's return, the CPA should consider whether to withdraw from preparing the return and whether to continue a professional or employment relationship with the taxpayer.

- *SSTS No. 7: Knowledge of Error (Administrative Proceeding).* When the CPA represents a taxpayer in an administrative proceeding regarding a return with an error known to the CPA that has resulted or may result in more than an insignificant effect on the taxpayer's tax liability, the CPA should notify the taxpayer and recommend corrective measures to be taken. The recommendations may be given orally. The CPA is not obligated to inform the IRS or other taxing authority, and may not do so without the taxpayer's permission, except where required by law. However, the CPA should request permission from the taxpayer to disclose the error to the IRS. Absent such permission, the CPA should consider withdrawing from the engagement.

The above discussion is just a brief introduction to the penalties and rules of practice that serve to define the proper conduct for taxpayers and preparers. In reality, there are a number of other penalties and rules that may apply in certain situations.[18] Nevertheless, this introduction may provide a sense of what are the most common ethical problems facing tax practitioners. Moreover, it underscores the importance of being able to find authoritative answers for questions, the subject of the next section.

✓ CHECK YOUR KNOWLEDGE

Review Question 1. The system of penalties provides an escape for taxpayers if the positions taken on their returns meet certain standards. In effect, meeting a certain standard enables the taxpayer to avoid a penalty. Practitioners generally associate a probability of success rate for each standard. What probabilities would you assign?

Frivolous	_____
Substantial authority	_____
Nonfrivolous	_____
More-likely-than-not	_____
Reasonable basis	_____
Realistic possibility of success	_____

None of these probabilities other than *realistic possibility of success* have been quantified by the law. However, practitioners would typically rank the standards in the following order with the associated probabilities of success. Although the probabilities might vary from firm to firm and practitioner to practitioner, the order would remain the same.

1.	More-likely-than-not	> 50%
2.	Substantial authority	≥ 40
3.	Realistic possibility of success	≥ 33
4.	Reasonable basis	≥ 20
5.	Nonfrivolous	≥ 5
6.	Frivolous	< 5

Review Question 2. Pete Hartman operates an accounting practice in northern Virginia just outside of Washington. One of his long-time clients is Jim Anderson. Last year the IRS audited Jim's 2001 tax return, and he ultimately had to pay additional taxes as well as interest on that amount. Jim now wants to deduct a portion of this interest as a business expense. He reasons that because business expenses are deductible and the interest was directly attributable to back taxes on business income, the deduction should be allowed. There has also been another development this year. Jim's daughter has been diagnosed to have dyslexia. The problem is not severe but it was enough to cause Jim to enroll his daughter in a private school that is better equipped to provide the additional help she needs.

---

[18] For a more complete discussion, see the related text, *Corporate Partnership, Estate and Gift Taxation, 2006 Edition*, Chapter 18.

The tuition for the school is $20,000, and Jim wants to deduct the cost as a medical expense. After some research, Pete believes that both positions are somewhat risky. Jim has asked Pete about the downside risk of taking this position on his return. Pete estimates that taking the deduction for the interest will reduce Jim's tax liability of $30,000 about $1,000. If he were to claim only the medical expense deduction by itself, it would reduce his tax liability by about $6,000. Try to answer the following questions.

a. What is the maximum penalty that Jim might pay if he deducts only the interest and it is considered erroneous but not fraudulent?

Jim would be subject to an accuracy-related penalty (negligence), which is 20 percent of the amount of the underpayment due to the overstatement of deductions. In this case, the penalty would be $200 (20% × $ 1,000). In addition, Jim would owe the additional $1,000 in tax plus interest on the underpayment *and* interest on the penalty.

b. True-False. Jim will not be subject to penalty with respect to the interest deduction as long as his position has a reasonable basis even if he does not specifically disclose the position on the return.

True. The negligence penalty will not be assessed as long as the taxpayer has a reasonable basis for the position regardless of whether the position is disclosed on the tax return.

c. True-False. Jim will not be subject to penalty with respect to the tuition deduction as long as his position has a reasonable basis even if he does not specifically disclose the position on the return.

False. In this situation, Jim's $6,000 understatement would be considered substantial since it exceeds the larger of $5,000 or 10 percent of the correct tax, $3,000 (10% × $30,000). When the understatement in question is substantial, the substantial understatement penalty applies. This penalty can be avoided only if the taxpayer has substantial authority for his position *or* he discloses the position and such position has reasonable basis. Here Jim will not have disclosed the position, so a reasonable basis for the position will not suffice.

d. Jim has indicated that he does not want to flag either position. Pete would not be subject to a preparer penalty with respect to the tuition deduction if the position is *not* disclosed as long as the position
    (1)   has a reasonable basis
    (2)   is nonfrivolous
    (3)   has a realistic possibility of success
    (4)   more than one of the above
    (5)   all of the above

(3). To avoid the $250 preparer penalty of § 6694(a), an undisclosed position must have a reasonable possibility of success, a higher standard than reasonable basis. However, if the position is disclosed, the preparer penalty will not apply as long as it is not a frivolous position.

e. True-False. By signing the tax return, Pete would not be violating the AICPA Statement on Standards for Tax Services assuming both positions have a reasonable basis.

False. The AICPA has also adopted the realistic possibility of success standard, suggesting that tax practitioners should not sign returns containing undisclosed positions that do not meet this standard.

f. Pete understands that the SSTS indicate that he is not supposed to sign the return where there is an undisclosed position unless the position has a realistic possibility of success. However, he has no real idea whether the chances are 20 percent, 30 percent, 40 percent, or whatever based on what he has found. Can Pete sign a return containing a position for which there is no reasonable basis without violating the AICPA statements if he discloses the position?

Yes. The SSTS provide that a practitioner can sign any return as long as the position is disclosed and it is not frivolous.

SOURCES AND APPLICATIONS OF TAX LAW

As stated at the outset of this chapter, before delving into the rules and regulations of taxation, it is important at a minimum to have an appreciation of not only the nature of tax practice but also the sources of the tax law and how they can be used for solving questions. The second half of this chapter identifies the various components of the tax law, explains how they can be accessed, and reviews the basic methods of tax research.

AUTHORITATIVE SOURCES OF TAX LAW

Sources of tax law can be classified into two broad categories: (1) the law, and (2) official interpretations of the law. The law consists primarily of the Constitution, the Acts of Congress, and tax treaties. In general, these sources are referred to as the *statutory* law. Most statutory law is written in general terms for a typical situation. Since general rules, no matter how carefully drafted, cannot be written to cover variations on the normal scheme, interpretation is usually required. The task of interpreting the statute is one of the principal duties of the Internal Revenue Service (IRS) as representative of the Secretary of the Treasury. The IRS annually produces thousands of releases that explain and clarify the law. To no one's surprise, however, taxpayers and the government do not always agree on how a particular law should be interpreted. In situations where the taxpayer or the government decides to litigate the question, the courts, as final arbiters, are given the opportunity to interpret the law. These judicial interpretations, administrative interpretations, and the statutory law are considered in detail below.

STATUTORY LAW

The Constitution of the United States provides the Federal government with the power to tax. Disputes concerning the constitutionality of an income tax levied on taxpayers without apportionment among the states were resolved in 1913 with passage of the Sixteenth Amendment. Between 1913 and 1939, Congress enacted revenue acts that amounted to a complete rewrite of all tax law to date, including the desired changes. In 1939, due primarily to the increasing complexity of the earlier process, Congress codified all Federal tax laws into Title 26 of the *United States Code*, which was then called the *Internal Revenue Code of 1939*. Significant changes in the Federal tax laws were made during World War II and the postwar period of the late 1940s. Each change resulted in amendments to the 1939 Code. By 1954, the codification process had to be repeated in order to organize all additions to the law and to eliminate obsolete provisions. The product of this effort was the *Internal Revenue Code of 1954*. After 1954, Congress took great care to ensure that each new amendment to the 1954 Code was incorporated within its organizational structure with appropriate cross-references to any prior provisions affected by a new law. In 1986, Congress again made substantial revision in the tax law. Consistent with this massive redesign of the 1954 Code, Congress changed the title to the *Internal Revenue Code of 1986*. Like the 1954 Code, the 1986 Code is subject to revisions introduced by a new law. Recent changes incorporated into the 1986 Code include the Job Creation and Worker Assistance Act of 2002 and the Jobs and Growth Tax Relief Reconciliation Act of 2003.

The legislative provisions contained in the Code are by far the most important component of tax law. Although procedure necessary to enact a law is generally well known, it is necessary to review this process with a special emphasis on taxation. From a tax perspective, the *intention* of Congress in producing the legislation is extremely important since the primary purpose of tax research is to interpret the legislative intent of Congress.

THE MAKING OF A TAX LAW

Article I, Section 7, Clause 1 of the Constitution provides that the House of Representatives of the U.S. Congress has the basic responsibility for initiating revenue bills.[19] The Ways and Means Committee of the House of Representatives must consider any tax bill before it is presented for vote by the full House of Representatives. On bills of major public interest, the Ways and Means Committee holds public hearings where interested organizations may send representatives to express their views about the bill. The first witness at such hearings is usually the Secretary of the Treasury, representing the President of the United States. In many cases, proposals for new tax legislation or changes in existing legislation come from the President as a part of his political or economic programs.

After the public hearings have been held, the Ways and Means Committee usually goes into closed session, where the Committee prepares the tax bill for consideration by the entire House. The members of the Committee receive invaluable assistance from their highly skilled staff, which includes economists, accountants, and lawyers. The product of this session is a proposed bill that is submitted to the entire House for debate and vote.

After a bill has been approved by the entire House, it is sent to the Senate and assigned to the Senate Finance Committee. The Senate Finance Committee may also hold hearings on the bill before its consideration by the full Senate. The Senate's bill generally differs from the House's bill. In these situations, both versions are sent to the Joint Conference Committee on Taxation, which is composed of members selected from the House Ways and Means Committee and from the Senate Finance Committee. The objective of this Joint Committee is to produce a compromise bill acceptable to both sides. On occasion, when compromise cannot be achieved by the Joint Committee or the compromise bill is unacceptable to the House or the Senate, the bill "dies." If, however, compromise is reached and the Senate and House approve the compromise bill, it is then referred to the President for his or her approval or veto. If the President vetoes the bill, the legislation is "killed" unless two-thirds of both the House and the Senate vote to override the veto. If the veto is overridden, the legislation becomes law.

It should be noted that at each stage of the process, information is produced that may be useful in assessing the intent of Congress. One of the better sources of Congressional intent is a report issued by the House Ways and Means Committee. This report contains the bill as well as a general explanation. This explanation usually provides the historical background of the proposed legislation along with the reasons for enactment. The Senate Finance Committee also issues a report similar to that of the House. Because the Senate often makes changes in the House version of the bill, the Senate's report is also an important source. Additionally, the Joint Conference Committee on Taxation issues its own report, which is sometimes helpful. Two other sources of intent are the records of the debates on the bill and publications of the initial hearings.

---

[19] Tax bills do not originate in the Senate, except when they are attached to other bills.

Committee reports and debates appear in several publications. Committee reports are officially published in pamphlet form by the U.S. Government Printing Office as the bill proceeds through Congress. The enacted bill is published in the *Internal Revenue Bulletin* and the *Internal Revenue Cumulative Bulletin*. The debates are published in the *Congressional Record*. In addition to these official government publications, several commercial publishers make this information available to subscribers.

The diagram below illustrates the normal flow of a bill through the legislative process and the documents that are generated in this process.

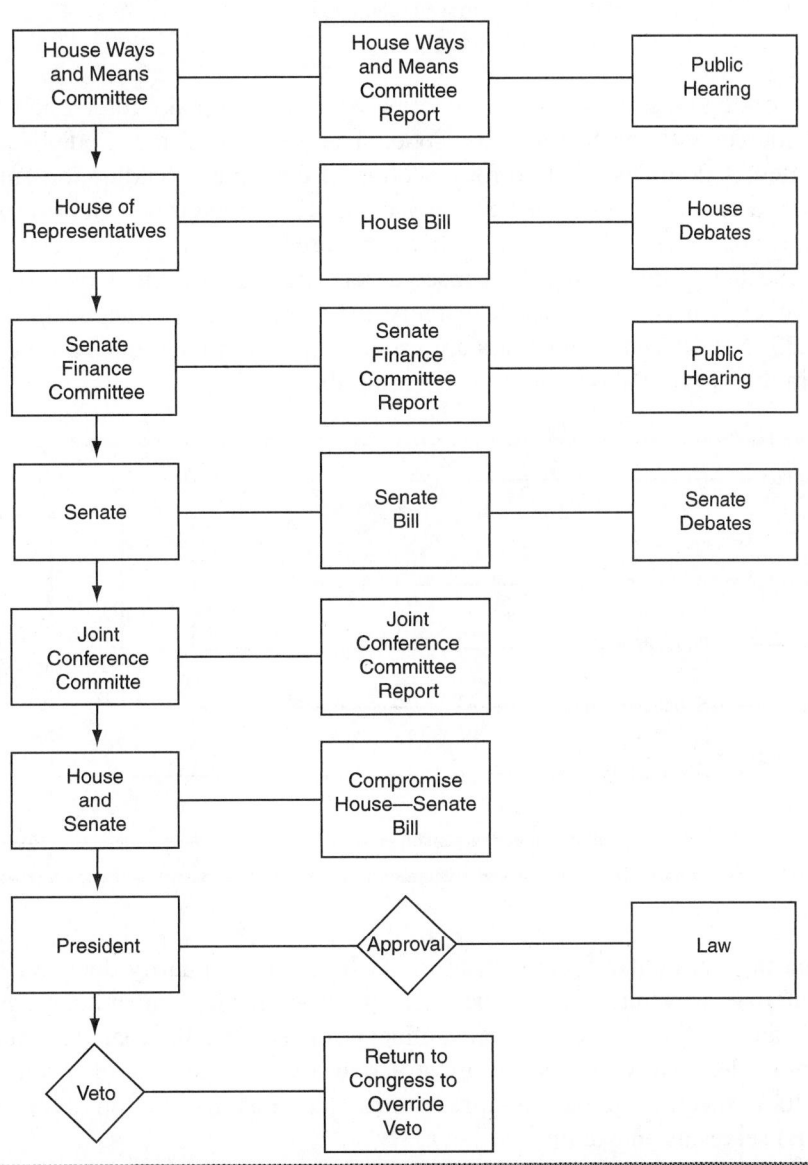

ORGANIZATION OF THE CODE

Once a tax bill becomes tax law, it is incorporated into the existing structure of the *Internal Revenue Code*.[20] The ability to use the Internal Revenue Code is essential for all individuals who have any involvement with the tax laws. It is normally the starting point for research.

---

[20]   All future use of the term Code or Internal Revenue Code refers to the *Internal Revenue Code of 1986*, as amended.

The following format is the basic organization of the Code.

Title 26 of the United States Code (referred to as the Internal Revenue Code)

Subtitle A—Income Taxes

Chapter 1—Normal Taxes and Surtaxes

Subchapter A—Determination of Tax Liability

Part I—Tax on Individuals
Sections 1 through 5

When working with the tax law, it is often necessary to make reference to, or *cite*, a particular source with respect to the Code. The *section* of the Code is the source normally cited. A complete citation for a section of the Code would be too cumbersome. For instance, a formal citation for Section 1 of the Code would be "Subtitle A, Chapter 1, Subchapter A, Part I, Section 1." In most cases, citation of the section alone is sufficient. Sections are numbered consecutively throughout the Code so that each section number is used only once. Currently the numbers run from Section 1 through Section 9833. Not all section numbers are used, so that additional ones may be added by Congress in the future without the need for renumbering.[21]

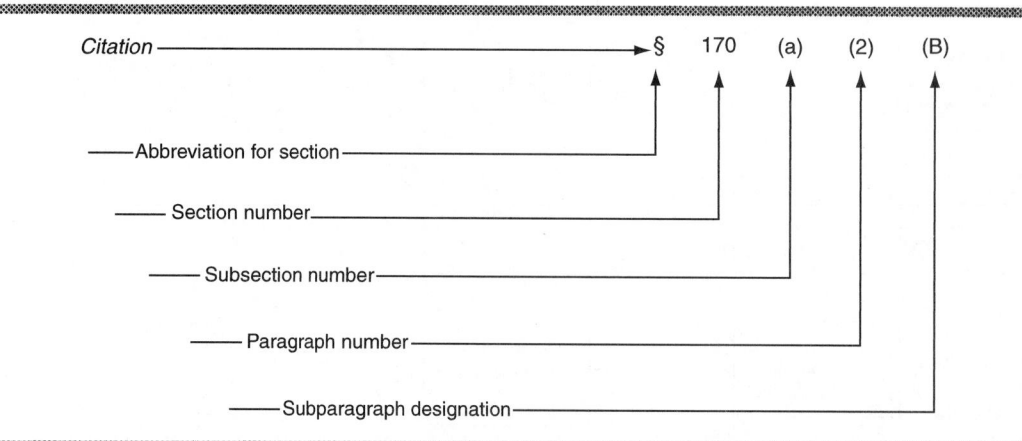

Citation of a particular Code section in tax literature ordinarily does not require the prefix "Internal Revenue Code" because it is generally understood that, unless otherwise stated, references to section numbers concern the Internal Revenue Code of 1986 as amended. However, since most Code sections are divided into subparts, reference to a specific subpart requires more than just its section number. Section 170(a)(2)(B) serves as an example.

All footnote references used throughout this text are made in the form given above. In most cases, the "§" or "§§" symbols are used in place of the terms "section" or "sections," respectively.

---

[21] It is interesting to note that when it adopted the 1954 Code, Congress deliberately left section numbers unassigned to provide room for future additions. Recently, however, Congress has been forced to distinguish new sections by alphabetical letters following a particular section number. See, for example, Sections 280, 280A, 280B, and 280C of the 1986 Code.

Single-volume or double-volume editions of the Internal Revenue Code are published after every major change in the law. Commerce Clearing House, Inc. (CCH) and the Research Institute of America (RIA) publish these editions. Additionally, the Code is included in each of the major tax services that are discussed in a later section of this chapter.

TAX TREATIES

The laws contained in tax treaties represent the third and final component of the statutory law. Tax treaties (also referred to as tax conventions) are agreements between the United States and other countries that provide rules governing the taxation of residents of one country by another. For example, the tax treaty between the United States and France indicates how the French government taxes U.S. citizens residing in France and vice versa. Tax treaties, as law, have the same authority as those laws contained in the Code.[22] Treaty provisions may override provisions of the Internal Revenue Code if the treaty was signed after August 16, 1954.[23] For this reason, persons involved with an international tax question must be aware of tax treaties and recognize that the Code may be superseded by a tax treaty.

ADMINISTRATIVE INTERPRETATIONS

After Congress has enacted a tax law, the Executive branch of the Federal government has the responsibility for enforcing it. In the process of enforcing the law, the Treasury interprets, clarifies, defines, and analyzes the Code in order to apply Congressional intention of the law to the specific facts of a taxpayer's situation. This process results in numerous administrative releases including the following:

1. Regulations

2. Revenue rulings and letter rulings

3. Revenue procedures

4. Technical advice memoranda

REGULATIONS

Regulations are the Treasury's official interpretation of the Internal Revenue Code. Code § 7805(a) authorizes the Secretary of the Treasury to "prescribe all needful rules and regulations for the enforcement of this title, including all rules and regulations as may be necessary of any alteration of law in relation to internal revenue." Section 7805(b) provides authority to the Secretary to prescribe the extent, if any, to which any ruling or regulation relating to the internal revenue laws will be applied without retroactive effect. In most cases the Secretary delegates the power to write the regulations to the Commissioner of the Internal Revenue Service. In practice, this means that the regulations are written by the technical staff of the IRS or by the office of the Chief Counsel of the IRS, an official who is also an assistant General Counsel of the Treasury Department.

Regulations are issued in the form of *Treasury Decisions* (often referred to as TDs), which are published in the *Federal Register* and sometimes later in the *Internal Revenue*

---

[22]   See Code § 7852(d)(1).

[23]   § 7852(d)(2).

Bulletin. The *Federal Register* is the official publication for regulations and legal notices issued by the executive branch of the Federal government. The *Federal Register* is published every business day. Before a TD is published in final form, it must be issued in proposed form, a *proposed regulation*, for a period of at least 30 days before it is scheduled to become final.

Section 7805(d) provides that any temporary regulation (see subsequent discussion) issued by the Secretary will also be issued as a proposed regulation. Any temporary regulation expires within three years after the date of issuance of such regulation.

Upon publication, interested parties have at least 30 days to comment on proposed regulations. In theory, at the end of this comment period, the Treasury responds in any one of three ways; it may withdraw the proposed regulation, amend it, or leave it unchanged. In the latter two cases, the Treasury normally issues the regulation in its final form as a TD, published in the *Federal Register*. The final version of any given regulation is quite frequently significantly different from the proposed version.

Afterwards, the new regulation is included in Title 26 of the *Code of Federal Regulations*. In fact, however, proposed regulations sometimes remain in proposed form for many years. Proposed regulations do not have the force of law and are not the Treasury's official position on a particular issue.

Temporary Regulations. The National Office of the Treasury issues temporary regulations as the need arises. Often such regulations are issued in response to substantive changes in the tax law when tax practitioners, in particular, need immediate guidance in applying a new or revised statute. Such regulations usually deal with immediate filing requirements or details regarding a mandated accounting method change. Temporary regulations are effective immediately; they are not given the 30-day period for public comment provided with proposed regulations. Generally, the IRS also issues temporary regulations as proposed regulations, however. Temporary regulations expire three years after issuance and are given the same respect and precedential value as final regulations.

The primary purpose of the regulations is to explain and interpret particular Code sections. Although regulations have not been issued for all Code sections, they have been issued for the great majority. In those cases where regulations exist, they are an important authoritative source on which one can usually rely. Regulations can be classified into three groups: (1) legislative; (2) interpretive; and (3) procedural.

Legislative Regulations. Occasionally, Congress will give specific authorization to the Secretary of the Treasury to issue regulations on a particular Code section. For example, under § 1502, the Secretary is charged with prescribing the regulations for the filing of a consolidated return by an affiliated group of corporations. There are virtually no Code sections governing consolidated returns, and the regulations in effect serve in lieu of the Code. In this case and others where it occurs, the regulation has the force and effect of a law, with the result that a court reviewing the regulation usually will not substitute its judgment for that of the Treasury Department unless the Treasury has clearly abused its discretion.[24]

Interpretative Regulations. Interpretative regulations explain the meaning of a Code section and commit the Treasury and the Internal Revenue Service to a particular position relative to the Code section in question. This type of regulation is binding on the IRS but not on the courts, although it is "a body of experience and informed judgment to which courts and litigants may properly resort for guidance."[25] Interpretive

---

[24]   *Anderson, Clayton & Co. v. U.S.,* 77-2 USTC ¶9727, 40 AFTR2d 77-6102, 562 F.2d 972 (CA-5, 1977), *Cert. den.* at 436 U.S. 944 (USSC, 1978).

[25]   *Skidmore v. Swift and Co.,* 323 U.S. 134 (USSC, 1944).

regulations have considerable authority and normally are invalidated only if they are inconsistent with the Code or are unreasonable.

Procedural Regulations. Procedural regulations cover such areas as the information a taxpayer must supply to the IRS and the internal management and conduct of the IRS in certain matters. Those regulations affecting vital interests of the taxpayers are generally binding on the IRS, and those regulations stating the taxpayer's obligation to file particular forms or other types of information are given the effect of law.

Citation for Regulations. Regulations are arranged in the same sequence as the Code sections they interpret. Thus, a regulation begins with a number that designates the type of tax or administrative, definitional, or procedural matter and is followed by the applicable Code section number. For example, Treasury Regulation Section 1.614-3(f)(5) serves as an illustration of how regulations are cited throughout this text.

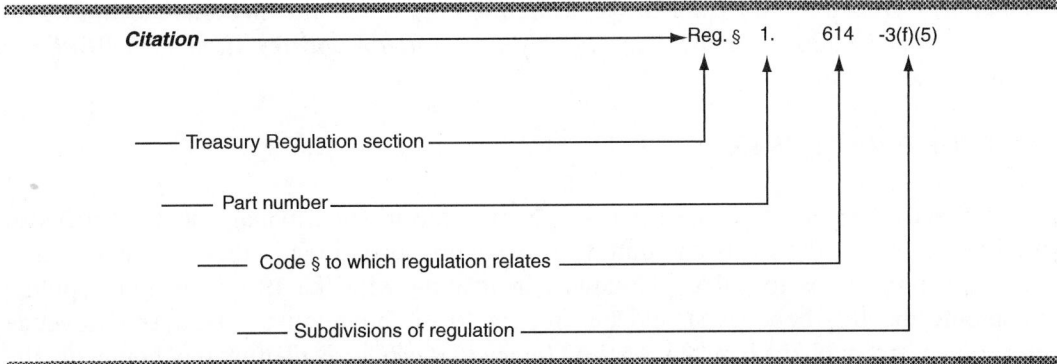

The part number of a Treasury regulation is used to identify the general area covered by the regulation as follows.

Part Number	Law Subject
1	Income Tax
20	Estate Tax
25	Gift Tax
31	Employment Tax
48–49	Excise Tax
301	Procedural Matters

The various subdivisions of a regulation are not necessarily related to a specific subdivision of the Code.

Sometimes the Treasury issues temporary regulations when it is necessary to meet a compelling need. For example, temporary regulations are often issued shortly after enactment of a major change in the tax law. These temporary regulations have the same binding effect as final regulations until they are withdrawn or replaced. Such regulations are cited as Temp. Reg. §.

Temporary regulations should not be confused with proposed regulations. The latter have no force or effect.[26] Nevertheless, proposed regulations provide insight into how the IRS currently interprets a particular Code section. For this reason, they should not be ignored.

---

[26] Federal law (i.e., the Administrative Procedure Act) requires any federal agency, including the Internal Revenue Service, that wishes to adopt a substantive rule to publish the rule in proposed form in order to give interested persons an opportunity to comment. Proposed regulations are issued in compliance with this directive.

REVENUE RULINGS

Revenue rulings also are official interpretations of the Federal tax laws and are issued by the National Office of the IRS. Revenue rulings do not have quite the authority of regulations, however. Regulations are a direct extension of the law-making powers of Congress, whereas revenue rulings are an application of the administrative powers of the Internal Revenue Service. In contrast to rulings, regulations are usually issued only after public hearings and must be approved by the Secretary of the Treasury.

Unlike regulations, revenue rulings are limited to a given set of facts. Taxpayers may rely on revenue rulings in determining the tax consequences of their transactions; however, taxpayers must determine for themselves if the facts of their cases are substantially the same as those set forth in the revenue ruling.

Revenue rulings are published in the weekly issues of the *Internal Revenue Bulletin*. The information contained in the *Internal Revenue Bulletins* (including, among other things, revenue rulings) is accumulated and usually published semiannually in the *Cumulative Bulletin*. The *Cumulative Bulletin* reorganizes the material according to Code section. Citations for the *Internal Revenue Bulletin* and the *Cumulative Bulletin* are illustrated below.

REVENUE PROCEDURES

Revenue procedures are statements reflecting the internal management practices of the IRS that affect the rights and duties of taxpayers. Occasionally they are also used to announce procedures to guide individuals in dealing with the IRS or to make public something the IRS believes should be brought to the attention of taxpayers. Revenue procedures are published in the weekly *Internal Revenue Bulletins* and bound in the *Cumulative Bulletin* along with revenue rulings issued in the same year. The citation system for revenue procedures is the same as for revenue rulings except that the prefix "Rev. Proc." is substituted for "Rev. Rul."

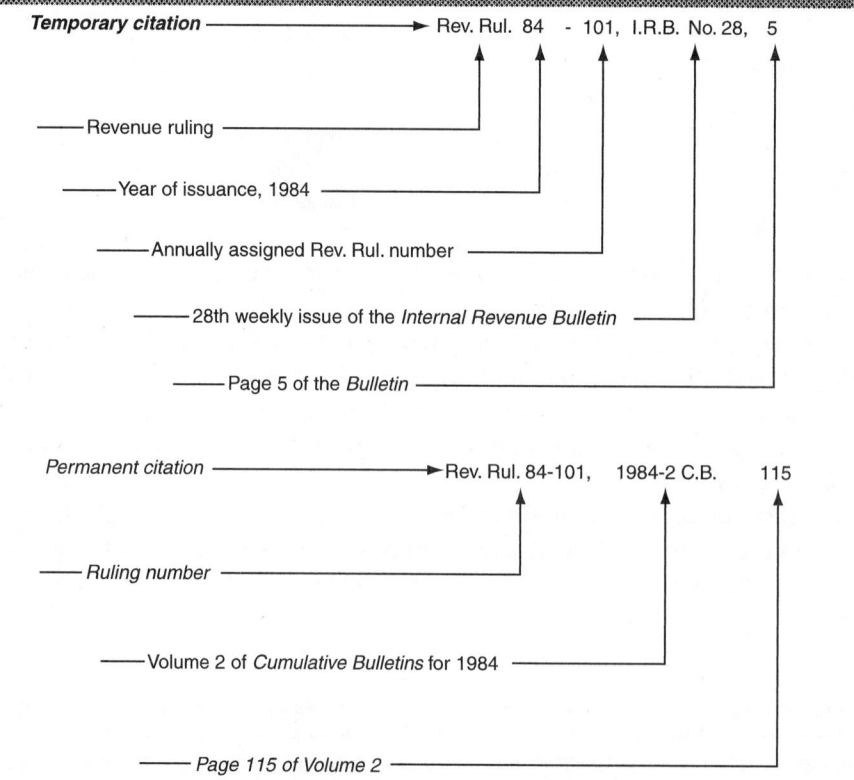

LETTER RULINGS

The term *letter ruling* actually encompasses three different types of rulings: private letter rulings, determination letters, and technical advice memoranda. These items are not published in an official government publication but are available from commercial sources.

Private Letter Ruling. Taxpayers who are in doubt about the tax consequences of a contemplated transaction can ask the National Office of the IRS for a ruling. Generally, the IRS has discretion about whether to rule or not, and it has issued guidelines describing the circumstances under which it will rule.[27]

Unlike revenue rulings, private letter rulings apply only to the particular taxpayer asking for the ruling and are thus not applicable to taxpayers in general. Section 6110(j)(3) specifically states that "unless the Secretary otherwise establishes by regulations, a written determination may not be used or cited as a precedent." Recently, however, the IRS has expanded the list of authorities constituting "substantial" authority for Section 6662 purposes to include private letter rulings. As discussed in the previous section, § 6662 imposes an accuracy-related penalty equal to 20 percent of the underpayment unless the taxpayer can cite "substantial authority" for his or her position.

For those requesting a ruling, the IRS's response might provide insurance against surprises. As a practical matter, a favorable ruling should preclude any controversies with the IRS on an audit of that transaction, at least with respect to the matters addressed in the private letter ruling. During the process of obtaining a private letter ruling, the IRS often recommends changes in a proposed transaction to assist the taxpayer in achieving the tax result he or she wishes. Since 1976 the IRS has made individual private letter rulings publicly available after deleting names and other information that would tend to identify the taxpayer. Private letter rulings are published by both CCH and RIA.

Determination Letter. A determination letter is similar to a private letter ruling, except that it is issued by the office of the local IRS district director, rather than by the National Office. Unlike private letter rulings, determination letters usually relate to completed transactions. Like private letter rulings, they are not published in any official government publication but are available commercially. In most instances, determination letters deal with issues and transactions that are not overtly controversial. Obtaining a determination letter in order to ensure that a pension plan is qualified is a typical use of a determination letter.

Technical Advice Memorandum. A technical advice memorandum ("tech advice") is typically requested by an IRS agent during an audit. The request is normally made to the National Office when the agent has a question that cannot be answered by sources in his or her local office. The technical advice memorandum only applies to the taxpayer for whose audit the technical advice was requested and cannot be relied upon by other taxpayers. Technical advice memoranda are available from private publishers but are not published by the government.

Citations for letter rulings and technical advice follow a multi-digit file number system. IRS Letter Ruling 200434039 serves as an example.

---

[27]   See Rev. Proc. 2004-1, I.R.B. 2004-1 (Appendix D), for a description of the areas in which the IRS has refused to issue advanced rulings. Note, also, that the IRS is required to charge taxpayers a fee for letter rulings, opinion letters, determination letters, and similar requests. The fees range from $50 to $1,000. See § 6591.

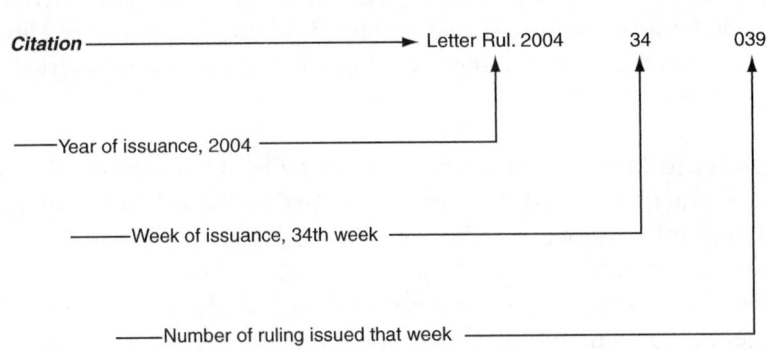

JUDICIAL INTERPRETATIONS

The Congress passes the tax law and the Executive branch of the Federal government enforces and interprets it, but under the American system of checks and balances, it is the Judiciary branch that ultimately determines whether the Executive branch's interpretation is correct. This provides yet another source of tax law—court decisions. It is therefore absolutely essential for the student of tax as well as the tax practitioner to have a grasp of the judicial system of the United States and how tax cases move through this system.

Before litigating a case in court, the taxpayer must have exhausted the administrative remedies available to him or her within the Internal Revenue Service. If the taxpayer has not exhausted his or her administrative remedies, a court will deny a hearing because the claim filed in the court is premature.

All litigation begins in what are referred to as *courts of original jurisdiction*, or *trial courts*, which "try" the case. There are three trial courts: (1) the Tax Court; (2) the U.S. District Court; and (3) the U.S. Court of Federal Claims. Note that the taxpayer may select any one (and only one) of these three courts to hear the case. If the taxpayer or government disagrees with the decision by the trial court, it has the right to appeal to either the U.S. Court of Appeals or the U.S. Court of Appeals for the Federal Circuit, whichever is appropriate in the particular case. If a litigating party is dissatisfied with the decision by the appellate court, it may ask for review by the Supreme Court, but this is rarely granted. The judicial system is illustrated and discussed on the following page.

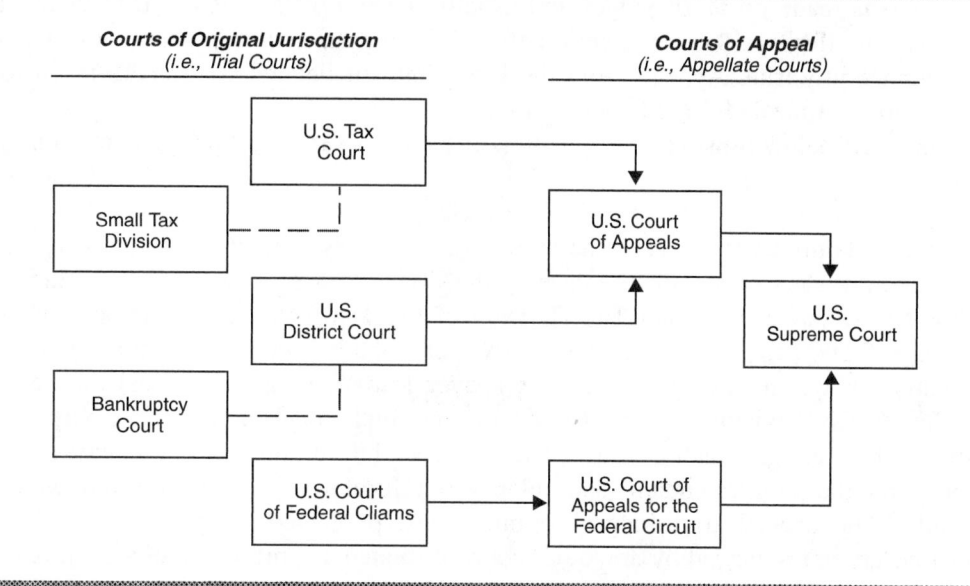

| Courts of Original Jurisdiction (i.e., Trial Courts) | Courts of Appeal (i.e., Appellate Courts) |

TRIAL COURTS

U.S. Tax Court. The Tax Court, as its name suggests, specializes in tax matters and hears no other types of cases. The judges on the court are especially skilled in taxation. Usually, prior to being selected as a judge by the President, the individual was a practitioner or IRS official who was noted for his or her expertise. This Court is composed of 19 judges who "ride circuit" throughout the United States (i.e., they travel and hear cases in various parts of the country). Occasionally, the full Tax Court hears a case, but most cases are heard by a single judge who submits his or her opinion to the chief judge, who then decides whether the full court should review the decision.

Besides its expertise in tax matters, two other characteristics of the Tax Court should be noted. Perhaps the most important feature of the Tax Court is that the taxpayer does not pay the alleged tax deficiency before bringing his or her action before the court. The second facet of the Tax Court that bears mentioning is that a trial by jury is not available.

U.S. District Courts. For purposes of the Federal judicial system, the United States is divided into 11 geographic areas called circuits, which are subdivided into districts. For example, the second circuit, which is composed of Vermont, Connecticut, and New York, contains the District Court for the Southern District of New York, which covers parts of New York City. Other districts may include very large areas, such as the District Court for the State of Arizona, which covers the entire state. A taxpayer may take a case into the District Court for the district in which he or she resides, but only after the disputed tax deficiency has been paid. The taxpayer then sues the IRS for a refund of the disputed amount. The District Court is a court of general jurisdiction and hears many types of cases in addition to tax cases. This is the only court in which the taxpayer may obtain a jury trial. The jury decides matters of fact but not matters of law. However, even in issues of fact, the judge may, and occasionally does, disregard the jury's decision.

U.S. Court of Federal Claims. The United States Court of Federal Claims hears cases involving certain claims against the Federal government, including tax refunds. The Court is made up of 16 judges and usually meets in Washington, D.C. A taxpayer must pay the disputed tax deficiency before bringing an action in this court, and may not obtain a jury trial. Appeals from the U.S. Court of Federal Claims are taken to the U.S. Court of Appeals for the Federal Circuit.

The chart below illustrates the position of the taxpayer in bringing an action in these courts.

Small Claims Cases. When the amount of a tax assessment is relatively small, the taxpayer may elect to submit the case to the division of the Tax Court hearing small claims cases, called the Small Tax Division of the Tax Court. If the amount of tax at issue is $50,000 per year or less, the taxpayer can obtain a decision with a minimum of formality, delay, and expense; but the taxpayer loses the right to appeal the decision. The Small Tax Division is administered by the chief judge of the Tax Court, who is authorized to assign small claims cases to special trial judges. These cases receive priority on the trial calendars, and relatively informal rules are followed whenever possible. The special trial judges' opinions are published on these cases, but the decisions are not reviewed by any other court or treated as precedents in any other case.

Bankruptcy Court. Under limited circumstances, it is possible for the bankruptcy court to have jurisdiction over tax matters. The filing of a bankruptcy petition prevents creditors, including the IRS, from taking action against a taxpayer, including the filing of a proceeding before the Tax Court if a notice of deficiency is sent after the filing of a petition in bankruptcy. In such cases, a tax claim may be determined by the bankruptcy court.

	U.S. Tax Court	U.S. District Court	U.S. Court of Federal Claims
Jurisdiction	Nationwide	Specific district in which court is sitting	Nationwide
Subject Matter	Tax cases only	Many different types of cases, both criminal and civil	Claims against the Federal government, including tax refunds
Payment of Contested Amount	Taxpayer does not pay deficiency, but files suit against IRS Commissioner to stop collection of tax	Taxpayer pays alleged deficiency and then files suit against the U.S. government for refund	Taxpayer pays alleged deficiency and then files suit against the U.S. government for refund
Availability of Jury Trial	No	Yes	No
Appeal Taken to	U.S. Court of Appeals	U.S. Court of Appeals	U.S. Court of Appeals for the Federal Circuit
Number of Courts	1	95	1
Number of Judges per Court	19	1	16

APPELLATE COURTS

U.S. Courts of Appeals. Which appellate court is appropriate depends on which trial court hears the case. Taxpayer or government appeals from the District Courts and the Tax Court are taken to the U.S. Court of Appeals that has jurisdiction over the court in which the taxpayer lives. Appeals from the U.S. Court of Federal Claims are taken to the U.S. Court of Appeals for the Federal Circuit, which has the same powers and jurisdictions as any of the other Courts of Appeals except that it only hears specialized appeals. Courts of Appeals are national courts of appellate jurisdiction. With the exceptions of the Court of Appeals for the Federal Circuit and the Court of Appeals for the District of Columbia, these appellate courts are assigned various geographic areas of jurisdiction as follows:

Court of Appeals for the Federal Circuit (CA-FC)	District of Columbia Circuit (CA-DC)	First Circuit (CA-1)		
U.S. Court of Federal Claims	District of Columbia	Maine Massachusetts New Hampshire Puerto Rico Rhode Island		

Second Circuit (CA-2)	Third Circuit (CA-3)	Fourth Circuit (CA-4)	Fifth Circuit (CA-5)	Sixth Circuit (CA-6)
Connecticut New York Vermont	Delaware New Jersey Pennsylvania Virgin Islands	Maryland N. Carolina S. Carolina Virginia W. Virginia	Louisiana Mississippi Texas	Kentucky Michigan Ohio Tennessee

Seventh Circuit (CA-7)	Eighth Circuit (CA-8)	Ninth Circuit (CA-9)	Tenth Circuit (CA-10)	Eleventh Circuit (CA-11)
Illinois Indiana Wisconsin	Arkansas Iowa Minnesota Missouri Nebraska N. Dakota S. Dakota	Alaska Arizona California Guam Hawaii Idaho Montana Nevada Oregon Washington	Colorado New Mexico Kansas Oklahoma Utah Wyoming	Alabama Florida Georgia

Taxpayers may appeal to the Courts of Appeal as a matter of right, and the Courts must hear their cases. Very often, however, the expense of such an appeal deters many from proceeding with an appeal. Appellate courts review the record of the trial court to determine whether the lower court completed its responsibility of fact finding and applied the proper law in arriving at its decision.

District Courts must follow the decision of the Appeals Court for the circuit in which they are located. For instance, the District Court in the Eastern District of Missouri must follow the decision of the Eighth Circuit Court of Appeals because Missouri is in the Eighth Circuit. If the Eighth Circuit has not rendered a decision on the particular issue involved, then the District Court may make its own decision or follow the decision in another Circuit.

The Tax Court is a national court with jurisdiction throughout the entire country. Prior to 1970, the Tax Court considered itself independent and indicated that it would not be bound by the decisions of the Circuit Court to which its decision would be appealed. In *Golsen*,[28] however, the Tax Court reversed its position. Under the *Golsen rule*, the Tax Court now follows the decisions of the Circuit Court to which a particular case would be appealed. Even if the Tax Court disagrees with a Circuit Court's view, it will decide based upon the Circuit Court's view. On the other hand, if a similar case arises in the jurisdiction of another Circuit Court that has not yet ruled on the same issue, the Tax Court will follow its own view, despite its earlier decision following a contrary Circuit Court decision.

The U.S. Courts of Appeals generally sit in panels of three judges, although the entire court may sit in particularly important cases. They may reach a decision that affirms the lower court or that reverses the lower court. Additionally, the Appellate Court could send the case back to the lower court (remand the case) for another trial or for rehearing on another point not previously covered. It is possible for the Appellate Court to affirm the decision of the lower court on one particular issue and reverse it on another.

Generally, only one judge writes a decision for the Appeals Court, although in some cases no decision is written and an order is simply made. Such an order might hold that the lower court is sustained, or that the lower court's decision is reversed as being inconsistent with one of the Appellate Court's decisions. Sometimes other judges (besides the one assigned to write the opinion) will write additional opinions agreeing with (concurring opinion) or disagreeing with (dissenting opinion) the majority opinion. These opinions often contain valuable insights into the law controlling the case, and often set the ground for a change in the court's opinion at a later date.

U.S. Supreme Court. The U.S. Supreme Court is the highest court of the land. No one has a *right* to be heard by this Court. It only accepts cases it wishes to hear, and generally those involve issues that the Court feels are of national importance. The Supreme Court generally hears very few tax cases. Consequently, taxpayers desiring a review of their trial court decision find it solely at the Court of Appeals. Technically, cases are submitted to the Supreme Court through a request process known as the "Writ of Certiorari." If the Supreme Court decides to hear the case, it grants the Writ of Certiorari; if it decides not to hear the case, it denies the Writ of Certiorari. It is important to note that there is another path to review by the U.S. Supreme Court—*by appeal*—as opposed to by Writ of Certiorari. This "review by appeal" may be available when a U.S. Court of Appeals has held that a state statute is in conflict with the laws or treaties of the United States. The "review by appeal" may also be available when the highest court in a state has decided a case on grounds that a Federal statute or treaty is invalid, or when the state court has held a state statute valid despite the claim of the losing party that the statute is in conflict with the U.S. Constitution or a Federal law. Review by the U.S. Supreme Court is still discretionary, but a Writ of Certiorari is not involved.

The Supreme Court, like the Courts of Appeals, does not conduct another trial. Its responsibility is to review the record and determine whether or not the trial court

---

[28] *Jack E. Golsen.* 54 T.C. 742 (1970).

correctly applied the law in deciding the case. The Supreme Court also reviews the decision of the Court of Appeals to determine if the court used the correct reasoning.

In general, the Supreme Court hears cases only when one or more of the following conditions apply:

1. When the Court of Appeals has not used accepted or usual methods of judicial procedure or has sanctioned an unusual method by the trial court;

2. When a Court of Appeals has settled an important question of Federal law and the Supreme Court feels such an important question should have one more review by the most prestigious court of the nation;

3. When a decision of a Court of Appeals is in apparent conflict with a decision of the Supreme Court;

4. When two or more Courts of Appeals are in conflict on an issue; or

5. When the Supreme Court has already decided an issue but feels that the issue should be looked at again, possibly to reverse its previous decision.

CASE CITATION

Tax Court Decisions. Prior to 1943, the Tax Court was called the Board of Tax Appeals. The decisions of the Board of Tax Appeals were published as the *United States Board of Tax Appeals Reports* (BTA). Board of Tax Appeals cases are cited as follows:

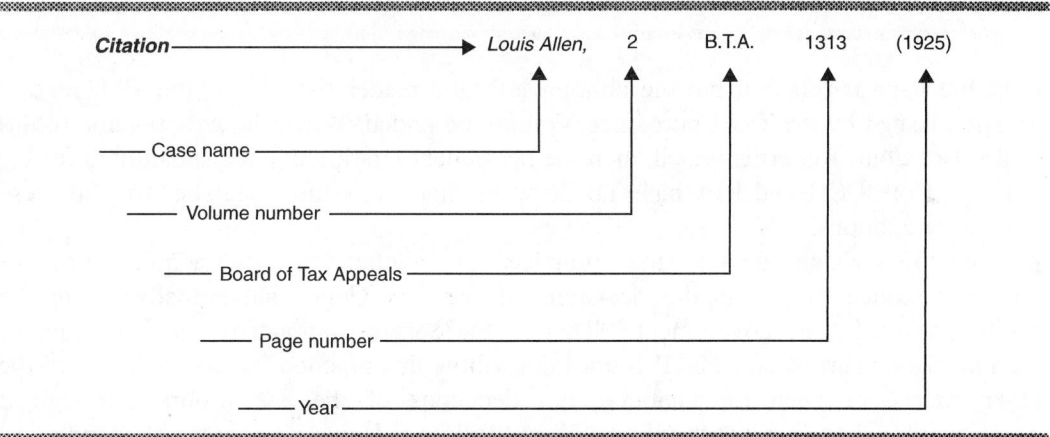

The Tax Court renders two different types or decisions with two different citation systems: regular decisions and memorandum decisions.

Tax Court *regular* decisions deal with new issues that the court has not yet resolved. In contrast, decisions that deal only with the application of already established principles of law are called *memorandum* decisions. The United States government publishes regular decisions in *United States Tax Court Reports* (T.C.). Tax Court regular decisions are cited as follows:

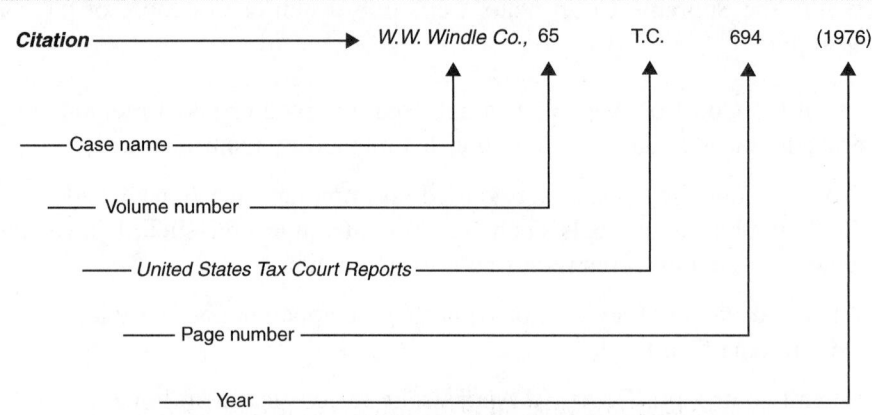

Like revenue rulings and the *Cumulative Bulletins*, there is a time lag between the date a Tax Court regular decision is issued and the date it is bound in a *U.S. Tax Court Report* volume. In this case, the citation appears as follows:

Temporary Citation:

W.W. Windle Co., 65 T.C. _____ , No. 79(1976).

Here the page is left out, but the citation tells the reader that this is the 79th regular decision issued by the Tax Court since Volume 64 ended. When the new volume (65th) of the Tax Court Report is issued, then the permanent citation may be substituted for the old one. Both CCH and RIA have tax services that allow the researcher to find these temporary citations.

The IRS has adopted the practice of announcing its acquiescence or nonacquiescence to the regular decisions of the Tax Court that are adverse to the position taken by the government.[29] That is, the Service announces whether it agrees with the Tax Court or not. The IRS does not follow this practice for the decisions of the other courts, or even for memorandum decisions of the Tax Court, although it occasionally announces that it will or will not follow a decision of another Federal court with a similar set of facts. The IRS may withdraw its acquiescence or nonacquiescence at any time and may do so even retroactively. Acquiescences and nonacquiescences are published in the weekly *Internal Revenue Bulletins* and the *Cumulative Bulletins*.

Although the U.S. government publishes the Tax Court's regular decisions, it does not publish memorandum decisions. However, both CCH and RIA publish them. CCH publishes the memorandum decisions under the title *Tax Court Memorandum Decisions* (TCM), while RIA publishes these decisions as *Tax Court Reporter and Memorandum Decisions* (T.C. Memo). In citing Tax Court memorandum decisions, some authors prefer to use both the RIA and the CCH citations for their cases.

In an effort to provide the reader the greatest latitude of research sources, this dual citation policy has been adopted for this text. The case of *Alan K. Minor* serves as an example of the dual citation of Tax Court memorandum decisions.

---

[29] The IRS's acquiescence is symbolized by "A" or "Acq." and its nonacquiescence by "NA" or "Nonacq."

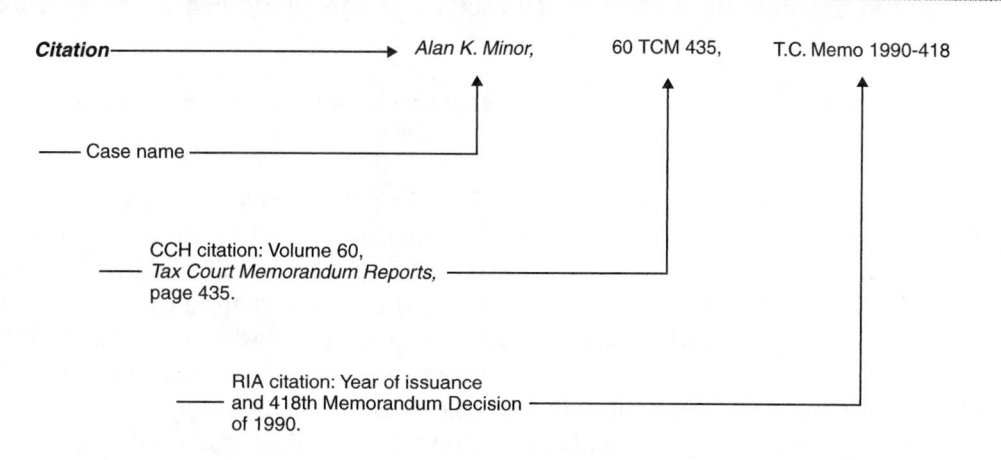

Citations for U.S. District Court, Court of Appeals, and Claims Court. Commerce Clearing House, Research Institute of America, and West Publishing Company all publish decisions of the District Courts, Courts of Appeals, and the Court of Federal Claims. When available, all three citations of a case are provided in this text.[30] CCH publishes the decisions of these courts in its *U.S. Tax Cases* (USTC—not to be confused with the *U.S. Tax Court Reports*) volumes, and RIA offers these decisions in its *American Federal Tax Reports* (AFTR) series.[31] West Publishing Company reports these decisions in either its *Federal Supplement Series* (F. Supp.—District Court decisions), or its *Federal Second Series* (F.2d—Court of Federal Claims and Courts of Appeals decisions).

The citation of the U.S. District Court decision of *Cam F. Dowell, Jr. v. U.S.* is illustrated for each of the three publishing companies as follows:

CCH Citation:

> *Cam F. Dowell, Jr. v. U.S.*, 74-1 USTC ¶9243, (D.Ct. Tx., 1974).

Interpretation: This case is reported in the first volume of the *U.S. Tax Cases*, published by CCH for calendar year 1974 (74-1), located at paragraph (¶) 9243, and is a decision rendered in 1974 by a U.S. District Court located in Texas (Tx.).

RIA Citation:

> *Cam F. Dowell, Jr. v. U.S.*, 33 AFTR2d 74-739, (D.Ct. Tx., 1974).

Interpretation: Reported in the 33rd volume of the second series of the *American Federal Tax Reports* (AFTR2d), published by RIA for 1974, and located at page 739.

West Citation:

> *Cam F. Dowell, Jr. v. U.S.*, 370 F.Supp. 69 (D.Ct. Tx., 1974).

---

[30] When all three publishers have not printed the case, only the citations to the cases published are provided.

[31] Until the acquisition of Prentice Hall by RIA, Prentice Hall published cases under its own name. Accordingly, researchers needing cases from before 1993 will often encounter Prentice Hall as publisher of these reporters now carried under RIA's name.

Interpretation: Located in the 370th volume of the *Federal Supplement Series* (F.Supp), published by West Publishing Company, and located at page 69.

The multiple citation of the U.S. District Court case illustrated above appears as follows:

Cam F. Dowell, Jr. v. U.S., 74-1 USTC ¶9243, 33 AFTR2d 74-739, 370 F.Supp. 69 (D.Ct. Tx., 1974).

Decisions of the Court of Federal Claims (Ct. Cls.), the Courts of Appeals (e.g., CA-1, CA-2, etc.), and the Supreme Court (USSC) are published by CCH and RIA in the same reporting source as District Court decisions (i.e., USTCs and AFTRs). Court of Federal Claims and Court of Appeals decisions are reported by West Publishing Company in its *Federal Second Series* (F.2d). Supreme Court decisions are published by West Publishing Company in its *Supreme Court Reports* (S.Ct.), and the U.S. Government Printing Office publishes Supreme Court decisions in its *Supreme Court Reports* (U.S.).

An example of the multiple citation of a Court of Appeals decision follows:

Citation:

Millar v. Comm., 78-2 USTC ¶9514, 42 AFTR2d 78-5246, 577 F.2d 212 (CA-3, 1978).

A multiple citation of a Supreme Court decision would appear as follows:

Citation:

Fausner v. Comm., 73-2 USTC ¶9515, 32 AFTR2d 73-5202, 413 U.S. 838 (USSC, 1973).

Note that in each of the citations above, the designation "Commissioner of the Internal Revenue Service" is simply abbreviated to "Comm." In some instances, the IRS or U.S. is substituted for Comm., and older cases used the Commissioner's name. For example, in *Gregory v. Helvering*, 293 U.S. 465 (USSC, 1935), Mr. Helvering was the Commissioner of the Internal Revenue Service at the time the case was brought to the Court. Also note that the citation contains a reference to the Appellate Court rendering the decision (i.e., CA-3, or USSC) and the year of issuance.

Exhibits 2-3 and 2-4 summarize the sources of case citations from various reporter services.

EXHIBIT 2-3
Reporters of Tax Court Decisions

Reporter	Abbr.	Type	Publisher
Tax Court Reports	TC	Regular	Government Printing Office
Tax Court Memorandum Decisions	TCM	Memorandum	Commerce Clearing House
Tax Court Memorandum Decisions	TC Memo	Memorandum	Research Institute of America

EXHIBIT 2-4
Reporters of Decisions Other Than Tax Court

Reporter	Abbr.	Courts Reported	Publisher
Supreme Court Reports	U.S.	Supreme Court	Government Printing Office
Supreme Court Reporter	S.Ct	Supreme Court	West Publishing
Federal Supplement	F.Supp	District Courts	West Publishing
Federal Reporter	F. F.2d	Cts. of Appeals and Ct. of Fed. Cls.	West Publishing
American Federal Tax Reports	AFTR AFTR2d	District Courts Ct. of Fed. Cls. Cts. of Appeals, and Supreme Ct.	Research Institute of America
United States Tax Cases	USTC	Same as AFTR and AFTR2d	Commerce Clearing House

SECONDARY SOURCES

The importance of understanding the sources discussed thus far stems from their role in the taxation process. As mentioned earlier, the statutory law and its official interpretations constitute the legal authorities that set forth the tax consequences for a particular set of facts. These legal authorities, sometimes referred to as *primary authorities*, must be distinguished from so-called *secondary sources* or *secondary authorities*. The secondary sources of tax information consist mainly of books, periodicals, articles, newsletters, and editorial judgments in tax services. When working with the tax law, it must be recognized that secondary sources are unofficial interpretations—mere opinions—that have no legal authority.

Although secondary sources should not be used as the supporting authority for a particular tax treatment (except as a supplement to primary authority or in cases where primary authority is absent), they are an indispensable aid when seeking an understanding of the tax law. Several of these secondary materials are discussed briefly below.

TAX SERVICES

"Tax service" is the name given to a set of organized materials that contains a vast quantity of tax-related information organized so as to make it useful and accessible to tax practitioners. In general, a tax service is a paper or electronic compilation of some or all of the following: the Code, regulations, court decisions, IRS releases, and explanations of these primary authorities by the editors. As the listing of contents suggests, a tax service is invaluable since it contains, all in one place, a wealth of tax information, including both primary and secondary sources. Most tax services are available on CD-ROM or the Internet, or both. Moreover, these materials are updated constantly to reflect current developments—an extremely important feature given the dynamic nature of tax law. The major tax services are

Publisher	Name of Publications
Commerce Clearing House	Standard Federal Tax Reporter—Income Taxes
Research Institute of America	United States Tax Reporter and Federal Tax Coordinator—2nd Series
The Bureau of National Affairs, Inc.	Tax Management Portfolios—U.S. Income

The widespread use of computers has found applications in tax research. For example, *LEXIS* is a computerized data base that a user can access through his or her personal computer. The *LEXIS* data base contains almost all information available in an extensive tax library. Suppliers of tax services currently make computer-based tax liabraries available to their customers. Undoubtedly computers are basic to tax research.

Commerce Clearing House, Research Institute of America, and other publishers issue weekly summaries of important cases and other tax developments that many practitioners and scholars find helpful in keeping current with developments in the tax field. The Bureau of National Affairs publishes the *Daily Tax Bulletin*, a comprehensive daily journal of late-breaking tax news that often reprints entire cases or regulations of particular importance. *Tax Notes*, published by Tax Analysts, is a weekly publication addressing legislative and judicial developments in the tax field. *Tax Notes* is particularly helpful in following the progress of tax legislation through the legislative process.

TAX PERIODICALS

In addition to these services, there are a number of quality publications (usually published monthly) that contain articles on a variety of important tax topics. These publications are very helpful when new tax acts are passed, because they often contain clear, concise summaries of the new law in a readable format. In addition, they serve to convey new planning opportunities and relay the latest IRS and judicial developments in many important sub-specialities of the tax profession. Some of the leading periodicals include the following:

Estate Planning	Taxes—The Tax Magazine
Journal of Corporate Taxation	The International Tax Journal
Journal of Partnership Taxation	The Review of Taxation of Individuals
Journal of Real Estate Taxation	The Tax Advisor
Journal of Taxation	The Tax Executive
Tax Law Journal	The Tax Lawyer
Tax Law Review	Trusts and Estates

In addition to these publications, many law journals contain excellent articles on tax subjects.

Several indexes exist that may be used to locate a journal article. Through the use of a subject index, author index, and in some instances a Code section index, articles dealing with a particular topic may be found. Three of these indexes are

Title	Publisher
Index to Federal Tax Articles	Warren, Gorham and Lamont
Federal Tax Articles	Commerce Clearing House
The Accountant's Index	American Institute of Certified Public Accountants

In addition, the *United States Tax Reporter*, published by RIA, contains a section entitled "Index to Tax Articles."

TAX RESEARCH

Having introduced the sources of tax law, the remainder of this chapter is devoted to working with the law—or more specifically, the art of tax research. Tax research may be defined as the process used to ascertain the optimal answer to a question with tax implications. Although there is no perfect technique for researching a question, the following approach normally is used:

1. Obtain all of the facts

2. Diagnose the problem from the facts

3. Locate the authorities

4. Evaluate the authorities

5. Derive the solution and possible alternative solutions

6. Communicate the answer

Each of these steps is discussed below.

OBTAINING THE FACTS

Before discussing the importance of obtaining all the facts, the distinction between closed fact research and open- or controlled-fact research should be noted. If the research relates to a problem with transactions that are complete, it is referred to as closed-fact research and normally falls within the realm of tax practice known as tax compliance. On the other hand, if the research relates to contemplated transactions, it is called controlled- or open-fact research and is an integral part of tax planning.

In researching a closed-fact problem, the first step is gathering all of the facts. Unfortunately, it is difficult to obtain all relevant facts upon first inquiry. This is true because it is essentially impossible to understand the law so thoroughly that all of the proper questions can be asked before the research task begins. After the general area of the problem is identified and research has begun, it usually becomes apparent that more facts must be obtained before an answer can be derived. Consequently, additional inquiries must be made until all facts necessary for a solution are acquired.

DIAGNOSING THE ISSUE

Once the initial set of facts is gathered, the tax issue or question must be identified. Most tax problems involve very basic questions such as these:

1. Does the taxpayer have gross income that must be recognized?

2. Is the taxpayer entitled to a deduction?

3. Is the taxpayer entitled to a credit?

4. In what period is the gross income, deduction, or credit reported?

5. What amount of gross income, deduction, or credit must be reported?

As research progresses, however, such fundamental questions can be answered only after more specific issues have been resolved.

Example 5. R's employer owns a home in which R lives. The basic question that must be asked is whether use of the home constitutes income to R. After consulting the various tax sources, it can be determined that § 61 requires virtually all benefits to be included in income unless another provision specifically grants an exclusion. In this case, § 119 allows a taxpayer to exclude the value employer-provided of housing if the housing is on the employer's premises, the lodging is furnished for the convenience of the employer, and the employee is required by the employer to accept the housing. Due to the additional research, three more specific questions must be asked:

1. Is the home on the employer's premises?

2. Is the home provided for the employer's convenience?

3. Is R required to live in the home?

As the above example suggests, diagnosing the problem requires a continuing refinement of the questions until the critical issue is identified. The refinement that occurs results from the awareness that is gained through reading and rereading the primary and secondary authorities.

Example 6. Assume the same facts as in *Example 5*. After determining that one of the issues concerns whether R's home is on the business premises, a second inquiry is made of R concerning the location of his residence. (Note that as the research progresses, additional facts must be gathered.) According to R, the house is located in a suburb, 25 miles from his employer's downtown office. However, the house is owned by the employer, and hence R suggests that he lives on the employer's premises. He also explains that he often brings work home and frequently entertains clients in his home. Having uncovered this information, the primary authorities are reexamined. Upon review, it is determined that in *Charles N. Anderson*,[32] the court indicated that an employee would be considered on the business premises if the employee performed a significant portion of his duties at the place of lodging. Again the question must be refined to ask: Do R's work and entertainment activities in the home constitute a significant portion of his duties?

LOCATING THE AUTHORITIES

Identification of the critical issue presented by any tax question begins by first locating, then reading and studying the appropriate authority. Locating the authority is ordinarily done using a tax service. With the issue stated in general terms, the subject is found in the index volume and the location is determined. At this point, the appropriate Code sections, regulations, and editorial commentary may be perused to determine their applicability to the question.

Example 7. In the case of R above, the problem stated in general terms concerns income. Using an index, the key word, *income*, could be located and a reference to information concerning the income aspects of lodging would be given.

Once information relating to the issue is identified, the authoritative materials must be read. That is, the appropriate Code sections, regulations, rulings, and cases must be examined and studied to determine how they relate to the question. As suggested above, this process normally results in refinement of the question, which in turn may require acquisition of additional facts.

---

[32] 67-1 USTC ¶9136, 19 AFTR2d 318, 371 F.2d 59 (CA-6, 1966).

EVALUATING THE AUTHORITY

After the various authorities have been identified and it has been *verified* that they are applicable, their value must be appraised. This evaluation process, as will become clear below, primarily involves appraisal of court decisions and revenue rulings.

The Code. The Internal Revenue Code is the final authority on most tax issues since it is the Federal tax law as passed by Congress. Only the courts can offset this authority by declaring part of the law unconstitutional, and this happens rarely. Most of the time, however, the Code itself is only of partial help. It is written in a style that is not always easy to understand, and it contains no examples of its application. Accordingly, to the extent the Code can be understood as clearly applicable, no stronger authority exists, except possibly a treaty. But in most cases, the Code cannot be used without further support.

Treasury Regulations. As previously discussed, the regulations are used to expand and explain the Code. Because Congress has given its authority to make laws to the Executive branch's administrative agency—the Treasury—the regulations that are produced are a very strong source of authority, second only to the Code itself. Normally, the major issue when a regulation is under scrutiny by a Court is whether the regulation is consistent with the Code. If the regulations are inconsistent, the Court will not hesitate to invalidate them.

Judicial Authority. The value of a court decision depends on numerous factors. On appraising a decision, the most crucial determination concerns whether the outcome is consistent with other decisions on the same issue. In other words, consideration must be given to how other decisions have evaluated the one in question. An invaluable tool in determining the validity of a case is a *citator*. A tax citator is a volume containing an alphabetical listing of virtually all tax cases. After the name of each case, there is a record of other decisions that have cited (in the text of their facts and opinions) the first case.

> **Example 8.** Assume the same facts as in *Example 6*. Examination of the *Anderson* case in a citator reveals that it has been cited by courts in other decisions numerous times. For example, two cases in which the *Anderson* decision was discussed are *U.S. Jr. Chamber of Commerce*[33] and *Jan J. Wexler*.[34]

It is important to note that tax citators often use abbreviations for subsequent case history. For example, the abbreviations *aff'g* and *aff'd* mean "affirming" and "affirmed" and indicate that an appeals court has upheld the decision in question. Similarly, *rev'g* and *rev'd* mean "reversing" and "reversed" and indicate that a trial court's decision was overturned. Finally, *rem'g* and *rem'd* mean "remanding" and "remanded" and indicate that the case has been sent back to a lower court for reconsideration.

The validity of a particular decision may be assessed by examining how the subsequent cases viewed the cited decision. For example, subsequent cases may have agreed or disagreed with the decision in question, or distinguished the facts of the cited case from those examined in a later case.

Another important factor that must be considered in evaluating a court decision is the level of the court that issued it. Decisions issued by trial courts have less value than those issued by appellate courts. And, of course, decisions of the Supreme Court are the ultimate authority.

---

[33] 64-2 USTC ¶9637, 14 AFTR2d 5223, 334 F.2d 660 (Ct. Cls., 1964).

[34] 75-1 USTC ¶9235, 35 AFTR2d 75-550, 507 F.2d 842 (CA-6, 1975).

A court decision's value rises appreciably if the IRS agrees with its result. As discussed earlier, the IRS usually indicates whether it acquiesces or does not acquiesce to regular Tax Court decisions. The position of the Service may also be published in a revenue ruling.

Rulings. The significance of revenue rulings lies in the fact that they reflect current IRS policy. Since agents of the IRS are usually reluctant to vary from that policy, revenue rulings carry considerable weight.

Revenue rulings are often evaluated in court decisions. Thus, a tax service should be used to determine whether relevant rulings have been considered in any decisions. By examining the Court's view of the ruling, possible flaws may be discovered.

Private letter rulings issued to the taxpayer must be followed for that taxpayer by the IRS as long as the transaction is carried out in the manner initially approved. Variation from the facts on which the ruling was based permits the Service to revise its position. As mentioned earlier, a private letter ruling applies only to the particular taxpayer to whom it was issued. However, such a ruling should prove helpful to any other taxpayer faced with a substantially identical fact pattern.

DERIVING THE SOLUTION

Once all the relevant authorities have been evaluated, a conclusion must be drawn. Before deriving the final answer or answers, however, an important caveat is warranted: the researcher must ensure that the research reflects all current developments. The new matters section of a tax service can aid in this regard. The new matters section updates the textual discussion with any late-breaking developments. For instance, the section will contain any new cases, regulations, or pronouncements of the Internal Revenue Service that may bear on the discussion of the topic covered in the main text.

COMMUNICATING THE FINDINGS

The final product of the research effort is a memorandum recording the research and a letter to the interested parties. Although many formats are suitable for the memorandum, one technique typically used is structured as follows:

1. Description of the facts

2. Statement of the issues or questions researched

3. Report of the conclusions (brief answers to the research questions)

4. Discussion of the rationale and authorities that support the conclusions

5. Summary of the authorities consulted in the research

A good tax memorandum is essential. If the research findings are not communicated intelligently and effectively, the entire research effort is wasted.

PROBLEM MATERIALS

DISCUSSION QUESTIONS

2-1 *Taxpayer Penalties.* In reviewing his last year's return, T noticed that he had inadvertently deducted the entire cost of a new air-conditioning system. Such cost should have been capitalized and depreciated.

    a. T wants to know what penalties, if any, might be assessed if his return is audited and the IRS uncovers his mistake.

    b. What should T do?

2-2 *Tax Positions.* R operates a small accounting practice in Columbus. While preparing the return for his long-time client C, he found out that C wants to deduct the cost of lawn care for her home. C is a landscape architect who recently started using a room at her home as an office. She feels that this is clearly a business expense. During the interview she seemed to have a point. "What if my clients came to my house and the yard was less than picture perfect? It would kill my business," she explained. R has reviewed the proposed regulations on the home office deduction, and they specifically state that lawn care is not deductible. Nevertheless, he understands C's point. R just cannot say no, and he is thinking about preparing the return and deducting a portion of lawn care allocable to C's home office.

    a. Assume the position is erroneous and is not disclosed. Will C be subject to any penalty? Explain.

    b. Assume the position is erroneous and is disclosed. Will C be subject to any penalty? Explain.

2-3 *Avoiding Preparer Penalties.* H recently quit a national public accounting firm and purchased the practice of a local accountant. Her first busy season with this new set of clients has been eye-opening. Some of the taxpayers have been taking very questionable positions on certain recurring items. Somewhat paranoid, H is now quite concerned about incurring penalties. What can she do to guard against possible preparer penalties?

2-4 *Knowledge of Error.* Last March, P put the finishing touches on the tax return of one of his most prized clients, Great Buy Corporation. When preparing the monthly financial statement for June, P noticed that $30,000 of sales somehow got left off of the return. What should P do?

2-5 *Knowledge of Error.* This year P got a new client from the firm down the street, Dewey, Cheatham and Howe. After reviewing the client's prior year return, he found, as he had expected, an error in the way Dewey had computed depreciation. What should P do?

2-6 *Making a New Tax Law.* Describe the Congressional process of making a tax bill into final law.

2-7 *Legislative vs. Interpretative Regulations.* Explain the difference between a legislative Treasury Regulation and an interpretative Regulation.

2-8 *Proposed vs. Final Regulations.* Distinguish between proposed and final Regulations. How would either type of Regulation involving Code § 704 be cited?

2-9 *Revenue Rulings and Revenue Procedures.* Distinguish between a Revenue Ruling and a Revenue Procedure. Where can either be found in printed form?

2-10 *Private vs. Published Rulings.* Distinguish between a private letter ruling and a Revenue Ruling. Under what circumstances would a taxpayer prefer to rely on either of these sources?

2-11 *Technical Advice Memoranda.* What are Technical Advice Memoranda? Under what circumstances are they issued?

2-12 *Trial Courts.* Describe the trial courts that hear tax cases. What are the advantages or disadvantages of litigating a tax issue in each of these courts?

2-13 *The Appeals Process.* A taxpayer living in Indiana has exhausted her appeals within the IRS. If she chooses to litigate her case, trace the appeals process assuming she begins her effort in each of the following trial courts:
  a. The U.S. Court of Federal Claims
  b. The U.S. District Court
  c. The U.S. Tax Court
  d. The Small Tax Division of the U.S. Tax Court

2-14 *Tax Court Decisions.* Distinguish between a Regular Tax Court decision and a Memorandum decision.

2-15 *Authority of Tax Law Sources.* Assuming that you have discovered favorable support for your position taken in a controversy with an IRS agent in each of the sources listed below, indicate how you would use these authoritative sources in your discussion with the agent.

  a. A decision of the U.S. District Court having jurisdiction over your case if litigated
  b. Treasury Regulation
  c. The Internal Revenue Code
  d. A decision of the Supreme Court
  e. A decision of the Small Claims Court
  f. A decision of the U.S. Tax Court
  g. A private letter ruling issued to another taxpayer
  h. A Revenue Ruling
  i. A tax article in a leading periodical

2-16 *Tax Services.* What materials are generally found in leading tax services? Which does your library have?

❓ YOU MAKE THE CALL

2-17 T is the owner of a small CPA firm that has developed a very good auditing and tax practice over the years. Recently, while visiting the home of S, his best client (revenues of about $15,000 annually for audit and tax services), T learned some very disturbing information about S's business practices. During a tour of her home, S accidentally revealed that some very expensive personal entertainment equipment acquired in 2003 had been charged to her corporation (cost of approximately $30,000). S stated that everyone she knew charged personal assets to their business accounts and that it appeared to be generally accepted practice. She said she hoped T would not mind.

When T returned to his office, he immediately checked S's 2003 corporate income tax return and found that depreciation had been taken on the $30,000 cost of assets listed simply as "Equipment." Of course, T never suspected the assets were for personal use in S's home.

What should T do? This client is too good to lose, but T is worried about the consequences of allowing this type of behavior to continue.

PROBLEMS

2-18 *Interpreting Citations.* Interpret each of the following citations:
  a. Reg. § 1.721-1(a).
  b. Rev. Rul. 60-314, 1960-2 C.B. 48.
  c. Rev. Proc. 86-46, 1986-2 C.B. 739.
  d. Rev. Rul. 98-36, I.R.B. No. 31, 6.
  e. § 351.

2-19 *Citation Abbreviations.* Explain each of the abbreviations below.

    a. B.T.A.

    b. Acq.

    c. D. Ct.

    d. CA-9

    e. F.Supp.

    f. NA.

    g. Ct. Cls.

    h. USTC

    i. AFTR

    j. *Cert. Den.*

    k. *aff'g* and *aff'd*

    l. *rev'g* and *rev'd*

    m. *rem'g* and *rem'd*

2-20 *Interpreting Citations.* Identify the publisher and interpret each of the following citations:

    a. 41 TCM 289.

    b. 93 S. Ct. 2820 (USSC, 1973).

    c. 71-1 USTC ¶9241 (CA-2, 1971).

    d. 236 F.Supp. 761 (D. Ct. Va., 1974).

    e. T.C. Memo 1977-20.

    f. 48 T.C. 430 (1967).

    g. 6 AFTR2d 5095 (CA-2, 1960).

    h. 589 F.2d 446 (CA-9, 1979).

    i. 277 U.S. 508 (USSC, 1928).

2-21 *Citation Form.* Record the following information in its proper citation form.

    a. Part 7, subdivision (a)(2) of the income tax Regulation under Code § 165

    b. The 34th Revenue Ruling issued March 2, 1987, and printed on pages 101 and 102 of the appropriate document

    c. The 113th letter ruling issued the last week of 1986

2-22 *Citation Form.* Record the following information in its proper citation form.

    a. A 1982 U.S. Tax Court case in which Roger A. Schubel sued the IRS Commissioner for a refund, published in volume 77 on pages 701 through 715 as a regular decision

    b. A 1974 U.S. Tax Court case in which H. N. Schilling, Jr. sued the IRS Commissioner for a refund, published by (1) Commerce Clearing House in volume 33 on pages 1097 through 1110 and (2) Prentice Hall as its 246th decision that year

    c. A 1966 Court of Appeals case in which Boris Nodiak sued the IRS Commissioner in the second Circuit for a refund, published by (1) Commerce Clearing House in volume 1 of that year at paragraph 9262, (2) Prentice Hall in volume 17 on pages 396 through 402, and (3) West Publishing Company in volume 356 on pages 911 through 919.

RESEARCH PROBLEMS

2-23 *Using a Citator.* Use either the Commerce Clearing House or Research Institute of America Citator in your library and locate *Richard L. Kroll, Exec. v. U.S.*

    a. Which Court of Appeals Circuit heard this case?

    b. Was this case heard by the Supreme Court?

    c. James B. and Doris E. Wallach are included in the listing below the citation for Kroll. In what court was the Wallach case heard?

2-24 *Using a Citator.* Using any available citator, locate the case of *Corn Products v. Comm.*, 350 U.S. 46. What effect did the decision in *Arkansas Best v. Comm.* (58 AFTR2d 86-5748, 800 F.2d 219) have on the precedential value of the *Corn Products* case?

2-25 *Locating Court Cases.* Locate the case of *Robert Autrey, Jr. v. United States*, 89-2 USTC ¶9659, and answer the following questions.
   a. What court decided the case on appeal?
   b. What court originally tried the case?
   c. Was the trial court's decision upheld or reversed?

2-26 *Locating Court Cases.* Locate the case of *Fabry v. Commissioner*, 111 T.C. 305, and answer the following questions.
   a. What court tried the case?
   b. Identify the various types of precedential authority the judge used in framing his opinion.

2-27 *Locating Court Cases.* Locate the cited court cases and answer the questions below.
   a. *Stanley A. and Lorriee M. Golanty*, 72 T.C. 411 (1979). Did the taxpayers win their case?
   b. *Hamilton D. Hill*, 41 TCM 700, T.C. Memo ¶71,127 (1971). Who was the presiding judge?
   c. *Patterson (Jefferson) v. Comm.*, 72-1 USTC ¶9420, 29 AFTR2d 1181 (Ct. Cls., 1972). What was the issue being questioned in this case?

2-28 *Completing Citations.* To the extent the materials are available to you, complete the following citations:
   a. Rev. Rul. 98-60, _____ C.B. _____ .
   b. *Lawrence W. McCoy*, _____ T.C. _____ (1962).
   c. *Reginald Turner* _____ TCM _____ T.C. Memo 1954-38.
   d. *RCA Corp. v. U.S.*, _____ USTC _____ (CA-2, 1981).
   e. *RCA Corp. v. U.S.*, _____ AFTR2d _____ (CA-2, 1981).
   f. *RCA Corp. v. U.S.*, _____ F.2d _____ (CA-2, 1981).
   g. *Comm. v. Wilcox*, _____ S. Ct. _____ (USSC, 1946).
   h. _____ , 79-1 USTC ¶9139 (USSC, 1979).
   i. _____ , 34 T.C. 842 (1960).
   j. *Brian E. Knutson*, 60 TCM 540, T.C. Memo _____ .
   k. *Samuel B. Levin v. Comm.*, 43 AFTR2d 79-1057 (_____).

2-29 *Examination of Tax Sources.* For each of the tax sources listed below, identify at least one of the tax issues involved. In addition, if the source has a temporary citation, provide its permanent citation (if available).
   a. *Battelstein Investment Co. v. U.S.*, 71-1 USTC ¶9227, 27 AFTR2d 71-713, 442 F.2d 87 (CA-5, 1971).
   b. *Joel Kerns*, 47 TCM, _____ T.C. Memo 1984-22.
   c. *Patterson v. U.S.*, 84-1 USTC ¶9315 (CA-6, 1984).
   d. *Webster Lair*, 95 T.C. 484 (1990).
   e. *Thompson Engineering Co., Inc.*, 80 T.C. 672 (1983).
   f. *Towne Square, Inc.*, 45 TCM 478, T.C. Memo 1983-10.
   g. Rev. Rul. 85-13, I.R.B. No. 7, 28.
   h. Rev. Proc. 85-49, I.R.B. No. 40, 26.
   i. *William E Sutton, et al. v. Comm.*, 84 T.C. _____ No. 17.
   j. Rev. Rul. 86-103, I.R.B. No. 36, 13.
   k. *Hughes Properties, Inc.*, 86-1 USTC ¶9440, 58 AFTR2d 86-5062, _____ U.S. _____ (USSC, 1986).
   l. Rev. Rul. 98-27, I.R.B. No. 22, 4.

2-30 *Office in the Home.* T comes to you for advice regarding the deductibility of expenses for maintaining an office in his home. T is currently employed as an executive vice president for Zandy Corporation. He has found it impossible to complete his job responsibilities during the normal forty-hour weekly period. Although the office building in which he works is open nights and weekends, the heating and air-conditioning systems are shut down at night (from 6 p.m.) and during the entire weekend. As a result, T has begun taking work home with him on a regular basis. The work is generally done in the den of T's home. Although T's employer does not require him to work at home, T is convinced that he would be fired if his work assignments were not completed on a timely basis. Given these facts, what would you advise T about taking a home-office deduction?

Partial list of research aids:

§ 280A

Proposed Reg. § 1.280A

M.G. Hill, 43 TCM 832, T.C. Memo 1982-143

2-31 *Journal Articles.* Refer to . Consult an index to periodicals (e.g., AICPA's *Accountants Index*; Warren, Gorham, and Lamont's *Index to Federal Tax Articles*; or CCH's *Federal Tax Articles*) and locate a journal article on the topic of tax deductions for an office in the home. Copy the article. Record the citation for the article (i.e., author's name, article title, journal name, publication date, and first and last pages of the article) at the top of your paper. Prepare a two-page summary of the article, including all relevant issues, research sources, and conclusions. Staple your two-page summary to the article. The grade for this exercise will be based on the relevance of your article to the topic, the accuracy and quality of your summary, and the quality of your written communication skills.

2-32 *Deductible Medical Expenses.* B suffers from a severe form of degenerative arthritis. Her doctor strongly recommended that she swim for at least one hour per day in order to stretch and exercise her leg and arm muscles. There are no swimming pools nearby, so B spent $15,000 to have a swimming pool installed in her back yard. This expenditure increased the fair market value of her house by $5,000. B consults you about whether she can deduct the cost of the swimming pool on her individual tax return. What do you recommend?

Hint: You should approach this problem by using the tax service volumes of either Commerce Clearing House or Research Institute of America. Both tax services are organized according to Code Sections, so you should start with Code § 213. You will find the Code Sections on the back binding of the volumes. Research Institute of America has a very extensive index, so look under the term "medical expenses."

2-33 *Deductible Educational Expenses.* T is a CPA with a large accounting firm in Houston, Texas. He has been assigned to the international taxation group of his firm's tax department. As a result of this assignment, T enrolls in an international tax law course at the University of Houston Law School. The authorities of the University require T to enroll as a regular law student; and, theoretically, if he continues to attend courses, T will graduate with a law degree. Will T be able to deduct his tuition for the international tax law course as a business expense?

Hint: Go to either the RIA or CCH tax service and use it to find the analysis of Code § 162. When you have found the discussion of § 162, find that part of the subsection dealing with educational deductions. Read the appropriate Regulations and then note the authorities listed after the Regulations. Read over the summaries provided and then choose those you think have the most relevance to the question asked above. Read these cases and other listed authorities, and formulate a written response to the question asked in light of these cases and other authorities Finally, for the authorities you choose, go to the RIA or CCH Citator and use it to ensure that your authorities are current.

Chapter 3

TAXABLE ENTITIES, TAX FORMULA, INTRODUCTION TO PROPERTY TRANSACTIONS

LEARNING OBJECTIVES

Upon completion of this chapter you will be able to:

▶ Identify the entities that are subject to the Federal income tax

▶ Explain the basic tax treatment of individuals, corporations, partnerships, S corporations, and fiduciary taxpayers (trusts and estates)

▶ Understand the basic tax formulas to be followed in computing the tax liability for individuals and corporations

▶ Define many of the basic terms used in the tax formula such as gross income, adjusted gross income, taxable income, exclusion, deduction, and credit

▶ Calculate the gain or loss on the disposition of property and explain the tax consequences, including the special treatment of capital gains and losses

CHAPTER OUTLINE

INTRODUCTION

The amount of income tax ultimately paid by any taxpayer is determined by applying the many rules comprising our income tax system. This chapter examines some of the fundamental features of this system. They are

- *Taxable Entities*—those entities that are subject to taxation and those that are merely conduits
- *Tax Formulas*—the mathematical relationships used to compute the tax for the various taxable entities
- *Property Transactions*—the tax treatment of sales, exchanges, and other dispositions of property

As will become clear, this chapter, in covering the essentials, provides a bird's-eye view of the entire income tax system. For many, this may be sufficient. This one chapter may contain enough tax law and have more than enough detail for some. Nevertheless, it is just part of the picture. Many of the details as well as the conceptual basis for some of these provisions are skipped and left to later chapters. This can be frustrating to those who want more or know that more exists, but the major purpose of this chapter is to establish the basic framework in which the implications of any particular transaction on taxable income can be assessed. To this end, the chapter gives not only a brief description of what is taxable and what is deductible but also a glimpse of such esoteric topics as the passive loss rules and the alternative minimum tax. Remember, the goal is not necessarily to provide a detailed discussion of all the rules but to provide a foundation so that problems, pitfalls, and opportunities can be recognized.

THE TAXABLE ENTITY

The income tax must be imposed on the income of some type of entity. Unfortunately, there is no uniform agreement on what is the theoretically correct unit of taxation. There are a variety of legal, economic, social, and natural entities that Congress could select: individuals (natural persons), family units, households (those living together), sole proprietorships, partnerships, corporations, trusts, estates, governments, religious groups, nonprofit organizations, and other voluntary or cooperative associations. Despite the disagreement over which of these or other entities are the proper choices, Congress has provided that only certain entities are responsible for actually paying the tax. According to the Code, individuals, most corporations, and fiduciaries (estates and trusts) are taxable entities. Other entities, such as sole proprietorships, partnerships, and so-called "S" corporations, are not required to pay tax on any taxable income they might have. Instead, the taxable income of these entities is allocated to their owners, who bear the responsibility for paying any tax that may be due.

> **Example 1.** R and S are equal partners in a partnership that had taxable income of $50,000 in the current year. The partnership does not pay tax on the $50,000. Rather, the income is allocated equally between R and S. Thus, both R and S will report $25,000 of partnership income on their individual returns and pay the required tax.

In the following sections, the general tax treatment of the taxable entities—individuals, corporations, and fiduciaries—is explained along with the treatment of partnerships and "S" corporations. The specific tax treatment of entities other than individuals is discussed separately in later chapters. However, it should be emphasized that many of the tax rules applying to one entity also apply to other entities. These similarities will be pointed out as the various rules are discussed.

TAXABLE ENTITIES

INDIVIDUAL TAXPAYERS

Citizens and Residents of the United States. Section 1 of the Internal Revenue Code provides that a tax is imposed on the taxable income of all individuals. As might be expected, the term *individual* generally applies to U.S. citizens. However, it also includes persons who are *not* U.S. citizens but who are considered residents, so-called *resident aliens.* Thus, if Prince Harry decides to move to New York to escape the tabloids of London, he could be subject to U.S. taxes even though he is not a U.S. citizen. The same could be said for a Japanese citizen working for Honda in Marysville, Ohio or a Canadian citizen who lives and works in Detroit. Whether these people are residents requires application of a complicated test.[1] The key point to remember is that foreign citizens who are not merely visiting but stay for an extended period must worry about the need for filing.[2] As discussed below, the tax would be levied on both their U.S. income and any foreign income.

Foreign Taxpayers. Individuals who are not U.S. citizens and who do not qualify as residents may be subject to U.S. tax. These persons, referred to as *nonresident aliens,* are taxed on certain types of income that are received from U.S. sources.[3] If the income is derived from a trade or business carried on in the United States, that income is taxed in the same way as it is for a citizen or resident. Most other income earned in the United States is taxed at a flat rate of 30 percent. However, there are a number of special rules that must be observed.

Age. It should be noted that the age of an individual is not a factor in determining if he or she is a taxpaying entity. Whether the individual is eight years old or eighty years old, he or she is still subject to tax on any taxable income received. Contrary to the belief of some people, a child's income is taxed to the child and not the parent. As explained later, age may have an impact on *both* the method of computing the tax and the amount of tax owed; it does not, however, affect the individual's status as a taxpayer.

Sole Proprietorship. Another aspect of individual taxation requiring consideration is the taxation of sole proprietorships. For financial accounting purposes, the business activities of the proprietor are treated as distinct from other activities. The sole proprietorship is considered a separate accounting entity for which separate records and reports are maintained. For tax purposes, however, the sole proprietorship is not a separate entity subject to tax. The sole proprietorship does not file its own tax return. Rather, the income and deductions of the proprietorship are reported on the individual's personal income tax return along with any other tax items. In essence, the sole proprietorship serves as a conduit; that is, any income it has flows through to the individual.

Example 2. K is employed as an accounting professor at State University, where she earns a salary of $42,000. K also operates a consulting practice as a sole

---

[1]   See § 7701(b) for a definition of the "substantial presence test" that is used to determine if an individual is a resident alien and subject to U.S. tax.

[2]   Reg. § 1.871-2(b).

[3]   § 871.

proprietorship, which earned net income of $10,000 during the year. The sole proprietorship does not file a separate return and pay tax. Instead, K reports the sole proprietorship's income along with her salary on her individual return (Form 1040) and pays both the income and self-employment taxes required. The operations of the sole proprietorship are reported on a special form, Schedule C, which accompanies Form 1040. (See Appendix for a copy of Schedule C.)

Worldwide Income. The Federal income tax on individuals applies not only to domestic (U.S.) source income, but also to income from foreign sources. It is therefore possible to have foreign source income taxed by more than one country (e.g., the foreign country and the United States). Several provisions exist to prevent or minimize double taxation, however. For example, U.S. citizens and residents living abroad may take either a direct reduction in U.S. tax (foreign tax credit)[4] or deduct such taxes.[5] In lieu of taking a credit or deduction for foreign taxes, a U.S. citizen who works abroad may exclude from his or her U.S. income certain amounts of income earned abroad.[6] This exclusion is limited to $80,000 for any 12-month period. To qualify, the taxpayer (referred to as an *expatriate*) must either be a bona fide resident of a foreign country (or countries) all year or be physically present in a foreign country for 330 days in any 12 consecutive months.

> **Example 3.** Z, a U.S. citizen, is an aircraft mechanic who was temporarily assigned to a lucrative job in Seoul, South Korea. Z lived in Seoul all of 2005 except for two weeks when he came back to the United States to visit relatives. From his Korean job, he earned $95,000 in 2005. Because Z was present in the foreign country for at least 330 days during 12 consecutive months, he meets the physical presence test and may exclude $80,000 of his $95,000 salary. The remaining $15,000 plus any other income, such as dividends and interest, are subject to tax.

In addition to the relief measures mentioned above, tax treaties often exist that deal with the problem of double taxation by the United States and foreign countries.

CORPORATE TAXPAYERS

Section 11 of the Code imposes a tax on all corporations. The tax applies to both domestic corporations and foreign corporations with trades or businesses operated in the United States.[7] Although § 11 requires all corporations to pay tax, other provisions in the law specifically exempt certain types of corporations from taxation. For example, a corporation organized not for profit, but for religious, charitable, scientific, literary, educational, or certain other purposes generally is not taxable.[8] However, if a nonprofit organization conducts a business unrelated to the purpose for which its exemption was granted, any taxable income resulting from that business would be subject to tax.[9] In addition to the special provisions governing taxation of nonprofit corporations, the rules applying to S corporations vary from those applying to C or "regular" corporations as explained below.

The overall income tax treatment of corporations is quite similar to that of individuals. In fact, all of the basic rules governing income, exclusions, deductions, and

---

4   § 901.

5   § 164(a).

6   § 911(a).

7   § 882(a). See Chapter 19 for more details.

8   § 501(a).

9   § 501(b).

credits apply to individuals as well as C corporations and, for that matter, fiduciaries. For example, the general rule concerning what is deductible, found in Code § 162, allows *all* taxpayers a deduction for trade or business expenses. Similarly, § 103 provides that *all* taxpayers are allowed to exclude interest income from state and local bonds. Although many of the general rules are the same for both individuals and corporations, there are several key differences.

The most obvious difference can be seen by comparing the corporate and individual formulas for determining taxable income as found in Exhibits 3-1 and 3-2. The concepts of adjusted gross income and itemized deductions common to the individual tax formula are conspicuously absent from the corporate formula. Other major differences in determining taxable income involve the treatment of particular items, such as dividend income and charitable contributions. These and other differences are discussed in detail in Chapter 19. It should be emphasized once again, however, that most of the basic rules apply whether the taxpayer is a corporation or an individual.

One difference in the taxation of individuals and corporations that is not apparent from the basic formula, but which should be noted, concerns the tax rates that each uses in computing the tax liability (see the inside back cover of the text). A comparison of the individual and corporate tax rates shows a somewhat similar progression: 10 to 35 percent for individuals and 15 to 39 percent for corporations. But note that the rates apply at quite different levels of income.

Perhaps the most critical aspect of corporate taxation that is generally not shared with any other taxable entity concerns the potential for double taxation. When a corporation receives income and subsequently distributes that income as a dividend to its shareholders, the effect is to tax the income twice: once at the corporate level and again at the shareholder level. Double taxation can occur because the corporation is not allowed to deduct any dividend payments to its shareholders. As one might suspect, many have questioned the equity of this treatment, arguing that it penalizes those who elect to do business in the corporate form. Note, however, that this treatment is consistent with the fact that the corporation is considered a separate legal entity. Moreover, it is often argued that the corporation and its owners in reality do not bear the burden of the corporate tax. According to the argument, corporations are able to shift the tax burden either to consumers by charging higher prices or to employees by paying lower wages. In addition, those who reject the double tax theory often note that closely held corporations, whose owners may also be employees of the business, are able to avoid double taxation to the extent they can characterize any corporate distributions as deductible salary payments rather than nondeductible dividends. Whether in fact double taxation does or does not occur, it appears that this feature, which has been part of the U.S. tax system since its inception, is unlikely to change in the immediate future.

Special rules apply to the formation of a corporation, corporate dividend distributions, and distributions made to shareholders in exchange for their stock. Penalty taxes also may be assessed against corporations that try to shelter income from high personal tax rates by accumulating it in the corporation, rather than making dividend distributions. These topics and others related to the income taxation of corporations and their owners are discussed in Chapters 19, 20, and 21.

FIDUCIARY TAXPAYERS

A *fiduciary* is a person who is entrusted with property for the benefit of another, the *beneficiary*. The individual or entity that acts as a fiduciary is responsible for managing and administering the entrusted property, at all times faithfully performing the required duties with the utmost care and prudence.

Two types of fiduciary relationships are the trust and the estate. The trust is a legal entity created when the title of property is transferred by a person (the *grantor*) to the fiduciary (the *trustee*). The trustee is required to implement the instructions of the grantor as specified in the trust agreement. Typically, the property is held in trust for a minor or some other person until he or she reaches a certain age or until some specified event occurs.

An estate is also recognized as a legal entity, established by law when a person dies. Upon the person's death, his or her property generally passes to the estate, where it is administered by the fiduciary until it is distributed to the beneficiaries. Both trusts and estates are treated as taxpaying entities.

The Code specifically provides for a tax on the taxable income of estates and trusts.[10] Determining the tax for such entities is very similar to determining the tax for individuals, with one major exception.[11] When distributions are made to beneficiaries, the distributed income is generally taxed to the beneficiary rather than to the estate or trust.[12] In essence, the trust or estate is permitted to reduce its taxable income by the amount of the distribution—acting as a *conduit,* since the distributed income flows through to the beneficiaries.

> **Example 4.** T is the trustee of a trust established for the benefit of A and B. The trust generated $4,000 of income subject to tax for the current year and no distributions were made to either A or B during the year. The trustee files an annual fiduciary tax return for the year and pays the tax based on the $4,000 taxable amount.

> **Example 5.** Assume that for the next year the trust in *Example 4* had $10,000 of income subject to tax and that distributions of $2,000 each were made to A and B. The trustee files an annual trust return for the year and pays a tax based on $6,000 ($10,000 taxable income − $4,000 distribution). A and B each include $2,000 in their income tax returns for the year.

Distributions made by a trust or estate from its corpus (also called the trust property or principal), including undistributed profits from prior years, generally are not taxable to the beneficiary.[13] This is because these distributions are part of a gift or inheritance or have been taxed previously. Similarly, the trust or estate is not entitled to deductions for these nontaxable distributions.[14]

PARTNERSHIPS

The partnership is a conduit for Federal income tax purposes. This means that the partnership itself is not subject to Federal income tax and that all items of partnership income, expense, gain, loss, or credit pass through to the partners and are given their tax effect at the partner level.[15] The partnership is required to file an information return (Form 1065) reporting the results of the partnership's transactions and how those results are divided among the partners. Using this information, the partners each report their respective shares of the various items on their own tax returns.[16] Because a partner pays

---

[10]   §§ 1(e) and 641(a).

[11]   § 641(b).

[12]   §§ 651 and 661.

[13]   § 662.

[14]   § 661. These and other provisions related to the Federal taxation of estates, trusts, and beneficiaries are discussed in Chapter 25.

[15]   § 701.

[16]   § 702(a).

taxes on his or her share of the partnership income, distributions made by the partnership to the partner generally are not taxable to the partner.[17]

> **Example 6.** For its current calendar year, EG Partnership had taxable income of $18,000. During the year, each of its two equal partners received cash distributions of $4,000. The partnership is not subject to tax, and each partner must include $9,000 in his annual income tax return, despite the fact that each partner actually received less than this amount in cash. The distributions normally are not taxable since they represent previously taxed income. The partnership must file an annual information return reporting the results of its operations and the effect of these operations on each partner.

A characteristic of a partnership (as well as an S corporation) that deserves special emphasis is the treatment of losses. If a business is typical, it will take several years of operation before it can be declared a profitable venture. Until that time, expenses normally exceed revenues and the result is a net loss. In the case of a conduit entity such as a partnership, that net loss flows through to the owners, who are generally allowed to offset it against any other income they may have. In contrast, if a regular C corporation sustains a loss, referred to as a net operating loss, or NOL, the shareholders do not benefit from that loss directly. A C corporation is allowed, like individuals, to use the loss to offset taxable income of prior or subsequent years. Generally, losses are carried back two years and forward 20 years. For example, the taxpayer would first carry back the loss to the second prior year and offset it against any taxable income. In such case, the taxpayer would file a claim for a tax refund. Any remaining loss is carried to the first prior year. Any remaining loss is carried forward for 20 years. The key point to remember is that the losses of a partnership flow through and thus may provide immediate benefit, whereas those of a C corporation do not flow through and can be used only if the corporation has income in other tax years.

In some respects, the partnership is treated as a separate entity for tax purposes. For example, many tax elections are made by the partnership,[18] and a partnership interest generally is treated as a single asset when sold.[19] In transactions between the partners and the partnership, the partners generally are treated like nonpartners.[20] However, an individual partner who performs services in his or her role as a partner is generally not considered an employee for tax purposes. As a result, a partner does not qualify for the favorable tax treatment of employee fringe benefits (see Chapter 6), and his or her share of any trade or business income is generally subject to self-employment taxes. These and other controlling provisions related to the Federal income tax treatment of partnerships are covered in detail in Chapter 22.

ELECTING SMALL BUSINESS CORPORATIONS: "S" CORPORATIONS

The Internal Revenue Code allows certain closely held corporations to elect to be treated as conduits (like partnerships) for Federal income tax purposes. The election is made pursuant to the rules contained in Subchapter S of the Code.[21] For this reason, such corporations are referred to as *S corporations*. Not all corporations are eligible to

---

[17] § 731(a).

[18] § 703(b).

[19] § 741 states that the sale or exchange of an interest in a partnership shall generally be treated as the sale of a capital asset.

[20] § 707(a).

[21] § § 1361 through 1379.

elect S status. The only corporations that qualify are those that have 100 or fewer shareholders and meet certain other tests.

If a corporation elects S corporation status, it is taxed in virtually the same fashion as a partnership. Like a partnership, the S corporation's items of income, expense, gain, or loss pass through to the shareholders to be given their tax effect at the shareholder level. Salaries and wages of shareholders who work for the corporation and other employees are reported on a Form W-2 and are subject to withholding of income taxes and FICA (that is matched by the employer corporation). Although employees generally qualify for favorable treatment of fringe benefits, shareholder-employees owning 2 percent or more of the corporation's stock do not. As a result, the value of any fringe benefits, such as medical insurance coverage, is taxable to the employee-shareholder.

The S corporation files an information return (Form 1120S) similar to that of a partnership, reporting the results of the corporation's transactions and how those results are allocated among the shareholders. The individual shareholders report their respective shares of the various items on their own tax returns. Chapter 23 contains a detailed discussion of the taxation of S corporations and their shareholders.

LIMITED LIABILITY COMPANIES

All 50 states and the District of Columbia have passed legislation creating a relatively new form of business entity: the limited liability company (LLC). What is this new creature and how is it taxed? Perhaps the best characterization of an LLC is that it is a cross between a partnership and a corporation. LLCs are created under state law by filing articles of organization. The owners of an LLC are called members and can be individuals, partnerships, regular corporations, S corporations, trusts, or other LLCs. Although some states allow single-member LLCs, two or more members usually form the entity. Like a corporation, an LLC can act on its own behalf and sue and be sued. Also like a corporation, members generally possess limited liability except that they may be liable for their own acts of malpractice in those states that allow professionals to form LLCs.

The tax law does not specifically address the tax treatment of an LLC. Initially, this omission caused some uncertainty as to whether an LLC should be taxed as a corporation or a partnership. To eliminate this confusion, the Treasury issued the so-called check-the-box regulations.[22] Under these rules, an LLC with two or more owners is treated as a partnership for tax purposes unless it elects to be treated as a corporation (i.e., the LLC is a partnership unless it checks the box on Form 8832 to be treated as a regular C corporation). LLCs with only one member are disregarded and treated as sole proprietorships.

The treatment of LLCs for self-employment tax purposes has also produced some confusion. As noted above, in the case of a partnership, a partner's share of partnership income is generally self-employment income subject to self-employment taxes. However, this rule is true only for general partners. Historically, limited partners have been treated differently on the theory that their role is similar to that of an investor rather than someone who is actively involved in the business. Consequently, a limited partner's share of partnership income has been viewed more similar to investment income (e.g., dividends and interest) than business income. Section 1402 (a)(13) reflects this line of reasoning, providing that a limited partner's share of partnership income is not subject to self-employment tax. However, based on this approach, it was not clear whether a member of an LLC was to be treated like a limited partner, in which case the LLC's income would escape employment taxes. Hoping to eliminate this potential loophole, recently proposed regulations created new rules to test limited partners as well

---

[22] Reg. § 301.7701-3.

as LLC members. A limited partner or LLC member must treat his or her share of income as self-employment income if any of the following tests are met:[23]

1. The individual has personal liability for the debts of or claims against the business by reason of being a partner. This rule should rarely apply to a member of an LLC.

2. The individual has authority to contract on behalf of the entity.

3. The individual participates in the entity's trade or business for more than 500 hours during the year.

4. Substantially all of the activities of the entity involve the performance of services in the fields of health, law, engineering, architecture, accounting, actuarial science, or consulting.

✓ CHECK YOUR KNOWLEDGE

Review Question 1. Section 1 of the Internal Revenue Code imposes a tax on all individuals. If taken literally, this would mean that the United States taxes not only Michael Jordan but also Fidel Castro and Vladimir Putin. Are these foreign citizens subject to U.S. tax? Explain and also comment on how the North American Free Trade Agreement (NAFTA) might make the definition of "individual" more important.

The U.S. income tax generally applies to the worldwide income of U.S. citizens and resident aliens. As a result, it would not apply to Castro and Putin since they are not citizens and do not live in the United States. The key question for an alien is whether the individual could be considered a resident. Whether a foreign citizen is considered a resident is normally based on the period of time he or she is present in the United States. For this purpose, an alien who is a mere transient (e.g., a foreigner who vacations in the United States) is not a resident.

Although foreign citizens such as Castro and Putin usually are not subject to U.S. tax, they can be. Nonresident aliens are taxed on their income from U.S. sources. Based on this rule, income earned from a job or a business in the United States is subject to U.S. tax. In addition, nonresident aliens who receive investment income from U.S. sources, such as dividends on U.S. stocks, normally must pay U.S. taxes on such income. The passage of NAFTA may mean that more Canadian and Mexican citizens could be living and working in the United States. Under the general rules, they could be considered residents subject to U.S. tax unless a treaty provision provides special treatment.

Review Question 2. Child actors and actresses have made millions of dollars from their movie appearances (e.g., Drew Barrymore, Macaulay Culkin).

a. Must these children file their own returns and report the income, or do their parents simply include it on their return?

Although there are some special rules that can apply, parents normally do not report the income of their children on their return. A child is treated as a taxable entity, separate and distinct from his or her parents. Consequently, if a child's income exceeds the filing requirement threshold, he or she must usually file a return.

---

[23] Prop. Reg. § 1.1402(a)-2(h).

b. Do you think there could be any advantage derived from the fact that a child is a separate taxpayer?

Besides all of the other things that children are—both good and bad—they can also be mini tax shelters. Since they are separate taxpayers, they have their own set of tax rates and other tax characteristics. Therefore, to the extent that parents are able to shift income from the parents' high bracket to the child's low bracket (and still control the use of the income), taxes can be saved. These opportunities and some limitations that restrict such schemes are discussed more fully in Chapter 4 and Chapter 5.

Review Question 3. After all these years, Dick and Jane have decided to start their own business: the Sumo Bar and Grill. They have everything lined up but still have to decide what form the business should take. Originally, the couple did not even think about it. They planned to simply operate the business as a sole proprietorship.

a. If they do pursue this course, will they need to file a separate return for the business?

A sole proprietorship is not considered a separate taxable entity. Instead, all of the information related to the proprietorship is included on the individual's personal tax return. The results of operation are summarized on Schedule C. The net profit or loss is transferred from Schedule C to page 1 of Form 1040. In addition, since such income is also subject to self-employment tax, the net profit is also transferred to Schedule SE, where the special computation is made. It is important to note that either Dick or Jane can be the proprietor—but not both. If Jane is to be the proprietor, she must own the business. If Jane wishes to compensate Dick, she can pay him a salary or wages. However, if Dick and Jane both wish to be owners, they must use another form of business.

b. After Dick and Jane talked to their attorney, it was clear that they did not want to be a general partnership (where each and every partner is liable for partnership obligations) or a sole proprietorship. Why?

Typically, individuals want to protect their personal assets from the liabilities of risky ventures. While insurance may provide some protection, most individuals want the added safety of limited liability that only the corporate or LLC form offers. A *limited* partnership allows some partners protection, but this business form requires that there must be at least one *general* partner (who would have unlimited liability).

c. At first Dick and Jane thought they would be a corporation. But according to their accountant, this new thing called an LLC allows business owners to achieve what he believes is tax nirvana. What is all the fuss about LLCs? Can you not get the same thing with S corporations? What do you think? How are LLCs taxed? What form of business organization seems best for Dick and Jane's business?

The beauty of an LLC is that all of the owners have limited liability yet the entity is usually taxed like a partnership. As a result, all of the income, as well as any loss, flows through to the partners. The significance of this treatment is twofold. First, if any loss occurs, it can be used to offset any other income Dick and Jane may have. If a C corporation is chosen, early losses do not provide any benefit until the business starts to make money. The NOL carryback feature for corporations is useless, because the business is brand new. Moreover, if it is like most businesses, Dick and Jane's operation will experience losses—at least until the clientele develop a love for Sumo wrestling. The second attraction of an LLC is the fact that its income avoids the double tax that can occur with C corporations. But why opt for an LLC? Is not this same treatment available with an S corporation? In this regard, the LLC is virtually identical to an S corporation, but there are many differences that some argue make the LLC more attractive. The only difference that can be gleaned from the discussion above is that an S corporation is limited to 75 shareholders while a partnership or LLC can have an unlimited number of owners. This may be irrelevant for Dick and Jane but could be extremely important for some businesses (e.g., a large public accounting firm). Another difference concerns the type of owner allowed. For example, an S corporation can generally have only individuals (and no nonresident aliens) as shareholders, but there are no restrictions on the type of partner or member that a partnership or an LLC can have. This too may be unimportant for Dick and Jane but there are still other considerations too technical to touch on here.

As a practical matter, prior to the advent of the LLC, most advisers would have suggested that Dick and Jane choose to be an S corporation. Since 1986 S corporations have generally been the most popular form of conducting business—at least when there were no more than the maximum shareholders allowed—because they were the only form of business that offered limited liability to all of its owners and a single level of tax. But the advent of the LLC changes all of this. In the next few years, it will be interesting to see if LLCs become more popular than S corporations. In any event, they provide yet one more option for the business owner to select.

TAX FORMULA

Computing an income tax liability is normally uncomplicated, requiring only a few simple mathematical calculations.[24] These steps, referred to as the tax formula, are shown in Exhibits 3-1 and 3-2. The tax formula is presented here in two forms: the simpler general formula that establishes the basic concepts as applicable to corporate taxpayers (Exhibit 3-1) and the more complex formula for individual taxpayers (Exhibit 3-2). The formulas in Exhibits 3-1 and 3-2 will be useful references while studying the various aspects of Federal income tax law in the subsequent chapters. To make such reference easier, both formulas are reproduced on the inside back cover of the text.

The tax formula for each type of entity is incorporated into the Federal income tax forms. Exhibit 3-1 may be compared with Form 1120 (the annual income tax return for corporations) and Exhibit 3-2 with Form 1040 (the return for individuals). These forms are included in Appendix B at the back of the text.

Examination of the two formulas reveals the importance of tax terms such as *gross income, deductions, and exemptions*. Each of these terms and countless others used in the tax law have very specific meanings. Indeed, as later chapters will show, taxpayers often have been involved in litigation solely to determine the definition of a particular term. For this reason, close attention must be given to the terminology used in taxation.

---

[24]   §§ 1 and 63.

EXHIBIT 3-1

Tax Formula for Corporate Taxpayers

Total Income (from whatever source)	$xxx,xxx
Less: Exclusions from gross income......................	−xx,xxx
Gross income..	$xxx,xxx
Less: Deductions	−xx,xxx
Taxable income	$xxx,xxx
Applicable tax rates	xx%
Gross tax	$ xx,xxx
Less: Tax credits and prepayments	−x,xxx
Tax due (or refund)	$ xx,xxx

EXHIBIT 3-2

Tax Formula for Individual Taxpayers

Total income (from whatever source)			$xxx,xxx
Less:	Exclusions from gross income		−xx,xxx
Gross income...			$xxx,xxx
Less:	Deductions *for* adjusted gross income		−xx,xxx
Adjusted gross income..................................			$xxx,xxx
Less:	1. The larger of:		
	a. Standard deduction......................	$x,xxx	
	or	or	−x,xxx
	b. Total itemized deductions	$x,xxx	
	2. Number of personal and dependency exemptions ×		
	exemption amount		−x,xxx
Taxable income			$xxx,xxx
Applicable tax rates			
(from Tables or Schedules X, Y, or Z)......................			xx%
Gross income tax......................................			$ xx,xxx
Plus:	Additional taxes (e.g., self-employment		
	taxes and recapture of tax credits).................		+x,xxx
Less:	Tax credits and prepayments.....................		−x,xxx
Tax due (or refund)			$ xx,xxx

ANALYZING THE TAX FORMULA

Income. The tax computation begins with a determination of the taxpayer's total income, both taxable and nontaxable. As the formula in Exhibit 3-2 suggests, income is defined very broadly to include income from any source.[25] The list of typical income

---

[25] § 61(a).

items in Exhibit 3-3 illustrates its comprehensive nature. A specific definition of income is developed in Chapter 5.

Exclusions. Although the starting point in calculating the tax is determining total income, not all of the income identified is taxable. Over the years, Congress has specifically exempted certain types of income from taxation, often in an attempt to accomplish some specific goal.[26] In tax terminology, income exempt from taxation and thus not included in a taxpayer's gross income is referred to as an "exclusion." Exhibit 3-4 shows a sample of the numerous items that can be excluded when determining gross income. Exclusions are discussed in detail in Chapter 6.

Gross Income. The amount of income remaining after the excludable items have been removed is termed *gross income*. When completing a tax return, gross income is usually the only income disclosed, because excluded income normally is not reported.

EXHIBIT 3-3
Partial List of Items Included in Gross Income

Alimony and separate maintenance payments	Income from rental operations
Annuities	Income in respect of a decedent
Awards	Interest
Bonuses	Pensions and other retirement benefits
Commissions	Prizes and gambling or lottery winnings
Debts forgiven to debtor by a creditor	Pro rata share of income of a partnership
Dividends from corporations	Pro rata share of income of an S corporation
Employee expense reimbursements	Punitive damages
Fees and other compensation for personal services	Rewards
	Royalties
Gains from illegal transactions	Salaries and wages
Gains from transactions in property	Tips and gratuities
Gross profit from sales	Trade or business income
Hobby income	Unemployment compensation
Income from an interest in an estate or trust	

EXHIBIT 3-4
Partial List of Exclusions from Gross Income

Amounts received from employer-financed health and accident insurance to the extent of expenses	Interest on most state and local government debt
	Meals and lodging furnished for the convenience of one's employer
Amounts received from health, accident, and disability insurance financed by the taxpayer	Personal damage awards
	Premiums paid by employer on group-term life insurance (for coverage up to $50,000)
Amounts received under qualified educational assistance plans	Proceeds of life insurance paid on death
	Proceeds of borrowing
Certain specified employee fringe benefits	Qualified transportation plan benefits
Child support payments received	Scholarship and fellowship grants (but only for tuition, fees, books, and supplies)
Contributions by employer to employer-financed accident and health insurance coverage	Social Security benefits (within limits)
Dependent care assistance provided by employer	Veteran's benefits
Gifts and inheritances	Welfare payments
Improvements by lessee to lessor's property	

---

[26] See Chapter 6 for a discussion of the social and economic reasons for excluding certain items of income from taxation.

Example 7. E is divorced and has custody of her only child. E's income for the current year is from the following sources:

Salary	$34,000
Alimony from former spouse	12,000
Child support for child	6,000
Interest from First Savings & Loan	1,200
Interest on U.S. Government Treasury Bonds	1,600
Interest on State of Texas Bonds	2,000
Total	$56,800

Even though E's total income is $56,800, her gross income for tax purposes is only $48,800 because the child support and the interest income from the State of Texas are excluded. All the other items are included in gross income. Note that the interest from the Federal government is taxable, even though interest from state and local governments is generally excluded from gross income.

Deductions. *Deductions* are those items that are subtracted from gross income to arrive at taxable income. The deductions normally allowed may be classified into two major groups:

1. *Business and Production-of-Income Expenses* — deductions for expenses related to carrying on a trade or business or some other income-producing activity, such as an investment.[27]

2. *Certain Personal Expenses* — deductions for a few expenses of an individual taxpayer which are primarily personal in nature, such as charitable contributions and medical expenses.[28]

Observe that the Code allows a deduction only for business or investment expenses. Personal expenses—other than a handful of special items—are not deductible. As someone once said, the Code's treatment of deductions is relatively simple: the costs of earning a living are deductible but the costs of living are not. The problem is determining into which category the expense falls.

A trade or business is an activity that is entered into for profit and involves significant taxpayer participation, either personally or through agents. It typically involves providing goods or services to customers, clients, or patients. If the activity qualifies as a trade or business, all the costs normally associated with operating a business are generally deductible. In most cases, it is easy to determine whether a taxpayer is engaged in a trade or business, but not always. For example, consider a taxpayer who travels around the world looking for antiques and incurs $10,000 of travel expenses but ultimately sells one item for a $100 profit. In this situation, the taxpayer might argue that he has a $9,900 loss from the activity that he should be able to offset against other income. On the other hand, it could easily be argued that the taxpayer was not really trying to make a profit. In such case, the IRS may deny the taxpayer's deduction. In these and similar situations, the determination of whether the taxpayer is truly in a trade or business must be based on all the facts and circumstances.

Interestingly, the Code also takes the view that an individual who is employed is in the business of being an employee. This is an extremely important assumption since it

---

[27] §§ 162 and 212.

[28] §§ 170 and 213.

enables employees to deduct their business expenses (e.g., professional dues, subscriptions, and similar costs). However, a number of special rules must be observed. For example, the Code allows an employee to deduct only 50 percent of the unreimbursed costs of business meals and entertainment. Similarly, there are restrictions on the deduction of expenses for education, travel, transportation, moving, and home offices. Most of these special rules are discussed in detail in Chapter 8.

The rental of real estate is generally not considered to be a trade or business, unless the tenants are transient (i.e., stay for short periods of time, as in a hotel or motel) or there are extraordinary services provided to tenants. Nevertheless, the expenses are normally deductible as expenses related to an income-producing activity and are classified as deductions for adjusted gross income.

As one might suspect at this point, Congress is quite cautious in granting deductions. There are rules, rules, and more rules that try to ensure that only true business expenses are deductible. The tax law is particularly concerned about deduction of losses (i.e., the excess of deductions over revenues) from activities in which the taxpayer may have an interest. The problem became particularly acute in the 1970s and 1980s, when certain activities were designed primarily to generate tax losses (tax shelter limited partnerships and rental real estate were the biggest culprits). In an attempt to eliminate widespread abuse, Congress enacted the so-called *passive loss* rules in 1986. These highly complex rules generally limit the deduction of losses from activities, including rental real estate, in which the taxpayer is a mere investor and does not materially participate. The passive loss rules are covered in detail in Chapter 12.

Classifying Deductions. A comparison of the general tax formulas used by corporations and by individuals reveals some differences in the treatment of deductions. For a corporate taxpayer, all deductions are subtracted directly from gross income to arrive at taxable income. In contrast, the individual formula divides deductions into two groups:[29] one group of deductions is allowed to reduce gross income, resulting in what is referred to as *adjusted gross income* (A.G.I.), while a second group is subtracted from A.G.I. As explained more fully below, the first group of deductions is generally composed of certain business expenses and other special items. The deductions in this group are referred to as deductions *for* adjusted gross income. The second group of expenses consists of two categories of allowable deductions: (1) deductions *from* adjusted gross income, and (2) deductions for personal and dependency exemptions. Deductions from adjusted gross income, normally referred to as *itemized deductions*, may be deducted only if they exceed a stipulated amount known as the *standard deduction* (e.g., $5,000 for single taxpayers in 2005). The deduction for any personal and dependency exemptions claimed (e.g., $3,200 per exemption in 2005) is deductible regardless of the amount of other deductions.

Dividing deductions into two groups is done primarily for administrative convenience. Congress substantially reduced the number of individuals who claim itemized deductions because such deductions need to be reported only if they exceed the taxpayer's standard deduction. This reduction in the number of tax returns with itemized deductions significantly reduced the IRS audit procedures involving individual taxpayers. Since corporate taxpayers have only business deductions, no special grouping was needed and thus the term *adjusted gross income* does not exist in the corporate formula.

Adjusted Gross Income. The amount of an individual taxpayer's adjusted gross income (A.G.I.) serves two primary purposes. First, it is simply a point of reference used for classifying deductions: deductions are classified as either for or from A.G.I. Second, the calculation of the amount of several itemized deductions is made with reference to A.G.I.

---

[29]   § 62.

For example, medical expenses are deductible only if they exceed 7.5 percent of A.G.I., while personal casualty losses may be deducted only if they exceed 10 percent of A.G.I. In addition, recent changes in the tax law make A.G.I. even more important for some taxpayers. As explained below, most itemized deductions and the deduction for exemptions are reduced if adjusted gross income exceeds certain levels.

Example 8. This year proved to be very difficult for T; his divorce became final, and shortly thereafter he became very sick. For the year, he earned $45,000 and paid $5,000 in alimony to his ex-wife and $10,000 for medical expenses that were not reimbursed by insurance. T's A.G.I. is $40,000 ($45,000 − $5,000) because alimony is a deduction for A.G.I. As computed below, T's medical expense deduction is limited to $7,000 because he is allowed to deduct only the amount that exceeds 7.5% of his A.G.I.

Medical expenses (unreimbursed).................		$10,000
Adjusted gross income..........................	$40,000	
Times:	×7.5%	
Threshold.....................................	$ 3,000	(3,000)
Deductible medical expenses		$ 7,000

Deductions for Adjusted Gross Income. Code § 62 specifically lists the deductions allowable in arriving at A.G.I. This listing is a potpourri of items, as illustrated in Exhibit 3-5. They have been given various names besides deductions for A.G.I. For example, practitioners often refer to this category of deductions as being "above the line"—the line being A.G.I. Some commentators and authors label these as deductions from gross income. This text will use the "deduction for" terminology. Classification of a deduction as one for A.G.I. is significant for numerous reasons, as explained fully in Chapter 7. The most important of these reasons, however, is that unlike itemized deductions, deductions for A.G.I. need not exceed a minimum level before they are subtracted when computing taxable income.

EXHIBIT 3-5
List of Deductions for Adjusted Gross Income

Alimony and separate maintenance payments paid

Attorney fees and court costs related to unlawful discrimination cases

Certain deductions of life tenants and income beneficiaries of property

Certain portion of lump-sum distributions from pension plans subject to the
    special averaging convention

Certain required repayments of supplemental unemployment compensation
    benefits

Contributions to health savings accounts and Archer Medical Savings Accounts

Contributions to pension, profit sharing, and other qualified retirement plans on
    behalf of a self-employed individual

Contributions to the retirement plan of an electing Subchapter S corporation on
    behalf of an employee/shareholder

Deductions attributable to property held for the production of rents and royalties

Individual retirement account contributions (within limits)

Losses from the sale or exchange of property

Moving expenses

One-half of any self-employment tax

Penalties for premature withdrawal of deposits from time savings accounts

Reforestation expenses

Reimbursed trade or business expenses of employees

State and local official's deductible expenses

Student loan interest

Trade or business deductions of self-employed individuals (including
    unreimbursed expenses of qualified performing artists)

Tuition payments up to $4,000 for some students

Itemized Deductions and the Standard Deduction. Itemized deductions are all deductions other than the deductions for A.G.I. and the deduction for personal and dependency exemptions.[30] While deductions for A.G.I. are deductible without limitation, itemized deductions are deducted only if their total exceeds the taxpayer's *standard deduction*. For example, if T has total itemized deductions of $3,500 and his standard deduction amount is $5,000, he normally would claim the standard deduction in lieu of itemizing deductions. In contrast, if T's itemized deductions were $6,000, he would no doubt elect to itemize in order to maximize his deductions.

The standard deduction was introduced along with the concept of adjusted gross income and deductions *for* and *from* A.G.I. as part of the overall plan to eliminate the need for every taxpayer to list or itemize certain deductions on his or her return. As suggested above, by allowing the taxpayer to claim some standard amount of deductions in lieu of itemizing each one, the administrative problem of verifying the millions of deductions that otherwise would have been claimed has been eliminated. The standard deduction also simplifies return preparation since most individuals no longer have to determine the amount of most of the deductions to which they are entitled. For this reason, the amount of the standard deduction is theoretically set at a level that equals or exceeds the average person's expenditures for those items qualifying as deductions from A.G.I. Consequently, the great majority of taxpayers claim the standard deduction in lieu of itemizing deductions.

The amount of each taxpayer's standard deduction differs depending on his or her filing status.[31] The amounts for each filing status are adjusted annually for inflation. For 2004 and 2005, the amounts are as follows:

---

[30] § 63.

[31] § 63(c) contains the standard deduction amounts for 1988. The amounts for subsequent years are adjusted
for inflation and announced by the IRS annually. Filing status is discussed in Chapter 4.

	Standard Deduction Amount	
Filing Status	*2004*	*2005*
Single.	$4,850	$ 5,000
Unmarried head of household	7,150	7,300
Married persons filing a joint return		
(and surviving spouse).	9,700	10,000
Married persons filing a separate return.	4,850	5,000

Exhibit 3-6 contains a partial list of itemized deductions. The most common itemized deductions are those granted for a few personal expenses: medical expenses, state and local property and income taxes, casualty and theft losses, and interest expense related to a home mortgage and investments.

Miscellaneous Itemized Deductions. Itemized deductions are also allowed for a group of other expenses referred to as *miscellaneous itemized deductions*. Miscellaneous itemized deductions include the deductions for unreimbursed employee business expenses (e.g., dues to professional organizations, subscriptions to professional journals, travel), tax return preparation fees and related costs, and certain investment expenses (e.g. safety deposit boxes, investment advice). The classification of an expense as a miscellaneous itemized deduction is extremely important because a limitation is imposed on their deduction. Only the portion of miscellaneous itemized deductions exceeding 2 percent of adjusted gross income is deductible. Congress imposed this limitation in hopes of simplifying the law. The floor is intended to relieve taxpayers of the burden of recordkeeping (unless they expect to incur substantial expenditures) and relieve the IRS of the burden of auditing these expenditures.

EXHIBIT 3-6
Partial List of Itemized Deductions

Not Subject to 3 Percent Cutback Rule

Medical expenses (amount in excess of 7.5 percent of A.G.I.):
    Prescription drugs and insulin
    Medical insurance premiums
    Fees of doctors, dentists, nurses, hospitals, etc.
    Medical transportation
    Hearing aids, dentures, eyeglasses, etc.
Investment interest (to extent of investment income)
Casualty and theft losses (amount in excess of 10 percent of A.G.I.)
Wagering losses (to the extent of wagering income)

Subject to 3 Percent Cutback Rule

Certain state, local, and foreign taxes:
    State, local, and foreign income taxes
    State, local, and foreign real property taxes
    State and local personal property taxes
Mortgage interest on personal residences (limited)
Charitable contributions (not to exceed 50 percent of A.G.I.)
Miscellaneous itemized deductions (amount in excess of 2 percent of A.G.I.):
    Costs of preparation of tax returns
    Fees and expenses related to tax planning and advice
    Investment counseling and investment expenses
    Certain unreimbursed employee business expenses (including travel and transportation, professional
        dues, subscriptions, continuing education, union dues, and special work clothing)

Example 9. R, single, is employed as an architect for the firm of J&B Associates, where he earned $25,000. His itemized deductions for the year were interest on his home mortgage, $5,000; charitable contributions, $900; tax return preparation fee, $200; and unreimbursed professional dues, $400. R's total itemized deductions are computed as follows:

Miscellaneous itemized deductions:	
Tax return preparation fee.	$ 200
Professional dues	400
Total miscellaneous itemized deductions	$ 600
A.G.I. limitation (2% × $25,000)	(500)
Total deductible miscellaneous itemized deductions.	$ 100
Other itemized deductions:	
Interest on home mortgage	5,000
Charitable contributions	900
Total itemized deductions	$6,000

Because R's itemized deductions of $6,000 exceed the standard deduction for single persons, $5,000 (2005), he will deduct the entire $6,000. Note that only $100 of R's miscellaneous itemized deductions is deductible, whereas all of his other itemized deductions are deductible.

Three Percent Cutback Rule. In search of more revenue, Congress imposed a new limitation on the amount of itemized deductions that high-income taxpayers may deduct in tax years after 1990. Currently, taxpayers must reduce total itemized deductions otherwise allowable (*other than* medical expenses, casualty and theft losses, and investment interest) by 3 percent of their A.G.I. in excess of $145,950 ($72,975 for married individuals filing separately). However, this reduction cannot exceed 80 percent of the deductions. This 80 percent limit ensures that taxpayers subject to the cutback rule can deduct at least 20 percent of their so-called 3 percent deductions. As a result, a taxpayer's itemized deductions are never completely phased out.

Example 10. J and K are married and file a joint return for 2005. Their combined adjusted gross income is $169,750 and they are entitled to itemized deductions of $16,500 and exemption deductions of $6,400. Due to the cutback rule, their deductible itemized deductions must be reduced (i.e., cutback) by $714 [($169,750 − $145,950) × 3%], leaving $15,786 ($16,500 − $714). J and K have taxable income calculated as follows:

Adjusted gross income.	$ 169,750
Minus: Deductible itemized deductions	−15,786
Minus: Exemption deductions ($3,200 × 2)	−6,400
Equals: Taxable Income	$ 147,564

The 3 percent cutback rule, which is scheduled to be phased out between 2006 and 2010, is discussed in detail in Chapter 11.

Additional Standard Deduction for Elderly or Blind Taxpayers. Congress has traditionally extended some type of tax relief to the elderly and blind, presumably to take into account their special situations. Currently, an unmarried taxpayer who is either blind or age 65 at the close of the taxable year is allowed to increase his or her standard deduction by an additional $1,250 (for 2005). If an unmarried taxpayer is *both* blind and 65 or older, he or she is allowed to increase the standard deduction by $2,500. A married couple is allowed $1,000 (for 2005) for each status for a maximum increase on a joint return of $4,000.

> **Example 11.** In 2005, S celebrated her sixty-fifth birthday. Instead of using the $5,000 standard deduction amount allowed for single taxpayers for 2004, S will be allowed a standard deduction of $6,250 ($5,000 basic standard deduction + $1,250 additional standard deduction) for 2005.
>
> If S were married filing a joint return for 2005, the standard deduction amount allowed would be $11,000 ($10,000 + $1,000). If both S and her husband were 65 or older, the standard deduction would be $12,000 [$10,000 standard deduction + (2 × $1,000 additional standard deduction)].

Both age and blindness are determined at the close of the taxable year. Guidelines are provided for determining whether an individual is legally blind, and specific filing requirements must be met.[32] An individual is considered to have attained age 65 on the day *preceding* his or her sixty-fifth birthday.[33] Thus, if a taxpayer's sixty-fifth birthday is January 1, 2006, he or she is considered to be 65 on December 31, 2005.

Limitations on Use of Standard Deductions. Not all individuals are entitled to the full benefit of the standard deduction. No standard deduction is allowed for the following individuals:

1. A married person filing a separate return if his or her spouse itemizes deductions;[34]

2. A nonresident alien;[35] and

3. An individual filing a return for a period of less than 12 months because of a change of accounting period.[36]

In addition, the standard deduction is limited for an individual who is claimed as a dependent on another taxpayer's return. This limitation is discussed in Chapter 4.

Exemptions. Congress has always recognized the need to insulate from tax a certain amount of income required by the taxpayer to support himself and others. For this reason, every individual taxpayer is entitled to a basic deduction for himself and his dependents. This deduction is called an *exemption*. For 2005, an individual taxpayer is entitled to a deduction of $3,200 for each *personal* and *dependency* exemption.[37] *Personal exemptions* are those allowed for the taxpayer. Generally, every taxpayer is entitled to claim a personal exemption for himself or herself. However, taxpayers *cannot* claim a personal exemption on their own return if they can be claimed as a dependent

---

[32]   §§ 151(d) and 151(d)(3). A taxpayer is legally blind if he or she cannot see better than 20/200 in the better eye with corrective lenses, or the taxpayer's field of vision is not more than 20 degrees. A statement must be attached to the tax return for the year. The statement must be prepared by a physician or optometrist when a taxpayer is less than totally blind. Reg. § 1.151-1(d)(2).

[33]   Reg. § 1.151-1(c)(2).

[34]   If one spouse elects to itemize deductions on a separate return, the other spouse *must* also itemize deductions. § 63(c)(6)(A).

[35]   § 63(c)(6)(B).

[36]   § 63(c)(6)(C).

[37]   §151(d)(1). For 1989 the exemption was $2,000. For years *after* 1989, the amount has been indexed for inflation.

on another taxpayer's return.[38] If husband and wife file a joint return, they are treated as two taxpayers and are therefore entitled to claim two personal exemptions. *Dependency exemptions* may be claimed for qualifying individuals who are supported by the taxpayer.[39] In addition to the 3 percent cutback in itemized deductions, high-income taxpayers are required to reduce the amount of their total deduction for personal and dependency exemptions. All the special rules governing deductions for exemptions are discussed in detail in Chapter 4.

Taxable Income and Tax Rates. After all deductions have been identified, they are subtracted from gross income to arrive at taxable income. Taxable income is the tax base to which the tax rates are applied to determine the taxpayer's gross tax liability (i.e., the tax liability before any credits or prepayments).

The tax rate schedule to be used in computing the tax varies, depending on the nature of the taxable entity. For example, one set of tax rates applies to all regular corporations (see inside back cover of text). In contrast, individuals use one of four tax rate schedules (see inside front cover) depending on their filing status, of which there are four. These are

1. Unmarried individuals (i.e., single) who are not surviving spouses or heads of household

2. Heads of household

3. Married individuals filing jointly and surviving spouses

4. Married individuals filing separately

These tax rate structures are all graduated with the rates of 10, 15, 25, 28, 33, and 35 percent. Although the rates in each schedule are identical, the degree of progressivity differs. For example, in 2005 the 28 percent marginal rate applies to single taxpayers when income exceeds $71,950, but this rate does not apply to married individuals filing jointly until income exceeds $119,950. The various filing statuses and rate schedules are discussed in Chapter 4.

The 2003 tax reforms include a reduction in marginal income tax rates to a point where the top marginal tax rate for individuals is 35 percent. The marginal tax rates for individuals are now 10, 15, 25, 28, 33, and 35 percent. More information related to these rates is provided in Chapter 4.

Example 12. Y and Z are married and file a joint return for 2005. They have adjusted gross income of $125,700, two dependents, and itemized deductions of $32,400. Their taxable income is $80,500, computed as follows:

Adjusted gross income.		$ 125,700
Minus: Itemized deductions.	$ 32,400	
Personal exemptions ($3,200 × 4).	+ 12,800	−45,200
Equals: Taxable income.		$ 80,500

The tax for a married couple filing jointly on this amount is $13,455, computed below.

Tax on $59,400	$ 8,180
Plus: Tax on excess at 25%	
[($80,500 − $59,400) × .25].	5,275
Equals: Total tax	$13,455

---

[38] § 151(d)(2).

[39] § 152.

Credits. Unlike a deduction, which reduces income in arriving at taxable income, a credit is a direct reduction in tax liability. Normally, when the credit exceeds a person's total tax, the excess is not refunded—hence, these credits are referred to as *nonrefundable* credits. In some instances, however, the taxpayer is entitled to receive a payment for any excess credit. This type of credit is known as a *refundable* credit.

Credits have frequently been preferred by Congress and theoreticians because they affect all taxpayers equally. In contrast, the value of a deduction varies with the taxpayer's marginal tax rate. However, credits often have complicated rules and limitations. A partial list of tax credits is included in Exhibit 3-7.

EXHIBIT 3-7
Partial List of Tax Credits

Foreign tax credit
Child tax credit
Earned income credit
Child and dependent care credit
Credit for adoption expenses
Hope scholarship credit
Lifetime learning credit
Credit for the elderly
Credit for producing fuel from a nonconventional source
Credit for increasing research activities
Welfare to work credit
Work opportunity credit
Low income housing credit
Credit for rehabilitating certain buildings

Prepayments. Attempting to accelerate the collection of revenues for the war effort in 1943, Congress installed a "pay-as-you-go" system for certain taxes. Under this system, income taxes are paid in installments as the income is earned.

Prepayment, or advance payment, of the tax liability can be made in several ways. For individual taxpayers, the two most common forms of prepayment are Federal income taxes withheld from an employee's salaries and wages and quarterly estimated tax payments made by the taxpayer. Certain corporate taxpayers must make quarterly estimated tax payments as well. Quarterly estimated tax payments are required for taxpayers who have not prepaid a specified level of their anticipated Federal income tax in any other way, and there are penalties for failure to make adequate estimated prepayments.

These prepayments serve two valuable purposes. As suggested above, prepayments allow the government to have earlier use of the tax proceeds. Secondly, prepayments reduce the uncertainty of collecting taxes since the government, by withholding at the source, gets the money before the taxpayer has a chance to put it to a different use. In effect, the government collects the tax while the taxpayer has the wherewithal (ability) to pay the tax.

Other Taxes. There are several types of other taxes that must be reported and paid with the regular Federal income tax. A partial list of these taxes is included in Exhibit 3-8. Two deserve special mention.

EXHIBIT 3-8
Partial List of Other Taxes

> Alternative minimum tax on corporations
> Alternative minimum tax on individuals and fiduciaries
> Self-employment tax
> Social security tax on tip income not reported to employer
> Tax on premature withdrawal from an Individual Retirement Account
> Tax from recapture of investment credit
> Uncollected employee F.I.C.A. and R.R.T. A. tax on tips

Self-Employment Tax. As explained in Chapter 1, self-employed individuals as well as general partners in partnerships are, like employees, required to pay FICA taxes (commonly known as self-employment taxes). Since the tax is paid on income from sole proprietorship and partnership businesses carried on by individual partners, it is convenient for the IRS to collect this tax along with the income tax on Form 1040. The individual calculates the tax on Schedule SE and claims the income tax deduction for one-half of the self-employment tax paid on page 1 of Form 1040.

Alternative Minimum Tax. In 1969 there was an outcry by the media and others that the rich did not pay their fair share of taxes. Indeed, the House Ways and Means Committee Report indicated that in 1964 over 1,100 returns with adjusted gross incomes over $200,000 paid an average tax of 22 percent. Moreover, it reported that there were a significant number of cases where taxpayers with economic income of $1 million or more paid an effective tax amounting to less than 5 percent of their income. As might be expected, faced with such facts Congress decided to take action. However, instead of risking the wrath of their constituents by simply repealing the various loopholes that enabled these taxpayers to avoid taxes, Congress elected to take a politically cautious approach: a direct tax on the loopholes. In effect, the taxpayer simply added up all of the loopholes and paid a flat tax on them. As a result, the minimum tax was born. The whole thrust of this new tax was to ensure that all individuals paid a minimum tax on their income. It currently applies to all taxpayers, individuals, corporations, and fiduciaries.

Over the years, the minimum tax evolved into a monster and was adorned with its current name, the alternative minimum tax (AMT). Despite the changes and increased complexity, it remains basically the same. The mathematical steps for computing the AMT are relatively simple:

	Regular taxable income
±	Adjustments and preferences
	Alternative minimum taxable income
−	Exemption (subject to phase-out)
	Tax base
×	Rate
	Tentative alternative minimum tax
−	Regular tax
	Alternative minimum tax

As the formula above illustrates, the taxpayer starts with taxable income and then adds back certain income that is excluded for regular tax purposes and subtracts certain deductions that are normally allowed. These modifications to regular taxable income are referred to as *preference items* and *adjustments*. In this regard, it is important to recognize that the AMT effectively functions as an entirely separate system with its own rules. For example, while most interest from state and local bonds is not taxable, such interest is taxable for AMT purposes if the bonds are used to fund some private activity such as a downtown mall. Similarly, deductions that are usually allowed for regular tax purposes, such as exemptions, miscellaneous itemized deductions, and state and local taxes, are not allowed in computing the AMT. In effect, there are two rules for some items: one rule for regular tax purposes and another for AMT purposes. After taking into account all of the special adjustments required under this alternative system, the new result is called alternative minimum taxable income. This amount is then reduced by an allowable exemption ($58,000 for married taxpayers filing jointly; $40,250 for single and head-of-household taxpayers) to arrive at the tax base. Note, however, that this exemption begins to phase-out when AMTI becomes large (e.g. $150,000 for joint filers, $112,000 for singles). A two-tier rate structure is then applied to the tax base (26 percent on the first $175,000 and 28 percent on the excess). The product is referred to as the tentative AMT. This amount is compared to the regular tax, and the taxpayer pays the higher. Technically, the excess of the tentative AMT over the regular tax is the AMT, but the bottom line is that the taxpayer pays the higher amount.

Example 13. H and W are married with four children. This year they filed a joint return, reporting gross income of $400,000 and regular taxable income of $100,000. Various adjustments required under the AMT were $48,000. The couple must pay an AMT of $5,070, computed as follows:

	Regular taxable income	$100,000
±	Adjustments	48,000
	Alternative minimum taxable income	$148,000
−	Exemption	(58,000)
	Tax base	$ 90,000
×	Rate	×26%
	Tentative alternative minimum tax	$ 23,400
−	Regular tax	(18,330)
	Alternative minimum tax	$ 5,070

Note that the AMT is only $5,070, but the taxpayer must pay a total of $23,400 (regular tax of $18,330 + AMT of $5,070).

There is no good rule of thumb as to when the AMT is triggered. For the vast majority of taxpayers it is simply not an issue. These individuals are not subject to the tax since they have low to moderate taxable incomes with few adjustments, causing them to fall below the $40,250 or $58,000 exemption. It is typically high-income taxpayers who have substantial adjustments, and other taxpayers who are successful in avoiding the regular tax, that fall prey to the AMT. Obviously the key lies in the nature of the adjustments. For now it is sufficient to say that beyond the few preferences and adjustments mentioned above there are several more such as those relating to depreciation, depletion, and stock options. Full coverage is deferred until Chapter 13. Nevertheless, even at this early juncture it is important to recognize that the AMT exists and often alters what appears to be very favorable tax treatment. In effect, the AMT makes some tax benefits more apparent than real. As these items come up throughout the text, the implications for the AMT are duly noted.

✅ *CHECK YOUR KNOWLEDGE*

Review Question 1. It's time for "Tax Jeopardy." Here are the answers; supply the questions.

a. The type of expenses all taxpayers can deduct.

What are business expenses? Around tax time, there is a single question that can be heard reverberating across the land: What can I deduct? The answer is business expenses. All taxpayers are allowed to deduct the ordinary and necessary expenses incurred in carrying on a trade or business. The vast majority of all deductions fall into this category. Note also that this rule allows the deduction of employee business expenses. In addition, taxpayers are entitled to deduct expenses related to investment activities (e.g., investment advice or repairs and maintenance on rental property).

The type of expenses taxpayers normally cannot deduct.

b. What are personal expenses? Although business expenses are deductible, personal expenses normally are not deductible. For example, the costs of food, shelter, clothing, and personal hygiene cannot be deducted. However, there are some exceptions.

c. Five notable exceptions to the rule that personal expenses are not deductible. (Hint: they are all reported on Schedule A of Form 1040, found in Appendix of this book.)

What are the following?

    1. Medical expenses (but only if they exceed 7.5 percent of A.G.I.)

    2. Taxes
- State and local income taxes (but not federal)
- Real estate taxes
- Personal property taxes

    3. Interest
- Home mortgage interest
- Student loan interest (maximum of $2,500)
- Investment interest (but only to the extent of investment income)

    4. Charitable contributions

    5. Casualty and theft losses

d. The type of business expenses that are deductible as itemized deductions.

What are unreimbursed employee business expenses? For example, if an employee pays for a business meal and his or her employer reimburses the cost of the meal, the expense is deductible in arriving at A.G.I. if the employer includes the reimbursement in the employee's gross income. However, when the expense is not reimbursed, it is allowable only as an itemized deduction. Other common examples of employee business expenses that are frequently deductible as itemized deductions are unreimbursed professional expenses (e.g., subscriptions, dues, license fees), union dues, and special clothing (when deductible).

e. The only type of tax-exempt income reported on the return. (Hint: see page 1 of Form 1040.)

What is tax-exempt interest income (reported on line 8b of page 1 of Form 1040)?

f. Something the individual tax formula has that the corporate tax formula does not have.

What is adjusted gross income? What is the standard deduction? What are exemptions?

g. A benefit received by the elderly and blind.

What is the increased standard deduction for taxpayers who are age 65 or over or who are blind?

h. Deductions that are deductible regardless of their amount.

What are deductions for A.G.I.? If a taxpayer's itemized deductions do not exceed the standard deduction, the taxpayer receives no benefit from the itemized deductions.

i. A deduction that may be claimed by virtually all individual taxpayers.

What is the exemption deduction, or the standard deduction? As explained above, however, certain persons are not entitled to a standard deduction. For example, a married person filing a separate return must itemize if his or her spouse does. In addition, as fully explained in Chapter 4, taxpayers cannot claim a personal exemption on their own return if they can be claimed as a dependent on another taxpayer's return.

j. A loss from this activity may not be deductible.

What are losses from rental real estate and any other activity in which the taxpayer does not materially participate? Before losses from an activity can be deducted (e.g., a loss that passes through from a partnership or a loss from renting a duplex), they must run through the gauntlet of tests prescribed by the passive loss rules covered in Chapter 12.

k. A separate tax intended to close loopholes.

What is the alternative minimum tax?

Review Question 2. Mabel just reached the age of 65 and was somewhat relieved because she remembered hearing of the tax she would save as a 65-year-old senior. What tax savings can Mabel expect?

Perhaps none. The only benefit for being 65 years old is an additional standard deduction ($1,250 for unmarried taxpayers for 2005). If Mabel itemizes her deductions rather than claiming the standard deduction, she receives no benefit. If she does not itemize and she is single, her standard deduction for 2005 is $6,250 (the basic standard deduction of $5,000 plus the extra $1,250).

Review Question 3. Robert and Kerry just learned that they are expecting their first child. What tax benefits can they expect after Junior is born?

Many. First are the dependency exemption deduction ($3,200 for 2005) and the child tax credit ($1,000 for 2005). In addition, Robert and Kerry can look forward to a credit for any job-related child care expenses that they pay.

Review Question 4. Are deductions of a sole proprietor deductible *for* or *from* adjusted gross income? (Hint: see Adjustments to Income on Page 1 of Form 1040 and Schedule C in Appendix of this book.)

The trade or business expenses of a sole proprietor or someone who is self-employed are deductible for A.G.I. Note that these are not shown as one of the adjustments to income on Page 1 of Form 1040. Instead, they are netted against the sole proprietor's income on Schedule C, and this net profit is included in the taxpayer's total income reported on Page 1 of Form 1040.

Review Question 5. A sole proprietor's income generally is subject to self-employment tax. Is the deduction for one-half of the self-employment tax deducted for or from adjusted gross income? Is it reported on Schedule C or Form 1040?

This is a deduction for A.G.I. and is reported as an adjustment to income on Form 1040 (and not Schedule C).

INTRODUCTION TO PROPERTY TRANSACTIONS

The tax provisions governing property transactions play a very important part in our tax system. Obviously, their major purpose is to provide for the tax treatment of transactions involving a sale, exchange, or other disposition of property. However, the basic rules covering property transactions can also impact the tax liability in other indirect ways. For example, the amount of the deduction granted for a charitable contribution of property may depend on what the tax result would have been had the property been sold rather than donated. As this example suggests, a basic knowledge of the tax treatment of property transactions is helpful in understanding other facets of taxation. For this reason, an overview of property transactions is presented here. Chapters 14, 15, 16, and 17 examine this subject in detail.

The tax consequences of any property transaction may be determined by answering the following three questions:

1. What is the amount of gain or loss *realized*?

2. How much of this gain or loss is *recognized*?

3. What is the *character* of the gain or loss recognized?

Each of these questions is considered in the following sections.

GAIN OR LOSS REALIZED

A realized gain or loss results when a taxpayer sells, exchanges, or otherwise disposes of property. In the simple case where property is purchased for cash and later sold for cash, the gain or loss realized is the difference between the purchase price and the sale price, adjusted for transaction costs. The determination of the realized gain or loss is more complicated when property other than cash is received, when liabilities are involved, or when the property was not acquired by purchase. As a result, a more formal method for computing the gain or loss realized is used. The formulas for computing the gain or loss realized are shown in Exhibits 3-9, 3-10, and 3-11. As these exhibits illustrate, the gain or loss realized in a sale or other disposition is the difference between the *amount realized* and the *adjusted basis* in the property given up.

EXHIBIT 3-9
Computation of Amount Realized

	Amount of money received (net of money paid)	
Add:	Fair market value of any other property received	
	Liabilities discharged in the transaction (net of liabilities assumed)	
Less:	Selling costs	
Equals:	**Amount realized**	

EXHIBIT 3-10
Determination of Adjusted Basis

Basis at time of acquisition:
For purchased property, use cost
Special rules apply for the following methods of acquisition:
  Gift
  Bequest or inheritance
  Nontaxable transactions
Add: Capital improvements, additions
Less: Depreciation and other capital recoveries
Equals: **Adjusted basis in property**

EXHIBIT 3-11
Computation of Gain or Loss Realized

Amount realized from sale or other disposition
Less: Adjusted basis in property (other than money) given up
Equals: **Gain or loss realized**

Amount Realized. The amount realized is a measure of the economic value received for the property given up. It generally includes the amount of any money plus the fair market value of any other property received, reduced by any selling costs.[40] In determining the amount realized, consideration must also be given to any liabilities from which the taxpayer is relieved or which the taxpayer incurs. From an economic standpoint, when a taxpayer is relieved of debt, it is the same as if cash were received and used to pay off the debt. In contrast, when a taxpayer assumes a debt (or receives property that is subject to a debt), it is the same as if the taxpayer gave up cash. Consequently, when a sale or exchange involves the transfer of liabilities, the amount realized is increased for the net amount of any liabilities discharged or decreased for the net amount of any liabilities incurred.

Adjusted Basis. The adjusted basis of property is similar to the concept of "book value" used for accounting purposes. It is the taxpayer's basis at the time of acquisition—usually cost—increased or decreased by certain required modifications.[41]

---

[40]   § 1001(b).

[41]   §§ 1011 through 1016.

The taxpayer's basis at the time of acquisition, or original basis, depends on how the property was acquired. For purchased property, the taxpayer's original basis is the property's cost. When property is acquired by gift, inheritance, or some form of tax-deferred exchange, special rules are applied in determining the original basis. Once the original basis is ascertained, it must be increased for any capital improvements and reduced by depreciation and other capital recoveries. The adjusted basis represents the amount of investment that can be recovered free of tax.

Example 14. This year, L sold 100 shares of M Corporation stock for $41 per share for a total of $4,100. He received a settlement check of $4,000, net of the broker's sales commission of $100. L had purchased the shares several years ago for $12 per share for a total of $1,200. In addition, he paid a sales commission of $30. L's realized gain is $2,770, computed as follows:

Amount realized ($4,100 − $100)	$ 4,000
Less: Adjusted basis ($1,200 + $30)	−1,230
Gain realized	$ 2,770

Example 15. During the year, T sold his office building. As part of the sales agreement, T received $20,000 cash, and the buyer assumed the mortgage on the building of $180,000. T also paid a real estate brokerage commission of $7,000. T originally acquired the building for $300,000 in 1980, but since that time had deducted depreciation of $230,000 and had made permanent improvements of $10,000. T's gain realized is computed as follows:

Amount realized:		
Cash received.	$ 20,000	
Liability assumed by buyer	+180,000	
Selling expenses.	−7,000	
		$ 193,000
Less: Adjusted basis		
Original cost	$ 300,000	
Depreciation claimed.	−230,000	
Capital improvements	+10,000	
		−80,000
Gain realized.		$ 113,000

GAIN OR LOSS RECOGNIZED

The gain or loss *realized* is a measure of the economic gain or loss that results from the ownership and sale or disposition of property. However, due to special provisions in the tax law, the gain or loss reported for tax purposes may be different from the realized gain or loss. The amount of gain or loss that affects the tax liability is called the *recognized* gain or loss.

Normally, all realized gains are recognized and included as part of the taxpayer's total income. In some instances, however, the gain recognition may be deferred or postponed until a subsequent transaction occurs.

Example 16. M exchanged some land in Oregon costing $10,000 for land in Florida valued at $50,000. Although M has realized gain of $40,000 ($50,000 − $10,000), assuming certain requirements are satisfied, this gain will not be recognized, but rather postponed. This rule was adopted because the taxpayer's economic position after the transaction is essentially unchanged. Moreover, the taxpayer has not received any cash or wherewithal with which she could pay any tax that might result.

Chapter 15 contains a discussion of the more common types of property transactions in which the recognition of an individual taxpayer's realized gains are postponed.

Any loss realized must be specifically allowed as a deduction before it is recognized. Individuals generally are allowed to deduct *three* types of losses. These are

1. Losses incurred in a trade or business (e.g., an uncollectible receivable)

2. Losses incurred in an activity engaged in for profit (e.g., sale of investment property such as stock at a loss)

3. Casualty and theft losses

Losses in the first two categories generally are deductions for adjusted gross income. Casualty and theft losses from property used in an individual's trade, business, or income-producing activity also are allowed as deductions for adjusted gross income. However, casualty and theft losses from personal use property are classified as itemized deductions and are deductible only to the extent they exceed $100 per casualty or theft and other specific limitations. Other than casualty and theft losses, all other losses from dispositions of personal use assets are *not* deductible. The rules governing the deductibility of losses in the first three categories are covered in Chapter 10. The special rules governing the deduction of "capital" losses are introduced below and covered in greater detail in Chapter 16.

CHARACTER OF THE GAIN OR LOSS

From 1913 through 1921, all includible income was taxed in the same manner. Since 1921, however, Congress has provided special tax treatment for "capital" gains or losses. As a result, in determining the tax consequences of a property transaction, consideration must be given to the character or nature of the gain or loss—that is, whether the gain or loss should be classified as a *capital* gain or loss or an *ordinary* gain or loss. Any *recognized* gain or loss must be characterized as either an ordinary or a capital gain or loss.

Capital Gains and Losses. Although capital gains and losses arise in numerous ways, they normally result from the sale or exchange of a *capital asset*. Any gain or loss due to the sale or exchange of a capital asset is considered a capital gain or loss.

Capital assets are defined in § 1221 of the Code as being anything *other* than the following:

1. Inventory, or other property held primarily for sale to customers in the ordinary course of a trade or business

2. Depreciable property or real property used in a trade or business of the taxpayer

3. Trade accounts or notes receivable

4. Certain copyrights, literary, musical, or artistic compositions, and letters or memoranda held by the person whose personal efforts created them, and certain specified other holders of these types of property

5. U.S. government publications acquired other than by purchase at the price at which they are sold to the general public

The term *capital assets,* therefore, includes most passive investments (e.g., stocks and bonds) and most personal use assets of a taxpayer. However, property used in a trade or business is not a capital asset and is subject to special tax treatment, as discussed later in this chapter.

Treatment of Capital Gains. For many years, Congress has attempted to encourage greater investment and savings by substantially cutting the rates on capital gains. Unfortunately, each change in the rules has added complexity. For example, capital gains qualifying for special treatment could now be taxed at one of five different rates (28%, 25%, 15%, 10%, or 5%).

Holding Period. The exact treatment of a capital gain or loss depends primarily on how long the taxpayer held the asset or what is technically referred to as the taxpayer's *holding period.* The holding period is a critical element in determining which of the rates will apply. As might be expected, the longer the holding period is, the lower the applicable tax rate will be. A *short-term* gain or loss is one resulting from the sale or disposition of an asset held *one year or less.* A *long-term* gain or loss occurs when an asset is held for *more than one year.* However, after this initial classification, individuals must subdivide the long-term group into additional subgroups: (1) the 28% group for long-term capital gains resulting from the sales of *collectibles* (e.g., antiques, coins, stamps) and *qualified small business stock* (often referred to as § 1202 stock); (2) the 25% group for long-term capital gains (and only gains) from the sale of depreciable real estate (e.g., office buildings, warehouses, apartment buildings) held for more than one year but only to the extent of the depreciation claimed on such property; and (3) the 15% group for other (most) long-term capital gains.

The effect of the new rules is to require taxpayers to assign their capital gains and losses into one of four different groups and net the amounts to determine the net gain or loss in each group as shown below.

	Short-term	Long-term		
Holding period (months)	≤12 Ordinary	Collectibles & § 1202 stock > 12 28%	Realty > 12 25%	> 12 15%
Gains	$xx,xxx	$x,xxx	Gains only	$xx,xxx
Losses	(xxx)	(x,xxx)	—	(x,xxx)
Net gain or loss	????	????	Gain only	????

As a practical matter, the capital gains of most individuals arise from the sales of stocks and bonds and mutual fund transactions. Rarely do individuals have gains from collectibles, § 1202, stock or depreciable realty. Consequently, for most individuals, the classification and netting process will indeed be much easier.

Applicable Capital Gains Rates. Generalizations about the treatment of capital gains and losses are difficult because the actual treatment can be determined only after the various groups (i.e., the four groups above) are combined, or netted, to determine the overall net gain or loss during the year. The details of this netting process are quite complex and left to Chapter 16. Suffice it to say here that the treatment of the net gains of each group—*before any netting between groups*—can be summarized as follows:

1. A net short-term capital gain (NSTCG) generally receives no special treatment and is taxed as ordinary income at the taxpayer's regular tax rate (up to 35%).

2. A net 28% capital gain (N28CG) is taxed at a maximum rate of 28%.

3. A net 25% gain (N25CG) from dispositions of realty is taxed at a maximum rate of 25% (generally only to the extent of any depreciation claimed). The balance of any gain is part of the 15% group.

4. A net 15% gain (N15CG) is taxed at a maximum rate of 15%. However, if the taxpayer's tax bracket (determined by *including* the net 15% gain) is 15% or less, the net gain in this group is taxed at a rate of 5%.

In applying these rules, it should be emphasized that they operate to set only the maximum rate at which the particular type of gain will be taxed. If the taxpayer's tax using the regular rates would be lower, the regular rates are used. For example, if the taxpayer is in the 15% tax bracket and has a 28% gain, the 15% rate would apply instead of the 28% rate.

Example 17. During the year, T, who is in the 35% tax bracket, reported the following capital gains and losses.

	Short-term	Long-term 28%	Long-term 15%
Gains.............	$10,000	$4,000	$10,000
Losses............	(4,000)	—	(3,000)
	$ 6,000	$4,000	$ 7,000

In this case, T has a NSTCG of $6,000, a N28CG of $4,000, and a N15CG of $7,000. As explained in Chapter 16, no further netting of these transactions occurs. T's NSTCG of $6,000 receives no special treatment and is taxed as ordinary income. T's N28CG is taxed at 28% while his N15CG is taxed at 15%.

Dividends Taxed at Capital Gain Rates. Beginning in 2003, most dividends received are subject to the long-term capital gains rates[42]: 15% generally and 5% for dividends that would otherwise be taxed at an ordinary rate of 15% or lower. The qualifying dividend is added to the net capital gain and is not subject to the capital gain and loss netting process. As a result, the dividends are subject to capital gains treatment regardless of whether the taxpayer has other capital gains or losses. The details related to calculating the tax on these dividends are presented in Chapter 16.

Treatment of Capital Losses. While capital gains receive favorable treatment, such is not the case with capital losses. As can be seen in *Example 17* above, capital losses are first netted with capital gains within the same group. A net capital loss from a particular group can then be combined with net capital gains from the other groups. As a general rule, the long-term groups are netted together before considering any short-term items. If after netting all of the groups together, the taxpayer has an overall net capital loss, the loss is deductible up to an annual limit of $3,000. The deductible capital loss is a deduction for adjusted gross income. Any losses in excess of the annual $3,000 limitation are carried forward to the following year where they are treated as if they occurred in such year. In effect, an unused capital loss can be carried over for an indefinite period.

---

[42] § 1(h)(11).

Example 18. During the year, B reported the following capital gains and losses.

	Short-term	Long-term 28%	Long-term 15%
Gains............	$ 10,000	$ 3,000	$ 5,000
Losses...........	(18,000)	(4,000)	(3,000)
	($8,000)	($1,000)	$ 2,000

B's only other taxable income included his salary of $50,000. He had no other deductions for A.G.I. After netting all of his gains and losses, B has a net capital loss of $7,000. T may deduct only $3,000 of the net capital loss in determining his A.G.I. Therefore, his A.G.I. is $47,000 ($50,000 – $3,000). The unused capital loss of $4,000 ($7,000 – $3,000) is carried forward to future years when it is treated as if it arose in the subsequent year. In such case, the loss can be used against other capital gains or ordinary income just as it was this year.

Details of capital gain and loss treatment and the capital loss carryover rules are discussed in Chapter 16.

Corporate Taxpayers. The taxation of capital gains for corporate taxpayers differs somewhat from that for individuals. Most important, the capital gains of a corporation receive no special treatment but are taxed as ordinary income. In addition, the capital losses of a corporation can never offset ordinary income but can be carried back three and forward five years to offset other capital gains. There are a number of other differences which are considered in a full discussion of a corporation's capital gains and losses in Chapter 19.

TRADE OR BUSINESS PROPERTY

Depreciable property and real property used in a trade or business are not capital assets, but are subject to several special provisions. Nevertheless, gain on the sale of these assets may ultimately be treated as capital gain while losses may be treated as ordinary losses. These rules are exceedingly complex and considered in Chapter 17.

☑ CHECK YOUR KNOWLEDGE

Try the following true-false questions.

Review Question 1. An individual always receives preferential treatment for his or her capital gains.

False. An individual can receive special treatment only for long-term capital gains. Short-term capital gains are treated just like ordinary income.

Review Question 2. J is interested in the stock market. This year she realized a $1,000 short-term capital gain and an $8,000 capital loss from stock she held for two years. She will report a $1,000 short-term capital gain and carry over the $8,000 long-term capital loss.

False. She first nets the short-term gain of $1,000 against her $8,000 15% loss, resulting in an overall long-term capital loss of $7,000. She may deduct $3,000 of this loss as a deduction for A.G.I. The remaining loss is carried over to the following year, when it will be treated as if she had realized a long-term (28%) capital loss of $4,000.

Review Question 3. K makes $300,000 a year and plays the stock market. So far this year she has realized a 15% capital gain of $3,000. It is now December 31. Should K sell stock and recognize a $3,000 15% loss?

Who knows! If she recognizes a $3,000 loss, the loss is offset against the gain and therefore reduces income that would have been taxed at a 15 percent rate. This would produce a tax benefit from the loss of only $450 ($3,000 × 15%). If she waits and uses the loss against ordinary income, it will produce a tax benefit of $1,050 (35% × $3,000), or $600 ($1,050 − $450) more. However, if she postpones the loss until some subsequent year hoping to use it to offset income taxed at a higher rate, she will lose the time value of the $450.

Review Question 4. A corporation receives no special treatment for its long-term capital gains.

True. The capital gains of a corporation are treated in the same manner as ordinary income.

Review Question 5. John Doe is the typical American taxpayer. He is married, has a dog and two kids. He also owns two cars: a brand new Ford and a 1996 Chevrolet. He bought the Ford for $17,000 and the Chevy for $10,000. Both of the cars were used for personal purposes. This year John and his family moved to New York and decided they did not need the cars, so he sold them. He sold the Chevy for only $3,000. The story on the Ford was different. The Ford happened to be a Mustang convertible, and because Mustangs were in demand and were on back order, a car nut was willing to give him $19,000, a $2,000 premium for not having to wait. How will these sales affect John's taxable income? Explain whether the taxpayer has a gain or loss, its character, and in the case of a loss whether it is deductible for or from A.G.I.

John reports a capital gain of $2,000. The first step is to determine John's gain or loss *realized.* In this case, the determination is simple. On the sale of the Chevy, John realized a loss of $7,000 ($3,000 − $10,000), and on the sale of the Mustang he realized a gain of $2,000 ($19,000 − $17,000). The second step is to determine whether he *recognizes* the gain and loss realized. John must recognize the gain. As a general rule, all income is taxable unless the taxpayer can point to a specific provision that specifically exempts the income from tax. In this case, there is no exclusion. On the other hand, the $7,000 loss is not deductible. Although all income is normally taxable, only those items specifically authorized are deductible. Only three types of losses are deductible: (1) losses incurred in carrying on a trade or business; (2) losses incurred in an activity engaged in for profit (e.g., investment losses); and (3) casualty and theft losses. In this case, the loss on the sale of the Chevy is purely personal, and therefore no deduction is allowed. Thus John is not allowed to net the loss against the gain but must report only the gain of $2,000. While this may seem like a surprising result, understand that tax is a one-way street: as a general rule, all income is taxable and only those expenses and losses specifically allowed are deductible. The final step is determining the character of the gain, that is, whether the gain is capital gain or ordinary income. In order for a taxpayer to have a capital gain, there must be a sale or exchange of a capital asset. The Code defines a capital asset as essentially everything but inventory and real or depreciable property used in a trade or business. In this case, the car is not used in business and it does not represent inventory, so it is a capital asset. As a result, John reports a capital gain of $2,000.

Review Question 6. Indicate whether the following assets are capital assets.

    a. 2,000 boxes of Frosted Flakes held by a grocery store
    b. A crane used in the taxpayer's bungee-jumping business
    c. A warehouse owned by Wal-Mart
    d. IBM stock held for investment
    e. The personal residence of Jane Doe

The Code generally defines a capital asset as essentially everything but inventory, business receivables, and real or depreciable property used in a trade or business. Based on this definition, the Frosted Flakes are not a capital asset since they are held as inventory by the grocery; the crane is not a capital asset since it is depreciable property used in a business; and the warehouse is not a capital asset since it is real property used in a business. The personal residence and IBM stock are both capital assets since they are neither inventory nor property used in a trade or business.

TAX PLANNING CONSIDERATIONS

CHOICE OF BUSINESS FORM

One of the major decisions confronting a business from a tax perspective concerns selecting the form in which it conducts its operations. A taxpayer could choose to operate a business as a sole proprietorship, a partnership, a limited liability company, an S corporation, or a regular C corporation. Each of these entities has its own tax characteristics that make it more or less suitable for a particular situation. The following discussion highlights a number of the basic factors that should be considered.

Perhaps the most important consideration in choosing a business form is the outlook for the business. A business that expects losses will typically opt for a business form different from the one that expects profits. A key advantage of a conduit entity (i.e., partnership or S corporation) applies in years in which a business suffers losses. Like income, losses flow through to the owners of the entity and generally can be used to offset other income at the individual level. In contrast, losses suffered by a regular C corporation are bottled up inside the corporate entity and can benefit only the corporation. Losses of a regular corporation generally are carried back two years and carried forward 20 years to offset income that the corporation has in prior or subsequent years.

A profitable business may also benefit from choosing the proper form of organization. To illustrate, consider a business that is generating taxable income of $1 million per year. If the taxpayer conducts the business as a sole proprietorship or through one of the conduit entities, the top tax rate applied to the income is 35 percent. In contrast, if a C corporation is used to operate the business, the top rate is 35 percent. Tax savings may also be generated at lower levels of income. This possibility can be seen in the tax rate schedules for corporations and individuals. A quick comparison reveals that the first $50,000 of income of a corporate taxpayer is taxed at a 15 percent rate, whereas married taxpayers receive the benefits of a 15 percent (or lower) rate on a maximum of $59,400. Obviously, the tax-wise individual might try to structure the activities so that the best of both worlds could be obtained. Consider a business that produces income of $90,000. If a corporation is used, the company could pay a deductible salary of $50,000 to the owner (assuming it is a reasonable amount), leaving $40,000 of taxable income in the corporation. By so doing, the maximum tax rate paid on the income would be 15 percent. Had the business been operated as a sole proprietorship or an S corporation, $30,600, the amount of taxable income in excess of $59,400, would have been taxed at a 25 percent rate, or 10 percentage points higher.

This may seem appealing, but it is a very simplistic analysis and leaves vital elements out of the equation. For example, this scheme completely ignores the problem of double taxation; it assumes that the taxpayer will be able to withdraw the $34,000 ($40,000 − $6,000 corporate income tax) left in the corporation at a later time in a deductible fashion so as to avoid the second tax. Unfortunately, doing so is not as easy as it may appear, and this plan as well as any other requires careful analysis. Suffice it to say here, however, that careful planning at the outset of a new business can save the taxpayer substantial taxes in the future.

A major disadvantage of partnerships and S corporations concerns the treatment of certain fringe benefits. As explained in Chapter 6, the Code contains a host of fringe benefits that generally are deductible by the employer and nontaxable to the employee. For example, a corporation is entitled to deduct the costs of group-term life insurance provided to an employee, and the benefit (i.e., the payment of the premiums) is not treated as taxable compensation to the employee but is tax-free. Note that if the employee purchases the insurance directly, it is purchased with compensation that has been previously taxed. As a result, the employee acquires the benefit with after-tax dollars. The favorable tax treatment of fringe benefits is generally available only to employees of a business. Unfortunately, partners and shareholders in S corporations who work in the business are not considered employees for this purpose and consequently cannot obtain many of the tax-favored fringe benefits. In contrast, shareholders in regular C corporations who work in the business are treated as employees and are therefore able to take advantage of the various benefits. Consideration should also be given to payroll and self-employment taxes.

ITEMIZED DEDUCTIONS VS. STANDARD DEDUCTION

A typical complaint of many taxpayers is that they have insufficient deductions to itemize and therefore cannot benefit from any deductions they have in a particular year. Nevertheless, with a little planning, not all of those deductions will be wasted. Taxpayers in this situation should attempt to bunch all their itemized deductions into one year. By so doing, they may itemize one year and claim the standard deduction the next. By alternating each year, total deductions over the two-year period are increased. This could be accomplished simply by postponing or accelerating the payment of expenses. Cash basis taxpayers have this flexibility because they are entitled to deduct expenses when paid.

Example 19. Last year, X, a widow age 61, made the final payment on her home mortgage. As a result, she no longer has the interest deductions that in the past enabled her to itemize. In fact, the only deductible expenses she anticipates are property taxes on the house and charitable contributions to her church. However, these expenses together do not exceed the standard deduction as her estimates below show.

	2005	2006
Property taxes	$1,400	$1,400
Charitable contributions	2,700	2,700
Total	$4,100	$4,100

If the pattern above continues, X will not benefit from any of the itemized deductions since they do not exceed the standard deduction for single taxpayers, $5,000. In short, she would obtain a total of $10,000 ($5,000 × 2) of deductions over the two-year period, assuming the standard deduction does not change. Note, however, what would happen if X simply shifted the payment of the charitable contributions from one year to the other by paying it either earlier or later. In such case, total itemized deductions in one year would be $6,800 ($4,100 + $2,700) and she could itemize, while in the other year she could claim the standard deduction. As a result, she would obtain total deductions over the two-year period of $11,800 ($6,800 + $5,000), or $1,800 more than if she merely claimed the standard deduction.

EMPLOYEE BUSINESS EXPENSES

Most employee business expenses are typically paid by the employer, either through direct payment or reimbursement. As such, the expenses are deductible by the employer. In the case of reimbursements, the employee has equal amounts of income and deduction if the reimbursement equals the expense. The net effect on adjusted gross income is zero.

If an employer requires employees to incur some business expenses, the employee can claim them only to the extent he or she itemizes and has miscellaneous itemized deductions in excess of 2 percent of A.G.I. As a result, the employee may receive little or no tax benefit from the expenses.

In reviewing the employee's compensation package, employers might consider changing their reimbursement policies. If an employer adopts more generous reimbursement policies in lieu of compensation increases, the employees may benefit.

Example 20. E is an employee with gross income of $20,000. She typically has annual employee business expenses of $750 that are not reimbursed. Since E does not itemize, she derives no tax benefit from the expenses.

If, instead of the above arrangement, E received a salary of $19,250 and the $750 were reimbursed, she would be in the same position before tax. However, she would pay $113 ($750 × 15% marginal tax on her salary) less in Federal income taxes.

PROBLEM MATERIALS

DISCUSSION QUESTIONS

3-1 *Taxable Entities.* List the classes of taxable entities under the Federal income tax. Identify at least one type of entity that is not subject to the tax.

3-2 *Double Taxation.* It has been stated that corporate earnings are subject to double taxation by the Federal government. Elaborate.

3-3 *Fiduciary.* In some regards, the fiduciary is a conduit for Federal income tax purposes. Explain.

3-4 *Partnership and S Corporation Returns.* The partnership and S corporation tax returns are often referred to as information returns only. Explain.

3-5 *Income from Partnerships.* Y is a general partner in the XYZ Partnership. For the current calendar year, Y's share of profits includes his guaranteed compensation of $55,000 and his share of remaining profits, which is $22,000. What is the proper income tax and payroll tax (F.I.C.A. or self-employment tax) treatment of each of the following to Y for the current calendar year?
a. The guaranteed compensation of $50,000
b. The remaining income share of $22,000

3-6 *Income from S Corporations.* K is the president and chief executive officer of KL, Inc., an S corporation that is owned equally by individuals K and L. K receives a salary of $83,000, and her share of the net income, after deducting executive salaries, is $50,000. What is the proper income tax and payroll tax (F.I.C.A. or self-employment tax) treatment of each of the following to K for the current calendar year?

    a. The salary, assuming it is reasonable in amount

    b. The net income of $50,000 that passes through to K

    c. The $3,600 that the company paid for group employee medical insurance for K and her family

3-7 *Tax Formula.* Reproduce the tax formula for individual taxpayers in good form and briefly describe each of the components of the formula. Discuss the differences between the tax formula for individuals and that for corporations.

3-8 *Gross Income.* How is gross income defined in the Internal Revenue Code?

3-9 *Deductions.* Distinguish between deductions *for* and deductions *from* adjusted gross income.

3-10 *Standard Deduction.* What is the standard deduction? Explain its relationship to itemized deductions. Which taxpayers are entitled to additional standard deductions?

3-11 *Itemized Deductions.* List seven major categories of itemized deductions. How and when are these reduced? Is the standard deduction reduced? If so, under what circumstances?

3-12 *Employee Business Expenses.* Expenses incurred that are directly related to one's activities as an employee are trade or business expenses. True or False?

3-13 *Additional Standard Deduction.* H and W are married and are 74 and 76 years of age, respectively. Assuming they have gross income of $16,400 for 2005 and file a joint return, determine their standard deduction and their personal exemption deductions.

3-14 *Exemptions.* Differentiate between personal exemptions and dependency exemptions. Which taxpayers are denied a personal exemption?

3-15 *Credits.* There are numerous credits that are allowed to reduce a taxpayer's Federal Income tax liability. List at least four such credits.

3-16 *Credits.* Credits of equal amount affect persons in different tax brackets equally, whereas deductions of equal amount are more beneficial to taxpayers in higher tax brackets. Explain.

3-17 *Prepayments.* What is meant by the concept of "wherewithal to pay" for tax purposes? How do prepayments of an individual's income taxes in the form of withholding and quarterly estimates represent the application of this concept?

3-18 *Alternative Minimum Tax.* What is the alternative minimum tax? Explain what is meant by *alternative* and *minimum* in this context.

3-19 *Amount Realized.* What is meant by "the amount realized in a sale or other disposition"? How is the amount realized calculated?

3-20 *Adjusted Basis.* Describe the concept of adjusted basis. How is the basis in purchased property determined?

3-21 *Gain or Loss Realized.* Reproduce the formula for determining the gain or loss realized in a sale or other disposition of property.

3-22 *Gain or Loss Recognized.* Differentiate between the terms "gain or loss realized" and "gain or loss recognized."

3-23 *Losses.* Which losses are deductible by individual taxpayers?

3-24 *Capital Assets.* Define the term "capital asset."

3-25 *Holding Period.* The determination of the holding period is important in determining the treatment of capital gains and losses. What is the difference between a long-term holding period and a short-term holding period?

3-26 *Capital Gains.* Briefly explain the favorable treatment given to capital gains and when such treatment applies.

3-27 *Capital Losses of Individuals.* There are "limitations" on the capital loss deduction for individuals. Identify these limitations.

3-28 *Capital Losses of Corporations.* What is the limitation on the deduction for capital losses of a corporate taxpayer?

3-29 *Carryover of Excess Capital Losses.* Excess capital losses of individuals may be offset against gains for other years. Specify the carryover and/or carryback period for such excess losses.

❓ *YOU MAKE THE CALL*

3-30 Shortly after Murray began working in the tax department of the public accounting firm of Dewey, Cheatham and Howe, he was preparing a tax return and discovered an error in last year's work papers. In computing the gain on the sale of the taxpayer's duplex, the preparer had failed to increase the amount realized by the $50,000 mortgage assumed by the buyer. Apparently, the mistake was overlooked during the review process. Upon discovering the mistake, Murray went to his immediate supervisor, Norm (who actually prepared last year's return), and pointed out the error. Norm, knowing that the client would probably flip if he found out he had to pay more tax, told Murray "let's just wait and see if the IRS catches it. Forget it for now." What should Murray do?

PROBLEMS

3-31 *To Whom Is Income Taxed?* In each of the following separate cases, determine how much income is to be taxed to each of the taxpayers involved:
  a. Alpha Partnership is owned 60 percent by William and 40 percent by Patricia, who agree to share profits according to their ownership ratios. For the current year, Alpha earned $12,000 in ordinary income and made no cash distributions.
  b. Beta Trust is managed by Susan for the benefit of Gregory. The trust is required to distribute all income currently. For the current year, Beta Trust had net ordinary income of $5,500 and made cash distributions to Gregory of $7,000.
  c. Gamma Corporation earned net ordinary income of $24,000 during the current calendar year. The corporation is a regular U.S. corporation. Heather and Kristie each own 50 percent of the stock and received dividend distributions of $1,350 each during the year.

3-32 *Selecting a Form of Doing Business.* Which form of business—sole proprietorship, partnership, S corporation, limited liability company, or regular corporation—is each of the following taxpayers likely to choose? An answer may include more than one business form.

    a. Edmund and Gloria are starting a new business that they expect to operate at a net loss for about five years. Both Edmund and Gloria expect to have substantial incomes during those years from other sources.

    b. Robin would like to incorporate her growing retail business for nontax reasons. Because she needs all of the net profits to meet personal obligations, Robin would like to avoid the corporate "double tax" on dividends.

3-33 *Income from C Corporations.* M is the president and chief executive officer of MN, Inc., a corporation that is owned solely by M. During the current calendar year, MN, Inc. paid M a salary of $80,000, a bonus of $22,000, and dividends of $30,000. The corporation's gross income is $350,000, and its expenses excluding payments to M are $225,000.

    a. Compute the corporation's taxable income and determine its gross income tax.

    b. Assuming M's only other income is interest income of $12,500, determine M's adjusted gross income.

    c. Does this situation represent double taxation of corporate profits? Explain.

3-34 *Income from Partnerships.* J is a one-fourth partner in JKLM Partnership. The partnership had gross sales of $880,000, cost of sales of $540,000, and operating expenses excluding payments to partners of $145,000 for the current calendar year. Partners' compensation for services of $90,000 ($45,000 to J) were paid, and distributions of $120,000 ($30,000 to J) were made for the year.

    a. Determine the partnership's net income for tax reporting purposes.

    b. Determine the amount of income J must report from the partnership for the year.

    c. Determine how much of the income in (b) is self-employment income.

3-35 *Income from Fiduciaries.* G created a trust for the benefit of B to be managed by T. For the current year, the trust had gross income of $45,000, income-producing deductions of $1,900, and cash distributions to B of $12,500.

    a. Determine the taxable income of the trust.

    b. Assuming B's only other income is interest of $22,300, determine B's adjusted gross income.

3-36 *Tax Treatment of Various Entities.* Office Supplies Unlimited is a small office supply outlet. The results of its operations for the most recent year are summarized as follows:

Gross profit on sales	$95,000
Cash operating expenses	43,000
Depreciation expense	16,500
Compensation to owner(s).	20,000
Distribution of profit to owner(s).	5,000

In each of the following situations, determine how much income is to be taxed to each of the taxpayers involved.

    a. The business is a sole proprietorship owned by T.

    b. The business is a partnership owned by R and S with an agreement to share all items equally. S is guaranteed a salary of $20,000 (see above).

    c. The business is a corporation owned equally by U and K. K is employed by the business and receives a salary of $20,000 (see above).

3-37 *Gross Income.* The following represent some of the more important items of income for Federal tax purposes. For each, indicate whether it is fully includible in gross income, fully excludable from gross income, or partially includible and partially excludable.

    a. Alimony received from a former spouse

    b. Interest from state and local governments

    c. Money and other property inherited from a relative

    d. Social security benefits

    e. Tips and gratuities

    f. Proceeds of life insurance received upon the death of one's spouse

3-38 *Classifying Deductions.* The following represent some of the more important deductions for Federal tax purposes. For each, indicate whether it is deductible for A.G.I. or as an itemized deduction.

    a. Alimony paid to one's former spouse

    b. Charitable contributions

    c. Trade or business expenses of a self-employed person

    d. Expenses of providing an apartment to a tenant for rent

    e. Interest incurred to finance one's principal residence

    f. Reimbursed trade or business expenses of an employee

    g. Unreimbursed trade or business expenses of an employee

3-39 *Determining Adjusted Gross Income and Taxable Income.* Fred and Susan are married and file a joint income tax return. Neither is blind or age 65. They have two children whom they support, and the following income and deductions for 2005:

Gross income	$46,800
Deductions for A.G.I.	1,200
Total itemized deductions	8,900
Credits and prepayments	3,050

Determine Fred and Susan's adjusted gross income and taxable income for the calendar year 2005.

3-40 *Tax Formula.* The following information is from the 2005 joint income tax return of Gregory and Stacy Jones, both of good sight and under 65 years of age.

Gross income	$65,400
Adjusted gross income	56,550
Taxable income	29,250
Number of personal exemptions	2
Number of dependency exemptions	2

Determine the amount of the Jones's deductions for A.G.I. and the amount of their itemized deductions.

3-41 *Tax Formula.* Complete the following table of independent cases for a single person with good eyesight and under age 65 in 2005:

	A	B	C
Gross income	$50,000	$65,250	$_____
Deductions for A.G.I.	_____	8,000	7,000
Adjusted gross income (A.G.I.)	42,000	_____	68,000
Itemized deductions	7,300	4,650	
Standard deduction	_____	_____	_____
Exemptions	2	1	1
Taxable income	_____	_____	$58,300

3-42 *Worldwide Income Subject to Tax.* T, a U.S. citizen, has income that was earned outside the United States. The income was $20,000, and a tax of $2,000 was paid to the foreign government. Determine the general treatment of this income and the tax paid under the following circumstances:

a. The tax paid was on income earned on foreign investments, and the U.S. tax attributable to this income is $2,800.

b. Same as (a), except the U.S. tax attributable to this income is $1,800.

c. Same as (a), except the income is from services rendered while absent from the United States for 13 successive months.

3-43 *Alternative Minimum Tax.* L is single, has no dependents, and uses the cash method and the calendar year for tax purposes. The following information was derived from L's records for 2005:

Taxable income (regular income tax).................	$22,000
AMT adjustments and preferences	32,000

Although L does have substantial gross income and deductions, she does not itemize. Calculate L's regular income tax and alternative minimum tax, if any.

3-44 *Asset Classification.* For each of the assets in the list below, designate the appropriate category using the symbols given:

C - Capital asset

T - Trade or business asset (§ 1231)

O - Other (neither capital nor § 1231 asset)

a. Personal residence

b. Stock in Xerox Corporation

c. Motor home used for vacations

d. Groceries held for sale to customers

e. Land held for investment

f. Land and building held for use in auto repair business

g. Trade accounts receivable of physician's office

h. Silver coins held primarily for speculation

3-45 *Gain or Loss Realized.* During the current year, W disposed of a vacant lot which he had held for investment. W received cash of $12,000 for his equity in the lot. The lot was subject to a $32,000 mortgage that was assumed by the buyer. Assuming W's basis in the lot was $23,000, how much is his realized gain or loss?

3-46 *Adjusted Basis.* M owns a rental residence that she is considering selling, but she is interested in knowing her exact tax basis in the property. She originally paid $39,000 for the property. M has spent $8,000 on a new garage, $2,500 for a new outdoor patio deck, and $4,500 on repairs and maintenance. M has been allowed depreciation on the unit in the amount of $7,500. Based on this information, calculate M's basis in the rental residence.

3-47 *Gain or Loss Realized, Adjusted Basis.* This year S sold her rental house. She received cash of $6,000 and a vacant lot worth $30,000. The buyer assumed the $36,000 mortgage loan outstanding against S's property. S had purchased the house for $52,000 four years earlier and had deducted depreciation of $12,000. How much are S's amount realized, her adjusted basis in the house sold, and her gain or loss realized in this transaction?

3-48 *Capital Gain and Loss.* Individual D is in the 35% tax bracket. This year he executed the following transactions.

Transaction	Sales Price	Adjusted Basis	Holding Period
Sale of 100 shares of XYZ............	$2,000	$1,000	15 months
Sale of land held for investment........	9,000	3,000	19 months
Sale of silver held for speculation	5,000	7,000	23 months
Sale of personal jewelry.............	4,000	6,000	60 months

Determine the tax consequences of these transactions.

3-49 *Excess Capital Loss.* This year, T, an individual taxpayer, had a short-term capital gain of $4,000 and a capital loss of $9,000 from stock he held for four years. How much is T's allowable capital loss deduction for the year? What is the treatment of the short-term gain?

3-50 *Individual's Tax Computation.* Richard Hartman, age 29, single with no dependents, received a salary of $31,750 in 2005. During the year, he received $1,300 interest income from a savings account and a $1,500 gift from his grandmother. At the advice of his father, Richard sold stock he had held as an investment for five years, for a $3,000 gain. He also sustained a loss of $1,000 from the sale of land held as an investment and owned for four months. Richard had itemized deductions of $4,900. For 2005 compute the following for Richard:
a. Gross income
b. Adjusted gross income
c. Taxable income
d. Income tax before credits and prepayments (use the appropriate 2005 tax rate schedule located on the inside front cover of this text)
e. Income tax savings that would result if Richard made a deductible $2,000 contribution to a qualified Individual Retirement Account

3-51 *Tax Treatment of Income from Entities.* The G family—Mr. G, Mrs. G, and G Jr.— owns interests in the following successful entities:

1. X Corporation is a calendar year regular corporation owned 60 percent by Mr. G and 15 percent by G Jr. During the year, it paid salaries to Mr. G of $80,000 to be its president and to G Jr. of $24,000 to be a plant supervisor. The company earned a net taxable income of $75,000, and paid dividends to Mr. G and G Jr. in the amounts of $42,000 and $10,500, respectively.

2. Mrs. G owned a 60 percent capital interest in a retail outlet, P Partnership. The partnership earned a net taxable income of $60,000 and made distributions during the year of $72,000. The profit and the distributions were allocated according to relative capital interests.

3. Mr. G and G Jr. each own 25 percent interest in H Corporation, an electing S Corporation. The corporation is a start-up venture and generated a net tax loss of $28,000 for the calendar year. No dividend distributions were made by H. Both Mr. G and G Jr. have bases in their H Corporation stock of $30,000.

4. G Jr. is the sole beneficiary of G Trust created by Mrs. G's father. The trust received dividends of $16,000 and made distributions of $4,500 to G Jr.

Determine the amount of income or loss from each entity that is to be reported by the following:

a. Mr. and Mrs. G on their joint calendar year tax return
b. G Jr. on his calendar year individual return

    c. X Corporation
    d. P Partnership
    e. H Corporation
    f. G Trust

3-52 *Comprehensive Taxable Income Computation.* Indy Smith, single, is an anthropology professor at State University. The tax records that he brought to you for preparation of his return revealed the following items.

Income

Salary from State University	$67,250
Part-time consulting	5,000
Dividend income	1,250
Reimbursement of travel to Denver by State University	200

Expenses

Interest on personal residence	$ 9,800
Travel expenses related to consulting	1,000
Tax return preparation fee	500
Safe deposit box to hold bonds	50
Travel and lodging to present academic paper in Denver related to his teaching position	450

In addition, Indy claims a dependency exemption for his father for whom he provides 60 percent support (including 60 percent of housing costs). Compute Indy's taxable income for calendar year 2005.

3-53 *Comprehensive Taxable Income Computation.* Eli and Lilly have been happily married for 30 years. Eli, 67, is a research chemist at Pharmaceuticals Inc. Lilly, 64, recently retired but stays busy managing the couple's investments, including a duplex. The majority of the couple's income is derived from Eli's employment, from which he received a salary of $95,000 this year. Other income includes interest on corporate bonds of $5,400 and interest on State of Illinois bonds of $1,000. In addition, rents collected from the duplex were $10,000 while rental expenses (e.g., maintenance, utilities, depreciation) were $6,000. During the year, the company transferred Eli to a new division located on the north side of town. As a result, the couple decided to move so that Eli would not have such a long commute. They paid deductible moving expenses of $2,000. The couple also paid the following expenses: unreimbursed medical expenses, $7,400; interest on the home mortgage, $11,900; property taxes on the home, $3,000; charitable contributions, $4,000; and rental of safe deposit box, $100. Determine the couple's taxable income for 2005.

3-54 *Alternative Minimum Tax.* H and W are married and file a joint return. The couple has five children between the ages of 3 and 13. Their records for the current year reveal the following:

Salary income	$100,000
State and local taxes (property and income)	12,600

Compute the alternative minimum tax, if any.

3-55 *Losses.* This year, B and J formed a partnership to operate a bar and grill. B was the brains behind the venture and J supplied the bulk of the financing. B contributed $30,000 to the partnership, receiving a 30 percent interest while J contributed $70,000 for a 70 percent interest. B received 30 percent of the profits and losses and J received 70 percent. During the year, B worked his fingers to the bone, running the business. J did little, sitting back and watching his investment. For the year, the partnership reported a $30,000 loss (revenues $60,000, deductible expenses $90,000). Can B and J use their share of the loss as a deduction to offset other income they might have on their own individual tax return (Form 1040) such as the salary income of their spouses? Explain.

INTRODUCTORY TAX RETURN PROBLEMS

3-56 *Continuous Tax Return Problem.* Larry and Cathy Zepp have been married 19 years. Larry is 62 years old (Social Security number 123-45-6789) while Cathy is 50 years old (Social Security number 123-45-6788). They live at 1234 Elm Dr. in Des Moines, Iowa 50311. Larry is a salesman employed by DSK Industries. This year he earned $110,000 (income tax withheld was $17,000). Cathy recently completed a graduate degree in computer technology. She continues to freelance as an independent contractor in computer graphics. Her earnings from various engagements were $12,000. Her only expenses were for miscellaneous office supplies of $3,000. She paid estimated taxes during the year of $1,000 ($250 on each due date). Other income earned by the couple included interest income of $3,000 from a certificate of deposit and $975 of interest from tax-exempt bonds issued by the State of Iowa. The couple owns a duplex that it rents out. Annual rentals were $8,000 and rental expenses (e.g., maintenance, utilities, depreciation) were $3,000. Other expenses paid during the year included:

Unreimbursed medical expenses....................	$ 9,000
Interest on home mortgage	12,000
Real property taxes on home......................	1,900
Charitable contributions...........................	1,000
Rental of safety deposit box to hold certain investments . . .	100
Unreimbursed employee business expenses of Larry	3,000

The couple paid $600 of interest on a loan they made three years ago, to help for Cathy's graduate degree. Cathy earned her MBA two years ago.

Prepare the 2004 individual income tax return for the Zepps. Complete Forms 1040, Schedules A, B, C, E and SE. Assume that all of the expenses except their business expenses are incurred jointly.

Prepare Form 1040 for the Zepps.

3-57 *Continuous Tax Return: Additional Questions.* Answer the following questions relating to the continuous tax return problem above. (Hint: consider using the "What-If Worksheet" in Turbo Tax in answering these questions.)

a. What is the Zepp's marginal tax rate? Average tax rate? Effective tax rate?

b. The Zepps recently heard that making a contribution to an individual retirement account (IRA) may be a wise tax move. It is their understanding that contributions to a traditional or conventional IRA is deductible and the earnings on the accounts are not taxable until withdrawn (see Chapter 18 for more information). Assuming both Larry and Cathy make the maximum deductible contribution of $3,000, what amount of tax will the couple save?

c. This question relates to the income tax of your state and may or may not be applicable. Check with your instructor for further instructions. Larry incurred $3,000 of expenses related to his employment while Cathy incurred $3,000 related to her freelancing activity (i.e., self-employment). Which of the following statements is (are) true regarding the treatment of the expenses for state income tax purposes?

1. Both expenses were deductible in full.

2. Neither of the expenses was deductible.

3. The employment related expenses were deductible but the expenses related to self-employment were not deductible.

4. The expenses related to self-employment were deductible but the employment related expenses were not deductible.

d. Assume that Larry-instead of Cathy-had the self-employment income of $9,000. Which of the following statements is true?

1. Larry paid 15.3% self-employment tax on self-employment income of $9,000.

2. Larry paid 15.3% self-employment tax on self-employment income of $8,312.

3. Larry paid the same amount of self-employment tax that Cathy would have paid had she earned the income.

4. Larry pays less than the amount of self-employment tax that Cathy would have paid had she earned the income.

RESEARCH PROBLEMS

3-58 *Using the Internal Revenue Code.* Locate a copy of the *Internal Revenue Code of 1986.* Read §§ 61 through 65, 67, 151, and 152. Read the titles of §§ 71 through 135, 161, and 162.

a. Describe how Congress defined "gross income."

b. Why is the "exemption deduction" properly called a deduction from adjusted gross income?

c. A taxpayer is self-employed and incurs an ordinary and necessary expense in his business endeavor. What is the authority for deducting the expense? Why is it considered a deduction *for* adjusted gross income?

d. A taxpayer pays alimony to her former husband. Within limits, it is deductible *for* adjusted gross income. Why?

Chapter 4

PERSONAL AND DEPENDENCY EXEMPTIONS; FILING STATUS; DETERMINATION OF TAX FOR AN INDIVIDUAL; FILING REQUIREMENTS

LEARNING OBJECTIVES

Upon completion of this chapter you will be able to:

▸ Identify the various requirements that a taxpayer must meet in order to claim a personal or dependency exemption

▸ Explain the phase-out of the deduction for personal and dependency exemptions

▸ Apply the rules to determine the taxpayer's filing status

▸ Compute the tax liability of an individual taxpayer using the tax rate schedules and the tax tables

▸ Explain the special approach used in computing the tax liability of certain children

▸ Describe the filing requirements for individual taxpayers and the role of the statute of limitations as it applies to the filing of tax returns

▸ Explain when taxes must be paid and the penalties that apply for failure to pay on a timely basis

CHAPTER OUTLINE

As seen in Chapter 3, numerous factors must be considered in the determination of an individual's net tax liability. Beginning in this chapter and continuing through Chapter 18, a detailed examination of these factors is conducted. This chapter is devoted to four particular concerns of individual taxpayers:

1. Personal and dependency exemptions;

2. Child tax credit;

3. Filing status;

4. Calculation of the tax liability using the tax rate schedules and tax tables; and

5. Filing requirements.

PERSONAL AND DEPENDENCY EXEMPTIONS

Since the inception of the income tax, policymakers have recognized the need to protect from tax some minimum amount of income that could be used for the support of the taxpayer and those who depend on him. The device used to accomplish this objective is the deduction allowed for exemptions. There are two types of exemptions for which deductions are allowed: personal exemptions and exemptions for a child or other dependent.[1] Taxpayers may deduct the *exemption amount* for each of their exemptions. The exemption amount for 2005 is $3,200.[2] Each type of exemption is discussed below.

---

[1] §§ 151(a), 151(b), and 151(c). For 2004, the deduction allowed for each personal and dependency exemption was $3,100.

[2] Since 1989 the exemption amount has been increased to reflect price level changes based on changes in the consumer price index. The exact amount is announced by the IRS in the fall of the preceding year. For instance, the exemption amount for 2006 will be announced by December 15, 2005. §§ 1(f) and 151(d)(3). If the exemption amount had been adjusted for inflation for real growth in income since 1948, when it was $600, it would have been about $8,650 for 1993. See Steurle, "Decline in the Value of the Dependent Exemption," 62 *Tax Notes* 109 (October 4, 1993).

PERSONAL EXEMPTIONS

There are *two* types of personal exemptions:

1. Exemption for the taxpayer

2. Exemption for the taxpayer's spouse

Each individual taxpayer normally is entitled to one personal exemption. When a *joint return* is filed by a married couple, *two* personal exemptions may be claimed. This occurs not because one spouse is the dependent of the other, but because the husband and wife are each entitled to his or her own personal exemption. If a married individual files a *separate return*, however, a personal exemption may be claimed for his or her spouse only if the spouse has no gross income and is not claimed as a dependent of another taxpayer.[3]

Disallowance of Personal Exemption. A taxpayer is denied a personal exemption if he or she qualifies as a dependent of another taxpayer (see discussion below).[4] This rule prevents two taxpayers (e.g., a child and his or her parent) from benefiting from two exemptions for the same person.

> **Example 1.** J is 21 years of age and a full-time college student. J receives a partial scholarship and works part-time, but the majority of his support is received from his parents. Assuming J is eligible to be claimed as a dependent on his parents' return, he is not entitled to a personal exemption deduction on his own return. This rule applies *regardless* of whether J's parents actually claim an exemption for him.

EXEMPTIONS FOR DEPENDENTS

For as long as most remember, an individual qualified as a taxpayer's dependent if he or she met one set of rules. Ironically, in an attempt toward simplicity, Congress added a second set of rules under which an individual might be considered a dependent. By virtue of the *Working Families Tax Relief Act of 2004*, § 152 now defines a dependent as either:

1. A qualifying child, or

2. A qualifying relative.

EXEMPTION FOR QUALIFYING CHILD

An individual is considered a *qualifying child* and can be claimed as a dependent of the taxpayer if he or she satisfies all of the following tests.

1. *Relationship Test.* The individual and the taxpayer must meet one of the following relationship tests:

   ‣ Natural child, stepchild, adopted child, certain foster children

   ‣ A sibling or step-sibling

   ‣ A descendant of either of the above

---

[3] § 151(b).

[4] § 151(d)(2).

Note that the scope of these rules goes far beyond the conventional definition of a taxpayer's "child." For example, a taxpayer's brother or sister is considered his or her child as are his nieces or nephews. Similarly, a taxpayer's "children" include a grandchild as well as great grandchildren and other descendants.

2. *Residence Test.* The "child" must have the *same principal place of abode* (i.e., residence) as the taxpayer for more than one half of the taxable year. For this purpose, temporary absences are permissible if due to special circumstances such as education, illness, business, vacation, or military service. Note that a child could live more than half of the taxable year with more than one person where several people live together, including the child. For example, the child could live with his mother, grandmother and grandfather. Thus this test could be met with respect to more than one person.

3. *Age Requirement.* The "child" must also meet one of the conditions concerning age:

   ▸ Has not reached age 19 by the close of the taxable year.

   ▸ Has not reached age 24 *and* is considered a full-time student at a qualifying educational institution. For this purpose, "full-time" is whatever is considered full-time under the rules and regulations of the institution. The individual must meet the full-time condition for any part of five calendar months during the calendar year.

   ▸ Is permanently and totally disabled at any time during the year. The age limitation does not apply to these individuals.

4. *Joint Return Test.* The "child" must not have filed a joint return with his or her spouse.

5. *Citizenship or Residency Test.* The "child" must be a U.S. citizen, resident or national, or a resident of Canada or Mexico.

6. *Not Self-Supporting Test.* To be a "qualifying child" the "child" may not be self-supporting; that is, the child must not have provided more than one-half of his or her own support. For this purpose, scholarships received from an educational institution are not considered an amount spent on support.

Tie Breaker Rules. Application of the tests above could result in an individual being a "qualifying child" for more than one taxpayer. For example, if a 10-year-old child lived with his father, grandmother and uncle in the same residence during the year, the father, grandmother, or uncle could potentially claim the child as a dependent since the child meets the relationship, age and residence test with respect to each. Such a situation is not surprising in an age when family structures are often unconventional due to divorce and remarriage, absentee parents, childbearing by unmarried individuals, and multi generational households. When a child is a qualifying child for more than one taxpayer, the following tie-breaker rules apply.

   ▸ If only one of the taxpayers is the child's parent, the parent claims the exemption for the child.

   ▸ If both taxpayers are the child's parents and they do not file a joint return, the parent with whom the child resided for the longest period of time during the tax year claims the exemption for the child.

   ▸ If the child resides with both parents for the same period of time during the tax year and the parents do not file a joint return, the parent with the highest adjusted gross income claims the exemption for the child.

▸ If none of the taxpayers are the child's parent, the taxpayer with the highest adjusted gross income for the tax year claims the exemption for the child.

Example 2. M and D, mom and dad, provide a home in which they live with their son, P, and P's daughter, G, for the current year. P is unmarried, 23 years of age and a full-time student. P earned $6,000 for the year, which is less than 50% of his total support. M and D may claim an exemption for P—he is their qualifying child since he meets all of the tests (age, residence and relationship). Under the tie-breaking rules, P, as parent, would be able to claim an exemption for his daughter G; however, P cannot claim G as a dependent because P is, himself, a dependent. In this case, M and D could claim an exemption for their granddaughter G because she is a qualifying child with respect to them.

EXEMPTION FOR QUALIFYING RELATIVE

The second type of dependent is a *qualifying relative*—generally a relative or member of the taxpayer's household that depends on the taxpayer for support. In contrast to the definition for qualifying children, this term permits exemptions for a broader class of individuals but only if the taxpayer provides for their support and the prospective dependent meets an income test.

Technically, an individual is considered a *qualifying relative* only if he or she is *not* a qualifying child and meets the following requirements.

1. *Support Test.* The taxpayer must provide more than 50 percent of the dependent's total support.

2. *Gross Income Test.* The dependent's gross income must be less than the exemption amount. An exception is provided for a child of the taxpayer who is under age 19 or a child of the taxpayer who is a full-time student and is under age 24.

3. *Relationship or Member of the Household Test.* The dependent must be a relative of the taxpayer or a member of the taxpayer's household for the entire taxable year.

4. *Joint Return Test.* The "child" must not have filed a joint return with his or her spouse.

5. *Citizenship or Residency Test.* The "child" must be a U.S. citizen, resident or national, or a resident of Canada or Mexico.

Although an individual could conceivably be a qualifying relative and a qualifying child, the Code makes it clear that in such case the individual is treated as a qualifying child, and therefore, he or she cannot be claimed as a dependent by someone under the qualifying relative rules.

Support Test. To satisfy the support requirement, the taxpayer must provide more than half of the amount spent for the dependent's total support.[5] Total support includes not only amounts expended by others on behalf of the dependent but also any amounts spent by the dependent. Note that only the amount *actually spent* for support is relevant. Income and other funds available to the dependent for spending are ignored unless they are spent.

---

[5]   § 152(a).

Example 3. During the year, C paid $10,000 to maintain her father, F, in a nursing home that provides all of his needs. No other amounts were spent for his support. C made these payments, even though her father could afford them since he has cash in the bank and tax-exempt bonds valued at $200,000. Although F has funds available for providing his own support, they are not considered in applying the support test because the funds were not spent. Consequently, the support test is satisfied.

Support is generally measured by the cost of the item to the individual providing it. However, when support is provided in a noncash form, such as the use of property or lodging, the amount of support is the fair market value or fair rental value.

What constitutes an item of support is not always clear. If, for example, a child receives a stereo or car, are these items considered support, or do only necessities qualify? The Regulations provide some guidance as to the nature of support, indicating that it includes food, shelter, clothing, medical and dental care, education, recreation, and transportation.[6] Support is not limited to these items, however. Examination of the numerous cases and rulings reveals a hodgepodge of qualifying expenditures as well as some that are not. For example, the costs for boats, life insurance, and lawn mowers are not considered support. Additionally, the value of any services performed for the dependent by the taxpayer is ignored.[7] Exhibit 4-1 presents a sampling of those items that constitute support.

The determination of support also is complicated by several items accorded special treatment. For example, scholarships and fellowships received by the taxpayer's child or stepchild are not considered support items. Accordingly, such amounts are not treated as being provided by either the taxpayer or the dependent.[8]

EXHIBIT 4-1
Partial List of Support Items

Automobile	Lodging
Care for a dependent's pet	Medical care
Charitable contributions by	Medical insurance premiums
or on behalf of dependent	Singing lessons
Child care	Telephone
Clothing	Television
Dental care	Toys
Education	Transportation
Entertainment	Utilities
Food	Vacations
Gifts	

Example 4. J was the recipient of an athletic scholarship that covered 100% of her tuition, books, supplies, room, and board. In addition, J was paid a small cash allowance. J's parents also provided her with $2,000 cash to be used for clothing, entertainment, and miscellaneous expenses.

The scholarship package, which was related to J's continued scholastic activity, was valued at $9,500 per year. Nevertheless, assuming the other four tests are met, J's parents are entitled to a dependency exemption, since the scholarship is not included in her support.[9]

---

[6]   Reg. § 1.152-1(a)(2)(i).

[7]   *Markarian v. Comm.*, 65-2 USTC ¶9699, 16 AFTR2d 5785, 352 F.2d 870 (CA-7, 1965).

[8]   Reg. § 1.152-1(c). Note that G.I. Bill benefits are not treated as scholarships and therefore are included as support items provided by the recipient.

[9]   Any part of a scholarship providing benefits other than tuition, fees and supplies, is *includible* in the recipient's gross income to the extent of those benefits. See Chapter 6 for a discussion of taxable scholarships.

Although social security benefits generally are not taxable income to the recipient, they are considered as support provided by the person covered by social security. Thus, social security benefits are included in determining support to the extent they are spent for support.[10] State welfare payments are considered provided by the state, and therefore are not treated as provided by the parent or any other taxpayer. This is true even though the parent is entrusted to oversee the prudent expenditure of the funds.[11]

Example 5. F received support during the current year from various sources, including amounts contributed by his son, S. The amounts spent toward F's support were provided as follows:

F's social security benefits	$ 7,500
Taxable interest income	900
Amount provided by S	4,100
Total	$12,500

S is not entitled to a dependency exemption for F because he did not provide more than 50% of F's total support ($4,100 is not greater than 50% of $12,500).

Example 6. This year K received social security benefits of $8,000, $5,500 of which was immediately deposited in a savings account. The amounts spent toward K's support were provided as follows:

K's social security benefits spent	$2,500
Taxable interest income	600
Amount provided by K's brother, B	4,000
Total	$7,100

Assuming the other tests are met, B is entitled to a dependency exemption for K since he provided more than one-half of her support expenditures ($4,000 is > 50% of $7,100).

In many instances, an individual who is not self-supporting is supported by more than one taxpayer. Generally, no dependency exemption is allowed for such persons because no *one* individual provides more than 50 percent of the total support provided. However, two exceptions exist. Exemptions may be allowed under multiple support agreements or to divorced or separated parents with respect to their children.

Multiple Support Agreements. A dependency exemption may be assigned to a taxpayer under a multiple support agreement if all of the following tests are met:[12]

1. No one person contributed over half the support of the individual.

2. Over half the support was provided by a group, all of whose members are qualifying relatives of the individual.

---

[10] Reg. § 1.152-1(a)(2)(ii).

[11] See Rev. Rul. 71-468, 1971-2 C.B. 115 and *N. Williams*, T.C. Memo 1996-126. A similar result was reached related to state payments for the care of a mentally retarded child. See *Trail*, T.C. Memo 1993-221, *aff'd* at 73 AFTR2d ¶ 94-931 (CA-5, 1994).

[12] § 152(c).

3. The citizenship, joint return, and gross income requirements are met by the individual.

4. The dependency exemption is assigned by agreement to a group member *who contributed more* than 10 percent of the total support.

The assignment is effective only if each of the members contributing more than 10 percent signs a declaration to the effect that he or she will not claim the exemption. This declaration is made on Form 2120 (see Appendix), which is then filed with the return of the taxpayer claiming the exemption.

> **Example 7.** M is single and received her support of $12,000 for the current year from the following sources:
>
> | | Amount | Percentage |
> |---|---|---|
> | Social security benefits | $ 4,000 | 33.33% |
> | Taxable interest income | 800 | 6.67 |
> | From D, M's daughter | 4,700 | 39.17 |
> | From S, M's son | 1,500 | 12.50 |
> | From G, M's grandchild | 1,000 | 8.33 |
> | | $12,000 | 100.00% |
>
> Together, D, S, and G contribute more than 50% of M's support for the year ($7,200 > 50% of $12,000). If a multiple support agreement is executed, either D or S may be allowed the exemption deduction. G is not eligible since he did not contribute more than 10% of the total support. Also, note that S may claim M as a dependent even though D provided more of M's support.

Gross Income Test. The second test that must be satisfied before an individual (other than a qualifying child) may be claimed as a dependent concerns his or her gross income. A dependency exemption generally is not allowed for a person whose gross income equals or exceeds the exemption amount ($3,200 for 2005).[13] In applying this test, the technical definition of "gross income" must be heeded.[14] It does not include items that are excluded from income. Accordingly, a person whose only sources of income are excluded from gross income (e.g., social security and municipal bond interest) may qualify as a dependent.

It also should be noted that gross income is not always synonymous with includible gross receipts. Regulation § 1.61-3 indicates that gross income for a merchandising business generally means the total sales less the cost of goods sold *plus* any income from investments or other sources. The importance of this distinction between gross receipts and gross income is demonstrated in the following example.

> **Example 8.** T provides 60% of the support for his single brothers, F and R, for the 2005 calendar year. F's sole source of income is from the sale of fireworks. During the year, he sold fireworks costing $4,000 for $6,500. R's sole source of income is derived from rental property. During the year, he collected rents of $4,200 while incurring expenses of $1,700 for repairs, maintenance, and interest. Although F and R each earned $2,500 (F: $6,500 − $4,000 = $2,500; R: $4,200 − $1,700 = $2,500),

---

[13] § 151(c)(1)(A). Note that there is no relief from the gross income test for qualifying relatives. Under prior law, this relief was reserved for children of the taxpayer.

[14] See Chapters 5 and 6 for detailed discussion of "gross income."

F's gross income was $2,500, whereas R's was $4,200. As a result, T can only claim an exemption for F, since F's *gross income* was less than the $3,200 exemption amount for 2005.

Relationship or Member of the Household Test. The third of the five hurdles that must be cleared before an individual can be claimed as a dependent concerns the individual's relationship to the taxpayer. Regardless of the amount of support that the taxpayer provides for another person, no exemption is allowed unless the prospective dependent is properly related to the taxpayer.[15] Apparently the authors of the dependency rules believed that the tax law should not grant an exemption unless there is some obligation on the part of the taxpayer to support an individual. Such an obligation normally exists between relatives or others who are members of the taxpayer's household. Therefore, to qualify as a dependent, an individual must satisfy one of nine qualifying relationship tests. All of these are *familial* (i.e., related by blood, marriage, or adoption) except one. These are:

1. A son or daughter (including an adopted child, a foster child who lives with the taxpayer the entire taxable year, or a child placed with the taxpayer by an authorized agency pending legal adoption by the taxpayer), or a descendant of either (e.g., a grandchild)

2. A stepson or stepdaughter

3. A brother, sister, stepbrother, or stepsister

4. The father or mother, or an ancestor of either (e.g., a grandparent)

5. A stepfather or stepmother

6. A niece or nephew[16]

7. An aunt or uncle[17]

8. A son-in-law, daughter-in-law, father-in-law, mother-in-law, brother-in-law, or sister-in-law

9. Any person who lives in the taxpayer's home and is a member of the taxpayer's household for the entire *taxable* year. Even though such a person is not legally related to the taxpayer (i.e., a familial relative), he or she is treated the same as one who satisfies one of the legal relationships as long as he or she lives with the taxpayer the entire taxable year; for this purpose, temporary absences due to illness, school, vacation, business, or military service are ignored; in addition, a person cannot be claimed as a dependent if the relationship with the taxpayer violated local law (e.g., cohabitation).[18]

A relationship created by marriage does not cease upon divorce or the death of the spouse. Thus, for tax purposes, a divorce would not terminate an individual's

---

[15] § 152(a). Note: Recall that there is no dependency exemption for a spouse. The exemption for a spouse is the *personal* exemption.

[16] A niece or nephew must be a daughter or son of a brother or sister of the taxpayer. § 152(a)(6).

[17] An aunt or uncle must be a sister or brother of the father or mother of the taxpayer. § 152(a)(7). For example, the person married to your mother's sister would be her brother-in-law, but he would not qualify as your uncle for purposes of this definition. Technically, such a person would be your "uncle-in-law," a relationship not defined in Code § 152.

[18] § 152(b)(5).

relationship with his or her mother-in-law.[19] Additionally, if a dependent dies before the close of the tax year, the taxpayer may still claim a dependency exemption.

> **Example 9.** This year F provided all the support for several individuals, none of whom had income in excess of the exemption amount. Each person and his or her status as a relative is shown below:
>
> 1. S, F's son, living in Los Angeles and attending UCLA. S is a relative; a son is a familial relative and such persons need not live in the home.
>
> 2. B, F's 29-year-old brother who moved in with F on November 1 after leaving the military. B is a relative; a brother is a familial relative and such persons need not live in the home.
>
> 3. C, F's 27-year-old cousin who moved in with F on October 1 after being unemployed for 10 months. C is not a relative; a cousin is not considered a familial relative and, therefore, qualifies only if he lives with the taxpayer the entire taxable year.
>
> 4. BL, the brother of F's former wife. BL is a relative; BL is F's brother-in-law, a familial relative; such a relationship continues to exist whether F is divorced or his wife dies.
>
> 5. Z, a friend who has been living with F since December 1 of the prior year. Z is a "relative"; a person who lives with the taxpayer the *entire* taxable year qualifies as a relative even though such person is not related by blood or marriage.

Joint Return Test. The dependent must not have filed a joint return with his or her spouse. This requirement is discussed further below.

Citizenship or Residency Test. The dependent must be a U.S. citizen, resident or national, or a resident of Canada or Mexico. Additional exceptions exist as noted below.

PROVISIONS COMMON TO ALL DEPENDENCY EXEMPTIONS

As is apparent from the discussion above, there are several important differences in the definitions of a qualifying child and a qualifying relative. For example, there is no gross income test or support test applicable to a "child" of the taxpayer. In a sense, these conditions are assumed to be met where the individual is the child of the taxpayer. Notwithstanding these differences, it is important to note that—as may be apparent–there are some rules common to both types of dependents. Each of these is considered in greater detail below.

No Joint Return. A taxpayer normally cannot claim a dependency exemption for a married individual if such person files a joint return.[20] This is true for both a qualifying child and a qualifying relative. This rule appears to reflect a presumption that married taxpayers usually rely on themselves for support rather than others. Note, however, that if a joint return is filed solely for a refund (i.e., the tax is zero and all withholding is refunded), the return is ignored and the individual may be claimed as a dependent (assuming the other tests are met).[21] Also observe that the test is met as long as a joint

---

[19]   Reg. § 1.152-2(d).

[20]   § 151(c)(2).

[21]   Rev. Rul. 54-567, 1954-2 C.B. 108.

return is *not* filed. If the married individual files a separate return, he or she may still be claimed as a dependent. In certain situations, parents of newlyweds and others may find it beneficial for their child to file a married, separate return.

Example 10. B and C were married on December 21, 2005. B, a budding 25-year-old attorney, earned $38,000 for the year. C, age 23, is a full-time graduate student. Because C was fully supported by her parents, she was eligible to be claimed as a dependent on her parents' return. However, C's parents may not claim C as a dependent if B and C elect to file a joint return. The family must determine whether they are better off if: (1) B and C file a joint return and C claims her exemption on their joint return; or (2) B and C each file married filing separately and they relinquish C's exemption to her parents. A partial analysis would suggest the first alternative is far superior. If a joint return is filed, all of B's income would be taxed at 15% or less (see inside front cover of text for rates). Alternatively, the filing of separate returns would cause a substantial portion of B's taxable income to be taxed at 25%. In this case, it would appear that the additional tax caused by filing separate returns would more than offset any savings to be derived from shifting the exemption to C's parents.

Example 11. D and E were married on December 28, 2005. During 2005 D, age 22, attended State University full time. In addition, she worked part-time, earning $9,500 for the year. E, age 21, was also a full-time student, fully supported by his parents. E had no income. In this case, E's parents are entitled to claim an exemption for E even if D and E elect to file a joint return. The joint return requirement would not be violated because the couple owes no tax (the couple's standard deduction eliminates their taxable income). Consequently, under the IRS view, they would be filing merely to obtain a refund of any withholding and not filing an actual return.

It should be emphasized that the fact that a person files his or her own tax return does not bar another taxpayer (who otherwise meets all the necessary tests) from claiming him or her as a dependent. This is true as long as the dependent does not file a joint return for any reason other than to claim a refund of the entire amount of taxes withheld. Otherwise, the joint return test would not be met and the dependency exemption would be denied.

Citizenship or Residency Test. A dependent must be a citizen or national (e.g., an American Samoan) of the United States or a resident of the United States, Canada, or Mexico. In addition, an adopted child of a citizen qualifies, even though not a resident, if he or she was a member of the taxpayer's household for the entire taxable year. For example, if a taxpayer's employment results in his relocation to London where he adopts a British child, this rule enables the taxpayer to claim the child as a dependent even though the child is not a U.S. citizen or resident.

Taxpayer Not a Dependent. A person who is a dependent cannot claim others as dependents. For example, if a child is a dependent of his or her parents, the child cannot claim his or her own children as dependents.

Social Security Number. In order to claim an exemption for a dependent, the taxpayer must list the dependent's Social Security number on the tax return. If the number is not listed or is listed incorrectly, the exemption may be disallowed and a $50 penalty may be imposed. More importantly, the taxpayer's filing status (head of household, surviving spouse) or child credit could be affected. Since it usually takes about two weeks to obtain a social security number, obtaining one by the extended due date of the return normally does not present a problem.[22]

CHILDREN OF DIVORCED OR SEPARATED PARENTS

If a married couple with children is divorced or separated, special rules may apply in determining who claims exemptions for the children.[23] These rules operate when the couple is:

- ▸ Legally separated under a decree of divorce or separate maintenance
- ▸ Separated under a written separation agreement; or
- ▸ Lived apart at all times during the last six months of the calendar year.

In these situations, the normal rules for assigning the exemption are initially used. However, if certain tests are met, the taxpayer who is entitled to the exemption may waive his or her right to the exemption, thereby transferring it to his or her spouse. The waiver is available only if

1. More than half of a child's support is provided either by one parent or collectively by both parents (including amounts contributed by the new spouse of a parent), and

2. The child is in custody of one or both parents for more than half of the year.[24]

If these conditions are met, the *noncustodial parent* may claim the exemption. In order for the waiver to be effective, it must be evidenced in a decree of divorce or separate maintenance or a written agreement between the parents. Absent one of these, the waiver can take the form of a signed declaration that the custodial parent will not claim the dependency exemption. It should also be noted that if the exemption is waived, the child credit (discussed below) is also waived.

PHASE-OUT OF PERSONAL AND DEPENDENCY EXEMPTIONS

Since 1989 Congress has reduced the benefits that high-income taxpayers receive from their personal and dependency exemptions. Under § 151(d), taxpayers must reduce their deduction for personal and dependency exemptions by 2 percent for each $2,500 or fraction thereof ($1,250 for married persons filing separate returns) by which a taxpayer's A.G.I. exceeds the applicable threshold. These thresholds depend on the taxpayer's filing status, and the amounts are adjusted for inflation annually.

Filing Status	*Threshold A.G.I.*	
	2004	*2005*
Single individuals (not surviving spouse or head of household)	$142,700	$145,950
Married filing jointly or surviving spouse	214,050	218,950
Head of household	178,350	182,450
Married filing separately	107,025	109,475

---

[22]   The year that this requirement became effective the number of exemptions dropped 7 million below what had been expected, resulting in about $2.8 billion in additional tax revenue. Interestingly, more than 48 percent of the drop was attributable to single taxpayers. See IRS Pub. 1500 (August 1991).

[23]   § 152(e).

[24]   § 152(e)(1).

The reduction in the exemption deduction may be computed as follows:

$$\frac{\text{A.G.I} - \text{Threshold}}{\$2,500 \text{ (or } \$1,250)} = \frac{\text{Factor}}{\text{(round-up)}} \times \frac{2}{\text{percentage points}} = \frac{\text{Percentage}}{\text{reduction}}$$

Example 12. H and W are married with four children. They are entitled to claim six exemptions. In 2005 their A.G.I. is $259,950. The reduction in the couple's exemption deduction is computed as follows:

A.G.I.	$ 259,950
Threshold	−218,950
Excess	$ 41,000

$$\frac{\$41,000}{\$2,500)} = 16.4, \text{ rounded to } 17 \times 2 = 34\%$$

1. H and W are required to reduce their exemption deduction by 34%. Assuming the total exemption deduction is $19,200 ($3,200 × 6), the deduction is reduced by $6,528 (34% × $19,200) to $12,672 ($19,200 − $6,528). In effect, the couple receives only 66% of their normal exemption deduction.

Note that the exemption deduction is completely eliminated if A.G.I. exceeds the threshold by more than $122,500. For example, if a married couple's A.G.I. exceeds $341,450, their total deduction for exemptions would be eliminated [($341,450 − $218,950 = $122,501) ÷ $2,500 = 49.0004, rounded up to 50 × 2 = 100% reduction].

CHILD TAX CREDIT

Although most credits are covered in Chapter 13, the child tax credit is addressed briefly here because it is so closely tied with exemptions.[25] Under § 24, the amount of the child tax credit is $1,000 for each *qualifying child*.[26] For example, if a taxpayer had four children, the potential credit would be $4,000 ($1,000 × 4). The definition of a qualifying child for purposes of the child credit piggybacks on the uniform definition of a child used in determining a taxpayer's dependency exemption (discussed earlier in this chapter). In other words, a *qualifying child* for the child credit is a *qualifying child* as that expression is defined for determining a taxpayer's dependents but with certain modifications. A qualifying child for the child credit is any person who meets the following conditions.

- ▸ The individual is a *qualifying child* as defined in § 152 relating to dependents (age, relationship, residence tests).
- ▸ The individual has not attained the age of 17 by the close of the taxable year.
- ▸ The individual is a U.S. citizen.

To summarize, a taxpayer normally can claim the $1,000 credit for each child under age 17. Also note that as mentioned above, if a divorced or separated taxpayer waives his or her right to an exemption, the child credit is also waived and transferred to the noncustodial spouse.

---

[25] § 24.

[26] §§ 24(c)(1)(C) and 32(c)(3)(B).

Example 13. M and D are the proud parents of a 16-year-old daughter, C. The parents file jointly, reporting gross income of $34,725 for 2005. After claiming a standard deduction of $10,000 and three exemptions of $3,200 each, their taxable income is $15,125. Their tax on $15,125 is $1,513. After claiming their child tax credit of $1,000 for C, M and D's gross income tax is $513.

Refundable Child Tax Credit. As a general rule, most credits are limited to the taxpayer's tax liability for the year. For example, if the taxpayer's tax liability before the child credit is $5,000 and the child credit is $3,000, the taxpayer's regular tax usually would be reduced to $2,000. If the taxpayer's regular tax liability before the credit is $3,000 and the child credit is $4,000, the credit would reduce the tax to zero and *normally* the $1,000 balance of the credit would not be used and the taxpayer would not receive a refund of the unused credit. However, the law permits a portion of the unused child credit to be refunded. In other words, in the situation above, all or a portion of the unused credit of $1,000 would be refunded. The amount of the refundable credit depends on several variables, including the number of children, the taxpayer's earned income, other credits and some additional factors. The actual calculation of the amount of refundable credit can be found in Chapter 13 in the discussion of refundable credits.

Phase-Out of Credit. Like many other tax benefits, the child tax credit is phased out for higher income taxpayers. Specifically, the allowable credit is reduced by $50 for each $1,000 (or fraction thereof) of A.G.I. in excess of specified thresholds. The thresholds are $75,000 for unmarried taxpayers and $110,000 for married taxpayers filing jointly ($55,000 for those filing separately).[27]

Example 14. R and S have two daughters, L and M (both under age 17). R and S are married and file jointly, reporting A.G.I. of $115,800 for 2005. After claiming a standard deduction of $10,000 and four exemptions of $3,200 each, their taxable income is $93,000. Their tax on $93,000 is $16,580. The child tax credit for two qualifying children is generally $2,000, but R and S must reduce their credit by $300 ($50 × 6, since $115,800 exceeds $110,000 by five thousand and a fraction) to $1,700. Consequently, their tax after the credit is $14,880 ($16,580 − $1,700).

✓ CHECK YOUR KNOWLEDGE

Try these 10 true-false questions concerning exemptions. If the statement is false, explain why.

Review Question 1. All individuals are entitled to claim a personal exemption.

False. An individual who may be claimed as a dependent on another taxpayer's return cannot claim a personal exemption. This prohibits two different taxpayers from claiming two separate exemptions for the same person.

Review Question 2. Certain people that are normally considered relatives (e.g., cousins) do not qualify as relatives for purposes of the exemption tests.

True. A cousin is not a familial relative.

Review Question 3. An individual, such as a cousin, can qualify as a "relative" even though he or she is not a familial relative.

---

[27]   § 24(b). For purposes of this phase-out, adjusted gross income is increased by the amount of the foreign earned income exclusions under §§ 911, 931, and 933.

True. An individual who lives in the taxpayer's home the entire taxable year is treated as a relative even though such person and the taxpayer would not be "related" under the statutory definition.

Review Question 4. T takes care of his mom. He satisfies the support test if he provides more than 10 percent of her total support.

False. A taxpayer must generally provide more than 50 percent of an individual's support in order to claim the individual as a dependent. However, an individual who provides more than 10 percent of a person's support may be able to claim a dependency exemption under a multiple support agreement.

Review Question 5. In determining whether T provides more than 50 percent of his mom's support, her savings of over $100,000, and any earnings from them, are not counted except to the extent they are actually spent.

True. Funds available for an individual's support are ignored in applying the support test. Only amounts spent (or the value of support items provided, such as lodging) are considered.

Review Question 6. T received a scholarship to attend Harvard worth more than $15,000. This amount is ignored in determining whether her parents provided more than one-half of her support.

True. Scholarships are not considered support.

Review Question 7. T's mom has no income other than social security benefits of $5,000 and interest from City of Duluth bonds of $6,000. T may claim an exemption for her mom.

True. A dependency exemption normally cannot be claimed for an individual if such person's gross income exceeds the exemption amount. For this purpose, gross income includes only income that is subject to tax. In this case, T's mom's income from social security is excluded as is the interest from the municipal bonds.

Review Question 8. T's 14-year-old son earned $5,000 from his paper route this year. T may not claim an exemption for his son.

False. As a general rule, an individual cannot be claimed as a dependent if he or she has gross income for the year that exceeds the personal exemption amount. However, the gross income test does not apply to a child of the taxpayer who has not reached the age of 19 or who is a full-time student and has not reached the age of 24.

Review Question 9. In the case of a divorced couple with children, the custodial parent normally receives the exemption for the children even if the noncustodial parent provides all of the child support.

True. The custodial parent is entitled to the exemption unless he or she assigns it to the noncustodial parent.

Review Question 10. H and W are married with three children ages 15, 16, and 17. The couple can normally claim a child tax credit of $3,000.

False. The child tax credit is generally available for dependent children less than 17 years old. Therefore the couple can claim a credit of $2,000 ($1,000 × 2).

FILING STATUS

EVOLUTION OF FILING STATUS

The tax rates that are applied to determine the taxpayer's tax liability depend on the taxpayer's filing status. From 1913 to 1948, there was only one set of tax rates that applied to individual taxpayers. During this period, each taxpayer filed a separate return, even if he or she were married. For example, if both a husband and wife had income, each would file a separate return, reporting their respective incomes. This system, however, proved inequitable due to the differing state laws governing the ownership of income (or property).

In the United States, the rights that married individuals hold in property are determined using either the common law or community property system. There are ten community property states: Alaska, Arizona, California, Idaho, Louisiana, Nevada, New Mexico, Texas, Washington, and Wisconsin. In a community property state, income generated through the personal efforts of either spouse is generally owned *equally* by the community (i.e., the husband and wife). In common law states, income belongs to the spouse that earns the income. The differing treatments of income by community property and common law states produced the need for a special rate schedule for married taxpayers.

Married Status. The category of married couples filing jointly and its unique rate schedule were added to the law because of an inequity that existed between married couples in community property states and non-community property jurisdictions (separate or common law property states). As noted above, earnings derived from personal services performed by married persons in community property states generally are owned jointly by the two spouses. Accordingly, both husband and wife in a community property state would file returns showing one-half of their earned income, even though only one may have been employed. Note that the total income of the couple would be split equally between the husband and wife regardless of who earned the income. If a couple in a non-community property state relied on one spouse's earnings, the employed spouse filed a return showing the entire amount of those earnings.

Since the tax rates are progressive, a married couple in a non-community property state would bear a larger tax burden than one in a community property state if only one spouse was employed outside the home or one spouse earned substantially more than the other. To eliminate this inequity, Congress elected to grant the benefits of income splitting to all married couples. This was accomplished by authorizing a new tax schedule for married persons filing jointly. A joint return results in the same amount of tax as would be paid on two "married, filing separate" returns showing half the total income of a married couple.

Example 15. L and M are married and reside in California with their two children. L is an executive with a major corporation and M works in the home. Under state law, L's salary of $70,000 is owned equally by L and M. Each may file a separate return and report $35,000 of the salary.

Example 16. S and T are married and reside in Virginia with their two children. S is an executive with a major corporation and T works in the home. S earns a salary of $70,000. If S were to file a separate return, she would report the entire $70,000 salary on that return. Since the tax rate schedules for individuals are progressive, S would pay a higher tax than the total paid by L and M in *Example 15*. Consequently, the total tax burden on S and T would be greater than that on L and M. By filing a joint return, S and T are placed in a position equivalent to that of L and M.

Head-of-Household Status. Introduction of the joint return in 1948 was not viewed by the public as merely a solution to a problem caused by differing state laws. Many saw it as a tax break for those who had family obligations. As a result, single parents and other unmarried taxpayers with dependents tried to persuade Congress that they should be entitled to some tax relief due to their family responsibilities. Their arguments were based on the fact that they suffered a greater tax burden than single-earner married couples. In 1957, a tax reduction was allowed in the form of a new tax rate schedule for taxpayers who qualify as a *head of household*. The rates were designed to be lower than the original rates, which applied to all taxpayers, but *higher* than the rates for married persons filing jointly.

Single Status. The most recent change in the overall tax rate structure was the addition of a separate tax rate schedule for single persons. This change was made because a single person was paying a higher rate of tax on the same income than married persons filing jointly and heads of households. The reduced rates for single taxpayers still are higher than those for a head of household, but lower than those in the original rate structure. As a result of this final change, the original tax rate structure that once applied to all taxpayers now applies only to married persons filing separately.

Summary. The Federal income tax on individuals is based on four tax rate schedules. Taxpayers must file under one of the following classifications, listed in order from lowest to highest in tax rates:

1. Married filing jointly (including surviving spouses)
2. Head of household
3. Single
4. Married filing separately

The 2005 tax rate schedules for these classifications are reproduced on the inside front cover of this text.[28]

MARRIED INDIVIDUALS

Marital status is determined on the last day of an individual's taxable year. A person is married for tax purposes if he or she is married under state law, regardless of whether he or she is separated or in the process of seeking a divorce.[29]

Joint Return. A husband and wife generally may file a return using the rates for married persons filing jointly.[30] If a joint return is filed, husband and wife are jointly and severally (individually) liable for any tax, interest or penalties related to *that* joint

---

[28] The 2005 tax tables had not been issued by the IRS at the date of publication of this text. However, the 2004 tax tables are reproduced in Appendix A.

[29] Special rules apply to a taxpayer whose spouse dies during the year. See §§ 7703(a)(1) and 6013(a)(2).

[30] § 6013(a). However, a special rule applies if the spouse is a nonresident alien. See § 6013(g). Also, both spouses must have the *same* taxable year.

return. As a result, one spouse may be held liable for paying the entire tax, even though the other spouse earned all the income. For this reason, a spouse should be cautious in signing a joint return. However, under the *innocent spouse rule*, a spouse will not be held liable for tax and penalties attributable to misstatements by the other spouse in two instances. The first provision allows relief if the innocent spouse establishes that he or she did not know and had no reason to know of the understatement, that it is inequitable to hold him or her liable for the deficiency, and that he or she elected the benefits of this provision within two years after the date collection activities began. The second provision limits the liability of a spouse to only the portion of the deficiency properly allocable to him or her if he or she is no longer married to, is legally separated from, or is no longer living with the spouse with whom the joint return was filed.[31]

Surviving Spouse. Certain widows and widowers may use the tax rates for married persons filing jointly. In order to use these lower rates, the person must qualify as a *surviving spouse*. There are two requirements. First, the spouse must have died within the two taxable years preceding the current taxable year. Second, the taxpayer must provide over half the cost of maintaining a home in which he or she and a *dependent* son, stepson, daughter, or stepdaughter live.[32] In determining whether the child is a dependent, the following modifications are made when applying the qualifying individual or qualifying relative tests.

▸ For purpose of determining whether the child is a dependent under the "qualifying relative" standard, the gross income test is ignored.

▸ In applying either test, the fact that the individual files a joint return is ignored.

▸ In applying either test, the fact that a dependent is ineligible to have dependents is ignored.

Remarriage terminates surviving spouse status. Of course, a joint return can be filed with the new spouse.

Example 17. H and W were married in 1992 and had two children, S and D. In 2005, H died. After H's death, W continued to provide a home and all the support of S and D. As a result, W is entitled to claim S and D as dependents. For 2005 H may file a joint return with W. W may file as a surviving spouse in 2006 and 2007, using the same rates as married persons filing jointly. In subsequent years, W may file as a head of household if she meets all the other requirements.

Separate Returns. Normally, it will be advantageous for married persons to file a joint return because it is simpler to file one return than it is to file two, and the tax will be as low or lower than the tax based on the rules for married persons filing separately. In some situations, a taxpayer may prefer to file a separate return. For example, a person may wish to avoid liability for the tax on the income—especially any unreported income—of his or her spouse. Similarly, a husband and wife who are separated and are contemplating divorce may wish to file separate returns.

Separate returns may be to the taxpayers' advantage in certain circumstances. Although rare, use of the separate rate schedules may result in a lower total tax than by using the rates applicable to a joint return. Filing of separate returns may also prove beneficial when the filing of a joint return would prevent another taxpayer (e.g., a parent) from claiming a dependency exemption deduction for either the husband or the

---

[31] § 6015(b) and (c).

[32] § 2(a).

wife (see *Example 10* above). State income tax laws may also make filing separately beneficial.

HEAD OF HOUSEHOLD

Head-of-household rates may be used if the taxpayer satisfies two conditions. First, the taxpayer must be unmarried or considered unmarried (i.e., an abandoned spouse) on the last day of the tax year. The second condition generally requires that the taxpayer provide more than one-half of the cost of maintaining the home in which an unmarried *qualifying child* or other *dependent familial relative* lives for more than half the taxable year.[33] As might be expected, the same individuals that are considered "relatives" for exemption purposes generally qualify as relatives when applying the head-of-household rules (e.g., children, grandchildren, parents, grandparents). However, there is an exception. Even though a person who is not truly related to the taxpayer but who lives in the taxpayer's home for the entire taxable year is treated as a relative for purposes of the dependency exemption, such is not the case here. In order for the taxpayer to qualify for head-of-household status, the individual living in the home must be a familial relative.[34] Exhibit 4-2 gives a listing of those who are normally considered relatives for purposes of meeting both the head-of-household and dependency rules. Note that they are all the same except for the nonfamilial relative.

EXHIBIT 4-2
Relatives for Dependency and Head-of-Household Tests

Relative	For Dependency Exemption	For Head-of-Household Test
Qualifying child	Yes	Yes
Familial relative	Yes	Yes
Other individuals—person who lives in taxpayer's home entire taxable year	Yes	No

An individual normally enables head of household status *only* if he or she is the taxpayer's dependent *and* lives in the taxpayer's household. Three exceptions exist to this general rule.

1. A parent must be a dependent but need not live in the taxpayer's home; however, the taxpayer still must pay more than half of the cost of keeping up a home for his or her mother or father.

For example, the taxpayer qualifies if he or she paid more than half the cost of the parent's living in a rest home or home for the elderly and the parent is a dependent.

Example 18. D, an unmarried individual, lives in San Francisco and pays more than half of the cost of maintaining a home in Reno for her dependent parents. Although her parents do not live with her in San Francisco, D qualifies for the head-of-household rates.

---

[33] § 2(b)(1).

[34] §§ 2(b)(3), 152(a)(9), and 152(c).

2. An *unmarried qualifying* child of the taxpayer need not be a dependent. This exception permits a divorced parent to qualify as head-of-household even though the former other parent claims the exemption for the child.

Example 19. M is divorced and maintains a household for herself and her 10-year-old daughter. Although M is the custodial parent, she allows her former husband to claim the exemption for the child. M still qualifies for the head-of-household rates.

3. A *married* child, grandchild, stepchild, or adopted child of the taxpayer who *could* be claimed as a dependent except for the fact that the taxpayer has signed a written declaration allowing the noncustodial parent to claim the dependent.

It should be noted that a person for whom a dependency exemption is claimed solely under a multiple support agreement (e.g., the taxpayer did not provide over half the cost of maintaining the home) is not considered a qualifying relative and the agreement *cannot* qualify the taxpayer as a head of household. In addition, a nonresident alien cannot be a head of household.[35]

Costs of Maintaining a Home. In determining whether a taxpayer qualifies for head-of-household status, it is necessary to determine whether he or she pays more than half of the cost of maintaining a home for the taxable year. This determination must also be made for surviving spouse filing status. The costs of maintaining the home include the costs for the mutual benefit of the occupants and include such expenses as property taxes, mortgage interest, rent, utilities, insurance, repairs, upkeep, and *food* consumed on the premises. The cost of maintaining a home does not include clothing, educational expenses, medical expenses, or transportation.[36]

Abandoned Spouse Provision. Without a special provision, an individual whose spouse has simply abandoned him or her might be forced to file using the high rates for married individuals filing separately. Aware of this problem, Congress has provided that a married individual who files a separate return may file as head of household if he or she qualifies as an *abandoned spouse*. To qualify, the individual must provide more than half the cost of maintaining a home that houses him or her and a child for whom a dependency exemption deduction is *either* claimed or could be claimed by the taxpayer except for the fact that the exemption was assigned to the noncustodial parent.[37] The child must live in the home with the taxpayer for more than half the taxable year and the taxpayer's spouse must not live in the home at any time during the last six months of the year. If each of these requirements is met, an abandoned spouse qualifies as a head of household.

Example 20. M and N are married with six children. In October, M stormed out of the house, saying he would never return. N was hopeful that M would return and consequently had not taken action to obtain a divorce by the end of the year. Although M and N are eligible to file a joint return, M indicated that he would not. Consequently, N's filing status is married filing separately. She does not qualify as an abandoned spouse since her husband lived in the home during the last six months of the year. In the following year, however, N could qualify and file as head of household.

---

[35]   *Supra*, footnote 34.

[36]   Reg. § 1.2-2(d).

[37]   § 2(c) and § 7703(b). An adopted child of the taxpayer is considered a son or daughter for this test.

Single. Single filing status is defined by exception. A single taxpayer is anyone who is unmarried and does not qualify as a head of household or surviving spouse. Even though these rates are somewhat lower, they may not be used by married persons filing separately.[38]

Marriage Tax Penalty. A well-known tax phenomenon faced by couples contemplating marriage is the possibility of the so-called marriage tax penalty. Whether matrimony is for better or for worse on the couple's tax return depends on a number of factors, such as how much each earns as well as whether either individual brings dependents into the marriage.

Joint filing originally was intended as a benefit to married couples. Prior to 1969, the joint return schedule was designed to tax one-half of total marital income at the tax rates applicable to single individuals. The resultant tax was then doubled to produce the married couple's tax liability. Note that this procedure produces a perfect split of a single earner's income between two spouses so that it is taxed at a lower marginal rate. While this approach is quite beneficial for married taxpayers, single taxpayers felt that they were paying an unjustifiable "singles penalty." To illustrate, consider the situation of a single taxpayer with taxable income of $24,000. In 1965, this taxpayer owed $8,030 of income tax, with the last dollar of income taxed at a 50 percent marginal tax rate. A married couple with the same 1965 taxable income owed only $5,660 (more than $2,000 less) and faced a marginal tax rate of only 32 percent.

In 1969 Congress attempted to alleviate the singles penalty by enacting a new (and lower) rate schedule for single taxpayers. While this action did reduce (but not eliminate) the singles penalty, it also created a marriage penalty for certain individuals as shown in the example below.

Example 21. Assume that H is single and his only source of income is his salary of $75,000. As shown below, his tax liability as a single taxpayer after taking into account the standard deduction and two exemptions is $12,565. If H marries W during the year and W has no taxable income of her own, the couple may file a joint tax return reflecting a larger standard deduction and two exemptions. Their tax liability as a married couple will be only $8,085. In this situation, marriage has saved H $4,480 and a *singles penalty* can be said to exist since others like H (except for being married) would pay a higher tax.

Now assume that W also earns a salary of $75,000. If she and H remain single, each will pay a separate tax of $13,365 for a combined total of $26,730. However, if they choose to marry, their tax liability will increase and a marriage penalty occurs. If they marry, their combined taxable income will remain the same at $133,600. However, their tax liability as a married couple will increase to $27,140 and they will pay a marriage tax penalty of $409.

---

[38]   Single filing status is referred to in Code § 1(c) as "Unmarried individuals (Other Than Surviving Spouses and Heads of Households)."

	H *Single No* *Dependent*	*H* *Single One* *Dependent*	*H & W* *One Earner* *Married*	*H & W* *Two Earners* *Married*
Gross income of H	$75,000	$75,000	$ 75,000	$ 75,000
Gross income of W	—	—	—	75,000
Standard deduction	(5,000)	(5,000)	(10,000)	(10,000)
Exemption	(3,200)	(6,400)	(6,400)	(6,400)
Taxable income	$66,800	$63,600	$ 58,600	$133,600
Tax	$13,365	$12,565	$ 8,085	$ 27,140
Tax for two singles (2 × $13,365)				(26,730)
Singles penalty ($12,565 − $8,085) . . .			$ 4,480	
Marriage penalty				$ 409

As a general rule, if a couple marries and only one spouse has income (or there is a large disparity between their incomes), marriage will be beneficial due to the splitting effect (i.e., the married, one earner effect above). In contrast, if a couple marries and they have similar incomes, there may be a marriage tax penalty (i.e., the married, two earners effect above).

Tax Reform and the Marriage Penalty. One of the goals of recent tax reforms was to reduce the marriage penalty. The specific provisions are summarized as follows:

- ▸ The standard deduction for a married couple was increased to an amount which is exactly double that for a single individual.

- ▸ The tax brackets are adjusted in a way to reduce the marriage penalty. First, the 10 percent bracket for married couples ($14,600) is double that for single individuals ($7,300). Next, the 15 percent bracket was adjusted to an amount which is double that for single taxpayers. Note, however, that the higher tax brackets are not adjusted and will remain in the same proportions that they are currently for married compared to unmarried persons.

EXHIBIT 4-3
Determination of Filing Status

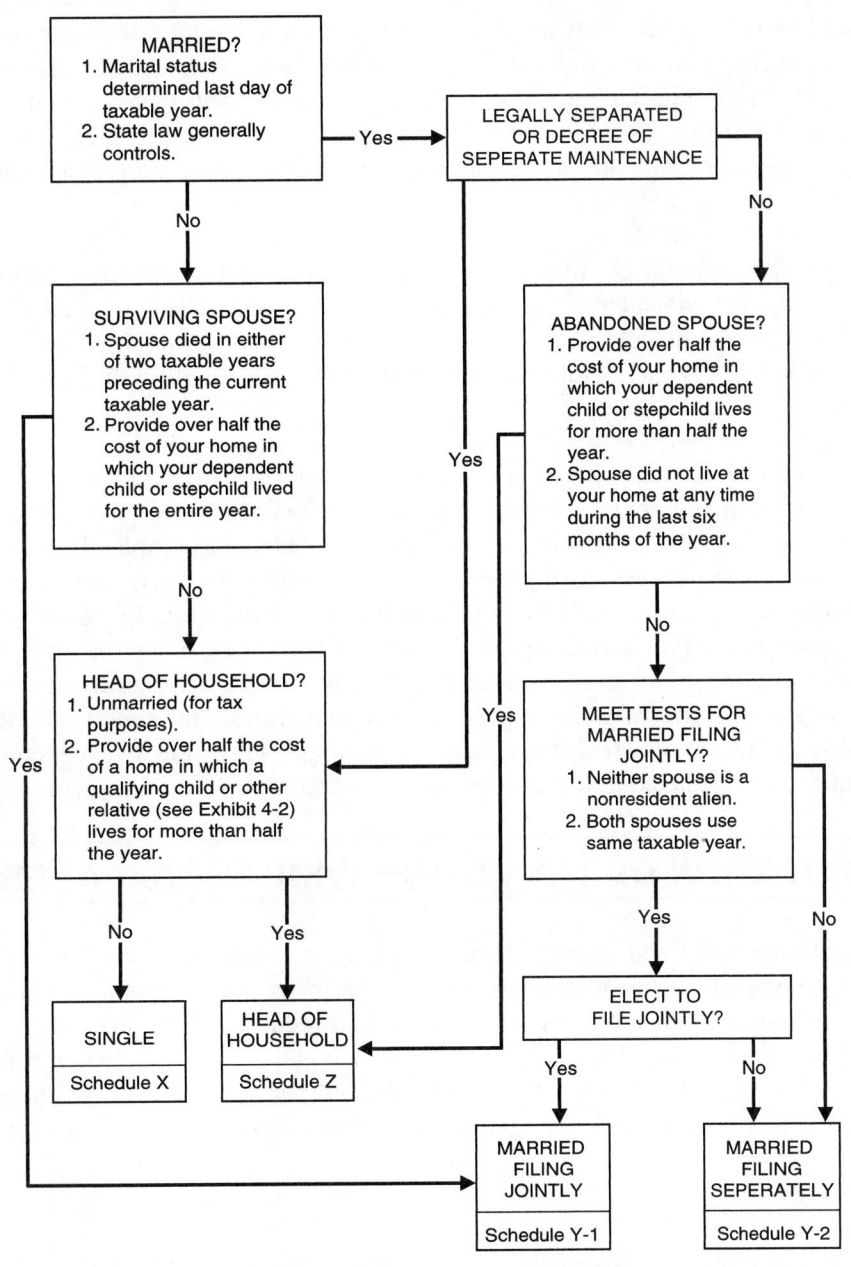

✓ CHECK YOUR KNOWLEDGE

Review Question 1. List the available rate schedules in the order of their progressivity (highest to lowest tax rates).

Married filing separately, single, head of household, and married filing jointly (including surviving spouses).

Review Question 2. H died in 2003, survived by his wife, W, and two young children, S and D. What rate schedule may W use in 2005 assuming she has not remarried?

She should be able to file as a surviving spouse and use the joint return rate schedule. A taxpayer qualifies as a surviving spouse if his or her spouse has died in either of the two taxable years preceding the current year (i.e., 2004 or 2005 in this case) and he or she provides over half the cost of a home in which he or she and a dependent child live. In this case, H died in 2003, and it appears that W provides a home in which she and her dependent children live.

Review Question 3. Q, divorced, is alive and well in Los Angeles. She has a 19-year-old daughter who attends school full-time at Arizona State. Q provides all her daughter's support, including payment of her dorm bill each month. Can Q file as a head of household? What additional questions must be asked before this question can be answered?

An individual can normally file as a head of household if he or she provides over *one-half* the cost of maintaining a home in which a dependent familial relative lives for more than *one-half* of the taxable year. In this case, it is not completely clear whether the half-and-half test is met. As a general rule, the relative must live in the home of the taxpayer one-half of the year. Here Q's daughter may only live in Q's home during the summer months, and it would therefore appear that Q could not qualify. However, temporary absences due to special circumstances such as those due to education, business, vacation, and military service are ignored. Since the daughter's absence is temporary, the test is satisfied. Note that Q's daughter need not be a dependent since this requirement is relaxed in the case of an unmarried child of the taxpayer.

COMPUTATION OF TAX FOR INDIVIDUAL TAXPAYERS

Once filing status and taxable income have been determined, the tax computation for most individuals is fairly straightforward. The gross tax is computed using the tax tables or the tax rate schedules. This amount is then reduced by any tax credits available to the taxpayer and any tax prepayments in arriving at the tax due or the refund. Children under age 14 with unearned income and all persons claimed as dependents are subject to special rules in the computation of their income tax.

TAX TABLES

The vast majority of individuals must determine their tax using *tax tables*, which are provided by the IRS along with the instructions for preparing individual income tax returns. The tables are derived directly from the rate schedules to simplify compliance and reduce taxpayer errors. The tax for any particular range of taxable income is determined by using the midpoint of the range and the appropriate rate schedule. For example, the tax in the 2004 tables for a single taxpayer with taxable income of $19,010 is $2,489, which is the tax computed on $19,025 (see Exhibit 4-4 for an excerpt and Appendix A for the complete 2004 Tax Tables).

EXHIBIT 4-4
Excerpts From Tax Tables for 2004

If line 40 (taxable income) is—		And you are—				If line 40 (taxable income) is—		And you are—			
At least	But less than	Single	Married filing jointly *	Married filing sepa- rately	Head of a house- hold	At least	But less than	Single	Married filing jointly *	Married filing sepa- rately	Head of a house- hold
			Your tax is—						Your tax is—		
19,000						**31,000**					
19,000	19,050	2,496	2,139	2,496	2,344	31,000	31,050	4,494	3,939	4,494	4,144
19,050	19,100	2,504	2,146	2,504	2,351	31,050	31,100	4,506	3,946	4,506	4,151
19,100	19,150	2,511	2,154	2,511	2,359	31,100	31,150	4,519	3,954	4,519	4,159
19,150	19,200	2,519	2,161	2,519	2,366	31,150	31,200	4,531	3,961	4,531	4,166
19,200	19,250	2,526	2,169	2,526	2,374	31,200	31,250	4,544	3,969	4,544	4,174
19,250	19,300	2,534	2,176	2,534	2,381	31,250	31,300	4,556	3,976	4,556	4,181
19,300	19,350	2,541	2,184	2,541	2,389	31,300	31,350	4,569	3,984	4,569	4,189
19,350	19,400	2,549	2,191	2,549	2,396	31,350	31,400	4,581	3,991	4,581	4,196
19,400	19,450	2,556	2,199	2,556	2,404	31,400	31,450	4,594	3,999	4,594	4,204
19,450	19,500	2,564	2,206	2,564	2,411	31,450	31,500	4,606	4,006	4,606	4,211
19,500	19,550	2,571	2,214	2,571	2,419	31,500	31,550	4,619	4,014	4,619	4,219
19,550	19,600	2,579	2,221	2,579	2,426	31,550	31,600	4,631	4,021	4,631	4,226
19,600	19,650	2,586	2,229	2,586	2,434	31,600	31,650	4,644	4,029	4,644	4,234
19,650	19,700	2,594	2,236	2,594	2,441	31,650	31,700	4,656	4,036	4,656	4,241
19,700	19,750	2,601	2,244	2,601	2,449	31,700	31,750	4,669	4,044	4,669	4,249
19,750	19,800	2,609	2,251	2,609	2,456	31,750	31,800	4,681	4,051	4,681	4,256
19,800	19,850	2,616	2,259	2,616	2,464	31,800	31,850	4,694	4,059	4,694	4,264
19,850	19,900	2,624	2,266	2,624	2,471	31,850	31,900	4,706	4,066	4,706	4,271
19,900	19,950	2,631	2,274	2,631	2,479	31,900	31,950	4,719	4,074	4,719	4,279
19,950	20,000	2,639	2,281	2,639	2,486	31,950	32,000	4,731	4,081	4,731	4,286

The tables cover taxpayers in each filing status with taxable incomes less than $100,000. A taxpayer who qualifies generally is required to use the tax tables.[39]

Example 22. William W. Bristol was single for 2004 and had no dependents. Bill's only income was wages of $26,610 and taxable interest of $350. Since his itemized deductions totaled only $1,650, Bill claims the $4,850 standard deduction allowed for 2004. Federal income tax of $2,820 was withheld from Bill's salary. Bill's taxable income and tax for 2004 are calculated as follows:

Salary			$26,610
Taxable interest			+ 350
Equals:	Adjusted gross income...............		$26,960
Less:	Standard deduction for 2004	$4,850	
	Personal exemption for 2004	3,100	– 7,950
Equals:	Taxable income		$19,010
Tax on $19,010 for 2004 (See Exhibit 4-4)			$ 2,496
Less:	Income tax withheld..................		– 2,820
Equals:	Tax due or (refund)		($ 324)

---

[39] § 3.

A completed Form 1040EZ for William W. Bristol, based on the information in this example, is shown in the Appendix at the end of the chapter.

Example 23. Clyde F and Delia C. Cooper were married during all of 2004 and had income from the following sources:

Salary, Clyde		$33,445
Federal income tax withheld	$1,170	
Part-time salary, Delia		22,200
Federal income tax withheld	780	
Interest from City Savings		950
Interest from U.S. Government		550

Clyde and Delia are the sole support for their two children, ages 2 and 7. During 2004 they paid job-related child care expenses of $3,500 and made deductible contributions of $4,000 to their Individual Retirement Accounts ($2,000 each). Their itemized deductions for the year do not exceed their standard deduction of $9,700. The Coopers' taxable income and tax for 2004 are calculated as follows:

Salary ($33,445 + $22,200)		$ 55,645
Plus: Taxable interest ($950 + $550)		+ 1,500
Less: Contributions to IRAs		− 4,000
Equals: Adjusted gross income		$ 53,145
Less: Standard deduction for 2004	$ 9,700	
Exemptions for 2004 ($3,100 × 4)	12,400	− 22,100
Equals: Taxable income		$ 31,045
Tax on $31,045 for 2004 (See Exhibit 4-4)		$ 3,939
Less: Child care credit (.20 × $3,500)		− 700
Child tax credit (2 × $1,000)		− 2,000
Equals: Net tax		$ 1,239
Less: Income tax withheld ($1,170 + $780)		− 1,950
Equals: Tax due or (refund)		
		($ 711)

A completed Form 1040A based on this information is included in the Appendix at the end of the chapter.

TAX RATE SCHEDULES

A taxpayer who is unable to use the tax tables uses the tax rate schedules in computing his or her income tax. These schedules contain the rates provided in § 1 of the Internal Revenue Code. The 2004 tax rate schedules are included, along with the 2004 tax tables, in Appendix A. The 2005 tax rate schedules are summarized in Exhibit 4-5. For future reference, the tax rate schedules for 2005 are also reproduced on the inside front cover of this text.

EXHIBIT 4-5
Individual Tax Rate Schedules for 2005

Single—Schedule X

If taxable income is		Tax liability			Of the amount over
Over	But not over				
$ 0	$ 7,300	—		10%	$ 0
7,300	29,700	$ 730	+	15%	7,300
29,700	71,950	4,090	+	25%	29,700
71,950	150,150	14,653	+	28%	71,950
150,150	326,450	36,549	+	33%	150,150
326,450	—	94,728	+	35%	326,450

Married filing jointly or Qualifying widow(er)—Schedule Y-1

If taxable income is		Tax liability			Of the amount over
Over	But not over				
$ 0	$ 14,600	—		10%	$ 0
14,600	59,400	$ 730	+	15%	14,600
59,400	119,950	7,450	+	25%	59,400
119,950	182,800	22,588	+	28%	119,950
182,800	326,450	40,186	+	33%	182,800
326,450	—	87,590	+	35%	326,450

Head of household—Schedule Z

If taxable income is		Tax liability			Of the amount over
Over	But not over				
$ 0	$ 10,450	—		10%	$ 0
10,450	39,800	$ 730	+	15%	10,450
39,800	102,800	5,133	+	25%	39,800
102,800	166,450	20,883	+	28%	102,800
166,450	326,450	38,705	+	33%	166,450
326,450	—	91,505	+	35%	326,450

Married filing separately—Schedule Y-2

If taxable income is		Tax liability			Of the amount over
Over	But not over				
$ 0	$ 7,300	—		10%	$ 0
7,300	29,700	$ 730	+	15%	7,300
29,700	59,975	4,090	+	25%	29,700
59,975	91,400	11,659	+	28%	59,975
91,400	163,225	20,458	+	33%	91,400
163,225	—	44,160	+	35%	163,225

A typical example illustrating the use of the tax rate schedules is given below.

Example 24. R, single, has taxable income of $175,000 for 2004. R's gross tax liability is $44,749, computed as follows:

Tax on $150,150	$36,549
Plus: Tax on income above $150,150	
[($175,000 – $150,150) × 33%]	8,200
Tax liability............................	$44,749

Tax Reform and the Tax Rates. As has been mentioned previously, recent tax reforms included a phased-in reduction in the marginal tax rates for noncorporate taxpayers.

- ► A new 10 percent bracket was carved out of the existing lowest rate 15 percent bracket as reflected in the 2005 tax schedules above.

- ► There are four tax brackets above the 15 percent bracket, all of which were reduced under tax reform. The phase-in of the rates is summarized as follows:

Tax Year	Rates			
2001	28.0%	31.0%	36.0%	39.6%
2002	27.5	30.5	35.5	39.1
After 2002	25.0	28.0	33.0	35.0

The post-2002 rates are reflected in the 2005 tax schedules above. All of the tax brackets continue to be indexed for inflation and are scheduled to remain in effect through 2010.

SPECIAL TAX COMPUTATION RULES

Unfortunately, the computation of the income tax is not always as straightforward as shown in *Example 24* above. For certain individuals, special rules must be followed.

Persons Claimed as Dependents. As one might deduce from the brief introduction to tax rates, one of the most fundamental principles of tax planning concerns minimizing the marginal tax rate that applies to the taxpayer's income. The significance of this principle is easily understood when it is recognized that Federal marginal tax rates have at times exceeded 90 percent. Even with the reduction of marginal rates to their current levels, minimizing the tax rate can provide benefits.

Historically, one of the most popular techniques to minimize the tax rate has been to shift income to a lower bracket taxpayer such as a child. As discussed in Chapter 5, this could be accomplished most easily by giving the child income-producing property. For example, a parent might establish a savings account for a child. In this way, the income would be taxed to the child at his or her low rate rather than the parents' high rate. In addition, this strategy—absent any special rules—takes advantage of the personal exemption and standard deduction available to a child.

Congress has long recognized the tax-saving potential inherent in such plans. For this reason, it is not surprising that it has taken steps to limit the opportunities. These are:

1. **Personal exemption.** A taxpayer who can be claimed as a dependent on another taxpayer's return is not entitled to a personal exemption. This rule effectively

prohibits all children from claiming a personal exemption. Observe that *without this rule*, a child could currently receive up to $3,200 (2005) income tax-free due to the exemption.

2. **Standard deduction.** The standard deduction available to a taxpayer who can be claimed as a dependent on another taxpayer's return is limited to the *greater* of $800 or $250 plus his or her earned income—but not to exceed the standard deduction amount ($5,000 for single taxpayers in 2005). Without this rule, a child could receive unearned income such as interest of up to $5,000 tax-free.

3. **Kiddie tax.** The *unearned income* of a child under age 14 is generally taxed as if the parent received it to the extent it exceeds $1,600 (2 × $800 standard deduction).[40] Absent this provision, affectionately known as the *kiddie tax*, a parent could shift up to $29,700 of taxable income to the child in 2005, who would pay taxes at a 15 percent or lower rate rather than at the parents' rate.

The effect of these provisions is to severely limit the success of any schemes designed to shift income.

Example 25. V, age 15, lives at home and may be claimed as a dependent on her parents' return. Several years ago, V's grandfather died, leaving her with a tidy sum to help send her to college. For 2005 V received interest income of $3,175. Her taxable income is computed as follows:

Adjusted gross income.		$ 3,175
Less: Standard deduction	$800	
Personal exemption	+0	– 800
Taxable income		$ 2,375

Note that, in computing V's taxable income, her standard deduction is limited to $800 (the larger of $250 plus her earned income, $250, or $800). The limitation is imposed because she is eligible to be claimed as a dependent on another taxpayer's return. For the same reason, she is not allowed to claim her own personal exemption deduction. Although the benefits of the normal standard deduction and personal exemption are denied, she avoids the kiddie tax because she is more than 13 years of age. Consequently, her tax is $238 (10% × $2,375). By escaping the kiddie tax, some tax savings are probably achieved since the income is taxed at her 10% rate rather than a higher rate had her parents actually received the income.

Example 26. Assume the same facts in *Example 25*, except that V also earns $2,000 from a part-time job. V's taxable income is determined as follows:

Adjusted gross income:		
Earned income	$ 2,000	
Interest income	+3,175	$ 5,175
Less: Standard deduction	$ 2,250	
Personal exemption	+0	–2,250
Taxable income		$ 2,925

---

[40] § 1(i).

As in *Example 25*, because V is a dependent, she is not allowed to claim her personal exemption deduction, nor may she claim the full standard deduction of $5,000. Note, however, that her standard deduction has increased because of her earned income. Her standard deduction is now $2,250 (the *larger* of $250 plus her earned income of $2,000, or $800). In effect, V is able to shelter income from tax with the standard deduction to the extent it is earned from personal services (plus another $250).

Kiddie Tax. The kiddie tax provisions apply only to children who have not attained the age of 14 before the close of the taxable year and who have at least one living parent (or foster parent). If the child becomes 14 before the close of the year, he or she is treated as being 14 for the entire taxable year and the rules do not apply. Moreover, the kiddie tax rules are triggered only when the affected child has *net unearned income*. For this purpose, unearned income generally includes dividends, interest, rents, and royalties. Net unearned income is unearned income in excess of $1,600 in 2005.[41] In short, when a child under 14 has unearned income exceeding $1,600, the special tax computation must be made. The effect of this calculation is that the first $800 of unearned income is offset by the standard deduction and the second $800 of unearned income is taxed at the child's rates (currently ten percent). Any unearned income exceeding $1,600 is taxed at the parents' top rates.

Example 27. J is 12 years old. Each year he receives interest income from a savings account and earned income from his paper route. The table below shows several sample calculations of J's taxable income assuming various amounts of earned and unearned income. In addition. the amount taxed at his rates and his parents' rates is computed.

	A	B	C	D
Unearned income.	$ 1,650	$ 500	$ 1,650	$ 3,100
Earned income.	350	700	700	5,150
Total.	$ 2,000	$ 1,200	$ 2,350	$ 8,250
Standard deduction:				
Greater of $800 or $250 plus earned income not to exceed $4,850 standard deduction	− 800	− 950	− 950	− 5,000
Personal exemption	—	—	—	—
Taxable income (a)	$ 1,200	$ 250	$ 1,400	$ 3,250
Taxed at parents' rates				
Unearned income > $1,600 (b).	$ 50	$ 0	$ 50	$ 1,500
Taxed at child's rates [(a) − (b)]	$ 1,150	$ 250	$ 1,350	$ 1,750

In case B, there is no net unearned income because J's unearned income was less than $1,600. J has net unearned income in cases A, C, and D. In each case, the amount taxed at the parents' rate is the amount by which the child's unearned income exceeded $1,600. Any other income is taxed at the regular rates for the child.

---

[41] § 1(i)(4). If greater than $1,600, the sum of $800 and the allowable itemized deductions specifically allocable to production of the unearned income are used.

When the child has net unearned income, the tax must be computed as if such income had been the parents' income. The child is required to pay the tax computed using his or her parents' rates except in rare cases where the tax computed in the normal manner is greater (in which case the higher tax must be paid).

Although the thrust of the kiddie tax is to tax income that would be taxed at a 10 or 15 percent rate at a higher rate, determination of the child's actual tax is somewhat complicated. The tax is computed on Form 8615 using the following approach:

Taxable income from parents' return	$xxx
Add: Net unearned income of child (children)	+ xxx
Equals: Total income taxed at parents' rate	$xxx
Tax on total income taxed at parents' rate	$xxx
Minus: Tax on parents' income	−xxx
Equals: Parental tax on child's net unearned income.	$xxx
Add: Tax on child's remaining taxable income at child's rate	+ xxx
Equals: Total tax on child's taxable income	$xxx

The first step in this process requires the calculation of the parental tax. This is accomplished by combining the income of the parents with the net unearned income of the child and then calculating the total tax on this combined income as if the parents had reported all the income. Then, by subtracting the tax on the parents' income (from the parents' return), the amount of tax that the parents would have paid on the child's net unearned income is determined. This *parental tax* is, therefore, the tax that the parents would have paid on the net unearned income had they reported it directly.

The final part of the calculation involves determining the tax on the child's remaining taxable income at the child's tax rate of 10 percent. This tax is added to the parental tax to arrive at the child's total tax.

In those situations where the parents are divorced, the parental tax is computed using the taxable income of the custodial parent (or joint income if he or she has remarried). Where the parents file separate returns, the tax is computed using the greater of the parents' two taxable incomes.

In computing the tax on the parent *including* the child's net unearned income, such income is not considered when computing any of the parents' deductions or credits (e.g., the deduction for miscellaneous itemized deductions, which is limited to the amount that exceeds two percent of adjusted gross income).

Where there is more than one child under 14 with net unearned income, the parental tax must be computed using the net unearned income of all children. As shown below, the tax so computed is then allocated pro rata based on each child's relative contribution to total net unearned income.

$$\frac{\text{Child's net unearned income}}{\text{All children's net unearned income tax}} \times \text{Parental tax} = \text{Child's share of parental tax}$$

Example 28. During 2005 T, age 11, received $5,000 in interest from a savings account created for him in 2000 by his now deceased grandfather. Similarly, his sister, V, age 6, had $2,200 of interest income. Since T and V are under 14 and have net unearned income of $3,400 ($5,000 − $1,600) and $600 ($2,200 − $1,600), respectively, their tax must be computed in the special manner. The children's parents had income of $101,000. In addition, due to special medical problems of the father, they incurred $12,575 of medical expenses. The couple also has other itemized deductions of $10,000. T's tax is computed as follows:

1. Tax on parents computed in the normal manner:

Adjusted gross income	$ 101,000
Deductions:	
Medical expenses [$12,575 − (7.5% × $101,000)]	−5,000
Other itemized deductions	−10,000
Exemptions (4 × $3,200)	−12,800
Taxable income computed in the normal manner	$ 73,200
Tax [$7,450 + 15% ($73,200 − $59,400)]	$ 10,900

2. Tax on parents including net unearned income of all children:

Parents' taxable income computed in the normal manner	$ 73,200
Net unearned income of children:	
($3,400 + $600)	+4,000
Taxable income including net unearned income	$ 77,200
Tax [$7,450 + 15% ($77,200 − $59,400)]	$ 11,900

3. Parental tax:

Tax on parents including net unearned income	$ 11,900
−Tax on parents computed in the normal manner	−10,900
= Parental Tax	$ 1,000

4. T's share of parental tax [$1,000 × ($3,400 ÷ $4,000)] = ... | $ 850 |

5. Tax on T excluding net unearned income:

Interest income	$ 5,000
− Net unearned income	−3,400
− Standard deduction (as limited for dependents)	− 800
− Exemption deduction (none for dependents)	−0
Taxable income	$ 800
Tax (10% × $800)	$ 80

6. Total tax on T:

Tax on T excluding net unearned income	$ 80
+ Parental Tax	+850
= T's total tax	$ 930

Note that in this case the total parental tax of $1,000 is simply the product of the net unearned income of $4,000 and the parents' marginal tax rate of 25%. Also note that the parents' deduction for medical expenses is computed without including the net unearned income of the children (i.e., the percentage limitation is based on $101,000 rather than $105,000).

Election to Report Child's Income on Parents' Return. In order to simplify the return filing process, parents may elect to include on their own return the unearned income of a child if certain conditions are satisfied.[42] Note that this is contrary to the normal procedure where the child files his or her own return and pays the tax computed with respect to the parents' rates. This election eliminates the hassle of filing separate returns for each child. However, the election can only be made where the child is under age 14, his or her income is between $800 and $8,000, and it consists *solely* of interest and dividends. The election is not available if estimated taxes have been paid or taxes have been withheld on dividend or interest income (i.e., the child is subject to back-up withholding).

DETERMINATION OF NET TAX DUE OR REFUND

Once the tax is determined using the tax tables, tax rate schedules, or the special tax computation procedures described above, it is reduced by the amount of any credits or prepayments. The primary prepayments are the Federal income tax withheld from the taxpayer's salary or wages by an employer, quarterly estimated tax payments, and the estimated tax paid when an extension of time to file a return is requested. Estimated tax payments and extensions of time to file are discussed later in this chapter.

Numerous credits are allowed in computing the Federal income tax. The credit most frequently encountered on an uncomplicated income tax return is the child care credit. This and other credits are discussed in detail in Chapter 13.

✓ CHECK YOUR KNOWLEDGE

Review Question 1. What are the top and bottom tax rates for individuals?

It depends on the year. For 2005, the lowest rate is 10 percent and the highest rate is 35 percent (on taxable income over $326,450).

Review Question 2. Several years ago Grandma gave her grandchild K, now 13, $20,000 to be used for her college education. All of the money was invested in stock. This year K's dad, acting on her behalf, sold some of the stock for a $4,000 short-term capital gain. K's parents are in the 35 percent tax bracket.

a. Compute K's taxable income and K's tax.

Income (unearned).	$ 4,000
Standard deduction:	
Greater of $800 or $250 plus earned income	– 800
Exemption	0
Taxable income	$ 3,200

K's personal exemption and standard deduction are limited since she can be claimed as a dependent on her parent's return. Consequently, she is not entitled to an exemption, and her standard deduction is $800 since she has no earned income. In computing K's tax, the amount of unearned income in excess of $1,600 is $2,400 ($4,000 − $1,600), which must be taxed at her parents' rates while the remainder is taxed at her rates. Thus her tax is $920 [(35% × $2,400) + ($800 × 10%)].

---

42   § 1(g)(7).

b. What suggestion might you give to K and her dad?

K should wait to sell the stock until next year, when she turns 14 and the kiddie tax does not apply. If she does so, the gain would be taxed at 10 percent rather than 35 percent (or 5 percent if it is a long-term gain), and the family could save either $240 [(15% − 5% = 10%) × $2,400] or $600 [(35% − 10% = 25%) × $2,400].

c. Assume there were no kiddie tax. How much unearned income could be shifted to a dependent child and taxed at the child's 15 percent or lower rate rather than the parents' rate?

The 10 percent bracket for 2005 extends from taxable income of $1 to $7,300 and the 15 percent bracket extends from $7,301 to $29,700 for single taxpayers. Plus, another $800 escapes tax all together due to the child's standard deduction.

FILING REQUIREMENTS

Individual taxpayers with extremely low levels of income are not required to file a Federal income tax return. In general, a taxpayer is not required to file an income tax return for the year if his or her gross income is less than the *total* of his or her standard deduction (including the additional amount for the elderly but not the blind) *plus* personal exemptions (but not dependency exemptions).[43] These taxpayers generally are not liable for any Federal income tax. The filing requirement is based on gross income, so taxpayers who have gross incomes exceeding specified thresholds *must* file even if they owe no Federal income tax. A partial list of filing requirements for 2005 and how they are computed is illustrated in Exhibit 4-6.

EXHIBIT 4-6
Gross Income Filing Requirements for 2005

	Personal Exemption	+	Standard Deduction	+	Elderly Standard Deductions	=	2005 Gross Income
Single person 65 years old	$3,200		$ 5,000		—		$ 8,200
Single person ≥65 years old	3,200		5,000		$1,250		9,450
Head of household 65	3,200		7,300		—		10,500
Head of household ≥ 65	3,200		7,300		1,250		11,750
Married filing jointly, both 65	6,400		10,000		—		16,400
Married filing jointly, both ≥ 65	6,400		10,000		2,000		18,400
Married filing separately	3,200						3,200
Surviving spouse 65	3,200		10,000		—		13,200
Surviving spouse ≥ 65	3,200		10,000		1,000		14,200
Dependents							Special Rules

---

[43]   § 6012(a)(1).

In addition to the general requirement for filing (gross income is at least as much as the taxpayer's standard deduction + personal exemptions), certain individuals *must* file returns. These include:

1. Any taxpayer who has self-employment income of $400 or more

2. An individual who is claimed as a dependent on another taxpayer's return *and* who has unearned income at least equal to his or her minimum standard deduction (i.e., generally $800, but increased by the additional amount for elderly or blind taxpayers)[44]

3. Any person who receives any advance payments of earned income credit

Form 1040. The individual taxpayer is required to file Form 1040, along with related forms and schedules. A complicated return involves many forms and schedules in addition to the Form 1040, whereas a simpler return may require only a few or no attached schedules.

Two simplified forms are provided for taxpayers with uncomplicated tax calculations. The Form 1040EZ is available for taxpayers who are single or married filing jointly and have no dependents. To qualify, the taxpayer's income must consist only of salaries and wages plus interest income of $1,500 or less. The only allowable deductions on this form are the personal exemption amount and the standard deduction.

The Form 1040A is available for a large number of taxpayers who do not itemize their deductions and have no income other than salaries and wages, dividends, interest, and unemployment compensation. This form provides for deductions for individual retirement account (IRA) contributions, personal and dependency exemptions, and the earned income credit.

Example 29. Jeremy S. Allen, a registered nurse, and Shelly R. Allen, an air traffic controller, are married and file a joint income tax return for 2004. They are the sole support of their three children: William, Susan, and Gregory (all under age 17). The following information is from their records for 2004:

Salaries and wages, Jeremy		$31,875
Federal income tax withheld	$1,700	
Salaries and wages, Shelly		44,900
Federal income tax withheld	2,400	
Interest income—Mercantile National Bank		1,800
Interest income—U.S. Government Bonds		700
Interest income—Ben Franklin Savings		500
Itemized deductions are as follows:		
Hospitalization insurance		700
Unreimbursed fees of doctors, hospitals, etc.		2,100
Unreimbursed prescription drugs		200
Real estate taxes on residence		1,200
State income taxes paid		3,400
Interest paid on original home mortgage		8,500
Investment interest		400
Charitable contribution—First Church		1,300
Charitable contribution—Home State University		200
Preparation of prior year's tax return		225

---

[44] § 6012(a)(1)(C)(i). As stated earlier, certain children under the age of 14 are not required to file a tax return *if* their parents *elect* to include the child's income on their return and pay the appropriate additional tax.

The Allens' adjusted gross income is $79,775 ($31,875 + $44,900 + $3,000 interest income) since there were no deductions for A.G.I. The deductible amount of their itemized deductions is $15,000, summarized as follows:

Medical expenses exceeding $5,983	
(i.e., 7.5% × $79,775 A.G.I.)	$ 0
Deductible taxes ($1,200 + $3,400)	4,600
Qualifying home mortgage interest	8,500
Investment interest	400
Charitable contributions	1,500
Miscellaneous itemized deductions	
exceeding $1,596 (i.e., 2% × $79,775 A.G.I.)	0
Total itemized deductions	$15,000

The Allens' taxable income, gross tax, and tax refund for 2004 are determined as follows:

Adjusted gross income.		$ 79,775
Less: Itemized deductions.	$ 15,000	
Personal and dependency		
exemptions ($3,100 × 5)	+15,500	−30,500
Equals: Taxable income.		$ 49,275
Gross Tax (from 2004 Tax Table)		$ 6,676
Less: Prepayments ($1,700 + $2,400).		−4,100
Child tax credit (3 × $1,000)		−3,000
Equals: Tax due or (refund).		($ 424)

The Allens' completed 2004 tax return is shown in the Appendix at the end of the chapter. It consists of a Form 1040 plus Schedules A and B.

The more common tax forms and schedules used by individual taxpayers are listed in Exhibit 4-7. Copies of these forms are contained in Appendix B at the end of the text.

EXHIBIT 4-7

List of Common Forms and Schedules Used by Individual Taxpayers

Form 1040	**U.S. Individual Income Tax Return**

Accompanying Schedules:

Schedule A	Itemized deductions
Schedule B	Interest and dividend income
Schedule C	Profit (or loss) from business or profession
Schedule D	Capital gains and losses
Schedule E	Supplemental income schedule (rents, royalties, etc.)
Schedule F	Farm income and expenses
Schedule R	Credit for the elderly
Schedule SE	Computation of social security self-employment tax

Accompanying Forms:

Form 2106	Employee business expenses
Form 2210	Underpayment of estimated tax by individuals
Form 2441	Credit for child and dependent care expenses
Form 3800	General business credit
Form 3903	Moving expense adjustment
Form 4562	Depreciation
Form 4684	Casualties and thefts
Form 4797	Supplemental schedule of gains and losses
Form 6251	Alternative minimum tax computation
Form 6252	Computation of installment sale income
Form 8582	Passive activity losses
Form 8615	Computation of tax for children under age 14 who have investment income of more than $1,600
Form 8814	Parents' election to report child's interest and dividends

Other Common Forms:

Form 1040A	U.S. Individual Income Tax Return
Form 1040EZ	Income tax return for single filers with no dependents
Form 4868	Application for automatic extension of time to file
Form 2688	Application for extension of time to file

DUE DATES FOR FILING RETURNS

The day on which a Federal return must be filed with the IRS depends upon what type of return is involved. Generally the tax returns must be filed on or before the due dates, which are as follows:[45]

---

[45]   § 6072(a).

Type of Return	*Due Date*
Annual Individual Income Tax Returns	Fifteenth day of the fourth month following the close of the tax year (April 15 for calendar year individuals)
Annual C Corporation and S Corporation Income Tax Returns	Fifteenth day of third month following the close of the tax year (March 15 for calendar year corporations)
Annual Partnership, Estate, and Trust Income Tax Returns	Fifteenth day of the fourth month following the close of the year (April 15 for calendar year entities)
Estate Tax Returns	Nine months after the date of the descedent's death
Gift Tax Returns	April 15 (All gift tax returns are for a calendar year)

Any return that is mailed via the U.S. Postal Service is deemed to be delivered when mailed, so any return postmarked on or before the above due dates is timely filed. If any of these due dates fall on Saturday, Sunday, or a legal holiday, the return must be filed on the succeeding day that is not a Saturday, Sunday, or legal holiday.

Extension of Time to File. The Internal Revenue Code provides extensions of time for filing returns. The extension must be requested on or before the due date of the return. Currently, there is an *automatic* four-month extension for filing the individual income tax return (Form 1040). Thus the extended due date for calendar year individuals is August 15. If the taxpayer desires to use the four-month extension, he or she simply fills out Form 4868 and mails it to the IRS by the original due date along with a check covering the estimated balance due. It should be noted that an extension of time to file is not an extension of time to pay. There is *no extension* of time to pay estimated tax due.[46]

If the taxpayer needs additional time to prepare the return after the automatic four-month extension, he or she must file Form 2688 or write a letter explaining the circumstances. This extension is discretionary with the IRS and probably will not be granted unless unusual circumstances indicate that the taxpayer is laboring under "undue hardship" in compiling the necessary records.

Example 30. As a result of a severe flood in early April, T lost all records necessary for the filing of his Federal income tax return for the prior year. T should file Form 4868 and pay any income tax he estimates to be due by April 15. If T requires more than four months to gather duplicate copies of his records (e.g., bank statements, cancelled checks, and prior years' Federal income tax returns), he should file Form 2688 or write a letter to the District Director of the IRS requesting an additional extension of time. Under these circumstances, there is no doubt that T will be granted his request.

Interest and Penalties. Whenever a taxpayer fails to pay the amount of tax owed by the due date of the return, interest is charged at a rate 2 percent higher than the Federal short-term rate. For the first quarter of 2004, the annual interest rate charge on such a

---

[46]   Reg. § 1.6081-4(a).

deficiency is 4 percent (2% + 2%), compounded daily on the unpaid balance.[47] An interest charge normally results when the taxpayer files for an extension and pays the estimated tax due that ultimately turns out to be less than that due when the return is actually filed. This *failure-to-pay* penalty is one-half of 1 percent (0.5%) per month (or any fraction of a month), up to a maximum of 25 percent of the amount due.[48] However, no penalty for failure to pay is assessed when there is reasonable cause or an extension of time to file is properly obtained and the tax due is less than 10 percent of the total tax shown on the return.

> **Example 31.** W was simply too busy to file his Federal tax return for the most recent calendar year. Thus on April 15 he requested an automatic extension of time to file until August 15. W had prepaid taxes of $5,800 in the form of withholding, and he estimated that his total tax would be $6,200. Therefore, he paid $400 when he filed the request for an extension. When he finally did file on June 15, W's return showed a total tax of $6,850 and a tax due of $650. W is not required to pay the penalty for failure to pay since his tax due is less than 10 percent of the total tax [$650 < 10% × $6,850]. However, assuming the current rate of interest on underpayments is 10%, W must pay interest of $11 ($650 at 10% annually, compounded daily for 61 days).

In the event a tax return is not filed by the due date (including extensions), the IRS will impose a *failure-to-file* penalty of 5 percent per month—up to a maximum of 25 percent—on the amount of tax due on the return.[49] Like the failure-to-pay penalty, any fraction of a month is counted as a full month. A minimum penalty of $100 (limited to the total tax on the return) applies if the return is not filed within 60 days of the due date.

When both of the preceding penalties apply, the penalty for failure to file is reduced by the amount of the penalty for failure to pay. Since both penalties are technically an addition to the tax, interest must be paid on the penalty as well as the unpaid tax.

> **Example 32.** K forgot to file her Federal tax return for the most recent calendar year. When she finally filed the return on November 1 (7 months late), her return showed a gross tax of $5,200 and a tax due after withholding of $600. Assuming the current rate of interest on underpayments is 10%, K must pay not only her tax due of $600 but also late penalties of $156 and interest on the tax and penalties of $41, for a total of $797, as computed below.

Tax due		$600
Penalties:		
Failure to pay ($600 × .005 × 7)		21
Failure to file:		
Failure-to-file penalty ($600 × .05 × 5)	$150	
Reduced by failure-to-pay penalty		
($600 × .005 × 5)	(15)	135
Total tax and penalties.		$756
Interest on tax and penalties ($756 × 10% × 199/365)		41
Total due		$797

---

[47] § 6601(a). The 5 percent rate is scheduled to remain in effect until April 2005, at which time it will be increased, reduced, or allowed to remain unchanged, based on a predetermined formula. Generally, the government pays interest to taxpayers in the case of overpayments, beginning on the due date for the tax (usually the due date for the tax return). The rate of interest is the same as that on underpayments for noncorporate taxpayers. See § 6621.

[48] § 6651(a)(2).

[49] § 6651(a)(1). If the failure to file is fraudulent, the penalty is 15 percent per month up to a maximum of 75 percent. § 6551(f).

Note that the minimum failure-to-file penalty is not triggered here since the penalty of $135 computed in the normal manner exceeds the minimum penalty of $100 (the lesser of the total tax due, $600, or $100).

As mentioned in Chapter 2, many other penalties exist to ensure proper compliance with the tax laws. For example, the Code provides for an *accuracy-related* penalty of 20 percent of the amount of understatement due to negligence or intentional disregard of the rules (e.g., failing to report income), or substantial valuation infractions.[50] In addition, severe penalties, both civil and criminal, exist for fraud.[51] Still another important penalty to be considered is that for failure to pay estimated taxes during the year. This penalty is discussed below.

Claim for Refund. After the original return has been filed, an individual taxpayer generally has until the later of three years from the date of filing the original return, or two years from the time the tax was paid, to file a claim for refund, usually by filing an amended individual income tax return (i.e., Form 1040X—see Appendix).[52]

Example 33. K filed a timely return for 2004 on April 12, 2005. The total tax on the return was $5,500, and after withholdings of $4,700, K owed $800. K's return was audited and she was required to pay a deficiency of $200 on June 3, 2006. K may file a claim for refund for any part of the tax of $5,700 ($5,500 on the original return plus the additional tax of $200) until April 12, 2008 (three years from the date filed). A claim for up to $200 could be filed up until June 3, 2008 (two years from the date the $200 was paid).

In a recent case, the Supreme Court upheld the two year rule. The taxpayers simply did not file on time, nor did they request an extension. After some time, the IRS calculated the tax based on available information. Later, a claim for refund, in the form of a delinquent tax return showing an overpayment, was filed. The tax had been paid in the form of withholding, which was deemed to have been paid on the original due date. Since the claim for refund was filed just over two years after the original due date for the return, no refund was required to be made.[53]

Example 34. C estimated his federal income tax for the calendar year 2002 to be $1,200. Since he had $1,350 withheld (deemed paid on April 15, 2003), C did not file on time and continued to procrastinate, realizing he owed no money. The IRS prepared a return for C from available information, showing a tax due of $125 on November 15, 2004. If C finally files a correct return showing $1,200 in tax on May 1, 2005, he will not owe the $125 (since in reality he owed no more taxes), but he also will not be entitled to the $150 ($1,350 − $1,200) that he could have claimed as a refund up until April 15, 2005.

In the case of a refund granted by the United States Tax Court, the period for filing the claim for refund ends three years after the date the tax was paid.[54]

---

[50] § 6653(a)(1).

[51] § 6653(b).

[52] § 6511(a).

[53] *Comm. v. Lundy*, 116 S. Ct. 647, 77 AFTR2d 406, 96-1 USTC ¶50,035 (USSC, 1996).

[54] § 6512(b)(3).

ESTIMATED TAX PAYMENTS

Under the "pay-as-you-go" system for collection of taxes, taxpayers are required to prepay Federal income taxes in the form of withholding from certain types of income and estimated tax payments. Withholding is normally adequate for taxpayers receiving only salaries and wages. However, those taxpayers with other income *must* estimate the tax that will be due (including the self-employment tax, the alternative minimum tax, and certain other taxes) and make periodic payments of the estimated tax during the year. Corporations are also required to make estimated tax payments.

A penalty is imposed for taxpayers who fail to make adequate estimates. This penalty is separate from the penalty for failure to pay the tax and the interest which is charged.[55] Interest and the failure-to-pay penalty apply to underpayments of tax due as of the due date (e.g., April 15) of the return. The estimated tax penalty is charged from the date the estimated tax installment was due (e.g., June 15th) until the tax is paid (or, if the tax is paid late, the due date of the return). The penalty is assessed at the same rate as the interest which is charged on tax deficiencies; however, it is not assessed where the net tax due after withholding is less than $1,000.

The estimates are due on April 15, June 15, September 15, and January 15 for a calendar year taxpayer. To avoid penalty, the total prepayments must *generally* equal or exceed the lesser of the following:

1. Ninety percent of the tax shown on the return, or

2. One hundred percent of the tax shown on the return for the individual for the preceding year [If A.G.I. in the prior year exceeded $150,000, the payment must be 110% of the prior year's tax].[56]

Example 35. For 2005 T, a single individual, reported an adjusted gross income of $165,000, a taxable income of $140,000, and a tax liability (after credits) of $40,000. In 2006 his tax liability is $60,000. Under the general rules T must have paid the lesser of 90% of the current year's tax, $54,000, or 100% of last year's tax, $40,000, in order to avoid underpayment penalty. However, because T's adjusted gross income exceeded $150,000 in the prior year, 2005, he is subject to the 110% rule regarding his estimated tax payments for the current year, 2006. As a result, he can avoid underpayment penalties with respect to 2006 only if he pays the lesser of the following:

1. 90% of the current year's tax of $60,000	$54,000
2. 110% of last year's tax of $40,000	44,000

Thus, if T pays at least $44,000 on a timely basis during 2006, he will not be subject to any penalty for failing to pay estimated taxes.

Whether the payments are adequate or not is determined at the end of each quarter. For this purpose, withholding is treated as if it occurred proportionately throughout the year. At the end of each quarter, the payments to date are compared to the appropriate portion of the amount required to be paid.

Example 36. For 2004 and 2005 G's gross tax was $12,000 and $16,000, respectively. G's withholding for 2005 was $6,500 and his estimated tax payments

---

[55] § 6654(a).

[56] § 6654(d).

were $1,500 on April 15 and June 15 and $500 on September 15 and January 15. G's underpayment is determined as follows:

	Payment Due Date			
	4/15	6/15	9/15	1/15
Percentage due	25%	50%	75%	100%
90% of current year's tax				
($16,000 × .90 × percentage due).	$ 3,600	$ 7,200	$ 10,800	$ 14,400
100% of prior year's tax				
($12,000 × percentage due)	$ 3,000	$ 6,000	$ 9,000	$ 12,000
Payments to date:				
Withholding.	$ 1,625	$ 3,250	$ 4,875	$ 6,500
Estimated tax payments	+ 1,500	+ 3,000	+ 3,500	+ 4,000
Total	$ 3,125	$ 6,250	$ 8,375	$ 10,500

G's payments are adequate for the first quarter and the second quarter, since the payments up to each date exceed the lesser of the two required amounts (the prior year's tax in both cases). As of the third payment date, G is underpaid by $625 ($9,000 − $8,375); and as of the last payment date, he is underpaid by $1,500 ($12,000 − $10,500). The penalty is computed based on these amounts from the due date until the day they are paid (or April 15, if earlier).

Assuming the current rate of penalty is 10% and G does not pay his tax early, G's penalty would be $58, which is the penalty on $625 from September 15 through January 15 [$625 × .1 × 122 days/365 days) = $21] *plus* that on $1,500 from January 15 through April 15 [$1,500 × (.1 × 90 days/365 days) = $37].

The penalty for failure to make adequate estimated tax payments is calculated on Form 2210 (see Appendix for a sample form). Unless a taxpayer can reduce the penalty by applying the annualized income installment or otherwise, he or she may simply let the IRS calculate this penalty and assess a deficiency for it. In addition, the IRS may waive the underpayment penalty in the event of a casualty or unusual circumstances where it might be inequitable to impose the additional tax. The IRS may also waive the penalty for retired taxpayers who are at least age 62 or disabled where the underpayment was due to reasonable cause rather than willful neglect.

Annualized Income Installment. If income for a year is earned disproportionately during the year, the taxpayer may be able to avoid penalty for one or more of the first three payments under the *annualized income installment* method.[57] Under this method, no penalty is imposed when the payment to date exceeds the tax which would be due on the income for the months preceding the payment date determined on an annualized basis.

Example 37. F, a calendar year individual, is engaged in a seasonal business that earns most of its income during the fourth quarter. F is able to demonstrate that the income was earned as follows:

---

[57] § 6654(d).

	Payment Due Date			
	4/15	6/15	9/15	1/15
Months preceding payment	3	5	8	12
Net income earned for the months preceding the payment	$10,000	$18,000	$25,000	$50,000
Annualized amount [Net income × (12 × No. of months to date)].	$40,000	$43,500	$37,500	$50,000

To apply this exception, the tax on the annualized income is determined. There is an underpayment only if the estimated tax payments are less than the appropriate portion of the tax on the annualized income.

The required payment for April 15 is the fraction 3 months ÷ 12 months times the tax on $40,000. If the tax on $40,000 is $8,000, F has no underpayment for the first payment so long as she paid $2,000 ($8,000 × 3/12) or more. If she had paid less, the underpayment would be the amount by which $2,000 exceeded the payments. A similar process would be followed for each quarter.

To apply the annualized income installment calculations, a taxpayer completes a worksheet that accompanies the Form 2210. If this method is used to the benefit of the taxpayer for one payment, it must be used for *all* four payments.

STATUTE OF LIMITATIONS

Even in the administration of the Federal tax laws, all things must finally come to an end. As the U.S. Supreme Court has stated:

> Congress has regarded it as ill advised to have an income tax system under which there would never come a day of final settlement and which required both a taxpayer and the Government to stand ready forever and a day to produce vouchers, prove events, and recall details of all that goes into an income tax contest.[58]

Accordingly, there are certain time periods within which the IRS must take action *against* a taxpayer. If the Service does not take action within the prescribed time period, it is *barred* from pursuing the matter further. Technically the period in which an action must be commenced is called the Statute of Limitations. If the Statute of Limitations runs (expires) without any action on the part of the IRS, then the government is prohibited from assessing additional taxes for the expired periods.

Under the general rule, the IRS has three years from the date a return is filed to assess an additional tax liability against the taxpayer. If the tax return is filed before its due date, the three-year period for assessment begins *on* the due date.

Example 38. R, a calendar year taxpayer, files a 2005 income tax return (due April 15) on March 8, 2006. The IRS will be prevented from assessing R additional taxes for 2005 any time after April 15, 2009.

Example 39. Refer to *Example 38*. If R files a 2005 income tax return on October 15, 2006, the IRS may assess additional taxes for 2005 at any time through October 15, 2009.

---

[58] *Rothensies v. Electric Storage Battery Co.*, 47-1 USTC ¶9106, 35 AFTR 297, 329 U.S. 296, 301 (USSC, 1946).

There are several important exceptions to the three-year time period for assessing additional taxes. First, if the taxpayer has filed a false or a fraudulent return with the intention to *evade* the tax, then the tax may be assessed (or a proceeding may be initiated in court without assessment) at *any time* in the future. Similarly, if the taxpayer fails to file a return, the Statute of Limitations will not begin to run. Interestingly, a willful failure to file, a negligent failure to file, or an innocent failure to file are all treated the same. Thus, under any of these circumstances there is no limit to the time in which the IRS may make an assessment or begin a court proceeding against the taxpayer.

In the case of a *substantial omission of income* from a tax return, the Statute of Limitations is extended to six years. A substantial omission is defined as an omission of income in excess of 25% of the gross income *reported* on the return.[59] If the omission of gross income was committed with the intent of evading the tax, however, the assessment period would be unlimited.

> **Example 40.** T, a calendar year taxpayer, unintentionally failed to include $8,000 of dividends in his 2004 tax return filed on April 15, 2005. If the $8,000 omitted is more than 25% of the gross income reported on T's 2004 return, the IRS may assess an additional income tax liability against him at any time until after April 15, 2011.

The periods within which assessments must be made are summarized in Exhibit 4-8, which follows.

EXHIBIT 4-8
Periods Within Which Assessments Must Be Made

Circumstances of Return	Period of Assessment
Normal return had been filed	Three years from date of filing or due date, whichever is later
Return filed with substantial omission of gross income	Six years from date of filing or due date, whichever is later
No return is filed	No time limit
False or fraudulent return	No time limit

INDEXATION AND THE FEDERAL INCOME TAX

Inflation has significant effects on a progressive tax rate structure stated in terms of a *constant* dollar. Taxpayers whose *real* incomes remain constant will have increasing levels of income, stated in terms of *nominal* dollars. Accordingly, their incomes will *creep up* into higher tax brackets. As an illustration, assume a taxpayer who earned $100,000 in 2004 is entitled to an annual raise at least equal to any increase in the Consumer Price Index (approximately four percent increase in 2004). Although his 2005 salary will creep up to $104,000, his before tax income in terms of 2004 prices remains at $100,000. At first glance, the taxpayer is as well off in 2005 as he was in 2004. Note, however, that the salary increase will be taxed at his marginal tax bracket, in which case he would have less after-tax income in real terms in 2005 than he had in 2004. Over

---

[59]   § 6501(e).

time, this *bracket creep*, as it has been labeled, results in a larger portion of the taxpayer's earnings being paid to the Federal government. In effect, unlegislated tax increases occur.

For many years, Congress simply ignored the bracket creep phenomenon, choosing instead to allow the hidden tax increases to occur. As might be expected, this was a very palatable approach to politicians, particularly considering the alternative. The concerns of the few who objected were mollified in part by tax reduction packages enacted in 1981 and 1986. Both the Economic Recovery Tax Act of 1981 and the Tax Reform Act of 1986 directly reduced tax rates. These specific tax rate adjustments have since been followed by a permanent remedy for bracket creep: indexation.

Congress began adding the concept of indexation to the tax law in 1985. In 1986 it specified the amounts of the standard deduction, exemption amounts, and tax brackets for 1987 and 1988 (and the exemption amount for 1989). Thereafter, each of these amounts and many others have been annually adjusted for price level changes as measured by the Consumer Price Index.[60]

✅ *CHECK YOUR KNOWLEDGE*

Review Question 1. Z, age 16, earned $2,000 from umpiring baseball games and refereeing soccer matches during the year. Z—rather Z's parents—wants to know whether he is required to file a tax return since this was his only income.

A taxpayer is not normally required to file a return if his or her income is less than the sum of the personal exemption amount and the standard deduction. However, this general rule does not apply to an individual who can be claimed as a dependent on another return since he or she is not entitled to claim a personal exemption and the standard deduction may be limited. In this case, all of Z's income is earned income and is therefore offset by his standard deduction of $2,250 (the greater of $800 or $250 plus earned income). Consequently, it seems that there is no need for him to file a return. However, even though he is not subject to the income tax, he still must consider self-employment taxes (assuming the income is self-employment income). A return is required if a taxpayer has self-employment income of at least $400. As a result, Z must file a return.

Review Question 2. After spending three years on the auditing staff of a large accounting firm, Norm took a job as controller of a small construction company. On the first day of the job, Norm looked around his new office and noticed a bunch of tax forms on the corner of his desk. One looked like the 1040 for his boss, and the others were corporate and partnership returns related to the company. At first he panicked. But then he realized that it was only the end of February and he had until April 15 to figure out what needed to be done. Should Norm relax?

Doubtful. Although returns for calendar year individuals and partnerships are normally due on April 15, the returns for C corporations or S corporations are due on March 15.

Review Question 3. As always, April 15 arrived and T had not even begun to prepare his tax return. Not to worry, he thought. He could simply file for an extension.

a.   Assume T does not file for an extension and simply files his return late. Are there any penalties?

---

[60]   See §§ 1(f), 1(g)(4), 639(c)(4), and 151(d)(3).

Maybe. A failure-to-file as well as a failure-to-pay penalty may be imposed. Both penalties apply only if there is a tax due. If T is entitled to a refund, there is no penalty. The failure-to-file penalty is 5 percent per month on the balance due, not to exceed 25 percent.

b. How long is the extension?

An automatic extension of four months until August 15 is available.

c. Is an extension for time to file the return also an extension of time to pay the tax?

No. If T does not pay a sufficient amount of his tax by April 15, he faces penalties and interest imposed on the balance due.

d. Assuming T's gross tax liability before withholding is $10,000, how much must he pay by April 15 in order to avoid penalty?

T must pay 90 percent of the gross tax, or $9,000, by April 15. Otherwise, a penalty of ½ of 1 percent per month is imposed (up to a maximum of 25 percent) on the entire underpayment from the due date of the return (April 15).

e. Assume that T's net tax due for the year is $10,000 and he never files a return or a proper extension. What is the maximum failure-to-file and failure-to-pay penalty that can be assessed (ignore fraud and interest)?

The maximum failure-to-file and failure-to-pay penalty in this case is $4,750 (47.5% × $10,000). The failure-to-file penalty is 5 percent per month up to a maximum of 25 percent reduced by .5 percent per month for any month in which the failure-to-pay penalty also applies. Thus, the maximum failure-to-file penalty when the failure-to-pay penalty also applies is 22.5 percent [(5 × 5% = 25%) − (5 × .05 = 2.5%)]. The maximum failure-to-pay penalty is .5 percent per month up to a maximum of 25 percent. Adding the two penalties together produces a maximum penalty for failure to file the return and failure to pay the tax of 47.5 percent (22.5% + 25%) of the amount due.

f. If T fails to pay his tax and he is subject to penalties, how does interest work? Must he pay interest on just the tax due or on both the tax and the penalties?

He pays interest not only on the tax due but also on the penalties since the penalties are considered an additional tax.

Review Question 4. Penalties for failing to file a return and failing to pay at least 90 percent of the tax due by the due date must be distinguished from penalties for failure to adequately make estimated tax payments during the year (underpayment penalties). Try the following true-false questions concerning estimated tax payments.

a. T finally filed her 2004 tax return and is now worrying about 2005. As a general rule, an individual taxpayer must pay 22.5 percent of her 2005 tax (even though she has no idea what it will be) 15 days after the end of each quarter (i.e., April 15, July 15, October 15, and January 15).

False. Although it is true that the taxpayer must normally pay 90 percent of the current tax due during the year (or 22.5 percent per installment), the installments are due on April 15, June 15, September 15, and January 15. Notwithstanding the fact that these payments are not truly paid on a quarterly basis, most people refer to them as "quarterly" estimated tax payments.

b. In lieu of paying 90 percent of their tax liability, individual taxpayers may avoid the underpayment penalty by paying 90 percent of last year's tax liability.

False. Penalty can be avoided if the taxpayer pays 90 percent of the current year's tax or 100 percent of last year's tax. However, the 100 percent rule is increased to 105 percent if the taxpayer's adjusted gross income in the prior year exceeded $150,000.

c. T earns a salary but also does some tinkering in the stock market. In October she realized that she should have paid estimated taxes throughout the year given what her income was going to be. Asking her employer to withhold an extra $36,500 in taxes during October, November, and December will help solve T's estimated tax problems for April, June, and September.

True. Withholding is treated as being paid ratably throughout the year. Therefore the additional $36,500 is not simply applied to the later due dates. Instead, T is treated as having paid $100 per day each day of the year. For example, she is treated as having paid an additional $10,500 (105 × $100) on April 15.

Review Question 5. T filed her 2005 tax return on March 15, 2006. The IRS is barred from assessing a deficiency after

    a. March 15, 2007
    b. March 15, 2008
    c. March 15, 2009
    d. April 15, 2008
    e. April 15, 2009

The statue of limitations runs out on April 15, 2009, three years from the later of the due date or the date of filing.

APPENDIX

TAX RETURN ILLUSTRATIONS

The following pages provide realistic examples of uncomplicated tax returns for individual taxpayers. The information from *Examples 22, 23,* and *29* of this chapter is used.

Form 1040EZ Return for William W. Bristol
(Example 22)

Form **1040EZ**

Department of the Treasury—Internal Revenue Service

Income Tax Return for Single and Joint Filers With No Dependents (99) **2004**

OMB No. 1545-0675

Label
(See page 11.)
Use the IRS label.
Otherwise, please print or type.

Presidential Election Campaign (page 11)

Your first name and initial: WILLIAMS W.
Last name: BRISTOL

If a joint return, spouse's first name and initial / Last name

Home address (number and street). If you have a P.O. box, see page 11.
651 SOUTH HAMPTON   Apt. no.

City, town or post office, state, and ZIP code. If you have a foreign address, see page 11.
BLUE SPRINGS, MO 64015

Your social security number: 187 52 9034
Spouse's social security number:

▲ **Important!** ▲
You **must** enter your SSN(s) above.

Note. Checking "Yes" will not change your tax or reduce your refund.
Do you, or your spouse if a joint return, want $3 to go to this fund? . . . . . . ▶

You: ☑Yes ☐No   Spouse: ☐Yes ☐No

Income

Attach Form(s) W-2 here.
Enclose, but do not attach, any payment.

Note. You **must** check Yes or No.

1 Wages, salaries, and tips. This should be shown in box 1 of your Form(s) W-2. Attach your Form(s) W-2.   **1** 26,610

2 Taxable interest. If the total is over $1,500, you cannot use Form 1040EZ.   **2** 350

3 Unemployment compensation and Alaska Permanent Fund dividends (see page 13).   **3**

4 Add lines 1, 2, and 3. This is your **adjusted gross income.**   **4** 26,960

5 Can your parents (or someone else) claim you on their return?
   Yes. Enter amount from worksheet on back. ☐
   No. ☑ If **single,** enter $7,950.
   If **married filing jointly,** enter $15,900.
   See back for explanation.   **5** 7,950

6 Subtract line 5 from line 4. If line 5 is larger than line 4, enter -0-. This is your **taxable income.**   ▶ **6** 19,010

Payments and tax

7 Federal income tax withheld from box 2 of your Form(s) W-2.   **7** 2,820

8a **Earned income credit (EIC).**   **8a**

b Nontaxable combat pay election.   **8b**

9 Add lines 7 and 8a. These are your **total payments.**   ▶ **9** 2,820

10 **Tax.** Use the amount on **line 6 above** to find your tax in the tax table on pages 24–32 of the booklet. Then, enter the tax from the table on this line.   **10** 2,496

Refund

Have it directly deposited! See page 18 and fill in 11b, 11c, and 11d.

11a If line 9 is larger than line 10, subtract line 10 from line 9. This is your **refund.**   ▶ **11a** 324

▶ b Routing number
▶ c Type: ☐ Checking ☐ Savings
▶ d Account number

Amount you owe

12 If line 10 is larger than line 9, subtract line 9 from line 10. This is the **amount you owe.** For details on how to pay, see page 19.   ▶ **12**

Third party designee

Do you want to allow another person to discuss this return with the IRS (see page 19)? ☐ **Yes.** Complete the following. ☐**No**

Designee's name ▶   Phone no. ▶ ( )   Personal identification number (PIN)

Sign here

Joint return? See page 11.
Keep a copy for your records.

Under penalties of perjury, I declare that I have examined this return, and to the best of my knowledge and belief, it is true, correct, and accurately lists all amounts and sources of income I received during the tax year. Declaration of preparer (other than the taxpayer) is based on all information of which the preparer has any knowledge.

Your signature: William W. Bristol   Date: 2/20/05   Your occupation: RESTAURANT MANAGER   Daytime phone number: (816) 229-1207

Spouse's signature. If a joint return, **both** must sign.   Date   Spouse's occupation

Paid preparer's use only

Preparer's signature ▶   Date   Check if self-employed ☐   Preparer's SSN or PTIN

Firm's name (or yours if self-employed), address, and ZIP code ▶   EIN   Phone no. ( )

For Disclosure, Privacy Act, and Paperwork Reduction Act Notice, see page 23.   Cat. No. 11329W   Form **1040EZ** (2004)

Form 1040A Return
for Ciyde F. Delia C. Cooper
(Example 23)

Form **1040A**

Department of the Treasury—Internal Revenue Service

U.S. Individual Income Tax Return (99) **2004** IRS Use Only—Do not write or staple in this space.

OMB No. 1545-0085

Label (See page 18.)

Use the IRS label.

Otherwise, please print or type.

LABEL HERE

Your first name and initial: **CLYDE F.** Last name: **COOPER**

Your social security number: **234 56 7890**

If a joint return, spouse's first name and initial: **DELIA C.** Last name: **COOPER**

Spouse's social security number: **345 67 8901**

Home address (number and street). If you have a P.O. box, see page 18. **1234 FINE STREET** Apt. no.

City, town or post office, state, and ZIP code. If you have a foreign address, see page 18. **DESIRABLE, OK 66987**

▲ **Important!** ▲
You **must** enter your SSN(s) above.

Presidential Election Campaign (See page 18.)

Note. Checking "Yes" will not change your tax or reduce your refund.
Do you, or your spouse if filing a joint return, want $3 to go to this fund?. . . ▶

You: ☑Yes ☐No   Spouse: ☑Yes ☐No

Filing status
Check only one box.

1 ☐ Single
2 ☑ Married filing jointly (even if only one had income)
3 ☐ Married filing separately. Enter spouse's SSN above and full name here. ▶
4 ☐ Head of household (with qualifying person). (See page 19.) If the qualifying person is a child but not your dependent, enter this child's name here. ▶
5 ☐ Qualifying widow(er) with dependent child (see page 19)

Exemptions

6a ☑ **Yourself.** If someone can claim you as a dependent, **do not** check box 6a.

b ☑ **Spouse**

c **Dependents:**

(1) First name Last name	(2) Dependent's social security number	(3) Dependent's relationship to you	(4) ☑ if qualifying child for child tax credit (see page 21)
GARY COOPER	777 99 6451	SON	☑
DEBORAH COOPER	564 99 8765	DAUGHTER	☑
			☐
			☐
			☐
			☐

If more than six dependents, see page 20.

Boxes checked on 6a and 6b: **2**

No. of children on 6c who:
• lived with you: **2**
• did not live with you due to divorce or separation (see page 21): ___
Dependents on 6c not entered above: ___

Add numbers on lines above ▶ **4**

d Total number of exemptions claimed.

Income

Attach Form(s) W-2 here. Also attach Form(s) 1099-R if tax was withheld.

If you did not get a W-2, see page 22.

Enclose, but do not attach, any payment.

7 Wages, salaries, tips, etc. Attach Form(s) W-2. — 7 — **55,645**

8a **Taxable** interest. Attach Schedule 1 if required. — 8a — **1,500**

b **Tax-exempt** interest. **Do not** include on line 8a. — 8b

9a Ordinary dividends. Attach Schedule 1 if required. — 9a

b Qualified dividends (see page 23). — 9b

10 Capital gain distributions (see page 23). — 10

11a IRA distributions. — 11a   11b Taxable amount (see page 23). — 11b

12a Pensions and annuities. — 12a   12b Taxable amount (see page 24). — 12b

13 Unemployment compensation and Alaska Permanent Fund dividends. — 13

14a Social security benefits. — 14a   14b Taxable amount (see page 26). — 14b

15 Add lines 7 through 14b (far right column). This is your **total income.** ▶ 15 — **57,145**

Adjusted gross income

16 Educator expenses (see page 26). — 16

17 IRA deduction (see page 26). — 17 — **4,000**

18 Student loan interest deduction (see page 29). — 18

19 Tuition and fees deduction (see page 29). — 19

20 Add lines 16 through 19. These are your **total adjustments.** — 20 — **4,000**

21 Subtract line 20 from line 15. This is your **adjusted gross income.** ▶ 21 — **53,145**

For Disclosure, Privacy Act, and Paperwork Reduction Act Notice, see page 57.   Cat. No. 11327A   Form **1040A** (2004)

Return of Clyde F. and Delia C. Cooper
continued

Form 1040A (2004)   Page **2**

Tax, credits, and payments	**22**	Enter the amount from line 21 (adjusted gross income).	22	*53,145*

23a Check if: ☐ **You** were born before January 2, 1940, ☐ Blind   ☐ **Spouse** was born before January 2, 1940, ☐ Blind   **Total boxes checked** ▶ 23a ☐

b If you are married filing separately and your spouse itemizes deductions, see page 30 and check here ▶ 23b ☐

Standard Deduction for—

- People who checked any box on line 23a or 23b **or** who can be claimed as a dependent, see page 31.
- All others:

Single or Married filing separately, $4,850

Married filing jointly or Qualifying widow(er), $9,700

Head of household, $7,150

24	Enter your **standard deduction** (see left margin).	24	*9,700*
25	Subtract line 24 from line 22. If line 24 is more than line 22, enter -0-.	25	*43,445*
26	If line 22 is $107,025 or less, multiply $3,100 by the total number of exemptions claimed on line 6d. If line 22 is over $107,025, see the worksheet on page 32.	26	*12,400*
27	Subtract line 26 from line 25. If line 26 is more than line 25, enter -0-. This is your **taxable income.** ▶	27	*31,045*
28	**Tax,** including any alternative minimum tax (see page 31).	28	*3,939*

29	Credit for child and dependent care expenses. Attach Schedule 2.	29	*700*
30	Credit for the elderly or the disabled. Attach Schedule 3.	30	
31	Education credits. Attach Form 8863.	31	
32	Retirement savings contributions credit. Attach Form 8880.	32	
33	Child tax credit (see page 36).	33	*2,000*
34	Adoption credit. Attach Form 8839.	34	

35	Add lines 29 through 34. These are your **total credits.**	35	*2,700*
36	Subtract line 35 from line 28. If line 35 is more than line 28, enter -0-.	36	*1,239*
37	Advance earned income credit payments from Form(s) W-2.	37	
38	Add lines 36 and 37. This is your **total tax.** ▶	38	*1,239*

39	Federal income tax withheld from Forms W-2 and 1099.	39	*1,950*
40	2004 estimated tax payments and amount applied from 2003 return.	40	

If you have a qualifying child, attach Schedule EIC.

41a	**Earned income credit (EIC).**	41a	
b	Nontaxable combat pay election. 41b		
42	Additional child tax credit. Attach Form 8812.	42	
43	Add lines 39, 40, 41a, and 42. These are your **total payments.** ▶	43	*1,950*

Refund	**44**	If line 43 is more than line 38, subtract line 38 from line 43. This is the amount you **overpaid.**	44	*711*

Direct deposit? See page 50 and fill in 45b, 45c, and 45d.

45a Amount of line 44 you want **refunded to you.** ▶ 45a *711*

▶ **b** Routing number [ ][ ][ ][ ][ ][ ][ ][ ][ ] ▶ **c** Type: ☐ Checking ☐ Savings

▶ **d** Account number [ ][ ][ ][ ][ ][ ][ ][ ][ ]

46 Amount of line 44 you want **applied to your 2005 estimated tax.** 46

Amount you owe	**47**	**Amount you owe.** Subtract line 43 from line 38. For details on how to pay, see page 51. ▶	47
	48	Estimated tax penalty (see page 51). 48	

Third party designee

Do you want to allow another person to discuss this return with the IRS (see page 52)? ☐ **Yes.** Complete the following. ☐ **No**

Designee's name ▶   Phone no. ▶ ( )   Personal identification number (PIN) ▶ [ ][ ][ ][ ][ ]

Sign here

Under penalties of perjury, I declare that I have examined this return and accompanying schedules and statements, and to the best of my knowledge and belief, they are true, correct, and accurately list all amounts and sources of income I received during the tax year. Declaration of preparer (other than the taxpayer) is based on all information of which the preparer has any knowledge.

Joint return? See page 18. Keep a copy for your records.

Your signature *Cylde F. Cooper*	Date 2/7/05	Your occupation *PROFESSIONAL MODEL*	Daytime phone number (821) 753–1968
Spouse's signature. If a joint return, **both** must sign. *Delia C. Cooper*	Date 2-8-05	Spouse's occupation *PROGRAMMER*	

Paid preparer's use only

Preparer's signature ▶	Date	Check if self-employed ☐	Preparer's SSN or PTIN
Firm's name (or yours if self-employed), address, and ZIP code ▶		EIN	
		Phone no. ( )	

✱

Form **1040A** (2004)

Return of Clyde F. and Delia C. Cooper
continued

Schedule 1
(Form 1040A)

Department of the Treasury—Internal Revenue Service

Interest and Ordinary Dividends for Form 1040A Filers   (99)   **2004**

OMB No. 1545-0085

Name(s) shown on Form 1040A

CLYDE F. AND DELIA C. COOPER

Your social security number

234 : 56 : 7890

Part I

Interest

(See back of schedule and the instructions for Form 1040A, line 8a.)

Note. If you received a Form 1099-INT, Form 1099-OID, or substitute statement from a brokerage firm, enter the firm's name and the total interest shown on that form.

1	List name of payer. If any interest is from a seller-financed mortgage and the buyer used the property as a personal residence, see back of schedule and list this interest first. Also, show that buyer's social security number and address.		Amount
	CITY SAVINGS	1	950
	U. S. GOVERNMENT		550
2	Add the amounts on line 1.	2	1,500
3	Excludable interest on series EE and I U.S. savings bonds issued after 1989. Attach Form 8815.	3	
4	Subtract line 3 from line 2. Enter the result here and on Form 1040A, line 8a.	4	1,500

Part II

Ordinary dividends

(See back of schedule and the instructions for Form 1040A, line 9a.)

Note. If you received a Form 1099-DIV or substitute statement from a brokerage firm, enter the firm's name and the ordinary dividends shown on that form.

5	List name of payer.		Amount
		5	
6	Add the amounts on line 5. Enter the total here and on Form 1040A, line 9a.	6	

For Paperwork Reduction Act Notice, see Form 1040A instructions.   Cat. No. 12075R   Schedule 1 (Form 1040A) 2004

Return of Clyde F. and Delia C. Cooper
continued

Schedule 2
(Form 1040A)

Department of the Treasury—Internal Revenue Service

**Child and Dependent Care
Expenses for Form 1040A Filers**   (99)   **2004**

OMB No. 1545-0085

Name(s) shown on Form 1040A

CLYDE F. AND DELIA C. COOPER

Your social security number

234 : 56 : 7890

Before you begin: You need to understand the following terms. See **Definitions** on page 1 of the separate instructions.
● **Dependent Care Benefits**   ● **Qualifying Person(s)**   ● **Qualified Expenses**

Part I

Persons or organizations who provided the care

You **must** complete this part.

1

(a) Care provider's name	(b) Address (number, street, apt. no., city, state, and ZIP code)	(c) Identifying number (SSN or EIN)	(d) Amount paid (see instructions)
HAPPY TRAILS PRESCHOOL	*2391 BRONCO STREET DESIRABLE, OK 66789*	*44-667892*	*3,500*

(If you need more space, use the bottom of page 2.)

Did you receive **dependent care benefits?**	**No** ────────→ Complete only Part II below.
	Yes ────────→ Complete Part III on the back next.

Caution. If the care was provided in your home, you may owe employment taxes. If you do, you must use Form 1040. See **Schedule H** and its instructions for details.

Part II

Credit for child and dependent care expenses

2   Information about your **qualifying person(s).** If you have more than two qualifying persons, see the instructions.

(a) Qualifying person's name		(b) Qualifying person's social security number	(c) Qualified expenses you incurred and paid in 2004 for the person listed in column (a)
First	Last		
GARY	*COOPER*	777 : 99 : 6451	*1,750*
DEBORAH	*COOPER*	564 : 99 : 8765	*1,750*

3	Add the amounts in column (c) of line 2. **Do not** enter more than $3,000 for one qualifying person or $6,000 for two or more persons. If you completed Part III, enter the amount from line 26.	3	*3,500*
4	Enter your **earned income.** See the instructions.	4	*33,445*
5	If married filing jointly, enter your spouse's earned income (if your spouse was a student or was disabled, see the instructions); **all others,** enter the amount from line 4.	5	*22,200*
6	Enter the **smallest** of line 3, 4, or 5.	6	*3,500*
7	Enter the amount from Form 1040A, line 22. 7 *53,145*		
8	Enter on line 8 the decimal amount shown below that applies to the amount on line 7.		

If line 7 is:			If line 7 is:		
Over	**But not over**	**Decimal amount is**	**Over**	**But not over**	**Decimal amount is**
$0—15,000		.35	$29,000—31,000		.27
15,000—17,000		.34	31,000—33,000		.26
17,000—19,000		.33	33,000—35,000		.25
19,000—21,000		.32	35,000—37,000		.24
21,000—23,000		.31	37,000—39,000		.23
23,000—25,000		.30	39,000—41,000		.22
25,000—27,000		.29	41,000—43,000		.21
27,000—29,000		.28	43,000—No limit		.20

8   × **.20**

9	Multiply **line 6** by the decimal amount on line 8. If you paid 2003 expenses in 2004, see the instructions.	9	*700*
10	Enter the amount from Form 1040A, line 28.	10	*3,939*
11	**Credit for child and dependent care expenses.** Enter the **smaller** of line 9 or line 10 here and on Form 1040A, line 29.	11	*700*

For Paperwork Reduction Act Notice, see Form 1040A instructions.   Cat. No. 107491   Schedule 2 (Form 1040A) 2004

Form 1040 Returns, and Schedules A and B,
for Jeremy S. and Shelly R. Allen
(Example 29)

Form **1040**

Department of the Treasury—Internal Revenue Service

U.S. Individual Income Tax Return 2004 (99) IRS Use Only—Do not write or staple in this space.

For the year Jan. 1–Dec. 31, 2004, or other tax year beginning , 2004, ending , 20

OMB No. 1545-0074

Label
(See instructions on page 16.)
Use the IRS label. Otherwise, please print or type.

Your first name and initial	Last name
JEREMY S.	ALLEN
If a joint return, spouse's first name and initial	Last name
SHELLY R.	ALLEN

Home address (number and street). If you have a P.O. box, see page 16. Apt. no.
8473 SMITHSON PLACE

City, town or post office, state, and ZIP code. If you have a foreign address, see page 16.
BORING OR 97832

Your social security number
123 45 9875

Spouse's social security number
456 85 2147

▲ **Important!** ▲
You **must** enter your SSN(s) above.

Presidential Election Campaign
(See page 16.)

Note. Checking "Yes" will not change your tax or reduce your refund.
Do you, or your spouse if filing a joint return, want $3 to go to this fund? . . . ▶

You ☐ Yes ☑ No   Spouse ☑ Yes ☐ No

Filing Status

Check only one box.

1 ☐ Single
2 ☑ Married filing jointly (even if only one had income)
3 ☐ Married filing separately. Enter spouse's SSN above and full name here. ▶
4 ☐ Head of household (with qualifying person). (See page 17.) If the qualifying person is a child but not your dependent, enter this child's name here. ▶
5 ☐ Qualifying widow(er) with dependent child (see page 17)

Exemptions

6a ☑ **Yourself.** If someone can claim you as a dependent, **do not** check box 6a . . . .
b ☑ **Spouse** . . . .

Boxes checked on 6a and 6b: 2

c Dependents:

(1) First name Last name	(2) Dependent's social security number	(3) Dependent's relationship to you	(4) ☑ if qualifying child for child tax credit (see page 18)
WILLIAM ALLEN	789 65 4321	SON	☑
SUSAN ALLEN	456 65 9879	DAUGHTER	☑
GREGORY ALLEN	321 72 9347	SON	☑
			☐

If more than four dependents, see page 18.

No. of children on 6c who:
● lived with you: 3
● did not live with you due to divorce or separation (see page 18)
Dependents on 6c not entered above
Add numbers on lines above ▶ 5

d Total number of exemptions claimed . . . .

Income

Attach Form(s) W-2 here. Also attach Forms W-2G and 1099-R if tax was withheld.

If you did not get a W-2, see page 19.

Enclose, but do not attach, any payment. Also, please use Form 1040-V.

7 Wages, salaries, tips, etc. Attach Form(s) W-2 . . . . | 7 | 76,775 |
8a Taxable interest. Attach Schedule B if required . . . . . . | 8a | 3,000 |
b Tax-exempt interest. **Do not** include on line 8a . . . | 8b |
9a Ordinary dividends. Attach Schedule B if required . . . . . | 9a |
b Qualified dividends (see page 20) . . . . . . | 9b |
10 Taxable refunds, credits, or offsets of state and local income taxes (see page 20) . . | 10 |
11 Alimony received . . . . | 11 |
12 Business income or (loss). Attach Schedule C or C-EZ . . . . | 12 |
13 Capital gain or (loss). Attach Schedule D if required. If not required, check here ▶ ☐ | 13 |
14 Other gains or (losses). Attach Form 4797 . . . . | 14 |
15a IRA distributions . . | 15a | b Taxable amount (see page 22) | 15b |
16a Pensions and annuities | 16a | b Taxable amount (see page 22) | 16b |
17 Rental real estate, royalties, partnerships, S corporations, trusts, etc. Attach Schedule E | 17 |
18 Farm income or (loss). Attach Schedule F . . . . | 18 |
19 Unemployment compensation . . . . | 19 |
20a Social security benefits | 20a | b Taxable amount (see page 24) | 20b |
21 Other income. List type and amount (see page 24) _____ | 21 |
22 Add the amounts in the far right column for lines 7 through 21. This is your **total income** ▶ | 22 | 79,775 |

Adjusted Gross Income

23 Educator expenses (see page 26) . . . . | 23 |
24 Certain business expenses of reservists, performing artists, and fee-basis government officials. Attach Form 2106 or 2106-EZ | 24 |
25 IRA deduction (see page 26) . . . . | 25 |
26 Student loan interest deduction (see page 28) . . . . | 26 |
27 Tuition and fees deduction (see page 29) . . . . | 27 |
28 Health savings account deduction. Attach Form 8889 . | 28 |
29 Moving expenses. Attach Form 3903 . . . . . | 29 |
30 One-half of self-employment tax. Attach Schedule SE . . | 30 |
31 Self-employed health insurance deduction (see page 30) | 31 |
32 Self-employed SEP, SIMPLE, and qualified plans . . . | 32 |
33 Penalty on early withdrawal of savings . . . . . | 33 |
34a Alimony paid b Recipient's SSN ▶ _____ | 34a |
35 Add lines 23 through 34a . . . . | 35 |
36 Subtract line 35 from line 22. This is your **adjusted gross income** . . . . . ▶ | 36 | 79,775 |

For Disclosure, Privacy Act, and Paperwork Reduction Act Notice, see page 75. Cat. No. 11320B Form **1040** (2004)

Return for Jeremy S. and Shelly R. Allen
continued

Form 1040 (2004)   Page **2**

Tax and Credits	37	Amount from line 36 (adjusted gross income)	37	79,775

38a Check if: □ **You** were born before January 2, 1940, □ Blind. □ **Spouse** was born before January 2, 1940, □ Blind. } **Total boxes** checked ▶ 38a [ ]

b If your spouse itemizes on a separate return or you were a dual-status alien, see page 31 and check here ▶ 38b □

Standard Deduction for—

39	**Itemized deductions** (from Schedule A) **or** your **standard deduction** (see left margin) . .	39	15,000
40	Subtract line 39 from line 37	40	64,775

● People who checked any box on line 38a or 38b **or** who can be claimed as a dependent, see page 31.

41	If line 37 is $107,025 or less, multiply $3,100 by the total number of exemptions claimed on line 6d. If line 37 is over $107,025, see the worksheet on page 33	41	15,500
42	**Taxable income.** Subtract line 41 from line 40. If line 41 is more than line 40, enter -0-	42	49,275
43	**Tax** (see page 33). Check if any tax is from: **a** □ Form(s) 8814 **b** □ Form 4972 . . .	43	6,676
44	**Alternative minimum tax** (see page 35). Attach Form 6251	44	
45	Add lines 43 and 44 . . . . ▶	45	6,676

● All others:

Single or Married filing separately, $4,850

Married filing jointly or Qualifying widow(er), $9,700

Head of household, $7,150

46	Foreign tax credit. Attach Form 1116 if required	46	
47	Credit for child and dependent care expenses. Attach Form 2441	47	
48	Credit for the elderly or the disabled. Attach Schedule R . .	48	
49	Education credits. Attach Form 8863	49	
50	Retirement savings contributions credit. Attach Form 8880 . .	50	
51	Child tax credit (see page 37)	51	3,000
52	Adoption credit. Attach Form 8839	52	
53	Credits from: **a** □ Form 8396 **b** □ Form 8859 . .	53	
54	Other credits. Check applicable box(es): **a** □ Form 3800 **b** □ Form 8801 **c** □ Specify _____	54	
55	Add lines 46 through 54. These are your **total credits**	55	3,000
56	Subtract line 55 from line 45. If line 55 is more than line 45, enter -0- . . . . . ▶	56	3,676

Other Taxes

57	Self-employment tax. Attach Schedule SE	57	
58	Social security and Medicare tax on tip income not reported to employer. Attach Form 4137 . .	58	
59	Additional tax on IRAs, other qualified retirement plans, etc. Attach Form 5329 if required .	59	
60	Advance earned income credit payments from Form(s) W-2	60	
61	Household employment taxes. Attach Schedule H	61	
62	Add lines 56 through 61. This is your **total tax** . . . . ▶	62	3,676

Payments

If you have a qualifying child, attach Schedule EIC.

63	Federal income tax withheld from Forms W-2 and 1099 . .	63	4,100
64	2004 estimated tax payments and amount applied from 2003 return	64	
65a	Earned income credit (EIC)	65a	
b	Nontaxable combat pay election ▶	65b	
66	Excess social security and tier 1 RRTA tax withheld (see page 54)	66	
67	Additional child tax credit. Attach Form 8812	67	
68	Amount paid with request for extension to file (see page 54)	68	
69	Other payments from: **a** □ Form 2439 **b** □ Form 4136 **c** □ Form 8885 .	69	
70	Add lines 63, 64, 65a, and 66 through 69. These are your **total payments** . . . . ▶	70	4,100

Refund

Direct deposit? See page 54 and fill in 72b, 72c, and 72d.

71	If line 70 is more than line 62, subtract line 62 from line 70. This is the amount you **overpaid**	71	424
72a	Amount of line 71 you want **refunded to you** . . . . ▶	72a	424

▶ **b** Routing number [ ] ▶ **c** Type: □ Checking □ Savings
▶ **d** Account number [ ]

73 Amount of line 71 you want **applied to your 2005 estimated tax** ▶ | 73 |

Amount You Owe

74	**Amount you owe.** Subtract line 70 from line 62. For details on how to pay, see page 55 ▶	74	
75	Estimated tax penalty (see page 55)	75	

Third Party Designee

Do you want to allow another person to discuss this return with the IRS (see page 56)? □ **Yes.** Complete the following. □ **No**

Designee's name ▶   Phone no. ▶ (   )   Personal identification number (PIN) ▶ [ ]

Sign Here

Joint return? See page 17.

Keep a copy for your records.

Under penalties of perjury, I declare that I have examined this return and accompanying schedules and statements, and to the best of my knowledge and belief, they are true, correct, and complete. Declaration of preparer (other than taxpayer) is based on all information of which preparer has any knowledge.

Your signature	Date	Your occupation	Daytime phone number
Jeremy S. Allen	2/14/05	REGISTERED NURSE	(605) 931–1786
Spouse's signature. If a joint return, **both** must sign.	Date	Spouse's occupation	
Shelley R. Allen	2/14/05	AIR TRAFFIC CONTROLLER	

Paid Preparer's Use Only

Preparer's signature ▶		Date	Check if self-employed □	Preparer's SSN or PTIN
Firm's name (or yours if self-employed), address, and ZIP code ▶			EIN	
			Phone no. ( )	

Form **1040** (2004)

Return for Jeremy S. and Shelly R. Allen
continued

SCHEDULES A&B
(Form 1040)

Department of the Treasury
Internal Revenue Service   (99)

Schedule A—Itemized Deductions

(Schedule B is on back)

▶ **Attach to Form 1040.**   ▶ **See Instructions for Schedules A and B (Form 1040).**

OMB No. 1545-0074

2004

Attachment
Sequence No. **07**

Name(s) shown on Form 1040

JEREMY S. AND SHELLY R. ALLEN

Your social security number
123 : 45 : 9875

Medical and Dental Expenses		**Caution.** Do not include expenses reimbursed or paid by others.					
	1	Medical and dental expenses (see page A-2)	**1**	*3,000*			
	2	Enter amount from Form 1040, line 37	**2**	*79,775*			
	3	Multiply line 2 by 7.5% (.075).	**3**	*5,983*			
	4	Subtract line 3 from line 1. If line 3 is more than line 1, enter -0-			**4**	*0*	
Taxes You Paid (See page A-2.)	5	State and local (check only one box):					
		a ☐ Income taxes, **or**	**5**	*3,400*			
		b ☐ General sales taxes (see page A-2)					
	6	Real estate taxes (see page A-3).	**6**	*1,200*			
	7	Personal property taxes	**7**				
	8	Other taxes. List type and amount ▶	**8**				
	9	Add lines 5 through 8			**9**	*4,600*	
Interest You Paid (See page A-3.)	10	Home mortgage interest and points reported to you on Form 1098	**10**	*8,500*			
	11	Home mortgage interest not reported to you on Form 1098. If paid to the person from whom you bought the home, see page A-4 and show that person's name, identifying no., and address ▶	**11**				
Note. Personal interest is not deductible.	12	Points not reported to you on Form 1098. See page A-4 for special rules	**12**				
	13	Investment interest. Attach Form 4952 if required. (See page A-4.)	**13**	*400*			
	14	Add lines 10 through 13			**14**	*8,900*	
Gifts to Charity	15	Gifts by cash or check. If you made any gift of $250 or more, see page A-4	**15**	*1,500*			
If you made a gift and got a benefit for it, see page A-4.	16	Other than by cash or check. If any gift of $250 or more, see page A-4. You **must** attach Form 8283 if over $500	**16**				
	17	Carryover from prior year	**17**				
	18	Add lines 15 through 17			**18**	*1,500*	
Casualty and Theft Losses	19	Casualty or theft loss(es). Attach Form 4684. (See page A-5.)			**19**		
Job Expenses and Most Other Miscellaneous Deductions (See page A-5.)	20	Unreimbursed employee expenses—job travel, union dues, job education, etc. Attach Form 2106 or 2106-EZ if required. (See page A-6.) ▶	**20**				
	21	Tax preparation fees.	**21**	*225*			
	22	Other expenses—investment, safe deposit box, etc. List type and amount ▶	**22**				
	23	Add lines 20 through 22	**23**	*225*			
	24	Enter amount from Form 1040, line 37	**24**	*79,775*			
	25	Multiply line 24 by 2% (.02)	**25**	*1,596*			
	26	Subtract line 25 from line 23. If line 25 is more than line 23, enter -0-			**26**	*0*	
Other Miscellaneous Deductions	27	Other—from list on page A-6. List type and amount ▶			**27**	*15,000*	
Total Itemized Deductions	28	Is Form 1040, line 37, over $142,700 (over $71,350 if married filing separately)?					
		☐ **No.** Your deduction is not limited. Add the amounts in the far right column for lines 4 through 27. Also, enter this amount on Form 1040, line 39. ▶			**28**		
		☐ **Yes.** Your deduction may be limited. See page A-6 for the amount to enter.					

For Paperwork Reduction Act Notice, see Form 1040 instructions.   Cat. No. 11330X   **Schedule A (Form 1040) 2004**

Return for Jeremy S. and Shelly R. Allen
continued

Schedules A&B (Form 1040) 2004

OMB No. 1545-0074   Page **2**

Name(s) shown on Form 1040. Do not enter name and social security number if shown on other side.

JEREMY S. AND SHELLY R. ALLEN

Your social security number

123 45 9875

Schedule B—Interest and Ordinary Dividends

Attachment Sequence No. **08**

Part I
Interest

(See page B-1 and the instructions for Form 1040, line 8a.)

1 List name of payer. If any interest is from a seller-financed mortgage and the buyer used the property as a personal residence, see page B-1 and list this interest first. Also, show that buyer's social security number and address ▶

	Amount
MERCANTILE NAT'L BANK	*1,800*
U.S. GOVERNMENT BONDS	*700*
BEN FRANKLIN SAVINGS	*500*

Note. If you received a Form 1099-INT, Form 1099-OID, or substitute statement from a brokerage firm, list the firm's name as the payer and enter the total interest shown on that form.

2 Add the amounts on line 1 . . . .   **2**   *3,000*

3 Excludable interest on series EE and I U.S. savings bonds issued after 1989. Attach Form 8815 . . . .   **3**

4 Subtract line 3 from line 2. Enter the result here and on Form 1040, line 8a ▶   **4**   *3,000*

Note. If line 4 is over $1,500, you must complete Part III.

Part II
Ordinary Dividends

(See page B-2 and the instructions for Form 1040, line 9a.)

5 List name of payer ▶

	Amount

Note. If you received a Form 1099-DIV or substitute statement from a brokerage firm, list the firm's name as the payer and enter the ordinary dividends shown on that form.

6 Add the amounts on line 5. Enter the total here and on Form 1040, line 9a . ▶   **6**

Note. If line 6 is over $1,500, you must complete Part III.

Part III
Foreign Accounts and Trusts

(See page B-2.)

You must complete this part if you **(a)** had over $1,500 of taxable interest or ordinary dividends; or **(b)** had a foreign account; or **(c)** received a distribution from, or were a grantor of, or a transferor to, a foreign trust.

	Yes	No
7a At any time during 2004, did you have an interest in or a signature or other authority over a financial account in a foreign country, such as a bank account, securities account, or other financial account? See page B-2 for exceptions and filing requirements for Form TD F 90-22.1.		✓
b If "Yes," enter the name of the foreign country ▶		
8 During 2004, did you receive a distribution from, or were you the grantor of, or transferor to, a foreign trust? If "Yes," you may have to file Form 3520. See page B-2		✓

For Paperwork Reduction Act Notice, see Form 1040 instructions.

Schedule B (Form 1040) 2004

PROBLEM MATERIALS

DISCUSSION QUESTIONS

4-1 *Personal and Dependency Exemptions.* Distinguish between personal and dependency exemptions.

4-2 *Dependency Exemption for a Qualifying Child.* List the requirements that must be met in order for one to claim a dependency exemption for a *qualifying child*.

4-3 *Relationship.* In addition to a natural child, which other *children* are included in the definition of a *qualifying child?*

4-4 *Tie-breaking.* Determine who gets the dependency exemption for D in each of the following independent situations. Assume any requirements that are not addressed (e.g., citizenship) are met.

    a. Q provides a home in which she lives with her daughter, C, and C's son, D. C is 25 years of age and has gross income of $6,500 for the current year.

    b. R provides a home in which she lives with her son, E, and E's son, D. E is 18 years of age and has gross income of $6,500 for the current year.

    c. S provides a home in which she lives with her daughter, F, and F's daughter, D. F is 25 years of age and has gross income of $3,000 for the current year.

4-5 *Tests for Dependency Exemptions.* List and briefly describe the five tests that must be met before a taxpayer is entitled to a dependency exemption for an individual other than a qualifying child. Must all five tests be met?

4-6 *Support.* Briefly describe the concept of support. As part of your definition, include examples of support items.

4-7 *Support—Special Items.* With respect to the support test, discuss survivor's treatment of each of the following items: athletic scholarships, social security survivors' benefits paid to an orphan, and aid to dependent children paid by the state government.

4-8 *Gross Income Test.* Describe the gross income test that is applied to the dependency exemption. Must all dependents for whom a dependency exemption is claimed meet this test?

4-9 *Gross Income Test—Dependency Exemption.* M provides more than half of the support for her father, F, who is single for tax purposes. F's other support is in the form of interest income of $5,000 and social security benefits of $9,000.
    a. May M claim a dependency exemption for supporting F in the current year?
    b. Would your answer differ if F's interest income were only $1,500?

4-10 *Relationship Test—Dependency Exemption.* Assuming Q provides more than 50 percent of their support and the dependent meets the gross income, relationship, and citizenship tests, which of the following relatives may be claimed as a dependent?
    a. Widow of Q's deceased son
    b. Q's husband's brother
    c. Daughter of Q's husband's brother
    d. Q's mother's brother
    e. Q's grandmother's brother
    f. Q's great grandson

4-11 *Joint Return Test—Dependency Exemption.* K and L were married in 2004 and elected to file a joint return. K had interest income of $5,000 and a salary of $30,000 for the year. L had interest income of $2,250 and received the remainder of her support from her mother and K.

    a. If L's mother provided more than 50 percent of L's support, can she claim a dependency exemption for L?

    b. If not, under what circumstances could the exemption be claimed?

4-12 This year P, 25, was accepted to medical school. P is a single parent. To save money, she and her one-year-old baby, B, moved in with P's mom and dad, M and D. The four lived together from May through December. May anyone claim an exemption for B? If so, whom?

4-13 *Community Property Law.* How does the treatment of earned income differ between a community property state and a non community property (i.e., separate property) state for Federal income tax purposes? Why?

4-14 *Filing Status, Tax Schedules.* List the four sets of rate schedules that apply to individual taxpayers. Refer to them by filing status and schedule designation (e.g., Schedule Z). Which taxpayers must use the rate schedules rather than the tax rate tables?

4-15 *Determination of Marital Status.* Married taxpayers are subject to a separate set(s) of tax rates. When is marital status determined? What authority (state or federal) controls marital status?

4-16 *Exceptions—Marital Status.* In certain instances, a person who is married may use the rates for unmarried persons. In another instance, a single person may use the rates for married persons filing jointly. Elaborate.

4-17 *Head of Household—Requirements.* What are the specific requirements for head-of-household status? List at least ten relatives who may qualify the taxpayer for head-of-household filing status.

4-18 *Head of Household—Divorced Parents.* May a divorced parent with custody of a child qualify as a head of household even though his or her former spouse is entitled to the dependency exemption for the child? Explain.

4-19 *Head of Household—Taxpayer's Home.* Must the person who qualifies a taxpayer as a head of household (i.e., the taxpayer's child or other dependent) live in the taxpayer's home? Are there any exceptions to this rule?

4-20 *Costs of Maintaining Home.* Which of the following expenses are included in determining the cost of a home when determining whether a taxpayer qualifies as a head of household?

    a. Food consumed on the premises

    b. Transportation for a dependent to and from school

    c. Clothing for a dependent

    d. Property taxes on residence

    e. Rent paid on residence

4-21 *Abandoned Spouse.* M is married and lives with her dependent son, S. M receives child support sufficient to provide 65 percent of S's support from S's father, who lived in a nearby city for the entire year. M provides more than one-half of the cost of providing the home in which she and S live.

    a. What is M's filing status and what is the number of exemption deductions that she may claim?

b. How would your answers differ if M agreed to let S's father claim the dependency exemption for S?

4-22 *Tax Tables.* Are taxpayers required to use the tax tables? Which taxpayers are ineligible to use the tables?

4-23 *Limited Standard Deduction.* W is 16 years old, single, and claimed as a dependent by his parents. His 2005 adjusted gross income is $5,850, and he claims the standard deduction.

a. If W's taxable income is $5,050, what is the character of his income, earned or unearned?

b. If W's taxable income is $3,700, what is the character of his income, earned or unearned?

c. If W's taxable income is $850, what is the character of his income, earned or unearned?

4-24 *Kiddie Tax.* G is 13 years old and claimed as a dependent by her parents. G's top marginal tax rate is 15 percent and her parents' is 25 percent. Calculate G's taxable income and the rate at which it will be taxed in the following instances:

a. Interest of $1,000

b. Interest of $1,800

c. Interest of $850 and wages of $4,650

d. Interest of $3,500 and wages of $450

4-25 *Filing Requirements.* Which individuals are exempted from filing a Form 1040 (or equivalent Form 1040A or Form 1040EZ)?

4-26 *Due Date.* P is a calendar year individual taxpayer with taxable income of $45,000 and a tax due of $350 for the current year.

a. When is P's tax return due?

b. Assuming P uses the fiscal year ending June 30, when is her annual income tax return due?

4-27 *Extensions.* Q is a calendar year individual taxpayer with taxable income of $25,000 and a tax refund of $150 for the current year.

a. If Q is unable to file on time, she may request an automatic extension of time to file her tax return. How long is the maximum extension period?

b. If Q is unable to complete her return by the extended due date and she has an appropriate reason, how long of an additional extension can she request?

c. How much is Q's penalty if she fails to file an extension?

4-28 *Due Dates for Estimated Tax Payments.* R is a calendar year taxpayer whose estimated tax liability for the current year is $4,000. What are the amounts and the due dates of R's estimated tax payments?

4-29 *Amount of Estimated Tax Payments.* H is a calendar year taxpayer who estimates his Federal income tax to be $5,500 and his self-employment tax to be $4,500 for 2005. For 2004, H's Federal income tax was $4,950, and his self-employment tax was $3,975. What is the amount of estimated tax that H must pay on each due date to avoid a penalty for failure to make adequate estimated tax payments?

4-30 *Penalties and Interest.* J is a calendar year individual whose gross tax for 2005 is $10,000. J had taxes of $5,750 withheld and made estimated tax payments of $500 each due date. She submitted $1,350 along with her request for an automatic extension on April 15. The remaining $900 was paid when J's tax return was filed on July 9. J's 2004 tax totaled $9,950.

a. Does J owe a penalty for failure to file for 2005?

    b. Does J owe a penalty for failure to pay for 2005? If so, for what period?

    c. Does J owe a penalty for failure to make adequate estimated tax payments for 2004? If so, over what period?

    d. Does J owe interest on any of the amounts paid? If so, for what period?

4-31 *Statute of Limitations.* What is the importance of the Federal Statute of Limitations to the taxpayer? To the IRS? Generally, how long is the statute of limitations on tax matters?

4-32 *Six-Year Statute of Limitations.* Under what circumstances will the regular three-year statutory period for assessments be extended to six years?

4-33 *Indexation and the Individual Income Tax.* Congress has provided for indexation of certain deductions. What items are subject to indexation? What index is to be used as an estimate of price-level changes?

PROBLEMS

4-34 *Exemptions.* In each of the following situations determine the proper number of personal and dependency exemptions available to the taxpayer. Unless otherwise implied, assume that all tests are satisfied.

    a. R's mother, age 85, lives in his home. R figures that including the value of the lodging, he provides support of about $6,000. The remainder of her support is paid for with her social security benefits of $4,000.

    b. This year D sent his father, F, monthly checks of $200, or $2,400 for the year. F used these checks along with $2,300 of rental income ($4,400 of rents less $2,100 of expenses) to pay all of his support.

    c. H and W are married with one daughter, D, age 7. D models children's clothing and earned $4,000 of wages this year. D also has a trust fund of $50,000 established by her grandparents. All of D's wages were saved and none were used to pay for her support. Similarly none of the funds of the trust were used to pay for D's support.

    d. Professor and Mrs. Smith participated in the foreign exchange student program at their son's high school. In December of 2004 a student, Hans, arrived from Germany, spent the spring of 2005 with the Smiths, then returned to Germany.

    e. B and C are happily married with one son, S. S, age 20, is a full-time student at the University of Cincinnati. S worked as a painter during the summer to help put himself through school. He earned wages of $4,000, $2,500 of which was used to pay for his room and board at school and $1,500 for miscellaneous living expenses (e.g., gas for his car, dates, laundry, etc.). He lived with his parents during the summer. The value of their support including meals and lodging was $5,000. He also received a National Merit Scholarship, which paid for his tuition of $8,000.

4-35 *Personal and Dependency Exemptions.* In each of the following situations determine the proper number of personal and dependency exemption deductions available to the taxpayer.

    a. A is single and 44 years of age. He provides full support for his mother, who is 67 and lives in a small retirement community in A's hometown.

    b. D and K are married and file a joint return for the year. D is 67 years of age and K is 62. They have no dependents.

    c. E and O are married and file a joint return for the year. They provide all the support for their two younger children for the entire year. E and O also provided all the support for their oldest child (age 19) for the eight months she was a full-time student. After graduating from high school, she accepted a job that paid $3,000 in salary. Nevertheless, her parents contributed more than one-half of her support for the entire year.

4-36 *Married Dependents.* In November of this year Jim Jenkins married his college sweetheart, Kate Brown. Jim was 24 and Kate was 22. Jim had graduated two years ago. Kate still had one more year of school. The majority of Kate's support this year was provided by her parents. Jim earned $15,000 during the year while Kate received $900 of interest from her savings account. Assume Kate's parents are in the 27 percent tax bracket and would give the couple any tax savings to be derived from claiming Kate as a dependent.

  a. May Kate's parents claim an exemption for Kate assuming the couple files a joint return?

  b. Would the couple be better off filing separate returns (and thus receiving any taxes saved by Kate's parents) or filing a joint return? Show all computations you must make to determine your answer.

4-37 *Itemized Deductions and Exemptions.* G and H are married and file a joint return for 2005. They have A.G.I. of $241,250 for the year and the following itemized deductions and personal and dependency exemptions:

State and local taxes	$ 5,300
Residence interest	14,500
Investment interest	500
Charitable contributions	6,200
Personal and dependency exemptions	4

  a. Calculate G and H's taxable income for 2005.

  b. Calculate G and H's taxable income for 2005 assuming their A.G.I. was $251,250, a $10,000 increase over (a).

  c. By what amount did taxable income increase due to this $10,000 increase in adjusted gross income? Why wasn't it $10,000?

4-38 *Multiple Support Agreements.* G's support is provided as follows:

Social security benefits	$3,600
Taxable interest income	800
Support from:	
A, G's oldest son—Cash for trip to Europe	1,600
B, G's daughter—Fair value of lodging and cash	2,300
C, G's youngest son—Cash	700
Total	$9,000

  a. Who is entitled to a dependency exemption for G in the absence of any agreement as to who gets the deduction?

  b. Who may claim a dependency exemption for G under a multiple-support agreement?

  c. How would your answer to (b) differ if A contributed $650 instead of $1,600?

4-39 *Children of Divorced Parents.* For each of the following, determine whether M or F is entitled to the dependency exemption in 2005 for their only child, S. M and F were divorced in 2002 and M has custody, except when F has visitation privileges. Together, M and F provide 100 percent of S's support.

  a. M was granted the dependency exemption under the divorce decree. F pays child support for the year totaling $1,500. Total support expenditures for S are $5,600.

  b. No mention of the dependency exemption was made in the divorce decree. F pays child support for S of $3,400, and the total support for S is $6,500.

  c. F was granted the dependency exemption in the divorce decree and he paid child support of $2,800 for the year. The total support for S for the year was $5,500.

4-40 *Filing Status and Standard Deduction.* Determine the most beneficial filing status and the standard deduction for each of the following taxpayers for 2005:

    a. M is a 54-year-old unmarried widow whose spouse died in 2002. During all of 2005 M's son, for whom she claims a dependency exemption, lives with her.

    b. S is a 67-year-old bachelor who lives in New York City. S pays more than half the cost of maintaining a home in Tampa, Florida for his 89-year-old mother. He is entitled to a dependency exemption under a multiple-support agreement executed by his brother, his sister, and himself.

    c. R is a widower whose wife died in 2004. R maintained a household for his three dependent children during 2005 and provided 100 percent of the cost of the household.

    d. J is divorced and has custody of his 9-year-old child. J provides more than half the cost of the home in which he lives with his child, but his ex-wife is entitled to the dependency exemption for the child for 2005.

4-41 *Head of Household.* Indicate whether the taxpayer would be entitled to file using the head-of-household rate schedule.

    a. Y is divorced from her husband. She maintains a home in which she and her 10-year-old son live. Her ex-husband pays child support to her that she uses to provide all of the support for the child. In addition, Y has relinquished her right to claim her son as a dependent to her former spouse.

    b. C is divorced from his wife. He provides 75 percent of the support for his mother, who lives in a nursing home. His mother receives $5,000 of interest income annually.

    c. J's grandson, L, had a falling-out with his parents and moved in with him early this year. J did not mind because he had grown lonely since his wife died three years ago. L is 17 years old and earned $5,000 this year as a part-time grocery clerk.

    d. B's wife died four years ago and he has not remarried. Last year his daughter, D, graduated from Arizona State University and moved to Hawaii. Unfortunately, D was unable to earn enough money to make ends meet and had to rely on checks from dad. B paid for D's own apartment and provided the majority of her support.

    e. M's wife died last year. This year he maintains a home for his 25-year-old daughter, E, who is attending graduate school. E earned $8,000 as a teaching assistant. Nevertheless, M provided the majority of E's support.

    f. Same as (e) except E is the taxpayer's sister.

    g. F's husband died this year. She continues to provide a home for her two children, ages 6 and 8.

4-42 *Dependent's Personal Exemption and Standard Deduction.* K is 16 years old and is claimed as a dependent on her parents' income tax return. She earned wages of $2,800 and collected interest of $1,450 for the year. What is the amount of K's taxable income for the year?

4-43 *Dependent's Personal Exemption and Standard Deduction.* B is 20 years old and is claimed as a dependent on his sister's tax return. B earned $3,000 from a part-time job during the year. What is B's taxable income?

4-44 *Computation of Tax.* R and S are married and have two dependents. Compute their 2005 tax liability before credits, assuming they file a joint return and their taxable income is

    a. $64,400

    b. $189,950

    c. $336,450

4-45 *High-Income Taxpayer.* H and W are married and file a joint return for 2005. They have no dependents and both are under age 40. H earned a salary of $120,000. W is self-employed and earned a net profit from business of $98,000. H and W have personal itemized deductions totaling $19,800 (all subject to the 3% cutback problem).

   a. What are the amounts of their adjusted gross income and taxable income on their joint income tax return?

   b. Calculate the 2005 tax liability, including W's self-employment tax. Assume that the 2005 self-employment tax is 15.3 percent on income up to $90,000 (2.9% MHI with no limit).

4-46 *Tax Tables.* S earned a salary during 2004 of $55,515. She is single and had no dependents for the year. Her only other income was taxable interest income of $560. Determine S's taxable income and her Federal income tax. (**Note:** This tax table computation is for 2004 because the 2005 tax tables will not be available until late 2005. See Appendix for the 2004 tax tables.)

4-47 *Tax Rate Schedules.* W and T were married and filed a joint return for 2005. Their adjusted gross income for the year was $141,350. Their total itemized deductions were $12,700 and they were entitled to three personal and dependency exemptions. Neither W nor T is 65 years old and both have good sight. Determine W and T's taxable income and their Federal income tax liability before prepayments and credits for 2005.

4-48 *Application of the Kiddie Tax.* For each of the following situations, determine the child's taxable income and the amounts that would be taxed at the child's and parents' rates for the 2005 tax year.

   a. When J's rich uncle died, he left her GM corporate bonds. This year J received $1,750 of interest from these bonds, her only income. J is seven years old and her parents claim an exemption for her.

   b. L, age 13, works in his father's music store on weekends. During the year, he earned $1,200 from this job. In addition, L had $800 of interest income attributable to a gift from his grandfather. L's father claims an exemption for him.

   c. Same as (b) except L's earned income was $2,150 and interest income was $1,850.

4-49 *Computation of the Kiddie Tax.* G's great aunt gave her a certificate of deposit that matures in ten years when she is 21. The certificate pays interest of $2,000 annually. G's parents file a joint return. Their 2005 taxable income is $127,250. Compute G's tax.

4-50 *Failure-to-File Penalty.* T, overwhelmed by other pressing concerns, simply forgot to file his tax return for 2004 until July 20, 2005. When filed, T's 2004 return showed a tax due before withholding and estimated taxes of $10,000.

   a. Will T be penalized for failure to file his return if the total income taxes withheld by his employer were $11,000?

   b. Assuming T's employer withheld $9,000, what is the amount of the failure-to-file penalty, if any?

4-51 *Failure-to-Pay Penalty.* On April 13, 2006 R, a calendar year taxpayer, sat down to prepare his 2005 tax return. Realizing that he simply did not have time to accumulate all of his records, R decided to file for an extension. R's tax liability for the previous year, 2004, was $8,000. During 2005 R's employer withheld $2,500 and R paid estimated taxes of $500. R estimates that his final gross tax liability for 2005 will be $12,000.

   a. Assuming R obtains an extension to file his 2005 return, when will his return normally be due?

   b. Based on the facts above, what amount must R pay by April 15 to avoid a failure-to-pay penalty?

c. R completed and filed his return on July 20, 2006. Unfortunately, his initial estimate of his tax was low and his final tax (before withholding and estimated tax payments) was $15,000. Assuming R paid the amount determined in part (b) above, what is the amount of the failure-to-pay penalty, if any?

4-52 *Estimated Taxes and Underpayment Penalty.* K works as a salesperson for the National Hospital Supply Corporation, selling surgical and other hospital supplies. He receives a salary plus a percentage commission on sales over a certain threshold. In 2005 K's tax liability before prepayments was $20,000. His 2004 tax liability was $12,000. In each year his A.G.I. was less than $150,000.

a. What is the lowest required tax installment (including withholding) that K can make and avoid the penalty for underpaying his taxes during the year? (Ignore the annualized income installment.)

b. Assume that K paid estimated taxes of $1,000 on each due date. In addition, K's employer withheld a total of $3,000 during the year. K filed and paid the balance of his liability on April 15, 2006. Assume the applicable interest rate charged on underpayments for each period in 2005 is 10 percent. Compute K's penalty, if any, for failure to pay estimated taxes. Compute the penalty for the first installment only.

c. Assume that K works solely for commissions and that he had no income through March 31, 2005 because he decided to take a winter vacation. Income for the remainder of the year was sufficient to generate a tax liability before prepayments of $20,000. What implications do these facts have on the calculation of the underpayment penalty for 2005?

4-53 *Penalties for Inadequate Estimated Tax Payments.* Z is a calendar year individual whose gross tax for 2005 is $40,000. Z had taxes of $8,000 withheld and did not make estimated tax payments. Z's tax due was paid with his timely filed return on April 15, 2006. His 2004 tax was $35,000 on adjusted gross income of $148,000.

a. Calculate Z's penalty for failure to make adequate estimated tax payments, if any.

b. Does Z owe interest on any of the amounts paid? If so, for what period?

c. Same as (a) above, except Z's adjusted gross income for 2004 was $160,000.

4-54 *Penalties and Interest.* Y filed her tax return for 2004 on April 15, 2005. Upon discovering an inadvertent error, Y filed an amended return and submitted additional tax of $1,250.

a. Does Y owe a penalty for failure to pay? If so, how much?

b. Does Y owe interest on the $1,250 paid with the amended return? If so, how much?

4-55 *Statute of Limitations.* T, a calendar year taxpayer, filed her 2004 Federal income tax return on January 29, 2005 and received a tax refund check for overpaid 2004 taxes on May 17, 2005.

a. Assuming that T did not file a false return or have a substantial omission of income, what is the last date on which the IRS may assess an additional income tax liability against her for the 2004 tax year?

b. If T unintentionally had a substantial omission of income from her 2004 return, what is the last day on which the IRS may assess her an additional 2004 income tax liability?

c. If T had never bothered to file her 2004 tax return, what is the last day on which the IRS may assess her an additional 2004 income tax liability?

TAX RETURN PROBLEMS

4-56 *Form 1040EZ.* Samuel B. White was single for 2005 and had no dependents. Sam's only income was wages of $20,850 and taxable interest of $215. Federal income tax of $1,430 was withheld from Sam's salary.

Calculate Sam's Federal income tax and his tax due or refund for 2005. A Form 1040EZ may be completed based on this information. Supply fictitious occupation, social security number, and address. (**Note:** If the 2005 tax forms are not available, use 2004 forms.)

4-57   *Form 1040A.* Charles D. and Alice A. Davis were married during all of 2005 and had income from the following sources:

Salary, Charles	$26,300
Federal income tax withheld	1,625
Part-time salary, Alice	16,000
Federal income tax withheld	880
Interest from Home Savings	320
Interest from U.S. Government Bonds	430

Charles and Alice provide the sole support of their two children (both under age 17). During the year, they paid job-related child care expenses of $2,200. Their itemized deductions for the year are insufficient for them to itemize, but a deductible $2,000 was deposited in each of their individual retirement accounts.

Calculate the Federal income tax and the tax due (or refund) for Mr. and Mrs. Davis, assuming they file a joint return. If the 2005 tax tables are not available, use the tax rate schedules on the inside front cover of the text. A Form 1040A may also be completed. Supply fictitious information for the address, occupations, social security numbers, and children's names. (**Note:** If the 2005 tax forms are not available, use 2004 forms.)

4-58   *Form 1040.* William A. Gregg, a high school educator, and Mary W. Gregg, a microbiologist, are married and file a joint income tax return for 2005. Neither William nor Mary is over 50 years old, and both have excellent sight. They provide the sole support of their three children: Barry, Kimberly, and Rachel (all under age 17). The following information is from their records for 2005:

Salaries and wages, William	$34,150
Federal income tax withheld	2,620
Salaries and wages, Mary	44,300
Federal income tax withheld	4,360
Interest income—Home Savings and Loan	690
Interest income—City Bank	220
Tax-exempt interest income	1,400
Itemized deductions as follows:	
Hospitalization insurance	320
Unreimbursed fees of doctors, hospitals, etc	740
Unreimbursed prescription drugs	310
Real estate taxes on residence	1,350
State income taxes paid	1,440
State sales taxes paid	720
Interest paid on original home mortgage	8,430
Charitable contribution—Faith Church	1,720
Charitable contribution—State University	200
Quarterly estimated taxes paid	3,500

Calculate the 2005 Federal income tax and the tax due (or refund) for the Greggs assuming they file a joint return. Form 1040, along with Schedules A and B, may be completed. Supply fictitious information for the address and social security numbers. (**Note:** If the 2005 tax forms are not available, use 2004 forms.)

4-59 *Continuous Tax Return Problem*

Previous Facts: Larry L. and Cathy C. Zepp have been married 19 years. Larry is age 62 (Social Security number 123-45-6789) while Cathy is age 50 (Social Security number 123-45-6788). They live at 1234 Elm Dr. in Des Moines, Iowa 50311. Larry is a salesman employed by DSK Industries. This year he earned $110,000 (income tax withheld was $17,000). Cathy recently completed a graduate degree in computer technology. She continues to freelance as an independent contractor in computer graphics. Her earnings from various engagements were $12,000. Her only expenses were for miscellaneous office supplies of $3,000. She paid estimated taxes during the year of $1,000 ($250 on each due date). Other income earned by the couple included interest income of $3,000 from a certificate of deposit and $975 of interest from tax-exempt bonds issued by the State of Iowa. The couple owns a duplex that it rents out. Annual rentals were $8,000 and rental expenses (e.g., maintenance, utilities, depreciation) were $3,000. Other expenses paid during the year included:

Unreimbursed medical expenses.....................	$ 9,000
Interest on home mortgage	12,000
Real property taxes on home.......................	1,900
Charitable contributions	1,000
Rental of safety deposit box to hold certain investments . . .	100
Unreimbursed employee business expenses of Larry	3,000

Assume that all of the expenses except their business expenses are incurred jointly.

New Facts:

Larry and Cathy Zepp (see *continuous tax return problem in* Chapter 3) just called and after a quick discussion the following additional information was obtained:

- Larry received a corrected W-2 in the mail that now shows that income taxes withheld were $7,000 (rather than $17,000).
- They forgot to note on the tax organizer that they had two children, a son and a daughter: Wrigley F. Zepp (111-33-4444, 12/1/1986)) and Apple A. Zepp (111-33-4445, 1/4/1992). Both children live with them the entire year. Apple is considered legally blind.
- Apple received interest income of $3,000.

Prepare Form 1040 for the Zepps.

4-60 *Continuous Tax Return: Additional Questions.* Using the facts above, prepare Form 1040 for Apple Zepp.

4-61 *Continuous Tax Return: Additional Questions.* Answer the following questions relating to the *continuous tax return problem* above.

   a. The Zepps generally could have avoided the estimated tax penalty by paying estimated taxes or by relying on their prior year's tax liability. Ignoring their prior year liability, how much should the couple have paid on each installment date to avoid the penalty? Alternatively, what would the amount of last year's tax liability have to be to avoid the penalty?

For purpose of the questions below, assume Cathy was also an employee and received wages of $100,000.

   b. Does the couple's *taxable* income increase by $100,000, more than $100,000 or less than $100,000? Explain what accounts for the change in taxable income and tax liability, if any.

   c. What would the Zepp's marginal tax rate be on the next $1,000 of income?

d. The Zepps heard that in their state it may benefit them to file separately rather than jointly. Would the couple's federal tax liability increase or decrease if they filed separately? What is the amount of the benefit (or cost)?

e. If Cathy had hired Apple as an employee and paid her $4,000 to help her on certain business-related projects, what effect would it have on the family's tax liability? For simplicity, assume that Apple had no other income.

RESEARCH PROBLEMS

4-62 *Support by Noncustodial Parent.* G incurred several expenses while exercising visitation rights with his children from a dissolved marriage. Determine which, if any, of the following expenses are treated as provided by G toward the support of his children: travel by G to visit the children, transportation and entertainment for children, lodging in G's residence, and gifts of toys and clothing.

Research aids:

Brandes v. Comm., 29 TCM 1436, T.C. Memo 1970-313.

Gilliam v. Comm., 28 TCM 956, T.C. Memo 1969-188.

Hout v. Comm., 25 TCM 1468, T.C. Memo 1966-281.

Hastings v. Comm., 16 TCM 928, T.C. Memo 1957-202.

4-63 *Nonresident Alien Spouse.* C is a citizen of the United States who resides indefinitely in Europe. C is married to N, a citizen of Greece. C has $32,000 of gross income subject to United States tax and would like to file jointly with N. Can C accomplish this goal? If so, what steps are necessary? How is the income of N treated?

Research aids:

Code § 6013(g) and Reg. § 1.6013-6.

Part II

GROSS INCOME

❖ **Contents** ❖

Chapter 5

GROSS INCOME

LEARNING OBJECTIVES

Upon completion of this chapter you will be able to:

▸ Define income for tax purposes and explain how it differs from the definitions given to it in accounting or economics

▸ Explain the concept of the taxable year and identify who is eligible to use fiscal years

▸ Apply the cash and accrual methods of accounting to determine the tax year in which items are reported

▸ Determine the effect of a change in accounting method

▸ Describe some of the special rules governing the treatment of prepaid income, interest income, interest-free loans, and income from long-term contracts

▸ Identify which taxpayer is responsible for reporting income and paying the taxes on such income

CHAPTER OUTLINE

INTRODUCTION

Determination of the final income tax liability begins with the identification of a taxpayer's gross income. Before that can be done, however, one obviously must understand what constitutes *income* for tax purposes. The primary purpose of this chapter is to examine the income concept and thus provide some general guidelines regarding what is and what is not subject to taxation. As a practical matter, income is normally easy to spot. Salary, interest, dividends, rents, gains from the sales of property, and most other items that one customarily thinks of as income are in fact income for tax purposes. In fact, these represent the bulk of all income that is reported. But what if a taxpayer is lucky enough to receive an inheritance, a gift, or a scholarship? Are these taxable? What about court-awarded damages? And if a taxpayer borrows $1,000, is there income? What happens if Publishers Clearing House gives you $10 million? Is the IRS as happy as you are? And how do hurricane victims treat their government aid? Is their relief taxable? The list of possible income items goes on and on. Fortunately, these items are more the exception than the rule. In any event, newcomers to tax should understand that there are no hard and fast rules that can be applied to every conceivable situation. The Supreme Court clearly stated the problem in a case concerning the income status of embezzled funds:

> In fact, no single conclusive criterion has yet been found to determine in all situations what is sufficient gain to support the imposition of an income tax. No more can be said in general than that all relevant facts and circumstances must be considered.[1]

Notwithstanding the Court's observations, three important generalizations developed in this chapter are

1. "Income" is broadly construed for tax purposes to include virtually any type of gain, benefit, or profit that has been realized.

2. Although the scope of the income concept is broad, certain types of income are exempted from taxation by statute, administrative ruling, or judicial decree.

3. Taxpayers who realize income may not be required to recognize and report it immediately but may be able to postpone recognition until some time in the future.

To sum up, there are three basic questions to address concerning income:

1. Did the taxpayer have income?

2. If the taxpayer had income, was it realized?

3. If the taxpayer has realized income, must it be recognized now or is it permanently excluded or perhaps temporarily deferred and reported at some future date?

The first part of this chapter examines the concept of income. Once one is sensitive to the concept of income, consideration must be given to *if and when* the income must be reported as well as *who* must report it. The latter part of the chapter focuses on the timing of income recognition and the identification of the reporting entity.

---

[1]   *Comm. v. Wilcox*, 46-1 USTC ¶9188, 34 AFTR 811, 327 U.S. 404 (USSC, 1946).

GROSS INCOME DEFINED

The definition of income found in the Internal Revenue Code reflects the language of the constitutional amendment empowering Congress to impose taxes on income.[2] Section 61(a) of the Code defines *gross income* as follows:

> Except as otherwise provided in this subtitle, gross income means all income from whatever source derived, including (but not limited to) the following items:
>
> 1. Compensation for services, including fees, commissions, fringe benefits, and similar items;
> 2. Gross income derived from business;
> 3. Gains derived from dealings in property;
> 4. Interest;
> 5. Rents;
> 6. Royalties;
> 7. Dividends;
> 8. Alimony and separate maintenance payments;
> 9. Annuities;
> 10. Income from life insurance and endowment contracts;
> 11. Pensions;
> 12. Income from discharge of indebtedness;
> 13. Distributive share of partnership gross income;
> 14. Income in respect of a decedent; and
> 15. Income from an interest in an estate or trust.

Despite the statute's detailed enumeration of income items, the list is not comprehensive. The items specified are only a sample of the more common types of income. Taxable income includes many other economic benefits not identified above.

As a practical matter, Code § 61 furnishes little guidance for determining whether a particular benefit should be treated as income. The statute provides no criteria or factors that could be used for assessment. For example, the general definition does not provide any clue as to whether a gift or an inheritance constitutes taxable income. Similarly, the statute is not helpful in determining whether income arises upon the discovery of buried treasure. These and similar issues, as will be seen, are often answered by reference to other, more specific, sections of the Code. On the other hand, many questions cannot be resolved by reference to the statute or the regulations. In situations where clear statutory guidance is absent, the difficult task of ascertaining how far the definitional boundary of income extends falls to the courts. To this end, the courts have utilized the meanings given income in both economics and accounting to mold a workable definition of income for tax purposes.

ECONOMIC CONCEPT OF INCOME

Economists define income as the amount that an individual could have spent for consumption during a period while remaining as well off at the end of the period as at the beginning of the period. This concept of income may be expressed mathematically as the sum of an individual's consumption during the period plus the change in the individual's net worth between the beginning and end of the period.[3] Note that an

---

[2]   See Chapter 1.

[3]   The economic definition of income given here is often referred to as the Haig-Simons definition as derived from the following works: Robert M. Haig, "The Concepts of Income—Economic and Legal Aspects," *The Federal Income Tax* (New York: Columbia University Press, 1921); Henry C. Simons, *Personal Income Taxation* (Chicago: University of Chicago Press, 1921).

increase in net worth is actually savings. Thus income can be defined as $I = C + S$ where I is income, C is consumption and S is savings.

Example 1. K's records revealed the following assets and liabilities as of December 31, 2005 and 2006:

	12-31-05	12-31-06
Assets (fair market value)	$100,000	$140,000
Liabilities	(20,000)	(30,000)
Net worth	$ 80,000	$110,000

During the year, K spent $25,000 on rent, food, clothing, entertainment, and other items. From an economic perspective, K's income for 2006 is $55,000 determined as follows:

Consumption	$25,000
Change in net worth ($110,000 − $80,000)	30,000
Economic income	$55,000

There are two key aspects of an economist's definition. The first is the emphasis on a change in net worth. According to the economist, a taxpayer has income under any circumstances that cause his or her net worth to increase. Note that this view is extremely broad. Taxpayers who receive an inheritance, are the beneficiaries of a life insurance policy, discover buried treasure, or have their debts cancelled have all had an increase in net worth and would therefore have income using this definition. Some may object to this comprehensive approach. It is nevertheless consistent with § 61, which states that income includes *all* income regardless of its source.

The second and perhaps more critical aspect of the economist's definition from a tax perspective is the notion that consumption and the change in net worth must be computed using market values on an accrual basis rather than on a realization basis. For example, economists include in income any increase in the value of an individual's shares of stock during the period, even though the shares are not sold and the individual does not *realize* the increase in value. In addition, economists would include in income the rental value of one's car or home, as well as the value of food grown for personal use, since such items constitute consumption. Gifts and inheritances would also be considered income by an economist since these items would affect an individual's net worth. Although the economist's approach to income is theoretically sound, it has significant drawbacks from a practical view.

For practical application, the meaning given to income must be objective to minimize controversies. The economist's reliance on market values to measure net worth and consumption violates this premise. Few assets have readily determinable and accurate values. Valuation of most assets would be a subjective determination. For example, an individual may be able to value shares of stock by referring to an active publicized market, but how is the value of a closely held business or work of art to be computed? The difficulty in making such valuations would no doubt lead to countless disputes and administrative hassles. These practical problems of implementing the economic concept of income have caused the courts to adopt a different interpretation.

It should be pointed out, however, that the economist's approach to measuring income—the so-called net worth method—is sometimes used when the IRS decides that the taxpayer's records do not adequately reflect income.[4] Application usually occurs where the taxpayer has not maintained records, or has falsified or destroyed any records that were kept. In these situations, the IRS reconstructs income by determining the change in net worth during the year and adding estimated living expenses.

Before leaving the economist's definition of income, a final observation is warranted. Over the years, some have argued that the income tax does not encourage savings and, therefore, the U.S. should switch to a consumption tax such as a national retail sales tax. Observe, however, that a similar result could be obtained under the current income tax law if taxpayers were given a deduction for savings. This can be demonstrated mathematically by simply manipulating the terms of the income equation above:

$$I = C + S$$

$$C = I - S$$

In light of President Bush's commitment to tax reform and simplification during his second term, it is not surprising that this concept has surfaced. Only time will tell what changes will be made.

ACCOUNTING CONCEPT OF INCOME

The principle of realization distinguishes the accountant's concept of income from that of the economist. Under this principle, accountants recognize income when it is *realized*. Income is generally considered realized when (1) the earnings process is complete, and (2) an exchange or transaction has taken place.[5] Normally, some type of *conversion* occurs that substantially changes the taxpayer's relationship to the asset. To illustrate, consider a taxpayer who discovers oil on his property. He may have "income" in the economic sense (at least to the extent that the value of his property and his net worth have increased). But he has not realized that increase in net worth and does not have income in the accounting sense until he converts his discovery into another asset (e.g., he sells the property or the oil). Observe that these two criteria provide the objective determination of value traditionally believed necessary for the work that accountants perform. As a result, accounting income usually does not recognize changes in market values of assets during a period (as would economic income) unless such changes have been realized.

INCOME FOR TAX PURPOSES: THE JUDICIAL CONCEPT

The landmark decision of the Supreme Court in *Eisner v. Macomber* in 1918 provided the first glimpse of how the concept of income would be interpreted for tax purposes.[6] In this case, the court embraced the realization principle of accounting, indicating that income must be *realized* before it can be taxed. As later decisions suggested, the primary virtue of the realization principle is not that it somehow yields a better or more theoretically precise income figure. Rather, it provides an objective basis for measuring income, eliminating the problems that would arise if income were determined using subjective valuations. In short, the realization principle is a well-entrenched part of the tax law because it makes the law so much easier to administer.

---

[4]   *Holland v. U.S.*, 54-2 USTC ¶9714, 46 AFTR 943, 348 U.S. 121 (USSC, 1954). Net worth, however, is to be determined using the tax basis in assets and not their fluctuating market values [*S. Bedeian,* 54 T.C. 295 (1970)].

[5]   "Basic Concepts and Accounting Principles Underlying Financial Statements of Business Enterprises," *Accounting Principles Board Statements No. 4* (New York: American Institute of Certified Public Accountants, 1970), ¶134.

[6]   1 USTC ¶32, 3 AFTR 3020, 252 U.S. 189 (USSC, 1920).

A second issue addressed by the *Eisner* decision concerned the scope of the income concept. How far did it reach? Did income include gifts, scholarships, court-awarded damages, a personal secretary, and other types of benefits? In essence, the Court again followed the accounting approach, stating that income was restricted to gains realized from property or personal services.

Hence, finding a $10 bill, receiving a prize or award, or profiting from a cancelled debt would not have been taxable under *Eisner*, since the benefits were obtained without any effort by the taxpayer. Later decisions, however, expanded the concept of income by rejecting the notion that only gains derived from capital or labor are recognized. The courts have taken what is often referred to as an "all-inclusive" approach; that is, *all* gains are presumed to be taxable except those specifically exempted. The Supreme Court's opinion in *Glenshaw Glass Co.* provides the definition of income that is perhaps most commonly accepted today.[7] This case involved the treatment of punitive damages awarded to Glenshaw Glass for fraud and antitrust violations of another company. In holding that such awards were income, the Court stated:[8]

> Here we have instances of undeniable accessions to wealth, clearly realized, and over which the taxpayer has complete dominion. The mere fact that the payments were extracted from wrongdoers as punishment for unlawful conduct cannot detract from their character as taxable income to the recipients.

Thus, income for tax purposes is construed to include any type of gain, benefit, profit, or other increase in wealth that has been realized and is not exempted by statute. Note that the courts have adopted key elements of both the economic and accounting definition of income: income is any increase in the taxpayer's *net worth* (i.e., wealth) that has been *realized*. Also note that, even though it all sounds very technical and precise, the rule, like so many rules in taxation, may be difficult to apply in a given situation. For example, if a tenant paints the walls of her apartment or plants some gladiolus in the garden, has the landlord realized income? Arriving at a solution for this and any particular set of facts can be quite frustrating, but one can generally take heart that these are rare and, moreover, a common sense approach generally works: if it seems as if the taxpayer is better off, there is probably income.

It should be emphasized that even though a taxpayer may have "income" that has in fact been realized, this by itself does not guarantee that it will be taxed. In tax parlance, the question still remains as to whether the taxpayer must "recognize" the income (i.e., report the income for tax purposes). There are *three* relatively common exceptions to the general rule that all income must be recognized immediately:

1. *Excluded income.* Income that has been realized need not be recognized if it is specifically exempted from taxation by virtue of some provision in the Code. For example, as discussed in Chapter 6, interest income from state and local bonds is specifically excluded under § 103 while gifts and inheritances (which obviously increase net worth) are excluded under § 102. In these cases, the income permanently escapes tax and normally creates a difference between taxable income and financial accounting income. It should be noted that, notwithstanding the Code's all-inclusive concept of income, the tax base is far from comprehensive because of the numerous exclusions and exemptions that have crept into the law over the years.[9]

---

[7]   55-1 USTC ¶9308, 47 AFTR 162, 348 U.S. 426 (USSC, 1955).

[8]   *Ibid.*

[9]   For an excellent discussion of the concept of income and the notion of a comprehensive tax base see Boris Bittker, "A Comprehensive Tax Base as a Goal of Income Tax Reform," 80 *Harvard Law Review* 925 (1967).

2. *Accounting methods.* A taxpayer may be able to defer recognition of income to a subsequent year by following some particular method of accounting (e.g., the installment sales method or the completed contract method).

3. *Nontaxable exchanges.* Income realized on a sale or exchange may be deferred under a special nonrecognition rule. For example, a taxpayer who swaps one parcel of land costing $10,000 for another parcel worth $50,000 is not required to recognize the $40,000 gain under the like-kind exchange rules. The theory underlying nonrecognition in this and similar situations is that the taxpayer has not liquidated his investment to cash but has continued it, albeit in another form. In effect, the law is willing to defer the tax until such time when the taxpayer does in fact convert the asset to cash and has the wherewithal to pay the tax. It is important to note, however, that in these and similar cases, the gain is only *deferred*; it does not escape tax permanently as is the case with excluded income.

In summary, income for tax purposes can generally be defined as any increase in wealth (net worth) or consumption that has been realized. In addition, such income normally must be recognized unless it is specifically excluded or postponed due to an accounting rule or deferral provision. A list of some of the common types of income—both taxable and nontaxable— can be found in Chapter 3-3 and Chapter 3-4 in Chapter 3.

Before leaving this subject, one final observation should be made. It is important to understand that this definition of gross income is the same for all types of taxpayers. In other words, § 61 and its many interpretations not only applies to individual taxpayers but also applies equally to business entities such as C corporations, S corporations, partnerships, and LLCs as well as trusts and estates.

REFINEMENTS OF THE GROSS INCOME DEFINITION

As one might imagine, in the early years of the tax law, when there were few specific rules, people found it easy to take the position that Congress never intended to tax their particular type of "income." To support such contentions, taxpayers, never lacking for imagination, often concocted ingenious arguments explaining why they should escape tax. In one memorable case, a taxpayer who received a gift (gifts are specifically excluded from income) argued that the income from the gifted property was also exempt since the income was merely an extension of the gift. Unfortunately, the court did not accept this gift-that-keeps-on-giving theory and taxed the income. But this was typical of the development of the tax law. As the courts dealt with this and other income issues, their decisions set a number of precedents that shaped and refined the concept of income. Because of their significance, some of the principles established by early court decisions were given statutory effect; that is, the rule evolving from the decision was subsequently enacted as part of the law, or codified. For example, § 102(b) now provides that income from gifted property is not part of the gift and is fully taxable.

Other court rulings have been incorporated into the Regulations either directly or by way of reference. Several of these rulings, however, have not found their way into the Code or Regulations. Nevertheless, they provide authoritative guidance for the determination of taxable income. This section examines three major principles that are relevant to the income concept. These concern:

1. *Form of Benefit.* Must income be realized in a particular form, such as cash, before it becomes taxable?

2. *Return of Capital.* Does gross income mean gross receipts or net gain after allowance for a tax-free recovery of the taxpayer's capital investment?

3. *Indirect Economic Benefits.* Are benefits provided by an employer (such as a company car) taxable where they are not intended as compensation?

FORM-OF-BENEFIT PRINCIPLE

Many taxpayers erroneously believe that income need be reported only when cash is received. The Regulations clearly state, however, that gross income includes income realized in any form.[10] Thus, income is not limited to receipts of cash but also extends to receipts of property, services, and *any other economic benefits*. For example, taxpayers may realize income when their debts are cancelled or they purchase property at a price less than its fair market value—a so-called *bargain purchase*. In situations where income is received in a form other than cash, a cash-equivalent approach is adopted.[11] Under this method, the measure of income is its fair market value at the time of receipt.

Example 2. Several years ago on the television show *60 Minutes*, a segment was devoted to what the commentators implied was a tax travesty. In truth, it was a sad tale. According to the story, a generous employer who wanted to reward his employees for their long years of service gave them stock in the company. At that time, the stock had a value of about $100 per share. The employees, as one might guess, were extremely pleased. Unfortunately, a sudden turn of events caused the value of the shares to plummet. By the close of the year, the stock was practically worthless. Some employees still holding the stock were upset but accepted their misfortune graciously. On April 15, however, those still holding the stock found themselves in tax shock. What was the problem? As may be apparent from the discussion of the form-of-benefit principle, the employees were required to report compensation income equal to the value of stock at the time of receipt, $100 per share. This meant that many employees had to report thousands of dollars of income even though the stock was currently worthless. They had income without any way to pay the tax. Although the employees might be able to claim a deduction for worthless stock, it might not provide total relief since such loss would be a capital loss, the deduction of which is limited.

Example 3. Borrower B owed Lender L $10,000, evidenced by a note payable due in six months. If L allows B to cancel the note for a payment of $9,000, B must normally recognize gross income of $1,000.

RETURN OF CAPITAL DOCTRINE

The return of capital doctrine is best illustrated by a simple loan transaction. When a taxpayer lends money and it is later repaid, no income is recognized since the repayment represents merely a *return of capital* to the taxpayer. Although there is no statutory provision to this effect, it is a well-recognized rule. Moreover, the taxpayer's net worth has not increased (one asset, a receivable, has simply been replaced by another, cash). However, any interest on the loan that is paid to the taxpayer would be income.

Sale or Disposition. The application of the return of capital doctrine is not limited to loans. One of the first refinements made to the income concept concerned the use of the return of capital principle to determine the income from a sale of property. In 1916 the

---

[10] Reg. § 1.61-1(a).

[11] Reg. § 1.446-1(a)(3).

Supreme Court held that the total proceeds received on a sale were not to be treated as income.[12] Rather, the portion of the proceeds representing the taxpayer's capital (i.e., adjusted basis) could be recovered tax free. Thus, it is the return of capital doctrine that allows the taxpayer to determine the income upon a sale or disposition of property by reducing the amount realized (cash + the fair market value of other receipts such as property) by the adjusted basis of the property. Using this approach—now contained in § 1001(a)—the taxpayer's income on dispositions of property is limited to the *gain* realized.

> **Example 4.** R sold XYZ stock for $10,000. He purchased the stock for $6,000. R's realized gain is $4,000 ($10,000 amount realized − $6,000 adjusted basis) rather than the gross amount of the sales price, $10,000, since the return of capital doctrine permits him to recover his $6,000 investment tax free.

The return of capital doctrine also stands for the important proposition that gross income is not the same as gross receipts. This is reflected in Regulations, which provide that in the manufacturing, merchandising, or mining business, *gross income* means total sales less costs of goods sold.[13]

Damages. The return of capital doctrine may also apply to amounts awarded for injury inflicted upon the taxpayer. Section 104, discussed in detail in the following chapter, specifically excludes from income the amount of any damages awarded for personal physical injury or physical sickness on the grounds that the amount received represents a return of the personal capital destroyed. In many cases, amounts are also awarded to penalize the party responsible for the wrongdoing. These so-called punitive damages are normally taxable.[14] Similarly, where the damages awarded represent reimbursement for lost profits, the amounts are considered taxable since they are merely substitutions for income.[15]

> **Example 5.** After ten consecutive losing seasons as head football coach at Trample University and a swing at his offensive line coach, Coach F was fired. Shortly thereafter, F developed an ulcer, which forced him to have surgery. It was subsequently determined that the operation had been improperly performed. F sued the university for lost wages and the court awarded him $25,000. The $25,000 is fully taxable since it represents a substitution of income. F also sued the surgeon for $200,000 for malpractice and won. If the $200,000 represents damages awarded for physical injury, the amount is excluded on the theory that it is a return of the taxpayer's personal capital. However, if the award represents punitive damages, it is taxable.

Damages awarded to businesses are generally subject to the same tests applied to individuals. Awards or settlements for antitrust violations or patent infringements are examples of substitutions for income and thus are taxable. This is true for both actual and punitive damages. Compensation for damages to property are taxable to the extent that amounts received exceed the adjusted basis of the assets. Where the award is for damages to the goodwill of the business, the entire amount is usually taxable since the taxpayer normally does not have any recoverable basis in the goodwill.[16]

---

[12] *Doyle v. Mitchell Bros.*, 1 USTC ¶17, 3 AFTR 2979, 247 U.S. 179 (USSC, 1918). See also *Southern Pacific Company v. Lowe*, 1 USTC ¶19, 247, 3 AFTR 2989, 247 U.S. 330 (USSC, 1918).

[13] Reg. § 1.61-3(a).

[14] § 104(a)(2); but see § 104(c) for an exception if only punitive damages can be awarded.

[15] *Phoenix Coal Co. v. Comm.*, 56-1 USTC ¶9366, 49 AFTR 445, 231 F.2d 420 (CA-2, 1956).

[16] *Raytheon Production Corp. v. Comm.*, 44-2 USTC ¶9424, 32 AFTR 1155, 144 F.2d 100 (CA-1, 1944).

Example 6. M left her car running and ran inside the bank to make a deposit. When she came back, she stopped in shock as she watched her car plunge through the front of a furniture store. The furniture store ultimately received $50,000 in damages for property for which it had a basis of $35,000. The store realized a gain of $15,000. This gain must be recognized unless certain special rules concerning involuntary conversions discussed in Chapter 15 are followed.

Other Considerations. The scope of the return of capital doctrine extends beyond situations involving damages and simple sales transactions. Numerous Code sections are grounded on this principle, and often contain detailed rules for ascertaining how a receipt should be apportioned between capital and income. For example, amounts received under a life insurance policy are not taxable on the theory that the proceeds—at least in part—represent a return of the taxpayer's premium payments.[17] Similarly, where the taxpayer purchases an annuity (i.e., an investment which makes a series of payments to the investor in the future), the return of capital doctrine provides that each payment is in part a tax-free return of capital.[18] In addition, somewhat intricate provisions exist to determine whether a corporate distribution represents a distribution of earnings (i.e., a dividend) or a tax-free return of the taxpayer's investment.[19] The special rules governing life insurance, annuities, and dividends are covered in detail in Chapter 6.

INDIRECT ECONOMIC BENEFITS

Another refinement to the otherwise all-inclusive definition of gross income concerns certain benefits provided by employers for employees. Early rulings and decisions exempted benefits conferred to employees that did not represent compensation and were provided for the convenience of the employer. For example, in 1919, the IRS ruled that lodging furnished seamen aboard ship was not taxable.[20] Similarly, in 1925, the Court of Claims held that the value of quarters provided an Army officer was not includible in income.[21] Explanations offered for exempting the lodging from income emphasized that the employee was granted the benefit solely because the employer's business could not function properly unless an employee was furnished that benefit on the employer's premises. The Court also observed that the benefits were not designed as a form of compensation for the employee, but rather were an outgrowth of business necessity. These early holdings established the view that certain benefits an employee receives indirectly from his or her employer are nontaxable. Current law grants an exclusion only if the employee can demonstrate that the benefit served a business purpose of the employer other than to compensate the employee.[22]

Example 7. In the following situations an employee is permitted to exclude the benefit received under the rationale discussed above.

1. An employer provides the employee with a place to work and supplies tools and machinery with which to do the work. Similarly, an employee is not taxed when his or her secretary types a letter.

---

17 § 101.

18 § 72.

19 §§ 301 and 316.

20 O.D. 265, 1 C.B. 71 (1919).

21 *Jones v. U.S.*, 1 USTC ¶129, 5 AFTR 5297, 60 Ct.Cls. 552 (1925). Section 119, discussed in Chapter 6, currently provides specific rules that must be satisfied before meals and lodging may be excluded.

22 *George D. Patterson v. Thomas*, 61-1 USTC 9310, 7 AFTR2d 862, 289 F.2d 108 (CA-2, 1960).

2. An employer provides tuition-free, American-style schools for its overseas employees.

3. An employer provides an executive with protection in response to threats made by terrorists.

4. An employer requires its employees to attend a convention held in a resort in Florida and pays the travel costs of the employees.

It is often difficult to determine whether a particular benefit represents compensation or, alternatively, serves the business needs of the employer. For example, free parking places and similar fringe benefits provided by an employer could arguably fall into either category, depending upon the circumstances. After many years of controversy concerning the taxation of fringe benefits, Congress addressed the problem in 1984. To emphasize that fringe benefits are taxable, Congress modified the listing of typical income items found in § 61 to specifically include "fringe benefits and similar items." However, several exceptions exempting certain benefits still exist. These exceptions are discussed in Chapter 6 concerning exclusions.

☑ CHECK YOUR KNOWLEDGE

Review Question 1. After exploring the cavernous pits of his patient's mouth, Dr. Will Floss, a dentist, concluded that the gentleman had to have a root canal. Floss explained to the patient the nature of the work and that it could very well be the first in a series of expensive steps required to put his teeth back in working order. He estimated the total cost at $5,000. At that moment, the patient, a wily floor-covering dealer, immediately recalled Floss's need for new carpeting. As a result, he suggested that he would be happy to make a deal: carpeting, pad, and installation in exchange for the dental work. The two agreed, the teeth were repaired, and the carpeting was installed. Is there a tax problem here?

The issue is whether either party must report income. Many individuals think that barter transactions, exchanges of property for services or property other than cash, are not taxable. However, taxpayers who believe bartering escapes the eye of the tax collector are in for a rude awakening by the IRS. Barter transactions are fully taxable under the form-of-benefit principle. It makes no difference whether the taxpayer's net worth is increased by cash or property. In either case, the taxpayer is better off and must recognize income. Here the dentist recognizes income equal to the value of the services rendered, $5,000, and the carpet salesman has revenue equal to the value of services received.

Review Question 2. Several years ago, Intel Corporation, a leading manufacturer of computer chips in the United States, sued another chip manufacturer, American Micro, for using its patented technology. The courts awarded Intel millions of dollars for the infringement. Another situation, perhaps more well-known, was the McDonald's coffee debacle. In this case, a jury awarded 79-year-old Stella Liebeck of Albuquerque, New Mexico $200,000 in compensatory damages and another $2.7 million in punitive damages for severe burns she suffered when she spilled McDonald's coffee in her lap. (Liebeck and McDonald's ultimately settled for unknown amounts out of court.) In a comparable story, Theresa Burke and more than 8,000 other women employees of the Tennessee Valley Authority claimed unlawful discrimination in the payment of salaries on the basis of sex. The TVA had increased the salaries in certain male-dominated pay schedules, but not in certain female-dominated pay schedules. Moreover, the TVA lowered salaries in the latter. The female employees asked for and were awarded back pay, costs, and attorney's fees. Burke and the other women each received amounts in settlement according to a formula based on their length of service and rates of pay. What tax treatment might be proposed for these taxpayers?

The basic question in all of these situations is the same: does Intel, Liebeck, or Burke have taxable income? The key is recognizing that the amounts received may be taxable or nontaxable depending on the application of the return of capital doctrine and perhaps other provisions of the Code. The problem that Intel faces is demonstrating that the award for the patent infringement is not merely a replacement of lost income. It would appear that the corporation would have a difficult time overcoming a long string of cases that indicates that patent infringement awards are taxable. Nevertheless, there is no certainty in these matters without knowledge of all of the facts and a great deal of research. On the other hand, Liebeck probably had an easier time excluding her compensatory damages for her physical injury since they represent a return of her personal capital. However, the treatment of the punitive damages, although clearly taxable now, was not as clear under prior law. And what about Ms. Burke? It would seem that the knife could cut either way. On the one hand, the amounts received reimbursed her for back pay and arguably should be taxable as a substitution of income. On the other hand, the amounts could be viewed as a nontaxable reimbursement for a personal injury, sexual discrimination. If this seems difficult, it was. The courts struggled with the issue. The Sixth Circuit Court of Appeals held that the amounts were not taxable, but that decision was reversed by the Supreme Court. In 1996, Congress clarified the treatment, providing in § 104 that emotional distress does not constitute physical injury or physical sickness, thereby making damages from sex or age discrimination taxable.

Review Question 3. There is little doubt that the CEOs of Chrysler and GM, receive the use of a company car. The same can probably be said for the owners of every car dealership in the country as well as their salespeople. (If only accountants could receive such a deal!) Assume that each individual can drive the car for only 3,000 miles, after which he or she must evaluate the experience then exchange the old car for a new one and do it all over again. This is a nice arrangement: use a Jeep Grand Cherokee one month and a Chrysler Town and Country Van the next. Great benefits, but what are the tax consequences?

Once again the question concerns income. Is the value of the use of the company car taxable? Can the taxpayers argue that their use (including all personal trips) is not compensation but simply an incidental benefit that they must endure in order to evaluate the car? Does the indirect benefit rule apply? Is there a special provision that exempts fringe benefits of this nature? In a long line of cases, it has been established that the value of a car provided by an employer is compensation to the extent of the employee's personal use. The twist on the basic fact pattern—the required evaluation—may, however, suggest a different conclusion. The fringe benefit rules enacted in 1984 and discussed more fully in Chapter 6 do allow an exclusion for certain full-time automobile salespeople who use demonstration vehicles in the sales area in which the automobile dealer's sales office is located. Note that this rule applies only to salespeople. Thus an owner or executive would not qualify for an exclusion under this exception unless he or she also is considered a salesperson. There may be another escape hatch for executives and other management personnel, however, buried in the Regulations concerning product testing.[23] These Regulations allow the employee to exclude the benefit if the employee receives goods for testing and evaluation if a laundry list of requirements is met. The key point to remember here is not necessarily knowing the specific answer to this question but recognizing that an important theory exists—the indirect benefit doctrine—that is a valuable weapon on which the taxpayer can sometimes rely to avoid taxation of what at first glance has all the characteristics of taxable income.

---

[23] Reg. § 1.132-5(n).

REPORTING INCOME: TAX ACCOUNTING METHODS

Once the taxpayer has realized an item of taxable income, he or she must determine *when* the income should be reported. This determination, however, requires an understanding of the nature of accounting periods and accounting methods that may be used for tax purposes. This section examines some of the fundamental rules of tax accounting and how they govern the timing of income recognition.

ACCOUNTING PERIODS

Taxable income is usually computed on the basis of an annual accounting period commonly known as the taxable year.[24] There are two types of taxable years: a calendar year and a fiscal year. A calendar year is a 12-month period ending on December 31, whereas a fiscal year generally is any period of 12 months ending on the last day of any month other than December.[25] Any taxpayer may use a calendar year. Fiscal years may be used only by taxpayers who maintain adequate books and records. A taxpayer filing his or her *first* return may adopt either a calendar year or a fiscal year without IRS consent simply by filing a return. After adoption, however, any change does require IRS consent.[26]

Income from Partnerships, S Corporations, Fiduciaries. Reporting income derived from an interest in a partnership, an S corporation, or an estate or trust presents a special problem. As explained in Chapter 3, income realized by a partnership or an S corporation is not taxable to either of these because they are not treated as separate taxable entities. Rather, the partnership or S corporation merely serves as a conduit through which the income flows. Consequently, partners or S shareholders report their distributive shares of the entity's income in their taxable year within which (or with which) the partnership or S corporation tax year ends. Partners or S shareholders must report their share of the income regardless of the amounts distributed to them.

> **Example 8.** DEF Company, a fiscal year taxpayer, is a partnership owned equally by D, E, and F. For the taxable year ending September 30, 2005, the company had net income of $90,000. During the 12-month period ending on September 30, 2005, D withdrew $20,000 from his capital account. For his year ending December 31, 2005, D must report his share of partnership income, $30,000 ($1/3$ of $90,000), even though he only received a distribution of $20,000. Note that any income earned by the partnership from October 2005 through December 2005 is not reported until D files his 2006 tax return, which is normally due on April 15, 2007.

Income realized by a trust or an estate is generally taxed to the beneficiaries to the extent it is actually distributed or required to be distributed. Income that is not taxed to the beneficiaries is taxed to the estate or trust.

Limitation on Fiscal Years. One effect of allowing fiscal years for reporting is to enable certain taxpayers to *defer* the taxation of income. For instance, in *Example 8* above, the election by the partnership to use a fiscal year creates an opportunity for D.

---

[24] § 441(a) and (b).

[25] Reg. § 1.441-1(d) and (e). The taxpayer may elect to end the tax year on a particular day of the week rather than a date, resulting in a tax year that varies in length between 52 and 53 weeks. See Reg. § 1.441-2.

[26] A request for a change is made on Form 1128. The initial selection of, or a change in, tax year may result in a short tax year, in which case the tax may have to be computed on an annualized basis. See §§ 442 and 443.

Note that D's share of the partnership's income for October 2005 through December 2005 is not reported until D files his 2006 tax return, which is normally filed on April 15, 2007. A small corporation that primarily provides personal services could obtain a similar deferral.

Example 9. G&H Inc., a law firm, is a regular C corporation owned by two attorneys, G and H. The corporation reports using a fiscal year ending on January 31. During 2005 the corporation paid G and H small salaries. Just before the close of its taxable year ending January 31, 2006, the corporation paid a bonus to G and H equal to its taxable income. By deducting the bonus, the corporation reports no income for its taxable year ending January 31, 2006, and G and H defer reporting the bonus until they file their 2006 tax return on April 15, 2007.

In 1986, Congress felt that the use of fiscal years to create deferral of income as shown above was improper. As a result, provisions were enacted that restrict the use of fiscal years by partnerships, S corporations, and so-called personal service corporations (i.e., corporations where the principal activity is the performance of services, substantially all of which are performed by employees who are also the owners of the business). Although certain exceptions enable these entities to use a fiscal year on a limited basis, as a general rule, these taxpayers normally must use the calendar year.[27]

Annual Accounting and Progressive Rates. The use of an annual accounting period in combination with other features of the taxation process causes numerous difficulties. For example, consider the effect of the tax system's use of both an annual accounting period and a progressive tax rate structure. Each year the taxpayer computes his or her taxable income for that period and applies a progressive rate structure to the income of that year. If income varies from one year to the next, taxes paid on the *total* income of those two years are likely to exceed the total taxes that would have resulted had the taxpayer earned the income equally each year. The problems that occur with so-called incoming-bunching are illustrated below.

Example 10. Taxpayer R is a salesperson whose income is derived solely from commissions. Taxpayer S earns a salary. Both taxpayers are single. In 19X1 and 19X2 R's taxable income was $80,000 and $20,000 respectively, while S had taxable income of $50,000 each year. The tax effect on R and S (rounded to the nearest dollar and using 2005 tax rates) is as follows:

	R		S	
	Taxable Income	Tax	Taxable Income	Tax
19X1	$ 80,000	$16,907	$ 50,000	$ 9,165
19X2	20,000	2,635	50,000	9,165
Total	$100,000	$19,542	$100,000	$18,330

Note that although R and S have the same total income of $100,000 for the two-year period, R's total tax bill of $19,542 exceeds S's bill of $18,330 by $1,212.

As the above example demonstrates, the use of an annual accounting period may create inequities. In this particular case, R could reduce his tax bite if he could defer some of his income from one year to the next so as to split his income between years as equally as possible. In other cases, Congress has responded by enacting special provisions. For example, where a taxpayer has a loss during the year, the net operating

---

[27] §§ 441(i), 444, 706(b), and 1378.

effect, the cash method allows taxpayers merely to refer to their checkbooks to determine taxable income.

In using the cash method, items of income need not be in the form of cash but need only be capable of valuation in terms of money. Under this rule, sometimes termed the *cash equivalent doctrine*, the taxpayer reports income when the equivalent of cash is received.[35] Thus, where property or services are received, the fair market value of these items serves as the measure of income.

Due to the cash equivalent doctrine, reporting of income arising from notes and accounts receivable differs. Notes received by a cash basis taxpayer are usually considered property and hence constitute income equal to the value of the note.[36] Where a promise to pay is *not* evidenced by a note (e.g., credit sales resulting in accounts receivable), income is normally not recognized by a cash basis taxpayer until payment is received.[37] This treatment results because unsupported promises to pay normally are not considered as having a fair market value.

Constructive Receipt Doctrine. Taxpayers using the cash method of accounting have substantial control over income recognition since they may control the timing of the actual receipt of cash. If the requirement calling for *actual* receipt were strictly adhered to, the cash basis taxpayer could easily frustrate the purpose of progressive taxation. For example, taxpayers could select the year with the lowest tax rate and simply cash their salary or dividend checks or redeem their interest coupons in that year. To curtail this practice, the doctrine of constructive receipt was developed. Under this principle, a taxpayer is *deemed* to have received income even though such income has not actually been received. It should be noted that there is no corresponding doctrine for deductions (i.e., there is no constructive payment doctrine).

The constructive receipt doctrine is currently expressed in Regulation § 1.451-2(a) as follows:

> Income, although not actually reduced to the taxpayer's possession, is constructively received by him in the taxable year in which it is credited to his account, set apart for him or otherwise made available so that he could have drawn upon it during the taxable year if notice of intention to withdraw had been given. However, income is not constructively received if the taxpayer's control of its receipt is subject to substantial limitations or restrictions.

As the Regulation indicates, the taxpayer is treated as having received income when three conditions are satisfied:

1. The taxpayer has control over the amount without substantial limitations and restrictions

2. The amount has been set aside or credited to the taxpayer's account

3. The funds are available for payment by the payer (i.e., the payer's ability to make payment must be considered)

Some of the common situations to which the rule is applied are illustrated in the following examples.

Example 11. B refereed a basketball game on Saturday night, December 31, 2005 and did not receive the check for his services until after the banks had closed. He

---

[35] Reg. § 1.446-1(a)(3).

[36] *A.W. Wolfson*, 1 B.T.A. 538 (1925).

[37] *Bedell v. Comm.*, 1 USTC ¶359, 7 AFTR 8469, 30 F.2d 622 (CA-2, 1929).

cashed the check on January 3, 2006. B must report the income in 2005. In the case of a check, a taxpayer is deemed to have received payment in the year the check is received rather than when it is cashed.[38]

Example 12. T mailed a check on December 29, 2005, which S received in January 2006. S is not in constructive receipt of the check since it was not available to him for his immediate use and enjoyment. However, if S requested that T mail him the check so that he receives it in 2006, or if S could have received the check by merely appearing in person and claiming it, S would be deemed to have received the payment in 2005.

Example 13. When G made a deposit on January 15, 2006, the bank updated her passbook on December 31, 2005 to show that $200 of interest was credited to her account for the last quarter of 2005. G withdrew the interest on January 31. G must report the interest in 2005. Interest credited to the taxpayer's account is taxable when credited, regardless of whether it is in the taxpayer's possession, assuming that it may be withdrawn.[39]

Example 14. B Corporation mailed dividend checks dated December 20 on December 28, 2005. R, a shareholder in B, received her check on January 4, 2006. R reports the dividend income in 2006 as long as the payer customarily pays dividends by mail so that the shareholder receives it after the end of the year.[40]

Example 15. R's secretary received several checks for services that R had performed. Payments received by a taxpayer's agent are considered constructively received by the taxpayer.[41]

Example 16. A taxpayer who agrees not to cash a check until authorized by the payer has not constructively received income if the payer does not have sufficient funds in the bank to cover the check.[42]

Limitations on the Use of the Cash Method. As a method of accounting, the cash method's principal advantage lies in its simplicity and objectivity. If a taxpayer uses the cash method, taxable income is easily computed merely by referring to cash receipts and disbursements. Moreover, the amount of taxable income computed in this manner is incontrovertible—it is not open to question or dispute and is readily verifiable. Unlike the accrual method, whether income has been "earned" or expenses have been "incurred" are simply not issues under the cash method.

On other counts, the cash method scores poorly, ranking a distant second to the accrual method. From an accounting perspective, the cash method is entirely inappropriate since income and expense are recognized without regard to the taxable year in which the economic events responsible for the income or expense actually occur. Similarly, when some parties to a transaction use different methods of accounting, there may be a mismatching of income and deductions. For example, an accrual basis

---

[38]   *C.F. Kahler,* 18 T.C. 31 (1952).

[39]   Reg. § 1.451-2(b).

[40]   *Ibid.; S.L. Avery,* 4 USTC ¶1277, 13 AFTR 1168, 292 U.S. 210 (USSC, 1934). See also *H.B. McEuen v. Comm.,* 52-1 USTC ¶9281, 41 AFTR 1169, 196 F.2d 127 (CA-5, 1952).

[41]   *T. Watson,* 2 TCM 863 (1943).

[42]   *A.V. Johnston,* 23 TCM 2003, T.C. Memo 1964-323.

corporation could accrue expenses payable to a cash basis individual. In such case, the corporation could obtain deductions without ever having to make a disbursement and, moreover, without the individual taxpayer recognizing any offsetting income.

While the above are clearly shortcomings, the major flaw found in the cash method is that it is easily abused. Taxpayers have often secured benefits by merely timing their transactions appropriately: recognizing income in one year, deductions in the next, or what is more likely, deductions in years in which the taxpayer is in a high tax bracket and income in years in which the taxpayer is in a low tax bracket.

To attack these problems, Congress has limited the use of the cash method of accounting. The following entities are normally prohibited from using the cash method:[43]

1. Regular C corporations;

2. Partnerships that have regular C corporations as partners (other than certain personal service corporations described below); and

3. *Tax shelters,* generally defined as any enterprise (other than a regular C corporation) in which interests have been offered for sale in any offering required to be registered under Federal or State security agencies.

Despite these general restrictions, Congress believed that the simplicity of the cash method justified its continued use in certain instances. For example, Congress felt that it would be costly for small businesses to switch to the accrual method. Similarly, it recognized that the accrual method would create undue complexity for farming businesses if such a method were required to account for growing crops and livestock. In addition, Congress believed that personal service corporations, which have traditionally used the cash method, should be allowed to continue their use. Accordingly, the following entities are allowed to use the cash method.[44]

1. Any corporation or partnership whose annual *gross receipts* for *all* preceding years do not exceed $5 million. This test is satisfied for any prior year only if the average annual gross receipts[45] for the three-year period ending with such year does not exceed $5 million. Once this average *exceeds* $5 million, the corporation cannot use the cash method for the following year.

2. Certain farming businesses.

3. Qualified personal service corporations. A regular C corporation is qualified if substantially all of the activities consist of performing services in the fields of health, law, engineering, architecture, accounting, actuarial science, performing arts, or consulting, *and* at least 95 percent of its stock is held by the employees who are providing the services.[46] The latter test is considered satisfied if the stock is owned by a retired employee or by the estate or heirs of a deceased employee.

---

[43] § 448(a).

[44] § 448(b).

[45] Gross receipts include total sales (net of returns and allowances but not reduced by costs of goods sold) and amounts received for services, interest, rents, royalties, and annuities. For sales of capital assets and real or depreciable property used in trade or business, gross receipts are reduced by the taxpayer's adjusted basis in such property. See Temp. Reg. § 1.448-1T(f)(2)(iv).

[46] § 448(d)(2).

Example 17. C's Video Rentals, a regular C corporation, started business in 19X1. Since that time it has grown to 20 locations and had annual gross receipts as follows:

Year	Gross Receipts	Average Annual Gross Receipts*
19X1	$ 4,000,000	$4,000,000
19X2	2,000,000	3,000,000
19X3	6,000,000	4,000,000
19X4	10,000,000	6,000,000

$$* \frac{\text{Current + Prior two years}}{3 \text{ (or if less, years in existence)}}$$

It initially adopted the cash method in 19X1. It was able to use the cash method through 19X4 because the average annual gross receipts for all prior years did not exceed $5 million. Note that although its gross receipts were $6,000,000 in 19X3, its *average annual* gross receipts for that year were only $4,000,000 [($4,000,000 + $2,000,000 + $6,000,000) ÷ 3]. Consequently, the cash method could be used for 19X4. It will be denied use of the cash method for 19X5 since the average annual gross receipts for 19X4 exceed $5 million [($2,000,000 + $6,000,000 + $10,000,000) ÷ 3 = $ 6,000,000].

It should be noted that the above exceptions do not apply to tax shelters. Any enterprise considered a tax shelter must use the accrual method. In addition, as discussed below, if the taxpayer maintains inventories, special rules apply.

Accounting for Inventory. As noted above, most businesses—other than large C corporations—are permitted to use the cash method. However, an important exception exists for taxpayers with inventories. According to the longstanding rule of Regulation §1.471-1 "[I]n order to reflect taxable income correctly, inventories . . . are necessary in every case in which the production, purchase, or sale of merchandise is an income producing factor." Regulation § 1.446-1(c)(2) adds that "in any case in which it is necessary to use an inventory the accrual method of accounting must be used with regard to purchases and sales . . ." In short, if a business sells "inventory," taxpayers must capitalize the cost of inventory purchases and can expense such costs only when the item is sold. Just as important, if not more so, businesses with inventories also must accrue and recognize income at the time of sale—regardless of when the cash is received. Both halves of the accrual requirement are significant since both effect the amount of income that the taxpayer ultimately reports in a particular year.

The reasoning behind the regulatory scheme requiring inventories is anchored in the matching principle that ensures income will be clearly reflected. The rationale was eloquently stated by the Appellate Court in *Knight-Ridder Newspapers Inc.*, a case involving whether a cash-basis corporation should inventory its costs of newsprint and ink.[47]

> According to accounting wisdom the income realized from the sale of merchandise is most *clearly measured* by matching the cost of the merchandise with the revenue from its sale. In order to achieve such matching of revenue and cost, it is necessary to keep an inventory account reflecting the costs of merchandise, raw materials, and

---

[47] 84 -2 USTC ¶9827, 54 AFTR 2d 84-6120, 743 F.2d 781 (CA-11, 1984).

The claim of right doctrine does not apply where the taxpayer receives the income but recognizes an obligation to repay.[67] For example, a landlord would not be required to report the receipt of a tenant's security deposit as income because the deposit must be repaid upon the tenant's departure if the apartment unit is undamaged.

In those situations where the taxpayer repays an amount that previously had been included in income, a deduction is allowed. Section 1341 provides a special rule for computing the deduction, which ensures that the tax benefit of the deduction is the equivalent to the tax paid on the income in the prior year.

PREPAID INCOME

Over the years, a web of exceptions and special rules have developed regarding the reporting of prepaid income by an *accrual basis* taxpayer. Absent these rules, the accrual basis taxpayer (in accordance with the all-events test) would defer recognition of prepaid income until it becomes earned, as is the case in financial accounting. For tax purposes, however, accrual basis taxpayers often report prepaid income in the year received. This treatment normally results from application of the claim of right doctrine, which requires income recognition when the taxpayer receives earnings under an unrestricted claim. For example, accrual basis taxpayers must report prepaid rental income when received (not when earned) since the taxpayer accepts the money under a claim of right without restrictions on its use. Unfortunately, no general rule is completely reliable to determine when prepaid income must be reported. Rather, the reporting procedure depends on the type of income received. As discussed below, special rules exist for prepaid income from rents, interest, services, warranties, goods, dues, subscriptions, and similar items. Note, however, these rules apply to *accrual basis* taxpayers only. A *cash basis* taxpayer reports all of these prepaid items of income in the year the cash is received.

Prepaid Interest, Rents, and Royalties. Several types of advance payments are included in income when received without question. For example, prepaid interest is income when received.[68] Prepaid rent and lump-sum payments, such as bonuses or advance royalties received upon execution of a lease or other agreement, are also income when received.[69] As subsequently explained, however, the term *rent* does not include payments for the use or occupancy of rooms or space where their use is ancillary to the services provided to the user of the property. (e.g., hotels, motels, and convalescent homes are not considered as having received rents).[70] Because of the significant service element, these prepayments are reported using the rules applying to prepaid service income. Prepaid rents must be distinguished not only from services but also from lease or security deposits. Amounts received from a lessee that are refundable provided the lessee complies with the terms of the lease are not income since the lessor recognizes an obligation to repay.[71] The deposits become income only when the lessor becomes entitled to their unrestricted use upon the lessee's violation of the agreement.

Prepaid Service Income. Over the years, the treatment of advance payments for services—prepaid service income—has been quite controversial. Disputes between the IRS and taxpayers began when the IRS argued that the claim of right doctrine required

---

[67] *Comm. v. Turney*, 36-1 USTC ¶9168, 17 AFTR 679, 82 F.2d 661 (CA-5, 1936).

[68] *Franklin Life Insurance v. U.S.*, 68-2 USTC ¶9459, 22 AFTR2d 5180, 399 F.2d 757 (CA-7, 1968).

[69] *South Dade Farms, Inc. v. Comm.*, 43-2 USTC ¶9634, 31 AFTR 842, 138 F.2d 818 (CA-5, 1943); *W.M. Scott*, 27 B.T.A. 951.

[70] Rev. Proc. 2004-34, 2004-22 I.R.B. 991.

[71] *Clinton Hotel Realty Corp. v. Comm.*, 42-2 USTC ¶9559, 29 AFTR 758, 128 F.2d 968 (CA-5, 1942).

accrual basis taxpayers to report prepayments for services as income in the year received. The IRS took this approach notwithstanding the fact that the taxpayer had not performed the services. After a great deal of litigation, the government relented and permitted limited deferral in certain circumstances. These rules were recently revised in 2004, with the issuance of Rev. Proc. 2004-34.[72]

Rev. Proc. 2004-34 now permits two acceptable methods of accounting for advanced payments for services. These are: a "full-inclusion method" and a "deferral method." The full-inclusion option is the easiest and the least desirable: all of the payments are reported in the year of receipt regardless of how the payments are reported for financial accounting purposes. In contrast, under the deferral method, taxpayers generally must report advanced payments as income in the year of receipt to the extent the payments are included in the revenues of the taxpayer's financial statements.[73] The balance of the advanced payments are deferred and reported as income in the following year. Thus, book income normally equals taxable income in the first year but may differ in subsequent years. This technique, unlike the previous approach, permits at least one year of deferral regardless of the length of the contract.

> **Example 26.** Murray Inc.—a calendar-year, accrual-method taxpayer—is in the business of providing ballroom dance lessons. On October 29 of year 1, Murray received $4,800 for a 48-month contract under which Murray would provide up to 96 lessons. Murray provides 8 lessons in year 1, 48 lessons in year 2, and 40 lessons in year 3. In its audited financial statements, the company reports the income as the lessons are provided. Therefore, for financial accounting purposes, Murray reports $400 ($4,800 × 8/96) in year 1. Similarly, under the deferral method of Rev. Proc. 2004-34, Murray would also report $400 of income for tax purposes since this procedure permits deferral equal to that reported for financial statement purposes. In year 2, for financial statement purposes, Murray would report $2,400 (48/96 × $4,800) based on the number of lessons provided. However, in year 2 for tax purposes, Murray would report the remaining balance of the advanced payment, $4,400, as income.

The advance payment rules allowing limited deferral for prepaid service income also apply to prepaid rental income if the occupancy or use of property is ancillary to the provision of services to the user of the property.[74] According to the procedure, advance payments for the use of hotel rooms or other quarters, booth space at a trade show, campsite space at a mobile home park, and recreational or banquet facilities are not considered rents but rather services. Note that this treatment permits hotels, motels and the like to enjoy the deferral provision as outline above for services.

Advance Payments for Goods. Normally, an accrual basis taxpayer reports advance payments for sales of merchandise when they are earned (e.g., when the goods are shipped). This treatment enables the taxpayer to defer recognition of the prepayments. However, this approach is allowed only if the taxpayer follows the same method of reporting for financial accounting purposes.[75]

---

[72] Rev. Proc. 2004-34, 2004-22 IRB 991 (effective for tax years ending after 5/5/04) superseding Rev. Proc. 71-21, 1971-2 C.B. 549.

[73] If "applicable" financial statements (a certified audited financial statement used for credit purposes, reporting to shareholders, or any other substantial nontax purpose) have not been prepared, the amount of the payment earned is reported in the first year. Rev. Proc. 2004-34 (4.06), 2004-22 I.R.B. 991.

[74] Rev. Proc. 2004-34 identifies other types of prepayments that do and do not qualify as an advanced payment for which limited deferral is permitted.

[75] Reg. § 1.451-5(b). See Reg. § 1.451-4(c)(1) for certain situations where the prepayments must be reported earlier.

Example 27. C Corporation, a calendar year taxpayer, manufactures kitchen appliances. In late December 2005, it received $50,000 for kitchen appliances that it will produce and ship in May 2006. The corporation may postpone recognition of the income until 2006, assuming that such income is also reported on the financial accounting income statement in 2006.

Long-Term Contracts. Section 460 contains special rules for the reporting of income from long-term contracts. A long-term contract is defined as any contract for the manufacture, building, installation, or construction of property that is not completed within the same taxable year in which it was entered into. However, a *manufacturing* contract is still not considered long-term unless it also involves either (1) the manufacture of a unique item not normally carried in finished goods inventory (e.g., a special piece of machinery), or (2) items that normally require more than 12 months to complete. If a manufacturing contract does not qualify as a long-term contract, deferral may still be available under the rules regarding advance payments for goods discussed above. Note that contracts for services normally do not qualify for treatment as long-term contracts.

The tax law has long allowed taxpayers who enter into a long-term contract to use the percentage of completion method or the completed contract method (subject to certain limitations) to account for advance payments.[76] The percentage of completion method requires the taxpayer to recognize a portion of the gross profit on the contract based on the estimated percentage of the contract completed. In contrast, the completed contract method allows the taxpayer to defer income recognition until the contract is complete and acceptance has occurred. When available, taxpayers usually opt to use the completed contract method in order to postpone recognition of income. In some extreme cases, however, taxpayers have been able to postpone income for many years on the claim that the contract was not complete.

Over the years, Congress became concerned about the opportunities for deferral as well as the potential for abuse. Consequently, it took various steps, slowly but surely limiting the use of the completed contract method. These actions culminated with the virtual repeal of the method in 1989. As a result, long-term contracts currently entered into normally must be accounted for using the percentage of completion method.[77] However, there are two situations where the completed contract method can still be used. These include[78]

1. *Home construction contracts.* Contracts in which 80 percent of the costs are related to buildings containing four or fewer dwelling units. Special rules apply to contracts if the buildings contain more than four units (i.e., so-called residential construction contracts).[79]

2. *Contracts of small businesses.* Construction contracts that are completed within two years of commencement and are performed by a contractor whose average annual gross receipts for the three preceding tax years do not exceed $10 million.

When using the percentage of completion method, the portion of the total contract price reported during the year and matched against current costs is computed as follows

$$\text{Total contract price} \times \frac{\text{Direct and allocable indirect costs incurred this period}}{\text{Total estimated costs of contract}}$$

[76]   Reg. § 1.451-3.

[77]   § 460(a).

[78]   § 460(e).

[79]   A 70 percent of completion method may be used for certain residential construction contracts.

Note that if less than 10 percent of the contract's costs have been incurred, the taxpayer may elect to defer reporting until the year in which the 10 percent threshold is reached.[80]

> **Example 28.** In October 2005, W Corporation entered into a contract to build a hotel to be completed by May 2007. The contract price was $1 million. The company's estimated total costs of construction were $800,000. W's average annual gross receipts exceed $10 million, and it is therefore required to use the percentage of completion method. Total costs incurred during 2005 were $600,000. In 2006, the contract was completed at a total cost of $840,000. The income reported in 2005 and 2006 is computed below:

	2005	2006
Revenue recognized	$ 750,000*	$ 250,000
Current costs	(600,000)	(240,000)
Total.	$ 150,000	$ 10,000

$$\frac{*\$600,000}{\$800,000} = 75\% \times \$1,000,000$$

Any contract for which the percentage of completion method is used is subject to the special *look-back* provisions.[81] Under these rules, once the contract is complete, annual income is recomputed based on final costs rather than estimated costs. Interest is then paid to the taxpayer if there was an overstatement of income. Conversely, the taxpayer must pay interest if income was understated.

> **Example 29.** Same facts as in *Example 28*, above. Based on total actual costs of $840,000, W's 2005 income should have been $114,000, computed as follows:

	2005
Revenue recognized	$ 714,000*
Current costs	(600,000)
Total	$ 114,000

$$\frac{*\$600,000}{\$840,000} = 71.4\% \times \$1,000,000$$

Because the contract was in reality only 71.4% complete and not 75% complete, W overstated income in 2005 by $36,000 ($150,000 − $114,000). Consequently, the IRS is required to pay the taxpayer interest on the overpayment of the related tax.

Prepaid Dues and Subscriptions. Amidst much controversy concerning the reporting of prepaid income, Congress provided specific rules for the reporting of prepaid dues and subscriptions. Section 455 permits the taxpayer to elect to recognize prepaid subscription income (amounts received from a newspaper, magazine, or

---

[80] § 460(b)(5).

[81] § 460(b)(2). The lookback rule is elective if the cumulative income (loss) determined using estimated contract price and cost is within 10 percent of actual.

periodical) ratably over the subscription period. Section 456 provides that taxpayers may elect to report prepaid dues ratably over the membership period.

INTEREST INCOME

The period in which a taxpayer recognizes interest income usually follows the basic tax accounting rules for cash and accrual basis taxpayers. In some cases, however, these taxpayers must observe special provisions that may cause reporting to vary from the normal pattern.

General Rules. As a general rule, cash basis taxpayers recognize interest income when received, while accrual basis taxpayers recognize the income when it is earned. As previously noted, both accrual and cash basis taxpayers that receive interest before it is earned (prepaid interest) must report the income when it is received.

Example 30. T operates a small business that manufactures pottery dishes. When one of her customers was unable to pay her bill, T accepted a $10,000 note, dated October 1, 2005, payable with 6% interest on October 1, 2006. Assuming T is a cash basis taxpayer, she will report $600 of interest income ($10,000 × 6%) when received in 2006. If T uses the accrual method, she would include $150 ($10,000 × 3/12 × 6%) in her gross income for 2005 and $450 ($10,000 × 9/12 × 6%) when received in 2006. Had the customer paid all of the interest, $600, in 2005 as a showing of good faith, T would report the entire $600 in 2005 regardless of whether she is a cash or accrual basis taxpayer.

In many instances, a taxpayer will purchase an interest-bearing instrument between payment dates. When this occurs, it is assumed that the purchase price includes the interest accrued to the date of the purchase. Thus, when the buyer later receives the interest payment, the portion accrued to the date of purchase is considered a nontaxable return of capital that reduces the taxpayer's basis in the instrument. On the other hand, the seller must include as interest income the amount accrued to the date of the purchase, regardless of the seller's method of accounting.

Example 31. S owned a $1,000, 12% AT&T bond that paid interest semiannually on November 1 and May 1. He purchased the bond at par several years ago. On September 1, 2005, S sold the bond for $1,540 including $40 of the accrued interest ($1,000 × 12% × 4/12). S must report $40 of interest income accrued to the date of sale. In addition, S will report a capital gain of $500 ($1,540 − $40 interest − $1,000 basis). The result is the same if S is a cash or accrual basis taxpayer.

Example 32. Assume B purchased for $1,540 the bond that S sold in the example above. On November 1, B receives an interest payment of $60 ($1,000 × 12% × 6/12). B treats the interest accrued to the date of purchase, $40, as a nontaxable return of basis. Thus, B's basis is reduced to $1,500 ($1,540 − $40). The remaining $20 of interest is included in B's gross income.

In practice, the broker's statement normally reflects the interest accrued to the date of the sale or purchase.

Discount. When accounting for interest income, any discount relating to the debt instrument—the excess of the face value of the obligation over the purchase price—must be considered. Discount typically results when the rate at which the instrument pays interest is less than the market rate. In such case, the discount essentially functions as a substitute for interest. Consistent with this view, the tax law attempts to ensure that the discount is treated as interest income and is normally reported currently. Special provisions have been introduced over the years to clarify the reporting of the discount income as well as to prohibit taxpayers from converting the discount income into capital gain.

> **Example 33.** During 2003, T purchased a $10,000, 8% corporate bond for $8,000, or a $2,000 discount. In 2005 the bond matured and the taxpayer redeemed the bond for its par value of $10,000. The redemption is treated as an exchange, and the taxpayer recognizes a long-term capital gain of $2,000 ($10,000 redemption price − $8,000 basis). In this case, the taxpayer has converted the discount of $2,000, which from an economic view is ordinary interest income, to capital gain. Moreover, the taxpayer has deferred the reporting of such income from the time it accrues to the time the bond is sold. Although this opportunity still exists for certain older bonds, some of the provisions discussed below (and in greater detail in Chapter 16) eliminate this possibility for bonds issued in the future.

The tax treatment of discount depends in part on when it arises. The discount often occurs at the time the instrument is issued. For example, certain instruments such as U.S. Savings Bonds, Treasury bills, and so-called zero coupon bonds do not bear interest and are usually *issued* at discounts. Other debt obligations that do bear interest (such as corporate bonds) also may be issued at a discount, usually if the coupon rate is set lower than the current rate. Discount could also result after the instrument is issued. For example, where interest-bearing instruments are issued at par, discount may arise upon a subsequent purchase. The specific treatment of discount is examined below.

Non-Interest-Bearing Obligations Issued at a Discount. The Code provides special rules for non-interest-bearing obligations that are issued at a discount and redeemable for a fixed amount that increases over time. The instruments to which these rules would normally apply are Series E and EE U.S. Savings Bonds. Series E Bonds were issued between 1941 and 1980, having maturities up to 40 years. Beginning in 1980, these bonds were replaced by Series EE Bonds. Beginning in 2001, Series EE Bonds are inscribed with the special legend "Patriot Bonds" inspired by the tragedy of September 11, 2001. Series EE bonds earn 90 percent of five-year Treasury security yields. They do not pay interest but are sold at a discount (half their face value), and are available in denominations ranging from $50 through $10,000. They have maturities of 30 years. The bonds are generally redeemable at any time up until the final maturity date at a price that increases with the passage of time. No interest payments are made while the bond is held. The holder's interest income is represented by the difference between the redemption price and purchase price. Note, however, that Series EE savings bonds stop increasing in value after 30 years. Savings bonds rates are adjusted semiannually on May 1 and November 1. For example, for bonds issued in November 2004, the rate was 3.25 percent (2.61 percent in 2003—see *www.savingsbonds.gov*).

For reporting purposes, taxpayers may elect to include in income the annual increase in the redemption price of the bond.[82] In essence, this election allows a cash basis taxpayer to use the accrual method with respect to these bonds. If income is not reported on an annual basis, the taxpayer reports the entire difference between the redemption and issue prices as income when the bond is redeemed.

> **Example 34.** S purchased Series EE Bonds with a face value of $10,000 at a cost of $8,000. The redemption price of the bonds increases during the year by $100. If S elects to report the income annually, she will include $100 in her gross income. Alternatively, S could wait until she redeems the bond to report the income. For

---

[82]   § 454(a).

example, if S later redeemed the bonds for $9,500, she would report $1,500 income (the difference between the redemption price of $9,500 and her cost of $8,000) at the time of redemption.

The taxpayer may make the election to report the interest annually at any time. When the election is made, all interest previously deferred on all Series E and EE Bonds must be reported. This procedure effectively allows the taxpayer to choose the year in which the interest income is to be reported. However, once the election is made, it applies to *all* Series E and EE Bonds subsequently acquired. Should the taxpayer desire to change to reporting the income at redemption, consent from the IRS is required.

Series E and EE Bonds may be exchanged within one year of their maturity date for Series HH Bonds that *pay* interest semiannually. By exchanging the Series E or EE Bonds for Series HH Bonds, the taxpayer is able to postpone the recognition of any unreported income attributed to the Series E or EE Bonds to the year in which the Series HH Bonds are redeemable.[83]

> **Example 35.** In June 1967, B purchased Series E Bonds at a cost of $6,000. He did not report the income annually. When the bonds mature in 2004, B will receive $40,000 and will have to report a gain of $34,000 ($40,000 − $6,000). B could effectively shift the $34,000 of income to a year of his choice by exchanging the Series E Bonds for Series HH and redeeming the Series HH Bonds at a later date. By so doing, B may be able to create a significant tax savings by recognizing the income in a year in which a lower tax rate would apply (e.g., his retirement years).

As discussed in Chapter 6, certain taxpayers who cash in Series EE Bonds and use the proceeds for educational expenses may be able to exclude the interest.

Government Obligations. Special rules also govern the treatment of the discount arising upon the purchase of short-term government obligations such as Treasury bills.[84] Typically, a taxpayer purchases a short-term Treasury bill at a discount and redeems it for par value shortly thereafter. In this instance, Code § 454(b) applies to cash basis taxpayers to ensure that the gain on the redemption—in effect, the discount—is treated as ordinary interest income. Specifically, any gain realized by cash basis taxpayers from the sale or redemption of non-interest-bearing obligations issued by governmental units that have a fixed maturity date that is one year or less from the date of issue is always ordinary income. This ordinary income is reported *in the year* of sale or redemption. In contrast, accrual basis taxpayers are required to amortize the discount (i.e., include it in income) on a *daily* basis under Code § 1281(a).

> **Example 36.** On December 1, 2004, B, a cash basis calendar year taxpayer, purchased a $10,000 non-interest-bearing Treasury bill. She purchased the bill at 97 ($9,700) and redeemed the bill on March 1, 2005 at par. B recognizes a $300 gain ($10,000 − $9,700) on the redemption, and the entire gain is treated as ordinary income in 2005. The same result would occur if B had *sold* the Treasury bill for $10,000 on January 15, 2005. Note that if B were an accrual basis taxpayer, the $300 discount would have been included in income on a daily basis. Consequently, a portion of the income would be reported in 2004 and the remainder in 2005.

> **Original Issue Discount.** When interest-bearing obligations such as corporate bonds are *issued* at a discount, a complex set of provisions operates to prevent taxpayers from

---

[83] § 454(c); Reg. § 1.454-1(a); § 1037.

[84] Special rules also apply to Treasury Inflation-Protection Bonds (TIPs) and Treasury Inflation-Indexed Securities.

not only deferring the discount income but also converting it to capital gain as depicted in *Example 30*. These rules apply only to discount that arises when the bonds are originally issued. This discount is technically referred to as *original issue discount* (OID) and is determined as follows:

Redemption price............................	$x,xxx
− Issue price.................................	− xxx
= Original issue discount........................	$x,xxx

The thrust of the provisions is to require the holder of the bond to amortize the discount into income during the period the bond is held. A complete discussion of the treatment of OID is provided in Chapter 16.

✓ CHECK YOUR KNOWLEDGE

Review Question 1. For financial accounting purposes, prepaid income is generally reported as it is earned. Does the same treatment apply for tax purposes? Explain the treatment of prepaid interest, rents, royalties, services, and advance payments for goods.

As a general rule, prepaid income must be reported when received. This is obviously true for cash basis taxpayers and surprisingly true for accrual basis taxpayers. The unusual treatment for accrual basis taxpayers stems from the claim of right doctrine, which requires recognition of income whenever the amount has been received and the taxpayer does not recognize an obligation to repay. This treatment applies to prepaid interest, rents, and royalties. It does not apply to prepaid service income (including prepaid rents if the property's use is secondary to the services provided) where the reporting follows that for books in the first year with the balance reported in the second year. It also does not apply to advance payments for goods, which are normally reported in the same manner as they are for financial accounting purposes (the normal accrual method).

A close look at the reporting requirements for prepaid income reveals that cash basis taxpayers report prepaid income when it is received and this approach is consistent with the cash method of accounting. In contrast, accrual basis taxpayers report—subject to certain exceptions—prepaid income as if they were on the cash basis. The table below summarizes the law's schizophrenic approach to prepaid income and—as seen in Chapter 7—prepaid expenses.

	Prepaid income	Prepaid expenses
Cash basis taxpayer	Report in year received *Consistent with cash method*	Deduct over appropriate period *Treat as if on accrual basis*
Accrual basis taxpayer	Report in year received *Treated as if on cash basis*	Deducted over appropriate period *Consistent with accrual method*

Review Question 2. After the changes made during the 1980s, some commentators pronounced the use of the completed contract method dead. Is this true? Are there any circumstances under which the completed contract method can be used?

The completed contract may be dead for large construction companies that build mammoth projects such as airplanes, stadiums, dams, office towers, and the like. But it is alive and well for the majority of construction companies. The completed contract

sum in those days) to be paid over a five-year period at a rate of $22,000 per year: $11,000 to Randy and $11,000 to his father, Cecil. The payment to Randy's father was pursuant to an oral agreement the two had made when Randy was 16. According to the agreement, Cecil, a former semiprofessional baseball player and coach, acted as Randy's coach and business manager in exchange for 50 percent of any bonus that Randy might receive if he should obtain a baseball contract.

At about the same time that the Cubs were striking a deal with Hundley, the Philadelphia Phillies reached an agreement with Richie Allen, another future star.[91] According to this arrangement, Allen was to receive a $70,000 bonus: $30,000 paid to him over five years and $40,000 paid to his mother. How should the bonuses be treated? Should they both be treated the same?

The question in both cases is whether the child has effectively split the income between himself and his parent or merely made an anticipatory assignment of income. If the latter is true, all of the income would be taxed to the child and none to the parent. In both cases, the IRS argued that the payment to Randy's father and Richie's mother should be treated as being first made to the child and then followed by a nondeductible gift. Despite the similarity of the cases, the Court believed that the services provided by Hundley's father were instrumental in his son's success, whereas Allen's mother made no tangible contribution. As a result, Hundley was allowed to deduct the payment to his father as a business expense and, therefore, split the income between them. In contrast, no deduction was allowed to Allen and he was required to pay taxes on the entire bonus.

Review Question 2. M wants to shift income to her 14-year-old daughter so that it will be taxed at the daughter's 10 percent rate rather than at M's 35 percent rate. M plans on loaning her daughter $10,000 interest-free for this purpose. Will her plan to shift income to the daughter work?

As a general rule, interest-free loans can no longer be used successfully to shift income, since interest income must be imputed to the lender. In this case, M would be treated as having received an interest payment from her daughter, thus defeating the entire plan. At first blush, some might believe that because the loan is less than $10,000, the de minimis rule operates and M is not required to impute interest; this is a typical misconception. It is true that imputation is not required if the loan is less than $10,000, but only if the borrower does not invest the loan amount in income-producing property. Of course, if the borrower does not invest in income-producing property there is no income and nothing is shifted. Therefore, the $10,000 de minimis rule does not create any opportunity. In this particular case, the $100,000 rule also would come into play. This exception provides that the maximum amount of interest to be imputed to the lender is equal to the net investment income of the borrower (zero, if net investment income is less than $1,000). This provision does provide a small opportunity. If the daughter invests the $10,000 to produce $900 of interest income, no income would be imputed to M and $900 would be successfully shifted. M would be treated as having made a gift of $900 to her daughter, but there would be no gift tax because of the annual exclusion of $11,000.

TAX PLANNING

TIMING INCOME RECOGNITION

The proper timing of income recognition can reap great benefits for the taxpayer. As a general rule, postponement of income recognition is wise since the tax on such income

---

[91] *Richard A. Allen*, 50 T.C. 466 (1968).

is deferred. The major advantage of tax deferral is that the taxpayer has continued use of the real funds that otherwise would have been used to pay taxes. Deferral of the tax is in essence an interest-free loan from the government.

When considering deferral, attention must be given to the marginal tax rates that may apply to the income. For example, taxpayers often postpone income until their retirement years, when they are usually in a lower tax bracket. Although deferral may be wise in this situation, it may be unwise where tax rates rise by operation of law or because of the taxpayer's increase in earnings. Ideally, the taxpayer should attempt to level out taxable income from one year to the next and equalize the tax rate that applies annually (to avoid the situation of R in *Example 11* and duplicate that of S).

The opportunities for most individuals to postpone income are limited, particularly in light of the constructive receipt doctrine. Several techniques do exist, however, as outlined below:

1. Installment sales of property enable the taxpayer not only to avoid the bunching of income in a single year but also to defer the tax.

2. Income on Series E and EE bonds, Treasury bills, and certain certificates of deposit may be deferred until they are redeemed.

3. Investments in Individual Retirement Accounts (IRAs), Keogh plans, and qualified retirement plans are all made with before-tax dollars (since these contributions are deductible), and earnings on these investments are not taxed until they are withdrawn.

4. Deferred compensation arrangements may be suitable, as in the case of a professional athlete, celebrity, or executive. (See Chapter 18.)

INCOME-SPLITTING TECHNIQUES

As stressed earlier, the most fundamental rule in tax planning concerns minimizing the marginal tax rate that applies to the taxpayer's income. Minimizing the applicable rate is usually accomplished through use of some type of income splitting or shifting technique.

> **Example 42.** Mr. and Mrs. J pay taxes at a rate of 35% in 2005. The couple helps support Mr. J's 67-year-old retired mother, M, by giving her $5,000 annually. Such gifts do not entitle the couple to claim M as a dependent. Consequently, in 2005, M may claim an exemption deduction of $3,200 and a standard deduction of $6,250 ($5,000 regular + $1,250 additional for unmarried and over 65 years of age), for total deductions of $9,450. In providing M's support through gifts, the couple is using after-tax dollars. That is, the couple would have to earn $7,692 to provide M with $5,000 in support [$7,692 − (35% of $7,692) = $5,000]. Instead, the couple could transfer income-producing property to M to provide the needed support. By so doing, the income would not be subject to tax (assuming M's only other income is tax-exempt such as social security benefits), and the cost of support would be far less expensive. Although this arrangement requires the couple to give up the property permanently (since any type of reversionary interest would cause the income to be taxed back to the couple), in many family situations, M would probably give the property back when she no longer needs it or when she dies. In addition, other techniques are available that can circumvent the problem of permanently departing with the property.

The above example demonstrates how income can be shifted successfully. Where income is to be shifted to children, however, the taxpayer must contend with the "kiddie" tax.

The "kiddie" tax clearly limits opportunities for shifting unearned income to children. However, it does not eliminate them. It should be emphasized that the "kiddie" tax does not apply to children 14 and over. Thus, tax savings similar to those illustrated in *Example 39* can be obtained with little difficulty where the children have reached 14. Moreover, the "kiddie" tax does not apply until unearned income exceeds $1,500 (in 2004). Consequently, for a child under 14, the first $750 of unearned income bears no tax because of the standard deduction, and the next $750 is taxed at the child's rates. Although the "kiddie" tax severely curtails the amount of tax that could otherwise be saved through shifting income to children, taxpayers attempting to shift modest amounts of income are not affected.

Example 43. In 2005, Father, who earns $90,000 and is in the 35% tax bracket decided to start a college fund for his seven-year-old, Son. To this end, he opened a savings account for Son and deposited $1,000 in the account annually. Assuming the account pays 10% interest annually and the standard deduction is $800, interest income for the next several years would be determined as follows:

Year	Son's Age	Balance	Interest	Son's Tax	After-Tax Income
1	7	$ 1,000	$ 100	$ 0	$ 100
2	8	2,100	210	0	210
3	9	3,310	331	0	331
4	10	4,641	464	0	464
5	11	6,105	611	0	611
6	12	7,716	772	0	772
7	13	9,487	949	15	934
8	14	11,421	1,142	34	1,108

As the table shows, Son pays no taxes at all for the first five years due to the $800 standard deduction. Moreover, for the next several years Son pays taxes at his low 10% rate because his unearned income does not exceed $1,600 and consequently is not subject to the "kiddie" tax. Note that in this case the "kiddie" tax never applies since Son's unearned income begins to exceed $1,600 only after he turns 14. In contrast, if Father had embarked on a similar program for himself, all income would have been taxed at a rate of 35%.

For taxpayers wanting to shift more unearned income to their children, other techniques are available. One way of coping with the "kiddie" tax is by making investments with income that is deferred until the child becomes 14 or older. For example, the taxpayer could give a child Series EE savings bonds. The income from these bonds can be deferred by not electing to report the accumulated interest until after the child turns 14. Interest thereafter would be reported annually. Similarly, discount bonds—those *without* original issue discount—could be purchased. In this case, the interest is not reported until the bond is sold.

The "kiddie" tax applies to unearned income and not earned income. As a result, earned income can be successfully shifted by paying the child for performing some task. Of course, shifting does not occur unless the payment is deductible by the parent. Such payments, when made by a parent directly to a child under 18, have the added benefit of not being subject to social security taxes.

EXCLUDED ECONOMIC INCOME

In arranging one's affairs, it should be observed that certain "economic" income does not fall within the definition of income for tax purposes and thus can be obtained tax-free.

Example 44. Taxpayer R received a gift from her rich uncle of $100,000, which she is considering investing in either a condominium or corporate stocks. The condominium in which she is interested is the one in which she currently lives and rents for $8,000 annually. In lieu of purchasing the condominium, she could continue to rent and invest the $100,000 in preferred stocks paying dividends of 10% annually, or $10,000 of income per year. Assume that R pays taxes at a marginal rate of 30%. The return after taxes on the preferred stock will be 7%, or $7,000. The return from the investment in the condominium is represented by the rent that she does not pay of $8,000, which is nontaxable. In essence, the condominium pays a dividend-in-kind (i.e., shelter), which is tax-exempt. Consequently, R would obtain a higher yield on her investment by purchasing the condominium. Note that income for tax purposes does not include the value of the condominium which would be considered income in the economic sense because the use of the condominium's shelter represents consumption. This same type of analysis applies to all types of investments in consumer goods that provide long-term benefits, such as washers and refrigerators.

PROBLEM MATERIALS

DISCUSSION QUESTIONS

5-1 *Economic versus Tax Concept of Income.* It has been said that the income tax discriminates against the person who lives in a rented home as compared with the person who owns his or her own residence. Comment on the truth of this assertion and why such discrimination may or may not be justified.

5-2 *Net Worth Method.* Explain the circumstances in which the economist's approach to measuring income might be used for tax purposes and what specific steps might be taken to implement such an approach.

5-3 *What Is Income?* Listed below are several items that may or may not constitute income for purposes of economics and income taxes. Indicate whether each item would be considered income for each of these purposes, including comments on why differences, if any, might exist.
   a. Beef raised and consumed by a cattle rancher.
   b. Interest received on state or local bonds.
   c. Air transportation provided by an airline to one of its flight attendants.
   d. Appreciation of XRY stock from $1,000 to $6,000 during the year.
   e. Proceeds collected from an insurance company for a casualty loss and reinvested in similar property.
   f. A loan obtained from a friend.
   g. $105 received from sale of stock purchased one year ago for $100; inflation during the past year averaged five percent.
   h. A gift received as a Christmas present.

5-4 *Cash Equivalent Doctrine.* A financial newsletter recently reported the many advantages that may be obtained from belonging to a barter club or organization. Would tax benefits be included among these advantages (e.g., no taxable income realized on the exchange of services)?

5-5 *Return of Capital Doctrine—General.* Explain the return of capital doctrine and discuss three situations in which the doctrine operates.

5-6   *Indirect Benefits.* A, an assistant manager for a department store, often is required to work overtime to help mark down merchandise for special sales. On these occasions, her employer pays the cost of her evening meal. Does the meal constitute income? Explain.

5-7   *Annual Accounting Period-Planning.* Briefly explain the notion of "income bunching" and why it is a problem.

5-8   *Relationship between Tax and Financial Accounting Methods.* Does conformity with generally accepted accounting principles satisfy the requirement of § 446(c) that income must be clearly reflected? Explain, including some illustrations where income for tax purposes will differ from that for financial accounting purposes.

5-9   *Cash Basis Taxpayer's Receipt of Notes.* Does a cash basis taxpayer recognize income when a note is received or when collections are made?

5-10 *Constructive Receipt Doctrine.* Discuss the planning opportunities related to the cash method of accounting and how these are affected by the constructive receipt doctrine.

5-11 *Accrual Method of Accounting.* Address the following questions:
   a.   When does a taxpayer using the accrual method of accounting normally report income?
   b.   Under what circumstances is an accrual basis taxpayer treated like a cash basis taxpayer for purposes of reporting income?

5-12 *Change in Accounting Method.* T Corporation is considering altering the way in which it accounts for a particular item.
   a.   If T wishes to make the change, how should it proceed?
   b.   Explain the Section 481 adjustment and how T must account for it.

5-13 *Change in Accounting Method—Pre-1954 Balances.* J has operated a furniture store in Littleville, Ohio since 1947. This year, he hired an accountant who immediately discovered that J was not using the accrual method to account for his inventory costs. According to the accountant, a change to this method will result in additional income of $200,000, a portion of which is attributable to the years 1947 through 1953. What would you advise J to do?

5-14 *Changing Accounting Methods: Procedures.* F files the tax returns for his three-year-old son, S. Up until this year, F had always reported the interest on S's Series EE savings bonds annually. F now wishes to report the interest income when the bonds are redeemed (e.g., when the child reaches age 14). Can F change the way he reports the interest? If so, how?

5-15 *What Is an Accounting Method?* This year, T hired a new accountant, A. As part of A's routine review procedures, A determined that T's previous accountant had improperly computed the gross profit percentage to be used in recognizing income on an installment sale. Based on the previous accountant's calculation, 40 percent of each year's receipts were to be included in income, whereas according to A's calculation the proper percentage was 50 percent. Explain what A should do upon finding the discrepancy.

5-16 *Claim of Right.* Consider the questions below.
   a.   Is the application of the claim of right doctrine limited to situations that involve only contested income? Explain.
   b.   Explain the difference between the claim of right and constructive receipt doctrines.

5-17 *Prepaid Rent.* In light of the tax treatment, should landlords of apartment complexes characterize an initial $500 deposit from their tenants as a security deposit or as a payment of the last month's rent in advance? Explain.

5-18 *Prepaid Services.* Identify several types of services where the accrual basis provider will not be permitted to defer any prepayments of income related to such services. Explain.

5-19 *Long-Term Contracts.* Indicate which method of accounting for long-term contracts—completed contract or percentage of completion—the taxpayer may use in the following situations. Assume each contract is considered a long-term contract unless otherwise implied.
   a. A contract to build an office building. The taxpayer's annual gross receipts for the past five years have exceeded $11 million.
   b. A contract to build a home to be finished next year. The taxpayer's annual gross receipts for the last five years have exceeded $11 million.
   c. A contract to build a high-rise apartment complex containing 120 units. The contractor's average gross receipts are $11 million.
   d. A contract to manufacture 15,000 seats for a football stadium. The taxpayer has several contracts for this type of seat. Average gross receipts are $12 million.
   e. A contract to manufacture a special part for NASA's space shuttles. Average annual gross receipts were $12 million.

5-20 *Taxpayer Identification—Family Trusts.* In recent years, many taxpayers have fallen victim to vendors of the so-called family trust tax shelter. Under this arrangement the taxpayer signs a contractual agreement entitling the trust to all of the taxpayer's income which is subsequently distributed to the beneficiaries of the trust. Explain how this arrangement is supposed to save taxes and why it fails.

5-21 *Income Reporting by Partnerships and S Corporations.* Explain how partners and shareholders in S corporations may defer the reporting of income by having their respective entities select fiscal years for reporting rather than calendar years.

5-22 *Income from Community Property.* Under what circumstances will knowledge of the community property system be relevant? Is it necessary for persons residing in common law states to understand the community property system?

5-23 *Planning—Timing Income Recognition.* Although it is generally desirable to defer income recognition and the related taxes. when would acceleration of income be preferred?

5-24 *Planning—Income Splitting.* How might R, who operates a shoe store as a sole proprietorship, reduce the taxes that are imposed on his family using income-splitting techniques?

5-25 *"Kiddie" Tax.* R has been advised that due to changes in the tax law over the years he can no longer save taxes by shifting income to his children.
   a. Explain the origin of such advice.
   b. Refer to *Example 43* in this chapter. Determine how much more Father is able to accumulate for Son's education by using the savings account over the period shown in the example.

❓ YOU MAKE THE CALL

5-26 In the last episode in the adventures of Dr. Will Floss, the tax-evading dentist identified earlier in this chapter, he was found exploring the cavities of his patient's mouth. As may be remembered, Dr. Floss had just made a deal with a patient whereby he exchanged a root canal for some carpet complete with pad and installation. Floss's accountant, Al, was faced with a dilemma. After dumping his records on Al's desk, Floss had proudly proclaimed that it was another great year. Al could remember his exact words: "Made over $200,000 but reported only $50,000. Not bad," said Floss. "Am I glad I talked to Dr. Moller!" Unfortunately, Al had to lower the boom on Floss's plan, explaining to him that he was required to report his barter income. However, Floss has stated flatly that he will not report the income. "If Moller doesn't report his, I'm not reporting mine," insists Floss. What should Al the accountant do about his client Floss and his friend Moller? If Floss goes to another accountant, does Al have any responsibilities?

PROBLEMS

5-27 *What Is Income?* In each of the following situations indicate whether taxable income should be recognized.

    a. Q purchased an older home for $20,000. Shortly after its purchase, the area in which it was located was designated a historical neighborhood, causing its value to rise to $50,000.

    b. R, a long-time employee of XYZ Inc., purchased one of the company's cars worth $7,000 for $3,000.

    c. I borrowed $10,000 secured by property that had an adjusted basis of $3,000 and a fair market value of $15,000.

    d. S, a 60 percent shareholder in STV Corporation, uses a company car 70 percent of the time for business and 30 percent for personal purposes. The rental value of the car is $200 per month.

5-28 *What Is Income?* In each of the following situations indicate whether taxable income should be recognized.

    a. R discovered oil on his farm, causing the value of his land to increase by $100 million.

    b. While jogging, L found a portable stereo radio valued at $200.

    c. E agreed to rent his lake cottage to F for $1,000 during the summer. After living there for two weeks, E and F agreed that E would only charge $700 if F made certain improvements.

    d. D borrowed $100,000, $20,000 each from S, T, U, V, and W. He gave them each a one-year note bearing interest at a rate of 25 percent. At the end of the year, D borrowed $200,000 from X, promising to pay him back in one year plus 30 percent interest. D used part of the $200,000 from X to pay the interest due to S, T, U, V, and W. D also convinced them to extend the original notes for another year. D has no intention of ever repaying the principal of the notes.

5-29 *What Is Income?* In each of the following situations indicate whether taxable income should be recognized.

    a. L sued her former employer for sex discrimination evidenced in his compensation policy. She was awarded $100,000, $39,000 of which represented reimbursement for mental anguish.

    b. M, a sales clerk for a department store, purchased a microwave oven from the store's appliance department. The store has a policy allowing employees a 10 percent discount. This discount results in $45 savings to M.

    c. R received a bottle of perfume and a case of grapefruit from her boss at the annual Christmas party. The items were valued at $25.

5-30 *Constructive Receipt.* When would a cash basis taxpayer recognize income in the following situations? Assume the taxpayer reports on a calendar year.

    a. R, a traveling salesperson, was out of town on payday, December 31. He picked up his check when he arrived back on January 3.

b. C owns a bond with interest coupons due and payable on December 31. C clipped the coupons and redeemed them on January 7.

c. R is an officer and controlling shareholder in XYZ Corporation. In December the corporation authorized bonuses for all officers. The bonus was paid in February of the following year.

5-31 *Constructive Receipt.* For each of the following situations, indicate whether the taxpayer has constructively received the income.

a. R received a bonus as top salesperson of the year. He received the check for $20,000 at 10 p.m. on December 31 at a New Year's Eve party. All the banks were closed.

b. On January 3, D received the check for January's rent of her duplex. The envelope was postmarked December 31.

c. On December 25, C Corporation rewarded its top executive, E, with 100 shares of stock for a job well done. E was unable to find a buyer until March 15 of the following year.

d. Immediately after receiving her check on December 31, Z went to her employer's bank to cash it. The bank would not cash it since the employer's account was overdrawn.

5-32 *Constructive Receipt.* For each of the following situations, indicate whether the taxpayer has constructively received the income.

a. X Corporation declared a dividend on December 15 and mailed dividend checks on December 28. R received her check for $200 on January 4.

b. F owns a small apartment complex. His son, S, lives in one of the units and manages the complex. Several tenants left their January rent checks with S during the last week of December. S delivered the checks to his father in January.

c. This year, the cash surrender value of L's life insurance policy increased by $500. In order to obtain the value, L must cancel the policy.

5-33 *Changes in Accounting Method.* JB and his sons have operated a small "general store" in Backwoods, Idaho, since 1960. This year, JB hired a new accountant, who immediately told him he should be using the accrual method to account for his inventories and related sales and receivables. The receivables were primarily attributable to sales of seed to farmers as well as appliances. JB has always used the cash method of accounting, reporting all of his income when he receives it and deducting all costs when paid. According to the accountant, as of the close of the current year, JB had $70,000 in receivables outstanding (none of which had been reported in income), inventory of $130,000 (all expensed), and outstanding accounts payable for recent purchases of inventory of $20,000.

a. If the IRS audits JB and requires him to change his method of accounting, what is the adjustment amount and when will JB report it?

b. Same as (a) except JB voluntarily changes his method of accounting prior to the audit.

c. If JB changes to the accrual method of accounting to account for inventories and sales, may he continue to report other items of income (e.g., interest income) and expense (e.g., supplies) using the cash method?

5-34 *Advanced Payments for Goods.* HIJ Furniture, an accrual basis company for both tax and financial accounting purposes, normally does not sell the items displayed in its showrooms, nor does it keep those items in stock. Instead, it obtains partial payment from the customer and orders the items directly from the manufacturer. During 2005, HIJ collected $60,000 with respect to furniture sales still on order at the close of the year. (The partial payments collected by HIJ do not exceed their cost for the items ordered.) Must HIJ report any of the $60,000 as income in 2005?

5-35 *Percentage of Completion.* THZ Corporation is a large construction company. This year it contracted with the city of Old York to build a new performing arts center for a price of $5,000,000. Estimated total costs of the project were $4,000,000. Annual costs incurred were as follows:

2006.	$2,000,000
2007.	500,000
2008.	1,000,000
Total.	$3,500,000

    a. What method(s) of accounting may the corporation use to report income from the project?

    b. How much income would be reported each year under the percentage of completion method?

    c. Would any interest be due to (or from) the IRS as a result of this contract? If so, compute for the first year only, assuming the taxpayer is in the 34 percent tax bracket and the interest rate is 10 percent.

5-36 *U.S. Savings Bonds.* During 2005, S purchased U.S. Government Series EE Bonds for $700. The redemption value of the bonds at the end of the year was $756.

    a. What options are available to S with respect to reporting the income from the bonds?

    b. What advantage might be obtained by exchanging the Series EE Bonds for Series HH Bonds?

5-37 *Contested Income.* In 2005, GLX Company, an accrual basis taxpayer, received $10,000 for supplying running shoes to T for sale in his sporting goods store. During 2005, T claimed the shoes had defective soles and requested GLX to refund the $10,000 payment.

    a. Must GLX report any of the $10,000 as income in 2005?

    b. Had GLX not received payment in 2005, would your answer in (a) change?

5-38 *Deposits and Prepaid Rents.* Q owns several duplexes. From each new tenant she requires a $150 security deposit and $300 for the last month's rent. The deposit is refundable assuming the tenant complies with all the terms of the lease. During the year, Q collected $1,000 in deposits and $2,400 of prepaid rents for the last month of occupancy. In addition, she refunded $400 to previous tenants but withheld $300 due to damages. How much must Q include in income assuming she is an accrual basis taxpayer?

5-39 *Prepaid Service Income: Accrual Method.*

    a. LL Corporation, a calendar year and accrual basis taxpayer, is engaged in the lawn care business, providing fertilizer treatments. It sells one-, two- and three-year contracts. Each contract provides that the customer will receive four treatments (fall, winter, spring and summer). An analysis of its customer contracts revealed that it received $200,000 during the fall for a one-year contract. Each of these customers will receive one treatment in 2005 and three treatments in 2006. In its financial accounting statements, the company reports the income as services are performed. What amount of income must the corporation report in 2005 and 2006?

    b. Same as (a) above except the contracts are for two years. The customers will receive one treatment in 2005, four treatments in 2006 and three treatments in 2007.

    c. A professional basketball team that reports on the calendar year and uses the accrual method collected $700,000 in pre-season ticket sales in August and September of 2005. Of its 41-game home season, 15 games were played *prior to* *the end* of the year. In its financial statements, the organization reports the income as the games are played. What amount must be included in income in 2005?

    d. A posh resort hotel in Florida reports on the calendar year and uses the accrual method. During 2005, it collected $10,000 in advance payments for rooms to be rented during January and February 2006. What amount of income must be included in 2005 and 2006?

5-40   *Income from Transferred Property.* E's grandmother owns several vending machines on campus. To help him through college, she allows E to collect and keep all the receipts from the machines. During the year, E spent approximately two hours a month to collect $5,000. Who must report the income and what is the amount to be included?

5-41   *Partnership Income.* QRS, a partnership, had taxable income of $120,000 for the fiscal year ended September 30, 2005. For the first quarter ending December 31, 2005, taxable income was $30,000. During 2005, Q, a partner with a 30 percent interest in profits and losses, withdrew $1,000 per month for a total of $12,000. What is Q's taxable income from QRS for 2005?

5-42   *Reporting Interest Income.* On November 1, 2004, G received a substantial inheritance and promptly made several investments. Indicate in each of the following cases the amount of interest income that he must report and the period in which the income is properly reported, assuming that G uses (1) the cash method of accounting, or (2) the accrual method of accounting. G reports using the calendar year.

    a. G purchased a $10,000, 90-day U.S. Treasury bill at 99. The bill matured on January 30, 2005, when G redeemed it at par.

    b. G purchased $100,000 of AFN Inc. 10 percent bonds for $95,000. The bonds were issued at par in 1996. The bonds pay interest semiannually on March 1 and September 1. On March 1, 2005, G received an interest payment of $5,000.

5-43   *Interest-Free Loans.* This year Dr. W, an orthopedic surgeon, and her husband, H, an attorney, established a trust for their five-year-old daughter, D. In conjunction with setting up the trust, the couple loaned the trust $200,000 payable on demand without interest. Assuming the interest that should have been charged under the applicable rate was $23,000, explain the effect of the loan on all of the parties.

5-44   *Shareholder Advances.* In 1978, J started ACC Corporation, a construction company. J owns all of the stock of the corporation and is also its president. Like many owners of closely-held corporations, J pretty much treats the corporation's checkbook as his own. He often asks the bookkeeper to make out checks to him that he ostensibly uses for business purposes. Over time, J does repay the amounts used for personal purposes, or turns in receipts for amounts used for business. In the meantime, the bookkeeper charges these checks to a special account titled "J Suspense." Upon the accountant's review this year, he noted that the account showed a balance of $15,000 (indicating an amount due from J). Explain the tax consequences.

5-45   *Interest-Free Loans.* F is chief executive officer of CVC Corporation and has taxable income in excess of $200,000 annually. During the year, he loaned his 20-year-old son, S, $30,000, payable on demand without interest. S promptly invested the $30,000 and earned $1,200, which was his only income during the year.

    a. Assuming the interest that should have been charged under applicable rate is $3,000, compute the effect of the loan on the taxable income of both F and S.

    b. Would F be able to shift income to his son if he had made a loan of only $9,000?

5-46   *Code § 7872: Exceptions.* For each of the following independent cases, indicate the income and gift tax consequences for both the lender and the borrower.

a. J loaned his 19-year-old son, K, $8,000 interest-free, which K used to purchase a car. K had $400 investment income from a savings account for the year.

b. Same as (a) except K decided to invest the money in a certificate of deposit yielding $800 of interest income producing a total net investment income of $1,200 for the year.

c. G loaned her 29-year-old daughter, D, $50,000 interest-free to help her acquire a franchise for a fast-food restaurant. All of D's funds were invested in the business and consequently she had no investment income for the year.

d. P Corporation loaned its sole shareholder, Q, $150,000 interest-free.

e. Same as (d) except Q owns no stock in P but is simply a key employee.

5-47 *Cash Method Eligibility.* Given the facts below, indicate whether the taxpayer may use the cash method for 2005 in the following situations.

a. Sweatshirt Corporation, a publicly traded corporation: annual gross receipts for 2002 and previous years were $1 million annually; gross receipts for 2003 were $3 million; and for 2004, $8 million.

b. Dewey, Cheatham, and Howe, a national public accounting firm, operated as a partnership. Annual gross receipts for the past five years have exceeded $50 million.

c. McSwane, McMillan, and McClain, Inc., an architectural firm, operated as a regular C corporation. Annual gross receipts for the past two years have exceeded $7 million. McSwane, McMillan, and McClain own all of the stock and perform services for the firm.

d. Buttons and Bows, Inc., an S corporation.

e. A trust established for John Doe.

f. Plantation Office Park, a publicly traded limited partnership: annual gross receipts have never exceeded $2 million. The partnership is a tax shelter.

5-48 *Accrual Method of Accounting.* Frank's Casing Crew and Rental Tools Inc. uses the accrual method of accounting and reports using the calendar year. The corporation sells oil pipes, leases equipment used in oil fields, and provides crews necessary to operate the leased equipment. The company's customers are primarily large oil companies. The company's contracts provide that payment is due when it sends the customer an invoice that includes all supporting documentation (i.e., job tickets, equipment tickets, and third party charges). In 2005, the company finished several jobs but did not invoice the customers until after year-end because it had not yet received a third party's invoice. When should the corporation report the income from these contracts?

5-49 *Accrual Method of Accounting.* N Corporation operates a chain of coffee shops in various locations throughout Indiana. It uses the accrual method of accounting and reports using the calendar year. In 2006, its expenses exceeded its revenue resulting in a net operating loss (NOL). Like federal law, Indiana's state law, permits corporations to carry back an NOL to prior years where it can be used to offset such year's taxable income, enabling the corporation to obtain a refund of previously paid Indiana state income taxes. (Note that state income taxes are deductible business expenses so a recovery of such expenses is taxable income.) The Indiana Department of Revenue has the right to examine any refund claim before determining whether to allow the claim and the refund amount. In 2007, the corporation filed the proper forms to carry back the NOL, seeking a refund of part of the state income taxes it had paid in previous years. In 2008, N received a refund of $100,000. When should N report the income?

5-50 *Accrual Method of Accounting.* Giant Corp. operates retail stores throughout the country. It uses the accrual method of accounting and reports using the calendar year. Each store offers film processing. Customers wanting film developed put the film in an order envelope and place the envelope in a drop box. Finished prints are produced primarily by Giant's own processing labs but also unrelated labs. The labs develop the film using highly specialized equipment and a complex chemical process, normally returning the finished prints within two days of when their couriers pick up the film. The finished prints are held for customer pick-up at the stores. Customers are not required to buy the prints unless they are completely satisfied. Store employees review the unsold prints on hand every 30 days and remind customers by phone or mail that their prints are available. Finished prints that are unclaimed after 120 days or customer rejects are discarded. Giant owns the finished prints until either a customer purchases them or they are discarded. Only a small percentage of customers do not purchase the finished prints. Upon audit, the IRS asserted that Giant should have to report the income when the stores receive the finished prints. Indicate whether the agent is correct or incorrect and explain the reasons for your answer.

5-51   *Continuous Tax Return Problem.*

Previous Facts: Larry and Cathy Zepp have been married 19 years. Larry is 62 years old (Social Security number 123-45-6789) while Cathy is 50 years old (Social Security number 123-45-6788). They live at 1234 Elm Dr. in Des Moines, Iowa 50311. Larry is a salesman employed by DSK Industries. This year he earned $110,000 (income tax withheld was $17,000). Cathy recently completed a graduate degree in computer technology. She continues to freelance as an independent contractor in computer graphics. Her earnings from various engagements were $12,000. Her only expenses were for miscellaneous office supplies of $3,000. She paid estimated taxes during the year of $1,000 ($250 on each due date). Other income earned by the couple included interest income of $3,000 from a certificate of deposit and $975 of interest from tax-exempt bonds issued by the State of Iowa. The couple owns a duplex that it rents out. Annual rentals were $8,000 and rental expenses (e.g., maintenance, utilities, depreciation) were $3,000. Other expenses paid during the year included:

Unreimbursed medical expenses....................	$9,000
Interest on home mortgage	12,000
Real property taxes on home......................	1,900
Charitable contributions..........................	1,000
Rental of safety deposit box to hold certain investments . .	100
Unreimbursed employee business expenses of Larry	3,000

Assume that all of the expenses except their business expenses are incurred jointly.

- The Zepps have two children, a son Wrigley F. Zepp (111-33-4444, 12/1/1986)) and a daughter: Apple A. Zepp (111-33-4445, 1/4/1992). Both children lived with them the entire year. Apple is considered legally blind.
- Apple received interest income of $3,000.

New Facts

This morning's mail contained a note from Larry Zepp (see *continuous tax return problem in* Chapter 3) including a Schedule K-1 from a calendar-year partnership in which he is a small investor. The relevant portions of the Schedule K-1 are shown below.

Prepare Form 1040 for the Zepps.

5-52   *Continuous Tax Return Problem. Additional Questions.* Answer the following questions relating to the *continuous tax return problem* above.

a. According to the Schedule K-1, Larry Zepp did not receive any distributions from the partnership. Is he required to include the Schedule K-1 income on his personal income tax return if he did not receive any income? Explain.

6511

Schedule K-1 (Form 1065)	2004			

Department of the Treasury
Internal Revenue Service

Tax year beginning _____ , 2004
and ending _____ , 20___

Partner's Share of Income, Deductions, Credits, etc. ▶ See back of form and separate instructions.

☐ Final K-1   ☐ Amended K-1   OMB No. 1545-0099

Part III	Partner's Share of Current Year Income, Deductions, Credits, and Other Items

Part I	**Information About the Partnership**

A Partnership's employer identification number
75-

B Partnership's name, address, city, state, and ZIP code

KLM Associates

3214 Memorial

Houston, TX 77452

C IRS Center where partnership filed return

D ☐ Check if this is a publicly traded partnership (PTP)

E ☐ Tax shelter registration number, if any _____

F ☐ Check if Form 8271 is attached

Part II	**Information About the Partner**

G Partner's identifying number
123-45-6789

H Partner's name, address, city, state, and ZIP code

Larry L. Zepp

1234 Elm Drive

Des Moines, IA 50311

I ☐ General partner or LLC member-manager   ☑ Limited partner or other LLC member

J ☐ Domestic partner   ☐ Foreign partner

K What type of entity is this partner? _____

L Partner's share of profit, loss, and capital:

	Beginning		**Ending**	
Profit		%		%
Loss		%		%
Capital		%		%

M Partner's share of liabilities at year end:

Nonrecourse . . . . $_____

Qualified nonrecourse financing . . $_____

Recourse . . . . $_____

N Partner's capital account analysis:

Beginning capital account . . . . $_____

Capital contributed during the year . $_____

Current year increase (decrease) . . $_____

Withdrawals & distributions . . . $(_____)

Ending capital account . . . . $_____

☐ Tax basis ☐ GAAP ☐ Section 704(b) book
☐ Other (explain)

1 Ordinary business income (loss) **600**		**15** Credits & credit recapture	
2 Net rental real estate income (loss)			
3 Other net rental income (loss)		**16** Foreign transactions	
4 Guaranteed payments			
5 Interest income **400**			
6a Ordinary dividends			
6b Qualified dividends			
7 Royalties			
8 Net short-term capital gain (loss)			
9a Net long-term capital gain (loss)		**17** Alternative minimum tax (AMT) items	
9b Collectibles (28%) gain (loss)			
9c Unrecaptured section 1250 gain			
10 Net section 1231 gain (loss)		**18** Tax-exempt income and nondeductible expenses	
11 Other income (loss)			
12 Section 179 deduction		**19** Distributions	
13 Other deductions		**20** Other information	
14 Self-employment earnings (loss)			

See attached statement for additional information.

For IRS Use Only

For Privacy Act and Paperwork Reduction Act Notice, see Instructions for Form 1065.   Cat. No. 11394R   Schedule K-1 (Form 1065) 2004

b. Is the partnership income considered self-employment income of Larry Zepp for purposes of computing any self-employment tax he might owe? Explain.

5-53 *Shifting Income to Children.* Mr. and Mrs. D wish to shift income to their seven-year-old son, C, to be used for his college education. Explain whether the following would serve their goals or, alternatively, how they affect any technique designed to shift income.

a. Paying C an allowance for making his bed and picking up his clothes.

b. Paying C for helping to wash cars at his dad's car wash.

c. Buying C Series EE Savings Bonds.

d. Arranging to have Mrs. D's employer pay C part of her salary.

e. The social security rules.

f. The rules governing personal exemptions.

CUMULATIVE PROBLEM

5-54 David K. Gibbs, age 37, and his wife Barbara, age 33, have two children, Chris and Ellen, ages 2 and 12. David is employed as an engineer for an oil company, and his wife recently completed a degree in accounting and will begin working for a public accounting firm next year. David has compiled the following information for your use in preparing his tax return for 2004.

1. For the current year, David received a salary of $50,000. His employer withheld Federal income taxes of $9,000 and the appropriate amount of FICA taxes.

2. At the annual Christmas party, he received a card indicating that he would receive a bonus of $3,000 for his good work during the year. The bonus check was placed in his mailbox at work on December 30. Since David was out of town for the holidays, he did not pick up the bonus check until January 2.

3. A bond issued by AM&T Inc. was sold on May 30, 2004 for $9,700, $700 of which represented interest accrued to the date of the sale. The Gibbs had purchased the bond (issued at par value of $10,000 on March 1, 1984) in 2000 for $10,000.

4. The couple has a $500 U.S. Savings Bond, which they purchased for $300 and gave to their daughter several years ago. The proper election to report the income from the bond annually was made. The bond's redemption value increased $30 this year.

5. David was an instant winner in the state lottery and won $50.

6. The Gibbs sold 100 shares of stock in JB Corporation for $10,000. They had purchased the stock on June 1, 1996 for $14,000.

7. During the year, Barbara prepared a number of tax returns for which she received $5,000. Her only deductible expense incurred in performing these services was $100 for some tax software.

8. The couple's only itemized deductions were medical expenses of $3,000, interest on their home mortgage of $7,500, and property taxes on their home of $900.

Compute Mr. and Mrs. Gibbs' Federal income tax liability (or refund) for 2004. If a tax return is required by your instructor, prepare Form 1040, including Schedules A and B.

RESEARCH PROBLEMS

5-55 During the year, J, a college accounting professor, received complimentary copies of various textbooks from numerous publishers. J gives some of these books to students and the school library. J also keeps some of the books for his personal use and reference. A few times during the year J sold an unwanted text to a wholesale book dealer who periodically checked with him and other professors for texts. Must J report any income related to receipt of these books?

5-56 R recently became a member of a religious order. As a member, she was subject to the organization's complete control. The organization often required its members to terminate their employment in order to work in other jobs consistent with the organization's philosophy. For example, the organization supplied personnel to missions, hospitals, and schools. The organization also requires all members to take an oath of poverty and pay over all their earnings to it. Members' living expenses are paid for by the organization out of its own funds. Is R taxed on her earnings?

5-57 In each of the following cases, indicate who is responsible for reporting the income.
   a. Dr. A instructed the hospital for which he worked to pay his salary to his daughter C.
   b. R, a famous entertainer, agreed to perform at a concert gratuitously (without fee) for the benefit of a charitable organization.
   c. In a contest for the best essay on why education is important, T, age 25, won the right to designate a person under 17 to receive $1,000.

5-58 M owed her good friend, F, $20,000. In addition, M planned on making a charitable contribution to her church of $10,000. Instead of using cash to pay her friend and to make the contribution, M is considering transferring stock to each in the appropriate amount. The stock is currently worth $100 per share. M had purchased the 300 shares of stock several years ago for $6,000 ($20 per share). Will M realize any income if she transfers the stock rather than paying cash?

5-59 Sam Sellit is a salesperson for Panoramic Pools of St. Louis, a construction company that builds and sells prefabricated swimming pools. Over the past several years, Sam has progressed to become the top salesperson for the St. Louis franchise. Sam has done so well that he is considering purchasing his own franchise and starting a company in San Antonio. This year he contacted the home office in Pittsburgh about the possibility of opening up his own shop. The vice president in charge of expansion, Greg Grow, suggested that the two of them meet at the company's annual meeting of franchisees in Orlando. Greg knew that Sam, although not a franchisee, would be attending because he was the top salesperson in the St. Louis office, and the company invites the top salesperson from each office as well as his or her spouse to attend the meeting.

   While at the four-day meeting (Tuesday through Friday) in Orlando, Sam and his wife, Sue, met with Greg and discussed the potential venture. In addition, Greg allowed Sam and Sue to attend the parts of the meeting that were only for franchisees so that they could get a glimpse of how the company operated. Of course, while they were in Orlando, Sam and his wife visited all of the tourist attractions. On Tuesday, there were no meetings scheduled and everyone spent the day at Disney World and Epcot Center. On Thursday afternoon, no meetings were scheduled and the couple went with Greg and his wife to Sea World. Sam attended meetings for several hours on Friday while his wife played golf. The couple stayed over through Sunday and continued their sightseeing activities.

   The company picked up the tab for the couple's trip, reimbursing Sam $3,500 which included the costs of air fare, meals, lodging, and entertainment. What are the tax consequences to Sam?

5-60 Large Corporation manufactures computers. Its total sales of computers last year were well over $100 million. With each computer it offers a three-year warranty, covering parts and labor. The company estimates the future costs of warranty work related to current-year sales and defers the recognition of income until such time that it expects the warranty work will be done. Currently, the corporation reports 60 percent of the warranty income in the year of sale because the majority of warranty work occurs shortly after the computer has been sold. Thirty percent of the warranty income is reported in the second year of the warranty, and the remaining 10 percent is reported in the last year of the warranty. The company's estimates were based on sophisticated statistical techniques. Such techniques have produced estimates that appear extremely accurate based on the past ten years of data. No insurance is purchased to cover the warranty risk. Upon audit this year, the IRS agent indicated that the company cannot defer the warranty income and assessed a large tax deficiency. Advise the taxpayer as to whether it should pay the additional tax or pursue the matter in court.

5-61 Several years ago, R started his own delivery company, RT Haulers Inc. (RTH). The corporation is an accrual basis taxpayer. The corporation grew quickly, in part because of the excellent service that it was able to offer. Historically, the company has accrued its income when its services were completed. If the customer objected to the manner in which the services were performed (e.g., late delivery, damaged goods), RTH gave the client a credit against any future services that it might provide. RTH is now considering changing its agreements with customers to provide for a seven day acceptance period during which the customer could reject the services, in which case the customer would not have any obligation to pay. Advise the client regarding when its income should be reported, specifically addressing how the change in terms might impact the reporting of future service revenues.

5-62 Basinger Hauling is a trucking company that does business primarily on the west coast and in Mexico and Canada. Its headquarters are in Portland, Oregon. The company generally pays its drivers a specific rate, depending on a variety of factors such as miles driven, load weight, weather, unloading, fuel costs and the like. The company treats eight percent of each driver's compensation as a reimbursement for meals and lodging. Consequently, the company does not pay employment taxes (social security and Medicare) on the portion considered a reimbursement and does not include the reimbursement on the driver's W-2 form, reporting the amount representing wage income. Advise the client regarding this practice.

Chapter 6

GROSS INCOME: INCLUSIONS AND EXCLUSIONS

LEARNING OBJECTIVES

Upon completion of this chapter you will be able to:

- Identify which items an individual taxpayer must include in the computation of gross income

- Determine which items an individual taxpayer can exclude from the computation of gross income

- Understand generally what goals Congress had in mind in passing the applicable rules and exceptions for inclusions and exclusions

- Recognize tax planning opportunities related to the more common types of income inclusions and exclusions available to individual taxpayers

CHAPTER OUTLINE

INTRODUCTION

While the tax law makes it clear that any type of gain, benefit, profit, or other increase in wealth is potentially taxable, in reality not all income is within the grasp of the IRS. As a practical matter, there are a number of special rules that must be observed before the final treatment of any particular benefit can be determined. For example, Congress has specifically exempted several types of income from tax such as interest on state and local bonds, scholarships, gifts, and inheritances. In addition, special provisions exist that clarify the treatment of a long list of possible income items such as annuities, alimony, and employee benefits. Because of these rules, the concept of income is not quite as comprehensive as perhaps suggested in Chapter 5. As a result, any particular item initially identified as "income" might ultimately fall into one of the following three categories:

- ▶ Taxable (i.e., totally includible)
- ▶ Nontaxable (i.e., excluded in full)
- ▶ Taxable in part and nontaxable in part

This chapter examines the more frequently encountered sources of income. To provide some order and logic to the presentation, the various sources of income are grouped and discussed as follows:

- ▸ Investment income (dividends, interest, annuities)
- ▸ Employee compensation and fringe benefits
- ▸ Personal transfers (gifts, inheritances, alimony)
- ▸ Transfers by unrelated individuals (life insurance, prizes, scholarships)
- ▸ Business income
- ▸ Miscellaneous items

INVESTMENT INCOME

As shown in Exhibit 6-1, the vast majority of the income reported by individuals comes in some form of employee compensation such as salaries and wages (75.8 percent of all reported income for 2000). However, the income of many individuals is also likely to contain some type of investment income. Common examples of investment income—sometimes referred to as unearned income—include

- ▸ Dividends
- ▸ Interest
- ▸ Annuities
- ▸ Rents

For the most part, these income items present little problem for taxpayers. Each is usually fully taxable as ordinary income. In addition, to make reporting and compliance easier, those who pay dividends, interest, and annuities during the taxable year normally must report such payments to both the taxpayer and the IRS on the appropriate Form 1099. Nevertheless, special rules often apply in determining not only the amount of income that must be reported but also when it must be reported. The treatment of each is discussed below.

EXHIBIT 6-1
Sources of Income 2000

Type of Income	Percent of Returns Showing	Percent of All Income Reported
Salaries and wages	85.52%*	75.80%
Taxable interest	48.95	2.30
Dividends	24.12	1.63
Pensions and annuities	17.69	5.99
Business or profession net income	10.55	4.11
Net capital loss	10.21	−.49
Social Security benefits	8.32	1.56
Net capital gain	8.31	4.07
Unemployment compensation	8.00	.71
Business or profession net loss	3.72	−.56
Tax-exempt interest	3.42	.89
Rent net loss	3.38	−.58
Rent net income	3.21	.80
Partnership and S corporation net income	3.08	4.69
Partnership and S corporation net loss	1.69	−.92
Farm net loss	1.10	−.33
Royalty net income	.82	.10
Sales of property other than capital assets, net loss	.68	−.14
Sales of property other than capital assets, net gain	.59	.11
Farm net income	.43	.10
Estate or trust net income	.39	.17
Estate or trust net loss	.03	−.01
Royalty net loss	.02	−.00

*Preliminary estimates based on samples taken from 130,201,415 individual returns filed in 2002.
Source: *Statistics of Income Bulletin*, Winter 2003–2004. Volume 23, Number 3, Internal Revenue Service, Washington, D.C. 2004.

DIVIDENDS

Today it is not uncommon for even the smallest investor to own stock in a corporation or an interest in a mutual fund. Those who do are likely to obtain part of their investment return in the form of dividends. One of the high-profile debates surrounding the Jobs and Growth Tax Relief Reconciliation Act of 2003 concerned the taxation of dividends. The original proposal of the administration called for the complete exclusion for dividends in order to address the potential problem of double taxation. However, the final legislation did not adopt such a sweeping measure. Instead, the Act reduced the tax rates imposed on dividends to what they are for capital gains, 5 percent for taxpayers whose income falls in the 10 percent and 15 percent ordinary income tax brackets and 15 percent for all other taxpayers. The reduced rate generally applies to dividends from all domestic corporations and foreign corporations whose stock is readily tradable on an established U.S. securities market. Dividends from other foreign corporations, however, may be subject to special rules. The new low rates apply *only* to dividends paid with respect to stock (common or preferred).

The definition of a dividend remains the same in applying the new rule. Only distributions made out of current or accumulated earnings and profits (E&P) qualify as dividends. Amounts distributed in excess of E&P are nontaxable returns of capital to the extent of the shareholder's basis in the stock and the balance is capital gain.

Dividends received from regulated investment companies (mutual funds) would generally be eligible for the reduced rate (if such dividends were received by the fund after 2002).

Dividends generally would not be eligible for the lower rate if the stock was held for 60 days or less. Special rules apply to dividends related to short sales. In addition, the lower rate does not apply if dividends are included as "investment income" for purposes of determining the amount of investment interest expense that can be deducted. If the taxpayer elects not to include the dividends for this purpose, the lower rate applies. Special rules also apply to § 306 stock and "extraordinary dividends" under § 1059. The reduced rates also apply for purposes of computing the alternative minimum tax.

Note that while dividends are taxed at the same rates as capital gains, they are not included in the capital gain and loss netting process.

Dividends received by tax deferred investment accounts [e.g., 401(k) plans, individual retirement accounts, Keogh plans] receive no special treatment and are taxed as ordinary income when distributed from the plan.

Note that this change represents a major philosophical shift that has little precedent in tax history. Dividends received by individuals have historically been taxed as ordinary income with little or no special treatment. Although a small exclusion for dividends once existed, dividends have otherwise been treated the same as ordinary income. It should also be observed that there is no special treatment for interest income.

The section that follows examines the tax treatment of the various dividends that a taxpayer is most likely to receive.

Corporate Dividends. The vast majority of all distributions made by corporations to their shareholders are considered dividends and are fully taxable as ordinary income. Technically, however, a distribution made by a corporation is treated as a *dividend* only to the extent that it is out of the corporation's current or accumulated *earnings and profits*, or *E&P* as it is commonly called.[1] Amounts not considered dividends because the distribution exceeds E&P are treated as nontaxable returns of capital to the extent of the shareholder's basis in the stock. In effect, the nondividend portion of the distribution is applied to and reduces the basis of the stock. Should the return of capital distribution exceed the shareholder's basis, the excess is capital gain. In applying these rules, all distributions by corporations are deemed to be distributions of E&P to the extent thereof.

> **Example 1.** C, Inc. distributes $100,000 to shareholders when its current E&P is $60,000 and it has no accumulated E&P. T, a 10% shareholder, has a basis in C, Inc. stock of $3,000. T receives $10,000, of which $6,000 (10% × $60,000) is from C's current E&P. Thus, T has a $6,000 taxable dividend; the $3,000 equal to his basis in the stock is a nontaxable return of investment, and the remaining $1,000 is capital gain. T's basis in the stock after the distribution will be zero.

As noted above, dividends are fully taxable as ordinary income.[2] However, as explained in Chapter 3, in order to prevent multiple taxation of dividends, corporate taxpayers are entitled to a special dividends-received deduction. This special deduction (discussed more fully in Chapter 19) normally entitles the corporation to deduct 70 percent of the dividend received.[3]

---

[1]   §§ 301 and 316.

[2]   Special rules apply to the rare distribution of noncash property (e.g., land). See §§ 301(b) and (d).

[3]   §§ 243 through 246. Generally, the deduction is a percentage of the dividends received from a domestic corporation determined as follows: (1) 70% when the stock ownership percentage (SOP) is less than 20%, (2) 80% when the SOP is 20% or more but less than 80%, and (3) 100% when the SOP is 80% or more.

The most critical variable in determining the treatment of a corporate distribution is the amount of the corporation's earnings and profits. The actual computation of E&P can be quite complex but the theory underlying it is relatively simple. The calculation attempts to measure the amount the corporation can pay out without impairing its capital account. In this regard, it is quite similar to the financial accounting concept of retained earnings. However, the two are not identical. Current E&P generally represents taxable income as adjusted for certain specified items.[4] Accumulated E&P is the sum of current E&P reduced by distributions. Using this information, a corporation determines the amount of its distribution that is considered a dividend (e.g., 60%) and reports this information to the shareholder on Form 1099-DIV or similar statement.

Mutual Fund Dividends. Millions of taxpayers now invest in stocks, bonds, and other securities indirectly through mutual funds. Mutual funds typically buy and sell investments realizing gains and losses as well as collect earnings from investments such as interest on bonds or dividends on stock.[5] Like corporations, mutual funds make distributions. However, the treatment of these distributions differs somewhat from regular corporate dividends in that they are generally characterized to reflect the nature of the income realized by the mutual fund. Mutual fund distributions are normally characterized as either *ordinary dividends* or *capital gain dividends*.[6] Ordinary dividends represent the individual's share of the fund's earnings from its own investments such as interest or dividends as well as any short-term gains the fund may realize. An individual reports all ordinary dividends as dividend income. Capital gain dividends represent the capital gains and losses actually realized by the mutual fund during the year. All capital gain dividends are treated as *long-term* capital gains. Corporate taxpayers are entitled to the dividends-received deduction for ordinary dividends but not capital gain dividends. Each fund reports the information regarding its distributions to its shareholders on Form 1099-DIV.

A few funds retain their capital gains, in which case they are required to pay tax on such amounts. Nevertheless, these gains are allocated to the shareholders who must include them in income as capital gain.[7] In such case, shareholders may claim a credit for any tax paid by the fund and increase their basis in their shares for the amount included in income less the tax paid.

Other "Dividends". There are a number of other distributions that taxpayers receive that are often called dividends. Technically, however, these are not "dividends" in the tax sense but receive special treatment. Some of these are listed below.

1. In some instances, earnings on deposits with banks, credit unions, investment companies, and savings and loan associations are referred to as dividends when they actually possess all the characteristics of interest. These dividends are reported as interest.[8]

2. Mutual insurance companies distribute amounts referred to as dividends to owners of unmatured life insurance policies. These dividends are treated as a nontaxable return of a portion of the insurance premium paid.[9]

---

[4]   E&P is not defined in the Code. See § 312 and the related regulations.

[5]   Funds are taxed like trusts, deducting income distributed and paying tax on income retained. Distributed income generally retains its character as either ordinary income or capital gain.

[6]   Reg. § 1.852-4(a) and (b).

[7]   § 852(b)(3)(D).

[8]   Reg. § 1.61-7(a).

[9]   § 316(b)(1).

3. Cooperatives distribute patronage dividends to cooperative members. These dividends are treated as a return of part of the original price paid for items purchased by members.[10]

4. As noted above, dividends from regulated investment companies (mutual funds) that represent gains on sales of investments from the fund are treated as long-term capital gains.[11]

Stock Dividends. From time to time, a corporation may make a distribution of its own stock. These so-called stock dividends are normally declared as a means to reduce the selling price of the stock or as simply a gesture of goodwill to the shareholders. As a practical matter, when a corporation distributes its own stock, it is not distributing an asset of the business; indeed, the corporation's assets remain completely intact and only the number of shares outstanding changes. From the shareholder's point of view, assuming all shareholders receive their proportionate shares of the stock distributed, they have essentially received nothing because their interest in corporate assets remains unchanged. Since the effect is to leave both the corporation and the shareholder in the same economic position as they held prior to the distribution, the stock dividend—a misnomer in this case—is nontaxable.[12] On the other hand, if the distribution is structured so that the shareholder's interest does change (e.g., the shareholder can elect to take stock or cash), the stock distribution is taxable.[13]

If the distribution of stock is nontaxable, the only responsibility of the shareholder is to determine the basis of the "new" and the "old" stock. Note that only the shareholder's per-share basis is altered. Total basis for all of the stock owned remains the same. Technically, the shareholder must allocate a portion of the basis of the original stock to the distributed stock. The basis is allocated between the old and the new in proportion to the relative values of the old and new stock on the date of the distribution.[14] When the old shares are identical to the new shares (e.g., a common on common stock dividend), the basis for each share is determined simply by dividing the basis of the old stock by the total number of shares held by the shareholder after the distribution. The holding period of the old shares carries over to the new shares.[15]

> **Example 2.** V owns 100 shares of Z common with a basis of $2,200 ($22 per share). He receives 10 shares of Z common as a stock dividend. If V did not have the right to receive cash or other assets in lieu of the stock, he has no taxable income and his $2,200 basis is allocated among the 110 shares of common for a $20 per share basis ($2,200 ÷ 110).

> **Example 3.** Q owns 100 shares of S common with a basis of $2,200. She receives 10 shares of S preferred as a stock dividend. The market value is $4,000 ($40 per share) for common and $1,000 ($100 per share) for preferred. If Q did not have the right to receive cash or other assets in lieu of the stock, she has no taxable income since her proportionate interest did not change. Her basis for the preferred stock is $440 [$1,000 ÷ ($4,000 + $1,000 = $5,000 total value) = 20% × $2,200] and her basis for the common stock is $1,760 [either ($2,200 − $440) or ($4,000 ÷ $5,000) × $2,200].

---

[10] § 1385(b).

[11] § 1382(b).

[12] § 305(a).

[13] § 305(b).

[14] § 307(a).

[15] § 1223(5).

INTEREST

The second most common item of income appearing on individual tax returns is interest (see Exhibit 6-1). More than 48 percent of all returns filed in 2002 reported some type of taxable interest. As a general rule, interest income is taxable. This is true regardless of its source (a bank, business, friend, or relative) or the form of the interest-bearing instrument (savings account, bond, or note). However, there are two notable exceptions to this rule: (1) the exclusion for interest on certain state and local government obligations, and (2) the exclusion for interest on educational savings bonds.

Interest on State and Local Government Obligations. From the inception of the Federal income tax law, interest on obligations of a state, a territory, a U.S. possession, or any of their political subdivisions has been *nontaxable*.[16] From time to time and even currently this exclusion has been criticized as an unwarranted loophole. Critics often characterize this exclusion as simply a tax shelter existing primarily for the rich. In truth, however, this treatment stems from an uncertainty about whether taxing this interest would be unconstitutional and also from political pressure exerted by the affected governments.[17] The exclusion is exceedingly beneficial to these governments because it means they can pay a lower interest rate and still attract investors, especially those investors who are subject to taxes at the highest marginal rates.

Example 4. K, Inc. invests $10,000 in corporate bonds that pay 13% annually and $10,000 in state bonds that pay 9% annually. If K, Inc.'s marginal tax rate is 34%, its after-tax earnings on the corporate bonds are less than its earnings on the state bonds.

	Corporate Bonds	State Bonds
Annual interest income	$1,300	$900
Federal income tax (34%)	442	0
After-tax income	$ 858	$900

If K's marginal tax rate is 15%, however, its after-tax earnings for the corporate bonds increase to $1,105 ($1,300 − $195).

A break-even point between taxable and nontaxable rates of return may be calculated with the following formula:

Taxable interest rate × (1 − Marginal tax rate) = Tax-free rate

Applying the numbers in the example above when K, Inc.'s tax rate is 34 percent, the breakeven point for the taxable bond is

13% × (1 − 0.34 = 0.66) = 8.58%

Thus, at the 34 percent marginal tax rate, a 13 percent taxable return is equal to an 8.58 percent tax-exempt return.

---

[16] § 103(a); § 103(c).

[17] The constitutional issue now seems to be moot. See *South Carolina v. Baker*, 109 S.Ct. 1355 (1988) where the Supreme Court noted that there was no constitutional prohibition barring the Federal government from taxing such interest. See also *National Life Insurance Co.*, 1 USTC ¶314, 6 AFTR 7801, 277 U.S. 508 (USSC, 1928), where the Supreme Court originally indicated that Federal taxation of *interest* paid by state and local governments was unconstitutional.

The formula can be converted to compute the break-even point for the tax-exempt bond as follows:

$$\text{Tax-free rate} \div (1 - \text{Marginal tax rate})$$

or

$$9\% \div (1 - 0.34 = 0.66) = 13.6\%$$

Thus, at the 34 percent marginal tax rate, a 9 percent tax-exempt return is equal to a 13.6 percent taxable return.

A comparison of the effective yield on tax-free versus taxable investments is provided in Exhibit 6-2 using the five marginal tax brackets for individuals. Given current market conditions, the effective yield on tax-exempt securities will be difficult to match with taxable investments. For example, if a taxpayer is in the 28 percent bracket and the current yield on tax-exempt securities is five percent, the after-tax return on taxable securities would be greater as long as the yield exceeded 6.94 percent.

Over the years, Congress has reacted to the criticism that this exclusion subsidizes the wealthy (i.e., those subject to the highest tax rates) and has also reacted to the increasing number and complexity of financial offerings developed by state and local governments. Originally, these governments sold securities to fund public projects. More recently, however, bonds have been issued to fund business construction and other industrial development projects. When this occurs, a governmental unit retains ownership of the facilities and leases them to a business. Because the interest rate on these bonds is lower than it would be on bonds issued by the corporation, the negotiated lease payments can be lower. Congress has curtailed the tax-exempt status of these so-called industrial development bonds. With certain specified exceptions, interest on industrial development bonds is taxable income.[18]

EXHIBIT 6-2
Comparison of Taxable vs. Tax-Free Investments

	If your tax-free investment is yielding:					
	4.50%	5.00%	5.50%	6.00%	6.50%	7.00%
Tax Bracket	Your taxable equivalent yield is:					
15%	5.29%	5.88%	6.47%	7.06%	7.65%	8.24%
28%	6.25%	6.94%	7.64%	8.33%	9.03%	9.72%
31%	6.52%	7.25%	7.97%	8.70%	9.42%	10.14%
36%	7.03%	7.81%	8.59%	9.38%	10.16%	10.94%
39.6%	7.45%	8.28%	9.11%	9.93%	10.76%	11.59%

In addition to the limitations imposed on industrial development bonds, there are still other restrictions intended to curb the use of state and local bonds to finance business activities. For example, tax-exempt bonds can no longer be issued to finance airplanes, gambling facilities, liquor stores, health clubs, sky boxes, or other luxury boxes. Nor can the bonds be issued to finance the acquisition of farmland or existing facilities, with certain exceptions.

Gain on Sale of Tax-Exempt Bonds. It should be noted that any exclusion on state and local obligations is for *interest* income received by the bondholder. Thus, *gain* on the sale of tax-exempt securities that does not represent interest is taxable income.[19]

---

[18] § 103 (b).

[19] *Willcuts v. Bunn*, 2 USTC ¶640, 9 AFTR 584, 282 U.S. 216 (USSC. 1931). (See footnote 17.)

Example 5. On January 1 of the current year N purchased at par a $30,000, 10-year tax exempt municipal bond, yielding 8%. On September 30 of the following year, she sold the bond for $32,000 plus accrued interest of $800. Although the accrued interest is tax-exempt, N must report $2,000 of capital gain ($32,000 − $30,000) subject to tax of up to 20%.

Educational Savings Bonds. In 1988 Congress took steps to help taxpayers finance the rising costs of higher education by offering a special tax break for those who save to meet such expenses. Code § 135 generally provides that accrued interest on Series EE savings bonds issued after 1989 is exempt from tax when the accrued interest and principal amount of such bonds are used to pay for *qualified educational expenses* of the taxpayer or the taxpayer's spouse or dependents (but only if these relationships are satisfied in the year of the redemption). For this purpose, qualified education expenses include those for tuition or fees to attend college or certain schools offering vocational education. Costs that otherwise qualify must be reduced by any scholarships or fellowships that may be received, as well as any employer-provided assistance.

The interest exclusion is allowed only to the extent that the taxpayer uses the proceeds of the bond redemption to pay qualified educational expenses during the year that he or she redeems a bond. If the redemption proceeds received during the year exceed the amount of education expenses paid during the same year, the amount of the interest exclusion must be reduced proportionately. The amount of the exclusion may be computed as follows:

$$\frac{\text{Qualified eductional expenses paid during the year}}{\text{Total redemption proceeds of qualified bonds during the year}} \times \text{Accrued interest} = \text{Exclusion}$$

Example 6. Mr. and Mrs. T purchased Series EE savings bonds in 2005 for $4,000. On June 2, 2018 they cashed in the bonds and received $10,000, $6,000 representing accrued interest and $4,000 representing their original investment. Three months later on September 2, they paid tuition of $9,000 for their dependent daughter, D, who attends a private university. In November, D received a scholarship of $1,000 for being an outstanding accounting major. Only $8,000 ($9,000 tuition − $1,000 scholarship) of D's expenses are considered qualified educational expenses. Since this amount represents only 80% ($8,000/$10,000) of the total redemption proceeds, Mr. and Mrs. T may exclude only 80% of the $6,000 accrued interest, or $4,800.

Note that to qualify for the exclusion, the savings bonds need not be transferred directly to the educational institution. The exclusion applies to interest on *any* post-1989 Series EE savings bond that is realized during the taxable year as long as the taxpayer pays sufficient qualified educational expenses during the same taxable year.

The special exclusion is designed to benefit only those who have moderate incomes. To achieve this objective, the exclusion is gradually reduced once the taxpayer's A.G.I. (as determined in the taxable year when the bonds are redeemed) reaches a certain level. The 2005 income level at which the phase-out begins depends on the taxpayer's filing status as shown below.

Filing Status	Phase-out Range Modified A.G.I.*
Single (including heads of household)	$61,200–$ 76,200
Married filing jointly	$91,850–$121,850

*Adjusted annually for inflation

The reduction of the exclusion otherwise allowed is computed as follows:

$$\frac{\text{Excess A.G.I}}{\$15,000} \times \text{Otherwise excludable interest} = \text{Reduction}$$

($30,000 for joint returns)

Married taxpayers filing separately are not eligible for the exclusion. Taxpayers who are married must file a joint return to secure the exclusion.

Example 7. Mr. and Mrs. B have an A.G.I., after proper modifications, of $101,850, before the exclusion. As a result, the amount of any interest that would otherwise be nontaxable must be reduced by one third:

$$\frac{(\$101,850 \text{ A.G.I} - \$91,850 \text{ threshold} = \$10,000)}{(\$121,850 - \$91,850 = \$30,000 \text{ phase-out range})}$$

Assume the couple redeemed qualified bonds this year with accrued interest of $10,000. Only 90% of the proceeds of the bonds (i.e., interest and principal) were spent on qualifying education expenses. They could exclude $6,000 of the interest, computed as follows:

Excludable interest (90% × $10,000)	$ 9,000
Exclusion phase-out (1/3 × $9,000).	– 3,000
Amount of interest excluded	$ 6,000

Note that the exclusion would not be available to the couple if their A.G.I. in the year they redeemed the bonds exceeded the phase-out range (e.g., $121,850 for 2005).

Without any special provision, taxpayers with high incomes might try to circumvent the income limitation to obtain the exclusion. For example, a father earning an income of $150,000 might give $10,000 to his 10-year-old daughter who would then be instructed to buy the bonds. When the daughter started college, she would redeem the bonds to pay for her tuition. Absent any restrictions, the daughter could secure 100 percent of the available exclusion since she would have little or no income. To prevent such schemes, the exclusion is available only for bonds that are *issued* to individuals who are at least 24 years old. In addition, the exclusion is available only to the original purchaser of the bond or his or her spouse. This rule prohibits gifts of qualified bonds.

Example 8. Mr. and Mrs. C have an A.G.I. of $150,000. Assume they currently hold qualified Series EE bonds with $10,000 of accrued interest. To avoid the income limitation, the bonds are given to Mr. C's father, GF, who has little income. This year, GF cashes the bonds in and pays for his grandson's tuition. The payment is sufficient to qualify the grandson as GF's dependent. Even though the redemption proceeds are used to pay for education expenses of the taxpayer's dependent, no exclusion is available for the interest since GF was not the original purchaser of the bond. Had GF originally purchased the bonds for his grandson, the exclusion would be allowed (assuming his grandson is his dependent).

ANNUITIES

An annuity is an investment contract that requires a fixed amount of money to be paid to the owner at specific intervals for either a certain period of time or for life.

Annuities are quite common in a number of situations. For example, retirees often receive their retirement benefits (i.e., their pensions) in the form of an annuity. In this case, employees and employers contribute to a retirement fund while the individual is employed. Upon retirement, the employee is usually given the choice of receiving his or her pension in the form of a lump-sum distribution or the accumulations are used to buy an annuity. The annuity option is often selected. Annuities are also a popular investment among elderly taxpayers. These taxpayers, often fearing that they may outlive their assets, purchase an annuity that will provide a steady stream of income until they die.

When the annuity is purchased by an individual, the interest earned on the investment is tax-deferred. This means the interest is taxable income but not during the current year when it is earned. Instead, the interest is included in gross income at some future date when the annuitant receives cash payments. Until then, the interest is automatically reinvested in full, without payment of Federal income taxes, to earn tax-deferred interest. Annuity payments are commonly scheduled to begin on retirement when the recipients' marginal tax rates are lower. Because of the lower rates, these individuals usually pay less total taxes in addition to receiving the benefits from tax deferral.

The taxation of annuities reflects the cost recovery principle. As discussed in Chapter 5, the portion that is a return of capital is nontaxable.[20] The formula for determining the portion that is a *nontaxable return of capital* for the current period is

$$\frac{\text{Investment in the contract}}{\text{Expected return from the contract}} \times \text{Amount received currently} = \text{Excluded portion}$$

The taxable portion is the amount received currently less the portion that is a return of capital (i.e., the excluded portion). When the annuity will be received over a stipulated number of years, the expected return from the contract is the amount to be received each year (or month) multiplied by the number of years (or months) payments are to be received.

Example 9. W invests $20,000 in a single-premium deferred annuity. At the end of 15 years, W elects to receive the $20,000 principal plus interest over the next ten years. She receives $7,000 in the current year and will receive $7,000 each of the following nine years. W's nontaxable return of capital each year is $2,000 computed as follows:

$$\frac{\$20,000}{\$7,000 \times 10 \text{ years} = \$70,000} \times \$7,000 = \$2,000$$

W's taxable income each year is $5,000 ($7,000 − $2,000).

Example 10. Refer to *Example 9*. If W receives only three payments in the first year totaling $1,750 ($7,000 × 3/12), the computation remains the same except the amount received currently is $1,750 (instead of $7,000). Consequently, her nontaxable return of capital in the first year is $500 [($20,000 ÷ $70,000) × $1,750] and her taxable income is $1,250 ($1,750 − $500).

Note that the solution to *Example 9* is the same if W had simply divided the $20,000 principal by the 10 years (and to *Example 10* if W adjusted the annual amount to months). This is not true, however, when an individual elects to receive the annuity payments over his or her lifetime. For these situations, the Regulations contain several tables based on contract payment terms and the annuitant's age.[21] For many years,

---

[20] § 72(b)(1).

[21] Reg. § 1.72-9.

separate tables existed for men and women on account of the differences in their life expectancies. However, because of a related Supreme Court decision, these separate tables were considered discriminatory.[22] Consequently, tables V through VIII were added to the Regulations; these tables ignore a taxpayer's gender in calculating the expected return. In general, these tables became effective July 1, 1986, and must be used by those taxpayers making post-June 1986 contributions to the annuity contract. A portion of table V, which contains the new multiples, is reproduced in Exhibit 6-3.

EXHIBIT 6-3
Ordinary Life Annuities—One Life—Expected Return Multiples

Age	Multiple	Age	Multiple	Age	Multiple
21	60.9	58	25.9	95	3.7
22	59.9	59	25.0	96	3.4
23	59.0	60	24.2	97	3.2
24	58.0	61	23.3	98	3.0
25	57.0	62	22.5	99	2.8
26	56.0	63	21.6	100	2.7
27	55.1	64	20.8	101	2.5
28	54.1	65	20.0	102	2.3
29	53.1	66	19.2	103	2.1
30	52.2	67	18.4	104	1.9

When the payments will be received over the life of the annuitant, the expected return from the contract is the amount to be received each year multiplied by the multiple that corresponds to the annuitant's age in the table. It also is important to note that the portion of any annuity payment to be excluded from gross income cannot *exceed* the unrecovered investment in the contract immediately before the receipt of the payment.[23] In addition, if the annuitant dies before the entire investment is recovered, the amount of the *unrecovered investment* is allowed as a *deduction* on his or her final tax return.[24]

> **Example 11.** T, 65 years old, purchased a single-premium immediate life annuity on January 1, 2005 for $11,400. It will pay $100 a month for the rest of her life (i.e., annual payment of $1,200). From Exhibit 6-3, her multiple is 20.0. T's nontaxable return of capital each year is
>
> $$\frac{\$11,400}{\$1,200 \times 20 = \$24,000} \times \$1,200 = \$570$$
>
> T's taxable income is $630 ($1,200 − $570). The $570 is considered a return of capital until T recovers her $11,400 investment. Note that if she lives 21 years, the total amount she excludes is limited to $11,400 ($570 × 20 years = $11,400). Thus, T's taxable income for year 21 is the entire $1,200 received. In contrast, if she lives just 15 years, the total amount she excludes is $8,550 ($570 × 15 years), and the unrecovered amount of $2,850 ($11,400 − $8,550) is allowed as a deduction on T's final tax return.

As noted above, employers with qualified pension or profit-sharing plans (see Chapter 18) purchase annuity contracts for their employees' retirement. The taxable

---

[22] *Arizona Governing Committee v. Norris.* 82-52 Slip Op. (USSC, 1983).

[23] § 72(b)(2).

[24] § 72(b)(3).

income to the employee is dependent on the employee's total *after-tax* investment in the annuity. After tax funds generally exclude contributions, for example, to certain Individual Retirement Accounts (when individuals are allowed a deduction for the contribution) and to qualified employer retirement plans (since these contributions are made from amounts that are excluded from gross income in the current year). Investments that are not from after-tax funds are ignored in determining the individual's capital investment in the annuity. In some situations, employees may not have invested any after-tax funds in the employer's plan. Consequently, their basis in the annuity contract is zero and all amounts are included in gross income when received by them. In all other instances, calculations for return of capital and taxable income are identical to the procedure outlined in the above paragraphs.

Simplified Treatment for Annuities from Qualified Plans. The 1996 tax legislation essentially codifies the simplified safe harbor method for determining the taxation of annuities as prescribed by the Internal Revenue Service in Notice 88-118.[25] The simplified method may be elected if the annuity payments

1. Start after November 18, 1996;

2. Depend on the life of the distributee or the joint lives of the distributee and his or her beneficiary;

3. Are made from a qualified employee plan [under § 401(a)], an employee annuity [under § 403(a)], or an annuity contract [under § 403(b)]; and

4. Start when the distributee is under age 75 or, if older, there are less than five years of guaranteed payments remaining.

A taxpayer electing to use the safe harbor method will find the computations less onerous than those previously described for computing the exclusion ratio under § 72. Under this method, the total number of monthly annuity payments expected to be received is based on the distributee's age at the annuity starting date. Consequently, the life expectancy tables (such as Exhibit 6-3) can be ignored. Instead, Exhibit 6-4 is used, and is applicable whether the annuity is single life or joint and survivor type.[26]

EXHIBIT 6-4
Monthly Payments Table

Age of Distributee	Number of Payments
55 and under	360
56–60	310
61–65	260
66–70	210
71 and over	160

The portion of each monthly annuity payment that is nontaxable is determined using the following formula:

$$\frac{\text{Investment in the contract}}{\text{Number of monthly payments}} = \text{Nontaxable return of capital}$$

---

[25] Notice 88-118, 1988-2 C.B. 450.

[26] A single life annuity pays a fixed amount at regular intervals for the remainder of one person's life. A joint and survivor annuity pays a fixed amount at regular intervals to one individual for life, and on his or her death, the payments continue over the life of a designated person such as a spouse or child.

Example 12. H, an employee, retired on January 1, 2005 at the age of 65. He started receiving retirement benefits in the form of a joint and 50% survivor annuity to be paid for the joint lives of H and W (his spouse), who is 60. H contributed $52,000 (after-tax contributions) to the plan and will receive a retirement benefit of $2,000 a month. Upon H's death, W will receive a survivor retirement benefit of $1,000 each month. The nontaxable portion of each monthly annuity payment to H is calculated as follows:

$$\frac{\$52{,}000 \text{ investment}}{260 \text{ payments (see Exhibit 6-4)}} = \$200 \text{ nontaxable return of capital}$$

Should H die prior to receiving his entire investment of $52,000, W will likewise exclude $200 from her $1,000 monthly payment. As explained earlier, after 260 annuity payments have been made, any additional payments will be fully taxable. Should both H and W die prior to receiving 260 payments, a deduction is allowed in the amount of the unrecovered investment in the last income tax return.

The safe harbor method should help reduce the number of requests the IRS receives each year from retirees and beneficiaries asking the Service to make the necessary computations.

Early Withdrawals of Annuities. Investors are discouraged from withdrawing funds before annuity benefits are scheduled to be received on contracts issued after August 13, 1982. Not only are early withdrawals treated as being distributions of the interest earned on the contract, a 10 percent penalty is assessed on the deferred income. The penalty is waived if the taxpayer satisfies certain requirements provided in the Code.[27]

PREPAID TUITION PLAN

In recent years, several states have established prepaid tuition plans to help individuals pay for the cost of a college education. Out-of-pocket costs for tuition, fees, books, supplies, equipment and room and board can be prepaid through a qualified state tuition program. Eligible educational institutions include not only colleges and universities, but also propriety and vocational institutions (e.g., trade schools).

Under a typical program, parents might prepay a university for tuition credits or certificates that entitled their child to waive tuition when the child attends college in the future. In effect, such programs enabled parents to freeze the cost of future tuition to the price currently charged by the institution. From the institution's standpoint, it provided a revenue stream that was not otherwise available.

The 2001 Act made vast improvements in the treatment of prepaid tuition plans. Under prior law, distributions from prepaid tuition plans were taxable, normally at the low rate of the beneficiary. Under the new law, distributions from qualified prepaid tuition plans will no longer be taxable. As long as the amounts are used to pay for qualified higher education expenses such as tuition, books, supplies, equipment required for enrollment or attendance and those incurred for "special needs beneficiaries," the distributions will be nontaxable. In addition, taxpayers may claim a deduction for the amount of a distribution from a qualified tuition plan that is not attributable to earnings under the new qualified tuition deduction provision (see discussion in Chapter 8). These changes represent a huge improvement over prior law.

---

[27] See § 72(q)(2).

Example 13. During the current year, F withdraws $1,000 from a qualified tuition plan to pay her undergraduate tuition at State University. F does not claim a credit for the amount spent. If the $1,000 consists of $800 of contributions to the plan and $200 of earnings, a deduction for the $800 of contributions may be claimed by F. Furthermore, the $200 of earnings is excluded from F's income.

Under prior law, only state governments were permitted to establish such qualified tuition plans (so-called 529 plans). The Act now allows individual universities, both state and private colleges and universities. Furthermore, under prior law, there was no provision in the Code that allowed a tax-free rollover from one state college savings program to another for the same beneficiary. Unused balances in the plan could only be rolled over without penalty to an account for another member of the taxpayer's family. A member of the family included the beneficiary's spouse, ancestor's or decedents, nieces or nephews, aunts or uncles and in-laws, as well as the spouse of any of the above individuals. Under the 2001 Act, unused balances can now be rolled over tax-free from one college savings program to another once every twelve months without a beneficiary change. In addition, the 2001 Act adds first cousins as qualified family members.

Estate and Gift Tax Treatment. Under current gift tax law, an annual exclusion allows individuals to transfer $11,000 per donee per year without tax as long as the gift represents a present interest (i.e, the donee's enjoyment commences immediately and not at a future date). In the past, there was some question whether payments to a prepaid tuition plan would qualify for the exclusion since the education would commence at a future date and arguably would not be a present interest. The new law clarifies the treatment of payments to prepaid tuition plans, indicating that such payments do qualify as present interests eligible for the annual exclusion. Thus, an individual could contribute to a prepaid tuition plan for a young child and such contributions would not be subject to the gift tax. Amounts contributed in excess of the annual exclusion would be considered taxable. However, a taxpayer may elect to have a contribution to a plan treated as if it had been made ratably over five years. In so doing, the amount may come under the annual exclusion. For example, a contributor could give $55,000 to a plan and treat the transfer as if he or she had made gifts of $11,000 per year over the next five years. A gift tax return must be filed for amounts contributed in excess of the exclusion. If the contributor should die before the five-year period has elapsed, the balance is included in his or her estate.

Example 14. In 2005 G made a $50,000 contribution to Indiana University's qualified tuition plan for the benefit of her grandson. She elected to treat the transfer as being made over a five-year period. In 2007, G died. In 2005, 2006, and the year of death, G may exclude $11,000 annually. The remaining $17,000 would be included in her gross estate.

The current gift tax law also permits an unlimited exclusion for tuition paid on someone's behalf if it is paid directly to an educational institution. This latter rule is not extended to payments made to qualified prepaid tuition plans. Consequently, only the basic $11,000 exclusion applies. For example, this prohibition bars a grandmother from prepaying a grandchild's tuition for four years (e.g., over $100,000 for some schools) and quickly removing substantial amounts from her estate tax-free.

The new law also clarifies the estate tax treatment of amounts accumulated in prepaid tuition plans. Such amounts are not included in an individual's taxable estate (i.e., neither the estate of the parent nor that of the student).

Interaction with HOPE and Lifetime Learning Credits. As discussed in Chapter 13, there are two credits related to education: (1) the HOPE credit available for the first two years of college, and (2) the Lifetime Learning credit for undergraduate, graduate and other educational courses. Interestingly, the new law makes it clear that taxpayers receiving qualified tuition plan distributions are also eligible to claim either the HOPE or Lifetime Learning credit for a taxable year as long as the distributions are not used for the same expenses for which a credit is claimed.

Recent Developments. The new law provides approximately $29 billion in tax relief to help taxpayers pay for education. Due to favorable tax treatment, many states along with individual colleges and universities are expected to get on the bandwagon and establish their own versions of prepaid tuition plans. The extension of the income-tax exclusion for employer-provided educational assistance to pay for graduate courses along with expanded breaks for education IRAs and the college tuition deduction should only add fuel to the fire. Taxpayers will have to carefully plan their educational expenditures, properly juggling tuition plans, employer-provided education assistance, education IRAs, and the HOPE and Lifetime Learning credits so as to maximize their tax benefits.

EMPLOYEE COMPENSATION AND OTHER BENEFITS

By far the most important source of income for individual taxpayers is compensation from their employment. As seen earlier in Exhibit 6-1, preliminary statistics from 2002 indicate that salaries and wages represent more than 75 percent of all income reported on returns. While the bulk of employee compensation consists of salaries and wages, compensation includes all payments received for personal services such as commissions, bonuses, tips, vacation pay, severance pay, jury fees, and director's fees.[28] In addition, employers typically provide a variety of fringe benefits for their employees such as health and life insurance, child care, discounts on merchandise or services, parking, and contributions to retirement plans.

Although most forms of compensation are taxable, Congress has exempted certain benefits (e.g., health insurance, group-term life insurance), hoping the exclusion would encourage employers to provide such benefits for their employees. It is important to emphasize that these benefits are typically exempt not only from income tax but also from social security and medicare taxes. The power of the exclusion feature is shown in the following example.

Example 15. T recently began working for B Corporation, which provides each of its employees with a number of fringe benefits. Among these benefits is payment of the premium on a health insurance policy for T and his family at an annual cost of $2,000 (a nontaxable fringe benefit). However, T may elect to receive $2,000 in cash instead. Assume that T's marginal tax rate is 15% and that he would buy the health insurance in any event. The table below compares the two options:

	Salary	Premium Payment
Amount	$2,000	$2,000
Income tax (15% × $2,000).	(300)	—
FICA (7.65% × $2,000)	(153)	—
After tax	$1,547	$2,000

---

[28] § 61(a)(1) and Reg. § 1.61-2(a). See Chapter 18 for the treatment of stock received for services.

Observe that T is much better off if he elects to have the employer pay for his health care. Electing the cash option would leave T with $453 less to pay for a similar insurance policy. Moreover, the employer is probably able to secure a better insurance rate than T could individually.

As the above example demonstrates, structuring a compensation package to include nontaxable fringe benefits provides a significant advantage to an employee. In effect, the employee is able to secure a particular benefit with before-tax or pre-tax rather than after-tax dollars. Employers also benefit because not only can they deduct the cost of the benefit just like cash compensation but they normally reduce their compensation cost since they are not required to pay social security, medicare, or unemployment taxes on such amounts.

Exhibit 6-5 provides a listing of the common examples of compensation grouped by whether they are ordinarily taxable or nontaxable.

EXHIBIT 6-5
Taxable and Nontaxable Employee Compensation

Generally included in gross income	*Generally excluded from gross income*
Salaries, wages	Premiums paid on
Commissions	Group-term life insurance (up to $50,000 coverage)
Bonuses	Health, accident, disability or long-term care insurance
Garnished wages	Life insurance proceeds
Tips	Meals and lodging if for employer's convenience
Director's fees	Adoption assistance
Jury fees	Educational assistance plans (both undergraduate and graduate)
Severance pay	Child or dependent care
Reimbursements for	Benefits otherwise deductible by the employee
Business transportation and travel	(i.e., working condition fringe benefits)
Business entertainment	Qualified employee discounts
Indirect moving expenses	No-additional cost services
Educational expenses	De minimus benefits
Employer gifts	Parking
Employer awards	Use of company facilities or services
	Qualified retirement planning services
	Supper money
	Tuition reduction by educational institutions

Most employee fringe benefit plans must meet rigid rules to enable the employer to deduct contributions to the plans and for employees to exclude these amounts. Basically, the plans must (1) not discriminate in favor of highly compensated employees, (2) be in writing, (3) be for the exclusive benefit of the employees, (4) be legally enforceable, (5) provide employees with information concerning available plan benefits, and (6) be established with the intent that they will be maintained indefinitely. In addition, several eligibility and benefit tests provide detailed rules that must be met to ensure that employer costs are nontaxable income for employees. Additional employment benefits involving stock option, profit-sharing, and pension plans are discussed in Chapter 18.

REIMBURSEMENT OF EMPLOYEE EXPENSES

Employers often reimburse employees for their business-related expenses. Commonly reimbursed items include expenses for transportation, out-of-town travel, entertainment, and moving expenses. Such reimbursements are generally considered taxable. However, the employee usually has an offsetting expense that is deductible for A.G.I., so the effect on the tax return is usually a wash. This is not always the case, however. If the employee is over-reimbursed or reimbursed for nondeductible expenses, there is a net increase in A.G.I. The effects of under-reimbursements and other aspects of reporting reimbursed expenses is considered in Chapter 8.

EMPLOYER GIFTS

Although § 102(a) allows taxpayers to exclude gifts from gross income, amounts transferred from an employer to an employee in the form of cash or other property are not excludable as a gift.[29] In effect, employers are prohibited from disguising compensation as a nontaxable gift. Consequently, employers interested in providing nontaxable benefits must look to other sections of the Code that offer exclusions. For example, as discussed below, an employee can exclude certain employee achievement awards (e.g., golf clubs for productivity)[30] and certain insignificant or de minimis fringe benefits such as inexpensive holiday gifts (e.g., a turkey at Thanksgiving).[31]

EMPLOYER AWARDS

It is quite common for an employer to award an employee for some type of achievement. An employee might receive a gold watch for many years of faithful service, a gift certificate for low absenteeism, or a free dinner for a great idea dropped in the suggestion box. For many years, employees argued that such awards were gifts rather than compensation and, therefore, were not taxable. Congress addressed this problem in two ways. As discussed above, the rules governing gifts were amended to make it clear that employers generally cannot make nontaxable gifts to employees. At the same time, Congress created a special rule allowing employees to exclude awards from their employer if certain conditions are met.

Employer awards to employees, other than de minimis fringe benefits (discussed later in this chapter), are generally treated as compensation with two exceptions: if they are provided (1) for length-of-service or safety achievements, or (2) under a nondiscriminatory qualified award plan. To be nontaxable, the awards must be made with tangible personal property. No exclusion is available for cash payments or the equivalent. The award must be given as part of a meaningful presentation and under conditions and circumstances that do not create a significant likelihood of the payment of disguised compensation. Also, no exclusion for the length-of-service award is available if it or a similar award is made within the individual's first five years of employment with the employer. To be nontaxable, safety awards cannot have been made to more than 10 percent of a company's eligible employees. All employees are considered to be eligible except those in managerial, professional, and clerical positions.[32]

Qualifying awards are deductible by the employer and nontaxable by the employee if the amount does not exceed the statutory limits. Under these limitations, the cost of property cannot exceed $400 per employee annually for length-of-service and safety achievements or $1,600 annually for all qualified plan awards, including length-of-service and safety achievements. For example, an employee achievement award (other than a qualified plan award) that costs the employer $390 and has a fair market value of $440 would be fully excluded from the employee's gross income. Excess costs are taxable

---

[29]   § 102(c).

[30]   §§ 74(c) and 274(j).

[31]   § 132(e).

[32]   See §§ 74(c) and 274(j).

income to the extent of the *greater* of (1) the nondeductible cost to the employer due to the limitations, or (2) the property's market value in excess of the limitations. This taxable income must be reported on the employee's Form W-2.

> **Example 16.** R, Inc. pays $525 ($640 market value) J for a brooch that it awards to L in recognition of her 15 years of service to the company. No other awards are given to L during the year. R's deduction is limited to $400, and L has taxable income of $240 (the greater of $525 − $400 = $125 and $640 − $400 = $240). The $240 will appear on L's Form W-2 as taxable income.

SOCIAL SECURITY BENEFITS

When most taxpayers collect social security benefits, these benefits can be excluded from gross income. This treatment can be traced to an early IRS ruling that granted the exclusion with little explanation in 1941.[33] Interestingly, the exclusion was allowed notwithstanding the fact that there was no statutory authority for it. In 1984, however, Congress apparently felt that this gracious treatment, while proper for those whose primary source of income was social security, was not appropriate for higher-income taxpayers. As a result, it created § 86 to address its concern.

Under the 1984 legislative formula, the social security benefits of most taxpayers continued to be nontaxable. However, upper-income taxpayers could have as much as 50 percent of their social security benefits taxed. Note that the effect of this provision is to tax these amounts—at least that portion representing the taxpayer's contributions—twice; first when included as gross wages and second when included as social security benefits are received. On the other hand, the portion received representing the contribution by the employer and any earnings on the amounts contributed are not taxable at all.

The treatment created in 1984 continued until 1993 when the Clinton administration, with the backing of Congress, increased the amount that could be taxed from 50 to 85 percent.[34] The thrust of the current rules is quite simple. As long as income remains below a certain threshold, social security benefits are completely nontaxable. But as income increases, the amount of social security that may be taxed increases. Unfortunately, the actual calculation of the amount that must be included in gross income is unduly cumbersome. The effect of the revised provisions is to establish two income thresholds:

	Married Filing Jointly	Married Filing Separately	Unmarried Taxpayers
Modified A.G.I. threshold #1	$32,000	$0	$25,000
Modified A.G.I. threshold #2	44,000	0	34,000

Notice that in determining whether a taxpayer's level of income warrants taxation of his or her social security benefits, an expanded notion of income referred to as *modified adjusted gross income* is used. Modified adjusted gross income is computed as follows:

	Adjusted gross income
+	½ of social security benefits
+	Tax-exempt income
+	Foreign earned income exclusion
	Modified A.G.I.

---

[33]   Rev. Rul 70-217, 1970-1 C.B. 12.

[34]   § 86.

Taxpayers whose modified A.G.I. is less than the first threshold ($32,000 for married filing jointly) are not taxed on their social security benefits. Those whose modified A.G.I. falls between the two thresholds ($32,000 − $44,000 for married filing jointly) must include the lesser of one-half of their social security benefits or one-half of the excess of their modified A.G.I. over the specified threshold. For those taxpayers whose modified A.G.I. *exceeds* the first threshold (e.g., $32,000 for married filing jointly), the calculation can be made using the following schedules:

Married filing jointly

If modified A.G.I. is

Over	But not over	Amount taxed:
$32,000	$44,000	Step 1: Lesser of (1) 50% of benefits, or (2) 50% × (Modified A.G.I. − $32,000)
$44,000		Step 2: Lesser of (1) Step 1 amount, not to exceed $6,000, + 85% × (Modified A.G.I. − $44,000), or (2) 85% of benefits

Unmarried taxpayers

If modified A.G.I. is

Over	But not over	Amount taxed:
$25,000	$34,000	Step 1: Lesser of 1. 50% of benefits, or 2. 50% × (Modified A.G.I. − $25,000)
$34,000		Step 2: Lesser of 1. Step 1 amount, not to exceed $4,500, + 85% × (Modified A.G.I. − $34,000), or 2. 85% of benefits

Example 17. George and Mildred, happily married for 45 years, received the following income:

Dividend income	$50,000
Social security benefits	16,000

In this case, the couple's modified A.G.I. is $58,000 [$50,000 + (50% × $16,000 = $8,000)]. Because the couple's $58,000 modified A.G.I. exceeds the second threshold of $44,000, the 85% rule is triggered. Their taxable social security is $13,600, computed as follows:

Step 1 amount

Lesser of
    50% × social security of $16,000 $ 8,000

            or

    50% × ($58,000 − $32,000 = $26,000) $13,000
Step 1 amount $ 8,000

Step 2 amount

Lesser of
    Step 1 amount ($8,000), not to exceed $6,000, $ 6,000
       + 85% × ($58,000 − $44,000 = $14,000)   11,900
                                            $17,900

            or

    85% × benefits of $16,000 $13,600
Step 2 amount and taxable social security benefits $13,600

Example 18. Assume the same facts as in *Example 17* above except that dividend income amounts to $30,000. Because the couple's $38,000 modified A.G.I. [$30,000 + (50% × $16,000)] falls below the second threshold ($44,000), their taxable social security is $3,000, computed as follows:

Lesser of
    50% × social security of $16,000 $8,000

            or

    50% × ($38,000 − $32,000 = $6,000) $3,000
Step 1 amount and taxable social security benefits $3,000

As indicated above, the base or threshold amount is zero for married filing separately. Consequently, married taxpayers who elect to file separately automatically expose social security benefits to taxation.

Taxpayers whose social security benefits are subject to taxation should give consideration to shifting money out of municipal bonds and into other investment vehicles such as growth stocks that do not pay dividends or into Series EE U.S. savings bonds, which generally do not produce taxable income until they are redeemed.

UNEMPLOYMENT BENEFITS

In any dynamic economy, the forces at work often leave individuals without a job. For example, in the United States, weekly unemployment claims during 1995 ranged from about 375,000 to 550,000. In order to help those workers who have lost their jobs through no fault of their own, Congress created the unemployment insurance system as part of the Social Security Act in 1935. Under this system, employers, not employees, are subject to Federal and State unemployment taxes, which they are entitled to deduct as ordinary business expenses. These taxes are then used to provide benefits for the unemployed, thus allowing them a period of time that they can seek a new job without major financial distress.

Prior to 1979, unemployment benefits received were not taxable. In 1979, however, Congress reversed direction and opted to tax such benefits. Apparently it believed that the exclusion might actually reduce the incentive to work, making unemployment more, rather than less, attractive. Currently, unemployment benefits received under a government program are fully taxable.[35]

While the new law does not change the tax treatment of unemployment benefits, it does allow states to extend current benefits. All states may extend the maximum 26-week period for unemployment benefits by 13 weeks for workers who filed their initial claims on or after March 15, 2001. States with an insured unemployment rate of at least four percent may extend benefits for an additional 13-week period.

EMPLOYEE INSURANCE

Over the years, Congress has created several exclusions for employer-provided life, health, accident, and disability insurance. The continuation for these exclusions can generally be found in the Congressional desire to ensure that all individuals are adequately protected against unforeseen hardships. As a result, it is quite common for employers to provide some type of group insurance for employees. Premiums for insurance coverage may be paid by the employer only, by the employee only, or by both the employer and employee under some shared cost arrangement. Generally, employer-paid premiums for health, accident, and disability insurance are deductible business expenses and are excluded from the employee's gross income. On the other hand, life insurance premiums paid by the employer generally are included by the employee and deductible by the employer. As may be expected, however, there are exceptions.

Recently, as discussed below, Congress extended tax-favored treatment to long-term care benefits.

Life Insurance Premiums and Proceeds. Employer-paid life insurance premiums are nontaxable by an employee but *only* for the first $50,000 of *group-term life insurance* protection.[36] Premiums paid by an employer for any other type of life insurance are fully included in each employee's gross income. In order to qualify as group insurance, the employer's plan generally must not discriminate. The employer must provide coverage for all employees with a few permitted exceptions based on their age, marital status, or factors related to employment. Examples of employment-related factors are union membership, duties performed, compensation received, and length of service.[37] Acceptable discrimination, however, is limited by the Regulations. Thus, employers may establish eligibility requirements that exclude certain types of employees, such as those who work part-time, who are under age 21, or who have not been employed at least six months. But omitting older employees or those with longer service records generally is not permitted.

When group-term insurance protection exceeds $50,000, the employee generally must include in income the premium attributable to the amount of coverage over $50,000. The actual amount to be included is set forth in the Regulations rather than

---

35 § 85(a).

36 § 79(a)(1). The $50,000 limit is eliminated for retired employees who are disabled.

37 Reg. §§ 1.79-0 and 1.79-1(a)(4).

actual premiums paid. The taxable amount for each $1,000 of insurance in excess of $50,000 is based on the employee's age as of the last day of his or her tax year. These amounts (which were recently lowered by the Treasury) are shown in Exhibit 6-6.[38]

EXHIBIT 6-6
Imputed Costs of Excess Group-Term Life Insurance

Employee's Age	Includible Income per $1,000	
	Monthly	Annually
Under 25	$0.05	$ 0.60
25 to 29	0.06	0.72
30 to 34	0.08	0.96
35 to 39	0.09	1.08
40 to 44	0.10	1.20
45 to 49	0.15	1.80
50 to 54	0.23	2.76
55 to 59	0.43	5.16
60 to 64	0.66	7.92
65 to 69	1.27	15.24
70 and over	2.06	24.72

Source: Reg. § 1.79-3, effective July 1, 1999.

Example 19. BC, Inc. provides all full-time employees with group-term insurance. Records for three of the employees show the following information. All three were employed by BC for the full year.

Employee	Age	Insurance Coverage	Coverage in Excess of $50,000
D	56	$80,000	$30,000
E	38	62,000	12,000
F	35	40,000	0

D's taxable income is $154.80 ($5.16 × $30,000 ÷ $1,000). E's taxable income is $12.96 ($1.08 × $12,000 ÷ $1,000). F has no taxable income from group-term life insurance, since the coverage does not exceed $50,000.

As explained further within, regardless of whether life insurance is provided by the employer, proceeds received by a beneficiary on the death of the insured ordinarily are excludable from gross income.[39]

Health Insurance Benefits. With few exceptions, all medical insurance benefits are excluded from income regardless of who pays the premiums.[40] Any reimbursement of medical costs simply reduces the amount of medical expenses that can be itemized (as deductions from A.G.I.—discussed in Chapter 11).[41] However, in some instances the expenses are paid in one year but reimbursement is not received until a later year. Taxpayers have a choice when this occurs. One, they may anticipate the reimbursement

---

[38]   Reg. § 1.79-3. Beginning in 1988, the cost of group-term life insurance that an employee must include in his or her gross income must also be treated as wages for social security withholding purposes.

[39]   § 101(a)(1).

[40]   § 106.

[41]   §§ 105(b) and 213.

and not deduct any of the reimbursable expenses. This decision means the reimbursement is nontaxable when received. Alternatively, these taxpayers may choose to itemize all medical costs in the year paid even though reimbursement is expected. This decision means the reimbursement is included in gross income when received to the extent a *tax benefit* was obtained for the prior year's deduction.[42] Since only the amount of medical expenditures that exceed 7.5 percent of A.G.I. provides a tax benefit (i.e., reduces an individual's taxable income), it is possible that part of the reimbursement is nontaxable.

> **Example 20.** J pays $4,000 medical expenses in 2005 and receives reimbursement of $1,100 in 2005 and $2,900 in 2006 from the insurance company. J's 2005 A.G.I. is $20,000, and her other itemized deductions exceed the standard deduction for the year. If J chooses to deduct all unreimbursed medical expenses in 2005, her itemized deduction is $2,900 ($4,000 − $1,100 reimbursed in 2005) and her *tax benefit* is $1,400 [$2,900 − (7.5% × $20,000 A.G.I. = $1,500)]. Thus, only $1,400 of the $2,900 reimbursement received in 2006 is included in gross income. Alternatively, if J decides to forgo the deduction in 2005, she has no taxable income in 2006. In this example, the important factors in J's decision are (1) her marginal tax rates for both years, and (2) the present value to her of the tax deferral for one year.

In contrast to the above, reimbursement received in one year for a medical expense not paid until a future year is nontaxable.

> **Example 21.** L pays medical expenses of $1,100 in 2005 and $2,900 in 2006. However, he is reimbursed in 2005 by the insurance company for the entire $4,000. L may not deduct the medical expenses, but he also does not have taxable income for the reimbursement.

If medical coverage is financed by the employer, any reimbursement in excess of medical expenses incurred by an employee for himself or herself, a spouse, and dependents is included in gross income.[43] These excess amounts, however, are not included if the premiums were paid by the individual.

Corporations that finance their own medical benefit plans from company funds (instead of through insurance) are required to establish plans that do not discriminate in favor of certain officers, shareholders, or highly paid employees. If the plan is discriminatory, individuals in these three categories must report taxable income equal to any medical reimbursement they received that is not available to other employees.[44] Thus, the purpose is to encourage corporations to extend medical coverage to all of their employees.

Qualified Long-Term Care Benefits. Under prior law, benefits received under long-term care insurance policies were not necessarily excluded. The new law makes it clear that insurance contracts for long-term care that provide services for chronically-ill individuals and meet a number of other requirements will be considered an accident and health insurance contract. As a result, taxpayers will be able to exclude benefits received under such policies. The amount excluded from gross income for 2004 is the greater of $230 per day ($220 in 2003) or the actual cost of the care.

---

[42] § 111 (a).

[43] § 105(b).

[44] § 105(h).

Under § 7702B(c), qualified long-term care services generally include necessary diagnostic, preventive, therapeutic, curing, treating, mitigating and rehabilitative services, and maintenance or personal care services that are required by a chronically-ill individual and provided pursuant to a plan of care prescribed by a licensed health care practitioner. A chronically-ill individual is generally a person who is unable to perform at least two activities of daily living (e.g., eating, toileting, transferring, bathing, dressing, and continence) for a period of at least 90 days due to a loss of some type of functional capacity.

As general rule, employees can exclude from income the value of employer-provided coverage under a long-term care plan. However, there is no exclusion if the coverage is provided through a cafeteria plan. Furthermore, long-term care services cannot be reimbursed on a tax-free basis under a flexible spending account.

Accident and Disability Insurance Benefits. As a general rule, all amounts received under an *employer-financed* accident or disability plan are taxable, with few exceptions. However, when payments are for permanent loss or use of a function or member of the body or for permanent disfigurement of the employee, employee's spouse or dependent, they are nontaxable.[45] Moreover, to be excludable, the payments must be computed with reference to the *nature* of the injury, and not on the *time* the employee is absent from work (i.e., a wage substitute).

> **Example 22.** G lost two fingers while making repairs to her automobile. She received $20,000 from her employer-provided accident insurance policy. The $20,000 is nontaxable to G because the payment was solely for loss of a function or member of the body.

In contrast with employer-financed disability plans, all disability income is *nontaxable* if the taxpayer paid for the disability coverage.[46] Consequently, those employees with long-term disabilities may incur substantial tax costs if their disability income is received from employer-financed plans.

> **Example 23.** After graduation from high school, R was employed by WW Manufacturing Company. The company's employee benefits included disability insurance. R's disability insurance premiums averaged $250 annually. After 15 years with WW, R became seriously ill. The illness left him permanently disabled. After a three-month wait, required by the insurance company, R began receiving $800 monthly disability income. Whether the $800 is taxable income depends on who paid the $250 annual premium on the disability policy. If WW paid the premium, the $800 monthly disability income is taxable income. If R paid the premium, the $800 is nontaxable. If R paid a portion of the premium, for example 40%, then that portion, $320 (40% × $800), is nontaxable, and the remaining $480 is attributable to the employer's contribution and is, therefore, taxable income.

EMPLOYER-PROVIDED MEALS AND LODGING

As explained in Chapter 5, early rulings and decisions exempted certain benefits given to employees when they did not serve as compensation but rather were for the "convenience of the employer." A classic example of this principle can be found in the working relationship between many apartment owners and their managers. Typically, owners require their managers to live on the premises without charge so that they are

---

[45] §§ 105(a) and (c).

[46] § 104(a)(3) and Reg. § 1.104-1(d).

immediately available should they be needed. While this is an obvious benefit to employees, the tax law allows employees to exclude the value of the housing because in this case it is not primarily a means of compensation but serves some overriding purpose of the employer. In 1954, Congress codified this principle for meals and lodging in § 119.

Under § 119, the value of meals and lodging provided by an employer to an employee and the employee's spouse and dependents is excluded from income if

1. Provided for the *employer's convenience*;

2. Provided on the employer's *business premises*; and

3. In the case of lodging, the employee is *required* to occupy the quarters in order to perform employment duties.[47]

Generally, meals and housing furnished to employees without charge are considered to be for the employer's convenience if a substantial noncompensatory business purpose exists.[48] The regulations provide some guidance in this regard, indicating that meals are usually considered noncompensatory if there are insufficient eating facilities in the vicinity of the employer's premises (e.g., an employee working on an oil rig in the North Sea) or the employee must be available for emergency calls during the meal period (a 911 operator). The regulations also specifically provide that meals provided to wait staff, and other food service employees are noncompensatory. Beyond the examples in the regulations, there are numerous court decisions on the subject. For example, the Tax Court found that there were substantial business reasons to provide meals and lodging to the manager of a motel who is on 24-hour call.[49] But, if the employee has the option to receive other compensation instead, the value of the meals and lodging is included in income.[50]

> **Example 24.** Z is a warden at a state prison in Northern Arizona. She must be on duty from 8:00 a.m. until 5:00 p.m. Monday through Friday. Z is given the choice of residing at the prison free of charge (value of $12,000 per year), or of residing elsewhere and receiving a cash allowance of $1,000 per month in addition to her regular salary. If she elects to reside at the prison, the value to Z of the lodging furnished by the prison will be taxable because her residence at the prison is not required in order for her to perform properly the duties of her employment.

Nontaxable meals and lodging must be furnished on the employer's premises. The term *business premises* has been interpreted to be either the primary place of business (e.g., the hotel, restaurant, or construction site) or elsewhere as long as it is near the place of business and where a significant portion of the business is conducted.[51] However, employer-owned housing located two blocks from the primary place of business, a motel, was disallowed because it was not considered to be on the employer's premises.[52] This contrasts with employer-owned housing located across the street from the primary place of business, a hotel, that was held to be on the premises.[53] Apparently,

---

[47] § 119(a)(2) and Reg. § 1.119-1(b).

[48] Reg. §§ 1.119-1(a)(2) and (b).

[49] *J.B. Lindeman*, 60 T.C. 609 (1973), *acq.*

[50] Reg. § 1.119-1(c)(2).

[51] Rev. Rul. 71-411, 1971-2 C.B. 103.

[52] *Comm. v. Anderson*, 67-1 USTC ¶9136, 19 AFTR2d 318, 371 F.2d 59 (CA-6, 1966), *cert. denied.*

[53] *J.B. Lindeman*, 60 T.C. 609 (1973), *acq.*

taxpayer success in this second case was based on the amount of business conducted in the home rather than its location.

Over the years, there has been a great deal of controversy about application of the exclusion where the employer did not provide the meals but rather reimbursed the employee for his or her meal cost. The landmark case in the area is *Kowalski*, which dealt with a New Jersey state trooper who was given meal allowances under the condition that he eat in his assigned duty area and remain on call.[54] In denying the deduction, the Supreme Court explained that the exclusion only applies to meals in kind and not to cash reimbursements. Despite the apparent clarity of this decision, controversy still arises over this issue.

Interestingly, the *Kowalski* court indicated in a footnote that its decision was not intended to address the treatment of so-called supper money, the term used to describe meal money given to employees who are required to work overtime. The IRS had historically allowed taxpayers to exclude such amounts.[55] This exclusion, as discussed later in this chapter, is now preserved in the Regulations as a de minimis fringe benefit. These rules specifically allow taxpayers to exclude supper money which is provided to overtime workers on an occasional basis.[56]

> **Example 25.** F Inc., a furniture retailer, has an exhibit each year at the local home show convention. Three of F's employees are asked to put in 12-hour days during the week-long convention. To help ease their burden, F provides each of the three employees $8 per day to cover the cost of their dinner. The $56 ($8 × 7 days) each employee receives is considered "supper money" and is therefore excluded as a de minimis fringe benefit.

Tax legislation passed in 1998 clarifies that meals provided to all employees will be excludable if provided to more than one-half of all employees for the convenience of the employer. This rule is important for employers as well since it enables employers to deduct all of such costs (e.g. the cost of a company cafeteria).

CHILD AND DEPENDENT CARE ASSISTANCE

A touchy issue over the years has been the treatment of child care expenses. Arguably, a taxpayer should be extended some tax relief because such costs are inevitable if he or she is to be gainfully employed. Currently, the tax law underwrites the cost of child care under these circumstances in two ways. Employees who receive reimbursements for their child care expenses or whose employer provides child care in kind (e.g., a day care facility) may exclude up to $5,000 annually.[57] In addition, the law allows gainfully employed individuals a limited credit for their child care expenses (20–35% of $3,000 – $6,000 of expenses depending on the taxpayer's income and the number of children).[58] While this might suggest that the taxpayer may be able to secure two benefits, the law effectively prohibits this by reducing any expenses that qualify for the credit by the amount of any benefits that are excluded. In order to claim either the exclusion or the credit, a laundry list of special rules must be followed. These are discussed in connection with the child care credit in Chapter 13.

---

[54] *Kowalski v. Comm.*, 77-2 USTC ¶9748, 40 AFTR2d 6128, 434 U.S. 77 (USSC, 1977).

[55] O.D. 514, 2 C.B. 90 (1920).

[56] Reg. § 1.132-6.

[57] § 129(a)(1).

[58] § 21.

Example 26. J works for the U.S. Group, Inc. J routinely drops off her two young children at a day care facility provided by her employer. This year the value of the service is worth approximately $5,000. J normally may exclude the full $5,000 from income. Had J paid $5,000 for child care which her employer reimbursed, she could also exclude the $5,000. However, in such case, the amount of her qualifying expenses for purposes of the child care credit would be zero ($5,000 expense − $5,000 exclusion). Alternatively, J could report the $5,000 as income and claim a credit equal to 20–35% of the maximum allowable expenses of $6,000. See Chapter 13 for a complete discussion.

ADOPTION ASSISTANCE PROGRAMS

To encourage adoptions, Code § 137 allows an employee a $10,630 per child (including special needs children) exclusion for qualified adoption expenses paid or incurred by an employer. The exclusion begins to be phased out for taxpayers with modified adjusted gross income (A.G.I.) above $159,450 and is not available once modified A.G.I. reaches $199,450. The Internal Revenue Code also provides an increased nonrefundable adoption credit of up to $10,630 per child adopted. Refer to Chapter 13 for a discussion of the adoption credit including the definition of the term "special needs."

Example 27. H and W incurred $10,630 of qualified adoption expenses in the current year to adopt a "child with special needs." The $10,630 was furnished to H under an adoption assistance program maintained by his employer. Assuming the couple's A.G.I. for the current year amounts to $179,450, the maximum exclusion of $10,630 will be reduced by 50% (i.e., $179,450 − $159,450/$199,450 − $159,450). As a result, the couple must include $5,315 of the $10,630 payment in their gross income (i.e., $10,630 − $5,315).

Foster Care Payments. Under Section 131, taxpayers are entitled to exclude "qualified foster care payments" made if they are eligible foster care providers. The new law expands the definition of qualified payments to include payments made by either a state or local governmental agency or any "qualified foster care placement agency" that is licensed or certified by a state or local government or an entity designated by a state or local government to make payments to foster care providers. This change enables payments from for-profit agencies contracting with state and local governments to provide nontaxable foster care payments to foster care providers. Prior to this change, payments made by licensed, private providers to qualified foster care providers were taxable. Certain other changes relating to age restrictions were also made.

EDUCATIONAL ASSISTANCE PLANS

The 2001 Act makes the annual exclusion of up to $5,250 for employer-provided educational assistance (i.e., tuition, fees, books, supplies and equipment) contained in § 127 permanent. Although prior law covered only expenses of undergraduate education, the Act extends the exclusion to include graduate level courses. Note that this rule generally relieves employers of the burden of establishing that payments for graduate courses would qualify as a non-taxable working condition fringe benefit discussed below. However, if the education provided exceeds this amount, this problem will still exist.

The 2001 Act also makes a number of other changes designed to help taxpayers pay for education including: (1) a new above-the-line deduction for up to $3,000 of qualified higher education expenses such as tuition and fees (see discussion in Chapter 8); (2) new rules for deducting student loan interest (see discussion in Chapter 11); (3) greatly expands the usefulness of education IRAs (see discussion in Chapter 18); and (4) the changes related to qualified prepaid tuition plans noted earlier.

SECTION 132 FRINGE BENEFITS

In 1984, Congress attempted to tackle what was a growing controversy over fringe benefits. During that time, more and more employers were finding innovative ways to reward their employees with benefits that many aggressive taxpayers argued were nontaxable fringe benefits. Congress responded to these potential abuses by inserting a clause in the definition of gross income in § 61 declaring that all fringe benefits were taxable. At the same time, however, § 132 was added and it not only sanctioned the exclusion for certain benefits that historically had escaped tax, but also created guidelines for evaluating others.

An overview of the nontaxable fringe benefits now provided under § 132 is given in Exhibit 6-7. These additional employee benefits include the following:

1. Working condition fringe benefits

2. No-additional-cost services

3. Qualified employee discounts

4. De minimis fringe benefits

5. On-premises athletic facilities

6. Qualified transportation fringe benefits

7. Qualified moving expense reimbursement

8. Qualified retirement planning services

Furthermore, employees of educational institutions receive special treatment under § 117 for reduction in tuition costs.

Working Condition Fringe Benefits. This exclusion provides that fringe benefits are nontaxable to the extent that employees could deduct the costs if they reimbursed their employer or otherwise paid the costs.[59] For example, if an accounting firm paid $100 for an employee's membership dues to the AICPA and $50 for a subscription to *The Wall Street Journal*, the employee could exclude the amounts since such costs could be deducted by the employee as routine business expenses had he or she paid them directly. Similarly, many businesses furnish some of their employees with company-owned automobiles. Expenses related to the business usage of the cars are deductible by employers and are excluded from income by the employees. In contrast, personal use of the cars, which includes commuting between the employees' home and work, is taxable compensation (unless it is nontaxable under the de minimis rule discussed later in this section).[60] This income is reported as other compensation, and thus not subject to withholding taxes.[61] If, however, employees reimburse their employers for all personal

---

[59] Such costs would have been deductible as business expenses under § 162 or as depreciation under § 167. § 132(d); Reg. § 1.132-5.

[60] § 61(a)(1) and Reg. § 1.61-2(d)(1).

[61] Reg. § 1.6041-2 and Ltr. Rul. 8122017. Although not subject to withholding taxes, this income is subject to social security taxes.

use of the automobiles, there is no auto-related taxable compensation. These benefits need not be provided to all employees (i.e., they may be reserved for officers, owners, and highly paid employees).

In addition to the above exclusions, this § 132 fringe benefit allows an exclusion for payments made for education by an employer if the employee could have deducted the cost as an education expense under § 162 as a business expense (e.g., the education enabled the taxpayer to improve his skills used in his business and was not necessary to meet the minimum education requirement imposed by the job). Under prior law, this rule generally enabled taxpayers to exclude employer-provided educational assistance which otherwise could not be excluded under the educational assistance rules of § 127 discussed above since such exclusion was limited to undergraduate courses. Under the new law, however, the exclusion of § 127 is extended to graduate education. As a result, the significance of the working condition fringe exclusion for graduate education has been diminished somewhat—at least to the extent that the annual assistance does not exceed $5,250. More important, the extension of the § 127 exclusion to graduate education relieves employers of the burden of establishing that payment for graduate courses would qualify as a nontaxable working condition fringe benefit before omitting such amounts from the employees W-2. Previously, uncertain employers would include the education reimbursements as W-2 income subject to both income and payroll taxes.

Also note that the working condition fringe benefit rules apply only if payments made by the employee would have been deductible as a business expense under § 162. As a result, the § 132 fringe benefit does not exclude employer payments for education that would have been deductible under the new qualified tuition deduction of § 222. The new rules create some complex interactions between the working condition fringe benefit provisions, the educational assistance exclusion, and the deduction for qualified higher education. These interactions are examined in greater detail in Chapter 8.

EXHIBIT 6-7
Nontaxable Fringe Benefits under § 132

Type of Benefit	Conditions	Examples
No additional cost service—§ 132(b)	Company incurs no substantial additional cost Service sold in normal course of business Same-line-of-business limitations Reciprocal agreements allowed Must be nondiscriminatory	Airplane tickets Hotel rooms Telephone services
Qualified employee discount—§ 132(c)	Offered for sale in normal course of business Same-line-of-business limitation Merchandise discounts limited to employer's gross profit Service discounts limited to 20% of normal price Must be nondiscriminatory Not applicable to investment property or real estate	Retail items
Working condition fringes—§ 132(d)	Nontaxable to extent employee would have deducted the cost had he or she paid for the property or service	Company car Club memberships Professional dues and subscriptions Seminar expenses

De minimus fringes—§ 132(e)	Benefits are so small that accounting for them is unreasonable or administratively impractical	Employee picnics
		Cocktail parties
		Holiday gifts
		Occasional use of:
		    Copying machine
		    Typing services
		    Meals
		    Coffee and donuts

Qualified transportation fringes—§ 132(f)	Valuation of parking: amount a person would pay in an arm's-length transaction to obtain parking at the same site
	
	Available only to employees—not "partners" and "independent contractors"
		Up to $105 per month:
		    Transit passes and
		      Vanpooling combined
		
		Up to $200 per month:
		    Parking

Moving expense reimbursement—§ 132(g)	Reimbursements or payments by an employer to an employee for qualified moving expenses (i.e., those that would be deductible under § 217)	Moving expenses in connection with:
		    Beginning employment
		    Changing job locations

Athletic facilities—§ 132(j)(4)	Located on employer's premises Operated by employer Substantially all use is by employees, spouses, and children	Tennis court Golf course Gym Pool

Qualified retirement planning services—§ 132(m)(1)	Any retirement planning services provided to an employee/spouse by an employer maintaining a "qualified" employer plan (i.e., pension plans)	Advice and information on retirement income planning
		Does not apply to:
		    Tax preparation
		    Accounting services
		    Legal or brokerage services

No-Additional-Cost Services. Some employers allow employees to use company facilities or services without charge or for a minimal maintenance fee. For example, an airline may allow its employees to fly stand-by for free because it loses nothing since the seat would have otherwise not been used. In this and similar situations, § 132(b) permits the employee to exclude the benefit as long as the company incurs *no substantial additional cost* as a result of the employee's usage. However, unlike the working condition fringe benefit, the exclusion is not allowed if the benefit discriminates in favor of officers or other highly compensated employees.

There are literally thousands of benefits that could qualify as no-additional-cost services. They range from use of company meeting rooms to free tickets in the entertainment industry for seats that would otherwise be empty. Note that the exclusion is limited to services sold in the normal course of business in which the employee works. For example, the value of a hotel room is nontaxable if used by an employee (and/or a spouse or dependent children) who works in the employer's hotel business. It is taxable, however, if the employee works for another line of business of an employer with diversified interests such as hotels and auto rentals. Those employees identified with more than one line of business (e.g., an accountant) may exclude the benefits received from all of them. The exclusion is extended to benefits provided under a written reciprocal agreement by another employer that is in the same line of business.[62] Thus, the hotel employee has nontaxable income for free use of a hotel room provided by another company that has a qualified reciprocal agreement with the employer.

Qualified Employee Discounts. It is common practice for companies to allow employees to purchase inventory items at a discount. For example, a department store may allow its employees to purchase merchandise at the selling price less a stipulated discount. Such discounts seldom result in taxable income unless they discriminate in favor of highly compensated employees.[63] The exclusion, however, is not available for discounts on investment property or on residential or commercial real estate.

The rules governing nondiscrimination, the requirement that items must be offered for sale in the normal course of business and line of business, and the rules governing coverage of spouses and dependent children discussed above for nontaxable services also pertain to nontaxable discounts. In contrast with services, however, discounts under reciprocal agreements are taxable income. The merchandise discount exclusion is limited to the employer's normal profit (i.e., the discount may not exceed the employer's gross profit). In the case of employer services, the discount may not exceed 20 percent of the price charged to customers. Any discount beyond that amount is taxable income to the employee.

Example 28. V, an employee of an auto mechanic business, has her automobile repaired by the company. Accounting records show the following information for the parts and service necessary to repair V's car:

	Normal Selling Price	Firm's Cost	V's Cost
Parts	$200	$120	$112
Service.	90	81	70

V's taxable income for the parts is $8 ($120 − $112) and for the service is $2 [($90 − $70 = $20) − ($90 × 20% = $18)].

---

[62] § 132(i). The line of business limitation is relaxed in certain instances if a special excise tax is paid.

[63] § 132(c).

De Minimis Fringe Benefits. Exclusion of employee benefits also extends to items of minimal value such as the occasional use of a company's photocopy machines, other equipment, or typing services; annual employee picnics, cocktail parties, or occasional lunches; and inexpensive holiday gifts such as a turkey at Thanksgiving. No dollar amount is specified in determining what qualifies as de minimis. The general guideline is that the value of these benefits is so small that accounting for them is unreasonable or administratively impractical.[64] The exclusion also covers discounts on food served in an eating facility provided by an employer *if* (1) the facility is located on or near the employer's business premises, (2) its revenue equals or exceeds its direct operating costs, and (3) the nondiscriminatory rules discussed above are met.[65] In addition, as noted earlier, supper money—cash meal allowances—given occasionally to employees who are required to work overtime may be excluded as a de minimis fringe benefit.

Under the 1997 Act, meals provided on the employer's premises for the convenience of the employer (and excluded from an employee's income under Code § 119) are now considered a de minimis fringe benefit under Code § 132. As a result, employers will be able to deduct the entire cost of the provided meals and they no longer will be subject to the 50 percent disallowance rule that normally applies for meals and entertainment (see Chapter 8).

Employer-Provided Transportation Benefits. Limits on the value of transportation benefits allow an employee to exclude up to $105 per month for qualified employer-provided (1) van pooling in a "commuter highway vehicle" between the employee's home and place of work and (2) transit passes. Furthermore, an employee can exclude up to $200 per month for (3) qualified parking. Categories (1) and (2) above are combined, regardless of the total value of both benefits. Category (3) has a separate limitation.[66] Both of these dollar limits are subject to an annual inflation adjustment. Generally, the value of employer-provided parking is based on the cost that an individual would incur in an arm's-length transaction to obtain parking at the same site.[67] Should employer-provided transportation benefits exceed the statutory limits, the excess value is includible in the employee's gross income for both income and employment tax purposes.

> **Example 29.** Each month Employer M provides a transit pass valued at $110 to Employee D. D does not reimburse M for any portion of the pass. Because the value of the monthly transit pass exceeds the statutory limit by $5, D is subject to both income and employment taxes on the $5 excess.

> **Example 30.** Each month Employer M provides parking valued at $215 to Employee E. Because the fair market value of the parking exceeds the statutory limit by $15, E is subject to both income and employment taxes on the $15 excess.[68]

Payments by employees for qualified transportation fringes must also be considered in determining if the value of the benefit exceeds the statutory limit.

> **Example 31.** Employer P provides qualified parking with a fair market value of $230 per month to its employees, but P charges the employees $30 per month. Because the amount paid ($30) by the employees plus the amount excludable ($200) for qualified parking equal the fair market value of the benefit, no amount is includible in the employee's gross income.[69]

---

[64]   § 132(e).

[65]   § 132(e)(2).

[66]   Pub. L. No. 102-486: § 132(f).

[67]   Notice 94-3, 1994-3 I.R.B., p. 17.

[68]   Notice 94-3, p. 15.

[69]   Notice 94-3. p. 15.

Under prior law, the exclusion for employer-provided parking was not available to employees if the employee could receive cash instead. Beginning in 1998, employers may offer employees a choice of free-parking or cash without jeopardizing the exclusion for those who opt for the parking. However, those who elect to receive cash must include the amount received in income. The change was prompted by Congress' belief that prior law encouraged individuals to drive and take advantage of tax-free parking. Under the current approach, presumably more people will opt for the cash and fewer will drive, resulting in a better environment!

Qualified Moving Expense Reimbursement. As provided by the Revenue Reconciliation Act of 1993, qualified moving expenses reimbursed by an employer (or paid directly by the employer) are excludable from an employee's gross income to the extent the moving expenses would be deductible under Code § 217 if paid or incurred by the employee. The term *qualified moving expense reimbursement* does not include payments for, or reimbursement of, expenses actually deducted by an individual in a prior taxable year.[70] The moving expense provisions are discussed in detail in Chapter 8.

On-Premises Athletic Facilities. The Code contains an exclusion for the use of athletic facilities provided on the employer's premises primarily for current or retired employees, their spouses, and their dependent children. Facilities that qualify for the exclusion include gyms, golf courses, swimming pools, tennis courts, and running and bicycle paths. Resorts are not qualifying facilities. Although the athletic facility must be located on premises owned or leased by the employer, it need not be located on the employer's business premises. Because the nondiscrimination rules are not applicable to on-premises athletic facilities, they may be made available to executives only.[71]

Qualified Tuition Reduction by Educational Institutions. Employees of educational institutions have nontaxable income for reduction in tuition costs provided by their employer or other educational institution *below* the graduate level. This exclusion is available to the employee, a spouse, and dependent children and is extended to these individuals even if the employee is retired, disabled, or deceased.[72]

Under § 117(d), *graduate* students who are engaged in teaching or research activities (e.g., graduate assistants) for an educational institution are allowed to exclude tuition costs provided by the institution for graduate level work as well as undergraduate work. In effect, this new rule extends favorable nontaxable treatment to tuition reduction arrangements for graduate students who teach or serve as research assistants.[73]

It should be emphasized that the regulations indicate that only the benefit in excess of the portion representing reasonable compensation for the graduate student's services can be excluded. Moreover, the amount received for services cannot be excluded solely because all candidates for the degree are required to perform such services.

Example 32. F is a doctoral student at State University. As part of her doctoral program she is required to teach one of the basic accounting courses each semester. For her efforts, she receives free tuition worth $17,000. Assuming other adjunct professors receive $3,000 for providing like services, F may only exclude $14,000. She must report $3,000 because it represents compensation for services.

---

[70] § 132(g).

[71] § 132(j)(4) and Reg. § 1.132-1T(e)(5).

[72] § 117(d)(1).

[73] § 117(d) is subject to the compensation limitation in 117(c).

Employer-Provided Retirement Advice. In order to help employees adequately prepare for retirement, the Act provides that "qualified retirement planning services" are an excludable fringe benefit [§ 132(a)(7)]. The exclusion is granted for retirement planning services provided to an employee and his or her spouse by an employer that maintains a qualified pension plan. The exclusion is not intended to apply to services that may be related to tax preparation, accounting, legal, or brokerage services. In Letter Ruling 199929043, the IRS concluded that financial counseling services provided to family members of terminally ill employees and survivors of deceased employees were taxable income. Presumably, the value of such services would not be taxable under the new law.

MILITARY PERSONNEL

Military personnel are employees subject to most of the same provisions as nonmilitary employees. However, the character and tax treatment of some military benefits differ from those of nonmilitary employee benefits. All compensation is taxable unless specifically excluded. Examples of taxable compensation are active duty and reservist pay, reenlistment bonuses, lump-sum severance and readjustment pay, and retirement pay. Examples of non-taxable benefits are allowances for subsistence, uniforms, and quarters; extra allowances for housing and living costs while on permanent duty outside the United States, and family separation allowances caused by overseas duty; moving and storage expenses; compensation received by *enlisted* service members (up to $500 per month for commissioned officers) for active duty in an area designated by the President as a combat zone (e.g., Operation Desert Storm); and all pay while a prisoner of war or missing in action.[74] Benefits provided to military veterans by the Veterans Administration also are nontaxable. Examples of these are allowances for education, training, and subsistence; disability income; pensions paid to veterans or family members; and grants for specially equipped vehicles and homes for disabled veterans. In addition, bonuses paid from general welfare funds by state governments to veterans are nontaxable.

REPARATIONS TO HOLOCAUST VICTIMS

Section 803(b) of the 2001 Act codifies an earlier IRS statement regarding amounts received as a result of an individual's persecution by Nazi Germany or any other Axis power during the Holocaust. Under the new law, amounts received by victims of the Holocaust or their heirs are generally nontaxable. In addition, property received by eligible individuals is deemed to have a basis equal to fair market value.

PERSONAL TRANSFERS BETWEEN INDIVIDUALS

While the bulk of all income is derived from the fruits of one's labor or invested capital, there are a number of items that still have significance for which special rules exist. Among these are the provisions covering the treatment of certain transfers between individuals, specifically gifts, inheritances, child support, and alimony. With the exception of alimony, each of these is nontaxable. In each case, the recipient does not include the amount in income and the payer is not entitled to a deduction.

---

[74] The TRA of 1986 consolidated existing military benefits and provided the Treasury with the authority to expand the list.

GIFTS AND INHERITANCES

Section 102 excludes the value of property received as a gift, bequest, devise, or inheritance from gross income.[75] This exclusion is normally justified on the theory that there is merely a redistribution of the donor's or decedent's after-tax income.

While gifts are nontaxable, it is not always easy to determine whether an amount received represents a gift or compensation. The problem was clearly revealed in the landmark case of *Comm. v. Duberstein.*[76] In this case, Duberstein, a businessman from Dayton, Ohio, provided the names of potential customers to Berman, an entrepreneur from New York City. The names proved to be very valuable to Berman and, to show his appreciation, he gave Duberstein a Cadillac. Although Berman's company deducted the cost of the car on its tax return as a business expense, Duberstein considered the Cadillac a gift and therefore nontaxable. The issue was ultimately reviewed by the Supreme Court, which announced its now famous distinction between gifts and compensation. According to the court, a gift is made out of a detached and disinterested generosity and not as a reward for past services or made in expectation of future services. Based on the Court's view, Berman intended the car to be remuneration for services rendered and consequently ruled that Duberstein had taxable compensation.

The exclusion for gifts does not extend to income earned on the property.[77] For example, the value of bonds inherited or received as a gift is nontaxable, but any interest income earned on the bonds by the new owner is taxable unless specifically exempted by the Code (e.g., interest on tax-exempt bonds issued by a municipality).

ALIMONY AND SEPARATE MAINTENANCE

As may be clear by now, virtually nothing is left untouched by the tax law and that includes the area of matrimonial disputes. Indeed, given the divorce rate in the United States (in 1987 about 2.4 million marriages and 1.2 million divorces), it should not be surprising that a thriving part of many tax practices relates to the tax consequences of divorce and separation. That this can be is attributable to the fact that a major element in the dissolution of many marriages is the financial arrangement of the settlement.

Typically, a divorcing couple must first split up their property and establish separate households. Under most state laws, each spouse is entitled to the property he or she brought into the marriage and an equal share of property accumulated during the marriage. In addition to the property settlement, the divorce decree may require one of the spouses to pay support for the children (i.e., child support), and in many cases make support payments—normally referred to as alimony or separate maintenance payments-to the ex-spouse. For tax purposes, the obvious questions concern the treatment of the property settlement, child support, and alimony. The general rules governing these transfers are quite straightforward:

> ▸ *Property Settlement.* The division of the property (i.e., the transfer of property from one spouse to the other in exchange for the release of that spouse's marital claim) is a nontaxable event.[78] Neither spouse has income for the property received or a deduction for the property transferred. Consistent with this

---

75 § 102(a).

76 60-2 USTC ¶9515, 5 AFTR2d 1626, 363 U.S. 278 (USSC, 1960).

77 Reg. § 1.102-1(a). Amounts paid out of an estate or trust may be taxable under certain circumstances. However, the end result should protect the exclusion for the gift or inheritance. See § 663.

78 § 1041(b)(2). Prior to 1985, transfers between spouses were taxable. See *U.S. v. Thomas Crawley Davis*, 62-2 USTC S ¶9509, 9 AFTR2d 1625, (USSC, 1962).

approach, the basis of the property received by either spouse under the property settlement remains the same, leaving any built-in gain or loss unchanged.[79]

▶ *Alimony.* Amounts designated as alimony (or equivalent payments) are considered a mere reallocation or sharing of the payer's income and, therefore, are taxable to the recipient and deductible by the payer.[80]

▶ *Child Support.* Amounts paid for child support, often covered in a separate agreement, are nontaxable to the recipient (regardless of how the money is used) and non deductible to the payer.

Example 33. H and W are divorced, and W was awarded custody of their only child. Pursuant to the divorce decree, this year H transferred his various investments in stock to W worth $24,000 (basis to H of $16,000). In addition, H paid W $18,000 in alimony and $10,000 in child support. Neither H nor W is affected by the transfer of stocks. H's basis of $16,000 carries over to W so that her basis is also $16,000. Thus the built-in appreciation of $8,000 shifts to W. H is entitled to deduct all $18,000 of the alimony as a deduction for A.G.I. while W must report the $18,000 as taxable income. H is not entitled to deduct the $10,000 paid as child support, but W is allowed to exclude the $10,000 from income.

Due to the drastically different tax treatments of these transfers, characterization of a particular payment as alimony, child support, or part of the property settlement is obviously crucial in structuring a divorce settlement. As might be expected, without some rules and coordination, a paying spouse might want to call something alimony while the recipient spouse may feel that it is either child support or part of the property settlement. Moreover, the two parties, despite their failure in marriage, may be able to work out a financial arrangement that works well for both but unfairly reduces the government's rightful share. To help eliminate controversy, a number of special rules must be observed when dealing in this area. In this regard, these rules normally do not apply to divorces occurring before 1985.[81]

Alimony. Prior to 1942, there was no specific statute governing the treatment of alimony or child support. As early as 1917, however, the Supreme Court ruled that alimony did not fall within the definition of income and, consequently, the recipient avoided tax. From the payer's perspective, the payments were not deductible since there was no provision that authorized the deduction. In some cases, this treatment could produce an inequitable result. For example, consider a taxpayer who earns $150,000 and is required to pay alimony of $100,000 to his ex-wife. Assuming the taxpayer pays taxes at a rate of 50 percent, he would have only $75,000 after-tax to meet his $100,000 alimony obligation! Because alimony seriously reduced the taxpayer's ability to pay, Congress believed it was more appropriate to view the payments of alimony as simply a splitting of the payer's income. Consequently, the law was changed to make payments of alimony deductible by the payer and taxable to the recipient.

Under current law, payments qualify as alimony or separate maintenance only if[82]

1. They are made in *cash*;

2. They are made as a result of a divorce or separation under a *written decree* of separate maintenance or support;

---

[79] § 1041(b)(2).

[80] § 215(a) and 71(a)(1).

[81] These rules apply to a pre-1985 divorce decree *only if* both parties expressly agree. Ltr. Rul. 8634040.

[82] § 71(a) and (b) and Reg. § 1.71-1.

3. They are *required* under a decree or a written instrument incident to a divorce or separation;

4. The spouses or court do *not* elect that they be designated as not qualifying as alimony;

5. The husband and wife do not live together nor do they file a joint return together; and

6. Payments cease with the death of the *recipient*.

Payments meeting these requirements, however, are not treated as alimony if the divorce or separation agreement clearly states they are not alimony for Federal income tax purposes. Note that this provision gives the parties a great deal of flexibility in structuring the divorce.

As noted above, payments only qualify as alimony if they are in cash. However, the payments need not be made directly to the ex-spouse.[83] Specifically, the following types of payments qualify as alimony:

1. Payments made in cash, checks, and money orders payable on demand.

2. Payments of cash by the ex-husband to the ex-wife's creditors in accordance with the terms of the divorce or separation instrument such as payments of the ex-wife's mortgage (i.e., on house ex-wife owns), taxes, rent, medical and dental bills, utilities, tuition, and other similar expenses.

3. Premiums paid by the ex-husband for term or whole life insurance on the ex-husband's life made pursuant to the terms of the divorce or separation instrument, provided the ex-wife is the owner of the policy.

4. Payments of cash to a third party on behalf of the ex-wife, if they are made at the written request of the ex-wife, such as a contribution to a charitable organization.

However, the following *do not* qualify as alimony or separate maintenance payments:[84]

1. Assets transferred as a part of the property settlement, such as a home, car, stocks and bonds, life insurance policies, annuity contracts, etc.

2. Any payments to maintain property owned by the ex-husband and used by the ex-wife, including mortgage payments, real estate taxes, insurance premiums, and improvements. Such payments increase the ex-husband's equity in the property.

3. Fair rental value of residence owned by ex-husband but used exclusively by ex-wife.

4. Repayment by the ex-husband of a loan previously made to him by his ex-wife as part of the general settlement.[85]

5. Transfers of services (i.e., professional or otherwise).[86]

6. Voluntary payments not required by the divorce or separation agreement.

7. Payments made prior to a divorce or separation.

---

[83] Temp. Reg. § 1.71-1T(b).

[84] Temp. Reg. § 1.71-1T(b), Questions 5 and 6.

[85] Reg. § 1.71-1(b)(4).

[86] Temp. Reg. § 1.71-1T(b), Question 5.

Example 34. D and G are divorced. The divorce decree requires D to transfer personal assets valued at $30,000 to G, to pay G $2,400 per year until G remarries or dies, and to pay G $50,000 over a period of 12 years. During the year. D pays G the following amounts:

1. $1,000 separate maintenance, voluntarily made prior to their separation or divorce

2. $2,400 separate maintenance, made in accordance with the divorce agreement

3. $30,000 of personal assets, transferred in accordance with the divorce agreement

4. $6,000 of the $50,000 to be paid over 12 years

G's alimony is $8,400 ($2,400 + $6,000). The $1,000 separate maintenance is not alimony because it was paid voluntarily and before any divorce or separate maintenance agreement was made. The $30,000 transfer of personal assets is not alimony since it is a property settlement. Since G has taxable alimony of $8,400, D has a deduction for A.G.I. of $8,400.

Limitations on Front Loading. Absent some limitations, *both* spouses might be better off if what is really a property settlement is treated as deductible alimony. To illustrate, consider the following example.

Example 35. H and W are in the process of negotiating the terms of their divorce. It is anticipated that after the divorce, H will be in the 50% bracket while W will pay taxes at a rate of 20%. If H pays $10,000 to his wife and the amount is *not* considered alimony, the after-tax cost of the payment to the husband is $10,000 while the after-tax benefit to the wife is $10,000. On the other hand, if the payment is considered deductible alimony, H could increase the payment to W to $20,000 and it would have the same $10,000 after-tax cost as the first payment. However, in such case, W would receive $16,000 after-tax, $6,000 more even though she has to pay taxes. As a result, both H and W are inclined to characterize any payment that is made as alimony.

As the above example illustrates, depending on the tax rates of the parties, a divorcing couple may be inclined to characterize a payment as alimony regardless of its actual substance. This is particularly true for the spouse required to make the payments since the value of the alimony deductions up front is normally far greater than their value if deferred to later years.

When an arrangement like this might provide an advantage, the divorce agreement normally calls for large "alimony" payments for the first few years followed by smaller payments later. As a practical matter, however, the large payments made initially that are purportedly alimony are in all likelihood simply part of what is a disguised property settlement. To prevent this so-called front loading, Congress created special rules.[87]

The front loading rules are triggered when there is a significant drop in alimony in either the second or third year after the divorce. If such a drop occurs, the alimony is *recaptured*, that is, the payment is no longer treated as alimony. As a result, the payer must include the amount in income and the recipient who previously reported the payment as income is entitled to a deduction. Unfortunately, the actual calculation of the amount to be recaptured is quite cumbersome.

---

[87] § 71(f).

Alimony paid in the first and second years must be recaptured in the third year if, during this three years, alimony payments decreased by more than $15,000. Amounts recaptured are included in gross income by the payor and deductible by the payee in arriving at A.G.I. To compute the recapture, the years must be considered in reverse order. Thus, the recapture formula for the second post-separation year is (1) total payments made in the second year less (2) payments made in the third year less (3) $15,000. The recapture formula for the first year is similar with one exception. In the second step, an *average* is computed of the second-year payments (less excess payments for that year, determined in the preceding computation above) plus the third-year payments.

Example 36. Alimony payments by W to H for the first three years after divorce are $25,000, $20,000, and $15,000. Since payments did not decrease by more than $15,000, no recapture is required. Both W's deductions for A.G.I. and H's taxable income are $25,000 the first year, $20,000 the second year, and $15,000 the third year.

Example 37. Alimony payments by M to F for the first three years after divorce are $50,000, $20,000, and $0. Since payments decrease by more than $15,000, recapture is required in the third year. As computed below, the recapture for the second year is $5,000 and for the third year is $27,500.

Drop from year 2 to year 3:	
Total payments made in second year	$ 20,000
−Payments made in third year	0
Drop from year 2 to year 3	$ 20,000
−$15,000 allowance	(15,000)
Year 3 recapture amount	$ 5,000

Drop from year 1 to year 2:	
Total payments made in first year	$ 50,000
−(Year 2 + year 3 payments − year 3 recapture)/2	(7,500)*
Drop from year 1 to year 2	$ 42,500
−$15,000 allowance	(15,000)
Recapture amount	$ 27,500

*($20,000 + $0 − $5,000 = $15.000)/2 = $7,500

M's deduction for A.G.I. and F's taxable income are $50,000 the first year and $20,000 the second year. In the third year, the recaptures exceed payments: thus, M's taxable income and F's deduction for A.G.I. is $32,500 ($5,000 + $27,500).

The recapture rules do not apply for post-1984 divorce instruments if payments

1. Cease because of the death of either spouse during the three-year period;

2. Cease because the payee remarries during the three-year period;

3. Are made under a support agreement, and thus do not qualify as alimony; or

4. Are a fixed portion of income to be paid for at least three years and based on revenues from a business, from property, or from employee or self-employment compensation.

Child Support. If there are children, it is reasonable to assume that a portion of the husband's payments will be for their care and support. Amounts that qualify as child support are nondeductible personal expenses for the husband and nontaxable income to the wife.[88] Funds qualify as child support *only* if

1. A specific amount is fixed or is contingent on the child's status (e.g., reaching a certain age);

2. Paid solely for the support of minor children; and

3. Payable by decree, instrument, or agreement.

If all three requirements are not met, the payments are treated as alimony with no part considered to be child support.[89] All other factors are irrelevant to the issue. For example, the intent of the parties involved, the actual use of the funds, and state or local support laws have no bearing on whether payments qualify as child support. Also, even though state law may be to the contrary, a minor child is anyone under age 21.[90]

Example 38. A divorce decree states that B is to pay $300 per month as alimony and support of two minor children. The agreement also states that the payments will decrease by one-third (1) if the former spouse dies or remarries, and (2) as each child reaches 21 years of age. This type of agreement meets the contingency rule for child support. Consequently, $100 per month qualifies as alimony and $200 per month qualifies as child support.

Once child support is established, no payments are considered to be alimony until all past and current child support payments are made.[91]

Example 39. A divorce decree states that H is to pay $100 per month as alimony and $200 per month as support of two minor children. The first payment was due October 1. H paid $150 in October, $300 in November, and $350 in December. These payments are allocated between child support and alimony as follows:

	Payment	Child Support	Alimony
October	$150	$150	$ 0
November	300	250	50
December	350	200	150
Total	$800	$600	$200

The above allocation is made even if H or state law stipulates that payments are to cover alimony first.

TRANSFERS BY UNRELATED PARTIES

The last section clearly revealed that the income concept can be quite broad and could, without special rules, encompass benefits normally derived from personal relationships. This section discusses a hodgepodge of provisions that are loosely

---

88 Reg. § 1.71-1(e).

89 See § 71(c)(2) and Temp. Reg. § 1.71-1T, Questions 16 and 17. Also, see *Arnold A. Abramo*, 78 T.C. 154 (1983) *acq.* and *Comm. v. Lester*, 61-1 USTC ¶9463, 7 AFTR2d 1445,366 U.S. 299 (USSC, 1961).

90 *W.E. Borbonus*, 42 T.C. 983 (1964).

91 Reg. § 1.71-1(e).

associated in that the benefits are received from unrelated or third parties. These include life insurance, prizes and awards, scholarships, cancellation of debts, and government transfer payments.

LIFE INSURANCE PROCEEDS AND OTHER DEATH BENEFITS

Life Insurance. Since its inception the tax law has contained an exclusion for life insurance proceeds received by a beneficiary after an insured person's death.[92] Congress apparently wanted to encourage individuals to buy life insurance to provide adequate resources for their survivors and, at the same time, provide tax-free funds in a time of need.

Many life insurance policies allow the beneficiary to take the life insurance proceeds in either a lump-sum payment or installments. The exclusion applies in either situation. However, the beneficiary is entitled to exclude only the face amount of the policy. Any excess (e.g., investment earnings while the proceeds were left with the insurance company) are taxable.

> **Example 40.** This year W's husband, H, died. Under the terms of a life insurance policy, W is to receive $500,000. Alternatively, W can elect to receive $55,000 per year for the next 10 years. If W takes the lump sum payment, she can exclude the entire $500,000. If she elects to take the installment payout of $55,000 annually, $50,000 of each payment is a nontaxable return of the life insurance proceeds, but the remaining $5,000 is taxable income [$55,000 − ($500,000/10)].

Although life insurance proceeds are normally nontaxable, there are several special rules that should be observed.

Cashing-In the Policy Before Death. Some life insurance policies, notably whole-life, enable the holder to cash the policy in before the taxpayer's death. Any amount received in excess of the premiums paid is taxable. No loss is recognized if the premiums paid exceed the amount received. The 1996 tax legislation provides, however, tax-favored treatment for accelerated death benefits.

Over the past several years, many terminally-ill individuals (e.g., AIDS patients) have surrendered their life insurance policies or sold the policies to a third party in exchange for the death benefits. These death benefits would then be used to pay for medical and other expenses. Although life insurance benefits that are payable on account of death are normally nontaxable, the treatment of accelerated death benefits, often referred to as "viatical settlements," was somewhat unclear. The new law clarifies their treatment by adding Code § 101(g). This section provides that accelerated death benefits (i.e., surrender of the policy to the insurer for a lump sum or sale to a third party) generally may be excluded if the individual is chronically or terminally ill. While the exclusion for terminally ill individuals is unlimited, the exclusion for a chronically ill individual (who is not also terminally ill) is restricted to the amount of long-term care services actually incurred.

An individual is considered terminally ill if he or she has been certified by a physician as having an illness or physical condition that can reasonably be expected to result in death in 24 months or less. A chronically-ill individual is generally a person who is unable to perform at least two activities of daily living (e.g., eating, toileting,

---

[92] § 101(a)(1). Insurance proceeds are also taxable if the policy is an investment contract with little or no *insurance risk* or the owner of the policy does not have an *insurable interest* in the insured. In addition to the insured, a spouse, dependents, business partners, and in some instances, creditors and employers are considered to possess the requisite insurable interest.

transferring, bathing, dressing, and continence) for a period of at least 90 days due to a loss of functional capacity.

> **Example 41.** C is 60 years old and has smoked two packs of cigarettes a day since he was a young man. Three years ago, C was diagnosed with lung cancer. His condition recently took a turn for the worse and his physician now expects that C will live less than a year. C owns a life insurance policy with a face value of $150,000. In order to pay for his medical expenses and home nursing care, C has elected to surrender the policy to his insurance provider for a lump sum of $130,000. Because C is expected to die in 24 months or less, the accelerated death benefit of $130,000 is excluded from his gross income.

Substitute for Taxable Income. In some instances, life insurance is used to protect a creditor against a bad debt loss on the death of the insured. However, the fact that the debt is offset by life insurance proceeds on the death of the insured does not cause otherwise taxable income to be nontaxable. For example, amounts equal to unreported interest due on the debt are taxable interest income.[93] Similarly, proceeds offsetting debt that was previously written off as uncollectible, or proceeds representing gain not previously reported, are included in gross income.[94]

Transfer for Valuable Consideration. If a policy is transferred to another party in exchange for valuable consideration, any *gain* from the proceeds on the insured's death is taxable income.[95] Gain is defined as the insurance proceeds less the owner's basis. Basis is the total purchase price plus all premiums paid by the subsequent owner after the transfer.

> **Example 42.** XY Corporation purchased a $15,000 life insurance policy from S, the insured, for $7,300. The corporation made five annual premium payments of $600 each on the policy. S died at the end of the fifth year and XY collected $15,000 insurance. since XY's basis in the policy is $10,300 [($600 × 5 payments) + $7,300], its taxable income is $4,700 ($15,000 − $10,300).

There are four exceptions to *Example 42.* All gain is nontaxable if the purchaser is (1) a partner of the insured, (2) a partnership in which the insured is a partner, (3) a corporation in which the insured is a shareholder or officer, or (4) the insured.[96]

EMPLOYEE DEATH BENEFITS

Under prior law, the first $5,000 of payments that qualified as death benefits was deductible by the employer but was excluded from income for the deceased's beneficiaries. The 1996 Act repeals this provision by making such payments taxable for decedents dying after August 20, 1996. The repeal of § 101(b) clearly reduces the after-tax value of employee death benefits. Consequently, in order to preserve the economic value of this benefit, employers must increase their payments to the beneficiaries or estate of a deceased employee.

---

[93] *Landfield Finance Co. v. Comm.,* 69-2 USTC ¶9680, 24 AFTR2d 69-5744, 418 F.2d 172 (CA-7, 1969), *aff'g.* 69-1 USTC ¶9175, 23 AFTR2d 69-601, 296 F. Supp. 1118 (DC, 1969).

[94] *St. Louis Refrigerating & Cold Storage Co. v. Comm.,* 47-2 USTC ¶9298, 35 AFTR 1477, 162 F.2d 394 (CA-8, 1947), *aff'g.* 46-2 USTC ¶9320, 34 AFTR 1574, 66 F. Supp. 62 (DC, 1946) and Rev. Rul. 70-254, 1970-1 C.B. 31.

[95] § 101(a)(2).

[96] § 101(a)(2)(B).

PRIZES AND AWARDS

The tax law provides no escape for those fortunate enough to receive prizes and awards. Prizes and awards are fully taxable. This is true regardless of the reason for the award. While this was not always the case, since 1986 winners of the Nobel Prize are taxed the same as those who win the grand prize from Publisher's Clearinghouse. Similarly, winners of sweepstakes, lotteries, employer service awards, contests, door prizes, and raffles held by charitable organizations have taxable income to the extent the fair market value of the winnings exceeds the cost of entering the contests.[97] Fair market value of property won is not necessarily the list price or even the cost to the purchaser. For example, the Tax Court held that the taxable amount for an automobile won was less than its purchase price but more than the amount allowed as a trade-in ten days later, after the car was driven several hundred miles.[98] When property won has no resale market or is nontransferable, the Tax Court has estimated the value that the particular winner could and would pay for similar goods.[99]

Taxpayers who have won a prize or award may avoid taxation if they immediately transfer the prize or award to charity. Although this may seem unnecessary given that taxpayers are entitled to a charitable contribution deduction, the deduction is generally limited to 50 percent of the taxpayer's A.G.I. Consequently, if the taxpayer received a $100,000 award that he or she wanted to donate to charity, an outright contribution might not necessarily offset the income. This treatment is available only for prizes and awards that are made in recognition of religious, charitable, scientific, educational, artistic, literary, or civic achievements, but only if

1. The recipient was selected without any direct action on his or her part to enter the contest or proceeding;

2. The recipient is not required to perform substantial future services as a condition of receiving the prize or award; and

3. The prize or award is given by the payor to a governmental unit or tax-exempt organization as designated by the recipient.[100]

When these rules are met, the award has no impact on the winner's tax liability; it is neither taxable income nor a deductible charitable contribution.

Example 43. After twenty years of medical research at the MNO Institute, E gained an international reputation for her computer studies of protein structures. As a result, she was recently awarded the Nobel Prize in Medicine. E gave the award, which amounted to $375,000, to the American Cancer Society. Because all of the conditions for exclusion are satisfied, the $375,000 prize is excludable from E's gross income.

SCHOLARSHIPS AND FELLOWSHIPS

Although scholarships and fellowships are considered to be prizes and awards, Congress has elected to specifically exempt them from the above provisions in order to promote and lower the cost of education. To this end, § 117 generally allows an exclusion of scholarships and fellowships for those individuals who are candidates under the following conditions:

---

[97] Reg. § 1.74-1(a)(2).

[98] *Lawrence W. McCoy*, 38 T.C. 841(1962), *acq.*

[99] *Reginald Turner*, 13 TCM 462, T.C. Memo. 1954-38.

[100] § 74(b).

- ▶ The individual is a candidate for a degree (either undergraduate or graduate).
- ▶ The degree granting organization is a qualified educational institution, that is, the organization has a faculty, curriculum, and an organized student body (e.g., obtaining a degree at correspondence schools would not qualify).
- ▶ The amount received is a scholarship. It must aid the individual in his or her pursuit of study or research and not represent compensation for services.
- ▶ The amounts received are used for tuition and related expenses, including fees, books, supplies, equipment, and other expenses that are required for either enrollment or attendance (but not room and board).

Example 44. C holds a Ph.D. in chemistry from the University of Michigan. This year the Gemini Foundation, a nonprofit research institution, awarded C a post-doctoral fellowship of $30,000 to do research for a semester at the University of Texas with a noted scientist. C must include the fellowship as taxable income since he is not a candidate for a degree.

As a practical matter, most scholarships easily meet these requirements. A few potential difficulties should be mentioned, however.

It should be emphasized that amounts received for room and board cannot be excluded; however, they are considered earned income for purposes of determining the individual's standard deduction, which should facilitate an offsetting deduction.

Example 45. J, a junior majoring in engineering at Private University, was awarded a $10,000 scholarship during the current year. She used the funds to pay the following school-related expenses: tuition $6,000, technology fee $100, athletic fee $25, books $875, room and board $2,500, and notebooks, pencils, and other supplies, $100. J used the remaining $400 to purchase a set of software products (word processor, spreadsheet, data base, presentation) that several of her professors said would be useful in their courses. J must report $2,900 of taxable income, representing the room and board of $2,500, and the equipment that was not required of $400. Assuming J had no other sources of income, her standard deduction would be equal to her earned income, which in this case is the $2,900 spent on room and board and the suggested equipment. As a result, J's standard deduction would offset her $2,900 of taxable income.

In some situations, amounts that are characterized as scholarships may be considered compensation for services rendered or to be rendered. In such case, the amounts received are taxable even if a current employment relationship does not exist. For example, a scholarship that was awarded a beauty contest winner was considered taxable, since much like an employee, she participated in a televised pageant and was expected to perform promotional services in the future.[101]

Note, however, that amounts received by an employee may qualify for exclusion under an educational assistance plan or as a working condition fringe benefit, as discussed earlier in this chapter. Similarly, employees of educational institutions, including graduate students engaged in teaching or research activities, are entitled to exclude any tuition reductions. In addition, amounts paid for education that are related to the taxpayer's employment may be deductible if certain conditions are met, as described in Chapter 8.

---

[101] Rev. Rul. 68-20, 1968-1 C.B. 55.

CANCELLATION OF INDEBTEDNESS

When a taxpayer borrows money, no income must be recognized since there has been no increase in the taxpayer's net worth. On the other hand, if a lender reduces or cancels a taxpayer's debt, there is a corresponding increase in net worth. In such case, the taxpayer is normally required to include the amount of debt forgiveness in gross income.[102] However, in certain situations the taxpayer may be able to exclude this so-called cancellation of debt income. Some of these include:

- ▸ The cancellation represents a gift or bequest (e.g., a father forgives his son's debt).
- ▸ The cancellation occurs when the taxpayer is insolvent or bankrupt.
- ▸ The cancellation represents a renegotiation of the purchase price.
- ▸ The cancellation of student loans.

Bankruptcy or Insolvency. If the taxpayer is *solvent* at the time a debt is cancelled, there is normally no exclusion and income must be recognized to the extent of the debt forgiveness. On the other hand, if the taxpayer is *bankrupt* or *insolvent* (liabilities exceed the value of the assets), the IRS does not add to the taxpayer's financial woes with more taxable income but provides a reprieve under § 108.

When a debt is cancelled pursuant to a bankruptcy proceeding, there is no taxable income.[103] However, the taxpayer is required to reduce certain tax attributes that normally would produce tax savings in the future. For example, the taxpayer must reduce any net operating loss carryovers by the amount of debt forgiveness. As a result, the taxpayer would lose the benefit of deducting the NOL in the future. In this sense, the income is not truly excluded but rather deferred. However, any debt reduction that exceeds the attributes identified below is ignored entirely, and the related income forever escapes tax. The attributes that must be reduced are:

1. Net operating losses (NOLs) and any NOL carryovers
2. General business credit carryovers
3. Minimum tax credit
4. Capital losses (current and carryovers)
5. Basis of the taxpayer's property (generally depreciable realty)
6. Passive activity loss and credit carryovers
7. Foreign tax credit carryovers

While the attributes normally must be reduced in the order shown, the taxpayer may elect to reduce the basis of property first (i.e., shift number 5 to number 1). By so doing, the taxpayer gives up a deferred deduction (i.e., the depreciation related to the property) for perhaps an immediate deduction (e.g., an NOL as soon as income is produced).

If the taxpayer is not bankrupt when the debt is cancelled, but insolvent, the approach is generally the same as shown above.[104] However, to the extent the taxpayer becomes solvent, taxable income results. Thus, an insolvent taxpayer reduces the attributes identified above until solvency results and the balance is included in gross income.

---

[102] § 61(a)(12).

[103] § 108(a)(1)(A).

[104] § 108(a)(1)(B).

Example 46. XYZ Inc. has assets of $375,000, liabilities of $500,000, and an NOL carryover of $100,000. If creditors forgive $90,000 of debt, none of the forgiveness will generate taxable income because, as shown below, XYZ is insolvent both before and after the debt cancellation. XYZ would be required to reduce the NOL carryover by $90,000 (from $100,000 to $10,000).

	Before	After
Total assets	$ 375,000	$ 375,000
Total liabilities	(500,000)	(410,000)
Insolvent	$(125,000)	$ (35,000)

If, on the other hand, the creditors forgive $140,000 of debt, XYZ will be solvent after the cancellation (i.e., $375,000 − $360,000 = $15,000). Consequently, the firm would report $15,000 of the forgiveness as taxable income in such case. In addition, XYZ would reduce the NOL carryover by $100,000 to zero.

Qualified Real Property Business Indebtedness. As explained above, if a business's debt is cancelled, the taxpayer normally must recognize income unless the business is bankrupt or insolvent. To provide relief to those engaged in the real estate business (other than corporations), Congress created a special exception. Under § 108, a taxpayer may elect to exclude the income resulting from the cancellation of indebtedness incurred or assumed in connection with real property used in a trade or business (*qualified real property business indebtedness*). This is true even though the taxpayer is neither bankrupt nor insolvent. The cancellation of debt income does not escape tax, however. The taxpayer must reduce the basis of the depreciable property for any income that is excluded. As a result, the taxpayer forgoes future deductions. The maximum amount of exclusion may not exceed the excess of the outstanding principal amount of the debt over the fair market value of the property.

Example 47. During 1989 T acquired an office building in Houston for $800,000. He borrowed $700,000 of the purchase price by giving First Bank of Houston a note payable with interest at a rate of 14%. The note was secured by the building. By 2005 the value of the building had dropped to $400,000. At that time, the balance on the note was $600,000. Instead of foreclosing and taking the property, the bank agreed it would be better to leave the real estate in the hands of T and renegotiate the terms of the note so that T could handle the payments. As a result, the bank reduced the principal of the note from $600,000 to $400,000. T may elect to exclude the cancellation of debt income of $200,000, but he must reduce the basis of the property by $200,000.

Seller Reduction of Purchaser's Debt. Another situation where § 108 allows the taxpayer to exclude cancellation of debt income relates to sales where the seller provides the financing for the buyer. If the seller/lender cancels the debt, the buyer may exclude the benefit but must reduce the basis of the property.[105] In effect, the Code treats the transaction as a renegotiation of the purchase price. Note that the result is identical to that discussed above for qualified real property business indebtedness. This rule does not apply if the buyer is bankrupt or insolvent.

---

[105]   § 108(e)(5)(A).

Example 48. Several years ago, B purchased an apartment building from S for $1,000,000. B gave S $200,000 cash and signed a note payable to S for the $800,000 balance. The note was secured by the building. B has recently fallen on hard times and may default on the note, which has a current balance of $700,000. S, not wanting to become a landlord again and not sure that he could find another buyer, reduced the note's principal to $400,000. Since S provided the financing and B is solvent, B may exclude the $300,000 cancellation of debt income but must reduce his basis in the building by $300,000.

Cancellation of Student Loans. Code § 108(f) allows individuals to exclude from income the amount of certain student loans that have been cancelled. This exclusion normally applies only if the forgiveness of the loan is issued by the government and the forgiveness is contingent on the student's fulfilling a public service work requirement. The 1998 law extends this rule to loans that refinance earlier loans that qualify. For example, assume a student receives federal financial aid and subsequently refinances this loan with one issued by the proper organization. If the organization subsequently cancels the new loan and the student agrees to fulfill a public service work requirement, the cancellation of indebtedness income is excluded.

GOVERNMENT TRANSFER PAYMENTS

Many government transfer payments are excluded from income. For example, earlier discussion in this chapter revealed that all or a portion of Social Security benefits are excluded from income. Since medicare benefits are considered to be Social Security, they also are nontaxable. Supplementary medicare payments received as reimbursement of medical expenses deducted in a prior year are taxable, however, to the extent the taxpayer received a *tax benefit* in that year.[106]

Worker's compensation received as a result of a work-related injury is excluded from income.[107] Similar to the typical accident insurance policy discussed earlier in this chapter, worker's compensation provides the injured employee with a fixed amount for the permanent loss or use of a function or member of the body. For example, an individual who loses a hand, fingers, or hearing in a work-related accident receives a nontaxable amount, according to a schedule of payments. This exclusion is extended to compensation received by the survivors of a deceased worker. Other worker's compensation benefits are taxable unless the requirements for accident or health plans, previously discussed, are met.

Both state and Federal government transfer payments that are classified as public assistance (e.g., food stamps) or paid from a general welfare fund (e.g., welfare payments) are nontaxable.[108] Among others, these include payments to foster and adoptive parents, to individuals who are blind, to victims of crimes, for disaster relief, to reduce energy costs for low-income groups, and for urban renewal relocation payments.[109]

Benefits to participants in government programs designated to train or retrain specified groups are frequently nontaxable. Whether these benefits are nontaxable or not is dependent upon the primary purpose of the programs. Thus, if the objective of the program is to provide unemployed or under-employed individuals with job skills that enhance their employment opportunities, amounts received are nontaxable.[110] But, if the

---

[106] Rev. Rul. 70-341, 1970-2 C.B. 31.

[107] § 104(a)(1).

[108] Rev. Rul. 71-425 1971-2 C.B. 76.

[109] Rev. Ruls. 78-80, 1978-1 C.B. 22; 74-153, 1974-1 C.B. 20; 77-323, 1977-2 C.B. 18; 74-74, 1974-1 C.B. 18; 76-144, 1976-1 C.B. 17; 78-180, 1978-1 C.B. 136; and 76-373, 1976-2 C.B. 16.

[110] Rev. Ruls. 63-136, 1963-2 C.B. 19; 68-38, 1968-1 C.B. 446; 71-425, 1971-2 C.B. 76; and 72-340, 1972-2 C.B. 31.

primary purpose is to provide compensation for services, participants are government employees with taxable wages.[111]

Most government transfer payments to farmers are included in income.[112] For example, gross income from farming includes government funds received for trees, shrubs, seed, and certain conservation expenditures, and for reducing farm production.[113] If materials are received instead of cash, their fair market value is taxable income. In addition, taxpayers receiving government funds under qualifying conservation cost-sharing plans may elect to exclude the reimbursement of capital improvements. However, the capitalized cost of the projects must be reduced by the excluded amount.[114]

BUSINESS GROSS INCOME

The amount to be included in gross income for proprietorships, partnerships, and corporations is total revenues plus net sales less cost of goods sold. This same concept is applicable even if the business conducted is illegal or if the activities do not qualify as a trade or business but constitute a hobby. Many of the other includible and excludable business gross income items are discussed earlier in this chapter. Additional income items peculiar to business that deserve discussion are classified as (A) generally includible in, or (B) generally excludable from, gross income.

A. *Generally Includible in Gross Income*
   Agreement not to compete
   Goodwill
   Business interruption insurance proceeds
   Damages awarded
   Lease cancellation payments

B. *Generally Excludable from Gross Income*
   Leasehold improvements (unless made in lieu of rent)
   Contributions to capital

AGREEMENT NOT TO COMPETE AND GOODWILL

The sale of a business often contains an agreement that the seller will not compete with the buyer in the same or similar business within a particular area or distance. In such case, the seller must treat any amount assigned to the agreement as ordinary income. The purchaser may amortize (deduct) this amount over 15 years on a straight-line basis regardless of its useful life.

When the net selling price of the business exceeds the fair market value of all identifiable net assets, the business generally is considered to possess *goodwill*. That is, its potential value exceeds its net assets because of the business name, location, reputation, or other intangible factor. Goodwill is considered a capital asset and, consequently any amounts received for goodwill are normally treated as capital gain. As provided in the Revenue Reconciliation Act of 1993, acquired goodwill can be amortized ratably over a period of 15 years. If the contract includes a single amount for both goodwill *and* a noncompetition agreement, the entire amount is treated as goodwill.

---

[111] Rev. Rul. 74-413, 1974-2 C.B. 333.

[112] Reg. § 1.61-4(a)(4).

[113] *R. L. Harding*, 29 TCM 789, T.C. Memo. 1970-179 and Rev. Rul. 60-32, 1960-1 C.B. 23.

[114] See § 126 and Temp. Reg. § 16A.126-1.

In negotiating the sale, the seller should consider the tradeoffs involved in an allocation of the sales price between the covenant not to compete and goodwill. As a general rule, a seller will normally prefer to allocate more of the sales price to assets that produce capital gain, such as goodwill, than to those that produce ordinary income, such as a covenant not to compete.

> **Example 49.** On January 1 of the current year, Ralph purchased all of the assets of Ed's Bowling Alley (a sole proprietorship) for $500,000. Included in the purchase contract is $60,000 allocable to goodwill and $45,000 to a covenant that prohibits Ed from opening another bowling alley in the next five years. Ed will report $60,000 as a long-term capital gain (taxed at no more than 28%) and the $45,000 as ordinary income. On the other hand, Ralph may amortize the amount paid for goodwill over 15 years (i.e., $60,000 ÷ 15 years = $4,000 per year), and the amount paid for the covenant not to compete over 15 years, notwithstanding it has a useful life of only five years ($45,000 ÷ 15 = $3,000 per year).

BUSINESS INTERRUPTION INSURANCE PROCEEDS

Some businesses carry insurance policies that provide for the loss of the use of property and of net profits sustained when the business property cannot be used because of an unexpected event such as fire or flood. The Regulations state that the insurance proceeds are included in gross income regardless of whether they are a reimbursement for the loss of the use of property or of net profits.[115] Similarly, insurance proceeds that are to reimburse the business for overhead expenses during the period of interruption are taxable.[116]

> **Example 50.** Jordan Manufacturing, Inc. (JMI) was the victim of arson during the current year. The fire destroyed the main office building and the company's warehouse and its contents. JMI received a check for $1.5 million from its insurance company covering the projected lost profit for six months during which operations at JMI ceased. Since the profits which were not generated would be taxed, the payment representing the lost profit is fully included in JMI's gross income.

DAMAGES AWARDED

Cash may be awarded by the courts or by insurance companies for damages suffered by businesses because of patent infringement, cancellation of a franchise, injury to a business's reputation (see later discussion concerning professional reputation), breach of contract, antitrust action, or unfair competition. The treatment of the damages depends on whether they are compensatory (i.e., those amounts making the taxpayer whole) or punitive (i.e., those amounts that serve as a penalty). Punitive damages are fully taxable.[117] On the other hand, compensatory awards may be used *first* to offset any litigation expenses or other expenditures in obtaining the award.[118] *Second*, funds that represent a recovery of capital when damages are awarded because of a loss in value to a business's goodwill or other assets are used to offset or write down the capitalized asset costs.[119] Remaining damages generally are considered to be a reimbursement for a

---

[115] Reg. § 1.1033(a)-2(c)(8).

[116] Rev. Rul. 55-264, 1955-1 C.B. 11.

[117] *Comm. v. Glenshaw Glass Co.*, 55-1 USTC ¶9308, 47 AFTR 162,348 U.S. 426 (USSC, 1955).

[118] *State Fish Corp.*, 49 T.C. 13 (1967), *mod'g* 48 T.C. 465 (1967).

[119] *Farmers' and Merchants Bank of Cattletsburg, Ky. v. Comm.*, 3 USTC ¶972,11 AFTR 619,59 F.2d 912 (CA-6, 1932) and *Thomson v. Comm.*, 69-I USTC ¶9199,23 AFTR2d 69-529,406 F.2d 1006 (CA-9, 1969).

loss of profits and are included in gross income.[120] An exception to the latter classification occurs when compensatory damages are awarded in an antitrust suit. While the punitive damages in these cases are taxable, the compensatory damages are taxable only to the extent that losses sustained by the business resulted in a tax benefit.[121]

> **Example 51.** Several years ago, Good Corporation contracted with Bad Corporation to build a condominium project. Good later identified defects in the construction and sued Bad. This year the court awarded Good $1,000,000; $750,000 for compensatory damages and $250,000 for punitive damages. Good incurred legal fees of $150,000. Good must treat the $250,000 punitive damages as ordinary taxable income. The compensatory damages are first reduced by the costs incurred to secure the award, $150,000. The remaining $600,000 is used to reduce the basis of the property, and any excess would be taxable.

LEASE CANCELLATION PAYMENTS

Early termination of lease agreements may result in a lease cancellation payment. Either a lessor or a lessee may receive these payments, depending on which party canceled the lease. In *Hort*, the Supreme Court held that lease cancellation funds received by a lessor are a substitute for rent.[122] Consequently, these receipts are taxable income. Amounts received by a lessee on cancellation of a lease are considered proceeds from the sale of the lease.[123] Thus, the gain is included in gross income. Whether the gain is ordinary or capital depends on the use of the property (see discussion in Chapter 16).

> **Example 52.** Alice owns a 50-unit apartment complex in Manhattan. Nancy, who rents one of Alice's units, has decided to purchase her own house. Consequently, Nancy paid Alice $1,100 in return for cancelling her lease. Alice must treat the payment as a substitute for rental income and, therefore, must include the amount as ordinary income.

> **Example 53.** This year Alice decided to convert her 50-unit apartment complex into a medical clinic for use by physicians and dentists. She paid one of her tenants $2,000 to cancel the lease. Because the lease agreement represents a capital asset to the tenants (i.e., the lease on a residence is a personal asset), the tenant will treat the $2,000 as capital gain.

LEASEHOLD IMPROVEMENTS

A lessee often makes improvements to leased real estate. These may range from minor improvements up to the construction of a building on the leased land. If these improvements are made in lieu of rent payments, they are included in the lessor's gross income.[124] Otherwise, the lessor has no taxable income either at the time the improvements are made or at the time the lease is terminated, even if the improvements substantially increase the property's value.[125] The lessor's only taxable income from these improvements will occur indirectly on the sale of the property to the extent the improvements result in a higher net selling price.

---

[120] *Durkee v. Comm.*, 1950-1 USTC ¶9283, 35 AFTR 1438, 162 F.2d 184 (CA-6, 1947), *rem'g.* 6 T.C. 773 (1946).

[121] § 186 and Reg. § 1.186-1.

[122] *Hort v. Comm.*, 41-1 USTC ¶9354, 25 AFTR 1207, 313 U.S. 28 (USSC, 1941).

[123] § 1241.

[124] Reg. § 1.109-1.

[125] § 109.

Example 54. For the past 10 years W had leased land to X. During the current year the lease expired and W became the owner of a three-stall garage (FMV $19,000) that X had constructed on the property seven years previously. Assuming the improvements were not made in lieu of rent, the FMV of the garage is not currently included in W's gross income.

Under new § 110, a retail tenant that receives cash or rent reductions from the lessor of retail space does not include such amounts in income if the cash (or equivalent) is used for qualified construction or improvement to the space. In order to qualify for the exclusion, the tenant must have a short-term lease (i.e., a lease of retail space for 15 years or less). The amount excluded cannot exceed the amount spent by the tenant for the improvement.

From time to time, lessors will make improvements on their property in order to attract lessees. If a lessor abandons a leasehold improvement in the year the lease terminates, the lessor is allowed a deduction equal to the landlord's adjusted basis of the improvement [§ 168(i)(8)]. This rule does not apply where the improvement is demolished in which case the landlord simply increases the basis of the property (§ 280B). This change is effective for abandonments and disposals after June 12, 1996.

CONTRIBUTIONS TO CAPITAL

Cash or other property received by a business in exchange for an ownership interest are nontaxable transactions for the business. These transfers are treated as contributions to capital and not income.[126] Contributions to capital that are not in exchange for an ownership interest also are nontaxable.

MISCELLANEOUS ITEMS

As stated in the first paragraph of this chapter, gross income includes *all* income unless specifically exempted. Although this chapter is not intended to discuss every income item, some additional items are classified for discussion purposes as miscellaneous.

FEES RECEIVED

Ordinarily, fees received for services performed are included in gross income. Thus, fees paid to corporate directors, jurors, and executors are reported as miscellaneous gross income. However, if executor fees are paid regardless of whether the taxpayer performs any services, they may qualify as nontaxable gifts.[127]

ASSET DISCOVERY

Cash or other assets found by a taxpayer are taxable income even if found accidentally, with no effort expended in discovering them.[128] For example, taxpayers were held to have taxable income equal to cash found in a used piano they had purchased.[129]

---

[126] §§ 118 and 721.

[127] Rev. Rul. 57-398, 1957-2 C.B. 93.

[128] Rev. Rul. 53-61, 1953-1 C.B. 17.

[129] *Cesarini v. Comm.*, 70-2 USTC ¶9509, 26 AFTR2d 70-5107. 428 F.2d 812 (CA-6, 1970).

CAR POOL RECEIPTS

One type of earned income is nontaxable. Vehicle owners operating car pools for fellow commuters may exclude all the revenues received.[130] Car pool expenses are *personal* commuting expenses, and therefore are not deductible. If, however, the car pool activities are sufficient to qualify a taxpayer as being in a trade or business, all revenues are taxable. How much activity constitutes a trade or business is a question of fact not easily answered, but in this type of situation, the definition of trade certainly requires considerably more activity than a single automobile or small van making one round trip daily.

INCOME TAX REFUNDS

All income tax refunds are nontaxable except to the extent the taxpayer received a tax benefit in a prior year.[131] A corporation receives a tax benefit for all business expenses, including state and local income taxes but not Federal income taxes, unless the corporation incurs a net operating loss for the year of deduction. State and local income taxes paid by individuals, however, provide a tax benefit only if the taxpayer itemized these deductions in the year paid. There is no tax benefit for the expense if the standard deduction was used instead of itemized deductions.

> **Example 55.** John and Lori Hansen are married and live in Kokomo, Indiana. The couple filed a joint return for 2004. Their total itemized deductions, including state income taxes withheld by their employers of $3,000, amounted to $12,100 in 2004. On June 12, 2005, the Hansens received a refund from the State of Indiana for $225 as a result of overpaying their 2004 Indiana income taxes. Because the Hansens received a tax benefit by deducting the state income taxes on their 2004 Federal income tax return, they must include the $225 refund in gross income on their 2005 Federal income tax return.

TEMPORARY LIVING COSTS

If an individual receives insurance proceeds to cover temporary living costs incurred because the principal residence was destroyed or damaged by fire, flood, or other casualty, the funds are nontaxable to the extent they are offset by *extra* living costs.[132] These funds also may be excluded if the government prevented the individual from using an undamaged residence because of the existence or threat of a casualty. Extra living costs are limited to those additional costs actually incurred for temporarily housing, feeding, and transporting the taxpayer and members of the household. Typical qualifying costs are hotel or apartment rent and utilities, extra costs for restaurant meals, and additional transportation necessitated by having to live outside the immediate area of the residence.

DAMAGES AWARDED TO INDIVIDUALS

The growing controversy over the treatment of punitive and compensatory damages awarded to individuals for personal injury and sickness sparked Congress to make clarifications in the law. Prior law contained two basic rules: (1) punitive damages were normally taxable and (2) compensatory damages received on account of physical injury

---

[130] Rev. Rul. 55-555, 1955-2 C.B. 20.

[131] § 111(a).

[132] § 123.

or sickness were not taxable. Interpretative problems plagued the application of both of these rules.

Punitive Damages. While punitive damages are normally taxable, the courts had reached differing opinions about the treatment of punitive damages related to cases involving physical injury or sickness. One theory allowed the taxpayer to exclude punitive damages related to physical injury or sickness while the other theory made all punitive damages taxable. As amended, § 104(a)(2) now makes it clear that all punitive damages are taxable even if they are related to physical injury or sickness.

Compensatory Damages. As noted above, damages awarded on account of physical injury or sickness (other than punitive damages) are not taxable. Problems arose in applying this rule to certain awards such as those involving age, sex, and race discrimination. Taxpayers artfully argued that these awards were at least in part related to physical injury and sickness, hoping to qualify for an exclusion. The seriousness of the situation could be seen in a class action suit brought by hundreds of IBM employees that had been laid off who argued for the exclusion of their severance pay on the grounds that such payments were made in part to allay future claims of discrimination.

The new law continues the old rule that damages awarded on account of physical injury and sickness are not taxable. However, § 104 is revised to emphasize that *emotional distress* is not considered a physical injury or sickness unless such distress had its origins from physical injury or sickness. Emotional distress includes physical symptoms such as insomnia, headaches or stomach disorders that may result from such emotional distress. According to the Committee Reports, this rule bars an exclusion for any damages received based on a claim of employment discrimination or injury to reputation accompanied by a claim of emotional distress. Thus it appears that awards made due to employment discrimination based on age, sex, race or similar factors would be fully taxable. The fact that the individual suffered emotional distress that produced physical symptoms would not enable the taxpayer to qualify for the exclusion. However, the law does explain that damages actually used to pay for medical expenses related to emotional distress are nontaxable.

The narrowing of this provision generally is effective for amounts received after August 20, 1996. However, settlements involving continuing payments will continue to be nontaxable if they were entered into on or before September 13, 1995.

Example 56. In July of 2003 K filed a sex discrimination lawsuit against Statewide University after being denied promotion to associate professor with tenure. In November of 2005 the parties entered into an out-of-state settlement pursuant to which the university awarded K $80,000 in lost wages, $5,000 for medical expenses related to emotional distress and $40,000 of punitive damages. Of the $125,000 she received, only the $5,000 payment for medical expenses would be excluded from K's gross income. Amounts allocated to lost wages and punitive damages are taxable.

TAX PLANNING

INVESTMENTS

Tax-planning strategy must be viewed in terms of each taxpayer's own financial position. When considering investments, both the after-tax return and the risk involved must be evaluated. Before-tax income frequently is lower for tax-exempt and tax-deferred investments than it is for taxable investments with the same degree of risk. Consequently, tax-exempt investments should be most attractive to those in the higher tax bracket. They may not be beneficial to those in the lower bracket. Tax-deferred investments should be most attractive to those expecting a lower tax bracket when the deferral period ends. In addition, investors must consider whether any gains will be taxed as ordinary income or capital gains (see Chapter 16), and whether capital gains will be needed to offset capital losses.

Taxpayers have a variety of investment opportunities available to them. In order to arrive at informed investment decisions, comparative evaluations are necessary. However, such evaluations must be viewed with caution. The very nature of this type of analysis means that tentative assumptions must be made about the future. For example, when comparing a possible stock purchase with an annuity purchase, assumptions must be made about (1) future cash flows for the two investments, (2) future marginal tax rates, and (3) the discount rate to be used in determining the present value of the expected cash flows. A decision should never be based on a simple nonmathematical tax comparison of the total of annual dividends plus capital gains for the stock, as opposed to the total deferred ordinary income for the annuity. A tax adviser should always remember that while taxation is a very important factor, it is just one of several that must be considered.

On the death of an insured person, life insurance companies ordinarily allow beneficiaries to receive the proceeds in one lump sum, or in installments for a stipulated period or over the beneficiary's life. Tax concerns aside, some beneficiaries may elect to leave the proceeds with the insurance company simply because they like the security of receiving a periodic payment from an established financial institution. Each installment contains a ratable portion of the proceeds plus interest. This interest is taxable income. Thus, life insurance proceeds received in installments are treated the same as annuities.

> **Example 57.** M is the sole beneficiary of her husband's $60,000 life insurance policy. She elects to receive the proceeds in monthly installments for 10 years. Her monthly installment is $500 plus interest on the unpaid principal. In the current year, she receives $6,000 plus $3,700 interest. Her taxable interest income is $3,700.

One feature of life insurance that has enticed many investors over the years is its tax-free cash build-up. Taxpayers have taken advantage of this by borrowing against the policy—in effect receiving use of the income without having to pay tax on it. To discourage the purchase of life insurance as a tax-sheltered investment vehicle, special rules have been established. As a result, taxpayers must closely scrutinize the type of insurance they purchase with respect to its tax treatment. Under the revised rules, a taxpayer who receives amounts before age 59½, including loans, from certain single premium and other investment-oriented life insurance contracts (modified endowment contracts) is treated as receiving income first and then a recovery of basis. In addition, the recipient is subject to an additional 10 percent income tax on the amounts received that are includible in gross income. This provision affects only "modified endowment contracts" entered into on or after June 21, 1988.

An investor who desires nontaxable income may choose to purchase assets such as

1. Qualifying state and local government bonds to obtain the full interest income exclusion

2. Stocks in companies with net income for accounting purposes, but no earnings and profits for tax purposes, to obtain the full exclusion for distributions that are treated as a return of capital

Investors who wish to defer income may choose to

1. Exchange Series E or EE bonds that are maturing for Series HH bonds in order to continue deferring the accrued interest on the surrendered E or EE bonds

2. Purchase annuities (or to elect that life insurance proceeds be received as annuities) to obtain the deferral of all interest income until received

3. Purchase assets that are expected to appreciate, such as stocks, real estate, and collectables, to obtain the deferral of all appreciation until it is realized

If the taxpayer does not dispose of the assets, the deferral becomes permanent. That is, no one recognizes the income and the assets are inherited at their market values, including the deferred income.

EMPLOYEE BENEFITS

Company fringe benefits can provide employees with tax consequences that range from excellent savings to actual disadvantages. From a tax viewpoint, the best fringe benefits are those that are deductible by the employer and convert otherwise taxable income to nontaxable income for the recipient. For example, most employee benefits that are provided in lieu of additional salary convert taxable compensation to nontaxable benefits.

> **Example 58.** W is a new employee of Z Corporation. Her compensation package is $20,000. However, she may choose to receive (a) $20,000 salary and no benefits, or (b) $19,000 salary and Z will pay premiums of $600 for medical insurance and $400 for group-term life insurance. If W chooses the first option, she has $20,000 taxable income, but if she selects the second option, she has $19,000 taxable income.

Another very valuable type of fringe benefit is one that is nontaxable income if provided by the employer but is a nondeductible expenditure if paid by the employee. Most fringe benefits are of this type. These include premiums paid for group-term life insurance up to $50,000, qualifying meals and lodging on the premises, supper money, company parking, use of company facilities, and employee discounts. All of these benefits are deductible costs by the employer but nontaxable income to the employee when the necessary requirements discussed in this chapter are met. If, however, the employees pay these costs instead of the employer, there is no tax deduction for them.

A third type of fringe benefit includes expenditures that are deductible expenses, when paid by individuals, but are subject to restrictions. For example, health insurance premiums are deductible for employees who itemize their deductions but *only* to the extent that all qualifying medical expenditures exceed 7.5 percent of A.G.I. (see Chapter 11). Thus, employer-paid health insurance represents different tax savings to different employees.

> **Example 59.** L's compensation includes a salary of $30,000 plus employer-paid health insurance premiums of $600. L's taxable income is $30,000 since the $600 is nontaxable. If the company policy is changed so that L pays the $600 health insurance premiums and the company increases his salary to $30,600, the tax effect on L depends on his individual tax situation.
>
> 1. If L does not itemize medical expenses, he has taxable income of $30,600 salary and no deduction for the $600.
>
> 2. If L itemizes deductions and his medical expenditures before the health insurance premiums exceed 7.5% of A.G.I., he still has taxable income of $30,600 salary but now has a deduction of $600.

Assume L has a 25% marginal tax rate. In situation 1 above, his tax benefit from employer-paid health insurance premiums is $150 ($600 × 25%). In the second situation, L appears to receive no tax benefit when his company pays the health insurance premiums. However, his A.G.I. is $600 higher when L pays the premium. Since medical expenses equal to 7.5% of A.G.I. are not deductible, this increases the nondeductible portion by $45 ($600 × 7.5%). Thus, at the 25% tax rate, his tax increases by $11.25 ($45 × 25%).

Some employer-provided benefits can be a disadvantage to employees. Recall, for example, that disability income is taxable if the premiums were paid by the employer but nontaxable if they were paid by the individual. The best tax-planning advice when employers pay disability insurance premiums is for employees to convince employers to provide another benefit and let employees pay their own disability premiums.

Considerable leeway in tax planning is available to those employees who are allowed to select their own fringe benefits. Simply looking at the cost of each benefit to the company, however, is inadequate. Each employee should carefully evaluate personal needs and the tax effect of each desirable benefit before selection is made.

EMPLOYEE VERSUS SELF-EMPLOYED

The numerous favorable tax results received with fringe benefits are available only if an employer/employee relationship exists. When all necessary requirements are met, it does not matter if the employees are major shareholders of the employer. This situation creates an incentive to operate some businesses as corporations rather than as proprietorships or partnerships or LLCs.

One of these fringe benefits, employer-furnished meals and lodging, has been of interest to closely held businesses for years. Farming represents a particularly good example of a business that requires someone to be available on the property 24 hours a day. When the working owner lives on the farm, a business deduction plus an employee exclusion for the cost of meals and lodging provided to the farmer can be significant.

Example 60. A farm owned by M has the following information for the current year:

Gross income.	$130,000
Cost of food consumed by M	2,000
Cost of lodging used by M	4,200
Salary to M.	20,000
Other farm expenses	85,000

If the farm is a proprietorship, net farming income is $25,000 ($130,000 − $20,000 − $85,000) and M has an A.G.I. of $45,000 ($25,000 + $20,000).[133] Similar results occur if the farm is a partnership, except M will report only his share of the $25,000. In contrast, if the farm is a corporation, net income is $18,800 ($130,000 − $2,000 − $4,200 − $20,000 − $85,000) and M has an A.G.I. of $20,000. Thus, M, the proprietor, has $45,000 A.G.I. compared with a combined income of $38,800 ($18,800 + $20,000) for the M Corporation and M, the employee.

Although the above example seems to result in a tax advantage for the corporate farm, such a conclusion is over-simplified. Other tax factors are important. For example, corporate net income is taxed to the corporation currently and again as dividend income to shareholders when distributed to them (see Chapter 20). Another important factor is that individuals and corporations are subject to different tax rates. Also, if farming

---

[133] Technically, a proprietor's salary is not a farming expense but is shown in the example for comparison purposes. Thus, net income is $45,000 ($130,000 − $85,000) and M's A.G.I. is $45,000.

losses occur, the results may be very unfavorable with a corporate entity. The important point to remember is that the tax advantage achieved with the corporation for meals and lodging (and other employee benefits) is just one of the necessary ingredients when evaluating whether a business should be incorporated.

DIVORCE

Insufficient attention usually is given to tax planning during separation and divorce. Of course, favorable tax results are easier to accomplish when the individuals are parting amicably, but good results still can occur amid animosity. The more disparate the husband's and wife's tax brackets, the greater the benefits to be achieved. This is because payments classified as alimony or separate maintenance are deductible by the payor and are taxable income to the recipient. In contrast, all other asset transfers are neither deductible expenses nor taxable income.

> **Example 61.** H and W are divorced. H's marginal tax rate is 35% while W's is 15%. Every $10 of alimony costs H $6.50 after taxes [$10 paid − $3.50 tax savings ($10 × 35%)] and is worth $8.50 to W after taxes [$10 received − $1.50 tax due ($10 × 15%)]. Thus, H pays $6.50 for W to receive $8.50. If W requires $425 after taxes each month, she must receive $500 if the payments qualify as alimony [$500 − ($500 × 15% = $75)] or $425 if they do not. On the surface, it seems that H would rather pay $425 a month than $500 but $500 in alimony results in an after-tax cost of $325 [$500 − ($500 × 35% = $175)] for a monthly savings of $100 ($425 − $325). Naturally, the closer the two marginal rates, the less there is in tax savings.

PROBLEM MATERIALS

DISCUSSION QUESTIONS

6-1 *Basic Concepts.* Determine whether each of the following statements is true or false. If false, rewrite the statement so that it is true. Be prepared to explain each statement.
   a. Receipts are included in gross income only if specifically listed in the Code.
   b. Tax returns show (1) gross receipts from all sources, less (2) excludable income, which equals (3) taxable income.
   c. Interest earned on tax-exempt municipal bonds is nontaxable income regardless of whether it is received by an individual or by a corporation.

6-2 *Investment—Stocks versus Bonds.* C has $10,000 to invest but is uncertain whether to purchase H, Inc. stocks or tax-exempt bonds issued by the State of Illinois. List the relevant types of information that C must obtain or estimate in order to make a mathematical calculation of her after-tax return on the two investments she is considering.

6-3 *Investments—Bonds.* D, Inc. bonds are selling for $1,000 each with an interest rate of 11 percent. Tax-exempt bonds issued by the State of Kentucky are selling for $1,000 each with an interest rate of 8 percent. Which bond provides a taxpayer with the higher after-tax return when the marginal tax rate is
   a. 36 percent?
   b. 15 percent?

6-4 *Investments—Dividend Income.* Corporate distributions may qualify as dividends, return of capital, or stock dividends. Explain the tax treatment of each of these three distributions. What determines whether a distribution is a dividend, a return of capital, or a stock dividend?

6-5 *Employee Benefits.* Z, Inc. owns and operates several businesses, including six hotels and two real estate agencies. R, an employee of Z, spends three nights free of charge in one of Z's hotels in Indiana. Is the value of the lodging nontaxable to R, assuming the information below? Explain.

    a. R works for one of the real estate agencies.

    b. R tends bar in one of the hotels in Maine.

    c. R is a tax accountant in Z's corporate headquarters where the tax records of all of Z's businesses are maintained.

6-6 *Employee Benefits—Comparison.* Compare the tax treatment for each of the items listed below assuming they are paid by (1) the employer, or (2) the employee.

    a. Parking in the company lot during working hours

    b. Health insurance premiums

    c. Disability insurance premiums

    d. Meals eaten in the company cafeteria when the employee must remain on the premises for job reasons

6-7 *Employee Benefits—Meals and Lodging.* Employer-provided meals and lodging that qualify as nontaxable income can be an exceedingly valuable employee benefit.

    a. When do employer-provided meals and lodging qualify as nontaxable income?

    b. List at least 10 types of occupations in which employer-provided lodging and/or meals could qualify for the exclusion. Explain why these occupations are appropriate for the exclusion.

6-8 *Employee Benefits.* Over the years, the list of employee benefits that qualify as deductible expenses by the employer and nontaxable income for the employee has expanded. Assume Congress is interested in further expanding the list of benefits available for this special tax treatment. Prepare a list for Congress of at least three items not discussed in this chapter that would provide many employees with valuable benefits. Explain why these three would be logical additions.

6-9 *Gifts.* How can gifts to family members reduce the family's income tax liability?

6-10 *Alimony and Child Support.* A husband and wife who are obtaining a divorce disagree whether certain periodic payments should be classified as alimony or child support.

    a. What difference does it make how the payments are classified?

    b. What if the agreement states the payments are for both alimony and child support without making a specific distinction in dollar allocation between the two?

    c. List three types of compromise offers that could be made by the husband to reach an allocation that might satisfy both the husband and wife. Explain the tax consequences of each of the three possible solutions.

6-11 *Alimony.* A husband (H) and wife (W) are obtaining a divorce. He agrees to pay alimony of $25,000 in each of the two years after the divorce to enable her to attend graduate school. No alimony will be paid after the second year.

    a. What are his deductible and her taxable amount of alimony for each of the two years, and what are the tax effects in year three?

    b. How could the payment schedule be restructured to maximize his deductions?

    c. How could the payment schedule be restructured to minimize her taxable income?

6-12 *Prizes and Awards.* Contest winners must report the value of prizes won as taxable income.

    a. What arguments could the taxpayer use to convince the IRS and the courts that the values of the prizes are less than their retail selling prices?

    b. Are any prizes or awards ever nontaxable? Explain.

6-13 *Scholarships and Fellowships.* CPA firms are interested in encouraging practical research that explores accounting issues with an objective of developing better accounting methods for the profession. Assume the XY firm decides to establish a fund that will support individual research efforts. Recipients of these grants will be selected based on the quality of their past work and on a written proposal of a specific research project to be completed with funds from the XY firm. Do recipients of these grants have taxable or nontaxable income? Explain.

6-14 *Goodwill versus Agreement Not to Compete.* A preliminary agreement covering the sale/purchase of a dental practice includes an allocation of $40,000 to goodwill and the agreement that the seller will not practice dentistry within a five-mile radius for five years.
  a. What are the tax consequences of this $40,000 allocation?
  b. What advice should a tax adviser give the seller?
  c. What advice should a tax adviser give the buyer?

6-15 *Damages Awarded.* As the result of a newspaper article, V claims his character was damaged beyond repair, he lost his job, and he incurred medical expenses for psychiatric care. His lawsuit requested that the court award him the following amounts: $500,000 for personal injury due to slander; $30,000 in lost wages; and $5,000 for psychiatric care.
  a. What are the tax consequences to V if he is awarded the $535,000?
  b. V decides to accept an out-of-court settlement of $150,000. The newspaper and its insurer are willing to allocate the $150,000 in any manner that V requests. How should V have the amount allocated?

PROBLEMS

6-16 *Basic Concepts.* Calculate the amount to be included in gross income for the following taxpayers.
  a. T is self-employed as a beautician. Her records show

Receipts	
Services	$21,000
Product sales	3,000

Expenditures	
Cost of products sold	1,800
Cost of supplies used	2,600
Utilities	2,400
Shop and equipment rent	3,600
Other expenses	1,000

  b. R owns rental property. His records show

Gross rents	$6,000
Depreciation expense	4,200
Repair expense	2,100
Miscellaneous expense	300

c. S is an employee with the following tax information:

Gross salary.	$15,000
Social security (FICA) taxes withheld (rounded for simplicity)	1,000
Federal income tax withheld	2,200
Health insurance premiums withheld	500
Net salary received in cash	11,300
Employer's share of social security taxes	1,000

6-17 *Investments—Cash Dividends.* Three years ago, Z purchased 50 shares of L common stock for $6,000. Although Z is married, the stocks are recorded in his name alone. The current market value of these shares totals $7,200. He and Mrs. Z file a joint return and neither of them owns any other stock. Mr. Z wants to know what effect each of the following totally separate situations has upon (1) his taxable income and (2) his basis in each share of stock.

a. L distributes a cash dividend and Z receives $330.

b. L distributes cash as a return of capital and Z receives $330.

6-18 *Investments—Stock Dividends.* A, who is single, purchased 100 shares of N Corporation common stock four years ago for $12,000. The stock has a current fair market value of $14,400. A asks how each of the following separate situations affects her (1) taxable income and (2) basis in each share of stock.

a. N distributes common stock as a dividend and A receives 10 shares.

b. N distributes nonconvertible preferred stock as a dividend and A receives ten shares. The preferred stock has a current fair market value of $100 per share.

6-19 *Investments—Cash Dividends.* D, Inc. had accumulated earnings and profits at January 1 of the current year of $20,000. During the taxable year, it had current earnings and profits of $10,000. On December 31 of the current year, D, Inc. made a cash distribution of $40,000 to its sole shareholder, G. G paid $25,000 for his stock three years ago.

a. How will G treat the $40,000 he received on December 31?

b. Assume G sold all of his stock for $36,000 on January 1 of the following year. Compute his capital gain.

6-20 *Investments—Interest.* Mr. K died at the beginning of the year. Mrs. K received interest during the year from the following sources:

Corporate bonds	$1,100
Bank savings account	200
Personal loan to a friend	500
City of Maryville bonds (issued to build a new high school) . .	600

In addition to the above, Mrs. K was the beneficiary of her husband's $50,000 life insurance policy. She elected to receive the $50,000 proceeds plus interest over the next 10 years. She receives $7,500 in the current year and will receive a like amount each of the following nine years. Calculate the taxable portion of the interest income received by Mrs. K during the year.

6-21 *Educational Savings Bonds Requirements.* H and W have twin sons, S and T, and two daughters, D and E. The couple purchased Series EE savings bonds, hoping to take advantage of the interest exclusion for their children's education. This year, they cashed in some of the bonds, receiving $5,000. Of this amount, $2,000 represented interest. For each of the following independent situations, indicate how much, if any, of the exclusion is allowed this year.

    a. D enrolled at Michigan State University and paid tuition of $4,000. To help defray some of these expenses, she used an academic scholarship of $1,000.

    b. While on her way to the first day of class, D fell and broke her leg. She withdrew from classes and received all of her money back.

    c. S is 25 and entered the Ph.D. program at the University of Texas this year. As a teaching assistant, he receives a salary of $7,000 during the year. His parents paid $1,000 of his tuition.

    d. H and W paid for all of T's tuition to attend Arizona State University. The couple's A.G.I. for this year was $110,000. When the couple purchased the particular bonds used to pay for T's tuition, their A.G.I. was $55,000.

    e. E, 22, redeemed bonds this year, receiving $5,000. E used all of the proceeds to pay for her tuition. She received the bonds as a gift from her parents last year. E's A.G.I. for this year is $3,000.

6-22 *Investments—Annuities.* P is single, 65 years old, and retired. On August 1, 1990 he purchased a single-premium deferred life annuity for $40,000 using after-tax funds. This year, P received $5,000 in annuity benefits. He will receive a like amount each year for the rest of his life. (**Note:** In answering the following questions, use the information in Exhibit 6-3 of this chapter.)

    a. Calculate P's taxable income from the annuity for the current year.

    b. Calculate P's taxable income from the annuity for year 5.

    c. Calculate P's taxable income from the annuity for year 22.

    d. Assume P lives just 15 more years. Calculate the deduction that would be allowed on P's final tax return.

    e. Assume the annuity was purchased by P and his employer jointly. P contributed $12,000 in after-tax funds, and the employer contributed $28,000. Calculate P's taxable income from the annuity for the current year.

6-23 *Annuities.* A, age 62, retired after 30 years of service as an employee of the XYZ Corporation. He started receiving retirement benefits in the form of a single life annuity on January 1 of the current year. A's total after-tax contributions to the plan amounted to $39,000, and his retirement benefit is $1,500 per month.

    a. Determine A's nontaxable portion of each monthly payment, assuming he elects the simplified safe-harbor method.

    b. Assume A lives another 25 years. Will there be a time period in which A will be required to fully include the monthly payments in gross income? If so, when?

6-24 *Prepaid Tuition Plan.* Z is a dependent beneficiary of a qualified prepaid tuition plan established by her parents. During the current year, Z received a $20,000 distribution and used it to pay $20,000 for tuition at a private university. Z's parents contributed $60,000 to the plan and earnings from investments total an additional $20,000.

    a. How much of the $20,000 distribution may Z exclude from gross income?

    b. Assume Z elects to join the work force rather than attend college and the entire $80,000 accumulated in the plan is distributed to Z's parents. How much is included in the parent's gross income?

6-25 *Prepaid Tuition Plan.* V, who is divorced, transfers $45,000 to Eastern University's qualified prepaid tuition plan for the benefit of his son, W, in 2005. W received no other gifts during 2005.

    a. Compute V's taxable gift for 2005 (assume no election was made).

    b. Assume V elects to treat the contribution as a gift made over five years. Does V owe any gift taxes?

    c. Assume V dies in 2008. How much of the $45,000 contribution made in 2005 will be included in V's gross estate?

6-26 *Investments—Life Insurance.* L is 65 years old and retired. Her husband died early in the year. L was the beneficiary of his $20,000 life insurance policy. L elected to receive $5,200 annually for five years rather than receive a single payment of $20,000 immediately. Calculate L's taxable income from the first payment.

6-27 *Social Security Benefits.* X, who is single and retired, has the following income for the current year:

Taxable interest	$12,000
Dividend income	10,000
Tax-exempt bond interest	8,000
Social security benefits	7,200

    a. Compute the taxable portion of X's social security benefits.

    b. Assume the above information remains the same, except X's taxable interest amounted to $10,000. Compute the taxable portion of his social security benefits.

6-28 *Group-Term Life Insurance.* E, age 55, is Vice President of QRS, Incorporated. His salary for 2005 amounted to $75,000. Employees at QRS receive group-term life insurance coverage equal to twice their annual salaries. Determine E's taxable income from his group-term life insurance protection for 2005.

6-29 *Employee Benefits.* Determine the (1) deductible employer amount, and (2) taxable employee amount for each of the following employer-provided benefits.

    a. Reimbursement of expenses paid by an employee to entertain a client of the business, $200.

    b. Bonus paid an employee when a sales quota was met, $300.

    c. Watches given employees at Christmas, $38 each.

    d. Free parking provided on company property, $500 market value and $220 cost per employee.

    e. Supper money of $15 paid to an employee for each of 10 nights that she worked past 6 p.m., $150.

6-30 *Employee Benefits.* Determine the (1) deductible employer amount, and (2) taxable employee (or beneficiary) amount for each of the following employer-provided benefits.

    a. A death benefit of $6,000 paid to the wife and $4,000 to the son of a deceased employee.

    b. Premiums of $700 paid on $70,000 of group-term life insurance for a 52-year-old woman employee.

    c. Ten percent employee discounts are allowed on the retail price of all merchandise purchased from the employer. During the year, sales to employees totaled $18,000 ($20,000 retail price − $2,000 discount) for merchandise that cost the employer $14,000. The employer reported the $18,000 as sales and the $14,000 as cost of goods sold.

6-31 *Employee Benefits—Medical Insurance.* F's $400 annual health insurance premium is paid by his employer. During the year, F received $870 reimbursement of medical expenses; $650 for this year's expenses and $220 for last year's expenses. Determine F's taxable income from the reimbursement in the current year if

    a. F never itemizes any medical expenses.

    b. F deducted medical expenses from his A.G.I. this year of $900 and last year of $450.

6-32   *Tax Benefit Rule.* During 2004 K had adjusted gross income of $30,000. A list of itemized deductions available to K in preparing her 2004 return is shown below:

State income taxes paid	$2,000
Property taxes on residence	600
Charitable contributions	400
Medical expenses	2,500
Interest paid on residence	1,200

K is single, and her son M, who is 8 years old, lives with her. She qualifies as a head of household. In 2005 K received $2,500 from an insurance company for reimbursement of her 2004 medical expenses. Is K required to include any of the $2,500 reimbursement in her gross income in 2005?

6-33   *Fringe Benefits versus Compensation.* P is a 46-year-old professor at Z University, a private school in the Midwest. P is married and has triplets who are freshmen at Z University. Among others, P is provided with the following fringe benefits during the current year:

Group-term life insurance coverage of $75,000. Premium cost to Z University is $300.
Tuition reduction of $30,000 for the triplets.

a.   How much does the group-term life insurance cost Professor P? Assume his marginal tax bracket is 31 percent.

b.   Would P be equally well off if the university simply paid him an additional $300 in compensation to cover the term insurance?

c.   Is the tuition reduction for the triplets taxable?

d.   Assuming tuition remains constant, how much will Professor P save in tuition payments by remaining on the faculty at Z University until the triplets graduate?

e.   What would be the result for the current year if the university increased Professor P's salary by $30,000 a year to pay for the triplets' tuition?

6-34   *Unemployment Compensation and Disability Income.* Mr. and Mrs. B are married filing jointly. Mrs. B was permanently disabled the entire year and Mr. B was unemployed part of the year. Both are 55 years old. Their receipts for 2005 were

Disability income—Mrs. B	$ 6,200
Social security income—Mrs. B	1,000
Salary—Mr. B	16,500
Unemployment compensation—Mr. B	4,500

Calculate their taxable income for 2005, assuming the disability insurance premiums were paid

a.   Entirely by Mrs. B.

b.   Entirely by Mrs. B's employer.

6-35   *Damages Awarded and Disability Income.* D works for the XYZ Tool and Die Shop. On March 1, 2005 a stamping press that D was operating malfunctioned, resulting in the loss of the index finger on his right hand. D, claiming the machine was not properly maintained, sued XYZ for the following damages:

Medical expenses during D's one-week stay in the hospital	$ 8,000
Loss of D's finger	50,000
Punitive damages	5,000
Total	$63,000

On April 1, 2006 the court awarded D $63,000.

a. Assuming D did not deduct the $8,000 of medical expenses he incurred in 2005, what portion of the $63,000 settlement is included in D's gross income in 2006?

b. D did not return to work for three months. During this time period, he received $3,000 in disability income payments. Assuming D paid the annual premium on the disability insurance, how much of the $3,000 is taxable income to D?

6-36 *Meals and Lodging.* Mr. and Mrs. G own and operate a small motel near Big Mountain resort area. Their only employees are two maids and one cook. The rest of the work is done by Mr. and Mrs. G. In order to be on 24-hour call, they live in a home next to the motel. The home is owned by the business. Both Mr. and Mrs. G eat most of their meals in the motel restaurant. Answer the questions below assuming the business is (1) a corporation, or (2) a partnership.

a. Are any of the costs for the meals and lodging deductible by either the business or Mr. and Mrs. G?

b. Is the value of the meals and lodging included in Mr. and Mrs. G's gross income?

c. Answer the questions in (a) and (b) again, but assume Mr. and Mrs. G paid the business for all their meals in the restaurant and for rent of the home.

6-37 *Adoption Assistance.* R and L are married and file a joint return. R is the controller of a tool and die firm and is paid a salary of $140,000. L is a grade school teacher and earns $27,500. Other income received during the current year includes $1,000 in interest on State of Indiana bonds owned by R and $2,500 in dividends on Procter & Gamble stock that L owns. R and L, who have no children of their own, incurred $9,000 in qualified adoption expenses (i.e, adoption fees, attorney fees and court costs) to adopt a 2-year-old "special needs" child. These expenses were covered by R's employer under the company's adoption assistance program.

a. Determine R and L's A.G.I. for the current year.

b. Assuming the couple elects the standard deduction, compute their taxable income for the current year.

6-38 *Transportation Fringes.* How much is includible in the employee's gross income in each of the following scenarios?

a. Employee A receives a transit pass each month from Employer X valued at $95.

b. Employer Y provides free parking each month to employee B valued at $215.

c. Employer Z provides parking each month to employee C valued at $195. Employee C pays Employer Z $40 per month for this parking fringe.

6-39 *Employer-Provided Parking.* Employer V operates a factory in a rural area in which no commercial parking is available. V provides ample parking for its employees on the business premises, free of charge.

a. What guidance does the Internal Revenue Service provide for determining the value of free parking?

b. Given the facts presented above, what value would the IRS place on the free parking provided by Employer V?

6-40 *Military Compensation.* After graduating from high school last year, K, who is single, joined the U.S. Air Force. Her military compensation for 2005 is

	Cash	Market Value
Salary	$10,000	
Military housing		$2,500
Computer training on the job		1,800
Uniforms		800
Meals on the base		3,600
Reimbursement of moving expenses	500	

Calculate K's taxable income for the year.

6-41 *Inheritances.* In each of the following independent situations. determine how much. if any, the taxpayer must include in gross income.

    a. At the beginning of this year, a taxpayer inherited rental property valued at $87,000 from his grandmother. Rental income from the property after the transfer of title totaled $6,000, and rental expenses were $5,200.

    b. A taxpayer inherited $50,000 from her employer. She was his housekeeper for ten years and was promised she would be provided for in his will if she continued employment with him until his death.

    c. A taxpayer lent $15,000 to a friend. To protect the loan, the taxpayer had his friend make him beneficiary on her $20,000 life insurance policy. Six months later the friend died and the taxpayer received $20,000 from the insurance company.

6-42 *Gifts.* In each of the following independent situations, determine how much, if any, the taxpayer must include in gross income.

    a. A taxpayer often visits her uncle in a nursing home. In addition, she manages his investment portfolio for him. To show his gratitude, he has given her stock valued at $5,000. He has also implied that if she continues these activities, he will transfer other shares of stock to her.

    b. A taxpayer saved a child's life during a fire. The child's parents gave him land valued at $5,000 to show their gratitude. They paid $2,200 for the land several years ago.

    c. Taxpayer's employer gave him $1,200 in recognition of his 20 years of service to the company. The employer deducted the $1,200 as a business expense.

6-43 *Awards.* In each of the following independent situations, determine how much, if any, the taxpayer must include in gross income.

    a. The taxpayer, a professional basketball player, was voted as the outstanding player of the year. In addition to the honor, he received an automobile with a sticker price of $16,000. He drove the car for six months and sold it for $12,000. The taxpayer's employer also gave him a gold watch worth $1,200. He wears the watch. Both donors deducted their respective costs for the automobile and the watch as business expenses. The costs of the automobile and watch were $13,500 and $800, respectively.

    b. The taxpayer was selected by the senior class as the most outstanding classroom teacher. The high school presented her with a $1,000 check in recognition of her significant accomplishments. She used the money to take a well-earned vacation to Cancun.

    c. M, Inc. gave T a watch in recognition of her 20 years of service to the company. The watch cost the employer $400.

6-44 *Child Support and Alimony.* Determine the effect on A.G.I. for the husband (H) and wife (W) in each of the following *continuous* situations. H and W are divorced and do not live in a community property state. They have three children.

    a. H pays W $400 per month as alimony and support of the three children.

    b. W discovers her attorney did not word the agreement correctly. H and W sign a statement that the *original* agreement is retroactively amended to hold that H pays $100 per month as alimony to W and $300 per month as support of the three children. All other language remains unchanged. What is the effect of this change on future and past payments?

    c. Assume the original agreement contained the wording in (b) above. In the first year, H makes only 10 of the 12 payments for a total of $4,000. In the second year, H pays the $800 balance due for the prior year and makes all 12 payments of $400 each on time.

d. On their divorce, W was awarded an automobile. H is required to pay the loan outstanding on the car, $94 per month for 20 months. During the year, H pays $94 for 12 months. This includes $130 interest and $998 loan principal.

e. H owns the home in which W and the children live free of charge. H's mortgage payments are $360 per month for the next 20 years. During the year, his expenses on the home are $2,900 interest, $800 property taxes, $340 insurance, $280 loan principal, and $218 repairs. The rental value of the home is $425 per month.

f. In addition to the monthly alimony and support payments above, H is to pay W $30,000 over a period of 11 years. H pays $2,500 of this amount the first year and $3,600 the second year.

g. H inherits considerable property. As a result, he voluntarily increases the alimony to $150 and child support to $450 per month. He makes 12 payments of $600 each during the year.

6-45   *Alimony.* Determine the effect on A.G.I. for the husband (H) and wife (W) in each of the three years. W is to pay H alimony of $100,000 as follows:

Year	Amount
1.	$56,000
2.	26,000
3.	18,000

6-46   *Divorce—Property Settlement.* Husband (H) and wife (W) are divorced this month. The divorce agreement states that all jointly owned property will be transferred as follows:

	Cost	Market Value	Transferred to
Home	$35,000	$65,000	W
Investments	3,000	5,000	W
Cash	7,000	7,000	H and W equally

W will occupy the home and H will rent an apartment. Determine the recognized gain or loss and the basis of the assets to H and W after the transfer. Explain.

6-47   *Divorce—Property Settlement.* H and W, who live in Michigan (a common law state), decided to end their troubled 30-year marriage. Pursuant to the divorce decree, the following assets are transferred from H to W on March 1, 2005:

	Basis to H	Market Value
Stocks (purchased by H on April 10, 1999)	$300,000	$400,000
Land (purchased by H on June 2, 1995)	200,000	500,000

In addition to the above, H transferred a life insurance policy on his life with a face value of $200,000 to W, who assumed responsibility for the annual premium.

W sold the stocks for $500,000 on November 1, 2005 and the land for $550,000 on December 1, 2005. H died on December 20, 2005.

a. Determine W's gain on the sale of the stocks and land in 2005.

b. Are any of the life insurance proceeds taxable to W? Explain.

6-48   *Accelerated Death Benefits.* T, a wife and mother of three, was diagnosed with throat cancer. Due to the complications from chemotherapy treatments, she resigned from her teaching position at a private university in Chicago on June 1, 2005. Having been certified by her medical doctor on July 7, 2005 as terminally ill, T is considering selling her life insurance policy with a face value of $200,000 to a viatical "settlement provider" (VSP) for a lump sum.

    a. Assuming T has paid $15,000 in premiums, how much must she include in her gross income if she sells her policy to VSP for $150,000 on August 1, 2005?

    b. Does your answer change if T lives longer than 24 months from the date of certification?

    c. If T dies 8 months later, how much must VSP include in its gross income? (Assume VSP paid additional premiums of $10,000 after purchasing the policy.)

6-49 *Employee Fringe Benefits.* For each of the following independent situations, indicate whether the fringe benefit the employee receives is taxable or nontaxable. Explain your answer.

    a. C is a ticket agent for North Central Airways. The airline has a nondiscriminatory policy that allows its employees to fly without charge on a standby basis only. The last week in July, C took a vacation and flew from Kansas City to San Francisco. The value of the round-trip ticket was $400.

    b. Assume that C [in part (a) above] also stayed, without charge, for the entire week at a hotel in San Francisco that North Central Airways owns. The value of a week's stay in the hotel was $2,000.

    c. Assume in part (a) above that C was unable to obtain an empty seat on North Central the last week in July. Consequently, utilizing the qualified reciprocal arrangement that North Central has with South Shore Airlines, C flew free to San Francisco on South Shore. The value of the round-trip ticket was $400.

    d. M is a sales clerk for J-mart department store. The store has a nondiscriminatory policy whereby its employees may purchase inventory items at a discount. In June, M purchased a microwave oven for $250 that J-mart sells to its customers for $300. J-mart's gross profit rate is 20 percent.

    e. F is a CPA and works for a public accounting firm. On F's behalf, the firm paid $375 in subscription fees for three professional accounting journals.

    f. Officers of the XYZ Corporation are provided free parking space in a public parking garage located across the street from the firm's office building. The monthly cost of the parking space to XYZ is $300 for each officer.

6-50 *Unrelated Party Transfers.* In each of the following independent situations, determine how much, if any, the taxpayer must include in gross income.

    a. Taxpayer has been very active as a volunteer hospital worker for many years. In the current year, the city named her as the Outstanding Volunteer of the Year. She later discovered that she was nominated for the award by two nurses at the hospital. The honor included a silver tray valued at $400. In addition, the two nurses collected $700 from hospital personnel and gave her a prepaid one-week vacation for two people.

    b. Taxpayer, an undergraduate degree candidate, was selected as one of five outstanding sophomore students in accounting by the Institute of Management Accountants. Selection was based on an application submitted by eligible students. The winner received $15,000. Although there was no stipulation of how the money was to be used, the award was given with the expectation that the money would be used for tuition, books, and fees in the student's junior and senior years.

    c. Taxpayer won the bowling league award for the highest total score over a five-week period. Taxpayer received a trophy valued at $65 and $100 cash.

    d. Taxpayer purchased church raffle tickets in her eight-year-old son's name and gave the tickets to him. One of the tickets was drawn. The prize was a $600 color television.

    e. Taxpayer receives a $20,000 grant from the National Association of Chiefs of Police to conduct a research study on crowd control. The grant stipulates that the research period is for eight months and that $8,000 of it is for travel and temporary living costs.

    f. An accounting student accepted an internship with a CPA firm and is paid $3,000. The stated purpose of the internship is to provide students with a basic understanding of how accounting education is applied. It is believed this understanding will help students in remaining course work and later job selection. Although the faculty believes internships would benefit all students, only 40 percent of the accounting majors participate in the program.

6-51 *Businesses.* In each of the following independent situations, determine how much, if any, the taxpayer must include in gross income.

    a. A taxpayer sold a beauty shop operated as a proprietorship for $60,000. The assets were valued as follows: tangible assets, $45,000; agreement not to compete, $10,000; and goodwill, $5,000. The seller's basis for the tangible assets is $45,000 but there is no basis for the other two assets.

    b. The building in which a drug store is located is damaged by fire. The store had to be closed for two weeks while repairs were made. As a result, the insurance company paid the store $50,000 for lost profits during the period and $15,000 to cover overhead expenses.

    c. E, Inc. leases land to V, Inc. The agreement states that the lease period is for five years and the annual lease payment is $1,000 per month. Under the terms of the lease, V immediately constructs a storage building on the land for $40,000. E receives $12,000 from V each year for three years. At the end of the third year, V cancels the lease and pays a cancellation penalty of $6,000. At this time, the building's market value is $30,000. Thus, in the third year, E received $18,000 cash and a building worth an additional $30,000. Determine E's taxable income from the lease for each of the three years.

    d. A corporation accepted $100,000 from an insurance company as an out-of-court settlement of a lawsuit for patent infringement.

6-52 *Debt Cancellation.* DEF, Inc. is in the van conversion business. Due to stiff competition and a declining economy in the region served by DEF, the company has incurred significant operating losses during the past year. As of December 31 of the current year, DEF's financial statements reflect the following pertinent information:

Total assets	$ 750,000
Total liabilities	1,000,000
Tax attributes	
Adjusted basis of depreciable assets	300,000
NOL carryover	100,000
Capital loss carryover	25,000

    In an attempt to rescue the company from going out of business, DEF's suppliers have agreed to forgive $180,000 of indebtedness.

    a. Assuming DEF is not in bankruptcy proceedings, what are the tax consequences to the corporation resulting from the cancellation of the debt?

    b. Would your answer to part (a) change if DEF makes an election under Code § 108(b)(5)?

    c. Would your answer to part (a) change if the $180,000 of debt is cancelled under bankruptcy proceedings?

    d. Assume that the facts in the problem remain the same, except that DEF has total assets of $1 million and total liabilities of $750,000. What impact does the cancellation of $180,000 in debt now have on DEF?

6-53 *Miscellaneous Items.* In each of the following independent situations, determine how much, if any, the taxpayer must include in gross income.

a. A taxpayer's round trip mileage to and from work is 50 miles. Five fellow employees live near him and pay to ride with him. The taxpayer's records for the current year show $3,900 receipts and $3,120 automobile expenses.

b. While walking across campus, a taxpayer found a diamond ring. She notified the authorities on campus and paid $10 for an ad in the lost-and-found section of the newspaper. When six weeks went by with no response, she had the ring appraised. It was valued at $1,200. After six more weeks with no response, she sold the ring for $850.

c. A taxpayer was injured on the job and was out of work for most of the year. He received the following government benefits during the year: $800 in food stamps; $1,500 worker's compensation for the injury; and $1,800 in welfare payments.

d. A taxpayer sued her neighbor for malicious slander. The court awarded her $30,000 for personal injury due to indignities suffered as a result of the slander; $3,500 in lost income; and $200 reimbursement for medical expenses incurred. The taxpayer does not itemize deductions.

6-54 *Ordinary v. Capital Gain Income.* In each of the following scenarios, determine the amount (if any) and type of income to be included in gross income by the recipient:

a. Denise acquired all of the net assets of Mary's CPA firm. Mary operated the practice as a sole proprietorship. The purchase price includes $20,000 allocable to goodwill and $15,000 allocable to a covenant not to compete for five years.

b. Ernie rents an apartment from Doug. Because Ernie is being transferred to another city by his employer, he paid Doug $800 to cancel his lease.

c. Mary Ann owns an apartment complex in Jacksonville, Florida. In an effort to convert the apartment into an office building, she pays Jean, one of her tenants, $900 to cancel the apartment lease.

d. John, who is single and lives in Detroit, had total itemized deductions in 2004 of $6,000 including $700 of state income taxes withheld by his employer. On May 14, 2005, John received a refund from the State of Michigan for $200 due to overpaying his Michigan income taxes in 2004.

6-55 *Miscellaneous Fringe Benefits.* In each of the following independent situations answer true if the ending sentence is correct and false if the ending sentence is incorrect. During the current year, A withdraws $2,000 from a qualified tuition plan to pay his undergraduate tuition at Ivy Tech. Of the $2,000 received, $1,600 represents contributions to the plan and $400 represents earnings. *The $400 of earnings is excluded from A's income.*

a. B is employed at the Tire Rack Company. She works the day shift and her two children, ages 3 and 4, stay at the company's day care facility. The current year's value of this service is approximately $4,000. *B may exclude the full $4,000 from income.*

b. C works for Ever Green, Inc. During the evenings C attends State University where she is working on her undergraduate degree in Marketing. During the current year Ever Green paid C's tuition ($3,000) and her textbooks ($800) out of the company's nondiscriminatory educational assistance program. *C may exclude the full $3,800 from income.*

c. D is an employee of Night Line, Inc. where he is covered under the company's qualified pension plan. During the current year D, who is 64 years old, and his wife attended several seminars related to retirement planning that were sponsored by Night Line. The value of this service is approximately $1,500. *The $1,500 will be reported on D's Form W-2 as taxable income.*

CUMULATIVE PROBLEMS

TurboTax

6-56 H, age 40, and W, age 38, are married with two dependent children: M, age 15, and N, age 16. H, who is president of a local bank, is paid a salary of $150,000. He also is the sole proprietor of a jewelry store that had a net profit for 2005 of $75,000. W, a registered nurse at a large hospital, is paid a salary of $50,000. In addition to the above income, H and W received the following during 2005:

a. $6,000 cash dividend on ABC, Inc. stock, which they own jointly. They paid $25,000 for the stock three years ago and it has a current market value of $40,000. ABC, Inc. has $300,000 of current and accumulated E&P.

b. $750 in interest on State of Michigan bonds that H owns.

c. $7,000 in interest on corporate bonds that H and W purchased two years ago at face value for $100,000.

d. W received a check for $400 from her employer in recognition of her outstanding service to the hospital during the past 10 years.

e. The bank provides H with $90,000 of group term life insurance protection. The bank provides all full-time employees with group term insurance.

f. 1,000 shares of XYZ common as a stock dividend. Prior to the distribution, H and W owned 9,000 shares of common with a basis of $15,000. H and W did not have the right to receive cash or other assets in lieu of the stock.

g. Because W must be available should an emergency arise, she is required to eat her lunches in the hospital cafeteria. The value of the free meals provided by her employer during 2005 was $1,100.

h. H's grandfather passed away in February 2005, leaving H a 400-acre farm in southern Illinois valued at $500,000. H rented the land to F, a neighboring farmer, for $13,000.

i. In order to drain off the excess surface water from 10 acres, F (see h above) installed drainage pipe at a cost of $1,500.

j. W sold 50 shares of DEF stock for $100 per share. She bought the stock four years ago for $1,800.

k. H received a dividend check for $280 from the MNO Mutual Life Insurance Company. H purchased the policy in 1983, and W is the primary beneficiary.

l. H and W's only itemized deductions were interest on their home mortgage, $18,000; property taxes on their home, $4,000; and charitable contributions, $6,000.

m. The hospital withheld $11,000 of Federal income taxes on W's salary and the appropriate amount of FICA taxes. The bank withheld $30,000 in Federal income taxes from H's salary and the appropriate amount of FICA taxes. Furthermore, H's quarterly estimated tax payments for 2005 total $35,000.

Part I: Computation of Federal Income Tax. Calculate H and W's 2005 Federal income tax liability (or refund) assuming they file a joint return.

Part II: Tax Planning Ideas. H and W are very concerned about the amount of Federal income tax they now pay. Because they want to send M and N to private universities, they have come up with the following strategies, which they hope will reduce their family's total tax liability.

1. In 2006 M and N will begin working at the jewelry store two nights a week and on Saturdays throughout the school year and 20 hours a week during the summer months. Each child will be paid $4,500 for services during the year.

2. On January 1, 2006 H and W will sell their corporate bonds for $100,000 and invest the cash proceeds in Series EE savings bonds. H and W will use the bonds to pay for M and N's qualified educational expenses.

3. On January 1, 2006 H and W will gift their stock in ABC, Inc. to M and N equally.

4. Beginning in 2006 H will instruct the farmer who is leasing his Illinois farm to pay the $13,000 in rent directly to M and N (i.e., $6,500 each).

H and W have asked for your opinion concerning the above strategies. For each idea, explain why it will or will not reduce the family's total tax liability. Assuming H and W implement only the strategies that will reduce taxes, how much will the family save in taxes in 2006 compared to 2005 (**Note:** Calculate the 2006 tax using the tax law and rates applicable to 2005 and assume all other data from Part I above is the same.)

6-57 A and B are married with two children, ages 15 and 16. A, who is 45 years old, is president of Greenville Savings & Loan (a large financial institution located in Greenville, Michigan). During 2005 his salary amounted to $400,000. Additional information pertaining to A and B's financial affairs for 2005 is summarized below:

a. A and B purchased 1,000 shares of GHI, Inc. common stock on January 1, 2005 for $22,000. On May 1, 2005 A and B received 100 shares of GHI, Inc. common as a stock dividend. They did not have the right to receive cash or other assets in lieu of the stock.

b. On November 15, 2004 A and B purchased a small farm (50 acres) five miles from Greenville for $50,000. Although A and B originally planned to move to the farm when A retires, they ended up selling it on October 20, 2005 to a large real estate developer for $200.000.

c. On August 1, 2005 A and B redeemed Series EE bonds that had matured for $30,000. They originally purchased the bonds for $14,000. During the period they held the bonds, A and B never elected to include in income the annual increase in the redemption price.

d. B's father passed away on September 1, 2005. She inherited $100,000, which they deposited in a savings account at the Greenville Savings & Loan. The interest on the deposit amounted to $2,000 for the year.

e. Greenville Savings & Loan provided A with the following benefit package:

Fringe Benefit	Annual Cost to Greenville S & L
Health insurance premium.	$2,400
Accident and disability premium.	600
Parking space	190
Group-term life insurance of $150,000.	800

f. A and B's only itemized deductions were mortgage interest on their personal residence, $40,000; state and local taxes, $30,000; and charitable contributions, $8,000.

g. The Greenville Savings & Loan withheld $100,000 of Federal income taxes on A's salary and the appropriate amount of payroll taxes. In addition, A's quarterly estimated tax payments for 2005 total $40,000.

Part I: Calculation of Taxable Income and Tax Due. Compute A and B's taxable income and Federal income tax liability for 2005 assuming they file a joint return.

Part II: Tax Planning Suggestions. Assume that A and B come to you on July 1, 2005 seeking your advice on ways in which they can reduce their 2005 Federal income tax liability. They provide you with the following additional information:

1. The real estate developer, who is interested in acquiring A and B's 50 acres, is willing to defer the purchase date to June 16, 2006. What would you recommend A and B do? Explain your answer.

2. A and B would like to get the best return possible on the money they will receive from the sale of their farm. Two options they are considering are (1) invest the

proceeds in corporate bonds paying 7% annually and (2) purchase State of Michigan bonds paying 5½% annually. What would you recommend A and B do? Explain your answer.

3. A and B have been informed that the Series EE bonds that mature on August 1, 2005 can be exchanged for Series HH bonds that pay interest semiannually. What would you recommend A and B do? Explain your answer.

6-58 *Continuous Tax Return Problem.*
Previous Facts:
Larry L. and Cathy C. Zepp have been married 19 years. Larry is age 62 (Social Security number 123-45-6789) while Cathy is age 50 (Social Security number 123-45-6788). They live at 1234 Elm Dr. in Des Moines, Iowa 50311. Larry is a salesman employed by DSK Industries. This year he earned $110,000 (income tax withheld was $17,000). A corrected W-2 is below. Cathy recently completed a graduate degree in computer technology. She continues to freelance as an independent contractor in computer graphics. Her earnings from various engagements were $12,000. Her only expenses were for miscellaneous office supplies of $3,000. She paid estimated taxes during the year of $1,000 ($250 on each due date). Other income earned by the couple included interest income of $3,000 from a certificate of deposit and $975 of interest from tax-exempt bonds issued by the State of Iowa. The couple owns a duplex that it rents out. Annual rentals were $8,000 and rental expenses (e.g., maintenance, utilities, depreciation) were $3,000. Other expenses paid during the year included:

Unreimbursed medical expenses.....................	$ 9,000
Interest on home mortgage	12,000
Real property taxes on home........................	1,900
Charitable contributions.............................	1,000
Rental of safety deposit box to hold certain investments	100
Unreimbursed employee business expenses of Larry	3,000

Assume that all of the expenses except their business expenses are incurred jointly.

- The Zepps have two children, a son Wrigley F. Zepp (111-33-4444, 12/1/1986)) and a daughter: Apple A. Zepp (111-33-4445, 1/4/1992). Both children lived with them the entire year. Apple is considered legally blind.
- Apple received interest income of $3,000.

New Facts

- This year Larry began receiving Social Security benefits. For the year, he received $12,000.
- The couple received a Form 1099 (see below) regarding an investment in a mutual fund.
- Cathy was unemployed for a short period and received unemployment compensation of $800.
- Larry paid $1,800 of alimony to his first wife.
- Cathy received $2,000 of alimony from her first husband.
- Cathy inherited $100,000 from her rich uncle.
- The corrected W-2 below reveals an item reported in Box 12 Code C of $125.

Prepare Form 1040 for the Zepps.

a Control number 0068251111		OMB No. 1545-0008	Safe, accurate, FAST! Use	IRS *e~file*	Visit the IRS website at www.irs.gov/efile.

b Employer identification number (EIN) 25-2222345	1 Wages, tips, other compensation 110,000.00	2 Federal income tax withheld 7,000.00

c Employer's name, address, and ZIP code DSK Industries 1635 Longest Drive Des Moines, IA 50311	3 Social security wages 90,000.00	4 Social security tax withheld 5,580.00
	5 Medicare wages and tips 110,000.00	6 Medicare tax withheld 3,190
	7 Social security tips	8 Allocated tips

d Employee's social security number 123-45-6789	9 Advance EIC payment	10 Dependent care benefits

e Employee's first name and initial Last name Larry L. Zepp 1234 Elm Dr. Des Moines, IA 50311	11 Nonqualified plans	12a See instructions for box 12
	13 Statutory employee ☐ Retirement plan ☐ Third-party sick pay ☐	12b
	14 Other	12c 125
		12d

15 State Employer's state ID number	16 State wages, tips, etc.	17 State income tax	18 Local wages, tips, etc.	19 Local income tax	20 Locality name

Form **W-2** Wage and Tax Statement   **2005**   Department of the Treasury—Internal Revenue Service

Copy B—To Be Filed With Employee's FEDERAL Tax Return.
This information is being furnished to the Internal Revenue Service.

9191   ☐ VOID   ☐ CORRECTED

PAYER'S name, street address, city, state, ZIP code, and telephone no. National Funds Box 2509 Santa Ana, CA 92799	1a Total ordinary dividends $ 3,000	OMB No. 1545-0110	Dividends and Distributions
	1b Qualified dividends $ 3,000	2004 Form 1099-DIV	
	2a Total capital gain distr. $ 1,400	2b Unrecap. Sec. 1250 gain $	**Copy A** For **Internal Revenue Service Center** File with Form 1096.
PAYER'S Federal identification number	RECIPIENT'S identification number		
RECIPIENT'S name Larry L. Zepp	2c Section 1202 gain $	2d Collectibles (28%) gain $	For Privacy Act and Paperwork Reduction Act Notice, see the **2004 General Instructions for Forms 1099, 1098, 5498, and W-2G.**
	3 Nontaxable distributions $	4 Federal income tax withheld $	
Street address (including apt. no.) 1234 ELM DR		5 Investment expenses $	
City, state, and ZIP code DES MOINES, IA 50311	6 Foreign tax paid $	7 Foreign country or U.S. possession	
Account number (optional) 2nd TIN not. ☐	8 Cash liquidation distributions $	9 Noncash liquidation distributions $	

Form **1099-DIV**   Cat. No. 14415N   Department of the Treasury - Internal Revenue Service

Do Not Cut or Separate Forms on This Page — Do Not Cut or Separate Forms on This Page

6-59   *Continuous Tax Return Problem. Additional Questions.* Answer the following questions relating to the *continuous tax return problem* above.

a.   What is the Zepp's marginal tax rate? Effective rate?

b.   At what rate were the dividends taxed?

c.   Which of the following statements is true regarding the tax treatment of Larry's social security benefits?

    1.   None of the social security payments was taxable

    2.   50% of the social security payments was taxable

    3.   85% of the social security payment was taxable

    4.   None of the above.

d.   The item in Box 12 Code C represents the taxable amount of $125.00.

    1.   Nontaxable combat pay

    2.   Employer paid adoption benefits

    3.   The taxable cost of group term life insurance exceeding $50,000

    4.   Amounts contributed to a 401(k) retirement plan (elective deferral of income)

6-60   *Continuous Tax Return Problem. Additional Questions.* Answer the following questions relating to the *continuous tax return problem* above.

a.   Assume that Apple received interest income of $3,000 and qualified dividend income of $1,000. Prepare Form 1040 for Apple. For simplicity purposes, assume that the taxable income of his parents was $200,000 and their return revealed qualified dividend income of $3,000.

b.   At what rates were Apple's interest and dividend income taxed?

RESEARCH PROBLEMS

6-61   *Divorce.* J and M are obtaining a divorce after ten years of marriage. They have two children. A draft of the divorce agreement and property settlement between them states that they will have joint custody of the children. They plan to live in the same general area and each child will live half of each year with each parent. Since J's A.G.I. is $40,000 and M's $15,000, he will pay her $100 per month for each child ($2,400 per year) and $500 per month for her support. The $500 ceases on his or her death, her remarriage, or when her A.G.I. equals his. In addition, J agrees to continue to pay premiums of $50 per month on his life insurance policy payable to her. All jointly owned property will be distributed as follows:

	Basis	Market Value	Transfer to
Home	$50,000	$80,000	M
Furnishings	20,000	15,000	M
Investments	10,000	30,000	J

Each will keep his or her individually owned personal items and an automobile. This is an amicable divorce and they both request your advice. Their objective is to maximize total tax benefits without making too many changes to the agreement. Use tax-planning techniques when possible in responding to the following questions.

a.   Who will be able to claim the children as dependents?

b.   What is each one's filing status for the current year if neither one remarries?

    c. Does the $500 per month qualify as alimony? Does the $50 per month qualify as alimony?

    d. J expects to make the $500 and $50 payments for three months while legally separated before the divorce. What are the tax effects during this period?

    e. What is the tax effect of the distribution of jointly owned property to J and to M?

    f. What tax planning advice could you give to J and M that would decrease their combined tax liability?

6-62 *Meals and Lodging.* H and W are married with three children. The children are 8, 10, and 15 years old. H and W are purchasing a 500-acre farm, which they will manage and operate themselves. In addition, they will employ one full-time farmer year round and several part-time people at peak times. H will be responsible primarily for management of the operations, the crops, and the dairy herd and other farm animals. W will be responsible primarily for the garden, the chickens, providing meals for the family and farm hands, and maintaining the family home. The children are assigned farm chores to help their parents after school and on weekends.

    The taxpayers prefer to operate the farm as a partnership but, after all factors are considered, are willing to incorporate the farm if it seems to provide greater benefits. Presently, they ask for detailed information about the residence on the farm and the groceries that will be purchased to feed them and their employees on the farm. Some of their specific questions are listed below.

    a. What are the benefits and requirements covering meals and lodging provided by the business?

    b. Is it possible to meet the requirements and obtain all or at least some of the benefits if the farm is operated as a proprietorship or partnership, or must it be operated as a corporation?

    c. If full benefits are obtained, are any adjustments required for the children, for personal entertainment and meals shared with friends and relatives in the farm home, or any other personal use? If any adjustments are required, which ones, and are they made at cost or market value?

    d. If full benefits are obtained, exactly what qualifies? For example, do all groceries qualify, including supplies that are not eaten, such as freezer bags to store frozen foods from the garden, soap, and bathroom supplies? Do all expenses for the home qualify, such as utilities, insurance, and repairs?

    e. Should the business or should H and W own the home?

    f. Is it acceptable for H and W to purchase the food and be reimbursed by the business?

6-63 *Discharge of Indebtedness.* T, who is single, purchased a new home in 1978 from the XYZ Construction Co. for $55,000. She received a 7.25 percent mortgage from the Federal Savings and Loan Association (FS&L). Currently, the home's fair market value is approximately double its original purchase price. Since interest rates have risen significantly in recent months, FS&L wants to rid itself of the low 7.25 percent mortgage. Lending to others at a much higher interest rate would clearly enhance FS&L's profits. Consequently, during the current year FS&L sent a letter to T offering to cancel the mortgage (which had a remaining principal balance of $35,000) in return for a payment of $29,000. T took advantage of the prepayment opportunity, thus receiving a discount equal to the difference between the remaining principal balance of $35,000 and the amount paid by T of $29,000, or $6,000.

    a. Although T is pleased she no longer has a monthly mortgage payment, she is concerned about the possible tax consequences resulting from the discharge of indebtedness. T has come to you for your advice.

    b. Assume that the fair market value of T's residence has declined to $25,000 due to the construction of a nearby land fill operation. Does this fact change your answer?

6-64 *Compensatory Damages.* T. J. Taxpayer, CLU, has owned an insurance agency in Santa Rosa, California since 1960. As an independent agent, he represented five companies selling auto, home, commercial, and life insurance. Because of his excellent reputation in the community, T. J. has built a very successful agency. Last year, T. J. applied for an agency license from the American Life Insurance Co. in order to broaden his life insurance business. In reviewing his application, American requested a credit report from Federal Credit. Federal Credit provided copies to American Life as well as other insurance companies.

The credit report contained numerous false accusations. In addition to questioning Taxpayer's integrity, the report stated that T. J. seldom returned phone calls from clients and lacked understanding of basic insurance practices and concepts. As a result, American Life denied T. J. a license to sell its life insurance. Because the report adversely affected his ability to work with existing clients and to attract new business, T. J.'s profits declined considerably.

T. J. sued Federal Credit for libel, claiming that the credit report was issued with intent to damage his business or professional reputation. The jury found that Federal Credit had committed libel and awarded him $100,000 in compensatory damages. T. J. has heard conflicting comments from various sources about whether the $100,000 is taxable and comes to you for help. What advice would you give T. J. Taxpayer concerning the taxability of the $100,000?

6-65 *Sex Discrimination.* Alice Johnson has worked for the AMAX Corporation for ten years. In March 1999, after talking with various company employees, Alice came to the realization that there was a significant pay differential between men and women. In fact, she discovered that the corporation had modified its compensation package in 1997 whereby the salaries of employees in certain male-dominated pay schedules were increased but those in certain female-dominated pay schedules were either unchanged or reduced.

As a result, Alice Johnson brought suit (under Title VII of the Civil Rights Act of 1964) in District Court against the AMAX Corporation alleging unlawful discrimination in the payment of wages based upon gender. Alice sought back pay from the company in the amount of $10,000 to eliminate the discrimination. Rather than incur substantial costs in litigating the issue, AMAX reached an out-of-court settlement with Alice on January 15, 2005. The settlement requires AMAX to pay Alice back pay of $8,000 and to develop gender-neutral pay schedules.

Is the $8,000 subject to tax?

Part III

DEDUCTIONS AND LOSSES

❖ Contents ❖

Chapter 7

OVERVIEW OF DEDUCTIONS
AND LOSSES

LEARNING OBJECTIVES

Upon completion of this chapter you will be able to:

- Recognize the general requirements for deducting expenses and losses
- Define the terms *ordinary*, *necessary*, and *reasonable* as they apply to business deductions
- Recognize tax accounting principles with respect to deductions and losses
- Explain the proper treatment of employee business expenses

- Describe the importance of properly classifying expenses as deductions *for* or *from* adjusted gross income
- Classify expenses as deductions *for* or *from* adjusted gross income
- Recognize statutory, administrative, and judicial limitations on deductions and losses
- Explain tax planning considerations for optimizing deductions

CHAPTER OUTLINE

As explained in Chapter 3, the income tax is imposed on taxable income, a quantity defined as the difference between gross income and allowable deductions.[1] The concept of gross income was explored in Chapters 5 and 6. This chapter and the following four chapters examine the subject of deductions.

There is little doubt that when it comes to taxation, the questions asked most frequently concern deductions. What is deductible? Can this expense be deducted? How much can I deduct? This is a familiar refrain around taxpaying time, and rightfully so, since any item that might be deductible reduces the tax that otherwise must be paid. Many of the questions concerning deductions are easily answered by merely referring to the basic criteria. On the other hand, many items representing potential deductions are subject to special rules. The purpose of this chapter is to introduce the general rules that are in fact used for determining the answer to that age-old question: Is it deductible?

DEDUCTION DEFINED

In the preceding chapters, the definition given for income was described as being "all-inclusive" (i.e., gross income includes *all* items of income except those specifically excluded by law). Given this concept of income, it might be assumed that a similarly broad meaning is given to the term deduction. Deductions, however, are defined narrowly. Deductions are only those *particular* expenses, losses, and other items for which a deduction is authorized.[2] The significance of this apparently meaningless definition is found in the last word—"authorized." *Nothing is deductible unless it is allowed by the Code.* It is a well-established principle that before a deduction may be claimed the taxpayer must find some statutory provision permitting the deduction. The

---

[1]   § 63.

[2]   § 161.

courts consistently have affirmed this principle, stating that a taxpayer has no constitutional right to a deduction. Rather, a taxpayer's right to a deduction depends solely on "legislative grace" (i.e., Congress has enacted a statute allowing the deduction).[3]

Although a taxpayer's deductions require statutory authorization, this does not mean that a particular deduction must be specifically mentioned in the Code. While several provisions are designed to grant the deduction for a specific item, such as § 163 for interest expense and § 164 for taxes, most deductions are allowed because they satisfy the conditions of some broadly defined category of deductions. For example, no specific deduction is allowed for the advertising expense of a restaurant owner, but the expense may be deductible if it meets the criteria required for deduction of *business expenses*.

The remainder of this chapter examines those provisions authorizing several broad categories of deductions: § 162 on trade or business expenses, § 212 on expenses of producing income, and § 165 on losses. In addition to these deduction-granting sections, several provisions that expressly deny or limit deductions for certain items are considered. The rules provided by these various provisions establish the basic framework for determining whether a deduction is allowed. Once the deductibility of an item is determined, an additional problem exists for individual taxpayers—the deduction must be classified as either a deduction *for* adjusted gross income or a deduction *from* adjusted gross income (itemized deduction). The classification process is also explained in this chapter.

DEDUCTIONS FOR EXPENSES: GENERAL REQUIREMENTS

Given that the taxpayer can deduct only those items that are authorized, what deductions does Congress in fact allow? The central theme found in the rules governing deductions is relatively straightforward: those expenses and losses incurred in business and profit-seeking activities are deductible while those incurred in purely personal activities are not. The allowance for business and profit-seeking expenses stems in part from the traditional notion that income is a *net* concept. From a conceptual perspective, income does not result until revenues exceed expenses. It generally follows from this principle that it would be unfair to tax the revenue from an activity but not allow deductions for the expenses that produced it.

In light of the Code's approach to deductions, many commentators have aptly stated that the costs of *earning* a living are deductible while the costs of living are not. Although this is a good rule of thumb, it is also an over-generalization. As will become clear, the Code allows deductions not only for the costs of producing income, but also for numerous personal expenses such as interest on home mortgages, property taxes, medical expenses, and charitable contributions. To complicate matters further, the line between personal and business expenses is often difficult to draw. For this reason, the various rules governing deductions must be examined closely.

GENERAL RULES: CODE §§ 162 AND 212

Two provisions in the Code provide the authority for the deduction of most expenses: § 162 concerning trade or business expenses and § 212 relating to expenses for the production of income. Numerous other provisions of the Code pertain to deductions. These other provisions, however, normally build on the basic rules

---

[3] *New Colonial Ice Co. v. Helvering*, 4 USTC ¶1292, 13 AFTR 1180, 292 U.S. 435 (USSC, 1934).

contained in §§ 162 and 212. For this reason, the importance of these two provisions cannot be overstated.

Section 162(a) on trade or business expenses reads, in part, as follows:

> In General.—There shall be allowed as a deduction all the ordinary and necessary expenses paid or incurred during the taxable year in carrying on any trade or business, including—
>
> 1) a reasonable allowance for salaries or other compensation for personal services actually rendered;
> 2) traveling expenses (including amounts expended for meals and lodging other than amounts which are lavish or extravagant under the circumstances) while away from home in the pursuit of a trade or business;
> 3) rentals or other payments required to be made as a condition to the continued use or possession, for purposes of the trade or business, of property to which the taxpayer has not taken or is not taking title or in which he has no equity.

Although § 162(a) specifically enumerates three items that are deductible, the provision's primary importance lies in its general rule: ordinary and necessary expenses of carrying on a trade or business are deductible.

Section 212 contains a general rule very similar to that found in § 162. Section 212, in part, reads as follows:

> In the case of an individual, there shall be allowed as a deduction all the ordinary and necessary expenses paid or incurred during the taxable year—
>
> 1) for the production or collection of income;
> 2) for the management, conservation, or maintenance of property held for the production of income...

Production of income expenses are normally those related to investments, such as investment advisory fees and safe deposit box rentals.

An examination of the language of §§ 162 and 212 indicates that a deduction is allowed under either section if it meets *four* critical requirements. The expense must have all of the following properties:

1. It must be related to carrying on a trade or business or an income-producing activity.

2. It must be ordinary and necessary.

3. It must be reasonable.

4. It must be paid or incurred during the taxable year.

It should be emphasized, however, that satisfaction of these criteria does not ensure deductibility. Other provisions in the Code often operate to prohibit or limit a deduction otherwise granted by §§ 162 and 212. For example, an expense may be ordinary, necessary, and related to carrying on a business, but if it is also related to producing tax-exempt income, § 265 prohibits a deduction. This system of allowing, yet disallowing, deductions is a basic feature in the statutory scheme for determining deductibility.

RELATED TO CARRYING ON A BUSINESS OR AN INCOME-PRODUCING ACTIVITY

The Activity. Whether an expense is deductible depends in part on the type of activity in which it was incurred. A deduction is authorized by § 162 only if it is paid or incurred in an activity that constitutes a trade or business. Similarly, § 212 permits a deduction only if it is paid or incurred in an activity for the production or collection of income. The purpose of each of these requirements is to deny deductions for expenses incurred in an activity that is *primarily personal* in nature. For example, the costs incurred in pursuing what is merely a hobby, such as collecting antiques or racing automobiles, normally would be considered nondeductible personal expenditures. Of course, this assumes that such activities do not constitute a trade or business.

The Code does not provide any clues as to when an activity will be considered a trade or business or an income-producing activity rather than a personal activity. Over the years, however, one criterion has emerged from the many court cases involving the issue. To constitute a trade or business or an income-producing activity, the activity must be *entered into for profit*.[4] In other words, for the taxpayer's expenses to be deductible, they must be motivated by his or her hope for a profit. For this reason, taxpayers who collect antiques or race automobiles can deduct all of the related expenses if they are able to demonstrate that they did so with the hope of producing income. In such case, they would be considered to be in a trade or business. If the required profit motive is lacking, however, expenses of the activity generally are not deductible except to the extent the activity has income.

As may be apparent, the critical question in this area is what inspired the taxpayer's activities. The factors to be used in evaluating the taxpayer's motivation, along with the special provisions governing activities that are not engaged in for profit—the so-called hobby loss rules—are considered in detail later in this chapter.

A profit motive is the only requirement necessary to establish existence of an *income-producing* activity. However, the courts have imposed an additional requirement before an activity qualifies as a *trade or business*. Business status requires both a profit motive and a sufficient degree of taxpayer involvement in the activity to distinguish the activity from a passive investment. No clear guidelines have emerged indicating when a taxpayer's activities rise to the level of carrying on a business. The courts, however, generally have permitted business treatment where the taxpayer has devoted a major portion of time to the activities or the activities have been regular or continuous.[5]

> **Example 1.** C owns six rental units, including several condominiums and townhouses. He manages his rental properties entirely by himself. His managing activities include seeking new tenants, supplying furnishings, cleaning and preparing the units for occupancy, advertising, and bookkeeping. In this case, C's involvement with the rental activities is sufficiently continuous and systematic to constitute a business.[6] If the rental activities were of a more limited nature, they might not qualify as a trade or business. The determination ultimately depends on the facts of the particular situation.[7]

> **Example 2.** H owns various stocks and bonds. Her managerial activities related to these securities consist primarily of maintaining records and collecting dividends and interest. She rarely trades in the market. These activities are those normally associated with a passive investor, and accordingly would not constitute a trade or business under § 162 (they would be considered an income-producing activity under § 212).[8] On the other hand, if H had a substantial volume of transactions, made personal investigations of the corporations in which she was interested in

---

[4]   *Doggett v. Burrett*, 3 USTC ¶1090, 12 AFTR 505, 65 F.2d 192 (CA-D.C., 1933).

[5]   *Grier v. U.S.*, 55-1 USTC ¶9184, 46 AFTR 1536, 218 F.2d. 603 (CA-2, 1955).

[6]   *Edwin R. Curphey*, 73 T.C. 766 (1980).

[7]   *Ibid.*

[8]   *Higgins v. Comm.*, 41-1 USTC ¶9233, 25 AFTR 1160, 312 U.S. 212 (UCSC, 1941).

purchasing, and devoted virtually every day to such work, her activities could constitute a trade or business.[9] Again, however, the answer depends on the facts.

Distinguishing between §§ 162 and 212. Prior to enactment of § 212, many investment-related expenses were not deductible because the activities did not constitute a business. The enactment of § 212 in 1942, allowing for the deduction of expenses related to production or collection of income, enabled the deduction of investment-oriented expenses. This expansion of the deduction concept to include so-called nonbusiness or investment-related expenses eliminates the need for an activity to constitute a business before a deduction is allowed. As a result, the issue of deductibility (*assuming* the other requirements are met) is effectively reduced to a single important question: Is the expense related to an activity engaged in for profit?

It may appear that the addition of § 212 completely removed the need for determining whether the activity resulting in the expense constitutes a business or is merely for the production of income. However, the distinction between business and production of income expenses remains important. For example, the classification of the expense as a deduction for or from adjusted gross income may turn on whether the expense is a trade or business expense or a production of income expense. Production of income expenses (other than those related to rents or royalties) are usually miscellaneous itemized deductions that can be deducted only to the extent they *exceed* two percent of adjusted gross income. In contrast, most business expenses are deductions for adjusted gross income and are deductible in full.

> **Example 3.** Refer to *Example 2*. In the first situation, where H is considered a passive investor, her investment related expenses (e.g., subscriptions to stock advisory services and investment newsletters) would be miscellaneous itemized deductions and deductible only to the extent they exceed 2% of adjusted gross income. In the second situation, however, the same type of expenses would be deductions for adjusted gross income since H's trading activities qualify as a trade or business.
>
> Another reason for ascertaining whether the activity constitutes a business relates to the use of the phrase "trade or business" in other Code Sections. The phrase "trade or business" appears in at least 60 different Code Sections, and the interpretation given to this phrase often controls the tax treatment. For example, whether an activity is an active business or a passive investment affects the tax consequences related to losses (deductible or limited), bad debts (short-term capital loss vs. ordinary loss), property sales (capital gain or loss vs. ordinary gain or loss), expenses for offices in the home (deductible vs. nondeductible), and limited expensing of depreciable property (allowed vs. disallowed).[10]

The Relationship. Before an expense is deductible under §§ 162 or 212, it must have a certain relationship to the trade or business or income-producing activity. The Regulations require that business expenses be directly connected with or pertain to the taxpayer's trade or business.[11] Similarly, production of income expenses must bear a reasonable and proximate relationship to the income-producing activity.[12] Whether an

---

[9] *Samuel B. Levin v. U.S.*, 79-1 USTC ¶9331, 43 AFTR2d 79-1057, 597 F.2d 760 (Ct. Cls., 1979). But see *Joseph Moller v. U.S.*, 83-2 USTC ¶9698, 52 AFTR2d 83-633 (CA-FC, 1983) where, for purposes of the home office deduction, the court held that the taxpayer's management of his substantial investment portfolio could not be a trade or business regardless of how continuous, regular, and extensive the activities were.

[10] See §§ 165, 166, 1221, 280A, and 179.

[11] Reg. § 1.162-1(a).

[12] Reg. § 1.212-1(d).

expenditure is directly related to the taxpayer's trade or business or income-producing activity usually depends on the facts. For example, the required relationship for business expenses normally exists where the expense is primarily motivated by business concerns or arises as a result of business, rather than personal, needs.[13]

> **Example 4.** While driving from one business to another, T struck a pedestrian with his automobile. He paid and deducted legal fees and damages in connection with the accident that were disallowed by the IRS. The Court found that the expenses were not directly related to, nor did they proximately result from, the taxpayer's business. The accident was merely incidental to the transportation and was related only remotely to the business.[14]

Whether a particular item is deductible often hinges on whether the expense was incurred for business or personal purposes. Consider the case of a law enforcement officer who is required to keep in top shape to retain his employment. Is the cost of a health club membership incurred for business or personal purposes? Similarly, can a disc jockey who obtains dentures to improve his speech deduct the cost as a business expense? Unfortunately, many expenses—like these—straddle the business-personal fence and the final determination is difficult. In both of the cases above, the Court denied the taxpayers' deductions on the theory that such expenses were inherently personal.

Another common question concerns expenses paid or incurred prior to the time that income is earned. In the case of § 212 expenses, it is not essential that the activity produce income currently. For example, expenses may be deductible under § 212 even though there is little likelihood that the property will be sold at a profit or will ever produce income.[15] Deductions are allowed as long as the transaction was entered into for profit.

> **Example 5.** B purchased a vacant lot three years ago as an investment. During the current year she paid $200 to have it mowed. Although the property is not currently producing income, the expense is deductible since it is for the conservation or maintenance of property held for the production of income.

ORDINARY AND NECESSARY EXPENSES

The second test for deductibility is whether the expense is ordinary and necessary. An expense is *ordinary* if it is normally incurred in the type of business in which the taxpayer is involved.[16] This is not to say that the expense is habitual or recurring.[17] In fact, the expense may be incurred only once in the taxpayer's lifetime and be considered ordinary. The test is whether other taxpayers in similar businesses or income-producing activities would customarily incur the same expense.

> **Example 6.** P has been in the newspaper business for 35 years. Until this year, his paper had never been sued for libel. To protect the reputation of the newspaper, P incurred substantial legal costs related to the libel suit. Although the taxpayer has never incurred legal expenses of this nature before, the expenses are ordinary since

---

13   *U.S. v. Gilmore*, 63-1 USTC ¶9285, 11 AFTR2d 758, 372 U.S. 39 (USSC, 1963).

14   *Julian D. Freedman v. Comm.*, 62-1 USTC ¶9400, 9 AFTR2d 1235, 301 F.2d. 359 (CA-5, 1962); but see *Harold Dancer*, 73 T.C. 1103 (1980), where the Tax Court allowed the deduction when the taxpayer was traveling between two locations of the *same* business. Note how the subtle change in facts substantially alters the result!

15   Reg. § 1.212-1(b).

16   *Deputy v. DuPont*, 40-1 USTC ¶9161, 23 AFTR 808, 308 U.S. 488 (USSC, 1940).

17   *Dunn and McCarthy, Inc. v. Comm.*, 43-2 USTC ¶9688, 31 AFTR 1043, 139 F.2d 242 (CA-2, 1943).

it is common in the newspaper business to incur legal expenses to defend against such attacks.[18]

It is interesting to note that the "ordinary" criterion normally becomes an issue in circumstances that are, in fact, unusual. For example, in *Goedel*,[19] a stock dealer paid premiums for insurance on the life of the President of the United States, fearing that his death would disrupt the stock market and his business. The Court denied the deduction on the grounds that the payment was not ordinary but unusual or extraordinary.

A deductible expense must be not only ordinary, but also *necessary*. An expense is necessary if it is appropriate, helpful, or capable of making a contribution to the taxpayer's profit-seeking activities.[20] The necessary criterion, however, is rarely applied to deny a deduction. The courts have refrained from such a practice since to do so would require overriding the judgment of the taxpayer.[21] The courts apparently feel that it would be unfair to judge *currently* whether a previous expenditure was necessary at the time it was incurred.

It should be emphasized that not all necessary expenses are ordinary expenses. Some expenses may be appropriate and helpful to the taxpayer's business but may not be normally incurred in that particular business. In such case, no deduction is allowed.

> **Example 7.** W was an officer in his father's corporation. The corporation B unable to pay its debts, was adjudged bankrupt. After the corporation was discharged from its debts, W decided to resume his father's business on a fresh basis. To reestablish relations with old customers and to solidify his credit standing, W paid as much of the old debts as he could. The Supreme Court held that the expenses were necessary in the sense that they were appropriate and helpful in the development of W's business. However, the Court ruled that the payments were not ordinary because people do not usually pay the debts of another.[22]

REASONABLE EXPENSES

The third requirement for a deduction is that the expense be reasonable in amount. An examination of § 162(a) reveals that the term "reasonable" is used only in conjunction with compensation paid for services (e.g., a reasonable allowance for salaries). The courts have held, however, that reasonableness is implied in the phrase "ordinary and necessary."[23] In practice, the reasonableness standard is most often applied in situations involving salary payments made by a closely held corporation to a shareholder who also is an employee. In these situations, if the compensation paid exceeds that ordinarily paid for similar services—that which is reasonable—the excessive payment may represent a nondeductible dividend distribution.[24] Dividend treatment of the excess occurs if the amount of the excessive payment received by each employee closely relates to the number of shares of stock owned.[25] The distinction between reasonable compensation and dividend is critical because characterization of

---

18   *Welch v. Helvering*, 3 USTC ¶1164, 12 AFTR 1456, 290 U.S. 111 (USSC, 1933).

19   39 B.T.A. 1 (1939).

20   *Supra*, Footnote 18. See also *Comm. v. Heininger*, 44-1 USTC ¶9109, 31 AFTR 783, 320 U.S. 467 (USSC, 1943).

21   *Supra*, Footnote 18.

22   *Supra*, Footnote 18.

23   *Comm. v. Lincoln Electric Co.*, 49-2 USTC ¶9388, 38 AFTR 411, 176 F.2d 815 (CA-6, 1949).

24   Reg. § 1.162-7(b)(1).

25   Reg. § 1.162-8.

the payment as a dividend results in double taxation (i.e., it is taxable to the shareholder-employee and not deductible by the corporation).

> **Example 8.** B and C own 70 and 30% of XYZ Corporation, respectively. Employees in positions similar to that of B earn $60,000 annually while those in positions similar to C's earn $20,000. During the year, the corporation pays B a salary of $130,000 and C a salary of $50,000. The excessive payment of $100,000 [($130,000 + $50,000) − ($60,000 + $20,000)] is received by B and C in direct proportion to their percentage ownership of stock (i.e., B's salary increased by $70,000 or 70% of the excessive payment). Because the payments are in excess of that normally paid to employees in similar positions and the excessive payment received by each is closely related to his stockholdings, the excessive payment may be treated as a nondeductible dividend.

Some of the factors used by the IRS when considering the reasonableness of compensation are[26]

1. Duties performed (i.e., amount and character of responsibility)
2. Volume and complexity of business handled (i.e., time required)
3. Individual's ability and expertise
4. Number of available persons capable of performing the duties of the position
5. Corporation's dividend policies and history

PAID OR INCURRED DURING THE TAXABLE YEAR

Sections 162 and 212 both indicate that an expense is allowable as a deduction only if it is "paid or incurred during the taxable year." This phrase is used throughout the Code in sections concerning deductions. Use of both terms, "paid" and "incurred," is necessary because the year in which deductions are allowable depends on the method of accounting used by the taxpayer.[27] The term *paid* refers to taxpayers using the cash basis method of accounting while the term *incurred* refers to taxpayers using the accrual basis method of accounting. Accordingly, the year in which a deduction is allowed usually depends on whether the cash or accrual basis method of accounting is used.

Cash Basis Taxpayers. For those taxpayers eligible to use the cash method (as discussed in Chapter 5), expenses are deductible in the taxable year when the expenses are actually paid.[28] However, there are numerous exceptions to this rule that are designed to restrict the flexibility a cash basis taxpayer would otherwise have in reporting deductions. Without these restrictions, a cash basis taxpayer could choose the year of deductibility simply by appropriately timing the cash payment. Before examining these restrictions, it is important to understand when the taxpayer is considered to have paid the expense.

Time of Payment. For the most part, determining when a cash basis taxpayer has paid an expense is not difficult. A cash basis taxpayer "pays" the expense when cash, check, property, or service is transferred. Neither a promise to pay nor a note evidencing such promise is considered payment. Consequently, when a cash basis taxpayer buys on

---

[26] Internal Revenue Manual 4233, § 232.

[27] § 461(a).

[28] Reg. § 1.446-1(a)(1).

credit, no deduction is allowed until the debts are paid. However, if the taxpayer borrows cash and then pays the expense, the expense is deductible when paid. For this reason, a taxpayer who charges expenses to a credit card is deemed to have borrowed cash and made payment when the charge is made. Thus, the deduction is claimed when the charge is actually made and not when the bank makes payment or when the taxpayer pays the bill.[29] If the taxpayer uses a "pay-by-phone" account, the expense is deductible in the year the financial institution paid the amount as reported on a monthly statement sent to the taxpayer.[30] When the taxpayer pays by mail, payment is usually considered made when the mailing occurs (i.e., dropping it in the post-office box).[31]

Restrictions on Use of Cash Method. Under the general rule, a cash basis taxpayer deducts expenses when paid. Without restrictions, however, aggressive taxpayers could liberally interpret this provision to authorize not only deductions for routine items, but also deductions for capital expenditures and other expenses that benefit future periods (e.g., supplies, prepaid insurance, prepaid rent, and prepaid interest). To preclude such an approach, numerous limitations have been imposed.

One of the more fundamental restrictions applying to cash basis taxpayers concerns inventories. For example, if no limitation existed, a cash basis owner of a department store could easily reduce or eliminate taxable income by increasing purchases of inventory near year-end and deducting their cost. To prevent this possibility, the Regulations require taxpayers to use the accrual method for computing sales and costs of goods sold if inventories are an income-producing factor.[32] In such cases, inventory costs must be capitalized, and accounts receivable and accounts payable (with respect to cost of goods sold) must be created. The taxpayer could continue to use the cash method for other transactions, however. It is also important to note that there are two relief provisions for small business owners that allow them to elect out of the accrual method and the requirement to account for inventories. As discussed in Chapter 5, taxpayers with average gross receipts of no more than $1 million, and certain taxpayers with average annual gross receipts of more than $1 million and up to $10 million may use the cash method of accounting even when inventory is an income producing factor.[33]

Provisions of both the Code and the Regulations limit the potential for deducting capital expenditures, prepaid expenses, and the like. As discussed later in this chapter, Code § 263 specifically denies the deduction for a capital expenditure; such costs as those for equipment, vehicles, and buildings normally are recovered through depreciation, as discussed in Chapter 9.

The Regulations—at least broadly—deal with other expenditures that are not capital expenditures per se but that do benefit future periods. According to the Regulations, any expenditure resulting "in the creation of an asset having a useful life which extends *substantially beyond the close of the taxable year* may not be deductible when made, or may be deductible only in part."[34] In this regard, the courts agree that "substantially beyond" means a useful life of more than one year.[35] Perhaps the simplest example of this rule as so interpreted concerns payments for supplies. Assuming the supplies would be exhausted before the close of the following tax year, a deduction should be allowable

---

[29] Rev. Rul. 78-39, 1978-1 C.B. 73.

[30] Rev. Rul. 80-335, 1980-2 C.B. 170.

[31] See Rev. Rul. 73-99, 1973-1 C.B. 412 for clarification of this general rule.

[32] Reg. § 1.446-1(c)(2).

[33] Rev. Proc. 2000-22, Rev. Proc. 2001-10, and Rev. Proc. 2002-28.

[34] Reg. § 1.446-1(a)(1).

[35] *Martin J. Zaninovich*, 69 T.C. 605, *rev'd* in 80-1 USTC ¶9342, 45 AFTR2d 80-1442, 616 F.2d 429 (CA-9, 1980).

when payment is made. In regard to other prepayments, however, the application of this principle has spawned a hodgepodge of special rules.

Prepaid Rent. An Appeals Court decision suggests that a cash basis taxpayer's prepayments for rents or services may be deducted in the year paid when two conditions are present: (1) the period for which the payment is made does not exceed one year following the end of the current tax year, and (2) the taxpayer is contractually obligated to prepay an amount for a period extending beyond the close of the year.[36] Other advanced payments of rentals can be deducted only during the period to which they relate.

Example 9. R, a farmer, is a cash-basis calendar-year taxpayer. In 2005 he leases farm-land for the twenty-year period December 1, 2005 to November 30, 2025. The lease agreement provides that annual rent for the period December 1 to November 30 is payable on December 20 each year. The yearly rent is $24,000. On December 20, 2005 R pays the $24,000 rental for the next year. The prepayment is deductible because it is for a period not exceeding a year and R is obligated to pay for the entire year in advance on December 20. However, if the lease agreement required only monthly rentals of $2,000 each (instead of an annual payment of $24,000), only $2,000 would be deductible (representing the rent allocable to the month of December) because the remainder of the payment was voluntary.[37]

Prepaid Insurance. Prepayments of insurance premiums normally are not deductible when paid. Instead, the IRS holds that this expense must be prorated over the period that the insurance covers.[38] However, the "one year" exception noted above with respect to prepaid rent may also apply here.

Example 10. On December 15, 2005 T purchased an insurance policy covering theft of his inventory. The policy cost $3,000 and covered 2006–2008. T may not deduct any of the cost in 2005. In each of the following three years, he will deduct $1,000.

Other Prepayments. Perhaps the Service's current view of the proper treatment of most prepayments is best captured in a ruling concerning prepaid feed. In this ruling, the taxpayer purchased a substantial amount of feed prior to the year in which it would be used.[39] The purchase was made in advance because the price was low due to a depressed market. The IRS granted a deduction for the prepayment because there was a business purpose for the advanced payment, the payment was not merely a deposit, and it did not materially distort income. Based on this ruling and related cases, prepayments normally should be deductible if the asset will be consumed by the close of the following year, there is a business purpose for the expenditure, and there is no material distortion of income.

Prepaid Interest. The Code expressly denies the deduction of prepaid interest. Prepaid interest must be capitalized and deducted ratably over the period of the loan.[40] The same is true for any costs associated with obtaining the loan. The sole exception is for "points" paid for a debt incurred by the taxpayer to purchase his or her *principal*

---

[36] *Supra*, Footnote 35.

[37] *Bonaire Development Co.*, 83-2 USTC ¶9428, 679 F.2d 159 (CA-9, 1983), *aff'g*, 76 T.C. 789 (1981).

[38] Rev. Rul. 70-413, 1970-2 C.B. 103.

[39] Rev. Rul. 79-229, 1979-2 C.B. 210. See also, *Kenneth Van Raden*, 71 T.C. 1083 (1979), *aff'd* in 81-2 USTC ¶9547, 48 AFTR2d 81-5607, 650 F.2d 1046 (CA-9, 1981).

[40] § 461(g).

residence. In this regard, the IRS has ruled that points incurred to refinance a home must be amortized over the term of the loan.[41] However, an Appeals Court case allowed a taxpayer to deduct the amount of points paid on refinancing a home. The proceeds were used to pay off a three-year, temporary loan that was made to allow the borrower time to secure permanent financing for the home.[42] The court stated that, since the temporary loan was merely an integrated step in securing permanent financing for the taxpayer's residence, the points were deductible currently.

> **Example 11.** K desires to obtain financing for the purchase of a new house costing $100,000. The bank agrees to make her a loan of 80% of the purchase price, or $80,000 (80% of $100,000) for thirty years at a cost of two points (two percentage "points" of the loan obtained). Thus, she must pay $1,600 (2% of $80,000) to obtain the loan. Assuming it is established business practice in her area to charge points in consideration of the loan, the $1,600 in points (prepaid interest) is deductible. However, if the house is not the principal residence of the taxpayer, then the prepaid interest must be deducted ratably over the 30-year loan period.

Accrual Basis Taxpayers. An accrual basis taxpayer deducts expenses when they are incurred. For this purpose, an expense is considered incurred when the *all events test* is satisfied and *economic performance* has occurred.[43] Two requirements must be met under the all-events test: (1) all events establishing the existence of a liability must have occurred (i.e., the liability is fixed); and (2) the amount of the liability can be determined with reasonable accuracy. Therefore, before the liability may be accrued and deducted it must be fixed and determinable.

> **Example 12.** In *Hughes Properties, Inc.*, an accrual basis corporation owned a gambling casino in Reno, Nevada that operated progressive slot machines that paid a large jackpot about every four months.[44] The increasing amount of the jackpot was maintained and shown by a meter. Under state gaming regulations, the jackpot amount could not be turned back until the amount had been paid to a winner. In addition, the corporation had to maintain a cash reserve sufficient to pay all the guaranteed amounts. At the end of each taxable year, the corporation accrued and deducted the liability for the jackpot as accrued at year-end. The IRS challenged the accrual, alleging that the all events test had not been met, and that the amount should be deducted only when paid. It argued that payment of the jackpot was not fixed but contingent, since it was possible that the winning combination may never be pulled. Moreover, the Service pointed out the potential for tax avoidance: the corporation was accruing deductions for payments that may be paid far in the future, and thus—given the time value of money—overstated the amount of the deduction. The Supreme Court rejected these arguments, stating that the probability of payment was not a remote and speculative possibility. The Court noted that not only was the liability fixed under state law, but it also was not in the interest of the taxpayer to set unreasonably high odds, since customers would refuse to play and would gamble elsewhere.

The all events test often operates to deny deductions for certain estimated expenditures properly accruable for financial accounting purposes. For example, the estimated cost of product guarantees, warranties, and contingent liabilities normally may

---

[41]   Rev. Rul. 87-22, 1987-1 C.B. 146. See also Rev. Proc. 94-27, 1994-1 I.R.B. 15.

[42]   *James R. Huntsman*, 90-2 USTC ¶50,340, 66 AFTR2d 90-5020, 905 F.2d 1182 (CA-8, 1990). In an *Action on Decision* issued on February 11, 1991, the IRS ruled that although it will not appeal the *Huntsman* decision, it will not follow this decision outside the Eighth Circuit.

[43]   § 461(h).

[44]   *Hughes Properties, Inc.*, 86-1 USTC ¶9440, 58 AFTR2d 86-5015, 106 S. Ct. 2092 (USSC, 1986).

not be deducted— presumably because the liability for such items has not been fixed or no reasonable estimate of the amount can be made.[45] However, the courts have authorized deductions for estimates where the obligation was certain and there was a reasonable basis (e.g., industry experience) for determining the amount of the liability.

The condition requiring *economic performance* was introduced in 1984 due to Congressional fear that the all events test did not prohibit so-called premature accruals. Prior to 1984, the courts—with increasing frequency—had permitted taxpayers to accrue and deduct the cost of estimated expenditures required to perform certain activities *prior* to the period when the activities were actually performed. For example, in one case, a strip-mining operator deducted the estimated cost of backfilling land that he had mined for coal.[46] The court allowed the deduction for the estimated expenses in the current year even though the back filling was not started and completed until the following year. According to the court, the liability satisfied the all-events test since the taxpayer was required by law to backfill the land and a reasonable estimate of the cost of the work could be made. A similar decision involved a taxpayer that was a self-insurer of its liabilities arising from claims under state and Federal worker's compensation laws.[47] Under these laws, the taxpayer was obligated to pay a claimant's medical bills, disability payments, and death benefits. In this situation, the taxpayer was allowed to accrue and deduct the estimated expenses for its obligations even though actual payments would extend over many years. In Congress' view, allowing the deduction in these and similar cases prior to the time when the taxpayer actually performed the services, provided the goods, or paid the expenses, overstated the true cost of the expense, because the time value of money was ignored. Perhaps more importantly, Congress recognized that allowing deductions for accruals in this manner had become the foundation for many tax shelter arrangements. Accordingly, the economic performance test was designed to defer the taxpayer's deduction until the activities giving rise to the liability are performed.

The time at which economic performance is deemed to occur—and hence the period in which the deduction may be claimed—depends on the nature of the item producing the liability. A taxpayer's liabilities commonly arise in three ways, as summarized below.

1. *Liability of taxpayer to provide property and services.* When the taxpayer's liability results from an obligation to provide goods or services to a third party (e.g., perform repairs), economic performance occurs when the taxpayer provides the goods or services to the third party.

2. *Liability for property or services provided to the taxpayer.* When the taxpayer's liability arises from an obligation to pay for services, goods, or the use of property provided to (or to be provided to) the taxpayer (e.g., consulting, supplies, and rent), economic performance occurs when the taxpayer receives the services or goods or uses the property. Note that in this case, economic performance occurs when the taxpayer *receives* the consideration bargained for, while in the situation above it occurs when the taxpayer *provides* the consideration.

3. *Liabilities for which payment represents economic performance.* There are a number of liabilities for which economic performance is deemed to occur only when the taxpayer actually makes payment. This rule effectively places the taxpayer on the cash basis for these liabilities. These include the following:[48]

---

[45] *Bell Electric Co.*, 45 T.C. 158 (1965).

[46] *Paul Harrold v. Comm.*, 52-1 USTC ¶9107, 41 AFTR 442, 192 F.2d 1002 (CA-4, 1951).

[47] *Crescent Wharf & Warehouse Co. v. Comm.*, 75-2 USTC ¶9571, 36 AFTR2d 75-5246, 518 F.2d 772 (CA-5, 1975).

- ▸ Refunds and rebates
- ▸ Awards, prizes, and jackpots
- ▸ Premiums on insurance
- ▸ Provision of work to the taxpayer under warranty or service contracts
- ▸ Taxes
- ▸ Liabilities arising under a worker's compensation act or out of any tort, breach of contract, or violation of law, including amounts paid in settlement of such claims

Example 13. In 2005 C, an accrual basis corporation, contracted with P, a partnership, to drill 50 gas wells over a five-year period for $500,000. Absent the economic performance test, C could accrue and deduct the $500,000 fee in 2005 because the obligation is fixed and determinable. However, because economic performance has not occurred (i.e., the services have not been received by C), no deduction is permitted in 2005. Rather, C may deduct the expense when the wells are drilled.

Example 14. Same facts as above. Although P is obligated to perform services for C for $500,000 over the five-year period (i.e., the obligation is fixed and determinable), P cannot prematurely accrue the cost of providing these services because economic performance has not occurred. Deduction is permitted only as the wells are drilled.

Example 15. C Corporation, a calendar year, accrual method taxpayer, owns several casinos across the country. Each contains progressive slot machines. These machines provide a guaranteed jackpot that increases as money is gambled through the machine until the jackpot is won or until a maximum predetermined amount is reached. On July 1, 2005, the guaranteed jackpot amount on one of C's slot machines reaches the maximum predetermined amount of $100,000. On February 1, 2006, the $100,000 jackpot is won by B. Although the all-events test is met in 2005 when the amount of the liability becomes fixed (i.e., guaranteed) and determinable, economic performance does not occur for prizes until payment is actually made. As a result, C is not allowed to accrue the deduction in 2005 but must wait and claim the expense when it pays the jackpot in 2006. (Note this rule reverses the decision in *Hughes Properties, Inc.*)

Note that even though payment of an expense may make it ripe for accrual, other rules may require deferral of the deduction.

Example 16. Kidco Products Corporation, a calendar year E accrual method taxpayer, manufactures car seats for children. On July 1, 2005 it purchased an insurance policy from INS Inc. for $360,000 under which INS must satisfy any liability arising during the next three years for any claims attributable to defects in the manufacturing. Although economic performance occurs when Kidco pays the premium, it has created an asset with a life that extends substantially beyond 2005. Under cash-basis principles, such expenses cannot be deducted currently but must be amortized. Consequently, Kidco should amortize the insurance premium over the term of the policy, deducting $60,000 ($360,000/36 × 6 months) in 2005 and the remaining $300,000 over the next 30 months.

To prohibit the disruption of normal business and accounting practices, certain recurring expenses are exempted from the economic performance rules. The expense may be accrued and deducted under the recurring item exception if all of the following conditions are met.[49]

1. The all-events test is satisfied.

2. Economic performance does in fact occur within eight and one-half months after the close of the taxable year or the filing of the return if earlier.

3. The item is recurring in nature, and the taxpayer consistently treats such items as incurred in the taxable year.

4. The item is immaterial or accrual in the earlier year results in a better match against income than accruing the item when economic performance occurs.

The recurring item exception does not apply to liabilities arising under a worker's compensation act or out of any tort, breach of contract, or violation of law.

Example 17. M Corporation, a calendar year, accrual method taxpayer, manufactures and sells automobile mufflers. Under the terms of an agreement with D Corporation, one of its distributors, D is entitled to a discount on future purchases (i.e., a rebate) from M based on the amount of purchases made by D from M during any calendar year. During 2005, purchases by D entitled it to future rebates of $20,000. M paid $12,000 of the rebate in January 2006 and the remaining $8,000 in October 2006. M filed its 2005 tax return on March 15, 2006. Although the all events test has been met in 2005 (i.e., the fact of the liability is fixed and the amount can be determined with reasonable accuracy), no deduction is allowed until economic performance occurs. Normally, economic performance for rebates is deemed to occur when the rebate is paid. Therefore, the expense would usually be deductible by M in 2006. However, under the recurring item exception M should be able to accrue $12,000 of the $20,000 in 2005 because all of the conditions are met: (1) the all events test is met, (2) economic performance occurs in a timely manner (i.e., the January payment occurs before the earlier of the filing of the tax return or 8½ months after the close of the year), (3) the item is recurring, and (4) accrual in the earlier year results in a better match against income. The remaining $8,000 is not eligible for the recurring item exception because economic performance (payment of the $8,000 liability) did not occur until October, which is beyond both the filing of the return and the 8½-month window.

Real Property Taxes. The addition of the economic performance test and the recurring item exception posed a problem for a great number of taxpayers who incur real property taxes.

Example 18. Oldco Corporation uses the accrual method and reports on the calendar year. It owns a warehouse in a state where the lien date (i.e., the date on which the corporation technically becomes liable) for real property taxes for 2004 is January 1, 2005. Payment is due in two installments, 40 percent due on June 1 and the remaining 60 percent due on December 1. Shortly after the close of 2004, the corporation received its bill for its 2004 taxes of $100,000, paying $40,000 on June 1 and $60,000 on December 1. For financial accounting purposes, the corporation accrues the entire $100,000 expense in 2004. For tax purposes, however, economic performance for taxes does not occur until payment is made. Therefore, accrual normally is not allowed until the payment is made (2005) unless the recurring item exception applies. In this case, the recurring item exception would apply. However,

---

[49] § 461(h)(3).

the corporation could deduct only the portion paid by the earlier of the filing of its tax return or September 15 (8½ months after the close of the taxable year). If the corporation delayed filing its return until the extended due date, September 15, it could accrue and deduct on its 2004 tax return the $40,000 paid on June 1. However, if it filed its return by March 15, none of the taxes could be accrued under the recurring item exception.

Recognizing the problem illustrated *Example 18* above, Code § 461(c) was created. Under this provision, taxpayers can elect to accrue real property taxes ratably over the period to which the taxes relate. Note that if the taxpayer makes the election, the treatment for tax purposes is consistent with that for financial accounting.

> **Example 19.** Same facts as *Example 18*. If the corporation makes the election under § 461(c), it may accrue and deduct the entire $100,000 in 2004 because all of the taxes related to such period.

RELATIONSHIP TO FINANCIAL ACCOUNTING

As may be apparent from the discussion above, the rules for accruing expenses for tax accounting purposes do not necessarily produce the same result as those for financial accounting. Differences often occur, particularly in the treatment of estimated expenses. As noted in Chapter 5, such differences are justified given the differing goals of financial and tax accounting. Financial accounting principles adopt a conservative approach in measuring income to ensure that income is not overstated and investors are not misled. Accordingly, financial accounting embraces the matching principle that encourages the accrual of estimated expenditures. In contrast, the objective of the income tax system is to ensure that taxable income is objectively measured so as to minimize controversy. Consistent with this view, the tax law allows a deduction only when a liability is actually fixed and economic performance has occurred. Estimates of future expenses are not sufficient to warrant a deduction for tax purposes (unless the recurring item exception should apply). Note, however, that these different accounting techniques produce differences only in *when* the expense is taken into account. The total amount of expense to be accounted for is not affected. Common examples of these so-called timing differences include:

- *Depreciation.* As discussed in Chapter 9, depreciation for tax purposes differs substantially from that for financial accounting purposes. Although the total amount of depreciation is often the same in both cases, the amount expensed in any one period may differ significantly.

- *Bad debts.* For tax purposes, bad debts normally may be deducted only in the year they actually become worthless. In contrast, financial accounting permits use of the reserve method, which allows an estimate of future bad debts related to current year sales to be charged against current year income. The tax treatment of bad debts is discussed fully in Chapter 10.

- *Vacation pay.* For financial accounting purposes, vacation pay accrues as it is earned by the employees. For tax purposes, however, vacation pay may be accrued and deducted only if it is paid within 2½ months following the close of the taxable year.

- *Warranty costs.* For financial accounting purposes, warranty costs are normally estimated and matched against current year sales. For tax purposes, no deduction is allowed until the warranty work is actually performed (unless the recurring item exception applies).

Timing differences should be distinguished from permanent differences. As seen throughout this text, there are a number of situations in which an expense for financial accounting purposes is not allowed as a deduction for tax purposes. For example, fines and penalties are expenses that must be taken into account in determining financial accounting income, as are expenses related to tax-exempt income. However, tax deductions for such costs are not allowed. Similarly, expenses for business meals and entertainment may be fully expensed for financial accounting but only 50 percent of such costs can be deducted for tax purposes.

The rules governing the accrual of deductions are summarized in Exhibit 7-1.

EMPLOYEE BUSINESS EXPENSES

The definition of *trade or business* also includes the performance of services as an employee. In other words, an employee is considered to be in the business of being an employee. As a result, the ordinary and necessary expenses incurred by an employee in connection with his or her employment are deductible under § 162 as business expenses. Examples of deductible expenses typically incurred by employees include union dues, dues to trade and professional societies, subscriptions to professional journals, small tools and supplies, medical exams required by the employer, and work clothes and uniforms as well as their maintenance (where required as a condition of employment and not suitable for everyday use).[50] Expenses such as travel, entertainment, and education may also be deducted as employee business expenses under certain conditions explained in Chapter 8. As explained later in this chapter, employee business expenses—other than those that are reimbursed—are considered miscellaneous itemized deductions and thus are deductible only to the extent they exceed 2 percent of A.G.I.

---

[50]   Rev. Rul. 70-474, 1970 C.B. 35.

EXHIBIT 7-1

Requirements for Accrual of Deduction

Requirements

▸ All events test is met.

All events have occurred that fix the fact of the liability.

The amount of the liability can be determined with reasonable accuracy.

▸ Economic performance has occurred as follows:

Event Producing Liability	Time When Economic Performance Occurs	Example
Taxpayer obligated to provide goods or services to a third party	When the taxpayer provides the property or services	Taxpayer to perform repairs, warranty work
Goods or services provided or to be provided to the taxpayer	When taxpayer actually receives the goods or services	Taxpayer buys supplies, contracts for consulting
Property provided or to be provided to the taxpayer	When taxpayer uses the property	Taxpayer rents property
Obligations to pay refunds, rebates, awards, prizes, insurance, warranty or service contracts, taxes	When taxpayer makes payment	Refunds, rebates, etc.
Claims under worker's compensation, tort, breach of contract	When taxpayer makes payment	Taxpayer incurs product liability
Real property taxes	When taxpayer makes payment unless he or she elects special accrual rule	Real estate taxes

DEDUCTIONS FOR LOSSES

The general rules concerning deduction of losses are contained in § 165. This provision permits a deduction for any loss sustained that is not compensated for by insurance. The deductions for losses of an individual taxpayer, however, are limited to

1. Losses incurred in a trade or business

2. Losses incurred in a transaction entered into for profit

3. Losses of property not connected with a trade or business if such losses arise by fire, storm, shipwreck, theft, or some other type of casualty

Note that personal losses—other than those attributable to a casualty—are not deductible. For example, the sale of a personal residence at a loss is not deductible.

Before a loss can be deducted, it must be evidenced by a closed and completed transaction. Mere decline in values or unrealized losses cannot be deducted. Normally, for the loss to qualify as a deduction, the property must be sold, abandoned, or scrapped, or become completely worthless. The amount of deductible loss for all taxpayers cannot exceed the taxpayer's basis in the property. Special rules related to various types of losses are discussed in Chapter 10.

CLASSIFICATION OF EXPENSES

Once the deductibility of an item is established, the tax formula for individuals requires that the deduction be classified as either a deduction *for* adjusted gross income or a deduction *from* adjusted gross income (itemized deduction).[51] In short, the deduction process requires that two questions be asked. First, is the expense deductible? Second, is the deduction for or from adjusted gross income (A.G.I.)? Additional aspects of the first question are considered later in this chapter. At this point, however, it is appropriate to consider the problem of classification.

The classification process arose with the introduction of the standard deduction in 1944. The standard deduction was introduced to simplify filing for the majority of individuals by eliminating the necessity of itemizing primarily personal deductions such as medical expenses and charitable contributions. In addition, the administrative burden of checking such deductions was eliminated. Although these objectives were satisfied by providing a blanket deduction in lieu of itemizing actual expenses, a new problem arose. The standard deduction created the need to classify deductions as either deductions that would be deductible in any event (deductions for A.G.I.), or deductions that would be deductible only if they exceeded the prescribed amount of the standard deduction (deductions from A.G.I.).

IMPORTANCE OF CLASSIFICATION

The classification problem is significant for several reasons. First, itemized deductions may be deducted only to the extent they exceed the standard deduction. For this reason, a taxpayer whose itemized deductions do not exceed the standard deduction would lose a deduction if a deduction for A.G.I. is improperly classified as a deduction from A.G.I. This would occur because deductions for A.G.I. are deductible without limitation.

A second reason for properly classifying deductions concerns the treatment of miscellaneous itemized deductions. As part of the tax overhaul in 1986, Congress limited the deduction of miscellaneous itemized deductions—defined below—to the amount that exceeds 2 percent of A.G.I. This new limitation is extremely important. Under prior law, taxpayers who itemized deductions could misclassify a deduction for A.G.I. as an itemized deduction with little or no effect, since the expense would be deductible either one place or the other. Under the current scheme, however, misclassification of a deduction for A.G.I. as a miscellaneous itemized deduction would subject the expense to the 2 percent floor, possibly making it wholly or partially nondeductible.

A third reason for properly classifying deductions concerns A.G.I. itself. Limitations on deductions such as medical expenses and charitable contributions are expressed in terms of the taxpayer's A.G.I. For example, miscellaneous itemized deductions are deductible only to the extent they exceed 2 percent of A.G.I., medical expenses are deductible only to the extent they exceed 7.5 percent of A.G.I., and charitable contributions are deductible only to the extent of various limitations (50, 30, or 20 percent) based on A.G.I.

As discussed in Chapter 3, Congress has created two relatively new limitations that are based on A.G.I. First, the amount of itemized deductions (other than for medical expenses, casualty and theft losses, and investment interest) must be reduced by

---

[51]   § 62.

3 percent of a taxpayer's A.G.I. in excess of $145,950 (2005). In addition, the deduction for personal exemptions is phased out as the taxpayer's A.G.I. exceeds a threshold amount (e.g., in 2005 $218,950 for joint returns and $145,950 for a single taxpayer). Thus, the misclassification of a deduction for A.G.I. as an itemized deduction would result in a higher A.G.I. and could result in a lower deduction for itemized deductions and personal exemptions.

Adjusted gross income for Federal income tax purposes also serves as the tax base or the starting point for computing taxable income for many state income taxes. Several states do not allow the taxpayer to itemize deductions. Consequently, misclassification could result in an incorrect state tax liability.

Still another reason for properly classifying expenses concerns the self-employment tax. Under the social security and Medicare programs, self-employed individuals are required to make an annual contribution based on their net earnings from self-employment. Net earnings from self-employment include gross income from the taxpayer's trade or business less allowable trade or business deductions attributable to the income. Failure to properly classify a deduction as a deduction for A.G.I. attributable to self-employment income results in a higher self-employment tax.

DEDUCTIONS FOR A.G.I.

The deductions for A.G.I. are specifically identified in Code § 62. It should be emphasized, however, that § 62 merely classifies expenses; it does *not* authorize any deductions. Deductions *for* A.G.I. are

1. Trade or business deductions except those expenses incurred in the business of being an employee (e.g., expenses of a sole proprietorship or self-employment normally reported on Schedule C of Form 1040)

2. Three categories of employee business deductions:

   a. Expenses that are reimbursed by an employee's employer (and included in the employee's income);
   b. Expenses incurred by a qualified performing artist (see below); and
   c. Expenses incurred by an official of a state or local government who is compensated on a fee basis

3. Losses from sale or exchange of property

4. Deductions attributable to rents or royalties

5. Educator expenses (K–12 teachers)

6. Deductions for reservists, performing artists, fee-basis government officials

7. Deductions for certain tuition and fees

8. Student loan interest expense

9. Deduction for certain legal expenses

10. Deductions for contributions to Individual Retirement Accounts or Keogh retirement plans

11. Alimony deductions

12. Deductions for penalties imposed for premature withdrawal of funds from a savings arrangement

13. Deduction for 50 percent of self-employment tax paid by self-employed persons

14. Deduction for contributions to Medical Savings Accounts (MSAs) and Health Savings Accounts (HSAs)

15. Moving expenses

16. Deduction for 100 percent of self-employed health insurance premiums

17. Certain other deductions

All of the above are deductible for A.G.I., while all other deductions are from A.G.I. (i.e., itemized deductions).

ITEMIZED DEDUCTIONS

As seen above, only relatively few expenses are deductible for A.G.I. The predominant expenses in this category are the deductions incurred by taxpayers who are self-employed (i.e., those carrying on as a sole proprietor). All other expenses are deductible from A.G.I. as itemized deductions.

Itemized deductions fall into two basic categories: those that are *miscellaneous itemized deductions* and those that are not. The distinction is significant because miscellaneous itemized deductions are deductible only to the extent they exceed two percent of A.G.I. Miscellaneous itemized deductions are all itemized deductions *other than* the following:

1. Interest

2. Taxes

3. Casualty and theft losses

4. Medical expenses

5. Charitable contributions

6. Gambling losses to the extent of gambling gains

7. Deduction where annuity payments cease before investment is recovered

8. Certain other deductions

The miscellaneous itemized deductions category is comprised primarily of *unreimbursed* employee business expenses, investment expenses, and deductions related to taxes such as tax preparation fees. Examples of these (assuming they are not reimbursed by the employer) include:

1. Employee travel away from home (including meals and lodging)

2. Employee transportation expenses

3. Outside salesperson's expenses [except that "statutory employees" (e.g., full-time life insurance salespersons, certain agent or commission drivers, and traveling salespersons) are allowed to report their income and expenses on a separate Schedule C and avoid the two percent of A.G.I. limitation]

4. Employee entertainment expenses

5. Employee home office expenses

6. Union dues

7. Professional dues and memberships

8. Subscriptions to business journals

9. Job-seeking expenses (in the same business) or employment-seeking expenses

10. Education expenses

11. Investment expenses, including expenses for an investment newsletter, investment advice, and rentals of safety deposit boxes

12. Tax preparation fees or other tax-related advice including that received from accountants or attorneys, tax seminars, and books about taxes

With respect to item 12 above, expenses related to tax preparation and resolving tax controversies normally are reported as miscellaneous itemized deductions. However, the IRS allows taxpayers who own a business, farm, or rental real estate or have royalty income to allocate a portion of the total cost of preparing their tax return to the cost of preparing Schedule C (trade or business income), Schedule E (rental and royalty income), or Schedule F (farm income) and deduct these costs "for" A.G.I.[52] The same holds true for expenses incurred in resolving tax controversies, including expenses relating to IRS audits or business or rental activities.

SELF-EMPLOYED VERSUS EMPLOYEE

Under the current scheme of deductions for and from A.G.I., an important—and perhaps inequitable—distinction is made based on whether an individual is an employee or self-employed. As seen above, employees generally deduct all unreimbursed business expenses as itemized deductions. In contrast, self-employed taxpayers (i.e., sole proprietors or partners) deduct business expenses for A.G.I. At first glance, the difference appears trivial, particularly for those taxpayers who itemize their deductions. Recall, however, that an employee's business expenses are treated as miscellaneous itemized deductions and thus are deductible only to the extent that these and all other miscellaneous itemized deductions collectively exceed 2 percent of the taxpayer's A.G.I. Due to this distinction, deductibility often depends on the employment status of the taxpayer.

> **Example 20.** T is an accountant. During the year she earns $30,000 and pays dues of $100 to be a member of the local CPA society. These were her only items of income and expense. If T practices as a self-employed sole proprietor (e.g., she has a small firm or partnership), the dues are fully deductible for A.G.I. However, if T is an employee, none of the expense is deductible since it does not exceed the 2% floor of $600 (2% × $30,000). If T's employer had reimbursed her for the expense and included the reimbursement in her income, the expense would have been completely deductible, totally offsetting the amount that T must include in income. If T is employed, but at the same time does some accounting work on her own, part-time, the treatment is unclear.

The logic for the distinction based on employment status is fragile at best. According to the committee reports, Congress believed that it was generally appropriate to disallow deductions for employee business expenses because employers reimburse employees for those expenses that are most necessary for employment. In addition, Congress felt that the treatment would simplify the system by relieving taxpayers of the burden of record keeping and at the same time relieving the IRS of the burden of auditing such deductions.

---

[52] Rev. Rul. 92-29, 1992-1 C.B.20.

Reimbursed Expenses. As emphasized above, an employee's business expenses are generally deductible as itemized deductions unless a reimbursement is received. Where the employee is fully reimbursed and the reimbursement is included in income, the deduction is fully deductible for A.G.I. If only a portion of the expense is reimbursed and included in income, that portion is deductible for A.G.I. and the remainder is a miscellaneous itemized deduction.

Example 21. Professor K is employed by State University in the finance department. The department has a policy of reimbursing up to $50 for each faculty member's costs of subscribing to finance journals. During the year, K spent $75 on subscriptions and received a $50 reimbursement. K's tentative A.G.I. is $40,000 (including the $50 reimbursement). He may deduct $50 for A.G.I., thereby leaving K with A.G.I. of $39,950. The remaining $25 is a miscellaneous itemized deduction that may or may not be deductible depending on whether the sum of this amount plus all other miscellaneous itemized deductions exceeds the 2% floor of $799 ($39,950 × 2%).

The discussion to this point assumes that all employee reimbursements are included by the employer in the employee's income. This is usually not the case, however. As discussed in Chapter 8, the employee may omit both the reimbursement and the expense from the return if, as is generally true, the reimbursement equals such expense and an adequate accounting is made to the employer. In fact, the IRS does not require the employer to file an information return under such circumstances.[53] As a result, an employee expense reimbursement generally is not included in income, and the related expense is not deductible either as a deduction for A.G.I. or as an itemized deduction.

Whether a reimbursement is or is not included in the income of the employee, the effect on A.G.I. is the same. That is, there is no effect on A.G.I. The transaction is a "wash" economically for the employee and is, therefore, a "wash" on the employee's tax return. This concept is demonstrated below.

Example 22. Dr. R is employed by General Hospital. The hospital reimburses employees for the cost of subscribing to medical journals. During the year, Dr. R spent $100 on subscriptions and, after an adequate accounting, received a $100 reimbursement. If the reimbursement is included in Dr. R's income, she is allowed an offsetting deduction for A.G.I. If the reimbursement is not included in her income, she does not take any deduction with respect to the subscription cost.

	Reimbursement Included in Income	Reimbursement Not Included in Income
Gross income	$100	$-0-
Deduction for A.G.I.	(100)	(-0-)
A.G.I.	$ -0-	$-0-

Expenses of Performing Artists. Most employee business expenses were relegated to second-class status in 1986 as they became subject to the 2 percent limitation. However, one group of employees, the struggling performing artists, escaped this restriction. These actors, actresses, musicians, dancers, and the like are technically employees but exhibit many attributes of the self-employed. They often work for several employers for little income yet incur relatively large unreimbursed expenses as they

---

[53] Reg. § 1.6041-3(i).

seek their fortunes. For these reasons, "qualified performing artists" are permitted to deduct their business expenses *for* A.G.I. To qualify, the individual must perform services in the performing arts as an employee for at least two employers during the taxable year, earning at least $200 from each. In addition, the individual's A.G.I. before business deductions cannot exceed $16,000. Lastly, the artist's business deductions must exceed 10 percent of his or her gross service income, otherwise they too are considered miscellaneous itemized deductions.

> **Example 23.** Z is an actress. This year she worked in two Broadway productions for two different employers, earning $7,000 from each for a total of $14,000. Her expenses, including the fee to her agent, were $2,000. She may deduct all of her expenses for A.G.I.

Self-Employed or Employee? The above discussion illustrates the importance of determining whether an individual is self-employed or is treated as an employee. However, whether an individual is self-employed or is an employee is often difficult to determine. An employee is a person who performs services for another individual subject to that individual's direction and control.[54] In the employer-employee relationship, the right to control extends not only to the result to be accomplished but also to the methods of accomplishment. Accordingly, an employee is subject to the will and control of the employer as to both what will be done and how it will be done. In the case of the self-employed person, the individual is subject to the control of another only as to the end result, and not as to the means of accomplishment. Generally, physicians, lawyers, dentists, veterinarians, contractors, and subcontractors are not employees. An insurance agent or salesperson may be an employee or self-employed, depending on the facts. The courts have developed numerous tests for differentiating between employees and self-employed persons. Each of the following situations would suggest that an employer-employee relationship exists.[55]

1. Complying with written or oral instructions (an independent contractor need not be trained or attend training sessions)

2. Regular written or oral reports on the work's status

3. Continuous relationship—more than sporadic services over a lengthy period

4. Lack of control over the place of work

5. No risk of profit or loss; no income fluctuations

6. Regular payment—hourly, weekly, etc. (an independent contractor might work on a job basis)

7. Specified number of hours required to work (an independent contractor is master of his or her own time)

8. Unable to delegate work—hiring assistants not permitted

9. Not independent—does not work for numerous firms or make services available to general public

---

[54] Reg. § 31.3401(c)-1(a).

[55] Rev. Rul. 87-41, 1987-1 C.B. 296. This Revenue Ruling actually contains 20 questions.

LIMITATIONS ON DEDUCTIONS

Some provisions of the Code specifically prohibit or limit the deduction of certain expenses and losses despite their apparent relationship to the taxpayer's business or profit-seeking activities. These provisions operate to disallow or limit the deduction for various expenses unless such expenses are specifically authorized by the Code. As a practical matter, these provisions have been enacted to prohibit abuses identified in specific areas. Several of the more fundamental limitations are considered in this chapter.

HOBBY EXPENSES AND LOSSES

As previously discussed, a taxpayer must establish that he or she pursues an activity with the objective of making a profit before the expense is deductible as a business or production of income expense. When the profit motive is absent, the deduction is governed by § 183 on activities not engaged in for profit (i.e., hobbies). Section 183 generally provides that hobby expenses of an individual taxpayer or S corporation are deductible only to the extent of the gross income from the hobby. Thus, the tax treatment of hobby expenses substantially differs from profit-seeking expenses if the expenses of the activity exceed the income, resulting in a net loss. If the loss is treated as arising from a profit-motivated activity, then the taxpayer ordinarily may use it to reduce income from other sources.[56] Conversely, if the activity is considered a hobby, no loss is deductible. Note, however, that hobby expenses may be deducted to offset any hobby income.

Profit Motive. The problem of determining the existence of a profit motive usually arises in situations where the activity has elements of both a personal and a profit-seeking nature (e.g., auto racing, antique hunting, coin collecting, horse breeding, weekend farming). In some instances, these activities may represent a profitable business venture. Where losses are consistently reported, however, the business motivation is suspect. In these cases all the facts and circumstances must be examined to determine the presence of the profit motive. The courts have held that the taxpayer simply is required to pursue the activity with a bona fide intent of making a profit. The taxpayer, however, need not show a profit. Moreover, the taxpayer's expectation of profit need not be considered reasonable.[57] The Regulations set out nine factors to be used in ascertaining the existence of a profit motive.[58] Some of the questions posed by these factors are

1. Was the activity carried on in a businesslike manner? Were books and records kept? Did the taxpayer change his or her methods or adopt new techniques with the intent to earn a profit?

2. Did the taxpayer attempt to acquire knowledge about the business or consult experts?

3. Did the taxpayer or family members devote much time or effort to the activity? Did they leave another occupation to have more time for the activity?

4. Have there been years of income as well as years of loss? Did the losses occur only in the start-up years?

---

[56] The limitations imposed on losses from passive activities should not be applicable in this situation since the taxpayer materially participates in the activity. See discussion in Chapter 12 and § 469.

[57] Reg. § 1.183-2(a).

[58] Reg. § 1.183-2(b).

5. Does the taxpayer have only incidental income from other sources? Is the taxpayer's wealth insufficient to maintain him or her if future profits are not derived?

6. Does the taxpayer derive little personal or recreational pleasure from the activity?

An affirmative answer to several of these questions suggests a profit motive exists.

Presumptive Rule. The burden of proof in the courts is normally borne by the taxpayer. Section 183, however, shifts the burden of proof to the IRS in hobby cases where the taxpayer shows profits in any three of five consecutive years (two of seven years for activities related to horses).[59] The rule creates a presumption that the taxpayer has a profit motive unless the IRS can show otherwise. An election is available to the taxpayer to postpone IRS challenges until five (or seven) years have elapsed from the date the activity commenced. Making the election allows the taxpayer sufficient time to have three profitable years and thus shift the burden of proof to the IRS. This election must be filed within three years of the due date of the return for the taxable year in which the taxpayer first engages in the activity, but not later than 60 days after the taxpayer has received notice that the IRS proposes to disallow the deduction of expenses related to the hobby. The election automatically extends the statute of limitations for each of these years, thus enabling a later challenge by the IRS. It should be emphasized that this presumptive rule only shifts the burden of proof. Profits in three of the five (or two of seven) years do not absolve the taxpayer from attack.

Example 24. T enjoys raising, breeding, and showing dogs. In the past, she occasionally sold a dog or puppy. In 2004 T decided to pursue these activities seriously. During the year, she incurred a loss of $4,000. T also had a loss of $2,000 in 2005. If T made no election for any of these years (i.e., within three years of the start of the activity), the IRS may assert that T's activities constitute a hobby. In this case, the burden of proof is on T to show a profit motive, since she has not shown a profit in at least three years. If T made an election, then the IRS is barred from assessing a deficiency until five years have elapsed. Five years need to elapse to determine whether T will have profits in three of the five years and, if so, shift the burden of proof to the IRS in any litigation that may occur. If an election is made, however, the period for assessing deficiencies for all years is extended until two years after the due date of the return for the last taxable year in the five-year period.[60] In T's case, an election would enable the IRS to assess a deficiency for 2004 and subsequent years up until April 15, 2011, assuming T is a calendar year taxpayer. If an election were not made, the statute of limitations would normally bar assessments three years after the return is due (e.g., assessments for 2004 would be barred after April 15, 2008).

Deduction Limitation. If the activity is considered a hobby, the related expenses are deductible to the extent of the activity's gross income as reduced by *otherwise allowable deductions*.[61] Otherwise allowable deductions are those expenses relating to the hobby that are deductible under other sections of the Code regardless of the activity in which they are incurred. For example, property taxes are deductible under § 164 without regard to whether the activity in which they are incurred is a hobby or a business. Similarly, interest

---

[59] § 183(d).

[60] § 183(d)(4).

[61] § 183(b). On classification of the deductions, see Rev. Rul. 75-14, 1975-1 C.B. 90 and Senate Finance Committee Report on H.R. 3838, S. Rep. No. 99-313 (5/29/86), p. 80, 99th Cong., 2nd. Sess.

on debt secured by the taxpayer's principal or secondary residence is deductible regardless of the character of the activity. Consequently, any expense otherwise allowable is deducted *first* in determining the gross income limitation. Any other expenses are deductible to the extent of any remaining gross income (i.e., other operating expenses are taken next, with any depreciation deductions, taken last). Otherwise allowable deductions are fully deductible as itemized deductions, while other deductible expenses are considered miscellaneous itemized deductions and are deductible only to the extent they exceed 2 percent of A.G.I. (including the hobby income).

Example 25. R, an actor, enjoys raising, breeding, and racing horses as a hobby. His A.G.I. excluding the hobby activities is $68,000. He has a small farm on which he raises the horses. During the current year, R won one race and received income of $2,000. He paid $2,300 in expenses as follows: $800 property taxes related to the farm and $1,500 feed for horses. R calculated depreciation with respect to the farm assets at $6,500. As a result, R has a net loss from the activity of $6,800 ($2,000 − $2,300 − $6,500). If the activity is *not* considered a hobby but rather a trade or business, R would report the loss on Schedule C and assuming it is not a passive loss, he could use it to offset his other income. However, if the activity is considered a hobby and R itemizes deductions, he would compute his deductions as follows:

Gross income.	$2,000	
Otherwise allowable deductions:		
Taxes	(800)	$ 800
Gross income limitation	$1,200	
Feed expense:		
$1,500 limited to remaining		
gross income		1,200
Total		$2,000

Note that because depreciation is taken last, there is no deduction for this item.

R would include $2,000 in gross income, increasing his A.G.I. to $70,000. Of the $2,000 in deductible expenses, the property taxes of $800 are deductible in full as an itemized deduction. The remaining $1,200 is considered a miscellaneous itemized deduction. In this case, none of the $1,200 is deductible since this amount does not exceed the 2% floor of $1,400 (2% of $70,000). No deduction is allowed for the remaining feed expense of $300 ($1,500 − $1,200) due to the gross income limitation.

Example 26. Assume the same facts as in *Example 25* except that R's expense for property taxes is $2,400 instead of $800. In this case, because the entire $2,400 is deductible as an otherwise allowable deduction and exceeds the gross income from the hobby, none of the feed expense is deductible. Thus, R would include $2,000 in gross income and the $2,400 of property taxes would be fully deductible from A.G.I.

PERSONAL LIVING EXPENSES

Just as the Code specifically authorizes deductions for the costs of pursuing income—business and income-producing expenses—it denies deductions for personal expenses. Section 262 prohibits the deduction of any personal, living, or family expenses. Only those personal expenditures expressly allowed by some other provision in the Code are deductible. Some of the personal expenditures permitted by other provisions are medical expenses, contributions, qualified residence interest, and taxes. Normally, these expenses are classified as itemized deductions. These deductions and their underlying rationale are discussed in Chapter 11.

The disallowance of personal expenditures by § 262 complements the general criteria allowing a deduction. Recall that the general rules of §§ 162 and 212 permit deductions for ordinary and necessary expenses *only where a profit motive exists*. As previously seen in the discussion of hobbies, however, determining whether an expense arose from a personal or profit motive can be difficult. Some of the items specifically disallowed by § 262 are:

1. Expenses of maintaining a household (e.g., rent, utilities)

2. Losses on sales of property held for personal purposes

3. Amounts paid as damages for breach of promise to marry, attorney's fees, and other costs of suits to recover such damages

4. Premiums paid for life insurance by the insured

5. Costs of insuring a personal residence

Legal expenses related to divorce actions and the division of income-producing properties are often a source of conflict. Prior to clarification by the Supreme Court, several decisions held that divorce expenses incurred primarily to protect the taxpayer's income-producing property or his or her business were deductible.[62] The Supreme Court, however, has ruled that deductibility depends on whether the expense arises in connection with the taxpayer's profit-seeking activities. That is, the *origin* of the expense determines deductibility.[63] Under this rule, if the spouse's claim arises from the marital relationship—a personal matter—then no deduction is allowed. Division of income-producing property would only be incidental to or a consequence of the marital relationship.

> **Example 27.** R pays legal fees to defend an action by his wife to prevent distributions of income from a trust to him. Because the wife's action arose from the marital relationship, the legal expenses are nondeductible personal expenditures.[64]

Legal expenses related to a divorce action may be deductible where the expense is for advice concerning the tax consequences of the divorce.[65] The portion of the legal expense allocable to counsel on the tax consequences of a property settlement, the right to claim children as dependents, and the creation of a trust for payment of alimony are deductible.

Over the years, there has been a great deal of controversy regarding the treatment of contingent attorney fees incurred in securing a damages award. To illustrate, assume a taxpayer receives an award of fully taxable punitive damages of $10 million and the attorney is to receive a contingent fee of 40 percent of that amount or $4 million. In this situation, the taxpayer typically asserted that the fees represent a splitting of the income and, therefore, he or she should be taxed only on the net amount received or $6 million.

---

[62]   *F.C. Bowers v. Comm.*, 57-1 USTC ¶9605, 51 AFTR 207, 243 F.2d 904 (CA-6, 1957).

[63]   *Supra*, Footnote 13, Also, compare *Comm. v. Tellier*, 66-1 USTC ¶9319, 17 AFTR2d 633, 383 U.S. 687 (USSC, 1966) with *Boris Nodiak v. Comm.*, 66-1 USTC ¶9262, 17 AFTR2d 396, 356 F.2d 911 (CA-2, 1966).

[64]   *H.N. Shilling, Jr.*, 33 TCM 1097, T.C. Memo 1974-246.

[65]   Rev Rul. 72-545, 1972-2 C.B. 179.

Conversely, the government argued that the full $10 million is included in gross income and the $4 million of attorney fees are a miscellaneous itemized deduction subject to the two percent limitation and the three percent cutback. But more importantly, since the attorney fees are classified as miscellaneous itemized deduction, they are not allowed in computing the alternative minimum tax (AMT). As a result, an AMT would normally result. In effect, the taxpayer pays tax on $10 million when he or she has only received $6 million.

Congress addressed this problem in 2004. Attorney's fees and court costs incurred for certain legal actions are deductible for AGI. This rule applies to most legal actions, but not necessarily all.[66] Apparently, certain types of tort actions, such as defamation, would not fall within the statute unless they occur within the employment context. By classifying these expenses as deductions for A.G.I., the AMT problem is eliminated since the AMT limitations generally apply only to certain itemized deductions.[67]

CAPITAL EXPENDITURES

A capital expenditure is ordinarily defined as an expenditure providing benefits that extend beyond the close of the taxable year. It is a well-established rule in case law that a business expense, though ordinary and necessary, is not deductible in the year paid or incurred if it can be considered a capital expenditure.[68] Normally, however, a capital expenditure may be deducted ratably over the period for which it provides benefits. For example, the Code authorizes deductions for depreciation or cost recovery, amortization, and depletion where the asset has a determinable useful life.[69] Capital expenditures creating assets that do not have a determinable life, however, generally cannot be deducted. For example, land is considered as having an indeterminable life and thus cannot be depreciated or amortized. The same is true for stocks and bonds. Expenditures for these types of assets are recovered (i.e., deducted) only when there is a disposition of the asset through sale (e.g., cost offset against sales price), exchange, abandonment, or other disposition.

As a general rule, assets with a useful life of one year or less need not be capitalized. For example, the taxpayer can write off short-lived assets with small costs such as supplies (e.g., stationery, pens, pencils, calculators), books (e.g., the Internal Revenue Code), and small tools (e.g., screwdrivers, rakes, and shovels).

Goodwill. Like land, goodwill is an example of an asset that does not have a determinable useful life. Because of this indeterminate life, acquired goodwill historically has been treated as a capitalized asset that could not be depreciated. The only way a taxpayer could receive a current tax benefit from acquired goodwill was to identify components separate and apart from goodwill that had an ascertainable value and limited useful life (e.g., client files and subscription lists). If a taxpayer was

---

[66] § 62 (a)(19) extends the deduction for actions in connection with unlawful discrimination claims, certain claims against the federal government, and private causes of action under the Medicare Secondary Payer law. Unlawful discrimination actions include those that claim violations of the Civil Rights Acts of 1964 and 1991, the Congressional Accountability Act of 1995, the National Labor Relations Act, the Family and Medical Leave Act of 1993, the Fair Housing Act, the Americans with Disabilities Act of 1990, and various whistle-blower statutes.

[67] The Jobs Act does apply to cases settled prior to October 23, 2004. The Supreme Court settled the issue for these cases, reversing pro-taxpayer decisions in the Sixth and Ninth Circuits, indicating that there had been an invalid assignment of income and, therefore the legal expenses were miscellaneous itemized deductions. See *Comm. v. John W. Banks II and Comm. v. Sigitas J. Banaitis*, (combined) 2005-1 USTC ¶50,595, AFTR 2d 2005-659, (USSC, 2005), *rev'g Banks II*, 92 2003-6298, 2003-2 USTC ¶50,675, AFTR 2d, 345 F3d 373 (CA-6, 2003), and *rev'g Banaitis*, 92 AFTR 2d 2003-5834, 2003-2 USTC ¶50,638; 340 F3d 1074 (CA-9, 2003).

[68] *Supra*, footnote 18.

[69] §§ 167, 168, 169, 178, 184, 188, and 611 are examples.

successful in establishing the requisite valuation and limited life for a goodwill component, the taxpayer could depreciate the cost of the intangible asset over its useful life using the straight-line method (known as amortization). However, in practice, taxpayers often faced challenges by the IRS, and many attempts to depreciate goodwill components were unsuccessful.

Congress enacted Code § 197 to reduce the uncertainty surrounding the depreciation of goodwill and its identifiable components. Effective August 10, 1994, the cost of acquiring intangible assets (including acquired goodwill) may, at the election of the taxpayer, be amortized over a 15-year period. If the election is not made, the cost of acquiring goodwill and related intangibles must be capitalized and no amortization will be allowed.

> **Example 28.** B has decided to purchase a newspaper business in a small town for $100,000. It can be determined that $80,000 of the purchase price is allocable to the assets of the business and $20,000 is attributable to goodwill (subscription lists and other intangibles). B may be able to recover all $100,000 of the cost through deductions for depreciation and amortization.

Capital Expenditures vs. Repairs. The general rule of case law disallowing deductions for capital expenditures has been codified for expenditures relating to property. Code § 263 provides that deductions are not allowed for any expenditures for new buildings or for permanent improvements or betterments made to increase the value of property.[70] Additionally, expenditures substantially prolonging the property's useful life, adapting the property to a new or different use, or materially adding to the value of the property are not deductible.[71] Conversely, the cost of incidental repairs that do not materially increase the value of the property nor appreciably prolong its life, but maintain it in a normal operating state, may be deducted in the current year.[72] For example, costs of painting, inside and outside, and papering are usually considered repairs.[73] However, if the painting is done in conjunction with a general reconditioning or overhaul of the property, it is treated as a capital expenditure.[74]

> **Example 29.** L operates his own limousine business. Expenses for a tune-up such as the costs of spark plugs, points, and labor would be deductible as routine repairs and maintenance since such costs do not significantly prolong the car's life. In contrast, if L had the transmission replaced at a cost of $600, allowing him to drive it for another few years, the expense must be capitalized.

Acquisition Costs. As a general rule, costs related to the acquisition of property must be capitalized. For example, freight paid to acquire new equipment or commissions paid to acquire land must be capitalized. In addition, Code § 164 requires that state and local general sales taxes related to the purchase of property be capitalized. The costs of demolition or removal of an old building prior to using the land in another fashion must be capitalized as part of the cost of the land.[75] Costs of defending or perfecting the title to property, such as legal fees, are normally capitalized.[76] Similarly,

---

[70]   § 263(a).

[71]   Reg. § 1.263(a)-1(b).

[72]   Reg. § 1.162-4.

[73]   *Louis Allen*, 2 BTA 1313 (1925).

[74]   *Joseph M. Jones*, 57-1 USTC ¶9517, 50 AFTR 2040, 242 F.2d 616 (CA-5, 1957).

[75]   § 280B.

[76]   Reg. § 1.263(a)-2.

legal fees incurred for the recovery of property must be capitalized unless the recovered property is investment property or money that must be included in income if received.[77]

INDOPCO and the Long-Term Benefit Theory. Interestingly, one of the most important and widely debated tax developments to occur in recent years concerns the capital expenditure area. The controversy stems from a Supreme Court decision involving the treatment of costs incurred by a target company as part of a friendly takeover. In 1977, Unilever approached one of its suppliers, INDOPCO, about the possibility of a takeover to which INDOPCO agreed. During the acquisition process, INDOPCO paid an investment banking company, Morgan Stanley, about $2.2 million for advice and a fairness opinion and another $500,000 to its own legal counsel for services related to the takeover. The IRS ultimately denied deduction of the expenses (as well as amortization) on the grounds that the expenses were capital in nature. In 1992, the Supreme Court concurred with the IRS, believing that INDOPCO would receive long-term benefits from the acquisition, including the opportunity for synergy with Unilever and the future availability of Unilever's financial and business resources.[78]

The effect of the INDOPCO decision would not be so great if it were confined to costs incurred as part of a friendly takeover. However, the IRS has used the broad language of the court to capitalize any expense to which it can associate any long-term benefit. In this regard, it is important to understand that the Supreme Court indicated that the long-term benefits need not be associated with any specific identifiable asset. As long as the expenditure leads to the permanent betterment of the business as a whole, capitalization may be in order. For example, the IRS has used this approach to deny a deduction for the costs of removing asbestos insulation from equipment if the removal is part of a general plan of rehabilitation, despite the fact that the expense did not extend the life of the asset.[79] Instead, the taxpayer was required to capitalize the expenditure on the grounds that the firm would derive long-term benefits from safer working conditions and reduced risk of liability. In another ruling concerning advertising costs, the IRS, while allowing a current deduction, warned that in certain instances advertising could produce long-term benefits, in which case such expenses must be capitalized.[80] In short, the INDOPCO decision has increased the tension between taxpayers and the IRS in the capital expenditure arena.

Over time, the intensity of the controversy and the level of uncertainty produced by INDOPCO escalated to an intolerable level. In response to the criticism, the IRS issued final regulations in 2004 to reign in the scope of INDOPCO and its "long-term-benefit" theory.[81] The regulations are quite extensive. There are over 50 pages and more than 80 examples all aimed at resolving whether a particular cost related to an intangible should be capitalized. Although a full discussion of these regulations is beyond the scope of this text, they are required reading whenever a taxpayer incurs an expense related to an intangible. Specifically, the regulations address amounts paid to

- *Acquire* an intangible (e.g., purchase a customer list, lease, patent, copyright, franchise, trademark, trade name, assembled workforce, or goodwill; most of these must be amortized over 15 years under § 197)
- *Create* an intangible (e.g., costs for prepaid items such as prepaid rents and insurance, membership privileges such as membership in a trade association, rights from governmental agencies such as the exclusive rights obtained from the

---

[77] Reg. § 1.212-1(k).

[78] *INDOPCO, Inc. v. Comm.*, 92-1 USTC ¶50,113, 69 AFTR2d 92-694, 503 U.S. 79 (USSC, 1992).

[79] *Norwest Corporation*, 108 T.C. No. 15 (1997).

[80] Rev. Rul. 92-80, 1992-2 C.B. 57.

[81] Reg. § 1.263(a)-4 and -5.

local government by a cable television company to serve a particular region, contract rights and contract terminations such as the rights to renew or renegotiate, licenses, and covenants not to compete)

▸ *Create* or enhance a separate and distinct intangible

▸ *Facilitate* the acquisition or creation of an intangible (e.g., legal expenses for negotiating commercial property lease, drafting agreements)

▸ *Facilitate* the acquisition of a trade or business, a change in the capital structure of a business entity, and certain other transactions (e.g., legal expenses to issue debt, payments to investment banker and outside legal counsel for evaluating alternative investments, performing due diligence, structuring the transaction, preparing SEC filings, and obtaining necessary regulatory approvals, hostile takeover defenses).

These regulations should bring to a close a period of great uncertainty that was not envisioned when the Supreme Court decided the INDOPCO case in 1992.

Environmental Remediation Costs. Under Code § 198 which took effect on August 5, 1997, a taxpayer may elect to treat certain environmental remediation expenditures that would otherwise be chargeable to a capital account as deductible in the year paid or incurred. To qualify for this special treatment, the expense must be incurred in connection with the abatement or control of hazardous substances at a qualified contaminated site. Prior to the enactment of this provision, the IRS took the view that costs incurred to clean-up the environment were controlled by the long-term benefit theory of INDOPCO and, therefore, were capital expenditures for which no deduction was allowed. The effect of § 198, then, is to override the IRS's reliance on the long-term benefit theory to deny deductions with respect to environmental remediation costs.

Elections to Capitalize or Deduct. Various provisions of the Code permit a taxpayer to treat capital expenditures as deductible expenses, as deferred expenses, or as capital expenditures. For example, at the election of the taxpayer, expenses for research and experimentation may be deducted currently, treated as deferred expenses and amortized over at least 60 months, or capitalized and included in the basis of the resulting property.[82]

BUSINESS INVESTIGATION EXPENSES AND START-UP COSTS

Another group of expenses that arguably may be considered capital expenditures are those incurred when seeking and establishing a new business, such as costs of investigation and start-up. Business investigation expenses are those costs of seeking and reviewing prospective businesses prior to reaching a decision to acquire or enter any business. Such expenses include the costs of analysis of potential markets, products, labor supply, and transportation facilities. Start-up or pre-opening expenses are costs that are incurred after a decision to acquire a particular business and prior to its actual operations. Examples of these expenses are advertising, employee training, lining up distributors, suppliers, or potential customers, and the costs of professional services such as attorney and accounting fees.

For many years, the deductibility of expenses of business investigation and start-up turned solely on whether the taxpayer was "carrying on" a business at the time the expenditures were incurred. Notwithstanding some modifications, the basic rule still remains: when the taxpayer is in the same or similar business as the one he or she is

---

[82]   § 174. See §§ 175 and 180 for other examples.

starting or investigating, the costs of investigation and start-up are wholly deductible in the year paid or incurred.[83] The deduction is allowed regardless of whether the taxpayer undertakes the business.[84] However, this rule often forces taxpayers to litigate to determine whether a business exists at the time the expenses are incurred. Prior to the enactment of § 195, if the taxpayer could not establish existence of a business, the expenditures normally were treated as capital expenditures with indeterminable lives.[85] As a result, the taxpayer could only recover the expenditure if and when he or she disposed of or abandoned the business.

In 1980 Congress realized that the basic rule not only was a source of controversy but also discouraged formation of new businesses. For this reason, special provisions permitting deduction of these expenses under certain conditions were enacted.[86] Before examining these provisions, it should be emphasized that the traditional rule continues to be valid. Thus, if a taxpayer can establish that the investigation and start-up costs are related to a similar existing business of the taxpayer, a deduction is allowed.

> **Example 30.** S owns and operates an ice cream shop on the north side of the city. A new shopping mall is opening on the south side of the city, and the developers have approached her about locating a second ice cream shop in their mall. During 2005 S pays a consulting firm $1,000 for a survey of the potential market on the south side. Because S is in the ice cream business when the expense is incurred, the entire $1,000 is deductible regardless of whether she undertakes the new business.

Amortization Provision. Section 195 sets out the treatment for the start-up and investigation expenses of taxpayers who are *not* considered in a similar business when the expenses are incurred *and* who actually enter the new business. Eligible taxpayers may elect to deduct up to $5,000 of business investigation and start-up expenses in the tax year in which the business begins. If the § 195 expenses exceed $5,000, the excess must be amortized over the 180-month period (15 years) beginning with the month in which the business begins.[87] If the expenses exceed $50,000, the $5,000 allowance is reduced one dollar for each dollar in excess of $50,000. Expenses for research and development, interest payments, and taxes are not considered start-up expenditures.[88] Consequently, these costs are not subject to §195 and may be deducted under normal rules.

> **Example 31.** J, a calendar year, cash basis taxpayer, recently graduated and received $10,000 from his wealthy uncle as a graduation gift. J paid an accountant $1,200 in September to review the financial situation of a small restaurant he desired to purchase. In December, J purchased the restaurant and began actively participating in its management. J may deduct $1,200 for the current year.

> **Example 32.** S, a famous bodybuilder, has decided to build his first health spa. While the facility is being constructed, a temporary office is set up in a trailer next to the site. The office is nicely decorated and contains a small replica of the facility. S hired a staff who will manage the facility but at this time are calling prospective customers. Elaborate brochures have been printed. All of these costs, including the salaries paid to the staff, the printing of the brochures, and the costs of operating the

---

[83] *The Colorado Springs National Bank v. U.S.*, 74-2 USTC ¶9809, 34 AFTR2d 74-6166, 505 F.2d 1185 (CA-10, 1974).

[84] *York v. Comm.*, 58-2 USTC ¶9952, 2 AFTR2d 6178, 261 F.2d 421 (CA-4, 1958).

[85] *Morton Frank*, 20 T.C. 511 (1953).

[86] § 195(a).

[87] § 195 expenses incurred prior to October 23, 2004 are amortized over 60 months.

[88] § 195(c)(1).

trailer such as depreciation and utilities, are start-up costs and must be amortized over a period of 180 months.

Example 33. Same facts as above except S incorporated and the corporation incurred $23,000 of start-up and investigation expenses. The corporation was formed in July of this year and adopted the calendar year. In this case, the corporation could deduct $5,000 immediately and amortize the remaining balance of $18,000 over 15 years (180 months) beginning in July. This would result in amortization of $100/month for 180 months. The deduction for start-up and investigation expenses for 2005 would be $5,600 computed as follows:

First-year allowance..	$5,000
Amortization ($18,000/180 = $100/month × 6 months)	600
Total deduction in first year	$5,600

In 2006, the corporation would continue to amortize the remaining expenses, resulting in a deduction of $1,200 ($100/month × 12).

Example 34. In March, 2005 LMN, LLC was formed and incurred start-up and investigation expenses of $52,000. LMN's immediate expensing allowance of $5,000 must be reduced one dollar for each dollar of § 195 expense exceeding $50,000. In this case, the allowance is reduced by $2,000 ($52,000 − $50,000) to $3,000. Thus LMN may deduct $3,000 plus amortization of the remaining $49,000, resulting in a deduction of $5,720 computed below.

First-year allowance [$5,000 − ($52,000 − $50,000 = $2,000)]		$3,000
Amortization:		
Total expense.....................................	$52,000	
First-year allowance	(3,000)	
Amortizable balance................................	$49,000	
Amortization ($49,000/180 = $272/month × 10 months)...		2,720
Total § 195 expense deduction in first year		$5,720

Note that if LMN had incurred $55,000 or more of § 195 expenses, the $5,000 immediate write-off would be reduced to zero and all $55,000 of the expenses would be amortized over 180 months.

As suggested above, the taxpayer must enter the business to qualify for amortization. Whether the individual is considered as having entered the business normally depends on the facts in each case.

If the taxpayer (who is not in a similar, existing business) does not enter into the new business, the investigation and start-up expenses generally are not deductible. The Tax Court, however, has held that a taxpayer may deduct costs as a loss suffered from a transaction entered into for profit if the activities are sufficient to be considered a "transaction."[89] The IRS has interpreted this rule to mean that those expenditures related to a *general search* for a particular business or investment are not deductible.[90] Expenses are considered general when they are related to whether to enter the transaction and which transaction to enter. Once the taxpayer has focused on the acquisition of a *specific* business or investment, expenses related to an unsuccessful acquisition attempt are deductible as a loss on a transaction entered into for profit.

---

[89] *Harris W. Seed*, 52 T.C. 880 (1969).

[90] Rev. Rul. 77-254, 1977-2 C.B. 63.

Example 35. L, a retired army officer, is interested in going into the radio business. He places advertisements in the major trade journals soliciting information about businesses that may be acquired. Upon reviewing the responses to his ads, L selects two radio stations for possible acquisition. He hires an accountant to audit the books of each station and advise him on the feasibility of purchase. He travels to the cities where each station is located and discusses the possible acquisition with the owners. Finally, L decides to purchase station FMAM. To this end, he hires an attorney to draft the purchase agreement. Due to a price dispute, however, the acquisition attempt collapses. The expenses for advertising, auditing, and travel are not deductible since they are related to the taxpayer's general search. The legal expenses are deductible as a loss, however, since they occurred in the taxpayer's attempt to acquire a specific business.

Job-Seeking Expenses. The tax treatment of job-seeking expenses of an employee is similar to that for expenses for business investigation. If the taxpayer is seeking a job in the same business in which he or she is presently employed, the related expenses are deductible as miscellaneous itemized deductions subject to the 2 percent floor.[91] The deduction is allowed even if a new job is not obtained. No deduction or amortization is permitted, however, if the job sought is considered a new trade or business or the taxpayer's first job.

Example 36. B, currently employed as a biology teacher, incurs travel expenses and employment agency fees to obtain a new job as a computer operator. The expenses are not deductible because they are not incurred in seeking a job in the profession in which she was currently engaged. Moreover, the expenses are not deductible even though B obtained the new job. However, the expenses would be deductible if she had obtained a new job in her present occupation.

PUBLIC POLICY RESTRICTIONS

Although an expense may be entirely appropriate and helpful, and may contribute to the taxpayer's profit-seeking activities, it is not considered necessary if the allowance of a deduction would frustrate sharply defined public policy. The courts established this longstanding rule on the theory that to allow a deduction for expenses such as fines and penalties would encourage violations by diluting the penalty.[92] Historically, however, the IRS and the courts were free to restrict deductions of any type of expense where, in their view, it appeared that the expenses were contrary to public policy—even if the policy had not been clearly enunciated by some governmental body. As a result, taxpayers were often forced to go to court to determine if their expense violated public policy.

Recognizing the difficulties in applying the public policy doctrine, Congress enacted provisions specifically designed to limit its use.[93] The rules identified and disallowed certain types of expenditures that would be considered contrary to public policy. Under these provisions no deduction is allowed for fines, penalties, and illegal payments.

Fines and Penalties. A deduction is not allowed for any fine or similar penalty paid to a government for the violation of any law.[94]

---

[91] Rev. Rul. 75-120, 1975-1 C.B. 55, as clarified by Rev. Rul. 77-16, 1977-1 C.B. 37.

[92] *Hoover Motor Express Co., Inc. v. U.S.*, 58-1 USTC ¶9367, 1 AFTR2d 1157, 356 U.S. 38 (USSC, 1958).

[93] S. Rep. No. 91-552, 91st Cong., 1st Sess. 273-75 (1969). Note, however, that the Tax Court continues to utilize the doctrine despite Congress's attempt to restrict its use—see *R. Mazzei*, 61 T.C. 497 (1974).

[94] § 162(f).

Example 37. S is a salesperson for an office supply company. While calling on customers this year, he received parking tickets of $100. None of the cost is deductible because the violations were against the law.

Example 38. Upon audit of T's tax return, it was determined that he failed to report $10,000 of tip income from his job as a maitre d', resulting in additional tax of $3,000. T was also required to pay the negligence penalty for intentional disregard of the rules. The penalty—20% of the tax due—is not deductible.

Fines include those amounts paid in settlement of the taxpayer's actual or potential liability.[95] In addition, no deduction is allowed for two-thirds of treble damage payments made due to a violation of antitrust laws.[96] Thus, one-third of this antitrust "fine" is deductible.

Illegal Kickbacks, Bribes, and Other Payments. The Code also disallows the deduction for four categories of illegal payments:[97]

1. Kickbacks or bribes to U.S. government officials and employees if illegal

2. Payments to governmental officials or employees of *foreign* countries if such payments would be considered illegal under the U.S. Foreign Corrupt Practices Act

Example 39. R travels all over the world, looking for unique items for his gift shop. Occasionally when going through customs in foreign countries, he is forced to "bribe" the customs official to do the necessary paperwork and get him through customs as quickly as possible. These so-called grease payments to employees of foreign countries are deductible unless they violate the Foreign Corrupt Practices Act. In general, such payments are not considered to be illegal.

1. Kickbacks, bribes, or other illegal payments to any other person if illegal under generally enforced U.S. or state laws that provide a criminal penalty or loss of license or privilege to engage in business

2. Kickbacks, rebates, and bribes, although legal, made by any provider of items or services under Medicare and Medicaid programs

Those kickbacks and bribes not specified above would still be deductible if they were ordinary and necessary. The payment, however, may not be necessary and thus will be disallowed if it controverts public policy.

Kickbacks generally include payments for referral of clients, patients, and customers. However, under certain circumstances, trade discounts or rebates may be considered kickbacks.

Example 40. M, a life insurance salesperson, paid rebates or discounts to purchasers of policies. Since such practice is normally illegal under state law, the rebate is not deductible.[98]

Expenses of Illegal Business. The expenses related to an illegal business are deductible.[99] Similar to the principle governing taxation of income from whatever source

---

[95]   § 162(g).

[96]   Reg. § 1.162-21(b).

[97]   § 162(c).

[98]   *James Alex*, 70 T.C. 322 (1978).

[99]   See *Max Cohen v. Comm.*, 49-2 USTC ¶9358, 176 F.2d 394 (CA-10, 1949) and *Neil Sullivan v. Comm.*, 58-1 USTC ¶9368, AFTR2d 1158, 356 U.S. 27 (USSC, 1958).

(including income illegally obtained), the tax law is not concerned with the lawfulness of the activity in which the deductions arise. No deduction is allowed, however, if the expense itself constitutes an illegal payment as discussed above. In addition, Code § 280E prohibits the deduction of any expenses related to the trafficking in controlled substances (i.e., drugs).

LOBBYING AND POLITICAL CONTRIBUTIONS

Although expenses for lobbying and political contributions may be closely related to the taxpayer's business, Congress has traditionally limited their deduction. These restrictions usually are supported on the grounds that it is not in the public's best interest for government to subsidize efforts to influence legislative matters.

Lobbying. Prior to 1962, no deduction was permitted for any type of lobbying expense. In 1962, however, Congress altered its position slightly with the addition of § 162(e), which carved out a narrow exception for certain lobbying expenses. This provision allowed a deduction for the expenses of appearing before or providing information to governmental units on legislative matters of *direct interest* to the taxpayer's business. Similarly, a deduction was permitted for expenses of providing information to a trade organization of which the taxpayer was a member where the legislative matter was of direct interest to the taxpayer and the organization. The portion of dues paid to such an organization attributable to the organization's allowable lobbying activities was also deductible. Beginning in 1994, however, these rules for deducting lobbying expenses are even more restrictive. Lobbying expenditures are now deductible only if incurred for the purpose of influencing legislation at the *local* level. Therefore, the expense of influencing national and state legislation (including the costs of hiring lobbyists to represent the taxpayer in these matters) is not deductible. This prohibition is extended to the costs of any direct communication with executive branch officials in an attempt to influence official actions or positions of such official.

The taxpayer must have a direct interest in the local legislation before lobbying expenses may be deducted. Although the definitional boundaries of the term "direct" are vague, a taxpayer is considered as having satisfied the test if it is reasonable to expect that the local legislative matter affects or will affect the taxpayer's business. However, a taxpayer does not have a direct interest in the nomination, appointment, or operation of any local legislative body.[100]

The deduction for lobbying *does not* extend to expenses incurred to influence the general public on legislative matters, elections, or referendums.[101] Expenses related to the following types of lobbying are not deductible:

1. Advertising in magazines and newspapers concerning legislation of direct interest to the taxpayer.[102] However, expenses for "goodwill" advertising presenting views on economic, financial, social, or similar subjects of a general nature, or encouraging behavior such as contributing to the Red Cross, are deductible.[103]

2. Preparing and distributing to a corporation's shareholders pamphlets focusing on certain legislation affecting the corporation and urging the shareholders to contact their representatives in Congress.[104]

---

[100] Reg. § 1.162-20(b).

[101] § 162(e)(2).

[102] Rev. Rul. 78-112, 1978-1 C.B. 42.

[103] Reg. § 1.162-20(a)(2).

[104] Rev. Rul. 74-407, 1974-2 C.B. 45, as amplified by Rev. Rul. 78-111, 1978-1 C.B. 41.

Example 41. T owns a restaurant in Austin, Texas. Legislation has been introduced by the City Council to impose a sales tax on food and drink sold in Austin, to be used for funding a dome stadium. T places an ad in the local newspaper stating reasons why the legislation should not be passed. He goes to the City Council and testifies on the proposed legislation before several committees. He pays dues to the Austin Association of Restaurant Owners organization, which estimates that 60% of its activities are devoted to lobbying for local legislation related to restaurant owners. T may deduct the cost of travel and 60% of his dues since the local legislation is of direct interest to him. He may not deduct the ad since it is intended to influence the general public.

Political Contributions. No deduction is permitted for any contributions, gifts, or any other amounts paid to a political party, action committee, or group or candidate related to a candidate's campaign.[105] This rule also applies to indirect payments, such as the payments for advertising in a convention program and admission to a dinner, hall, or similar affair where any of the proceeds benefit a political party or candidate.[106]

EXPENSES AND INTEREST RELATING TO TAX-EXEMPT INCOME

Section 265 sets forth several rules generally disallowing deductions for expenses relating to tax-exempt income. These provisions prohibit taxpayers from taking advantage of the tax law to secure a double tax benefit: tax-exempt income and deductions for the expenses that help to produce it. The best known rule prohibits the deduction for any *interest* expense or nonbusiness (§ 212) expense related to tax-exempt *interest* income.[107] Without this rule, taxpayers in high tax brackets could borrow at a higher rate of interest than could be earned and still have a profit on the transaction.

Example 42. D, an investor in the 25% tax bracket with substantial investment income, borrows funds at 9% and invests them in tax-exempt bonds yielding 7%. If the interest expense were deductible, the after-tax cost of borrowing would be 6.75% [(100% − 25% = 75%) × 9%]. Since the interest income is nontaxable, the after-tax yield on the bond remains 7%, or .25 percentage points higher than the effective cost of borrowing. Section 265, however, denies the deduction for the interest expense, thus eliminating the feasibility of this arrangement. It should be noted, however, that business (§ 162) expenses (other than interest) related to tax-exempt interest income may be deductible.

If the income that is exempt is not interest, none of the related expenses are deductible.[108]

Example 43. A company operating a baseball team paid premiums on a disability insurance policy providing that the company would receive proceeds under the policy if a player were injured. Because the proceeds would not be taxable, the premiums are not deductible even though the expenditure would apparently qualify as a business expense.[109] Note, however, that such expenses would enter into the calculation of net income for financial accounting purposes.

---

[105] § 162(e).

[106] § 276.

[107] § 265(2).

[108] § 265(1).

[109] Rev. Rul. 66-262, 1966-2 C.B. 105.

As a practical matter, it would appear difficult to determine whether borrowed funds (and the interest expense) are related to carrying taxable or tax-exempt securities. For example, an individual holding tax-exempt bonds may take out a mortgage to buy a residence instead of selling the bonds to finance the purchase price. In such case, it could be inferred that the borrowed funds were used to finance the bond purchase. Generally, the IRS will allow the deduction in this and similar cases unless the facts indicate that the primary purpose of the borrowing is to carry the tax-exempt obligations.[110] The facts must establish a *sufficiently direct relationship* between the borrowing and the investment producing tax exempt income before a deduction is denied.

> **Example 44.** K owns common stock with a basis of $70,000 and tax-exempt bonds of $30,000. She borrows $100,000 to finance an investment in an oil and gas limited partnership. The IRS will disallow a deduction for a portion of the interest on the $100,000 debt because it is presumed that the $100,000 is incurred to finance all of K's portfolio including the tax-exempt securities.[111]

> **Example 45.** R has a margin account with her broker. This account is devoted solely to the purchase of taxable investments and tax-exempt bonds. During the year, she buys several taxable and tax-exempt securities on margin. A portion of the interest expense on this margin account is disallowed because the borrowings are considered partially related to financing of the investment in tax-exempt securities.[112]

Business Life Insurance. Absent a special rule, premiums paid on insurance policies covering officers and employees of a business might be deductible as ordinary and necessary business expenses. However, to ensure that the taxpayer is not allowed to deduct expenses related to tax-exempt income (i.e., life insurance proceeds), a special provision exists. Under § 264, the taxpayer is not allowed any deduction for life insurance premiums paid on policies covering the life of any officer, employee, or any other person who may have a financial interest in the taxpayer's trade or business, if the taxpayer is the *beneficiary* of the policy. Thus, premiums paid by a business on a key-person life insurance policy where the company is beneficiary are not deductible. Note that this differs from the financial accounting treatment, where the premiums would be considered routine operating costs that should be expensed in determining net income. In contrast, payments made by a business on group-term life insurance policies where the employees are beneficiaries are deductible.

RELATED TAXPAYER TRANSACTIONS

Without restrictions, related taxpayers (such as husbands and wives, shareholders and their corporations) could enter into arrangements creating deductions for expenses and losses, and not affect their economic position. For example, a husband and wife could create a deduction simply by having one spouse sell property to the other at a loss. In this case, the loss is artificial because the property remains within the family and their financial situation is unaffected. Although the form of ownership has been altered, there is no substance to the transaction. To guard against the potential abuses inherent in

---

[110] Rev. Proc. 72-18, 1972-1 C.B. 740, as clarified by Rev. Proc. 74-8, 1974-1 C.B. 419, and amplified by Rev. Rul. 80-55, 1980-2 C.B. 849.

[111] *Ibid.*

[112] *B.P. McDonough v. Comm.*, 78-2 USTC ¶9490, 42 AFTR2d 78-5172, 577 F.2d 234 (CA-4, 1978).

transactions between related taxpayers, Congress designed specific safeguards contained in § 267.

Related Taxpayers. The transactions that are subject to restriction are only those between persons who are considered "related" as defined in the Code. Related taxpayers are[113]

1. Certain family members: brothers and sisters (including half-blood), spouse, ancestors (i.e., parents and grandparents), and lineal descendants (i.e., children and grandchildren)

2. Taxpayer and his or her corporation: an individual and a corporation if the individual owns either directly or *indirectly* more than 50 percent of the corporation's stock.[114]

3. Personal service corporation and an employee-owner: a corporation whose principal activity is the performance of personal services that are performed by the employee-owners (i.e., an employee who owns either directly or indirectly *any* stock of the corporation)

4. Certain other relationships involving regular corporations, S corporations, partnerships, estates, trusts, and individuals

In determining whether a taxpayer and a corporation are related, the taxpayer's direct and indirect ownership must be taken into account for the 50 percent test. A taxpayer's indirect stock ownership is any stock that is considered owned or "constructively" owned but not actually owned by the taxpayer. Section 267 provides a set of constructive ownership rules, also referred to as *attribution rules*, indicating the circumstances when the taxpayer is considered as owning the stock of another. Under the constructive ownership rules, a taxpayer is considered owning indirectly[115]

1. Stock owned directly or indirectly by his or her family as defined above

2. His or her proportionate share of any stock owned by a corporation, partnership, estate, or trust in which he or she has ownership (or of which he or she is a beneficiary in the case of an estate or trust)

3. Stock owned indirectly or directly by his or her partner in a partnership

In using these rules, the following limitations apply: (1) stock attributed from one family member to another *cannot* be reattributed to members of his or her family, and (2) stock attributed from a partner to the taxpayer *cannot* be reattributed to a member of his or her family or to another partner.[116]

Example 46. H and W are husband and wife. HB is H's brother. H, W, and HB own 30, 45, and 25% of X Corporation, respectively. H is considered as owning 100% of X Corporation, 30% directly and 70% indirectly (25% through HB and 45% through W, both by application of attribution rule 1 above). W is considered as owning 75% of X Corporation, 45% directly and 30% indirectly through H by application of attribution rule 1 (note that HB's stock cannot be attributed to H and

---

[113] § 267(b).

[114] A partner and a partnership in which the partner owns more than a 50 percent interest are treated in the same manner. See § 707(b).

[115] § 267(c).

[116] § 267(c)(5).

reattributed to W). HB is considered as owning 55% of X Corporation, 25% directly and 30% indirectly through H by application of attribution rule 1 and the reattribution limitation.

Losses. The taxpayer is not allowed to deduct the loss from a sale or exchange of property directly or indirectly to a related taxpayer (as defined above).[117] However, any loss disallowed on the sale may be used to offset any gain on a subsequent sale of the property by a related taxpayer to an unrelated third party.[118]

Example 47. A father owns land that he purchased as an investment for $20,000. He sells the land to his daughter for $15,000, producing a $5,000 loss. The $5,000 loss may not be deducted because the transaction is between related taxpayers. If the daughter subsequently sells the property for $22,000, she will then realize a $7,000 gain ($22,000 sales price − $15,000 basis). However, the gain may be reduced by the $5,000 loss previously disallowed, resulting in a recognized gain of $2,000 ($7,000 realized gain − $5,000 previously disallowed loss). If the daughter had sold the property for only $19,000, the realized gain of $4,000 ($19,000 − $15,000) would have been eliminated by the previous loss of $5,000. The $5,000 loss previously disallowed is used only to the extent of the $4,000 gain. The remaining portion of the disallowed loss ($1,000) cannot be used. Had the father originally sold the property for $19,000 to an outsider as his daughter subsequently did, the father would have recognized a $1,000 loss ($19,000 sales price − $20,000 basis). Note that the effect of the disallowance rule does not increase the basis of the property to the related taxpayer by the amount of loss disallowed.

The results of these transactions are summarized below.

Original sale between related parties

Sales price	$ 15,000
Adjusted basis	(20,000)
Disallowed loss	($5,000)

Subsequent sale	1	2
Sales price	$ 22,000	$ 19,000
Adjusted basis	(15,000)	(15,000)
Realized gain (loss)	$ 7,000	$ 4,000
Usage of disallowed loss	(5,000)	(4,000)
Recognized gain	$ 2,000	$ 0

Example 48. S owns 100% of V Corporation. She sells stock with a basis of $100 to her good friend T for $75, creating a $25 loss for S. T, in turn, sells the stock to V Corporation for $75, thus recouping the amount he paid S with no gain or loss. The $25 loss suffered by S, however, is not deductible because the sale was made *indirectly* through T to her wholly owned corporation.

Unpaid Expenses and Interest. Prior to enactment of § 267, another tax avoidance device used by related taxpayers involved the use of different accounting methods by each taxpayer. In the typical scheme, a taxpayer's corporation would adopt the accrual basis method of accounting while the taxpayer reported on a cash basis. The taxpayer

---

[117] § 267(a)(1).

[118] § 267(d).

could lend money, lease property, provide services, etc., to the corporation and charge the corporation for whatever was provided. As an accrual basis taxpayer, the corporation would accrue the expense and create a deduction. The cash basis individual, however, would report no income until the corporation's payment of the expense was actually received. As a result, the corporation could accrue large deductions without ever having to make a disbursement and, moreover, without the taxpayer recognizing any offsetting income. The Code now prohibits this practice between "related taxpayers" as defined above. Code § 267 provides that an accrual basis taxpayer can deduct an accrued expense payable to a related cash basis taxpayer *only* in the period in which the payment is included in the recipient's income.[119] This rule effectively places all accrual basis taxpayers on the cash method of accounting for purposes of deducting such expenses.

Example 49. B, an individual, owns 100% of X Corporation, which manufactures electric razors. B uses the cash method of accounting while the corporation uses the accrual basis. Both are calendar year taxpayers. On December 27, 2005 the corporation accrues a $10,000 bonus for B. However, due to insufficient cash flow, X Corporation was not able to pay the bonus until January 10, 2006. The corporation may not deduct the accrued bonus in 2005. Rather, it must deduct the bonus in 2006, the year in which B includes the payment in his income.

Example 50. Assume the same facts as above, except that B owns only a 20% interest in X. In addition, X is a large law firm in which B is employed. The results are the same as above because B and X are still related parties: a personal service corporation and an employee-owner.

PAYMENT OF ANOTHER TAXPAYER'S OBLIGATION

As a general rule, a taxpayer is not permitted to deduct the payment of a deductible expense of another taxpayer. A deduction is allowed only for those expenditures satisfying the taxpayer's obligation or arising from such an obligation.

Example 51. As part of Q's rental contract for his personal apartment, he pays 1% of his landlord's property taxes. No deduction is allowed because the property taxes are the obligation of the landlord.

Example 52. P is majority stockholder of R Corporation. During the year, the corporation had financial difficulty and was unable to make an interest payment on an outstanding debt. To protect the goodwill of the corporation, P paid the interest. The payment is not deductible, and P will be treated as having made a contribution to the capital of the corporation for interest paid.

An exception to the general rule is provided with respect to payment of medical expenses of a dependent. To qualify as a dependent for this purpose, the person needs only to meet the relationship, support, and citizen tests.[120] If the taxpayer pays the medical expenses of a person who qualifies as a dependent under the modified tests, the expenses are treated as if they were the taxpayer's expenses and are deductible subject to limitations applicable to the taxpayer.

---

[119] § 267(a)(2).

[120] § 213(a)(1).

SUBSTANTIATION

The Code requires that taxpayers maintain records sufficient to establish the amount of gross income, deductions, credits, or other matters required to be shown on the tax return.[121] As a practical matter, record keeping requirements depend on the nature of the item. With respect to most deductions, taxpayers may rely on the "*Cohan* rule."[122] In *Cohan*, George M. Cohan, the famous playwright, spent substantial sums for travel and entertainment. The Board of Tax Appeals (predecessor to the Tax Court) denied any deduction for the expenses because the taxpayer had no records supporting the items. On appeal, however, the Second Circuit Court of Appeals reversed this decision, indicating that "absolute certainty in such matters is usually impossible and is not necessary."[123] Thus, the Appeals Court remanded the case to make some allowance for the expenditures. From this decision, the "*Cohan* rule" developed, providing that a reasonable estimation of the deduction is sufficient where the actual amount is not substantiated. In 1962, however, Congress eliminated the use of the *Cohan* rule for travel and entertainment expenses and established rigorous substantiation requirements for these types of deductions. Substantiation for other expenses, however, is still governed by the *Cohan* rule. Despite the existence of the *Cohan* rule, records should be kept documenting deductible expenditures since estimates of the expenditures may be substantially less than actually paid or incurred.

TAX PLANNING CONSIDERATIONS

MAXIMIZING DEDUCTIONS

Perhaps the most important step in minimizing the tax liability is maximizing deductions. Maximizing deductions obviously requires the taxpayer to identify and claim all the deductions to which he or she is entitled. Many taxpayers, however, often overlook deductions that they are allowed because they fail to grasp and apply the fundamental rules discussed in this chapter. To secure a deduction, the taxpayer needs only to show that the expense paid or incurred during the year is ordinary, necessary, and related to a profit-seeking activity. Notwithstanding the special rules of limitation that apply to certain deductions, most deductions are allowed because the *taxpayer* is able to recognize and establish the link between the expenditure and the profit-seeking activity. The taxpayer is in the best position to recognize that an expenditure relates to his or her trade or business, not the tax practitioner. Practitioners typically lack sufficient insight into the taxpayer's activities to identify potential deductions. Thus, it is up to the taxpayer to recognize and establish the relationship between an expenditure and the profit-seeking activity. Failure to do so results in the taxpayer's paying a tax liability higher than what he or she is required to pay.

The taxpayer should maximize not only the absolute dollar amount of deductions, but also the value of the deduction. A deduction's value is equal to the product of the amount of the deduction and the taxpayer's marginal tax rate. Because the taxpayer's marginal rate fluctuates over time, the value of a deduction varies depending on the period in which the deduction is claimed. When feasible, deductions should normally be accelerated or deferred to years when the taxpayer is in a higher tax bracket. In timing deductions, however, the time value of money also must be considered. For example, in

---

[121]   Reg. § 1.6001-1(a).

[122]   *Cohan v. Comm.*, 2 USTC ¶489, 8 AFTR 10552, 39 F.2d 540 (CA-2, 1930).

[123]   *Ibid.*

periods of inflation, the deferral of a deduction to a high-bracket year may not always be advantageous, since a deduction in the future is not worth as much as one currently.

An individual taxpayer's timing of itemized deductions is particularly important in light of the standard deduction and the floor on miscellaneous itemized deductions. Many taxpayers lose deductions because their deductions do not exceed the standard deduction in any one year. These deductions need not be lost, however, if the taxpayer alternates the years in which he or she itemizes or uses the standard deduction. For example, in those years where the taxpayer itemizes, all tax deductible expenditures from the prior year should be deferred while expenditures of the following year should be accelerated. By so doing, the taxpayer bunches itemized deductions in the current year to exceed the standard deduction. In the following year, the taxpayer would use the standard deduction. Itemized deductions are considered in detail in Chapter 11.

Maximizing deductions also requires shifting of deductions to the taxpayer who would derive the greatest benefit. For example, if two sisters are co-obligors on a note, good tax planning dictates that the sister in the higher tax bracket pay the deductible interest expense. In this case, either sister may pay and claim a deduction.

TIMING OF DEDUCTIONS

In the previous section, the importance of maximizing the absolute amount of deductions was emphasized. However, because of the time value of money it is equally important to consider the timing of deductions.

> **Example 53.** R, who pays Federal, state, and local taxes equal to 50% of his income, makes a cash expenditure of $10,000. If the $10,000 is deductible immediately, R will realize a tax benefit of $5,000 ($10,000 × 50%). Moreover, because the tax savings were realized immediately, the present value of the benefit is not diminished. On the other hand, if R is not able to deduct the $10,000 for another five years, the benefit of the deduction is substantially reduced. Specifically, assuming the annual interest rate is 10%, the present value of the $5,000 tax savings decreases to $3,105 ($5,000 × [1 ÷ (1 + 0.10)^5]), a decrease of almost 38%.

As the above example illustrates, accelerating a deduction from the future to the present can substantially increase its value. Awareness of the provisions permitting acceleration of deductions allows taxpayers to arrange their affairs so as to reap the greatest rewards. For example, a taxpayer may choose an investment that the tax law allows him or her to deduct immediately rather than an investment that must be capitalized and deducted through depreciation over the asset's life.

EXPENSES RELATING TO TAX-EXEMPT INCOME

Although expenses related to tax-exempt income are not deductible, expenses related to tax-deferred income are deductible.[124] For example, income earned on contributions to Individual Retirement Accounts is not taxable until the earnings are distributed (usually at retirement). If the taxpayer borrows amounts to contribute to his or her Individual Retirement Account, interest paid on the borrowed amounts may be deductible (if the general rules for deductibility are met) because the income to which it relates is only tax-deferred, not tax-exempt.

---

[124] *Hawaiian Trust Co., Ltd. v. U.S.*, 61-1 USTC ¶9481, 7 AFTR2d 1553, 291 F.2d 761 (CA-9, 1961). See also Letter Rul. 8527082 (April 2, 1985).

"POINTS" ON MORTGAGES

"Points" paid to secure a mortgage to acquire or improve a principal residence normally are deductible in the year paid or incurred. In some cases, however, the points are not paid out of independent funds of the taxpayer but are withheld from the mortgage proceeds. For example, where a lender is charging two points on a $50,000 loan, or $1,000 (2% of $50,000), the $1,000 is withheld by the lender as payment while the remaining $49,000 ($50,000 − $1,000) is advanced to the borrower. The Tax Court has ruled that in these situations, the taxpayer has not prepaid the interest (as represented by the points) and thus must amortize the points over the term of the loan.[125] To avoid this result and obtain a current deduction, the taxpayer should pay the points out of separate funds rather than having them withheld by the lender. This requirement will be met if the cash paid by the borrower up to and at the closing (including down payments, escrow deposits, earnest money, and amounts paid at closing) is at least equal to the amount deducted for points.[126] In this regard, the IRS has ruled that points paid by the seller on behalf of a borrower will be treated as paid directly from the funds deposited by the borrower.[127] Thus, the borrower will be entitled to a deduction. However, in determining the basis of the residence, the borrower must subtract the amount of seller paid points from the purchase price.

HOBBIES

Several studies suggest that the factor on which the hobby/business issue often turns is the manner in which the taxpayer carries on the activity.[128] For business treatment, it is imperative that the taxpayer have complete and detailed financial and nonfinancial records. Moreover, such records should be used in decision making and in constructing a profit plan. The activity should resemble a business in every respect. For example, the taxpayer should maintain a separate checking account for the activity, advertise where appropriate, obtain written advice from experts and follow it, and acquire some expertise about the operation.

Although the taxpayer is not required to actually show profits, profits in *three* of *five* consecutive years create a substantial advantage for the taxpayer. Where the profit requirement is satisfied, it is presumed that the activity is not a hobby and the IRS has the burden of proving otherwise. For this reason, the cash basis taxpayer might take steps that could convert a loss year into a profitable year. For example, in some situations it may be possible to accelerate receipts and defer payment of expenses. However, the taxpayer should be cautioned that arranging transactions so nominal profits occur has been viewed negatively by the courts.

PROBLEM MATERIALS

DISCUSSION QUESTIONS

7-1 *General Requirements for Deductions.* Explain the general requirements that must be satisfied before a taxpayer may claim a deduction for an expense or a loss.

7-2 *Deduction Defined. Consider the following:*

---

[125] *Roger A. Schubel*, 77 T.C. 701 (1982).

[126] Rev. Proc. 92-12, 1992-3, I.R.B. 27.

[127] Rev. Proc. 94-27, 1994 I.R.B. 15, 6.

[128] See, for example, Burns and Groomer, "Effects of Section 183 on the Business Hobby Controversy," *Taxes* (March 1980) pp. 195-206.

    a. It is often said that income can be meaningfully defined while deductions can be defined only procedurally. Explain.

    b. The courts are fond of referring to deductions as matters of "legislative grace." Explain.

    c. Although deductions may only be defined procedurally, construct a definition for a deduction similar to the "all inclusive" definition for income.

    d. Will satisfaction of the requirements of your definition ensure deductibility? Explain.

7-3 *Business versus Personal Expenditures.* Consider the following:

    a. If the taxpayer derives personal pleasure from an otherwise deductible expense, will the expense be denied? Explain.

    b. Name some of the purely personal expenses that are deductible, and indicate whether they are deductions for or from A.G.I.

7-4 *Business versus Investment Expenses.* Two Code sections govern the deductibility of ordinary and necessary expenses related to profit-motivated activities. Explain why two provisions exist and the distinction between them.

7-5 *An Employee's Business.* Is an employee considered as being in trade or business? Explain the significance of your answer.

7-6 *Year Allowable.* The year in which a deduction is allowed depends on whether the taxpayer is a cash basis or accrual basis taxpayer. Discuss.

7-7 *Classification of Expenses.* F is a self-employed registered nurse and works occasionally for a nursing home. G is a registered nurse employed by a nursing home. Their income, exemptions, credits, etc. are identical. Explain why a deductible expense, although paid in the same amount by both, may cause F and G to have differing tax liabilities.

7-8 *Above- and Below-the-Line Deductions.* At a tax seminar, F was reminded to ensure that he properly classified his deductions as either above- or below-the-line. After the seminar, F came home and scrutinized his Form 1040 to determine what the instructor meant and why it was important. Despite his careful examination of the form, F could not figure out what the instructor was talking about or why it was important. Help F out by explaining the meaning of this classification scheme.

7-9 *Performing Artists.* V hopes to become a movie star someday. Currently, she accepts bit parts in various movies, waiting for her break. What special tax treatment may be available for V?

7-10 *Classification of Deductions.* J and K are both single, and each earns $30,000 of income and has $2,000 of deductible expenses for the current year. J's deductions are for A.G.I. while K's deductions are itemized deductions.

    a. Given these facts, and assuming that the situation of J and K is identical in every other respect, will their tax liabilities differ? Explain.

    b. Same as (a) except their deductions are $5,000.

7-11 *Constructive Distributions.* D owns all of the stock of DX Inc., which manufactures record jackets. Over the years, the corporation has been very successful. This year, D placed his 16- and 14-year-old sons on the payroll, paying them each $10,000 annually. The boys worked on the assembly line a couple of hours each week. Explain D's strategy and the risks it involves.

7-12 *Disguised Distributions.* E owns all of the stock of EZ Inc., which operates a nursery. During the past several years, the company has operated at a deficit and E finally sold all of his stock to C. C drew a very low salary before he could turn things around. Now the business is highly profitable, and C is paying himself handsomely. As C's tax adviser, what counsel if any should be given to C?

7-13 *Income and Expenses of Illegal Business.* B is a bookie in a state where gambling is illegal. During the year, he earned $70,000 accepting bets. His expenses included those for rent, phone, and utilities. In addition, he paid off a state legislator who was a customer and who obviously knew of his activity.

    a. Discuss the tax treatment of B's income and expenses.

    b. Same as (a) except B was a drug dealer.

7-14 *Permanent and Timing Differences.* Financial accounting and tax accounting often differ in the manner in that certain expenses are treated. Identify several expenditures that, because of their treatment, produce permanent or timing differences.

7-15 *Capital Expenditures.* Can a cash basis taxpayer successfully reduce taxable income by purchasing supplies near year-end and deducting their cost?

7-16 *Independent Contractor versus Employee.* Briefly discuss the difference between an independent contractor (self-employed person) and an employee and why the distinction is important.

7-17 *Hobby Expenses.* Discuss the factors used in determining whether an activity is a hobby and the tax consequences resulting from its being deemed a hobby.

7-18 *Public Policy Doctrine.* A taxpayer operates a restaurant and failed to remit the sales tax for August to the city as of the required date. As a result, he must pay an additional assessment of 0.25 percent of the amount due. Comment on the deductibility of this payment.

7-19 *Constructive Ownership Rules.* Explain the concept of constructive ownership and the reason for its existence.

7-20 *Expenses Relating to Tax-Exempt Income.* Discuss what types of expenses relating to tax exempt income may be deductible.

7-21 *Substantiation.* Explain the Cohan rule.

PROBLEMS

7-22 *General Requirements for Deduction.* For each of the following expenses identify and discuss the general requirement(s) (ordinary, necessary, related to business, etc.) upon which deductibility depends.

    a. A police officer who is required to carry a gun at all times lives in New York. The most convenient and direct route to work is through New Jersey. The laws of New Jersey, however, prohibit the carrying of a gun in the car. As a result, he must take an indirect route to the police station to avoid New Jersey. The indirect route causes him to drive ten miles more than he would otherwise. The cost of the additional mileage is $500. (**Note:** commuting expense from one's home to the first job site generally is a nondeductible personal expense.)

    b. The current president of a nationwide union spends $10,000 for costs related to reelection.

    c. The taxpayer operates a lumber business. He is extremely religious and consequently is deeply concerned over the business community's social and moral responsibility to society. For this reason, he hires a minister to give him and his employees moral and spiritual advice. The minister has no business background although he does offer solutions to business problems.

d. The taxpayer operates a laundry in New York City. He was recently visited by two "insurance agents" who wished to sell him a special bomb policy (i.e., if the taxpayer paid the insurance "premiums," his business would not be bombed). The taxpayer paid the premiums of $500 each month.

7-23 *Accrual Basis Deductions.* In each of the following situations assume the taxpayer uses the accrual method of accounting and indicate the amount of the deduction allowed.

a. R sells and services gas furnaces. As part of his sales package, he agrees to turn on and cut off the buyer's furnace for five years. He normally charges $35 for such service, which costs him about $20 in labor and materials. Based on 2005 sales, R sets up a reserve for the costs of the services to be performed, which he estimates will be $4,500 over the next five years.

b. At the end of 2005, XYZ, a regular corporation, agreed to rent office space from ABC Leasing Corp. Pursuant to the contract, XYZ paid $10,000 on December 1, 2005 for rent for all of 2006.

c. RST Villas, a condominium project in a Vermont ski resort, reached an agreement with MPP Pop-Ins providing that MPP would provide maid services in 2006 for $20,000. RST transferred its note payable for $20,000 at the end of 2006 to MPP on December 1, 2005.

7-24 *Economic Performance.* KKO Printing, a calendar year, accrual method taxpayer, leases a number of copying machines. In conjunction with the lease, it typically purchases a one-year maintenance contract covering service on the machines. On July 20, 2005, KKO paid $6,000 for a one-year service contract that runs from July 1, 2005 through June 30, 2006. Ignoring the recurring item exception, when may KKO deduct the expense?

7-25 *Recurring Items.* M Corporation is an accrual basis taxpayer and uses the calendar year for both financial accounting and tax purposes. The corporation manufactures car stereo equipment and provides a one-year warranty. Based on an analysis of its sales for 2005, it estimates that its warranty expense for equipment sold in 2005 will be $500,000. For financial accounting purposes, M plans to accrue the expense in 2005. The corporation is in the process of finishing its 2005 tax return, which it plans on filing by the extended due date, September 15, 2006. According to the company's latest figures, as of August 31, it had incurred $200,000 in parts and labor costs in honoring warranties on 2005 sales. How should the corporation treat the $500,000 estimated warranty cost on its 2005 tax return?

7-26 *Accrual of Real Property Taxes.* M Corporation owns a chain of hamburger restaurants located all across the country. In one state where the company has several outlets, it paid real property taxes of $12,000 for the period October 1 through September 30, 2005 on January 10, 2006. M is an accrual basis taxpayer and uses a calendar year-end for reporting.

a. When is the corporation entitled to a deduction for the real estate taxes assuming it has not made an election under § 461(c) and the recurring item exception does not apply?

b. Same as (a) except the corporation makes an election under § 461(c).

7-27 *Accrual versus Cash Method of Accounting.* D operates a hardware store. For 2005, D's first year of operation, D reported the following items of revenue and expense:

Cash receipts.	$140,000
Purchase of goods on credit	90,000
Payments on payables.	82,000

By year-end, D had unsold goods on hand with a value of $25,000.

    a. Using the cash method of accounting, compute D's taxable income for the year.

    b. Using the accrual method of accounting, compute D's taxable income for the year.

    c. Which method of accounting is required for tax purposes? Why?

7-28 *Prepaid Interest.* In each of the following cases, indicate the amount of the deduction for the current year. In each case, assume the taxpayer is a calendar year, cash basis taxpayer.

    a. On December 31, P, wishing to reduce his current year's tax liability, prepaid $3,000 of interest on his home mortgage for the first three months of the following taxable year.

    b. On December 1 of this year, T obtained a $100,000 loan to purchase her residence. The loan was secured by the residence. She paid two points to obtain the loan bearing a 6 percent interest rate.

    c. Same as (b) except the loan was used to purchase a duplex, which she will rent to others. The loan was secured by the duplex.

7-29 *Prepaid Rent.* This year F, a cash basis taxpayer, secured a ten-year lease on a warehouse to be used in his business. Under the lease agreement he pays $12,000 on September 1 of each year for the following twelve months' rental.

    a. Assuming F pays $12,000 on September 1 for the next 12 months' rental, how much, if any, may he deduct? How would your answer change if F were an accrual basis taxpayer?

    b. In order to secure the lease, F also was required to pay an additional $12,000 as a security deposit. How much, if any, may he deduct?

7-30 *Prepaid Expenses.* D, a cash basis taxpayer, operates a successful travel agency. One of her more significant costs is a special computer form on which airline tickets are printed as well as stationery on which itineraries are printed. Typically, D buys about a three-month supply of these forms for $2,000. Knowing that she will be in a lower tax bracket next year. D would like to accelerate her deductions to the current year.

    a. Assuming that D pays $12,000 on December 15 for forms that she expects to exhaust before the close of next year, how much can she deduct?

    b. Same as above except D purchases the larger volume of forms because D's supplier began offering special discounts for purchases in excess of $3,000.

7-31 *Expenses Producing Future Benefits.* B took over as chief executive officer of Pentar Inc., which specializes in the manufacture of cameras. As part of his strategy to increase the corporation's share of the market, he ran a special advertising blitz just prior to Christmas that cost more than $1,000,000. The marketing staff estimates that these expenditures could very well increase the company's share of the market by 10 percent over the next three years. Speculate on the treatment of the promotion expenses.

7-32 *Capital Expenditure or Repair.* This year, Dandy Development Corporation purchased an apartment complex with 100 units. At the time of purchase, it had a 40 percent vacancy rate. As part of a major renovation, Dandy replaced all of the carpeting and painted all of the vacant units. Discuss the treatment of the expenditures.

7-33 *Identifying Capital Expenditures.* K, a sole proprietor, made the following payments during the year. Indicate whether each is a capital expenditure.

    a. Sales tax on the purchase of a new automobile

    b. Mechanical pencil for K

    c. Mops and buckets for maintenance of building

    d. Freight paid on delivery of new machinery

    e. Painting of K's office

    f. Paving of dirt parking lot with concrete

    g. Commissions to leasing agent to find new office space

    h. Rewiring of building to accommodate new equipment

7-34 *Hobby Expenses—Effect on A.G.I.* C is a successful attorney and stock car racing enthusiast. This year she decided to quit watching the races and start participating. She purchased a car and entered several local races. During the year, she had the following receipts and disbursements related to the racing activities:

Race winnings	$3,000
Property taxes	2,800
Fuel, supplies, maintenance	1,000

Her A.G.I. exclusive of any items related to the racing activities is $100,000.

    a. Indicate the tax consequences assuming the activity is not considered to be a hobby.

    b. Assuming the activity is treated as a hobby, what are the tax consequences?

    c. Assuming the activity is deemed a hobby and property taxes are $4,000, what are the tax consequences?

    d. What is the critical factor in determining whether an activity is a hobby or a business?

    e. What circumstances suggest the activity is a business rather than a hobby?

7-35 *Hobby-Presumptive Rule.* In 2003 R, a major league baseball player, purchased a small farm in North Carolina. He grows several crops and maintains a small herd of cattle on the farm. During 2003 his farming activities resulted in a $2,000 loss, which he claimed on his 2003 tax return, filed April 15, 2004. In 2005 his 2003 return was audited, and the IRS pro posed an adjustment disallowing the loss from the farming activity, asserting that the activity was merely a hobby.

    a. Assuming R litigates, who has the burden of proof as to the character of the activity?

    b. Can R shift the burden of proof at this point in time?

    c. Assume R filed the appropriate election for 2003 and reported losses of $3,000 in 2004 and profits of $14,000 in 2005, $5,000 in 2006, and $6,000 in 2007. What effect do the reported profits have?

7-36 *Hobby Losses and Statute of Limitations.* Assume the same facts as in *Problem 7-35.* When does the statute of limitations bar assessment of deficiencies with respect to the 2003 tax return?

7-37 *Investigation Expenses.* H currently operates several optical shops in Portland. During the year he traveled to Seattle and San Francisco to discuss with several doctors the possibility of locating optical shops adjacent to their practices. He incurred travel costs to Seattle of $175 and to San Francisco of $200. The physicians in Seattle agreed to an arrangement and H incurred $500 in legal fees drawing up the agreement. The physicians in San Francisco, however, would not agree, and H did not pursue the matter further.

    In the following year, H decided to enter the ice cream business. He sent letters of inquiry to two major franchisers of ice cream stores and subsequently traveled to the headquarters of each. He paid $400 for travel to Phoenix for discussions with X Corporation and $500 for travel to Los Angeles for discussions with Y Corporation. He also paid an accountant $1,200 to evaluate the financial aspects of each franchise ($600 for each evaluation). H decided to acquire a franchise from Y Corporation. He paid an attorney $800 to review the franchising agreement.

    a. Discuss the tax treatment of H's expenses associated with the attempt to expand his optical shop business.

b. Discuss the tax treatment of the expenses incurred in connection with the ice cream business, assuming H acquires the Y franchise and begins business.

c. Same as (b). Discuss the tax treatment of these expenses, assuming H is forced to abandon the transaction after being informed that there is no franchise available in his city.

7-38 *Investigation Expenses.* P incurred significant expenses to investigate the possibility of opening a Dowell's Hamburgers franchise in Tokyo, Japan. Her expenditures included hiring a local firm to perform a feasibility study, travel, and accounting and legal expenses. Her 2005 expenditures total $25,000. With respect to this amount:

a. Assuming this was P's first attempt at opening a business of her own, how much may she deduct in 2005 if she decides not to acquire the franchise?

b. Assuming this was P's first attempt at opening a business of her own, how much may she deduct in 2005 if she decides to acquire the franchise?

c. Assuming P was already in the fast-food business (she owns a Dowell's franchise in Toledo, Ohio), how much may she deduct in 2005 to acquire the franchise?

7-39 *Capital Expenditures.* Consider the following:

a. A corporate taxpayer reimbursed employees for amounts they had loaned to the corporation's former president, who was losing money at the racetrack. Comment on the deductibility of these payments as well as those expenditures discussed in *Example 7* of this chapter (relating to payments of debts previously discharged by bankruptcy) in light of the rules concerning capital expenditures.

b. How are the costs of expenditures such as land and investment securities recovered?

c. How are the costs of expenditures for goodwill recovered?

d. Distinguish between a capital expenditure and a repair.

7-40 *Classification of Deductions.* M works as the captain of a boat. His income for the year is $20,000. During the year, he purchased a special uniform for $100. Indicate the amount of the deduction and whether it is for or from A.G.I. for the following situations:

a. M's boat is a 50-foot yacht, and he operates his business as a sole proprietorship (i.e., he is self-employed).

b. M is an employee for Yachts of Fun Inc.

c. M is an employee for Yachts, which reimbursed him $70 of the cost (included in his income on Form W-2).

7-41 *Computing Employee's Deductions.* T, who is single, is currently a supervisor in the tax department of a public accounting firm in Milwaukee. T's total income for the year consisted of compensation of $42,000 and dividend income of $2,100. During the year, she incurred the following expenses:

AICPA dues	$ 200
State Society of Accountants dues	280
Subscriptions to tax journals	300
Tax return preparation	200
Pen and pencil set	50
Cleaning of suits	389
Safe deposit box (holds investment documents)	90
Annual fee on brokerage account	130
Qualified residence interest	6,000

T's employer reimbursed her $100 for the AICPA dues (included in her income).

a. Compute T's taxable income.

b. Assuming T expects her expenses to be about the same for the next several years, what advice can you offer?

7-42 *Computing Employee's Deductions.* Z, a single taxpayer, is employed as a nurse at a local hospital. Z's records reflect the following items of revenue and expense for 2005:

Gross wages	$20,000
Expenses:	
Employee travel expenses, not reimbursed	1,100
Cost of commuting to and from work,	
reimbursed (included in gross wages).	520
Charitable contributions	700
Interest and taxes on personal residence	3,900
Nurse's uniform, reimbursed (included in	
gross wages)	250

a. What is Z's A.G.I.?

b. What is Z's total of itemized deductions?

7-43 *Interest.* Mr. E operates a replacement window business as a sole proprietorship. He uses the cash method of accounting. On November 1, 2005 he secured a loan in order to purchase a new warehouse to be used in his business. Information regarding the loan and purchase of the warehouse is shown below. All of the costs indicated were paid during the year.

Term	20 years
Loan origination fee	$ 2,000
Points.	6,000
One year's interest paid in advance.	20,000
Legal fees for recording mortgage lien.	500

What amount may E deduct in 2005?

7-44 *Insurance.* Hawk Harris owns and operates the Waterfield Mudhens, a franchise in an indoor soccer league. Both Hawk and the corporation are cash basis, calendar year taxpayers. During 2005 the corporation purchased the following policies:

Policy Description	Cost	Date Paid
Two-year fire and theft effective 12/1/05.	$2,400	12/15/04
One-year life insurance policy on Jose Greatfoot, star forward; the corporation is beneficiary; effective 11/1/05	1,000	11/1/04
One-year group-term life insurance policy covering entire team and staff; effective 1/1/05.	9,000	1/15/04

| One-year policy for payments of overhead costs should the team strike and attendance fall; effective 11/1/05 . . . . | 3,600 | 9/1/04 |

In addition to the policies purchased above, the corporation is unable to get insurance on certain business risks. Therefore, the corporation has set up a reserve—a separate account—to which it contributes $5,000 on February 1 of each year.

How much may the corporation deduct for 2005?

7-45   *Life Insurance.* The Great Cookie Corporation is owned equally by F and G. Under the articles of incorporation, the corporation is required to purchase the stock of each shareholder upon his or her death to ensure that it does not pass to some undesirable third party. To finance the purchase, the corporation purchased a life insurance policy on both F and G, naming the corporation as beneficiary. The annual premium is $5,000. Can the corporation deduct the premiums?

7-46   *Business Life Insurance.* L, 56, has operated her sole proprietorship successfully since its inception three years ago. This year she has decided to expand. To this end, she borrowed $100,000 from the bank, which would be used for financing expansion of the business. The bank required L to take out a life insurance policy on her own life that would serve as security for the business loan. Are the premiums deductible?

7-47   *Public Policy-Fines, Lobbying, etc.* M is engaged in the construction business in Tucson. Indicate whether the following expenses are deductible.
   a.   The Occupational Safety and Health Act (OSHA) requires contractors to fence around certain construction sites. M determined that the fences would cost $1,000 and the fine for not fencing would be only $650. As a result, he did not construct the fences and paid a fine of $650.
   b.   M often uses Mexican quarry tile on the floors of homes that he builds. To obtain the tiles, he drives his truck across the border to a small entrepreneur's house and purchases the materials. On the return trip he often pays a Mexican customs official to "expedite" his going through customs. Without the payment, the inspection process would often be tedious and consume several hours. This year he paid the customs officials $200.
   c.   M paid $100 for an advertisement supporting the administration's economic policies, which he felt would reduce interest rates and thus make homes more affordable. In addition, he paid $700 for travel to Washington, D.C. to testify before a Congressional Committee on the effects of high interest rates on the housing industry. While there, he paid $100 to a political action committee to attend a dinner, the proceeds from which went to Senator Q.

7-48   *Limitations on Business Deductions.* This is an extension of Problem 7-22(d) In that problem, you are asked to determine if the case contains expenditures that are ordinary, necessary, and reasonable under the provisions of Code § 162. Assume the positive criteria of § 162 are met (i.e., the expenditures are ordinary, necessary, and reasonable). Are there any additional provisions in § 162 that will cause the expenditures to be disallowed?

7-49   *Related Taxpayers—Sale.* E sold stock to her son for $8,000. She purchased the stock several years ago for $11,000.
   a.   What amount of loss will E report on the sale?
   b.   What amount of gain or loss will the son report if he sells the stock for $12,000 to an unrelated party?
   c.   If the son sells for $10,000?
   d.   If the son sells for $4,000?

7-50 *Related Taxpayers-Different Accounting Methods.* G, a cash basis, calendar year taxpayer,—owns 100 percent of XYZ Corporation. XYZ is a calendar year, accrual basis taxpayer engaged in the advertising business. G leases a building to the Corporation for $1,000 per month. In December, XYZ accrues the $1,000 rental due. Indicate the tax treatment to XYZ and G assuming the payment is

a. Made on December 30 of the current year; or

b. Made on April 1 of the following year.

c. Would your answers above change if G owned 30 percent of XYZ?

7-51 *Constructive Ownership Rules.* How much of RST Corporation's stock is B considered as owning?

Owner	Shares Directly Owned
B	20
C, B's brother	30
D, B's partner	40
E, B's 60-percent-owned corporation	100
Other unrelated parties	10

7-52 *Expenses of Another Taxpayer.* B is the only child of P and will inherit the family fortune. P, who is in the 28 percent tax bracket, is willing to give B and his wife $500 a month. Comment on the advisability of P paying the following directly in lieu of making a gift.

a. Medical expenses of B, who makes $20,000 during the year; P (the father) provides 55 percent of B's support.

b. Interest and principal payments on B's home mortgage, on which B and his wife are the sole obliges.

c. Same as (b) except that P is also an obligee on the note.

7-53 *Losses.* This year was simply a financial disaster for Z. Indicate the effects of the following transactions on Z's taxable income. Ignore any limitations that may exist.

a. After the stock market crash, Z sold her stock and realized a loss of $1,000.

b. Z sold her husband's truck for $3,000 (basis $2,000) and her own car for $5,000 (basis $9,000). Both vehicles were used for personal purposes.

c. Z's $500 camera was stolen.

d. The land next to Z's house was rezoned to light industrial, driving down the value of her home by $10,000.

7-54 *Planning Deductions.* X, 67, is a widow, her husband having died several years ago. Each year, X receives about $30,000 of interest and dividends. Because the mortgage on her home is virtually paid off, her only potential itemized deductions are her contributions to her church and real estate taxes. Her anticipated deductions are:

Year	Contribution
2005	$2,000
2006	3,000
2007	1,000

What tax advice can you offer X?

7-55 *Timing Deductions.* T currently figures that Federal, state, and local taxes consume about 30 percent of his income at the margin. Next year, however, due to a tax law change his taxes should increase to about 40 percent and remain at that level for at least five or six years. Assuming T buys a computer for $4,000 and he has the option of deducting all of the cost this year or deducting it ratably through depreciation over the next five years, what advice can you offer?

7-56 *Classification and Deductibility.* In each of the following independent situations, indicate for the current taxable year the amounts deductible *for* A.G.I., *from* A.G.I., or *not deductible* at all. Unless otherwise stated, assume all taxpayers use the cash basis method of accounting and report using the calendar year.

a. M spent $1,000 on a life insurance policy covering her own life.

b. G is an author of novels. His wife attempted to have him declared insane and have him committed. Fearing the effect that his wife's charges might have on him and his book sales, G paid $11,000 in legal fees, resulting in a successful defense.

c. Taxpayer, a plumber employed by XYZ Corporation, paid union dues of $100.

d. Q Corporation paid T, its president and majority shareholder, a salary of $100,000. Employees in comparable positions earn salaries of $70,000.

e. L operates a furniture business as a sole proprietorship. She rents a warehouse (on a month-to-month basis) used for storing items sold in her store. In late December, L paid $2,000 for rental of the warehouse for the month of January.

f. M is a self-employed security officer. He paid $100 for uniforms and $25 for having them cleaned.

g. N is a security officer employed by the owner of a large apartment complex. He pays $150 for uniforms. In addition, he paid $15 for having them cleaned. His employer reimbursed him $60 of the cost of the uniforms (included in his income on Form W-2).

h. K owns a duplex as an investment. During the year, she paid $75 for advertisements seeking tenants. She was unable to rent the duplex, and thus no income was earned this year.

i. P paid $200 for subscriptions to technical journals to be used in his employment activities. Although P was fully reimbursed by his employer, his employer did not report the reimbursement in P's income.

7-57 *Classification and Deductibility.* In each of the following independent situations, indicate for the current taxable year the amounts deductible *for* A.G.I., *from* A.G.I., or *not deductible* at all. Unless otherwise stated, assume all taxpayers use the cash basis method of accounting and report using the calendar year.

a. O paid the interest and taxes of $1,000 on his ex-wife's home mortgage. The divorce agreement provided that he could claim deductions for the payments.

b. P paid an attorney $1,500 in legal fees related to her divorce. Of these fees, $600 is for advice concerning the tax consequences of transferring some of P's stock to her husband as part of the property settlement.

c. R paid $10,000 for a small warehouse on an acre of land. He used the building for several months before tearing it down and erecting a hamburger stand.

d. H and his wife moved into the city and no longer needed their personal automobiles. They sold their Chevrolet for a $1,000 loss and their Buick for a $400 gain.

e. C is employed as a legal secretary. This year he paid an employment agency $300 for finding him a new, higher-paying job as a legal secretary.

f. X operates his own truck service. He paid $80 in fines for driving trucks that were overweight according to state law.

g. T, an employee, paid $175 to an accountant for preparing her personal income tax returns.

7-58 *Classification and Deductibility.* In each of the following independent situations, indicate for the current taxable year the amounts deductible for A.G.I., from A.G.I., or not deductible at all. Unless otherwise stated, assume all taxpayers use the cash basis method of accounting and report using the calendar year.

a. B sold stock to his mother for a $700 loss. B's mother subsequently sold the stock for $400 less than she had paid to B.

b. Same as (a) but assume the mother sold the stock for $500 more than she had paid to B.

c. D operates three pizza restaurants as a sole proprietorship in Indianapolis. In July he paid $1,000 in air fares to travel to Chicago and Detroit to determine the feasibility of opening additional restaurants. Because of economic conditions, D decided not to open any additional restaurants.

d. T owns and operates several gun stores as a sole proprietorship. In light of gun control legislation, he traveled to the state capital at a cost of $80 to testify before a committee. In addition, he traveled around the state speaking at various Rotary and Kiwanis Club functions on the pending legislation at a cost of $475. T also placed an advertisement in the local newspaper concerning the merit of the legislation at a cost of $50. He pays dues to the National Rifle Association of $100.

e. D is employed as a ship captain for a leisure cruise company. He paid $1,000 for rent on a warehouse where he stores smuggled narcotics, which he sells illegally.

f. M, a plumber and an accrual basis taxpayer, warrants his work. This year he estimates that expenses attributable to the warranty work are about 3 percent of sales, or $3,000.

g. G, a computer operator, pays $75 for a subscription to an investment newsletter devoted to investment opportunities in state and municipal bonds.

7-59 *Employee Business Expenses:* Planning. J is employed as a salesman by Bigtime Business Forms Inc. He is considering the purchase of a new automobile that he would use primarily for business. Are there any tax factors that J might consider before purchasing the new car?

CUMULATIVE PROBLEMS

7-60 Tony Johnson (I.D. No. 456-23-7657), age 45, is single. He lives at 5220 Grand Avenue, Brooklyn, NY 10016. Tony is employed by RTI Corporation, which operates a chain of restaurants in and around New York City. He has supervisory responsibilities over the managers of four restaurants. An examination of his records for 2005 revealed the following information.

1. During the year, Tony earned $33,000. His employer withheld $2,200 in Federal income taxes and the proper amount of FICA taxes. Tony obtained his current job through an employment agency to which he paid a $150 fee. He previously was employed as a manager of another restaurant. Due to the new job, it was necessary to improve his wardrobe. Accordingly, Tony purchased several new suits at a cost of $600.

2. On the days that Tony works, he normally eats his meals at the restaurants for purposes of quality control. There is no charge for the meals, which are worth $2,000.

3. He provides 60 percent of the support for his father, age 70, who lived with Tony all year and who has no income other than social security benefits of $7,000 during the year. Tony provided more than one-half of the cost of maintaining the home.

4. Dividend income from General Motors Corporation stock that he owned was $350. Interest income on savings was $200.

5. Tony and other employees of the corporation park in a nearby parking garage. The parking garage bills RTI Corporation for the parking. Tony figures that his free parking is worth $1,000 annually.

6. Tony subscribes to several trade publications for restaurants at a cost of $70.

7. During the year, he paid $200 to a bank for a personal financial plan. Based on this plan, Tony made several investments, including a $2,000 contribution to an individual retirement account, and also rented for $30 a safety deposit box in which he stores certain investment related documents.

8. Tony purchased a new home, paying three points on a loan of $70,000. He also paid $6,000 of interest on his home mortgage during the year. In addition, he paid $650 of real property taxes on the home. He has receipts for sales taxes of $534.

9. While hurrying to deliver an important package for his employer, Tony received a $78 ticket for violating the speed limit. Because his employer had asked that he deliver the package as quickly as possible, Tony was reimbursed $78 for the ticket, which he paid.

Compute Tony's taxable income for the year. If forms are used for the computations, complete Form 1040 and Schedule A. (Use 2004 tax forms if the 2005 forms are not available.)

7-61 Wendy White (I.D. No. 526-30-9001), age 29, is single. She lives at 1402 Pacific Beach Ave., San Diego, CA 92230. Wendy is employed by KXXR television station as the evening news anchor. An examination of her records for 2005 revealed the following information.

1. Wendy earned $150,000 in salary. Her employer withheld $22,000 in Federal income taxes and the proper amount of FICA taxes.

2. Wendy also received $10,000 in self-employment income from personal appearances during the year. Her unreimbursed expenses related to this income were: transportation and lodging, $523; meals, $120; and office supplies, $58.

3. Wendy reports the following additional deductions: home mortgage interest, $6,250; charitable contributions, $1,300; state and local income taxes, $3,100; and employment-related expenses, $920.

Compute Wendy's taxable income for 2005 and her tax due (including any self-employment tax). If forms are used for the computations, complete Form 1040, Schedule A, Schedule C, and Schedule SE.

Reminder: FICA and self-employment taxes are composed of two elements: social security (old age, survivor, and disability insurance) and Medicare health insurance (MHI). In 2005, social security is paid at a rate of 6.2 percent (12.4 percent for self-employed individuals) on the first $90,000 of earned income; MHI is paid at a rate of 1.45 percent (2.9 percent for self-employed individuals) on all earned income.

7-62 *Continuous Tax Return Problem.*
Previous Facts: Larry L. and Cathy C. Zepp have been married 19 years. Larry is age 62 (Social Security number 123-45-6789) while Cathy is age 50 (Social Security number 123-45-6788). They live at 1234 Elm Dr. in Des Moines, Iowa 50311. Larry is a salesman employed by DSK Industries. This year he earned $110,000 (income tax withheld was $17,000). A corrected W-2 is below. Cathy recently completed a graduate degree in computer technology. She continues to freelance as an independent contractor in computer graphics. Her earnings from various engagements were $12,000. Her only expenses were for miscellaneous office supplies of $3,000. She paid estimated taxes during the year of $1,000 ($250 on each due date). Other income earned by the couple included interest income of $3,000 from a certificate of deposit and $975 of interest from tax-exempt bonds issued by the State of Iowa. The couple owns a duplex that it rents out. Annual rentals were $8,000 and rental expenses (e.g., maintenance, utilities, depreciation) were $3,000. Other expenses paid during the year included:

Unreimbursed medical expenses.	$ 9,000
Interest on home mortgage	12,000
Real property taxes on home.	1,900
Charitable contributions.	1,000
Rental of safety deposit box to hold certain investments	100
Unreimbursed employee business expenses of Larry	3,000

Assume that all of the expenses were incurred jointly except their business expenses.

- The Zepps have two children, a son Wrigley F. Zepp (111-33-4444, 12/1/1986)) and a daughter: Apple A. Zepp (111-33-4445, 1/4/1992). Both children lived with them the entire year. Apple is considered legally blind.
- Apple received interest income of $3,000.
- This year Larry began receiving Social Security benefits. For the year, he received $12,000.
- The couple received a Form 1099 (see below) regarding an investment in a mutual fund.
- Cathy was unemployed for a short period and received unemployment compensation of $800.
- Larry paid $1,800 of alimony to his first wife.
- Cathy received $2,000 of alimony from her first husband.
- Cathy inherited $100,000 from her rich uncle.
- The corrected W-2 below reveals an item reported in Box 12 Code C of $125.

New Facts

- Cathy paid medical insurance premiums of $4,000
- The couple paid $1,000 for tax preparation of last year's return. Before last year, Larry did the return but since last year involved filing a Schedule C for Cathy he decided to get professional tax help.
- Cathy continued her hobby of breeding and selling terriers. This year she sold 10 puppies for $6,000. Her expenses for raising the dogs (food, shots, etc.) were $2,000.

Prepare Form 1040 for the Zepps.

7-63 *Continuous Tax Return Problem. Additional Questions.* Answer the following questions relating to the *continuous tax return problem* above.

a. Larry incurred $3,000 of expenses related to his employment while Cathy incurred $3,000 related to her freelancing activity (i.e., self-employment). Which of the following statements is true regarding the treatment of the expenses for federal income tax purposes?

  1. The expenses of both Larry and Cathy were subject to the 2% limitation.

  2. The expenses of both Larry and Cathy were fully deductible as deductions for A.G.I. (i.e., deductible in arriving at adjusted gross income).

  3. The expenses of both Larry and Cathy were considered itemized deductions but only the employment expenses were subject to the 2% limitation.

  4. The expenses of Cathy affected the amount of Larry's expenses that are deductible.

  5. None of the above is correct.

b. Assume Larry is considered a statutory employee (see Box 13 of his W-2 in an earlier chapter). Indicate the amount, if any, by which the couple's taxable income increases or decreases.

c. Did Cathy's payment for medical insurance affect her self-employment tax?

RESEARCH PROBLEMS

7-64 T and two associates are equal owners in LST Corporation. The three formed the corporation several years ago with the idea of capitalizing on the fitness movement.

After a modest beginning and meager returns, the corporation did extremely well this year. As a result, the corporation plans on paying the three individuals salaries that T believes the IRS may deem unreasonable. T wonders whether he can avoid the tax consequences associated with an unreasonable compensation determination by paying back whatever amount is ultimately deemed a dividend.

a. What would be the effect on T's taxable income should he repay the portion of a salary deemed a dividend?

b. Would there be any adverse effects of adopting a payback arrangement?

Partial list of research aids:

Vincent E. Oswald, 49 T.C. 645.

Rev. Rul. 69-115, 1969-1 C.B. 50.

7-65 C, a professor of film studies at State University, often meets with her doctoral students at her home. In her home, C has a room that she uses solely to conduct business related to the classes she teaches at the university. In the room she and her students often review the movies the students have made to satisfy requirements in their doctoral program. Can C deduct expenses related to her home office?

7-66 R moved to St. Louis in 2004 and purchased a home. After living there for a year, his family had grown and required a much larger home. On August 1, 2005 they purchased their dream house, which cost far more than their first home. Shortly before he closed on the new residence, he put his first house on the market to sell. After two months had passed, however, he had received no offers. Fearing that he would be unable to pay the debt on both homes, R decided to rent his old home while trying to sell it. Surprisingly, he was able to rent the house immediately. However, in order to secure the party's agreement to rent monthly, he was required to perform a few repairs costing $500. Seven months after he had rented the home, R sold it. During the rental period, R paid the utilities and various other expenses. R has come to you for your advice on how these events in 2005 would affect his tax return.

7-67 In November 2005 B, employed as a life insurance salesperson for PQR Insurance Company in Newark, New Jersey, purchased a personal computer for use in his work. B has come to you for help in deciding how to handle this purchase on his 2005 tax return. He, of course, wants to expense the full price of the computer under Code § 179.

B relates the following salient information to you with respect to this purchase:

1. B files a joint return with his wife, L. They have a combined A.G.I. of $65,000 before considering this item. They have sufficient qualified expenditures to itemize deductions on Schedule A, but they have no miscellaneous itemized deductions.

2. B paid $3,000 for the laptop computer, which will be used 100 percent for business use.

3. B bought the computer to analyze client data. He figures this will help him increase his sales because he can analyze the results of various insurance options at the client's home or office (all personalized, of course).

4. PQR does not provide B with company-owned computing equipment. In fact, they refused to pay for B's computer because the expense of providing computers for all of PQR's agents would be too great.

How should B treat this purchase on his 2005 tax return?

7-68 On January 28, 2005 S comes to you for tax preparation advice. She has always prepared her own return, but it has become somewhat complicated and she needs professional advice.

During your initial interview, you discover that S is a teacher at a high school in Chicago, Illinois. She is also the coach of the golf team. In 2002 S decided she wanted to be a professional golfer. So, when she was 32 years old, she began a part-time apprenticeship program with the Professional Golfers' Association of America (PGA), where she was an unpaid assistant to the pro at a local country club. Then, in 2003 she became a member of the PGA and began her professional career.

S has not made much money as a professional golfer. In fact, her expenses exceeded her income in both 2003 and 2004 ($4,000 loss in 2003; $3,500 loss in 2004). Believing she was actively engaged in a trade or business (she kept separate records for her golf activities, practiced about 10 hours each week, and worked with a pro whenever she could), S deducted her golf-related expenses on Schedule C and reported her losses from this activity on her prior returns.

The IRS has challenged S's 2003 and 2004 loss deductions, calling them nondeductible "hobby" losses. Is the IRS correct in this matter? Would she win if the matter is taken to court? What planning steps can S take to ensure that any future losses are deductible trade or business losses?

Chapter 8

EMPLOYEE BUSINESS EXPENSES

LEARNING OBJECTIVES

Upon completion of this chapter you will be able to:

► Discuss the rules governing the deduction of several common expenses incurred by employees and self-employed persons

► Recognize when educational expenses are deductible

► Explain the rules concerning the deduction of moving expenses

► Describe when expenses of maintaining a home office are deductible

► Distinguish between deductible transportation expenses and nondeductible commuting costs

► Understand the differences between deductible travel expenses and deductible transportation costs

► Determine when entertainment expenses can be deducted

► Describe the 50 percent limitation on the deduction of meals and entertainment

► Explain the special record-keeping requirements for travel and entertainment expenses

► Discuss the two types of reimbursement arrangements: accountable and nonaccountable plans

CHAPTER OUTLINE

Over the years, many rules have been developed to govern the deductibility of specific business expenses. These rules normally augment the general requirements of § 162 (identified in Chapter 7) by establishing additional criteria that must be satisfied before a deduction may be claimed. As a practical matter, the primary purpose of many of these rules is to prohibit taxpayers from deducting what are in reality personal expenditures. For example, consider a taxpayer who uses a room at home to work or a taxpayer who takes a customer to lunch. In both cases, the expenses incurred very well may be genuine business expenses and deductible under the general criteria. On the other hand, such expenses could simply be *disguised* personal expenditures. As these examples suggest, some of the expenses that are likely to be manipulated are those often incurred by employees in connection with their employment duties. Such common employee expenses as those for travel and entertainment, education, moving, and home offices have long been the source of controversy. Of course, such costs are incurred by a self-employed person as well as by employees and raise similar problems. This chapter examines the special provisions applicable to these items.

EDUCATION EXPENSES

Historically, the tax law has taken the view that most education expenses are personal and, therefore, not deductible. For example, an art appreciation course for the taxpayer's cultural enrichment is purely personal in nature. Consequently, its cost is not deductible.[1] Similarly, no deduction is granted for expenses of a college education as a business expense on the theory that they are costs of preparing the taxpayer to enter a new business—not the costs of carrying on a business. Therefore, such general education expenses are nondeductible capital expenditures for which no amortization is allowed. Other education expenses, however, such as those incurred by an accountant to attend a seminar on a new tax law, are considered essential costs of pursuing income and are deductible like other ordinary and necessary business expenses. To ensure that deductions are permitted only for education expenses that serve current business objectives and are not personal or capital in nature, special tests must be met.

The Regulations allow a deduction if the education expenses satisfy *either* of the following conditions *and* are not considered personal or capital in nature, as discussed below.[2]

1. The education maintains or improves skills required of the taxpayer in his or her employment or other trade or business.

2. The education meets the express requirements imposed by either the individual's employer or applicable law, and the taxpayer must meet such requirements to retain his or her job, position, or rate of compensation.

Education expenses that meet either of these conditions are still not deductible if they are considered personal or capital expenditures under either of the following two tests:[3]

1. The education is necessary to meet the minimum educational requirements of the taxpayer's trade or business.

2. The education qualifies the taxpayer for a new trade or business.

REQUIREMENTS FOR DEDUCTION

Maintain Skills. For the expense to qualify under the first criterion, the education must be related to the taxpayer's present trade or business and maintain or improve the skills used in such business. The taxpayer must be able to establish the necessary connection between the studies pursued and the taxpayer's current employment. For example, a personnel manager seeking an M.B.A. degree was allowed to deduct all of her education expenses when she ingeniously related each course taken to her job (e.g., a computer course enabled her to be more effective in acquiring information from and communicating with computer personnel).[4] In contrast, the U.S. Tax Court denied the deductions of a research chemist's cost of an M.B.A., indicating that courses such as advanced business finance, corporate strategy, and business law were only remotely related to the skills needed for his job.[5]

Refresher and continuing education courses ordinarily meet the skills maintenance test.

Example 1. T repairs appliances. To maintain his proficiency, he often attends training schools. The costs of attending such schools are deductible because the education is necessary to maintain and improve the skills required in his job.

---

[1]   As discussed below, beginning in 2002, § 222 permits a deduction for qualified expenses.

[2]   Reg. § 1.162-5(a).

[3]   Reg. §§ 1.162-5(b)(2) and (3).

[4]   *Frank S. Blair, III*, 41 TCM 289, T.C. Memo 1980-488.

[5]   *Ronald T. Smith*, 41 TCM 1186, T.C. Memo 1981-149.

Required by Employer or Law. Once the minimum education requirements are met to obtain a job, additional education may be required by the employer or by law to retain the taxpayer's salary or position. Costs for such education are deductible as long as they do not qualify the taxpayer for a new trade or business.

> **Example 2.** This year, R took a new job as a high school instructor in science. State law requires that teachers obtain a graduate degree within five years of becoming employed. Expenses for college courses for this purpose are deductible even though they lead to a degree since such education is mandatory under state law.

New Trade or Business. If education prepares the taxpayer to enter a new trade or business, no deduction is permitted. In this regard, a mere change of duties usually is not considered a new business.[6] For example, a science teacher may deduct the cost of courses enabling him or her to teach art since the switch is a mere change in duties. The taxpayer becomes qualified for a new occupation if the education enables the taxpayer to perform substantially different tasks, regardless of whether the taxpayer actually uses the skills acquired.

> **Example 3.** R was hired as a trust officer in a bank several years ago. His employer now requires that all trust officers must have a law degree. R may not deduct the cost of obtaining a law degree because the degree qualifies him for a new trade or business.[7] No deduction is allowed even though it is required by his employer and R does not actually engage in the practice of law.

Minimum Education. Expenses of education undertaken to gain entry into a business or to meet the minimum standards required in a business are not deductible. These standards are determined in light of the typical conditions imposed by the particular job. For example, the U.S. Tax Court denied a $21,000 deduction for the cost of a Northwestern University "MBA" on the taxpayer's 1998 return because the degree not only enabled her to meet the minimum education requirements for her position at Merrill Lynch and Raymond James but also prepared her for a new trade or business.[8] This rule also operates to prohibit the deduction of such expenses as those for a review course for the bar or C.P.A. exam and fees to take such professional exams.[9] Similarly, education expenses related to a pay increase or promotion may not be deductible under this rule if the increase or promotion was the primary objective of the education. However, as discussed below, a special provision allows a deduction for qualified tuition expenses.

TRAVEL AS A FORM OF EDUCATION

Prior to 1986, travel in and of itself was considered a deductible form of education when it was related to a taxpayer's trade or business. For example, an instructor of Spanish could travel around Spain during the summer to learn more about the Spanish culture and improve her conversational Spanish. In such case, the travel cost would have been deductible since it was related to the taxpayer's trade or business. In 1986, Congress became concerned that many taxpayers were using this rule to deduct what were essentially the costs of a personal vacation. Moreover, Congress believed that any business purpose served by traveling for general education purposes was insignificant.

---

6   Reg. § 1.162-5(b)(3).

7   Reg. § 1.162-5(b)(3)(ii), Ex.1.

8   *Will M. McEuen III*, TC Summary Opinion 2004-107.

9   Rev. Rul. 69-292, 1969-1 C.B. 84.

To eliminate possible abuse, no deduction is allowed simply because the travel itself is educational.[10] Deductions are allowed for travel only when the education activity otherwise qualifies and the travel expense is necessary to pursue such activity. For example, a deduction for travel would be allowed where a professor of French literature travels to France to take courses that are offered only at the Sorbonne.

TYPES AND CLASSIFICATION OF EDUCATION DEDUCTIONS

Education expenses normally deductible include costs of tuition, books, supplies, typing, transportation, and travel (including meals, lodging, and similar expenses). Typical education expenses are for college or vocational courses, continuing professional education programs, professional development courses, and similar courses or seminars.

The costs of transportation between the taxpayer's place of work and school are deductible. If the taxpayer goes home before going to school, however, the expense of going from home to school is deductible, but only to the extent that it does not exceed the costs of going directly from work. The cost of transportation from home to school on a nonworking day represents nondeductible commuting.

Unreimbursed educational expenditures of an employee are treated as miscellaneous itemized deductions subject to the 2 percent floor. In contrast, if an employer reimburses an employee for such expenses under an *accountable plan* (discussed later in this chapter), the reimbursement is excludable from gross income. Any reimbursement not made under an accountable plan must be included in the employee's gross income, and qualifying deductions must be treated as miscellaneous itemized deductions. Finally, education expenses incurred by a self-employed person are deductible *for* A.G.I.

DEDUCTION FOR QUALIFIED TUITION AND RELATED EXPENSES

The general rules governing the deduction of education expenses normally prohibit taxpayers from deducting the costs of obtaining a college education since such expenses are considered personal (i.e., incurred to meet minimum education requirements). However, to help subsidize the increasing cost of higher education, Congress created a special provision. Section 222 allows a deduction for *qualified tuition and related expenses* incurred in connection with enrollment or attendance at an *eligible educational institution.* The amount of the deduction is $4,000. The deduction is generally available to all taxpayers since it may be claimed for A.G.I. However, the deduction is not available for single taxpayers with modified adjusted gross income exceeding $65,000 ($130,000 for joint filers). Note that there is no phase-out of the deduction, but rather a cliff effect. If A.G.I. exceeds the applicable dollar limit, no deduction is allowed. The deduction can be claimed for expenses of the taxpayer, the taxpayer's spouse, and the taxpayer's dependents. Consistent with this approach, the law prohibits taxpayers who are eligible to be claimed as dependents from claiming the deduction. In addition, married taxpayers must file jointly in order to claim the deduction. Finally, to prohibit a double benefit, the deduction is not allowed if the taxpayer or any other person claims the Hope Scholarship credit or the Lifetime Learning credit (see below) with respect to that individual for that particular year. Moreover, the deduction is reduced by distributions used for educational expenses that are otherwise excludable such as those from a prepaid tuition plan or educational savings account (see below). Unless action is taken, the deduction is set for repeal after 2005.

Only qualified tuition and related expenses may be deducted. This definition normally encompasses the tuition and fees charged by most universities. It should be

---

[10]   § 274(m)(2).

noted, however, that fees for course-related books, supplies, and equipment normally do not qualify unless—according to the IRS—the fees must be paid *to the institution* as a condition of enrollment or attendance.[11] For example, a student activity fee, a special technology or lab fee charged by a university should qualify. On the other hand, qualified expenses do not include the cost of: insurance, medical expenses (including student health fees), room and board, transportation, or similar personal, living, or family expenses. This is true even if the fee must be paid to the institution as a condition of enrollment or attendance. In addition, qualified tuition and related expenses generally do not include expenses that relate to any course of instruction or other education that involves sports, games or hobbies, or any noncredit course unless the course is part of the student's degree program. Note that both undergraduate and graduate courses qualify and it makes no difference whether the course is part of a program that leads to a degree.

Only qualified expenses paid to *eligible educational institutions* are deductible. An eligible education institution is defined as any accredited post secondary institution that offers credit toward a bachelor's degree, an associate's degree or other recognized post-secondary credential. Thus tuition for most colleges and universities as well as junior colleges qualify. Some vocational institutions (e.g., trade schools) and proprietary for-profit organizations may qualify as well.

Example 4. In August 2005, Mr. and Mrs. Smith paid the tuition for their son's attendance at State University, a cost of $1,900. In December 2005, the Smiths paid the tuition for the second semester of $2,000. The second semester began in January 2006. Mr. and Mrs. Smith have an A.G.I. of $120,000. The son is a junior at State and, consequently, the expenses do not qualify for the Hope Scholarship credit discussed below. In addition, because their A.G.I. exceeds $100,000, the couple is not entitled to claim either the Hope or Lifetime Learning credit. While the credits are not available, a deduction is allowed since the expenses are paid during the year and are for education for such year or education that begins within three months after the close of the year. The deduction is limited to $4,000 and may be claimed for A.G.I.

Example 5. This year R started law school. He is a part-time student and has a part-time job. He paid tuition of $12,000 for the year. He may deduct $4,000 of the tuition for A.G.I. Alternatively, he could elect to use the Lifetime Learning credit of $2,000 ($10,000 maximum qualified expenses × 20%). However, as noted above, he can either deduct the expenses or claim the credit but not both. If his marginal rate was 25%, the $4,000 deduction would be worth only $1,000 so in this case, he would be better off claiming the credit.

RELATIONSHIP TO EDUCATION CREDITS AND QUALIFIED PREPAID TUITION

In addition to the deduction for education expenses, the Code provides other benefits for education related expenses. There are two credits related to education: (1) the Hope Scholarship credit, and (2) the Lifetime Learning credit. Special benefits are also extended to Educational Savings Accounts and Qualified Tuition Programs (§ 529 plans). These credits and tax-favored savings arrangements, discussed in detail in Chapters 13 and 18, are designed to help middle America fund the ever-increasing cost of higher education.

The Hope Scholarship credit and the Lifetime Learning credit are both available for education expenses paid on behalf of the taxpayer, the taxpayer's spouse, or a

---

[11] See *Tax Benefits for Higher Education*, IRS Publication 970 (Rev. 2004, p. 35).

dependent. The Hope Scholarship credit is 100 percent of the first $1,000 of education expenses and 50 percent of the next $1,000 of expenses for each student. Thus the maximum credit is $1,500 per year per student. The Hope Scholarship credit generally can be claimed only for the first two years of post-secondary education (e.g., college). The Lifetime Learning credit can be claimed for 20 percent of up to $10,000 of qualified tuition and fees annually. Thus the maximum credit per taxpayer return would be $2,000. In contrast to the Hope Scholarship credit, the Lifetime Learning is available for virtually any type of education for an unlimited number of years. For any one particular student, a taxpayer could elect *either* the Hope credit or a Lifetime Learning credit but not both. As noted above, if the taxpayer elects either credit, the deduction is not allowed. Both credits are phased out for high-income earners. Under the phase-out rules, married taxpayers filing joint returns cannot claim either credit if their A.G.I. exceeds $107,000 in 2005 ($53,500 for other taxpayers).

The tax law also provides favorable treatment for two savings arrangements: (1) Educational Savings Accounts (Coverdell Accounts described in § 530) and (2) Qualified Tuition Programs (so-called § 529 plans). Contributions to these plans are not deductible. However, income on amounts contributed are nontaxable when earned. In addition, amounts distributed from the plans are nontaxable if such amounts are used for certain expenses for higher education.

It is important to note that the law prevents taxpayers from trying to double dip; that is, the law specifically prohibits taxpayers from claiming both a deduction and a credit for the same education expenses. For example, if a CPA spends $300 to attend a continuing education course, he could claim a deduction of $300 as a business expense under § 162, qualified tuition under § 222, or as the basis for the Lifetime Learning credit of $60. Observe, however, that due to limitations, differing phase-out amounts, definitions of qualifying expenditures, and the interaction with other educational provisions such as the exclusion for educational assistance of § 127 and the working condition fringe benefit rules of § 132, a single expense could be covered by multiple provisions and results in mind-boggling complexity.

> **Example 6.** J recently completed his undergraduate degree at the University of Texas and took a job with a brokerage firm in Dallas. The firm agreed to reimburse him for a portion of the cost of an M.B.A. program. In January, J enrolled as a part-time student in the M.B.A. program at a local university. This year he paid tuition of $22,250 and the firm reimbursed him $8,250 of this amount. In addition, J withdrew $1,000 from an Educational Savings account to help pay the tuition. He paid for the remaining $13,000 from a student loan.
>
> Under the revised educational assistance rules of § 127 (see Chapter 6), J could exclude $5,250 reimbursement for the coursework (both undergraduate and graduate courses qualify) and neither he nor his employer would be required to pay FICA or Medicare taxes on this amount. J also could exclude $1,000 withdrawn from the Educational Savings Account since it was used for qualified higher education expenses. Note that J could not deduct the amount for which he was reimbursed or the withdrawal since both were excluded. The treatment of the remaining $16,000 ($22,250 − $5,250 − $1,000) is not clear. In order to exclude the $3,000 balance reimbursed by his employer as a working condition fringe benefit under § 132, the expense must qualify as a deductible business expense under § 162. The IRS might take the position that none of the remaining amount paid is deductible under § 162 since J has not met the minimum education requirement of the brokerage firm and, therefore, the $3,000 reimbursement would not qualify for exclusion. In any event, J could deduct $4,000 as a qualified tuition expense under § 222. (Observe, that to exclude the $3,000 reimbursement as a working condition fringe under § 132, the item must be deductible under § 162—not § 222.) J could utilize the Lifetime

Learning credit instead of the deduction. If it is assumed that he could not exclude the additional reimbursement under § 132 and he did not deduct *any* amount under § 222, he could claim a Lifetime Learning credit of $2,000 (20% × up to $10,000). Whether J utilizes the amount paid as a basis for claiming the credit or as a deduction under § 222 depends on any phase-outs and his tax bracket. However, he cannot use the expenses for claiming both the deduction and the credit. Also note that the new § 222 deduction is a deduction for AGI and not a miscellaneous itemized deduction subject to the 2% floor.

DEDUCTION FOR EXPENSES OF PRIMARY AND SECONDARY SCHOOL TEACHERS

In 2002, the Bush administration reached out to the teaching profession by creating a special deduction. The deduction originated from a 1996 National Education Association study which found that the average kindergarten–12th grade teacher spent approximately $400 per year out of their personal funds for unreimbursed classroom supplies (e.g., a first grade teacher may incur expenses for the decoration of his or her classroom). Although such expenses were deductible, because they were miscellaneous itemized deductions, it was unlikely that most teachers could deduct such expenses. In supporting the deduction, President Bush asserted that if a businessperson could deduct a meal, "a teacher certainly ought to be able to deduct the cost of pencils or a Big Chief tablet." To this end, §62(a)(2)(D) allows a deduction of up to $250 per year for unreimbursed business expenses incurred in connection with books, supplies, computer equipment, other equipment and supplementary materials used in the classroom. The deduction is for A.G.I. and, therefore, all qualifying teachers benefit. Qualifying teachers are defined as "eligible educators" who for at least 900 hours during a school year is a kindergarten–12th grade teacher, instructor, counselor, principal or aide. The educator is eligible only if he or she works at a school that provides elementary or secondary education (kindergarten–12th grade). The Working Families Tax Relief Act of 2004 extended the deduction through 2005.

✔ *CHECK YOUR KNOWLEDGE*

For each of the following situations, indicate whether the expenditures are deductible as education expenses.

Review Question 1. Last June, D graduated magna cum laude from the University of Virginia. This fall he entered Johns Hopkins Medical School, paying tuition of thousands of dollars.

The costs of medical school are not deductible under § 162 as business expenses for two reasons. First, the education is necessary to meet the minimum educational requirements to become a doctor. Second, the education qualifies the taxpayer to carry on a new trade or business. Nevertheless, D could deduct a portion under § 222 as qualified tuition or claim the Lifetime Learning credit, but not both.

Review Question 2. H, a practicing tax accountant, is taking a series of correspondence courses to become a certified financial planner.

As may be clear by now, very little is black or white in the tax law; here is yet another case. The IRS would probably take the position that the expenses are not deductible because the education qualifies the taxpayer to carry on a new trade or business. From the accountant's perspective, however, the course work simply improves or maintains the skills that he is already using in his business. It would appear that the education does not necessarily enable the taxpayer to do anything that he could not do before except to hold himself out as a certified financial planner. The accountant would deduct the expense. In addition, the Lifetime Learning credit and qualified tuition deduction may also be available if the courses are taken at an eligible educational institution (e.g., as part of a university sponsored program).

Review Question 3. Ms. McClain, an elementary school teacher, took a sabbatical to Ireland, where she studied the art of storytelling.

Whether her expenses are deductible ultimately depends on the facts and circumstances. As noted above, changes made in 1986 aimed to eliminate deductions for travel that were primarily personal in nature. In this case, the taxpayer appears to be pursuing that which might not be available at home. Assuming she spent a reasonable amount of time studying and researching, the expense would be deductible. In contrast, consider an architect who travels all over Europe simply taking pictures of classic architectural styles that he may incorporate in his work. Without more, a court would probably view his trip as merely a disguised vacation and deny a deduction for his travel expenses. As in the previous question, the Lifetime Learning credit and qualified tuition deduction may also be available if the courses are taken at an eligible educational institution (e.g., as part of a university sponsored program).

MOVING EXPENSES

For many years, moving expenses were viewed as nondeductible personal expenses. In 1964, however, Congress revised its position, believing that moving expenses necessitated by the taxpayer's employment should be regarded as a deductible cost of earning income. To this end, Code § 217 was enacted, expressly authorizing a deduction for moving expenses. Section 217 allows self-employed individuals and employees to deduct moving expenses incurred in connection with beginning employment or changing job locations. To ensure that the deduction is allowed only for moves required by the taxpayer's employment, the taxpayer must satisfy *both* a distance test and a time test in order to qualify for the deduction.

DISTANCE REQUIREMENT

The thrust of § 217 is to allow a taxpayer to deduct moving expenses only if there is a change in job location *and* the new location is sufficiently far away that it essentially requires the taxpayer to uproot and move his or her residence. This idea is captured in a somewhat misleading 50-mile distance test. The taxpayer does not satisfy the requirement simply by moving 50 miles to a new residence in connection with a new job location. If this were the case, the taxpayer could meet the requirement by simply moving his office down the hall and at the same time moving his residence 50 miles. Instead, the distance test is constructed to determine if the taxpayer's commute to the new job site *without the move* would have increased at least 50 miles. Technically, the condition is satisfied if the distance between the old residence and the new job site is at least 50 miles greater than the distance between the old residence and the old job site. Note that both distances are measured from the taxpayer's *former residence* . Thus, if the taxpayer's old commute was four miles, the new commute (absent a move) would have to be at least 54 miles (54 − 4 = 50) before the test is satisfied.

Example 7. During the year, R was promoted to district sales manager, requiring her to move from Tucson to Phoenix. To determine whether the 50-mile test is met, the distances shown below must be compared.

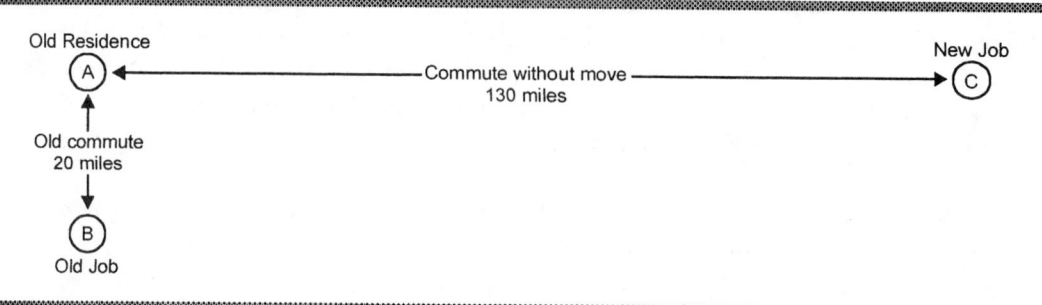

Since the distance between R's old residence and new job (AC = 130 miles) exceeds the distance between R's old residence and old job (AB = 20 miles) by at least 50 miles (130 − 20 = 110), the distance requirement is satisfied. In this case, it is quite clear that if the taxpayer had not moved, her commute would have increased significantly (110 miles). Consequently, § 217 grants her a deduction for the costs of moving her residence to a place where the commute is more reasonable. In applying the test, note that the location of the new residence is irrelevant.

If the taxpayer has no old job site, the distance test is satisfied if the new job site is 50 miles from the old residence.[12]

TIME TEST

If taxpayers were not required to maintain employment at the new job site for a minimum amount of time, they could move from place to place, taking temporary jobs in each location to justify the deduction of what in effect are personal travel expenses. To prohibit this possibility, the second test generally requires the taxpayer to work for a *sustained period* of time upon arrival at the new job location. This condition is met if the taxpayer is a *full-time* employee in the area of the new job location for at least 39 weeks during the 12-month period immediately following arrival.[13] Alternatively, the taxpayer may satisfy the test by being an employee or self-employed on a *full-time* basis for at least 78 weeks during the 24-month period after arrival. Note, however, that—like the first test—39 of these 78 weeks must be during the first 12-month period. In either case, the taxpayer need not work for the same employer or for 39 weeks in a row. The time requirement is waived if the taxpayer dies, becomes disabled, is involuntarily dismissed, or is transferred by the new employer.[14]

> **Example 8.** N, an accountant, left his job in Boston to take a new job with a firm in Orlando. After working for the firm for eight months, he became dissatisfied and quit to open his own practice as a sole proprietor. Due to the poor economy, N closed the business after six months and moved to Denver. N may not deduct his expenses of moving to Orlando. since he was employed for only 32 weeks (eight months) during the 12-month period after arrival in Orlando, he does not meet the 39-week test for employees. Similarly, he does not meet the alternative 78-week test since he was employed or self-employed only 56 weeks (14 months) of the 24-month period in Orlando after his arrival. Whether the costs of moving to Denver are deductible depends on whether either of the tests can be satisfied.

---

[12]   § 217(c)(1).

[13]   § 217(c)(2).

[14]   § 217(d).

In many instances, taxpayers do not know by the end of the tax year whether they will be able to satisfy the time test. Accordingly, the law permits the taxpayer to claim the deduction on the assumption that the test will be satisfied. If the test is subsequently failed, the taxpayer must increase income in the year of failure by the amount of the previous deduction. In lieu of claiming the deduction prior to satisfaction of the test, the taxpayer may wait until the test is satisfied and file an amended return for the year of the moving expense.

DEDUCTIBLE MOVING EXPENSES

For many years, taxpayers were allowed to deduct a variety of moving expenses. These included not only direct expenses such as the cost of moving the taxpayer's personal belongings and the cost of traveling to the new location but also a limited amount of indirect expenses (up to $3,000). For example, a taxpayer could deduct expenses for house-hunting trips, temporary living at the new location, and expenses related to disposing of the taxpayer's former residence. In 1993, however, Congress eliminated the deduction for all indirect moving expenses. Beginning in 1994, only direct moving expenses are deductible. They are:[15]

1. Costs of moving household goods and personal belongings; and

2. Costs of traveling from the old location to the new location.

Costs of Moving Household Goods and Personal Belongings. This category of direct moving expenses includes the following:[16]

- Packing, crating, and transporting the taxpayer's personal possessions (e.g., the cost of hiring a moving company or renting a truck)
- Storage and insurance of goods and personal effects while "in-transit" (i.e., any consecutive 30-day period after the day the items are moved from the former home and before they are delivered to the new home)
- Connecting and disconnecting utilities required by the moving of the taxpayer's appliances
- Moving a pet
- Shipping a car

Losses sustained on dispositions of memberships in clubs, expenses of refitting rugs and drapes, mortgage prepayment penalties (although these are usually deductible as interest), and similar expenses are not deductible.

Costs of Traveling. Once the taxpayer's furniture and other items are out the door, the taxpayer's household must follow. Only the costs of moving a taxpayer's family members (including pets) are deductible. Those for such nonfamily members as servants, chauffeurs, governesses, or nurses do not qualify. The following travel expenses are deductible:

- Transportation costs. The taxpayer may use actual expenses (i.e., the costs of oil, gasoline, tolls, and parking—but not those for general repairs or maintenance) or 15 cents per mile in 2005.

---

[15]   §§ 217(b)(1)(A) and (B).

[16]   Reg. § 1.217-2(b)(3).

▶ Lodging expenses. The taxpayer may deduct the costs of lodging incurred in traveling to the new location. No deduction is allowed for any meal expenses related to the move.[17]

Nondeductible Expenses. As noted above, in 1993 Congress eliminated the deduction for so-called "indirect" moving expenses. As a result, expenses for the following are no longer deductible:

▶ House-hunting trips

▶ Temporary living at the new job location (e.g., an apartment or motel)

▶ Sale, purchase, or lease of a residence (e.g., appraisals, attorney's fees, points, or payments to a lessor to cancel a lease)

▶ Meals

Example 9. J, who was employed by the San Francisco 49ers, was traded to the Kansas City Chiefs during the year. Although he had lived in San Francisco for years, J decided he would move permanently to Kansas City. Prior to the move, J and his wife made several trips to Kansas City looking for a new home. After finding just the right one, they hired a moving company to pack and move all their belongings. During the summer, the entire family made the long trek to Kansas City. Upon arrival, however, complications arose and they were not able to move in immediately. They ended up staying at a hotel for three weeks before they were able to take possession. J incurred the following expenses in making the move:

Costs of traveling to Kansas City to look for a house.............	$ 900
Costs of moving van (including costs of $500 for packing and crating)	15,000
Costs of storage in Kansas City.............................	1,000
Transportation costs (2,000 miles @ 15 cents per mile)	300
Three-week hotel stay (meals and lodging)	3,000
Real estate commission on sale of former residence.............	30,000

J is allowed to deduct only the direct expenses related to the move: the van, storage, and transportation, for a total of $16,300 ($15,000 + $1,000 + $300). The indirect expenses, house-hunting, temporary living, and selling expenses are not deductible. However, J may treat the costs of selling his home as a reduction in the amount realized on the sale of the home, decreasing any gain realized or increasing any loss realized. Note that if J's new employer reimburses J for any of the expenses, he must include the reimbursement in income.

CLASSIFYING AND REPORTING THE MOVING EXPENSE DEDUCTION

Moving expenses of an employee or a self-employed person are deductible for A.G.I. All moving expenses are reported on Form 3903.

In many cases, the employer will either pay the moving expenses directly or reimburse the employee for such expenses. When the latter occurs, the employee excludes the payment from gross income as a qualified fringe benefit under § 132. However, the exclusion is allowed only to the extent that the moving expenses meet the requirements for deductibility. It is not unusual for the employer to pay for a number of moving expenses that are not deductible (e.g., house-hunting and temporary living expenses); in such case, these amounts are included in the employee's W-2 as other

---

[17] § 217(b)(1)(B).

income. Similarly, no exclusion is allowed for any moving expenses actually deducted by the employee in the prior year.

✅ CHECK YOUR KNOWLEDGE

Review Question 1. After 15 years with the firm, J was finally promoted to partner. The substantial raise that came along with the promotion enabled him to build the house of his dreams. The new home is nestled in the woods near Lake Lemon, 60 miles from his old condo in the city. His new commute is 58 miles. Will J be able to deduct his moving expenses?

No. The distance requirement focuses on what would have happened to the taxpayer's commute had he not moved. As a general rule, J's commute absent the move must have increased by at least 50 miles. In other words, the distance between the old home and the *new job site* must exceed the distance between the old home and the *old job site* by at least 50 miles. Note that in order to satisfy this requirement there normally must be a change in job location. In this case, his commute without the move does not increase since the job location did not change. Therefore, his moving expenses are not deductible.

Review Question 2. Mitch's three grueling years in law school finally paid off. This year he graduated from Harvard and took a job with a firm in Memphis for $80,000 a year. He does not itemize his deductions. Can he deduct any of his moving expenses?

Yes. Deduction of moving expenses normally requires the taxpayer to change job sites. However, if the taxpayer is not currently employed and has no former job site, the distance test is met if the new job site is at least 50 miles from the taxpayer's old residence. Also note that because moving expenses are deductible for A.G.I., Mitch can claim the deduction even though he does not itemize.

Review Question 3. Grandma and Grandpa retired this year and moved from Detroit to Florida at a cost of $15,000. Both took part-time jobs at a local fast-food restaurant. Can they deduct their moving expenses?

No. In order to meet the time test, the taxpayer must be employed on a *full-time* basis for 39 weeks of the 12-month period immediately following arrival at the new location.

Review Question 4. Indicate whether the following moving expenses are deductible.

   a.   Rental of moving truck
   b.   Boxes to pack household items
   c.   Brake job for car while en route to new location
   d.   40.5 cents per mile for each mile driven to the new job location
   e.   Meals on the three-day, 900-mile trip to the new location
   f.   Trip to look for a new house after the new job was secured but before the move

Only (a) and (b) are deductible. Unusual costs incurred in traveling to the new location such as repairs are not deductible. In lieu of deducting actual transportation expenses, 15 cents per mile is allowed. Meals and house-hunting trips are not deductible.

HOME OFFICE EXPENSES

It is currently estimated that more than 39 million Americans—39 percent of the labor force—work at home either full or part time. However, simply working at home does not automatically enable a taxpayer to write off the costs of owning or renting. Very narrow standards must be met before a deduction is permitted.

For many years, expenses relating to use of a portion of the taxpayer's home for business purposes were deductible without limitation when they were merely appropriate and helpful in the taxpayer's business. In 1976, however, Congress felt that the appropriate and helpful test was insufficient to prevent the deduction of what were really personal expenses. For example, under the helpful test, a university professor who was provided an office by his employer could convert personal living expenses into deductions by using a den or some other room in his residence for grading papers. In such a situation, it was unlikely that any additional expense was incurred due to the business use. To prevent the deduction of disguised personal expenses, Congress enacted § 280A, severely limiting the deduction of expenses related to the home. Section 280A generally disallows deduction of any expenses related to the taxpayer's home except those otherwise allowable, such as qualified residence interest and taxes, and those for *certain* business and rental use (the exception for rental use is discussed in Chapter 12).

REQUIREMENTS FOR DEDUCTIBILITY

Under the business use exception, a deduction is allowed for a home office if a portion of the home is "exclusively" used on a "regular" basis for any of three types of business use:[18]

1. As the principal place of business for *any* business of the taxpayer;

2. As a place of business used regularly by patients, clients, or customers in meeting or dealing with the taxpayer in the normal course of his or her trade or business; or

3. In connection with the taxpayer's trade or business when the office is located in a separate structure.

Beyond these basic requirements applicable to all taxpayers, there is one additional test that must be met if the taxpayer is an employee. Employees are entitled to claim a home office deduction only if the home office is for the *convenience of the employer*. Each of these prerequisites is considered below.

Exclusive Use. Under prior law, a taxpayer might write off his whole kitchen just because he opened his briefcase there. The exclusive use requirement was intended to put an end to such shenanigans. A deduction is allowed only when the space in the home is devoted solely to business use. The authors of § 280A apparently did not believe a deduction should be allowed where the space was used for both personal and business purposes. The exclusive use requirement does not mean that the home office must be physically separated from the remainder of the home. It is not necessary that the portion of the room be marked off by a permanent partition. It is sufficient if the home office activities are confined to a particular space in a room that is used only for business purposes.[19] To what extent, if any, the IRS will permit personal activities to be

---

[18] § 280A(c).

[19] *George Weightman*, 42 TCM 104, T.C. Memo 1981-301.

carried on in the home office (e.g., making personal phone calls, reading for pleasure, taking care of investments as well as business) is not clear. In any event, the taxpayer should be reminded that the key word is *exclusive*. Two exceptions to the exclusive use test, storage and daycare use, are discussed below.

Regular Use. Section 280A also requires the home office to be used on a regular basis. Fortunately, the Code and Regulations have not adopted precise rules that require the taxpayer to punch a time clock every time he or she steps into the home office. Currently, there is no requirement to keep track of the hours spent in the office. The little guidance that does exist on the issue can be found in IRS publications. The Service does not specifically define *regular* but does explain that occasional or incidental use does not meet the regular use test even if that part of the home is used for no other purpose.[20]

Convenience of the Employer. As noted above, if the taxpayer is an employee, he or she must jump one additional hurdle before claiming the home office deduction. An employee must work at home for the *convenience of the employer*. To meet this condition, the home office must be more than appropriate and helpful. The U.S. Tax Court has suggested that satisfaction of this test requires the taxpayer to show that he or she was unable to do the work performed at home at the employer's office.[21] For example, the Second Circuit has held in *Weissman* that this standard is met if the employer does not provide the employee with space to properly perform his or her employment duties.[22] In this case, a college professor who shared an office and did extensive research at home satisfied the test because in the Court's view the home office was necessitated by lack of suitable working space on campus.

Principal Place of Any Business. A taxpayer satisfies the first business use test if the home office is the principal place of business for *any* business of the taxpayer. Most taxpayers, as employees, fail this test since their only business is that of being an employee and the principal location of that business is at the employer's office. This rule is not foolproof, however. In one decision, the court held that the principal place of business of a taxpayer employed as a concert musician was his home practice room rather than where he gave performances.[23] In contrast, employees who have a *second* business (e.g., selling cosmetics or vitamins) or self-employed persons who operate these activities out of their home normally satisfy the first business use test as long as they can show that the home is in fact the principal place of business.

For years, taxpayers and the IRS have squabbled over when a home office constitutes a taxpayer's *principal* place of business.[24] The leading case was the Supreme Court's 1993 decision in *Nader E. Soliman*.[25] Soliman was an anesthesiologist who worked for three hospitals. However, none of the hospitals provided him an office so he spent 10 to 15 hours a week at his home office doing his billing and scheduling. To Soliman's chagrin, the IRS denied his deductions for his home office expenses. Upon review, the U.S. Tax Court was more sympathetic, allowing the deductions on the grounds that the home office was essential to Soliman's business, he had spent substantial time there, and there was no other location available to perform the office function of the

---

[20]   § 280A(c)(1). See *Business Use of Your Home*, IRS Publication 587 (2004), p. 2.

[21]   *Robert Chauls*, 41 TCM 234, T.C. Memo 1980-471.

[22]   *Weissman v. Comm.*, 85-1 USTC ¶9106, 55 AFTR2d 85-539, 751 F.2d (CA-2, 1984).

[23]   *Drucker v. Comm.*, 83-2 USTC ¶9550, AFTR2d 83-5804 (CA-2, 1983); but see *Popov v. Comm.*, T.C. Memo 1998-374.

[24]   For example, see *Rudolph Baie*, 74 T.C. 105 (1980).

[25]   *Comm. v. Soliman*, 93-1 USTC ¶50,014 (USSC, 1993), rev'g *Nader E. Soliman*, 94 T.C. 20 (1990).

business. Although the Fourth Circuit agreed with the U.S. Tax Court, the Supreme Court did not. The high court stated that it is not sufficient that the work done in the home office is essential to the business. The court explained that to satisfy the principal place of business test, the home office must be the most important place of business as compared to all the other locations where the taxpayer carries on business. In determining whether the home office is the *most important place of business,* the court identified two factors that should be considered: (1) the relative importance of the functions performed at each of the business locations, and (2) the amount of time spent at each location. In this case, the court believed that the hospital, where Soliman performed his services and treated patients, was his most important place of business.

As might be expected, a huge backlash erupted after the *Soliman* decision since it operated to deny the home office deduction to millions of taxpayers. Most affected were those who performed essential business functions in their homes but who spent most of their time at the locations of their clients and customers (e.g., salespeople, consultants, repair people, personal trainers, caterers, etc.). In response, Congress acted in 1997 to reverse the restrictive approach of *Soliman.* As revised, the taxpayer may now meet the principal place of business test if both of the following tests are met:

1. The office is used by the taxpayer to conduct *administrative and management activities* of a trade or business; and

2. There is no other fixed location of the trade or business where the taxpayer conducts *substantial* administrative and management activities of the trade or business.

Under the new test, taxpayers who manage or administer their businesses out of a home office should be allowed a deduction even if the taxpayer conducts substantial non-administrative or nonmanagement business activities at a fixed location of the business outside the home. For example, this new approach would allow taxpayers like the doctor in *Soliman* a deduction for their home office expenses even though they conduct significant activities away from home at a fixed location (e.g., surgery at a hospital). Similarly, outside salespeople who spend the majority of their time calling on customers can claim the deduction if they use their home office to conduct administrative activities such as receiving orders, setting up appointments, or writing-up orders. In some cases, taxpayers may have an office available to perform administrative activities but opt to perform these tasks at home. In such case, the test is still met assuming the taxpayer does not actually perform substantial management or administrative activities at the other location. At all times, however, it must be emphasized that in the case of an employee, the *convenience of the employer test* must still be met. For this reason, an *employee* may be denied the deduction of expenses for a home office used for administrative activities if suitable space is available for performing such duties at the employer's office.

> **Example 10.** T is a manufacturer's representative. He promotes the products of several companies, selling to both wholesalers and retailers all over the state of Ohio. None of the companies he represents provide him an office, so he maintains an office at home. T spends an average of 30 hours a week visiting customers and 12 hours a week working in his home office. Under the *Soliman* rule, T would not be allowed to deduct the costs of maintaining a home office since his clients' premises would be his most important place of business.[26] Using the revised approach, however, T could claim the deduction since he conducts management

---

[26] Notice 93-12, 1993-1 C.B. 202; see also, Rev. Rul. 94-24, 1994-1 C.B. 87 for how the IRS will apply the *Soliman* tests.

activities in the home and there is no other fixed location where he conducts substantial management activities related to his business.

It should be emphasized that taxpayers who cannot qualify for the home office deduction under the principal place of business test may still find relief if they meet one of the other—more liberal—tests discussed below (i.e., regularly meet with clients or separate structure tests).

Trade or Business. No deduction is permitted for home office expenses if the activities to which they relate do not constitute a business.[27]

Example 11. B, an engineer, regularly uses a room in his home exclusively for evaluating his investments. No deduction is permitted since the activity does not constitute a business.

Meeting Place. The second exception for business use is less restrictive than the first. Under this exception, the home office qualifies if clients regularly meet with the taxpayer there. Interestingly, in *John W. Green,* the taxpayer ingeniously argued that this exception should be satisfied where he regularly received phone calls in his home office. Although a majority of the U.S. Tax Court agreed with the taxpayer, the decision was reversed on appeal. The Appellate Court believed that the statute required that the taxpayer *physically* meet with clients in the home office.[28]

Separate Structure. The third exception for business use is the least restrictive of the three. If a separate structure is the site of the home office, it need be used only in connection with the taxpayer's work (e.g., a converted detached garage or barn).

AMOUNT DEDUCTIBLE

If the taxpayer qualifies for the home office deduction, an allocable portion of expenses related to the home may be deducted. The allocation of expenses generally must be based on square footage. Typical expenses include utilities, depreciation, insurance, security systems, repairs (e.g., furnace repair), interest, taxes, and rent. It should be emphasized that the home office deduction is limited to the gross income from the home business as reduced by allowable deductions. This computation is very similar to that for determining deductible hobby expenses. The taxpayer may deduct expenses equal to the extent of gross income reduced by (1) expenses allowable without regard to the use of the dwelling unit (e.g., interest—assuming it is a primary or secondary residence—and taxes), and (2) business or rental expenses incurred in carrying on the activity other than those of the home office (e.g., supplies and secretarial expenses).[29] Any home office expenses that are not deductible due to this limitation may be carried over and used to offset income from the business which led to the deduction, even if the taxpayer does not use the unit in the business in subsequent years.

When the taxpayer is self-employed (i.e., a sole proprietor), all of the taxpayer's expenses, including those attributable to the home office, are deductible for A.G.I. In contrast, if the taxpayer is an employee, the *otherwise allowable* expenses (e.g., interest and taxes) are deductible in full as itemized deductions. The other business expenses, including the home office expenses, are considered miscellaneous itemized deductions and are subject, along with other miscellaneous itemized deductions, to the 2 percent

---

[27]   S. Rep. No. 94-938, 94th Cong., 2d Sess. 147-49 (1976).

[28]   78 T.C. 428 (1982).

[29]   See § 280A(c)(5).

floor. All expenses for business use of a home office must be reported on Form 8829 (see Appendix for a sample form).

Example 12. K maintains a qualifying home office. During this year, she earned only $2,000 from the home office activities. Her expenses included the following: interest and taxes allocable to the home office, $600; secretarial services, miscellaneous supplies and postage, $900; and expenses directly related to the home office including insurance, utilities, and depreciation, $1,700. K's potential deduction is $2,000 computed as follows:

Gross income.............................	$2,000	
Otherwise allowable deductions:		
Interest and taxes......................	(600)	$ 600
Other business expenses................	(900)	900
Gross income limitation	$ 500	
Home office expenses:		
$1,700 limited to remaining gross income ...		500
Total potential deduction		$2,000

Whether the $2,000 of deductible expenses are deductible for or from A.G.I. depends on whether K is self-employed or an employee. If K is self-employed, the entire $2,000 is deductible for A.G.I. If the taxpayer is an employee, the $600 of interest and taxes allocable to the home office are deductible as itemized deductions and would be subject to the 3% cutback provision. The remaining $1,400 is considered a miscellaneous itemized deduction subject (along with other miscellaneous itemized deductions) to the 2% floor. Of course, any miscellaneous itemized deductions exceeding the 2% floor are still subject to the 3% cutback provision. The home office expenses that are not deductible this year, $1,200 [($600 + $900 + $1,700 = $3,200) − $2,000], may be carried over to the following years to be offset against future home office income.

DAYCARE AND STORAGE USE

The home office rules for taxpayers who use their home as a daycare center or as a place to store inventory or product samples of a home-based business receive special attention from the Code. In both cases, the normal rules apply except that the exclusive use test is relaxed.

Daycare Use. If a portion of the taxpayer's home doubles as both a living space and a daycare center it would appear that no deduction would be allowed since the exclusive use test would not be satisfied. When the home is used as a daycare center, however, the exclusive use test does not apply.[30] Instead, the expenses attributable to the room are prorated between personal and daycare use based on the number of hours of use per day. Thus, if the taxpayer uses a family room for daycare 40 percent of the time, 40 percent of the expenses allocable to that room would be deductible. A portion of the home qualifies for this special treatment if the taxpayer uses the home to provide daycare services for children, individuals over age 65, or those who are physically or mentally incapable of taking care of themselves.

Storage Use. If the taxpayer regularly uses part of the home to store product samples or goods sold at retail or wholesale *and* the home is the sole fixed location of

---

[30] § 280A(c)(4).

that business, expenses related to the storage space are deductible.[31] More important, the space need not be used exclusively for this purpose. However, the space should be a specific area (e.g., a particular part of a basement or closet).

RESIDENTIAL PHONE SERVICE

For many years, taxpayers who used their home phone for business or income-producing purposes deducted a portion of the basic charge for local service on the grounds that it was business-related. In 1988, however, Congress saw the issue differently. Apparently it believed that in this day and age the cost of basic phone service to a taxpayer's residence would have been incurred in any event—without regard to any business that the taxpayer might otherwise conduct. As a result, a taxpayer may no longer deduct any charge (including taxes) for local phone service for the *first* phone line provided to any residence. The taxpayer may still deduct the costs of long-distance phone calls or optional phone services such as call waiting or call forwarding, when such costs are related to business. In addition, taxpayers may deduct the costs of additional phone lines into the home that are used for business (e.g., a separate line for a fax machine or modem).

✅ CHECK YOUR KNOWLEDGE

Review Question 1. Indicate whether the following taxpayers would be allowed to deduct expenses attributable to a home office.

a. T is on the tax staff of a public accounting firm. From time to time, he brings home returns and does a little work in his home office. In addition, he does most of his technical reading in the home office.

T would not be allowed a deduction since he does not meet the principal place of business or convenience of the employer tests. He fails the first of these tests since his principal place of business is his employer's office. He fails the convenience of the employer test since the employer provides him an office and he could do at the office what he does at home. His work at home appears to be for his own convenience.

b. R is a decorator. She works out of an office in her home. She spends about 10 hours per week visiting her client's homes and another 10 visiting businesses that carry furniture and home accessories. The remainder of her 40-hour week is spent at her home office doing sketches, ordering, keeping books, and the like.

R may deduct her home office expenses since she conducts management activities in the home and there is no other fixed location used by her to perform substantial management activities related to her business.

c. J operates a floral shop in town. He grows the plants for his shop in a greenhouse behind his home.

Even though the principal place of J's business is arguably at J's shop, J would still qualify for the deduction under the separate structure exception.

Review Question 2. With the kids starting college, income from their regular jobs was not enough, so this year N and her husband started a small blind and drapery

---

[31] § 280A(c)(2).

operation. They run it out of an office in their home. N orders the fabric and sews the drapes while her husband installs. In their first year of business, the couple had gross income of $2,000. Interest and taxes allocable to the home office were $600. Various supplies and equipment, including a file cabinet, table, Rolodex, sewing machine, and scissors, cost $1,000. Depreciation, utilities, insurance, and similar expenses allocable to the home office were $900. According to their friend Norm, they should be able to deduct all $1,900 since they are all ordinary and necessary business expenses. Is Norm correct? How much can they deduct?

Norm is only partially right. Section 280A limits the deduction of home office expenses. Home office expenses are essentially deductible to the extent of net income from the business before taking into account the home office expenses (other than the interest and taxes). The home office expenses cannot create a loss from the activity. As a result, the couple can deduct $400 ($2,000 − $1,000 − $600), and the couple's net income from the business after the home office deductions is zero. Note that § 280A limitations do not apply to the $1,000 of expenses for items directly used in the business. These costs relate directly to the business (rather than the home) and, therefore, are fully deductible (or depreciable, as explained in Chapter 9).

TRANSPORTATION EXPENSES

If there ever was a contest for the most popular tax deduction or at least the one that arouses the most attention, it would be easy to pick the winner. Virtually everyone who tumbles out of bed each morning and makes the daily trip to work has the same question at tax time: can I deduct the costs of getting there and getting back? In a world where commuting is routine for millions of taxpayers, it would seem that the answers would be clear-cut. But this is not necessarily the case.

Before examining the deduction for transportation expenses, the distinction between transportation expenses and travel expenses should be explained. In tax jargon, transportation and travel are not synonymous. Travel expenses are broadly defined to include not only the costs of transportation but also related expenses such as meals, lodging, and other incidentals when the taxpayer is in a travel status. As discussed below, the taxpayer is in travel status when he or she is *away from home overnight* on business.[32] In contrast, transportation expenses are defined narrowly to include only the actual costs of transportation—expenses of getting from one place to another while in the course of business when the taxpayer is *not* away from home overnight.[33] Transportation expenses normally occur when the taxpayer goes and returns on the same day. The most common transportation expense is the cost of driving and maintaining a car, but the term also includes the cost of traveling by other forms of transportation such as bus, taxi, subway, or train.[34]

> **Example 13.** M is an architect in Cincinnati. At various times during the year, he drove to Cleveland to inspect one of his projects. He often ate lunch and dinner in Cleveland before returning home. M is allowed to deduct only the costs of transportation. The costs of the meals are not deductible since he was not away from home overnight. Had he spent the night in Cleveland and returned the next day, the costs of meals and lodging as well as transportation would be deductible.

---

[32] § 162(a)(2).

[33] Reg. § 1.62-1(g).

[34] *Ibid.*

The deduction for transportation is allowed under the general provisions of §§ 162 and 212. Therefore, to qualify for deduction, the transportation expense must be ordinary, necessary, and related to the taxpayer's trade or business or income-producing activity. Personal transportation, of course, does not qualify for deduction. Like many other expenses, however, the boundary between business and personal transportation is often difficult to identify. Some of the common problem areas are discussed below.

DEDUCTIBLE TRANSPORTATION VERSUS NONDEDUCTIBLE COMMUTING

The cost of transportation or commuting between the taxpayer's home and his or her place of employment may appear to be a necessary business expense. It is settled, however, that commuting expenses generally are nondeductible personal expenses. This rule derives from the presumption that the commuting expense arises from the taxpayer's *personal preference* to live away from the place of business or employment. This presumption persists even though there often is no place to live within walking distance of employment, much less one that is suitable or within the taxpayer's means. The fact that the taxpayer is forced to live far away from the place of employment is irrelevant and does not alter the personal nature of the expenses.

Example 14. In *Sanders v. Comm.*, the taxpayers were civilian employees working on an Air Force base.[35] Despite the fact that they were not allowed to live on the base next to their employment and could only live elsewhere and commute, the transportation costs were not deductible. The Court found it impossible to distinguish between these expenses and those of a suburban commuter, both being personal in origin.

Example 15. In *Tauferner v. Comm.*, the taxpayer worked at a chemical plant that was located 20 miles from any community due to the dangers involved.[36] The taxpayer was denied deductions for his commuting even though he lived in the nearest habitable spot. Arguably, the nature of his job—not personal convenience—produced additional transportation costs. Nevertheless, the Court did not believe that such hardship changed the personal character of the expenses.

While the costs of commuting normally are not deductible, there are several exceptions. These exceptions are discussed below.

Commuting with Tools and Similar Items. The fact that the taxpayer hauls tools, instruments, or other equipment necessary in pursuing business normally does not cause commuting expenses to be deductible. The Supreme Court has ruled that only the *additional* expenses attributable to carrying the tools are deductible.[37] The IRS determines the taxpayer's "additional expenses" by applying the so-called "same mode" test.[38] Under this test, a deduction is allowed for the extra cost of commuting by one mode with the tools over the cost of commuting by the same mode without the tools. Thus, a carpenter who drives a truck would not be allowed a transportation deduction simply by loading it with tools since carrying the tools created no additional expense. The fact that tools may have caused the carpenter to drive a truck, which is more expensive than some other type of transportation, is irrelevant under the IRS view. The courts, however, have rejected this test in certain cases.[39]

---

[35]   71-1 USTC ¶9260, 27 AFTR2d 71-832, 439 F.2d 296 (CA-9, 1971).

[36]   69-1 USTC ¶9241, 23 AFTR2d 69-1025, 407 F.2d 243 (CA-10, 1969).

[37]   *Fausner v. Comm.*, 73-2 USTC ¶95-15, 32 AFTR2d 73-5202, 413 U.S. 838 (USSC, 1973).

[38]   Rev. Rul. 75-380, 1975-2 C.B. 59.

[39]   *J.F. Grayson*, 36 TCM 1201, T.C. Memo 1977-304. See also *H.A. Pool*, 36 TCM 93, T.C. Memo 1977-20.

Example 16. M plays third trumpet in the Dallas orchestra. During the year, his employer indicated that they did not need the third trumpet and that M would have to switch to his second instrument, the tuba, to retain his job. If, in order to transport the tuba, M had to change from driving to work in a small car costing $3 per day to driving to work in a van costing $5 per day, the IRS would not allow a deduction for the additional cost. Under the same mode test, the cost of driving the van with the tuba is the same as without the tuba. The courts, however, may allow a deduction for the $2 increase in cost. On the other hand, if M rented a trailer to carry the tuba at a cost of $2 per day, the IRS would allow the deduction because the cost of driving the van with the tuba is now $2 more than without the tuba.

The IRS view on the treatment of local transportation is summarized in Exhibit 8-1.

EXHIBIT 8-1
When Are Local Transportation Expenses Deductible?

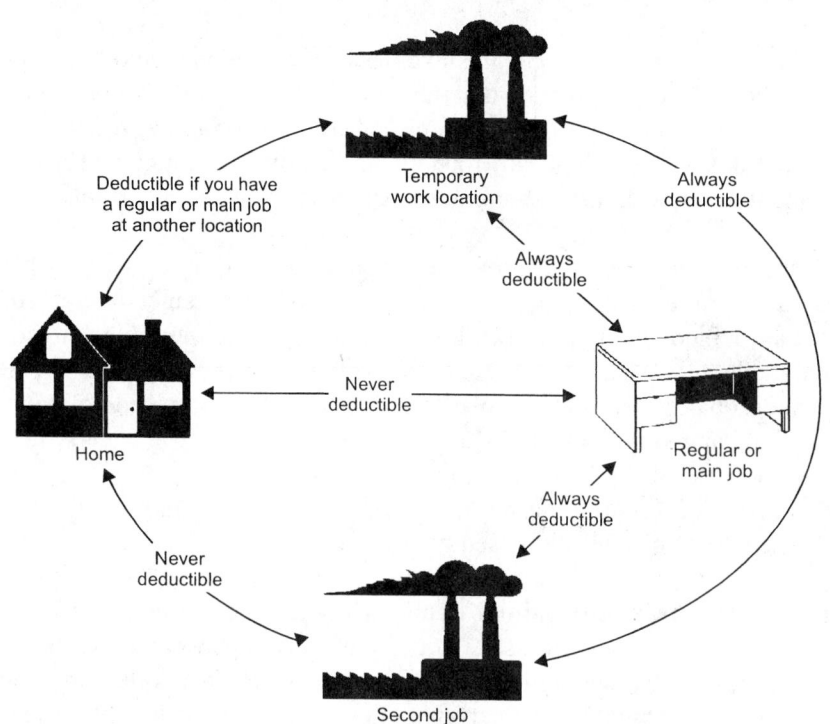

Home: The place where you reside. Transportation expenses between your home and your main or regular place of work are personal commuting expenses.

Regular or main job: Your principal place of business. If you have more than one job, you must determine which one is your regular or main job. Consider the time you spend at each, the activity you have at each, and the income you earn at each.

Temporary work location: A place where your work assignment is realistically expected to last (and does in fact last) one year or less. Unless you have a regular place of business, you can only deduct your transportation expenses to a temporary location *outside* your metropolitan area.

Second job: If you regularly work at two or more places in one day, whether or not for the same employer, you can deduct your transportation expenses of getting from one workplace to another. You cannot deduct your transportation costs between your home and a second job on a day off from your main job.

Source: *Travel, Entertainment, Gift and Car Expense*, IRS Publication 463 (Rev. 2001), p. 14.

Commuting between Two Jobs. The transportation cost of going from one job to a second job is deductible.[40] The deduction is limited to the cost of going *directly* from one job to the other.

Example 17. R works for X Corporation on the morning shift and for Y Corporation on its afternoon shift. The distances he drives are diagrammed below.

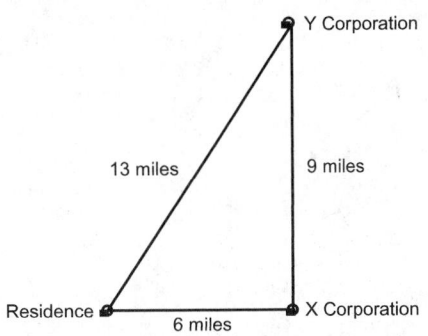

If R leaves X and goes home to eat lunch before going to Y, he actually drives 19 miles to get to Y, or 10 more miles than if he had driven directly (19 − 9). However, only the cost of driving directly, 9 miles, is deductible.

Commuting to a Temporary Assignment. Individuals are often assigned to work at a location other than where they regularly work. When a taxpayer commutes to a *temporary work location,* the commuting expenses are deductible transportation costs if either of the following tests are satisfied:

1. The temporary assignment is *within* the general area of the taxpayer's employment and he or she otherwise has a *regular* place of business (e.g., an office);[41] or

2. The temporary assignment is *outside* the general area of the taxpayer's employment (i.e., his or her tax home).[42]

Example 18. C is an auditor for a public accounting firm that has its office in downtown Chicago. C works about 30% of the time in her employer's office, and the remaining 70% is spent at various clients' offices around the city. C may deduct the costs of commuting between her residence and a client's office because the client's office is a temporary work location and C otherwise has a regular place of business (i.e., her employer's office).

Example 19. M is a carpenter. He works for a construction company that builds houses in subdivisions in various areas of Houston. Most of his assignments are located within about 25 miles of downtown Houston. During the year, M worked at two different locations, one on the north side of Houston and the other on the west side. Although M is assigned to temporary work locations, he is not allowed to deduct any of his commuting expenses because he does not otherwise have a regular place of business.

---

40   *Supra*, Footnote 38.

41   Rev. Rul. 99-7, 1999-1 C.B. 361.

42   *Ibid.*

Example 20. Assume the same facts as above except that M was temporarily assigned to a job in Galveston, 60 miles from Houston. He drove to Galveston daily and returned home in the evenings. Under these circumstances, M may deduct the cost of driving the entire 120-mile round trip from his home to Galveston. The following diagram illustrates this approach.

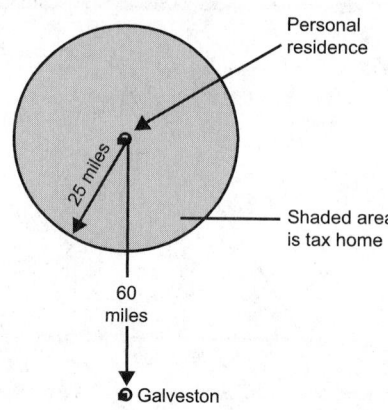

The IRS draws an important distinction between temporary and regular work locations. A work location is temporary if employment at the location is realistically expected to last and does in fact last for one year or less.[43] In contrast, a work location is considered a *regular* place of business if—as one might expect—the taxpayer performs services there on a regular basis. According to the IRS, a taxpayer may have more than one regular place of business even though he or she does not perform services at that location every week or on a set schedule. When the taxpayer commutes to these different locations on a "regular" basis, the costs of commuting would not be deductible because such locations are not temporary.

Example 21. Dr. T, a podiatrist, has an office on both the north side and south side of Indianapolis. In addition, she performs services at a clinic and a hospital with which she is associated. T may not deduct the costs of transportation between her residence and these various locations because each is considered a regular place of business and not a temporary work location. As discussed below, however, the costs of going between two business locations (e.g., a clinic and a hospital) are deductible.

Transportation between Job Sites. While the transportation costs between a taxpayer's home and the first and last job sites generally are considered nondeductible commuting expenses, transportation costs between two job sites are deductible.[44] Accordingly, once the taxpayer arrives at the first job site any business travel thereafter usually is deductible.

Example 22. R is employed as a tax accountant and works primarily in his employer's office downtown. R drives 34 miles round-trip from his home to the office. After arriving at work one day, R drove 6 miles to a client's office and returned to his employer's office. In this case, R may deduct the cost of driving 12 miles.

43   *Ibid.*

44   Rev. Rul. 55-109, 1955-1 C.B. 261 and Rev. Rul. 99-7, 1999-1 C.B. 361.

Example 23. Assume R drives 17 miles to work in the morning. In the afternoon, he drives 15 miles to a client's office where he conducts some business. From the client's office he drives 9 miles home. In this situation, R may deduct the cost of driving 15 miles because transportation between two job sites is deductible. In addition, it appears that he may deduct the cost of driving 9 miles since transportation between the taxpayer's residence and a temporary work location (i.e., the client's office) is deductible.

Although transportation expenses between the taxpayer's home and work normally are not deductible, the rule concerning travel between job sites creates a favorable exception for taxpayers who maintain a separate trade or business at home. For these taxpayers, the transportation from the first job site—the home—and the second job site in the same trade or business would be deductible.

Example 24. V is a landscape engineer and works out of his home. Transportation costs from his home to a client's place of business are deductible since the expenses are incurred in traveling from his principal place of business to a job site.[45]

COMPUTING CAR EXPENSES

Deductions relating to driving and maintaining a car may be computed using actual expenses or a standard mileage rate (automatic mileage method). Under either method, if the car is used for both business and personal purposes, only the car expenses attributable to business or income production are deductible.

Actual Expenses. Actual car expenses normally deducted include the costs for gas, oil, repairs, insurance, depreciation, interest on loans to purchase the car (other than that of an employee), taxes, licenses, garage rent, parking fees, and tolls. Calculating actual expenses usually requires determining the portion of the nondeductible expenses attributable to personal use. Under the actual expense method, the total actual expense is allocated based on mileage.

Example 25. R, self-employed, drove 20,000 miles during the year: 16,000 on business and 4,000 for personal purposes. Total actual expenses were as follows:

General expenses:	
Gas	$1,200
Maintenance (oil, repairs)	200
Insurance	1,100
Interest expense	600
Depreciation	1,900
Total	$5,000
Other business expenses:	
Tolls incurred on business trips	$ 10
Parking fees when calling on clients	90
Total	$ 100

---

[45] See *Raymond Garner*, 42 TCM 1181, T.C. Memo 1981-542, and *Joe J. Adams*, 43 TCM 1203, T.C. Memo 1982-223. See also, *Charles Walker*, 101 T.C. 36 (1993) and Rev. Rul. 94-47, 1994-2 C.B. 18.

Since R used the car 80% (16,000 ÷ 20,000) for business, he may deduct 80% of the general expenses, $4,000 (80% × $5,000). In addition, he may deduct the entire $100 cost for the parking and tolls since they were incurred solely for business purposes, for a total deduction of $4,100. Note that the nonbusiness portion of the interest expense would not be deductible, assuming it is not attributable to a loan secured by his first or second home. If R were an employee, *none* of the interest would be deductible because business interest of an *employee* is not deductible.

Standard Mileage Rate. The automatic mileage method allows a deduction of 40.5 cents per mile (2005) for *all* business miles driven during the year.[46] The business portion of expenses for interest (if self-employed), state and local property taxes, parking, and tolls also may be added to the amount computed using the mileage rate. Other expenses such as depreciation, insurance, and maintenance are built into the mileage rate and cannot be added.

Example 26. Same facts as in *Example 25*. R's deduction using the standard mileage rate would be $7,060, as computed below.

Business mileage (16,000 × $0.405)	$6,480
Interest ($600 × 80%)	480
Parking and tolls	100
Total	$7,060

Note that in arriving at the deduction, gas, maintenance, insurance, and depreciation are not added to the amount computed using the standard rate since they are built into the rate. Conversely, interest (if self-employed), parking, and tolls are added since they are not included in the rate.

Taxpayers who lease their cars may also use the standard mileage rate. If a taxpayer elects to use the rate for a leased car, it must be used for the entire lease period.[47]

The standard mileage rate may be used *only* if it is adopted in the first year the car is placed in service. In addition, the following conditions must be satisfied:[48]

1. The car must not be one of two or more cars being used simultaneously in a business, such as in a fleet operation. When a taxpayer alternates in using different cars on different occasions, the cars are treated as one and the mileage is combined.

2. The car must not be for hire, such as a taxi.

3. Additional first-year depreciation or depreciation using an accelerated method must not have been claimed in a prior year.

If these conditions are met, the taxpayer may switch methods from year to year. However, use of the standard mileage method precludes the taxpayer from using the Modified Accelerated Cost Recovery System (MACRS) for computing depreciation in a subsequent year, and depreciation must be computed under one of the alternative methods (e.g., straight-line).[49] Note that selecting the actual method in the first year

---

[46]   Rev. Proc. 2004-64, 2004-49 I.R.B.

[47]   Prop. Reg. § 1.274-5(g).

[48]   *Ibid.*

[49]   *Supra*, footnote 46.

generally *prohibits* the taxpayer from ever using the standard mileage rate for that automobile.

Taxpayers who use the standard mileage rate are required to reduce the adjusted basis of their automobiles just as if they had claimed depreciation. The rate per mile varies by year. For example, the rate for miles driving during 2003–2004 was 16 cents per mile and increased to 17 cents per mile for 2005.[50]

CLASSIFICATION OF TRANSPORTATION AND TRAVEL EXPENSES

The *unreimbursed* transportation and travel expenses of an employee are treated as miscellaneous itemized deductions subject to the 2 percent floor. In contrast, if an employee is reimbursed for such expenses under a qualified arrangement known as an *accountable plan* (discussed later in this chapter), the reimbursement is excludable from gross income. Any reimbursement not made under such a plan must be included in the employee's gross income, and any qualifying deductions must be treated as miscellaneous itemized deductions. If the expenses are incurred by a self-employed person, the expenses are deductible for A.G.I. An employee reports the expenses on Form 2106, a copy of which is reproduced in the last section of this chapter.

Travel and transportation expenses related to property held for the production of income are also considered miscellaneous itemized deductions unless the income is rents or royalties, in which case the deductions would be for A.G.I. In addition, the deduction for meals may be limited to 50 percent of their cost. This limitation is discussed in detail with entertainment expenses later in this chapter.

TRAVEL EXPENSES

Section 162 of the Code provides for the deduction of travel expenses while "away from home" in the pursuit of a trade or business.[51] A similar deduction is allowed for travel expenses connected with income-producing activities not constituting a business.[52] The definition of travel expenses is not as narrow as that of transportation expenses. Travel expenses include not only the costs of transportation but also the costs of meals (but limited to 50 percent of actual costs, as discussed later), lodging, cleaning and laundry, telephone, and other similar expenses related to travel.[53] Whether these additional expenses such as meals and lodging are deductible depends on whether the taxpayer is considered "away from home."

AWAY-FROM-HOME TEST

The taxpayer must be *away from home* before travel expenses are deductible. The "away from-home" test poses two questions: for what period does the taxpayer need to be away from home, and where is the taxpayer's home for tax purposes? With respect to the first question, the Supreme Court has ruled that the away-from-home test generally requires the taxpayer to be away from home *overnight*.[54] Later interpretations of this decision have indicated that the taxpayer will be considered to be "overnight" when it is reasonable for the taxpayer to stop for needed sleep or rest. A trip where the taxpayer

---

[50] For previous rates see *Travel, Entertainment, Gift and Car Expenses*, IRS Publication 463 (Rev. 2004) p. 25.

[51] *Supra*, Footnote 33.

[52] §§ 212(1) and (2).

[53] Reg. § 1.162-2(a).

[54] *U.S. v. Correll*, 68-1 USTC ¶9101, 20 AFTR2d 5845, 389 U.S. 299 (USSC, 1967).

leaves and returns the same day is not travel and, consequently, only the transportation cost would be deductible. Meals eaten during the trip, lodging, etc., would not be deductible.

The second and more critical aspect of the away-from-home test concerns the determination of the taxpayer's *tax home*. The IRS and the Tax Court have defined the term *tax home* to mean the business location of the taxpayer or the general vicinity of the taxpayer's employment, regardless of the location of the taxpayer's personal residence.[55] The Court of Appeals in several circuits, however, has held that "home" should be interpreted in the normal fashion (i.e., as the place where the taxpayer normally maintains his or her residence;[56] see *Example 28*). The interpretation problems usually arise when taxpayers live in one location but also conduct substantial business at another location where they often stay because it is impractical to return to the residence. To illustrate, consider a construction worker who lives with his family in Milwaukee but obtains a job to work on the construction of a nuclear power plant near Chicago. During the week, he stays in a motel in Chicago and eats his meals. The issue here is the location of the taxpayer's tax home. If the taxpayer normally works in Chicago, the IRS would take the position that the taxpayer's tax home is in Chicago and deny the deductions for meals and lodging. On the other hand, if the taxpayer normally works in Milwaukee and takes a job in Chicago, he may be able to secure a deduction for his Chicago expenses if he could demonstrate that the Chicago job is only a *temporary* assignment. The IRS permits taxpayers to deduct travel expenses incurred away from the principal place of business if an assignment away from home is temporary and not indefinite. Under § 162(a), assignments in a single location lasting a year or more are not temporary but indefinite.[57] Consequently, if a taxpayer anticipates an assignment to last more than a year or it actually exceeds one year, none of the taxpayer's travel expenses are deductible (not even those for the first 12 months). According to the IRS, the nature of assignments lasting less than a year depends on the facts and circumstances of each case. In most cases, however, the IRS treats assignments lasting less than a year as temporary.

> **Example 27.** D is employed as an engineer, living and working in Kansas city. D's employer assigned her to a job in El Paso that D expected to complete in five months. In reality, D lived and worked in El Paso for ten months before completing the job and returning to Kansas city. Because she realistically expected the assignment to last for one year or less and it in fact did not exceed this period, D may deduct her travel expenses for the entire ten months. What would be the result if at the end of four months it became clear that D's stay in El Paso would exceed a year? In such case, the IRS takes the position that she would be able to treat the first four months as temporary and deduct her expenses for those months. However, the expenses for the remainder of the job assignment would not be deductible.

If the taxpayer has no principal place of employment, the tax home is normally his regular place of abode.[58] However, if the taxpayer has no permanent place of residence, the courts have consistently denied the taxpayer's deductions for meals and lodging since there is no "home" to be away from. This rule has been applied to itinerant construction workers and salespeople whom the courts view as being *at home* wherever their work may take them.[59]

---

[55] G.C.M. 23672, 1943 C.B. 66, superseded by Rev. Rul. 74-291, 1974-1 C.B. 42.

[56] For example, see *Rosenspan v. U.S.*, 71-1 USTC ¶9241, 27 AFTR2d 71-707, 438 F.2d 905 (CA-2, 1971).

[57] *Supra*, Footnote 43 and Rev. Rul 93-86, 1993-2 C.B. 71. Federal employees providing services related to investigating or prosecuting a Federal crime are not subject to this rule. See § 162(a), last sentence.

[58] Criteria exist for determining whether a taxpayer has a regular place of abode. See Rev. Rul. 73-529, 1973-2 C.B. 37.

[59] *George H. James v. U.S.*, 62-2 USTC ¶9735, 10 AFTR2d 5627, 308 F.2d 204 (CA-9, 1962).

The purpose of the away-from-home provision is to reduce the burden of the taxpayer who, because of business needs, must maintain two places of abode and consequently incurs additional and duplicate living expenses. The rule is based on the principle that a taxpayer normally lives and works in the same general vicinity. Thus, when taxpayers choose to live in an area other than where they work, the resulting expenses normally are considered personal. This rule often is difficult to apply in particular situations. For this reason, the deduction of travel expenses ultimately depends on the facts.

Example 28. C works at a testing laboratory in a remote mountain area of New Mexico, 70 miles from his home. His residence, however, is the closest place to the laboratory to live. C normally commutes to work but sometimes stays at the testing facilities' quarters overnight when he works overtime. In this situation, the IRS would not allow a deduction for travel expenses since C's tax home is at the testing laboratory, and when staying there he is not away from home. Some Appellate Courts, however, may permit the deduction for meals and lodging since he is away from his residence.[60]

COMBINED BUSINESS AND PLEASURE TRAVEL

As discussed above, travel costs are deductible only while away from home in pursuit of business or income-producing activities. When traveling away from home, however, taxpayers often combine business with pleasure with the hope that they can deduct what is really a personal vacation. With an eye to this possibility, the Regulations provide special guidance as to how much can be deducted in this situation. The rules governing combined business and pleasure travel differ depending on whether the taxpayer is traveling inside or outside of the United States.

Domestic Travel. The taxpayer who travels within the United States (all 50 states and the District of Columbia) may deduct *all* of the costs of travel to and from the destination if the trip is *primarily* for business.[61] If the trip is primarily for business, the taxpayer will not lose all or even a part of the deduction merely because he or she takes a personal side-trip or extends the trip for a short vacation. However, the costs of any personal side-trips are not allowed. Travel which is primarily for personal purposes is not deductible even though some business is conducted. Note that the taxpayer either deducts *all* of the *to-and-from* travel expenses or deducts *none* of them—there is no allocation. Of course, any travel expenses (e.g., meals and lodging) directly related to business upon arriving at the destination qualify.

Example 29. F, a CPA, flew from Dallas to Denver for the annual convention of the Texas Society of Certified Public Accountants. The air fare was $500. Meals and lodging for the three days she attended were $150 and $230, respectively. Upon conclusion of the convention, F drove to the mountains and skied for two days before returning home. The travel to the mountains, including meals and lodging, cost $350. F may deduct all of the air fare, $500, because costs of transportation are fully deductible without allocation when the trip is primarily for business. In addition, F may deduct 50% of the meal costs, $75 (50% × $150), and $230 for lodging because these travel expenses are directly related to business. The expenses of $350 for the ski trip are nondeductible personal expenses.

---

[60]   For example, see *Lee E. Coombs*, 79-2 USTC ¶9719, 45 AFTR2d 80-444, 608 F.2d 1269 (CA-9, 1979).

[61]   Reg. § 1.162-2(b)(1).

Example 30. Assume the same facts as in *Example 29*, except that F skied for five days. In this case, the trip may be treated as primarily personal thus preventing any deduction of the $500 air fare from Dallas to Denver. Fifty percent of the expenses for meals and all of the lodging costs while at the convention on business are still deductible.

Obviously the most troublesome question concerning domestic travel is whether the nature of the trip is primarily business or pleasure. In this regard, the Regulations, Rulings, and reported decisions offer little guidance—saying only that the answer depends on the facts and circumstances in each case. Among the factors normally considered, the amount of time devoted to business as compared to personal activities is often decisive. Another factor emphasized is the type of location where the business occurs (e.g., a resort hotel or a more businesslike setting). The increasing number of professional organizations that schedule their conventions and seminars in resort areas has caused the IRS to closely scrutinize deductions for alleged business trips which are merely disguised vacations. Congress took action regarding expenses related to nonbusiness conventions (e.g., investment and tax seminars), completely disallowing their deduction after 1986.[62] For a business meeting, however, if it can be clearly shown that the expenses were incurred for business purposes, the deduction is not disallowed merely because the meeting occurs at a resort.

Example 31. This year, Dr H, a surgeon, attended a week-long course on arthroscopic surgery in Palm Beach. His wife accompanied him and attended a seminar on personal financial planning. H may deduct his costs of transportation as well as the travel expenses incurred after arriving in Palm Beach because the expenses are related to business. None of his wife's expenses are deductible because they relate not to her trade or business but to investments and taxes.

Travel Expense of Spouse and Dependents. The IRS has always taken a dim view of taxpayers who combine business travel with pleasure and in the process deduct the cost of taking their families with them. For years, the Service attacked this abuse with a longstanding regulation that denied the deduction of a family member's travel expenses unless the taxpayer could demonstrate that the family member's presence served a bona fide business purpose.[63] Apparently this ammunition was incapable of adequately policing the problem. Consequently, Congress provided the IRS more help with new legislation in 1994.[64] Currently, no deduction is allowed for any travel expenses paid or incurred with respect to a spouse, dependent, or other individual accompanying the taxpayer (or an officer or employee of the taxpayer) on business unless (1) the individual is an employee of the person paying or reimbursing the expenses, (2) the travel of such individual has a bona fide business purpose, and (3) such expenses are otherwise deductible. The rule does not apply to deductible moving expenses.

Example 32. T is the owner and president of TDI Corporation, which owns seven car dealerships in and around Des Moines. This year General Motors held a meeting for all of its dealers in Maui, and T took his wife and 18-year-old daughter. TDI reimbursed T for all of his traveling expenses including those of his wife and daughter. TDI is not allowed to claim a deduction for the travel expenses of T's wife and daughter unless they are both employees of the company and it can establish that their presence had a bona fide business purpose. Note that T and TDI

---

[62] § 274(h)(7).

[63] Reg. § 1.162-2(c); Rev. Rul. 55-57, 1955-1 C.B. 315.

[64] § 274(m).

may be able to overcome the first requirement by employing both his wife and daughter. Satisfying the second test is more difficult. In this regard, the regulations provide that performance of incidental services does not cause a family member's expenses to qualify. The courts, however, have allowed a deduction for a spouse's expenses when the facts have shown that the spouse's presence enhanced the image of the taxpayer or the spouse acted as a business assistant.[65]

Foreign Travel. When the taxpayer travels outside the United States, the travel expenses must satisfy more stringent requirements for deduction. Generally, the costs of transportation to and from the foreign destination and other travel expenses must be allocated between business (or income-producing activities) and personal activities. If the travel is *primarily* business, the costs of transportation are fully deductible without allocation if *one* of the following conditions is satisfied:[66]

1. *Travel outside the United States does not exceed one week* (seven consecutive days). In counting the days out of the United States, the day of departure from the United States is excluded while the day of return to the United States is included. (For example, leaving on Sunday and returning on the following Sunday is exactly seven days.)

2. *More than 75 percent of the days on the trip were devoted to business.* A day is treated as a business day if during any part of the day the taxpayer's presence is required at a particular place for a business purpose. Moreover, the day is considered a business day even though the taxpayer spends more time during normal working hours on nonbusiness activity than on business activity. Weekends, holidays, or other "standby" days that fall between the taxpayer's business days are also considered business days. However, such days are not business days if they fall at the end of the taxpayer's business activities and the taxpayer merely elects to stay for personal purposes. The day of departure and the day of return are both treated as business days.

3. Taxpayer has no substantial control over arranging the business trip.

4. Personal vacation is not a major consideration in making the trip.

If the travel is not primarily for business or fails to satisfy one of the above conditions, an *allocation* of the to-and-from travel expenses must be made. In such cases, the deductible travel expenses are determined by the following allocation formula:

$$\frac{\text{Business days on trip}}{\text{Total days on trip}} \times \begin{array}{c} \text{Total} \\ \text{to-and-from} \\ \text{Travel Expenses} \end{array} = \begin{array}{c} \text{Deductible} \\ \text{to-and-from} \\ \text{Travel Expenses} \end{array}$$

A deduction for the to-and-from travel expenses is not allowed if the trip is primarily personal. However, travel costs (e.g., meals and lodging) directly related to business upon arriving at the destination are deductible.

Example 33. B, an executive, arranged a trip to Japan primarily for business. He left Chicago for Tokyo on July 1 and returned on July 20. During his trip, he spent 15 days on business (including the two travel days) and five days sight-seeing. His air fare was $1,000 and his lodging plus 50% of the meal costs totaled $100 per day.

---

[65]   See *Fraser Wilkins*, 72-2 USTC ¶9707, 30 AFTR2d 72-5639, 348 F. Supp. 1282 (D.Ct. Neb., 1972); *Pierre C. Warwick*, 64-2 USTC ¶9864, 14 AFTR2d 5817, 236 F. Supp. 761 (D.Ct. Va., 1974).

[66]   § 274(c); Reg. § 1.274-4.

Unless B can show that a personal vacation was not a major consideration for the trip, he must allocate his expenses because none of the other conditions are satisfied. In such case, B may deduct $2,250 [(15 business days ÷ 20 total days = 75%) × $3,000 total expenses]. If B had returned July 8 or spent one less day sight-seeing, no allocation would be required since he would have been out of the United States less than a week or would have spent more than 75% of his time on business activities.

Luxury Water Travel. When lawmakers lowered the boom on entertainment and meal expenses in 1986, they also took a swipe at unhurried business people who travel by cruise ships, ocean liners, and other luxury water transportation. As a general rule, deductions for transportation by water are limited to *twice* the highest per diem amount allowed to Federal employees while away from home but serving in the 48 contiguous states.[67]

Example 34. To conduct a business meeting in London, T traveled by ocean liner, taking five days at a total cost of $3,000. Assuming the top per diem rate for Federal employees serving in the United States is $200 per day, T's deduction is limited to $2,000 ($200 × 2 × 5).

FOREIGN CONVENTIONS

Notwithstanding the restrictions imposed on deductions related to foreign travel, substantial abuse existed until 1976. Most of this abuse involved travel to foreign conventions, seminars, cruises, etc., which if properly scheduled amounted to government-subsidized vacations. To eliminate this possibility, specific safeguards were enacted. Currently, no deduction is allowed for travel expenses to attend a convention, seminar, or similar meeting *outside* of North America *unless* the taxpayer establishes the following:[68] (1) the meeting is directly related to the active conduct of his or her trade or business, and (2) it is as reasonable to hold the meeting outside North America as within North America. North America includes the United States, its possessions, Canada, Mexico, the Trust Territory of the Pacific Islands, Bermuda and qualifying Caribbean countries.

Example 35. B, a professor of international business, traveled to Spain to present a paper on tax incentives for exports at the International Accounting Convention. Since it is as reasonable to hold an international meeting in Spain as in North America, and presentation of the paper is directly related to B's business, she may deduct her travel expenses subject to the normal rules for travel outside the United States.

CRUISE SHIPS

No deduction is allowed for the cost of attending a meeting conducted on a cruise ship unless the following requirements are met:[69] (1) the ship is a vessel registered in the United States and it sails *only* between ports in the United States or its possessions; (2) the meeting is directly related to the taxpayer's business; and (3) certain detailed information regarding the cruise is submitted with the return. For qualifying cruises, the maximum deduction is $2,000 per calendar year for each taxpayer. An employer,

---

[67] § 274(m)(1).

[68] See § 274(h)(1), (3), and (6).

[69] § 274(h)(2).

however, may deduct the cost of sending an individual to a foreign convention or on any type of cruise if the amount is included in the employee's income.

✅ *CHECK YOUR KNOWLEDGE*

Review Question 1. Try the following true-false questions. F is director of sales for QVS in Los Angeles but chooses to live 90 miles away in Santa Barbara. Each day he drives to and from work. Once in a while he will leave the office to call on a customer and then return. F may not deduct his cost to commute but can deduct the cost of driving to make calls.

True. As a general rule, commuting is not deductible regardless of the distance traveled. However, the cost of going from one job site to another site is deductible.

Review Question 2. A taxpayer must have a regular work location in order to deduct the costs of commuting to a temporary work assignment outside his tax home.

False. In order to deduct the cost of commuting to a work location *within* the taxpayer's tax home, the taxpayer must have a regular place of business. The same requirement does not apply to commuting outside the taxpayer's tax home.

Review Question 3. The costs of depreciation and insurance for an automobile vary significantly depending on the type of car and driver. Consequently, these items are not reflected in the standard mileage rate; however, the taxpayer can add the appropriate amount of depreciation and insurance expense to the amount computed using the standard rate in computing deductible automobile expenses.

False. Depreciation and insurance are included in the rate.

Review Question 4. T is the district manager for Mississippi Catfish, a fast-food chain with more than 100 stores. He lives in New Orleans. On Monday he traveled to Baton Rouge and returned the same day. On Tuesday he traveled to Houston, spent the night, and returned on Wednesday. T may deduct the costs of lunch both in Baton Rouge and in Houston.

False. In order to deduct the costs of meals and lodging, the taxpayer must be in a travel status (i.e., away from home overnight). Thus T cannot deduct the cost of lunch on his day trip to Baton Rouge. He is allowed to deduct the cost of his lunch while in Houston since he was there overnight.

Review Question 5. This year, Dr. F, an ophthalmologist, attended a four-day meeting of his professional organization in Cancun. He remained another three days to lie on the beach and fish. Dr. F may deduct 4/7 of his airfare.

False. If the trip is primarily for business, the taxpayer is allowed to deduct all of the transportation costs to and from the destination.

ENTERTAINMENT EXPENSES

Perhaps no single deduction has created as much controversy as that for entertainment expenses. The difficulty lies in the fact that there is no simple way to distinguish entertainment expenses incurred out of business necessity from those incurred for personal purposes. The problem is the "dual personality" of entertainment.

Entertainment can be purely for fun and amusement. Or it can be used to break the ice with a potential customer, to relax, or to create an engaging atmosphere for closing the sale or getting the contract. Over the years, Congress and various administrations have continually struggled to devise the proper test that would prohibit taxpayers from deducting what might be a personal expenditure. As recently as 1993, Congress made major changes affecting entertainment expenses.

The Kennedy administration was the first to have some success in limiting the entertainment deduction. In 1961, President Kennedy recommended abolishing the deduction for entertaining customers at parties, nightclubs, etc., as well as disallowing the deduction for country club dues. Although Kennedy's suggestions were not enacted, Congress did move to make it more difficult to deduct entertainment expenses with the enactment of Code § 274. This provision—discussed below—still stands as the major hurdle that must be overcome before entertainment expenses may be deducted. Under § 274, entertainment expenses must not only satisfy the normal criteria for business and income-producing expenses but also several additional requirements, including certain record keeping standards. Despite these additional conditions, the so-called *Kennedy rules* still were viewed by many to be inadequate.

President Carter's administration ventured into the battle over entertainment deductions in 1977, blasting the taxpayer's right to deduct the cost of what is now the infamous "three-martini lunch." The Carter attacks were generally unsuccessful, however. It was not until President Reagan's term that the entertainment deduction was drastically curtailed. Present law now presumes that virtually every entertainment and meal expense contains a personal element that is not deductible. As discussed below, only 50 percent of the cost of allowable meals and entertainment is currently deductible.

DEDUCTION REQUIREMENTS

To be deductible, an entertainment expense must first survive the gauntlet of tests applied to all potential deductions by § 162. That is, the expense must be reasonable, ordinary, and necessary, and incurred in carrying on a trade or business.

> **Example 36.** D is a sales representative of M Corporation, a manufacturer of cookware. Twice a month, she takes buyers from the leading retail department stores to lunch where they discuss the corporation's new products. Business meals are customary, appropriate, and helpful in commissioned sales and thus are deductible.

As a practical matter, most entertainment expenses satisfy the ordinary and necessary tests with little difficulty. It is the additional requirements of § 274 that provide the greatest obstacles.

The restrictions contained in § 274 apply to any expense related to an activity customarily considered to provide entertainment, amusement, or recreation.[70] The provision applies to expenses for entertaining guests such as those for the following: food, liquor, sporting events, movie and theater productions, social, athletic and country clubs, yachts, hunting and fishing trips, and company-provided vacations. Business gifts also are governed by this provision.[71] It should be emphasized that expenses ostensibly for other purposes also are subject to the requirements of § 274 if they are of an entertaining nature.

> **Example 37.** A national magazine desiring publicity often sends the company president flying in a hot air balloon emblazoned with the corporation's logo.

---

[70] § 274(a)(1).

[71] § 274(d).

Although the expense is for advertising, § 274 applies since the activity constitutes entertainment.

As might be expected, when the IRS questions the taxpayer about his or her deductions for entertainment, the auditor does not ask whether the taxpayer had a good time. Unfortunately, the agent is concerned with whether the taxpayer has satisfied either of two principal tests. Under § 274, no deduction is allowed unless the taxpayer can adequately substantiate that the entertainment expense is *either* "directly related to" or "associated with" the taxpayer's business or falls within one of ten exceptions.

Directly-Related-to Expenses. The Regulations set forth what the taxpayer must establish for an entertainment expenditure to be considered *directly related* to the taxpayer's business or income-producing activity. Expenses are treated as directly related under the so-called *general test* if the taxpayer shows all of the following:[72]

1. More than a general expectation of deriving some income or other specific benefit (other than goodwill) existed as a result of making the expenditure; no resulting benefit must be shown, however.

2. Business was actually discussed or engaged in during the entertainment.

3. The combined business and entertainment was principally characterized by business.

Business Benefit. Prior to the enactment of § 274, entertainment deductions were liberally granted where they were shown to promote the customer's goodwill. Section 274 rejects this prior standard. Under current law, the taxpayer must have more than just a general expectation of deriving some income or some specific business benefit. Although this standard is hardly the epitome of clarity, it is clear that the likelihood of a benefit must be greater than a remote possibility.

Example 38. T, an insurance salesperson, sees his old college chum, C, in a bar. T buys his buddy a few drinks and then takes him to a ball game, using an extra ticket T has. Before the night is over, T mentions that if C ever needs insurance he should give T a call. In this case, T's prospect of a business benefit is slight, too distant, and thus not directly related. It simply creates goodwill, which is insufficient to obtain a deduction. However, T may be able to benefit from hindsight. If C later calls him about insurance, T could rightfully claim the deduction.

Actively Engage in Business. Under the general test, the taxpayer must actually discuss or engage in business. This means that at some point during the entertainment— at halftime, during the intermission, between innings—the taxpayer must forsake the merriment of the moment and get down to business, negotiating, dealing, bargaining with respect to a bona fide business transaction. Since this is obviously difficult to police, the Regulations have given the IRS two helpful presumptions.[73] First, it is presumed that no business can take place if the taxpayer is not present. If the taxpayer is at home mowing the lawn while the client is enjoying the game using tickets given to him by the taxpayer, the implication is that no business can take place. (In such case, the taxpayer may be able to deduct the cost of the tickets as a business gift as discussed below.) Second, it is presumed that no business can take place where there are substantial distractions. The Regulations insist that such distractions are present at night

---

[72] Reg. § 1.274-2(c)(3).

[73] Reg. § 1.274-2(c)(7).

clubs, sporting events, social gatherings, cocktail lounges, theaters, and wherever the taxpayer meets with a group including not only business associates but others. Despite these presumptions, a deduction is still allowed if the taxpayer can establish to the contrary that he or she actively engaged in the discussion of business. As a practical matter, most taxpayers take advantage of this latitude, claiming the deduction and hoping that they will never be called upon to justify it.

Principal Character Is Business. During the entertainment, business must predominate. This does not mean that the taxpayer must spend more time on business than enjoying the activity. It does mean that the business aspects must be more than incidental. As above, the Regulations rest on the rebuttable presumption that the primary character of certain activities—those on a hunting or fishing trip, a yacht or pleasure boat—is not business.

The Regulations also specify several other situations where the entertainment expense will be considered directly related. For example, entertainment is directly related if it is provided in a clear business setting—a setting where the guest recognizes the taxpayer's business motive (e.g., a hospitality room provided by a book publisher at a convention of accounting professors).[74] Expenditures for entertainment provided for those who render services for the taxpayer also are regarded as directly related. For example, a vacation trip awarded by a manufacturer to the retailer selling a number of its products qualifies.[75]

Associated-with Expenses. It is often difficult to qualify the entertainment under the directly-related-to test, generally due to the presumption regarding distractions or simply because the taxpayer could not squeeze in any business during the show or game. However, the entertainment may still qualify for deduction if it satisfies the *associated-with test.* Entertainment expenses are considered *associated with* the taxpayer's business if the entertainment is immediately before or after a substantial business discussion.[76] The key distinction between associated-with and directly-related-to expenses concerns when the business activity occurs. The associated-with test allows the business to occur immediately preceding or following the entertainment while the directly-related-to standard requires business during the entertainment. Note that to satisfy the "immediately preceding or following" requirement it is sufficient that the entertainment merely takes place on the same day as business. In some cases, the entertainment may be on the day before or after the business activity.

> **Example 39.** B operates a chain of sporting goods stores in Dallas. Before school begins each fall, he invites area coaches to one of his stores, where he presents his new lines of equipment. Immediately afterward, he takes them to a Cowboys football game. B may deduct the costs of tickets to the game since there was substantial business activity immediately before the entertainment. Note that due to the distractions presented by the game no deduction would be permitted if B merely took the coaches to the game and discussed business there.

Business Meals. For many years, taxpayers were allowed to deduct the cost of meals with business associates regardless of whether they satisfied the directly-related-to or associated-with requirements. More importantly, the costs could be deducted even if business was not discussed. The effect of these rules was to allow a deduction for entertaining that created goodwill. In 1986, Congress believed that this favorable treatment was no longer justified and therefore tightened the rules.

---

[74]   Reg. § 1.274-2(d)(4).

[75]   Reg. § 1.274-2(d)(5).

[76]   *Supra,* Footnote 70; Reg. § 1.274-2(d).

Currently, expenses for meals, like other entertainment expenses, are not deductible unless they satisfy the directly-related-to or associated-with tests.[77] Under these criteria, the business meal is not deductible unless there is a substantial and bona fide business discussion either before, after, or during the meal.[78] In addition, the taxpayer or an employee of the taxpayer normally must be present at the meal.[79] For example, if the taxpayer merely reserves a table for dinner at a restaurant for a customer, but neither the taxpayer nor one of his or her employees attends the dinner, no deduction is allowed. For purposes of this rule, an independent contractor who performs significant services for the taxpayer such as an attorney or accountant is considered an employee.

A common question regarding the deduction for business meals concerns the costs of the taxpayer's own meals. From a purely theoretical view, the cost would presumably be a nondeductible personal expense since the taxpayer has to eat in any event. In *Richard A. Sutter,* the U.S. Tax Court took just such a view in disallowing a taxpayer's deduction for his own meals at business lunches.[80] The Court said:

> We think the presumptive nondeductibility of personal expenses (the taxpayer's meals) may be overcome only by clear and detailed evidence as to each instance that the expenditure in question was *different from or in excess* of that which would have been made for the taxpayer's personal purposes (emphasis supplied).

Despite the Court's holding, the IRS has been quite gracious. The Service permits the taxpayer to deduct the *entire cost* of his or her own meal except in abusive situations where it is evident that a substantial amount of personal expenditures are being deducted.[81] Where abuse is apparent, the IRS would invoke the *Sutter* rule and allow a deduction only to the extent it exceeds the amount the taxpayer would normally spend.

Another common question concerns the costs of entertaining those who are not directly involved in the business activities to which the entertainment relates. The portion of any entertainment expense attributable to the customer's and the taxpayer's spouses is deductible where the purpose is business rather than personal or social.[82] For example, when the taxpayer entertains a business client and it is impractical to entertain the client without the spouse, the expenses of both the taxpayer's spouse and the client's spouse are deductible. Any expenses of other persons not closely connected with those who attended the business discussion are not deductible.

ENTERTAINMENT FACILITIES

For many years, the costs of owning and maintaining such status symbols as airplanes, luxury skyboxes, yachts, and hunting and fishing lodges could be subsidized by deducting them as entertainment expenses. Typically, taxpayers would deduct expenses like depreciation, utilities, maintenance, insurance, and salaries (e.g., that of the yacht's captain) that were allocable to business usage of the property. In 1978, however, Congress imposed severe restrictions. Currently, costs such as those listed above that are related to *any entertainment facility* are not deductible.[83] Additional special rules apply to expenses incurred in using a luxury skybox.[84]

---

77   An individual who is away from home on business and eats alone need not satisfy these tests.

78   §§ 274(a) and (b).

79   § 274(k)(1)(B).

80   21 T.C. 170 (1953).

81   Rev. Rul. 63-144, 1963-2 C.B. 129.

82   Reg. § 1.274-2(d)(4).

83   § 274(a)(1)(B); Reg. § 1.274-2(e)(2).

84   § 274(l)(2).

These rules governing entertainment facilities do not prohibit the deduction of out-of-pocket expenses incurred while at the entertainment facility. Expenses for such items as food or beverage would be deductible, assuming they meet the directly-related-to or associated-with tests. In addition, the various exceptions of § 274 discussed below may enable an employer to deduct expenses connected with entertainment facilities. For example, an employer may deduct the costs of vacation condominiums, swimming pools, tennis courts, and similar facilities if such entertainment facilities are provided primarily for employees.[85]

Club Dues. For years, the tax law contained an exception to the facility rule that allowed taxpayers to deduct their dues or fees paid for a membership in country clubs, etc., if the club was primarily used for business. In the never-ending attack on entertainment expenses, Congress eliminated the deduction for club dues in 1993. Currently no deduction is allowed for the cost of membership in any club organized for business, pleasure, recreation, or any other social purpose.[86] The new rule extends not only to country club dues but to all types of clubs, including luncheon, social, athletic, airline, and hotel clubs. The prohibition does not apply to dues paid to civic organizations, such as the Kiwanis or Rotary Club, or to professional organizations, such as the bar association, as long as the principal purpose of the organization is not entertainment. Note that specific expenses incurred at a club such as a business meal continue to be deductible to the extent that they satisfy any other applicable requirements.

EXCEPTIONS TO DIRECTLY-RELATED-TO AND ASSOCIATED-WITH TESTS

In certain innocent situations, entertainment and meal expenses need not meet either the directly-related-to or associated-with requirements. These include expenses for the following:[87]

1. Food and drink furnished on the business premises primarily for employees (e.g., costs of a holiday office party)

2. Recreational or social activities, including facilities primarily for employees (e.g., a summer golf outing, a company health club, an annual picnic)

3. Entertainment and meal expenses for an employee if the employee reports their value as taxable compensation (e.g., a company-provided vacation for the top salesperson)

4. Entertainment and meal expenses at business meetings of employees, stockholders, and directors (e.g., refreshments at a directors' meeting)

5. Costs of items made available to the general public (e.g., soft drinks at a grand opening, free ham to the first 50 customers)

6. Costs of entertainment and meals sold to customers (e.g., costs of food sold at an event)

FIFTY PERCENT LIMITATION ON ENTERTAINMENT AND MEAL EXPENSES

Opponents of the deduction for entertainment and meal expenses have long argued that, despite their business relationship, such expenses are inherently personal and

---

[85] § 274(e)(5).

[86] § 274(a)(3).

[87] § 274(e)(1)-(9).

should not be deductible. These same critics typically declare that business persons should not be able to live high-on-the-hog at the expense of the government. In 1986 the critics got their way, cutting the deduction to 80 percent of the actual cost. In 1993, they did it again, slashing the deduction even further.[88]

Currently, § 274(n) generally limits the amount that can be deducted for meals and entertainment to 50 percent of their actual cost. In effect, 50 percent of the cost is disallowed. For employees whose entertainment expenses are *not reimbursed,* the 50 percent limitation is applied before the 2 percent floor for itemized deductions.

> **Example 40.** B, an employee, pays $3,000 for business entertainment for which he is not reimbursed. B's A.G.I. is $50,000 for the year and he has no other miscellaneous itemized deductions. B's deduction is $500, computed as follows:
>
> | | |
> |---|---:|
> | Total unreimbursed entertainment expenses | $ 3,000 |
> | Less 50% reduction (50% × $3,000) | (1,500) |
> | | |
> | Miscellaneous itemized deductions | $ 1,500 |
> | Less 2% of A.G.I. (2% × $50,000) | (1,000) |
> | | |
> | Itemized deduction | $ 500 |

Expenses subject to the 50 percent limitation include the costs of taxes, tips, and parking related to a meal or an entertainment activity. In contrast, the costs of transportation to and from the activity are not subject to limitation.

> **Example 41.** B is the agent of G, who recently signed a lucrative contract with the Milwaukee Bucks. After successfully negotiating G's contract, B and G took a cab to a local restaurant where they toasted their success. After dinner, they walked to a nearby nightclub. For the night, B spent $207 for the following:
>
> | | Limited Expenses | Other |
> |---|---:|---:|
> | Meal | $120 | |
> | Tax | 12 | |
> | Tips | 30 | |
> | Cover charge | 38 | |
> | Cab | | $7 |
> | | | |
> | Total | $200 | $7 |

The cost of the cab ride, $7, is not subject to limitation and thus can be deducted in full. Of the remaining $200, only $100 is deductible (50% of $200).

It should be emphasized that the percentage reduction rule applies to meals while away from home overnight on business as well as the traditional quiet business meal. The 50 percent limitation does not apply in several situations, thus allowing the taxpayer to deduct the meal or entertainment in full. These exceptions are discussed below.

---

[88] § 274(n). Taxpayers subject to the hours of work limitations of the Department of Transportation (e.g., pilots and flight attendants) and workers at remote seafood processing facilities (e.g., Alaskan whale boat captains) may deduct a greater portion.

Reimbursed Expenses. When the taxpayer is reimbursed for the meal or entertainment, the limitation is imposed on the party making reimbursement, not the taxpayer.[89]

Example 42. N, a sales representative for Big Corporation, took a customer to lunch after he secured a large order. He paid $30, for which he was totally reimbursed. N includes the $30 in income and may deduct the entire $30. The corporation can deduct only $15 (50% of $30).

If an employee has a reimbursement or expense allowance arrangement with the employer, but under the arrangement the full amount of business expenses is not reimbursed, special problems arise. These problems are considered along with record keeping requirements later in this chapter.

Excludable Fringe Benefit. The 50 percent limitation does not apply where the food or beverage provided is excludable as a de minimis employee fringe benefit (e.g., holiday turkeys, hams, fruitcakes, etc., given to employees, subsidized cafeterias, or to meals provided on the employer's premises for the convenience of the employer).[90]

Code § 274(e) Exceptions. The percentage reduction rule generally is not imposed on entertainment and meal costs which are exempted from the directly-related-to and associated-with tests noted above.[91] For example, there is no reduction required for the deductible costs of an annual employee Christmas party, summer golf outings, or company-provided vacations treated as compensation. Similarly, the costs of promotional items made available to the general public (e.g., 100 baseball tickets given by a radio to the first 100 callers) or the salaries of comedians paid by a nightclub are not subject to the 80 percent limitation.

Charitable Sporting Event. The costs of tickets to a sporting event are not subject to the reduction rule if the event is related to charitable fund-raising.[92] Specifically, the event must be organized for the primary purpose of benefiting a tax-exempt charitable organization, must contribute 100 percent of the proceeds to the charity, and must use volunteers for substantially all work performed in putting on the event. For example, the cost of tickets to attend a golf or tennis celebrity tournament sponsored by the local chapter of the United Way would normally satisfy these requirements and would be fully deductible. Tickets for high school, college, or other scholastic events (e.g., a football game or theater tickets) do not qualify for this exception on the grounds that volunteers do not do all the work (e.g., coaches, their assistants, and other paid individuals provide substantial work such as coaching and recruiting).

LIMITATIONS ON DEDUCTIONS FOR TICKETS

In the entertainment fracas of 1986, lawmakers also struck a blow at the deductible costs of tickets. This deduction is limited to the face value of the ticket (e.g., 50% of the normal ticket price).[93] This rule is aimed at amounts paid to a ticket scalper in excess of the regular price of the ticket. Such excess is not deductible. The rule also makes

---

[89] §§ 274(n)(2) and 274(e)(3).

[90] § 274(n)(2)(B).

[91] § 274(n)(2).

[92] § 274(n)(2)(C).

[93] § 274(1)(1).

nondeductible any fee paid to a ticket agency for arranging tickets. Note, however, that this rule does not apply to tickets to qualified charitable fundraisers.

BUSINESS GIFTS

In hopes that their generosity will someday be rewarded, taxpayers often make gifts to customers, clients, and others with whom they have a business relationship. Such business connected gifts are deductible under the general rules of § 162. Under prior law, taxpayers wanting to create goodwill could shower their business associates with gifts and deduct these instruments of goodwill. Moreover, the recipient of such bounty could arguably exclude the presents. Currently, § 274(b) curbs such practice by limiting the deduction for business gifts to $25 per donee per year.[94] For this purpose, the following items *are not* considered gifts:

1. An item costing $4 or less imprinted with the taxpayer's name (e.g., pens)

2. Signs, display racks, or other promotional materials to be used on the business premises of the recipient

Incidental costs such as engraving, mailing, and wrapping are not considered part of the cost of an item for purposes of the $25 limit. However, husband and wife are treated as *one* recipient for purposes of the $25 limitation.

Example 43. J, a saleswoman of hospital supplies, computes her deduction for business gifts during the year in the following manner.

Description of Gift	Amount	Deduction
H, head of purchasing at St. Jude hospital:		
Perfume	$10	
Solar calculator	30	
Total	$40	$25
Dr. Z:		
Box of golf balls	$18	
Gift wrap	2	
Total	$20	20
Total business gift deduction		$45

Assuming J is an employee, she may deduct the $45 as a miscellaneous itemized deduction.

Employee Achievement Awards. When a business expresses its gratitude for an employee's performance with a gift, special rules allow amounts greater than $25 to be transferred. The effect of these rules is to allow an employer to make and deduct gifts of up to $1,600 to an employee who is allowed to *exclude* the amount of the gift. The Code generally allows an employer to deduct up to $400 per employee for an *employee achievement award*.[95] An employee achievement award is defined as an item of tangible

---

[94]   § 274(b).

[95]   § 274(j).

personal property (e.g., a television or watch, not cash or a gift certificate) transferred to the employee for *length of service* or for *safety* achievement. To help ensure that such awards are not merely disguised compensation, the award must be transferred as part of a meaningful presentation. When the employer has a qualified plan in effect—a nondiscriminatory written plan where the average annual award to all employees does not exceed $400—a deduction of up to $1,600 for a particular award is allowed.

TRAVEL AND ENTERTAINMENT RECORD KEEPING REQUIREMENTS

Travel and entertainment expenses (including business gifts) are not deductible unless the taxpayer properly substantiates the expenses.[96] The *Cohan* rule permitting a deduction for an unsupported but reasonable estimation of an expense does not apply in regard to travel and entertainment.[97]

Section 274(d) specifically requires the taxpayer to substantiate each of the following five elements of an expenditure:

1. Amount

2. Time

3. Place

4. Business purpose

5. Business relationship (for entertainment only)

In most cases, each item must be supported by adequate records such as a diary, account book, or similar record, *and* documentary evidence including receipts or paid bills. Where adequate records have not been maintained, the taxpayer's personal statement will suffice—but only if there is other corroborating evidence, such as the testimony of the individual who was entertained.[98] Congress has indicated that oral evidence would have the least probative value of any evidence and has also authorized the IRS to ask certain additional questions concerning substantiation on the return (see Part II, lines 19-21 of Form 2106, discussed below). In addition, the legislative history makes it clear that the IRS and the courts will invoke the negligence and fraud penalties in those cases where the taxpayer claims tax benefits far in excess of what can be justified.

A receipt is necessary only for lodging expenses and any other expenses of $75 or more. Cancelled checks, without other evidence, may not be sufficient. In the well-known blizzard case of 1975, the importance of properly substantiating each element of the expense was made clear.[99] In this case, the taxpayer did not keep a diary or other record of his substantial travel and entertainment expenses, but he presented the District Court with over 1,700 bills, chits, and memos, as well as 20 witnesses. The District Court allowed the deduction holding that the virtual "blizzard" of bills, etc., met the required tests. The Appellate Court, however, disagreed, indicating that the District Court did not determine whether the elements of each expense were substantiated. Lacking sufficient information on the specific purpose of each expenditure, deductions were denied. A written statement of the purpose is unnecessary,

---

[96]   § 274(d).

[97]   Reg. § 1.274-5T(a)(4).

[98]   Reg. § 1.274-5(c)(3).

[99]   *Cam F. Dowell, Jr. v. U.S.*, 75-2 USTC ¶9819, 36 AFTR2d 75-6314, 522 F.2d 708 (CA-5, 1975), *vac'g. and rem'g.* 74-1 USTC ¶9243, 33 AFTR2d 74-739, 370 F. Supp. 69 (D.Ct. Tex., 1974).

however, where the business purpose or business relationship is obvious from other surrounding facts.

In lieu of substantiating the *amount* of meals and lodging expenses while away from home on business, employees and self-employed individuals may elect to compute the deduction using a standard daily allowance rate. For example, in 2005 the standard meal and incidental expense rate (M&IE rate) is usually $31 per day and is reduced by the 50 percent limit on meals. The standard lodging rate is $60 per day. These rates vary based on location. For example, for 2005 the lodging rate in Indianapolis is $87 per day ($47 M&IE) while in Manhattan it is $208 (for 9/1–12/31) ($51 M&IE).[100]

✓ CHECK YOUR KNOWLEDGE

Review Question 1. P, the public defense attorney of South City, occasionally takes all of his staff to lunch. Q, an attorney in private practice, occasionally takes all of her staff to lunch. Can P and Q deduct the costs of the meals?

Too bad, P. This question illustrates the relatively rare situation when the taxpayer's entertainment expenses may fail the ordinary and necessary criterion or perhaps be considered lavish or extravagant. Q, the attorney in private practice, would have no trouble deducting her expenses. However, the IRS denied (with the U.S. Tax Court's support) a public defender's deduction since public defenders do not commonly take their staffs to lunch!

Review Question 2. To illustrate the problems with entertainment expenses, consider the case of Danville Plywood Corporation,[101] a custom manufacturer of plywood. In 1981, Danville sponsored a four-day excursion for 116 people to the Super Bowl in New Orleans. The so-called Super Bowl Sales Seminar cost $103,444 including tickets, airfare, food, and lodging. On its 1981 tax return, the corporation claimed a deduction for the entire amount, euphemistically calling it "advertising expense." The list of attendees included 55 customers, 37 of their spouses, and two of their children. The remainder consisted of a few employees of the corporation and their spouses, as well as the owner, a few of his friends, and two of his children. According to the corporation, the goal of the seminar was to have discussions with the customers over a period of days in order to ascertain how Danville could do a better job as well as cut down on the travel expenses its salespeople incurred on customer visits. In the past, customers had rarely participated in plant visits so the corporation thought some type of sales meeting held in conjunction with a sporting event might boost attendance. In preparation for the trip, the company instructed its employees regarding some new products and provided other information that they were to share with the customers during the Super Bowl or a side trip to the French Quarter. The company also arranged a display showing some of its products in an area adjacent to the lobby of the hotel where everyone stayed. However, when Danville invited its guests, the letter made no reference to business meetings of any kind, nor did the company reserve rooms where business could be conducted. The corporation did hold a dinner in the hotel for all of its guests, but other individuals were also present. Danville had sponsored a similar trip to the 1980 Super Bowl and had deducted about $98,000. Was Danville able to deduct the expenses of all of the attendees?

---

[100] Rev. Proc. 2005-10, I.R.B. 2005-3. See also *www.policyworks.gov/perdiem.*

[101] *Danville Plywood Corp. v. U.S.* 65 AFTR 2d 90-982, 899 F2d 3, 90-1 USTC ¶50,161 (CA-FC, 1990) aff'g 63 AFTR 2d 89-1036, 16 Cl Ct 584, 89-1 USTC ¶9248 (Cl Ct, 1989). Contrast with *Townsend Industries, Inc. v. U.S..* 92 AFTR 2d 2003-6096 342 F3d 890 (CA-8, 2003) rev'g 90 AFTR 2d 2002-6588 (Southern D. Ct. IA, 2002), where a fishing trip for employees had "a bona fide business purpose" for the trip and it enabled informal conversation about employer's business.

Unfortunately, Danville got sacked on this play and none of the costs were deductible. In denying the deduction, the court emphasized that the expenses not only had to meet the tests of § 162 (i.e., ordinary and necessary business expenses) but also had to pass the rigorous requirements of § 274. The court found little difficulty in concluding that these tests were not met. It found incredible the corporation's attempt to deduct not only the expenses of the president's children but also those of the customers, explaining that their presence did not serve a bona fide business purpose. The court felt similarly about the president's friends as well as the spouses of both the customers and the employees. With respect to the customers and employees, it noted that there was little if any business discussed—a few idle conversations at most. Moreover, the letters to the customers never mentioned the possibility of business discussions or meetings. Nor were meeting rooms reserved for such purpose. In addition, the court believed that such trips were not commonplace in the industry. Based on these observations, the court concluded that the central focus of the trip was entertainment, not business. Unfortunately, it appears that Danville could have won this contest if it had a better game plan. For example, the deduction may have been secured if only the company's correspondence had properly explained the business nature of the weekend and it had actually conducted a business meeting in a separate room devoted to such purpose. No doubt, it also did not sit well with the IRS that the corporation was so aggressive that it deducted the expenses of the children and the friends. Simply bypassing these deductions may have saved the day.

Review Question 3. Although there appears to be one test after another that taxpayers must meet before they deduct entertainment expenditures, there are some basic requirements. Describe them.

The entertainment must be either directly related or associated with business. This means that a taxpayer must discuss business either before, after, or during the entertainment activity.

Review Question 4. D, an attorney in Indianapolis, is an avid Hoosier fan. Somehow he managed to obtain season tickets to the IU basketball games. From time to time, he is unable to attend a game, so he calls a client and surprises him or her with a pair of tickets. Can D deduct the cost of the tickets for his clients?

D can continue to make his friends happy. As a general rule, no deduction is allowed unless the taxpayer or his representative (e.g., an employee) is present, since business cannot take place. However, D could deduct up to $25 as a business gift.

Review Question 5. E runs an advertising firm and is constantly taking people to lunch. Just yesterday he took the ad director at Channel 12 to dinner at his favorite gourmet restaurant. They both had drinks, salad, prime rib, dessert, and coffee: a total of $30 each. When E eats alone, he typically eats a value meal at the local fast-food place. Can E deduct the cost of his client's meal? Can he deduct the entire cost of his own meal or only the amount in excess of what he normally spends?

E can eat, drink, and be merry. As long as E and his friend discussed business in between bites or the meal followed or preceded a business meeting, he can deduct the entire $60 subject to the 50 percent limitation.

Review Question 6. This year F was admitted to the partnership of her accounting firm. Not only was F required to contribute $50,000 to the partnership but she was also required to join a country club. She joined the plush Meridian Lakes Country Club at a cost of $25,000. In addition, she must pay monthly dues of $300. Assuming F uses the club exclusively for business, can she deduct the membership and dues?

Sorry, F, but it is the price of being a partner. The Code denies a deduction for the costs of both the membership and the club dues.

Review Question 7. True or False: Taxpayers are generally allowed to deduct only 50 percent of their unreimbursed travel and entertainment expenses.

False. Do not be fooled. A typical mistake is to lump travel and entertainment together. Only meals and entertainment expenses are subject to the 50 percent rule. Travel (other than meals) is not subject to the limitation.

Review Question 8. G&H, a public accounting firm, provides continuing education for its tax staff at a resort in Florida. During the week, the employees spend hour upon hour in seminars devoted to the tax law. The firm pays for the meals and lodging of the participants. Is G&H entitled to deduct the entire costs of the meals or only 50 percent?

The 50 percent limitation normally applies to the costs of all meals and entertainment. However, the limitation does not apply if any of the various exceptions contained in § 274(e) apply. One of these concerns business meetings of employees. Consequently, the firm is allowed to deduct 100 percent of the meal costs.

Review Question 9. This year the School of Business at X University created an annual award of $100 given to three staff members (e.g., secretaries) for outstanding performance during the year. The School's bookkeeper is uncertain as to whether taxes are to be withheld on such awards. How should the awards be handled?

Unfortunately, what appears to be an award of $100 is probably closer to $60 since the award is fully taxable and both income and employment taxes must be withheld. No exclusion is available since the award is given in cash and is not for length of service or safety.

REPORTING BUSINESS EXPENSES AND LOSSES

SOLE PROPRIETORS AND SELF-EMPLOYED PERSONS

Sole proprietors and self-employed persons are not treated as separate taxable entities. Rather, their income and expenses are compiled and reported simply as a part of their individual return. This information is reported on Schedule C or C-EZ of Form 1040. Page 1 of Schedule C appears below. An examination of Schedule C reveals that it is relatively straightforward and self-explanatory. The net income or loss as reported on line 31 of Schedule C is transferred to Page 1 of Form 1040 and is added to the taxpayer's income. The net income or loss on Schedule C also is used in the computation of self-employment tax. Accordingly, the net amount on Schedule C must also be transferred to Schedule SE.

Schedule C Form 1040

| SCHEDULE C (Form 1040)
Department of the Treasury
Internal Revenue Service | **Profit or Loss From Business**
(Sole Proprietorship)
► **Partnerships, joint ventures, etc., must file Form 1065 or 1065-B.**
► **Attach to Form 1040 or 1041.**   ► **See Instructions for Schedule C (Form 1040).** | OMB No. 1545-0074
20**04**
Attachment
Sequence No. **09** |

Name of proprietor

A Principal business or profession, including product or service (see page C-2 of the instructions)

B Enter code from pages C-7, 8, & 9 ►

C Business name. If no separate business name, leave blank.

D Employer ID number (EIN), if any

E Business address (including suite or room no.) ►
City, town or post office, state, and ZIP code

F Accounting method: **(1)** ☐ Cash   **(2)** ☐ Accrual   **(3)** ☐ Other (specify) ►

G Did you "materially participate" in the operation of this business during 2004? If "No," see page C-3 for limit on losses   ☐ Yes   ☐ No

H If you started or acquired this business during 2004, check here . . . . ► ☐

Part I   Income

1	Gross receipts or sales. **Caution.** If this income was reported to you on Form W-2 and the "Statutory employee" box on that form was checked, see page C-3 and check here . . . . . ► ☐	**1**
2	Returns and allowances	**2**
3	Subtract line 2 from line 1	**3**
4	Cost of goods sold (from line 42 on page 2)	**4**
5	**Gross profit.** Subtract line 4 from line 3. . . .	**5**
6	Other income, including Federal and state gasoline or fuel tax credit or refund (see page C-3) . . .	**6**
7	**Gross income.** Add lines 5 and 6 . . . . ►	**7**

Part II   Expenses. Enter expenses for business use of your home **only** on line 30.

8	Advertising	**8**	**19** Pension and profit-sharing plans	**19**	
9	Car and truck expenses (see page C-3).	**9**	**20** Rent or lease (see page C-5):		
			a Vehicles, machinery, and equipment	**20a**	
10	Commissions and fees . .	**10**	**b** Other business property. . .	**20b**	
11	Contract labor (see page C-4)	**11**	**21** Repairs and maintenance . .	**21**	
12	Depletion	**12**	**22** Supplies (not included in Part III) .	**22**	
13	Depreciation and section 179 expense deduction (not included in Part III) (see page C-4) .	**13**	**23** Taxes and licenses	**23**	
			24 Travel, meals, and entertainment:		
			a Travel	**24a**	
14	Employee benefit programs (other than on line 19). .	**14**	**b** Meals and entertainment		
15	Insurance (other than health) .	**15**	**c** Enter nondeductible amount included on line 24b (see page C-5) .		
16	Interest:				
a	Mortgage (paid to banks, etc.) .	**16a**	**d** Subtract line 24c from line 24b	**24d**	
b	Other	**16b**	**25** Utilities	**25**	
17	Legal and professional services	**17**	**26** Wages (less employment credits) .	**26**	
18	Office expense	**18**	**27** Other expenses (from line 48 on page 2)	**27**	

28	**Total expenses** before expenses for business use of home. Add lines 8 through 27 in columns . ►	**28**

29	Tentative profit (loss). Subtract line 28 from line 7	**29**
30	Expenses for business use of your home. Attach **Form 8829**	**30**
31	**Net profit or (loss).** Subtract line 30 from line 29.	
	• If a profit, enter on **Form 1040, line 12,** and **also** on **Schedule SE, line 2** (statutory employees, see page C-6). Estates and trusts, enter on Form 1041, line 3.	**31**
	• If a loss, you **must** go to line 32.	
32	If you have a loss, check the box that describes your investment in this activity (see page C-6).	
	• If you checked 32a, enter the loss on **Form 1040, line 12,** and **also** on **Schedule SE, line 2** (statutory employees, see page C-6). Estates and trusts, enter on Form 1041, line 3.	**32a** ☐ All investment is at risk.
	• If you checked 32b, you **must** attach **Form 6198.**	**32b** ☐ Some investment is not at risk.

For **Paperwork Reduction Act Notice,** see Form 1040 instructions.   Cat. No. 11334P   Schedule C (Form 1040) 2004

EMPLOYEES

Both the treatment and reporting of an employee's business expenses vary significantly depending on whether the expenses are reimbursed. As explained in Chapter 7, employee business expenses that are *not* reimbursed are treated as miscellaneous itemized deductions, and are therefore deductible only to the extent that total miscellaneous itemized deductions exceed 2 percent of A.G.I. In addition, such deductions would be subject to the 3 percent cutback. On the other hand, expenses reimbursed under an accountable plan (discussed below) are *not deductible* by the employee, *but* the reimbursement is excludable from his or her gross income. In such case, there is no effect on the taxpayer's return. This latter treatment normally applies to most employee expense accounts, including those arrangements where the employer reimburses an employee for a particular expense as well as those where the employer gives the employee a fixed allowance (e.g., a per diem amount such as $15 per day for meals and $25 per day for lodging). It should be emphasized, however, that even though an expense may appear to be reimbursed in the normal sense, it may not be treated as reimbursed for determining whether the expense is deductible from A.G.I. or the reimbursement is excludable from gross income.

Accountable and Nonaccountable Plans. Since 1989, an employee's business expenses are treated as reimbursed only if his or her employer has a reimbursement or allowance arrangement that qualifies as an *accountable plan*. An arrangement generally qualifies as an accountable plan if the employee properly substantiates the expenses to the employer, and, in the case of advances or allowances, is required to return to the employer any amount in excess of that which is substantiated.[102] If the arrangement does not meet the accountable plan requirements, it is considered a *nonaccountable plan*. As might be expected, the tax treatment of payments under the two different plans differs drastically.

Reimbursements or advances made under an accountable plan are treated far more favorably than those under a nonaccountable plan. Amounts paid under an accountable plan are normally excluded from gross income, not reported on the employee's Form W-2, and are exempt from employment taxes (i.e., social security and unemployment). In contrast, reimbursements and advances made under a nonaccountable plan must be reported in the employee's gross income, included on Form W-2, and are subject to employment taxes. More importantly, the expenses for which the employee is reimbursed under a nonaccountable plan must be claimed as miscellaneous itemized deductions subject to the 2 percent floor. Under either plan, the employee normally summarizes employee business expenses on Form 2106 (shown on pp. 8–51 and 8–52). When this form is properly completed, expenses not considered reimbursed flow to Schedule A and are deducted as miscellaneous itemized deductions. The reporting of employee business expenses is summarized in Exhibit 8-2, which follows.

---

[102] Temp. Reg. § 1.62-2T.

EXHIBIT 8-2
Reporting Travel, Transportation, Meal, and Entertainment Expenses and Reimbursements

Type of Reimbursement or Other Expense Allowance Arrangement	Employer Reports on Form W-2	Employee Shows on Form 2106	Employee Claims on Schedule A
Accountable			
1. Adequate accounting and excess returned	Not reported	Not shown	Not claimed
2. Per diem or mileage allowance (up to government rate)	Not reported	All expenses and reimbursements only if excess expenses are claimed. Otherwise, form is not filed	Expenses the employee can prove and which exceed the reimbursements received
Adequate accounting and excess returned			
3. Per diem or mileage allowance (exceeds government rate)	Excess reported as wages in Box 1. Amount up to the government rate is reported only in a Box 13—it is not reported in Box 1	All expenses, and reimbursements equal to the government rate, only if expenses in excess of the government rate are claimed.[1] Otherwise, form is not filed	Expenses the employee can prove and which exceed the government rate[2]
Adequate accounting up to the government rate only and excess not returned			
Nonaccountable			
4. Adequate accounting or return of excess either not required or required but not met	Entire amount is reported as wages in Box 1.[3]	All expenses[1]	Expenses the employee can prove[2]
5. No reimbursement	Normal reporting of wages, etc.	All expenses[1]	Expenses the employee can prove[2]

[1]These amounts are subject to income tax withholding and to all employment taxes such as FICA and FUTA.

[2]Any allowable expense is carried to line 20 of Schedule A and deducted as a miscellaneous itemized deduction.

[3]These amounts are subject to the applicable limits including the 50 percent limit on meals and entertainment expenses and the two percent of adjusted gross income limit on the total miscellaneous itemized deductions.

Source: *Travel, Entertainment, Gift and Car Expense*, IRS Publication 463 (Rev 2004), p. 35.

Under an accountable plan, an employee who substantiates his or her expenses and returns any excess reimbursement reports neither the reimbursements nor the expenses because there is a complete wash. (See Exhibit 8-2 Item 1.) *However,* if the employee fails to return any excess reimbursement, a different accounting is required. In this case, the excess reimbursement is treated as *if* paid under a nonaccountable plan. Therefore, the employer must report the *excess* in the employee's Form W-2 as well as pay the related employment taxes. On the other side, the employee must include the excess in gross income. (See Exhibit 8-2, Item 3).

Example 44. R is a sales representative for C Corporation and has an expense account arrangement. Under this arrangement, R fills out an expense report every two weeks, documenting all of his expenses, and submits it for reimbursement. This year R submitted travel expenses of $5,000, all of which were reimbursed. Assuming this is an accountable plan and R has properly substantiated expenses of $5,000, there is nothing included on his Form W-2 and none of the expenses are reported on his return. In effect, there is no effect on R because the reimbursement and expenses wash. (See Exhibit 8-2 Item 1.)

Example 45. Assume the plan in *Example 44* was not properly structured and did not require R either to substantiate his expenses or to return any excess reimbursement. In this case, the arrangement would be a nonaccountable plan. Consequently, the $5,000 reimbursement would be included as income in R's Form W-2 and he could deduct the $5,000 as a miscellaneous itemized deduction. In this case, the income and deduction do not necessarily wash (e.g., if R does not itemize), and R ends up with taxable income that economically he does not have. (See Exhibit 8-2 Item 4. The Form 2106 shown on pp. 8–51 and 8–52 reveals how this information would be reported.)

As the above examples illustrate, most employers should opt to establish reimbursement arrangements that meet the accountable plan requirements so that employees are not unduly penalized. Nevertheless, as noted above, even if the employer has an accountable plan, the employee must still substantiate any expenses and return any reimbursements in excess of the expenses substantiated to avoid unfavorable treatment.

Substantiation. A plan generally satisfies the substantiation requirement if the employee meets the normal rules for substantiation of expenses. For example, travel and entertainment expenses must be substantiated under the special rules of § 274(d) discussed earlier in this chapter. Note that an employee whose reimbursement is based on some type of fixed allowance (e.g., a per diem for meals and lodging or a mileage allowance) is *deemed* to have substantiated the amount of his or her expenses up to the amount set by the IRS for per diem, mileage, or other expense allowances.[103] Generally, the only expense substantiation for such plans is the number of business miles traveled and the number of days away from home spent on business. Due to this rule, employees who receive allowances within the IRS guidelines will have no reimbursements in excess of their substantiated expenses and, therefore, will not have any excess to return.

Example 46. K works as an accountant for a public accounting firm in Tampa. This year she attended a continuing education course in Jacksonville. The firm gives its employees a meal allowance of $12 per diem, which is within the IRS guidelines. K attended the course for five days. When she returned from the trip, she submitted

---

[103]   See Temp. Regs. §§ 1.62-2T(e)(2) and 1.274-5T(g).

her expense report requesting reimbursement for meals of $60 (5 × $12). In reality, K, wanting to save as much as she could, spent only $40 on meals. Although K has actually received $20 more than she spent ($60 − $40), she does not have to return the excess because she is deemed to have substantiated expenses of $60.

If an employee has expenses that the employer did not reimburse, the employee should file Form 2106 to claim a deduction for the unreimbursed expenses. Proper completion of this form results in the unreimbursed expenses being claimed as miscellaneous itemized deductions on Schedule A. (See Exhibit 8-2 Item 2.)

Form 2106

Form **2106** Department of the Treasury Internal Revenue Service (99)	**Employee Business Expenses** ▶ See separate instructions. ▶ Attach to Form 1040.	OMB No. 1545-0139 **2004** Attachment Sequence No. **54**

Your name R. EMPLOYEE	Occupation in which you incurred expenses SALES REPRESENTATIVE	Social security number 456 78 9102

Part I   **Employee Business Expenses and Reimbursements**

Step 1   Enter Your Expenses

		Column A Other Than Meals and Entertainment	Column B Meals and Entertainment
1	Vehicle expense from line 22 or line 29. (Rural mail carriers: See instructions.)		
2	Parking fees, tolls, and transportation, including train, bus, etc., that **did not** involve overnight travel or commuting to and from work		
3	Travel expense while away from home overnight, including lodging, airplane, car rental, etc. **Do not** include meals and entertainment.	5,000	
4	Business expenses not included on lines 1 through 3. **Do not** include meals and entertainment.		
5	Meals and entertainment expenses (see instructions)		
6	**Total expenses.** In Column A, add lines 1 through 4 and enter the result. In Column B, enter the amount from line 5	5,000	

Note: *If you were not reimbursed for any expenses in Step 1, skip line 7 and enter the amount from line 6 on line 8.*

Step 2   Enter Reimbursements Received From Your Employer for Expenses Listed in Step 1

7	Enter reimbursements received from your employer that were **not** reported to you in box 1 of Form W-2. Include any reimbursements reported under code "L" in box 12 of your Form W-2 (see instructions)	–0–	

Step 3   Figure Expenses To Deduct on Schedule A (Form 1040)

8	Subtract line 7 from line 6. If zero or less, enter -0-. However, if line 7 is greater than line 6 in Column A, report the excess as income on Form 1040, line 7	5,000	
	Note: *If **both** columns of line 8 are zero, you cannot deduct employee business expenses. Stop here and attach Form 2106 to your return.*		
9	In Column A, enter the amount from line 8. In Column B, multiply line 8 by 50% (.50). (Employees subject to Department of Transportation (DOT) hours of service limits: Multiply meal expenses incurred while away from home on business by 70% (.70) instead of 50%. For details, see instructions.)	5,000	
10	Add the amounts on line 9 of both columns and enter the total here. **Also, enter the total on Schedule A (Form 1040), line 20.** (Reservists, qualified performing artists, fee-basis state or local government officials, and individuals with disabilities: See the instructions for special rules on where to enter the total.) ▶	5,000	

For Paperwork Reduction Act Notice, see instructions.   Cat. No. 11700N   Form **2106** (2004)

Form 2106 Continued

Form 2106 (2004)   *R.EMPLOYEE*   Page **2**

Part II   Vehicle Expenses

Section A—General Information (You must complete this section if you are claiming vehicle expenses.)

		(a) Vehicle 1	(b) Vehicle 2
11	Enter the date the vehicle was placed in service	11 / /	/ /
12	Total miles the vehicle was driven during 2004	12 miles	miles
13	Business miles included on line 12	13 miles	miles
14	Percent of business use. Divide line 13 by line 12	14 %	%
15	Average daily roundtrip commuting distance	15 miles	miles
16	Commuting miles included on line 12	16 miles	miles
17	Other miles. Add lines 13 and 16 and subtract the total from line 12	17 miles	miles

18	Do you (or your spouse) have another vehicle available for personal use?	☐ Yes	☐ No
19	Was your vehicle available for personal use during off-duty hours?	☐ Yes	☐ No
20	Do you have evidence to support your deduction?	☐ Yes	☐ No
21	If "Yes," is the evidence written?	☐ Yes	☐ No

Section B—Standard Mileage Rate (See the instructions for Part II to find out whether to complete this section or Section C.)

22	Multiply line 13 by 37.5¢ (.375)	22	

Section C—Actual Expenses

		(a) Vehicle 1		(b) Vehicle 2	
23	Gasoline, oil, repairs, vehicle insurance, etc.				
24a	Vehicle rentals				
b	Inclusion amount (see instructions)				
c	Subtract line 24b from line 24a				
25	Value of employer-provided vehicle (applies only if 100% of annual lease value was included on Form W-2—see instructions)				
26	Add lines 23, 24c, and 25				
27	Multiply line 26 by the percentage on line 14				
28	Depreciation (see instructions)				
29	Add lines 27 and 28. Enter total here and on line 1				

Section D—Depreciation of Vehicles (Use this section only if you owned the vehicle and are completing Section C for the vehicle.)

		(a) Vehicle 1		(b) Vehicle 2	
30	Enter cost or other basis (see instructions)				
31	Enter section 179 deduction and special allowance (see instructions)				
32	Multiply line 30 by line 14 (see instructions if you claimed the section 179 deduction or special allowance)				
33	Enter depreciation method and percentage (see instructions)				
34	Multiply line 32 by the percentage on line 33 (see instructions)				
35	Add lines 31 and 34				
36	Enter the applicable limit explained in the line 36 instructions				
37	Multiply line 36 by the percentage on line 14				
38	Enter the **smaller** of line 35 or line 37. Also enter this amount on line 28 above				

Form **2106** (2004)

Example 47. Under an accountable plan, T is reimbursed 32.5 cents per mile for all business miles driven. For the year, he received $1,000. After consulting his records, T determined that his actual expenses exceed 32.5 cents per mile for a total of $1,200. None of the reimbursement is included on T's Form W-2 because this is an accountable plan and the allowance does not exceed the government rate. T should report the $1,200 of expenses on lines 1–6 of Form 2106. The $1,000 reimbursement is entered on line 7 and subtracted from the $1,200 expense amount to leave $200. The $200 (the amount for which T did not receive a reimbursement) flows through to Schedule A and is treated as a miscellaneous itemized deduction. (See line 10 of Form 2106 and Exhibit 8-2, Item 2).

Example 48. J's employer pays her a flat $100 per month to cover her car expenses. The employer does not have an accountable plan. Thus the employer must include the $100 as income in J's Form W-2, and J may deduct her car expenses as miscellaneous itemized deductions. (See Exhibit 8-2. Item 4.)

In certain instances, the employer may give the employee a per diem allowance that exceeds the Federal government allowable rate (e.g., 40 cents per mile instead of the allowable standard mileage rate). In such cases, special reporting rules apply.[104] Similarly, special allocation rules must be observed when the amount of the reimbursement covers only a portion of the employee's expenses.[105]

TAX PLANNING CONSIDERATIONS

MOVING EXPENSES

Upon retirement, many individuals move to another location. Normally, the moving expenses would not be deductible. If the taxpayer can obtain a *full-time* job at the new location, however, the costs of moving become deductible. In this regard, the taxpayer must be sure to satisfy the 39- or 78-week test.

TRAVEL AND ENTERTAINMENT EXPENSES

The rules governing deductions for combined business and pleasure travel permit some vacationing on business trips without jeopardizing the deduction. As long as the trip is primarily for business, the entire cost of traveling to the business/vacation destination is deductible. Although the expenses of personal side-trips are not allowed, these expenses may be incidental to the major costs of getting to the desired location. For example, a taxpayer living in New York can deduct a major portion of the cost of a vacation in Florida—the cost of getting there—by properly scheduling business in Miami. In those situations where vacation time exceeds time spent on business, the taxpayer must be prepared to establish that the trip would not have been taken *but for* the business need.

When traveling, the taxpayer may also be able to deduct the expenses of a spouse if a business purpose for the spouse's presence can be established. Even where a spouse's travel expenses are clearly not deductible, only the *incremental* expense attributable to the spouse's presence is not allowed. When an automobile is used for transportation, there is no incremental expense. In the case of lodging, the single room rate would be fully deductible and only the few extra dollars added for a double room rate, if any, would not be deductible.

---

[104] *Supra*, Footnote 100, p. 15.

[105] Reg. § 1.62-1(f).

The importance of adequate records for travel and entertainment expenses cannot be over emphasized. However, the *actual* cost of travel expenses need not be proved when a per diem or a fixed mileage allowance arrangement exists between the employee and the employer. In these situations, the other elements of the expense—time, place, and business purpose—must still be substantiated by the employer and employee. Moreover, the taxpayer must substantiate the cost of travel where the employee is "related" to the employer (an employee is considered related when he or she either owns more than 10 percent of a corporate employer's stock or is the employer's spouse, brother, sister, ancestor, or lineal descendant). Notwithstanding the relaxation of the substantiation requirements for travel costs, it is advisable to maintain receipts and other records to substantiate the other elements of the expenditure.

The taxpayer should get in the habit of contemporaneously recording the required elements for each expenditure. Although a bothersome task, this must be done to secure deductions for travel and entertainment expenses. *Each* element of each expenditure must be established.

With respect to vehicle expenses, the taxpayer cannot simply deduct the expenses and hope that he or she will never be asked to produce evidence supporting the deduction. Form 2106 (Part II, line 21) specifically asks whether the taxpayer has proper written evidence. Thus, failure to maintain such documentation would mean that the taxpayer could not answer this question in the affirmative, increasing the probability of audit. Of course, indicating that such evidence exists when it in fact does not could subject the taxpayer to negligence or fraud penalties.

PROBLEM MATERIALS

DISCUSSION QUESTIONS

8-1 *Requirements for Education Expenses.* J has been told that, as a practical matter, most education expenses are considered nondeductible personal expenses. Under what conditions. if any, may J deduct expenses for education?

8-2 *Education: Degrees, Promotion, and Employer Assistance.* Y is currently employed as the manager of a fast-food restaurant, earning $29,000. In order to improve her upward mobility in the company, Y decides that she should go to college and earn her degree.

   a. Can Y deduct any of the cost of obtaining her bachelor's degree in business?

   b. Same as above, except Y already has her bachelor's degree and now decides to take courses which could lead to her receiving an M.B.A.

   c. What is the effect on Y if her employer pays for her education costs this year of $6,000? Answer for both a bachelor's degree and an M.B.A.

8-3 *Expenses of Education.* F, vice president of sales for a large corporation, is in the executive M.B.A. program at the University of Michigan. F lives in Chicago and travels to Ann Arbor and Detroit to take certain courses.

   a. F's employer reimburses F for the tuition, which is $8,000 per year. Explain how F will treat the reimbursement and the expense. What if F was not reimbursed? Indicate whether the following expenses incurred by F would be deductible:

   b. Meals and lodging when he stays overnight

   c. Transportation costs from Chicago and back

   d. Books

   e. Secretarial fees for typing term projects

   f. Copying expenses

   g. Value of vacation time used to take classes

   h. Tutor

8-4 *Qualifying Educational Expenses.* Indicate whether education expenses would be deductible in the following situations:

   a. J is currently an elementary school teacher. State law requires beginning teachers to have a bachelor's degree and to complete a master's degree within five years after first being hired. This year he took two courses toward the master's degree.

   b. R is a full-time engineering student and has a part-time job as an engineer with a firm that will employ him as an engineer when he graduates.

   c. C is an airline pilot and is presently taking lessons to become a helicopter pilot.

   d. H retired from the finance department of the Army and now is getting his M.B.A. He plans to get a job with a financial institution.

8-5 *Moving Expenses.* Address the following:

   a. What two tests must be satisfied before moving expenses may be deducted?

   b. What moving expenses are deductible?

   c. Are moving expenses deductible *for* or *from* adjusted gross income?

8-6 *Moving Expenses: Real Estate Commissions.* B's employer transferred him during the year. As a result, B sold his home in North Dakota and moved to New York, where he lives in an apartment. He does not plan to move into a new home. B's real estate commissions were $6,000. B has asked how he should treat the real estate commissions.

8-7 *Home Office Expenses.* The enactment of the restrictive rules related to home office deductions caused many commentators to conclude that the home office deduction had been essentially eliminated. Which particular requirement(s) of § 280A prompted such a conclusion?

8-8 *Computing Car Expenses.* Briefly answer the following:

   a. With respect to a business car, can the taxpayer claim depreciation in addition to the expense determined using the standard mileage rate?

   b. Can a taxpayer switch to the automatic mileage method after using MACRS to compute depreciation? If so, when does the car become fully depreciated?

8-9 *Transportation vs. Travel.* Explain the distinction between transportation expenses and travel expenses.

8-10 *U.S. Travel vs. Foreign Travel.* Compare and contrast the rules governing travel in the United States to those rules governing travel outside of the United States.

8-11 *Limitations on Entertainment and Meals.* T is employed by KL Publishing Corporation. He is a sales representative with responsibility for college textbook sales in Alabama, Florida and Georgia. T lives in Atlanta. For each of the following situations, indicate whether T's or the corporation's deduction for entertainment or meals would be limited, and if so, how?

   a. T flew to Birmingham on a Tuesday night. After checking in at the hotel, he caught a cab to his favorite restaurant where he ate by himself. The cost of the meal was $20, including a $1 tax and a $3 tip. The cost of the cab ride was $10. The next day he called on a customer.

   b. Same as (a), except that T's employer reimbursed him under an accountable plan for all of his costs.

   c. Same as (a), but further assume that T's A.G.I. for the year was $30,000 and that he has other miscellaneous itemized deductions of $700.

   d. At the year-end Christmas party for employees, the corporation gave T a 10-pound, honey-baked ham, costing $40. The cost of the party (excluding the ham), which was held at a local restaurant, was $300.

e.   During the annual convention of college marketing professors in New Orleans, the corporation rented a room in the convention hotel for one night and provided hors d'oeuvres. The room cost $200 while the food and drink cost $1,000.

8-12   *Reimbursed Expenses.* Explain the reporting requirements relating to expenses that are reimbursed.

8-13   *Entertainment Expenses.* Distinguish between entertainment expenses that are considered "directly related to" the taxpayer's business and those that are "associated with" the taxpayer's business.

8-14   *Business Meals.* Can the taxpayer deduct the cost of his or her own meal when he or she pays for the lunch of a customer and no business is discussed?

8-15   *Entertainment Facilities.* Under what circumstances are expenses related to an entertainment facility deductible?

8-16   *Substantiation of Travel and Entertainment Expenses.* What information must the taxpayer be prepared to present upon the audit of his or her travel and entertainment expenditures? Does the taxpayer need to maintain records if he or she has a per diem arrangement with the employer?

8-17   *Foreign Convention.* Dr. B recently learned that a world famous plastic surgeon will be making a presentation concerning her area of expertise at a convention of physicians in Switzerland. If B attends, can she deduct the costs of airfare, meals, lodging, and registration? Explain.

8-18   *Cruise Ship Seminars.* The American Organization of Dental Specialists is offering a seven-day seminar on gum disease aboard a cruise ship. Dr. D, a dentist. would like to attend. If D attends, can he deduct his expenses?

8-19   *Reporting Reimbursements.* R is regional sales manager for a large steel manufacturing corporation. His job requires him to travel extensively to call on customers and salespeople. As a result, he incurs substantial expenses for airfare, hotel, meals, and entertainment, for which he is reimbursed. Under what conditions may R simply ignore reporting the reimbursements and the expenses for tax purposes?

8-20   *Reporting Employee Business Expenses.* T is a salesperson for Classy Cosmetics Inc. During the year, she incurred various business expenses for which she was reimbursed under an accountable plan. Discuss the problems T encounters when reporting the reimbursements and expenses in the following situations, assuming an adequate accounting was made.
a.   T was reimbursed $3,800 for expenses totaling $3,000.
b.   T was on a per diem of $25 per day for lodging and $15 per day for meals. She received $2,000 under the per diem arrangement for expenses totaling $2,200.

8-21   *Per Diem Arrangement.* A1 was recently hired by a public accounting firm as a staff accountant. When A1 is out of town on business (e.g., staff training or an audit at a client's place of business), the firm gives him $12 a day for dinner. A1 normally spends $5 and banks the rest. What are the tax consequences?

8-22   *Substantiation Requirements.* Indicate whether each of the following is required in order to properly substantiate a deduction:
a.   Purpose of an entertainment expenditure
b.   Date of entertainment expenditure
c.   Receipt for business meal with client, which cost $15
d.   Receipt for lodging at Motel Cheap, which cost $12

e. Description of what the taxpayer wore on the day he lunched with client

f. Diary detailing information normally required for substantiation of entertainment expenses

g. Canceled check for $12 for tickets to baseball game that was attended with customer

h. Social security number of client entertained

YOU MAKE THE CALL

8-23 The unfortunate experience of Danville Plywood Corporation and its deduction for the Super Bowl trip described earlier in this chapter raises another issue. The corporation booked what clearly seemed to be entertainment expenses as advertising expenses, perhaps with the hope that the expense would be forever buried. Assume that you were the accountant on the job, noted this, and proposed a reclassification entry to the client who objected. What action should you take?

PROBLEMS

8-24 *Education Expenses.* Indicate the amount, if any, of deductible education expenses in each of the following cases. Comment briefly on your answer and state whether the deduction is deductible *for* or *from* adjusted gross income:

a. C is employed as a plumber, but is training to become a computer programmer. During the year, he paid $500 for tuition and books related to a college course in programming.

b. E is a licensed nurse. During the year, she spent $300 on courses to become a registered nurse.

c. R paid a $75 fee to take the C.P.A. exam and $800 for a C.P.A. review course. R currently is employed by a public accounting firm.

d. R is an IRS agent. This year, he began taking courses toward a law degree emphasizing tax. Tuition and books cost $1,000.

e. H is a high school instructor teaching European history. On a one-year sabbatical leave from school, he traveled to Europe, taking slides which he planned on using in his classes. The trip cost $7,000, including $1,000 for meals.

8-25 *Moving Expenses.* In May of the current year. M found a new job, forcing him to move from Tulsa to Seattle. On June 1, the moving company picked up all of M's possessions. M and his family stayed in a hotel on June 1, left the morning of June 2, and arrived in Seattle on June 4. They incurred the following expenses.

1. Airfare and meals for him and his wife while traveling to Seattle to look for a new house, $260 and $50 respectively. They failed to find a home. Consequently, they moved into an apartment, from which they continued their search.

2. Lodging in Tulsa on the day they moved out of their house, $70.

3. Expenses on the way to Seattle included meals, $80, and lodging, $100.

4. Mileage to Seattle, 2,000 miles.

5. Car repair on trip to Seattle, $175.

6. Moving van, $4,000.

7. Storage charges for furniture that would not fit in the apartment: $3 per day for the period June 5–July 31.

8. Temporary living expenses for period June 5–July 31: apartment, $10 per day; meals, $20 per day; and cleaning and laundry, $25.

9. Realtor's commission on sale of old home. $1,000.

Compute M's moving expense deduction (Form 3903 may be helpful).

8-26 *Home Office.* In each of the following independent situations, indicate whether the taxpayer is entitled to deduct expenses related to the home office:

a. C, a dermatologist employed by a hospital, also owns several rental properties. He regularly uses a bedroom in his home solely as an office for bookkeeping and other activities related to management of the rental properties.

b. R, an attorney employed by a large law firm, frequently brings work home from the office. She uses a study in her home for doing this work as well as paying bills, sorting coupons and conducting other personal activities.

c. M is a research associate employed by the Cancer Research Institute. His duties include designing and carrying out experiments, reviewing data, and writing articles and grant proposals. His employer furnishes M a laboratory but due to insufficient space cannot provide an office for him. Thus, for about three hours each day, M uses a portion of his bedroom (where he and his wife sleep) to do the writing, reviewing, and other related activities.

d. T is a self-employed tax consultant. He has an office downtown and a home office. He occasionally meets with his clients in the home office since it is often more convenient for the clients to meet there.

e. S, an artist, converted a detached garage to a studio for painting. She sells her paintings at her own gallery located in town.

f. D has four toddlers. Since her home is virtually a nursery already, she decided to turn her family room into a daycare center.

8-27 *Home Office.* R is considering purchasing a home priced somewhat over her budget. Her brother has suggested that converting a room to a home office would enable her to deduct a substantial part of the costs related to the home, thus making the purchase feasible. R is a sales manager for X Corporation, which transfers its middle management employees frequently.

Comment on the following advice given to R by her brother:

a. Establishing a home office is an effective method for reducing the costs of home ownership by the amount of the tax benefits received.

b. There are no disincentives for claiming the home office deduction.

8-28 *Home Office Computations.* T is employed as a law professor at State University. Outside of her university work she teaches continuing education courses for attorneys and occasionally provides legal services. T does all her work for these outside pursuits in her home office. Income and expenses relating to these were

Income:	
Fees for services	$2,000
Expenses:	
Depreciation on home office furniture and computer	400
Miscellaneous supplies, books, etc.	500
Expenses attributable to home office:	
Depreciation	500
Insurance and utilities	700
Taxes	300
Interest	700

Determine the tax consequences resulting from T's part-time activities.

8-29 *Deductible Moving Expenses.* Indicate whether the following expenses qualify as deductible moving expenses:

a. Costs of meals and lodging while en route to new location.

b. Insurance on household and personal effects being transported—an option provided by the moving company.

c. Costs of driving the family car to new location.

d. Costs of storing items that would not fit in apartment at the new location; the apartment served as a temporary residence until a home was purchased.

e. Costs of new carpeting and wallpaper to prepare old home to be sold.

    f.   Real estate commission on sale of former residence.

    g.   Loss on sale of residence.

    h.   Payment of six months' rent to settle lease obligation at old location; the lease had six more months to run.

    i.   Cost of appraisal of new home required as part of loan application.

8-30 *Moving Expenses: Time Test.* On September 1, 2005, L left her former employment in Indianapolis to seek her fortune in Cincinnati. Indicate whether L could deduct the cost of her moving expenses to Cincinnati under the following conditions.

    a.   L found a teaching job with the public school system for which she worked ten months, September through June. After school was out, L took a three-month vacation. She then decided to leave Cincinnati and move to Atlanta.

    b.   Same as (a) except L found a job as a substitute teacher and was considered self-employed.

    c.   L moved to take a new position as product manager with P&G Corporation. After working three months, she and her new employer had a falling out over what she considered unethical advertising. She quit her job and moved to New York.

8-31 *Moving Expenses: Distance Test.* P is an accountant for L Corporation. This year, his employer moved from its downtown Manhattan location to a new office in New Jersey. As a result, P decided to move to be closer to the office.

    a.   Assuming P did not change jobs, is he allowed to deduct any moving expenses?

    b.   Regardless of your answer to (a), indicate whether P satisfies the distance test in light of the following information:

        – Old office building to new building: 60 miles

        – Old home to new home: 65 miles

        – New home to old office: 51 miles

        – Old home to old office: 30 miles

        – New home to new office: 15 miles

        – Old home to new office: 58 miles

8-32 *Standard Mileage Rate.* R, self-employed, leases her car. She elects to compute her deduction for car expenses using the standard mileage rate. Indicate whether the following expenses may be deducted in addition to expenses computed using the standard rate:

    a.   Depreciation

    b.   Interest on car loan

    c.   Insurance

    d.   Parking while calling on customers

    e.   Parking tickets incurred while on business

    f.   Major overhaul

    g.   Personal property taxes on car

    h.   Tolls

8-33 *Transportation Expenses.* Indicate the amount, if any, deductible by the taxpayer in each of the following cases. (Ignore the floor on miscellaneous itemized deductions.)

    a.   R works in downtown Denver, but chooses to live in the mountains 90 miles away. During the year, he spent $2,700 for transportation expenses to and from work.

    b.   Q, a high school basketball coach, liked to scout his opposition. On one Friday afternoon, he left school and drove 40 miles to attend the game of the team he played next. On the way, he stopped for a meal ($5). He watched the game and returned home.

    c.   R, a carpenter, commutes to work in a truck. He drives the truck in order to carry the tools of his trade. During the year, R's total transportation costs were $5,000.

R estimates that his costs of transportation without the tools would have been $4,000, since he otherwise would have taken public transportation.

d. G, an attorney, works downtown. She is on retainer, however, with a client who has offices two miles from her home. G often stops at the client's office before going to work. The distance between these locations is as follows: home to office, 20 miles; home to client, 2 miles; and client to office, 22 miles. During the year, G drove directly to work 180 days and via the client's office 50 days.

8-34 *Transportation to Temporary Assignments.* For each of the following cases, indicate the number of business miles driven by the taxpayer. (Ignore the floor on miscellaneous itemized deductions.)

a. K is employed as a salesperson for Midwest Surgical Supply Company. The company's offices are in downtown Chicago. K's sales territory is the northwest side of Chicago and the adjacent suburbs. During Monday through Thursday, K drives directly from her residence to call on various customers. She sees each customer about once a month. On Friday of each week, she goes directly from her home to her office downtown to turn in orders, attend the weekly sales meeting, and do any other miscellaneous work. A portion of K's trip diary appears below.

| | | Odometer Reading | | |
Date	Destination	Begin	End	Mileage
3-17	Springmill Clinic	470	482	12
	Dr. J	482	485	3
	Home	485	500	15
3-18	Office	500	530	30
	Home	530	560	30

b. F, an electrician, works for EZ Electrical. He lives and works in the Los Angeles area. For 200 days of this year, he was assigned to do the wiring on a 30-story office building in downtown Los Angeles. His mileage from his home to the building was 20 miles. For 50 days during the year, he was assigned to a job in San Diego. Most of F's assignments are 20 miles closer than San Diego. F commuted 70 miles from his home to San Diego.

8-35 *Travel Expenses.* Indicate the amount, if any, deductible by the taxpayer in each of the following situations. (Ignore the floor on miscellaneous itemized deductions.)

a. P, a steelworker, obtained a job with XYZ Corporation to work on a nuclear reactor 200 miles from his residence. P drove to the site early on Monday mornings and returned home late Friday nights. While at the job site he stayed in a boarding house. P anticipates that the job will last for eight months. During the year, he traveled 4,000 miles in going to and from the job. Other expenses while away from home included the following: meals, $1,000; lodging, $900; and laundry, $75.

b. Same as (a), except P anticipates the job to last for more than a year.

c. W plays professional football for the Minnesota Vikings. He has an apartment in St. Paul but he and his wife's permanent personal residence is in Tucson. During the season, W usually stays in St. Paul. In the off-season he returns to Tucson. Expenses for the year include travel between St. Paul and Tucson, $2,000; apartment in St. Paul, $1,800; meals while in St. Paul, $900.

d. R took a trip to New York primarily for business. R's husband accompanied her. She spent two weeks on business and one week sight-seeing in the city. Her train fare was $400 and meals and lodging cost $30 and $50 per day, respectively. R's husband incurred similar expenses.

e. L flew from Cincinnati to Chicago for $300 round-trip. She spent one day on business and four days shopping and sight-seeing. Her meals and lodging cost $30 and $50 per day, respectively.

8-36 *Car Expense Computation.* E, a salesperson for T Corporation, incurred the following expenses for transportation during the year:

Gas and oil.	$1,200
Repairs	200
Insurance.	700
Interest on car loan	400
Depreciation.	2,000
License	100

In addition, he spent $70 on parking while calling on customers. E drove the car 20,000 miles during the year, 18,000 for business.

a. Compute E's deduction, assuming the standard mileage rate is elected.

b. Compute E's deduction, assuming he claims actual expenses.

8-37 *Travel Outside of the United States.* S, an executive for an automotive company, traveled to Paris this year for business meetings with a European subsidiary. Prior to the trip, she thought that the meetings presented an ideal opportunity for her to vacation in Paris as well as to conduct business. For this reason, she scheduled the trip. S's airfare to Paris was $1,000 and her daily meals and lodging were $30 and $50 respectively. Given the additional facts below, indicate the amount, if any, of the deduction that S may claim.

a. S's trip was primarily business. She spent two days on business (including travel days) and four days sight-seeing.

b. Her itinerary revealed the following:

Thursday May 1:	Depart New York, arrive Paris
Friday, May 2:	Business 9–11 a.m.; remainder of day sight-seeing in Paris
Saturday and Sunday, May 3–4:	Tour French countryside
Monday and Tuesday, May 5–6:	Business 9–5
Wednesday-Sunday, May 7–11:	Tour Germany
Monday, May 12:	Business 9–5
Tuesday, May 13:	Depart Paris, arrive New York

c. Same as (a) except the travel was to Paris for the International Car Exposition, a foreign convention.

d. Same as (a) except the business meetings took place on a luxury liner cruising the Caribbean.

e. Same as (a) except S had no control over arranging the trip.

f. Same as (a) except the trip was primarily personal.

8-38 *Entertainment Expenses.* R is president of X Corporation, a company that manufactures and distributes office supplies. During the year, he and the company incurred various expenses relating to entertainment. In each of the following situations, indicate the amount of the deduction for entertainment expenses. Briefly explain your answer and classify the deduction as either *for* or *from* adjusted gross income. (Assume all the substantiation requirements are satisfied.)

a. R and his wife took a potential customer and his wife to a night club to hear a popular singer. Tickets for the event cost $10 each. R was unable to discuss any business during the evening.

b. After agreeing in the afternoon to supply S's company with typing paper, R took S to a baseball game that evening. Tickets were $8 each. X Corporation reimbursed R $16 for the tickets under an accountable plan.

c. R and S, a client, went to lunch at an expensive restaurant. R paid the bill for both his meal, $30, and S's meal, $40. No business was discussed during lunch.

d. X Corporation purchased a vacation condominium for use primarily by its employees. Expenses relating to the condominium, including depreciation, maintenance, utilities, interest, and taxes, were $7,000.

e. R joined an exclusive country club this year. The membership fee, which is not refundable, was $1,000. In addition, R paid annual dues of $3,600. During the year, R used the club 100 days, 70 days for entertainment directly related to business and 30 days for personal use.

f. R gave one of the company's best customers a $100 bottle of wine.

g. X Corporation gave one of its retailers 1,000 golf balls ($1 each) to distribute for promotional purposes. X Corporation's name was imprinted on the balls.

8-39 *Convention and Seminar Expenses.* Dr. F, a pediatrician, is employed at a hospital located in Chicago. He also operates his own practice. During the year, he attended the following seminars and conventions. In each case, he incurred expenses for registration, travel, meals, and lodging. Indicate whether such expenses would be deductible assuming he attended.

a. "The Care and Feeding of Newborns," a seminar in Honolulu sponsored by the American Family Medical Association.

b. While Dr. F was attending the meeting above, his wife attended a concurrent seminar entitled "Tax Planning for Physicians and their Spouses."

c. "The Economics of a Private Practice: Make Your Investment Count," sponsored by the American Management Corporation in Chicago.

d. "Investing and Inside Information," sponsored by the National Association of Investment Specialists in Orlando.

CUMULATIVE PROBLEM

8-40 George (445-42-5432) and Christina Campbell (993-43-9878) are married with two children, Victoria, 7, and Brad, 2. Victoria and Brad's social security numbers are 446-75-4389 and 449-63-4172, respectively. They live at 10137 Briar Creek Lane, Tulsa, OK 74105. George is the district sales representative for Red Duck, a manufacturer of sportswear. His principal job is to solicit orders of the company's products from department stores in his territory, which includes Oklahoma and Arkansas. The company provides no office for him. Christina is a maker of fine quilts which she sells in selected shops in the surrounding area. The couple uses the cash method of accounting and reports on the calendar year. Their records for the year reveal the following information:

1. George received a salary of $45,000 and a bonus of $5,000. His employer withheld Federal income taxes of $5,000 and the proper amount of FICA taxes.

2. Christina's income and expenses of her quilting business, Crazy Quilts, include

Quilt sales	$7,000
Costs of goods sold	600
Telephone (long-distance calls)	100

Christina makes all of the quilts at home in a separate room that is used exclusively for her work. This room represents 10 percent of the total square footage of their home. Expenses related to operating the entire home include utilities, $2,000; and insurance, $500. Depreciation attributable solely to the home office is $800. Christina computes her deduction relating to use of her car using actual expenses, which included gas and oil, $900; insurance, $300; and repairs, $100. The car is fully depreciated. Her daily diary revealed that, for the year, she had driven the car a total of 20,000 miles, including the following trips:

Trip Description	Miles
Home to sales outlets and return	10,000
Between sales outlets	2,000
Miscellaneous personal trips	8,000

3. George incurs substantial expenses for travel and entertainment, including meals and lodging. He is not reimbursed for these expenses. This is the second year that George has used the standard mileage rate for computing his automobile expenses. During the year he drove 50,000 miles; 40,000 of these were directly related to business. Expenses for parking and tolls directly related to business were $90. Total meal and lodging costs for days that he was out of town overnight were $600 and $1,200, respectively. Entertainment expenses were $400.

4. This is George's second marriage. He has one child, Ted (age 11), from his first marriage to Hazel, who has custody of the child. He provides more than 50 percent of the child's support. The 1983 divorce agreement between George and Hazel provides that George is entitled to the exemption for Ted. George paid Hazel $4,800 during the year, $1,600 as alimony and the remainder as child support. Ted's Social Security number is 122-23-3221.

5. The couple's other income and expenses included the following:

Dividends (IBM stock owned separately by George)	$ 400
Interest on redeemed Treasury bills.	700
Interest on City of Reno bonds	566
Interest paid on home mortgage	10,000
Real property taxes on home.	900
Safety deposit box fee	50

6. Both taxpayers elect to give to the Presidential campaign fund.

Compute the couple's tax liability for the year. If forms are used, complete Form 1040 for the year, including Schedules A, B, C, SE, and Form 2106.

RESEARCH PROBLEMS

8-41   *Travel Away from Home.* M is a traveling salesperson who lives with his family in Cincinnati. His sales territory consists of Indiana, Illinois, and Kentucky. Most of his business, however, is in the Louisville area. For this reason, he normally travels to Louisville weekly and spends three or four days there living in a hotel. He also spends considerable time traveling throughout his territory. M completes the paperwork and other tasks incidental to his work at his home in Cincinnati. M's wife has a good job in Cincinnati and consequently M has never considered moving to Louisville. May M deduct the costs of traveling between his residence in Cincinnati and Louisville (including the costs of meals and lodging while in Louisville)?

8-42   *Business Gifts.* R is product manager for a large pharmaceutical company. At the annual Christmas party, he handed out $50 gifts (checks from his personal account) to each of the 10 employees that work in his division under his supervision. R's group had been highly successful during the year and he felt that each person contributed to the division's profitability. He also gave his secretary $100. What amount, if any, may R deduct?

Chapter 9

CAPITAL RECOVERY: DEPRECIATION, AMORTIZATION, AND DEPLETION

LEARNING OBJECTIVES

Upon completion of this chapter you will be able to:

- Identify the various depreciation methods and accounting conventions available under the Modified Accelerated Cost Recovery System (MACRS)

- Make recommendations concerning the selection of an appropriate depreciation method and accounting convention

- Compute a taxpayer's depreciation deduction under each of the various depreciation methods and accounting conventions

- Explain the depreciation rules for listed property

- Identify property eligible for the election to currently expense rather than depreciate its cost

- Determine the current depletion deduction for various assets

- Explain the options available in selecting the appropriate tax treatment of research and experimentation expenditures

- Recognize tax planning opportunities related to depreciation, amortization, and depletion deductions

CHAPTER OUTLINE

The concept of capital recovery originated with the basic premise that income does not result until revenues exceed the capital expended to produce such revenues. For example, consider the situation where a taxpayer purchases an asset at a cost of $1,000 and subsequently sells it. Generally, the sale produces no income unless the asset is sold for a price exceeding $1,000. This result derives from the principle that the taxpayer first must *recover* his or her $1,000 of capital invested (basis) before he or she can be considered as having income. Here, the recovery occurs as the taxpayer offsets the basis of the asset against the amount realized on the sale. This same principle operates when an asset, instead of being sold and providing a readily identifiable benefit, provides benefits indirectly (e.g., a machine used for many years as part of a process to manufacture a product). In this case, the cost of the asset or the capital invested is *recovered* by offsetting (deducting) the asset's cost against the revenues the asset helps to produce. Thus, in the absence of a sale or other disposition of an asset, capital recovery usually occurs when the taxpayer is permitted to deduct the expenditure. Certain capital expenditures such as research and experimental costs are recovered in the year of the expenditure since the tax law allows immediate deduction. For other types of capital expenditures, the taxpayer is allowed to deduct or recover the cost over the years for which the asset provides benefits.

This chapter examines the various cost allocation methods allowed by the Code. These are depreciation, amortization, and depletion. Although each of these methods relates to a process of allocating the cost of an asset over time, different terms for the same process are used because each method relates to a different type of property. Depreciation concerns *tangible property,* amortization concerns *intangible property,* and depletion concerns *natural resources*. Tangible property means any property having physical existence (i.e., property capable of being touched such as plant, property, and equipment). Conversely, intangible property has no physical existence but exists only in connection with something else, such as the goodwill of a business, stock, patents, and copyrights. There are two types of tangible property: real property and personal property. Real property (or *realty*) is land and anything attached to the land such as buildings, curbs, streets, fences, and other improvements. Personal property is property that is not realty and is usually movable. The concept of personal property or *personalty* should be distinguished from property that a person owns and uses for his or her benefit—usually referred to as *personal-use* property.

In addition to the cost recovery methods mentioned above, this chapter discusses the tax treatment of other capital expenditures such as those for research and experimentation, and certain expenses of farmers.

DEPRECIATION AND AMORTIZATION FOR TAX PURPOSES

GENERAL RULES FOR DEPRECIATION DEDUCTIONS

The Code allows as a depreciation deduction a reasonable allowance for the exhaustion, wear and tear, and obsolescence of property that is either used in a trade or business or held for the production of income.[1] This rule makes it clear that not all capital expenditures for property are automatically eligible for depreciation. Rather, like all other expenditures, only those that satisfy the initial hurdles can be deducted.

Exhaustion, Wear and Tear, and Obsolescence. Only property that wears out or becomes obsolete can be depreciated. As normally construed, this requirement means that depreciation is allowed only for property that has a *determinable life*.[2] Property such as land that does not wear out and that has no determinable life cannot be depreciated. Similarly, works of art cannot be amortized or depreciated since they normally have an indefinite life. In contrast, intangible assets with definite lives, such as patents, copyrights, and licenses that cover a fixed term, can be amortized.

Business or Income-Producing Property. Like other expenses, no deduction is allowed for depreciation unless the property is used in a trade or business or an income-producing activity. Property used for personal purposes cannot be depreciated. In many instances, however, a single asset may be used for *both* personal purposes and profit-seeking activities. In these cases, the taxpayer is permitted to deduct depreciation on the portion of the asset used for business or production of income.

Example 1. N is a salesperson who uses his car for both business and personal purposes. He purchased the car this year for $18,000. During the year, N drove the car 50,000 miles: 40,000 miles for business and 10,000 miles for personal purposes. Under these circumstances, 80% (40,000 ÷ 50,000) of the cost of the car is subject to depreciation in the current year. Note that the business-use percentage may vary from year to year. If so, the depreciation allowed each year will vary accordingly.

Property held for the production of income, even though not currently producing income, may still be depreciated. For example, a duplex held out for rental that is temporarily vacant may still be depreciated for the period during which it is not rented.

---

[1] § 167(a).

[2] Reg. §§ 1.167(a)-2 and 1.167(a)-3.

Similarly, if the taxpayer's trade or business is suspended temporarily, rather than indefinitely, depreciation can be continued despite the suspension of activity.

Depreciable Basis. The basis for depreciation is the adjusted basis of the property as used for computing gain or loss on a sale or other disposition.[3] This is usually the property's cost. Where property used for personal purposes *is converted* to use in business or the production of income, the basis for depreciation purposes is the lesser of the fair market value or the adjusted basis at the time of conversion.[4] This ensures that no deduction is claimed for declines in value while the property was held for personal purposes.

Example 2. R purchased a home computer for $1,000 while attending college. He used it solely for personal purposes. After graduation, R went into the consulting business and began using the computer for business purposes. At the time he converted the computer to business use, its value was $400. R may compute depreciation using a basis of $400 (the lesser of the adjusted basis, $1,000, or its value, $400, at the time of conversion).

Commencement of Depreciation. The date on which depreciation begins can be quite important. Depreciation may not begin until an asset is *placed in service*. This is not necessarily the time when the asset is purchased. According to the Regulations, an asset is placed in service when it is in a "state of readiness and availability for the assigned function" of the activity.[5] For those assets acquired for a new business, the depreciation period starts when the business begins.

Example 3. In 1981, William and Lois Walsh[6] leased a building and immediately began making substantial repairs and improvements to prepare it to open as a restaurant. Although the restaurant did not open until 1982, the couple claimed depreciation deductions in 1981 that were denied by the IRS. At trial, the taxpayers asserted that their restaurant business began in 1981 when they acquired assets for use in the restaurant and executed a lease for the premises. Although the taxpayers purchased the assets in 1981, the court denied the taxpayers' 1981 depreciation deductions. According to the court, the restaurant had not yet begun to function as a going concern and to perform those activities for which it was organized. For this reason, the assets had not been placed in service until the restaurant opened in 1982.

HISTORICAL PERSPECTIVE

Prior to 1981, taxpayers could compute depreciation using either of two approaches: (1) the facts-and-circumstances method or (2) the Class Life System. Depreciation methods such as straight-line, declining balance, and sum-of-the-years'-digits were available for most assets under each system. The facts-and-circumstances method enabled taxpayers to choose useful life and salvage value estimates for depreciable assets based on their experience and judgment of all surrounding facts and circumstances. There were no predetermined or prescribed guidelines. Conflicts often arose between taxpayers and the IRS over useful life selections because taxpayers were motivated to employ short useful lives in order to maximize the present value of tax savings from depreciation deductions.

---

[3]   § 167(g).

[4]   Reg. § 1.167(g)-1.

[5]   Reg. §§ 1.46-3(d)(1) and § 1.167(a)-11(e)(1)(i).

[6]   William J. Walsh, TC Memo 1988-242.

As an alternative to the facts-and-circumstances system, the Class Life System became part of the law in 1971. It was developed primarily to minimize IRS-taxpayer conflicts over useful life estimates. The system prescribed depreciable life ranges for numerous categories of assets. For example, office furniture and fixtures could be depreciated using lives from 8 years to 12 years under the Class Life System.[7] Taxpayers electing this system were not challenged by the IRS. However, IRS-taxpayer conflicts were not eliminated because many taxpayers continued to employ the facts-and-circumstances system, seeking depreciable lives that were shorter than those available with the Class Life System.

In 1981, the facts-and-circumstances system and Class Life System were all but eliminated for assets placed in service after 1980. In the Economic Recovery Tax Act of 1981 (ERTA), Congress substantially revised the method for computing depreciation by enacting Code § 168 and the Accelerated Cost Recovery System (ACRS). Altered several times since 1981, the current version of this system is known as the Modified Accelerated Cost Recovery System (MACRS). An alternative to MACRS, called the Alternative Depreciation System (ADS), is also available.

A major benefit of MACRS and ADS is the elimination of previous areas of dispute between taxpayers and the IRS. Under these systems, the taxpayer is required to choose from a small set of predetermined options regarding depreciable life and depreciation method. Salvage value is ignored in all cases. Thus, depreciation calculations are more uniform for all taxpayers.

It should be emphasized, however, that some assets may not be depreciated using either of these systems. For this reason, the facts-and-circumstances approach and the Class Life System have continuing validity in certain instances.

MODIFIED ACCELERATED COST RECOVERY SYSTEM

AN OVERVIEW OF MACRS

Once it is determined that property is eligible for depreciation, the amount of the depreciation deduction must be computed. Under current law, taxpayers are required to calculate depreciation for most property using the Modified Accelerated Cost Recovery System (MACRS) or what is sometimes referred to as the General Depreciation System or GDS. As suggested earlier, MACRS is a radical departure from traditional approaches to depreciation. Under MACRS, useful lives for assets are termed *recovery periods* and are prescribed by statute. Regardless of the effects of nature and outside forces, each asset is deemed to have a particular useful life of 3, 5, 7, 10, 15, 20, 27.5, or 39 years. In addition, salvage value is ignored under MACRS. By assuming there is no salvage value, taxpayers can depreciate the basis of each asset to zero. With these rules, possibilities for abuse using unrealistic values for useful life and salvage value are essentially eliminated. Finally, certain assumptions—so-called *accounting conventions*—exist regarding about how much depreciation is allowed for the year of acquisition and disposition (e.g., a half-year or something more or less).

The basic machinery of MACRS that is used to compute depreciation can be summarized as follows:

1. The system establishes eight classes or categories of property (e.g., three-year property).

---

7   Rev. Proc. 77-10, 1977-1 C.B. 548.

2. For each class of property, a specific useful life and depreciation method are prescribed (e.g., for three-year property the useful life is three years and either the 200 percent declining-balance or straight-line method must be used).

To actually compute depreciation, taxpayers must first determine when the asset is placed in service, whether the property is subject to MACRS, then—based on the property's classification—determine the applicable method, recovery period, and accounting convention. These elements of the depreciation calculation are discussed below.

PROPERTY SUBJECT TO MACRS

Taxpayers generally must use MACRS to compute depreciation for all *tangible* property, both real and personal, new or used.[8] MACRS is not used to amortize *intangible* assets such as patents or copyrights, which are amortized using the straight-line method. In addition, MACRS may not be used with respect to the following property:[9]

1. Property depreciated using a method that is not based on years (e.g., the units-of production or income forecast methods)

2. Automobiles if the taxpayer has elected to use the standard mileage rate (such an election precludes a depreciation deduction)

3. Property for which special amortization is provided and elected by the taxpayer in lieu of depreciation (e.g., amortization of pollution control facilities)

4. Certain motion picture films, video tapes, sound recordings, and public utility property

5. Generally, any property that the taxpayer—or a party related to the taxpayer—owned or used (e.g., leased) prior to 1987

As a practical matter, MACRS is mandatory for all tangible property. But as explained below, the taxpayer has several alternatives under MACRS, including the option to elect out entirely and use the Alternative Depreciation System. In addition, in lieu of depreciation, the taxpayer may be allowed to expense up to $105,000 annually of certain assets placed in service during the year. Observe, however, that there are no elections available enabling the taxpayer to use the facts-and-circumstances method typically used for financial accounting purposes. Exhibit 9-1 identifies the depreciation methods and accounting conventions available under the MACRS and ADS systems.

---

[8]   § 168(a).

[9]   § 168(f).

EXHIBIT 9-1

Depreciation Methods and Accounting Conventions under MACRS and ADS

8 MACRS Property Classes	Modified Accelerated Cost Recovery System (MACRS): Use MACRS Property Class Life	Alternative Depreciation System (ADS): Use ADS Life	Accounting Convention[1]
3-year, 5-year, 7-year, 10-yr[2]	Choices: 200% DB, 150% DB, or SL[3]	SL	Half-year or mid-quarter
15-year, 20-year	Choices: 150% DB or SL	Choices: 150% DB or SL	Half-year or mid-quarter
Residential rental real estate	27.5 years SL	40 years SL	Mid-month
Nonresidential real estate	39 years SL	40 years SL	Mid-month

Notes:

(1) Taxpayers do *not* have the option of choosing either the half-year or mid-quarter convention. As explained later in this chapter, either the half-year or mid-quarter convention is *required* depending on the timing of asset purchases during the year.

(2) Under certain conditions, $105,000 immediate expensing under Code § 179 is available for most 3-, 5-, 7-, and 10-year assets (i.e., depreciable tangible personal property).

(3) Abbreviations:

DB = declining balance

SL = straight-line

CLASSES OF PROPERTY

As indicated in Exhibit 9-1, all property subject to MACRS is assigned to one of eight classes.[10] Classification is important because the recovery periods, methods, and accounting conventions to be used in calculating depreciation can vary among the different classes of property. Property is assigned to a particular class based on its *class life* as prescribed in Revenue Procedure 87-56.[11] This Revenue Procedure, an excerpt of which is provided in Exhibit 9-2, specifies not only the class lives of various assets but also the recovery periods to be used for both MACRS and ADS. Note that the "General Depreciation System" column of Exhibit 9-2 pertains to MACRS. Exhibit 9-3 provides examples of property in each of the eight MACRS property classes.

In examining Exhibit 9-2, it is important to emphasize that many classes of assets and their descriptions are omitted. Only by examining Revenue Procedure 87-56 can one truly appreciate its scope. Nevertheless, it is impossible to identify the useful life of every asset. For this reason, as can be seen in Exhibit 9-2, Revenue Procedure 87-56 divides assets into two major categories: *Specific Depreciable Assets Being Used in All Business Activities* (such as computers and automobiles) and *Depreciable Assets Used in the Following Activities.* Thus if a particular asset is not assigned a recovery period—a common occurrence, its life is determined by the activity in which it is used.

---

[10] § 168(e).

[11] 1987-2 C.B. 674, as modified by Rev. Proc. 88-22, 1988-1 C.B. 785.

EXHIBIT 9-2
Excerpt from Revenue Procedure 87-56

Asset Class	Description of Assets Included	Class Life (in years)	Recovery Periods (in years) General Depreciation System	Recovery Periods (in years) Alternative Depreciation System
SPECIFIC DEPRECIABLE ASSETS USED IN ALL BUSINESS ACTIVITIES, EXCEPT AS NOTED:				
00.11	**Office Furniture, Fixtures, and Equipment:** Includes furniture and fixtures that are not structural components of a building. Includes such assets as desks, files, safes, and communications equipment. Does not include communications equipment that is included in other classes	10	7	10
00.12	**Information Systems:** Includes computers and their peripheral equipment.	6	5	5
00.13	**Data Handling Equipment, except Computers:** Includes only typewriters, calculators, adding and accounting machines, copiers, and duplicating equipment	6	5	6
00.21	**Airplanes (airframes and engines), except those used in commercial or contract carrying of passengers or freight, and all helicopters (airframes and engines) . .**	6	5	6
00.22	**Automobiles, Taxis**	3	5	5
00.23	**Buses**	9	5	9
00.241	**Light General Purpose Trucks:** Includes trucks for use over the road (actual unloaded weight less than 13,000 pounds)	4	5	5
00.242	**Heavy General Purpose Trucks:** Includes heavy general purpose trucks, concrete readymix trucks, and ore trucks, for use over the road (actual unloaded weight 13,000 pounds or more)	6	5	6

EXHIBIT 9-2
Excerpt from Revenue Procedure 87-56 (continued)

Asset Class	Description of Assets Included	Class Life (in years)	Recovery Periods (in years) General Depreciation System	Recovery Periods (in years) Alternative Depreciation System
	DEPRECIABLE ASSETS USED IN THE FOLLOWING ACTIVITIES:			
01.1	**Agriculture:** Includes machinery and equipment, grain bins, and fences but no other land improvements, that are used in the production of crops or plants, vines, and trees; livestock; the operation of farm dairies, nurseries, greenhouses, sod farms, mushroom cellars, cranberry bogs, apiaries, and fur farms; the performance of agriculture, animal husbandry, and horticultural services.	10	7	10
01.11	**Cotton Ginning Assets**	12	7	12
01.21	**Cattle, Breeding or Dairy**	7	5	7
01.4	**Single-Purpose Agricultural or Horticultural Structures**	15	10	15
15.0	**Construction** Includes assets used in construction by general building, special trade, heavy and marine construction contractors, operative and investment builders, real estate subdividers and developers, and others except railroads.	6	5	6
20.1	**Manufacture of Grain and Grain Mill**	17	10	17
27.0	**Printing, Publishing, and Allied Industries**	11	7	11
36.0	**Manufacture of Electronic Components, Products, and Systems**	6	5	6
37.11	**Manufacture of Motor Vehicles**	12	7	12
39.0	**Manufacture of Athletic, Jewelry and Other Goods:** Includes assets used in the production of jewelry; musical instruments; toys and sporting goods; motion picture and television films and tapes; pens, pencils, office and art supplies, brooms, brushes, caskets, etc.	12	7	12
45.0	**Air Transport**	12	7	12
48.2	**Radio and Television Broadcastings:** Includes assets used in radio and television broadcasting, except transmitting towers	6	5	6
48.42	**CATV-Subscriber Connection and Distribution Systems**	10	7	10
79.0	**Recreation** . . . . Includes assets used in the provision of entertainment services on payment of a fee or admission charge, as in the operation of bowling alleys, billiard and pool establishments, theaters, concert halls, and miniature golf courses. Does not include amusement and theme parks and assets which consist primarily of specialized land improvements or structures, such as golf courses, sports stadia, race tracks, ski slopes, and buildings which house the assets used in entertainment services	10	7	10
		10	7	10
80.0	**Theme and Amusement Parks**	12.5	7	12

Example 4. FunSpot Inc. operates a chain of bowling alleys all over New Jersey. During the year, it purchased furniture, computers, automatic pin-setters, bowling balls and shoes. In determining the recovery period of these assets, the only assets to which a specific life has been assigned are the furniture (Asset Class .11, 7 years) and the computers (Asset Class .12, 5 years). The life of the pin-setters, bowling balls and shoes would be determined based on the activity in which they are used, (Asset Class 80.0, 7 years).

CALCULATING DEPRECIATION

Under MACRS, depreciation is a function of *three* factors: the recovery period, the method, and the accounting convention.

Recovery Periods. As seen in Exhibit 9-1, recovery periods run various lengths of time depending on the class of property.[12] In examining the different classes, several features should be observed. First, certain property is assigned to a class without regard to its class life. The most notable example of this is cars, which are assigned to the five-year class (see asset class 00.22 in Exhibit 9-2). Note also that the current structure provides different recovery periods for real property, depending on whether it is residential (27.5 years) or nonresidential (39 years) real estate. As a result, when a building is used for both residential and nonresidential purposes (e.g., a multilevel apartment building with commercial space on the bottom two floors) it must be classified as one or the other. For this purpose, realty qualifies as residential real estate if 80 percent of the gross rents are for the dwelling units.[13]

EXHIBIT 9-3
Examples of MACRS Property

MACRS Property Class	Examples
3 years	Special tools, race horses, tractors, and property with a class life of 4 years or less
5 years	Automobiles, trucks, computers and peripheral equipment (such as printers, external disk drives, and modems), typewriters, copiers, R&E equipment, and property with a class life of more than 4 years and less than 10 years
7 years	Office furniture, fixtures, office equipment, most machinery, property with a class life of 10 years or more but less than 16 years, and property with no assigned class life
10 years	Single-purpose agricultural and horticultural structures, assets used in petroleum refining and manufacturing of tobacco and certain food products, and property with a class life of 16 years or more but less than 20 years
15 years	Land improvements (such as sidewalks, roads, parking lots, irrigation systems, sewers, fences, and landscaping), service stations, billboards, telephone distribution plants, and property with a class life of 20 years or more but less than 25 years
20 years	Municipal sewers and property with a class life of 25 years or more
27.5 years	Residential rental real estate, including apartment buildings, duplexes, etc.
39 years	Nonresidential real estate, including office buildings, warehouses, factories, and farm buildings

---

[12]   § 168(c).

[13]   § 168(e)(2).

Depreciation Method. The depreciation method to be used—like the recovery period—varies depending on the class of the property. A closer look at Exhibit 9-1, however, reveals that the variation is actually between real and personal property. Real property is depreciated using the straight-line method, while personal property is depreciated using either straight-line or a declining balance method. If a declining-balance depreciation method is elected, a switch to straight-line is made in the first year in which a larger depreciation would result. *Example 5* illustrates this procedure, and the IRS depreciation tables presented later in this chapter incorporate the switch to straight-line.

Accounting Conventions. For assets placed in service or disposed of during the year, an assumption is made regarding the amount of depreciation that is allowed for the year (e.g., a half-year).[14] These assumptions are referred to as depreciation or accounting conventions. The conventions apply only in the years of acquisition and disposition. The applicable convention generally depends on the type of property: realty or personalty. As discussed further below, they are:

Type of Property	Convention
Real property	Mid-month convention
Tangible personal property	Half-year convention
Tangible personal property	Mid-quarter convention

Half-Year Convention. The half-year convention applies to all property *other than* nonresidential real property and residential rental property. From a practical perspective, the half-year convention applies to *all depreciable tangible personal property*. Under the half-year convention, one-half year of depreciation is allowed regardless of when the asset is placed in service or sold during the year (e.g., ½ × the annual depreciation as normally computed).[15] Since only one-half year's depreciation is allowed in the first year, the recovery period is effectively extended one year so that the remaining one-half may be claimed.

Example 5. On March 1, 2005 T purchased a car to be used solely for business for $10,000. It was his only acquisition during the year. The car had an estimated useful life of four years and an estimated salvage value of $2,000. Although these estimates might be used for financial accounting purposes, under MACRS, salvage value is ignored and T is required to use the recovery period, depreciation method, and accounting convention prescribed for five-year property, the class to which cars are assigned under MACRS. T elects to compute his depreciation using the 200% declining-balance method (switching to straight-line where appropriate), a five-year recovery period, and the half-year convention. The 200% declining-balance rate would be 40% (200% × straight-line rate, 15 or 20%). The declining balance method would be used until 2008, when a switch to straight-line maximizes the depreciation deduction. Due to the half-year convention, the cost is actually recovered over six years rather than the five-year recovery period. Depreciation would be computed as follows:

---

[14]   § 168(d).

[15]   § 168(d)(4).

Year	Depreciation Method	Basis for Depreciation Computation	Rate	Depreciation
2005	200% D.B.	$10,000	20%*	$ 2,000
2006	200% D.B.	8,000	40%	3,200
2007	200% D.B.	4,800	40%	1,920
2008	200% D.B.	2,880	40%	1,152**
2009	S.L.	1,730	1.0/1.5	1,152***
2010	S.L.	1,730	0.5/1.5	576
				$10,000

* Half-year allowance (40% × ½ = 20%).

** Note that straight-line depreciation is the same ($2,880 ×2/5).

*** Declining-balance depreciation would have been $692 ($1,730 × 40%); since straight-line depreciation over the remaining 1.5 years is $1,152 and greater than $692, the switch to straight-line is made.

Example 6. Same facts as above except the property was sold on December 20, 2007. In computing depreciation for personal property in the year of sale or disposition, the half-year convention must also be used. Thus, depreciation for 2007 would be $960 ($4,800 × 40% × ½).

To simplify the computation of depreciation, the IRS provides optional tables as shown in Exhibit 9-4 to Exhibit 9-7.[16] The percentages (or rates) shown in the tables are the result of combining the three factors used in determining depreciation—method, rate, and convention—into a single, composite percentage to be used for each class of property.[17]

EXHIBIT 9-4

MACRS Accelerated Depreciation Percentages Using the Half-Year Convention for 3-, 5- and 7-year property

Recovery Year	Property Class		
	3-Year	5-Year	7-Year
1	33.33%	20.00%	14.29%
2	44.45	32.00	24.49
3	14.81	19.20	17.49
4	7.41	11.52	12.49
5		11.52	8.93
6		5.76	8.92
7			8.93
8			4.46

Source: Rev. Proc. 87-57, Table 1.

Appendix C has additional depreciation tables.

---

[16] Rev. Proc. 87-57, 1987-2 C.B. 687.

[17] Depreciation percentages in the tables are rounded to one-hundredth of a percent for recovery property with a recovery period of less than 20 years, and one-thousandth of a percent for all other property. See Rev. Proc. 87-57 *supra*.

Example 7. The depreciation rates shown in Exhibit 9-4 for 5-year property for the year that it is placed in service and for the following year is determined as follows:

Year 1

	Straight-line rate (1/5)	20%
×	Declining-balance rate	× 200%
	200% declining-balance rate	40%
×	Half-year allowance	× ½
	Depreciation rate per table.....................................	20%

Year 2

	Basis of asset remaining (100% − 20%)	80%
×	200% declining-balance rate	× 40%
	Depreciation rate per table.....................................	32%

In studying *Example 7* above, note how the table percentage for the second year, 32 percent, is derived. This percentage takes into account the requirement of the declining-balance method that the annual rate must be applied to the cost of the asset less previous depreciation [i.e., the second-year percentage of 32 percent is the product of the annual rate of 40 percent and the balance of the asset not yet depreciated, 80% (100% − 20%)]. Similarly, the percentages given for declining-balance methods also incorporate a switch to the straight-line method whenever the straight-line rate would yield a higher depreciation amount. Because these various considerations are already reflected in the tables, depreciation is computed by simply applying the appropriate percentage to the *unadjusted basis* of the property. The general formula for computing depreciation can be expressed as follows.

Unadjusted basis of the property × Recovery percentage = Annual depreciation

Example 8. Same facts as in *Example 5*. Depreciation computed using the table in Exhibit 9-4 would be the same as above, computed as follows:

Year	Unadjusted Basis	×	Accelerated Recovery Percentage	Annual Depreciation
2005	$10,000		20.00%	$ 2,000
2006	10,000		32.00	3,200
2007	10,000		19.20	1,920
2008	10,000		11.52	1,152
2009	10,000		11.52	1,152
2010	10,000		5.76	576
			100.00%	$10,000

Example 8 illustrates the basic steps necessary to compute annual depreciation. These steps are as follows:

1. Identify the *depreciable basis* of the asset (generally its cost): $10,000 in *Example 8*

2. Determine the MACRS *property class:* five-year property in *Example 8*

3. Identify the *depreciation convention* (either half-year or mid-quarter for personal property; mid-month for real estate): half-year convention in *Example 8*

4. Determine the *recovery period* and *method*. See Exhibit 9-1 for a summary of the available choices: five-year 200 percent declining balance in *Example 8*

5. Locate the *appropriate table* based on the depreciation convention, recovery period, and method: Exhibit 9-4 for *Example 8* (Note the depreciation convention is already reflected in the table percentages for the year of acquisition, but *not* for the year of disposition.)

6. Choose the *table percentages* relating to the recovery period of the asset: five-year property percentages for *Example 8* (i.e., 20 percent, 32 percent, etc.).

7. Multiply the table percentages by the depreciable (cost) basis of the asset to *compute annual depreciation* amounts: $10,000 multiplied by 20 percent provides $2,000 of depreciation for 2005 in *Example 8*

When using the depreciation tables, a special adjustment must be made if there is a disposition of the property before its cost is fully recovered. As noted above, under the half-year convention the taxpayer is entitled only to a half-year of depreciation in the year of disposition. Therefore, where the half-year convention applies and the property is used for only a portion of the disposition year, only one-half of the amount of depreciation determined using the table is allowed.

Example 9. Same facts as *Example 8* except the taxpayer sold the property on December 1, 2007. Since the taxpayer did not hold the property the entire taxable year and the half-year convention is in effect, only one-half of the amount of depreciation using the table is allowed. Therefore, depreciation for 2007 would have been $960 ($10,000 × 19.2% × ½). Note that this is the same result as obtained in *Example 6* above.

Mid-Month Convention. This convention applies only to real property (i.e., nonresidential real property and residential rental property).[18] Under the mid-month convention, one-half month of depreciation is allowed for the month the asset is placed in service or sold and a full month of depreciation is allowed for each additional month of the year that the asset is in service.[19] For example, if a calendar year taxpayer places a building in service on April 3, the fraction of the annual depreciation allowed is 8.5/12 (half-month's depreciation for April and eight months' depreciation for May through December).

Example 10. The first-year depreciation rate for residential rental realty that is placed in service in April is determined as follows:

Straight-line rate (1/27.5)	3.636%
× Mid-month convention	×8.5/12
Depreciation rate per table	2.576%

Due to the mid-month convention, the recovery period must be extended one month to claim the one-half month of depreciation that was not claimed in the first month. For example, the entire cost of residential rental property is recovered over 331 months (27½ years is 330 months + 1 additional month to claim the half-month of depreciation not claimed in the first month). As a result, depreciation deductions are actually claimed over either 28 or 29 years depending on the month in which the property was placed in

---

[18]   § 168(d)(2).

[19]   § 168(d)(4)(B).

service. This can be seen by examining the composite depreciation percentages for real property reflecting the mid-month convention given in Exhibit 9-5 and Exhibit 9-6.

EXHIBIT 9-5
MACRS Depreciation Percentages for Residential Rental Property

Month Placed in Service	Recovery Year					
	1	2	3-26	27	28	29
1	3.485%	3.636%	3.636%	3.636%	1.970%	0.000%
2	3.182	3.363	3.636	3.636	2.273	0.000
3	2.879	3.636	3.636	3.636	2.576	0.000
4	2.576	3.636	3.636	3.636	2.879	0.000
5	2.273	3.636	3.636	3.636	3.182	0.000
6	1.970	3.636	3.636	3.636	3.485	0.000
7	1.667	3.636	3.636	3.637	3.636	0.152
8	1.364	3.636	3.636	3.637	3.636	0.455
9	1.061	3.636	3.636	3.637	3.636	0.758
10	0.758	3.636	3.636	3.637	3.636	1.061
11	0.455	3.636	3.636	3.637	3.636	1.364
12	0.152	3.636	3.636	3.637	3.636	1.667

Source: IRS Publication No. 534. Appendix C of this book has additional depreciation tables.

EXHIBIT 9-6
MACRS Depreciation Percentages for Nonresidential Real Property Placed in Service after May 12, 1993

Month Placed in Service	Recovery Year		
	1	2–39	40
1	2.461%	2.564%	0.107%
2	2.247	2.564	0.321
3	2.033	2.564	0.535
4	1.819	2.564	0.749
5	1.605	2.564	0.963
6	1.391	2.564	1.177
7	1.177	2.564	1.391
8	0.963	2.564	1.605
9	0.749	2.564	1.819
10	0.535	2.564	2.033
11	0.321	2.564	2.247
12	0.107	2.564	2.461

Source: IRS Publication No. 534.
Appendix C of this book has additional depreciation tables.

Example 11. S purchased a duplex as an investment for $110,000 on July 17, 2005. Of the $110,000 cost, $10,000 is allocated to the land. The estimated useful life of the duplex is 30 years—the same period as her mortgage—and the estimated salvage value is $15,000. Despite these estimates, under MACRS salvage value is ignored and S is required to use the recovery period, depreciation method, and convention prescribed for residential rental property, the class to which the duplex is assigned. Therefore, S uses a 27.5-year life, the straight-line method, and the mid-month convention. Using the table in Exhibit 9-5, depreciation for the first year would be $1,667 ($100,000 × 1.667%).

When using the depreciation tables, an adjustment must be made if there is a disposition of the real property before its cost is fully recovered. This adjustment is similar to that required where the half-year convention applies, but not identical. In the year of disposition, the taxpayer may deduct depreciation only for those months the property is used by the taxpayer. In addition, under the mid-month convention, the taxpayer is entitled to only a half-month of depreciation for the month of disposition.

> **Example 12.** Same facts as *Example 11* except the taxpayer sold the property on May 22, 2007. Depreciation for 2006 would be $1,363 ($100,000 × 3.636% × 4.5/12).

Mid-Quarter Convention. The mid-quarter convention applies only to *personal property*. However, it applies only if more than 40 percent of the aggregate bases of all personal property placed in service during the taxable year is placed in service during the last three months of the year.[20] Property placed in service and disposed of during the same taxable year is not taken into account. Also not taken into account is any amount immediately expensed under § 179 (discussed below) or property used for personal purposes. If the 40 percent test is satisfied, the mid-quarter convention applies to *all* personal property placed in service during the year (regardless of the quarter in which it was actually placed in service).

> **Example 13.** During the year, K Company, a calendar year taxpayer, acquired and placed in service the following assets:
>
> | Assets | Acquisition Date | Cost |
> | --- | --- | --- |
> | Office furniture | March 28 | $20,000 |
> | Machinery | October 9 | 80,000 |
> | Warehouse | February 1 | 90,000 |
>
> Of the total *personal* property placed in service during the year, more than 40% [$80,000 ÷ ($20,000 + $80,000)] occurred in the last quarter (i.e., October through December). As a result, K must use the mid-quarter convention for computing the depreciation of both the furniture and the machinery.

When applicable, the mid-quarter convention treats all personal property as being placed in service in the middle of the quarter of the taxable year in which it was actually placed in service.[21] Therefore, one-half of a quarter's depreciation—in effect one-eighth (½ × ¼) or 12.5 percent of the annual depreciation—is allowed for the quarter that the asset is placed in service or sold. In addition, a full quarter's depreciation is allowed for each additional quarter that the asset is in service. For example, personal property placed in service on March 3 would be treated as having been placed in service in the middle of the first quarter and the taxpayer would be able to claim 3½ quarters—3.5/4 or 87.5 percent—of the annual amount of depreciation. The percentages of the annual depreciation allowed under the mid-quarter convention for a year in which an asset is placed in service are

	Quarter Placed in Service			
	First January–March	Second April–June	Third July–September	Fourth October–December
Percentage of annual depreciation allowed	87.5%	62.5%	37.5%	12.5%

---

[20] § 168(d)(3).

[21] *Ibid.*

The above chart illustrates that where an asset is placed in service in the first quarter and the mid-quarter convention applies, the taxpayer is allowed to deduct 87.5 percent of the annual depreciation. In contrast, for personal property placed in service during the fourth quarter only 12.5 percent of the annual depreciation may be deducted. Note that the recovery period must be extended by one year so that the balance of the depreciation not claimed in the first year may be deducted. Composite depreciation percentages to be used for 3-year and 5-year property where the mid-quarter convention applies are provided in Exhibit 9-7. Appendix C has depreciation tables for all categories of personal property under the mid-quarter convention.

EXHIBIT 9-7
MACRS Accelerated Depreciation Percentages Using the Mid-Quarter Convention for 3- and 5-Year Property

3-Year Property:

	Quarter Placed in Service			
Recovery Year	1	2	3	4
1	58.33%	41.67%	25.00%	8.33%
2	27.78	38.89	50.00	61.11
3	12.35	14.14	16.67	20.37
4	1.54	5.30	8.33	10.19

5-Year Property:

1	35.00	25.00	15.00	5.00
2	26.00	30.00	34.00	38.00
3	15.60	18.00	20.40	22.80
4	11.01	11.37	12.24	13.68
5	11.01	11.37	11.30	10.94
6	1.38	4.26	7.06	9.58

Source: Rev. Proc. 87-57. Appendix C has additional depreciation tables.

Example 14. In 2005 T, a calendar year taxpayer, purchased five trucks to use in his business at a cost of $20,000 each. These purchases were his only acquisitions of personal property during the year. Four of the trucks were purchased in December while the other truck was purchased in January. Since more than 40% of the property placed in service during the year was placed in service in the last quarter ($80,000 ÷ $100,000 = 80%), the mid-quarter convention applies in computing depreciation. Thus, the depreciation allowed on the truck purchased in January would be limited to 87.5% of a full year's depreciation, and the depreciation allowed on the three trucks purchased in December would be limited to 12.5% of a full year's depreciation. Since a full year's depreciation would be 40% of cost (straight-line rate of 20% per year × 200% declining-balance = 40%), the depreciation for the January purchase would be limited to 35% of cost (40% × 87.5%), or $7,000 (35% × $20,000). Similarly, the depreciation for the December purchases would be limited to 5% of cost (40% × 12.5%), or $4,000 (5% × $80,000). Total depreciation under the mid-quarter convention is limited to $11,000 ($4,000 + $7,000). These amounts are easily computed using the tables in Exhibit 9-7.

Note that had the mid-quarter convention not applied, the depreciation percentage would have been 20%—reflecting the half-year allowance for 5-year property (40% × ½ = 20%), or $20,000 ($100,000 × 20%). Due to the timing of the acquisitions, T's depreciation for the year is reduced by $9,000 ($20,000 − $11,000).

When using the depreciation tables, a special adjustment must be made if there is a disposition of the property before its cost is fully recovered. This adjustment is similar to that for the half-year and mid-month conventions. As noted above, under the mid-quarter convention, the taxpayer is entitled to only one-half of a quarter's depreciation—in effect one-eighth ($\frac{1}{2} \times \frac{1}{4}$) or 12.5 percent of the annual depreciation—for the quarter that the asset is sold. In addition, a full quarter of depreciation is allowed for each quarter that the asset is in service. For example, if property was sold on August 2, the taxpayer could claim 2½ quarters—2.5/4 or 62.5 percent—of the annual amount of depreciation. The percentages of annual depreciation allowed under the mid-quarter convention for the year an asset is sold are

	Quarter Property Sold			
	First	Second	Third	Fourth
	January–March	April–June	July–September	October–December
Percentage of annual depreciation allowed ..	12.5%	37.5%	62.5%	87.5%

Example 15. Same facts as in *Example 14* above, except the truck acquired in January 2005 was sold on August 9, 2007. Since T did not hold the property the entire taxable year and the mid-quarter convention is in effect, only 62.5% of the amount of depreciation using the table is allowed. Therefore, using the table in Exhibit 9-7, T's depreciation for this truck would have been $1,950 ($20,000 × 15.6% × 62.5%).

OTHER METHODS

The accelerated depreciation methods prescribed by MACRS are normally desirable since they allow taxpayers to recover their costs more rapidly than the straight-line method. However, there may be circumstances where the slower-paced straight-line method may be more advantageous. For example, if the taxpayer is currently in the 10 or 15 percent tax bracket, he or she may want to defer depreciation deductions to years when he or she is in a higher tax bracket. By doing this, the taxpayer may be able to maximize the present value of the tax savings from depreciation deductions (depending upon the taxpayer's discount rate).

Perhaps a more common reason for using straight-line depreciation concerns the alternative minimum tax (AMT). As discussed briefly in Chapter 3 and in detail in Chapter 13, the AMT is an alternative system for computing the tax, using certain modifications. For AMT purposes, depreciation is generally computed using a method slower than MACRS (e.g., 150% rather than 200% declining balance). This difference can lead to an AMT liability. To avoid this, taxpayers often elect to use a straight-line method for regular tax purposes. If a taxpayer elects to use the straight-line method in lieu of the accelerated method, two different approaches are available: straight-line under MACRS, or straight-line under ADS.

MACRS Straight-Line. Although it may seem inconsistent, the *Modified Accelerated Cost Recovery System* offers taxpayers a straight-line method of depreciation.[22] If the taxpayer so elects, the straight line method is used in conjunction with all of the other rules that normally apply under MACRS; that is, the taxpayer simply uses the straight-line method (in lieu of the accelerated method) along with the applicable recovery period and accounting convention. The depreciation percentages to be used where the taxpayer elects the straight-line method are contained in Exhibit 9-8 (half-year convention property) for 3-, 5-, and 7-year property. Appendix C has straight-line depreciation tables for all categories of personal property under the half-year

---

[22]   § 168(b)(3)(C).

convention. The depreciation percentages for the straight-line method when the mid-quarter convention applies can be found in Revenue Procedure 87-57.[23]

> **Example 16.** On June 1, 2005 L purchased 5-year property (to which the half-year convention applies) for $50,000. Using the table in Exhibit 9-8, depreciation for the year would be $5,000 ($50,000 × 10%). Depreciation for 2006 would be $10,000 (20% × $50,000). If L sold the property on January 22, 2007, depreciation would be $5,000 ($50,000 × 20% × ½).

EXHIBIT 9-8
MACRS and ADS Straight-Line Depreciation Percentages Using the Half-Year Convention for 3-, 5-, and 7-year Property

Recovery Year	Property Class		
	3-Year	5-Year	7-Year
1	16.67%	10.00%	7.14%
2	33.33	20.00	14.29
3	33.33	20.00	14.29
4	16.67	20.00	14.28
5		20.00	14.29
6		10.00	14.28
7			14.29
8			7.14

Source: Rev. Proc. 87-57

Appendix C has additional depreciation tables.

The election to use the straight-line method is made annually by class (recall the straight-line method must be used for realty). For example, if in 2005 the taxpayer makes the election for 7-year property, *all* 7-year property placed in service during the year must be depreciated using the straight-line method. The election does not obligate the taxpayer to use the straight-line method for any other class. Similarly, the taxpayer need not use the straight-line method for such class of assets placed in service in the following year.

Alternative Depreciation System. The Alternative Depreciation System (ADS) is an option for taxpayers.[24] This system is similar to MACRS in two ways: salvage value is ignored, and the same averaging conventions must be followed. The major differences between MACRS and ADS are the longer recovery periods provided by ADS for most assets and in some cases, slower rates of depreciation. The recovery period to be used for ADS is normally the property's class life. The class life—which is usually longer than the MACRS life—is used unless no class life has been prescribed for the property or a specific class life has been designated in Code § 168. For example, as shown in Exhibit 9-2, the ADS class life for copiers (asset class 00.13) is six years, whereas the MACRS life is five years. Thus, depreciation under ADS would be computed using a six-year life, whereas depreciation for MACRS would be computed using a five-year life. The recovery periods to be used for ADS are summarized in Exhibit 9-9.

Taxpayers electing ADS for real property are restricted to straight-line depreciation. Thus, an office building (nonresidential real property) would be depreciated using straight-line and a 40-year recovery period under ADS. The ADS depreciation percentages for real property are found in Exhibit 9-10.

---

[23]   1987-2 C.B. 687.

[24]   § 168(g).

In contrast, either straight-line or 150 percent declining balance depreciation may be chosen for depreciable tangible personal property. The ADS straight-line depreciation percentages for such property, which in fact have class lives of three, five and seven years, are the same as those for MACRS straight-line and can be found in Exhibit 9-8.

EXHIBIT 9-9

Alternative Depreciation System Recovery Periods

General Rule: Recovery period is the property's class life unless
1. There is no class life (see below), or
2. A special class life has been designated (see below).

Type of Property	Recovery Period
Personal property with no class life	12 years
Nonresidential real property with no class life	40 years
Residential rental property with no class life	40 years
Cars, light general-purpose trucks, certain technological equipment, and semiconductor manufacturing equipment	5 years
Computer-based telephone central office switching equipment	9.5 years
Railroad track	10 years
Single-purpose agricultural or horticultural structures	15 years
Municipal wastewater treatment plants, telephone distribution plants	24 years
Low-income housing financed by tax-exempt bonds	27.5 years
Municipal sewers	50 years

EXHIBIT 9-10

ADS Straight-Line Depreciation Percentages for Real Property Using the Mid-Month Convention

Month Placed in Service	Recovery Year		
	1	2–40	41
1	2.396%	2.500%	0.104%
2	2.188	2.500	0.312
3	1.979	2.500	0.521
4	1.771	2.500	0.729
5	1.563	2.500	0.937
6	1.354	2.500	1.146
7	1.146	2.500	1.354
8	0.938	2.500	1.562
9	0.729	2.500	1.771
10	0.521	2.500	1.979
11	0.313	2.500	2.187
12	0.104	2.500	2.396

Source: Rev. Proc. 87-57, Table 13.

Taxpayers have as many as four options for depreciating personal property—straight line or accelerated depreciation over the MACRS recovery period, or straight line over a longer ADS recovery period. Accelerated depreciation options are 200 percent or 150 percent declining balance. For example, the ADS option for a copier consists of straight-line over six years. The MACRS alternatives allow for a five-year write-off using either 200 percent or 150 percent declining balance or straight line. Which of these four choices would be best for depreciating the typewriter? In general, the taxpayer should select the depreciation method that maximizes the present value of tax savings from depreciation deductions. For taxpayers who expect their future marginal tax rate to either remain constant or decline, the fastest depreciation method over the shortest time period will maximize the present value of tax savings from depreciation.

The mechanics of the election to use ADS—except for real property—are identical to those of MACRS discussed above. Except for real property, the taxpayer may elect to use ADS on a class-by-class, year-by-year basis.[25] For realty, the election is made on a property-by-property basis. In addition, the taxpayer *must* use ADS straight-line for depreciating the following:[26]

- Certain "listed property" that is not used predominately for business (see discussion below)
- Foreign use property (i.e., property used outside the U.S. more than half of a taxable year)
- Property leased to a tax-exempt entity
- Property leased to foreign persons (unless more than 50 percent of the income is subject to U.S. tax)
- Property financed by the issuance of tax-exempt bonds (i.e., tax-exempt bond-financed property).

ADS is also used for computing depreciation for purposes of the alternative minimum tax (discussed in Chapter 13) and a corporation's earnings and profits (discussed in Chapter 20).

CHANGES IN DEPRECIATION

There are many situations where the taxpayer incorrectly computes depreciation, resulting in too much or too little depreciation. For example, a corporation may discover it mistakenly classified an asset initially and the wrong recovery period was used. Similarly, the IRS may change the recovery period of an asset. For example, in 2003, the Service ruled that the life of canopies at gas stations that protect the pumps and customers from inclement weather are five-year rather than 15-year property.[27] When the taxpayer is entitled to additional depreciation, the IRS permits a change in accounting method and the taxpayer may deduct all of the unclaimed depreciation for years that are closed by the statute of limitations as well as open years. This is normally done through a § 481(a) adjustment that reduces income in the year of the change (a single year adjustment).[28] If the adjustment increases the taxpayer's income, the increase is normally spread over four years.

✅ CHECK YOUR KNOWLEDGE

Review Question 1. Indicate whether the following statements concerning tax depreciation are true or false.

a. During the year, Mr. L purchased a computer that he uses to track how his stocks and bonds are doing. L can depreciate the computer even though it is not used in a trade or business.

---

[25]   § 168(g)(7).

[26]   § 168(g)(1).

[27]   Rev. Rul. 2003-54, 2003-23 I.R.B. 982.

[28]   Rev. Proc. 96-31, 1996-1 C.B. 714. But see *Brookshire Brothers Holding, Inc.*, 320 F.3d 507 (CA-5, 2003) where the court held that it was not a change in accounting method and the government was barred from reducing depreciation in closed years. See also *Green Forest Manufacturing Inc.*, T.C. Memo 2003-75.

True. An asset generally may be depreciated to the extent that it is used in a trade or business or an income-producing activity. Since the computer is used to monitor investments, an income-producing activity, it is depreciable. Thus if L uses the computer 30 percent of the time to monitor his stocks and bonds and 70 percent for playing solitaire (i.e., personal use), 30 percent of the cost of the computer could be depreciated.

b. Land and goodwill are never depreciable or amortizable since neither has a determinable life

False. Assets without a determinable life normally cannot be depreciated or amortized. Under normal circumstances, neither of these assets would be considered as having a determinable life and, therefore, neither could be depreciated. However, § 197 of the Code creates a specific exception to this rule for goodwill, allowing taxpayers to amortize goodwill over 15 years. Land normally is not depreciable.

c. This year Z Corporation purchased a new car to be used in its business. For financial accounting purposes, the company computed depreciation assuming the car had an estimated useful life of three years and an approximate salvage value of $1,000. In computing depreciation for tax purposes, the company will also use a three-year life and a salvage value of $1,000.

False. The computation of tax depreciation ignores the asset's actual useful life and salvage value. For tax purposes, a car is deemed to have a five-year life and salvage value is always ignored. Note that because different depreciation methods are used annual depreciation for financial accounting will normally differ from tax depreciation.

Review Question 2. In November of this year, Park and Ride Inc., a calendar year taxpayer, purchased five new vans to use in its limousine service for $100,000. In February, the company closed on the acquisition of a new maintenance facility. Indicate whether the following are true or false.

a. Assuming the cost of the maintenance facility was $50,000, the corporation must use the mid-quarter convention to depreciate the facility.

False. The mid-quarter convention applies only to personal property and not realty. The mid-month convention must be used in computing depreciation for realty. The mid-quarter convention must be used for the vans.

b. Assuming the cost of the maintenance facility was $500,000, the corporation must use the *half-year* convention in depreciating the vans.

False. The mid-quarter convention applies if more than 40 percent of the *personal property* placed in service during the year is placed in service during the last three months. For purposes of making this calculation, only personal property—the vans—is considered and the realty (i.e., the maintenance facility) is ignored. Moreover, any personal property that is expensed under § 179 (discussed below) is also ignored. In this case, all of the personal property was placed in service during the last quarter of the year and, therefore, the corporation must use the mid-quarter convention.

Review Question 3. During the year, C Corporation purchased equipment that qualifies as five-year property. Due to other purchases of personal property during the year, the mid-quarter convention must be used in computing depreciation. Compute the first-and second-year depreciation rates that should be used assuming the asset was placed in service in February. Check your answers by using the table in Exhibit 9-7.

The depreciation rates are 35 percent for the first year and 26 percent for the second year, which are computed as follows:

Year 1:

	Straight-line rate (1/5)	20%
×	Declining-balance rate.	×200%
	200% declining-balance annual rate	40%
	Mid-quarter percentage	×87.5%
		35%

Year 2:

	Basis of asset remaining (100% − 35%)	65%
×	200% declining-balance annual rate	×40%
	Depreciation rate per table.	26%

Review Question 4. On February 15 of this year, K Corporation purchased a warehouse for $250,000 ($50,000 allocable to the land). For financial accounting purposes, the building is treated as having a 40-year life and a salvage value of $20,000.

a. Compute the depreciation deduction for the year.

Depreciation for the year is $4,494 as computed below. Note that the useful life and the salvage value that are used for financial accounting purposes are irrelevant for tax purposes.

	Unadjusted basis of the building	$200,000
×	Recovery percentage for month placed in service (February) . .	×2.247%
	Depreciation.	$4,494

b. Assuming the corporation sold the building on March 10 of the following year, compute the depreciation deduction for the year.

	Unadjusted basis of the building	$200,000
×	Recovery percentage for second year.	×2.564%
×	Mid-month convention in year of disposition	×2.5/12
	Depreciation.	$1,068

LIMITED EXPENSING ELECTION: CODE § 179

When Congress introduced ACRS in 1981, it also created § 179. This provision allows taxpayers (other than estates or trusts) to *elect* to treat the cost of qualifying property as a currently deductible expense rather than a capital expenditure subject to depreciation. Initially, the maximum amount that could be expensed under § 179 was $5,000. Over the years, Congress has gradually increased that amount and in 2005 it is $105,000 (adjusted annually for inflation). This measure was intended primarily to stimulate investment; however, its corollary effect was to eliminate the need for maintaining depreciation records where the taxpayer's annual acquisitions were not substantial.

Although the maximum amount that can be expensed by a taxpayer is $105,000 for 2005, two limitations may restrict the amount that the taxpayer may otherwise expense:

1. *Acquisitions of Eligible Property Exceeding $420,000.* Where the aggregate cost of *qualifying* property placed in service during the year exceeds $420,000 (in 2005), the $105,000 amount must be reduced $1 for each $1 of cost in excess of $420,000. For example, taxpayers purchasing $431,000 of property could expense up to $94,000 of the cost while taxpayers purchasing in excess of $525,000 ($420,000 + $105,000) could not benefit from § 179 at all.

2. *Taxable Income Limitation.* The deduction under § 179 cannot exceed the amount of taxable income derived from all of the taxpayer's trades or businesses (including wage income).[29] Any amount that cannot be deducted can be carried over indefinitely to following years to be used against future income. The $105,000 maximum amount that can be expensed in subsequent years is not increased by the carryover amount, however. Rather than carry over the amount that could not be expensed because of the taxable income limitation, the taxpayer has the option of not reducing the property's basis by the carryover amount so it can be depreciated along with the rest of the property's cost.

As explained later in this chapter, additional limitations on the use of § 179 apply in the case of luxury automobiles, sports utility vehicles (SUVs) and "listed" property.

The taxpayer may elect to expense all or a portion of an asset so long as the total amount expensed does not exceed the dollar limitation. If only a portion of an asset is expensed, the remaining portion is subject to depreciation.

> **Example 17.** T Corporation purchased 5-year property for $100,000 and 7-year property for $155,000 during the current year. Both assets are eligible to be expensed subject to the limitations of § 179. Assume T expects its future marginal tax rate to remain constant. To maximize the present value of the tax savings from limited expensing and depreciation deductions, T should expense $105,000 of the 7-year property rather than the 5-year property since the cost of the 5-year property could be recovered more quickly, thus resulting in higher depreciation deductions in the current year. Assuming T elects to expense $105,000 of the 7-year property, its deduction for such property would be $112,145 computed as follows:

	Original cost.	$ 155,000	
−	Expensed portion.	−105,000	$105,000
	Remaining depreciable basis.	$ 50,000	
×	Depreciation percentage	× 14.29%	
	Depreciation deduction	$ 7,145	7,145
	Total deduction		$112,145

> In addition, the taxpayer could claim a deduction for *depreciation* of the 5-year property.

Assume these two assets were the only depreciable assets T purchased during the year. Further assume that the five-year property was purchased in August (the third quarter of the year) and the seven-year property was purchased in November (the fourth quarter of the year). If immediate expensing had *not* been elected, T would be required

---

[29] Taxable income is computed with § 1231 gains and interest from working capital but not deductions allowable for § 179, one half of self-employment tax, net operating loss carrybacks or carryforwards and deductions suspended under other Code sections (e.g., passive losses, partnership or S corporation losses limited for lack of basis). Note that taxable income presumably reflects depreciation for the § 179 property without considering § 179. [See § 179(b)(3)(C) and Reg. § 1.179-2(c)(1) and -(2)(c)(5)].

to use the mid-quarter convention for both assets since more than 40 percent of the cost was placed in service during the fourth quarter [$155,000 is about 60% of $255,000 ($100,000 + $155,000)]. Because T expenses $105,000 of the $155,000 asset, the cost of the asset placed in service in the fourth quarter is deemed to be $50,000, not $155,000. Thus, the mid-quarter convention is avoided and the taxpayer can maximize depreciation for the year using the half-year convention.

Eligible Property. Only property that satisfies certain requirements is eligible for expensing. To qualify, the property may be new or used and must be[30]

1. Recovery property;

2. Property that would have qualified for the investment credit (e.g., most property other than buildings and their components);

3. Property used in a trade or business, as distinguished from property held for the production of income; and

4. Property acquired by purchase from someone who is generally not a "related party" under § 267 (e.g., gifted or inherited property usually does not qualify nor would property acquired from a spouse or parent).

Certain property is designated as *ineligible* for expensing. Such property includes

1. Property used predominantly to furnish lodging or in connection with furnishing lodging unless the business is a hotel or motel that provides accommodations used primarily by transients. Presumably, this rule prohibits taxpayers who provide long-term rentals (e.g., apartments, duplexes, etc.) from expensing such items as furniture and appliances.

2. Air conditioning and heating units;

3. Property that is primarily used by a tax-exempt organization; and

4. Property used outside the U.S. (But there are a number of exceptions).

Recapture. Without any special rule, taxpayers could use an asset in business for a short period (e.g., one day), expense it for tax purposes, then convert it to nonbusiness use. To prohibit this possible abuse, a special rule applies. If the property is converted to *nonbusiness* use *at any time*, the taxpayer must *recapture* the benefit derived from expensing.[31] Recapture requires the taxpayer to *include* in income the difference between the amount expensed and the MACRS deductions that would have been allowed for the actual period of business use.

Example 18. On January 1, 2005 F purchased a computer for $5,000. He used it for business for one year, then gave it to his teenage son as a graduation present and bought himself another computer. F may expense the entire $5,000 cost of the computer. However, in 2006 he must recapture and include in income the difference between the expensed amount and the deduction computed under MACRS, $4,000 [$5,000 expensed − MACRS deduction of $1,000 ($5,000 × 20%)]. Note that the net effect in this case is to allow F a deduction equal to what he otherwise could have claimed under MACRS, $1,000.

---

[30] §§ 179(d)(1) and (2).

[31] § 179(d)(10).

ADDITIONAL FIRST-YEAR DEPRECIATION ALLOWANCE (BONUS DEPRECIATION)

For new property placed in service after September 10, 2001 and before January 1, 2005, the law permitted taxpayer's to claim additional first-year depreciation (30% or 50 percent of the cost depending on when the asset was placed in service). This provision terminated at the close of 2004 and is no longer available except for certain noncommercial aircraft.

LIMITATIONS FOR AUTOMOBILES

Over the years, Congress has become more and more concerned about taxpayers who effectively use the benefits of the tax law to reduce the cost of what are essentially personal expenses. For example, a taxpayer may justify the purchase of a luxury rather than standard automobile on the grounds that the government is helping to defray the additional cost through tax deductions and credits allowed for the purchase. In 1984 Congress enacted Code § 280F to reduce the benefits of depreciation and limited expensing for certain automobiles and other properties that are often used partially for personal purposes. In addition, the record keeping requirements for travel and entertainment were tightened and extended to certain property used for personal purposes.

Section 280F sets forth a special set of limitations for *passenger automobiles*. A passenger automobile is defined as any four-wheeled vehicle manufactured primarily for use on public streets, roads, and highways that weighs 6,000 pounds or less unloaded. For purposes of § 280F, the term *passenger automobiles* does not include vehicles for hire, such as taxis, rental trucks, and rental cars.[32] Ambulances and hearses directly used in a trade or business are also unaffected by the § 280F limitations. Temporary regulations create certain exceptions to the definition of passenger automobile. Excluded is any "qualified nonpersonal use vehicle" defined as any vehicle which, by reason of its nature (i.e., design or modification), is not likely to be used more than a *de minimis* amount for personal purposes.[33] This category would include police and fire vehicles, ambulances, qualified moving vans, and delivery and utility repair trucks.

For passenger automobiles, § 280F generally imposes a ceiling on the amount of annual depreciation and first-year expensing deductions. The *maximum* depreciation and/or § 179 expense for autos is shown in Exhibit 9-11. The limits for a particular auto are determined by the year the auto is placed in service by the taxpayer. Thus, annual limits for autos placed in service in 2004 are determined by the 2004 column in Exhibit 9-11.[34] For example, the deduction for depreciation and § 179 expensing cannot exceed $2,560 for the year placed in service.

A comparison of the first-year limitation for 2002 and 2003 to other years shows a significant increase. The increase is attributable to the enactment of the additional first-year depreciation allowance created in 2001, expiring in 2004.

The 2004 limitations under § 280F restrict the annual depreciation amounts for autos costing $14,800 or more (assuming 200 percent declining-balance depreciation and no bonus depreciation was claimed). The $14,800 amount reflects the $2,960 first-year depreciation limitation ($14,800 × 20% regular depreciation rate for five-year property).

---

[32] § 280F(d)(5).

[33] Regs. § 1.274-5T(k)(2)).

[34] Rev. Proc. 2003-75, 2003-45 I.R.B. 1018. Additional tables are provided for autos for which bonus depreciation was elected.

EXHIBIT 9-11

Section 280F Depreciation Limits for Autos (Bonus Depreciation Elected for 2002 and 2003)

	Limits for Autos Based on Year Placed in Service					
	1999	2000	2001	2002*	2003*	2004
First year of service	$3,060	$3,060	$3,060	$7,660	$10,710	$2,960
Second year of service	5,000	4,900	4,900	4,900	4,900	4,800
Third year of service	2,950	2,950	2,950	2,950	2,950	2,850
Thereafter	1,775	1,775	1,775	1,775	1,775	1,675

*Limit if bonus depreciation was claimed.

Where the car is used less than 100 percent of the time for business—including the portion of time the car is used for production of income purposes—the maximum amounts given above must be reduced proportionately.

Example 20. T purchased a car for $20,000 in 2004. She used it 60% of the time for business purposes and 20% of the time traveling to her rental properties. Depreciation and limited expensing may not exceed $8,568 (80% × $10,710) for the first year, $3,920 (80% × $4,900) for the second year, and so on.

If the property's basis has not been fully deducted by the close of the normal recovery period (i.e., normally the extended recovery period of six years), a deduction for the *unrecovered basis* is allowed in subsequent years. Deductions for the property's unrecovered basis are limited to $1,775 annually until the entire basis is recovered.

Example 21. On December 1, 2004 R purchased a new automobile for $18,000 which he uses solely for business. R's regular depreciation for the first year initially is $3,600 but is limited to $2,960 as shown below.

Original cost.	$18,000	
Depreciation percentage	× 20%	
Depreciation before limitation.		3,600
Limitation		$2,960

The calculation of regular depreciation for the first year and subsequent years is summarized below.

In examining the schedule below, note that the recovery period is extended from six to eight years due to the limitations. Also, understand that the unadjusted depreciable basis used for computing depreciation is $18,000 for each year even though only $2,960 of the depreciation was deducted in the first year.

	1	2	3	4	5	6	7	8
	2004	**2005**	**2006**	**2007**	**2008**	**2009**	**2010**	**2011**
Unadjusted basis ..	$18,000	$18,000	$18,000	$18,000	$18,000	$18,000	$18,000	$18,000
Depreciation Percentage	20.00%	32.00%	19.20%	11.52%	11.52%	5.76%		
MACRS depreciation	$ 3,600	$ 5,760	$ 3,456	$ 2,074	$ 2,074	$ 1,037	$ 1,675	$ 1,675
Limit	$ 2,960	$ 4,800	$ 2,850	$ 1,675	$ 1,675	$ 1,675	$ 1,675	$ 1,675
Deduction........	$ 2,960	$ 4,800	$ 2,850	$ 1,675	$ 1,675	$ 1,037	$ 1,675	$ 1,328
Cumulative depreciation	$ 2,960	$ 7,760	$10,610	$12,285	$13,960	$14,997	$16,672	$18,000
Adjusted basis	$15,040	$10,240	$ 7,390	$ 5,715	$ 4,040	$ 3,003	$ 1,328	0

Trucks, Vans, and SUVs. Responding to criticisms that the limitations for passenger automobiles did not fairly reflect the higher price that must be paid for trucks and vans, in 2003 the IRS created a separate set of limitations for these vehicles as shown in Exhibit 9-12.

EXHIBIT 9-12

Section 280F Depreciation Limits for Trucks and Vans

Year	2004*
1	$3,360
2	5,400
3	3,250
Thereafter	1,975

*Limits if bonus depreciation was not claimed.

For this purpose, a vehicle qualifies as a truck or van if it is built on a truck chassis. Since most Sport Utility Vehicles (SUVs) are built on a truck chassis these higher limits would apply (assuming these vehicles do not have a gross vehicle weight exceeding 6,000 pounds).

Electric Cars. To encourage the purchase of electric vehicles, the depreciation limits (as shown in Exhibit 9-13) are about triple the limits for passenger automobiles.

Depreciation limits are also tripled in the case of a passenger vehicle designed to be propelled primarily by electricity and built by an original equipment manufacturer. Another depreciation limit exception is intended to encourage the use of clean burning fuels. There is no depreciation limitation on the portion of a vehicle's cost that enables it to burn clean burning fuels.

EXHIBIT 9-13
Section 280F Depreciation Limits for Electric Automobiles

Year	2004*
1	$ 8,880
2	14,300
3	8,550
Thereafter	5,125

*Limits if bonus depreciation was not claimed.

Leasing. Without any special rule, the taxpayer could lease a car and circumvent the limitations on depreciation since the restrictions would appear to apply only to the deduction for depreciation and not lease payments. For instance, in *Example 22* on page 9-31, the taxpayer might lease the car for $400 per month and claim a deduction of $4,800 for the year—far in excess of the amount allowed for depreciation after the first year. To prohibit this possibility, lessees may deduct the amount of the lease payment (applicable to business or income-producing use)—but must *include* certain amounts in income to bring their deductions for use of the car in line for owners. In practice, these inclusion amounts are not actually added to income but simply reduce the deduction for the lease payment.

The amount that the taxpayer must include in income is generally based on the automobile's fair market value and is determined in the following manner.[35]

1. Using the value of the automobile for the taxable year in which the auto is first used under the lease, identify the annual inclusion amount from the table found in Exhibit 9-14. Note that for the last year of the lease, the dollar amount for the preceding year is used unless the lease term begins and ends in the same year.

---

[35] § 280F(c) and Reg. § 1.280F-7(a). Note that these limitations do not apply to cars leased for 30 or fewer days or to lessors who regularly engage in the auto-leasing business.

EXHIBIT 9-14

Leased Passenger Automobile: Income Inclusion Amounts for Automobile Leases Beginning in 2004

Fair Market Value of Automobile		Tax Year during Lease				
Over	Not Over	1st	2nd	3rd	4th	5th and Later
$ 17,500	$ 18,000	11	23	33	42	48
18,000	18,500	13	26	40	49	56
18,500	19,000	14	31	46	55	65
19,000	19,500	16	35	51	63	73
19,500	20,000	18	39	57	70	81
20,000	20,500	20	43	63	77	89
20,500	21,000	22	47	69	84	97
21,000	21,500	23	51	75	91	106
21,500	22,000	25	55	81	98	114
22,000	23,000	28	61	90	109	126
23,000	24,000	32	69	102	123	142
24,000	25,000	35	77	114	137	159
25,000	26,000	39	85	126	151	176
26,000	27,000	43	93	137	166	192
27,000	28,000	46	101	149	180	209
28,000	29,000	50	109	161	194	225
29,000	30,000	54	116	174	208	242
30,000	31,000	57	125	185	223	257
31,000	32,000	61	133	197	237	274
32,000	33,000	64	141	209	251	291
33,000	34,000	68	149	221	265	307
34,000	35,000	72	157	232	280	323
35,000	36,000	75	165	244	294	340
36,000	37,000	79	173	256	308	357
37,000	38,000	83	181	268	322	373
38,000	39,000	86	189	280	337	389
39,000	40,000	90	197	292	351	405
40,000	41,000	94	204	304	365	423
41,000	42,000	97	213	316	379	438
42,000	43,000	101	221	327	394	455
43,000	44,000	105	228	340	408	471
44,000	45,000	108	237	351	422	488
45,000	46,000	112	245	363	436	504
46,000	47,000	115	253	375	451	520
47,000	48,000	119	261	387	464	538
48,000	49,000	123	269	398	479	554
49,000	50,000	126	277	411	493	570
50,000	51,000	130	285	422	508	586
*						
*						
*						
240,000	250,000	838	1,840	2,732	3,276	3,784

Source: Rev Proc. 2004-25, 2004-13 I.R.B. 642. Note that this table extends to values of $250,000.

1. Prorate the dollar amount for the number of days of the lease term included in the taxable year.

2. Multiply the prorated dollar amount by the business and investment use for the taxable year.

Taxpayers who lease (1) trucks and vans or (2) electric vehicles do not use the tables above for passenger automobiles but must use separate tables designed specifically for these two categories.

> **Example 22.** On April 1, 2004, M, a calendar year taxpayer, signed a three-year lease on a new passenger automobile with a value of $29,800. For 2004 and 2005, M used the car exclusively in his business. During 2006 and 2007, his business use dropped to 40%. The amounts that M must include in income for 2004 through 2007 are computed as follows:

Tax Year	Dollars Amount	Proration	Business Use%	Inclusion Amount
2004	$ 54	275/365	100%	$ 41
2005	116	366/366	100%	116
2006	174	365/365	40%	70
2007	208	90/365	40%	21

Observe that dollar amounts are based on the value of the car in the first year of the lease. Subsequent declines in the car's value are ignored. Also note that in computing the inclusion amount for 2008, the $208 amount for the preceding year (2007) is used because the lease did not begin and end in the same year.

Deducting SUVs. As noted above, a truck or van—including an SUV or minivan— is *not* treated as a passenger automobile subject to annual depreciation limits if it has *a gross vehicle weight* (GVW) of more than 6,000 pounds. "GVW" is the weight of the vehicle plus its maximum load (typically printed on the inside of the driver's door).[36] This exception was created for taxpayers who need to use large vehicles in their businesses such as farmers, construction workders and others—but not white-collare professionals. However, without further limitations, any taxpayer would be able to expense "heavy" SUVs (assuming they were used for business). When the limited expensing amount was raised to $100,000 (now $105,000), this enabled taxpayers to deduct the entire cost of a qualified SUV. Believing that many of these SUVs were in reality luxury automobiles, Congress decided to close what had become the so-called Hummer loophole.

As revised, §179 now limits the first-year write-off for vehicles considered SUVs. The maximum deduction is limited to $25,000. Taxpayers may still claim regular depreciation for the balance.

The limitation applies only to SUVs as defined in §179(b)(6)(B). This provision defines an SUV as any four-wheeled vehicle that is primarily designed or that can be used to carry passengers over public streets, roads, or highways and that weighs more than 6,000 pounds unloaded gross weight and not more than 14,000 pounds gross vehicle weight. Thus heavier vehicles, weighing 14,000 pounds or more (e.g., refrigerated trucks) are not subject to the new limitation. Absent some exceptions, the definition of SUVs would include heavy pickup trucks, vans and small buses. To allow the deduction in these cases, the following vehicles are not considered SUVs and therefore, the $25,000 limitation does not apply.

- A vehicle designed to have a seating capacity of more than nine persons behind the driver's seat.
- A vehicle equipped with a cargo area of at least six feet in interior length which is an open area or is designed for use as an open area but is enclosed by a cap and is not readily accessible directly from the passenger compartment.

---

[36] PLR 9520034.

▸ A vehicle having an integral enclosure, fully enclosing the driver compartment and load carrying device, does not have seating rearward of the driver's seat.

▸ A vehicle having no body section protruding more than 30 inches ahead of the leading edge of the windshield.

Note that the exceptions would permit deductions for large pick-up trucks weighing more than 6,000 pounds under the cargo area exception or because it as no seats behind the driver. Similarly, cargo vans should qualify under the exception. These rules apply for SUVs placed in service after October 22, 2004.

> **Example 23.** In 2005, T purchased a Lexus LX 470 for $65,000. The SUV has a GVW exceeding 6,000 pounds and is used 100% for business. In such case, the § 179 deduction is $25,000 and regular depreciation would be $8,000 [20% × ($65,000 − $25,000 = $40,000)] for a total deduction of $33,000 ($25,000 + $8,000). If T were in the 35% tax bracket, the deduction would save him $11,550. Note that the limitation on the § 179 deduction is $25,000 and there is no limit on depreciation since the SUV is not a passenger automobile because it weighs more than 6,000 pounds.

Below is a list of the SUVs with GVWs more than 6,000 pounds and the manufacturer's suggested retail price (MSRP):

SUV	MSRP
BMW X5	$ 39,500
Cadillac Escalade	53,855
Chevrolet Suburban	39,750
Chevrolet Tahoe	35,015
Dodge Durango	28,995
Ford Expedition	34,390
Ford Excursion	39,690
Hummer H2	48,455
Hummer H1	105,160
GMC Yukon	35,725
Land Rover Discovery	34,350
Land Rover Range Rover	71,200
Lexus LX 470	63,625
Lexus GX 470	44,925
Lincoln Navigator	49,225
Mercedes-Benz M Class	37,320
Mercedes-Benz G 500	74,320
Porsche Cayenne	55,900
Toyota Land Cruiser	54,465
Toyota Sequoia	32,135

LIMITATIONS FOR PERSONAL USE

Section 280F also restricts the amount of depreciation that may be claimed for so-called listed property that is not used predominantly—more than 50 percent—for business. If the property is not used more than 50 percent *for business* in the year it is placed in service, the following restrictions are imposed:[37]

1. Limited expensing under § 179 is not allowed.

---

[37] § 280F(b).

2. MACRS may *not* be used in computing depreciation. Property not qualifying must be depreciated using the straight-line method of ADS and the asset's class life (except in the case of certain property such as automobiles and computers, where the life to be used is specifically prescribed as five years).

Note that these restrictions are imposed if the property is not used primarily for business in the *first* year. Subsequent usage in excess of 50 percent does not permit the taxpayer to amend the earlier return or later use accelerated depreciation or limited expensing. On the other hand, if qualified usage initially exceeds 50 percent but subsequently drops to 50 percent or below, benefits previously secured must be relinquished. The recapture of these benefits is discussed below. Exhibit 9-15 identifies the depreciation methods available for listed property.

These restrictions apply only to *listed property*. Listed property includes the following:[38]

1. Passenger automobiles (as defined above)

2. Any other property used as a means for transportation (e.g., motorcycles and trucks)

3. Any property generally used for purposes of entertainment, recreation, or amusement (e.g., yacht, photography equipment, video recorders, and stereo equipment) *unless* used exclusively at a regular business establishment (e.g., at the office or at a home office) or in connection with the taxpayer's principal trade or business

4. Any computer or peripheral equipment *unless* used exclusively at a regular business establishment

5. Any cellular telephones and similar communications equipment

---

[38]   § 280F(d)(4).

EXHIBIT 9-15
Depreciation Methods Available for Listed Property

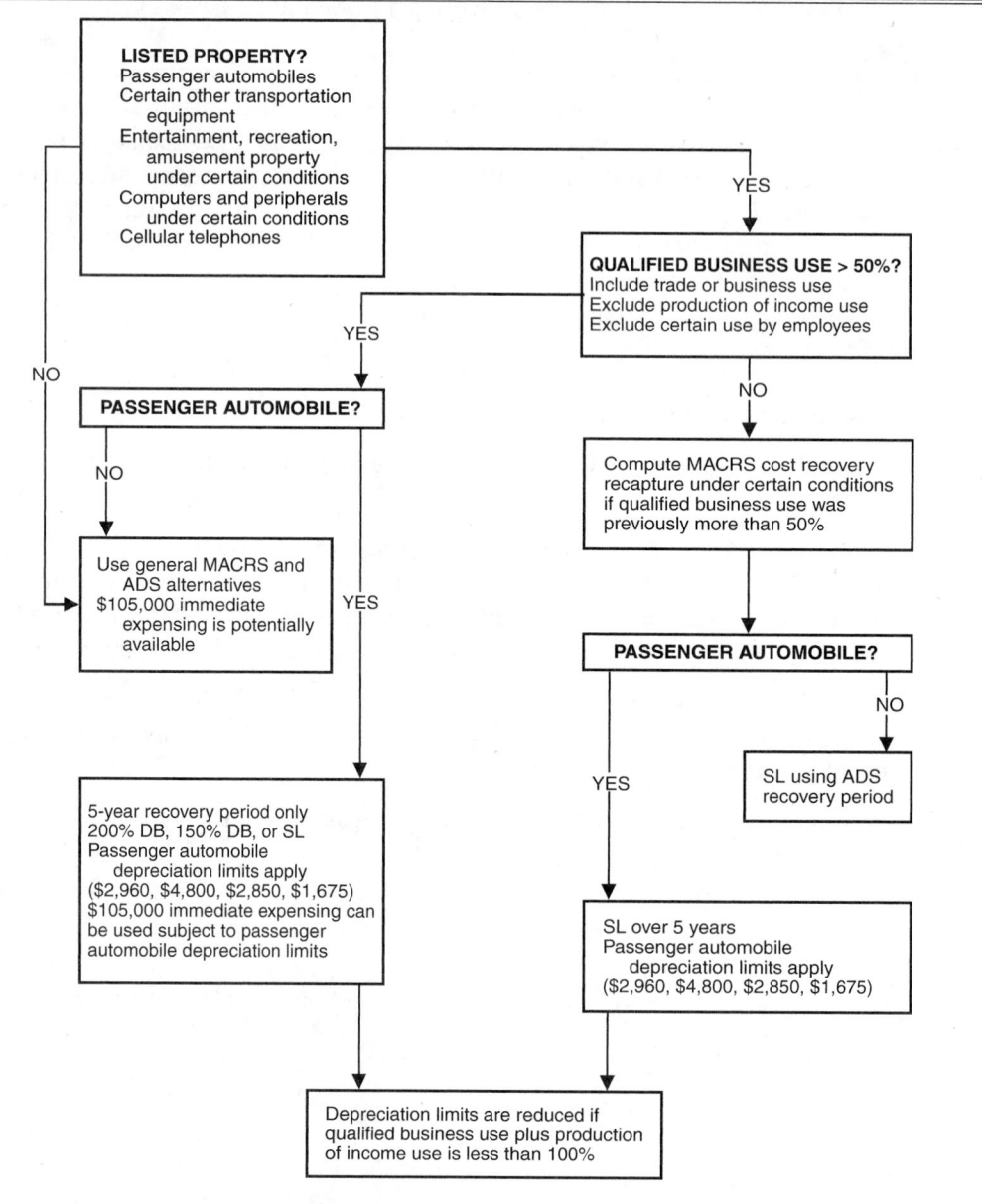

Example 24. K, self-employed, purchased a car for $20,000 in 2004. She uses her car 40% of the time for business and the remaining time for personal purposes. Since the property is a car, the limitations on depreciation are first reduced in light of the personal usage. In the first year depreciation would initially be limited to $1,184 ($2,960 maximum allowed × 40% business use.) In addition, since the car is listed property and is not used more than 50% for business, K must use ADS to compute depreciation. Therefore, depreciation in the first year is $800 ($20,000 cost × 40% business use = $8,000 × 10% ADS rate).

Qualified Business Use. In determining whether the property is used more than 50 percent for business, only *qualified business use* is considered.[39] Generally, qualified

---

[39] § 280F(b)(1) and (2).

business use means any use in a trade or business of the taxpayer.[40] Thus, for this test *only*, use in an activity that does not constitute a trade or business is ignored (e.g., use of a computer to monitor the taxpayer's investments does not count toward the 50 percent threshold since the activity is not a business).[41] Additionally, an employee's use of his or her own property in connection with employment is not considered business use unless it is for the *convenience of the employer* and is *required as a condition of employment.*[42] According to the Regulations, these two requirements generally have the same meaning for § 280F as they have for § 119 relating to the exclusion for meals or lodging.[43] Given this interpretation, a mere statement by the employer expressly requiring the employee to use the property is insufficient. Ordinarily, the property is considered required only if it enables the employee to properly perform the duties of his or her employment.

> **Example 25.** T is employed by X, a newspaper company, to deliver papers in a rural area where the homes are widely scattered. The company does not provide T with a car and does not require T to own a car for employment. Since the car enables T to properly perform his duties and is for the convenience of X, T's use should qualify for purposes of the 50% test even though he is not explicitly required to own a car.

> **Example 26.** J is a budget analyst in the accounting department of a large construction firm. She owns a personal computer that is identical to the one she uses at work. Instead of staying late at the office, J occasionally brings home work for which she uses her computer. J's use of her computer for her work is not qualified business use.

The IRS takes a very narrow view regarding what satisfies the convenience-of-the-employer and condition-of-employment tests. In one instance, the Service held that a professor's use of her home computer for writing related to her research—which was required for continued employment—did not satisfy the tests.[44] Although the Service agreed that the use of the computer was related to her work, it found no evidence that employees who did not use home computers were professionally disadvantaged. The Service also felt that her employer did not explicitly require use of the home computer before she was hired. Apparently, the Service will require taxpayers to demonstrate that the work could not properly be performed without the computer or at least that they will be professionally disadvantaged if they do not use the computer. In addition, under the IRS view, taxpayers will be obliged to show that use of the computer was mandatory and not optional.

The reach of this and other rulings goes farther than it first appears. As brought out by the Service, a literal interpretation of the statute indicates that if an employee does not satisfy the convenience-of-the-employer and condition-of-employment tests, *none* of the employee's use is treated as business use. This view does *not* mean that the employee is merely relegated to using ADS for depreciation. Rather, with no business use, the employee is prohibited from claiming any deductions relating to the listed property. Only time will tell whether this interpretation is consistent with Congressional intent.

In those cases where qualified business use exceeds 50 percent, any usage for the production of income or other business purposes is included in determining the

---

40 § 280F(d)(6).

41 Temp. Reg. § 1.280F-6T(d)(2).

42 § 280F(d)(3).

43 Temp. Reg. § 1.280F-6T(a)(2).

44 Letter Ruling 8615024.

percentage of the asset that may be depreciated using MACRS. Similarly, if business use is 50 percent or less, the usage for production of income or other nonqualified business purposes is still included in determining the percentage of the asset that may be depreciated using ADS. Note that depreciation is still allowed where the 50 percent test is not met, assuming there is business or investment usage.

Example 27. V, a financial consultant, purchased a car for $20,000. She uses the car 25% of the time for business and 55% for production of income activities that do not qualify as a business. V must use ADS since business usage is only 25%. Although the time spent for the production of income cannot be counted toward the 50% test, it may be considered in the depreciation computation. Thus, V's depreciation would be $1,600 [$20,000 × (55% + 25%) × 10%]. It should be noted that where the listed property is an automobile, the limitations on depreciation also apply. Here the depreciation limitation is $2,368 [(55% + 25%) × $2,960]; note that the production of income usage is considered in making the proper reduction]; thus it does not restrict the amount of the depreciation deduction. Had the usage percentages been reversed (i.e., 55% for business), the depreciation and limited expensing deduction would still have been limited to $2,368.

Employer-Provided Cars. The qualified business use rules directly address the problems of the company-owned car and other company-owned property used by employees. In the case of automobiles, employers typically provide company-owned cars to their employees principally for use in the employer's business. Normally, however, the employee also uses the car for personal purposes if only to commute to work. Under prior law, the employer claimed deductions and credits for the car without limitation (i.e., 100 percent of the car's basis was taken into account) while employees were required to treat the personal use as compensation. In most cases, the compensation income was avoided as long as the employee reimbursed the company for the value of the personal use, which the company in turn reported as income. Section 280F now prescribes specific rules governing depreciation where listed property is used by someone *other than* the owner—such as an employer-provided automobile. The following discussion examines these rules as they apply to employer-provided automobiles; however, such rules extend to other listed property as well.

Where an employee uses an automobile, an *employer* is able to secure 100 percent qualified business use—and thus depreciate the entire cost of the automobile—in one of four ways.[45]

1. The employee's actual business usage is disregarded and the *entire value* of using the vehicle is included in the employee's income.

2. The employee's actual business usage is combined with inclusion of the value of any personal use by the employee as income.

3. The employee's actual business usage is combined with a reimbursement arrangement where the employee reimburses the employer for any personal use (i.e.. a fair rent is paid).

4. The use falls under one of four exceptions.

Conditions 2 and 3 cannot be applied to qualify the use of a person owning greater than a 5 percent interest in the business (e.g., the company president, who is also a 30 percent shareholder). In this case, the employer can depreciate the car based only on the employee's actual business usage.

---

[45] Temp. Reg. § 1.280F-6T(d)(4)(iv).

Before looking at several examples of these rules, it should be noted that each requires a valuation of the vehicle's use to the employee. The value can be determined using a facts-and-circumstances approach (e.g., considering such variables as geographic location, make and model, etc.) or one of several safe harbors provided by Temporary Regulations.[46] For example, the Regulations provide a table (i.e., a lease value table) based on the car's total value which provides values for personal use. Another alternative that can be used to value personal use under certain circumstances is the standard mileage allowance.

Example 28. During the year, X Corporation provided T, an employee, with a new car costing $10,000. T drove the company car 15,000 miles, 9,000 miles or 60% for business purposes, and 6,000 miles or 40% for personal purposes. X Corporation may use any of the first three alternatives to account for the car.

Alternative No. 1. Under this full inclusion method, the employee's actual use is disregarded and the employee must include 100% of the value of the car's use in income, $6,075 (15,000 × 40.5 cents—the standard mileage rate for 2005)[47] just as if it were salary (i.e., X Corporation includes it on T's Form W-2 and withholds income and FICA taxes). Therefore, all of T's use qualifies and X may depreciate 100% of the car using MACRS. T may then deduct any substantiated business use as a miscellaneous itemized deduction subject to the 2% floor. One advantage of this method for the employer is that it shifts all of the substantiation burden to the employee.

Alternative No. 2. Under this partial inclusion method, only T's personal use is treated as income, or $2,430 (6,000 × 40.5 cents). X could depreciate the car in the same manner as above. T may be better off under this method since the amount of compensation is reduced. This may have an effect on the amount of deductions or credits T may otherwise claim (e.g., the 2% floor on miscellaneous itemized deductions would be smaller due to the lower amount of income). In this case, X must be able to substantiate the employee's actual business use.

Alternative No. 3. Under the rental reimbursement method, T would pay X Corporation for his personal use, $2,430. X could depreciate the car in the same manner as above. T would be worse off in this situation. Each dollar of reimbursement costs T one dollar, while inclusion of the value of the personal use costs the employee only the tax on the value. Again, X must be able to substantiate the employee's actual business use.

Five Percent Owner. If T owns 5% or more of the business (i.e., X Corporation), the only alternative is to compute depreciation using T's actual business mileage. In this case, X could depreciate 60% of the car using MACRS. Had T's business usage been 50% or less, X would be required to use ADS to compute depreciation.

Additional rules for determining qualified business usage exist for other situations. For example, leasing the property to a 5 percent owner of the business or a related person is not considered qualified business use. Similarly, special rules are provided for aircraft.

Recapture Provisions. If the 50 percent test is satisfied in the year property is placed in service but failed prior to the time when the cost of the asset would be completely recovered using the listed property recovery rules, the taxpayer is required to relinquish the benefits of MACRS. Technically, the taxpayer must recompute the

---

[46]   Temp. Reg. § 1.61-2T(d)(2)(iii).

[47]   Rev. Proc. 2004-64, 2004-49 I.R.B.

depreciation in the prior years using ADS and include in income the excess of the depreciation actually claimed over the ADS amounts. Depreciation in future years is computed using the straight-line method.

> **Example 29.** In 20X1 G purchased a car for $10,000 and used it entirely for business. Depreciation for 20X1 was $2,000 ($10,000 × 20%). In 20X2 G's business usage dropped to 40%. Since G's business usage is no longer greater than 50%, he must recapture the benefits of accelerated depreciation. Depreciation using the straight-line method in 20X1 would have been $1,000 ($10,000 × 10%). Thus, G must include $1,000 ($2,000 original depreciation—$1,000 straight-line depreciation) in income in 20X2. Depreciation for 20X2 and all subsequent years must be computed using the straight-line method.

Record keeping Requirements. Not only has Congress severely restricted tax benefits for listed property, it also has imposed strict record keeping requirements for such property. The substantiation rules contained in Code § 274(d), which were formerly reserved solely for travel and entertainment expenses, now extend to expenses related to "listed property." For listed property, the taxpayer is required to substantiate the following:[48]

1. The amount of each expenditure related to the property, including the cost of acquisition, maintenance, and repairs

2. The date of the use of the property

3. The amount of each business or investment use as well as total use [the number of miles—in the case of a car or other means of transportation—or the amount of time that the property was used for other listed property (e.g., a computer)]

4. The purpose of the use of the property

In those cases where the overall use of the property for a taxable year can be definitely determined without entries, nonbusiness use need not be recorded. For example, in the case of a car, total miles can be determined by comparing the odometer readings at the beginning and the end of the taxable year. Consequently, the taxpayer needs to make entries only for business and investment use.

✅ CHECK YOUR KNOWLEDGE

Review Question 1. This year Y purchased new property. Indicate whether the following questions are true or false.

a. Assuming the property is a duplex that Y rents to others, she may not expense any of the cost.

True. Only eligible property may be expensed. As a general rule, only personal property such as machinery and equipment are eligible. Buildings are normally not eligible.

b. Assuming the property is a $125,000 dental chair, Y may expense $105,000, and the $20,000 balance may be carried over to the following years to be expensed to the extent the maximum amount is not used in such years.

False. Y may expense $105,000, and the balance is subject to depreciation.

---

[48] Temp. Reg. § 1.274-5T(b)(6).

c. Assuming the property is a $20,000 passenger automobile that is used 70 percent for business, Y may deduct $14,000.

False. Depreciation and expensing for automobiles are limited. The maximum amount of depreciation or expense claimed in the year the automobile is placed in service is limited to $2,072 ($2,960 × 70%). This amount could be deducted for the current year, and the remaining balance could be depreciated beginning next year.

d. Assuming the property is a $40,000 car that is used 30 percent for business, Y may deduct $888 ($2,960 × 30%).

False. If the property is listed property and qualified business use does not exceed 50 percent, the taxpayer is not allowed to expense any of the car and must use straight-line depreciation. Therefore, Y could claim a deduction of $300 ($10,000 × 30% × 10%). Note that bonus depreciation is not allowed since ADS is required.

e. If the property is listed property, such as a passenger automobile or a computer, and the property is not used more than 50 percent of the time for business, the restrictions of § 280F do not affect the total amount of cost deducted but simply alter the time when it is deducted.

True. The total depreciation is not changed. If the property is restricted and qualified business use does not exceed 50 percent, the taxpayer is simply forced to use the straight-line method in lieu of the accelerated methods of MACRS and the expensing allowance of § 179 that are normally available.

OTHER CONSIDERATIONS

Anti-Churning Rules. In some cases, a taxpayer's depreciation deductions under MACRS would be higher than those that the taxpayer may currently have. For this reason, Congress believed that some taxpayers would engage in transactions that might enable them to secure the advantages of MACRS.

Example 30. In 1980 H acquired an apartment building as an investment that she chose to depreciate using the straight-line method over 35 years. H made this decision because the use of accelerated depreciation caused a portion of any gain from the subsequent sale of such property to be treated as ordinary income rather than favorable capital-gain. With the elimination of favorable capital-gain treatment in 1986, there no longer was any disincentive to use the accelerated method. Therefore, H created a plan to benefit from the change. She sold the property to her son, who immediately leased it back to her. The rental payments to be paid by H were structured in light of the higher depreciation deductions (27.5-year life instead of 35 years) that her son would be able to take as the new owner of the property.

Sales, exchanges, and other dispositions of assets such as that illustrated above are referred to as "churning" transactions—exchanges of used property solely to obtain the benefits of MACRS.

The thrust of the anti-churning rules is to preclude the use of MACRS for property placed in service prior to the enactment of either version of MACRS, unless the property is transferred in a transaction where not only the owner changes but also the user.[49] In *Example 30* the anti-churning rules prohibit H's son from using MACRS since ownership did not truly change.

---

[49] § 168(e)(4).

There are three sets of rules designed to police churning. For practical purposes these provisions should be given close review whenever the taxpayer is involved in a leasing or nontaxable transaction. For example, a taxpayer would typically be subject to the anti-churning rules in the following situations:

1. Sale followed by immediate leaseback

2. Like-kind exchange

3. Formation and liquidation of a corporation or partnership, including transfers of property to and distributions from these entities

Expensing Costs of Qualified Film and Television Productions. Over the years, production of American film projects has migrated to foreign locations often lured by tax and other incentives offered by foreign countries. To encourage producers to bring feature film and television production projects back to the U.S., Congress created § 181 in 2004. Section 181 allows immediate deduction for costs of qualified film or television productions. To qualify, one condition requires that at least 75 percent of the total compensation expended on the production is for services performed in the U.S.. The special expensing allowance is limited to smaller productions in that it does not apply if the aggregate production costs exceed $15 million. In other words, if the total costs exceed $15 million, none can be expensed. Instead the amount must be capitalized and amortized. The $15 million amount is increased to $20 million if a significant amount of the production expenditures are incurred in areas eligible for designation as a low-income community or eligible for designation by the Delta Regional Authority as a distressed county or isolated area.

Property Leased to Tax-Exempt Entities. For a variety of reasons, tax-exempt entities, such as schools, hospitals, or government organizations, lease property from taxable entities rather than purchase it. One incentive for this type of transaction is that the taxable entity can benefit from depreciation deductions, whereas the tax-exempt entity cannot. Thus, a tax plan might be devised under which a taxable lessor and a tax-exempt lessee "share" the tax benefits of the depreciation deductions. This would be accomplished through discounted lease payments. The taxable lessor would be willing to accept discounted lease payments "in exchange" for receiving all of the tax benefits from depreciation deductions. To reduce the incentive for this type of tax plan, depreciation of "tax-exempt use property"—most property leased to a "tax-exempt entity"—must be depreciated using ADS with special rules to determine the applicable recovery period.[50] This rule applies regardless of the tax planning motives of the lessor and lessee. The result of the rule is to lower the present value of the tax savings from the depreciation deductions. There are several types of leasing transactions that are exempted from the rule. For example, the rule does not apply to "short-term leases."

AMORTIZATION

As previously discussed, MACRS does not apply to intangible property. Therefore, intangibles are subject to the rules existing prior to enactment of ACRS and MACRS. Generally, intangibles are amortized using the straight-line method over their estimated useful life. Special amortization and depreciation rules apply to certain expenditures, however.

---

[50]   § 168(g)(1)(C).

GOODWILL AND COVENANTS NOT TO COMPETE

As mentioned in Chapter 6, buyers of a going concern often pay an amount in excess of the fair market value of the concern's tangible assets. This excess purchase price normally is attributable to intangible assets such as goodwill and/or a covenant not to compete. The tax treatment for such intangible assets was changed dramatically by the Revenue Reconciliation Act of 1993 for acquisitions occurring after August 10, 1993. Acquisitions taking place on or before August 10, 1993 continue to be treated under prior law, which held that goodwill could not be amortized because it was considered as having an unlimited life. Thus, recovery of a taxpayer's basis in goodwill could occur only when the business was subsequently sold or abandoned. In contrast, a covenant not to compete usually has an ascertainable life because the seller typically agrees to refrain from conducting similar business or some other activity for a certain number of years. As a result, prior law held that any cost attributable to the covenant may be amortized over the appropriate period using the straight-line method.

Under prior law, taxpayers attempted to allocate the purchase price to assets other than goodwill since goodwill could not be amortized. In this regard, accountants were quite creative, assigning the purchase price to a variety of intangibles such as covenants not to compete, favorable contracts, customer lists, accounting control systems, and a long list of other items. As long as the taxpayer was able to establish that the intangible was separate and distinct from goodwill and had a determinable useful life, the taxpayer was entitled to amortize the cost. For example, a taxpayer might allocate a substantial portion of the purchase price of a business to a covenant not to compete and amortize the cost over three years, producing a significant benefit where otherwise there would be no benefit at all if the cost were allocated to goodwill.

Post–August 10, 1993 Acquisitions. As might be expected, the IRS did not sit idly by and allow taxpayers to do as they pleased. In case after case, the IRS challenged the taxpayer's allocation, and there was a great deal of controversy and litigation. To put an end to the disputes and clear up the uncertainty, Congress enacted § 197. Effective for acquisitions after August 10, 1993 all "Section 197 intangibles" must be amortized over 15 years. (A taxpayer may elect to have the rules of § 197 apply to intangibles acquired after July 15, 1991.) Much like MACRS, § 197 forces the taxpayer to use the 15-year period even if the useful life is actually more or less than 15 years. Section 197 intangibles include a number of items such as goodwill, going-concern value, covenants not to compete, information bases such as customer or subscription lists, know-how, customer-based intangibles, governmental licenses and permits (e.g., liquor licenses, taxicab medallions, landing or takeoff rights, regulated airline routes, television or radio licenses), franchises, trademarks, and trade names.

To further prohibit the deduction of an intangible obtained as part of an acquisition, special rules govern disposition. No loss is allowed on the disposition of an intangible if the business retains other intangible assets acquired in the same or a series of related transactions. Instead, any remaining basis is reallocated among the bases of other § 197 intangibles. Although losses are not recognized, the same treatment does not apply to gains.

If § 197 intangibles are sold at a gain, the gain is recognized. The tax character of the entire gain is ordinary income if the intangible is held one year or less. Gains from sales of intangibles held more than one year are treated as gains from sales of § 1245 property. As explained in Chapter 17, gains from dispositions of § 1245 property are "recaptured" and treated as ordinary income up to the amount of amortization on the intangible deducted through the time of sale. Any excess gain is a § 1231 gain.

Example 31. Buyer allocates $150,000 to intangible assets in a purchase. Under § 197 Buyer would claim $10,000 per year for 15 years as an amortization deduction. The deduction would not be affected by breaking the $150,000 into separate portions for goodwill, a covenant not to compete, or any other specifically identified intangibles.

Assume that the purchase occurred on January 1, 2005. Buyer will claim a $10,000 deduction every year for 15 years through 2019. Assume that Buyer allocates $105,000 to goodwill and the remaining $45,000 to a covenant not to compete that would expire on January 1, 2008. From 2005 through 2007. Buyer claims an annual amortization deduction of $3,000 ($45,000/15) on the covenant and $7,000 ($105,000/15) on the goodwill. On January 1, 2008, Buyer will have an unrecovered basis of $36,000 on the covenant, which has expired [$45,000 − $9,000 amortization ($3,000 amortization per year for three years)]. However, Buyer must add the $36,000 unrecovered basis to the basis of goodwill and continue to deduct $10,000 per year as amortization of the goodwill.

A number of anti-churning rules exist to prohibit taxpayers from creating and amortizing goodwill and going-concern value. Other intangibles are not covered by these rules.

FIVE-YEAR ELECTIVE AMORTIZATION

To accomplish certain economic and social objectives, Congress has enacted various optional five-year (60-month) amortization procedures from time to time over the last 40 years. During certain periods, a five-year amortization election (in lieu of regular depreciation) has been available for expenditures made in connection with child care facilities (§ 188), pollution control facilities (still an option under § 169), railroad rolling stock (§ 184), and rehabilitation of low-income housing [§ 167(k)].

LEASEHOLD IMPROVEMENTS

Taxpayers often lease property and improve the property while leasing it. In this situation, the lessee is entitled to recover the investment in the improvement.[51] After 1986, the cost of any leasehold improvement made by a lessee is depreciated in the normal manner without regard to the term of the lease. Note that bonus depreciation may apply if certain conditions are met. Any unrecovered cost at the end of the lease term would increase the taxpayer's basis for determining gain or loss. The recovery of the costs of acquiring a lease is determined under special rules in Code § 178.

DEPLETION

A taxpayer who invests in natural resources that are exhausted over time is entitled to recover his or her capital investment. Depletion is the method of recovering this cost and is similar to depreciation.[52] Depletion usually is claimed for investments in oil, gas, coal, copper, and other minerals. Land is not subject to depletion.

To qualify for depletion, the taxpayer must have an economic interest in the mineral deposits.[53] Typically, both the owner of the land who leases the property and the

---

[51] § 168(i)(8); also see § 178(a) when the lease permits renewals.

[52] § 611.

[53] Reg. § 1.611-1(b).

operator to whom the land is leased have the requisite interest since they both receive income from the severance or extraction of the minerals.

COMPUTING THE DEPLETION DEDUCTION

Taxpayers generally are permitted to compute their depletion deduction using either the cost or percentage (statutory) depletion method. The taxpayer computes both cost and percentage depletion and is required to claim the higher amount.[54]

Cost Depletion. Using cost depletion, the taxpayer recovers the actual investment (adjusted basis in the natural resource) as the mineral is produced. The following formula is used:[55]

$$\frac{\text{Annual cost}}{\text{depletion}} = \frac{\text{Unrecovered adjusted basis}}{\text{Estimated recoverable units}} \times \frac{\text{Number of units sold}}{\text{during the year}}$$

This formula generally matches the cost of the investment against the revenues produced.

Example 32. A coal producer, T, paid $150,000 to acquire the mineral rights in a property which contains coal. He estimates that 90,000 tons of coal are recoverable from the property. During the year, 58,000 tons of coal were produced and 30,000 were sold. T's cost depletion would be $50,000 computed as follows:

$$\frac{\$150,000 \text{ basis}}{90,000 \text{ units}} \times \frac{30,000}{\text{units sold}} = \frac{\$50,000}{\text{depletion}}$$

Similar to depreciation, total cost depletion can never exceed the taxpayer's adjusted basis in the property.

Percentage Depletion. For large oil and gas producers, cost depletion is the only depletion method allowed. However, both cost depletion and percentage depletion are available to small "independent" oil and gas producers as well as royalty owners.[56] Both cost depletion and percentage depletion are also allowed for *all* producers of certain types of minerals (e.g., gold, silver, gravel).

Under the percentage depletion method, the taxpayer's depletion deduction is computed *without reference* to the taxpayer's cost of the investment. Rather, percentage depletion is based on the amount of income derived from the property.[57] For this reason, the taxpayer may deduct percentage depletion in excess of the adjusted basis of the investment. Thus, the taxpayer is entitled to a deduction for percentage depletion as long as the property continues to generate income.

To compute percentage depletion, a percentage specified in the Code (see Exhibit 9-16) is applied to the *gross* income from the property. The resulting product is the amount of percentage depletion unless limited. For oil and gas properties, percentage depletion is generally limited to the taxpayer's *taxable* income before depletion. Percentage depletion is limited to 50 percent of the taxpayer's taxable income from mineral properties. Gross income is the value of the natural resource when severed from the property before any processing. Taxable income from the property is the difference between income and operating expenses including overhead.

---

[54]   § 613(a); Reg. § 1.611-1(a).

[55]   Reg. § 1.611-2(a).

[56]   § 613A(c).

[57]   § 613.

EXHIBIT 9-16
Summary of Various Percentage Depletion Rates

Natural Resource	Percentage Rate
1. Gravel, sand, and other items	5
2. Shale and clay used for sewer pipes; or brick and clay, shale, and slate used for lightweight aggregates	7.5
3. Asbestos, coal, sodium chloride, etc.	10
4. Gold, silver, oil and gas, oil shale, copper, and iron ore from deposits in the United States	15
5. Sulfur and uranium and a series of minerals from deposits in the United States	22
6. Metals, other than those subject to 22% or 15% rate.	14

Example 33. Assume the same facts in *Example 32* and that the 30,000 tons sold were sold for $10 per ton (gross income of $300,000). Further, operating expenses attributable to the coal operation were $260,000. Percentage depletion is computed as follows:

Gross income.	$300,000
Statutory percentage for coal.	×10%
Percentage depletion before limitation.	$ 30,000

Taxable income limitation:

Gross income	$300,000
Less: Operating expenses	−260,000
Taxable income before depletion	$ 40,000
Limitation percentage	×50%
Percentage depletion limit.	$ 20,000
Percentage depletion allowable	$ 20,000

In this situation, T would use cost depletion of $50,000 as computed in *Example 32* because it exceeds allowable percentage depletion.

Example 34. Assume the same facts in *Example 33* except that barrels of oil are being produced, rather than tons of coal. Cost depletion computations are the same as in *Example 33*. Percentage depletion is computed as follows:

Gross income.	$300,000
Statutory percentage for oil	×15%
Percentage depletion before limitation.	$ 45,000
Gross income.	$300,000
Less: Operating expenses	−260,000
Taxable income before depletion.	$ 40,000
Percentage depletion limit	$ 40,000
Percentage depletion allowable	$ 40,000

T would use cost depletion of $50,000 (computed in *Example 32*) rather than percentage depletion of $40,000 because cost depletion is larger.

Whether percentage or cost depletion is used, the taxpayer must reduce the property's basis (but not below zero) by the amount of depletion claimed. Note that once the basis of the property is reduced to zero, only percentage depletion may be claimed (when the taxpayer is permitted to take percentage depletion), and *no* adjustment is made to create a negative basis.

RESEARCH AND EXPERIMENTAL EXPENDITURES

At first glance, it may appear that the proper tax treatment for research and development expenses requires their capitalization as part of a project's cost. This approach seems appropriate since these costs normally yield benefits only in future periods. Under this theory, the capitalized costs could be recovered over the period during which the project provides benefits or when the project is disposed of or abandoned. Upon closer examination, however, it becomes apparent that this approach is fraught with problems. Since it is difficult to establish any direct relationship between costs of research and development and the actual period benefited, it may be impossible to determine the appropriate period for recovery. For example, establishing a useful life for a scientific discovery that has numerous applications and which continually contributes to later research would be guesswork at best. A similar problem exists for unsuccessful efforts. Although a particular effort may not prove fruitful, it may at least indicate what does not work and thus lead to other, perhaps successful, research. In such case, it is not clear whether the costs should be written off or capitalized as part of the subsequent project.

Due to the administrative difficulties inherent in these determinations, the IRS historically granted research and experimental costs favorable treatment by generally allowing the taxpayer to deduct the expenses as incurred or to capitalize the expenses and amortize them over whatever period the taxpayer desires. Although this approach encountered difficulties in the courts, Congress eliminated the problems with enactment of special provisions in 1954.

RESEARCH AND EXPERIMENTAL EXPENDITURES DEFINED

The Code provides separate rules for research and experimental costs.[58] It should be emphasized that the provisions apply to research and *experimental* costs, not to research and *development* costs. The term *experimental* was used instead of *development* to limit the special treatment to laboratory costs.[59] Qualified costs generally include those incident to the development or improvement of a product, a formula, an invention, a plant process, an experimental or pilot model, or similar property. Research and experimental costs do *not* include expenditures for ordinary testing or inspection of materials or products for quality control, efficiency surveys, management studies, consumer surveys, advertising, or promotion. Costs of obtaining a patent, such as legal fees, qualify. However, the costs of acquiring an existing patent, model, or process are not considered research and experimental costs. Expenditures for depreciable property do not qualify but the depreciation allowable on the property is eligible for special treatment.

---

[58]   § 174.

[59]   Reg. § 1.174-2(a).

ALTERNATIVE TAX TREATMENTS

Three alternative methods may be used to account for research and experimental expenditures. The expenses may be deducted as they are paid or incurred, deferred and amortized, or capitalized. Immediate deduction usually is the preferred method since the present value of the tax benefit is greater using this method. Deferral may be preferable in two instances, however. If the taxpayer's income is low in the current year, the tax benefit of the deduction might be increased by deferring the deduction to high-income years when the taxpayer is in a higher marginal tax bracket. Deferral also may be better if an immediate deduction creates or adds to a net operating loss since such losses may be carried over and used only for a limited period of time. The general rule for selecting the best alternative is to choose the one that maximizes the present value of the tax savings from the research and experimental expenditures.

Expense Election. The taxpayer can elect to deduct all research and experimental expenditures currently.[60] Note, however, that expenditures for depreciable property cannot be expensed currently.[61] If the taxpayer adopts this method in the first tax year in which research and experimental expenses are incurred, the method must be used for all such expenditures in all subsequent years, unless permission is secured to change methods of part or all of the expenditures.[62] The IRS does not need to approve the method the taxpayer adopts initially. Consent is required, however, if the taxpayer wishes to change methods.

Deferral Option. Research and experimental expenditures may be deferred and amortized at the election of the taxpayer.[63] The expenses must be amortized ratably over a period not less than 60 months beginning in the period in which benefits from the expenditures are first realized. It should be emphasized that costs of depreciable property are not deferred expenses; rather, the depreciation expense must be capitalized and amortized over 60 months. Also, if the taxpayer elects to defer the expenditures and a patent is subsequently obtained, the cost must be amortized over the life of the patent, 17 years. If the deferral method is initially elected, the taxpayer must use this method for all future expenses in subsequent tax years unless permission to change methods is obtained.[64]

Election to Capitalize. A taxpayer who does not elect either to amortize research and experimental expenditures over 60 months or to deduct them currently must capitalize them. Capitalizing the expenditure increases the basis of the property to which the expense relates. No deduction is permitted for the capital expenditure until the research project is considered worthless or abandoned. A disposition of the research project such as a sale or an exchange enables the taxpayer to offset the capitalized expenditures—the basis of the project—against any amount realized.

Example 35. L Corporation, a drug manufacturer, is an accrual basis, calendar year taxpayer. During 2005 the corporation performed research to improve various cold and flu medications. On December 1, 2005 a new cold and flu product line was successfully introduced on the market. In connection with this project, L incurred the following costs:

---

[60] § 174(a).

[61] § 174(c).

[62] § 174(a)(2).

[63] § 174(b).

[64] § 174(b)(2).

Lab equipment (5-year property)	$50,000
Salaries	90,000
Laboratory materials	5,000

If L Corporation elects to expense the research and experimental costs, it may deduct $105,000 in 2005 as follows:

MACRS depreciation on lab equipment	
(20% of $50,000)	$ 10,000
Salaries	90,000
Laboratory materials	5,000
Total deductions	$105,000

Note that only the depreciation on the lab equipment may be deducted as a research and experimental cost, not the entire cost of the equipment. If L Corporation elects to defer the expense, its monthly amortization beginning December 1, 2005 would be

$$\frac{\$105,000}{60} = \$1,750$$

Alternatively, L could capitalize all the expenses as an asset (including the $10,000 of depreciation) and receive no deduction until a later disposition or abandonment.

OTHER RELATED PROVISIONS

Several other provisions exist relating to the treatment of research and experimental expenditures, such as a tax credit for research and experimentation. Generally, the credit is 20 percent of the current year's expenditures after adjustments (see Chapter 13).[65] Taxpayers electing the credit are generally required to reduce their research and experimentation expenses by 50 percent of the credit for purposes of computing the amount to either be expensed, deferred, or capitalized.[66] Special rules also exist for contributions of research property by corporations (see Chapter 11).[67]

EXPENSES OF FARMERS AND RANCHERS

Special provisions exist for certain types of expenditures incurred by those engaged in farming and ranching. The rules examined below generally differ from the treatment of expenses that normally would be considered capital expenditures subject to depreciation.

EXPENSES RELATED TO LIVESTOCK

Costs of acquiring animals used for breeding, dairy, work, or sport are treated as capital expenditures and are depreciable under MACRS unless such animals are primarily held for sale and would be appropriately included in inventory. If a farmer raises his or her own livestock, however, expenses incurred such as feed normally can be deducted as paid, assuming the taxpayer uses the cash basis method of accounting.[68]

---

[65] § 41.

[66] § 280C(c).

[67] § 170.

[68] Reg. § 1.162-12

This rule is in sharp contrast to that applying to other self-production costs. Costs incurred by farmers and others in constructing their own equipment and buildings must be capitalized and depreciated.

SOIL AND WATER CONSERVATION, FERTILIZER, LAND CLEARING

Farmers often incur expenses for soil and water conservation. Examples of these expenses are the costs of leveling or terracing the soil to control the flow of water, irrigation and drainage ditches, ponds, dams, eradication of brush, and planting windbreaks. Although normal tax rules would require these expenses to be capitalized, Code § 175 permits a deduction when such expenses are paid or incurred as long as such expenses are consistent with a conservation plan approved by the Soil Conservation Service of the Department of Agriculture. To encourage these practices and still restrict the availability of this benefit, the Code requires that the taxpayer be engaged in the business of farming. In addition, the annual deduction for these expenses is limited to 25 percent of the taxpayer's gross income from farming. This limitation prohibits a taxpayer from using the deductions to reduce nonfarm income. Expenditures exceeding this limitation may be carried over to subsequent years.

Like soil and water conservation expenditures, Code § 180 provides that the cost of fertilizer, lime, and other materials used to enrich farmland can be deducted in the year paid or incurred by those engaged in the business for farming. There is no limitation imposed on the amount of the deduction.

Taxpayers engaged in the farming business must capitalize expenses of clearing land in preparation for farming. These expenses include any cost of making the land suitable for farming such as those for removing and eradicating brush or tree stumps and the treating or moving of earth. Routine brush clearing and other ordinary maintenance related to the land may be expensed, however.

DEVELOPMENT EXPENSES

Expenses incurred in the development of farms and ranches prior to the time when production begins may be capitalized or expensed at the election of the taxpayer.[69] Examples of these expenses are costs of cultivation, spraying, pruning, irrigation, and management fees.

The expensing of development and other farm-related costs prior to the period in which the farm begins to produce income provides an attractive device for high-bracket taxpayers—who have no interest in farming—to shelter their income from other nonfarm sources. These and other tax advantages offered by farming in the 1960s brought such an influx of "urban cowboys" to the farming industry that several farm groups protested and demanded protection. Congress first responded to these groups in 1969. Currently, this provision prohibits the immediate expensing of any amount attributable to the planting, cultivation, maintenance, or development of any citrus or almond grove. Any of these development costs that are incurred in the first four years of the grove's life must be capitalized.

Congress adopted additional safeguards in 1976. Section 447 generally requires that corporations (and partnerships having a corporate partner) engaged in the business of farming must use the accrual method of accounting. Since this provision was intended to protect small farmers and family-owned farms, the following are not treated as corporations: (1) S corporations; (2) family-owned corporations (at least 50 percent of the stock is owned by family members); and (3) any corporation that did not have gross receipts exceeding $1 million in any prior year. In addition, farming syndicates may

---

[69] *Ibid.*

deduct the costs of feed, seed, fertilizer, and similar farm supplies only as they are actually used.[70] A farming syndicate generally is defined to include partnerships and S corporations where the sale of their interests is specifically regulated by state or local securities laws, or more than 35 percent of their losses during any period are allocated to limited partners or persons who do not actively participate in the management of the business.

In 1986 the prohibition against the deduction of prepaid farming expenses was extended to all farmers that prepay more than 50 percent of their expenses such as feed, seed, and fertilizer.[71] Farmers cannot deduct such expenses until the items are consumed or used. Several exceptions exist, however.

TAX PLANNING CONSIDERATIONS

DEPRECIATION AND AFTER-TAX CASH FLOW

Many taxpayers, when analyzing an investment, fail to consider the tax aspects. For example, a taxpayer who looks solely to the cash flow projections of investing in a rental property might overlook the effect of depreciation. The depreciation deduction does not require an outlay of cash, but does produce a tax benefit.

Example 36. In January of the current year, L purchased a duplex for $80,000, which she rented to others. Of the $80,000 purchase price, $70,000 was allocable to the building and $10,000 was allocable to the land. L financed the purchase with a $5,000 downpayment and a mortgage calling for monthly payments of interest and principal of $400. During the year, L rented the property for $7,000. Expenses for the year were as follows:

Mortgage interest	$4,000
Taxes	1,200
Insurance	500
Maintenance and utilities	300
Depreciation (MACRS: $70,000 × 3.485%)	2,440
Total expenses	$8,440

The net taxable loss from the real property would be

Rental income	$ 7,000
Less: Rental expenses	−8,440
Net taxable loss	$ 1,440

Note that the taxable loss contains depreciation expense of $2,440, a noncash expenditure. Assuming L is in the 28 percent tax bracket, the net cash flow from the project would be computed as follows:

---

[70] § 464.

[71] § 464(f).

Cash inflow:

Rental income..................		$ 7,000
Tax saving from loss ($1,440 × 28%)		403
Total cash inflow...............		$ 7,403
Cash outflow:		
Total expenses	$8,440	
Less: Depreciation	−2,440	
....	$6,000	
Debt service		
Mortgage payments ($400 × 12)	$ 4,800	
Less: Interest (included in expenses above)	−4,000	+ 800
Total cash outflow...............		(6,800)
After-tax cash flow		$ 603

Therefore, L has a positive cash flow of $603 on the project notwithstanding the taxable loss that she suffered of $1,440.

Under certain circumstances, limitations are imposed on the deduction of losses from rental property. These limitations are discussed in Chapter 12.

ACCELERATING DEPRECIATION WITH COST SEGREGATION

Prior to 1981, some taxpayers used a technique called "component depreciation" to accelerate real estate depreciation deductions. These taxpayers separated the costs of their depreciable buildings into various components with useful lives shorter than the rest of the building. For example, structural components such as wiring, plumbing, and roofing were depreciated over periods of 10 or 15 years rather than the much longer periods typically associated with the useful life of the building shell.

Although MACRS rules do not allow component depreciation for structural components of buildings, taxpayers may still be able to accelerate depreciation on some costs that might otherwise be depreciated over 27.5 or 39 years with the rest of the building's cost. Examples of assets that taxpayers should segregate from the cost of the building and depreciate over five or seven years include movable partitions, computers, separate fire protection systems, manufacturing equipment, and built-in desks and cabinets. Separate humidity-control and air conditioning systems installed specifically for special equipment can also be depreciated over seven years. A rule of thumb for identifying these separate depreciable assets is to assess whether the items would be removed if the business were to relocate. If so, the removable assets can have their own depreciation schedules.

Land improvements represent another set of costs that should be separated since they can be depreciated over 15 years. These include parking lots, landscaping, sewers and irrigation systems.

To segregate costs successfully, taxpayers or their advisers should work closely with building contractors to document the costs of fast-depreciating assets. Early involvement with the contractor or architect could even lead to building designs that maximize the number of separate depreciable assets while not reducing the productive use of the building.

GOODWILL AMORTIZATION RULE BENEFITS BUYERS AND SELLERS

Prior to August 10, 1993 the goodwill portion of the cost of acquiring a business provided no tax benefit to the buyer until the buyer later sold the business because the basis assigned to goodwill could not be amortized. Now that goodwill can be amortized over 15 years, its value is greater because the present value of a series of tax deductions received throughout a 15-year period is higher than the present value of a single deduction received many years in the future (assuming constant or declining marginal tax rates over time). Buyers and sellers will share this increase in value as they negotiate purchase/sale prices of their businesses.

Typically, buyers and sellers have some flexibility regarding the allocation of purchase price between goodwill (a capital asset that produces capital gain for the seller) and other intangibles. Two factors encourage increased allocations to goodwill. First, the seller will recognize capital gain income instead of ordinary income (assuming the allocation choice is between goodwill and a covenant not to compete). Second, for buyers concerned about earnings per share, goodwill may be preferable to payments for a covenant not to compete due to the treatment of goodwill under generally accepted accounting principles (GAAP). Under GAAP, goodwill normally is not amortized unless it is found to be impaired. Thus, as long as there is no reduction in the value of goodwill, no amortization is required. In contrast, the covenant may be amortized over its economic life. Buyers not concerned about GAAP should be indifferent between allocations to goodwill versus a covenant not to compete because *all* intangibles are amortizable over 15 years for tax purposes. Thus, at best, increased allocations to goodwill could benefit both buyers and sellers of businesses. At worst, increased goodwill allocations will neither help nor harm buyers or sellers.

PROBLEM MATERIALS

DISCUSSION QUESTIONS

9-1 *Requirements for Depreciation.* Indicate the basic requirements that must be satisfied before property may be depreciated.

9-2 *Depreciation and Amortization: Eligible Property.* Indicate whether a taxpayer could claim deductions for depreciation or amortization of the following property:
   a. Land used in the taxpayer's farming business.
   b. A duplex—the taxpayer lives in one half while he rents the other half out.
   c. The portion of the taxpayer's residence that she uses as a home office.
   d. The taxpayer's former residence, which he listed for rental temporarily until he is able to sell it. The residence was listed in late November and was not rented as of the end of the taxable year.
   e. A mobile home that the taxpayer initially purchased and used while he was in college and this year began renting to several students.
   f. The costs attributable to goodwill and a covenant not to compete.
   g. An automobile used for business. The taxpayer accounts for his deductible car expenses using the standard mileage rate.

9-3 *Definitions: Cost Allocation Methods and Types of Property.* Explain the terms depreciation, amortization, and depletion. Include in your discussion an explanation of tangible and intangible property as well as personal and real property.

9-4 *Depreciation Systems.* Briefly describe the depreciation systems (e.g., MACRS) for computing tax depreciation that one may encounter in practice.

9-5 *Ineligible Property.* What types of property are not depreciated using MACRS? How can the taxpayer avoid MACRS?

9-6 *Depreciation Methods and MACRS Statutory Percentages.*
  a. Indicate the first-year depreciation percentage applicable to office furniture and show how it is determined.
  b. Same as (a) except the property is an apartment building.

9-7 *MACRS and Straight-Line Depreciation.* Assuming a taxpayer desires to use the straight-line method of depreciation, what alternatives, if any, are available?

9-8 *Alternative Depreciation System.* Typically, all depreciation is computed using MACRS. However, Code § 168 also establishes an alternative depreciation system (ADS). As a practical matter, when will use of ADS be most likely?

9-9 *Depreciating Recovery Property.* During the year, X purchased land and a building for a total of $500,000 and furniture for the building for $100,000. He intends to lease the building. Indicate whether the following factors are taken into account in computing the depreciation of these assets.
  a. Each asset's useful life as estimated by the taxpayer in light of industry standards.
  b. Salvage value.
  c. The month in which the property was placed in service.
  d. The use of the building by the lessee.
  e. The taxpayer is a corporation.
  f. The property is used for investment rather than business use.
  g. The acquisition cost of the building including the land.
  h. The lessee.

9-10 *Half-Year Convention.* Indicate whether the following statements are true or false regarding the half-year convention.
  a. Depreciation can be claimed for the *entire* year if the asset has been in service for more than six months.
  b. The half-year convention applies to *all* property placed in service during the year.
  c. The half-year convention applies *both* in the year of acquisition and the year of disposition of the asset.
  d. The convention must be considered when expensing an asset under Code § 179.

9-11 *Acquiring a Business.* L has worked as a salesperson in the outdoor advertising business for ten years. This year he decided to go into business for himself. To this end he purchased all of the assets of Billboards Unlimited Corporation for $2 million. The value of the tangible assets such as the office building, furniture, and equipment was $1.4 million. Explain how L will recover the cost of his investment.

9-12 *Luxury Cars.* Indicate whether the following statements are true or false. If false, explain why.
  a. W purchased a new car used solely for business for $12,000. The limitations imposed by Code § 280F on deductions related to automobiles do not alter what W could claim in the year of acquisition.
  b. P Corporation is a distributor of hospital supplies. During the year, it purchased a $20,000 car for its best salesperson. Section 280F does not alter the total amount of depreciation deducted while P owns the car. Section 280F alters only the timing of the depreciation deductions.

9-13 *Leasing and Luxury Automobiles.* D is a manufacturer's representative for several different companies. His sales territory covers all of Indiana, Kentucky and Ohio. Recently, he decided it was time to get rid of his old car, which had just passed the 100,000-mile mark. Many of his friends have told him that he should lease his next car rather than buy it. Assuming D plans on using the car exclusively for business, briefly discuss the tax factors that should be considered in making the decision.

9-14 *Listed Property.* Indicate whether the following statements are true or false. If false, explain why.

    a. J is a part-time photographer. This year she purchased a camera that cost $1,000 for her videocassette recorder. Thirty percent of her usage was for business while the remainder was personal. J may use the accelerated depreciation recovery percentages of MACRS.

    b. P, a proprietor of a lighting store, purchased computer equipment for $10,000 which he uses 50 percent of the time for business. Under Code § 280F, the maximum deduction for depreciation and limited expensing in the first year is $500, while without § 280F the deduction would be $5,000.

    c. C purchased computer equipment that he uses 60 percent of the time for managing his investments and 35 percent of the time in connection with a mail-order business he operates out of his home. C may claim straight-line depreciation deductions based on 95 percent of the cost of the asset.

    d. G is employed as a research consultant for RND Corporation, a research institute. G uses the company's computer at the office but often takes home work, which she does on her home computer. G's use of her home computer for work done for her employer is considered qualified business use.

    e. T is a college professor who uses a computer, for which he properly claims deductions, to write textbooks in his home office. It is unnecessary for T to maintain records on business usage of the computer.

9-15 *Employer-Provided Automobiles.* WS Corporation, a large clothing manufacturer, provides a company car for each of its salespeople. Indicate whether the following statements are true or false. If false, explain why.

    a. An employee must generally include the value of any personal use of the automobile as income; however, he or she is allowed to depreciate the car to the extent of any business use and to deduct any other business-related operating expenses.

    b. This year B, an employee, used a new company-owned vehicle 55 percent of the time for personal purposes and 45 percent of the time for business. The corporation can only depreciate 45 percent of the car, and, since qualified business use is less than 50 percent, it cannot use limited expensing and must use straight-line depreciation.

    c. This year C, an employee, used a company car, driving it 50,000 miles: 40,000 for business and 10,000 for personal purposes. Under the arrangement with C, the company includes $20,250 (50,000 × 40.5 cents) in C's W-2 as additional income. C may deduct any business expenses incurred related to operation of the car.

    d. Assuming WS charges all of its employees 40.5 cents per mile for each mile of personal use, the corporation may ignore any personal use of the cars by its salespeople and depreciate 100 percent of the cost of the cars.

    e. WS Corporation also provides a car for its chief executive officer, C, who owns 10 percent of the company's stock. All of C's use is for business except for commuting to work, which represents 60 percent of the car's use. C reimburses the company for the personal use. WS may claim accelerated depreciation for the car based on 40 percent of the car's cost.

9-16 *Amortization.* How are the costs of patents, copyrights, and goodwill recovered?

9-17 *Leasing Restrictions.* Address the following:

    a. Construct a numerical example illustrating why a tax-exempt entity would rather lease than buy.

    b. R acquired a ten-year ground lease on three acres on which it constructed a small office building. Explain how R will recover its cost of the building.

9-18 *Depreciation—Allowed or Allowable.* R inherited her mother's personal residence in 1979 and converted it to rental property. Her basis for depreciation was $100,000. The residence had an estimated useful life of 30 years. This year, R sold the residence for $170,000. During the time R held the property, she never claimed a deduction for depreciation on the residence. What amount of gain will R report upon the sale?

9-19 *Salvage Value.* How is salvage value used in computing the depreciation deduction using MACRS?

9-20 *Depreciable Basis and Limited Expensing.* Explain how the taxpayer's depreciable basis may be affected by the amount expensed under the limited expensing election of § 179.

9-21 *Anti-Churning Rules.* Explain the purpose of the anti-churning rules and when they normally will apply.

9-22 *Component vs. Composite Depreciation.* Answer the following:
a. Distinguish component depreciation from composite depreciation.
b. May the taxpayer use either method? Explain.

9-23 *Mid-Quarter Convention.* T Company, a calendar year taxpayer, purchased $300,000 of equipment on December 3 of this year.
a. Under what circumstances will the mid-quarter convention apply in computing depreciation of the equipment?
b. Assume that T can purchase the equipment at any time during the year. How will T time the acquisitions if it wants to maximize the firm's depreciation deductions for the year?

9-24 *Additional First-Year (Bonus) Depreciation.* Assume the same facts in Question 9-23.
a. If T Company elects to claim bonus depreciation on the equipment, what is the total depreciation deduction allowed for the year?
b. If T elects to take the maximum § 179 expense option *and* claim bonus depreciation, what is the total depreciation deduction allowed for the year?

9-25 *Depletion.* Address the following:
a. Briefly describe how cost and percentage depletion are computed and determine which is used in a particular year.
b. Assuming the taxpayer has completely recovered her depletable cost basis (e.g., her basis is zero), is she entitled to further depletion deductions?

9-26 *Farming Expenses.* N plans on stepping down from his position as president of a large energy company in five years. At that time, he and his wife would like to move to the country where they would retire and perhaps operate a small dairy farm. N has spotted some land through which a sparkling creek runs. His accountant has suggested that he purchase the land now and begin to operate it despite initial losses. Explain the rationale behind the accountant's advice.

PROBLEMS

9-27 *Depreciation of Converted Personal-Use Property.* F purchased a mobile home to live in while at college. The home cost $20,000. When he graduated, he left the home in the trailer park and rented it. At the time he converted the home to rental property, it had a fair market value of $15,000.
a. What is F's basis for depreciation?
b. F now lives 75 miles away from his alma mater. Can he deduct the cost of traveling back to check on his rental property (including those trips on which he also attended a football game)?

9-28   *MACRS Accelerated Depreciation.* In 2005 T, a calendar year taxpayer, decided to move her insurance business into another office building. She purchased a used building for $70,000 on March 15. T also purchased new office furniture for the building. The furniture was acquired for $20,000 on May 1. Compute MACRS depreciation. Ignore first-year expensing and bonus depreciation. MACRS depreciation tables are located in the Appendix.

   a.   Compute T's depreciation deduction for 2005.

   b.   Compute T's depreciation deduction for 2006.

   c.   Assuming that T sold the office building and the furniture on July 20, 2007, compute T's depreciation for 2007.

   d.   Answer (a), (b), and (c) above assuming that the furniture was purchased on October 20.

9-29   *Mid-Quarter Convention.* Q Corporation anticipates purchasing $300,000 of office furniture and fixtures (seven-year property) next year. This will be Q's only personal property acquisition for the year. Q Corporation management is willing to purchase and place the property in service any time during the year to accelerate its depreciation deductions. In addition, management wants to depreciate the property as rapidly as possible. MACRS depreciation tables are located in the Appendix. Ignore bonus depreciation and limited expensing.

   a.   Compute depreciation for the first two years of ownership assuming *all* of the property is purchased and placed in service on February 2.

   b.   Compute depreciation for the first two years of ownership assuming *all* of the property is purchased and placed in service on December 6.

   c.   Compute depreciation for the first two years of ownership assuming $177,000 (59%) of the property is purchased and placed in service on February 2 and $123,000 (41%) is purchased and placed in service on December 6.

   d.   Based on the results of (a) through (c) above, what course of action do you recommend for Q Corporation?

9-30   *MACRS Straight-Line Depreciation.* G Corporation operates a chain of fast-food restaurants. On February 7, 2005 the company purchased a new building for $100,000. In addition, on May 5, 2005 G purchased a used stove for $5,000 and refrigeration equipment for $30,000 (both seven-year property). G does not elect to use the limited-expensing provision. The company does elect to compute depreciation using the straight-line method under MACRS. MACRS depreciation tables are located in the Appendix. Ignore bonus depreciation and limited expensing.

   a.   Why might G elect to use the straight-line method?

   b.   Assuming G elects to use the straight-line method and a seven-year recovery period for depreciating the stove applies, can it use MACRS accelerated recovery percentages for the refrigeration equipment? For the building?

   c.   Compute G's depreciation for the stove and building in 2005 assuming it elects the straight-line method for the seven-year property.

   d.   Compute the depreciation for the stove and building in 2006.

   e.   If G does not dispose of either the stove or building, what is the final (i.e., last year's) depreciation deduction for the stove and the building?

   f.   Assuming G disposes of both the stove and the building on October 18, 2006, what is the depreciation for each of these assets in 2006?

9-31   *ADS Depreciation.* P retired several years ago to live on a small farm. To supplement his income, he cuts wood and sells it in the nearby community. This year he purchased a used light duty truck to haul and deliver the wood. He used the truck 20 percent of the time for business. Assuming the truck cost $9,000, compute P's depreciation for the year.

9-32   *Section 179 Election.* Although K is currently a systems analyst for 3L Corporation, her secret desire is to write a best-selling novel. To this end, she purchased a computer for $3,000 this year. She used the computer only for writing her novel. Can she deduct the entire cost of her computer this year even though she has not yet received any income from the novel? Next year?

9-33 *Limitations on § 179 Expensing.* In each of the following situations, indicate whether T may elect to use the limited-expensing provisions of § 179. Assume the acquisition qualifies unless otherwise indicated.

a. T is a corporate taxpayer.

b. This year, T purchased a $500,000 building and $50,000 of equipment.

c. T suffered a net operating loss of $40,000 this year before consideration of the § 179 deduction.

d. T purchased the asset on the last day of the taxable year.

9-34 *Limited-Expensing Election: Eligible Property.* For each of the following assets, indicate whether the taxpayer may elect to expense a portion or all of the asset's cost.

a. A $40,000 car used 75 percent of the time for business purposes and 25 percent of the time for personal purposes.

b. A home computer used by the taxpayer to maintain records and perform financial analyses with respect to her investments.

c. An apartment building owned by a large property company.

d. A roll-top desk purchased by the taxpayer's father, who gave it to the taxpayer to use in her business.

9-35 *Limited-Expensing Election Calculations.* N, a single taxpayer, purchased duplicating equipment to use in his business. He purchased the equipment new on June 3 of the current year for $300,000. N elects to expense the maximum amount allowable with respect to the equipment.

a. What portion of the cost of the equipment may N expense for this year?

b. Compute N's depreciation deduction for the current year.

9-36 *Leasing Automobiles.* On May 27, 2005 J signed a three-year lease on a new Corvette with a list price of $40,000. His lease payments are $600 a month beginning on June 15. Assuming J is self-employed and uses the car exclusively for business, how does the lease affect his taxable income in 2005 and 2006?

9-37 *Section 280F Calculations.* In the current year, H purchased a new automobile for $30,000. The first-year expensing election is not made. Use the most current limits from Exhibit 9-11 in responding to the questions below.

a. Assuming the car is used solely for business, prepare a depreciation schedule illustrating the amount of annual depreciation to which H is entitled assuming he holds the car until the entire cost is recovered.

b. Assume the same facts as (a) except the car is used 80 percent of the time for business and 20 percent of the time for personal purposes. Compute the current year's depreciation deduction.

c. Same as (b) except the car is used 70 percent of the time for business, 10 percent of the time for production of income activities, and 20 percent of the time for personal purposes.

d. Same as (a) except the car is used 40 percent of the time for business and 60 percent of the time for personal purposes.

9-38 *Section 280F Calculations.* M purchased a new automobile for $40,000. The first year expensing election is not made. The car is used solely for business. M is in the 25 percent tax bracket. The present value factors for a 10 percent discount rate are as follows: year 1, .91; 2, .83; 3, .75; 4, .68; 5, .62; 6, .56; 7, .51; 8, .47; 9, .42; 10, .39; 11, .35; 12, .32; 13, .29; 14, .26; 15, .24; 16, .22; 17, .20.

a. Prepare a depreciation schedule.

b. Compute the total tax savings M will receive throughout the recovery period from depreciation deductions.

c. Using an after-tax discount rate of 10 percent, compute the present value of tax savings from depreciation deductions under § 280F.

d. Using an after-tax discount rate of 10 percent, compute the present value of tax savings from depreciation deductions under MACRS as if § 280F were repealed.

e. Compare the results of (b) and (c) above. What impact does discounting have in assessing the tax benefits of depreciation?

f. Compare the results of (c) and (d) above. What is the discounted after-tax cost of the § 280F limitations for this taxpayer?

9-39 *Research and Experimental Expenditures.* ABC Corporation is developing a new process to develop film. During the year, the company had the following expenditures related to research and development:

Salaries	$60,000
Laboratory equipment (5-year property).	30,000
Materials and supplies	10,000

Compute ABC's deduction for research and experimental expenditures under each of the alternative methods.

9-40 *Depletion.* DEF Company produces iron ore. It purchased a property for $100,000 during the year. Engineers estimate that 50,000 tons of iron ore are recoverable from the property. Given the following information, complete DEF's depletion deduction and undepleted cost basis for each year.

Year	Units Sold (tons)	Gross Income	Taxable Income before Depletion
1	15,000	$300,000	$124,000
2	20,000	400,000	50,000
3	10,000	250,000	90,000

9-41 *Depletion.* Assume the same facts in *Problem 9-42* except that barrels of oil are being produced rather than tons of iron ore. Compute DEF's depletion deduction and undepleted cost basis for each year.

CUMULATIVE PROBLEMS

9-42 David and Lauren Hammack are married with one child, Jim, age 12. The couple lives at 2006 Rolling Drive, Indianapolis, IN 46222. David is a product manager for G&P Corporation, a food company. Lauren operates a clothing store as a sole proprietorship (employer identification number 35-123444). The couple uses the cash method of accounting except where the accrual method is required. They report on the calendar year.

David earned a salary of $60,000 during the year. G&P also provides health insurance for David and his family. Of the total insurance premium, the company paid $750. Income taxes withheld from David's salary were $7,000. The couple paid $9,000 in estimated taxes during the year.

Lauren's father died on June 20. As a result, Lauren received $40,000 as beneficiary of a life insurance policy on her father. In addition, her father's will provided that she receive all of his shares of IBM stock. The stock was distributed to her in October when it was worth $30,000.

On August 1 of this year, the couple purchased a six-month Treasury Bill for $9,700. They redeemed it on February 1 of the following year for its face value,

$10,000. In addition, the couple purchased a previously issued AT&T bond with the face value of $1,000 for $890 on June 1. The bond pays interest at 6 percent per year on January 1 and July 1. On July 1 they received an interest payment of $30, which was also reported on Form 1099-INT, sent to them shortly after year-end. The couple plans on reporting any accrued market discount in taxable income when they sell or redeem the bond, in some future year.

Each year, Lauren travels to Paris to attend the annual fashion shows for buyers. When scheduling her trip for this year, Lauren decided to combine business with pleasure. On Thursday, March 6, Lauren departed for Paris, arriving on Friday morning. Friday afternoon was devoted to business discussions with several suppliers. Since the shows began on Monday, she spent the weekend touring Paris. After attending the shows Monday through Wednesday, she returned to Indianapolis on Thursday, arriving late that night. The cost of her round-trip air fare to Paris was $500. Meals were $30 per day and lodging was $100 per day for Friday through the following Wednesday.

In addition to running her own shop, Lauren teaches an M.B.A. course in retailing at the local university. She received a $5,400 salary for her efforts this year. The university withheld $429 in FICA taxes, but did not make additional tax withholdings related to the salary. The school is ten miles from her office. Normally, she goes home from her office to get dinner before she goes to the school to teach (16 miles from her home). According to her log, she made 80 trips from home to school. In addition, the log showed that she had driven 20,000 miles related to her clothing business. She uses the standard mileage rate to compute her automobile expenses.

Lauren's records, which she maintains for her business using the cash method of accounting, reveal the following additional information:

Sales	$120,000
Cost of goods sold	(50,000)
Gross profit	$ 70,000
Advertising	6,000
Insurance	1,400
Rent	9,000
Wages	15,000
Employment taxes	2,000

The insurance included (1) a $200 premium paid in September for coverage of her car from October through March of the following year; and (2) a $1,200 payment for fire insurance for June 1 through May 31 of the following year. Similarly, rent expense includes a $4,500 payment made on November 1 for rent from November through April. She has a five-year lease requiring semiannual rental payments of $4,500 on November 1 and May 1.

During the year, David purchased a new automobile for $30,000, which he uses 60 percent of the time for business (i.e., "qualified business usage" is 60 percent). His actual operating expenses, excluding depreciation, were $3,000.

In addition to the information provided earlier in this problem, the couple paid the following amounts during the year:

State income taxes	$5,500
County income taxes	500
Real estate taxes	2,400
Mortgage interest on their home	3,600
Charitable contributions	2,000

David and Lauren's social security numbers are 445-54-5565 and 333-44-5789, respectively. Their son Jim's social security number is 464-57-4681.

Compute David and Lauren's tax liability for the year. Make all computations (including any special elections required) to minimize the Hammacks' tax liability based on *current* tax law. If a tax return is to be prepared for this problem, complete the following forms: 1040 (including Schedules A, C, and SE), and 2106. There is no alternative minimum tax liability. (**Note:** If the § 280F limitations apply to any auto depreciation, you should use the most current numbers from Exhibit 9-11.)

9-43   Michelle Kay purchased a small building on February 1 of the current year for $650,000. In addition, she paid $15,000 for land. Ms. Kay obtained a $640,000 mortgage for the acquisition. She and five of her employees use the property solely to store and sell a variety of gift items under the business name of "Michelle's Gifts." The following information pertains to the business:

Sales	$950,000
Cost of goods sold	625,000
Wages for employees ($20,000 each)	100,000
Payroll taxes for five employees	?
Depreciation	?
Advertising	25,000
Mortgage interest	60,000
Legal services	20,000
Real estate taxes	4,000
Fire insurance	3,000
Meals and entertainment	2,500

During the year, Ms. Kay purchased the following assets for the business. She wants to depreciate all business assets as rapidly as the law allows.

	Cost	Month/Day of Acquisition
Personal computer	$14,000	March 31
Printer for computer	2,000	April 2
Office furniture and fixtures	20,000	April 29
Machinery (7-year property)	30,000	May 12

Michelle Kay was divorced from Benjamin Kay two years ago. The divorce decree stipulates that Benjamin Kay would receive the dependency exemption for their son, Eric (now 12 years old), even though Eric lives full-time with Ms. Kay in a home she maintains. During the year, Ms. Kay provided 25 percent of Eric's support and Mr. Kay provided 75 percent. Ms. Kay received $15,000 of alimony and $10,000 of child support from Mr. Kay during the year. Ms. Kay's social security number is 333-46-2974. Her address is 567 North Hollow Drive, Grimview, IL 48124. For business purposes, her employer ID number is 66-2869969. She uses the cash method of accounting for all purposes.

Unrelated to her business, Ms. Kay paid the following amounts during the year:

Estimated federal income taxes.	$16,000
State income taxes	3,500
County income taxes	1,500
Real estate taxes.	2,000
Mortgage interest on her home	5,600
Charitable contributions	2,900
Deductible contribution to individual retirement account (Note: This is a deduction for A.G.I. It is one of the "adjustments to income" on page 1 of Form 1040.).	2,000
Health insurance for Ms. Kay.	1,000

Compute Ms. Kay's tax liability for the year based on *current* tax law. (**Hint:** Ms. Kay's adjusted gross income is less than $100,000.) If a tax return is to be prepared for this problem, complete the following forms: 1040 (including Schedules A, C, and SE) and 4562. There is no alternative minimum tax liability. For grading purposes, attach a sheet to Schedule C showing supporting calculations for payroll taxes.

RESEARCH PROBLEMS

9-44 *Depreciation.* S is a land developer. During the year, he finished construction of a complex containing a new shopping mall and office building. To enhance the environment of the complex, substantial landscaping was done including the planting of many trees, shrubs, and gardens. In addition, S acquired a massive sculpture that served as the focal point of the complex. S also purchased numerous pictures, which were hung in the shopping center and office building. Can S claim depreciation deductions for any of the items noted above?

9-45 *Amortization.* During the year, the metropolis of Burnsberg accepted bids from various cable television companies for the right to provide service within its city limits. The accepted bid was submitted by Cabletech Inc. in the amount of $500,000. For this amount, the city granted the company a license to operate for 10 years. The terms of the agreement further provided that the company's license would be renewed if the city was satisfied with the services provided. May Cabletech amortize the cost of the license?

Chapter 10

CERTAIN BUSINESS DEDUCTIONS AND LOSSES

LEARNING OBJECTIVES

Upon completion of this chapter you will be able to:

- Determine when a deduction is allowed for a bad debt
- Understand the different tax treatment for business and nonbusiness bad debts
- Explain what constitutes a deductible casualty or theft loss
- Compute the amount of the deduction for casualty and theft losses
- Determine the net operating loss deduction and explain how it is treated
- Explain the basic tax accounting requirements for inventories

- Identify the costs that must be capitalized as part of inventory and the role of the uniform capitalization rules in making this determination
- Explain how inventory costs are assigned to costs of goods sold using the FIFO and LIFO assumptions
- Compute ending inventory using double-extension dollar-value LIFO
- Apply the lower of cost or market rule in valuing ending inventory

CHAPTER OUTLINE

The rules governing the treatment of expenses and losses discussed in Chapter 7 set forth the general requirements that must be met if the taxpayer wishes to claim a deduction. As already seen, the basic test—whether the item was incurred in carrying on business or profit-seeking activities—is often just the initial hurdle in obtaining a deduction. Other provisions in the Code may impose additional conditions or limitations that must be considered. This chapter examines some of the special rules that relate to certain business losses and expenses of the taxpayer, including the provisions for bad debts, casualty losses, the net operating loss deduction, and inventories.

BAD DEBTS

Loans are made for a variety of reasons. Some are made in connection with the taxpayer's trade or business while others are made for purely personal purposes. People also make loans hoping to make a profit. Regardless of the motive, with the extension of credit comes the possibility—as every lender knows—that the loan will never be repaid. When the borrower, in fact, cannot repay the loan, the taxpayer has what is termed a *bad debt* and may be entitled to a deduction. For tax purposes, a bad debt is considered a special form of loss subject to the specific rules of Code § 166. This provision governs the treatment of all types of bad debts: those that arise from the sale of goods or services such as accounts receivable, as well as those resulting from a direct loan of money. Moreover, § 166 applies regardless of the form of the debt (e.g., a secured or unsecured note receivable or a mere oral promise to repay).[1]

---

[1] Notes issued by a corporation (with interest coupons or in registered form) that are considered capital assets in the hands of the taxpayer are treated as worthless securities, as discussed in Chapter 12.

TREATMENT OF BUSINESS VERSUS NONBUSINESS BAD DEBTS

The tax treatment of a bad debt vastly differs depending on whether it is a *business* or *nonbusiness* bad debt. Business bad debts may be deducted without limitation. In contrast, nonbusiness bad debts are deductible only as *short-term* capital losses and are therefore subject to the limitation on deductions of capital losses (i.e., to the extent of capital gains plus $3,000).[2] Congress provided this distinctive treatment for nonbusiness bad debts in part to ensure that investments cast in the form of loans are handled in virtually the same manner as other investments that become worthless. As a general rule, an investment in a company's stock or bonds that becomes worthless also receives capital loss treatment.

Another difference between business and nonbusiness bad debts concerns the method allowed to claim a deduction. For some debts, it may be apparent that a portion of the loan will become uncollectible but determination of the exact amount must await final settlement. In the case of a nonbusiness bad debt, there is no deduction for partial worthlessness.[3] A deduction is postponed until the ultimate status of the debt is determined.

> **Example 1.** R loaned his neighbor $5,000 in 2004. During 2005 his neighbor declared bankruptcy, and it is estimated that R will recover no more than 20 cents on the dollar or a maximum of $1,000 from the debt. Although R can establish that he has a bad debt of at least $4,000 ($5,000 − $1,000), no deduction is permitted in 2005 since the debt is nonbusiness, and it is partially worthless. If in 2006 R settles for $500, he will realize a loss of $4,500. Assuming he has no capital gains or other capital losses, he may deduct $3,000 of this loss as a *short-term* capital loss and carry over the remaining $1,500 ($5,000 − $3,000 − $500) to the following year. On the other hand, if the debt had arisen from R's *business*, R could deduct $4,000 in 2005 based on his estimate of the uncollectible amount, and the $500 remainder of the loss in 2006, all against ordinary income.

Because of their significantly different treatments, the determination of whether a particular debt is a business or nonbusiness bad debt has produced substantial controversy.

Business Bad Debts. Business bad debts are defined as those that arise in connection with the taxpayer's trade or business.[4] To qualify, the loan must be closely related to the taxpayer's business activity. Simply making a loan to a business associate does not make the loan business-related; it must support the business activity. Common business bad debts include the following:

1. Uncollectible accounts receivable (for accrual basis taxpayers only)

2. Loans to suppliers to ensure a reliable source of materials

3. Loans to customers, clients, and others to preserve business relationships or nurture goodwill

4. Loans to protect business reputation

5. Loans or advances to employees

6. Loans by employees to protect their employment

7. Loans made by taxpayers in the business of making loans

---

[2] § 166(d)(1)(B). See Chapter 16 for a detailed discussion of capital gains and losses.

[3] Reg. § 1.166-5(a)(2).

[4] § 166(d)(2).

It is important to note that C corporations are not subject to the nonbusiness bad debt rules.[5] All loans made by a C corporation are deemed to be related to its trade or business. Thus, any bad debt of a corporation is considered to be a *business* bad debt.

Nonbusiness Bad Debts. A nonbusiness bad debt is defined as any debt other than one acquired in connection with the taxpayer's trade or business.[6] From a practical perspective, nonbusiness bad debts are simply those that do not qualify as business bad debts.

The most common nonbusiness bad debts are losses on personal loans, such as those made to friends or relatives. As suggested above, however, nonbusiness bad debt treatment also extends to loans that are made to make a profit and that essentially function as investments. For example, a loan to an acquaintance to start a new business is in effect an investment and thus a nonbusiness debt. Similarly, a loan to a business to protect an investment in such enterprise would be considered a nonbusiness debt. For instance, an investor may loan funds to a struggling corporation in which he owns stock, hoping that the infusion of cash might sustain it and save the original investment.

Although the dividing line between business and nonbusiness bad debts usually is clear, controversy typically arises in several common situations. One troublesome area involves taxpayers who frequently make loans to make a profit but who do not make such loans their full-time occupation. In such cases, the Service takes the view that the taxpayers are not in the business of making loans and thus any bad debts are not business bad debts. These situations can become even more difficult when the taxpayer devotes substantial time and energy to establishing and developing the business.

> **Example 2.** In *Whipple v. Comm.*, Whipple had made sizable cash advances to the Mission Orange Bottling Co., one of several enterprises that he owned.[7] He spent considerable effort related to these enterprises but received no type of compensation, either salary, interest, or rent. When these advances subsequently became worthless, Whipple deducted them as a business bad debt. The Supreme Court held that the loans made by the shareholder to his closely held corporation were nonbusiness bad debts even though Whipple had worked for the company. According to the Court:
>
> > Devoting one's time and energies to the affairs of a corporation is not of itself, and without more, a trade or business of the person so engaged. Though such activities may produce income, profit or gain in the form of dividends—this return is distinctive to the process of investing—as distinguished from the trade or business of the taxpayer himself. When the only return is that of an investor, the taxpayer has not satisfied his burden of demonstrating that he is engaged in a trade or business.

Despite the Court's holding in *Whipple*, taxpayers have achieved limited success where they have shown that they were in the business of organizing, promoting, and financing businesses.

The other prominent area of controversy concerns a situation common to many new struggling corporations: loans made to corporations by employees who are also shareholders. Here, the issues are similar to that above. Is the taxpayer making the loan to protect an investment or to protect his or her job (i.e., the business of being an employee)? When employee-shareholders have been able to show that a loan was made to protect their jobs rather than their investment, they have been able to secure business bad debt treatment.

---

5   § 166(d)(1).

6   § 166(d)(2).

7   63-1 USTC ¶9466, 11 AFTR2d 1454, 373 U.S. 193 (USSC, 1963).

GENERAL REQUIREMENTS

To be deductible, the debt must not only be partially or totally worthless but must also represent a bona fide debt and have a basis.[8]

Bona Fide Debt. A debt is considered bona fide if it arises from a true debtor-creditor relationship. For this relationship to exist, there must be a promise to repay a fixed and determinable sum, and the obligation must be enforceable under local law.

The question of whether there is valid debtor-creditor relationship usually arises when it appears that the taxpayer made the loan with little expectation of being repaid. This is typically the case when there is a close relationship between the taxpayer and the borrower. For example, loans to relatives or friends are likely to be viewed as nondeductible gifts rather than genuine debts. Such treatment is most likely where the lender makes little attempt to enforce repayment of the loan—a common occurrence when the borrower is a child or parent. In a similar fashion, advances to a closely held corporation that are not repaid may be considered nondeductible contributions to capital. On the other hand, loans made by a corporation may be something other than what they purport to be. For example, a loan to a shareholder may be treated as a disguised dividend distribution while a loan to an employee could be considered compensation.

To determine whether a bona fide debtor-creditor relationship exists requires an assessment of all of the facts and circumstances related to the debt. Besides the relationship of the parties, factors typically considered are (1) whether the debt is evidenced by a note or some other written instrument (in contrast to a mere oral promise to repay that has not been reduced to writing); (2) whether the debt is secured by collateral; (3) whether the debt bears a reasonable interest rate; and (4) whether a fixed schedule for repayment has been established.

Basis. A taxpayer may deduct a loss from a bad debt only if he or she has a basis in the debt.[9] For this reason, cash basis taxpayers who normally do not report income until it is received are not entitled to deductions for payments they cannot collect. Their loss is represented by the unrecovered expenses incurred in providing the goods or services. Conversely, accrual basis taxpayers who engage in credit transactions usually report income as it is earned. Accordingly, they may deduct bad debts for those amounts previously included in income. Uncollectible loans (as distinguished from accounts receivable) made by either cash or accrual basis taxpayers may be deducted, assuming the taxpayer has a basis for the loan.

Example 3. R is an orthodontist and uses the cash method of accounting. This year he completed some dental work for B for $3,000, which he never collected. In addition, he loaned $1,000 to a material supplier who left the country. Assuming both debts are worthless, R may deduct only the loan to the supplier for $1,000. No deduction is allowed for the uncollected $3,000 since R does not report the amount as income until he collects it and, therefore, has no basis in the debt. However, any expenses incurred in doing the dental work (i.e., materials. etc.) are deductible.

Worthlessness. Whether a debt is worthless ultimately depends on the facts. The Regulations indicate that a taxpayer does not have to undertake legal action to enforce payment or obtain an uncollectible judgment with respect to the debt to prove its worthlessness.[10] It is sufficient that the surrounding circumstances suggest that legal

---

[8]   Reg. §§ 1.166-1(c) and (e).

[9]   Reg. §§ 1.166-1(d) and (e).

[10]   Reg. §§ 1.166-2(a) and (b).

action would not result in recovery. Among the circumstances indicating a debt's worthlessness are the debtor's bankruptcy or precarious financial position, consistent failure to pay when requested, or poor health or death. As noted above, a *business* bad debt need not be totally worthless before a deduction is allowed. When events occur which suggest that the debt will not be recoverable in full, a deduction for partial worthlessness is granted.

DEDUCTION METHODS

As a general rule, deductions for bad debts must be claimed using the specific charge-off method.[11] This method—often called the direct write-off method—allows a deduction only in the year when the debt actually becomes worthless. The reserve method, which allows deductions for estimated bad debts and is typically used for financial accounting purposes, was repealed for all businesses except certain financial institutions and service businesses by the Tax Reform Act of 1986.

The direct write-off method provides some flexibility in accounting for business bad debts. When the facts indicate that a specific debt is *partially* worthless, the portion considered uncollectible may be deducted, but only if such portion is actually written off the taxpayer's books for financial accounting purposes.[12] Any remaining portion of the debt that later becomes worthless can be deducted in subsequent years. Using this approach, taxpayers need not wait until the debt becomes totally worthless before any deduction is claimed. Alternatively, taxpayers can wait until the debt becomes totally worthless and claim the entire deduction at that time. Note that when the debt is totally worthless (in contrast to partially worthless), there is no requirement that the debt actually be written off the taxpayer's books.

> **Example 4.** K Company is a major supplier of lumber to homebuilders. One of its customers, which owed the company $10,000, fell on hard times in 2005 and declared bankruptcy. Because this event suggests that the debt is partially worthless, a deduction is permitted. K estimated that it would recover $7,000 of the debt, and therefore claimed a $3,000 bad debt deduction in 2005. The $3,000 amount was also charged off the taxpayer's books as required. In 2007 K Company actually received $1,000 and deducted the remainder of the loss, $6,000 ($10,000 − $3,000 previously deducted − $1,000 actually received). Alternatively, K may opt to claim no deduction for 2005 and deduct the entire $9,000 loss in 2007. Note that when the debt becomes totally worthless in either case, the taxpayer is not required to write the debt off its books for financial accounting purposes. The company should take heed, however. If the IRS later determines that the debt is partially worthless, no deduction would be allowed since the debt was not written off on the books.

Experience Method for Service Businesses. Although the 1986 Act ostensibly eliminated the reserve method of accounting for bad debts, it provided an equivalent—but not identical—technique for service businesses. If a business uses the *accrual method* to account for income from services, the business is not required to accrue any amount that, *based on experience*, it knows will not be collected.[13] Businesses can take advantage of this exception only if they do not charge interest or a late charge on the amount billed. The experience method is available only for businesses that (1) have average annual gross receipts of less than $5,000,000 or (2) perform services in the

---

[11] § 166(a).

[12] Reg. § 1.166-3(a).

[13] § 448(d)(5).

following eight areas: health, law, engineering, architecture, accounting, actuarial science, performing arts, or consulting.

As a practical matter, the actual use of this technique may be limited, since most service businesses are allowed and often do use the cash method rather than the accrual method of accounting. Service businesses usually are exempt from the rule requiring use of the accrual method,[14] falling under the exceptions for sole proprietorships, S corporations, qualifying partnerships, personal service corporations, or taxpayers with gross receipts that generally do not exceed $5 million.

☑ CHECK YOUR KNOWLEDGE

Review Question 1. Over the years Dr. D has done extremely well financially and has made a number of investments. Several years ago, her good friend T started a small amusement park with such attractions as a water slide and a miniature golf course. Needing some venture capital, T convinced D to lend the new business $50,000, which he would repay to D in three years with 15 percent interest. This year the note came due and T was unable to repay because his business had failed. How will D treat the bad debt?

D's loan did not arise during the ordinary course of business but rather was in the nature of an investment. Therefore, the debt is considered a nonbusiness bad debt and is deductible as a short-term capital loss (limited annually to $3,000 plus capital gains).

Review Question 2. T worked for P Corporation for 25 years. When the company began struggling this year, she worked without pay. The company finally went out of business this year, owing T six months of back pay. Does T have a business or nonbusiness bad debt?

Neither. Although most taxpayers would believe that they have a deductible loss, such is not the case. As a cash basis taxpayer, which T no doubt is, no deduction is allowed because she has no basis in her debt. Had she reported the income (i.e., had she been on the accrual basis), the IRS would be happy to allow a bad debt deduction.

Review Question 3. At the close of 2004, Z Corporation, a lumber company, estimated that based on current year sales about $30,000 of its accounts receivable would be uncollectible. Therefore, in accordance with generally accepted accounting principles, the company adjusted its reserve account, charging bad debt expense for $22,000. May Z claim a $22,000 bad debt deduction for tax purposes?

For most businesses, the reserve method is not permitted for tax purposes. Since 1986 the law has generally required the use of the direct write-off method. Under this method, a taxpayer can claim a deduction for a bad debt only when the debt actually becomes totally or partially worthless. This requirement is relaxed for service businesses that are allowed to use a method based on their experience. Consequently, since Z is not a service business, it is not allowed to deduct $22,000 but only the amount that represents debts that are actually worthless.

---

[14] Subject to certain exceptions, § 448 requires corporations, partnerships with corporate partners, or tax shelters to use the accrual method of accounting.

CASUALTY AND THEFT LOSSES

GENERAL RULES

Unfortunately, as everyone knows, disaster may strike at any moment. Hurricanes hit, volcanoes erupt, and rivers overflow. Thieves steal, and people are mugged. The list of possible calamities is endless. Luckily, Congress has recognized that when such events occur they may seriously impair a taxpayer's ability to pay taxes. For this reason, taxpayers are generally allowed to deduct losses arising from casualty or theft. The special rules governing this deduction are the subject of this section.

The Code generally provides that an individual's losses arising from casualty or theft are deductible regardless of the activity in which the losses are incurred. An individual's casualty and theft losses related to profit-seeking activities may be deducted under the general rules, which provide that losses incurred in a trade or business or a transaction entered into for profit are deductible.[15] In addition, § 165(c)(3) expressly allows a deduction for losses related to property used for *personal* purposes where the loss arises from fire, storm, shipwreck, theft, or other casualty.

A deduction is allowed only for casualty losses related to property owned by the taxpayer; no deduction is allowed for damages the taxpayer may be required to pay for inflicting harm upon the person or property of another.[16] Further, the casualty must damage the property itself. A casualty that indirectly reduces the resale value of the property normally does not create a deductible loss (e.g., a mud slide near the taxpayer's residence).[17] Any expenses of cleanup, or similar expenses such as repairs to return the damaged property to its condition prior to the casualty, are usually deductible as part of the casualty loss. Incidental expenses that arise from the casualty, such as the cost of temporary housing or a rental car, are considered personal expenses and are not deductible as part of the casualty loss.

CASUALTY AND THEFT DEFINED

Casualties. The Code permits a deduction for losses arising not only from fire, storm, or shipwreck, but also from other casualties. While the terms *fire*, *storm*, and *shipwreck* are easily construed and applied, such is not the case with the phrase "other casualty." Interpretation and application of this phrase is a continuing subject of conflict. The courts and the IRS generally have agreed that to qualify as a casualty the loss must result from some *sudden, unexpected, or unusual event, caused by some external force*.[18] Losses deductible under these criteria include those resulting from earthquakes, floods, hurricanes, cave-ins, sonic booms, and similar natural causes.[19] On the other hand, losses resulting from ordinary accidents or normal everyday occurrences (e.g., breakage due to dropping) are not considered unusual and consequently are not deductible.[20] Similarly, no deduction is allowed for losses due to a gradual process, since such losses are not sudden and unexpected.[21] For this reason, losses suffered because of rust, corrosion, erosion, disease, insect infestation, or similar types of

---

[15] §§ 162 and 212.

[16] *Robert M. Miller*, 34 TCM 528, T.C. Memo 1975-110.

[17] *Pulvers v. Comm.*, 48 T.C. 245, *aff'd.* in 69-1 USTC ¶9272, 23 AFTR2d 69-678, 407 F.2d 838 (CA-9, 1969).

[18] *Matheson v. Comm.*, 2 USTC ¶830, 10 AFTR 945, 54 F.2d 537 (CA-2, 1931).

[19] *Your Federal Income Tax*, IRS Publication 17 (Rev. Nov. 96), p. 190.

[20] *Diggs v. Comm.*, 60-2 USTC ¶9584, 6 AFTR2d 5095, 281 F.2d 326 (CA-2, 1960).

[21] *Supra*, Footnote 18.

progressive deterioration, generally are not deductible. Unfortunately, the casualty criteria are vague, and the taxpayer may be forced to litigate to determine if his or her loss is sufficiently sudden or unusual to qualify. For example, the IRS has ruled that termite damage does not occur with the requisite swiftness to be deductible.[22] The courts, however, have found the necessary suddenness to be present in several termite cases and have allowed a deduction for the resulting losses.[23]

Thefts. Losses of business or personal property due to theft are deductible. The term *theft* includes, but is not limited to, larceny, embezzlement, and robbery.[24] If money or property is taken as the result of kidnapping, blackmail, threats, or extortion, it also may be a theft. Seizure or confiscation of property by a foreign government does not constitute a casualty or theft loss but may be deductible if incurred in profit-seeking activities.[25] Losing or misplacing items is not considered a theft but may qualify as a casualty if it results from some sudden, unexpected, or unusual event.[26]

Example 5. H slammed a car door on his wife's hand, dislodging the diamond from her ring, never to be found. The Tax Court held that the loss was deductible as an "other" casualty.[27]

LOSS COMPUTATION

The loss computation is the same whether the casualty or theft relates to property connected with profit-seeking activities or personal use.[28] As explained below, however, limitations on the amount of deductible loss may differ depending on the property's use.

The *amount* of the loss is the difference between the fair market value immediately before the casualty and the fair market value immediately after the casualty as reduced by any insurance reimbursement. Of course, when the property is completely destroyed or stolen, the loss is simply the fair market value of the property as reduced by any insurance reimbursement. Although appraisals are the preferred method of establishing fair market values, costs of repairs to restore the property to its condition immediately before the casualty may be sufficient under certain circumstances.[29]

For many years, a controversy existed concerning the deductibility of insured casualty losses for which taxpayers chose not to file a claim. The problem typically arises when taxpayers avoid filing a claim for fear that their insurance coverage may be cancelled or its cost may increase. When this occurs, the Treasury is effectively acting as an insurance company, partially subsidizing the taxpayer's loss. In 1986 Congress eliminated the controversy for *nonbusiness* property by providing that no deduction is permitted for casualty losses of insured property unless a timely insurance claim is filed.[30]

The amount of the deductible loss generally is limited to the lesser of the property's adjusted basis or fair market value (decline in value if a partial casualty).[31] The lesser of these two amounts is then reduced by any insurance reimbursements. There are two exceptions to this general rule, however. First, for property used in a trade or business or

---

22   Rev. Rul. 63-232, 1963-2 C.B. 97.

23   *Rosenberg v. Comm.*, 52-2 USTC ¶9377, 42 AFTR 303, 198 F.2d 46 (CA-8, 1952).

24   Reg. § 1.165-8(d).

25   *W.J. Powers*, 36 T.C. 1191 (1961).

26   Rev. Rul. 72-592, 1972-2 C.B. 101.

27   *John P. White*, 48 T.C. 430 (1967).

28   Reg. § 1.165-7(a).

29   Reg. § 1.165-7(a)(2)(ii).

30   § 165(h)(4)(E).

31   Reg. § 1.165-7(b)(i).

for the production of income that is *completely* destroyed or stolen, the deductible loss is the property's adjusted basis reduced by insurance reimbursements. Second, losses to property *used for personal* purposes are deductible only to the extent they exceed a $100 floor. The $100 floor does not apply to property used in a trade or business or for the production of income. The $100 floor applies to each event, not each item. Further, if spouses file a joint return, they are subject to a single $100 floor. If spouses file separately, each one is subject to a $100 floor for each casualty.[32]

In 1982 Congress added a further limitation on the deduction for casualty or theft losses of property used for personal purposes. In addition to the $100 floor on personal losses, only total losses (after reduction by the $100 floor) in excess of 10 percent of adjusted gross income are deductible.[33] This limitation does not apply to property used in a trade or business or an income-producing activity. The computation of the casualty and theft loss deduction is summarized in Exhibit 10-1.

EXHIBIT 10-1
Computation of Casualty and Theft Loss Deduction

Smaller of

    1. Decline in value; or
    2. Adjusted basis*

Less:

    ▸ Insurance reimbursement
    ▸ $100 floor/casualty if personal
    ▸ 10% of A.G.I. if personal

Equals: Deductible casualty loss

*Adjusted basis, rather than decline in value, must be used if business or income property is completely destroyed or stolen.

Example 6. R had four casualties during the year:

	Casualty	Property	Adjusted Basis	Fair Market Value Before Casualty	Fair Market Value After Casualty
1.	Accident	Business car	$ 3,000	$ 9,000	$ 5,000
2.	Robbery	Ring	500	800	0
		Suit	95	75	0
3.	Tornado	Residence	50,000	60,000	57,000
4.	Fire	Business computer	3,000	4,000	0

R received a $600 insurance reimbursement for his loss on the residence. The deductible loss for each casualty is as follows:

    1. The loss for the business car is $3,000 [lesser of the decline in value $4,000 ($9,000 − $5,000) or the adjusted basis of $3,000]. The deduction is *for* adjusted gross income unless it is related to R's business as an employee, in which case the deduction would be an itemized deduction.

[32] Reg. § 1.165-7(b)(4)(iii).

[33] § 165(h)(2).

2. The loss for the ring and suit is $475. The loss for the ring is $500 [lesser of decline in value of $800 ($800 − $0) or the adjusted basis of $500]. The loss for the suit is $75 [lesser of decline in value of $75 ($75 − $0) or the adjusted basis of $95]. The total loss attributable to the robbery is $575 ($500 + $75). This loss must be reduced by the $100 floor to $475 ($575 − $100). Note that the $100 floor is applied to the event, not to each item of loss. The loss, subject to the ten percent overall limitation, is deductible *from* adjusted gross income.

3. The loss for the residence is $2,300 [lesser of decline in value of $3,000 ($60,000 − $57,000) or the adjusted basis of $50,000, reduced by the insurance reimbursement of $600 and the $100 floor]. The loss, subject to the ten percent overall limitation, is deductible *from* adjusted gross income. Assuming R's adjusted gross income is $20,000, $775 is deductible [$2,300 + $475 − $2,000 (10% × $20,000)].

4. The loss for the computer is $3,000. Since the computer is used for business and is completely destroyed, the loss is the adjusted basis of the property regardless of its fair market value. The loss is deductible *for* adjusted gross income.

CASUALTY GAINS AND LOSSES

When the claims for some casualties are settled, the insurance reimbursement may exceed the taxpayer's adjusted basis for the property resulting in a gain. As discussed in Chapter 15, the Code provides some relief in this case, permitting the taxpayer to postpone recognition of the gain if the insurance proceeds are reinvested in similar property. When the gain must be recognized, however, Code § 165(h) sets forth special treatment.

Under § 165(h), all gains and losses arising from a casualty unrelated to business or a transaction entered into for profit—*personal casualty gains and losses*—must first be netted. For this purpose, the personal casualty loss is computed after the $100 floor but before the 10 percent limitation. If personal casualty gains exceed personal casualty losses, each gain and each loss is treated as a gain or loss from the sale or exchange of a capital asset. The capital gain or loss would be long-term or short-term depending on the holding period of the asset. In contrast, if losses exceed gains, the net loss is deductible as an itemized deduction to the extent it exceeds 10 percent of the taxpayer's adjusted gross income.

Example 7. T had three separate casualties involving personal use assets during the year:

	Casualty	Property	Adjusted Basis	Fair Market Value Before Casualty	Fair Market Value After Casualty
1.	Accident	Personal car	$12,000	$ 8,500	$ 6,000
2.	Robbery	Jewelry	1,000	4,000	0
3.	Hurricane	Residence	60,000	80,000	78,000

T received insurance reimbursements as follows: (1) $900 for repair of the car; (2) $3,200 for the theft of her jewelry; and (3) $1,500 for the damages to her home. Assuming T does not elect (under § 1033) to purchase replacement jewelry, her personal casualty gain exceeds her personal casualty losses by $300, computed as follows:

1. The loss for the car is $1,500 [(lesser of $2,500 decline in value or the $12,000 adjusted basis = $2,500) − $900 insurance recovery − $100 floor].

2. The gain for the jewelry is $2,200 ($3,200 insurance recovery − $1,000 adjusted basis).

3. The loss from the residence is $400 [(lesser of $2,000 decline in value or the $60,000 adjusted basis = $2,000) − $1,500 insurance recovery − $100 floor].

T must report each separate gain and loss as a gain or loss from the sale or exchange of a capital asset. The classification of each gain and loss as short-term or long-term depends on the holding period of each asset.

> **Example 8.** Assume the same facts as in *Example 7* except the loss for the personal car was not insured. In this case the loss on the car is $2,400 and the personal casualty losses exceed the gain by $600 ($2,400 + $400 − $2,200). T must treat the $600 net loss as an itemized deduction subject to the limitation of 10% of A.G.I.

YEAR DEDUCTIBLE

A casualty loss usually is deductible in the taxable year in which the loss occurs.[34] A theft loss is deductible in the *year of discovery*. If a claim for reimbursement exists and there is a reasonable prospect of recovery, the loss must be reduced by the amount the taxpayer *expects* to receive.[35] If later receipts are less than the amount originally estimated and no further reimbursement is expected, an amended return is *not* filed. Instead, the remaining loss is deductible in the year in which no further reimbursement is expected. If the casualty loss deduction was reduced by the $100 floor in the prior year, the remaining loss need not be further reduced. However, the remaining loss is subject to the 10 percent limitation of the later year.

> **Example 9.** G's diamond bracelet was stolen on December 4, 2005. Her loss was $700 before taking into account any insurance reimbursement. She expects the insurance company to reimburse her $400 for the loss. In 2005 G may deduct $200 ($700 loss less the expected reimbursement of $400 and reduced by the $100 floor) subject to the 10% limitation for 2005. If G actually receives only $300 in the following year, she may deduct an additional $100 (the difference between the expected reimbursement of $400 and the $300 received) subject to the 10% limitation for 2006. If the reimbursement was greater than that expected, the excess is included in gross income.

A special rule exists for the reporting of casualty losses sustained within an area designated by the President as a "disaster area." This rule permits the taxpayer to accelerate the tax relief provided for casualty losses by electing to deduct the disaster loss in the taxable year immediately preceding the year of the disaster loss.[36]

> **Example 10.** F, a calendar year taxpayer, suffered a loss in a "disaster area" from a flood on March 4, 2005. F may elect to deduct the loss on his 2004 return. If he has not filed the return by the casualty date, he may include the loss on the original 2004 return. If the 2004 return has been filed prior to the casualty, an amended return or refund claim is required. Alternatively, F could claim the loss on his 2005 return. In determining which year to claim the loss, F should consider the effect of the 10% limitation. For example, assume F had no other casualty losses in 2005 and his casualties in 2004 exceeded 10% of his 2004 adjusted gross income. F would derive greater tax benefits by deducting the loss in 2004 since the *entire* loss would be deductible, while the loss deduction in 2005 would be reduced by 10% of his 2005 adjusted gross income.

---

[34] Reg. § 1.165-7(a).

[35] Reg. § 1.165-1(d)(2)(i).

[36] § 165(i).

✔️ *CHECK YOUR KNOWLEDGE*

Review Question 1. While acting like a couch potato and channel surfing one rainy day, S felt a drop on the end of his nose. Then, all of a sudden, water started gushing out of the ceiling. S later determined that squirrels had eaten a hole in his roof. Can S claim a casualty loss deduction for any damage caused by the squirrels? What must S demonstrate before he can claim a casualty loss deduction?

In order to claim a deduction for an "other casualty," S must establish that the damage is sudden, unexpected, and unusual. As can be imagined, these standards are often difficult to apply. In this case, the IRS has ruled that no deduction was allowed since it is common knowledge that squirrels are destructive and because the roof holes caused by the rodents were not unexpected or unusual.[37]

Review Question 2. In 1996 B purchased a music box as a Christmas present for his wife at a cost of $1,000. This year the box was stolen. It turned out that the music box was an antique worth more than $5,000. Because of the deductible on his homeowner's insurance policy, B received only $400 for his loss.

a. Before considering *any* limitation, what is the amount of B's casualty loss deduction?

In the case of a casualty of personal use property, a taxpayer is generally allowed to deduct the lesser of the property's value or basis as reduced by any insurance reimbursement. As a result, B is allowed to deduct a loss of $600 ($1,000 − $400).

b. After B found out that his loss in the eyes of the tax law was only $600, he went crazy. He said it was ridiculous to allow a deduction of only $600 when in fact his economic loss was really $4,600 ($5,000 − $400). Is B right or wrong?

B's belief that he has a $4,600 loss rather than a $600 loss is based on the value of the property. It is true that he has had an economic loss of $4,600, but he never had to recognize the increase in value from $1,000 to $5,000 as income for tax purposes. Therefore, the loss is measured from his basis.

c. Answer (a) assuming the music box had been worth only $700.

In this case, the deduction would be $300 [(lesser of fair market value, $700, or basis, $1,000) − $400]. Note that B would probably believe this is unfair since he paid $1,000 for the box and was reimbursed only $400. However, the starting point for measuring the loss is the value; Congress did not want to allow a deduction for the loss in value that is not attributable to the casualty since to do so would allow the taxpayer to deduct a personal expense.

d. Even though B has a casualty loss, he will probably not receive any tax relief. Why?

Despite the loss, the deduction for *personal* casualty losses is subject to two limitations. The amount of the casualty (as measured above) must exceed the $100 floor per casualty and 10 percent of the taxpayer's adjusted gross

---

[37] Ltr. Rul. 8133097.

income. After the 10 percent floor was added to the law in 1982, reported casualty loss deductions fell by 97 percent. Because of this limitation, a personal casualty loss must be almost catastrophic before a taxpayer receives any tax relief.

e. Answer (a) and (c) assuming that B was in the business of selling music boxes.

If the property is used in a trade or business, the taxpayer is entitled to a deduction equal to the basis of the property reduced by an insurance reimbursement. Consequently, in (a), where the box is worth $5,000 and has a basis of $1,000, the deduction would be $600 (adjusted basis $1,000 − insurance reimbursement $400). The same rationale provided for the solution in (b) above applies here. The deduction is limited since the taxpayer has never recognized the appreciation as income. In (c), where the box is worth $700 and has a basis of $1,000, the taxpayer is also allowed a deduction for $600 (rather than $300 as was the case when the property was used for personal purposes). Note that even though the value of the property is less than its basis, the business taxpayer is allowed to deduct the entire basis in the property. This treatment is allowed since the taxpayer would have been able to deduct the $1,000 in any event because the property is used in a trade or business. For example, the taxpayer would be able to claim a deduction when the property was sold or if the property was depreciable, through depreciation.

Review Question 3. Checkers Pizza delivers. This year one of its cars was stolen. Does the $100 floor and 10 percent of adjusted gross income limitation apply in determining the amount of its casualty loss?

The $100 floor and 10 percent rule do not apply to casualties of property used in a trade or business or an income-producing activity. These limitations apply only to casualties of personal use property.

Review Question 4. During 2004, the Smiths' house was destroyed by a hurricane. As a result, the Smiths moved into a motel until their home was rebuilt six months later. The cost of their motel stay was $2,700. May the couple deduct the $2,700 cost as a casualty loss?

No deduction is allowed. This is considered an incidental personal expense and is not deductible as part of the casualty loss.

NET OPERATING LOSSES

As someone once said, life is not always a bed of roses. This chapter, at least in part, is a testimonial to that. Debts do go bad, lightning may strike, and casualties can happen. Perhaps taxpayers can take some consolation in that in both of these cases, the government shares in the taxpayer's misfortune and provides some relief. Unfortunately, this section also dwells on the negative. For some taxpayers, income does not always exceed deductions. Businesses are not always profitable and catastrophic events may give rise to large expenses. In those lean or rotten years, the taxpayer may actually have a negative taxable income, usually referred to as a loss. When this happens, as might be expected, the taxpayer to his or her joy does not have to pay taxes. More importantly, the taxpayer may be able to use the loss to reduce his or her tax in a previous or subsequent year. This section examines this possibility.

In a year during which the taxpayer's deductions exceed gross income, the taxpayer is allowed to use the excess deductions to offset taxable income of prior or subsequent years.[38] Technically, the excess of deductions over income, as modified for several complex adjustments, is referred to as the taxpayer's *net operating loss* (NOL).[39] The Code generally permits the taxpayer to carry back the NOL two years and forward 20 years to redetermine taxable income.[40]

Allowance of the net operating loss deduction reduces the inequity that otherwise exists due to the use of an annual reporting period and a progressive tax rate structure. For example, consider a situation involving two taxpayers, R and S, who over a two-year period have equivalent taxable incomes of $100,000 each. R earned $50,000 each year while S earned $300,000 in the first year and had a loss of $200,000 in the second year. Without the NOL provisions, S would *not* be able to offset his $200,000 loss against his $300,000 income and consequently would pay a substantially greater tax than R. Such a result clearly would be unfair since both taxpayers had identical taxable incomes over the two-year period. The NOL provision partially eliminates this inequity by allowing a loss in one year to offset income in other years.

CARRYBACK AND CARRYFORWARD YEARS

As mentioned above, an NOL resulting in the current year is generally carried back two years and forward 20 years. The loss is first carried back to the second prior year (i.e., the earliest year first) and taxable income is recomputed for that year. If any loss remains after reducing that year's tax liability to zero, the remaining loss is carried to the first prior year. If a loss still remains, the taxpayer carries it forward to the first year after the loss and so on up to the 20th year following the loss year. For example, a loss occurring in 2005 would be applied to taxable income of these years as follows: 2003, 2004, 2006, 2007, . . . , 2024, 2025.

The taxpayer may *elect* to forego the carryback period and carry forward the loss instead.[41] The election is made simply by attaching a statement to the tax return for the year to indicate the taxpayer's intention of forgoing the carryback period. This election must be made by the due date of the return (including extensions) in which the net operating loss is reported. The election *cannot* be subsequently claimed or revoked by filing an amended return. This election normally is appropriate only where the taxpayer expects future profits. If future profits are anticipated, the taxpayer must determine whether carrying the loss back or forward will yield the greater tax benefit. This decision is often difficult since the taxpayer may be unable to predict the future with any certainty.

When the taxpayer carries the loss back to a prior year, the loss deduction is claimed on an amended return for the earlier year (Form 1040X). For this purpose, the statute-of-limitations period for returns of the earlier years normally is extended to three years after the due date (including extensions) of the return in which the loss is reported.[42] Alternatively, the loss may be claimed using Form 1045 (Form 1139 for corporations) for a so-called quick refund. This form must be filed *after* the return of the loss year is filed and *within* one year after the *close* of the loss year. If the taxpayer fails to file Form 1045, an amended return (Form 1040X) may still be filed.

---

[38]   § 172.

[39]   § 172(c).

[40]   § 172(b)(1). Pre-1998 NOLs are carried back three and forward 15 years. NOLs arising in 2001 and 2002 may be carried back five rather than two years.

[41]   § 172(b)(3)(c).

[42]   § 6511(d)(2).

Example 11. B, a calendar year taxpayer, reported a loss for 2005. He filed his 2005 return April 15, 2006. Under normal conditions, B must file an amended return for 2003 (the year to which the loss is carried) by April 15, 2007 (three years after April 15, 2004, the due date for the 2003 return). The Code, however, extends the period for filing an amended return for 2003 until April 15, 2009, three years after the due date of the return for the loss year. Alternatively, B may claim the loss using Form 1045 by filing the form before December 31, 2006, one year after the close of the loss year.

Where the taxpayer carries the loss forward, the loss deduction is claimed on the subsequent year's normal return (Form 1040).

If the taxpayer has losses occurring in two or more years, the loss occurring in the earliest year is used first. When the loss from the earliest year is absorbed, the losses from later years may be claimed.

NET OPERATING LOSS COMPUTATION

The term *net operating loss* (NOL) is defined as the excess of the deductions allowed over gross income, computed with certain modifications.[43] The purpose of the modifications is twofold. First, the net operating loss provisions are designed to permit a taxpayer a deduction for his or her true *economic* loss. Thus, certain artificial deductions that do not require cash outlays (such as the deductions for personal and dependent exemptions) are added back to negative taxable income. Second, the net operating loss provisions were enacted to provide relief only in those cases where there is a business or casualty loss. As a practical matter, a net operating loss is caused by one of the following:

- ► Loss from operating a sole proprietorship (e.g., a loss on Schedule C)
- ► Loss from rental operations in which the taxpayer actively participates subject to certain limitations
- ► Share of an S corporation or partnership loss
- ► A casualty or theft loss

Since the NOL provisions generally allow only for the carryback or carryforward of losses attributable to business or casualty, restrictions are imposed on the amount of nonbusiness expenses that may be deducted in computing the NOL. As will be seen, it is these limitations on the deduction of nonbusiness expenses and losses that make the computation of the NOL deduction so complex.

The net operating loss deduction of an individual taxpayer is computed by making the following modifications in computing taxable income.[44]

1. Any net operating loss deduction carried forward or carried back from another year is not allowed.

2. The deduction for personal and dependent exemptions is not allowed.

3. Deductions for capital losses and nonbusiness expenses are limited as explained below.

To determine the extent of any deduction for capital losses and nonbusiness expenses, gross income must be classified into *four* categories: (1) capital gains from business; (2) other income from business; (3) capital gains not from business; and

---

[43]   *Supra*, Footnote 39.

[44]   § 172(d)(1) through (4).

(4) other income not from business. With income so classified, the following rules are applied with respect to nonbusiness expenses and capital losses in the following order:[45]

1. Nonbusiness capital losses may be deducted to the extent of any nonbusiness capital gains; thus, any excess is added back to taxable income.

2. Nonbusiness expenses may be deducted to the extent of any nonbusiness income, including any excess of nonbusiness capital gains over nonbusiness capital losses (as determined in step 1); thus, any excess is added back to taxable income.

3. Business capital losses may be deducted to the extent of any business capital gains; any excess business capital losses may be deducted to the extent of any excess of nonbusiness capital gains over nonbusiness capital losses and nonbusiness expenses (as determined in step 2).

A general formula for computing the NOL deduction is set forth in Exhibit 10-2. As may be surmised from the previous discussion and the formula, the critical first step when actually calculating the deduction is classifying income and deductions and gains and losses as either business or nonbusiness. Exhibit 10-3 identifies and classifies the most common items appearing on tax returns.

EXHIBIT 10-2
Computation of Net Operating Loss

Taxable loss shown on return

Add back:
- Exemptions

- Nonbusiness deductions
    Less:
        Nonbusiness ordinary income
        Nonbusiness net capital gain

- Nonbusiness capital losses
    Less:
        Nonbusiness capital gains

- Business capital losses
    Less:
        Nonbusiness net capital gains
        Less: (Nonbusiness deductions − nonbusiness income)

Equals: Net Operating Loss Deduction

---

[45] § 172(d)(4).

EXHIBIT 10-3

Calculation of Net Operating Loss Deduction: Classification of Business and Nonbusiness Income and Expenses

Business income	Nonbusiness income
Salaries and wages	Interest income
Schedule C income	Dividends
Rental income	Pension income
Farm income	Annuity income
Partnership and S corporation income if not passive	Partnership and S corporation income if passive
Gains from sale of business assets	Gain from sale of capital assets not used in business (such as stocks)

Business deductions	Nonbusiness expenses
Schedule C expenses	Standard deduction
Rental expenses	Itemized deductions including medical, interest, taxes, contributions
Farm expenses	
Partnership and S corporation loss if not passive	Partnership and S corporation loss if passive
Casualty or theft losses (business and personal)	IRA contribution
Loss on sale of § 1244 stock	Contribution to self-employed retirement plan
Miscellaneous itemized deductions for business	Alimony
Moving expenses	

Example 12. In 2005 G quit his job and opened a car repair shop. G's filing status is married, filing jointly, and he reported the following income and deductions for the year:

Income

Business income.	$ 40,000
Salary from previous job	10,000
Business capital gains—long term	7,000
Business capital losses—long term	(2,000)
Nonbusiness capital gains—long term	5,000
Nonbusiness capital losses—long term	(3,000)
Interest income on nonbusiness investments	1,000

Expenses

Business expenses.	70,000
Casualty loss on personal car.	5,100
Interest on home mortgage.	8,000

Taxable income is computed as follows:

Net business loss ($40,000 − $70,000)		($ 30,000)
Salary		10,000
Interest earned		1,000
Net long-term capital gain.		7,000
Adjusted gross income (loss)		($ 12,000)
Less: Itemized deductions		
Casualty loss	$5,000*	
Mortgage interest paid	8,000	(13,000)
Less: Personal exemptions ($3,200 × 2)		(6,400)
Taxable income (loss).		($ 31,400)

*$5,100 − $100 floor. Note that the 10 percent limitation does not apply since A.G.I. is a negative number.

Following the format of Exhibit 10-2, G's net operating loss for 2005 is computed as follows:

Taxable income (loss)			($31,400)
Modifications			
Add back:			
Personal exemptions			6,400
Excess nonbusiness expenses:			
Mortgage interest		$ 8,000	
Nonbusiness income:			
Interest.........................	$ 1,000		
Nonbusiness net capital gain ($5,000 − $3,000)	+ 2,000	(3,000)	5,000
Net operating loss for 2005			($20,000)

Computation of the real dollar loss or economic loss results in a similar deduction:

Business loss...	($30,000)
+ Salary..	10,000
+ Business capital gains	5,000
− Casualty loss.......................................	(5,000)
Net operating loss	($20,000)

Note that the nonbusiness income (capital gains of $2,000 and interest income of $1,000) is not considered in this computation of economic loss since it is offset by nonbusiness expenses.

RECOMPUTING TAXABLE INCOME FOR YEAR TO WHICH NET OPERATING LOSS IS CARRIED

Once the net operating loss deduction is computed, it is carried to the appropriate year and used in the recomputation of taxable income for that year. The net operating loss deduction is a deduction *for* A.G.I. As a result, the deduction may have an effect on the amount of the deduction for certain items such as medical expenses, which are based on the taxpayer's A.G.I. All expenses based on A.G.I. except charitable contributions must be *recomputed* in determining the revised taxable income.[46] The net operating loss deduction also may have an effect on any tax credits originally claimed. For example, if a year 2007 net operating loss deduction completely eliminates the taxable income of 2005, any credit originally claimed in 2005 becomes available for use in another year.

After the effect on the tax of the earliest year is computed, the amount of any loss remaining to be carried forward must be determined. In other words, a computation is required to determine how much of the net operating loss is absorbed in the year to which it is carried and how much may be carried to subsequent years. Although this calculation is somewhat similar to that explained above, additional nuances exist making the computation somewhat complex. For this reason, further reference should be made to the Regulations and Form 1045.

---

[46] Reg. § 1.172-5(a)(3)(ii).

☑ **CHECK YOUR KNOWLEDGE**

During 2005, C. D. opened his own computer store, specializing in sales of multimedia. He operated the business as an S corporation. Upon his first crack at computing his taxable income for the year, C. D. determined that he had a negative taxable income of $15,000 (see line 37, page two of Form 1040).

Review Question 1. Assuming C. D. has a net operating loss for the year, how is it treated?

An NOL is generally carried back two years and forward 20 years. The 2005 loss is carried back to the second prior year (i.e., the earliest year, 2003), where taxable income is recomputed and a refund claim is filed. If any loss remains after reducing the taxable income of 2003 to zero, the loss is carried forward to the first prior year (i.e., 2004). If a loss still remains, C. D. may carry it forward for up to 20 years, after which any remaining loss expires and is lost. Alternatively, C. D. may elect not to carry the loss back but to carry the loss forward for 20 years. Carrying forward the loss may make more sense if he expects to be in a tax bracket in the future that is higher than past years. In such case, the loss would produce greater benefit.

Review Question 2. A review of C.D.'s tax return reveals that his negative taxable income of $15,000 includes several items of income and deductions. For example, his only income other than that related to his business was interest and dividends of $5,000. Indicate whether the following deductions would be allowed in computing C. D.'s net operating loss deduction and, if so, how much could be used.

   a. Personal exemption
   b. Dependency exemption
   c. Net loss from S corporation operations (sales less operating expenses)
   d. Casualty loss to personal residence from earthquake damage
   e. Interest expense on the mortgage on his personal residence of $7,000
   f. Net capital loss $8,000 ($3,000 used to offset ordinary income and $5,000 carried over)

In computing his net operating loss deduction, C. D. must make certain adjustments to negative taxable income to arrive at the taxpayer's true economic loss that the law allows to be carried over. No deduction is allowed for personal or dependency exemptions since these are artificial deductions. Therefore, the exemption deduction must be added back to negative taxable income. The net loss from his business (i.e., the S corporation) does reduce taxable income in calculating the NOL, so there is no adjustment. The casualty loss is also allowable in computing the NOL. Nonbusiness expenses such as mortgage interest and taxes are considered personal expenses and can be deducted only to the extent of nonbusiness income. Therefore, only $5,000 of the $7,000 expense is deductible, requiring an addback of $2,000. Finally, a capital loss can generally be used only to offset capital gains. Thus the $3,000 deduction attributable to the capital loss is not allowed and must be added back.

INVENTORIES

As might be expected, taxpayers who buy or produce merchandise for subsequent sale are not allowed to deduct the costs of the merchandise *at the time* the goods are produced or purchased. Instead, such costs normally must be capitalized (i.e., inventoried) and deducted when the goods are sold. The following example illustrates what might occur if taxpayers were not required to capitalize the costs of inventory.

Example 13. C Corporation began business in 2005 and purchased 10,000 gizmos at $10 each for a total of $100,000. In 2005 the corporation sold 6,000 gizmos for $120,000. In 2006 the corporation made no further purchases and sold the remaining 4,000 gizmos for $80,000. Gross profit reported with and without inventories is computed below.

	No Inventories		Inventories	
	2005	2006	2005	2006
Sales	$120,000	$80,000	$120,000	$80,000
Cost of good sold:				
Beginning inventory	—	—	—	$40,000
+ Purchases	$100,000	—	$100,000	—
− Ending Inventory	—	—	(40,000)	—
Costs of goods sold (4,000 @ $10)	$100,000	—	$ 60,000	$40,000
Gross profit	$ 20,000	$80,000	$ 60,000	$40,000

Although the total income for the two-year period is the same under either method ($100,000), the time when it is reported differs significantly. The use of inventories produces higher income and higher taxes in the first year because only the costs of goods actually sold are deducted.

As the preceding example shows, the lack of inventories causes a mismatching of revenues and expenses and with it the possibility of widely fluctuating incomes. Without inventories, the income reported in any one year would in most cases represent a distorted picture—not a clear reflection—of how well the firm was doing. Perhaps what is more crucial, at least from the Treasury's point of view, is that taxpayers would be able to postpone the payment of taxes if inventories were not required. Note in *Example 13* that absent inventories, the taxpayer is able to defer $40,000 ($60,000 − $20,000) of income and the corresponding tax from 2005 to 2006. Congress recognized these possibilities at an early date and in 1918 took corrective action that is still intact today. Currently, Code § 471 provides the following:

> Whenever in the opinion of the Secretary the use of inventories is necessary in order clearly to determine the income of any taxpayer, inventories shall be taken by such taxpayer on such basis as the Secretary may prescribe as conforming as nearly as may be to the best accounting practice in the trade or business and as most clearly reflecting income.

With the enactment of § 471, Congress delegated its rulemaking authority concerning inventories to the IRS. The IRS has responded with a number of regulations indicating when inventories are necessary as well as what methods are acceptable for tax purposes.

The Regulations require taxpayers to maintain inventories whenever the production, purchase, or sale of merchandise is an income-producing factor.[47] As a practical matter, this means virtually all manufacturers, wholesalers, and retailers must keep track of inventories while service businesses are usually exempt. Note that inventories are required regardless of the taxpayer's method of accounting. Cash basis taxpayers must account for inventories as do accrual basis taxpayers. However, the mandatory use of

---

[47]   Reg. § 1.471-1 and Reg. § 1.446-1(a)(4)(i).

the accrual method for purchases and sales does not prohibit taxpayers from using the cash method to account for other items such as advertising costs or interest income.[48]

EXCEPTIONS TO THE INVENTORY REQUIREMENT

While the inventory rule seems relatively straightforward, it has led to a significant amount of controversy. To understand the problem, it is necessary to recall that where inventory exists, the taxpayer not only must capitalize inventory costs, it also must accrue income from credit sales. The difficulty stems from the requirement that only those items representing merchandise *inventory* must be capitalized. In contrast, under Regulation § 1.162-3, materials and supplies that are considered *incidental* to the primary function of the business may be expensed currently. In contrast, *nonincidental* materials and supplies can be deducted only as they are consumed—much like inventory. Therefore, according to these rules, if a taxpayer can successfully argue that items are merely incidental materials or supplies, the items can be expensed immediately and the taxpayer may defer recognition of income from their sale until cash is received. On the other hand, if the IRS can prove that the items are inventory, the items must be capitalized and the income from their sale must be accrued. Note how much is at stake in the definition of inventory. If the items are considered incidental, the taxpayer wins the entire battle: deductions now and income in the future. If the items are nonincidental, the IRS secures a partial victory in that nonincidental items cannot be deducted immediately but only as they are consumed; however, income is still deferred. But if the items are considered inventory, the IRS has won the entire war since such characterization not only prevents an immediate write-off of the items' costs but also forces the taxpayer to accrue income currently. The difficulty is that there is no clear definition of inventory.

The problem is particularly acute with service providers. In *Wilkinson-Beane*, a mortuary provided funeral services, including supplying the caskets.[49] The taxpayer did not separately bill for the caskets but merely charged a flat fee for the services. Consistent with this approach, the taxpayer did not treat the caskets as inventory even though the costs represented 15.1 percent of total cash receipts. Unfortunately for the taxpayer, the court held that the caskets must be capitalized and any income forthcoming from the services to be accrued. A different approach was taken in the recent decision in *Osteopathic Medical Oncology and Hematology P.C.*[50] In this situation, the taxpayer provided chemotherapy treatment for cancer patients. In so doing, it used certain drugs. The IRS argued that the drugs were inventory and, therefore, the taxpayer could not expense the drugs and had to report the income when the treatments were provided (rather than when the cash was received—usually much later). However, the Tax Court sided with the taxpayer, ruling that the drugs were not inventory but rather an indispensable and inseparable part of the service of treating patients.

Due to the growing controversy about the definition of inventory and the ensuing problems, the government reacted. In 2000, the IRS began to relax its position on the mandatory use of inventories and at the same time the mandatory use of the accrual method. In a series of Revenue Procedures, the IRS has carved out two major exceptions, allowing taxpayers with inventories to escape the clutch of the accrual method. As may be grasped from the discussion above, the exceptions are of huge importance primarily because they permit the taxpayers—at least small businesses—to defer income.

1. *Gross Receipts of $1,000,000 or Less.* Taxpayers with average annual gross receipts of $1,000,000 or less are not required to use the accrual method for

---

[48]   Reg. § 1.446-1(c)(1)(iv).

[49]   70-1 USTC ¶9173, 25 AFTR 2d 70-418 420 F.2d 352 (CA-1, 1970).

[50]   113 T.C. 376.

inventories. This does not mean that taxpayers can simply expense inventory purchases. Instead, as discussed above, the items must be accounted for as nonincidental materials and supplies and expensed as they are used or consumed. While the treatment of inventory *costs* is essentially the same whether the costs are treated as inventory or nonincidental materials and supplies, the treatment of *income* significantly differs. Taxpayers who fall under this exception need not recognize accounts receivable income until they collect the receivables. In other words, they may defer the recognition of income until they receive payment for the merchandise.[51]

2. *Gross Receipts Less Than $10,000,000.* The above rule carves out a special exception only for small businesses: taxpayers with gross receipts of $1,000,000 or less. Revenue Procedure 2002-28 extends the same rule discussed above to taxpayers with average annual gross receipts exceeding $1,000,000 but less than $10,000,000 but only if they are not in certain industries, including manufacturing, wholesale, retail and information industries (e.g., newspapers, books, periodicals, database publishers and sound recording industries) or meet certain other exceptions. These businesses also need not use the accrual method for purchases and sales but inventory must be accounted for as nonincidental materials and supplies and expensed as they are used or consumed. Note that this rule does not override § 448 discussed above. Farming businesses, C corporations having gross receipts exceeding $5,000,000 and partnerships with a tainted C corporation partner do not qualify for this exception. This rule should benefit small businesses primarily in service businesses.[52]

Example 14. Golf Accessories Inc. (GAI) sells a variety of items for golfers, such as golf balls, tees, headcovers, ball marks, towels, clothing, training tapes and devices. The company sells direct to the public through its Internet site as well as to golf shops around the country. It has average annual gross receipts (e.g., sales) of $700,000. GAI began the year with $80,000 of merchandise on hand. During the year it purchased $300,000 of new merchandise, and at the end of the year had $70,000 on hand. Sales during the year were $650,000 but at the end of the year it had $40,000 of receivables outstanding. It also collected $15,000 of the receivables outstanding from the prior year. Because GAI averages gross receipts of less than $1,000,000 it need not use the accrual method to account for purchases and sales. As a result, it has revenues of $625,000 ($15,000 + $650,000 − $40,000) and costs of good sold of $310,000 ($80,000 + $300,000 − $70,000). Note that under the exception GAI is able to defer the $40,000 of income from the uncollected receivables until it is collected next year—a very valuable benefit. Also note that the inventory costs were still capitalized and could not be expensed until the items were sold or consumed.

Example 15. Same facts as above except GAI Inc. had average annual gross receipts of $4,000,000. Under these revised circumstances, the company would not qualify for the first exception since its gross receipts exceed $1,000,000. Moreover, it also would not qualify for the second exception even though its gross receipts are less than $10,000,000 since it is in one of the prohibited businesses of retail and wholesale trade.

---

[51] Rev. Proc. 2000-22, 2000-1 C.B. 1008 *modified* and *superseded* by Rev. Proc. 2001-10, I.R.B. 2001-2, 272. Note that Rev. Proc. 2001-10 eliminated the book conformity requirement.

[52] Rev. Proc. 2002-28, 2002-18 I.R.B. 2002-18, 815 clarifying and implementing Notice 20001-76, I.R.B. 2001-52, 613. See Rev. Proc. 2002-28 for exceptions where the principal business activity is the provision of services or fabrication or modification of or property to meet customer specifications.

Example 16. Same facts as in *Example 14* above except that GAI Inc. had average annual gross receipts of $8,000,000 and provided heating and air conditioning services. GAI meets the requirements of the second exception in that it is in the business of providing services and its gross receipts are less than $10,000,000. It would appear that GAI could avoid use of the accrual method and defer income from credit sales. However, if GAI is a C Corporation, it must still use the accrual method in accounting for purchases and sales because its gross receipts exceed $5,000,000.

INVENTORY ACCOUNTING IN GENERAL

A close reading of § 471 reveals that Congress has given the IRS two criteria to be followed in determining what inventory accounting methods are acceptable for tax purposes: (1) the method should conform as nearly as possible to the best accounting practice used in the taxpayer's trade or business; and (2) the method should clearly reflect income. Because of these requirements, the tax rules for inventory are quite similar to those used for financial accounting. Nevertheless, it is important to recognize that the IRS is the ultimate authority on determining what method represents the "best accounting practice" as well as what method most clearly reflects income. Consequently, as will be seen, taxpayers are sometimes required to adopt methods that vary from generally accepted accounting principles and cause differences between book income and taxable income.

There are three steps that must be followed in accounting for inventories and computing costs of goods sold: (1) identifying what costs (e.g., direct and indirect) are to be inventoried or capitalized; (2) evaluating the costs assigned to the ending inventory and determining whether reduction is necessary to reflect lower replacement costs (i.e., lower of cost or market); and (3) allocating the costs between ending inventory and costs of goods sold (e.g., specific identification, FIFO, LIFO). Each of these steps is discussed below.

COSTS TO BE INVENTORIED

The first step in determining costs of goods sold and ending inventory is identifying the costs that should be capitalized as part of inventory. Without guidance, taxpayers no doubt would be inclined to expense as many costs as possible. However, over the years, the IRS with help from Congress has established strict guidelines concerning what can be deducted currently (i.e., period costs) and what must be capitalized (i.e., product costs). The most recent development in this continuing debate was the enactment of the *uniform capitalization rules* (unicap) in 1986. As discussed below, the unicap provisions narrow further what the taxpayer is able to treat as a period cost.

As a general rule, the costs that must be capitalized depend on whether the taxpayer manufactures the goods (e.g., a producer of razor blades) or purchases the items for later resale (e.g., a wholesaler or a retailer such as a department store). When merchandise is bought for resale, the taxpayer must capitalize as a cost of inventory the invoice price less trade discounts plus freight and other costs of acquisition. Cash discounts may be deducted from the inventory cost or reported as a separate income item. In addition, certain retailers and wholesalers are subject to the unicap rules that require capitalization of particular indirect costs as discussed below. For manufactured items, inventory cost includes costs of raw materials, direct labor, and certain indirect costs. The unicap rules apply to all manufacturers.

Many of the problems concerning inventory involve the treatment of indirect costs. Various methods have been devised to account for these costs. For example, under the *prime costing* method only the costs of direct materials and direct labor are capitalized;

all indirect costs are expensed. Another method, often advocated by cost accountants, is the *variable* or *direct costing* approach. This method capitalizes only those costs varying with production and expenses all fixed costs. Despite the acceptance of these methods for managerial and internal reporting, the IRS has outlawed their use. In 1974, the IRS issued regulations requiring all manufacturers to use the *full absorption costing* method.[53] Retailers and wholesalers were not subject to the full absorption rules, and, therefore, were not required to capitalize any indirect costs.

Under the full absorption method, direct costs of material and labor must be capitalized. The treatment of indirect costs depends on which of three categories they fall into: *Category 1* includes costs that must be capitalized; *Category 2* includes costs that can be expensed; and *Category 3* includes costs whose tax treatment must conform with their financial accounting treatment. A summary of these categories and what they include appears in Exhibit 10-4.

The search for additional tax revenues brought about a substantial revision of the treatment of indirect costs in 1986 with the enactment of § 263A containing the *uniform capitalization rules*. The unicap rules apply to all manufacturers. They also apply to any retailers and wholesalers if their average annual gross receipts for the past three years exceed $10 million. Although these rules replace the full-absorption costing method, in practice many manufacturers continue to use the full-absorption method with certain modifications to meet the unicap requirements.

Section 263A requires the capitalization of direct material, direct labor costs, and, most important, any indirect costs that, in the words of the Regulations, "directly benefit or are incurred by reason of the performance of a production or resale activity."[54] The effect of these rules is to require taxpayers to capitalize many costs that they previously deducted. The Regulatory scheme is shown in Exhibit 10-4. In general, the Regulations categorize costs as (1) those that benefit only production and resale activities (must capitalize); (2) those that benefit only policy and management functions (do not capitalize); and (3) those that benefit both production and resale activities and policy and management functions, referred to as mixed service costs (capitalized by using any reasonable basis to allocate costs between production and policy functions).

The practical effect of the enactment of the uniform capitalization rules was to require taxpayers to adjust their accounting systems to capture the additional costs required to be capitalized. This was no small task, particularly for retailers and wholesalers that previously had never had to capitalize any indirect costs. As can be seen in Exhibit 10-4, the current scheme requires large retailers and wholesalers to capitalize any costs related to offsite storage (e.g., operating a warehouse), purchasing, or handling and an allocable portion of general and administrative costs. To provide all affected taxpayers with some relief, the IRS has provided several simplified techniques to account for these costs detailed in the Regulations.

---

[53]   Reg. § 1.471-11. Absorption costing is currently used for financial statement purposes.

[54]   Reg. § 1.263A-1T(b)(2)(ii).

EXHIBIT 10-4
Capitalizable Costs Full-Absorption vs. Uniform Capitalization

Direct costs	Full absorption	Unicap
Direct material	C	C
Direct labor	C	C

Indirect costs		
Repairs/maintenance (equipment and facilities)	C	C
Utilities (equipment and facilities)	C	C
Rent (equipment and facilities)	C	C
Indirect labor	C	C
Indirect material and supplies	C	C
Small tools and equipment	C	C
Quality control and inspection	C	C
Taxes other than income taxes	F	C
Depreciation and depletion for books	F	C
Depreciation and depletion: excess tax	E	C
Insurance (facilities, contents, equipment)	F	C
Current pension costs	F	C
Past service pension costs	E	C
Bidding expenses—successful bids	E	C
Engineering and design	E	C
Warehousing, purchasing, handling and general and administrative related to such functions	E	C

Policy and Management		
Marketing, selling, advertising, and distribution	E	E
Bidding expenses—unsuccessful bids	E	E
Research and experimental expenses	E	
Losses	E	E
Depreciation on idle equipment or facilities	E	E
Income taxes	F	C
Strike costs	F	E

Interest		
	E	*

Mixed Service Costs		
Administrative/coordination of production or resale	F	C
Personnel department	E	C
Purchasing department	E	C
Materials handling and warehousing	E	C
Accounting and data servicing departments	E	C
Data processing	E	C
Security services	E	C
Legal department providing services to production	E	C
Overall management and policies	E	E
General business planning	E	E
Financial accounting	E	E
General financial planning	E	E
General economic analysis and forecasting	E	E
Internal audit	E	E
Shareholder and public relations	E	E
Tax department	E	E

C: Capitalize
E: Expense currently
F: Follows financial statement treatment

*Capitalized if the produced property has a life of 20 years or more, if the property has an estimated production period of more than two years, or if the production period exceeds one year and the cost exceeds $1 million. Does not apply to property acquired for resale.

ALLOCATING INVENTORIABLE COSTS

After total product costs for the year have been identified, these costs along with the cost of beginning inventory must be allocated between the goods sold during the year and ending inventory. If each item sold could be identified (e.g., a car or jewelry) or all items had the same cost, there would be little difficulty in determining the cost of items sold and those still on hand. As a practical matter, these conditions rarely exist. Consequently, the taxpayer must make some assumptions regarding which costs should be assigned to costs of goods sold. Like financial accounting, the tax law does not require the cost flow assumption to be consistent with the physical movement of goods. There are several acceptable approaches for allocating costs: specific identification, first-in first-out (FIFO), last-in first-out (LIFO), and weighted averaged.

Example 17. K Corporation's inventory records revealed a beginning inventory of 300 units acquired at a cost of $3 per unit. This year the corporation purchased 400 units for $4 per unit, and it sold 500 units for $5,000. Gross profit using FIFO and LIFO are computed below.

	FIFO	LIFO
Sales (500 units @ $10)	$5,000	$5,000
Costs of goods sold:		
Beginning inventory (300 @ $3)	$ 900	$ 900
Purchase (400 @ $4)	1,600	1,600
Goods available	$2,500	$2,500
Ending inventory:		
FIFO (200 @ $4)	(800)	
LIFO (200 @ $3)		(600)
Costs of goods sold	$1,700	$1,900
Gross profit	$3,300	$3,100

If K uses FIFO it is assumed that goods are used in the order that they are purchased (i.e., the first goods in are the first goods to be sold). Thus, the ending inventory consists of the most recent purchases, $800 (200 at $4 per unit). The effect of FIFO is to assign the oldest costs to costs of goods sold. In contrast, LIFO assumes that the last goods purchased are the first sold. As a result, under LIFO the most recent costs are assigned to costs of goods sold and the oldest costs to ending inventory. Thus, ending inventory under LIFO is $600 (200 at $3).

The preceding example illustrates the principal advantage of LIFO. In periods of rising prices, LIFO matches current costs against current revenue. From a financial accounting perspective, it can be reasoned that this produces a better measure of current income since both revenues and costs are stated on a comparable price basis, thereby reducing the inflationary element of earnings.[55] From a tax perspective, LIFO appears preferable because taxable income is typically lower and the corresponding tax is reduced. In effect, taxable income is not "overstated" by fictitious gains. Interestingly,

---

[55] Arguably, income results only to the extent that the sales price exceeds what it will cost to buy a replacement item for the merchandise sold. LIFO approximates this approach.

LIFO became part of the tax law in 1939 for just this reason—to help businesses reduce the "paper profits" that conventional methods were yielding and that were being taxed at wartime rates of close to 80 percent.

It must be noted, however, that the advantage of LIFO is lost to the extent that sales in any one year exceed purchases (see *Example 17* above). In this case, the lower prices of goods purchased in previous periods are charged to costs of goods sold. This dipping into the past LIFO layers creates inventory profits, the specific problem that LIFO was designed to address. In a worst case scenario, a company that adopted LIFO in 1942 might unexpectedly liquidate all of its LIFO layers, matching 1942 costs with 2005 revenues. This would no doubt lead to an unforeseen tax liability with little "real" income to pay the tax. This is a significant risk when LIFO is used. At the same time, it may represent an opportunity. Companies may be able to create income, if desirable, by liquidating LIFO layers (e.g., to absorb an expiring net operating loss).

DOLLAR VALUE LIFO

As a practical matter, applying the LIFO procedure to specific goods can be quite cumbersome and costly. In contrast to the simple one-item example above, most firms have hundreds or thousands of individual inventory items, and the number of units purchased and sold each period may amount to hundreds of thousands or more. Pricing each separate unit at the oldest costs and properly accounting for the liquidation of any LIFO layers might be a recordkeeping nightmare. Moreover, the major advantage of LIFO could be lost if old LIFO layers had to be liquidated because a specific item was discontinued or replaced. To address the problems of specific-goods LIFO, variations of LIFO have been developed. Perhaps the most widely used version of LIFO is the dollar-value method.

The dollar-value method reaches the desired result—eliminating the inflationary element of earnings attributable to inventory—in a unique way. Ending inventory is priced using the prices at the time LIFO was originally adopted (base-year). This value is then compared to beginning inventory to determine if there is a real increase or decrease in the pool of dollars invested in inventory. If there is no real change (i.e., ending inventory at base-year prices is the same as beginning inventory at base-year prices), the effect is to charge costs of goods sold with an amount reflecting current prices. On the other hand, if there is a real increase in inventory in terms of base-year dollars, the increase is valued at current prices and added to beginning inventory as a separate LIFO layer to determine ending inventory.

> **Example 18.** T Corporation had an ending inventory on December 31, 2004 of 10,000 units at a cost of $20,000. During the year, T sold the original units and purchased another 10,000 units for $24,000. On December 31, 2005 ending inventory valued at current prices was $24,000. In such case, costs of goods sold would be $20,000, computed as follows.

Beginning inventory	$ 20,000
Purchases	24,000
Ending inventory	(24,000)
Costs of goods sold	$ 20,000

But what if, as the facts suggest, prices have increased by 20%? If so, the real amount invested in inventory has not changed ($24,000 ÷ 120% = $20,000). Consequently, valuing ending inventory at current-year prices of $24,000 (as above) effectively assigns the oldest costs of $20,000 to costs of goods sold, resulting in an

inflationary profit of $4,000. Dollar-value LIFO eliminates this artificial gain—the objective of LIFO—by restating ending inventory at base-year prices. In this case, ending inventory would be restated at $20,000 ($24,000 ÷ 120%). This restatement would yield a cost of goods sold of $24,000, and would properly match current-year costs against current-year revenues.

The important difference between dollar-value and specific-goods LIFO is that increases and decreases in inventory are measured in terms of dollars rather than physical units. This approach allows goods to be easily combined into pools and effectively treated as a single unit. Consequently, the likelihood of liquidating LIFO layers is reduced.

Although there are various methods of dollar-value LIFO, the most frequently used is the *double-extension method*.[56] The steps to be used in applying the double-extension method are summarized in Exhibit 10-5 and applied to the following example.

Example 19. In 2005 T Corporation elected to value inventories using double-extension dollar-value LIFO. Beginning inventory for 2005 consisted of the following:

Date	Pool Items	Ending Quantity	Current Cost Per Unit	Total at Current Cost
1-1-05	A	3,000	$3	$ 9,000
	B	4,000	6	24,000
Total base-year cost				$33,000

Inventory information for 2005–2007 and the computation of ending inventory using the steps in Exhibit 10-5 are shown on the following page.

---

[56] Taxpayers may use the link-chain method or certain simplified procedures. See Code §§ 472(f) and 474 and the applicable regulations.

EXHIBIT 10-5

Double-Extension Dollar-Value LIFO Computation of Ending Inventory

Step 1.   *Extension #1.* Value ending inventory at current-year prices (actual cost of most recent purchases, average cost, or other acceptable method).

Step 2.   *Extension #2.* Value ending inventory at base-year prices.

Step 3.   Compute current-year quantity increase or decrease by comparing beginning and ending inventories at base-year prices.

Ending inventory at base-year price (Step 2)
$$\underline{-\quad \text{Beginning inventory at base-year price}}$$
Curent-year quantity increase (decrease) at base-year price

Step 4.   Calculate current-year price index.

$$\text{Index} = \frac{\text{Ending inventory at current-Year price (Step 1)}}{\text{Ending inventory at base-year price (Step 2)}}$$

Step 5.   Compute the quantity increase or decrease to be added to or subtracted from beginning inventory.

   a. For a quantity increase: convert the increase measured at base-year prices (Step 3) to current year's prices using the current-year price index (Step 4).

$$\begin{array}{ccc}\text{Quantity increase at} & & \text{New} \\ \text{Base-year price} \quad \times & \text{Index} & = \quad \text{LIFO} \\ \text{(Step 3)} & \text{(Step 4)} & \text{layer}\end{array}$$

   b. For a quantity decrease: a current-year decrease consumes the layer(s) of inventory in LIFO fashion (i.e., the decrease must be subtracted from the most recently added layer). Previous layers are peeled off at the prices at which they were added.

Step 6.   Ending LIFO inventory is the beginning inventory increased by the new LIFO layer [Step 5(a)] or decreased by any liquidation of LIFO layers [Step 5(b)].

Steps 1 and 2: Double extend ending inventory.

Date	Pool Items	Ending Quantity	Current Cost Per Unit	Total at Current Cost	Base-Year Cost Per Unit	Total at Base-Year Cost
			Ending Inventory at Current-Year Prices		Ending Inventory at Base-Year Prices	
12-31-05	A	2,000	$ 4	$ 8,000	$3	$ 6,000
	B	5,000	7	35,000	6	30,000
				$43,000		$36,000
12-31-06	A	6,000	$ 5	$30,000	$3	$18,000
	B	7,000	9	63,000	6	42,000
				$93,000		$60,000
12-31-07	A	4,000	$ 6	$24,000	$3	$12,000
	B	5,000	10	50,000	6	30,000
				$74,000		$42,000

realizable value. For tax purposes, a write-down below this value is allowed only for what are often referred to as "subnormal" goods.[59]

Subnormal goods are those items in inventory that cannot be sold at normal prices because of damage (e.g., a dent in a file cabinet), imperfections (e.g., a thousand sweatshirts with the logo improperly spelled), shop wear, changes of style, odd or broken lots, and so on. The Regulations allow the taxpayer to value these "subnormal" goods at a bona fide selling price less direct costs of disposition. However, this lower value is acceptable *only* if the goods are actually offered for sale at such price 30 days after the inventory date (e.g., cars with severe hail-damage are actually on the lot with a sales price slashed below replacement cost within 30 days of when inventory is taken).

> **Example 21.** In the landmark decision of *Thor Power Tool Co.*,[60] the taxpayer manufactured power tools consisting of 50 to 200 parts. Thor followed the common practice of producing additional parts at the same time it manufactured the original tool. This practice helped the company to avoid expensive retooling and special production runs as replacement parts were actually required. When accounting for these spare parts, the company initially capitalized their costs and—consistent with GAAP—subsequently wrote them down to reflect the decline in their expected sales price. The Supreme Court ultimately denied the write-down because Thor could not show that the parts (i.e., the excess inventory) were a subnormal good, and even if they had, the company had not actually offered the parts for sale at the lower price. The effect of this decision is to prohibit companies from writing down the value of slow-moving inventory.

QUALIFIED PRODUCTION ACTIVITIES DEDUCTION

Over the years, Congress has adopted a number of measures that it hoped would attract, create and maintain manufacturing jobs in the U.S. For the most part, these provisions were designed to encourage businesses to increase its exports. Most of these approaches, however, resulted in a permanent reduction of U.S. tax and were held to constitute an illegal export subsidy under the U.S. trade agreements with the World Trade Organization. Congress addressed the problem with a different tactic in the *American Jobs Creation Act of 2004* (Jobs Act) with the creation of § 199.

In short, the law now provides direct tax breaks for domestic production activities. The focus has shifted to what companies are doing in the United States, not what they are exporting or moving overseas. For tax years beginning *after* 2004, § 199 allows taxpayers to claim a special deduction relating to production and manufacturing activity undertaken in the U.S., regardless of whether the items are exported. When fully effective in 2010, eligible taxpayers will be able to claim a deduction equal to 9 percent of the taxpayer's *qualified production activities income* (QPAI) or if less, the taxpayer's taxable income (modified A.G.I. in the case of an individual). The deduction percentage allowed is phased in as follows:

Year	Deduction Percentage
2005–2006	3%
2007–2009	6
2010 and thereafter	10

---

[59] See Reg. § 1.471-2(c). Note that reduction of net realizable value by an allowance for a normal profit margin is not allowed for tax purposes.

[60] 79-1 USTC ¶9139, 43 AFTR2d 79-362, 439 U.S. 522 (USSC, 1979).

All taxpayers are entitled to the deduction (C corporations, S corporations, partnerships, sole proprietorships, estates and trusts). For individual taxpayers, the deduction is for A.G.I. but is not deductible in computing self-employment tax. The effect of the deduction is to reduce a corporation's effective tax rate by about 3 percent (35% × 9% = 3.15%).

Limitations on Deduction. There are two critical limitations impacting the deduction. QPAI cannot exceed the taxable income limitation and the § 199 deduction itself cannot exceed 50 percent of the employer's wages.

Taxable Income Limitation. As noted above the deduction is generally 9 percent of QPAI or if smaller, the taxpayer's taxable income. For individual taxpayers, A.G.I. with certain modifications is substituted for taxable income. The taxable income limitation normally applies when a taxpayer has current losses from activities other than production sufficient to offset production income or no current income because of a carryback or carryforward of losses. In such case, the taxpayer receives no benefit from the manufacturing deduction, either currently or by an increase in its NOL carryback or carryforward.

For pass-through entities, the taxable income limitation is determined at the individual, not the entity, level. Therefore, partnerships, S corporations, trusts and estates must separately state the amount of QPAI that flows through to the owners or beneficiaries.

W-2 Wages Limitation. The § 199 deduction itself cannot exceed 50 percent of the W-2 wages of the employer for the taxable year. W-2 wages are defined as the sum of wages and elective deferrals [e.g., contributions to 401(k) plans that must be reported on Form W-2]. Wages presumably include production and nonproduction employees, as well as key executive officers and staff, in-house counsel, and research and marketing staff. Partners, S shareholders and other pass-through beneficiaries are treated as having been allocated W-2 wages from the entity in an amount equal to the lower of their allocable share of the wages or two times 9 percent or 18 percent of QPAI for the year. In light of this rule, it would appear that "one-person" sole proprietorships do not qualify for the deduction because the income from such businesses is not paid to the owner in the form of wages. This may encourage "one-person" operations to be conducted in the form of an S corporation that pays its owner/sole-employee wages.

Qualified Production Activities Income (QPAI). QPAI and the § 199 deduction are computed in the following manner:

> "Domestic production gross receipts"
> − Allocable costs of goods sold
> − Directly allocable deductions
> − Ratable allocation of other deductions not directly allocable to another class of income
> = Qualified production activities income (QPAI) not to exceed taxable income
> × 3% (6% in 2007–2009, 9% in 2010 and thereafter)
> = Qualified production activities deduction not to exceed 50% of W-2 wages

Under §199(c)(4), the term *domestic production gross receipts* means the gross receipts derived from:

1. Any lease, rental, license, sale, exchange, or other disposition of *qualifying production property* which includes tangible personal property, computer software, and sound recordings which is:
   - *Manufactured, produced, grown or extracted **by the taxpayer** in whole or in significant part* within the U.S. For this purpose, production includes production of electricity, natural gas and potable (drinking) water. Production also includes farming, food storage, and food processing—meat packing plant but not a chef's creation of a western omelet; or

- *Any qualified film* produced by the taxpayer. This includes any motion picture, television production or video tape if at least 50 percent of the total compensation relating to the production of such property is compensation for services performed in the U.S. by actors, production personnel, directors, and producers.

2. Construction performed in the U.S. (erection or substantial renovation of residential or nonresidential buildings and infrastructure); or

3. Engineering or architectural services performed in the U.S. for construction projects in the U.S.

Domestic production gross receipts do not include gross receipts derived from

1. Sale of food and beverages prepared by the taxpayer at a retail establishment (e.g., restaurants).

2. Transmission or distribution of electricity, natural gas, or potable water.

3. Property leased, licensed, or rented by the taxpayer for use by any related person.

Observe that QPAI is the *net* result of subtracting allocable expenses from qualified gross receipts. For this reason, the allocation of expenses becomes extremely important. Section 199 gives the IRS the power to write rules for proper allocation of income and deduction to determine QPAI. According to the Committee reports, those rules should be consistent with the uniform capitalization rules of § 263A and the income sourcing rules found in § 861 used to determine the foreign tax credit.

Example 22. G Inc. manufactures razor blades in a plant in Columbus, Ohio and Munich, Germany. The blades from both factories are sold all over the world. Gross receipts from the sales of blades from the Columbus operation qualify as domestic production gross receipts for purpose of calculating the production deduction since they are derived from the sale of qualifying production property—tangible personal property (the razor blades)—that is manufactured by the taxpayer, G, entirely in the U.S. Note that all of the gross receipts qualify as domestic notwithstanding the fact that a portion could be attributable to sales in foreign countries (e.g., Canada and Mexico).

Example 23. Same facts as above. For the current year, the company reported taxable income of $4,000,000. Total wages for all employees were $3,500,000. The company's records reveal the additional information below. Based on this information the production deduction is $1,200,000 computed as follows:

Qualifying domestic production gross receipts	$15,000,000	
Allocable costs:		
Costs of good sold	$4,000,000	
Directly allocable expenses.	3,000,000	
Indirect expenses	1,000,000	
Total allocable costs	(8,000,000)	
Qualified production activities income	$ 7,000,000	
Taxable income before the production deduction.	$ 4,000,000	
Lesser of QPAI $7,000,000 or taxable income $4,000,000	$4,000,000	
2005 rate	×3%	
Tentative production deduction	$1,200,000	
Wage limitation (50% × $3,500,000 wages)	$1,750,000	
Production deduction (lesser of tentative production deduction or wage limitation)		$1,200,000

Note that the production deduction is permitted for AMT purposes. However, the taxable income limitation is based on AMTI rather than taxable income.

Unresolved Issues. Unfortunately, the artificial simplicity of the examples above masks the many obstacles that make application of § 199 troublesome. To appreciate the difficulty, simply consider the basic requirements that must be met in order to secure the deduction: *qualified property must be manufactured, produced, grown, or extracted by the taxpayer in whole or in significant part within the U.S.* At the start, § 199 provides no definition of manufacturing or production. Does assembly of vacuum cleaners or conversion of orange concentrate into orange juice constitute production? What about mixing water and concentrate to produce soft drinks or French Vanilla coffee? When McDonald's sells a hamburger is it providing a service or is it combining inputs to manufacture a product? There are two sets of provisions, those contained in the uniform capitalization rules of § 263A and those in the international area, that can be drawn upon to answer these questions. In part, the problem is which of these different approaches will apply.

The international provisions generally have a much narrower interpretation of "production activity" than the unicap rules. In order to have production in the international context, a substantial transformation is normally required to occur; that is, activities occur from which emerges a new and different article that has a distinctive name, character and use. Alternatively, there must be substantial conversion costs incurred to constitute production. The assembly of vacuum cleaners and conversion of orange concentrate were not considered production under the international rules. Leasing computers was a production activity where the lessor customized the computer for the customer. Mixing water and concentrate to produce soft drinks was considered manufacturing but was a service if done in a snack bar. On the other hand, the unicap rules define produce (e.g., to construct, build, install, manufacture, develop, improve, create, or grow) but do not define production activity, although there is some guidance in the regulations and several cases. In general, production is construed much more broadly under unicap. Regardless of the approach, the more serious problem is that it is unlikely that a definition of these critical terms can be fashioned to prevent controversy.

A second issue concerns the requirement that the activity must be done *by the taxpayer*. How is subcontracting treated? How will minor assembly, packaging, repackaging and labeling be treated? The issue here is whether activities undertaken on behalf of the taxpayer by subcontractors can be treated as production by the taxpayer. While there is some case law in the international area concerning this issue, there has been mixed results.

Another area requiring clarification concerns the requirement that the activity must be accomplished *in significant part* in the U.S. The Senate version of § 199 provided a numerical bright line test, stating that the "significant part" condition was satisfied if more than 50 percent of the total development and production costs were incurred by the taxpayer in the U.S. However, this test was left out of the final law, leaving a significant void.

Still another complication involves the complexity in distinguishing between qualified and nonqualified gross receipts and the problem of allocating expenses between them. The already famous "Starbucks footnote" found in the Conference Report acknowledges the difficulty.

Example 24. Coffee Inc. operates a chain of coffee shops all over the world. It buys coffee beans and roasts and packages them at its own central processing facility. It distributes the packages of roasted coffee to its own retail stores which the stores brew for selling to customers. In addition, the stores sell the packaged coffee directly to consumers and to other retail stores. How are the gross receipts from a single sale of coffee classified? How much is attributable to the qualifying production activity, the roasting of the beans, and how much is attributed to the nonqualifying activity, the processing in the retail establishment. An even more daunting question concerns how the various costs of operating the company are to allocated between these activities. According to the footnote, only the sales receipts attributable to the off-site roasting function can be taken into account in computing QPAI. The balance of the receipts is not qualified.

There are many other issues worthy of consideration but are beyond the scope of this overview. Nevertheless, it should be emphasized that § 199 can have a major impact not simply on the accounting systems that must be designed to capture the required information but also on how a company structures itself and conducts its business.

TAX PLANNING CONSIDERATIONS

CASUALTY AND THEFT LOSSES

Much of the controversy surrounding casualty losses results from insufficient documentation of the loss. For this reason, taxpayers should give careful attention to accumulating the evidence necessary to establish the deduction. Such evidence would include, where appropriate, pictures, eyewitnesses, police reports, and newspaper accounts. The taxpayer also should gather evidence regarding the value of the property damaged or destroyed. In situations where an item is not repaired or replaced, an appraisal may be the only method of adequately valuing the loss.

In some cases, a taxpayer may suffer a casualty loss and in seeking insurance reimbursement incur appraisal costs. Even if the casualty loss is not deductible due to the 10 percent limitation, the appraisal costs are deductible as a cost of preparing the tax return and are therefore claimed as a miscellaneous itemized deduction.

Taxpayers often measure the amount of their casualty losses by the amount paid for repairs that are necessary to bring the property back to its condition before the casualty. This method of measuring may be inappropriate, however, if the repairs do not restore the property to its same condition before the casualty. In such case, an additional loss representing the decline in value should be claimed.

The rules for determining the deductible casualty loss have important implications for the amount of insurance that a taxpayer should maintain.

> **Example 25.** T purchased a home in Boston for $70,000 15 years ago. This year, the home burned to the ground and the taxpayer received a $70,000 reimbursement from the insurance company. The cost of rebuilding the house was $200,000. Although T's economic loss was $130,000 ($200,000 − $70,000), none of the loss is deductible as a casualty loss. The casualty loss deduction is the *lesser* of the decline in value, $200,000, or the taxpayer's adjusted basis, $70,000, less the insurance reimbursement. Since the insurance reimbursement of $70,000 completely offset T's basis, there is no deductible loss.

BAD DEBTS

It is not uncommon for family members or friends to make loans to each other that are never repaid. This often occurs when a son or daughter is embarking on a business venture in which a parent is willing to invest. If the taxpayer wishes to claim a deduction if the debt is not paid, steps should be taken upon making the loan to ensure that the loan is not considered a gift. For example, the taxpayer should document the transaction in such a way that it is clear that both parties intend that repayment of the loan will occur. The best method of documenting the parties' wishes is to have a formal note drafted. Such a note would lend support to the argument that a debtor-creditor relationship existed between the parties. The note also should have a definite payment schedule, and each payment should be made on time. Collateral could be included as well. In addition, the note should call for a reasonable amount of interest. Failure to charge adequate interest could cause the imputed interest rules discussed in Chapter 5 to operate.

> **Example 26.** In 2004 F loaned his friend K $10,000 to start a chocolate chip cookie business. The business struggled along, requiring K to ask F for another $5,000, which he gladly loaned her. The business failed after six months. If F documented the loans and sought repayment, he may claim a deduction for a nonbusiness bad debt. If he failed to do so, any deduction may be disallowed.

NET OPERATING LOSSES

When a taxpayer suffers a net operating loss, a decision must be made whether to carry the loss back or elect to carry it forward only. Due to the time value of money, a carryback is usually more advantageous since an immediate tax refund can be obtained. However, this gain must be weighed against the future benefits to be obtained by a carryforward. If the taxpayer expects to be in a higher tax bracket in the future, the present value of the higher savings may be greater than the value of an immediate refund.

PROBLEM MATERIALS

DISCUSSION QUESTIONS

10-1   *Business vs. Nonbusiness Bad Debts.* R is employed as the chief executive officer of XYZ Corporation. Believing the company's future to be bright, he has acquired 75 percent of XYZ's stock. During the year, R loaned XYZ $10,000. Explain the tax consequences assuming XYZ is unable to repay all or a portion of the loan.

10-2   *Bad Debt Requirements.* Under what circumstances, if any, is a cash basis taxpayer allowed to claim a deduction for a bad debt? An accrual basis taxpayer?

10-3   *Identifying Bad Debts.* For each of the following situations, indicate whether the taxpayer would be able to claim a deduction for a bad debt.
   a.   Several years ago, F advanced $30,000 to his wholly owned corporation, which was experiencing financial difficulties. Last year he loaned it another $10,000. No notes were executed and no payments have been made. During the current year, the company declared bankruptcy.
   b.   E quit his old job as a salesperson to become a sales manager for K Corporation this year. As part of his arrangement with K, he was to receive a $10,000 bonus if the company reached $1 million in sales for the year. Sales for the year were $900,000, and K Corporation did not pay E a bonus.
   c.   B and C each own 50 percent of ABC Incorporated. Over the years, ABC made loans to C. When C died he was penniless. He owed the company $20,000.

10-4   *Is There a Bad Debt?* Several years ago, R's son, S, got into the restaurant business. R loaned S $10,000 to help him get the business going. No note was signed nor was any interest charged. The business was initially a huge success but as time passed, it began having financial problems. This year the son's business failed.
   a.   Can R claim a bad debt deduction? If so, is the debt a business or nonbusiness bad debt and how much is the deduction?
   b.   Same as (a) except R obtained a signed note from his son.

10-5   *Bad Debt of Related Party.* H loaned her son $10,000 to enter the car repair business. If the son subsequently abandons the business and does not repay the loan, what are the tax consequences to H?

10-6   *Casualty Losses.* Explain the rationale underlying the rules (lower of basis or value with certain exceptions) for computing the amount of the deduction for a casualty loss.

10-7   *Casualty Losses.* During the year, R had various losses. Explain whether each of the following would qualify as a casualty loss.
   a.   Loss of stove due to electrical fire.
   b.   Damage to water pipes from freezing temperatures in Southern California.
   c.   Loss of tree from Dutch elm disease.
   d.   Ruined carpeting from clogged sewer line.
   e.   Hole in his suit from cigarette ashes he dropped; ruined shirt from pen leaking.
   f.   Damage to both his and his neighbor's car while R's son drove R's car.
   g.   Luggage and contents seized by a foreign government during a European vacation.

10-8   *Theft Loss Calculation.* If taxpayers could plan their taxes to account for thefts of their own personal use property (e.g., theft of their stereo and television), would they want the burglar to take all the property at once or take some property the first time and return for more later?

10-9   *Net Operating Losses in General.* Comment on each of the following:
   a.   The purposes of the net operating loss deduction.
   b.   The rationale underlying the complex calculation of the net operating loss deduction.
   c.   How a net operating loss occurring in 2005 is utilized (i.e., the carryover process).

10-10   *Inventoriable Costs: § 263A.* HHG operates a chain of retail appliance stores. The company has grown tremendously over the past several years. It expects that its gross receipts will exceed $10 million this year. What are the implications of this growth for the company's method of accounting for inventories?

10-11   *LIFO vs. FIFO.* During the 1970s, there was a tremendous shift from the FIFO method of inventory to LIFO. Nevertheless, not every company shifted to the LIFO method. Discuss why some might shift to LIFO although others might not.

PROBLEMS

10-12   *Treatment of Bad Debts.* AAA Computer Company, an accrual basis corporation, installed a new computerized accounting system for a customer and billed him $1,500 in June, 2005. When aging its accounts receivable at year-end, the company found that the customer was experiencing financial difficulties.
   a.   Assuming the company estimated that only $1,000 of the account would be collected, what is the amount of the bad debt deduction, if any, that it can claim in 2005?
   b.   Would the answer to (a) change if the debt were a nonbusiness bad debt?
   c.   In 2006 the company actually collected $200 and the remainder of the debt was worthless. What is the amount of the bad debt deduction, if any, that it can claim in 2006?

10-13   *Bad Debts and Accounting Methods.* Dr. D, a dentist, performed a root canal for a patient and charged him $300. The patient paid $100, then left town, never to be seen again. What is the amount of bad debt deduction, if any, that D may claim assuming that she is a cash basis taxpayer?

10-14 *Uncollectible Loan.* Several years ago, L loaned his old high-school friend B $5,000 to help him start a new business. Things did not go as well as B planned, and late in 2005 B declared bankruptcy. L expects to collect 40 cents on the dollar. In 2006 all of B's affairs were settled and L received $1,000. What are the tax consequences to L in 2005 and 2006?

10-15 *Personal Casualty.* When the waters of the Mississippi began to overflow their banks and flood the surrounding area, M was forced to leave her home and head for higher ground. On December 2, she returned to her home to find that it had been vandalized as well as damaged from the flood. After cleaning up, she determined that the following items had been stolen or damaged:

Item	Adjusted Basis	FMV Before	FMV After	Insurance Reimbursement
Fur coat	$6,000	$7,000	$0	$7,000
Computer	4,000	3,000	0	Uninsured
Couch	1,200	800	See below	500
Van	7,000	5,000		

The couch had been damaged and M had it reupholstered for $700. The insurance company reimbursed her for the amounts shown on December 27. Under M's insurance policy, the company did not reimburse her for loss on the car until 45 days had passed. M expected to recover $4,000 but, after several delays, finally received a check for $2,000 on April 25, 2006. While she was waiting for reimbursement for her van, she rented a car at a total cost of $700. Although M received value for the coat, she did not replace it. In addition to the losses shown above, her real estate broker advised that even though her house had not been damaged by the flood, the value had dropped by $20,000 since it was evident that it was located in an area prone to flooding.

a. Compute M's casualty loss deduction, assuming her A.G.I. in 2005 was $18,000 and in 2006, $20,000.

b. Assume the loss occurred on January 2, 2006 and the location was officially designated a disaster area by the President. Explain when the loss could be deducted.

10-16 *Casualty Loss: Business and Investment Property.* H is a private detective. While sleuthing this year, his car was stolen. The car, which was used entirely for business, was worth $7,000 and had an adjusted basis of $12,000. H received no insurance reimbursement for his car. Also this year, his office was the victim of arson. The fire destroyed only a painting that had a basis of $1,500 and was worth $3,000. H received a reimbursement of $800 from his insurance company for the painting. H suffered yet another misfortune this year as his rental property was damaged by a flood, the first in the area in 70 years. Before the casualty, the property—which had greatly appreciated in value—was worth $90,000 and afterward only $40,000. The rental property had an adjusted basis of $30,000. He received $20,000 from the insurance company, the maximum amount for which homes in a flood plain could be insured. Compute H's casualty loss deduction assuming his A.G.I. is $30,000. Can a casualty loss create a net operating loss?

10-17 *Casualty Gains and Losses.* This year, C's jewelry, which cost $10,000, was stolen from her home. Luckily, she was insured and the insurance company reimbursed her for its current value, $19,000. In addition, while she was on vacation all of her camera equipment was stolen. The camera equipment had cost her $3,500 and was worth $3,100. She received no reimbursement since she carried a large deductible on such items. C's A.G.I. for the year was $15,000.

a. What is the effect of the casualty losses on C's taxable income?

b. Same as above except the jewelry was worth $11,000.

10-18 *Casualty and Theft Loss Computation.* In each of the following cases, compute the taxpayer's casualty loss deduction (before percentage limitations) and indicate whether it is deductible *for* or *from* adjusted gross income.

    a. While G was at the theater, his house (adjusted basis $60,000, fair market value $80,000) was completely destroyed by fire. The fire also completely destroyed both his skiing equipment (cost $300, fair market value $90) and a calculator (adjusted basis $110, fair market value $80) used for business. He was reimbursed for $30,000 with respect to the house.

    b. B owned a duplex which she rented. A tornado demolished the roof but did not damage the remainder of the duplex. The duplex's value before the tornado was $45,000 and after the tornado was $40,000. B's adjusted basis in the property was $30,000. The President declared the entire city a "disaster area."

    c. Assume the same facts in (b) except that instead of B's duplex being partially damaged it was her personal cabin cruiser, and she received a $2,000 reimbursement from the insurance company.

    d. L backed his car out of the garage and ran over his 10-speed bicycle (cost $400, fair market value $300). The bicycle is worthless.

10-19 *NOL Items.* Indicate whether the following items can create a net operating loss for an individual taxpayer.

    a. Business capital loss
    b. Nonbusiness bad debt
    c. Casualty loss
    d. Interest expense on mortgage secured by primary residence
    e. Employee business expenses
    f. Contribution to Individual Retirement Account
    g. Alimony
    h. Personal exemption

10-20 *Items Considered in Computing an NOL.* Indicate whether the following items are considered in computing the net operating loss deduction for an individual.

    a. Salary
    b. Capital gain on the sale of investment property
    c. Interest income
    d. Interest on a mortgage on a primary residence

10-21 *Net Operating Loss Computation.* R, a single taxpayer, operates a bicycle shop. For the calendar year 2005 he reports the following items of income and expense:

Gross income from business	$150,000
Business operating expenses	210,000
Interest income from investments	7,000
Casualty loss	4,000
Interest expense on home mortgage	9,000
Long-term capital gains (nonbusiness)	3,000
Long-term capital loss (nonbusiness)	5,000
Long-term capital gains (business)	1,000

The casualty loss represented the uninsured theft of R's personal auto worth $4,100 ($9,000 adjusted basis).

    a. Compute R's net operating loss for 2005.

    b. Assuming R carries the loss back to 2003, when must the corrected return for 2003 be filed?

10-22 *Net Operating Loss Computation.* V, married with two dependents, owns a hardware store. For the current year, her records reveal the following:

Gross income from sales	$180,000
Business operating expenses	230,000
Royalties from investment	6,000
Nonbusiness expenses	9,000
Long-term capital gain (nonbusiness)	5,000
Long-term capital gain (business)	3,000
Long-term capital loss (business)	3,500

What is V's net operating loss?

10-23 *Valuing Inventories.* Chapters Inc., a large publishing house, prints a variety of titles, some of which are best sellers and others of which are duds. Because it is very difficult for Chapters to estimate with any accuracy which books will be successful, and because the marginal cost of printing an additional book is small, it typically prints 5,000 more copies than it expects to sell. Books that are not sold within a year of release are stored. The company's experience has shown that 95 percent of the books stored are never sold. Consequently, the company writes off any excess copies once they are delivered to storage. This practice appears permissible for financial accounting purposes. Can the same procedure be used for tax purposes?

10-24 *Applying Lower of Cost or Market.* Fitness Galore specializes in selling physical fitness equipment. The company's inventory at the close of this year revealed the following:

Mercandise	Cost	Replacement Cost
Weight machines	$40,000	$43,000
Stationary bicycles	10,000	8,000
Stair climbers	24,000	27,000

a. Compute the company's inventory assuming it uses the lower of FIFO cost or market.

b. Assume the company adopts LIFO next year. Explain the tax consequences.

10-25 *Double Extension Dollar-Value LIFO.* Unwound Sound has recently engaged an accountant to evaluate its inventory procedures and determine whether it should change from using FIFO to LIFO to account for inventories. The company's inventory records for 2004 and 2005 are shown below. Assume that the company had adopted double-extension dollar-value LIFO in 2004, and compute the ending inventory for:

a. 2004
b. 2005

	1-1-04		12-31-04	
Inventory Pool	Units	Cost Per Unit	Units	Cost Per Unit
Records	5,000	$2	3,000	$2
Tapes	4,000	3	6,000	4
Compact discs	2,000	6	5,000	7

	12-31-05	
Inventory Pool	Units	Cost Per Unit
Records	2,000	$3
Tapes	3,000	5
Compact discs	4,000	7

10-26 *LIFO Pooling.* As shown in above, the inventory of Unwound Sound consists of records, tapes, and compact discs. Over the last 15 years, the components of the company's inventory have changed dramatically. Whereas once the company only carried records, now it also carries tapes and CDs. Unwound Sound expects that in the very near future it will discontinue selling records. Assuming the company uses LIFO, explain the advantages of having one single pool containing all three items rather than three different pools.

10-27 *Accounting for Inventories.* VE Trucking Inc., an S Corporation and a cash-basis taxpayer, buys and transports sand and gravel for its customers, primarily contractors and developers. The contractors and developers use the materials in the construction of foundations for streets, houses, buildings and other construction projects. Normally, a customer contacts VE and orders a load of sand or gravel which VE subsequently buys from another source. VE then picks up the materials and delivers them to the customer's job site. VE bills the customer a flat sum, representing the costs of the materials and transportation. To determine the amount of the charge, the total cost is marked up for a reasonable profit. Because VE acquires and delivers the sand and gravel to its customers during the same business day, it does not possess any sand and gravel at the beginning or end of its business day. VE has been very profitable over the past ten years, averaging annual earnings of about $4,000,000 on annual revenues of about $15,000,000.

a. Must VE use the accrual method? If so, will the accrual method have any impact given that VE has no materials at the beginning and end of each business day?

b. Same as (a) except VE has average annual gross receipts of $8,000,000.

c. Same as (b) except VE is a C corporation

d. Same as (a) except VE has average annual gross receipts of $700,000.

10-28 *Production Deduction.* For each of the following situations, explain how the facts affect application and determination of § 199 deduction related to qualified production activities affect.

a. BAH is a strategic management and technology consulting firm that provides advisory services to companies around the world.

b. AMZ Corporation sells books and other products over the Internet throughout the world. All of its products that are purchased for resale are manufactured or produced by U.S. companies in the U.S.

c. MSFT Inc. distributes software written by its employees.

d. RYL Corporation, located in Detroit, is a construction company that primarily builds residential homes. It also is in the business of selling and assembling prefabricated steel buildings used primarily by businesses. The materials for these metal buildings are supplied by another corporation. RYL simply pours the foundation and bolts the materials in place. In addition, RYL's engineers and architects provide consulting services. One of RYL's subsidiaries is in the remodeling business.

e. CSC is currently a single member limited liability company operated by Jim Smith. The LLC has seven employees. It is in the advertising business, producing commercials for television, radio, the Internet, and print media.

f. PNA Inc. operates several restaurants in Houston. Their menu consists primarily of soup and sandwiches. Their baked products such as bread and cookies are also popular. In fact, PNA has its own central baking operation that produces bread and other pastry items that are sold to some of the finest restaurants in the area.

RESEARCH PROBLEMS

10-29 R has had several minor automobile accidents in the last two years. During the current year, R demolished his car (value, $7,000; adjusted basis, $8,000) when he ran into a telephone pole. He used the car solely for business. R decided not to report the accident to the insurance company and claim his reimbursement because he believes his insurance rates will be raised if he does. Will R's deduction of his unreimbursed casualty loss be allowed?

10-30   T, a cash basis taxpayer, paid a swimming pool contractor, C, the sum of $10,000 in advance for improvements that C agreed to make to T's personal residence. C performed part of the contract and then ceased activity, leaving much of the work uncompleted.

T seeks your advice concerning whether she may claim a deduction for a bad debt.

10-31   Ten years ago Mac and Beth left the stress of city life and moved to a beautiful home near Davenport overlooking the Mississippi River. Mac took a job as a dealer at a local riverboat gambling casino while Beth became a full-time mom. The couple was happily raising their four children until 2004, the year of the great flood. Their home, although several miles from the river, suffered thousands of dollars of water damage. Other homes in their small subdivision that were on somewhat lower ground had far worse damage. Mac and Beth and their neighbors were quite shocked that this could happen to them since they lived in an area where it had not flooded for more than 100 years. But then some were calling this the 100-year flood. After cleaning up, several of the owners decided to move, not willing to take any more chances. Unfortunately, those people who were able to sell their homes sold them for far less than what they thought they were worth, presumably because they lived in what was now perceived as a flood-prone area. Although Mac was not planning on selling his home, he did decide it was time to refinance his mortgage, the second time in 18 months. As part of the process, he got an appraisal that revealed that the value of his home had dropped substantially from the last time it was appraised. In 2001, when he refinanced for the first time, it appeared that he had made a great investment since he had purchased the house for $150,000 and the house was appraised at a value of $225,000. However, the most recent appraisal revealed that the house was worth only $120,000. What is the amount of the couple's casualty loss deduction, if any?

10-32   In 1986, Michael Malone, a professor of computer science and a specialist in digital technology, realized that it was only a short time before the computer would change the way people lived. Although he was 59 and quite happy with his $70,000 annual salary, he decided that this was an opportunity he just could not pass up. In 1986, he formed a new corporation, investing virtually all of his accumulated wealth, $200,000, in exchange for 51 percent of its stock. Three other individuals contributed additional cash for the remaining 49 percent of the stock. In the first few years of operation, the corporation was immensely successful. In 1988 Mike retired from the university and turned all of his attention to the business. All went well. In fact, things went so well that, by 1995, Mike turned over the supervision of everyday operations to several trusted employees; he began spending more time at the golf course and less time at the office. He was completely content working 20 hours a week and drawing an annual salary of $70,000. That income combined with his pension from the university of $20,000 a year was more than enough to keep him happy. During 2004, however, the competition in the computer business became fierce and the corporation had cash flow problems. As a result, Michael loaned the corporation $150,000 to keep it afloat. Unfortunately, the corporation was not able to survive and declared bankruptcy in 2006. How should Michael treat the worthless loan?

Chapter 11

ITEMIZED DEDUCTIONS

LEARNING OBJECTIVES

Upon completion of this chapter you will be able to:

- Identify the personal expenses that qualify as itemized deductions

- Explain the rules regarding deductible medical expenses and compute the medical expense deduction

- Distinguish between deductible taxes and nondeductible fees or other charges

- Explain the rules regarding deductible state income taxes, including the proper treatment of such taxes by married persons filing joint or separate returns

- Distinguish between currently deductible and nondeductible interest expenses

- Explain the requirements for the deductibility of charitable contributions and compute the contribution deduction

- Identify the personal expenditures that qualify as either miscellaneous itemized deductions or other itemized deductions

- Explain the cutback rule applicable to certain itemized deductions of high-income taxpayers and compute their total deduction allowed

CHAPTER OUTLINE

Although the vast majority of deductions are those for trade or business expenses, a taxpayer's deductions are not confined to these alone. As noted in Chapter 7, since 1942 Congress has also allowed taxpayers to deduct expenses relating to profit-seeking activities—thus creating a *second* category of so-called investment or nonbusiness expenses. In addition, despite the fact that Code § 262 expressly prohibits the deduction of personal expenditures, Congress has created various exceptions. As a result, a *third* category of deductible expenses exists, which contains such personal items as medical expenses, casualty losses, interest on home mortgages, taxes on real and personal property, charitable contributions, and tax return preparation costs. The last four chapters have focused primarily on business expenses. This chapter continues the discussion of the three types of deductions by examining the specific statutory and administrative authority relating to personal itemized deductions. As defined in Chapter 3, these personal expenses are deducted by a taxpayer only if (1) they exceed the available standard deduction, or (2) the taxpayer is not eligible for the standard deduction.

Before considering these deductions in detail, it should be emphasized that a particular type of expense (e.g., interest) does not necessarily receive the same treatment in all situations. More often than not, the expense is treated differently depending on whether it is business, investment, or personal in nature. For example, the deductibility of interest expense generally depends on whether it is related to a loan that was used to make a business, investment, or personal expenditure. In contrast, real property taxes are deductible regardless of whether the property is used for business, investment, or personal purposes. The character of the expense may also affect the deduction's classification. Generally, trade or business expenses (other than the unreimbursed expenses of an employee) and expenses related to producing rents or royalties are deductions *for* A.G.I., while other expenses are *itemized deductions* which may or may not be subject to the 2 percent floor.

MEDICAL EXPENSES

IN GENERAL

Deductible medical expenses include amounts paid for the diagnosis, cure, relief, treatment, or prevention of disease of the taxpayer, his or her spouse, and dependents.[1] The status of a person as the taxpayer's spouse or dependent must exist *either* at the time the medical services are rendered *or* at the time the expenses are paid.[2] A spousal relationship does not exist if the taxpayer is legally separated from his or her spouse under a decree of separate maintenance because the two parties are not considered married.[3] For purposes of dependency status, however, *both* the gross income test and the joint return test are waived.[4]

> **Example 1.** T pays all the medical expenses of his mother, M, during the current year. Although M had gross income in excess of the exemption amount ($3,200 in 2005) for the current year, all other dependency tests are met by T. Even though T cannot claim M as a dependent, he will be allowed to deduct all medical expenses paid on her behalf (assuming T itemizes his deductions and they exceed the percentage limitations imposed on medical deductions).

Medical expenses for children of divorced parents are deductible by the parent who pays for them, regardless of which parent is entitled to the dependency exemption. Additionally, if a taxpayer is entitled to a dependency exemption under a multiple support agreement, the taxpayer will be allowed to deduct any medical expenses which he or she actually pays on behalf of the claimed dependent.[5]

Medical expenses also include payments for treatment affecting any part or function of the body,[6] expenditures for certain medicines and drugs,[7] expenses paid for transportation primarily *for* and *essential* to the rendition of the medical care,[8] and payments made for medical care insurance for the taxpayer, his or her spouse, and dependents.[9] Again, the term *dependent* includes any person who would otherwise qualify as the taxpayer's dependent even though the gross income or separate return tests are not met, and any person claimed as a dependent under a multiple support agreement.

---

[1]   See §§ 213(a) and 213(d)(1).

[2]   Reg. § 1.213-1(e)(3).

[3]   § 143(a).

[4]   See Reg. § 1.213-1(a)(3)(i) and Chapter 4 for a discussion of the dependency tests.

[5]   See § 213(d)(5) and Reg. § 1.213-1(a)(3)(i). Medical expenses taken into account under § 21 in computing a credit for the care of certain dependents are not allowed to be treated as deductible medical expenses. See § 213(e) and Reg. § 1.213-1(f) and Chapter 13 for a discussion of the tax credit allowed under § 21.

[6]   § 213(d)(1)(A) and Reg. § 1.213-1(e)(1)(i).

[7]   § 213(d)(2) and Reg. § 1.213-1(e)(2).

[8]   § 213(d)(1)(B) and Reg. § 1.213-1(e)(1)(iv).

[9]   § 213(d)(1)(C) and Reg. § 1.213-1(e)(4).

Partial lists of deductible and nondeductible medical expenses are presented in Exhibits 11-1 and 11-2. The most recent addition to the list of nondeductible medical expenses involves cosmetic surgery or other similar procedure. Cosmetic surgery is defined as any procedure that is directed at improving the patient's appearance and does not meaningfully promote the proper function of the body or prevent or treat disease. Thus, the costs of face lifts, liposuction, hair transplants, and other similar elective procedures undertaken primarily to improve the taxpayer's physical appearance are not deductible. However, deductions are allowed for procedures necessary to ameliorate a congenital deformity, a personal injury arising from an accident or trauma, or a disfiguring disease.

EXHIBIT 11-1
Partial List of Deductible Medical Expenses[10]

Fees paid for doctors, surgeons, dentists, osteopaths, ophthalmologists, optometrists, chiropractors, chiropodists, podiatrists, psychiatrists, psychologists, and Christian Science practitioners

Fees paid for hospital services, therapy, nursing services (including nurse's meals while on duty), ambulance hire, and laboratory, surgical, obstetrical, diagnostic, dental, and X-ray services

Meals and lodging provided by a hospital during medical treatment, and meals and lodging provided by a center during treatment for alcoholism or drug addiction

Medical and hospital insurance premiums

Medicines and drugs, but only if prescribed by doctor (includes vitamins, iron, and pills or other birth control items)

Special foods and drinks prescribed by doctor, but only if for the treatment of an illness

Special items, including braces for teeth or limbs, false teeth, artificial limbs, eyeglasses, contact lenses, hearing aids, crutches, wheelchairs, and guide dogs for the blind or deaf

Smoking cessation programs

Transportation expenses for needed medical care, including air, bus, boat, railroad, and taxi fares

EXHIBIT 11-2
Partial List of Nondeductible Expenditures[11]

Accident insurance premiums

Bottled water

Care of a normal and healthy baby by a nurse*

Cosmetic surgery (with limited exceptions)

Diaper service

Funeral and burial expenses

Health club dues

Household help*

Illegal operation or treatment

Maternity clothes

Social activities, such as dancing lessons, for the general improvement of health, even though recommended by doctor

Toothpaste, toiletries, cosmetics, etc.

Trip for general improvement of health

Vitamins for general health

Note: A portion of these expenditures may qualify as expenses for the child or dependent care tax credit allowed under § 21. See Chapter 13 for further discussion of this credit.

---

[10]   See *Your Federal Income Tax*, IRS Publication 17 (Rev. 2004), p. 154.

[11]   *Ibid.*

WHEN DEDUCTIBLE

In computing the medical expense deduction for a given tax year, the taxpayer is allowed to take into account *only* those medical expenses *actually paid* during the taxable year, regardless of when the illness or injury that occasioned the expenses occurred, and regardless of the method of accounting used by the taxpayer in computing his or her taxable income (i.e., cash or accrual).[12] Consequently, if the medical expenses are incurred but not paid during the current tax year, the deduction for such expenses will not be allowed *until* the year of payment. The IRS has ruled, however, that the use of a bank credit card to pay for medical expenses *will* qualify as payment in the year of the credit card charge regardless of when the taxpayer actually repays the bank.[13]

The *prepayment* of medical expenses does not qualify as a current deduction unless the taxpayer is required to make the payment as a condition of receiving the medical services.[14] Accordingly, the IRS has ruled that a taxpayer's nonrefundable advance payments required as a condition for admission to a retirement home or institution for future lifetime medical care are deductible as expenses in the year paid.[15]

> **Example 2.** As a prerequisite for prenatal care and the delivery of her child, M prepays $3,150 to her doctor on November 15, 2005. Even though much of the prenatal care and the delivery of the child does not occur until 2006, M will be allowed to treat the prepayment as a medical expenditure in 2005.

DEDUCTION LIMITATIONS

The medical expense deduction was created by Congress with the stated social objective of providing individual taxpayers relief from a heavy tax burden during a period of medical emergency and thereby encouraging the maintenance of a high level of public health. However, the deduction was designed to provide relief for only those expenditures in excess of a normal or average amount. Currently, the medical expense deduction is allowed only to the extent medical expenditures exceed 7.5 percent of the taxpayer's adjusted gross income. This limitation ensures that only extraordinary medical costs will result in a deduction.

In addition to the percentage limitation imposed on the medical expense deduction, it is important to note that most of the everyday type of expenditures incurred by an individual for items incident to his or her general health and hygiene are excluded from the definition of qualifying medical expenses. For example, medicine and drug expenditures are deductible only if they are for insulin and *prescribed* drugs.[16] Over-the-counter medicines and drugs such as aspirin, cold remedies, skin lotions, and vitamins are not deductible. Other nondeductible expenditures are listed in Exhibit 11-2.

---

[12] Reg. § 1.213-1(a)(1).

[13] Rev. Rul. 78-39, 1978-1 C.B. 73.

[14] See *Robert S. Basset*, 26 T.C. 619 (1956). Absent such a prohibition, a taxpayer could maximize the tax benefits of medical deductions simply by timing the year of payment.

[15] Rev Rul. 75-303, 1975-2 C.B. 87.

[16] § 213(b) and Reg. § 1.213-1(b)(2)(i).

Example 3. F had adjusted gross income of $30,000 for 2005 and paid the following medical expenses:

Doctors	$ 500
Dentist	600
Hospital	1,300
Medical insurance premiums	800
Medicines and drugs:	
Prescription drugs	300
Nonprescription medicines	150

Assuming F is not reimbursed for any of the medical expenditures during 2005, her medical expense deduction is computed as follows:

Medical insurance premiums	$ 800
Fees paid doctors and dentist	1,100
Hospital costs	1,300
Prescription drugs only	300
Total medical expenses taken into account	$ 3,500
Less: 7.5% of $30,000 (A.G.I.)	−2,250
Allowable medical deduction for 2005	$ 1,250

SPECIAL ITEMS AND EQUIPMENT

The term *medical care* includes not only the diagnosis, treatment, and cure of disease, but the mitigation and prevention of disease as well. Thus, a taxpayer's expenditures for special items such as contact lenses, eyeglasses, hearing aids, artificial teeth or limbs, and ambulance hire would also qualify as medical expenditures.[17] Similarly, the cost of special equipment (e.g., wheelchairs and special controls or other equipment installed in an auto for use by a physically handicapped person) purchased *primarily* for the prevention or alleviation of a physical or mental defect or illness will be allowed as medical deductions. If the purchase of special equipment qualifies as a medical expenditure, the cost of its operation and maintenance is also a deductible medical expense.[18]

Capital expenditures generally are not deductible for Federal income tax purposes (i.e., depreciation is allowed only for property or equipment used in a taxpayer's trade or business or other income-producing activity). However, if a capital expenditure would otherwise qualify as a medical expense (i.e., it is incurred primarily for medical care), it will not be disqualified as a deduction. If the capital expenditure is for the permanent improvement or betterment of property such as the taxpayer's home, *only* the amount of the expenditure which *exceeds* the increase in value of the property improved will qualify as a medical expense.[19]

---

[17] Reg. § 1.213-1(e)(1)(ii). The IRS has ruled that the costs to acquire, train, and maintain a dog that assists a blind or deaf taxpayer are deductible medical expenses (see Rev. Rul. 55-216, 1955-1 C.B. 307 and Rev. Rul. 68-295, 1968-1 C.B. 92). In the Committee Reports for the Technical and Miscellaneous Revenue Act of 1988, Congress indicated its approval of this IRS position and stated that similar costs incurred with respect to a dog *or* other service animal used to assist individuals with *other physical disabilities* would also be eligible for the medical expense deduction.

[18] *Supra,* Footnote 10.

[19] Reg. § 1.213-1(e)(1)(iii).

Example 4. After suffering a heart attack, T is advised by his physician to install an elevator in his residence rather than continue climbing the stairs. If the cost of installing the elevator is $6,000 and the increase in the value of his residence is determined to be only $1,000, the difference of $5,000 will be deductible by T as a medical expense in the year paid. Annual operating costs (i.e., utilities) and maintenance of the elevator also qualify as deductible medical expenses.

In two specific situations, any increase in value of the improved property is ignored (or deemed to be zero) for purposes of measuring the medical expense deduction. First, if permanent improvements are made to property *rented* by the taxpayer, the *entire* costs are deductible (subject to the 7.5% floor).[20] Likewise, the entire cost of certain home-related capital expenditures incurred by a physically handicapped individual qualifies as a medical expense. Qualifying costs include expenditures for (1) constructing entrance or exit ramps to the residence; (2) widening doorways at entrances or exits to the residence; (3) widening or otherwise modifying hallways and interior doorways to accommodate wheelchairs; (4) railings, support bars, or other modifications to bathrooms to accommodate handicapped individuals; (5) lowering of or other modifications to kitchen cabinets and equipment to accommodate access by handicapped individuals; and (6) adjustment of electrical outlets and fixtures.

SPECIAL CARE FACILITIES

Expenses paid for emergency room treatment or hospital care of the taxpayer, his or her spouse, or dependents qualify for the medical deduction.[21] However, the deductibility of expenses for care in an institution other than a hospital depends upon the medical condition of the individual *and* the nature of the services he or she receives. If the *principal reason* an individual is in an institution (such as a nursing home or special school) is the availability of medical care, the *entire cost* of the medical care qualifies as a medical expenditure. This includes the cost of meals and lodging as well as any tuition expenses of special schools.[22]

Example 5. T enrolled his dependent son, S, in a special school for children with hearing impairments. If the principal reason for S's attendance at the school is his medical condition *and* the institution has the resources to treat or supervise training of the hearing impaired, the entire cost of S's attendance at the school qualifies as a medical expense. This includes tuition, meals and lodging, and any other costs that are incidental to the special services furnished by the school.

If an individual's medical condition *is not* the principal reason for being in an institution, only that part of the cost of care in the institution which is attributable to medical care will qualify as a medical expense.[23]

Example 6. T placed her dependent father, F, in a nursing home after F suffered a stroke and partial paralysis. Of the $6,000 total nursing home expenses, only $2,500 is attributable to the medical care and nursing attention furnished to F. If F is not in

---

20   Rev. Rul. 70-395, 1970-2 C.B. 65.

21   This includes the cost of meals and lodging incurred as an in-patient of a hospital. See Reg. § 1.213-1 (e)(1)(v).

22   Reg. § 1.213-1(e)(1)(v)(a). See also *Donald R. Pfeifer*, 37 TCM 817, T.C. Memo 1978-189; *W.B. Counts*, 42 T.C. 755 (1963); Rev. Rul. 78-340, 1978-2 C.B. 124; and Rev. Rul. 58-533, 1958-2 C.B. 108.

23   Reg. § 1.213-1(e)(1)(v)(b). This *excludes* meals and lodging and any other expenses not directly attributable to the medical care or treatment.

the nursing home for the principal reason of the medical and nursing care, only $2,500 will be deductible by T.

LONG-TERM CARE COSTS

Prior to 1996, it was unclear whether the costs of long-term care qualified as a medical expense. The IRS commonly challenged such costs as personal and denied their deduction. Tax legislation passed in 1996 clarified the treatment of such expenses by providing that unreimbursed amounts paid for qualified long-term care services provided to a chronically-ill taxpayer (or his or her spouse or dependents), as well as the premiums paid for long-term care insurance that meets certain requirements, are eligible for deduction as medical expenses. The amount deductible for insurance premiums is subject to limitations, but also is adjusted annually for inflation. The limits for 2005 are as follows:

Age before close of tax year	Limitation
40 or less	$ 270
More than 40 but less than 50	510
More than 50 but less than 60	1,020
More than 60 but less than 70	2,720
More than 70	3,400

Qualified long-term care services generally include necessary diagnostic, preventive, therapeutic, curing, treating, mitigating and rehabilitative services, and maintenance or personal care services that are required by a chronically-ill individual and provided pursuant to a plan of care prescribed by a licensed health care practitioner. A chronically-ill individual is generally a person who is unable to perform at least two activities of daily living (e.g., eating, toileting, transferring, bathing, dressing, and continence) for a period of at least 90 days due to a loss of functional capacity.

Amounts paid to relatives for long-term care services normally are not eligible for deduction unless such person is a licensed professional with respect to the services that he or she is providing.

In addition, § 7702B allows an income exclusion for long-term care benefits received by an individual. For 2005, the exclusion from gross income is the greater of $240 per day or the actual cost of the care.

MEDICAL TRAVEL AND TRANSPORTATION

Expenses paid for transportation to and from the office of a doctor or dentist or to a hospital or clinic usually are deductible as medical expenses. This includes amounts paid for bus, taxi, train, and plane fares, as well as the out-of-pocket expenses for use of the taxpayer's personal vehicle (i.e., gas and oil, parking fees, and tolls). If the taxpayer uses his or her personal automobile for medical transportation and does not want to calculate actual expenses, the IRS allows a deduction of 15 cents a mile *plus* parking fees and tolls paid while traveling for medical treatment.[24]

Travel costs include *only* transportation expenses and the cost of lodging. For these expenses to qualify as a medical deduction, a trip beyond the taxpayer's locale *must* be "primarily for and essential to medical care."[25] Meal costs are deductible only if

---

[24]   Rev. Proc. 2004-64, 2004-49 I.R.B.

[25]   See § 213(d)(2), Reg. § 1.213-1(e)(1)(iv), and *Comm. v. Bilder*, 62-1 USTC ¶9440, 9 AFTR2d 1355, 369 U.S. 499 (USSC, 1962).

provided by a hospital or similar institution as a necessary part of medical care. Thus, meals consumed while en route between the taxpayer's home and the location of the medical care are not deductible.

If an individual receives medical treatment as an outpatient at a clinic or doctor's office, the cost of lodging while in the new locality may be deductible—but not the cost of meals. The cost of lodging will qualify as a medical expense if (1) the lodging is not lavish or extravagant under the circumstances; and (2) there is no significant element of personal pleasure, recreation, or vacation in the travel away from home. If deductible, the amount of lodging costs includible as a medical expense may not exceed *$50* for *each night* for each individual.[26] It is important to note that travel costs of a companion (including parents or a nurse) are included as medical expenses if the individual requiring medical treatment could not travel alone, or if the companion rendered medical treatment en route.[27] Thus, the lodging costs of such a person while in the new locality should also be treated as a part of any medical expenses (subject to the $50 per night limitation).

> **Example 7.** At the advice of a doctor, T travels with his three-year-old daughter, D, from Lincoln, Nebraska to Houston, Texas. D has a rare blood disease and a hospital in Houston is the nearest facility specializing in treatment of her disorder. The transportation costs and lodging for both T and his daughter while en route to and from Houston are deductible. If they stay at a nearby hotel while D receives treatment as an outpatient, the costs of lodging (but not meals) incurred in Houston—up to $100 per night—are also deductible.

MEDICAL INSURANCE COSTS AND REIMBURSEMENTS

Amounts paid for medical care insurance for the taxpayer, his or her spouse, and dependents qualify as medical expenses. If premiums are paid under an insurance contract which offers coverage beyond medical care (e.g., coverage for loss of life, limb, or sight, or loss of income), only the portion of the premiums paid that is attributable to medical care is deductible. To be deductible, however, the medical care portion of the premiums paid must either be separately stated in the contract itself, or included in a separate bill or statement from the insurer.[28]

Taxpayers receiving reimbursements for medical expenses in the *same year* in which the expenses were paid must reduce any medical expense deduction to a net amount. However, if the reimbursement is for medical expenses in a prior year, the income tax treatment of the reimbursement depends upon whether the taxpayer claimed a medical expense deduction for the year in which the expenses were actually paid. If no medical expense deduction was taken in the year in which the expenses were paid (e.g., taxpayer used the standard deduction or total medical expenses did not exceed the required percentage of A.G.I.), any reimbursement for such expenses will not be included in gross income. If the taxpayer claimed a deduction for the medical expenses in the prior year, however, the reimbursement must be included in gross income to the extent of the *lesser* of: (1) the previous medical expense deduction, or (2) the excess of the taxpayer's itemized deductions over his or her standard deduction. The inclusion in gross income of all or a part of the reimbursement is in accordance with the tax benefit rule.

---

[26]   § 213(d)(2).

[27]   See Rev. Rul. 75-317, 1975-2 C.B. 57.

[28]   Reg. § 1.213-1(e)(4). Participants in the Federal Medicare program are entitled to treat as medical care insurance premiums the amounts withheld for voluntary doctor-bill insurance.

Example 8. T has adjusted gross income of $30,000 for 2005. During the year, T pays the following medical expenses:

Hospitalization insurance premiums	$1,900
Doctor and dental bills	800
Eyeglasses	175
Medical transportation	25

T's medical expense deduction is computed as follows:

Total medical expenses	$ 2,900
Less: 7.5% of $30,000 (A.G.I.)	−2,250
Medical expense deduction for 2005	$ 650

T's itemized deductions (including the $650 medical expense deduction) for 2005 exceeded his standard deduction by $1,500. In 2006 T received $400 as a reimbursement from his insurance company. T must include the *entire* $400 in gross income for 2006. If T had received the $400 reimbursement in 2005, his medical expense deduction would have been limited to $250.

Example 9. Assume the same facts as in *Example 8* except that the medical expense reimbursement was $900 instead of $400. If the reimbursement was received in 2006, T would be required to include only $650 in gross income—the amount of the medical expenses included in his itemized deductions. If the amount by which T's itemized deductions exceeded his standard deduction was *less* than $650 for 2005, he would include in gross income for 2006 only so much of the reimbursement represented by the prior year's itemized deductions in excess of the standard deduction amount. However, if T had used the standard deduction in 2005, none of the $900 reimbursement would be included in 2006 gross income because T received no tax benefit in 2005.

The situations illustrated in *Examples 89* occur quite often because taxpayers are *not required* to reduce a current year's medical expense deduction by *anticipated* insurance reimbursements. Notice that this can result in a taxpayer receiving reimbursements early in the next tax year and not being required to pay income taxes on the reimbursement until April 15 of the following year.

MEDICAL SAVINGS ACCOUNTS

The Health Insurance Act of 1996 established a new experimental program, the Medical Savings Account (now known as Archer MSAs), that enables a limited number of individuals to pay for unreimbursed medical expenses on a before-tax basis. For those familiar with flexible spending accounts for medical expenses now used by many employers and their employees, MSAs are virtually identical without the *use it or lose* it rule. For those familiar with Individual Retirement Accounts, MSAs are quite similar.

Beginning in 1998, § 220 permits individuals to deduct for A.G.I. a limited amount of contributions to an MSA. Similarly, § 106(b) allows individuals to exclude limited contributions to such accounts made on their behalf by their employers. Amounts contributed to the MSA may be invested and the earnings are nontaxable. Distributions from the account are nontaxable as long as they are used for medical expenses that normally would be deductible other than those for health insurance.

Note that no deduction is allowed for expenses paid for with dollars out of the MSA. However, the deduction for amounts *contributed* and the exclusion for amounts distributed essentially provide the same benefit. The end result of these rules effectively enables an individual to pay for medical expenses not covered by insurance with dollars that have never been subject to tax. Observe that if the taxpayer pays for unreimbursed medical expenses using dollars that do not come from the MSA, they normally are not deductible due to the 7.5 percent limitation. In such case, the payments are effectively made with after-tax dollars.

> **Example 10.** Assume M is in the 30% tax bracket with an adjusted gross income of $60,000. He is covered by health insurance that pays for most but not all of his medical expenses. During the year, M contributed $1,000 to an MSA. Later during the year he withdrew the entire $1,000 to pay for medical expenses related to knee surgery that were not covered by his insurance. As shown by the following analysis (ignoring exemptions and the standard deduction and assuming M itemized deductions), by using an MSA, M saves $300, the tax that otherwise would have been paid on the amounts used to pay for the unreimbursed medical expenses.

	Employee Pays	MSA Pays	
Income	$ 60,000	$ 60,000	
Deduction for contribution to MSA	—	(1,000)	
Adjusted gross income	$ 60,000	$ 59,000	
Medical expense deduction [$1,000 −(7.5% × $60,000)]	0	—	
Income	$ 60,000	$ 59,000	
Tax @ 30%	(18,000)	(17,700)	
Cost of medical expense	(1,000)	—	(MSA pays)
After-tax income	$ 41,000	$ 41,300	

Another advantage of contributions provided by an employer to an MSA is that they are not subject to FICA or FUTA taxes.

Penalty for Distributions Not Used for Medical Expenses. If the taxpayer withdraws amounts from the MSA and uses them for something other than qualified medical expenses before age 65 (or death or disability), a penalty equal to 15 percent of the amount withdrawn is imposed. Amounts withdrawn after age 65 are not subject to penalty but will be taxed as ordinary income to the extent they are not used to pay for medical expenses.

Contribution Limitations. The amount that can be contributed to an MSA is a function of the "deductible" of the "high-deductible" health plan. For individual coverage, the annual contribution limit is 65 percent of the deductible while it is 75 percent of the deductible for family coverage. As explained below, the deductible of a high-deductible plan for single coverage ranges from $1,750 to $2,650 in 2005. Therefore, the contribution for a single coverage plan would be limited to 65 percent of these amounts or $1,137 to $1,722. Similarly, the deductible for family coverage is $3,500 to $5,250 resulting in maximum contributions ranging from $2,625 to $3,937. Contributions are further limited to the individual's compensation, or in the case of a self-employed person, the amount of net earnings from self-employment.

Treatment of MSAs at Death. If the taxpayer dies before using the amount in the MSA, the balance may be passed on to a beneficiary who can use the amount for their own medical expenses. If no beneficiary is named, the MSA is terminated and its value (reduced by final medical expenses of the decedent paid within one year) is taxed as income to the estate. Any balance in the MSA at the taxpayer's death is included in the decedent's gross estate subject to estate taxes (unless such amount is left to the surviving spouse in which case it qualifies for the marital deduction).

Eligible Individuals. Under the initial version of the MSA program, everyone would have been eligible to establish an MSA. But the authors of the final bill rejected this position and decided to treat the MSA as an experiment. As a result, at this juncture, not everyone is permitted to take advantage of MSAs. An individual is eligible for the MSA deduction only if he or she is self-employed or elects to be covered under a so-called high-deductible health plan that is sponsored by a "small employer" (i.e., one who on average employs 50 or fewer workers). A plan qualifies as a high-deductible health plan if it has the following deductibles and limitations on out of pocket expenses:

- ▸ *Individual coverage*: An annual deductible not less than $1,750 and not more than $2,650 and the maximum annual out-of-pocket expenses required to be paid under the plan for covered benefits (other than premiums) does not exceed $3,500.

- ▸ *Family coverage*: An annual deductible not less than $3,500 and not more than $5,250 and the maximum annual out-of-pocket expenses required to be paid under the plan for covered benefits (other than premiums) does not exceed $6,450.

To further limit the number of persons using MSAs, only the first 750,000 individuals who establish MSAs are eligible. To determine whether the limit has been met, custodians of these accounts (e.g., banks and savings and loans) must report the creation of the accounts to the IRS which will decide whether to continue, expand, or eliminate the program. The number of reported MSAs is still significantly less than 750,000. New Archer MSAs may not be established after 2005 [§ 220(I)(2)]. Beginning in 2004, individuals and employees can establish Health Savings Accounts (HSAs). HSAs differ from MSAs in that HSAs are not limited only to small employer employees or self-employed. HSAs are available on a wider range of high-deductible plans than MSAs. Contribution to HSAs may be made by the taxpayer, their family or employer [§ 223(C)(2)(A)].

HEALTH INSURANCE COSTS OF SELF-EMPLOYED TAXPAYERS

Self-employed individuals are allowed to treat the amounts paid for health insurance on behalf of a self-employed individual, his or her spouse, and dependents as a deductible business expense.[29] A more than two percent owner-employee of S Corp. stock can deduct 100% of the amount paid for medical insurance for himself, spouse and dependents [§ 162 (I)I)(S)]. The deduction is allowed in determining adjusted gross income (i.e., a deduction *for* A.G.I.) rather than being treated as an itemized medical expense deduction subject to the 7.5 percent floor. No deduction is allowable to the extent it *exceeds* the taxpayer's net earnings from self-employment.[30] Thus, the deduction cannot create a loss. More important, the deduction does not reduce the income base for which the taxpayer is liable for self-employment taxes.

Example 11. K, a self-employed individual, paid $2,600 during 2005 for health insurance for himself, his wife, and their two children. K had no employees during the year. K is entitled to deduct the entire $2,600 in determining adjusted gross income, provided the deduction does not exceed his net earnings from self-employment, and his A.G.I. before the deduction is at least $2,600.[31]

---

[29]   § 162(I).

[30]   § 162(I)(2)(A).

[31]   § 162(I)(3).

Absent a special rule, self-employed individuals who are also employees might be tempted to opt out of an employer-provided medical insurance plan. By so doing, the 7.5 percent floor on medical expenses could be avoided and taxpayers could deduct a portion of what normally would be nondeductible premium payments. To prevent this course of action, the deduction is not allowed if a self-employed individual or spouse is eligible to participate in a health insurance plan of an employer.[32]

PERSONAL CASUALTY AND THEFT LOSSES

As discussed in Chapter 10, Congress has provided for a deduction of losses related to property used for *personal* purposes where the loss arises from fire, storm, shipwreck, or other casualty, or theft.[33] Like the medical expense deduction, the deduction for personal casualty and theft losses is designed to provide relief for only extraordinary losses. Thus, an individual taxpayer's deduction for personal casualty and theft losses is allowed only to the extent such losses exceed $100 per occurrence *and* the sum of all losses (after reduction by the $100 floor) for a given tax year exceeds 10 percent of the taxpayer's adjusted gross income. These deduction limitations were discussed and illustrated in Chapter 10.

YEAR DEDUCTIBLE

A personal casualty loss is generally deductible in the taxable year in which the loss occurs. Recall, however, that a theft loss is deductible only in the year of discovery. If a claim for insurance reimbursement (or any other potential recovery) exists and there is a reasonable prospect of recovery, the loss must be reduced by the amount *expected* to be received.[34] If later receipts are *less* than the amount originally estimated and no further reimbursement is expected, an amended return is not filed. Instead, the remaining loss is deductible in the year in which no further reimbursement is expected. Most important, if the casualty loss deduction claimed in the prior year was reduced by the $100 floor and exceeded the 10 percent A.G.I. limitation, the remaining loss is not further reduced. However, the remaining loss is subject to the 10 percent limitation of the later year.[35]

REPORTING CASUALTY LOSSES

Individual taxpayers are required to report and compute casualty losses on Form 4684,[36] which is to be filed with Form 1040. The casualty loss deduction, if any, is reported with other itemized deductions on Schedule A, Form 1040.

TAXES

Code § 164 is the statutory authority that permits taxpayers to deduct several types of taxes for Federal income tax purposes. If the taxes are related to an individual taxpayer's trade or business or income-producing activity, the deduction is generally allowed in arriving at adjusted gross income. However, both the IRS and the courts have taken the position that state, local, and foreign *income* taxes are deductible by an individual taxpayer *from* his or her adjusted gross income—even though it could be

---

[32]   § 162(l)(2)(B).

[33]   § 165(c)(3).

[34]   Reg. § 1.165-1(d)(2)(i).

[35]   See *Example 9* of Chapter 10.

[36]   See Appendix B for a sample of this form.

argued that such taxes are related to his or her trade or business. Likewise, if *property* taxes are related to personal use property (e.g., residence, car, etc.), such taxes are deductible only if the individual itemizes his or her deductions. If taxes are deductible by taxpayers other than individuals, the deductions simply reduce gross income to taxable income.[37]

The types of taxes specifically allowed as deductions under § 164 are:

1.   State, local, and foreign real property taxes;

2.   State and local personal property taxes;

3.   State and local general sales taxes;

4.   State, local, and foreign income, war profits, and excess profit taxes; and

5.   The generation-skipping transfer tax.[38]

The generation-skipping transfer tax is imposed on income distributions from certain trusts. Discussion of this tax is beyond the scope of this text. However, each of the other types of deductible taxes is discussed in detail below.

GENERAL REQUIREMENTS FOR DEDUCTIBILITY

A tax is deductible *only* if (1) it is imposed on the taxpayer's income or property; and (2) it is paid or incurred by the taxpayer in the taxable year for which a deduction is being claimed. Even if these two requirements are met, deductions for certain Federal, state, and local taxes are expressly denied. Exhibit 11-3 contains a list of nondeductible taxes.

In addition to the nondeductible taxes listed in Exhibit 11-3, deductions for *fees* (whether or not labeled as taxes) paid by taxpayers usually are denied *unless* the fees are incurred in the taxpayer's trade or business or for the production of income. Fees paid or incurred in connection with a trade or business, if ordinary and necessary, are deductible as business expenses under § 162. Similarly, fees related to the production of income generally are deductible expenses under § 212.[39]

EXHIBIT 11-3
Nondeductible Taxes[40]

Nondeductible Federal taxes:
   Federal income taxes (including those withheld from an individual's pay)
   Social security or railroad retirement taxes withheld from an individual by his or her employer (includes self-employment taxes)
   Social security and other employment taxes paid on the wages of the taxpayer's employee who performed domestic or other personal services
   Federal excise taxes or customs duties unless they are connected with the taxpayer's business or income-producing activity
   Federal estate and gift taxes

Nondeductible state and local taxes:
   Motor vehicle taxes (unless they qualify as ad valorem taxes on personal property)
   Inheritance, legacy, succession, or estate taxes
   Gift taxes
   Per capita or poll taxes
   Cigarette, tobacco, liquor, beer, wine, etc., taxes

---

[37]   See the later section in this chapter entitled "Reporting Deductions for Taxes."

[38]   § 164(a).

[39]   See Chapter 7 for a discussion of the requirements that must be met in order to deduct business and nonbusiness expenses of this nature.

[40]   See § 275, Reg. § 1.164-2, and *Your Federal Income Tax*, IRS Publication 17 (Rev. 2004), p. 161.

The IRS distinguishes a "tax" from a "fee" by looking to the *purpose* of the charge.[41] If a particular charge is imposed upon the taxpayer for the purpose of *raising revenue* to be used for public or government purposes, the IRS will consider the charge to be a tax. However, if the charge is imposed because of either *particular acts or services* received by the taxpayer, such charge will be considered as a *fee*. Thus, fees for driver's licenses, vehicle registration and inspection, license tags for pets, hunting and fishing licenses, tolls for bridges and roads, parking meter deposits, water bills, sewer and other service charges, and postage fees are not deductible *unless* related to the taxpayer's trade or business, or income-producing activity.[42]

Since most individual taxpayers use the cash receipts and disbursements method of accounting for tax purposes, the following discussion of income and property tax deductions concentrates on cash-basis taxpayers and the requirement that taxes be *paid* in the year of deduction. Bear in mind throughout this discussion, however, that accrual method taxpayers are allowed a deduction for taxes in the tax year in which the obligation for payment becomes fixed and determinable (i.e., the all-events test is met).

INCOME TAXES

Most state, local, or foreign income taxes paid or accrued by a taxpayer are deductible in arriving at taxable income. For individual taxpayers, however, a deduction for state and local income taxes is allowed only if the taxpayer itemizes his or her deductions. Although the income taxes may be related solely to the individual's business income (e.g., income from a sole proprietorship or partnership), or income from rents and royalties, these taxes are considered personal in nature. Since income taxes paid to a foreign country or a U.S. possession may either be deducted as an itemized deduction or claimed as a credit against the U.S. income tax, an individual who does not itemize deductions should elect to claim foreign income taxes as credits.[43]

Cash-basis taxpayers are allowed to deduct state and local income taxes *paid* during the taxable year, including those taxes imposed on interest income that is exempt from Federal income taxation. Amounts considered paid during the taxable year include:

1. State and local income or foreign taxes withheld from an individual's salary by his or her employer;

2. Estimated payments made by the taxpayer under a pay-as-you-go requirement of a taxing authority; and

3. Payments made in the current year on an income tax liability of a prior year.

Example 12. During 2005 Z, a cash basis taxpayer, had $1,500 of Illinois state income taxes withheld by her employer. In 2005 she paid the remaining $450 in state income taxes due on her 2004 Illinois tax return, and also paid $300 in estimated state income tax payments during 2005. If Z itemizes her deductions for Federal income tax purposes, she is entitled to a $2,250 ($1,500 + $300 + $450) state income tax deduction for 2005.

---

[41]   See § 275 and Reg. § 1.164-2.

[42]   *Your Federal Income Tax*, IRS Publication 17 (Rev. 2004), p. 162. No matter how strong an argument a taxpayer can make that his or her marriage was for business or income-producing purposes, fees for marriage licenses are considered non-deductible personal expenses.

[43]   § 27.

If a cash basis taxpayer receives a refund of state, local, or foreign income taxes in the current year, the refund must be included in the current year's gross income to the extent a deduction in an earlier tax year provided a tax benefit.[44]

Example 13. Assume the same facts as in *Example 12*. While preparing her 2005 Illinois state income tax return in early 2006, Z determined she had overpaid the state tax liability by $375. She received a refund of the entire overpayment on August 10, 2006. If Z claimed the total $2,250 state income taxes paid as a deduction on her 2005 Federal income tax return and her itemized deductions exceeded the standard deduction amount by at least $375, she must include the entire refund in gross income on her 2006 Federal income tax return.

Married taxpayers filing *separate* state or Federal income tax returns are subject to the following rules regarding the deduction for state income taxes:[45]

1. If separate state *and* Federal returns are filed, each spouse may deduct on his or her Federal income tax return the amount of state income tax imposed on and paid by such spouse during the tax year.

2. If separate state returns *but* a joint Federal return will be filed, the married couple may deduct on the joint Federal income tax return the sum of the state income tax imposed on both husband and wife, regardless of which spouse actually paid the tax.

3. If a joint state return *but* separate Federal returns are filed, each spouse is allowed to deduct on his or her Federal income tax return that *portion* of the total state tax imposed and paid during the year that the gross income of each spouse contributes to their total combined gross income.

PROPERTY TAXES

Personal property taxes paid to a state, local, or foreign government are deductible *only* if they are *ad valorem* taxes.[46] Ad valorem taxes are taxes imposed on the *value* of property. Quite often, state and local taxing authorities impose a combination tax and fee on personal property. In such cases, only that portion of the charge based on value of the property will qualify as a deductible tax.[47]

Example 14. State A imposes an annual vehicle registration charge of 60 cents per hundredweight. X, a resident of the state, paid $24 in 2005 for the registration of his personal automobile. Since this charge is not based on the value of the auto, X has not paid a deductible tax.

Example 15. State B imposes an annual vehicle registration charge of 1% of value plus 50 cents per hundredweight. Y, a resident of the state, owns a personal use automobile having a value of $10,000 and weighing 4,000 pounds. Of the $120 [(1% × $10,000) + (50¢ × 40 hundredweight)] total registration charge paid by Y, only $100 would be deductible as a personal property tax.

---

[44] § 111.

[45] *Your Federal Income Tax*, IRS Publication 17 (Rev. 2004), p. 159.

[46] § 164(b)(1) and Reg. § 1.164-3(c).

[47] § 164(b)(2)(E). States known to include some ad valorem tax as part of auto and boat registration fees are Arizona, California, Colorado, Indiana, Iowa, Maine, Massachusetts, Nevada, New Hampshire, Oklahoma, Washington, and Wyoming.

Real property (real estate) taxes are generally deductible only if imposed on property owned by the taxpayer and paid or accrued by the taxpayer in the year the deduction is claimed. If real property taxes are imposed on jointly held real estate, each owner may claim his or her portion of the taxes. For example, if cash basis, married taxpayers file separate Federal income tax returns and real property taxes are imposed on jointly held real estate, each spouse may claim *half* of the taxes paid.

If real estate is sold during the year, the deduction for real estate taxes *must be apportioned* between the buyer and seller according to the number of days in the year each held the property, regardless of which party actually paid the property taxes.[48] The taxes are apportioned to the seller up to (but not including) the date of sale, and to the buyer beginning with the date of sale.

> **Example 16.** The real property tax year in Colorado County is April 1 to March 31. X, the owner on April 1, 2005 of real property located in Colorado County, sells the real property to Y on June 30, 2005. Y owns the real property from June 30, 2005 through March 31, 2006. The real property tax is $730 for the county's tax year April 1, 2005 to March 31, 2006. For purposes of § 164(a), $180 (90 ÷ 365 × $730 = $180 taxes for April 1, 2005 through June 29, 2005) of the real property tax is treated as imposed on X, the seller. The remaining $550 (275 ÷ 365 × $730 = $550 taxes for June 30, 2005 through March 31, 2006) of such real property tax is treated as imposed on Y, the purchaser.[49]

When both buyer and seller of real property are cash-basis taxpayers and only one of the parties *actually* pays the real property taxes for the period in which both parties owned the property, *each* party to the transaction is entitled to deduct the portion of the real property taxes based on the number of days he or she held the property. As a practical matter, real property taxes are usually allocated during the closing process, and the details are provided in the closing statement for real property sales. A taxpayer need only acquire the closing statement to ascertain the proper allocation and how the sales price has been affected by the allocation.

Unless the actual real property taxes are apportioned between buyer and seller as part of the sale/purchase agreement, adjustments for the taxes must be made to determine the amount realized by the seller, as well as the buyer's cost basis of the property.[50] The treatment of the adjustments depends upon which party actually paid the real estate taxes.

> **Example 17.** Assume that buyer and seller are both cash basis, calendar year taxpayers, and real estate taxes for the entire year are to be paid at the end of the year. Real property is sold on October 1, 2005 for $30,000, and B, the buyer, pays the real estate taxes of $365 on December 31, 2005. The real estate taxes attributable to and deductible by B are $92 (92 ÷ 365 × $365). The remaining $273 ($365 −$92) of the taxes will be apportioned to and deductible by S, the seller. As a result of this apportionment, the seller must increase the amount realized from the sale to $30,273, and the buyer will have an adjusted cost basis for the property of $30,273.

> **Example 18.** Assume the same facts as in *Example 17*, except that the real property taxes are payable in advance for the entire year and that S, the seller, paid $365 in January 2005. The real estate taxes are apportioned in the same manner, and the

---

[48]   § 164(d) and Reg. § 1.164-6(b).

[49]   Reg. § 1.164-6(b)(3), *Example 1*.

[50]   Reg. § 1.164-6(d); Reg. § 1.1001-1(b); and Reg. § 1.1012-1(b). A similar result should occur if buyer and seller are using different accounting methods.

buyer, B, will be entitled to deduct $92. However, B must adjust his cost basis of the property to $29,908 ($30,000 purchase price − $92 taxes paid by seller). The seller, S, is entitled to deduct $273 of the taxes and reduce his amount realized from the sale to $29,908.

Real property taxes assessed against local benefits of a kind tending to increase the value of the property assessed (e.g., special assessments for paved streets, street lights, sidewalks, drainage ditches, etc.) are not deductible.[51] Instead, the property owner simply adds the assessed amount paid to his or her cost basis of the property. However, if assessments for local benefits are made for the purpose of maintenance or repair, or for the purpose of meeting interest charges with respect to such benefits, they are deductible.[52] If an assessment is in part for the cost of an improvement and in part for maintenance, repairs or for interest charges, only *that* portion of the tax assessment relating to maintenance, repairs, or interest charges will be deductible. Unless the taxpayer can show the allocation of the amounts assessed for the different purposes, *none* of the amount paid is deductible.[53]

DEDUCTION FOR STATE AND LOCAL GENERAL SALES TAX

For 2004 and 2005, the American Jobs Creation Act allows taxpayers to deduct state and local sales and use taxes instead of state and local income taxes.[54] Interestingly, prior to 1987 taxpayers could deduct both. The deduction is classified as an itemized deduction but not a miscellaneous itemized deduction. It is subject to the 3 percent cutback discussed in a later part of this chapter. In addition, the deduction for state and local sales and use taxes is not allowed for alternative minimum tax purposes.

Only "general" sales taxes are deductible. Section 164(b)(5)(B) defines a general sales tax as a tax imposed at one rate with respect to the sale at retail of a broad range of classes of item. In determining whether a tax is a "general" sales tax, the fact that it does not apply to food, clothing, medical supplies and motor vehicles, or applies at a different rate is disregarded. If other items are taxed at a different rate, such taxes are not deductible. If the rate of tax on a motor vehicle exceeds the general rate, the excess is disregarded. If the amount of the general sales tax is separately stated, to the extent it is paid by the consumer, the amount is treated as a tax imposed on and paid by the consumer.

Taxpayers may deduct their actual sales taxes as substantiated by accumulated receipts or use IRS-published tables. These tables are contained in Appendix A of this text. The tables take into account the number of exemptions, "available" income (A.G.I. increased by any tax-exempt income such as social security and tax-exempt interest) and rates of state and local general sales taxation. Since sales tax rates vary from state to state (and even by localities within a state), there are 51 different tables for the 50 states and the District of Columbia. The tables extend to available income as high as $200,000 in 2004 (2005 tables are to be released before the end of the year).

The tables include only general *state* sales taxes and do not include any additional *local sales taxes*. A special calculation must be made to determine the amount of local sales taxes that may be added to the table amount. In addition to the amount determined using the table, taxpayers may add the taxes on cars, motorcycles, motor homes, recreational vehicles, sport utility vehicles, trucks, vans, and off-road vehicles, aircraft, boats, homes (including mobile and prefabricated), or home-building materials, if the

---

[51] § 164(c)(1), Reg. § 1.164-2(g), and Reg. § 1.164-4(a).

[52] § 164(c)(1) and Reg. § 1.164-4(b)(1).

[53] Reg. § 1.164-4(b)(1).

[54] See § 165(b)(5).

tax rate was the same as the general sales tax rate. Special rules apply when a taxpayer lives in more than one state during the year. A portion of the tables appears below.

2004 Optional State Sales Tax Tables

Alaska residents only. If you paid any local sales taxes, you must use your actual expenses to figure your deduction.

Income At least	Income But less than	Alabama 1	2	3	4	5	Over 5	Arizona 1	2	3	4	5	Over 5	Arkansas 1	2	3	4	5	Over 5	California 1	2	3	4	5	Over 5
$0	$20,000	288	344	381	410	434	468	332	374	402	422	439	463	430	510	564	605	640	688	363	416	451	477	499	529
20,000	30,000	366	434	481	517	547	590	430	485	520	547	568	598	542	641	708	760	803	863	469	537	581	615	643	681
30,000	40,000	416	494	547	587	621	669	496	558	599	629	654	688	616	727	802	860	908	976	540	617	668	706	738	782
40,000	50,000	460	545	602	647	684	736	552	621	666	699	727	765	678	800	882	945	998	1072	600	685	741	784	819	867
50,000	60,000	498	590	652	700	740	796	603	678	726	763	792	833	734	864	952	1021	1077	1157	654	747	807	854	892	944
60,000	70,000	532	630	695	747	789	849	648	728	780	819	851	895	783	922	1015	1088	1148	1232	702	801	866	916	956	1012
70,000	80,000	565	667	737	791	835	898	690	776	831	872	906	952	829	976	1074	1150	1214	1302	748	853	922	974	1017	1077
80,000	90,000	593	701	773	830	877	942	728	818	876	920	955	1004	871	1023	1126	1206	1272	1365	789	899	971	1027	1072	1134
90,000	100,000	621	733	809	868	916	985	765	859	920	965	1003	1054	910	1070	1177	1260	1328	1425	828	944	1019	1077	1124	1189
100,000	120,000	657	775	855	917	968	1040	814	913	977	1026	1065	1119	962	1130	1242	1330	1402	1503	880	1002	1082	1143	1193	1262
120,000	140,000	706	832	916	982	1037	1114	878	985	1054	1106	1148	1206	1031	1210	1330	1422	1499	1607	949	1080	1166	1232	1285	1359
140,000	160,000	749	881	971	1040	1098	1179	935	1048	1122	1177	1222	1283	1093	1280	1407	1504	1585	1699	1010	1149	1240	1310	1366	1445
160,000	180,000	789	928	1022	1095	1155	1240	990	1109	1186	1244	1292	1357	1151	1347	1479	1582	1667	1785	1069	1215	1311	1384	1444	1526
180,000	200,000	827	972	1070	1146	1209	1298	1041	1166	1247	1308	1357	1425	1205	1410	1548	1654	1743	1866	1123	1277	1377	1454	1516	1602
200,000 or more		995	1166	1281	1371	1445	1549	1267	1417	1514	1587	1647	1728	1443	1684	1846	1971	2074	2220	1365	1549	1669	1761	1835	1939

Example 19. A family of four living in Arizona has available income of $51,800 for 2004. If the election is made to claim a deduction for their general sales taxes rather than state and local income taxes, the family will be allowed a deduction of $763. If the taxpayers paid a sales tax of $450 on a new truck purchased in 2004, the sales tax table amount would be increased to $1,213 ($763 + $450).

In the seven states that do not impose an income tax — Alaska, Florida, Nevada, South Dakota, Texas, Washington and Wyoming – taxpayers will now have an additional itemized deduction and, therefore, now may be able to itemize. For taxpayers in the other 43 states, which levy at least some form of state or local income tax, they will be forced to make a decision about whether an election should be made.

REPORTING DEDUCTIONS FOR TAXES

Deductible state and local taxes are reported on different forms depending on the taxpaying entity claiming the deduction. Corporations report their deductions for these taxes on Form 1120. Fiduciaries (trusts and estates) report deductible taxes on Form 1041. Partnerships and S corporations report deductible taxes on Forms 1065 and 1120S, respectively. Individuals report deductible taxes on Form 1040, but the particular schedule used depends upon whether the taxes are business expenses or personal itemized deductions.

An individual's deduction for taxes (other than income taxes) related to his or her trade or business is reported on Schedule C of Form 1040 (Schedule F for farmers and ranchers). Deductible taxes (other than income taxes) related to rents and royalties are reported on Schedule E. All other deductible taxes, including state and local general sales taxes or state and local income taxes on business income or income from rents or royalties, are reported by an individual taxpayer on Schedule A of Form 1040.

INTEREST EXPENSE

Interest expense is an amount paid or incurred for the use or forbearance of money.[55] Under the general rule of Code § 163(a), all interest paid or accrued on indebtedness within the taxable year is allowed as a deduction. As with most general rules in the tax law, however, there are limitations imposed on the deduction of certain interest expense as well as the complete disallowance of deductions for interest related to certain items. These restrictions are discussed below.

LIMITATIONS ON DEDUCTIONS OF INTEREST EXPENSE

Prior to 1987, interest expense for most taxpayers was totally deductible. As part of the tax reform package of 1986, however, Congress substantially limited the deduction for interest. Over the years, Congress became concerned that by allowing a deduction for all interest expense the tax system encouraged borrowing and, conversely, discouraged savings. This problem was exacerbated by the fact that the "economic" income arising from the ownership of housing and other consumer durables is not subject to tax. For example, when a taxpayer purchases a residence, the return on the investment—the absence of having to pay rent for the item—is not subject to tax. Had the taxpayer invested in assets other than housing or other durables, the return (e.g., interest or dividends) would have been fully taxable. In those situations where the investment is financed by borrowing, allowing a deduction is equivalent to allowing a deduction for expenses related to tax-exempt income—which is expressly prohibited under Code § 265. The net result of this system is to provide an incentive to consume rather than save.

In rethinking the approach to interest in 1986, Congress believed that it would not be advisable to impute income on investments in durables and tax it. However, Congress did feel that it was appropriate and practical to address situations where consumer expenditures are financed by borrowing. Accordingly, Congress enacted rules that prohibit the deduction for personal interest (other than certain home mortgage interest and interest on certain education loans). As a result, interest expenses on personal auto loans, credit card purchases, etc., are no longer deductible.

In eliminating the deduction for personal interest, Congress effectively established *six* categories of interest expense, each of which is subject to its own special set of rules. The different categories of interest expense are (1) personal interest, (2) qualified residence interest, (3) trade or business interest, (4) investment interest, (5) passive-activity interest, and (6) qualified student loan interest. As explained in detail below, interest (other than qualified residence interest) is classified according to how the loan proceeds are *spent*. Consequently, taxpayers are required to determine the nature of an expenditure from loan proceeds before the amount of the interest deduction can be determined.

Personal Interest. Today, taxpayers are not allowed to deduct any *personal interest*. Personal interest is defined as all interest arising from personal expenditures *except* the following:[56]

1. Interest incurred in connection with the conduct of a trade or business (other than the performance of services as an employee);

2. Investment interest;

---

[55] *Old Colony Railroad v. Comm.*, 3 USTC ¶880, 10 AFTR 786, 284 U.S. 552 (USSC, 1936).

[56] § 163(h)(1).

3. Qualified residence interest;

4. Interest taken into account in computing the income or loss from passive activities;

5. Interest on qualified education loans; and

6. Interest related to payment of the estate tax liability where such tax is deferred.

The effect of these rules is to severely limit the deduction for interest on consumer debt. For example, if a taxpayer borrows $3,000 from the bank and uses it to take a Caribbean cruise, none of the interest on the loan is deductible. Similarly, interest and finance charges would not be deductible on the following:

1. Automobile loans;

2. Furniture and appliance loans;

3. Credit card debt;

4. Life insurance loans;

5. Loans from qualified pension plans [including § 401(k) plans]; and

6. Delinquent tax payments and penalties.

It should be emphasized that interest incurred by an *employee* in connection with his or her trade or business is treated as consumer interest and is not deductible. In contrast, interest incurred by a self-employed person in his or her trade or business is fully deductible.

> **Example 20.** K sells cosmetics for Fantastic Faces, Incorporated. Her job involves calling on department stores all over the state of Ohio and soliciting their orders. She uses her car entirely for business. Interest on her car loan for the year was $2,000. Since K is an employee, none of the interest is deductible.

> **Example 21.** R is a real estate agent working for Bungalow Brokers. All of his compensation is based on the number of homes he sells during the year. He uses his car entirely for business. Under the employment tax rules (Code § 3508), real estate agents and direct sellers are not considered employees where their remuneration is determined by sales. Since R would not be considered an employee, all of the interest on his car loan would be deductible.

> **Example 22.** P is a reporter for the *News-Gazette*. She purchased a portable computer for $1,000, charging it on her bank credit card. She uses the computer entirely for business. Finance charges attributable to the purchase are $25. Even though the finance charges are incurred in connection with P's business, they are not deductible since she is an employee.

Qualified Residence Interest. The elimination of the deduction for personal interest in 1986 did not extend to interest on most home mortgages. As a general rule, interest on any debt *secured* by a taxpayer's first or second home is deductible. The interest is normally deductible whether the interest is on an original, second, or refinanced mortgage. Moreover, the interest is deductible regardless of how the taxpayer uses the money as long as the debt is *secured* by a mortgage on his or her primary or secondary residence. Unfortunately, tucked behind these seemingly simple rules are several complex restrictions.

Qualifying Indebtedness. Technically, only "qualified residence interest" is deductible. There are two types of qualified residence interest:[57]

1. Interest on *acquisition indebtedness:* Interest on debt that is incurred in acquiring, constructing, or improving a qualified residence *and* that is secured by such residence.

2. Interest on *home equity indebtedness:* Interest on debt secured by a qualified residence to the extent that the debt does not exceed the property's fair market value reduced by its acquisition debt.

Note that in both cases, the crucial element in determining whether the interest qualifies is whether the debt is secured by a residence. Unsecured debt and debt secured by other property does not qualify even though the debt proceeds may be used to acquire a personal residence.

> **Example 23.** J borrowed $50,000 from her pension plan and $10,000 from her father to buy a new home. None of the interest on the debt is deductible because neither of the debts is secured by the residence. This is true even though the borrowed amounts were used to buy a residence.

Also observe that in the case of both acquisition and home equity debt, the debt must be secured by a *qualified* residence. A qualified residence is the taxpayer's principal home and one other residence of the taxpayer.[58] This rule effectively allows taxpayers to deduct the interest on only two homes: their first home and a second of their choosing. A taxpayer with more than two homes must designate which is the second home when the return is filed. Different homes can be selected each year.

> **Example 24.** After winning the New York State lottery, T retired from her job and purchased a home in Tampa, Florida. She also purchased a motor home and a condominium in Vail, Colorado. All purchases were debt-financed and secured by the property. Within certain dollar limitations, T can treat the interest paid on her home in Tampa *and* the interest paid on *either* the motor home *or* the condominium as qualified residence interest.

> **Example 25.** Assume the same facts as above except that T converted the condominium into rental property at the advice of her tax accountant. In this case, the condominium will not qualify as T's secondary residence.[59]

In determining the deductibility of interest on a second home, special rules must be considered if the taxpayer *rents* it out. These rules are examined in conjunction with vacation homes discussed later in this chapter. If the second home is not rented out, no personal use is actually needed in order to meet the qualified residence test.

Congress also took steps to ensure that a taxpayer could not convert nondeductible interest into qualified residence interest simply by pitching a tent on the property and calling it a second home (e.g., vacant land or a car). In determining whether the debt is incurred with respect to a qualified residence, the term *residence* includes a vacation home, condominium, mobile home, boat, or recreational vehicle as long as the property

---

[57]   § 163(h)(3).

[58]   § 163(h)(4).

[59]   This does not mean that a taxpayer's interest expense on rental property is not deductible. As discussed later, however, losses from rental property (including interest expense) may be subject to deduction limitations.

contains basic living accommodations (i.e., sleeping space, toilet, and cooking facilities).

Limitations on Deductible Amount. To prevent taxpayers from taking undue advantage of the deductibility of home mortgage interest, Congress imposed limits on the maximum amount of debt qualifying under either definition. The aggregate amount of debt that can be treated as acquisition indebtedness for any taxable year cannot exceed $1 million ($500,000 in the case of a married individual filing a separate return),[60] whereas the aggregate amount of debt that will be treated as home equity indebtedness for any taxable year cannot exceed $100,000 ($50,000 if married and filing separately).[61] Collectively, the total amount of debt in any one year on which the interest paid or accrued will be treated as qualified residence interest cannot exceed $1.1 million.

> **Example 26.** During the current year, T purchases a principal residence in Boston for $900,000 and a vacation home in Tampa for $500,000. Mortgages secured by both properties total $1.3 million. T may treat *only* the interest paid on $1 million of acquisition indebtedness as qualified residence interest. In addition, he may treat $100,000 of the loans as home equity indebtedness and, therefore, the related interest is deductible as qualified residence interest. Whether interest on the balance of the debt, $200,000, is deductible depends on how the funds are used.

> **Example 27.** C purchased his present residence several years ago at a cost of $1.9 million. The present balance on his home mortgage is $800,000 and the property is valued at $2.5 million. This year, C borrowed $300,000 secured by a second mortgage on his home. Even though the total indebtedness does not exceed $1.1 million, C may deduct the interest on the $800,000 unpaid acquisition indebtedness and the interest on only $100,000 of the home equity mortgage. Any excess interest paid during the year will be treated as personal interest.

It is important to note that the interest paid on qualifying home equity indebtedness is allowed as a deduction *regardless* of how the taxpayer uses the loan proceeds. Thus, the obvious reason for the $100,000 limit on qualifying home equity debt is to impose a limit on the amount of an interest deduction the taxpayer may claim on loan proceeds used for personal purposes.

> **Example 28.** K purchased her present residence 10 years ago at a cost of $70,000. The present balance on her home mortgage is $40,000 and the property is appraised at a value of $150,000. This year, K borrowed $80,000 secured by a second mortgage on her home. She used the loan proceeds to purchase new clothes and a new automobile, and to take a vacation to Hawaii. The interest on the $80,000 loan is deductible since it is qualified residence interest. The fact that K used the loan proceeds for personal purposes is irrelevant. Also note that K's original cost of $70,000 is not used to limit the amount of her $80,000 home equity loan.

Finally, any attempt to refinance acquisition indebtedness should be undertaken with caution. A qualifying residence's acquisition debt is *reduced* by principal payments and *cannot be increased* unless the loan proceeds are used for home improvements. Thus, the acquisition debt can be refinanced only to the extent that the principal amount of the

---

[60] Any qualified residence indebtedness incurred before October 14, 1987—whether it is acquisition debt, home equity debt, or a combination of both—is to be treated as acquisition debt and is not subject to the $1 million limitation. If the property is later refinanced, however, the new indebtedness will be subject to this limitation. § 163(h)(3)(D).

[61] § 163(h).

refinancing does not exceed the principal amount of the acquisition debt immediately before the refinancing.[62] The interest paid on any excess refinanced debt will not be treated as acquisition indebtedness. However, any excess may be treated as home equity indebtedness. As noted above, the total qualifying indebtedness (acquisition and home equity) cannot exceed the value of the residence.

> **Example 29.** In 1970, G purchased her California bungalow for $25,000. The house is now worth $350,000. G paid off the mortgage on the home several years ago. This year, G mortgaged her house for $120,000 and subsequently loaned the money to her grandson to enable him to buy his first home. None of the loan qualifies as acquisition debt because the balance of acquisition debt refinanced was zero. However, G may deduct interest on $100,000 of the loan, which qualifies as home-equity debt.

> **Example 30.** R purchased his present residence in 1997 for $250,000 and borrowed $210,000 on a 11% mortgage secured by the property. In 2005 R refinanced the balance of his mortgage, $190,000, by securing a new mortgage of $230,000 at 6%. Unless R used the additional loan proceeds to substantially improve the residence, only $190,000 of the new mortgage constitutes acquisition indebtedness, and the corresponding interest is therefore deductible. In addition, the $40,000 balance of the debt may be treated as home-equity debt. In such case, the interest on the entire $230,000 mortgage would be deductible as qualified residence interest.

Trade or Business Interest. While the taxpayer normally cannot deduct interest of a personal nature, interest related to a trade or business expenditure is totally deductible. Perhaps the most common example of business interest is that arising from loans used to acquire fixed assets such as buildings and equipment that are used in the business. Business interest also includes that attributable to loans used to acquire an interest in an S corporation or a partnership in which the taxpayer materially participates. Recall, however, that interest incurred in connection with performing services as an employee is not considered business interest, and thus is considered nondeductible personal interest.

As explained below, the fact that a business incurs interest expense does not necessarily mean that such interest is classified as business interest. If interest expense incurred by a business arises from an investment considered unrelated to the business, it will not be business interest (e.g., a closely held corporation purchases stock on margin).

Investment Interest. The fourth category of interest expense subject to limitation is investment interest. This limitation is imposed on taxpayers, other than regular corporations, who have paid or incurred interest expense to purchase or carry investments.[63] Common examples include interest on loans to purchase unimproved land and interest incurred on margin accounts used to purchase stocks and other securities. Congress imposed the investment interest limitation to eliminate what it perceived was an unfair advantage to certain wealthy investors. For example, consider the taxpayer who borrows to acquire or carry investments that produce little or no income currently but pay off handsomely when the investment is sold. This is commonly the hoped-for result with investments in such assets as growth stock or land. Without any restrictions, the taxpayer would be able to claim an immediate deduction for interest expense yet postpone any income recognition until the property was ultimately sold. Moreover, the income that the taxpayer would realize on the sale would normally be favorable capital gain. Congress apparently felt that this mismatching of income and expense was

---

[62]   § 163(h)(3)(B).

[63]   § 163(d).

unwarranted and reacted by limiting the taxpayer's deduction for investment interest to the taxpayer's current investment income.

Before examining the investment interest limitation, the definition of investment interest should be clarified. *Investment interest* is generally any interest expense on debt used to finance property held for investment. It does not include, however, qualified residence interest or any interest related to a passive activity. As discussed in Chapter 12, interest related to a passive activity is allocated to the passive activity and is taken into account in computing the activity's income or loss. As a result, such interest is effectively limited by the passive-loss rules. Note, however, that any interest incurred by a passive activity that is related to its portfolio income (i.e., interest and dividend income) would normally be considered investment interest subject to the investment interest limitation. Because rental activities are usually treated as a passive activity, interest expense allocable to a rental activity is normally subject to the passive-loss rules.

The annual deduction for investment interest expense is limited to the taxpayer's *net investment income*, if any, for the tax year.[64] Any investment interest that exceeds the limitation and is disallowed may be carried forward until it is exhausted. Operationally, the disallowed interest is carried forward to the subsequent year, where it is combined with current year interest and is once again subject to the net investment income limitation. (Note that a sale of the financed property does not trigger the allowance of any disallowed interest.)

Net Investment Income. Net investment income is the excess of the taxpayer's investment income over investment expenses. For this purpose, *investment income* is generally defined as the gross income from property held for investment. Common examples of investment income include:

1. Interest;

2. Dividends;

3. Royalties;

4. Ordinary income from the recapture of depreciation or intangible drilling costs under §§ 1245, 1250, and 1254;

5. Portfolio income under the passive loss rules; and

6. Income from a trade or business in which the taxpayer did not materially participate (but which is not a passive activity, e.g., a working interest in an oil or gas property).

Note that income from rental property and income from a passive activity (other than portfolio income) are not considered investment income. As noted above, any interest expense incurred in rental or passive activities is allocated to those activities and is used in computing the passive income or loss of such activity.[65] For example, mortgage interest on rental property would be deductible only to the extent of passive income. It is also important to note that a net capital gain from the disposition of an asset producing investment income (e.g., stocks or bonds) is not normally included in investment income. However, a taxpayer currently facing a limitation on the deduction for investment interest expense because of a limited amount of investment income may elect to include all or a part of such a gain as investment income. Basically, such an election results in net capital gain being taxed as ordinary income in order to increase

---

[64]   § 163(d)(1).

[65]   § 163(d)(4)(E). See Chapter 12 for a detailed discussion of the passive loss rules.

the electing taxpayer's ordinary deduction for investment interest expense. Likewise, the lower tax rate for qualifying dividends does not apply if the dividends are included as investment income for purposes of determining the amount of deductible investment interest expense.

Investment expenses are generally all those deductions (except interest) that are directly connected with the production of the investment income. Any investment expenses that are considered miscellaneous itemized deductions are considered only to the extent they exceed the 2 percent floor. For this purpose, the 2 percent floor is first absorbed by all other miscellaneous expenses.

Example 31. G's records for 2005 revealed the following information:

Salary	$ 40,000
Dividends and interest	3,500
Share of partnership income:	
Partnership ordinary income	700
Portfolio income:	
Dividends	50
Interest	80
Rental income from duplex	15,000
Rental expenses	(14,000)
Adjusted gross income	$ 45,330
Qualified residence interest	$ 8,000
Real estate taxes on home	4,000
Property tax on land held for investment	1,000
Miscellaneous itemized deductions:	
Safety deposit box rental	50
Financial planner	1,500
Fee to maintain brokerage account	100
Unreimbursed employee business expenses	725

G is a limited partner in the partnership and thus treats the partnership as a passive activity. G also paid $7,700 of interest expense on the land held for investment. G's net investment income is computed as follows:

Investment income:

Dividends and interest	$3,500	
Partnership income:		
Portfolio income:		
Dividends	50	
Interest	80	
Total investment income		$ 3,630
Investment expenses:		
Property tax on land	$1,000	
Safe deposit box rental	50	
Financial planner	1,500	
Fee to maintain brokerage account.	100	
Miscellaneous itemized deductions disallowed		
2% floor (2% × $45,330)	$ 907	
Unreimbursed employee business expenses	(725)	
Investment expenses classified as		
miscellaneous itemized deductions disallowed	(182)	
Total investment expenses		(2,468)
Net investment income		$ 1,162

For 2005 G may deduct $1,162 of investment interest expense (*not* subject to the three percent cutback). The balance of $6,538 ($7,700 −$1,162) is carried over to the next year, 2006, and is treated as if it were paid in 2006. There is no limit on the carryover period. Note that in computing investment expenses, only investment expenses exceeding the 2% floor are allowed. In computing the disallowed portion, investment expenses are deemed to come last. Also note that rental income is not considered investment income.

Passive Activity Interest. Deductions attributable to so-called *passive activities* (e.g., those in which a taxpayer does not participate in a material fashion) are subject to special rules. Interest expense incurred by a passive activity itself (e.g., a limited partnership), or by investment in a passive activity, is treated as a deduction relating to the passive activity and is limited by the passive loss rules.[66] The passive activity loss rules are discussed in Chapter 12.

Interest on Student Loans. One of several measures enacted by the Taxpayer Relief Act of 1997 to help taxpayers finance the cost of higher education concerns the treatment of interest on student loans. As noted earlier, without a special rule, interest paid on loans to help pay college tuition and the like would be nondeductible personal interest. Beginning in 1999, however, § 221 altered this treatment by granting a deduction for interest on qualified educational loans. The maximum amount of interest that can be deducted annually is limited to $2,500. Before 2001, the deduction was allowed only with respect to interest paid on the loan during the first 60 months in which interest payments were required. However, the 2001 Tax Act repealed this 60-month limit.

---

[66]   § 163(d)(3)(B).

If the interest qualifies for deduction, it is deductible *for* adjusted gross income. Therefore taxpayers are not required to itemize in order to benefit from the deduction. (It is also true that the deduction would not be subject to the three-percent cutback; however, those taxpayers subject to the cutback would not be able to deduct the expense due to the phase-out rules discussed below.)

Like many of the relief provisions created by the new law, the deduction for interest on qualified educational loans is not extended to high-income taxpayers. To accomplish this objective, the maximum deduction is phased out once the taxpayer's A.G.I. (computed with certain modifications) exceeds $105,000 for joint returns ($50,000 for other returns). The reduction occurs over a $30,000 income range for married filing jointly ($15,000 for all others), producing a complete phase-out as follows.

Student Loan Interest Deduction Phase-out

$$\text{Reduction of deductible Portion of student loan interest} = \text{Deductible amount of interest (\$2,500 maximum in 2005)} \times \frac{\text{Modified A.G.I.} - \text{threshold}}{\text{Income range}}$$

	Modified A.G.I. Phase-Out Begins	Modified A.G.I. Phase-Out Complete
Married filing jointly	$105,000	$135,000
Other taxpayers	50,000	65,000

For this purpose, modified A.G.I. is A.G.I. before the exclusions for (1) foreign earned income and housing; (2) income from American Samoa, Guam and the Northern Mariana Islands; and after the exclusions for (1) Series EE savings bonds interest used to pay for education; (2) employer provided adoption benefits; (3) social security; (4) the deduction for contributions to IRAs; and (5) the deduction for losses on passive activities.

> **Example 32.** In 2005, S, single, graduated from Notre Dame with a law degree. During the year, she paid student loan interest of $5,000 and reported adjusted gross income before consideration of the interest of $56,000. Since S's adjusted gross income exceeds the $50,000 threshold for single taxpayers by $6,000 (40% of the $15,000 range), the maximum allowable deduction is reduced in 2005 to $1,500 [$2,500 − ($6,000/$15,000 × $2,500 = $1,000)]. Therefore, S may deduct $1,500 of the $5,000 interest for adjusted gross income.

Only interest on qualified education loans is deductible. Such loans are defined as any debt (other than a loan from a related party) incurred to pay qualified educational expenses for the taxpayer, the taxpayer's spouse, or other individuals who were the taxpayer's dependents at the time the debt was incurred. No deduction is allowed for interest paid by the taxpayer if the taxpayer is claimed as a dependent on another's return. For example, a child who pays interest on his student loans could not deduct the interest if his parents claim an exemption for him. Married taxpayers must file a joint return to claim the deduction.

Interest is deductible only if the education is furnished to an eligible student. An eligible student is generally one who is enrolled in a degree, certificate, or other program leading to a recognized credential at an eligible institution of higher education. In addition, the student must have been attending at least half-time (i.e., one-half of the normal full-time work load for the course of study that the student is pursuing).

Qualified educational expenses include the costs of attendance at an eligible educational institution. They include tuition, fees, room and board, and related expenses, such as books and supplies. Such amounts must be reduced by any amounts excluded under § 127 concerning employer educational assistance plans, § 135 concerning interest excluded on Series EE bonds, or § 530 excluding distributions from education IRAs (see discussion in Chapter 6).

CLASSIFICATION OF INTEREST EXPENSE

The different rules for different types of interest expense force taxpayers to classify and allocate their interest expense among appropriate categories. The classification procedure established by the Treasury is very straightforward in principle. Under the Temporary Regulations, interest is generally classified according to how the loan proceeds are spent—that is, the character of the expenditure determines the character of interest.[67] The type of collateral that may secure the loan is irrelevant in the classification process—except in the case of the qualified residence interest which is deductible regardless of how loan proceeds are spent.[68]

> **Example 33.** This year, T pledged IBM stock held as an investment as collateral for a loan which he uses to purchase a personal car. Any interest expense on the loan is considered nondeductible personal interest since the debt proceeds were used for personal purposes. The fact that the debt is secured by investment property is irrelevant. If the loan were secured by T's primary residence, the interest could be deductible as qualified residence interest.

The classification scheme demands that the taxpayer trace how any loan proceeds were used. To simplify this task, specific rules exist for debt proceeds that are (1) deposited in the borrower's account, (2) disbursed directly by the lender to someone other than the borrower, or (3) received in cash.

Proceeds Deposited in the Borrower's Account. In most cases, taxpayers borrow money, deposit it in an account, and write checks for various expenditures. Since money is fungible (that is, one dollar cannot be distinguished from another) it would be impossible without special rules to determine how the loan proceeds were spent, and therefore, how the related interest should be allocated. The Temporary Regulations create such rules.[69]

The first presumption created by the Regulations concerns the treatment of interest on funds that have not been spent. To the extent borrowed funds are deposited and not spent, interest attributable to such a period is considered *investment interest* regardless of whether the account bears interest income.[70]

> **Example 34.** On November 1, K borrowed $1,000 which she intends to use to fix up her boat. She deposited the $1,000 in a separate account. No expenditures were made during the remainder of the year. In this case, K is subject to the interest allocation rules since the interest expense is considered attributable to an investment, and is therefore, investment interest.

---

[67] Temp. Reg. § 1.163-8T.

[68] Temp. Reg. § 1.163-8T(c)(1). For purposes of the alternative minimum tax, however, qualified housing interest is deductible only if the debt is spent on the residence. See Chapter 13 for further discussion.

[69] Temp. Reg. § 1.163-8T(c)(4).

[70] *Ibid.*

Example 35. Same as above except K makes several personal expenditures during the next three months. Interest must be allocated between investment interest and personal interest.

Example 36. A borrows $100,000 on January 1 and deposits it in a separate account where it remains until April 1 when he purchases an interest in a limited partnership for $20,000. On September 1, R purchases a new car for $30,000. Interest expense attributable to the $100,000 is allocated in the following manner:

| | Debt Proceeds | | |
Period	Investment Interest	Passive Interest	Personal Interest
1/1–3/31	$100,000		
4/1–8/31	80,000	$20,000	
9/1–12/31	50,000	20,000	$30,000

Commingled Funds. In most situations, a taxpayer has one account in which all amounts are deposited. When this occurs, all expenditures from the account after the loan is deposited are deemed to come first from the borrowed funds.

Example 37. On October 1, B borrowed $1,000 to purchase a snowplow attachment for the front of his truck. He plans to make some extra money this winter by plowing driveways and parking lots. B deposited the $1,000 in his only checking account. On October 20, he bought the attachment for $1,500. Prior to October 20, he wrote $700 in checks for groceries and other personal items. Of the $1,000 loan, $700 is deemed to have been spent for personal items while the remaining $300 is allocated to the snow plow. Consequently, B may deduct only the interest expense on $300.

If proceeds from more than one loan are deposited into an account, expenditures are treated as coming from the borrowed funds in the order in which they were deposited (i.e., first-in, first-out).

Example 38. Dr. T has a personal checking account with a current balance of $3,000. On November 1, T obtained a $1,000 one-year Loan (Debt A) from her bank, which it credited to her personal account. She planned to use the loan to purchase a small copier for her dental practice. After shopping, T determined she would need additional funds. Therefore, on November 30 she obtained another $1,000 loan (Debt B). On December 12, T wrote a check for $800 to pay for her husband's Christmas present, a diamond ring. On December 19, she wrote a check for $2,100 to purchase the copier. These transactions are summarized as follows:

Date	Transaction	
11/1	Borrowed (Debt A)	$ 1,000
11/30	Borrowed (Debt B)	1,000
12/12	Purchased ring	(800)
12/19	Purchased copier	(2,100)

For purposes of determining the deduction for the interest on the loan, $800 of Debt A is deemed to be used for personal purposes (i.e., the ring purchase) and $200 toward the copier. All of Debt B is used for the copier. Thus, interest attributable to

$800 of Debt A is nondeductible personal interest while that attributable to $200 is totally deductible. All of the interest on Debt B is deductible business interest. This may be summarized as follows:

| | 11/1 Debt A $1,000 | | 11/30 Debt B $1,000 | | |
Expenditure	Personal	Business	Personal	Business	Other
$ 800 ring	$800				
2,100 copier		$200		$1,000	$900

Fifteen-Day Rule. In lieu of allocating the debt proceeds in the above manner, an alternative method is available. A borrower can elect to treat any expenditure made within 15 days after the loan proceeds are deposited as having been made from the proceeds of that loan.

Example 39. C borrowed and deposited $5,000 in his checking account on December 1. On December 2, he wrote a check for $6,000 for his estimated income taxes. On December 10, he wrote a check for $5,000 for furniture for his business. Under the normal allocation rule, the entire $5,000 proceeds from the debt would be considered spent for personal purposes. Under the 15-day rule, however, C may treat the $5,000 as used to purchase the furniture since the proceeds were spent within 15 days of deposit.

Loan Proceeds Received Indirectly. In many transactions, a borrower incurs debt without receiving any loan proceeds directly. For example, if the taxpayer borrowed $100,000 from a bank to purchase a building, the bank typically disburses the $100,000 directly to the seller rather than to the borrower. Similarly, the borrower may purchase the building and assume the seller's $100,000 mortgage. In this and similar situations, the borrower is treated as having received the proceeds and used them to make the expenditure for the property, services, or other purpose.[71]

Loan Proceeds Received in Cash. When the borrower receives the loan proceeds in cash, the taxpayer may treat any cash expenditure made within 15 days after receiving the cash as made from the loan. If the loan proceeds are not spent within 15 days, however, the loan is deemed to have been spent for personal purposes.

Debt Repayments, Refinancings, and Reallocations. Loans that are used for several purposes present a unique problem when a portion of the loan is repaid. In this case, repayments must be applied in the following order:[72]

1. Personal expenditures;

2. Investment expenditures and passive activity expenditures (other than rental real estate in which the taxpayer actively participates);

3. Rental real estate expenditures;

4. Former passive activity expenditures; and

5. Trade or business expenditures.

---

[71]   Temp. Reg. § 1.163-8T(c)(3).

[72]   *Ibid.*

Example 40. R borrows $10,000, $6,000 of which is used to purchase a personal automobile and $4,000 of which is used to invest in land. On June 1 of this year she paid $7,000 on the loan. Of the $7,000 repayment, $6,000 reduces the portion of the loan allocated to personal expenditures and the remaining $1,000 reduces the portion allocated to investment.

If the taxpayer refinances an old debt, interest on the new debt is characterized in the same way as that on the old debt.

Example 41. In 2004 S borrowed $10,000 at an annual interest rate of 14%. He used $8,000 to purchase a new boat and $2,000 to purchase a computer to use in his business. This year, he borrowed $6,000 from another bank at 10% to pay off the balance of the old loan. At the time the original loan was paid off, $4,000 of the $6,000 balance was allocated to the boat purchase and $2,000 was allocated to the computer purchase. The new debt will be allocated in the same manner as the old debt.

If the taxpayer borrows to finance a business asset, the debt must be recharacterized whenever the asset is sold or the nature of the use of the asset changes.

Example 42. Several years ago B, a traveling salesperson, borrowed $12,000 to buy a car that he used entirely for business. This year, B gave his car to his wife who uses it solely for personal use. The loan and interest thereon must be reclassified.

Computation and Allocation of Interest Expense. The special rules governing the taxpayer's deduction for interest expense do not affect its computation. Interest is computed in the normal manner. However, allocation of the interest expense among the different categories does present certain difficulties. As a general rule, interest expense accruing on a debt for any period is allocated in the same manner as the debt. Interest which accrues on interest—that is, compound interest—is allocated in the same manner as the original interest.[73]

Example 43. On January 1, R borrowed $100,000 at an interest rate of 10%, compounded semiannually. She deposited the loan in a separate account and on July 1 used the funds to purchase a yacht. On December 31, R paid the accrued interest of $10,250, computed as follows:

Period	Principal		Rate		Time		Interest
1/1–6/30	$100,000	×	10%	×	6/12	=	$ 5,000
7/1–12/31	105,000	×	10%	×	6/12	=	5,250
							$10,250

Under the allocation rules, R's loan is classified as an investment loan from January 1 through June 30 and, therefore, the interest accruing for that period of $5,000 is investment interest. In addition, the interest expense which accrues on this $5,000 from July 30 through December 31 of $250 ($5,000 × 10% × 612) is considered investment interest for a total of $5,250. This $250 of "compound interest" accruing from July 31 through December 31 is allocated to the investment category even though the original loan has been assigned to a new category for the same period. The remaining $5,000 of interest expense accruing from July 1 through December 31 ($100,000 × 10% × 612) is personal interest.

---

[73] Temp. Reg. § 1.163-8T(c)(2).

To simplify the allocation of interest expense, the taxpayer may use a straight-line method. Using this technique, an equal amount of interest is allocated to each day of the year. For this purpose, the taxpayer may treat a year as consisting of twelve 30-day months.

> **Example 44.** Assume the same facts as in *Example 43* above, except that R elects to allocate the interest expense on a straight-line basis, treating the year as consisting of twelve 30-day months. As a result, interest expense of $5,125 ($\frac{180}{360} \times \$10,250$) would be investment interest while the remaining $5,125 of interest expense would be personal interest.

WHEN DEDUCTIBLE

The taxpayer's method of accounting generally controls the timing of an interest expense deduction. Accrual method taxpayers generally may deduct interest over the period in which the interest accrues, regardless of when the expense is actually paid. However, cash-basis taxpayers must *actually* pay the interest before a deduction is allowed. Many situations arise in which the "actual payment" requirement imposed on cash-basis taxpayers delays the timing of a deduction. Other situations concern measurement of the amount of interest actually paid. The most common of these situations are briefly discussed below.

Interest Paid in Advance. If interest is paid in advance for a time period that extends beyond the end of one tax year, *both* accrual method and cash-basis taxpayers generally are required to spread the interest deduction over the tax years to which it applies.[74] An important exception is made for cash-basis individual taxpayers who are required to pay interest "points" in connection with indebtedness incurred to *purchase* or *improve* the taxpayer's principal residence (i.e., taxpayer's home).[75] The term *points* is often used to describe charges imposed on the borrower under such descriptions as "loan origination fees," "premium charges," and "maximum loan charges." Such charges usually are stated as a percentage (point) of the loan amount. If the payment of any of these charges is *strictly* for the use of money *and* actual payment of these charges is made out of *separate funds* belonging to the taxpayer, an interest deduction is allowed in the year of payment.[76]

> **Example 45.** R borrowed $15,000 from State Bank to make improvements on his home. The loan is payable over a 10-year period, and the bank charged R a loan origination fee of $300 (2 points). If R pays the $300 charge from separate funds, it is currently deductible as an interest expense (assuming R itemizes his deductions). However, if the $300 charge is added to the amount of the loan, R has not currently paid interest. Instead, R will be required to treat the charge as note-discount interest (see discussion below).

Note-Discount Interest. Taxpayers often sign notes calling for repayment of an amount greater than the loan proceeds actually received. This occurs when the creditor subtracts (withholds) the interest from the face amount of the loan and the taxpayer receives the balance, or when the face amount of the note simply includes add-on interest. In either case, cash-basis taxpayers are not allowed a deduction until the tax

---

[74] § 461(a).

[75] § 461(g).

[76] See *Roger A. Schubel*, 77 T.C. 701 (1982), and *James W. Hager*, 45 TCM 123, T.C. Memo 1982-663. Note, however, that this interest deduction is subject to the rules regarding qualified residence interest.

year in which the interest is actually paid. Accrual-method taxpayers are allowed to deduct the interest over the tax years in which it accrues.

Graduated Payment Mortgages. A creature of the high interest rate mortgage market of recent years, graduated payment mortgages provide for increasing payments in the early years of the mortgage until the payments reach some level amount. Under these plans, the payments in the early years are less than the amount of interest owed on the loan. The unpaid interest is added to the principal amount of the mortgage and future interest is computed on this revised balance. As should be expected, cash-basis taxpayers may deduct *only* the interest actually paid in the current year; the increases in the principal balance of the mortgage are treated much the same as note-discount interest.

Installment Purchases. Individual taxpayers who purchase personal property or pay for educational services under a contract calling for installment payments in which carrying charges are separately stated but the interest charge cannot be determined are allowed to *impute* an interest expense. The imputed expense is allowed whether or not a payment is actually made during the tax year, and is computed at a rate of 6 percent of the *average unpaid balance* of the contract during the year.[77] The average unpaid balance is the sum of the unpaid balance outstanding on the first day of each month of the tax year, divided by 12 months.[78] Credit card and revolving charge account finance charges are generally much greater than 6 percent. Fortunately, these charges are usually stated separately at a *predetermined* interest rate (e.g., finance charge of 1½% of unpaid monthly balance). Recall, however, that this type of interest expense is generally personal interest and thus nondeductible!

WHERE REPORTED

Like the deductions for taxes, the appropriate tax form or schedule on which deductible interest is reported depends upon the entity entitled to the deduction and the nature of the indebtedness to which the interest relates. A corporation's deductible interest is reported on its annual tax return Form 1120. Estates and trusts report interest deductions on Form 1041; partnerships and S corporations claim interest deductions on Forms 1065 and 1120S, respectively. Individuals claiming a deduction for interest expense must report the amount on the appropriate schedule of Form 1040. If the interest is related to business indebtedness—and the business is self-employment—the individual will claim his or her deduction on Schedule C (Schedule F for farmers and ranchers). Interest on debt incurred in connection with the production of rents or royalties is reported on Schedule E. Deductible interest on indebtedness incurred for personal use must be reported as an itemized deduction on Schedule A (with the exception of qualifying student loan interest which is deductible for A.G.I.). However, any individual who has refinanced his or her home, or is otherwise subject to the limitations imposed on qualified residence interest, should see IRS Publication 936 for instructions in computing the home mortgage interest deduction.

An individual's current deduction for investment interest expense should be calculated on Form 4952 (see Appendix B), and any disallowed deduction reported as a carryover amount. The deductible amount from Form 4952 should be transferred to and claimed as a deduction on the individual's Schedule E, Form 1040, if the interest relates to the production of royalties; otherwise, the deductible amount is reported on Schedule A. Partnerships and S corporations are not allowed to deduct investment interest

---

[77]   § 163(b)(1).

[78]   *Ibid.*

expense in determining income or loss. Instead, these conduit entities are required to set out and separately report each partner's or shareholder's share of *both* investment interest expense *and* net investment income for the current year. Each partner or shareholder must claim his or her deduction subject to the previously described limitations. Recall, however, that a partner that is a regular corporation will not be subject to the investment interest expense limitation.

CHARITABLE CONTRIBUTIONS

To encourage the private sector to share in the cost of providing many needed social services, Congress allows individuals, regular corporations, estates, and trusts deductions for charitable contributions (or gifts) of money or other property to certain qualified organizations. Partnerships and S corporations are not allowed to deduct charitable contributions. Instead, these conduit entities pass the contributions through to the partners and shareholders who must claim the deduction on their own Federal income tax returns.[79]

Code § 170 contains the rules regarding deductions for charitable contributions made by individuals and regular corporations. Code § 642(c) sets forth the rules regarding the amount and timing of charitable contribution deductions claimed by estates and trusts. The rules related to the measurement, timing, and qualification of contribution deductions claimed by individuals and corporations are discussed below. A discussion of the percentage limitations imposed on current deductions by individual taxpayers is also included. The specific rules regarding limitations imposed on a corporation's annual charitable contribution deduction are discussed in Chapter 19.

DEDUCTION REQUIREMENTS

Individual taxpayers are allowed a deduction for contributions of cash or other property *only if* the gift is made to a qualifying donee organization. Additionally, individuals are required to actually pay cash or transfer property before the close of the tax year in which the deduction is claimed. An exception to the payment requirement is made in the case of contribution deductions which, due to deduction limitations, have been carried over from prior years. The deduction limitations and carryover rules are discussed later in this chapter. Finally, for any contribution of $250 or more, special substantiation requirements must be met. Basically, a deduction for any contribution of $250 or more will be denied unless the taxpayer substantiates the contribution with a written acknowledgment of the contribution by the charitable organization. For this purpose, a cancelled check is not sufficient. However, separate payments (e.g., a weekly contribution to the church of $50) are not aggregated for purposes of applying the $250 threshold.

Qualifying Donees. To be deductible, contributions of cash or other property must be made to or for the use of one of the following:[80]

1. A state, a U.S. possession, a political subdivision of a state or possession, the United States, or the District of Columbia, if the contribution is made solely for public purposes;

2. A community chest, corporation, trust, fund, or foundation that is organized or created in, or under the laws of, the United States, any state, the District of Columbia, or any possession of the United States *and* is organized and operated

---

[79] See §§ 702(a)(4) and 1366(a)(1).

[80] See § 170(c).

exclusively for religious, charitable, scientific, literary, or educational purposes or for the prevention of cruelty to children or animals;

3. A war veterans' organization;

4. A nonprofit volunteer fire company or civil defense organization;

5. A domestic fraternal society operating under the lodge system, but only if the contribution is to be used for any of the purposes stated in item 2 above; and

6. A nonprofit cemetery company, if the funds are to be used solely for the perpetual care of the cemetery as a whole, and not for a particular lot or mausoleum crypt.

If the taxpayer has not been informed by the recipient organization that it is a qualifying donee, he or she may check its status in the *Cumulative List of Organizations* (IRS Publication 78). This publication contains a frequently updated listing of organizations which have applied to and received tax-exempt status from the IRS. To be a qualifying donee, however, the organization is not required to be listed in this publication.

Disallowance Possibilities. Direct contributions to needy or worthy individuals are not deductible. In addition, contributions to qualifying organizations must not be restricted to use by a specific person; if so, deductions generally are disallowed.

Example 46. F contributed cash of $10,000 to his son, S. S is a missionary for a church that is a qualified organization, and the gift proceeds were used exclusively by S to further the charitable work of the church. F is not entitled to a charitable contribution deduction since the gift was not made to a qualifying donee. Similarly, F would be denied a deduction if he made the gift to the church but restricted the use of the funds only for his missionary son.[81]

A taxpayer's contribution to a qualified organization that is motivated by the taxpayer's expectation and receipt of a significant economic benefit will not be deductible as a charitable contribution. The receipt of an unexpected and indirect economic benefit as a result of the gift should not disqualify the taxpayer's deduction, however.

Example 47. T donated two parcels of land to a nearby city for use as building sites for new public schools. The location of the building sites was such that the city had to construct two access roads through the taxpayer's remaining undeveloped land in order to make use of the gifted property. Construction of the access roads significantly enhanced the value of T's remaining acreage, and as a result, his charitable contribution deduction may be denied.[82]

Apparently, because Congress does not believe that the benefit received by a taxpayer is of great significance, 80 percent of the amount paid by a taxpayer to a college or university that either directly or indirectly entitles the taxpayer to purchase tickets to the institution's athletic events is allowed as a deduction.[83] However, any amount actually paid for the tickets will not be deductible.

---

[81] *White v. U.S.*, 82-1 USTC ¶9232, 49 AFTR2d 82-364, 514 F. Supp. 1057 (D.Ct. Utah, 1981). For a similar result, see *Babilonia v. Comm.*, 82-2 USTC ¶9478, 50 AFTR2d 82-5442 (CA-9, 1982).

[82] See *Ottawa Silica Co. v. U.S.*, 83-1 USTC ¶9169, 51 AFTR2d 83-590, 699 F.2d 1124 (CA-Fed. Cir., 1983) where, under similar circumstances, the taxpayer's claimed contribution deduction was disallowed.

[83] See § 170(m), introduced into the Code by the Technical and Miscellaneous Revenue Act of 1988. This provision was made retroactive to tax years beginning after 1983, and set aside a longstanding position of the IRS that denied any portion of such payments as deductions.

LIMITATIONS ON DEDUCTIONS

Unlike the requirement that an individual's medical expenses and casualty losses *exceed* some minimum percentage of adjusted gross income (referred to as the *floor* amount) *before* any deductions are allowed, deductions for charitable contributions are subject to *ceiling* limitations (i.e., not to *exceed* a percentage of A.G.I.). Generally, an individual's current deduction for charitable contributions is limited to 50 percent of the taxpayer's adjusted gross income. A 30 percent ceiling limitation is imposed on an individual's contributions of *certain appreciated property*, and a 20 percent overall limitation is imposed on an individual's contributions to *certain qualifying organizations*.

Under the general rule, the amount of a taxpayer's charitable deduction (before any percentage limitation) is the *sum* of money *plus* the fair market value of any property other than money which is contributed to a qualifying donee. However, both the gift of property to certain organizations and the gift of certain types of property other than money may result in a deduction of an amount *less than* the property's fair market value. These exceptions to the general rule are explained below, followed by a discussion of the various percentage limitations imposed on an individual's deduction for charitable contributions.[84]

Contributions Other Than Money or Property. No charitable contribution deduction is allowed for the value of time or services rendered to a charitable organization.[85] Likewise, no deduction is allowed for any "lost income" associated with the rent-free use of a taxpayer's property by a qualifying charity. However, *unreimbursed* (out-of-pocket) *expenses* incurred by the taxpayer in rendering services to a charitable institution or allowing rent-free use of property by such an organization *qualify* as charitable contributions.[86] For example, a taxpayer is allowed a deduction for the cost and upkeep of uniforms required to be worn while performing the charitable services, but only if the uniforms are not suitable for everyday use. Similarly, a taxpayer is generally allowed to deduct amounts paid for transportation to and from his or her home to the place where the charitable services are performed.[87] This includes the costs for gasoline, oil, parking, and tolls incurred by a taxpayer using his or her own vehicle in connection with the charitable services. In lieu of deducting the actual expenses for gasoline and oil, a taxpayer is allowed to use a standard mileage rate of 14 cents per mile in calculating the cost of using an automobile in charitable activities.[88] In either case, no deduction is allowed for insurance, depreciation, or the costs of general repairs and maintenance.

Example 48. T is the scoutmaster of a local troop of the Boy Scouts of America. During the current year, T incurred the following expenses in rendering his services to this charitable organization:

---

[84] Regular corporations are subject to an overall limitation of 10 percent of taxable income, determined without regard to certain deductions. See Chapter 19 for more details.

[85] Reg. § 1.170A-1(g).

[86] *Ibid.*

[87] The Tax Reform Act of 1986 added § 170(k) to the Code to disallow a deduction for travel expenses related to charitable services where there is a significant element of personal pleasure, recreation, or vacation in such travel.

[88] See § 170(j) and Rev. Proc. 2004-64, 2004-49 I.R.B.

Cost and upkeep of uniforms	$ 80
Gasoline and oil expenses	200
Parking and tolls	30
Estimated value of rent-free use of den in home	1,000
Estimated value of services (500 hours @ $50 per hour)	25,000
Total	$26,310

T is entitled to a $310 charitable contribution deduction for his out-of-pocket expenses ($80 + $200 + $30) incurred in rendering the charitable services as a scoutmaster. No deduction is allowed for the estimated value of his services or the rent-free use of his home.

Example 49. Assume the same facts as in *Example 48*, except that T drove his automobile 3,000 miles in connection with the charitable services. If he did not keep records of the actual expenses for gasoline and oil, T could use the standard mileage rate of 14 cents per mile. In this case, he will be allowed to deduct $530 [(3,000 miles × 14¢ per mile for charitable use of auto = $420) + $30 for parking and tolls + $80 related to uniforms].

Fair Market Value Determination. The IRS defines fair market value as "the price at which the property would change hands between a willing buyer and a willing seller, neither being under any compulsion to buy or sell and both having reasonable knowledge of relevant facts."[89] Determination of this amount usually means the taxpayer must make an educated guess or incur the cost of an independent appraisal. Since the IRS requires that the taxpayer attach a statement to his or her return when a deduction exceeding $500 is claimed for a charitable gift of property (Form 8283, Noncash Charitable Contributions), many taxpayers seek independent appraisals to support their claimed deductions. Independent appraisals are *required*—and the donee must *attach* a summary of the appraisal to his or her return—if the claimed value of the contributed property exceeds $5,000.[90] Appraisal fees are not deductible as contributions. However, they are deductible by individuals as miscellaneous itemized deductions (subject to the 2% floor).[91]

Ordinary Income Property. The term *ordinary income property* is used to describe any property which, if sold, would require the owner to recognize gain *other than* long-term capital gain. As such, ordinary income property includes a donor/taxpayer's property held primarily for sale to customers in his or her trade or business (i.e., inventory items), a work of art created by the donor, a manuscript prepared by the donor, letters and memoranda prepared by or for the donor, and a capital asset held by the taxpayer for not more than one year (i.e., short-term capital gain property). The term also includes property which, if sold, would result in the recognition of ordinary income under any of the depreciation recapture provisions.[92]

The charitable deduction (without regard to any percentage limitations) for the gift of ordinary income property is equal to the property's fair market value *reduced* by the

---

[89] Reg. § 1.170-1(c)(1).

[90] § 6050L. A donee charity that sells or otherwise disposes of such property within two years of the donation *must* report the disposition (and amount received, if any) to the IRS and the donor.

[91] Under § 212(3), individuals are allowed to deduct expenses associated with the determination of their tax liability. This includes appraisal fees paid in valuing property contributions.

[92] See § 170(e)(1), Reg. §§ 1.170A-4(b)(1) and (b)(4).

amount of ordinary income that would be recognized if the property had been sold at its fair market value (this amount is often called the *ordinary income potential*).[93]

> **Example 50.** F donated 100 shares of IBM stock to his church on December 15, 2005. F had purchased the stock for $9,000 on August 7, 2005, and it was worth $12,000 on the date of the gift. Since F would have recognized a short-term capital gain if the stock had been sold on December 15, 2005 (i.e., holding period not more than one year), the stock is ordinary income property. As a result, F's charitable contribution deduction is limited to $9,000 ($12,000 fair market value −$3,000 ordinary income potential).

In most cases, the charitable deduction for ordinary income property will be limited to the taxpayer's adjusted basis in the property since its fair market value is reduced by the *unrealized appreciation* in value (fair market value − adjusted basis), which would not result in long-term capital gain if the property were sold. There are, however, four important instances when this would not be the case. First, the charitable deduction for *any property* which, if sold, would result in a *loss* (i.e., adjusted basis > fair market value) is limited to the property's fair market value. Second, any depreciable property held by the taxpayer for more than one year and used in his or her trade or business is *§ 1231 property*. The amount of gain from the sale of such property that exceeds any depreciation recapture is referred to as "§ 1231 gain." Potential § 1231 gains are treated as long-term capital gains for purposes of measuring a taxpayer's charitable contribution deduction.[94] As such, any unrealized appreciation in the value of property that is attributable to § 1231 gain will not be considered ordinary income potential for purposes of the limitation described above.

The two remaining exceptions apply to the deduction allowed a corporation that contributes inventory items (ordinary income property) to certain qualifying charities. In one situation, the inventory must be donated to a public charity or private operating foundation *and* used by the charitable organization for the care of children, the ill, or the needy.[95] The other situation requires that the inventory item be manufactured by the corporate taxpayer, constitute scientific property, and be donated within two years of its construction to an educational institution for use in research.[96] In each of these situations, the corporate taxpayer is permitted to claim a contribution deduction in excess of the property's adjusted basis.

Capital Gain Property. Any property which, if sold by the donor/taxpayer, would result in the recognition of a long-term capital gain or § 1231 gain is *capital gain property*.[97] A taxpayer is generally allowed to claim the fair market value of such property as a contribution deduction. There are two important exceptions to this rule, however. *First*, if capital gain property is contributed to or for the use of a private nonoperating foundation [as defined in § 509(a)], the donor must *reduce* the contribution deduction by the *entire* amount of any long-term capital gain or § 1231 gain that would be recognized if the property were sold at its fair market value.[98] In effect, this exception treats the contribution of capital gain property to private

---

[93]   § 170(e)(1). For an application of this rule, see *William Glen*, 79 T.C. 208 (1982).

[94]   Reg. § 1.170A-4(b)(4).

[95]   § 170(e)(3).

[96]   § 170(e)(4).

[97]   § 170(e)(1).

[98]   § 170(e)(1)(B)(ii). An exception is provided for contributions of publicly traded stock to private foundations. Taxpayers making such contributions are allowed to deduct the full fair market value of such stock.

nonoperating foundations exactly like contributions of ordinary income property, since the donor must reduce the contribution deduction to the basis of the property.

> **Example 51.** G donates land worth $10,000 to a private nonoperating foundation on November 17, 2005. G had purchased the land for $4,000 on August 23, 2002. G's charitable contribution deduction must be reduced to $4,000 ($10,000 fair market value − entire $6,000 appreciation).

It is important to note that this limitation *generally* does not apply to donations of capital gain property to public charities.

> **Example 52.** Assume the same facts as in *Example 51*, except that G donated the land to her alma mater, State University (a public charity). G's charitable contribution would be $10,000 because the reduction requirement applies only to contributions to private foundations.

The *second* exception to the general rule that taxpayers are allowed to claim a deduction for the fair market value of contributed capital gain property involves contributions of tangible personalty.[99] If tangible personalty is contributed to a public charity (i.e., a university, museum, church, etc.) and the property is put to an *unrelated use* by the donee organization, the charitable contribution must be reduced by the entire amount of the property's unrealized appreciation in value (i.e., to the property's basis). For purposes of this limitation, the term *unrelated use* means that the property could not be used by the public charity in its activities for which tax-exempt status had been granted. For example, if antique furnishings are donated to a local museum that either stores, displays, or uses the items in its office in the course of carrying out its functions, the use of such property is a related use.[100] The fact that the charity later sells or exchanges the property does not alter the contribution deduction. Thus, if the taxpayer can reasonably anticipate that the tangible personalty donated to the charitable organization will be put to a related use, this limitation will not be applicable.[101]

> **Example 53.** J contributes a painting to the local university. He had purchased the painting in 1991 for $10,000, and it was appraised at $60,000 on the date of the gift. The painting was placed in the university's library for display and study by art students. J's charitable contribution will be measured at $60,000 (the painting's fair market value) since the property was not put to an unrelated use. This is true even if the university later sells the painting.

> **Example 54.** R donates her gun collection to the YWCA (a public charity). R had paid $8,000 for the collection 10 years ago, and the guns were appraised at $18,000 on the date of the gift. The YWCA immediately sold the collection for $18,000 to a local gun dealer. Although the property had appreciated by $10,000, R's charitable contribution must be reduced to $8,000 (the property's basis) since the property was not (and most likely could not be) put to a related use.

Fifty Percent Limitation. An individual's deduction for contributions made to public charities may not exceed 50 percent of his or her adjusted gross income for the

---

[99] As described in Chapter 9, tangible personalty is all tangible property *other than* realty (i.e., land, buildings, structural components).

[100] Reg. § 1.170A-4(b)(3).

[101] Reg. § 1.170A-4(b)(3)(ii).

year.[102] This "ceiling" deduction limitation applies to contributions made to the following types of public charities:[103]

1. A church or a convention or association of churches;

2. An educational organization that normally maintains a regular faculty and curriculum;

3. An organization whose principal purposes or functions are providing medical or hospital care (hospitals) or medical education or medical research (medical schools);

4. An organization that receives support from the government and is organized and operated exclusively to receive, hold, invest, and administer property for the benefit of a college or university;

5. A state, a possession of the United States, or any political subdivision of any of the foregoing, or the United States or the District of Columbia;

6. An organization that normally receives a substantial part of its support from a government unit (described in item 5 above) or from the general public; and

7. Certain types of private foundations discussed below.

Private foundations are organizations that, by definition, do not receive contributions from the general public. Examples of well-known private foundations include the Ford, Carnegie, Cullen, and Mellon Foundations. For charitable deduction purposes, private foundations are classified as either operating or nonoperating foundations. Contributions to *all* private operating foundations are subject to the 50 percent ceiling limitation.[104] The 50 percent limit also applies to contributions to certain private, nonoperating foundations if the organizations

1. Distribute the contributions they receive to public charities and private operating foundations *within* 2½ months following the year the contributions were received; or

2. Pool all contributions received into a common fund, and distribute *both* the income and the principal from the fund to public charities.

An individual's contributions of cash and ordinary income property to public charities, private operating foundations, and the above described nonoperating foundations that exceed the 50 percent limitation are carried forward and deducted in subsequent years. The carryover rules are discussed in a later section of this chapter. Contributions of capital gain property *and* contributions to private nonoperating foundations (other than those described above) are subject to *either* the 30 percent or 20 percent limitation. These limitations are discussed below.

Thirty Percent Limitation. There are *two* situations in which the 30 percent limitation may apply. The first situation involves the following types of contributions:

1. Contributions for the *use* of any charitable organization;

---

[102] § 170(b) and Reg. § 1.170A-8(b).

[103] § 170(b)(1).

[104] See § 4942(j) for the requirements for classification as a private operating foundation. For all practical purposes, an operating foundation is recognized as a public charity.

2. Contributions to veterans' organizations, fraternal societies, and not-for-profit cemetery companies; *and*

3. Contributions to most private nonoperating foundations.

The annual deduction for these contributions is limited to the *lesser of*

1. Thirty percent of adjusted gross income, *or*

2. An amount equal to 50 percent of adjusted gross income, *reduced* by contributions qualifying for the 50 percent limitation.[105]

Example 55. R has adjusted gross income of $50,000 for the current year and contributes $5,000 cash to his church and $20,000 cash to the Veterans of Foreign Wars. R's deduction for the contribution to his church will not be limited because it does not exceed 50% of A.G.I. (i.e., $5,000 < $25,000). However, only $15,000 of the contribution to the veterans' organization will be allowed as a deduction for the current year because this donation is subject to the 30% limitation.

```
Contribution to church ............................. $ 5,000

    Plus:  Lesser of
           (1)  30% × $50,000 = $15,000
                or
           (2)  50% × $50,000 = $25,000, reduced
                by $5,000 gift to church = $20,000
                                                    15,000
    Total contribution deduction......................... $20,000
```

Example 56. Assume the same facts in *Example 55*, except that the contribution to the church was $20,000 and the contribution to the veterans' organization was $8,000. Again, the contribution to the church will not be limited because it does not exceed 50% of A.G.I. However, the contribution to the veterans' organization will be limited to $5,000, computed as follows:

```
Contribution to church ............................. $20,000

    Plus:  Lesser of
           (1)  30% × $50,000 = $15,000
                or
           (2)  50% × $50,000 = $25,000, reduced
                by $20,000 gift to church = $5,000
                                                    5,000
    Total contribution deduction......................... $25,000
```

Note that it is not the 30% of A.G.I. Limitation that causes R's contribution to the veterans' organization to be limited. Instead, it is the fact that the overall limitation on the annual contribution deduction amount is 50% of adjusted gross income, and the contribution to the public charity is considered first.

---

[105] See § 170(b)(1)(C).

The *second* situation in which the 30 percent limitation may apply involves contributions of capital gain property. The annual deduction allowed for contributions of capital gain property that have not been reduced by the unrealized appreciation will generally be limited to 30 percent of the taxpayer's adjusted gross income.[106] As in the first situation discussed above, these contributions subject to the 30 percent limit are considered only after the amount of contributions allowed under the 50 percent limitation has been determined. Contributions in excess of the 30 percent limit can be carried forward and deducted in subsequent years.

> **Example 57.** K has adjusted gross income of $30,000 for the 2005 tax year. The only contribution made by K in 2005 consisted of stock worth $10,000, which she had purchased for $4,000 in 2000. The stock was given to her church. Although the contribution does not exceed 50% of her adjusted gross income, K's deduction is limited to $9,000 (30% × $30,000 A.G.I.) since the stock is capital gain property. The $1,000 excess contribution can be carried over to subsequent years.

> **Example 58.** Assume the same facts as in *Example 57*, except that K's 2005 adjusted gross income is $40,000 and she also gave $14,000 cash to her church. In this case, her deduction for the gift of the stock is limited to $6,000 (50% × $40,000 A.G.I. = $20,000 − $14,000 cash contribution) since the 50% overall limitation is applied before the 30% limitation. The remaining $4,000 ($10,000 fair market value of stock − $6,000 deduction allowed) will be carried forward to subsequent years.

When capital gain property has been contributed, the 30 percent limitation can be avoided if the taxpayer *elects* to reduce his or her claimed deduction for the capital gain property by the property's unrealized appreciation.[107] This may result in a larger deduction in the current year since the reduced amount will be subject to a higher ceiling limitation (i.e., 50 percent of A.G.I. rather than 30 percent). It is important to note that this election, if made, applies to all contributions of capital gain property made during the year.

> **Example 59.** T has adjusted gross income of $50,000 for the current year and contributes stock worth $23,000 to the American Heart Association (a public charity). T had purchased the stock for $19,000 two years earlier. Assuming this is T's only contribution for the current year, he can either claim his deduction subject to the 30% limitation and carry over any excess, or *elect* to reduce the claimed deduction by the capital gain property's unrealized appreciation and forgo any carryover. T's deduction choices are:
>
> 1. $15,000 current deduction (30% × $50,000 A.G.I.) and $8,000 ($23,000 − $15,000) contribution carryover; or
>
> 2. $19,000 current deduction ($23,000 − $4,000 unrealized appreciation) and no carryover.

Obviously, the decision to reduce a current deduction by the property's unrealized appreciation *or* to claim the deduction subject to the 30 percent limit and carry over any excess amount will depend on several factors. Among the factors to be considered are:

1. The difference between the capital gain property's fair market value and its adjusted basis to the taxpayer (i.e., unrealized appreciation);

---

[106] § 170(b)(1)(C)(i).

[107] § 170(b)(1)(c)(iii).

2. The taxpayer's current marginal income tax bracket compared to his or her anticipated future marginal tax rates; and

3. The expected remaining life of the taxpayer and his or her anticipated future contributions.

Twenty Percent Limitation. The 50 percent ceiling limitation imposed on an individual's annual charitable contribution deduction is an "overall" limitation. The 30 percent limitation applies to most contributions of capital gain property and to contributions of cash and ordinary income property contributed to nonqualifying private nonoperating funds. However, a more severe restriction is imposed on deductions for contributions of capital gain property to such private nonoperating foundations. In addition to the required *reduction* of the contribution by any unrealized appreciation in value, the deduction allowed for contributions to *private charities* (i.e., organizations not included in the seven categories listed earlier) is limited to the *lesser of*:

1. Twenty percent of adjusted gross income; or

2. An amount equal to 50 percent of adjusted gross income, and reduced by contributions qualifying for the 50 percent and 30 percent limitations, including any amount in excess of the 30 percent limitation.[108]

Like excess contributions to public charities, any contributions to private nonoperating foundations that exceed the 20 percent limitation are carried forward and deductible subject to the 20 percent limit, in subsequent years.[109]

Example 60. D contributed $8,000 to his church (a public charity) and land worth $15,000 to a private nonoperating foundation in 2005. D had purchased the land for $11,000 in 1999. His adjusted gross income for the year is $20,000. D's contribution deduction for 2005 is $10,000 [$8,000 contribution to church + $2,000 of the eligible $11,000 contribution to private foundation ($15,000 market value − $4,000 unrealized "appreciation" = $11,000)]. The deduction allowed for the contribution to the private foundation is limited to the *lesser* of:

1. $4,000 (20% × $20,000 A.G.I.); or

2. $2,000 [(50% × $20,000 A.G.I. = $10,000) − $8,000 contribution qualifying for the 50% limitation].

Note that D's total contribution deduction of $10,000 does not exceed 50 percent of his 2005 adjusted gross income. If D had contributed $10,000 or more to his church, *none* of the $11,000 contribution to the private foundation would have been allowed. In either case, the excess contributions can be carried over to subsequent years.

CONTRIBUTION CARRYOVERS

An individual's contributions that exceed either the 20 percent limitation, the 30 percent limitation, or the 50 percent overall limitation may be carried over for five years.[110] All excess contributions due to the 20 and 30 percent limitations will *again* be

---

[108] § 170(b)(1)(B)(i).

[109] § 170(d)(1).

[110] § 170(d)(1)(A) and Reg. § 1.170A-10(a).

subject to these limitations in the carryover years.[111] Although contribution carryovers are treated as having been made in the year to which they are carried, contributions *actually* made in the carryover year must be claimed before any carryover amounts are deducted.[112]

> **Example 61.** In 2005 D contributes $10,000 cash to State University (a public charity). Her adjusted gross income for 2005 is $15,000. D's contribution deduction for 2005 is limited to $7,500 (50% × $15,000 A.G.I.) and she may carry over the remaining $2,500 to 2006. If she does not make contributions in 2006 that exceed the 50% limitation, D can claim the $2,500 carryover as a deduction. If the contributions actually made in 2006 exceed 50% of D's 2006 adjusted gross income, she must carry over the 2006 excess contributions *and* the $2,500 carryover from 2005.

> **Example 62.** Assume the same facts as in *Example 61*, except that D's contribution was a capital gain property worth $10,000 instead of cash. Her 2005 deduction would be limited to $4,500 (30% × $15,000 A.G.I.) and she would have a $5,500 contribution carryover. Since this carryover resulted from the 30% limitation, it will be subject to the 30% limit in any carryover year. Thus if D has adjusted gross income of $10,000 and does not make contributions in 2006, she can claim a deduction of $3,000 (30% × $10,000 A.G.I.) and carry over the remaining $2,500.

All charitable contribution carryovers are applied on a first-in, first-out basis in determining the amount of any carryovers deductible in the current year.[113] Since such carryovers will expire if not deducted within five succeeding tax years, taxpayers obviously should limit actual contributions until the carryovers are used.

MISCELLANEOUS ITEMIZED DEDUCTIONS

As discussed in Chapter 7, two major changes regarding miscellaneous itemized deductions were introduced into the tax laws in 1986. Perhaps the most significant change involves the inclusion in this category of all *unreimbursed* employee business expenses. Prior to 1987, an employee's unreimbursed travel and transportation expenses were allowed as deductions in arriving at adjusted gross income. Since 1986, *both* unreimbursed employee expenses *and* those not reimbursed under an accountable plan must be treated as miscellaneous itemized deductions.[114] Additionally, an employee's unreimbursed costs for business entertainment and meals (whether or not incurred in connection with travel) must first be reduced by a 50 percent disallowance since only 50 percent of these costs qualify for deduction.[115] It is also important to remember that interest on any indebtedness to finance an employee's business expenses is treated as *nondeductible* personal interest expense.

The second major change involves the introduction of a deduction *floor* on the total of all expenses in this category similar to the approach taken for medical and casualty loss deductions. After 1986, miscellaneous itemized deductions are deductible only to the extent they *exceed* 2 percent of A.G.I.[116] The obvious intent of this change in the law is to limit the number of taxpayers who will be able to deduct miscellaneous itemized

---

[111] Reg. § 1.170A-10(b)(2).

[112] Reg. § 1.170A-10(c)(1).

[113] Reg. § 1.170A-10(b)(2).

[114] Reg. § 1.62-2.

[115] § 274(n).

[116] § 67(a).

deductions—and thereby reduce the administrative cost of policing such deductions. Exhibit 11-4 contains a partial list of items qualifying as miscellaneous itemized deductions.

EXHIBIT 11-4
Partial List of Miscellaneous Itemized Deductions

Reimbursed employee expenses under
    A nonaccountable plan

Unreimbursed employee expenses for
    Travel away from home (lodging and 50% of meals)
    Transportation expenses
    Entertainment expenses (after 50% reduction)
    Home office expenses
    Outside salesperson's expenses
    Professional dues and memberships
    Subscriptions to business journals
    Uniform costs, cleaning, and maintenance expenses
    Union dues

Investment expenses for
    Investment advice
    Investment newsletter subscriptions
    Management fees charged by mutual funds
    Rentals of safe deposit boxes

Qualifying education expenses

Job seeking expenses (in the same business)

Tax determination expenses for
    Appraisal costs incurred to measure deductions for medical expenses (capital
        improvements), charitable contributions, and casualty losses
    Tax return preparation fees
    Tax advice, tax seminars, and books about taxes

Example 63. T has $40,000 of adjusted gross income in 2005. His unreimbursed employee business expenses and other miscellaneous itemized deductions include:

Unreimbursed business travel expenses	$ 90
Subscription to *The Wall Street Journal*	110
Professional dues	250
Safe deposit box rental	50
Tax return preparation fee	250
Total	$750

Since T's total miscellaneous itemized deductions of $750 do not exceed $800 (2% × $40,000 A.G.I.), he will not be able to claim any deduction for these expenses.

OTHER ITEMIZED DEDUCTIONS

The final category of itemized deductions includes certain personal expenses and losses that cannot be classified in any of the other categories discussed thus far. Some of the items in this category—referred to as "Other Miscellaneous Itemized Deductions"—are discussed in other chapters.

1. Unrecovered investment in an annuity where the taxpayer's death prevents recovery of the entire investment. As discussed in Chapter 6, this deduction is allowed on the taxpayer's final tax return.

2. Impairment-related work expenses of persons with disabilities.

3. Amortizable premium on bonds purchased before October 23, 1986. Amortization of bond premium is discussed in Chapter 16.

4. Gambling losses to the extent of gambling winnings.

It is important to note that each of these items may be subject to its own unique set of limitations (e.g., gambling losses). Unlike miscellaneous itemized deductions, however, these deductions *are not* subject to the two percent limit.

THREE PERCENT CUTBACK RULE

As mentioned in Chapter 3, the total itemized deductions of certain high-income taxpayers are subject to another limitation. Basically, taxpayers must reduce total itemized deductions otherwise allowable (*other than* medical expenses, casualty and theft losses, investment interest, and gambling losses) by three percent of their A.G.I. in excess of $145,950 ($72,975 for married individuals filing separately).[117] However, this reduction cannot exceed 80 percent of the deductions. Again, this ensures that taxpayers subject to the cutback rule can deduct at least 20 percent of their so-called "three-percent" deductions. Consequently, a taxpayer's itemized deductions are never completely phased out.

Exhibit 11-5 identifies the itemized deductions that are subject to the cutback rule. Again, it is important to note that a taxpayer's medical expenses, investment interest expense, casualty and theft losses, and gambling losses are not subject to this limitation.

EXHIBIT 11-5
Itemized Deductions Subject to Cutback Rule

Taxes paid, including
    State, local, and foreign income taxes
    State and local general sales taxes
    State, local, and foreign real property taxes
    State and local personal property taxes
Mortgage interest on personal residences
Charitable contributions
Miscellaneous itemized deductions (in excess of 2% of A.G.I.)

Example 64. Z is single and has adjusted gross income of $295,950 for the current year. Z has the following itemized deductions: medical expenses ($1,200 after the 7.5% limitation), real estate taxes paid ($3,000), state income taxes ($7,400), home mortgage interest ($10,300), charitable contributions ($2,500), and miscellaneous itemized deductions ($800 after the 2% limitation). The amount of itemized deductions that Z may deduct for the current year is computed as follows:

---

[117] § 68. These threshold amounts were $142,700 and $71,350, respectively, for 2004, and they are adjusted annually for inflation. Phase-out of the cutback rule is scheduled to begin in 2006 and be completed in 2010. § 68(f).

Itemized deductions subject to cutback:

Taxes paid ($3,000 + $7,400)	$ 10,400
Home mortgage interest	10,300
Charitable contributions	2,500
Miscellaneous itemized deductions.	800

Deductions subject to 3% cutback rule $24,000

Tentative cutback:

Adjusted gross income	$ 295,950
Threshold amount.	(145,950)
Excess A.G.I.	$ 150,000
Times: 3%	×3%

Tentative cutback. . . . . $ 4,500

Cutback limit:

Itemized deductions subject to cutback	$ 24,000
Times: 80%	×80%

Maximum cutback . . . . $ 19,200

Cutback:	*Lesser* of tentative cutback or maximum cutback.	(4,500)

Amount deductible after 3% cutback $19,500

Plus:	Itemized deductions not subject to cutback (medical expenses)	1,200

Total deduction for itemized deductions. $20,700

Example 65. Assume the same facts as in *Example 64* above, except that Z's adjusted gross income for the current year is $845,950.

Total itemized deductions subject to cutback. . . . . $ 24,000

Tentative cutback:

Adjusted gross income	$ 845,950
Threshold amount.	(145,950)
Excess A.G.I.	$ 700,000
Times: 3%	×3%

Tentative cutback. . . . . $ 21,000

Cutback limit:

Itemized deductions subject to cutback	$ 24,000
Times: 80%	×80%

Maximum cutback . . . . $ 19,200

Cutback:	*Lesser* of tentative cutback or maximum cutback.	(19,200)

Amount deductible after 3% cutback . . . . $ 4,800

Plus:	Itemized deductions not subject to cutback (medical expenses)	1,200

Total deduction for itemized deductions. . . . . $ 6,000

Note that in this case Z's tentative cutback ($21,000) exceeds the maximum cutback ($19,200). Thus, Z is allowed to deduct at least 20% ($24,000 × 20% = $4,800) of the itemized deductions subject to the cutback rule.

It should be obvious from the above examples that relatively few taxpayers will suffer drastic cutbacks in their itemized deductions. However, those taxpayers with adjusted gross incomes above the annual threshold amount will find that they face another complexity in computing their itemized deductions.

TAX PLANNING CONSIDERATIONS

MAXIMIZING PERSONAL DEDUCTIONS

Each year the taxpayer must choose between taking the standard deduction and itemizing actual deductions. If the standard deduction is chosen, then legitimate itemized deductions are lost. If the taxpayer chooses to itemize actual deductions, then the standard deduction is lost. One technique used to minimize the loss of personal deductions is to shift actual itemized deductions from one year to another (to the extent allowed by law) so that they are high in one year and low in the next.

Example 66. S is single and has itemized deductions that are expected to be constant in 2005 and 2006 as follows:

Mortgage interest	$ 400
Dental expense (deductible portion)	1,400
State and local taxes	350
Charitable contributions	1,350
Total	$3,500

S cannot itemize actual deductions in 2005 or 2006 because actual deductions are less than the standard deduction for single status (assumed to be $4,000 in each year for illustration purposes). Over the two-year period, S will deduct $8,000 for personal expenses by claiming the standard deduction. However, if S were able to shift $1,000 of elective dental expenses from 2006 into 2005, and to accelerate the 2006 charitable contribution into 2005, then she would receive a greater tax benefit in the two-year period for personal expenses. Actual expenses in each year would be:

	2005	*2006*
Mortgage interest	$ 400	$ 400
Dental expense (deductible portion)	2,400	400
State taxes	350	350
Charitable contributions	2,700	0
Total	$5,850	$1,150

Although actual personal expenses still total $7,000 over the two-year period, S now has itemized deductions of $5,850 in 2005 and a standard deduction of $4,000 in 2006. During the two-year period S will deduct $9,850 for personal expenses and will receive $1,850 more in deductions than if personal expenses had not been shifted.

Personal expenses should be shifted into years when adjusted gross income is lower. Not only will the 7.5 percent medical expense threshold and the two percent miscellaneous expense threshold be lower, but the effect of the three percent cutback on itemized deductions may be less. If adjusted gross income is under the prevailing threshold amount if the year that the itemized deductions are bunched, the three percent limitation will be avoided altogether.

MEDICAL EXPENSES

The dependency exemption under a multiple support agreement should be assigned to the taxpayer who pays the medical expenses of the dependent. The medical expenses are deductible only by the family member entitled to the dependency exemption and only if that family member actually pays on behalf of the claimed dependent. Medical expenses paid by other family members on behalf of the dependent will not be allowed as deductions.

Often expenditures incurred in the care of an ill or handicapped child may qualify for either a medical expense deduction or for the child care credit (discussed in Chapter 13). When this happens, the tax liability should be computed under each alternative to determine which is more advantageous. Usually the choice depends on the taxpayer's marginal tax rate as compared to the credit percentage rate. The choice will also depend on the 7.5 percent threshold and whether the taxpayer is itemizing or taking the standard deduction.

Example 67. In 2005 T and W spend $2,000 for care of their handicapped child. The $2,000 qualifies both as a medical expense and for the child care credit. T and W have other medical expenses that exceed the 7.5% threshold amount. T and W file a joint tax return, and their marginal tax rate is 31%. The applicable percentage for the child care credit is 20%. If T and W are able to itemize deductions, they will receive a $620 tax benefit ($2,000 × 31%) for claiming the expenditure as a medical expense, whereas they will receive only a $400 tax benefit ($2,000 × 20%) if they claim the expenditure for the child care credit. If T and W are not able to itemize deductions or if they cannot exceed the 7.5% medical expense threshold amount, then the expenditure should be claimed for the child care credit.

CHARITABLE CONTRIBUTIONS

When a taxpayer makes noncash donations of property having a fair market value lower than the adjusted tax basis, it may be more advantageous to sell the property and donate the proceeds. If the property is held for investment, the sale will yield a deductible capital loss in addition to the charitable deduction. No loss will result, however, if the property itself is donated. To recognize a loss when selling depreciated property, the property must be held for investment or business use rather than for personal use.

Example 68. T owns 100 shares of X Corporation stock that he bought for $5,000 in 2003. The stock currently has a fair market value of $2,000. If T donates the stock to a qualified charity, he will only be entitled to a $2,000 charitable deduction.

If T sells the stock and donates the $2,000 proceeds to a qualified charity, he will be entitled to a $3,000 capital loss as well as a $2,000 charitable deduction.

MISCELLANEOUS DEDUCTIONS

Because certain miscellaneous itemized deductions are deductible only to the extent that they aggregately exceed 2 percent of the adjusted gross income, it is important that expenses that can be properly classified into another, nonlimited category be identified and separated. For example, if a taxpayer supplements his or her regular salary with self-employed consulting income, it may be proper to deduct some of the cost of professional publications, professional journals, and educational expenses on Schedule C rather than as a miscellaneous itemized deduction.

Some unreimbursed employee business expenses that are not presently deductible because of the 2 percent limit might be converted into deductible reimbursed employee business expenses by agreement with the employer.

> **Example 69.** K incurs $500 of unreimbursed employee business expenses each year. Her miscellaneous itemized deductions do not exceed the 2 percent limit; she is therefore unable to deduct any of this expense. K's employer agrees, as part of next year's compensation increase, to reimburse her for $500 of employee business expenses. K will now be able to deduct the $500 of expenses against the reimbursement.

PROBLEM MATERIALS

DISCUSSION QUESTIONS

11-1 *Medical Expenses and Dependency Status.* Under what circumstances is a taxpayer entitled to deduct medical expenses attributable to other people?

11-2 *Medical Expenses.* F and M are the divorced parents of three minor children. M, the custodial parent, has proposed to F that the current child-support payments be increased in order to pay the expected dental costs of having braces put on their oldest son's teeth. F's tax advisor has suggested that F agree to pay these costs directly to the dentist rather than increasing the support payments. From a tax perspective, why has F's advisor made this suggestion?

11-3 *Medical Expenses.* K and her two brothers currently provide more than half the support of their mother. For the past several years, they have taken turns claiming a dependency exemption deduction for their mother under a multiple support agreement. This year, K will be entitled to the exemption, and her mother needs money for cataract surgery and new eyeglasses. K's accountant has suggested that she can double up on the tax benefits by directing her share of her mother's support toward these expenses. How is this possible?

11-4 *Medical Expenses.* For the past several years, L's total itemized deductions have barely exceeded his standard deduction amount, and this pattern is not expected to change in the near future. L is currently faced with elective surgery to repair a hernia, and the procedure is not covered under his health insurance policy. Strictly from a tax perspective, and assuming that this ailment is not life-threatening, what advice would you give to L concerning the timing of the surgery?

11-5 *Prepaid Medical Expenses.* What is the requirement imposed on taxpayers who wish to deduct prepaid medical expenses? What potential abuse is prevented by this requirement?

11-6 *Medical Deductions—Percentage Limitation.* The only medical expenditures made by taxpayer T during 2005 were for prescription drugs costing $800 and new eyeglasses costing $150. If T has adjusted gross income of $10,000 for the year and itemizes his deductions, how much, if any, medical expense deduction will he be allowed?

11-7 *Medical Travel Expenses.* W resides in Gary, Indiana and suffers from chronic bronchitis. At the advice of her doctor, W spends three months each year in Flagstaff, Arizona. Under what circumstances would W be entitled to claim the costs incurred for these trips as deductible medical expenses? If deductible, which costs?

11-8 *Casualty Losses.* Taxpayer F has adjusted gross income of $20,000 during the current year and he asks you the following questions regarding the deductibility of damages to his home caused by a recent hurricane. (**Hint:** See Chapter 10 for discussion of limitations on casualty loss deductions.)

   a. If F does not have home insurance, how much must his loss be before any deduction is available?

   b. If F repairs the damage himself, what amount can he deduct for the value of his time?

   c. If the area in which he resides is declared a disaster area, what options are available to F as to when to claim a deduction for the casualty loss?

11-9 *Taxes versus Fees.* What is the distinction between a deductible tax and a fee? If an individual taxpayer paid appraisal fees in connection with the determination of his personal casualty loss and charitable contribution deductions, would these payments be deductible?

11-10 *Deductible Income Taxes.* Which income taxes are deductible by an individual taxpayer? Does it make any difference whether the taxes are paid directly by the taxpayer as opposed to being withheld from his or her salary and paid by an employer to the appropriate taxing authority?

11-11 *Filing Status and State Income Taxes.* If married taxpayers file separate state or Federal income tax returns, how is the Federal tax deduction for state income taxes determined?

11-12 *State and Local Sales Tax Deduction.* Your brother has called you for advice concerning the deductibility of the $1,460 state sales taxes that he paid on the purchase of his new Ford F250 truck. What other information would you need from you brother to properly answer his question?

11-13 *Personal Property Taxes.* What is an ad valorem tax? What difference does it make to a taxpayer if he or she pays a tax on nonbusiness property and the tax is based on weight or model year as opposed to value?

11-14 *Real Estate Tax Apportionment.* How are real estate taxes apportioned between the buyer and seller in the year real property is sold? What effect does the apportionment have on the seller if the buyer pays the real estate taxes for the entire year?

11-15 *Special Tax Assessments.* Under what circumstances can a property owner claim a deduction for a special tax assessment?

11-16 *Personal Interest.* What is the current limitation imposed on the deductions of personal interest? What impact do you suppose this restriction might have on debt-financed consumer purchases?

11-17 *Deductible Interest.* Your neighbor has come up with an excellent tax plan and he asks you for advice on structuring his scheme. He plans to give each of his five children a $10,000 promissory note, due in 20 years and bearing interest at 10 percent per year. The interest will be paid annually and he plans to claim a $5,000 interest expense deduction. Do you see any flaws in this plan? What advice would you give to your neighbor?

11-18 *Classifying Interest Expenses.* The local bank has just introduced a new loan program entitled "Home Equity Credit Line" under which individuals can either borrow funds or finance credit card purchases based on the equity they have in their homes. What is the tax incentive offered by this arrangement?

11-19 *Investment Interest Expense.* What is the investment interest expense limitation? Which taxpayers are not subject to this limitation? What is the purpose of the limitation?

11-20 *Types of Interest Expense.* D is a spender, not a saver. In fact, he spends money he doesn't even have. This year he borrowed more than $50,000 and paid interest of close to $7,000. D was shocked when his accountant told him that only certain types of interest were deductible.
  a. Identify the different types of interest expense and explain the treatment of each.
  b. How will D classify the interest expense that he paid?

11-21 *Charitable Contribution Requirements.* What are the basic requirements imposed on an individual taxpayer's deduction for charitable contributions?

11-22 *Contributions of Ordinary Income Property.* What is ordinary income property? Does this contribution deduction limitation apply to all taxpayers? Explain.

11-23 *Contributions of Capital Gain Property.* Under what circumstances must a taxpayer reduce his or her contribution deduction by the unrealized appreciation in value of capital gain property donated to a qualifying charity? How might this limitation be avoided?

11-24 *Contribution Deduction Percentage Limitations.* What are the percentage limitations imposed on an individual taxpayer's annual charitable contribution deduction? In what order must these percentage limitations be applied to current contributions?

11-25 *Contribution Carryovers.* Which excess contributions may be carried forward by an individual taxpayer? For how many years? In determining the amount of his or her contribution deduction for the current year, how must the taxpayer treat the carryovers from prior years?

11-26 *Miscellaneous Itemized Deductions.* E's employer has offered her the option of a $50 monthly pay raise or a reimbursement plan to cover her current subscriptions to professional journals ($200) and her dues to professional organizations ($350). E files a joint return with her husband, and they expect their adjusted gross income to be $50,000 for the upcoming year. Assuming that their only miscellaneous itemized deductions are from E's subscriptions and professional dues, is this a good offer? Explain.

11-27 *Three-Percent Cutback Rule.* Explain the difference between the tentative cutback and the maximum cutback amounts related to the total deduction allowed for itemized deductions. Which itemized deductions are not subject to the cutback rule?

PROBLEMS

11-28 *Medical Expense Deduction.* R, an unmarried taxpayer, has adjusted gross income of $20,000 for 2005. During the year, he paid the following amounts for medical care: $300 for prescription medicines and drugs, $600 for hospitalization insurance, and

$1,100 to doctors and dentists. R filed an insurance reimbursement claim in December 2005 and received a check for $1,200 on January 24, 2006.

a. Assuming R itemizes deductions, determine the deduction allowed for the medical expenses paid in 2005.

b. What effect does the insurance reimbursement have on R's deduction for 2005? How should the reimbursement be treated in 2006 if R's itemized deductions for 2005 (including the medical expense deduction) were $4,500 greater than his standard deduction?

c. How should the reimbursement be treated in 2006 if R's itemized deductions for 2005 were $400 greater than his standard deduction?

11-29 *State Income Taxes.* During 2005 K paid $500 in estimated state income taxes. An additional $400 in state income taxes was withheld from her salary by K's employer and remitted to the state. K also received a $200 refund check during 2005 for excess state income taxes paid in 2004. She had claimed a deduction for $750 of state income taxes paid in 2004. K uses the cash method of accounting and has adjusted gross income of $50,000 for the year.

a. If K itemizes her deductions, how much may she claim as a deduction for state income taxes on her 2005 Federal tax return?

b. If K's itemized deductions for 2004 were $1,900 greater than her standard deduction, how must the $200 refund be treated for Federal income tax purposes?

11-30 *General Sales Tax Deduction.* Rob and Lisa are married and file a joint return for 2004. They have three dependent children ages 7, 9, and 12 and the family lived in Orlando Florida for the entire year. For each of the questions below, assume that the couple has A.G.I. of $87,900 and no other available income.

a. Using the optional sales tax tables located in Appendix A of this text, determine the couple's state sales tax deduction for 2004.

b. How would your answer in (a) above change if Rob and Lisa also paid $1,250 sales tax on the purchase of a new car and an additional $350 on the purchase of new furniture?

c. Assume that the family lived in Georgia rather than Florida for the entire year. Also assume that Rob and Lisa paid $3,200 in state income taxes in 2004. How does this additional information change your answer to (b) above?

11-31 *Real Estate Tax Apportionment.* S sells her home located in Blue Springs, Missouri, on March 1, 2005. Blue Springs assesses real property taxes at the beginning of each calendar year for the entire year, and the property tax becomes a personal liability of the owner of real property on January 1. The tax is payable on April 1, 2005. Buyer B paid $80,000 for the home on March 1, 2005 and also paid the $1,200 real estate taxes on April 1. Both S and B are cash basis, calendar year taxpayers.

a. How much of the $1,200 in real estate taxes is deductible by S? What adjustment must S make to the amount she realized from the sale?

b. How much of the $1,200 in taxes is deductible by B? How will he treat any of the taxes paid which are attributable to S?

11-32 *Interest Expense Limitations.* Indicate in each of the following cases the amount of interest expense, if any, that the taxpayer is allowed to deduct.

a. During the year, H used his bank credit card to purchase a new stereo for his teenage daughter. Finance charges for the year were $70.

b. Over the years, G has consistently borrowed against her insurance policies because of their low rates. This year, she paid interest of $1,100 on the loans.

c. D lives and works in Birmingham. He owns a house there as well as a summer home at Hilton Head and a condominium at Sun Valley. He paid interest expense of $6,000 on loans on each unit.

d. B owns a home in Denver that she purchased in 1989 for $70,000. The current balance on B's mortgage loan is $60,000 and the property is worth $150,000.

During the year, B obtained a second mortgage on her home, receiving $20,000 which she used to pay off her two outstanding car loans. Interest on the first mortgage was $4,000 while interest on the second mortgage was $1,000.

e. M is a heavy trader of stocks and bonds, using his margin account frequently. This year, interest expense charged on his margin purchases was $1,200. M's investment income was $900.

f. R is an employee of a television repair shop. He uses his own truck solely for business, making customer service calls. During the year, he paid $900 interest on a loan on his truck.

11-33 *Investment Interest Expense.* R, a cash basis, single taxpayer, paid $17,000 of investment interest expense during 2005. R uses the calendar year for tax purposes and reports the following investment income: $1,500 interest income, and $3,500 dividends.

a. How much of the investment interest expense is deductible by R in 2005?

b. What must R do with any investment interest expense deduction which is disallowed for 2005?

11-34 *Investment Interest Expense Limitation.* L is an engineer. This year, she borrowed $300,000 and purchased 40 acres south of Houston. For the year, L paid interest of $30,000 on the loan. Her tax records revealed the following additional information:

Income:	
Salary	$50,000
Qualifying dividends	8,000
Share of partnership income:	
Ordinary loss	(3,000)
Portfolio income:	
Interest	1,000
Rental income	8,000
Expenses:	
Rental expenses	7,000
Qualified residence interest	10,000
Property tax on land	5,000
Investment publications	400
Professional dues, licenses, and subscriptions	1,100

The items noted concerning the partnership result from L's limited partnership interest in Country Homes, a real estate development. The rental income is derived from a four-unit apartment complex that is currently filled with tenants with one-year leases. The related rental expenses include $2,000 of interest expense on the debt to acquire the apartments. Compute L's deduction for investment interest expense this year, assuming that she includes the qualifying dividends in the calculation of net investment income.

11-35 *Interest Expense—Note Discount.* Taxpayer T signed a note for $2,000 on August 30, 2005, agreeing to pay back the loan in 12 equal installments beginning September 30, 2005. The 12 percent interest charge ($2,000 × 12% = $240) was subtracted from the face amount of the note and T received $1,760, all of which was used to purchase furniture for his business. T uses the calendar year as his taxable year.

a. If T is a cash-basis taxpayer and he makes the four payments scheduled for 2005, what is his deduction for interest on the note in 2005? In 2006?

b. Would your answers to (a) change if T were an accrual method taxpayer? Explain.

11-36 *Charitable Contributions.* Determine the amount of the charitable deduction (without regard to percentage limitations) allowed in each of the following situations:

a. Rent-free use of building for three months allowed for the United Way fund drive. The building normally rents for $900 per month, and the owner paid $1,100 for utilities during this period.

b. Gift of General Motors stock valued at $9,000 to State University. Taxpayer purchased the stock five months ago for $11,000.

c. Donation of stamp collection valued at $4,000 to local museum for display to the general public. Taxpayer had paid $1,000 for the stamps many years ago.

d. Gift of paintings to local hospital to be placed on the walls of a remodeled floor. The paintings were painted by the donor and were appraised at $20,000.

e. Donation of Civil War relics to American Heart Association to be sold at its current fund-raising auction. Taxpayer paid $1,000 for the relics ten years ago and an expert appraiser valued them at $7,000 on the day of the gift.

11-37 *Contribution Deductions—Percentage Limitations.* J contributed $10,000 to the University of Southern California and a long-term capital asset worth $10,000 (basis of $5,000) to a private nonoperating foundation during 2005. Assuming his adjusted gross income for the year is $24,000, answer the following:

a. What is the amount of J's contribution deduction for 2005?

b. How must any excess contributions be treated?

c. If J had come to you for advice before making the gifts, what advice would you have offered?

11-38 *Contribution Deductions—Percentage Limitations.* During 2005 R donated land to her church (a public charity) to be used as a building site for a new chapel. R had purchased the land as an investment in 1994 at a cost of $10,000. The land was appraised at a fair market value of $30,000 on the date of the gift. Assuming R's adjusted gross income for 2005 is $60,000, answer the following:

a. If R made no additional charitable contributions during 2005, what is the amount of her contribution deduction for the year?

b. If R contributed cash of $20,000 to her church in addition to the land, what is the amount of her charitable contribution deduction for 2005?

c. Calculate the amount of R's excess contributions from (a) and (b) and explain how these amounts are to be treated.

11-39 *Contribution Deductions—Percentage Limitations.* T, a single taxpayer, had adjusted gross income of $20,000 for 2005. During the year, T contributed cash of $1,000 and Xerox Corporation stock worth $10,000 to his church (a public charity). T inherited the stock during 2004 when it was valued at $8,000.

a. Calculate T's total contribution deduction for 2005.

b. How must any excess contributions be treated?

c. If T does not anticipate being able to itemize his deductions in any future years, what might he do in 2005 to increase his current contribution deduction?

11-40 *Miscellaneous Itemized Deductions.* R, single, has the following miscellaneous itemized deductions for the current year:

Unreimbursed employee business expenses..........	$1,350
Professional dues and subscriptions	650
Job-seeking expenses...........................	800
Tax return preparation fee	250
Safe-deposit box rental (for stocks and bonds)	50

Assume that R itemizes his deductions for the current year.

a. What is the amount of R's deduction for the above items if his adjusted gross income is $70,000 for the current year?

b. What is the amount of R's deduction for these items if his adjusted gross income is $100,000 for the current year?

11-41   *Three-Percent Cutback Rule.* H and W are married and file a joint return for the current year. They have the following itemized deductions (before any percentage limitations) for the year:

Medical and dental expenses....................	$8,000
Real estate taxes on home	3,500
Deductible interest on home mortgage	9,000
State income taxes paid.........................	5,500
Charitable contributions........................	4,000
Miscellaneous itemized deductions	2,500

Determine H and W's itemized deductions, assuming the following levels of adjusted gross income for the current year.

a. $100,000

b. $400,000

c. $800,000

11-42   *Calculating Itemized Deductions.* Robert and Jean Snyder have an adjusted gross income of $30,000 for 2005. Their expenses for 2005 are:

Prescription drugs	$ 300*
Medical insurance premiums	900
Doctor and dental bills paid	1,400*
Eyeglasses for Robert	155
Hospital and clinic bills paid.............................	450*
Property taxes paid on home............................	900
State income taxes paid:	
Remaining 2004 tax liability	125
Withheld from wages during year	1,850
State and local sales taxes paid:	
Amount paid on new automobile.......................	800
Amount paid on new widiscreen television	280
Personal property taxes paid	100
Interest on home mortgage**.............................	4,750
Interest paid on personal auto loan	1,100
Interest paid on credit card purchases....................	400
Interest paid on E.F. Hutton margin account***	120
Cash contributions to church	2,000
Fair market value of Hightech Corp. stock contributed	
to church (purchased for $1,000 three years ago)	5,000
Labor union dues paid by Robert.........................	200
Qualifying education costs paid by Jean	300
Safe deposit box rental (for stocks and bonds)	50
Fee paid accountant for preparation of 2004	
state and Federal tax returns	350

*   These amounts are net of insurance reimbursements received during 2005.

**   This mortgage was created at the time the home was purchased.

*** This investment interest expense is related to the production of $1,500 of net investment income.

The Snyders drove their personal automobile 500 miles for medical and dental treatment and an additional 1,000 miles in connection with charitable services performed for their church. Assuming Robert and Jean are both under age 40, lived in Virginia for the entire year, and plan to file a joint income tax return, determine their total itemized deductions. If a tax form is used for the computations, complete Schedule A (Form 1040).

RESEARCH PROBLEM

11-43 Sam Simpson transferred stock, real estate, and his principal residence to his former wife, Shirley, under the terms of the property settlement agreement. In exchange, Shirley agreed to pay Sam $250,000 down and another $750,000 at 10 percent per year for 10 years. Can Shirley deduct any of the interest she expects to pay over the next 10 years? Explain.

Chapter 12

DEDUCTIONS FOR CERTAIN INVESTMENT EXPENSES AND LOSSES

LEARNING OBJECTIVES

Upon completion of this chapter you will be able to:

- Discuss the basic rules governing the deduction of investment expenses

- Explain the limitations imposed on the deduction of losses incurred in an activity in which a taxpayer does not materially participate (i.e., passive losses)

- Understand the special treatment for interest expense related to a passive activity

- Discuss the restrictions imposed on deductions related to vacation homes

---

CHAPTER OUTLINE

Since 1942 Congress has generally allowed taxpayers to deduct expenses and losses incurred in connection with investment activities. As explained in Chapter 7, Code § 212 currently authorizes the deduction of investment-oriented expenses. This provision specifically allows a deduction for expenses incurred for the production or collection of income or for the management, conservation, or maintenance of property held for the production of income. Deductible investment expenses typically include such items as fees paid to rent a safety deposit box to hold securities, cost of financial advice, and travel expenses incurred in managing property. Expenses incurred in operating rental property such as those for maintenance, depreciation, utilities, and insurance are also deductible under § 212. Similarly, deductions for interest expense incurred by taxpayers to finance their investments also are deductible under § 212, although certain restrictions apply (as discussed in Chapter 11). Most important, the law generally allows the deduction of losses flowing through to the taxpayer from investments in partnerships and S corporations. Specific investment expenses incurred by the taxpayer are normally classified as miscellaneous itemized deductions and are subject to the two percent limitation and the 3 percent cutback. However, expenses related to property held for the production of rents or royalties are deductible *for* A.G.I. In addition, losses flowing from a partnership or S corporation are generally deductible for A.G.I.

For many years, the general rules adequately governed the deduction of most investment expenses and losses. In time, these rules became insufficient to police growing abuse. As a result, Congress enacted special provisions to restrict investment-type deductions where it found the general rule to be lacking. This chapter examines four additional measures: the at-risk rules, the passive activity limitations, the restrictions on the deduction for interest expense related to passive activities, and the provisions related to the rental of vacation homes.

INTRODUCTION TO TAX SHELTERS

Historically, the tax law has generally allowed taxpayers to use deductions from one activity to offset the income of another. Similarly, most credits could be used to offset tax attributable to income from any of the taxpayer's activities.

Example 1. R earns $50,000 annually working as vice president of marketing at Plentiful Products, Inc. Over the years, he has accumulated a modest portfolio of stocks which generates dividends of about $10,000 a year. In addition, he is a 10% limited partner in a partnership that owns an apartment complex consisting of 200 units. During the year, the apartment complex had operating expenses that exceeded rental income, creating a $100,000 loss. Prior to 1987, R could use his share of the loss, $10,000, to offset his other income, both salary and dividends. Assuming R's marginal tax rate was 30%, the loss produced tax savings of $3,000.

The above example illustrates the essentials of what is now a well-publicized phenomenon: under prior law, an individual could reduce his or her tax liability—even eliminate it—by investing in "tax shelters" that produced losses which could be offset against other income. The attraction of such losses for taxpayers wishing to avoid taxes was so great that the tax shelter business grew into a thriving industry.

A tax shelter is simply an investment which takes advantage of certain tax rules to enhance its rate of return. Like any investment, there is an outlay of cash (or credit) for something that hopefully will yield income year after year and produce gain on its disposition. The ultimate reward or potential loss is usually commensurate with the risk that the investor is willing to assume. It is the tax treatment of the various pieces of the investment that converts an ordinary investment to a potential tax shelter. For example, in the broadest sense, an investment in municipal bonds may be considered a type of tax shelter because the return paid on the investment—the interest—is tax exempt. In the real world, however, the term *tax shelter* is usually not associated with tax-exempt bonds—tax-favored probably would be a more appropriate label. The words "tax shelter" typically conjures up images of complex investments that—as in *Example 1*— throw off losses to "shelter" the investor's other income.

STRUCTURE OF THE TAX SHELTER

In the heyday of the industry, a tax shelter was organized as a limited partnership. From a tax perspective, the partnership form is the perfect structure for the shelter because it is not a separate taxable entity. Instead, a partnership acts as a conduit, enabling the tax benefits produced by the activity to flow through to the investing partners. Operating losses from the partnership's business flow through to the partners who may be able to offset the losses against their other income. Long-term capital gains realized by the partnership flow through, retaining their favorable character to be reported by the partners on their own returns. Special credits generated by the partnership's activity (e.g., the rehabilitation and low-income housing credits) might pass through to the partners to be used to reduce the tax on other taxable income. Observe the vital role that the flow-through characteristic of a partnership plays in a tax shelter. Such results could not be obtained with a C corporation. A C corporation, which is a separate taxable entity, pays taxes on its own income which may be taxed again when distributed to the shareholders as a dividend. More important, at least in a tax shelter sense, the losses of a C corporation can only be used by the corporation to offset its own income and, therefore, produce no benefits to the investing shareholders. For these reasons, tax shelters are not organized as C corporations. Indeed, it is not surprising that as tax shelters became more popular, the IRS tried to halt their growth by arguing that tax shelters posing as limited partnerships were not really partnerships but—because of their limited liability and their close resemblance to a corporation— were corporations. However, the government had little success with this theory and had to devise other techniques to eliminate the perceived abuse.

Promoters of tax shelters historically used limited partnerships—rather than general partnerships—as the vehicle of choice. The promoter, the one who put the deal together and got a fee for his efforts, normally acted as the general partner. To lure an investor, the promoter had to limit an individual's exposure to risk. By structuring the investment as a "limited" partnership, individuals could invest and limit the possibility of financial loss to the amount of their investment. Any liability in excess of that borne by the limited partners was the responsibility of the general partner. This ceiling on an individual's exposure was an extremely attractive feature in the promotion of tax shelters, paving the way for otherwise wary investors to make a financial commitment to the activity.

ELEMENTS OF A TAX SHELTER

Most tax shelters are constructed to offer three basic benefits: tax deferral, conversion of ordinary income into capital gain, and leverage. Each of these characteristics on its own can produce significant benefits. But when the three are combined into a single package, the result is almost too good to be true.

Deferral. Deferral is one of the most important tools in tax planning. Postponing the time at which taxes must be paid is the equivalent of an interest-free loan from the government. To illustrate, consider a taxpayer who can defer the payment of $10,000 of taxes for a five-year period. Assuming an after tax rate of return of ten percent, the present value of the tax payment is only $6,210 [$10,000 × (1/(1.10)^5]. In this case, postponing payment of tax saves $3,790, a decrease of almost 38 percent!

A typical tax shelter achieves deferral through a mismatching of revenues and expenses. Mismatching occurs because of the timing of income and deductions. Normally a tax shelter produces deductible expenses prior to the period in which the investment produces income in sufficient amounts to offset the deductions. In the appropriately structured tax shelter, taxpayers may be able to use these excess deductions, in effect losses from the shelter, to offset income from other sources thus producing immediate benefits. Most tax shelters were built around this same modus operandi: deduct expenses now while the gain accrues and is not taxed until later. This approach, "deduct now, pay later," is still the foundation of many current tax planning ideas.

> **Example 2.** R, S, and T formed a partnership for the purpose of breeding cattle. Each contributed $15,000 for a one-third interest. The partnership uses the cash to purchase a herd of cattle consisting primarily of cows, heifers and a few bulls. The partnership's only cash expenses during the year were the costs for breeding and maintaining the cattle totaling $45,000. No income was produced since none of the cattle were sold. Assuming the partnership uses the cash method of accounting and ignoring depreciation, the partnership has a loss of $45,000 which is allocated equally among R, S and T. As a result, R, S and T each have a $15,000 deduction for the losses attributable to their investment in the partnership, and this loss can be offset against income from other sources. Assuming each is in the 50% tax bracket (federal, state and local), each saves taxes of $7,500 ($15,000 × 50%).

Note in the above example that the tax savings occur because the cash method of accounting results in a mismatching of expenses and revenues. Had the partnership been required to use the accrual method or simply prohibited from deducting the expenses until the partnership *sold* the cattle, revenue and expenses would have been properly matched—at least in the financial accounting sense—and no tax savings would result (unless the cattle are later sold at a loss). It also should be emphasized that the taxes saved in this situation are not permanently avoided but only *deferred* until the future when the cattle are sold.

> **Example 3.** Refer to the situation in *Example 2* where expenses during the first year of operations were $45,000, producing a $45,000 deductible loss. Now assume that the cattle that were born and raised are sold for $45,000 on the first day of the next accounting period. If there were no other expenses, the partnership would have income of $45,000, each partner reporting $15,000. Since each partner is in the 50% tax bracket each pays taxes of $7,500. Note that the taxes paid in this period are the same as the taxes saved in the prior period. Thus, the taxpayer has not escaped $7,500 in taxes; nevertheless, the taxpayer has benefited since he deferred payment of the tax for one year. In addition, the taxpayer has benefited even though he had no gain or loss on the transaction as a whole ($45,000 income was equal to the $45,000 cost of breeding and raising). Of course, whether the taxpayers are happy with the result depends on the return that they could have otherwise received had the $45,000 been invested elsewhere.

The cattle example typifies the classic tax shelter but there were many more. Taxpayers could invest in partnerships created to explore for oil and gas, produce a movie or broadway show, buy art masters from which lithographs and prints could be made, or lease equipment (e.g., railroad boxcars, barges, cable TV systems, houseboats, executive jets and any other item someone might be willing to rent). Perhaps the shelter of all shelters is real estate. Here the partnership buys an office or apartment building for which current depreciation deductions can be claimed even though the value of the building is holding or increasing. Despite their differences, all tax shelters had one common thread: claim deductions this year for expenses that add value that will not be taxed until next year.

While deferral is a huge advantage, the opportunities increase dramatically when the element of conversion can be added to the mix.

Conversion. The second element of the successful tax shelter involves conversion. Conversion is a two-step process. The first step concerns the treatment of deductions arising from the tax shelter activity. These expenses are deductible and reduce ordinary operating income that would otherwise be taxed at ordinary tax rates. The second step is where the conversion takes place. When the tax shelter activity is sold, any gain on the sale is taxed as long-term capital gain, which is taxed at the far more favorable capital gain rates.

Example 4. Recall *Example 3* where the cattle were purchased, bred and raised at a cost of $45,000. Assume now that the cattle are sold after they were held for more than two years—the holding period necessary for cattle if gain is to qualify for long-term capital gain treatment. Given this additional fact, the $45,000 gain would be treated as long-term capital gain and thus each partner would (using the tax rates in effect today) pay taxes at a capital gains rate of 20%, producing a tax of $3,000 (20% × $15,000) for each of the partners. Contrast the tax paid on the gain, $3,000, with the $7,500 of taxes saved from deducting the costs (50% × $15,000 share of the loss = $7,500). Most important, note that there was no real economic gain on the transaction: the cattle cost $45,000 to raise and then were sold for $45,000. However, because of the difference between the tax rates applying to ordinary income and capital gains, each partner is better off by $4,500 ($7,500 − $3,000). Note that in the previous example the $7,500 of taxes initially saved by each partner were entirely recouped by the government when the cattle were sold. In this situation, however, the government recoups only $3,000 of the original savings because the ordinary income was converted to capital gain. Thus, in this case, the taxpayer has not only benefited from deferral—deductions now, income later—but also earned $4,500 from the conversion of ordinary income into capital gain.

Leverage. The third element of most tax shelters is leverage. In physics, a strategically placed lever provides a mechanical benefit, enabling people to lift more than they would be able to with their own physical strength. The principle is the same in the world of finance. In investing, borrowing money enables an individual to obtain a larger return than otherwise could be obtained. For example, assume an individual purchases land for $100,000, $10,000 of her own money and $90,000 borrowed from a lender. If the investment is sold a year later for $120,000, there has been a 20 percent return on the total $100,000 investment. But for the individual investor, after paying back the lender $90,000 and $10,000 for the use of the money (i.e., interest), the $20,000 remaining means that she has doubled her money, a return of 100 percent! In tax terminology, the term *leverage* means that by borrowing money, a taxpayer can obtain a disproportionately large benefit from a small investment. The most common use, sometimes referred to as "tax leverage" concerns depreciation. For example, a tax shelter partnership might purchase a railroad boxcar for $25,000 down and finance the balance with a $75,000 note (i.e., the leverage). The law allows depreciation on the entire $100,000 not just the $25,000—creating much larger depreciation deductions than could have been obtained had depreciation been allowed only on the amount not borrowed.

Example 5. Assume the same facts as in the previous examples concerning the cattle breeding tax shelter except that the partnership acquired the original herd using an initial investment of $5,000 each—$15,000 total—and $30,000 of funds borrowed from the bank for which the partners are personally liable. Note the result when the taxpayer leverages a small investment with borrowed funds: each taxpayer receives a deductible loss providing a tax saving of $7,500 ($45,000 deduction × 13 = $15,000 × 50%) which is more than his $5,000 original investment!

Note in the example above that by using leverage the taxpayers are able to generate $45,000 of deductions for an investment of only $15,000. In the language of tax shelters, this means that the taxpayers got a 3:1 write-off, $3 of deduction for each $1 invested. If the taxpayer is in the 50 percent tax bracket, a $3 deduction produces a benefit of $1.50 in tax savings at a cost of $1—clearly a miracle. When tax shelters were at the peak of their popularity, some investments boasted far greater benefits, 5:1, 10:1 and higher.

While the principle of leverage can work miracles, it can also spell disaster. If a taxpayer invests in a tax shelter where the write-off is 10:1, this means that the deal is highly leveraged—a large amount is being borrowed. If the investment goes sour, the lender still must be repaid. In such cases, the cost of the deductions could result in a severe financial loss. However, tax shelter promoters usually solved this problem by using a magical tool: *nonrecourse financing.*

A nonrecourse note is a loan for which the borrower bears no liability for the debt. If the borrower defaults on the loan, the lender can foreclose on the property (i.e., the collateral). However, if the funds derived from foreclosure and sale of the property are not sufficient to satisfy the loan obligation, the lender is out of luck—there is no recourse against the borrower. In a partnership, if the financing for the tax shelter activity was provided using nonrecourse debt (e.g., an office building or other real estate), the investing partners were only liable for the debt to the extent of their investment. As might be imagined, promoters took advantage of this phenomenon. In the most outrageous deals, the promoter would overstate the value of the investment and then act as the banker, providing the financing, all nonrecourse. The investors' cash investment would cover any real costs of the promoter and the nonrecourse financing simply served to create deductions.

Example 6. P put together a limited partnership to create deductible losses for the investors. Ten doctors invested $10,000 each for a partnership interest. The partnership used the $100,000 to buy a building from P for $1,000,000. The partnership signed a nonrecourse note to P for $900,000, payable with interest only for 20 years and a balloon payment of $900,000 at the end of the term. Before consideration of depreciation, operation of the office building broke even. The partnership proceeded to depreciate the property (a noncash expenditure), producing net losses that could be passed through and deducted by the partners. At the end of 20 years, the partnership might default on the note. In this case, P would take back his property and each partner would have received essentially $100,000 of deductions at a cost of $10,000. If the partners were in the 50% tax bracket, the deductions would be worth $50,000 and the arrangement would have provided a terrific return on the partners' investments. On the other side of the deal, P would pocket the $100,000 for his trouble. Note that the value of the building could have been whatever the partnership wanted to set, $1 million, $1.5 million, $2 million, or whatever, since the debt was nonrecourse and no one was ever going to pay!

In order to prevent what it considered the harmful and excessive use of tax shelters, Congress took action—albeit indirect—with enactment of the at-risk rules in 1976 and the passive loss rules in 1986. Perhaps fearing that it would alienate certain constituencies, Congress opted not to eliminate or limit the provisions on which shelters are built (e.g., special benefits for low-income housing and rehabilitation of old and historic buildings). Instead, the new legislation, placed limitations on the losses created by these special provisions.

AT-RISK RULES

As can be seen in *Example 6*, the linchpin that held many tax shelters together was nonrecourse financing. From the outset, the government believed that investors should not be entitled to deductions unless they actually incurred a cost—something that was not necessarily present when a tax shelter was structured with nonrecourse financing. Consequently, to eliminate the possibility of artificial deductions, as part of the Tax Reform Act of 1976, Congress enacted § 465 and the so-called at-risk rules. Section 465 generally limits the deductions of individuals and closely held businesses to the amount which they could actually lose from the investment—the amount at-risk. Consequently, to secure the deduction, investors generally must commit personal funds to the venture's activities or be personally liable for debt incurred by the venture in carrying on its activities. The at-risk rules were subsequently amended in the Revenue Act of 1978 and the Tax Reform Act of 1986.

Initially, the at-risk rules were limited to four specific types of activities: (1) holding, producing, or distributing motion picture films or tapes; (2) farming; (3) leasing personal property; and (4) oil and gas exploration and development. As the list suggests, all of these were ripe for sheltering income. In 1978, legislation extended the rules to cover all other activities with one blatant omission: real estate. Real estate was added in 1986 but a huge exception was created in 1987. This exception essentially allowed real estate ventures to escape the at-risk limitations when they were financed using funds from a third-party commercial lender. Consequently, as the law currently reads, the at-risk rules apply to all trade or business or the production of income activities operated by individuals and closely held businesses. Real estate placed in service before 1987 (e.g., an office building or an apartment complex) is exempt as is a separate activity that involves the leasing of equipment by a closely held C corporation. It is important to realize that the at-risk rules cover *any* trade or business or investment activity. Unlike the passive loss rules discussed below, they are not limited to those investments that produce portfolio income or loss, or to those that produce passive income or loss.

AT-RISK COMPUTATION

Under § 465(a), the at-risk provisions limit the deduction of losses incurred in an activity to the amount *at-risk* in the activity at the close of the tax year. Any loss in excess of the amount at-risk cannot be deducted in the current year but can be carried forward and used when there is an increase in the amount at-risk. The following formula can be used to compute the amount at-risk (see Form 6198).

Beginning at-risk balance

+ Contributions of cash and property (adjusted basis)

+ Increases in recourse debt (taxpayer is personally liable and the lender has no interest in the venture)

+ Increases in debt for which the taxpayer has pledged property which is not used in the activity as security

+ Increases in qualified nonrecourse debt related to realty

+ Income (taxable and tax-exempt)

− Cash or property withdrawals or distributions

− Nondeductible expenses related to tax-exempt income

− Decreases in qualified nonrecourse debt related to realty

− Decreases in recourse debt (T/P personally liable)

− Losses

= Amount at-risk

Observe that the calculation attempts to measure the amount of the taxpayer's economic investment that could be lost from the activity. Accordingly, a taxpayer's at-risk basis includes cash and other assets committed to the activity. Similarly, adjustments are made for income that is retained within the activity and not distributed since such amounts represent additional investments that might be lost. In addition, the at-risk amount includes amounts borrowed for use in the activity for which the taxpayer is personally liable for repayment—recourse debt—as well as amounts borrowed for which the taxpayer has pledged property as security (other than property used in the activity). Finally, as discussed further below, Congress appeased the real estate industry by including in the amount at-risk certain nonrecourse debt related to the holding of real property. Note that while the taxpayer's at-risk basis increases as these items increase, conversely, the at-risk amount is reduced as these items decrease (e.g., amounts are withdrawn, losses are incurred, recourse debt is reduced).

Example 7. This year, G started a business, designing web pages and providing connections to the Internet. He operated the business as a sole proprietorship. His first step was to purchase a server from a computer manufacturer for $100,000. He gave the company $10,000 cash and agreed to pay the manufacturer $90,000 over the next 10 years. In addition, he put up 20 shares of stock that he owned in his father's business worth $20,000 as collateral. The company agreed to accept the stock and equipment as security for the loan. G also borrowed $150,000 from the local bank. The bank required S to sign a note for the loan for which he is personally liable for repayment. During the year, he contributed another $50,000 of his own money to keep the business running. The first year the business turned a small profit of $30,000 and G left the money in the business for working capital. G's at-risk basis includes, the $50,000 of his own money contributed to the business, the $10,000 used to purchase the equipment, the $20,000 of stock that he pledged to secure the equipment loan, the debt of $150,000 for which he is personally obligated, and the $30,000 of income that he left in the business for a total of $260,000. It does not include the $90,000 to be paid to the manufacturer since the note is nonrecourse and the property is used in the business. Note that the pledged property is included since the property is not used in the business as is the case with the equipment.

In the second year of operations, the business turned sour and produced a loss of $10,000. In addition, G withdrew $50,000 for personal use. He also made a $20,000 payment on the principal of the loan. Since G's at-risk basis is $260,000 the loss is not limited and G may use the loss to offset his other income (assuming he satisfies the passive loss rules discussed later in this chapter). G must adjust his beginning at-risk basis of $260,000 by reducing it for the loss of $10,000, the distribution of $50,000 and the $20,000 payment of the debt, leaving an at-risk basis of $180,000.

While the at-risk rules went a long way to eliminate abusive tax shelters, one industry was able to escape—real estate. After much controversy, the real estate lobby convinced Congress to provide relief for real estate deals to the extent that they used arm's length, third-party commercial financing (e.g., savings and loan provides loan and charges interest at a reasonable market rate). Consequently, a taxpayer's at-risk amount includes so-called qualified nonrecourse financing. Section 465(b)(6) sets forth the specific requirements.

1. The financing is secured by the real property used in the activity.

2. No person is personally liable for the debt (nonrecourse debt).

3. The amounts are borrowed from a person who is regularly engaged in the lending business (e.g., a commercial lender such as a bank or savings and loan or a federal, state, or local governmental unit).

4. The lender is not related to the taxpayer. Note that financing made by a lending institution that has an equity interest in the venture is permissible if the loan is commercially reasonable and similar to those made to unrelated parties.

5. The lender is not the seller of the property or the promoter of the deal (i.e., receives a fee for the taxpayer's investment) or related to the seller or promoter.

Example 8. J was one of 10 investors to contribute $100,000 to Silver Queen Partnership. Each investor received a 10% partnership interest. The partnership used the cash and $900,000 borrowed from First National Bank to purchase an office building for $1,000,000. The debt was secured by a mortgage on the building and was payable over 20 years with interest at 7%, the current market rate. None of the partners were personally liable on the obligation. This year J's share of the partnership's loss was $200,000. J's at-risk amount is $190,000, including the $100,000 cash contribution and 10% of the $900,000 nonrecourse loan. The loan is considered qualified nonrecourse financing since it was borrowed from an unrelated commercial lender and not the seller. Although J's share of the loss is $200,000, her deduction is limited to the amount she has at-risk, $190,000, and the balance is carried over. Her at-risk basis is reduced to zero and she may not deduct the $10,000 carryover until her amount at-risk increases.

Despite the at-risk rules, wily tax shelter promoters were able to structure investments that could avoid them. As might be expected, many of these deals involved real estate since real estate was effectively exempt if the financing was properly structured. To the chagrin of Congress, the tax shelters industry continued to grow. Perhaps one of the most revealing testimonials of the popularity of tax shelters can be found on the cover of the February 1986 issue of *Money* magazine. The cover pictured three highly successful individuals, and indicated that each had made more than a million dollars but paid no taxes. In light of this and other similar reports, it is not surprising that taxpayer confidence in the fairness of the tax system had badly eroded. Many taxpayers had come to believe that tax was paid only by the naive and the unsophisticated. This belief, in turn, was leading to noncompliance and providing incentives for expansion of the tax shelter market, often diverting investment capital from productive activities to those principally or exclusively servicing tax avoidance goals. Consequently, Congress took aim at tax shelters again in 1986 and enacted yet another hurdle to be cleared before losses could be deducted: the passive loss rules of § 469. These rules go beyond the at-risk provisions, placing far-reaching restrictions on when deductions, losses, and credits of a passive activity can be used to offset the income of another activity. Although these restrictions were designed principally for losses from a limited partnership interest, they also limit losses from rental activities, as well as losses from any trade or business in which the taxpayer does not materially participate.

PASSIVE ACTIVITY LOSS LIMITATIONS

GENERAL RULE

The thrust of § 469 is to divide a taxpayer's income into three types: (1) wages, salaries, and other income from activities in which the taxpayer materially participates (e.g., income from an S corporation that the taxpayer owns and operates); (2) portfolio income (e.g., interest, dividends, capital gains and losses); and (3) passive income—the sort deemed to be produced by most tax shelters and rental activities. Expenses related to passive activities can be deducted only to the extent of income from *all* such passive activities. Any excess expenses of these passive activities—the passive activity loss— may not be deducted against portfolio income or wages, salaries, or any other income from activities in which the taxpayer materially participates. Losses that cannot be used are held in suspension and carried forward to be used to offset passive income of future years.[1] Suspended losses from a passive activity can be used in full to offset portfolio or active income *only* when the taxpayer disposes of his or her entire interest in the activity. Upon disposition, any current and suspended losses (including any loss realized on the disposition) are used to offset income in the following order:[2]

1. Any gain on the disposition of the interest

2. Any *net* income from all passive activities (after taking into account any suspended losses)

3. Any other income or gain (i.e., active and portfolio income)

Observe that this special ordering rule requires the taxpayer to use up the suspended losses against gain on the disposition and any passive income (net of any passive losses) before offsetting such losses against active or portfolio income. Without this rule, a taxpayer would use all of the suspended loss against active income, thus freeing up the passive gain on the disposition to absorb other passive losses.

> **Example 9.** T owned and operated her own construction company as a sole proprietorship. For the year, the company had net income of $120,000. T has a substantial portfolio that produced dividends of $15,000 and a short-term capital loss from the sale of stock of $7,000. In addition, her investment in LP1, a limited partnership, produced a passive loss. T's share of the loss was $30,000. Her investments in LP2 and LP3, two other limited partnerships, generated passive activity income. T's share of the income was $5,000. Under the capital gain and loss provisions, T may deduct $3,000 of the capital loss and carry over the remaining $4,000. The $30,000 passive loss is deductible only to the extent of passive income,

---

[1] Suspended losses are carried forward to the following year, where they are treated as if they were incurred in such year. Temp. Reg. § 1.469-1T(f)(4)(B).

[2] § 469(g). To date, Regulations have not been issued on dispositions, leaving many unanswered questions. See Erickson, "Passive Activity Disposition," *The Tax Adviser* (May 1989), p. 338. See TAM 9742002 where the taxpayer did not have to offset current and suspended losses from sold activities with passive income from only those activities that produced net incomes.

which is $5,000. In effect, income and loss from the passive activities are netted, and the net loss attributable to LP1, $25,000, is carried over to the following year.

Example 10. Same facts as above. T held on to her investment in LP1 until this year, when she sold her entire interest, producing a gain of $40,000. Total suspended losses attributable to her investment in LP1 were $70,000. Net income from LP2 was $30,000 for the year while LP3 produced a net loss of $10,000. T may deduct the entire $70,000 loss: $40,000 against the gain, $20,000 against the net passive income from LP2 and LP3 ($30,000 − $10,000), and $10,000 against any other income.

As a practical matter, many taxpayers will have investments in several passive activities, some that produce income and some that produce losses. If the taxpayer has losses from more than one activity, the suspended loss for *each* activity must be determined in the event that the taxpayer subsequently disposes of one of the activities. The suspended loss of each activity is determined by allocating the total loss disallowed for the year, including any suspended losses, pro rata among the loss activities using the following formula.[3]

$$\text{Total disallowed loss for year} \times \frac{\text{Loss for this activity}}{\text{Total losses from all activities with losses}} = \frac{\text{Suspended loss}}{\text{for this activity}}$$

Note that this fraction simply represents the percentage of losses attributable to a particular activity. For example, if a loss from a particular activity represents 10 percent of all losses, 10 percent of the disallowed loss is allocated to such activity and carried over to the following year. Alternatively, it could be said that the particular activity absorbs 10 percent of any passive income. In effect, each loss activity absorbs this fraction of any passive income from other activities.

Example 11. T owns an interest in three passive activities: A, B, and C. For 2005, activity B reports income of $2,000 while activities A and C report losses of $10,000, $6,000 from A and $4,000 from C. T is allowed to deduct the passive losses from A and C to the extent of the passive income from B. Thus he may deduct $2,000 of the losses. The remaining loss of $8,000 cannot be used to offset T's income from other sources (e.g., wages, dividends, or interest income) but must be suspended and carried forward to the following year. The suspended loss of $8,000 must be allocated between the loss activities pro rata. Since 60% ($6,000/$10,000) of the net loss was attributable to A, the suspended loss for A is $4,800 (60% × $8,000). Similarly, the suspended loss for C is $3,200 [($4,000/$10,000) × $8,000]. Alternatively, the loss activities could be viewed as absorbing the passive income. Using this approach, the suspended losses would be computed somewhat differently but with the same result.

	A	C	Total
Loss for the year	$(6,000)	$(4,000)	$(10,000)
Loss absorbed:			
$2,000 × ($6,000/$10,000).	1,200	—	1,200
$2,000 × ($4,000/$10,000).	—	800	800
Suspended loss	$(4,800)	$(3,200)	$ (8,000)

---

[3]   Temp. Reg. § 1.469-1T(f)(2).

These losses are carried over and treated as if they were a deduction in the following year.

Example 12. Assume the same facts as in *Example 11*. The income and loss for 2006 of the three activities is shown below.

Activity	Current Net Income (Loss)	Carryforward from Prior Years	Total
A	$ (5,200)	$(4,800)	$(10,000)
B	12,000	—	12,000
C	(1,800)	(3,200)	(5,000)
Total	$ 5,000	$(8,000)	$ (3,000)

The total passive loss disallowed in 2006 is $3,000. The $3,000 disallowed loss is allocated among the activities with total losses (taking into account both current operations and losses suspended from prior years) as follows:

Activity	Total Disallowed Loss	×	Percentage of Total Loss	=	Allocable Portion of Loss
A	$3,000	×	$10,000/($10,000 + $5,000)	=	$2,000
C	3,000	×	5,000/($10,000 + $5,000)	=	1,000

In making the allocation, the disallowed loss is allocated based on an activity's net loss *including* suspended losses (e.g., $10,000 for A) rather than the loss that actually occurred in the current year (e.g., $5,200 for A).

Example 13. J has three passive activities: R, S, and T. The suspended losses and current income and losses for each activity for 2005 are shown below. In addition, J sold activity S for a $10,000 gain in 2005. Because there has been a complete disposition of S, J is able to deduct all of the suspended losses for S as shown below.

	R	S	T
Suspended loss	$ (9,000)	$(12,000)	$(15,000)
Current income (loss).	(5,000)	(6,000)	(7,000)
Total.	$(14,000)	$(18,000)	$(22,000)
Gain on disposition of S.		10,000	
Excess loss of S deducted against other income		$ (8,000)	

J must first offset the suspended and current losses of $18,000 from activity S against the $10,000 gain on the sale of S. The next step is to offset the $8,000 balance of losses against any net passive income for the year. In this case, the activities have no income, and thus none of the loss is absorbed by passive income. At this point, the remaining loss of $8,000 is no longer considered passive and can be used to offset any active or portfolio income that J may have.

Example 14. K has three passive activities: X, Y, and Z. The suspended losses and current income and losses for each activity for 2005 are shown below. In addition, in 2005 K sold activity Y for a $21,000 gain. K is able to deduct all of the suspended losses of Y as shown below.

	X	Y	Z
Suspended loss	$ (7,000)	$(10,000)	$(18,000)
Current income (loss)	(8,000)	(6,000)	8,000
Total	$(15,000)	$(16,000)	$(10,000)
Gain on disposition of Y	—	21,000	—
	$(15,000)	$ 5,000	$(10,000)
Loss absorbed:			
$5,000 × ($15,000/$25,000)	3,000		
$5,000 × ($10,000/$25,000)			2,000
Suspended loss	$(12,000)		$ (8,000)

K must first offset Y's current and suspended losses of $16,000 against the $21,000 gain on the sale. Note that the balance of the gain ($5,000) is considered passive income that can be combined with the net losses (the sum of current income or loss and suspended losses) from the other passive activities for the year.[4]

Rules similar to those for passive losses apply to tax credits produced by passive activities (e.g., the low-income housing credit, rehabilitation credit, research credit, and jobs credit). Passive credits can be used *only* to offset any tax attributable to passive income. Any unused credit may be carried forward to the next taxable year to offset future taxes arising from passive income. In contrast to passive losses, however, credits being carried over are not fully triggered when a passive activity is sold. In the year of disposition, like any other year, the credit can be used only if there is tax attributable to passive income (including gain on the sale of the activity). If the credit cannot be used, it can continue to be carried over to offset tax from other passive activities. However, the credit is subject to its own rules concerning carryover and expiration.

> **Example 15.** T invested in a limited partnership that rehabilitated a historic structure. In 2005, T sold his interest, realizing a gain of $5,000. At that time, T had suspended losses of $20,000 and credits of $10,000. T is able to use $5,000 of the losses to offset the gain and the other $15,000 to offset other active or portfolio income. None of the credit can be used, however, because there is no income from the passive activity. Had T sold the property for a gain of $50,000, he would have had $30,000 of passive income. Assuming T is in the 28% tax bracket, he could have used $8,400 ($30,000 × 28%) of the credit. The remaining credit of $1,600 may be carried over to offset tax that may arise from passive income.

TAXPAYERS SUBJECT TO LIMITATIONS

The passive loss rules apply to individuals, estates, trusts, personal service corporations, and certain closely held C corporations.[5] Partnerships and S corporations are not subject to the limitations per se. However, their activities flow through to the owners who are subject to limitation.

---

[4]   § 469(g)(1)(A) and Temp. Reg. § 1.469-2T(c)(2)(i)(A)(2).

[5]   § 469(a)(2).

The passive loss rules generally do not apply to regular C corporations. Presumably, their immunity is based on the theory that individuals generally do not benefit from losses locked inside the corporate form. Congress, however, did not want taxpayers to be able to circumvent the passive loss rules merely by incorporating. Absent a special rule, a taxpayer could utilize corporate immunity to shelter income derived from personal services. Taxpayers would simply incorporate as a personal service corporation and acquire tax shelter investments at the corporate level. The losses produced by the tax shelters would offset not only the service income but also income from any investments made at the corporate level. Consequently, the passive loss rules apply to *personal service corporations* (PSC). A PSC is one where the principal activity is the performance of personal services and such services are primarily performed by employee-owners who, *in the aggregate*, own more than 10 percent of the stock of the corporation either directly or indirectly (e.g., through family members). Common examples of personal service corporations are professional corporations such as those of doctors, accountants, attorneys, engineers, actors, architects, and others where personal services are performed.

Without additional restrictions, any taxpayer—not just one who derives income from services—could incorporate his or her portfolio and offset the investment income with losses from tax shelters. To prohibit this possibility, the passive loss rules also apply in a limited fashion to all closely held C corporations (i.e., a regular C corporation where five or fewer individuals own more than 50 percent of the stock either directly or indirectly). Note that some personal service corporations that might escape the tests above may still be subject to the rules due to their status as closely held corporations. A closely held corporation may not use passive losses to offset its portfolio income. However, such corporations may offset losses from passive activities against the income of any active business carried on by the corporation.[6]

> **Example 16.** R and his two brothers own Real Rustproofing Corporation. This year the corporation suffered a loss from operations of $10,000. In addition, it received interest income from short-term investments of working capital of $20,000. The corporation also had a passive loss from a real estate venture of $30,000. In determining taxable income, the passive activity limitation rules apply since the corporation is closely held (i.e., five or fewer individuals own more than 50%). As a result, none of the loss can be deducted since the loss cannot offset portfolio income of the corporation and the corporation did not have any income from operations. Had the corporation had $50,000 of operating profit, the entire loss could be deducted since passive losses can be used by a closely held corporation to offset active income—but not portfolio income.

PASSIVE ACTIVITIES

Assuming the taxpayer is subject to the passive activity rules, the most important determination is whether the activity in which the taxpayer is engaged is *passive*. The characterization of an activity as passive generally depends on the level of the taxpayer's involvement in the activity, the nature of the activity, or the form of ownership. Section 469(c) provides that the following activities are passive:

1. Any activity (other than a working interest in certain oil and gas property) that involves the conduct of a trade or business in which the taxpayer *does not materially participate*; and

2. *Any* rental activity regardless of the level of the taxpayer's participation.

---

[6] § 469(e)(2).

Given these definitions, several questions must be addressed to determine whether a particular endeavor of the taxpayer is a passive activity.

1. What is an activity?

2. Is the activity a rental or nonrental activity?

3. What is material participation?

Unfortunately, none of these questions are easily answered. An exceedingly complex set of Regulations exists that, in large measure, creates intricate definitions designed to prohibit wily taxpayers from deducting their passive losses. The basic rules are considered below.

DEFINITION OF AN ACTIVITY

The definition of an activity serves as the foundation for the entire structure of the passive loss rules. Virtually all of the important determinations required in applying the passive loss rules are made at the activity level. Perhaps the most significant of these concerns the taxpayer's level of participation. As discussed later in this chapter, if the taxpayer participates for more than 500 hours per year in a nonrental activity, he or she is deemed to materially participate in the activity, and the activity is therefore not passive. As the following example illustrates, this 500-hour test requires an unambiguous definition of an activity.

> **Example 17.** Mr R. Rock owns and operates 10 restaurants in 10 different cities. In addition, in each of those 10 cities he owns and operates 10 movie theaters. R spends 80 hours working in each restaurant during the year for a total of 800 hours. R spends 70 hours working in each movie theater for a total of 700 hours. If *each* restaurant and each movie theater are treated as separate activities, it would appear that R would not be treated as a material participant in any one of the businesses because he devoted only a minimum amount of his time during the year, 80 or 70 hours, to each. On the other hand, if all the restaurants are aggregated and deemed a *single activity*, R's total participation in all the restaurants, 800 hours would, in fact, be considered material. A similar conclusion could be reached for the movie theaters. In addition, if the restaurants are adjacent to the movie theaters (or in fact are concession stands in the theaters), it might be appropriate to treat the restaurant operation and the movie theater operation as a single activity.

The definition of an activity is not only important for the material participation test, but it is also significant should there be a disposition. As noted above, a complete disposition of an activity enables a taxpayer to deduct any suspended losses of the activity.

> **Example 18.** Same facts as in *Example 17* above. Also assume that there are suspended losses for each restaurant. If each restaurant is treated as a separate activity, a sale of one of the restaurants would enable R to deduct the suspended loss for that restaurant. In contrast, if the restaurant is not considered a separate activity, none of the loss would be recognized on the tax return for the year of sale.

Examples 17 and *18* demonstrate not only the importance of the definition of an activity but also the problems inherent in defining what constitutes an activity.

The authors of § 469 obviously anticipated the difficulty in defining an activity and therefore provided no working definition in the Code. As a result, the formidable task of defining an activity fell in the laps of those who write the Regulations. Defining an activity would not be difficult if all taxpayers were engaged in a single line of business at one location. As a practical matter, this is not always the case. Some taxpayers, such as Mr. Rock in *Example 17*, are involved in several lines of business at multiple locations. Consequently, any definition of an activity had to consider such situations. In fixing the scope of an activity, the Treasury feared that a narrow definition would allow taxpayers to generate passive income at will that could be used to offset passive losses. For example, if Mr. Rock were able to treat each restaurant as a separate activity, he could easily manipulate his participation at each restaurant to obtain passive or active income as he deemed most beneficial. To combat this problem, the IRS initially designed a broad definition that generally required a taxpayer to aggregate various endeavors into a single activity. By establishing a broad definition that treats several undertakings as a single activity, the IRS made the material participation test easier to meet, resulting in active rather than passive income. Unfortunately, the initial definition was quite complicated, as evidenced by the Temporary Regulations, which contained 196 pages of intricate rules and examples devoted to the subject.[7] In a refreshing change of direction, however, the IRS allowed these Temporary Regulations to expire, creating a far simpler approach all contained in only four pages![8]

Appropriate Economic Unit. Under the final regulations, taxpayers are required to treat one or more trade or business activities or one or more rental activities as a single activity if the activities constitute an *appropriate economic unit* for measuring gain or loss.[9] Whether two or more activities constitute an appropriate economic unit (AEU) is determined by taking into account all of the relevant facts and circumstances. Five factors are to be given the greatest weight in making the determination. These are as follows:

1. Similarities and differences in *types* of business;

2. The extent of common control;

3. The extent of common ownership;

4. Geographical location; and

5. Interdependencies between activities (e.g., they have the same customers or same employees, are accounted for with a single set of books, purchase or sell goods between themselves, or involve products or services that are normally provided together).

A taxpayer may use *any* reasonable method of applying the relevant facts and circumstances.

Example 19. C operates several businesses as a sole proprietor. These include a bakery and a movie theater at a shopping mall in Santa Fe and a bakery and a movie theater in Albuquerque. Reasonable groupings, depending on the facts and circumstances. may be as follows.

- ▸ A single activity
- ▸ A movie theater activity and a bakery activity
- ▸ A Santa Fe activity and an Albuquerque activity
- ▸ Four separate activities

---

[7] Temp. Reg. § 1.469-4T(a)(2).

[8] Reg. § 1.469-4.

[9] Reg. § 1.469-4(c)(1).

Consistency Requirement. To ensure that taxpayers do not bounce from one grouping to another to fit their needs, the proposed regulations impose a consistency requirement. Once the activities have been grouped in a particular manner, the grouping may not be changed unless the original grouping was clearly inappropriate or there has been a material change in the facts and circumstances that makes the original grouping inappropriate.[10] For instance, in *Example 19* above, once one of the groupings is selected, the taxpayer is required to continue using the grouping unless a material change in the facts and circumstances makes it clearly inappropriate.

In addition, to prevent a taxpayer from misusing the facts-and-circumstances approach, the IRS has the power to regroup activities if the taxpayer's grouping fails to reflect one or more appropriate economic units and one of the primary purposes of the taxpayer's grouping is to circumvent the passive loss rules.[11]

Activities Conducted through Conduit Entities. As a practical matter, many taxpayers will conduct activities through a partnership or an S corporation. In this case, the grouping is done at the partnership or S corporation level. Partners and S corporation shareholders then determine whether they should aggregate the entity activities with those they conduct directly or through other partnerships or S corporations.[12]

Grouping of Rental and Nonrental Activities. Rental activities and nonrental activities normally may *not* be grouped together and treated as a single activity. This rule is consistent with the basic provision that all rental activities are passive regardless of the taxpayer's participation. Therefore, it makes sense that rental and nonrental activities should not be aggregated. The practical significance of the rule is to prohibit taxpayers from sheltering active income with passive rental losses. Nevertheless, the Regulations do carve out an exception, allowing aggregation of rental and nonrental activities whenever either activity is *insubstantial* in relation to the other.[13]

> **Example 20.** PB&K, an accounting firm, operates its practice out of an office building that it owns. The firm occupies two floors of the building and leases the other three floors to third parties. This year, 90% of the firm's income is from its accounting practice and 10% is from rental of the office space. Because the rental operation is insubstantial in relation to the nonrental operation, the rental and nonrental operations are aggregated into a *single nonrental* activity. Note that in this case any net loss on the rental activity is effectively combined with the income of the accounting operation.

It should also be noted that the rental of real property and the rental of personal property cannot be grouped unless the personal property is provided in connection with the real property.[14]

> **Example 21.** T owns a small apartment building with eight units that he rents completely furnished. In addition, the building contains a small room with coin-operated laundry facilities. As a general rule, the laundry rental and apartment rental cannot be aggregated because the rental of real property cannot be grouped with the rental of personal property. In this case, however, the rental income and laundry

---

[10]   Reg. § 1.469-4(g).

[11]   Reg. § 1.469-4(h).

[12]   Reg. § 1.469-4(j).

[13]   Reg. § 1.469-4(d).

[14]   Reg. § 1.469-4(e).

income can be grouped since the personal property is provided in connection with the real property.

Rental and nonrental operations normally must be separated because they are subject to different rules. For example, rental activities are always passive, whereas nonrental activities are passive only if the taxpayer does not materially participate in such activities. In addition, owners of rental real estate are normally entitled to deduct up to $25,000 of rental losses annually without limitation, whereas there is no comparable rule for nonrental activities.

RENTAL VERSUS NONRENTAL ACTIVITIES

Under the general rule described above, all rental activities are deemed to be passive, *regardless* of whether the taxpayer materially participates. Congress adopted this view based on the belief that there is seldom any significant participation in rental activities. Therefore, it created a presumption that all rental activities would be passive. For this purpose, a rental activity is defined as any activity whereby a taxpayer receives payments that are principally for the use of property owned by the taxpayer (e.g., apartments or equipment).

Observe that this blanket rule effectively classifies many rental activities as passive even though an owner might render significant services in connection with the rental. For example, renting video tapes would be considered passive under the general rule even though the owner might perform substantial services. This approach would be unfair to those who participate yet suffer losses. Moreover, the rule creates a huge planning opportunity for those seeking passive income given that many rental businesses are profitable. Recognizing these problems, the authors of the Regulations identified six situations where what is normally a rental is to be treated as a nonrental activity.[15]

1. *1–7 Days Rental.* The activity is not a rental if the average rental period is seven days or less. Under this exception, short-term rentals of such items as cars, hotel and motel rooms, or videocassettes are not considered rental activities.

2. *8–30 Days Rental.* The activity is not a rental if the average rental period is 30 days or less and significant services are performed by the owner of the property. In determining whether *significant services* are provided, consideration is given to the type of service performed and the value of the services relative to the amount charged for the use of the property. In this regard, the Regulations indicate that telephone service and cable television are to be ignored as are those services commonly provided in connection with long-term rentals of commercial and residential property (e.g., janitorial services, repairs, trash collection, cleaning of common areas, and security services provided by landlords of shopping malls and centers). Unfortunately, the Regulations provide few other clues as to what constitutes significant services.

Example 22. T owns and rents a resort condominium in Florida. He provides telephone, cable, trash removal, cleaning of the common areas, and daily maid and linen service. The cost of the maid and linen services is less than 10% of the amount charged to tenants occupying the apartments. In determining whether significant services are provided, the telephone, cable, trash, and cleaning services are disregarded. Moreover, according to the Regulations, the maid and linen services would not be considered significant in this case. Because there are no significant

---

[15] Temp. Reg. § 1.469-1T(e)(3)(ii).

services under the Regulations' view, the activity would be considered a rental (*assuming* the average rental use exceeds seven days) and, therefore, a passive activity.

3. *Extraordinary Services.* The activity is not a rental if extraordinary personal services are provided by the owner of the property. Services are considered extraordinary if the use of the property is merely incidental to the services performed.

Example 23. Nathan Hale Military Academy, a private college preparatory school, provides housing for its students. The school's rental of such facilities would be considered incidental to the educational services provided and thus be treated as a nonrental activity.

4. *Incidental Rentals.* The activity is not a rental activity if the rental of the property is merely incidental to the nonrental activity.

Example 24. S owns unimproved land that she is holding for future appreciation. To defray the costs of the land, she leases the land to a rancher for grazing his cattle. According to the Regulations, if the rent is less than 2% of the basis of the property (or value if less), the activity is not treated as a rental.

5. *Nonexclusive Use.* The activity is not a rental activity if the taxpayer customarily makes the property available during defined business hours for the nonexclusive use of various customers. For example, this exception would apply to a golf course that sells annual memberships but which is also open to the public on a daily basis.

6. *Property Made Available for Use in a Nonrental Activity.* The activity is not a rental activity if the taxpayer owns an interest in a partnership, S corporation, or joint venture to which the property is rented. For example, if T rents equipment to a partnership in which he is a partner, the rental is treated as a nonrental activity.

Similarly, rental of property to a C corporation in which the taxpayer materially participates is not considered a rental.

Example 25. Mr. F, an attorney, owns and operates F&H Corporation, a law firm. This year F and his wife leased a building that they owned jointly to F&H Inc. The corporation was the sole tenant. Mr. F would like to treat the rent as passive and use it to absorb the couple's passive activity losses. Unfortunately, the regulations provide that rental to a C corporation in which the taxpayer materially participates is a nonrental activity. Therefore, the amounts received for leasing the building are not considered passive income.[16]

As noted above, any activity constituting a " rental" is a passive activity. Note, however, that those activities not classified as rentals (i.e., nonrental activities) may still be considered passive. Whether a *nonrental* activity is a passive activity depends on whether the taxpayer has materially participated in the activity.

---

[16] See *Remy Fransen, Jr.*, 99-2 USTC ¶50,882 (CA-5, 1999), *aff'g* 98-2 USTC ¶50,776 (D.C., E.D. La., 1998) where the Court upheld the validity of Reg. § 1.469-2(f)(6), recharacterizing the activity as active and not passive. See also *Schwalbach*, 111 T.C. No. 9 (1998).

MATERIAL PARTICIPATION

Material participation serves a crucial role in the application of the passive loss rules. It is the criterion that distinguishes between "passive" and "active" nonrental activities. The Code provides that an individual meets the material participation test only if he or she is involved in the operation of the activity on a regular, continuous, and substantial basis. Without further guidance, applying this nebulous criterion would essentially be left to the subjective interpretation of the taxpayer. However, the Regulations establish objective standards that look to the actual number of hours spent in the activity.

Under the regulatory scheme, a taxpayer materially participates in an activity if he or she meets one of seven tests.[17]

1. *More Than 500 Hours.* An individual materially participates if he or she spends more than 500 hours in the activity during the taxable year. Apparently the authors of the Regulations believed that this threshold (e.g., about 10 hours per week) appropriately distinguished those who truly were involved in the business from mere investors. Note that the work of a spouse is counted if it is work typically done by owners. For example, if B owned an S corporation that suffered losses (e.g., a football team), he would materially participate if he devoted more than 500 hours to the activity. However, if he spent only 300 hours and hired his wife as a receptionist who spent 250 hours, the test is not met because her work is not normally done by owners.

2. *Substantially All of the Participation.* The individual and his or her spouse materially participate if they are the sole participants or their participation constitutes substantially all of the participation of all individuals (including nonowners and nonemployees) who participate in the activity. This test, as well as the next, takes into account the fact that not all businesses require 500 hours to operate during the year. For example, if S operates a snow removal service by himself and spends only 50 hours in the activity this year because of light snow, the test is met because he was the sole participant.

3. *More Than 100 Hours and Not Less Than Anyone Else.* An individual materially participates if he or she participates for more than 100 hours and no other individual spends more time on the activity. For example, assume that S, above, occasionally hires E to help him remove snow. If S spent 160 hours and E 140, S qualifies because he spent more than 100 hours and not less than anyone else. Had S spent only 60 and E 40, S arguably would not qualify under either this or the previous test.

4. *Significant Participation in Several Activities.* An individual materially participates if his or her total participation in all *significant participation activities* (SPAs) exceeds 500 hours. A significant participation activity is defined as a trade or business in which the taxpayer participates more than 100 hours, but fails the other six tests for material participation. Thus a taxpayer must spend more than 100 hours in each activity and greater than 500 in all. The rule derives from the view that an individual who spends more than 500 hours in several different activities should be treated the same as those who spend an equivalent amount of time on a single activity.

---

[17] Temp. Reg. § 1.469-5T(a).

Example 26. T spends 140 hours overseeing his car wash, 160 hours supervising his quick-lube operation, and 499 hours managing his gas station. Each activity qualifies as a SPA because T spends more than 100 hours in each. More importantly, T is treated as materially participating in each because the total hours in all SPAs exceeds 500. However, if T spent two more hours in his gas station, then he would not be a material participant in either the car wash or quick-lube business. This occurs because the gas station would no longer be a SPA since the activity by itself satisfies the more-than-500-hours test. As a result, T's total hours in all SPAs, 300 (160 + 140), would not exceed the 500-hour benchmark. Obviously, this is a strange result.

The Regulations provide what at first glance is a curious treatment of SPAs. As expected, losses from SPAs failing to meet the 500-hour test are passive and generally not deductible. However, income from SPAs failing to meet the 500-hour test is *not* passive. Note that the IRS obtains the best of both worlds when a taxpayer is unable to combine his or her SPAs to get over the 500-hour threshold: passive loss but not passive income. This "heads I win, tails you lose" approach was designed to prevent taxpayers from creating passive income that could be used to absorb passive losses by spending small amounts of time in unrelated activities that are profitable.[18]

5. *Prior Participation.* An individual materially participates if he or she has materially participated (by tests 1 through 4) in an activity for five of the past ten years. This test prevents the taxpayer from moving in and out of material participation status. For example, D and son are partners in an appliance business that D started 30 years ago. D has essentially retired, leaving the day-to-day operations to his son. Without a special rule, D could tailor his participation year by year to obtain passive or nonpassive income as fits his needs.

6. *Prior Participation in a Personal Service Activity.* An individual materially participates in a personal service activity if he or she has materially participated in the activity for at least three years. Like the previous test, this rule eliminates the flexibility those working for personal service businesses have in tailoring their participation to obtain passive or nonpassive income as they need. For example, if a general partner in a law firm retired and converted her interest to a limited partnership interest, she would still be treated as a material participant in that law firm.

7. *Facts and Circumstances.* An individual materially participates if, based on the facts and circumstances, he or she participates in the activity on a regular, continuous, and substantial basis.

Rental Real Estate Exception. An extremely important exception to the passive activity rules is carved out in § 469(i) for rental real estate activities of the small investor. In many cases, the rental real estate held by a taxpayer is a residence that is used part-time, was formerly used, or may be used by the taxpayer in the future. Relief was provided for this type of rental real estate because it is often held to provide financial security to individuals with moderate incomes. In such a case, these individuals share little common ground with the tax shelter investors. The relief is provided solely to individuals and certain trusts and estates. Regular C corporations are ineligible.

Under the exception, a taxpayer who *actively* participates (in contrast to materially participates) may deduct up to $25,000 of losses attributable to rental real estate

---

[18] See Reg. § 1.469-2T(f)(2).

annually. The $25,000 allowance is reduced by 50 percent of the excess of the taxpayer's A.G.I. over $100,000. This relationship may be expressed as follows:

$$\text{Reduction in \$25,000 allowance} = 50\% \ (\text{A.G.I.} - \$100,000)$$

Based on this formula, high-income taxpayers (i.e., those with A.G.I. of $150,000 or more) cannot take advantage of this provision. A.G.I. for this purpose is computed without regard to contributions to individual retirement accounts, taxable social security, and any net passive losses that might be deductible. Any portion of the rental loss that is not deductible may be carried over and deducted subject to the same limitations in the following years.

> **Example 27.** L moved to a new home this year. Instead of selling his old home, L decided to rent it out to supplement his income. During the first year, rents were $3,000 while expenses including maintenance, depreciation, interest, utilities, and taxes were $10,000. L's A.G.I. is $40,000. L may deduct the $7,000 loss for A.G.I. Had L's A.G.I. been $140,000, he could have deducted only $5,000 and carried over $2,000 to the following year. This computation is illustrated below.

Loss allowance		$ 25,000
Phase-out:		
A.G.I.	$ 140,000	
Threshold	(100,000)	
Excess A.G.I.	$ 40,000	
Rate	×50%	
Phase-out		(20,000)
Maximum loss allowed		$ 5,000

It should be emphasized that the taxpayer can use this exception only if the property is considered rental real estate. It cannot be used for losses from rental of personal property. More important, the real estate is not considered a "rental" activity where the rental period is either 1 to 7 days or between 8 and 30 days and significant services are performed.[19] For example, consider the typical investor who owns a vacation condominium. If the average rental of the condominium is 1 to 7 days, the condominium is not considered rental property and the $25,000 exception does not apply. The result is the same if the average rental period is between 8 and 30 days and significant services are provided. Note that even though the $25,000 exception is not available in either case, all is not necessarily lost. In both situations, the condominium is treated as a nonrental activity. In such case, the taxpayer will be able to deduct all losses if there is material participation.[20]

> **Example 28.** M lives in Orlando, where she practices law. M owns a condominium, which she rents out on a daily basis to tourists. M runs ads in the local newspaper, makes arrangements for the rental, and cleans the unit as needed. In this case, it appears that the activity is not a rental business because of the short-term rental. As a result, the $25,000 exception for rentals does not apply. However, M still may be able to deduct a loss. Since the property by definition is not a rental activity due to

---

[19] For an excellent discussion of this topic and issue see Bomyea and Marucheck, "Rental of Residences," *The Tax Adviser* (September 1990), p. 543.

[20] See *Steven D. Rapp*, T.C. Memo 1999-249, 78 TCM 175 and *Walter A. Barniskis*, T.C. Memo 1999-258, 78 TCM 226.

the short-term rental period, it is—by default—a nonrental activity. Accordingly, the loss would be deductible if she materially participates in the activity. For example, if M spent more than 100 hours in the activity and more than anyone else or met any of the other six material participation tests, the loss would be deductible.

As noted above, the Code draws a distinction between material and active participation. The primary difference concerns the taxpayer's degree of involvement in operations. For example, a taxpayer is actively involved if he or she participates in management decisions such as approving new tenants, deciding on rental terms, approving capital or repair expenditures, or if he or she arranges for others to provide services such as repairs. In all cases, the taxpayer is not treated as actively participating in the activity if less than a 10 percent interest is owned. On the other hand, the taxpayer is not presumed to actively participate if the interest is 10 percent or more. The above standard still must be satisfied.

Real Estate Developer Exception. Under the basic rules described above, taxpayers who are engaged in the rental real estate business (e.g., owners of warehouses, shopping centers, or office buildings) cannot deduct losses from such business activities since the law presumes that virtually all long-term rental real estate activities are passive. Note that this treatment occurs regardless of the amount of time and energy spent by the taxpayer in such activities. The level of the taxpayer's participation is irrelevant. After much debate, however, Congress finally agreed in 1994 that the passive loss rules were aimed at passive investors in real estate and not those who were in the real estate business. For this reason, it took steps to enable these individuals to deduct losses arising from these activities. This special relief is granted only if the individual can pass certain tests that effectively establish that he or she is truly in the real estate business.

An individual is *eligible* to deduct losses from rental real estate if both of the following conditions are met:[21]

1. Services representing more than 50 percent of the total personal services performed by the individual in all trades or businesses during the tax year are performed in *real property trades or businesses* in which the taxpayer materially participates during the year. For this purpose, real property trades or businesses include real property development, redevelopment, construction, acquisition, conversion, rental, operation, management, leasing, and brokerage. In the case of a closely held C corporation, this test is met if more than 50 percent of the gross receipts of such corporation are derived from real property businesses in which the corporation materially participates.

2. The individual performs more than 750 hours of services in *real property trades or businesses.*

If a joint return is filed, the special relief is available if either spouse separately satisfies the requirements. Note that for this purpose, the couple *cannot* aggregate their hours.

Observe that satisfaction of these two tests merely opens the door for possible deduction of losses. In order to treat the losses as nonpassive, the taxpayer must still meet the material participation requirements (e.g., spend more than 500 hours in the activity). For this purpose, each activity is normally treated as a separate activity. However, the taxpayer may elect to aggregate such activities. In most cases, it would seem that those who are eligible and who elect to aggregate their real property businesses should be able to meet the material participation tests. It should also be emphasized that personal services as an *employee* in a real property business are not

---

[21] § 469(c)(7).

treated as performed in the real property business unless the individual owns at least 5 percent of the business.

> **Example 29.** G graduated from the Vanderbilt law school in 1961 and has been practicing his trade ever since. Over the years, however, he has accumulated a number of properties. As a result, he is increasingly spending more time being a real estate magnate and less time being a lawyer. Currently, he owns, operates, and manages a small shopping center and several duplexes. Each of these rental activities produces a loss, primarily due to depreciation. According to G's detailed diary of how he spends his time, he worked 40 hours a week for 50 weeks during the year for a total of 2,000 hours. The majority, 1,100 hours, was devoted to his real estate ventures. The other 900 hours related to his law practice. In this case, G meets both tests that enable him to treat the rental operations as nonrental activities: (1) more than 50% of his personal services were performed in real property businesses, and (2) his 1,100 hours of service in these businesses exceeded the 750-hour threshold. Although the rental taint is removed, this does not necessarily mean G is allowed to deduct the losses. He must still satisfy the material participation tests. Whether this final requirement is met depends on whether G elects to aggregate all of the activities. If so, his 1,100 hours of participation is greater than the 500 hours required and he would be entitled to deduct all of the losses.

RECHARACTERIZED PASSIVE INCOME

As is evident throughout the passive loss Regulations, the IRS was concerned that taxpayers might create passive income which could be used to absorb otherwise nondeductible passive losses. Nowhere is this more evident than in the recharacterization rules. In certain situations, income that is characterized under the general rules as passive is recharacterized under a special rule and treated as active. An example of the type of recharacterization that can occur was discussed earlier in connection with SPAs. As noted in that discussion, income from SPAs that fail to meet the 500-hour test would normally be treated as passive, but under the special recharacterization rule it is treated as active. There are several other situations when this might occur. Consequently, before it can be concluded that income is passive, the recharacterization rules must be considered. These rules operate to convert the following types of income to nonpassive or active income (rather than passive).[22]

1. *Significant Participation Activities:* Income from "significant participation activities" that fail to meet the 500-hour test.

2. *Rental of Nondeductible Property:* Income from rental activities is active if less than 30 percent of the basis of the property rented is not depreciable (e.g., rental of land). (Losses are passive.)

3. *Developer Sales of Rental Property:* Rental income, including gain on the sale of rental property, if (1) gain on the sale is included in income during the taxable year; (2) rental of the property commenced less than 24 months before the date of disposition; and (3) the taxpayer performed sufficient services that enhanced the value of the rental property.

4. *Self-Rented Property:* Income from rental of property to an activity in which the taxpayer materially participates, other than related C corporations.

---

[22] Temp. Reg. § 1.469-2T(f).

5. *Licensing of Intangible Property:* Royalty income from a pass-through entity that the taxpayer acquired after the entity created the intangible property.

6. *Equity-Financed Lending Activity:* Income from the trade or business of lending money if certain conditions are satisfied.

Example 30. Dr. S owns a dental practice that he operates through a corporation, Family Dentistry, Inc. He also has substantial passive losses derived from two rental properties, an apartment and shopping center. Hoping to generate some passive income to absorb such losses, he purchased a building and leased it to his corporation for $25,000 this year. The corporation uses the building to house the doctor's dental practice. The self-rental rule treats the rental income received by Dr. S as portfolio income since S materially participates in the corporation to which the property is rented.[23]

In a similar move, S and his brother, B, formed an LLC to establish a trailer park. The LLC purchased the land for $300,000 and made depreciable improvements on the land of $100,000. Any rental income derived from the park is treated as portfolio income rather than passive income since the basis of the nondepreciable property (unadjusted for depreciation) is less than 30% of the basis of all the property used in the rental activity ($100,000/$400,000 = 25%). Any gain on the sale of the partnership interest would also be treated as portfolio income. Note that this recharacterization rule is usually triggered when the bulk of the rental property's cost is in the land rather than the improvements.

PASSIVE-ACTIVITY INTEREST EXPENSE

One aspect related to the passive loss rules that requires special attention is the treatment of interest expense. As discussed in Chapter 11, Congress has imposed severe limitations on the deduction of interest. Interest expense incurred by a taxpayer to finance an investment in a passive activity is subject to the passive loss rules and is not considered investment interest. Similarly, interest expense incurred by an activity that is considered passive (e.g., a partnership if the taxpayer is a limited partner) is subject to the passive loss rules.[24]

Example 31. Dr. P borrowed $50,000 and invested it by acquiring an interest in a limited partnership that produces movies. Interest on the loan for the year is $5,000. P can deduct the interest only to the extent of any passive income that he may have.

Example 32. Assume the partnership above incurs interest expense related to loans obtained to acquire equipment used in its operations. The interest is treated as a normal deduction and is used in arriving at the partnership's net income or loss for the year. This year, the partnership suffered a net loss including deductions for interest expense. Dr. P is allowed to deduct his share of the loss only to the extent he has passive income from other activities.

---

[23] *Krukowski*, 114 T.C. 366 (2000).

[24] § 163(d)(3)(B).

✅ *CHECK YOUR KNOWLEDGE*

Try the following true-false questions.

Review Question 1. This year T's tax records revealed that he had income consisting of a salary of $90,000, dividends of $10,000, and a capital gain from the sale of stock of $5,000. In addition, he received a Schedule K-1 from a partnership in which he is a limited partner. According to the K-1, his share of the partnership's loss for the year was $50,000. T can deduct $15,000 of this loss (i.e., to the extent of his passive dividend and capital gain income).

False. While a taxpayer is entitled to deduct passive losses to the extent of passive income, passive income does not include dividends, interest, capital gains, etc., which are considered portfolio income.

Review Question 2. A passive loss that cannot be deducted in the current year is generally suspended. The suspended loss is deductible only in the year in which the property to which the loss relates is sold, since the sale affirms the fact that the taxpayer has actually suffered an economic loss.

False. The above is true for the most part, but suspended passive losses are not frozen to thaw only when the taxpayer sells his or her interest. Passive losses that cannot be deducted in a particular year are carried over to the following year and treated as if they occurred in that subsequent year. Accordingly, the suspended loss can be deducted to the extent that the taxpayer has passive income in the following year. In addition, the taxpayer is allowed to deduct the suspended losses whenever the property to which the loss relates is sold.

Review Question 3. A capital gain from the sale of stock in an S corporation in which the taxpayer does not materially participate is considered portfolio income.

False. Capital gains are normally considered portfolio income, but when such gain arises from the sale of the taxpayer's interest in a passive activity, it is treated as passive income.

Review Question 4. The passive loss rules do not apply to regular C corporations since the losses do not flow through and are not available to the individual shareholders.

False. The passive loss rules do apply to personal service corporations and closely held corporations (i.e., corporations where five or fewer individuals own more than 50 percent of the stock). Personal service corporations must play by the same rules applicable to individuals. Closely held corporations, however, are allowed to offset passive losses against income from operations *other than* portfolio income.

Review Question 5. Moe, Larry, and Curly pooled all of their savings to start a new restaurant, Stooges. Stooges is operated as an S corporation, and its stock is owned equally by the threesome. In its first year, the restaurant produced a loss. Depending on the circumstances, Moe may be able to deduct his share of the loss this year while Larry and Curly may not be able to deduct their shares.

True. Whether a deduction is allowed for the loss depends on whether the taxpayer materially participates in the activity. Moe may be actively involved on a daily basis, and Larry and Curly may be passive investors. In such a case, only Moe would be able to deduct the loss currently.

Review Question 6. D operates a small bed-and-breakfast motel. Most of his customers rent rooms for one or two days. D's operation is not considered a rental activity for purposes of the passive-loss rules.

True. An activity is not considered a rental for purposes of the passive-loss rules if the average period of customer use is seven days or less.

Review Question 7. T owns a duplex and rents it out. She normally signs six-month leases with her tenants. Any loss related to the rental is considered a passive loss and is not deductible regardless of T's participation.

True. This activity is considered a rental since the average period of customer use exceeds 30 days and T does not provide any extraordinary services. Losses on long-term rental real estate are normally not deductible except to the extent of passive income unless the taxpayer can qualify under one of two exceptions. First, she is permitted to deduct up to $25,000 of losses from rental real estate if she actively participates and her adjusted gross income is less than $150,000. In addition, a special exception allows individuals who spend more than 50 percent of their time in real property businesses and more than 750 hours in such businesses to treat the activities as nonrental and deduct any losses if they materially participate in such activities.

Review Question 8. Several years ago, Q purchased an interest in a limited partnership. This year his share of the partnership's loss was $10,000. Assuming Q's adjusted gross income is $80,000, he may deduct the loss since it is less than $25,000.

False. The loss would be treated as a passive loss since Q does not materially participate in the partnership activity. The de minimis exception that enables a taxpayer to deduct up to $25,000 of passive losses annually applies only to losses from rental real estate activities in which the taxpayer actively participates.

Review Question 9. B opened her first Planet Jupiter Cafe five years ago in Aspen. Now she has five restaurants, each located in a different resort. Since each store is located in a separate city, she must treat each store as a separate activity.

False. A taxpayer is required to treat one or more activities as a single activity if the activities constitute an appropriate economic unit (AEU). The Regulations give the taxpayer a great deal of flexibility in determining what constitutes an AEU. Thus, the taxpayer could treat each as a separate activity, combine all and treat as a single activity, or use some other grouping that may be appropriate under the Regulations.

Review Question 10. B is a college professor who recently got involved in a mail-order smoke alarm business. This year he spent about 100 hours in the activity, taking orders and arranging to fill them. B materially participates in the business.

True. Under the general rule, a taxpayer is considered a material participant if he or she spends more than 500 hours in the activity during the year. Although B does not meet the general rule, he does meet an alternative test; that is, his participation constitutes substantially all of the participation in the activity. Therefore the activity is not a passive activity.

Review Question 11. G owns two businesses, a convenience grocery store and a dry cleaners. For the past several years, the grocery has not done as well as G had hoped and she has lost money. This year, G did not play as much golf as usual and spent about 400 hours trying to turn the business around. She spent about 300 hours at the cleaners.

Each business has a number of full-time employees. G may offset any loss attributable to the grocery store against the profits from her dry cleaners.

True. The restaurant and the dry cleaners are considered significant participation activities since G spends more than 100 hours in each. If the total participation in all SPAs exceeds 500 hours, the taxpayer is deemed to materially participate in each of the activities. In this case, the total participation in all SPAs exceeds the 500-hour threshold, and G is therefore deemed to materially participate in each of the activities. Thus, she can use the loss in the grocery activity to offset the income from the cleaning business.

Review Question 12. Same as above, except G spends 100 hours at the cleaners, 300 hours at the grocery, and the remaining time at the beach. G may offset any loss attributable to the grocery against the profits from her dry cleaners.

False. In this case, G's combined participation in the SPAs does not exceed 500 hours. This is the "heads we win, tails you lose" situation: the loss is passive, the income is nonpassive, and the two cannot be combined.

Review Question 13. J borrowed $100,000 to purchase an interest in the Lockwood Limited Partnership, which operates several apartment complexes. This year J paid $8,000 interest on the loan to acquire his interest. In addition, J's share of the partnership's losses was $10,000. J has no passive income. The loss is a passive loss and cannot be deducted, but the interest is treated as investment interest and is deductible to the extent of J's investment income.

False. J simply treats the $8,000 of interest expense as another operating expense of the partnership, increasing the loss from $10,000 to $18,000. None of the loss, including the interest, is deductible.

RENTAL OF RESIDENCE (VACATION HOME RENTALS)

Section 280A imposes restrictions on the deduction of expenses related to rental of a residence if the taxpayer is considered as using the residence primarily for personal purposes rather than for making a profit. These restrictions are aimed at the perceived abuse existing in the area of vacation home rental. Prior to the enactment of § 280A, many felt that personal enjoyment was the predominant motive for purchasing a vacation home. Any rental of the vacation home served merely to minimize the personal expense of ownership and not to produce income.

BASIC RULES

In 1976, Congress prescribed an objective method for ascertaining the purpose of the rental activity as well as the amount of the deduction. According to this approach, the expenses incurred by the taxpayer in owning and operating the home (e.g., interest, taxes, maintenance, utilities, and depreciation) must first be allocated between personal use and rental use. The deductibility of the expenses allocated to each then depends on whether the home is considered the taxpayer's *residence or rental property*. This latter determination is made based on the owner's personal use and the amount of rental activity.[25]

---

[25] §§ 280A(c)(5) and 280A(d) through (g).

1. *Nominal Rentals:* If the residence is rented out fewer than 15 days, all rental income is excluded from gross income and no deduction is allowed for rental expenses. Otherwise allowable deductions, such as those for qualified residence interest, real estate taxes, and casualty losses may be deducted *from* A.G.I.

2. *Used as a "Residence":* If the taxpayer uses the vacation home for more than 14 days or 10 percent of the number of days the property is actually rented out, whichever is greater, the home is treated as his or her residence and deductions are restricted as explained below. A typical taxpayer caught by this rule is the owner of a vacation home who uses it for more than two weeks and rents it out to defray the cost.

   a. *Expenses allocable to the rental use:* These expenses are deductible to the extent of gross income less otherwise allowable deductions. Any deductions in excess of gross income can be carried over and deducted to the extent of any future income. These expenses are deductible *for* A.G.I. since they are related to rental use. Note that the passive-loss rules do not apply since the property is used as a residence and not a rental.

   b. *Expenses allocable to personal use:* Since these expenses are considered personal, they may be deducted only if they are specifically authorized by the Code. Allocable property taxes are deductible without limitation as an itemized deduction since such expenses are fully deductible regardless of the activity in which they are incurred. Interest expense *may* be deductible as an itemized deduction. Allocable interest is normally qualified residence interest since the home—*in this case*—is considered the taxpayer's residence (e.g., because it is used more than 14 days). However, if the home is not the primary or secondary residence of the taxpayer (e.g., the taxpayer has several vacation homes), no deduction would be available. The other operating expenses are not deductible.

3. *Used as "Rental Property":* If the taxpayer does not use the property extensively (i.e., more than the greater of 14 days or 10 percent of the number of days rented out), then the property is effectively treated as rental property.

   a. *Expenses allocable to the rental use:* These expenses are deductible subject only to the restrictions on passive losses. If the property's average rental period is either (1) 1–7 days or (2) 8–30 days *and* significant services are provided, the property is not rental property under the passive loss rules. Thus, the treatment of any loss depends on whether the taxpayer materially participates in this "nonrental activity." If the taxpayer materially participates, any loss would not be passive and would therefore be fully deductible. (See *Example 20* earlier in this chapter.) If the property is considered a rental (e.g., perhaps under the facts-and-circumstances test or if the rental is 8–30 days and no significant services are provided) and the taxpayer is considered as having met the active participation standard, the taxpayer may qualify for the rental exception under the passive loss rules. This would allow the taxpayer to deduct up to $25,000 in losses annually. Any deductions would be for A.G.I.

   b. *Expenses allocable to personal use:* As noted above, since these expenses are personal, they may be deducted only if they are specifically authorized by the Code. In this case, property taxes would continue to be fully deductible. On the other hand, none of the interest expense would be deductible as qualified residence interest since the vacation home is not considered a "residence" (because the taxpayer did *not* use it more than 14 days). However, the excess interest expense would be treated as investment interest and could be deducted to the extent of investment income. Other operating expenses would not be deductible.

This treatment is summarized in Exhibit 12-1.

EXHIBIT 12-1
Vacation Homes—Summary of § 280A Rules

Character of vacation home:	Residence	Rental property

Characterization:
  Personal use exceeding the greater of
    1. 14 days, or
    2. 10 percent of days rented out
	Yes	No

Expenses allocable to rental use:	Limited to gross income by § 280A	Limited by passive-loss rules Rental exception may apply

Expenses allocable to personal use:
  Taxes
  Interest
  Other
	Deductible
	Qualified residence interest
	Not deductible
		Deductible
		Investment interest
		Not deductible

For purposes of the owner use test, the number of days a unit is rented out does not include any day the unit is used for personal purposes. The unit is generally treated as used for personal purposes on any day where the owner or a member of his or her family uses it for any portion of the day for personal purposes or the unit is rented at less than a fair rental.[26] A day on which the taxpayer spends at least two-thirds of the time at the unit (or if less than two-thirds then at least eight hours) on repairs is not counted as a personal day. This is true even though individuals who accompany the taxpayer do not perform repairs or maintenance.[27]

> **Example 33.** In 1985 Floyd Toups and his wife purchased a vacation home for $120,000. The unit was one of 155 individually owned "cottages" located at Callaway Gardens, a favorite vacation resort in Pine Mountain, Georgia, about 70 miles south of Atlanta. The units were marketed and managed by a development company that received 50% of the net rental income for its services. Each owner was entitled to rent-free use of the cottage for no more than 14 days during the year. On their 1988, 1989, and 1990 returns, the Toupses took the position that the cottage, which was generating losses, was a *nonrental* activity since the average period of customer use of the cottage was seven days or less, and accordingly the Toupses deducted the losses on their Schedule C on the grounds that they materially participated in the activity. However, the IRS disagreed and assessed deficiencies exceeding $3,000 for each year. In the Tax Court, the Toupses attempted to justify their position, explaining that they had spent 341 hours each year in activities related to the rental of the unit. They listed 13 activities, which they believed supported their claim. According to the couple they (1) provided funds for the purchase; (2) prepared an annual budget; (3) prepared a cash flow analysis; (4) provided a rental agency for renting their unit; (5) marketed the resort and rental of the cottage; (6) met with other owners; (7) established rental rates for the cottages with other owners; (8) inspected the cottage and common areas at least twice a year;

---

[26] § 280A(d)(2).

[27] Prop. Reg. § 1.280A-1(e)(4) and § 280A(d)(2).

(9) reviewed monthly reports received from the rental agent; (10) reviewed other correspondence from the rental agent; (11) reviewed advertising brochures about the resort received from the rental agent; (12) received and deposited net revenues received from the rental; and (13) issued checks for expenses of the cottage. The Tax Court agreed that the property was not "rental property" under the passive-loss rules and, therefore, did not qualify for the $25,000 allowance available for rental real estate. Unfortunately, the court did not agree with the taxpayers' claim that they materially participated in the activity. The court found that the activities of the taxpayer did not constitute material participation because they were not involved in the day-to-day operation of their cottage or in its management. The activities of the taxpayers were considered to be activities of an investor, and therefore their losses were passive.[28]

ALLOCATION OF EXPENSES

As discussed above, the treatment of expenses incurred in operating a vacation home varies depending on whether the expenses are allocated to rental or personal use. Consequently, the critical first step in applying the vacation home rules is allocation of the expenses. Once expenses are properly allocated between rental and personal use, the appropriate limitations can be applied.

Vacation home expenses can be classified as either direct and indirect. Direct expenses are those that are *not* related to the general operation or maintenance of the unit but which are incurred to obtain tenants.[29] For example, advertising, brokers' fees, office supplies, and depreciation on office equipment used in the rental activity are considered directly related to the rental. These direct expenses reduce gross rental receipts to arrive at gross rental income. All other expenses are considered indirect expenses—including otherwise allowable deductions such as interest and taxes—and must be allocated *between* personal and rental use.

In allocating the expenses between personal and rental use, two different methods are used. Under the so-called *Bolton* approach, otherwise allowable deductions such as interest and taxes are assumed to *accrue daily* regardless of use.[30] Consequently, the fraction for allocating these items to the rental use was

$$\text{Otherwise allowable deduction} \times \frac{\text{Number of rental days}}{365} = \text{Portion attributable to rental use}$$

In contrast, expenses such as utilities, maintenance, and depreciation are considered a *function of use*. As a result, the fraction used for allocating these items to the rental use was

$$\text{Operating expenses} \times \frac{\text{Number of rental days}}{\text{Rental + Personal days}} = \text{Portion attributable to rental use}$$

The method of allocating expenses and their treatment is summarized in Exhibit 12-2 below.

Note that the court's approach in *Bolton* (which uses a denominator of 365 rather than total personal and rental days used) allocates less interest and taxes to the rental portion and, therefore, more to the residential or personal portion. This approach enables the taxpayer to deduct a larger amount of expenses allocable to the rental. At the same time, this method increases the amount of the itemized deduction for interest and taxes. The end result is that a larger deduction can be secured using the *Bolton* approach.

---

[28]   *Floyd A. and Joanna Toups*, 66 T.C.M. 370, T.C. Memo 1993-359.

[29]   Prop. Reg. § 1.280A-3(d)(2).

[30]   *Dorance D. Bolton*, 77 T.C. 104 (1982), *aff'd.* at 82-2 USTC ¶9699, 51 AFTR2d 83-305 (CA-9, 1982).

Unfortunately, the IRS continues to oppose *Bolton* so taxpayers must proceed with caution.[31] The example below follows *Bolton*.

EXHIBIT 12-2
Vacation Homes—Expense Allocation Rules

Type of Expense	Personal Use	Rental Use
Directly related (advertising, brokers' fees)	None allocated	Gross rental receipts − Directly related expenses Sch. E
Otherwise allowable (qualified residence interest, taxes, etc.)	Itemized deduction*	Gross rental income − Otherwise allowable Sch. E Limit on indirect rental expenses
Indirect (maintenance, depreciation, utilities, etc.)	Not deductible	− Indirect expenses Sch E**

*Interest allocated to personal use:

(1) if the property is treated as a residence, deductible as qualified residence interest;
(2) if not a residence, the interest may be deductible as investment interest to the extent of investment income.

Taxes allocated to personal use are fully deductible in either case.

**Indirect expenses allocated to rental use:

(1) if the property is treated as a residence, such expenses are limited to remaining rental income;
(2) if not a residence but a rental, passive loss rules apply unless not considered a rental (i.e., average customer use does not exceed seven days);
(3) if rental for passive loss purposes, limited to passive income and $25,000 allowance may be available;
(4) if not a rental for passive activity purposes, loss deductible if materially participate

> **Example 34.** A owns a condominium in a ski resort. During the year, A uses the condominium as a secondary residence for 30 days and rents it out for 90 days. The condominium is not used the remainder of the year. During the year, A's rental agent, R, collected rents of $5,000. The agent's standard fee was 30% of rents; therefore the charge was $1,500 and R sent Form 1099 to A showing net rental income of $3,500. Total expenses for the entire year include maintenance and utilities of $1,000, interest of $6,200, taxes of $1,100, and $2,000 depreciation on the entire cost of the unit.
>
> A's use for 30 days is more than 14 days, the greater of 14 or 9 days (10% of the 90 days rented). Therefore, the unit is treated as a residence. For this reason, expenses attributable to the rental are deductible to the extent of gross income as reduced by otherwise allowable deductions (the interest and taxes). Deductions are computed and deducted in the *following order:*

---

[31]   § 280A(e). The IRS continues to take the position that all expenses should be allocated based on use. See *Residential Rental Property* (IRS Publication 527, 2004, p. 5).

Gross rental receipts	$ 5,000
Deduct directly related expenses (brokerage fee).	−1,500
Gross rental income.	$ 3,500
Deduct allocable portion of otherwise allowable deductions:	
Interest and taxes [$7,300 × (90 ÷ 365)]	−1,800
Gross income limitation	$ 1,700
Deduct allocable portion of deductions other than	
those otherwise allowable and depreciation:	
Utilities and maintenance	
[$1,000 × 90 ÷ (30 + 90)]	− 750
Gross income limitation	$ 950
Deduct allocable portion of depreciation:	
Depreciation [$2,000 × 90 ÷ (30 + 90)] = $1,500	
but limited to $950 balance of gross income	−950
Net income.	$ 0

All of the above deductions are *for* A.G.I. The balance of interest and taxes not allocated to the rental use, $5,500 ($7,300 − $1,800), is deductible if the taxpayer itemizes deductions. Note that the interest in this case is qualified residence interest since the unit is treated as A's residence. The deduction for maintenance and utilities is not limited by gross income since all of these expenses attributable to the rental activity are deductible. The $250 ($1,000 − $750) remaining balance of maintenance and utilities would not be deductible in any case since it represents the expenses attributable to personal use. Of the remaining depreciation balance of $1,050 ($2,000 − $950), $550 ($1,500 − $950) attributable to the rental is not deductible due to the gross income limitation but may be carried over to subsequent years. The other $500 of depreciation is not deductible since it is the portion attributable to personal use. Also note that only the $950 of depreciation allowed is treated as a reduction in the basis of A's condominium.

Example 35. Assume the same facts as in *Example 34*, except that A used the condominium for 10 days rather than 30. Also assume that the rental is on a three-month basis to locals and no services are provided. In such case, the condominium would be treated as rental property rather than as a residence since A stayed less than 14 days. In addition, the $25,000 rental exception of the passive loss rules would apply since there is a long-term rental and no significant services are provided. A's deduction would be computed as follows:

Gross rental receipts	$ 5,000
Deduct directly related expenses (brokerage fee).	−1,500
Gross rental income.	$ 3,500
Deduct allocable portion of otherwise allowable deductions	
($7,300 × 90 ÷ 365)	−1,800
Deduct allocable portion of utilities and maintenance	
[$1,000 × 90 ÷ (90 + 10)]	−900
Deduct allocable portion of depreciation	
[$2,000 × 90 ÷ (90 + 10)]	−1,800
Loss.	$ (1,000)

In this case, a loss is created that may offset any other income of the taxpayer under the $25,000 rental loss exception. In contrast to *Example 34* above, however, the balance of the interest expense, $5,500 ($7,300 − $1,800), would not be deductible as qualified residence interest since the property does not qualify as a residence. Nevertheless, the taxpayer may be able to deduct the amount as investment interest to the extent of any net investment income that he or she may have from other investments. Lacking investment income, the taxpayer would be better off using the condominium more in order that he could qualify as a second residence and deduct the interest. The balance of the other expenses would not be deductible.

The vacation home rules, as discussed above, could operate to eliminate legitimate deductions for those taxpayers who convert their personal residence for rental during the year. In these cases, the owner usually uses the residence for more than 14 days and thus deductions are limited. However, § 280A(d) provides relief for taxpayers in these situations. The provision accomplishes this goal by not counting as personal use days any days of personal use during the year immediately before (or after) the rental period begins (or ends). This rule, often referred to as the *qualified rental period exception*, applies only if the rental period is at least a year (or if less than a year, the house is sold at the end of the rental period).

Example 36. B lived in her home from January through July. In August, she moved into a condominium and decided to convert her old home to rental property. B was able to find a tenant who leased the old home for a year. Under the normal rules of § 280A, B's deductions related to the old home would be limited to gross income since her personal use exceeded 14 days. The relief measure of § 280A(d) removes this limitation because the seven months of personal use preceding the one-year rental period are not counted as personal use days. As a result, B would treat the lease as a rental activity and could deduct expenses subject to the passive loss rules, possibly qualifying for the $25,000 exception.

✓ CHECK YOUR KNOWLEDGE

Review Question 1. During the Olympics held in Atlanta during 1996, many Georgians left town and rented their homes out for the two weeks the games were in town. It was rumored that some of the mansions were rented for more than $100,000 during this time. How would these temporary landlords treat the income?

Under § 280A, if the home is rented out for less than 15 days, all of the rental income is excluded and none of the expenses allocable to the rental period are deductible. Consequently, these temporary landlords received a real windfall because they were allowed to exclude all of the income.

Review Question 2. T owns a condominium in Vail. This year his rental agent was able to rent it out for 100 days (most guests stayed for six days). Unfortunately, he was able to use the condo for personal purposes for only one week in January because of a skiing accident in which he broke his shoulder. Interest expense and taxes allocable to the personal use were $500. The net loss attributable to the rental during the remainder of the year was $4,000. What amount can T deduct? Is the property considered rental property subject to the passive loss rules?

Since the personal use was nominal (i.e., not more than the greater of ten percent of the number of days rented or two weeks), the property is not considered a residence. Moreover, it is not considered rental property under the passive loss rules since the average rental period was less than eight days. Thus, it is considered a nonrental activity with the treatment dependent on whether T materially participates in the activity. Since he does not materially participate, the loss is a passive loss and is not deductible unless he has other passive income. The interest attributable to the period of personal use is not qualified residence interest since the unit did not qualify as a residence. Instead the interest is treated as investment interest and is deductible to the extent of investment income.

Review Question 3. W owns a condominium in St. John in the Caribbean. She rented it out for seven months (one month at a time) during the year but used it personally for the entire month of January. Can W treat the activity as a rental activity and take advantage of the $25,000 de minimis exception that would allow her to deduct a loss from the property?

No. If a taxpayer uses a home for more than two weeks or 10 percent of the number of days the unit is rented, she treats the home as a residence. In this case, the taxpayer used the home 31 days for personal purposes, thereby exceeding the threshold and converting the property to a residence. Any interest is deductible as qualified residence interest, assuming this is a first or second home. On the other hand, rental expenses can be deducted only to the extent of rental income. The excess expenses may be carried over and deducted in subsequent years to the extent the unit generates income. The passive loss rules do not apply, and the $25,000 allowance is not available.

PROBLEM MATERIALS

DISCUSSION QUESTIONS

12-1 *Tax Shelters and the Solution.* In 1982, T purchased for $10,000 an interest in Neptune III, a limited partnership created by Dandy Development Company to finance and build a 25-story office building in downtown Houston. T, who was in the 50 percent tax bracket, hoped that this investment would significantly cut her taxes.
   a. Explain the features of the investment that during that period made such investments attractive and might produce the benefits desired by T.
   b. Explain what steps Congress took in 1986 to eliminate the benefits of investments in such activities as Neptune III. Comment in some detail on the approach used by Congress to accomplish its objective.
   c. What steps might you have suggested had you been advising Congress on the restriction of tax shelter?

12-2 *Effect of Code § 469.* D owns and operates several ski rental shops in Vail, Aspen, Beaver Creek, and Steamboat Springs. Over the years, the shops have had their ups and downs, with profits in some years, losses in others. Recently, D has spent less and less time at the shop, letting his employees do most of the work.
   a. What is the significance should the business be characterized as a passive activity?
   b. Should D worry about his business being treated as a passive activity? When is an activity considered passive?
   c. Does the fact that D's business is a rental operation have any bearing on the nature of the activity?
   d. What are the aggregation or grouping rules and why might they be important in D's case?

12-3 *Taxpayers Subject to § 469* Dr. R has been quite successful over the years. She left St. James hospital in 1981 and started her own sports medicine practice, The Sports Institute Inc., a regular C corporation. After building this operation into a thriving practice, she branched out. In 1990, she and a good friend opened their own restaurant, The Diner, a partnership. In 1993, her college roommate persuaded R to invest and buy stock in a new venture, Compatible PCS, a corporation that manufactured personal computers. Compatible PCS was owned by R and three other individuals and operated as a regular C corporation until this year, when it converted to S status. Dr. R's other investments include a single family house that she rents out, a limited partnership interest in an oil and gas operation, and a limited partnership interest in a business that develops land into shopping centers. Explain how R is affected by the passive loss rules.

12-4 *Definition of an Activity and Planning.* D owns several businesses, including an indoor soccer facility, a gas station adjacent to the soccer facility (he bought it with the intention of someday expanding the soccer facility), and a fast-food restaurant across the street from the soccer facility. Within the soccer facility, he has rented space to a local soccer retail store. He also rents space in the facility to another company, which operates a small bar and restaurant. In any one year, each business may be profitable or may have losses. For simplicity, assume each business is operated as a sole proprietorship.

   a. Assuming one of the businesses is profitable, would D prefer passive or active income?

   b. Assuming one of the businesses has losses, would D prefer a passive or active loss?

   c. Discuss the passive loss rules, how they might apply to D, and what planning might be considered. Identify as many questions as possible that might be asked in determining how the passive loss rules apply to D.

12-5 *Aggregating Activities.* Aggregation of activities may be required for purposes of the material participation tests.

   a. Explain the general rules concerning aggregation and their purpose.

   b. Explain when this rule is beneficial and when it is detrimental for the taxpayer.

12-6 *Rental Activities and Material Participation.* T owns a 10-unit apartment complex. He not only manages the apartments but also performs all of the routine maintenance and repairs as well as keeping the books. Most of the leases that he signs with tenants are for one year. This year the complex produced a loss of $30,000. How will T treat the loss, assuming his adjusted gross income from other sources is $90,000?

12-7 *Recharacterization.* Briefly explain the purpose of the recharacterization rules and why they must not be overlooked when dealing with passive activities.

12-8 *Credits from a Passive Activity.* P is considering rehabilitating a home in a historic neighborhood. She hopes to qualify for both the rehabilitation credit and the low-income housing credit.

   a. Assuming she qualifies, explain how she will compute the amount of credit that she may claim.

   b. P's accountant has explained the limitations that apply to losses and has indicated to P that any losses on the rental that are denied currently will ultimately be allowed once P sells the property. Can the same be said of credits?

12-9 *Grouping Activities.* Urged by their accountants to reduce their tax liability, a group of orthopedic surgeons invested in real estate that produced passive losses. Prior to 1986, these losses did in fact serve as tax shelters. After 1986, however, the passive loss rules significantly restricted the tax benefits of the investments. Consequently, the accountants prodded the doctors to form a partnership to acquire and operate X-ray equipment. The doctors do not participate in the X-ray partnership, and, therefore, any income produced by the partnership is passive income. Most of the income from operation of the partnership is derived from services provided to the doctors themselves. Will this scheme successfully produce passive income that can be used to absorb passive losses?

12-10 *Interest Expense.* This year Dr. Z purchased a 20 percent interest in a partnership that is building an office building in downtown Dallas. To finance the acquisition, he used his line of credit at the bank and borrowed $100,000. As a result, he paid $10,000 in interest during the year.

    a. How will Dr. Z treat the interest expense?

    b. After the building was completed, the partnership secured permanent financing. This year the partnership paid mortgage interest of $700,000, of which $14,000 represented Dr. Z's allocable share. How will Dr. Z treat the interest?

PROBLEMS

12-11 *Identifying Activities.* For each of the following situations, indicate the number of activities in which the taxpayer participates.

    a. S owns and operates an ice cream store in Southwoods Mall. He is also a camera buff and owns a camera shop in the same mall.

    b. T owns a small "strip" shopping center that houses 10 businesses, including T's own video store. This year T received $40,000 in income from renting out space in the shopping center and grossed $60,000 from her video store.

    c. O owns five greeting card stores spread all around Denver.

    d. P owns 10 gas stations throughout the state of Georgia. Each station not only sells gas but also sells groceries. Seven of the stations derive 60 percent of their income from gas sales and 40 percent from food sales. Two of the stations derive 55 percent of their income from food sales and 45 percent from gas sales. One station also provides auto repair services and derives one-third of its income from each operation.

    e. E owns a beer distributorship and ten liquor stores throughout Minneapolis. Sixty percent of the distributorship sales are to the liquor stores.

12-12 *Combining Activities.* T owns a 70 percent interest in each of three partnerships: a radio station (WAKO), a minor league baseball team (the Harrisville Hippos), and a video and film company (Dynamite Productions) that produces short subjects for television, including advertisements. In any particular year, one business may be profitable while another may be unprofitable. Each business is at a different location. Each business also prepares its own financial statements and has its own management, although T participates extensively in the management of all three partnerships. Any financing needed for the three partnerships is usually obtained from Second National, a local bank. The radio station broadcasts all of the Hippo games, and the production company often prepares material for local television spots on the Hippos. Occasionally, some employees in one partnership assist the other partnership in periods of peak activity or emergency. Explain how the passive loss rules apply to T in this case.

12-13 *Material Participation.* During the week, A is a mild-mannered reporter for the local paper. On the weekends, he is a partner with his brother-in-law, B, in a small van-conversion operation in Elkhart. The two typically work seven or eight hours on most Saturdays during the year. This year, the partnership suffered a loss of $10,000.

    a. How will A treat the loss?

    b. What planning might you suggest?

12-14 *Participation Defined.* Three recent Purdue graduates—C, D, and E—formed their own lawn treatment company. Each of the three participates on a part-time basis because each is otherwise employed on a full-time basis. In this, their first year of operations, C spent 40 hours, D spent 70 hours, and E contributed 80 hours. E's wife also kept the books for the partnership. Explain whether C, D, and E satisfy the material participation test.

12-15 *Material Participation.* F is an accountant with a large C.P.A. firm. She also has an interest in two partnerships: a night club and a family-owned drugstore. F maintains the accounting records for each partnership, spending 200 hours working for the night club and 400 hours for the drugstore.
   a. How will F treat any losses that the partnerships might have?
   b. How will F treat any income that the partnerships might have?

12-16 *Material Participation.* In 1986 H started his own replacement window business, Sting Construction, an S corporation. Up until 1999 H had been the sole shareholder. In 1999 he sold 90 percent of his stock to J and K, who continued the business. From time to time, H still provides advice to J and K. This year, H spent 300 hours working for the company. J and K each devoted 1,500 hours to the business. Unfortunately, the corporation suffered a loss this year because of a downturn in the economy. How will H treat the loss?

12-17 *Rental or Nonrental Activities.* Indicate whether the following are rental or nonrental activities.
   a. P owns an airplane. She has an arrangement with a flying club at a small airport to lease the plane out on a short-term basis to its students. Most of the time the plane is rented for two to three hours.
   b. Q owns a condominium in Aspen that he rents out during the year. The average stay is one week. Q has arranged to provide daily maid and linen service for the unit. In addition, his monthly condominium fee pays for maintenance of the common areas.
   c. S and his wife, T, own White Silver Sands, a posh resort on the coast of Florida. As part of its package, the resort provides everything a vacationer could want (daily maid service, free use of the golf, tennis, and pool facilities, an on-site masseuse, etc.). The average stay is two weeks.
   d. Z owns a duplex near the University of Texas that she normally rents out to students on a long-term basis. The average stay is nine months. Z provides typical landlord services such as repairs and maintenance.
   e. B owns Quiet Quarters, a retirement home for the elderly. The home's staff includes a physician and several nurses.
   f. C owns and operates Body Beautiful, a fitness club. The club has over 1,000 members who have use of the club daily from 6 a.m. to 11 p.m.
   g. D owns a 200-acre parcel of land on the outskirts of Lubbock. The land is worth $700,000 (basis $200,000). During the year, D leased the land to a local car enthusiast who used it as a raceway. D collected rents of $5,000.

12-18 *Passive Activities.* G is the head chef for Half-Way Airlines, making a salary of $70,000 a year. In addition, his portfolio income is about $20,000 a year. Over the years, G has made numerous investments and has been a participant in many ventures. Indicate whether the passive activity rules would apply in each of the following situations.
   a. A $10,000 loss from G's interest in Flimsy Films, a limited partnership. G is a limited partner.
   b. A $5,000 loss from G's interest as a shareholder in D's Bar and Grill, an S corporation. G and his wife operate the bar. Each spent 300 hours working there in the current year.
   c. G and his friend, F, are equal partners in a partnership that produces and markets a Texas-style barbecue sauce. G leaves the management of the day-to-day operations to F. However, G spent 130 hours working in the business during the current year. For the year, the partnership had income of $15,000. Assume that this is G's only investment.

    d. Same as (c) except G has an ownership interest in three other distinctly different activities (e.g., construction and consulting). He spends 130 hours in each of the four activities.

    e. G is a 10 percent partner in a restaurant consulting firm. The firm operates the business on the bottom floor of a three-story building it owns. The firm leases the other two floors to a law firm and a real estate company. The consulting side of the business reported a $100,000 profit from consulting, $5,000 in interest income, and had a loss from the rental operation.

    f. G is the sole owner of Try, Inc., a regular C corporation that produces G's special salad dressing. The corporation had an operating profit of $4,000. In addition, Try, Inc. had interest income of $5,000 and a $7,000 loss from its investment in a real estate limited partnership in which it was a limited partner.

12-19 *Passive-Activity Limitations.* M is a successful banker. Two years ago, M's 27-year-old son, J, asked his dad to become his partner in opening a sporting goods store. M agreed and contributed $50,000 for a 50 percent interest in the partnership. J operates the store on his own, receiving little advice from his father. Information regarding M's financial activities reveals the following for the past two years:

Year	Salary	Interest Income	Partnership Income (Loss)
2005	$100,000	$20,000	$(40,000)
2006	100,000	20,000	12,000

All parties are cash basis, calendar year taxpayers. Answer the following questions.

    a. How did M's investment in the partnership affect his A.G.I. in 2005?

    b. How did M's investment in the partnership affect his A.G.I. in 2006?

    c. Would your answer to (b) change if the partnership had a loss in 2006 and the income shown was from M's interest as a limited partner in a real estate venture?

    d. On January 1, 2007, M sold his interest in the partnership to his son for a $40,000 gain. What effect?

12-20 *Passive-Activity Limitations: Rental Property.* L, single, is the chief of surgery at a local hospital. During the year, L earned a salary of $120,000. L owns a four-unit apartment building that she rents out unfurnished. The current tenants have one-year leases, which expire at various times. This year, the property produced a loss of $30,000 due to accelerated depreciation. L is actively involved in the rental activity, making many of the decisions regarding leases, repairs, etc.

    a. How much of the loss may L deduct?

    b. Would the answer to (a) change if L materially participated?

12-21 *Rental Real Estate.* M and H are real estate moguls. Together they have created a number of partnerships that own more than 50 shopping malls as well as a few office buildings, apartments, and warehouses. Most of their lease agreements with their mall tenants are tied to the tenant's gross receipts. Unfortunately, with the downturn in the economy, several of the mall projects have produced substantial losses. How will M and H treat their share of the losses?

12-22 *Suspended Losses.* When tax shelter activity was at its highest, G was one of its biggest proponents. Currently, she still owns an interest in several limited partnerships. She is now considering what she should do in light of the passive loss rules. To help her make this decision, she has put together her best guess as to the performance of her investments over the next two years. These are shown below.

Activity	2005	2006
X	$(7,000)	$(2,000)
Y	(3,000)	(9,000)
Z	6,000	1,000

    a. Determine the amount of suspended loss for each activity at the end of 2005 and 2006.

    b. Assume the same facts as in (a) above, except assume that in 2006 G sells the Y activity for a $4,000 gain. Explain the effect of the disposition on any suspended losses G might have, including the amount of suspended losses to be carried forward to 2007.

12-23 *Characterizing Income.* Indicate whether the income in the following situations is passive or nonpassive.

    a. Ten years ago, T purchased a strip of land for $300,000. Shortly thereafter, he built an office building on the land for $100,000. He currently leases the entire building to a large corporation on a ten-year lease for $90,000 annually. This year he sold the building for $700,000.

    b. Q owns a real estate development business that she operates as an S corporation. In 2004 she purchased a vacant lot for $100,000. Q proceeded to put in roads, sewers, and other amenities at a cost of $50,000. Shortly thereafter, she contracted for the construction of a warehouse at a cost of $1 million. Upon completion of the building in September 2004, Q began leasing the space. It was completely leased by June 2005. In December 2006 she sold the property for $2 million.

    c. T owns 100 percent of the stock of Z Corporation, an S corporation that operates a construction company. This year T purchased and leased a crane to the corporation. T received total rents of $10,000.

    d. X operates a travel agency and an office supply store to which she devotes 300 and 100 hours, respectively. The travel agency produced a profit of $10,000 while the office supply business sustained a loss of $40,000.

12-24 *Rental versus Nonrental Activities.* Identify rental activities that would not be considered "rental activities" for purposes of the passive loss rules.

12-25 *Vacation Home Rental.* S owns a condominium in Florida, which he and his family use occasionally. During the year, he used the condominium for 20 days and rented it for 40 days. The remainder of the year, the condominium was vacant. S compiled the following information related to the condominium for the entire year:

Rental income	$1,000
Expenses:	
Interest on mortgage.	3,650
Maintenance	900
Depreciation	6,000

    a. Compute the tax effect of the rental activity on S.

    b. Assuming S only used the condominium personally for ten days, compute the tax effect.

    c. Assuming S only rented the condominium for 14 days, compute the tax effect.

12-26 *Vacation Home-Personal Use Days.* Indicate the number of personal use days in each of the following situations.

    a. Saturday morning, March 3, S drove to Vail to replace a water heater in his vacation home. He arrived in Vail at 9 a.m. and skied until late afternoon, when he retired to his condominium at 6 p.m. After dinner, he worked on replacing the water heater until midnight, when he went to sleep. The following morning he awoke and went skiing until 5 p.m., when he returned home.

b. Same as (a) except S's wife and family accompanied him. S's family also skied but did not perform any repairs or maintenance related to the vacation home.

c. T owns a duplex, which he rents. On February 1 of this year, the one-year lease of the tenant living upstairs expired and she moved. Unable to rent the upstairs unit, T moved in on December I and remained through the end of the year.

12-27 *Participation in Real Estate.* When D reached age 60 several years ago, he decided to cut back on the number of hours he devoted to his dental practice. He figured that the income from a mini-warehouse, a trailer park, and a duplex that he owned would sufficiently supplement the income that he derived from his practice. Unfortunately, this year all of these rental activities produced losses. Assuming D has no passive income, indicate whether each of the following statements is true or false. If false, explain why.

a. D is not allowed to deduct the losses since rental real estate activities are considered passive regardless of the taxpayer's participation.

b. D is allowed to deduct the losses if most of his working hours are spent managing the real estate properties.

c. Assuming D works 700 hours managing the properties and his wife spends 200 hours helping him, the couple will be able to deduct the losses on their joint return.

12-28 *At-Risk Computation.* Ajax Construction builds apartments and condominiums. It has developed a unique construction technique. It created forms in the shape of a U in which concreted is poured. The U forms are then inverted and set on top of each other to form the walls and floors of a building. A crane is needed to hoist a U out of the concrete forms and stack it on top of another U. The owners of Ajax Construction, A and B, formed the AB Partnership to purchase the crane and other heavy equipment that would be rented to Ajax and other parties. The partnership is formed on January 1, 2004 by equal partners A and B who each contribute $100,000. The AB Partnership reports on a calendar year and is engaged in activities subject to § 465. The following transactions occurred during 2004 and 2005:

07/01/2004	AB Partnership borrows $120,000 from a bank using a recourse note.
10/01/2004	AB Partnership acquires equipment at a cost of $400,000 by giving a nonrecourse note to the vendor.
12/01/2004	AB Partnership reduces the recourse note balance to $30,000 and the nonrecourse note balance to $380,000.
12/31/2004	AB Partnership reports a taxable loss of $420,000 for 2004.
12/31/2004	Partners A and B each withdraw $40,000 from the partnership.
04/01/2005	Partners A and B each contribute $50,000 to the partnership.
12/31/2005	AB Partnership reports taxable income of $120,000

a. Computer partner A's amount at risk on 12/31/2004.
b. Compute partner A's amount at risk on 12/31/2005.

12-29 *At-Risk: Real Estate.* Kingsmill is a limited partnership. The partnership has three equal partners and it deals exclusively in rental real estate. S is the only general partner. On January 1, all three capital accounts were zero. No changes in the accounts occurred during the year. The partnership incurred losses of $75,000 during the year. As of the close of the year, the partnership had liabilities in the form of $20,000 of accounts payable and a $30,000 nonrecouse mortgage obtained from a commercial lender.

a. What losses can the partners claim as deductions on their returns for the year?

b. Would the result be the same if the partnership were engaged in equipment leasing rather than rental real estate?

Part IV

ALTERNATIVE MINIMUM TAX
AND TAX CREDITS

❖ Contents ❖

Chapter 13

THE ALTERNATIVE MINIMUM TAX AND TAX CREDITS

LEARNING OBJECTIVES

Upon completion of this chapter you will be able to:

- Explain the tax policy reasons underlying the Alternative Minimum Tax (AMT) system

- Understand the conceptual framework of the AMT system and understand the terminology necessary to communicate AMT issues or concerns to a tax professional

- Determine the amount of AMT adjustments, preferences, and exemptions, and calculate the alternative minimum taxable income, the tentative minimum tax, and the AMT

- Complete Form 6251, Alternative Minimum Tax—Individuals

- Explain the tax policy reasons for enacting recent tax incentives in the form of tax credits rather than deductions

- Distinguish between nonrefundable tax credits subject to dollar limitations and refundable tax credits, which have no such limitations

- Understand the components of the general business credit and be able to calculate the amount of credit allowable with respect to separate components

- Identify and calculate the nonbusiness tax credits, including the child tax credit, the dependent care credit, the educational tax credits, the earned income credit, and the minimum tax credit

- Understand and apply the tax credit carryover, carryback, and recapture rules

CHAPTER OUTLINE

INTRODUCTION

As may be abundantly clear at this point, the U.S. tax system is replete with rules whose purpose is not simply to raise revenue but also to shape the behavior of its citizens.[1] These so-called tax incentives—or *tax preferences*—are sprinkled throughout the Code, and they come in several forms. There are exclusions, deductions, and credits that stimulate economic activity and/or modify social behavior. For example, accelerated depreciation stimulates the acquisition of machinery and equipment, and percentage depletion boosts investment in natural resources. Research is encouraged through a quick write-off as well as a credit. There are also credits to attract investment in low-income housing and the rehabilitation of old buildings. Still other credits exhort taxpayers to use certain fuels, buy electric cars, and hire certain people. Even more tax benefits await those who invest in empowerment zones, enterprise communities, and small corporations.

Unfortunately, using the Code to solve some of the country's ills has created problems of its own. As the number of tax preferences began to grow, astute tax advisers and promoters saw an opportunity. They began to structure business and investment deals—all perfectly legal—that took advantage of the favorable treatment

---

[1] See "Goals of Taxation" discussion in Chapter 1.

extended to particular investments. In fact, tax professionals did their jobs so well that it was not unusual to find wealthy individuals with large economic incomes who paid little or no income tax. Indeed, in 1966 it was determined that 154 individuals with adjusted gross incomes in excess of $200,000 were able to completely escape tax by using the various incentives. Although the revenue lost from these high-income, no-tax individuals was slight, concerns started to surface. By the late 1960s Congress recognized that an increasing number of people were losing faith in the system, believing that it was unfairly tipped in favor of the rich. Finally, amidst cries that only the poor and middle class paid taxes, the Johnson administration responded.

In 1969 legislation was enacted to guarantee that all wealthy individuals paid at least some amount of Federal income tax. The method adopted, however, was circuitous. Instead of repealing the tax preferences that created the opportunities, Congress chose to add another layer of taxation: the minimum tax. Since 1969 the minimum tax has come a long way, steadily growing in scope and importance. The first part of this chapter takes a look at these complex provisions.

The second part of this chapter is devoted to the world of credits. Over the years, Congress has established a number of credits that attempt to accomplish a variety of objectives. In addition to the business credits noted above, there are also several credits reserved for individuals. For example, there are credits to aid individuals with child care, help the elderly and disabled, and encourage individuals to get off welfare and go to work. Each of the common credit provisions is discussed below.

ALTERNATIVE MINIMUM TAX

POLICY OBJECTIVES

Since its enactment in 1969, the minimum tax has gone through a virtual metamorphosis. Substantial revisions occurred in 1976, 1978, 1981, and 1982, and a complete overhaul took place in 1986. Throughout, however, the rationale behind the tax has remained virtually unchanged. The policy underlying the minimum tax was well-summarized in the following excerpt from the Senate Finance Committee Report on the Tax Reform Act of 1986:

Reasons for Change

The committee believes that the minimum tax should serve one overriding objective: to ensure that no taxpayer with substantial economic income can avoid significant tax liability by using exclusions, deductions, and credits. Although these provisions may provide incentives for worthy goals, they become counterproductive when taxpayers are allowed to use them to avoid virtually all tax liability. The ability of high-income individuals and highly profitable corporations to pay little or no tax undermines respect for the entire tax system and, thus, for the incentive provisions themselves. In addition, even aside from public perceptions, the committee believes that it is inherently unfair for high-income individuals and highly profitable corporations to pay little or no tax due to their ability to utilize various tax preferences.[2]

Guided by these goals, Congress revised the AMT to ensure that the tax liability is at least a minimum percentage of a broad-based concept of income, less related expenses and certain personal or unavoidable expenditures. The intent of the legislation is to increase tax levies on certain wealthy taxpayers.

Under the current AMT rules, taxpayers must make a completely separate tax calculation to determine the *tentative minimum tax*; if the tentative minimum tax is

---

[2]   Senate Finance Committee Report. H.R. 3838, Page 518, U.S. Government Printing Office, May 29, 1986.

greater than the regular tax liability, the taxpayer will have to pay the higher amount. The upshot of these rules is that the separate tax calculations force taxpayers to keep a separate set of books just to compute the AMT.

OVERVIEW OF AMT

The AMT applies to all of the separate taxable entities: individuals, estates, trusts, and regular C corporations. Partnerships and S corporations are not subject to the AMT per se; but if either has items of AMT significance, such items flow through to the partners or shareholders, who must consider them in calculating their own AMT. Consequently, these flow-through entities, like any other taxpayer, cannot ignore the AMT. The Taxpayer Relief Act of 1997 significantly impacted the AMT system. One ramification is discussed here and the others have been integrated with their related rules discussed later in this chapter. In an attempt at simplification, the new law exempts "small corporations" from the AMT for taxable years beginning after December 31, 1997.[3] For this purpose, a small corporation is one that has less than $5,000,000 in average annual gross receipts for the first three-taxable year period (or portion thereof) of the corporation beginning after December 31, 1993. Subsequent to the first 3-taxable year period the corporation's average gross receipts for all three-taxable-year periods ending before the current taxable year cannot exceed $7,500,000.[4]

The basic formula for computing the AMT, like the basic formula for determining taxable income, is relatively uncomplicated. As can be seen from Exhibit 13-1, the calculation starts with the taxpayer's final taxable income computed in the normal fashion.[5] This amount, regular taxable income, is increased by any *tax preferences* and further modified—increased or decreased—by certain *adjustments* (see Exhibits 13-3 and 13-5 for a list and brief explanation). The resulting amount is termed *alternative minimum taxable income* (AMTI). However, AMTI is not the amount subject to tax. AMTI is further reduced by an *exemption* to arrive at the tax base or "taxable excess." The appropriate rate is then applied to produce the gross AMT. This amount is reduced by an available AMT foreign tax credit to yield the *tentative minimum tax*. Finally, the tentative minimum tax is compared to the regular tax and the taxpayer pays the higher. Technically, the excess of the tentative minimum tax over the regular tax is the AMT, but as can be seen from the formula, the effect is to require the taxpayer to pay the higher amount.[6] It is important to observe that, in computing the AMT, the general business tax credits normally cannot be used to reduce the tentative minimum tax (TMT).[7] This can be quite a surprise for taxpayers who have a large general business credit that wipes out their regular tax liability but does nothing to shield them from the AMT. For tax years beginning in 2004 and 2005, all nonrefundable personal credits may be offset against both regular tax and the AMT.[8]

---

[3] § 55(e).

[4] See § 448 and Chapter 5. This test is the same as the one applied in determining whether a corporation must use the accrual method of accounting. Note that once a corporation is classified as a small corporation, special rules apply when the gross receipts exceed $7,500,000 because the corporation will lose its status as a small corporation [§ 55(e)].

[5] § 55(b)(2).

[6] § 55(a).

[7] The empowerment zone credit can offset 25 percent of the tentative minimum tax as authorized by § 38(c)(2)(A). The 2001 Tax Act made the nonrefundable portion of the Child Tax Credit offset against the AMT permanent [See § 24(b)(3)]. .

[8] The regular tax must be reduced by the amount of any applicable foreign tax credit. See §§ 904(h) and 26(a)(2) as amended by the Working Families Tax Relief Act of 2004.

EXHIBIT 13-1
The Alternative Minimum Tax Formula

Start with:	Regular taxable income		$xxx,xxx
Plus/Minus:	AMT adjustments (see Exhibit 13-3)	±	xx,xxx
Equals:	AMT adjusted taxable income		$xxx,xxx
Plus:	Sum of tax preference items (see Exhibit 13-5)	+	xx,xxx
Equals:	Alternative minimum taxable income (AMTI)		$xxx,xxx
Less:	Exemption amount (adjusted for phase-out)	−	xx,xxx
Equals:	AMT base (taxable excess)		$xxx,xxx
Times:	AMT rate	×	xx%
Equals:	Gross alternative minimum tax		$ xx,xxx
Less:	AMT foreign tax credit	−	x,xxx
Equals:	Tentative minimum tax (TMT)		$ xx,xxx
Less:	Regular tax liability.	−	x,xxx
Equals:	Alternative minimum tax.		$ xx,xxx

The last concern that is not revealed in the AMT formula concerns some Congressional largess. In an attempt to protect taxpayers from being taxed under both the regular tax system and the AMT system, Congress introduced the minimum tax credit. As explained later, the minimum tax credit provision essentially allows any alternative minimum tax paid in one year to be used (with some modifications) as a credit in subsequent years against the taxpayer's regular tax liability.

Example 1. K is single and has taxable income of $92,500, on which she is required to pay a regular income tax of $20,407. In computing her regular taxable income, she utilized regular tax incentives that resulted in $55,000 of AMT adjustments (including her personal exemption) and $35,000 of AMT tax preference items. K's alternative minimum taxable income is $182,500 ($92,500 + $55,000 + $35,000).

As might be suspected, it is not the AMT formula that causes problems. The difficulty lies in the determination of the various adjustments and preferences that must be computed to arrive at AMTI. The next several sections examine each of the items entering into the AMT calculation.

AMT RATES AND EXEMPTIONS

Tax Rates. Until 1993 the AMT was computed with two flat rates, one rate for corporations and a different rate for noncorporate taxpayers. But the increase in individual tax rates by the Revenue Reconciliation Act of 1993 (RRA) apparently necessitated a change in this approach for individuals, estates, and trusts. Consequently, these entities must use a two-tier rate system. Today, the rates for individuals, estates, and trusts are

If the AMT base is

Over	But not over	Tax liability is	Of the amount over
$ 0	$175,000	26%	$ 0
175,000	—	$45,500 + 28%	175,000

In addition, to help ensure that taxpayers are not snared by the AMT due to the new lower rates on capital gains, Congress conformed the AMT and regular tax. The new lower rates for unrecaptured § 1250 gain (25%) and long-term capital gains (15%) now apply for AMT purposes.[9] In contrast, the rate for corporate taxpayers is a flat 20 percent.

AMT Exemptions. In order to shield taxpayers with small amounts of tax preferences from the AMT, the Code provides an exemption.[10] As shown in Exhibit 13-2, the exemption amount varies depending on the entity and, in the case of an individual, his or her filing status. The exemption effectively removes the vast majority of taxpayers from the AMT rolls, but its benefit to high-income taxpayers is limited. Apparently the authors of the minimum tax rules did not want high-income taxpayers to profit from the exemption. To this end, they provided for a phase-out. Specifically, the exemption amount for each taxpayer is reduced (but not below zero) by 25 cents for each $1 of AMTI exceeding a certain threshold. These thresholds are identified in Exhibit 13-2. Note that the phase-out rule completely eliminates the exemption as AMTI increases beyond a certain amount. For example, the $58,000 exemption for married taxpayers is completely eliminated when AMTI reaches $382,000 [($382,000 − $150,000 = $232,000) × .25 = $58,000]. The various points at which the phase-out is complete are also shown in Exhibit 13-2.

EXHIBIT 13-2
Alternative Minimum Tax Exemptions and Phase-Out Levels for 2004 and 2005

Taxpayer	Exemption Amount	Phase-Out Begins	Phase-Out Complete
Married filing jointly	$58,000	$150,000	$382,000
Single individuals[11]	40,250	112,500	273,500
Married filing separately, estates, trusts	29,000	75,000	191,000
Estates and trusts	22,500	75,000	165,000
C corporation	40,000	150,000	310,000

Example 2. Assume the same facts as in *Example 1*. Since K is single, her initial AMT exemption is $40,250. However, because K's $182,500 alternative minimum taxable income exceeds the $112,500 threshold for single individuals by $70,000, her exemption amount must be reduced by $17,500 ($70,000 × 0.25). Thus, the allowable exemption for the year is $22,750 ($40,250 − $17,500).

---

[9]   § 55(b)(3).

[10]   § 55(d).

[11]   The exemption amount for children under age 14 is the lesser of $40,250 or earned income plus $5,850. The phase-out range is the same as that for single individuals. Rev. Proc. 2004-71, 2004-71 I.R.B.

K's AMT is $21,128, computed as follows:

Regular taxable income	$ 92,500
Plus: AMT adjustments	+55,000
AMT adjusted taxable income	$147,500
Plus: AMT preference items	+35,000
AMTI	$182,500
Less: Exemption amount	−22,750
AMTI base	$159,750
Times: AMT rate	×26%
Gross AMT	$ 41,535
Less: AMT foreign tax credit	−0
Tentative AMT	$ 41,535
Less: Regular tax liability	−20,407
AMT	$ 21,128

ADJUSTMENTS AND TAX PREFERENCE ITEMS IN GENERAL

Once taxable income is determined, the search for AMTI can begin. As noted above, there are two types of modifications that must be made to regular taxable income to arrive at AMTI: adjustments and preferences. Although both of these modifications serve a similar purpose (i.e., provide a more "realistic" measure of the taxpayer's economic income), they are not identical. *Preferences* generally require only an add-back to income. For example, one tax preference item requires the taxpayer to add back certain private activity bond income that was excluded from regular tax gross income under § 103. In contrast, *adjustments* generally call for the complete substitution of some special AMT treatment for the regular tax treatment. For instance, instead of using the regular tax rules to compute depreciation, the taxpayer must use the slower-paced methods for the AMT. Note that, when this occurs, depreciation for regular tax purposes may be more or less than AMT depreciation, resulting in either a positive or a negative adjustment. In short, AMT adjustments may increase or decrease taxable income whereas preferences only increase taxable income.

Another important distinction between adjustments and preferences concerns their effect on the taxpayer's basis in property. Adjustments, such as those for AMT depreciation, usually cause the property's basis for AMT purposes to differ from that for regular tax purposes. Consequently, when the taxpayer later disposes of the property, gain or loss for AMT purposes will normally not be the same as the gain or loss reported for regular tax purposes.[12] As might be imagined, this system effectively requires the taxpayer to maintain a separate set of records for AMT purposes. These separate records are used to compute the annual adjustments as well as the adjustment when the asset is subsequently sold. Note that adjustments can generally be thought of as timing differences between regular taxable income and AMTI. In early years the adjustment normally produces an increase in AMTI. In later years, however, the trend reverses and a negative adjustment is required, actually reducing AMTI.

---

[12]   § 56(b)(1)(F).

Although adjustments affect a property's basis, preferences do not. This approach makes accounting for preferences somewhat easier than it is for adjustments. In many cases, only a side calculation is necessary to determine the preference. The preference amount is then simply added to taxable income in the determination of AMTI. Generally, tax preference items are analogous to permanent differences between the regular tax and the minimum tax.

AMT ADJUSTMENTS

AMT adjustments can be classified into four groups. As shown in Exhibit 13-3, not all adjustments apply to all taxpayers; some apply to all taxpayers while others apply only to individuals or only to corporations.[13] In addition, there are special adjustments concerning losses from tax shelters. Although all of the adjustments are listed in Exhibit 13-3, only the more common adjustments are discussed below.

AMT ADJUSTMENTS APPLICABLE TO ALL TAXPAYERS

Depreciation. For AMT purposes, depreciation of property *placed in service after 1986* must be computed using the Alternative Depreciation System (ADS) with an exception for personal property discussed below.[14] As is probably apparent, this substitution of ADS for the taxpayer's normal method (e.g., MACRS) creates a difference between AMT depreciation and regular tax depreciation, and an adjustment must be made. The amount of the AMT adjustment is merely the difference between regular tax and AMT depreciation, which may be positive or negative as illustrated below.

As discussed in Chapter 9, depreciation under ADS is computed using the straight-line method, the appropriate convention, and the ADS life (the class life for personal property and 40 years for real property). While this same approach generally applies for AMT purposes, there is an exception for tangible personal property. ADS must be applied using a 150 percent declining-balance rate over the class life of the property for personal property placed in service prior to 1999. For personal property placed in service after 1998, Congress simplified the depreciation system and the AMT adjustments by allowing the MACRS recovery periods to be used for AMT purposes. The 150 percent declining-balance method does not apply to assets for which the taxpayer has elected the straight-line method for regular tax purposes. The allowable methods of depreciation for regular tax and AMT purposes are shown in Exhibit 13-4. The exhibit reveals that there are four methods of depreciation available for regular tax purposes, two of which are also suitable for AMT purposes. Two observations should be made that are not obvious from this table. The first concerns realty: note that even though the straight-line method must be used for both AMT and regular tax purposes, an adjustment is still necessary since the AMT class life is longer than the normal recovery period (40 years vs. 27.5 or 39 years). The second concerns avoidance of the AMT adjustment. Observe that the taxpayer can avoid the AMT adjustment by electing regular tax depreciation, which uses a slower rate (150% declining-balance or straight-line).[15]

Fifty Percent Additional Depreciation Allowance. The recently enacted 50 percent additional depreciation allowance for new property acquired after May 5, 2003 and before 2005 is also allowed for the AMT system. In addition, if the taxpayer takes the 50 percent additional allowance on property placed in service, any

---

[13] § 56.

[14] § 56(a)(1).

[15] The TRA of 1997 allows AMT depreciation to be computed using the same recovery periods as are used for regular tax purposes. For property placed in service prior to 1999, the AMT system required tangible personal property to be depreciated over the longer ADS class life of the property.

depreciation computed under the regular MACRS rules on the remaining cost basis (after reduction for any applicable first year expensing and after the reduction for the additional 50 percent depreciation), will not generate an AMT adjustment.[16]

EXHIBIT 13-3
AMT Adjustments

Applicable to All Taxpayers		Brief Explanation
§ 56(a)(1)	Depreciation	Use ADS or 150% DB
§ 56(a)(2)	Mining exploration and development costs	Capitalize and amortize over 10 years
§ 56(a)(3)	Income reported on the completed contract method	Use percentage completion
§ 56(a)(4)	Alternative tax net operating loss deduction	Recompute with AMT rules
§ 56(a)(5)	Pollution control facilities	Use ADS
§ 56(a)(6)	Gains or losses on asset dispositions	Differing AMT basis
§ 56(a)(7)	Alcohol fuel credit	Do not include as income
Applicable Only to Individuals		
§ 56(b)(1)(A)	Itemized deductions	No taxes, miscellaneous itemized deductions (MIDs); adjust interest, medical
§ 56(b)(1)(E)	Standard deduction	Not allowed
§ 56(b)(1)(E)	Personal dependent exemptions	Not allowed
§ 56(b)(1)(D)	Income tax refunds	Do not include
§ 56(b)(2)	Circulation and research expenditures	Capitalize and amortize
§ 56(b)(3)	Incentive stock options	Include spread (FMV − option price)
Applicable Only to Corporations		
§ 56(c)	ACE (adjusted current earnings)	Add 75% (ACE − AMTI)
Specialized Tax Shelter Loss Adjustments		
§ 56(b)	Passive activity losses	Recompute with AMT rules
§ 56(a)	Farm shelter losses	Deduct in following year, if income

EXHIBIT 13-4
Allowable Depreciation Methods for AMT and Regular Tax Purposes
for Property Placed in Service after 1998

Method	Depreciable Life	Regular Tax	AMT	AMT-ACE
200% DB	Recovery period	✓		
150% DB	Recovery period	✓	✓	✓
Straight line	Recovery period	✓		
Straight line	Class life	✓	✓	✓

---

[16] § 168(k)(2)(F).

Example 3. T placed an asset costing $100,000 in service on February 5, 2005. Assume the asset is "3-year property" and has an ADR class life of 3 years. The effect on the minimum tax is computed below assuming that the 150 percent declining-balance method was used for AMT purposes.

	2005	2006	2007	2008
Regular tax deduction (200%)	$33,330	$44,450	$14,810	$7,410
AMT deduction (150%)	−25,000	−37,500	−25,000	−12,500
Effect of adjustment on AMTI.	$ 8,330	$ 6,950	($10,190)	($5,090)
	increase	increase	decrease	decrease

Note that in the first two years regular depreciation exceeds what is allowed for AMTI—requiring the taxpayer to increase AMTI—a positive adjustment. In the third year, however, the trend reverses itself, and AMT depreciation is greater than what was actually deducted for regular tax purposes. Consequently, the taxpayer is allowed to decrease AMTI—a negative adjustment. Also note that the differences in regular and AMT depreciation cause the property's basis for AMT purposes to be different from the regular tax basis. Accordingly, if the property is sold, the amount of gain or loss for AMT and regular tax purposes may differ.

Recognizing the burdensome task of maintaining one set of depreciation books for each tax system, Congress took steps to coordinate the two. As shown in Exhibit 13-4, taxpayers may eliminate the AMT adjustment by electing the appropriate method for regular tax purposes.[17] For example, the taxpayer could, for regular tax purposes, elect to use the 150 percent declining balance method, which would be the same as AMT depreciation. Alternatively, if the taxpayer elects to use the ADS life and the straight-line method for regular tax purposes, that same method must be used for the AMT. Either approach eliminates the AMT adjustment.

Example 4. Assume the same facts as in *Example 3* above, except T elects to use the 150 percent modification. In this case, the need for an AMT adjustment is eliminated, as shown below:

	2005	2006	2007	2008
Regular tax depreciation (150%, ADS life) . . .	$25,000	$37,500	$25,000	$12,500
AMT depreciation (150%, ADS life) . . .	−25,000	−37,500	−25,000	−12,500
AMT adjustment.	$ 0	$ 0	$ 0	$ 0

Section 179 Limited Expensing. Given the elaborate scheme to curtail accelerated depreciation deductions for AMT purposes, it is surprising that the election to expense property under § 179 does not give rise to an AMT adjustment. Currently, first-year § 179 expensing deductions are allowed for both AMT and regular tax purposes.[18]

---

[17]   §§ 168(g)(7) and 56(a)(1)(A)(ii).

[18]   See Footnote 2, *supra*, page 552, note 5.

Mining Exploration and Development Costs. For regular tax purposes, mining exploration and development costs related to mineral property are currently expensed. For AMT purposes, however, such costs must be capitalized and amortized ratably over a 10-year period.[19]

Long-Term Contracts. As explained in Chapter 5, for regular tax purposes, taxpayers normally must use the percentage of completion method to account for long-term contracts. However, the Code carves out two exceptions. The completed contract method may be used to account for home construction contracts and by small contractors who have gross receipts less than $10 million. AMT treatment is similar, but it is not identical. For AMT purposes, there is no exception for small contractors. Consequently, the percentage of completion method must be used for computing AMTI in all cases except in accounting for home construction contracts.[20]

Pollution Control Facilities. While taxpayers are permitted to amortize expenditures related to pollution control facilities over 60 months for regular tax purposes, the AMT requires use of ADS.[21]

Alternative Tax Net Operating Loss (ATNOL) Deduction. An ATNOL is allowed as a deduction for minimum tax purposes.[22] The procedure for computing the ATNOL parallels its cousin, the regular tax NOL, but the ATNOL must be determined taking into consideration all of the AMT adjustments and tax preference items. In addition, the amount of the ATNOL is *limited* to 90 percent of the AMTI determined without regard to this deduction. Note, however, as part of the Job Creation and Worker Assistance Act of 2002, taxpayers are entitled to deduct 100 percent of the AMT NOLs generated in 2001 or 2002 as well as any AMT NOLs that are carried forward into 2001 or 2002. Also, an election to forgo the NOL carryback period for regular tax purposes is likely to control the treatment for the ATNOL.[23]

AMT ADJUSTMENTS APPLICABLE ONLY TO INDIVIDUALS

All of the adjustments applicable only to individual taxpayers are listed in Exhibit 13-3. Each of these is discussed below. But first it is important to note that the IRS, while routinely taking the position that the AMT and the regular tax system are two distinct and separate systems, has issued regulations governing the computation of AMTI for noncorporate taxpayers. These regulations provide that, in determining the AMTI of noncorporate taxpayers, all references to the taxpayer's A.G.I. or modified A.G.I. in determining the amount of items of income, exclusion, or deduction in the AMT system must be treated as references to the taxpayer's modified A.G.I. as determined for regular tax purposes.[24] For example, in the AMT system the medical expense deduction is subject to a 10 percent limitation just as the regular tax medical expense deduction is limited to a 7½ percent limitation. The important but apparently inconsistent point is that the limitation for the AMT system is not subject to 10 percent of AMTI (as it should be if the AMT were a separate system), but rather the regulation specifies that the AMT limitation will be subject to 10 percent of the taxpayer's regular

---

[19]   §§ 616 and 617; but see Footnote 52, *infra*, for the election under § 59(e) that allows taxpayers to avoid an AMT adjustment with respect to these expenditures.

[20]   § 56(a)(3).

[21]   § 169 and § 56(a)(5).

[22]   § 56(a)(4).

[23]   *Branum v. Comm.*, 94-1 USTC ¶50, 163, (CA-5, 1994).

[24]   Reg. § 1.55-1(e).

tax system A.G.I. The purported goal of the regulations is to reduce the complexity and to ease the record keeping burdens that are imposed on noncorporate taxpayers under a completely separate and parallel system that would require a computation of a separate adjusted gross income for alternative minimum tax purposes.

Itemized Deductions. For the most part, itemized deductions allowed for regular tax purposes are also allowed for AMT purposes (sometimes referred to as alternative minimum tax deductions, or ATIDs). However, there are several important exceptions and modifications. These adjustments differ from those above (e.g., depreciation) in that they serve to increase the tax base as permanent adjustments instead of merely altering the timing of the item.

Two itemized deductions are totally disallowed for AMT purposes:[25]

1. Miscellaneous itemized deductions (MIDs). For example, unreimbursed employee business expenses and tax preparation expenses are not allowed for the AMT.[26]
2. Itemized deductions related to the payment of any tax. For example, state, local, and foreign income taxes and real and personal property taxes are not allowed as deductions for AMT purposes.

In computing the itemized deductions allowed for AMT purposes, the limitations for regular tax purposes normally apply (e.g., the 10% limitation on personal casualty losses or the 50% limitation for charitable contributions). However, the 3 percent cutback rule that applies to certain itemized deductions *does not* apply for AMT purposes.[27] In addition, as noted below, special rules exist for medical expenses and interest.

ATIDs generally include the following:[28]

1. Medical expenses, but *only in excess* of 10 percent of taxpayer's regular tax A.G.I.
2. Interest expense, but only for
    a. Qualified housing interest
    b. Investment interest expense to the extent of net investment income
3. Charitable contributions
4. Theft, casualty, and wagering losses
5. Estate tax deductions resulting from reporting income in respect of a decedent under § 691
6. Impairment-related work expenses
7. Bond premium amortization deductions

The above list is self-explanatory with the exception of the amount of interest that will be allowed as an ATID. Several new terms and concepts regarding the deduction for interest were developed and incorporated into the alternative minimum tax system. *Qualified housing interest* is interest paid or accrued on indebtedness incurred after June 30, 1982, in acquiring, constructing, or substantially rehabilitating property that is a principal residence (within the meaning of Code § 121) or qualified dwelling, including

---

[25] § 56(b)(1)(A).

[26] Beginning in 1998, employee business expenses relating to service as an official of a state or local government or political subdivision thereof are deductible for A.G.I. provided the official is compensated on a fee basis. Thus, these expenses become deductible for the AMT system.

[27] § 56(b)(1)(F).

[28] See § 67(b) for a complete list of itemized deductions that are allowed as ATIDs. Also note that a standard deduction is not allowed for AMT purposes.

a secondary residence.[29] For indebtedness incurred *before* July 1, 1982, a deduction can be taken for interest paid or accrued on a debt that, at that time, was secured by a qualified dwelling without regard for the purpose or use of the proceeds of the indebtedness. The essence of these rules is that interest on home second mortgages—home equity loans—established after 1982 will not be deductible for AMT purposes as qualified housing interest *unless* the proceeds were used to improve the principal residence.

When interest rates fall, taxpayers often refinance their homes, and a question arose about the interest paid on a loan (new loan) the proceeds of which were used to pay off the original qualified housing indebtedness (old loan). The TRA of 1986 resolved the issue by allowing an interest expense deduction for AMT purposes on the new loan used to refinance the principal residence, but only to the extent that the new loan does not exceed the outstanding balance of the old loan.[30]

Investment interest expense is allowed as an ATID, but only to the extent of qualified *adjusted* net investment income.[31] The adjustment in computing the net investment income is required for AMT purposes as a result of including a portion of the tax-exempt interest income from specified private activity bonds (SPAB) as a tax preference item that increases the AMTI (see *Example 10* for details relating to the tax-exempt income preference item). If exempt interest income from SPABs is included as a preference item for AMT purposes, the interest expense incurred with respect to it will be allowed as a deduction for AMT purposes. These adjustments for tax-exempt income and its related interest expenses are also allowed in computing the "adjusted" net investment income for AMT purposes.

Circulation and Research Expenditures. Amounts paid or incurred that are allowable as a deduction for circulation[32] expenditures in computing the regular tax must be capitalized and amortized over a three-year period beginning with the taxable year in which the expenditures were made. The same rule applies to research and experimental expenditures, except the amortization period is ten years.[33] However, the Revenue Reconciliation Act of 1989 repealed the AMT adjustment for research expenses of individuals who materially participate in the activity in which research expenses are incurred. The repeal is effective for taxable years beginning after December 31, 1990.[34] As with other adjustments that create a disparity between basis for regular tax and basis for AMT, *separate records must be maintained* to determine the allowable amortization deduction in subsequent years or the gain or loss on disposition or abandonment.

Gains from Incentive Stock Options (ISOs). For regular tax purposes, the bargain element of ISOs is *not* required to be included in income either at the time the option is granted or when the option is exercised;[35] however, an income adjustment may be required for the AMT. The income adjustment with respect to stock received from options exercised after December 31, 1987 is determined under the principles of Code § 83. Assuming the stock acquired is not subject to substantial risk of forfeiture, the adjustment to AMTI is equal to the amount by which the value of the share at the time

---

29   A qualified dwelling is a house, apartment, condominium, or mobile home (not used on a transient basis). Qualified dwelling for AMT is a narrow definition and differs from that of Code § 280A(f)(1), which broadly defines a dwelling unit as a house, apartment, condominium, mobile home, boat, or similar property.

30   § 56(e)(1).

31   See Chapter 11 for a discussion of the investment interest deduction limitation.

32   § 173. See Footnote 52, *infra*, for an optional tax accounting method for circulation expenditures.

33   § 56(b)(2)(A)(ii). See Footnote 52, *infra*, for an optional tax accounting method for research and experimental expenditures.

34   § 56(b)(2)(D).

35   See Chapter 18 for a discussion of ISOs and § 83.

of exercise exceeds the option price.[36] If the stock is disposed of in the option year, however, this income adjustment is not required because the income attributable to the bargain element will be reported under the regular tax system in the same year.

> **Example 5.** D receives an incentive stock option to purchase 1,000 shares of her employer's stock at $50 per share. Three years after the receipt of the option, D exercises her option when the stock is selling for $70 per share. When D exercises the option, she has an AMT adjustment of $20,000 ($70,000 − $50,000).

Since the AMT adjustment amount computed above increases the AMTI, an upward basis adjustment in the stock of an equal amount is allowed for AMT purposes. This disparity in the stock's basis for regular tax and the AMT requires the *extra set of books* to determine the amount of gain recognized upon a subsequent disposition of the stock for AMT purposes.

> **Example 6.** Assume the same facts as in *Example 5* and that D holds the stock until it further increases in value to $85,000. If D sells the stock for $85,000, she has a $35,000 gain for regular tax purposes ($85,000 − $50,000), and an AMT gain of $15,000 ($85,000 − $70,000).

Standard Deduction Not Allowed. Individuals are not permitted to take into account the standard deduction in computing the alternative minimum taxable income.[37]

Personal Exemptions. Personal exemptions authorized under § 151 are not allowed as deductions in computing the AMTI.[38]

Adjustment to Income for Tax Refunds. Generally, taxpayers who itemize deductions must report a refund of a prior year's state or local income tax as gross income in the year of receipt.[39] However, since itemized deductions for all tax expenditures are not allowed for AMT purposes, the refund or recovery in *all cases* is excluded from AMTI.

ADJUSTMENT APPLICABLE ONLY TO CORPORATIONS

The only adjustment applicable solely to corporate taxpayers[40] is the adjustment based on a corporation's adjusted current earnings—commonly referred to as the *ACE adjustment*.[41] The ACE adjustment, like the minimum tax itself, was the Congressional response to what seemed an increasingly frequent phenomenon: corporations were reporting substantial earnings for financial accounting purposes yet paying little or no income tax. Curiously, this occurred despite the existence of the AMT. To address the problem, Congress created the ACE adjustment. This special adjustment is designed to ensure that all corporations pay some minimum tax on economic income.

In theory, the ACE adjustment is relatively simple. It requires a corporation to compare its economic income to taxable income to determine the amount of economic income, if any, that escaped tax. Part of this elusive income is then included in the

---

[36] § 56(b)(3). Although no direct authority exists, arguably a § 83(b) election may be made for AMT purposes.

[37] § 56(b)(1)(E).

[38] *Ibid.*

[39] See § 56(b)(1)(D) and Chapter 6 for an exception based on the tax benefit rule.

[40] Recall, however, that the TRA of 1997 exempted small corporations from the AMT system. *See* supra, Footnote 3, for the related discussion and the authority for this exemption.

[41] This adjustment *does not* apply to certain corporations, including S corporations, regulated investment companies, real estate investment trusts, or real estate mortgage investment conduits. § 56(g)(6).

corporation's AMTI. Technically, the ACE adjustment is equal to 75 percent of the difference between *adjusted current earnings* and AMTI.[42] In this calculation, adjusted current earnings essentially serve as a substitute for economic income. The actual computation of adjusted current earnings is quite technical. It begins with AMTI, to which a laundry list of adjustments are made.[43] A discussion of the various adjustments is beyond the scope of this text. Suffice it to say that their collective purpose is to yield the corporation's economic income so its true ability to pay tax can be determined.

> **Example 7.** T Corporation has AMTI of $200,000 without regard to the ACE adjustment. T's adjusted current earnings are determined to be $400,000. T's regular income tax liability is $41,750. T has an ACE adjustment of $150,000, AMTI of $350,000, a tentative AMT of $70,000, and AMT of $28,250, computed as follows:

AMTI before ACE.	$200,000
Plus: Ace adjustment [($400,000 − $200,000) × 75%].	+150,000
AMTI	$350,000
Less: Exemption amount (completely phased out)	−0
AMTI base	$350,000
Times: AMT rate	× 20%
Gross AMT	$ 70,000
Less: AMT foreign tax credit	−0
Tentative AMT	$ 70,000
Less: Regular tax liability	−41,750
AMT	$ 28,250

This portion of the alternative minimum tax system has been crafted to make certain the AMT is imposed on corporate taxpayers having an economic ability to pay.

SPECIAL TAX SHELTER LOSS ADJUSTMENTS

Certain losses that may be deductible for regular tax are *denied* for purposes of the AMT. Specifically, tax shelter farm losses and passive-activity losses allowed as deductions for regular tax purposes must be recomputed under the AMT system, taking into account all of the AMT tax accounting rules.[44] Clearly, a separate set of books will be required for each activity. The amount of the AMT adjustment required by the statute is the difference between the loss allowed for the regular tax system and the loss allowed under the AMT system.

Tax Shelter Farm Losses. Noncorporate taxpayers and personal service corporations are not allowed to deduct losses from a tax shelter farm activity in computing AMTI.[45] For the AMT system, the disallowed loss will be treated as a deduction allocable to such activity in the *first* succeeding taxable year, and will be allowed to offset income from that activity in any succeeding year. Under this rule, each farm is treated as a separate activity. In the year that the taxpayer disposes of his or her

---

[42]   § 56(g)(1).

[43]   § 56(g)(4).

[44]   These rules are specified in §§ 56 and 57.

[45]   § 58(a).

entire interest in any tax shelter farm activity, the amount of previously disallowed loss related to that activity is allowed as a deduction for the year under the AMT system.

Passive-Activity Losses. As discussed in Chapter 12, there are limitations on the use of losses from passive activities to offset other income of the taxpayer for regular tax purposes.[46] For AMT purposes, similar rules apply, except for AMT purposes a loss generated from a passive activity must be recomputed to reflect the AMT rules. This means that depreciation, certain intangible drilling and development costs, certain percentage depletion, and other adjustments and preferences must be reflected in computing the loss for AMT purposes.[47] Because of the differences in the treatment of such items, the amount of suspended losses relating to an activity may differ for minimum tax and regular tax purposes and may require that two sets of books be kept in order to track the passive-loss carryover on each activity.[48]

Example 8. C has $200,000 of salary income, $50,000 of gross income from passive activities, and $170,000 of deductions from passive activities for the current year. C's loss with respect to the passive activities is $120,000 for regular tax purposes. Because the recomputed expenses for AMT purposes are only $130,000, the passive-activity loss is $80,000 for minimum tax purposes. For regular tax purposes, the taxpayer has taxable income of $200,000 and a suspended passive loss in the amount of $120,000 ($170,000 passive deductions − $50,000 passive income). For minimum tax purposes, the taxpayer has AMTI of $200,000 and a suspended passive loss of $80,000 ($130,000 − $50,000).

As illustrated in the example above, the recomputed passive loss using the AMT rules can be significantly different from the regular tax passive loss with respect to an activity. In fact, in some situations it is possible to have a regular tax passive-loss amount *and* an AMT passive income amount on the same activity!

Example 9. Assume that taxpayer C in the example above had passive-activity deductions of $80,000 for regular tax purposes and $40,000 for minimum tax purposes. C would have regular taxable income of $200,000 and a suspended passive loss of $30,000 ($80,000 − $50,000) for regular tax purposes. For AMT purposes, C has alternative minimum taxable income of $210,000 [$200,000 salary + ($50,000 − $40,000)] and no suspended passive loss for minimum tax purposes.

TAX PREFERENCE ITEMS

Since tax preference items are required to be identified and computed for both corporate and noncorporate taxpayers, all the current preference items are listed in Exhibit 13-5; however, only the most common items are explained below.[49]

EXHIBIT 13-5
AMT Tax Preference Items

Percentage depletion in excess of cost basis on certain mineral properties
Certain intangible drilling and development costs
Specified tax-exempt interest *private activity Bond*
Exclusion for gain on sale of certain small business stock

---

[46]   See Chapter 12 for a discussion of passive losses.

[47]   § 58(b).

[48]   P.L. 99-514, Tax Reform Act of 1986, Conference Committee Report, Act § 701.

[49]   § 57 sets forth all of the tax preference items and the specifics of each calculation.

Excess Depletion. The amount of the preference item is the excess (if any) of the percentage depletion claimed for the taxable year over the adjusted basis of the property at the end of the taxable year (determined without regard to the depletion deduction for the taxable year).[50] This computation must be made for each unit of property.

Intangible Drilling and Development Costs. In general, the amount of the tax preference is equal to the intangible drilling costs (IDC) incurred and deducted on productive oil, gas, and geothermal wells reduced by the sum of

1. The amount allowed as if the IDCs had been capitalized and amortized over a ten-year period, and
2. Sixty-five percent of the net income for the year from these properties.[51]

If the intangible drilling and development costs are capitalized and amortized in accord with special rules contained in § 59(e), they are not treated as a preference item.[52]

Private Activity Bond Interest. This preference item pertains to interest income on specified private activity bonds (SPABs) issued after August 7, 1986.[53] The term *private activity bond* means any bond issued if 10 percent of the proceeds of the issue is used for private business use in any trade or business carried on by any person that is not a governmental unit. Where interest income on SPABs is includible in AMTI under the above rule, the regular tax rule of Code § 265 (denying deductions for expenses and interest relating to tax-exempt income) does not apply, and expenses and interest incurred to carry SPABs are deductible for minimum tax purposes.

> **Example 10.** Taxpayer P is required to include in AMTI $10,000 of otherwise tax-exempt interest income on SPABs as a preference item. She incurred $900 of interest expense on a temporary loan in order to purchase the bonds. Code § 265 disallows a deduction of this $900 for regular tax purposes, but it is deductible for minimum tax purposes.

Gain on the Sale of Qualified Small Business Stock. As explained in detail in Chapter 16, the Revenue Reconciliation Act of 1993 created a special incentive to encourage taxpayers to invest in the stock of qualified small businesses (i.e., stock of a C corporation with gross assets of $50 million or less at the time the stock was issued and that was held by the original owner for more than five years prior to sale). Under this special rule, a taxpayer is entitled to exclude 50 percent of the gain on the sale of the stock. However, what Congress gives with the right hand it takes away with the left. Seven percent of this exclusion (or 3.5% of the entire gain) is treated as a tax preference item.[54]

---

50   § 57(a)(1). This preference was repealed for certain independent producer and royalty interest owners of oil and gas properties for taxable years beginning after 1992.

51   § 57(a)(2)(E)(ii). The CNEPA of 1992 repealed this preference item for taxpayers (other than certain integrated oil and gas companies) for years beginning after December 31, 1992. However, the repeal of the excess IDCs preference "may not result in more than a 40 percent reduction in the amount of the taxpayer's AMTI computed as if the present-law excess IDC preference had not been repealed."

52   Code § 59(e) was enacted to provide relief to taxpayers that are subject to the AMT, but through proper planning want to maximize the regular tax deductions and at the same time minimize the impact of the AMT. This section provides an election to capitalize "qualified expenditures" and deduct them ratably over a 10-year period (three years in the case of circulation expenditures). Qualified expenditures include IDCs, circulation, research and experimentation, and mining exploration and development costs.

53   § 57(a)(5)(C)(iv).

54   § 57(a)(7), as amended by the TRA of 1997.

Example 11. On October 31, 2004 J sold qualified small business stock and recognized a gain of $80,000. Only 50 percent of the gain, $40,000, is subject to regular tax, and the remaining $40,000 is excluded. For AMT purposes J has a tax preference of $2,800 (7% × $40,000).

ALTERNATIVE MINIMUM TAX COMPUTATIONS

Before the alternative minimum tax calculations can be made, the taxpayer's current taxable income and Federal income tax liability must first be determined. As shown in Exhibit 13-1, a taxpayer's AMT liability is the excess of the tentative minimum tax over the regular tax liability. To further examine this interaction, a factual situation is presented below in *Example 12*, where the taxpayer's regular tax liability is determined. The same facts are then used to compute the ATIDs in *Example 13* and the taxpayer's AMT liability in *Example 14*.

Example 12. T is a married taxpayer filing a joint return for 2005. He had the following items of income, expenses, and regular tax liability for the year.

Income:		
Salary	$88,000	
Interest	12,000	
Adjusted gross income		$ 100,000[1]
Itemized deductions:		
Medical expenses [$9,500 total − (7.5% of $100,000 A.G.I.)]	$ 2,000	
Real property taxes on home	12,000	
Real property taxes on mountain range property	8,000	
Personal property taxes	4,000	
Interest expense:		
Residence interest	20,000[2]	
Investment interest on mountain range property ($12,000 total, but limited to)	4,000[3]	
Charitable contributions	10,000	
Casualty loss [$13,000 total − (10% of A.G.I.)]	3,000	
Miscellaneous itemized deductions [$11,000 total − (2% of A.G.I.)]	9,000	
Total itemized deductions		− 72,000
Personal exemptions (2 × $3,200)		− 6,400
Taxable income		$ 21,600
Regular tax		$ 2,510

[1]Although not required to be included in his taxable income, T exercised an incentive stock option for $20,000 when the fair market value of the stock was $80,000.

[2]Residence interest includes $18,000 of qualified housing interest (interest on mortgage to acquire home) and $2,000 of interest on a home equity loan to buy a boat.

[3]The mountain range property was acquired as a speculative investment and was 90 percent debt-financed. Recall that interest on investment indebtedness is allowed as a deduction under § 163(d) to the extent of net investment income. Net investment income = $12,000 interest − $8,000 property taxes = $4,000. Thus the $12,000 interest expense is limited to $4,000.

Example 13. Refer to *Example 12*. T's 2005 alternative tax itemized deductions (ATIDs) and the resulting AMT adjustments are determined as follows:

	Allowed ATIDs for AMT	Allowed Itemized Deductions for Regular Tax	AMT Adjustments
Medical expenses (in excess of 10% of A.G.I.)	$ 0*	$ 2,000	$ 2,000
Itemized deductions for taxes (not allowed)....	0	24,000	24,000
Qualified housing interest	18,000	18,000	0
Home equity loan.......................	0	2,000	2,000
Other qualified interest (limited to net investment income, = $12,000)...........	12,000**	4,000	(8,000)**
Casualty losses	3,000	3,000	0
Charitable contributions	10,000	10,000	0
Miscellaneous itemized deductions (not allowed)........................	0	9,000	9,000
Totals for 2004........................	$43,000	$72,000	$29,000

*$9,500 does not exceed 10% of $100,000, or $10,000.

**The real property taxes on the investment mountain property are not deductible for AMT purposes. § ?56(b)(1)(C)(v).

Note that the computations for ATIDs are similar to those in *Example 12* for itemized deductions except (1) the reduction in medical expenses is 10% of the regular tax A.G.I. rather than 7.5%, (2) deductions for state and local taxes are not allowed, (3) the miscellaneous itemized deductions are not allowed, (4) the interest on the home equity loan to purchase the boat is not allowed and (5) in the calculation of net investment income, the real property taxes on the mountain property are excludable for AMT purposes. The differences between the ATIDs allowed for AMT purposes and the itemized deductions allowed for regular tax purposes result in AMT adjustments. These adjustments are added back to T's regular taxable income to arrive at AMT adjusted taxable income and are reported on Form 6251, Computation of Alternative Minimum Tax for Individuals.

Example 14. Refer to *Examples 12* and *13*. T's alternative minimum tax (AMT) 2005 is computed as follows:

Regular taxable income		$ 21,600
Plus:	Net adjustment for itemized deductions	+ 29,000[1]
	Net adjustment for exercise of ISO	+ 60,000[2]
	Adjustment for personal exemptions	+ 6,400
AMT adjusted taxable income		$117,000
Plus:	Tax preference items	+ 0
Alternative minimum taxable income (AMTI)		$117,000
Less:	Exemption amount (married filing jointly)	− 58,000
AMT base (taxable excess)		$ 59,000
Times:	AMT rate	× 26%
Gross alternative minimum tax		$ 15,340
Less:	AMT foreign tax credit	− 0
Tentative minimum tax		$ 15,340
Less:	Regular tax liability	− 2,510
AMT liability for 2004		$ 12,830

[1]Regular tax itemized deductions	$ 72,000
ATIDs allowed for AMT	(43,000)
Disallowed itemized deductions increase in the AMTI	$ 29,000
[2]Stock FMV when ISO exercised	$ 80,000
Option price	(20,000)
Excess is AMT adjustment that increases AMTI	$ 60,000

Since the tentative minimum tax of $15,340 *exceeds* his $2,510 regular tax liability (computed in *Example 12*), T must pay the difference of $12,830 for 2005 because of the alternative minimum tax. Note that T must pay a total of $15,340 in taxes for 2005 ($2,510 regular income tax + $12,830 alternative minimum tax).

The previous example illustrates an unfortunate consequence of the strict application of the AMT provisions. The tax benefits of longstanding regular-tax incentive provisions such as home ownership (e.g., deductibility of interest and real property taxes) and medical expenses are either decreased or totally eliminated by the AMT. Although Congress continues to support the objectives of these incentives, their use by individuals to avoid all or most of their Federal income tax liability is not the intent of the law. Recent changes to the AMT are an attempt to minimize such perceived abuses. As illustrated in *Example 14*, because of the limited definition of ATIDs and the decreasing Federal income tax rates, it is possible that many unsuspecting individuals (like T) will be subject to the AMT.[55] Consequently, tax planning to avoid or minimize the AMT is becoming more important for a growing number of taxpayers. As an adjunct to planning for the impact of the AMT, it should be remembered that each taxpayer has the responsibility to maintain adequate records to support the accuracy of the amounts of tax preferences and adjustments used in the AMT computation [as required by Reg. § 1.57-5(a)].

---

[55]   *N. Holly v. Comm.*, T.C. Memo 1998-55.

A completed Form 6251, based on the facts from *Examples 12, 13,* and *14,* is contained in Exhibit 13-6. Note that the 2004 form is used because the 2005 form was not available at the publication date of this text.

With all of the potential complexity and extra reporting work required by the AMT provisions, it is noteworthy that Congress once made an attempt to make another area of the Federal tax laws more orderly—the part specifying credits against the tax liability. The remainder of this chapter is devoted to the tax incentives provided by the tax credit provisions. However, at the risk of upsetting what otherwise is an orderly presentation of the various credits, it seems only appropriate that the special minimum tax credit should be considered before we leave the AMT.

MINIMUM TAX CREDIT

One significant feature of the AMT system is that many taxpayers are required to pay the AMT long before they would have had to pay the regular income tax from certain investments. For example, taxpayers with substantial investments in depreciable personal property are *denied* the tax reduction benefits of MACRS for purposes of computing the AMT.[56] Likewise, a taxpayer who exercises an ISO must recognize income for AMT purposes to the extent the fair market value of the stock exceeds its option price, but for regular income tax purposes the taxpayer does not recognize income until the stock acquired with the ISO is sold. Without some form of relief, a taxpayer could be subject to the AMT in one year and the regular tax in a later year on the same item.

In order to limit the possibility of double taxation under the two tax systems, Congress introduced an alternative minimum tax credit. Basically, the alternative minimum tax paid in one year may be used as a credit against the taxpayer's *regular* tax liability in subsequent years. The credit may be carried forward indefinitely until used; however, the credit cannot be carried back *nor* can it be used to offset any future AMT liability.[57]

---

[56]   Recall that depreciable personal property placed in service after 1986 can be depreciated using either the 150 percent declining balance or the ADS straight-line method over the asset's class life for AMT purposes.

[57]   § 53(a).

EXHIBIT 13-6

Form **6251**	**Alternative Minimum Tax—Individuals**	OMB No. 1545-0227
Department of the Treasury Internal Revenue Service (99)	► See separate instructions. ► Attach to Form 1040 or Form 1040NR.	20**04** Attachment Sequence No. **32**

Name(s) shown on Form 1040 MR. AND MRS. T

Your social security number 324 : 91 : 0070

Part I   **Alternative Minimum Taxable Income** (See instructions for how to complete each line.)

1	If filing Schedule A (Form 1040), enter the amount from Form 1040, line 40, and go to line 2. Otherwise, enter the amount from Form 1040, line 37, and go to line 7. (If less than zero, enter as a negative amount.)	**1**	28,000 *
2	Medical and dental. Enter the **smaller** of Schedule A (Form 1040), line 4, **or** 2½% of Form 1040, line 37 .	**2**	2,000
3	Taxes from Schedule A (Form 1040), line 9	**3**	24,000
4	Enter the home mortgage interest adjustment, if any, from line 6 of the worksheet on page 2 of the instructions	**4**	2,000
5	Miscellaneous deductions from Schedule A (Form 1040), line 26	**5**	9,000
6	If Form 1040, line 37, is over $142,700 (over $71,350 if married filing separately), enter the amount from line 9 of the **Itemized Deductions Worksheet** on page B-1 of the Instructions for Schedules A & B (Form 1040)	**6**	( )
7	Tax refund from Form 1040, line 10 or line 21 .	**7**	( )
8	Investment interest expense (difference between regular tax and AMT)	**8**	(8,000)
9	Depletion (difference between regular tax and AMT) .	**9**	
10	Net operating loss deduction from Form 1040, line 21. Enter as a positive amount	**10**	
11	Interest from specified private activity bonds exempt from the regular tax	**11**	
12	Qualified small business stock (7% of gain excluded under section 1202) .	**12**	
13	Exercise of incentive stock options (excess of AMT income over regular tax income) .	**13**	60,000
14	Estates and trusts (amount from Schedule K-1 (Form 1041), line 9) .	**14**	
15	Electing large partnerships (amount from Schedule K-1 (Form 1065-B), box 6) .	**15**	
16	Disposition of property (difference between AMT and regular tax gain or loss) .	**16**	
17	Depreciation on assets placed in service after 1986 (difference between regular tax and AMT) .	**17**	
18	Passive activities (difference between AMT and regular tax income or loss) .	**18**	
19	Loss limitations (difference between AMT and regular tax income or loss) .	**19**	
20	Circulation costs (difference between regular tax and AMT) .	**20**	
21	Long-term contracts (difference between AMT and regular tax income) .	**21**	
22	Mining costs (difference between regular tax and AMT) .	**22**	
23	Research and experimental costs (difference between regular tax and AMT) .	**23**	
24	Income from certain installment sales before January 1, 1987 .	**24**	( )
25	Intangible drilling costs preference .	**25**	
26	Other adjustments, including income-based related adjustments .	**26**	
27	Alternative tax net operating loss deduction .	**27**	( )
28	**Alternative minimum taxable income.** Combine lines 1 through 27. (If married filing separately and line 28 is more than $191,000, see page 6 of the instructions.) .	**28**	117,000

Part II   **Alternative Minimum Tax**

29   Exemption. (If this form is for a child under age 14, see page 6 of the instructions.)

IF your filing status is . . .	AND line 28 is not over . . .	THEN enter on line 29 . . .		
Single or head of household	$112,500	$40,250		
Married filing jointly or qualifying widow(er) . .	150,000	58,000	**29**	58,000
Married filing separately	75,000	29,000		

If line 28 is **over** the amount shown above for your filing status, see page 6 of the instructions.

30	Subtract line 29 from line 28. If zero or less, enter -0- here and on lines 33 and 35 and stop here . .	**30**	59,000
31	• If you reported capital gain distributions directly on Form 1040, line 13; you reported qualified dividends on Form 1040, line 9b; **or** you had a gain on both lines 15 and 16 of Schedule D (Form 1040) (as refigured for the AMT, if necessary), complete Part III on the back and enter the amount from line 55 here. • **All others:** If line 30 is $175,000 or less ($87,500 or less if married filing separately), multiply line 30 by 26% (.26). Otherwise, multiply line 30 by 28% (.28) and subtract $3,500 ($1,750 if married filing separately) from the result.	**31**	15,340
32	Alternative minimum tax foreign tax credit (see page 7 of the instructions) .	**32**	
33	Tentative minimum tax. Subtract line 32 from line 31 .	**33**	15,340
34	Tax from Form 1040, line 43 (minus any tax from Form 4972 and any foreign tax credit from Form 1040, line 46). If you used Schedule J to figure your tax, the amounts for lines 43 and 46 of Form 1040 must be refigured without using Schedule J (see page 8 of the instructions) .	**34**	2,510
35	**Alternative minimum tax.** Subtract line 34 from line 33. If zero or less, enter -0-. Enter here and on Form 1040, line 44 .	**35**	12,830

For Paperwork Reduction Act Notice, see page 8 of the instructions.   Cat. No. 13600G   Form **6251** (2004)

*Taxable income before subtracting the exemption amounts.

Example 15. In 2004 J paid an alternative minimum tax, and his AMT credit after making the appropriate adjustments was $20,000. In 2005 J's regular tax liability before considering the minimum tax credit, is $45,000 and his *tentative* minimum tax is $40,000. Since J's regular tax exceeds his tentative minimum tax, there is no AMT for 2005. In computing his final tax liability, J is entitled to use the minimum tax credit against his regular tax liability but only to the extent that it does not create an AMT (i.e., bring his regular tax liability below his tentative minimum tax). Consequently, he may use $5,000 of the credit, reducing his regular tax liability to $40,000, as shown below. The remaining $15,000 of the minimum tax credit may be carried forward indefinitely.

Regular tax liability.		$45,000
Minimum tax credit:		
Limitation		
Regular tax	$45,000	
Tentative minimum tax . .	−40,000	
Allowable minimum tax credit		− 5,000
Total tax due		$40,000

Note that the minimum tax credit effectively converts the AMT from a permanent out-of-pocket tax to a prepayment of regular tax to the extent the AMT is attributable to deferral or timing preferences and adjustments rather than to exclusion items.[58]

For noncorporate taxpayers, the minimum tax credit for any year is the amount of the taxpayer's *adjusted net minimum tax* for all tax years after reduction for the minimum tax credit utilized for all such prior years. The adjusted net minimum tax, generally the amount of the minimum tax credit, is the difference between the AMT actually paid and the amount of AMT that would have been paid if only exclusion items were taken into account. The exclusion items are listed below:

1. Itemized deductions or standard deduction

2. Personal exemptions

3. Percentage depletion treated as a preference

4. Tax-exempt interest treated as a preference

Example 16. J is married and files a joint return for the current year on which she reports $80,000 of taxable income and claims the standard deduction. In computing her taxable income, J excluded $56,000 of tax-exempt interest from SPABs, which creates a $56,000 AMT preference item, and she claimed a $100,000 deduction for research expenses from an activity in which she does not materially participate, which creates a $90,000 AMT adjustment for research and experimental expenditures. J's minimum tax credit to be carried forward is $30,056, as computed below.

The amount of AMT actually required to be paid is $41,270, determined as follows:

---

[58]   § 53(d)(1)(B)(iv) authorizes corporate taxpayers to use the entire minimum tax liability as the minimum tax credit.

Regular taxable income			$ 80,000
Plus:	AMT adjustment for research expenses		+ 90,000
	AMT adjustment for personal exemptions		+ 6,400
	AMT adjustment for standard deduction		+ 10,000
	AMT preference item for SPAB income		+ 56,000
AMTI			$ 242,400
Less:	Exemption amount [$58,000 − $23,100 phase-out ($242,400 − $150,000 = $92,400 × 0.25)]		− 34,900
AMT base			$ 207,500
Tentative minimum tax [$45,500 + 28% ($207,500 − $175,000)]			$ 54,600
Less:	Regular tax liability		− 13,330
AMT liability for current year			$ 41,270

The amount of AMT that would have been required to be paid if only exclusion items were taken into account is $11,214 determined as follows:

Regular taxable income			$ 80,000
Plus:	AMT adjustment for personal exemptions		+ 6,400
	AMT adjustment for standard deduction		+ 10,000
	Tax preference item for SPAB income		+ 56,000
AMTI			$ 152,400
Less:	Exemption amount (no phase-out)		− 58,000
AMT base			$ 94,400
Times:	AMT rate		× 26%
Tentative AMT			$ 24,544
Less:	Regular tax liability		− 13,330
AMT using only exclusions			$ 11,214

The minimum tax credit is computed as follows:

AMT liability for current year	$ 41,270
AMT using only exclusion items	− 11,214
Minimum tax credit	$ 30,056

The $30,056 minimum tax credit may be carried forward and used to offset (reduce) the regular tax liability in subsequent years.

✅ CHECK YOUR KNOWLEDGE

Review Question 1. After completing his tax return for the year, C has a regular tax liability of $30,000, a tentative minimum tax of $45,000, and an alternative minimum tax of $15,000. How much does C actually owe the IRS?

C owes $45,000 in taxes, consisting of a regular tax liability of $30,000 and an AMT liability of $15,000.

Review Question 2. True-False. Jack is a professional golfer, earning more than $800,000 on the tour this year. After deducting expenses, taxable income for the year is $400,000. He and his wife are entitled to a $58,000 exemption in computing their alternative minimum tax liability.

False. The exemption phases out once their AMTI exceeds $150,000 and is completely phased out when AMTI reaches $382,000. Based on the size of his earnings, it would appear that his AMTI exceeds $382,000 so that the exemption would provide no benefit.

Review Question 3. True-False. In determining AMTI, the taxpayer begins with taxable income and then adds back all of the deductions allowed by so-called loopholes. There are no negative adjustments.

False. Although the effect of the AMTI is to fill in the loopholes, adjustments may be positive or negative (e.g., when AMT depreciation exceeds regular tax depreciation). All tax preference items are positive.

Review Question 4. True-False. In 2005, Steelco Corporation acquired several new copying machines for its offices and depreciated them under MACRS, using the 200 percent declining-balance method and a five-year recovery period. For AMT purposes, Steelco must use the straight-line method and a six-year class life. (**Hint:** See Revenue Procedure 87-56 contained in Exhibit 9-2).

False. Steelco may use the recovery period of five years, but is only allowed to use 150 percent declining-balance in computing depreciation for personal property for AMT purposes.

Review Question 5. Fred and Ethel are married with two children. Fred is a partner in a public accounting firm. Ethel recently retired as a traveling salesperson for an athletic shoe manufacturer. After completing their return, Fred and Ethel realized that they may have to pay the alternative minimum tax. Indicate whether an adjustment is required for AMT purposes for the following items that the couple reported for regular tax purposes.

    a. Personal exemptions for Fred and Ethel
    b. Dependent exemptions for their children
    c. Social security benefits that were nontaxable, $10,000
    d. Contribution to individual retirement account, $2,000
    e. Fred's membership dues to the Indiana C.P.A. Society reimbursed by his employer, $200
    f. Straight-line depreciation on their newly acquired duplex, which they are currently renting out, $6,000
    g. State income taxes, $10,000
    h. Property taxes on their personal residence, $4,000
    i. Tax-exempt interest from City of Indianapolis bonds used to finance its downtown mall, $2,000 (the bonds were issued after August 7, 1988)
    j. State income tax refund, $500
    k. Interest on the mortgage on their personal residence, $22,000
    l. Interest on a second mortgage on their residence (proceeds used to add a porch), $3,600
    m. Ethel's unreimbursed travel and entertainment expenses related to her employment, $1,000
    n. Alimony to Fred's ex-wife, Luci, $4,000

An adjustment is required for (a) and (b) (exemptions not allowed), (f) (40- vs. 39-year life), (g) and (h) (taxes), (i) (private activity bond), (j) (no AMT income for tax refunds), and (m) (miscellaneous itemized deduction). No adjustment is required for (c), (d), (e) (reimbursed employee business expense deductible for A.G.I.), (k) (qualified housing interest), (l) (home equity loan used for improvement to house is qualified housing interest), or (n) (no adjustment required).

Review Question 6. GHI Construction Corporation, a calendar year taxpayer, specializes in building warehouses. Its annual gross receipts average about $8 million. The corporation began work on a building in November 2005 and finished construction in February 2006. The contract was approximately 40 percent complete as of the close of the year. For regular tax purposes, the corporation uses the completed contract method. Consequently, it reported all of the income from the contract, $100,000, in 2006.

a. What is the amount of the AMT adjustment for 2005, if any?

GHI must use the percentage of completion method for AMT purposes. Therefore, the AMT adjustment would be a positive $40,000 (40% of $100,000).

b. Assume that the AMT attributable to the above contract was $8,000 (20% × $40,000) and that GHI paid this amount as AMT when it filed its 2005 tax return. In 2006 GHI reported the entire $100,000 profit for regular tax purposes. Is the $40,000 of profit earned in 2005 taxed twice, once under the AMT system when it is included as a $40,000 adjustment in 2005 and once under the regular tax system when it is included in the $100,000 reported in 2006?

No. The AMT paid in 2005 may be credited against the regular tax in 2006. The minimum tax credit ensures that the income is not taxed twice. Note that in this case the AMT effectively operates to accelerate the income tax paid on a portion of the $100,000 profit.

INCOME TAX CREDITS

One reason tax credits are popular is that a credit is viewed as providing a more equitable benefit than a comparable deduction. This is because a credit is a direct reduction of the tax liability, while a deduction merely reduces the amount of taxable income. This difference is illustrated in *Example 17*.

Example 17. Hi is in the 36% tax bracket, and Lo is in the 15% tax bracket. A credit of $100 is worth the *same* to both taxpayers since it reduces the tax liability of each by $100. On the other hand, a deduction of $100 provides a *different* benefit for each: $36 (36% × $100) for Hi and only $15 (15% × $100) for Lo.

The results from *Example 17* can be generalized for tax policy as (1) all taxpayers receive the *same dollar benefit* from credits, regardless of marginal tax rates; (2) taxpayers with higher marginal tax rates benefit more from tax deductions than do those with lower marginal rates; and (3) taxpayers receive more benefit from tax credits than from tax deductions of the same amount. In addition, the argument has been made that credits are of more benefit to those with lower incomes. This is based on the reasoning that the $100 tax saved has more relative value for those with low incomes than it has for those with high incomes. However, this line of reasoning is questionable since taxable income is just one inexact measure of a person's economic situation.

OVERVIEW OF TAX CREDITS

In recent years, the number of tax credits has been significantly increased by Congress. Most of them have been enacted into law to achieve a specified social, economic, or political goal. These goals range from encouraging taxpayers to engage in scientific research (the research credit) and the conservation of energy (energy tax credits) to providing compensatory tax reductions for those individuals who may carry greater burdens than others (credits for the elderly and for individuals with low earned incomes).

As the table in Exhibit 13-7 illustrates, the credit provisions are divided into *five* major groups or subparts. Subpart A consists of nonrefundable individual tax credits and Subpart B contains certain other nonrefundable credits. All of these nonrefundable credits may be used to reduce the tax liability, but *only* to the extent of the "regular tax liability." Subpart C contains the *refundable* credits. Subpart D consists of 13 separate credits, which are combined to form the "general business credit." Finally, the minimum tax credit is contained in Subpart G.

Limitation on Nonrefundable Credits. The TRA of 1986 amended the definition of *regular tax liability* for purposes of applying the credits. This definition is significant because the nonrefundable credits may only be used to reduce the § 26 tax liability. Under revised § 26, a taxpayer's "regular tax liability" does not include (1) the alternative minimum tax (§ 55); (2) the additional tax imposed on distributions from certain annuities [§ 72(m)]; (3) the additional tax imposed on distributions from educational IRAs [§ 530(d)]; (4) the accumulated earnings tax (§ 531); (5) the personal holding company tax (§ 541); (6) the tax on certain capital gains of S corporations (§ 1374); or (7) the tax on passive income of S corporations (§ 1375). Thus, the nonrefundable credits cannot be used to offset penalty taxes imposed by the Code (e.g., personal holding company tax, accumulated earnings tax, etc.). The practical impact of defining the "regular tax liability" in this manner is that the regular tax credits cannot offset the alternative minimum tax. Note, however that for taxable years 1999 through 2005 Congress has authorized the nonrefundable personal credits to offset the AMT as well as the regular tax liability.[59]

For taxpayers to whom two or more credits apply, generally the Code specifies an ascending order for the use of nonrefundable credits. Nonrefundable credits are to be used to reduce the § 26 tax liability in the following order: §§ 21, 22, 25A, 25, 25B, 24, 27, 23, 29, 30, 30A, 38 and 53.[60] This order is important because some of the credits may be carried forward or back and utilized in different tax years, while others "fall through the cracks" (i.e., provide no tax benefit) if they exceed the § 26 tax liability in the year they originate.

---

[59] *Huntsberry v. Comm.*, 83 T.C. 742 Also see Footnote 7, *supra* but see Footnote 8 for an amendment to § 26(a) that allows personal credits to offset the AMT for the years 2004 and 2005

[60] The order in which credits are absorbed can be pieced together by reading §§ 25(e), 23(b), 25B(g) and 53(c).

EXHIBIT 13-7
Table of Tax Credits

	Code Section	Specific Credit	Termination Date
Subpart A:	§ 21	Child and Dependent Care Credit	None
	§ 22	Credit for the Elderly	None
	§ 23	Credit for Adoption Expenses	None
	§ 24	Child Tax Credit	None
	§ 25	Credit for Interest on Certain Home Mortgages	None
	§ 25A	HOPE and Lifetime Learning Credits	None
	§ 25B	IRA Contribution Credit	12/31/2006
Subpart B:	§ 27	Possession and Foreign Tax Credit	None
	§ 29	Credit for Nonconventional Fuel Production	1/1/2008
	§ 30	Credit for Qualified Electric Vehicle	12/31/2006
	§ 30A	Puerto Rico Economic Activity Credit	12/31/2005
Subpart C:	§ 31	Credit for Taxes Withheld on Wages	None
	§ 32	Earned Income Credit	None
	§ 33	Credit for Taxes Withheld at Source on Nonresident Aliens and Foreign Corporations	None
	§ 34	Credit for Certain Uses of Gasoline and Special Fuels	None
Subpart D:	§ 38	General Business Credit Includes	
		1. Investment Credit (§ 46)	None
		2. Welfare to Work Credit (§ 51A)	12/31/2005
		3. Work Opportunity Tax Credit (§ 51)	12/31/2005
		4. Alcohol Fuels Credit (§ 40)	12/31/2010
		5. Research Credit (§ 41)	12/31/2005
		6. Low-Income Housing Credit (§ 42)	None
		7. Enhanced Oil Recovery Credit (§ 43)	None
		8. Disabled Individual Access Credit (§ 44)	None
		9. Renewable Electricity Production (§ 45)	None*
		10. Empowerment Zone Employment Credit (§ 1396)	12/31/2009
		11. Indian Employment Credit (§ 45A)	12/31/2005
		12. Employer Social Security Credit (§ 45B)	None
		13. Credit for Clinical Testing of Certain Drugs (§ 45C)	None
		14. New Markets Tax Credit (§ 45D)	12/31/2007
		15. Small Employer Pension Plan Start Up Costs (§ 45E)	12/31/2010
		16. Employer Provided Child Care Credit (§ 45F)	12/31/2010
		17. Railroad Track Maintenance Credit (§ 45G)	12/31/07
		18. Credit for production of low sulfur diesel fuel (§ 45H)	None
		19. Credit for producing oil and gas from marginal wells (§ 451)	None
		20. Energy Credit (§ 48)	None
Subpart G:	§ 53	Credit for Prior Year Minimum Tax Liability	None

*A qualified facility must be placed in service on or before 12/31/2005.

Refundable Credits. Refundable credits—listed in Exhibit 13-7 under Subpart C—are accounted for *after* the nonrefundable ones and may be applied against *any* income tax imposed by the Code-including the penalty taxes. As the name suggests, refundable credits may result in the taxpayer receiving a refund check for an amount in excess of any Federal taxes paid or withheld. In a sense, these credit provisions may result in a "negative income tax."

Due to the magnitude and relative importance of the business credits, they are examined first. A discussion of the tax credits available only to individual taxpayers immediately follows.

GENERAL BUSINESS CREDIT

As shown in Exhibit 13-7, the general business credit actually consists of 13 separate credits that are commonly available to business. Each of these credits is separately computed under its own set of rules. The various credits are then combined to determine the current year's total business credit. The credits are combined in order to determine an overall limitation on the amount of credit that can be used.

In order to prevent taxpayers from using business credits to avoid paying all income taxes, the general business credit is limited each year by the taxpayer's *net regular tax liability*. The net regular tax liability is the § 26 tax liability reduced by the credits allowed in §§ 21 through 30A. In addition, taxpayers with a net regular tax liability exceeding $25,000 are subject to an additional limitation. The business credit is limited to $25,000 *plus* 75 percent of the net regular tax liability in excess of $25,000.[61] It should also be recalled that the business credits normally are not allowed to offset the AMT. Generally, credits arising in tax years beginning after December 31, 1997 that are unused because of these limits can be carried back one year and then forward 20 years, applied on a first-in, first-out basis.[62]

> **Example 18.** In 2005 F has a potential general business credit of $92,000 and a net regular tax liability of $100,000. The maximum allowable business credit for 2005 is $81,250 [$25,000 + (75% × $75,000 = $56,250)]. The unused credit of $10,750 ($92,000 − $81,250) is subject to the carryover rules.

When the general business credit is limited and two or more components of the credit are applicable, special ordering rules apply to determine which credits will be utilized currently and which credits will be subject to the carryback and carryover rules. As specified in § 38(d), the order in which such credits are used is determined in the same order in which they are listed in Exhibit 13-7.

The common rules for computing the separate components of the general business credit beginning with the investment tax credit, are detailed in the following sections.

INVESTMENT CREDIT

In 1962 Congress enacted the investment tax credit in hopes of stimulating the economy by encouraging taxpayers to purchase certain assets—generally tangible personal property used in a trade or business. Although application of the provision became quite difficult, the essence of the law was simple. It allowed a credit equal to a particular percentage of the cost of the property. For example, taxpayers who purchased equipment at a cost of $100,000 might be entitled to a credit equal to 10 percent of the cost, or $10,000—but only as long as they met a host of requirements.

Since its enactment, the investment tax credit has had a tortuous history, in the law one year and out the next. It most recently was part of the Code in 1985 before it fell victim to the Tax Reform Act of 1986. In order to partially offset the significant loss of

---

[61]   § 38(c)(1). Married taxpayers filing separate returns are limited to $12,500 plus 75 percent of the tax liability in excess of $12,500 [§ 38(c)(4)].

[62]   § 39(a). Note that credits arising in years prior to 1998 generally could be carried back three years and then forward for 15 years.

Federal tax revenues resulting from the 1986 tax rate reductions, Congress terminated the regular investment tax credit for assets placed in service after December 31, 1985. However, Congress allowed certain portions of the old credit to continue as the investment credit (IC). Under current law, the IC is made up of two distinct parts: (1) the credit for rehabilitation expenditures and, (2) the energy credit. Each part of the IC is computed separately under its own specific rules. The actual amount of each part of the IC is the function of two factors: the taxpayer's basis in property qualifying for the credit, and the rate of the credit. The two components of the IC—the rehabilitation and energy credits—are discussed below.[63]

Rehabilitation investment Credit. The Economic Recovery Tax Act of 1981 grafted onto the regular investment credit an additional tax credit designed to encourage the restoration of buildings constructed prior to 1936. The credit represents a unique tax incentive for the restoration of old buildings.

With an emphasis on urban renewal, the rehabilitation investment credit is limited to substantial *rehabilitation expenditures* (excluding the purchase price) of *commercial buildings* and *historic structures.*[64] *Substantial* is defined to mean qualifying expenditures that exceed the greater of (1) the property's basis, or (2) $5,000. To prevent destruction of these buildings, the amended legislation requires that

1. Fifty percent or more of the existing external walls of the buildings is retained in place as external walls;

2. Seventy-five percent or more of the external walls of the building is retained in place as internal or external walls; and

3. Seventy-five percent or more of the existing internal structural framework of the building is retained in place.

If these requirements are met, the credit is available for qualified expenditures on *both* nonresidential real property and residential rental property or an addition or improvement to either type of property. However, if the rehabilitation credit is taken, the property *must* be depreciated under the straight-line method over the MACRS recovery period or the alternative depreciation system.[65]

The rate of rehabilitation credit is

Rate	*Type of Structure*
10%	Commercial building originally placed in service prior to 1936
20	All certified historic structures[66]

Example 19. On January 3, 2005 R purchases a commercial building that was constructed in 1920. In addition to the $300,000 of the purchase price allocated to the building, the entire core of the building is renovated at a cost of $600,000. R's rehabilitation credit is $60,000. computed as follows:

---

[63]   The reforestation credit allows a 10 percent credit for qualified reforestation expenditures. See §§ 48(b) and 194 for details.

[64]   § 47(a).

[65]   § 47(c)(2)(B).

[66]   § 47(c)(3). The designation as a certified historic structure is made by the Secretary of the Interior.

Qualified investment	$600,000
Rate of credit	× 10%
Current credit (before limitations)......................	$ 60,000

In some instances, rehabilitation expenditures also qualify for the energy investment credit (discussed below). When this occurs, taxpayers *must choose* between the two credits because both credits cannot be claimed for the same expenditure.[67]

Energy Investment Credit. With rising concern about conservation of energy use, Congress added the *energy credit* provisions to the Code. The objective of this credit is to encourage taxpayers to incur certain expenditures that decrease energy consumption or change the type of energy used. As originally enacted, this credit provision applied to a broad range of alternative energy sources and was available for expenditures related not only to business property but also to residential property (e.g., insulation for one's house).

In 1986, however, Congress narrowed the credit's application. Currently, the credit is available only for expenditures for solar or geothermal property that is used in a trade or business. The credit for both solar and geothermal property is 10 percent.[68]

Example 20. S is the owner of a deluxe print shop. In March 2005 S installed four solar panels to heat water to be used in a photographic development process. The panels, pumps, valves, storage tanks, control system, and installation cost a total of $80,000. S's energy tax credit is $8,000.

Qualified investment	$80,000
Rate of credit	× 10%
Current credit (before limitations).....................	$ 8,000

Basis Reduction of Qualified Property. At one time, taxpayers were allowed to take a full 10 percent IC or any applicable energy tax credit and still recover their entire cost basis of qualifying property under ACRS. In 1986 Congress decided that this treatment was too liberal with respect to rehabilitation property and required the basis of the property to be reduced by the amount of IC taken with respect to the property.[69] A similar rule requires that the basis of energy property be reduced by *one-half* of the amount of the IC taken on such energy property.[70]

Example 21. Refer to the facts in *Example 19*, where R's rehabilitation credit is $60,000. R purchased the property for $300,000 and incurred $600,000 of rehabilitation expenditures. R's basis in the rehabilitated property is $840,000 ($300,000 + $600,000 − $60,000).

---

[67]   § 48(a)(2)(B).

[68]   § 48(a)(3).

[69]   § 50(c)(1). Note that for determining the amount and character of gain on the disposition of the property, the downward basis adjustment is treated as a deduction allowed for depreciation. Accordingly, the amount of the basis adjustment will be subject to the § 1245 depreciation recapture rules discussed in Chapter 7.

[70]   § 50(c)(3).

Example 22. Refer to the facts in *Example 20*, where S's energy tax credit is $8,000. S purchased the solar property for $80,000. S's basis in the energy property is $76,000 ($80,000 − $4,000).

The investment credit calculations discussed here provide the background for computing the recapture of IC on early dispositions required by the Code.[71] The amount of IC recapture should be an economic consideration in planning the disposition of any asset upon which the IC was claimed.

IC Recapture. When taxpayers place qualified investment property into service, they claim the full amount of IC regardless of how long they intend to use the property. However, if an asset ceases to be qualified property during a five-year period (due to a sale or other disposition, or a change in the purpose or use of the asset), taxpayers are required to recapture a portion of the "unearned" IC. The recapture percentages illustrated in Exhibit 13-8 must be used to calculate the amount of unearned credit that is recaptured as an additional tax in the year of early disposition. As a general rule, 20 percent of the credit is "earned" for each full year the property is held. For example, a qualified rehabilitation property placed in service on December 20, 2004 qualified for the rehabilitation credit in 2004 and was taken on the taxpayer's return for the year. However, none of the credit was *earned* until December 21, 2005. On that date, 20 percent of the credit allowed in 2004 was earned and thus no longer subject to recapture.

EXHIBIT 13-8
ITC Recapture Percentages[72]

If qualified property ceases to be qualified property—	The recapture percentage is:
Before one full year, after placed in service	100%
After one year, within two full years	80
After two years, within three full years	60
After three years, within four full years	40
After four years, within five full years	20

Example 23. Assume that the commercial building (acquired on January 3, 2005) in *Example 19* was sold by R on September 1, 2006. The IC recapture is computed as follows:

Property	IC Claimed	×	Recapture Percentage	=	Amount Recaptured
Commercial bldg.	$60,000	×	80%	=	$48,000

This amount is reported on Form 4255 and is treated as an additional tax imposed on the taxpayer in the year in which an early disposition occurs. Because the building's basis was originally decreased by the entire credit claimed, its basis is increased by the amount of the recapture for purposes of computing the gain or loss to be recognized on the sale.[73]

---

[71] § 50(a).

[72] § 50(a)(1)(B).

[73] § 50(c)(2). A similar rule applies to energy property, but only one-half of the amount of recapture is added to the basis of the property.

In addition to sales and exchanges (including like-kind exchanges), dispositions generally include gifts, dividend distributions from corporations, cessation of business usage, and involuntary conversions.[74] Even though the recaptured IC is referred to as an "other tax" on Form 1040, the amount recaptured will not be treated as a tax for purposes of determining the amount of nonrefundable tax credits allowed under § 26.[75]

The recapture rules do not apply to transfers by reason of death or to assets transferred in certain corporate acquisitions.[76] The recapture rules also will not apply to transfers of property between spouses, even if the transfer is made incident to divorce.[77] Finally, property is not treated as ceasing to be qualified property when a mere change in the form of conducting the trade or business occurs, so long as the property continues to be qualified property in the new business and the taxpayer retains a substantial interest in this trade or business.[78]

IC Carryovers. Like the other components of the general business credit, the IC allowed in tax years beginning after December 31, 1997 but not utilized because of the tax liability limitation can be carried forward for 20 years. Finally, in determining the extent to which an investment credit is used in a taxable year, the regular investment credit is deemed to be used *before* the rehabilitation credit and the energy credit.[79]

WORK OPPORTUNITY CREDIT

For many years Congress has tried to spur employment by granting businesses a tax credit for hiring new workers that otherwise had a hard time finding employment. Since 1979, businesses have been able to claim the credit if they hire individuals from certain targeted groups. The targeted groups have been most recently redefined to include[80]

- ► recipients of a state law providing assistance for needy families with minor children,
- ► qualified veterans,
- ► qualified ex-felons,
- ► high-risk youth,
- ► vocational rehabilitation referrals,
- ► qualified summer youth employees,
- ► qualified food stamp recipients, or
- ► qualified SSI recipients.

To be eligible, each individual must obtain certification from a designated local agency, specifying that the individual meets the established criteria and therefore qualifies as a member of one of the targeted groups.

Amount of Credit. The work opportunity tax credit is 40 percent of the first $6,000 of first-year wages paid to a qualified individual.[81] Thus, the maximum credit is $2,400

---

[74] Reg. § 1.47-2.

[75] § 50(a)(5)(C).

[76] § 50(a)(4).

[77] § 50(a)(5)(B).

[78] § 50(a)(4) and Reg. § 1.47-3(f).

[79] See § 38(d).

[80] §§ 51(d) and 51(c)(4). This credit was extended through December 31, 2005 by the Working Families Tax Relif Act of 2004.

[81] See § 51(i) for other limitations based on the number of hours worked.

for each new employee. Note that, without any restriction, the employer would be able not only to claim a credit for the wages paid to the employee but also to deduct those wages. However, employers who elect to take the credit must reduce their wage expense by the amount of the credit; this eliminates the potential windfall. Note also that, as part of the general business credit, the § 38 rules limiting the amount of the credit ($25,000 + 75% of the tax liability in excess of $25,000) are applicable, as are the one-year carryback and 20-year carryover rules.

Special Rule for Qualified Summer Youth Employees. Employers are allowed to claim the jobs credit for wages paid for the summer employment of teenagers that are members of economically disadvantaged families. These individuals must be 16 or 17 years of age on the hiring date and must not have worked previously for the employer. To qualify for the credit, the services must be attributable to any 90-day period between May 1 and September 15. The summer youth employment credit is 40 percent of the first $3,000 of eligible wages, for a maximum credit of $1,200 per youth.[82] If a summer youth employee continues to work after the 90-day period, his or her wages may qualify for the general targeted jobs credit previously discussed. However, certification of this employee as a member of a second target group must be determined as of the date of the second certification rather than on the basis of the employee's original certification as a qualified summer youth employee. In addition, the $6,000 wage limit for the targeted job credit must be reduced by the qualified summer wages.

> **Example 24.** On July 29, 2005 the owners of a farm hired 10 youths that were certified as qualified summer employees to help harvest crops. The owners paid the youths $150 a week for eight weeks (through September 22). The amount of targeted jobs credit in 2005 without regard to additional certifications is $4,200, computed in the following manner:

Qualifying wages ($150 × 10 youths × 7 weeks)	$10,500
Percent of credit.	× 40%
Amount of credit.	$ 4,200

> The wage expense deduction attributable to the youths' salaries would be $7,800, computed as follows:

Total wages paid ($150 × 10 youths × 8 weeks).	$ 12,000
Reduced by allowable credit	− 4,200
Allowable wage expense	$ 7,800

> Note that the eighth week does not qualify for the credit since it occurs after the September 15 cutoff date.

WELFARE TO WORK CREDIT

To encourage employers to hire those who are making the transition off welfare, the new law provides employers with another employee related tax credit. The credit is available on the first $20,000 of eligible wages paid to qualified long-term family assistance recipients (e.g., individuals receiving aid under the Aid to Families with Dependent Children program) during the first two years of employment. The credit is 35

---

[82]   § 51(d)(12)(B).

percent of the first $10,000 of eligible wages in the first year and 50 percent of the first $10,000 of eligible wages in the second year. The maximum credit per new employee over the two year period is $8,500.[83]

ALCOHOL FUEL CREDIT

The fourth component of the general business credit is the alcohol fuel credit. To foster the production of gasohol, an income tax credit for alcohol and alcohol-blended fuels applies to fuel sales and uses before January 1, 2011. The alcohol fuel credit is computed and reported on Form 6478. Generally, the credit is $0.60 per gallon of alcohol used in a qualified alcohol mixture or as a straight alcohol fuel.[84] Although taxpayers are entitled to a credit, they must include an amount equal to the credit claimed in income.[85]

RESEARCH AND EXPERIMENTAL (R&E) CREDIT

The fifth component of the general business credit is the research credit—commonly referred to as the R&E credit. Created in 1981 and amended several times since, the R&E credit provisions generally allow taxpayers a credit equal to 20 percent of their *incremental* expenditures that constitute either (1) qualified research expenditures or (2) basic research payments.[86] The method for identifying what qualifies as an incremental expenditure is considered in detail below, as are the types of qualifying research. First, however, the relationship of the R&E credit and the deduction for R&E must be addressed.

Impact of R&E Credit on Current Deductions. The research credit is the second part of Congress's two-prong approach for stimulating research. The first part of this plan, as might be recalled from Chapter 9, allows taxpayers either to deduct research and experimental expenditures immediately or capitalize the expenditures and amortize them over 60 months. As might be expected, taxpayers are not allowed to have their research cake and eat it too—they must reduce their R&E deduction for the amount of R&E credit determined for the year.[87] For those taxpayers who normally expense R&E costs, this means that their deduction for R&E is simply smaller. For those taxpayers who capitalize and amortize the costs, the amount capitalized is reduced. Note that if the credit is not utilized by the taxpayer within the 20-year carryover period, a deduction equal to the amount of the expiring credit is allowed in the year following the expiration of the tax credit carryover period.[88]

Without additional rules, the cutback of the deduction for the credit could prove unduly harsh for taxpayers subject to the AMT, which generally does not allow the use of credits. For this reason taxpayers are allowed to *elect* to claim a reduced credit.[89] This election effectively enables the taxpayer to trade a credit that is not allowed to reduce the AMT for a deduction that could be used to reduce the AMT.

---

[83] § 51A. This credit was extended through December 31, 2005 by the Working Families Tax Relief Act of 2004.

[84] § 40. A similar credit applies to small ethanol producers.

[85] § 87.

[86] § 41(a). The credit currently extends only to amounts paid on or before June 30, 1995, and on or after July 1, 1996 through December 31, 2005.

[87] § 280C(c).

[88] § 196. The deduction allowed is 50 percent of the expired R&E credits attributable to taxable years beginning before 1990.

[89] § 280C(c)(3).

Qualified Research Expenditures. The R&E credit is allowed for both in-house research and contract (outside) research. *Qualified research expenditures* are those incurred in carrying on a trade or business for in-house research expenses (e.g., wages, supplies, rental of equipment, overhead) and 65 percent of *contract research expenses* (those paid to any person other than an employee of the taxpayer for qualified research).[90] To be eligible for the credit, the expenditures must meet the same criteria that must be met for their deduction. As a general rule, these criteria extend special treatment only for research and development in the experimental or laboratory sense. This includes (1) the development of an experimental or pilot model, plant process, formula, invention, or similar property, and (2) the improvement of such types of property already in existence.[91] In addition, the expenditures must be technological in nature *and* must relate to establishing a new or improved function, or improving the performance, reliability, or quality of a product.[92] Finally, the credit is *denied* for certain expenditure items,[93] including

1. Research undertaken outside the United States

2. Research conducted in the social sciences or humanities

3. Ordinary testing or inspection of materials or products for quality control

4. Market and consumer research

5. Research relating to style, taste, cosmetic, or seasonal design

6. Advertising and promotion expenses

7. Management studies and efficiency surveys

8. Computer software for internal use of the taxpayer

9. Research to locate and evaluate mineral deposits, including oil and gas

10. Acquisition and improvement of land and of certain depreciable or depletable property used in research (including the annual depreciation deduction)

Amount of Credit. The 20 percent credit is extended only to taxpayers who increase their research activities. As shown in the formula in Exhibit 13-9, this is accomplished by allowing a credit only for qualified research expenditures for the current year that exceed the taxpayer's base amount.[94] The base amount is a fixed percentage of the taxpayer's average gross receipts for the four previous years.[95] As a result, those taxpayers who continually increase their research benefit the most from this special incentive.

The fixed-base percentage is computed differently for firms with a history of doing research than for firms that do not have such a history. For taxpayers reporting both qualified research expenses and gross receipts during each of at least three years from 1984 to 1988, the "fixed-base percentage" is the ratio that its total qualified research expenses for the 1984 to 1988 period bears to its total gross receipts for this period, subject to a maximum ratio of 16 percent. "Start-up companies" and those taxpayers

---

[90] § 41(b)(4). The trade or business requirement may be met by certain start-up companies even though they are not currently in business.

[91] Reg. § 1.174-2(a).

[92] § 41(d)(1)(B).

[93] § 41(d)(4).

[94] § 41(a)(1).

[95] § 41(c).

not meeting the R&E expenditures and gross receipt requirements above are assigned a fixed-base percentage of 3 percent for the first five years in which qualified research expenditures are incurred.[96]

EXHIBIT 13-9
Calculation of R&E Credit

R&E Credit = 20% × (qualified R&E expenditures − base amount)

Base amount = Fixed-base percentage × Average gross receipts for four previous years

$$\text{Fixed-base percentage} * = \frac{\text{Total research expenses (1984 − 1988)}}{\text{Total gross receipts (1984 − 1988)}}$$

*Subject to special rules for start-up companies and limited to a maximum of 16 percent.

Example 25. Assume R Corporation reported the following research expenditures and gross receipts:

	1986	1987	1988
Research expenditures	$ 90,000	$100,000	$110,000
Gross receipts	700,000	900,000	800,000

	2001	2002	2003	2004	2005
Research expenditures	$120,000	$130,000	$ 140,000	$ 150,000	$ 180,000
Gross receipts	700,000	800,000	1,000,000	1,100,000	1,200,000

R Corporation's R&E credit for 2005 is computed as follows:

1. Fixed-base percentage = $300,000/$2,400,000 = .125

2. Base amount = .125 × $3,600,000/4 = $112,500

3. Qualified R&E expenditures for 2004 = $180,000

4. R&E Credit = 20% × ($180,000 − $112,500) = $13,500

Note that R's fixed-base percentage is based on the research activity and gross receipts during 1984–1988, whereas the average annual gross receipts number is based on receipts for the four previous years, 2001–2004 ($700,000 + $800,000 + $1,000,000 + $1,100,000 = $3,600,000). Also note that in 2005 R must reduce its current deduction for research expenditures by $13,500, or if the deferred asset method of accounting is used, the $180,000 R&E costs must be reduced to $166,500 ($180,000 − $13,500) before being capitalized and amortized over a period of not less than 60 months.[97]

Basic Research Expenditures. The second category of expenditures qualifying for the research credit is the *incremental* amount of *basic research payments* made to universities and other qualified organizations. Basic research means any original investigation for the advancement of scientific knowledge not having a specific commercial

---

[96] Special rules apply to start-up companies after the sixth taxable year in which they incur qualified research expenditures. See § 41(c)(3)(B).

[97] See the Tax Relief Extension Act of 1999, Act § 502 for special rules applicable to Research Tax Credits arising from expenditures made in 2000 and 2001.

objective. The term "basic research payment" means any amount paid in cash during the taxable year by a corporation to a qualified organization for basic research, but only if such payment is made pursuant to a written agreement and the basic research is to be performed by the qualified organization. Qualified organizations include educational institutions, certain scientific research organizations, and certain grant organizations.

The R&E credit applies to the *excess* of corporate cash expenditures in a year over the qualified organization base period amount. The qualified organization base period amount is the *sum* of (1) the minimum basic research amount, plus (2) the maintenance-of-effort amount. The *maintenance-of-effort amount* prevents the corporation from shifting its historical charitable contribution to any qualifying educational organization over to a creditable basic research payment. It is an amount equal to the *average* nondesignated university contributions paid by the corporation during the base period, increased by the cost of living adjustment for the calendar year over the amount of nondesignated university contributions paid by the taxpayer during that year. Any portion of the basic research payment that does not exceed the qualified organization base period amount will be treated as contract research expenses for computing the incremental qualified research expenditures discussed above under "qualified research expenditures" above.[98]

Alternative Incremental Credit. For taxable years beginning after June 30, 1996, a taxpayer may make an election to compute the research credit utilizing three tiers of reduced fixed base percentages and reduced credit rates.[99] This election may be beneficial for companies that have average gross receipts increasing at a faster rate than the increases in qualified research expenditures. This election is mentioned here only to round out the discussion of this credit but further analysis of the election is beyond the scope of this text.

Credit Limitations. As part of the general business credit, the tax liability limitation ($25,000 + 75% of the tax liability in excess of $25,000) applies, as do the one-year carryback and 20-year carryover rules. Additional limitations are imposed in an effort to prevent the research credit from being exploited by tax shelter promoters. For individuals with ownership interests in unincorporated businesses (i.e., partners of a partnership), trust or estate beneficiaries, or S corporation shareholders, any allowable pass-through of the credit cannot exceed the *lesser of* (1) the individual's net regular tax liability limitation discussed earlier, or (2) the amount of tax attributable to the individual's taxable income resulting from the individual's interest in the entity that earned such credit.[100]

The final unique characteristic of the R&E credit is applicable to changes in business ownership. Special rules apply for computing the credit when a business changes hands, under which qualified research expenditures for periods prior to the change of ownership generally are treated as transferred with the trade or business that gave rise to those expenditures.[101]

LOW-INCOME HOUSING CREDIT

The next component of the general business credit is the low-income housing credit. This credit is available for low-income housing that is constructed, rehabilitated, or acquired after 1986. The credit is claimed over a 10-year period, with an annual credit

---

[98]   § 41(e)(1)(B).

[99]   § 41(c)(4).

[100]   § 41(g).

[101]   § 41(f)(3).

of approximately 9 percent of the qualifying basis of low-income units placed in service. If federal subsidies are used to finance the project, the credit is limited to approximately 4 percent.[102] For property placed in service after 1987, the exact percentage is determined by the IRS on a monthly basis. The percentages for any month are calculated to yield, over a 10-year credit period, amounts of credit that have a present value equal to (1) 70 percent of the qualified basis of new buildings that are not federally subsidized for the tax year, and (2) 30 percent of the qualified basis of existing buildings and new buildings that are federally subsidized.[103]

> **Example 26.** In January 2005 H, an individual, constructed and placed in service a qualified low-income housing project. The qualified basis of the project was $1 million. The 70% present value credit for buildings placed in service in January 2005 is 7.99%.[104] Thus, the annual credit that H could claim is $79,900.

Each year, the sum of allowed low-income housing credits is subject to a nationwide cap. The cap amount is allotted among all of the states so that each state will have a cap on the amount of low-income housing credits it can authorize. A credit allocation from the appropriate state credit authority must be received by the owner of the property eligible for the low-income housing credit. The credit is available on a per-unit basis; thus, a single building may have some units that qualify for the credit and some that do not. In order to qualify, a low-income housing project must meet a host of exacting criteria throughout a 15-year compliance period.[105]

DISABLED ACCESS CREDIT

Another component of the general business credit is the disabled access credit. This credit was established in 1994 primarily as a relief measure for those businesses that are required under the Americans with Disabilities Act of 1990 to make improvements that make existing facilities accessible to the disabled. Under Code § 44, an eligible small business can elect to take a nonrefundable tax credit equal to 50 percent of the amount of the eligible access expenditures for any taxable year that exceed $250 but do not exceed $10,250. An eligible small business is defined as one having gross receipts for the preceding taxable year that did not exceed $1,000,000, or having no more than 30 full-time employees during the preceding taxable year. Eligible access expenditures are defined as amounts paid or incurred by an eligible small business to comply with applicable requirements of the Disabilities Act. Eligible access expenditures generally include amounts paid or incurred for the following:

1. Removing architectural, communication, physical, or transportation barriers that prevent a business from being accessible to, or usable by, individuals with disabilities

2. Providing qualified interpreters or other effective methods of making aurally delivered materials available to individuals with hearing impairments

3. Providing qualified readers, taped texts, and other effective methods of making visually delivered materials available to individuals with visual impairments

---

[102] § 42(b)(1).

[103] § 42(b)(2)(B). A formula for making such computations is provided in Rev. Rul. 88-6, 1988-1 C.B. 3.

[104] Rev. Rul. 2005-2, 2005-2 I.R.B.

[105] See §§ 42(g) and 42(l).

4. Acquiring or modifying equipment or devices for individuals with disabilities

5. Providing other similar services, modifications, materials, or equipment

In cases where the eligible business is being conducted as a partnership or an S corporation, the dollar limitations are applied at both the entity and the owner level. Any portion of the unused general business credit attributable to the disabled access credit may not be carried back to any taxable year ending before 1990.

> **Example 27.** J, a sole proprietor, had gross receipts of $700,000 last year and incurred $5,250 of eligible access expenditures this year. J's disabled access credit for this year is $2,500 [($5,250 − $250) × 50%].

As is the case with other components of the general business credit, the depreciable basis of assets acquired subject to the credit using access expenditures must be reduced by the amount of credit claimed with respect to those expenditures. Alternatively, any current deduction attributable to the access expenditures must be reduced by the amount of credit claimed.[106]

EMPOWERMENT ZONE EMPLOYMENT CREDIT

To help rebuild distressed urban and rural areas, the RRA of 1994 created several tax incentives. The hope is that these incentives will encourage businesses to locate in these areas and hire individuals who live there. The goal is carried out in § 1396, which authorizes the Secretary of Housing and Urban Development and the Secretary of Agriculture to identify 95 *enterprise communities* and 29 *empowerment zones* where the tax benefits will be offered. The regions must meet certain criteria concerning population, size (urban areas cannot exceed 20 square miles and rural areas cannot exceed 1,000 square miles), and poverty (a minimum rate of 20 percent).[107]

Businesses that operate within the designated areas are entitled to a variety of benefits. Perhaps the most important of these is the empowerment zone employment credit (EZEC). All employers located in an empowerment zone are entitled to a 20 percent credit for the first $15,000 of wages paid to full-time as well as part-time employees who are residents of the empowerment zone. The maximum credit per employee is $3,000 per year. If an employer is entitled to both a work opportunity credit (WOC) and an EZEC, the first $6,000 of wages paid qualify for the higher WOC of 40 percent, and the next $9,000 qualify for the EZEC of 20 percent. Thus, the payment of $15,000 of wages could enable the employer to claim a credit as high as $4,200 ($6,000 × 40% = $2,400) + ($9,000 × 20% = $1,800). Of course, the employer's deduction for wages must be reduced by the amount of credits allowed.

Like the WOC, the EZEC is part of the general business credit and is consequently subject to the tax liability limitation as well as the carryback and carryover rule. Unlike the WOC, the EZEC can offset 25 percent of the employer's AMT liability.

In addition to the EZEC, businesses within an enterprise community are entitled to increase the amount they can expense under § 179. The limit was $102,000 in 2004 and will be adjusted annually until December 31, 2007, after which it goes back to $25,000.[108] Note that buildings do not qualify for limited expensing in any event. The increase in the § 179 amount is also allowed for the AMT, so no AMT adjustment is required.

---

[106] § 44(c)(7).

[107] §§ 1391(a), 1391(g) and 1396.

[108] § 1397A.

CREDIT FOR EMPLOYER-PROVIDED CHILD-CARE

To encourage employers to provide quality child care for its employees, Congress established a special credit. The employer-provided child care credit became effective in 2002. The credit will be considered a part of the general business credit.

Under new § 45F, employers may claim a credit equal to 25 percent of the cost of qualified child care expenditures and 10 percent of qualified child care resource and referral expenditures. The maximum total amount of credit is limited to $150,000 per year. In addition, the basis of any property is reduced by the amount of credit claimed. Similarly, any other deduction or credit must be reduced by the amount of credit claimed.

Qualifying expenditures include the costs of (1) building, acquiring, rehabilitating or expanding property that is used as part of a *qualified child care facility* of the taxpayer for its employees, (2) operating such facilities, and (3) a contract with a qualified child care facility. A qualified child care facility is a facility whose principal use is to provide child care assistance and meets the requirements of all applicable laws and regulations of the state and local government in which it is located, including the licensing requirements applicable to a child care facility. The definition does not include a facility which is the principal residence of the taxpayer, any employee of the taxpayer, or the operator of the facility. Thus day care centers will be qualified only if they are separate and distinct from the operator's personal residence.

In addition, expenses incurred in providing child-care resource and referral services are eligible for a 10 percent credit. Usage of a facility cannot favor high-income earners, and at least 30 percent of the children in the center must be children of employees. Finally, if the facility is no longer used as a child care center or there is a disposition of the taxpayer's interest (e.g., the taxpayer sells the property), § 45F(d)(2) requires the taxpayer to recapture (i.e., pay back to the government) a percentage of the tax savings from prior years as shown below:

If the Recapture Event Occurs in Years	Percentage Recapture
1–3	100%
4	85
5	70
6	55
7	40
8	25
9–10	10
11	0

OTHER COMPONENTS OF THE GENERAL BUSINESS CREDIT

There are several other credits that make up the general business credit:

▸ *Indian Employment Credit.* Added by the RRA of 1994 to encourage the hiring of Native Americans, the Indian employment credit (authorized in § 45A) generally entitles employers conducting businesses located on Indian reservations to claim a credit of 20 percent for up to $20,000 of wages and insurance benefits paid to employees who are members of an Indian tribe and who work and live on the reservation.

▸ *Employer Social Security Credit.* This credit represents a relief measure (or perhaps a peace offering) for the restaurant industry, which presumably was detrimentally impacted by the 1994 cut in the deduction for business meals from 80 to 50 percent. Section 45B allows employers operating food and beverage establishments to claim a credit against their income tax liability for their FICA obligation (7.65%) on tips in excess of those treated as wages for purposes of satisfying the minimum wage provisions. To prevent a double benefit, no deduction is allowed for any FICA taxes taken into account in determining the credit.

▸ *Renewable Electricity Production Credit.* Section 45 provides a credit for taxpayers who produce electricity from qualified wind energy or certain other renewable resources from facilities placed in service after 2003 and before 2006.

▸ *Enhanced Oil Recovery Credit.* This is a special credit directed at owners of oil and gas properties requiring secondary or tertiary methods of production.

▸ *Orphan Drug Credit.* The credit for qualified clinical testing expenses for certain drugs for rare diseases or conditions has been made a permanent part of the general business credit. The credit is equal to 50 percent of the qualified clinical testing expenses for the taxable year.

▸ *Credit for Plan Start-up Costs of Small Employers.* Small employers with no more than 100 employees will receive a tax credit for some of the costs of establishing new retirement plans, effective for costs paid or incurred in tax years beginning after December 31, 2001. The credit equals 50 percent of the start-up costs incurred to create or maintain a new employee retirement plan. The credit is limited to $500 in any tax year and it may be claimed for qualified costs incurred in each of the three years beginning with the tax year in which the plan becomes effective [Code § 45E(b).]

In addition to those credits that make up the general business credit, there are still other credits available to business. The foreign tax credit and the credit for qualified electric vehicles, available to both businesses and individuals, are discussed briefly below. Another credit, one for producing fuel from a nonconventional source (§ 29), has limited applicability and is not discussed in this text.

GENERAL BUSINESS CREDIT CARRYOVER RULES

Recall that the carryback period is one year and the carryforward period is 20 years for business credits incurred in years beginning after 1997. If the business credit carryover cannot be used within the stipulated time period, the credit expires. Without special rules, this would be a double loss for taxpayers who claimed the full investment tax credit percentages or other credits and who decreased the basis of property for ACRS computations. Not only have they lost the credit but they also were unable to depreciate the full cost of the assets. Because of this possibility, taxpayers are allowed to take a deduction equal to the amount of the previous reductions from basis stipulated by the expired IC or other credits. This deduction may be taken in the year *following* the expiration of the tax credit carryover period.[109]

> **Example 28.** Q originally claimed an IC of $10,000 and reduced the basis in the assets by $5,000. After the expiration of the carryforward period, an unused IC of $3,000 expires. In the first taxable year after the expiration of the credit carryover period, Q may deduct $1,500 (½ of $3,000). This amount equals the original decrease in basis for the expired investment credit.

---

[109] § 196.

FOREIGN TAX CREDIT

The new emphasis on the global economy and global investing is making the treatment of foreign income and foreign taxes a concern for far more taxpayers than ever before. As explained in Chapter 3, U.S. citizens (including U.S. corporations) and resident aliens must pay U.S. taxes on their worldwide income: income earned in the United States as well as income from foreign sources. In many cases, they pay not only U.S. taxes but also foreign taxes on the same income. To alleviate the burden of two taxes on the same income, § 27 generally allows taxpayers to claim a credit for income taxes paid or accrued to a foreign country. Alternatively, taxpayers may elect to claim a deduction for the taxes. Also note that if the taxpayer elects to use the $74,000 earned income exclusion (see Chapter 3), any foreign taxes paid on such income cannot be claimed as a credit.

Although the taxpayer is normally allowed a credit for any foreign taxes paid, the amount of the credit may be limited in some cases. As a general rule, the credit for the foreign taxes cannot exceed the U.S. tax that would otherwise be paid on the same income. For example, assume a U.S. taxpayer earns $10,000 while living abroad and pays a foreign tax on such income of $3,000. If the U.S. tax on such income is only $2,000, the taxpayer's credit is limited to $2,000, and she consequently pays a foreign tax of $3,000 and no U.S. tax because her $2,000 U.S. tax liability is reduced to zero by the $2,000 FTC. Note that, without the limitation, the United States could effectively lose $1,000 of taxes on other U.S. income that it would otherwise receive. As this example illustrates, the limitation is generally triggered when the foreign tax rate exceeds the U.S. tax rate. The actual limitation is computed using the following formula:

$$\frac{\text{Foreign source taxable income}}{\text{Worldwide taxable income*}} \times \text{U.S. tax before credits} = \text{Foreign tax credit limitation}$$

*U.S. source taxable income + Foreign source taxable income + Personal exemptions

Any unused foreign tax credits may be carried back two years and carried forward five years. However, the credits may be carried over only to years where the foreign tax credit limitation has not been exceeded.

> **Example 29.** This year Mr. and Mrs. T took their financial consultants, advice on global investing. As a result, they received $10,000 of dividends from several foreign stocks. The couple's taxable income including the dividends was $94,250, producing a tax before credits of $16,893. The maximum foreign tax credit would be $1,678, computed as follows:
>
> $$\frac{\$10,000}{\$94,000 + \$6,400 = \$100,650} \times \$16,893 = \$1,678$$

One caveat is in order before leaving the foreign tax credit. Although the above rules normally apply, taxpayers must be careful. Not only are the rules complex (they are applied separately to different classes of income), but tax treaties with a particular country may provide special rules for income earned in that country by U.S. citizens. Such treaties must be examined when dealing with foreign income.

CREDIT FOR QUALIFIED ELECTRIC VEHICLES

One of the energy conservation provisions in the National Energy Policy Act of 1992 created an incentive for the manufacture and purchase of electric cars. Section 30 authorizes a tax credit equal to 10 percent of the cost of any qualified electric vehicle placed in service by the taxpayer after 1992 and before 2007. The maximum credit in a single year is $4,000 and under the American Jobs Creation Act of 2004, the maximum credit is $1,000 for a qualified electric vehicle placed in service after 2005. The phase out will continue through 2007. The credit is available to both individuals and businesses but is limited to the original owner of the vehicle.

NONBUSINESS CREDITS

In addition to the numerous business credits discussed thus far, there are several nonbusiness credits available to individual taxpayers only. These credits include (1) the child tax credit, (2) the child and dependent care credit, (3) the HOPE and Lifetime learning credits, (4) the credit for adoption expenses, (5) the credit for the elderly, (6) the credit for interest on certain home mortgages, and (7) the earned income credit and other refundable credits. Each of these credits is discussed below.

CHILD TAX CREDIT

One of the major changes made by the TRA of 1997 is the creation of a special tax credit for taxpayers with children. Section 24 was modified by the Working Families Tax Relief Act of 2004 and allows most taxpayers to claim a credit of $1,000 for each qualifying child. The amount of the credit will remain at $1,000 per qualifying child for tax years 2005 through 2009.

In order to be considered a qualifying child, the individual in question must meet the following conditions:

- ▸ The individual must be the child of the taxpayer. For this purpose, a stepson or stepdaughter or an eligible foster child qualifies as a child. Descendants of these individuals are also treated as a qualifying child.
- ▸ The child must not have attained the age of 17 before the close of the taxable year.
- ▸ The taxpayer is eligible to claim a dependency exemption for the child.
- ▸ The child is a citizen, or a national of the U.S., or a resident of the U.S.

Like many of the other tax relief provisions contained in the TRA of 1997, the benefits of the credit are not extended to wealthy individuals. To accomplish this policy objective, the credit is reduced by $50 for each $1,000 (or part thereof) of adjusted gross income (computed with certain modifications) exceeding the following levels of income for 2005.

EXHIBIT 13-10
2005 Child Tax Credit Phase-out

Taxpayer	Phase-out begins When Modified A.G.I. Exceeds	Phase-Out Ends when Modified A.G.I. Exceeds			
		One child	Two children	Three children	Four children
Single	$ 75,000	$ 86,000	$ 98,000	$110,000	$122,000
Married filing jointly	$110,000	$121,000	$133,000	$145,000	$157,000

Modified A.G.I. is A.G.I. determined before any exclusion for foreign earned income and foreign housing costs and income from certain possessions. These thresholds are not indexed for inflation. In order to claim the credit, the taxpayer must disclose the TIN of each qualifying child on the return and the taxable year of the taxpayer must include a 12 month period.

> **Example 30.** H and W are married with three children. At the close of 2005, the children, X, Y, and Z, were ages 12, 16 and 18 respectively. H and W claim a dependency exemption for each of the children. This year H and W reported adjusted gross income of $114,200. H and W may claim a child credit for X and Y since they are both dependents and did not attain the age of 17 before the close of the year. The amount of the credit is limited to $1,750 determined as follows:

Tentative credit for each child		$1,000
Qualifying children		× 2
Total credit before phase-out		$2,000
Reduction:		
Adjusted gross income	$ 114,200	
Threshold for joint return	(110,000)	
Excess adjusted gross income	$ 4,200	
Reduction [($4,200/$1,000 = 4.2 rounded up to 5) × $50]		(250)
Child credit allowed for children		$1,750

The amount of the child tax credit that can be claimed by a taxpayer for any taxable year shall not exceed the excess of the sum of the § 26 regular tax liability plus the AMT over the sum of the credits allowed by the Child and Dependent Care Credit (§ 21), the Credit for the Elderly (§ 22), the Credit for Interest on Certain Home Mortgages (§ 25), the HOPE and Lifetime Learning credit (§ 25A) and the foreign tax credit (§ 27). Note: The 2001 Tax Act made permanent the allowance of the nonrefundable portion of the child tax credit to be claimed against both regular and AMT tax liability. In addition the act provides that at least a portion of the child tax credit will be refundable for taxpayers with qualifying children. Since this credit is a refundable credit, it is discussed near the end of the "Earned Income Credit" section of this chapter.

CHILD AND DEPENDENT CARE CREDIT

The emergence of the working wife and two-earner couples during the post-World War II era produced a new tax issue. The dilemma concerned the treatment of the costs for the care of children and other dependents. The question posed was whether taxpayers who were forced to pay such costs in order to work should be entitled to deduct them as business expenses. Early court cases denied a deduction for these expenses on the grounds that they were personal in nature. In the court's view, the expenses stemmed from a personal choice by married couples to employ others to discharge their domestic duties, a purely personal expense. Congress, however, became sensitive to the issue in the late 1960s and responded with a limited deduction in 1971. After several alterations and amendments, the deduction received a complete makeover and was converted into a credit in 1976—a far better deal for those who did not itemize. It now appears that, almost 20 years after its creation, the credit is a permanent part of the tax law, presumably justified as both a relief measure for those who have differing abilities to pay and as a stimulant that reduces the costs of entering the work force.

As the statute is now drawn, taxpayers are able to claim a credit for a portion of their child and dependent care expenses if they meet two requirements: (1) the taxpayer maintains a household for a qualifying individual and (2) the expenses—so-called *employment-related expenses*—are incurred to enable the taxpayer to be gainfully employed.[110] Each of these requirements and the computation of the credit are discussed below.

Qualifying Individual. What many believe is simply a credit for child care actually has a far broader scope. True to its name, the *child and dependent care credit* is available not only to those who have children but also to those who take care of other dependents, such as an aging parent or other relative. A taxpayer (or in the case of divorced parents, only the custodial parent) can claim the credit only if he or she maintains a household for one of the following individuals:[111]

- A dependent under the age of 13 (e.g., taxpayer's child)
- An incapacitated dependent
- An incapacitated spouse

Note that the year in which a dependent turns 14 is an important factor in determining the applicability of the credit. First, if the individual becomes 13 during the year, he or she normally qualifies only for the part of the year he or she was under 13. Second, once the individual reaches age 14, expenses do not qualify unless the individual is incapable of self-care.

Employment-Related Expenses. Only certain expenses that enable the taxpayer to be gainfully employed or *seek* gainful employment qualify for the credit.[112] The work can be either full-time or part-time, but it must be work. Volunteer work for a nominal salary does not constitute gainful employment. For example, expenses for a baby-sitter while the taxpayer works at a church or hospital do not qualify. Note, however, that expenses incurred when one spouse works and the other attends school on a full-time basis are eligible.

Only certain types of expenses qualify as employment-related expenses. The expenses generally must be for the care of the qualifying individual (e.g., the cost of a baby-sitter). In this regard, the costs of household services qualify if the expenses are attributable at least in part to the care of a qualifying individual. Thus the IRS generally takes the position that the costs of a maid, nanny, or cook can qualify, but not those of a gardener or chauffeur. Eligible expenses normally do not include amounts paid for food, clothing, or entertainment. Similarly, the costs of transportation to a place for care do not qualify unless the qualifying individual is incapacitated. In addition, educational

---

[110] § 21.

[111] §§ 21(b)(1) and 21(e)(5).

[112] § 21(b)(2).

expenses incurred for a child in the first or higher grade level do not qualify. Observe, however, that the costs of pre-school or nursery school are eligible for the credit.

As a general rule, expenses for services both inside and outside the home qualify for the credit. However, there are several notable exceptions for the outside services:

▸ Care provided by a dependent care facility (e.g., a day care center) qualifies only if the facility provides care for more than six individuals.[113]

▸ Services outside the home for qualifying individuals other than a dependent under 13 (e.g., nursing home services for a spouse or an over-13-year-old dependent who is incapable of self-care) are eligible only if the individual spends at least eight hours a day in the employee's household.[114]

▸ Overnight camps do not qualify (day camps, however, can qualify).[115]

A final note on eligible expenses concerns payments made to relatives. Can the credit be claimed if the taxpayer simply pays his mother to baby-sit while he works? Payments to individuals do qualify as long as the individual is not a dependent of the taxpayer.[116] Thus payments to a child's grandparents would probably qualify since the grandparents normally are not dependents. Conversely, payments to a child's older brothers or sisters normally would not qualify since such individuals would be dependents. However, payments to the taxpayer's child can qualify if the child is not a dependent and is at least 19 years of age.

Computation of the Credit. The credit is generally computed by multiplying the applicable percentage times employment-related expenses. A general formula for the calculation is shown in Exhibit 13-11.

Applicable Percentage. The applicable percentage begins at 35 percent but is reduced (but not below 20 percent) by one percentage point for each $2,000 (or fraction thereof) that the taxpayer's adjusted gross income exceeds $15,000. For example, the rate for a taxpayer with an A.G.I. of $17,001 is 33 percent, one point reduction for the first $2,000 over $15,000 and another point reduction for the fractional part of the next $2,000. Based on this scheme, taxpayers with adjusted gross incomes exceeding $43,000 have a rate of 20 percent.[117]

EXHIBIT 13-11
Computations of the Child and Dependent Care Credit

Employment-related expenses
    Lesser of:
      1. Amount paid,
      2. Earned income or imputed earned income if full-time student or incapacitated spouse, or
      3. $3,000 (if one qualifying individual) or $6,000 (if more than one)

×   Applicable percentage (20-35%)
=   Child and dependent care credit

---

[113] § 21(b)(2)(C).

[114] § 21(b)(2)(B).

[115] Last sentence of § 21(b)(2)(A).

[116] § 21(e)(6).

[117] § 21(a)(2).

Limitations on Employment-Related Expenses. The Code imposes several limitations on the amount of expenses eligible for the credit. The first limitation simply sets a maximum dollar amount of expenses that may be taken into account in computing the credit. These amounts are based on the number of qualifying individuals: $3,000 for one qualifying individual and $6,000 for two or more individuals.[118] Thus, the maximum credits would be $1,050 (35% × $3,000) and $2,100 (35% × $6,000). As explained below, however, these amounts may be reduced. The computation of the credit requires a three-step approach, as illustrated in the following example.

Example 31. F is a widower and maintains a household for his two small children. He incurs $5,000 of employment-related expenses and reports A.G.I. of $27,300 for the current year. F's child care credit is determined as follows:

Step 1: Determining the applicable percentage:

Adjusted gross income	$27,300
Less: Ceiling on 35% rate	(15,000)
Adjusted gross income over $15,000 limit	$12,300
Divided by $2,000 and rounded up: ($12,300 ÷ $2,000) = 6.15% Rounded up to 7%	
Maximum rate	35%
Percentage reduction	(7%)
Allowable percentage	28%

Step 2: Determine the allowable employment-related expenses:

Lesser of $5,000 paid or $6,000 limit	$ 5,000

Step 3: Determine the dependent care credit:

Allowable employment-related expenses	$5,000
Times: Applicable percentage	× 28%
Dependent care credit	$1,400

Earned Income Limitation. In addition to the $3,000 and $6,000 limitations, employment-related expenses are limited to the individual's earned income for the year.[119] For this purpose, earned income generally includes such items as salaries, wages, and net earnings from self-employment, but not investment income such as dividends and interest.

The earned income limitation is a bit more cumbersome for married couples. If an individual is married, a joint return is required to claim the credit, and the amount of the exclusion may not exceed the lesser of the taxpayer's earned income or the earned income of the taxpayer's spouse.[120] In addition, in determining the lesser earned income

---

[118] § 21(c).

[119] § 21(d)(1).

[120] § 21(e)(2) and 21(d)(2).

for married couples, special rules apply if one spouse is either a *full-time student*[121] or an incapacitated person. The student or incapacitated spouse will be deemed to have earned income of $250 a month if there is one qualified dependent or $500 a month if there are two or more qualified dependents for each month a taxpayer is incapacitated or is a full-time student. This deemed income does not increase A.G.I. when determining the applicable percentage. These rules are illustrated in the following example.

> **Example 32.** B and G are married, have one dependent child, age 9, incur employment-related expenses of $2,700, and have A.G.I. of $22,500 for the current taxable year. G is employed full-time and earns $27,000 a year. B returned to graduate school and was a full-time student for 10 months during the year. He was not employed during the year.
>
> *Step 1:* The applicable percentage is determined to be 31%
> [35% − ($22,500 − $15,000 = $7,500 ÷ $2,000 = 3.75%, rounded up to 4%)].
>
> *Step 2:* The allowable employment-related expenses are $2,500. This is determined by the lesser of three amounts: (1) the $2,700 spent, (2) the $3,000 limit, and (3) B's deemed earned income of $2,500 ($250 for one dependent × 10 months).
>
> *Step 3:* Determine the dependent care credit:
>
> | | |
> |---|---:|
> | Allowable employment-related expenses . . . . | $2,500 |
> | Applicable percentage (35% − 4%) . . . . | × 31% |
> | Dependent care credit . . . . | $ 775 |

Filing Requirements for the Child and Dependent Care Credit. In order to claim the credit for taxable years beginning after 1996, married couples must file a joint return and the taxpayer ID numbers of *both* the day care service provider and of the child must be disclosed on the return.

Relationship to Other Credits. The child and dependent care credit is nonrefundable and is used to offset the tax liability determined under § 26. It is the *first* credit to be used in reducing an individual's tax liability, and there is no carryover or carryback available for unused credits.

Relationship to Dependent Care Assistance Programs. Congress has addressed the problem of child and dependent care in two ways: the child care credit and the exclusion for dependent care assistance. As mentioned in Chapter 6, since 1981 employers have been allowed to establish qualified dependent care assistance plans.[122] These plans allow employers a current deduction for contributions to the plans and allow employees to exclude from gross income up to $5,000 of payments (e.g., reimbursements) received under the plan to the extent that the expenses would qualify as employment-related expenses for purposes of the child and dependent care credits. If the taxpayer elects to exclude a reimbursement for care, the limit on the amount of employment-related expenses that qualify for the credit ($3,000 or $6,000) is reduced

---

[121] § 21 (d)(2). For this purpose, a full-time student is defined exactly the same as for the dependency test (i.e., for at least five months, partial months count as full months).

[122] See § 129 and the discussion in Chapter 6.

dollar for dollar by the amount excluded.[123] Whether the taxpayer is better off using the exclusion or the credit requires careful analysis of the taxpayer's situation, and some tax planning may be in order.

> **Example 33.** H and W are married with two children. H works full-time as an accountant, and he estimates his earnings for the year will be $50,000. W is employed part-time and estimates her earnings will be $20,000 for the year. H and W estimate that they will incur $4,000 of qualified employment-related expenses for the year. H and W are in the 28 percent tax bracket.
>
> At the beginning of H's employer's plan year, H has a decision to make. He can elect to have $1,000 excluded from his gross income in accordance with his employer's qualified dependent care assistance plan, which will be distributed to him as a reimbursement for qualified expenses, or he can elect to have the $1,000 included in his gross income as part of his salary. If the couple elects not to exclude the reimbursement, the child care credit is $800 (20% × $4,000), and they must pay taxes of $280 on the $1,000 of income, a net benefit of $520 ($800 − $280). On the other hand, if the couple elects to exclude the reimbursement, they pay no income tax on the $1,000 reimbursement, and their credit and net benefit is $800, computed as follows:

Employment-related expenses.	$4,000
Dollar limit: maximum allowable expenses for two individuals	$6,000
Reduction for employer-provided dependent care excluded from income .	(1,000)
Limit on expenses eligible for credit.	$5,000
Amount of credit (20% × lesser of $4,000 or $5,000)	$ 800

> Note that only the dollar limit eligible for the credit is reduced by the excluded income. The employment-related expenses total of $4,000 is still eligible for the credit.

EDUCATION CREDITS

A major thrust of the TRA of 1997 was to provide tax incentives to help reduce the cost of higher education and life-long learning. The new law adds six different provisions directed at this policy objective. The new rules are often conflicting, some are mutually exclusive, and taken together they can be confusing.

While interest income on Series E bonds has received favorable tax treatment by being excluded from gross income when the interest is used to pay qualified educational expenditures, the 1997 Act pushes educational incentives to the brink and makes the planning for higher education more complex than it should be. Taxpayers planning for the cost of educational programs or college degrees now must consider the following tax incentives:

- ▸ The exclusion for interest on Series E bonds.[124]
- ▸ The deductibility of certain interest on student loans.[125]

---

[123] § 21(c).

[124] See § 135 and Chapter 6.

[125] § 222. With respect to tax incentives directed toward students, also see § 117 (exclusion for scholarships and fellowships) and § 127 (employer paid educational expenses).

▸ Participation in qualified state tuition programs.[126]

▸ Distributions from regular IRAs to pay educational expenses.[127]

▸ Establishing an education IRA.[128]

▸ The HOPE scholarship credit.[129]

▸ The Lifetime Learning credit.[130]

New § 25A contains two credits: the HOPE Scholarship and Lifetime Learning credits. These credits are directly aimed at subsidizing the costs of pursuing undergraduate and graduate degrees as well as vocational training. While there are two credits, for any one particular student, a taxpayer could elect either the HOPE credit or a Lifetime Learning credit but not both. Like most of the other tax incentives provided for in the TRA of 1997, these credits are phased out at specific income levels and, therefore, are not available to high income or wealthy taxpayers. The following discussion first looks at each credit individually and then at requirements common to each credit.

HOPE Scholarship Credit. The HOPE Scholarship credit was born out of Congressional desire to enable all students to continue to pursue their education once they have completed high school. It is a nonrefundable credit for qualified tuition and certain related expenses for post secondary education furnished to an eligible student. The HOPE credit is effective for expenses paid after December 31, 1997 for academic periods beginning after that date. The taxpayer may elect to claim a credit for 100 percent of the first $1,000 of qualifying expenses and 50 percent of the next $1,000 of expenses for each student. These $1,000 limits are subject to an inflation adjustment beginning in 2006, but the limits for 2005 remain at $1,000. Thus the maximum credit is $1,500 per year per student (e.g., the taxpayer whose triplets enroll at the local state college could claim a maximum credit for the year of $4,500). The HOPE credit can be claimed for only two taxable years. In addition, it is permitted only if the student has not completed the first two years of post-secondary education as of the beginning of the taxable year. Normally, these rules should provide a credit for each student of $1,500 per year for two years for a total benefit of $3,000. Presumably Congress settled on this amount on the belief that $1,500 per year for two years was sufficient to cover the cost of the typical two-year community college.

The credit is available only for expenses paid on behalf of the taxpayer, the taxpayer's spouse, or a dependent. In the case of a dependent's expenses, the eligible student is not entitled to claim a credit if he or she is claimed as a dependent by the parent or another taxpayer. Instead, if a parent or other taxpayer claims a student as a dependent, any qualified tuition and related expenses paid by the student are treated as paid by the parent and the parent benefits from the credit![131]

The credit is generally available only for expenses paid during the taxable year for education that begins during such year.[132] For this purpose, education that begins during the first three months of the next year is treated as having started in the previous year. This special three-month rule allows a credit for prepaid expenses. Observe that these rules require careful planning to take advantage of the full credit. Because the credit is tied to the taxable year rather than the typical academic year (i.e., a year that begins

---

[126] § 529.

[127] § 72(t).

[128] § 530.

[129] § 25A.

[130] *Ibid.*

[131] § 25A(g)(3).

[132] § 25A(b)(1)(A).

with the fall semester and ends with the spring semester), taxpayers may lose some of the credit's benefits without taking advantage of the prepayment privilege.

> **Example 34.** H is a typical high school graduate who enrolled for the 2005 fall semester of a local two-year community college. He plans to finish in the spring semester of 2007. The school charges $1,000 tuition per semester. Assuming H elects to claim the credit in 2005 and 2006, he can claim a total credit of $2,500 ($1,000 + $1,500). In such case, he does not benefit from the entire $3,000 credit available. In order to avoid this result, H should prepay his 2006 tuition in December of 2005. Since prepayments qualify for the credit as long as the education occurs within the first three months of the following year, he would be eligible for the full $1,500 credit in 2005. He should also prepay in 2006 his tuition for the spring 2007 semester so that he will have paid at least $2,000 in 2006.

Note that qualifying expenses paid with loan proceeds are eligible for both credits in the year the expenses are paid, not when the loan is repaid.

Eligible Student. Expenses qualify for the credit only if they are for an eligible student. An eligible student is one who is enrolled in a program leading to a degree, certificate or other recognized educational credential at an eligible education institution. In addition, the student must carry one-half the load that a normal full-time student carries for at least one academic period per year. For example, if a student goes part-time during the spring semester (i.e., presumably one academic period) and carries one-half the full time load, his expenses for the summer and fall semesters will qualify even if he takes less than one-half the full time load during these later periods. Note also that the credit is not available for students that have been convicted of a federal or state felony offense consisting of the possession or distribution of a controlled substance.

Qualified Tuition and Expenses. Qualified tuition and related expenses include tuition and fees required for the enrollment or attendance at an eligible institution. Expenses that do not directly relate to the student's education such as student activity fees, athletic fees, insurance expenses, transportation, or other expenses unrelated to an individual's academic course of instruction do not qualify for either credit. Similarly, expenses related to courses involving sports, games, or hobbies do not qualify unless such course is part of the individual's degree program. In addition, neither the HOPE credit nor the Lifetime Learning credit is available for expenses incurred to purchase books or for room and board.

For both the HOPE credit and the Lifetime Learning credit, the amount of qualifying expenses must be reduced by amounts covered by excludable scholarships or educational assistance plans.[133] However, amounts withdrawn from a qualified prepaid tuition plan and used to pay eligible expenses qualify for the credit.

Eligible Institutions. Only expenses paid to eligible institutions qualify for the credit. While most colleges and universities would be considered eligible, other providers of courses may also qualify. Technically, an eligible institution includes accredited post-secondary educational institutions offering credit toward a bachelor's degree, an associate's degree, or another recognized post-secondary credential. Certain proprietary institutions and post-secondary vocational institutions also are eligible. The bright line test is whether the institution is eligible to participate in Department of Education student aid programs.

---

[133] § 25(g)(2).

Phase-out for High Income Taxpayers. The HOPE credit (like the Lifetime Learning credit discussed below) is not extended to high income taxpayers. To accomplish this objective, the total maximum credit allowed for all eligible students is phased out once the taxpayer's modified adjusted gross income exceeds certain thresholds: $87,000 for joint returns and $43,000 for other returns (adjusted for inflation). The reduction occurs over a $20,000 *income range* for joint filers and $10,000 for other taxpayers. If the taxpayer is married, a joint return must be filed to claim the credits. The formula for determining the phase-out and the levels at which a complete phase-out occurs are shown below.

EXHIBIT 13-12
Phase-Out of HOPE and the Lifetime Learning Credits for 2005

$$\text{Reduction of total allowable credits} = \text{HOPE credit allowable credits} \times \frac{\text{Modified A.G.I.*–threshold}}{\text{Income range}}$$

Taxpayer	Modified A.G.I.* Phase-out begins	Modified A.G.I.* Phase-out complete
Married filing joint	$87,000	$107,000
Other taxpayers	$43,000	$ 53,000

*Modified A.G.I. is A.G.I. increased by income earned outside the U.S. which normally is excluded under § 911. The income phase-out threshold amounts are indexed annually for inflation.

Example 35. M, a single mother, has modified A.G.I. of $45,000. In 2005, M's daughter, D, begins studying for her bachelor's degree as a full-time student at City University. On September 1, M pays $4,000 in qualified tuition for D's first semester. Without the income limitations, M would be entitled to the maximum HOPE credit of $1,500 (100% of $1,000 plus 50% of $1,000). However, taking into account the income limitations, M's credit is reduced by $300, computed below.

$$\text{Reduction of total allowable credits} = \$1,500 \times \frac{\$45,000 - \$43,000}{\$10,000} = \$300$$

Thus, M is entitled to a $1,200 HOPE credit.

Lifetime Learning Credit. In addition to the HOPE credit, § 25A creates the Lifetime Learning credit. This credit can be claimed for 20 percent of qualified tuition and fees incurred during the taxable year on behalf of the taxpayer, the taxpayer's spouse, or any dependents. The provision becomes effective for expenses paid after June 30, 1998 for education furnished in academic periods beginning after that date. For expenses paid after December 31, 2002, up to $10,000 of qualified tuition and fees per taxpayer return will be eligible for the credit (i.e., the maximum credit per return will be $2,000). For any one particular student, a taxpayer could elect either the HOPE credit or a Lifetime Learning credit but not both.

In contrast to the HOPE credit, a taxpayer may claim the Lifetime Learning credit for a unlimited number of taxable years. Also in contrast to the HOPE credit, the maximum amount of the Lifetime Learning credit that may be claimed on a taxpayer's return is not related to the number of students in the taxpayer's family. The key variable is the amount of qualified expenses incurred during the year and not the number of eligible individuals.

Qualified Tuition and Related Expenses for Lifetime Learning Credit. Qualified tuition and fees for purposes of the Lifetime Learning credit are defined in the same manner as for the HOPE credit but with several important additions. As noted above, the HOPE credit is available only for two taxable years and ceases after the year the student has completed two years of post-secondary education. In contrast, the Lifetime Learning credit—true to its name—applies not only to these same expenses but also such expenses incurred in any taxable year during the taxpayer's lifetime. For example, the Lifetime Learning credit would be applicable to expenses incurred in obtaining an undergraduate degree (all four years or whatever is required) or a graduate degree (e.g., a law degree, a medical degree, an M.B.A., and similar graduate degrees). In addition, the definition of qualified tuition and expenses is expanded for the Lifetime Learning credit to include any course of instruction at an eligible educational institution to acquire or improve job skills of the taxpayer. Thus expenses need not be incurred in a degree program but could be simply a continuing education course (e.g., a C.P.A. takes a course on the new tax law). Note, however, that for the course to qualify it must be provided by a qualifying educational institution (e.g., one that is eligible to participate in student aid programs of the Department of Education).

Like the HOPE credit, the amount of qualifying expenses for the Lifetime Learning credit must be reduced by amounts covered by scholarships or educational assistance plans (assuming such amounts are excludable from gross income). Expenses taken into account for the HOPE credit cannot be taken into account for the Lifetime Learning credit.

These credits will automatically be available to the taxpayer unless the taxpayer elects not to take the credit with respect to the qualified tuition and related expenses of an individual for any taxable year. Previously, the taxpayer had to elect to claim the credit.[134]

Interaction of HOPE Credit, Lifetime Learning Credit, Education IRAs and Series EE Savings Bonds. Special rules exist to prohibit the taxpayer from obtaining multiple benefits from the credits and nontaxable withdrawals from education individual retirement accounts. For each eligible student in each taxable year, the taxpayer must elect one of the three tax benefits: (1) the HOPE credit, (2) the Lifetime Learning credit, or (3) the exclusion from gross income for withdrawals from education IRAs. The election is separate for each student. Thus a parent could elect the HOPE credit for one child, the Lifetime Learning credit for another child, and the exclusion for IRA withdrawals for a third child. Any educational expenses taken into account for purposes of the credits or the IRA withdrawal cannot again be taken into account in determining the exclusion for interest on Series EE savings bonds that are used to pay for educational expenses.

CREDIT FOR ADOPTION EXPENSES

To encourage adoptions, § 23 was added to the Code in 1996 and amended in 2001. In general, it provides a maximum nonrefundable credit of $10,630 per child for qualified adoption expenses paid or incurred by the taxpayer. Qualified adoption expenses are reasonable and necessary adoption fees, court costs, attorney's fees and other expenses that are directly related to the legal adoption of an eligible child. An eligible child is an individual (1) who has not attained age 18 as of the time of the adoption, or (2) who is physically or mentally incapable of caring for himself or herself. No credit is allowed for expenses incurred (1) in violation of state or federal law, (2) in carrying out any surrogate parenting arrangement, or (3) in connection with the adoption of a child of the taxpayer's

---

[134] § 25A(e), as amended by the 2001 Tax Act, makes the credits applicable to the taxpayer unless the taxpayer *elects out* of the credit provisions.

spouse. The credit is phased out ratably for taxpayers with modified adjusted gross income above $159,450, and is fully phased out at $199,450 of modified A.G.I. For these purposes modified A.G.I. is computed by increasing the taxpayer's A.G.I. by the amount otherwise excluded from gross income of citizens or residents living abroad.[135] Both the dollar limitation and the income limitation amounts are subject to a cost-of-living adjustment in tax years beginning after December 31, 2002.

The $10,630 limit is a per child limit, not an annual limitation. If adoption expenses are paid during a tax year prior to the tax year in which the adoption is final, the credit is allowed for the year the adoption is made final. If adoption expenses are paid during or after the tax year in which the adoption is finalized, the credit is allowed for the tax year in which the expense is paid. For example, in the case of an adoption which is finalized in 2005, if a taxpayer pays or incurs $3,500 of otherwise allowable qualified adoption expenses with respect to the child in year 2004 and $7,500 of otherwise allowable qualified adoption expenses with respect to that same child in 2005, then the taxpayer would receive a $3,500 credit with respect to expenses incurred in 2004 and a $7,130 credit with respect to expenses incurred in 2005 (both credits are allowed on the 2005 tax return).

When the adoption credit is attributable to amounts chargeable to a capital account (e.g., the costs of constructing an elevator at the taxpayer's house to accommodate a wheelchair that is required as a condition of the adoption), the taxpayer is not allowed additional basis in the house to the extent of the adoption credit allowed. An ordering rule specifies that qualified adoption expenditures not chargeable to a capital account (the legal fees) are allowed for the credit before any amounts that are chargeable to a capital account.

A special rule applies to the adoption of a child with special needs. "Special needs" include the child's ethnic background, age, or membership in a minority or sibling group, or the presence of such factors such as medical conditions or physical, mental or emotional handicaps. In the case of a special needs child, $10,630 is allowed as an adoption credit regardless of whether the taxpayer has qualified adoption expenses. The credit for a special needs child is only allowed if the adoption becomes final and the credit is only allowed in the year in which the adoption becomes final.

Interaction with the New Exclusion for Qualified Adoption Expenses. A companion but separate $10,630 exclusion from gross income is also available to employees for qualified adoption expenses paid by the employer in accordance with a qualified adoption assistance program.[136]

Adoption expenses paid or reimbursed under an adoption assistance program may not be taken into account in determining the adoption credit. A taxpayer may, however, satisfy the requirements of the adoption credit *and* the exclusion with different expenses paid or incurred by the taxpayer and the employer, respectively. For example, in the case of an adoption that costs $14,000 with $7,000 of expenses paid by the taxpayer and $7,000 paid by the taxpayer's employer under an adoption assistance program, the taxpayer may qualify for the adoption credit and the exclusion.

There are special rules that apply to the adoption of foreign children, with no credit allowed until the year in which the adoption is final.

In order to claim the adoption credit, married couples must file a joint return and include the child's taxpayer I.D. number on the tax return claiming the adoption credit.[137] Recall that this credit can be used to offset the tentative minimum tax. If the credit is limited, it can be carried over for five years.

---

[135] § 23(b)(2)(B).

[136] § 137.

[137] § 23(f).

CREDIT FOR THE ELDERLY AND PERMANENTLY DISABLED

A nonrefundable tax credit is available to certain taxpayers who are either 65 years of age or older or are permanently and totally disabled.[138] The credit is 15 percent of an individual's earned and investment income that does not exceed the taxpayer's appropriate § 22 amount.[139] The maximum § 22 amount is

1. $5,000 for single individuals

2. $5,000 for a joint return where only one spouse is at least 65 years old

3. $7,500 for a joint return where both spouses are 65 years or older

4. $3,750 for a married individual filing separately

The maximum amount from above is then reduced by excludable pension and annuity income received during the year, including social security and railroad retirement benefits, and by one-half of the taxpayer's A.G.I. that exceeds

1. $7,500 for unmarried individuals

2. $10,000 if married filing jointly

3. $5,000 if married filing separately

Example 36. P is single, 65 years old, and has A.G.I. of $8,300 from interest and dividends. During the taxable year, she also received social security of $1,500. Her credit for the elderly is computed as follows:

Maximum § 22 amount			$ 5,000
Less:	Social security received	$1,500	
	50% of A.G.I. over $7,500 ($8,300 − $7,500 = $800 × 50%)	+400	(1,900)
Section 22 amount available for credit			$ 3,100
Multiply by rate			× 15%
Amount of credit			$ 465

There are a number of additional special rules, and because these rules are quite complicated, individuals are allowed to file their return with a request that the IRS compute their tax liability and tax credit. However, few people are able to take advantage of the credit for the elderly since social security receipts commonly exceed the maximum § 22 amount.

The credit for the elderly or permanently disabled is limited to the § 26 tax liability reduced by the child and dependent care credit. Like the child and dependent care credit, this credit is nonrefundable and may not be carried back or forward.

CREDIT FOR INTEREST ON CERTAIN HOME MORTGAGES

In order to help provide financing for first-time home buyers, Congress has created several special programs. One of these allows state and local governments to issue

---

[138] Limited rules apply to taxpayers who are under 65 years old if they are certain governmental retirees subject to the Public Retirement System and elect to have this section apply [see § 22(c)].

[139] § 22(a).

mortgage credit certificates (MCCs).[140] Taxpayers who receive such certificates are allowed to claim a nonrefundable credit for a specified percentage of interest paid on mortgage loans on their principal residence. Each certificate must specify the principal amount of indebtedness that qualifies for the credit as well as the applicable percentage rate of the credit. The credit percentage may differ with each certificate but must be between 10 and 50 percent. If the credit exceeds 20 percent, the maximum credit is limited to $2,000. Of course, the amount of the taxpayer's interest deduction must be reduced by the amount of the credit claimed during the year. Any credit that cannot be used may be carried over for three years.

> **Example 37.** After saving for years, R and his wife, W, decided to buy their first house. In order to finance the purchase, R applied for and received from the state an MCC. The certificate specifies that the rate is 15% and the maximum loan amount is $70,000. The couple purchased a house for $75,000 and obtained a loan of $65,000 from a savings and loan. For the year, R and W paid interest of $5,000 on the loan. They may claim a credit of $750 ($5,000 × 15%). In addition, they may deduct interest of $4,250 ($5,000 − $750).

While the credit can provide a significant benefit, it is not available to everyone. Under the MCC program, state and local governments are limited in the volume of credits they may dispense and in the individuals to whom they may be issued. Taxpayers are eligible to receive a certificate only if they meet certain narrowly defined criteria. For example, the purchaser's income cannot generally exceed 115 percent of the area's median gross income, the price of the home cannot exceed 90 percent of the average purchase price of homes in the area, and the homes may be available only in targeted areas. Still other constraints exist that restrict the credit's use.

REFUNDABLE CREDITS

Refundable credits are those credits that are recoverable even though an individual has no income tax liability in the current year. They are treated as payments of taxes. Included in this category are the credit for taxes withheld at the source (§ 31), the earned income credit (§ 32), the credit for tax withheld at the source on nonresident aliens and foreign corporations (§ 33), and the gasoline and special fuels credit (§ 34).

Refundable credits may be used to offset all taxes imposed by the Code, including penalty taxes. This result is accomplished by combining all the refundable credits and accounting for them after all the nonrefundable credits have been used to offset the § 26 tax liability.

TAX WITHHELD AT THE SOURCE

The first and most important of the refundable credits is styled "Credit for Tax Withheld on Wages" and obviously includes the amount withheld by an employer as a tax on wages earned.[141] However, the credit has broader application with respect to certain taxes withheld by the payor at the source of payment, including

1. Tax on pensions and annuities withheld by the payor

2. Overpaid FICA taxes (in cases where a taxpayer has two or more employers in the same year)

---

[140] § 25.

[141] §§ 31(a) and 3401.

3. Amounts withheld as backup withholding in cases where the taxpayer fails to furnish a taxpayer identification number to the payor of interest or dividends[142]

4. Quarterly estimated tax payments

EARNED INCOME CREDIT

In 1975 Congress introduced the earned income credit to eliminate some of the disincentives that discouraged low-income taxpayers with children from working.[143] The credit was specifically designed to alleviate the increasing burden of social security taxes. In many cases, income taxes were not a concern for these low-income taxpayers since they were protected by personal and dependent exemptions as well as the standard deduction. However, they were not exempt from social security taxes. Consistent with its purpose, the credit is refundable (e.g., the taxpayer would receive the credit amount even if he or she is not required to pay income taxes since it is viewed as a refund of the social security taxes).

Since its creation, the earned income credit has been the subject of a great deal of Congressional tinkering. The most recent round of adjustments was introduced by the Clinton administration in 1993. These changes not only increased the benefits of the credit but also expanded its coverage. Beginning in 1994, the credit may apply even if the taxpayer does not have children.

Computation of the Credit. The starting point for determining the credit is determination of the taxpayer's earned income. As might be expected, *earned income* consists of wages, salaries, tips, and other employer compensation plus earnings from self-employment included in gross income for the taxable year. It does not include pension and annuity income even if provided by an employer for past services. Amounts received similar to compensation that are excluded are not treated as earned income. For example, excludable dependent care benefits, the value of meals and lodging furnished for the convenience of the employer, excludable educational assistance benefits and salary deferrals [contributions to a § 401(k) plan] are not included in earned income.

The initial credit is computed by multiplying the earned income of the taxpayer (limited by a ceiling amount) by a statutory percentage; however, this initial credit amount is phased out as the taxpayer's income increases above a phase-out amount. As can be seen from Exhibit 13-13, the maximum amounts of earned income that qualify for the credit as well as the statutory credit percentages vary depending on the number of children the taxpayer has.[144] Observe that the credit for an individual with no children is essentially designed to give the taxpayer back the FICA taxes on the first $5,220 of wages (7.65% rate × $5,220). The maximum credits for eligible individuals for 2005 are shown in Exhibit 13-13.

---

[142] §§ 31(c) and 3406.

[143] § 32(a).

[144] § 32(b)(1).

EXHIBIT 13-13
Earned Income Credit: Credit and Phase-Out Percentages

Tax Year	Number of Qualifying Children	Credit Percentage	Ceiling on Earned Income Amounts	Phase-Out Starts at	Phase-Out Percentage
2005	0	7.65%	$ 5,220	$ 6,530	7.65%
	1	34.00	7,830	14,370	15.98
	2 or more	40.00	11,000	14,370	21.06

*The threshold phase-out amounts for married filing jointly are $8,530, $16,370 and $16,370, respectively.

As noted above, the credit begins to phase out once the taxpayer's income increases above the phase-out amount. The credit is reduced if *either* the earned income or the A.G.I. of the taxpayer exceeds certain specified amounts shown in Exhibit 13-13.[145]

The phase-out is computed by multiplying the applicable phase-out rate by the excess of A.G.I. or earned income (whichever is greater) over the phase-out amounts. The credit can be computed using the following formula:

Maximum credit
   Applicable percentage × earned income (not to exceed the ceiling amounts}
− Reduction
   Applicable percentage × (larger of earned income or A.G.I. − Phase-out amount)
= Earned income credit

For example, the maximum 2005 earned income credit for a taxpayer with one child is $2,662 ($7,830 × 34%). This credit is completely eliminated when the taxpayer's modified A.G.I. or earned income exceeds $31,030 [15.98% × ($31,030 − $14,370) = $2,662]. The levels at which the credit is completely phased out are shown in Exhibit 13-14.

EXHIBIT 13-14
Earned Income Credit Maximum Credits, Phase-Out Completion Amounts for 2005

Qualified Children	Maximum Credit	Phase-Out Completion Amounts*
0	$ 399 (7.65% × $5,220)	$11,750
1	2,662 (34% × $7,830)	31,030
2 or more	4,400 (40% × $11,000)	35,263

*The threshold phase-out amounts for married filing jointly are $8,530, $16,370 and $16,370, respectively.

Example 38. D and M are married, file a joint return for 2005, and maintain a household for their dependent son, who is three years old. D has earned income of $16,000 and M has none. The couple own investments that produce $1,475 of

---

[145] Prior to 2002, taxpayers had to make a complicated calculation to determine the modified AGI, which was used as part of the calculation for the EIC phase-out. The 2001 Tax Act simplified the calculation of the EIC by eliminating the concept of modified adjusted gross income.

includible income for the year and have an A.G.I. of $17,475 ($16,000 + $1,475). The earned income credit is computed as follows:

Maximum credit (34% × $7,830)		$2,662
Less: Reduction for A.G.I. over $16,370		
($17,475 − $16,370 = $1,105 × 15.98%)		−177
Earned income credit		$2,485

To help taxpayers compute the credit, the IRS provides a worksheet and an earned income credit table to aid taxpayers in determining the correct amount of the earned income credit. The work sheet and table are included with the instructions for completing Form 1040 and Form 1040A (see the Appendix for a copy of the 2004 Table).[146]

As a refundable credit, qualified individuals may receive tax refunds equal to their earned income credit even in years when they have no tax liability.[147]

> **Example 39.** Y has earned income and A.G.I. of $10,000, has three exemptions (including two qualified children), and files as head of household. As a result, she has no income tax liability for the year. However, she is entitled to a tax refund equal to the earned income credit of $4,000 ($10,000 × 40%) plus any taxes (other than FICA taxes) withheld from her wages.

Eligibility Requirements. Because the earned income credit was a mechanical calculation under the former rules, some wealthy taxpayers inadvertently qualified for the earned income credit in years in which they reported a small amount of earned income. To preclude such taxpayers from taking advantage of the earned income credit, a major change was made. The earned income credit is now disallowed for taxpayers that have too much investment income. Taxpayers are not allowed to claim the earned income credit if they have more than $2,700 of disqualified income.[148] The definition of disqualified income includes:

- interest,
- dividends,
- tax-exempt interest,
- the net income from rents or royalties not derived in ordinary course of a trade or business,
- capital gain net income,
- the excess of aggregate passive income over aggregate passive losses.

Finally, in an attempt to cut down on fraud and abuse relating to this credit, the taxpayer identification number required to be disclosed on the return means a Social Security number issued to an individual by the Social Security Administration.

Until 1993, the earned income credit was available only to taxpayers who had children. In a major change, the RRA of 1993 extended the earned income credit to certain individuals without children. In so doing, the act significantly broadened the availability of the credit. In either situation, if the taxpayer is married a joint return must

---

[146] § 32(f) Note that the earned income credit table prepared annually by the IRS reflects the credit based on a midpoint of each $25 increment of an income range.

[147] The taxpayer is required to reduce his or her earned income credit by the amount of the alternative minimum tax imposed on that individual.

[148] See § 32(i) and Rev. Proc. 2004-71, I.R.B. 2004-50.

be filed as a requirement to obtain the EIC.[149] The eligibility requirements for taxpayers with and without children are set forth below.

Taxpayers without Children. Taxpayers without a qualifying child are eligible to claim the credit if the taxpayer meets three conditions:[150]

1. The taxpayer (or the spouse of the taxpayer) must be at least 25 years old and not more than 64 years old at the end of the taxable year.

2. The taxpayer is not a dependent in the same year the credit is claimed.

3. The taxpayer has a principal residence in the United States for more than one-half of the taxable year.

Taxpayers with Children. Taxpayers are entitled to claim the credit if they have a qualifying child. The child need not be a dependent but must meet the following tests:

1. *Relationship.* The individual must be a child, stepchild, foster child, a legally adopted child of the taxpayer, or a descendant of any such individual. A married child does not meet this test unless the taxpayer can claim the child as a dependent.

2. *Age.* The child must be either (1) less than 19 years old at the close of the calendar year, (2) less than 24 years old and a full-time student at the close of the calendar year, or (3) permanently and totally disabled any time during the year.

3. *Residency.* The child must share the same principal place of abode as the taxpayer for more than one-half of the taxable year, and that abode must be located in the United States.

Assuming all of the above requirements are met and the taxpayer properly identifies the child on the return (i.e., name, age, taxpayer identification number), the credit is allowed.

REFUNDABLE CHILD TAX CREDITS

Taxpayers who qualify for the regular child credit may also qualify for a refundable Child Tax Credit which is authorized in § 24(d). Any amount allowed as a refundable credit will reduce the Child Tax Credit (CTC) that would otherwise be allowed under § 24.

One of the principal policy goals of the Child Tax Credit for low-income taxpayers is to offset not only the taxpayer's regular income tax but also the employee's share of FICA (or for those who are self-employed, one-half of the taxpayer's self-employment tax). To accomplish this goal, a portion of the Child Tax Credit must be refundable.

The overall limit on the amount of the CTC that will be refundable is the amount of the CTC determined as if the tax liability limitation did not apply. Recall that the CTC is limited to an amount not to exceed the excess of the sum of the § 26 regular tax liability plus the AMT over the sum of the credits allowed by the Child and Dependent Care Credit (§ 21), the Credit for the Elderly (§ 22), the credit for Interest on Certain Home Mortgages (§ 25), the HOPE and Lifetime Learning credit (§ 25A) and the foreign tax credit (§ 27). Generally this limitation will be equal to the full CTC computed by multiplying the per child amount by the number of qualifying children.

---

[149]   § 32(d).

[150]   § 32(c)(1)(A)(ii).

The amount of the refundable Child Tax Credit is the lessor of:

1. The child credit allowed without regard to the tax liability limitation of § 26, or

2. The amount by which the nonrefundable personal credits allowed would increase if the tax liability limitation were increased 15 percent of the taxpayer's earned income in excess of $11,000

Referred to as the 15 percent rule, for tax years beginning in 2004 and thereafter, the CTC is refundable to the extent that the nonrefundable personal credits allowed would increase if the tax liablity limitation was increased by 15 percent of the taxpayer's earned income in excess of $11,000. For purposes of computing earned income as applicable to the refundable CTC, combat pay excludable from gross income under §112, is treated as earned income.

Taxpayers with three or more children may calculate the refundable portion of the credit using the excess of their social security taxes (i.e., the taxpayer's share of the FICA taxes and one-half of self-employment taxes) over the earned income credit if this calculation results in a greater amount than computed under the 15 percent rule.

In summary, the refundable portion of the CTC is the lesser of:

1. the CTC determined as if the tax liability limitation did not apply,
    or
2. the amount by which the nonrefundable personal credits would increase if the tax liability were increased by 15 percent of the earned income over $11,000.*

*Note: For taxpayers with three or more children the excess of the employee's FICA and ½ of the self employment tax over the taxpayer's EIC can be used as a substitute for the 15 percent rule if this calculation results in a larger amount than the 15 % rule.

Finally, the refundable portion of the CTC will reduce the amount of the total CTC that can be claimed as a nonrefundable credit.

Example 40. D, a single parent, is raising two children at home and earns a 2005 salary of $22,000. The CTC is the only nonrefundable personal tax credit that D is entitled to.

Income.	$22,000
Standard deduction	(7,300)
Personal exemptions	(9,600)
Taxable income	$ 5,100
Tax on $5,100	$ 510
Earned income credit.	$ 2,793
FICA paid (7.65% × $22,000)	$ 1,683

The refundable portion of the CTC is the lesser of:

1. CTC determined as if the tax liability limitation did not apply = $2,000,
    or
2. the amount by which the nonrefundable personal credits would increase if the tax liability were increased by 15 percent of the earned income over $11,000, or $1,650 [15% × ($22,000 − $11,000)].

If D's tax liability were increased by $1,650, D's tax liabiity would be $2,160 and the amount of nonrefundable credits would go from $510 to $2,000 (the entire amount of the CTC). This is an increase of $1,490 which is D's allowable refundable portion of the CTC for 2005.

Thus D's refundable portion of the CTC is $1,490. D's nonrefundable CTC is $510 and she will be allowed to reduce her regular tax liability.

D's total tax refund is $4,283, computed as follows:

Tax liability.		$ 510
Less: CTC.		(510)
Tax liability before refundable credits.		$ 0
Less: Refundable credits:		
CTC	$1,490	
EIC	2,793	(4,283)
Total refund		$4,283

Example 41. H and W have three children and earned income of $27,000. For 2004 their tax liability would be $1,000. The CTC is the only nonrefundable personal credit that H and W are entitled to

Income.	$ 27,000
Standard deduction	(10,000)
Personal exemptions	(16,000)
Taxable income	$ 1,000
Tax on $1,000	$ 100
Earned income credit.	$ 2,161
FICA paid (7.65% × $27,000)	$ 2,066

The refundable portion of the CTC is the lesser of:

1. CTC determined as if the tax liability limitation did not apply = $3,000
   or
2. the amount by which the nonrefundable personal credits would increase if the tax liability were increased by 15 percent of the earned income over $11,000, or $2,400 [15% × ($27,000 − $11,000)].

If H & W's tax liability were increased by $2,400, their nonrefundable CTC would also increase by $2,400; therefore, $2,400 of the CTC will be a refundable credit.

Since H and W have at least three children, they should compute the excess of their FICA taxes over their EIC and compare it to $2,400. In this case, there is no excess and H and W will be able to treat $2,400 as the refundable portion of their CTC. Thus their nonrefundable CTC is $600 ($3,000 − $2,400).

H and W's total refund is $4,561, computed as follows:

Tax liability.		$ 100
Less: CTC.		(100)
Tax liability after refundable credits		$ 0
Less: Refundable credits:		
CTC	$2,400	
EIC	2,161	(4,561)
Total refund		$4,561

Although the total amount of the child credit is the same whether or not part of it is treated as a refundable credit, it is advantageous for taxpayers to claim a refundable credit rather than a nonrefundable child credit. As noted above, nonrefundable credits are subtracted from the total tax for the year and may *only* reduce the regular tax and the AMT tax to zero; any excess is not refunded. In contrast, refundable credits are treated as tax payments, and are added to the amounts of federal income taxes that have been withheld and any estimated tax payments that have been made. If this sum is more than the total tax due, the excess is refunded.

OTHER REFUNDABLE CREDITS

Three other refundable credits are allowed. Code § 33 allows as a credit the amount of tax withheld at the source for nonresident aliens and foreign corporations. Code § 34 provides an income tax credit for the amount of excise tax paid on gasoline, where the gasoline is used on a farm, for other nonhighway purposes, by local transit systems, and by operators of intercity, local, or school buses. Finally, Code § 35 provides that an overpayment of taxes resulting from filing an amended return will be treated as a refundable credit.

PROBLEM MATERIALS

DISCUSSION QUESTIONS

13-1 *Alternative Minimum Tax.* It has been said that a taxpayer must maintain a second set of books to comply with the AMT system. Why is the extra set of books necessary?

13-2 *Alternative Minimum Tax.* The AMT requires taxpayers to keep an extra set of books for several adjustment items. What action can a taxpayer take to minimize the recordkeeping requirements with respect to depreciation deductions?

13-3 *Alternative Minimum Tax.* Assume a taxpayer has a regular tax liability of $25,000, a tentative AMT of $28,000, and an AMT of $3,000 for the current year. How much does the taxpayer actually owe the IRS?

13-4 *Alternative Minimum Tax.* A taxpayer has an AMT liability of $50,000 and a general business credit of $50,000. He is not concerned about paying the AMT because he thinks the general business credit can be used to offset the AMT. Is he correct? What if the taxpayer were a corporation?

13-5 *Alternative Minimum Tax.* Is it safe to assume that only wealthy individuals who have low taxable incomes are subject to the alternative minimum tax? Are any taxpayers whose marginal rates exceed 26 percent subject to the alternative minimum tax? Explain.

13-6 *Alternative Minimum Tax.* G will be subject to the alternative minimum tax in 2005 but not in 2006. G's property tax on her residence is due November 15, 2005. If she defers payment of the property tax until 2006, she must pay a 5 percent penalty. When should G pay the property tax? Explain.

13-7 *Alternative Minimum Tax.* Some interest expense can be taken as an itemized deduction for regular tax purposes but different rules control the interest expenses allowable as an AMT itemized deduction. Explain the differences in these rules and note which rules are more restrictive.

13-8 *Alternative Minimum Tax.* Is the § 179 (first-year expensing) deduction allowed as a deduction for the AMT system?

13-9 *Credits vs. Deductions.* Assume taxpayers have a choice of deducting $1,000 for A.G.I. or taking a $250 tax credit for the current year. Which taxpayers should choose the deduction? Why?

13-10 *Rehabilitation and Energy Credits.* A taxpayer purchased an old train station, which was placed in service in 1935, for $20,000. He plans to tear the building down and erect a new office building for $100,000. Will any of this qualify for the rehabilitation or energy investment credit? What tax advice could you give the taxpayer for his consideration in maximizing these credits?

13-11 *Rehabilitation and Energy Credit.* When a taxpayer claims a rehabilitation credit, what impact does the credit have on the basis of the property for cost recovery purposes? What is the impact on the basis when a business energy credit is claimed? What if the disabled access credit is claimed?

13-12 *IC Recapture.* Explain two possible consequences if a taxpayer claims an investment credit on property and then makes an early disposition of the property.

13-13 *Minimum Tax Credit.* If a taxpayer pays an AMT in the current year, what consequences does that payment have on the AMT liability that may be owed in subsequent years? What impact does the payment of the AMT in the current year have on the regular tax liability in subsequent years?

13-14 *Dependent Care Credit.* A husband and wife both work and employ a babysitter to watch the children during their work hours. How much of the babysitter's salary qualifies for the child and dependent care credit if
a. The babysitter performs cooking and cleaning services while she is watching the children.
b. The babysitter also performs services around the house including gardening, bartending, and chauffeuring.

13-15 *Earned Income Credit.* A husband and wife with A.G.I. and earned income of $7,000 maintained a household for their son but were unable to claim him as a dependent because he was 20 years old and earned $3,500. Can the son or his parents qualify for the earned income credit? Explain.

13-16 *Research Credit.* An entrepreneur works in a garage during 2004 doing research for a new patent. He spends $15,000 on the research in 2004. In January 2005 he forms an S corporation and applies for the patent, which is granted in 2005. How much credit for research expenditures will the taxpayer be allowed and in what year?

13-17   *Work Opportunity Credit.* The purpose of the work opportunity credit is to encourage the employment of certain groups of people with high unemployment rates. The credit has not quite achieved the desired objectives. What changes should be made to the present credit to increase its effectiveness?

PROBLEMS

13-18   *Alternative Minimum Tax—Computation.* T is single and has taxable income of $56,550 and a regular tax liability of $10,803 for the current year. T uses the standard deduction for regular tax purposes and has $60,000 of positive adjustments (excluding the adjustment for the standard deduction) for AMT purposes.
   a.   Determine T's tentative minimum tax and her AMT.
   b.   Determine the amount that T actually has to pay the IRS this year.

13-19   *Alternative Minimum Tax—Computation.* V and W are married and file a joint return for the current year. They have no other dependents and they take the standard deduction. V and W's taxable income is $94,250 and their regular tax liability is $16,893. They have $60,000 of AMT preference items and $32,050 of AMT positive adjustments. Determine V and W's tentative AMT and their AMT liability.

13-20   *AMT and Qualified Small Business Stock.* T is an avid investor, always looking for that one stock that will make him rich and famous. On January 4, 1997 BC Corporation, a fast food chain, went public, and T thought this could be the one. He purchased 10,000 shares of stock for $100,000. One of the benefits from buying this initial offering was that BC's stock was eligible for treatment as qualified small business stock. After enduring the ups and downs of the market, T sold 5,000 shares of the stock for $250,000 on January 9, 2003.
   a.   Determine the gain recognized on the sale of the BC stock and the amount included in T's regular taxable income.
   b.   Determine the amount of tax preference or adjustment, if any, that T must take into account in computing his alternative minimum tax.

13-21   *Alternative Minimum Tax—Charitable Contribution Preference.* During the year, J contributed stock to the local university. He had purchased the stock in 1984 for $10,000, and it was appraised at $60,000 on the date of gift. The stock was sold shortly after the contribution was made, and a painting was purchased by the university with the proceeds from the sale. The university placed the painting in its Art Building for display and study by art students. J's A.G.I. in the year of contribution is $300,000.
   a.   Determine J's allowable charitable contribution deduction for the regular tax system.
   b.   Based solely on these facts, determine any AMT adjustments or preference items that apply to J.

13-22   *Alternative Minimum Tax—Computation.* B is single and reports the following items of income and deductions for the current year:

Salary	$ 50,000
Net long-term capital gain on sale of investment property	200,000
Medical expenses	17,500
Casualty loss	4,500
State and local income taxes	15,000
Real estate taxes	20,000
Charitable contributions (all cash)	15,000
Interest on home mortgage	12,000
Interest on investment loans (unimproved real property)	10,000

The only additional transaction during the year was the exercise of an incentive stock option of her employer's stock at an option price of $12,000 when the stock was worth $100,000. Compute B's tax liability and AMT, if any.

13-23   *Alternative Minimum Tax.* Refer to the facts in *Problem 13-22* and assume B holds the stock acquired by exercising her ISO for two years and sells it for $105,000. Determine the amount of gain that must be reported for regular tax purposes and the gain that must be reflected in the AMT calculations in the year the stock was sold.

13-24   *Alternative Minimum Tax—Cost Recovery Adjustment.* In 2005 T placed a light-duty truck in service at a cost of $40,000. T uses the applicable MACRS method of depreciation for all his assets and does not elect the § 179 first-year expensing option. Identify and calculate the minimum tax adjustment that must be made for AMT purposes in 2005.

13-25   *Alternative Minimum Tax—Cost Recovery.* Refer to the facts in *Problem 13-24,* but assume the truck that was placed in service this year at a cost of $40,000 was a heavy-duty truck. Identify and calculate the minimum tax adjustment that must be made for AMT purposes in 2005.

13-26   *Alternative Minimum Tax—Cost Recovery Adjustment.* In January 2005 A purchases residential rental property for $200,000, excluding the cost of the land. For regular tax purposes, the 2005 depreciation on the building is $6,970. For AMT purposes, depreciation is $4,792. Determine the AMT adjustment for cost recovery for 2005 and 2006.

13-27   *Alternative Minimum Tax—Computation.* O is married to G and they file a joint return for 2004. O and G have A.G.I. of $70,000. One of the deductions from gross income was $50,000 of percentage depletion. Cost depletion on their gold mine was zero because the cost basis of the property was reduced to zero by prior years' depletion deductions. They do not itemize deductions. Determine O and G's tax liability for 2005.

13-28   *Alternative Minimum Tax.* T is an unmarried entrepreneur. In 2002 he purchased several rental properties and leased them to tenants on long-term leases. In 2005, T has $100,000 of rental losses on his real estate activities in which he actively participates and income of $100,000 from his brokerage business. T also has a $25,000 general business credit carryover from 2004. Determine T's tax liability for 2005, assuming he does not itemize his deductions.

13-29   *Minimum Tax Credit.* Refer to the facts in *Problem 13-22* and determine the minimum tax credit, if any, that is available to offset the regular tax liability in 2006.

13-30   *General Business Credit—Limited by Tax Liability.* K's tax liability before credits is $35,000. She earned a general business credit of $40,000. Determine K's tax liability after credits and any general business credit carryback or carryforward that may exist.

13-31   *Energy Credit.* In May of the current year, J invested $60,000 in a solar system to heat water for a production process.
   a.   Determine the amount of business energy credit available to J.
   b.   Determine the basis of the energy property that J must use for cost recovery purposes.

13-32   *Rehabilitation Credit.* During the current year, T incurred $300,000 of qualified rehabilitation expenditures with respect to 75-year-old property. Prior to these expenditures, T had a $100,000 cost basis in the depreciable building.
   a.   Determine the amount of rehabilitation credit available to T.

b. Determine the basis of the rehabilitated property that T must use for cost recovery purposes.

13-33 *Rehabilitation Credit—Computation.* During the current year, K incurred $200,000 of qualified rehabilitation expenditures with respect to property constructed in 1930. The entire block where his property is located has been designated as a Certified Historical District.

a. Determine the amount of credit allowable to K if his structure is recognized as a historical structure.

b. Assuming that K paid $180,000 for his building in the current year and that he would claim MACRS depreciation, calculate his adjusted basis in the building at the end of the year. Assume that the property was placed in service in July of the current year.

13-34 *IC Recapture.* Assume D claimed a business energy credit of $30,000 for property placed in service on December 18, 2002 and that D sold this property on January 7, 2005. Determine the amount, if any, of IC recapture that D should report as an additional tax in 2005.

13-35 *IC Recapture.* Assume L claimed rehabilitation credit of $80,000 on property placed in service on February 18, 2002 and that L exchanged this rehabilitated property for like-kind property (a § 1031 exchange) on March 17, 2005. Determine the amount of IC recapture that L should report as an additional tax in 2005, if any.

13-36 *Research and Experimentation Credit.* M, a sole proprietor, has been in business only two years but is very successful. He has average annual gross receipts of $150,000 for this period and incurred $40,000 in qualified R&E expenses this year.

a. Determine M's R&E credit for the current year.

b. Determine the current deduction for R&E expenditures that M is entitled to, assuming he elects to deduct R&E expenditures currently.

13-37 *Disabled Access Credit—Computation.* P Corp. had gross receipts of $500,000 last year and incurred $9,000 of eligible access expenditures to build a wheelchair ramp this year.

a. Determine P's disabled access credit.

b. Determine the basis of the wheelchair ramp that will be eligible for cost recovery deductions.

13-38 *Child Tax Credit.* H and W are married with three children. At the close of 2005, the children, A, B, and C, were ages 2, 6, and 8, respectively. H and W claim a dependency exemption for each of the children. This year H and W reported adjusted gross income of $125,000. Determine the allowable child tax credit for H and W.

13-39 *Child Tax Credit.* M is a single mom raising one child, age 16, at home. M may claim a dependency exemption for her child. This year M earned $70,000 as salary and had investment income of $12,500. Determine the allowable child tax credit for M.

13-40 *Dependent Care Credit.* V and J are married and file a joint return for the current year. Because they both work, they had to pay a babysitter $5,200 to watch their three children (ages 7, 8, and 9). V earned $17,000 and J earned $21,200 during the year. They do not have any other source of income nor do they claim any deductions for adjusted gross income. Determine the allowable dependent care credit for V and J.

13-41 *Dependent Care Credit.* M and B are married, have a son three years old, and file a joint return for the current year. They incurred $500 a month for day care center expenses. During the year, B earned $23,000 but M did not work outside the home.

They do not have any other source of income nor do they claim any deductions for adjusted gross income. Determine the allowable dependent care credit for the year if

a. M enrolled as a full-time student in a local community college on September 6 of the current year.

b. M was in school from January through June, and from September through December of the current year.

13-42 *Dependent Care Credit.* C is a single parent raising a son who is eight years old. During the current year, C earned $19,500 and paid $3,000 to a sitter to watch her son after school. Determine C's dependent care credit for the current year.

13-43 *HOPE Scholarship Credit.* D is a single dad and has modified A.G.I. of $42,000. This year D's son begins studying for his bachelor's degree as a half-time student at Arapahoe County Community College. On September 1, D pays $2,000 in qualified tuition for his son's first semester. Determine the amount of HOPE credit available to D.

13-44 *HOPE Scholarship Credit.* H and W are married and have twins who are attending the State University as freshmen this year. State University is on the semester system and charges $1,000 tuition per semester. H and W pay State University $2,000 this year. H and W have adjusted gross income of $83,000.

a. Determine the allowable HOPE Scholarship credit for H and W.

b. If H and W ask your advice in terms of maximizing the HOPE Scholarship credit, what advice would you give them?

13-45 *Earned Income Credit.* R is 43, divorced, and maintains a household for his 7-year-old dependent daughter. R was laid off in 2004 and his unemployment benefits have run out. During 2005 he worked at part-time jobs earning $5,500. He has no other sources of income.

a. Determine R's allowable earned income credit.

b. Determine R's tax payment due or his refund, assuming that nothing was withheld from his wages and that he did not make any quarterly estimated tax payments.

13-46 *Earned Income Credit.* S, who is 24 and a single parent, maintains a household for her 3-year-old dependent daughter and her 10-month-old son. S earned $16,000 during this calendar year. S has no other source of income and does not itemize her deductions.

a. Determine S's allowable earned income credit.

b. Determine S's tax payment due or her refund, assuming that $200 was withheld from her wages and that she did not make any quarterly estimated tax payments.

13-47 *Additional Child Tax Credit.* H and W have four children and earned $24,000 for 2005 H and W paid $1,836 in FICA taxes but neither had any income tax withheld from their wages. Determine the amount of refund they should receive from the IRS.

13-48 *Integrative Credit Problem.* J, who is 32 and a single parent, maintains a household for his six-year-old dependent son. J earned $20,000 and paid $3,000 in child care payments during the calendar year. J did not have any Federal income tax withheld from his check. Determine the amount of J's refund from the IRS, if any, or the amount that J must pay the IRS, if required.

13-49 *Credit for the Elderly.* P and D are 66 years old, married, and file a joint return. The only sources of income they have are dividend income of $14,000 and social security of $2,500.

a. Determine the allowable credit for the elderly for the current year.

b. Determine the tax payable or refund due, assuming that no withholding was made on the dividends and that no quarterly estimated payments were made.

CUMULATIVE PROBLEM

TurboTax **13-50** R and S, married and the parents of two children ages 10 months and 6 years, file a joint return. R is a college professor of civil engineering and teaches at State University. R applied for a one-year visiting professorship with International Engineering Corporation (IEC) and was selected for the position. The visiting professor position was available from July 1 to May 31 of the following year and required R to relocate his family from Detroit to Los Angeles at a total cost of $6,500 during the last week in June. IEC reimbursed R only $5,000 for these expenses. R rented his Detroit home for the last six months of the calendar year at a net loss of $6,000 for regular tax purposes. Due to the longer life of the residential real property for AMT purposes, and therefore a smaller cost recovery deduction, the net loss for AMT purposes was only $4,000.

S was employed by the government and was able to get a temporary transfer to Los Angeles. S earned $12,000 for the calendar year. During the calendar year, R and S paid $6,000 in child care expenses.

R and his family incurred expenses of $2,500 a month to rent a furnished apartment (assume $1,000 a month was attributable to R and $1,000 a month was attributable to S) for the last six months of the calendar year. R and his family incurred expenses of $800 a month for food during the last six months of the year (assume 25% of the food is specifically attributable to R and that 25% is attributable to S). In addition, R incurred transportation expenses, parking fees, and laundry expenses of $2,500, and he spent $1,200 on lunches on work days during the last half of the year. S incurred transportation expenses of $500 and took her lunch to work with her. R earned $25,000 from State University for teaching half of the calendar year and $60,000 from IEC for practicing half of the year. Together, R and S had $12,000 of Federal income tax withheld from their paychecks.

During the year, R and S also incurred the following expenses:

Unreimbursed medical expenses.	$7,000
Charitable contribution of stock	
to State University (adjusted basis $1,000).	5,000
State and local income taxes	4,000
Real estate taxes on lake property	3,000
Real estate taxes on principal residence (one-half year) .	2,000
Interest on principal residence (one-half year).	4,800

The couple also had these additional income items:

State tax refund from previous year.	$1,500
Interest income from private activity bonds	7,000

R and S have a minimum tax credit carryover from last year of $5,000. Determine R and S's tax liability for the year.

RESEARCH PROBLEMS

13-51 *Rehabilitation Credit.* Taxpayer S, a real estate developer, rehabilitated an old commercial building and was entitled to an investment credit based on the rehabilitation expenses incurred. Prior to placing the new offices into service, S is approached by P, who is interested in purchasing the building. As an inducement to get P to buy the property, S offers to transfer the IC to P. That is, S agrees not to claim the credit on his tax return with the expectation that P can claim the credit instead. Will P be allowed to take credit on her tax return in the year she places the office building into service?

13-52 *Dependent Care Credit.* B is a single parent and his child is enrolled in a public school. The school administrators have scheduled a supervised trip to Dearborn,

Michigan for one full week for the students to see Greenfield Village and the Henry Ford Museum. Total trip cost per student is $800. If B pays for his child to make the trip, will he be entitled to a child care credit for the expenditures? If so, how much of the costs will qualify?

13-53 *Alternative Minimum Tax.* This year T was the victim of his company's restructuring and downsizing. Midway through the year his employer, ABC Corporation, offered him early retirement on the condition that he would provide consulting services when needed. The offer proved so lucrative that T accepted. T ended up working for the company for the first six months of the taxable year and earned $50,000 during this period. Prior to his retirement he exercised an incentive stock option he had received several years earlier. At the time he exercised the option, the market price of the stock was $140,000 and the purchase price under the option was $50,000. After he retired, T began a new business of building toys for disabled children. He materially participated in the business and incurred a loss of $60,000, which he properly reported on Schedule C of his Form 1040 tax return. T is married and files a joint return with his wife. The couple paid $18,000 in qualified housing interest and $6,000 in real estate taxes, and made a $25,000 cash contribution to Children's Hospital during the year. Determine T's regular tax liability and AMT, if any.

13-54 *Child Care Credit.* K recently divorced and decided to go back to school full-time to get her Masters of Taxation at Central University. She has a four-year-old child who attends nursery school at a cost of $4,000 per year. As a single parent, K finds it difficult just to get by. However, she maintains her home using her alimony payments, some dividend and interest income, and her child support. She also works as a volunteer for 10 hours a week at the library and receives $15 per week. This year she attended school for 11 months. Is K eligible for the child care credit?

Part V

PROPERTY TRANSACTIONS

❖ Contents ❖

Chapter Fourteen

Chapter Fifteen

Chapter Sixteen

Chapter Seventeen

Chapter 14

PROPERTY TRANSACTIONS: Basis Determination and Recognition of Gain or Loss

---

LEARNING OBJECTIVES

Upon completion of this chapter you will be able to:

- Understand the concepts of realized and recognized gain or loss from the disposition of property

- Explain the process of determining gain or loss required to be recognized on the disposition of property, including computation of the following:

    - Amount realized from a sale, exchange, or other disposition

    - Effect of liabilities assumed or transferred

    - Adjusted basis of property involved in the transaction

- Identify the most common types of adjustments to basis of property

- Define an installment sale and identify taxpayers eligible to use the installment method of reporting gain

- Compute the amount of gain required to be recognized in the year of installment sale and the gain to be reported in any subsequent year

- Explain the limitations imposed on certain installment sales, including

    - The imputed interest rules

    - Related-party installment sales

    - Gain recognition on the disposition of installment obligations

    - Required interest payments on deferred Federal income taxes

- Identify various transactions in which loss recognition is prohibited

CHAPTER OUTLINE

Section 61(a)(3) of the Code provides that gross income includes gains derived from dealings in property. Similarly, § 165 allows a deduction, subject to limitations, for losses incurred in certain property transactions. The term *dealings in property* includes sales, exchanges, and other types of acquisitions or dispositions of property. This chapter examines the determination of the amount of gains and losses from dealings in property. Specific rules regarding gain recognition are addressed, as are the gain-deferral possibilities associated with certain installment sales. Various limitations on the deductibility of losses also are addressed.

Other topics dealing with property transactions are examined in the next three chapters. Chapter 15 deals with certain nontaxable exchanges. Chapter 16 covers the special treatment accorded gains and losses from sales or exchanges of capital assets. The unique rules governing the disposition of property used in a trade or business, including depreciable property, are examined in Chapter 17.

DETERMINATION OF GAIN OR LOSS

INTRODUCTION

Determining the gain or loss realized in a property transaction is usually a simple computation. It is the mathematical difference between the amount realized in a sale or other disposition and the adjusted basis of the property surrendered (See Exhibit 14-1). The amount realized is a measure of the consideration received in the transaction. It represents the economic value *realized* by the taxpayer.

EXHIBIT 14-1
Computatin of Gain or Loss Realized

	Amount realized (See Exhibit 14-3)
−	Adjusted basis
=	Gain or loss realized

Sale or other disposition essentially refers to any transaction in which a taxpayer realizes benefit in exchange for property. It is not necessary that there be a sale transaction or that cash be received for gain or loss to be realized by the taxpayer surrendering property other than cash.

The adjusted basis of purchased property is generally cost, plus or minus certain adjustments. Computing gain or loss realized is similar to determining gain or loss for accounting purposes, and adjusted basis is similar in concept to book value. However, the adjusted basis of a property will not always be, and frequently is not, equal to its book value for accounting purposes.

In effect, the adjusted cost, or adjusted basis, of a given property is the amount that can be recovered tax-free upon its disposition. For example, if property is sold for exactly its cost, as adjusted, there is no gain or loss realized. This concept is referred to as the *recovery of capital or recovery of basis* principle. If a taxpayer receives more than the adjusted basis in exchange for property, gain is realized only to the extent of that excess. The adjusted basis is recovered tax-free. The following examples illustrate this concept:

Example 1. K transferred 30 acres of land to ZX Company for $42,000 cash. K had purchased the 30 acres five years earlier for $35,000, which is his adjusted basis. As a result of this "sale or other disposition," K has a realized gain of $7,000 ($42,000 − $35,000). His $35,000 basis in the land is recovered tax-free.

Example 2. In 2003 L purchased 300 shares of W Corporation stock for $3,600 cash, including brokerage fees. When the market outlook for W Corporation's product began to weaken in 2005, L sold her shares for $3,100. The broker deducted a commission of $48 and forwarded $3,052 cash to her. L has a realized loss on this transaction of $548 ($3,052 − $3,600) in 2005.

Example 3. R transferred 200 shares of C Corporation stock worth $4,000 and $2,000 cash for an auto he will use for personal purposes. The C Corporation stock had been purchased two years earlier for $4,600. R realizes a loss of $600 [($6,000 − $2,000) − $4,600] on the "sale or other disposition" of the stock.

GENERAL RULE OF RECOGNITION

Any gain or loss realized must be recognized unless some provision of the Internal Revenue Code provides otherwise. A *recognized gain* is reported on a tax return. For example, a gain on the sale of stock generally is recognized in full in the year of sale (i.e., the gain is reported on a tax return, included in gross income, and considered in determining the tax liability for the year). In determining taxable income, the recognized gain is either offset against losses for the year or included in the computation of taxable income.[1]

A *recognized loss* also is generally given its full tax effect in the year of realization. Depending on the type of loss, it may be either offset against gains or deducted against

---

[1]   Capital gains must be offset by capital losses, and only net capital gains are included in taxable income. See the discussion of capital gains and losses in Chapter 16.

other forms of income in determining taxable income. Some losses, however, are not deductible[2] and others are limited.[3] For example, losses on the sale of property used for personal purposes are disallowed. Certain other losses are deferred to later tax years. Some examples of nontaxable exchanges are listed in Exhibit 14-2.

EXHIBIT 14-2
Partial List of Nontaxable Exchanges

Types of Transaction	Action Required	Tax Result
Casualty, theft, condemnation (involuntary conversion)	Reinvest in similar property	Gain may be deferred see Chapter 15 and § 1033
Like-kind exchange	Exhchange directly for like-kind property	Gain or loss is deferred* see Chapter 15 and § 1031
Formation of a corporation or subsequent stock issues	Transfer property exchange for stock by controlling shareholders	Gain or loss is deferred* see § 351
Corporate reorganizations	Examples include mergers, consolidations divisions, recapitalizations	Gain or loss is deferred* see § 368
Partnership formation	Transfer property in exchange for a partnership interest	Gain or loss is deferred* see § 721

When gain or loss is deferred, the deferral is only until the replacement property is sold or otherwise transferred (i.e., the deferred gain or loss is recognized along with any subsequent gain or loss when the replacement property is sold).

COMPUTING AMOUNT REALIZED

The amount realized from a sale or other disposition of property includes the amount of money received plus the fair market value of any other property received in a transaction. Other property includes both tangible and intangible property.

Example 4. P received $20,000 and a motor home worth $80,000 in exchange for a sailing yacht that she had used for personal enjoyment. P's amount realized on the disposition of the yacht is $100,000 ($20,000 + $80,000).

The amount realized also includes any debt obligations of the buyer, and if the contract provides for inadequate interest or no interest, interest must be imputed and the sales price reduced accordingly.

Example 5. Y sold his vintage Dodge automobile to C for $10,000 and a note payable from C to Y for $15,000 plus interest compounded monthly at 9%. Y's amount realized in this transaction is $25,000, the down payment plus the value of C's note.

---

[2] Losses on certain sales to related parties are disallowed under § 267, and losses on the sale of personal use property are not allowed under § 165(c).

[3] The deduction for capital losses is limited under § 1211(b).

Example 6. Z sold a parcel of real estate for $100,000. Her basis in the land was $60,000. The sales contract called for $10,000 to be paid upon transfer of the property and the remaining $90,000 to be paid in full two years later.

Since no interest was provided for in the contract, interest must be imputed on the buyer's $90,000 obligation (in this case, 9% interest, compounded semiannually, is used).[4] Accordingly, the sales price is reduced to $85,471 [$10,000 cash down payment + $75,471 (the discounted present value of the $90,000 payment in two years)]. Z will report an amount realized of $85,471 and a gain realized of $25,471 ($85,471 − $60,000 basis). When Z collects the $90,000, she must report interest income of $14,529 ($90,000 face value − $75,471 present value on date of sale).

The amount realized also includes the amount of any existing liabilities of the seller discharged in the transaction. Specifically, it includes any debts assumed by the buyer and any liabilities encumbering the property transferred that remain with the property in the buyer's hands.[5] Exhibit 14-3 illustrates the computation of *both* the amount realized and the gain or loss realized from the sale or other disposition of property.

EXHIBIT 14-3
Computation of Amount Realized and Gain or Loss Realized

Amount realized:		
Amount of money received		$xxx,xxx
Add:	Fair market value of other property received	+x,xxx
	Liabilities discharged:	
	Liabilities assumed by the buyer	+xx,xxx
	Liabilities encumbering the property transferred	+x,xxx
Less:	Selling expenses	−xx,xxx
	Amount of money given up	−x,xxx
	Liabilities incurred:	
	Liabilities assumed by the taxpayer	−xx,xxx
	Liabilities encumbering the property received	−x,xxx
Equals:	Amount realized	$xxx,xxx
Less:	*Adjusted basis* in property other than money given up	−xx,xxx
Equals:	*Gain or loss realized*	$xxx,xxx

Example 7. B purchased a rental house for $40,000 in 1997. She paid $8,000 down and signed a mortgage note for the balance. During the years she owned the property, B deducted depreciation totaling $16,000 and made principal payments on the note of $4,000, leaving a mortgage balance of $28,000.

During 2005 B sold the house for $62,000. The buyer paid $34,000 cash and assumed the $28,000 mortgage liability. B's amount realized is $62,000 ($34,000 cash + $28,000 relief of liability), and her adjusted basis is $24,000 ($40,000 cost reduced by $16,000 depreciation). Her gain realized is therefore $38,000 ($62,000 amount realized − $24,000 adjusted basis).

Any expenses of selling the property reduce the amount realized. Selling costs include many costs, paid by the seller, associated with offering a property for sale and transacting the sale. For example, selling costs include advertising expenses, appraisal

---

[4]   The actual rate is determined with reference to current market rates and is announced periodically by the IRS. For transactions involving $2.8 million or less, the rate cannot exceed 9 percent compounded semiannually.

[5]   Reg. § 1.1001-2. Also, see the following discussion of the effect of liabilities in property transactions.

fees, sales commissions, legal fees, transfer taxes, recording fees, and mortgage costs of the buyer paid by the seller.

BASIS DETERMINATION RULES

The adjusted basis of property may be determined in several ways, depending on how the property is acquired and whether any gain or loss is being deferred in the transaction. Various methods of acquiring property and their specific basis determination rules are discussed below.

PROPERTY ACQUIRED BY PURCHASE

Cost Basis. In a simple purchase transaction, basis is the cost of the property acquired. Cost is the amount of money paid and the fair market value of any other property transferred in exchange for a given property.[6] The cost basis includes any payments made by the buyer with borrowed funds and any obligations (i.e., promissory notes) of the buyer given to the seller or any obligations of the seller assumed by the buyer in the exchange.[7]

Any costs of acquiring property are included in basis. For stock and securities, commissions, transfer taxes, and other acquisition costs are included. For other property, many types of acquisition costs, including commissions, legal fees related to purchase, recording fees, title insurance, appraisals, sales taxes, and transfer taxes, are added to basis.[8] Any installation and delivery costs also are part of basis.

> **Example 8.** C purchased a new machine for his auto repair business during 2005. He paid $16,500 for the machine, $8,500 of which was made possible by a bank loan. In addition, C paid state sales taxes of $660, delivery charges of $325, and installation charges of $175. C's cost basis in the equipment is $17,660 ($16,500 purchase price + $660 sales taxes + $325 delivery charges + $175 installation charges).

Periodic operating costs such as interest and taxes are generally deducted in the year paid. However, a taxpayer may elect to *capitalize* (i.e., include in basis) certain taxes and interest related to unproductive and unimproved real property or related to real property during development or improvement rather than take a current tax deduction.[9]

> **Example 9.** T purchased a small parcel of unimproved land near a lake known for its excellent fishing. She uses the property as a weekend retreat and plans someday to build a log cabin. T annually pays $150 for local property taxes but does not itemize deductions. T should elect to capitalize the property taxes paid each year as a part of her basis in the land.

Identification Problems. Generally, the adjusted basis of property sold or otherwise transferred is easily traced to the acquisition of the property and certain subsequent events. However, identification of cost may be difficult if a taxpayer has multiple homogeneous assets. For example, if a taxpayer owns identical shares of stock in a corporation that were acquired in more than one transaction and sells less than his

---

[6]   Reg. § 1.1012-1(a).

[7]   § 1001 and *Crane v. Comm.*, 47-1 USTC ¶9217, 35 AFTR 776, 331 U.S. 1 (USSC, 1947).

[8]   § 1012 and Reg. § 1.1012-1(a).

[9]   § 266 and Reg. § 1.266-1(b)(1).

or her entire investment in that stock, it is necessary to identify which shares are sold. For tax purposes, the owner must use the *first-in, first-out* (FIFO) method of identification if it is impossible to identify which shares were sold. Specific identification of the shares sold is appropriate if the shares can be identified.[10]

Example 10. K purchased the following lots of G Corporation stock:

50 shares	Purchased 1/10/02	Cost $5,500
75 shares	Purchased 8/15/02	Cost $9,000
40 shares	Purchased 6/18/04	Cost $4,600

K sold 60 shares of her G Corporation stock in 2005 for $8,700. Unless she can specifically identify the shares sold, her basis will be determined using the FIFO method. Therefore, her basis in 50 shares sold is $5,500 and her basis in 10 shares sold is $1,200 [10 shares × $120 ($9,000 ÷ 75 shares)]. Her total gain is $2,000.

Example 11. Assuming the same facts in *Example 10*, the gain would be different if K could specifically identify the shares sold. If she directed her broker to deliver to the buyer the shares purchased on 8/15/02, referring to them by certificate number and date of purchase, her gain would be $1,500 [$8,700 sale price − $7,200 ($120 basis per share × 60)].

PROPERTY ACQUIRED BY GIFT

Generally, the basis of property received by gift is the same as the basis was to the donor.[11] This basis is *increased* by that portion of the gift tax paid by the donor, which is attributable to the appreciation in the property's value, if any, up to the date of the gift. The appreciation is measured by the difference between the fair market value of the property and the donor's adjusted basis in the property immediately before the gift.[12] The appropriate increase in basis for a given property is determined using the following formula:

$$\frac{\text{Fair market value date of gift} - \text{Donor's basis date of gift}}{\text{Fair market value date of gift}} \times \text{Gift taxes paid}$$

Gift tax returns must be filed annually. If there is more than one gift on the annual gift tax return, then the taxes paid on a *particular gift* bear the same proportion to the total gift taxes for the year as the value of that taxable gift bears to the total taxable gifts for the year.[13]

Example 12. In 2005 P received a diamond necklace as a gift from her grandmother. The necklace had an adjusted basis to her grandmother of $12,000 and had a fair market value of $36,000 on the date of the gift. Gift taxes of $9,000 were paid. P's basis in the necklace is $18,000, including an adjustment for gift taxes of $6,000 ($9,000 gift taxes paid × [($36,000 − $12,000) ÷ $36,000]. If P sells the necklace for $39,000 in 2005, her gain will be $21,000 ($39,000 − $18,000).

Example 13. If P, from the previous example, had sold the necklace for $15,000, she would have realized a loss of $3,000. The tax treatment of the loss depends on

[10]   Reg. § 1.1012-1(c).

[11]   § 1015(a).

[12]   § 1015(d)(6).

[13]   § 1015(d)(2).

how she used the necklace. If she used the necklace for personal (rather than business or investment) purposes, then P would not be allowed to recognize the loss for tax purposes.

Loss Limitation Rule. Where the fair market value of the property *at the time of the gift* is less than the donor's basis, special rules must be applied to determine the basis for the donee. Perhaps the clearest expression of the rules in this case is as follows: the basis for *determining gain* is the donor's basis, while the basis for *determining loss* is the lower of either (1) the donor's basis or (2) the property's fair market value at the date of the gift.[14] Due to the way the rule for determining loss is stated, the donee will not recognize any gain or loss if the property is disposed of for any amount that is *less than* the donor's basis *but greater than* the value of the property at the date of the gift. These rules are illustrated in the following examples.

> **Example 14.** S received 200 shares of X Corporation stock as a gift from his uncle. The stock had a basis to the uncle of $32,000 and a fair market value on the date of the gift of $29,000. Gift taxes of $1,400 were paid on the transfer.
>
> During 2005 S sold all of the shares for $24,000. His loss realized on the sale is $5,000 ($24,000 sale price − $29,000 fair market value at date of gift). Note that S was not permitted to add any of the $1,400 gift taxes to his basis since such adjustments are allowed only if the fair market value is more than the donor's basis on the date of the gift (i.e., the property appreciated in the donor's hands).

> **Example 15.** Assuming the same facts as in *Example 14*, if S had sold his stock for $31,000 he would not realize gain or loss on the sale. His basis for gain is $32,000 (the donor's basis) and his basis for loss is limited to $29,000 (fair market value on the date of the gift). Since the $31,000 sales price does not exceed the gain basis and is not less than his loss basis, neither gain nor loss is realized on the sale.

> **Example 16.** Assuming the same facts as in *Example 14*, if S's stock had been sold for $36,000, his realized gain would have been $4,000 ($36,000 sales price − $32,000 gain basis). There is no adjustment for gift taxes paid because the property did not appreciate in the donor's hands.

Application of these special rules illustrates *three* important points. First, *any gain* realized by the donee on a subsequent sale of the property is limited to the amount of gain that the donor would have realized had he or she sold it at the donee's sales price. Second, *any loss* allowed on a subsequent sale of the property is limited to the decline in the property's value that occurs while owned by the donee. Third, although the payment of a gift tax may be required as a result of the gift, the donee is not allowed to adjust the donor's basis in the property by any gift taxes paid because there is no appreciation in value of the property in the donor's hands (i.e., the fair market value of the property at the time of the gift is less than the donor's basis).

Gifts before 1977. For gifts before 1977, the addition to the basis of property acquired by gift is the entire amount of gift taxes paid. The gift taxes, however, cannot be used to raise the basis above the fair market value of the property on the date of the gift.

> **Example 17.** B received a painting as a gift from her mother in 1975. The art work had a basis to her mother of $4,000 and a fair market value of $4,500. Gift taxes of $900 were paid on the gift. After further appreciation in the value of the painting, it

---

[14] § 1015(a). It also should be noted that total depreciation claimed using the gain basis for computation cannot exceed the property's fair market value at date of gift. Reg. § 1.167(g)-1.

was sold by B for $5,500 during the current year. Her realized gain is $1,000 [$5,500 sales price − $4,500 ($4,000 donor's basis + $500 of the gift taxes paid)].

Example 18. Assuming the same facts as in *Example 17*, if the painting had a fair market value of $5,000 on the date of the gift, the entire $900 gift taxes paid would be allowed as a basis adjustment. If B sold the painting for $5,500, her realized gain would now be $600 ($5,500 sales price − $4,900 basis).

PROPERTY ACQUIRED FROM A DECEDENT

The adjusted basis of property acquired from a decedent generally is its fair market value on the date of the decedent's death.[15] This also is the value used in determining the taxable estate for estate tax purposes.[16] The fiduciary (executor or administrator) of the estate may, however, *elect* to value the estate for estate tax purposes six months after the date of death.[17] This election is available only if (1) the estate is required to file a Federal estate tax return (Form 706), and (2) the alternate valuation reduces *both* the gross estate and the Federal estate tax.[18] If the fiduciary elects to use this alternate valuation date, the fair market value on the later date must also be used as the income tax basis to the heir or estate.[19]

Example 19. D inherited some gold jewelry from his grandmother during 2004. The fair market value of the jewelry on the date of her death was $4,000 and its adjusted basis to the grandmother was $3,050. If D sells the jewelry in 2005 for $4,350, his realized gain will be $350 ($4,350 sale price − $4,000 basis).

Example 20. If D, from the previous example, sells the jewelry for $3,000, he will have a realized loss of $1,000 ($3,000 − $4,000).

Exceptions to this basis rule are provided for *income in respect of a decedent* under § 691[20] and for certain property acquired by the decedent by gift. Income in respect of a decedent (often referred to as IRD) includes all items of income that the decedent had earned or was entitled to as of the date of death, but which were not included in the decedent's final income tax return under his or her method of accounting. For example, if a cash basis individual performed all the services required to earn a $3,000 consulting fee but had not collected the fee before his or her death, the $3,000 would be income in respect of a decedent. All IRD items are includible in the decedent's gross estate at fair market value for Federal estate tax purposes. Whoever receives the right to collect these items of income must report them in the same manner as the decedent would have been required to report them had he or she lived to collect the income. As a result, IRD items generally are fully included in the gross income of the recipient when received.[21]

If appreciated property was acquired by the decedent by gift within one year before his or her death and the property passes *back* to the donor or the donor's spouse, the recipient's adjusted basis is the decedent's adjusted basis.[22]

---

[15] § 1014(a).

[16] § 2031(a).

[17] § 2032(a).

[18] § 2032(c).

[19] § 1014(a)(2).

[20] § 1014(c).

[21] § 691(a)(1).

[22] § 1014(e).

Example 21. H transferred a parcel of lake-front real estate to his elderly grandmother when the property had an adjusted basis to H of $3,000 and a fair market value of $40,000. No gift taxes were paid on the transfer.

H's grandmother died three months after the gift and left the lake-front property to H in her will. H's basis in the property is $3,000 (the rules used for gifted property apply rather than those for inherited property). If his grandmother had lived for more than a year after the gift was made, H's basis would have been determined under the general rule for property acquired from a decedent.

Another exception is provided in the case of real property subject to special use valuation for Federal estate tax purposes. In such cases, the basis to the heir is the special value used for estate tax purposes. This special use valuation applies only to certain real property used in a trade or business and held by the heir more than 10 years.[23]

PROPERTY ACQUIRED IN A NONTAXABLE EXCHANGE

Most nontaxable exchanges provide deferral, rather than permanent nonrecognition of gain or loss. The mechanism for such deferral is typically an adjustment to the basis in some replacement property.[24] This adjustment is a reduction in basis in the case of a deferred gain and an increase in basis in the case of a deferred loss.

The specific rules for determining the basis of property acquired in nontaxable transactions, along with the requirements of each nontaxable transaction, are discussed in various parts of this text. Several such transactions are discussed in the next chapter. The following example illustrates one such transaction:

Example 22. T exchanged a five-acre residential lot for a 100-acre tract of farmland. He realized a $70,000 gain on the exchange because the farmland was worth $90,000 and his basis in the residential lot was $20,000. Since T met all the requirements for nonrecognition of gain in a like-kind exchange under § 1031, his basis in the farmland is $20,000 ($90,000 fair market value − $70,000 deferred gain).

PROPERTY CONVERTED FROM PERSONAL USE TO BUSINESS USE

Losses on the disposition of personal use properties are clearly not deductible. Absent some provision to the contrary, business owners could simply convert personal use assets to business use before disposing of them in order to generate business deductions for losses on their sale. Accordingly, when property is converted from personal use to trade or business use, its basis is limited for determining realized loss and for depreciation purposes. For each of those purposes, fair market value on the date of conversion is used as the property's basis if it is less than its adjusted basis.[25]

Example 23. J owned a single-family home that had been her personal residence for four years. When J discontinued use of the house as her residence, she converted it to rental property. J's original basis in the property was $90,000, and the property was worth $86,000 on the date of conversion. J must determine any depreciation using the fair market value of $86,000, since it is less than her $90,000 adjusted basis. If the property is later sold, J's *gain basis* will be the original $90,000 adjusted basis reduced by the depreciation allowed after the conversion. Her *loss basis* will be the lower fair

---

[23] § 2032A(b).

[24] See, for example, § 1031(d), dealing with like-kind exchanges.

[25] Reg. §1.167(g)-1.

market value on the date of conversion, $86,000, reduced by the allowed depreciation. Note the similarity to the basis rules that would have applied if J had received the residence as a gift (see *Examples 14*, *15*, and *16*).

PROPERTY CONVERTED FROM BUSINESS USE TO PERSONAL USE

Once property is converted from business use to personal use, it is treated as personal use property. Any loss on the disposition of such property would, therefore, be disallowed; and, in the event that the property was subsequently converted back to business use, the limitations discussed above would apply.

> **Example 24.** W has a photocopier used exclusively for business. The copier cost $4,000 and depreciation of $1,800 has been allowed, making its basis $2,200. If W converts the copier to personal and family use and later sells it for $500, no loss will be deductible. Of course, if W had immediately sold the copier at a loss rather than converting it to personal use, he would have a business loss.

ADJUSTMENTS TO BASIS

Regardless of the method used in determining a property's basis initially, certain adjustments are made to that basis. Generally, the adjustments can be broken down into three groups. Basis is *increased* by *betterments* or *improvements*[26] and *reduced* by *depreciation allowed* or *allowable*[27] and by *other capital recoveries.*[28]

Depreciation reduces basis regardless of whether it is actually deducted by the taxpayer. The *allowable depreciation* is determined using the straight-line method if no method is adopted by the taxpayer.[29]

Various types of *capital recoveries* also reduce a property's adjusted basis. The following are some of the specific items that reduce basis:

1. Certain dividend distributions that are treated as a return of basis[30]

2. Deductible losses with respect to property, such as casualty loss deductions[31]

3. Credits for rehabilitation expenditures related to older commercial buildings and certified historic structures[32]

Numerous other events have an impact on a property's adjusted basis. Many of them are discussed in the remaining chapters of this text, which deal with specific types of transactions.

Exhibit 14-4 summarizes the rules for determining a property's adjusted basis.

EFFECT OF LIABILITIES ON AMOUNT REALIZED

Mention has been made of the fact that the amount realized in a sale or other disposition of property includes the amount of any liabilities of the seller assumed by the buyer plus any liabilities encumbering the transferred property that remain with the

---

26   § 1016(a)(1).

27   § 1016(a)(2).

28   See following examples.

29   § 1016(a)(2).

30   § 1016(a)(4).

31   See Reg. § 1.1016-6 and Rev. Rul. 74-206, 1974-1 C.B. 198.

32   See §§ 46(a), 48(q), and 1016(a)(22).

property.[33] The amount realized from a transaction is reduced by any liabilities assumed by the seller plus any liabilities encumbering property received in the transaction that remain with the property. The basis of any property received includes the portion of the cost represented by the liabilities assumed by the seller or encumbering the property.[34]

> **Example 25.** B exchanges a vacant lot with an adjusted basis of $20,000 for a mountain cabin worth $75,000. B's vacant lot has a fair market value of $50,000 and is subject to a $15,000 mortgage. The mountain cabin B receives is subject to a mortgage of $40,000. B assumes the $40,000 mortgage on the mountain cabin and the other party to the exchange assumes the $15,000 mortgage on the vacant lot.
>
> B's amount realized on this exchange is $50,000 ($75,000 fair market value of cabin received + $15,000 mortgage on vacant lot assumed by the other party − $40,000 mortgage on the mountain cabin assumed by B). If this exchange does not qualify for tax deferral, B has a realized and recognized gain of $30,000 ($50,000 amount realized − $20,000 adjusted basis of the vacant lot given up); and his basis in the mountain cabin is $75,000 (i.e., its fair market value).

EXHIBIT 14-4
Determination of Adjusted Basis

Method of Acquisition	Basis	Exceptions
General Rule		
Purchase cost	See special rules	
Special Rules		
Acquired by gift	Donor's basis + gift taxes paid on appreciation	If fair market value at date of gift is less than donor's basis use fair market value to determine loss
Acquired from a decedent	Fair market value at date of death (or alternate valuation date, if elected)	1. Income in respect of a decedent 2. Property given to the decedent by the donor/heir within one year of decedent's death 3. Property subject to special § 2032A
Converted from personal use	Adjusted basis before conversion	For determining loss and depreciation, use fair market value date of conversion if lower than original adjusted basis
Acquired in a nontaxable exchange	Fair market value less any gain not recognized or plus any loss deferred	

Note: The basis as determined under any of the above methods is subject to adjustments as provided by other provisions of the Code. Basis is increased by betterments or improvements and reduced by depreciation allowed or allowable and by other capital recoveries.

---

[33]   Reg. § 1.1001-2(a)(1).

[34]   *Crane v. Comm.*, 47-1 USTC ¶9217, 35 AFTR 776, 331 U.S. 1 (USSC, 1947). Such liabilities are not included if they are contingent or not subject to valuation. Rev. Rul. 78-29, 1978-1 C.B. 62.

Example 26. D, the other party to the exchange in *Example 25*, had an adjusted basis in her mountain cabin of $65,000. D's amount realized on the exchange is $75,000 ($50,000 fair value of vacant lot received + $40,000 mortgage assumed by B − $15,000 mortgage on the vacant lot). If the exchange does not qualify for tax deferral, D has a realized and recognized gain of $10,000 ($75,000 amount realized − $65,000 adjusted basis in the mountain cabin given up); and her basis in the vacant lot is $50,000 (i.e., its fair market value).

The amount realized on a sale or exchange of property is affected by liabilities even though neither the buyer nor the seller is personally obligated for payment.[35] The rationale for such treatment is that the owner benefits from the nonrecourse liabilities as owner of the property because his or her basis in the property, or some other property, is properly increased because of the liability.[36]

CONCEPTS RELATED TO REALIZATION AND RECOGNITION

SALE OR OTHER DISPOSITION

Realization of gain or loss occurs upon any sale or other disposition of property. Whether such an event has occurred generally is not difficult to ascertain. A typical sale or exchange obviously constitutes a sale or other disposition, but other transactions in which the taxpayer surrenders property other than cash also may be so classified. The timing of such realization is determined according to the taxpayer's method of accounting. Under the accrual method, realization generally occurs when a transaction is closed and the seller has an unqualified right to collect the sales price.[37] Under the cash method, the taxpayer realizes gain or loss upon the receipt of cash or cash equivalents.[38] In any case, a sale is consummated and realization occurs if beneficial title or possession of the burdens and benefits of ownership are transferred to the buyer.[39]

Transactions Involving Certain Securities. Generally, a sale or other disposition occurs any time a taxpayer surrenders property in exchange for some consideration. Accordingly, if a taxpayer exchanges securities of one type for securities of another type, a taxable event has occurred.[40]

Example 27. F exchanged X Corporation 12% bonds with a face value of $100,000 for Z Corporation 9% bonds with a face value of $120,000. Each group of bonds was worth $105,000 at the time of the exchange. If the X Corporation bonds that F exchanged had a basis of $100,000, he has a $5,000 gain on the exchange.

Several exceptions to this scheme do exist. In some instances, the exchange of *substantially identical* bonds of state or municipal governments has been declared a nontaxable transfer.[41] The condition of being substantially identical is usually

---

[35] *Ibid.*

[36] See *Tufts v. Comm.*, 83-1 USTC ¶9328, 51 AFTR2d 1983-1132, 461 U.S. 300 (USSC, 1983) for an excellent discussion of nonrecourse liabilities and their impact on basis.

[37] See *Alfred Scully*, 20 TCM 1272, T.C. Memo 1961-243 (1961), and Rev. Rul. 72-381, 1972-2 C.B. 581.

[38] See, for example, *Comm. v. Union Pacific R.R. Co.*, 36-2 USTC ¶9525, 18 AFTR 636, 86 F.2d 637 (CA-2, 1936).

[39] *Ibid.*

[40] Rev. Rul. 60-25, 1960-1 C.B. 283, and Rev. Rul. 78-408, 1978-2 C.B. 203.

[41] *Motor Products Corp. v. Comm.*, 44-1 USTC ¶9308, 32 AFTR 672, 142 F.2d 449 (CA-6, 1944), and Rev. Rul. 56-435, 1956-2 C.B. 506.

determined in terms of rate of return and fair market value. If the bonds received do not meet this test, the exchange may be taxable.[42]

It is clearly established that converting bonds into stock under a conversion privilege contained in the bond instrument does not result in the recognition of gain.[43] Similarly, the conversion of stock into some other stock of the same corporation pursuant to a right granted under the stock certificate does not result in recognition of gain or loss.[44]

Transfer Related to Taxpayer's Debt. When property is transferred to a creditor, the transfer may or may not be a disposition. The mere granting of a lien against property to secure a loan is not a disposition.[45] The transfer of property in satisfaction of a liability, however, is a taxable disposition.[46] Similarly, the loss of property in a foreclosure sale[47] and the voluntary transfer of mortgaged property to creditors in satisfaction of debt[48] are dispositions of property.

Example 28. M purchased a commercial property for $20,000, paying $4,000 down and signing a note secured by a mortgage for the $16,000 difference. Three years later, when M had reduced the balance on the note to $7,000, the lender accepted 300 shares of T Corporation stock in satisfaction of the obligation. The T Corporation stock had a fair market value of $7,000 and an adjusted basis to M of $5,000. Because of this disposition of stock, M has a $2,000 realized gain. Note that this result is the same as if M had sold the stock for $7,000 cash and paid the balance on the note.

Example 29. K purchased a warehouse for use in her business for $30,000, paying $5,000 down and signing a nonrecourse note (K is not personally liable) secured by a mortgage lien for the $25,000 difference. Over a three-year period, K's business suffered a decline and as a result she was able to make payments of only $3,000 on the note. During the same three-year period, K deducted depreciation of $12,000, thereby reducing her basis in the warehouse to $18,000.

After the three years, K reduced the size of her business substantially and voluntarily transferred the warehouse to the lender. Upon the transfer, K's amount realized from the discharge of the remaining indebtedness is $22,000 ($25,000 original note − $3,000 payments). Since her basis in the warehouse was $18,000, K has a $4,000 realized gain on the disposition of the property.

Abandonment. The abandonment of property used in a business or income-producing activity, whether depreciable or not, results in realization of loss to the extent of the property's adjusted basis. A loss deduction is allowed if the taxpayer takes action that demonstrates that he or she has no intention of retrieving the property for use, for sale, or other disposition in the future.[49]

Example 30. While working in a logging operation, R's truck became unoperational, and it was clear that the cost of having the truck moved to a repair site exceeded its

42 See *Emery v. Comm.*, 48-1 USTC ¶9165, 36 AFTR 741, 166 F.2d 27 (CA-2, 1948), and Rev. Rul. 81-169, 1981-25 I.R.B. 17. Also, see *Mutual Loan and Savings Co. v. Comm.*, 50-2 USTC ¶9420, 39 AFTR 1034, 184 F.2d 161 (CA-5, 1950) for an example of nonrecognition where the state Supreme Court held the new bonds with a lower interest rate to be a mere continuation of the original issue.

43 Rev. Rul. 57-535, 1957-2 C.B. 513.

44 Ltr. Rul., 2-23-45, ¶76,130 P-H Fed. 1945.

45 See *Dorothy Vickers*, 36 TCM 391, T.C. Memo 1977-90.

46 *Carlisle Packing Co.*, 29 B.T.A. 514 (1933), and Rev. Rul. 76-111, 1976-1 C.B. 214 (1976).

47 *O'Dell & Sons Co., Inc.*, 8 T.C. 1165 (1947).

48 *Estate of Delman*, 73 T.C. 15 (1979).

49 Reg. §§ 1.165-2 and 1.167(a)-8.

value. R abandoned the truck with no intention of seeking its return. If R has a $2,500 adjusted basis in the truck, he is entitled to an abandonment loss deduction of $2,500.

Demolition. No deduction is allowed for expenses related to the demolition of a building or for a loss where the adjusted basis of the building exceeds any salvage value. Both the cost of the demolition and any disallowed loss are added to the basis of the land on which the building stood.[50]

> **Example 31.** T purchased a rezoned commercial lot with a small house for $75,000. The structure was worth $2,000. In order to expedite construction of a new car wash, T simply razed the house at a cost of $1,500. No deduction is allowed for the loss of the house or the razing cost, and T's basis in the vacant lot is $76,500 ($73,000 lot + $2,000 house + $1,500 demolition costs).

Spousal Transfers. The transfer of property to one's spouse while married or as a result of dissolution of the marriage does not constitute a taxable event. This is true even if the transfer is in exchange for the release of marital rights under state law or for some other consideration. This rule applies to *any* transfer made to one's spouse during the marriage or within *one year* after the marriage is terminated. It also applies to later transfers to a former spouse if the transfers are made incident to the divorce (e.g., under a provision of the divorce decree).[51] In a consistent manner, the basis of the transferred property for the transferee (recipient) is the same as the transferor's basis.[52]

It is important to note that this nonrecognition provision applies to all transfers between spouses—including the sale of property at a fair market price. Additionally, the transferor is required to provide the transferee with records needed to determine the basis and holding period of the property.[53]

> **Example 32.** H and W were divorced this year. Under the terms of their agreement, H received marketable securities with a basis of $16,000 and a value of $10,000. W received the house with a basis of $80,000, valued at $96,000 and subject to a mortgage of $60,000. No gain or loss is recognized by either party regardless of who owned the property before the transfer. H and W have bases in their separate properties of $16,000 and $80,000, respectively.

> **Example 33.** Under an option provided in their divorce agreement, W (from the previous example) sold the house to H six months later (subject to the mortgage obligation) for $36,000. W still recognizes no gain and H's basis in the residence is $80,000.

Gift or Bequest. A transfer of property by gift or bequest generally does not constitute a sale or other disposition. Accordingly, there is no gain or loss recognized by the donor or decedent, respectively. An exception exists, however, in the case of a sale of property at a price below its fair market value. In such a *part-gift* and *part-sale*, the donor recognizes gain *only* to the extent the sales price exceeds the adjusted basis of the property transferred.[54]

---

[50]   § 280B.

[51]   §§ 1041(a) and (c).

[52]   § 1041(b)(2).

[53]   Temp. Reg. § 1.1041-1T(e).

[54]   Reg. § 1.1015-4(d).

Example 34. M sold her personal automobile to her brother for $4,000. She had a basis of $12,000 in the auto which was worth $6,000 on the date of sale. M has made a gift of $2,000 in this part-sale/part-gift transaction and she recognizes no gain or loss.

Example 35. Assume the same facts above, except that M's basis in the auto had been reduced to $3,000 from depreciation deductions allowed in prior years. Although M has still made a $2,000 gift in this transaction, she must now recognize a $1,000 gain on the sale ($4,000 amount realized − $3,000 adjusted basis).

If the donee/buyer pays some cash and assumes debt of the donor/seller, or takes the property subject to encumbrances, the amount of the liabilities must be included by the donor/seller in the amount realized from the transaction.[55] Even if no cash changes hands, the part-gift and part-sale rules apply if there are liabilities associated with the transfer. Accordingly, if the donee assumes liabilities that exceed the donor's basis in the transferred property, the donor has taxable gain to the extent the liabilities exceed such basis.[56] Also, the donee/purchaser will take as his or her basis in the property acquired the *greater* of the basis under the gift rules or the purchase (cost) basis.

Example 36. F gave a duplex rental unit to her grandson for his 18th birthday so he could develop property management skills. The duplex had a basis to F of $22,000 and a fair market value on the date of the gift of $40,000. The property was subject to a mortgage of $25,000, for which the grandson is now responsible. F has an amount realized on the gift transaction of $25,000 (transfer of the mortgage). Since the adjusted basis of the duplex was $22,000, F has a $3,000 taxable gain. If no gift taxes were paid, the grandson's basis in the duplex will be $25,000, the greater of the basis under the gift rules ($22,000) or the purchase (cost) basis.

Example 37. If the property in the previous example had been subject to a mortgage of only $8,000, the general rule would have applied, and F would not have recognized gain or loss. The exception only applies when the discharged liabilities exceed the adjusted basis of the gifted property. Note also that the grandson's basis in the duplex would be $22,000, the same basis F had in the property.

Transfer of Property to Charities. The transfer of property to a charity generally is not treated as a sale or other disposition. Accordingly, no gain or loss is realized or recognized. However, an exception is provided for *bargain sales* of property to charities that result in a charitable contribution deduction to the seller. In such a case, the adjusted basis of the transferred property must be allocated between the sale portion and the contribution portion based on the fair market value of the property—and any resulting gain must be recognized.[57]

Example 38. P sold land to her church for $30,000. P had an adjusted basis in the land of $25,000. The land was appraised at $50,000 at the time of the bargain sale. P is entitled to a charitable contribution deduction of $20,000 ($50,000 fair market value − $30,000 sale price). She also has taxable gain of $15,000 on the sale ($30,000 amount realized − the $15,000 pro rata share of the adjusted basis allocable to the sale portion [($30,000 sale price ÷ $50,000 fair market value) × $25,000 basis]).

---

[55] *Reginald Fincke*, 39 B.T.A. 510 (1939).

[56] *Levine Est. v. Comm.*, 80-2 USTC ¶9607, 46 AFTR2d, 80-5349, 634 F.2d 12 (CA-2, 1980).

[57] § 1011(b); Reg. § 1.1011-2(a).

A charitable contribution of encumbered property is also treated as a bargain sale. The amount realized includes the amount of cash and the fair market value of any other property received plus the amount of the liabilities transferred. Accordingly, the property's adjusted basis must be allocated between the sale portion (represented by the amount realized) and the contribution portion.[58] This is true even if no cash or other property is received by the taxpayer.[59]

> **Example 39.** E made a gift of land to his alma mater. The land had a fair market value of $50,000 and was subject to a $22,000 mortgage which was assumed by the university. If the land is a long-term capital asset, E is entitled to a charitable contribution deduction of $28,000 ($50,000 fair market value reduced by the $22,000 mortgage).[60]

Additionally, E's $20,000 adjusted basis in the property must be allocated between the contribution of $28,000 and the amount realized of $22,000. The basis allocated to the sale portion is $8,800 [$20,000 basis × ($22,000 amount realized ÷ $50,000 fair market value)]. The result of the bargain sale is a taxable gain to E of $13,200 ($22,000 amount realized − $8,800 allocated basis).

ALLOCATIONS OF PURCHASE PRICE AND BASIS

Properties purchased in a single transaction are often sold separately. In such a situation, the total basis must be allocated between the various items in order to determine gain or loss on the independent sales. Generally, relative fair market values at the time of acquisition are used to allocate the total basis among the various properties.[61] Similarly, allocation is necessary when a single sale involves properties acquired at different times in separate transactions. It may be necessary to allocate the sales price to individual assets; in such a situation, the relative fair market values on the date of sale are used for the allocation. Generally, an allocation in the sale agreement between buyer and seller will sufficiently establish the relative values unless it is shown that such assigned values were arbitrary or unreasonable.[62]

> **Example 40.** T purchased a commercial lot in 1998 for $30,000 and built a warehouse on the site in 1999 at a cost of $60,000. During the six years he used the warehouse in his business, T deducted depreciation of $32,000. The property was sold this year for $110,000. T must allocate the $110,000 sale price between the building and the land to determine the gain or loss on each. If $40,000 is allocated to the land and $70,000 is allocated to the building based on relative fair market values, T has a gain of $10,000 ($40,000 − $30,000) and $42,000 [$70,000 − ($60,000 − $32,000)], respectively, on the properties.

Sale of a Business. When a business operated as a sole proprietorship is sold, the sale is treated as a sale of each of the individual assets of the business. Accordingly, allocations of sales price and basis must be made to the individual assets of the business.[63] The various gains and losses have separate impact, according to their character, on the taxable income of the owner.

---

[58] See Reg. § 1.1011-2(a).

[59] *Winston Guest*, 77 T.C. 9 (1981) and Rev. Rul. 81-163, 1981-1 C.B. 433.

[60] See Chapter 11 for a discussion of charitable contributions involving long-term capital gain property.

[61] See, for example, *Fairfeld Plaza, Inc.*, 39 T.C. 706 (1963), and Rev. Rul. 72-255, 1972-1 C.B. 221.

[62] See *John B. Resler*; 38 TCM 153, T.C. Memo 1979-40.

[63] See Rev. Rul. 55-79, 1955-1 C.B. 370, and *Williams v. McGowan*, 46-1 USTC ¶9120, 34 AFTR 615, 152 F.2d 570 (CA-2, 1945).

Example 41. F has owned and operated a convenience store for 12 years. F's increased interest in her grandchildren and in fishing prompted her to sell the store and retire. The sales agreement with the buyer allocated the total sales price to the individual assets as follows:

	Value per Sales Agreement	F's Adjusted Basis
Inventory	$16,000	$18,000
Furniture and fixtures	14,000	6,000
Leasehold and leasehold improvements	20,000	3,000
Goodwill	0	0
Total	$50,000	$27,000

F has a $2,000 loss on the sale of inventory, and gains on the furniture and fixtures of $8,000 and on the leasehold and improvements of $17,000, each of which has its separate impact on taxable income.

The sale of an interest in a partnership or in a corporation that operates a business is generally treated as the sale of such interest, rather than of the underlying assets. Therefore, no allocation is necessary and gain or loss is recognized on the sale of the interest. For each type of entity, major exceptions to this treatment exist and are discussed in a later chapter.[64]

INSTALLMENT SALE METHOD

The general rule of Federal taxation is that all gains or losses are recognized in the year of sale or exchange. This rule could place a severe burden on taxpayers who sell their property for something other than cash, particularly deferred payment obligations. Without some relief, taxpayers would be required to pay their tax liability before obtaining the sale proceeds with which they could pay the tax. If the tax is substantial, a requirement to pay before sufficient cash collections occur might necessitate the sale of other assets the taxpayer wished to retain.

Because of the potential hardship placed on taxpayers from reporting gain without the corresponding receipt of cash, Congress enacted the installment sale method of reporting in 1926. The installment method has been significantly modified over the years, with each modification further restricting *both* the types of gains and the taxpayers eligible for its use. The eligibility requirements are discussed below.

GENERAL RULES

The installment method is used to report *gains*—not losses—from qualifying installment sales of property. An *installment sale* is defined as any sale of property whereby the seller will receive at least one payment after the close of the tax year in which the sale occurs. Unfortunately, not all gains from installment sales qualify for installment reporting.

---

[64] See Chapter 19 for a discussion of corporate taxation, and Chapter 22 for partnership taxation.

Ineligible Sales. Currently, use of the installment method is denied for reporting gains from sales of the following:[65]

1. Property held for sale in the ordinary course of the taxpayer's trade or business (e.g., inventories)

2. Stocks or securities that are traded on an established securities market

In addition, the portion of any gain from the sale of depreciable property that must be reported as ordinary income under the depreciation recapture rules is not eligible for installment reporting. These rules are discussed in Chapter 17.

Mandatory Reporting Requirement. Generally, gains from eligible sales *must* be reported under the installment method regardless of the taxpayer's method of accounting.[66] Thus, the installment method is considered to be *mandatory* rather than elective. However, Congress recognized the fact that for some taxpayers the installment method of reporting would not be the relief measure that it was intended to be. Consequently, taxpayers are allowed to *elect out* of the installment method simply by reporting the entire gain in the year of sale.[67]

ELECTION OUT OF INSTALLMENT REPORTING

There are various reasons why a taxpayer might wish to elect not to use the installment method of reporting gain from the sale of property. Such reasons might include the following:

1. The taxpayer's income in the year of sale is quite low and income is expected to be higher in subsequent years.

2. The taxpayer might have a large capital loss with which to absorb the capital gain in the year of sale.

3. The taxpayer might have an expiring net operating loss.

4. It might be necessary for the taxpayer to report the gain in order to utilize a tax credit carryover.

5. The burden of complying with the installment sale rules might outweigh the advantage of the installment reporting of the gain.

If a taxpayer *elects not to use* the installment method for a given sale, the amount of gain must be computed under his or her usual method of accounting (i.e., cash or accrual) and reported in the year of sale.[68] A cash basis taxpayer must use the *fair market value* of any installment obligation received in determining the amount realized from the installment sale.[69] On the other hand, an accrual basis taxpayer must account for an installment obligation at its *face value* in computing the amount realized.[70]

Example 42. S, a cash basis taxpayer, sold land to B on December 15, 2005. S received $100,000 cash and a note from B payable in five equal annual installments

---

[65]   §§ 453(b), (i), and (l). See § 453(l)(2) for certain limited exceptions.

[66]   § 453(a).

[67]   See § 453(d) and Temp. Reg. 15a.453-1(d)(2)(ii).

[68]   *Ibid.*

[69]   § 1001(b).

[70]   Rev. Rul. 79-292. 1979-2 C.B. 287.

of $80,000 (i.e., face value), bearing a 9% interest rate. The note has a fair market value of $300,000 and S has a $75,000 basis in the land. If S elects not to use the installment method, his gain to be reported in 2005 is computed as follows:

Amount realized:	
Cash received..	$100,000
FMV of installment obligations	300,000
	$400,000
Less: Basis of land	(75,000)
Gain to be reported in 2005................................	$325,000

In addition to the interest income that S will recognize when the installment payments are collected, he must recognize additional income on the collection of each installment payment as follows:

Amount realized (installment payment)	$ 80,000
Less: Basis in each installment	
($300,000 FMV of note ÷ 5 installments)	(60,000)
Ordinary income to be reported	$ 20,000

Example 43. Assume the same facts as in *Example 42*, except that S is an accrual basis taxpayer. His gain to be reported in the year of sale is computed as follows:

Amount realized:	
Cash received..	$100,000
Face value of installment obligations	400,000
	$500,000
Less: Basis in land	(75,000)
Gain to be reported in 2005................................	$425,000

In this case, S will not be required to report any income other than the interest received as each of the payments are collected because his basis in each installment obligation is $100,000 (i.e., its face amount).

GAIN REPORTED UNDER THE INSTALLMENT METHOD

The following *six* factors must be taken into account by a taxpayer using the installment method of reporting gain:

1. The gross profit on the sale

2. The total contract price

3. The gross profit percentage

4. The payments received in the year of sale

5. The gain to be reported in the year of sale

6. The gain to be reported in the following years

Determining Gross Profit. A taxpayer's gross profit is nothing more than the total gain that will be reported (excluding interest) from the installment sale. It is determined by subtracting the *sum* of the seller's adjusted basis and expenses of sale from the selling price:[71]

Selling price.	$xxx,xxx
Less: Adjusted basis in property plus selling expenses	– xx,xxx
Gross profit on sale	$ xx,xxx

Determining the Total Contract Price. The total contract price is the total amount of cash (excluding interest) that the seller expects to collect from the buyer over the term of the installment sale. It is usually equal to the selling price less any liabilities of the seller that are transferred to the buyer. However, if the liabilities assumed by the buyer *exceed* the seller's adjusted basis in the property and the selling expenses, the excess must be treated as a *deemed payment* received in the year of sale. Because a deemed payment is treated as cash collected in the year of sale, it must be added to the contract price.[72]

Determining Gross Profit Percentage. The taxpayer's gross profit percentage is the percentage of each dollar received that must be reported as gain. It is equal to the gross profit divided by the total contract price.[73]

$$\frac{\text{Gross profit}}{\text{Total contract price}} = \text{Gross profit percentage}$$

Determining Payments Received in Year of Sale. Payments received in the year of sale include the following:[74]

1. Money received at the time of closing the sale, including any selling expenses *paid* by the buyer

2. Deemed payments (i.e., excess of seller's liabilities transferred over the property's adjusted basis plus selling expenses)

3. The fair market value of any third-party obligations received at the time of closing and the fair market value of any other property received

4. Installment payments received in the year of sale, excluding interest income

Gain Reported in Year of Sale. Gain reported in the year of sale is computed as follows:

$$\frac{\text{Gross profit}}{\text{Total contract price}} \times \text{Payments received} = \text{Recognized gain}$$

---

[71]   Temp. Reg. § 15a.453-1(b)(2)(v).

[72]   § 453A(a)(2) and Temp. Reg. § 15a.453-1(b)(2)(ii).

[73]   § 453(c) and Temp. Reg. § 15a.453-1(b)(2)(i).

[74]   Temp. Reg. § 15a.453-1(b)(3)(i).

Gain Reported in Following Years. Gain to be reported in the years following the year of sale equals the taxpayer's gross profit percentage multiplied by the principal payments received on the purchaser's note in that year.

Example 44. T sold a 70-acre tract of land that she had held as an investment on March 1, 2005. The facts concerning the sale are as follows:

Sales price:		
Cash payment.	$120,000	
Mortgage assumed by buyer	200,000	
Buyer's notes payable to T	480,000	$ 800,000
Less: Selling expenses	$ 50,000	
T's basis in land	250,000	(300,000)
Gross profit on sale		$ 500,000

The contract price is $600,000 ($800,000 sales price − $200,000 debt assumed by buyer). Assuming the $120,000 payment is the only payment received in 2005, T's gain to be reported for the year is computed as follows:

$$\frac{\$500,000 \text{ (gross profit)}}{\$600,000 \text{ (contract price)}} \times \$120,000 = \$100,000 \text{ gain to be recognized}$$

As T collects the remaining $480,000 of the total contract price, she will report the remaining $400,000 gross profit from the sale (i.e., $480,000 × 5/6 gross profit percentage = $400,000).

Example 45. Assume the same facts as in *Example 44*, except that T's basis in the land is only $100,000. In this case, the gross profit on the sale is $650,000 [$800,000 − ($50,000 + $100,000)]. T's payments received in the year of sale are computed as follows:

Cash payment		$120,000
Plus: deemed payment received:		
Mortgage assumed by buyer.	$ 200,000	
Less: Selling expense	(50,000)	
T's basis in land	(100,000)	50,000
Total payments received in 2005		$170,000

The total contract price is $650,000 ($800,000 selling price − $200,000 mortgage transferred + $50,000 excess of mortgage assumed over T's basis in property and selling expenses). T's gain to be reported in 2005 is computed as follows:

$$\frac{\$650,000 \text{ (gross profit)}}{\$650,000 \text{ (contract price)}} \times \$170,000 \text{ payments} = \$170,000$$

Note that the excess of the mortgage transferred over T's basis in the land and the selling expenses (i.e., the deemed payment) causes the gross profit percentage to become 100%. This adjustment to *both* the total contract price and the payments received in the year of sale must be made to ensure that the entire gain from the sale is ultimately reported by the seller. As a result, all payments received by T in subsequent years (excluding interest) will be reported as gain from the sale [$650,000 total gross profit − $170,000 gain reported in year of sale = $480,000 gain to be reported in subsequent years ($480,000 buyer's notes × 100%)].

LIMITATIONS ON CERTAIN INSTALLMENT SALES

As mentioned earlier, the installment sales provisions have been modified over the years to limit or stop perceived taxpayer abuse of what was intended to be simply a relief from immediate taxation of all gain from deferred payment sales. These modifications have created the following problem areas:

1. Imputed interest rules

2. Related-party rules

3. Gain recognition on dispositions of installment note

4. Required interest payments on deferred taxes

Each of these problem areas is discussed below.

Imputed Interest Rules. Without some limitation, a taxpayer planning a deferred payment sale of a capital asset could require the buyer to pay a higher sales price in return for a lower than prevailing market rate of interest on the deferred payments, thereby converting into capital gain what would have been ordinary (interest) income. The imputed interest rules were designed to prevent just such a scheme. Under these rules, any deferred payment sale of property with a selling price exceeding $3,000 must provide a *reasonable* interest rate.[75] Thus, in a deferred payment sale providing little or no interest, the selling price must be *restated* to equal the sum of payments received on the date of the sale and the discounted present value of the future payments. The difference between the face value of the future payments and this discounted value (i.e., the imputed interest) generally must be reported as interest income under the accrual method of accounting, regardless of the taxpayer's regular accounting method.[76]

If the sales contract does not provide for interest equal to the *applicable Federal rate* (AFR), interest will be imputed at that rate.[77] The AFR is the interest rate the Federal government pays on borrowed funds, and the actual rate varies with the terms of the loan. Loans are divided into short-term (not over three years), mid-term (over three years but not over nine years), and long-term (over nine years).[78]

Example 46. S, a cash basis taxpayer, sold land held as an investment on July 1, 2005 for $1 million cash and a non-interest-bearing note (face value of $4 million) due on July 1, 2007. At the time of the sale, the short-term AFR was 10% (compounded semiannually). Because the sales contract did not provide for interest of at least the AFR, the selling price must be restated and interest must be imputed at 10% (compounded semiannually).

Sale price:	
Cash payment.	$1,000,000
Present value of $4,000,000 note due	
July 1, 2007 (0.8227 × $4,000,000)	3,290,800
Recomputed sale price.	$4,290,800

---

[75] See §§ 483 and 1274.

[76] See §§ 1272(a), 1273(a), and 1274(a). Also see §§ 483 and 1274(c) for various exceptions to this requirement.

[77] § 1274(d)(1).

[78] These three Federal rates are published monthly by the IRS.

S must use this recomputed sale price in determining the total contract price, gross profit percentage, gain to be reported in the year of sale, and gain to be reported (excluding interest) when the $4 million deferred payment is received. In addition, S must report $164,540 of imputed interest income in 2005, computed as follows:

Period	Present Value	×	10% Compounded Semiannually	=	Imputed Interest
7/1/05 to 12/31/05	$3,290,800	×	0.05	=	$164,540

S must also compute and report her imputed interest for 2006 and 2007. When the $4 million note payable is collected on July 1, 2007, S will report only the gain on the sale remaining after that portion reported in 2005.

Related-Party Sales. Generally, installment sales between related parties are subject to the same rules as other such sales *except* (1) when the related-party purchaser resells the property before payment of the original sales price;[79] and (2) when the property sold is depreciable property.[80] The primary purpose of the *resale* rule is to prevent a related-party seller from deferring his or her gain on the first sale while the related-party purchaser enjoys the use of proceeds from its resale.

Example 47. M plans to sell a capital asset (basis $40,000) to B, an unrelated party, for $200,000. Instead of selling the asset to B, she sells it to her son, S, for $10,000 cash and a $190,000 note due in five years and bearing a reasonable interest rate. Shortly after his purchase, S sells the asset to B for $200,000.

Without the resale rule, M would report a gain of $8,000 in the year of sale, computed as follows:

$$\frac{\$200,000 - \$40,000}{\$200,000} \times \$10,000 = \$8,000$$

M would have a deferred gain of $152,000 ($160,000 gross profit − $8,000 gain reported in year of sale). More important, S would have a cost basis of $200,000 in the asset and report no gain on the subsequent resale to B. The net result of the two transactions is a $152,000 deferred gain and the immediate use of the sales proceeds by a family member.

Under the resale rule, any proceeds collected by the related-party purchaser on the subsequent sale are treated as being collected by the related-party seller. Consequently, M must report her $152,000 deferred gain when S resells the property, even though she has not yet collected the $190,000 note.

For purposes of the resale rule, the term *related party* includes the spouse, children, grandchildren, and parents of the seller.[81] Any controlled corporation, partnership, trust, or estate in which the seller has an interest is also considered related under these rules.[82] It is also important to note that the resale rule does not apply when the second sale occurs (1) more than two years after the first sale, or (2) after the death of the related-party seller."[83]

The installment method is generally not allowed to be used to report a gain on the sale of depreciable property to an entity controlled by the taxpayer.[84] This rule is

---

[79] § 453(e).

[80] § 453(g).

[81] §§ 453(f) and 267(b).

[82] §§ 453(f) and 318(a).

[83] § 453(e)(2).

designed to prevent a related-party seller from deferring gain on a sale that will result in the purchaser's being able to use a higher (cost) basis to claim depreciation deductions. For this purpose, a *controlled entity* is a partnership or corporation in which the seller owns a more than 50 percent direct or indirect interest. Indirect ownership includes any interest owned by the seller's spouse and certain other family members.[85] It is important to note that this rule is based on a presumption that the related-party installment sale is motivated by tax avoidance. Thus, the related-party seller can use the installment method of reporting the sale if he or she can establish that tax avoidance *was not* the principal motive of the transaction. This makes such a sale subject to a facts and circumstances review and approval of the Internal Revenue Service.

Dispositions of Installment Obligations. After deciding to report a deferred payment sale under the installment method, rather than *electing out*, sellers ordinarily collect the payments in due course and report the remaining gain in full. However, if this process is interrupted by a sale, gift, or other transfer of some or all of the installment obligations, rules require that any unreported gain be reported at the time of the transfer. Consequently, if an installment obligation is satisfied at other than its face value or is distributed, transmitted, sold, or otherwise disposed of, the taxpayer is generally required to recognize gain or loss.

The amount of gain or loss is the difference between the obligation's basis and *either* the amount realized, if the obligation is satisfied at an amount other than its face value because it is sold or exchanged, *or* its fair market value when distributed, transmitted, or disposed of, if the transfer is not a sale or exchange.[86] The obligation's basis is its face amount less the amount of gain that would have been reported if the obligation had been satisfied in full.[87]

Taxable dispositions include most sales and exchanges. Also included are gifts, transfers to trusts, distributions by trusts and estates to beneficiaries, distributions from corporations to shareholders, net proceeds from the pledge of an installment obligation, and cancellation of the installment obligation.

The obvious purpose of the disposition rules is to prevent the seller from *either* shifting the income to another taxpayer (e.g., by gift) *or* enjoying the use of the sales proceeds prior to gain recognition (e.g., by pledging an installment obligation for borrowed funds). However, there are several exceptions to the requirement of immediate gain recognition. Transfers of installment obligations upon the death of the seller, transfers incident to divorce, transfers to or distributions from a partnership, certain transfers to controlled corporations, and certain transfers incident to corporate reorganization are among the exceptions to these rules.[88]

Required Interest Payments on Deferred Taxes. Another rule designed to reduce the benefits of installment reporting for certain taxpayers is the requirement to pay interest to the government on the deferred taxes. This rule applies if *two conditions* are met. First, the taxpayer must have outstanding installment obligations from the sale of property (other than farming property) for more than $150,000. Second, the outstanding obligations from such sales must exceed $5 million at the close of the tax year.[89] Only the deferred taxes attributable to the installment obligations in *excess* of $5 million are subject to this annual interest payment. The interest must be calculated using the tax underpayment rate in § 6621.

---

[85]   §§ 1239(b) and (c).

[86]   § 453B(a).

[87]   § 453B(b).

[88]   See §§ 453B(c), (d), and (g).

[89]   § 453A.

Example 48. T has $9 million of installment obligations outstanding on December 31, 2005. These obligations arose from the sale of a vacant lot located in the downtown area of Chicago. T's gross profit percentage on the installment sale was 40%. Assuming the underpayment rate in § 6621 is 10% and T's 2005 marginal tax rate is 31%, the required interest payment on the deferred taxes is computed as follows:

Outstanding installment obligations	$9,000,000
Less: Amount not subject to rule	(5,000,000)
Excess installment obligations	$4,000,000
Times: Gross profit percentage	× 40%
Deferred gross profit	$1,600,000
Times: T's marginal tax rate	× 31%
Deferred Federal income taxes	$ 496,000
Times: § 6621 underpayment rate	× 10%
Required interest payment	$ 49,600

Because taxpayers are allowed to have up to $5 million of installment obligations outstanding without being subject to the required interest payment rule, it is apparent that only those taxpayers with one or more substantial installment sales need be concerned with this rule.

REPORTING GAIN ON INSTALLMENT SALES

Taxpayers reporting gain on the installment sale method should attach Form 6252, Computation of Installment Sale Income, to the tax return for the year of sale and each subsequent year in which a payment is collected. A sample of this form is contained in Appendix A.

DISALLOWED LOSSES

Various limitations exist regarding gain and loss recognition in certain property transactions. Several such limitations have already been discussed. Recall that any losses on the sale of personal use assets are disallowed. Similarly, losses on the sale of property acquired by gift are limited to the decline in its value subsequent to the transfer by gift. This results because the basis for determining loss is the fair market value on the date of gift, if that fair market value is less than the donor's basis (which would otherwise be the donee's basis).[90] Likewise, a loss on the disposition of property that has been converted from personal use to business use is limited to the decline in its value subsequent to the conversion. In determining any loss on such a disposition, the adjusted basis is the lesser of the taxpayer's adjusted basis or the fair market value on the date of conversion.[91]

There are several other limitations on the deductibility of losses arising from sales or other dispositions of property. As discussed in Chapter 7, losses incurred in sales between related taxpayers are not deductible. Also, certain losses incurred from the sale of stock or securities will not be allowed as a deduction.

---

[90]   § 1015(a).

[91]   Reg. § 1.165-9(b).

WASH SALES

A *wash sale* occurs when a taxpayer sells stock or securities at a loss and reinvests in substantially identical stock or securities within 30 days before or after the date of sale. Any loss realized on such a wash sale is not deductible.[92] In essence, a taxpayer who has a wash sale has not had a *change* in economic position—thus the transaction resulting in a loss is ignored for tax purposes. The loss is, however, taken into consideration in determining the adjusted basis in the new shares.[93]

> **Example 49.** C, a calendar year taxpayer, owns 400 shares of X Corporation stock (adjusted basis of $9,000), all of which he sells for $5,000 on December 28, 2005. On January 7, 2006 C purchases another 400 shares of X Corporation stock for $5,500. C's realized loss of $4,000 in 2005 will not be deductible because it resulted from a wash sale. Instead, his basis in the 400 shares purchased in 2006 is increased to $9,500 ($5,500 purchase price + $4,000 disallowed loss).

The *numbers* of shares purchased and sold are not always the same. When the number of shares reacquired is less than the number sold, the deduction for losses is disallowed only for the number of shares purchased.[94]

> **Example 50.** Assume the same facts as in *Example 49*, except that C purchased only 300 shares of X Corporation stock for $4,125. Because C replaced only 300 of the shares previously sold at a loss, only 75% (300 ÷ 400) of the $4,000 realized loss is disallowed. Consequently, C will report a $1,000 loss ($4,000 × 25%) in 2005 and will have a basis of $7,125 ($4,125 purchase price + $3,000 disallowed loss) in the 300 shares purchased.

When the number of shares repurchased is greater than the number of shares sold, none of the loss is deductible and the basis in a number of shares equivalent to the number of shares sold is affected by the disallowed loss.[95]

Any loss also will be disallowed if the "substantially equivalent" stock or securities are acquired by certain related parties. For example, the U.S. Supreme Court held that the wash sale provisions apply if replacement stock is acquired by a taxpayer's spouse *and* they file a joint return for the tax year of the loss.[96]

SALES BETWEEN RELATED PARTIES

The Code places numerous limitations on gain or loss recognition from transactions between certain related parties. The purpose of such restrictions is to prevent related taxpayers from entering into various property transactions solely for the tax reduction possibilities. For example, a father could sell land to his daughter at a loss, deduct the loss, and the property would still remain within the family unit. Similarly, a taxpayer could sell depreciable property to her spouse and report a long-term capital gain on their joint return. For many years thereafter, she and her husband could claim ordinary deductions for depreciation on this higher basis. To control such potentially abusive situations, Congress enacted Code §§ 267 and 1239.

---

[92] § 1091(a).

[93] § 1091(d).

[94] Reg. § 1.1091-1(c).

[95] Reg. § 1.1091-1(d).

[96] *Helvering v. Taft*, 40-2 USTC ¶9888, 24 AFTR 1976, 311 U.S. 195 (USSC, 1940).

Section 267 disallows deductions for any losses that result from the sale or exchange of property between related parties.[97] Such losses may, however, be used by the related purchaser to offset any gain realized from a subsequent disposition of the property.[98] For purposes of § 267, related parties include the following:[99]

1. Members of an individual's family—specifically, brothers and sisters (including by half blood), spouses, ancestors (i.e., parents and grandparents), and lineal descendants (i.e., children and grandchildren)

2. A corporation owned more than 50 percent in value by the taxpayer (directly or indirectly)

3. Two corporations owned more than 50 percent in value by the taxpayer (directly or indirectly) if either corporation is a personal holding company or a foreign personal holding company in the tax year of the transaction

4. Various partnership, S corporation, grantor, fiduciary, and trust relationships with regular corporations and individual taxpayers

Example 51. M sells stock (adjusted basis of $10,000) to her daughter, D, for its fair market value of $8,000. D sells the stock two years later for $11,000. M's $2,000 loss is disallowed as a deduction. However, D's realized gain of $3,000 ($11,000 sales price − $8,000 cost basis) is reduced by the $2,000 previously disallowed loss, and she will report only $1,000 of gain.

Note the similarity between the results in *Example 51* and the situation that would result if D had received the stock as a gift from M. First, D's basis for gain would be $10,000 (M's basis) if the stock had been received as a gift; its subsequent sale for $11,000 would have resulted in the same $1,000 recognized (reported) gain. Although the disallowance of a loss deduction might discourage many related-party transactions, some taxpayers prefer to sell rather than give property to a related party in order to avoid paying state or Federal gift taxes.

Section 1239 provides that any gain realized from the sale of depreciable property between specified related parties will be taxed as ordinary income.[100] In effect, this statute precludes the possibility that any gain on the sale might be taxed as a long-term capital gain since the sale results in a higher basis in the depreciable property to a related party. Furthermore, recall that such related-party sales of depreciable property are not eligible for installment sale treatment.[101] Transactions subject to § 1239 treatment are discussed in Chapter 19 (Corporate Taxation) and Chapter 22 (Partnership Taxation).

TAX PLANNING CONSIDERATIONS

GIFT VERSUS BEQUEST

In devising a plan for transferring wealth from one family member to another, several considerations related to the income tax, the transfer taxes, and the wishes of the parties involved must be evaluated. If there is a desire to transfer properties, there are

---

[97] § 267(a)(1).

[98] § 267(d).

[99] See §§ 267(b) and (c).

[100] § 1239(a).

[101] § 453(g).

relative advantages and disadvantages to lifetime transfers as opposed to testamentary transfers (transfers by will). Some of the specific factors that should be considered are as follows:

1. The income tax rate of each individual (decedent and heirs) relative to the estate and gift tax rates.

2. Whether the property is highly appreciated. If so, a testamentary transfer may be preferred since the property's basis to the heirs or the estate will be its fair market value at date of death or alternate valuation date. If the property is gifted, its basis will be the donor's basis increased by a fraction of any gift taxes paid. If the property has declined in value, only the *original owner* (donor) can benefit from any tax loss by disposing of the property to an unrelated party, due to the basis for determination of loss under § 1015(a).

3. Whether the property is expected to appreciate rapidly in the foreseeable future. If so, a current gift might be considered because the amount subject to gift taxes would be the current market value. If the property were held until death, the higher fair market value at that time would be used in calculating estate taxes. This action is, of course, speculative in nature.

4. Whether the transferee is likely to hold the property for a long period of time. If so, the basis considerations are not as important as they would be if the property were to be sold immediately upon its receipt.

5. Whether the property is income-producing property. If the property produces income, and the owner (donor) is in a high income tax bracket, a lifetime transfer could result in the profits being taxed at a lower tax rate to another family member. If the donee is in a significantly lower income tax bracket, substantial income tax savings can be accomplished.

These factors, as well as the health of the parties involved and other personal considerations, must all be considered. It is possible that the personal factors will outweigh the tax factors, or that significant amounts of taxes cannot be saved.

CHARITABLE TRANSFERS INVOLVING PROPERTY OTHER THAN CASH

Taxpayers who are considering making major charitable transfers and who have property other than cash that they would consider transferring must consider both the effects of any gain or loss if property is sold and the effects of any allowable charitable deduction. If a property has declined in value, its owner may benefit from selling the property and deducting the loss and later contributing the cash proceeds to the charity.

Planning can be even more important when the property is appreciated, since in certain instances a charitable deduction is allowed equal to the fair market value of the property. This is true when the property is long-term capital gain property that is used in the exempt function of the charity, is intangible, or is real estate (see Chapter 11). In such a case, the taxpayer will avoid paying tax on the property's unrealized appreciation and still receive full benefit from the charitable deduction.

CHANGES IN THE USE OF PROPERTY

A taxpayer who converts business property to personal use when its value is less than its adjusted basis should consider selling the asset in order to trigger a deduction for the loss. Also, a taxpayer who buys property that he or she intends to use in a business should think carefully before using the asset for personal purposes. For example, a taxpayer who purchases a new auto and drives it for personal purposes for two years before converting it to business use must use the fair value upon conversion—if less than adjusted basis—in determining both depreciation and any loss on disposition.

SALES TO RELATED PARTIES

Care must be exercised to avoid the undesirable effects of transactions between related parties. If a loss on the sale of property to a related party is disallowed, the tax benefit of a loss deduction is permanently lost unless the value of the property subsequently increases. The only way to generate a tax deduction for the loss is for the original owner to sell the property to an unrelated party. Also, characterizing gain on the sale of depreciable property as ordinary income under § 1239 should normally be avoided.

USE OF INSTALLMENT SALES

Installment sale treatment provides an excellent opportunity for deferring the tax on gain (other than depreciation recapture) when a taxpayer is willing to accept an installment obligation in exchange for property. Actually, installment reporting may provide such attractive tax deferral and tax savings possibilities that the taxpayer is induced to accept an installment obligation, even though he or she would not do so otherwise. In short, this is a tax variable that must be considered by a prudent taxpayer in planning sales of property.

A taxpayer may benefit in at least two ways from the installment method. First, benefits accrue from the deferral of the tax. The time value of money works to the taxpayer's benefit, assuming the sales contract provides for a fair rate of interest. The second benefit from installment reporting is the spreading of the gain over more than one tax year. If the gain on a sale is unusual and moves the taxpayer into a higher tax bracket, spreading the gain over several years tends to allow the overall gain to be taxed in lower tax brackets.

It is important to remember, however, that taxpayers may face several limitations on certain installment sales. First, if a reasonable interest rate is not provided in the deferred payment sale, the seller will be required to impute interest at the appropriate Federal rate. Second, a taxpayer unaware of the rules relating to related-party sales may find that he or she is required to report all the gain on such a sale long before the actual collection of cash from the installment obligations. Third, taxpayers with installment obligations must be informed of the rules requiring immediate gain recognition on certain dispositions of such obligations. These rules include treating borrowed funds as collections on the installment notes if such notes are used as collateral for a loan. Finally, taxpayers with significant amounts of installment obligations outstanding at the end of a particular tax year (i.e., in excess of $5 million) may find that the required interest payment on the deferred income taxes is greater than the interest currently being collected.

PROBLEM MATERIALS

DISCUSSION QUESTIONS

14-1 *Realization vs. Recognition.* In a few sentences, distinguish realization from recognition.

14-2 *Return-of-Capital Principle.* What is the return-of-capital principle?

14-3 *Computing Amount Realized.* Reproduce the formula for computing the amount realized in a sale or exchange.

14-4 *Impact of Liabilities.* What impact do liabilities assumed by the buyer or liabilities encumbering property transferred have on the amount realized? How are they treated if both parties to the transaction incur new liabilities?

14-5 *Cost Basis.* How does one determine cost basis for property acquired? How is this basis affected if property other than money is transferred in exchange for the new property?

14-6 *Gift Basis.* Reproduce the formula for the general rule for determining basis of property acquired by gift.

14-7 *Gift Basis Exception.* When does the general rule for determining basis of property acquired by gift (Question 14-6) not apply?

14-8 *Basis of Inherited Property.* The basis of property acquired from a decedent is generally fair market value at date of death. What are the two exceptions to this rule (do not include property subject to special-use valuation)?

14-9 *Basis Adjustments.* List the three broad categories of adjustments to basis.

14-10 *Transfers Pursuant to Divorce.* In general, do transfers of property in a divorce action result in the realization of gain or loss? Under what circumstances might gain recognition be required?

14-11 *Part-Sale/Part-Gift.* When does a bargain sale to a donee (part-gift) result in gain to the donor? Does the assumption of the donor's liabilities by the donee have any impact? Explain.

14-12 *Bargain Sales.* How is a bargain sale of property to a charitable organization treated for tax purposes?

14-13 *Allocating Sales Price.* Allocations are generally necessary when a sole proprietorship is sold as a unit. What method is normally used for such allocation? What impact does the sales agreement have if it allocates the price to the individual assets?

14-14 *Installment Sales Method—General Rules.* What is the purpose of the installment sale method of reporting gains? Is it an elective provision? How does one elect out of the installment sale method? What sales do not qualify for installment sale treatment?

14-15 *Installment Sales Method—Key Terms.* Explain how each of the following factors related to an installment sale is determined.
  a. Gross profit on deferred payment sale
  b. Total contract price
  c. Gross profit percentage
  d. Payments received in the year of sale
  e. Gain to be reported in the year of sale

14-16 *Imputed Interest Rules.* Under what circumstances must a taxpayer impute interest income from an installment sale? How is the applicable Federal rate (AFR) determined?

14-17 *Related-Party Installment Sales.* Under what circumstances will a taxpayer be faced with the related-party installment sale rules? Explain how a resale of the property by the related-party purchaser before the seller has collected the balance of the installment obligation affects the seller.

14-18   *Dispositions of Installment Obligations.* Your neighbor has $30,000 of installment obligations from a recent sale of land held for investment. He asks you for advice concerning his planned gift of these obligations to his children to be used for their future college expenses. An examination of Form 6252 attached to his most recent tax return reveals a gross profit percentage of 60 percent and a reasonable market rate of interest related to these installment obligations. What tax advice would you give regarding this plan?

14-19   *Wash Sale.* What is a wash sale? How is a wash sale treated for tax purposes?

14-20   *Timing of Recognition.* Under what circumstances is a realized gain actually recognized? What event generally controls the timing of gain recognition?

PROBLEMS

14-21   *Sale Involving Liabilities.* C sold a cottage in which his basis was $32,000, for cash of $12,000 and a note from the buyer worth $28,000. The buyer assumed an existing note of $30,000 secured by an interest in the property.
  a.   What is C's amount realized in this sale?
  b.   What is C's gain or loss realized on this sale?

14-22   *Exchange Involving Liabilities.* D exchanged a mountain cabin for a leisure yacht and $30,000 cash. The yacht was worth $25,000 and was subject to liabilities of $10,000, which were assumed by D. The cabin was subject to liabilities of $32,000, which were assumed by the other party.
  a.   How much is D's amount realized?
  b.   Assuming D's basis in the cabin was $42,000, what is his gain or loss realized?

14-23   *Identification of Stock Sold.* T purchased the following lots of stock in Z Corporation:

50 shares	1/12/96	Cost	$1,200
100 shares	2/28/01	Cost	$3,000
75 shares	10/16/02	Cost	$2,500

T sold 75 shares on January 16, 2005 for $2,800. His only instruction to his broker, who actually held the shares for T, was to sell 75 shares.
  a.   How much gain or loss does T recognize on this sale?
  b.   How could this result be altered?

14-24   *Sale of Property Acquired by Gift.* J received a set of silver flatware as a gift from her grandmother in 2001, when the set was worth $5,000. The silver had a basis to the grandmother of $2,000, and gift taxes of $500 were paid.
  a.   How much gain does J recognize when she sells the set for $5,000 during the current year?
  b.   What would be your answer if the sale price were $4,200?
  c.   What would be your answer if the sale price were $1,500?

14-25   *Sale of Property Acquired by Gift.* In 2002 F gave his son, S, 100 shares of IBM stock, which at that time were worth $30,000. F paid a gift tax on the transfer of $5,000. Assuming F had purchased the stock in 1996 for $40,000, what are the tax consequences to S if he sells the stock for the following amounts?
  a. $25,000
  b. $37,000
  c. $45,000

14-26 *Sale of Property Acquired by Gift.* For each of the following situations, determine the gain or loss realized by the taxpayer (donee), assuming the property was acquired by gift after 1976:

Case	Donor's Basis	Fair Market Value(*)	Gift Taxes Paid	Sales Price
A	$3,000	$4,000	$400	$4,100
B	3,000	2,500	500	3,200
C	1,200	1,400	280	1,100
D	2,000	1,600	400	1,700
E	2,400	1,800	600	1,500

*Date of gift

14-27 *Sale of Inherited Property.* D inherited two acres of commercial real estate from her grandmother, who had a basis in the property of $52,000, when it had a fair market value of $75,000. For estate tax purposes, the estate was valued as of the date of death, and estate and inheritance taxes of $8,250 were paid by the estate on this parcel of real estate.
   a. How much gain or loss will be realized by D if she sells the property for $77,000?
   b. What would be your answer if the sale price were $66,000?

14-28 *Basis of Inherited Property.* H inherited a parcel of real estate from his father. The property was valued for estate tax purposes at $120,000, and the father's basis was $45,000 immediately before his death. H had given the property to his father as a gift six weeks before his death. The proper portion of the gift taxes paid by H are included in his father's basis.
   a. What is H's basis in the real estate?
   b. What would be your answer if H had given the property to his father two years before his father's death?

14-29 *Basis of Converted Property.* K converted his 2002 sedan from personal use to business use as a delivery vehicle in his pizza business. The auto had an adjusted basis to K of $4,200 and a fair market value on the date of the conversion of $2,400. K properly deducted depreciation on the auto of $900 over two years before the auto was sold.
   a. How much is K's gain or loss if he sells the auto for $800?
   b. What would be your answer if the auto were sold for $3,500?

14-30 *Part-Sale/Part-Gift.* G sold a personal computer to his son for $2,000. The computer was worth $3,000, and G had a basis in the unit of $2,200. G has made a gift of $1,000 in this part-sale/part-gift.
   a. How much gain, if any, must G recognize on this sale?
   b. Would your answer differ if G's basis had been $1,700?

14-31 *Bargain Sale to Charity.* F sold a parcel of land to the city to be used as a location for a new art museum. The land had a market value of $70,000 and was sold for $40,000. F's adjusted basis in the property was $35,000. How much is F's charitable contribution deduction on this transfer? How much gain does F recognize on this sale?

14-32 *Installment Sale.* On July 1, 2005 G sold her summer cottage (basis $70,000) for $105,000. The sale contract provided for a payment of $30,000 at the time of sale and payment of the $75,000 balance in three equal installments due in July 2006, 2007, and 2008. Assuming a reasonable interest rate is charged on this deferred payment sale, compute each of the following:

    a. Gross profit on the sale

    b. Total contract price

    c. Gross profit percentage

    d. Gain to be reported (excluding interest) in 2005

    e. Gain to be reported (excluding interest) in 2006

    f. Gain to be reported in 2005 if G elects not to use the installment method

14-33 *Imputed Interest on Installment Sale.* On January 1, 2005 S sold a 100-acre tract of land for $200,000 cash and an $800,000 non-interest-bearing note due on January 1, 2008. On the date of sale, the land had a basis of $400,000. Assuming the applicable Federal rate is ten percent compounded semiannually, calculate the following:

    a. Gain, excluding interest, to be reported in 2005

    b. The imputed interest to be reported by S for 2005

    c. Gain, excluding interest, to be reported in 2008

14-34 *Wash Sale.* R purchased 500 shares of Y Corporation common stock for $12,500 on August 31, 2004. She sold 200 shares of this stock for $3,000 on December 21, 2005. On January 7, 2006 R purchased an additional 100 shares of Y Corporation common stock for $1,600.

    a. What is R's realized loss for 2005?

    b. How much of the loss realized can R report in 2005?

    c. What is R's adjusted basis in the 100 shares purchased on January 7, 2006?

14-35 *Related-Party Sale.* J sold 2,000 shares of T Corporation stock, in which he had an adjusted basis of $3,000, to his brother, F, for $1,200.

    a. How much of the realized loss is recognized (reported) by J?

    b. How much gain or loss to F if he subsequently sells the stock for $1,000? For $2,000?

14-36 *Property Settlements.* H was divorced from W this year. H was required to transfer stock, which was his separate property, to W in satisfaction of his obligation for spousal support. The stock was worth $5,700 and had an adjusted basis to H of $2,900.

    a. How much gain, if any, does H recognize on the transfer?

    b. How much gain or loss does W recognize? What is her basis in the property received?

14-37 *Property Tax Allocation.* J purchased a rental property during the current year for $45,000 cash. He was required to pay all of the property taxes for the year of sale, and under the law of the state $47 is allocable to the period before J purchased the property (see Chapter 11).

    a. How much is J's property tax deduction if the total payment made during the tax year of acquisition is $700?

    b. What is J's adjusted basis in the property?

14-38 *Sales of Inherited Properties.* Each of the following involves property acquired from a decedent. None of the properties include income in respect of a decedent. Determine the gain or loss for each.

Case	Decedent's Basis	Death Taxes Paid	Fair Market Value (*)	Sales Price
A	$3,000	$600	$4,000	$6,000
B	6,000	600	4,000	5,000
C	6,000	400	4,000	3,000

*Date of decedent's death.

14-39   *Nontaxable Dividends.* M owned 300 shares of X Corporation common stock, in which her basis was $6,000 on January 1, 2005. With respect to her stock, during 2005 M collected dividends of $600 and tax-free distributions of $400. What is M's basis in the stock as of December 31, 2005?

RESEARCH PROBLEMS

14-40   *Gain Realized from Transferred Debt.* H owns a small office building and commercial complex, which he purchased for $175,000 in 1999. H invested $20,000 and signed a nonrecourse note secured by an interest in the property for the difference. The note provided for 9 percent interest, compounded annually and payable quarterly.

After six years, H decided his property was not as good an investment as he had originally thought. He found a buyer who offered him $1,000 cash for the property, subject to the existing liabilities. H eventually accepted the offer and sold the property. During the six years he owned the property, H made timely interest payments and no payments of principal. He was allowed depreciation deductions of $34,000, using the straight-line method of depreciation and a 39-year recovery period.

Required:
1.   How much is H's gain or loss realized on this sale?
2.   Would your answer differ if H's building was only worth $150,000 and instead of selling the building he had voluntarily transferred it to the obligee on the note?

Partial list of research aids:

   Reg. § 1.1001-2.

   Crane v. Comm., 47-1 USTC ¶9217, 35 AFTR 776, 331 U.S. 1 (USSC, 1947).

   Tufts v. Comm., 83-1 USTC ¶9328, 51 AFTR2d 1983-1132, 461 U.S. 300 (USSC, 1983).

   Millar v. Comm., 78-2 USTC ¶9514, 42 AFTR2d 78-4276, 577 F.2d 212 (CA-3, 1978).

14-41   *Bargain Sale to Charity.* K sold a mountain cabin for $55,000 to State University (her alma mater) for use in an annual fund-raising auction. The cabin was worth $85,000. K had purchased the cabin five years earlier as an investment for $40,000, and no depreciation has been allowed.

Required:
1.   What is K's charitable contribution deduction and her gain or loss realized on this bargain sale?
2.   Would your answers differ if the property were a painting instead of a mountain cabin?

Research aids:

   § 170(e)(1).

   § 1011(b).

   Reg. §§ 1.170A-4(a)(2) and (c)(2).

   Reg. § 1.1011-2.

Chapter 15

NONTAXABLE EXCHANGES

LEARNING OBJECTIVES

Upon completion of this chapter you will be able to:

- Understand the rationale for deferral of gains and losses on certain property transactions
- Explain how gain or loss deferral is accomplished through adjustment to basis of the replacement property
- Apply the nonrecognition rules to the following transactions:
  - Sale of a taxpayer's principal residence

- Involuntary conversion of property
- Like-kind exchange of business or investment property
- Identify other common nontaxable transactions
- Recognize tax planning opportunities related to the more common types of gain-deferral transactions available to individual taxpayers

CHAPTER OUTLINE

INTRODUCTION

"If I could show you a perfectly legal way to pyramid your wealth to $1 million without paying tax, would you be interested?" Although this sounds like it came straight out of the con artist's guide to tax scams, its source is far more reputable.[1] More important, the assertion is entirely true. If a taxpayer is able to make the right investments—obviously a big if—the Internal Revenue Code is willing to lend a helping hand. The key to this wonderland without taxes can be found in the provisions concerning nontaxable exchanges, the subject of this chapter.

By now, the basic recipe for determining the tax treatment of any sale or exchange is fairly familiar. Whenever a taxpayer disposes of property, three questions must be addressed: (1) what is the gain or loss *realized*, (2) how much of this realized gain or loss is *recognized*, and (3) what is its character. This chapter focuses on the second of these questions, examining a handful of property transactions—such as the sale of a residence or a like-kind exchange—where all or at least a portion of the gain or loss realized is not recognized.

As a general rule, any gain or loss realized on a sale or other disposition of property must be recognized unless an exception is specifically provided. For the most part, this means taxpayers must include all of their realized gains and losses in determining their taxable income. However, there are a number of transactions that the Code has singled out for *nonrecognition*. In many cases, the property sold or exchanged is replaced with new property. For example, a taxpayer might trade in an old business car for a new one. When this occurs, any gain or loss realized is usually not taxed—at least immediately—on the theory that the taxpayer's economic situation has not changed sufficiently to warrant taxation. Nonrecognition is deemed appropriate since the taxpayer has not

---

[1] Robert J. Bruss, "Real Estate Exchange Provides a Way to Build Net Worth," *The Palm Beach Post*, February 19, 1989, p 57H.

liquidated her investment to cash but has continued it, albeit in another form. In substance, the taxpayer's investment has remained intact. For these situations, Congress is willing to allow a taxpayer to postpone the tax (or perhaps defer the deduction for a loss) until such time when the taxpayer does in fact convert the asset to cash and has the wherewithal to pay the tax.

When the recognition of a gain or loss is deferred, it is normally recognized later, when the replacement property from the deferred transaction is sold in a taxable transaction. This deferral is usually achieved by building the gain or loss not recognized into the basis of the replacement property.

> **Example 1.** D exchanged a vacant lot in San Jose that had been held for investment for unimproved farmland near Fresno. The city lot had cost $35,000 fifteen years earlier and had not been improved. Both the city lot and the rural property were worth $120,000. D recognizes no gain on the exchange and his basis in the farmland is $35,000.[2] Of course, if D later sells the farm for $130,000, his recognizable gain will be $95,000, the gain on the farm of $10,000 plus the gain deferred from the city lot of $85,000.

It is important to observe that nonrecognition can take one of two forms: permanent exclusion or temporary deferral. The world of permanent exclusions, first introduced in Chapter 6, is relatively small. It includes such items as interest paid on state and local government bonds, insurance proceeds paid on account of death, gifts, inheritances, scholarships, child support, and a number of fringe benefits. On the other side of the ledger, losses and expenses that are personal in nature (other than casualty losses) are generally disallowed. Note that if nonrecognition is permanent, the gain or loss never affects taxable income.

One instance in which the permanent exclusion of gain is allowed in property transactions is upon the sale of one's principal residence. This benefit, which was widely expanded by the *Taxpayer Relief Act of 1997*, allows a taxpayer who has owned and used his or her residence for two years to simply avoid tax on part or all of any gain.

> **Example 2.** F, an elderly widow, sold her personal residence of 30 years for $92,000 (basis $21,000) and moved into a rented unit in a retirement community. Under Code § 121, F is allowed to exclude her gain of $71,000 from gross income. Since the gain is excluded, F will never be required to pay tax on the gain from that residence.[3]

TYPES OF NONTAXABLE EXCHANGES

There are several types of nontaxable exchanges allowed under the Internal Revenue Code. Three are discussed in detail in this chapter. The sale of a personal residence is covered initially. Separate discussions of the deferral of gain on involuntary conversions and the deferral of gain or loss on like-kind exchanges follow. Then several other types of nontaxable transactions are discussed briefly.

SALE OF A PERSONAL RESIDENCE

While one's home may be one's castle, in the United States it is also a tax shelter. The tax law contains several provisions that encourage home ownership. Two of these,

---

[2]   See discussion of § 1031 following.

[3]   See discussion of § 121 following.

the deductions for interest and property taxes, were discussed in Chapter 11. A third, considered in detail below, concerns the sale of a residence. The effect of these provisions, whether intended or not, is to provide what is clearly a tax bonanza. If an individual sells a residence, any gain may be totally excluded from income up to $250,000 ($500,000 for certain married persons filing jointly) if the taxpayer qualifies under § 121. Gain in excess of the limit will generally be recognized.

> **Example 3.** T sold his principal residence for $300,000 on July 22, 2005. He has lived in the home since 1995. His basis in the property was $225,000 and his realized gain on the sale is $75,000 ($300,000 − $225,000). T may exclude all of the $75,000 in gain from his taxable income.

COMPUTATION OF BASIS OF RESIDENCE AND GAIN OR LOSS REALIZED

The calculation of the gain recognized on the sale of the house begins in the normal fashion. As usual, the computation starts with the sales price, which is then reduced by selling expenses to determine the amount realized. The sales price is usually easy to determine and presents no difficulties. Selling expenses are generally those costs paid to bring about the sale of the property. Although they are not directly deductible, they do reduce the potential gain. A few of the more common selling expenses incurred when selling a home are

Realtor's commission	Legal fees
Advertising	Title fees (abstracts, certificate, opinion)
Surveys	Transfer taxes
Buyer's points paid by the seller	Mortgage title insurance
Inspection fees (termites, radon, etc.)	Escrow fees

Gain or Loss Realized. The amount of the gain or loss realized is merely the difference between the amount realized and the adjusted basis. In computing the basis for the home, any improvements the owner has made should be included. Improvements include anything that adds value to the house and prolongs its useful life. Some of these are

Additions (rooms, porch, deck)	Flooring (carpeting, tile, vinyl)	Driveway, walks
Roof, siding, insulation	Fences	Curtains
Appliances, attic fan, grill	Air conditioning, furnaces, water	Well
Landscaping, sprinkling system	heaters	Mailbox, house numbers
Garage	Alarm system	Septic system
Basement improvement	Basketball goal post	Sewer assessment
Shed	Solar or geothermal heating	Smoke detector

Gain or Loss Recognized. The next concern, and no doubt the most important, is the determination of the amount of the gain or loss to be recognized. Losses are not subject to any special provision. Accordingly, since a personal residence is not held for either trade or business or investment purposes, any recognized loss is not deductible.[4] While losses are not deductible, gains receive far more favorable treatment. As explained below, if certain requirements are met, most homeowners will be able to exclude all or at least part of their gain.

---

[4] § 165(c).

SECTION 121 EXCLUSION OF GAIN

On the sale of a principal residence, § 121 generally allows a taxpayer to exclude any gain realized up to a maximum of $250,000 ($500,000 for married taxpayers). Any realized gain in excess of this threshold is taxable as capital gain. This relief provision applies to taxpayers of all ages and as frequently as every two years. To obtain this special treatment, taxpayers must meet several requirements as discussed below.

Principal Residence. The exclusion applies only to the sale of the taxpayer's *principal* residence. Most taxpayers have one residence, and if they move, they simply change their principal residence. However, it is sometimes difficult to determine which residence is the *principal residence* for taxpayers with multiple residences. This is a facts and circumstances determination. Some of the factors to be considered are the amount of time each residence is used, the taxpayer's place of employment, where other family members live, the addresses used (for things like tax returns, driver's licenses, car and voter registration, bills and correspondence), and the location of banks, religious organizations and recreational clubs.[5]

The exclusion only applies if the property is a *residence*. A residence not only includes a conventional home but also a condominium, a cooperative apartment, a mobile home, and a fully equipped recreational vehicle (e.g., plumbing, kitchen, sleeping facilities) notwithstanding that it is a means of transportation.[6] The residence also includes the land on which the residence sits and any gain attributable to the land is eligible for exclusion.[7] Land adjacent to the home qualifies if it is regularly used by the owner as part of the residential property, and it is sold along with the home or within two years before or after the sale of the home.[8]

It is not that uncommon for the seller of a home to also sell property that is technically not part of the residence such as furniture, lawn equipment, pool table, hot tub, or similar property. Unless such personalty is treated as a fixture under local law it is not considered part of the residence and, therefore, is not eligible for the exclusion. In most cases, however, sales of such items would result in nondeductible losses.

Ownership and Occupancy Tests. The § 121 exclusion is applicable to the sale of a residence which was owned by the taxpayer and used as his or her principal residence for at least two of the five years preceding its sale.[9] Note that these requirements are two separate tests. First, the exclusion is available only if the taxpayer *owned* the residence for two of the five years prior to the sale. Normally, ownership is not an issue.[10] However, whether the taxpayer *uses* the property as a principal residence for the requisite two years during the five-year window can be a bit more troubling. The question as to whether a residence is used as one's principal residence is a question of facts and circumstances, and as previously suggested, an individual can only have one principal residence at any given time.

---

5 Reg. § 1.121-1.

6 See Reg. § 1.121-1(b)(1) and (e)(2), § 280A(f)(1)(A); Prop Reg § 1.280A-1(e)(7), Ex (2) and *Ronald Haberkorn* 75 T.C. 259 (1980). See also *Richard Dougherty*, T.C. Memo 1994-597, T.C. Memo ¶94597 where a 32-foot charter cruiser that berthed six was considered a home.

7 But see where a taxpayer who moved his house and sold the land was not entitled to the exclusion for the land. See also IRS Publication 523 (2004) p. 3.

8 Reg. § 1.121-1(b)(3).

9 § 121(a).

10 See Reg. § 1.121-1(c)(3) allowing the exclusion where the residence is owned by grantor trusts and disregarded entities such as a single member LLC.

Example 4. Y purchased a home in 1983 and lived in it until she was transferred by her employer on April 30, 2001. From May 1, 2001 until the house was sold on May 1, 2005, it was used by Y only on occasional days off and she lived in a rented apartment in a nearby city. Since Y owned the house but did not use it as her principal residence during at least two of the five years before its sale, she does not qualify for the § 121 exclusion.

If, taking into account all facts and circumstances, the house, and not the apartment, had been Y's principal residence, she would have qualified. She would have to be able to demonstrate that she lived in the house, with only temporary visits to the apartment.

In applying the use test, short temporary absences, such as for vacation or other seasonal absence are counted as periods of use. For this purpose, temporary rental of the property is ignored.

Example 5. T purchased his home in South Bend in 1995. He used the house as his principal residence until January 31, 2002, when he moved to Chicago. Upon moving, T rented his house to tenants until April 18, 2004, when he sold it. T is eligible for the exclusion because he has owned and used the house as his principal residence for at least two of the five years preceding the sale.

Example 6. B owned and used her house in Houston as her principal residence from 1986 to the end of 1999. On January 4, 2000, she moved to Denver. Shortly thereafter, B's son moved into the house in March 2000 and used the residence until it sold on July 1, 2005. B may not exclude gain from the sale because she did not use the property as her principal residence for at least two years out of the five years preceding the sale. Use by her son is not counted as the mother's use.

Maximum Exclusion. The maximum amount excludable with respect to any sale or exchange is $250,000. This amount is doubled to $500,000 for most married taxpayers filing joint returns. In such cases, the ownership requirement only needs to be met by one spouse. So if either spouse meets the ownership test and both spouses meet the use test, the $500,000 exclusion applies.[11] However, if only one spouse satisfies the use test, the exclusion is allowable but limited to $250,000 (or the sum of the amount excludable by each spouse individually).

Example 7. H and W sold their jointly owned and occupied family residence on June 3, 2005, for $650,000. Their basis in the property, that they had owned for thirty years, was $125,000, so their gain was $525,000. If H and W file a joint return for their calendar year 2005, they may exclude $500,000 of the gain and must recognize a long-term capital gain of $25,000.

Example 8. Q purchased a home for use as her principal residence in 1991. On March 31, 2002, Q was transferred by her employer, so she moved away, rented an apartment and left her residence unused. When Q sells the residence at a gain of $200,000 on March 1, 2005, she may exclude the entire gain. During the five years preceding the sale—March 1, 2000 to February 28, 2005—Q *owned* the property for all five years and *used* it as her principal residence for 25 months (i.e., more than the requisite two years).

---

[11]   § 121(b)(1) and (2).

Example 9. L purchased a residence for use as his principal residence for $123,000 on July 12, 2003. Presented with an attractive offer on the property, L sold the residence on February 2, 2005 for $198,000 (net of selling costs). L must report a long-term capital gain of $75,000 since L does not meet the two of five year tests.

Example 10. F purchased a new personal residence in 1982 for $40,000 and lived in it until June 30, 1994. The house was rented out until January 1, 2002, with depreciation of $8,500 being claimed. On January 1, 2002, F moved back into the house and occupied it as her principal residence until February 5, 2005, when it was sold for $280,000. Since F owned and lived in the home for at least two of the five years preceding the sale, she may exclude up to $250,000 of gain (see subsequent discussion of depreciation recapture).

FREQUENCY LIMITATION: ONE SALE EVERY TWO YEARS

The benefits of the § 121 exclusion are so great that without some prohibition taxpayers might utilize the provision in unintended ways. One could easily envision a taxpayer selling one principal residence and excluding the gain, buying and selling another residence and excluding the gain, and continuing this pattern, using the exclusion as a tax shelter. To restrict this possibility, the Code imposes a limitation on the frequency with which the exclusion may be used. The exclusion cannot be used for sales occurring within two years of its last use. In other words, the law allows the exclusion for one sale every two years. To ensure that this rule does not unfairly penalize taxpayers who may be forced to sell their homes before the two-year period has elapsed, special rules concerning sales for unforeseen circumstances exist and are discussed below.[12]

Example 11. M purchased a residence for use as her principal residence for $70,000 on January 2, 2000, and lived in it until March 15, 2002. On March 16, 2002, M rented the original residence and purchased and moved into another residence costing $85,000. Upon retiring, M sold the original residence for $90,000 on December 31, 2003, and excluded most of her gain on the sale (see subsequent discussion of depreciation recapture). Even though M would otherwise be eligible to exclude any gain on the sale of the other residence on March 16, 2004, due to this one sale every two years rule, M will not be eligible until January 1, 2006 (see subsequent discussion related to electing out of § 121).

EXCEPTIONS TO OWNERSHIP, USE AND FREQUENCY TESTS

At times, taxpayers may be forced to sell their homes due to events beyond their control. For example, an individual may be forced take a job in another location or move because of health reasons. In these and similar situations, taxpayers may run afoul of the ownership and use requirement or the frequency limitation. Without relief, any realized gain on the sale of the house would be *fully* taxable notwithstanding the fact that there was nothing the taxpayer could do to avoid the sale. Recognizing this problem, § 121 provides some assistance.[13] A taxpayer may qualify for a *portion* of the exclusion if the sale were due to unforeseen circumstances. In many cases the reduced exclusion would be more than sufficient to offset any appreciation that occurred.

---

[12]   § 121(b)(3).

[13]   § 121(c).

Computation of the Reduced Exclusion. The portion of the exclusion allowed is the percentage of the required 24 months for which the taxpayer satisfies the ownership and use test or if lower the number of months used since the last sale.[14]

$$\begin{array}{c}\text{Exclusion} \times \\ (\$250,000 \text{ or } \$500,000)\end{array} \quad \frac{\text{Lesser of time owned and used or time since last sale}}{24 \text{ months}} = \begin{array}{c}\text{Reduced}\\\text{Exclusion}\end{array}$$

> **Example 12.** H and W have one son, S, who suffers from a rare disease. After living in their home only six months, the couple sold their home in Kansas City and moved to Memphis to obtain special treatment only available at St. Jude's Children's Research Hospital. H and W do not meet the ownership and use test since they did not own and use the home as their principal residence for two of the five years prior to the sale. However, because the sale is due to unforeseen circumstances, they qualify for a reduced exclusion of $125,000 [(6/24 = 25%) × $500,000].

This rule is often misconstrued. Taxpayers are not entitled to a portion of the exclusion just because they meet the ownership and use test for a few months. The reduced exclusion is granted only if the sale is due to unforeseen circumstances. If a taxpayer simply decides to sell before meeting the tests (e.g., because of market conditions) and without cause, the entire gain is taxable.

Unforeseen Circumstances. The Code provides that the reduced exclusion is available only if due to[15]

- Change in place of employment
- Health concerns
- Unforeseen circumstances

The tests regarding employment and health can be met by the

- Taxpayer
- Taxpayer's spouse
- Member of the taxpayer's household
- Co-owner of the residence

Change in place of employment. In applying the change of employment test, the Regulations contain a safe harbor, providing that the reduced exclusion is available due to a change in employment if the new place of business is at least 50 miles farther from the old residence than was the old job.[16] This is the same test that must be met to deduct moving expenses (the taxpayer's new commute without the move would exceed the old commute by more than 50 miles). If the taxpayer was not employed and moves to obtain employment, the distance between the new job and the residence sold must be at least 50 miles.

Health Reasons. A second safe harbor exists for residence sales for health reasons.[17] If the sale is necessary to obtain medical care or if a physician recommends a change of location for health reasons, the safe harbor is met. In contrast, sales that are merely beneficial to the general health or well-being of an individual do not qualify.

---

[14] § 121(c)(1).

[15] § 121(c)(2).

[16] Reg. § 1.121-3(c)(2).

[17] Reg. § 1.121-3(d).

Unforeseen Circumstances. If there is an occurrence of event that could not reasonably have been anticipated *before* purchasing the residence, the reduced exclusion can be used. According to the Regulations, unforeseen circumstances include[18]

- Involuntary conversion of the residence
- Natural or man-made disasters
- Acts of war or terrorism resulting in a casualty to the residence
- Death
- Unemployment so as to qualify for unemployment compensation
- Change in employment or self-employment status that results in the taxpayer's inability to pay housing costs and reasonable basic living expenses for the taxpayer's household
- Divorce
- Multiple births resulting from the same pregnancy

If a safe harbor is not met, the reduced exclusion may still be available.[19] The Regulations identify certain factors to be considered.

> **Example 13.** F purchased a personal residence on March 15, 2004 for $125,000. F must have been living right—he was transferred by his employer to his favorite city, received a big raise, and sold his house in two weeks time for $200,000 (on September 15, 2005). Even though F did not meet the two of five years test, he may exclude his entire $75,000 gain. Because the sale was related to a change of place of employment, F can exclude up to $187,500 [$250,000 × (18 months / 24 months)].

EXHIBIT 15-1
Section 121 Exclusion Basics

Taxpayer Qualifies If

- The residence was *owned* and *used as a principal residence* for two of the five years preceding the sale
  and
- No gain was excluded under § 121 in a qualifying sale made within the two years preceding the sale

Maximum Amount Excluded

- Generally $250,000
- $500,000 for married taxpayers filing jointly if either spouse meets the ownership test and both spouses meet the use test
- A fraction of these amounts is allowed if the sale is related to a change in the taxpayer's work location, health, or other qualifying unforeseen circumstances

Effects of Marriage. In applying the two of five year test, a widow or widower (who has not remarried) selling a residence is treated as having owned and occupied a

---

[18]   Reg. § 1.121-3(e).

[19]   In PLR 200403049, the IRS found that hostilities between the taxpayers and their neighbors qualified as unforeseen circumstances for purposes of §121.

residence for the period of time it was owned and occupied by his or her deceased spouse.[20]

> **Example 14.** R married S on November 27, 2003, and moved into a home that had been owned and occupied by S since 1996. S died on March 15, 2004, leaving the residence to R. Since R is deemed to have owned and lived in the residence since 1996, she qualifies for the $250,000 exclusion when the residence is sold on February 12, 2005.

Homes owned by one spouse before marriage or held as separate property during a marriage could also present problems in applying the two of five year rule. To prevent inequities, if a property is transferred to a spouse or former spouse in a transaction that is tax-free under § 1041 (e.g., in a divorce), the transferee is deemed to have owned the residence for the period of time it was owned by the transferor.

> **Example 15.** D lived in a residence owned as separate property by his spouse, E, for the duration of their four-year marriage. Upon their divorce, D received the residence. Fifteen months after the divorce, D married G and sold the residence (on December 24, 2005), realizing a gain of $280,000. D lived in the residence four years and is deemed to have owned the residence all of the five years preceding the sale. He may, therefore, exclude gain of $250,000 and recognize long-term capital gain of $30,000. D and G cannot exclude $500,000 since G does not meet the residential use test with respect to the residence.

Incapacitated Taxpayers. A taxpayer who purchases a residence and is soon forced to move to a rest home or similar facility may never be able to meet the time requirement for the § 121 exclusion. Fortunately, if a person in this situation lives in the residence for at least one year, he or she will be treated as having lived in that residence during any period of time that he or she has lived in a licensed facility for incapacitated individuals.[21] Thus, anyone who purchases a home, lives in it one year, and spends at least a year in a rest home while still owning the home will meet all the tests for § 121.

Involuntary Conversions. For purposes of § 121, an involuntary conversion of a qualifying residence will be treated as the sale of that residence.[22] Thus, a person who meets the use and ownership tests can exclude at least a portion of any gain from the destruction, theft, or condemnation of his or her residence. Involuntary conversions are discussed in detail later in this chapter.

Depreciation Recapture. Since a residence qualifying for the § 121 exclusion may have at times been used as rental property or business property, it may have been subject to the allowance for depreciation. To be able to depreciate a property, resulting in a basis reduction, and subsequently exclude any gain is to good to be true. Realizing this, Congress requires that the gain be recognized to the extent of any depreciation allowed after May 6, 1997.[23]

> **Example 16.** P purchased a home for use as a residence in 1992 for $60,000 and made improvements costing $18,000 in 2001. On June 30, 2004, P retired, moved out and converted the house to rental property. Between that date and the day the

---

[20] § 121(e)(1) and (2).

[21] § 121(d)(9).

[22] § 121(d)(5)(A).

[23] § 121(e)(6).

property was sold for $200,000, September 30, 2005, P claimed depreciation of $3,600, making the basis in the property $74,400 [$60,000 + $18,000 − $3,600]. P's realized gain is $125,600 ($200,000 − $74,400). P must recognize $3,600 of the gain and may exclude the remaining $122,000 under § 121.

Example 17. Assume the same facts as in the prior example, except the sales price is $77,000. P's gain is $2,600 ($77,000 − $74,400). Since the gain realized is less than the depreciation claimed after May 6, 1997, none of the gain may be excluded under § 121. P must, therefore, recognize a $2,600 gain (i.e., the lesser of the gain realized or the depreciation claimed).

When only a portion of a dwelling was used for business purposes, including use as an office in the home, gain is recognized only to the extent of the depreciation recapture that is required.[24] Any additional gain qualifies for the exclusion.

Example 18. B purchased a residence for use as his principal residence for $125,000 in 1991. After the children moved out, he converted a bedroom (ten percent of the residence) to a business office. Depreciation of $1,350 was claimed over three years before the residence was sold during the current year for $375,000. The total gain realized is $251,350 [$375,000 − ($125,000 − $1,350)]. One way to look at the sale would be to treat the sale as that of two separate properties.

	Business 10%	Personal 90%
Sales price....................	$ 37,500	$ 337,500
Adjusted basis	(11,150)*	(112,500)
Gain	$ 26,350	$ 225,000

*$125,000 × 10% − $1,350

Fortunately, the IRS chose not to require this two separate sales approach, and B is required to recognize gain of only $1,350. The remaining gain of $250,000 ($251,350 − $1,350) qualifies for exclusion since B owned and occupied the residence for the required period.

Sale After a Like-kind Exchange. Several references have been made to property that for some period of time was rental property. Rental property, but not personal use property, qualifies for like-kind exchange treatment. Owners of rental property might be interested in exchanging their rental property(s) for other rental property(s) in a tax-deferred exchange (see subsequent coverage in this chapter), later converting the replacement to a principal residence, and then (after at least two years) selling the replacement and excluding up to $250,000 (or $500,000 for some married couples). This possibility remains, but the § 121 exclusion will not apply to a property unless five years have passed since the like-exchange occured.

Example 19. B owned a four-plex of rental units that were purchased for $240,000 in 1990. Depreciation of $98,000 was claimed, so B's basis is $142,000. On November 16, 2003, B exchanged the units for a residential property worth $450,000 that was used as rental property. In October of 2004, the tenant moved out and B moved into the residence. Under the general rule, B would qualify for the

---

[24]   Temp. Reg. § 1.121-2.

§ 121 exclusion in October 2006, but under the special rule for like-kind exchange property B will not qualify until November 16, 2008 (five years after the exchange).

If B sells the property, after November 15, 2008, for $490,000, the gain realized is $348,000 [$490,000 − ($240,000 − $98,000)]. B can exclude $250,000.

If the sale had occurred earlier, none of the gain is excludable.

Electing Out. A taxpayer may elect not to have § 121 apply to an otherwise qualifying sale. The election is made by reporting the gain on the tax return for the year of the sale.[25] Presumably (unless future guidance provides otherwise) the election can be made on an amended return.

Example 20. A purchased her first residence on May 1, 2000. She lived there until she was transferred by her employer on August 1, 2002. She rented the original residence and purchased a second residence which she occupied beginning on September 1, 2002. On December 15, 2004, A sold the second residence, realizing at a gain of $5,000. Then on January 31, 2005, she sold her original residence at a gain of $177,000 ($2,000 of which is attributable to depreciation allowed). Only $175,000 can qualify for exclusion due to the depreciation claimed.

Both residences meet the two of five years ownerships and use tests. If A excludes the $5,000 gain from the second residence in 2004, she cannot exclude the $175,000 gain from the original residence in 2005 because of the one sale every two years rule. It would, therefore, be in her best interest to elect out of the benefits of § 121 exclusion with respect to the $5,000 gain, in order to take advantage of the § 121 exclusion with respect to the $175,000 gain.

✓ CHECK YOUR KNOWLEDGE

Review Question 1. True-False. Helen excluded $250,000 of gain from the sale of her primary residence which was sold on August 4, 2004. Helen cannot exclude her $23,000 gain from the sale of another primary residence on November 1, 2006 even though she has owned and used this home for more than two years.

False. Since more than two years transpired from the first sale to the second sale, Helen qualifies to exclude gain on both sales. The fact that the sale was in the second tax year after the original sale is not determinative.

Review Question 2. True-False. Mick purchased a residence on March 1, 2001 and lived in it until July 31, 2002. He rented it from August 1, 2002 until June 30, 2004 (claiming depreciation of $7,000), and then lived in it again from July 1, 2004 until it was sold on June 1, 2005. Mick cannot exclude any of his gain of $40,000 under § 121.

False. Mick qualifies for the § 121 exclusion because he lived in the residence more than two years during the five years preceding the sale (i.e., June 1, 2000 to May 31, 2005). Specifically, he lived there 25 months. However, Mick can only exclude $36,000, since the first $7,000 of gain must be recognized due to the depreciation claimed.

Review Question 3. Lin purchased a residence on June 1, 2004, for $235,000. On December 1, 2005, she sold the residence for $295,000, so she could move to a nearby city where she was transferred by her employer. How much gain, if any, may Lin exclude under § 121?

---

[25] See § 121(f) and I.R.S. Publication 523, p.2.

All $60,000. Even though Lin did not meet the two of five years ownership and use requirements, she qualifies for a reduced exclusion limit since the sale is related to a change in the place of employment. The reduced limit if $187,500 [$250,000 × (18 months / 24 months)].

Review Question 4. J and K were married on June 1, 2004, and K moved into the home that J had owned and occupied for ten years. On September 1, 2005, J and K sold the residence, recognizing a gain of $295,000. How much of the gain may J and K exclude on their joint return for 2005?

Only $250,000. In order to qualify for the increased $500,000 exclusion, both husband and wife must have used the residence for two of the five years preceding the sale. K only lived there for 15 months.

Review Question 5. After living together for ten years, L and M finally married on June 1, 2004. After their marriage, the couple continued to live in L's home. L never retitled the property and held it separately primarily for estate planning purposes. On September 1, 2005, L sold the residence, recognizing a gain of $360,000. How much of the gain may L and M exclude on their joint return for 2005?

All $360,000. In order to qualify for the increased $500,000 exclusion, only one spouse must have owned the residence for two of the preceding five years, but both husband and wife must have used the residence for two of the five years. They must file a joint return, but there is no requirement that the property be jointly owned or that they be married during the two years that they lived there.

INVOLUNTARY CONVERSIONS

Taxpayers occasionally lose their property from casualty or theft or are forced to sell their property because of some type of condemnation proceeding. When an *involuntary conversion* like this occurs, the taxpayer usually receives some form of compensation such as insurance proceeds or a condemnation award. In some cases, the compensation may actually cause the taxpayer to realize a gain from the "loss." Without any special rule, the tax resulting from this gain could produce a real hardship since the taxpayer typically uses the compensation received to acquire a replacement property. Recognizing that taxpayers may not have the wherewithal to pay the tax in this situation—which was totally beyond their control—Congress provided some relief. Special rules allow taxpayers to defer any gain realized from an involuntary conversion if they acquire qualified replacement property within a specified period of time.

Example 21. J operates a fishing boat in Miami. Unfortunately, the boat was totally destroyed when Hurricane Charley hit the Florida coast. J's basis in the boat was $40,000 (cost of $60,000 less depreciation of $20,000). Luckily, J was insured. He filed an insurance claim and received $75,000 based on the fair market value of the boat. As a result, he realized a gain of $35,000 ($75,000 − $40,000). J may defer the entire gain if he reinvests at least $75,000 in similar-use property within the allowable period.

INVOLUNTARY CONVERSION DEFINED

An involuntary conversion is defined in the Code as the compulsory or involuntary conversion of property "as a result of its destruction in whole or in part, theft, seizure, or requisition or condemnation or threat or imminence thereof.''[26] The terms *destruction* and *theft* have the same basic meaning as when they are used for casualty and theft losses. The IRS has ruled, however, that the destruction of property for purposes of § 1033 need not meet the *suddenness* test, which has been applied to casualty loss deductions.[27]

Typical involuntary conversions involve accidents, natural disasters, and other events beyond the control of the taxpayer. This has been found to include damages caused by other parties such as poisoning of cattle by contaminated feed and destruction of crops and soil by chemicals.[28] In each case, the taxpayer was allowed to defer recognition of gain upon the receipt of damages by reinvesting in qualified property.

Seizure, Requisition, or Condemnation. It is not as simple to determine what qualifies as a "seizure, or requisition or condemnation" as it is to identify theft or destruction. The property must be taken without the taxpayer's consent and the taxpayer must be compensated.[29]

Not all types of forced dispositions will qualify. For example, the courts have found that a foreclosure sale[30] and a sale after continued insistence by a Chamber of Commerce[31] did not constitute involuntary conversions. Similarly, the IRS has ruled that the condemnation of rental properties due to structural defects or sanitary conditions does not constitute an involuntary conversion since the sale was made to avoid making property improvements necessary to meet a housing ordinance.[32] Generally, a transfer must be made to an authority that has the power to actually condemn the property, and the property must be taken for a public use.

In the case of the conversion of part of a single economic unit, § 1033 applies not only to the condemned portion, but also to the part not condemned if it is *voluntarily sold*. When a truck freight terminal was rendered virtually useless because the adjoining parking lot for the trucks was condemned, a single economic unit was found to exist and § 1033 applied to the sale of the terminal as well as the condemnation of the parking area.[33] In a similar situation when a shopping center was partially destroyed by fire and the owner chose to sell the entire shopping center rather than reconstruct the destroyed portion, the IRS ruled that no conversion existed with respect to the remaining portion since the undamaged portion could still be used and the damaged portion repaired. The fire insurance proceeds, but not the sale proceeds, qualified for deferral under § 1033.[34]

Threat or Imminence of Condemnation. The possibility of a condemnation may very well cause a taxpayer to sell property before the actual condemnation occurs. For example, a farming corporation may discover that its property is being considered as the site for a new airport and sell the property. Section 1033 extends deferral to these *voluntary* sales to someone other than the condemning authority if they are due to the *threat or imminence* of condemnation. It should be emphasized that newspaper reports, magazine articles, or rumors that property is being considered for condemnation are not

---

[26] § 1033(a).

[27] Rev. Rul. 59-102, 1959-1 C.B. 200.

[28] Rev. Rul. 54-395, 1954-2 C.B. 143 and Ltr. Rul. 9615041.

[29] See, for example, *Hitke v. Comm.*, 62-1 USTC ¶9114, 8 AFTR2d 5886, 296 F.2d 639 (CA-7, 1961).

[30] See *Cooperative Publishing Co. v. U.S.*, 40-2 USTC ¶9823, 25 AFTR 1123, 115 F.2d 1017 (CA-9, 1940), and *Robert Recio*, 61 TCM 2626, T.C. Memo. 1991-215.

[31] *Davis Co.*, 6 B.T.A. 281 (1927), *acq.* VI-2 C.B. 2.

[32] Rev. Rul. 57-314, 1957-2 C.B. 523.

[33] *Harry Masser*, 30 T.C. 741 (1958), *acq.* 1959-2 C.B. 5; Rev. Rul. 59-361, 1959-2 C.B. 183.

[34] Rev. Rul. 78-377, 1978-2 C.B. 208, distinguishing Rev. Rul. 59-361, Footnote 27.

sufficient.[35] Threat or imminence exists only after officials have communicated that they intend to condemn the property and the owner has good reason to believe they would.

> **Example 22.** LSA Corporation has owned a department store in downtown Indianapolis for more than 50 years. The property has a value of about $2 million and a basis of only $400,000 (since the building is completely depreciated). Recently, the corporation learned that the city fathers, in an attempt to revive the downtown area, plan to build a new mall that may result in the condemnation of the building. Fearing that interest rates may rise before the city gets around to condemning the property, the corporation sold the building to another investor, who wanted to try to preserve the building as a historic structure. The corporation quickly used the sales proceeds to build another store in a nearby suburb. Unfortunately, the corporation's sale may not qualify for deferral since it has not been officially notified that the building will be condemned. The threat or imminence does not exist merely because the city is considering plans that may lead to condemnation. Nevertheless, the corporation may be able to produce evidence that clearly suggests otherwise.

As noted above, the sale to a third party after the threat exists is permissible.[36] If the third party realizes gain when the property is later sold to the condemning authority, the new transaction may also qualify for involuntary conversion treatment if the proceeds are reinvested in qualified property after the condemnation of the property, even though the threat existed before the property was acquired.[37]

> **Example 23.** T has owned and operated a successful automobile dealership for many years. This year he received legal notice from the City of New Orleans indicating that it planned to condemn his showroom and car lot for use as the site of a new convention center in approximately five years. As a result, T began searching for an acceptable new location. After finding a suitable location, T sold the old property to a person who could use it for just four or five years.
>
> T's sale and reinvestment qualifies for involuntary conversion treatment and his gain can be deferred so long as all other requirements are met. When the property is finally purchased by the city, the new owner can also qualify for involuntary conversion treatment if he or she realizes a gain and the proceeds are reinvested in qualifying property within the replacement period.

REPLACEMENT PROPERTY

To qualify for deferral of gain on an involuntary conversion, the taxpayer must reinvest in property that is *similar or related in service* or *use* to the property that is converted.[38] The IRS and taxpayers often disagree as to what qualifies as replacement property. It is clear, however, that the new property must replace the converted property, and therefore, property that was already owned by the taxpayer will not qualify.[39]

Generally, the replacement property must serve the same functional use as that served by the converted property. This *functional use* test requires that the character of service or use be the same for both properties.

---

[35]   Rev. Rul. 58-557, 1958-2 C.B. 402.

[36]   *Creative Solutions, Inc. v. U.S.*, 63-2 USTC ¶9615, 12 AFTR2d 5229, 320 F.2d 809 (CA-5, 1963); Rev. Rul. 81-180, 1981-2 C.B. 161.

[37]   Rev. Rul. 81-181, 1981-2 C.B. 162.

[38]   § 1033(a).

[39]   § 1033(a)(1)(A)(i).

Example 24. N has successfully owned and operated a bowling alley for many years. This year the bowling alley was destroyed by fire, and N replaced it with a billiard parlor. The billiard parlor is not qualified replacement property since services provided by each are not functionally equivalent. Although they both provide recreational services, the IRS believes bowling balls and billiard balls are not the same.[40]

When tangible trade or business personalty is destroyed in a Presidentially declared disaster area, the taxpayer is given more flexibility. The destroyed property may be replaced with *any* tangible trade or business personalty.[41]

A different and more liberal test has been applied to rental properties involved in involuntary conversions. This test is the *taxpayer use* test, which basically requires that the replacement property be used by the taxpayer/lessor as rental property regardless of the lessee's use.[42]

Example 25. Several years ago J purchased 30 acres of land and built a large warehouse that he leased to an appliance store. This year the warehouse site was condemned, and J used the proceeds to purchase a gas station that he currently leases to an oil company. The gas station is qualified replacement property since both properties are rental properties. The fact that the tenants use the properties for different purposes is irrelevant. From the owner's perspective each property is being used in the same way.

Control of Corporation. The replacement property in an involuntary conversion may be controlling stock in a corporation owning property that is "similar or related in use or service."[43] Control consists of owning at least 80 percent of all voting stock plus at least 80 percent of all other classes of stock.[44]

Condemned Real Estate. Congress provided special relief in the situation where real property is condemned by an outside authority. A more liberal interpretation of "similar or related in use" is allowed for the replacement of condemned real property if it is held by the taxpayer for use in a trade or business or for investment. The Code provides that the *like-kind* test shall be applied.[45] This is the test used for § 1031 like-kind exchanges. As explained later in this chapter, these rules allow nonrecognition whenever a taxpayer exchanges real estate for real estate regardless of the real estate's use. Thus, if the taxpayer's unimproved real estate (e.g., raw land) is condemned and replaced with improved real estate (e.g., shopping center), deferral would be granted.

Conversion of Personal Residence. Section 1033 applies to the involuntary conversion of a principal residence. Also, if he or she qualifies, a taxpayer may elect to use § 121 instead of, or along with, § 1033 for the involuntary conversion of a personal residence.[46]

Special rules apply if the residence was destroyed in a Presidentially declared disaster area. First, no gain is recognized with respect to amounts received for any

---

[40]   Rev. Rul. 76-319, 1976-2 C.B. 242.

[41]   § 1033(h).

[42]   Rev. Rul. 71-41, 1971-1 C.B. 223.

[43]   § 1033(a)(2)(A).

[44]   § 1033(a)(2)(E)(i).

[45]   § 1033(g)(1). The similar or related in use test must be applied if the real property is destroyed or the replacement property is stock in a controlled corporation.

[46]   § 121(d)(4).

contents other than those specifically listed in an insurance policy (e.g., expensive jewelry or artwork). Second, with respect to amounts received for listed contents and the residence, they are treated as a single asset. Accordingly, so long as the entire amount realized from the residence and the listed contents are reinvested in similar residential property (including listed contents), any gain is deferred.[47]

Conversion of Livestock. Section 1033 includes certain special provisions related to sales of livestock. Livestock sold because of disease[48] or solely because of drought, flood or other weather-related conditions[49] are considered involuntarily converted. Furthermore, if livestock are sold because of soil contamination or environmental contamination and it is not feasible for the owner to reinvest in other livestock, then other farm property, including real property, will qualify as replacement property.[50]

Property Acquired from a Related Party. Congress was concerned that the replacement property would conveniently be acquired from a related party. In order to prevent this, C corporations, partnerships with C corporations as partners, and other taxpayers deferring gains in excess of $100,000, will not be allowed the deferral under § 1033 if the replacement is purchased from a related party. For this purpose, a related party includes certain close family members and most entities where there is more than 50 percent control.[51]

REPLACEMENT PERIOD

The taxpayer is entitled to deferral only if reinvestment in the replacement property occurs within the proper time period. The replacement period usually begins on the date of disposition of the converted property; but in the case of condemnation or requisition, it begins at the earliest date of threat or imminence of the requisition or condemnation. The replacement period ends on the last day of the second taxable year after the year in which a gain is first realized,[52] but may be extended by the IRS if the taxpayer can show reasonable cause for being unable to replace within the specified time limit.[53] In the case of condemned real property used in a trade or business or held for investment, the replacement period is extended. The extension is one year, causing the replacement period to remain open until the end of the third taxable year after the first year in which gain is first realized.[54] These time periods are diagrammed below.

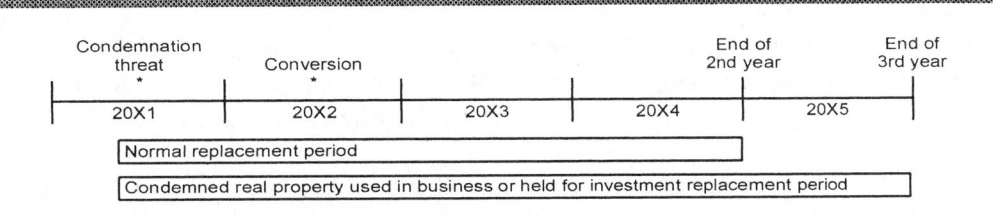

---

47   § 1033(h).

48   § 1033(d).

49   § 1033(e).

50   § 1033(f).

51   § 1033(i).

52   § 1033(a)(2)(B).

53   Reg. § 1.1033(a)-2(c)(3).

54   § 1033(g)(4).

Example 26. E's rental house was condemned for public use by the county during 2005. Her basis in the residence was $32,000 and the county paid her $46,000. E is a calendar year taxpayer and her replacement period begins the day of the condemnation, or threat thereof, and ends on December 31, 2008.

Example 27. If the residence in the previous example had been used as E's personal residence, the replacement period would end on December 31, 2007. The replacement period is extended only for real estate held for productive use or for investment, so the usual two-year rule applies.

Earlier reference was made to specific provisions dealing with replacement property upon the destruction of one's principal residence. A special reinvestment period is also provided. When the destruction is in a Presidentially declared disaster area, the reinvestment period is extended to the last day of the fourth year following the year in which gain is first realized.[55]

Example 28. U's principal residence was destroyed in an earthquake. U's insurance policy included limits of $100,000 for the residence, $40,000 for contents, and an additional $20,000 for U's prized musical instruments. U realized gains on the residence and musical instruments and a small loss on the contents. The region affected by the earthquake was declared a disaster area by the President and U's insurer paid the maximum amounts under the policy. U may defer his gain on the structure and musical instruments by reinvesting $120,000 in similar (residence or contents) property. The reinvestment must take place by the end of U's fourth taxable year after receiving the insurance settlement.

ELECTION REQUIRED

As a general rule, taxpayers are allowed to elect whether or not they want to defer any gain realized from an involuntary conversion. The election is made simply by not reporting any of the deferred gain on the tax return for the year in which the gain is realized. However, deferral of gain is mandatory if the property is converted directly into property that is similar or related in use.[56]

Example 29. G owned 100 acres of land next to an airport. He had farmed the land for 25 years. All of that changed this year when the city condemned G's land to expand the airport. Pursuant to the condemnation agreement, the city transferred similar farmland to G. In this case, nonrecognition is mandatory since there was a direct conversion into similar property. Had the city paid G for the land, G would have had the option to elect deferral or recognize any gain realized.

The return for the year of conversion must include detailed information relating to the involuntary conversion,[57] and if the taxpayer has not yet reinvested when the return is filed, he or she is required to notify the IRS when replacement property has been acquired or that no replacement will occur.[58] If after an election has been made under § 1033 *and* the taxpayer fails to reinvest all of the required amount within the allowable

---

[55]   § 1033(h)(1)(B).

[56]   § 1033(a).

[57]   Reg. § 1.1033(a)-2(c)(2).

[58]   Reg. § 1.1033(a)-2(c)(5).

period, the tax return for the year (or years) in which gain was realized must be *amended to include the recognized gain* and the tax deficiency must be paid.[59]

Statute of Limitations. The statute of limitations is extended for involuntary conversions when the taxpayer elects to defer his or her gain but has not replaced the property by the time the return for the year of the conversion is filed. The IRS may audit the transaction and assess a deficiency any time within three years after the taxpayer notifies the IRS that he or she has replaced the converted property or has failed to replaced the property triggering the recognition of gain.[60]

AMOUNT OF GAIN RECOGNIZED

No gain is recognized by an electing taxpayer on an involuntary conversion if the amount reinvested in replacement property equals or exceeds the amount realized from the converted property (i.e., the taxpayer does not "cash out" on the transaction). If the amount reinvested is less than the amount realized, the taxpayer has "cashed out" on the transaction and *must* recognize gain to the extent of the amount *not* reinvested (see Exhibit 15-2).[61] No gain is recognized in a direct conversion.[62]

The *amount reinvested* is the *cost* of the replacement property. The property may not have been acquired by gift, inheritance, or any other method resulting in other than a cost basis.[63] The cost basis would include the amount of any debt incurred in the purchase.

The taxpayer will determine his or her basis in property acquired in an involuntary conversion by taking into consideration the deferred gain. In the case of a direct conversion, the basis of the replacement property is the same as the basis in the converted property. In conversions into money and other property, the basis in the replacement property is its cost *reduced* by the amount of gain realized but not recognized (see Exhibit 15-2).[64]

---

58   Reg. § 1.1033(a)-2(c)(5).

59   Special rules extend the statute of limitations. § 1033(a)(2)(C): Reg. § 1.1033(a)-2(c)(5).

60   § 1033(a)(2)(C).

61   § 1033(a)(2)(A).

62   § 1033(a)(1).

63   Reg. § 1.1033(a)-2(c)(4).

64   § 1033(b); Reg. § 1.1033(b)-1.

EXHIBIT 15-2

Involuntary Conversion: Computation of Recognized Gain and Basis of Replacement Property

1. Gain realized

    Amount realized (net proceeds)

    Less: Adjusted basis

    Gain (loss) realized

2. Gain recognized

    Amount realized

    Less: Cost of replacement property

    Gain recognized (not to exceed gain realized)*

3. Basis of replacement property

    Cost of replacement property

    Less: Gain not recognized

    Adjusted basis of replacement property

*If this amount is negative, the taxpayer has reinvested more than the amount realized and no gain is recognized.

Example 30. M owned a rented industrial equipment warehouse that was adjacent to a railway. The warehouse was destroyed by fire on January 15, 2005, and M received $240,000 from her insurance carrier on March 26, 2005. Her basis in the warehouse was $130,000. M constructed a wholesale grocery warehouse on the same site since the predicted demand for such space was superior to equipment storage. The new warehouse was constructed at a cost of $280,000 and was completed May 7, 2006.

Leased (rental) property is subject to the more liberal *taxpayer use* test, rather than the *functional use* test that is applied to other properties. Therefore, the new warehouse meets the similar or related in use test since it is rental property to M.

As calculated below, M reports no gain on her 2005 return since she reinvested a sufficient amount within the reinvestment period, which ends December 31, 2007. She is required to give the IRS the details of the conversion with her 2005 return and provide a description of the replacement property when it is completed. The basis in the replacement property is $170,000 (cost of $280,000 − the gain not recognized of $110,000).

Amount realized.	$ 240,000
Less: Adjusted basis.	(130,000)
Gain (loss) realized	$ 110,000
Amount realized.	$ 240,000
Less: Cost of replacement property	(280,000)
Gain recognized (not to exceed gain realized).	None
Cost of replacement property.	$ 280,000
Less: Gain not recognized	(110,000)
Adjusted basis of replacement property	$ 170,000

Example 31. Assume the same facts as in *Example 30*, except that M reinvested $200,000. In this case she would be required to recognize a gain since she did not reinvest all of the insurance proceeds of $240,000. As a result, her recognized gain would be $40,000 and her basis in the replacement property would be $130,000, calculated as follows:

Amount realized.	$ 240,000
Less: Cost of replacement property	− 200,000
Gain recognized (not to exceed gain realized).	$ 40,000
Cost of replacement property.	$ 200,000
Less: Gain not recognized ($110,000 − $40,000).	−70,000
Adjusted basis of replacement property.	$ 130,000

Interaction of §§ 121 and 1033. When a taxpayer who has made a § 121 election has a gain greater than the maximum that may be excluded, then he or she may be able to defer the amount of excess gain by using § 1033 (involuntary conversions). In this situation, the amount realized for purposes of § 1033 is *reduced* by the gain excluded under § 121. This reduces the amount that must be reinvested in order to defer any remaining gain.[65]

Example 32. D's principal residence that he had owned and occupied for 22 years was involuntarily converted for $476,000 during the current year. D, an unmarried individual, had purchased the residence for $86,000. Six months after the sale, D located and purchased a smaller home for $260,000.

The interaction between the § 121 exclusion and § 1033 can be seen in the following calculations.

Amount realized on involuntary conversion	$ 476,000
Less: Adjusted basis.	−86,000
Gain (loss) realized	$ 390,000
Gain realized	$ 390,000
Less: § 121 exclusion	−250,000
Remaining gain realized	$ 140,000
Amount realized.	$ 476,000
Less: § 121 exclusion	−250,000
New amount realized for § 1033	$226,000
New amount realized for § 1033	$ 226,000
Less: Cost of replacement residence	−260,000
Gain recognized (if greater than zero)	$ None
Cost of replacement residence	$ 260,000
Less: Gain not recognized under § 1033	−140,000
Adjusted basis of new residence	$ 120,000

---

[65] § 121(d)(7).

In this case D receives the best of all possible treatments. He has his exclusion and defers his gain too! The end result is that none of his $390,000 is gain recognized. Note that when D takes advantage of the exclusion, the computations for § 1033 simply treat D as if he had never received the amount excluded (i.e., $250,000). In this case, the effect is to reduce both the gain realized and the adjusted sales price by $250,000. Consequently, D must reinvest $250,000 less in order to exclude the entire gain.

Example 33. Assume the same facts as in *Example 32*. Had D reinvested only $210,000 (instead of $260,000), he would be required to recognize a $16,000 gain and his basis in the new residence would be $86,000, computed as follows:

New amount realized from § 1033	$ 226,000
Less: Cost of replacement residence	−210,000
Gain recognized	$ 16,000
Cost of replacement residence	$ 210,000
Less: Gain not recognized under § 1033	
($390,000 − $250,000 − $16,000)	−124,000
Adjusted basis of new residence	$ 86,000

The end result is that D reports only $16,000 of the total $390,000 gain.

✓ CHECK YOUR KNOWLEDGE

Over the last several years, Rock and Roller Blades Inc. opened two new roller skating rinks to capitalize on the in-line skating craze. In February 2005, however, one of the rinks was destroyed by fire. At that time, the building had a basis of $300,000. The insurance proceeds awarded to the company amounted to $360,000.

Review Question 1. If the corporation uses the insurance proceeds to build a new indoor soccer facility, will the soccer facility be considered qualified replacement property?

Probably not. In order to qualify for deferral, the replacement property must be similar to or related in service or use to the converted property. This generally means that the replacement property must provide the same functional use as the converted property. Based on the IRS ruling that a billiard parlor is not functionally equivalent to a bowling alley, it would appear that a soccer facility does not provide the same services as a roller rink.

Review Question 2. By what date must the calendar year corporation invest in qualified replacement property?

The corporation must reinvest by the close of the second taxable year following the year in which the conversion takes place, in this case December 31, 2007.

Review Question 3. Assuming the corporation immediately erects another roller rink at the cost of $390,000 and elects to defer any gain realized, the company's gain (or loss) recognized will be

    a. $60,000
    b. $30,000
    c. $90,000
    d. $0

  e. $30,000 loss

  f. None of the above

The answer is (d). As shown in the following computations, the corporation is allowed to defer the entire gain realized since it reinvested all of the insurance proceeds.

Amount realized..	$ 360,000
Less: Adjusted basis....................................	−300,000
Gain (loss) realized	$ 60,000
Amount realized..	$ 360,000
Less: Cost of replacement property	−390,000
Gain recognized (not to exceed gain realized)....................	None

  Review Question 4. Same facts as in Question 3 The basis of the replacement property is

  a. $300,000

  b. $390,000

  c. $370,000

  d. $0

  e. $360,000

  f. None of the above

The answer is (f). The basis is $330,000, determined as follows:

Cost of replacement property.....................................	$ 390,000
Less: Gain not recognized	−60,000
Adjusted basis of replacement property..........................	$ 330,000

LIKE-KIND EXCHANGES

  Section 1031 of the Code provides that a taxpayer may exchange certain types of property *in kind* without the recognition of a taxable gain or loss. Specifically, no gain or loss is recognized when qualifying property is exchanged *solely* for other qualifying property that is of like-kind.

  Example 34. E traded in his 2001 automobile that was worth $4,500 and was used entirely for business purposes and also paid $15,000 cash for a new auto worth $19,500. E's basis in the old auto was $8,200, based on an original cost of $16,000 less depreciation of $7,800. E recognizes no gain or loss on the transaction since it is a qualifying like-kind exchange. His basis in the new auto is $23,200 ($8,200 basis of trade-in + $15,000 cash paid).

  If property other than like-kind property—commonly called *boot*—is received in the exchange, a gain may be recognized.[66] Losses, however, are never recognized.

---

[66] § 1031(b).

In order for a transaction to qualify as a nontaxable exchange, it must meet four separate requirements:

1. Both the property exchanged and the property received must be held for business or investment purpose.

2. Both the items exchanged and received must not be specifically excluded from §1031 treatment.

3. The property is like-kind.

4. There must be an exchange.

Each of these requirements are discussed below.

QUALIFIED PROPERTY

Holding Purpose. In order to qualify for like-kind exchange treatment, a property must be held *either* for use in a trade or business *or* for investment. A qualified exchange may, however, involve the transfer of investment property for trade or business property, or vice versa.[67] No personal use properties qualify.

It is important to note that it is the taxpayer's purpose for holding that is critical. The purposes or plans of the other party to the exchange are irrelevant. For example, if the taxpayer held the property exchanged for business or investment, the taxpayer has met the holding-purpose requirement even if the other party plans to sell the property, has a contract to sell it before the exchange, or is helped by the taxpayer in finding a buyer.

Excluded Properties. Certain properties are specifically excluded from like-kind exchange treatment. These are:[68]

- Inventory or other property held primarily for sale
- Stocks, bonds, or notes
- Other securities or evidences of indebtedness
- Partnership interests
- Interest in trusts (e.g., the beneficiary's interest)
- Livestock of different sexes

Whether an item is inventory (i.e., held primarily for sale to customers in the ordinary course of a trade or business) is discussed in Chapter 16. Several courts have interpreted the phrase *held for sale* to include any property that is acquired in an exchange only to be resold shortly thereafter.[69]

Example 35. K exchanged a parcel of real estate held for investment for another parcel and immediately offered the parcel received for sale. The parcel was sold on the installment basis. Since K held the new property for sale rather than for use in a trade or business or for investment, the entire gain realized on the exchange must be recognized at the time of the exchange.

LIKE-KIND PROPERTY

The term like-kind is not defined in the Code. However, the Regulations provide that "the words like-kind have reference to the nature or character of the property and not to its

---

[67]   Reg. § 1.1031(a)-1(a).

[68]   § 1031(a)(2).

[69]   *Ethel Black*, 35 T.C. 90 (1960); *George M. Bernard*, 26 TCM 858, T.C. Memo. 1967-176.

grade or quality."[70] This interpretation has been applied to allow exchanges of realty for realty and personalty for personalty. Exchanges of realty for personal property (nonrealty) or vice versa, are not considered exchanges of like-kind property and are fully taxable.

Real Estate. Generally, any exchange of realty for realty will meet the like-kind test. It is immaterial whether the real property is improved or unimproved.[71] No distinction is made between improved or unimproved, productive or unproductive, or similar differences since these relate to the grade or quality of the property and are to be specifically ignored. The IRS has ruled that a lease of real property with a remaining term of at least 30 years will be treated as real property for purposes of determining whether a like-kind exchange has occurred.[72] Accordingly, a realized loss from the exchange of property that had declined in value for a lease interest in that property with a life of 30 years or more resulted in a nondeductible (nonrecognized) loss.[73] Recall that condemned real estate in an involuntary conversion is also subject to the like-kind test.

Tangible Depreciable Personalty. In determining the meaning of "like-kind" for personalty, the IRS, with some support, has adopted a much narrower interpretation than its view toward realty.[74] This stems from the fact that personalty includes a far greater variety of assets than realty. From the Service's perspective, adoption of a lenient "like-kind" test for personalty would enable exchanges that violate the spirit of § 1031 (e.g., a car for a horse, a railroad boxcar for an airplane). As noted earlier, deferral is granted on the theory that the taxpayer's economic position has not changed sufficiently to warrant taxation. In the government's opinion, this principle would be seriously undermined if taxpayers were permitted to exchange any type of personalty. Thus, a restrictive approach is understandable. Unfortunately, this approach (i.e., determining whether replacement property represents a continuing interest or a conversion to a wholly new endeavor) is very subjective and difficult to implement.

Notwithstanding support for its position, the IRS became concerned about what it believed could be endless debate over what personalty was like-kind. Consequently, the government issued new Regulations in 1991.[75] These Regulations put taxpayers on alert that the government would continue to take its narrow view of whether one item of personalty is considered the equivalent of another, but, at the same time, offered safe harbors that would provide the taxpayer with some certainty.

Under the current Regulations, personal property qualifies for § 1031 treatment if the properties are either:

1. like-kind or

2. like-class.

---

[70] Reg. § 1.1031(a)(1)(A).

[71] Reg. § 1.1031(a)-1(b). It is also important to note that § 1250 may supersede § 1031 and cause the recognition of gain. Effectively, § 1250 property (generally depreciable realty) must be acquired in an amount at least as great as the § 1250 recapture potential—§ 1250(d)(4)(C). See Chapter 17 for a discussion of § 1250 recapture of depreciation.

[72] Rev. Rul. 76-301, 1976-2 C.B. 241.

[73] *Century Electric Co. v. Comm.*, 51-2 USTC ¶9482, 41 AFTR 205, 192 F.2d 155 (CA-8, 1951).

[74] In *California Federal Life Insurance Co.*, 50 AFTR 2d 82-5271, 680 F2d 85, 82-2 USTC ¶9464 (CA-9, 1982), aff'g 76 TC 107 (1981) the courts upheld the government's argument that Swiss francs and U.S. double-eagle gold coins were not like-kind. In explaining its holding, the Ninth Circuit noted that it was Congressional concern for lenient interpretation of the like-kind standard that prompted it to amend § 1031 to say that livestock of different sexes are not like-kind. According to the Ninth Circuit, in so acting, Congress was suggesting that personal property was to be accorded different treatment.

[75] Reg. § 1.1031(a)-2(b)(1).

The definition of "like-kind" remains the same, nebulous as it may be. In contrast, the *like-class* definition offers a more practical approach to determine if properties have the requisite similarity. The like-class definition utilizes a two class system: (1) General Asset Classes and (2) Product Classes. If the properties are within the same General Asset Class or the same Product Class, they are considered like-class and, therefore, like-kind for § 1031 purposes. Note that if the properties meet the like-class standard, they are considered like-kind regardless of whether the exchanged properties would be considered like-kind under general § 1031 standards. The like-class system is significant in that it provides taxpayers the certainty they need before engaging in a transaction. This is particularly true given the absence of authority on like-kind characterizations for personal property.

The General Asset Classes are identified and defined in Revenue Procedure 87-56. There are 13 classes of assets, as shown in Exhibit 15-3. If two assets fall in the same class, they are considered like-class. For instance, a computer, printer, monitor, and modem used in a trade or business would qualify as like-class properties since they are all part of the information systems class (General Asset Class .12). Note that these classes are quite narrow. For example, an automobile and a light-duty truck would not be considered like-class since they are not in the same Class. Recall, however, that these classes serve only as safe harbors in which taxpayers have guaranteed like-kind treatment.[76]

If a General Asset Class is not provided for a particular asset, the Product Classes are to be used to determine if the exchanged properties are like-class. Observe that it is possible—but not likely—that the properties may be in two different General Asset Classes but in the same Product Class. In such case, the items are not like-class since the Product Classes cannot be used if the properties can be found in the General Asset Classes which were designed by the government.

Assets are within the same Product Class if they have the same four-digit product code as listed in the *North American Industrial Classification System* (NAICS) *Manual* published by the Department of Commerce.

EXHIBIT 15-3
General Asset Classes: Revenue Procedure 87-56

	Asset Class	Class Number
1.	Office furniture, fixtures, and equipment	.11
2.	Information systems (computers and peripheral equipment)	.12
3.	Data handling equipment, except computers	.13
4.	Airplanes and helicopters (airframes and engines), except those used in commercial or contract carrying of passengers or freight	.21
5.	Automobiles, taxis	.22
6.	Buses	.23
7.	Light general-purpose trucks	.241
8.	Heavy general-purpose trucks	.242
9.	Railroad cars and locomotives	.25
10.	Tractor units for use over the road	.26
11.	Trailers and trailer-mounted containers	.27
12.	Vessels, barges, tugs, and similar water-transportation equipment, except those used in marine construction	.28
13.	Industrial steam and electric generation and/or distribution systems	.4

As noted above, if the property does not qualify as like-class under the safe harbors created by the Regulations, it may still be treated as like-kind. The IRS historically has allowed like-kind exchange treatment for personal property when the properties were

---

[76] PLR 200450005 provides that sport utility vehicles (SUVs) and passenger automobiles are like-kind. Note, however, that for depreciation purposes heavy SUVs are not subject to the depreciation limitations applicable to passenger automobiles under § 280F.

substantially the same. The courts have ruled that livestock used in a trade or business, but not held for sale, may qualify as like-kind. However, the Code does explain that livestock of different sexes are not like-kind.[77] While it may be obvious that a bull is not a cow, the treatment of bullion-type coins (e.g., decorative gold coins) has created a great deal of controversy. For some investors, collecting and trading gold and silver coins is a popular investment strategy. The IRS has ruled that an exchange of gold bullion held for investment for silver bullion held for the same purpose is not a like-kind exchange since gold and silver are intrinsically different minerals.[78] On the other hand, bullion-type coins of different countries constitute like-kind property.[79] Currency exchanges are not like-kind exchanges. Similarly, legal tender coins (currency) are not of like-kind with bullion-type noncurrency coins.[80]

Intangibles. The like-class rules apply only to tangible depreciable personalty. There are no like classes for intangible personal property. Whether intangibles such as patents and copyrights are like-kind depends on the nature of the property to which the rights relate. For example, copyrights on two novels are like-kind; but a copyright on a novel and a copyright on a song are not like-kind.[81] Similarly, the IRS has ruled that the contracts of professional athletes are like-kind.

Multiple Property Exchanges. In some cases an exchange may involve more than one property. When this occurs, as in an exchange of one business for another, the Regulations provide a somewhat complex set of rules. The effect of these rules is that the various assets are matched with those of the same kind or class. Note that if two businesses are exchanged, the IRS guidelines provide that the goodwill and going concern values of similar businesses are not considered like-kind properties."[82]

Property Outside the United States. Generally, real property located outside the U.S. is not like-kind with respect to real property located within the U.S. Similarly, personal property used predominately outside the U.S. is not like-kind with respect to personalty used predominantly within the U.S. In determining where property is predominately used, the two years before the exchange are considered for the property given up and the two years after the exchange are considered for the property received.[83]

RECEIPT OF PROPERTY NOT OF A LIKE-KIND (BOOT)

As a general rule, an exchange is nontaxable only if property is exchanged *solely* for like-kind property. But in many cases, taxpayers wanting to make an exchange do not have like-kind property of equal values. Consequently, one of the parties typically throws in cash or some other non-like-kind property—commonly called *boot*—to equalize the values exchanged. Fortunately, the receipt of boot does not totally disqualify the transaction. Instead, § 1031(b) provides that the taxpayer must recognize any gain realized to the extent of any boot received. For these purposes, *boot* includes

---

[77] § 1031(e). Apparently, if male calves could be exchanged for female calves, a breeding herd of females could be built up more quickly and sold for capital gain treatment.

[78] Rev. Rul. 82-166, 1982-2 C.B. 190.

[79] Rev. Rul. 76-214, 1976-1 C.B. 218.

[80] Rev. Rul. 79-143, 1979-1 C.B. 264; *California Federal Life Insurance Co. v. Comm.*, 82-2 USTC ¶9464, 50 AFTR2d 82-5271, 680 F.2d 85 (CA-9, 1982), aff'g. 76 T.C. 107 (1981). It is interesting that the Revenue Ruling states that U.S. gold coins are currency, while the courts in these cases state that they are more like "other property" than "money."

[81] Reg. § 1.1031(a)-2(c)(3), *Examples 1* and 2.

[82] Reg. § 1.1031(a)-2(c)(2).

[83] § 1031(h).

any money received in the exchange *plus* the fair market value of any property that is either nonqualified or not like-kind. Under § 1031(c), the receipt of boot does not cause the recognition of any realized losses in such an exchange.[84]

> **Example 36.** J transferred a vacant lot held as an investment and worth $8,000 to another party in exchange for a similar lot worth $6,000. J received $2,000 cash in addition to the new lot. J's basis in her old lot was $5,500. J's realized gain is $2,500 ($8,000 amount realized − $5,500 basis). If she holds the new lot as an investment, J still must recognize gain on this exchange in the amount of $2,000 because she received *cash boot* of $2,000.

> **Example 37.** If J's basis in the property given up in the prior example had been $6,500, her realized gain would have been $1,500 ($8,000 amount realized − $6,500 basis). Although she received $2,000 of boot, J's recognized gain is $1,500 (recognized gain is *never* more than the realized gain).

> **Example 38.** If J's basis in the vacant lot exchanged in the previous two examples had been $9,000, she would have a realized loss of $1,000 and a recognized loss of zero. Losses in like-kind exchanges are never recognized.

Liabilities as Boot. In many exchanges, a taxpayer transfers property encumbered by indebtedness (e.g., land subject to a mortgage) or has liabilities assumed as part of the exchange agreement. When a taxpayer is relieved of a liability, the tax law takes the view that such relief is the economic equivalent of receiving cash and paying off the liability. In essence, the party assuming the liability is treated as having paid cash for the property. Consistent with this view, any liabilities from which the taxpayer is relieved in a like-kind exchange are treated as boot received (or boot paid in the case of the party assuming the debt).[85] Note that without these rules, taxpayers could mortgage property shortly before the exchange, receive cash, and then transfer the property along with liability without having to recognize any gain. The treatment of liability relief as boot thwarts such plans.

> **Example 39.** Wanting to move his business out of the city, R exchanged his downtown warehouse encumbered by a mortgage of $200,000 for a new suburban building worth $700,000. R's basis in the warehouse was $600,000. As a result, R realized a gain of $300,000 ($700,000 + $200,000 − $600,000). Although R received only the building, the relief of the $200,000 liability is treated as boot received. Therefore, R must recognize a gain of $200,000.

Relief and Assumption of Liabilities. If both parties to the exchange assume a liability (e.g., the taxpayer is relieved of a liability of $100,000 but also incurs a liability of $90,000), the process becomes a bit more confusing. In this case, the taxpayer first nets the assumption and the relief. If the taxpayer has net relief (i.e., net decrease in liabilities), such amount is treated as boot received, which in turn may trigger gain recognition.[86] If the taxpayer has net incurred (i.e., net increase in liabilities), such amount is treated as boot paid and no gain is recognized. Note that liabilities are the only type of boot paid or received that can be netted. Other types of boot are not netted. But what if a taxpayer receives cash and incurs liabilities? Can the taxpayer offset any

---

[84]   If a note is received as boot, the gain may be reported using the installment sales rules. See § 453(h)(6) and (7).

[85]   § 1031(d).

[86]   See Reg. §§ 1.1031(b)-1(c) and 1.1031(d)-2. It is important to note that liabilities incurred in anticipation of a like-kind exchange will not qualify for this netting treatment. See Prop. Reg. § 1.1031(b)-1(c).

cash received (and the gain that goes with it) by any liabilities incurred? And what if a taxpayer is relieved of liabilities? Can the taxpayer offset any liability relief by giving cash? The Regulations have addressed these possibilities. A taxpayer cannot offset boot received by liabilities incurred. However, liability relief can be offset by boot given (since the taxpayer could presumably pay off the debt with the boot, thereby reducing the liability relief).[87] These various situations are addressed in the next three examples.

Example 40. S exchanged a tractor worth $11,000 for a lighter duty tractor worth $9,000, both held for use in his landscaping business. The tractor given up was subject to a secured obligation of $8,000 and S incurred a liability secured by the new tractor of $6,000. S's basis in the tractor given up was $6,500, his cost of $13,500 less depreciation allowed of $7,000. S's realized gain on this exchange is $4,500, computed as follows:

Fair market value of property received............................	$ 9,000
Plus: Liabilities encumbering the property transferred	+8,000
Less: Liabilities assumed by tax payer	−6,000
Amount realized...	$ 11,000
Less: Adjusted basis of property given up	−6,500
Gain realized	$ 4,500

S's recognized gain is $2,000 since his net liability relief ($8,000 liability relief − $6,000 liability assumed) is treated as boot.

Example 41. Use the facts in *Example 40*, but assume that instead of receiving a $9,000 tractor and incurring a $6,000 liability, S received a tractor worth $7,500 and paid $4,500 cash. S's realized gain is $4,500 computed as follows:

Fair market value of property received............................	$ 7,500
Plus: Liabilities encumbering the property transferred	+8,000
Less: Amount of money given up	−4,500
Amount realized...	$ 11,000
Less: Adjusted basis of property given up	−6,500
Gain realized	$ 4,500

S's recognized gain is $3,500, the amount of his liability relief ($8,000) less the other boot paid ($4,500 cash).

Example 42. If S had received a tractor worth $3,000 and incurred no liabilities and paid no cash in the transaction, his realized gain is still $4,500, computed as follows:

Fair market value of property received............................	$ 3,000
Plus: Liabilities encumbering the property transferred	+8,000
Amount realized...	$ 11,000
Less: Adjusted basis of property given up	−6,500
Gain realized	$ 4,500

---

[87] Reg. 1.1031(d)-2, Ex. 2.

The amount of boot received is $8,000, the amount of his liability relief. The recognized gain is $4,500, since the gain is recognized to the extent of boot received, but never more than the gain realized.

BASIS IN PROPERTY RECEIVED

Exhibit 15-4 presents two ways of computing the basis of property received in a like-kind exchange. The first method (Method 1), prescribed by the Code, is based on the notion that the like-kind property received in the exchange is merely a continuation of the taxpayer's investment in the like-kind property given up. Thus, the basis of the property received should be the same as the property given up—a so-called *substituted* basis. This basis is *increased* by any gain recognized and by any additional consideration given or to be paid in the future, or *decreased* by the fair market value of any boot received and by any liabilities transferred.[88] The second method is derived from the basis determination method used for replacement property in involuntary conversions and sales of principal residences. Under this method, the fair market value of the like-kind property received (i.e., its cost if purchased) is *reduced* by a deferred gain or *increased* by deferred loss in determining its basis. This adjustment is made so that if the newly acquired property is later sold, any realized gain or loss that is not recognized (deferred amount) from the previous like-kind exchange will be automatically considered in the computation of the realized gain or loss. Under either method, the basis of any boot received is its fair market value.

EXHIBIT 15-4
Basis of Property Received in a Like-Kind Exchange

Method 1:

Adjusted basis of property given up.			$xxx,xxx
Plus:	Gain recognized	$xx,xxx	
	Boot paid	x,xxx	
	Liabilities assumed by the taxpayer	xx,xxx	
	Liabilities encumbering the property received.	xx,xxx	+xx,xxx
			$xxx,xxx
Less:	Boot received	$xx,xxx	
	Liabilities assumed by the other party (transferee)	xx,xxx	
	Liabilities encumbering the property transferred	xx,xxx	−xx,xxx
Basis of property received			$xxx,xxx

Method 2:

Fair market value of like-kind property received.		$xxx,xxx
Less:	Deferred gain (realized gain − recognized gain).	−xx,xxx
Plus:	Realized loss (deferred)	+xx,xxx
Basis of property received		$xxx,xxx

Example 43. J operates a charter flight business out of Ft. Lauderdale. This year he put together a deal with one of his flying buddies whereby he traded his old plane,

---

[88] § 1031(d).

with a basis of $40,000, for another smaller plane worth $53,000 and a hangar to park it in, worth $7,000. J's realized gain is $20,000 [($53,000 + $7,000 = $60,000) − $40,000]. Since the hangar is realty, it is treated as boot. Thus, J must recognize a gain of $7,000 (lesser of the gain realized or boot received). The basis of the boot received, the hangar, is its fair market value of $7,000. J's basis in the new plane is $40,000, computed as follows:

Method 1:

Adjusted basis of property given up.	$ 40,000
Plus: gain recognized.	7,000
Less: boot received	−7,000
Basis of property received	$ 40,000

Method 2:

Fair market value of like-kind property received.	$ 53,000
Less: Deferred gain ($20,000 − $7,000)	−13,000
Basis of property received	$ 40,000

At first glance, the basis calculations may not make sense. In the substituted basis computation, the basis of the new property is initially the same as the property given up, $40,000. However, any gain recognized, in this case $7,000, must be added to ensure that upon subsequent sale of the property such gain is not taxed again. The sum of these two amounts ($40,000 + $7,000 = $47,000) represents the basis for the like-kind property and the boot received. A portion of this total is then allocated to the boot by subtracting the value of the boot, $7,000. In effect, the basis assigned to the boot is its $7,000 value, leaving the remaining $40,000 to be assigned to the like-kind property. Note how a subsequent sale of the like-kind property for its $53,000 value would cause the taxpayer to recognize the previously postponed gain of $13,000 ($53,000 − $40,000). This same result is accomplished in a much more obvious manner in the second calculation, where the deferred gain is simply subtracted from the value of the property. The following example is a comprehensive review of the like-kind exchange rules.

Example 44. E exchanged a rental house for T's rental condominium. E's house was worth $36,000 and her adjusted basis was $27,000. The house was not subject to any liabilities. T's condominium was worth $82,000 and was subject to a mortgage of $54,000. T also transferred $8,000 worth of Alpha Corp. stock to E in order to equalize the transaction. T's adjusted basis in his condominium and the Alpha stock were $64,000 and $5,600, respectively. The gains realized by E and T are computed as follows:

E

Fair market value of property received	
Rental condominium (like-kind property)...............	$ 82,000
Alpha Corp. stock (boot received)................	+8,000
	$ 90,000
Less: Liabilities (mortgage) assumed by taxpayer	−54,000
Amount realized...........................	$ 36,000
Less: Adjusted basis of rent house given up.................	−27,000
Gain realized	$ 9,000

T

Fair market value of rental house received		$ 36,000
Plus: Liabilities discharged (assumed by E)		+54,000
Amount realized...........................		$ 90,000
Less: Adjusted basis of properties given up:		
Rental condominium..........................	$64,000	
Alpha Corp. stock (boot paid)	5,600	−69,600
Gain realized		$ 20,400

E's gain recognized is $8,000, the amount of boot (stock) received. The amount of boot received by T is $54,000 (the amount of liabilities discharged), which is reduced by his boot paid of $8,000 (fair market value of Alpha stock). Therefore, T's net liabilities discharged are $46,000. T's recognized gain, however, is $20,400, since recognized gain never exceeds realized gain. T's recognized gain consists of $2,400 ($8,000 fair market value − $5,600 basis) for the taxable exchange of the Alpha stock, and the remaining $18,000 is attributable to the exchange of his house.

E and T's bases in their like-kind property received are determined as follows:

		E's Condominium	T's House
Adjusted basis of like-kind property given up...............		$ 27,000	$ 64,000
Plus:	Gain recognized........................	+8,000	+20,400
	Boot paid	+0	+5,600
	Liabilities assumed......................	+54,000	+0
Less:	Boot received.........................	−8,000	−0
	Liabilities discharged	−0	−54,000
Basis of property received		$ 81,000	$ 36,000

E's basis in the Alpha Corp. stock is $8,000, its fair market value.[89] E and T could have computed their bases in the like-kind property received by using the alternative method (Method 2) discussed previously.

---

[89]   Reg. §§ 1.1031(d)-1(c) and 1.1031(d)-1(d).

	E	T
Fair market value of like-kind property received:		
Rental house..........................		$ 36,000
Rental condominium.....................	$ 82,000	
Less: Deferred gain	−1,000	−0
Basis of like-kind property received	$ 81,000	$ 36,000

EXCHANGE REQUIREMENT

Generally, the determination of whether an exchange has occurred is not difficult. All that is required is a reciprocal transfer of qualifying properties. An exchange of one real estate investment for another would normally qualify. Similarly, a trade-in of a business auto along with some cash for another auto is a qualifying exchange. However, an argument can be made for collapsing seemingly independent transactions that might appear to be an exchange in substance.[90]

Example 45. B, a traveling salesperson, "sold" his business auto to a car dealership for $3,200 cash. Shortly thereafter, he purchased another auto from the same dealer for $12,000 cash. The IRS could collapse the *two* transactions (sale and purchase) between the same parties in *one* like-kind exchange. Thus, if B's basis in the old vehicle was $6,000, his loss would be disallowed, and his basis in the new auto would be $14,800 ($12,000 fair market value of new auto + $2,800 deferred loss).

Three-Corner Exchanges. It is not always easy for two parties with properties of equal value, both of which are suitable to the other party, to get together. Even so, it may be possible for a taxpayer who cannot find an exchange partner to qualify for like-kind treatment through a three-corner exchange.

Several forms of multiple-party exchanges have qualified for like-kind exchange treatment. The IRS has ruled that when three property owners entered into an exchange in which each gave up and received qualifying property, like-kind exchange treatment was appropriate.[91] However, a three-corner exchange must be part of a single, integrated plan.[92]

Example 46. X, Y and Z each own rental property. They exchange the properties as follows:

X gets Y's property, Y gets Z's property, and Z gets X's property. X, Y, and Z pay or receive boot in order to equalize the difference in the values of the properties.

This three-party transaction qualifies as a like-kind exchange under §1031. Each party receiving boot must recognize gain up to the amount of the boot received.

Perhaps a more common situation involves a taxpayer who is willing to "sell" property but does not want to recognize gain. In this situation, the interested buyer purchases like-kind property identified by the "seller" and then exchanges it for the seller's property.

---

[90]   Rev. Rul. 61-119, 1961-1 C.B. 395.

[91]   Rev. Rul. 57-244, 1957-1 C.B. 247; Rev. Rul. 73-476, 1973-2 C.B. 300.

[92]   Rev. Rul. 75-291, 1975-2 C.B. 332; Rev. Rul. 77-297, 1977-2 C.B. 304.

Example 47. C owned rental property worth $70,000 (adjusted basis of $34,000), which she was willing to dispose of only if she could do so without recognizing any gain. B wanted to purchase C's property, but in order that C might defer her potential gain of $36,000, he agreed to purchase another rental property of equal value that was suitable to C. As long as she receives no boot, C would recognize no gain and her basis in the replacement property would be $34,000 ($70,000 fair market value of property received − $36,000 deferred gain). B will not qualify for § 1031 treatment since he purchased the property specifically for the exchange and thus never held it for business use or investment.[93] However, B will not have any realized gain or loss as a result of the transaction since his amount realized of $70,000 (fair market value of rental property received from C) is equal to his cost basis of the property given up.

Delayed Exchanges. The property to be accepted by the taxpayer in a like-kind exchange need not be received *simultaneously* with the transfer of his or her property. Delayed exchanges are popularly referred to as *Starker* exchanges, after a 1979 appellate case in which a taxpayer transferred significant real property in exchange for a promise by a corporation to deliver the replacement property over five years.[94] These exchanges qualify currently for tax deferral only if specific timing requirements are met. In order to qualify for nonrecognition treatment, the property to be acquired must be

1. Identified within 45 days after the date the taxpayer surrenders his or her property; and

2. Received within 180 days of the transfer, but no later than the due date (including extensions) of the tax return for the year of transfer.[95]

Example 48. R has agreed to purchase any real property worth $120,000 that is acceptable to S if S will immediately transfer his commercial parking lot, which is adjacent to R's store, to R. S agrees to the plan. S later identifies a duplex worth $120,000 and directs R to purchase it for him. This delayed exchange will qualify under § 1031 if the duplex is specified as the replacement property within 45 days and is transferred to S within 180 days of the transfer of the parking lot to R. Note how the taxpayer has effectively sold the property for $120,000 cash and then reinvested the cash without having to pay tax.

Delayed exchanges are frequently expedited by an escrow company that holds money that is to be used to purchase a property for the transferor. It is possible that a property would be identified within 45 days but, due to circumstances beyond the taxpayer's control, cannot be acquired. To prevent this misfortune, the taxpayer may identify one or more additional properties within the 45-day period to be acquired if the acquisition of the first property cannot be completed.[96]

Related-Party Exchanges. For many years, related parties used a clever device to reduce gain on the sale of appreciated property. At the heart of the scheme were the substituted basis rules applied in like-kind exchanges. These rules effectively enabled

---

[93] *Biggs v. Comm.*, 81-1 USTC ¶9114, 47 AFTR2d 81-484, 632 F.2d 1171 (CA-5, 1980).

[94] *Starker v. U.S.*, 79-2 USTC ¶9541, 44 AFTR 2d 79-5525, 602 F.2d 1341 (CA-9, 1979).

[95] § 1031(a)(3).

[96] Reg. § 1.1031(k)-1. Also see Rev. Proc. 2000-37, 2000 I.R.B. 40, where the IRS provides a safe harbor for exchanges that occur through an intermediary in a reverse order.

the taxpayer to create a high basis for what otherwise was low-basis property that the taxpayer planned to sell.

> **Example 49.** T owns all of the stock of D Corporation, which is planning to sell 100 acres of land for $700,000 (basis $100,000). Accordingly, D anticipates that it will recognize a gain of $600,000. To minimize the gain on the sale, however, T transfers one of his real estate investments worth $700,000 (basis $500,000) to the corporation in exchange for the land and subsequently sells the land. T's gain on the sale of the land is only $200,000 ($700,000 − $500,000) since the like-kind exchange rules enabled him to substitute the higher basis of his realty, $500,000, as the basis for the land.

To put an end to the so-called basis-swapping illustrated in *Example 49*, Congress created a special rule. If a taxpayer exchanges property with a *related party* and either taxpayer disposes of the transferred property within two years, the like-kind exchange rules do not apply to the original exchange and any deferred gain must be recognized in the year of the subsequent disposition.[97] For this purpose, the definition of a related party is the same as that used for the loss disallowance rules of §§ 267 and 707(b)(1), which generally includes the taxpayer's family (spouse, brothers, sisters, ancestors, lineal descendants) and certain entities (e.g., corporations and partnerships) in which the taxpayer owns more than a 50 percent interest.

> **Example 50.** Assume the same facts as in *Example 49* above. Under current law T's plan would not work since T and his corporation are considered related parties and he sold the property within two years of the exchange. As a result, both T and D must recognize their deferred gains on the original exchange in the year of the sale. T recognizes a gain of $200,000 ($700,000 − $500,000) and D recognizes a gain of $600,000 ($700,000 − $100,000). T recognizes no gain on the sale itself because his basis in the land is now treated as $700,000 since the original transaction became taxable. Note that T's plan would have worked had T been patient and sold the land more than two years after the exchange.

TREATMENT MANDATORY

Like-kind exchange treatment is mandatory. Therefore, no gain or loss is recognized on any transaction that meets the like-kind exchange requirements even if the taxpayer desires otherwise. Since the provision applies to losses as well as gains, like-kind treatment may work to the disadvantage of a taxpayer, and it may be to his or her benefit to avoid exchange status.

> **Example 51.** This year B swapped her rental property in Malibu worth $200,000 (basis $230,000) for rental property in Vail worth $175,000 and cash of $25,000. B has realized a loss of $30,000 ($200,000 − $230,000). Although she received boot of $25,000, none of the loss is recognized. In this case, B would probably be better off selling the Malibu property and purchasing the Vail property so that she could recognize her loss.

HOLDING PERIOD

The holding period of like-kind property received in a § 1031 exchange includes the holding period of the property given up on the exchange.[98] This also applies to the

---

[97] § 1031(f).

[98] § 1223(1).

holding period of replacement property in an involuntary conversion. However, the holding period of any property received as boot in a § 1031 exchange *begins* on the date of its receipt. In effect, when boot received is property other than money (or liability relief), it is treated as if the taxpayer received money (equal to the property's fair market value) and used it to purchase the property. Consequently, the property's holding period starts on the day of the exchange *and* the basis of the property is its fair market value.

✅ CHECK YOUR KNOWLEDGE

Review Question 1. This year H retired. He decided to continue to live in Chicago but wanted to get rid of his rental property (fair market value $240,000, basis $140,000) and buy a condominium in Florida. H is now entertaining an offer to sell the property to a real estate mogul who loves the property and is hot to buy. What would you advise?

Without good advice, most taxpayers would sell the property, recognize a $100,000 gain, and pay a capital gains tax of $25,000, leaving them with only $72,000 to invest. There is a much better approach. H is a perfect candidate for a delayed like-kind exchange. He could "sell" the property and have the buyer transfer the funds to an escrow agent, who would hold the money while H identifies the property in Florida he wants. He must do this within 45 days after the sale. As long as he closes on the new property within 180 days of the transfer (but no later than the due date of the return for the year of the transfer, including extensions), the like-kind exchange provisions will apply and H does not have to recognize the gain!

Review Question 2. At the outset of this chapter, it was indicated that there is a way to pyramid one's wealth to $1 million without ever having to pay tax. How could this be done?

The first step is to make wise investments (typically real estate). If the investor desires to sell after the property has appreciated, he or she may "sell" the property using the delayed like-kind exchange technique just as H did in the previous question. The effect is to invest in replacement property without having to pay any tax. If H can continue to invest successfully, he never has to pay tax along the way to $1 million (and beyond). Note that H does not necessarily have to find a property of equal value, assuming the amount escrowed is reinvested in like-kind property. As long as all of the cash is used and none passes to H, he does not recognize any gain. Thus, H could effectively use the property as a down payment for new property and use additional leverage to accelerate the process.

Note that the property must be qualifying property. Since like-kind exchange treatment does not apply to stocks and bonds, this scheme would not work with respect to stock market investments.

Review Question 3. True-False. This year D swapped her billiard parlor building for a bowling alley building. The transaction qualifies as a like-kind exchange.

True. Although the properties are not considered similar or related in use according to the functional use test applied to involuntary conversion rules, the two investments are considered like-kind property since they are both realty.

Review Question 4. True-False. During the year, E exchanged her personal residence for a rental house. The swap qualifies as a like-kind exchange.

False. The properties exchanged must be held for productive use or investment. In this case, E is not holding her home for investment, and therefore the exchange is taxable.

Review Question 5. True-False. Under the like-kind exchange rules, a taxpayer must receive cash before any gain realized is recognized.

False. Although this may appear to be true, the taxpayer is taxed whenever boot is received. Any property other than the like-kind property received is treated as boot. For example, the boot could take the form of stock, a note, or even liability relief.

Review Question 6. True-False. This year, F swapped her investment land for a friend's land and $10,000 of cash. As a result, F realized a $20,000 loss. F may recognize a loss of $10,000.

False. Losses are never recognized on a like-kind exchange even if the taxpayer receives boot.

Review Question 7. True-False. G sold her rental property in Galveston for $100,000 and realized a $25,000 gain. Two months later, she used the $100,000 plus an additional $50,000 to purchase another rental property on Padre Island for $150,000. G does not recognize gain since she has not liquidated her investment but continued it in another rental property.

False. Although G seems to have met the spirit of the law, there must, as a general rule, be a direct exchange in order to qualify for nonrecognition under the like-kind exchange provisions. Note that G could have postponed the gain had she taken advantage of the delayed like-kind exchange rules or had she simply had the buyer of her property buy the Padre Island property and then done an exchange.

Review Question 8. During the year, Fred traded one of his buddies a tractor used solely in his construction business for another tractor for the same use. On the date of the trade, the old tractor had an adjusted basis of $3,000. He received in exchange $500 in cash and a smaller tractor with a fair market value of $2,800. Fred should recognize a gain on the exchange of:

    a. $800
    b. $500
    c. $300
    d. $0
    e. None of the above

The answer is (c). Fred realized a gain of $300 [($2,800 + $500 = $3,300) − $3,000]. Since he received boot of $500, he must recognize the lesser of the gain realized, $300, or the boot received, $500.

Review Question 9. Assuming the same facts as above, the basis of the new tractor to Fred would be

    a. $3,300
    b. $3,000
    c. $2,800
    d. $2,300
    e. None of the above

The answer is (c), as determined below.

Method 1:

Adjusted basis of property given up..........................	$3,000
Plus: Gain recognized..................................	300
Less: Boot received	−500
Basis of property received	$2,800

Method 2:

Fair market value of like-kind property received..................	$2,800
Less: Deferred gain	−0
Basis of property received	$2,800

OTHER NONTAXABLE TRANSACTIONS

CHANGES IN FORM OF DOING BUSINESS

Several provisions in the Internal Revenue Code are intended to allow mere changes in the form of carrying on a continuing business activity without the recognition of gain or loss. Section 721, for example, allows the transfer of property to a partnership in exchange for a partnership interest without the recognition of taxable gain or loss. Section 351 allows a similar treatment when property is transferred to a corporation solely in exchange for its stock by persons possessing control, and § 355 provides for nontaxability in certain corporate reorganizations. These specific topics are addressed in subsequent chapters.

CERTAIN EXCHANGES OF STOCK IN SAME CORPORATION

No gain or loss is recognized by the shareholder who exchanges common stock for common stock or preferred stock for preferred stock in the same corporation under § 1036. The exchange may be voting stock for nonvoting stock, and it is immaterial whether the exchange is with another shareholder or with the issuing corporation.[99] If the exchange is not solely in kind, the rules of § 1031(b) (applicable to like-kind exchanges) are applied to determine the amount of any gain recognized.[100]

CERTAIN EXCHANGES OF U.S. OBLIGATIONS

Gain may be deferred in the case of certain exchanges of U.S. obligations between the taxpayer and the U.S. Government. Section 1037 applies to exchanges of bonds of the government issued under Chapter 31 of Title 31 (the Second Liberty Bond Act). The Treasury regulations for § 1037 discuss the application of this section.

REPOSSESSION OF REAL PROPERTY

Section 1038 provides that the seller of real property will recognize a gain on the repossession of real property only to the extent the sum of the money and other property besides the repossessed realty received exceeds the gain from the transaction previously

---

[99] Reg. § 1.1036-1(a).

[100] Reg. § 1.1036-1(b).

reported. This provision applies only to repossessions to satisfy debt obligations received in exchange for the sold property (e.g., foreclosure for nonpayment of mortgage). Such purchase-money obligations must be secured by an interest in the property. If any part of these obligations has previously been deducted as a bad debt, the amount of such deductions is included in income in the year of the repossession.

CERTAIN EXCHANGES OF INSURANCE POLICIES

Section 1035 allows the deferral of gain on the exchange of a life insurance contract for another insurance policy. Additionally, it allows certain exchanges involving annuity contracts and endowment contracts.

TAX PLANNING CONSIDERATIONS

CURRENT RECOGNITION VERSUS DEFERRAL

A basic concept in tax planning, as discussed in earlier chapters, is the deferral of tax payments. Each of the provisions discussed in this chapter (as it relates to gains) is a perfect example of such a deferral. A taxpayer is usually better off by deferring any gain—unless he or she expects to be in a much higher effective tax bracket in the later year when the deferred gain would be recognized. Of course, a taxpayer is *always* better off if he or she can avoid tax altogether, as is the case under § 121. However, if a loss is deferred under § 1031, taxes are accelerated. Thus, if the adjusted basis of business or investment property being disposed of exceeds its fair market value, the nonrecognition treatment of § 1031 should be avoided.

CURRENT GAIN RESULTING IN FUTURE REDUCTIONS

In each case of deferred gain, the mechanism is a reduced basis in the replacement property. If this replacement property is depreciable property, the depreciation deductions will also be smaller. It may be advantageous to report a large gain *currently* if the tax cost is low, and reap the benefit of the larger depreciation deductions in later years.

> **Example 52.** W plans to dispose of a building that would result in capital gain if sold, and acquire similar property in a different location. W could defer gain by arranging an exchange, but his basis in the new property would be low. W also has a large capital loss carryforward that he has been deducting at the rate of $3,000 per year.
> If W sells the property, the gain would offset the capital loss carryforward and he would pay no tax. His basis in the new building would be its cost, resulting in larger future depreciation deductions.

SECTION 121 CONSIDERATIONS

The § 121 exclusion presents numerous planning opportunities. The simplest is planning so as to meet the tests. For example, a taxpayer owning a rental property can move into that property, making it his or her principal residence for two years, and qualify to exclude the gain. Similarly, homeowners who are close to meeting the two year requirements can defer closing dates and move-out dates until after the time requirements are met.

Retirees who have moved out of their residence, but have been unable to sell it, may want to move back in after three years or so in order to keep from having the property no longer qualify under § 121. If they have been away for three years, they can still meet the two of five years test.

In another situation, the timing of a move into a retirement home can be planned so as to take maximum advantage of § 121. For example, an elderly person may want to delay moving into a retirement home until he or she has lived in their new home for a year. Then, they are deemed to have lived in the home for the period of time they are in the retirement home.

Many other planning opportunities may present themselves. For example, the $250,000 limit may present a problem in some markets. A homeowner who has accrued a $250,000 gain may want to sell his or her residence and purchase a new one. Then— $250,000 can be excluded on the first residence and any gain accruing with respect to its replacement can also be excluded. It is somewhat ironic that this limit might cause a taxpayer—who would not otherwise sell—to dispose of their residence.

IMPORTANCE OF CAPITAL BUDGETING IN DECISION MAKING

In any decision of whether to defer taxes when subsequent tax years are affected, capital budgeting techniques are appropriate in making the decision. When considering possible investment opportunities, a taxpayer must *compare* current investment requirements and tax effects with the future returns from the investment and their tax effects. Some form of present-value analysis will help the taxpayer to make a sound decision. A similar analysis should be applied in deciding the appropriateness of entering into any nontaxable (tax-deferred) transaction.

PROBLEM MATERIALS

DISCUSSION QUESTIONS

15-1 *Repair vs. Improvement.* H owned her personal residence for ten years before she had to incur a cost of $4,000 due to a leaking roof. Is this roof maintenance a nondeductible repair or a capitalized improvement? Explain.

15-2 *Principal Place of Residence.* V lived in Milwaukee and worked in Chicago for many years. Finally, V rented an apartment in Chicago, where she stayed on weeknights. Weekends and holidays were spent in Milwaukee. Where is V's *principal* place of residence for purposes of § 121?

15-3 *Section 121 Exclusion.* List the two principal requirements that must be met before one can qualify for the § 121 exclusion upon the sale of a residence.

15-4 *Limit on Amount of Exclusion.* What is the maximum amount of gain that can be excluded under § 121?

15-5 *Loss on Sale of Personal Assets.* Y sold his principal residence and realized a $12,000 loss. What is the proper tax treatment of this loss?

15-6 *Conversion of Residence.* Y purchased a property to be used as a rental on September 15, 1995. Y moved into this house on May 1, 2005 so it would qualify for the § 121 exclusion.
  a. Can the residence eventually qualify for the § 121 exclusion?
  b. If so, how long must Y live in it before the gain can qualify for the exclusion?
  c. Can the entire gain be excluded?

15-7   *Two of Five Years Test.* F sold her primary residence on June 2, 2004, and excluded her $22,500 gain. She purchased and moved into another primary residence on August 5, 2004. On what date can F first qualify for the § 121 exclusion with respect to the second residence?

15-8   *One Sale Every Two Years Rule.* G sold a qualifying residence on June 2, 2004, and excluded his $22,500 gain on his calendar year 2004 return. G had previously purchased and moved into another residence on December 7, 2003. On what date may G first qualify for the § 121 exclusion with respect to the second residence?

15-9   *Sale Due to Unanticipated Events.* S purchased her dream home on April 17, 2004 for $120,000. Then, much to her surprise, she was given a promotion and transferred by her employer. So she sold the home on January 2, 2005, for $170,000.

   a.   Does S qualify for the exclusion of gain under § 121?

   b.   If so, what is the maximum amount S can exclude?

   c.   If so, under what other circumstances might S be able to qualify for this partial exclusion?

15-10   *Marriage and § 121.* D gave E a one-half interest in D's home of 10 years as a wedding gift. E moved into the home after the wedding. Eighteen months later, on December 2, 2005, the residence was sold at a gain of $314,500. How much of the gain may be excluded by D and E on their joint return for 2005?

15-11   *Divorce and § 121.* F and G lived in a home that was F's separate property during the duration of their five-year marriage. Upon their divorce, G received title to the property. How much, if any, of the $200,000 gain may G exclude upon the sale of the house one year later on April 22, 2005?

15-12   *Death of a Spouse and § 121.* X and Y were married on November 14, 2005, after which Y moved into the home that had been owned and occupied by X for more than 30 years. Upon X's death, Y inherited the home that had cost $40,000 and was worth $300,000. How much gain must Y recognize when she sells the home one year after X's death for $315,000?

15-13   *Condemnation.* What is required in order to have "threat or imminence" of condemnation?

15-14   *Replacement Property under § 1033.* How does the concept of "similar or related in service or use" differ between an owner/user of property and an owner/lessor?

15-15   *Replacement Period.* B's beauty salon was destroyed by fire on April 21, 2005. The building was covered by current value insurance, and B realized a gain of $70,000. When must B reinvest in order to defer this gain under § 1033?

15-16   *Making the § 1033 Election.* How does a taxpayer elect to defer gain under § 1033 in involuntary conversions?

15-17   *Interaction of §§ 121 and 1033.* G and H had an amount realized of $800,000 and a gain of $520,000 in 2004 on the insurance recovery from the fire that totally destroyed their residence of ten years. How much must G and H reinvest to avoid recognizing any gain on their joint return for their calendar year 2005?

15-18   *Ineligible Property.* Property "held for sale" is not eligible for like-kind exchange treatment. Elaborate.

15-19   *Real Property under § 1031.* K proposes to exchange a downtown office building she holds as rental property for a 450-acre ranch in Virginia that she would operate as a horse ranch. Will this transaction qualify for like-kind exchange treatment?

15-20 *Personal Property under § 1031.* What constitutes personal property of "like-kind"?

15-21 *Boot.* What is the meaning of "boot" in § 1031 like-kind exchanges?

15-22 *Liabilities.* Are liabilities discharged always treated as boot received in a like-kind exchange under § 1031? Explain.

15-23 *Basis of Property Received.* How is the basis in the property received in a like-kind exchange under § 1031 determined? What is the basis in any boot received?

15-24 *§ 1031 Elective or Mandatory.* Is like-kind exchange treatment elective with the taxpayer? If not, how could such treatment be avoided if the taxpayer was so inclined?

15-25 *Holding Period.* In the current year, R received a rental house and 300 shares of IBM common stock in exchange for a vacant lot he had held as an investment since April 16, 2001. When does the holding period for the rental house begin? For the IBM stock?

PROBLEMS

15-26 *Calculation of Gain Realized.* M purchased a residence on May 1, 1989 for $195,000. M lived in the residence until June 1, 1996 and from December 1, 2002, until it was sold on May 6, 2005. In between, the property was rented. The following information was derived from M's records:

Purchase closing costs	$ 1,450
Depreciation claimed while the property was rented	22,250
Addition of family room (January 2003)	23,500
Painting of interior (April 2005)	4,200

The property sold for $289,000, and M incurred realtor's commissions of $16,340 and other closing costs of $2,300. The depreciation claimed after May 6, 1997 was $750.

   a. How much is M's basis in the residence at the time of the sale?

   b. How much is M's gain realized on the sale?

15-27 *Section 121 Exclusion.* P and Q, who are married, sold their residence of 19 years on February 12, 2005. The house had cost $120,000 and improvements of $22,000 had been made. The house sold for $750,000. Selling costs of $37,500 were incurred and deferred maintenance costs of $4,500 were paid weeks before the sale. P and Q have taxable income not including this gain of $50,000 on their joint return for the year.

   a. How much is P and Q's gain realized on this sale?

   b. How much of that gain, if any, must be recognized? How will it be taxed?

15-28 *Section 121 Exclusion.* C lived in a sail boat that had cost $225,000 and was usually kept in a slip at Sarasota for three years, but frequent long trips were undertaken. Various improvements costing $22,300 were made and repairs totaling $32,000 were made to the boat in order for it to be sold for $345,000. How is this sale treated on C's income tax return for the calendar year of sale?

15-29 *Section 121 Exclusion with Depreciation.* V owned a house that cost $200,000 in which she lived from July 1, 1992 until June 30, 2004. From July 1, 2004 until September 30, 2005, the home was rented, and depreciation of $8,000 was claimed. How will the sale of the residence for $325,000 on October 1, 2005 be treated?

15-30 *Limitation on Amount Excluded.* In each of the following situations, determine the maximum amount that may be excluded under § 121.

a. H and W sold their home on October 31, 2005. The home was owned as separate property and lived in by W for six years. H lived in the home since they were married three years ago.

b. K owned a rental property which she rented to J for several years. Upon marrying J on June 1, 2004, K moved into the house. The house was sold on August 1, 2005, and J and K file a joint return for 2005.

c. L, an unmarried individual, purchased and moved into a residence on March 15, 2004 for $650,000. One June 16, 2004, L sold the residence for $825,000 because she was transferred to a new work location.

15-31   *Sale of Principal Residence—Costs.* U received and accepted an offer to purchase her principal residence for $78,000 on March 12 and completed the sale on May 8 (all in the current year). She later purchased a replacement residence. Specify whether each of the following is properly classified as a nondeductible expense, a selling expense, an addition to the basis of the residence that was sold, or none of these.

a. New garage built during February of the current year at a cost of $12,500 because the city requires that every residence that is sold in the subdivision have a garage.

b. Real estate transfer taxes of $780 assessed by the city government.

c. Steam cleaning of carpets for $125 on April 22 and paid for upon completion.

d. Painting interior of residence completed and paid for in February.

e. Commissions of $4,680 paid to listing and selling real estate brokers.

15-32   *Sale Due to Unanticipated Events.* Q purchases a new residence on April 17, 2003 for $720,000. Upon receiving a very lucrative offer of employment, Q moved to another city and sold the residence on January 17, 2005, for $1,000,000. How much gain must Q recognize on this sale?

15-33   *Sale of Principal Residence.* During the current year, H and W ended their stormy marriage of 20 years. They had jointly owned a residence valued at $330,000 with a basis of $95,000. As part of their divorce settlement, H sold his interest in the home to W for $165,000. Assuming that there were no selling costs or fixing-up expenses, answer the following:

a. How much gain must H recognize?

b. What is W's basis in the residence?

15-34   *Involuntary Conversion.* The business office of K, a real estate broker, was destroyed by fire on August 22, 2004.

a. By what date must K reinvest to avoid recognizing gain from the insurance proceeds received as a result of the fire?

b. What type of property must K purchase to avoid recognition?

c. Would your answers differ if, rather than being destroyed by fire, the office building had been condemned by the state for highway right of way?

15-35   *Involuntary Conversion.* L owned a leased warehouse that was totally destroyed by fire on October 31, 2005. The building had a basis to L of $45,000 and his insurance paid the replacement cost of $75,000. L completed construction of a new warehouse on the same land on December 2, 2007 at a cost of $80,000.

a. How much gain must L recognize on this conversion?

b. What is L's basis in the replacement warehouse?

c. Summarize L's reporting requirements.

d. How would your answers to parts (a), (b), and (c) differ if L had invested only $65,000 in the replacement property?

15-36   *Involuntary Conversion.* Complete the following table involving certain involuntary conversions in which the taxpayer elects to defer gain. The property is converted into cash and the cash is invested in qualifying replacement property in each case. Each case is independent of the others.

Case	Amount Realized	Adjusted Basis	Amount Reinvested	Gain Recognized	Basis in Replacement
A	$3,000	$1,600	$1,200	$	$
B	3,000	1,300	1,400	$	$
C	6,000	4,000	5,500	$	$
D	7,500	3,400	7,900	$	$
E	8,400	9,000	8,700	$	$

15-37 *Involuntary Conversion Replacement Period.* For each of the following involuntary conversions, state the beginning date and the ending date of the permissible replacement period.

   a. The city of Lemon Tree announced plans to condemn D's rental property on March 15, 2004 and completed condemnation proceedings on June 12, 2005 for $330,000.

   b. Assume the same facts as in part (a), except that the property was D's principal residence.

   c. A fire destroyed G's bike shop on November 7, 2004. G received an insurance settlement on April 12, 2005.

15-38 *Involuntary Conversion—Condemned Real Estate.* The city of Orange Grove condemned T's automobile parts warehouse for use as a community park. Plans to condemn the property were announced on June 14, 2004, instituted on December 12, 2004, and completed on May 1, 2005. T's basis in the warehouse was $235,000, and the condemnation award was $366,000.

   a. Describe the type of property with which T must replace this warehouse in order to qualify for involuntary conversion treatment.

   b. Specify the reinvestment period during which T must reinvest in order to qualify for involuntary conversion treatment.

   c. Determine the amount of gain that T must recognize and T's basis in the replacement property, which costs $387,000.

15-39 *Involuntary Conversion—Destroyed Residence.* B's residence and contents were totally destroyed when a nearby gas main burst. The gas company paid B $90,000 for the building (with a basis of $65,000) and $35,000 for the contents as follows:

	Fair Value	Adjusted Basis
Clothing, personal effects	$10,000	$22,000
Furniture and fixtures.	8,000	16,500
Appliances, utensils, etc.	7,000	11,000
Art collection	10,000	4,500

   a. What requirements must be met for B to defer all of his gain under § 1033?

   b. How would your answer differ if the loss had been caused by a fire which was a Presidentially declared disaster and the payments were made by B's insurer (the art collection was not separately listed in the insurance policy)?

15-40 *Interaction of §§ 121 and 1033.* B's home was totally destroyed by fire on May 22, 2005. B, an unmarried individual, received $1,050,000 for the house which had cost $700,000 five years earlier.

   a. How much gain may B exclude under § 121?

    b. Can B defer the remaining gain, if any, under § 1033? If so, how much is the minimum amount that B must reinvest in order to exclude all of the gain?

    c. Assuming that B reinvests $760,000 in another personal residence, what is the amount of gain B must recognize and what is his basis in the replacement residence?

15-41 *Like-Kind Exchange.* F traded in an automobile that was used 100 percent of the time for business for a new auto for the same use. F had fully depreciated the old auto. The auto received was worth $12,000 and F paid $5,000 cash in addition to giving up her old auto.

    a. How much gain must F recognize on the trade-in?

    b. What is F's adjusted basis in the new auto?

15-42 *Like-Kind Exchange.* T transferred his farmland (100 percent business) to V in exchange for a parcel of unimproved urban real estate held by V as an investment. The farm was valued at $400,000 and was subject to a mortgage obligation of $260,000. T's basis in the farm was $340,000. The urban real estate was valued at $450,000 and was subject to a mortgage of $310,000.

    a. How much gain must T recognize on this exchange?

    b. What is T's basis in the urban real estate received?

15-43 *Like-Kind Exchange.* Refer to *Problem 15-42*. Assume that V had a basis of $360,000 in the urban real estate transferred to T.

    a. How much gain must V recognize on the exchange?

    b. What is V's basis in the farm property received?

15-44 *Like-Kind Exchange.* B exchanged undeveloped land worth $245,000 with C for developed land worth $225,000 and DEF corporation stock worth $20,000. B's adjusted basis in the land was $176,000. C's adjusted bases in the land and stock were $243,000 and $17,500, respectively.

    a. How much gain or loss must B recognize in this exchange, and what are his bases in the land and stock received?

    b. How much gain or loss must C recognize in this exchange, and what is her basis in the land received?

15-45 *Like-Kind Exchange.* F exchanged undeveloped land worth $45,000 with G for land worth $42,000 and a personal automobile worth $3,000. F's adjusted basis in the land was $36,000. G's adjusted bases in the land and automobile were $39,500 and $2,500, respectively.

    a. How much gain or loss must F recognize in this exchange, and what are his bases in the land and automobile received?

    b. How much gain or loss must G recognize in this exchange, and what is her basis in the land received?

15-46 *Like-Kind Exchange: Installment Reporting.* D entered into an agreement on December 15, 2004 under which he will immediately receive an apartment complex worth $300,000 and an installment obligation of the buyer for $200,000 with interest at 12 percent annually. D is to give up another apartment complex in which he has a basis of $320,000.

    a. What is the minimum gain that D must recognize on this exchange in 2004?

    b. How much gain must D report when he receives his first principal installment of $20,000 (plus accrued interest) in 2005?

15-47 *Like-Kind Exchanges.* Complete the following table for exchanges that qualify for like kind exchange treatment under § 1031.

Case	Adjusted Basis of Property Given Up	FMV of Property Received	Cash Boot Received	Cash Boot Paid	Gain or Loss Recognized	Basis of Property Received
A	$3,000	$2,500	$ 0	$ 0	$ ___	$ ___
B	5,000	5,000	0	1,000	$ ___	$ ___
C	4,000	6,000	1,000	0	$ ___	$ ___
D	7,000	5,900	600	0	$ ___	$ ___
E	5,000	4,000	2,500	0	$ ___	$ ___
F	3,000	3,200	200	0	$ ___	$ ___
G	4,000	3,600	500	0	$ ___	$ ___

RESEARCH PROBLEMS

15-48 *Exchange of Businesses.* T has owned and operated a taxi service (T's Taxi) for many years, but he now wishes to move to a new city. If T sells his business, he will have a substantial gain. Through a business broker, T has arranged to exchange his business for a limousine service (U's Limos) in the other city. In order to strike the deal, U insists that T sign a covenant-not-to-compete that U and T value at $25,000. The balance sheets (representing fair market values) of the two businesses are as follows:

	T's Taxi	U's Limos
Automobiles...............................	$700,000	$750,000
Computers and data handling equipment	60,000	30,000
Covenant-not-to-compete	25,000	
Goodwill................................	65,000	60,000
Totals...................................	$850,000	$840,000

In order to equalize the transaction, U will pay T $10,000 cash. T's bases are as follows: in the automobiles, $675,000; in the computers, etc., $65,000; and in the covenant and goodwill, $0. T has asked you to determine the tax effect of this proposed exchange before he completes it.

Chapter 16

PROPERTY TRANSACTIONS: CAPITAL GAINS AND LOSSES

LEARNING OBJECTIVES

Upon completion of this chapter you will be able to:

► Define a capital asset and use this definition to distinguish capital assets from other types of property

► Explain the holding period rules for classifying a capital asset transaction as either short-term or long-term

► Apply the capital gain and loss netting process to a taxpayer's capital asset transactions

► Understand the differences in tax treatment of an individual's capital gains and losses

► Explain the differences in tax treatment of the capital gains and losses of a corporate taxpayer versus those of an individual taxpayer

► Identify various transactions to which capital gain or loss treatment has been extended

► Discuss the tax treatment of investments in corporate bonds and other forms of indebtedness

CHAPTER OUTLINE

The final piece of the property transaction puzzle concerns the treatment of the taxpayer's gains and losses. In the infancy of the tax law, solving this puzzle was relatively easy. Taxpayers who sold or otherwise disposed of property needed only to determine their gain or loss realized and how much, if any, they had to recognize. The actual treatment of the gain or loss recognized—or more precisely, the rate at which it was taxed—was identical to that for other types of income. The simplicity of treating all income and loss the same was short-lived, however, lasting a mere eight years, from 1913 to 1921. Since 1921, the taxation of property transactions has been complicated by the additional need to determine not only the amount of the taxpayer's gain but also its character. Virtually all of this complication can be traced to one source: Congress's desire to provide some type of preferential treatment for capital gains.

Whether capital gains should be taxed more leniently than wages and other types of income is the subject of what seems to be a never-ending debate. When the first income tax statute was enacted, there was nothing in the definition of income to indicate that gains on dealings in property were taxable. Seizing on the omission, taxpayers relied on somewhat abstract tax theory and ingeniously argued that a gain on a sale of property (e.g., a citrus grove) was not the same as income derived from such property (e.g., sale of the fruit) and should not be taxed at all. Moreover, taxpayers who sold property and reinvested in similar property argued that they had not altered their economic position and that taxation was therefore not appropriate. While detractors cried "nonsense!" champions of favorable treatment offered additional justification, explaining that capital gain is often artificial, merely reflecting increases in the general price level. Perhaps the most defensible argument can be found in the Ways and Means Committee Report that accompanied the Revenue Act of 1921. As the following quotation shows, Congress believed that the progressive nature of the tax rates was unduly harsh on capital gains, particularly when the rate (at that time) could be as high as 77 percent.

> The sale of . . . capital assets is now seriously retarded by the fact that gains and profits earned over a series of years are under present law taxed as a lump sum (and the amount of surtax greatly enhanced thereby) in the year in which the profit is realized. Many of such sales . . . have been blocked by this feature of the present law. In order to permit such transactions to go forward without fear of a prohibitive tax, the proposed bill . . . adds a new section [providing a lower rate for gains from the sale or dispositions of capital assets].[1]

Although the top rate is currently much lower than it has been historically, the bunching effect is still cited as one of the major justifications for lower rates for capital gains. Proponents also reason that taxing capital gains at low rates encourages taxpayers to make riskier investments and also helps stimulate the economy by encouraging the mobility of capital. Without such rules, taxpayers, they believe, would tend to retain rather than sell their assets.

Of course, opponents of special treatment are equally vocal in their objections to the benefits extended capital gains. They reject the proposition that capital gain should not be taxed. They maintain that income is income regardless of its form. Opponents also doubt the stimulus value of preferential treatment and complain about the uneven playing field that such treatment creates. Finally, opponents offer one argument for which there is no denial. As will become all too clear in this and the following chapter, the special treatment reserved for capital gains and losses creates an inordinate amount of complexity in the tax law.

Despite the various objections, Congress has generally sided with those in favor of preferential treatment. But, as history shows, there is little agreement on exactly what that treatment should be. From 1922 to 1933, taxpayers were given the option of paying a flat 12.5 percent tax on their capital gains and the normal rate on ordinary income. From 1934 to 1937, the treatment was altered to allow an exclusion for capital gains ranging from 20 to 80 percent, depending on how long the asset was held. After some tinkering with the exclusion in 1938, Congress moved again in 1942. This time it replaced the exclusion with a deduction equal to 50 percent of the gain. The 50 percent deduction—increased in 1978 to 60 percent—made capital gains the most popular game in town for almost 45 years. In 1986, however, Congress had a complete change of heart. After lowering the top rate on ordinary income to 28 percent, it apparently believed that special treatment for capital gains was no longer needed. Accordingly, favorable capital gain treatment was repealed. This period of low rates, however, proved to be only temporary, as Congress raised the top rate to 31 percent in 1991 and 39.6 percent in 1993. The increase prompted Congress to resurrect favorable treatment for capital gains, in this case providing that the gains of an individual would be taxed at a maximum rate not to exceed 28 percent. In 2003, Congress decided, once again, to improve the tax advantage extended to capital gains. Under the new rules, capital gains qualifying for special treatment can be taxed at one of four different rates (28 percent, 25 percent, 15 percent, or 5 percent).

The current rates applying to capital gains, like their predecessors, can produce substantial savings. The table below illustrates the benefit of the 15 percent capital gains rate (5 percent for taxpayers in the 10 percent or 15 percent brackets).

---

[1]   House Rep. No. 350, 67th Cong. 1st Sess., pp. 10–11, as quoted in Seidman, *Legislative History of the Income Tax Laws, 1938–1961*, 813 (1938).

Ordinary Rate	Capital Gains Rate	Differential Rate	Percentage Savings
35.0%	15%	20.0%	57.14%
33.0	15	18.0	54.55
28.0	15	13.0	46.43
25.0	15	10.0	40.00
15.0	5	10.0	66.67
10.0	5	5.0	50.00

As should be apparent capital gain treatment is clearly desirable. But as the remainder of this chapter explains, this favorable treatment is not extended to just any gain. The taxpayer must jump through a few hoops, turn a couple of cartwheels, and clear innumerable hurdles before he or she reaches the pot of gold at the end of the capital gains rainbow.

GENERAL REQUIREMENTS FOR CAPITAL GAIN

A gain or loss is considered a capital gain or loss and receives special treatment only if each of several elements is present. The asset being transferred must be a *capital asset* and the disposition must constitute a *sale or exchange*. In addition, the exact treatment of any net gain or loss can be determined only after taking into consideration the *holding period* of the property transferred. Each of these elements is discussed below.

CAPITAL ASSETS

DEFINITION OF A CAPITAL ASSET

In order for a taxpayer to have a capital gain or loss, the Code generally requires a sale or exchange of a *capital asset*. Obviously, the definition of a capital asset is crucial. Sales involving property that qualifies as a capital asset are eligible for a reduced tax rate while sales of assets that have not been so blessed may not be as lucky.

The Internal Revenue Code takes a roundabout approach in defining a capital asset. Instead of defining what a capital asset is, the Code identifies what is not a capital asset. Under § 1221, all assets are considered capital assets unless they fall into one of five excluded classes. The following are *not* capital assets:

1. Inventory or property held primarily for sale to customers in the ordinary course of a trade or business

2. Accounts and notes receivable acquired in the ordinary course of a trade or business for services rendered or from the sale of inventory

3. Depreciable property and land used in a trade or business

4. Copyrights, literary, musical, or artistic compositions, letters or memoranda, or similar property held by the creator, or letters or memoranda held by the person for whom the property was created; in addition, such property held by a taxpayer whose basis is determined by reference to the creator's basis (e.g., acquired by gift), or held by the person for whom it was created

5. Publications of the United States Government that are received from the Government by any means other than purchase at the price at which they are offered to the public, and which are held by the taxpayer who received the publication or by a transferee whose basis is found with reference to the original recipient's basis (e.g., acquired by gift)

Before looking at some of these categories, one should appreciate the statutory scheme and the rationale behind it.

As noted above, the Code starts with the very broad premise that all property held by the taxpayer is a capital asset. Thus the sale of a home, car, jewelry, clothing, stocks, bonds, inventory, and plant, property, and equipment used in a trade or business would produce, *at least initially*, capital gain or loss since all assets are by default capital assets. However, § 1221 goes on to alter this general rule with several significant exceptions. It specifically excludes from capital asset status inventory, property held for resale, receivables related to the sales of services and inventory, and certain literary properties. As may be apparent, the purpose of these exclusions, as the Supreme Court has said, "is to differentiate between the 'profits and losses arising from the everyday operation of business' on the one hand ... and 'the realization of appreciation in value accrued over a substantial period of time' on the other."[2] In essence, the statute is drawn to deny capital gain treatment for income from regular business operations. Income that is derived from the taxpayer's routine personal efforts and services is treated as ordinary income and in effect receives the same treatment as wages, interest, and all other types of income. In contrast, capital gain, at least in the general sense, is limited to gains from the sale of investment property.

Based on the above analysis, it might seem strange that § 1221 also excludes from capital asset status a class of assets that most people would consider capital assets: the fixed assets of a business (depreciable property and land used in a business). Although it is true that these assets are not "pure" capital assets, as will be seen in Chapter 17, these assets can, if certain tests are met, sneak in the back door and receive capital gain treatment. Also observe that this rule does not exclude intangibles from capital asset treatment even though they may be amortizable. For example, goodwill is a capital asset even though it may be amortized.

One final note: it should be emphasized that the classification of an asset as a capital asset may affect more than the character of the gain or loss on its sale. For example, the amount of a charitable contribution deduction also may be affected in certain instances. Recall that the deduction for charitable contributions of appreciated capital gain property is generally based on fair market value, but is limited to a percentage of adjusted gross income.[3]

INVENTORY

The inventory exception has been the subject of much litigation and controversy. Whether property is held primarily for sale is a question of fact. The Supreme Court decided in *Malat v. Riddell*[4] that the word "primarily" should be interpreted as used in an ordinary, everyday sense, and as such, means "principally" or of "first importance." As a practical matter, such interpretations provide little guidance. In many cases, it simply boils down to whether the court views the taxpayer as a "dealer" in the particular property or merely an investor. Unfortunately, the line of demarcation is far from clear.

The determination of whether an item is inventory or not frequently arises in the area of sales of real property. In determining whether a taxpayer holds real estate, or a particular tract of real estate, primarily for sale, the courts seem to place the greatest emphasis on the frequency, continuity, and volume of sales.[5] Other important factors

---

[2]   *Malat v. Riddell*, 66-1 USTC ¶9317, 17 AFTR2d 604, 383 U.S. 569 (USSC, 1966).

[3]   See § 170(e)(1) and Chapter 11 for a discussion of these charitable contribution limitations.

[4]   *Supra*, Footnote 2.

[5]   See, for example, *Houston Endowment, Inc. v. U.S.*, 79-2 USTC ¶9690, 44 AFTR2d 79-6074, 606 F.2d 77 (CA-5, 1979) and *Reese v. Comm.*, 80-1 USTC ¶9350, 45 AFTR2d 80-1248, 615 F.2d 226 (CA-5, 1980).

considered by the courts are subdivision and improvement,[6] solicitation and advertising,[7] purpose and manner of acquisition,[8] and reason for and method of sale.[9]

DISPOSITION OF A BUSINESS

The treatment of the sale of a business depends on the form in which the business is operated and the nature of the sale. If the business is operated as a sole proprietorship, the sale of the proprietorship business is not, as one taxpayer argued, a sale of a single integrated capital asset.[10] Rather, it is treated as a separate sale of each of the assets of the business. Accordingly, the sales price must be allocated among the various assets and gains and losses determined for each individual asset. Any gain or loss arising from the sale of inventory items and receivables would be treated separately as ordinary gains and losses. Gains and losses from the sale of depreciable property and land used in the business would be subject to special treatment discussed in Chapter 17 and may qualify for capital gain treatment. Finally, gains and losses from capital assets would of course be treated as capital gains and losses.

If the business is operated in the form of a corporation or partnership, the sale could take one of two forms: (1) a sale of the owner's interest (e.g., the owner's stock or interest in the partnership) or (2) a sale of all the assets by the entity followed by a distribution of the sales proceeds to the owner. An owner's interest—stock or an interest in a partnership—is a capital asset. Consequently, a sale of such interest normally produces capital gain or capital loss (although there are some important exceptions for sales of a partnership interest). On the other hand, a sale of assets by the entity would be treated in the same manner as the sale of a sole proprietorship, a sale of each individual asset.

✓ CHECK YOUR KNOWLEDGE

Review Question 1. Lois Price operates an office supply store, Office Discount, and owns the property listed below. Indicate whether each of the following assets is a capital asset. Respond yes or no.

    a. Refrigerator in her home used solely for personal use
    b. The building that houses her business
    c. A picture given to her by a well-known artist
    d. 100 shares of Chrysler Corporation stock held as an investment
    e. Furniture in her office
    f. A book of poems she has written
    g. The portion of her home used as a qualifying home office
    h. 1,000 boxes of 3 ½-inch floppy disks
    i. Goodwill of the business

The following are capital assets: (a), (d), and (i). All assets are capital assets except inventory (item h), real or depreciable property used in a trade or business (items b, e, g), literary or artistic compositions held by the creator (item f), or property received by

---

[6] See, for example, *Houston Endowment, Inc.* , and *Biedenharn Realty Co., Inc. v. U.S.*, 76-1 USTC ¶9194, 37 AFTR2d 76-679, 526 F.2d 409 (CA-5, 1976).

[7] See, for example, *Houston Endowment, Inc.*

[8] See, for example, *Scheuber v. Comm.*, 67-1 USTC ¶9219, 19 AFTR2d 639, 371 F.2d 996 (CA-7, 1967), and *Biedenharn Realty Co., Inc. v. U.S.*

[9] See, for example, *Voss v. U.S.*, 64-1 USTC 9290, 13 AFTR2d 834, 329 F.2d 164 (CA-7, 1964).

[10] *Williams v. McCowan*, 46-1 USTC ¶9120, 34 AFTR 615, 152 F.2d 570 (CA-2, 1945); Rev. Rul. 55-79, 1955-1 C.B. 370.

gift from the creator (item c). Note that the Code does not exclude intangible assets from capital assets status. Such assets as goodwill are treated as capital assets.

Review Question 2. Slam-Dunk Corporation manufactures collapsible basketball rims in Houston, Texas. Because of its tremendous growth, Mr. Slam and Ms. Dunk, the owners of the company, brought in a highly skilled executive to manage it, the famous Sam Jam. As part of the employment agreement, the company agreed to buy Sam's house if it should terminate his contract. As you might expect, Slam and Dunk did not get along with Sam and his creative management techniques. Consequently, the corporation dismissed Sam after two years and purchased his house at Sam's original cost of $300,000. Needing the cash, the corporation decided to unload the house immediately. Unfortunately, in the depressed housing market of Houston, the corporation sold the house for only $200,000. Explain the tax problems associated with the sale by the corporation. What important issue must be resolved and why?

In this situation, the corporation has realized a loss of $100,000. The critical issue is determining whether the loss is an ordinary or capital loss. The treatment, as explained below, is quite different. If the loss is ordinary, the corporation may deduct the entire loss in computing taxable income. In contrast, if the loss is a capital loss, the corporation can deduct the loss only to the extent of any capital gains that it has during the year or a three-year carryback and five-year carryforward period. The determination turns on the definition of a capital asset.

SALE OR EXCHANGE REQUIREMENT

Before capital gain or loss treatment applies, the property must be disposed of in a "sale or exchange." In most cases, determining whether a sale or exchange has occurred is not difficult. The requirement is met by most routine transactions and as a practical matter is often overlooked. Nevertheless, there are a number of situations when a sale or exchange does not actually occur but the Code steps in and creates one, thus converting what might have been ordinary income or loss to capital gain or capital loss. Several of these are considered below.

WORTHLESS AND ABANDONED PROPERTY

When misfortune strikes, leaving the taxpayer with worthless property, the taxpayer normally has a loss equal to the adjusted basis of the property. Note, however, that the loss in these situations does not technically arise from a sale or exchange, leaving the taxpayer to wonder how the loss is to be treated.

Worthless Securities. The Code has addressed this problem with respect to worthless securities (e.g., stocks and bonds). In the event that a qualifying security becomes worthless at any time during the taxable year, the resulting loss is treated as having arisen from the sale or exchange of a capital asset on the last day of the taxable year.[11] Losses from worthlessness are then treated as either short-term or long-term capital losses depending on the taxpayer's holding period.

Example 1. After receiving a hot tip, N bought 200 shares of Shag Carpets Inc. for $2,000 on November 1, 2004. Just three months later, on February 1, 2005, N received a shocking notice that the company had declared bankruptcy and her investment was worthless. Because of the worthlessness, N is treated as having sold

---

[11] § 165(g).

the stock for nothing on the last day of her taxable year, December 31, 2005. Because the sale is deemed to occur on December 31, 2005 (and not February 1), N is treated as if she actually held the stock for more than a year. As a result, she reports a $2,000 long-term capital loss.

The sale or exchange fiction applies only to qualifying securities. To qualify, the security must be (1) a capital asset and (2) a security as defined by the Code. Under § 165, the term *security* means stock, stock rights, and bonds, notes, or other forms of indebtedness issued by a corporation or the government. When these rules do not apply (e.g., property other than securities), the taxpayer suffers an ordinary loss. Whether a security actually becomes worthless during a given year is a question of fact, and the burden of proof is on the taxpayer to show that the security became worthless during the year in question.[12]

Worthless Securities in Affiliated Corporations. The basic rule for worthless securities is modified for a corporate taxpayer's investment in securities of an affiliated corporation. If securities of an affiliated corporation become worthless, the loss is treated as an ordinary loss and the limitations that normally apply if the loss were a capital loss are avoided.[13] A corporation is considered affiliated to a parent corporation if the parent owns at least 80 percent of the voting power of all classes of stock and at least 80 percent of each class of nonvoting stock of the affiliated corporation. In addition, to be treated as an affiliated corporation for purposes of the worthless security provisions, the defunct corporation must have been truly an operating company. This test is met if the corporation has less than 10 percent of the aggregate of its gross receipts from passive sources such as rents, royalties, dividends, annuities, and gains from sales or exchanges of stock and securities. This condition prohibits ordinary loss treatment for what are really investments.

Example 2. Toy Palace Corporation is the parent corporation for more than 100 subsidiary corporations that operate toy stores all over the country. Each subsidiary is 100 percent owned by Toy Palace. This year the store in Chicago, TPC Inc., declared bankruptcy. As a result, Toy Palace's investment in TPC stock of $1 million became totally worthless. Toy Palace is allowed to treat the $1 million loss as an ordinary loss since TPC was an affiliated corporation (i.e., Toy Palace owned at least 80 percent of TPC's stock and TPC was an operating corporation). Observe that without this special rule, Toy Palace would have a $1 million capital loss that it could deduct only if it had capital gains currently or within the three-year carryback or five-year carryforward period.

Abandoned Property. While the law creates a sale or exchange for worthless securities, it takes a different approach for abandoned business or investment property. When worthless property (other than stocks and securities) is abandoned, the abandonment is not considered a sale or exchange.[14] Consequently, any loss arising from an abandonment is treated as an ordinary loss rather than a capital loss, a much more propitious result. Note, however, that the loss is deductible only if the taxpayer can demonstrate that the business or investment property has been truly abandoned and not simply taken out of service temporarily.

---

[12]   *Young v. Comm.*, 41-2 USTC ¶9744, 28 AFTR 365, 123 F.2d 597 (CA-2, 1941). Code § 6511(d) extends the statute of limitations from three years to seven years because of the difficulty of determining the specific tax year in which stock becomes worthless.

[13]   § 165(g)(3).

[14]   Reg. §§ 1.165-2 and 1.167(a)-8.

CERTAIN CASUALTIES AND THEFTS

Still another exception to the sale or exchange requirement involves *excess* casualty and theft gains from the involuntary conversion of *personal use assets*. As discussed in Chapter 10, § 165(h) provides that if personal casualty or theft gains *exceed* personal casualty or theft losses for any taxable year, each such gain and loss must be treated as a gain or loss from the sale or exchange of a capital asset. Each separate casualty or theft loss must be reduced by $100 before being netted with the personal casualty or theft gains.

> **Example 3.** T had three separate casualties involving personal-use assets during the year:

| | | | Fair Market Value | |
Casualty	Property	Adjusted Basis	Before Casualty	After Casualty
1. Accident	Personal car	$12,000	$ 8,500	$ 6,000
2. Robbery	Jewelry	1,000	4,000	0
3. Hurricane	Residence	60,000	80,000	58,000

> T received insurance reimbursements as follows: (1) $900 for repair of the car; (2) $3,200 for the theft of her jewelry; and (3) $21,500 for the damages to her home. Assuming T does not elect (under § 1033) to purchase replacement jewelry, her personal casualty gain exceeds her personal casualty losses by $300, computed as follows:
>
> 1. The loss for the car is $1,500 [(lesser of $2,500 decline in value or the $12,000 adjusted basis = $2,500) − $900 insurance recovery − $100 floor].
>
> 2. The gain for the jewelry is $2,200 ($3,200 insurance recovery − $1,000 adjusted basis).
>
> 3. The loss from the residence is $400 [(lesser of $22,000 decline in value or the $60,000 adjusted basis = $22,000) − $21,500 insurance recovery − $100 floor].
>
> T must report each separate gain and loss as a gain or loss from the sale or exchange of a capital asset. The classification of each gain and loss as short-term or long-term depends on the holding period of each asset.

It is important to note that this exception *does not* apply if the personal casualty losses exceed the gains. In such case, the *net* loss, subject to the 10 percent limitation, is deductible *from* A.G.I. Recall, however, that casualty and theft losses are among those itemized deductions that are not subject to the 3 percent cutback rule imposed on high-income taxpayers. (See Chapter 11 for a discussion of this cutback rule.)

> **Example 4.** Assume the same facts in *Example 3* except the insurance recovery from the hurricane damage to the residence was only $11,500. In this case, the loss from the hurricane is $10,400 ($22,000 − $11,500 − $100), and the personal casualty losses exceed the gain by $9,700 ($1,500 + $10,400 − $2,200). T must treat the $9,700 net loss as an itemized deduction subject to the 10% of A.G.I. limitation, but not subject to the 3% cutback rule.

OTHER TRANSACTIONS

There are still other situations where the sale or exchange requirement is an important consideration. For example, foreclosure, condemnation, and other involuntary events are treated as sales even though they may not qualify as such for state law purposes. Similarly, as discussed in greater detail later in this chapter, the collection of the face value of a corporate bond (i.e., bond redemption) at maturity is treated as a sale or exchange.

HOLDING PERIOD

The exact treatment of a capital gain or loss depends primarily on how long the taxpayer held the asset or what is technically referred to as the taxpayer's *holding period*. The holding period is a critical element in determining which of the various tax rates will apply. As might be expected, the longer the holding period is, the lower the applicable tax rate will be. A *short term* gain or loss is one resulting from the sale or disposition of an asset held *one year or less.*[15] A *long-term* gain or loss occurs when an asset is held for *more than one year*.

In computing the holding period, the day of acquisition is not counted but the day of sale is. The holding period is based on calendar months and fractions of calendar months, rather than on the number of days.[16] The fact that different months contain different numbers of days (i.e., 28, 30, or 31) is disregarded.

> **Example 5.** P purchased 10 shares of EX, Inc. on March 16, 2005. Her gain or loss on the sale is short-term if the stock is sold on or before March 16, 2006 but long-term if sold on or after March 17, 2006.

> **Example 6.** T purchased 100 shares of FMC Corp. stock on February 28, 2005. His gain or loss will be long-term if he sells the stock on or after March 1, 2006.

The holding period runs from the time property is acquired until the time of its disposition. Property is generally considered *acquired* or *disposed* of when title passes from one party to another. State law usually controls the passage of title and must be consulted when questions arise.

STOCK EXCHANGE TRANSACTIONS

The holding period for securities traded on a stock exchange is determined in the same manner as for other property. The trade dates, rather than the settlement dates, are used as the dates of acquisition and sale.

Generally, both cash and accrual basis taxpayers must report (recognize) gains and losses on stock or security sales in the tax year of the trade, even though cash payment (settlement) may not be received until the following year. This requirement is imposed because the installment method of reporting gains is not allowed for sales of stock or securities that are traded on an established securities market.[17]

> **Example 7.** C, a cash basis calendar year taxpayer, sold 300 shares of ARA stock at a gain of $5,000 on December 29, 2005. The settlement date was January 3, 2006. C must report the gain in 2005 (the year of trade).

---

[15] § 1222.

[16] Rev. Rul. 66-7, 1966-1 C.B.188.

[17] § 453(k)(2). See Chapter 14 for a detailed discussion of the installment sale method.

SPECIAL RULES AND EXCEPTIONS

Section 1223 contains a number of special provisions that must be used for determining the holding period of certain properties. The rules address the holding period of property acquired (1) in a tax-deferred exchange; (2) by gift; (3) by inheritance; (4) in a wash sale; (5) as a stock dividend; or (6) by exercising stock rights or options.

Property Acquired in Tax-Deferred Transaction. The holding period of property received in an exchange *includes* the holding period of the property given up in the exchange if the basis of the property is determined by reference, in whole or in part, to the basis in that property given up (e.g., a substituted basis in a like-kind exchange).[18] This rule applies only if the property exchanged is a capital asset or a § 1231 asset (e.g., real or depreciable property used in a trade or business) at the time of the exchange. For this purpose, an involuntary conversion–where the taxpayer normally purchases replacement property for that which was involuntarily converted—is treated as an exchange.[19]

As suggested above, this rule commonly can be found operating when there is a like-kind exchange. For example, if a taxpayer purchased land on May 16, 1981 and swapped it for other land in 2003, the taxpayer's holding period for the new land would begin in 1981 since the basis of the new land is the same as the old land, $50,000, (i.e., the basis of the new land was "determined by reference" to the property given up). Normally, if any gain or loss is deferred, the holding period of the replacement property includes the holding period of the property that was converted or exchanged.

> **Example 8.** In 2004, the city of Milwaukee condemned 10 acres of M's farm land (a § 1231 asset) in order to build an exit for an interstate highway. M had acquired the land on May 1, 1992 for $20,000. M received $120,000 for the land and therefore realized a gain of $100,000. On July 7, 2006 M replaced the property by purchasing new land for $120,000. As a result, he was able to defer all of the realized gain, producing a basis for the new property of $20,000 ($120,000 cost less $100,000 deferred gain). Since an involuntary conversion is treated as an exchange, M's holding period begins on the date that he acquired the original property, May 1, 1992.

Property Acquired by Gift. Another exception provides that if a taxpayer's basis in property is the same basis as another taxpayer had in that property, in whole or in part, the holding period will include that of the other person.[20] Therefore, the holding period of property acquired by gift generally will include the holding period of the donor. This will not be true, however, if the property is sold at a loss and the basis in the property for determining the loss is fair market value on the date of the gift.

> **Example 9.** G received a gold necklace from her elderly grandmother as a birthday gift on August 31, 2005. The necklace was worth $5,200 at that time and had a basis to the grandmother of $1,300. Grandmother had bought the necklace in 1976. Contrary to her grandmother's wishes, G sold the family heirloom for $5,000 on December 13, 2005. G will recognize a gain of $3,700 ($5,000 − $1,300). Her holding period will begin in 1976 since her $1,300 basis is determined (under § 1015) by reference to her grandmother's basis, *and* her holding period includes the time the necklace was held by her grandmother.

---

[18]   § 1223(1).

[19]   § 1223(1)(A).

[20]   § 1223(2).

Example 10. If G's grandmother had a basis in the necklace of $6,000, G's basis for determining loss would be $5,200, the fair market value at the date of the gift (see discussion in Chapter 14). Because G's basis is *not* determined by reference to her grandmother's basis, the grandmother's holding period is not added to G's holding period. Since G only held the necklace for three months, she will have a $200 short-term capital loss ($5,200 basis − $5,000 sales price).

Property Acquired From a Decedent. A special rule is provided for the holding period of property acquired from a decedent. The holding period formally begins on the date of death. However, the Code provides that, if the heir's basis in the property is its fair market value under § 1014 and the property is subsequently sold after the decedent's death, the property is deemed to have a long-term holding period.[21]

Example 11. P sold 50 shares of Xero Corp. stock for $11,200 on July 27, 2005. The stock was inherited from P's uncle who died on May 16, 2005, and it was included in the uncle's Federal estate tax return at a fair market value of $12,000. Since P's basis in the stock ($12,000) is determined under § 1014, the $800 loss on the sale will be a capital loss from property deemed to be held more than 12 months. This would be the case even if P's uncle had purchased the stock within days of his death. The decedent's prior holding period is irrelevant.

Other Holding Period Rules. There are various other provisions that contain special rules for determining holding periods. The holding period of stock acquired in a transaction in which a loss was disallowed under the "wash sale" provisions (§ 1091) is added to the holding period of the replacement stock.[22] Also, when a shareholder receives stock dividends or stock rights as a result of owning stock in a corporation, the holding period of the stock or stock rights includes the holding period of the stock already owned in the corporation.[23] The holding period of any stock acquired by exercising stock rights, however, begins on the date of exercise.[24]

The holding period of property acquired by exercise of an option begins on the day after the option is exercised.[25] If a taxpayer sells the property acquired by option within one year after exercising the option, then he or she will have a short-term gain or loss.

Example 12. N owned an option to purchase ten acres of land. She had owned the option more than one year when she exercised it and purchased the property. Her holding period for the property begins on the day after she exercises the option. Had she sold the option, her gain or loss would have been long-term. If she had sold the property immediately, her gain or loss would have been short-term.

The holding period of a commodity acquired in satisfaction of a commodity futures contract includes the holding period of the futures contract. However, the futures contract must have been a capital asset in the hands of the taxpayer.[26]

---

[21] § 1223(11).

[22] § 1223(4); Reg. § 1.1223-1(d).

[23] § 1223(5); Reg. § 1.1223-1(e).

[24] § 1223(6); Reg. § 1.1223-1(f).

[25] See, for example, *Helvering v. San Joaquin Fruit & Inv. Co.*, 36-1 USTC ¶9144, 17 AFTR 470, 297 U.S. 496 (USSC, 1936), and *E.T. Weir*, 49-1 USTC ¶9190, 37 AFTR 1022, 173 F.2d 222 (CA-3, 1949).

[26] § 1223(8); Reg. § 1.1223-1(h).

TREATMENT OF CAPITAL GAINS AND LOSSES

The Taxpayer Relief Act of 1997 and the amendments of the Jobs and Growth Tax Relief Reconciliation Act of 2003 significantly cut the tax rates on capital gains but not without introducing an inordinate amount of complexity. The adventure begins below.

THE PROCESS IN GENERAL

The first step in determining the treatment of a taxpayer's capital gain or loss is identifying the applicable holding period. Once the holding period is determined, the gain or loss can normally be assigned to an appropriate group to determine its taxation. Historically, there have only been two groups: short-term and long-term. However, beginning in 1997, the law made the classification process a bit more cumbersome, producing the following groups for individual taxpayers.

- *Short-Term group.* Gains and losses from properties held not more than one year
- *Long-Term group.* Generally gains and losses from properties held more than one year. However, individual taxpayers must subdivide the long-term group into additional subgroups according to the rate at which they are to be taxed. The long-term group includes:

1. The 28% group

    - Capital gains and losses from collectibles (e.g., works of art, antiques, gold and silver bullion, etc.)[27]
    - Capital gains from qualified small business stock (taxable portion of § 1202 gains discussed below)

2. The 25% group.

    - Capital *gains* (and only gains) from the sales of depreciable real estate (e.g., office buildings, warehouses, apartment buildings) that are held for more than 12 months but only to the extent of any unrecaptured straight-line depreciation on such property (25CG). (See Chapter 17 for discussion of depreciation recapture.)

3. The 15% group

    - Capital gains and losses from the dispositions of other assets held more than 12 months (15CG and 15CL).

The effect of the new rules is to require taxpayers to assign their capital gains and losses into one of four different groups and net the amounts to determine the net gain or loss in each group as shown below.

Holding period (months)	Short-Term	Long-Term		
	≤12	Collectibles & § 1202 stock > 12	Realty > 12	> 12
	Ordinary	28%	25%	15%
Gains	$xx,xxx	$x,xxx	Gains only	$xx,xxx
Losses	(xxx)	(x,xxx)	—	(x,xxx)
Net gain or loss	????	????	Gain only	????

---

[27] § 1(h)(1)(C) and (h)(4).

As a practical matter, the capital gains of most individuals arise from the sales of stocks and bonds and mutual fund transactions. Rarely do individuals have gains from collectibles, § 1202 stock, or depreciable realty. Consequently, for most individuals, the classification and netting process will indeed be much easier.

NETTING PROCESS

Generalizations about the treatment of capital gains and losses are difficult because the actual treatment can be determined only after the various groups (i.e., the four groups above) are combined, or netted, to determine the overall net gain or loss during the year. This process is described below.[28]

Netting Within Groups. The first step in the netting process is to combine the gains and losses within each group to produce one of the following:

1. Net short-term capital gain or net short-term capital loss (NSTCG or NSTCL).

2. Net 28% capital gain or net 28% capital loss (N28CG or N28CL).

3. Net 15% capital gain or net 15% capital loss (N15CG or N15CL).

Note that the first step requires no netting in the 25% group since this group initially contains only gains.

Netting Between Groups. The second step requires the combination of the net capital loss positions in any particular group against any net capital gain positions. The treatment of these different groups is explained below.

1. *Short-Term Capital Gains and Losses.* A NSTCG receives no special treatment and is taxed as ordinary income. If a NSTCL results, it may be used to offset net gains of the long-term group in the following order: (1) the net 28% gains; (2) any 25% gains; and (3) the net 15% gain. Any remaining NSTCL not absorbed by the capital gains in the groups above is deductible subject to limitations on the deduction of capital losses discussed below.

2. *28% Group.* A N28CG is taxed at a maximum 28%.[29] Any net loss in the 28% group (N28CL) is applied in the following order: (1) 25% gains; (2) net 15% gain; and (3) NSTCG. Any remaining N28CL that is not absorbed is deductible subject to limitations on the deduction of capital losses discussed below.

3. *25% Group.* The 25% group generally includes *only* capital *gains* from the sales of depreciable real estate held for more than 12 months. Such gains are generally only included to the extent of any unrecaptured straight-line depreciation on such property. The net 25% capital gain (N25CG) is taxed at a maximum rate of 25%.[30] Note that there can be no net loss in the 25% group.

4. *15% Group.* A N15CG is taxed at a maximum of 15%. However, if the taxpayer's tax bracket (determined by *including* the N15CG) is only 10 or 15%, the net gain falling into these brackets is taxed at 5%.[31] Any N15CL is applied in the following order: (1) the net 28% gains; (2) any 25% gains; and (3) any

---

[28]   § 1(h)(1).

[29]   § 1(h)(1)(C).

[30]   § 1(h)(1)(B).

[31]   § 1(h)(1)(D) and (E).

NSTCGs. Any remaining N15CL not absorbed is deductible subject to limitations on the deduction of capital losses discussed below.

It should be noted that the three *long-term* groups (the 28%, 25% and 15% groups) are always netted together before taking into accounting any short-term items. Also observe that Congress has generally given taxpayers the best possible treatment of net capital losses in that a NSTCL offsets the net capital gain from the highest taxed group, then the next highest taxed and so on.

Example 12. During the year, T, who is in the 35 percent tax bracket, reported the following capital gains and losses.

	Short-Term	Long-Term 28%	Long-Term 15%
	$10,000	$ 5,000	$4,000
	(4,000)	(1,000)	3,000
	$ 6,000	$ 4,000	$7,000

In this case, T first nets the items within each group. She nets the $10,000 STCG and $4,000 STCL to arrive at a NSTCG of $6,000; she nets a $5,000 28CG and a $1,000 28CL to produce a N28CG of $4,000; and she adds the $4,000 15CG and the $3,000 15CG resulting in a N15CG of $7,000. No further netting of these groups can occur since they each group contains a positive amount. T's NSTCG of $6,000 will receive no special treatment and is taxed as ordinary income. T's N28CG is taxed at 28% while her N15CG is taxed at 15%.

Example 13. This year, L, who is in the 28% tax bracket, reported the following capital gains and losses.

	Short-Term	Long-Term 28%	Long-Term 15%
	$ 10,000	$ 5,000	$ 4,000
	(15,000)	(1,000)	3,000
	($5,000)	$ 4,000	$ 7,000
Netting	5,000	(4,000)	(1,000)
Net	$ 0	$ 0	$ 6,000

Here L has a NSTCL of $5,000 which is netted *first* against N28CG of $4,000, reducing it to zero. The remaining NSTCL of $1,000 would next be offset against N25CG, if any. In this case, there is no N25CG, therefore the remaining NSTCL of $1,000 is offset against the N15CG of $7,000, reducing it to $6,000 which would be taxed at a rate of 15%.

Example 14. This year, X, who is in the 35% tax bracket, reported the following capital gains and losses

	Short-Term	Long-Term 28%	Long-Term 25%	Long-Term 15%
	$14,000	$ 1,000	$ 600	$ 3,000
	(4,000)	(9,000)	400	1,000
	$10,000	($ 8,000)	$ 1,000	$ 5,000
Netting	(2,000)	8,000	(1,000)	(5,000)
Net	$ 8,000	$ 0	$ 0	$ 0

Here X has a N28CL of $8,000 which is netted first against the 25CGs of $1,000, reducing this group to zero. X next uses the remaining $7,000 N28CL to offset his $5,000 N15CG, reducing it to zero. The remaining N28CL of $2,000 ($7,000 – $5,000) is offset against NSTCG, producing a NSTCG of $8,000 which will be treated as ordinary income. Note that the effect of the rules is to net the long-term groups before considering any short-term items. Absent these rules, X would prefer to use the N28CL loss against the NSTCG which would leave $5,000 to be taxed at 15% and $2,000 to be taxed as ordinary income, a far more beneficial result. Unfortunately, X must net the long-term groups first.

Treatment of Capital Losses. While capital gains receive favorable treatment, such is not the case with capital losses. As can be seen above, capital losses are first netted with capital gains within the same group (rather than reducing ordinary income). A net capital loss from a particular group can then be combined with net capital gains from the other groups as explained above. If after netting all of the groups together, the taxpayer has an overall net capital loss, the loss is deductible against ordinary income. This deduction is limited to the lesser of (1) $3,000 ($1,500 in the case of a married individual filing a separate return) or (2) the net capital loss. In either case, the capital loss deduction cannot exceed taxable income before the deduction.[32] The deductible capital loss is a deduction *for* adjusted gross income. Any losses in excess of the annual $3,000 limitation are carried forward to the following year where they are treated as if they actually occurred in such year. In effect, an unused capital loss can be carried over for an indefinite period.[33] However, should the taxpayer die, any unused capital loss is normally lost.

If the netting process results in a NSTCL and either a N28CL or N15CL or both, the NSTCL is applied first toward the maximum $3,000 limit. For example, if the taxpayer has a NSTCL of $5,000 and a N15CL of $4,000, the NSTCL is used first. Any NSTCL in excess of the $3,000 limit along with any other unused losses may be carried forward to subsequent years indefinitely. In this case, the NSTCL carryover retains its character to be treated just as if it had occurred in the subsequent year. The N15CL or N28CL are both carried over as N28CLs. In other words, any long-term capital loss carryover is carried over as a 28CL. In the example above, $3,000 of the $5,000 NSTCL would be used first against ordinary income and the $2,000 remaining would be carried over as a STCL while the $4,000 N15CL would be carried over as a 28CL. In the absence of a NSTCL or, if after deducting any existing NSTCL, the taxpayer has not reached the annual $3,000 limit for the capital loss deduction, the taxpayer uses any other net capital losses (e.g., the excess of N15CL over N28CG and N25CG or the excess of N28CL

---

[32]   § 1212(b).

[33]   Reg. § 1.211-1(b)(4)(i).

over 25 CG and N15CG) to reduce ordinary income up to the $3,000 limit.[34] In this regard, the order in which the remaining net capital losses are used is irrelevant since any remaining losses (i.e., the long-term losses) are carried over as a N28CL which is treated as if it occurred in the subsequent year.

Example 15. During the year, B reported the capital gains and losses revealed below. B's only other taxable income included his salary of $50,000. He had no other deductions for A.G.I. The combination of gains, losses, and ordinary income is shown in the following table.

| | | Long-Term | |
	Short-Term	28%	15%
	$ 10,000	$ 5,000	$ 9,000
	(18,000)	(7,000)	(6,000)
	($ 8,000)	($ 2,000)	$ 3,000
Netting (long-term against long-term)		2,000	(2,000)
		$ 0	$ 1,000
Netting (long-term against short-term)	1,000		(1,000)
	($ 7,000)		$ 0
Deduction	3,000		
Carryover	($ 4,000)		

B first nets the long-term items, that is, the N28CL of $2,000 is netted against the N15CG of $3,000. This produces a N15CG of $1,000 ($3,000 − $2,000). B then combines the $8,000 NSTCL and the remaining N15CG of $1,000, leaving a NSTCL of $7,000. In determining his A.G.I., B may deduct only $3,000 of the NSTCL. Therefore his A.G.I. is $47,000 ($50,000 − $3,000). The unused NSTCL of $4,000 ($7,000 − $3,000) is carried forward to future years as a STCL where it is treated as if it arose in the subsequent year.

Example 16. This year, Q reported the capital gains and losses as shown below. He had no other deductions for A.G.I. The combination of gains, losses, and ordinary income is revealed in the following table.

| | | Long-Term | |
	Short-Term	28%	15%
	$ 1,000	$ 5,000	$ 4,000
	(2,000)	(3,000)	(9,000)
	($ 1,000)	$ 2,000	($ 5,000)
Netting (long-term against long-term)	0	(2,000)	2,000
Net	($ 1,000)	$ 0	($ 3,000)
Deduction	1,000		2,000
Carryover	$ 0		($ 1,000)

Here Q has a NSTCL of $1,000 and a net $5,000 N15CL. He first combines the long-term groups, using $2,000 of the $5,000 N15CL to offset the N28CG of $2,000, reducing it to zero. The remaining $3,000 normally would be netted against 25CG if

---

[34] § 1211(a).

there were any. No further netting is allowed. Therefore, J first uses the NSTCL of $1,000 and then $2,000 of the $3,000 N15CG remaining toward the $3,000 offset against ordinary income. The remaining N15CL of $1,000 is carried over and is treated as a *28CL*. It should be emphasized that the N15CL of $1,000 does not retain its character but becomes a capital loss in the 28% group. Note that the carryover rule is quite favorable. If next year J had $1,000 of N28CG and $1,000 of N15CG, the carryover would wipe out the N28CG, leaving the most favorable gain to be taxed.

Example 17. W's records for 2004 and 2005 revealed substantial ordinary income and the following capital gains and losses.

	Short-Term	Long-Term 28%	Long-Term 15%
2004 gains	$ 1,000	$ 5,000	$ 4,000
2004 losses	(2,000)	(9,000)	(9,000)
	$ (1,000)	$ (4,000)	$ (5,000)
2005	$10,000	$12,000	$15,000

In 2004, there can be no further netting. Therefore, W first uses the NSTCL of $1,000 against ordinary income and then uses $2,000 of the $9,000 in long-term losses, leaving a long-term capital loss carryover of $7,000. Note that it makes no difference which long-term loss is used (i.e., the 28% loss or the 15% loss) since all long-term capital loss carryovers are treated as 28CLs.

In 2005, W treats the $7,000 long-term capital loss carryover as a N28CL. As a result, W would report a N28CG of $5,000 ($12,000 − the $7,000 loss carryover), N15CG of $15,000 and a NSTCG of $10,000.

DIVIDENDS TAXED AT CAPITAL GAIN RATES

In negotiations related to the *Jobs and Growth Tax Relief Reconciliation Act of 2003*, Congress and the Bush administration considered a number of alternative statutory schemes to reduce or eliminate the double taxation of corporate dividends. Somewhat as a surprise, apparently in the interest of simplification, the 2003 Act allows noncorporate taxpayers to treat qualifying dividends similarly to long-term capital gains when calculating their tax. The dividends are now taxed at the reduced 15 percent capital gain rate (5 percent for lower bracket taxpayers) and appears to reduce significantly the toll of the double tax.

The new law provides that most dividends received after 2002 will be subject to the revised capital gains rates[35]: 15 percent generally and 5 percent for dividends that would otherwise be taxed at an ordinary rate of 15 percent or lower. The qualifying dividend is added to the net capital gain and is not subject to the capital gain and loss netting process. As a result, the dividends are subject to capital gains treatment regardless of whether the taxpayer has other capital gains or losses.[36]

Qualified dividends are dividends from domestic corporations and qualified foreign corporations.[37] *Qualified foreign corporations* are those that are incorporated in

---

[35] § 1(h)(11).

[36] Like other long-term capital gains, dividends qualifying for capital gain treatment are not investment income for purposes of the investment interest limitation. However, a taxpayer can elect to treat the dividends as investment income and forego the capital gain treatment. See § 1(h)(11)(D)(i).

[37] § 1(h)(11)(B).

possessions of the United States, those subject to a treaty with the U.S. (involving the exchange of tax information by the governments) and others, the stocks of which are traded on a U.S. stock exchange (certain foreign corporations that are not subject to U.S. tax are not included).

CORPORATE TAXPAYERS

The capital gains and losses of corporate taxpayers are treated a bit differently from those of individual taxpayers. Corporations separate all of their capital gains and losses into only two groups: short-term and long-term (holding period of more than one year). Unlike individuals, there is no further subdividing of the long-term group. Items within the groups are then netted, producing one of the following: NLTCG, NLTCL, NSTCG or NSTCL. If the taxpayer has a NSTCG and a NLTCG, no further netting is allowed. However, if the taxpayer has either a NSTCL and NLTCG or a NSTCG and a NLTCL, these results can be combined to produce a final position. This can be illustrated as follows:

	Short-Term	Long-Term	Result
Holding period (months)	≤ 12	> 12	
Gains	$xx,xxx	$xx,xxx	
Losses	(xxx)	(x,xxx)	
Net gain or loss	????	????	
Possibilities	NSTCG	NLTCG	No further netting
	NSTCG	NLTCL	NLTCL or NSTCG
	NSTCL	NLTCG	NSTCL or NLTCG
	NSTCL	NLTCL	No further netting

A corporate taxpayer receives no special treatment for either a NSTCG or NLTCG. They are treated just like ordinary income. If after netting, the corporation has a NSTCL or a NLTCL, such losses receive special treatment. Unlike an individual taxpayer, a corporation is not allowed to offset capital losses against ordinary income. A corporate taxpayer's capital losses can be used only to reduce its capital gains.[38] Any excess losses are first carried back to the three preceding years as *short-term capital losses* and offset against any net short-term capital gains and then any net long-term capital gains. Absent any capital gains in the three prior years, or if the loss carried back exceeds any capital gains, the excess may be carried forward for five years.[39]

> **Example 18.** An examination of C Corporation's records for 2005 revealed $200,000 of net ordinary taxable income, a long-term capital loss of $9,000 and a short-term capital gain of $2,000. The corporation nets the loss against the gain to produce a NLTCL of $7,000. The corporation cannot offset the loss against ordinary income and, therefore, reports $200,000 of taxable income (undiminished by the NLTCL). Instead the NLTCL is carried back to the third prior year, 2002, as a STCL where it can be used to first offset any NSTCG and then any NLTCG. If there are no capital gains in 2002, the corporation would carryover the loss, now a STCL of $7,000, to 2003 to use against capital gains. This process would continue until the loss is entirely used or it expires at the end of 2010. Note that when the loss is used in prior years, a refund can be obtained.

---

[38] § 1212(a).

[39] *Ibid.*

CALCULATING THE TAX

Section 1(h) provides a special tax calculation to ensure that an individual's capital gains will not be taxed at a rate greater than the applicable preferred rate (i.e., in 2004 the 28%, 25%, 15%, or 5% rate). This calculation can only reduce the tax, not increase it.

Example 19. H and W are married. For 2005, their sole source of income was a 15CG of $78,000 from the sale of assets held five years. Their taxable income is computed as follows:

15CG	$ 78,000
Standard deduction	(10,000)
Exemption deduction	(6,400)
Taxable income	$ 61,600

The 10% and 15% bracket for taxpayers filing jointly in 2005 runs to $59,400 at which point any dollar of income in excess of that amount is taxed at 25%. Since all of the couple's income is from capital gain, however, none of it is taxed at the 15% or 25% brackets. The effect of the special capital gains calculation is to tax the portion of the N15CG that falls into the 10% and 15% bracket at a 5% rate and the portion that falls into the 25% bracket at 15%. Therefore, $59,400 of the N15CG is taxed at 5% and the remaining $2,200 is taxed at 15%. The total tax is $3,300 [($59,400 × 5%) + ($2,200 × 15%)].

It may be clear from the above example that whenever an individual's ordinary taxable income exceeds the amount that would be taxed at 10 or 15 percent (e.g., $59,400 in 2005 for a joint return), none of the N15CG is taxed at 5 percent. In such case, the taxpayer computes the tax liability by first calculating the regular tax on ordinary taxable income and adding to that a tax of 15 percent on the N15CG. On the other hand, if ordinary taxable income does not exceed the amount that is taxed at 10 or 15 percent, a portion of the N15CG is taxed at the 5 percent rate until the 10 and 15 percent brackets are exhausted. A similar approach applies for N25CGs and N28CGs.

Before proceeding, it is important to understand some statutory terms. The first term is *net capital gain*—the excess of the net long-term capital gain over the net short-term capital loss for a year. If there is no net short-term capital loss, the net capital gain is simply the net gain from the 15 percent group, the 25 percent group, and the 28 percent group combined. If there is a short-term loss, it is the excess of the combined long-term gains minus the net short-term capital loss. The second term is *adjusted net capital gain*—the net capital gain reduced (but not below zero) by the 25 percent gain and the net 28 percent gain (reduced by any net short-term capital loss).

The actual steps to compute the capital gains tax are built into Schedule D of Form 1040. They are also summarized in Exhibit 16-1.

EXHIBIT 16-1
Tax Computation Involving Capital Gains

Step 1. Calculate the regular income tax using the regular rates on the taxpayer's taxable income

Step 2. Determine the tax on the *ordinary income*

    a. Select the greater of—

        ▸ Ordinary taxable income (taxable income − net capital gain), or

        ▸ The lesser of—

            ▸ The maximum amount that would be taxed at 15 percent, or

            ▸ Taxable income − the adjusted net capital gain

    b. Compute the regular income tax on this amount

Step 3. Determine the tax on the *net capital gain* by adding the following together

    a. *Tax on 5 Percent Gains*—5 percent of the portion of the adjusted net capital gain that would have been taxed at 10 or 15 percent when added to ordinary income [i.e., the lesser of (1) the adjusted net capital gain or (2) the maximum amount that would normally be taxed at 10 or 15 percent minus the amount of ordinary income].

    b. *Tax on 15 Percent Gains*—15 percent of (the adjusted net capital gain minus any 5 percent gains).

    c. *Tax on 25 Percent Gains*—The lesser of

        ▸ 25 percent of the 25 percent gains, or

        ▸ If less, (1) 10 or 15 percent (respectively) of the amount of the 25 percent gains that, when added to ordinary income and any 5 percent gains, would be taxed at 10 or 15 percent*, plus (2) 25 percent of any remaining 25 percent gains.

    d. *Tax on 28 Percent Gains*—The lesser of

        ▸ 28 percent of the 28 percent gains, or

        ▸ If less, (1) 10 or 15 percent (respectively) of the amount of the 28 percent gains that, when added to ordinary income, any 5 percent gains, and any 25 percent gains, would be taxed at 10 or 15 percent**, plus (2) 28 percent of any remaining 28 percent gains.

Step 4. Add the tax on the ordinary income (Step 2) to the tax on the net capital gain (Step 3) to get the total capital gains tax.

Step 5. The final tax is the lesser of the taxes computed in Step 1 and Step 4.

---

*This is the amount that would otherwise be taxed at 10 or 15 percent when added to ordinary income and any 5 percent gains (or stated differently, it is the maximum amount that would be taxed at 10 or 15 percent minus the amount of ordinary income and the amount of 5 percent gains).

**This is the amount that would otherwise be taxed at 10 or 15 percent when added to ordinary income, any 5 percent gains, and any 25 percent gains (or, stated differently, it is the maximum amount that would be taxed at 15 percent minus the amount of ordinary income and the amount of 5 percent gains).

Example 20. J and K are married and file a joint return for 2005. They have taxable income of $74,400, including a N15CG of $15,000. Thus they have ordinary taxable income of $59,400. Their tax is computed as follows:

Step 1: Regular tax on $74,400 = $11,930

Regular tax on $74,400:
Tax on $59,400 (10% and 15% brackets)	$ 8,180
Plus: Tax on excess at 25%	
[($74,400 − $59,400) × 25%]	+3,750
Equals: Total tax	$11,930

Step 2a: Ordinary income = $59,400 ($74,400 − $15,000)
Step 2b: Regular tax on ordinary income of $59,400 = $8,180

Regular tax on $59,400. . . . . $8,180

Step 3: Tax on the net capital gain = $2,250

   a. Tax on 5% Gains = 5% of zero (All of the net capital gain would have been taxed at a rate exceeding 15% since V's ordinary income plus 25% gains and 28% gains equaled or exceeded $59,400—the limit of the 15% bracket)
   b. Tax on 15% Gains = 15% × $15,000 = $2,250
   c. Tax on 25% Gains = 25% of zero
   d. Tax on 28% Gains = 28% of zero

Step 4: Total capital gains tax = $10,430 ($8,180 + $2,250)

Step 5: The final tax is $10,430. The savings is $1,500 ($11,930 − $10,430). Note that this $1,500 is the 10% difference (25% − 15%) on the $15,000 gain.

Example 21. V is single for 2005 and has taxable income for the year of $100,000 including the following:

Loss from stock held 11 months	($2,000)
Gain from gold bullion held 3 years	3,000
Gain from land held 9 years	16,000
Loss from stock held 2 years	(3,000)

V would summarize his gains and losses as follows:

		Long-Term	
	Short-Term	*28%*	*15%*
	($2,000)	$ 3,000	$16,000
	—	—	(3,000)
	($2,000)	$ 3,000	$13,000
Netting	2,000	(2,000)	—
	$ 0	$ 1,000	$13,000

The loss is a STCL since it was held for not more than a year. The gain on the sale of the gold bullion is treated as a 28CG since it is a collectible. Collectibles are treated as 28CGs even though they may have been held more than 12 months. The gain and loss from the land and stock are both classified as 15% items since they were held more than 12 months. Thus V's overall capital gain is $14,000, consisting of a N28CG of $1,000 and a N15CG of $13,000. V's tax is computed as follows.

Step 1:   Regular tax on $100,000 = $22,507

Tax on $71,950 (10%, 15% and 25% bracket)	$14,653
Plus: Tax on excess at 30% [($100,000 − $71,950) × 28%]	7,854
Equals: Total tax	$22,507

Step 2a: Ordinary income = $86,000 ($100,000 − $14,000)
Step 2b: Regular tax on ordinary income of $86,000 = $18,587

Tax on $71,950	$14,653
Plus: Tax on excess at 28% [($86,000 − $71,950) × 28%]	3,934
Equals: Total tax	$18,587

Step 3:   Tax on the net capital gain = $2,230 ($280 + $1,950)

   a. Tax on 5% Gains = 5% of zero (All of the net capital gain would have been taxed at a rate exceeding 15% since V's ordinary income exceeded $29,050—the limit of the 15% bracket)
   b. Tax on 15% Gains = 15% × $13,000 = $1,950
   c. Tax on 25% Gains = 25% of zero
   d. Tax on 28% Gains = 28% × $1,000 = $280

Step 4:   Total capital gains tax = $20,817 ($18,587 + $2,230)

Step 5:   The final tax is $20,817 (the lesser of *Step 1* or *Step 4*). The difference between the regular tax and the capital gains tax is $1,690 ($22,507 − $20,817). Note that this $1,690 is the 13% difference (28% − 15%) on $13,000 (13% × $13,000 = $1,690).

Example 22. Same as *Example 21*, except V's total taxable income is $35,000.

Step 1:   Regular tax on $35,000 = $5,415

Tax on $29,700	$4,090
Plus: Tax on excess at 25% [($35,000 − $29,700) × 25%]	1,325
Equals: Total tax	$5,415

Step 2a: Ordinary income = $21,000 ($35,000 − $14,000)

Step 2b: Regular tax on $21,000 = $2,785 ($7,300 × 10% + $13,700 × 15%)

Step 3:   Tax on the net capital gain = $1,330 ($435 + $645 + $250)

   a. Tax on 5% Gains = $435 [$8,700 × 5%—The N15CG is taxed at 5% to the extent the limit on the 15% tax bracket exceeds the ordinary income ($29,700 − $21,000 = $8,700)]

> **b.** Tax on 15% Gains = $645 [($13,000 − $8,700 = $4,300) × 15%—
> The adjusted net capital gain reduced by the portion taxed at 5%
> multiplied by 15%]
>
> **c.** Tax on 25% Gains = 25% of zero
>
> **d.** Tax on 28% Gains = 25% × $1,000 = $250 [Since ordinary income
> plus the 5% gains, 15% gains, and 25% gains are more than the limit
> on the 15% tax bracket ($21,000 + $8,050 + $4,950 > $29,700) but
> less than the top of the 25% bracket amounts, the 28% gains are
> taxed at 25%.]

Step 4: Total capital gains tax = $4,115 ($2,785 + $1,330)

Step 5: The final tax is $4,115 (the lesser of *Step 1* or *Step 4*). The difference
between the regular tax and the capital gains tax is $1,300 ($5,415 −
$4,115). Note that this $1,300 is the sum of the 10% difference (15% −
5%) on $8,700 and the 10% difference (25% − 15%) on $4,300 [10% ×
$8,700 + 10% × $4,300 = $1,300], but there is no difference on the 28%
gain that was taxed at the ordinary income rate.

REPORTING CAPITAL GAINS AND LOSSES

Individual taxpayers report any capital gains or losses on Schedule D of Form 1040.[40]
This form is designed to facilitate the netting process, with one part used for reporting
short-term gains and losses and another part used to report long-term transactions. A
third part of the form is available for the second step of the netting process in the event
the taxpayer has either NSTCGs and NLTCLs *or* NLTCGs and NSTCLs.

Regular corporations must report capital gains and losses on Schedule D of Form
1120 in much the same manner as individual taxpayers. Partnerships and S corporations
must also report capital gains and losses on a separate schedule (Schedule D of Form
1065 for partnerships and Schedule D of Form 1120S for S corporations). However,
these conduit entities are limited to the *first* step of the netting process. Each owner
(partner or S corporation shareholder) must include his or her share of the results from
the entity with the appropriate capital transactions being netted on the owner's Schedule
D, Form 1040.

✓ CHECK YOUR KNOWLEDGE

Review Question 1. For 2005 Ms. Reyes earned a salary of $70,000 from her job
as an art curator. In addition, she sold stock, realizing the following capital gains and
losses:

15CG	$ 10,000
15CL	(7,000)
STCL	(11,000)

In 2006 she changed jobs, becoming a tax accountant and earning a salary of $300,000. In
addition, she realized a 15CG of $12,000.

Compute Ms. Reyes's adjusted gross income for 2005 and 2006 and indicate the
amount, if any, that is eligible for preferential treatment as long-term capital gain.

---

[40] See Appendix for a sample of this form.

other hand, the IRS wants to do just the opposite. To eliminate the potential controversy and prohibit taxpayers from using their hindsight, Congress enacted § 1236, which simply requires the dealer to identify that a particular security is held for investment (and is therefore a capital asset) by the end of the day on which it was acquired.[52] If the security is not properly identified on a timely basis, the dealer must characterize any gain or loss as ordinary.

SUBDIVIDED REAL ESTATE

The dealer vs. investor debate also raises its ugly head for taxpayers selling land. Is the land held for investment or primarily for resale?

It is not uncommon for a taxpayer to hold land for investment for many years and then subdivide or improve it just before selling it. If the subdivision and improvements are significant, the property will probably be deemed to be held primarily for sale to customers in a trade or business. If the activities are minor, the land probably retains its character as a capital asset. As was pointed out earlier in this chapter, the determination usually is made based on the frequency, continuity, and volume of sales, but development activities are also very important.

In an attempt to prevent disputes, Congress created a safe harbor that guarantees capital gain treatment where there is a limited amount of subdivision activity. This rule allows the taxpayer, as someone once said, to subdivide and conquer the ordinary income problem. Under § 1237, real estate is not treated as held primarily for sale if all of the following conditions are met:[53]

1. The tract of land has been held at least five years prior to the sale (except in the case of inheritance).

2. The taxpayer has made no substantial improvements to the property that increase the value of the lots sold while the property was owned.

3. The parcel sold, or any part thereof, had not previously been held by the taxpayer primarily for resale.

4. No other real property was held by the taxpayer primarily for sale during the year of the sale.

Even if the requirements are met, the taxpayer may still be required to report a portion of the gain as ordinary income. If five or fewer lots are sold from the same tract of land, the entire gain is capital gain. However, in the year that the sixth lot is sold, all lots sold in that year and later years become the target of § 1237(b). This special rule provides that 5 percent of the sales price (not gain) is ordinary income.[54] In addition, any selling expenses reduce the ordinary income portion of the gain (limited to the amount of ordinary income), rather than the amount treated as capital gain.[55]

> **Example 31.** Twenty years ago X bought 100 acres 20 miles south of Tulsa for $100,000. This year he retired and decided to sell the land. In order to sell the property, he subdivided it into 10 lots of 10 acres each. This year X sold 5 lots for $310,000 and paid a real estate commission of $10,000. As a result, he recognized a gain of $250,000 ($310,000 − $10,000 − $50,000 basis). Since he sold only 5 lots, the gain on each sale is treated as long-term capital gain. Had X sold 6 lots for the

---

[52] § 1236(a).

[53] § 1237(a).

[54] § 1237(b)(1).

[55] § 1237(b)(2).

same total price, 5% of his selling price, $15,500 (5% × $310,000), would be considered ordinary income and he could reduce this amount by the selling expenses of $10,000, for net ordinary income on the sale of $5,500.

Note that § 1237 applies to property that has been subdivided, but it is of no help where significant improvements have been made to the property.

OTHER RELATED PROVISIONS

NONBUSINESS BAD DEBTS

Bad debt losses from nonbusiness debts are deductible as short-term capital losses. Nonbusiness bad debts are deductible only in the year they become totally worthless since no deduction is allowed for partially worthless debts.[56] These rules and others related to the allowable deduction for bad debts were discussed in Chapter 10.

FRANCHISE AGREEMENTS, TRADEMARKS, AND TRADE NAMES

Section 1253 includes specific guidelines for the treatment of both the transferee and the transferor of payments with respect to franchise, trademark, and trade name agreements. The transfer of such rights is *not* treated as the sale or exchange of a capital asset by the transferor *if* he or she retains significant power, right, or continuing interest with respect to the property.[57] Capital gain and loss treatment also is denied for periodic payments that are contingent on the productivity, use, or sale of the property.[58]

"Significant power, right, or continuing interest" is defined in the Code by example. Some of the characteristics listed in the Code as indicative of such power, right, or interest retained by the transferor of the franchise are as follows:[59]

1. The right to terminate the franchise at will;

2. The right to disapprove any assignment;

3. The right to prescribe quality standards;

4. The right to require that the transferee advertise only products of the transferor;

5. The right to require that the transferee acquire substantially all of his or her supplies or equipment from the transferor; and

6. The right to require payments based on the productivity, use, or sale of the property.

The transferee is allowed current deductions for amounts paid or accrued that are contingent on the productivity, use, or sale of the property transferred.[60] Other payments must be at least partially deferred. They generally are amortized over the shorter of 10 years or the period covered by the transfer agreement.[61]

---

[56] See § 166(d) and related discussion in Chapter 10.

[57] § 1253(a).

[58] § 1253(c).

[59] § 1253(b)(2).

[60] § 1253(d)(1).

[61] § 1253(d)(2).

Example 32. M, Inc. and R enter into a franchise agreement that allows R to operate a hamburger establishment using the trade name and products of M, Inc. According to the contract, M, Inc. has retained all six rights that are listed above. R is required to pay M $50,000 upon entering the contract and 2% of all sales. The term of the contract is 25 years with provision for renewals. R must also pay for any supplies provided by M. Both the $50,000 payment and the percentage royalty payment are ordinary income to M, Inc.

R may treat the royalty payments to M, Inc. as ordinary deductions incurred in his trade or business. The initial fee of $50,000 is amortized equally over 10 years beginning with the year in which the payment is made.

SHORT SALES

Investors who believe that the price of a security will fall rather than rise may bank on their belief by using short sales. Selling short essentially means selling shares that are not actually owned. To accomplish this, the seller typically borrows shares from a broker, sells such shares, and agrees to return an equivalent number of substantially identical shares to the broker within a certain period of time. For example, an investor may sell 100 shares of borrowed stock for $100 per share, or $10,000. If the stock price falls to $80 per share, the investor can purchase 100 shares in the market for $8,000, replace the 100 borrowed shares, and have a tidy profit of $2,000. Of course, if the price goes up to $110, it costs the investor $11,000 to *cover* the short position and a loss is realized.

The tax consequences of short sales are triggered at the time the seller replaces the borrowed shares (i.e., the short position is closed or covered). No gain or loss is recognized until this time.[62] The character of the gain or loss realized depends on whether the asset involved (normally stock) is a capital asset. Determination of the holding period is more confusing. If the replacement securities have been held for a year or less before the *short sale* or are acquired after the sale, the gain or loss realized on closing the position is short term.[63] Moreover, if the taxpayer does not use such stock to replace the borrowed shares, the holding period of such securities starts again, beginning on the date the short position was closed.[64] If the replacement property has been held for more than a year prior to the short sale, the gain or loss recognized on closing is long-term, regardless of the holding period of the actual shares used to close the short position.

Example 33. On March 15, 2004 T purchased 100 shares of S stock for $4,000. On February 15, 2005 T sold 100 shares of S stock short for $5,000. On June 15, 2005 T closed out her short position by delivering the March 15, 2004 shares. Because T held the replacement shares less than one year before she shorted the stock (March 15, 2004 to February 15, 2005), she reports a $1,000 short-term capital gain.

Example 34. Same facts as *Example 33*, except T closed out her position by purchasing 100 new shares on June 15, 2005 for $6,500. In addition, she sold the original shares on August 15, 2005 for $7,000. T reports a capital loss of $1,500 ($5,000 − $6,500) upon covering her short position, and it is short-term since she held substantially identical stock less than a year before she shorted the stock (March 15, 2004 to February 15, 2005). In addition, T reports a *short-term* capital gain on the sale of the original stock of $3,000 ($7,000 − $4,000) even though she has held the stock for more than one year (March 1, 2004 to August 15, 2005). The holding period for the original stock begins again on the date the short sale was

---

[62]   Reg. § 1.1233-1(a)(1).

[63]   § 1233(b).

[64]   *Ibid.*

closed by virtue of the fact that she owned such stock less than one year before the short sale.

Constructive Sale Treatment for Appreciated Financial Positions. For many years, investors often wanted to lock in their gain positions without having to recognize them for tax purposes. To accomplish this, an investor would sell stock short and close out the position at a later time. This was referred to as selling short against the box. The tax benefit of this technique was eliminated in 1997. Now, if a taxpayer undertakes a short sale or similar disposition of property that he or she owns, the taxpayer must treat the short sale as the disposition of the underlying property and recognize gain as if the underlying property had been sold.[65]

Example 35. P owns 200 shares of BDF Corporation that was purchased at a cost of $24 per share. On November 14 of the current year, P sold 50 shares of BDF short for $50 per share. P is treated as selling the shares for $2,500 on November 14 and must recognize a gain of $1,300 ($2,500 − $1,200).

This rule does not apply if the transaction is closed within 30 days after the close of the year of the short sale or similar disposition.

OPTIONS

Options of one variety or another have become commonplace in the business and investment world. They can be used in a variety of ways (e.g., an option to buy a house or buy land), but they are probably best known as a technique—sometimes a speculative one—to invest in the stock and commodities markets. The popularity of options has skyrocketed since the Chicago Board Options Exchange began organized trading in listed options in 1973. Currently, listed options on hundreds of securities can be bought and sold just like the securities themselves. One need only glance at the daily quotes in the *Wall Street Journal* or similar financial newspapers to appreciate this everyday phenomenon. This growth in the use of options requires tax advisers to have some appreciation of how they work and how they are taxed.

For some, however, options are shrouded in a cloud of mystery, an esoteric investment tool too sophisticated for the common investor. In reality, the basic operation of options is not that complicated. An option simply gives the holder the right to buy or sell a specific asset at a certain price by a specified date. A taxpayer who owns an option may either exercise the option, sell the option, or allow it to expire. The tax treatment of these actions is just as straightforward as the operation of the option itself.

Treatment of Option Buyer. If the taxpayer exercises the option, the amount paid for the option is treated as a capital expenditure and added to the taxpayer's basis for the property. If the taxpayer sells the option or allows it to expire, the tax treatment depends on the nature of the underlying property.[66] In other words, if the taxpayer sells the option, the sale is treated as a sale of the option property. Therefore, any gain or loss recognized is a capital gain or loss only if the option property is a capital asset.

Example 36. On May 1, J purchased for $500 an option to buy 100 shares of Wells Fargo common stock at a price of $100 per share at any time before August 2nd. On August 1, when Wells Fargo was trading at $130 per share, J exercised his

---

[65] § 1259.

[66] § 1234(a). Note that the lapse of an option is treated as a sale or exchange [§ 1234(b)].

option and bought 100 shares for $10,000. Although J is immediately better from his purchase, he has no income. The basis of his stock is $10,500 (the $500 cost of the option + the $10,000 cost of the stock) and the holding period begins on August 2nd.

Example 37. On January 2, Compaq common stock was trading at what K thought was a bargain price of $65 per share. Consequently, K purchased for $700 an option to buy 100 shares of Compaq at a price of $80 on or before March 15. After the corporation reported its earnings, the stock value jumped, and by March 1 the price was bouncing between $95 and $100 per share. The value of K's option had also increased, and he sold it for $3,000. Since the option property, the stock, is a capital asset, K reports a short-term capital gain of $2,300 ($3,000 − $700).

Example 38. Same facts as *Example 37*, except Compaq's earnings were disappointing and the value of the stock as well as the value of K's option decreased. On March 15, the stock was trading at $60 per share and K decided to let the option expire. K recognizes a short-term capital loss of $700.

Options are generally billed as a way to secure a potentially large profit from a relatively small investment with a known risk. The option buyer knows in advance that the most that can be lost is the amount paid for the option. There are generally two types of options: puts and calls. A *call* is simply the shorthand term given to an option that gives the holder the right to purchase a particular security at a fixed price. All of the discussion and examples above deal with call options. For example, if an individual believes the price of IBM will rise from $50 to $70 over the next several months, she might purchase a call that enables her to buy 1,000 shares at a price far lower than the $50,000 that would be required to actually buy the stock. The ultimate tax treatment of the call depends, as explained above, on whether the taxpayer sells or exercises the option or allows it to lapse.

Treatment of Option Writer (Seller). In any option agreement, there are two parties, the party who buys the option and the person who "writes," or sells, the option. Individuals who write, or sell, call options obligate themselves to deliver a certain number of shares at a particular price in exchange for the payment of some amount referred to as the call premium. If the call is written by a person who owns the underlying stock (a "covered" call), the individual can deliver such stock if the call is exercised. If the writer does not own the stock (a "naked" call), the stock must be purchased to meet the obligation—a very risky situation. Writers of covered calls generally view the call premium as an additional source of income or as a hedge against a possible decline in the value of the stock. If the buyer exercises the call, the writer of the option adds the premium to the amount realized in determining the gain or loss realized on the stock sold. The gain or loss is long-term or short-term depending on the holding period of the underlying stock. If the buyer allows the call to expire, the writer of the call treats the premium received for the option as a short-term capital gain regardless of the actual holding period.[67] The gain is reported at the time the option expires.

Example 39. After discussing it with her broker, W decided to write call options on her 100 shares of Colgate that she bought several years ago for $3,000. She deposited the stock with her broker and instructed him to write a call that allows an investor to purchase 100 shares of Colgate at $40 per share at a premium of $5 per share. Within a few business days, W's account was credited with $500 for writing

---

[67] If the writer of the call is in the trade or business of granting options, the gain would be ordinary rather than capital gain. § 1234(b).

the call. If the call is not exercised, W has a $500 short-term capital gain. If the call is exercised, W sells her stock and realizes a long-term capital gain of $1,500 ($4,000 + $500 − $3,000).

Puts. To understand puts, one has to mentally shift gears. Puts are the exact opposites of calls. Whereas a buyer of a call buys the right to purchase stock at a fixed price, a buyer of a put buys the right to sell stock at a fixed price. As in short sales, the buyer of a put typically believes that the price of the underlying stock will drop. If the put is sold, the taxpayer reports a short-term capital gain or loss regardless of the holding period. If the put is exercised (i.e., the taxpayer does in fact sell the underlying stock), the amount realized on the sale is decreased by the premium paid for the put. If the put lapses, a loss is allowable as of the date the option expires. As a practical matter, most puts are bought with the intention of selling them.

Example 40. After seeing reports on television that the airline industry was falling on hard times, P believed the current $47 price on Boeing stock would fall. He immediately called his broker and bought a put at a price of $200 on March 4. The put enables him to sell 100 shares of the stock at a price of $45 per share before August 24. The price did in fact fall and bottomed at $40 per share. As a result, his put, that is, his right to sell the stock at $45, became more valuable, and he sold the put for $500. P must report a short-term capital gain of $300 ($500 − $200).

CORPORATE BONDS AND OTHER INDEBTEDNESS

Investments in corporate bonds and other forms of indebtedness present several unique problems that must be considered by taxpayers who choose this form of investment. Under the general rules, mere collection of principal payments does not constitute a sale or exchange and, therefore, a capital gain or capital loss cannot result. However, the Code creates an exception for certain forms of debt. This special rule provides that any amounts received by the holder on retirement of any debt are considered as amounts received in exchange for the debt.[68] Consequently, capital gain or loss is normally recognized when the debt is redeemed or sold for more or less than the taxpayer's basis in the debt.

Example 41. B purchased a $1,000, 10% bond issued by Z Corporation for $990. Assuming the bond is held to maturity and redeemed by the corporation, B will recognize a capital gain of $10. If B had sold the bond prior to redemption for $995, he would recognize a capital gain of $5.

A second and more difficult problem to be considered concerns the *interest element* that may be inherent in the purchase price of a corporate bond. For example, if the rate at which a bond pays interest—the stated rate—is less than the current market rate, the bond will sell for less than its face value, or at a discount. In this case, the *discount* effectively functions as a substitute for interest income. Conversely, if the stated rate exceeds the market rate, the bond will sell for more than its face value, or at a premium. Here, the *premium* essentially reduces the amount of interest income. Without special rules, the proper amount of interest income would not be captured and reported in a timely manner.

Example 42. Several years ago when interest rates were 10%, T purchased a $10,000, 8% corporate bond for $8,000, or a $2,000 discount. This year the bond matured and T redeemed the bond for its par value of $10,000. Under normal accounting procedures, the redemption is treated as an exchange and the taxpayer

---

[68] § 1271.

would recognize a long-term capital gain of $2,000 ($10,000 − $8,000). In this case, the taxpayer would have converted the discount of $2,000, which from an economic view is ordinary interest income, to capital gain. Moreover, this income would be deferred until T sold the bond.

The example above illustrates the problems that the special tax rules governing bond transactions address. The provisions ensure that any premium or discount is not treated as part of the capital gain or loss realized on disposition of the bond, but rather is treated as an *adjustment* to the taxpayer's interest income received from the bond. In addition, the Code provides rules for determining how much of the premium or discount will affect interest income and *when* the additional interest income (in the case of discount) or the interest expense (in the case of premium) will be reported.

The Code provides a separate set of rules governing the treatment of premium and discount. In the case of discount, the rules differ depending on when the discount arises. One set applies when the bonds were *originally issued* at a discount (the "original issue discount" provisions) and another set applies if the discount arises when the bonds are purchased later in the open market (the "market discount" rules). The rules governing premium are the same regardless of when the premium arises.

ORIGINAL ISSUE DISCOUNT

When corporate bonds are *issued* at a price less than the stated redemption price at maturity (i.e., the bond's face value), the resulting discount is referred to as *original issue discount*, or more commonly OID. The amount of OID is easily computed as follows:

Redemption price (face value)	$x,xxx
− Issue price	−xxx
= Original issue discount	$x,xxx

The OID provisions generally require the holder of the bond to amortize the discount and include it in income during the period the bond is held.[69] For purposes of computing the gain or loss on disposition of the bond, the holder must increase the basis of the bond by the amount of any amortized discount. Any gain or loss on the disposition of the bond normally is capital gain. However, if at the time of issue there was an intention to call the bond before maturity, any gain on the bond is treated as ordinary income to the extent of any unamortized discount.[70]

Before examining the amortization methods, it should be emphasized that the Code furnishes a de minimis rule that may exempt the debt from the OID amortization requirements. OID is considered to be zero when the bond discount is less than one-fourth of one percent of the redemption price at maturity multiplied by the number of complete years to maturity.[71] This may be expressed as follows:

Redemption price at maturity	$x,xxx
× Percentage	×0.25%
× Number of complete years to maturity	×x
= De minimis amount	$x,xxx

---

[69]   §§ 1271–1275.

[70]   § 1271(a)(2).

[71]   § 1273(a)(3).

In most cases, new bond issues do not create OID because the stated interest rate is set near the market rate so that the amount of discount that arises, if any, does not exceed the de minimis amount. As a result, no amortization is required.

For bonds issued after July 1, 1982, the discount is amortized into income using a technique similar to the effective interest method used in financial accounting.[72] To determine the includible OID, the OID attributable to an accrual period must be computed. This is done by multiplying the *adjusted issue price* at the beginning of the *accrual period* by the *yield to maturity* and reducing this amount by any interest payable on the bond during the period. The adjusted issue price is the bond's original issue price as increased for previously amortized OID. The accrual period is generally the six-month period ending on the anniversary date of the bond (date of original issue) and six months before such date. The yield to maturity must be determined using present value techniques or may be found in bond tables designed specifically for this purpose.[73]

Once the OID attributable to the entire bond period is computed, this amount is allocated ratably to each day in the bond period. The bondholder's includible OID is the sum of the daily portions of OID for each day during the taxable year that the owner held the bond.

Example 43. On July 1, 2005 R purchased 100 newly issued 30-year, 8% bonds with a face value of $1,000 for $800 each or $80,000. The bonds pay interest semiannually on July 1 and December 31. The OID rules apply since the $200 discount per bond exceeds the de minimis amount of $75.

Redemption price at maturity	$1,000
× Percentage	×0.25%
× Number of complete years to maturity	×30
= De minimis amount	$ 75

Using present value calculations, the annual yield to maturity for this bond is 10.14% (or 5.07% semiannually). The OID that R must include in income in 2005 and 2006 for all of the bonds is computed in the aggregate as follows.

	7/1–12/31 2005	1/1–6/30 2006	7/1–12/31 2006
Adjusted issue price..........................	$80,000	$80,056*	$80,115
Semiannual yield............................	×5.07%	×5.07%	×5.07%
Total effective interest......................	$ 4,056	$ 4,059	$ 4,062
Less: Interest received....................	−4,000	−4,000	−4,000
Includible OID............................	$ 56	$ 59	$ 62

*$100,000 × 4% = $4,000
*$80,000 + $56 = $80,056

R would include the amount of OID in income in addition to the interest income actually received. Note that the issuer of the bond would include in its annual deduction for interest expense the amount of OID that must be amortized.

---

[72]   § 1272(a). For bonds issued after July 1, 1982, and before January 1, 1985, the accrual period is one year.

[73]   Given the issue price, the redemption price, and the number of periods to maturity, the yield to maturity may be approximated by reference to appropriate present-value tables.

Example 44. Assume the same facts as above, except that R sells all of the bonds for $85,000 on July 1, 2006. Assuming there was no intention to call the bonds when issued, R will report a capital gain of $4,885 ($85,000 − $80,115).

Additional computations are required when the purchase price exceeds the original issue price as increased by OID amortized by previous holders. As a practical matter, the issuer of the bond is obligated to provide the taxpayer a Form 1099-OID, Statement of Original Issue Discount, disclosing the amount of interest income to be reported annually. For those who do not receive such a form, the IRS provides a special publication with the necessary information.

For bonds issued before July 2, 1982, the OID is generally included in the income of the holder ratably over the term of the bond (i.e., a straight-line method is used).[74]

Example 45. Assume the bond in *Example 43* was issued prior to July 2, 1982. The original issue discount included annually would be $667 ($20,000 ÷ 30).

Although the OID rules are to apply to virtually all debt instruments, there are several notable exceptions:[75]

1. U.S. Savings Bonds (which are treated as discussed in Chapter 5)

2. Tax-exempt state and local obligations (although the discount income is not included as taxable income, the taxpayer increases the basis of the instrument)

3. Debt instruments that have a fixed maturity date not exceeding one year [unless held by certain parties identified in § 1281(b), including accrual basis taxpayers]

4. Obligations issued by individuals before March 2, 1984

5. Nonbusiness loans between individuals of $10,000 or less.

In 1984 the coverage of the OID rules was substantially extended to help curb abuses that occurred when a taxpayer sold property and received a note in exchange. The application of the OID rules in this area was discussed in Chapter 14 in conjunction with unstated interest.

MARKET DISCOUNT

As previously noted, without special rules, amortization of discount would not be required where the security was treated as having no OID (e.g., where the discount on the bond when originally issued was small). For example, if a bond having a $10,000 face value bearing 10 percent interest over a 30-year term was issued for $9,500, there would be no OID since the discount is less than $750 (0.25% × 30 × $10,000). In subsequent years, however, interest rates might rise, causing the bond to sell at a substantially greater discount (i.e., lower value), say $8,000 (e.g., if rates rose to 14 percent the bond's price might fall to $8,000). In such case, an investor could purchase the bond and ultimately report the built-in appreciation as capital gain—the $2,000 rise from the discounted price to face value at maturity—notwithstanding the fact that a portion of the increase in value actually represents interest income. Moreover, the investor could borrow amounts to purchase the investment and obtain an immediate deduction for interest on the debt, although the income from the bond was deferred until it was redeemed or sold. This highly publicized and extremely popular investment technique was foreclosed by the Deficit Reduction Act of 1984 for newly issued bonds.

---

[74] § 1272(a); for bonds issued before May 28, 1969, special rules apply. See § 1272(b).

[75] §§ 1272(a)(2) and 1274(c)(2).

Changes made in 1993 make the rules applicable to *all* bonds purchased after April 30, 1994. Code § 1276 provides that any gain on the disposition of a bond is treated as ordinary income to the extent of any accrued *market discount*. Market discount, in contrast to OID, is measured at the time the purchaser acquires the bond. Hence, market discount is the excess of the stated redemption price over the basis of the bond immediately after *acquisition*.[76] Like OID, market discount is considered to be zero if it is less than one-fourth of one percent of the stated redemption price multiplied by the number of complete years to maturity after acquisition. The portion of market discount that is considered ordinary income upon disposition of the bond is computed assuming the discount accrues ratably over the number of days from the purchase of the bond to the bond's maturity date.

> **Example 46.** On January 1, 2004 T purchased a bond issued in 2003 having a face value of $10,000 for $8,000. The bond matures four years later on January 1, 2008. The market discount on the bond is $2,000, the difference between the stated redemption price of $10,000 and the taxpayer's $8,000 basis in the bond immediately after acquisition (assuming there was no OID). The $2,000 is deemed to accrue on a daily basis over the 1,460 days remaining on the bond's term. Assuming T sells the bond for $9,000 on January 2, 2005, her gain is $1,000, of which $500 is ordinary interest income [$2,000 × (365 ÷ 1,460)] and the remaining $500 is long-term capital gain.

In lieu of using the daily method of computing the accrued market discount, the taxpayer may use the effective interest method similar to that used for amortizing OID. In addition, the taxpayer may elect to report accrued market discount in taxable income annually rather than at the date of disposition. If this election is made, the taxpayer increases the basis of the bond by the amount of market discount included in income.

Congress also enacted provisions limiting the taxpayer's interest deduction on loans to purchase market discount bonds. Section 1277 requires the taxpayer to defer the deduction for interest expense until that time when income from the bond is reported.

CONVERSION TRANSACTIONS

The original issue discount and market discount provisions exist in order to prevent taxpayers from converting ordinary interest income into capital gain when the interest element is in the form of a discount. In certain instances, taxpayers may still be able to avoid this treatment by structuring the transactions somewhat differently. Congress refers to these as *conversion transactions*.

Conversion transactions are certain investments on which the return is attributable to the time value of money, or for which the sales price of the investment is known at the time the investment is made. Upon the sale or disposition of such investments, any gain is treated as ordinary income, rather than capital gain, to the extent of a return on the investment calculated at 120 percent of the applicable federal rate.[77] Any gain in excess of the ordinary income or any loss realized on the investment is treated as capital gain or loss, assuming the contract is a capital asset to the taxpayer.

BOND PREMIUM

The treatment of premium depends in part on whether the interest income on the bond is taxable.[78] When the interest income is taxable, the taxpayer *may* elect to

---

[76] § 1277(a)(2). If the bond also has OID, the market discount is reduced by the amortized portion of OID.

[77] § 1258.

[78] § 171.

16-4 *Holding Period.* What is the rule for determining the holding period for property acquired by gift?

16-5 *Holding Period.* What is the holding period of property acquired from a decedent?

16-6 *Holding Period—Stock Exchange Transactions.* T placed an order with her stock broker to sell 100 shares of Kent Electronics, Inc. stock on December 23, 2005. Because the sale order was received after the close of the market on the 23rd, the sale was executed at 9:00 A.M. on December 30, 2005. T received a settlement check from the brokerage house on January 5, 2006. What is the date of sale and what is the last date of T's holding period?

16-7 *Holding Period—Worthless Securities.* D purchased 1,000 shares of H, Inc. for $4,450 in a speculative investment on October 25, 2004. Weeks later, on January 5, 2005, D received notice that the H, Inc. stock was worthless. What are the amount and character of D's loss in 2005?

16-8 *Capital Gain and Loss Netting Process.* Describe the three possible results of the capital gain and loss netting process. How are the gains treated for tax purposes?

16-9 *Capital Gains Tax.* D is single and has taxable income for the current year of $72,000, including a $7,000 capital gain on the sale of stock held for two years. Describe how D will determine the tax on his income for the year.

16-10 *Capital Loss Deduction: Individuals.* How is the capital loss deduction limited for individual taxpayers?

16-11 *Capital Gains and Losses: Corporations.* The tax rules governing a corporation's capital gains and losses differ somewhat from those for an individual.
    a. Explain how a corporation treats capital gains and losses and how this treatment differs from that of an individual.
    b. Some commentators are fond of saying that corporations rarely have capital gains and losses to worry about. Why might this be true?

16-12 *Capital Loss Carryover.* Capital losses in excess of the annual limit can be carried forward to the subsequent year. How long may losses be carried forward by individual taxpayers? What is the character of the loss carryover and what happens if net losses from each of the groups (short-term, 28 percent, and 15 percent) are carried forward?

16-13 *Patents.* What is necessary for a patent to qualify for capital gain or loss treatment under § 1235?

16-14 *Ordinary v. Capital Loss Treatment.* What are the tax consequences to P, a bachelor, of a $70,000 loss occurring on June 1 of the current year attributable to the following:
    a. An uncollectible nonbusiness loan to XYZ Corporation
    b. Worthless bonds of XYZ Corporation acquired on November 30 of the prior year
    c. The sale of XYZ stock qualifying as § 1244 stock when acquired two years ago

16-15 *Section 1244 Stock.* When is a taxpayer's stock considered § 1244 stock? Why is the designation significant?

16-16 *Fifty Percent Exclusion.* S purchased qualified small business stock in U Corp. on October 27, 2005 for $35,000 with hopes to later qualify for the 50 percent exclusion.
    a. What two major requirements must U Corp. meet throughout S's holding period?
    b. What is the first day on which S may sell the stock and qualify for the 50 percent exclusion?
    c. What is the rollover provision and why is it important?

16-17 *Rollover of Gain on Sales of Publicly Traded Securities.* Q sold common stock in K Corp., a publicly traded corporation, for $140,000, realizing a gain of $60,000.

   a. How much must Q reinvest in a corporation or partnership that is licensed by the Small Business Administration under § 301(d) of the Small Business Investment Act of 1958 (as in effect on May 13, 1994) in order to defer all of the $60,000 gain?

   b. By what day must Q reinvest to qualify for this gain rollover (deferral)?

16-18 *Dealers in Securities.* How does a dealer in securities guarantee that a particular "investment" will qualify for capital gain or loss treatment?

16-19 *Original Issue Discount—Deep Discount Bonds.* Financial consulting services often advise investment in so-called *deep discount bonds* (e.g., a $1,000 par value bond maturing in 10 years with coupon rate of six percent that sells at a discounted price of $400). Explain how such an investment could provide any tax savings in light of the original issue discount rules.

16-20 *Bond Premium.* This year, G purchased a $1,000 bond for $1,100. The bond matures in 2011 and pays interest at a rate of 10 percent. Interest is paid semiannually on February 1 and August 1. Explain the treatment of the premium on the bond if the bond was issued by:

   a. General Motors

   b. City of Sacramento

PROBLEMS

16-21 *Identifying Capital Assets.* Which of the following items are capital assets?

   a. An automobile held for sale to customers by Midtown Motors, Inc.

   b. An automobile owned and used by Sherry Hartman to run household errands

   c. An automobile owned and used by Windowwashers, Inc.

   d. The private residence of Robert Hamilton

   e. Letters from a famous U.S. President written to Jane Doe (Jane Doe has the letters.)

   f. A warehouse owned and used by Holt Packing Company

   g. Gold bullion

16-22 *Identifying Capital Assets.* Which of the following properties are capital assets? Briefly explain your answers.

   a. A house built by a home-building contractor and used by her as her principal residence

   b. A house, 80 percent of which is used as a residence and 20 percent of which is used to store business inventory

   c. The same house in (b) above, used as stated for 10 years, and now used exclusively as a residence

   d. Undeveloped land held for investment by a real estate broker

   e. Stock held for investment by a stock broker

16-23 *Capital Gain Netting Process.* D sold the following capital assets during 2005:

Description	Date Acquired	Date Sold	Sales Price	Adjusted Basis
100 shares XY Corp.	1/10/84	1/12/05	$14,000	$1,000
50 shares LM Inc.	9/14/03	1/12/05	1,900	4,000
140 shares CH Corp.	11/20/03	4/10/05	3,400	3,000
Gold necklace	4/22/92	6/30/05	5,000	1,300
Personal auto	5/10/01	8/31/05	4,000	6,500

Explain the effects of the transactions above on D's taxable income and final tax liability.

16-24 *Calculation of Capital Gains Tax.* Refer to the facts in *Problem 16-23* above. Assuming D, single, also has taxable income of $72,000 (net of her standard deduction and exemption), compute her tax liability.

16-25 *Capital Gain Netting Process.* Each of the following situations deals with capital gains and losses occurring during the current year for an individual taxpayer. For each case, determine the change in adjusted gross income and the maximum tax to be imposed on any gain.

> **Note:** N15CG(L) = Net 15 percent capital gain or (loss)
> NSTCG(L) = Net short-term capital gain or (loss)

Case	N15CG(L)	NSTCG(L)
A	$ 1,200	$ 1,200
B	1,600	(1,000)
C	(1,200)	1,800
D	4,500	(800)
E	2,400	1,800

16-26 *Gain and Losses on Property Acquired by Gift.* In each of the following independent situations, assume that the taxpayer received the capital asset as a gift on March 19, 2005, that the donor had held the property since 2001, and that the property was sold during 2005. No gift taxes were payable on the transfer. Determine the gain or loss recognized in each case.

Case	Date of Sale	Sales Price	Donor's Basis	FMV Date of Gift
A	4/19	$1,000	$ 400	$ 600
B	6/3	1,000	1,400	1,200
C	11/20	1,000	900	1,100

16-27 *Capital Gains and Losses.* K, a single individual, earned salaries and wages of $56,000 and interest and dividends of $3,700 for the current year. In addition, K sold the following capital assets:

100 shares of GHJ common stock, held 14 months.	$3,400 gain
1955 Ford pickup, used five years for personal purposes	4,500 gain
30 acres of land, held three years for investment	6,200 loss

a. Compute K's net capital gain or loss.
b. Compute K's adjusted gross income.

16-28 *Capital Gains and Losses.* L earned salaries and wages of $47,000 and interest and dividends of $6,700 for the current year. In addition, L sold the following capital assets:

10 shares LMN common stock, held ten months	$1,400 gain
1990 Dodge sedan, used four years for personal purposes. .	2,600 loss
10 acres of land, held six years for investment	9,200 loss

    a. Compute L's overall capital gain or loss.

    b. Compute L's adjusted gross income.

16-29   *Capital Gains Tax.* During her calendar year 2005, G, a single individual with no dependents, had the following capital gains and losses:

Asset	Gain/Loss	Holding Period
200 shares of Western Airlines	$1,400 loss	11 months
Land held for appreciation	12,300 gain	8 years
Silver held for appreciation	1,800 loss	15 months

    a. Assuming G's taxable income (properly calculated) is $29,000, calculate G's gross tax.

    b. Same as above, except G's taxable income is $55,000.

16-30   *Capital Gains Tax.* R is a single, calendar year taxpayer. During 2005, R recognized a $20,000 capital gain from the sale of stock held for three years. Calculate R's tax liability (before credits and prepayments) for each of the following levels of taxable income, assuming that the net capital gains have been included in the taxable income numbers.

    a. $39,700

    b. $81,950

    c. $500,000

16-31   *Capital Gains Tax.* H and J are married, calendar year taxpayers who elect to file jointly. They have no dependents and do not itemize their deductions. Their income and deductions for 2005 are summarized below.

Salaries and wages	$105,000
Interest income	15,500
Qualifying dividends received	4,500
Short-term capital loss	5,000
Long-term capital gains (held > 12 months) . . .	20,000

Determine H and J's tax liability (before credits and prepayments).

16-32   *Effective Tax Rate on Net Capital Gains.* T is an unmarried, calendar year taxpayer. He provides more than one-half the support of his elderly mother, who is living in a nearby nursing home. T's income and deductions for 2005 are summarized below.

Salary	$132,000
Interest income	7,000
Itemized deductions (all subject to the 3% cutback rule)	12,500
Personal and dependency exemptions	2

    a. Calculate T's taxable income and income tax liability (before credits and prepayments) for the year.

    b. How would your answers to (a) above change if T also had a $20,000 capital gain during the year from the sale of stock held 15 months?

    c. Is the additional income tax from the capital gain limited to $4,000 ($20,000 × 20%)? If not, explain why.

16-33   *Tax Treatment of Dividends as Capital Gain.* P and H, married, cash basis, calendar year taxpayers who file a joint return have the following income and expenses for 2005:

Salaries and wages	$80,000
Qualifying dividends.	4,000
Long-term capital gains	5,000
Short-term capital gains or (losses)	0
Itemized deductions.	31,700
Dependents—None	

a. Calculate the federal income tax for P and H for the year.

b. How would you answer differ if P and H also had short-term capital losses of $6,000?

16-34 *Netting Process and Capital Losses.* T, an unmarried taxpayer, sold the following capital assets during her calendar year 2005:

	Date Acquired	Date Sold	Sales Price	Adjusted Basis
100 shares CZ Corp.	1/10/05	9/17/05	$14,000	$18,000
75 shares PC, Inc.	7/6/05	9/17/05	5,200	4,300
Silver coins (held as an investment)	12/2/00	11/20/05	2,000	5,000

Complete each of the following requirements based on T's taxable income of $15,000 before capital gains and losses:

a. T's net 15 percent capital gain or loss

b. T's net 28 percent capital gain or loss

c. T's net short-term capital gain or loss

d. T's capital loss deduction in arriving at adjusted gross income

e. T's capital loss carryover to 2006 (describe amount and character)

f. How would your answers to (d) and (e) differ if T's basis in the PC stock had been $1,000?

16-35 *Capital Loss and Carryover.* N earned a salary of $55,000 and interest and dividends of $6,500 for the current year. N also has the following capital gains and losses for the current year:

30 shares MNO common stock, held ten months . . .	$ 400 gain
50 shares NOP common stock, held four years.	3,600 loss
Long-term capital loss carryforward from prior year. .	11,600 loss
10 acres of land, held six years for investment	9,200 gain

a. Compute L's overall capital gain.

b. Compute L's adjusted gross income.

16-36 *Capital Gains and Losses.* Each of the following independent cases involves capital gains and losses occurring during the calendar year 2005 for an unmarried individual taxpayer.

> **Note:** N15CG(L) = Net 15 percent capital gain or (loss)
> NSTCG(L) = Net short-term capital gain or (loss)

Case	N15CG(L)	NSTCG(L)
A	$ 1,200	$(4,300)
B	(5,000)	200
C	(1,200)	(2,300)

D	(7,000)	200
E	(5,000)	(200)

a. Determine the amount deductible in arriving at adjusted gross income in each case for 2005.

b. Which, if any, of the above case(s) generate(s) a capital loss carryover to 2006? Give the amount and character.

16-37 *Capital Loss Deduction and Capital Loss Carryover.* W, an unmarried calendar year individual, had numerous capital asset transactions during the years listed. Determine the amount deductible in each year and the amount and character of any carryover.

Year	N15CG(L)	NSTCG(L)
2004	$(8,000)	$ 1,000
2005	(1,500)	(2,000)
2006	0	(4,000)
2007	2,000	(3,000)

16-38 *Capital Loss Deduction and Capital Loss Carryover.* M, an unmarried calendar year individual, had numerous capital asset transactions during the years listed. Determine the amount deductible in each year and the amount and character of any carryover.

Year	N15CG(L)	NSTCG(L)
2004	$ 1,000	$(5,000)
2005	(6,000)	0
2006	3,000	(3,000)
2007	(3,000)	(3,000)

16-39 *Capital Loss Carryovers.* For her calendar year 2004, H, a single individual with no dependents, had unused short-term capital losses of $10,000. For 2005, her gains and losses were as follows:

Asset	Amount	Holding Period
Corporate stock	$ 1,400 loss	11 months
Land held for appreciation	14,300 gain	8 years
Silver held for appreciation	1,800 gain	25 months

After completing the netting process, how much are H's 15 percent gains and 28 percent gains?

16-40 *Requirements for § 1244 Stock.* During the year, X, who is single, sold stock and realized a loss. For each of the following situations, indicate whether § 1244 would apply to the taxpayer's stock loss. Unless otherwise indicated, Code § 1244 applies.

a. The stock was that issued to X when she incorporated her business several years ago.

b. The stock was that of General Motors Corporation and was purchased last year.

c. X inherited the stock from her grandfather, who had started the company ten years ago.

d. X is a corporate taxpayer.

e. X acquired her stock interest in 2000. The other four owners had acquired their interest for $250,000 each in 1995.

f. The loss was $60,000.

16-41 *Section 1244 Stock Computation.* S is a bachelor. During the year, he sold stock in X Corporation that qualifies as § 1244 stock at a loss of $70,000. In addition, S sold stock in Y Corporation, realizing a $4,000 15 percent capital gain. Compute the effect of these transactions on S's A.G.I.

16-42 *Short Sales.* K purchased 400 shares of Intel common five years ago for $7,000. During the current year, she sold short 200 shares for $17,500. Her plan is to either buy new shares to cover the short sale or deliver 200 of the original shares in one year. Assuming the stock drops, and as planned, K purchases 200 shares for $16,000 to cover the short sale, how are these transactions treated for tax purposes?

16-43 *Worthless Securities.* Several years ago, T was persuaded by his good friend W to invest in her new venture, Wobbly Corporation. T purchased 100 shares of Wobbly stock from W for $60,000. He also purchased Wobbly bonds, which had a face value of $20,000 for $18,000. This year, Wobbly declared bankruptcy and T's investment in Wobbly became worthless. What are the tax consequences to T?

16-44 *Sale of Stock.* B owned 50 percent of the stock in a small incorporated dress shop. The business was successful for several years until a new freeway diverted nearly all of the traffic away from the location. The shop was moved, but to no avail, and the stock continued to quickly decline in value. Other than small interest payments, the income of the business came exclusively from sales of women's apparel.

The total paid-in capital of the corporation was $250,000, all in the form of cash. B's basis in the stock was always $125,000. In an attempt to prevent further losses, the shop was sold to a larger competitor during 2005. B received $50,000 for all of her stock.

a. How will B report the loss on the joint return she files with her husband for 2005?

b. How would your answer to (a) differ if the stock became totally worthless rather than being sold in 2005?

16-45 *Worthless Securities.* Y purchased 30 shares of BCD Corporation common stock on March 2, 2004, for $2,475. On February 26, 2005 Y was notified by her broker that the stock was worthless.

a. What are the amount and character of Y's loss?

b. Could this loss qualify as an ordinary deduction under § 1244? Explain.

16-46 *Fifty Percent Gain Exclusion.* E purchased qualified small business stock in P, Inc. on October 27, 1999 for $75,000. The stock continued to qualify until E sold it for $400,000 on December 15, 2005.

a. How much is E's gain realized upon this sale?

b. How much of this gain may E exclude from gross income?

c. What is the maximum amount of tax that E could pay on this gain (assuming no change in tax rates)?

d. How could E avoid recognizing the gain realized?

16-47 *Rollover of Gain on Sale of Publicly Traded Securities.* R sold common stock in L Corp., a publicly traded corporation, on March 13, 2005 for $160,000, realizing a gain of $40,000. On April 1, 2005 R reinvested $200,000 in M Partnership, a partnership licensed by the Small Business Administration under § 301(d) of the Small Business Investment Act of 1958 (as in effect on May 13, 1993).

a. How much gain must R recognize on the sale of the L Corp. stock?

b. What is R's basis in his interest in M Partnership?

16-48 *Combining the Exclusion and Rollover.* Y sold common stock in X Corp., a publicly traded corporation, on October 1, 1999 for $200,000, realizing a gain of $35,000. On October 15, 1999 Y reinvested $250,000 in N, Inc., a corporation licensed by the Small Business Administration under § 301(d) of the Small Business Investment Act of 1958 (as in effect on May 13, 1993), the stock of which is qualified small business stock. On December 1, 2005 Y sold all of the N, Inc. stock for $625,000.

   a. How much is Y's gain realized on the sale of the N, Inc. stock?

   b. How much of this gain is excludable from gross income?

16-49   *Lease Cancellation Payment.* L rents a house to T for $450 per month under a two-year lease. When T is transferred, he offers L $675 to terminate the lease. If L accepts, what is the tax treatment of the transaction to L and T?

16-50   *Franchise Agreements.* J entered into a franchise agreement with Box, Inc. under which J will operate a fast food restaurant bearing the trademark and using the products of Box. Box retained "significant power, right and continuing interest" related to the franchise agreement.

     J made an initial payment under the contract of $40,000, which entitles him to the rights under the contract for 15 years with indefinite extensions at the agreement of both parties. J also is required to pay for all supplies used plus a royalty of 1.5 percent of gross sales. J's sales were $112,000 during the first year. All of the payments described, totaling $41,680, were made during the current year.

   a. How will J report these payments on his cash basis tax return for the current year?

   b. How would Box, Inc. treat the payments from J on its return for the current year? The corporation reports on the cash basis.

16-51   *Original Issue Discount.* On January 1, 2005 B purchased from XYZ Corporation a newly issued, $1 million, 30-year, 4 percent bond for $300,000. The bond produces a semiannual yield to maturity of 7 percent. Interest is paid semiannually on January 1 and July 1. What is B's income with respect to the bond in 2005 and 2006?

16-52   *Market Discount.* D purchased a $10,000, 7 percent bond, for $6,350, on January 1, 2005. The bond was issued at par on January 1, 2004 and matures January 1, 2009. On January 1, 2006 D sold the bond for $8,000. What is D's income from the sale?

16-53   *Conversion Transaction.* J purchased a non-interest-bearing financial instrument on June 1, 2004 for $60,000. It was purchased subject to a contract that allows J to redeem the instrument for $66,000 on May 31, 2005, but it may not be redeemed early. The applicable federal rate is 5 percent throughout J's holding period. What are the amount and character of J's gain recognized in 2005?

16-54   *Comprehensive Capital Gain Problem.* P is an unmarried full-time investor with no dependents. Her income for the year 2005 is as follows:

Taxable interest income.	$25,750
Excludable municipal bond interest	8,600
Qualifying dividends.	11,650
Consulting fees	6,400
Social security benefits	8,400

Although P does not have sufficient deductions to itemize, her records reveal the following:

Investment expenses.	$ 850
Expenses related to consulting	1,200

In addition to the above, P recognized the following gains and losses during the year:

Loss on sale of 100 shares of A, Inc., held three years	$ (1,200)
Loss on sale of personal automobile	(1,800)

Sales price of 100 shares of B Corp., sold short   8,200
    (This short sale was closed the following year with newly
    purchased shares costing $9,600. P owned no B Corp. stock at
    the time of the short sale.)
Gain on sale of unimproved land held as an investment for six years   45,000

Calculate P's adjusted gross income, taxable income, and gross income tax based on the above for 2005. Begin by calculating P's self-employment tax.

RESEARCH PROBLEMS

16-55 *Transfer of Patents.* G has just completed a successful invention of a new automotive fuel conservation device. He is willing to sell his patent rights for all areas of the United States east of the Rocky Mountains.

In 2005 G entered into an agreement with a marketing firm, giving it exclusive rights to market his invention anywhere east of the Rockies. In exchange, he received a principal sum and is to receive royalties based on sales volume.

Is G entitled to capital gain treatment on this sale under § 1235? Would it make any difference if the transferee of the patent was given exclusive rights to the patent and was given the right to "sublease" the patent?

Research aids:

Kueneman v. Comm., 80-2 USTC ¶9616, 46 AFTR2d 80-5677, 628 F.2d 1196 (CA-9, 1980).

Klein Est v. Comm., 75-1 USTC ¶9127, 35 AFTR2d 75-457, 507 F.2d 617 (CA-7, 1974).

Rouverol v. Comm., 42 T.C. 186 (1964), *non. acq.*, 1965-2 C.B. 7.

16-56 *Sale of Subdivided and Improved Real Property.* D, a full-time physician, has owned 15 acres of unimproved suburban real estate for 10 years. The property was originally purchased for $30,000 and has been held solely for investment. D is now interested in selling the property and has several alternatives. She has come to you for advice concerning the tax treatment of these alternatives. What is the proper tax treatment of each of the following?

a. A sale of the entire acreage to an unrelated party in a single transaction for $150,000.

b. Recording the property with the county as 30 single residential lots, adding roads and improvements at a cost of $100,000, and selling the lots for $25,000 each.

c. Recording the property with the county as 30 single residential lots, and then selling them to an unrelated developer in a single transaction for $190,000.

d. Recording the property with the county as 30 single residential lots and then selling them for $190,000 in a single transaction to a partnership in which D is a 40 percent partner. The partnership then adds roads and improvements at a cost of $100,000 and sells the lots for $25,000 each.

Chapter 17

PROPERTY TRANSACTIONS: DISPOSITIONS OF TRADE OR BUSINESS PROPERTY

LEARNING OBJECTIVES

Upon completion of this chapter you will be able to:

▸ Trace the historical development of the special tax treatment allowed for dispositions of trade or business property

▸ Apply the § 1231 gain and loss netting process to a taxpayer's § 1231 asset transactions

▸ Determine the tax treatment of § 1231 gains and losses

▸ Explain the purpose of the depreciation recapture rules

▸ Compute depreciation recapture under §§ 1245 and 1250

▸ Explain the additional recapture rule applicable only to corporate taxpayers

▸ Identify tax planning opportunities related to sales or other dispositions of trade or business property

---

CHAPTER OUTLINE

INTRODUCTION

As is no doubt clear by now, the treatment of property transactions is a complex story that seeks to answer three questions: (1) What is the gain or loss realized? (2) How much is recognized? and (3) What is its character? This chapter, the final act in the property transaction trilogy, addresses the problems in determining the character of gains or losses on the dispositions of *property used in a trade or business.*

In an uncomplicated world, it might seem logical to assume that gains or losses from property dispositions—be it stock, equipment, buildings, or whatever—would be treated just like any other type of income or deduction. But, as shown in the previous chapter, treating all items alike apparently was not part of the grand plan. Congress forever changed the process with the institution of preferential treatment for capital gains in 1921. Since that time taxpayers have been required to determine not only the gain or loss realized and recognized but also whether a disposition involved a capital asset. It is important to understand that these rules did not simply tip the scales in favor of capital gain. In the interest of fairness and equity, they also established a less than friendly environment for capital losses. The limitations on the deductibility of capital losses is clearly a major disadvantage, particularly considering that ordinary losses are fully deductible. The end result of Congress's handiwork was the creation of a system in which the preferred result is capital gain treatment for gains and ordinary treatment for losses. This chapter contains the saga of what happens when Congress attempts to provide taxpayers with the best of both worlds.

SECTION 1231

The road to tax heaven—capital gain and ordinary loss—begins at § 1231 (in tax parlance properly pronounced as "twelve thirty-one"). While § 1231 can be a completely bewildering provision, its basic operation is relatively simple. At the close of the taxable year, the taxpayer nets all gains and losses from so-called § 1231 property (e.g., land and depreciable property used in a trade or business). If there is a net gain, it is treated as a long-term capital gain. If there is a net loss, it is treated as an ordinary loss. In short, § 1231 allows taxpayers to have their cake and eat it, too. Unfortunately, this is accomplished only with a great deal of complexity, much of which makes sense only if the historical events that shaped § 1231 are considered.

HISTORICAL PERSPECTIVE

At first glance, it seems that the productive assets of a business—its property, plant, and equipment—would be perfect candidates for capital gain treatment and would therefore be considered capital assets. Indeed, that was exactly the case initially. From 1921 to 1938, real or depreciable property used in business was in fact treated as a capital asset. At that time, the classification of such property as a capital asset seemed not only appropriate but desirable—particularly as the economy grew during the early 1920s and taxpayers were realizing gains. However, the opposite became true with the onset of the Great Depression. As the economy deteriorated, businesses that had purchased assets at inflated prices during the booming 1920s found themselves selling such properties at huge losses during the depression-plagued 1930s. To make matters worse, the tax law treated such losses as capital losses, severely limiting their deduction. But Congress apparently had a sympathetic ear for these concerns. Hoping that a change would help stimulate the economy, Congress enacted legislation that removed business properties from the list of capital assets. The legislative history to the Revenue Act of 1938 provides some insight into Congressional thinking, explaining that "corporations will not, as formerly, be deterred from disposing of partially obsolescent property, such as machinery or equipment, because of the limitations imposed ... upon the deduction of capital losses."[1] With the 1938 changes in place, business got the ordinary loss treatment it wanted but at the same time was saddled with ordinary income treatments for its gains.

Although these rules worked well during the Depression years as businesses were reporting losses, they produced some unduly harsh results once the country moved to a wartime economy. By 1942 the build-up for World War II had the economy humming and inflation had once again set in. Businesses that earlier had sold assets for 10 cents on the dollar now found themselves realizing gains. Of course, under the 1938 changes these gains no longer benefited from preferential treatment but were taxed at extraordinarily high tax rates (88 percent for individuals and 40 percent for corporations). The shipping industry was particularly hard hit by the new treatment. Shippers not only had gains as the enemy destroyed their insured ships but also profited when they were forced to sell their property to the government for use in the war. Other businesses that had their factories and equipment condemned and requisitioned also felt the sting of higher ordinary rates. Although these companies could have deferred their gains had they replaced the property under the involuntary conversion rules of § 1033, qualified reinvestment property was in short supply, making § 1033 virtually useless. Understanding the plight of business, Congress once again came to the rescue. In 1942 Congress enacted legislation generally reinstating capital gain treatment but preserving ordinary loss treatment.

The changes in 1942 stemmed primarily from a need to provide relief for those whose property was condemned for the war effort. But in the end they went much further. For consistency, capital gain treatment was extended not only to condemnations of a business property but to other types of involuntary conversions as well. Under the new rules, casualty and theft gains from business property and capital assets also received capital gain treatment. In addition, the new legislation unexpectedly extended capital gain treatment to regular sales of property, plant, and equipment. Apparently, Congress felt that capital gain treatment was also appropriate for taxpayers who were selling out in anticipation of condemnation or simply because wartime conditions had made operations difficult. While Congress thought capital gain treatment was warranted for these gains, it also knew that other businesses had not profited from the war and were still suffering losses from their property transactions. Accordingly, it acted to preserve ordinary loss treatment. The end result of these maneuvers was the enactment of § 1231, an extremely complex provision that provides taxpayers with the best of all possible tax worlds: capital gain and ordinary loss.

The product of Congressional tinkering in 1942 still remains today. To summarize, real and depreciable property used in a trade or business is specifically denied capital asset status. But this does not necessarily mean that such property will be denied capital gain treatment. As explained at the outset, § 1231 generally extends capital gain treatment to gains and losses from these assets if the taxpayer realizes a net gain from all § 1231 transactions. On the other hand, if there is a net loss, ordinary loss treatment applies. But this summary lacks a great deal of precision. The specific rules of § 1231 are described below.

SECTION 1231 PROPERTY

The special treatment of § 1231 is generally granted only to certain transactions involving assets normally referred to as *§ 1231 property*.[2] Section 1231 property includes a variety of assets, but among them the most important is *real or depreciable property that is used in the taxpayer's trade or business* and that is held for more than

---

[1]   House Ways and Means Committee, H.R. Rep. 1860, 75th Cong., 3d Sess. (1938).

[2]   As explained below, § 1231 also applies to involuntary conversions of pure capital assets held more than one year that are used in a trade or business or held for investment. Involuntary conversions by theft or casualty of personal assets are not included under § 1231 but are subject to a special computation.

one year.[3] This definition takes in most items commonly identified as a business's fixed assets, normally referred to as its property, plant, and equipment. For example, the reach of § 1231 includes depreciable personal property used in business, such as machinery, equipment, office furniture, and business automobiles. Similarly, realty used in a business, such as office buildings, warehouses, factories, and farmland, is also considered § 1231 property.

The Code specifically excludes the following assets from § 1231 treatment:

1. Property held primarily for sale to customers in the ordinary course of a trade or business, or includible in inventory, if on hand at the close of the tax year;

2. A copyright; a literary, musical, or artistic composition; a letter or memorandum; or similar property held by a taxpayer whose personal efforts created such property or by certain other persons; or

3. A publication of the United States Government received from the government other than by purchase at the price at which the publication is offered to the general public.[4]

Note that the excluded assets are also excluded from the definition of a capital asset. As a result, gains or losses on the disposition of inventory, property held primarily for resale, literary compositions, and certain government publications always yield ordinary income or ordinary loss.

One of the critical conditions for § 1231 treatment requires that the property be used in a trade or business. Although this test normally presents little difficulty, from time to time it has created problems, particularly for those with rental property. As an illustration, consider the common situation of a taxpayer who sells rental property such as a house, duplex, or apartment complex. Is the property sold a capital asset or § 1231 property? If a taxpayer sells rental property at a gain, the gain would normally receive capital gain treatment regardless of whether the property is a capital asset or § 1231 property. On the other hand, if the taxpayer sells the rental property at a loss, § 1231 treatment is usually far more desirable. Although the Code does not provide any clear guidance on the issue, the courts have generally held that property used for rental purposes is considered as used in a trade or business and is therefore eligible for § 1231 treatment.[5]

OTHER § 1231 PROPERTY

From time to time, Congress has been convinced that particular industries deserve special tax relief. As a result, it has added a number of other properties to the § 1231 basket. Those eligible for capital gain and ordinary loss are

1. Timber, coal, and iron ore to which § 631 applies;[6]

2. Unharvested crops on land used in a trade or business and held for more than one year;[7] and

3. Certain livestock.[8]

---

[3] The holding period is determined in the same manner as it is for capital assets. See § 1223 discussed in Chapter 16.

[4] § 1231(b)(1).

[5] See, for example, *Mary Crawford*, 16 T.C. 678 (1951) A. 1951-2 C.B. 2, and *Gilford v. Comm.*, 53-1 USTC ¶9201, 43 AFTR 221, 201 F.2d 735 (CA-2, 1953).

[6] § 1231(b)(2).

[7] § 1231(b)(4).

[8] § 1231(b)(3).

Timber. Under § 631, the mere cutting of timber by the owner of the timber, or by a person who has the right to cut the timber and has held the timber or right more than one year, is to be treated, at his or her election, as a sale or exchange of the timber that is cut during the year. The timber must be cut for sale or for use in the taxpayer's trade or business. In such case, the taxpayer would report a § 1231 gain or loss and potentially receive capital gain treatment for what otherwise might be considered the taxpayer's inventory—a very favorable result. It may appear that the timber industry has secured an unfair advantage, but timber's eligibility is arguably justified on the grounds that the value of timber normally accrues incrementally as it grows over a long period of time.

The amount of gain or loss on the "sale" of the timber is the fair market value of the timber on the first day of the taxable year minus the timber's adjusted basis for depletion. For all subsequent purposes (i.e., the sale of the cut timber), the fair market value of the timber as of the beginning of the year will be treated as the cost of the timber. The term *timber* not only includes trees used for lumber and other wood products, but also includes evergreen trees that are more than six years old when cut and are sold for ornamental purposes (e.g., Christmas trees).[9]

> **Example 1.** B owned standing timber that he had purchased for $250,000 three years earlier. The timber was cut and sold to a lumber mill for $410,000 during 2005. The fair market value of the standing timber as of January 1, 2005 was $320,000. B has a § 1231 gain of $70,000 if he makes an election under § 631 ($320,000 fair market value of the timber on the first day of the taxable year less its $250,000 adjusted basis for depletion). The remainder of his gain on the *actual* sale of the timber, $90,000 ($410,000 selling price − $320,000 new "cost" of the timber), is ordinary income. Any expenses incurred by B in cutting the timber would be deductible as ordinary deductions.

An election under § 631 with respect to timber is binding on all timber owned by the taxpayer during the year of the election *and* in all subsequent years. The IRS may permit revocation of such election because of significant hardship. However, once the election is revoked, IRS consent must be obtained to make a new election.[10]

Section 631 also applies to the sale of timber under a contract providing a retained economic interest (i.e., a taxpayer sells the timber, but keeps the right to receive a royalty from its later sale) for the taxpayer in the timber. In such a case, the transfer is considered a sale or exchange. The gain or loss is recognized on the date the timber is cut, or when payment is received, if earlier, at the election of the taxpayer.[11]

Coal and Iron Ore. When an owner disposes of coal or domestic iron ore under a contract that calls for a retained economic interest in the property, the disposition is treated as a sale or exchange of the coal or iron ore. The date the coal or ore is mined is considered the date of sale and since the property is § 1231 property, the gain or loss will be treated under § 1231.[12]

The taxpayer may not be a co-adventurer, partner, or principal in the mining of the coal or iron ore. Furthermore, the coal or iron ore may not be sold to certain related taxpayers.[13]

---

9   § 631(a).

10   *Ibid.*

11   § 631(b).

12   § 631(c).

13   §§ 631(c)(1) and (2).

Unharvested Crops. Section 1231 also addresses the special situation where a farmer sells land with unharvested crops sitting upon the land. In this case, it seems logical that the farmer should allocate the sales price between the crops and the land to ensure ordinary income or loss for the sale of the farmer's inventory and capital gain or ordinary loss on the sale of the land. While this may be the theoretically correct result, Congress wanted to eliminate potential controversy over the allocation. Accordingly, for administrative convenience it brought the entire transaction into the § 1231 fold in 1951. Currently, whenever land used in a trade or business and unharvested crops on that land are sold at the same time to the same buyer, the gain or loss is subject to § 1231 treatment as long as the land has been held for more than a year.[14] It is worth noting that the benefits of § 1231 were not extended to farmers free of charge. At the same time, Congress eliminated the current deduction for production expenses. The law now provides that any expenses related to the production of crops cannot be deducted currently but must be capitalized as part of the basis of the crops.[15] Such treatment, in a year when land and crops are sold, reduces the farmer's capital gain on the sale rather than any other ordinary income.

Example 2. F sold 100 acres of land that she used in her farming business just days before the corn on the land was harvested. For the "package" deal, she received $600,000, including an estimated $70,000 for the unharvested crops that she figured had cost her $20,000 to produce. F had purchased the land many years ago for $200,000. In determining the character of her gain, F is not required to allocate the sales price between the crops and the land since she sold both at the same time to the same buyer, therefore qualifying for § 1231 treatment. As a result, she reports a § 1231 gain of $380,000 computed as follows:

Sales price..............................	$ 600,000
Adjusted basis ($200,000 + $20,000).........	− 220,000
§ 1231 gain	$ 380,000

Note that in the year of the sale F has effectively turned the $50,000 ($70,000 − $20,000) profit from the sale of her crops from ordinary income into potential capital gain.

Livestock. As a general proposition, livestock that are used for breeding and other purposes are depreciable assets much like machinery and equipment and therefore qualify for § 1231 treatment. In many situations, however, livestock is used for these purposes for only a short period of time and then sold. If this is the farmer's or rancher's normal practice, the IRS is inclined to argue that the animals are held primarily for resale, in which case the law specifically denies § 1231 treatment. To help end this controversy, Congress specifically made all livestock (other than poultry) used for draft, breeding, dairy, or sporting purposes eligible for § 1231 treatment as long as they are held for over a year.[16] In the case of cattle and horses, however, the holding period is extended to two years. Note that this treatment is extremely beneficial since the taxpayer effectively gets capital gain from animals pulled out of the breeding process and sold. Moreover, the farmer or rancher is allowed to deduct the costs of raising such animals currently against ordinary income. The extension of the holding period for cattle and horses was in part, an attempt to cut back on the benefits of this favorable treatment.

---

[14] § 1231(b)(4).

[15] § 268.

[16] § 1231(b)(3).

SECTION 1231 NETTING PROCESS

The treatment of § 1231 gains or losses ultimately depends on the outcome of a netting process that is far more complicated than outlined earlier.[17] As can be seen from the flowchart in Exhibit 17-1, the taxpayer must first identify all of the gains and losses that enter into the netting process. As might be expected, these include gains and losses from what has been described above as § 1231 property. In addition, the § 1231 hodgepodge includes *involuntary conversions* of certain *capital assets*. Surprisingly, gains or losses recognized from casualties, thefts, or condemnations of capital assets that are used in a trade or business or held for investment are part of the § 1231 netting process. Involuntary conversions of capital assets that are held for *personal use* are not considered under § 1231 but are subject to special rules.

After identifying all of the § 1231 transactions, the taxpayer must segregate the § 1231 gains and losses arising from casualty and theft from those attributable to sale, exchange, and condemnation. The end result is that there are two sets of § 1231 transactions:

1. Involuntary conversions due to casualty and theft of
   - § 1231 property
     - Real and depreciable property used in business and held more than one year
     - Timber, coal, iron ore, unharvested crops, and livestock
   - Capital assets
     - Used in a trade or business or held for investment in connection with business and held more than one year
2. Sales and exchanges of
   - § 1231 property
     - Real and depreciable property used in business
     - Timber, coal, iron ore, unharvested crops and livestock

Involuntary conversion due to condemnation of
   - § 1231 property
     - Real and depreciable property used in business and held more than one year
     - Timber, coal, iron ore, unharvested crops, and livestock
   - Capital assets
     - Used in a trade or business or held for investment in connection with business and held more than one year

---

[17] § 1231(a).

EXHIBIT 17-1
Section 1231 Netting Process

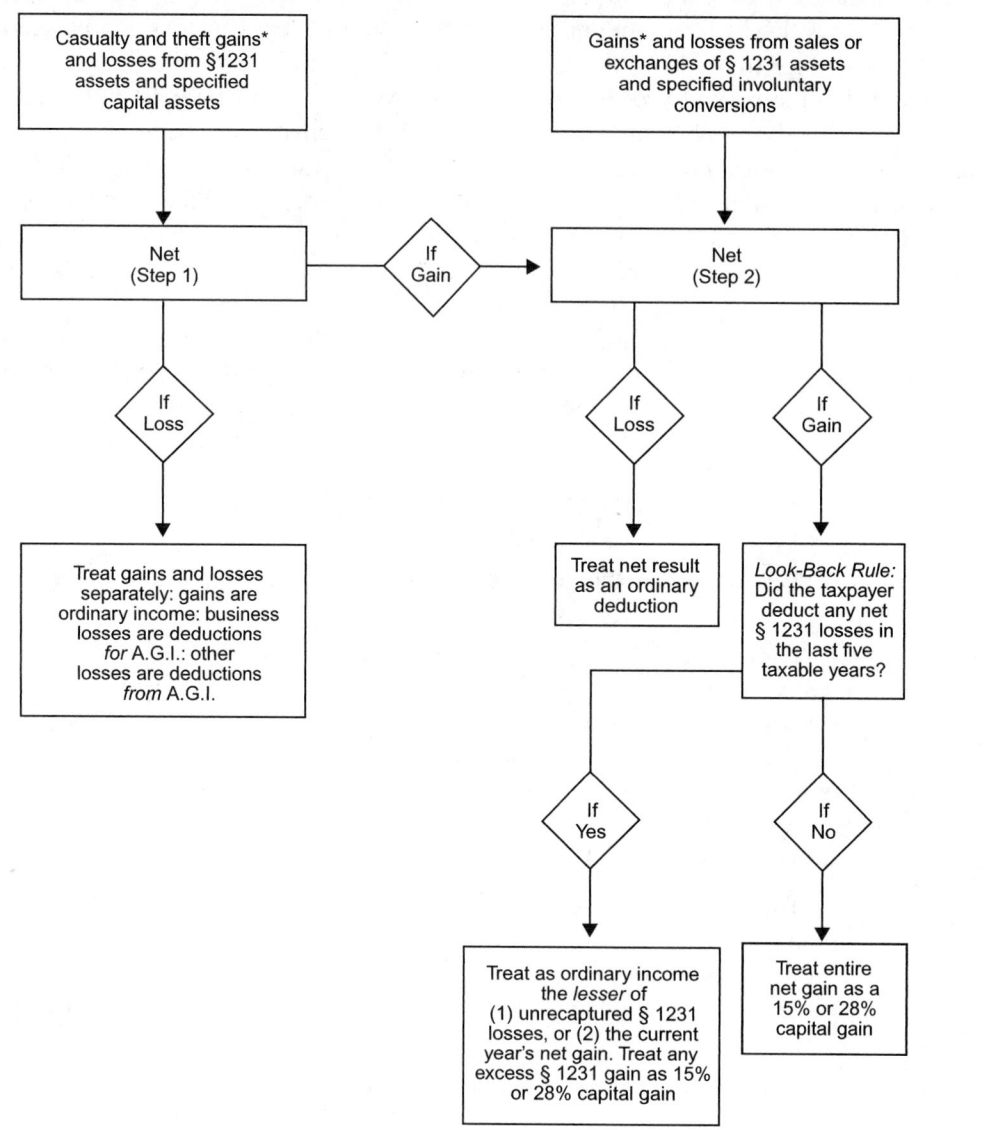

* Gains remaining after reduction for any depreciation recapture

Within each of these two categories, each gain and loss must be assigned to one of the three *potential* long-term capital gain groups and netted just as if they had been 28%, 25% or 15% capital gains or losses (see Chapter 16). This means that each § 1231 gain or loss is assigned to one of the following three categories: (1) 15% group for § 1231 gains and losses (15G or 15L); (2) 25% group for unrecaptured § 1250 depreciation related to gains from § 1231 assets (25G discussed below); and (3) 28% group for gains and losses from collectibles (28G or 28L). Once all of the appropriate transactions have been poured into the § 1231 process, the netting process can begin. There are three steps.

1. First, all of the gains and losses in the first category of § 1231 transactions (casualties and thefts) are netted. Specifically, gains and losses within the 15% and 28% groups are netted to arrive at one of the following: (1) a net gain or loss on 15% § 1231 assets (N15G or N15L); and (2) a net gain or loss on 28% § 1231 assets (N28G or N28L). Any net loss positions are then combined with

the net gain positions using the rules discussed for netting the three groups for capital asset transactions:

▸ A N28L first offsets 25G, then N15G.

▸ A N15L first offsets a N28G, then 25G.

▸ There can be no net loss in the 25G group since this group contains only gains.

This netting process is summarized as follows:

	Section 1231 Gains and Losses from Casualty and Theft		
	Collectibles	Unrecaptured Depreciation	Other
	28%	25%	15%
Gains	$x,xxx	Gains only	$xx,xxx
Losses	(x,xxx)	–	(x,xxx)
Net gain or loss	????	Gain only	????
Possibilities:			
1	N28G	25G	N15G
2	N28G	25G	N15L
3	N28L	25G	N15G
4	N28L	25G	N15L

If the netting process results in a net gain position(s) (e.g., a N28G, N25G, and a N15G) the net gains from casualties and thefts become § 1231 gains and become part of the second category of other § 1231 transactions (each assigned to either the 28%, 25%, or 15% groups).

Example 3. During the year, T, who is in the 35% tax bracket, reported the following § 1231 gains and losses from casualties of § 1231 assets (including casualties of capital assets used in a trade or business) and netted them as shown below.

	Section 1231 Gains and Losses		
	Collectibles	Unrecaptured Depreciation	Other
	28%	25%	15%
Gains	$10,000	$4,000	$ 2,000
Losses	(4,000)	—	(7,000)
Net gain or loss	$ 6,000	$4,000	($5,000)
Netting	(5,000)	—	5,000
To Section 1231 Other	$ 1,000	$4,000	$ 0

In this case, T has a N28G of $1,000 and a N25G of $4,000. Since the end results are net gains, each of these net gains is assigned to its appropriate group in the second category of other § 1231 transactions.

If a net loss results, the casualty and theft gains and losses are removed from the § 1231 process and treated separately. The gains are treated as ordinary income, and the losses on business use assets are deductible for A.G.I. Any other casualty and theft losses are deductible from A.G.I.

2. The second step of the process is to combine any net casualty or theft gains from the first step with the gains or losses in the second set of § 1231 transactions. In this regard, the net casualty and theft gains must be assigned to the appropriate group (15%, 25%, or 28% group) in the second category of § 1231 transactions (sales and exchanges of § 1231 assets and certain condemnations). For example, if the taxpayer had a net 15% gain from § 1231 casualties, this gain would become a 15% gain in the second category of § 1231 transactions. These transactions are then netted just as if they had been 28%, 25%, or 15% capital gains or losses to determine if there is a net gain or loss.

3. The third and final step in the § 1231 netting process is to characterize the gain or loss resulting from netting the transactions in the second step. If the net result is a loss, the net loss is treated as an ordinary deduction for adjusted gross income. It is not treated as a capital loss. If the net result is a gain (e.g., a N25G and a N15G), these gains are normally treated as capital gains and become part of the capital gain and loss netting process.

The § 1231 netting process is illustrated in Exhibit 17-1 and the following examples.

Example 4. During the current year, D sold real estate used in her business for $45,000. She had purchased the property several years ago for $36,000. D also sold a business car (held for more than 15 months) at a loss of $1,200. D's gain on the real estate is computed as follows:

Selling price	$ 45,000
Less: Adjusted basis	(36,000)
Gain realized and recognized	$ 9,000

D nets the gain and loss as follows:

15% Gain from sale of § 1231 asset	$ 9,000
15% Loss from sale of § 1231 asset	(1,200)
Net 15% § 1231 gain for year	$ 7,800

D's net 15% § 1231 gain of $7,800 is treated as a 15% capital gain. If she had other capital gains or losses during the year, they will be subject to the capital gain and loss netting process discussed in Chapter 16.

Example 5. During the year R, a sole proprietor, sold a business computer for $32,000. His basis at the time of the sale was $44,000. He also sold land used in his business at a gain of $1,400 and had an uninsured theft loss of works of art used to decorate his business offices (i.e., capital assets held in connection with a trade or business). R had purchased the artwork for $1,500 and it was valued at $5,000 before the burglary. All of the assets were acquired more than 12 months ago.

R nets his gains and losses as follows:

Step 1:   The net loss from the casualty is $1,500 (adjusted basis). Since R has a net 15% casualty loss, it is not treated as a § 1231 loss. Instead, the loss is treated as an ordinary loss (which is fully deductible for A.G.I. since the art works were business property).

Step 2: Combine gains and losses from sales of § 1231 assets:

15% loss from sale of business computer	($12,000)
15% gain from sale of business land	1,400
Net § 1231 loss for year.	($10,600)

Step 3: A net § 1231 loss is treated as an ordinary deduction. Thus, R's $10,600 loss can be used to offset other ordinary income.

Note that the theft loss of the works of art is included in the first step of the netting process even though these items are capital assets. This loss would have offset, dollar for dollar, any casualty or theft gains (net of depreciation recapture) from § 1231 assets as well as any casualty or theft gains from other capital assets held in connection with R's business. Also note that the current year's deductible § 1231 loss may result in a change in the character of any net § 1231 gains in the next five years due to the look-back rule.

LOOK-BACK RULE

For many years, taxpayers took advantage of the § 1231 netting process. For example, assume a taxpayer in the 35 percent tax bracket currently owns two § 1231 assets, both held for 15 months. One asset has a built-in gain of $3,000 and the other has a built-in loss of $2,000. If both assets are sold during the year, the loss offsets the gain and the taxpayer pays a capital gain tax of $150 [($3,000 − $2,000 = $1,000) × 15%]. If the taxpayer had sold the assets in different years, the loss would *not* have reduced the gain, and the tax after both transactions would have been $450 in one year ($3,000 × 15%) and $700 ($2,000 × 35%) of savings in the other year, for a net tax savings of $250 ($700 − $450). As might be imagined, taxpayers carefully planned their transactions to maximize their tax savings.

In an effort to prevent taxpayers from cleverly timing their § 1231 gains and losses to ensure that § 1231 losses reduced ordinary income and not potential capital gain, Congress enacted the so-called *look-back* rule in 1984. Under this rule, a taxpayer with a net § 1231 gain in the current year must report the gain as ordinary income to the extent of any *unrecaptured net* § 1231 losses reported in the past five taxable years.[18] In recapturing the § 1231 gains, recapture occurs in the following order: 28% gains, 25% gains, and 15% gains. Unrecaptured net § 1231 losses are simply the *net* § 1231 losses that have occurred during the past five years that have not been previously recaptured (i.e., the excess of net § 1231 losses of the five preceding years over the amount of such loss that has been recaptured in the five prior years).

Example 6. Assume the same facts in *Example 5* and that R's 2005 net § 1231 loss of $10,600 is the only loss he has deducted in the past five years. In 2006 R has a net 15% § 1231 gain of $15,000. R is subject to the look-back rule since in the prior year he reported a § 1231 loss of $10,600 that has not been recaptured. He must report $10,600 of ordinary income and $4,400 of net 15% § 1231 gain. Should R have a § 1231 gain in the following year, he will not be subject to the look-back rule since he has recaptured all prior year's net § 1231 losses.

---

[18] § 1231(c).

APPLICABILITY OF LOWER RATES

Five potential tax rates apply to long-term capital gains; six, to ordinary income, which includes short-term capital gains. How can the calculation of the capital gains tax, including any § 1231 gain, be completed in such a way as to arrive at a single right answer?

Caution must be exercised so as to complete the netting process in the prescribed order, as elaborated so far in this chapter and in Chapter 16.

- ▸ The first step is to complete the § 1231 netting process.

  - If there is a net § 1231 loss, that loss must be treated as an ordinary loss and it is left out of the capital gain and loss netting process entirely.
  - If there is a net § 1231 gain, it is treated as a long-term capital gain and is entered into the capital gain and loss netting process in the next step. In order to do this, a determination must be made as to which part of the gain, if any, is 25% gain, and which part, if any, is 15% gain.

- ▸ Netting of capital gains and losses occurs in each of the various groups of assets.

  - Short-term gains are netted against short-term losses and long-term gains are netted against long-term losses.
  - Within the long-term netting process, gains and losses are further broken down in the various sub-groups with 15% gains and losses, and 28% gains and losses being netted. Since there are no 25% losses, the 25% gains are not reduced.
  - The net gains and losses from these three groups are netted against one another as prescribed in Chapter 16 (e.g., 28% losses are first offset against 25% gains, then 15% gains, and 15% losses are first offset against 28% gains, then 25% gains.

- ▸ Short-term gains and losses are netted/combined with long-term gains and losses. Short-term losses are first netted against 28% gains, then 25% gains, and finally 15% gains. Net long-term losses are netted against short-term gains.
- ▸ The net results are subject to the capital gain tax.

  - Short-term gains are treated like ordinary income
  - Long-term gains are subject to tax at the appropriate specified capital gains rates (5%, 10%, 15%, 25%, and 28%)
  - Losses are subject to the $3,000 annual limit with the excess being carried forward.

Numerous possibilities exist, therefore, for any net § 1231 gain. Perhaps, the gain would be offset by capital losses, receiving no favorable treatment at all. However, if the § 1231 gain survives the netting process to be included in a net capital gain, it is subject to the preferred rates right along with any other long-term capital gains with surviving unrecaptured § 1250 gain being treated as 25% gain and any other surviving gain treated as 15% gain.

✅ CHECK YOUR KNOWLEDGE

Review Question 1. Indicate whether the following gains and losses are § 1231 gains or losses or capital gains and losses or neither. Make your determination prior to the § 1231 netting process and assume any holding period requirement has been met.

    a. Gain on the sale of General Motors stock held as a temporary investment by Consolidated Brands Corporation.

    b. Gain on the sale of a four-unit apartment complex owned by Lorena Smith. This was her only rental property.

    c. Loss on the sale of welding machinery used by Arco Welding in its business.

    d. Loss on theft of welding machinery used by Arco Welding in its business.

    e. Gain on sale of diamond bracelet by Nancy Jones.

    f. Income from sale of electric razors by Razor Corporation, which manufactures them.

    g. Gain on condemnation of land on which Tonya Smith's personal residence is built.

    h. Gain on condemnation of land owned by Tonya Smith's business.

    i. Loss on sale of personal automobile.

Answer. The § 1231 hodgepodge contains not only gains and losses from § 1231 property but also those from involuntary conversions by casualty, theft, or condemnation of capital assets that are used in a trade or business or held as an investment in connection with a trade or business.

    a. The sale of the GM stock is not included in the § 1231 pot since it is a sale of a capital asset and not an involuntary conversion.

    b. The rental property is generally considered property used in a trade or business and thus § 1231 property even if the owner owns only a single property.

    c. The welding machinery is depreciable property used in a business and is therefore considered § 1231 property.

    d. The theft of the welding machinery is also a § 1231 transaction. Note, however, that in processing the § 1231 gains and losses, the casualties must be segregated from the sales.

    e. The sale of the diamond bracelet produces capital gain since it is a pure capital asset and not trade or business property.

    f. The razors are inventory and are therefore neither capital assets nor § 1231 property.

    g. The condemnation of the land near the residence is considered a personal involuntary conversion gain. Since the land is not held in connection with a trade or business, it does not qualify as § 1231 property, but it is a capital asset.

    h. The condemnation of the land held for business does enter into the § 1231 hodgepodge as a regular § 1231 gain.

    i. Although the personal automobile is a capital asset, no loss is allowed from the sale.

Review Question 2. During his senior year at the University of Virginia, Bill decided that he never wanted to leave Charlottesville. After some thought, he opened his own hamburger joint, Billy's Burgers. That was 20 years ago and Bill has had great success, owning a number of businesses all over Virginia and North Carolina. Not believing in corporations, Bill and his wife, Betty, operate all of these as partnerships.

    a. Information from the partnerships and his own personal records revealed the following transactions during the current year:

        1. Sale of one of 50 apartment buildings that one of their partnerships owns: $50,000 gain (ignore depreciation)

        2. Sale of restaurant equipment: $20,000 loss

Assuming both assets have been held for several years, how should Bill and Betty report these transactions on their current year return?

Answer. Under § 1231, the taxpayer generally nets gains and losses from the sale of § 1231 property. If a net gain results, the gain is treated as a long-term capital gain, while a net loss is treated as an ordinary loss. For this purpose, § 1231 property generally includes real or depreciable property used in a trade or business. In this case, both the apartment complex and the restaurant equipment are § 1231 property and both are in the 15 percent group. As a result, the couple should net the gain and loss and report a 15 percent capital gain of $30,000.

    b.   The couple's records for the following year revealed several gains and losses:

        1.   Office building burned down: $20,000 loss

        2.   Crane for bungee jumping business stolen: $35,000 gain (assume no depreciation had been claimed)

        3.   Parking lot sold: $14,000 loss

        4.   Exxon stock sold: long-term capital loss of $10,000

        5.   Condemnation of Greensboro land held for use in the business: $15,000 gain.

Assuming each of the assets was held for several years, determine how much 15 percent capital gain or loss as well as the amount of ordinary income or loss that Bill and Betty will report for the year.

Answer. The § 1231 netting process requires the taxpayer to separate § 1231 casualty gains and losses from other § 1231 transactions (sometimes referred to as regular § 1231 items). The casualty loss on the office building and the casualty gain on the crane are both considered § 1231 15 percent casualties since they involve § 1231 property (i.e., real or depreciable property used in business). Note that the condemnation—even though it is an involuntary conversion—is not treated as a § 1231 casualty. The casualty items are netted to determine whether there is a net gain or loss. Here, there is a net casualty 15 percent gain of $15,000 ($35,000 − $20,000). This net gain is then combined with any "regular" § 1231 items, in this case the $14,000 loss on the sale of the parking lot (real property used in a business) and the $15,000 gain on the condemnation of the land (a capital asset). Note that both "regular" § 1231 items are also in the 15 percent group. After netting these items, the partnership has a net gain of $16,000. This $16,000 net § 1231 gain is treated as a 15 percent capital gain and is combined with $10,000 15 percent capital loss on the sale of the stock. The end result is a $6,000 15 percent capital gain. This process can be summarized as follows (see also Exhibit 17-3):

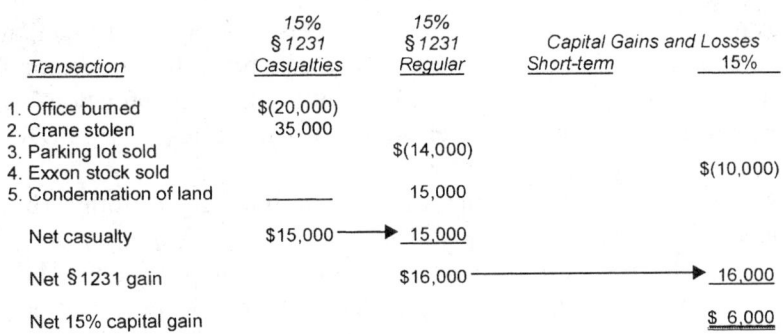

Transaction	15% § 1231 Casualties	15% § 1231 Regular	Capital Gains and Losses Short-term	15%
1. Office burned	$(20,000)			
2. Crane stolen	35,000			
3. Parking lot sold		$(14,000)		
4. Exxon stock sold				$(10,000)
5. Condemnation of land	_____	15,000		
Net casualty	$15,000 ⟶	15,000		
Net § 1231 gain		$16,000 ⟶		16,000
Net 15% capital gain				$ 6,000

c. Same as in (b), except Bill and Betty reported a net § 1231 loss of $3,000 in the previous year.

Answer. In this case, the look-back rule applies, causing $3,000 of the net 15 percent § 1231 gain to be treated as ordinary income. As a result, the couple's 15 percent capital gain from the § 1231 netting process is $13,000 and their net 15 percent capital gain is only $3,000.

DEPRECIATION RECAPTURE

HISTORICAL PERSPECTIVE

For many years, taxpayers have taken advantage of the interaction of § 1231 and the depreciation rules to secure significant tax savings. Prior to 1962 there were no substantial statutory restrictions on the depreciation methods that could be adopted. Consequently, a taxpayer could quickly recover the basis of a depreciable asset by selecting a rapid depreciation method such as declining balance and using a short useful life. If the property's value did not decline as quickly as its basis was being reduced by depreciation deductions, a gain was ensured if the property was disposed of at a later date. The end result could be quite beneficial.

Example 7. During the current year T purchased equipment for $1 million. After two years, T, using favorable depreciation rules, had claimed and deducted $600,000 of depreciation, leaving a basis of $400,000. Assume that the property did not truly depreciate in value and T was able to sell it in the third year for its original cost of $1 million. In such case T would report a gain of $600,000 ($1,000,000 − $400,000). Except for time value of money considerations, it appears that the $600,000 gain and the $600,000 of depreciation are simply a wash. However, the depreciation reduced ordinary income that would be taxed at ordinary rates while the gain would be a § 1231 gain and taxed at capital gain rates. As an illustration of the savings that could be achieved, assume that the law at this time provided for a top capital gain rate of 20% and the taxpayer's ordinary income was taxed at a 40%. In this case the depreciation would offset ordinary income and provide tax savings of $240,000, but the $600,000 gain on the sale would be treated as a capital gain and produce a tax of only $120,000. Thus, even though the taxpayer has had no economic gain or loss with respect to the property—he bought and sold the equipment for $1,000,000—he was able to secure a tax benefit of $120,000 ($240,000 − $120,000).

The above example clearly illustrates how taxpayers used rapid depreciation and the favorable treatment of § 1231 gains to effectively convert ordinary income into capital gain. In fact, this strategy—deferring taxes with quick depreciation write-offs at ordinary rates and giving them back later at capital gains rates—was the foundation of many tax shelter schemes.

Legislation to limit these benefits came in a number of forms, but the most important was the enactment of the so-called *depreciation recapture* rules. These rules strike right at the heart of the problem, generally treating all or some portion of any gain recognized as ordinary income, based on the amount of depreciation previously deducted. Thus, in the above example, the taxpayer's $600,000 gain, which was initially characterized as a § 1231 gain, is treated as ordinary income because of the $600,000 of depreciation previously claimed. In this way, all of the tax savings initially given away by virtue of the ordinary depreciation deductions are recaptured. Unfortunately, much like § 1231 in general, the recapture rules can become quite complex. The operations of the specific provisions are discussed below.

WHEN APPLICABLE

Before specific recapture rules are examined, there are two very important points to keep in mind. First, depreciable assets held for one year or less do not qualify for § 1231 treatment. Thus, any gain from the disposition of such assets is always reported as ordinary income. Second, the depreciation recapture rules *do not apply* if property is disposed of at a *loss*. Remember that losses from the sale or exchange of depreciable assets are treated as § 1231 losses if the property is held more than a year. In addition, casualty or theft losses of such property are included in the § 1231 netting process. Any loss from a depreciable asset held one year or less is an ordinary loss regardless of whether it was sold, exchanged, stolen, or destroyed.

TYPES OF DEPRECIATION RECAPTURE

There are essentially *three* depreciation recapture provisions in the Code. These are

1. Section 1245 Recapture—commonly called the *full recapture rule*, and applicable primarily to depreciable personalty (rather than realty)

2. Section 1250 Recapture—commonly called the *partial recapture rule*, and applicable to most depreciable realty if a method of depreciation other than straight-line was used

3. Section 291 Recapture—commonly called the *additional recapture rule*, and applicable *only* to corporate taxpayers

Each of these recapture rules is discussed below.

FULL RECAPTURE—§ 1245

The recapture concept was first introduced with the enactment of § 1245 by the Revenue Act of 1962. Section 1245 generally requires any gain recognized to be reported as ordinary income to the extent of *any* depreciation allowed on § 1245 property after 1961.

Definition of § 1245 Property. The recapture of depreciation under § 1245 applies only to *§ 1245 property*, normally *depreciable personal property*.[19] Because the definition of personal property itself is so broad, § 1245 generally covers a wide variety of depreciable assets such as:

- Machinery and equipment used in production of goods and services
- Office furniture and equipment
- Automobiles, vans, trucks, and other transportation equipment
- Livestock used for breeding or production
- Intangibles such as patents, copyrights, trademarks, and goodwill that have been amortized under § 197 or otherwise.

Essentially the amortization is treated the same as depreciation, just like any portion of the cost of a depreciable asset that is expensed under § 179 is treated as depreciation allowed.[20] It is important to understand that § 1245 applies only if the property is depreciable or amortizable. Consequently, it pertains only to property that is used in a trade or business and property held for the production of income. For example, livestock that are considered inventory are not subject to depreciation and are therefore not § 1245 property, although any gain or loss from the disposition of inventory is ordinary income.

Although the above definition is usually sufficient, § 1245 property actually includes a number of other assets besides depreciable personalty, including the following:[21]

1. Property used as an integral part of manufacturing, production, or extraction, or in furnishing transportation, communications, electrical energy, gas, water, or sewage disposal services.

    a. However, any portion of a building or its structural components is not included.
    b. A research facility or a facility for the bulk storage of commodities related to an activity listed above is included.

2. A single-purpose agricultural or horticultural structure (e.g., greenhouses).

3. A storage structure used in connection with the distribution of petroleum or any primary product of petroleum (e.g., oil tank).

4. Any railroad grading or tunnel bore.

5. Certain other property that is subject to a special provision allowing current deductibility or rapid amortization (e.g., pollution control facilities and railroad rolling stock).

Operation of § 1245. Section 1245 generally requires any gain recognized to be treated as ordinary income to the extent of *any* depreciation allowed.[22] To state the rule in another way: any gain on the disposition of § 1245 property is ordinary income to the extent of the *lesser* of the gain recognized or the § 1245 recapture potential, generally the depreciation claimed and deducted. Although both statements say the same thing,

---

[19]   § 1245(a)(3).

[20]   See § 197(f)(7) for intangibles and § 1245(a)(3)(D) for expensed property and certain other properties subject to unique expensing rules.

[21]   The definition parallels that of § 38 property, which qualified for the investment tax credit. § 48(a)(1).

[22]   § 1245(a).

the latter helps focus attention on two points and eliminates some misconceptions. First, a taxpayer is never required to report more income than the amount of gain realized regardless of the amount of depreciation claimed and deducted (i.e., regardless of the amount of recapture potential). For example, if the taxpayer realizes a gain of $10,000 and has deducted depreciation of $15,000, the taxpayer reports only $10,000 of income, all of which would be ordinary. Note that the depreciation recapture rules do not affect the amount of gain or loss, only the character of any gain to be recognized. Second, using the term *recapture potential* helps emphasize that sometimes the amount that must be recaptured may include more than mere depreciation.

Section 1245 *recapture potential* includes *all* depreciation or amortization allowed (or allowable) with respect to a given property—regardless of the method of depreciation used. This is why § 1245 is often called the full recapture rule. Recapture potential also includes adjustments to basis related to items that are expensed (e.g., under § 179 expense election) or where tax credits have been allowed under various sections of the Code.[23]

To summarize, determining the character of gain on the disposition of § 1245 property is generally a two-step process:

1. The gain is ordinary income to the extent of the *lesser* of the gain recognized or the § 1245 recapture potential (all depreciation allowed or allowable).

2. Any recognized gain in excess of the recapture potential retains its original character, usually § 1231 gain.

Recall that there is no § 1245 depreciation recapture when a property is sold at a loss, so any loss is normally a § 1231 loss.

Example 8. T owned a printing press that he used in his business. Its cost was $6,800 and T deducted depreciation in the amount of $3,200 during the three years he owned the press. T sold the press for $4,000 and his realized and recognized gain is $400 ($4,000 sales price − $3,600 adjusted basis). T's recapture potential is $3,200, the amount of depreciation taken on the property. Thus, the entire $400 gain is ordinary income under § 1245.

Example 9. Assume the same facts as in *Example 8*, except that T sold his press for $7,000. In this case, T's realized and recognized gain would be $3,400 ($7,000 − $3,600). The ordinary income portion under § 1245 would be $3,200 (the amount of the recapture potential), and the remaining $200 of the gain is a § 1231 gain. Note that in order for any § 1231 gain to occur, the property must be sold for more than its original cost since all of the depreciation is treated as ordinary income.

Example 10. Assume the same facts as in *Example 8*, except that the printing press is sold for $3,000 instead of $4,000. In this case, T has a loss from the sale of $600 ($3,000 − $3,600 adjusted basis). Because there is a loss, there is no depreciation recapture. All of T's loss is a § 1231 loss.

Exceptions and Limitations. In many ways, § 1245 operates much like the proverbial troll under the bridge. It sits ready to spring on its victim whenever the proper moment arises. Section 1245 generally applies whenever there is a transfer of property. However, § 1245 does identify certain situations where it does not apply, most

---

[23] See § 1245(a)(2) for a listing of these adjustments and their related Code sections, including the basis adjustment related to the earned portion of any investment credit.

of which are nontaxable events. For example, there is no recapture on a transfer by gift or bequest since both of these are nontaxable transfers.[24]

In involuntary conversions and like-kind exchanges, the depreciation recapture under § 1245 is limited to the *gain recognized*.[25] Similarly, in nontaxable business adjustments such as the formation of partnerships, transfers to controlled corporations, and certain corporate reorganizations, § 1245 recapture is limited to the gain recognized under the controlling provisions.[26] In any situation where recapture is not triggered, it is generally not lost but carried over in some fashion.

PARTIAL RECAPTURE—§ 1250

As originally enacted in 1961, the concept of recapture as set forth in § 1245 generally applied only to personalty. Gains derived from dealing in realty were not subject to recapture. In 1963, however, Congress eliminated this omission by enacting § 1250, a special recapture provision that applied to most buildings. Since that time § 1245 has generally been associated with depreciation recapture for personal property while § 1250 served that role for buildings. Although the two provisions are similar, § 1250 is far less damaging. Specifically, § 1250 calls for the recapture of only a *portion* of any *accelerated* depreciation allowed with respect to *§ 1250 property*. Note that while §§ 1250 and 1245 are essentially the same—they both convert potential capital gain into ordinary income—§ 1250 differs from § 1245 in several important ways: (1) it applies only if an accelerated method is used; (2) it does not require recapture of all the depreciation deducted but only a portion—generally only the *excess of accelerated depreciation over what straight-line would have been*; and (3) it applies to a different type of property, *buildings and their components*, rather than personal property. Each of these aspects is considered below.

Section 1250 Property. Section 1250 property is generally any real property that is depreciable and is not covered by § 1245.[27] For the most part, § 1250 applies to all of the common forms of real estate such as office buildings, warehouses, apartment complexes, and low-income housing. As explained earlier, however, nonresidential real estate (e.g., warehouse and office buildings) placed in service after 1980 and before 1987 for which an accelerated method was used is covered by the full recapture rule of § 1245.[28]

Depreciation of Real Property. Section 1250 applies only if an accelerated method of depreciation is used. If the straight-line depreciation method is used, § 1250 does not apply and there is no depreciation recapture for noncorporate taxpayers.[29] For this reason, a critical first step in determining the relevance of § 1250 is determining how the taxpayer has depreciated the realty.

For many years, taxpayers could choose to use either an accelerated or straight-line method to compute depreciation for realty. This was an extremely important decision, for it affected not only the amount of depreciation the taxpayer claimed but also the

---

[24] §§ 1245(b)(1) and (2). Recapture of depreciation under § 1245 is required, however, to the extent § 691 applies (relating to income in respect to a decedent).

[25] § 1245(b)(4).

[26] § 1245(b)(3). See Chapter 19 for further discussion of nontaxable business adjustments.

[27] § 1250(c).

[28] It is important to note, however, that such properties are § 1250 property if the optional straight-line method is used. § 1245(a)(5).

[29] As explained within, corporate taxpayers are still required to recapture 20 percent of any straight-line depreciation under § 291. Also, any unrecaptured straight-line depreciation is taxed at a maximum rate of 25 percent.

character of any gain on a subsequent disposition of the property. For example, a taxpayer could accelerate depreciation deductions but only at the possible expense of recapture. Alternatively, the taxpayer could accept the slower-paced straight-line method and avoid the § 1250 recapture rules. But the Tax Reform Act of 1986 ended this flexibility and at the same time simplified the law. Taxpayers who place realty in service *after 1986* must use the straight-line method. As a result, § 1250 does not apply to property acquired after 1986. However, much of the existing inventory of real property was acquired before 1987 and may therefore be subject to § 1250, depending on the depreciation method used.

Realty Placed in Service from 1981 through 1986. For real property acquired between 1981 and the end of 1986, the taxpayer could either use the accelerated depreciation method allowed under ACRS or elect an optional straight-line method. Of course, a taxpayer would normally select the accelerated method. In fact, that was the normal recommendation with respect to residential property. However, with respect to nonresidential property, electing to use the accelerated method resulted in the property that would normally be § 1250 property being classified as § 1245 property—subject to full, rather than partial, recapture.

Realty Placed in Service before 1981. All depreciable real property acquired before 1981 is classified as § 1250 property. For such property acquired before 1981 (non-ACRS property), taxpayers were required to estimate useful lives and salvage values. Although various methods could be used, the annual deduction (during the first two-thirds of the useful life) generally could not exceed that arrived at by using the following maximum rates and methods:[30]

Maximum Allowable Deduction Type of Property	Method/Rate
New residential real estate	Declining-balance using 200% of the straight-line rate
Used residential real estate:	
If estimated useful life at least 20 years	Declining-balance using 125% of the straight-line rate
If estimated useful life less than 20 years	Straight-line
New nonresidential real estate	Declining-balance using 150% of the straight-line rate
Used nonresidential real estate:	Straight-line

Operation of § 1250. The two critical factors in determining the amount, if any, of *§ 1250 recapture* are the gain realized *and* the amount of *excess depreciation*. Excess depreciation refers to depreciation deductions in excess of that which would be deductible using the straight-line method. For property held one year or less, all depreciation is considered excess depreciation.[31]

As a general rule, § 1250 requires recapture of the excess depreciation, that is, the excess of accelerated over straight-line. Consequently, even if the taxpayer uses an accelerated method to compute the amount of depreciation deducted on the return, the hypothetical amount of straight-line depreciation must still be computed in order to determine the excess of accelerated over straight-line when the property is sold. In determining the hypothetical amount of straight-line depreciation, the taxpayer uses the same life and salvage value, if any, that were used in computing accelerated depreciation.[32] Because of this approach, a taxpayer who uses the straight-line method

---

[30] § 167(j).

[31] § 1250(b).

[32] § 1250(b)(5).

would have no excess depreciation and no recapture. Because the § 1250 recapture rule applies only to any excess depreciation claimed by a taxpayer, it is sometimes referred to as the partial recapture rule. However, it should be emphasized that beginning in 1997, the unrecaptured § 1250 depreciation (e.g., the straight-line depreciation) on § 1250 property held more than 12 months is subject to a special 25 percent tax rate (assuming it survives the § 1231 netting process).

Determining the taxation of any gain recognized on the disposition of § 1250 property is a three-step process:

1. The gain is ordinary income to the extent of the *lesser* of the gain recognized or the § 1250 recapture potential (generally the excess depreciation allowed).[33]

2. Any recognized gain in excess of the recapture potential is usually treated as § 1231 gain.

3. Any gain recognized on § 1250 property held more than 12 months that is due to depreciation that is not recaptured and which survives the applicable netting processes is taxed at a maximum rate of 25 percent to the extent of any unrecaptured depreciation. Any additional gain is generally 15 percent gain.

There is no § 1250 depreciation recapture when a property is sold at a loss, so any loss is normally a § 1231 loss.

Unrecaptured § 1250 Gain. As may be apparent from step 3 above, under § 1250, taxpayers are required to recapture depreciation only if an accelerated method is used to depreciate the property. Consequently, individual taxpayers never recapture depreciation on § 1250 property if the straight-line method is used. Without some special rule, any gain attributable to straight-line depreciation for § 1250 property held more than 12 months would normally qualify for taxation at a 15 percent rate. However, Congress felt this treatment was too generous and created a special rule for *unrecaptured § 1250 gain.* The unrecaptured § 1250 gain is the lesser of (1) the gain recognized, or (2) the depreciation allowed after each (the gain recognized and the depreciation allowed) is reduced by any § 1250 recapture. The resulting amount will equal the amount of straight-line depreciation that was claimed or would have been claimed had the straight-line method been used (or, if less, the gain recognized minus the § 1250 recapture).

> **Example 11.** About 10 years ago, F purchased some residential rental property for $100,000. This year he sold the property for $110,000. He had claimed straight-line depreciation of $30,000 over this time, resulting in a basis of $70,000 (do not attempt to verify this amount). As a result, F recognized a gain of $40,000. Since the property is realty and a straight-line depreciation method was used there is no § 1250 recapture. Consequently, the entire gain is a § 1231 gain. However, the § 1231 gain will be treated as a 25% gain to the extent of any straight-line depreciation claimed. Therefore, $30,000 of the gain is a 25% § 1231 gain while $10,000 is a 15% § 1231 gain (i.e., in the capital gain netting process these will be 15% and 25% long-term gains, respectively). If F had sold the property for $90,000, he would have had a gain of $20,000, all of which would have been a 25% gain (i.e., the lesser of the gain realized, $20,000, or the unrecaptured straight-line depreciation, $30,000).

> **Example 12.** Same facts and $110,000 sales price from *Example 11* above, except that F also has a $400 gain on the sale of K Corporation stock held 26 months. F is

---

[33] See § 1250(a) and discussion following dealing with recapture of only a portion of the excess depreciation for certain properties.

single and has taxable income, excluding these transactions, of $76,000. F's tax would be computed as follows (using the 2004 tax rates for single taxpayers):

Regular tax on $76,000:	
Tax on $70,350..................................	$14,325
Tax on excess at 28%	
[($76,000 − $70,350 = $5,650) × 28%]...........	1,582
	$15,907
Tax on 15% gains (15% × $10,400)	1,560
Tax on 25% gains (25% × $30,000)	7,500
Total tax.....................................	$24,967

Combined Results. The net gain from the disposition of § 1250 property can be treated as ordinary income subject to the regular tax rate, 15 percent capital gain, and/or 25 percent capital gain (and rarely 28 percent capital gain). Each step in the netting and tax calculation processes has been covered. *Example 13 through Example 16* and *Comprehensive Example 18* illustrate how they work in combination.

Example 13. During the current year, L sold a small office building for $38,000. The building had cost her $22,000 in 1980, and she had deducted depreciation of $12,000 using an accelerated method. Straight-line depreciation would have been $10,600. L's gain recognized on the sale is $28,000 ($38,000 amount realized − $10,000 adjusted basis). Of that amount, $1,400 ($12,000 − $10,600 = $1,400 excess depreciation) is ordinary income under § 1250 and the remainder, $26,600, is § 1231 gain. Of the $26,600 § 1231 gain, the unrecaptured depreciation of $10,600 is a 25% gain. The $16,000 excess of the amount realized over the original basis is 15% gain.

Example 14. M purchased a rental duplex during 1986 for $60,000. He deducted $36,500 depreciation using the 19-year realty ACRS tables. Depreciation using the straight-line recovery percentages for 19-year realty would have resulted in total depreciation of $31,440.

On January 3, 2005 M sold the property for $87,000. His gain is reported as follows:

Sales price..		$ 87,000
Less: Adjusted basis		
Cost	$ 60,000	
Depreciation (accelerated)	(36,500)	(23,500)
Gain to be recognized		$ 63,500
Accelerated depreciation claimed and deducted		$ 36,500
Straight-line depreciation (hypothetical).........................		(31,440)
Excess depreciation subject to recapture......................		$ 5,060
Character of gain:		
Ordinary income (partial recapture).......................		$ 5,060
§ 1231 gain subject to 25% rate		31,440
§ 1231 gain subject to 15% rate		27,000
Total gain recognized.......................................		$ 63,500

Note that without a special rule, the gain not recaptured under § 1250 might be subject to the 15% capital gains rate. However, the balance of the depreciation that has not been recaptured $31,440 ($36,500 − $5,060) is carved out and is considered a 25% § 1231 gain. Note that the $31,440 25% § 1231 gain is the amount of straight-line depreciation. The remaining gain (i.e., the amount above the original cost) of $27,000 is a 15% § 1231 gain.

Example 15. Assume the same facts as in *Example 14*, except that M elected to recover his basis in the duplex using the 19-year straight-line method. Consequently she recognizes gain of $58,440 computed as follows:

Sales price				$ 87,000
Less:	Adjusted basis			
	Cost		$ 60,000	
	Depreciation (straight-line)		(31,440)	
				(28,560)
Gain				$(58,440)

None of the gain is subject to § 1250 recapture since M used straight-line depreciation (a requirement after 1986). However, the amount representing the unrecaptured depreciation (i.e., the straight-line depreciation) of $31,440 is considered a 25% § 1231 gain and the $27,000 balance is considered a 15% § 1231 gain.

Example 16. Assume the same facts as in *Example 14*, except that the property is an office building rather than a duplex. In this case, because the property is nonresidential real property and the accelerated method was used, the asset is treated as § 1245 property rather than § 1250 property. Thus, M is subject to full rather than partial depreciation recapture. All of the $36,500 depreciation is recaptured and treated as ordinary income. The balance of the gain, $27,000 is treated as a 15% § 1231 gain.

History of § 1250. Over the years, § 1250 has been changed frequently, with a general trend toward an expanded scope. The rules explained above apply only to depreciation allowed on nonresidential property after 1969 and residential property (other than low-income housing) after 1975. Only a *portion* of any other excess depreciation on § 1250 property is included in the recapture potential. The following percentages are applied to the gain realized in the transaction or the excess depreciation taken during the particular period, whichever is less:

1. For all excess depreciation taken after 1963 and before 1970, 100 percent less 1 percent for each full month over 20 months the property is held.[34] Any sales after 1979 would result in no recapture of pre-1970 excess depreciation since this percentage, when calculated, is zero.

2. For all excess depreciation taken after 1969 and before 1976, as follows:

    a. In the case of low-income housing, 100 percent less 1 percent for each full month the property is held over 20 months.
    b. In the case of other residential rental property (e.g., an apartment building) and property that has been rehabilitated [for purposes of § 167(k)], 100 percent less 1 percent for each full month the property is held over 100 months.[35]

---

[34]   § 1250(a)(3).

[35]   § 1250(a)(2).

All sales from this group of real property after August 1992 will have no recapture of excess depreciation claimed before 1976.

3. For excess depreciation taken after 1975 on low-income housing and property that has been rehabilitated [for purposes of § 167(k)], 100 percent less 1 percent for each full month the property is held over 100 months.[36]

In summary, 100 percent of the excess depreciation allowed with respect to § 1250 property after 1975 is subject to recapture unless it falls into one of the above categories. Any gain recognized to the extent of any unrecaptured depreciation will be considered 25% gain. The rules for the various categories are provided in § 1250(a).

Exceptions and Limitations under § 1250. Generally, the exceptions and limitations that apply under § 1245 also apply under § 1250. Thus, gifts, inheritances, and most nontaxable exchanges are allowed to occur without triggering recapture.[37] This exception is extended to any property to the extent it qualifies as a principal residence and is subject to deferral of gain under § 1034 or nonrecognition of gain under § 121.[38] In such nontaxable exchanges, the excess depreciation (that is not recaptured) taken prior to the nontaxable exchange on the property transferred carries over to the property received or purchased.[39] Similarly, in the case of gifts and certain nontaxable transfers in which the property is transferred to a new owner with a carryover basis, the excess depreciation carries over to the new owner.[40] In the case of inheritances in which basis to the successor in interest is determined under § 1014, no carryover of excess depreciation occurs.[41]

Certain like-kind exchanges and involuntary conversions may result in the recognition of gain solely because of § 1250 if insufficient § 1250 property is acquired. Since not all real property is depreciable, it is possible that the replacement property would not be § 1250 property and would still qualify for nonrecognition under the appropriate rules of §§ 1033 or 1034. In such situations, gain will be recognized to the extent the amount that would be recaptured exceeds the fair market value of the § 1250 property received (property purchased in the case of an involuntary conversion).[42]

Example 17. D completed a like-kind exchange in the current year in which he transferred an apartment complex (§ 1250 property) for rural farmland (not § 1250 property). The apartment had cost D $175,000 in 1980 and depreciation of $89,000 has been taken under the 200% declining-balance method. D would have deducted $62,000 under the straight-line method.

The farm land was worth $200,000 at the time of the exchange. There were no improvements on the farm property. D's realized gain on the exchange is $114,000 ($200,000 amount realized − $86,000 adjusted basis in property given up). If there had been no § 1250 recapture, then D would have had no recognized gain. Because the property acquired was not § 1250 property, § 1250 supersedes (overrides) § 1031. D has a recognized gain of $27,000 [($89,000 − $62,000), the amount of excess depreciation], which is all ordinary income under § 1250.

---

[36] § 1250(a)(1).

[37] §§ 1250(d)(1) through (d)(4).

[38] § 1250(d)(7).

[39] Reg. §§ 1.1250-3(d)(5) and (h)(4).

[40] Reg. §§ 1.1250-3(a), (c), and (f).

[41] Reg. § 1.1250-3(b).

[42] § 1250(d)(4)(C). A similar rule is provided for rollovers (deferral) of gains from low-income housing under § 1039 [see § 1250(d)(8)].

Exhibit 17-2 provides an overview of the handling of sales and exchanges of business property. Exhibit 17-3 provides a chart that may be useful in summarizing property transactions. Note that for purposes of this Exhibit 17-3, no distinction is made between 15%, 25% and 28% § 1231 gains and losses or 15%, 25% and 28% capital gains and losses. A comprehensive example of sales and exchanges of trade or business property is presented below.

EXHIBIT 17-2
Stepwise Approach to Sales or Exchange of Trade or Business Property—An Overview

Step 1: Calculate any depreciation recapture on the disposition of § 1245 property and § 1250 property sold or exchanged at a taxable *gain* during the year.

Step 2: For any remaining gain (after recapture) on depreciable property held for more than one year, add to other § 1231 gains and losses and complete the § 1231 netting process.

> ► The § 1231 gain must be broken down into the portions that qualify as 15%CG and 25%CG (and rarely 28%CG).

Step 3: Complete the netting process for capital assets, taking into consideration the net § 1231 gain, if any.

> ► The § 1231 gain is combined with other long-term capital gains and losses (with separate netting for 15%CG, 25%CG, and 28%CG. Then the long-term capital gain or loss is combined with the short-term capital gain or loss.

Example 18. Ted and Carol Smith sold the following assets during the current year:

Description	Holding Period	Selling Price	Adjusted Basis	Recognized Gain (Loss)
Land and building				
(straight-line depreciation)	3 years	$14,000	$9,000	$5,000
Cost, $13,000				
Depreciation allowed, $4,000				
Photocopier	14 months	2,600	2,000	600
Cost, $2,500				
Depreciation allowed, $500				
Business auto	2 years	1,800	1,920	(120)
Cost, $4,000				
Depreciation allowed, $2,080				

In determining the tax consequences of these sales, the Smiths must start with gains and losses from § 1231 transactions. The ultimate treatment of the gains, the character of the gain and any possible depreciation recapture must be considered.

> ► On the sale of the land and the building, there is no depreciation recapture for the building since straight-line depreciation was used. However, there is unrecaptured depreciation of $4,000 which is accounted for as a 25% § 1231 gain. The balance of the gain on the land and building, $1,000, is a 15% § 1231 gain.

> ► On the sale of the photocopier, $500 of the § 1231 gain of $600 is recaptured and treated as ordinary income. The balance of the gain, $100, is a 15% § 1231 gain.

▸ On the sale of the automobile, there is no recapture since it is sold at a loss. The $120 loss is treated as a 15% § 1231 loss. This information can be summarized as follows:

	Section 1231 Gains and Losses		
	Collectibles	Unrecaptured Depreciation	Other
	28%	25%	15%
Land and building.	$ 0	$4,000	$1,000
Photocopier			100
Automobile.			(120)
Capital gains from § 1231	$ 0	$4,000	$ 980

In this situation, the Smiths net the various groups, resulting in net gains in each of the groups as shown above. These amounts are then combined with the appropriate capital gain groups to determine the final treatment. Note that if the Smiths had unrecaptured § 1231 losses, they would first offset the 28% gains, then 25% gains, and finally 15% gains. The information is summarized in Exhibit 17-3.

EXHIBIT 17-3
Summary of Property Transactions

Recognized Gains (Losses)	Depreciation Recapture	Section 1231 Casualty and Theft*	Section 1231 Other *	Capital Gains/Losses Long-term* Short-term		Ordinary Income (Loss)
	§1245 Full recapture Personalty	Casualty and theft	Sale or exchange	Sale or exchange		
		1. §1231 property	§1231 property	Capital assets		
	§1250 Partial recapture Realty	Real or depreciable property used in business Timber, coal, iron ore, livestock, unharvested crops	Real or depreciable property used in business Timber, coal, iron ore, livestock, unharvested crops	All property except inventory, property held for resale, real and depreciable property used in trade or business, literary compositions, and government publications		
	§291 Corporations only 20% straight-line	2. Capital assets used in trade or business or held for investment in connection with business more than a year	Condemnation 1. §1231 property 2. Capital assets used in trade or business or held for investment in connection with business more than a year			

* These catagories must be subdivided into 15%, 25% and 28% groups.

Example 19. Assume that the Smiths, from the previous example, had the following capital asset transactions during the same year:

Description	Holding Period	Selling Price	Adjusted Basis	Description of Gain or (Loss)
100 shares XY Corp.	4 months	$ 3,200	$4,200	$(1,000) STCL
100 shares GB Corp.	3 years	3,200	4,600	(1,400) LTCL
1 acre vacant land	5 years	12,000	5,000	7,000 LTCG

Taking into consideration the § 1231 gains from *Example 18*, the Smith's summarize their transactions as follows:

	Short-Term	Capital Gains and Losses		
		Collectibles	Unrecaptured Depreciation	Other
	Ordinary	28%	25%	15%
Capital gains from § 1231		$ 0	$ 4,000	$ 980
XY stock loss	(1,000)			
GB stock loss				(1,400)
Vacant land gain				7,000
	$(1,000)	$ 0	$ 4,000	$ 6,580
Netting	1,000		(1,000)	
Total.	$ 0	$ 0	$ 3,000	$ 6,580

Ted and Carol Smith would report a $3,000 N25CG and a $6,580 N15CG.

A Form 4797 and Schedule D containing the information from *Examples 18* and *19* are included in Exhibit 17-4 which follows. In using the forms, it should be pointed out that neither the Form 4797 nor Schedule D Parts I, II, and III (i.e., the form for reporting capital gains and losses) require the taxpayer to distinguish 25% gains from 28% or 15% gains. The 25% distinction comes into play only when the taxpayer computes the tax as can be seen on Schedule D, Part IV, Lines 25 and 47. The tax is computed assuming the taxpayers have taxable income of $126,830 (including the capital gains).

ADDITIONAL RECAPTURE—CORPORATIONS

Corporations generally compute the amount of § 1245 and § 1250 ordinary income recapture on the sales of depreciable assets in the same manner as do individuals. However, Congress added Code § 291 to the tax law in 1982 with the intent of reducing the tax benefits of the accelerated cost recovery of depreciable § 1250 property available to corporate taxpayers. For sales or other taxable dispositions of § 1250 property, corporations must treat as ordinary income 20 percent of any § 1231 gain *that would have been* ordinary income if § 1245 rather than § 1250 had applied to the transaction.[43] The effect of this provision is to require the taxpayer to recapture 20 percent of any straight-line depreciation that has not been recaptured under some other provision. Technically, the amount that is treated as ordinary income under § 291 is computed in the following manner:

Amount that would be treated as ordinary income under § 1245	$xx,xxx
Less: Amount that would be treated as ordinary income § 1250 . . .	(x,xxx)
Equals: Difference between recapture amounts	$xx,xxx
Times: Rate specified in § 291	×20%
Equals: Amount that is treated as ordinary income	$xx,xxx

---

[43]   § 291(a)(1).

EXHIBIT 17-4
Completed Form 4797

Form **4797**	**Sales of Business Property**
Department of the Treasury Internal Revenue Service (99)	(Also Involuntary Conversions and Recapture Amounts Under Sections 179 and 280F(b)(2)) ▶Attach to your tax return. ▶See separate instructions.

OMB No. 1545-0184

2004

Attachment Sequence No. **27**

Name(s) shown on return: **TED AND CAROL SMITH**

Identifying number: **467-42-6030**

1. Enter the gross proceeds from sales or exchanges reported to you for 2004 on Form(s) 1099-B or 1099-S (or substitute statement) that you are including on line 2, 10, or 20 (see instructions). . . . . | **1** |

Part I Sales or Exchanges of Property Used in a Trade or Business and Involuntary Conversions From Other Than Casualty or Theft—Most Property Held More Than 1 Year (see instructions)

(a) Description of property	(b) Date acquired (mo., day, yr.)	(c) Date sold (mo., day, yr.)	(d) Gross sales price	(e) Depreciation allowed or allowable since acquisition	(f) Cost or other basis, plus improvements and expense of sale	(g) Gain or (loss) Subtract (f) from the sum of (d) and (e)
2						
AUTO	3-1-02	10-2-05	1,800	2,080	4,000	(120)

3 Gain, if any, from Form 4684, line 39	**3**	
4 Section 1231 gain from installment sales from Form 6252, line 26 or 37	**4**	
5 Section 1231 gain or (loss) from like-kind exchanges from Form 8824	**5**	
6 Gain, if any, from line 32, from other than casualty or theft	**6**	5,100
7 Combine lines 2 through 6. Enter the gain or (loss) here and on the appropriate line as follows:	**7**	4,980

Partnerships (except electing large partnerships) and S corporations. Report the gain or (loss) following the instructions for Form 1065, Schedule K, line 10, or Form 1120S, Schedule K, line 9. Skip lines 8, 9, 11, and 12 below.

All others. If line 7 is zero or a loss, enter the amount from line 7 on line 11 below and skip lines 8 and 9. If line 7 is a gain and you did not have any prior year section 1231 losses, or they were recaptured in an earlier year, enter the gain from line 7 as a long-term capital gain on Schedule D and skip lines 8, 9, 11, and 12 below.

8 Nonrecaptured net section 1231 losses from prior years (see instructions)	**8**	
9 Subtract line 8 from line 7. If zero or less, enter -0-. If line 9 is zero, enter the gain from line 7 on line 12 below. If line 9 is more than zero, enter the amount from line 8 on line 12 below and enter the gain from line 9 as a long-term capital gain on Schedule D (see instructions)	**9**	4,980

Part II Ordinary Gains and Losses

10 Ordinary gains and losses not included on lines 11 through 16 (include property held 1 year or less):

11 Loss, if any, from line 7	**11** (	)
12 Gain, if any, from line 7 or amount from line 8, if applicable	**12**	
13 Gain, if any, from line 31	**13**	500
14 Net gain or (loss) from Form 4684, lines 31 and 38a	**14**	
15 Ordinary gain from installment sales from Form 6252, line 25 or 36	**15**	
16 Ordinary gain or (loss) from like-kind exchanges from Form 8824	**16**	
17 Combine lines 10 through 16	**17**	500

18 For all except individual returns, enter the amount from line 17 on the appropriate line of your return and skip lines a and b below. For individual returns, complete lines a and b below:

a If the loss on line 11 includes a loss from Form 4684, line 35, column (b)(ii), enter that part of the loss here. Enter the part of the loss from income-producing property on Schedule A (Form 1040), line 27, and the part of the loss from property used as an employee on Schedule A (Form 1040), line 22. Identify as from "Form 4797, line 18a." See instructions . . . . | **18a** |

b Redetermine the gain or (loss) on line 17 excluding the loss, if any, on line 18a. Enter here and on Form 1040, line 14 . . . . | **18b** | 500 |

For Paperwork Reduction Act Notice, see page 8 of the instructions.   Cat. No. 13086I   Form **4797** (2004)

EXHIBIT 17-4
Completed Form 4797—Continued

Form 4797 (2004) *TED AND CAROL SMITH* Page **2**

Part III Gain From Disposition of Property Under Sections 1245, 1250, 1252, 1254, and 1255

19	(a) Description of section 1245, 1250, 1252, 1254, or 1255 property:	(b) Date acquired (mo., day, yr.)	(c) Date sold (mo., day, yr.)
A	*LAND / BUILDING*	*7-14-02*	*11-21-05*
B	*PHOTOCOPIER*	*6-12-04*	*8-31-05*
C			
D			

	These columns relate to the properties on lines 19A through 19D. ▶		Property A	Property B	Property C	Property D
20	Gross sales price (**Note:** See line 1 before completing.)	20	*14,000*	*2,600*		
21	Cost or other basis plus expense of sale	21	*13,000*	*2,500*		
22	Depreciation (or depletion) allowed or allowable	22	*4,000*	*500*		
23	Adjusted basis. Subtract line 22 from line 21	23	*9,000*	*2,000*		
24	Total gain. Subtract line 23 from line 20	24	*5,000*	*600*		
25	**If section 1245 property:**					
a	Depreciation allowed or allowable from line 22	25a		*500*		
b	Enter the **smaller** of line 24 or 25a	25b		*500*		
26	**If section 1250 property:** If straight line depreciation was used, enter -0- on line 26g, except for a corporation subject to section 291.					
a	Additional depreciation after 1975 (see instructions)	26a				
b	Applicable percentage multiplied by the **smaller** of line 24 or line 26a (see instructions)	26b				
c	Subtract line 26a from line 24. If residential rental property **or** line 24 is not more than line 26a, skip lines 26d and 26e	26c				
d	Additional depreciation after 1969 and before 1976	26d				
e	Enter the **smaller** of line 26c or 26d	26e				
f	Section 291 amount (corporations only)	26f				
g	Add lines 26b, 26e, and 26f	26g	*0*			
27	**If section 1252 property:** Skip this section if you did not dispose of farmland or if this form is being completed for a partnership (other than an electing large partnership).					
a	Soil, water, and land clearing expenses	27a				
b	Line 27a multiplied by applicable percentage (see instructions)	27b				
c	Enter the **smaller** of line 24 or 27b	27c				
28	**If section 1254 property:**					
a	Intangible drilling and development costs, expenditures for development of mines and other natural deposits, and mining exploration costs (see instructions)	28a				
b	Enter the **smaller** of line 24 or 28a	28b				
29	**If section 1255 property:**					
a	Applicable percentage of payments excluded from income under section 126 (see instructions)	29a				
b	Enter the **smaller** of line 24 or 29a (see instructions)	29b				

Summary of Part III Gains. Complete property columns A through D through line 29b before going to line 30.

30	Total gains for all properties. Add property columns A through D, line 24	30	*5,600*
31	Add property columns A through D, lines 25b, 26g, 27c, 28b, and 29b. Enter here and on line 13	31	*500*
32	Subtract line 31 from line 30. Enter the portion from casualty or theft on Form 4684, line 33. Enter the portion from other than casualty or theft on Form 4797, line 6	32	*5,100*

Part IV Recapture Amounts Under Sections 179 and 280F(b)(2) When Business Use Drops to 50% or Less (see instructions)

			(a) Section 179	(b) Section 280F(b)(2)
33	Section 179 expense deduction or depreciation allowable in prior years	33		
34	Recomputed depreciation. See instructions	34		
35	Recapture amount. Subtract line 34 from line 33. See the instructions for where to report	35		

Form **4797** (2004)

EXHIBIT 17-5
Completed Schedule D

SCHEDULE D (Form 1040)	Capital Gains and Losses	OMB No. 1545-0074
Department of the Treasury Internal Revenue Service (99)	▶ Attach to Form 1040. ▶ See Instructions for Schedule D (Form 1040). ▶ Use Schedule D-1 to list additional transactions for lines 1 and 8.	2004 Attachment Sequence No. **12**

Name(s) shown on Form 1040

TED AND CAROL SMITH

Your social security number: 467 42 6030

Part I Short-Term Capital Gains and Losses—Assets Held One Year or Less

	(a) Description of property (Example: 100 sh. XYZ Co.)	(b) Date acquired (Mo., day, yr.)	(c) Date sold (Mo., day, yr.)	(d) Sales price (see page D-6 of the instructions)	(e) Cost or other basis (see page D-6 of the instructions)	(f) Gain or (loss) Subtract (e) from (d)
1	100 SHS. XY CORP	6-1-05	10-15-05	3,200	4,200	(1000)

2	Enter your short-term totals, if any, from Schedule D-1, line 2	2		
3	**Total short-term sales price amounts.** Add lines 1 and 2 in column (d)	3	3,200	
4	Short-term gain from Form 6252 and short-term gain or (loss) from Forms 4684, 6781, and 8824	4		
5	Net short-term gain or (loss) from partnerships, S corporations, estates, and trusts from Schedule(s) K-1	5		
6	Short-term capital loss carryover. Enter the amount, if any, from line 8 of your **Capital Loss Carryover Worksheet** on page D-6 of the instructions	6	( )	
7	**Net short-term capital gain or (loss).** Combine lines 1 through 6 in column (f)	7	(1000)	

Part II Long-Term Capital Gains and Losses—Assets Held More Than One Year

	(a) Description of property (Example: 100 sh. XYZ Co.)	(b) Date acquired (Mo., day, yr.)	(c) Date sold (Mo., day, yr.)	(d) Sales price (see page D-6 of the instructions)	(e) Cost or other basis (see page D-6 of the instructions)	(f) Gain or (loss) Subtract (e) from (d)
8	100 SHS. XY CORP	6-1-02	11-1-05	3,200	4,600	(1,400)
	VACANT LAND	6-1-00	12-1-05	12,000	5,000	7,000

9	Enter your long-term totals, if any, from Schedule D-1, line 9	9		
10	**Total long-term sales price amounts.** Add lines 8 and 9 in column (d)	10	15,200	
11	Gain from Form 4797, Part I; long-term gain from Forms 2439 and 6252; and long-term gain or (loss) from Forms 4684, 6781, and 8824	11	4,980	
12	Net long-term gain or (loss) from partnerships, S corporations, estates, and trusts from Schedule(s) K-1	12		
13	Capital gain distributions. See page D-1 of the instructions	13		
14	Long-term capital loss carryover. Enter the amount, if any, from line 13 of your **Capital Loss Carryover Worksheet** on page D-6 of the instructions	14	( )	
15	**Net long-term capital gain or (loss).** Combine lines 8 through 14 in column (f). Then go to Part III on the back	15	10,580	

For Paperwork Reduction Act Notice, see Form 1040 instructions.   Cat. No. 11338H   Schedule D (Form 1040) 2004

EXHIBIT 17-5
Schedule D—Continued

Schedule D (Form 1040) 2004   *TED AND CAROL SMITH*   Page **2**

Part III   **Summary**

16 Combine lines 7 and 15 and enter the result. If line 16 is a loss, skip lines 17 through 20, and go to line 21. If a gain, enter the gain on Form 1040, line 13, and then go to line 17 below . . | **16** | *9,580* |

17 Are lines 15 and 16 **both** gains?
   ☒ **Yes.** Go to line 18.
   ☐ **No.** Skip lines 18 through 21, and go to line 22.

18 Enter the amount, if any, from line 7 of the **28% Rate Gain Worksheet** on page D-7 of the instructions . . . . ▶ | **18** |

19 Enter the amount, if any, from line 18 of the **Unrecaptured Section 1250 Gain Worksheet** on page D-8 of the instructions . . . . ▶ | **19** | *3,000* |

20 Are lines 18 and 19 **both** zero or blank?
   ☐ **Yes.** Complete Form 1040 through line 42, and then complete the **Qualified Dividends and Capital Gain Tax Worksheet** on page 34 of the Instructions for Form 1040. **Do not** complete lines 21 and 22 below.
   ☒ **No.** Complete Form 1040 through line 42, and then complete the **Schedule D Tax Worksheet** on page D-9 of the instructions. **Do not** complete lines 21 and 22 below.

21 If line 16 is a loss, enter here and on Form 1040, line 13, the **smaller** of:

   ● The loss on line 16 or
   ● ($3,000), or if married filing separately, ($1,500) } . . . . | **21** | (|) |

Note. When figuring which amount is smaller, treat both amounts as positive numbers.

22 Do you have qualified dividends on Form 1040, line 9b?
   ☐ **Yes.** Complete Form 1040 through line 42, and then complete the **Qualified Dividends and Capital Gain Tax Worksheet** on page 34 of the Instructions for Form 1040.
   ☐ **No.** Complete the rest of Form 1040.

Schedule D (Form 1040) 2004

Example 20. K Corporation sells residential rental property for $500,000 in 2005. The property was purchased for $400,000 in 1986. Assume that K claimed ACRS depreciation of $140,000 (i.e., do not attempt to verify this estimate). Straight-line depreciation would have been $105,000. K Corporation's depreciation recapture and § 1231 gain are computed as follows:

Step 1: Compute realized gain:

Sales price		$ 500,000
Less: Adjusted basis		
Cost	$ 400,000	
ACRS depreciation	(140,000)	(260,000)
Realized gain		$ 240,000

Step 2: Compute *excess* depreciation:

Actual depreciation	$ 140,000
Straight-line depreciation	(105,000)
Excess depreciation	$ 35,000

Step 3: Compute § 1250 depreciation recapture:

Lesser of realized gain of $240,000

or

Excess depreciation of $35,000

§ 1250 depreciation recapture	$ 35,000

Step 4: Compute depreciation recapture if § 1245 applied:

Lesser of realized gain of $240,000

or

Actual depreciation of $140,000

Depreciation recapture if § 1245 applied	$ 140,000

Step 5: Compute § 291 ordinary income:

Depreciation recapture if § 1245 applied	$ 140,000
§ 1250 depreciation recapture	(35,000)
Excess recapture potential	$ 105,000
Times: § 291 rate	×20%
§ 291 ordinary income	$ 21,000

Step 6: Characterize recognized gain:

§ 1250 depreciation recapture	$ 35,000
Plus: § 291 ordinary income	21,000
Ordinary income	$ 56,000
Realized gain	$ 240,000
Less: Ordinary income	(56,000)
§ 1231 gain	$ 184,000

Note that without the additional recapture required under § 291, K Corporation would have reported a § 1231 gain of $205,000 ($240,000 total gain − $35,000 § 1250 recapture). If the property had been subject to § 1245 recapture, K Corporation would have only a $100,000 § 1231 gain ($240,000 − $140,000 § 1245 recapture). Section 291 requires that the corporation report 20% of this difference ($205,000 − $100,000 = $105,000 × 20%), or $21,000, as *additional* recapture.

Note that this is 20% of the straight-line depreciation that is normally not recaptured on the disposition of nonresidential or residential real estate.

Example 21. Assume the same facts as in *Example 20*, except that the property is an office building rather than residential realty *and* straight-line depreciation was elected. An individual taxpayer would report the entire gain of $205,000 [$500,000 − ($400,000 basis − $105,000 straight-line depreciation)] as a § 1231 gain. However, the corporate taxpayer must recapture $21,000 (20% × $105,000 depreciation) as ordinary income under § 291. The remaining $184,000 ($205,000 − $21,000) would be a § 1231 gain.

OTHER RECAPTURE PROVISIONS

There are several other recapture provisions that exist. They include the recapture of farmland expenditures,[44] recapture of intangible drilling costs,[45] and recapture of gain from the disposition of § 126 property (relating to government cost-sharing program payments for conservation purposes).[46] Another type of recapture is investment credit recapture.[47] This is discussed in detail in Chapter 13.

✔ CHECK YOUR KNOWLEDGE

Review Question 1. True-False. This year T sold equipment for $6,000 (cost $15,000, depreciation $10,000), recognizing a gain of $1,000 ($6,000 − $5,000). To ensure that all of the ordinary deductions obtained from depreciation are recaptured, T must report ordinary income of $10,000 and a capital loss of $9,000, ultimately producing net income of $1,000.

False. This novel approach may seem consistent with Congressional intent, but it is incorrect. Under § 1245 any gain realized is treated as ordinary income to the extent of any depreciation allowed. As a result, the entire $1,000 is ordinary income. It may be useful to think of the depreciation recapture as an adjustment to the depreciation claimed. Depreciation of $10,000 was claimed, but the value of the equipment dropped by $9,000 ($15,000 cost − $6,000 sales price). T claimed an ordinary depreciation deduction of $10,000, and recognized ordinary income of $1,000, for a net ordinary deduction of $9,000.

Review Question 2. True-False. This year L sold a machine and recognized a small gain. Assuming L claimed straight-line depreciation, there is no depreciation recapture.

False. The machine is § 1245 property since it is depreciable personalty. Under the full recapture rule of § 1245, all depreciation is subject to recapture regardless of the method used.

Review Question 3. Several years ago Harry purchased equipment at a cost of $10,000. Over the past three years he claimed and deducted depreciation of $6,000. Assuming that Harry sold the equipment for (1) $7,000, (2) $13,000, or (3) $1,000, determine the amount of gain or loss realized and its character (i.e., ordinary income or § 1231 potential capital gain).

---

[44]   § 1252.

[45]   § 1254.

[46]   § 1255.

[47]   § 47.

	1	2	3
Amount realized	$ 7,000	$ 13,000	$ 1,000
Adjusted basis ($10,000 − $6,000)	−4,000	−4,000	−4,000
Gain (loss) recognized	$ 3,000	$ 9,000	$ (3,000)

The equipment is § 1245 property since it is depreciable personalty. As a result, the full recapture rule operates and any gain recognized is ordinary income to the extent of any depreciation deducted. In the first case, the entire $3,000 is ordinary income (the lesser of the gain recognized, $3,000, or the recapture potential, $6,000). In the second situation, $6,000 is ordinary income (the lesser of the gain recognized, $9,000, or the recapture potential, $6,000) and $3,000 is § 1231 gain. In the final case, § 1245 does not apply because the property is sold at a loss. Therefore, Harry has a § 1231 loss that is potentially an ordinary loss. Its ultimate treatment depends on the outcome of the § 1231 netting process.

Review Question 4. True-False. In 1990 Sal purchased an office building to rent out. This year she sold the building, recognizing a large gain. The entire gain is a § 1231 gain since there is no recapture under either § 1245 or § 1250.

True. The office build is § 1250 property. The recapture rules of § 1250 apply only when the taxpayer uses an accelerated method, in which case the excess of accelerated depreciation over straight-line is treated as ordinary income. However, since 1987 taxpayers have been required to use the straight-line method in computing depreciation on real estate. As a result, § 1250 is inapplicable and Sal's gain retains its original § 1231 character. Nevertheless, the gain will not be treated as a 15 percent gain to the extent of any unrecaptured § 1250 depreciation (i.e., all of the straight-line depreciation) but rather 25 percent gain.

Review Question 5. True-False. In 1992 Z Corporation purchased an office building to rent out. This year the corporation sold the building, recognizing a large gain. The entire gain is a § 1231 gain since there is no recapture under either § 1245 or § 1250.

False. There is no recapture under § or § 1250. However, under § 291, corporate taxpayers are required to recapture up to 20 percent of any straight-line depreciation. The 25 percent rate does not apply to corporate taxpayers

Review Question 6. True-False. In 1984 the Rose Partnership purchased a new office building to use as its headquarters. This year the partnership sold the building, recognizing a gain of $100,000. The partnership claimed and deducted accelerated depreciation of $40,000. Straight-line depreciation would have been $15,000. The partnership will report ordinary income of $25,000 and § 1231 gain of $75,000.

False. This would be true if the building were § 1250 property, but § 1250 does not apply. Nonresidential real estate such as this office building that was acquired from 1981 through 1986 is treated as § 1245 property and is subject to the full recapture rule if accelerated depreciation was used. In this case, the taxpayer opted for accelerated depreciation, so $40,000 is ordinary income and the remaining $60,000 is a 15% § 1231 gain.

Review Question 7. In 1984 the Daisy Partnership purchased a new apartment complex to rent out. This year the partnership sold the building, recognizing a gain of $100,000. The partnership claimed and deducted straight-line depreciation of $15,000.

Accelerated depreciation would have been $40,000. The partnership will report ordinary income of $15,000 and § 1231 gain of $85,000.

False. In contrast to question 6, the property is residential real estate and is consequently treated as § 1250 property. The partial recapture rule of § 1250 applies only if the taxpayer actually uses an accelerated method. In this case the taxpayer used straight-line, so the recapture rules of § 1250 are not triggered. As a result, the entire $100,000 gain is a § 1231 gain. However, the gain will be a 25 percent gain to the extent of any unrecaptured § 1250 gain (i.e., the straight-line depreciation).

RELATED BUSINESS ISSUES

INSTALLMENT SALES OF TRADE OR BUSINESS PROPERTY

As discussed in Chapter 14, gains on sales of trade or business property may be deferred using the installment sale method. However, depreciation recapture does not qualify for installment sale treatment. Thus, ordinary income from depreciation recapture must be reported in the year of sale—*regardless* of whether the seller received any payment in that year.[48] Consequently, only the § 1231 gain from such sales will qualify for installment gain deferral.

> **Example 22.** During 2005 K sold a rental house for $90,000. According to the terms of the sale, K received $30,000 down and the balance in two equal installments of $30,000 over the next two years. K had purchased the house in 1986 for $60,000 and deducted $20,000 of accelerated depreciation. Had she used the straight-line method, the straight-line depreciation would have been $15,000. K realizes a gain of $50,000 and has $5,000 of § 1250 recapture, computed as follows:

Amount realized.	$ 90,000
Adjusted basis ($60,000 − $20,000)	−40,000
Gain realized	$ 50,000
Accelerated depreciation on residential real estate acquired before 1987	$ 20,000
Hypothetical straight-line depreciation	−15,000
Excess depreciation.	$ 5,000

> K must report all of the depreciation recapture, $5,000, as ordinary income in the year of the sale. In addition, she must report $15,000 of the remaining gain of $45,000 as a § 1231 gain under the installment sale rules for the year of sale, computed as follows:

$$\frac{\text{Remaining gain, } \$45,000}{\text{Contract price, } \$90,000} \times \$30,000 \text{ Payment received} = \$15,000 \text{ Gain recognized}$$

> Note that in computing the gross profit ratio, only the remaining gain is used in the numerator and not the entire $50,000 gain realized, as would normally be the case.

---

[48] § 453(i). See Chapter 14 for a detailed discussion of installment reporting.

INTANGIBLE BUSINESS ASSETS

Historically, many purchased intangible assets were not subject to amortization for tax purposes. This was because the life of the assets was indefinite and the amortization deduction was indeterminable. However, § 197 currently allows the amortization (over 15 years) of most *purchased* intangibles acquired after August 11, 1993. No amortization is allowed, of course, for intangibles *developed* by the taxpayer.

For years, conventional thinking was that goodwill and similar intangibles were capital assets. A taxpayer who purchased or developed goodwill and similar intangibles generally recognized capital gain (or loss) to the extent the proceeds of the sale of a business were allocated to them.

All this became much more complex with the passage of § 197. Section 197(e) stipulates that upon the sale or disposition of § 197 assets, they are to be treated as depreciable property.

Private Letter Ruling [PLR] 200243002 brings clarity to this change. Under this ruling, intangible assets that are not subject to amortization are still treated as capital assets. This applies to assets placed in service on or before August 11, 1993, and presumably, self developed goodwill and other intangibles (with no basis). However, intangibles purchased after August 11, 1993 (i.e. amortizable "§ 197 intangibles") are to be treated as depreciable assets and upon sale they are subject to § 1245 and § 1231 treatment.

Under § 1245, any gain recognized will be ordinary income to the extent of amortization allowed. Any remaining gain or loss will be subject to the netting process under § 1231 and whatever treatment is required after the netting process.

DISPOSITIONS OF BUSINESS ASSETS AND THE SELF-EMPLOYMENT TAX

Gains and losses on the disposition of business assets do not increase or decrease self-employment income. So, even though gains are ordinary income for income tax purposes to the extent of depreciation recapture under § 1245 and § 1250, these amounts are not included in self-employment income.

TAX PLANNING CONSIDERATIONS

TIMING OF SALES AND OTHER DISPOSITIONS

Timing the sale of trade or business properties is very important and, from a tax perspective, can be critical. In the simplest case, if a taxpayer has a tax loss or is in a lower tax bracket, any contemplated sales at a gain should be considered to take advantage of the favorable tax result under § 1231. If tax rates are particularly high in the current year, loss transactions should be considered. Any net § 1231 loss is treated as an ordinary deduction for A.G.I. and avoids the $3,000 deduction limit imposed on net capital losses.

In addition, a net § 1231 gain qualifies as a long-term capital gain. For high-income taxpayers with no capital asset transactions or with a net capital gain in the current year, the net § 1231 gain qualifies for the maximum capital gains tax rate of 15 percent. The benefit can be even greater for a taxpayer with substantial capital losses for the year. Because the losses in excess of $3,000 would otherwise be suspended, any net § 1231 gain that would be offset by these losses can be currently recognized at no additional tax cost.

If a taxpayer has recognized or could recognize a § 1231 gain for the year and benefit from § 1231 treatment, additional sales of § 1231 property at a loss should be avoided. Because such losses must be netted against the gains, the favorable treatment of the gains is lost.

The look-back rule must be considered whenever a taxpayer is contemplating the timing of sales of § 1231 gain and loss assets. If no § 1231 losses have been recognized in the past five years, the gain assets should be sold in the current year to receive the favorable treatment of net § 1231 gains. The loss assets can then be sold in the next year and be treated as ordinary losses. This plan will not work, however, if the loss assets are sold first.

Finally, the timing of casualty and theft gains and losses should be considered. Obviously, a taxpayer cannot control the timing of such losses—not legally, anyway. However, the § 1033 gain deferral rules discussed in Chapter 15 may offer some tax planning opportunity. Because this deferral provision is generally elective, the taxpayer should consider existing § 1231 gains or losses before making a decision to defer gain. For example, a taxpayer with substantial capital losses may decide not to defer a capital gain or § 1231 gain under § 1033 even though the involuntarily converted asset is to be replaced. Immediate recognition of the gain will not have any negative tax consequences because it can be offset by the existing capital losses. The replacement property will have a higher (cost) basis for future depreciation. This plan is much more important to corporate taxpayers because excess capital losses can be carried forward only five years.

SELECTING DEPRECIATION METHODS

The accelerated cost recovery system provides taxpayers with several choices of depreciation methods and conventions. For example, a taxpayer with depreciable personalty may elect to use the straight-line method and either the class life or a longer alternative life. For real estate, an alternative 40-year life may be used.

Effect of Recapture. Generally, a taxpayer should adopt the most rapid method of depreciation available because this results in a deferral of income taxes. Unless tax rates are expected to change significantly in the near future, the tax benefits produced by large depreciation deductions currently allow the taxpayer the use of the money that would otherwise have been used to pay income taxes. In addition, the availability of the like-kind exchange and involuntary conversion provisions eliminates the risk of depreciation recapture when the taxpayer plans to continue in business. It is also important to remember that, for noncorporate taxpayers, there is no depreciation recapture possibility for real estate placed in service after 1986. Because only the straight-line depreciation method can be used, there will be no excess depreciation. However, the unrecaptured § 1250 depreciation is taxed at 25 percent.

Section 179. As discussed in Chapter 9, any § 179 expense amount is treated as depreciation allowed. As a result, the comments above may also apply in deciding whether to claim the option to expense the cost of qualifying property. If more than one qualifying asset is placed in service during the year and their total cost exceeds the annual limit (or reduced limit), the taxpayer must select the assets to be expensed. Obviously, only the assets not expected to be sold should be considered for this option. Given the time value of money, however, it seems unlikely that any taxpayer should forgo the § 179 expense option—unless the additional record keeping is considered to outweigh the current tax benefit.

INSTALLMENT SALES

Installment sales provide an excellent tax deferral possibility. Caution must be exercised, however, if trade or business property is to be sold under a deferred-payment arrangement. Because any depreciation recapture must be reported as income in the year of sale regardless of the amount of money received, taxpayers should require a cash down payment sufficient to pay any income taxes resulting from the depreciation recapture.

SALES OF BUSINESSES

The sale of a business typically involves some recognition of intangible assets, whether it be goodwill, or some similar asset, or other assets such as customer lists. The buyer is generally entitled to amortize the intangibles over 15 years. The seller may have ordinary income, capital gain, and/or § 1231 gain.

The IRS generally is required to recognize agreements between the buyer and the seller as to the value of the various assets in the sale of a business so long as they are reasonable. Thus in negotiating the value of the underlying assets, the buyer should consider the possible deductions related to the purchased assets. For depreciable assets and purchased intangibles, the deductions come in the form of depreciation and amortization. With respect to these assets, the buyer should also evaluate the effects of the depreciation recapture of the assets if they are to be sold in a short period of time.

DISPOSITIONS OF BUSINESS ASSETS AND THE SELF-EMPLOYMENT TAX

Gains on the disposition of business assets do not increase self-employment income. Similarly, losses do not reduce self-employment income. Generally speaking, foregoing allowable depreciation is not really optional since the basis of the depreciable assets must be reduced by depreciation allowed or allowable. So a taxpayer who does not feel like he or she needs the deduction, and realizes that the resulting gain if the asset is sold at a gain will be depreciation recapture, should claim it anyway!

> **Example 23.** D purchased a machine for $4,000 in the current year. The machine qualifies for expensing under § 197. D is uncertain as to whether she should claim the entire $4,000 since she expects to sell the machine for $3,200 the next tax year. Her dilemma involves the fact that the $4,000 is an ordinary deduction and the $3,200 is an ordinary gain. Why not just depreciate the machine? The reason is that by claiming the entire amount, she defers the tax on $3,200 for a year—assuming no change in her marginal tax rate.

Taxpayers paying self-employment tax should normally depreciate assets as rapidly as possible since the depreciation allowed will reduce the self-employment tax, but the future gain on the disposition of the asset is not includible in self-employment income.

> **Example 24.** D, in the prior example, can deduct the full $4,000, reducing her income tax and her self-employment tax. However, when she sells the machine the next year, the gain is subject only to income tax (as ordinary income).

PROBLEM MATERIALS

DISCUSSION QUESTIONS

17-1 *Section 1231 Assets.* What are § 1231 assets? What is the required holding period? Does the § 1231 category of assets include § 1245 and § 1250 assets as well? Elaborate.

17-2 *Excluded Assets.* What type of property is excluded from § 1231 treatment?

17-3 *Section 1231 Netting Process.* Briefly describe the § 1231 netting process. Are personal use assets included in this process?

17-4 *Net § 1231 Gains.* What is the appropriate tax treatment of net § 1231 gains? Are they offset by short-term capital losses? Can they be offset by capital loss carryovers from prior years?

17-5 *Net § 1231 Losses.* What is the appropriate tax treatment of net § 1231 losses? Are they subject to any annual limitation? Can they be used to create or increase a net operating loss for the year?

17-6 *Certain Casualty or Theft Gains and Losses.* Which casualty or theft gains and losses are included in the § 1231 netting process? What is the proper treatment of a net casualty or theft gain? What is the proper treatment of a net casualty or theft loss?

17-7 *Section 1231 Look-Back Rule.* Describe how the § 1231 look-back rule operates. Why do you think Congress enacted such a rule?

17-8 *Section 1245 Property.* What category of trade or business property is subject to § 1245? What depreciable real property has been included in this category?

17-9 *Full Depreciation Recapture—§ 1245.* What is meant by § 1245 recapture potential? Why is this rule sometimes called the full recapture rule? What is the lower limit of § 1245 recapture?

17-10 *Section 1245 Recapture Potential.* During the current year Z sold a vacuum used in his pool-cleaning business. The vacuum had cost $3,600 three years ago, and he had expensed the entire amount under § 179.
  a. How much is the § 1245 recapture potential with respect to this vacuum?
  b. If the vacuum was sold for $900, what is the character of the gain?

17-11 *Asset Classification.* When will the sale or other disposition of depreciable equipment be subject to both § 1231 and § 1245? What is the appropriate treatment of any loss from the sale of such equipment?

17-12 *Section 1245 Property.* F gave property with § 1245 recapture potential to his daughter, D. Will F be required to recapture any of the depreciation previously claimed? How must D characterize any gain she might recognize on a subsequent disposition of the property?

17-13 *Section 1245 Recapture Potential.* What happens to the § 1245 recapture potential when property is disposed of in a like-kind exchange?

17-14 *Section 179 Expense Treatment.* Explain the proper tax treatment of any gain recognized on the disposition of an asset that the taxpayer had earlier elected to expense under § 179. Does this mean that any amounts ever deducted under § 179 will always be subject to recapture? Explain.

17-15   *Section 1250 Property.* Is land included in the definition of § 1250 property? Is any real property depreciated under the straight-line method included in this definition?

17-16   *Section 1250 Property.* Is nonresidential real estate acquired after 1980 always § 1250 property? Explain.

17-17   *Section 1250 Property.* Why will depreciable real property placed in service after 1986 never be subject to § 1250 recapture? How is the unrecaptured depreciation treated?

17-18   *Section 1250 Recapture Potential.* Why is § 1250 sometimes called the partial recapture rule? Will the § 1250 recapture potential ever simply disappear? Explain.

17-19   *Section 1250 Recapture Potential.* This year Y sold a duplex that she had rented out for several years. The house had cost $40,000 20 years earlier and depreciation expense of $27,000 has been claimed. Straight-line depreciation would have been $24,500.
    a.   How much is the § 1250 recapture potential with respect to the duplex?
    b.   If the duplex was sold for $75,000, what is the character of Y's gain and how is it taxed?

17-20   *Additional Recapture—§ 291.* Briefly describe the additional depreciation recapture rule of § 291.
    a.   Which taxpayers are subject to this rule?
    b.   Compare this to the special rate for unrecaptured depreciation on § 1250 property for individual taxpayers.

17-21   *Section 291 Recapture.* Can a corporation that has always elected to use the straight-line depreciation method for all real property ever be subject to additional recapture under § 291? Explain.

17-22   *Reporting § 1231 Transactions.* What tax form does a taxpayer use to report the results of § 1231 transactions? How is any depreciation recapture reported on this form?

17-23   *Planning § 1231 Transactions.* Under what circumstances should a taxpayer with an in voluntary conversion gain from business property consider not electing to defer the gain under § 1033?

17-24   *Planning § 1231 Transactions.* A taxpayer plans to trade in depreciable property in order to acquire new property but is quite disappointed to find that his old equipment is worth less than its unrecovered cost basis. He is currently in the top marginal tax bracket and has no capital gains or losses or other § 1231 transactions for the year. What tax advice would you offer this taxpayer concerning the planned exchange?

17-25   *Installment Sales and Depreciation Recapture.* Briefly describe how recapture is reported when either § 1245 property or § 1250 property is disposed of in an installment sale. What tax planning should a taxpayer undertake concerning such sales?

PROBLEMS

17-26 *Characterizing Assets.* Indicate whether the following gains and losses are § 1231 gains or losses or capital gains and losses or neither. Make your determination prior to the § 1231 netting process.

   a. Printing press used in A's business; held for three years and sold at a loss.

   b. Goodwill sold as part of the sale of B's business

   c. Vacant lot used five years as a parking lot in C's business; sold at a gain

   d. House, 80 percent of which is D's home and 20 percent of which is used as a place of business; held 15 years and sold at a gain

   e. Camera used in E's business; held for 10 months and sold at a gain

   f. Land used by F for 10 years as a farm and sold at a loss

   g. Personal residence sold at a loss

17-27 *Section 1231.* During the year H sold the following assets, both of which had been held for several years:

Asset	Gain (Loss)
Vacant land held for investment	$ 52,000
Equipment used in his business	(12,000)

Determine how much capital gain or loss as well as the amount of ordinary income or loss that H will report for the year. At what rate will the gain, if any, be taxed?

17-28 *Section 1231 Netting.* G operates the Corner Bar and Grill as a sole proprietorship. During the year he sold the following assets, all of which had been held for several years:

Asset	Gain (Loss)
IBM stock	$(12,000)
Land and building used in the business	34,000
Equipment used in the business	(3,000)

The building had been acquired in 1993. Straight-line depreciation claimed and deducted with respect to the building was $8,000. Straight-line depreciation on the equipment was $4,000. Determine how much capital gain or loss as well as the amount of ordinary income or loss that G will report for the year and explain how they will be taxed.

17-29 *Involuntary Conversions and § 1231.* Assume the same facts as in *Problem 17-28.* In addition, G's records revealed the following information:

   ► A portion of the grill's parking lot was condemned by the city when it decided to expand the adjacent street. G pocketed the cash and recognized a gain of $5,000.

   ► A pool table was destroyed as part of a barroom brawl. G realized a casualty loss of $2,000.

Determine how much capital gain or loss as well as the amount of ordinary income or loss that G will report for the year. At what rate will the gain, if any, be taxed?

17-30 *Section 1231 Hodgepodge.* For 30 years Rae has operated The General Store, a hardware store in Columbus. Rae runs the business as a sole proprietorship. During the year, she recognized the following gains and losses from assets held several years:

1. Uninsured warehouse burned down: $10,000 loss

2. Equipment stolen: $190,000 gain (ignore depreciation)

3. Parking lot sold: $120,000 gain

4. IBM stock sold: capital loss of $70,000

5. Condemnation of land: $1,000 gain

Determine how much capital gain or loss as well as the amount of ordinary income or loss that Rae will report for the year. At what rate will the gain, if any, be taxed?

17-31 *Section 1231 Lookback.* J has recognized the following § 1231 gains and losses in the current year (2005) and since the inception of his business:

Year	Net § 1231 Gain (Loss)
2005	$ 50,000
2004	12,000
2003	(35,000)
2002	0
2001	65,000
2000	(13,000)

How will J treat the $50,000 gain for the current year?

17-32 *Section 1231—Timber.* A owns timber land that she purchased in 1991. During 2005, the timber was cut and A elected § 631 treatment for the gain. Her cost assignable to the timber was $25,000 and its fair market value on January 1, 2005 was $40,000. The actual sales price of the cut timber when it was sold in 2006 was $55,000.
a. How much is A's gain or loss recognized and what is its character?
b. Can A deduct the costs of cutting the timber?

17-33 *Section 1231—Unharvested Crops.* This year L sold her farmland, which she had owned for 20 years. L had made minor improvements to the farm and had used straight-line depreciation to depreciate them. No personal property was sold with the farm.

The sales price was $80,000 and L's adjusted basis was $36,000. The unharvested crops on the land represented $8,000 of the sales price, and L had spent $3,200 in producing the crop to the point of sale.
a. How does L report the gain or loss from the sale of the farm?
b. If L has no other sales of trade or business property or of capital assets, how much of the gain is included in her taxable income?

17-34 *Section 1245 Recapture.* During the year D sold a drill press he had used in his wood shop business for three years. D had purchased the press for $820 and had deducted depreciation of $476. Straight-line depreciation would have been $410. Determine the amount and character of gain or loss to D under each of the following circumstances below:
a. The press is sold for $500.
b. The press is sold for $100.
c. The press is sold for $900.

17-35 *Section 1245 Recapture.* This year N sold three different pieces of equipment used in her business:

Description	Holding Period	Sales Price	Cost	Depreciation Allowed
Processing machine	3 years	$1,200	$1,400	$600
Work table	4 years	1,600	1,300	500
Automatic stapler	2 years	500	900	300

What are the amount and character of N's gain or loss from these transactions?

17-36 *Section 1245 Recapture.* Fill in the missing information for each of the three independent sales of § 1245 assets identified below. Enter a dollar amount or n/a (for not applicable) in each blank space.

	Assets		
	A	B	C
Sales price.	$105	$ 90	$ ___
Cost.	100	125	100
Depreciation allowed	30	___	30
Depreciation recapture.	___	___	20
§ 1231 gain or (loss)	___	(10)	___

17-37 *Basis Reductions.* Dr. T purchased a treadmill for use in his cardiology practice for $13,000 on August 14, 2003. T claimed § 179 expense of $10,000 and depreciation of $429 in 2003. The depreciation for 2004 and 2005 is $735 and $524, respectively. T sold the treadmill on January 13, 2005 for $3,500,

a. What are the amount and character of T's gain on the sale?

b. What would be your answer if the unit had been sold for $13,500?

17-38 *Section 1250 Recapture.* Fill in the missing information for each of the three independent sales of § 1250 assets identified below. Enter a dollar amount or n/a (for not applicable) in each blank space.

	Assets		
	X	Y	Z
Sales price.	$100	$ ___	$200
Cost.	135	100	100
Depreciation allowed	55	___	30
Straight-line depreciation	___	20	___
Depreciation recapture.	0	10	___
§ 1231 gain or (loss)	___	30	120

17-39 *Real Property Acquired after 1986.* V sold an office building in the current year that she had purchased for $60,000 in 2003. Depreciation of $4,127 was claimed before the building was sold for $75,000.

a. What are the amount and character of V's gain on this sale?

b. At what rate will the gain be treated?

17-40 *Section 1245, § 1250, and § 291 Recapture.* K purchased a mini-warehouse unit on January 3, 1986 for $40,000. The unit was sold on January 15, 2005 for $41,000. Assume that K deducted ACRS depreciation of $26,480 for the period 1986–2005.

    a. How much is K's gain and what is its character? At what rate will the gain be treated?

    b. If K had used the optional straight-line method and a 19-year life under ACRS, the depreciation deductions would have totaled $23,120. What would be the amount and character of K's gain using this method? At what rate will the gain be treated?

    c. What would be your answer to (b) if K were a corporation?

17-41 *Section 1250 Recapture.* Z sold an apartment unit during 2005 for $75,000. Z purchased the property for $42,000 in 1986 and has deducted ACRS depreciation of $28,040. Straight-line depreciation using the same life and salvage value would have been $24,134. What are the amount and character of Z's gain if he receives the entire proceeds in 2005? At what maximum rate will the gain be taxed?

17-42 *Recapture and Installment Sales.* Assume the same facts as in *Problem 17-41* except that Z sold the property under an installment contract with $15,000 down and $15,000 in each of the next four years along with reasonable interest. How much gain would Z report in 2005 and 2006, and what is its character?

17-43 *Unrecaptured § 1250 Gain.* B purchased a small warehouse for $45,000 in 2003. This year he sold the property for $62,000. He had claimed and deducted straight-line depreciation of $6,500 on the property prior to the sale. What is the amount of gain, if any, and how will it be taxed?

17-44 *Twenty-Five Percent Gains.* V had the following gains and losses for the current year:

§ 1250 recapture	$ 2,000
Net § 1231 gains	6,000
Net short-term capital loss	(3,000)

V's § 1231 gain was from a building that was held 15 years. The total depreciation allowed was $5,000. How much are V's *15 percent gains* and *25 percent gains*, respectively?

17-45 *Section 1231 Gain and Look-Back Rule.* R sold land and a building used in farming for many years at a gain of $30,000 during 2005. No other sales or dispositions of § 1231 assets were made during the year. The § 1250 depreciation recapture for the building was $4,500 and the unrecaptured depreciation was $10,000.

    a. How is R's gain to be reported if he had a net § 1231 gain of $10,000 in 2002, a net § 1231 loss of $12,000 in 2003, and no § 1231 transactions in 2004?

    b. How would your answer to (a) differ if the sale of the property had resulted in a loss of $7,500?

17-46 *Section 1231 and Depreciation Recapture.* Fill in the missing information for each of the separate sales of § 1231 assets indicated below. Enter a dollar amount or n/a (for not applicable) in each blank space.

	Land	Building	Machine	Machine
Sales price	$100	$___	$ 90	$___
Cost	140	100	125	100
Depreciation allowed	0	30	___	30
Straight-line depreciation	0	20	___	___
Depreciation recapture	___	___	___	___
§ 1231 gain or (loss)	___	30	(10)	5

17-47 *Depreciation Recapture and the § 1231 Netting Process.* T had three § 1231 transactions during the current year. All of the assets were held for several years.

   a. Theft of electric cart used on business premises. The cart was worth $600, originally cost $800, and had an adjusted basis of $425.

   b. Sale of equipment used in manufacturing. The equipment sold for $5,500, originally cost $8,000, and had an adjusted basis of $4,250.

   c. Sale of land and a small building used for storage. The property was sold for $60,000, originally cost $56,000, and had an adjusted basis of $42,500. Straight-line depreciation was claimed on the building.

Determine the amount of ordinary income or loss and capital gain or loss that T must report from these transactions for the current year.

17-48 *Section 1231 Transactions.* K has the following business assets that she is interested in selling in either 2005 or 2006.

	Fair Market Value	Basis
Manufacturing equipment	$220,000	$400,000
Factory building	350,000	220,000
Land used for factory	450,000	120,000

Straight-line depreciation of $60,000 was claimed on the factory. K has never sold any other § 1231 assets.

   a. What are the tax results if K sells the land and building in 2005 and the equipment in 2006?

   b. What are the tax results if K sells the equipment in 2005 and the land and building in 2006?

   c. What are the tax results if K sells all the assets in 2005?

17-49 *Comprehensive Problem for Capital Asset and Trade or Business Property Transactions.* T owned a number of apartment units and sold several properties related to that trade or business during the current year as follows:

Description	Holding Period	Sales Price	Cost	Depreciation Allowed	Method
Apartment unit, including land (straight-line depreciation = $2,400)	3 years	$65,000	$24,000	$3,000	DB
Lawn tractor	5 years	1,000	3,000	2,600	SL
Spray painter	2 years	500	1,400	600	SL

During a severe winter storm, T also lost a depreciable motor scooter used in his business. The scooter, which was owned by T for two years and used exclusively in the business, had cost $2,600 and had an adjusted basis of $1,750.

   In addition, T sold several capital assets during the current year as follows:

Description	Holding Period	Sales Price	Adjusted Basis
100 shares LM Corp.	16 months	$2,000	$1,000
75 shares PL, Inc.	8 months	1,600	6,000
Silver ingots	6 years	2,600	6,000

Assuming T has never deducted § 1231 losses before, calculate the following amounts based on the above information:

a. The amount of § 1245 recapture and § 1250 recapture, if any.

b. The net § 1231 gain or loss.

c. The capital gain or loss and the rate at which it is taxed.

d. The net short-term capital gain or loss.

e. The overall impact of the above transactions on T's adjusted gross income.

17-50 *Netting Gains and Losses.* G had the following gains and losses for the current calendar year:

DFG Corporation stock held 3 years	$ 4,000
Gold held 6 years	(5,000)
Sale of business building:	
§ 1250 recapture	1,500
§ 1231 gain	7,000

Depreciation of $7,500 had been claimed on the building. What is the character of these gains in calculating the capital gains tax?

17-51 *Capital Gains Tax.* C, an unmarried head of household, has the following gains and losses for the current taxable year:

GHJ, Inc. stock held 16 months	($3,000)
Land held for investment 15 years	4,000
Sale of business real estate held 15 years:	
§ 1250 recapture	1,800
Net § 1231 gain	7,250

Depreciation claimed on the real estate was $7,800. C's taxable income (properly calculated and including the information above) is $110,550. How much is C's income tax for the calendar year 2005?

17-52 *Comprehensive Problem with Sales of Business Use Assets.* O and P are married. They have no dependents and elect to file jointly for the current year. They recently decided to retire, sell their home, and try renting for a while. Their income and related transactions for the year follow:

Ordinary income from business	$ 45,000
Interest income	3,700
Sale of personal residence of 20 years:	
Sales price	$760,000
Selling costs	43,000
Adjusted basis	195,000
Sale of business:	
§ 1245 recapture	15,000
§ 1250 recapture	26,000
§ 1231 gain	90,000
Gain on sale of stock held 5 years	16,000
Itemized deductions (after 3 percent cutback)	23,400

O and P had claimed depreciation on the § 1245 property and the § 1250 property in the amount of $25,000 and $56,000, respectively. Calculate O and P's adjusted gross income, taxable income, and gross income tax for the year.

17-53 *Sections 1231 and 1245 Property.* The terms § 1231 property and § 1245 property are often used interchangeably. However, there are times when a specific asset can be classified as (1) *both* § 1231 and § 1245 property; (2) only § 1231 property; or

(3) only § 1245 property. Based on the values assigned to the letters below, indicate the appropriate classification for each of the following mathematical expressions.

Let

X = asset's original cost
Y = depreciation claimed
Z = asset's adjusted basis
T = amount realized on sale

a. If T < Z, asset is § _____ property.
b. If T > X, asset is § _____ property.
c. If X > T < Z, asset is § _____ property.
d. If Y > T > Z, asset is § _____ property.

17-54 *Section 1231 and § 1250 Property.* It is possible that (1) *both* § 1231 and § 1250 apply to the sale of depreciable real property, (2) only § 1250 applies, or (3) only § 1231 applies. Based on the values assigned to the letters below, indicate which Code sections apply for each of the following mathematical expressions.

Let

X = asset's original cost
Y = depreciation claimed
Z = asset's adjusted basis
T = amount realized on sale
S = amount of straight-line depreciation

a. If Y > S and T < Z, § _____ applies.
b. If Y > S and T > X, § _____ applies.
c. If Y = S, § _____ applies.
d. If Y > S and (T–Z) < (Y–S), § _____ applies.

17-55 *Sale of Property Converted from Personal Use—Comprehensive Problem.* L owned and used a house as her personal residence since she purchased it in 2000 for $110,000. On February 11, 2003, when it was worth $85,000, L moved out and converted the property into a rental property. She rented the house until December 15, 2005, when it was sold for $104,500.

a. Determine L's depreciation deductions for the rental property from the time it was converted in 2003 until it was sold in 2005. Ignore land value.

b. What are the amount and character of L's gain or loss to be recognized from the sale?

17-56 *Sale of Property Converted to Personal Use—Comprehensive Problem.* Z purchased a computer system with peripherals for $14,500 on August 12, 2002. The system was used exclusively in his business. In October 2005, when the computer was worth $8,200, Z closed the business and began using the unit for personal purposes.

a. Determine Z's depreciation deductions for the computer system from the time it was purchased until it was converted to personal use, assuming that he elected the maximum § 179 expensing option for other assets placed into service in 2002.

b. Assume the computer system was sold for $5,400 on May 15, 2005 rather than being converted to personal use. What are the amount and character of Z's loss?

RESEARCH PROBLEMS

17-57 *Capital Assets versus § 1231 Assets.* R inherited a residence that had been used exclusively by her grandmother as a principal residence for 30 years. Upon receiving the property, R immediately offered the property for rent and rented to several tenants. After several months, R encountered an interesting potential business venture that would require a substantial capital investment. After an agonizing decision, she proceeded to sell her inherited rental unit. The unit was sold at a loss and R deducted the loss under § 1231. Since she had no § 1231 gains, the loss was deducted as an ordinary deduction. Is the treatment R chose the appropriate treatment for the loss? Does the character of the property to her grandmother carry over to R, resulting in disallowance of the loss or capital loss treatment?

Research aids:

Campbell v. Comm., 5 T.C. 272 (1945).
Crawford v. Comm., 16 T.C. 678 (1951), *acq.* 1951-2 C.B. 2.

17-58   *Business Use of Personal Residence.* J purchased a home in March 1987 for $120,000. Twenty percent of its cost was attributable to the land. From the date of purchase until March 2001, 20 percent of the house was used as a home-office, the costs of which were properly deducted annually (including depreciation). The home was used exclusively as J's residence from March 2001 until the house was sold for $325,000 on November 15, 2005.

   a.   Assuming J used the declining-balance method at a 5 percent rate and a useful life of 25 years, what amount of depreciation did he claim over the 15-year period that the property was used as a home-office?

   b.   Is there any depreciation recapture to be reported if gain is reported on the sale?

   c.   Is there depreciation recapture to be reported if all or part of the gain is excluded?

Part VI

EMPLOYEE COMPENSATION
AND
RETIREMENT PLANS

❖ **Contents** ❖

Chapter 18

EMPLOYEE COMPENSATION AND RETIREMENT PLANS

LEARNING OBJECTIVES

Upon completion of this chapter you will be able to:

- Distinguish between taxable and nontaxable employee fringe benefits

- Determine the tax consequences of the issuance and exercise of both nonqualified and qualified stock options

- Explain the advantages and disadvantages of nonqualified deferred compensation arrangements, including

  - The deferral of both the employee's recognition of income and the employer's deduction

  - The economic risk associated with unfunded arrangements

- Specify the two basic tax benefits of qualified retirement plans

- Distinguish between a defined benefit plan and a defined contribution plan

- Calculate the limitations on annual contributions to the various types of qualified plans

- Compute the annual amount of deductible contribution to an Individual Retirement Account

- Describe the characteristics of a Simplified Employee Pension

CHAPTER OUTLINE

INTRODUCTION

For a large majority of individual taxpayers, compensation received for services rendered as an employee is the most significant, if not the only, source of taxable income. Because of this significance, the topic of taxation of employee compensation is of primary interest to the tax-paying public. Employee compensation consists not only of cash wage and salary payments but an incredible variety of compensation "packages" designed to accommodate the needs and desires of employer and employee alike.

The tax consequences to both the employer and employee of various types of employment compensation are examined in this chapter. Because the concept of compensation includes provisions for employee retirement income, the chapter also includes a discussion of the numerous types of retirement income plans available to both employees and self-employed taxpayers.

TAXATION OF CURRENT COMPENSATION

Under the broad authority of § 61, a taxpayer's gross income includes all compensation for services rendered including wages, salaries, fees, fringe benefits, sales commissions, customer tips, and bonuses. Compensatory payments may be made in a medium other than cash. For example, payment for services rendered may be made with property, such as marketable securities. In such cases, the fair market value of the property is the measure of the gross compensation income received.[1]

Payment for services performed by Taxpayer A for Taxpayer B could consist of services performed by Taxpayer B for Taxpayer A. For example, a lawyer might agree to draft a will for a carpenter, who in turn agrees to repair the lawyer's roof. As a result of such a *service swap*, both taxpayers must recognize gross income equal to the value of the services received.[2]

STATUTORY FRINGE BENEFITS

As a general rule, any economic benefit bestowed on an employee by his or her employer that is intended to compensate the employee for services rendered represents gross income. This is true whether the benefit is in the form of a direct cash payment or an indirect noncash benefit that nonetheless improves the recipient's economic position.

Certain indirect or *fringe benefits*, however, are excludable from gross income under specific statutory authority. The following is a list of nontaxable fringe benefits and the authority for their exclusion from income. The details of these exclusions are discussed in Chapter 6.

1. Employer payment of employee group-term life insurance premiums (up to $50,000 of coverage)—§ 79

2. Employer contributions to employee accident or health plans—§ 106

3. Amounts paid to an employee under an employer's medical expense reimbursement plan—§ 105(b)

4. Employee meals or lodging furnished for the convenience of the employer—§ 119

5. Amounts received under an employer's group legal services program—§ 120

6. Amounts received under an employer's educational assistance program—§ 127

7. Amounts received under an employer's dependent care assistance program—§ 129

8. No-additional-cost services, qualified employee discounts, working condition fringes, and de minimis fringes—§ 132

The length of the above list demonstrates Congressional tolerance for the use of innovative fringe benefits to attract employees. Employers who want to design the most flexible compensation package for employees who have differing compensation needs may use a *cafeteria plan* of employee benefits. Under a cafeteria plan, an employee is allowed to choose among two or more benefits consisting of both cash and statutory nontaxable benefits.[3]

---

[1]   Reg. § 1.61-2(d).

[2]   *Ibid.*

[3]   § 125.

DEFERRED COMPENSATION

Deferral of compensation can be accomplished under a variety of methods that includes both "qualified" and "nonqualified" plans. A qualified plan is one that meets the requirements of Code § 401(a) and offers the employer a current deduction for money set aside for the eventual benefit of the employee. In this manner, the employees are not taxed on the amount set aside until it is distributed to them, and the income earned on the funds is exempt from tax. A nonqualified plan, on the other hand, does not possess all the specialized tax benefits, but offers a plan that is easier to administer and allows for discrimination among employees. Some of the more popular types of each of these plans are listed in Exhibit 18-1.

The purpose of deferred compensation plans is to allow employees to receive income at a later date when, presumably, they will have much less income. The employee's tax objective in participating in such an arrangement is to ensure that they will be taxed only when payments are received under the plan or agreement. The employer's tax objective is to offer a vehicle that will attract and compensate key personnel while obtaining a current tax deduction for any funds set aside for these employees.

Changes in the tax law, specifically the 1986 Tax Reform Act, reduced some of the glamour of deferred arrangements through its repeal of the capital gains differential and compression of the individual-corporate tax rate structure. However, subsequent legislation has reinstated a modest resurgence in plan activity due to the prospects of a widening capital gain differential and a probable increase in tax rates. Nevertheless, while the 1986 Act reduced the tax benefits of qualified plans, it is still possible to achieve both deferral of taxation and capital gains treatment on the eventual distribution of funds to the employee. However, most deferred compensation arrangements are not ordinarily utilized as vehicles to recharacterize the form of income.

EXHIBIT 18-1
Types of Deferred Compensation Plans

Qualified Plans

Defined Contribution Plans
Defined Benefit Plans
Money Purchase Plans
Stock Bonus Plans
Employee Stock Ownership Plans
Cash or Deferred Arrangements (401k)
Simplified Employee Plans
Individual Retirement Accounts
Incentive Stock Options
SIMPLE Plans

Nonqualified Plans

Restricted Stock
Deferred Payments
Rabbi Trusts
Secular Trusts
Nonqualified Stock Options

While numerous deferred compensation arrangements focus on tax benefits, most qualified plans are flexible and have a wide range of purposes other than reducing an

and the specific features of each, it will be useful to analyze the two basic tax benefits associated with qualified plans for employees—the tax-free nature of employer contributions and the tax-free growth of these contributions.

TAX BENEFITS OF QUALIFIED PLANS

When an employer makes a current contribution to a *qualified* retirement plan on behalf of an employee, §§ 402(a) and 403(a) provide that the value of the contribution is not includible gross income to the employee, even though the employee has obviously received additional compensation in the form of the contribution. In contrast, if the contribution was made by the employer to a *nonqualified* retirement plan in which the employee had a vested interest, the employee would have additional gross income equal to the value of the contribution. As a result, the net amount saved toward retirement by the employee participating in a nonqualified plan is less than the amount saved by the employee participating in a qualified plan.

The second major benefit of qualified retirement plans is that the earnings generated by employer contributions are nontaxable. Sections 401(a) and 501(a) provide that a trust created to manage and invest employer contributions to a qualified retirement plan is exempt from tax.

The effect of these two benefits on the total amount of savings available to an employee at retirement is illustrated in Exhibit 18-2. The exhibit compares two retirement plans, A and B. The plans are identical in every respect but one—A is a nonqualified personal savings plan while B is a qualified employer's trust. The exhibit is based on the following assumptions:

1. The employer will make an annual $10,000 contribution to the plan on behalf of the employee.

2. The employee has a 25 percent marginal tax rate. Therefore, the net amount saved by the employee in Plan A is only $7,500 ($10,000 − $2,500 tax on the current compensation represented by the contribution). The net amount saved in Plan B is $10,000.

3. Funds invested in both plans can earn a 12 percent before-tax return. The earnings from Plan A are taxable to the employee so that the plan's after-tax rate of return is 9 percent. Plan B is in the form of a qualified trust and therefore its earnings are tax-exempt.

EXHIBIT 18-2
Comparison of Nonqualified vs. Qualified Retirement Plans'
Year-End Values of Employer Contributions

	Nonqualified Plan A	Qualified Plan B
Year 1	$ 7,500	$ 10,000
Year 2	15,675	21,200
Year 15	220,208*	372,800**

*$7,500 × 29.361 (factor for the sum of an annuity of $1.00 at 9% for 15 years)
**$10,000 × 37.280 (factor for the sum of an annuity of $1.00 at 12% for 15 years)

The difference in the amounts available to an employee after 15 years of participation in either plan is dramatic. It is not difficult to understand why qualified retirement plans have become such an attractive fringe benefit to employees concerned with providing for their retirement years. However, before the analysis presented in Exhibit 18-2 is complete, it is necessary to examine the general rule as to the taxability of benefits paid out of a qualified plan upon an employee's retirement.

When an employee begins to withdraw funds from a nonqualified retirement savings plan, such funds represent *after-tax* dollars, and he or she will not be taxed on these funds a second time. In comparison, benefits received by an employee out of a qualified plan funded solely by employer contributions are fully taxable to the employee. It is important to understand that the retirement dollars available under Plan A of Exhibit 18-2 are excludable (as a return of capital), while the retirement dollars available under Plan B are fully includible in the recipient's gross income.

TAXABILITY OF QUALIFIED PLAN LUMP-SUM DISTRIBUTIONS

If an employee who has made no contributions to the employer's qualified retirement plan receives a distribution from the plan, the employee has no investment in the distribution and therefore must include the entire amount in adjusted gross income.[6] When the distribution is made by a series of payments (i.e., an annuity), the taxability of the distribution is spread over a number of years.[7] If the distribution is made in a lump sum, all the retirement income is taxed in one year.[8] Given the progressive rate structure of the Federal income tax, the normal tax on a large lump sum distribution could be prohibitive.

To mitigate this problem, Congress provided two relief provisions that benefit the recipient of a lump-sum distribution from a qualified retirement plan. First, an employee could treat the portion of a distribution attributable to the employee's participation in the retirement plan prior to 1974 as long-term capital gain.[9] The Tax Reform Act of 1986 generally repealed such capital gain treatment. However, a taxpayer who was age 50 before January 1, 1986 may elect to utilize this relief provision. In such case, the long-term capital gain portion of a distribution will be taxed at a flat 20 percent rate.[10] Note that in 2001, individuals who turned 65 before the close of the year would be eligible for this special treatment.

A second relief provision is a special procedure for computing the amount of current tax on a lump sum distribution. Prior to the Tax Reform Act of 1986, the procedure involved a 10-year forward averaging computation; for distributions made after December 31, 1986, the averaging period has been reduced to five years.[11] A taxpayer who was age 50 before January 1, 1986 may elect to use the 10-year forward averaging computation based on 1986 income tax rates for distributions received after 1986.[12]

While the original intent of the averaging rules was to prevent a bunching of income, Congress felt that taxpayers now have more control in determining the year that benefits are received. In addition, the averaging rules were perceived to be overly burdensome and the responsibility for this burden lay directly with the taxpayer. As a result, the special five-year averaging option under § 402(d) was repealed under the Small Business Job Protection Act of 1996. The repeal is effective for tax years beginning after December 31, 1999.

Under pre-2000 law, the averaging computation could be elected only for lump sum distributions received on or after the taxpayer had reached 59½ years of age, and a

---

6   If the employee has made contributions to the plan, he or she will have an investment in the plan, which may be recovered tax-free under the rules of § 72.

7   § 402(a).

8   § 402(e)(1).

9   § 402(a)(2), repealed by the Tax Reform Act of 1986.

10 Tax Reform Act of 1986, Act § 1122(h)(3).

11 § 402(e).

12 Tax Reform Act of 1986, Act § 1122(h)(5).

taxpayer could only make one such election.[13] Note that those who were born before 1936 continue to be eligible for ten-year averaging even after the five-year averaging is repealed.

ADDITIONAL TAXES ON PREMATURE OR EXCESS DISTRIBUTIONS

Congress intended for the tax-favored status of qualified plans to serve as an inducement for taxpayers to provide for a source of retirement income. Therefore, if a taxpayer makes a premature withdrawal from a qualified plan, a 10 percent penalty tax is imposed on the amount of the distribution included in the taxpayer's gross income.[14] However, the Code does permit penalty-free withdrawal from IRAs before age 59½ if any of the distributions are:

- On account of death or permanent disability.
- In the form of annuity payments over the taxpayer's lifetime.
- For medical expenses of the individual, his or her spouse and dependents that exceed 7.5 percent of A.G.I.
- For medical insurance of the individual, his or her spouse and dependents (without regard to the 7.5% of A.G.I. floor) if the individual has received unemployment compensation for at least 12 weeks, and the withdrawal is made in the year such unemployment compensation is received or the following year.
- For qualified education expenses. For this purpose, the term qualified higher education expenses is defined in § 529(e)(3) and generally means tuition, fees, books, supplies, and equipment required for enrollment or attendance at an eligible educational institution. It also includes the reasonable costs of room and board. In order to qualify, the expenses must be for education furnished to the taxpayer, the taxpayer's spouse, or any child or grandchild of the taxpayer or the taxpayer's spouse at an eligible education institution. Such expenses are reduced by amounts excluded from gross income that are used for such education.
- For first-time homebuyer expenses. The penalty waiver applies only to the first $10,000 withdrawn during the taxpayer's lifetime. The withdrawals must be used within 120 days of withdrawal to acquire, construct, or reconstruct a home that is the principal residence of the individual, his or her spouse, or any child, grandchild, or ancestor of the individual or spouse. Acquisition costs include any usual settlement, financing, or other closing costs. Although the name of the law suggests that it applies only to the purchase of a taxpayer's first home (and therefore is a once-in-a-lifetime opportunity), such is not the case. A first time homebuyer is defined as an individual (or if married, such individual's spouse) who had no present ownership interest in a principal residence during the two-year period ending on the date of acquisition. Thus, as long as the taxpayer has not owned a home in the past two years, withdrawals may be made from an IRA to help pay for the "new" home even though it is not the taxpayer's first home.

ROLLOVER CONTRIBUTION

There are many situations in which taxpayers receive lump-sum distributions from qualified plans prior to retirement. For example, a taxpayer who quits his job with his current employer to accept a position with a new employer may have a right to a

---

[13]   § 402(e)(4)(B).

[14]   § 72(t).

distribution from his current employer's qualified plan. Any taxpayer who receives a qualified plan distribution but does not need additional disposable income can exclude the distribution from gross income (and thus avoid both the income tax and any penalty tax on the distribution) by making a *rollover contribution* of the distributed funds. A rollover contribution must be made into another qualified employer plan, a Keogh plan, or an IRA, and it must be made within 60 days of the receipt of the distribution.[15] Note that in the case of a withdrawal, an employer is normally required to withhold 20 percent of the distribution as an estimated tax payment. However, withholding can be avoided if the amount is rolled directly into another qualified retirement plan, Keogh plan, or an IRA on a timely basis.[16] Failure to observe these rules can create a severe hardship and may lead to a penalty.

> **Example 4.** T is 45 years old. This year his employer laid-off 200 employees and, unfortunately, T lost his job. T decided to take a lump-sum distribution from his retirement plan of $200,000. Absent a direct rollover, T's employer will withhold $40,000 (20% × $200,000) and T will receive $160,000. Note that in order to avoid taxation on the $200,000 as well as the ten percent early withdrawal penalty, T must rollover the entire $200,000 to a qualified plan, even though he only received $160,000. Consequently, he would have to find an additional $40,000 to go along with the $160,000 to avert a catastrophe!

PLAN LOANS

Plan participants can avoid making taxable withdrawals from qualified plans while indirectly utilizing their retirement funds by borrowing money from their qualified plans. There is a very complex limit on the amount of a plan loan. In very general terms, a plan loan to a participant is limited to the lesser of (1) one-half the participant's vested accrued benefit (but not less than $10,000) or (2) $50,000. Any amount of a loan in excess of this limit is considered a taxable distribution.[17] Currently, owners of any small business (those with fewer than 100 employees) are generally permitted to make participant loans.

> **Example 5.** R and S are members of P's small business qualified plan. R has accrued vested benefits of $14,000, and S has accrued vested benefits of $80,000. R can borrow up to $10,000 even though this amount exceeds 50% of his vested benefits. If S, on the other hand, borrows $62,000 from the fund, $22,000 will be treated as a taxable distribution to her because this exceeds 50% of her benefits (which is more severe than the $50,000 ceiling violation).

In order to avoid being treated as a taxable distribution, a loan must be repaid in quarterly installments with interest within five years of the loan. However, if a taxpayer uses the loan to purchase a principal residence, any reasonable repayment period is allowed. The treatment of the interest expense depends on how the loan proceeds were used and whether the taxpayer is a key employee. If the plan loan is secured by the residence, the interest is qualified residence interest and is fully deductible as an itemized deduction. If the loan is used for investment purposes, the interest is considered investment interest and is normally deductible to the extent of any investment income. Unlike regular employees, key employees are not allowed to deduct any interest on plan loans.

---

[15]   § 402(a)(5).

[16]   § 3405(c)(2).

[17]   § 72(p).

TYPES OF QUALIFIED PLANS

Qualified plans fall into two basic categories, defined benefit plans and defined contribution plans. A *defined benefit plan* is one designed to systematically provide for the payment of definitely determinable benefits to retired employees for a period of years or for life. The focus of the plan is on the eventual retirement benefit to be provided. The amount of the benefit is usually based on both an employee's compensation level and years of service to the company. Defined benefit plans are commonly referred to as pension plans. The current amount of employer contributions that are required to fund future pension benefits under a given plan must be determined actuarially.[18]

Defined contribution plans provide for annual contributions to each participating employee's retirement account. Upon retirement, an employee will be entitled to the balance accumulated in his or her account. Defined contribution plans are designed to allow employees to participate in the current profitability of the business. Generally, in profitable years, an employer will make a contribution to a qualified trust and such contribution will be allocated to each employee's retirement account. However, contributions may be made to a qualified profit sharing plan without regard to current or accumulated profits of the employer corporation.[19] Although the employer may have the discretion as to the dollar amount of an annual contribution, such contributions must be recurring and substantial if the plan is to be qualified.[20]

While most defined contribution plans constitute "profit sharing plans," other types of defined contribution arrangements exist. These arrangements include *money purchase plans*, *stock bonus plans*, and *employee stock ownership plans*. Each of these is briefly discussed below.

In an effort to encourage small businesses to establish qualified retirement plans, Congress enacted a special credit as part of the 2001 Tax Act. The credit is 50 percent of up to $1,000 of the administrative and retirement education costs incurred during the first three years of the plan to create or maintain the plan. The special credit is only available for new plans established for years 2002 through 2006.

Money Purchase Plans. A money purchase plan is a defined contribution plan that is treated like a defined benefit plan. The employer's annual contribution is determined by a specific formula that involves either a percentage of compensation of covered employees or a flat dollar amount. Under a money purchase plan, unlike a defined benefit plan, a definite pension amount is not guaranteed. Rather, a participant's retirement benefit will be determined by his or her vested account balance at retirement.

Because an employee's account balance will be fashioned according to a definite formula under a money purchase plan, a certain amount of flexibility is permitted in structuring the plan's contribution formula.

Example 6. Under a company's money purchase plan formula, an employer is required to contribute to the plan 3% of an employee's compensation plus an extra 1% for each year of prior service up to a maximum of 10%. Thus, an employee with 12 years of service would receive a contribution equal to 13% [3 + (12 limited to 10)] of his covered compensation. A new employee would receive only 3%.

Note that under a money purchase plan an employer is required to make a contribution. If an employer fails to make these required contributions under the plan,

---

[18]   Reg. § 1.401-1(b)(1)(i).

[19]   § 401(a)(27).

[20]   Reg. § 1.401-1(b)(1)(ii).

the employer will be subject to certain excise taxes. This minimum funding standard does not apply to stock bonus or profit-sharing plans.[21]

Stock Bonus Plans. A stock bonus plan is another type of deferred compensation arrangement in which the employer establishes a plan in order to contribute shares of the company's stock. A stock bonus plan is subject to the same requirements as a profit sharing plan; therefore, a stock bonus plan must have a predetermined formula for allocating and distributing the stock among the employees. All benefits paid from the plan must be distributed in the form of the employer company's stock. An exception is made for fractional shares distributed from the plan, which may be paid in the form of cash.[22]

Employee Stock Ownership Plans. Another variety of qualified plans is the Employee Stock Ownership Plan (ESOP). As the name suggests, the major purpose of the ESOP legislation was to encourage stock ownership by all employees by giving employers and employees a host of tax incentives. Supporters of ESOPs believe in the fundamental principle that ownership of a business by its employees can help cure many of the ills of a market-based economy. A major proponent of this principle, former Senator Russell Long now deceased, endlessly extolled the virtues of ESOPs, saying that they could eliminate all of what is wrong with capitalism. According to Long and his followers, ESOPs increase worker productivity, improve labor relations, promote economic justice, provide a source of low-cost capital and are basically a savior for our economic system. On the other hand, critics of ESOPs say such claims are merely snake oil. Regardless of the view, ESOPs are now plentiful and have been a part of the system for more than 25 years.

Technically, an ESOP is a defined contribution plan. Like other qualified plans, a company that wants an ESOP first establishes a trust to which it makes annual contributions. The employer contributes either cash or its own stock. If the employer contributes cash, the ESOP uses the cash to purchase stock or securities of the sponsoring employer (rather than stocks or bonds of other companies). Regardless of how the stock or securities are obtained, they are then allocated to individual employee accounts within the trust using some type of formula. For example, the allocation may be in proportion to the employee's compensation or according to years of service or some combination of compensation and years of service. As a result, the company's employees—rather than outsiders—wind up owning a portion or all of the company. Any income earned by the ESOP is treated like that in other plans; that is, the income is completely tax-exempt. When the employee retires, he or she typically sells his or her shares of stock back to the trust and receives cash.

The tax benefits of this arrangement, once huge, have been whittled back by Congress over the years. Nevertheless, ESOPs still offer significant advantages. If the employer contributes stock, it receives a deduction for the value of the stock contributed.[23] Since it costs the employer little or nothing to issue the stock, the employer increases its cash flow by the taxes saved from the deduction. If the employer contributes cash that is subsequently used by the ESOP to purchase stock from the employer, the same benefit is obtained.

Example 7. This year P Corporation established an ESOP. Under the terms of the plan, P transferred 30,000 shares of unissued stock valued at $90,000 to the trust. Under § 1032, the issuance of the stock is nontaxable to P. However, P is entitled to a deduction for the value of the stock contributed, $90,000. Assuming P's marginal

---

21 § 412(h)(1).

22 Regs. § 1.401-1(b)(1)(iii).

23 § 1032.

rate is 34 percent, the contribution provides tax savings of $30,600 ($90,000 × 34%) with little or no cash drain.

The deductibility of contributions to an ESOP becomes even more attractive in the case of a *leveraged* ESOP. In a leveraged ESOP, the ESOP typically borrows money from a lender (e.g., a bank) and uses the cash to purchase the sponsoring corporation's stock. In subsequent years, the company makes contributions to the ESOP that are used to repay the interest and principal on the loan. When the contributions are used to pay the loan, such contributions are deductible. Observe that the effect is to allow the company to deduct the payments of not only the interest but also the principal. This feature makes the ESOP a very attractive form of debt financing for the employer. Similarly, the Code allows the company to deduct any dividends paid on ESOP stock which are used to repay the loan or which are passed through to the employees (a special feature of ESOPs).

Another significant benefit of the ESOP—no doubt the one that attracts the most attention—is the tax-free rollover permitted by § 1042. If the conditions of this provision are met, a shareholder who sells stock to an ESOP and who has owned the stock for at least three years may defer recognition of any gain realized on the sale by reinvesting in other stocks or bonds. This enables a retiring owner to get out of the business at the cost of one capital gains tax (rather than two taxes in most cases) that is deferred until the replacement property is sold.

SIMPLE Plans. As a general rule, retirement plan coverage is lower for small employers than among medium and larger employers. Congress believed that one of the reasons for this result stemmed from the complexity of the rules relating to establishment of tax-qualified retirement plans as well as the high costs associated with complying with those rules. In an effort to encourage small employers to adopt retirement plans for its employees, Congress created a simplified retirement plan option known as SIMPLE (the Savings Incentive Match Plan for Employees).[24]

Under a SIMPLE plan, employers with 100 or fewer employees and no other employer-sponsored retirement plan are permitted to establish a savings incentive match plan for their employees. Deductible contributions may be made either to individual IRA accounts established for each employee or to accounts established as part of a 401(k) plan. One of the key benefits of adopting a SIMPLE plan is that those plans which satisfy the SIMPLE plan contribution requirements are not required to satisfy the nondiscrimination and top-heavy requirements that other qualified plans must continue to meet.

Under a SIMPLE plan, an employer generally must either match elective employee contributions dollar-for-dollar up to 3 percent of compensation or make a 2 percent of compensation contribution on behalf of each eligible employee. The limitation on employee contributions is reflected in the table below. Contributions to a SIMPLE account are deductible by the employer and excluded from the employee's income. Distributions are generally taxed under the rules applicable to IRAs. All employees with W-2 income of at least $5,000 annually must be allowed to participate.

The annual contribution limit to a SIMPLE plan is as follows:

Year	Amount
Prior to 2002	$ 6,000
2002	7,000
2003	8,000
2004	9,000
2005 and thereafter	10,000

---

[24] §§ 1421 and 1422 of the Small Business Job Protection Act of 1996 amending § 401(k) and § 408(p).

Catch-up contributions. A SIMPLE plan can permit participants who are age 50 or over at the end of the calendar year to make catch-up contributions. The catch-up contribution limit for 2003 is $1,000. This limit increases by $500 each year thereafter until it reaches $2,500 in 2006. The limit is subject to cost-of-living increases after 2006. The amount of a catch-up contribution that a participant can make for a year cannot exceed the lesser of the following amounts:

- The catch-up contribution limit; or
- The excess of the participant's compensation over the salary reduction contributions that are not catch-up contribution.

QUALIFICATION REQUIREMENTS

In order for a retirement plan to be *qualified* and therefore eligible for preferential tax treatment, it first must comply with a long list of requirements set forth in §§ 401 through 415. These requirements are extremely complex and can prove burdensome to the employer wishing to establish a qualified plan for his or her employees. The rigorous requirements are intended to ensure that a qualified retirement plan operates to benefit a company's employees in an impartial and nondiscriminatory manner.

The current requirements for plan qualification came into the law in 1974 with the enactment of the Employees Retirement Income Security Act (ERISA). Prior to ERISA, many qualified plans were designed to benefit only those employees who were officers of the company, shareholders, or highly compensated executives. Since the passage of ERISA, such discriminatory plans are no longer qualified.

EXISTENCE OF A QUALIFIED TRUST

Under § 401 and the accompanying Treasury Regulations, contributions made as part of a qualified plan must be paid into a domestic (U.S.) trust, administered by a trustee for the exclusive benefit of a company's employees. The plan must be in written form and its provisions must be communicated to all employees. The plan must be established by the employer. Any type of employer—sole proprietor, partnership, trust, or corporation—may establish a plan.

ANTIDISCRIMINATION RULES

A retirement plan will not qualify if the contributions to or benefits from the plan discriminate in favor of the *prohibited group*. The prohibited group is defined as employees who are highly compensated or who are officers or shareholders of the company. If a plan provides for contributions or benefits to be determined under an equitable and reasonable formula, the fact that the prohibited group receives a greater dollar amount of contributions or benefits than employees in the nonprohibited group will not constitute discrimination.[25]

The Small Business Job and Protection Act of 1996 substantially simplified the definition of a "highly compensated employee." Currently, a highly compensated employee is a 5 percent owner during the current or prior year, or an employee with compensation during the prior year over $95,000 (2005). Employers may also elect to limit the pool of highly compensated employees to anyone who satisfies the basic definition and is in the top 20 percent of employees by compensation.[26]

---

[25]   §§ 401(a)(4) and (5).

[26]   § 414(q).

An important aspect of the statutory antidiscrimination rules for qualified plans is the fact that such plans may be integrated with public retirement benefits.[27] Under the integration rules, the calculation of plan benefits may take into account the extent to which an employee is covered by social security or a state retirement program. In effect, an employer can credit a portion of its social security contribution toward the amount it is required to contribute to the qualified plan. Without any limitations, integration could be used to pay substantially more benefits to a highly compensated employee. For example, assume H owns a corporation that has two employees, H who earns $150,000 and L who earns $20,000. Also assume that the corporation's qualified plan contribution rate was 6.2 percent of compensation. Using integration and ignoring current limitations, the corporation would not be required to contribute any amounts for L since all of its required contribution is met by its payment for L's social security. On the other hand, it would contribute 6.2 percent for H for every dollar above the social security wage base, $90,000 in 2005. As might be expected, special rules exist to prohibit such abuse. Nevertheless, integration can be used in a limited fashion to increase the benefits to highly compensated employees at the expense of other employees.

SCOPE OF PLAN PARTICIPATION AND COVERAGE

A qualified retirement plan must provide that a substantial portion of a company's employees are eligible to participate in the plan. Specifically, any employee who has reached age 21 must be eligible to participate after completing one year of service for the employer.[28] The plan may not exclude an employee from participation on the basis of a maximum age.[29]

In addition to these *minimum* and *maximum* age and service conditions, a qualified plan must meet complex minimum coverage requirements. A qualified plan must satisfy one of the following three minimum coverage tests: the *percentage test*, the *ratio test*, or the *average benefits test*.[30]

Under the percentage test, a plan must benefit 70 percent or more of all of the employer's non-highly compensated employees. For this test, all eligible employees are considered to benefit under the plan. A plan that has no coverage requirements or highly compensated employees will automatically satisfy this test.

> **Example 8.** P Corporation has two divisions, R and S. P Corporation adopts a plan that covers only the employees of division S. If R division has 2 highly compensated and 20 non-highly compensated employees and S division has 18 highly compensated and 80 non-highly compensated employees, P satisfies the percentage test. This is because the plan covers 80% [80% of (20 + 80)] of the nonhighly paid employees.

The ratio test requires that the plan benefit a classification of employees that does not allow more than a reasonable difference between the percentage of an employer's highly compensated employees who are covered and a similarly computed percentage for non-highly compensated employees. In other words, the ratio test allows the percentage test to be proportionately reduced.

> **Example 9.** Assume the same facts as *Example 8*. Because only 90% of the highly compensated employees are covered (18 of 20), only 90% of the percentage test

---

[27] § 401(a)(5).

[28] § 410(a)(1). The plan may defer participation for two years if it provides immediate 100 percent vesting.

[29] § 410(a)(2).

[30] § 410(b)(1).

must be met. Thus, the plan would meet the ratio test if as few as 63% of the non-highly compensated employees are covered (90% of 70%).

A plan will satisfy the average benefits test if (1) it benefits employees under a classification that the IRS finds does not discriminate and (2) the average benefit percentage for non-highly compensated employees is at least 70 percent of the average benefit percentage for highly compensated employees. The average benefit percentage, with respect to any group of employees, is the sum of all employer contributions and benefits under the plan provided to the group, expressed as a percentage of pay for all group members. An employer may compute the average benefit percentage based on either the current plan year or on a rolling average of three plan years that includes the current year. Once the employer makes this choice, it must obtain IRS consent to revoke it.[31]

The 50/40 Rule. While this rule is not a separate coverage rule, the 50/40 rule deserves attention because of the significance of the law involved. Basically, a plan will lose its qualification unless on each day of the plan year, it benefits the lesser of (1) 50 employees or (2) 40 percent of all employees of the employer. The 50/40 requirement applies separately to each qualified plan, and the Regulations exempt certain plans from this rule.[32]

VESTING REQUIREMENTS AND FORFEITURES

Once an employee is participating in an employer-sponsored retirement plan, he or she may not be entitled to any benefits under the plan for a certain period of time. After the requisite period of time, the employee's benefits *vest* and become nonforfeitable regardless of his or her continued employee status.

Under a qualified plan, vesting for non-top heavy employees must occur according to one of two statutory schedules designed to guarantee that an employee obtains a right to plan benefits within a reasonable time.[33] These two schedules are often referred to as "Cliff" vesting and "Graded" vesting.

Cliff Vesting. This schedule derived its name from the tendency, before ERISA, of some employers to push off the employment "cliff" (terminate) those employees just about to become vested in the retirement plan. Effective for years beginning after 1988, plans are no longer permitted to be more restrictive than five-year cliff vesting. Beginning in 2002, the cliff vesting must be complete within three years. Under three-year cliff vesting, an employee would not be entitled to any vesting before completing three years of service. At the end of the third year, the employer would have to vest the employee 100 percent in his or her accrued benefit attributable to employer contributions.[34]

Graded Vesting. The second permissible non-top heavy vesting schedule is graded vesting. Under such a schedule, employees must become proportionately vested over a two- to six-year vesting period. Under six-year graded vesting, a plan must provide at a minimum the following:

---

[31]   § 410(b)(2)(C).

[32]   § 401(a)(26) and Prop. Regs. § 1.401(a)(26)-2.

[33]   § 411(a)(2).

[34]   § 411(a)(2)(A).

20%	vesting after two years service;
40%	vesting after three years service;
60%	vesting after four years service;
80%	vesting after five years service; and
100%	vesting after six years service.

Under this schedule, the potential for discrimination diminishes because vesting occurs at a more gradual rate and, after three years of service, all employees are entitled to some vesting.[35]

If an employee leaves the job before some or all of the retirement benefits have vested, he or she forfeits the right to such benefits. Previous employee contributions toward these forfeited benefits are not returned to the employer, but instead transfer to remaining plan participants in a nondiscriminatory manner.[36]

FUNDING AND CONTRIBUTION LIMITATIONS

Qualified retirement plans must be *funded*. Consequently, an employer is required to make current payments into a qualified trust. For a defined benefit plan, an actuarially determined minimum current contribution is required by statute.[37] For a defined contribution plan, the annually determined contribution must be *paid* to the trustee. Because of these rules, an employer must back up its promises to the employees with actual plan contributions.

The Code limits the amount of contributions or benefits that are provided for employees. If these amounts should be exceeded, the plan will terminate.[38] In addition, § 404 establishes a limit on the amount that an employer may deduct. Sometimes the deductibility issue may have an impact on the amount that an employer may contribute on behalf of an employee.

Defined Contribution Plans. Under a defined contribution plan, the maximum contribution that can be made to the account of an employee is limited to the lesser of the following:

1. $42,000 (in 2005); or

2. 100 percent of the employee's compensation (subject to limits described in Exhibit 18-3 below).

EXHIBIT 18-3
Maximum Annual Inflation-Adjusted Dollar Amounts

Plan Type	2004	2005
Defined Benefit Plan	$165,000	$170,000
Defined Contribution Plan	41,000	42,000
Annual Compensation Limit	205,000	210,000
Cash or Deferred (401k)	13,000	14,000
Highly Compensated Employees	90,000	95,000
SIMPLE Contribution Limit	9,000	10,000

---

35 § 411(a)(2)(B).

36 Rev. Rul. 71-149, 1971-1 C.B. 118.

37 § 412.

38 §§ 415(a) and (b).

Example 10. S is a participant in Summa Inc.'s qualified profit sharing plan. If S's annual salary is $275,000, her employer can make a maximum annual contribution for 2005 on her behalf of $42,000 (the *lesser* of $42,000 or 100% of S's first $210,000 of compensation).

Example 11. If S's current salary is $35,000, the annual contribution is limited to $35,000 (the *lesser* of $42,000 or 100% of S's compensation).

Defined Benefit Plans. Under a defined benefit plan, the maximum annual benefit that can accrue to a participant is limited to the lesser of the following:[39]

1. $170,000 for 2005; or

2. 100 percent of the participant's average compensation for his or her three most highly compensated consecutive years of service with the employer.

Section 401(a)(17) was amended in 1993 to reduce the annual compensation limit to $150,000. Proposed regulations provide illustrations of how these new compensation limits affect *average compensation* for defined benefit plans.[40]

The limit is indexed annually for inflation, and adjustments to this figure are to be made if benefit payments are to begin before or after Social Security retirement age. Adjustments will be downward if payments begin before Social Security retirement age and upward if they begin after that age. The amount of the adjustment is determined actuarially based upon a straight-life annuity.[41] The current limitation is $170,000 for 2005.

TOP HEAVY PLANS

Section 416 contains additional requirements for qualified status of retirement plans that are deemed to be "top heavy." A *top heavy plan* is one in which more than 60 percent of the cumulative benefits provided by the plan are payable to *key employees*. Key employees include officers of the employer and highly compensated owner-employees. If a top heavy plan exists, § 416 provides an extra measure of assurance that the plan does not discriminate against non-key employees. To maintain qualified status a top heavy plan *must provide* a more rapid vesting schedule (generally 100% vesting after three years of service) and a minimum benefit to *all* employees regardless of social security or similar public retirement benefits.

DEDUCTIBILITY OF CONTRIBUTIONS BY EMPLOYER

Section 404(a) allows a deduction for employer contributions to qualified retirement plans if the contributions represent an ordinary and necessary business expense. In addition, § 404 contains complex rules that limit the dollar amount of the annual deduction. (Note that the statutory limitations on employer deductions are independent of the previously discussed limitations on the amount of contributions.) For example, the deduction for an employer's contribution to a qualified profit sharing plan is subject to a general limitation of 25 percent of total annual compensation paid to participating employees.[42] If an employer makes a contribution that exceeds this percentage

---

[39]   § 415(b)(1)(A).

[40]   Prop. Regs. § 1.401(a)(17)-1(b).

[41]   § 415(b)(2)(B).

[42]   § 404(a)(3).

limitation, the excess may be carried forward and deducted in succeeding years (subject to the percentage limitation for each succeeding year).[43]

DETERMINATION LETTERS

At this point, it should be obvious to the beginning tax student that the qualification rules for employer-sponsored plans are many and complex. As a result, employers are well advised to request a determination letter from the IRS before a plan is put into effect. Such determination letter is a *written approval* of the plan verifying that the plan, as described to the IRS, complies with all requirements for qualified status. If a plan treated by an employer as qualified is disqualified in an IRS audit, the employer could be liable for a considerable amount of unwithheld income and payroll taxes on employer contributions.

QUALIFIED PLANS FOR SELF-EMPLOYED INDIVIDUALS

Unincorporated taxpayers who earn money through self-employment are often precluded from retirement benefits afforded employees. To mitigate this result, Keogh (H.R. 10) plans were developed whereby contributions to such a plan are tax deductible, earnings accrue tax-free, and the self-employed individual is not taxed on any of the benefits until retirement. While Keogh plans provide substantial benefits, there are specific requirements that must be followed.

A self-employed individual who establishes an employer qualified retirement plan for his employees is not an employee eligible for participation in the plan. Self-employed individuals include sole proprietors and the partners in a business partnership. These taxpayers, however, may use the *Keogh* rules to obtain the tax benefits of a qualified plan.[44] A Keogh plan must benefit both the self-employed taxpayer and his or her employees in a nondiscriminatory manner under the wide range of rules for qualified plans previously discussed. In addition, the top heavy rules of § 416 apply to Keogh plans.[45]

To be eligible for a Keogh plan, the sole proprietor or partner must be an individual who satisfies one of the following conditions:[46]

1. Has "earned income" for the taxable year;

2. Would have had "earned income" for the year, but the trade or business being carried on had no net profits; or

3. Has been self-employed for any prior taxable year.

Generally, net earnings from self-employment will be the gross income from the trade or business less any related deductions; plus any distributive share of income or loss (if any) from a partnership. More specific definitions that are required for the tax computations are found in Exhibit 18-4.

---

43   *Ibid.*

44   See § 410(c)(1). It is interesting to note that retirement plans for self-employed individuals often are referred to as Keogh *or* H.R. 10 plans. Actually, the descriptions are interchangeable since H.R. 10 designated the legislative bill introduced by Congressman Keogh and passed by Congress in 1962.

45   § 416(i)(3).

46   § 415(c)(1)(B).

EXHIBIT 18-4
Special Definitions for KEOGH Plans

Earned Income	Self-employment income reduced by the self-employment tax deduction *and* the amount of the allowable Keogh deduction.
Net Earnings from Self-Employment	Earnings from self-employment without regard to the self-employment tax deduction or the allowable Keogh deduction.
Modified Net Earnings from Self-Employment	Net earnings from self-employment reduced by the self-employment tax deduction.
Self-Employment Tax Deduction	One-half of the self-employment taxes due for the year.

CONTRIBUTION LIMITATIONS

Annual contributions to Keogh plans are generally subject to the same limitations that apply to employer plans. For a defined contribution plan, the annual contribution by a self-employed taxpayer is limited to the lesser of $42,000 (2005) or 100 percent of *earned income*.[47] As seen in Exhibit 18-4, the definition of earned income includes the deduction for the allowable Keogh contribution, so the computation is a circular one.[48] The computation of the allowable contribution can best be expressed in the following formula:

$$
\begin{array}{cl}
 & \text{Net Earnings from Self-Employment (NE)} \\
- & \underline{\text{Self-Employment Tax Deduction}} \\
\\
 & \text{Modified Net Earnings from Self-Employment (MNE)} \\
- & \underline{\text{Allowable Contribution (AC)}} \\
\\
 & \text{Earned Income (EI)} \\
\times & \underline{100\%} \\
\\
= & \underline{\text{Allowable Contribution (AC)}}
\end{array}
$$

The results of this formula can now be restated in the form of the equation found in Exhibit 18-5. Notice that the solution to this equation demonstrates that the actual limit on a self-employed taxpayer's annual contribution to a defined contribution Keogh plan is just 50 percent of *modified net earnings*. For individuals who have self-employment income but no liability for employment taxes (e.g., they have exceeded the maximum FICA through other employment), the allowable contribution will be 50 percent of their *net earnings* from self-employment not to exceed the dollar limit for the year.

---

[47] §§ 415(c)(1) and (3)(B).

[48] § 401(c)(2).

EXHIBIT 18-5
Circular Computation of Allowable KEOGH Contribution

$$AC = 1.00(EI) = 1.00(MNE-AC) = 1.00MNE-1.00AC$$
or
$$2.00AC = MNE$$
thus
$$AC = [MNE/2.00 = .50MNE \ (50\% \text{ of } MNE)]$$

Example 12. During the current year, Mr. T earned $75,924 and paid $7,848 in self-employment taxes. The maximum contribution T can make to his defined contribution plan is 100% of $72,000 [$75,924 − (½ of $7,848)] less the contribution itself. Therefore, the maximum contribution is $36,000 [100% of ($75,924 − $3,924 − $36,000)]. Note that this contribution is actually 50% of the modified net earnings of $72,000.

A different limitation applies to a Keogh plan if it is purely a discretionary profit sharing plan as opposed to the defined contribution plan discussed above. In this case, § 404(a)(3) limits the deductible contribution to only 15 percent of *modified net earnings* from self-employment. Once again, because the computation is a circular one, a calculation similar to Exhibit 18-5 would be necessary. While the computation is not illustrated, the results of such a determination indicate that the actual limit is 13.043 percent of *modified net earnings* (net earnings if no self-employment taxes are paid) from self-employment. For those self-employed individuals who desire to make a deductible contribution equal to the maximum, a defined contribution plan that combines a discretionary profit sharing plan with a money purchase plan that requires an annual contribution can be established.

QUALIFIED PLANS FOR EMPLOYEES

Since the establishment of employer-qualified plans as part of the Internal Revenue Code of 1954, Congress has expanded the scope of the law to provide similar plans for individual taxpayers who are not covered by an employer plan or who wish to supplement their employer plan.

CASH OR DEFERRED ARRANGEMENTS [§ 401(K) PLANS]

Cash or deferred arrangements (CODAs), also known as salary reduction plans or 401(k) plans, have attained enormous popularity because these plans offer all the tax advantages of a qualified retirement plan and allow employees to make tax excludable contributions to the plan from their own funds. Contributions made on behalf of the employee can come in the form of bonuses paid to the employee, additional salary, or an agreement by the employee to reduce his or her normal salary.[49]

One of the major benefits of a CODA is the flexibility it offers an employee. For example, a plan may be designed to allow an employee to defer up to 6 percent of his or her compensation. If the employee elects, he can defer 6 percent, or any smaller amount

---

[49] Regs. § 1.401(k)-1(a).

such as 1, 2, or 3 percent. This gives employees greater control of their taxable income in as much as they may choose annually how much they want in salary and how much they want to place in trust. In addition, loans from the trust are available to the plan participants.

The amount that an employee may elect to defer under a CODA many not exceed $14,000 for 2005 as shown in the table below.[50] While this figure is adjusted annually for inflation, it must be reduced by contributions to other retirement plans such as tax sheltered annuities and simplified employee plans. Any amounts in excess of this limit must be included in the individual's gross income. Furthermore, the limitations apply to the plan year and not to the calendar year of the individual. Thus, a CODA on a noncalendar year could theoretically allow an employee on a calendar year to defer up to $27,000 ($14,000 + $13,000), for example, in a single year.

Section 401(k) Plan Contributions Limitations

Year	Amount
2001	$10,500
2002	11,000
2003	12,000
2004	13,000
2005	14,000
2006 and thereafter	15,000

Employer Contributions. One of the major benefits of a CODA to an employer is that it provides a low-cost method of financing retirement benefits to the employee. Thus, amounts that would have been paid in salaries or wages can now be directed toward the retirement plan. The offsetting administrative expenses of initiating and operating the plan should be relatively low so that they do not detract from its overall benefits. When establishing a CODA, contributions made to the trust should be treated as employer contributions as opposed to employee contributions. This is necessary to ensure the exclusion from income that is available only to contributions made by the employer.[51]

> **Example 13.** An employee's election form to fund a CODA should not state that she elects to contribute $5,000 of her salary to a CODA. Instead, the election should request that the employer reduce her salary by $5,000 in exchange for the employer's agreement to fund a CODA by the amount of $5,000.

An employer is entitled to take a deduction for a contribution to a CODA of up to 25 percent of an employee's compensation. This 25 percent limit is reduced by the employee's active contribution. Compensation for this purpose is net compensation after considering the employee's contribution.

> **Example 14.** E, an employee of Z Corporation, desires to make an elective contribution of $8,000 to a qualified CODA. If E's compensation for the year is $110,000, the available contribution that Z Corporation can make for the year is determined as follows:

---

[50] § 402(g)(5).

[51] § 414(h)(1).

Compensation	$110,000
Less: E's contribution.	(8,000)
Net Compensation.	$102,000
Employer limit	× 25%
Maximum Contribution.	$ 25,500
Less: E's contribution.	(8,000)
Available Contribution	$ 17,500

Catch-up Adjustment for Individuals Over Age 50. Beginning in 2002, taxpayers who are over the age of 50 are permitted to make additional elective deferrals in excess of the otherwise permissible limits in order to compensate for the increased limits. These additional amounts can be contributed to § 401(k) plans, § 403(b) plans, SEPs, and SIMPLE plans. These additional deferrals may be made without regard to the qualification requirements or limitations that usually apply to these provisions. The amount of the catch-up adjustments (by year) are illustrated in the table below:

Year	§ 401(k)	§ 403(b)	SEPs	SIMPLE	IRAs
2002	$1,000	$1,000	$1,000	$ 500	$ 500
2003	2,000	2,000	2,000	1,000	500
2004	3,000	3,000	3,000	1,500	500
2005	4,000	4,000	4,000	2,000	500
2006 and thereafter	5,000	5,000	5,000	2,500	1,000

Plan Requirements. In order to secure the benefits of a CODA, specific requirements must be satisfied. While a detailed explanation is beyond the scope of this coverage, a synopsis of these rules summarizes their features.[52]

1. A CODA must meet the qualification requirements of a profit sharing or stock bonus plan including its participation and coverage requirements.

2. A CODA must provide for an election by each eligible participant to have their employer make payments to a qualified trust or directly to them in cash.

3. Amounts held under a qualified CODA are restricted as to when the funds may be distributed to the employee, and the employee's right to those benefits must be nonforfeitable.

4. Under complicated rules, amounts available for tax deferral may not discriminate in favor of highly compensated employees.[53]

Roth 401(k) Plans. The new law allows taxpayers to create Roth 401(k) plans beginning in 2006. Amounts contributed to such plans (i.e., salary reductions), like those to Roth IRAs, would not be deferred but would be reported on a participant's Form W-2. For all practical purposes, these Roth 401(k) plans will be identical to Roth IRAs

---

[52] § 401(k)(2) and (3).

[53] Regs. § 1.401(k)-1(a)(4)(iv).

with certain limited differences. For example distributions for first-time home-buyers before age 59½ are not permitted tax-free. A detailed discussion of this plan is not warranted at this time.

INDIVIDUAL RETIREMENT ACCOUNTS

Prior to 1974, the benefits of qualified retirement plans were generally limited to employees of companies that opted to incur the expense of establishing plans. In 1974, however, Congress decided to provide an incentive for retirement savings in situations where there was no employer-provided plan and created the Individual Retirement Account (IRA). Since their creation, IRAs have been immensely popular.

The basic operation of a conventional IRA then and now mirrors that for employer-provided plans. Under the IRA provisions, an individual is generally entitled to make an annual tax-deductible contribution to the IRA. The contribution is a deduction for A.G.I., making it available to those who do not itemize deductions as well as those who do. Contributions are then invested and the income earned on such investments is not taxable currently. However, when amounts are withdrawn from the IRA they are fully taxable (both the earnings and the amounts representing the contributions). From an investment perspective, the tremendous advantages of the IRA relative to a traditional savings arrangement are the same as discussed earlier for employer-provided retirement plans. As explained above, the benefits of an IRA can be traced to two key factors: (1) the amounts invested are before-tax, providing a greater initial investment and (2) the tax is deferred until the amounts are withdrawn, resulting in greater earnings over the life of the investment.

The popularity of the IRA and the need to stimulate savings for retirement has caused Congress to expand the IRA concept over the years. Currently, there are three types of savings arrangements that bear the IRA name. They are:

1. The traditional or conventional IRA (discussed above).

2. The Roth IRA

3. The Educational IRA

Unfortunately, even though each of these savings vehicles is called an IRA, their treatment can be quite different.

TRADITIONAL IRA

The traditional IRA is currently the most common type of IRA since they have been in existence since 1974. Individuals are permitted to make three types of contributions to a traditional IRA.

1. Deductible contributions

2. Nondeductible contributions

3. Rollover contributions (i.e., contributions of amounts withdrawn from other qualified retirement plans)

Deductible Contributions to a Traditional IRA. As a general rule, an individual who is not covered by an employer-sponsored retirement plan can deduct contributions to a traditional IRA of up to $4,000 per year (in 2005). The contribution limit increases as illustrated in the table below. However, the deduction cannot exceed the taxpayer's compensation for the year.[54] In addition, taxpayers over 70½ cannot make contributions to a traditional IRA.

Increase in IRA Contribution Limit

Year	Amount
2002–2004	$3,000
2005–2007	4,000
2008 and thereafter	5,000

Similar to the § 401(k) rules discussed earlier, individuals age 50 and over are permitted to make additional annual IRA contributions in the following amounts:

▸ $500 for years 2002–2005 and
▸ $1,000 for 2006 and thereafter.

Example 15. H and W are married with two kids, Z and K. H's mom, M, also lives with the family. This year, Z, 14, received $500 of interest income from a savings account and earned $1,500 from sacking groceries at the local supermarket. K, 17, earned $5,000 delivering pizzas. M, age 75, earned $7,000 from a part-time job at a fast-food restaurant and had $40,000 of interest and dividends. Since Z's earned income is only $1,500, the maximum amount that he can deduct for contributions to an IRA is limited to $1,500 (his compensation). In contrast, K is able to contribute and deduct the maximum amount of $4,000 since she has compensation of at least $4,000. On the other hand, M cannot make contributions to an IRA since she is more than 70½ years old.

Example 16. Assume the same facts as *Example 15* except that M is 55 years old. In this case, her contribution to an IRA is limited to $3,500 for 2005. This includes the $3,000 that was available because of her compensation, as well as the $500 additional *catch-up adjustment* due to her age.

Deduction Phase-out Rules for Plan Participants. If a taxpayer or his or her spouse is an active participant in an employer-sponsored retirement plan *and* has A.G.I. in excess of a specified *applicable dollar amount*, the maximum deductible amount is phased out.[55] The applicable dollar amounts differ depending on which of following four categories the taxpayer is in.

1. Files jointly and is an active participant in an employer-sponsored plan.
2. Files jointly, is not active in another employer-sponsored plan but has a spouse that is active in an employer-sponsored plan.
3. Files married filing separately and is active in an employer-sponsored plan.
4. Files as a single or head of household taxpayer and is active in another employer-sponsored plan.

The applicable dollar amounts at which the phase-out begins and the IRA deduction ends are shown for each group in Exhibit 18-6. Note that the applicable dollar amounts increase over the next several years (except in the latter two cases). Also observe that if

---

[54] § 219(b)(l).

[55] § 219(g) and (g)(3)(B).

A.G.I. exceeds the applicable dollar amount by more than $10,000, none of the contribution is deductible. For excess A.G.I. amounts between $0 and $10,000, the phase-out is proportional. For example, if the excess A.G.I. is $4,000, the taxpayer loses 40 percent of the $3,000 deduction or $1,200. The amount of the phase-out can be computed using the following formula:

$$\frac{\text{A.G.I.} - \text{Applicable Dollar Amount}}{\$10,000} \times \text{IRA Deduction} = \text{Reduction in Dedcutible Allowance}$$

EXHIBIT 18-6
Applicable Dollar Amount Phase-out Ranges

	Married Joint Active Participant Phase-out	Single or Head of Household Active Participant Phase-out	Married Inactive but Active Spouse Phase-out	Married Separate Active Participant Phase-out
2002	$54,000 – $64,000	$34,000 – $44,000	$150,000 – $160,000	$0 – $10,000
2003	60,000 – 70,000	40,000 – 50,000	150,000 – 160,000	0 – 10,000
2004	65,000 – 75,000	45,000 – 55,000	150,000 – 160,000	0 – 10,000
2005	70,000 – 80,000	50,000 – 60,000	150,000 – 160,000	0 – 10,000
2006	75,000 – 85,000	50,000 – 60,000	150,000 – 160,000	0 – 10,000
Thereafter	80,000 – 100,000	50,000 – 60,000	150,000 – 160,000	0 – 10,000

Example 17. Q, a single taxpayer, is a salesperson for C Corporation. She actively participates in her employer's qualified retirement plan. In 2005, her compensation and A.G.I. were $28,000. Even though she participates in her employer's plan, her maximum deductible contribution is $4,000 since her A.G.I. does not exceed the applicable dollar amount of $50,000. In 2006, her compensation and A.G.I. were $54,000. Since she participates in an employer plan and her A.G.I. exceeds the applicable dollar amount of $50,000, the amount that she can deduct is subject to the phase-out rules. Her maximum deductible IRA contribution for 2006 is $2,400 [$4,000 (2006 amount) − $1,600 as calculated below].

$$\frac{\$54,000 \text{ A.G.I.} - \$50,000 \text{ Applicable Dollar Amount}}{\$10,000} = 40\% \times \$4,000 = \frac{\text{Reduction in Deductible Allowance}}{\$1,600}$$

Example 18. T, a single taxpayer, is an accountant for a small corporation. He received compensation of $70,000 in 2005. T's employer does not maintain a retirement plan. Since T is not an active participant in a qualified plan, he is not subject to the phase-out rules and can deduct contributions to a traditional IRA of up to $4,000.

Special Rules for Married Couples. Traditional IRAs provide a special rule for married couples where one spouse is the major breadwinner. Each spouse may make a deductible IRA contribution of up to $4,000 (2005) provided the couple's combined compensation exceeds the amount of the contributions. In effect, this allows a married couple to contribute up to $8,000 even though only one spouse works (assuming the working spouse has A.G.I. of at least $8,000).

Example 19. H and W are married. H had compensation income of $22,000 while W had no compensation and stayed at home taking care of the family's children. Although W had no compensation for the year, she may make a deductible IRA contribution of $3,000 to her own account in addition to H's contribution to his account since their combined compensation of $22,000 exceeded their total contributions for the year of $6,000.

As noted above, if one spouse is an active participant in an employer-provided plan but the other spouse is not, the nonworking spouse may still contribute to a traditional deductible IRA but the nonworking spouse's contribution is subject to phase-out if the couple's A.G.I. exceeds $150,000. The active participant's phase-out begins at $70,000 for 2005.

Example 20. H and W are married. W is covered by a qualified plan sponsored by her employer. H is not employed. The couple files a joint return for 2005 reporting A.G.I. of $135,000. Even though H is married to an active participant in a qualified plan, he may make a deductible IRA contribution of $4,000 since the applicable dollar amount for the spouse of an active participant begins at $150,000. On the other hand, W may not make a deductible IRA contribution since the couple's adjusted gross income exceeds the $70,000 applicable dollar amount for married plan participants in 2005 by more than $10,000.

Example 21. Assume the same facts as the *Example 20* above except that the couple's A.G.I. is $180,000. In this case, neither spouse could make a deductible contribution because their A.G.I. exceeds the applicable dollar amounts ($150,000 and $70,000) by more than $10,000 for each spouse.

Nondeductible IRA Contributions to a Traditional IRA. Individuals are permitted to make *nondeductible* contribution to their IRAs. These contributions can be made only to the extent that the maximum deduction for IRA contributions is not claimed (i.e., $4,000 or 100 percent of compensation).[56] Note that there is no phase-out or compensation income limitation that applies to nondeductible contributions.

Example 22. G, single, had compensation and A.G.I. for 2005 of $59,000. G is covered by his employer's qualified plan. Since G's A.G.I. exceeds the threshold by $9,000 ($59,000 − $50,000) his maximum deductible contribution is $400 [$4,000 − (90% × $4,000)]. However, he is still permitted to make nondeductible contributions of $3,600.

Excess Contributions. Since the earnings generated by contributions into an IRA are tax deferred, taxpayers might be tempted to contribute amounts in excess of the contribution limit. To prohibit this possibility, a 6 percent penalty tax is imposed on any excess contribution left in an IRA after the close of the taxable year.

Rollover Contributions. As alluded to earlier, one reason for establishing an IRA is for the purpose of *rolling over* a lump-sum distribution from a qualified retirement plan. In addition, individuals who receive distributions from an IRA may also make rollovers of distributions into another IRA. By rolling over a distribution to an IRA, the taxpayer avoids taxation as well as any early withdrawal penalty.

Rollovers generally take one of two forms: (1) the distribution is paid to the plan participant who then must roll the distribution into an IRA within 60 days; or (2) the

---

[56]   § 408(o).

distribution is paid directly to the IRA. Failure to transfer the funds to an IRA within the 60-day period makes the distribution taxable and also subject to the early withdrawal penalty. Note that by having the distribution paid directly to the IRA, the participant avoids the provision that requires the employer to withhold 20 percent of the distribution as an estimated tax payment. It should also be noted that taxpayers who choose to roll over a lump-sum distribution forego the right to use any beneficial capital gain or forward averaging rules for computing the tax on the distribution when it is ultimately withdrawn from the IRA.

Withdrawals from a Traditional IRA. Income earned in an IRA is tax-exempt, regardless of the deductibility of the contributions to the IRA.[57] When funds are withdrawn from an IRA, an amount of the withdrawal proportionate to any unrecovered nondeductible contributions in the account is not subject to tax; the balance of the withdrawal is fully includible in gross income.[58]

Example 23. In the current year, taxpayer A, age 61, withdrew $9,000 from his IRA, after which the account balance was $26,000. A has made $1,500 of unrecovered nondeductible contributions to the IRA. The nontaxable portion of the withdrawal is $386, computed as follows:

$$\frac{\substack{\$1,500 \\ \text{(nondeductible contributions)}}}{\substack{\$26,000 + \$9,000 \\ \text{(account balance before withdrawal)}}} \times \$9,000 \text{ withdrawal} = \$386$$

For subsequent years, A's unrecovered nondeductible contribution balance is $1,114 ($1,500 − $386).

Distribution Requirements. Without special rules, IRA owners might postpone distributions for as long as possible hoping to take advantage of tax deferral to build their estate. However, the law requires taxpayers to take the entire IRA balance or start taking periodic distributions from their IRAs no later than April 1 of the year following the year in which the taxpayer reaches age 70½. The minimum distribution is generally based on either the life expectancy of the taxpayer or the joint life expectancies of the taxpayer and his or her spouse or another designated beneficiary. The actual calculation of required distribution is somewhat complex and beyond the scope of this text. However, it is important to note that if the distributions received are less than the required distribution amount, a penalty equal to 50 percent of the shortage may apply. Note that Roth IRAs are not subject to these distribution requirements.

For years beginning after December 31, 1996, Congress liberalized the required distribution rules of § 401(a)(9) for certain taxpayers. For those individuals other than 5 percent owners of a business, distributions are now required to commence by April 1 following the later of the year the employee reaches age 70½ or retires. Benefit payments delayed past age 70½ would have to be actuarially increased to reflect the distributions that the employee would have received if he or she had retired at age 70½. A special transition rule permits (but does not require) plans to temporarily cease benefit payments for individuals currently in pay status who are no longer required to receive distributions because of the enactment of this provision.

---

[57] § 408(c).

[58] § 408(d).

ROTH IRAS

The 1997 Tax Act created a nondeductible IRA called the Roth IRA. Under this plan honoring Senator Roth of Delaware, individuals may make nondeductible contributions of up to $3,000 annually. However, the $3,000 maximum contribution limit is reduced to the extent of any contributions to another IRA in the same taxable year. In addition, the maximum annual contribution that can be made to a Roth IRA is phased out for single individuals with A.G.I. between $95,000 and $110,000 and for joint filers with A.G.I. between $150,000 and $160,000. The increase in contribution limits for the Roth IRA is the same as the traditional IRA over the next several years.

A Roth IRA is an IRA which is designated at the time of establishment as a Roth IRA. The major benefits of a Roth IRA are that distributions from a Roth IRA are generally not taxable, and unlike a deductible or nondeductible IRA, contributions to a Roth IRA may be made even after the individual for whom the account is established reaches the age of 70½.

Technically, only qualified distributions are nontaxable. A qualified distribution is any distribution that:

▸ Is made after the taxable five-year period beginning with the first taxable year in which the individual made a contribution to a Roth IRA and

▸ Meets *one* of the following conditions:

  1. Is made on or after the date on which the individual attains age 59½

  2. Is made to a beneficiary (or to the individual's estate) on or after the death of the individual

  3. Is attributable to the individual being disabled

  4. Is a distribution for first-time homebuyer expenses (see earlier discussion)

  5. Is used for certain education expenses

Distributions from a Roth IRA that are *not* qualified distributions are includible in income to the extent they are not attributable to contributions. In addition, these distributions are subject to the 10 percent early withdrawal tax that also applies to other IRAs. An ordering rule applies for purposes of determining what portion of a distribution is not a qualified distribution and is includible in income. Under the ordering rule, distributions from a Roth IRA are treated as made from contributions *first*. For purposes of determining the amount of contributions, all of an individual's Roth IRAs are treated as a single Roth IRA. Thus, no portion of a distribution from a Roth IRA is treated as attributable to earnings until the total of all distributions from a Roth IRA exceeds the sum of all contributions as well as rollover contributions. In effect, a taxpayer can make withdrawals of previous *contributions* without penalty or tax at any time—even within the mandatory five-year holding period.

> **Example 24.** L first opened a Roth IRA at his bank on November 1, 2004, making a contribution of $3,000. He continued to make $4,000 contributions in 2005, 2006, 2007, and 2008. On May 1, 2008, L celebrated his 65th birthday, retired and took a distribution of $11,000 from his Roth IRA to take a trip to Europe. Under the ordering rule, the $11,000 withdrawal represents his contributions in 2004, 2005, and 2006 and, therefore, is neither taxable nor subject to the 10 percent penalty that

otherwise applies to distributions during the five-year holding period. Note that he can begin withdrawing distributions in excess of previous contributions (without penalty) once the five-year holding period requirement is met in 2009. Observe that the five-year holding period begins in 2004, the first taxable year that L contributed to the Roth IRA.

Credit for Contributions to Plans by Low-Income Individuals. To encourage low and middle-income taxpayers to save for their retirement, the 2001 Tax Act created a nonrefundable credit for contributions to certain retirement saving plans (§ 25B). Credits are available for contributions to § 401(k) plans, § 403(b) plans, § 457 state and local government plans, SIMPLE plans, SEP plans, traditional IRAs, and Roth IRAs. The credit is in addition to the deduction to which the taxpayer is normally entitled. The amount of the credit is generally equal to 50 percent of the individual's retirement savings contributions not to exceed $2,000. Thus the maximum credit is $1,000 (50% × $2,000). On a joint return, the maximum credit would be $2,000, however, the credit decreases as the taxpayer's income increases. The allowable credit percentage is a function of the taxpayer's modified adjusted gross as follows:

MODIFIED ADJUSTED GROSS INCOME CREDIT DETERMINATION

Joint Return		Head of Household		All Others		
Over	Not Over	Over	Not Over	Over	Not Over	Percentage
$ 0	$30,000	$ 0	$22,500	$ 0	$15,000	50%
30,000	32,500	22,500	24,375	15,000	16,250	20%
30,000	50,000	24,375	37,500	16,250	25,000	10%
50,000		37,500		25,000		0%

The credit is *not* available to the following individuals:

1. Individuals who have not attained the age of 18 by the close of the tax year;

2. Individuals for whom a dependency exemption my be claimed; and

3. Full-time students.

Example 25. T, single, graduated from college last year and took a job with a national accounting firm. His adjusted gross income for the year was $24,000. If T contributes $3,000 to a Roth IRA, he may claim a credit of $200 (10% credit percentage × $2,000 ceiling amount). Had T been a full-time college student for the year, he would not have been eligible for the credit.

EDUCATION IRAS (COVERDELL EDUCATION SAVINGS ACCOUNTS)

In an effort to encourage savings and provide a vehicle to promote higher education, the Tax Reform Act of 1997 created a special type of IRA known as an education IRA or Coverdell Education Savings Account (CESA).[59] Although the creation of such an account has nothing to do with retirement planning, as the name might suggest, the tax treatment of this arrangement is very similar to that for nondeductible contributions to traditional or Roth IRAs—thus its classification as an IRA.

---

[59] § 530.

Currently, taxpayers may make *nondeductible* contributions of up to $2,000 ($500 for years before 2002) in cash per year into a CESA for certain qualified beneficiaries. A CESA is a trust account that is created for the purpose of paying *qualifying higher education* expenses. A qualified beneficiary is any individual under the age of 18 years, or any special needs child regardless of age. Qualifying higher education expenses include tuition, fees, books, supplies and equipment required for enrollment that are incurred during the taxable year for a student who attends an eligible education institution. The term also includes amounts contributed to a prepaid tuition plan. In certain circumstances, *room and board* are also included in these expenses. An eligible educational institution means any post-secondary education courses (e.g., undergraduate or graduate courses), and beginning in 2002, includes the cost of elementary, secondary, private and parochial schools.

Similar to retirement IRAs, earnings on the amounts contributed to a CESA are not taxed as they accumulate. Withdrawals from a CESA are totally nontaxable to the extent that they are used exclusively for the purpose of paying qualifying higher education expenses. Furthermore, no contribution may be made during a taxable year in which a contribution is made by *anyone* to a qualified prepaid tuition program on behalf of the same beneficiary. Note also that for any year in which an exclusion from gross income is claimed with respect to distribution from an education IRA, neither a Hope credit nor a Lifetime Learning credit may be claimed with respect to education expenses incurred during that year on behalf of the same beneficiary.

Contribution Limit. The $2,000 annual contribution limit, computed at the donor level, is phased out ratably for contributors with A.G.I. (computed with certain modifications) between $95,000 and $110,000 ($190,000 and $220,000 for contributors filing joint returns). The term "Modified A.G.I." means A.G.I. increased by income earned outside the U.S. that normally is excluded under § 911. Individuals with modified A.G.I. greater than the upper phase-out range are not allowed to make contributions to an education IRA established on behalf of any other individual.

EXHIBIT 18-7
Phase-out for CESAs

$$\frac{\text{Reduction of the}}{\$2,000 \text{ Contribution}} = \$2,000 \text{ Contribution} \times \frac{\text{Modified A.G.I. - threshold}}{\text{Income Range}}$$

	Modified A.G.I. Phase-out begins	Modified A.G.I. Phase-out complete
Married filing jointly:	$190,000	$220,000
Other taxpayers:	$ 95,000	$110,000

Multiple CESAs for a Single Beneficiary. Taxpayers contributing more than $2,000 per year to an a CESA for a single beneficiary are subject to a penalty. Section 4973 imposes a six percent excise tax on excess contributions. An excess contribution consists of two parts:

1. the amount by which contributions to all CESAs for a single beneficiary exceed $2,000, plus

2. the amount contributed during the year to a qualified tuition plan.

Note that this rule prohibits a taxpayer from contributing to both a qualified tuition plan and a CESA without penalty. These rules do not appear to prohibit parents from contributing $2,000 to a CESA for one child while the grandparents contribute to a prepaid tuition plan. Moreover, there is no rule requiring that the person contributing be related to the beneficiary. Similarly, there is no restriction on the number of CESAs an individual may establish as long as each has a different beneficiary.

Distributions. Distributions from a CESA that are used to pay qualifying education expenses are generally nontaxable. In reality, this general rule is a bit more complex. Technically, distributions from a CESA are deemed to consist of a proportionate part of both the original contributions and the earnings on such contributions. Distributions representing contributions are always nontaxable. Distributions of earnings are excludable from gross income only to the extent that the distribution does not exceed qualified higher education expenses incurred by the beneficiary during the year the distribution is made. In effect, all of the earnings on a CESA are nontaxable as long as they are used for qualified education expenses. Distributions of earnings in excess of qualified expenses cause a ratable portion of the entire distribution to be taxable. In addition, an excise tax of 10 percent is imposed on the portion not used for education.

Rollovers. If any balance remains in a CESA at the time a beneficiary becomes 30 years old, such amount *must* be distributed, and the amount representing the account's earnings will be taxable. In addition, the distribution will be subject to a 10 percent penalty tax because the distribution was not for educational purposes. Prior to the time the beneficiary reaches 30, the 1997 Act allows tax-free (and penalty-free) transfers and rollovers of account balances from one CESA benefiting one beneficiary to another education IRA benefiting a different beneficiary (as well as redesignations of the named beneficiary), provided that the new beneficiary is a member of the family of the old beneficiary. For this purpose, a family member includes the beneficiary's spouse or a familial relative described in the rules governing dependency exemptions. These would include a child, sibling, parent and certain other individuals. For example, if the taxpayer's son did not fully utilize the amount in the CESA, the unused balance could be converted to an account for his daughter or his grandchild.

Gift and Estate Tax Treatment. Contributions made to CESAs are considered completed gifts and qualify for the annual exclusion. Distributions are not treated as gifts nor is a rollover to another beneficiary and, therefore, not subject to gift tax. Amounts in a CESA are not includible in the estate of any individual. If a beneficiary dies and the interest passes to a spouse, the spouse simply becomes the beneficiary of the CESA. If the interest passes to someone other than a spouse, the CESA terminates at death and the account balance is includible in the beneficiary's income (e.g., a child).

SIMPLIFIED EMPLOYEE PENSIONS

The concept of a Simplified Employee Pension (SEP) was added to the law in 1978 to provide employers with a way to avoid the fearsome complexities involved in establishing and maintaining a qualified retirement plan. By following the relatively simple rules of § 408(k), which are designed to prevent discrimination in favor of the prohibited group, an employer may establish a SEP. This qualified plan allows the employer to make contributions directly into an employee's existing IRA, thereby avoiding the necessity of a qualified trust.

The annual limit on SEP contributions is the lesser of 25 percent of employee compensation (subject to compensation limits) or $42,000 (2005). Employer contributions to a SEP are excludable from an employee's gross income.[60]

RETIREMENT PLANNING USING NONQUALIFIED DEFERRED COMPENSATION

For many years employers have designed total compensation packages for valued employees that combined both a current compensation element and a *deferred* compensation element. A *nonqualified* deferred compensation arrangement typically is one in which the employee is compensated for current services rendered by the employer's promise to pay a certain amount at some future date. Although nonqualified deferred compensation plans do not receive the favorable tax treatment given to qualified plans, such arrangements are often attractive to employers because of their flexibility. Many employers find that what may be lost in tax benefits is more than made up in the savings derived from not having to comply with restrictive rules concerning the discrimination, participation, vesting, and funding that apply to qualified plans. The two questions that must be answered about a deferred compensation arrangement are

1. When is the employee taxed on deferred compensation that is earned currently but will be received in a later year?

2. When is the employer entitled to a business deduction for deferred compensation that will be paid in a later year?

Note that if a plan is a qualified plan, an employer is entitled to a current deduction for contributions and the employee is taxed on such contributions only when they are distributed. For nonqualified plans, however, the timing of the deduction and income is not quite as clear.

In order to completely answer the first question, an examination of the constructive receipt doctrine is necessary. To thoroughly answer the second, an examination of funded and unfunded plans is required.

CONSTRUCTIVE RECEIPT

The Regulations state that income (both current and deferred) is to be included in gross income for the taxable year in which it is actually or constructively received by the taxpayer.[61] Thus for a cash basis taxpayer, all items that constitute gross income (whether in the form of cash, property, or services) are to be included for the taxable year in which they are actually or constructively received. Consequently, the question to be resolved is whether deferred compensation is constructively received in the taxable year when it is authorized or in the year of actual receipt.

A mere promise to pay, not represented by notes or secured in any way, is not regarded as a receipt of income under the cash receipts and disbursements method. This should not be construed to mean that under the cash receipts and disbursements method income may be taxed only when realized in cash. Income, although not actually received, is constructively received by an individual in the taxable year during which it is credited to his account or set aside for him so that he may draw upon it at a later date.[62] Thus, under the doctrine of constructive receipt, a taxpayer may not deliberately

---

[60]   § 402(h).

[61]   Regs. § 1.451-1(a).

[62]   Regs. § 1.451-2(a).

turn his back upon income, nor may a taxpayer, by a private agreement, postpone receipt of income from one year to another.

Income is not constructively received if the taxpayer's control of its receipt is subject to substantial limitations or restrictions. Consequently, if a corporation credits its employees with bonus stock, but the stock is not available to those employees until some future date, the mere crediting on the books of the corporation does not constitute constructive receipt. In most cases, speculating whether an employer would have been willing to relinquish a payment earlier or determining a taxpayer's control over funds is not an easy task. As a result, in each case involving a deferral of compensation (especially nonqualified plans), the determination of whether the constructive receipt doctrine is applicable must be made on a fact-and-circumstances basis.

> **Example 26.** T, a football player, entered into a two-year contract to play football for the California Condors. In addition to his salary, as an inducement for signing the contract, T would be paid a signing bonus of $150,000. Although T could have demanded and received his bonus at the time of signing the contract, T's attorneys suggested that the $150,000 be transferred to an escrow agent to be held for five years and then paid to T over the next five years as an annuity. If T should die, the escrow account would become part of his estate. Because the bonus is set aside for T, the $150,000 bonus must be included in T's gross income in the year in which the club unconditionally paid the amount to the escrow agent. The employer's obligation for payment terminated when the amount of the bonus was fixed at $150,000 and irrevocably set aside for T's sole benefit.[63]

TREATMENT OF NONQUALIFIED DEFERRED COMPENSATION PLANS

Persuaded by corporate scandals at companies such as Enron, the *American Jobs Creation Act of 2004* imposes new restrictions and limitations on the design of nonqualified deferred compensation plans.[64] Under the new law, in order for deferred compensation to be excluded from gross income, the deferred compensation plan must meet specific guidelines. These guidelines include: (1) a distribution requirement, (2) an acceleration of benefits requirement, and (3) certain election requirements.

Restrictions on Distributions. Under Code § 409A(a)(2)(A), a nonqualified deferred compensation plan may not permit distributions from the plan earlier than:

- the participant's separation from service, as determined by the IRS, subject to a special rule for separation from service of any "specified employee";
- the date the participant becomes "disabled";
- the participant's death;
- a time specified, or a schedule fixed, under the plan at the date of the deferral of the compensation;
- to the extent allowed by the IRS, a change in the ownership or effective control of the corporation, or in the ownership of a substantial portion of the corporation's assets; or
- the occurrence of an "unforeseeable emergency" as defined in §409A(a)(2)(B)(ii).

Additionally, specified employees (referred to as "key employees") of publicly traded corporations generally may not receive their distributions earlier than six months after

---

[63]   Rev. Rul. 55-527, 1955-2 C.B. 25.

[64]   § 409A.

separation. A key employee is defined as an officer with compensation greater than $130,000 (adjusted for inflation and limited to 50 employees); 5 percent owners; and 1 percent owners with compensation greater than $150,000. Furthermore, taking a distribution with a "haircut" (i.e., forfeiture of a portion of the account balance in exchange for access to the plan account) is no longer a distribution option.

Acceleration of Benefits. Section 409A does not permit a plan to allow for the acceleration of benefits. However, under the anticipated IRS regulations, a nonqualified deferred compensation plan would not violate the prohibition on accelerations in certain limited situations. For example, a plan could provide that upon separation from service of a participant, account balances less than $10,000 will be automatically distributed (except in the case of specified key employees).

Election Requirements. Under the new law, the flexibility of a participant to change his or her deferral elections generally must be made in the tax year preceding the year in which the services are performed, or within 30 days of becoming eligible for plan participation. If the award is performance-based (e.g., an incentive bonus), the election must be made no later than six months before the end of the performance period.

In addition to the above rules, a deferred compensation plan may not provide that the deterioration in the financial status of the employer will trigger payment of the deferred compensation. Offshore Rabbi trusts and Rabbi trusts that are convertible into Secular trusts (protecting the assets from general creditors) are also prohibited under the new law.

Effective Date of New Rules. The new rules generally apply to amounts deferred after December 31, 2004. If a plan fails to meet the requirements, or is not operated in accordance with any of these three requirements, all compensation earned and deferred must be included in income for the first tax year that the nonqualified deferred compensation plan fails to meet the requirements, to the extent not subject to a "substantial risk of forfeiture" and not previously included in gross income.[65] A 20 percent penalty will also be imposed on the amount required to be included in income. Interest will also be assessed on the underpayment, at the underpayment rate plus one percentage point. Any compensation that becomes taxable will be subject to income tax withholding.

UNFUNDED DEFERRED COMPENSATION PLANS

If an employer contractually promises to pay deferred compensation to an employee and does not set aside current funds in some type of trust arrangement, the employee is put in the position of an unsecured creditor of the employer. If the employee is a cash basis taxpayer and does not have any current right to payment under the deferred compensation plan, there is no constructive receipt of the compensation and thus no current taxable income to the employee. The employee will not be taxed until the year in which the deferred compensation is actually paid.[66]

From the employer's point of view, such unfunded arrangements are attractive because they do not require any current cash outflow from the business. However, neither a cash basis nor an accrual basis employer may take a deduction for deferred compensation until the deferred amount is includible in the employee's gross income.[67]

---

[65] § 409A(a)(1)(A)(i).

[66] Rev. Rul. 69-649, 1969-2 C.B. 106.

[67] Rev. Rul. 69-650, 1969-2 C.B. 106.

FUNDED DEFERRED COMPENSATION PLANS

Employees who agree to a nonqualified deferred compensation arrangement normally prefer that their employers secure the promise of future compensation by transferring current funds into an independent trust for the employee's benefit. While these employees desire the protection of a funded plan, they do not wish to subject those funds to current taxation. Therefore, innovative methods have been devised to allow deferral of an employee's income under a funded method by making the employee's interest in those funds forfeitable. To this end, an employer can establish one of many types of trusts. Two of the more common nonqualified arrangements are the *Rabbi trust* and the *Secular trust*. The rules of § 83, discussed earlier in the chapter, apply to these funded deferred compensation plans.[68]

Rabbi Trusts. Rabbi trusts are so named because the first IRS ruling that approved this arrangement involved a fund established by a congregation for its rabbi. In the typical Rabbi trust arrangement, the rights of employees are forfeitable, so an employee will not recognize taxable income until he or she actually receives a distribution from the trust. If a deferred compensation arrangement provides that employees' rights in the retirement fund eventually become nonforfeitable (i.e., vested), an employee must recognize taxable income in the year his or her rights vest. In both cases, the employer will receive a deduction only in the taxable year in which the deferred compensation is includible in the gross income of the employee.[69]

> **Example 27.** As part of a deferred compensation arrangement, employer X agrees to place $10,000 annually into a trust account for employee Y. Y's rights to the trust funds are forfeitable until he completes 10 years of service for X. In the year in which Y's risk of forfeiture lapses, the value of the trust funds is included in Y's gross income. Subsequent payments into the fund by X are fully taxable to Y.[70]

A disadvantage of the Rabbi trust is that if the employer gets into financial difficulty, the trust assets are subject to the claims of the employer's creditors. In addition, any income that is generated by the trust will be taxable to the employer.

Secular Trusts. Designed in 1988, the Secular trust is a variation of the Rabbi trust.[71] Under a Secular trust, the employee receives a vested interest in the full amount of the transfer to the trust. Because the employee has a nonforfeitable interest, the employee is taxed immediately on the transfer of funds to the trust even though he or she has not actually received the funds. In return for the transfer, the employer receives an immediate deduction. The advantage of this arrangement is that the trust assets are not subject to the claims of the employer's creditors. The disadvantage, of course, is that the funds are immediately taxable to the employee. A Secular trust differs from a Rabbi trust, because the assets of the Rabbi trust will not be protected from the creditors of the employer in the event of bankruptcy.

---

[68]   § 402(b).

[69]   § 404(a)(5).

[70]   Reg. § 1.402(b)-1(b).

[71]   PLR8841023.

STOCK OPTIONS

As an alternative to the payment of compensation in the form of corporate stock, corporate employers may issue *options* to purchase stock at a specified price to employees whom the company wants to retain. As a general rule, stock options have no value on the date they are issued because the option price is equal to or greater than the market price of the stock. Consequently, the options will have value to the recipient (and become a cost to the employer) *only if* the market price of the shares increases.

If an option has no value upon date of grant to an employee, the employee obviously has not received taxable income. However, in certain unusual cases options may have a value at date of grant. If such value can be determined with reasonable accuracy under criteria provided in Regulation § 1.83-7(b)(2), the value represents compensation income to the recipient of the option. If an option is actively traded on an established market, it is deemed to have an ascertainable value at date of grant.[72]

> **Example 28.** Corporation C grants employee D an option to purchase 100 shares of C common stock for $11 a share at any time over the next ten years. If C stock is selling at $9 per share, D's option has no readily ascertainable value. Therefore, D has no taxable income at date of grant, and a zero-tax basis in the option. If, however, D's option is actively traded on an established market and as a result can be valued at $5, D has received taxable compensation of that amount, and will have a $5 basis in the option.

OPTION EXERCISE

When the owner of a stock option that had no ascertainable value at date of grant exercises the option, the difference between the option price and the market price (bargain element) of the stock purchased represents ordinary income to the owner. If the option had an ascertainable value at date of grant, so that the recipient recognized taxable income upon receipt of the option, no additional income is recognized when the option is exercised.[73]

> **Example 29.** In 2002 employee M received certain stock options as part of her compensation from Corporation Q. At date of grant, the options had no ascertainable value. However, in 2005 M exercised the options and purchased 1,000 shares of Q stock, market value $90 per share, for the option price of $60 per share. In 2005 M must recognize $30,000 of ordinary income ($30 per share bargain element × 1,000 shares). M's tax basis in her shares is $90,000.

From the employer's point of view, the value of a stock option can be taken as a deduction under the previously discussed rule of § 83(h). Generally, an employer will receive a deduction at date of grant if the option has a readily ascertainable value. If the option has no value at date of grant, the deduction will equal the income recognized by the owner of the option when the option is exercised.

---

[72]   Reg. § 1.83-7(b)(1).

[73]   Reg. § 1.83-7(a).

INCENTIVE STOCK OPTIONS

In the past, Congress has experimented with a variety of *qualified stock options—* options afforded preferential tax treatment under § 421. Currently there is only a single type of qualified option, the Incentive Stock Option (ISO) of § 422A.[74]

Under § 421(a), the exercise of an ISO will not result in any income recognition to the owner. Correspondingly, the corporate employer who issued the option will never receive any deduction for the spread between option and market price at date of exercise. If and when the stock received upon exercise is sold, the employee will realize capital gain equal to the difference between the option price and selling price. The difference in tax consequences between a nonqualified stock option and an ISO is presented in the example below.

Example 30. Employee T was granted an option in 1999 to purchase one share of his corporate employer's stock at any time within the two succeeding calendar years. At the time the option was granted, the option price was $150 and the market price was $140. Assume that T exercised the option in 2001 when the stock had a market price of $200, and the stock acquired was sold in 2005 for $375. The tax consequences for each tax year would be as follows:

	Nonqualified Stock Option	*Incentive Stock Option*
1999	None	None
2001	Market price of $200 – $150 option price = $50 ordinary income and $200 basis in purchased stock ($150 cost + $50 income recognized). Employer deduction = $50	No income and $150 basis in purchased stock
2004	Sale price of $375 – $200 basis = $175 capital gain	Sale price of $375 – $150 basis = $225 capital gain

It should be noted that § 83 will apply to a tax-free transfer of an incentive stock option in determining a taxpayer's AMTI. Under § 83(a), the taxpayer will include in AMTI the excess of the stock's fair market value at the first time it is transferable over the amount paid for the stock under the option. See Chapter 13 for a discussion of the alternative minimum tax (AMT).

HOLDING PERIOD REQUIREMENTS

For the beneficial rule of § 421(a) to apply, an individual may not dispose of the stock purchased upon exercise of the ISO within two years from the date of the granting of the option and within one year from the date of exercise.[75] Additionally, the individual must be an employee of either the corporation granting the ISO or a parent, subsidiary, or successor corporation from the date of grant until the day three months before the date of exercise.[76]

If an individual violates the holding period requirement by disposing of his or her stock too quickly after purchase, § 421(b) provides that the *compensation income*

---

[74] The rules of § 422A apply to options granted on or after January 1, 1976 and outstanding on January 1, 1981.

[75] § 422A(a)(1).

[76] § 422A(a)(2).

(ordinary income) the individual did not recognize at date of exercise must be recognized in the year of disposition. Any gain so recognized increases the cost basis of the stock.[77] In such a situation the employer will be entitled to a corresponding deduction.

> **Example 31.** Beta Corporation grants an ISO to employee Z on November 1, 1999. The option allows Z to purchase 500 shares of Beta stock at $3 per share. Z exercises the option on December 1, 2004, when Beta stock is selling for $7 per share. Z sells his 500 shares on March 1, 2005 for $9 per share. Because of the premature disposition (less than one year from date of exercise), Z must recognize $2,000 ordinary income [500 shares × $4 bargain price ($7 market price − $3 option price)] and a $1,000 capital gain in 2005. Additionally, Beta Corporation may claim a $2,000 deduction in 2005.

If the amount realized on a premature sale is less than the value of the stock at date of exercise, only the excess of the amount realized over the option price is recognized as ordinary income.[78]

> **Example 32.** Refer to the facts in *Example 31*. If Z sold his Beta stock for $6 rather than $9 a share, his ordinary income (and Beta's deduction) would be limited to $1,500 [500 shares × $3 bargain price ($6 selling price − $3 option price)].

QUALIFICATION REQUIREMENTS

An employee stock option must meet a number of statutory requirements set forth in § 422A(b) to qualify as an ISO. The primary requirements are as follows:

1. The option is granted pursuant to a plan that specifies the total number of shares that may be issued under options and the class of employees eligible to receive the options. The shareholders of the corporation must approve the plan within twelve months before or after the date the plan is adopted.

2. The options are granted within ten years of the date of adoption or the date of shareholder approval, whichever is earlier.

3. The option price is not less than the market value of the stock at date of grant.

4. The option must be exercised within ten years of date of grant.

5. The option can only be exercised by the recipient employee during his or her lifetime and can only be transferred at the employee's death.

6. The recipient of the option does not own stock possessing more than 10 percent of the total combined voting power of all classes of stock of the employer corporation or of its parent or subsidiary corporation.[79]

A major restriction on the use of ISOs is the statutory requirement that the value of stock with respect to which ISOs are *exercisable* shall not exceed $100,000 per calendar year per employee. For purposes of this requirement, the value of the stock is determined at date of grant.[80]

---

[77] Reg. § 1.421-5(b)(2).

[78] § 422A(c)(2).

[79] § 422A(c)(6) waives this requirement in certain cases.

[80] § 422A(b)(7).

Example 33. In calendar year 2004, Corporation Q granted Employee F an ISO to purchase 1,000 shares of Q stock with a current aggregate value of $200,000. In calendar year 2005, Corporation Q granted Employee F a second ISO to purchase 1,200 shares of Q stock with a current aggregate value of $300,000. If Employee F decides to exercise any of her ISOs in 2005, she may only purchase 500 shares through exercise of her 2004 option or 400 shares through exercise of her 2005 option.

Exclusion from Wages. The *American Jobs Creation Act of 2004* eliminated the uncertainty as to employer withholding obligations upon the exercise of statutory stock options. The Act provides a specific exclusion from the FICA/FUTA payroll tax withholding obligations for remuneration on account of the transfer of stock pursuant to the exercise of an incentive stock option or under an employee stock purchase plan, or any disposition of such stock.[81] The new law also provides that federal income tax withholding is not required on a disqualifying disposition of stock acquired from ISO and employee stock purchase plans (ESPP), nor when compensation is recognized in connection with an ESPP discount.

NONQUALIFIED STOCK OPTIONS

A Nonqualified Stock Option (NQSO), also referred to as a nonstatutory stock option, is generally any option that does not meet the statutory requirements in the Code to be treated as an Incentive Stock Option (ISO). NQSOs are often used as implements of deferred compensation because the corporation can avail itself of a tax deduction without a cash outlay and the options themselves can be issued with more flexible terms than ISOs. The only major disadvantage of using an NQSO is the potential for income recognition to the employee. That potential is, in turn, dependent upon whether the option has a readily ascertainable fair market value.

Readily Ascertainable Fair Market Value. If an option is actively traded on an established exchange (e.g., American Stock Exchange or Chicago Board of Options Exchange), it is deemed to have a readily ascertainable fair market value. An option that is not traded on an established exchange will not have a readily ascertainable fair market value unless it can be measured with reasonable accuracy. The Regulations support this presumption with detailed conditions for determining value.[82]

Determining value is important because, if the option has a readily ascertainable fair market value at the time of grant, the employee will be taxed immediately. Any gain or loss that accrues after the time of the grant will be recognized as capital gain or loss on the disposition of the underlying stock. When gain is recognized, the employee's basis in the stock includes any amounts paid for the stock plus the amount that was recognized as ordinary income at the time of the grant. The corporate employer takes a deduction in the same year (and for the same amount) income is recognized by the employee.[83] It is important to notice that the result of these options is conditioned on establishing a value for the option and not establishing a value for the stock of the corporation.

No Readily Ascertainable Fair Market Value. If an option does not have a readily ascertainable fair market value, the transaction will remain "open," and the employee will not be taxed when the option is granted. Instead, the employee recognizes ordinary

---

81 §§ 3121(a)(22), 3306(b)(19), 421(b), and 423(c).

82 Regs. § 1.83-7(b)(2).

83 Regs. § 1.421-6(c), (d), (e), and (f).

income when the option is exercised. The amount of income to be recognized is the spread between the value of the stock purchased and the price paid at the date of exercise. Any appreciation in the stock after the exercise date will be recognized as capital gain. The corporate employer takes a corresponding tax deduction in the same year and to the extent of ordinary income recognized by the employee.

> **Example 34.** On January 1, 2005 R Corporation grants S, an employee, the option to purchase 1,000 shares for $12 per share on or before August 15, 2006. At the time of the grant, R stock is valued at $20 per share. On June 3, 2006, when the value of R stock is $35, S exercises the option and acquires the stock for $12,000 (1,000 × $12). On November 1, 2006 S sells the stock for $48,000 (1,000 × $48). If the option granted has no readily ascertainable fair market value, S will recognize $23,000 ($35,000 − $12,000) of ordinary income and a $13,000 ($48,000 − $35,000) capital gain, both in 2006. R takes a deduction of $23,000 in 2006. If on the other hand, the option has a readily ascertainable value (for example $8 per share), S must recognize $8,000 of ordinary income in 2005 (the grant date) and a capital gain of $28,000 in 2006 (the sale date). R will take an $8,000 deduction in 2005.

STOCK APPRECIATION RIGHTS

Occasionally, NQSOs can create a problem for employees when they generate taxable income without providing resources to pay the tax. Unfortunately, when this occurs, some employees find it necessary to sell the stock to raise the capital, and this defeats the purpose of providing equity compensation. To ameliorate this dilemma, some employers wrap an NQSO with a Stock Appreciation Right (SAR).

An SAR is a type of right (similar to an option) that entitles the employee to a cash payment equal to the difference between the fair market value of one share of the common stock of the corporation on the date of the *exercise* of the SAR over its fair market value on the date it was *granted*. An employee need not own any stock of the corporation to receive an SAR, and SARs are granted without cost to the employee. An SAR cannot be exercised before one year after it was granted and must be exercised by the fifth year, or the SAR will be deemed exercised and cash will be paid to the employee. An SAR is not included in taxable income until the year the right is exercised. The IRS has ruled that an employee who receives an SAR will not be in constructive receipt of income in the year it was granted.[84]

TAX PLANNING CONSIDERATIONS

The area of employment compensation and retirement planning offers tremendous opportunity for creative tax planning. During a taxpayer's productive years, he or she needs to be able to analyze and appreciate the tax consequences of the various types of compensation alternatives that may be offered. The taxpayer must be aware of the tradeoff between types of compensation that will be taxed currently and fringe benefits that may not be taxable upon receipt. Sophisticated forms of compensation such as § 83 property and incentive stock options should be considered in designing a specialized compensation package.

---

[84]   Rev. Rul. 80-300. 1980-2 C.B. 165.

Taxpayers should also appreciate the necessity for long-range retirement planning. An understanding of the different tax consequences of qualified and nonqualified retirement plans is essential to effective planning for post-employment years. Exhibit 18-8 contains a comparison of the plans discussed in this chapter.

PLANNING FOR RETIREMENT INCOME

One of the central features of an individual's financial plan should be a provision for some source of retirement income. As the life span of the average American lengthens, the number of prospective retirement years increases. As a result, many individuals realize that some amount of current investment is necessary in order to ensure that their retirement years can be a period of financial security.

In analyzing a particular retirement plan, two basic questions must be answered:

1. Are payments into the plan deductible for Federal income tax purposes by the taxpayer?

2. To what extent are retirement benefits received from a plan includible in the recipient taxpayer's gross income?

ADVANTAGES OF IRAS

IRAs used to be among the best retirement saving plans around until Congress clipped some of their more generous features in 1986. Today they are still a useful part of many retirement portfolios; however, some limitations will apply.

Prior to 1987, IRAs were available to anyone who had not reached the age of 70½. Contributions were allowable up to the $3,000 annual limit and were fully tax deductible. Today, these rules apply to only two types of people:

▸ Those who are not eligible for an employer-sponsored retirement plan; or

▸ Those whose incomes fall below specified levels.

For individuals with company retirement plans, deductible IRAs are still available, provided certain tests can be satisfied. The first test of IRA deductibility is income. A taxpayer may still make a fully deductible IRA contribution as long as A.G.I. does not exceed certain levels. Exhibit 18-8 provides a list of eligible individuals and the limitations on IRA deductions.

> **Example 35.** H and W have A.G.I. of $152,000 and file a joint tax return. Their table amount indicates they are entitled to a partial deduction. To determine their deduction, subtract their A.G.I. from the limit for that particular row ($160,000 − $152,000 to get $8,000). Next, divide that amount ($8,000) by $10,000 to get a percentage ($8,000/$10,000 = 80%). This is the percentage of the IRA base, $4,000, that may be deducted. Accordingly, H and W may deduct $3,200.
>
> *Note* that the taxpayers may still *contribute* the full $4,000, but cannot deduct the extra $800.

EXHIBIT 18-8

IRA Deductions for Active Participants in Qualified Plans for 2005

A.G.I. Before IRA Deduction	Single or Head of Household	Filing Jointly or Widower	Married, Filing Separately
$0 – $10,000	full	full	partial
$10,000 – $50,000	full	full	NONE
$50,000 – $60,000	partial	full	NONE
$60,000 – $160,000	NONE	partial	NONE
$160,000 +	NONE	NONE	NONE

*Locate income and filing status. If the word *full* appears, a $4,000 deduction is available; if *NONE* appears, no deduction is available; and if *partial* appears, a prorated amount is deductible.

SPOUSAL IRAS

Holding a job is not a prerequisite to opening and deducting an IRA. A nonworking spouse may start a *spousal IRA*, as long as both taxpayers file jointly and the combined total of both spouse's earned income equals $8,000. When these two requirements are met, each spouse may make contributions to an IRA. Together, they may contribute as much as $8,000 in any single year. No more than $4,000 of that amount, however, may go to either account. If the combined total earned income is less than $8,000, the deduction is not lost. The combined total of the IRA's is limited to the amount of combined income (limited to $4,000 per spouse).

WHAT IS AN ACTIVE PARTICIPANT?

As discussed earlier, an individual may not be eligible for a deductible IRA if he or she is an active participant or eligible to participate in a pension or profit sharing plan. As a general rule, the IRS considers a taxpayer an active participant in a defined plan if the plan's guidelines state that the taxpayer is covered, even if they decline to participate. As a result, just being eligible for a plan makes the taxpayer an active participant.

If an individual is not sure if he is an active participant, he can look at his W-2 form, provided by his employer. It provides a box for the taxpayer's employer to check. If this box is blank, additional research may be necessary. Exhibit 18-9 provides aid in determining whether a taxpayer is eligible to participate.

EXHIBIT 18-9
Active Participation

Participation in any of the following plans can make a taxpayer an active participant and not eligible to deduct IRA contributions.

- ▶ Qualified pension, profit sharing, or stock bonus plans, including Keogh plans
- ▶ Qualified annuity plans simplified employee pension plans (SEPs)
- ▶ Retirement plans for Federal, state, or local government employees
- ▶ Certain union plans [so-called § 501(c)(18) plans]
- ▶ Tax-sheltered annuities for pubic school teachers and employees of charitable organizations.
- ▶ § 401(k) plans

MAKING A NONDEDUCTIBLE CONTRIBUTION TO AN IRA

Even if a taxpayer is not eligible, for whatever reason, to make deductible contributions to an IRA, a nondeductible contribution is available. Whether a taxpayer should make a nondeductible IRA contribution depends on the circumstances. Some of the following pros and cons should be considered before a taxpayer makes a decision.

The most obvious pro is that even though a taxpayer may not deduct his or her annual IRA contribution, the earnings from IRA investments accumulate and compound tax-deferred. This means a faster fund build-up compared to a taxable savings account. (See Exhibit 18-10 for a similar comparison.)

The most obvious con is that once money is put into an IRA, it is locked in until the taxpayer attains the age 59½. Otherwise, the taxpayer is subject to pay a 10 percent penalty for early withdrawal. The penalty applies to the deductible portion of the IRA contribution and to any earnings that may have accumulated tax-deferred in the account. However, no penalty applies when nondeductible contributions are withdrawn.

Many investment counselors suggest tax-free bonds as a reasonable alternative to making a nondeductible IRA contribution. The earnings from the bonds are tax-free and are not subject to a penalty if the taxpayer needs to withdraw any of the money. Moreover, a taxpayer is not limited to investing $4,000 ($8,000 for spousal IRAs).

Bonds, however, come with two potential drawbacks. First, a taxpayer can possibly get locked into the bonds until maturity. If interest rates rise, the value of the bonds generally declines, and a taxpayer would potentially have to sell the bonds at a loss. Second, depending on the market, the yields on bonds are sometimes low compared to the after-tax yields of other securities. So, potentially, bonds can be a very poor investment.

EXHIBIT 18-10
Comparison of Corporate Retirement Plans

Description	Corporate Plan	Keogh [HR 10]	Roth or Traditional IRA	SEP	CODA (401(k))	Funded	
						Rabbi	Secular
Qualified	Yes	Yes	Yes	Yes	Yes	No	No
Participation	21 years old or > 1 year = 100% vested	21 years old or > 1 year = 100% vested	Limited by AGI	21 years old or 3 out of 5 year's service	1 year's service	No Requirements	
Limitations	100% | $42,000 or 100% of $210,000 | 100% average.	100% | $42,000 or 13.043% of $210,000 | 100% average.	$ 4,000 or 100% Earned Income	$ 42,000 or 15% Earned Income	$14,000 (for 2005)	No limitations if paid as reasonable compensation	
Vesting	3 years Cliff or 6 years Graded	3 years Cliff or 6 years Graded	100%	100%	100% of employee's contribution	Subject to claims of creditors	100%
Premature Distributions	Rollover or 10% Penalty	Rollover or 10% Penalty	Rollover or 10% Penalty	Rollover or 10% Penalty	Rollover or 10% Penalty	Taxable only if not previously taxed	
Lump-Sum 5/10 year Averaging Available	Yes	Yes	No, taxed as Ordinary Income or Tax free	No, taxed as Ordinary Income	Yes	Not available: in some cases funds previously taxed	
Date Plan Must Be Established	By last day of plan year	By last day of plan year	Regular tax due date	Regular tax due date	By last day of plan year	By last day of plan year	
Required Date to Contribute	Extended due date	Extended due date	Regular due date	Regular due date	Extended due date	Year end	
Employee Loans from the Plan	Yes	None: Owner-Employees	None	None	Limited	Yes, but very risky	Yes

PROBLEM MATERIALS

DISCUSSION QUESTIONS

18-1 *Taxation of Barter Transactions.* Your friend who is a practicing dentist tells you that he filled a tooth for a friend's child "for no payment" because the friend had prepared the dentist's income tax return for the previous year. Must the dentist recognize taxable income because of this arrangement? Explain.

18-2 *Taxation of Fringe Benefits.* Define the term *fringe benefit*. As a general rule are fringe benefits taxable?

18-3 *Taxation of Fringe Benefits.* Every year, Employer E gives each employee the choice of a turkey or ham as a Christmas "gift." Is the value of this fringe benefit taxable to the employees? Would your answer be different if each employee received a Christmas bonus of $500 cash?

18-4   *Fringe Benefits—Cafeteria Plans.* What is a cafeteria plan of employee benefits?

18-5   *Reasons for Stock Options.* How does a corporation benefit from compensating valuable employees with shares of stock in the corporation rather than a cash wage or salary?

18-6   *Receipt of Restricted Property for Services.* What factors should a taxpayer consider when deciding to make an election under § 83(b) with regard to restricted property?

18-7   *ISO Plans.* An ISO (incentive stock option) allows the recipient both a deferral of income and a conversion of ordinary income into capital gain. Explain.

18-8   *Funded versus Unfunded Deferred Compensation Arrangements.* Why would an employee normally prefer a funded rather than an unfunded deferred compensation arrangement? Which would the employer normally prefer?

18-9   *Deferred Compensation and the Constructive Receipt Doctrine.* Explain the doctrine of constructive receipt as it relates to a cash basis employee who has a deferred compensation arrangement with his or her employer.

18-10   *Tax Advantages of Qualified Retirement Plans.* Discuss the tax advantages granted to qualified retirement plans.

18-11   *Defined Benefit versus Defined Contribution Plans.* Differentiate between a defined benefit retirement plan and a defined contribution retirement plan.

18-12   *Retirement Plan Qualification Requirements.* Any employee of Trion Ltd. Partnership can participate in the company's pension plan after they have been employed by Trion for 36 consecutive months. Can Trion's plan be a qualified retirement plan? Discuss.

18-13   *The Meaning of Vested Benefits.* Explain the concept of vesting as it relates to qualified retirement plans. How does it differ from the concept of participation?

18-14   *Profit-Sharing Plans versus Pension Plans.* Many small, developing companies will choose to establish a qualified profit-sharing plan rather than a pension plan. Why?

18-15   *Spousal IRAs.* Discuss the purpose of a spousal IRA (individual retirement account).

18-16   *Lump-Sum Distribution Rollovers.* Why might an employee who receives a lump-sum distribution from a qualified retirement plan choose to roll over the distribution into an IRA? What are the negative tax consequences of doing so?

18-17   *Roth IRAs vs. Traditional IRAs.* In 1998, Congress provided taxpayers wanting to establish an IRA a choice. Taxpayers may now use either a Roth IRA or a traditional IRA or both.
   a.   Identify the major differences between Roth IRAs and traditional IRAs.
   b.   Identify circumstances when a Roth IRA may be preferred over a traditional IRA and vice versa.

18-18   *Education IRAs.* One of the tax incentives created for higher education in 1998 was the Education IRA.
   a.   Explain how an education IRA works.
   b.   Compare an education IRA to a qualified prepaid tuition and how it relates to the Hope and Lifetime Learning credits.

PROBLEMS

18-19   *Receipt of Restricted Property for Services.* D, a calendar year taxpayer, is an employee of M Corporation, also on a calendar year for tax purposes. In 2005 M Corporation transfers 100 shares of its own common stock to D as a bonus for his outstanding work during the year. If D quits his job with M within the next three years, he must return the shares to the corporation. At date of transfer, the shares are selling on the open market at $35 per share. Three years later, when the risk of forfeiture lapses, the stock is selling at $100 per share.

   a.   Assume D does not make the election under § 83(b). How much income must he recognize in 2005 because of his receipt of the stock? In 2008 when his restriction lapses?

   b.   Assume D does elect under § 83(b). How much income must he recognize in 2005? In 2008?

   c.   Refer to questions (a) and (b). In each case how much of a deduction may M Corporation claim and in which year should the deduction be taken?

18-20   *Tax Consequences of a Nonqualified Stock Option Plan.* In 2005 Z Corporation grants a nonqualified stock option to employee M. The option allows M to purchase 100 shares of Z Corporation stock for $20 per share at any time during the next four years. Because the current market value of Z stock is $22 per share, the option has a readily ascertainable value of $200 ($2 per share bargain element × 100 shares) at date of grant. M exercises the option in 2007 when the market value of the Z stock has increased to $28 per share.

   a.   How much income does M recognize in 2005 because of the receipt of the option?

   b.   How much income does M recognize in 2007 upon exercise of the option?

   c.   What amount of deduction is available to Corporation Z because of the option granted to M? In what year is the deduction claimed?

18-21   *Tax Consequences of a Nonqualified Stock Option Plan.* In 2005 X Corporation grants a nonqualified stock option to E, a valued employee, as additional compensation. The option has no value at date of grant, but entitles E to purchase 1,000 shares of X stock for $20 per share at any time during the next five years. E exercises the option in 2006, when X Corporation's stock is selling on the open market at $48 per share.

   a.   How much income does E recognize in 2005 because of her receipt of the option?

   b.   How much income does E recognize in 2006 upon exercise of the option?

   c.   What amount of deduction is available to X Corporation because of the option granted to E? In what year is the deduction claimed?

18-22   *Nonqualified Stock Option Plans.* Refer to the facts in *Problems 18-20* and *18-21*. In each case, what tax basis does the employee have in the purchased corporate stock?

18-23   *Incentive Stock Options (ISO) versus Nonqualified Stock Options.* Refer to the facts in . If the stock option issued by X corporation had been an ISO rather than a nonqualified option, how much income would E recognize in 2006 upon option exercise?

18-24   *Incentive Stock Option Plans.* In May 2004 employee N exercised an ISO that entitled him to purchase 50 shares of Clay Corporation common stock for $120 a share. The stock was selling on the open market for $210 per share. N sold the 50 shares in 2007 for $390 per share.

   a.   How much income must N recognize in 2004 upon exercise of the option?

   b.   How much income must N recognize in 2007 upon sale of the Clay stock?

18-25 *Incentive Stock Options—Early Disposition of Stock*. Refer to the facts in *Problem 18-24*. What would be the tax consequences if N sold the Clay stock in August 2004 for $250 per share? For $190 per share?

18-26 *Tax Computation on Lump Sum Distributions*. T participated in his employer's qualified profit sharing plan from 1981 until his retirement at age 64 in the current year. T made no contributions to the plan. In the current year, T received a lump sum distribution of $75,000 from the plan.

    a. How much of the distribution is taxable to T in the current year?

    b. Assuming T is single with no dependents, does not itemize deductions, and has only $13,000 of other taxable income (including exemptions and the standard deduction), use the five-year forward averaging method to compute his current-year tax liability.

18-27 *Tax Computation on Lump-Sum Distributions*. In the current year, Mrs. Z, age 61, retired after a 35-year career with the same corporate employer. She received her entire $51,000 account balance from her employer's qualified profit sharing plan. In the current year, Mrs. Z and her husband will file a joint return on which they will report $21,000 of other taxable income (net of all deductions and exemptions). If Mrs. Z elects five-year averaging, compute the tax liability on the joint return.

18-28 *Qualified Pension Plan—Maximum Annual Benefits*. During his last three years as president of R Corporation, G was paid $200,000 in 2003, $230,000 in 2004, and $280,000 in 2005 as total compensation for his services. These were the three highest compensation years of his employment. What is the maximum retirement benefit payable to G from the corporation's qualified pension plan (a defined benefit plan)?

18-29 *Qualified Profit Sharing Plans—Maximum Annual Contribution*. In the current year, Mr. W, a corporate vice president, earned a base salary of $350,000. His corporate employer maintains a qualified retirement plan that provides for an annual contribution equal to 10 percent of each employee's base level of compensation. Based on these facts. compute the maximum current-year contribution to Mr. W's retirement account.

18-30 *Additional Taxes on Plan Distributions*. In the current year, Mr. L, age 51 and in perfect health, resigns as President of Meta Industries, Inc. Mr. L receives a $300,000 lump sum distribution from Meta's qualified retirement plan. Before consideration of this distribution, Mr. L's taxable income for the year is over $200,000. If Mr. L decides not to "roll over" the contribution into another qualified plan or IRA, compute the net after-tax amount of the distribution that Mr. L will be able to spend.

18-31 *Maximum Annual Contributions to Keogh Plans*. H is a self-employed business person with several employees. He has established a profit-sharing plan for himself and his employees. The annual net earned income from his business is $132,000. What is the maximum amount of a deduction available to H for his contribution to the plan for the year?

18-32 *Maximum Annual Contributions to IRAs*. H and W file a joint tax return. W is a lawyer with current-year earned income of $65,000. H works part-time as a landscape architect and earned $22,000 in the current year.

    a. Assume that W is an active participant in the firm's qualified profit-sharing plan. How much may W and H contribute to their IRAs for the current year? How much of the contribution is deductible?

    b. Assume neither H nor W is an active participant in a qualified retirement plan. How does this assumption change your answers to (a) above?

18-33 *Maximum Deductible Contributions to IRAs*. In the current year, Ms. A, a single taxpayer, contributed $1,400 to her IRA. She also is an active participant in her employer's qualified money purchase pension plan. Ms. A's adjusted gross income (before any deduction for her IRA contribution) is $29,640. How much of the IRA contribution is deductible in 2004?

18-34 *Taxability of IRA Distributions.* Taxpayer B, age 66, makes his first withdrawal of $8,800 from his IRA in the current year and uses the money to make a down payment on a sailboat. At the end of the year, B's IRA balance is $36,555. During previous years, B had made nondeductible contributions to the IRA totaling $13,400. Based on these facts, what amount of the $8,800 withdrawal must B include in current-year gross income?

18-35 *Simplified Employee Pensions.* Z is an employee of a company that has established a SEP. Z's current-year salary is $18,000.
  a. How much may Z's employer contribute to her IRA during 2004?
  b. May Z make any additional deductible contribution herself to her IRA?

RESEARCH PROBLEMS

18-36 *Current versus Deferred Compensation.* Roy Hartman is a 55-year-old executive of the Robco Oil Tool Corporation. The corporation does not have any type of qualified pension or profit-sharing plan, nor does it intend to adopt one in the near future. However, in an effort to ensure the continuing services of Mr. Hartman, Robco Corporation has offered him a choice between two different compensation arrangements. One pays $40,000 additional annual salary; and the other provides for $50,000 a year deferred compensation for 10 years beginning when Roy retires at age 65. Currently, Hartman's marginal tax rate is 31 percent. Roy does not expect to be in a lower tax bracket within his last 10 years of employment or after retirement. Since he does not need the $28,800 which would remain after paying current taxes on the $40,000 additional annual salary, Mr. Hartman asks you to evaluate his alternative compensation proposals. Assuming a 10 percent pre-tax return on savings will prevail over the entire 20-year period (10 years before and 10 years after retirement), and assuming that he would save the entire $28,800 annual after-tax salary under the $40,000 additional annual compensation arrangement, which alternative would you recommend? Why?

18-37 *Qualified Retirement Plans.* Shelly Carol is the sole shareholder of Gills Corporation. The corporation has been in business since 1989 manufacturing dog food. Profits have averaged about $300,000 per year for the past five years. Shelly projects that with the purchase of additional manufacturing equipment costing $700,000, he can double his production of dog food, resulting in additional profits of $200,000. Unfortunately, Shelly does not have the funds readily available to make the additional capital purchases, so in order to implement the plan he intends to borrow the entire $700,000.

Required:

1. How can Gills Corporation achieve its goal of financing the capital improvements while providing an incentive benefit to its employees?

2. Assume that Gills Corporation's payroll is approximately $600,000 and that Shelly intends to set aside $100,000 for the benefit of the employees. Compare the plan selected in (1) above with an ordinary pension or profit-sharing plan.

3. What are some of the disadvantages that Shelly should consider in using the plan established in (1)?

Research aids
  § 401(a)(28)(C)
  § 404(a)(3)
  § 404(a)(9)
  § 409(h)
  § 4975(e)(7)

Part VII

CORPORATE TAXATION

❖ Contents ❖

Chapter 19

CORPORATIONS:
Formation and Operation

LEARNING OBJECTIVES

Upon completion of this chapter you will be able to:

▸ Define a corporation for Federal income tax purposes

▸ Compare and contrast corporate and individual taxation

▸ Compute the corporate income tax, including the tax for personal service corporations

▸ Describe the corporate tax forms and filing requirements

▸ Explain the basic tax consequences of forming a new corporation, including:

   ▸ Determination of the gain or loss recognized by the shareholders and the corporation

   ▸ Determination of the basis of the shareholder's stock in the corporation and the corporation's basis in the property received

▸ Describe the requirements for qualifying a transfer to a corporation for tax-free treatment

▸ Understand the effects of transferring liabilities to an existing corporation

CHAPTER OUTLINE

INTRODUCTION

As discussed in Chapter 3, there are several types of taxable entities. The individual taxpayer has already been discussed at length. Various aspects of the corporate entity are covered in this chapter and the next two chapters. S corporations, partnerships, and fiduciaries are covered in later chapters.

WHAT IS A CORPORATION?

A corporation is an artificial "person" created by state law. The state may impose restrictions on the issuance of shares and the type of business conducted. The state also specifies the requirements for incorporation, such as the filing of articles of incorporation, the issuance of a corporate charter, and the payment of various fees (e.g., franchise taxes).

Federal tax law provides that a tax will be imposed upon the taxable income of every corporation. For this purpose, a *corporation* is a business entity organized under a Federal or state statute, if the statute refers to the entity as incorporated or as a corporation, body corporate, or body public.[1] This definition includes entities such as insurance companies, state-statute authorized joint-stock companies or associations, banks with any FDIC-insured deposits, businesses wholly owned by state or political subdivisions, and business entities, such as publicly traded partnerships, that are treated

---

[1] § 7701(a)(3).

as corporations. The regulations also classify a list of specified foreign entities as corporations.

ASSOCIATIONS

Historically, an association that was not treated as a corporation under state or Federal law (e.g., a partnership) could be classified as a corporation for Federal income tax purposes and thus be inadvertently exposed to the disadvantages of the regular (C) corporate form of doing business. The aspects that were addressed in determining whether an association should be classified and taxed as a corporation included:[2]

1. Continuity of life,

2. Centralized management,

3. Limited liability, and

4. Free transferability.

If three of these four characteristics were satisfied, an entity would be taxed as a corporation, even if the entity was treated differently under state law. For example, a limited liability partnership (LLP) or a limited liability company (LLC) could be treated as a corporation for tax purposes if it had, along with limited liability, two of the other three characteristics (e.g., centralized management and no restrictions on the transfer of interests).

It is important to note what could happen to any anticipated tax benefits if an organization was unexpectedly classified as an association. For example, if the owners of a real estate business expected losses in the early years of operations, the corporate tax entity would not be the best choice of business form unless the organization qualified for and elected S corporation status. If the business was treated as a partnership or an S corporation, the losses flowed through to the owners and could be deductible on their personal tax returns, subject to the passive activity loss rules. However, if the entity was classified as an association and was thereby taxable as a regular corporation, the losses simply accumulated at the corporate level in the form of net operating loss carryovers, the tax benefit of which expired at the end of 20 years.[3] Obviously, if the organization's owners did not think that the business was a corporation, they certainly would not file the required election to be treated as an S corporation for Federal income tax purposes. Thus, unless the organization qualified as a partnership for tax purposes, any anticipated tax benefits would *either* be lost or, at best, unduly delayed.

Naturally, the above classification rules led to a great number of conflicts between the IRS and taxpayers. To simplify this process, the IRS issued regulations in 1998 that replace the old rules for classifying entities with a "check-the-box" system.[4] Under the new rules, an entity organized as a corporation under state law, or an entity classified under the Code as a corporation, will be treated as a corporation and will not be allowed to make an election. However, any other business entity (e.g., an LLC) that has at least two members may elect to be treated as a corporation or a partnership for tax purposes (an entity with only one member will be treated as a corporation or a sole proprietorship). In general, existing entities will continue to operate as they are as long as there is a reasonable basis for the current classification. These rules greatly simplify the process of selecting the form of business in which the owners wish to operate.

---

[2]   Reg. § 301.7701-2.

[3]   See § 172(b)(1)(B).

[4]   Reg. § 301.7701-1.

An important exception to the classification rules, however, is the so-called *publicly traded partnership* (PTP). A partnership meeting the definition of a PTP will be treated *and* taxed as a regular corporation. Basically, a partnership is a PTP if it (1) is a limited partnership, (2) was organized after December 17, 1987 and (3) has interests that are traded on an established securities market or are readily tradeable on a secondary market. Certain exceptions exist for PTPs in existence on December 17, 1987 and for those with income consisting primarily of interest, dividends, rental income from real property and gains from the sale of such property, gains from the sale of capital or § 1231 assets, and income and gains from development, mining or production, refining, transportation, or marketing of any mineral or natural resource (see Chapter 22 for further discussion).

LIMITED LIABILITY COMPANIES

The "check-the-box" rules eliminate the need for LLCs to create artificial features (e.g., limits on centralized management, restrictions on transferability, limits on life of the entity) to receive the desired entity classification. Under a default system, a newly formed LLC will automatically be classified as a partnership if it has at least two members unless it affirmatively elects to be taxed as a corporation. Thus, LLCs can easily and effectively provide limited liability to their members while still being treated as a partnership for Federal tax purposes.

SHAM CORPORATIONS

In some instances, the IRS will ignore the fact that an entity is considered a corporation as defined by its state law. This may happen when a corporation's only purpose is to reduce taxes of its owners or to hold title to property. If the corporation has no real business or economic function, or if it conducts no activities, it may be a "sham," or "dummy," corporation.[5] Generally, as long as there is a business activity carried on, a corporation will be considered a separate taxable entity.[6]

> **Example 1.** M owns a piece of real estate. To protect it from his creditors, M forms X Corporation and transfers the land to it in exchange for all of X Corporation's stock. The only purpose of X Corporation is to hold title to the real estate, and X Corporation conducts no other business activities. It is properly incorporated under state law. The IRS is likely to designate X Corporation as a sham corporation and to disregard its corporate status. Any income and expenses of X Corporation will be considered as belonging to M.
>
> If X Corporation had conducted some business activities (such as leasing the property and collecting rents), it is likely that it will not be considered a sham corporation.

Generally the IRS, but not the taxpayer, is allowed to disregard the status of a corporation. The courts have frequently agreed that if a taxpayer has created a corporation, he or she should not be allowed to ignore its status (i.e., in order to reduce taxes). However, the Supreme Court has ruled that a taxpayer could use a corporate entity as the taxpayer's agent in securing financing.[7] Thus, under certain conditions, taxpayers may use a corporation for a business purpose and not have it treated as a corporation for Federal tax purposes.

---

[5]   See *Higgins v. Smith*, 40-1 USTC ¶9160, 23 AFTR 800, 308 U.S. 473 (USSC, 1940).

[6]   *Moline Properties, Inc.*, 43-1 USTC ¶9464, 30 AFTR 1291, 319 U.S. 436 (USSC, 1943).

[7]   *Jesse C. Bollinger*, 88-1 USTC ¶9233, 61 AFTR2d 88-793, 108 S.CT. 1173 (USSC, 1988).

COMPARISON OF CORPORATE AND INDIVIDUAL INCOME TAXATION

A corporation's taxable income is computed by subtracting various deductions from its gross income. Although this appears to be the same basic computation as for individual taxpayers, there are numerous important differences. In order to highlight these differences, Exhibits 19-1 and 19-2 contain the tax formulas for corporate and individual taxpayers.

GROSS INCOME

The definition of gross income is the same for both corporations and individuals.[8] However, there are some differences in the exclusions from gross income. For example, capital contributions to a corporation (i.e., purchase of corporate stock by shareholders) are excluded from gross income.[9]

EXHIBIT 19-1
Tax Formula for Corporate Taxpayers

Income (from whatever source)	$xxx,xxx
Less: Exclusions from gross income	− xx,xxx
Gross income	$xxx,xxx
Less: Deductions	− xx,xxx
Taxable income	$xxx,xxx
Applicable tax rates	xx%
Gross tax	$ xx,xxx
Less: Tax credits and prepayments	− x,xxx
Tax due (or refund)	$ xx,xxx

---

[8] § 61(a).

[9] § 118(a).

EXHIBIT 19-2

Tax Formula for Individual Taxpayers

Total income (from whatever source)		$xxx,xxx
Less: Exclusions from gross income		− xx,xxx
Gross income		$xxx,xxx
Less: Deductions for adjusted gross income		− xx,xxx
Adjusted gross income		$xxx,xxx
Less: **1.** The larger of		
a. Standard deduction	$x,xxx	
or	*or*	− x,xxx
b. Total itemized deductions	$x,xxx	
2. Number of personal and dependency exemptions × exemption amount		− x,xxx
Taxable income		$xxx,xxx
Applicable tax rates (from Tables or Schedules X, Y, or Z)		xx%
Gross income tax		$ xx,xxx
Plus: Additional taxes (e.g., self-employment taxes and recapture of tax credits)		+ x,xxx
Less: Tax credits and prepayments		− x,xxx
Tax due (or refund)		$ xx,xxx

DEDUCTIONS

Corporations have no "Adjusted Gross Income." Thus, for corporations there are no "deductions for A.G.I." or "deductions from A.G.I." All corporate expenditures are either deductible or not deductible. All allowable deductions are subtracted from gross income in arriving at taxable income.

Although corporations are considered to be "persons" under the tax law, they are not entitled to the following "personal" deductions that are available for individuals:

1. Personal and dependency exemptions

2. Standard deduction

3. Itemized deductions

All activities of a corporation are considered to be business activities. Therefore, corporations usually deduct all their losses since they are considered business losses.[10] In addition, corporations do not have to reduce their casualty losses by either the $100 statutory floor or by 10 percent of adjusted gross income. (Corporations have no A.G.I., as mentioned.)

Corporations do not have "nonbusiness" bad debts, since all activities are considered business activities. All bad debts of a corporation are business bad debts.[11]

---

[10] § 165(a). Like individuals, certain corporations are subject to the passive-loss rules discussed in Chapter 12.

[11] § 166.

Several deductions are available only for corporations.[12] These are deductible in addition to the other business deductions and include the dividends-received deduction and the amortization of organizational expenditures.

DIVIDENDS-RECEIVED DEDUCTION

No doubt the most salient tax aspect of operating a business in the corporate form is that double taxation occurs when corporate profits are distributed in the form of dividends to the shareholders. The corporation is not allowed a deduction for the dividends paid, and an individual shareholder is not entitled to an exclusion. Therefore, when one corporation is a shareholder in another corporation, *triple* taxation might occur. To alleviate this, Congress provided corporations with a deduction for dividends received.[13]

Generally, the dividends-received deduction (DRD) is 70 percent of the dividends received from taxable domestic (U.S.) corporations.[14] However, a corporation that owns at least 20 percent—but less than 80 percent—of the dividend-paying corporation's stock is allowed to deduct 80 percent of the dividends received.[15] In addition, members of an *affiliated group* are allowed to deduct 100 percent of the dividends that are received from another member of the same group. A group of corporations is generally considered affiliated when at least 80 percent of the stock of each corporation is owned by other members of the group.[16]

Taxable Income Limitation. The 70 percent dividends-received deduction may not exceed 70 percent of the corporation's taxable income computed without the deduction for dividends received, net operating loss carrybacks or carryforwards, and capital loss carrybacks.[17] However, if the dividends-received deduction adds to or creates a net operating loss for the current year, the 70 percent of taxable income limitation does not apply.

Like the dividends-received deduction percentage, the taxable income limitation percentage becomes 80 rather than 70 percent if the dividend-paying corporation is at least 20 percent owned by the recipient corporation. In the unlikely event a corporation receives dividends subject to *both* the 70 and 80 percent rules, a special procedure must be followed. First, the 80 percent limitation is applied by treating the "70 percent dividends" as other income. The 70 percent limitation is then applied by treating the "80 percent dividends" as if they had not been received.[18]

Exhibit 19-3 contains a format for the computation of the 70 percent dividends-received deduction, and *Example 2*, *Example 3*, and *Example 4* illustrate this computational procedure.[19]

---

[12]   § 241.

[13]   §§ 243 through 246.

[14]   § 243(a)(1).

[15]   § 243(c).

[16]   §§ 243(a)(3), 243(b)(5), and 1504.

[17]   § 246(b)(2).

[18]   § 246(b)(3).

[19]   To apply the 80 percent rules, simply substitute 80 for 70 percent in this exhibit and accompanying examples.

EXHIBIT 19-3
Computation of Corporate Dividends-Received Deduction

Step 1:   Multiply the dividends received from taxable domestic (U.S.) corporations by 70 percent.* This is the *tentative* dividends-received deduction (DRD).

Step 2:   Compute the tentative taxable income for the current year, using the tentative DRD (from Step 1):

> Total revenues (including dividend income)
> Less: Total expenses
> Equals: Taxable income (before DRD)
> Less: Tentative DRD (Step 1)
> Equals: Tentative taxable income (loss)

> *If* the tentative taxable income is *positive*, the taxable income limitation may apply. Go to Step 3.

> *If* the tentative taxable income is *negative*, there is no taxable income limitation. The dividends-received deduction is the amount computed in Step 1.

Step 3:   Compute the taxable income limitation:

> Taxable income (before DRD) (Step 2)
> Add: Any net operating loss carryovers from other years that are reflected in taxable income
> Add: Any capital loss carrybacks from later years that are reflected in taxable income
> Equals: Taxable income, as adjusted
> Multiply by 70 percent*
> Equals: Taxable income limitation

Step 4:   Compare the tentative DRD (Step 1) to the taxable income limitation (Step 3). Choose the *smaller* amount. This is the corporate dividends-received deduction.

*To apply the 80 percent rules, simply substitute 80 for 70 percent in Steps 1 and 3 above.

Example 2. R Corporation has the following items of revenue and expenses for the year:

Dividends received from domestic corporations.	$40,000
Revenue from sales.	60,000
Cost of goods sold and operating expenses	54,000

The dividends-received deduction is computed as follows:

Step 1: $40,000 dividends received
 × 70%

 $28,000 *tentative* DRD

Step 2:

Dividend income	$ 40,000
Revenue from sales.	+60,000
Total revenues.	$100,000
Less: Total expenses	− 54,000
Taxable income (before DRD)	$ 46,000
Less: Tentative DRD.	−28,000
Tentative taxable income.	$ 18,000

Since tentative taxable income is positive, the taxable income limitation may apply. Go to Step 3.

Step 3: Compute the taxable income limitation:

Taxable income (before DRD)	$ 46,000
Multiply by 70%.	×70%
Taxable income limitation	$ 32,200

Step 4: Compare the tentative DRD ($28,000) to the taxable income limitation ($32,200). Choose the *smaller* amount ($28,000). In this case, R Corporation's dividends-received deduction is $28,000 (not subject to limitation).

Example 3. Assume the same facts as in *Example 2* except that the revenue from sales is $50,000. The dividends-received deduction is computed as follows:

Step 1: $40,000 dividends received
× 70%
$28,000 *tentative* DRD

Step 2:

Dividend income	$ 40,000
Revenue from sales.	+50,000
Total revenues.	$ 90,000
Less: Total expenses	−54,000
Taxable income (before DRD)	$ 36,000
Less: Tentative DRD (Step 1).	−28,000
Tentative taxable income.	$ 8,000

Since tentative taxable income is *positive*, the taxable income limitation may apply. Go to Step 3.

Step 3: Compute the taxable income limitation:

Taxable income (before DRD)	$ 36,000
Multiply by 70%.	×70%
Taxable income limitation	$ 25,200

Step 4: Compare the tentative DRD ($28,000) to the taxable income limitation ($25,200). Choose the smaller amount ($25,200). In this case, R Corporation's dividends-received deduction is $25,200 (limited to 70% of taxable income).

Example 4. Assume the same facts as in *Example 2* except that the revenue from sales is $41,000. The dividends-received deduction is computed as follows:

Step 1:	$40,000 dividends received	
	$\times$ 70%	
	$28,000 *tentative* DRD	

Step 2:	Dividend income	$40,000
	Revenue from sales.	+41,000
	Total revenues.	$81,000
	Less: Total expenses	−54,000
	Taxable income (before DRD)	$27,000
	Less: Tentative DRD.	− 28,000
	Tentative taxable income.	($1,000)

Because the tentative taxable income (loss) is *negative*, there is no taxable income limitation. The dividends-received deduction is $28,000.

The taxable income limitation discussed above *does not* apply to dividends received from affiliated corporations that are subject to the 100 percent dividends-received deductions.[20]

Other Restrictions on Dividends-Received Deduction. The dividends-received deduction will be limited if the purchase price of the stock was debt-financed or the stock was refinanced and any portion of the debt remains unpaid during the period dividends are received on that stock.[21] In taxable years before 1984, a corporation could increase its cash flow and decrease its tax liability by purchasing stock with borrowed funds. Under prior law, the interest paid on the debt was fully deductible, whereas the dividends were only partially taxable because of the dividends-received deduction. Currently, corporations must reduce the dividends-received deduction if the stock was debt-financed. The dividends-received deduction for debt-financed stock equals the 70 percent deduction multiplied by the percentage of the stock price that is *not* debt-financed.[22]

Example 5. T Corporation purchased 100 shares of XYZ stock for $ 100,000. T borrowed $60,000 of the purchase price. Therefore, the corporation used $40,000 of its own funds or 4% of the purchase price. The dividends-received deduction for dividends from XYZ will be limited to 28% (70% × 40%). As T Corporation *reduces* the debt, the dividends-received deduction will increase. For instance, if T reduces the debt to $50,000 before the next dividends are received from XYZ, the dividends-received deduction *increases* to 35% (70% × 50% of stock price no longer debt-financed). When the debt is retired, the dividends-received deduction is restored to the full 70%.

The dividends-received deduction may also cause a reduction in the basis of the stock. If a corporation receives an *extraordinary dividend* within the first two years that the stock is owned, the basis of the stock must be reduced by the nontaxable portion of the extraordinary dividend.[23] An extraordinary dividend is any dividend that equals or

---

20   § 246(b)(1).

21   § 246A.

22   § 246A(a)(1); 80 percent in the case of any dividends received from a 20 percent or more owned corporation. This limitation does not apply to dividends that are eligible for the 100 percent dividends-received deduction.

23   § 1059(a).

exceeds 10 percent of the taxpayer's basis of common stock, or 5 percent of the basis of preferred stock.[24] If the taxpayer can prove the fair market value of the stock, then the taxpayer can use such value instead of basis to determine if the dividend is extraordinary.

> **Example 6.** P Corporation purchases 100 shares of Y Corporation common stock on January 1, 2005 for $100,000. On December 31, 2005 Y Corporation declares and pays a $30,000 dividend to P. Since the dividend exceeds 10% of the basis of the stock, it is an extraordinary dividend. P Corporation must reduce its basis of the Y Corporation stock by $21,000 (70% × $30,000), the amount of the dividends-received deduction.

ORGANIZATIONAL EXPENDITURES

When a corporation is formed, various expenses directly related to the organization process are incurred, such as attorneys' fees, accountants' fees, and state filing charges. Although some of the attorneys' and accountants' fees may be ordinary and necessary business expenses which do not benefit future periods (and are therefore deductible), most of these expenditures will benefit future periods and are therefore capitalized as *organizational expenditures*. These organizational expenditures are intangible assets that have value for the life of the corporation.

Generally, assets with indefinite lives may not be amortized for Federal income tax purposes. However, Congress has given corporations the option of expensing some of the organization expenditures and amortizing the remainder. The amount that can be expensed is limited to $5,000 reduced by the amount of the expenditures over $50,000. The amortizable amount is amortized over 180 months.[25] The 180-month period starts in the month in which the corporation begins business.

The Regulations give the following examples of organizational expenditures:[26]

1. Legal services incident to the organization of the corporation, such as drafting the corporate charter, by-laws, minutes of organizational meetings, and terms of original stock certificates

2. Necessary accounting services

3. Expenses of temporary directors and of organizational meetings of directors or stockholders

4. Fees paid to the state of incorporation

The Regulations also give several examples of items that are *not* considered organizational expenditures, such as costs of issuing stock.[27] The costs of issuing stock are considered to be selling expenses, and therefore are reductions in the proceeds from selling the stock. They reduce stockholders' equity and do not create any tax deduction.

> **Example 7.** N Corporation was formed and began business on July 1, 2005 and incurred and paid qualifying organizational expenditures of $8,600. N Corporation has chosen to use the calendar year for tax purposes. On its first tax return (2005),

---

[24] Amounts distributed to corporate shareholders on certain preferred stock or as part of a partial liquidation or non-pro rata redemption that are treated as dividends are also considered extraordinary dividends. See Chapter 20 for a discussion of redemptions and partial liquidations.

[25] See § 248.

[26] Reg. § 1.248-1(b)(2).

[27] Reg. § 1.248-1(b)(3).

N Corporation will expense $5,000 and claim an amortization deduction of $120, computed as follows:

$$\frac{\text{Organizational expenditures}}{180 \text{ months}} = \text{Amortization per month}$$

$$\frac{\$3,600}{180 \text{ months}} = \$20 \text{ Amortization per month}$$

$$\$20 \times 6 \text{ months in 2005 (July} - \text{December)} = \underline{\underline{\$120}}$$

The amortization deduction for organizational expenditures for 2006 will be $240 ($20 per month $\times$ 12 months).

An election to amortize organizational expenditures is made by attaching a statement to the corporation's first tax return.[28] If the election is not made, the organizational expenditures may not be amortized.

NET OPERATING LOSS

Corporations, like individuals, are entitled to deduct net operating loss carryovers in arriving at taxable income. As discussed in Chapter 8, numerous modifications are considered in computing an individual's net operating loss. However, only two modifications are considered in computing a corporation's net operating loss. These two modifications are the net operating loss deductions[29] and the dividends-received deduction.[30] Net operating loss deductions for each year are considered separately. Therefore, the net operating loss deductions for other years are omitted from the computation of the current year's net operating loss. The modification relating to the dividends-received deduction is that the 70 percent (or 80 percent) taxable income limitation is ignored (i.e., the dividends-received deduction is allowed in full).

A corporate net operating loss may be carried back two years and carried forward 20 years.[31] The loss is first carried back to the earliest year. Any unabsorbed loss is carried to the first prior year, the first year after the loss was created, and then forward until the loss is completely used or the 20-year period expires.

A corporation may elect not to carry the loss back.[32] If a corporation makes this election, the loss would be carried forward for 20 years. No loss would be carried back. This election is irrevocable.[33]

Example 8. T Corporation had the following items of revenue and expense for 2005:

Revenue from operations.	$42,000
Dividends received from a less than 20% owned corporation	40,000
Expenses of operations	63,000

---

[28] Reg. § 1.248-1(c).

[29] § 172(d)(1).

[30] § 172(d)(5).

[31] § 172(b)(1). For NOLs generated in 2001 and 2002 the carryback period is five years.

[32] § 172(b)(3)(C).

[33] *Ibid.*

T Corporation's net operating loss for 2005 is computed as follows:

Revenue from operations.		$42,000
Dividend income		40,000
Total revenue.		$82,000
Less:	Total expenses	−63,000
Less:	Dividends-received deduction (ignore the taxable income limitation).	−28,000
Net operating loss (negative taxable income)		($ 9,000)

The 2005 net operating loss is carried back two years to 2003. If T Corporation's taxable income for 2003 is $3,000, the 2005 net operating loss is treated as follows:

2003 taxable income	$ 3,000
Less: NOL carryback	−9,000
NOL carryover to 2004.	($ 6,000)

A corporate net operating loss is carried back by filing either Form 1120X (Amended U.S. Corporation Income Tax Return) or Form 1139 (Corporation Application for Tentative Refund). T Corporation should receive a refund of its 2003 income tax paid.

CHARITABLE CONTRIBUTIONS

A corporation's charitable contribution deduction is much more limited than the charitable contribution deductions of individuals. As with individuals, the charitable contributions must be made to qualified organizations.[34] The amount that can be deducted in any year is the amount actually donated during the year plus, *if the corporation is on the accrual basis*, any amounts that are authorized during the year by the board of directors, provided the amounts are actually paid to the charity by the 15th day of the third month following the close of the tax year.[35]

> **Example 9.** C Corporation donated $3,000 cash to United Charities (a qualified charitable organization) on June 3, 2005. On December 20, 2005 the board of directors of C Corporation authorized a $2,500 cash donation to United Charities. This $2,500 was actually paid to United Charities on March 12, 2006. C Corporation uses the calendar year as its accounting period.
>
> If C Corporation is a *cash basis* corporation, only the $3,000 contribution to United Charities made in 2005 may be deducted in 2005. The additional $2,500 authorized contribution may not be deducted until 2006.
>
> If C Corporation is an *accrual basis* corporation, then $5,500 ($3,000 + $2,500) may be deducted in 2005.
>
> *Note:* If the $2,500 donation authorized on December 20, 2005 had been paid after March 15, 2006, the $2,500 contribution deduction would not be allowed until 2006.

Contributions of Ordinary Income Property. The amount deductible when property is contributed generally is the fair market value of the property at the time it is

---

[34] § 170(c).

[35] §§ 170(a)(1) and (2).

donated. There are, however, several exceptions to this general rule. One exception involves donations of *ordinary income property*.[36] The Regulations define ordinary income property as property that would produce a gain *other than* long-term capital gain if sold by the contributing corporation for its fair market value. The charitable contribution deduction for ordinary income property generally may not exceed the corporation's basis in the property.

> **Example 10.** G Corporation donates some of its inventory to a church. The inventory donated is worth $5,000 and has an adjusted basis to G Corporation of $2,000. G Corporation's deduction for this contribution is $2,000, its adjusted basis in the inventory.

There is an exception that permits corporate taxpayers to claim contribution deductions in excess of the basis of the ordinary income property. A corporation is allowed to deduct its basis *plus* one-half of the unrealized appreciation in value (not to exceed twice the basis) of any inventory item donated to a qualifying charity and used solely for the care of the ill, the needy, or infants.[37] This rule also applies in two other situations: (1) the gift to a college or university of a corporation's newly manufactured scientific equipment if the donee is the original user of the property and at least 80 percent of its use will be for research or experimentation;[38] and (2) computer equipment donated to a primary or secondary school (i.e. grades K through 12), provided the property is not more than two years old.[39] In either case, the corporation is required to obtain a written statement from the charity indicating that the use requirement has been met.

Contributions of Capital Gain Property. As discussed in Chapter 11, there are limitations on an individual's deduction for contributions of appreciated property (property which has increased in value). In *two* situations, a corporation also is limited in the amount of deduction when appreciated long-term capital gain property is contributed.[40] The *first* situation is when tangible personal property donated to a charity is put to a use that is not related to the charity's exempt purpose. The *second* situation in which a limitation will apply is the donation of appreciated property to certain private foundations. The limitation applied in these cases is that the fair market value of the property must be reduced by the unrealized appreciation (i.e., the deduction is limited to the property's adjusted basis). For other types of capital gain property, the contributions deduction is the fair market value of the property.

> **Example 11.** L Corporation donated a painting to a university. The painting was worth $10,000 and had an adjusted basis to L Corporation of $9,000. If the painting is placed in the university for display and study by art students, this is considered a use related to the university's exempt purpose.[41] The limitation mentioned above would not apply, and L Corporation's charitable contribution deduction would be $10,000, the fair market value of the painting.
>
> If, however, the painting is immediately sold by the university, this is considered to be a use that is not related to the university's exempt purpose. L Corporation's contribution deduction would be limited to $9,000, its basis in the painting ($10,000 fair market value − $1,000 unrealized appreciation).

---

[36]   Reg. § 1.170A-4(b)(1).

[37]   § 170(e)(3).

[38]   § 170(e)(4).

[39]   § 170(e)(6).

[40]   § 170(e)(1).

[41]   Reg. § 1.170A-4(b)(3).

Annual Deduction Limitations. In addition to the limitations based on the type of property contributed, there is a maximum annual limitation. The limitation is 10 percent of the corporation's taxable income before certain deductions.[42] The 10 percent limitation is based on taxable income without reduction for charitable contributions, the dividends-received deduction, net operating loss carrybacks, and capital loss carrybacks. Amounts contributed in excess of this limitation may be carried forward and deducted in any of the five succeeding years.[43] In no year may the total charitable contribution deduction exceed the 10 percent limitation. In years in which there is both a current contribution and a carryover, the current contribution is deductible first. At the end of the five-year period, any carryover not deducted expires.

Example 12. M Corporation has the following for tax year 2005:

Net income from operations	$100,000
Dividends received (subject to 70% rules)	10,000
Charitable contributions made in 2005	8,000
Charitable contribution carryforward from 2004	5,000

M Corporation's contribution deduction for 2005 is limited to $11,000, computed as follows:

Net income from operations	$100,000
Dividends received	+ 10,000
Taxable income without the charitable contribution deduction and the dividend-received deduction	$110,000
Multiply by 10% limitation	×10%
Maximum contribution deduction for 2005	$ 11,000

Taxable income for the year will be $92,000, computed as follows:

Net income from operations		$100,000
Dividends received		+ 10,000
		$110,000
Less: Special corporate deductions:		
Charitable contributions (maximum)	$ 11,000	
Dividends received (70% of $10,000)	+7,000	
Total special deductions		– 18,000
M Corporation's 2005 taxable income		$ 92,000

Example 13. Based on the facts in *Example 12*, M Corporation has a $2,000 charitable contribution carryover remaining from 2004. The first $8,000 of the $11,000 allowed deduction for 2005 is considered to be from the current year's

---

[42] § 170(b)(2).

[43] § 170(d)(2).

contributions, and the $3,000 balance is from the 2004 carryover. Thus, the remaining (unused) $2,000 of the 2004 contributions must be carried over to 2006.

CAPITAL GAINS AND LOSSES

Like individuals, corporate taxpayers receive special treatment for capital gains and losses. The definition of a capital asset, the determination of holding period, and the treatment of net short-term capital gains are the same for corporations as they are for individuals. Prior to 1988, corporate taxpayers could obtain favorable treatment for their net long-term capital gains by electing to tax such gains at an alternative rate. For example, in 1986, the alternative tax rate was 28 percent while the top rate applying to ordinary income was 46 percent. Beginning in 1988, however, a corporation's net long-term capital gain is taxed in the same manner as ordinary income. Although such treatment suggests that there is no reason to distinguish capital gains and losses from ordinary income, such is not the case. Like an individual, a corporation's deduction for capital losses is limited.

Net capital losses of corporations may *only* be used to offset corporate capital gains.[44] A corporation is never permitted to reduce income from operations or investment by a capital loss. As a result, corporations may not deduct their excess capital losses for the year. Instead, a corporation may carry back the excess capital losses for three years and forward for five years,[45] and use them to offset capital gains in those years. The losses are *first* carried back three years. They may reduce the amount of capital gains reported in the earliest year. Any amount not used to offset gain in the third previous year can offset gain in the second previous year and then the first previous year. If the sum of the capital gains reported in the three previous years is less than the capital loss, the excess is carried forward. Losses carried forward may be used to offset capital gains recognized in the succeeding five tax years. Losses unused at the end of the five-year carryforward period expire.

Example 14. B Corporation has income, gains, and losses as follows:

	2002	2003	2004	2005
Ordinary income	$100,000	$100,000	$100,000	$100,000
Net capital gain (or loss)	4,000	3,000	2,000	(10,000)
Total income..............	$104,000	$103,000	$102,000	$ 90,000

B reported taxable income in years 2002, 2003, and 2004 of $104,000, $103,000, and $102,000, respectively, since net capital gains are added into taxable income. In 2005, B must report $100,000 taxable income because capital losses are nondeductible. However, B Corporation is entitled to carry the net capital loss back to years 2002, 2003, and 2004 and file a claim for refund of the taxes paid on the capital gains for each year. Because the 2005 capital loss carryback ($10,000) exceeds the sum of the capital gains in the prior three years ($9,000), B has a $1,000 capital loss carryforward. This loss carryforward can be used to offset the first $1,000 of capital gains recognized in years 2006 through 2010.

Corporations treat all capital loss carrybacks and carryovers as short-term losses. At the present, this has no effect on the tax due and it is often immaterial whether the carryover is considered long-term or short-term. However, if Congress ever reinstates

---

[44]   § 1211(a).

[45]   § 1212(a).

special treatment for corporate long-term capital gains, keeping short-term and long-term carryovers separate will once again have meaning.

SALES OF DEPRECIABLE PROPERTY

Corporations generally compute the amount of § 1245 and § 1250 ordinary income recapture on the sales of depreciable assets in the same manner as do individuals. As discussed in Chapter 17, however, Congress added Code § 291 to the tax law in 1982 with the intent of reducing the tax benefits of the accelerated cost recovery of depreciable § 1250 property available to corporate taxpayers. As a result, corporations must treat as ordinary income 20 percent of any § 1231 gain which would have been ordinary income if Code § 1245 rather than § 1250 had applied to the transaction. In effect, a corporation must recapture 20 percent of the straight-line depreciation claimed on residential or nonresidential realty. Similar rules apply to amortization of pollution control facilities and intangible drilling costs incurred by corporate taxpayers.

Example 15. C Corporation sells residential rental property for $500,000 in 2005. The property was purchased for $400,000 in 1986, and C claimed ACRS depreciation of $120,000. Straight-line depreciation would have been $65,000. C Corporation's depreciation recapture and § 1231 gain are computed as follows:

Step 1:	Compute realized gain:			
	Sales price.			$500,000
	Less: Adjusted basis			
	Cost	$400,000		
	ACRS depreciation	−120,000	−280,000	
	Realized gain.			$220,000
Step 2:	Compute *excess* depreciation:			
	Actual depreciation.			$120,000
	Straight-line depreciation			− 65,000
	Excess depreciation.			$ 55,000
Step 3:	Compute § 1250 depreciation recapture:			
	Lesser of realized gain of $220,000			
	or			
	Excess depreciation of $55,000			
	§1250 depreciation recapture			$ 55,000
Step 4:	Compute depreciation recapture if § 1245 applied:			
	Lesser of realized gain of $220,000			
	or			
	Actual depreciation of $120,000			
	Depreciation recapture if			
	§1245 applied			$120,000

Step 5:	Compute § 291 ordinary income:		
	Depreciation recapture if		
	§ 1245 applied	$120,000	
	§ 1250 depreciation recapture	−55,000	
	Excess recapture potential.	$ 65,000	
	Multiplied by § 291 rate.	×20%	
	§ 291 ordinary income	$ 13,000	
Step 6:	Characterize recognized gain:		
	§ 1250 depreciation recapture	$ 55,000	
	Plus: § 291 ordinary income	+13,000	
	Ordinary income	$ 68,000	
	Realized gain.	$220,000	
	Less: Ordinary income	− 68,000	
	§ 1231 gain	$152,000	

TRANSACTIONS BETWEEN CORPORATIONS AND THEIR SHAREHOLDERS

As discussed in Chapter 7, no deduction is allowed for a loss incurred in a transaction between related parties.[46] A corporation may be subjected to this rule. For example, a loss on the sale of the property from a corporation to a shareholder who owns more than 50 percent of the corporation is nondeductible. In such case, the unrecognized loss must be suspended and may be used by the shareholder to offset gain when the property is sold. A corporation also may be subjected to the prohibition of deductions for *accrued* but *unpaid* expenses incurred in transactions between related parties. For example, an accrual basis corporation will be denied a deduction for accrued expenses payable to cash basis related parties *until* the amount actually is paid.[47] In calculating ownership, stock owned by family members and other entities owned by the taxpayer are included.[48] With respect to the matching of income and deduction provisions only, the Tax Reform Act of 1986 expanded the definition of a related party in the case of a *personal service corporation* to include any employee that owns any of the corporation's stock. For this purpose, a personal service corporation is one where the principal activity of the corporation is the performance of personal services *and* such services are substantially performed by employee-owners. This rule applies to firms engaged in the performance of services in the fields of health, law, engineering, architecture, accounting, actuarial science, performing arts, or consulting.

The sale of property at a *gain* between a corporation and its controlling shareholders is not affected by the disallowance rules. Instead, the gain is *reclassified* as ordinary income rather than capital or § 1231 gain if the property is depreciable by the purchaser.[49] For purposes of this rule, a controlling shareholder is defined the same as under the disallowed loss rule (i.e., more than 50 percent ownership).[50] In addition, sales

---

[46]   § 267(a)(1).

[47]   § 267(a)(2).

[48]   §§ 267(b) and (c).

[49]   § 1239(a).

[50]   § 1239(c).

of depreciable property between a corporation and a more than 50 percent shareholder generally are ineligible for the installment method.[51]

DEDUCTION ATTRIBUTABLE TO DOMESTIC PRODUCTION

In an attempt to make U.S. corporations more competitive in the world market, Congress has enacted a special deduction for corporations engaged in production activities within the United States. The deduction is 9 percent times the lesser of *qualified production activity income* or taxable income. Qualified income is gross receipts from domestic production less cost of goods sold, direct expenses allocated to this income and a ratable share of indirect expenses allocated to this income. The deduction may not exceed 50 percent of the taxable wages paid during the year.

COMPUTATION OF CORPORATE INCOME TAX

For many years the maximum individual tax rate exceeded the maximum corporate tax rate. The Tax Reform Act of 1986 reversed this situation. This led many advisers to consider entities other than corporations. The Revenue Reconciliation Act of 1993 raised the maximum individual rate, making it once again greater than the maximum corporate rate. This may have the effect of encouraging the formation of corporations. The corporate tax rates for 1993 and subsequent years are as follows:[52]

Taxable Income	Tax Rate
$ 1–50,000	15%
50,001–75,000	25
75,001–10,000,000	34
More than $10,000,000	35

CORPORATE SURTAX

In an effort to restrict the tax benefit of the lower graduated rates to small corporate businesses with taxable incomes of $100,000 or less, a 5 percent *surtax* is imposed on corporate taxable income in excess of $100,000, up to a maximum surtax of $11,750—the net "savings" of having the first $75,000 of corporate income taxed at the lower rates rather than at 34 percent. For corporations with taxable income in excess of $15 million, an additional surtax is imposed equal to the lesser of $100,000 or 3 percent of the taxable income in excess of $15 million.[53] The purpose of this additional surtax is to eliminate the tax "savings" arising from taxing the first $10 million at 34 percent rather than 35 percent (i.e., 1% of $10 million = $100,000 additional surtax).

---

[51] § 453(g). The sale can qualify for installment treatment if the taxpayer can prove absence of tax avoidance motive.

[52] § 11(b).

[53] *Ibid.*

Example 16. L corporation has taxable income of $120,000 for its 2005 calendar year its tax liability is computed as follows:

15%	×	$50,000	=	$ 7,500
25%	×	25,000	=	6,250
34%	×	45,000	=	15,300

Tax liability before surtax	$29,050
Plus: 5% surtax on $20,000 ($120,000 − $100,000)	+ 1,000
Total tax liability for 2005	$30,050

Example 17. P Corporation has taxable income of $335,000 for its 2005 tax year. Its tax liability is computed as follows:

15%	×	$ 50,000	=	$ 7,500
25%	×	25,000	=	6,250
34%	×	260,000	=	88,400

Tax liability before surtax	$102,150
Plus: 5% surtax on $235,000	+ 11,750
Total tax liability for 2005	$113,900

Note that the 5% surtax on the $235,000 income in excess of $100,000 completely offsets the benefit of the lower graduated tax rates of 15 and 25%.

Example 18. R Corporation has taxable income of $20 million for its 2005 tax year. Its tax liability is computed as follows:

15%	×	$ 50,000	=	$ 7,500
25%	×	25,000	=	6,250
34%	×	9,925,000	=	3,374,500
35%	×	10,000,000	=	3,500,000

Tax liability before surtaxes		$6,888,250
Plus:	5% surtax	11,750
	3% surtax on $3,333,333	100,000
Total tax liability for 2005		$7,000,000

Note that the combined effect of the 5 and 3% surtaxes results in a flat tax rate of 35% for corporations with taxable income of $18,333,333 or more.

Taking the 5 percent and 3 percent surtaxes into account, a corporate tax rate schedule applicable to *most* corporations would be as follows:

Taxable Income	Tax Rate
$ 1–$ 50,000	15%
50,001– 75,000	25
75,001– 100,000	34
100,001– 335,000	39
335,001– 10,000,000	34
10,000,001– 15,000,000	35
15,000,001– 18,333,333	38
More than $18,333,333	35

This rate structure is not available to so-called personal service corporations or to certain related corporations. The specific rules applicable to these corporations are discussed below.

PERSONAL SERVICE CORPORATIONS

As described earlier, a personal service corporation (PSC) is a corporation where the principal activity is the performance of services in the fields of health, law, engineering, architecture, accounting, actuarial science, the performing arts, or consulting, *and* substantially all of the stock is owned by employees, retired employees, or their estates.[54] Apparently concerned that PSCs were being used to shield income from the employee-owners' higher individual tax rates, Congress denied the benefits of the lower tax rates to such corporations for taxable years after 1987. As a result, the taxable income of a PSC is subject to a flat rate of 35 percent.[55]

ALTERNATIVE MINIMUM TAX

As discussed in Chapter 13, corporations are subject to the alternative minimum tax. This tax is computed at a 20 percent rate on alternative minimum taxable income (AMTI) in excess of $40,000.[56] The $40,000 exemption is reduced by 25 percent of the amount of AMTI in excess of $150,000.[57] Consequently, the exemption is completely eliminated for AMTI in excess of $310,000.

Corporations are required to use many of the tax preferences and adjustments that individuals use in arriving at AMTI. However, there is one very important additional adjustment for corporations. The adjustment is 75 percent of the difference between adjusted current earnings (ACE) and alternative minimum taxable income.[58] In general, adjusted current earnings will equal current earnings and profits. The adjustment will be added to taxable income in arriving at AMTI.[59]

In an attempt at simplification, the Taxpayer Relief Act of 1998 exempts small corporations from the AMT. All corporations are exempt their first year of existence. In its second year, a corporation is exempt if its gross receipts for the first year were less than $5,000,000. Starting in its third year, the corporation is exempt if its average

---

[54] § 448(d)(2).

[55] § 11(b)(2). Note that a PSC is not subject to the 5 or 3 percent surtax since it does not benefit from the lower corporate tax rates.

[56] See §§ 55(b)(1)(B) and (d)(2).

[57] § 55(d)(3)(A).

[58] § 56(g).

[59] See Chapter 13 for a detailed discussion of the required adjustments and tax preferences used in computing the alternative minimum tax.

annual gross receipts for all prior three year periods are less than $7,500,000. Once a corporation fails this test, it may not claim exemption as a small corporation even if its gross receipts decline to less than $7,500,000. A corporation that fails to meet the $7.5 million gross receipts test becomes subject to the corporate AMT only with respect to preferences and adjustments that relate to transactions and investments entered into after the corporation loses its status as a small corporation. For example, if a corporation fails the test in 2004, it is not required to calculate AMT depreciation for assets placed in service in previous years but only for those placed in service in 2005 (i.e., the year in which they become subject to the AMT).

TAX CREDITS

Most of the same tax credits available to individuals are also available to corporations. However, corporations are not entitled to the earned income credit, the child care credit, or the credit for the elderly.[60]

ACCOUNTING PERIODS AND METHODS

A corporation is generally allowed to choose either a calendar year or fiscal year for its reporting period.[61] However, a personal service corporation (PSC) must use a calendar year for tax purposes unless it can satisfy IRS requirements that there is a business purpose for a fiscal year.[62] Special rules apply to deductions for year-end payments made by a fiscal year PSC to its employee-owners.[63] Like PSCs, S corporations generally must use a calendar year for tax purposes.[64]

Unlike individuals, most corporations are denied the use of the cash method of accounting for tax purposes. There are three basic exceptions, however. The cash method may be used by the following:

1. Corporations with average annual gross receipts of $5 million or less in all prior taxable years

2. S corporations

3. Personal service corporations[65]

CORPORATE TAX FORMS AND FILING REQUIREMENTS

Corporations are required to report their income and tax liability on Form 1120 (or on Form 1120-A for those corporations with gross receipts, total income, and total assets all under $500,000). Page 1 of this form contains the summary of taxable income and tax due the Federal government or the refund due the corporation. There are separate schedules for the computation of cost of goods sold, bad debt deduction, compensation of officers, dividends-received deduction, and tax computation.

In addition to the computational schedules, Form 1120 also has several schedules that contain additional information. For example, Schedule L requires the corporation to

---

[60] §§ 32 and 22.

[61] § 441.

[62] § 441(i).

[63] § 280H.

[64] § 1378(b). But see § 444 for an exception, and Chapter 23 for further discussion.

[65] § 448.

provide a balance sheet as prepared for book purposes as of the beginning and end of the year. Form 1120 also contains two schedules of reconciliation, Schedules M-1 and M-2.

Schedule M-1 is a reconciliation of income per books and income per tax return. Both permanent and timing differences will appear in this schedule.

Schedule M-2 reconciles opening and closing retained earnings. This schedule uses accounting rather than tax data. Corporations without any special transactions will show an increase in retained earnings for net income and a decrease for distributions (i.e., dividends) as the major items in Schedule M-2. The use of these schedules is illustrated in an example of a corporate tax return presented later in this chapter.

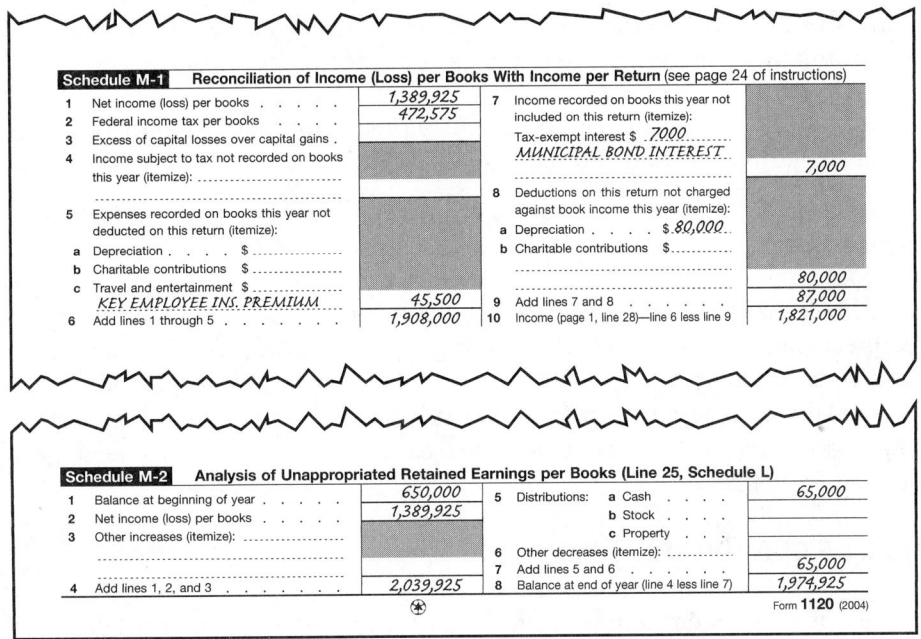

FILING REQUIREMENTS

Form 1120 is required to be filed by the 15th day of the third month following the close of the corporation's tax year.[66] As mentioned previously, a corporation is permitted to elect either a calendar or fiscal year. The decision generally is unaffected by the tax years of its shareholders.[67] The selection is made by filing the first return by the appropriate due date. For calendar year corporations, the due date is March 15. The return must be signed by an officer or other authorized person.[68]

Corporations may obtain an automatic six-month extension of time to file the tax return.[69] The extension covers only the return—not the tax due. The request for extension (Form 7004) must be accompanied by the full amount of estimated tax due. The extension can be terminated by the government on ten days' notice.

---

[66] § 6072(b).

[67] Although a regular corporation's selection of a calendar or fiscal year is not affected by the tax years of its shareholders, a corporation electing to be treated as a conduit (flow-through) entity under Subchapter S of the Code generally is required to use the calendar year for tax purposes. See Chapter 23 for greater details.

[68] § 6062.

[69] § 6081(b).

ESTIMATED TAX PAYMENTS

Corporations are required to file and pay estimated tax (including any estimated AMT liability).[70] The estimates are due the 15th day of the 4th, 6th, 9th, and 12th months of the tax year. For a calendar year corporation, the payment dates for estimated taxes are April 15, June 15, September 15, and December 15. One-fourth of the estimated tax due is to be paid on each payment date.

To avoid a penalty for underpayment of the estimated tax, at least 100 percent of the corporation's tax due for the year must be paid as estimated taxes. Specifically, the corporation must pay *one-fourth* of this amount—25 percent (100% ÷ 4) of the tax shown on its return—by the due date of each installment.[71] However, the underpayment penalty is normally not imposed where the installment for any period is

1. At least 25 percent of the tax shown on the prior year's return (if such return was for 12 months and showed a tax liability); or

2. Equal to 100 percent or more of the tax due for each quarter based on annualized taxable income.[72]

A so-called *large* corporation—one with taxable income of $1 million or more in any of its three preceding taxable years—is not allowed to use exception (1) above *except* for its first estimated tax payment of the year.[73] In addition, a corporation whose tax liability for the year is less than $500 is not subject to the underpayment penalty.[74] If a corporation does not qualify for any of the exceptions, its underpayment penalty is computed on Form 2220.

EXAMPLE OF CORPORATE TAX RETURN

The next few pages contain an illustration of a corporation's annual Federal income tax return (Form 1120). This return is based on the following information:

R Corporation is a calendar year, accrual method taxpayer, which operates as a men's clothing store. John Beyond owns 100 percent of R Corporation's stock and is employed as the company's only officer. The corporation had the following items of income and expense for the current year:

---

[70]   § 6655.

[71]   § 6655(b).

[72]   See §§ 6655(d) and (e) for these exceptions.

[73]   § 6655(d)(2).

[74]   § 6655(f).

Gross sales	$3,900,000
Sales returns	20,000
Inventory at beginning of year	120,000
Purchases	1,100,000
Inventory at end of year	140,000
Salaries and wages:	
Officers	400,000
Other	150,000
Rent expenses	120,000
Interest expense	50,000
Interest income:	
Municipal bonds	7,000
Other	10,000
Charitable contributions	79,000
Depreciation	110,000
Dividend income	30,000
Advertising expenses	50,000
Professional fees paid	20,000
Taxes paid (state income and payroll taxes)	40,000
Premiums paid on key employee life insurance policy	45,500

R Corporation timely paid $600,000 in estimated income tax payments based on its prior year's tax liability of $595,200. All dividends received by the corporation qualify for the 70 percent dividends-received deduction. The corporation declared and paid dividends of $65,000 to its sole shareholder. Additional information is provided in the balance sheets in Schedule L.

R Corporation's 2005 tax liability is $612,000 ($1,800,000 × 34%).

Note: The sample corporate tax return is shown on 2004 tax forms because the 2005 forms were not available at the publication date of this text.

Form 1120

Form **1120**	U.S. Corporation Income Tax Return	OMB No. 1545-0123
Department of the Treasury Internal Revenue Service	For calendar year 2004 or tax year beginning ...., 2004, ending ...., 20 .... ▶ See separate instructions.	2004

A Check if:
1 Consolidated return (attach Form 851) . . ☐
2 Personal holding co. (attach Sch. PH) . . ☐
3 Personal service corp. (see instructions) . . ☐
4 Schedule M-3 required (attach Sch. M-3) . . ☐

Use IRS label. Other-wise, print or type.

Name **R.CORPORATION**
Number, street, and room or suite no. If a P.O. box, see page 9 of instructions. **123 JONES AVENUE**
City or town, state, and ZIP code **ANYWHERE, U.S.A. 98765**

B Employer identification number **74 : 0987650**
C Date incorporated **1-1-2002**
D Total assets (see page 8 of instructions) $ **2,184,925**

E Check if: (1) ☐ Initial return (2) ☐ Final return (3) ☐ Name change (4) ☐ Address change

Income

1a	Gross receipts or sales **3,900,000**	**b** Less returns and allowances **20,000**	**c** Bal ▶ 1c **3,880,000**
2	Cost of goods sold (Schedule A, line 8)		2 **1,080,000**
3	Gross profit. Subtract line 2 from line 1c		3 **2,800,000**
4	Dividends (Schedule C, line 19)		4 **30,000**
5	Interest		5 **10,000**
6	Gross rents		6
7	Gross royalties		7
8	Capital gain net income (attach Schedule D (Form 1120))		8
9	Net gain or (loss) from Form 4797, Part II, line 17 (attach Form 4797)		9
10	Other income (see page 11 of instructions—attach schedule)		10
11	**Total income.** Add lines 3 through 10 ▶		11 **2,840,000**

Deductions (See instructions for limitations on deductions.)

12	Compensation of officers (Schedule E, line 4)		12 **400,000**
13	Salaries and wages (less employment credits)		13 **150,000**
14	Repairs and maintenance		14
15	Bad debts		15
16	Rents		16 **120,000**
17	Taxes and licenses		17 **40,000**
18	Interest		18 **50,000**
19	Charitable contributions (see page 14 of instructions for 10% limitation)		19 **79,000**
20	Depreciation (attach Form 4562)	20 **110,000**	
21	Less depreciation claimed on Schedule A and elsewhere on return	21a **-0-**	21b **110,000**
22	Depletion		22
23	Advertising		23 **50,000**
24	Pension, profit-sharing, etc., plans		24
25	Employee benefit programs		25
26	Other deductions (attach schedule) *PROFESSIONAL FEES*		26 **20,000**
27	**Total deductions.** Add lines 12 through 26 ▶		27 **1,019,000**
28	Taxable income before net operating loss deduction and special deductions. Subtract line 27 from line 11		28 **1,821,000**
29	**Less:** **a** Net operating loss deduction (see page 16 of instructions)	29a	
	b Special deductions (Schedule C, line 20)	29b **21,000**	29c **21,000**

Tax and Payments

30	**Taxable income.** Subtract line 29c from line 28 (see instructions if Schedule C, line 12, was completed)		30 **1,800,000**
31	**Total tax** (Schedule J, line 11)		31 **612,000**
32	Payments: **a** 2003 overpayment credited to 2004	32a	
	b 2004 estimated tax payments	32b **600,000**	
	c Less 2004 refund applied for on Form 4466	32c ( ) d Bal ▶ 32d **600,000**	
	e Tax deposited with Form 7004	32e	
	f Credit for tax paid on undistributed capital gains (attach Form 2439)	32f	
	g Credit for Federal tax on fuels (attach Form 4136). See instructions.	32g	32h **600,000**
33	Estimated tax penalty (see page 17 of instructions). Check if Form 2220 is attached ▶ ☐		33
34	**Tax due.** If line 32h is smaller than the total of lines 31 and 33, enter amount owed		34 **12,000**
35	**Overpayment.** If line 32h is larger than the total of lines 31 and 33, enter amount overpaid		35
36	Enter amount of line 35 you want: **Credited to 2005 estimated tax** ▶ Refunded ▶		36

Sign Here ▶ Under penalties of perjury, I declare that I have examined this return, including accompanying schedules and statements, and to the best of my knowledge and belief, it is true, correct, and complete. Declaration of preparer (other than taxpayer) is based on all information of which preparer has any knowledge.

John Beyond
Signature of officer | Date **3-14-05** | Title **PRESIDENT**

May the IRS discuss this return with the preparer shown below (see instructions)? ☐ Yes ☐ No

Paid Preparer's Use Only	Preparer's signature *Sherry L. Hartman*	Date **3/12/05**	Check if self-employed ☐	Preparer's SSN or PTIN **454-24-9464**
	Firm's name (or yours if self-employed), address, and ZIP code	**ROY W. HARTMAN & DAUGHTERS** **11318 KINGSLAND BLVD, SEALY, TX**	EIN **74 : 2735841**	Phone no. (**281**) **489-6443**

For Privacy Act and Paperwork Reduction Act Notice, see separate instructions. | Cat. No. 11450Q | Form **1120** (2004)

Form 1120 continued

Form 1120 (2004)   Page **2**

Schedule A   Cost of Goods Sold (see page 17 of instructions)

1	Inventory at beginning of year	1 120,000
2	Purchases	2 1,100,000
3	Cost of labor	3
4	Additional section 263A costs (attach schedule)	4
5	Other costs (attach schedule)	5
6	**Total.** Add lines 1 through 5	6 1,220,000
7	Inventory at end of year	7 140,000
8	**Cost of goods sold.** Subtract line 7 from line 6. Enter here and on page 1, line 2	8 1,080,000

9a   Check all methods used for valuing closing inventory:

     (i) ☐ Cost as described in Regulations section 1.471-3

     (ii) ☑ Lower of cost or market as described in Regulations section 1.471-4

     (iii) ☐ Other (Specify method used and attach explanation.) ▶ --------------------------------

   b   Check if there was a writedown of subnormal goods as described in Regulations section 1.471-2(c)   ▶ ☐

   c   Check if the LIFO inventory method was adopted this tax year for any goods (if checked, attach Form 970)   ▶ ☐

   d   If the LIFO inventory method was used for this tax year, enter percentage (or amounts) of closing inventory computed under LIFO | 9d |

   e   If property is produced or acquired for resale, do the rules of section 263A apply to the corporation?   ☐ Yes ☑ No

   f   Was there any change in determining quantities, cost, or valuations between opening and closing inventory? If "Yes," attach explanation   ☐ Yes ☑ No

Schedule C   Dividends and Special Deductions (see page 18 of instructions)

		(a) Dividends received	(b) %	(c) Special deductions (a) × (b)
1	Dividends from less-than-20%-owned domestic corporations that are subject to the 70% deduction (other than debt-financed stock)	30,000	70	21,000
2	Dividends from 20%-or-more-owned domestic corporations that are subject to the 80% deduction (other than debt-financed stock)		80	
3	Dividends on debt-financed stock of domestic and foreign corporations (section 246A)		see instructions	
4	Dividends on certain preferred stock of less-than-20%-owned public utilities		42	
5	Dividends on certain preferred stock of 20%-or-more-owned public utilities		48	
6	Dividends from less-than-20%-owned foreign corporations and certain FSCs that are subject to the 70% deduction		70	
7	Dividends from 20%-or-more-owned foreign corporations and certain FSCs that are subject to the 80% deduction		80	
8	Dividends from wholly owned foreign subsidiaries subject to the 100% deduction (section 245(b))		100	
9	**Total.** Add lines 1 through 8. See page 19 of instructions for limitation			21,000
10	Dividends from domestic corporations received by a small business investment company operating under the Small Business Investment Act of 1958		100	
11	Dividends from affiliated group members and certain FSCs that are subject to the 100% deduction		100	
12	Dividends from controlled foreign corporations subject to the 85% deduction (attach Form 8895)		85	
13	Other dividends from foreign corporations not included on lines 3, 6, 7, 8, 11, or 12			
14	Income from controlled foreign corporations under subpart F (attach Form(s) 5471)			
15	Foreign dividend gross-up (section 78)			
16	IC-DISC and former DISC dividends not included on lines 1, 2, or 3 (section 246(d))			
17	Other dividends			
18	Deduction for dividends paid on certain preferred stock of public utilities			
19	**Total dividends.** Add lines 1 through 17. Enter here and on page 1, line 4 ▶	30,000		
20	**Total special deductions.** Add lines 9, 10, 11, 12, and 18. Enter here and on page 1, line 29b ▶			21,000

Schedule E   Compensation of Officers (see instructions for page 1, line 12, on page 13 of instructions)

Note: *Complete Schedule E only if total receipts (line 1a plus lines 4 through 10 on page 1) are $500,000 or more.*

(a) Name of officer	(b) Social security number	(c) Percent of time devoted to business	Percent of corporation stock owned (d) Common	(e) Preferred	(f) Amount of compensation
1 JOHN BEYOND, PRESIDENT	451-54-6184	100 %	100 %	%	400,000
714 ENDEL CIRCLE		%	%	%	
ANYWHERE, U.S.A. 78765		%	%	%	
		%	%	%	
		%	%	%	

2	Total compensation of officers	400,000
3	Compensation of officers claimed on Schedule A and elsewhere on return	
4	Subtract line 3 from line 2. Enter the result here and on page 1, line 12	400,000

Form **1120** (2004)

Form 1120 continued

Form 1120 (2004)   Page **3**

Schedule J   Tax Computation (see page 20 of instructions)

1	Check if the corporation is a member of a controlled group (see sections 1561 and 1563). . . . . ▶ ☐		
	Important: Members of a controlled group, see page 20 of instructions.		
2a	If the box on line 1 is checked, enter the corporation's share of the $50,000, $25,000, and $9,925,000 taxable income brackets (in that order):		
	(1) $ _____ **(2)** $ _____ **(3)** $ _____		
b	Enter the corporation's share of: **(1)** Additional 5% tax (not more than $11,750) $ _____		
	(2) Additional 3% tax (not more than $100,000) $ _____		
3	Income tax. Check if a qualified personal service corporation under section 448(d)(2) (see page 21) . ▶ ☐	3	612,000
4	Alternative minimum tax (attach Form 4626)	4	
5	Add lines 3 and 4	5	612,000
6a	Foreign tax credit (attach Form 1118)	6a	
b	Possessions tax credit (attach Form 5735)	6b	
c	Check: ☐ Nonconventional source fuel credit ☐ QEV credit (attach Form 8834)	6c	
d	General business credit. Check box(es) and indicate which forms are attached: ☐ Form 3800 ☐ Form(s) (specify) ▶ _____	6d	
e	Credit for prior year minimum tax (attach Form 8827)	6e	
f	Qualified zone academy bond credit (attach Form 8860)	6f	
7	**Total credits.** Add lines 6a through 6f	7	0
8	Subtract line 7 from line 5	8	612,000
9	Personal holding company tax (attach Schedule PH (Form 1120))	9	
10	Other taxes. Check if from: ☐ Form 4255 ☐ Form 8611 ☐ Form 8697 ☐ Form 8866 ☐ Other (attach schedule) . . .	10	
11	**Total tax.** Add lines 8 through 10. Enter here and on page 1, line 31	11	612,000

Schedule K   Other Information (see page 23 of instructions)

		Yes	No
1	Check accounting method: a ☐ Cash		
	b ☐ Accrual c ☑ Other (specify) ▶ *HYBRID*		
2	See page 25 of the instructions and enter the:		
a	Business activity code no. ▶ *448110*		
b	Business activity ▶ *MEN'S CLOTHING STORE*		
c	Product or service ▶ *CLOTHING*		
3	At the end of the tax year, did the corporation own, directly or indirectly, 50% or more of the voting stock of a domestic corporation? (For rules of attribution, see section 267(c).)		✓
	If "Yes," attach a schedule showing: **(a)** name and employer identification number (EIN), **(b)** percentage owned, and **(c)** taxable income or (loss) before NOL and special deductions of such corporation for the tax year ending with or within your tax year.		
4	Is the corporation a subsidiary in an affiliated group or a parent-subsidiary controlled group?		✓
	If "Yes," enter name and EIN of the parent corporation ▶ _____		
5	At the end of the tax year, did any individual, partnership, corporation, estate, or trust own, directly or indirectly, 50% or more of the corporation's voting stock? (For rules of attribution, see section 267(c).) *SEE SCHEDULE E* If "Yes," attach a schedule showing name and identifying number. (Do not include any information already entered in **4** above.) Enter percentage owned ▶ *100%*	✓	
6	During this tax year, did the corporation pay dividends (other than stock dividends and distributions in exchange for stock) in excess of the corporation's current and accumulated earnings and profits? (See sections 301 and 316.) . .		✓
	If "Yes," file **Form 5452,** Corporate Report of Nondividend Distributions.		
	If this is a consolidated return, answer here for the parent corporation and on **Form 851,** Affiliations Schedule, for each subsidiary.		

		Yes	No
7	At any time during the tax year, did one foreign person own, directly or indirectly, at least 25% of **(a)** the total voting power of all classes of stock of the corporation entitled to vote or **(b)** the total value of all classes of stock of the corporation?		✓
	If "Yes," enter: **(a)** Percentage owned ▶ _____		
	and **(b)** Owner's country ▶ _____		
c	The corporation may have to file **Form 5472,** Information Return of a 25% Foreign-Owned U.S. Corporation or a Foreign Corporation Engaged in a U.S. Trade or Business. Enter number of Forms 5472 attached ▶ _____		
8	Check this box if the corporation issued publicly offered debt instruments with original issue discount . ▶ ☐		
	If checked, the corporation may have to file **Form 8281,** Information Return for Publicly Offered Original Issue Discount Instruments.		
9	Enter the amount of tax-exempt interest received or accrued during the tax year ▶ $ *7,000*		
10	Enter the number of shareholders at the end of the tax year (if 75 or fewer) ▶ *1*		
11	If the corporation has an NOL for the tax year and is electing to forego the carryback period, check here ▶ ☐ If the corporation is filing a consolidated return, the statement required by Temporary Regulations section 1.1502-21T(b)(3)(i) or (ii) must be attached or the election will not be valid.		
12	Enter the available NOL carryover from prior tax years (Do not reduce it by any deduction on line 29a.) ▶ $ _____		
13	Are the corporation's total receipts (line 1a plus lines 4 through 10 on page 1) for the tax year **and** its total assets at the end of the tax year less than $250,000? . . .		✓
	If "Yes," the corporation is not required to complete Schedules L, M-1, and M-2 on page 4. Instead, enter the total amount of cash distributions and the book value of property distributions (other than cash) made during the tax year. ▶ $ _____		

Note: *If the corporation, at any time during the tax year, had assets or operated a business in a foreign country or U.S. possession, it may be required to attach* **Schedule N (Form 1120),** *Foreign Operations of U.S. Corporations, to this return. See Schedule N for details.*

Form **1120** (2004)

Form 1120 continued

Form 1120 (2004)   Page **4**

Note: *The corporation is not required to complete Schedules L, M-1, and M-2 if Question 13 on Schedule K is answered "Yes."*

Schedule L — Balance Sheets per Books

		Beginning of tax year		End of tax year	
Assets		**(a)**	**(b)**	**(c)**	**(d)**
1	Cash		30,000		320,000
2a	Trade notes and accounts receivable	180,000		210,000	
b	Less allowance for bad debts	( )	180,000	( )	210,000
3	Inventories		120,000		140,000
4	U.S. government obligations				100,000
5	Tax-exempt securities (see instructions)				104,425
6	Other current assets (attach schedule)				
7	Loans to shareholders				
8	Mortgage and real estate loans				
9	Other investments (attach schedule)		200,000		970,500
10a	Buildings and other depreciable assets	420,000		420,000	
b	Less accumulated depreciation	(50,000)	370,000	(80,000)	340,000
11a	Depletable assets				
b	Less accumulated depletion	( )		( )	
12	Land (net of any amortization)				
13a	Intangible assets (amortizable only)				
b	Less accumulated amortization	( )		( )	
14	Other assets (attach schedule)				
15	Total assets		900,000		2,184,925
Liabilities and Shareholders' Equity					
16	Accounts payable		150,000		110,000
17	Mortgages, notes, bonds payable in less than 1 year				
18	Other current liabilities (attach schedule)				
19	Loans from shareholders				
20	Mortgages, notes, bonds payable in 1 year or more				
21	Other liabilities (attach schedule)				
22	Capital stock: **a** Preferred stock				
	b Common stock	10,000	10,000	10,000	10,000
23	Additional paid-in capital		90,000		90,000
24	Retained earnings—Appropriated (attach schedule)				
25	Retained earnings—Unappropriated		650,000		1,974,925
26	Adjustments to shareholders' equity (attach schedule)				
27	Less cost of treasury stock		( )		( )
28	Total liabilities and shareholders' equity		900,000		2,184,925

Schedule M-1 — Reconciliation of Income (Loss) per Books With Income per Return (see page 24 of instructions)

1	Net income (loss) per books	1,389,925	7	Income recorded on books this year not included on this return (itemize):	
2	Federal income tax per books	472,575			
3	Excess of capital losses over capital gains			Tax-exempt interest $ 7000	
4	Income subject to tax not recorded on books this year (itemize):			*MUNICIPAL BOND INTEREST*	
	....				7,000
5	Expenses recorded on books this year not deducted on this return (itemize):		8	Deductions on this return not charged against book income this year (itemize):	
a	Depreciation . . . . $		a	Depreciation . . . . $ 80,000	
b	Charitable contributions $		b	Charitable contributions $	
c	Travel and entertainment $			....	80,000
	KEY EMPLOYEE INS. PREMIUMS	45,500	9	Add lines 7 and 8	87,000
6	Add lines 1 through 5	1,908,000	10	Income (page 1, line 28)—line 6 less line 9	1,821,000

Schedule M-2 — Analysis of Unappropriated Retained Earnings per Books (Line 25, Schedule L)

1	Balance at beginning of year	650,000	5	Distributions: **a** Cash	65,000
2	Net income (loss) per books	1,389,925		**b** Stock	
3	Other increases (itemize):			**c** Property	
	....		6	Other decreases (itemize):	
	....		7	Add lines 5 and 6	65,000
4	Add lines 1, 2, and 3	2,039,925	8	Balance at end of year (line 4 less line 7)	1,974,925

Form **1120** (2004)

CORPORATE FORMATION

When a corporation is formed, property generally is transferred to the corporation and the transferors receive stock in exchange for their property. If the fair market value of the stock received is more than the transferor's adjusted basis in the property transferred, that person has a *realized gain*. Without any special provisions in the Code, this realized gain would be recognized.[75] However, Congress did not wish to prevent or discourage incorporation because of tax reasons. Moreover, this treatment was justified since the taxpayer had not "cashed in" but continued to have an indirect interest in and control over the property transferred. Therefore, Congress enacted Code § 351 permitting the nonrecognition of gain or loss on incorporation.

Section 351(a) provides that

> No gain or loss shall be recognized if *property* is transferred to a corporation by *one or more persons solely* in exchange for *stock* in such corporation and immediately after the exchange such person or persons are in *control* of the corporation. (Emphasis added.)

This nonrecognition treatment is mandatory and not optional. Thus, if the transferor meets all the requirements, neither gain nor loss will be recognized. Only by failure to meet prescribed conditions will there be recognition of gain or loss.

TRANSFER OF PROPERTY

The first requirement in § 351(a) is that *property* must be transferred to a corporation. The Code states that property does not include services rendered.[76] From this it is inferred that property includes money,[77] real property, and tangible and intangible personal property.

A person who receives stock in exchange for services is required to recognize income from services rendered. In this case, the corporation is entitled to deduct the amount as an expense or capitalize it depending on the nature of services rendered.

> **Example 19.** T incorporates his grocery store. He transfers all the assets for stock. The corporation issues additional stock to S, an attorney, in payment of her fee for legal services rendered in connection with the incorporation. T has neither gain nor loss recognized. S, however, is required to report the value of the stock as income. Note that this is the economic equivalent of paying S cash for her services followed by her investment of the amount received in stock of the corporation. The corporation must capitalize the value of the stock issued to S as an organization expense.

The rule that property but not services can be transferred under § 351 is generally applied to persons who transfer both. Such transferors are required to allocate the stock received between the property and services transferred and report the value of the stock received for services as income. Although the shareholder who contributes services is required to report some income, he or she can generally count *all* of the shares received in the determination of control.

---

[75]   § 1001(c).

[76]   § 351(d)(1).

[77]   Rev. Rul. 69-357, 1969-1 C.B. 101.

BY ONE OR MORE PERSONS

For purposes of § 351(a), the term *persons* includes individuals, trusts, estates, partnerships, associations, corporations, or any combination of these.[78] Examples of transactions that might qualify for nonrecognition under § 351 include

1. Starting a new business

2. Incorporating a business already in existence

3. The formation of a subsidiary corporation by an existing corporation

4. Additional contributions to an existing corporation by an existing shareholder or a new shareholder

SOLELY FOR STOCK

Section 351 generally applies only if the transferor receives *solely* stock in exchange for property. The stock received by the transferor must be issued by the transferee (new) corporation. This requirement ensures that nonrecognition is granted only where the transferor has a continuing interest in the assets transferred. Stock may be common or preferred, voting or nonvoting, participating or nonparticipating. Stock rights and warrants are not considered stock since these represent only the right to obtain an equity interest.[79] In addition, preferred stock that is redeemable or whose dividend varies with interest rates or commodity prices is not considered stock.

CONTROL

One of the conditions imposed by § 351 is that the transferors be in *control* of the corporation immediately after the transfer. Under § 368(c), control exists if the transferor(s) own at least 80 percent of the total voting power and at least 80 percent of the total number of shares of all other classes of stock.[80]

The phrase *"immediately after the exchange"* has raised several questions. The first question is *when* to measure control. Transfers by two or more transferors do not have to be simultaneous to fall under this nonrecognition provision provided the transfers are part of one transaction. Therefore, control is measured at the conclusion of the intended transaction and not after each transfer. Another question that has been raised is whether the transferor must obtain control with the transfer or simply have control afterward. The wording of § 351(a) indicates that the transferor(s) must simply have control *after* the exchange.

> **Example 20.** B owns all the outstanding stock of R Corporation. In the current year, he transfers real estate to the corporation as an additional capital contribution. B does not receive any additional stock from the corporation. The transfer qualifies, therefore, under § 351. B has control of R Corporation *after* the transfer. He did not have to acquire control as a result of the transfer. B did not receive anything other than stock, but the fact that he did not receive anything is immaterial.

The final question raised by the phrase "immediately after the exchange" concerns the *loss of control* after the transfer. Is it necessary for the transferors to maintain control of the corporation or is it sufficient if they have control momentarily? There is

---

78 Reg. § 1.351-1(a)(1).

79 Reg. § 1.351-1(a)(1)(ii).

80 See Rev. Rul. 59-259, 1959-2 C.B. 115, for specific rules regarding voting power.

no specified length of time for which the transferor must maintain control. Instead, the courts have looked at whether the loss of control is an integral part of the initial transfer.[81] As long as the transaction in which control is lost is not arranged and enforceable prior to the transfer, the receipt of the corporation's stock should be nontaxable. The subsequent transfer of stock and loss of control will be considered a separate transaction.

RECEIPT OF BOOT

Although § 351(a) states that the transferor(s) may receive only stock, § 351(b) deals with the receipt of property other than stock (e.g., money). This cash and other nonqualified property is referred to as *boot*. The receipt of boot does *not* invalidate the § 351(a) nonrecognition treatment. Section 351(a) still applies to the extent that stock is received. However, any realized gain must be recognized to the extent that boot is *received* by the transferor.[82] This treatment is similar to the receipt of nonqualifying property in a like-kind (§ 1031) exchange.

The amount of gain recognized is the lesser of the realized gain or the fair market value of the boot received. The receipt of boot does not cause the recognition of loss.[83] The gain recognized may be either long- or short-term. The nature of the gain is determined by the property transferred to the corporation. If the property was a capital asset in the hands of the transferor, the gain is capital. If the property was ordinary income property, the gain is ordinary.

> **Example 21.** T transfers land to X Corporation in return for all of the common stock and $5,000 cash. T had purchased the land three years ago as a speculative investment for $40,000. At the time of transfer, the land was worth $100,000. The stock received is worth $95,000. The corporation plans on subdividing and selling the property.
>
> T's realized and recognized gains are computed as follows:
>
> | | | |
> |---|---|---:|
> | Value of the stock received | | $ 95,000 |
> | Plus: Boot (cash) received | | +5,000 |
> | Amount realized | | $100,000 |
> | Less: T's adjusted basis in the land | | −40,000 |
> | Realized gain | | $ 60,000 |
> | Gain recognized equals *lesser* of | | |
> | **a.** | Realized gain | $ 60,000 |
> | | or | |
> | **b.** | Boot received | $ 5,000 |
>
> Thus, T's recognized gain is $5,000.
>
> The gain is a long-term capital gain because the land was a capital asset in the hands of T. The fact that the land will be inventory to the corporation is immaterial. If no boot had been received by T, no gain would have been recognized.

---

[81] *American Bantam Car Co.*, 11 T.C. 397; *aff'd.*, 49-2 USTC ¶9471, 38 AFTR 820, 177 F.2d 513 (CA-3, 1949).

[82] § 351(b)(1).

[83] § 351(b)(2).

ASSUMPTION OF LIABILITIES

Transfers to a corporation often include the transfer of liabilities as well as assets. Normally, the relief of a liability is treated the same as if cash had been received and the liability paid off. In a transaction otherwise qualifying under § 351, such treatment would result in the taxpayer receiving boot and having to recognize gain. However, for § 351 transactions, Code § 357(a) carves out a special *exception.*

The general rule of § 357(a) states that the assumption of the transferor's liability by the transferee corporation will not be considered *boot.* Therefore, under the general rule of this special exception, the assumption of liabilities by the transferee corporation will not cause recognition of gain.

However, there are two exceptions to this general rule. First, if the reason for the transfer of any of the liabilities is *tax avoidance*, then the total amount of the liabilities transferred will be considered as boot received.[84]

Example 22. K transferred land to a corporation in exchange for all of its common stock, worth $85,000. The land cost $40,000 and had a fair market value of $100,000. The day before the § 351 transfer, K mortgaged the land, receiving $15,000. The corporation assumed the $15,000 mortgage. The loan and its transfer were principally entered into to avoid tax. K's realized gain is computed as follows:

Fair market value of stock received	$ 85,000
Plus: Liabilities assumed by transferee corporation	+ 15,000
Amount realized	$100,000
Less: Basis in land transferred	−40,000
Realized gain	$ 60,000

Because the primary purpose of the transfer was tax avoidance, the liabilities assumed by the transferee corporation are treated as boot received.

Gain recognized equals *lesser* of

a.	Realized gain	$60,000
	or	
b.	Boot received	$15,000

Thus, K's recognized gain is $15,000.

The second exception to the general rule concerning the assumption of liabilities operates when the amount of the liabilities transferred *exceeds* the adjusted basis of all property (including money) transferred. This situation produces a recognized gain, computed as follows:

Liabilities assumed by the transferee corporation		$xx,xxx
Minus:	Adjusted basis of all property transferred (by that transferor) including money	−xx,xxx
Equals:	Recognized gain	$xx,xxx

---

[84]   § 357(b).

Example 23. N transfers land to a corporation in exchange for all of its common stock (worth $50,000). N's adjusted basis in the land is $10,000 and has a fair market value of $90,000. The land is subject to a $40,000 mortgage, which the corporation assumes. N's recognized gain is computed as follows:

Liabilities assumed by transferee corporation	$40,000
Minus: Adjusted basis in property transferred.	−10,000
Recognized gain	$30,000

If tax avoidance is not the motivation, and the basis of the assets equals or exceeds the amount of the liabilities, the transferor will not be treated as having received boot.

EFFECT OF § 351 ON THE TRANSFEREE CORPORATION

Section 1032 provides that a corporation will not recognize gain or loss when it issues its own stock in exchange for money or other property. Therefore, gain or loss is not recognized by the transferee corporation in a § 351 transfer.

BASIS TO SHAREHOLDERS

Following a transfer to which § 351 applies, the transferors (shareholders) must determine the basis of the stock and property received. To preserve the gain or loss not recognized on the transfer, the shareholder's basis in any stock received is generally the same as the basis of the property transferred (i.e., a substituted basis). Technically, the basis of the stock and other property received by a shareholder is determined under § 358, computed as follows:

Basis of property transferred			$xxx,xxx
Plus:	Gain recognized by transferor		+ x,xxx
Less:	Money received by transferor		− x,xxx
	Fair market value of any other property		
	(except stock) received by transferor		− x,xxx
	Liabilities assumed by transferee corporation		− xx,xxx
Equals:	Shareholder's (transferor's) basis in stock received.		$xxx,xxx

If several classes of stock are received, the total basis is allocated among the several classes based on the relative fair market value of the stock. The shareholder's basis in any other property (boot) received is its fair market value.[85] The holding period of the stock will include the holding period of the assets transferred to the corporation if the transferred property would have produced a capital or § 1231 gain on sale.[86] Otherwise, the holding period starts with the date of transfer.

Example 24. J owns MNO, Inc. In the current year, he transfers land and building to the corporation in return for 50 shares of common stock and 10 shares of preferred stock. The corporation also assumes mortgage of $40,000. J's adjusted basis in the land is $10,000 and $90,000 in the building. The land and building

---

[85] § 358(a)(2).

[86] § 1223.

together have a current fair market value of $200,000. The common stock has a fair market value of $120,000, and the preferred stock has a value of $40,000.

J's basis in the stock received is		
Basis of property transferred		$ 100,000
Less: Liabilities assumed by transferee corporation		−40,000
J's basis in the stock received		$ 60,000

The $60,000 total basis is allocated based on the relative fair market value of the stock. Thus, J's basis in each class of stock is computed as follows:

Common Stock:

$$\$60{,}000 \text{ total basis } \times \frac{\$120{,}000 \text{ value of common stock}}{\$160{,}000 \text{ value of all stock}} = \$45{,}000 \text{ basis}$$

Preferred Stock:

$$\$60{,}000 \text{ total basis } \times \frac{\$40{,}000 \text{ value of preferred stock}}{\$160{,}000 \text{ value of all stock}} = \$15{,}000 \text{ basis}$$

BASIS TO TRANSFEREE CORPORATION

The transferee corporation must also determine the basis of the property it has received from the transferor(s). This is computed under § 362 as follows:

Transferor's basis in property	$xx,xxx
Plus: Gain recognized to transferor on transfer.	+ x,xxx
Equals: Transferee corporation's basis in property received	$xx,xxx

If the corporation receives assets under §§ 351 or 118 with a built-in loss, then the corporation's basis in the assets will be their fair market value. As an alternative, the transferor can elect to reduce his or her stock basis by the built-in loss instead of the corporation taking the lower basis.

DEPRECIATION RECAPTURE

If the transferor has no recognized gain in a § 351 transfer, then there will be no recapture of depreciation.[87] However, the transferee corporation is responsible for recapturing depreciation when the asset is later sold or disposed of in a taxable transaction. If there is gain recognized in a § 351 transfer, the depreciation recapture provisions apply to the recognized gain.

Exhibit 19-4 contains a summary of the computations required in a § 351 transfer. A comprehensive example of § 351 transfers follows Exhibit 19-4.

---

[87]   §§ 1245(b)(3) and 1250(d)(3).

EXHIBIT 19-4
Computation in a § 351 Transfer

Step 1: Compute the amount realized by the transferor [§ 1001(b)].

Fair market value of stock received			$xxx,xxx
Plus:	Amount of money received	$xx,xxx	
	Fair market value of other property received	xx,xxx	
	Liabilities assumed by transferee corporation	xx,xxx	+ xx,xxx
Less:	Amount of money given up (paid)	$xx,xxx	
	Expenses of transfer	x,xxx	
	Liabilities assumed by the transferor	x,xxx	– xx,xxx
Equals:	Amount realized.		$xxx,xxx

Step 2: Compute gain realized by transferor [§ 1001(a)].

Amount realized.		$xxx,xxx
Less:	Adjusted basis in property transferred	– xx,xxx
Equals:	Gain realized	$ xx,xxx

Step 3: If any *boot* was *received*, compute transferor's gain recognized [§ 351 (b)].
Gain recognized equals *lesser* of
   a. Gain realized,
      or
   b. Boot received
If no boot was received, then there is no gain recognized by the transferor.

Step 4: Compute shareholder's basis in stock received (§ 358).

Basis of property plus any money transferred			$ xx,xxx
Plus:	Gain recognized by transferor		+ x,xxx
Less:	Money received by transferor	$ x,xxx	
	Fair market value of any other property		
	(except stock) received by transferor.	x,xxx	
	Liabilities assumed by transferee corporation	x,xxx	– x,xxx
Equals:	Shareholder's (transferor's) basis in stock received.		$ xx,xxx

The shareholder's basis in any other property (boot) received is its fair market [see § 358(a)(2)].

Step 5: Compute the transferee corporation's basis in the property transferred to it (§ 362).

Transferor's basis in property		$ xx,xxx
Plus:	Gain recognized to transferor on transfer	+ xx,xxx
Equals:	Transferee corporation's basis in property received.	$ xx,xxx

Example 25. R and S pooled their assets to form a new corporation, T Incorporated. R transferred the following:

1. Land (adjusted basis of $54,000, fair market value of $75,000).

2. A mortgage of $52,000 which the land was subject to.

3. Cash of $7,000.

S transferred the following:

1.   Patent (adjusted basis of $24,000, fair market value $31,000)

R received the following:

50 shares of T Corporation stock, fair market value* $30,000

S received the following:

50 shares of T Corporation stock, fair market value* $30,000
$1,000 cash

*The value of the T Corporation stock is computed as follows:

R's investment:

Land, FMV.	$ 75,000	
Less: Mortgage.	(52,000)	
Cash paid.	7,000	

S's investment:

Patent, FMV.	31,000	
Less: Cash received	(1,000)	
Value of T Corporation stock	$ 60,000	

Step 1:   Compute amount realized.

	R	S
FMV of stock received	$ 30,000	$ 30,000
Plus: Money received	0	1,000
Liabilities assumed by transferee corporation . . .	52,000	0
Less: Amount of money given up	(7,000)	0
Amount realized.	$ 75,000	$ 31,000

Step 2:   Compute gain realized.

	R	S
Amount realized.	$ 75,000	$ 31,000
Less: Adjusted basis in property transferred	(54,000)	(24,000)
Gain realized	$ 21,000	$ 7,000

Step 3:   Compute gain recognized.

Gain recognized equals lesser of

	R	S
a. Gain realized	$ 21,000	$ 7,000
b. Boot received.	0	1,000
Gain recognized is	$ 0	$ 1,000

Step 4:   Compute shareholder's basis in property received.

	R	S
Basis of property and money transferred ($54,000 + $7,000)	$ 61,000	$ 24,000
Plus: Gain recognized.	0	1,000
Less: Money received, ...	0	(1,000)
Less: Liabilities assumed by the transferee.	(52,000)	0
Shareholder's basis in stock received	$ 9,000	$ 24,000

Step 5:   Compute corporation's basis in property received.

	R	S
Transferor's basis in property	$ 54,000	$ 24,000
Plus: Gain recognized to transferor on transfer	0	1,000
Basis in land received	$ 54,000	
Basis in patent received.		$ 25,000

CAPITAL CONTRIBUTIONS

MADE BY SHAREHOLDERS

A corporation recognizes neither gain nor loss on the issuance or sale of its stock.[88] It is immaterial whether the stock is a newly authorized issue, previously unissued stock, or treasury stock that the corporation had previously acquired. If it is treasury stock that was purchased for a price different from its sale price, the difference is merely an increase or decrease in the stockholders' equity. If it is a new sale of stock, the discount or premium also is a stockholders' equity adjustment. The contingent liability associated with issuing par value stock at a discount has no counterpart in tax.[89] The sale of stock at a discount is treated as the issuance of stock for the amount received. This provision, however, does not prevent a corporation deducting as an expense the value of stock issued for services. However, no gain or loss is recognized.

The provision against recognizing gain or loss afforded a corporation applies only to the issuance or sale of the corporation's own stock. Sale or exchange of stock in another corporation will be treated as any other sale or exchange of an asset. The difference between cost and sale price will produce realized gain or loss. This general rule applies to stock acquired as a short-term investment as well as stock in related corporations.

In addition to the exclusion of gain or loss on the issuance of stock, contributions to capital are excluded from the corporation's income.[90] This exclusion applies to contributions from shareholders and nonshareholders. Although nonshareholder contributions are not as frequent as shareholder contributions, communities occasionally donate land and/or buildings in return for the relocation of a corporation's facilities.

MADE BY NONSHAREHOLDERS

There are special rules for contributions by nonshareholders.[91] Property contributed by a nonshareholder will have a *zero* basis. This prevents a corporation from obtaining a tax deduction either through depreciation or expense for the property. The provision was placed in the law because the value of the property is not treated as income to the corporation. This provision also guarantees that any amount received by the corporation upon sale of the property will be a taxable gain. The exclusion from income applies only to the receipt of property by the corporation as a contribution to capital, however.

If the property received by the corporation is money, the above rule does not apply. It is impossible to assign a zero basis to cash. Instead, the corporation is required to reduce the basis of property purchased using the cash by the amount of the contribution.[92] If the corporation does not acquire property with the contributed cash within 12 months, it is required to reduce the basis of property it already owns by the amount of the contribution.

---

[88] § 1032.

[89] In many states, it is *illegal* for a corporation to issue its own stock below par value.

[90] § 118.

[91] § 362(c)(1).

[92] § 362(c)(2).

PROBLEM MATERIALS

DISCUSSION QUESTIONS

19-1   *What Is a Corporation?* Although an entity may be a corporation under state law, what characteristics must the entity possess to be treated as a corporation for Federal tax purposes? What difference will it make in the Federal tax classification if the entity possesses *all* or only a few of these characteristics?

19-2   *Disregard of Corporate Form.* Why might the IRS try to disregard the corporate status of an entity that meets the state law requirements for a corporation? Under what circumstances might shareholders try to use the corporate form but attempt to disregard it for Federal tax purposes?

19-3   *Corporate vs. Individual Taxation.* What are the differences in income tax treatment of corporations and individuals for the items below?
a.   Dividends received
b.   Classification of deductions
c.   Casualty losses
d.   Charitable contribution limitations
e.   Capital loss deduction
f.   Capital loss carryovers and carrybacks
g.   Gain on sale of depreciable realty

19-4   *Dividends-Received Deduction.* Why is a corporation allowed a dividends-received deduction? Under what circumstances is the recipient corporation allowed an 80 percent rather than the usual 70 percent dividends-received deduction?

19-5   *Limitations on Dividends-Received Deduction.* What are the limitations imposed on a corporation's dividends-received deduction? Under what circumstances can one of these limitations be disregarded?

19-6   *Charitable Contribution Carryovers.* Under what circumstances must a corporation carry over its qualifying contributions to subsequent years? If contributions are made in the current prior year, which contributions are deducted first? Why do you suppose Congress imposes this ordering of contribution deductions?

19-7   *Five-Percent Surtax.* Which corporations are subject to the five percent surtax? What is the marginal tax rate on the last dollar of taxable income of a corporation with taxable income of $170,000? What is the flat tax rate imposed on a corporation with taxable income of $335,000?

19-8   *Property Requirement of § 351.* What constitutes property for purposes of § 351? If an individual receives stock for both property and services, what are the tax consequences?

19-9   *What Are Transferring Persons?* What types of entities are "persons" for purposes of § 351? When might such "person" or "persons" make use of the § 351 nonrecognition provision?

19-10   *Solely for Stock.* What is considered stock for purposes of § 351? Why do you suppose Congress imposes as a requirement for nonrecognition treatment the receipt of only stock by the transferor?

19-11 *Control Requirement.* What is the control requirement for purposes of § 351? What is the meaning of the term "immediately" when used to qualify the control requirement?

19-12 *Taxable § 351 Transfers.* Under what circumstances may a transferor be subject to gain recognition even though his or her transfer is subject to § 351?

19-13 *Transfer of Liabilities.* Unlike Code § 1031 transactions (like-kind exchanges), the transfer (discharge) of a liability generally is not treated as boot for purposes of Code 351. Explain.

19-14 *Transfer of Liabilities and Tax Avoidance.* A transferor is considering whether to receive some cash in addition to stock when she transfers appreciated property to a corporation, or to mortgage the property for a similar amount of money and then transfer the property and the liability to the corporation. What difference will either alternative make?

19-15 *Basis of Stock Received.* How does a shareholder determine basis in stock received in a § 351 transfer? If both common stock and preferred stock are received, how is basis in each determined?

19-16 *Corporation's Basis.* What is the corporation's basis in property received in a § 351 transfer? If due to his current tax situation a transferor will not incur additional income taxes on any gain recognized, would it benefit the corporation to have a partially taxable § 351 transfer? Explain.

19-17 *Depreciation Recapture.* How do the depreciation recapture rules (i.e., §§ 1245, 1250, 291) apply to a § 351 transfer?

PROBLEMS

19-18 *Comparison of Corporate vs. Individual Taxation.* In each of the situations below, explain the tax consequences if taxpayer T were either a corporation or a single individual.

a. For the current year, T has gross income of $60,000, including $10,000 dividends from Ford Motor Company. Without regard to taxable income, how much of the dividend income will be subject to tax?

b. During the current year, T sustains a total loss of an asset. The asset was valued at $2,000 shortly before the loss and had an adjusted basis of $2,700. If the casualty loss were incurred by T as an individual, it would be a personal rather than business loss. Without regard to any taxable income limitation, what is the measure of the casualty loss deduction?

c. During 2005, T had $8,000 of long-term capital gains and $3,000 of short-term capital gains. During 2004, the only prior year with capital asset transactions, T had a short-term capital loss of $6,000. How much of T's 2005 gross income will consist of capital gains?

d. T's taxable income for 2005, before any deduction for charitable contributions, is $50,000. If T were an individual, adjusted gross income would be $60,000. If T made cash contributions of $40,000 during the year, what is the maximum amount that could be claimed as a deduction for 2005?

19-19 *Dividends-Received Deduction.* K Corporation has the following items of revenue and expense for the current year:

Sales revenue, net of returns	$100,000
Cost of sales	30,000
Operating expenses	40,000
Dividends (subject to 70% rules)	20,000

[handwritten margin note: Refer to EXHIBIT 10-1 p. 10-10]

a. What is K Corporation's dividends-received deduction for the current year?

b. Assuming that K Corporation's operating expenses were $72,000 instead of $40,000, what is its dividends-received deduction for the current year?

19-20 *Dividends-Received Deduction.* During 2005 R Corporation (a cash method, calendar year taxpayer) has the following income and expenses:

Revenue from operations.	$170,000
Operating expenses.	178,000
Dividends (subject to 70% rules)	40,000

a. What is R Corporation's 2005 dividends-received deduction?

b. Assuming R Corporation's 2005 tax year has not yet closed, what would be the effect on its dividends-received deduction if R accelerated to 2005 $5,000 of operating expenses planned for 2006?

19-21 *Organizational Expenditures.* G Corporation incurred and paid $6,800 of qualifying organizational expenditures in 2005. Assuming G Corporation makes an election under § 248 to expense and amortize these costs, what is the maximum amount that may be deducted for each of the following years if G Corporation adopts a calendar tax year?

a. For 2005, during which G Corporation began business on September 1?

b. Calendar year 2006?

c. Calendar year 2010? *2020 !*

19-22 *Charitable Contributions Deductions.* T Corporation has the following for tax year 2005:

Net income from operations.	$600,000
Dividends received (subject to 70% rules)	100,000

a. What is T Corporation's maximum charitable contribution deduction for 2005?

b. Assuming T Corporation made charitable contributions of $68,000 during 2005 and had a $10,000 charitable contribution carryover from 2004, how much of its 2004 contributions will be carried over to 2006?

19-23 *Computation of Corporate Tax Liability.* L Corporation had taxable income of $150,000 for 2005. What is L Corporation's 2005 income tax liability before credits or prepayments?

19-24 *Corporate Tax Computation.* T Corporation had the following items of income for its calendar year 2005:

Net income from operations.	$150,000
Dividends received (subject to 70% rules)	10,000
Charitable contributions	30,000
Net operating loss carryover from 2004	30,000
Long-term capital gains	8,000
Long-term capital losses	6,000
Short-term capital gains.	3,000
Capital loss carryover from 2004	9,000

a. Compute T Corporation's 2005 income tax liability before credits or prepayments.

b. What is the nature and amount of any carryovers to 2006?

19-25 *Corporate Formation.* Individuals J and R form the JR Corporation. J transfers land with a basis of $50,000 and a fair market value of $100,000. R transfers all the depreciable property from his former business, which has a basis of $80,000 and a fair market value of $70,000. In order to be an equal shareholder, R also transfers cash of $30,000 to the corporation. J and R each receive 100 shares of JR Corporation stock.

a. What is J's realized gain or loss? Recognized gain or loss?

b. What is R's realized gain or loss? Recognized gain or loss?

c. What basis will J have in the JR Corporation stock?

d. What basis will JR Corporation have in the land?

e. What basis will R have in the JR Corporation stock?

f. What basis will JR Corporation have in the depreciable property?

19-26 *Corporate Formation.* Individuals K, L, and M form the KLM Corporation. K transfers land with a basis of $30,000, with fair market value of $100,000, and which is subject to a $20,000 mortgage in exchange for 80 shares of KLM common stock. L transfers $50,000 cash and equipment with a basis of $25,000 and fair market value of $40,000 in exchange for 90 shares of KLM common stock. M transfers $18,000 cash and renders services incident to the organization of KLM Corporation in exchange for 30 shares of its common stock.

Net of the mortgage transferred by K and assumed by the corporation, KLM issued 188 shares of common stock in exchange for money and other property with a net fair market value of $188,000 [$80,000 from K ($100,000 fair market value of land − $20,000 mortgage) + $90,000 from L ($50,000 cash + $40,000 fair market value of equipment) + $18,000 cash from M]. The additional 12 shares of common stock issued to M were in exchange for services.

a. What is K's realized and recognized gain?

b. What basis will K have in the KLM stock?

c. What basis will KLM Corporation have in the land?

d. How much gain must L recognize?

e. What basis will L have in the KLM stock?

f. What basis will KLM Corporation have in the equipment?

g. How much income, if any, must M recognize?

h. What basis will M have in the KLM stock?

i. Assume that KLM Corporation incurred and paid $6,800 of organizational costs, in addition to its payment of stock in exchange for M's services incident to organization. If the corporation begins business on October 1, 2005, adopts a calendar tax year, and elects to expense and amortize its organizational expenditures, what amount can KLM Corporation deduct for 2005?

19-27 *Transfer of Liabilities.* Each of the transfers below qualifies as a § 351 transaction, and in each case the transferee corporation assumes liabilities involved in the transfer. For each transfer, compute the transferor shareholder's recognized gain, the transferor's basis in any stock or securities received, and the transferee corporation's basis in any property received.

a. T transfers land with a basis of $60,000 and subject to a mortgage of $20,000 in exchange for stock worth $55,000.

b. A transfers machinery with a basis of $4,000 and subject to a mortgage of $9,000 in exchange for stock worth $6,000. The $9,000 mortgage was created two weeks before the transfer and A used the loan proceeds to take her husband on a vacation trip to Europe.

c. Assume the same facts in (b) except that the $9,000 liability is the balance remaining on a five-year $40,000 mortgage loan created to acquire the machinery transferred by A.

d. X transfers equipment with a basis of $30,000 and subject to a liability of $10,000 in exchange for stock worth $80,000 and a $20,000 security (bond) maturing in 10 years and paying 15 percent interest annually.

RESEARCH PROBLEMS

19-28 *Corporate Formation.* T, an individual taxpayer, plans to incorporate his farming and ranching activities currently operated as a sole proprietorship. His primary purpose of incorporating is to transfer a portion of his ownership in land to his son and daughter. T believes that gifts of stock rather than land will keep his business intact. T's current thought is to incorporate and immediately transfer 40 percent of the corporate stock to his two children. In fact, he has promised his children that he would make the stock gifts as soon as the corporation is created. What potential tax problems might result if T pursues his current plans? Would it make any difference if T received all voting stock and had the new corporation transfer nonvoting stock to the children?

Research aid:

Rev. Rul. 59-259, 1959-2 C.B. 115.

19-29 *Admission of New Shareholder.* RST Corporation is currently owned by three individuals, R, S, and T. The corporation has a net worth of $750,000 and has 500 shares (1,000 shares authorized) of common stock outstanding. R owns 200 shares (40 percent), and S and T each own 150 shares (30 percent). Individual E owns land worth $90,000 which the corporation could use as a new plant site. However, E is not interested in selling the land now because it would result in a large capital gain tax. E is willing to transfer the land to the corporation in exchange for 60 shares of its common stock or securities of equivalent value, but only if the transfer will be nontaxable. How would you advise the parties to structure the transaction?

Research aids:

Rev. Rul. 73-472, 1973-2 C.B. 115.

Rev. Proc. 76-22, 1976-1 C.B. 562.

Reg. § 1.351-1(a)(1)(ii).

Chapter 20

CORPORATE DISTRIBUTIONS, REDEMPTIONS AND LIQUIDATIONS

LEARNING OBJECTIVES

Upon completion of this chapter you will be able to:

- Determine the tax consequences of dividend distributions to shareholders and the distributing corporation

- Compute a corporation's earnings and profits

- Identify the more common types of constructive dividends

- Explain the tax consequences of taxable and nontaxable stock dividends

- Define a redemption and distinguish it from other types of nonliquidating distributions

- Explain the tax consequences of a redemption to a shareholder and the distributing corporation

- Define a liquidation and determine its tax consequences to shareholders and the liquidating corporation

- Discuss the special rules that apply when a corporation liquidates a subsidiary

CHAPTER OUTLINE

INTRODUCTION

The life cycle of a corporation starts with its formation. This is followed by a period of operation and growth. During the growth stage, the corporation generally makes distributions to its shareholders, called *dividends*. Shareholders not only expect to receive dividends, but also expect their stock to appreciate in value. Following the growth phase, the corporation enters a period of maturity. In the maturity stage profits may stabilize, but eventually business may start to decline. A decline may force the corporation to redeem stock, reorganize, or possibly liquidate.

This chapter deals with the Federal income tax aspects of corporate dividends, redemptions of stock, and liquidations as they relate to both the shareholders and the corporations.

DIVIDENDS

A distribution by a corporation of cash or property to a shareholder is income to the shareholder to the extent it is a *dividend*.[1] A dividend is defined as a distribution by a corporation out of either its accumulated earnings and profits since 1913 (the inception of corporate income tax) or its earnings and profits for the current year.[2] If the distribution exceeds the corporation's earnings and profits, the excess is treated as a nontaxable reduction of the shareholder's basis in his or her stock. If the distribution exceeds both the corporation's earnings and profits and the shareholder's adjusted basis in his or her stock, the excess is treated as a gain on the sale of the shareholder's stock.

> **Example 1.** J purchased 100 shares of M Corporation common stock on January 1, 1998 for $1,000. On February 3, 2005 M Corporation distributed to J $5,000 with respect to its stock, of which $2,300 is a dividend. (The amount of M Corporation's earnings and profits allocable to J is $2,300.)
>
> J is required to include this $2,300 of dividend income in gross income. The remaining $2,700 is applied first to reduce the $1,000 basis of J's stock to zero, and the rest ($1,700) is treated as a gain on the sale of his stock. It will be a long-term capital gain since he has held the stock as an investment for more than one year. J still has the 100 shares of stock, but his basis is reduced to zero.

EARNINGS AND PROFITS

The term *earnings and profits* (also referred to as "E&P") is not defined in either the Internal Revenue Code or the Regulations. Instead, the effect of certain transactions on earnings and profits is described.[3] From an examination of these transactions, however, it is possible to create a general definition of earnings and profits. Basically, corporate earnings and profits equal taxable income *increased* by nontaxable income and *decreased* by nondeductible expenses. Although earnings and profits are similar to retained earnings as used in financial accounting, there are often significant differences between the two. These differences are caused by differences in the treatment of various items (e.g., stock dividends) for financial accounting purposes as opposed to the items' tax treatment. Therefore, the computation of earnings and profits should be completely independent of any computation of retained earnings.

---

[1] § 301.

[2] § 316(a).

[3] § 312.

As mentioned previously, earnings and profits generally consist of taxable income plus nontaxable income minus nondeductible expenses. Exhibit 20-1 contains a partial list of the adjustments that must be made to determine earnings and profits for a taxable year.

Although most are self-explanatory, several items in Exhibit 20-1 require further clarification. For example, while there is an adjustment for tax-exempt interest income, there is no adjustment for the portion of a gain that is realized but not recognized in a like-kind exchange. A gain on the sale of assets affects earnings and profits only to the extent that the gain is recognized.[4]

Depreciation. The use of accelerated depreciation is not permitted in computing earnings and profits.[5] The corporation generally must use the straight-line method. Specifically, depreciation for E&P purposes must be computed under the Alternative Depreciation System (ADS), using the straight-line method and the property's class life. Because taxable income reflects any accelerated methods used, an adjustment in determining earnings and profits is to *add* to taxable income the excess of the accelerated depreciation over straight-line. In the later years of the asset's class life, the corporation would be required to *subtract* from taxable income the excess of straight-line depreciation over accelerated depreciation.

Example 2. N Corporation uses the 150% declining balance method to compute the depreciation on its warehouse. (Assume that all other assets are depreciated using the straight-line method and that there are no other adjustments to earnings and profits.) The depreciation claimed on the warehouse for the current year (2005) was $7,350. Straight-line depreciation using ADS on the warehouse would have been $5,000. N Corporation's taxable income for 2005 was $19,000. Earnings and profits for 2005 are computed as follows:

Taxable income for 2005		$19,000
Plus: Excess of accelerated over straight-line depreciation:		
Accelerated depreciation	$ 7,350	
Straight-line depreciation	(5,000)	+ 2,350
Earnings and profits for 2005		$21,350

---

[4]   § 312(f)(1).

[5]   § 312(k)(1).

EXHIBIT 20-1

Partial List of Adjustments Used in Computing Current Earnings and Profits

Taxable Income

Plus:

Tax-exempt interest income

Deferred gain on installment sales

Dividends-received deduction

Excess of accelerated depreciation over straight-line depreciation

Excess of ACRS depreciation over straight-line depreciation [§312(k)(3)]

Excess of LIFO cost of goods sold over FIFO cost of goods sold

Four-fifths (⅘) of deduction for immediate expensing of assets under § 179 taken during
the current year [§312(k)(3)(B)]

Excess of depletion taken over cost depletion

Increases in cash surrender value of life insurance when the corporation is the beneficiary
(directly or indirectly)

Proceeds of life insurance when the corporation is the beneficiary (directly or indirectly)

Net operating loss deductions carried over from other years

Federal income tax refunds

Recoveries of bad debts and other deductions, but only if they *are* not included in taxable
income under the tax benefit doctrine

Income based on the percentage-of-completion rather than the completed contract method

In the year they are reflected in taxable income: charitable contribution carryovers, capital loss
carryovers, and other timing differences (since they reduced E&P in the year that
they originated)

Minus:

Federal income taxes

Nondeductible expenses:

Penalties and fines

Payments to public officials not reflected in taxable income

Expenses between related parties not deductible under § 267

Interest expense related to the production of tax-exempt income

Life insurance premiums when the corporation is the beneficiary (directly or indirectly)

Travel, entertainment, and gift expenses that do not meet the substantiation
requirements of § 247(d)

Fifty percent of meals and entertainment disallowed as a deduction under § 274(n)

Other expenses disallowed to the corporation as the result of an IRS audit

Nondeductible losses between related parties under § 267

Charitable contributions in excess of the 10 percent limitation

Excess capital losses for the year that are not deductible

Gains on sales of depreciable property to the extent that accelerated depreciation or ACRS
exceeds the straight-line depreciation method used for computing increases in E&P

Gains on sales of depletable property to the extent that depletion taken exceeds cost depletion

One-fifth (⅕) of any immediate expensing deduction under §179 taken during the previous
four years [§ 312(k)(3)(B)]

Foreign taxes paid that have been treated as credits on the corporations tax return

Equals: **Current Earnings and Profits**

Note: This exhibit does not include the effect of corporate distributions and dividends on E&P,
which is discussed later in the chapter.

Code § 179 Expense. If a corporation has elected the immediate expensing option of § 179, E&P adjustments are made for the year in which the asset is expensed and also for the four following years.[6] The effect of a § 179 election on earnings and profits is that the amount expensed is an earnings and profits deduction in equal installments over the five-year period.

Example 3. X Corporation elected to expense a $5,000 asset under § 179 in 2005. X Corporation's taxable income for 2005 was $20,000. Although the entire $5,000 deduction is reflected in X Corporation's taxable income, the amount that affects E&P is $1,000 per year for five years. Therefore, taxable income must be adjusted as follows (assume there are no other adjustments to earnings and profits):

2005 Taxable income.	$20,000
Plus: $4/5$ of immediate expensing deduction ($4/5$ of $5,000).	4,000
2005 Earnings and profits	$24,000

In 2006 through 2009, $1,000 per year ($1/5$ of the 2005 immediate expensing deduction) is subtracted when computing E&P.

Adjustments to More Accurately Reflect Income. Over the years, Congress has required additional adjustments to be made in the computation of a corporation's earnings and profits in an attempt to have E&P more accurately reflect the corporation's current economic gain or loss.[7] One of the most important of these adjustments affects corporations using the LIFO method of inventory valuation. These firms must adjust E&P for the *difference* between the inventory as valued by LIFO and the value the inventory would have if FIFO had been used.[8]

Another similar adjustment applies to corporations that use the installment method for any asset sale. The corporation's E&P must include the full amount of the gain in the year of sale as if the corporation had not used the installment method.[9]

DISTRIBUTIONS FROM EARNINGS AND PROFITS

A special approach has been designed for determining whether a distribution is made out of E&P and therefore treated as a dividend. This approach treats E&P as consisting of two distinctly separate pools of earnings from which distributions may be made: current E&P and accumulated E&P. Using this approach, the law creates a presumption that any distribution made during the year is deemed to come *first* from any current E&P that may exist.[10] If distributions during the year *exceed* current E&P, the distribution is treated as having been paid from any accumulated E&P. Note that under this "two-pot" process, it is possible for a distribution to be a taxable dividend out of current E&P even though the corporation has a deficit in accumulated E&P that, in fact, exceeds current E&P. In addition, a distribution may be treated as a taxable dividend even though it is distributed at a time during the year when the firm had a current loss. This result can occur because current E&P is computed at the close of the taxable year, without reduction for any distributions.

---

[6]   § 312(k)(3)(B).

[7]   § 312(n).

[8]   § 312(n)(5).

[9]   § 312(n)(6).

[10]   Reg. § 1.316-2(a).

Example 4. T Corporation distributed $10,000 cash on February 1 and $10,000 on November 1. The corporation has $25,000 of current earnings and profits and $15,000 of accumulated earnings and profits. The entire $20,000 distributed is a taxable dividend from current earnings and profits, since distributions are considered to come first from current earnings and profits and then from accumulated earnings and profits.

Example 5. Assume the same facts as in *Example 4* except that there is a deficit in accumulated earnings and profits of $15,000. The $20,000 distributed is still a taxable dividend since there are current earnings and profits of $25,000. Accumulated earnings and profits will still have a deficit of $15,000.

Example 6. R Corporation made a $15,000 distribution to its shareholders on December 31. R Corporation has $3,000 earnings and profits for the current year and $18,000 accumulated earnings and profits. The entire $15,000 distribution is a taxable dividend. Accumulated earnings and profits are reduced to $6,000 as a result of the distribution.

In applying this basic scheme to determine whether a distribution is in fact a dividend, the following additional rules must be observed:[11]

1.   Current E&P is allocated among *all* distributions made during the year on a pro rata basis, as follows:

$$\frac{\text{Amount of the distribution}}{\text{Total current distributions}} \times \frac{\text{Amount of}}{\text{current E\&P}} = \frac{\text{Distribution's share}}{\text{of current E\&P}}$$

Example 7. During the current year, P Corporation distributed $12,000 to its shareholders on March 1 and an other $12,000 to its shareholders on October 1. Current E&P was only $10,000. Each distribution would be treated as consisting of $5,000 of current E&P [($12,000 ÷ $24,000) × $10,000]. The balance of each distribution would be deemed to come from any accumulated E&P that may exist at the time of the distribution.

2.   Accumulated E&P is allocated among distributions made during the year in *chronological order*.

Example 8. Same facts as in *Example 7*. In addition, the corporation had accumulated E&P of $7,000. Earnings and profits are allocated as follows:

	$12,000 March Distribution	$12,000 October Distribution	Total
Current earnings and profits [allocated pro rata to all distributions: ($12,000 ÷ $24,000) × $10,000 current E&P = $5,000]	$ 5,000	$5,000	$10,000
Accumulated earnings and profits (allocated in chronological order: first to the March distribution and then to the October distribution)	7,000	0	7,000
Taxable dividend	$12,000	$5,000	$17,000

The entire amount of the March distribution ($12,000) is a taxable dividend, but only $5,000 of the October distribution is a taxable dividend to the shareholders. The

---

[11]   Reg. § 1.316-2.

remaining $7,000 of the October distribution is a return of capital to the shareholders and will first be applied to reduce their bases in their stock. Any amount in excess of their stock bases will be treated as a gain from the sale of their stock.

This allocation process becomes especially important if there is a change of ownership during the year, since each shareholder is concerned with how much of each distribution he or she receives is taxable as dividends. However, the *total* amount of taxable dividends is not affected by the allocations.

3. If there is a deficit in current E&P for the year (e.g., a current operating loss), it is treated as occurring *ratably* during the year (unless it can be shown that the loss did not occur evenly during the year).[12] Accordingly, the loss is allocated on a daily basis against any accumulated E&P.

Example 9. T Corporation distributed $10,000 to its shareholders on February 1 and $10,000 to its shareholders on October 1. T Corporation had a $6,000 loss for its current calendar tax year and accumulated earnings and profits from prior years of $20,000. The $6,000 loss is assumed to have occurred evenly throughout the year (assume $500 per month). The tax treatment of the distributions is determined as follows:

February distribution: Since there are no current earnings and profits, the distribution is presumed to come from accumulated earnings and profits. Accumulated earnings and profits as of February 1 are considered to be $19,500 [$20,000 − $500 (one month of the current loss)]. The entire February distribution of $10,000 is a taxable dividend since accumulated earnings and profits are applied chronologically.

The balance in accumulated earnings and profits after the February distribution is $9,500 ($20,000 − $500 − $10,000).

October distribution: Since there are no current earnings and profits, the next step is to look at accumulated earnings and profits. Accumulated earnings and profits as of October 1 are $5,500 [$9,500 remaining after the February 1 distribution − $4,000 (8 months of current loss @ $500 per month from February through September)]. Therefore, $5,500 of the October distribution is a taxable dividend to the shareholders. The remaining $4,500 is a return of capital to the shareholders. After the October 1 distribution, the balance in accumulated earnings and profits is zero.

At the end of the year, the balance in accumulated earnings and profits is a deficit of $1,500 (the remaining 3 months of current loss at $500 per month).

CASH DIVIDENDS

Shareholders are required to include in income the amount of any distribution that is a dividend. If the distribution is cash, the amount of the distribution is simply the amount of the cash. As demonstrated in the above examples, earnings and profits are reduced by the amount of the cash distribution, but not below zero.[13]

PROPERTY DIVIDENDS

Corporations make distributions of property as well as distributions of cash. Code § 317(a) defines property as "money, securities, and any other property," but excludes

---

[12]   *Ibid.*

[13]   § 312(a)(1).

from the definition stock and stock rights in the distributing corporation. Special rules must be followed when a property distribution is made. Basically, the thrust of the property distribution rules is to treat the corporation and shareholders as if the corporation had sold the property and distributed to the shareholders the cash proceeds from the sale.

Code § 311 provides that a corporation must recognize gain—*but not loss*—upon the distribution of property other than its own obligations.[14] Thus, when a corporation distributes property that has a value exceeding its basis, gain must be recognized. In contrast, a corporation is not allowed to recognize loss on a distribution of property whose value is less than its basis. This rule prohibits a corporation and its shareholders from circumventing the gain recognition requirement by distributing loss property that would offset the gain on appreciated property. When the corporation distributes appreciated property and recognizes gain, its E&P is first increased by the gain and then reduced by the fair market value of the property distributed.[15] In contrast, if the corporation distributes depreciated property, no loss is recognized and the corporation decreases its E&P by the basis of the property distributed.[16]

Both corporate and noncorporate shareholders that receive a distribution of property report the fair market value of the property as a dividend to the extent it is out of the corporation's E&P.[17] The shareholder's basis in the property is also its fair market value.[18]

> **Example 10.** P Corporation distributed land worth $100,000 (basis $20,000) and equipment worth $30,000 (basis $45,000) to its sole shareholder, individual X. The corporation must recognize the $80,000 ($100,000 − $20,000) gain realized on the distribution of the land. Although P also realizes a loss on the distribution of the equipment, the loss is not recognized. Assuming the corporation has adequate E&P, X reports a dividend of $130,000 (the fair market values of the property, $100,000 + $30,000). X's basis in the land and equipment is $100,000 and $30,000, respectively. The net effect of the distribution on the corporation's E&P is to decrease it by $65,000 ($80,000 gain − $100,000 value of the land − $45,000 basis of the equipment).

Adjustments for Liabilities. The above discussion ignores the possibilities that the property may be distributed subject to a liability or that the shareholder may assume a liability in conjunction with the property distribution. In such case, the rules regarding the amount of the distribution and the adjustment to E&P must be modified to account for any liabilities.[19] When a liability is distributed in connection with property, the amount of the distribution is decreased by the liability. Similarly, the reduction in E&P is decreased (i.e., E&P is increased by the amount of the liability). There is no adjustment to the basis of the property to the shareholder.

CONSTRUCTIVE DIVIDENDS

In addition to actual distributions of cash and property, a shareholder can be charged with the *constructive receipt* of a dividend. For example, excessive salaries to the shareholder or a member of the shareholder's family can be treated as a dividend. The

---

[14]   §§ 311(a) and (b).

[15]   § 312(b).

[16]   § 312(a)(3).

[17]   § 301(b)(1).

[18]   § 301(d).

[19]   § 301(b)(2).

corporation is limited to deducting only those salaries that are reasonable. The amount in excess of the reasonable standard will be considered a constructive dividend. Other transactions that have given rise to constructive dividends are:

1. Loans to shareholders where there is no intent to repay the amounts loaned

2. Bargain purchases and rentals of corporate property by shareholders

3. Excess payment for corporate use of shareholder property

4. Payment of shareholder's loans or expenses by the corporation

5. Personal use by shareholder of corporate assets

As indicated by the above types of transactions, constructive dividends usually arise in closely held corporations, especially those with only one or two shareholders. Constructive dividends are not planned by the corporations. They usually arise in an IRS audit as the result of lack of formality in dealing with the corporate entity and a lack of transactions at "arm's length" (for fair market value). Therefore, it is possible for a shareholder to be considered as having received a dividend even though the corporation did not declare one.

As with other dividends, the corporation must have sufficient earnings and profits for a constructive dividend to be taxable to the shareholders. Also, the dividends-received deduction is available to corporate shareholders with respect to constructive dividends.

STOCK DIVIDENDS AND STOCK RIGHTS

Occasionally, a corporation may want to pay a dividend but does not have sufficient cash or property to distribute. In this situation, the corporation may declare a dividend of its stock or of rights to acquire its stock.

Stock Dividends. As a general rule, a shareholder does not have any income as the result of receiving a distribution of the distributing corporation's own stock.[20] Instead, the shareholder simply allocates the basis of his or her old stock between the old stock and the new stock. There are several exceptions to this general rule, however. If the shareholder is given a choice between receiving stock or receiving property or money, the distribution will be taxable.[21] It does not matter which form of distribution the shareholder actually selects. The ability to select makes the distribution taxable. In fact, the ability of *any* of the shareholders to select property or stock will make the distribution taxable to all of the shareholders.[22]

Another case in which a stock dividend will be taxable is if the distribution is *disproportionate*.[23] The Code defines *disproportionate* in this situation as the receipt of cash or other property by some shareholders with an increase in the proportionate interests of other shareholders in the corporation. The determination as to whether or not a distribution is disproportionate is made at the end of the distribution or series of distributions and is made based on the result of the transactions.

Distributions of preferred stock to common stockholders are covered by the general rule of nontaxability. However, a distribution or a series of distributions that results in some shareholders receiving common and others receiving preferred is a taxable transaction.[24] In addition, any distribution (e.g., common stock) to a preferred

---

[20] § 305(a).

[21] § 305(b)(1).

[22] Reg. § 1.305-2.

[23] § 305(b)(2).

[24] § 305(b)(3).

stockholder is taxable.[25] A special rule applies for distributions of convertible preferred stock. The distribution will be taxable unless it can be shown that the result will not be disproportionate[26] (see above for definition of disproportionate).

Taxable stock dividends can be either actual or deemed dividends.[27] Actual dividends require distributions of stock. Deemed-dividend transactions include changes in conversion ratios, changes in redemption price, an excess redemption price over issue price, or any other transaction that increases the proportionate ownership of one or more shareholders. Deemed dividends can be totally unintentional. For example, in a corporate reorganization the issuance of preferred stock with a redemption value greater than its current issue price is a possible taxable stock dividend.[28]

Nontaxable Stock Dividends. If the taxpayer receives a nontaxable distribution of stock, the basis of the shares received is determined by allocation. The basis of the shares upon which the dividend is received is allocated between the old stock and the new stock based on their relative fair market values at the time of distribution.[29] If the shares received are identical to the shares owned (i.e., both the old and new stock are the same class of common stock), the allocation can be accomplished simply by dividing the basis of the old stock by the total number of shares owned after the distribution. If the type of shares received differs from the shares originally owned (e.g., old stock was common stock and new stock is preferred stock), the allocation of basis between the old stock and new stock is computed based on relative fair market value. The holding period of the new stock includes the holding period of the old stock.[30]

Example 11. Q owned 100 shares of common stock of V Corporation. His basis in the V Corporation stock was $1,300 ($13 per share). Q received a stock dividend of 25 additional shares of V Corporation common stock in a nontaxable distribution. Q's $1,300 basis in the old stock is allocated between his old stock (100 shares) and his new stock (25 shares) as follows:

$$\frac{\text{Basis in old stock}}{\text{Number of shares after distribution}} \times \frac{\$1,300}{125 \text{ shares}} = \underline{\$10.40} \text{ per share}$$

Q's basis in his stock is still $1,300, which is $10.40 per share, since he now has 125 values of V Corporation common stock.

Example 12. Assume the same facts as in *Example 11* except that Q received 25 shares of preferred stock instead of common stock. On the date of distribution, the fair market value of V Corporation common stock was $15 per share and the fair market value of V Corporation preferred stock was $5 per share. Q's $1,300 basis in his stock is allocated between the old stock and the new stock as follows:

Step 1: Determine fair market value of stock:

Fair market value of Q's common stock (100 shares × $15), ...	$1,500
Fair market value of Q's preferred stock (25 shares × $5)	125
Total fair market value of Q's stock.	$1,625

---

25 § 305(b)(4).

26 § 305(b)(5).

27 § 305(c).

28 See Rev. Rul. 83-119, 1983-2 C.B. 57.

29 Reg. § 1.307-1.

30 § 1223(5).

Step 2: Compute basis in each type of stock based on relative fair market value:

(a) $\dfrac{\text{Fair market value of Q's common stock}}{\text{Total fair market value of Q's stock}} \times \text{Old basis} = \begin{array}{l}\text{New basis in}\\\text{common stock}\end{array}$

$\dfrac{\$1,500}{\$1,625} \times \$1,300 = \underline{\underline{\$1,200}} \quad \begin{array}{l}\text{New basis in}\\\text{common stock}\end{array} \quad (\$12 \text{ per share})$

(b) $\dfrac{\text{Fair market value of Q's preferred stock}}{\text{Total fair market value of Q's stock}} \times \text{Old basis} = \begin{array}{l}\text{New basis in}\\\text{preferred stock}\end{array}$

$\dfrac{\$125}{\$1,625} \times \$1,300 = \underline{\underline{\$100}} \quad \begin{array}{l}\text{Basis in}\\\text{preferred stock}\end{array} \quad (\$4 \text{ per share})$

A nontaxable stock dividend *does not affect* the earnings and profits of the distributing corporation.[31]

Taxable Stock Dividends. The recipient shareholder must treat a taxable distribution of stock the same as a property distribution. If the stock distribution is taxable, the shareholder must report dividend income equal to the *lesser* of the fair market value of the stock received or the distributing corporation's earnings and profits.[32] The basis of the stock received is the amount of income reported.[33] The holding period of the shares received would start on the date of distribution. The basis of the original stock is not affected by a taxable stock dividend. Taxable stock dividends have the same effect on the earnings and profits of a corporation as property dividends. However, the distributing corporation does not recognize gain or loss from taxable distribution of its stock.

Stock Rights. Instead of stock, corporations may distribute stock rights to their shareholders. The taxation of the receipt of stock rights is governed by the same general principles as stock dividends.[34] In determining whether the distribution is taxable, it is often easier to assume that the stock that can be acquired by exercise of the rights was distributed instead of the rights. If the distribution of the stock to which the stock rights apply would have been taxable, the rights are taxable. If a distribution of the related stock would not have been taxable, the rights are not taxable.

Example 13. N Corporation had 100 shares of common stock and 100 shares of nonvoting preferred stock outstanding. The corporation distributed rights to acquire a new issue of nonvoting preferred stock to all of its existing shareholders. The common shareholders have received a nontaxable distribution, whereas the preferred shareholders have received a taxable distribution. Since the distribution of the new preferred stock to the common shareholders would have been nontaxable, the rights received by the common shareholders are nontaxable. However, since preferred shareholders receive only taxable stock dividends, the rights received by the preferred shareholders also are taxable.

Nontaxable Stock Rights. If the stock rights are not taxable, there is a basis allocation similar to the one for stock dividends.[35] The basis of the old stock is allocated between the old stock and the new rights based on the relative fair market values at the

---

[31]   § 312(d)(1).

[32]   Reg. § 1.305-1(b)(1); Code §§ 301(b) and 316(a).

[33]   § 301(d).

[34]   § 305(a).

[35]   § 307(a).

date of distribution. There is no allocation of basis to the rights if the shareholder allows them to lapse[36] (and consequently no recognized loss on the lapse of the rights). Therefore, although the allocation uses the fair market values as of the date of distribution, the actual allocation generally is not made until the rights are sold or exercised.

Example 14. T Corporation distributed nontaxable stock rights to its shareholders on January 3. C received 100 rights on the 100 shares of common stock he purchased three years ago for $1,000. On the date of distribution, T Corporation's common stock had a value of $15 per share and the rights had a value of $5 each. On March 1, C sold the rights for $7 each. The stock had a value of $17 per share on March 1. C allocates the basis of his old stock between the stock and the rights based on their relative fair market values as of January 3, the date of the distribution. The March 1 value of the stock is irrelevant. The basis allocation is computed as follows:

Step 1:

Fair market value of C's common stock (100 × $15)	$1,500
Fair market value of C's stock rights (100 × $5)	500
Total fair market value of stock and stock rights	$2,000

(a) $\dfrac{\text{Fair market value of C's common stock}}{\text{Total fair market value of stock and stock rights}} \times \text{Old basis}$

$$= \frac{\$1,500}{\$2,000} \times \$1,000 = \underline{\$750} \quad (\$7.50 \text{ per share})$$

(b) $\dfrac{\text{Fair market value of C's stock rights}}{\text{Total fair market value of stock and stock rights}} \times \text{Old basis}$

$$\frac{\$500}{\$2,000} \times \$1,000 = \underline{\$250} \quad (\$2.50 \text{ per stock right})$$

C's gain on the sale of his stock rights is computed as follows:

Selling price of stock rights (100 × $7)	$700
Less: Basis in stock rights.	−250
Gain on sale of stock rights	$450

Example 15. Assume the same facts as in *Example 14* except that C does not sell the stock rights, but allows them to lapse on June 1. Since the stock rights lapsed, rather than being exercised or sold, there is no basis allocated to them. C has no recognized loss (since the rights have no basis) and the basis of the old shares remains $1,000.

If the taxpayer sells or exercises his or her rights, basis is allocated to the rights. The holding period of the rights includes the holding period of the old stock.[37] The fair market value of stock rights is frequently small in relation to the value of the stock on which it was distributed. As a result, an allocation of basis between the old stock and the new rights would produce a very small basis in the stock rights. For this reason,

---

[36]   Reg. § 1.307-1(a).

[37]   § 1223(5).

there is an exception to the rule regarding allocation of basis. If the fair market value of the stock rights is *less than* 15 percent of the value of the stock at the date of distribution, no basis is *required* to be allocated to the rights.[38] The basis of the rights is zero and the basis of the old stock remains unchanged. However, even though the basis of the rights is zero, the holding period of the rights includes the holding period of the old stock.[39] If a taxpayer wishes, he or she may elect to allocate basis to the rights even though there is no requirement to allocate basis to the rights under this 15-percent rule.[40] This election to allocate is made by filing a statement with the taxpayer's tax return for the year in which the rights are received. The election applies to all the stock rights received in the distribution and is irrevocable

Example 16. Assume the same facts as in *Example 14* except that the fair market values of the stock and rights on January 3 were $19 and $1, respectively. Since the value of the rights ($100) is less than 15% of the value of the stock (15% of $1,900 = $285), no allocation is required. C would have a $700 gain on the sale of the stock rights since their basis was zero. The gain would be long-term since the holding period of the rights includes the holding period of the stock.

Example 17. Assume the same facts as in *Example 16* except that C elects to allocate basis between the stock and the stock rights. The basis of the rights is computed as follows:

$$\frac{\text{Fair market value of stock rights}}{\text{Fair market value of stock and stock rights}} \times \text{Old basis}$$

$$= \frac{(100 \text{ rights} \times \$1)}{(100 \text{ rights} \times \$1) + (100 \text{ shares} \times \$19)} \times \underline{\$1,000} \text{ Old basis}$$

$$\frac{\$100}{\$2,000} \times \$1,000 = \underline{\$50} \text{ basis in stock rights}$$

In this situation, the sale of the rights for $700 would result in a $650 gain.

Taxable Stock Rights. The taxable receipt of stock rights, like a taxable stock dividend, is treated as a property dividend by the shareholder. The shareholder would have dividend income equal to the lesser of the fair market value of the rights on date of receipt or the distributing corporation's earnings and profits.[41] The rights would have a basis equal to the fair market value[42] and the holding period starts on the date of distribution. If the rights lapse, the taxpayer will have a loss equal to the basis of the rights. Stock rights have the same effect on a corporation's earnings and profits as stock dividends. Additionally, the corporation does not recognize gain or loss from taxable distributions of its stock rights.

NONDEDUCTIBILITY OF DIVIDENDS TO CORPORATION

A corporation is not permitted a deduction for distributions to its shareholders with respect to its stock. It does not matter whether the distribution is cash, property, stock, or stock rights. As mentioned in Chapter 19, this produces "double taxation." The shareholders are taxed individually on dividends (distributed corporate earnings and

---

[38] § 307(b)(1).

[39] § 1223(5).

[40] § 307(b)(2) and Reg. § 1.307-2.

[41] Reg. § 1.305-1(b)(1): Code §§ 301(b) and 316(a).

[42] § 301(d).

profits), but the distributing corporation may not take a corresponding deduction for the dividends.

STOCK REDEMPTIONS

Corporations occasionally will acquire their own shares. Sometimes the acquisition is motivated by a desire to eliminate an issue of stock. In these cases, the corporation might cancel the stock after its acquisition. Alternatively, the corporation might reacquire its own shares in order to issue the shares as additional compensation to hire or retain qualified employees or to acquire additional assets or even a whole business. The stock may be kept as treasury stock until needed. Such an acquisition is called a *stock redemption*. A redemption is defined in the Code as the acquisition by a corporation of its own stock from its shareholders in exchange for cash or other property, regardless of whether the shares are canceled, retired, or held as treasury stock.[43]

IN GENERAL

The taxation of the acquisition of the shares from an existing shareholder could take either of two forms. It could be treated as a sale of stock, with the corporation treated as an independent purchaser. This generally would result in a capital gain or loss for the shareholder. Alternatively, the sales price could be treated as a distribution. In this situation, the shareholder would have dividend income to the extent of the corporation's earnings and profits. Generally, the key factor as to whether a stock redemption is treated as a sale or a dividend distribution is whether or not the shareholder's proportionate interest in the corporation is significantly reduced.

As a general rule, if a shareholder's interest is basically the same or nearly the same after a redemption, the redemption is treated as a distribution. The tax treatment is based on whether the distribution is of cash or other property. The taxability of cash and property dividends was discussed previously in this chapter.

There are *five* situations in which stock redemptions are treated as a sale by the shareholder instead of as a dividend distribution. These five situations are as follows:

1. Redemptions not equivalent to dividends [§ 302(b)(1)]
2. Substantially disproportionate redemptions of stock [§ 302(b)(2)]
3. Terminations of shareholders' interests [§ 302(b)(3)]
4. Redemptions from noncorporate shareholders in partial liquidation [§ 302(b)(4)]
5. Distributions in redemption of stock to pay death taxes (§ 303)

In the above five situations, a shareholder recognizes gain or loss equal to the difference between the redemption proceeds and the basis of the stock surrendered.

REDEMPTIONS NOT EQUIVALENT TO DIVIDENDS

The Code states that a stock redemption is treated as a sale or exchange of the shareholder's stock "if the redemption is not essentially equivalent to a dividend."[44] The Regulations refer to *dividend equivalency* as meaning that the redemption has "the same effect as a distribution without any redemption of stock."[45] Several cases have

---

[43] § 317(b).

[44] § 302(b)(1).

[45] Reg. § 1.302-2(a).

helped to further clarify this provision. The most significant litigation over this issue was *U.S. v. Davis,*[46] decided by the Supreme Court in 1970. The case involved the redemption of all of the corporation's outstanding preferred stock from the sole shareholder (directly and indirectly)[47] of the corporation. The Court ruled that the redemption was a distribution and not a sale. In reaching this decision, the Court rejected the taxpayer's argument that since there was a business purpose for the issuance and redemption of the preferred stock, the transaction was not equivalent to a dividend. Instead, the Court decided that to meet the requirement of § 302(b)(1), there must be a meaningful reduction in the shareholder's interest in the corporation. There are *no other* relevant considerations. One of the outgrowths of this decision is that no redemption from a sole shareholder will qualify as being "not equivalent to a dividend." A sole shareholder remains a 100 percent owner after *any* redemption. Therefore, there can never be a meaningful reduction in a sole shareholder's interest.

Following the decision in *Davis,* it was generally felt that the "not essentially equivalent to a dividend" exception was effectively canceled. Subsequent litigation has shown that this is not so. Taxpayers have been successful in those cases in which they were able to convince the court that there was a meaningful reduction in their interest in the corporation. Unfortunately, no precise definition of "meaningful reduction" has emerged from the litigation. Consequently, all subsequent taxpayers must prove the significance of the reduction based on the facts and circumstances of each specific case.

When a stock redemption is determined to be essentially equivalent to a dividend, the shareholder's basis in the stock redeemed is *added* to the basis of the stock that was not redeemed.[48]

> **Example 18.** R owned 1,000 shares (100%) of the common stock of T Corporation. (T Corporation had no other classes of stock outstanding.) R's basis in the stock was $20,000 ($20 per share). T Corporation redeemed 500 shares of R's common stock for $15,000. Since R owned 100% of T Corporation, both before and after the redemption, the redemption was essentially the same as a dividend. (There was no meaningful reduction in R's interest in the corporation.) R, therefore, has a distribution of $15,000, a taxable dividend if T Corporation has sufficient earnings and profits. R's basis of $10,000 ($20 per share) in the 500 shares redeemed is added to the basis in his remaining 500 shares. After the redemption. R's basis in his remaining 500 shares is $20,000 ($40 per share).

SUBSTANTIALLY DISPROPORTIONATE REDEMPTIONS

A stock redemption is treated as a sale if it is *substantially disproportionate.*[49] In order for a redemption to be substantially disproportionate with respect to a shareholder, the shareholder must, after the redemption, own less than 80 percent of the voting stock owned prior to the redemption and own less than 80 percent of the common stock owned prior to the redemption.[50] By requiring the shareholder's ownership of both *voting* and *common stock* to be less than 80 percent of his or her former ownership, the law prevents redemption of solely preferred stock from meeting the § 302(b)(2) requirements. Redemptions of preferred stock may qualify only if there is also a redemption of common stock. In addition to the above requirements, a shareholder is not eligible for sale or exchange treatment unless the shareholder's ownership of voting

[46]   70-1 USTC ¶9289. 25 AFTR 2d 70-827. 397 U.S. 301 (USSC. 1970).

[47]   The provisions regarding constructive ownership of stock are discussed later in this chapter.

[48]   Reg. § 1.302-2(c).

[49]   § 302(b)(2).

[50]   § 302(b)(2)(C).

stock after the redemption is less than 50 percent of the total voting stock.[51] Basically, satisfaction of these three mathematical tests provides a safe harbor for qualifying a redemption as not equivalent to a dividend (i.e., sale or exchange treatment).

Example 19. M owned 100 shares of Q Corporation's voting common stock. M's basis in this stock was $500 ($5 per share). Q Corporation had 200 shares of common stock (its only class of stock) issued and outstanding. The corporation redeemed 40 shares of M's stock for $300. The tax treatment of the redemption is determined as follows:

Test 1: Does M own less than 80% of the voting stock that she owned prior to the redemption?

Before the redemption M owned 50% of the voting stock. $\left(\dfrac{100}{200}\right)$

After the redemption M owned 37.5% of the outstanding voting stock. $\left(\dfrac{60}{160}\right)$

$$\frac{\text{M's percentage interest in the voting stock after the redemption}}{\text{M's percentage interested in the voting stock prior to the redemption}} = \frac{37.5\%}{50\%} = \underline{75\%}$$

(**Alternative Computation:** 80% of 50% = 40%; therefore, Test 1 is met because 37.5% is less than 40%.)

Test 2: Does M own less than 80% of the common stock that she owned prior to the redemption? Since the voting stock in this example is the same as the common stock, Test 2 is a repetition of Test 1. Therefore, Test 2 is also met.

Test 3: Is M's ownership of voting stock after the redemption less than 50% of the total voting stock? (This is measured in voting *power* if different classes of stock have unequal voting rights.)

$$\frac{\text{Number of shares of voting stock owned by M after the redemption}}{\text{Total number of shares of voting stock after the redemption}} = \frac{60}{160} = \underline{37.5\%}$$

37.5% is less than 50% of the voting stock, so Test 3 is met.

(**Alternative Computation:** 160 shares × 50% = 80 shares; therefore, Test 3 is met since 60 shares is less than 80 shares.)

All three tests must be met in order for a stock redemption to be "substantially disproportionate." Since all three tests are met in this example, the redemption of 40 shares of M's stock meets the requirements of § 302(b)(2) and is, therefore, treated as a sale or exchange of the stock. M's gain is computed as follows:

Proceeds from redemption.	$300
Less: M's basis in the 40 shares redeemed (40 × $5)	(200)
Gain from redemption	$100

The gain will be long-term or short-term depending on how long the stock was held.

Note: All computations regarding ownership after the redemption were made using 160 shares, the number of shares outstanding after 40 of the 200 originally outstanding shares had been redeemed by Q Corporation.

---

[51] § 302(b)(2)(B).

Example 20. X owned 150 of the 200 outstanding shares of W Corporation's voting common stock. (W Corporation has no other classes of stock.) The corporation redeemed 100 shares of X's stock. The tax treatment of the redemption is determined as follows:

Test 1: Does X own less than 80% of the voting stock that he owned prior to the redemption?

Before the redemption X owned 75% of the voting stock. $\left(\dfrac{150}{200}\right)$

After the redemption X owned 50% of the voting stock. $\left(\dfrac{50}{100}\right)$

$$\frac{50\%}{75\%} = \underline{\underline{67\%}}$$

67% is less than 80%, so Test 1 is met.

Test 2: Does X own less than 80% of the common stock that he owned prior to the redemption? Since the voting stock in this example is the same as the common stock, Test 2 is a repetition of Test 1. Therefore, Test 2 is also met.

Test 3: Is X's ownership of voting stock after the redemption less than 50% of the total voting stock?

$$\frac{50\%}{100\%} = \underline{\underline{50\%}}$$

Exactly 50% is not less than 50%. Therefore, Test 3 is not met.

Because *all three tests* must be met in order for a stock redemption to be "substantially disproportionate," the redemption is treated as a distribution, not a sale. Any proceeds from the redemption are treated as a dividend to the extent of earnings and profits, and X's basis in the 100 shares redeemed is added to the basis in his remaining 50 shares.

To prevent abuses in cases of multiple redemptions, the law requires that the tests be applied at the end of the series of redemptions if the redemptions are all part of one plan. Without this limitation, it would be possible to meet the substantially disproportionate rules after each redemption while leaving the redeeming shareholders' relative interests unaffected at the close of the intended transactions.[52]

Example 21. A, B, and C each owned 50 shares (⅓) of F Corporation's common stock. There are no other classes of stock. On January 2, pursuant to an overall plan, the corporation redeemed 40 shares of stock from A. On February 1, pursuant to the same plan, the corporation redeemed 40 shares from B. Finally, on March 3, the corporation redeemed 40 shares from C. Independently, each redemption is disproportionate. However, combining the series, A, B, and C each end up with the same ⅓ ownership of F Corporation. Consequently, the redemptions are not substantially disproportionate.

TERMINATION OF A SHAREHOLDER'S INTEREST

The third case in which a redemption can qualify as a sale is if the redemption completely terminates the shareholder's interest.[53] A *complete termination* requires the corporation to redeem all of the shares that the stockholder owns. If a shareholder is

---

[52] § 302(b)(2)(D).

[53] § 302(b)(3).

completely terminating his or her interest in a corporation in which various close relatives own stock, special rules apply to the termination of the shareholder's interest.[54] These special rules regarding constructive ownership of stock are discussed later in this chapter.

REDEMPTION FROM NONCORPORATE SHAREHOLDER IN PARTIAL LIQUIDATION

The fourth case in which a redemption can qualify as a sale is a redemption from a noncorporate shareholder in partial liquidation.[55] A *partial liquidation* is a distribution that is not essentially equivalent to a dividend, determined at the corporate level rather than at the shareholder level.[56] To qualify, the distribution must be made in accordance with a plan of partial liquidation and made either in the year the plan is adopted or in the following year.

The Code specifically provides that a distribution in partial liquidation shall include (but not be limited to) distributions attributable to the termination of a business.[57] To satisfy this test, the distribution must be the result of the corporation ceasing to conduct a trade or business that had been in existence for at least five years prior to the distribution. The corporation, following the distribution, must be conducting a trade or business that also has been in existence for at least five years. Neither the continuing nor the terminated business may have been acquired during the five-year period in a transaction in which a gain or loss was recognized.[58] This provision was included to prevent the corporation from purchasing a business in order to convert a dividend into a partial liquidation.

There is no exact definition of a "trade or business." The Regulations state that a trade or business consists of a group of activities that includes every step in the process of earning income.[59] Owning investment assets or real estate used in a trade or business is not a trade or business by itself. The Regulations are helpful but do not eliminate all the questions as to what constitutes a trade or business.

REDEMPTIONS OF STOCK TO PAY DEATH TAXES

The fifth provision in the Code that classifies a redemption as a sale rather than as a distribution deals with the redemption of stock to pay death taxes.[60] This provision only applies to stock included in a decedent's gross estate and was designed to provide a way to obtain cash needed for the administration of an estate. It permits the redemption of stock in an amount equal to the taxes imposed as a result of decedent's death and to the funeral and administration expenses deductible by the estate.[61] There is no restriction in the law that the redemption proceeds actually be used to pay taxes or expenses. The limitation refers simply to the maximum amount that can be redeemed under the provision. The tax treatment of any amount redeemed in excess of the amount of the above expenses is determined by applying the rules previously discussed regarding taxability of stock redemptions.

In order to be eligible to redeem stock using this provision, the value of the stock that the decedent owned in the redeeming corporation must exceed 35 percent of the

---

54 § 302(c)(2).

55 § 302(b)(4).

56 § 302(e)(1).

57 § 302(e)(2).

58 § 302(e)(3).

59 Reg. § 1.355-1(c).

60 § 303(a).

61 Ibid.

value of the decedent's gross estate reduced by expenses and losses of the estate.[62] This condition effectively limits the use of this exception to estates of which the stock of the redeeming corporation is a substantial part. It is also possible to use this provision when two or more corporations comprise a substantial part of a decedent's estate. In this situation, if 20 percent or more of the value of the outstanding stock of each of two or more corporations is included in the decedent's gross estate, the corporations are treated as a single corporation for the purpose of determining the 35 percent requirement.[63]

CONSTRUCTIVE OWNERSHIP OF STOCK

As demonstrated above, one of the primary factors distinguishing a stock redemption qualifying for sale or exchange treatment from a dividend distribution is whether there has been a change in the taxpayer's proportionate interest in the corporation. Ownership in a corporation refers to both *actual* and *constructive* ownership.[64]

Under the rules of constructive ownership of stock, a taxpayer is considered to own not only those shares of stock he or she personally owns, but also to own those shares of stock owned by certain relatives and entities in which the taxpayer has an interest. The only family members considered relatives for these constructive ownership rules are the taxpayer's spouse, children, grandchildren, and parents.[65] Excluded from the list are siblings (i.e., brothers and sisters) and grandparents.

> **Example 22.** F, an individual, owns 60% of the stock of G Corporation. The remaining 40% is owned by S, F's son. F is considered to own 100% of G Corporation, 60% directly and 40% by the application of the constructive ownership rules.

> **Example 23.** H is married to W. They have one son, C, and a grandchild, G. H owns 100 shares of ABC Corporation. Either W or C can be considered to constructively own H's stock. G is not considered to be a constructive owner of H's stock, since an individual is not considered to constructively own his or her grandparent's stock.

Under the constructive ownership rules (also called the *attribution rules*), a person is deemed to own a proportionate share of the stock owned by a partnership, estate, or trust in which he or she has an interest.[66] Partnerships, estates, and trusts are also deemed to own the stock owned by persons who have an ownership interest in them.[67]

> **Example 24.** Y and Z are equal (50% each) partners in the YZ Partnership. The YZ Partnership owns 300 shares of A Corporation. Since Y and Z each own one-half of the partnership, they are each considered to constructively own one-half of the 300 shares of A Corporation owned by the YZ Partnership, or 150 shares each.

> **Example 25.** Assume the same facts as in *Example 24* except that the 300 shares of A Corporation stock are owned by Y instead of by the partnership. Since a partnership is considered to constructively own all of the stock of its partners, the YZ Partnership is deemed to own the entire 300 shares of A Corporation stock. Z

[62] § 303(b)(2)(A).

[63] § 302(b)(2)(B).

[64] § 318.

[65] § 318(a)(1).

[66] §§ 318(a)(2)(A) and (B).

[67] §§ 318(a)(3)(A) and (B).

does not constructively own any of the stock unless Y and Z are related family members.

In order for there to be attribution (constructive ownership) between a shareholder and a corporation, the shareholder must own, actually or constructively, at least 50 percent of the value of the corporation's stock.[68] Once this requirement is met, a shareholder is deemed to own a proportionate share of the stock owned by the corporation.

> **Example 26.** C Corporation is owned 60% by B and 40% by W. C Corporation owns 1,000 shares of Z Corporation stock. B constructively owns 600 (1,000 shares × 60%) shares of the Z Corporation stock. W does not constructively own any shares of Z Corporation stock since he does not own at least 50% of C Corporation.

A corporation is deemed to own all of the stock owned by shareholders who have a 50 percent or more interest in the corporation.[69]

There are rules against *double* attribution. Specifically, stock may not be attributed to a family member from a family member and then reattributed to another family member.[70] In addition, stock attributed to an entity from an owner may not then be attributed to another owner.[71] These rules prevent attribution between unrelated individuals.

> **Example 27.** P has two children, R and S. R owns 100 shares of H Corporation. Therefore, P constructively owns R's 100 shares of H Corporation. Without the rules against double attribution, the 100 shares could be reattributed from P to S, resulting in sibling attribution, which is not authorized by the definition of relatives.

Complete Termination of Interest. The stock attribution rules could make it very difficult for a redemption by a family-owned corporation to qualify as a complete termination of interest under § 302(b)(3). Any constructively owned stock would prevent the shareholder from qualifying as having completely terminated his or her interest. To eliminate this problem, the Code permits the redeeming shareholder to ignore the family attribution rules (but not attribution from other entities) in determining whether there has been a complete termination of the shareholder's interest.[72] To qualify for this provision, the shareholder must not have any interest in the corporation after the redemption other than that of a creditor. Specifically, the shareholder may not be an officer, director, or even an employee of the corporation. In addition, the shareholder must not acquire one of the prohibited interests in the corporation during the 10 years following the redemption. This provision makes it much easier for a shareholder to qualify a redemption as a complete termination of interest.

REDEMPTIONS THROUGH RELATED CORPORATIONS

As stated earlier, a stock redemption is defined as the acquisition by a corporation of its own stock. The limitations on sale treatment discussed thus far could be avoided by an individual who controls two or more corporations. Instead of having a corporation redeem its stock, the shareholder could *sell* the stock of one controlled corporation to another controlled corporation. To prevent this type of transaction from avoiding the

---

[68] § 318(a)(2)(C).

[69] § 318(a)(3)(C).

[70] § 318(a)(5)(B).

[71] § 318(a)(5)(C).

[72] § 302(c)(2).

redemption limitations, Code § 304 reclassifies the "sale" of one controlled corporation's stock to another controlled corporation as a stock redemption.[73] Two different transactions are included in the reclassification provision. First, the sale of stock of a corporation controlled by one or more persons to another corporation controlled by the *same persons* is reclassified as a redemption.[74] Control is defined as ownership of either 50 percent or more of the combined voting power or 50 percent or more of the value of the outstanding stock.[75] The second reclassified transaction is the sale of stock of a parent corporation to its controlled subsidiary.[76]

> **Example 28.** A, B, and C, unrelated individuals, each own equal shares of T Corporation's outstanding stock. These same individuals own 100% of V Corporation's stock. If either A, B, or C sells shares of T Corporation to V Corporation, the transaction will be treated as a stock redemption.

> **Example 29.** Individual D owns all of the stock of P Corporation. P Corporation owns all of the stock of S Corporation. If D sells some of her P Corporation stock to S Corporation, the transaction will be treated as a stock redemption.

The fact that a transaction is reclassified as a stock redemption does not mean that the shareholder will be denied sale treatment. Instead, it requires that the selling shareholder meet one of the special rules relating to stock redemptions in § 302 (i.e., being not essentially equivalent to a dividend, substantially disproportionate, a complete termination of an interest, or a partial liquidation from a noncorporate shareholder) to qualify for sale treatment. In measuring the change in ownership under § 302, the stock of the issuing corporation—not the purchasing corporation—is used.[77] In addition, stock owned by attribution is counted.

> **Example 30.** Individual G owns 80 of the 100 shares of X Corporation and 90 of the 100 shares of Y Corporation. G "sells" 10 shares of X Corporation stock to Y Corporation. Since G controls both corporations, the transaction is reclassified as a redemption. Before the transaction, G owns 80% of X Corporation. After the transaction, G owns 79% of X, computed as follows:
>
> | | |
> |---|---|
> | Actual ownership (70 × 100 shares) | 70% |
> | Constructive ownership: | |
> | (90% ownership of Y corporation × | |
> | Y Corporation's 10% ownership of × Corporation) | 9% |
> | Total direct and indirect ownership | 79% |

Since G's ownership of X Corporation has only declined from 80% to 79%, the redemption does not meet any of the tests for sale treatment. Consequently, G must treat the "sale" proceeds as a dividend.

If the transaction is treated as a dividend rather than a sale, the amount of dividend income is measured by the earnings and profits of *both* the issuing corporation and the purchasing corporation.[78] This deemed dividend is considered as having been paid first

---

[73] § 304.

[74] § 304(a)(1).

[75] § 304(c)(1).

[76] § 304(a)(2).

[77] § 304(b)(1).

[78] § 304(b)(2).

from the E&P of the purchasing (acquiring) corporation to the extent thereof, and then from the E&P of the issuing corporation.

> **Example 31.** Assume the same facts as in *Example 30*. Since the transaction is treated as a dividend, it is considered to come from Y Corporation's E&P first and then, if necessary, from X Corporation's E&P.

EFFECT OF REDEMPTIONS ON REDEEMING CORPORATION

In a stock redemption, the stockholders are concerned with whether the redemption is treated for tax purposes as a sale or as a distribution. The redeeming corporation, however, is concerned with whether or not it has income on the redemption and what effect there is on earnings and profits.

Gain or Loss. The tax effect of redemption distributions on the corporation is identical to that arising from property distributions discussed earlier. As previously explained, the corporation must recognize gain—but not loss—on the distribution of property.[79]

Effect of Redemption on E&P. The E&P of a corporation must be adjusted to reflect any redemption distributions. First, if the corporation must recognize gain on the distribution under § 311, E&P must be increased for the gain. The amount of the reduction of E&P on account of the distribution depends on whether the distribution qualifies for sale treatment. If the distribution does not qualify for sale treatment but rather is treated as a dividend, the rules discussed earlier for cash and property dividends must be followed. If the redemption qualifies for sale treatment, only a portion of the distribution is charged against E&P. In such case, E&P is reduced by the redeemed stock's proportionate share of E&P but not by more than the amount of the redemption distribution.[80]

> **Example 32.** B Corporation had the following capital accounts on January 2:
>
> | | |
> |---|---:|
> | Common stock............................... | $100,000 |
> | Paid-in capital in excess of par .... | 300,000 |
> | Earnings and profits............................ | 500,000 |
>
> The common stock outstanding consisted of 1,000 shares of $100 par value stock. On January 2, B Corporation redeemed 100 shares for $700 per share (a total of $70,000). The corporation therefore redeemed 10% of its stock (100 ÷ 1,000). Of the $70,000 paid for the shares, B Corporation must charge $50,000 to its earnings and profits (10% × $500,000). The remaining $20,000 is charged to the capital accounts [$10,000 to common stock (10% × $100,000) and the remaining $10,000 to paid-in capital in excess of par].
>
> **Note:** This example assumes that this redemption meets the requirements for sale or exchange treatment.

---

[79] § 311.

[80] § 312(n)(7).

COMPLETE LIQUIDATIONS

INTRODUCTION

As discussed earlier in the chapter, in a partial liquidation or stock redemption the corporation redeems only a portion of its stock. In these situations, the corporation continues to operate all or part of its business. In other situations, however, a corporation may wish to terminate its existence by liquidating completely. A complete liquidation of a corporation occurs when, under a plan of complete liquidation, the corporation redeems *all* of its stock using a series of distributions.[81] In addition, the corporation must be in a status of liquidation throughout the life of the liquidation. The Regulations state that a status of liquidation exists when a corporation ceases to be a going concern and is engaged in activities whose sole function is the winding up of the business affairs.[82] There is one set of rules that governs most liquidations and one special set of rules that governs liquidations of a subsidiary.

COMPLETE LIQUIDATIONS: THE GENERAL RULES

Shareholder Gain or Loss. When a shareholder receives a liquidating distribution, the treatment of the shareholder—except where a parent liquidates a subsidiary—is governed solely by Code § 331. This rule provides that shareholders treat property received in liquidation of a corporation as full payment for their stock. Therefore, the shareholder must recognize gain or loss equal to the difference between the *net* fair market value of the property received (fair market value of the assets received less any liabilities assumed by the shareholder) and the basis of the stock surrendered. Special rules must be followed where a shareholder receives an installment note arising from a sale by the corporation within the 12-month period after the corporation has adopted a plan of liquidation.[83] If the stock was purchased at different times and for different amounts, the gain or loss is computed on each separate lot. The gain or loss normally is capital gain or loss since the shareholder's stock is usually a capital asset.

Basis to Shareholder. When a shareholder uses the general rule of § 331 to determine gain or loss on the liquidation, the shareholder's basis in the property received in the liquidation is its fair market value on the date of distribution.[84]

Example 33. K owned 100 shares of stock in L Corporation. K's adjusted basis in the stock was $400. L Corporation completely liquidated and distributed to K $200 cash and office equipment worth $700 in exchange for his stock. K's recognized gain is computed as follows:

Cash received by K	$200
Fair market value of property distributed to K	700
Amount realized	$900
Less: K's adjusted basis in his stock	(400)
Realized gain	$500

---

[81] § 346(a).

[82] Reg. § 1.332-2(c).

[83] § 453(h).

[84] § 334(a).

K's entire realized gain of $500 is recognized under § 1001(c). K's basis in the cash received is, of course, $200. K's basis in the office equipment received is $700, its fair market value on the date of distribution.

Gain or Loss to the Liquidating Corporation. A corporation generally must recognize gain *and* loss on the distribution of property as part of a complete liquidation.[85] The gain or loss is computed as if such property were sold to the shareholder for its fair market value.

> **Example 34.** Sleepwaves Corporation, a waterbed retailer, fell on hard times and decided to dissolve the business. During the year, the corporation adopted a plan of liquidation and completely liquidated. The furniture that the corporation was unable to move in their going-out-of-business sale was distributed to its sole shareholder. This inventory was worth $5,000 (basis $1,000). In addition, the corporation distributed land held for investment worth $8,000 (basis $10,000). The corporation must recognize $4,000 of ordinary income ($5,000 − $1,000) on the distribution of the inventory and a $2,000 capital loss ($8,000 − $10,000) on the distribution of the land.

If the shareholder assumes a corporate liability or takes the property subject to a liability, the fair market value of the property is treated as being no less than the liability.[86] Therefore, where the liability exceeds the value of the property, gain must be recognized to the extent the liability exceeds the basis of the property.

> **Example 35.** T Corporation's only asset is a building with a basis of $100,000 and which is subject to a liability of $400,000. The low basis is attributable to accelerated depreciation. The property is currently worth $250,000. During 2005, T distributed the land to its sole shareholder, R. T Corporation must recognize a gain of $300,000 ($400,000 liability − $100,000 basis). Had the liability been $200,000, T would have ignored the liability and recognized a gain of $150,000 ($250,000 value − $100,000 basis).

The treatment of distributions in liquidation differs from that of nonliquidating distributions in that the corporation is normally allowed to recognize loss on a liquidating distribution. This is not true for all liquidating distributions, however. As with nonliquidating distributions, Congress was concerned that taxpayers might use the loss recognition privilege to circumvent the gain recognition rule. To prohibit possible abuse, § 336(d) provides two exceptions concerning the treatment of losses.

The first exception prohibits the deduction of the loss if certain conditions are satisfied. Section 336(d)(1) provides that the liquidating corporation cannot recognize any loss on the distribution of property to a *related party* if the distribution is either (1) non-pro rata or (2) the property was acquired by the corporation during the five-year period prior to the distribution, either in a nontaxable transfer under § 351 (relating to transfers to a controlled corporation) or as a contribution to capital. For this purpose, a related party is the same as that defined in Code § 267 (e.g., an individual who owns either directly or constructively more than 50 percent of the distributing corporation).

> **Example 36.** J is the sole shareholder of Z Corporation. In anticipation of the corporation's liquidation, J contributed a dilapidated warehouse to the corporation, with a built-in loss of $100,000 (value $200,000, basis $300,000). Shortly thereafter, Z Corporation distributed the warehouse along with land worth $90,000 (basis

---

[85] § 336.

[86] § 336(b).

$20,000). Absent the special rule, the corporation would recognize a loss of $100,000, which would offset the $70,000 gain on the land that it must recognize ($90,000 − $20,000). Under the exception, however, no loss is recognized since the distribution is to a related party, J, and the property was acquired as a contribution to capital within five years of the liquidation.

The second provision concerning losses limits the amount of loss that can be deducted—assuming the loss is not disallowed entirely under the related-party rule above. Under § 336(d)(2), the amount of loss recognized by a liquidating corporation on the sale, exchange, or distribution of any property acquired in a § 351 transaction or as a contribution of capital is reduced. This rule applies only if the principal purpose for the acquisition was the recognition of a loss by the corporation in connection with the liquidation. It is generally presumed that any property acquired in the above manner during the period starting two years prior to the date on which a plan of liquidation is adopted was acquired for the purpose of recognizing a loss. When the tax-avoidance motive is found, the rule effectively limits the loss deduction to the decline in value that occurs while the property is in the hands of the corporation. In other words, any built-in loss existing at the time of contribution is not deductible. To ensure that any built-in loss is not deducted, the Code provides a special computation. For purposes of determining the *loss* on the disposition of the tainted property, the basis of such property is reduced (but not below zero) by the amount of the built-in loss (i.e., the excess of the property's basis over its value at the time the corporation acquired it). By reducing the basis, any subsequent loss recognized is reduced.

> **Example 37.** R, S, T, and U own the stock of Q Corporation. Knowing that the corporation planned to liquidate, R contributed land to the corporation with a built-in loss of $100,000 (value $200,000, basis $300,000) in exchange for shares of Q stock that qualified for nonrecognition under § 351. During the liquidation, the corporation sold the property for $160,000. Under the general rule, the corporation would recognize a loss of $140,000 ($160,000 amount realized − $300,000 carryover basis). However, since the property was acquired in a § 351 exchange and the principal purpose of the transaction was to recognize loss on the property in liquidation, the special rule applies. The loss recognized is limited to that which occurred in the hands of the corporation $40,000 ($200,000 value at contribution − $160,000 amount realized). In other words, the loss computed in the normal manner, $140,000, must be reduced by the built-in loss of $100,000. Technically, Q Corporation would compute the loss by reducing its basis in the property by the amount of built-in loss as follows:

Amount realized.			$ 160,000
Adjusted basis:			
Carryover basis.		$ 300,000	
− Basis reduction:			
Carryover basis	$300,000		
− Value at contribution	−200,000		
Built-in loss		−100,000	
Adjusted basis			(200,000)
Loss recognized.			($ 40,000)

LIQUIDATION OF A SUBSIDIARY

A parent corporation generally recognizes no gain or loss on property it receives from the liquidation of a subsidiary corporation.[87] In order to qualify to use this provision (Code § 332), the parent corporation must own at least 80 percent of the voting power and this stock must have a value at least equal to 80 percent of the total value of the subsidiary corporation's stock.[88] For purposes of these computations, nonvoting preferred stock is excluded.[89] This minimum amount of stock must be owned on the date of adoption of the plan of liquidation and at all times thereafter until the liquidation is completed. All of the property of the subsidiary must be distributed in complete cancellation of the subsidiary's stock within three years following the close of the tax year in which the first distribution takes place.[90] It also is important to note that Code § 332 is not elective. If the above conditions are met, no gain or loss is recognized.

Effect on Subsidiary. Under § 337, a subsidiary recognizes no gain or loss on the distribution of its assets to its parent in a liquidation under § 332.[91] This rule only applies to property transferred to the parent corporation in the liquidation. Property transferred to minority shareholders will result in the recognition of gain but not loss.[92]

Ordinarily, when one taxpayer is indebted to another and the debt is canceled, the indebted taxpayer has income to the extent of the debt due to the relief of the indebtedness. Section 337(b) contains an exception to this general rule. The exception states that when a subsidiary corporation is indebted to its parent corporation and the subsidiary liquidates under § 332, no gain or loss is recognized when the subsidiary transfers property to the parent to satisfy the debt.

Basis of Assets—General Rule. When a subsidiary is liquidated by its parent corporation, the basis of the assets transferred from the subsidiary to the parent must be determined. Generally, the basis of each of the assets transferred is the same for the parent corporation as it had been for the subsidiary.[93] This rule applies not only to property transferred in cancellation of the subsidiary's stock, but also to property transferred in order to satisfy the subsidiary's debt to the parent.[94] The amount of the parent's investment in the subsidiary's stock is ignored. The parent's basis is determined solely by the subsidiary's basis.

Example 38. T Corporation had assets with a basis of $1 million and no liabilities. P Corporation bought all of the stock of T Corporation for $1.2 million. Several years later, when T Corporation's assets had a basis of $800,000, P Corporation liquidated T Corporation in a tax-free liquidation under § 332. P Corporation's basis in the assets received from T Corporation is $800,000, the same basis as T Corporation had in the assets. The $400,000 difference between the basis of the assets and P Corporation's basis in the stock of T Corporation is lost.

---

[87] § 332.

[88] §§ 332(b)(1) and 1504(a)(2).

[89] § 1504(a)(4).

[90] § 332(b)(3).

[91] § 337(a).

[92] §§ 337(a) and 336(d)(3).

[93] § 334(b)(1).

[94] §§ 337(b)(1) and 334(b)(1).

Example 39. Assume the same facts as in *Example 38* except that P Corporation had paid $700,000 (instead of $1,200,000) for T Corporation's stock. P Corporation's basis in the assets received from T Corporation is still $800,000, the same as T Corporation's basis in the assets. In this example, rather than losing a $400,000 investment, P Corporation received a $100,000 tax-free increase in its basis in T Corporation and its assets ($800,000 basis in T Corporation's assets − $700,000 basis that P Corporation had in T Corporation's stock).

As demonstrated above, this carryover of the basis of assets from a subsidiary to its parent can be either beneficial (*Example 39*) or detrimental (*Example 38*) to the parent corporation.

Basis of Assets—Exception. The carryover basis rule was challenged in the case of *Kimbell-Diamond Milling Co. v. Commissioner:*[95] In this case, Kimbell-Diamond's plant was destroyed by fire. The corporation wished to purchase replacement property to avoid recognizing gain on the involuntary conversion. The only plant that they wanted was owned by a corporation that would not sell. To acquire the asset, Kimbell-Diamond purchased the corporation's stock and then liquidated the corporation. Kimbell-Diamond used the basis of the assets of the liquidated corporation as its basis for the assets. The amount that Kimbell-Diamond paid for the stock of the corporation was *much less* than the liquidated corporation's basis in the assets, so that by using the carryover basis, Kimbell-Diamond received much larger depreciation deductions (and therefore had much smaller taxable income) than if it had actually purchased the plant. Upon review, however, the IRS reclassified the transaction as a purchase of assets, rather than a purchase of stock followed by a separate liquidation. The Tax Court agreed with the IRS that the two transactions should be treated as one. This decision created the *Kimbell-Diamond* exception. Under this exception, if the original purpose of the stock acquisition was to acquire assets, the purchaser's basis in the assets acquired was the cost of the stock rather than the liquidated corporation's basis.

Congress incorporated the Kimbell-Diamond exception into the Internal Revenue Code,[96] effectively allowing an acquiring corporation such as Kimbell-Diamond to select the basis to be used for the subsidiary's assets: either a basis equal to the purchase price of the assets or the same basis as that of the subsidiary. As might be expected, many acquiring corporations attempted to take advantage of this latitude provided by the Code. Consequently, to curb potential abuses, Congress enacted § 338 in 1982. Although § 338 is still a codification of the *Kimbell-Diamond* exception, its requirements are much more specific than the previous law.

Code § 338—Purchase of Assets. To qualify for a purchase price basis offered under § 338, the parent corporation must purchase stock having at least 80 percent of the voting power and at least 80 percent of the value of all stock (except nonvoting, nonparticipating, preferred stock).[97] To qualify as a purchase, the stock may not be acquired from a related party, in a transaction that qualifies under Code § 351, or in any transaction that will result in the purchaser using a carryover basis.[98] This acquisition of control may occur in a series of transactions; however, no more than 12 months may elapse between the first purchase and the acquisition of the required 80 percent control.[99]

---

[95] 14 T.C. 74 (1950), aff'd., 51-1 USTC ¶9301, 40 AFTR 328, 187 F2d 718 (CA-5, 1951).

[96] The Kimbell-Diamond exception was formerly § 334(b)(2).

[97] § 338(d)(3).

[98] § 338(h)(3).

[99] § 338(d) and (h).

If the parent corporation meets the purchase requirement, it must elect to treat the acquisition as an asset purchase by the 15th day of the ninth month following the month of acquisition.[100] The election, once made, is irrevocable. Failure to make the election results in the parent being treated as having purchased stock and thus prohibits the subsidiary from adjusting the basis of its assets. After the election, the subsidiary generally increases or decreases the basis of its assets to their fair market value.

Code § 338 does not require a liquidation. As a result, both the parent and the subsidiary may continue to exist. Section 338 takes a *two-step* approach to achieve the basis step-up. First, the subsidiary is treated as having sold in a single transaction all of its assets at fair market value on the close of the acquisition date. Any gain or loss realized on this hypothetical sale must be recognized *and* reported on the subsidiary's final tax return. Second, the subsidiary is treated as a new corporation that is deemed to have purchased all of the assets of the old subsidiary (i.e., the acquired or target corporation) on the day after the date the parent obtained the necessary control. For purposes of determining the subsidiary's new basis in its assets, the deemed purchase price is generally equal to the price the parent corporation paid for the subsidiary's stock adjusted for ownership less than 100 percent (i.e., the portion not owned by the parent) as well as liabilities of the subsidiary and other relevant items.[101] Note that in increasing the purchase price of the stock for liabilities of the subsidiary, such liabilities include the tax liability attributable to income arising from the deemed sale.

> **Example 40.** During 2005 P Corporation purchased all of the stock of T Corporation for $1 million. T's only asset is land with a basis of $200,000. It had no liabilities. Assuming P makes the appropriate election under § 338, T is deemed to have sold its assets, in this case the land, for its fair market value, $1 million. Thus, T must recognize a gain of $800,000 ($1,000,000 − $200,000). The tax liability arising from the deemed sale is $272,000 ($800,000 × 34%). After the hypothetical sale and repurchase, P's basis in the land is $1,272,000, its purchase price of the stock ($1 million) increased by the liability arising on the deemed sale of $272,000. Note that P, as the new owner of T, bears the economic burden of the tax liability. Consequently, assuming the value of the land is truly $1 million, P would no doubt desire to reduce the purchase price of the stock by the liability that arises with a § 338 election; that is, it probably would try to buy the stock for $728,000 ($1,000,000 − $272,000). If P did buy the stock for $728,000, presumably the gain on the deemed sale would still be $800,000, since the land is considered sold for its value of $1 million. In such case, the tax liability would still be $272,000 and the basis of the land under § 338 would be $1 million ($728,000 purchase price of the stock + $272,000 tax liability). Note that the effect of these rules is to reduce the value of the target subsidiary by an amount equal to the tax liability that would arise if § 338 is elected.

Under § 338, the subsidiary is considered to have purchased all of its assets from itself at the deemed price. The subsidiary must increase or decrease the basis of its assets so that its new basis in its assets equals the deemed purchase price. The method of allocating the basis among the assets is outlined by the Regulations.[102]

Allocation of Deemed Purchase Price. The temporary regulations under Code § 338 provide that the deemed purchase price of the stock is to be allocated to the

---

[100] § 338(g).

[101] § 338(a). § 338(b) provides that the basis is the sum of the grossed-up basis of stock purchased during the 12-month acquisition and the basis of stock not purchased during the period, adjusted as necessary.

[102] § 338(b)(3).

subsidiary's assets using the "residual value" approach.[103] Under this technique, assets must be grouped into seven classes for purposes of making the allocation:

1. *Class I:* Cash, demand deposits, and other cash equivalents
2. *Class II:* Certificates of deposit, U.S. government securities, readily marketable securities, and other similar items
3. *Class III:* Accounts receivable;
4. *Class IV:* Inventory;
5. *Class V:* All assets other than those in Classes I, II, III, or IV, such as accounts receivable, inventory, plant, property, and equipment
6. *Class VI:* Section 197 intangibles other than goodwill or going concern value
7. *Class VII:* Intangible assets in the nature of goodwill and going-concern value

According to the system, the purchase price is first allocated to Class I assets in proportion to their relative fair market values as determined on the date following the acquisition. Because Class I assets are either cash or cash equivalents, the basis assigned to them is their face value. Once this allocation is made, any excess of the purchase price over the amount allocated to Class I assets is allocated to Class II assets, again based on relative fair market values. Any excess purchase price remaining after making the allocation to Class II assets is allocated to Class III assets based on relative values. Then amounts are allocated to Classes IV, V and VI in order. Any excess of purchase price over amounts allocated to Classes I, II, III, IV, V and VI is allocated to Class VII assets based on relative fair market values. In allocating such excess to Class II through Class VI assets, the amount allocated *cannot exceed the fair market value* of the asset. Thus, any purchase price which remains after the allocation to Class I, II, III, IV, V and VI assets is assigned to Class VII assets—hence the reason for calling this method the *residual* value approach. By limiting the allocation to Class I, II, III, and IV, V and VI assets to the assets' fair market values, the rules generally seek to ensure that corporate taxpayers allocate the proper amount to goodwill.

For the purpose of these allocation rules, the temporary regulations provide that the fair market value of the asset is its gross value computed without regard to any mortgages, liens, or other liabilities related to the property. These rules are illustrated in the following example.

Example 41. P Corporation purchases from an unrelated person 100% of the stock of T Corporation on June 1, 2005. Assume the purchase price adjusted for all relevant items is $100,000. T's assets at acquisition date are as follows:

	Basis	Fair Market Value
Cash	$10,000	$10,000
Accounts receivable.	20,000	20,000
Inventory	25,000	55,000
Total	$55,000	$85,000

The purchase price is first allocated to cash in the amount of $10,000. This leaves $90,000 to be allocated. Since there are no Class II assets, the allocation is to Class III. Thus $20,000 is allocated to the accounts receivable. If the residual approach was not required, the taxpayer might allocate all of the remaining $70,000 to the inventory, despite the fact that its value is only $55,000. If this were allowed,

---

[103] Temp. Reg. § 1.338-6T.

the subsequent sale of the inventory would result in a loss. However, since the remaining purchase price ($70,000) exceeds the fair market value of the Class IV assets, the basis of the assets in this class is their fair market value, $55,000 for the inventory. This leaves $15,000 of the purchase price which has not been allocated. It is all assigned to goodwill since there are no Class VII intangibles.

If the parent corporation owns less than 100 percent of the subsidiary, the deemed price must be "grossed up" to take into account the minority interest. The adjustment for a minority interest results in a deemed purchase price called the "grossed-up basis." This grossed-up basis is obtained by multiplying the actual purchase price of the stock by a ratio, the numerator being 100 percent and the denominator equal to the percentage of the subsidiary stock owned by the parent.[104] This computation can be expressed as follows:

$$\text{Grossed-up basis} = \frac{\text{Parent corporation's basis in the subsidiary's stock on the acquisition date}}{1} \times \frac{100\%}{\text{Percentage of subsidiary's stock held by parent on the acquisition date}}$$

Example 42. P Corporation purchased 90% of the outstanding stock of T Corporation for $900,000. T Corporation had only one asset, land with a basis of $900,000. Assume there are no liabilities or other relevant items that affect the deemed purchase price. Since P owns less than 100% of T, a grossed-up basis must be calculated. The result is $1 million [$900,000 purchase price × (100 ÷ 90, the percentage of T owned by P)]. If P elects § 338, T's basis for the land is $1 million. Note, however, that it is likely that the Regulations require the deemed sales price to be increased by any liabilities of the subsidiary. In such case, the deemed purchase price here would include the tax liability resulting from the fact that P purchased less than 100% of the stock, which in turn causes T to recognize income.

Section 338 not only entitles the subsidiary to a stepped-up basis for its assets, it also treats the subsidiary as a new corporation in every respect. As a result, the subsidiary may adopt any tax year it chooses, unless it files a consolidated return with the parent corporation, in which case it must adopt the parent's tax year. It may adopt new accounting methods if it desires. MACRS depreciation may be used for all of the hypothetically purchased property—the antichurning rules being inapplicable since the old and new subsidiary are considered unrelated. The new subsidiary acquires none of the other attributes of the old subsidiary. The earnings and profits of the old subsidiary are eliminated and any net operating loss carryovers of the old subsidiary are unavailable to the new subsidiary.

In most situations, the target subsidiary has some assets that have appreciated in value (i.e., fair market value exceeds the asset's basis) and other assets where the value is less than the asset's basis. In such cases the acquiring corporation, desiring the highest possible basis for the assets, might first purchase the appreciated property, then purchase the subsidiary's stock and liquidate the subsidiary under § 332. By so doing, the acquiring corporation would obtain the best of both worlds: a basis for the appreciated property equal to its fair market value and a carryover basis for the other assets. In the latter case, the basis is higher than it would have been had the assets themselves been purchased or the stock purchased followed by an election under § 338. To prohibit the acquiring corporation from effectively selecting the basis that is most desirable for each separate asset, the Code contains the so-called consistency provisions. According to these rules, an acquiring corporation is required to use a carryover basis for purchased assets unless a § 338 election is made for the acquired corporation. The consistency

---

[104] § 338(b)(2). This approach is modified when the parent holds stock not acquired during the 12-month period.

period begins one year before the date of the first acquisition that comes within § 338 and ends one year after the acquisition date (i.e., the date on which the corporation obtains 80 percent control).

> **Example 43.** P Inc. purchased 60% of T Corporation's stock on March 7, 2005 and the remaining 40% on December 4, 2005. The consistency period runs from March 7, 2004 through December 4, 2006. If P acquires any assets of T during this period, it will be required to use carryover basis unless a § 338 election is made.

As mentioned above, § 338 is an elective provision. If the election is not made and the subsidiary is liquidated, § 332, the general rule for the nontaxable liquidation of a subsidiary, applies. If § 332 is used, the parent corporation carries over the subsidiary's basis for its assets, whereas under § 338 the basis of the assets is their deemed purchase price (based upon the parent corporation's investment in the subsidiary).

PROBLEM MATERIALS

DISCUSSION QUESTIONS

20-1 *Dividends.* Define the term *dividend*.

20-2 *Earnings and Profits.* What are "earnings and profits"? Are earnings and profits the same as "retained earnings"? Why or why not?

20-3 *Earnings and Profits.* In addition to taxable income, what types of items affect earnings and profits?

20-4 *Earnings and Profits.* How does the use of an accelerated method of depreciation affect a corporation's earnings and profits?

20-5 *Earnings and Profits.* How does the § 179 immediate expensing option affect a corporation's earnings and profits?

20-6 *Distributions.* Is it possible for a distribution to be a taxable dividend even if there is a deficit in accumulated earnings and profits? If so, how?

20-7 *Cash Dividends.* What is the amount of distribution when cash is distributed?

20-8 *Property Dividends.* What is the amount of the distribution when property other than cash is distributed?

20-9 *Property Dividends and Liabilities.* What effect does a liability have on the amount and basis of property distributed if the property is subject to the liability?

20-10 *Constructive Dividends.* What are constructive dividends? When do they arise?

20-11 *Effect of Property Dividend on the Corporation.* In what situations must a corporation recognize income as a result of a distribution?

20-12 *Effect of Property Dividends on Earnings and Profits.* How do property dividends affect earnings and profits?

20-13 *Stock Dividends.* What is a stock dividend?

20-14 *Stock Dividends.* In what situations may a stock dividend be taxable? When is it not taxable?

20-15 *Stock Dividends.* How is the shareholder's basis in a stock dividend determined?

20-16 *Stock Dividends.* How do stock dividends affect earnings and profits?

20-17 *Stock Rights.* What are stock rights? How does their tax treatment differ from stock dividends?

20-18 *Dividends.* What is the effect of a dividend on the distributing corporation's taxable income?

20-19 *Stock Redemptions.* What is a stock redemption?

20-20 *Stock Redemptions.* List the situations in which a stock redemption will be treated as a sale of stock.

20-21 *Constructive Ownership.* What is constructive ownership of stock? How may stock be constructively owned?

20-22 *Effect of Redemption on Redeeming Corporation.* How do stock redemptions affect the redeeming corporation? In what situations must gain or loss be recognized when stock is redeemed? How do stock redemptions affect earnings and profits?

20-23 *Complete Liquidations.* What is a complete liquidation?

20-24 *Code § 331.* Generally explain the treatment of the shareholders in a complete liquidation.

20-25 *Code § 336.* Generally explain the treatment of the liquidating corporation in a complete liquidation.

20-26 *Liquidation of a Subsidiary.* What conditions must be met in order for § 332 to apply to the liquidation of a subsidiary?

20-27 *Liquidation of a Subsidiary—Basis.* What is the general rule for determining the parent corporation's basis in the assets received from its liquidated subsidiary?

20-28 *Kimbell-Diamond Exception.* What is the *Kimbell-Diamond* exception?

20-29 *Code § 338—Purchase of Assets.* When does § 338 apply to the liquidation of a subsidiary? How does it differ from the general rule for determining basis in the liquidation of a subsidiary?

PROBLEMS

20-30 *Dividends.* A's basis in his 50 shares of Q Corporation stock is $3,000. A purchased the Q Corporation stock in 1999. On November 11, 2005 Q Corporation distributed $8,000 to A with respect to the Q Corporation stock. The portion of Q Corporation's earnings and profits allocable to A is $3,500. What is the tax treatment of the $8,000 distribution to A?

20-31 *Earnings and Profits.* D Corporation's taxable income for the year was computed as follows:

Gross income from operations.		$1,000,000
Less: Operating expenses		(900,000)
Net income from operations.		$100,000
Dividend income		20,000
Long-term capital gain	$15,000	

Less: Capital loss carryover	(7,000)	8,000

Income before special deductions		$ 128,000
Net operating loss carryover	$ 9,000	
Dividends-received deduction	16,000	
Total of special deductions		(25,000)
Taxable income.		$ 103,000

Additional information:

1. The corporation received $5,000 in tax-exempt interest income.
2. Included in operating expenses is depreciation of $130,000. Straight-line depreciation of the depreciable assets would have been $50,000.

Compute the earnings and profits of D Corporation for the current year.

20-32 *Earnings and Profits.* V Corporation's taxable income for the year included the following items:

1. A $12,000 charitable contributions deduction. Actual charitable contributions made by V Corporation were $20,000, but only $12,000 was deductible this year due to the 10 percent charitable contributions limitation.
2. An 80 percent dividends-received deduction of $8,000. The amount of dividend income received by V Corporation was $10,000.
3. Percentage depletion of $4,000 was deducted by V Corporation. Cost depletion would have been $800.
4. $2,000 of assets purchased by V Corporation this year were expensed using the § 179 immediate expensing option.
5. MACRS depreciation of $1,500 was taken on a new heavy-duty truck (five-year property) purchased this year. The cost of the automobile was $10,000.

Compute the effect of the above items on V Corporation's current earnings and profits.

20-33 *Distributions.* For each of the following independent situations, compute the amount of dividend income to the shareholder as a result of the distribution(s), and specify the source of each distribution (current and/or accumulated earnings and profits).

Distributions

	April 1	October 1	Current E&P	Accumulated E&P
a.	$5,000	$5,000	$ 15,000	$ 10,000
b.	9,000	9,000	15,000	10,000
c.	2,000	4,000	7,000	(20,000)
d.	6,000	2,000	0	11,000
e.	3,000	5,000	(12,000)	30,000
f.	3,000	2,000	1,000	0
g.	1,000	3,000	(6,000)	8,000

20-34 *Cash and Property Dividends.* A Corporation is owned by J (an individual) and B Corporation. A Corporation declared and paid the following dividends: $10,000 cash and a printing press with a fair market value of $10,000 and an adjusted basis of $6,000. A Corporation's current and accumulated earnings and profits exceed $20,000. Consider each alternative independently.

a. If B Corporation received the cash and J received the printing press, how much dividend income would each report?

b. If J received the cash and B Corporation received the printing press, how much dividend income would each report?

    c.   What are the tax consequences to A Corporation of the distribution?

    d.   What is the effect of the distribution on corporate earnings and profits?

20-35   *Property Dividends—Installment Obligations.* G Corporation distributed installment notes with a face value of $20,000 to its shareholders. The gross profit percentage of the notes was 20 percent, and the fair market value of the notes was $18,000 when they were distributed. Compute G Corporation's recognized gain on the distribution of the installment notes.

20-36   *Stock Dividends.* P owns 100 shares of Z Corporation common stock, which she purchased in 1997 for $50 a share. Z Corporation declared and paid a 100 percent stock dividend to all common stockholders. At the date of record, the selling price of a share of common stock was $200. Immediately following the distribution, the stock was selling for $225 per share.

    a.   How much income must P recognize on the receipt of the 100 shares of common stock as a dividend?

    b.   What is the basis of the dividend shares?

    c.   Assume that P received the dividend on June 1 and sold 50 shares of stock (25 new and 25 old) on July 1 for $150 per share. What is P's recognized gain or loss? Is it long-term or short-term?

20-37   *Stock Dividends.* R owns 50 shares of A Corporation common stock, which he purchased in 2001 for $100 per share. On January 1 of the current year, A Corporation declared a dividend of one share of new preferred stock for each share of common. The shares were distributed on March 1. On that date, the common stock was selling for $150 per share and the preferred stock had a value of $50 per share.

    a.   How much income must R recognize on the receipt of the preferred stock?

    b.   What is R's basis in the preferred stock?

    c.   On June 1, R sells 25 shares of common stock for $175 per share and 25 shares of preferred stock for $75 per share. What is R's recognized gain or loss? Is it long-term or short-term?

20-38   *Stock Dividends.* N owns 200 shares of M Corporation preferred stock. She purchased the stock for $200 per share in 2003. On February 1 of the current year, the corporation declared and paid a 50 percent stock dividend. At date of declaration, the preferred stock was selling for $220 per share. Immediately following the distribution (June 1), the preferred stock was selling for $150 per share.

    a.   How much income will N have as a result of the dividend?

    b.   What is her basis of the dividend shares?

    c.   If N sells 25 shares of the old and 25 shares of the new for $180 per share on August 1, what is her recognized gain or loss? Is it long-term or short-term?

20-39   *Stock Rights.* Y Corporation's profits had taken a deep dive in recent years. To encourage purchase of its stock, the corporation issued one stock right for each share of outstanding common stock. The rights allow the holder to purchase a share of stock for $1. The common stock was selling for $1.50 when the rights were issued (June 1). The value of the stock rights on June 1 were $0.50 each. A owns 1,000 shares of common stock for which he paid $20 per share 10 years ago, and therefore received 1,000 stock rights. A sold 100 rights on July 1 for $175. He exercised 100 rights on August 1 when the stock was selling for $1.80 per share. The remaining rights lapsed on December 30.

    a.   How much dividend income must A recognize?

    b.   How much gain or loss must A recognize on the July 1 sale of the stock rights? Is it long-term or short-term?

    c.   What is A's recognized loss when the remaining rights lapse?

    d.   What is the basis of the original 1,000 shares on December 31?

20-40   *Stock Redemptions.* B owned 100 shares (100%) of the common stock of C Corporation. C Corporation has no other classes of stock outstanding. B's basis in his 100 shares was $3,000 ($30 per share). C Corporation redeemed 20 of B's shares for $1,000.

  a.   What is B's recognized gain or loss on the redemption? What is the character of B's recognized gain or loss?

  b.   What is B's basis in his remaining shares of C Corporation stock?

20-41   *Stock Redemptions.* W has owned 500 shares of X Corporation's 1,000 outstanding shares of voting common stock since 1997. X Corporation has no other classes of stock outstanding. W's basis in her 500 shares was $1,500 ($3 per share). X Corporation redeemed 200 shares of W's stock for $800.

  a.   Is this redemption treated as a sale or a distribution?

  b.   What is W's recognized gain or loss on the redemption? What is the character of W's recognized gain or loss?

  c.   What is the basis of W's remaining shares after the redemption?

20-42   *Stock Redemptions.* Assume the same facts as in *Problem 20-41* except that X Corporation redeemed 100 shares of W's stock instead of 200 shares. Answer the above questions a, b, and c for this situation.

20-43   *Stock Redemptions.* T Corporation is owned by the following unrelated individuals:

K	60 shares
L.	20 shares
M	10 shares
N	10 shares
Total	100 shares

If T Corporation redeems 30 shares owned by K, will the transaction qualify as a sale? Why or why not?

20-44   *Stock Redemptions—Constructive Ownership.* Use the same facts as in Problem 20-43. Would this redemption qualify as a sale if L is K's son? Why or why not?

20-45   *Constructive Ownership of Stock.* Q, an individual, owns 20 percent of A Corporation. Mrs. Q owns 60 percent of A Corporation and 50 percent of BC Partnership. R, Q's daughter, owns 30 percent of BC Partnership and 10 percent of A Corporation. What is Q's ownership (directly and indirectly) in A Corporation and BC Partnership, if the constructive ownership rules of § 318 apply?

20-46   *Constructive Ownership of Stock.* D is a 30 percent partner in DE Partnership. DE Partnership owns 10 percent of F Corporation. Using the § 318 constructive ownership rules, what percentage of F Corporation is D considered to own?

20-47   *Constructive Ownership of Stock.* G owns 200 shares of H Corporation stock. G is a 50 percent partner in GJ Partnership. Using the § 318 constructive ownership rules, how many shares of H Corporation is the GJ Partnership considered to own?

20-48   *Liquidations—General Rule (§§ 331 and 336).* S, an individual, owns all of the stock of B Corporation. S purchased the stock 10 years ago for $300,000. S decided to completely liquidate B Corporation, and all of the assets of B Corporation were distributed to S. The balance sheet for B Corporation immediately prior to the liquidation was as follows:

	Basis	Fair Market Value
Cash	$ 40,000	$ 40,000
Marketable securities (acquired after 1953)....	40,000	80,000
Equipment .... $ 300,000		
Less: Accumulated depreciation.......... (150,000)	150,000	200,000
Land.................................	520,000	880,000
Total assets	$750,000	$1,200,000
Retained earnings	$450,000	$ 0
Common stock........................	300,000	1,200,000
Total equity........................	$750,000	$1,200,000

   a.   What is S's recognized gain or loss?

   b.   What is S's basis in the assets received?

   c.   How much, if any, income or loss will B Corporation recognize as a result of the liquidation?

20-49   *Liquidations (§ 332).* Assume the same facts as in *Problem 20-48* except that the stock is owned by S, Inc.

   a.   How much, if any, gain or loss must S, Inc. recognize?

   b.   What is the basis of the assets received by S, Inc.?

   c.   How much, if any, income must B Corporation recognize as a result of the liquidation?

20-50   *Section 338 Election.* Assume the same facts as in *Problem 20-48* except that all the stock was purchased by Z Corporation during the past 12 months for $1 million. Assume Z makes a § 338 election and pays taxes at a 34 percent rate.

   a.   What is Z's recognized gain or loss?

   b.   What, if any, income must B recognize?

   c.   What is the total basis of the assets to B after the election?

Chapter 21

TAXATION OF CORPORATE ACCUMULATIONS

LEARNING OBJECTIVES

Upon completion of this chapter you will be able to:

- Understand the rationale for the two corporate penalty taxes: the accumulated earnings tax and the personal holding company tax

- Identify the circumstances that must exist before the accumulated earnings tax will apply

- Recognize when earnings have accumulated beyond the reasonable needs of the business

- Explain how the accumulated earnings tax is computed

- Indicate when the personal holding company tax applies

- Apply the stock ownership and income tests to determine if a corporation is a personal holding company

- Explain how the personal holding company tax is computed and how it might be avoided

CHAPTER OUTLINE

INTRODUCTION

In addition to the regular tax, a corporation may be subject to two penalty taxes—the *accumulated earnings tax* and the *personal holding company tax*. As the label "penalty" suggests, the primary goal of these taxes is not to raise revenues but rather to prohibit certain activities. The objective of the accumulated earnings tax and the personal holding company tax is to discourage individual taxpayers from using the corporate entity solely for tax avoidance. These taxes contend with potential abuse by imposing limitations on the amount of earnings a corporation may retain without penalty. The rationale for these taxes is readily apparent when some of the opportunities for tax avoidance using the corporate structure are considered.

Perhaps the best illustration of how the corporate entity could be used to avoid taxes involves the 70 percent dividends-received deduction. As discussed in Chapter 1, this deduction is available only to corporate taxpayers. Nevertheless, individuals could take advantage of the deduction by establishing a corporation and transferring their dividend-paying stocks to it. By so doing, all dividend income would be taxable to the corporation instead of the individual. Using this arrangement, the corporation would pay tax on dividends at an effective rate of 10.5 percent or lower [35% × (100% − 70%)] in 2005. Most individual taxpayers with taxable dividend income would reap substantial tax savings from this arrangement since all individual marginal rates are 15 percent or higher. This is but one of the alluring features of the corporate entity.

Another corporate advantage that individuals previously used to avoid taxes concerned the difference between individual and corporate tax rates. Until the current year, because the highest individual tax rate exceeded the top corporate tax rate, individuals operating a business in the corporate form could benefit by leaving earnings in the corporation and reinvesting at this lower tax rate. The savings obtained by utilizing this disparity, the dividends-received deduction, and other advantages of the corporate entity, illustrate that individuals could achieve wholesale tax avoidance if not for some provision denying or discouraging such plans.

The two penalty taxes were developed to battle avoidance schemes such as those above by attacking their critical component: the accumulation. This can be seen by examining the two previous examples. The fate of both tax savings schemes rests on whether the shareholder can reduce or totally escape the second tax normally incurred when the income is ultimately received. In other words, the success of these arrangements depends on the extent to which double taxation is avoided. Herein lies the role of corporate accumulations. As long as the earnings are retained in the corporation, the second tax is avoided and the taxpayer is well on the way to obtaining tax savings. To foil such schemes, Congress enacted the accumulated earnings tax and the personal holding company tax. Both taxes are imposed on unwarranted accumulations of income—income that normally would have been taxable to the individual at individual tax rates if it had been distributed. By imposing these taxes on unreasonable accumulations, Congress hoped to compel distributions from the corporation and thus prevent taxpayers from using the corporate entity for tax avoidance.

Although these penalty taxes are rarely incurred, each serves as a strong deterrent against possible taxpayer abuse. However, with the reduction in the tax rate on dividends to 15 percent, imposition of these penalties or change in corporate behavior is even less likely. This chapter examines the operation of both the accumulated earnings tax and the personal holding company tax.

Mitigation of the double tax penalty and any resulting tax savings are not achieved solely through corporate accumulations. The effect of double taxation can be reduced or avoided in other ways. The most common method used to avoid double taxation is by making distributions that are deductible. Typical deductible payments include compensation for services rendered to the corporation, rent for property leased to the corporation by the shareholder, and interest on funds loaned to the corporation. All of these payments are normally deductible by the corporation (thus effectively eliminating the corporate tax) and taxable to the shareholder. Avoidance of the double tax penalty does not ensure tax savings, however. All of these payments are taxable to the shareholder; thus, savings through use of the corporate entity may or may not result. For example, savings could occur if the payments are made to shareholders after they have dropped to a tax bracket lower than the one in which they were when the earnings were initially realized by the corporation. In addition, even if the shareholder's tax bracket remains unchanged, deferral of the tax could be beneficial.

> **Example 1.** L operates a home improvement company, specializing in kitchen renovations. He is in the 35% bracket in 2005. Assume that he incorporates his business in 2005 and it earns $100,000, of which $50,000 is paid to him as a salary and $50,000 is accumulated. In 2005 L saves $10,000 [(35% − 15%) × $50,000] in taxes on the $50,000 not distributed. However, if the $50,000 accumulated is distributed to L as a salary in 2010 when he is still in the 35% bracket, the $10,000 of taxes originally saved is lost. Although no taxes have been saved, L continues to benefit because he has been able to postpone the $10,000 in tax for five years. Assuming his after-tax rate of return is 10%, the present value of the $10,000 tax is reduced to $6,209—a savings of $3,791, or almost 38%. Note that the savings would have increased if the distribution had been made to L when his tax bracket dropped below 35%.

ACCUMULATED EARNINGS TAX

The accumulated earnings tax, unlike most taxes previously discussed, is not computed by a corporation when filing its annual income tax return. There is no form to file to determine the tax. Normally, the issue arises during an audit of the corporation. Consequently, the actual tax computation is made only after it has been determined that the penalty must be imposed.

AN OVERVIEW

The accumulated earnings tax applies whenever a corporation is "formed or availed of" for what is generally referred to as the *forbidden purpose*, that is, "for the purpose of avoiding the income tax with respect to its shareholders ... by permitting earnings and profits to accumulate instead of being ... distributed."[1] Whether a corporation is in fact being used for the forbidden purpose and thus subject to penalty is an elusive question requiring a determination of the taxpayer's *intent*. Without guidance from the law, ascertaining the taxpayer's intent might prove impossible. However, the Code states that the required intent is deemed present whenever a corporation accumulates earnings beyond its reasonable needs unless the corporation can prove to the contrary by a preponderance of evidence.[2] The problems concerning intent are considered in detail below.

Not all corporations risk the accumulated earnings tax. The Code specifically exempts tax-exempt corporations, personal holding companies, and passive foreign investment companies.[3] In addition, the tax normally does not apply to an S corporation since it does not shield shareholders from tax. An S corporation's earnings are taxed to its shareholders annually.

---

[1]   § 532(a).

[2]   § 533(a).

[3]   § 532.

If it applies, the accumulated earnings tax is imposed on the annual increment to the corporation's total accumulated earnings, not on the total accumulated earnings balance. This annual addition is referred to as *accumulated taxable income*. The tax is 15 percent of the corporation's accumulated taxable income.[4] This tax does not replace any other taxes (e.g., the corporate income tax or the alternative minimum tax) but is imposed in addition to these taxes.

> **Example 2.** In an audit of P Corporation, it was determined that the company had accumulated earnings beyond the reasonable needs of its business. In addition, the corporation's accumulated taxable income was $150,000. Since evidence of the forbidden purpose is present and the corporation has accumulated taxable income, the accumulated earnings tax must be paid. P Corporation's accumulated earnings tax is $22,500 ($150,000 × 15%).

In short, the corporation actually pays the accumulated earnings tax only if the forbidden purpose is found and it has accumulated taxable income. The following sections examine the determination of the taxpayer's intent and the computation of accumulated taxable income.

INTENT

The accumulated earnings tax is imposed only if the corporation is formed or used for the purpose of avoiding income tax on its shareholders by accumulating earnings.[5] Unfortunately, the Code provides no objective, mechanical test for determining whether a corporation is in fact being used for the forbidden purpose. As a result, application of the accumulated earnings tax rests on a subjective assessment of the shareholders' intent. The Code and regulations offer certain guidelines for making this assessment. Section 533 provides that a corporation is deemed to have been formed or used for the purpose of avoiding tax on its shareholders in two situations:

1. If the corporation has accumulated earnings beyond the reasonable needs of the business; or

2. If the corporation is a mere holding or investment company.

The first situation is the most common cause of an accumulated earnings tax penalty. Consequently, avoidance of the accumulated earnings tax normally rests on whether the corporation can prove that its balance (i.e., the amount in excess of the $250,000 or $150,000 threshold) in accumulated earnings and profits is required by the reasonable needs of the business. Before discussing what constitutes a "reasonable need" of the business, it should be noted that other circumstances may indicate that the forbidden purpose does or does not exist.

According to the Regulations, the following factors are to be considered in determining whether the corporation has been used to avoid tax:[6]

1. Loans to shareholders or expenditures that benefit shareholders personally;

2. Investments in assets having no reasonable connection with the corporation's business; and

3. Poor dividend history.

---

[4] § 531.

[5] § 532(a).

[6] § 1.533-1(a)(2).

Although these factors are not conclusive evidence, their presence no doubt suggests improper accumulations.

In determining whether the requisite intent exists, the courts have considered not only the criteria mentioned above but also whether the corporation's stock is widely held. As a general rule, the accumulated earnings tax does not apply to publicly held corporations. Publicly held corporations normally are protected since the number and variety of their shareholders usually preclude the formation of a dividend policy to minimize shareholder taxes. Nevertheless, the tax has been applied to publicly held corporations in which management was dominated by a small group of shareholders who were able to control dividend policy for their benefit.[7] Moreover, in 1984, Congress eliminated any doubts as to whether publicly held corporations are automatically exempt from the penalty tax. Section 532(c) currently provides that the tax be applied without regard to the number of shareholders of the corporation. Thus, the tax may be imposed on a publicly held corporation if the situation warrants.

While publicly held corporations usually are immune from the penalty tax, closely held corporations are particularly vulnerable since dividend policy is easily manipulated to meet shareholders' desires. Indeed, it may be a formidable task to prove that the corporation was not used for tax avoidance in light of the *Donruss* decision.[8] In that case, the Supreme Court held that the tax avoidance motive need not be the primary or dominant motive for the accumulation of earnings before the penalty tax is imposed. Rather, if tax avoidance is but one of the motives, the tax may apply.

As a practical matter, it is difficult, if not impossible, to determine the actual intent of the corporation and its shareholders. For this reason, the presumption created by § 533(a) looms large in virtually all accumulated earnings tax cases. Under this provision, a tax avoidance purpose is deemed to exist if earnings were accumulated beyond the reasonable needs of the business.[9] As might be expected, most of the litigation in this area has concerned what constitutes a reasonable need of the business. In fact, many cases do not even mention intent, implying that the accumulated earnings tax will be applied in all cases in which the accumulation exceeds business needs. Except in the unusual case in which a corporation's intent can be demonstrated, a corporation should be prepared to justify the accumulations based on the needs of the business.

REASONABLE NEEDS OF THE BUSINESS

The Code does not define the term "reasonable needs of the business." Instead it states that the reasonable needs of the business include the *reasonably anticipated needs* of the business.[10] The Regulations clarify the term reasonably anticipated needs.[11] First, the corporation must have specific, definite, and feasible plans for the use of the accumulation. The funds do not have to be expended in a short period of time after the close of the year. In fact, the plans need only require that the accumulations be expended within a *reasonable* time in the future. However, if the plans are postponed indefinitely, the needs will not be considered reasonable. As a general rule, the plans

---

7   See *Trico Products*, 42-2 USTC ¶9540, 31 AFTR 394, 137 F.2d 424 (CA-2, 1943). In *Golconda Mining Corp.*, 58 T.C. 139 (1972), the Tax Court held that the tax applied where management controlled 17 percent of the outstanding stock of a publicly held corporation but the Ninth Circuit reversed, suggesting the tax should be applied solely to closely held corporations, 74-2 USTC ¶9845. 35 AFTR2d 75-336, 507 F.2d 594 (CA-9, 1974). Tax applied to publicly held corporation in *Alphatype Corporation v. U.S.* 76-2 USTC ¶9730, 38 AFTR2d 76-6019 (Ct. Cls., 1976). In Rev. Rul. 73-305, 1975-2 C.B. 228 the IRS confirmed its position that it will apply the tax to publicly held corporations.

8   *U.S. v. Donruss*, 69-1 USTC ¶9167, 23 AFTR2d 69-418, 393 U.S. 297 (USSC, 1969).

9   § 533(a).

10   § 537(a)(1).

11   Reg. § 1.537-1(b).

must not be vague and uncertain. If the plans are based on specific studies containing dollar estimates and are approved by the board of directors, the corporation is in a better position to prove that the plans qualify as reasonable business needs.

In addition to reasonably anticipated needs, the Code and Regulations identify certain specific reasons for accumulations that are considered to be reasonable needs of the business.[12] Several of these reasons are discussed below.

Stock Redemptions from an Estate. A corporation is allowed to temporarily accumulate earnings in order to redeem the stock of a deceased shareholder in conjunction with Code § 303 (discussed in Chapter 20).[13] The accumulations may commence *only after* the death of a shareholder. The fact that a shareholder dies after accumulations have been made and the corporation redeems his or her stock under § 303 is ignored in evaluating pre-death accumulations.[14] If the shareholder owned stock in two or more corporations, each corporation is entitled to accumulate only a portion of the total redeemable amount unless the estate's executor or administrator has indicated that more shares of one of the corporations will be offered for redemption than will those of another corporation.[15] The requirements of § 303 (relating to redemption of stock to pay death taxes) must be met in order for this provision to apply.

Product Liability Loss Reserves. The Code also allows accumulations to cover product liability losses.[16] Product liability is defined as damages for physical or emotional harm as well as damages and loss to property as a result of the use of a product sold, leased, or manufactured by the taxpayer.[17] The amount accumulated can cover both actual and reasonably anticipated losses.

Business Expansion or Plant Replacement. Perhaps the most common reason for accumulating earnings that the Regulations specifically authorize is for *bona fide* expansion of business or replacement of plant.[18] This provision includes the purchase or construction of a building.[19] It also includes the modernization, rehabilitation, or replacement of assets.[20] However, this provision does not shield a corporation which has not adequately specified and documented its expansion needs.[21]

Acquisition of a Business Enterprise. A second reason offered in the Regulations for accumulating earnings is for the acquisition of a business enterprise through the purchase of stock or assets.[22] This provision appears to encourage business expansion, since the Regulations state that the business for which earnings can be accumulated includes any line of business the corporation wishes to undertake, and not just the line of business previously carried on.[23] However, this provision for accumulation is limited by the statement in the Regulations that investments in properties or securities that are

---

[12]   See § 537(a) and (b), and Reg. § 1.537-2.

[13]   § 537(b)(1).

[14]   § 537(b)(5).

[15]   Reg. § 1.537-1(c)(3).

[16]   § 537(b)(4).

[17]   § 172(f).

[18]   Reg. § 1.537-2(b)(1).

[19]   *Sorgel v. U.S.*, 72-1 USTC ¶9427, 29 AFTR2d 72-1035, 341 F. Supp. 1 (D. Ct. Wisc., 1972).

[20]   *Knoxville Iron*, 18 TCM 251, T.C. Memo 1959-54.

[21]   *I.A. Dress Co.*, 60-1 USTC ¶9204, 5 AFTR2d 429, 273 F.2d 543 (CA-2, 1960), aff&g. 32 T.C. 93; *Herzog Miniature Lamp Works, Inc.*, 73-2 USTC ¶9593, 32 AFTR2d 73-5282, 273 F.2d 543, (CA-2, 1973).

[22]   Reg. § 1.537-2(b)(2).

[23]   Reg. § 1.537-3(a).

unrelated to the activities of the business of the corporation are unacceptable reasons for accumulations.[24] The statements in the Regulations raise a question as to the validity of accumulations for diversification. On one hand the corporation can acquire an enterprise or expand its business into any field. On the other hand the acquisition should be related to the corporation's activities. This apparent conflict in the Regulations is reflected in court decisions. A corporation that manufactured automobile clutches was permitted to accumulate income to acquire a business that would make use of the corporation's metal-working expertise, whereas a corporation in the printing business was not permitted to accumulate income to acquire real estate.[25] The extent to which a corporation can diversify is uncertain. It appears that diversification into passive investments is unacceptable whereas diversification into an operating business, no matter how far removed from the original line of business, is acceptable.

Retirement of Indebtedness. The Regulations also provide for the accumulation of earnings to retire business indebtedness.[26] The debt can be to either a third party or a shareholder as long as it is a bona fide business debt.

Investments or Loans to Suppliers or Customers. The Regulations state that earnings may be accumulated to provide for investments or loans to suppliers or customers.[27] However, loans to shareholders, friends and relatives of shareholders, and corporations controlled by shareholders of the corporation making the loan indicate that earnings are possibly being accumulated beyond reasonable business needs.[28]

Contingencies. Although the Regulations do not specifically allow accumulations for contingencies, they do imply approval of such accumulations as long as the contingencies are not unrealistic.[29] Unfortunately, the distinction between realistic and unrealistic contingencies is difficult to define. However, the more specific the need, the more detailed the cash estimate, and the more likely the occurrence, the easier it will be to prove the accumulation is reasonable.

Redemption of Stock. As noted above, accumulations to redeem stock from a decedent's estate under § 303 constitute a reasonable need of the business. This provision does not cover any other stock redemption. Several cases have held that a redemption may be a reasonable need provided the redemption is for the benefit of the corporation and not the shareholder.[30] For example, the redemption of a dissenting minority shareholder's stock can be for the corporation's benefit whereas the redemption of a majority shareholder's stock would be for the shareholder's benefit. It might also be possible to prove that the redemption was necessary to reduce or eliminate disputes over management or conduct of the business.

Working Capital. Another reason mentioned in the Regulations for a reasonable accumulation of earnings and profits is the need for working capital.[31] This is one of the

---

24 Reg. § 1.537-2(c)(4).

25 *Alma Piston Co.*, 22 TCM 948, T.C. Memo 1963-195; *Union Offset*, 79-2 USTC ¶9550, 44 AFTR2d 79-5652. 603 F.2d 90 (CA-9, 1979).

26 Reg. § 1.537-2(b)(3).

27 Reg. § 1.537-2(b)(5).

28 Reg. §§ 1.537-2(c)(1), (2), and (3).

29 Reg. § 1.537-2(c)(5).

30 See *John B. Lambert & Assoc. v. U.S.*, 38 AFTR2d 6207 (Ct. Cls., 1976); *C.E. Hooper, Inc. v. U.S.*, 38 AFTR2d 5417, 539 F.2d 1276 (Ct. Cls.,1976); *Mountain State Steel Foundries, Inc. v. Comm.*, 6 AFTR2d 5910, 284 F.2d 737 (CA-4, 1960); and *Koma, Inc. v. Comm.*, 40 AFTR 712, 189 F.2d 390 (CA-10, 1951).

31 Reg. § 1.537-2(b)(4).

primary justifications corporations use for the accumulation of earnings. A corporation is permitted to retain earnings to provide necessary working capital. Initially, the courts tried to measure working capital sufficiency by using rules of thumb. A current ratio of 2.5 to 1 generally meant that the corporation had not accumulated income unreasonably.[32] The courts considered a current ratio more than 2.5 to 1 an indication of unreasonable accumulation.

In the 1965 case of *Bardahl Mfg. Corp.*, the Tax Court utilized a formula to compute the working capital needs of a corporation.[33] Under this approach (called the *Bardahl* formula), the working capital needed for one operating cycle is computed. This amount in essence represents the cash *needed* to meet expenses incurred during the operating cycle—the period required for a business to convert cash into inventory, sell the merchandise, convert the customer's accounts receivable into cash, and pay its accounts payable. This necessary working capital is then compared to actual working capital. If necessary working capital is greater than actual working capital, an accumulation of earnings to meet the necessary working capital requirements is justified. If actual working capital is greater than the working capital needed, the corporation must show other reasons for the accumulation of earnings in order to avoid the accumulated earnings tax.

The initial step of the *Bardahl* formula is to calculate the inventory, accounts receivable, and accounts payable cycle ratios. These ratios are computed as follows:

1. *Inventory cycle ratio* $= \dfrac{\text{Average inventory}}{\text{Cost of goods sold}}$

2. *Accounts receivable cycle ratio* $= \dfrac{\text{Average accounts receivable}}{\text{Net sales}}$

3. *Accounts payable cycle ratio* $= \dfrac{\text{Average accounts payable}}{\text{Purchases}}$

The ratios resulting from these calculations represent the cycle expressed as a percentage of the year. In other words, if the accounts receivable cycle ratio is 10 percent, then it normally takes about 36 days (10% × 365) to collect a receivable once it has been generated by a sale.

Instead of using the *average* inventory and the average receivables, a corporation can use *peak values* if it is in a seasonal business. If the corporation uses peak values for the other ratios, it may be required to use peak payables.

Once computed, the three ratios are combined. The result represents the number of days—expressed as a fraction of the year—during which the corporation needs working capital to meet its operating expenses. The operating cycle ratio is computed as follows:

$$
\begin{array}{l}
\text{Inventory cycle ratio} \\
+ \text{ Accounts receivable cycle ratio} \\
\underline{- \text{ Accounts payable cycle ratio}} \\
= \text{Operating cycle ratio}
\end{array}
$$

The operating cycle ratio is multiplied by the *annual operating expenses* to compute the necessary working capital. Operating expenses are defined as the cost of goods sold plus other annual expenses (i.e., general, administrative, and selling expenses). The operating expense category does not include depreciation since depreciation does not require the use of cash. However, the category can include income taxes if the corporation pays estimated taxes and will make a tax payment during the next operating cycle.[34] Other expenses should be included if they will require the expenditure of cash during the next operating cycle.

---

[32] *J Scripps Newspaper*, 44 T.C. 453 (1965).

[33] *Bardahl Mfg. Corp.*, 24 TCM 1030, T.C. Memo 1965-200.

[34] *Empire Steel*, 33 TCM 155, T.C. Memo 1974-34.

The required working capital computed by the *Bardahl* formula is compared to actual working capital to determine if there have been excess accumulations. Since the computed working capital is based on accounting data, it is normally compared to actual working capital (current assets − current liabilities) computed from the corporation's financial statements. There are exceptions to this rule. Financial statements are not used if they do not clearly reflect the company's working capital. The Supreme Court authorized the use of fair market value instead of historical cost to value a firm's current assets in *Ivan Allen Co.*[35] The assets in question were marketable securities that had appreciated. The decision is broad enough to permit the Internal Revenue Service to determine actual working capital based on current value any time there is a significant difference between cost and market.

Any corporation whose actual working capital does not exceed required working capital (per the *Bardahl* formula) should be exempt from the accumulated earnings tax. If the actual working capital exceeds required working capital, the excess is considered an indication of unreasonable accumulations. This excess is compared to the reasonable needs of the business (other than working capital) to determine if the accumulations are unreasonable. To the extent that the corporation has needs, it may accumulate funds. If all of the excess working capital is not needed, the tax is imposed. The tax is based on the accumulated taxable income and not the excess working capital.

Example 3. K owns and operates K's Apparel, Inc. (KAI). After hearing that a friend's corporation was recently slapped with an accumulated earnings tax penalty, she asked her accountant to determine the vulnerability of her own business. The following is a balance sheet and income statement for 2004 and 2005 for KAI.

Balance Sheet

	2004	2005
Current Assets:		
Cash	$ 55,000	$ 67,000
Marketable securities	10,000	8,000
Accounts receivable (net)	45,000	55,000
Inventory	30,000	20,000
Total Current Assets	$ 140,000	$ 150,000
Property, plant, and equipment (net)	300,000	425,000
Total Assets	$ 440,000	$ 575,000
Current Liabilities:		
Notes payable	$ 5,000	$ 4,000
Accounts payable	50,000	30,000
Accrued expenses	8,000	16,000
Total Current Liabilities	$ 63,000	$ 50,000
Long-term debt	37,000	40,000
Total Liabilities	$ 100,000	$ 90,000
Stockholders' Equity:		
Common stock	10,000	10,000
Earnings and profits	330,000	475,000
Total Liabilities and Stockholders' Equity	$ 440,000	$ 575,000

---

[35] *Ivan Allen Co. v. U.S.*, 75-2 USTC ¶9557, 36 AFTR2d 75-5200, 422 U.S. 617 (USSC, 1975).

Income Statement

Sales	$ 400,000	$ 500,000
Cost of goods sold:		
Beginning inventory	$ 40,000	$ 30,000
Purchases	300,000	320,000
Ending inventory	(30,000)	(20,000)
Total	$ 310,000	$ 330,000
Gross profit	$ 90,000	$ 170,000
Other expenses:		
Depreciation	$ 40,000	$ 55,000
Selling expenses	10,000	15,000
Administrative	20,000	50,000
Total	$ 70,000	$ 120,000
Net income before taxes	$ 20,000	$ 50,000
Income tax expense	(2,000)	(5,000)
Net income	$ 18,000	$ 45,000

In addition to this information, K indicated that at the end of 2005 the securities were worth $15,000 more than their book value, or $23,000. K also estimates that her reasonable needs for the current year 2005 amount to $20,000.

Under the *Bardahl* formula, her working capital needs are determined as follows:

Step 1: Operating cycle expressed as a fraction of the year (in thousands):

	Inventory cycle	$=$	$\dfrac{\text{Average inventory}}{\text{cost of goods sold}}$	$= [(30+20)/2]/330 =$	0.0758
$+$	Receivable cycle	$=$	$\dfrac{\text{Average receivables}}{\text{Sales}}$	$= [(45+55)/2]/500 =$	0.1000
$-$	Payables cycle	$=$	$\dfrac{\text{Average payables}}{\text{Purchases}}$	$= [(50+30)/2]/320 =$	(0.1250)

$=$ Operating cycle expressed as percentage of the year $\qquad = \quad$ 0.0508

Step 2: Computation of operating expenses:

Operating expenses:	
Cost of goods sold	$330,000
Selling expenses	15,000
Administrative expenses	50,000
Taxes	5,000
Total operating expenses	$400,000

Step 3: Working capital needs:

	Operating expenses (Step 2)	$400,000
$\times$	Operating cycle (Step 1)	$\times$ 0.0508
$=$	Working capital needs	$ 20,320

K's working capital needs, $20,320, must be compared to actual working capital using the assets' fair market value. Any excess of actual working capital over required working capital must be compared to the current year's needs to determine if unwarranted accumulations exist. Assuming the marketable securities are actually worth $23,000, the comparison is made as follows:

	Actual working capital:	
	Current assets	
	($150,000 + $15,000)......	$165,000
−	Current liabilities	(50,000)
=	Actual working capital	$115,000
−	Required working capital (Step 3)	(20,320)
=	Excess working capital..................	$ 94,680
−	Reasonable needs.....................	(20,000)
=	Accumulations beyond current needs	$ 74,680

The accumulated earnings tax focuses on whether the corporation has accumulated liquid assets beyond its reasonable needs that could be distributed to shareholders. In this case, actual working capital exceeds required working capital and other needs of the business by $74,680, implying that the accumulated earnings tax applies. If so, the actual penalty tax is computed using accumulated taxable income, as explained below.

COMPUTATION OF THE ACCUMULATED EARNINGS TAX

The purpose of the accumulated earnings tax is to penalize taxpayers with unwarranted accumulations. To accomplish this, a 15 percent tax is imposed on what the Code refers to as accumulated taxable income. Accumulated taxable income is designed to represent the amount that the corporation could have distributed after funding its reasonable needs. In essence, the computation attempts to determine the corporation's dividend-paying capacity. Exhibit 21-1 shows the formula for computing accumulated taxable income.[36]

---

[36] § 535.

EXHIBIT 21-1
Accumulated Taxable Income[37]

Taxable income:

Plus:
1. The dividends-received deduction
2. Any net operating loss deduction that is reflected in taxable income
3. Any capital-loss carryovers from other years that are reflected in taxable income

Minus:
1. Federal income taxes for the year, but not the accumulated earnings tax or the personal holding company tax
2. The charitable contributions for the year in excess of the 10 percent limitation
3. Any net capital loss incurred during the year reduced by net capital gain deductions of prior years that have not previously reduced any net capital loss deduction
4. Any net capital gain (net long-term capital gain – the net short-term capital loss) for the year minus the taxes attributable to the gain and any net capital losses of prior years that have not reduced a net capital gain deduction in determining the accumulated earnings tax

Equals: *Adjusted taxable income*

Minus:
1. Accumulated earnings credit (see Exhibit 21-2)
2. Dividends-Paid deduction (see Exhibit 21-3)

Equals: *Accumulated taxable income*

The computation of accumulated taxable income begins with an imperfect measure of the corporation's ability to pay dividends-taxable income. To obtain a more representative measure of the corporation's dividend-paying capacity, taxable income is modified to arrive at what is often referred to as *adjusted taxable income*.[38] For example, the deduction allowed for dividends received is added back to taxable income since it has no effect on the corporation's ability to pay dividends. The same rationale can be given for the net operating loss deduction. In contrast, charitable contributions in excess of the 10 percent limitation may be deducted in determining adjusted taxable income since the corporation does not have the nondeductible amount available to pay dividends. For the same reason, Federal income taxes may be deducted in computing adjusted taxable income.

The deduction for capital gains stems from the assumption that these earnings are used to fund the corporation's needs and consequently may be accumulated with impunity. Capital losses are deductible since these amounts are unavailable for payment of dividends and are not reflected in taxable income. As shown in Exhibit 21-1, however, the deductions for capital gains as well as capital losses must be modified.

Prior to 1984, corporations were entitled to reduce taxable income not only by the amount of their net capital gains (reduced by related taxes) but also by the full amount of their net capital losses, depending on whether a net capital gain or loss occurred. Consequently, there was an advantage in recognizing capital gains in one year and capital losses in another year in order to avoid netting and thus permit both gains and losses to be deductible in full. For example, if the corporation had a capital loss of $1,000 this year and a capital gain of $5,000 next year (ignoring taxes), both could be deducted in full each year in computing adjusted taxable income. However, if they occurred in the same year, the deduction would be limited to $4,000. To eliminate this planning opportunity, corporations are now required to reduce their net capital losses by any net capital gain deductions that have been used to arrive at adjusted taxable income

---

[37] § 535. Several additional adjustments are required for computing accumulated taxable income of a holding or investment company.

[38] This term is not found in the Code; it is used here solely for purposes of exposition.

in prior years. Under these rules, it is immaterial in what order or in what year gains and losses are recognized. In effect, taxable income is reduced only by the overall net gain or loss that the corporation has recognized to date.

Example 4. T Corporation has the following income and deductions for 2005:

Income from operations	$150,000
Dividend income (from less than 20% owned corporations)	40,000
Charitable contributions	25,000

T Corporation computes its taxable income as follows:

Income from operations		$150,000
Dividend income		40,000
Income before special deductions		$190,000
Special deductions:		
Charitable contribution (limited)	$ 19,000	
Dividend-received deduction	28,000	
Total special deductions		(47,000)
Taxable income		$143,000

T Corporation's Federal income taxes for 2005 are $39,020. T Corporation's adjusted taxable income is computed as follows:

Taxable income		$143,000
Plus: Dividend-received deduction		28,000
		$171,000
Minus the sum of		
Federal income taxes	$39,020	
Actual charitable contributions for the year minus the charitable contribution deduction reflected in taxable income ($25,000 − $19,000)	6,000	(45,020)
Equals: Adjusted taxable income		$125,980

Two additional deductions are permitted in computing accumulated taxable income: the accumulated earnings credit and the dividends-paid deduction. The deduction allowed for dividends is consistent with the theory that the tax should be imposed only on income that has not been distributed. The accumulated earnings credit allows the taxpayer to accumulate without penalty $250,000 or an amount equal to the reasonable needs of the business, whichever is greater.

ACCUMULATED EARNINGS CREDIT

In creating the accumulated earnings tax, Congress realized that a corporation should not be penalized for keeping enough of its earnings to meet legitimate business needs. For this reason, in computing accumulated taxable income, a corporation is allowed—in effect—a reduction for the amount out of current year's earnings necessary to meet such needs. This reduction is the *accumulated earnings credit*.[39] Note that despite its name, the credit actually operates as a deduction. As a practical matter, it is this credit that insulates most corporations from the accumulated earnings tax.

Specifically, the credit is the greater of two amounts as described in Exhibit 21-2 and discussed further below. Generally, however, the credit for the current year may be determined as follows:

Reasonable business needs (or $250,000 if larger)...................	$xxx,xxx
Less: Beginning Accumulated E&P	(xx,xxx)
Accumulated earnings credit..................................	$xxx,xxx

EXHIBIT 21-2
Accumulated Earnings Credit[40]

The accumulated earnings credit is the greater of

1. *General Rule:* Earnings and profits for the taxable year that are retained to meet the reasonable needs of the business, minus the net capital gain for the year (reduced by the taxes attributable to the gain),

    or

2. *Minimum Credit:* $250,000 ($150,000 for personal service corporations) minus the accumulated earnings and profits of the corporation at the close of the *preceding* taxable year, adjusted for dividends paid in the current year *deemed* paid in the prior year.

Part 1 of Exhibit 21-2 contains the general rule authorizing accumulations. It permits corporations to accumulate earnings to the extent of their reasonable needs without penalty.[41] In determining the amount of the earnings and profits for the taxable year that have been retained to meet the reasonable needs of the business, it is necessary to consider to what extent the accumulated earnings and profits are available to cover these needs.[42] In effect, prior accumulations reduce the amount that can be retained in the current year. If the corporation's accumulated earnings and profits are sufficient to meet the reasonable needs of the business, *none* of the current earnings and profits will be considered to be retained to meet the reasonable needs of the business.

Part 2 of Exhibit 21-2 is the so-called *minimum credit*.[43] For most corporations the amount of the minimum credit is $250,000. For personal service corporations, the minimum credit is $150,000. Personal service corporations are corporations that provide services in the area of health, law, engineering, architecture, accounting, actuarial science, performing arts, or consulting. The lower credit for personal service corporations reflects the fact that their capital needs are relatively small when compared to retail or manufacturing businesses.

To determine the amount of the minimum credit available for the current year, the base amount, $250,000 ($150,000), must be reduced by the accumulated earnings and profits at the close of the preceding tax year. For purposes of this computation, the accumulated earnings and profits at the close of the preceding year are reduced by the

---

[39]   § 535(c).

[40]   § 535(c)(1).

[41]   *Ibid.*

[42]   Reg. § 1.535-3(b)(1)(ii).

[43]   § 535(c)(2).

dividends that were paid by the corporation within 2½ months after the close of the preceding year.[44]

Example 5. X Corporation, a calendar year retail department store, had current earnings and profits for 2005 of $75,000. Its accumulated earnings and profits at the close of 2004 were $200,000. X Corporation has paid no dividends for five years. X Corporation's taxable income for 2005 included a net capital gain of $20,000. [The taxes related to this net capital gain were $6,800 (34% × $20,000).] The reasonable needs of X Corporation are estimated to be $240,000. The amount of X Corporation's current earnings and profits that are retained to meet reasonable business needs is computed as follows:

Estimated reasonable needs of X Corporation.	$ 240,000
Less: Accumulated earnings and profits as of 12/31/04	(200,000)
Extent to which current earnings and profits are needed to cover the reasonable needs of the business	$ 40,000

Even though the current earnings and profits are $75,000, only $40,000 of the current earnings and profits are needed to meet the reasonable needs of the business.

The accumulated earnings credit is the greater of

1.	Current earnings and profits to meet the reasonable needs of the business.		$ 40,000
	Minus: Net capital gain	$20,000	
	Reduced by the taxes attributable to the gain.	(6,800)	(13,200)
	General rule credit		$ 26,800
	or		
2.	$250,000		$ 250,000
	Minus: Accumulated earnings and profits as of 12/31/04.		(200,000)
	Minimum credit		$ 50,000

X Corporation's accumulated earnings credit is $50,000, the greater of the general rule credit ($26,800) or the minimum credit ($50,000).

Example 6. Assume the same facts as in *Example 5*, except that X Corporation is an engineering firm. The general rule credit would still be $26,800, but the minimum credit would be computed as follows:

$150,000	$ 150,000
Minus: Accumulated earnings and profits as of 12/31/04.	(200,000)
Minimum credit (the minimum credit cannot be a negative number)	$ 0

In this situation the accumulated earnings credit is $26,800, the greater of the general rule credit ($26,800) or the minimum credit ($0).

Two aspects of the accumulated earnings credit deserve special mention. First, the minimum credit has a very limited role. Since the $250,000 (or $150,000 for service

---

[44] § 535(c)(4).

corporations) is reduced by the prior accumulations, the minimum credit will always be zero for firms that have greater than $250,000 of accumulated earnings. In other words, accumulations in excess of $250,000 must be justified by business needs.

The second aspect involves capital gains. As discussed previously, capital gains (net of related taxes) are subtracted from taxable income in arriving at adjusted taxable income. Therefore, a corporation can accumulate all of its capital gains without the imposition of the accumulated earnings tax. At the same time, however, capital gains are subtracted from business needs in arriving at the general credit (see Exhibit 21-2). As a result, a capital gain may cause accumulations of ordinary income to be subject to the special tax even though the capital gain itself escapes penalty. In effect, the computations are based on the assumption that business needs are funded first from capital gains and then from income from operations.

DIVIDENDS-PAID DEDUCTION

Exhibit 21-1 indicated that both the accumulated earnings credit and the dividends-paid deduction are adjustments in computing accumulated taxable income. Exhibit 21-3 lists the types of dividends that constitute the dividends-paid deduction.

EXHIBIT 21-3
Dividends-Paid Deduction[45]

1. Dividends paid during the taxable year,[46]
2. Dividends paid within 2½ months after the close of the taxable year,[47]
3. Consent dividends,[48] plus
4. Liquidating distributions,[49]

Equals: **Dividends-Paid Deduction**

To qualify for the dividend deduction, the distribution must constitute a "dividend" as defined in § 316.[50] As previously discussed, § 316 limits dividends to distributions out of current earnings and profits and accumulated earnings and profits since 1913. Property distributions qualify only to the extent of their adjusted basis.[51]

Throwback Dividends. The dividends-paid deduction includes not only dividends paid during the year, but also so-called *throwback dividends*, dividends paid during the 2½ months following the close of the tax year.[52] Amounts paid during the 2½-month period *must* be treated as if paid in the previous year.[53] This treatment is mandatory and not elective by the shareholders or the corporation.

Consent Dividends. In addition to actual dividends paid, the corporation is entitled to a deduction for consent dividends.[54] Sometimes a corporation may have a large amount of accumulated earnings, but insufficient cash or property to make a dividend

---

[45] §§ 561 through 565.

[46] § 561(a)(1).

[47] § 563(a).

[48] § 565.

[49] § 562(b)(1).

[50] § 562(a).

[51] Reg. § 1.562-1(a).

[52] § 563.

[53] § Reg. 1.563-1.

[54] § 565.

distribution. In order to avoid the accumulated earnings tax, the corporation may obtain a dividends-paid deduction by using consent dividends—so called because the shareholders consent to treat a certain amount as a taxable dividend on their tax returns even though there is no distribution of cash or property. Not only are the shareholders deemed to receive the amount to which they consent, but they also are treated as having reinvested the amount received as a contribution to the corporation's capital.

To qualify a dividend as a consent dividend, the shareholders must file a consent form (Form 972) with the corporate income tax return. The consents must be filed by the due date (including extensions) of the corporate tax return for the year in which the dividend deduction is requested. Only shareholders who own stock on the last day of the tax year need file consent forms. On the forms, each shareholder must specify the amount of the consent dividend and then include this amount as a cash distribution by the corporation on his or her individual income tax return. Consent dividends are limited to the amount that would have qualified as a dividend under Code § 316 had the dividend been distributed in cash.[55] Only shareholders of common and participating preferred stock may consent to dividends.[56]

Liquidating Distributions. If the distribution is in liquidation, partial liquidation, or redemption of stock, the portion of the distribution chargeable to earnings and profits is included in the dividend deduction.[57] For partial liquidations and redemptions, this is the redeemed stock's proportionate share of accumulated E&P. For complete liquidations, any amount distributed within the two years following the adoption of a plan of liquidation and that is pursuant to the plan is included in the dividends-paid deduction, but not to exceed the corporation's current earnings and profits for the year of distribution.[58]

PERSONAL HOLDING COMPANY TAX

As mentioned earlier in this chapter, the accumulated earnings tax is not the only penalty tax applicable to corporations. Congress has also enacted the personal holding company tax. This tax evolved in 1934 from the need to stop the growing number of individuals who were misusing the corporate entity despite the existence of the accumulated earnings tax. The personal holding company tax was designed to thwart three particular schemes prevalent during that period.

The first two schemes specifically aimed to take advantage of the disparity between individual and corporate tax rates. At that time, the maximum individual tax rates were approximately 45 percentage points higher than the maximum corporate rates. A typical plan used to take advantage of this differential involved the formation of a corporation to hold an individual's investment portfolio. This plan allowed an individual's interest and dividends to become taxable to the corporation rather than to the individual and consequently to be taxed at the lower corporate rates. Another, somewhat more sophisticated, technique enabled the transfer of an individual's service income to a corporation. The blueprint for this plan required the formation of a corporation by an individual (e.g., movie star) who subsequently became an employee of the corporation. With the corporation in place, parties seeking the individual's services were forced to contract with the corporation rather than with the individual. The individual would then perform the services, but the corporation would receive the revenue. Finally, the corporation would pay the individual a salary that was less than the revenue earned.

---

[55]   Reg. § 1.565-2(a).

[56]   § 565(f).

[57]   § 562(b)(1).

[58]   § 562(b)(1)(B).

Through this plan, the individual succeeded in transferring at least some of the revenue to the corporation, where it would be taxed at the lower corporate rates.

The final scheme was not specifically designed to take advantage of the lower corporate rates. Instead, its attraction grew from the practical presumption that all corporate activities are business activities. Given this presumption, an individual would transfer his or her personal assets (e.g., a yacht, race car, or vacation home) along with other investments to the corporation. Under the veil of the corporation, the expenses relating to the personal assets, such as maintenance of a yacht, would be magically transformed from nondeductible personal expenses to deductible business expenses which could offset the income produced by the investments. In short, by using the corporate form, individuals were able to disguise their personal expenses as business expenses and deduct them.

Although the Internal Revenue Service tried to curb these abuses using the accumulated earnings tax, such attempts often failed. These failures normally could be attributed to the problem of proving that the individuals actually intended to avoid taxes. Aware of this problem, Congress formulated the personal holding company tax, which could be applied without having to prove that the forbidden purpose existed. In contrast to the accumulated earnings tax, which is imposed only after a subjective assessment of the individual's intentions, the personal holding company tax automatically applies whenever the corporation satisfies two objective tests.

Not all corporations that meet the applicable tests are subject to the penalty tax, however. The Code specifically exempts certain corporations. These include S corporations, tax-exempt corporations, banks, life insurance companies, surety companies, foreign personal holding companies, lending and finance companies, and several other types of corporations.[59]

If the personal holding company tax applies, the tax is 15 percent of undistributed personal holding company income.[60] Like the accumulated earnings tax, the personal holding company tax is levied in addition to the regular tax.[61] The personal holding company tax differs from the accumulated earnings tax however, in that the corporation is required to compute and remit any personal holding tax due at the time it files its annual return. Form 1120-PH is used to compute the tax and must be filed with the corporation's annual Form 1120. In those cases where both the accumulated earnings tax and the personal holding company tax are applicable, only the personal holding company tax is imposed.[62]

PERSONAL HOLDING COMPANY DEFINED

The personal holding company tax applies only if the corporation is considered a personal holding company (PHC). As might be expected in light of the schemes prevalent at the time the tax was enacted, a corporation generally qualifies as a personal holding company if it is closely held and a substantial portion of its income is derived from passive sources or services. Specifically, the Code provides that a corporation is deemed to be a personal holding company if it satisfies both of the following tests.[63]

1. *Ownership*—At any time during the last half of the taxable year, more than 50 percent of the value of the corporation's outstanding stock is owned by five or fewer individuals.[64]

---

[59]   § 542(c).

[60]   § 541.

[61]   *Ibid.*

[62]   § 532(b)(1).

[63]   § 542.

[64]   § 542(a)(2).

2. *Passive income*—At least 60 percent of the corporation's adjusted ordinary gross income consists of personal holding company income (PHCI).[65]

Before each of these tests is examined in detail, the distinction between the personal holding company tax and the accumulated earnings tax should be emphasized. The accumulated earnings tax applies only when it is proven that it was the shareholder's intention to use the corporation to shield income from individual tax rates. In contrast, application of the personal holding company tax requires only that two mechanical tests be satisfied. As a result, a corporation may fall victim to the personal holding company tax where there was no intention to avoid tax by misusing the corporation. For example, consider a closely held corporation in the process of liquidating. During liquidation, the corporation may have income from operations and passive income from temporary investments (investments made pending final distributions). If the passive income is substantial—60 percent or more of the corporation's total income—the corporation will be treated as a personal holding company subject to the penalty tax even though there was no intention by the shareholders to shelter the passive income. As this example illustrates, the mechanical nature of the personal holding company tax, unlike the subjective nature of the accumulated earnings tax, presents a trap for those with the noblest of intentions.

PHC OWNERSHIP TEST

As indicated above, the first part of the two-part test for personal holding company status concerns ownership. Apparently it was Congressional belief that the tax-saving schemes described above succeeded primarily in those cases where there was a concentration of ownership. For this reason, the ownership test is satisfied only if five or fewer individuals own more than 50 percent of the value of the corporation's outstanding shares of stock at any time during the last half of the taxable year.[66] As a quick study of this test reveals, a corporation having less than ten shareholders always meets the ownership test since there will always be a combination of five or fewer shareholders owning more than 50 percent of the stock (e.g., $100\% \div 9 = 11\%$; $11\% \times 5 > 50\%$). Thus, it becomes apparent that closely held corporations are extremely vulnerable to the tax.

In performing the stock ownership test, the shareholder's *direct and indirect* ownership must be taken into account.[67] Indirect ownership is determined using a set of constructive ownership rules designed specifically for the personal holding company area.[68] According to these rules, a taxpayer is considered owning indirectly the following:

1. Stock owned directly or indirectly by his or her family, including his or her brothers, sisters, spouse, ancestors, and lineal descendents;[69]

2. His or her proportionate share of any stock owned by a corporation, partnership, estate, or trust in which he or she has ownership (or of which he or she is a beneficiary in the case of an estate or trust);[70] and

3. Stock owned indirectly or directly by his or her partner in a partnership.[71]

---

[65] § 542(a)(1).

[66] § 542(a)(2).

[67] *Ibid.*

[68] § 544.

[69] § 544(a)(2).

[70] § 544(a)(1).

[71] § 544(a)(2).

In using these rules, the following guidelines must be observed: (1) stock attributed from one family member to another cannot be reattributed to yet another member of the family,[72] (2) stock attributed from a partner to the taxpayer cannot be reattributed to a member of his or her family or to yet another partner,[73] (3) stock on which the taxpayer has an option is treated as being actually owned,[74] and (4) convertible securities are treated as outstanding stock.[75] In addition, Code § 544 contains other rules that may affect an individual's stock ownership.

INCOME TEST

Although the stock ownership test may be satisfied, a corporation is not considered a personal holding company unless it also passes an income test. In general terms, this test is straightforward: at least 60 percent of the corporation's income must be derived from either passive sources or certain types of services. Unfortunately, the technical translation of this requirement is somewhat more complicated. According to the Code, at least 60 percent of the corporation's adjusted ordinary gross income must be *personal holding company income*.[76] This relationship may be expressed numerically as follows:

$$\frac{\text{Personal holding company income}}{\text{Adjusted ordinary gross income}} \geq 60\%$$

As will be seen below, the definition of each of these terms can be baffling. However, the general theme of each term and the thrust of the test should not be lost in the complexity. Personal holding company income is generally passive income, while adjusted ordinary gross income is just that, ordinary gross income with a few modifications. Performing the income test is, in essence, a matter of determining whether too much of the corporation's income (adjusted ordinary gross income) is passive income (personal holding company income).

> **Example 7.** K, a high-bracket taxpayer, wished to reduce her taxes. Upon the advice of an old friend, she transferred all of her stocks and bonds to a newly formed corporation of which she is the sole owner. During the year, the corporation had dividend income of $40,000 and interest income of $35,000. In this case, the corporation is treated as a personal holding company because both the stock ownership test and the income test are satisfied. The stock ownership test is met since K owned 100% of the stock in the last half of the year. The income test is also met since all of the corporation's income is passive income—or more specifically, its personal holding company income, $75,000 ($40,000 dividends + $35,000 interest) exceeds 60% of its adjusted ordinary gross income, $45,000 (60% of $75,000).

The technical definitions of adjusted ordinary gross income and personal holding company income are explored below.

ADJUSTED ORDINARY GROSS INCOME

The first quantity that must be determined is adjusted ordinary gross income (AOGI).[77] As suggested above, the label given to this quantity is very appropriate since

---

[72] § 544(a)(5).

[73] *Ibid.*

[74] § 544(a)(3).

[75] § 544(b).

[76] § 542(a)(1).

[77] § 543(b)(2).

the amount which must be computed is just what the phrase implies; that is, it includes only the ordinary gross income of the corporation with certain adjustments. In determining AOGI, the following amounts must be computed: (1) gross income, (2) ordinary gross income, and (3) the adjustments to ordinary gross income to arrive at AOGI. Therefore, the starting point for the calculation of AOGI is gross income.

Gross Income. The definition of gross income for purposes of the personal holding company provisions varies little from the definition found in § 61. Accordingly, gross income includes all income from whatever source except those items specifically excluded. In addition, gross income is computed taking into consideration cost of goods sold. The only departure from the normal definition of gross income concerns property transactions. Only the net gains from the sale or exchange of stocks, securities, and commodities are included in gross income.[78] Net losses involving these assets do not reduce gross income. Similarly, any loss arising from the sale or exchange of § 1231 property is ignored and does not offset any § 1231 gains.

Ordinary Gross Income. In applying the income test, capital-gain type items are ignored and consequently have no effect on whether the corporation is treated as a personal holding company. Therefore, since the quantity desired is adjusted "ordinary" gross income, the second step of the calculation requires the removal of capital-gain type items from gross income. As seen in Exhibit 21-4, all capital gains and § 1231 gains are subtracted from gross income to arrive at ordinary gross income.[79] It should be noted that this amount, "ordinary gross income," is not simply a subtotal in arriving at AOGI. As discussed below, ordinary gross income (OGI) is an important figure in determining whether certain types of income are treated as personal holding company income.

EXHIBIT 21-4
Ordinary Gross Income[80]

Gross income		
Minus:	**a.**	Capital gains
	b.	(b) Section 1231 gains
Equals:	**Ordinary gross income (OGI)**	

Adjustments to OGI. For many years, OGI generally served as the denominator in the income-test fraction shown above. In 1964, however, modifications were necessary to discourage the use of certain methods taxpayers and their advisors had forged to undermine the income test. The popular schemes capitalized on the fact that $1 of gross rental income could shelter 60 cents of passive personal holding company income. This particular advantage could be obtained even though the rental activity itself was merely a break-even operation. Consequently, a taxpayer could easily thwart the income test and reap the benefits of the corporate entity by investing in activities that produced substantial gross rents or royalties, notwithstanding the fact that these activities were not economically sound investments.

Example 8. Refer to the facts in *Example 7*. Absent special rules, K could circumvent the income test by purchasing a coin-operated laundry which generated

---

[78] Prop. Reg. § 1.543-12(a). Also see Reg. §§ 1.542-2 and 1.543-2.

[79] § 543(b)(1).

[80] *Ibid.*

gross rents of more than $50,000 (e.g., $51,000) and transferring it to the corporation. In such case, assuming the rents would not be treated as personal holding income, the personal holding company income would still be $75,000 (dividends of $40,000 + interest of $35,000). However, when the laundry rents are combined with the personal holding company income to form the new AOGI, personal holding company income would be less than 60% of this new AOGI [$75,000 60% × ($40,000 + $35,000 + $51,000) = $75,600]. Although the laundry business might not show a profit, this would be irrelevant to K since she would have gained the advantage of the dividends-received deduction and avoided personal holding company status.

To deter the type of scheme illustrated above, the calculation now requires rental and royalty income to be reduced by the bulk of the expenses typically related to this type of income: depreciation, interest, and taxes. This requirement reduces the ability of the activities to shelter income. For instance, in *Example 8* above, K would be required to reduce the gross rental income by depreciation, interest, and taxes—which would severely curtail the utility of purchasing the laundry business.[81] The specific modifications that reduce ordinary gross income to arrive at adjusted ordinary gross income are shown in Exhibit 21-5.[82] Exhibit 21-6 and Exhibit 21-7 illustrate the adjustments required to be made to gross income from rents and mineral, oil, and gas royalties for purposes of computing adjusted ordinary gross income.

EXHIBIT 21-5
Adjusted Ordinary Gross Income[83]

Ordinary gross income (OGI)

Minus:
    a. Depreciation, property taxes, interest expense, and rents paid related to gross rental income. These deductions may not exceed gross rental income. (Gross rental income is income for the use of corporate property and interest received on the sales price of real property held as inventory.)

    b. Depreciation and depletion, property and severance taxes, interest expense, and rents paid related to gross income from mineral, oil, and gas royalties. These deductions may not exceed the gross income from the royalties.

    c. Interest on tax refunds, on judgments, on condemnation awards, and on U.S. obligations (only for a dealer in the obligations).

Equals: ***Adjusted ordinary gross income* (AOGI)**

EXHIBIT 21-6
Adjusted Income from Rents[84]

Gross rental income

Minus:
    a. Depreciation
    b. Property taxes
    c. Interest expense
    d. Rents paid

Equals: **Adjusted income from rents**

---

[81] Under current law, it is also likely that the rents would be treated as PHCI, thus further spoiling the plan.

[82] § 543(b)(2).

[83] § 543(a)(1).

[84] § 543(a)(1).

EXHIBIT 21-7
Adjusted Income from Mineral, Oil, and Gas Royalties[85]

Gross income from mineral, oil, and gas royalties (including production payments and overriding royalties)		
Minus:	**a.**	Depreciation
	b.	Property and severance taxes
	c.	Interest expense
	d.	Rents paid
Equals:		**Adjusted income from mineral, oil, and gas royalties**[86]

PERSONAL HOLDING COMPANY INCOME (PHCI)

Following the computation of AOGI, the corporation's personal holding company income must be measured to determine whether it meets the 60 percent threshold. Although personal holding company income can be generally characterized as passive income and certain income from services, the Code identifies eight specific types of income which carry the personal holding company taint.[87] These are listed in Exhibit 21-8. Selected items of PHCI are discussed below.

Dividends, Interest, Royalties, and Annuities. The most obvious forms of PHCI are those usually considered passive in nature: dividends, interest, royalties, and annuities.[88] Generally, identification and classification of these items present little problem. The most noteworthy exception concerns royalties. Mineral, oil, gas, copyright, and computer software royalties generally are included in this category of PHCI. However, as seen in Exhibit 21-8, items b, c, and d, these royalties are not treated as PHCI if certain additional tests are satisfied.

---

[85]   *Ibid.*

[86]   § 543(b)(4).

[87]   § 543.

[88]   § 543(a)(1).

EXHIBIT 21-8

Personal Holding Company Income (PHCI)

Dividends, interest, royalties (except mineral, oil, or gas royalties, copyright royalties, and certain software royalties), and annuities.

Plus: **a.** Adjusted income from rents, *but* the adjusted income from rents is not added to PHCI *if*

        1. The adjusted income from rents is 50 percent or more of AOGI, and

        2. The dividends paid, the dividends considered paid, and the consent dividends equal or exceed

            i. PHCI computed without the adjusted income from rents

            ii. Minus 10 percent of OGI.

    b. Adjusted income from mineral, oil, and gas royalties, *but* the adjusted income from these royalties is not added to PHCI *if*

        1. The adjusted income from the royalties is 50 percent or more of AOGI,

        2. PHCI computed without the adjusted income from these royalties does not exceed 10 percent of OGI, and

        3. The § 162 trade or business deductions equal or exceed 15 percent of AOGI.

    c. Copyright royalties, *but* the copyright royalties are not added to PHCI *if*

        1. The copyright royalties are 50 percent or more of OGI,

        2. PHCI computed without the copyright royalties does not exceed 10 percent of OGI, and

        3. The § 162 trade or business deductions related to the copyright royalties equal or exceed 25 percent of

            i. The OGI minus the royalties paid, plus

            ii. The depreciation related to the copyright royalties.

    d. Software royalties, *but* these are not added to PHCI *if*

        1. The royalties are received in connection with the licensing of computer software by a corporation which is actively engaged in the business of developing, manufacturing, or production of such software,

        2. The software royalties are 50 percent or more of OGI,

        3. Research and experimental expenditures, § 162 business expenses, and § 195 start-up expenditures allocable to the software business are generally 25 percent or more of OGI computed with certain adjustments, and

        4. Dividends paid, considered paid, and the consent dividends equal or exceed

            i. PHCI computed without the software royalties and certain interest income

            ii. Minus 10 percent of OGI.

    e. Produced film rents, but the produced film rents are not added to PHCI if the produced film rents equal or exceed 50 percent of OGI.

    f. Rent (for the use of tangible property) received by the corporation from a shareholder owning 25 percent or more of the value of the corporation's stock. This rent is only included in PHCI if PHCI computed without this rent and without the adjusted income from rents exceeds 10 percent of OGI.

    g. Income from personal service contracts *but only if*

        1. Someone other than the corporation has the right to designate who is to perform the services or if the person who is to perform the services is named in the contract, and

        2. At some time during the taxable year, 25 percent or more of the value of the corporation's outstanding stock is owned by the person performing the services.

    h. Income of estates and trusts taxable to the corporation.

Equals: **Personal holding company income (PHCI)**

Example 9. B Corporation has three stockholders. Its income consisted of

Gross income from a grocery	$52,000
Interest income	38,000
Capital gain	6,000

B Corporation's OGI (see Exhibit 21-4) is $90,000, computed as follows:

Gross income ($52,000 + $38,000 + $6,000)	$96,000
Minus: Capital gains	(6,000)
OGI	$90,000

In this example, AOGI is the same as OGI since the amounts which are subtracted from OGI to arrive at AOGI are zero (see Exhibit 21-5).

B Corporation's PHCI is $38,000, the amount of the interest income (see Exhibit 21-8). Since the corporation's PHCI ($38,000) is not 60 percent or more of its $90,000 AOGI ($90,000 × 60% = $54,000), it does not meet the income requirement.

Although B Corporation meets the stock ownership requirement since it has only three shareholders, it does not meet *both* the ownership requirement and the income requirement. As a result, it is not a personal holding company and is not subject to the personal holding company tax.

Example 10. Assume the same facts as in *Example 9* except that B Corporation had received $88,000 of interest income.

B Corporation's OGI and AOGI would be computed as follows:

Gross income ($52,000 + $88,000 + $6,000)	$146,000
Minus: Capital gains	(6,000)
OGI (also AOGI)	$140,000

B Corporation's PHCI is now $88,000, the amount of the interest income. Since the corporation's $88,000 of PHCI is more than 60% of the $140,000 AOGI ($140,000 × 60% = $84,000), it meets the income requirement.

Since B Corporation meets both the ownership requirement and the income requirement, *it is* a personal holding company.

Adjusted Income from Rents. Rental income presents a special problem for the personal holding company provisions. Normally, rents—generally defined as compensation for the use of property—represent a passive type of income. However, for many corporations, most notably those involved in renting real estate and equipment, rental operations are not merely a passive investment but represent a true business activity. If all rental income were considered personal holding income, closely held corporations involved in the rental business could not escape PHI status. To provide these corporations with some relief, rental income is not treated as PHCI under certain circumstances.

The amount of rental income potentially qualifying as PHCI is referred to as the *adjusted income from rents*.[89] As seen in Exhibit 21-6, adjusted income from rents consists of the corporation's gross rental income reduced by the adjustments required for

---

[89]   § 543(b)(3).

determining AOGI—depreciation, property taxes, interest expense, and rental payments related to such income (e.g., ground lease payments). The corporation's adjusted income from rents is treated as PHCI unless it can utilize the relief measure suggested above. Specifically, adjusted income from rents is PHCI unless: (1) it is 50 percent or more of the corporation's AOGI, and (2) the corporation's dividends during the taxable year as well as dividends paid within the first 2½ months of the following year *and* consent dividends are not less than the amount by which nonrental PHCI (e.g., dividends and interest) exceeds 10 percent of OGI.[90]

These relationships may be expressed as follows:

1. Adjusted income from rents $\geq$ (50% $\times$ AOGI); *and*

2. Dividends $\geq$ [nonrental PHCI $-$ (10% $\times$ OGI)].

As the latter expression indicates, when rents represent a substantial portion of OGI relative to nonrental PHCI (as typically would be the case where a corporation is truly in the rental "business"), no dividends are required. In other words, as long as nonrental income is not a major portion of the corporation's total income—does not exceed 10 percent of the corporation's OGI—dividends are unnecessary. Otherwise, a corporation in the rental business is forced to make dividend distributions to avoid penalty.

> **Example 11.** D Corporation had four shareholders in 2005 and therefore met the stock ownership requirement. The following information is available for D Corporation for 2005:
>
> | | |
> |---|---:|
> | Interest income | $10,000 |
> | Gross rental income | 25,000 |
> | Depreciation, property taxes, and interest expense related to rental income | 24,000 |
> | Maintenance and utilities related to rental income | 3,000 |
> | Dividends paid during 2005 | 8,000 |
>
> OGI (Exhibit 21-4) is $35,000 ($10,000 + $25,000). AOGI (see Exhibit 21-5) is computed as follows:
>
> | | |
> |---|---:|
> | OGI | $ 35,000 |
> | Minus: Depreciation, property taxes, and interest expense related to rental income | (24,000) |
> | AOGI | $ 11,000 |
>
> D Corporation's adjusted income from rents is computed as follows (see Exhibit 21-6):
>
> | | |
> |---|---:|
> | Gross rental income | $ 25,000 |
> | Minus: Depreciation, property taxes, and interest expense related to rental income | (24,000) |
> | Adjusted income from rents | $ 1,000 |

Note that in determining AOGI and adjusted income from rents, the maintenance and utility expenses are ignored. Such expenses are also not taken into account in determining gross income or OGI. The next step is to determine if the adjusted income from rents is to be added to PHCI. It is *not* added to PHCI if *both* of the following tests are met.

---

[90] *Ibid.*

Test 1. (50% test): Is the adjusted income from rents 50% or more of AOGI?

The adjusted income from rents ($1,000) is not 50% or more of AOGI ($11,000), so Test 1 is *not* met.

The adjusted income from rents is excluded from PHCI only if *both* Test 1 and Test 2 are met. Since Test 1 is not met, the adjusted income from rents *is* included in PHCI, and there is no need to go on to Test 2. However, Test 2 is done here for illustrative purposes.

Test 2. (10% test): Does the total of the dividends paid, the dividends considered paid, and the consent dividends equal or exceed PHCI (computed without the adjusted income from rents) reduced by 10% of OGI? This test can also be expressed as:

Dividends $\geq$ [nonrental PHCI – (OGI $\times$ 10%)]. Nonrental PHCI is $10,000 (interest income). OGI $\times$ 10% = $35,000 $\times$ 10% = $3,500. Therefore, nonrent PHCI ($10,000) minus OGI $\times$ 10% ($3,500) is $6,500. Since the total dividends ($8,000) were more than $6,500, Test 2 is met.

However, as mentioned above, *both* Test 1 and Test 2 must be met if the adjusted income from rents is to be excluded from PHCI. Therefore, the adjusted income from rents *is part of PHCI.*

D Corporation's PHCI is computed as follows (see Exhibit 21-8):

Interest income	$10,000
Adjusted income from rents	1,000
PHCI	$11,000

D Corporation's $11,000 PHCI is more than 60% of the $11,000 AOGI. In this example, in fact, PHCI is 100% of AOGI since all of the income is personal holding company income. D Corporation, therefore, meets *both* the ownership requirement and the income requirement, and thus is a personal holding company.

The rules relating to mineral, oil, gas, copyright, and software royalties are very similar to those discussed above for rents. See Exhibit 21-7 and Exhibit 21-8, items b, c, and d.

Income from Personal Service Contracts. The shifting of service income to a corporation by highly compensated individuals, such as actors and athletes, is sharply curtailed by the personal holding company provision. The PHC provisions attack the problem by treating service income as PHCI under certain conditions. Generally, amounts received by a corporation for services provided are treated as PHCI if the party desiring the services can designate the person who will perform the services and that person owns 25 percent or more of the corporation's stock[91] (see Exhibit 21-8, item g).

Example 12. T Corp., a producer of motion pictures, wanted RK to act in a new movie it was producing. Assume that RK's services could be obtained only by contracting with his wholly owned corporation, RK Inc. Accordingly, a contract is drafted providing that RK Inc. will provide the services of RK to T Corp. for $500,000. All of the income is PHCI to RK Inc. since RK owns at least 25% of the corporation *and* he is actually designated in the contract to perform the services.

Given the general rule, it would appear that virtually all service corporations are likely candidates for the PHC tax. This problem was considered in Revenue Ruling

---

[91]   § 543(a)(7).

75-67.[92] According to the facts of the ruling, a corporation's primary source of income was attributable to the services of its only employee, a doctor, who also owned 80 percent of the corporation's stock. In this case, all the facts suggested that the income would be PHCI. The only question was whether the doctor's patients formally designated him as the one to perform the services. Although a formal designation was lacking, it was implicit since the doctor was the only employee of the corporation and the patients never expected someone other than the doctor to perform the services. Despite evidence to the contrary, the IRS ruled that the income was not PHCI on the theory that there was no indication that the corporation was obligated to provide the services of the doctor in question. In addition, the ruling emphasized that the services to be performed were not so unique as to prohibit the corporation from substituting someone else to perform them. The Service also relied on the uniqueness rationale in situations involving a CPA who had incorporated his or her practice and a musical composer who had incorporated his or her song-writing activities.[93] Apparently, as long as the services are not so unique as to preclude substitution and there is no formal designation of the individual who will perform the services, a service business can escape PHC status.

COMPUTATION OF THE PHC TAX

The personal holding company penalty tax is 15 percent of the *undistributed personal holding company income*. Undistributed personal holding company income is defined as adjusted taxable income minus the dividends-paid deduction.[94] The computation of adjusted taxable income and undistributed PHCI is shown in Exhibit 21-9.

EXHIBIT 21-9
Undistributed Personal Holding Company Income[95]

Taxable income

Plus:
- **a.** Dividends-received deduction.
- **b.** Net operating loss deduction (but not a net operating loss of the preceding year computed without the dividends-received deduction).
- **c.** The amount by which the § 162 (trade or business) deductions and the § 167 (depreciation) deductions related to rental property exceed the income produced by the rental property, unless it can be shown that the rent received was the highest possible and that the rental activity was carried on as a bona fide business activity.

Minus:
- **a.** Federal income taxes (but not the accumulated earnings tax or the personal holding company tax).
- **b.** The amount by which actual charitable contributions exceeds the charitable contributions deduction reflected in net income.
- **c.** Net capital gain reduced by the taxes attributable to the net capital gain.

Equals: ***Adjusted taxable income***

Minus: *Dividends-Paid Deduction*

Equals: ***Undistributed Personal Holding Company Income***

---

[92] Rev. Rul. 75-67, 1975-1 C.B. 169.

[93] Rev. Rul. 75-290, 1975-1 C.B. 172; Rev. Rul. 75-249, 1975-1 C.B. 171; and Rev. Rul. 75-250, 1975-1 C.B. 179.

[94] § 545(a). The term "adjusted taxable income" is not found in the Code.

[95] § 545.

Like the computation of accumulated taxable income, the calculation attempts to determine the corporation's dividend-paying capacity. As a practical matter, the tax is rarely paid because of a deduction allowed for "deficiency dividends," which can be made once it has been determined the PHC tax applies.

Dividends-Paid Deduction. The dividends-paid deduction for personal holding companies is similar to the one for the accumulated earnings tax. It includes the following types of distributions:

1. Dividends paid during the taxable year;

2. Throwback dividends: dividends paid within 2½ months after the close of the taxable year (but subject to limitation as discussed below);

3. Consent dividends;

4. Liquidating distributions; and

5. Deficiency dividends.

Note that this list of qualifying distributions is identical to that provided in Exhibit 21-3 for the accumulated earnings tax, except for the special deficiency dividend. In addition, personal holding companies are entitled to a dividend carryover, which is not available for accumulated earnings tax purposes.[96]

Throwback dividends. As in the accumulated earnings tax computation, a personal holding company is allowed a deduction for throwback dividends (i.e., dividends paid within 2½ months after the close of the taxable year).[97] However, the PHC throwback dividend differs from that for the accumulated earnings tax in two ways. First, it is included in the dividends-paid deduction only if the corporation makes an election at the time the corporate tax return is filed to treat the dividends as applying to the previous year.[98] Second, the amount treated as a throwback dividend is limited to the smaller of the following:[99]

1. Twenty percent of the dividends actually paid during the taxable year in question; or
2. Undistributed PHCI (computed without the dividends paid during the 2½-month period).

Consent dividends. The rules for consent dividends are the same for personal holding companies as for the accumulated earnings tax.[100] As mentioned previously, a consent dividend is an amount that a shareholder agrees to consider as having been received as a dividend even though never actually distributed by the corporation. Consent dividends are limited to shareholders who own stock on the last day of the tax year. Their shares must be either common stock or participating preferred stock. Consent dividends do not include preferential dividends. A shareholder who consents to a dividend is treated as having received the amount as a cash dividend and contributing the same amount to the corporation's capital on the last day of the year.

---

96   § 561(a)(3).

97   § 563.

98   § 563(b).

99   *Ibid.*

100   § 565.

Dividend carryover. A personal holding company is also entitled to a dividend carryover as part of its dividends-paid deduction.[101] If the dividends paid in the two prior years exceed the adjusted taxable incomes (see Exhibit 21-9) for those years, the excess may be used as a dividend carryover (and therefore as part of the dividends-paid deduction) for the year in question.

Deficiency dividends. Once a determination has been made that a corporation is subject to the personal holding company tax, the tax can still be abated by the use of a *deficiency dividend.*[102] Following the determination of the personal holding company tax, the corporation is given 90 days to pay a deficiency dividend. A deficiency dividend must be an *actual cash dividend* which the corporation elects to treat as a distribution of the personal holding company income for the year at issue, and it is taxable to the shareholders. It does not reduce the personal holding company income of any year other than the year at issue. A deficiency dividend effectively reduces the amount of the penalty tax. However, interest and penalties are still imposed as if the deduction were not allowed. Thus, the corporation may be able to escape the tax itself— but not any interest or penalties related to such tax. It should also be noted that the deficiency dividend is available *only* to reduce the personal holding company tax. This escape is not available to those corporations subject to the accumulated earnings tax.

Example 13. C Corporation determined that it was a personal holding company and had to file Form 1120-PH. Its records for 2005 reveal the following:

Gross profit from operations	$ 150,000
Dividend income	400,000
Interest income	350,000
Long-term capital gain	30,000
Gross income	$ 930,000
Compensation	(30,000)
Selling and administrative	(100,000)
	$ 800,000
Dividends-received deduction	(280,000)
Charitable contributions	(80,000)
Taxable income	$ 440,000
Federal income tax @ 34%	$ 149,600

Charitable contributions actually made during the year were $90,000, but are limited to $80,000 (10% × $800,000 taxable income before the deductions for contributions and dividends received). C paid dividends of $20,000 in 2005 and $10,000 during the first 2½ months of 2005, which it *elects* to throw back to 2005 in computing the dividends-paid deduction. The personal holding company tax is computed as follows:

---

[101] § 564.

[102] § 547.

	Taxable income	$ 440,000
+	Dividends-received deduction	280,000
–	Excess charitable contributions	(10,000)
–	Federal income taxes.	(149,600)
–	Long-term capital gain net of tax [$30,000 – (34% × $30,000)]	(19,800)
	Adjustable taxable income	$ 540,600
–	Dividends paid deduction:	
	2005	(20,000)
	2006 Throwback (Limited to 20% of 2005 dividends)	(4,000)
	UPHCI	$ 516,600
	Times: PHC tax rate	× 15%
	PHC tax	$ 77,490

C Corporation's tax liability for 2005 is $227,090 ($149,600 regular tax + $77,490 PHC tax). The PHC tax could be avoided by paying a deficiency dividend equal to UPHCI ($516,600). However, the payment of the dividend would not eliminate any penalties or interest that might be assessed on the $77,490 PHC tax due if Form 1120-PH is not filed in a timely manner.

TAX PLANNING

ACCUMULATED EARNINGS TAX

For taxpayers wanting to use the corporate form to shield their income from individual taxes, the accumulated earnings tax represents a formidable obstacle. Although there is an obvious cost if the tax is incurred, that cost may be far more than expected. This result often occurs because the imposition of the tax for one year triggers an audit for all open years. In addition, the IRS usually takes the position that the negligence penalty of Code § 6653 should be imposed whenever the accumulated earnings tax is applicable. Moreover, in contrast to the personal holding company tax which can normally be averted using the deficiency dividend procedure, the accumulated earnings tax, once levied, cannot be avoided. At the time of the audit, it is too late for dividend payments or consent dividends!

Despite the potential cost of the tax, the rewards from avoidance—or at least the deferral—of double taxation are often so great that the shareholders are willing to assume the risk of penalty. Moreover, many practitioners believe that with proper planning the risk of incurring the accumulated earnings tax is minimal, particularly since the tax is not self-assessed but dependent on the audit lottery. In addition, it is possible to shift the burden of proof to the IRS. The discussion below examines some of the means for reducing the taxpayer's exposure to the accumulated earnings tax.

Liquid Assets and Working Capital. Normally, the accumulated earnings tax is not raised as an issue unless the corporation's balance sheet shows cash, marketable securities, or other liquid assets that could be distributed easily to shareholders. The absence of liquid assets indicates that any earnings that have been retained have been reinvested in the business rather than accumulated for the forbidden purpose. It is a rare occasion, however, when such assets do not exist. Consequently, most IRS agents routinely assess whether the level of the corporation's working capital is appropriate by applying the *Bardahl* formula.

The courts have made it clear that the *Bardahl* formula serves merely as a guideline for determining the proper amount of working capital. In *Delaware Trucking Co., Inc.*, the court held that the amount needed using the *Bardahl* formula could be increased by 75 percent due to the possibility of increased labor and other operating costs due to inflation.[103] Nevertheless, in those instances where working capital appears excessive, the Internal Revenue Manual directs agents to require justification of such excess. Therefore, the corporation should closely control its working capital to ensure that it does not exceed the corporation's reasonable needs.

One way to reduce working capital is to increase shareholder salaries, bonuses, and other compensation. Since these payments are deductible, double taxation is avoided. This technique also has the benefit of reducing taxable income, which in turn reduces the accumulated earnings tax should it apply. However, this method of reducing working capital may not be feasible if the compensation paid exceeds a reasonable amount. To the extent that the compensation is unreasonable, the payments are treated as dividends and double taxation results. In addition, if the unreasonable compensation is not pro rata among all shareholders, the dividend will be considered preferential and no deduction will be allowed for the dividend in computing adjusted taxable income.

Another method for reducing working capital is for the corporation to invest in additional assets. However, the taxpayer must be careful to avoid investments that are of a passive nature or that could be considered unrelated to the corporation's existing or projected business. With respect to the latter, the courts have ruled that the business of a controlled subsidiary is the business of the parent while the business of a sister corporation normally is not the business of its brother.[104]

Reasonable Needs. The courts have accepted a variety of reasons as sufficient justification for the accumulation of earnings. On the one hand, the needs deemed reasonable have been both certain and well-defined, such as the repayment of corporate debt. On the other hand, the courts have approved needs as contingent and unknown as those arising from possible damage from future floods.

One contingency that seemingly could be asserted by all corporations as a basis for accumulating funds is the possibility of a business reversal, depression, or loss of major customer. Interestingly, the courts have often respected this justification for accumulations, notwithstanding the fact that it is a risk assumed by virtually all business entities. Acceptance of this need, however, appears to be dependent on the taxpayer's ability to establish that there is at least some chance that a business reversal could occur that would affect the taxpayer. For example, in *Ted Bates & Co.*, the corporation was in the advertising business and received 70 percent of its fees from only five clients.[105] In ruling for the taxpayer, the court held that the corporation was allowed to accumulate amounts necessary to cover its fixed costs for a period following the loss of a major client. Much of the court's opinion was based on its view that the advertising business was extremely competitive and the possibility of losing a client was not unrealistic. A similar decision was reached where a manufacturer sold all its products to one customer and had to compete with others for that customer's business. The court believed that accumulations were necessary to enable the corporation to develop new markets if it lost its only customer. Relying on a possible downturn in business as a basis for accumulations has not always sufficed. In *Goodall*, the company accumulated earnings in light of the prospect that military orders would be lost.[106] The court upheld the

---

[103] 32 TCM 104, T.C. Memo 1973-29.

[104] For example, see *Latchis Theatres of Keene, Inc. v. Comm.*, 54-2 USTC ¶9544, 45 AFTR 1836, 214 F.2d 834 (CA-1,1954).

[105] 24 TCM 1346, T.C. Memo 1965-251.

[106] *Robert A. Goodall Estate v. Comm.*, 68-1 USTC ¶9245, 21 AFTR2d 813, 391 F.2d 775, (CA-8.1968).

penalty tax, indicating that even if the loss occurred, it would not have a significant effect because the corporation's business was expanding.

Although the courts have sustained various reasons for accumulations, a review of the cases indicates that the taxpayer must demonstrate that the need is realistic. This was made clear in *Colonial Amusement Corp.*[107] In this case, the corporation's accumulations were not justified when it wanted to construct a building on adjacent land and building restrictions existed that prohibited construction.

In establishing that a need is realistic, a taxpayer's self-serving statement normally is not convincing. Proper documentation of the need is critical. This is true even when the need is obvious and acceptable. In *Union Offset*, the corporation stated at trial that its accumulations were necessary to retire outstanding corporate debt, a legitimate business need.[108] To the taxpayer's dismay, however, the Tax Court still imposed the tax because the corporation had failed to document in any type of written record its plan to use the accumulations in the alleged manner. In this case, a simple statement in the Board of Directors' minutes concerning the proposed use of the funds would no doubt have saved the taxpayer from penalty.

S Corporation Election. In those cases where it is difficult to justify accumulations, the shareholders may wish to elect to be treated as an S corporation. Since the earnings of an S corporation are taxed to the individual shareholders rather than the corporation, S corporations cannot be used to shelter income and thus are immune to the accumulated earnings tax. However, the election insulates the corporation only prospectively (i.e., only for that period for which it is, an S corporation). Prior years open to audit are still vulnerable. In addition, the S election may raise other problems. The shareholders will be required to report and pay taxes on the income of the corporation even though it may not be distributed to them. As a result, cash flow problems may occur. Further, because the corporation has accumulated earnings and profits, the excess passive income tax specifically designed for C corporations that have elected S status may apply. In addition, the corporation may be subject to the built-in gains tax.[109] For these reasons, an S election should be carefully considered.

PERSONAL HOLDING COMPANY TAX

The personal holding company tax, like the accumulated earnings tax, is clearly a tax to be avoided. Unfortunately, the personal holding company tax differs from the accumulated earnings tax in that it is not reserved solely for those whose intent is to avoid taxes. Rather, it is applied on a mechanical basis, regardless of motive, to all corporations that fall within its purview. For this reason, it is important to closely monitor the corporation's activities to ensure that it does not inadvertently become a PHC.

One important responsibility of a practitioner is to recognize potential personal holding company problems so that steps can be taken to avoid the tax or the need to distribute dividends. This responsibility not only concerns routine operations but extends to advice concerning planned transactions that could cause the corporation to be converted from an operating company to an investment company. For example, a corporation may plan to sell one or all of its businesses and invest the proceeds in passive type assets. Similarly, a planned reorganization may leave the corporation holding stock of the acquiring corporation. Failure to identify the possible personal holding company difficulty which these and other transactions may cause can lead to serious embarrassment.

---

[107] 7 TCM 546.

[108] 79-2 USTC ¶9550, 603 F.2d 90 (CA-9, 1979).

[109] See Chapter 23 for a discussion of these special taxes that may be imposed on S corporations.

Although the thrust of most tax planning for personal holding companies concerns how to avoid the tax, there are certain instances when a planned PHC can provide benefits. Both varieties of personal holding companies, the planned and the unplanned, are discussed below.

PHC Candidates. All corporations could fall victim to the PHC tax. However, some corporations are more likely candidates than others. For this reason, their activities and anticipated transactions should be scrutinized more carefully than others.

Potential difficulties often concern corporations that are involved in rental activities and those that have some passive income. In this regard, it should be noted that the term "rent" is defined as payments received for the use of property. As a result, "rental companies" include not only those that lease such items as apartments, offices, warehouses, stadiums, equipment, vending machines, automobiles, trucks, and the like, but also those that operate bowling alleys, roller and ice skating rinks, billiards parlors, golf courses, and any other activity for which a payment is received for use of the corporation's property. All of these corporations are at risk since each has rental income which could be considered passive personal holding company income unless it satisfies the special two-prong test for rental companies.

There are several other types of corporations that must be concerned with PHC problems. Investment companies—corporations formed primarily to acquire income producing assets such as stock, bonds, rental properties, partnership interests, and similar investments—clearly have difficulties. Corporations that derive most of their income from the services of one or more of their shareholders also are vulnerable. In recent years, however, the Service has taken a liberal view toward the professional corporations of doctors, accountants, and several others. Another group of corporations that are probable targets of the PHC tax includes those that collect royalty income. The royalty income might arise from the corporation's development and licensing of a product (e.g., patent on a food processor or franchises to operate a restaurant). Other logical candidates for the PHC tax are banks, savings and loans, and finance companies since the majority of their income is interest income from making loans and purchasing or discounting accounts receivable and installment obligations. Banks and savings and loans need not worry, however, since they are specifically excluded from PHC status. Finance companies are also exempt from the penalty tax, but only if certain tests—not discussed here—are met. Consequently, those involved with finance companies should review their situation closely to ensure such tests are satisfied.

Avoiding PHC Status. In general, if a corporation is closely held and 60 percent of its income is derived from passive sources or specified personal services, the PHC tax applies. Thus, to avoid the PHC tax *either* the stock ownership test or the income test must be failed.

Stock Ownership Test. The stock ownership test is satisfied if five or fewer persons own more than 50 percent of the stock. This test is the most difficult to fail since it requires dilution of the current shareholders' ownership. Moreover, dilution is very difficult to implement in practice due to the constructive ownership rules. The rules make it virtually impossible to maintain ownership in the family since stock owned by one family member or an entity in which the family member has an interest is considered owned by other family members. Therefore, to fail the ownership test, sufficient stock must be owned by unrelated parties to reduce the ownership of the five largest shareholders to 50 percent or less. Unfortunately, it is often impossible to design an arrangement that meets these conditions yet is still desirable from an economic viewpoint.

Passive Income Test. The corporation is deemed to satisfy the passive income test if 60 percent of its adjusted ordinary gross income (AOGI) is personal holding company income (PHCI)—income from dividends, interest, annuities, rents, royalties, or specified shareholder services. The potential for failing this test is perhaps more easily seen when this test is expressed mathematically:

$$\frac{\text{PHCI}}{\text{AOGI}} \geq 60\%$$

The steps that can be taken to fail this test fall into three categories: (1) increasing operating income or AOGI, (2) reducing PHCI, and (3) satisfying the exceptions to remove the PHC taint from the income.

Increasing Operating Income. One way to fail the 60 percent test is to increase the denominator in the income test fraction, AOGI, without increasing the numerator. This requires the corporation to increase its operating income without any corresponding increase in its passive income. Obtaining such an increase is not easy since it is essentially asking that the corporation generate more gross income. This does not necessarily mean that sales must increase, however. The corporation might consider increasing its profit margin. Although this could reduce sales, the resulting increase in gross income could be sufficient to fail the test. Alternatively, the corporation might consider expanding the operating portion of the business. Expansion not only in increases AOGI but also may have the effect of reducing PHCI if the investments generating the PHCI are sold to invest in the expansion.

Reducing Personal Holding Income. Failing the income test normally is accomplished by reducing personal holding company income. It is sometimes asserted that merely reducing PHCI is not sufficient since both the numerator and the denominator in the test fraction are reduced by the same amounts. (This occurs because AOGI includes PHCI.) A mathematical check of this statement shows that it is incorrect and that a simple elimination of PHCI aids the taxpayer.

Example 14. Z Corporation has $100,000 of AOGI, including $70,000 of interest income that is PHCI. Substituting these values into the test fraction reveals that the corporation has excessive passive income.

$$\frac{\text{PHCI}}{\text{AOGI}} = \frac{\$70,000}{\$100,000} = 70\%$$

If Z Corporation simply reduces its interest income by $30,000, the corporation would fail the income test despite the fact that both the numerator and the denominator are reduced by the same amounts.

$$\frac{\text{PHCI}}{\text{AOGI}} = \frac{\$40,000}{\$70,000} = 57.1\%$$

One way a corporation could eliminate part of its PHCI is by paying out as shareholder compensation the amounts that otherwise would be invested to generate PHCI. Alternatively, the corporation could eliminate PHCI by switching its investments into growth stocks where the return is generated from capital appreciation rather than dividends. Of course, the taxpayer would not necessarily want to switch completely out of dividend-paying stocks since the advantage of the dividends-received deduction would be lost.

The corporation could also reduce its PHCI by replacing it with tax-exempt income, capital gains, or § 1231 gains. This would have the same effect as simply eliminating the PHCI altogether.

Example 15. Same as *Example 14* above except the corporation invests in tax-exempt bonds which generate $20,000 of tax-exempt, rather than taxable, interest. In addition, the corporation realizes a $10,000 capital gain instead of taxable interest. The effect of replacing the taxable interest of $30,000 with capital gains of $10,000 and tax-exempt income of $20,000 would produce results identical to those above. This derives from the fact that the tax-exempt interest and capital gains are excluded from both the numerator, PHCI, and the denominator, AOGI, creating fractions identical to those shown above.

Removing the PHC Taint. In some situations, income which is normally considered PHCI (e.g., rental income) is not considered tainted if certain tests are met. For example, the Code provides escape hatches for rental income; mineral, oil, and gas royalties; copyright royalties; and rents from the distribution and exhibition of produced films. Although additional tests must be met to obtain exclusion for these types of income, there is one requirement common to each. *Generally*, if a corporation's income consists predominantly (50 percent or more) of only one of these income types, exclusion is available. More importantly, this condition can normally be obtained without great difficulty. To satisfy the 50 percent test, the taxpayer should take steps to ensure that a particular corporation receives only a single type of income. This may require forming an additional corporation that receives only one type of income, but by so doing the 50 percent test is met and the PHC tax may be avoided.

With proper control of their income, these corporations will have no difficulty in satisfying the income test since at least 50 percent of their AOGI is from one source. For corporations with rental income, however, dividends equal to the amount that their nonrental PHC income exceeds 10 percent of their OGI still must be paid. Note, however, that if a corporation has little or no nonrental PHC income, no dividends are necessary to meet the test. Also note that each additional dollar of gross rents, unreduced by expenses, decreases the amount of dividend that must be paid.

Example 16. G Corporation has $60,000 of OGI, including $53,000 of rental income and $7,000 of dividend income. In this case, dividends of only $1,000 are necessary since nonrental PHCI exceeds the 10% threshold by only $1,000 [$7,000 − (10% of OGI of $60,000)]. If the taxpayer wants to avoid distributing dividends, consideration should be given to increasing gross rents. Note how an increase of $10,000 in gross rents to $63,000 would increase OGI and concomitantly eliminate the need for a dividend. This increase in gross rents would be effective even if the typical adjustments for depreciation, interest, and taxes reduce the taxpayer's net profit to zero or a loss. This is true because such adjustments are not included in determining OGI, but only AOGI. Thus, an incentive exists for the corporation to invest in breakeven or unprofitable activities as a means to eliminate the dividend.

Reducing the PHC Tax with Dividends. If the tests for PHC status cannot be avoided, the penalty can be eliminated or minimized by the payment of dividends. Although a similar opportunity exists for the accumulated earnings tax, the treatment of dividends differs in several important respects.

On the one hand, the PHC tax requires quicker action than the accumulated earnings tax. For accumulated earnings tax purposes, all dividends paid within the 2½-month period after the close of the taxable year are counted as paid for the previous year. However, for purposes of the PHC tax, the after-year-end dividends are limited to 20 percent of the amount actually paid during the year. Thus, if no dividends are paid during the year, then none can be paid during the 2½-month period. On the other hand, the PHC tax can almost always be avoided through payment of a deficiency dividend, which is not available for the accumulated earnings tax. The deficiency dividend may come at a high price, however. As previously mentioned, any interest and penalties that would have been imposed had the penalty tax applied must be computed and paid as if the PHC tax were still due.

Planned Personal Holding Companies. Treatment of a corporation as a personal holding company is normally considered a dire consequence. Yet, in certain cases, PHC status may not be detrimental and at times can be beneficial. Two of these situations are outlined below.

Certain taxpayers seeking the benefits of the corporate form are unable to avoid characterization as a personal holding company. For example, an athlete or movie celebrity may seek the benefits reserved solely for employees, such as group-term life insurance, health and accident insurance, medical reimbursement plans, and better pension and profit-sharing plans. In these situations, if the individual incorporates his or her talents, the corporation will be considered a PHC since all of the income for services will be PHCI. This does not mean that the PHC tax must be paid, however. The PHC tax is levied only upon undistributed PHCI. In most cases, all of the undistributed PHCI can be eliminated through the payments of deductible compensation directly to the individual or deductible contributions to his or her pension plan. As a result, the individual can obtain the benefits of incorporation without concern for the PHC tax. This technique was extremely popular prior to 1982, when the benefits of corporate pension plans were significantly better than those available to the self-employed (i.e., Keogh plans).

Over the years, personal holding companies have been used quite successfully in estate planning in reducing the value of the taxpayer's estate and obtaining other estate tax benefits. Under a typical plan, a taxpayer with a portfolio of securities would transfer them to a PHC in exchange for preferred stock equal to their current value and common stock of no value. The exchange would be tax free under Code § 351. The taxpayer would then proceed to give the common stock to his or her children at no gift tax cost since its value at the time is zero. The taxpayer would also begin a gift program, transferring $10,000 of preferred stock annually to heirs, which would also escape gift tax due to the annual gift tax exclusion. There were several benefits arising from this arrangement.

First and probably foremost, any appreciation in the value of the taxpayer's portfolio would accrue to the owners of the common stock and thus be successfully removed from the taxpayer's estate, avoiding both gift and estate taxes. Second, the corporation's declaration of dividends on the common stock would shift the income to the lower-bracket family members. Dividends on the preferred stock would also be shifted to the extent that the taxpayer has transferred the preferred stock. The dividends paid would in part aid in eliminating any PHC tax. Third, the taxpayer's preferred stock in the PHC would probably be valued at less than the value of the underlying assets for estate and gift tax purposes. Although the IRS takes the position that the value of the stock in the PHC is the same as the value of the corporation's assets, the courts have consistently held otherwise. The courts have normally allowed a substantial *discount* for estate and gift tax valuation, holding that an investment in a closely held business is less desirable than in the underlying shares since the underlying securities can easily be traded in the market while the PHC shares cannot.[110]

---

[110] For example, see *Estate of Maurice Gustane Heckscher*, 63 T.C. 485 (1974). Also, see Chapter 26 for possible limitations on this estate planning technique.

PROBLEM MATERIALS

DISCUSSION QUESTIONS

21-1 *Double Taxation.* List four approaches that corporations use to avoid the effects of double taxation.

21-2 *Accumulated Earnings Tax.* What is the purpose of the accumulated earnings tax?

21-3 *Accumulated Earnings Tax.* What is the accumulated earnings tax rate? Why do you suppose Congress chose this particular tax rate?

21-4 *Accumulated Taxable Income.* What is the difference between accumulated taxable income and taxable income?

21-5 *Accumulated Earnings Credit.* What is the accumulated earnings credit? How does it affect the accumulated earnings tax?

21-6 *Dividends-Paid Deduction.* What constitutes the dividends-paid deduction for purposes of the accumulated earnings tax?

21-7 *Throwback Dividend.* What is a throwback dividend?

21-8 *Consent Dividends.* What is a consent dividend? What is its purpose?

21-9 *Intent of Accumulations.* What situations are considered to indicate the intent of a corporation to unreasonably accumulate earnings?

21-10 *Reasonable Needs.* List six possible reasons for accumulating earnings that might be considered reasonable needs of the business.

21-11 *Reasonable Needs—The Bardahl Formula.* What is the *Bardahl* formula? How is it used?

21-12 *Personal Holding Company Tax.* What is the purpose of the personal holding company tax?

21-13 *Personal Holding Company.* What requirements must be met by a corporation in order for it to be a personal holding company?

21-14 *Ownership Requirement.* What is the ownership requirement for personal holding companies? What constructive ownership rules apply?

21-15 *Income Requirement.* What is the income requirement for personal holding companies? What terms must be defined in order to determine if a corporation meets the income requirement?

21-16 *Income Requirement.* What tests must be met in order to determine whether the adjusted income from rents is included in personal holding company income?

21-17 *Computing the Personal Holding Company Tax.* How is the personal holding company penalty tax computed?

21-18 *Adjusted Taxable Income.* How does adjusted taxable income differ from taxable income?

21-19   *Dividends-Paid Deduction.* How does the dividends-paid deduction for personal holding company tax purposes differ from the dividends-paid deduction for accumulated earnings tax purposes?

21-20   *Deficiency Dividends.* What is a deficiency dividend? What is its purpose? What effect does it have on the personal holding company tax?

PROBLEMS

21-21   *Computing the Accumulated Earnings Tax.* Z Corporation had accumulated taxable income of $180,000 for the current year. Calculate Z Corporation's accumulated earnings tax liability.

21-22   *Computing Adjusted Taxable Income.* R Corporation has the following income and deductions for the current year:

Income from operations	$200,000
Dividend income (from less than 20% owned corporations)	60,000
Charitable contributions	40,000

Compute R Corporation's adjusted taxable income.

21-23   *Minimum Accumulated Earnings Tax Credit.* B Corporation, a calendar year manufacturing company, had accumulated earnings and profits at the beginning of the current year of $60,000. If the corporation's earnings and profits for the current year are $270,000, what is B Corporation's minimum accumulated earnings tax credit?

21-24   *Accumulated Earnings Tax Credit.* Assume the same facts in *Problem 21-23* above, except that B Corporation has estimated reasonable business needs of $170,000 at the end of the current year.
   a.   Compute B Corporation's accumulated earnings tax credit for the current year.
   b.   Would your answer differ if B Corporation was an incorporated law practice owned and operated be one person? If so, by how much?

21-25   *Computing the Accumulated Earnings Tax.* T Corporation had accumulated earnings and profits at the beginning of 2005 of $300,000. It has never paid dividends to its shareholders and does not intend to do so in the near future. The following facts relate to T Corporation's 2005 tax year:

Taxable income	$200,000
Federal income tax	61,250
Dividends received (from less than 20% owned corporations)	40,000
Reasonable business needs as of 12/31/05	356,850

   a.   What is T Corporation's accumulated earnings tax?
   b.   If T Corporation's sole shareholder wanted to avoid the accumulated earnings tax, what amount of consent dividends would be required?

21-26   *Dividends-Paid Deduction.* J Corporation, a small oil tool manufacturer, projects adjusted taxable income for the current year of $200,000. Its estimated reasonable business needs are $500,000; and the corporation has $380,000 of prior years' accumulated earnings and profits as of the beginning of the current year. Using this information, answer the following:
   a.   Assuming no dividends-paid deduction, what is J Corporation's accumulated earnings tax for the current year?
   b.   If J Corporation paid $50,000 of dividends during the year, what is J Corporation's accumulated earnings tax liability?

    c. If J Corporation's shareholders are willing to report more dividends than the $50,000 actually received during the year, what amount of consent dividends is necessary to avoid the accumulated earnings tax?

    d. If the corporation's shareholders are not interested in paying taxes on hypothetical dividends, what other possibility is available to increase the dividends-paid deduction?

21-27 *Working Capital Needs—The* Bardahl *Formula.* X Corporation wishes to use the Bardahl formula to determine the amount of working capital it can justify if the IRS agent currently auditing the company's records raises the accumulated earnings tax issue. For the year under audit, X Corporation had the following:

Annual operating expenses	$285,000
Inventory cycle ratio	.41
Accounts receivable cycle ratio	.61
Accounts payable cycle ratio	.82

    a. How much working capital can X Corporation justify based on the above facts?

    b. If X Corporation's turnover ratios are based on annual averages, what additional information would you request before computing working capital needs based on the *Bardahl* formula?

21-28 *Working Capital Needs—Bardahl Formula.* B owns and operates BKA Inc., which is a retail toy store. One Wednesday morning in January 2006, she noticed in the *Wall Street Journal's* tax column an anecdote about a small corporation that was required to pay the accumulated earnings tax. Concerned, B presented the following information to her tax advisor to evaluate her exposure as of the end of 2005.

Balance Sheet

	2004	2005
Current Assets:		
Cash	$ 15,000	$ 30,000
Marketable securities (cost)	10,000	23,000
Accounts receivable (net)	55,000	45,000
Inventory	30,000	50,000
Property, plant, and equipment (net)	500,000	552,000
Total Assets	$610,000	$700,000
Current Liabilities:		
Accounts payable	$ 13,000	$ 31,000
Long-term debt	147,000	119,000
Common stock	50,000	50,000
Earnings and profits	400,000	500,000
Total Liabilities and Equity	$610,000	$700,000

Income Statement

Sales		$ 400,000
Cost of goods sold:		
Beginning inventory	$ 30,000	
Purchases.	220,000	
Ending inventory	(50,000)	
Total		(200,000)
Gross profit		$ 200,000
Other Expenses:		
Depreciation	$ 70,000	
Selling expenses and administrative	25,000	
Interest	5,000	
Total		(100,000)
Net income before taxes		$ 100,000
Income taxes		(25,750)
Net income.		$ 74,250

B noted that the market value of the securities was $40,000 as of December 31, 2005. In addition, B estimates the future expansion of the business (excluding working capital) will require $25,000. Determine whether the accumulated earnings tax will apply to B.

21-29 *Personal Holding Company—Income Requirement.* K Corporation is equally owned and operated by three brothers. K Corporation's gross income for the current year is $80,000, which consists of $10,000 of dividend income, interest income of $40,000, and a long-term capital gain of $30,000.
  a. Calculate ordinary gross income.
  b. Calculate adjusted ordinary gross income.
  c. Is K Corporation a personal holding company?

21-30 *Personal Holding Company—Rent Exclusion.* T Corporation has gross income of $116,000, which consists of gross rental income of $86,000, interest income of $20,000, and dividends of $10,000. Depreciation, property taxes, and interest expense related to the rental property totaled $16,000. Assuming T Corporation has seven shareholders and has no dividends-paid deduction, answer the following:
  a. What is T Corporation's ordinary gross income?
  b. Adjusted ordinary gross income?
  c. Does the rental income constitute personal holding company income?
  d. Is T Corporation a personal holding company?

21-31 *Personal Holding Company Income.* V Corporation is equally owned by two shareholders. The corporation reports the following income and deductions for the current year.

Dividend income	$30,000
Interest income	15,000
Long-term capital gain	10,000
Rental income (gross)	80,000
Rental expenses:	
Depreciation	10,000
Interest on mortgage.	9,000
Property taxes.	3,000
Real estate management fees	8,000

    a. Calculate ordinary gross income.

    b. Calculate adjusted ordinary gross income.

    c. Calculate adjusted income from rentals.

    d. Calculate personal holding company income.

    e. Is V Corporation a personal holding company?

    f. If V Corporation paid $3,000 of dividends to each of its two shareholders during the current year, how would this affect your answers to (d) and (e) above?

21-32 *Items of PHC Income.* Indicate whether the following would be considered personal holding company income.

    a. Income from the sales of inventory

    b. Interest income from AT&T bond

    c. Interest income from State of Texas bond

    d. Dividend income from IBM stock

    e. Long-term capital gain

    f. Short-term capital gain

    g. Rental income from lease of office building (100% of the corporation's income is from rents)

    h. Fees paid to the corporation for the services of Jose Greatfoot, internationally known soccer player.

21-33 *PHC Income Test.* All of the stock of C Corporation is owned by B. Next year, the corporation expects the following results from operations:

Sales	$500,000
Costs of goods sold	200,000
Other operating expenses	40,000
Interest income	10,000

What is the maximum amount of dividend income that the corporation can have without being classified as a personal holding company?

21-34 *Computing the Personal Holding Company Tax.* P Corporation is owned by five individuals. For the current year P had the following:

Taxable income	$200,000
Federal income tax	60,750
Dividends received (from less than	
20% owned corporations)	40,000
Long-term capital gain	10,000

Compute P Corporation's personal holding company tax assuming that P meets the income test, P did not pay dividends, and the long-term capital gain was taxed at 34 percent.

21-35 *Personal Holding Company—Dividend Deduction.* H, a personal holding company, anticipates having undistributed personal holding company income of $120,000 before any dividend deduction for 2005. The company wishes to distribute all of its income to avoid the penalty. Because of cash flow problems, it wishes to pay as much of this dividend as it can in the 2½ months after the close of the tax year.

    a. What is the *maximum* amount that H can distribute during 2006 to accomplish its task if dividends of $50,000 were paid during 2005?

    b. What is the *minimum* amount that H must distribute during 2005 and still be able to defer until 2006 the payment of any additional dividends?

21-36 *Personal Holding Company—Service Income.* J, an orthopedic surgeon, is the sole owner of J Inc. The corporation employs surgical nurses and physical therapists in addition to J. The nurses assist Dr. J on all operations, and the therapists provide all follow-up treatment. J Inc. bills all clients for all services rendered and pays the employees a stated salary. Will any of J Inc.'s fee be personal holding company income?

21-37 *PHC Dividends—Paid Deduction.* Indicate whether the following distributions would qualify for the personal holding company dividends-paid deduction for 2005. Assume that the corporation is a calendar year taxpayer.
a. Cash dividends paid on common stock in 2005.
b. Dividend distribution of land (value $20,000, basis $5,000) paid on common stock in 2005.
c. Cash dividends paid on common stock March 3, 2006.
d. Cash dividends paid on common stock in 2004.
e. Consent dividend; the 2005 corporate tax return was filed on March 3, 2006; the consents were filed on May 15, 2006.
f. Cash dividend paid in 2008 shortly after it was determined that the corporation was a personal holding company.
g. The corporation adopted a plan of liquidation in 2003 and the final liquidating distribution was made during 2005.

21-38 *Accumulated Earnings Tax Dividends-Paid Deduction.* Indicate whether the distributions identified in *Problem 21-37* would qualify for the accumulated earnings tax dividends-paid deduction for 2005.

21-39 *Understanding the PHC Tax.* Indicate whether the following statements regarding the personal holding company tax are true or false.
a. The PHC tax is self-assessed and, if applicable, must be paid in addition to the regular income tax.
b. An S corporation or partnership may be subject to the PHC tax.
c. A corporation that can prove that its shareholders did not intend to use it as a tax shelter is not subject to the PHC tax.
d. A publicly traded corporation normally would not be subject to the PHC tax.
e. A corporation that derives virtually all of its income from leasing operations does not risk the PHC tax, even though such income is normally considered passive.
f. Federal income taxes reduce the base on which the PHC tax is assessed.
g. Long-term capital gains are not subject to the PHC tax.
h. A corporation that consistently pays dividends normally would not be subject to the PHC tax.
i. Throwback dividends are available to reduce the corporation's potential liability without limitation.
j. Corporations without cash or property that they can distribute cannot benefit from the dividends-paid deduction.
k. The PHC tax is not truly a risk because of the deficiency dividend procedure.
l. A corporation may be required to pay both the accumulated earnings tax and the personal holding company tax in the same year.

21-40 *Understanding the Accumulated Earnings Tax.* Indicate whether the statements in *Problem 21-39* are true or false regarding the accumulated earnings tax.

RESEARCH PROBLEMS

21-41 H Corporation is owned and operated by William and Wilma Holt. The corporation's principal source of income for the past few years has been net rentals from five adjacent rent houses located in an area that the city has condemned in order to expand its freeway system. The Holts anticipate a condemnation award of approximately $400,000, and a resulting gain of $325,000. Although convinced that they will have the corporation reinvest the proceeds in other rental units, the Holts would like to invest the corporation's condemnation proceeds in a high-yield certificate of deposit for at least three years. They have come to you for advice.

a. What advice would you give concerning the reinvestment requirements of Code § 1033?

b. If H Corporation will have substantial interest income in the next few years, could the § 541 tax be a possibility?

c. If the Holts have considered liquidating the corporation and reinvesting the proceeds in rental units, what additional information would you need in order to advise them?

21-42 Stacey Caniff is the controlling shareholder of Cotton, Inc., a textile manufacturer. She inherited the business from her father. In recent years earnings have fluctuated between $0.50 and $3.00 per share. Dividends have remained at $0.10 per share for the past ten years with a resulting increase in cash. On audit, the IRS agent has raised the accumulated earnings tax issue. In your discussion with Stacey, she has indicated that the dividends are so low because she is afraid of losing the business (as almost happened to her father during the Depression), of decreased profitability from foreign competition, and of the need to modernize if OSHA were to enforce the rules concerning cotton dust. Evaluate the possibility of overcoming an accumulated earnings tax assessment.

Part VIII

FLOW-THROUGH ENTITIES

❖ **Contents** ❖

Chapter 22

TAXATION OF PARTNERSHIPS AND PARTNERS

LEARNING OBJECTIVES

Upon completion of this chapter you will be able to:

- Define the terms *partner* and *partnership* for federal income tax purposes

- Distinguish between the entity theory and the aggregate theory of partnerships

- Analyze the tax consequences of forming a new partnership

- Determine the tax basis of a partnership interest

- Compute partnership taxable income or loss and identify any separately computed items of partnership income, gain, loss, deduction, or credit

- Explain how the tax consequences of partnership operations are reported on the tax returns of the partners and how the partners' bases in their partnership interests are adjusted to reflect these tax consequences

- Identify the tax consequences of various transactions between a partner and a partnership

- Determine the tax consequences of both current and liquidating distributions from a partnership

- Analyze the tax consequences of a sale of a partnership interest to both the seller and purchaser

- Apply the family partnership rules to partnership interests created by gift

- Recognize a termination of a partnership and summarize the tax consequences of the termination to the partners

CHAPTER OUTLINE

When two or more parties agree to go into business together, they must first decide which form of business to use. Should the business be incorporated or should it operate as a partnership? Although the corporate form predominates for large companies, it is certainly not appropriate for all businesses. Consequently, partnerships are widely used throughout the business world.

Partnerships come in a wide assortment of shapes and sizes. For example, two accountants may form a professional partnership through which to conduct their business, or a family may organize a partnership to manage real estate or operate a corner delicatessen. In contrast, two international corporations may form a partnership to develop a new product or to conduct research. Partnerships may also be used as investment vehicles. For instance, hundreds or thousands of people may invest in partnerships that drill for oil, construct office buildings, or make movies. For whatever reason, when two or more parties decide to pool their resources in order to carry on a profit-making activity, they often choose to do so as partners in a partnership.

The federal tax consequences of business activities that meet the statutory definition of a partnership are governed by the provisions of Subchapter K of the Internal Revenue Code (§§ 701 through 777). This chapter begins with an analysis of this definition and a brief introduction to several other important concepts that underlie Subchapter K. The chapter also includes discussions of the formation and operation of a partnership, the mechanics by which partnership income or loss is allocated to and taken into account by each partner, and the tax consequences of common transactions between partners and partnerships. The more advanced topics of current and liquidating partnership distributions and dispositions of partnership interests are also introduced.

DEFINITIONS

WHAT IS A PARTNERSHIP?

The Uniform Partnership Act defines a partnership quite simply as "an association of two or more persons to carry on as co-owners a business for profit."[1] This basic definition is expanded in the Code to include a syndicate, group, pool, joint venture, or any other unincorporated organization.[2] For an organization to constitute a partnership, it must have at least two partners. Note that there are no restrictions on either the maximum number of partners or on the type of entity that may be a partner. Individuals, corporations, trusts, estates, and even other partnerships may join together as partners to carry on a profit-making activity.

As a practical matter, determining whether an organization qualifies as a partnership is rarely a problem. For example, any organization formed under the Uniform Partnership Act or the Uniform Limited Partnership Act should expect to be treated as a partnership. However, as explained in Chapter 19, certain unincorporated organizations may or may not be treated as partnerships for tax purposes. Under the "check the box" regulations, all business entities incorporated under a state law providing for a separate corporation, a joint stock company, an insurance company, a bank, or certain foreign entities will be classified as corporations for federal tax purposes.[3] All other business entities, known as associations, which are not automatically defined as a corporation can *elect* to be taxed as a corporation. Any association, including any limited liability company having two or more owners and that does not make the election, will be treated as a partnership.[4]

A foreign entity in which all owners have limited liability will be treated as a corporation. A foreign entity in which one or more owners have unlimited liability will be treated as a partnership unless it makes the election to be taxed as a corporation.[5]

Other treasury regulations clarify that certain arrangements are not treated as partnerships for federal tax purposes. A joint undertaking is not a partnership if the only joint activity is the sharing of expenses. For example, if two adjacent property owners share the cost of a dam constructed to prevent flooding, no partnership exists. Similarly, joint ownership of property is not a partnership if the co-owners merely rent or lease the property and provide minimal services to the lessees. In such case, the co-owners are not actively conducting a trade or business. If, however, these co-owners provide substantial tenant services, they may elevate their passive co-ownership to active partnership status.[6]

ELECTING OUT OF SUBCHAPTER K PARTNERSHIPS

Section 761(a) allows certain unincorporated organizations that potentially constitute partnerships for federal tax purposes to be excluded from the application of the statutory rules of Subchapter K. An organization may elect out of the statutory rules governing the taxation of partners and partnerships if it is formed for (1) investment purposes only and not for the active conduct of a business, or (2) the joint production,

---

[1]   Uniform Partnership Act, § 6(1).

[2]   § 761(a).

[3]   Reg. §§ 301.7701-1(b) and 301.7701-4.

[4]   A limited liability company with only one owner cannot be considered a partnership for tax purposes. Instead, such an entity will be treated as either a corporation or sole proprietorship.

[5]   See Reg. §§ 301.7701-1(b) and 301.7701-4.

[6]   Reg. § 1.761-1(a).

extraction, or use of property. The members of such an organization must be able to compute their separate incomes without the necessity of computing partnership taxable income (i.e., income for the organization as a whole). The election is made by attaching a statement to a properly filed Form 1065 (U.S. Partnership Return of Income) for the first taxable year for which the organization desires exclusion from Subchapter K. The statement must identify all members of the organization and indicate their consent to the election.[7]

GENERAL AND LIMITED PARTNERSHIPS

There are two types of partnerships: *general* partnerships and *limited* partnerships. The two differ primarily in the nature of the rights and obligations of the partners; the major differences can be summarized as follows.

1. General partnerships are owned solely by general partners, whereas limited partnerships must have at least one general partner and one or more limited partners.

2. General partners have *unlimited liability* for partnership debt, whereas limited partners are usually liable only to the extent of their capital contributions to the partnership.

3. General partners participate in the management and control of the partnership business, whereas limited partners are not allowed to participate in such business.[8]

4. General partners are subject to self-employment taxes on partnership business earnings even if they do not perform services for the partnership, whereas limited partners are not.

Two other types of entities that are usually taxed as partnerships are limited liability companies (LLC) and limited liability partnerships (LLP). In an LLC, all members (i.e., owners) have limited liability. Generally, the partners in an LLP have better liability protection than general partners, but more liability exposure than limited partners. LLP partners usually have unlimited liability, except any particular partner is not personally liable for claims arising from a tort that was committed by a different partner. Nevertheless, the partner committing the tort is personally liability for the claims resulting from his or her actions.

All references throughout the text are to general partners and general partnerships unless otherwise stated.

ENTITY AND AGGREGATE THEORIES

Most rules governing the taxation of partnerships are based on either the entity or aggregate theory of partnerships.[9] According to the *entity theory*, partnerships should be regarded as entities distinct and separate from their owners. As such, partnerships may enter into taxable transactions with partners, may hold title to property in their own names, are not legally liable for debts of partners, are required to file annual returns

---

[7]   Reg. § 1.761-2(b)(2).

[8]   A limited partner who takes part in the control of the partnership business may become liable to the creditors of the partnership by doing so. Revised Uniform Limited Partnership Act (1976), § 303(a).

[9]   For an interesting historical discussion of the development of these conflicting theories, see Arthur B. Willis, John S. Pennell, and Philip F. Postlewaite, *Partnership Taxation* (Colorado Springs, CO.: Shepard's/ McGraw-Hill, Inc.), Chapter 4.

(Form 1065) that report the results of operations, and can make tax elections concerning partnership activities that apply to all partners.

In contrast, the *aggregate theory* views a partnership as a collection of specific partners, each of which indirectly owns an undivided interest in partnership assets. Under this theory, the partnership itself has no identity distinct from that of its partners. The fact that a partnership is a pass-through rather than a taxable entity, functioning only as a conduit of income to the partners, is a clear reflection of the aggregate theory. The aggregate theory also prevents the recognition of gain or loss on several types of transactions between partners and their partnerships.

The inconsistent application of the entity and aggregate theories throughout Subchapter K certainly complicates the taxation of partners and their partnerships. In extreme cases, a single Code section may contain elements of both theories. In spite of this confusion, taxpayers and their advisers who can determine which theory underlies a particular rule of partnership tax law will gain valuable insight into the proper application of that rule to a specific fact situation.

FORMING A PARTNERSHIP

The first step in the formation of any partnership is the drafting of a partnership agreement by the prospective partners. A *partnership agreement* is a legal contract stipulating the rights and obligations of the co-owners of the business. Ideally a partnership agreement should be drafted by a competent attorney, should be in writing, and should be signed by each partner. However, even oral partnership agreements between business associates have been respected as binding contracts by the courts.[10]

A partner's *interest in a partnership* is an intangible asset—an equity interest in the partnership business, the exact nature of which is defined in the partnership agreement. Under the typical agreement, each partner has a specified interest in partnership cash and property. The dollar amount of such interest at any time is reflected by the balance in each partner's *capital account* in the equity section of the partnership balance sheet. In addition to his or her capital interest, each partner has an interest in any income or loss generated by the partnership's activities. This interest is usually expressed as a *profit-and-loss sharing ratio* among the partners. If the partners consent, the terms of their agreement may be modified with respect to a particular taxable year at any time before the unextended due date by which the partnership return for such year must be filed.[11]

Partners may certainly agree to share profits and losses in different ratios. They may also agree that these ratios will be independent of the relative amounts of capital to which the partners are entitled.

> **Example 1.** Doctors J and K decide to form a general partnership to carry on a medical practice. Both individuals contribute $50,000 of cash to the partnership so that both have an initial capital account balance of $50,000. The partnership will use the cash to purchase equipment and supplies and to lease office space. Doctor J has been in local practice for several years and has an established reputation, while Doctor K recently graduated from medical school. Consequently, the partnership agreement provides that Doctor J will be allocated 65% of profits and losses, while Doctor K will be allocated 35%. The agreement stipulates that J and K will renegotiate this profit-and-loss sharing ratio after three years.

---

[10]   See, for example, *Elrod*, 87 T.C. 1046 (1986).

[11]   § 761(c).

CONTRIBUTIONS OF PROPERTY

Partners may make initial contributions to partnership capital in the form of cash, property, or a combination of both. When a partner transfers property to a partnership in exchange for an ownership interest, § 721 provides that neither the partner nor the partnership recognizes any gain or loss on the exchange.[12] The partner's tax basis in the transferred property carries over to become the partnership's basis in the property (i.e., a *carryover* basis).[13] The tax basis in the transferring partner's newly acquired partnership interest equals the basis of the transferred property plus any amount of cash contributed to the partnership (i.e., a *substituted* basis).[14] Tax professionals who specialize in the partnership area have coined the term *inside basis* to refer to the tax basis of assets owned by a partnership. In contrast, the term *outside basis* refers to the tax basis of a partner's interest in a partnership. Although neither term is used in the Code or Regulations, they provide a descriptive and easy way to differentiate between these two basis concepts.

The partnership's holding period for contributed assets includes the holding period of the assets in the hands of the contributing partner.[15] If the assets were either capital assets or § 1231 assets to the contributing partner, the partner's holding period for these assets becomes the holding period for his new partnership interest.[16] If the contributed assets were not capital or § 1231 assets, the partner's holding period for his interest begins on the date the interest is acquired.

> **Example 2.** A contributes § 1231 assets with a fair market value of $25,000 and an adjusted basis of $15,500, and B contributes $25,000 cash to the AB Partnership. The capital accounts on the partnership books are credited to reflect the equal $25,000 contributions of each partner. A does not recognize any gain on the exchange of the appreciated business assets for his interest in the AB Partnership. However, A's initial outside basis in his partnership interest is only $15,500. A's holding period for this interest includes the period of time for which A owned the contributed § 1231 assets. Even though the partnership recorded the contributed assets on its books at their $25,000 fair market value, the partnership's inside basis in these assets is only $15,500. B's initial tax basis in her partnership interest is $25,000, and her holding period for this interest begins on the date of contribution.

The above example illustrates two important points. First, a partner's outside basis is not necessarily equal to the balance in his or her capital account on the partnership's financial books and records. The partnership book capital accounts reflect the economic value of contributions to the partnership, while the partners' outside bases in their partnership interests reflect the tax basis of their respective contributions. Second, the tax rules governing contributions to partnerships result in an initial equilibrium between the partners' aggregate outside bases and the total inside basis of partnership assets. In *Example 2*, A and B have aggregate outside bases of $40,500. The AB Partnership has total inside basis in its assets of $40,500 ($25,000 cash + $15,500 carryover basis of its § 1231 assets). This equilibrium reflects the aggregate theory of partnerships under

---

[12] This nonrecognition rule does not apply to gain realized on transfer of appreciated stocks and securities to an investment partnership. § 721(b). Also, special rules—beyond the scope of this text—apply to transfers to partnerships with foreign persons and transfers of intangibles to foreign partnerships. See §§ 721(c) and 721(d).

[13] § 723. If contributed property is depreciable, the partnership will continue to use the cost recovery method and life used by the contributing partner. § 168(i)(7).

[14] § 722.

[15] § 1223(2).

[16] § 1223(1).

which A and B are considered to own indirect interests in AB's assets. However, it is possible that during the partnership's existence the aggregate outside basis will differ at times from the total inside basis.

A partner may have a divided holding period in his or her partnership interest in two circumstances. If a divided holding period occurs, the portion of a partnership interest to which a holding period relates is based on the relative fair market values of the properties contributed.[17] This will occur if the partner acquired portions of the partnership interest at different times.[18]

> **Example 3.** R purchased a 10% interest in Z Partnership for $10,000 on January 1, 2005. She purchased another 5% interest in Z for $5,000 on November 1, 2005. As of January 1, 2006, R has a one-year holding period in two-thirds of her partnership interest ($10,000/$15,000), and a two-month holding period for one-third ($5,000/$15,000) of her interest.

A partner will also have a divided holding period in his or her partnership interest if the partner contributed more than one property for the partnership interest, and these properties had different holding periods in the hands of the partner.[19]

> **Example 4.** E contributes cash of $2,000 and a capital asset (basis = $1,000; value = $2,000) held for five years for a 25% interest in Partnership Y. The portion of E's interest attributable to the cash, 50% [$2,000/($2,000 + $2,000)], will have a holding period beginning the day after the contribution. The portion of his interest attributable to the capital asset (50%) has a five-year holding period.

EFFECT OF PARTNERSHIP LIABILITIES ON BASIS

When a partnership borrows money, the general partners typically have unlimited liability for repayment of the debt to the partnership's creditors. If the partnership itself is unable to repay its debts, each partner must contribute personal funds to satisfy the unpaid balance. As a result, a partner's economic investment in a partnership consists not only of the contribution of cash or property reflected in his or her capital account, but also of the share of partnership debt for which the partner might ultimately be held responsible.

Section 752(a) acknowledges this responsibility by providing that any increase in a partner's share of the liabilities of a partnership or any assumption of a partnership debt by a partner is treated as a contribution of money to the partnership. This constructive cash contribution increases the partner's outside basis in his or her partnership interest. Conversely, § 752(b) provides that any decrease in a partner's share of the liabilities of a partnership or any assumption of a partner's debt by a partnership is treated as a distribution of money from the partnership to the partner. This constructive cash distribution reduces the partner's outside basis.[20]

> **Example 5.** M and N are equal partners in the M&N Partnership. On January 1 of the current year, both M and N had a $25,000 outside basis in their partnership interests, and the partnership had no debt on its balance sheet. On January 31, the partnership borrowed $15,000 from a local bank and used the funds to buy business assets. Because this transaction increased M and N's respective shares of the

---

[17] Reg. § 1.1223-3(b)(1).

[18] Reg. § 1.1223-2(a); for transfers of partnerships interests after September 20, 2000.

[19] Reg. § 1.1223-3(a)(2).

[20] § 733.

partnership's liabilities by $7,500, each was considered to have contributed this amount of cash to the partnership. As a result, their outside bases as of January 31 increased to $32,500.

On June 1, the partnership repaid $6,000 of the outstanding debt. Because this payment decreased M and N's respective shares of partnership debt, each was considered to have received a $3,000 cash distribution from the partnership. As a result, their outside bases as of June 1 decreased to $29,500.

			M	N
January 1 outside basis			$25,000	$25,000
Plus:	Increase in share of partnership debt on 1/31		7,500	7,500
Less:	Decrease in share of partnership debt on 6/1		(3,000)	(3,000)
June 1 outside basis			$29,500	$29,500

Note that in the above example, the inclusion of partnership debt in the partners' outside bases maintained the equilibrium between inside and outside basis. Between January 1 and June 1, M and N's aggregate outside bases increased by a net amount of $9,000. During this same period, the basis of partnership assets also increased by $9,000 ($15,000 debt proceeds − $6,000 cash distribution).

Partner's Share of Partnership Liabilities. The combined result of § 752(a) and (b) is that on any particular date, a partner's outside basis includes a share of the various debts reflected on the partnership balance sheet as of that date. The Treasury Regulations under § 752 provide a lengthy and complex set of rules for determining a partner's share of partnership liabilities. Under these regulations, each partner's share of any specific debt depends on the classification of the debt itself and whether the partner is a general or limited partner. All partnership debts are classified as either recourse or nonrecourse. A debt is *recourse* if the creditor can look to the personal assets of any general partner to satisfy the unpaid portion of the debt in the event the partnership does not have sufficient assets for repayment. A debt is *nonrecourse* if the creditor cannot look beyond the assets of the partnership for repayment.

A partner's share of recourse debt equals the portion of such debt for which that partner bears the *economic risk of loss*.[21] Because limited partners generally bear no responsibility for the repayment of partnership liabilities, they have no risk of loss with respect to partnership recourse debt. Consequently, no amount of such debt is apportioned to any limited partner. The extent to which general partners are deemed to bear the economic risk of loss for partnership recourse debt is generally determined by using the results from a hypothetical *constructive liquidation scenario*.[22] The basic idea behind these rules is to consider which partners would have to actually satisfy these liabilities if the absolute worst scenario imaginable (i.e., all liabilities are due but all partnership assets are worthless) happened to the partnership. The following transactions are assumed to occur, simultaneously, at the end of the partnership's taxable year:

1. All liabilities must be paid immediately in full.

2. All partnership assets, including cash, are assumed to have a fair market value of zero.

---

[21] Reg. § 1.752-2(a).

[22] Reg. § 1.752-2(b). In so-called straight-up partnerships in which the partners' profit-and-loss sharing ratios correspond to the ratios of their respective capital account balances, the application of this analysis has the same result as an apportionment based on loss-sharing ratios.

3. All partnership assets are sold for no consideration, which results in a recognized loss for each asset equal to the asset's adjusted basis.

4. These losses are allocated to the partners according to the loss sharing ratios in the partnership agreement.

5. The partners reduce their respective capital accounts by the amount of the losses.

6. The partnership liquidates. Consequently, any partner having a negative capital account after step five is deemed to make a cash contribution to the partnership, equal to this negative amount, so that his or her ending capital account will be zero.

7. The partnership is deemed to use this cash to pay off the recourse liabilities of the partnership.

8. Any remaining cash is deemed to be distributed to partners that have positive capital account balances.

The amount of cash that is deemed to be contributed to the partnership under step six is the partner's share of the recourse liabilities.

Example 6. Individuals W and X are general partners and individuals Y and Z are limited partners in the WXYZ Partnership. Partnership losses are allocated 20% to W, 30% to X, and 25% respectively to Y and Z. As of December 31 of the current year, the partnership has $100,000 of recourse debt. The partnership's balance sheet as of December 31 is as follows:

	Basis	Fair Market Value
Cash	$ 50,000	$ 50,000
Inventory	75,000	200,000
Machinery and equipment	75,000	150,000
	$200,000	$400,000
Recourse liabilities	$100,000	$100,000
W, capital	20,000	60,000
X, capital	30,000	90,000
Y, capital	25,000	75,000
Z, capital	25,000	75,000
	$200,000	$400,000

If the assets were worthless and sold for no consideration, a $200,000 loss would be recognized. In allocating this loss to the partners, the limited partners cannot have a negative capital account since they have limited liability. Therefore, whereas Y and Z would otherwise each be allocated $50,000 of loss ($200,000 × 25%), each is limited to a loss allocation of $25,000. The remaining $150,000 of loss is allocated to W and X based on their relative loss sharing ratios, as follows:

W: $150,000 × 20%/(20% + 30%)=$60,000

X: $150,000 × 30%/(20% + 30%)=$90,000

After allocation of these losses, the capital accounts are as follows:

	W	X	Y	Z
Capital, 12/31	$ 20,000	$ 30,000	$ 25,000	$ 25,000
Loss allocation	(60,000)	(90,000)	(25,000)	(25,000)
	$(40,000)	$(60,000)	-0-	-0-

The WXYZ Partnership is now assumed to liquidate. W and X must contribute $40,000 and $60,000 to the partnership, respectively, to restore their capital accounts to zero. This $100,000 is then used to pay the $100,000 recourse liability. Therefore, W and X are allocated $40,000 and $60,000 of the recourse liability, respectively, while Y and Z are not allocated any of the liability.

If a partnership defaults on the repayment of a nonrecourse debt and partnership assets are insufficient to satisfy the debt, the creditor cannot look to the personal assets of any partner for satisfaction. Therefore, no partner—general or limited—bears any economic risk of loss with regard to partnership nonrecourse debt. As a result, separate rules are provided for the allocation of nonrecourse debt. In general, the Regulations provide that nonrecourse debt is apportioned to all partners based on their profit-sharing ratios. However, an exception is provided to this rule if a partner has contributed property to the partnership encumbered with nonrecourse debt that has a built-in gain. In this case, the contributing partner is first allocated nonrecourse debt to the extent of the lower of 1) the built-in gain on the contributed property, or 2) the excess of the non-recourse debt over the adjusted basis of the contributed property. Any remaining gain is then allocated to all the partners based on their profit-sharing ratios.[23] This apportionment rule reflects the fact that such debt will be repaid from partnership profits and that both general and limited partners alike will pay tax on their allocated shares of such profits.

> **Example 7.** Individuals G and H are general partners and individuals I and J are limited partners in the GHIJ Partnership. Partnership profits are allocated 10% to G, 20% to H, and 35% respectively to I and J. As of December 31 of the current year, the partnership has $100,000 of nonrecourse debt. This $100,000 debt is attached to property that was contributed by G. At the time of contribution, the property had an adjusted basis to G of $80,000 and a fair market value of $120,000. The first $20,000 of the $100,000 debt is allocated to G as follows:
>
> Lower of
> 1. the built-in gain on the property, $40,000 ($120,000 − $80,000),
>
>   *or*
> 2. the excess of the non-recourse debt over the adjusted basis of the contributed property, $20,000 ($100,000 − $80,000)
>
> The remaining $80,000 of nonrecourse debt is allocated based on the profit sharing ratios.
>
> In summary, the $100,000 nonrecourse debt is allocated as follows:
>
> | | G | H | I | J |
> |---|---|---|---|---|
> | Built-in gain | $ 20,000 | $ 0 | $ 0 | $ 0 |
> | Profit ratio | 8,000 | 16,000 | 28,000 | 28,000 |
> | | $ 28,000 | $ 16,000 | $ 28,000 | $ 28,000 |

---

[23] Reg. § 1.752-3(a); these regulations also include the concept of minimum gain for allocations of nonrecourse debt, but that discussion is beyond the scope of this book.

Consequently, G, H, l, and J may include $28,000, $16,000, $28,000, and $28,000 of the debt respectively in the outside bases of their partnership interests.

Liabilities Transferred to the Partnership. A partner who contributes property to a partnership in exchange for an ownership interest may negotiate for the partnership to assume a recourse liability of the partner as part of the exchange transaction. Similarly, the property contributed to the partnership may be subject to a nonrecourse liability. In both cases, the rules of § 752 have an impact on the computation of the contributing partner's outside basis.

Any debt from which the contributing partner is relieved of personal liability reduces that partner's basis in his or her new partnership interest. However, this outside basis is also increased by any amount of such debt apportioned to the contributor in his or her capacity as partner. Because this decrease and increase occur simultaneously as the result of a single transaction, only the net increase or decrease is taken into account in computing the contributing partner's basis.[24] The net increase or decrease for the contributing partner's basis can be computed as: amount of liability transferred × (100% − partner's percentage share of debt).

Example 8. Individual T contributes business assets with an adjusted basis of $50,000 to a partnership in exchange for a 25% general interest in partnership capital, profits, and losses. As part of the contribution, the partnership assumes $12,000 of T's business recourse debt, relieving T of personal liability. The partnership has no other debts. Although T is relieved of the $12,000 debt in her individual capacity, she continues to bear the economic risk of loss for 25% of the debt in her capacity as general partner. Accordingly, T's outside basis in her partnership interest immediately subsequent to her contribution is $41,000 ($50,000 basis of contributed property − $9,000 *net* relief of debt).

Basis of contributed property		$ 50,000
Less:	Relief of personal liability	(12,000)
Plus:	Liability for debt as general partner	
	(25% × $12,000)	3,000
T's outside basis in partnership interest		$ 41,000

A partnership's assumption of a contributing partner's debt has tax consequences not only to the contributor but to the other partners as well. The outside bases of the noncontributing partners will increase by the amount of newly assumed debt apportioned to them and decrease by the amount of existing partnership debt apportioned to the newly admitted partner.

Example 9. Individual L contributes business assets with a fair market value of $23,600 and adjusted basis of $10,000 to a partnership in exchange for a one-third general interest in partnership capital, profits, and losses. As part of the contribution, the partnership assumes $3,600 of L's business recourse debt, relieving L of personal liability. Consequently, L's contribution has a net value of $20,000 ($23,600 − $3,600) and a net basis of $6,400 ($10,000 − $3,600). The partnership has $6,000 of existing debt as of the date of contribution. Immediately after the contribution, the partnership has the following balance sheet:

---

[24]   Reg. § 1.752-1(f).

	Inside Basis	Fair Market Value
Contributed assets.	$10,000	$23,600
Existing assets.	30,000	46,000
	$40,000	$69,600
Assumed debt	$ 3,600	$ 3,600
Existing debt	6,000	6,000
Capital: Partner L (33.3%)	6,400	20,000
Partner M (33.3%).	12,000	20,000
Partner N (33.3%)	12,000	20,000
	$40,000	$69,600

L's outside basis in his new partnership interest is $9,600 ($10,000 basis of contributed property − $2,400 ($3,600 × 66.7%) net relief of the assumed debt + $2,000 ($6,000 × 33.3%) assumption of one-third of existing partnership debt).

Prior to L's admission to the partnership, partners M and N each had $15,000 of outside basis in his partnership interest. This basis number represented a one-half interest in the $24,000 net inside basis of existing partnership assets plus one-half of the $6,000 of existing partnership debt. Upon L's admission, M and N are each apportioned $1,200 of the assumed debt. However, they are each relieved of $1,000 of existing debt. Subsequent to L's admission, their outside bases have each increased to $15,200 ($15,000 + $200 net increase in share of partnership liabilities).

Note that in *Example 9*, the inclusion of $9,600 of total partnership debt in the partners' outside bases maintains the equilibrium between the $40,000 aggregate outside basis (L's $9,600 basis + M's $15,200 basis + N's $15,200 basis) and the $40,000 total inside basis of the partnership assets.

CONTRIBUTION OF SERVICES

The nonrecognition rule of § 721 does not apply when an incoming partner contributes personal services to a partnership in exchange for an ownership interest. The tax consequences of such an exchange to both parties depend on whether the service partner receives an interest in partnership *capital* or merely an interest in the *future profits* of the partnership business.

Receipt of a Capital Interest. If a service partner receives an interest in the existing capital of a partnership, the partner must recognize ordinary compensation income to the extent of the value of such interest.[25] The amount of income recognized becomes the partner's initial outside basis in the interest received.[26]

Example 10. G agrees to perform services for the AB Partnership in exchange for a 20% interest in partnership capital, profits, and losses. On the date that C is admitted to the partnership, the net value of the partnership assets is $250,000. The value of C's newly acquired interest is $50,000 (20% of $250,000), which equates to the value of the assets that C would receive if the partnership were to

---

[25] Reg. § 1.721-1(b)(1). The partnership can usually deduct the value of the capital interest given for services as an ordinary business expense. A complete analysis of the tax consequences of this payment by the partnership is beyond the scope of this chapter.

[26] Reg. § 1.722-1.

immediately liquidate and distribute its assets to each partner based on their relative capital account balances. C must recognize $50,000 of compensation income on the exchange and will have a $50,000 outside basis in her partnership interest.

Receipt of a Profits Interest. The partners in an established partnership may be reluctant to give up any part of their equity in existing partnership assets (i.e., a capital interest) as compensation to a newly admitted service partner. These partners might be more willing to give the service partner an interest in the future profits of the business—profits partially attributable to the new partner's efforts on behalf of the partnership.

Example 11. J agrees to perform services for the GHI Partnership in exchange for a 25% interest in future partnership profits and losses. On the date that J is admitted to the partnership, the net value of the partnership's assets is $800,000. However, J is not given an initial capital account and has no legal interest in these assets. If the partnership were to immediately liquidate and distribute its assets to the partners based on their relative capital account balances, J would receive nothing. If the partnership generates income subsequent to J's admission, J will be entitled to 25% of such income.

The tax consequences to a service partner who receives nothing more than an interest in future partnership profits have been the subject of heated debate among tax experts for many years. The courts have also struggled with this issue with confusing and inconclusive results.[27] Currently, the uneasy consensus of opinion is that a service partner does not recognize current income upon the receipt of a profits interest because the interest has no immediate liquidation value. Consequently, the service partner's initial basis in the interest is zero. The partner will, of course, recognize income to the extent of his or her share of future partnership profits.

OPERATING THE PARTNERSHIP

Section 701, the first section in Subchapter K, states that "a partnership as such shall not be subject to the income tax imposed by this chapter. Persons carrying on business as partners shall be liable for income tax only in their separate or individual capacities." Even though partnerships are not taxable entities, they are required to file an annual information return, Form 1065 (U.S. Partnership Return of Income).[28] Basically, this return shows the computation of partnership taxable income and how such income is allocated to each partner. Form 1065 is due by the 15th day of the fourth month following the close of the partnership taxable year.[29]

In order to compute its annual taxable income, a newly formed partnership must make a number of initial elections, including the adoption of both an accounting method (or methods) by which to compute income and the partnership taxable year. The fact that these important elections are made by the partnership itself rather than by each partner is a very practical application of the entity theory of partnerships.[30] As a general rule, partnerships are free to elect the cash receipts and disbursements method, the

---

[27]   See *Sol Diamond*, 56 T.C. 530 (1971), *aff'd* 74-1 USTC ¶9306, 33 AFTR2d 74-852, 492 F.2d 286 (CA-7, 1974), *William G. Campbell*, 59 TCM 236, T.C. Memo 1990-162, *rev'd* 1991-2 USTC ¶50,420 (CA-8, 1991), and Rev. Proc. 93-27, 1993-2 C.B. 343.

[28]   § 6031.

[29]   § 6072(a).

[30]   § 703(b).

accrual method, or a hybrid method of accounting for tax purposes.[31] As explained in the next section of the chapter, they have much less flexibility in the choice of a taxable year.

THE PARTNERSHIP'S TAXABLE YEAR

Income generated by a partnership is included in the taxable income of a partner for the partner's year in which the partnership's taxable year ends.[32] If partnerships had no restrictions as to their choice of taxable year, this simple timing rule could be used to achieve a significant deferral of income recognition.

> **Example 12.** R and S, calendar year individuals, decide to operate a business as equal partners. The RS Partnership begins business on February 1, 2005. During its first year of operations the partnership generates $3,000 of taxable income each month. If the partnership could adopt a fiscal year ending January 31, its $36,000 of first-year income ($33,000 of which was earned in 2005) would be included in the partners' 2006 tax returns because 2006 is the partners' taxable year in which the partnership's fiscal year ends. For each subsequent year that the RS Partnership remains in existence, eleven months of income earned in one calendar year would not be taxed at the partner level until the following calendar year.

Subchapter K contains a set of complex rules designed to minimize the potential for income deferral through use of a partnership. A partnership must adopt the taxable year used by one or more partners who own more than a 50 percent aggregate interest in partnership capital and profits. If no such *majority interest taxable year* exists, the partnership must adopt the taxable year used by its principal partners (those partners owning at least a 5 percent interest in partnership capital or profits).[33] If the principal partners use different taxable years, the partnership must adopt a taxable year resulting in the least aggregate deferral of income to the partners. The taxable year resulting from the application of these rules is known as the "required taxable year."

Under the *least aggregate deferral method*,[34] all year-ends that any of the partners have must be tested, and the one that produces the least amount of deferral for the partners as a group is the required tax year. The deferral for each partner is computed as the time from the year-end being tested until the next year-end of the partner. The months of deferral are then weighted by each partner's profits interest. The least aggregate deferral method is illustrated by the following example:

> **Example 13.** M and N are equal corporate partners in the MN Partnership. M has a year-end of March 31 and N has a year-end of November 30. Since M and N each own 50% of the partnership, no partner, or group of partners, that have the same year-end own a more than 50% interest in the partnership. MN Partnership has two principal partners, but the principal partners do not have the same year end. Therefore, the least aggregate deferral method must be used. The two months that must be tested are March and November.

---

[31] § 446(c). Section 448(a) limits the use of the cash method for a partnership that (1) is a tax shelter, or (2) has a C corporation as a partner. However, § 448(b) provides several important exceptions to this restrictive limitation.

[32] § 706(a).

[33] § 706(b)(1)(A).

[34] Reg. § 1.706-1(b)(3).

Test of March 31 Year-End

Partner	Year-End	Profit Interest	×	Months of Deferral	Weighted Deferral
M	3/31	50%	×	0	0.0
N	11/30	50%	×	8	4.0
				Aggregate Deferral	4.0

Test of November 30 Year-End

Partner	Year-End	Profit Interest	×	Months of Deferral	Weighted Deferral
M	3/31	50%	×	4	2.0
N	11/30	50%	×	0	0.0
				Aggregate Deferral	2.0

Therefore, the required year end is November 30 since it produces the least amount of deferral for the partners as a group.

If the partners wish to use a year different from the "required tax year," the Code offers relief from these mechanistic rules by allowing a partnership to adopt any taxable year (without reference to the taxable years of its partners) if it can convince the IRS that there is a valid business purpose for such year.[35] The IRS will generally agree that a partnership has a *business purpose* for adopting a taxable year that conforms to its natural business year. For example, a partnership operating a ski resort might have a natural business year that ends on April 30. The IRS should allow this partnership to adopt this fiscal year for tax purposes, regardless of the taxable years used by the various partners. A partnership can also use a different year-end from its required year-end if it meets the 25 percent test. This test holds that a partnership may change its tax year if at least 25 percent of the taxpayer's annual gross receipts are recognized in the last two months of the tax year to which the partnership wishes to change, and this 25 percent test is met for three consecutive years.[36]

ORGANIZATION COSTS AND SYNDICATION FEES

Any costs incurred to organize a partnership, such as legal fees for drafting the partnership agreement and filing fees charged by the state in which the partnership is formed, must be capitalized and are not deductible as ordinary and necessary business expenses. The partnership may expense up to $5,000 of these *organization costs* and elect to amortize the remainder over a period of 180 months, beginning with the month in which the partnership begins business.[37] Any *syndication fees* connected with the issuance and marketing of partnership interests must also be capitalized. These fees may not be amortized and will remain as an intangible asset on the partnership books until the partnership is liquidated.[38]

---

[35]   § 706(b)(1)(B).

[36]   Rev. Proc. 2002-39, 2002-22 I.R.B. 1046, provides guidelines for changing from the required tax year because of the business purpose test and the 25 percent gross receipts test. Also see Rev. Rul. 87-57, 1987-2 C.B. 117 for other examples of circumstances that may or may not be considered valid business purposes.

[37]   § 709(b). The $5,000 amount to be expensed must be reduced (but not below zero) by the amount of organizational costs in excess 0f $50,000.

[38]   § 709(a).

COMPUTATION OF PARTNERSHIP TAXABLE INCOME

Partnership taxable income is computed in the same manner as the taxable income of an individual.[39] However, a partnership must make a separate accounting of any item of income, gain, deduction, loss, or credit that is potentially subject to special treatment at the partner level.[40] Separately stated items include capital gains and losses, § 1231 gains and losses, investment income and expenses, net rental income or loss, and charitable contributions. As a result, partnership taxable income is the net of all items that are not separately stated, which can be narrowly defined as gross receipts from services or gross profits from sales of inventory less deductible business expenses incurred by the partnership during the year. This net number is computed on page 1 of Form 1065 and is labeled *ordinary income (loss)*. In contrast, all separately stated items are listed as such on page 3, Schedule K of Form 1065. (Appendix contains a copy of Form 1065 and accompanying Schedule K.)

The character of any item of partnership income, gain, deduction, or loss is determined with reference to the activities of the partnership rather than the activities of the individual partners.[41] For example, gain on the sale of land held by a partnership as an investment for two years is long-term capital gain. This characterization holds even if some of the partners to whom the gain will be taxed are real estate developers in whose hands the land would have been inventory. Similarly, the gain is long-term even if some of the partners have owned their partnership interests for less than one year.[42]

Section 724 contains three exceptions to the general rule that tax characteristics are determined at the partnership level.

1. In the case of unrealized receivables contributed to the partnership by a partner, any gain or loss recognized when the partnership disposes of the receivables must be treated as ordinary gain or loss.

2. In the case of inventory contributed to the partnership by a partner, any gain or loss recognized on disposition within the five-year period subsequent to contribution must be treated as ordinary gain or loss.

3. In the case of a capital asset contributed to the partnership by a partner, any loss recognized on disposition within the five-year period subsequent to contribution must be treated as capital loss to the extent the basis of the asset exceeded its fair market value at date of contribution.

Example 14. Three years ago, D exchanged land that he held as an investment ($50,000 fair market value and $65,000 basis) and an inventory asset from his sole proprietorship ($20,000 fair market value and $18,000 basis) for an interest in the DEF Partnership. Both assets had a carryover basis to the partnership under § 723. Both contributed assets were used in the partnership business, and therefore were characterized as § 1231 assets at the partnership level. During the current year, the partnership sold both assets, realizing a $22,000 loss on the sale of the land and a $3,500 gain on the sale of the former inventory asset.

Because the sales took place within the five-year period subsequent to contribution, the partnership must recognize $15,000 of the loss on the land sale

---

[39] § 703(a).

[40] § 702(a). Reg. § 1.702-1(a)(8)(ii) explains that each partner must be able to take into account separately his or her distributive share of any partnership item that results in an income tax liability different from that which would result if the item were not accounted for separately.

[41] § 702(b).

[42] Rev. Rul. 67-188, 1967-1 C.B. 216.

(excess of $65,000 contributed basis over $50,000 contributed value) as capital loss and the $7,000 remainder as § 1231 loss. The partnership must recognize the entire gain on the sale of the former inventory as ordinary income. If the sales had taken place after the expiration of the five-year period, both the recognized loss and gain would have been § 1231 in nature.[43]

REPORTING OF PARTNERSHIP ITEMS BY PARTNERS

Partners must take into account their distributive shares of partnership taxable income and any separately stated partnership items in computing their taxable incomes.[44] This passthrough of partnership items to the partners is deemed to occur on the last day of the partnership's taxable year. Consequently, the passthrough items are included in each partner's return for the partner's taxable year within which the partnership year ends.[45]

Each partner's distributive share of every partnership item is reported on a Schedule K-1 for that partner. Partnerships must include a copy of each Schedule K-1 with the annual partnership return filed with the IRS. A second copy is transmitted to each partner. Upon receipt, partners must incorporate the information reported on the Schedule K-1 into their tax returns.

> **Example 15.** Individual A and Corporation B are calendar year taxpayers and equal partners in the AB Partnership, which uses a September 30 fiscal year end for tax purposes. During December 2005 each partner received a Schedule K-1 showing the following results of partnership operations from October 1, 2004 through September 30, 2005.
>
> | | |
> |---|---:|
> | Ordinary income from business activities (partnership taxable income) | $42,300 |
> | Dividend income | 2,300 |
> | Net long-term capital loss | (4,000) |
> | Investment interest expense | (5,500) |
> | Charitable contributions | (1,900) |

Individual A will include his $42,300 share of ordinary business income on Schedule E, his $2,300 share of dividend income on Schedule B, and his $4,000 share of the long-term capital loss on Schedule D of his 2005 Form 1040. Per § 163(d), A's $5,500 share of investment interest expense is deductible only to the extent of his net investment income for 2005. Furthermore, the deductible portion of the interest expense and A's $1,900 share of the charitable contribution must be reported as itemized deductions on Schedule A, Form 1040.

Corporation B will include both its $42,300 share of ordinary business income and its $5,500 share of investment interest expense on page 1, and its $4,000 share of long-term capital loss on Schedule D of its 2005 Form 1120. [Corporations are not subject to the § 163(d) limitation.] B will include its $2,300 share of dividend income on Schedule C (Dividends and Special Deductions) and will compute an appropriate dividends-received deduction. B's $1,900 share of the charitable contribution may be deducted on page 1 of Form 1120 to the extent that the

---

[43] § 704(c) also requires a special allocation of both loss and gain among the partners. This allocation rule is discussed in a later section of the chapter.

[44] § 702(a). Section 772(a) provides a simplified reporting system for certain electing *large* partnerships. Large nonservice partnerships with 100 or more members can elect to reduce the number of items that must be separately reported to their numerous partners. See §§ 771 through 777.

[45] § 706(a).

corporation's total charitable contributions for 2005 do not exceed 10% of taxable income.

ADJUSTMENTS TO PARTNER'S BASIS

A partner's distributive share of annual partnership income is determined without reference to actual cash distributions made by the partnership to its partners. If a partner's share of annual partnership income exceeds any cash received from the partnership during the year, the undistributed income will be recorded as an increase in that partner's capital account balance (his or her equity in the partnership) at year-end. On the other hand, in a year in which a partnership operates at a loss, a partner's share of such loss will be recorded as a capital account decrease.

The fluctuating nature of a partnership investment is also reflected in the basis of the partner's interest in the partnership. Outside basis is *increased* by a partner's distributive share of both taxable and nontaxable partnership income.[46] Outside basis is *decreased* by distributions made by the partnership to the partner and by the partner's distributive share of partnership losses and nondeductible current expenditures.[47] These basis adjustments are made in the above order at the end of the partnership taxable year.[48] Even if cash distributions representing advances or draws against a partner's share of current income are made at various dates throughout the year, the effect of these distributions on basis is determined as of the last day of the year.[49]

> **Example 16.** M owns a 40% interest in the capital, profits, and losses of the KLMN Partnership. Both M and KLMN use a calendar year for tax purposes. At the beginning of the current year, M's outside basis in her partnership interest was $35,000. During the year, M received four cash distributions of $5,000 each as advances against her share of current-year income. At the end of the year, the partnership has $20,000 of nonrecourse debt. M's Schedule K-1 for the current year showed the following distributive shares:
>
> | | |
> |---|---:|
> | Ordinary income | $33,000 |
> | Tax-exempt interest income | 4,000 |
> | Net long-term capital gain | 8,100 |
> | Nondeductible penalty | (1,700) |
> | Nondeductible 50% business meals and entertainment | (600) |
>
> As of the last day of the current year, M's outside basis is increased by $8,000 ($20,000 × 40%) for her share of the debt and by $45,100 (her share of partnership taxable and tax-exempt income), decreased by the $20,000 of cash distributions made during the year, and decreased by $2,300 (her share of the partnership nondeductible current expenses). Consequently, M's outside basis as of the first day of the next taxable year is $65,800.

PARTNERS' DISTRIBUTIVE SHARES

The income or loss generated by a business conducted in partnership form is measured and characterized at the partnership level, then allocated to the various

---

[46] § 705(a)(1).

[47] § 705(a)(2).

[48] Reg. § 1.705-1(a).

[49] Reg. § 1.731-1(a)(1)(ii).

partners for inclusion on their income tax returns. Each partner's *distributive share* of any item of partnership income, gain, loss, deduction, or credit is determined by reference to the partnership agreement.[50] Consequently, the partners themselves can decide exactly how the profits or losses from their business are to be shared. The sharing arrangement as specified in the partnership agreement can be an equal allocation of profits and losses to each partner or a more elaborate arrangement under which different items of gain or loss are shared in different ratios among different categories of partners.

Although partners certainly have a great deal of flexibility in determining the allocation of partnership income and loss, § 704(b) warns that such allocations must have *substantial economic effect* if they are to be respected by the Internal Revenue Service. If the IRS concludes that the allocation of any partnership item lacks substantial economic effect, it may reallocate the item among the partners. Such reallocation will be based upon the partners' true economic interests in the partnership, as determined by the IRS upon examination of all relevant facts and circumstances.

SUBSTANTIAL ECONOMIC EFFECT

Treasury regulations provide an intricate set of rules for determining whether partnership allocations meet the substantial economic effect test of § 704(b). The basic objective of the regulations is to "ensure that any allocation is consistent with the underlying economic arrangement of the partners. This means that in the event there is an economic benefit or economic burden that corresponds to an allocation, the partner to whom the allocation is made must receive such economic benefit or bear such economic burden."[51] The economic benefit or burden of an allocation equates to the impact of the allocation on a partner's interest in partnership capital. In other words, an allocation of income or loss for tax purposes must correspond to an allocation of dollars to or from a partner's capital account on the partnership books.

The regulations attempt to ensure this correspondence through a three-pronged test for economic effect.[52] Any allocation for tax purposes will have economic effect only if the following three conditions are met.

1. The allocation is reflected in the partners' capital accounts for book purposes.

2. Upon liquidation of the partnership, liquidating distributions of cash and property are made to the partners based upon the balances in their capital accounts.

3. Partners with deficit balances in their capital accounts upon liquidation are unconditionally required to restore such deficit balance to the partnership. (This obligation may be expressly stated in the partnership agreement or imposed by state law.)[53]

Example 17. The RST Partnership agreement provides that taxable income or loss will be allocated 50% to R and 25% respectively to S and T. The agreement provides that this allocation will be reflected in the partnership capital accounts, that liquidating distributions will be based on capital account balances, and that any partner with a deficit capital account balance must restore the deficit immediately prior to liquidation.

---

[50]   § 704(a).

[51]   Reg. § 1.704-1(b)(2)(ii)(a).

[52]   The additional requirement that economic effect be *substantial* is discussed in Reg. § 1.704-1(b)(2)(iii). Any discussion of this difficult regulation is beyond the scope of an introductory text.

[53]   Reg. § 1.704-1(b)(2)(ii)(c).

For the current year, the RST Partnership generated $48,000 taxable income, $24,000 of which was reported as R's distributive share on his Schedule K-1 and $12,000 of which was reported as S and T's respective distributive shares on their Schedules K-1. Each partner's capital account was increased by the amount of income reported as his distributive share for tax purposes. Because the allocation meets the three-pronged test, it has economic effect and should be respected by the IRS.

Note that in the above example, the taxable income allocated to each partner matched the increase in each partner's capital account balance for the year. Moreover, upon liquidation of the partnership, the partners will receive an amount of dollars (or property) equal to the balances in their capital accounts. Contrast this result with that in the following example.

Example 18. The XYZ partnership agreement provides that taxable income or loss will be allocated 50% to X and 25% respectively to Y and Z. The agreement states that for book purposes income will be allocated equally to each partner. For the current year, the XYZ Partnership generated $48,000 of taxable income, $24,000 of which was reported as X's distributive share on his Schedule K-1 and $12,000 of which was reported as Y and Z's respective distributive shares on their Schedules K-1. However, each partner's capital account on the partnership books was increased by $16,000.

In this example, the allocation of taxable income fails to reflect the allocation of dollars to the partners. Because this tax allocation obviously lacks economic effect, the IRS can reallocate the taxable income to the partners based upon its determination of how the partners actually intend to share the economic benefit of the income. The facts of this simple example indicate that X, Y, and Z intend to share the dollars generated by their partnership business equally. Consequently, the IRS will allocate $16,000 of current-year taxable income to each partner.

ALLOCATIONS WITH RESPECT TO CONTRIBUTED PROPERTY

When a partner contributes property to a partnership and the value of such property is more or less than the contributing partner's tax basis in the property, subsequent allocations of taxable income, gain, loss, and deduction with respect to the contributed property will lack substantial economic effect within the meaning of § 704(b).

Example 19. M contributed an asset (fair market value $20,000, adjusted basis $14,000) and N contributed $20,000 cash to M&N Partnership in exchange for a one-half interest in partnership capital, profits, and losses. The asset contributed by M was recorded on the partnership books at $20,000 but had a carryover tax basis to the partnership of $14,000. The capital accounts for both M and N were credited with the $20,000 values of their respective contributions. Three months after its formation, the partnership sold the contributed asset for $20,000. For tax purposes, the partnership recognized a $6,000 gain on sale. For book purposes, the partnership realized no gain and made no entry to either partner's capital account.

Because of the initial difference between the contributed *value* and the contributed *basis* of the asset in the above example, the taxable gain on the sale is not equal to the gain realized for book purposes. Consequently, any allocation of the taxable gain to the partners does not have substantial economic effect because the allocation cannot be reflected in book capital accounts.

Section 704(c) solves this problem by mandating a special allocation rule for items of income, gain, loss, and deduction attributable to contributed assets. Essentially, any difference between the amount of the item for tax purposes and for book purposes at the time of contribution must be allocated to the contributing partner when the partnership disposes of the asset. The remainder of the item is allocated for both tax and book purposes according to the sharing ratios specified in the partnership agreement. The application of this special rule to the $6,000 taxable gain recognized in *Example 19* results in an allocation of the entire $6,000 gain to contributing partner M. Note that this amount of gain equals the deferred gain that M was not required to recognize upon the contribution of the appreciated asset to the partnership.

> **Example 20.** O contributed an asset (FMV $20,000, adjusted basis $26,000) and P contributed $20,000 cash to O&P Partnership in exchange for a one-half interest in partnership capital, profits, and losses. The asset contributed by O was recorded on the partnership books at $20,000 but had a carryover tax basis to the partnership of $26,000. The capital accounts for both O and P were credited with the $20,000 values of their respective contributions. Seven months after its formation, the partnership sold the contributed asset for $17,000. For tax purposes, the partnership recognized a $9,000 loss on sale, while for book purposes it realized only a $3,000 loss (the decline in the value of the asset subsequent to its contribution to the partnership). The first $6,000 of the tax loss must be allocated to contributing partner O. The remaining $3,000 loss is allocated equally between O and P.

Section 704(c) affects the allocation of depreciation deductions attributable to contributed property as well as allocations of gains and losses recognized by the partnership upon disposition of the property. These depreciation deductions are first allocated to the noncontributing partners in an amount equal to their allocable share of book depreciation (depreciation computed on the contributed value of the property). Any remaining tax depreciation is allocated to the partner who contributed the property.

> **Example 21.** D contributed a depreciable asset (fair market value $60,000, adjusted basis $48,000) and E contributed $120,000 cash to DEF Partnership in exchange for a one-third and a two-thirds interest respectively in partnership capital, profits, and losses. The partnership will depreciate the asset over five years on a straight-line basis. In each year, tax depreciation on the contributed asset is $9,600 (20% of the $48,000 contributed basis), while book depreciation is $12,000 (20% of the $60,000 contributed value). One-third and two-thirds of the book depreciation is allocated to D and E respectively. Each year noncontributing partner E is allocated the first $8,000 of tax depreciation (her two-thirds share of the $12,000 book depreciation). The remaining $1,600 of the annual tax depreciation is allocated to contributing partner D.

RETROACTIVE ALLOCATIONS

In addition to the substantial economic effect requirement of § 704(b) and the special allocation rule of § 704(c), the determination of each partner's annual distributive share of partnership income, gain, loss, deduction, or credit must take account of any change in the partner's equity interest in the partnership during the year.[54] This *varying interest rule* was enacted to prevent retroactive allocations of partnership items to new partners who were admitted to the partnership after the items were recognized or incurred.

---

[54] § 706(d)(1).

Example 22. K and L have been equal partners in the calendar year cash basis K&L Partnership since 2001. On November 1 of the current year, M contributed $100,000 cash in exchange for a one-third interest in partnership capital. The partnership generated a $108,000 operating loss for the current taxable year. The maximum amount of this loss that can be allocated to M under the revised partnership agreement among K, L, and M is $18,049, the portion of the loss attributable to the last 61 days of the year during which M owned an interest in the partnership.

BASIS LIMITATION ON LOSS DEDUCTIBILITY

Under § 704(d), a partner's distributive share of partnership loss is deductible only to the extent of the partner's outside basis in his or her partnership interest as of the end of the partnership year in which the loss was incurred. Any nondeductible portion of a current year loss is carried forward indefinitely into future years and can be deducted if and when sufficient outside basis is restored. This loss limitation rule is applied only after a partner's basis has been increased by any distributive share of current-year partnership income and decreased by any distributions made to the partner for the year.[55]

Example 23. F is a partner in the calendar year DEFG partnership. At the beginning of the current year, F's outside basis in her partnership interest was $14,500. During the year, F received a $3,000 cash distribution from DEFG. At the close of the year, Schedule K-1 showed that her distributive share of the partnership's current-year operating loss was $20,000, while her shares of current-year dividends and long-term capital gains were $3,400 and $1,300 respectively. F will increase her outside basis by $4,700 (her share of partnership income) and decrease it by the $3,000 cash distribution. Under § 704(d), F may deduct her allocated partnership loss only to the extent of her $16,200 remaining outside basis, thereby reducing her year-end basis to zero. The $3,800 nondeductible portion of F's loss will carry forward into subsequent taxable years.

F's January 1 outside basis	$ 14,500
Plus: Allocated share of income.	4,700
Less: Distributions	(3,000)
Deductible share of allocated loss	(16,200)
F's December 31 outside basis	-0-
F's loss carryforward	$ 3,800

If a partner is allocated a distributive share of more than one type of loss and the partner's outside basis is insufficient to absorb the aggregate amount of losses, the § 704(d) limitation is applied proportionately to each type of loss.[56]

Example 24. Refer to the facts in *Example 23*, but assume that F is allocated a $6,000 § 1231 loss in addition to the $20,000 operating loss. F's currently deductible amounts of each type of loss are computed as follows:

Operating loss:	($20,000 ÷ $26,000) × $16,200 = $12,462
§ 1231 loss:	($6,000 ÷ $26,000) × $16,200 = $3,738

---

[55]   Reg. § 1.704-1(d)(2).

[56]   Reg. § 1.704-1(d)(2).

The nondeductible $7,538 operating loss and $2,262 § 1 231 loss are carried forward into subsequent years.

TRANSACTIONS BETWEEN PARTNERS AND PARTNERSHIPS

Under the entity theory, a partner and a partnership are separate and distinct entities that can transact with each other at arm's length. This perspective is adopted in § 707(a), which states that "if a partner engages in a transaction with a partnership other than in his capacity as a member of such partnership, the transaction shall, except as otherwise provided in this section, be considered as occurring between the partnership and one who is not a partner." Because of this general rule, a partner can assume the role of unrelated third party when dealing with the partnership. For example, a partner can lend money to or borrow money from a partnership, rent property to or from a partnership, buy property from or sell property to a partnership, or provide consulting services to a partnership as an independent contractor. The tax consequences of all the above transactions will be determined as if the partnership were dealing with a nonpartner.[57]

The major exception to the general rule of § 707(a) concerns partners who work in the partnership business on a regular and ongoing basis. The point was made earlier in the chapter that general partners are considered self-employed individuals, rather than employees of their partnership. Consequently, partners cannot be paid a salary or wage by the partnership, even if they perform exactly the same duties as nonpartner employees. However, partners who work in a partnership business certainly expect to be compensated for their time and effort. The tax consequences of compensatory payments made by partnerships to partners in their capacities as such are governed by § 707(c). The annual amounts of such payments are typically determined with reference to the extent and nature of the services performed, without regard to the income of the partnership for that year. Such *guaranteed payments* must be recognized as ordinary income by the recipient partner. The partnership will either deduct the guaranteed payment as a § 162 business expense or capitalize it to an appropriate asset account as required by § 263.[58]

> **Example 25.** P has a one-third interest in the calendar year OPQ Partnership. Unlike partners O and Q, P works in the partnership business on a full-time basis. The partnership agreement provides that for the current year P will receive a monthly guaranteed payment of $4,000 from the partnership. The partnership business generates $175,000 of annual income before consideration of P's guaranteed payment.
>
> Based on the nature of the work performed by P, the partnership may claim a current deduction for the guaranteed payment; accordingly its net income for the year is $127,000 ($175,000 − $48,000 total guaranteed payments), and each partner's one-third distributive share is $42,333. P will report total partnership income for the year of $90,333 ($48,000 guaranteed payment + $42,333 distributive

---

[57] Under § 267(a)(2), a payment made by an accrual basis taxpayer to a cash basis related party may not be deducted by the payor until the taxable year in which the payee includes the payment in gross income. Per § 267(e), a partnership and any partner are related parties for purposes of this matching rule. The rule does not apply to § 707(c) guaranteed payments.

[58] Guaranteed payments can also be made with respect to a partner's capital account. Such payments are functionally equivalent to interest, always represent ordinary income to the recipient partner, and will be either deducted or capitalized by the partnership.

share), while O and Q will each report only their $42,333 distributive shares of income.

> **Example 26.** Assume the same facts as in *Example 25*, except that the OPQ Partnership generates only $30,000 of annual income before consideration of P's guaranteed payment. In this case, the deduction of the payment results in an $18,000 net *loss* of which each partner's distributive share is $6,000. P will report total partnership income for the year of $42,000 ($48,000 guaranteed payment − $6,000 loss), while O and Q will each report only their $6,000 distributive shares of loss.

From an economic perspective, a guaranteed payment received by a partner is functionally equivalent to a salary received by an employee. Nonetheless, for tax purposes several important differences distinguish the two. An employer is required by law to withhold federal, state, and local income taxes and employee payroll taxes from an employee's salary. Guaranteed payments are not subject to any similar withholding requirement. At the end of each calendar year, employees receive a Form W-2 on which gross annual compensation and various withheld amounts are summarized. Guaranteed payments are reported only as a line item on the recipient partner's Schedule K-1 issued by the partnership. Finally, while cash basis employees must recognize salary payments as gross income in the year the payments are received, guaranteed payments are deemed to be paid to partners on the last day of the tax year, regardless of when they are actually paid during the year.[59]

> **Example 27.** Refer to the facts in *Example 26*, but assume the OPQ Partnership is on a fiscal year ending September 30. As a result, P actually received three $4,000 guaranteed payments in October, November, and December of the prior calendar year and only nine $4,000 payments during the current calendar year. Notwithstanding, P will report the entire $48,000 of guaranteed payments in the current year because all twelve months of guaranteed payments are deemed to be paid on September 30. Note that this result holds regardless of the amount of any renegotiated guaranteed payment that P may receive during the last three months of the current year.

SALES BETWEEN PARTNERS AND CONTROLLED PARTNERSHIPS

Section 707(b) defines two situations in which the general rule of § 707(a) is overridden and the tax consequences of transactions between partners and partnerships are not determined as if the transaction were negotiated at arm's length between independent parties. Both situations involve a sale of property between (1) a partnership and any person owning more than a 50 percent interest in either partnership capital or profits, or (2) two partnerships in which the same persons own more than a 50 percent interest in either capital or profits.[60] If such a sale results in a recognized loss to the seller, such loss is disallowed. If the purchaser of the property subsequently disposes of the property at a gain, the originally disallowed loss may be used to offset such gain.[61]

> **Example 28.** T owns a 60% interest in the TV Partnership. During the current year, T sells investment land to TV for $100,000; T's basis in the land is $145,000.

---

[59] Reg. § 1.707-1(c).

[60] Percentage ownership is determined with reference to the constructive ownership rules of § 267(c) other than paragraph (3) of such section. § 707(b)(3).

[61] § 707(b)(1). Note the similarity to the more general loss disallowance rule of § 267(a)(1).

T may not recognize his $45,000 loss realized on the sale, and TV will take a $100,000 cost basis in the land. If the partnership subsequently sells the land for more than $100,000, T's $45,000 disallowed loss may be used to offset the amount of taxable gain the partnership must recognize. If the partnership sells the land for less than $100,000, T's disallowed loss will have no effect on the amount of the taxable loss the partnership will recognize.

If a sale of property between a partner and a related partnership results in a recognized gain, and the property is *not* a capital asset in the hands of the purchaser, the gain must be characterized as ordinary income.[62]

Example 29. Refer to the facts in *Example 28*, but assume that T's basis in the investment land was $70,000. If the TV Partnership uses the land in its trade or business, rather than holding it as a capital asset, T's $30,000 recognized gain on the sale must be characterized as ordinary income.

PARTNERSHIP DISTRIBUTIONS

This next section of this chapter is an analysis of the broad set of rules applicable to partnership distributions to which the specialized provision of § 751(b) does not apply. (Any discussion of disproportionate distributions is beyond the scope of this chapter.) All partnership distributions can be classified as either current or liquidating. A *current distribution* reduces a partner's interest in partnership capital but does not extinguish the interest. In other words, subsequent to the receipt of a current distribution, a partner is still a partner. In contrast, a *liquidating distribution* extinguishes the recipient partner's entire equity interest in the partnership. An ongoing partnership may make liquidating distributions to any of its partners who terminates an interest. When a partnership itself terminates, it will make a final liquidating distribution to all its partners.

The aggregate theory of partnerships predominates in the sections of Subchapter K (§§ 731–737) devoted to distributions. Under this theory, a partner's interest in a partnership represents an indirect ownership interest in partnership assets. Therefore, a partner who receives a distribution of cash or property is merely converting his or her indirect interest in partnership assets to direct ownership of the distributed assets. This change in ownership form should not be a taxable event and should have no effect on the tax basis of the distributed assets. This theoretical foundation is clearly discernible in the set of rules explained in the following paragraphs.

CURRENT DISTRIBUTIONS

Cash Distributions. Partners may withdraw cash from their partnerships at various times throughout the partnership's taxable year in order to meet their personal short-term liquidity needs or as advance payments of their anticipated distributive shares of current-year partnership income. Partners may also receive periodic cash distributions as guaranteed payments for ongoing services rendered to the partnership. Finally, partners may receive constructive cash distributions in the form of reductions in their respective shares of partnership liabilities.[63]

Regardless of the nature of a current cash distribution, § 731(a) provides that the recipient partner does not recognize gain upon its receipt. The cash distribution is instead treated as a nontaxable return of capital that reduces the recipient's outside basis

---

[62] An almost identical (and therefore redundant) gain characterization rule can be found in § 1239(a).

[63] § 752(b).

in his or her partnership interest.[64] However, the basis of a partnership interest can never be reduced below zero. Consequently, a partner who receives a cash distribution in excess of outside basis must recognize the excess as gain derived from sale of the partnership interest.[65]

Guaranteed payments and other cash distributions representing advances against the recipient's share of current-year partnership income are taken into account as of the last day of the partnership year.[66] This timing rule minimizes the possibility that distributions will trigger gain recognition at the partner level.

Example 30. Partnership WXYZ and 25% partner Z both use a calendar year for tax purposes. At the beginning of the current year, Z's outside basis was $50,000, and partnership debt totaled $60,000 ($15,000 of which was properly included in Z's outside basis). On July 7, the partnership made a $75,000 cash distribution to Z. As of the last day of the year, partnership debt totaled $80,000. Partnership income for the current year consisted of $109,000 ordinary income and a $5,600 capital loss. Z's outside basis at the end of the year is computed as follows:

Basis on January 1		$ 50,000
Increased by:	25% share of ordinary income	27,250
	25% share of $20,000 increase in partnership debt	5,000
Decreased by:	July 7 cash distribution.	(75,000)
	25% share of capital loss	(1,400)
Basis on December 31.		$ 5,850

The effect of the July 7 distribution is determined as if the distribution had occurred on the last day of the partnership year. Because Z's outside basis is first increased by his distributive share of partnership income and his share of WXYZ's increased debt load, the distribution is treated as a nontaxable return of capital.

If the $75,000 distribution had not been a guaranteed payment or advance against income, its tax effect would have been determined on July 7. Assuming that the partnership debt on this date was still $60,000, Z must recognize a $25,000 capital gain equal to the excess of the distribution over his $50,000 basis. Subsequent to the distribution, Z's outside basis would have been reduced to zero.

Property Distributions. As a general rule, a current distribution of partnership property to a partner does not cause gain or loss recognition at either the partnership or the partner level.[67] The recipient partner simply takes a *carryover* basis in the distributed property and reduces the outside basis in her partnership interest by a corresponding amount.[68]

Example 31. S receives a current distribution of property from the STUV Partnership. At date of distribution, the property has a fair market value of $14,000 and an inside basis to the partnership of $7,500. Immediately prior to the distribution, S's outside basis in her partnership interest was $12,000. Neither the

---

[64]   § 733.

[65]   § 731(a)(1). This gain is capital gain per § 741.

[66]   Reg. § 1.731-1(a)(1)(ii).

[67]   § 731(a) and (b). Section 731(c) provides that certain marketable securities are treated as money rather than property for purposes of § 731(a). Consequently, the distribution of such securities by a partnership may trigger gain recognition to the recipient partner. Discussion of this special rule is beyond the scope of this text.

[68]   §§ 732(a)(1) and 733.

partnership nor S recognizes a gain on the distribution. S's basis in the property becomes $7,500 and her outside basis is reduced to $4,500 ($12,000 − $7,500).

Note that in the above example, the $7,500 inside basis of the distributed property (i.e., the carryover basis) was preserved by shifting $7,500 of S's outside basis to the property. If the recipient partner's outside basis is less than the inside basis of the distributed property, the distribution is referred to as a *substituted* basis transaction. In such a situation, the basis of the distributed property in the hands of the partner is limited to his or her outside basis amount.[69]

> **Example 32.** Refer to the facts in *Example 31*. If S's predistribution outside basis had been only $6,000, S's basis in the distributed property would be $6,000 and her postdistribution outside basis would be zero ($6,000 − $6,000). Note that S simply substitutes her outside basis as the basis in the distributed asset.

If a partnership distribution consists of multiple assets and the recipient partner's outside basis is less than the aggregate inside bases of the assets, the outside basis must *first* be reduced by any amount of cash included in the distribution. The remaining basis is allocated between two categories of noncash assets in the following order of priority:

1. To any unrealized receivables and inventory (Category 1) in an amount not to exceed the basis of these assets in the hands of the partnership.[70]

2. To any other distributed properties (Category 2).

Basis is allocated to multiple assets within either of these two categories under a *basis decrease formula*. The basis decrease is first allocated to property with unrealized depreciation (i.e., inside basis greater than fair market value) to the extent of the unrealized depreciation in each property.[71]

> **Example 33.** J receives a current distribution from the JKL Partnership consisting of the following:
>
> | | JKL Basis | FMV |
> | -------------------- | --------: | ------: |
> | Cash | $4,000 | $4,000 |
> | Accounts receivable | 0 | 3,000 |
> | Inventory | 2,000 | 2,900 |
> | Capital asset 1 | 1,000 | 1,500 |
> | Capital asset 2 | 3,000 | 1,000 |
>
> Immediately prior to the distribution, J's outside basis in his partnership interest was $8,000. This basis must first be reduced by the $4,000 cash distribution. The $4,000 remaining basis is allocated to the Category 1 assets in an amount not to exceed JKL's inside basis:
>
> | | Partner J's Basis |
> | --------------------- | ----------------: |
> | Unrealized receivables | $ 0 |
> | Inventory | 2,000 |

---

[69]   § 732(a)(2).

[70]   An unrealized receivable is any right to payment for goods or services provided to customers in the ordinary course of business that has not been recognized by the partnership as ordinary income. Reg. § 1.732-1(c)(1) and § 751(c).

[71]   § 732(c)(3)(A).

Because J's $2,000 remaining outside basis is less than the aggregate inside bases of the Category 2 assets distributed, the basis decrease formula must be used to allocate this amount to the two capital assets received. First, the amount of the basis decrease is computed to be $2,000 by subtracting J's remaining outside basis amount ($2,000) from the aggregate inside bases ($1,000 + $3,000 = $4,000) of these assets. The $2,000 basis decrease is then allocated to any of these assets with unrealized depreciation; in this case only Capital asset 2. Thus J's basis in Capital asset 2 is $1,000 ($3,000 − $2,000). J's resulting basis in each of these assets is reflected below:

	Inside Basis	FMV	Unrealized Depreciation	Partner J's Basis
Capital asset 1	$1,000	$1,500	$ 0	$1,000
Capital asset 2	3,000	1,000	2,000	1,000

Subsequent to this distribution, J's outside basis in his partnership interest has been reduced to zero.

If more than one of the distributed assets from the same category has depreciated in value, the basis decrease is allocated based on relative depreciation.

Example 34. Assume the same facts in *Example 33* above, except that the fair market value of Capital asset 1 is $500 instead of $1,500. In this case, the basis decrease is allocated between the two capital assets based on relative depreciation. J's basis in each of these assets is determined as follows:

	Inside Basis	FMV	Unrealized Depreciation
Capital asset 1	$1,000	$ 500	$ 500
Capital asset 2	3,000	1,000	2,000

	J's Basis
Capital asset 1:	
$1,000 carryover basis − $400 [($500/$2,500) × $2,000 basis decrease] =	$ 600
Capital asset 2:	
$3,000 carryover basis − $1,600 [($2,000/$2,500) × $2,000 basis decrease] =	1,400

Finally, if the required basis decrease exceeds the unrealized depreciation of the assets, any further decrease is allocated in proportion to the assets relative bases (as previously adjusted).[72]

Example 35. Assume the same facts as in *Example 34* above, except that the total amount of the required basis decrease is $2,800 instead of $2,500. In this case, the bases of Capital assets 1 and 2 would first be reduced by the existing depreciated amount to $500 and $1,000, respectively. The $300 remaining basis decrease would be allocated between these assets in proportion to these reduced bases. J's basis in each of the capital assets would be computed as follows:

	JKL Basis	Depreciation	Reduced Basis	$300 Basis Decrease	J's Basis
Capital asset 1	$1,000	$ 500	$ 500	$100 [($500/$1,500) × $300]	$400
Capital asset 2	3,000	2,000	1,000	200 [($1,000/$1,500) × $300]	800

---

[72] § 732(c)(3)(B).

LIQUIDATING DISTRIBUTIONS

Cash Distributions. When a partner's entire interest in a partnership is extinguished upon receipt of a liquidating cash distribution, the partner will recognize capital gain to the extent of any amount of cash in excess of the outside basis in his partnership interest. Conversely, if the cash distribution is less than outside basis, the partner may recognize the amount of unrecovered basis as capital loss.

Example 36. C receives a liquidating distribution of $20,000 cash from the ABC Partnership. (This distribution equals the $20,000 value of C's capital account as of the date of distribution.) Because she is no longer a partner, C is relieved of $13,000 of partnership debt. C's total cash distribution is $33,000 ($20,000 actual cash + $13,000 constructive cash in the form of debt relief).

If C's outside basis immediately prior to distribution is $24,500, she must recognize a $8,500 capital gain equal to the excess of the $33,000 cash distribution over this basis.

If C's outside basis immediately prior to distribution is $35,000, she may recognize a $2,000 capital loss equal to the excess of this basis over the $33,000 cash distribution.

Property Distributions. Liquidating distributions of property generally do not result in gain or loss recognition to either partnership or partner.[73] When a partnership distributes property as a liquidating distribution, the recipient partner's outside basis (reduced by any amount of cash included in the distribution) is allocated to the distributed property.[74] In most cases, this substituted basis rule defers the recognition of any economic gain or loss realized by the partner upon liquidation.

Example 37. M receives a liquidating distribution of $6,000 cash and a partnership § 1231 asset with a fair market value of $25,000 and a $14,600 inside basis to the partnership.

Assume M's predistribution outside basis is $40,000. This basis is reduced by the $6,000 cash distribution and the remaining $34,000 basis is substituted as the basis of the distributed asset to M. Neither M nor the partnership recognizes gain or loss because of the distribution.

Assume M's predistribution outside basis is $9,000. This basis is reduced by the $6,000 cash distribution and the remaining $3,000 basis is substituted as the basis of the distributed asset to M. Neither M nor the partnership recognizes gain or loss because of the distribution.

Assume M's predistribution outside basis is only $4,000. M must recognize the $2,000 cash distribution in excess of basis as capital gain. The distributed asset will have a zero basis to M.

If a liquidating distribution includes multiple assets, the recipient partner's outside basis (reduced by any cash distributed) is allocated between two categories of noncash assets in the following order of priority:

1. To any unrealized receivables and inventory (Category 1) in an amount not to exceed the basis of these assets in the hands of the partnership.

2. To any other distributed properties (Category 2).

---

[73] See Footnote 67, *supra.*

[74] § 732(b).

Unlike the current (nonliquidating) distribution rules that limit the distributee partner's bases in *any* assets to the distributing partnership's inside basis (i.e., a carryover basis), only the bases of unrealized receivables or inventory (Category 1 assets) are subject to this rule in a liquidating distribution. If the distributee partner's outside basis exceeds the partnership's inside basis of any unrealized receivables or inventory distributed, the remaining outside basis must be assigned to any asset received from Category 2.[75] If the partner does not receive any Category 2 assets, then the excess of the outside basis over the inside basis of the Category 1 assets is recognized as a loss by the partner.[76] However, if Category 2 assets are received, the partner can never recognize a loss.

Example 38. R receives a liquidating distribution from the RST Partnership that consists of the following:

	RST Basis	FMV
Cash	$2,500	$2,500
Accounts receivable	0	2,000
Inventory	3,000	4,000
Capital asset	5,000	9,000

R's predistribution outside basis in his partnership interest was $12,000. This basis must first be reduced by the $2,500 cash distribution. The $9,500 remaining basis is allocated to the Category 1 assets in an amount not to exceed RST's inside basis:

	Partner R's Basis
Unrealized receivables	$ 0
Inventory	3,000

The $6,500 remaining basis is allocated to the capital asset (Category 2 asset), even though this substituted basis exceeds the RST Partnership's $5,000 inside basis. In addition, neither R nor the RST Partnership recognizes gain or loss because of the distribution.

Example 39. N receives a liquidating distribution from the MNOP Partnership that consists of the following:

	MNOP Basis	FMV
Cash	$ 700	$ 700
Accounts receivable	0	800
Inventory asset 1	1,000	1,300
Inventory asset 2	2,100	2,500

Immediately prior to the distribution, N's outside basis is $4,000. This basis must first be reduced by the $700 cash distribution. Only $3,100 of the $3,300 remaining basis is allocable to the Category 1 assets.

	Partner N's Basis
Unrealized receivables	$ -0-
Inventory asset 1	1,000
Inventory asset 2	2,100

N may recognize her $200 unrecovered outside basis as a capital loss.

---

[75] § 732(c).

[76] § 731(a)(2).

Note that in *Example 39* partner N received a liquidating distribution with a total fair market value of $5,300 so that she realized an economic gain upon termination of her partnership interest. The Subchapter K rules governing the tax consequences of partnership property distributions ensure that a partner's economic gain or loss with respect to the distribution is deferred until subsequent disposition of the property.

Example 40. Refer to the facts in *Example 39*. Although N recognized a $200 tax loss upon receipt of the liquidating distribution, she realized a $1,300 economic gain ($5,300 value of assets received in excess of $4,000 basis in N's liquidated partnership interest). However, N's basis in the distributed assets is only $3,100. If N were to sell the unrealized receivables and inventory for their aggregate value of $4,600, she would recognize a $1,500 taxable gain.

This result is consistent with the aggregate theory of partnerships under which N has not severed her interest in the MNOP Partnership until she no longer owns any interest in partnership *assets*. When N finally sells the distributed MNOP assets, her $1,500 recognized gain on sale netted against her $200 recognized loss upon distribution equates to her $1,300 economic gain attributable to the termination of her partnership interest.

Finally, when a partner receives more than one Category 2 asset in a liquidating distribution, his or her remaining outside basis must be allocated between the assets using one of the following:

1. *Basis decrease formula*—where the sum of the bases of the distributed Category 2 assets *exceeds* the distributee partner's outside basis remaining after reduction for any cash received and basis allocated to any unrealized receivables or inventory (Category 1 assets).

2. *Basis increase formula*—where the sum of the bases of the distributed Category 2 assets is *less* than the distributee partner's outside basis remaining after reduction for any cash received and basis allocated to any unrealized receivables or inventory (Category 1 assets).

Example 41. After reduction for a distribution of cash and the required allocation of basis to unrealized receivables and inventory received in a liquidating distribution from the RST Partnership, partner T's remaining outside basis of $25,000 must be allocated to the following capital assets:

	RST's Basis	FMV
Capital asset 1	$10,000	$20,000
Capital asset 2	30,000	10,000

Because T's $25,000 remaining outside basis is less than the aggregate bases of the Category 2 assets, the basis decrease formula must be used. First, the amount of the basis decrease is computed to be $15,000 by subtracting T's outside basis amount ($25,000) from the aggregate inside bases ($40,000) of these assets. The $15,000 basis decrease is then allocated to any of the assets with unrealized depreciation; in this case only Capital asset 2. T's basis in each of these assets is reflected below:

	Inside Basis	FMV	Unrealized Depreciation	Partner T's Basis
Capital asset 1	$10,000	$20,000	$ 0	$10,000
Capital asset 2	30,000	10,000	20,000	15,000

Note that even though the depreciation in value of Capital asset 2 is $20,000, the total basis decrease is only $15,000. Thus, the $30,000 inside basis in that asset is reduced to $15,000 in T's hands.

If more than one of the distributed assets from the same category has depreciated in value, the basis decrease is allocated based on relative depreciation.

Example 42. Assume the same facts in *Example 41* above, except that the fair market value of Capital asset 1 is $5,000 instead of $20,000. In this case, the $15,000 total basis decrease is allocated between the two capital assets based on relative depreciation as follows:

		J's Basis
Capital asset 1:		
$10,000 carryover basis − $3,000 [($5,000/$25,000) × $15,000 basis decrease] =		$ 7,000
Capital asset 2:		
$30,000 carryover basis − $12,000 [($20,000/$25,000) × $15,000 basis decrease] =		18,000

Example 43. After reduction for a distribution of cash and the required allocation of basis to unrealized receivables and inventory received in a liquidating distribution from the RST Partnership, partner T's remaining outside basis of $25,000 must be allocated to the following capital assets:

	RST's Basis	*FMV*
Capital asset 1............................	$10,000	$20,000
Capital asset 2............................	5,000	25,000

Because the aggregate bases of the Category 2 assets is *less* than T's remaining outside basis, the basis *increase* formula must be used. First, the amount of the basis increase is computed to be $10,000 by subtracting the aggregate inside bases ($15,000) of these assets from T's outside basis amount ($25,000). The $10,000 basis increase is then allocated to the assets based on relative unrealized appreciation. T's basis in each of these assets is reflected below:

	Inside Basis	FMV	Unrealized Appreciation	Basis Increase
Capital asset 1	$10,000	$20,000	$10,000	$3,333
Capital asset 2	5,000	25,000	20,000	6,667

T's basis in Capital asset 1 will be $13,333 ($10,000 carryover basis + $3,333 basis increase) and his basis in Capital asset 2 will be $11,667 ($5,000 carryover basis + $6,667 basis increase). Note that the total of T's bases in these assets ($13,333 + $11,667 = $25,000) equals his $25,000 remaining predistribution outside basis.

If only one of the assets in *Example 43* above had unrealized appreciation, it would have been allocated all of the basis increase up to its total fair market value. In the event that the basis increase exceeded the unrealized appreciation, any remaining basis increase amount would be allocated between the assets based on relative fair market values.

Closing of Partnership Year. When a partner's entire interest in a partnership is liquidated, the partnership taxable year closes with respect to that partner.[77] As a result, the partner may have to include a proportionate share of more or less than 12 months of partnership income in his or her taxable year in which the liquidation occurs.

---

[77] § 706(c)(2)(A)(ii).

Example 44. The BCD Partnership and partner B both use a calendar year for tax purposes. On September 30, 2005 B received a liquidating distribution from BCD that terminated his interest in the partnership. BCD's taxable year closed with respect to B on September 30. As a result, B will include his proportionate share of BCD's income from January 1 through September 30 (nine months) in his 2005 tax return. BCD's taxable year does not close with respect to the remaining partners, who will include their proportionate shares of BCD's income for the full calendar year on their respective returns.

Example 45. Refer to the facts in *Example 44*. If BCD uses a fiscal year ending May 31 for tax purposes, two partnership years (June 1, 2004 through May 31, 2005 and the short year June 1, 2005 through September 30, 2005) ended within partner B's 2005 taxable year. As a result, B will include his proportionate share of BCD's income from June 1, 2004 through May 31, 2005 (12 months) and from June 1, 2005 through September 30, 2005 (four months) in his 2005 tax return.

In *Example 44* and *Example 45*, B's outside basis in his partnership interest immediately prior to the receipt of his liquidating distribution should reflect his distributive share of BCD's income or loss through September 30, 2005.[78] Therefore, B cannot determine the tax consequences of the distribution itself until he receives his final Schedule K-1 from the BCD Partnership.

SECTION 736 PAYMENTS

The amount of a liquidating distribution paid to a partner who is terminating an interest in an ongoing partnership should theoretically equal the partner's proportionate interest in the value of the partnership assets. In reality, partners may negotiate for and partnerships may agree to pay liquidating distributions in excess of such amount. In such case, § 736 provides that only the portion of the total distribution attributable to the partner's interest in partnership assets is subject to the statutory rules dealing with partnership distributions. The remainder of the distribution (labeled a *§ 736(a) payment*) is not subject to the normal distribution rules. Instead, § 736(a) payments that are determined without regard to the income of the partnership are classified as *guaranteed payments*. Section 736(a) payments determined with reference to partnership income are classified as *distributive shares* of such income.

Example 46. R, a 20% general partner in the RSTU Partnership, retired from the partnership business during the current year. As of the date of R's retirement, the partnership had the following balance sheet.

	Inside Basis	FMV
Cash	$ 50,000	$ 50,000
Business assets	65,000	90,000
	$115,000	$140,000
Debt	$ 5,000	$ 5,000
Capital: R	22,000	27,000
Other partners	88,000	108,000
	$115,000	$140,000

---

[78] § 705(a).

Even though R's capital account balance was only $27,000, the other partners agreed to pay R $40,000 cash in complete liquidation of his equity interest. The additional $13,000 payment was in grateful recognition of R's long years of faithful service to the business.

The total liquidating payment to R consisted of $41,000 ($40,000 actual cash + $1,000 relief of 20% of the partnership debt). R's 20% interest in the value of partnership assets was $28,000 (as evidenced by the $27,000 value of his capital account and 20% share of the partnership debt). Therefore, only $28,000 of the liquidating payment is treated as a distribution. If R's outside basis in his partnership interest was $23,000, R must recognize a $5,000 capital gain equal to the excess of the cash distribution over this basis.

The $13,000 § 736(a) payment to R was determined without regard to partnership income. Consequently, it is classified as a guaranteed payment, which R must recognize as ordinary income and the partnership may deduct as a current expense.

Payments for Unrealized Receivables and Unspecified Goodwill. Section 736 contains a special rule concerning liquidating payments made with respect to a partner's interest in certain partnership assets. Payments made with respect to unrealized receivables must be considered § 736(a) payments rather than distributions.[79] Payments made with respect to goodwill are similarly classified unless the partnership agreement specifies that a withdrawing partner will be paid for his or her share of goodwill. Prior to the enactment of the Revenue Reconciliation Act of 1993, this special rule applied to liquidating payments made to any partner by any partnership. The 1993 Act limited its application to payments made to *general* partners by partnerships in which capital is not a material income-producing factor.[80]

Example 47. E is a 10% general partner in the Beta Partnership, a professional service partnership in which capital is not a material income-producing factor. During the current year, E had a serious disagreement with the other partners and decided to withdraw from the partnership. As of the date of E's withdrawal, the partnership had the following balance sheet.

	Inside Basis	FMV
Cash	$ 35,000	$ 35,000
Accounts receivable	0	24,000
Business assets	100,000	145,000
	$135,000	$204,000
Debt	$ 15,000	$ 15,000
Capital: E	12,000	18,900
Other partners	108,000	170,100
	$135,000	$204,000

---

[79] § 751(c) provides that, for § 736 purposes, the term *unrealized receivables* includes only zero basis accounts receivable and not § 1245, § 1250, or other types of ordinary income recapture.

[80] § 736(b)(3). Capital is not a material income-producing factor if substantially all of the partnership's income consists of fees, commissions, or other compensation for personal or professional services performed by individuals.

After considerable negotiation, the other partners agreed to pay E $20,000 cash in complete liquidation of her equity interest. The partners determined that this was a fair price for E's 10% capital interest because the partnership business has considerable goodwill and going concern value that is not recorded as an asset on its balance sheet. The Beta Partnership agreement does not provide for specific payments with respect to partnership goodwill.

The total liquidating payment to E consisted of $21,500 ($20,000 actual cash + $1,500 relief of 10% of the partnership debt). E's 10% interest in the value of the recorded partnership assets was $20,400 (as evidenced by the value of her $18,900 capital account and 10% share of the partnership debt). However, the $2,400 payment made with respect to E's 10% interest in Beta's unrealized receivables must be classified as a § 736(a) payment. Consequently, only $18,000 of the liquidating payment ($20,400 − $2,400) is treated as a distribution. If E's outside basis in her partnership interest was $13,500, E must recognize a $4,500 capital gain equal to the excess of the cash distribution over this basis.

The $3,500 § 736(a) payment to E represents the value of her 10% interest in Beta's accounts receivable and unspecified goodwill. Because the payment was determined without regard to partnership income, it is classified as a guaranteed payment, which E must recognize as ordinary income and Beta may deduct as a current expense.

DISPOSITIONS OF DISTRIBUTED PROPERTY

If a partner who received either a current or liquidating distribution of partnership unrealized receivables subsequently collects the receivables or disposes of them in a taxable transaction, that partner must recognize the excess of the amount realized over the zero basis in the receivables as ordinary income.[81] Similarly, if a partner sells inventory distributed from a partnership within five years of the date of distribution, any gain or loss recognized must be characterized as ordinary gain or loss.[82] A partnership's holding period for a distributed asset is included in the recipient partner's holding period.[83]

> **Example 48.** Two years ago, G received a current distribution of land from the EFG Partnership, which operates a real estate development business. The land was an inventory asset to EFG and took a carryover basis of $140,000 in G's hands. G held the land as an investment and sold it in the current year for $200,000. Because she sold the land within five years of the date of its distribution by EFG, G must recognize her gain as ordinary income, even though the land was a capital asset in her hands.

BASIS ADJUSTMENTS TO PARTNERSHIP PROPERTY

Under the general rules governing the tax consequences of partnership distributions, no gain or loss is recognized at either the partnership or the partner level and distributed assets simply take a carryover basis in the hands of the recipient partner. However, in certain circumstances, a partner may be required to recognize either capital gain or loss

---

[81] § 735(a)(1). This paragraph provides that both gain or loss realized on a partner's disposition of partnership unrealized receivables is characterized as ordinary gain or loss. Except in unusual circumstances, such receivables will have a zero basis in the hands of a distributee partner; consequently, their disposition can only trigger gain recognition.

[82] § 735(a)(2).

[83] § 735(b).

because of a distribution. In other cases, the inside basis of a distributed partnership asset does not carry over to the recipient partner.

These exceptions to the general rules can be viewed as anomalies that violate the aggregate theory of partnerships. Subchapter K provides a mechanism to correct these anomalies in the form of an adjustment to the inside basis of undistributed partnership property. Specifically, if a partnership has a *§ 754 election* in effect, it is allowed to *increase* the basis of partnership property by (1) any amount of gain recognized by a partner as the result of a distribution, or (2) any reduction of the inside basis of a distributed partnership asset in the hands of the recipient partner.[84]

> **Example 49.** Partner L received a current distribution from the LMNO Partnership that consisted of $5,000 cash and partnership inventory with an inside basis of $1,500. Because L's predistribution outside basis was only $3,600, L recognized a $1,400 capital gain and took a zero basis in the distributed inventory. If LMNO has a § 754 election in effect, it may increase the inside basis in its remaining assets by $2,900 ($1,400 gain recognized by L + $1,500 reduction in the basis of the distributed inventory).

In *Example 49*, $1,400 of the positive basis adjustment counterbalances the current gain recognized at the partner level by decreasing the amount of future gain the partnership will recognize on a sale of assets (a $1,400 basis increase is equivalent to a $1,400 decrease in gain potential). The remaining $1,500 positive basis adjustment to LMNO's assets compensates for the $1,500 lost basis in the distributed inventory.[85]

A partnership with a § 754 election in effect is required to *decrease* the basis of partnership property by (1) any amount of loss recognized by a partner as the result of a distribution, or (2) any increase in the basis of a distributed partnership asset in the hands of the recipient partner.[86]

> **Example 50.** Partner E received a liquidating distribution of $5,000 cash from the EFGH Partnership. Because E's predistribution outside basis was $7,000, E recognized a $2,000 capital loss. Partner F received a liquidating distribution from EFGH consisting of a capital asset with an inside basis of $10,000. Because F's predistribution outside basis was $14,500, F took a $14,500 substituted basis in the distributed asset.
>
> If EFGH has a § 754 election in effect, it must decrease the basis in its remaining assets by $6,500 ($2,000 loss recognized by E + $4,500 increase in the basis of the distributed capital asset).

In *Example 50*, $2,000 of the negative basis adjustment counterbalances the current loss recognized at the partner level by decreasing the amount of future loss the partnership will recognize on a sale of assets (a $1,400 basis decrease is equivalent to a $1,400 decrease in loss potential). The remaining $4,500 negative basis adjustment to EFGH's assets compensates for the $4,500 additional basis in the distributed capital asset.

The optional basis adjustment is allocated to the same asset class in which the distributed property falls. For purposes of this adjustment, the partnership's assets are divided into two property classes:

1. Capital assets and § 1231 property (i.e., capital gain property), and

2. All other assets (i.e., ordinary income property).

---

[84] § 734(b)(1).

[85] The rules for allocating a § 734(b) basis adjustment to specific partnership assets are found in § 755 and the regulations thereunder.

[86] § 734(b)(2).

However, any loss resulting from the distribution of cash, unrealized receivables, and inventory, must be allocated to the partnership's capital gain property. Further, any gain recognized from the distribution of cash must also be allocated to the capital gain property.

For allocations of increases in basis within a class, the increase must be allocated first to any properties in that class with unrealized appreciation. If more than one property has unrealized appreciation, the increase is allocated in proportion to each asset's unrealized appreciation. However, in no case can the allocated increase for an asset exceed that asset's unrealized appreciation. If any increase remains after this allocation, it is allocated to properties within that class in proportion to their fair market values.

The rules are similar for a decrease in basis. The decrease must be allocated first to any properties in that class with unrealized depreciation. If more than one property has unrealized depreciation, the decrease is allocated in proportion to each asset's unrealized depreciation. However, in no case can the allocated decrease for an asset exceed that asset's unrealized depreciation. If any decrease remains after this allocation, it is allocated to properties within that class in proportion to their adjusted bases. The adjusted bases used for this allocation include any adjustments already made as part of the overall allocation process.[87] In no case can the adjusted basis for an asset be reduced below zero. If the bases of all assets within a class have been reduced to zero, any remaining decreases are suspended until the partnership acquires property in that class.[88]

It is important to note that the rules for increases and decreases are similar, except that any remaining adjustment after the initial allocations are based on relative *fair market values* for increases, but on relative *adjusted bases* for decreases.

Example 51. Refer to the facts in *Example 49*. The § 734 adjustment was $2,900: $1,400 for the gain from the cash distribution and $1,500 due to the reduction in basis for the distributed inventory. The $1,400 for the gain must be allocated to capital gain property. Since inventory is an ordinary asset, the $1,500 for the inventory basis must be allocated to the ordinary income class.

Assume that LMNO Partnership owns the following two capital assets:

	Adjusted Basis	FMV	Unrealized Appreciation
Capital Asset A	$1,000	$3,000	$2,000
Capital Asset B	1,000	1,000	-0-

Since the only capital asset with unrealized appreciation is asset A, its basis is increased by $1,400 to $2,400.

Alternatively, assume that LMNO Partnership owns the following two capital assets:

	Adjusted Basis	FMV	Unrealized Appreciation
Capital Asset A	$1,000	$2,200	$1,200
Capital Asset B	1,000	1,800	800

The $1,400 basis increase is allocated to the assets based on the relative unrealized appreciation. Therefore, asset A receives a basis increase of $840 ($1,200/$2,000 × $1,400). Asset B receives a basis increase of $560 ($800/$2,000 × $1,400). Note that these basis increases are allowed because neither exceeds the unrealized

---

[87] Reg. § 1.755-1(c)(2).

[88] Reg. § 1.755-1(c)(4).

appreciation for the respective asset. Asset A's basis is increased from $1,000 to $1,840, and asset B's basis is increased from $1,000 to $1,560.

Example 52. Refer to the facts in *Example 50*. The § 734 adjustment was $6,500: $2,000 for the loss recognized and $4,500 for the increase in basis of the capital asset. This results in a $6,500 decrease in the basis of capital assets, because all losses due to distributions are allocated to capital assets, as are adjustments due to the distribution of capital assets.

Assume that LMNO Partnership owns the following two capital assets:

	Adjusted Basis	FMV	Unrealized Depreciation
Capital Asset A	$12,000	$ 4,000	$8,000
Capital Asset B	10,000	12,000	-0-

Since the only capital asset with unrealized depreciation is asset A, its basis is decreased by $6,500 to $5,500.

The Section 754 Election. A partnership will adjust the inside basis of its assets as the result of a distribution to a partner only if it has a § 754 election in effect for the year of the distribution. A partnership makes a § 754 election simply by attaching a statement to that effect to its Form 1065 for the first taxable year for which the election is to be effective. Once made, the election applies for all subsequent years unless the Internal Revenue Service agrees to its revocation.[89]

Substantial Basis Reduction. Even if a § 754 election is not in effect, the rules discussed above will apply if there is a substantial basis reduction to partnership property as the result of a distribution. A substantial basis reduction occurs if the sum of 1) the partner's loss on the distribution, and 2) the basis increase to the distributed properties is more than $250,000.[90]

Example 53. Partner B has a basis of $4,000,000 in her partnership interest in Partnership AB. Partnership AB does not have a §754 election in effect. She receives a liquidating distribution of land from the partnership having a fair market value of $3,500,000 and a basis of $1,800,000. She will recognize no gain or loss on the distribution. Her basis in the land will be $4,000,000 and the basis in her partnership interest will be reduced to zero. Since the basis of the land has increased by more than $250,000 (by $2,200,000, from $1,800,000 to $4,000,000) a substantial basis reduction has occurred. Therefore, Partnership AB will have to reduce the basis of its other properties by $2,200,00 according to the rule §755.

DISPOSITIONS OF PARTNERSHIP INTERESTS

The most common way for a partner to dispose of a partnership interest is through a liquidating distribution from the partnership itself. There are, however, a number of other types of dispositions, each of which has a unique set of tax consequences to both partner and partnership.

---

[89]   Reg. § 1.754-1.

[90]   See § 734(d)(1). These rules apply for distributions made after October 22, 2004

SALES OF PARTNERSHIP INTERESTS

Partnership agreements typically place restrictions on the partners' right to sell their equity interests in the partnership to third parties. For example, an agreement might provide that a partner must offer his or her interest to the partnership itself or to the existing partners before offering it to a third-party purchaser. The agreement may also provide that a prospective purchaser must be approved by the general partners or by a majority of all partners. Because of such limits on transferability, partnership interests are considered illiquid assets.

When a partner sells his or her entire interest in a partnership, the partnership's taxable year closes with respect to that partner.[91] The selling partner's outside basis in the partnership interest immediately prior to sale includes his or her distributive share of partnership income or loss through date of sale. The tax consequences of the sales transaction itself to both seller and purchaser are governed by specific rules in Subchapter K.

Tax Consequences to Seller. Upon sale of a partnership interest, the seller recognizes gain or loss to the extent the amount realized exceeds or is less than the outside basis of the interest. Section 741 contains a general rule that such gain or loss is capital in nature. This rule reflects the entity theory under which a partnership interest represents the partner's equity in the partnership as a whole rather than a proportionate interest in each specific asset owned by the partnership. Literally in mid sentence, § 741 shifts to the aggregate theory by cautioning that the general rule is inapplicable to the extent provided in § 751(a). This subsection applies only if the partnership owns unrealized receivables or inventory, which for convenience' sake tax practitioners have simply labeled *hot assets*.

Hot Assets. The term *unrealized receivables* includes zero basis trade accounts receivables generated by a cash basis partnership. The term also includes the § 1245 and § 1250 ordinary income recapture potential inherent in depreciable partnership assets.[92] All partnership unrealized receivables are deemed to have a zero tax basis.[93] Partnership inventory includes not only stock in trade and property held primarily for sale to customers in the ordinary course of business, but also any other property that is not a capital asset or a § 1231 asset to the partnership.[94]

Example 54. The accrual basis MNO Partnership owns the following assets:

		Tax Basis	FMV
Cash		$ 7,000	$ 7,000
Accounts receivable		29,000	27,000
Stock in trade		330,000	410,000
Equipment cost	$100,000		
Accumulated depreciation	(30,000)	70,000	80,000
Other 1231 assets		250,000	390,000
Total		$686,000	$914,000

---

[91] § 706(c)(2)(A)(i). Refer to the discussion of the closing of a partnership year with respect to a partner at Footnote 77, *supra*.

[92] § 751(c). The term *unrealized receivables* also includes many esoteric types of ordinary income recapture potential, such as § 1254 recapture of intangible drilling and development costs of oil and gas wells and mining development and exploration expenditures.

[93] Reg. § 1.751-1(c)(5).

[94] § 751 inventory also includes any partnership property that would be inventory if held by a selling or distributee partner [§ 751(d)(2)(D)].

If MNO were to sell its equipment for market value, it would recognize a $10,000 gain, all of which would be recaptured as § 1245 ordinary income. Consequently, the partnership has $10,000 of unrealized receivables.

Both MNO's accounts receivable and stock in trade are inventory assets because accounts receivable are not a capital or § 1231 asset to the partnership.[95]

Under § 751 (a) the amount of gain or loss for the hot assets (unrealized receivables and inventory) is determined by assuming that these assets are sold by the partnership in a fully taxable transaction for cash in an amount equal to the fair market value of the properties. The partner selling his partnership interest is allocated the portion of the ordinary income that would have been allocated to him if these assets had actually been sold by the partnership.[96]

Example 55. K sold her 10% interest in the KLM Partnership to P for $45,000 cash. KLM used the cash method of accounting and had the following balance sheet as of the date K sold her interest. K's outside basis in her interest was $35,500.

	Inside Basis	FMV
Cash	$ 40,000	$ 40,000
Accounts receivable	0	30,000
Stock in trade	90,000	100,000
Section 1231 assets (no recapture)	225,000	300,000
	$355,000	$470,000
Debt	$ 20,000	$ 20,000
Capital: K	33,500	45,000
Other partners	301,500	405,000
	$355,000	$470,000

At date of sale, the partnership had both unrealized receivables of $30,000 (zero basis accounts receivable) and $100,000 of inventory.

If the hot assets were sold by the partnership at fair market value the partnership would recognize $40,000 of ordinary income ($130,000 fair market value − $90,000 basis). Ten percent of this income, or $4,000, would be allocated to K. Therefore, on the sale of her partnership interest K must recognize $4,000 of ordinary income under § 751(a).

Subsequent to the application of § 751(a), the amount realized on the sale of K's partnership interest has been reduced to $34,000 ($47,000 total amount realized − $13,000 attributable to hot assets). K's outside basis in her partnership interest has been reduced to $26,500 ($35,500 predistribution basis − $9,000 basis allocated to hot assets). Under the general rule of § 741, K recognizes a $7,500 capital gain on the sale of her partnership interest.

These computations can be summarized as follows:

	Total	Hot Assets [§ 751(a)]	Other (§ 741)
Amount realized	$ 47,000	$13,000	$ 34,000
Adjusted basis	(35,500)	(9,000)	(26,500)
Recognized gain/loss	$ 12,500	$ 4,000	$ 7,500
		Ordinary Income	Capital Gain

---

[95] Accounts receivable of a cash basis partnership are both an unrealized receivable and an inventory item for purposes of § 751.

[96] Reg. § 1.751-1(a)(2).

In addition to the recognition of ordinary income if the partnership has hot assets, the seller of a partnership interest may also have special tax treatment in three other situations: collectibles gain, § 1250 capital gain, and residual long-term capital gain or loss.

First, if at the time of the sale of a partnership interest (which has been held for more than one year) the partnership holds collectibles with unrealized appreciation, the gain attributable to this appreciation is taxed at 28 percent.[97] A collectible includes any work of art, rug, antique, metal, gem, stamp, coin, or alcoholic beverage.[98]

> **Example 56.** H and G are individuals that have been equal partners in HG for the last three years. The partnership owns gems that qualify as collectibles that have an adjusted basis of $500 and a fair market value of $1,100. H sells her interest in HG to I. As a result, $300 of H's gain from the sale will be characterized as collectibles gain (50% of the $600 gain that HG would have realized if it sold its collectibles in a fully taxable transaction).

Second, unrecaptured § 1250 gain is taxed at a 25 percent maximum rate. Unrecaptured § 1250 gain is the capital gain that would be treated as ordinary income if § 1250(b)(1) required all depreciation to be recaptured as ordinary income. If a partner sells an interest in a partnership, and the partnership has unrecaptured § 1250 gain, then the partner must take into account his or her portion of that gain in computing the tax results.[99]

> **Example 57.** Assume in *Example 56* above that HG also owns residential rental property. At the time of H's sale, the property had a fair market value of $110,000 and adjusted basis of $60,000. The property's original cost basis was $100,000. Straight-line depreciation of $40,000 had been claimed on the property. At the time of H's sale, one must compute what H's share of unrecaptured § 1250 gain would be if the property was sold. Since the property is realty and straight-line depreciation was used there would be no § 1250 recapture. Consequently, the entire gain ($50,000) would be a § 1231 gain. However, the § 1231 gain would be treated as a 25% gain to the extent of any straight-line depreciation claimed ($40,000). H's share of the 25% gain is $20,000. Consequently, of the total gain recognized by H on the sale of his partnership interest, $20,000 will be 25% gain due to the § 1250 unrecaptured gain.

The collectibles gain and § 1250 unrecaptured gain that are allocable to a partner that has sold his or her partnership interest are together known as the look-through capital gain.[100] The residual long-term capital gain or loss is computed as follows:

> Residual long-term capital gain/loss =
>
> § 741 long-term capital gain or loss (after application of § 751),
>
> −,
>
> Look-through capital gain or loss.

> **Example 58.** G and H are individuals that have been equal partners in Partnership B for the last two years. B owns collectibles with a basis and fair market value of

---

[97]   § 1(h)(6)(B); for transfers of partnership interests after September 20, 2000.

[98]   § 408 (m)(3).

[99]   Reg. § 1.1(h)-1(b)(3)(ii); for transfers of partnership interests after September 20, 2000.

[100]   § 1(h)(1)(D); Reg. § 1.1(h)-1(b)(1).

$3,000 and $5,000, respectively. G sells his interest in partnership B to R and has a total recognized gain of $500. After the application of the § 751 hot assets rules, assume that G recognizes ordinary income of $2,000 and § 741 long-term capital loss of $1,500 (i.e., the pre-look through long-term capital loss). G's share of the collectibles gain (i.e., the look-through capital gain) is $1,000 [($5,000 − $3,000) × 50%].

Total gain.	$ 500
§ 751 Hot asset ordinary income	(2,000)
Pre-look through long-term capital loss	(1,500)
Gain from collectibles.	1,000
Residual long-term capital loss	$(2,500)

To summarize, G has $2,000 of ordinary income, $1,000 collectibles gain taxed at 28%, and a $2,5000 capital loss.

Tax Consequences to Purchaser. Section 742 states that the basis of a partnership interest acquired other than by contribution shall be determined under the normal basis rules provided in §§ 1011 and following. Thus, the purchaser of a partnership interest takes a *cost* basis in the interest. The *cost basis* includes the amount of cash and the value of any noncash property paid to the seller plus the amount of any partnership liabilities assumed by the purchaser in his or her role as a new partner.

The fact that a purchaser is given a cost basis in the partnership interest rather than in a proportionate share of partnership assets reflects the entity theory of partnerships. Section 743(a) reinforces this perspective by specifying that the basis of partnership property shall not be adjusted as the result of a transfer of an interest in a partnership by sale or exchange. This general rule typically results in an imbalance between a purchasing partner's outside basis and the inside basis of his or her proportionate share of partnership assets.

Example 59. P purchased a 10% interest in the accrual basis KLM Partnership from K for $45,000 cash. As of the date of sale, the partnership had the following balance sheet:

	Inside Basis	FMV
Cash	$ 40,000	$ 40,000
Accounts receivable.	30,000	30,000
Stock in trade.	90,000	100,000
Depreciable assets	225,000	300,000
	$385,000	$470,000
Debt.	$ 20,000	$ 20,000
Capital: K (replaced by P)	36,500	45,000
Other partners.	328,500	405,000
	$385,000	$470,000

P's cost basis in his new partnership interest is $47,000 ($45,000 cash + 10% of KLM's debt). The transaction between P and K had no effect on the basis of the partnership assets, so that P's aggregate inside basis in 10% of KLM's assets is only $38,500.

The imbalance between P's outside and inside bases in *Example 59* has several negative implications for P. If the partnership sells its entire stock in trade for $100,000, P will be allocated $1,000 of ordinary income (the excess of the $10,000 value of 10 percent of the stock in trade over its $9,000 basis), even though P indirectly paid $10,000 to acquire his share of this asset. Similarly, P will be allocated tax depreciation computed on the $22,500 inside basis of 10 percent of KLM's depreciable assets, even though P indirectly paid $30,000 to acquire his share of these assets.

Special Basis Adjustment for Purchaser. Strict adherence to the entity theory is relaxed if a purchaser acquires an interest in a partnership with a § 754 election in effect.[101] In this case, § 743(b) provides that any excess of the purchaser's outside basis over the inside basis of his or her proportionate share of partnership assets becomes a *positive* adjustment to that partner's inside basis.[102] Conversely, any excess of a purchaser's inside basis in his or her proportionate share of partnership assets over outside basis becomes a *negative* adjustment to that partner's inside basis.

Any positive or negative adjustment to the inside basis of the partnership property must be allocated to specific assets in such a manner as to reduce the difference between the fair market value and the tax basis of the asset. For purposes of this adjustment, the partnership's assets are divided into two property classes:[103]

1. Capital assets and § 1231 property (i.e., capital gain property), and

2. All other assets (i.e., ordinary income property).

The allocation of the optional basis adjustment between these two classes is based on the gain or loss that would be allocated to the transferee partner based on a hypothetical sale of all the partnership's assets. Therefore, it is possible that a positive adjustment could be made to the capital assets and a negative adjustment to the other assets, or vice-versa.

The adjustment to the ordinary income class is the amount of income, gain, or loss allocated to the transferee partner from the hypothetical sale of all ordinary income property at fair market value for cash. The adjustment to the capital asset class is then the difference in the total adjustment less the adjustment to the ordinary income class. However, any decrease in basis adjustment for the capital asset class cannot reduce the basis of the capital assets below zero. Once the basis of the capital assets is reduced to zero, any remaining negative adjustment must be used to reduce the basis of ordinary income property.[104]

The adjustment to each class must then be allocated to assets within that class. Generally, the adjustment to each item of ordinary income property equals the amount of income, gain, or loss allocated to the transferee partner in a hypothetical sale of the item. The adjustment for each item in the ordinary income class is determined as shown below.

Example 60. G sells his 25% interest in the JJG Partnership to D on March 15, 2005. JJG Partnership previously made a § 754 election. D paid $50,000 to G and assumed G's share of partnership liabilities. JJG's balance sheet at the date of sale is as follows:

---

[101] The § 754 election is discussed at Footnote 87, *supra*.

[102] § 743(b)(1).

[103] § 755.

[104] Reg. § 1.755-1(b).

	Inside Basis	FMV
Cash	$ 40,000	$ 40,000
Accounts receivable........	20,000	15,000
Inventory	42,000	50,000
Building	70,000	85,000
Land..................	20,000	40,000
	$192,000	$230,000
Debt..................	$ 30,000	$ 30,000
Capital: G (replaced by D) ..	40,500	50,000
Other partners	121,500	150,000
	$192,000	$230,000

Since the JJG Partnership has a § 754 election in effect, D is entitled to a $9,500 basis adjustment [the excess of his $57,500 outside basis over the $48,000 inside basis of his 25% share of JJG's assets ($192,000 × 25%)]. Note that his outside basis is computed as the $50,000 cash payment plus 25% of the partnership's debt. The $9,500 is labeled as a § 743(b) adjustment.

The § 743(b) adjustment is allocated between classes and among properties based on the allocations of income, gain, or loss that the transferee partner would receive from a hypothetical sale of all partnership assets.

Allocation Between Classes:

D's Allocable Share (25%)

Ordinary Income Property	Adjusted Basis	FMV	Gain/(Loss)
Accounts receivable	$ 5,000	$ 3,750	$(1,250)
Inventory	10,500	12,500	2,000
Total	$ 15,500	$ 16,250	$ 750

Capital Gain Property	Adjusted Basis	FMV	Gain/(Loss)
Building	$ 17,500	$ 21,250	$ 3,750
Land	5,000	10,000	5,000
Total	$ 22,500	$ 31,250	$ 8,750

Therefore, the § 743(b) adjustment is allocated $750 to the ordinary income property and $8,750 to the capital gain property.

Allocation Within Classes:

If a hypothetical sale occurred, D would be allocated a loss of $1,250 from the sale of the receivables and a gain of $2,000 from the sale of the inventory. D would also be allocated a gain of $3,750 for the building and a gain of $5,000 for the land. Therefore, these amounts are D's basis adjustment for each of these assets.

To summarize, D's allocation of the inside basis of JJG's assets is as follows:

	Inside Basis	25% of Basis	§ 743(b) Adjustment	Adjusted Inside Basis
Cash	$40,000	$10,000	$ 0	$10,000
Accounts receivable	20,000	5,000	(1,250)	3,750
Inventory	42,000	10,500	2,000	12,500
Building	70,000	17,500	3,750	21,250
Land	20,000	5,000	5,000	10,000
				$57,500

Note that D's total outside basis of $57,500 is now equal to his allocation of the inside basis of the partnership's assets.

Effect of the Adjustment. A § 743(b) special basis adjustment belongs only to the purchasing partner and has no effect on the other partners. Although any benefit of a § 743(b) basis adjustment accrues only to the purchasing partner, the burden of record keeping for the adjustment falls upon the partnership. This disparity is one reason partnerships may be reluctant to make the § 754 election necessary to activate § 743(b). If a partner has a special basis adjustment with respect to an asset disposed of by the partnership in a taxable transaction, the adjustment will be taken into account in calculating that partner's distributive share of gain or loss.

Example 61. If the JJG Partnership in the previous example sells its inventory for $50,000 and recognizes $8,000 of ordinary income, D's 25% share of that is $2,000. However, D's $2,000 special basis adjustment in the inventory reduces his distributive share of the partnership ordinary income to zero.

If a partner has a special basis adjustment with respect to a depreciable or amortizable asset, the adjustment will generate an additional cost recovery deduction for that partner.[105] Therefore, D can depreciate the $3,750 step-up in basis for the building in *Example 60.*

Substantial Built-in Loss. Even if a §754 election is not in effect, the rules discussed above will apply if there is a substantial built-in loss to the partnership immediately after the transfer of the partnership interest. A substantial built-in loss occurs if the partnership's basis in its assets exceeds the fair market value of those assets by more than $250,000.[106]

Example 62. Partner M sells his partnership interest for $500,000 at a time when the MN partnership has a basis and fair market value in it is assets of $3,000,000 and $2,500,000, respectively. Since the basis of the partnership's assets exceeds the fair market value by more than $250,000 [by $500,000 [($3,00,000 – $2,500,000)], a substantial built-in loss exists. Therefore, even if Partnership MN does not have a §754 election in effect, the partnership must reduce the basis of its properties by $500,000 accordin §755.

GIFTS OF PARTNERSHIP INTERESTS AND FAMILY PARTNERSHIPS

Dispositions of partnership interests by gift generally have no income tax consequences to either donor or donee, although the donor may be liable for a gift tax on the transfer.[107] The donee will take a basis in the partnership interest as determined under § 1015.

Transfers of partnership interests by gift usually involve donors and donees who are members of the same family, and therefore often result in the creation of *family partnerships.* Such partnerships can be an effective way to divide the income from a family business among various family members. To the extent the income can be allocated and taxed to individuals in the lower marginal tax brackets, family partnerships can also achieve a significant tax savings.

---

[105]   A § 743(b) basis adjustment to depreciable property is considered a newly purchased asset placed in service in the year in which the adjustment arises. Prop. Reg. § 1.168-2(n).

[106]   See § 743(d)(1). These rules apply for distributions made after October 22, 2004.

[107]   If the donor's relief of partnership liabilities attributable to the gift of the partnership interest exceeds the donor's outside basis in the interest, the excess relief over basis must be recognized as a gain on sale of the interest. Reg. § 1.1001-1(e).

Not surprisingly, the tax laws restrict the use of family partnerships as income shifting devices. If the income earned by a partnership is primarily attributable to the individual efforts and talents of its partners, any allocation of that income to nonproductive partners would be an unwarranted assignment of earned income. Accordingly, a family member generally cannot be a partner in a personal or professional service business unless he or she is capable of performing the type of services offered to the partnership's clientele.[108]

A family member can be a partner in a business in which capital is a material income-producing factor.[109] In contrast to a service partnership, the mere ownership of an equity interest in a capital intensive partnership entitles a partner to a share of partnership income. Under the general rules of § 704, a partner's allocable share of income does not have to be in proportion to his or her interest in partnership capital as long as the allocation has substantial economic effect. However, § 704(e)(2) provides that in the case of any partnership capital interest *created by gift*, the income allocable to such interest cannot be proportionally greater than the income allocated to the donor's capital.

> **Example 63.** M creates a partnership with his son S and daughter D by giving each child an equity interest in his business. M is in the highest marginal tax bracket, while his children are in the 15% marginal tax bracket. The initial MSD Partnership balance sheet appears as follows:
>
> Contributed business assets $300,000
>
> | | | |
> |---|---|---|
> | Capital: | M . . . . | $200,000 |
> | | S . . . . | 50,000 |
> | | D . . . . | 50,000 |
> | | | $300,000 |

If S and D's interests had not been created by gift, the partnership agreement could allocate any amount of partnership income to S and D as long as the allocation had substantial economic effect. Because the interests were created by gift, the maximum percentage of income allocable to S and D respectively is 16.7% ($50,000 donee's capital ÷ $300,000 total capital of both donor and donees).

Section 704(e)(2) also requires that any allocation of income with respect to donor and donee partners take into account the value of services rendered to the partnership by the donor. This statutory requirement prevents a donor partner from forgoing reasonable compensation from the partnership in order to maximize the amount of income shifted to the donee partners.

> **Example 64.** Refer to the facts in *Example 63*. If M performs services for MSD during its first taxable year that are reasonably worth $25,000, he must be compensated for the services before any amount of partnership income may be allocated to S and D. If the partnership earns $145,000 of operating income during its first year, the maximum amount of such income allocable to S and D respectively is $20,000 [16.7% of ($145,000 operating income − $25,000 compensation to M)].

---

[108] See *Comm. v. Culbertson*, 337 U.S. 733 (USSC, 1949).

[109] § 704(e)(1). Capital is a material income-producing factor if the operation of the partnership business requires substantial inventories or a substantial investment in plant, machinery, or equipment. Reg. § 1.704-1(e)(1)(iv).

Note that the restrictions illustrated in *Example 63* and *Example 64* technically apply to any partnership interest created by gift, regardless of any familial relationship between donor and donee. Realistically, these restrictions most frequently apply to family partnerships. In order to prevent families from circumventing these restrictions, the statute states that a partnership interest purchased from a family member is considered to have been acquired by gift.[110]

DEATH OF A PARTNER

When an individual partner dies, his or her partnership interest passes to a *successor in interest* in the partnership.[111] The partner's gross estate for federal estate tax purposes includes the fair market value of the partnership interest at date of death, and the decedent's successor takes an outside basis in the interest equal to such fair market value.[112] Because the death of a partner causes a closing of the partnership's tax year with respect to that partner, items of income, gain, loss, deduction, or credit attributable to the deceased partner's interest up to date of death will be included on the final tax return of the decedent. Any amounts for the remainder of the partnership's tax year must be reported by the deceased partner's successor in interest.[113]

Example 65. Individual Z, who owned a 40% interest in the capital, profits, and loss of the calendar year XYZ Partnership, died on November 3 of the current year. Under the terms of Z's will, all his assets (including his interest in XYZ) passed to his estate. Because the partnership's tax year closes with respect to Z on the date of his death, XYZ's income or loss attributable to this interest from January 1 to November 3 will be included in Z's final tax return. Income or loss attributable to this 40% interest for the remainder of the year must be included in the first fiduciary income tax return filed on behalf of Z's estate.

PARTNERSHIP TERMINATION

One of the important legal characteristics of the partnership form of business is *limited life*. Under state law, a partnership is dissolved whenever any partner ceases to be associated in the carrying on of the partnership business.[114] From a legal perspective, a partnership's identity, and therefore its existence, is dependent upon the continued association of a particular group of partners. This perspective is consistent with the aggregate theory of partnerships. Nevertheless, it would be totally impractical to require a partnership to close its taxable year and make a final accounting of its business activities every time an existing partner left or a new partner joined the partnership.

Section 708(a) adopts the entity theory by providing that a partnership does not terminate for tax purposes simply because it may be dissolved under state law. In other words, a partnership shall continue in existence as an entity for purposes of Subchapter

---

[110] § 704(e)(3). For purposes of this rule, a partner's family members include a spouse, ancestors, and lineal descendants.

[111] The successor in interest is named under the decedent partner's will or determined by reference to state intestacy laws if the decedent died without a will.

[112] § 1014(a). Any imbalance between a successor in interest's outside basis and inside basis in the partnership assets is remedied if the partnership has a § 754 election in effect. In such case § 743(b) permits a special adjustment with respect to the inside basis of the partnership assets.

[113] § 706(c)(2)(A)(ii). Prior to 1998, the death of a partner did not cause the partnership's tax year to close with respect to the deceased partner. As a result, income or loss attributable to the interest for the entire year was usually included on the tax return of the successor in interest.

[114] Uniform Partnership Act, § 29.

K even if the association of partners changes. Section 708(b) provides that a partnership shall terminate for tax purposes *only if*:

1. No part of any business, financial operation, or venture is being conducted by the partnership (*natural termination*), or

2. Within a 12-month period there is a sale or exchange of 50 percent or more of the total interest in partnership capital and profits (*technical termination*).

TECHNICAL TERMINATIONS

When a partnership ceases to conduct any type of economic activity, its termination for federal tax purposes marks the natural end of its life as a business entity. In contrast, a partnership that is terminated because of a sale or exchange of more than a 50 percent interest may be conducting a vital, ongoing business. Moreover, the partners who were not involved in the sale or exchange may be unaware that the terminating transaction even occurred!

Only sales or exchanges of partnership interests can trigger a technical termination. Other types of dispositions, such as gifts or transfers at death, are ignored. Similarly, changes in the relative ownership interests of partners because of contributions to or distributions from a partnership cannot result in termination. Sales or exchanges will not cause termination unless *at least* a 50 percent cumulative interest in both capital and profits changes hands within a 12-month period.

> **Example 66.** Partners A, B, and C have owned equal interests in the capital and profits of the ABC Partnership since 1995.
>
> - On January 12, 2004, A sold her one-third interest to new partner D.
> - On July 8, 2004, B sold 10% of his interest to new partner E.
> - On November 22, 2004, C gave his one-third interest to new partner F.
> - On January 9, 2005, F exchanged this interest for stock in a new corporation; the exchange was nontaxable under § 351.
>
> The January 12 sale did not terminate the ABC Partnership because only a 33.3% interest in capital and profits was sold. The July 8 sale did not terminate the partnership because at that point in time only a 43.3% cumulative interest in capital and profits had been sold within a 12-month period. The November 22 gift did not enter into the termination calculation. The January 9 exchange did result in a termination of the ABC Partnership; within the 12-month period beginning on January 12, 2004, a cumulative 76.6% interest in the partnership was sold or exchanged. If F had delayed his exchange until after January 11, 2005, the transaction would have not triggered a termination.

In determining whether a cumulative 50 percent interest has been sold or exchanged within the crucial 12-month time period, multiple transfers of the *same interest* are counted only once.[115] In *Example 66*, if D (rather than F) had exchanged his one-third interest for corporate stock on January 9, 2005, the exchange would not have resulted in a technical termination.

---

[115]   Reg. § 1.708-1(b)(2).

EFFECT OF TERMINATION

Upon termination, a partnership's taxable year closes with respect to all its partners. If the partnership and any partner use different taxable years, a bunching of more than 12 months of income may occur.

> **Example 67.** The QRS Partnership uses a calendar year for tax purposes, while corporate partner A uses a fiscal year ending June 30. The partnership terminated on March 31, 2005 and closed its taxable year on that date. Because two partnership years (calendar year 2004 and the short taxable year from January 1–March 31, 2005) ended within its fiscal year ending June 30, 2005, Q must include its distributive share of 15 months of partnership income in its taxable income for the year.

Pursuant to a natural termination, a partnership typically will wind up its affairs and distribute all remaining cash and assets to the partners in complete liquidation of their interests.[116] In a technical termination, the partnership contributes all of its assets and liabilities to a new partnership in exchange for an interest in the new partnership. The terminated partnership then distributes interests in the new partnership to the purchasing partner and all other remaining partners.[117] The result of the application of these rules is that the technical termination does not automatically result in adjustments to the bases of the partnership assets because no assets are treated as being distributed.[118]

PROBLEM MATERIALS

DISCUSSION QUESTIONS

22-1 *Partnership versus Corporation.* List both tax and nontax advantages or disadvantages of operating a business as a partnership rather than as a corporation.

22-2 *General versus Limited Partners.* Distinguish between the legal rights and responsibilities of a general partner and a limited partner.

22-3 *Aggregate versus Entity Theory.* How does the aggregate theory of partnerships differ from the entity theory of partnerships? Give a specific example of a Subchapter K rule that reflects each theory.

22-4 *Contributions of Property.* True or false: neither a partner nor a partnership ever recognizes gain or loss on the contribution of property in exchange for a partnership interest. Explain your conclusion.

22-5 *Partnership Liabilities as Basis.* What is the economic rationale for including a portion of partnership recourse debt in the partners' bases of their partnership interests? What is the rationale for the inclusion of nonrecourse debt?

22-6 *Contributions of Services.* Distinguish between the tax consequences to a partner who contributes services in exchange for a capital interest in a partnership and one who contributes services in exchange for an interest in future profits.

22-7 *Organization Costs versus Syndication Fees.* Compare the tax treatment of partnership organization costs to that of syndication fees.

---

[116] Reg. § 1.708-1(b)(1).

[117] Reg. § 1.708-1(b)(1)(iv).

[118] A complete analysis of the potential tax consequences of technical terminations is beyond the scope of an introductory text.

22-8 *Partnership Taxable Year.* What choices are available to a business partnership when selecting a taxable year?

22-9 *Basis Adjustments.* Indicate whether each of the following occurrences increases, decreases, or has no effect on a general partner's basis in his partnership interest. Assume all liabilities are recourse liabilities.
   a. The partnership borrows cash that will be repaid in two years.
   b. The partnership earns tax-exempt interest on municipal bonds.
   c. The partnership generates an operating loss for the year.
   d. The partnership distributes cash to its partners.
   e. The partnership incurs a nondeductible penalty.
   f. The partnership makes a principal payment on a mortgage secured by partnership property.
   g. The partnership recognizes a long-term capital gain on the sale of marketable securities.

22-10 *Partners' Transactions with Partnerships.* Give three examples of a transaction between a partnership and a partner that will be treated as a transaction between the partnership and a nonpartner for tax purposes. Does such arm's length treatment reflect the aggregate or the entity theory of partnerships?

22-11 *Partners as Employees.* May a general partner be an employee of the partnership for federal tax purposes? Explain your conclusion.

22-12 *Current versus Liquidating Distributions.* Explain the difference between a current distribution and a liquidating distribution from a partnership.

22-13 *Current Distributions.* Is the statement that a partner never recognizes a loss upon the receipt of a current distribution true or false? Explain your conclusion.

22-14 *Liquidating Distributions.* Under what circumstances will a partner recognize a capital loss upon the receipt of a liquidating distribution?

22-15 *Closing of Partnership Year.* Partner Z received a liquidating distribution from a calendar year partnership on April 3 of the current year. Explain why Z could not determine the tax consequences of the distribution until the end of the year.

22-16 *Partnership Goodwill.* Explain the difference in tax consequences to both partner and partnership of liquidating payments with respect to (1) specified and (2) unspecified partnership goodwill.

22-17 *Sale of a Partnership Interest.* Is the statement that the sale of an interest in a partnership owning hot assets can result in either ordinary gain or loss recognition true or false? Explain your conclusion.

22-18 *Sale of a Partnership Interest.* Does the fact that a partner recognizes capital gain or loss on the sale of an interest in a partnership with no hot assets reflect the entity or aggregate theory of partnerships?

22-19 *Tax Consequences to Purchaser.* Explain why the outside basis in a purchased interest in a partnership without a § 754 election in effect is usually different than the purchaser's proportionate share of the inside basis of partnership assets. Does this result reflect the entity or aggregate theory of partnerships?

22-20 *Family Partnerships.* In what ways does the tax law restrict the use of a family partnership as a device to shift income to individuals in the lower marginal tax brackets?

22-21   *Death of a Partner.* How is any partnership income, gain, loss, deduction, or credit attributable to a deceased partner's interest allocated between that partner's final tax return and that of the successor in interest? Assume for purposes of your answer that death occurred on August 15th and that both the partnership and the deceased were calendar year taxpayers.

22-22   *Partnership Terminations.* Distinguish between the dissolution of a partnership under state law and the termination of a partnership for federal tax purposes.

PROBLEMS

22-23   *Formation—No Liabilities.* J and G form the JG Partnership and contribute the following business assets:

Asset	Fair Market Value	Basis	Contributed by
Land	$60,000	$30,000	J
Inventory	50,000	28,000	G
Auto	10,000	14,000	G

J and G will share profits and losses equally.
a.   Calculate each partner's realized and recognized gain or loss.
b.   Calculate each partner's basis in his or her partnership interest.
c.   Calculate the partnership's basis in each asset.

22-24   *Formation—No Liabilities.* The A-E Partnership is being formed by five individuals who each contribute assets in exchange for a 20 percent capital and profit/loss interest. Calculate the following for each partner: (1) recognized gain or loss, (2) each partner's basis in his or her partnership interest, (3) the partnership's basis for each asset, and (4) the holding period of the partnership interest for the partner and the assets for the partnership. Assume all contributed assets will be used in the partnership's trade or business.
a.   A contributes business furniture with a market value of $10,000. The furniture cost $16,000 when purchased four years ago, and A's adjusted basis in the furniture is $5,000.
b.   B contributes business equipment with a market value of $10,000. The equipment cost $20,000 when purchased two years ago, and B's adjusted basis in the equipment is $12,000.
c.   C contributes business inventory with a market value of $10,000. The inventory cost $9,000 when purchased 16 months ago.
d.   D and E contribute $10,000 cash each.

22-25   *Formation—Liabilities.* Refer to *Problem 22-24*, but assume that D and E made the following contributions *instead* of cash. How do these new facts change your answers for each partner?
a.   D contributes land with a market value of $16,000. The land was acquired 10 months ago for $9,000 cash and a $6,000 note payable (recourse debt). The $6,000 note payable is also transferred to the partnership.
b.   E contributes land with a market value of $18,000. E received the land three years ago as a gift from a relative and has a basis of $5,000. In addition, E transfers an $8,000 mortgage (nonrecourse debt) on the land to the partnership.

22-26   *Partner's Holding Period.* Individuals X and Y contributed $50,000 each to the equal Z Partnership on January 1, 2005. On July 1, 2005, X contributed land with an adjusted basis of $10,000 and fair market value of $25,000 to Z for an increased interest in the partnership. X had owned the property as an investment for six months.

On October 1, 2005, Y contributed land with an adjusted basis of $30,000 and fair market value of $25,000 to Z for an increased interest in the partnership. Y, a dealer in real property, had owned the land for three years. As of December 31, 2005, what are the partners' holding period in their partnership interests?

22-27 *Allocation of Recourse Debt.* Individuals A and B are general partners and individual L is a limited partner in the ABL Partnership. Partnership losses are allocated 40 percent to A, 35 percent to B, and 25 percent to L. As of December 31 of the current year, the partnership has $50,000 of recourse debt. The partnership's balance sheet as of December 31 is as follows:

	Basis	Fair Market Value
Cash	$ 25,000	$ 25,000
Receivables	50,000	75,000
Land	25,000	40,000
	$100,000	$140,000
Recourse liabilities	$ 50,000	$ 50,000
A, capital	20,000	36,000
B, capital	20,000	36,000
L, capital	10,000	18,000
	$100,000	$140,000

How would the $50,000 of recourse debt be allocated to A, B, and L?

22-28 *Relief of Debt in Excess of Basis.* Corporation C contributed land used in its business to the Beta Partnership in exchange for a 40 percent general interest in partnership capital, profits, and loss. The land had a $320,000 basis to the corporation and an appraised fair market value of $850,000, and was subject to a $635,000 recourse mortgage. Beta assumed the mortgage in the exchange transaction; as of the date of the exchange, Beta had no other liabilities.

a. What are the tax consequences to Corporation C of its contribution of the land to Beta? What initial basis does Corporation C have in its partnership interest?

b. How would your answers to (a) change if the $635,000 mortgage were nonrecourse rather than recourse?

c. How would your answers to (a) change if Beta had $200,000 of other recourse liabilities on its books as of the date of Corporation C's contribution of the land?

22-29 *Receipt of Partnership Interest for Services.* In return for services rendered to the AX Partnership, T receives a 20 percent unrestricted interest in partnership capital. On the day T receives her interest, the partnership owned the following assets:

	Basis	Fair Market Value
Inventory	$ 5,000	$10,000
Equipment	10,000	14,000
Land	15,000	21,000
Building	40,000	50,000
Totals	$70,000	$95,000

Assuming the partnership has no liabilities and that before T's admission it is owned 60 percent by partner A and 40 percent by partner X, answer the following questions.

a. How much compensation income must be reported by T?

b. What is T's basis in the partnership interest received?

22-30 *Required Taxable Year.* F, G, and H are partners in the FGH Partnership. F, G, and H have profit-sharing ratios of 30 percent, 50 percent, and 20 percent, respectively. F has a year-end of December 31, G of February 28, and H of September 30. What is the required year-end for FGH Partnership?

22-31 *Computation of Partnership Taxable Income.* N is a 10 percent general partner in the KLMN Partnership. The partnership's records for the current year show the following:

Gross receipts from sales	$ 670,000
Cost of sales	(500,000)
Operating expenses.	(96,000)
Net income from rental real estate.	48,000
Dividend income	10,000
Business meals and entertainment	(6,700)
Section 1231 loss	(13,500)

N's outside basis in his partnership interest was $125,000 at the beginning of the year. During the year, partnership recourse liabilities increased by $55,000; the partnership has no nonrecourse liabilities. KLMN made no distributions during the year to its partners.

a. Calculate the partnership's taxable income (Form 1065, page 1) for the current year.

b. Calculate N's basis in the partnership at the end of the year.

22-32 *Organization and Syndication Costs.* The Sigma Limited Partnership was organized during May and June of the current year. During these two months, the partnership paid $25,000 to a law firm to draft the partnership agreement and $13,000 to a CPA to set up an accounting system for the partnership business. The partnership also paid a $2,500 filing fee to the state of Illinois and $18,000 to advertise and market the sale of limited interests to potential investors. Sigma began business in August of the current year and properly adopted a fiscal year ending September 30 for tax purposes. Based on these facts, what portion of the above expenses may be expensed and amortized on Sigma's first Form 1065?

22-33 *Contributed Property—Allocations.* At the beginning of the current year, S contributed depreciable business property (market value $90,000 and basis $67,200) and T contributed investment land (market value $180,000 and basis $145,000) to form the ST Partnership. S has a one-third interest and T has a two-thirds interest in partnership capital, profits, and loss.

a. The ST Partnership will depreciate the property contributed by S on a straight-line basis over six years. Compute the amount of first year tax depreciation on the property and allocate the depreciation between partners S and T.

b. Assume the partnership sells the property contributed by S on the first day of the partnership's third taxable year. The amount realized on sale is $65,000. Compute the taxable gain or loss recognized on the sale and allocate the gain or loss between partners S and T.

c. How would your answer to (b) change if the amount realized on sale had been $54,000 rather than $65,000?

d. During its fourth taxable year, the ST Partnership sells the land contributed by T for $200,000. Compute the taxable gain recognized on sale and allocate the gain between partners S and T.

22-34 *Sale of Contributed Property—Allocations.* Two years ago, X contributed property, which was part of his proprietorship inventory, to the D Partnership in exchange for a one-third partnership interest. At the date of contribution, the property had a basis of $120,000 and a value of $145,000. The property was used in the partnership's business as a nondepreciable § 1231 asset. The partnership sold the property for $160,000 in the current year.

    a. Calculate the amount and character of the taxable gain recognized on the sale allocable to X.

    b. How would the answer for (a) change if the sale occurred six years rather than two years after contribution?

    c. How would the answer for (a) change if the property had been sold for $100,000 rather than $160,000?

22-35 *Retroactive Loss Allocations.* On September 1 of the current year, Corporation M contributed $125,000 cash to the calendar year, accrual basis Topper Partnership. For the current year, Topper recognized a $180,000 net operating loss; $82,000 of this loss had accrued as of August 31. In June of the current year, Topper sold marketable securities, recognizing a $63,000 capital gain.

    a. If Topper does not make an interim closing of its books on August 31, what is the maximum amount of current-year net operating loss and capital gain that can be allocated to Corporation M? Explain your conclusion. (In answering the question, you may assume that any allocation will have substantial economic effect.)

    b. If Topper does make an interim closing of its books on August 31, what is the maximum amount of current-year net operating loss and capital gain that can be allocated to Corporation M? Explain your conclusion. (In answering the question, you may assume that any allocation will have substantial economic effect.)

22-36 *Losses—Section 704(d).* Z has a 60 percent interest in the capital, profits, and losses of the Zeta Partnership. Both Z and Zeta are calender year taxpayers. At the beginning of the current year, Z's basis in her partnership interest was $100,000. For the current year, Zeta incurred a $200,000 ordinary loss from its business operation, earned $14,600 of dividend and interest income on its investments, and recognized a $62,000 capital gain on the sale of a partnership capital asset. On March 12 of the current year, Z received a $15,000 cash distribution from Zeta. Assume that there was no change in the amount of Zeta's liabilities during the current year.

    a. How much of the $200,000 operating loss may Z deduct on her current-year tax return? In answering this question, ignore any impact of the at-risk or passive activity loss limitations.

    b. Calculate Z's basis in her partnership interest at the end of the year.

22-37 *Losses—Section 704(d).* Corporation Q owns a 50 percent interest in the capital, profits, and loss of the QRST Partnership. Both Q and QRST are calendar year taxpayers. At the beginning of the current year, Q's outside basis in its partnership interest was $30,000. For the current year, the partnership earned $14,000 of tax-exempt interest on its investment in municipal bonds, incurred a $106,000 ordinary loss from its business operation, and recognized a $42,000 capital loss on the sale of a partnership capital asset. QRST made no distributions to partners during the year and did not change the amount of partnership debt on its books. Based on these facts, how much of the partnership's operating loss and capital loss may Corporation Q deduct in the current year? (In answering this question, assume that Q has sufficient current-year capital gains against which to deduct any amount of partnership capital loss.)

22-38 *Transactions between Partners and Partnerships.* A calendar year, accrual basis partnership rents property from a calendar year, cash basis partner, paying an arm's-length rent of $4,000 per month. The December rent payment for the current year was not received by the partner until January 5 of the subsequent year. The partnership pays this same partner a guaranteed payment for services rendered to the partnership of $10,000 per month. The December guaranteed payment was not received by the partner until January 10 of the subsequent year.

    a. In what year should the partnership deduct the December rent payment, and in what year should the partner include this payment in gross income?

    b. In what year should the partnership deduct the December guaranteed payment, and in what year should the partner include this payment in gross income?

22-39 *Guaranteed Payments.* B and G are partners in the DR Partnership. B oversees the daily operations of the business and therefore receives compensation of $50,000, regardless of the amount of the partnership's net income. In addition, his distributive share of profits and losses is 50 percent.

    a. If the partnership had $75,000 ordinary income before any payments to partners, determine the amount and character of B's total income.

    b. Same as (a), but assume the partnership had $30,000 ordinary income before payments to partners.

    c. Same as (a), except assume the partnership had $25,000 ordinary income and $50,000 long-term capital gain before payments to partners.

22-40 *Sale to Related Partnership—Loss.* V, a 60 percent partner, sells land to the partnership for $8,000. V's basis in the land is $9,000.

    a. Determine (1) V's recognized loss and (2) the partnership's basis in the land after the transaction.

    b. What are the tax consequences to the partnership if it sells the land six months later for (1) $7,500, (2) $8,600, or (3) $9,300?

    c. How would your answers to (a) and (b) differ if V were a 40 percent partner?

22-41 *Sale to Related Partnership—Gain.* During the current year, Corporation J sold investment land with a $400,000 basis to the Kappa Partnership for a selling price of $525,000. Determine the amount and character of Corporation J's recognized gain on the sale under each of the following sets of assumptions.

    a. Corporation J owns a 75 percent interest in the capital, profits, and loss of Kappa, and Kappa also holds the land as an investment asset.

    b. Corporation J owns a 35 percent interest in the capital, profits, and loss of Kappa, and Kappa uses the land in its business operation.

    c. Corporation J owns a 75 percent interest in the capital, profits, and loss of Kappa, and Kappa uses the land in its business operation.

22-42 *Contribution of Inventory with Built-in Gain.* V is a 40 percent partner in the TUV Partnership. V is a dealer in computer equipment, and V contributes computers to TUV that the partnership will use in its business operations. The computers have a basis to V of $10,000 and a fair market value of $16,000. What are the tax consequences to V and to TUV under the following circumstances?

    a. TUV sells the computers six months later for $15,000. Assume the basis is the same.

    b. TUV sells the computers six years later for $3,000. Assume the basis is zero at that time.

    c. What would your answer be if the facts are the same as in part a, except that TUV also is a dealer in computer equipment?

22-43 *Contribution of Capital Asset with Built-in Loss.* W is a 20 percent partner in the WXY Partnership. W has owned a parcel of land as an investment for three years. W contributes this land to WXY. WXY is a dealer in land. The land has a basis to W of $120,000 and a fair market value of $100,000. What are the tax consequences to W and to WXY under the following circumstances?

    a. WXY sells the land six months later for $100,000.

    b. WXY sells the land six months later for $90,000.

    c. WXY sells the land six years later for $90,000.

    d. WXY sells the land six years later for $150,000.

22-44 *Current Distributions—Proportionate.* X is a 50 percent partner in XY, a calendar year partnership. X had a basis in her partnership interest of $10,000 at the beginning of the year. On October 1, she and the other partner withdrew $15,000 cash each as an advance against their anticipated share of partnership income for the year. The partnership's ordinary, taxable income for the year was $60,000.

    a. How much gain or loss must X recognize on October 1?

    b. What is X's distributive share of partnership taxable income for the year, and what is her basis in her partnership interest at the end of the year?

    c. How would the answers to (a) and (b) change if partnership taxable income had been $6,000 instead of $60,000?

22-45 *Current Distribution—Proportionate.* During the current year, partner J received a proportionate distribution from HIJK Partnership, consisting of $13,000 cash and land (an investment asset to the partnership). The land had a basis to the partnership of $20,000 and FMV of $33,000. Prior to the distribution, J's basis in his partnership interest was $40,000. The distribution had no effect on J's profit and loss sharing ratio.

    a. How much gain or loss must J recognize because of this distribution? What basis will J have in the land? What basis will J have in his partnership interest after the distribution?

    b. Does the partnership recognize any gain on the distribution of the appreciated land to J?

    c. How would the answer to (a) change if J's basis in his interest prior to distribution had been $25,000 rather than $40,000?

22-46 *Current Distribution of Inventory.* C received a current proportionate distribution consisting of partnership inventory with an inside basis of $25,000 and a FMV of $31,000. C's predistribution outside basis in his partnership interest was $22,500.

    a. How much gain or loss must C recognize because of this distribution?

    b. What basis will C take in the distributed inventory and what will be C's postdistribution outside basis?

    c. How would your answers to (a) and (b) change if C's predistribution outside basis had been $29,000 rather than $22,500?

22-47 *Dispositions of Distributed Inventory.* Refer to the facts in *Problem 22-46*.

    a. What will be the tax consequences to C if he sells the distributed inventory for $30,000 in the first year following the distribution?

    b. How does your answer to (a) change if C waits for six years and then sells the distributed inventory for $40,000?

22-48 *Optional Adjustment to Basis—Current Proportionate Distribution.* Refer to *Problem 22-46(b)* and *(c)*. The partnership has a § 754 election in effect. Determine the § 734(b) basis adjustment for the partnership assets.

22-49 *Basis of Distributed Property—Current Distribution.* R receives a current distribution from the RST Partnership consisting of the following:

	Inside Basis	Fair Market Value
Cash	$10,000	$10,000
Accounts receivable.	0	7,500
Inventory	4,000	5,000
Capital Asset 1.	5,000	4,000
Capital Asset 2.	8,000	6,000

Immediately prior to the distribution, R's outside basis in her partnership interest was $22,000. What are R's bases in the distributed assets, and what is her basis in his partnership interest after the distribution?

22-50 *Liquidating Distribution—Proportionate.* Immediately prior to its termination, the FN Partnership owned the following assets:

	Inside Basis	Fair Market Value
Cash	$ 40,000	$40,000
Equipment	100,000	70,000
Accumulated depreciation	(60,000)	
Capital asset	10,000	30,000

F, a 50 percent owner, receives one-half of all the assets in complete liquidation of her partnership interest. F's outside basis in this interest is $45,000.

a. Calculate F's basis for each asset received in the distribution.

b. How would your answer to (a) change if F's outside basis in her partnership interest is $95,000?

22-51 *Basis of Distributed Property—Liquidating Distribution.* After reduction for a distribution of cash and the required allocation of basis to unrealized receivables and inventory received in a liquidating distribution from the HIJ Partnership, Partner J has an outside basis of $100,000. J also receives the following capital assets as part of the liquidating distribution:

	Inside Basis	Fair Market Value
Capital asset 1...................	$25,000	$60,000
Capital asset 2...................	50,000	20,000

What basis does J have in the capital assets?

22-52 *Section 734 Basis Adjustment.* Partner F received a liquidating distribution of $9,000 cash from the EFG Partnership. F's predistribution outside basis was $12,000. Assume that EFG has a § 754 election in effect. Partnership EFG owns the following assets after the distribution to F:

	Inside Basis	Fair Market Value
Cash	$20,000	$20,000
Inventory	12,000	15,000
Capital asset M	14,000	10,000
Capital asset N	10,000	8,000

a. What is F's gain or loss from the distribution?

b. What are the § 734 basis adjustments for the partnership's remaining assets?

22-53 *Payments to a Retiring Partner.* The balance sheet of RST Partnership shows the following:

	Inside Basis	Fair Market Value
Cash	$120,000	$120,000
Accounts receivable.	20,000	20,000
Inventory	105,000	112,000
§ 1231 assets	4,000	57,000
	$249,000	$309,000
Liabilities	$ 9,000	$ 9,000
R, capital	80,000	100,000
S, capital	80,000	100,000
T, capital	80,000	100,000
	$249,000	$309,000

During the current year, partners S and T agree to liquidate R's interest in the partnership for $115,000 cash. Capital is a material income-producing factor to the RST Partnership and the partnership has no unrecorded goodwill. R's basis in his interest (including his one-third share of partnership liabilities) is $83,000.

a. What are the tax consequences to R of the cash distribution from the partnership?

b. What are the consequences to the partnership of the liquidating distribution?

22-54 *Section 754 Election and Partnership Distributions.* Refer to the facts in *Problem 22-53*. What are the tax consequences to the continuing partnership if a § 754 election is in effect for the year in which R's interest is liquidated?

22-55 *Sale of a Partnership Interest.* Refer to the facts in *Problem 22-53*. Assume that U, an unrelated party, will purchase R's interest in RST Partnership for a lump sum payment of $115,000

a. What are the tax consequences of the sale to R?

b. Compute U's basis in his newly purchased partnership interest.

c. What is the effect of U's purchase of R's partnership interest on the inside basis of partnership assets if RST Partnership does not have a § 754 election in effect?

22-56 *Consequences of a § 754 Election to a Purchasing Partner.* Refer to the facts in *Problem 22-55*. What are the tax consequences to new partner U and to RST Partnership if a § 754 election is in effect for the year in which U purchases R's partnership interest?

22-57 *Sale of Partnership Interest with Hot Assets.* T, a general partner in the accrual basis TUV Partnership, sells her one-third partnership interest to D at the end of the current year for $50,000 cash. The partnership's balance sheet at the end of the year is as follows:

	Basis	FMV		Basis	FMV
Cash	$61,000	$ 61,000	T, capital	$30,000	$ 50,000
Inventory	21,000	39,000	U, capital	$30,000	$ 50,000
Land.	8,000	50,000	V, capital	$30,000	$ 50,000
	$90,000	$150,000		$90,000	$150,000

  a. What is T's gain or loss from this sale?

  b. What basis does D have in her partnership interest?

  c. If the partnership sells the land for $50,000 immediately after D purchases her interest, what is the tax effect to D?

  d. What should D request that the partnership do to prevent the result in part (c) from occurring?

22-58 *Section 754 Election.* Based on the facts from *Problem 22-57*, what would the tax result be to D upon the sale of the land if the partnership had a § 754 election in effect?

22-59 *Dispositions of Partnership Interests.* K owns a limited interest in the Kappa Investment Partnership. The interest has a FMV of $50,000 and a basis to K of $37,000. No amount of partnership debt is included in this basis number. What are the tax consequences to K in each of the following situations?

  a. K exchanges the interest for a general interest in Kappa that is worth $50,000.

  b. K exchanges the interest for investment land worth $50,000.

  c. K dies and bequeaths the interest to her nephew.

  d. K exchanges the interest for newly issued stock in Gamma Inc. Immediately after the exchange, K owns 12 percent of Gamma's outstanding stock.

  e. K determines that the value of the interest is not $50,000 but is zero. Consequently, she abandons the interest.

22-60 *Partnership Termination.* At the beginning of 2005, Beta Partnership was owned by four equal partners. On June 8, 2005 Partner A sold her one-fourth interest to B, one of the other three partners. On November 19, 2005 new partner G contributed cash and property in exchange for a 55 percent interest in partnership capital and profits. On March 31, 2006 G sold a 30 percent interest to a new partner P. Beta and all its partners use the calendar year for tax purposes.

  a. Do any of the capital transactions described above terminate the Beta partnership?

  b. What is the effect of any termination on Beta's taxable year?

Chapter 23

S CORPORATIONS

LEARNING OBJECTIVES

Upon completion of this chapter you will be able to:

▸ Identify the requirements necessary to elect S status

▸ Recognize the actions that terminate S status

▸ Compute the net operating income or loss for an S corporation and the impact of S corporate operations on shareholders' taxable income

▸ Recognize transactions between shareholders and their S corporations that are subject to special treatment

▸ Determine the shareholders' basis in the S corporation stock

▸ Determine the appropriate taxable year for an S corporation

▸ Explain the unique concepts relevant to family members

▸ Calculate gain or loss for the S corporation and its shareholders when asset distributions are made and the S corporation (1) has no AE&P or (2) has AE&P

▸ Calculate the special taxes on excessive passive income and on built-in gains

▸ Understand how dispositions of S corporate stock differ from those of C corporate stock

▸ Compare the four business organizations—proprietorships, partnerships, S corporations, and C corporations (see Appendix)

CHAPTER OUTLINE

INTRODUCTION

Congress added Subchapter S to the Internal Revenue Code in 1958, giving birth to a unique tax entity: the S corporation. The S corporation is taxed in a manner very similar to a partnership, while retaining the legal characteristics of a corporation. In providing this distinctive treatment, Congressional intent was to allow small businesses to have "the advantages of the corporate form of organization without being made subject to the possible tax disadvantages of the corporation."[1] As this statement suggests, Congress recognized that many taxpayers who normally would incorporate their businesses to secure limited liability were reluctant to do so because of the possibility of double taxation. Accordingly, one of the major objectives of the Subchapter S legislation was to minimize taxes as a factor in the selection of the form of business organization. To accomplish this objective, a complete set of special rules were designed, most of which are contained in Subchapter S.

Although the treatment of S corporations was intended to be similar to that for partnerships, this goal was not achieved under the 1958 legislation. As originally written, the rules governing S corporations (or Subchapter S corporations as they were initially called) bore little resemblance to partnership rules. Many of these differences were eliminated, however, with the substantial modifications introduced by the Subchapter S Revision Act of 1982. Under the revised rules, Federal income tax treatment of S corporations and their shareholders is similar to that of partnerships and their partners. The S corporation generally is not subject to the corporate *Federal*

---

[1]   S. Rept. No. 1622, 83rd Cong., 2d Sess., 119 (1954).

income tax. Rather, like a partnership, the S corporation is merely a conduit. The income, deductions, gains, losses, and credits of the S corporation flow through to its shareholders. An S corporation, however, may be subject to a special tax such as the tax on excessive passive income or on built-in gains.

Even though the Federal income tax treatment of an S corporation resembles that of a partnership, the corporation is subject to many rules that apply to regular corporations. For example, since an S corporation is formed in the same manner as a regular corporation (defined as "C" corporations), the basic rules governing organization (i.e., the nonrecognition rules contained in § 351 concerning transfers to a controlled corporation discussed in Chapter 19) of all corporations also apply to S corporations. Similarly, redemptions of an S corporation's stock, as well as liquidation and reorganization of an S corporation, generally are taxed according to the rules applying to regular corporations. As a practical matter, however, each provision must be closely examined to determine whether special treatment is provided for S corporations.

S CORPORATION ELIGIBILITY REQUIREMENTS

The special tax treatment provided for S corporations is available only if the corporation is a *small business corporation* and its shareholders *consent* to the corporation's election to be taxed under Subchapter S. A small business corporation must[2]

1. Be an *eligible domestic* corporation;

2. Not have more than 100 *eligible* shareholders; and

3. Have only *one class of stock* outstanding.

All of these requirements must be met when the election is made and at all times thereafter. Failure at any time to qualify as a small business corporation terminates the election, and as of the date of termination, the corporation is taxed as a regular corporation (hereafter referred to as a C corporation).[3]

The phrase *small business corporation* may be a misnomer. As the requirements for this status indicate, the sole restriction on the size of the corporation is the limitation imposed on the *number* of shareholders. Corporations are not denied use of Subchapter S due to the amount of their assets, income, net worth, or any other measure of size. In addition, the S corporation is not required to conduct an active business. Merely holding assets does not bar the corporation from Subchapter S.

ELIGIBLE CORPORATIONS

Subchapter S status is reserved for *eligible domestic corporations.*[4] Thus, foreign corporations do not qualify. In addition, certain types of domestic corporations are considered ineligible. These ineligible corporations include insurance companies, banks that use the reserve method of accounting for bad debts, corporations electing the special possessions tax credit under Code § 936 and domestic international sales corporations (DISCs).[5]

It should be emphasized that only corporations or entities that are considered corporations may take advantage of Subchapter S. As a practical matter, this is rarely an

---

[2] § 1361. For S corporations' taxable years beginning before January 1, 2005, the limit was 75.

[3] § 1362(d)(2). As discussed later, however, a corporation may avoid loss of its election by applying for "inadvertent termination" relief.

[4] § 1361(b); Reg. 301.7701-5(b) includes any U.S. territory as well as states.

[5] § 1361(b)(2).

issue. A limited liability company (LLC) or other unincorporated entity can qualify as an S corporation if it elects to be treated as a corporation under the check-the-box regulations (see Chapter 19).[6] Under these rules, the entity could only be considered an S corporation if it opts to be taxed as a corporation *and* subsequently makes a valid S election. In other words, an LLC that elects to be treated as a corporation is treated as a C corporation until an S election is made.

Until 1997, an S corporation could not own 80 percent or more of the stock of another corporation. However, beginning in 1997, S corporations may own stock in *C corporations* without limitation. This new approach gives S corporations the freedom to structure their ownership in C corporations to meet the needs of their organization. For example, an S corporation may establish a wholly owned C corporation as a subsidiary to hold a risky business thereby protecting the assets of the parent. Although S corporations may now have C corporations as subsidiaries, S and C corporations cannot file a consolidated return.[7]

Example 1. D Inc., an S corporation, is interested in purchasing T Inc., a C corporation. T operates a hazardous waste disposal business that is quite profitable but also quite risky. D would like to structure the acquisition in such a way that it does not expose its current business to the risks associated with T's operation. D may own as little or as much of T stock that it wants since there are no rules prohibiting an S corporation from owning the stock of a C corporation.

While S corporations may own stock of C corporations, the reverse is not allowed. As discussed below, S corporations generally are not allowed to have any corporate shareholders. However, an S corporation may own the stock of another corporation, and treat the wholly-owned corporation as a qualified subchapter S subsidiary (QSub).

Qualified Subchapter S Subsidiary (QSub). A QSub is a corporation that is 100 percent owned by an S corporation (i.e., the parent) that elects to treat the subsidiary as a QSub.[8] The QSub is a corporation that exists as a separate entity for nontax purposes but is not treated as a separate entity under Federal income tax laws. By electing to treat the subsidiary as a QSub, the parent corporation agrees to report all of the income and deductions of the QSub along with its own tax items. Note that if a parent S corporation acquires all of the stock of an existing corporation (C or S), it must treat the subsidiary as if it were liquidated for tax purposes when it elects QSub status for the subsidiary.[9] Alternately, the parent S corporation could treat the subsidiary corporation as a C corporation, regardless of the amount of stock it owned.

SHAREHOLDER REQUIREMENTS

Subchapter S imposes several restrictions on S corporation shareholders. Not only is the total number of shareholders limited to 100, but certain parties are prohibited from owning stock of the corporation.

Type of Shareholder. The stock of an S corporation may be owned only by

1. Individuals who are citizens or resident aliens of the United States,

2. Estates,

---

[6]   Rev. Proc. 2004-48, 2004-32 I.R.B.

[7]   § 1504(b)(8).

[8]   § 1361(b)(3)(B).

[9]   Use Form 8869. The liquidation is nontaxable under §§ 332 and 337.

3. Certain trusts, and

4. Charitable organizations, pension trusts (not IRAs), and employee stock ownership plans.

Nonresident aliens (i.e., generally foreign citizens residing outside the United States), C corporations, other S corporations, partnerships, and most trusts are *not* allowed to hold stock in an S corporation.

Over the years, rules prohibiting trusts as shareholders have proved unduly inflexible, often intruding on sensible planning. This prohibition has been particularly troublesome in the estate and retirement planning area. For example, an individual may not want to leave the shares of his or her S corporation outright to a young child in his or her will but rather in trust for the benefit of a child. Without special rules, this obviously prudent action would be barred. Consequently, the current provisions allow some freedom in using trusts.

Eligible Trusts. The list of trusts that are eligible shareholders and a brief description of each follows below. In examining the list, note the concern for the shareholder limitation issue and how the shareholders are counted when an eligible trust holds shares.[10]

Grantor Trusts. A grantor trust is a trust that is disregarded under the trust taxation rules because of the power, control and benefits retained by the individual who established the trust (i.e., the grantor). All of the income of a grantor trust (e.g., a revocable trust that is used to avoid probate) is normally taxed to the grantor rather than the trust. If the grantor dies, the S shares normally have to be distributed to the beneficiaries within two years after the death. A grantor trust has one deemed shareholder. (See Chapter 26 for a discussion of these trusts.)

Beneficiary Controlled Trust or § 678 trust. A § 678 trust is similar to the grantor trust, except the income of the trust is taxed to the beneficiary (rather than the grantor) because of the power that the beneficiary holds over trust property. A § 678 trust has one deemed shareholder.

Qualified Subchapter S Trust (QSST). A QSST is a trust that has *only one* beneficiary (who must be a U.S. citizen or resident) to whom all of the income of the trust must be distributed annually and for which a proper election to be treated as a QSST has been filed in a timely manner. The trust's beneficiary (or legal guardian thereof) must file an election to include all of the trust's share of the S corporation's income, deductions and other tax items directly on the beneficiary's return as if he or she were the shareholder of the trust's stock. The beneficiary must file this election within two months and 15 days from the date the trust acquires the stock. (If the trust owns shares on the date the corporation elects to become an S corporation, the beneficiary must file this election within two months and 15 days after the corporation files its S election. In practice the two elections are often made concurrently.) In addition to this election, there are certain other restrictions on the QSST. The trust may not be able to distribute any of its income or property to any person other than the current income beneficiary during his or her lifetime. In addition, the trust must distribute (or be required to distribute) all of its income to this beneficiary annually. Note that failure to adhere to these rules properly results in an ineligible shareholder and loss of the S election.

---

[10] § 1361(c)(2).

In practice, the QSST election is often misunderstood. The result has been a multitude of private letter rulings allowing a corporation's S election to take effect, or continue in effect, after a trust has acquired the stock and the beneficiary has failed to make a timely QSST election. Accordingly, the IRS has issued an automatic relief rule for a QSST election that is no more than 24 months late.[11] If the QSST election is not filed within the 24-month period, the corporation must apply for inadvertent termination or inadvertent invalid election relief. Relief is sought from the National Office of the IRS in the form of a letter ruling request, which must be accompanied by a user fee.

For all purposes of subchapter S, the beneficiary of the QSST is treated as the shareholder. This treatment applies to consents, allocations of income, other items, and the 100-shareholder limit.

Electing Small Business Trust (ESBT). In contrast to the QSST that has only a single beneficiary, an *ESBT* can have more than one potential current beneficiary. The trustee can have the right to accumulate or distribute income to any of the beneficiaries. The trustee must file a timely election for the trust to qualify. A price is paid for use of this trust since all of the income flowing from the S corporation to the trust is taxed to the trust itself (i.e., there is no deduction for distributions of the trust) and such income is taxed at the highest marginal rate (35 percent for ordinary income in 2004 and 2005). In addition, the ESBT must pay tax on any capital gains in the same manner as an individual taxpayer who is in the highest marginal tax bracket. This rule applies both to any capital gains passing through from the S corporation to the trust and to any gain recognized by the trust on the disposition of the S corporation stock. However, a distribution from the trust to a beneficiary is tax-free to the beneficiary and is nondeductible to the trust. In counting shareholders, each potential income beneficiary is considered to own stock in the S corporation.

Testamentary Trusts. A testamentary trust is one that is created by the decedent's last will and testament. A testamentary trust may only be an eligible shareholder for two years unless it also qualifies under one of the other trust rules. The estate is treated as the owner of the stock in the case of one or more testamentary trusts that are established (e.g., if three trusts are created, the estate is considered the single owner).

Charitable Organizations, Pension Trusts, and Employee Stock Ownership Plans. For taxable years beginning after 1997, these organizations (generally tax-exempt) can be shareholders in S corporations. However, individual retirement accounts are not allowed to hold stock in an S corporation.[12]

Charitable organizations and pension trusts may find S corporations unappealing since they must include their share of income from the S corporation as unrelated business taxable income. Thus these organizations would be subject to income tax on their income from the S corporation. However, the S corporation will usually make sufficient cash distributions to enable all shareholders to pay their income taxes on their portions of the S corporation's income. In contrast, these organizations are not subject to taxation on interest or dividend income derived from an investment in a C corporation. In addition, they are normally not taxable on gains from the disposition of stock or securities of a C corporation. ESOPs may also view investment in an S corporation unattractive since they may lose some special tax breaks to which they are entitled if they own stock in a C corporation.

---

[11] Rev. Proc. 2003-43, 2003-23 I.R.B. 998.

[12] There is an extremely narrow exception for certain IRAs that held stock in banking corporations on October 22, 2004. Under a special rule, these IRAs (and no others) are permitted shareholders. See §1361(c)(2)(A).

Voting Trusts. A voting trust is a trust created primarily to hold the shares and exercise the voting power of the stock transferred to it. For a voting trust, each beneficiary is treated as a shareholder.

Number of Shareholders. As a general rule, a corporation does not qualify as an S corporation if the number of shareholders exceeds 100 at any moment during the taxable year. For purposes of counting the number of shareholders in an S corporation, stock owned by a husband and wife is treated as owned by one shareholder.[13] If either the husband or wife dies, the one-shareholder rule includes the estate. The one-shareholder rule applies whether the stock is owned by the spouses separately or jointly. Consequently, it is possible for an S corporation to have 200 shareholders if all stock is owned by married couples. This treatment is not extended to couples who are divorced but continue to own the stock jointly. Similarly, other persons who are co-owners of the stock but who are not married are counted as separate shareholders.

Beginning in 2005, members of a single family may elect to have some rather broad attribution rules treat a family unit as a single shareholder. Specifically, the law now permits six generations of descendants from common ancestors to elect to be treated as a single shareholder, for purposes of the shareholder count.[14] There is no requirement that members of each generation must be living. Thus it is possible to have extended generations of second, third and fourth cousins all be treated as one shareholder. A spouse (or former spouse) of any of the lineal family members is also included in this attribution. However, any of these individuals that holds stock at the time a corporation files an election for S status would have to consent to the election in his or her individual capacity. At press time of this edition, the IRS has not released any guidance on this new rule.

When a permissible trust is a shareholder of the S corporation, the number of shareholders counted depends on the type of trust. As discussed above, all qualifying trusts, *except* ESBTs and voting trusts, represent one shareholder. For ESBTs and voting trusts, each beneficiary is counted as a shareholder.

When stock is held in the name of a nominee, agent, guardian, or custodian, the beneficial owner of the stock is treated as the shareholder.

Example 2. XYZ Bank and Trust, a corporation, holds legal title to stock in an S corporation. The XYZ corporation holds the stock for the benefit of R, a minor child. In this case, R, the beneficial owner, is treated as the shareholder rather than XYZ whether the trust qualifies as a QSST, an ESBT, or a § 678 trust. As a result, the S corporation is not denied the benefits of Subchapter S because of a corporate shareholder.

Example 3. F holds stock in an S corporation as custodian for his two minor children. For purposes of counting shareholders, F is ignored and the children are counted as two separate shareholders.

ONE CLASS OF STOCK

In order to minimize the problems of allocating income of the S corporation among shareholders, the corporation is allowed only one class of stock outstanding. Stock that is authorized but unissued does not invalidate the election. For example, an S corporation may have authorized but unissued preferred stock. Similarly, stock rights, options, or convertible debentures may be issued without affecting the election. A

---

[13]   § 1361(c)(1).

[14]   §1361(c)(1)(B)(ii).

corporation that has issued a second class of stock may qualify if the stock is reacquired and cancelled or held as Treasury stock.

Outstanding shares generally must provide identical distribution and liquidation rights to all shareholders. However, differences in *voting rights* are expressly authorized by the Code.[15] This exception enables control of the organization to be exercised in a manner that differs from stock ownership and income allocation.

> **Example 4.** R organized MND, an S corporation. MND issued two classes of common stock to R: class A voting and class B nonvoting stock. The rights represented by the stock are identical except for voting rights, and thus do not invalidate the S election. Shortly after the organization of the corporation, R gives the class B nonvoting stock to her two children. Although R has shifted income and future appreciation of the stock to her children (assuming certain other requirements are satisfied), she has retained all of the voting control of the corporation.

Debt as a Second Class of Stock. In the past, the second class of stock issue has arisen where the IRS or the courts have stepped in and reclassified an S corporation's debt as stock. As discussed in Chapter 19, reclassification might occur when the corporation is thinly capitalized (e.g., the debt to equity ratio exceeds 4:1). If this were to happen to an S corporation, the result would be particularly disastrous since the S corporation might be considered as having two classes of stock, resulting in loss of its S election. To provide S corporations and their shareholders with some certainty in this area, Congress created a safe-harbor for debt meeting certain requirements. Under these rules, an S corporation's *straight debt* will not be classified as a second class of stock if [16]

1. The interest rate and interest payment dates are not contingent on either the corporation's profits, management's discretion, or similar factors;

2. The debt instrument is written and cannot be converted into stock; and

3. The creditor is an individual, estate or trust, (but only if the trust is a grantor trust, QSST or ESBT) that is eligible to hold stock in an S corporation, or any person that is actively and regularly engaged in the business of lending money (e.g., a bank).

Straight debt is defined as any written unconditional promise to pay on demand, or on a specified date, a certain sum of money. Also included as straight debt are any short-term unwritten advances from a shareholder less than $10,000 in the aggregate—if treated as debt by the parties, and if expected to be repaid in a reasonable period of time.[17]

Whether an S corporation has more than one class of stock is determined by the corporate charter, articles of incorporation, bylaws, applicable state law, and binding agreements relating to distributions and liquidation. Unintended unequal distributions will generally not cause a second class of stock. For example, excessive compensation paid to an owner-employee may be recharacterized as a distribution by the IRS. However, regulations for § 1361 hold that this type of distribution normally will not result in a second class of stock.[18] The Regulations also permit unequal distributions that occur in states that require the S corporation to withhold state taxes from distributions made to some or all of its shareholders, but only if there is a compensating distribution

---

[15] § 1361(c)(4).

[16] § 1361(c)(5).

[17] Reg. § 1.131-1(1)(4)(ii)(B).

[18] Reg. § 1.1361-1(1)(2)(vi), Example 3.

to shareholders who are not subject to the state withholding. Generally, the facts and circumstances of each situation will be considered.

ELECTION OF S CORPORATION STATUS

A corporation that qualifies as a small business corporation is taxed according to the rules of Subchapter S only if the corporation elects to be an S corporation. This election exempts the business from the corporate income tax and all other Federal income taxes normally imposed on corporations except for (1) the tax on excessive passive investment income, (2) the tax on built-in gains, and (3) the LIFO recapture tax. In addition, the corporation normally is exempt from the personal holding company tax and the accumulated earnings tax. Although the S corporation generally avoids taxation as a regular corporation, most rules governing regular corporations such as those concerning organization, redemptions, and liquidations apply.

MAKING THE ELECTION: MANNER AND PERIOD OF EFFECT

In order for a corporation to be taxed according to the rules of Subchapter S, an election must be filed on Form 2553. The effective date of the election, as well as the required shareholder consents that must be evidenced on the form, generally depend on when the election is filed. The election must be filed with the IRS center where the S corporation files its tax returns.

Time of the Election. To be effective for the corporation's current taxable year, the election must be filed within two months and 15 days of the beginning of the corporation's taxable year.[19] Note that well-meaning shareholders or tax professionals trying to ensure a prompt election might file an election before the corporation has actually started business. Unfortunately, an election cannot be made before the corporation is in existence and any election filed before such date would be invalid. Since the election must be filed in a particular time period—neither too early nor too late—the starting date is critical. For this purpose, the first taxable year starts on the earliest date that the corporation (1) issues shares; (2) acquires property; or (3) commences business.[20] Once the starting date begins, the election may be filed any time on or before the two months and 15 days deadline. For many years, there was no relief for taxpayers who filed a late election even if there were good reasons for the failure. However, the IRS is now allowed to treat a late election as being timely filed if there is reasonable cause.[21]

> **Example 5.** J and B decided to start a publishing corporation in 2005. The corporation issued shares on December 13, 2005 in exchange for $20,000. On January 15, 2006 the corporation opened a bank account and deposited the $20,000. On February 1, 2006 the corporation started operations. In this case, the corporation is considered to have started business on December 13, 2005 (the earliest of the dates that it issued shares, acquired property or commenced business). Consequently, the election must be filed on or before February 27, 2006. If the start date was May 1, June 23 or November 8, 2005 the election must be filed on or before July 15, September 6 or January 22, 2006 respectively. Note that in all of these examples, the third month and the start of the 15-day count begins on the

---

[19] §§ 1362(b)(1)(B) and (b)(2) and Reg. § 1.1362-6(a)(2)(ii).

[20] Reg. § 1.1362-6(a)(2)(ii)(c).

[21] § 1362(b)(5).

same numerical day as the year began (i.e., February 13, July 1, August 23, and January 8 plus 14 days yields the critical date).

If the corporation does not file a timely election or secure recognition of a late election, it will be considered a C corporation for the taxable year in question and the S election will be effective for the following tax year. Failure to make a timely election can be a crucial blunder. For instance, any losses that occurred during the C year would not flow through and any distributions could be treated as fully taxable dividends. However, since enactment of the legislation specifically enabling the acceptance of late elections, such mistakes have not been quite as costly.

Under current law, the IRS has been reasonable, if not outright lenient, in granting late elections. In 2003, the IRS authorized its Service Centers to accept S elections that are up to a year late as long as the extended due date of the return for the first year of desired S status has not passed and the corporation states a "reasonable cause" for the lateness of the election.[22]

> **Example 6.** This year J and B formed a calendar year corporation on May 1, 2005. Unfortunately, J and B were unaware that they needed to file the S election by July 15 (i.e., two months and 15 days after May 1) and their error was not discovered until they visited an accountant in January 2006. Under the current approach, the IRS would accept an election up to September 15, 2006, the extended due date of the return for the first year it desired S status.

If an S corporation does not meet these criteria and still wishes to validate a late election, it must apply to the National Office of the IRS for a private letter ruling—a process that can be a very costly (e.g., the IRS fee for the ruling, currently $6,000, plus the expense of the accounting or law firm that prepares the ruling request). The IRS frequently grants favorable rulings on these requests. The fee is reduced to $500 if the corporation has no more than $1,000,000 of gross receipts.[23]

It should also be noted that the law instructs the IRS to accept a timely filed but defective election (e.g., second class of stock outstanding) if the reason for the defect is inadvertent. Inadvertence is a higher standard than reasonable cause and only the National Office of the IRS can approve a defective election.[24]

Shareholder Consent. In order for the election to be valid, the corporation must secure and file the consents of the shareholders along with the election. Consent to the election must be obtained not only from *all* shareholders (both husband and wife) holding stock at the time of election, but also from former shareholders who have held stock during the earlier portion of that taxable year.[25] The consent of former shareholders is required since they will be allocated a share of the income, losses, and other items applicable to the time they held the stock. The IRS may grant an extension for filing the consent for one or more shareholders if reasonable cause can be shown.[26] If a *former* shareholder will not or does not sign the consent, the election is effective for the following taxable year. Similarly, if the corporation fails to meet any of the Subchapter S requirements during the pre-election portion of the year, the election is effective for the following taxable year.

---

[22] Rev. Proc. 2003-43, 2003-23 I.R.B. 998.

[23] See Rev. Proc. 2004-1, 2004-1 I.R.B. 1, Appendix A for the most recent schedule of user fees.

[24] § 1362(f).

[25] §§ 1362(a)(2) and (b)(2)(B)(ii).

[26] Reg. § 1.1362-6(b)(3)(iii).

Example 7. At the beginning of 2004, D, E, and F owned the stock of GHI Corporation, a calendar year taxpayer. On February 15, 2004 F sold all of her shares in GHI to C. On March 1, 2004 an S corporation election is desired. In order for the election to be effective for 2004, all shareholders on the date of election (C, D, and E), as well as any shareholders in the pre-election portion of the year (F), must consent. Failure to obtain F's consent would cause the election to become effective for 2005. Consent is required from both C and D even if they are married and qualify as one shareholder.

Election Effective for Subsequent Years. Elections made after the first two months and 15 days of the current taxable year are effective for the following taxable year.[27] When the election becomes effective in the following taxable year, only shareholders holding stock on the date of election must consent. The consent of shareholders who acquire stock after the election is not required.

Example 8. On November 1, 2005, J Corporation filed an S election on Form 2553, including all of the shareholder consents. The election was to be effective for its next taxable year beginning on January 1, 2006. Unknowing to those handling the incorporation, one of the consenting shareholders, V, was a Canadian citizen, living in Vancouver. On December 15, 2005 the corporation discovered the problem and V agreed to sell all of his stock to one of the other shareholders. Since the corporation had a nonresident alien shareholder on the date that the election was filed, the election is not valid. The fact that the problem was corrected before the year in which the election was to be effective is irrelevant. Note, however, that if the corporation recognized the error, it could cure it by filing another Form 2553 by March 15, 2006. As an alternative, the corporation could file—at a cost—a ruling request asking the IRS to accept the inadvertently invalid election. Such requests are routinely granted.

TERMINATION OF THE ELECTION

An election to be taxed as an S corporation is effective until it is terminated. The election may be terminated when the corporation[28]

1. Revokes the election;

2. Fails to satisfy the requirements; or

3. Receives excessive passive income.

Revocation. The S corporation election may be revoked if shareholders holding a *majority* of the shares of stock (voting and nonvoting) consent.[29] A revocation filed by the fifteenth day of the third month of the taxable year (e.g., March 15 for a calendar year corporation) normally is effective for the current taxable year.[30] In contrast, if the revocation is filed after this two months and 15-day period has elapsed, it usually becomes effective for the following taxable year.[31] In both situations, however, a date on or after the date of revocation may be specified for the termination to become effective.[32]

---

[27]   § 1362(b)(3).

[28]   § 1362(d).

[29]   § 1362(d)(1)(B).

[30]   § 1362(d)(1)(C)(i).

[31]   § 1362(d)(1)(C)(ii).

[32]   § 1362(d)(1)(D).

Example 9. A calendar year S corporation is owned equally by C, D, and E. On February 12, 2005 C and D consent to revoke the S corporation election. Since C and D own a majority of the outstanding shares of stock, the election is effective beginning on January 1, 2005 unless the revocation specifies February 12, 2005 or some later date.

Example 10. Same as *Example 9* above except the revocation was made on May 3, 2005. The election is effective for the following taxable year beginning January 1, 2006. If the revocation had specified, however, that the termination was to become effective May 3, 2005, the S corporation year would end on May 2, 2005.

Example 11. An S corporation has 100 shares of outstanding stock, 75 owned by J and 25 owned by B. On June 1 of this year, J sold 60 of her 75 shares to D. Since D owns a majority of the outstanding shares, he may cause the corporation to revoke the election, even if J and B are opposed to the revocation. However, the corporation must file the revocation. A statement filed by a shareholder is insufficient to revoke the election.

Failure to Meet the Eligibility Requirements. If the S corporation fails to satisfy any of the Subchapter S requirements at any time, the election is terminated on the date the disqualifying event occurs.[33] In such case, the corporation is treated as an S corporation for the period ending the day before the date of termination. This often causes the corporation to have two short taxable years: one as an S corporation and one as a C corporation. As a result, income and loss for the entire year must be allocated between the two years. The tax returns for both the short S year and short C year must be filed by the due date of the short year C corporate return.[34]

Example 12. C, D, and E own a calendar year S corporation. On June 3 of this year, E sold her stock to a corporation. The S corporation's year ends on June 2. The same result would be obtained if the sale had been to a partnership or to an individual who became the 101st shareholder. The S short year includes January 1 through June 2. The C short year is June 3 through December 31. Both returns are due on March 15 of the next year, although they may be extended to September 15.

Unless the S election termination occurs on the first day of the corporation's tax year, the termination year is split into two short periods. There are some special rules governing the allocation of income between the two short periods. The two methods that the corporation may use are the pro-rata allocation and the interim closing method.

Using the pro-rata method, each item required to be reported to the shareholders is assigned equally to each day in the entire tax year.[35] If the corporation uses the interim closing method it must separately account for activities during the S and C portions of the year.[36]

Example 13. On March 14, 2005, X Corporation terminates its S election. S uses the calendar year for tax purposes. Its income and loss items for 2005 occurred during the following periods.

---

[33] § 1362(d)(2).

[34] § 1362(e)(6)(B).

[35] § 1362(e)(1).

[36] § 1362(e)(3).

	S Short Year	C Short Year	Total
Ordinary income	$80,000	$40,000	$120,000
Long-term capital gain	16,000	0	16,000
Dividend income (X holds 20% stock in payor)	0	5,000	5,000

If the corporation uses the interim closing method, it will report $80,000 of ordinary income and $16,000 of long-term capital gain to the shareholders, who will include these items on their 2005 tax returns. X would include $45,000 income, less a 70% dividends-received deduction of $3,500, on its Form 1120 for the C short year ending December 31, 2005. If the corporation pro rates all of the items, the allocation would be as follows:

	S Short Year (73/365)	C Short Year (292/365)	Total
Ordinary income	$24,000	$96,000	$120,000
Long-term capital gain	3,200	12,800	16,000
Dividend income	1,000	4,000	5,000

The corporation must use the pro-rata method unless it elects to use the interim closing, or there is a change of ownership of 50 percent or more of the corporation's shares within the S termination year.[37] The election is filed with the corporation's Form 1120 for the C short year. The election must be accompanied by consents of all persons who are shareholders at any time during the S short year, as well as all shareholders on the first day of the C short year.[38]

The corporation must annualize its income and tax for the C short year. This is accomplished by grossing up the income as if it were earned ratably for a year of 365 days (366 in a leap year), and then apportioning the tax for the number of days in the C short year.

Example 14. Refer to *Example 13*, above. Assume that the corporation elects to use the interim closing method. X would report the following annualized income and tax.

Ordinary income	$40,000
Dividend income	5,000
Less dividends received deduction	(3,500)
Taxable income	$41,500
Annualization	(365/292)
Annualized taxable income	$51,875
Tax on $51,875	$7,969
Annualization	(292/365)
Annualized tax	$6,375

---

[37] § 1362(e)(6)(D).

[38] Reg. § 1.1362-6(a)(5).

When termination is *inadvertent*, the Code authorizes the IRS to allow a corporation to continue its S status uninterrupted if the disqualifying action is corrected.[39] It is possible, for example, that if stock is transferred to an ineligible shareholder, the IRS might allow the corporation to correct the violation and continue its S status uninterrupted. Inadvertent termination relief can only be granted to a corporation that applies to the IRS National Office and pays the user fee for a letter ruling.

> **Example 15.** On the advice of his attorney, a majority shareholder transferred his S corporation shares to an ineligible trust. When the shareholder discovered the transfer terminated the S corporation election, the trust transferred the stock to the previous shareholder. The IRS has ruled, under similar circumstances, that the S election was not lost since the termination of the S status was inadvertent, it occurred as the result of advice from counsel, and it was corrected as soon as the violation of S status was discovered.[40]

Excessive Passive Income. Without special rules relating to passive income, owners of C corporations might convert to S status to avoid problems they face as a C corporation. To illustrate, consider the retiring owner of a C corporation who causes the corporation to sell all of its operating assets. After paying the corporate level tax on the sale, the owner could distribute the after tax proceeds in liquidation, resulting in yet a second tax at the shareholder level. The owner could then take what is left of the original sales price after paying two taxes (one by the C corporation and one by the shareholder on the liquidation) and invest it. Alternatively, the owner could opt not to liquidate and elect S status. Using this latter approach, the tax on the liquidation is avoided, the owner has more capital to invest, yet the investment income is taxed only once—the same as it would have been taxed if the owner held the investments personally. Moreover, the owner need not be concerned with the accumulated earnings tax or the personal holding company tax since these penalty taxes are reserved solely for C corporations. To foil this plan and others, Congress created two provisions that are triggered when evidence of this scheme are present. In short, if an S corporation has E&P accumulated while it was a C corporation (i.e., evidence of conversion) and too much passive income (i.e., investment income), the S corporation will have to pay a corporate level tax and could lose its S election. In this section, the rules governing termination of the S election are considered. A later section examines the passive investment income tax.

Under the passive income test, the election is terminated if the corporation has[41]

1. Passive investment income exceeding 25 percent of its gross receipts for three consecutive years, *and*

2. C corporation accumulated earnings and profits (AE&P) at the end of each of the three consecutive years.

If both of these conditions are satisfied, the termination becomes effective at the beginning of the first year following the end of the three-year period.[42]

As reflected in the second condition above, the excessive passive income test is reserved for corporations that were C corporations prior to becoming S corporations. In addition, the test applies to these former C corporations only if they have AE&P from C years. Accordingly, corporations that have never been C corporations as well as

---

[39]   § 1362(f).

[40]   Rev. Rul. 86-110, 1986-38 I.R.B. 4. Also, see Ltr. Ruls. 8550033 and 8608006.

[41]   § 1362(d)(3).

[42]   § 1362(d)(3)(A)(ii).

corporations that have distributed all AE&P cannot lose their S election because of passive investment income.

Passive investment income generally is defined as gross receipts from royalties, rents, dividends, interest (including tax-exempt interest but excluding interest on notes from sales of inventory and interest derived from a lending business), annuities, and gains on sales or exchanges of stock or securities.[43] For this purpose, rents are not considered passive income if significant services are provided (e.g., room rents paid to a hotel) or if the rents are received in the ordinary course of a rental business.[44] In computing total gross receipts, costs of goods sold, returns and allowances and deductions are ignored. Receipts from the sale or exchange of stocks and securities are included to the extent of gains [i.e., gross receipts = amount realized − adjusted basis = gain (but not loss)]. In contrast, receipts from the sale or exchange of capital assets other than stocks and securities are included only to the extent of net gains (i.e., capital gains less capital losses).[45]

> **Example 16.** OBJ, an S corporation, was a C corporation for several years before it elected to be taxed under Subchapter S beginning in 2003. For 2003 and 2004 the corporation had excessive passive income. In addition, at the close of 2003 and 2004, OBJ reported a balance in its AE&P that was attributable to its years as a C corporation. OBJ's income and expenses for 2005 are shown below. No distributions from its AE&P were made during the year. The corporation's passive investment income and total gross receipts, based on its reported items, are determined as follows:

	Reported	Gross Receipts	Passive Income
Sales	$ 200,000	$200,000	$ 0
Cost of goods sold	(150,000)	0	0
Interest income	30,000	30,000	30,000
Dividends	15,000	15,000	15,000
Rental income (passive)	40,000	40,000	40,000
Rental expenses	(28,000)	0	0
Gain on sale of stock ($20,000 − $5,000)	15,000	15,000	15,000
Loss on sale of stock ($10,000 − $12,000)	(2,000)	0	0
Total		$300,000	$100,000
25% of gross receipts		$ 75,000	

Because OBJ's passive investment income exceeds 25% of its gross receipts for the third consecutive year and it also has a balance of AE&P at the end of each of those years, the election is terminated beginning on January 1, 2006.

Even though a corporation may avoid having its election terminated by failing the excessive passive income test once every three years, a corporation still may be required to pay a tax on its excessive passive investment income. This tax is explained in detail later in this chapter.

---

[43]   § 1362(d)(3)(D).

[44]   Reg. § 1.1362-2(c)(5)(ii)(B)(2).

[45]   §§ 1362(d)(3)(C) and 1222(9).

ELECTION AFTER TERMINATION

When the election is terminated, whether voluntarily through revocation or involuntarily through failure to satisfy the Subchapter S or passive income requirements, the corporation normally may not make a new election until the fifth taxable year following the year in which the termination became effective.[46] The five-year wait is unnecessary, however, if the IRS consents to an earlier election. Consent usually is given in two instances: (1) when the corporation's ownership has changed such that more than 50 percent of the stock is owned by persons who did not own the stock at the time of termination, or (2) when the termination was attributable to an event that was not within the control of the corporation or its majority shareholders.[47] A corporation must apply to the IRS National Office for an early re-election. It must request a ruling and pay the user fee.

> **Example 17.** KLZ, an S corporation, was wholly owned by G. The corporation revoked its S election effective on July 17, 2005. KLZ may not make an election until 2010 unless it obtains permission from the IRS. Permission to reelect S status prior to 2010 would ordinarily be denied unless G divested himself of at least 50% of the KLZ stock.

OPERATING THE S CORPORATION

Once an S election is effective, a corporation officially becomes an S corporation and is subject to a special set of rules governing the measurement and reporting of its income. Under the provisions of Subchapter S, S corporations, like partnerships, are pass-through entities. While S corporations may pay taxes in certain situations (e.g., the passive investment income tax or the built-in gains tax discussed below), they primarily serve as conduits. Items of income, expense, gain, loss, and credit are measured at the S corporation level and then passed through to shareholders who report them on their own returns.[48] The focus of this section is on three questions:

- ▸ What items at the corporate level must be reported to the shareholder?
- ▸ How much of each item is reported to each shareholder?
- ▸ When does the shareholder report the items on his or her own tax return?

DETERMINING S CORPORATION NET INCOME

S corporations generally compute net income, gains, and losses in a manner similar to a partnership. The following discussion examines some of the more important aspects that should be considered in measuring S corporation income, particularly the differences between S corporations and partnerships.

Elections. Consistent with the partnership provisions, most special elections that must be made in determining the amount of income are made at the S corporation level and not by the shareholder.[49] Among the elections that must be made by the corporation are the corporation's overall method of accounting (e.g., cash or accrual), the inventory

---

[46]   § 1362(g).

[47]   Reg. § 1.1362-5(a).

[48]   § 1366(a).

[49]   § 1363(c).

method (e.g., FIFO or LIFO), depreciation methods, § 179 limited expensing ($102,000 in 2004 and $105,000 in 2005), the installment method, and deferral of gain on involuntary conversions. The exceptions to this general approach are the same as those for partnerships and affect few taxpayers.

Payments to a Shareholder-Employee. The treatment of payments to an S shareholder who works for the corporation is markedly different from that of a partner who works for the partnership. S corporation shareholders who work for the corporation are treated as *employees*. As a result, salary paid to a shareholder-employee as well as payroll taxes related to the salary are deductible by the S corporation. In contrast, a partner who works for a partnership is not considered an employee and the payment received for work for the partnership is not technically considered a salary. As discussed in Chapter 22, compensation paid to partners is referred to as a guaranteed payment. Like salaries, partnerships normally deduct guaranteed payments. However, unlike salaries, guaranteed payments are not subject to withholding or payroll taxes.[50] Instead, a partner's compensation is treated as self-employment income.

> **Example 18.** H and W own their own company. This year the company made net income of $60,000 before consideration of any payments to H and W. Assume that H and W each receive a salary of $10,000 for total salary payments of $20,000. If the business is an S or C corporation, the salary is subject to withholding taxes and the corporation must pay FICA and unemployment taxes on it. If, however, the business is a partnership, there are no payroll taxes for owner compensation and partnership net income is $40,000 ($60,000 − $20,000), which is usually self-employment income and is subject to self-employment tax at the partner level. In addition, the salaries of $20,000 (i.e., guaranteed payments in the context of a partnership) would be subject to self-employment taxes.
>
> A comparison of the two business forms reveals the following:

	Partnership	S Corporation
Net income before compensation	$ 60,000	$ 60,000
Guaranteed payment or salary.	(20,000)	(20,000)
Employer FICA tax (7.65% × $20,000)	0	(1,530)
Federal unemployment tax (6.2% × $7,000 × 2).	0	(868)
Flow-through income	$ 40,000	$ 37,602
Add guaranteed payment or salary	20,000	20,000
Withheld FICA tax (.0765 × $20,000)		(1,530)
Self-employment tax (15.3% × $60,000 × .9235)	(8,478)*	0
Net income after taxes.	$ 51,522	$ 56,072

*The partner claims a deduction for 50% of these taxes.

As this example demonstrates, the S corporation is preferred to the partnership if capital is to be retained in the business. This derives from the fact that the partners are subject to self-employment tax on their portions of partnership income, whether or not it is distributed. The S corporation and its shareholders, by contrast, are only subject to the FICA tax on money actually distributed to the shareholders as compensation.

---

[50]   Reg. § 1.707-1(c) and Rev. Rul. 69-148, 1969-1 C.B. 256.

Employment Taxes and Undercompensation. It is important to note that, unlike partnerships, no self-employment income passes from an S corporation to its shareholders. In the S corporation setting, the only amounts subject to employment taxes are the salaries paid. In light of this treatment, owners of S corporations are tempted to undercompensate themselves in order to avoid social security and other payroll taxes. To illustrate, consider the example above. In this situation, the owners took only $20,000 in salary, paying employment taxes of $3,898 ($1,530 + $1,530 + $838). This is far less than the $8,478 in self-employment tax that the owners would pay if they were partners in a partnership even though the amounts paid in both cases were identical ($20,000). The difference is due to the fact that the net income of the S corporation, $37,602, is not subject to employment taxes. However, there is another mitigating factor that reduces this difference. Each partner is allowed a deduction for A.G.I. for one-half of the self-employment tax paid on partnership income. Indeed, it would appear that the owners could avoid all employment taxes using an S corporation by not paying themselves any salary but simply distributing the profits. As might be expected, the IRS, with the support of the courts, frowns on this technique. In situations when this occurs, that is, when shareholders are undercompensated for their services, the Service generally recharacterizes all or a part of any distributions as compensation thereby securing the applicable payroll taxes.[51]

Social Security Benefit Cutback. With the graying of America, the treatment of payments to S corporation owners is also becoming an increasingly important issue for social security purposes. An individual who retires before "normal" retirement age, must reduce his or her social security benefits if he or she earns income above a certain level. In 2005, the *normal retirement* age is 65 plus six months. A person who has not reached normal retirement age by the end of 2005 will be required to reduce his or her social security benefit by $1 for each $2 of earned income in excess of $12,000. After normal retirement age, an individual may receive full social security benefits regardless of the amount of earned income. For this reason, some owners of S corporations are tempted to take distributions from an S corporation rather than salary for services rendered. In a number of cases involving such attempts, however, the courts have upheld the Social Security Administration's bid to reclassify the distributions as wages.[52]

Employee Benefits. One of the most important differences concerning the taxation of C corporations, partnerships, and S corporations is the treatment of fringe benefits provided to the owners (e.g., health and accident insurance, group-term life insurance). The taxation of a number of these benefits depends on whether the individual is an "employee" of the business. If the individual is an employee, the employer normally is allowed to deduct the cost of the benefit and its value is never subject to income or employment taxes. On the other hand, if the individual is not an employee, the benefit is usually considered compensation deductible by the employer but is subject to income and employment taxes to the payees. In the case of C corporations, an owner who works for the business, is always considered an employee. Therefore, shareholder-employees of C corporations enjoy the best of all possible worlds: the corporation is allowed to deduct the cost of these benefits yet their value to the shareholder-employees is never subject to income or employment taxes. In contrast, a partner (much like a sole proprietor) is normally not considered an employee of the business. Consequently, several of the key fringe benefits provided by partnerships to their partners are considered compensation (i.e., guaranteed payments) that are deductible by the partnership but subject to income and self-employment taxes to the partners.

---

[51] See Rev. Rul 74-44, 1974-1 C.B. 287, *Radtke v. U.S.*, 90-1 USTC ¶50,113 and *Spicer Accounting, Inc., v. U.S.*, 918 F.2d 90 (CA-9, 1990).

[52] *Ludeking v. Finch*, 421 F.2d 499 (CA-8, 1970).

Unfortunately, the treatment of these key fringe benefits by an S corporation for the most part mirrors that for partnerships rather than that for C corporations.[53]

In determining the treatment extended to S corporations, shareholder-employees are divided into two groups: those who own more than 2 percent of the stock and those who own 2 percent or less.[54] The treatment for the two groups is summarized below.

Shareholders owning 2 percent or less. For those S shareholders who own 2 percent or less, the treatment follows the C corporation rules: the benefits are deductible by the corporation and nontaxable (both income and employment) to the employee.

Shareholders owning more than 2 percent. More-than-2 percent shareholders are treated much like partners.[55] The fringe benefits requiring employee status are considered compensation: the benefits are deductible by the corporation but are included in the shareholder's gross income.[56] Unlike a partnership where these benefits are subject to self-employment tax, the value of health insurance provided to an S corporation employee is not subject to FICA or FUTA.[57] Note also that while the more-than-2 percent shareholder is required to include the benefit in income, he or she is also entitled to treat such amount as if he or she paid for the benefit. For example, in the case of medical insurance premiums paid by the S corporation on behalf of a more-than-2-percent shareholder, the shareholder is entitled to deduct 100 percent of the premiums as a deduction for A.G.I.[58]

In determining whether an individual owns more than 2 percent of an S corporation's stock, the constructive ownership rules of § 318 are applied.[59] For example, § 318 provides that an individual is deemed to own the stock of his or her spouse, children, parents or grandchildren. This rule prevents an owner (e.g., a husband) from employing a family member that does not own stock (e.g., a wife) in order to provide tax-free fringe benefits from the corporation to the family unit.

There are currently six fringe benefits which are nontaxable to owners of C corporations but which are treated as compensation to partners and more-than-2 percent shareholders. They are:

- ► Group-term life insurance (§ 79)
- ► Amounts received under accident and health (medical reimbursement) plans (§ 105)
- ► Premiums on employer-paid accident and health insurance (§ 106)
- ► Meals and lodging provided by the employer (§ 119)
- ► Value of transit passes (but this qualifies as a de minimis fringe if not greater than $21 per month) [§ 132(f)(5)(E)]
- ► Parking provided by the employer (except that provided away from the business such as at a client's) [§ 132(f)(5)(E)]

---

53   § 1372(a)(1) and (2).

54   § 1372(a) and (b).

55   § 1372(a)(2).

56   Rev. Rul. 91-26, 1991-1 C.B. 184, § 162(a) (subject to the capitalization rules of § 263), and § 61(a), respectively.

57   Announcement 92-16, 1992-5 I.R.B. 53.

58   §§ 162(l) and 106, respectively.

59   § 1372(b). See Chapter 20 for discussion of § 318.

The value of all of these is included in the shareholder-employee's Form W-2 as noncash compensation. Premiums on accident and health insurance are not subject to FICA tax.

The remaining fringe benefits are eligible for exclusion not only by shareholder-employees of C corporations but also to partners and, therefore, more-than-2 percent shareholders of S corporations. In effect, the statutes governing these particular benefits specifically explain that, for purpose of the given exclusion, partners are considered employees, thereby enabling exclusion not only for partners but also all S corporation shareholders. These include:

- Child and dependent care assistance (§ 129)
- Educational assistance plans (§ 127)
- No additional cost services [§ 132(b)]
- Qualified employee discounts [§ 132(c)]
- Working condition fringe benefits [§ 132(d)]
- De minimis fringes [§ 132(e)]
- Company dining room [§132(e)]
- On-premise athletic facilities [§132(h)]
- Employee achievement awards [§74(c)]

Subdivision of Real Estate. Under the "subdivide and conquer" rules of § 1237, *individual* taxpayers are ensured capital gain rather than ordinary income treatment when they subdivide and sell land if they meet a number of requirements. To qualify, the land must be held more than five years (unless inherited); there must be no substantial improvements to the property; and the parcel sold, or any part thereof must not have previously been held by the taxpayer primarily for resale. An S corporation (as well as a partnership) is treated in the same manner as an individual and is entitled to this special treatment.[60]

Section 291 Recapture. In most cases, an S corporation is not subject to the special rules of § 291 that require the recapture as ordinary income 20 percent of any straight-line depreciation claimed on residential or nonresidential real estate (see Chapter 19 for an example). However, an S corporation that was a C corporation for any of the three immediately preceding taxable years is subject to the special depreciation recapture rules of § 291(a)(1).[61]

Accounting Methods. Certain entities are prohibited from using the cash method of accounting, and consequently are required to use the accrual method. The cash method normally cannot be used by a C corporation unless its annual gross receipts average $5 million or less for the past three years, or it is a qualified personal service corporation. In contrast, an S corporation can use the cash method (unless it is required to maintain inventories to clearly reflect income).[62]

Charitable Contributions. Charitable contributions made by an S corporation are treated as if they are made directly by the shareholder. Consequently, unlike C corporations, an S corporation that uses the accrual method of accounting is not

---

[60] § 1237(a).

[61] See § 1363(b)(4).

[62] § 448. However, see Rev. Proc. 2001-10, which allows any taxpayer with no more than $1 million gross receipts to use the cash method. Also see Rev. Proc. 2002-28, which allows certain taxpayers with up to $10 million gross receipts to use the cash method.

entitled to deduct accrued contributions.[63] Like an individual, contributions made by an S corporation can be deducted by the shareholders only in the tax year in which the contribution is made. Similarly, the special rule allowing C corporations to deduct the adjusted basis plus one-half of the foregone gross profit of inventory contributed to a organization for the care of the needy, the ill, or infants is not available to S corporations.[64]

Qualified Production Activities Income Deduction. The deduction for Qualified Production Activities Income (QPAI) is allowed to all tax entities. However, for the S corporation, this deduction is to be computed at the shareholder level.[65] At press time for this edition, the IRS has not released any guidance for the application of this rule.

REPORTING S CORPORATION INCOME

Once an S corporation identifies and measures the relevant items of income, deduction and credit, such items must be passed through to the shareholders for reporting on their own returns. The approach used is similar to that used by partnerships. Consistent with the conduit concept, the items normally retain their character when they are allocated to the shareholders. For example, charitable contributions made by the S corporation flow through and are reported as charitable contributions by the shareholders subject to all the special tax rules that apply to individuals. The amounts allocated to the shareholders are based on their percentage of stock owned during the year. Unlike partnerships, Subchapter S contains no provision for special allocations among owners. This can be a disadvantage if special allocations are desirable.

To accomplish the pass-through, the S corporation must file an annual information return, Form 1120S. Indeed, the similarity between the taxation of S corporations and partnerships becomes readily apparent when Forms 1120S and 1065 are compared. (See Exhibit 23-1 for an illustration of Form 1120S.) There are some differences in computing the net ordinary income on page one of the two tax forms, however. Unlike Form 1065, Form 1120S has a section for computing any taxes due on excessive passive investment income and Schedule D built-in gains (both are discussed in a later section of this chapter).

All income, expenses, gains, losses, and credits that may be subject to special treatment by one or more of the shareholders are reported separately on Schedule K, which is filed with Form 1120S.[66] Schedule K-1 is then prepared for the shareholders' use. (See Exhibit 23-1 for an illustration. Also see Exhibit 23-2 for a summary of items.) Again, these schedules are quite similar to the schedules applicable to partnerships and partners. There are differences, including the following:

▸ There are no guaranteed payments on the S corporation schedule.

▸ There is no self-employment income on the S corporation schedule.

▸ There are no reconciliations of capital accounts on the S corporation schedule.

▸ There is no allocation of liabilities on the S corporation schedule.

Finally, the S corporation schedule includes a section for reporting distributions. These are divided into two categories: (1) distributions from earnings of the S corporation, and (2) if it has been operated as a C corporation in previous years, distributions from

---

[63] See § 1363, which incorporates the rules of § 702 that disallow the deduction of charitable contributions to partnerships.

[64] § 170(e)(3)(A). Also see Rev. Rul. 2000-43, 2000-41 I.R.B. 333.

[65] §199(d)(1).

[66] § 1366(a)(1)(A).

earnings of the C corporation. (Distributions are discussed in a later section of this chapter.)

Filing Requirements. Form 1120S, with the attached Schedule K-1s, must be filed for the S corporation on or before the 15th day of the third month following the close of its taxable year. An automatic extension of six months may be obtained. Thus a calendar year S corporation's normal due date is March 15 but may be extended until September 15. In order to obtain the extension, the corporation must file Form 7004 on or before March 15 (or two months and 15 days after the close of the corporation's fiscal year). In contrast, partnership returns are due on the 15th day of the fourth month following the close of the taxable year (e.g., April 15 for a calendar year partnership). So even though an S corporation is treated much like a partnership, its return is due at the same time as a C corporation return.

In addition to attaching the Schedule K-1s to Form 1120S, the S corporation is required to provide shareholders with Schedule K-1 by the due date of the return. The shareholder need not attach the K-1 to his or her Form 1040.

EXHIBIT 23-1
Form 1120S

Form **1120S**	**U.S. Income Tax Return for an S Corporation**
Department of the Treasury Internal Revenue Service	▶ Do not file this form unless the corporation has timely filed Form 2553 to elect to be an S corporation. ▶ See separate instructions.

OMB No. 1545-0130

2004

For calendar year 2004, or tax year beginning _____ , 2004, and ending _____ , 20 ___

A Effective date of S election   *1-1-04*

B Business code number (see pages 36–38 of the Insts.)   *448110*

Use the IRS label. Otherwise, print or type.

Name   *T COMPANY*

Number, street, and room or suite no. (If a P.O. box, see page 12 of the instructions.)   *8122 SOUTH 8TH STREET*

City or town, state, and ZIP code   *NORFOLK, VA 23508*

C Employer identification number   *88 : 9138761*

D Date incorporated   *1-1-04*

E Total assets (see page 12 of instructions) $ *322,000*

F Check applicable boxes: (1) ☑ Initial return (2) ☐ Final return (3) ☐ Name change (4) ☐ Address change (5) ☐ Amended return

G Enter number of shareholders in the corporation at end of the tax year . . . . ▶

Caution: Include **only** trade or business income and expenses on lines 1a through 21. See page 13 of the instructions for more information.

Income

1a Gross receipts or sales _____	**b** Less returns and allowances _*–0–*_	**c** Bal ▶ **1c**	*470,000*
2 Cost of goods sold (Schedule A, line 8)		**2**	*300,000*
3 Gross profit. Subtract line 2 from line 1c		**3**	*170,000*
4 Net gain (loss) from Form 4797, Part II, line 17 *(attach Form 4797)* .		**4**	
5 Other income (loss) *(attach schedule)*		**5**	
6 **Total income (loss).** Add lines 3 through 5. . . . . ▶		**6**	*170,000*

Deductions (see page 14 of the instructions for limitations)

7 Compensation of officers *$ 24,000 + $ 700. EMPLOYEE BENEFITS*	**7**	*24,700*
8 Salaries and wages (less employment credits)	**8**	*48,000*
9 Repairs and maintenance	**9**	*12,000*
10 Bad debts	**10**	
11 Rents.	**11**	
12 Taxes and licenses *$ 3,000 PROPERTY TAXES + $ 6,000 PAYROLL TAXES* .	**12**	*9,000*
13 Interest	**13**	*3,300*
14a Depreciation *(attach Form 4562)* **14a** *15,000*		
b Depreciation claimed on Schedule A and elsewhere on return . . **14b** *–0–*		
c Subtract line 14b from line 14a	**14c**	*15,000*
15 Depletion **(Do not deduct oil and gas depletion.)**	**15**	
16 Advertising	**16**	
17 Pension, profit-sharing, etc., plans	**17**	
18 Employee benefit programs. *LIFE INSURANCE COVERAGE*	**18**	*1,400*
19 Other deductions *(attach schedule)* *UTILITIES & PHONE = $ 2,500 + $ OFFICE 1,000 + INSURANCE CO. $ 3,100*	**19**	*6,700*
20 **Total deductions.** Add the amounts shown in the far right column for lines 7 through 19 ▶	**20**	*120,100*
21 Ordinary business income (loss). Subtract line 20 from line 6	**21**	*49,900*

Tax and Payments

22 **Tax: a** Excess net passive income tax *(attach schedule)* . . . **22a**		
b Tax from Schedule D (Form 1120S) **22b**		
c Add lines 22a and 22b (see page 18 of the instructions for additional taxes)	**22c**	*NONE*
23 **Payments: a** 2004 estimated tax payments and amount applied from 2003 return **23a**		
b Tax deposited with Form 7004. . . . . **23b**		
c Credit for Federal tax paid on fuels *(attach Form 4136)* **23c**		
d Add lines 23a through 23c	**23d**	*NONE*
24 Estimated tax penalty (see page 18 of instructions). Check if Form 2220 is attached. . ▶ ☐	**24**	
25 **Tax due.** If line 23d is smaller than the total of lines 22c and 24, enter amount owed. .	**25**	*NONE*
26 **Overpayment.** If line 23d is larger than the total of lines 22c and 24, enter amount overpaid .	**26**	
27 Enter amount of line 26 you want: **Credited to 2005 estimated tax ▶** _____ Refunded ▶	**27**	*NONE*

Sign Here

Under penalties of perjury, I declare that I have examined this return, including accompanying schedules and statements, and to the best of my knowledge and belief, it is true, correct, and complete. Declaration of preparer (other than taxpayer) is based on all information of which preparer has any knowledge.

▶ *adolph Z. T*   ▶ *3-10-05*   ▶ *PRESIDENT*
Signature of officer   Date   Title

May the IRS discuss this return with the preparer shown below (see instructions)? ☐ Yes ☐ No

Paid Preparer's Use Only

Preparer's signature ▶	Date	Check if self-employed ☐
Firm's name (or yours if self-employed), address, and ZIP code ▶	EIN :	Preparer's SSN or PTIN
	Phone no. ( )	

For Privacy Act and Paperwork Reduction Act Notice, see the **separate instructions.**   Cat. No. 11510H   Form **1120S** (2004)

EXHIBIT 23-1
Continued

Form 1120S (2004)   Page **2**

Schedule A Cost of Goods Sold (see page 18 of the instructions) * *SEE NOTE BELOW* *

1	Inventory at beginning of year	1	
2	Purchases	2	
3	Cost of labor	3	
4	Additional section 263A costs *(attach schedule)*	4	
5	Other costs *(attach schedule)*	5	
6	**Total.** Add lines 1 through 5	6	
7	Inventory at end of year	7	
8	**Cost of goods sold.** Subtract line 7 from line 6. Enter here and on page 1, line 2	8	*300,000*

9a Check all methods used for valuing closing inventory: *(i)* ☑ Cost as described in Regulations section 1.471-3

    (ii) ☐ Lower of cost or market as described in Regulations section 1.471-4

    (iii) ☐ Other (specify method used and attach explanation) ▶ ....

  b Check if there was a writedown of subnormal goods as described in Regulations section 1.471-2(c) . . . . ▶ ☐

  c Check if the LIFO inventory method was adopted this tax year for any goods (if checked, attach Form 970) . . . . . ▶ ☐

  d If the LIFO inventory method was used for this tax year, enter percentage (or amounts) of closing inventory computed under LIFO . . . . **9d** |

  e If property is produced or acquired for resale, do the rules of Section 263A apply to the corporation? . . . . ☐ Yes ☑ No

  f Was there any change in determining quantities, cost, or valuations between opening and closing inventory? . . ☐ Yes ☑ No
    If "Yes," attach explanation.

Schedule B Other Information (see page 19 of instructions)

		Yes	No
1	Check method of accounting: **(a)** ☐ Cash **(b)** ☑ Accrual **(c)** ☐ Other (specify) ▶		
2	See pages 36 through 38 of the instructions and enter the: **(a)** Business activity ▶ *RETAIL SALES* **(b)** Product or service ▶ *MENS CLOTHING*		
3	At the end of the tax year, did the corporation own, directly or indirectly, 50% or more of the voting stock of a domestic corporation? (For rules of attribution, see section 267(c).) If "Yes," attach a schedule showing: **(a)** name, address, and employer identification number and **(b)** percentage owned		✓
4	Was the corporation a member of a controlled group subject to the provisions of section 1561?		✓
5	Check this box if the corporation has filed or is required to file **Form 8264**, Application for Registration of a Tax Shelter ▶ ☐		
6	Check this box if the corporation issued publicly offered debt instruments with original issue discount . . ▶ ☐ If checked, the corporation may have to file **Form 8281**, Information Return for Publicly Offered Original Issue Discount Instruments.		
7	If the corporation: **(a)** was a C corporation before it elected to be an S corporation **or** the corporation acquired an asset with a basis determined by reference to its basis (or the basis of any other property) in the hands of a C corporation **and (b)** has net unrealized built-in gain (defined in section 1374(d)(1)) in excess of the net recognized built-in gain from prior years, enter the net unrealized built-in gain reduced by net recognized built-in gain from prior years . . . . ▶ $		
8	Check this box if the corporation had accumulated earnings and profits at the close of the tax year . . ▶ ☐		
9	Are the corporation's total receipts (see page 19 of the instructions) for the tax year **and** its total assets at the end of the tax year less than $250,000? If "Yes," the corporation is not required to complete Schedules L and M-1.		✓

Note: *If the corporation had assets or operated a business in a foreign country or U.S. possession, it may be required to attach* **Schedule N (Form 1120)**, *Foreign Operations of U.S. Corporations, to this return. See Schedule N for details.*

Schedule K Shareholders' Shares of Income, Deductions, Credits, etc.

	Shareholders' Pro Rata Share Items			Total amount
1	Ordinary business income (loss) (page 1, line 21)		1	*49,900*
2	Net rental real estate income (loss) *(attach Form 8825)*		2	
3a	Other gross rental income (loss)	**3a**		
b	Expenses from other rental activities *(attach schedule)*	**3b**		
c	Other net rental income (loss). Subtract line 3b from line 3a		3c	
4	Interest income		4	
5	Dividends: **a** Ordinary dividends		5a	*2,000*
	b Qualified dividends	**5b** *2,000*		
6	Royalties		6	
7	Net short-term capital gain (loss)		7	
8a	Net long-term capital gain (loss)		8a	*1,000*
b	Collectibles (28%) gain (loss)	**8b**		
c	Unrecaptured section 1250 gain *(attach schedule)*	**8c**		
9	Net section 1231 gain (loss) (attach Form 4797)		9	
10	Other income (loss) *(attach schedule)*		10	

(left margin label: Income (Loss))

* Note: Lines 1 through 6 of schedule a must be completed before return is filed.

Form **1120S** (2004)

EXHIBIT 23-1
Continued

Form 1120S (2004)   Page **3**

	Shareholders' Pro Rata Share Items (continued)		Total amount	
Deductions	**11** Section 179 deduction (attach Form 4562)	**11**		
	12a Contributions	**12a**	7,000	
	b Deductions related to portfolio income (attach schedule) . . .	**12b**		
	c Investment interest expense	**12c**		
	d Section 59(e)(2) expenditures **(1)** Type ▶ _____ **(2)** Amount ▶	**12d(2)**		
	e Other deductions (attach schedule)	**12e**		
Credits & Credit Recapture	**13a** Low-income housing credit (section 42(j)(5))	**13a**		
	b Low-income housing credit (other)	**13b**		
	c Qualified rehabilitation expenditures (rental real estate) (attach Form 3468) . . .	**13c**		
	d Other rental real estate credits	**13d**		
	e Other rental credits	**13e**		
	f Credit for alcohol used as fuel (attach Form 6478)	**13f**		
	g Other credits and credit recapture (attach schedule). *REHABILATION CRERDIT* .	**13g**	2,000	
Foreign Transactions	**14a** Name of country or U.S. possession ▶ _____			
	b Gross income from all sources	**14b**		
	c Gross income sourced at shareholder level	**14c**		
	Foreign gross income sourced at corporate level:			
	d Passive	**14d**		
	e Listed categories (attach schedule)	**14e**		
	f General limitation	**14f**		
	Deductions allocated and apportioned at shareholder level:			
	g Interest expense	**14g**		
	h Other	**14h**		
	Deductions allocated and apportioned at corporate level to foreign source income:			
	i Passive	**14i**		
	j Listed categories (attach schedule)	**14j**		
	k General limitation	**14k**		
	Other information:			
	l Foreign taxes paid	**14l**		
	m Foreign taxes accrued	**14m**		
	n Reduction in taxes available for credit (attach schedule). . . .	**14n**		
Alternative Minimum Tax (AMT) Items	**15a** Post-1986 depreciation adjustment	**15a**		
	b Adjusted gain or loss	**15b**		
	c Depletion (other than oil and gas)	**15c**		
	d Oil, gas, and geothermal properties—gross income	**15d**		
	e Oil, gas, and geothermal properties—deductions.	**15e**		
	f Other AMT items (attach schedule)	**15f**		
Items Affecting Shareholder Basis	**16a** Tax-exempt interest income	**16a**		
	b Other tax-exempt income	**16b**		
	c Nondeductible expenses	**16c**		
	d Property distributions . *LAND: FMV. = $ 10,000 + $ 12,000 CASH* . . .	**16d**	22,000	
	e Repayment of loans from shareholders	**16e**		
Other Information	**17a** Investment income *DIVIDENDS*	**17a**	2,000	
	b Investment expenses	**17b**		
	c Dividend distributions paid from accumulated earnings and profits	**17c**		
	d Other items and amounts (attach schedule)			
	e **Income/loss reconciliation.** (Required only if Schedule M-1 must be completed.) Combine the amounts on lines 1 through 10 in the far right column. From the result, subtract the sum of the amounts on lines 11 through 12e and lines 14l or 14m, whichever applies	**17e**		

Form **1120S** (2004)

EXHIBIT 23-1
Continued

Note: The corporation is not required to complete Schedules L and M-1 if question 9 of Schedule B is answered "Yes."

Schedule L	Balance Sheets per Books	Beginning of tax year		End of tax year	
SEE NOTE BELOW **Assets**		(a)	(b)	(c)	(d)
1	Cash . * .				
2a	Trade notes and accounts receivable . . .				
b	Less allowance for bad debts				
3	Inventories				
4	U.S. government obligations.				
5	Tax-exempt securities				
6	Other current assets (attach schedule) . .				
7	Loans to shareholders		*FIRST*		
8	Mortgage and real estate loans . . .		*YEAR*		
9	Other investments (attach schedule) . . .		*CORPORATION*		
10a	Buildings and other depreciable assets . .				
b	Less accumulated depreciation				
11a	Depletable assets				
b	Less accumulated depletion.				
12	Land (net of any amortization)				
13a	Intangible assets (amortizable only) . .				
b	Less accumulated amortization.				
14	Other assets (attach schedule)				
15	Total assets				322,000
	Liabilities and Shareholders' Equity				
16	Accounts payable				
17	Mortgages, notes, bonds payable in less than 1 year .				
18	Other current liabilities (attach schedule) . .				
19	Loans from shareholders.				
20	Mortgages, notes, bonds payable in 1 year or more				
21	Other liabilities (attach schedule) . . .				
22	Capital stock				
23	Additional paid-in capital.				
24	Retained earnings				
25	Adjustments to shareholders' equity (attach schedule).				
26	Less cost of treasury stock		( )		( )
27	Total liabilities and shareholders' equity . .				322,000

Schedule M-1	Reconciliation of Income (Loss) per Books With Income (Loss) per Return		
1	Net income (loss) per books.	*SEE NOTE BELOW*	5 Income recorded on books this year not included on Schedule K, lines 1 through 10 (itemize):
2	Income included on Schedule K, lines 1, 2, 3c, 4, 5a, 6, 7, 8a, 9, and 10, not recorded on books this year (itemize):		a Tax-exempt interest $ ....
3	Expenses recorded on books this year not included on Schedule K, lines 1 through 12, and 14l or (14m) (itemize):		6 Deductions included on Schedule K, lines 1 through 12, and 14l or (14m), not charged against book income this year (itemize):
a	Depreciation $		a Depreciation $ ....
b	Travel and entertainment $		
			7 Add lines 5 and 6. . . . . . .
4	Add lines 1 through 3.		8 Income (loss) (Schedule K, line 17e). Line 4 less line 7

Schedule M-2	Analysis of Accumulated Adjustments Account, Other Adjustments Account, and Shareholders' Undistributed Taxable Income Previously Taxed (see page 32 of the instructions)		
	* SEE NOTE BELOW	(a) Accumulated adjustments account	(b) Other adjustments account	(c) Shareholders' undistributed taxable income previously taxed
1	Balance at beginning of tax year . . .			
2	Ordinary income from page 1, line 21. . .	49,900		
3	Other additions . . . $ 2,000 DIVIDENDS	3,000		
4	Loss from page 1, line 21 +$ 1,000 CAP GAIN . . .	( )		
5	Other reductions	( )	( )	
6	Combine lines 1 through 5			
7	Distributions other than dividend distributions	29,000 ←	← $ 22,000 + $ 7,000	*CHARITABLE*
8	Balance at end of tax year. Subtract line 7 from line 6			*CONTRIBUTION*

EXHIBIT 23-1
Continued

☐ Final K-1   ☐ Amended K-1   OMB No. 1545-0130

Schedule K-1
(Form 1120S)
20**04**

Department of the Treasury
Internal Revenue Service

Tax year beginning _____ , 2004
and ending _____ , 20__

Shareholder's Share of Income, Deductions, Credits, etc.   ► See back of form and separate instructions.

Part I	**Information About the Corporation**

A Corporation's employer identification number
88 9138761

B Corporation's name, address, city, state, and ZIP code

T COMPANY

1822 SOUTH 8TH STREET

NORFOLK, VA 23508

C IRS Center where corporation filed return
MEMPHIS, TN

D ☐ Tax shelter registration number, if any _____

E ☐ Check if Form 8271 is attached

Part II	**Information About the Shareholder**

F Shareholder's identifying number
467–63–5052

G Shareholder's name, address, city, state and ZIP code

ADOLF Z.T

1291 MAPLE STREET

NORFOLK, VA 23508

H Shareholder's percentage of stock
ownership for tax year . . . . _____ 100 %

For IRS Use Only

Part III	**Shareholder's Share of Current Year Income, Deductions, Credits, and Other Items**

1	Ordinary business income (loss)	**13**	Credits & credit recapture
	49,900		
2	Net rental real estate income (loss)		2,000
3	Other net rental income (loss)		
4	Interest income		
5a	Ordinary dividends		
	2,000		
5b	Qualified dividends	**14**	Foreign transactions
	2,000		
6	Royalties		
7	Net short-term capital gain (loss)		
8a	Net long-term capital gain (loss)		
	1,000		
8b	Collectibles (28%) gain (loss)		
8c	Unrecaptured section 1250 gain		
9	Net section 1231 gain (loss)		
10	Other income (loss)	**15**	Alternative minimum tax (AMT) items
	CHARITABLE CONTRIBUTIONS = 7,000		INVESTMENT INCOME = 7,000
11	Section 179 deduction	**16**	Items affecting shareholder basis
12	Other deductions		
	CHARITABLE		
	CONTRIBUTIONS		
	= 7,000		
		17	Other information
			INVESTMENT
			INCOME = 2,000

* See attached statement for additional information.

For Privacy Act and Paperwork Reduction Act Notice, see Instructions for Form 1120S.   Cat. No. 11520D   Schedule K-1 (Form 1120S) 2004

EXHIBIT 23-2
Separately and Nonseparately States Items

For each of the following items of income, deduction, loss, and credit, and "X" in the appropriate column indicates whether the item is includible in an S corporation's combined ordinary income or loss (reported on Form 1120S, page 1; Schedule K, line 1; and Schedule K-1, line 1) or whether the item must be separately stated (reported on Schedules K and K-1, and lines 2 and following).

		Combined Ordinary Income or (Loss) (Form 1120S, p.1)	Separately Stated Item (Schedule K)	Reason
a.	Sales	X		No special shareholder treatment
b.	Income or loss from rental activities		X	Passive income for § 469 purposes
c.	Dividends		X	Investment (portfolio) income
d.	Taxable interest		X	Investment (portfolio) income
e.	Tax-exempt interest		X	May affect shareholder interest deductions (§ 265), or tax on social security benefits
f.	Cost of sales	X		No special shareholder treatment
g.	State and local taxes	X		Generally, no special shareholder treatment
h.	Net long-term capital gain or loss		X	Requires netting at shareholder level
i.	Net short-term capital gain or loss		X	Requires netting at shareholder level
j.	Net gain from sales of collectibles		X	Requires netting at shareholder level
k.	Net unrecaptured § 1250 gain		X	Requires netting at shareholder level
l.	Gain from sales of qualified small business stock		X	Requires netting at shareholder level
m.	Charitable contribution		X	Subject to A.G.I. limitation of shareholder
n.	Foreign income		X	Required for foreign tax credit computation at shareholder level
o.	Foreign taxes		X	Subject to election to credit or deduct
p.	Medical expenses		X	Includible by shareholder; deductible by shareholder subject to A.G.I. limitation; deductible by S corporation
q.	Investment interest		X	Subject to investment interest limitation
r.	MACRS or ACRS on plant and equipment	X	X	Subject to AMT tax liability at shareholder level[a]
s.	Section 179 expensing		X	Subject to § 179 shareholder limit
t.	Research and experimentation expenditures		X	Subject to special election by shareholder
u.	Work opportunity credit		X	Subject to tax liability limitation at shareholder level
v.	Recovery of a bad debt		X	Subject to § 111 determination at shareholder level
w.	Advertising	X		No special shareholder treatment
x.	Repairs and maintenance	X		No special shareholder treatment
y.	Expenses for production of income (§ 212)		X	Miscellaneous itemized deduction at shareholder level
z.	QPAI information		X	Deductions claimed at shareholder level

[a]Any preference or adjustment resulting from the use of accelerated depreciation must be separately reported, along with any § 179 expense.

ALLOCATIONS TO SHAREHOLDERS

All S corporation items (except distributions) are allocated among the shareholders based on their *ownership percentage* of the outstanding stock on each day of the year.[67] Thus, a shareholder owning 20 percent of the outstanding stock all year is deemed to have received 20 percent of *each item*. The allocation rate can be changed only by increasing or decreasing the percentage of stock ownership. This precludes shareholders from dividing net income or losses in any other manner. Of course, a certain amount of special allocation can be achieved through salaries and other business payments to owners. If there is no change in stock ownership during the year, each item to be allocated is multiplied by the percentage of stock owned by each shareholder. In contrast, actual distributions of assets are assigned to the shareholder who receives them.

Example 19. M owns 100 of an S corporation's 1,000 shares of common stock outstanding. Neither the number of shares outstanding nor the number owned by M has changed during the year. The S corporation items for its calendar year are allocated to M, based on her 10% ownership interest, as follows:

	Totals on Schedule K	M's 10% on Schedule K-1
Ordinary income (from Form 1120S, page 1)	$70,000	$7,000
Net capital gain	2,000	200
Charitable contributions	4,000	400

If the ownership of stock changes during the year, there are two methods for determining the allocations for those shareholders whose interests have changed. These are (1) the *per day allocation method* and (2) the *interim closing of the books* method. Generally, the per day allocation method must be used. However, the S corporation may elect to use either method if

1. A shareholder's ownership interest is *completely* terminated;

2. There is a disposition by one shareholder of *more than* 20 percent of the outstanding shares of the corporation within 30 days; or

3. The corporation issues shares to one or more new shareholders and the new shares are at least 25 percent of the number previously outstanding.

Per Day Allocation. This method assigns an equal amount of the S items to each day of the year.[68] When a shareholder's interest changes, the shareholder *must* report a pro rata share of each item for each day that the stock was owned. For this purpose, the seller is deemed to own the stock on the day of the sale. This computation may be expressed as follows:

$$\text{Percentage of shares owned} \times \text{Percentage of year stock was owned} = \text{Portion of item to be reported}$$

Example 20. Assume the same facts as in *Example 19*, except that M sold all of her shares on August 7 to T. Because the S corporation uses the calendar year, M has held 100 shares for 219 days, or 60% of the year (219 ÷ 365). (The day of sale is considered an ownership day for the seller, M.) Thus M is allocated 6% (60% × 10%) of each corporate item while T is allocated 4% (40% × 10%). Based on the

---

[67]   §§ 1366(a) and 1377(a).

[68]   § 1377(a)(1).

per day allocation method, M's and T's shares of the S corporation items are as follows:

	Totals on Schedule K	10 Percent to M & T	M's Portion (10% × 219/365)	T's Portion (10% × 146/365)
Ordinary income	$70,000	$7,000	$4,200	$2,800
Net capital gain	2,000	200	120	80
Charitable contributions	4,000	400	240	160

The per day allocation method also is applicable for a shareholder whose stock interest varies during the year; however, the computation is more complex.

Example 21. Assume the same facts as in *Example 20*, except M only sold 20 shares on August 7 to T. Thus, she owned 10% of the business the first 219 days and 8% the remaining 146 days. Based on the per day allocation method. M's and T's shares of the S corporation items are as follows:

		M's Share			T's Share
	Totals Schedule K	1/1–8/7 (10% × 219/365)	8/8–12/31 (8% × 146/365)	Schedule K-1	Schedule K-1
Ordinary income	$70,000	$4,200	$2,240	$6,440	$560
Net capital gain	2,000	120	64	184	16
Charitable contributions .	4,000	240	128	368	32

Interim Closing of the Books. As noted above, the per day method must be used unless there is either (1) a complete termination of a shareholder's interest, (2) a disposition of more than 20 percent of the outstanding stock of the corporation by one shareholder within a 30-day period, or (3) issuance of shares to persons who were not previously shareholders equal to at least 25 percent of the number previously outstanding. In any of these situations, the corporation may elect to use the interim closing of books method instead of the per day allocation method.[69] If the corporation elects, the year is divided into two short taxable years for allocation purposes and all owners report the actual dollar amounts that were accumulated while they owned their shares. A valid election must be filed by the corporation with Form 1120S. All parties who are affected by the transaction must consent to the election. This election does not require the corporation to file separate returns for each portion of the year.

Example 22. Assume the same facts as in *Example 20*, except the interim closing of books method is elected. since M sells *all* of her shares on August 7 to T, the S corporation's year ends the day before on August 6. Corporate records show the following amounts for the first 219 days, for the last 146 days, and M's share for the first 219 days.

	First 219 days	Last 146 days	M's 10% on Schedule K-1	T's 10% on Schedule K-1
Ordinary income (from Form 1102S, page 1)	$15,000	$55,000	$1,500	$5,500
Net capital gain	1,000	1,000	100	100
Charitable contributions	0	4,000	0	400

---

[69] § 1377(a)(2).

The computations for M's share are the amounts for the first 219 days *multiplied* by her 10% ownership interest. T's share are the amounts for the last 146 days *multiplied* by his 10% ownership interest. The combined amounts for M and T equal the amount for M in *Example 19*.

It is also possible for an S corporation to have an ordinary loss for part of the year and ordinary income for the remaining period.

LOSSES OF THE S CORPORATION

One of the most common reasons a corporation elects Subchapter S status is because of the tax treatment for corporate losses. Recall that the C corporation's benefits are limited to those available from carrying the losses to another year to offset its own income. Refunds may be obtained to the extent *prior* year income is offset while losses carried to future years reduce the taxes due in those years. Frequently, these carryover benefits provide little or no value to the corporation. For example, many businesses report losses in the first few years so the carryback privilege is useless. In addition, many new businesses are never successful. But, even those that are successful receive no tax benefit from their losses currently—generally when the need is the greatest.

The pass-through feature of S corporations can be a significant advantage when a corporation has a net loss. Based on the flow-through concept, shareholders include their distributive shares of the S corporation's losses in their taxable income currently. Thus, the deduction for losses is transferred to the shareholder and generally results in tax savings for the current year. Even if a shareholder is unable to use the loss currently, carryover provisions may provide the shareholder with tax benefits in the near future.

Limitations. Each shareholder's deductible share of net losses may not exceed that shareholder's basis in the corporation's stock and the basis in any debt that the corporation owes to the shareholder. (Shareholder basis is discussed in more depth later in this chapter.) Any losses that exceed a shareholder's basis may be carried forward indefinitely to be used when the shareholder's basis is increased.[70] When basis is insufficient and there is more than one item that reduces basis, the flow-through of each item is determined in a pro rata manner.[71] In addition, any income items that increase basis flow through to the owner before any items that reduce basis, including distributions on stock.[72]

Example 23. G owns 200 of an S corporation's 1,000 shares of common stock outstanding and has a basis of $10,000 at the beginning of the year. Neither the number of shares outstanding nor those owned by G has changed during the year. The S corporation items for its calendar year are allocated to G, based on his 20% ownership interest, as follows:

	Totals on Schedule K	*G's 20% on Schedule K-1*
Ordinary loss (from Form 1120S, page 1)	($70,000)	($14,000)
Net capital loss	(5,000)	(1,000)
Section 1231 gain	10,000	2,000

---

[70] § 1366(d)(2). Losses may also be subject to limitation under § 465 at-risk rules and § 469 passive activity rules.

[71] Reg. § 1.1366-2(a)(4).

[72] §§ 1366(d)(1) and 1367(a). After positive adjustments, basis is reduced by distributions and nondeductible items, before separately stated deductions and losses. See discussion below.

G's share of the S corporation's losses is limited as follows:

	Basis	Loss Carryover
G's beginning basis	$ 10,000	
Section 1231 gain	2,000	
Limitation on losses	$ 12,000	
Ordinary loss*	(11,200)	$2,800
Net capital loss**	(800)	200
G's ending basis	$ 0	

*($14,000/$15,000 × $12,000)
**($1,000/$15,000 × $12,000)

Because G's basis is less than the $15,000 total loss, G may report ordinary loss of only $11,200 and net capital loss of $800. The remaining ordinary loss of $2,800 and net capital loss of $200 are carried forward to be used at the end of the first year that G's basis increases.

The above allocation of losses is applicable to all losses and separate deductions (e.g., investment interest and state income taxes) for owners of both the S corporation and the partnership.

Carryovers from C Corporation Years. Generally, no carryovers from a C corporation may be used during the years it is taxed as an S corporation (or vice versa). For example, a C corporation with a net operating loss may not use it to offset income in an S year. There is one exception: C corporate NOL carryforwards may be used to offset the S corporation's built-in gains (discussed later in this chapter).[73] The S years are counted, however, when determining the expiration period of the carryover. Thus, a carryback of two years means two fiscal or calendar years regardless of whether the corporation was a C corporation or an S corporation.[74]

DETERMINING SHAREHOLDER BASIS

A shareholder's basis in his or her stock as well as any debt owed to the shareholder is critical for three principal purposes. First, upon a sale of stock, shareholders must know the basis of the stock to compute gain or loss on the sale. Second, the treatment of distributions depends on the basis of a shareholder's stock. Third, shareholders must know their stock basis as well as their debt basis in loss years since losses are deductible only to the extent of the basis in their stock and debt.

BASIS IN S CORPORATE STOCK

Conceptually, the computation of a shareholder's stock basis is similar to that for a partner's interest in a partnership. Both calculations are designed to ensure that there is neither double taxation of income nor double deduction of expenses. Consider a typical

---

[73] § 1374(b)(2).

[74] §§ 1371(b) and 1362(e)(6)(A).

situation where two individuals form a business. Assume both parties contribute $10,000 for a 50 percent interest in an S corporation which immediately takes the money and invests it in land that it subsequently sells for $22,000. In this case, the S corporation has income of $2,000 ($22,000 − $20,000) and each shareholder reports his $1,000 share. Note that the shareholders report their share of the S corporation's income even if they receive no distributions from the S corporation. However, to ensure that an S corporation's income is not taxed again when it is distributed, each shareholder must keep track of his or her investment, that is, basis in the S corporation. In this case, each shareholder has an original basis equal to the amount contributed to the S corporation, $10,000. Upon the reporting of S corporation income, each shareholder adjusts basis in the S corporation interest for his or her share of income, increasing it from $10,000 to $11,000. When a shareholder actually receives the $1,000 share of the income, the distribution is treated as tax-free to the extent of basis. Each shareholder would then reduce basis by $1,000 back to the original basis of $10,000. The end result is that the shareholders have reported and received income that has been subject to only one tax. The same rationale can be applied to situations involving tax-exempt income, deductible losses and nondeductible expenses to ensure the proper result is reached.

The steps for calculating a shareholder's stock basis are shown and compared to that for a partner in Exhibit 23-3.[75] Generally, both computations begin with the owner's initial investment, increased by items of taxable and tax-exempt income then decreased by distributions, nondeductible expenditures,[76] deductible expenses and losses in that order. As may be apparent in Exhibit 23-3, the primary difference between the two calculations is that an S corporation shareholder does not include a proportionate share of corporate debt to other lenders. In addition, as illustrated later, the treatment of the distribution of noncash property differs from that of a partnership.

---

[75]   § 1367.

[76]   With respect to the order of nondeductible and deductible expenditures, there is no special rule for partnerships and in absence of sufficient basis, presumably a pro rata portion of each type of expenditure is deducted as shown in *Example 23*. In contrast, S corporation shareholders must use the order shown unless they make a special election to reverse the order and agree to carry forward any disallowed expenses which exceed basis to reduce basis in future years. See Reg. § 1.1367-1(g).

EXHIBIT 23-3
Adjustments to Ownership Basis

Shareholder's Basis in S Corporation Stock	*Partner's Basis in Partnership Interest*
Original Basis	**Original Basis**
Cost	Generally same as S unless received in
Substitute for property contributed in § 351 exchange	exchange for property contributed to
Donor's basis	partnership where partner assumed or
	reduced liabilities
Inherited basis (estate tax value from deceased shareholder)	
Increased by	**Increased by**
Taxable income (ordinary or separately stated)	Same
Tax-exempt income	Same
Decreased (but not below zero) by	**Decreased (but not below zero) by**
Nondeductible expenses (unless election)*	Same
Losses (ordinary and separately stated)	Same
Distributions of cash	Same
Distributions of property at fair market value	Partnership basis of distributed property (in most cases)
No effect	**Additional effect**
Increase in corporate liabilities	Increase partner's basis for share of liabilities
Decrease in corporate liabilities	Decrease partner's basis for share of liabilities

*Nondeductible expenses must be used to offset basis before deductible items unless a special election is made to reverse the order. Reg. § 1.1367-1(f).

BASIS IN S CORPORATION DEBT

If a shareholder's portion of the corporation's losses exceeds his or her stock basis, the shareholder must next turn to debt basis. Unlike a partnership, in which a partner increases basis for his or her portion of the organization's debt to outsiders, a shareholder in an S corporation must actually loan money to the corporation in order to receive debt basis. This issue has been frequently litigated by shareholders with little success. The loan must represent an actual economic outlay on the shareholder's part, rather than a mere paper shuffling of debt instruments.[77] The loan must be made directly by the shareholder, rather than indirectly through a related party.[78] A shareholder guarantee of the corporation's debt to the lender does not create shareholder basis.[79] Thus there must be a receivable from the corporation to the shareholder, based on the shareholder's economic outlay. Quite logically, the shareholder's basis, before any adjustments, is the amount loaned by the shareholder.

A shareholder's basis in the loan is adjusted *only* (1) when the actual indebtedness itself changes due to additional loans or repayment of loans, (2) when corporate net losses exceed the shareholder's basis in S stock, and (3) to restore any basis reduction

---

[77] *Wilson*, T.C. Memo. 1991-544.

[78] *Hitchins*, 103 T.C. 40 (1994).

[79] *Raynor*, 50 T.C. 762 (1968).

due to the prior flow-through of net losses. The application of these latter two rules is somewhat tricky. As a general rule, losses first reduce the shareholder's stock basis (but not below zero). (Note that nondeductible expenses reduce basis before deductible expenses and losses unless a special election is made.) If there is insufficient stock basis to absorb the loss, the loss is deducted to the extent of the shareholder's debt basis. If there is insufficient stock and debt basis, the loss is carried over and used once there is sufficient basis to absorb the loss.

> **Example 24.** An S corporation incurs a net operating loss of $30,000 in 2005. L, its sole shareholder, has a basis in the stock of $24,000 and a note due him from the corporation totals $10,000.

	Stock Basis	Debt Basis
Balance 12/31/2004.....................	$ 24,000	$10,000
Loss to extent of stock basis	(24,000)	
Loss to extent of debt		(6,000)
Balance 12/31/2005.....................	$ 0	$ 4,000

> The $30,000 loss flows through to L, first to the extent of his $24,000 stock basis and the remaining $6,000 because of the $10,000 note owed to him.
>
> If the 2005 loss had been $36,000, only $34,000 would be deductible by L, reducing his basis in both stock and debt to zero. The remaining $2,000 loss would be carried forward indefinitely until a positive basis adjustment occurs in stock or debt.

As the corporation earns income, the shareholder restores stock and debt basis. Debt basis is increased only for income in excess of current year distributions and deductible and nondeductible expenses and losses.[80] Thus if there are no distributions or losses during the year, the basis of the debt is increased first. However, in years where there are distributions and/or losses, the effect is to first allocate income to the stock's basis equal to the amount of any current year losses and distributions with any excess to the debt. While these rules are obviously confusing, failure to properly understand their operation may cause the shareholder to inadvertently have gain on the repayment of any corporate debt.

> **Example 25.** Refer to *Example 24*. The S corporation has net income of $3,000 in 2006 and $8,000 in 2007. There were no losses or distributions in either of these years.

	Stock Basis	Debt Basis
Balance 12/31/2005.....................	$ 0	$ 4,000
2006 net income	0	3,000
2007 net income	5,000	3,000
Balance 12/31/2007.....................	$5,000	$10,000

---

[80] § 1367(b)(2).

In 2006, the excess of income over distributions and losses is $3,000 ($3,000 − $0 − $0) and, therefore, the basis of the note is increased by $3,000. In 2007, the excess of income over distributions and losses is $8,000 ($8,000 − $0 − $0). Consequently, the basis of the debt is increased first by $3,000 to its original $10,000 face amount ($7,000 + $3,000). The remaining income of $5,000 ($8,000 − $3,000) is used to increase the basis of the stock.

Example 26. The records of X, an S corporation, reveal the information below for 2005 and 2006. In addition, at the beginning of 2005, X's sole shareholder had a basis of $10,000 in her stock and $12,000 in the loan she had made to the corporation during 2004.

	2005	*2006*
Tax-exempt income	$ 5,000	
Loss	(30,000)	
Income		$21,000
Distribution		14,000

In 2005, the shareholder first increases the basis in her stock by the tax-exempt income of $5,000, resulting in a stock basis of $15,000. The $30,000 loss is then applied: first to the extent of her stock basis, $15,000, and then to the extent of her debt basis, $12,000. The remainder of the loss, $3,000, is carried over to 2006. These calculations are shown below.

	Stock Basis	*Debt Basis*
Begin 2005	$ 10,000	$ 12,000
Tax-exempt income	5,000	
Loss $30,000	(15,000)	(12,000)
End 2005	$ 0	$ 0
Loss in excess of basis		$ 3,000

In 2006 the corporation reports taxable income of $21,000 and distributes $14,000. The $21,000 income is applied in the following order.

	Stock Basis	*Debt Basis*
Begin 2006	$ 0	$ 0
2006 income . . . . $ 21,000		
2006 distribution . . . . (14,000)		7,000
Loss from 2005		(3,000)
End 2006	$ 0	$ 4,000

The shareholder deducts $27,000 of the 2005 loss in 2005 and carries the remaining $3,000 forward. In 2006, the shareholder reports $21,000 of income and deducts the remaining $3,000 of the 2005 loss.

After a shareholder's basis in the indebtedness is reduced, repayments of the debt in excess of basis result in taxable income. If the debt is a note, bond, or other written debt instrument, the shareholder recognizes capital gain to the extent the payment exceeds basis.[81] If the debt is an *open* account, the shareholder recognizes ordinary income.[82] This ordinary income can be recharacterized as capital gain by converting the open account to a capital contribution; no gain is recognized for this conversion, even if the open account has been reduced by net losses (i.e., its basis is less than its face or market value).[83]

In accounting for repayments, the following rules must be followed:[84]

1. Only the bases of loans outstanding at the close of the year are reduced.

2. Only loans outstanding at the beginning of the year are restored.

The operation of these rules generally favors the taxpayer. Observe that the basis of any loan that is completely paid off during the year may be increased for income earned during the year but is not reduced for losses.

> **Example 27.** J owns all of the stock of H, an S corporation. At the beginning of 2005, J had a basis in his S stock of $13,000 and a loan outstanding to the corporation of $10,000. On July 1, the corporation paid J the $10,000 it owed to him on the loan. As of July 1, the corporation's books and records revealed a loss of $15,000. The loss for the entire year was $20,000. J recognizes no gain on repayment of the loan since his basis is $10,000. Even though the losses suffered by the corporation at the date of the repayment, $15,000, and at the close of the year, $20,000, exceeded J's stock basis, there is no reduction in the basis of the loan since only the basis of a loan outstanding at the close of the year is reduced. However, J can only deduct $13,000 of the loss, the amount equal to his stock basis.

> **Example 28.** Assume the same facts above except that the corporation repaid the loan on June 1 of the following year, 2006. In this case, J's basis in the loan at the beginning of 2006 would be $3,000 computed as follows:

	Stock Basis	Debt Basis
Begin 2005.	$ 13,000	$10,000
Loss for year $20,000	(13,000)	(7,000)
End 2005	$ 0	$ 3,000

> If the corporation had no income for 2006, J would report a gain on the repayment of $7,000 ($10,000 − $3,000). On the other hand, if the corporation had income for the year of $6,000 *and* no distributions were made, the basis of the loan would be increased by the income of $6,000 to $9,000 and the gain on the repayment would be $1,000 ($10,000 − $9,000). Notice that in this latter case the basis of the loan is increased by income for the entire year even though the loan is paid off during the year. This follows from the rule that calls for loans outstanding at the first of the year to be restored.

---

[81]   § 1232 and Rev. Rul. 64-162, 1964-1 C.B. 304.

[82]   Rev. Rul. 68-537, 1968-2 C.B. 372 and *Cornelius v. U.S.*, 74-1 USTC ¶9446, 33 AFTR2d 74-1331, 494 F.2d 465 (CA-5, 1974).

[83]   §§ 108(e)(6) and (d)(7)(C). The holding period of the capital asset (the note) begins with the creation of the note—not the date of the unwritten loan.

[84]   Reg. § 1.1367-2(d).

RELATIONSHIP BETWEEN AN S CORPORATION AND ITS SHAREHOLDERS

The S corporation is a legal entity, distinctly separate from its owners. As a result, transactions between an S corporation and its shareholders are treated as though occurring between unrelated parties unless otherwise provided. Of course, these transactions must be conducted in an arm's-length manner, based on market values that would be used by unrelated parties.

TRANSACTIONS BETWEEN S CORPORATIONS AND THEIR SHAREHOLDERS

Owners may engage in *taxable transactions* with their S corporations. For example, shareholders may lend money, rent property, or sell assets to their S corporations (or vice versa). With few exceptions, owners include the interest income, rent income, or gain or loss from these transactions on their tax returns. Meanwhile, the S corporation is allowed a deduction for the interest, rent, or depreciation expense on assets purchased (if applicable).

> **Example 29.** During the year, K received the following amounts from an S corporation in which she owns 30% of the stock outstanding:
>
> 1. $2,750 interest on a $25,000 loan made to the corporation;
>
> 2. $3,600 rental income from a storage building rented to the corporation; and
>
> 3. $6,300 for special tools sold to the corporation; the tools were acquired for personal use two years ago for $5,800.

Assume that the S corporation's net ordinary income, excluding the above items, is $40,000, and the depreciation deduction for the tools is $900. K's income is computed as follows:

	S Corporation	Shareholder K
Ordinary income (before items below)	$40,000	
Gain on sale of tools ($6,300 − $5,800)		$ 500
Depreciation of tools	(900)	
Interest.	(2,750)	2,750
Rent.	(3,600)	3,600
Ordinary income:		
Corporation.	$32,750	
K ($32,750 × 30%).		9,825

There is a restriction, however, on when an S corporation may deduct expenses owed but not paid to a shareholder, regardless of the amount of stock owned. An accrual basis business (whether an S corporation or partnership) may not deduct expenses owed to a cash basis owner until the amount is paid.[85]

> **Example 30.** Assume the same facts as in *Example 29*, except that $2,000 of the $2,750 interest is accrued but not paid at the end of 2005, the S corporation is on the

---

[85] §§ 267(a)(2) and 267(e). This same restriction applies to a C corporation only if a cash basis shareholder owns more than 50 percent of its stock. § 267(b)(10).

accrual basis, and K is on the cash basis. The corporation paid K the accrued interest of $2,000 on January 15, 2006. Because K is a shareholder the corporation cannot deduct the $2,000 of accrued interest in 2005 but must wait until it pays the amount. Consequently, the corporation will deduct the interest when it is paid in 2006. K will report the payment when she receives it in 2006.

Two special rules governing related-party transactions affect all business forms. Both are discussed in Chapter 22. *First*, realized *losses* on sales between related parties are disallowed.[86] This is not a deferral; therefore, there is no carryover of basis or holding period. However, if this property is later sold at a gain, the gain is offset by the previously disallowed losses.[87] *Second*, recognized gains on sales between related parties of *property* that will be *depreciable* to the new owner are taxed as ordinary income.[88] A related party is defined as one who owns directly or indirectly more than 50 percent of the business when losses are disallowed or when depreciable property is involved. (See the discussion and examples in Chapter 22 regarding these transactions and the definitions of related parties.) A *third* restriction, affecting transactions between partners and their 50 percent owned partnerships, is *not* applicable to either S or C corporations. For these partners, recognized gains on sales of capital assets that will not be capital assets to the partnership are taxed as ordinary income.[89] In contrast, shareholders may sell capital assets to their more than 50 percent owned S or C corporations and the gain is capital, as long as the assets will not be depreciable property to the corporation. Note that this rule may favor the S corporation over the partnership or LLC for certain activities such as real estate development.

SELECTING A TAXABLE YEAR

Shareholders report their shares of S corporation income, deductions, and credits in their tax years in which the corporation's year ends regardless of when distributions of assets are actually made.[90] This timing requirement makes the selection of a year-end for the owners and the business an important tax planning decision. Under current law, an S corporation normally must use the calendar year. Fiscal years are available but only if very strict conditions are met.

Currently an S corporation may have as its taxable year:

- A calendar year.
- A fiscal year if it is a natural business year.
- A fiscal year if its majority shareholders are on the same year.
- A fiscal year under the special election of § 444.

Calendar Years. An S corporation is allowed to have a calendar year.[91] No permission is needed to adopt the calendar year. As will become evident, the severe requirements that must be met to obtain a fiscal year force the vast majority of S corporations to use the calendar year.

---

[86] §§ 267 and 707(b)(1).

[87] § 267(d).

[88] § 1239.

[89] § 707(b)(2).

[90] § 1366(a); § 706 provides a similar rule for partnerships.

[91] § 1378.

Natural Business Year. Section 1378 permits an S corporation to adopt a fiscal year if it "establishes a business purpose to the satisfaction of the Secretary." In this regard, the IRS has indicated that it will allow a fiscal year only in the case of a *natural business year*. An S corporation can qualify for use of a fiscal year end if it considered to have a "natural business year-end." There are two general categories of the natural business year end for S corporations: fiscal year-ends that meet a "25 percent gross receipts test" and fiscal year ends that meet an "annual business cycle" or "seasonal business" test. Year-ends qualifying under the gross receipts test can be adopted automatically by the S corporation. The other category requires permission of the IRS.

Automatic Adoption. A corporation that is electing S status, or a corporation that already has an S election in effect may automatically retain, adopt or change to a natural business year-end if it meets the "25 percent" test for its gross receipts of the past four years. To determine if this test is met, the corporation selects its desired year end (for example June 30) and determines its receipts for the two months ended on June 30 (May and June), and for the twelve months ending on that date in its most recent history (e.g. July through June). If the gross receipts for the final two months (e.g. May and June) exceed 25 percent of its gross receipts for the twelve months ending on that date (e.g. July through June), the S corporation meets the test. The S corporation must meet the test for its past three years ending on that date. A corporation that qualifies under this test may claim its fiscal year without receiving permission for the IRS, although it must file Form 1128 if it is changing its year.[92]

Annual Business Cycle or Seasonal Business Tests. An S corporation may also qualify to apply for a natural business year-end under the annual business cycle test, or the seasonal business test. The annual business cycle test is for a corporation that has a "peak" period of receipts. The seasonal business test exists when there is a period of inactivity due to the nature of the business. Thus a retailer with peak sales during December holiday periods may qualify for the business cycle test, and a ski resort may qualify for the seasonal business test. However, the S corporation may not automatically claim a year-end based on either of these tests, but must apply to the National Office of the IRS and pay a ruling request fee.[93]

Example 31. An S corporation is organized November 1, 2004. Its net ordinary income for the first 14 months is as follows:

November 1, 2004–December 31, 2004	$ 20,000
January 1, 2005–October 31, 2005	200,000
November 1, 2005–December 31, 2005	40,000

All shareholders report on the calendar year. If the S corporation's year-end also is December 31, the owners have includible income of $20,000 in 2004 and $240,000 ($200,000 + $40,000) in 2005. If, however, the S corporation meets the natural business year requirements and receives permission for an October 31 year-end, the owners have no includible income in 2004 but have includible income of $220,000 ($20,000 + $200,000) in 2005. The $40,000 will be combined with the net income or loss for the first ten months in 2006 and reported in 2006.

Majority Ownership Year. Consistent with its concern about deferral, the IRS permits an S corporation to adopt a tax year that is identical to that of owners holding a majority of the corporation's stock.[94] For example, if an individual who operated a farm

---

[92] See Rev. Proc. 2002-37, 2002-22 I.R.B. 1030, § 5.06, Rev. Proc. 2002-38, 2002-22 I.R.B. 1037, § 5.05 and Rev. Proc. 2002-39, 2002-22 I.R.B. 1046, § 5.03(3).

[93] See Rev. Proc. 2002-39, 2002-22 I.R.B. 1046 for details.

[94] Rev. Proc. 2002-37, § 5.05 and Rev. Proc. 2002-38, § 5.06.

used a March 31 year-end, his wholly owned S corporation could use the same year-end since it conformed to the year of its majority owner. However, as a practical matter, this option is seldom used since most shareholders are individuals and certain trusts and they rarely use a fiscal year (e.g., trusts must use a calendar year).

Section 444 Year. A partnership or an S corporation may elect to adopt or change its tax year to any fiscal year that does not result in a deferral period longer than three months—or, if less, the deferral period of the year currently in use.[95] This election requires the electing partnership or S corporation to make a single deposit on or before May 15 of each year computed on the deferred income at the highest tax rate imposed on individual taxpayers *plus* one percent (currently 35% + 1% = 36%).[96] This deposit does *not* flow through to the shareholders. In essence, the partnership or S corporation must maintain a non-interest-bearing deposit of the income taxes that would have been deferred without this requirement. Since this option eliminates some tax benefits of income deferral and has burdensome compliance requirements, few S corporations make the election. The deposit is refunded if the S corporation's income declines in the future.

Since restrictions on C corporation year-end choices are much more lenient than those for S corporations, an election by a fiscal year C corporation to become an S corporation also may require a change in the corporate year-end. This new year is applicable to all future years, even if the Subchapter S election is cancelled and the business reverts to a C corporation.

FAMILY OWNERSHIP

Many of the benefits available to family businesses from *income splitting* are dependent on which organizational form is selected. Some income splitting, however, may be achieved by employing relatives in the business regardless of the organizational form. For example, owners may hire their children to work for them. All reasonable salaries are deductible business expenses and includible salary income to the children. In addition to the tax benefits, some owners believe this provides personal advantages, including encouraging the children to take an interest in the business at an early age.

In some instances, family businesses are formed primarily for tax reasons. The most common example includes both a parent and one or more otherwise dependent children as owners. The basic tax rate structure provides considerable incentive for this type of arrangement when the child is at least 14 years of age.[97]

Rules similar to those affecting the family partnership (discussed in Chapter 22) are applicable to family S corporations.[98] Thus, if reasonable compensation is not paid for services performed or for the use of capital contributed by a family member, the IRS may reallocate S corporation income or expenses.[99] Unlike the partnership, this rule extends to all family members, including those who are *not* owners and when there is no donee/donor relationship.

---

[95]   § 444 and Temp. Reg. § 1.444-1T(b). Partnerships and S corporations in existence before 1987 are allowed to continue their fiscal years even if the deferral period exceeds three months (i.e., the fiscal year is "grandfathered").

[96]   § 7519 and Temp. Reg § 1.7519-2T(a)(4)(ii).

[97]   Recall that many of the income-splitting advantages involving passive income are not available with children under 14 years of age.

[98]   § 1366(e) and Reg. § 1.1366-3(a).

[99]   Family member, as defined by the Code, is the same for the partnership and the S corporation. §§ 704(e)(3) and 1366(e).

Example 32. This year, Dr. F created LME Corporation, an S corporation whose business is leasing medical equipment. He gave all of the stock in LME to his son and daughter. For the year, LME has $20,000 of net rental income. If Dr. F performs services for LME and is not adequately compensated, the IRS may adjust the income of the parties to force Dr. F to include reasonable compensation in his income, and reduce LME's income accordingly. The IRS is not required to make this adjustment.

CURRENT DISTRIBUTIONS OF CORPORATE ASSETS

The treatment of distributions by an S corporation borrows from the rules applying to distributions from partnerships and C corporations. Normally, distributions from an S corporation, like those from a partnership, represent accumulated income that has been previously taxed to its owners. Accordingly, this income should not be taxed again when it is distributed. Consistent with this approach, most distributions by an S corporation are considered nontaxable to the extent of the shareholder's stock basis. Any distribution in excess of the shareholder's stock basis is treated as gain from the sale of the underlying stock, producing capital gain.

Problems arise if the retained earnings of an S corporation consist of any C corporation earnings and profits (i.e., AE&P as discussed in Chapter 20). As might be expected, when this occurs, clarification is required regarding how the S and C corporation rules interact. Consequently, one of the first questions that must be considered before the treatment of a distribution can be determined is whether an S corporation has AE&P. Beyond this first concern, however, still other considerations may be relevant. For example, special rules can operate if the S corporation distributes property (i.e., assets other than cash) or the distribution occurs shortly after the S corporation election terminates. Each of these issues and several others are examined below.

THE E&P QUESTION

As noted above, the treatment of an S corporation distribution can depend on whether the corporation has any AE&P. Normally a corporation that has been an S corporation since its inception will not have AE&P since it never operated as a C corporation.[100] Nevertheless, AE&P could be found in the retained earnings of a life-long S corporation if a C corporation was merged or liquidated into the S corporation. An election to treat a subsidiary corporation as a QSub is a deemed liquidation of the subsidiary, governed by Code §§ 332 and 337. Accordingly, any AE&P of the subsidiary becomes AE&P of the parent S corporation.

An S corporation is far more likely to have AE&P if it operated as a C corporation before it elected S status. This is not at all uncommon. For example, it is estimated that due to substantial changes made by the Tax Reform Act of 1986, about 500,000 C corporations made S elections. Many of these converted C corporations are alive and operating today. There are also many other C corporations that for one reason or another have opted for S status. In these cases, AE&P is likely to exist. In any event, whether the corporation has always been an S corporation or is a converted C corporation, it is crucial to ascertain whether the corporation has AE&P. This determination often requires a long detailed study.

---

[100] Prior to 1983, it was possible for an S corporation to generate AE&P while it was an S corporation. Starting in 1997, an S corporation's C earnings and profits do not include any AE&P that was produced while it was an S corporation prior to 1983. See § 1311 of the Small Business Jobs Protection Act. (P.L. 104-88).

S CORPORATIONS WITH NO AE&P

All cash distributions by S corporations that have no AE&P are nontaxable unless they exceed the shareholder's basis in the stock.[101] It should be emphasized that the shareholder's stock basis is the critical variable in measuring the taxability of the distribution. The basis of any debt is irrelevant in this regard.

In determining whether a distribution exceeds the shareholder's stock basis, all distributions are deemed to be made on the last day of the tax year. For this purpose, the basis in the stock is increased for all positive adjustments before accounting for distributions. Like partnerships, distributions reduce the owner's basis before consideration of losses.[102] If the shareholder owns stock on the last day of the taxable year, all of the basis adjustments are made on the last day of the corporation's taxable year (or on the last day of ownership for a shareholder whose interest completely terminates). The general approach used by S corporations in accounting for distributions is illustrated below.

	Original basis (purchase, formation, inherited, gift, etc.)
+	Additional capital contributions
+	Separately stated income items (taxable and tax-exempt)
+	Nonseparately stated income items (taxable and tax-exempt)
−	Distributions
−	Nondeductible, non-capital, expenses
−	Separately and nonseparately stated deduction and loss items
=	Ending basis of stock

Example 33. D and F have been equal owners of an S corporation for five years. D has a basis in his stock of $40,000 while F's stock basis is $10,000. The corporation's records for the year revealed the following:

Ordinary taxable income	$50,000
Tax-exempt income	10,000
Nondeductible portion of meals and entertainment	2,000
Capital loss (not fully deductible by shareholder)	30,000

---

[101] § 1368(b).

[102] Prior to 1997, distributions of S corporations were the final item absorbed (i.e., distributions were after losses and separately stated items of deductible and nondeductible expenses).

During the year, the corporation distributed $100,000, $50,000 to D and $50,000 to F. Based on these facts, the distribution to D would be nontaxable while the distribution to F would result in a capital gain of $10,000 as determined below.

	D's Share		F's Share	
	Taxable Income	Basis	Taxable Income	Basis
Beginning basis		$40,000		$ 10,000
Positive adjustments:				
Exempt income		5,000		5,000
Ordinary taxable income $25,000	25,000	$25,000	25,000	
Basis before $50,000 distribution to each		$70,000		$ 40,000
Nontaxable portion of distribution		(50,000)		(40,000)
Taxable portion of distribution (capital gain)	0	—	10,000	—
Basis before negative adjustments		$20,000		$ 0
Negative adjustments:				
Nondeductible meals and entertainment		(1,000)		—
Capital loss		(15,000)		—*
Ending basis		$ 4,000		$ 0

*The capital loss would be allowed to F in any future year if F's basis were to increase.

In determining the treatment of the distributions, the stock basis for each shareholder is first adjusted for all positive adjustments before accounting for the distribution. In this case, the positive adjustments boost D's basis to $70,000 so that his $50,000 distribution is completely tax-free. After accounting for the distribution, D reduces his basis for his share of the nondeductible expenses and then the capital loss. The reduction to basis for the capital loss is made even though D is not able to fully deduct the loss on his own return. Any portion of the capital loss that D cannot deduct is carried over to subsequent years until it is exhausted.

The distribution to F results in a capital gain of $10,000 since his basis after positive adjustments, $40,000, is insufficient to absorb the entire $50,000 distribution. Note also that F cannot deduct any of the capital loss since losses are deductible only to the extent of the shareholder's basis. However, the capital loss carries over until such time that F has sufficient basis to enable its flow-through. Contrast the treatment of the capital loss with that of the nondeductible portion of meals and entertainment. There is no requirement that F must carryover the nondeductible expenses and reduce his basis. When it is known that distributions will exceed a shareholder's basis, the recognition of capital gain can be avoided if the shareholder increases his or her stock basis before the year ends. This may be done by (1) contributing capital to the S corporation, or (2) having debt owed this shareholder converted to capital.

S CORPORATIONS WITH AE&P

The distribution rules for S corporations that have AE&P—regardless of the amount—are far more complex than that for S corporations without AE&P. This derives from the fact that the distributions that are out of an S corporation's earnings that were accumulated while it was a C corporation (C AE&P) are treated much differently from those out of its earnings accumulated while it was an S corporation. Distributions out of the S corporation's AE&P are treated as dividends, and are fully taxable as ordinary income to the shareholder. In contrast, distributions out of the S corporation's earnings accumulated while it was an S corporation are generally nontaxable to the extent of the shareholder's stock basis. As a result, the source of the distribution is extremely important. This distinction—and a special concern about a potential abuse—requires the corporation to break down its retained earnings into several components. It is important to remember that while each of these components have their own special characteristics, all of them are simply part of the S corporation's total earnings that have been accumulated and not distributed over the years. There are four corporate level equity accounts. They are referred to as (1) the accumulated adjustments account (AAA); (2) previously taxed income (PTI); (3) AE&P; and (4) the other adjustments account (OAA). The treatment of the distributions from such accounts, as discussed below, can be summarized as follows:

Order	Source	Description	Treatment	Effect on Basis
1.	AAA	All S corps to the extent of AAA	Nontaxable unless exceeds shareholder's stock basis	Reduces stock basis to the extent thereof
2.	PTI	Distributions to shareholders who have personal pre-1983 PTI accumulations	Nontaxable unless exceeds shareholder's stock basis	Reduces stock basis to the extent thereof
3.	AE&P	S corps that have C AE&P	Ordinary dividend income	No effect
4.	OAA	All remaining distributions from S corp's tax-exempt income	Nontaxable unless exceeds shareholder's stock basis	Reduce basis to the extent thereof
5.	Paid-in Capital	All remaining distributions	Nontaxable unless exceeds shareholder's stock basis	Reduce basis to the extent thereof

Accumulated Adjustments Account. The *accumulated adjustments account* (AAA) is the initial reference point for determining the source of a distribution and therefore its treatment. All distributions are assumed to first come out of AAA to the extent thereof. While neither the name of the account nor its acronym are descriptive, this account generally represents post-1982 income of the S corporation that has been taxed to shareholders but has not been distributed. Consequently, distributions from the account are a *nontaxable* return of the shareholder's basis in his or her stock. Distributions from the AAA that exceed the shareholder's stock basis are capital gain.[103]

The AAA is a corporate-level equity account that must be maintained if the S corporation has accumulated E&P from years when it was operated as a C corporation.[104] The AAA is the cumulative total of the S corporation's post-1982 income and gains (other than tax-exempt income) as reduced by all expenses and losses (both deductible and nondeductible other than those related to tax-exempt income) and any distributions deemed to have been made from the account. The specific formula for computing the balance in the AAA is shown in Exhibit 23-4. Note that the adjustments to the AAA are similar to those made by shareholders to their basis in their stock with some exceptions:[105]

---

[103] § 1368(b).

[104] § 1368(c).

[105] § 1368(e)(1).

1. Tax-exempt income increases the shareholder's stock basis but has no effect on the AAA. These items are posted to the OAA discussed below.

2. Expenses and losses related to tax-exempt income decrease the shareholder's stock basis but have no effect on the AAA. [However, other nondeductible expenditures reduce the AAA as they do the shareholder's stock basis (e.g., the 50 percent of meal and entertainment expenses that is not deductible, fines, and penalties).]

3. The various adjustments to the AAA (other than distributions) can create either a positive or negative balance in the AAA account. In contrast, the shareholder's stock basis can never be negative.

4. The ordering rules for the AAA are somewhat different than for basis. The corporation adjusts for income, then subtracts deductions and losses (but *only* to the extent of income items) before it calculates the balance available for distributions. In a year in which the corporation has deductions and losses in excess of income items, it reduces the AAA for this excess (called the "net negative adjustment") *after* reduction for distributions.

EXHIBIT 23-4
Accumulated Adjustments Account Computations

Beginning Balance (S years beginning after 1982)
Add income items:
Taxable income
Separately stated gains and income (not including tax-exempt income)
Less losses and deductions (not to exceed income items above)
Nondeductible losses and expenses (excluding expenses relating to tax-exempt income)
Ordinary loss
Less distributions (to extent of beginning balance plus income less losses and deductions)
Less losses and deductions, to the extent they exceed income items (the net negative adjustment)
Equals AAA end of the year

Example 34. In 1985 T formed ABC Inc. and operated it as a calendar year C corporation until 1992, when it elected to be treated as an S corporation. T has owned 100% of the stock since the corporation's inception. T's basis in his stock at the beginning of 2005 was $10,000. Other information related to the S corporation for 2005 is shown below.

Net ordinary income..............................	$50,000
Charitable contribution...........................	9,000
Tax-exempt interest income.......................	10,000
Expenses related to tax-exempt interest income	1,000
Disallowed portion of meal expenses................	2,000
Cash distributions	20,000
Beginning accumulated adjustments account	10,000

The first five items listed above flow through to T. Of these, T must include the $50,000 of ordinary taxable income on his 2005 tax return. In addition, T is allowed to report the $9,000 charitable contribution made by the corporation as an itemized deduction on his return.

T's basis and the balances in the AAA and OAA accounts at the end of the year are computed in the following manner:

	Basis	AAA	OAA
Beginning balance	$ 10,000	$ 10,000	$ 0
Positive adjustments:			
Taxable income	50,000	50,000	0
Tax-exempt income	10,000	0	$10,000
Basis before distributions.	$ 70,000	—	—
Negative items to AAA:			
Disallowed meal expense	—	(2,000)	
Charitable contributions		(9,000)	
AAA before distribution		$ 49,000	
Less distribution.	(20,000)	(20,000)	
Basis and AAA after distribution.	$ 50,000	$ 29,000	
Negative items to basis:			
Disallowed meal expense	(2,000)		
Expenses related to tax-exempt income	(1,000)		(1,000)
Charitable contribution	(9,000)		
Final balances	$ 38,000	$ 29,000	$ 9,000

Note that for purposes of the determining the treatment of the distribution, the shareholder's stock basis is determined after the positive adjustment but before the negative adjustments. In contrast, the AAA balance available for distributions is determined after the nondeductible and deductible items (including losses) but only to the extent of the positive adjustments. Also observe that the $9,000 ($38,000 − $29,000) difference between the increase in T's basis in his stock and the corporation's AAA is attributable to the tax-exempt interest income of $10,000 less the $1,000 of expenses related to this income, neither of which affects the AAA. These items are reflected in the OAA account.

As noted above, distributions from the AAA are nontaxable to the shareholder unless they exceed the shareholder's stock basis. However, it is rare for shareholders to receive distributions from the AAA that exceed the basis in their stock. Most of the time, the aggregate basis of the shareholders will equal or exceed the AAA (e.g., see *Example 34* above). Note also that the AAA is a corporate-level account and is unaffected by either shareholder transactions or shareholder basis in the stock. Therefore, if a shareholder sells stock, new shareholders are entitled to distributions from the AAA, which will be reductions of basis. On rare occasions a distribution from the AAA will exceed a shareholder's stock basis. In such case, the excess is treated as a gain from the sale of stock.

Previously Taxed Income. The second account from which a distribution may come consists of undistributed income that has been previously taxed for S years before 1983, commonly referred to as previously taxed income (PTI).[106] As a practical matter, this account may be viewed as the AAA for years prior to 1983. The balance in this account represents taxable income that was earned by the corporation while it was an S corporation prior to 1983 and which has not been distributed to shareholders. Distributions from this account, like those from the AAA, are considered to be a

---

[106] § 1368(c).

nontaxable return of the shareholder's basis in his or her stock. Unlike AAA, PTI is considered a personal account and is nontransferable. Therefore buyers of a shareholder's interest do not obtain any of that shareholder's PTI.

Accumulated E&P of C Years. The third account from which a distribution may come represents earnings and profits accumulated in years when the corporation was a C corporation. Distributions from AE&P are taxable as dividend income. There is no schedule or reconciliation of AE&P on Form 1120S.

Other Adjustments Account. Schedule M-2 of Form 1120S creates a fourth classification, entitled *other adjustments account* (OAA). The OAA represents post-1982 tax-exempt income and expenses related to such income that do not flow into the AAA. Thus, the OAA is used to show amounts that affect shareholder bases but not the AAA.

Schedule M-2. Schedule M-2 on page 4 of Form 1120S is a reconciliation of the beginning and ending balances in these corporate accounts: the AAA, the OAA, and shareholders' undistributed taxable income previously taxed (i.e., PTI). Interestingly, the M-2 does not reflect the ordering rules (i.e., distributions before losses and other expenses); nor does the M-2 provide for any reconciliation of AE&P.

Example 35. Same facts as in *Example 34* above. The corporation's Schedule M-2 for the year would appear as follows:

Schedule M-2 Analysis of Accumulated Adjustments Account, Other Adjustments Account, and Shareholders' Undistributed Taxable Income Previously Taxed (see page 32 of the instructions)			
	(a) Accumulated adjustments account	**(b)** Other adjustments account	**(c)** Shareholders' undistributed taxable income previously taxed
1 Balance at beginning of tax year	10,000		
2 Ordinary income from page 1, line 21	50,000		
3 Other additions		10,000	
4 Loss from page 1, line 21	( )		
5 Other reductions	(11,000)	(1,000)	
6 Combine lines 1 through 5	49,000	9,000	
7 Distributions other than dividend distributions	20,000		
8 Balance at end of tax year. Subtract line 7 from line 6	29,000	9,000	

Form **1120S** (2004)

Source of Distribution. As discussed above, the treatment of a distribution depends on its source. For this purpose, distributions are presumed to flow out of the various accounts in the following order with the treatment as described.[107]

1. *Accumulated Adjustments Account (AAA).* Distributions are first considered distributions out of the AAA and, therefore, are nontaxable to extent of the shareholder's stock basis. Any amount received out of the AAA that is in excess of the shareholder's basis is treated as a sale of the underlying stock, resulting in capital gain.

2. *Previously Taxed Income (PTI).* Distributions of PTI are nontaxable to the extent of the shareholder's stock basis with any excess treated as capital gain.

3. *Accumulated Earnings and Profits (AE&P).* Distributions of AE&P are treated as dividends income just as if distributed from a C corporation and, therefore, are fully taxable as dividend income to the shareholder.

4. *Other Adjustments Account (OAA).* Distributions out of the OAA are nontaxable to the extent of the shareholder's stock basis with any excess treated as capital gain.

---

[107] § 1368(c).

5. *Remaining Distributions.* Distributions in excess of the amounts in the accounts described above (i.e., the other accounts are exhausted) are treated as returns of the shareholder's capital and are nontaxable to the extent of the shareholder's stock basis. Any excess is treated as capital gain.

Note that all of the distributions above reduce the shareholder's stock basis except amounts out of the corporation's AE&P.

Example 36. J and W have been equal owners of a calendar year S corporation for several years. It has been operated as a C and an S corporation in the past. Balances at the beginning of the year are shown below in the schedule. Operations for the year show $12,000 net ordinary income, $2,000 tax-exempt interest income, and $24,000 cash distributions. Based on the approach described above, the $24,000 cash distribution exhausts (1) all of the $18,000 AAA, (2) all of the $4,000 PTI, and (3) $2,000 ($24,000 − $18,000 − $4,000) of the AE&P. The balances at the end of the year are determined as follows:

	Corporate Accounts				Stock Basis	
	AAA	PTI	AE&P	OAA	J	W
Beginning balances	$ 6,000	$ 4,000	$ 3,000	$ 0	$10,000	$ 6,000
Net ordinary income	12,000				6,000	6,000
Tax-exempt interest income				2,000	1,000	1,000
Cash distributions:						
AAA	(18,000)				(9,000)	(9,000)
PTI		(4,000)			(2,000)	(2,000)
AE&P			(2,000)		0	0
Ending balances	$ 0	$ 0	$ 1,000	$ 2,000	$ 6,000	$ 2,000

Both J and W have $6,000 net ordinary income (from S operations) and $1,000 dividend income (from AE&P). Note that J and W recognize dividend income because tax-exempt income does not increase AAA. Also note that there is no longer any need to maintain an account for PTI once the corporation has distributed its PTI.

Example 37. Refer to *Example 36.* Operations for the following year show net ordinary income of $9,400 and cash distributions of $16,000. The balances at the end of this year are determined as follows:

	Corporate Accounts			Stock Basis	
	AAA	AE&P	OAA	J	W
Beginning balances	$ 0	$ 1,000	$ 2,000	$ 6,000	$ 2,000
Net ordinary income	9,400			4,700	4,700
Cash distributions:					
AAA	(9,400)			(4,700)	(4,700)
AE&P		(1,000)		0	0
OAA			(2,000)	(1,000)	(1,000)
Remaining (basis)				(2,800)	(1,800)	(1,000)
Remaining (gain) to W				(800)		
Ending balances	$ 0	$ 0	$ 0	$ 3,200	$ 0

Both J and W have $4,700 net ordinary income and $500 dividend income (from AE&P). In addition, W has $800 capital gain since the distributions that reduce basis exceed her basis in the stock by $800. Because this S corporation no longer has AE&P, any future distributions will be nontaxable unless they exceed a shareholder's basis in the stock. Note that in this case there is no PTI component because the S corporation has no PTI.

DISTRIBUTIONS OF PROPERTY

Although most distributions consist solely of cash, an S corporation may distribute property. Rules governing property distributions of an S corporation are a unique blend of both the partnership and C corporation provisions.

Like C corporations, the amount of any property distributed by an S corporation is the fair market value of the property less any associated liabilities. Also like a C corporation, an S corporation must recognize gain—but not loss—on the distribution of property. Any gain recognized by the S corporation on the distribution passes through to be reported by the shareholders. In addition, this gain increases each shareholder's stock basis. Upon receipt of the distribution, the shareholder reduces his or her basis by the fair market value of the property received (but not below zero). Any amount in excess of the shareholder's basis is capital gain. The shareholder's basis in the property is its fair market value. The treatment of property distributions is identical to the approach described above for cash distributions.[108]

Example 38. After using the following equipment for four years of its five-year MACRS life, an S corporation distributes it to H, its sole owner.

Asset	Cost	Accumulated Depreciation	Basis	Fair Market Value
Equipment	$10,000	$7,900	$2,100	$4,300

H's stock basis, after all adjustments except the equipment distribution, is $1,800.

	Includible Income	Stock Basis
H's basis, before		$ 1,800
S gain recognized (§ 1245)	$2,200	2,200
Balance		$ 4,000
Tax-free distribution		(4,000)
Taxable distribution	$ 300	
H's basis, after		$ 0

H must also recognize a $300 capital gain since the $4,300 FMV of the equipment exceeds his $4,000 stock basis. His basis in the equipment becomes $4,300.

SPECIAL RULES RELATING TO SOURCE OF DISTRIBUTIONS

While the normal rules for the sourcing of distributions usually is favored by shareholders, this is not always the case. For example, recall that an S election is terminated if an S corporation has excess passive income and AE&P for three

---

[108]   Under current IRS instructions to Form 1120S, both property and cash reduce PTI.

consecutive years. In this situation and others, the corporation may want to purge itself of its AE&P to avoid losing its election. Note, however, that under the normal rules, the corporation must distribute all of its AAA before it can begin distributing its AE&P. Fortunately, the law provides possible relief and makes a special election available to the corporation to alter the source of the distribution. If all of the shareholders affected consent, § 1368(e)(3) allows the corporation to make the so-called bypass election. As shown in Exhibit 23-5, this election enables the corporation to bypass AAA and treat accumulated E&P as being distributed before AAA.[109] The election is made annually by attaching an appropriate statement to a timely filed or extended return.

When an S corporation has PTI and needs to eliminate AE&P, the election under § 1368(e)(3) is not sufficient. The corporation must also exhaust PTI before it can start distributing AE&P. The Regulations make this possible by allowing the corporation to elect to bypass PTI when determining the treatment of its distributions.[110] If the elections to bypass both AAA and PTI are made (as shown in Exhibit 23-5), AE&P is deemed to be the first item distributed by the S corporation.

In many cases, an S corporation identifies the need to distribute its AE&P after the close of the taxable year—normally a time when it would be too late to take action. However, the Regulations rescue the corporation in this situation with a very valuable tool: the deemed dividend election.[111] When this election is consented to by all of the corporation's shareholders, the corporation is treated as having made a distribution of its AE&P on the last day of its taxable year. The shareholders must first include the deemed dividend in their income and then are treated as having contributed the amount to the corporation as a contribution to capital increasing the basis in their stock.

EXHIBIT 23-5
Sources of Distributions

Distribution Order	Normal Treatment	AAA and PTI Bypass Elections	Post-Termination Transition Period
1	AAA	AE&P	AAA
2	PTI	AAA	CE&P
3	AE&P	PTI	AE&P
4	OAA	OAA	NOT PTI or OAA

POST-TERMINATION TRANSACTIONS

Distributions. When a corporation election terminates its S election, the entity is immediately treated as a C corporation. Without special rules, this transition could be particularly severe. Recall that distributions for a C corporation are dividends to the extent of E&P. This is true even though the C corporation may have undistributed nontaxable income from S years. This could create a special hardship on a person who had been a shareholder during the corporation's final S corporation year and who had received an allocation of income from the corporation attributable to that period. In such a situation, the shareholder would not be able to withdraw money from the corporation, even to the extent necessary to pay taxes on his or her portion of the S corporation's taxable income, without the possibility of dividend treatment. To address this problem, special rules allow a shareholder to treat distributions as being from the AAA during the post-termination transition period (PTTP).

---

[109] Reg. § 1.1368-1(f)(2).

[110] Reg. § 1.1368-1(f)(4).

[111] Reg. § 1.1368-1(f)(3).

The PTTP begins the day after the S corporation's final tax year and lasts at least one year and perhaps longer.[112] During the PTTP, cash—but not property—distributions are deemed to come from AAA to the extent thereof.[113] But this is where the normal pattern of distributions ends. Any PTTP distributions in excess of AAA are *not* considered as having come from PTI or OAA but rather current or accumulated E&P. As shown in Exhibit 23-5, any distributions during the PTTP in excess of AAA would be fully taxable as dividends to the extent of the corporation's E&P. Note that this special ordering rule for distributions during the PTTP is deemed to occur unless the corporation elects not to have it apply. Also observe that a distribution during the PTTP is only treated as coming from the AAA if it is received by a person who was a shareholder on the corporation's final day as an S corporation.[114]

Losses. In some cases, a shareholder who had sustained losses prior to the termination of an S election may have lacked sufficient basis to deduct those losses. Without some relief, those losses would provide no tax benefit after the termination since the corporation is no longer an S corporation but a C corporation. However, the Code enables shareholders to secure those losses by allowing them to increase their stock basis during the PTTP.[115] Note that a loan during this period does not create basis for prior losses. Only increases in stock basis can secure losses. For example, shareholders could cancel any corporate debt owed to them and treat the cancellation as a contribution to capital with a corresponding increase in basis. Similarly, a shareholder could exchange the debt for additional stock. A shareholder could also increase the stock's basis by simply contributing additional cash or property to the capital of the corporation.

TAXES IMPOSED ON THE S CORPORATION

S corporations, like partnerships, normally are considered nontaxable entities. Unlike partnerships, however, S corporations may be required to pay one of the following taxes:

1.   Excessive passive investment income tax

2.   Tax on built-in gains

3.   LIFO recapture tax

TAX ON EXCESSIVE PASSIVE INCOME

As discussed earlier, when Congress revised Subchapter S in 1982, it was concerned that C corporations with a potential accumulated earnings tax or personal holding company tax, particularly those that are mere holding companies (i.e., those whose principal assets are investment properties such as stocks, securities, and real estate projects), would attempt to escape these penalty taxes by electing to be treated as S corporations. Subchapter S can provide a refuge for these corporations since S corporations normally are exempt from both penalty taxes. To guard against this possibility, two steps were taken. First, as previously explained, when a corporation has AE&P *and* excessive passive income in three consecutive years, the corporation's S

---

[112]   § 1377(b).

[113]   § 1371(e).

[114]   Reg. § 1.1377-2(b).

[115]   § 1366(d)(3).

election is terminated.[116] Second, an S corporation must pay a special tax on its passive income if (1) it has AE&P at the close of its tax year, *and* (2) passive investment income exceeds 25 percent of its gross receipts that year.[117] Note that this tax, as well as the termination provision for excessive passive income (discussed early in this chapter), only applies to corporations that have been operated as C corporations and have AE&P at the end of the taxable year. Consequently, the tax is not imposed on corporations that have distributed all of their AE&P or that have never been C corporations.

The tax on excessive passive income is equal to the maximum corporate rate for the year (35 percent) multiplied by *excess net passive income* (ENPI). ENPI is computed as follows:

$$\text{ENPI} = \text{Net passive income} \times \frac{\text{Passive investment income} - 25\% \text{ of gross receipts}}{\text{Passive investment income}}$$

In computing the tax, several rules must be observed.

1. For any taxable year, *ENPI* cannot exceed the corporation's taxable income, computed as though it were a C corporation but before reduction for the dividends-received deduction and net operating loss deduction.[118]

2. *Passive investment income* is defined the same as it is for the termination provisions of § 1362(d) discussed previously:[119] generally gross receipts from dividends, interest (including tax-exempt interest), rents, royalties, and annuities, and gains from sales of stocks and securities (not netted with losses).

3. *Net passive income* is passive investment income reduced by any allowable deductions directly connected with the production of this income. These deductions include such expenses as property taxes and depreciation related to rental property but exclude such deductions as the dividends-received deduction.[120]

The amount of any tax paid reduces the amount of each item of passive investment income that flows through to shareholders. The tax is allocated proportionately based on net passive investment income.[121]

Example 39. PTC is owned equally by R and S. At the close of the year, PTC, an S corporation, reports gross receipts of $200,000 and a balance in its AE&P account of $24,000. Gross receipts include $25,000 interest and $50,000 of passive rent. Deductions directly attributable to rents were $30,000, including depreciation, maintenance, insurance, and property taxes. Using this information, PTC has excess net passive investment income of $15,000 determined as follows:

---

[116] § 1362(d)(3).

[117] § 1375(a).

[118] § 1375(b)(1)(B) and Reg. § 1.1375-1(b)(1)(ii).

[119] §§ 1375(b)(3) and 1362(d)(3).

[120] § 1375(b)(2).

[121] Reg. § 1.1366-4(c).

Total gross receipts:

Gross receipts:	
Interest	$ 25,000
Rent (passive).	50,000
Total passive gross receipts	$ 75,000
Active gross receipts.	125,000
Total gross receipts	$200,000

Permitted passive portion (25% × $200,000)	$ 50,000

Excess passive gross receipts ($75,000 − $50,000)	$ 25,000
Net Passive Income:	
Passive gross receipts	$ 75,000
Deductions connected with rent	(30,000)
Net passive income	$ 45,000

Excess net passive income:	
Excess passive gross receipts	$ 25,000
Divide by total passive gross receipts	75,000
Excess fraction ($25,000/$75,000)	$\frac{1}{3}$
Times net passive income.	45,000
Excess net passive income	15,000

Since the corporation has passive investment income exceeding 25% of its gross receipts ($25,000) *and* it has AE&P at the end of the taxable year, the tax on excessive passive income is imposed.

PTC's excessive passive investment income tax is $5,250 (35% × $15,000). This amount is allocated as follows:

	Interest	Rent	Total
Gross receipts	$25,000	$ 50,000	$ 75,000
Expenses.	0	(30,000)	(30,000)
. . . .	$25,000	$ 20,000	$ 45,000
Tax allocation.	(2,916)	(2,334)	(5,250)
. . . .	$22,084	$ 17,666	$ 39,750
To each shareholder (50%)	$11,042	$ 8,833	$ 19,875

TAX ON BUILT-IN GAINS

Without special rules, C corporations planning sales or distributions of appreciated property (e.g., as a dividend or in liquidation) could avoid double taxation by electing S status before making the distributions.

Example 40. R, a regular C corporation, owns land worth $50,000 (basis $10,000). If R Corporation distributes the land to its sole shareholder, D, as a dividend, the corporation recognizes a gain of $40,000 ($50,000 − $10,000) and D recognizes dividend income of $50,000. Therefore, two taxes are imposed. In contrast, compare the result that occurs if R Corporation has S status. R still recognizes a $40,000 gain. However, that gain is not taxed at the corporate level, but flows through to D to be taxed. In addition, D increases his basis in his stock by $40,000. On receipt of the property, D does not report any income but simply reduces the basis in his stock. As a result, there is only a *single tax* if R Corporation has S status.

To eliminate the tax-avoidance possibility of electing S status before the distribution (or a sale), Congress enacted § 1374. This section imposes a special corporate-level tax—the *built-in gains tax*—on gains recognized by an S corporation that accrued while it was a C corporation. The tax applies *only* to gains recognized during the 10-year period following the S election.

Under § 1374, it is presumed that *any* gain recognized on the sale or distribution of any property by a "converted" S corporation is subject to the built-in gains tax. However, the corporation may rebut this presumption and avoid the tax by proving either of the following: (1) the asset sold or distributed was not held on the date that the corporation elected S status; or (2) the gain had not accrued at the time of the election. As a practical matter, this approach requires every C corporation electing S status to have an independent appraisal of its assets on the date the S election becomes effective (i.e., the conversion date) in order to rebut the presumption. Note that for purposes of this tax, built-in gains are applicable to *all* assets, including inventory, unrealized receivables of a cash basis taxpayer, any gain on a long-term contract that has not been recognized (e.g., the taxpayer uses the completed contract method of accounting), and any goodwill.

As a general rule, the special tax applies only to S corporations having a *net unrealized built-in gain*. A net unrealized built-in gain is defined as the difference between the value and basis of all assets held on the conversion date. This difference represents the *maximum* amount that may be subject to the built-in gains tax.

Example 41. On November 3, 2005 T Corporation made an S election. The election was effective for calendar year 2006. On January 1, 2006 its balance sheet revealed the following assets.

	Adjusted Basis	Fair Market Value	Built-in Gain (Loss)
Equipment	$ 50,000	$ 75,000	$25,000
Land.	30,000	70,000	40,000
Stock	20,000	15,000	(5,000)
	$100,000	$160,000	$60,000

T Corporation's net unrealized built-in gain is $60,000. Note that the built-in loss on the stock effectively limits the taxpayer's future exposure to the built-in gains tax.

Only the *net recognized built-in gain* (NRBIG) is subject to tax.[122] According to the regulations, NRBIG is the lesser of:

1. The *Pre-Limitation Amount* (PLA). The PLA is the S corporation's taxable income as if its *only* recognized items for the year were its recognized built-in gains and losses. The S corporation must observe the C corporation rules in making this computation. However, in using the C rules, the corporation is not permitted to claim any dividends-received deduction or any loss carryforward.

2. The *Taxable Income Limit* (TIL). The TIL is the S corporation's taxable income computed in the same manner as a C corporation, including *all* of its recognized gross income and deductions for the taxable year. Again, it is not allowed to

---

[122] § 1374(b).

claim the dividends-received deduction or any loss carryforward. Due to this rule, NRBIG cannot exceed the taxable income that the corporation would have had if it had been a C corporation.

3. The *Net Unrealized Built-in Gain Limit* (NUL). In its first S corporation year, the NUL is the same as the net *unrealized* built-in gain (i.e., the maximum net built-in gain that could be recognized). In subsequent years, the NUL is the original net unrealized built-in gain reduced by all net recognized built-in gains in prior years. In this manner, the net unrealized built-in gain acts as the limiting factor on the total net recognized built-in gains that could be reported during the ten year recognition period.

The corporation computes each of these amounts and the lowest is the NRBIG for the year. After the corporation computes this amount, it is then allowed to reduce it by any unused net operating loss carryforwards from years in which it was a C corporation. The corporation applies a flat rate of 35 percent to this amount, which in turn may be offset by certain credit carryforwards from prior years.

> **Example 42.** Refer to the facts in *Example 41*. During 2006 T Corporation sold the equipment and the stock for $77,000 and $15,000, respectively. Although T recognizes a gain of $27,000 ($77,000 − $50,000) on the sale of the equipment, T's built-in gain recognized is limited to the amount accrued on the date of conversion from a C corporation to S status, $25,000. T's net recognized built-in gain that is potentially subject to tax is $20,000 (the built-in gain of $25,000 less the $5,000 built-in loss recognized.)

> **Example 43.** Refer to the facts in *Examples 41* and *42*. Assume that during 2006, T Corporation's taxable income, including the equipment and stock sales, is $38,000. This figure is computed using the modified C corporation rules. At this point, the TIL is greater than the PLA of $20,000, so the PLA is treated as the taxable built-in gain. The corporation then computes its NUL. In its first S corporation year, the NUL is the same as the net unrealized built in gain, $60,000. As a result, the net realized built-in-gain (NRBIG) for the year is $20,000 (the lesser of PLA of $20,000, TIL $38,000, and NUL $60,000).
>
> If the corporation had sold the land at a gain of $40,000 instead of selling the stock, the total gain for the first S corporation year would have been $67,000 ($40,000 gain from land + $27,000 gain from equipment). However, only $60,000 of this gain would be potentially subject to the § 1374 tax because T's NUL is the maximum amount subject to the tax. Moreover, assuming that its TIL is $38,000, the gain would be further limited to $38,000.
>
> In subsequent years, the NUL is computed by subtracting all net recognized built-in gains to date from the original net unrealized built-in gain. In this manner, the net unrealized built in gain may act as the limiting factor on the total net recognized built-in gains during the ten year recognition period.

In determining the built-in gains tax, the net recognized built-in gain (after applying all limitations) is reduced by any NOL and capital loss carryforward from C corporate years. In addition, business tax credit carryforwards arising in a C year can be used to reduce the tax.[123] Any net recognized built-in gain not subject to tax because of the TIL is carried over to the following year and treated as if it occurred in that year. The calculation of the tax is summarized below.

---

[123] § 1374(b)(2) and (3).

	Net recognized built-in gain	$ x,xxx
−	NOL carryforward from C year	(xxx)
=	Tax base	$ x,xxx
×	Top corporate tax rate	× xx%
=	Potential tax	$ x,xxx
−	Business credit and AMT carryforward from C year	(xxx)
=	Tax	$ x,xxx

Example 44. Refer to the facts in *Example 42*. Assume that T sold the land for $70,000 in its first S corporation year, but did not sell the equipment or stock. T recognizes a $40,000 gain, which is also the total PLA for the year. The TIL is $38,000 and the NUL is $60,000. Assume T also has a NOL carryforward of $3,000 from C corporation years. The corporation's built in gains tax is:

Lesser of:		
PLA	$40,000	
NUL	$60,000	
TIL	$38,000	$38,000
Less NOL carryforward		(3,000)
Taxable amount		$35,000
Tax rate		× 35%
Built in gains tax		$12,250

After the S corporation calculates its built-in gains tax for the year, it needs to make some additional computations:

1. If the TIL is the least of the three net recognized built-in gain measures, the corporation will need to determine its recognized built-in gain carryforward to the next year.

2. The corporation must apportion the tax as a reduction to the income items flowing through to the shareholders, as well as the year's increment to the AAA.

3. The corporation must compute its NUL for its next taxable year.

For the corporation in *Example 44* above, the calculations are shown below.

Adjustment to next year's PLA to reflect the gain carryforward arising from the TIL for the current year.

Lesser of NUL ($60,000) or PLA ($40,000)	$ 40,000
Subtract TIL, if less	(38,000)
Gain carryforward to add to next year's PLA	$ 2,000

Adjustment to next year's NUL:

NUL at beginning of current year	$ 60,000
Less net recognized built-in gain of current year	(38,000)
NUL for next year	$ 22,000

The corporation must then subtract its built-in gains tax from the income items that created the built-in gain in order to determine the pass-through of items to the shareholders. Assuming that the recognized built-in gain of $40,000 was a § 1231 gain, the corporation would reduce this gain by the tax of $12,250 and pass through $27,750 of § 1231 gain ($40,000 − $12,250) to its shareholders. Assuming that the corporation had a net ordinary loss of $2,000, to yield the TIL of $38,000, the corporation would pass the loss of $2,000 through to its shareholder's and the year's net addition to the AAA would be $25,750 computed as follows:

§ 1231 gain	$ 40,000
Built in gains tax	(12,250)
Ordinary loss	(2,000)
Net increment to AAA	$ 25,750

LIFO RECAPTURE TAX

A corporation using the LIFO method of accounting for inventories in its last taxable year before an S election becomes effective must include in taxable income for its last C corporation year an additional amount, called the LIFO recapture amount.

The LIFO recapture amount is the excess of the inventory's value under FIFO (lower of cost or market) over its actual LIFO basis as of the end of the corporation's last C corporation taxable year.[124] The increase in tax liability is referred to as the LIFO recapture tax and is payable in four equal installments, with the first installment due on the due date of the corporation's last C corporation return and the subsequent payments due on the due dates of the first three S corporation returns.[125] No interest is due if the required installments are paid on a timely basis, and there is no requirement that estimated tax payments be made with respect to any LIFO recapture tax due.[126] Finally, the inventory's basis is increased by the LIFO recapture amount. Any additional appreciation attributable to the inventory (i.e., excess of fair market value over its FIFO basis) will be subject to the built-in gains tax as the inventory is sold. However, if the corporation does not report a decrement from its initial S corporation LIFO layer during its recognition period, it will not recognize income as a built-in gain.

> **Example 45.** H Corporation converts to S corporation status for 2005. H used the LIFO method of accounting for its inventory in 2004 and had an ending LIFO inventory basis of $90,000. At the end of 2004, the inventory's actual fair market value was $175,000 and its FIFO value was $150,000. H must add the $60,000 LIFO recapture amount (FIFO value of $150,000 − $90,000 LIFO value) to its 2004 taxable income. Assuming a 35 percent corporate tax rate, H Corporation's 2004 tax liability is increased by $21,000, the LIFO recapture tax. Thus, H must pay $5,250 (one-fourth) of the LIFO recapture tax with its 2004 corporate tax return and the remaining three installments of $5,250 each must be paid with H's next three tax returns. Note also that after adjusting the inventory's basis to $150,000, there is $25,000 of remaining unrealized appreciation that may be subject to the built-in gains tax as the inventory is sold. However, the future gains will be calculated by the LIFO method.

---

[124] § 1363(d)(3).

[125] § 1363(d)(2)(B).

[126] § 6655(g)(4).

ESTIMATED TAXES

S corporations are required to pay estimated taxes for (1) excessive passive investment income taxes (§ 1375), and (2) taxes on built-in gains (§ 1374). The computations of estimated taxes generally follow the rules applicable to C corporations.[127]

DISPOSITION OF OWNERSHIP INTEREST

Based on the entity theory, sales of stock by shareholders of an S corporation result in capital gain or loss. This, of course, is identical to how stock sales of a C corporation are treated. However, the amount of the gain or loss will differ since an S shareholder's basis is adjusted for income, losses, and distributions whereas a C shareholder's basis is not. All other stock transfers also follow the rules of an exchange or gift of a capital asset. This is a significant advantage for the S (or C) corporate shareholder when compared with the complicated and often unfavorable rules of the partnership. Shareholders who sell or otherwise dispose of their stock must report their share of the S corporation's current-year items, based either on the per-day allocation method or the interim closing-of-the-books method.

WORTHLESS SECURITIES

S and C shareholders who hold worthless securities, including stock and debt, are subject to the same provisions with one exception. The S corporation's flow-through rules apply *before* the deduction for worthless stock or debt. The loss on worthless securities is treated as though it occurred on the last day of the *shareholder's* taxable year (not the S corporation's year) from the sale or exchange of a capital asset. Thus, it is possible for stock to become worthless before corporate activities are completed. In addition, if the S corporation's year ends *after* the stockholder's year ends, worthlessness could occur before the flow-through is available. This potential loss of deduction could be a serious disadvantage to shareholders.

The deduction for worthless stock is a capital loss unless the stock qualifies for ordinary loss treatment under § 1244.[128] Bad debts also are capital losses unless the shareholder can establish that they are business bad debts.[129] For example, the debts may have arisen as a result of a business transaction or the shareholder's employment status with the corporation. Business bad debts are ordinary losses. Nonbusiness bad debts are short-term capital losses.

CORPORATE LIQUIDATION

Generally, provisions governing liquidations and reorganizations for C corporations are applicable to S corporations (see Chapter 20)

---

[127] See § 6655 for estimated taxes applicable to C corporations.

[128] Compare §§ 165(g) and 1367(b)(3) with § 1244(a).

[129] Compare §§ 166(a) and (d).

TAX PLANNING

CHOICE OF ENTITY: COMPARING S CORPORATIONS, C CORPORATIONS, PARTNERSHIPS, AND LLCS

No doubt one of the most common questions asked by a taxpayer who is anticipating starting a new business or has an existing business concerns the form of organization that should be used. That decision has probably never been as confusing as it is today. For years, nontax factors, specifically the desire to limit an individual's liability, often was the key determinant in the choice of entity decision. Professional advisors, wishing to minimize the owner's personal liability, usually encouraged the owner to incorporate and secure the liability protection that the corporate entity offered. Assuming the owner took the advice, the only decision left from a tax perspective was whether the corporation would elect to be treated under the rules of Subchapter S or operate as a regular corporation subject to the rules of Subchapter C.

But the introduction of the limited liability company (now authorized in all 50 states) has made the choice of entity decision far more difficult. This new creature, which provides limited liability yet is taxed as a partnership, has added an important new dimension to the business organization question. Business owners who seek limited liability are no longer constrained to accept the corporate form and the C or S tax treatment that accompanies it. They may now opt for partnership tax treatment provided by limited liability companies and still obtain the protection that was formerly available only with a corporation. In short, the limited liability company has for the most part made the liability factor moot. Consequently, the decision now turns on other critical factors, which for small business owners include tax considerations.

A complete comparison of these entities and the advantages and disadvantages of operating each can fill volumes and is beyond the scope of this text. Nevertheless, Exhibit 23-6 identifies some of the key transactions in the life of a business and explains how each of the various entities would be treated.

EXHIBIT 23-6
Comparative Analysis of Business Forms

Items for Comparison	Proprietorship / Proprietor	Partnership / Partner	S Corporation / Shareholder	C Corporation / Shareholder
1. What are the restrictions on the number of owners or who may be an owner?	One owner who must be an individual	None, except there must be at least two owners	No more than 100 shareholders who must be individuals, estates, certain trusts, charities, pensions and ESOPs	None.
2. Are owners liable for business debts that they have not personally guaranteed?	Yes, except if single-member LLC	Yes, for general partners but no for limited partners or LLC members	No	No
3. What are the appropriate tax forms and schedules and who files them?	Schedules C, SE, and all supporting schedules and forms	Form 1065 and Schedules K-1 are prepared by partnership; partners report on Schedules E, SE, and other supporting schedules	Form 1120S and its Schedules K-1 are prepared by corporation; shareholders report on Schedule E and other supporting schedules	Form 1120 and all supporting schedules are filed for the C corporation; shareholders report dividend income on Schedule B
4. Who is the taxpayer?	Proprietor	Partners	Shareholders except tax on built-in gains, excess passive investment income, and LIFO recapture	C corporation: its shareholders are also taxed on dividend income when corporate earnings are distributed
5. Do owners have self-employment (SE) income from the business?	Yes, the net income from Schedule C	Yes, each *general* partner's share of net (SE) income plus guaranteed payments; for *limited* partners, only guaranteed payments from services	No	No
6. Must the business's taxable year be the same as that of the majority owners?	Yes	Generally, but a different year may be used if the partnership has natural business year or pays a tax on deferred income	Same as partnership	No, any period may be used except for personal service corporation
7. Are contributions of assets for an ownership interest taxable transactions?	No	No, same as proprietorship	No, *if* parties to the exchange own more than 80 percent of the corporation after the contribution, but otherwise, a taxable exchange with no carryover of tax attributes	Same as S corporation

EXHIBIT 23-6
Continued

Items for Comparison	Proprietorship / Proprietor	Partnership / Partner	S Corporation / Shareholder	C Corporation / Shareholder
8. Are distributions of cash includible income to owners?	No	No, except a distribution in excess of the partner's basis in the partnership is treated as a partial sale of the ownership interest	No, unless distribution exceeds shareholder's basis or from accumulated E&P	Yes, if from the C corporation's earnings and profits
9. Do property distributions result in taxable income to the business or the owners?	No: basis is preserved in distributed property	No, with several exceptions	Yes, S corporation must recognize realized gain—but not loss—if a nonliquidating distribution; shareholders have dividend income if the FMV of the property exceeds AAA	Yes. Corporation recognizes gain, but not loss: shareholders have dividend income to extent of property's value or E&P
10. May an owner enter into taxable transactions (sales, loans, etc.) with the business?	No	Yes, when acting in a nonpartner capacity, but subject to related-party restrictions	Yes, subject to related-party restrictions	Same as S corporation percentage owners
11. May an accrual basis business deduct accrued expenses to cash basis owners?	No, not applicable	No, deductible only when paid (except see 12 below)	Same as partnership	Same as partnership and S corporation for more than 50 percent owners
12. Are accrued expenses of the business includible income to cash basis owners? If yes, when?	No, not applicable	Yes, when received, except guaranteed salary and interest on capital are includible when accrued	Yes, when received	Yes, when received
13. Can owners be employees of the business and be paid salaries subject to employment taxes and withholding?	No	No	Yes	Yes
14. Are fringe benefits for owner/ employees deductible expenses?	No	Yes, but partner must include in gross income	Yes, but a more than 2 percent shareholder must include in gross income	Yes

EXHIBIT 23-6
Continued

Items for Comparison	Proprietorship / Proprietor	Partnership / Partner	S Corporation / Shareholder	C Corporation / Shareholder
15. May the business use the cash method?	Yes	Yes, depending on income and type of business unless it qualifies as a tax shelter or has a C corporation as a partner	Yes, depending on income and type of business unless it qualifies as a tax shelter	No, unless gross receipts do not exceed $5 million or it qualifies under "type of business" exception
16. Is the business a conduit with the original character of the items flowing through to its owners as of the last day of the business's taxable year?	Yes	Yes	Yes	No, the business is an entity and the flow-through concept is not applicable
17. How are capital gains and losses of the business treated?	As though received by the proprietor	Flow through to each partner	Same as partnership	Net capital gain includible in corporate taxable income and taxed at regular rates; net capital losses carried back 3, forward 5 years, with no deduction against ordinary income
18. How is dividend income received by the business treated?	Includible income as though received by the proprietor (may be subject to reduced rate)	Flows through to each partner as dividend income (may be subject to reduced rate)	Same as partnership	Includible income with a dividend-received deduction
19. How are charitable contributions treated?	An itemized deduction as though contributed by the proprietor	Flow through to each partner as an itemized deduction	Same as partnership	Deductions may not exceed 10 percent of taxable income before certain deductions
20. Who pays state and local income taxes on the business net income and how are they treated?	Proprietor; an itemized deduction as though paid by the proprietor	Each partner; an itemized deduction	Same as partnership, except some state and local income taxes are assessed on the S corporation	Deductible expense
21. How are tax credits treated?	Offsets proprietor's tax	Qualifying credits flow through to each partner subject to any limitations applicable at the partner level	Same as partnership	Computed at the corporate level and reduces corporate tax liability
22. How is net ordinary income treated?	Includible with proprietor's A.G.I.	Flows through to each partner	Same as partnership	Included in corporate taxable income
23. How is net ordinary loss treated?	Reduction of proprietor's A.G.I.	Flows through to each partner, potentially deductible up to that partner's basis in the partnership; any excess is carried forward	Same as partnership except that basis rules differ	Subject to carryover rules (back two years and forward 20 years or forward 20 years only) and deductible against net ordinary income

EXHIBIT 23-6
Continued

Items for Comparison	Proprietorship / Proprietor	Partnership / Partner	S Corporation / Shareholder	C Corporation / Shareholder
24. How are AMT adjustments and preferences treated?	Included on proprietor's return	Flow through to partners	Same as partnership	Included in corporation's AMTI; ACE adjustment required: small corporations exempt
25. Is § 291(a)(1) applicable?	No	No	Yes, if C corporation for any of three prior tax years	Yes
26. How are items allocated among the owners?	Not applicable	According to profit and loss ratio or may be specially allocated	According to stock ownership ratio; special rules for years of termination or dispositions	Not applicable
27. Is the basis of business assets adjusted when an ownership interest is sold?	Not applicable	Yes, if partnership has elected the optional adjustment to basis	No, unless § 338(h)(10) election is in effect	No, unless § 338(h)(10) election is in effect
28. Is basis affected by business liabilities?	Not applicable	Yes, a partner's basis includes his or her share of partnership liabilities	No, except for loans directly from shareholders	No
29. Is basis affected by business income, gains, deductions, and losses?	Not applicable	Yes, all income and gains increase basis and all expenses and losses (that flow through) decrease basis	Yes, same as partnership	No
30. What is the character of gains and losses on the sale of a business interest?	Each asset is treated as sold individually and the character of the gain or loss is dependent on that asset	Capital gain or loss except ordinary income to the extent of partner's share of unrealized receivables, depreciation recapture, or inventory. Some gain may be taxed at 25 percent of 28 percent	Capital gains and losses, except losses may qualify as § 1244 ordinary losses if the corporation meets certain requirements. Some gain may be taxed at 28 percent (but not at 25 percent).	Same as S corporation, except no 28 percent portion. Special rules apply if stock is § 1202 stock.
31. Must a reasonable salary be allocated to family members performing services for the business?	No	Yes	Yes	No

PROBLEM MATERIALS

DISCUSSION QUESTIONS

23-1 *Eligibility Requirements.* May the following corporations elect Subchapter S? If not, explain why.

   a. A corporation is 100 percent owned by another corporation.

   b. A corporation has 101 shareholders, including Mr. and Mrs. V and Mr. and Mrs. Z.

   c. A family corporation is owned by a father and his three children. Since the children are under age 18, their shares are held in a trust fund.

   d. A corporation has 1,000 shares of common stock outstanding and 500 shares of authorized but unissued preferred stock.

   e. A corporation has 70 unrelated shareholders, and 35 shareholders who are all descendants of Mr. and Mrs. A.

23-2 *Eligibility Requirements.* Y corporation's shareholders want to elect S status. Do any of the following facts about the corporation prevent the election? Why?

   a. It has a wholly owned subsidiary.

   b. It has 99 shareholders who own their shares solely in their own name and a married couple who own the stock jointly.

   c. It has 10 shareholders, and one is the estate of a former shareholder. It is expected that the shares held by the estate will be distributed to three U.S. citizens and one Englishman who is a U.S. resident.

   d. It has 73 shareholders plus L, who owns no shares but serves as custodian for shares owned by her two minor children.

   e. It has 15 owners of common stock and no owners of its authorized preferred stock.

   f. It has 10 owners of voting common stock and five owners of nonvoting common. Except for voting, all other rights of the two sets of common stock are identical.

   g. A corporation was formed many years ago by X, Y and Z. Several generations later there are 210 shareholders, 150 of whom are descendants of X, Y and Z.

23-3 *Eligibility Requirements and Termination.* Refer to *Problem 23-2* and assume Y corporation made its S election in 2002. Do the following facts about the corporation terminate the election? When? Why? Can the shareholders prevent the termination?

   a. Refer to a above. It has $5 billion in sales with various customers in the United States and $10,000 sales that it places through its subsidiary.

   b. Refer to b above. The married couple is divorced December 29, 2005, and each receives one-half the shares in Y that were owned jointly by them prior to that date.

   c. Refer to c above. The Englishman decides it is time to return home and moves to London England, on March 3, 2005. He continues to own five shares of Y and gives up his residency in the United States.

   d. Refer to e above. M exchanges her 500 shares of Y common for 700 shares of Y preferred. Although the number of shares differs, the dollar value of M's holdings remains the same.

   e. The corporation elects to revoke its S election. Holders of 70 percent of the stock consent to the revocation. The other shareholders do not consent.

   f. On June 5, 2005 a 20 percent shareholder transfers her stock to a C corporation she owns.

   g. Y has $15,000 accumulated earnings and profits (AE&P) from C corporate years, and 30 percent of its gross receipts in 2003, 2004, and 2005 are from dividends and interest on investments.

23-4 *Stock Requirements.* A mother wishes to establish an S corporation with her two children. However, she is concerned about the one class of stock requirement. She does not want to provide her children with voting control but does wish to give them 60 percent of the stock. Can she achieve her wishes? Explain.

23-5 *Election.* F, M, and T are shareholders of a calendar year corporation. On February 15, 2005 they are advised they should elect Subchapter S status. All agree to the election. However, they state that they purchased a 10 percent ownership interest from V on January 4, 2005. V sold his interest because he said he never wanted to have any contact with F, M, or T again. Can the corporation make an S election for 2005? Explain.

23-6 *Election.* B, C, and D are shareholders, each owning 1,000 shares. On February 20, 2005 they are advised to elect S status for 2005. Can they make the election for all of 2005 under the following circumstances? Explain.

    a. B purchased 10 shares from R on January 5, 2005. R is hitchhiking across Europe and cannot be located until April 1, 2005.

    b. C sells 10 percent of her interest (after the election) July 7, 2005 to X. X refuses to agree to the S election and wants it terminated.

23-7 *Elections.* This year, RJ, an individual, formed ABC Corporation. ABC commenced business on April 17, 2005. The corporation issued its first shares on March 2, 2005. RJ transferred property (fair market value $100,000, adjusted basis $20,000) to the corporation March 28, 2005 in a nontaxable § 351 exchange. ABC intends to use the calendar year for tax purposes. For the years in question ABC does not have any attribute that would disqualify it from S status.

    a. By what date must ABC make an election to be an S corporation if the election is to be in effect for the corporation's first taxable year, assuming the corporation does not utilize any relief provisions?

    b. Assume that ABC discovers, on February 15, 2006 that it has not made a timely S election for its year ended December 31, 2005. Could the corporation make an election to take effect for its taxable year beginning January 1, 2006?

    c. If the corporation made an S election for its taxable year beginning January 1, 2006, would it have any exposure to the built-in gains tax?

    d. Assume that on February 15, 2006 ABC discovered that no S election had been made. What would be needed for the corporation to make an S election to take effect for its year 2005 tax year?

    e. Assume the same facts in (b) above except that the corporation discovered that it had not made an S election as of April 15, 2006. What would be required for the corporation to make an S election for its 2005 taxable year?

23-8 *Termination of the Election.* Compare the effects of an intentional revocation, an unintentional violation of the eligibility requirements, and a termination due to the receipt of excessive passive investment income.

23-9 *Termination of the Election.* A calendar year S corporation unexpectedly receives a government contract on April 3, 2005. The profits from the contract in 2005 will be substantial. The three equal shareholders wish to revoke the election for 2005. Can they? Explain.

23-10 *Passive Investment Income.* An S corporation with AE&P of $5,000 is expected to receive 30 percent of its gross income from rents but only 18 percent of its net income from these rents. Will the excess passive investment income test be violated? Assume the S corporation's taxable year does not end for seven months and all income is earned equally over the year.

    a. Can any action be taken during the next seven months to ensure the test will not be violated?

b. Could the corporation take any corrective action if it does not determine the nature of its gross receipts until after the end of its tax year?

23-11 *Employee-Owner.* Which of the three organizational forms—S corporation, C corporation, or partnership—treats owners who work for the business in the following manner?

a. The owner's compensation is a deductible business expense.

b. The owner's compensation is subject to FICA withholding.

c. The employee benefits are deductible expenses.

d. The employee benefits are excluded from the owner-employee's gross income.

23-12 *Schedule K-1.* Why must each shareholder of an S corporation be provided with a Schedule K-1?

23-13 *Business Income.* How is each of the following items treated by an S corporation?

a. Dividend income

b. Accrued rental expense to a shareholder

c. Net capital gain

d. Distribution of assets with a market value in excess of basis

23-14 *Family Ownership.* A taxpayer operates a retail store as an S corporation. He has a 16-year-old daughter and an 11-year-old son.

a. Can he employ either or both of them in the business and deduct their salaries?

b. Can they be shareholders in the S corporation?

c. Can a trust be formed to hold the shares of stock owned by a minor child?

23-15 *Family Ownership.* A mother wants to transfer a substantial portion of her ownership in an S corporation to a trust for her son and daughter. She wants to transfer value but retain voting control. She also wants to be able to exercise some control over how the assets of the trust are distributed. However, she is willing to use an independent trustee to manage the assets.

a. Can she transfer nonvoting stock to the children and retain voting shares without creating a second class of stock?

b. If she transfers stock to a trust, but retains the ability to remove the shares from the trust, will she disqualify the corporation from S status?

c. How could she create a QSST for each child? What restrictions would the trust face? Who would pay the tax on the income of the corporation allocated to the trusts' shares?

d. What would be the advantages of using an ESBT? Who would pay the tax on the income of the corporation allocated to the trust's shares?

23-16 *Stock and Debt Basis.* What is the significance of stock basis and debt basis to a shareholder? How does a shareholder adjust basis for the activity of an S corporation for a year? How does a shareholder obtain debt basis?

23-17 *Property Distributions.* What effect do noncash distributions have on the S corporation and on the shareholder if the S corporation has no AE&P, and:

a. The property's market value exceeds its basis, or

b. The property's basis exceeds its market value?

23-18 *Distributions.* When do cash distributions result in includible income to the S shareholder?

23-19 *Post-Termination Transition Period.* What is a post-termination transition period? How is it useful?

23-20 *Basic Comparison.* List the tax advantages and the tax disadvantages of an S corporation when compared with:

    a. A partnership.

    b. A C corporation.

PROBLEMS

23-21 *Termination of Election.* T, the sole shareholder and president of T, Inc., had operated a successful automobile dealership as a regular C corporation for many years. In 2001, however, the corporation elected S corporation status. After T's unexpected illness in 2002, the corporation sold most of its assets and retained only a small used car operation. In 2003 and 2004 T, Inc. had paid the tax on excessive passive income and had AE&P (from its C corporation years) at the end of both years. In 2005 the corporation paid no dividends and had the following income and expenses:

Interest income	$50,000
Dividend income	5,000
Gain from prior installment sale	30,000
Used car sales	40,000
Cost of sales	20,000

Is the S election terminated, and if so, when?

23-22 *Consequences of Revocation of an S Election.* In July 2005 S Inc., a calendar year corporation, revoked its S election as of August 1, 2005. The corporation's taxable income for January through December 2005 is $432,000, and the shareholders do not elect to perform an interim closing of the corporate books.

    a. What tax return(s) must S file for the year, and what are the due dates of the return(s)?

    b. Compute S's corporate taxable income for the short year for the (1) S corporation and (2) C corporation.

    c. Compute the C corporation's Federal income tax.

23-23 *Net Income from Operations.* A and B are MDs in the AB partnership. Because of limited liability considerations, their attorney has advised them to incorporate. A typical year for the MDs (who are equal partners) is as follows:

Revenues	$400,000
Operating expenses	190,000
Charitable contributions	10,000
Owner compensation	200,000

    a. Calculate AB's ordinary net income if it is taxed as (1) a partnership or (2) an S corporation.

    b. Calculate the effect on A's ordinary income if AB is taxed as (1) a partnership; (2) and S corporation; or (3) a C corporation.

    c. Ignoring limited liability considerations, should the partners incorporate? If so, should they elect S status?

    d. If A and B desire partnership tax treatment, is there any business entity that would meet their needs?

23-24 | *Net Income.* A calendar year S corporation has the following information for the current taxable year:

Sales	$180,000
Cost of goods sold	(70,000)
Dividend income	5,000
Net capital loss	(4,000)
Salary to Z	12,000
Life insurance for Z	500
Other operating expenses	40,000
Cash distributions to owners	20,000

Assume Z is single and her only other income is $30,000 salary from an unrelated employer. She is a 20 percent owner with a $10,000 basis in the S stock at the beginning of the year. Calculate the S corporation's net ordinary income and Z's adjusted gross income and ending basis in the S corporation stock.

23-25 | *Net Losses.* A calendar year S corporation has the following information for the current taxable year:

Sales	$ 180,000
Cost of goods sold	(130,000)
Net capital loss	(6,000)
Salary to Z	18,000
Charitable contributions	1,000
Other operating expenses	65,000
Dividend income	4,000

Assume Z is single and her only other income is $30,000 salary from an unrelated employer. She is a 40 percent owner with a $10,000 basis in the S stock and no corporate debt owed to her. Calculate the S corporation's net ordinary loss, Z's adjusted gross income, and the character and amount of S corporate items that flow through to her.

23-26 | *Net Income/Loss and Basis.* For 2005, an S corporation reported an ordinary loss of $100,000, a net capital loss of $10,000, and a § 1231 gain of $20,000. M owns 10 percent of the stock and at the beginning of the year had a basis in her stock of $7,500. In addition, M loaned the corporation $5,000 during the year. She materially participates in the S corporation.

a.   Compute her deductible loss.

b.   The following year, the corporation reported ordinary income of $70,000 and made no distributions. How does this income affect M's basis in the stock and the debt?

23-27   *Allocations.* V owns 500 shares of stock of an S corporation with 2,000 shares outstanding. The calendar year S corporation's records show the following information:

Net ordinary income	$200,000
Net capital loss	(10,000)

Calculate V's share of the items if on March 15 he sells:

a.   200 of his shares of stock;

b.   All 500 shares of his stock and the per-day allocation method is used; or

c.   All 500 shares of his stock and the interim closing of the books method is used. The records reveal that through March 15, net ordinary income was $60,000 and net capital loss was $ 10,000.

23-28 *Allocations.* D owns 25 percent of Corp stock. Corp has ordinary income (from page 1 of Form 1120S) of $60,000 through July 31 of the current year and $40,000 for the remainder of the year. Calculate D's includible income in the following cases:

    a. D sells 10 percent of Corp on July 31 and keeps 15 percent.

    b. D sells all of her Corp stock July 31 and (1) no election is made or (2) the interim closing of books method is elected.

23-29 *Basis.* A calendar year business reports the following information as of the end of 2004 and 2005:

	2004	2005
Accounts payable to suppliers	$10,000	$11,000
Note payable to City Bank	40,000	37,000
Note payable to H	12,000	10,000
Cash distributions to owners		20,000
Net ordinary income	15,000	

H, a 30 percent owner, had a basis in the business at the end of 2004 of $9,000. Calculate H's basis in his ownership interest at the end of 2005 assuming the business is

    a. A partnership

    b. An S corporation

23-30 *Deductibility of Losses by Shareholders.* B, Inc. was incorporated and its shareholders made a valid S election for B's first taxable year. At the beginning of the current year, Shareholder Z had a basis of $14,500 in his B stock and held a $10,000 note receivable from B with a $10,000 basis. For the current year Z was allocated a $32,000 ordinary loss and a $4,000 capital loss from the corporation. B did not make any distributions to its shareholders during the current year.

    a. How much of each allocated loss may Z deduct in the current year?

    b. What happens to any losses in excess of the limits in (a) above?

    c. How much basis will Z have in his B stock and his note receivable at the end of the current year?

23-31 *Basis Adjustments—Restoration.* Refer to the facts in *Problem 23-30* above. In the next year Z is allocated $7,000 of ordinary income and $5,500 of tax-exempt income from B. B did not make any distributions to its shareholders during the year. What effect will these income allocations have on Z's basis in his B stock and note receivable?

23-32 *Losses and Basis.* J, Inc. is an S corporation that reported the following selected items as of December 31, 2005.

Ordinary loss (from Form 1120S, page 1)	$(30,000)
Long-term capital gain	500
Tax-exempt interest income	1,000
Notes payable to banks	30,000
(1/1/05 balance = $20,000)	
Notes payable to LJ	5,000
(1/1/05 balance = $0)	

The corporation is owned 60 percent by LJ and 40 percent by RS. At the beginning of the year, they had a basis in their *stock* of $12,000 and $10,000, respectively. How much income or loss will each of the shareholders report for 2005?

23-33   *Basis.* M, a 40 percent owner, has a basis in the S corporate stock of $15,000 and in a note receivable from the S corporation of $8,000. Compute the basis of the stock and the note and the amount of the ordinary loss and income that flow through to M in 2005 and 2006.

    a.   The S corporation has a net operating loss of $45,000 in 2005.

    b.   The S corporation has a net operating income of $20,000 in 2006.

23-34   *Basis.* A calendar year S corporation has the following information for 2005 and 2006:

	2005	2006
Net ordinary income (or loss)...............	$(50,000)	$10,000
Dividend income	5,000	2,000

X, an unmarried 60 percent shareholder, has a basis in the stock on January 1, 2005 of $18,000 and a note receivable from the corporation for $12,000. X's only other income is salary from an unrelated business.

    a.   Calculate X's basis in the stock and in the note after the above income and loss are recorded for 2005.

    b.   Calculate X's basis in the stock and in the note after the above income items are recorded for 2006.

    c.   Assume the corporation paid the $12,000 note on April 3, 2006. Calculate X's basis in the stock after the above income distributions are recorded for 2006, and calculate the effect on X's adjusted gross income for all 2006 items, including the payment of the note.

23-35   *Inside and Outside Basis.* XYZ is an S corporation owned equally by three shareholders. X has often disagreed with the other shareholders over business matters and now believes he should withdraw from the corporation. X's basis in his stock is $50,000. The corporation's balance sheet appears as follows:

Cash	$100,000
Accounts receivable..................................	50,000
Land..	30,000
Equipment (net).....................................	10,000
Accounts payable	30,000
Note payable to X	10,000
Shareholders' equity	150,000

The equipment's market value is approximately the same as its net book value, but the land is now valued at $60,000. X sells all of his stock to W for $60,000.

    How much gain must X recognize?

23-36   *Family Ownership.* K operates a small retail store as a proprietorship. Annual net ordinary income is expected to be $60,000 next year. The estimated value of her services to the business is $25,000. K's 14-year-old son is interested in the business. She is considering giving him a 30 percent ownership interest in the business. If she does this, she will be paid a salary of $25,000. K files as head of household and does not itemize deductions. Neither she nor her son has any other includible income. Ignore all payroll and self-employment taxes in the following computations.

    a.   Determine next year's tax savings that will be achieved if K establishes an S corporation with her son at the beginning of the year compared with continuing the business as a proprietorship.

    b.   Will K or her son have any includible income if they exchange the appreciated proprietorship assets for the 70 and 30 percent ownership interests, respectively, in the S corporation?

    c.   What advice should you give K on establishing and operating the S corporation?

23-37 *Property Distributions.* M receives the following equipment from an S corporation as a distribution of profits.

Asset	Cost	Accumulated Depreciation	Basis	Fair Value Market
Equipment	$10,000	$7,900	$2,100	$2,280

The equipment was used in the business for four years of its five-year MACRS life and will be a nonbusiness asset to M. M is a 60 percent owner and has a basis in the stock of $11,000 before the property distribution. Calculate the following amounts.

a. The S corporation's recognized gain
b. M's basis in the equipment
c. The effect on M's basis in the stock
d. The effect on M's adjusted gross income

23-38 *Property Distributions.* Refer to *Problem 23-37.* Calculate the same amounts if M's basis in the S corporation, before the distribution, is $1,200 instead of the $11,000.

23-39 *Property Distribution.* J purchases 20 percent of an S corporation's stock for $50,000 when its records show the following:

	Fair Market Value	Basis
Cash	$ 40,000	$ 40,000
Inventory	60,000	45,000
Land—investment	80,000	20,000
Other operating assets	100,000	80,000
Liabilities	(30,000)	(30,000)
Net assets	$250,000	$155,000

Six months later, all of the land is distributed in equal plats to the shareholders. What is the effect of this distribution on J?

23-40 *Cash and Property Distributions—No AE&P.* An S corporation with no AE&P distributes $10,000 cash, land ($7,000 FMV and $4,000 basis), and desks ($3,000 FMV and $4,500 basis) to *each* of its three equal shareholders. (That is, $30,000 in cash, $21,000 in land, and $9,000 in desks was distributed in total.) One of the shareholders, T, has a basis in the stock before the distribution of $12,000 and a long-term note from the corporation of $5,000. The other two shareholders have a basis in the stock before the distribution of $40,000 and no debt from the corporation. Calculate the effect of the distribution on the A.G.I. of each of the shareholders.

23-41 *Computation of AAA and Basis.* J formed R Corporation in 1986. The corporation operated as a C corporation from 1986 until 1995, when it elected to be taxed as an S corporation. At the beginning of the current year, J had a basis in his stock of $100,000. The corporation's balance in the AAA at the beginning of the current year was $143,000. R's records for the current year reveal the following information:

Sales	$ 300,000
Cost of goods sold	(120,000)
Miscellaneous operating expenses	50,000
Salary to J	40,000
Nondeductible portion of entertainment	4,000
Tax-exempt interest income	13,000
Expenses related to tax-exempt interest income	3,000
Capital gain	7,000
Capital loss	(2,000)
Charitable contribution	5,000
Cash distribution to J	10,000

The corporation also had AE&P from C years of $4,000.

Compute J's basis in his stock and the corporation's balance in the AAA as of the end of the taxable year. Assume J is the sole shareholder.

23-42 *Treatment of Distributions: Converted C Corporation.* Assume the same facts as in *Problem 23-41* above. Explain the tax treatment to J if he receives the following distributions during the year.
a. $100,000
b. $220,000
c. $260,000

23-43 *Cash and Property Distributions—AE&P.* S, Inc. had previously been a regular C corporation, but elected to be taxed as an S corporation in 1982. It is owned equally by J and G, who have a basis in their stock of $100,000 each at the beginning of the current year. Also at the beginning of the current year, the corporation had the following balances:

Accumulated adjustments account	$50,000
Previously taxed income	40,000
Accumulated earnings and profits	30,000
Other adjustments account	0

During the current year, the corporation had ordinary income of $35,000 and distributed IM stock worth $75,000 to J and cash of $75,000 to G. The stock was purchased four years ago for $50,000.
a. What are the tax effects of the distribution on the corporation?
b. What are the consequences to each of the shareholders?

23-44 *Cash Distributions—AE&P.* A calendar year S corporation has the following balance on January 1, 2005:

Accumulated adjustments account	$13,000
Previously taxed income	2,000
Accumulated earnings and profits	6,000
Other adjustments account	0

The S corporation records show $12,000 net ordinary income, $4,000 tax-exempt income net of related expenses, and $55,000 cash distributions for 2005. Y owns 70 percent of the stock. Her basis in the stock on January 1, 2005 was $7,000, and she has a note receivable from the corporation of $5,000. Y is single, and her only other income is salary from an unrelated business.

a. Calculate the balances in the corporate accounts as of December 31, 2005.

b. Calculate the effect on Y's adjusted gross income for 2005.

c. Calculate the basis in Y's stock and note as of December 31, 2005.

23-45 *Property Distributions—AE&P.* Assume the same facts as in *Problem 23-44* except the distribution is stock held more than one year as an investment with a market value of $55,000 and a basis of $53,000.

a. Calculate the balances in the corporate accounts as of December 31, 2005.

b. Calculate the effect on Y's adjusted gross income for 2005.

c. Calculate the basis in Y's stock and note as of December 31, 2005.

23-46 *Cash Distributions—AE&P.* D, Inc. was incorporated in 1999, and its shareholders made a valid S election for D's 2002 calendar year. At the end of the current year but before the distribution is considered, D had $19,000 of accumulated earnings and profits from 1999 through 2003, and an accumulated adjustments account of $11,000. D made only one cash distribution of $20,000 during the year, $5,000 of which was paid to shareholder M, who owns 25 percent of D's stock. After all adjustments *except* any required for the distribution, M's basis in his stock was $18,000.

a. What are the tax consequences of the distribution to M, and what is M's basis in his D stock after the distribution?

b. What are the balances in D's accumulated earnings and profits account and accumulated adjustments account after the distribution?

23-47 *Cash Distribution—AE&P.* M and J have been equal owners of an S corporation for several years. It was operated as a C corporation its first two years and as an S corporation since then. In 2005 it has $12,000 ordinary income, $2,000 tax-exempt interest income, $24,000 cash distributions, and the following balances at the end of 2004 (prior year):

Accumulated adjustments account	$8,000
Previously taxed income ($1,000 to M, $1,000 to J)	2,000
AE&P from C years	3,000

M's stock basis at the end of 2004 was $8,500 and J's was $13,000.

a. Calculate the balances in the corporate accounts as of December 31, 2005.

b. Calculate the effect on M's and J's adjusted gross income for 2005.

c. Calculate the basis in M's and J's stock as of December 31, 2005.

23-48 *Property Distribution—AE&P.* Refer to *Problem 23-47*, but assume the $24,000 distribution is of land that has a $23,000 basis.

23-49 *Excess Passive Investment Income.* A calendar year S corporation has AE&P of $15,000 from years when it was operated as a C corporation. Its records show the following:

Sales	$100,000
Cost of goods sold	(55,000)
Operating expenses.	(15,000)
Dividend income	20,000
Rental income (passive)	40,000
Rental expenses	(25,000)

The corporation is owned equally by three brothers. Determine the tax effect on the S corporation and on each brother.

23-50 *Tax on Built-in Gains.* A corporation, organized in 1983, was operated as a C corporation until Subchapter S was elected as of January 1, 2001, when it had total assets of $240,000 FMV and $185,000 basis. Assets held on that date ($80,000 market value and $50,000 basis) are distributed in 2005 when the market value is $90,000. Calculate the 2005 tax on built-in gains if 2005 taxable income, based on computations for a C corporation, is

a. $60,000

b. $20,000

23-51 *Tax on Built-in Gains.* On February 5, 2005 L Corporation, a cash basis calendar year C corporation, elected S status effective for January 1, 2005. On January 1, L's balance sheet revealed the following assets:

	Adjusted Basis	Fair Market Value
Inventory	$20,000	$85,000
Land.	30,000	70,000
Equipment	45,000	15,000

During the current year, L sold all of its inventory for $90,000. It also sold the equipment for $9,000 (L did not claim any more depreciation on the equipment this year, so its basis at the time of sale was $45,000). L's taxable income limitation is $100,000 for the current year. Compute L Corporation's built-in gains tax.

23-52 *LIFO Recapture Tax.* T Corporation converts to S corporation status for 2005. T used the LIFO method of accounting for its inventory in 2004 and had an ending LIFO inventory basis of $540,000. The ending inventory's FIFO value was $650,000 and its fair market value was $800,000.

a. What is T Corporation's LIFO recapture amount?

b. Assuming its corporate tax rate is 35 percent, what is T Corporation's LIFO recapture tax?

c. How is the LIFO recapture tax required to be paid?

23-53 *Worthless Securities.* A calendar year S corporation is bankrupt. E, a 60 percent owner for several years, will not receive any assets from the business. His basis in the stock as of January 1, 2005 was $70,000, and he has a note receivable of $25,000 from the corporation. Both are determined to be uncollectible July 1, 2005. The S corporation has a net ordinary loss during 2004 of $30,000; $20,000 before July 1 and $10,000 after July 1. E lent the corporation the $20,000 last year and $5,000 four months ago in an effort to protect his ownership interest in the business. Calculate E's adjusted gross income and capital loss carryovers if his adjusted gross income from other sources totals $120,000.

TAX RETURN PROBLEMS

23-54 *Tax Return Problem.* Individuals P and K formed P&K Corporation on March 1, 1993 to provide computer consulting services. The company has been an S corporation since its formation, and the stock ownership is divided as follows: 60 percent to P and 40 percent to K. The business code and employer identification numbers are 7389 and 24-3897625, respectively. The business office is located at 3010 East Apple Street, Atlanta, Georgia 30304. P and K live nearby at 1521 South Elm Street and 3315 East Apple Street, respectively. Their social security numbers are 403-16-5110 for P and 518-72-9147 for K.

The calendar year, cash basis corporation's December 31, 2003 balance sheet and December 31, 2004 trial balance contain the following information:

	Balance Sheet 12/31/03		Trial Balance 12/31/04	
	Debit	Credit	Debit	Credit
Cash	$ 12,000		$ 22,000	
Note receivable[(1)]...............	14,000		14,000	
Equipment[(2,3)]	150,000		190,000	
Accumulated depreciation		$ 38,000		$ 63,500
Notes payable[(3,4)]		94,000		17,200
Capital stock		10,000		10,000
Accumulated adjustments account.....................		34,000		34,000
Cash distributed to P			25,440	
Cash distributed to K			16,960	
Revenues......................				235,000
Interest income[(1)]...............				1,400
§ 1245 gain				3,500
Salary expense[(5)]...............			110,000	
Rent expense..................			12,000	
Interest expense			16,600	
Tax expense (property and payroll) ..			13,800	
Repair expense			5,800	
Depreciation expense			29,200	
Health insurance expense[(6)]			1,600	
Property insurance expense.....................			1,500	
Office supplies expense...........			3,000	
Utility expense			2,200	
Charitable contributions			500	
Totals	$ 176,000	$ 176,000	$ 464,600	$ 464,600

(1)   The note receivable is from K and is due December 31, 2009. The annual interest rate is 10 percent and K paid $1,400 on December 28, 2005.

(2)   Equipment was sold May 12, 2004 for $9,800. It was purchased new on May 1, 2003 for $10,000 and its basis when sold was $6,300.

(3)   New equipment was purchased March 1, 2004 with $5,000 cash and a $45,000 three-year note payable. The first note payment is March 1, 2005.

(4)   Notes payable are long-term except for $20,000 of the note to be paid next year.

(5)   Salary expense is composed of salary of $30,000 each to P and to K and $50,000 to unrelated employees.

(6)   Health insurance premiums paid were for the unrelated employees.

Prepare Form 1120S (including Schedules K, L, and M), and Schedule K-l for shareholder P. Complete all six pages, including responses to all questions. If any necessary information is missing in the problem, assume a logical answer and record it. Do not prepare Schedule K-l for shareholder K or other required supplemental forms at this time.

23-55   *Tax Return Problem.* During 2004 Lisa Cutter and Jeff McMullen decided they would like to start their own gourmet hamburger business. Lisa and Jeff believed that the public would love the recipes used by Lisa's mom, Tina Woodbrook. They also thought that they had the necessary experience to enter this business, since Jeff currently owned a fast-food franchise business while Lisa had experience operating a small bakery. After doing their own market research, they established Slattery's Inc. and elected to be taxed as an S corporation. The company's address is 5432 Partridge Pl., Tulsa, Oklahoma 74105 and its employer identification number is 88-7654321.

The company started modestly. After refurbishing an old gas station that it had purchased, the company opened for business on February 25, 2005. Shortly after business began, however, business boomed. By the end of 2005, the company had established two other locations.

Slattery's has three shareholders who own stock as follows:

Shareholder	Shares
Lisa Cutter	500
Jeff McMullen	200
Tina Woodbrook	300
Total outstanding	1,000

Slattery's was formed on February 1, 2005. On that date, shareholders made contributions as follows:

▸ Lisa Cutter contributed $30,000 in cash and 200 shares of MND stock, a publicly held company, which had a fair market value of $20,000. Lisa had purchased the MND stock on October 3, 1997 for $8,000.

▸ Jeff McMullen contributed equipment worth $35,000 and with a basis of $29,000.

▸ Tina Woodbrook contributed $30,000 in cash.

Assume 2005 depreciation for tax purposes is $11,500 and omit the detailed computations for depreciations from Form 4562.

The company is on the accrual basis and has chosen to use the calendar year for tax purposes. Its adjusted trial balance for *financial accounting* purposes reveals the following information:

	Debit	Credit
Cash	$279,800	
Ending inventory	16,000	
Equipment	35,000	
Land	10,000	
Building	15,000	
Improvements to building	55,000	
Accumulated depreciation		$ 9,000
Notes payable		93,000
Accounts payable		40,000
Taxes payable		8,000
Salaries payable		20,000
Capital stock		100,000
Sales		400,000
Gain on sale of MND stock		18,000
Dividend from MND Corporation		2,000
Cost of goods sold	84,000	
Legal expenses	500	
Accounting expenses	400	
Miscellaneous expenses	2,100	
Premium on life insurance policy	800	
Advertising	8,600	
Utilities	8,000	
Payroll taxes	12,500	
Salary expenses	120,000	
Insurance	9,000	
Repairs	6,500	
Charitable contributions	17,600	
Depreciation per books	9,000	
Interest expense	200	

The company has provided additional information below.

The company took a physical count of inventory on December 31, 2005 and determined that ending inventory was $16,000. Ten percent of the notes payable are due each year for the next ten years.

The legal costs were for work done by Slattery's attorney in February for drafting the articles of incorporation and by-laws. Accounting fees were paid in May for setting up the books and the accounting system. Miscellaneous expenses included a one-time $100 fee paid in February to the State of Oklahoma to incorporate.

The MND stock was sold for $38,000 on April 3, 2005. Shortly before the sale, MND had declared and paid a dividend. Slattery's received $2,000 on April 1, 2005. MND was incorporated in Delaware.

Slattery's has elected *not* to use the limited expensing provisions of Code § 179 but has otherwise claimed the maximum depreciation with respect to all assets. Any other elections required to minimize the corporation's tax liability were made.

Lisa Cutter (Social Security No. 447-52-7943) is president of the corporation and spends 90 percent of her working time in the business. She received a salary of $60,000. No other officers received compensation. Social security numbers are 306-28-6192 for Jeff and 403-34-6771 for Tina. The life insurance policy covers Lisa's life, and she has the right to name the beneficiary.

Prepare Form 1120S and other appropriate forms and schedules for Slattery's. On separate schedule(s), show all calculations used to determine all reported amounts except those for which the source is obvious or which are shown on a formal schedule to be filed with the return. If information is missing to answer a question on the return, make up an answer and circle it.

RESEARCH PROBLEMS

23-56 *Expanding an S Corporation.* L Inc., an S corporation, manufactures computers. Most of its computers are sold through individually owned retail computer stores. This year it decided it wanted to expand its operations into the retail market. To this end, it has decided to acquire Micros Unlimited, which operates a chain of computer retail stores nationwide.

If L Inc. acquires all of the stock of Micro, may it operate Micro as a C corporation? May it operate Micro as a QSub? What would be some major considerations with each form of business?

23-57 *Basis and Losses.* J and K, individuals, are equal shareholders in JK, Inc., an S corporation. For the current year, the corporation anticipates a loss of approximately $200,000. Neither shareholder has any substantial stock basis. The corporation has a $200,000 loan from First National Bank. J and K have personally guaranteed the loan. They are concerned about their ability to deduct the loss in the current year. Please advise if they have debt basis due to the current arrangement. If they do not have basis, explain how they might create basis without any outlay of additional funds.

Research aids:

Raynor, 50 T.C. 762 (1968).

Rev. Rul. 75-144, 1975-1 C.B. 277.

23-58 *Losses and Basis.* Q, an individual, is the sole shareholder of QR Corporation, an S corporation. In past years, Q's losses have exceeded her basis by $100,000. Now QR Corporation is insolvent and is $100,000 in debt. The lenders realize that they will have no possibility of collecting the full amount and are writing down the $100,000. After the debt reduction, QR will not be solvent. QR's tax advisors have told Q that the write-down of debt will not result in taxable income to QR due to the insolvency exception of § 108. Q understands that tax-exempt income flows through to shareholders in S corporations and increases stock basis. She asks you to find out if any income realized by QR due to the cancellation of debt will give her basis to deduct her prior suspended losses.

Research aids:

§ 108(d)(7).

Prop. Reg. § 1.1366-1(a)(2)(viii).

23-59   *Distribution Problems.* Dr. A has operated his medical practice as a sole proprietor. He has heard that there is no self-employment income passing through from an S corporation to a shareholder. He has also heard that distributions from corporations are not subject to social security tax. Accordingly, he intends to incorporate his medical practice. He will take no salary or other compensation for his services. Instead, he will cause the corporation to declare dividends each quarter and withdraw the profits as distributions from the corporation. He believes he will not be subject to self-employment tax or social security tax. Do you see any problems with this scheme?

Research aid:

Rev. Rul. 74-44, 1974-1 C.B. 287.

Part IX

FAMILY TAX PLANNING

❖ Contents ❖

Chapter 24

THE FEDERAL TRANSFER TAXES

LEARNING OBJECTIVES

Upon completion of this chapter you will be able to:

- Characterize the types of transfers that are subject to the Federal gift tax

- Compute a donor's total taxable gifts for the current year, including

  - Determination of all available $11,000 exclusions

  - Calculation of any available marital or charitable deduction

- Explain the mechanics of the calculation of the gift tax, including the role of the unified credit

- List the three basic steps involved in the computation of a decedent's taxable estate

- Specify the various types of property interests that must be valued for inclusion in a decedent's gross estate

- Describe any deductions from the gross estate

- Explain the mechanics of the calculation of the estate tax, including the role of the unified credit

- Discuss the purpose of the generation-skipping transfer tax

CHAPTER OUTLINE

INTRODUCTION

Since 1916 Congress has imposed taxes aimed solely at an individual's transfer of wealth: the estate tax (1916), the gift tax (1932), and the generation-skipping transfer tax (1976). As a practical matter, these taxes have produced relatively little revenue—about 1 percent of total revenues—and affected few individuals—also around 1 percent. Despite their limited impact, the taxes have survived. But that may all be coming to an end. In 2000, Congress repealed all of the transfer taxes by a wide margin but President Clinton vetoed the legislation and Congress was unable to muster sufficient votes to overturn the veto. However, with the inauguration of President Bush in 2001, the tide changed. Under the Economic Growth and Tax Relief Reconciliation Act of 2001, the estate tax—but not the gift tax—is scheduled to die. The estate tax is scheduled for phase-out and complete elimination in 2010. However, the gift tax remains with an exemption of $1,000,000 and a top rate of 35 percent. It should be emphasized that without further action by Congress, many of the rules enacted by the 2001 Act are effectively repealed beginning in 2011. In other words, in 2011, the tax law will revert to the rules that existed prior to enactment of the 2001 Act. In such case, the estate tax would be reinstated in 2011 as would all of the other rules that existed prior to the 2001 Act. Consequently, good tax planning suggests that taxpayers should die in 2010! Interestingly, commentators have noted that before the estate tax expires in 2010 there will be another presidential election (2008) and two congressional elections (2006 and

2008). Most believe that it is highly unlikely that the estate tax will be completely repealed. But only time will tell whether Congress has the nerve to reinstate it. In any event, until that time, the transfer taxes will continue to be an important consideration in estate planning.

HISTORY AND OVERVIEW

The estate tax became a permanent part of the tax system in 1916. In short, it is merely an excise tax on the transfer of the decedent's *net* wealth (fair market value of total assets less debts and expenses) that passes to his or her heirs at death. For example, if a taxpayer dies with a home worth $1,000,000 and a mortgage of $200,000, he or she is potentially taxed on the net amount of $800,000. Whether or not the taxpayer is actually taxed on such amount depends in part on a number of variables including who receives the property. For example, the law currently provides deductions for transfers to a spouse or qualifying charitable organizations.

Shortly after the enactment of the estate tax it became clear that without additional rules a taxpayer could easily avoid the estate tax simply by giving away property before he or she died. As might be expected, to prevent full scale avoidance of the estate tax Congress enacted a gift tax in 1924. A unique feature of the gift tax is the fact that unlike the income tax where the current year's tax is based on the current's year's income, the gift tax is computed on the cumulative amount of gifts made by an individual during his or her lifetime. Because of the progressive transfer tax rates, this approach makes every gift more expensive in terms of tax dollars than the last. Another important characteristic of the gift tax is the annual exclusion. To eliminate the vast administrative problems that would result if the gift tax were imposed on all gifts (e.g., birthday and Christmas presents) the gift tax is imposed only on those that exceed a certain threshold, currently $11,000 (2005) per donee per year (previously $3,000 from 1932 to 1981).

Until 1976, the estate and gift tax were separate and distinct taxes. Although both taxes imposed a tax on transfers of wealth, one on lifetime transfers and one on transfers at death, they differed in several important ways. One important difference could be found in the rate structures. For many years, the gift tax rates were 25 percent less than estate tax rates, presumably to encourage taxpayers to transfer their assets during their lifetime rather than hoarding them until death. Another difference involved the amount of transfers exempted from tax. The gift tax had its own lifetime exemption of $30,000 while the estate tax exemption was $60,000. Any of the exemption for gifts that was not used during the taxpayer's lifetime could not be carried over and used at death but was lost. Another distinction concerned the tax computation. Transfers made during the taxpayer's lifetime (i.e., taxable gifts) did not enter into the calculation of the tax on the taxpayer's transfers at death (i.e., the taxable estate). However, these distinctions came to an end with the passage of the Tax Reform Act of 1976 when the two taxes were unified. Although current practice still refers to these transfer taxes as the estate tax and the gift tax, they are really part of what is a unified transfer tax system.

The unification of the estate and gift tax eliminated the differences between the two taxes, completely integrating the two systems into the one that exists today. The new law replaced the two separate rate schedules with a single, unified transfer tax rate schedule used to compute both the estate and the gift tax. Moreover, since 1976 a decedent's taxable estate is effectively treated as an individual's final taxable gift. This is accomplished by computing the estate tax on a base that includes not only the taxable estate but also any taxable gifts made during the decedent's life. The changes in 1976 also replaced the separate exemptions with a single unified credit. The credit is unified in the sense that whatever amount is used to offset the gift tax during life is unavailable to reduce the estate tax at death. Beginning in 2004, however, the exemption for the estate tax slowly increases to $3.5 million by 2009 ($1.5 million for 2004–2005 and $2 million for 2006-2008). In contrast, the gift tax exemption remains at $1 million.

Another change made in 1976 was the introduction of a third Federal transfer tax on generation-skipping transfers. This tax, designed to complement the gift and estate taxes, is quite complex and highly controversial. It is discussed later in this chapter.

The Economic Recovery Tax Act of 1981 (ERTA 1981) continued the restructuring of the transfer tax system begun in 1976. The most important feature of this legislation was the unlimited marital deduction. This deduction makes gifts between spouses completely nontaxable and allows the first spouse to die to leave the family wealth to the surviving spouse at no Federal transfer tax cost. Thus, after 1981, the taxable unit for the imposition of the gift or estate tax is no longer the individual but the marital unit.

PROPERTY INTERESTS

Since the estate and gift taxes concern transfers of property, understanding the two taxes requires an appreciation of the nature of property interests and the different forms of property ownership. In the United States, each of the 50 states has its own system of *property law*—statutory rules that govern an individual's right to own and convey both real and personal property during his or her lifetime. Unfortunately, the specific property laws of each state vary considerably and therefore generalizations about property laws can be dangerous. However, the various state legal systems can be divided into two basic categories: *common law systems* and *community property systems*. The common law system, derived from English laws of property ownership, focuses on individual ownership of assets, regardless of the marital status of the individual. This system has been adopted in 41 states. The community property system is a derivation of Spanish property law and is followed in nine states: Arizona, California, Idaho, Louisiana, Nevada, New Mexico, Texas, Washington, and Wisconsin. Under either system, an individual may own property alone or jointly with another. In addition, an individual may own only a partial interest in the property such as an income interest. The different forms of co-ownership and various types of partial interests are considered below.

FORMS OF CO-OWNERSHIP

The consequences of holding property jointly with another can vary substantially, depending on the type of co-ownership. There are four forms of co-ownership: (1) tenancy in common, (2) joint tenancy, (3) tenancy by the entirety, and (4) community property ownership.

Tenancy in Common. A tenancy in common exists when two or more persons hold title to property, each owning an undivided fractional interest in the whole. The percentage of the property owned by one tenant need not be the same as the other co-tenants but can differ as the co-tenants provide. The most important feature of this type of property interest is that it is treated in virtually all respects like property that is owned outright. Thus, the interest can be sold, gifted, willed, or, when there is no will, passed to the owner's heirs according to the laws of the state. Another important characteristic of a tenancy in common is the *right of partition*. This right permits co-owners who disagree over something concerning the property to go to court to secure a division of the property among the owners. In some cases, however, a physical division is impossible (e.g., 50 acres of land where each acre's value is dependent on the whole), and consequently, the property must be sold with the proceeds split between the owners.

Joint Tenancy. Under a joint tenancy arrangement, two or more persons hold title to property, each owning the same fractional interest in the property. Joint tenancy normally implies the right of survivorship (joint tenancy with right of survivorship, or JTWROS). This means that upon the death of one joint tenant, the property automatically passes to the surviving joint tenants. Consequently, the disposition of the property is *not* controlled by the decedent's will. Like tenants in common, joint tenants have the right to sever their interest in the property. This is a particularly valuable right since the tenant may wish to disinherit the other joint tenants.

Tenancy by the Entirety. A tenancy by the entirety is a JTWROS between husband and wife. The critical difference between a tenancy by the entirety and a JTWROS is that in most states a spouse cannot sever his or her interest without the consent of the other spouse. In addition, in some states the husband has full control over the property while alive and is entitled to all the income from it.

Community Property. In a community property system, married individuals own an equal, undivided interest in all wealth acquired during the course of the marriage, regardless of which spouse made any individual contribution to the marital wealth. In addition to a half interest in such "community property," a spouse may also own property in an individual capacity as "separate property." Generally, assets acquired prior to marriage and assets received by gift or inheritance are separate property. However, in all nine community property states there exists a strong legal presumption that all property possessed during marriage is community, and that presumption can only be overcome by convincing proof of the property's separate nature.

Marital Property. Before leaving the subject of joint ownership, the concept of marital property deserves attention. Except in community property states, it is a common mistake to assume that all property acquired during marriage is jointly held. State laws vary widely on this issue. In some states, only property specifically titled as JTWROS is treated as jointly held. In these and other states, it is not unusual that property acquired during marriage belongs to the husband regardless of whose earnings were used to acquire the property. In other states, each spouse is deemed to own that which can be traced to his or her own earnings. Because of the problems with marital property, transfers of such property should be evaluated carefully to ensure that the rights of either spouse are not violated.

LIFE ESTATES, REVERSIONS, AND REMAINDERS

Persons who own property outright have virtually unlimited rights with respect to their property. They can sell it, mortgage it, or transfer it as they wish. In addition, they can divide the ownership of the property in any number of ways. In this regard, it is not uncommon for property owners to transfer ownership in property to someone temporarily. During the period of temporary ownership, the beneficiary could have the right to use, possess, and benefit from the income of the property. Assuming that the beneficiary's interest is limited to the income from the property, he or she would be treated as having an *income interest*. The time to which the beneficiary is entitled to the income from the property could be specified in any terms, such as common measures of time: days, weeks, months, or years. Alternatively, the time period could be determined by reference to the occurrence of a specific event. For example, when an individual has an income interest for life, the interest is referred to as a life estate. In this case, the person entitled to the *life estate* is called the life tenant.

The owner of property has the right to provide for one or more temporary interests, subject only to the *rule against perpetuities*. This rule requires that the property pass outright to an individual within a certain time period after the transfer. Normally, ownership of the property must vest at a date no later than 21 years after the death of persons alive at the time the interest is created. After any temporary interests have been designated, the owner has the right to provide for the outright transfer of the property. If the owner specifies that the property should be returned to the owner or his or her estate, the interest following the temporary interest is referred to as a *reversionary interest*. If the property passes to someone other than the owner, the interest is called a *remainder interest*. The holder of the remainder interest is the *remainderman*.

Life estates, remainders, and reversions are property interests that can be transferred, sold, and willed (except for life estates) like other types of property. These interests can also be reached by creditors in satisfaction of their claims. However, a person can establish a trust with so-called *spendthrift* provisions, which prohibit the beneficiary from assigning or selling his or her interest (e.g., a life estate) or using the assets to satisfy creditors.

THE GIFT TAX

The statutory provisions regarding the Federal gift tax are contained in §§ 2501 through 2524 of the Internal Revenue Code. These rules provide the basis for the gift tax formula found in Exhibit 24-1. The various elements of this formula are discussed below.

EXHIBIT 24-1
Computation of Federal Gift Tax Liability

Fair market value of all gifts made		
in the current year		$xxx,xxx
Less the sum of		
Annual exclusions ($11,000 per donee in 2004–2005)	$xx,xxx	
Marital deduction.	xx,xxx	
Charitable deduction	x,xxx	−xx,xxx
Taxable gifts for current year		$xxx,xxx
Plus: All taxable gifts made in prior years		+ xx,xxx
Taxable transfers to date		$xxx,xxx
Tentative tax on total transfers to date.		$ xx,xxx
Less the sum of		
Gift taxes computed at current		
rates on prior years' taxable gifts.	$ x,xxx	
Unified transfer tax credit	x,xxx	−xx,xxx
Gift tax due on current gifts		$ xx,xxx

TRANSFERS SUBJECT TO TAX

Section 2511 states that the gift tax shall apply to transfers in trust or otherwise, whether the gift is direct or indirect, real or personal, tangible or intangible. The gift tax is imposed only on transfers of property; gratuitous transfers of services are not subject to tax.[1] The types of property interests to which the gift tax applies are virtually unlimited. The tax applies to transfers of such common items as money, cars, stocks, bonds, jewelry, works of art, houses, and every other type of item normally considered

---

[1]   Rev. Rul. 56-472, 1956-2 C.B. 21.

property. It should be emphasized that no property is specifically excluded from the gift tax. For example, the transfer of municipal bonds is subject to the gift tax, even though the income from the bonds is tax free.

The gift tax reaches transfers of partial interests as well. One example is a transfer of property in trust where the income interest is given to someone—the income beneficiary—for his or her life, while the trust property or remainder interest is given to another person—the remainderman—upon the income beneficiary's death. In this case, the donor would be treated as having made two separate gifts, a gift of the income interest and a gift of the remainder interest.

The application of the gift tax to both direct and indirect gifts ensures that the tax reaches all transfers regardless of the method of transfer. Direct gifts encompass the common types of outright transfers (e.g., father transfers bonds to daughter, or grandmother gives cash to grandson). On the other hand, indirect gifts are represented primarily by transfers to trusts and other entities. When a transfer is made to a trust, it is considered a gift to the beneficiaries of the trust. Similarly, a transfer to a corporation or partnership is considered a gift to the shareholders or partners. However, if the donor owns an interest in a partnership or corporation, he or she is not treated as making a gift to the extent it would be a gift to himself or herself. An individual may also be treated as making a gift if he or she refuses to accept property and the property passes to another person on account of the refusal.

Most taxpayers understand that the gift tax is imposed on transfers of property motivated by affection and generosity. However, the tax may also be imposed on a transfer of property not intended as a gift within the commonly accepted definition of the word. The tax is intended to apply to any transfer of wealth by an individual that reduces his or her potential taxable estate. Therefore, § 2512 provides that any transfer of property, in return for which the transferor receives *less than adequate or full consideration* in money or money's worth, is a transfer subject to the gift tax.

Adequate Consideration. Revenue Ruling 79-384 provides an excellent example of a transfer for insufficient consideration.[2] The taxpayer in the ruling was a father, who had made an oral promise to his son to pay him $10,000 upon the son's graduation from college. The son graduated but the father refused to pay him the promised amount. The son then successfully sued the father, who was forced to transfer the $10,000. The IRS ruled that the father had received no consideration in money or money's worth for the transfer and therefore had made a taxable gift to his son.

Revenue Ruling 79-384 illustrates two important concepts. First, *donative intent* on the part of a transferor of property is *not necessary* to classify the transfer as a taxable gift.[3] Second, anything received by the transferor in exchange for the property must be subject to valuation in monetary terms if it is to be consideration within the meaning of § 2512.[4] The father did receive the satisfaction resulting from his son's graduation, and this consideration was sufficient to create an enforceable oral contract between father and son. However, because the consideration could not be objectively valued in dollar terms it was irrelevant for tax purposes.

The question of sufficiency of consideration normally arises when transfers of assets are made between family members or related parties. When properties are transferred or exchanged in a bona fide business transaction, the Regulations specify that sufficiency of consideration will be presumed because of the arm's-length negotiation between the parties.[5]

---

[2]   1979-2 C.B. 12.

[3]   Reg. § 25.2511-1(g)(1).

[4]   Reg. § 25.2512-8.

[5]   *Ibid.*

Transfers of wealth to dependent family members that represent support are not taxable gifts. The distinction between support payments and gifts is far from clear, particularly when the transferor is not legally obligated to make the payments. Section 2503(e) specifies that amounts paid on behalf of any individual for tuition to an educational organization or for medical care shall not be considered taxable gifts to such individual. However, this rule only applies if the payments are made directly to the educational institution or the health care provider.

Payments that a divorced taxpayer is legally required to make for the *support* of his or her former spouse are not taxable gifts.[6] However, Regulation § 25.2512-8 specifies that payments made prior to or after marriage in return for the recipient's relinquishment of his or her *marital property rights* are transfers for insufficient consideration and subject to the gift tax. Section 2516 provides an exception to this rule. If a transfer of property is made under the terms of a written agreement between spouses and the transfer is (1) in settlement of the spouse's marital property rights, or (2) to provide a reasonable allowance for support of any minor children of the marriage, no taxable gift will occur. For the exception to apply, divorce must occur within the three-year period beginning on the date one year before such agreement is entered into.

Retained Interest. The final criterion of a taxable transfer is that the transfer must be complete. A transfer is considered complete only if the donor has surrendered all control over the property. For this reason, when the donor alone retains the right to revoke the transfer, the transfer is incomplete and the gift tax does not apply. For example, creation of a joint bank account is not considered a completed gift since the depositor is free to withdraw the money deposited in the account. Similarly, the donor must not be able to redirect ownership of the property in the future; nonetheless, to have a completed gift it is not necessary that the donees have received the property or that the specific donees even be identified.[7]

> **Example 1.** Donor D transfers $1 million into an irrevocable trust with an independent trustee. The trustee has the right to pay the income of the trust to beneficiaries A, B, or C *or* to accumulate the income. After 15 years, the trust will terminate and all accumulated income and principal will be divided among the surviving beneficiaries. Because D has parted with all control over the $1 million, it is a completed gift, even though neither A, B, or C has received or is guaranteed any specified portion of the money.

VALUATION

The value of a transfer subject to the Federal gift tax is measured by the fair market value of the property transferred less the value of any consideration received by the transferor. Determining fair market value can be the most difficult aspect of computing a gift tax due. Fair market value is defined in the Regulations as "the price at which such property would change hands between a willing buyer and a willing seller, neither being under any compulsion to buy or to sell, and both having reasonable knowledge of relevant facts."[8]

The determination of an asset's fair market value must be made on the basis of all relevant facts and circumstances. The Regulations under § 2512 are quite detailed and extremely useful in that they prescribe methods for valuation of a variety of assets.

---

6   Rev. Rul. 68-379, 1968-2 C.B. 414.

7   Reg. § 25.2511-2(a).

8   Reg. § 25.2512-1.

Example 2. Donor S transfers 10 shares of the publicly traded common stock of XYZ Corporation on June 8, 2005. On that date, the highest quoted selling price of the stock was $53 per share. The lowest quoted selling price was $48 per share. Regulation § 25.2512-2(b)(1) specifies that the fair market value of the XYZ stock on June 8, 2005 shall be the mean between the highest and lowest quoted selling price [($53 + $48) ÷ 2], or $50.50 per share.

Valuation of Income and Remainder Interests. In estate planning, it is quite common for individuals to make gifts of only a partial interest of property. These arrangements usually involve transfers to a trust such as the following:

- An individual transfers property to a trust, giving away an income interest to one beneficiary and a remainder interest to another beneficiary. In this case, the taxpayer has actually made two gifts—the income interest and the remainder interest—each of which must be valued for gift tax purposes.
- An individual transfers property to a trust, retaining the income interest and giving away the remainder interest. Here there is only a single gift of the remainder interest.
- An individual transfers property to a trust, giving the income interest to a beneficiary but providing that the remainder interest reverts or returns to the individual once the income interest has expired. In this case, the taxpayer has made a single gift of the income interest.

Gifts of income and remainder interests are valued using actuarial tables. These tables take into consideration current interest rates and, if necessary, current mortality rates. In valuing the various types of transfers, the tables assume that property transferred produces income at a certain rate, regardless of the actual amount of income that is produced.

For transfers after April 30, 1989, § 7520 requires valuations using the interest rate prevailing at the time of the transfer. Specifically, the rate to be used is 120 percent of the applicable Federal midterm rate in effect under § 1274(d)(1) for the month in which the transfer is made. These rates are published monthly. Using the appropriate rate, the values can be found in actuarial tables published by the IRS. The tables were first issued in 1989 in Notice 89-60.[9] Section 7520(c)(3) requires that the tables be revised at least once every 10 years thereafter to reflect the most recent mortality experience available. They were most recently revised in 1999 and can be found in IRS Publications 1457, 1458 or 1459.[10] These three massive volumes provide factors for interest rates of 2.2 percent to 26 percent and annuity factors for ages 0–110. The IRS issues monthly announcements indicating which of these tables applies for the month.[11] For example, the § 7520 rate for January 2005 was 4.6 percent.[12] Table S shows the factors for determining the value of an annuity, a life estate, or a remainder interest based on a single life. Table B shows the factors for determining the value of an annuity, a life estate or a remainder interest for a term of years Selected portions of the tables can be found in Appendix A in this book.

---

[9] 1989-1 C.B. 700.

[10] IRS Publication 1457, Actuarial Values, Aleph Volume (2001); IRS Publication 1458, Actuarial Values, Beth Volume (2001); IRS Publication 1459, Actuarial Values, Gimel Volume (2001).

[11] These rates are published monthly. For transfers after December 31, 1970 and before December 1, 1983 the interest rate used to compute the value of reversions and other interests was six percent. The factors can be found in the appropriate table contained in Reg § 20.2031-10(f) . For transfers after November 30, 1983, and before May 1, 1989, the interest rate used to compute the value of reversions and other interests was 10 percent.

[12] Rev. Rul. 2005-2, 2005-2 I.R.B.

In examining the tables, observe that if the value of the property is split between an income interest and a remainder interest, there are two factors and the sum of those two factors equals one. In a case where the remainder factor is known but the income factor is unknown or vice-versa, the income factor can be determined as follows:

Income factor = 1.000000 − Remainder factor.

Example 3. In May, 19X9, H transferred $100,000 to a trust for his son, S, and his grandson, GS. According to the terms of the trust, S is to receive the income for life and upon his death, the remainder is to be paid to GS, if living, otherwise to GS's estate. S was 40 years old at the time the trust was created. H has made two gifts. The value of S's income interest is a function of three factors determined at the time of the gift: (1) S's life expectancy, (2) the current interest rate, and (3) the value of the trust property. Assume the applicable rate for valuing the interest is five percent (120% of the May Federal mid-term rate). Using the table for valuing a remainder interest (Table S in Appendix A-1), the value of the remainder interest is $19,519 ($100,000 × .19516). The value of the income interest is $80,484 [$100,000 × (1 − .19516 = .80484)]. Note that the sum of the remainder interest and the income interest equals the total value of the property.

Example 4. In June, 19X2, M transferred $100,000 to a trust for her daughter, D. Under the terms of the trust, D is to receive the income for 20 years at which time the trust will terminate and the property will revert to M. Assume the applicable rate for valuing the interest is 5.2% (120% of the June Federal mid-term rate). In this case, the factor for the income interest must be determined by subtracting the factor for the remainder interest from 1. Using the table for valuing a term certain remainder interest (Table B in Appendix A-2), the value of D's income interest for 20 years is $63,719 ($100,000 × .637185).

The valuation of a gift of a partial interest in property is subject to special rules when the donor retains an income interest. These rules are considered in Chapter 16 in conjunction with the discussion on special estate planning techniques [e.g., grantor retained income trusts, annuity trusts, and unitrusts (GRITS, GRATS, and GRUTS)].

BASIS

The basis of an asset in the hands of a donee is calculated under the rules of § 1015. Generally, the basis of property received as a gift is the basis of the asset in the hands of the donor, increased by the amount of any gift tax paid attributable to the excess of fair market value over the donor's basis at the date of gift. This general rule applies only if the asset is sold at a gain by the donee. If the carryover basis rule would result in a realized loss upon subsequent sale, the basis of the asset will be considered the *lesser* of the carryover basis (donor's basis) *or* the asset's fair market value at date of gift. If the asset is sold at a price greater than the fair market value at date of gift but less than its carryover basis, no gain or loss is recognized.

THE GIFT TAX EXCLUSION

When the gift tax was enacted in 1932, Congress wanted to "eliminate the necessity of keeping an account of and reporting numerous small gifts." To this end, it created an annual exclusion designed to exempt gifts under a certain threshold from the gift tax.[13]

---

[13] § 2503(b).

The annual exclusion was initially set at $3,000 until it was raised to $10,000 in 1981. The annual exclusion is now adjusted annually for inflation and is $11,000 for 2005.

A donor is entitled to exclude $11,000 per year per donee. Note, however, that not all gifts are eligible for the annual exclusion. Congress was concerned about the problems that could arise in determining the number of exclusions when there was only a remote possibility that a donee would receive a gift (e.g., remote and contingent beneficiaries). For this reason, to qualify for the exclusion the gift must be constitute a *present* interest. Regulation § 25.2503-3(b) defines a present interest as one that gives the donee "an unrestricted right to the immediate use, possession, or enjoyment of property or the income from property." Therefore, the annual exclusion is not available for a gift that can only be enjoyed by the donee at some future date, even if the donee does receive a present ownership interest in the gift.

> **Example 5.** Donor D gifts real estate worth $20,000 to donees M and N. M is given a *life* estate (the right to the income from the property for as long as M lives) worth $8,000. N receives *the remainder interest* (complete ownership of the property upon the death of M) worth $12,000. Although both M and N have received legal property interests, D may claim only one exclusion for his gift to M. The gift to N is a gift of a future rather than a present interest. Thus D has made a taxable gift of $12,000.

Securing the obvious tax benefit of the annual exclusion can be difficult if the gift in question is made to a minor or an incapacitated donee. In such cases the donor may be reluctant to give an unrestricted present interest in the donated property. A complete discussion of strategies for making gifts to minors or incapacitated donees is included in Chapter 26.

GIFT SPLITTING

Because of the progressivity of the gift tax and the availability of the annual $11,000 exclusion, gift taxes on a transfer can be minimized by increasing the number of donors. A gift made by a married individual residing in a community property state may have two donors (husband and wife) because of state property law. Property laws in the 41 noncommunity property states do not produce this *two donor* result. To compensate for this difference, § 2513 provides a *gift splitting* election to a married donor.

If a donor makes the proper election on his or her current gift tax return, one-half of all gifts made during the year will be considered to have been made by the donor's spouse. Both spouses must consent to gift splitting for the election to be valid. Since evidence of the spouse's consent is necessary when gift splitting is used, a gift tax return must be filed.

> **Example 6.** In 2005, husband H makes two gifts of $100,000 each to his son and daughter. His wife, W, makes a gift of $5,000 to their daughter. H and W elect gift splitting on their current gift tax returns. As a result, H will report a gift to the daughter of $52,500 and a gift to the son of $50,000, and will claim two $11,000 gift tax exclusions. W will report exactly the same gifts and claim two $11,000 exclusions.
>
> Without gift splitting, H would still be entitled to $22,000 of exclusions, but W could only claim an exclusion of $5,000 for her gift to the daughter.

GIFTS TO POLITICAL AND CHARITABLE ORGANIZATIONS

Code § 2501(a)(5) excludes gifts of money or other property to a political organization from the statutory definition of taxable transfers. If a gratuitous donation is made to a qualified charitable organization, § 2522 provides a deduction for such gift from the donor's taxable gifts for the calendar year. Thus, transfers made without sufficient consideration to qualifying political or charitable groups are not subject to the Federal gift tax.

THE GIFT TAX MARITAL DEDUCTION

Under § 2523, gifts to spouses are fully deductible by the donor. The marital deduction is permitted only if certain requirements are satisfied. A full discussion of these requirements is considered in conjunction with the discussion of the marital deduction for estate tax purposes.

The gift tax marital deduction allows an individual to make tax-free transfers of wealth to his or her spouse. This opportunity to equalize the wealth owned by husband and wife plays an essential role in family tax planning, a role that will be discussed in Chapter 26.

COMPUTATION AND FILING

Unlike the income tax, which is computed on annual taxable income, the Federal gift tax is computed on cumulative taxable gifts made during a donor's lifetime. This is done by adding taxable gifts for the current year to all taxable gifts made in prior years, calculating the gross tax on the sum of cumulative gifts, and subtracting the amount of gift tax calculated on prior years' gifts.[14] The transfer tax rate schedule currently in effect is reproduced in Exhibit 24-2. Consistent with the ultimate repeal of the estate tax in 2010, the maximum estate and gift tax rate is gradually reduced as follows:

Year	Top Rate
2002	50%
2003	49%
2004	48%
2005	47%
2006	46%
2007–09	45%

EXHIBIT 24-2
2005 Estate and Gift Tax Rates

If taxable transfer is			Of the
Over	But not over	Tax liability	Amount over
$ 0	$ 10,000	18%	$ 0
10,000	20,000	$ 1,800 + 20%	10,000
20,000	40,000	3,800 + 22%	20,000
40,000	60,000	8,200 + 24%	40,000
60,000	80,000	13,000 + 26%	60,000
80,000	100,000	18,200 + 28%	80,000
100,000	150,000	23,800 + 30%	100,000
150,000	250,000	38,800 + 32%	150,000
250,000	500,000	70,800 + 34%	250,000
500,000	750,000	155,800 + 37%	500,000
750,000	1,000,000	248,300 + 39%	750,000
1,000,000	1,250,000	345,800 + 41%	1,000,000
1,250,000	1,500,000	448,300 + 43%	1,250,000
1,500,000	2,000,000	555,800 + 45%	1,500,000
	Over 2,000,000	780,800 + 47%	

---

[14] § 2502(a). The amount of gift tax calculated on prior years' gifts is based on current gift tax rates, regardless of the rates in effect when the gifts were actually made.

Example 7. In 1995, X made his first taxable gift of $100,000 (after the exclusion). The tax (before credits) on this amount was $23,800. X made a second taxable gift of $85,000 in 2005. The tax (before credits) on the second gift is $26,200, computed as follows:

1995 taxable gift	$100,000
2005 taxable gift	+85,000
Cumulative gifts	$185,000
Tax on $185,000	$ 50,000
Less: Tax on 1995 taxable gift	−23,800
Tax on 2005 gift	$ 26,200

This cumulative system of gift taxation and the progressive rate schedule of § 2003 causes a higher tax on the 2005 gift, even though the 2005 gift was $15,000 *less* than the 1995 gift.

Unified Credit. Both the estate and gift tax provisions have long contained exemptions to ensure that the taxes do not apply to modest transfers of wealth. As noted earlier, prior to their unification in 1976, each tax had its own separate exemption: the estate tax provided for an exemption of $60,000 while the gift tax allowed a lifetime exemption of $30,000 for otherwise taxable gifts (i.e., those not otherwise exempt by the annual exclusion). The unification in 1976 led to the creation of the unified credit. The unified credit is a lifetime credit available for offsetting the tax on all taxable transfers (i.e., the taxes imposed on taxable gifts or the taxable estate). In 2005, the credit is $555,800 for the estate tax and $345,800 for the gift tax. This amount of credit completely offsets the tax on $1,000,000 of taxable transfers. For example, consider a taxpayer whose first *taxable* gift is $1,000,000. The tax on the $1,000,000 taxable transfer would be $345,800. However, the credit of $345,800 would completely eliminate the tax, effectively providing an exemption from tax for transfers of up to $1,000,000.

As can be seen in Exhibit 24-3, the amount of the credit has been increased over the years. In 1976, the credit was originally set so that when it was completely phased in by 1981 it would exempt from tax transfers of up to $175,625. However, by 1981, Congress and the Reagan administration viewed that amount as inadequate. Consequently, legislation was passed to gradually increase the credit so that it would reach $192,800 in 1987 where it would exempt $600,000 of transfers from tax. The credit remained at that level for more than 10 years until Congress acted again in the Taxpayer Relief Act of 1997. Beginning in 1998, the credit began to increase gradually. However, before the increase was complete, Congress changed course and moved toward ultimate repeal of the estate tax. Beginning in 2004, the exemption amounts for the estate tax and the gift tax are no longer the same. The gift tax is not scheduled for repeal and the exemption is set permanently at the $1,000,000 level. On the other hand, the exemption for the estate tax gradually increases to $3,500,000 by 2009 before the tax is eliminated in 2010 as shown below.

EXHIBIT 24-3
Credit and Exemption Equivalent

	Credit		Exemption Equivalent	
Year	**Estate Tax**	**Gift Tax**	**Estate Tax**	**Gift Tax**
1/1/77–6/30/77	$ 6,000	Same	$ 30,000	Same
7/1/77–12/31/77	30,000	Same	120,666	Same
1978	34,000	Same	134,000	Same
1979	38,000	Same	147,333	Same
1980	42,500	Same	161,563	Same
1981	47,000	Same	175,625	Same
1982	62,800	Same	225,000	Same
1983	79,300	Same	275,000	Same
1984	96,300	Same	325,000	Same
1985	121,800	Same	400,000	Same
1986	155,800	Same	500,000	Same
1987–97	192,800	Same	600,000	Same
1998	202,050	Same	625,000	Same
1999	211,300	Same	650,000	Same
2000–01	220,550	Same	675,000	Same
2002–03	345,800	Same	1,000,000	Same
2004–05	555,800	$345,800	1,500,000	$1,000,000*
2006–08	780,800	345,800	2,000,000	1,000,000
2009	1,455,800	345,800	3,500,000	1,000,000
2010	Repealed	345,800	Repealed	1,000,000

*Gift tax exemption is frozen at $1,000,000 for all subsequent years and the credit is no longer unified.

The unified credit is the only credit available to offset the Federal gift tax. As noted above, the credit offset the tax on $1,000,000 of taxable gifts. Thus, an individual may make substantial transfers of wealth before any tax liability is incurred. The unified credit must be used when available—a taxpayer may not decide to postpone use of the credit if he or she makes a taxable gift during the current year.[15]

Example 8. In 1995, Y made her first taxable gift of $350,000. The tax calculated on this gift is $104,800, and Y must use $104,800 of her available unified credit so that the actual gift tax due is reduced to zero. In 2005, Y makes her second taxable gift of $2,000,000. The tax on this gift is $599,500, computed as follows:

Taxable gift for 2005		$ 2,000,000
Plus: 1995 taxable gift		+ 350,000
Taxable transfers to date		$ 2,350,000
Tentative tax on total transfers to date (See Exhibit 24-2)		$ 945,300
Less: Gift taxes calculated on 1995 gift		− 104,800
Tentative tax on 2005 gift		$ 840,500
Less: Remaining unified transfer tax credit:		
Total credit available for 2005	$ 345,800	
Less: Unified transfer tax credit used in 1995	− 104,800	− 241,000
Gift tax due on 2005 gift		$ 599,500

---

[15] Rev. Rul. 79-398, 1979-2 C.B. 338.

Filing Requirements. The Federal gift tax return, Form 709, is filed annually on a calendar year basis. The due date of the return is the April 15th after the close of the taxable year. If a calendar year taxpayer obtains any extension to file his or her Federal income tax return, such extension automatically applies to any gift tax return due. If the donor dies during a taxable year for which a gift tax return is due, the gift tax return must be filed by the due date (nine months after death) plus any extensions of the donor's Federal estate tax return.[16]

THE OVERLAP BETWEEN THE GIFT AND ESTATE TAXES

A beginning student of the Federal transfer tax system might reasonably assume that an inter vivos (during life) transfer of property that is considered complete and therefore subject to the gift tax would also be considered complete for estate tax purposes, so that the transferred property would not be included in the decedent's taxable estate. This, however, is not the case. The gift tax and the estate tax are not mutually exclusive; property gifted away in earlier years can be included in the donor's taxable estate. The relationship between the two taxes is illustrated in the following diagram:

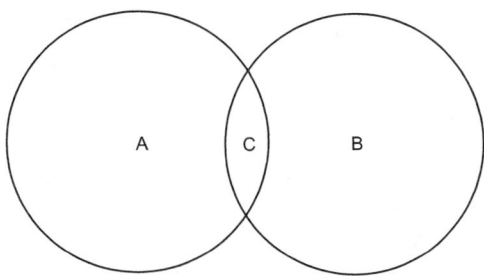

Circle A represents property transferred by the decedent during his or her lifetime and subject to the gift tax. Circle B represents the decedent's taxable estate. Overlap area C represents property already subject to a gift tax that is nevertheless included in the donor/decedent's taxable estate.

Examples of transfers that fall into the overlap area above will be presented later in the chapter. At this point, however, it is important to note that any gift tax paid on a transfer which is considered incomplete for estate tax purposes reduces the amount of estate tax payable.[17]

TRANSFERS OF PROPERTY AT DEATH

ROLE OF A WILL

Each of the 50 states gives its citizens the right to transfer the ownership of their property at death by means of a valid will. State law provides various formal requirements for valid wills, and as a result great care must be taken that a will is drafted in strict accordance with such requirements. There are few restrictions on the right of an individual to dispose of property at death in any manner he or she chooses. The most common restriction is the right under state law of a surviving spouse to receive a specified statutory share of the deceased individual's wealth. The statutory

---

[16] § 6075(b).

[17] § 2001(b)(2).

share rules effectively prevent an individual from completely disinheriting a surviving spouse.[18]

INTESTACY

When a person dies with no will or an invalid will, the transfer of his or her wealth is determined under the intestacy laws of the deceased's state of residence. Again, the particulars of the intestacy laws of each state are different. As a general rule, property will pass in order in prescribed shares to a decedent's surviving spouse, children and lineal descendants, parents and lineal ancestors, collateral relatives, and finally, if no relatives of any degree can be located, to the state of residence itself. For example, in Indiana if the decedent has a surviving spouse but no children, $\frac{1}{3}$ of the property generally passes to the spouse and $\frac{1}{4}$ passes to the decedent's parents. If there were two children, the spouse normally would receive $\frac{1}{2}$ while the children would receive $\frac{1}{2}$ of the property.

PROBATE

Probate is the legal process whereby a decedent's will is established as genuine and valid, and during which creditors of the decedent may submit their claims for payment from the estate. A decedent's probate estate consists of property interests owned at death that will pass under the terms of a decedent's will (or under the laws of intestacy if no valid will exists). It is extremely important for an individual engaged in estate planning to be aware of any property interests that he or she owns but which will *not* be included in the probate estate at death. A major example of such a property interest is a joint tenancy with right of survivorship (JTWROS). As previously explained, upon the death of one of the joint tenants, ownership of the asset automatically shifts to the surviving joint tenant or tenants. This is true *regardless* of the provisions of the deceased joint tenant's will. Similarly, survivor benefits, such as those from a life insurance policy or an annuity, or payments from pension and profit sharing plans, usually pass directly to the beneficiary and are not controlled by the will.

It should be apparent that those individuals who have amassed any amount of wealth and who wish to control the disposition of that wealth at death should have a validly executed will. However, there are compelling reasons why *every* responsible adult should have a will. When an individual dies intestate (without a valid will), the resulting legal and administrative complications can cause unnecessary hardship and confusion for the surviving family. Finally, one of the most critical functions of a will is to name a guardian for the decedent's minor children; failure to have a will can result in years of family discord and distress.

THE TAXABLE ESTATE

Code §§ 2001 through 2056A contain the statutory rules providing for the imposition of a tax on the transfer of the taxable estate of every decedent who is a citizen or resident of the United States. Sections 2101 through 2108 provide for an estate tax on the value of assets located within the United States owned by a nonresident alien decedent. Discussion of this latter tax is beyond the scope of an introductory text.

Computation of a decedent's taxable estate involves three basic steps:

1. Identification and valuation of assets includible in the gross estate;

---

[18]   Modern statutory share laws have their origins in the English common law property concepts of the "dower" rights of a widow and the "curtesy" rights of a widower.

2. Identification of deductible claims against the gross estate and deductible expenses of estate administration; and

3. Identification of any deductible bequests out of the gross estate.

The formula for computing the estate tax is shown in Exhibit 24-4 below.

EXHIBIT 24-4
Estate Tax Formula

Gross estate (§§ 2031 through 2046)		$x,xxx,xxx
Less the sum of		
Expenses, indebtedness,		
and taxes (§ 2053).	$xx,xxx	
Losses (§ 2054)	x,xxx	
State death taxes (§ 2058)	x,xxx	
Charitable bequests (§ 2055)	xx,xxx	
Marital deduction (§ 2056)	xxx,xxx	−xxx,xxx
Taxable estate (§ 2051).		$ xxx,xxx
Plus: Taxable gifts made after		
December 31, 1976 [§ 2001(b)].		+ xx,xxx
Total taxable transfers		$ xxx,xxx
Tentative tax on total transfers (§ 2001)		$ xxx,xxx
Less the sum of		
Gift taxes paid on post-1976		
taxable gifts (§ 2001).	$ x,xxx	
Unified transfer tax credit (§ 2010)	xx,xxx	
Other tax credits (§§ 2012 through 2016)	x,xxx	−xx,xxx
Estate tax liability		$ xx,xxx

THE GROSS ESTATE CONCEPT

Section 2031 broadly states that "the value of the gross estate of the decedent shall be determined by including to the extent provided for in this part the value at the time of his death of all property, real or personal, tangible or intangible, wherever situated." The Regulations under this section make it clear that property located in a foreign country is included in this definition.[19]

Sections 2033 through 2044 identify the various types of property that are includible in a decedent's gross estate. Section 2033 is the most commonly applied of these Code sections. It requires the inclusion of any property interest owned by the decedent at date of death. The property interests specified in § 2033 correspond to the legal concept of a decedent's *probate estate*, property interests that will pass to the beneficiaries under the terms of the decedent's will.[20] If the decedent dies without a valid will, these interests will be distributed to the decedent's heirs under the state intestacy laws.

---

[19] Reg. § 20.2031-1(a).

[20] Reg. § 20.2031-1(a)(1).

All individuals are, in a sense, on the accrual method of accounting for estate tax purposes. Any legal claim to or interest in an asset that exists at death is includible in the gross estate. For example, a cash basis taxpayer who performed substantial services and was to be paid $20,000 would not report the fee as income until collected. However, if death occurred before collection, the decedent is considered to have owned a $20,000 asset, the right to the fee which would be includible in his or her gross estate.

The concept of the gross estate is much broader than the legal probate estate. Exhibit 24-5 lists the various types of property interests and assets includible in the gross estate and the statutory authority for each inclusion. These various inclusions are discussed in more detail later in the chapter.

Although the estate tax reaches virtually all types of property interests, it does not extend to property in which the decedent owned a life estate created by another. Section 2033 does not require inclusion of such property since the decedent's only legal interest in the property terminated upon death.

> **Example 9.** Upon W's death, she transferred stock worth $300,000 in trust, giving her son, S, a life estate and the remainder to her grandson. Several years later, S died when the property was worth $900,000. However, his estate does not include the stock, since his interest terminates at his death and he is not transferring the property to the grandson.

The above example illustrates why the life estate is one of the most important devices used in estate planning. Note that the son is entitled to use the property for his life, yet the property and all of the appreciation escapes taxation in his estate. In other words, the property was taxed in the first and third generations (i.e., in their estates) but not the second generation. Congress addressed this problem by enacting the generation-skipping transfer tax, discussed later in this chapter. This special tax, however, has not eliminated all of the benefits of using the life estate for family tax planning purposes.

VALUATION OF GROSS ESTATE AND BASIS

Once an asset is identified as part of the gross estate, its fair market value at date of death must be determined. Practically, valuation of assets is the most difficult and subjective problem in computing a decedent's gross estate. Many assets, such as stock in a closely held corporation, have no readily ascertainable fair market value. Fortunately, the estate tax Regulations, like their gift tax counterparts, provide detailed guidelines to the valuation of many types of assets.[21]

In the 41 common law states, a surviving spouse may have a legally enforceable claim against assets owned by a decedent that cannot be defeated by the terms of the decedent's will. Section 2034 states that the value of property included in the decedent's gross estate is not diminished by such a claim. In the nine community property states, most property owned by a married individual is community property in which both spouses have equal interests. Only one-half the value of such community property is included in a decedent's gross estate.

Although the gross estate is normally valued as of the decedent's date of death, § 2032 allows the executor to elect an alternative valuation date of six months after death. If the election is made, the alternative valuation date must be used for every asset in the gross estate. If an asset is disposed of within six months of death, its value at date of disposition is used. This choice of two possible dates for valuation gives the executor some flexibility in minimizing the value of the gross estate and any estate tax liability.

---

[21]   Reg. § 20.2031.

EXHIBIT 24-5
Property Included in the Gross Estate

Property	Statutory Authority
Any property interest owned by the decedent at death	Section 2033

Includes
    cash
    stocks, bonds, other investment securities
    personal assets
    personal residence
    collectibles (antiques, etc.)
    investment real estate
    business interests (sole proprietorship, partnership interest)	

Certain gifts made within three years of death (limited application after 1981)	Section 2035
Assets transferred during life in which the decedent retained an income interest or control over the enjoyment of the assets or the income therefrom	Section 2036
Assets transferred during life in which the decedent retained more than a 5 percent reversionary interest and possession of which could only be obtained by surviving the decedent	Section 2037
Assets transferred during life if, at death, the decedent possessed the right to alter, amend, revoke, or terminate the terms of the transfer	Section 2038
Certain survivor benefits and annuities	Section 2039
Joint tenancies with right of survivorship	Section 2040
Assets over which the decedent held a *general* power of appointment	Section 2041
Insurance proceeds on the decedent's life if 1. payable to the decedent's estate; *or* 2. the decedent possessed any incident of ownership in the policy at death.	Section 2042
Assets in a QTIP trust in which the decedent had the income interest	Section 2044

BASIS

For income tax purposes, the basis of property in the hands of a person acquiring the property from a decedent is the property's fair market value at date of death or on the alternate valuation date under Code § 2032.[22] Under § 1223(11), assets acquired from a decedent are presumed to have a holding period in excess of one year. In the case of community property, the adjustment to fair market value is available for the *entire property* rather than just the one-half interest that is included in the gross estate of the decedent spouse.[23] Note that if the estate tax is repealed in 2010, the basis rule is

---

[22] § 1014(a). This rule does not apply to items of property that constitute income in respect of a decedent. § 1014(c). For a complete discussion of income in respect of a decedent, see Chapter 25.

[23] § 1014(b)(6).

modified to limit the amount of basis increase to $1.3 million ($4.3 million in the case of a surviving spouse).

In situations in which the Federal estate tax to be imposed on a particular estate is minimal, an executor might actually elect the alternate valuation date in order to increase the valuation of assets included in the gross estate, thus achieving maximum step-up in the basis of the assets for income tax purposes. Section 2032(c) eliminates this particular tax planning option by providing that no § 2032 election may be made unless such election will decrease the value of the gross estate *and* the amount of the Federal estate tax imposed.

SPECIAL USE VALUATION: § 2032A

The requirement that property in a decedent's gross estate be valued at fair market value can create hardship if a principal estate asset is real property used in a family business. The value of such real property as it is used in the business may be considerably less than its potential selling price on the open market. As a result, an estate might be forced to sell the real estate and terminate the family business in order to pay the Federal estate tax.

Section 2032A provides that qualifying real estate used in a closely held business may be valued based on its business usage rather than market value. The requirements for qualification under this section are formidable, but can be summarized as follows:

▸ *Location.* The realty must be located in the United States.

▸ *Qualified Heir.* The realty must pass from the decedent to a "qualified heir" (generally a family member including the taxpayer's spouse, siblings, parents, grandparents and other ancestors, or children, grandchildren and other lineal descendants).

▸ *Qualified Farming or Business Use.* During the eight years prior to death (or disability or the time at which he begins to receive social security), there were at least 5 years when the realty was used for farming or in business and the decedent or a member of his family materially participated in the operation of the farm or business.

▸ *Realty and Personal Property Value (50 percent Test).* The *adjusted value* of the real and personal property used in farming or business must be at least 50 percent of adjusted value of the gross estate. For purpose of this test and the test below, the adjusted value of the realty is the value of the property less any related debt while the adjusted value of the gross estate is the value of the gross estate less any debts related to property included in the estate.

▸ *Realty Value (25 percent Test).* The adjusted value of the real property taken by itself is at least 25 percent of the adjusted value of the gross estate.

If these requirements are met, the maximum reduction from highest and best use value was originally $750,000, but is now adjusted for inflation. For 2005 the amount is $870,000. Note also that when special valuation is elected, the basis of the realty to the heirs is the reduced value.

> **Example 10.** F died in 2005. He owned a large farm south of a major urban center. As farming property, F's real estate was worth $4,000,000; however, developers wanting to acquire the real estate for future use as commercial and residential property had offered F $7,000,000 for the real estate. If all the qualifications of § 2032A can be met, F's real property would be valued at $6,130,000 ($7,000,000 − $870,000) in his gross estate, and would take an income tax basis of $6,130,000.

Recapture of Tax Savings. The estate tax savings offered by the election of qualified-use valuation is conditional upon the continued use of the qualified real property in the family farm or other business. If the heirs of the decedent dispose of the real property or discontinue its qualified use within 10 years of the decedent's death, Code § 2032A(c) requires that the heirs repay the estate tax saved by the original use of the § 2032A election.

GROSS ESTATE INCLUSIONS

The Federal estate tax is not a property tax levied on the value of property owned at death. Instead, it is a transfer tax levied on the value of any shift in a property interest that occurs because of a decedent's death. As a result, a decedent's gross estate may include assets not owned by a decedent at death, the transfer of which is not controlled by the terms of the decedent's will.

INSURANCE ON THE LIFE OF THE DECEDENT

The proceeds of an insurance policy on the life of a decedent do not come into existence until the death of the insured and are paid to the beneficiaries specified in the insurance contract, not the beneficiaries named in the decedent's will. However, § 2042 provides that such proceeds shall be included in the decedent's gross estate if either of the following is true:

1. The decedent's estate is the beneficiary, or

2. The decedent, at his or her death, possessed any incident of ownership in the life insurance policy, alone or in conjunction with any other person.

The term *incident of ownership* implies any economic interest in the policy and is broadly interpreted by the IRS. The Regulations under § 2042 list the power to change the policy's beneficiary, the right to cancel or assign the policy, and the right to borrow against the policy as incidents of ownership.[24]

Example 11. In 1999 T purchased a term insurance policy on his own life. Under the terms of the policy, beneficiary B would receive $150,000 upon T's death. In 2005 T died. Immediately before T's death the policy had no value since it was term insurance. Nevertheless, the $150,000 paid to B is includible in T's gross estate.

SURVIVOR BENEFITS

Section 2039 requires that the value of an annuity or any payment receivable by a beneficiary by reason of surviving a decedent be included in the decedent's gross estate. This rule only applies to the extent that the value of the annuity or payment is attributable to contributions made by the decedent or the decedent's employer. A second condition for applicability is that the payment or annuity be payable to the decedent or that the decedent possess the right to payment at death. For example, social security death benefits paid to a decedent's family are not covered by § 2039 because the decedent had no right to the payments during his or her lifetime.

The value of an annuity includible under § 2039 is the replacement cost to the beneficiary of a comparable commercial annuity.[25]

---

[24]   Reg. § 20.2042-1(c)(2).

[25]   Reg. § 20.2031-8(a).

Example 12. H purchased a self and survivor annuity contract that was to pay him $1,500 a month for his life and, upon his death, $1,000 a month to his widow, W. At the date of H's death, W would have to pay $24,000 to purchase a $1,000 a month lifetime annuity for herself. Under § 2039, the value of the annuity received by W, $24,000, is includible in H's gross estate.

JOINT INTERESTS

Nonspousal Joint Tenancies. As discussed earlier in the chapter, a joint tenancy with right of survivorship is a form of equal co-ownership of an asset that causes full ownership of the asset to vest automatically in the survivor when the first joint tenant dies. The decedent's will cannot change this result; property owned in joint tenancy is not included in a decedent's probate estate. However, some portion of the value of this property may be includible in the decedent's gross estate. Under § 2040, it is necessary to determine the proportion of the decedent's original contribution toward the acquisition of the asset. This same proportion of the value of the asset at date of death must be included in the decedent's gross estate.

Example 13. Brothers A and B decided to purchase a tract of real estate as equal joint tenants with right of survivorship. A contributed $40,000 and B contributed $10,000 toward the $50,000 purchase price. At A's death, the real estate was worth $150,000. A's gross estate must include $120,000, 80% [$40,000 ÷ ($40,000 + $10,000)] of the real estate's value. If B had died before A, only $30,000, 20% of the real estate's value, would be includible in B's gross estate.

Note in *Example 13* that in the year the real estate was acquired, A made a taxable gift to B of $15,000, the difference between half the value of the asset when purchased, $25,000, and B's $10,000 contribution. In spite of this completed gift, a portion of the property is taxed in A's gross estate under the authority of § 2040 if he dies before B.

Spousal Joint Tenancies. If a husband and wife own property as joint tenants with right of survivorship, § 2040(b) contains a rule that requires 50 percent of the value of the property to be included in the gross estate of the first spouse to die, regardless of the original contribution of that spouse.

GENERAL POWERS OF APPOINTMENT

A *power of appointment* is a right to dispose of property that the holder of the power does not legally own. It is normally created by the will of a decedent in conjunction with a transfer of property in trust. Typically, the decedent's will provides for the transfer of property in trust, giving an individual a life estate and a power to appoint the remainder interest during his or her life or at death through a will. By so doing, the decedent transfers the ability to control the property's disposition to the holder of the power, even though the holder does not own the property. In effect, a power of appointment gives a person the right to fill in the blanks of another person's will.

A power of appointment may be *specific*, meaning that the holder of the power may only give the property to members of a specified eligible group of recipients which does *not* include the holder. Alternatively, the power may be *general*, so that the holder may appoint the property to himself or herself, or his or her creditors, estate, or creditors of that estate. The terms of the power should specify to whom ownership of the property will go if the holder deliberately or inadvertently fails to exercise the power.

A *general power of appointment* over property is tantamount to actual ownership of the property. If the holder appoints the property to another person, the exercise is treated as a taxable gift per § 2514.[26] Section 2041 provides that if a decedent holds a general power over property at his or her death, the value of the property must be included in the gross estate.

> **Example 14.** P has the right to appoint ownership of certain real estate to any of P's children or grandchildren. He may exercise the right during life or by will. Upon P's death, his will appoints the property to his daughter, D. Because P held only a *specific power*, the value of the appointed property is not included in P's gross estate.

> **Example 15.** M has the right to appoint ownership of certain real estate to *himself* or any of his brothers and sisters. He may exercise the right during life or by will. However, M dies without exercising the power. The terms of the power provide that if the power is not exercised the property shall go to M's uncle. Because M possessed a *general power* of appointment, the date of death value of the property must be included in M's gross estate.

Nontaxable Powers. As indicated above, a specific power of appointment over property will not result in inclusion of the property in the holder's gross estate. There are other situations where a power does not cause taxation. If the holder's power to appoint property for his or her benefit is limited to an *ascertainable standard*, it is not a general power of appointment and inclusion is not required. A power is considered limited to a standard if appointments of property may be made solely for the holder's health, education, maintenance, or support in his or her accustomed manner of living. The language used to describe the scope of the holder's power is extremely important. For example, a power is not considered limited if it permits appointments for the holder's comfort, happiness, or well-being.

> **Example 16.** H's will provided for the transfer of $600,000 in trust, giving his wife a life estate and a power to appoint the property to herself for her support. Upon the wife's death, nothing is included in her gross estate since she does not have a general power of appointment. The power does not cause inclusion since it is limited to an ascertainable standard.

Another nontaxable power which offers great planning flexibility is the so-called five and five power. Section 2041 generally does not require inclusion if the amount that the holder can appoint for his or her use in any one year does not exceed the greater of $5,000 or 5 percent of the value of the property. As long as the power is drawn within these limits, the power need not be restricted in any other manner to avoid taxation. However, in the year of the holder's death, the power is considered a general power to the extent of the greater of the two amounts and thus causes inclusion in the holder's estate to that extent.

> **Example 17.** R created a $1,000,000 trust for his wife, giving her the income for life and the remainder to the children. R wanted to give his wife access to the corpus of the trust without causing it to be included in her estate. Therefore, he gave his wife the annual right to withdraw for her use any time during the year the greater of $5,000 or five percent of the aggregate value of the trust. As a result, assuming the value of the trust remained at $1,000,000, his wife could withdraw up to $50,000 (5% of $1,000,000) annually without having the entire corpus included in her estate. However, in the year of the wife's death, she must include $50,000 in her estate, the amount over which she might have exercised the power at death.

---

[26] If the holder of a general power releases the power or allows it to lapse, the transfer of ownership is still considered a taxable gift made by the holder. See §§ 2514(b) and (e).

TRANSFERS TAKING EFFECT AT DEATH

Taxpayers who are reluctant to give away property during life but who also want to minimize the tax burden on their estate have designed a variety of inter vivos gifts with "strings attached." Such gifts are subject to a condition or restriction that enables the donor to continue to benefit from or enjoy the property until death. Such a transfer may be complete for gift tax purposes. Nevertheless, for estate tax purposes it may be classified as a transfer taking effect at death, with the result that the date of death value of the property is includible in the donor's gross estate.

Code §§ 2036, 2037, and 2038 govern transfers taking effect at death. Because these three sections were added to the Code at different times, there is a confusing amount of overlap in their coverage. The sections' requirements are very complex and difficult to apply. However, a brief description of each section can give the beginning tax student an idea of their general functions.

One important rule to remember is that all three sections can only require the inclusion in a decedent's gross estate of property that was originally owned by the decedent. A second rule is that the sections are inapplicable if the transfer of the property by the decedent was for sufficient consideration.

Code § 2036. This section requires that the value of any property given away by the decedent, but to which the decedent retained the right to the property's income or the right to designate who may possess or enjoy the property, shall be included in the decedent's gross estate. Section 2036 also specifies that the retention of the voting rights of shares of stock in a controlled corporation represents a retention of enjoyment.[27]

> **Example 18.** In 2001, F made a completed gift of rental property to his son, S, subject to the condition that F was to receive the net rent from the property for the rest of his life. Upon F's death in the current year, the date of death value of the rental property must be included in F's gross estate since he retained a right to income (i.e., rentals), even though S is the owner of the property.

> **Example 19.** In the current year, M transferred assets into an irrevocable trust for the sole benefit of her grandchildren. Under the terms of the trust instrument, M reserved the right to designate which of the grandchildren should receive the annual income of the trust. Because M retained the right to designate the persons who shall possess the income from the trust assets, the value of the trust assets will be included in M's gross estate upon her death.

The IRS is very aggressive in applying § 2036. For example, in a situation in which a parent gifts a family residence to a child but continues to occupy the residence rent free, the parent is considered to have retained a beneficial interest in the residence, with the result that the value of the residence will be includible in the parent's gross estate.[28]

Code § 2037. This statute requires inclusion in a decedent's gross estate of the value of previously transferred property if two conditions are met:

1. Possession or enjoyment of the property can only be obtained by surviving the decedent,

---

[27]   § 2036(b)(2) defines a controlled corporation as a corporation in which the decedent controlled (directly or indirectly) at least 20 percent of the voting power of all classes of stock.

[28]   Rev. Rul. 70-155, 1970-1 C.B. 189; and *Estate of Linderme*, 52 T.C. 305 (1966).

2. The decedent owns a reversionary interest in the property, the value of which exceeds 5 percent of the value of the property. The value of the reversion is computed as of the moment immediately before death, based on actuarial tables.[29]

Regulation § 20.2037-1(e) gives the following example of the application of Code § 2037.

Example 20. The decedent transferred property in trust, with the income payable to his wife for life and with the remainder payable to the decedent or, if he is not living at his wife's death, to his daughter or her estate. The daughter cannot obtain possession or enjoyment of the property without surviving the decedent. Therefore, if the decedent's reversionary interest immediately before death exceeded 5% of the value of the property, the value of the property less the value of the wife's outstanding life estate is includible in the decedent's gross estate.

Note in *Example 20* that the decedent's reversionary interest was extinguished at death and did not constitute an interest in property that would be transferred under the terms of the decedent's will. However, it is the event of the decedent's death that completes the transfer of the remainder interest in the trust to the daughter or her estate.

Code § 2038. If, on the date of death, the decedent had the power to alter, amend, or revoke the enjoyment of any property previously given away by the decedent, § 2038 requires that the date of death value of the property be included in the decedent's gross estate. Obviously, a revocable transfer falls within § 2038. However, the scope of the section is broad enough to apply to much less obvious types of powers.

Example 21. Individual Z creates an irrevocable trust for the benefit of her children and names the trust department of a national bank as trustee. The only right retained by Z allows her to replace the trustee with a different trust department. Upon Z's death, Revenue Ruling 79-353[30] states that Code § 2038 applies and the value of the trust corpus must be included in Z's gross estate.

GIFTS IN CONTEMPLATION OF DEATH

For many years, Code § 2035 required that the date of death value of any gift made by the decedent during the three years prior to death, plus the amount of any gift tax paid on such gifts, be included in the decedent's gross estate. In 1981, Congress drastically altered this section so that it currently applies only to gifts of interests described in the sections governing transfers taking effect at death (§§ 2036, 2037, and 2038) and § 2042, relating to gifts of life insurance. In addition, § 2035 applies for determining the applicability of provisions such as § 2032A, concerning special use valuation (e.g., any property given away within three years of death is added back to the gross estate in applying the 50 and 25 percent tests). Notwithstanding the limited application of the general rule, § 2035(c) continues to require the inclusion in the gross estate of any gift tax paid within three years of death.

Example 22. Refer to the facts in *Example 18*. Assume that one year prior to his death, F made a gift of his retained income interest in the rental property to his granddaughter, D. Section 2035 applies to the transfer of the income interest, with

---

[29]   Reg. § 20.2037-1(c)(3).

[30]   1979-2 C.B. 325.

the result that the date of death value of the rental property and any gift tax paid on the gift are included in F's gross estate.

TRANSFERS FOR INSUFFICIENT CONSIDERATION

A transfer for which the donor received consideration less than the value of the transferred property is vulnerable to the application of §§ 2035, 2036, 2037, or 2038 upon the donor's death. However, 2043 does allow the estate an offset for the consideration received.[31]

> **Example 23.** A transferred her 100 shares of stock in Famco Corporation to her daughter, D, subject to the condition that A would retain the voting rights in the shares. At date of transfer, the fair market value of the stock was $500,000, and D paid A only $300,000 cash in exchange. The transfer constituted a taxable gift of $200,000. Upon A's death, the value of the stock, $1.2 million, is includible in A's gross estate under § 2036. However, A's estate may reduce this value by $300,000, the amount of the consideration received by A.

The § 2043 consideration offset equals the value of the consideration at date of receipt. Therefore, in *Example 23* only 40 percent ($200,000 ÷ $500,000) of the value of the property was transferred without consideration, but 75 percent [($1.2 million − $300,000) ÷ $1.2 million] of the date of death value of the property must be included in the gross estate.

DEDUCTIONS FROM THE GROSS ESTATE

Not all of the value of a decedent's gross estate will be available for transfer to estate beneficiaries or other individuals. Some of the value must first be used to pay off debts of the decedent and other claims against the estate. The second step in computing an individual's taxable estate is to identify the debts and claims that are deductible against the gross estate.

EXPENSES, INDEBTEDNESS, AND TAXES

The estate tax is based on the *net* wealth that is actually transferred by the decedent. Consistent with this concept, the law permits deductions for expenses associated with death as well as costs of settling the estate and other claims against the property in the estate. As might be expected, the executor cannot spend and borrow willy-nilly and expect to deduct these items. Section 2053(a) generally allows deductions for funeral and administrative expenses, mortgages on property included in the gross estate and other personal debts owed by the decedent. Under § 2053(a), these items are deductible *only* if allowed by local law and *only* to the extent they are incurred in administering property subject to claims (i.e., creditors of the decedent can seek satisfaction of their claims from these assets). This normally encompasses those expenses relating to administering the probate estate. In addition, Section 2053(b) grants deductions for expenses incurred in administering property that is included in the gross estate but which is *not* subject to the claims of the estate's creditors. For example, expenses related to a revocable trust would be deductible even though creditors cannot seek satisfaction of their claims from the trust property. These deductions are allowed because the assets of the trust are included in the gross estate [§ 2053(b)].

---

[31] See Reg. § 20.2043-1(a).

Funeral Expenses. Deductible funeral expenses include costs for the funeral service, clergy, mortuary, hearse, limousines, casket, cremation, pianist, singers, flowers and the like. In addition, a deduction is allowed for costs of a tombstone, monument, or mausoleum crypt, or for a burial lot, either for the decedent or his family. If the decedent had acquired the burial lots prior to death, no deduction is allowed but the lots are not included in the gross estate. Deductions are also allowed for a reasonable expenditure for the future care of the lot. Transportation costs of the person bringing the body to the burial site also are deductible as funeral expenses (e.g., a corpse is flown home). Traveling expenses for beneficiaries or others to attend the decedent's funeral are not deductible (e.g., costs of flying decedent's grandchildren to the funeral are not deductible).

Administrative Expenses Section 2053 also permits deductions for administering and settling the decedent's estate. Deductions normally include all probate costs such as those incurred in collection and preservation of probate assets (bank charges), payment of debts and distribution of property (e.g., cost of wire transfer). Common administrative expenses are fees paid to the executor or administrator of the estate, accounting and legal expenses, court costs, and appraisal fees. In addition, expenses incurred in preserving the estate, including the costs of maintaining and storing property (e.g., utility bills on the decedent's home after death) are deductible.

It should be emphasized that deductions are limited for those expenses in the administration of the estate. Those that are not "essential" to the proper settlement of the estate, but are incurred for the benefit of the heirs or others, may not be claimed as deductions. In this regard, selling expenses are deductible administrative expenses, if the assets must be sold to pay debts, expenses or taxes. Regulation § 20.2053-3(d)(2) authorizes the deduction of the expenses of selling assets of the estate only if the sale is necessary (1) to pay debts, administrative expenses or tax; (2) to preserve the estate; or (3) to effect distribution.

Example 24. In *Estate of David Smith*, a famous sculptor died and left over 425 pieces of his work.[32] The executors of his estate paid commissions in excess of $1,000,000 to a gallery for selling the decedent's work presumably to raise money to pay expenses of the estate. However, only $290,000 of those commissions were identified as attributable to sales needed to pay the decedent's debts, taxes, and other administration expenses. The Court held that only $290,000 of commissions were attributable to the estate's liquidity needs and denied a deduction for the remainder. Moreover, the court found no evidence that it was necessary to sell all of the works promptly. Presumably, such expenses could be claimed as selling expenses on the estate's income tax return. Note that *Smith* also stands for the proposition that assets cannot be valued in the gross estate at their value net of any expected selling expenses.

Adminstrative expenses incurred after death can be claimed as either a deduction on the estate tax return (Form 706) or on the estate's income tax return but not on both.[33]

The executor must be careful not to waste any deductions for administration expenses. This is a major concern when the estate owes no estate tax (e.g., due to the unlimited marital or charitable deductions or the unified credit) since the only potential benefit could be derived from deducting the expense for income tax purposes. Even if the executor properly waives the deduction for estate tax purposes, this does not ensure that an income tax benefit will be derived since the estate may have little or no income that could be

---

[32]   75-1 USTC ¶13,046, AFTR 2d 75-1594, 510 F.2d 479 (CA-2, 1975) aff'g 57 TC 650 (1972) cert. denied.

[33]   § 642(g).

reduced by the deduction. However, if the deduction exceeds income *in the year the estate terminates*, §642(h) provides that all excess deductions pass through to the beneficiaries succeeding to the decedent's property who can then deduct them on their individual tax returns as itemized deductions. This is allowed only for the excess deductions that occur in the year of termination. If excess deductions occur in earlier years (e.g., because the estate chooses the wrong time to pay the expense) the deduction is generally lost.

Claims Against the Estate. Deductions are allowed for any debts that the decedent owed at the time of death. The deduction for these items reflects the fact that the estate must pay these amounts before the property is distributed thereby reducing the amount that is transferred to the heirs by the decedent. Debts of the estate typically include unpaid mortgages or liens on property included in the gross estate, unpaid income taxes on income received by the decedent before he or she died, property taxes accrued before death as well as personal obligations of the decedent. Examples of personal liabilities are balances due on credit card accounts, utility bills, interest on mortgages accrued before death, margin accounts, and other loans outstanding at the date of death. Interest accrued after the date of death is not deductible on the Form 706 even if the alternate valuation date is elected.[34]

Medical expenses of the decedent are deductible as a claim against the estate. However, if such expenses are paid within one year of death, they may be claimed as income tax deduction on the final return. The expenses cannot be claimed on both returns, however.

LOSSES

Section 2054 allows deductions for casualty and theft losses occurring while the estate is being settled and are deductible in computing the taxable estate. For example, the decedent's car may be stolen or his home destroyed by fire. The amount of the deductible loss is the value of the property reduced for any insurance proceeds received. If the alternate valuation date is elected, the property is valued at zero when determining the value of the gross estate. Therefore no loss deduction is allowed.

Although casualty and theft losses are also deductible for income tax purposes, there is no double deduction allowed.[35] The loss can be deducted on either the estate tax return or the estate's income tax return, but not both. In most cases, a greater benefit could be secured by deducting the expenses on the estate tax return since such expenses may be subject to limitations for income tax purposes.

STATE DEATH TAXES

In addition to the Federal estate tax, decedents must be concerned about state death taxes. Most states impose some type of death tax. These usually take the form of an inheritance tax, an estate tax or both. On the other hand very few states impose any type of gift tax. However, gifts made in contemplation of death (e.g., a deathbed transfer) are usually subject to the state's death tax.

State Inheritance Taxes. Many states and some local jurisdictions impose an inheritance tax on the right to receive property at death. Unlike an estate tax, which is imposed on the estate according to the value of property transferred by the decedent at death, an inheritance tax is imposed on the recipient of property from an estate (although it is typically paid out of the estate). The amount of an inheritance tax payable

---

[34] Reg. § 20.2053-7.

[35] *Supra* Footnote 34.

usually is directly affected by the degree of kinship between the recipient and the decedent. The inheritance tax typically provides an exemption from the tax, which increases as the relationship between the recipient (e.g., the surviving spouse, children, grandchildren, etc.) and the decedent becomes closer. For example, under the Indiana inheritance tax rules, transfers to a surviving spouse are exempt while transfers to a child under 21 are entitled to an exemption of $100,000. The rate of tax also differs depending on the relationship. For example, the Indiana rates for transfers to children range from 1 to 10 percent while transfers to nonrelatives range from 10 to 20 percent. Observe that the small exemptions, at least in Indiana, make even modest estates subject to state inheritance taxes even though they may be exempt from the Federal estate tax.

State Estate Taxes. These taxes are similar to the Federal estate tax and are based on the value of the property held by the decedent at the date of death.

Deduction for State Death Taxes. Prior to 2005, the estate was allowed a credit for state death taxes. Beginning in 2005, however, the state death tax credit is repealed and replaced by a deduction. Note that the deduction is for state death taxes. There is no deduction for Federal estate taxes.

Technically, § 2058 allows a deduction for the amount of any estate, inheritance, legacy, or succession taxes actually paid to any state or the District of Columbia, in respect of property included in the gross estate. The amount must be actually paid to the estate, not merely estimated or accrued. Observe that many states permit a discount for prompt payment. For example, Indiana allows a five percent discount if the tax is paid within 9 months of date of death. In such case, the amount paid, not the amount assessed, is the amount of the deductible state death tax.

CHARITABLE CONTRIBUTIONS

An estate may deduct the value of any transfer of assets to a qualified charitable organization under § 2055. Qualifying organizations are specifically defined in the statute. If an individual is willing to leave his or her entire estate for public, charitable, or religious use, there will be no taxable estate.

For a charitable contribution to be deductible, it normally must consist of the decedent's entire interest in the underlying property. For example, if a decedent bequeaths a life interest in real estate to his son and the remainder interest in the property to charity, the value of the remainder interest is not deductible. Similarly, if the decedent bequeaths the interest in the real estate to a charity for a term of years (e.g., 20 years), and the remainder to his son, the value of the income interest is not deductible. However, this restriction does not apply if the transfer is in a specific statutory form: a *charitable lead trust*, where an income interest is given to the charity, or a *charitable remainder trust*, where a remainder interest is given to the charity.[36] A detailed description of such trusts is beyond the scope of this text, but they do allow a decedent to create both a charitable and a noncharitable interest in the same property and secure a deduction for the charitable interest. The restriction also is inapplicable to a charitable contribution of a remainder interest in a personal residence or farm and to certain contributions for conservation purposes.[37]

If an individual taxpayer is considering making bequests to charity upon his or her death, his or her tax adviser should certainly explore the possibility of having the individual make such charitable contributions during his or her life. Such inter vivos contributions would serve a dual purpose: the donated assets would be removed from

---

[36] § 2055(e)(2).

[37] *Ibid.*

the individual's potential taxable estate, and the donation would create a deduction for income tax purposes.

THE MARITAL DEDUCTION

Code § 2056 provides an unlimited deduction for the value of property passing to a surviving spouse. If a married taxpayer, no matter how wealthy, is willing to leave all his or her property to the surviving spouse, no transfer tax will be imposed on the estate.[38] Only upon the subsequent death of the spouse will the couple's wealth be subject to taxation. Planning for maximizing the benefit of the unlimited marital deduction is discussed in Chapter 26.

In certain instances, interests transferred to the surviving spouse are not deductible— so-called *nondeductible terminable interests*. If a decedent leaves an interest in property to his or her spouse that can or will terminate at a future date *and* if after termination another person receives an interest in the property from the decedent, the value of the interest passing to the spouse is ineligible for the marital deduction.[39] Absent this rule, the interest would escape taxation entirely, since it terminates prior to or with the death of the surviving spouse and thus is not included in his or her gross estate.

> **Example 25.** Decedent H leaves a life estate in real property to his surviving spouse, W, with the remainder after W's death left to their daughter. The interest passing to W is a terminable interest ineligible for the marital deduction. Note that without this rule barring a marital deduction, the value of the property would completely escape estate taxation since it would not be taxed in either H's estate (due to the marital deduction) or W's estate (since W's life estate terminates at her death).

The property need not pass directly to the surviving spouse to qualify for the marital deduction. Section 2056(b)(5) generally allows the deduction if the surviving spouse is entitled to annual payments of all of the income from the property for life and has a general power of appointment over the property exercisable during life or at death. In this case, the entire value of the property will be included in the estate of the surviving spouse because of his or her general power of appointment.

For many years, these two methods of leaving property to a spouse (outright or in trust with a general power of appointment to the surviving spouse) were essentially the only two techniques available if the decedent wanted to qualify the transfer for the marital deduction. This often left a married couple with a perplexing problem. Notice that in both situations, the decedent surrenders control of the property to the surviving spouse. When the surviving spouse is given a general power of appointment over the property, he or she has complete control over the ultimate disposition of the property— the same control that would have been obtained if he or she had received the property outright. Under either scenario, the surviving spouse is left with the choice of who will be the beneficiaries of the decedent's property. In other words, the decedent could not be assured that property that had been accumulated during marriage would reach the desired beneficiaries, typically the couple's children. For example, if the surviving spouse remarried, the decedent's property could end up being used for the benefit of the new spouse and new children, usually not the result desired by the decedent. Unfortunately, more suitable arrangements from a nontax point of view normally did not qualify for the marital deduction. Consequently, the tax law put taxpayers in a very awkward position, requiring them to either give up control or face higher taxes.

---

[38]   No marital deduction is allowed for the value of property passing to a surviving spouse who is not a U.S. citizen unless the property is placed in a "qualified domestic trust."

[39]   § 2056(b).

In 1981, Congress addressed this problem by sanctioning the marital deduction for a life estate for the surviving spouse. Observe that without this relief provision the life estate would be considered a nondeductible terminable interest. However, as explained below, the deduction is allowed only if the property (that would normally escape tax by virtue of the life estate rules) is included in the surviving spouse's estate upon his or her death. The special rules enabling this treatment are contained in § 2056(b)(7).

Under § 2056(b)(7), a marital deduction is allowed for the value of *qualifying terminable interest property* left to a surviving spouse. Qualifying terminable interest property is property from which the entire income must be paid to the spouse at least annually. During the spouse's lifetime, no one else must be able to receive any interest in the property. Upon the spouse's death, the property may pass to anyone. If the executor elects, the entire value of the property is deductible on the decedent's estate tax return. In most cases, these requirements are met by transferring property to a trust from which the spouse receives the income for life. Such arrangements are normally referred to as QTIPs, reflecting the fact that they are created to enable to the property to be considered Qualifying Terminable Interest Property.

Without further requirements, the interest described above is simply a life estate that would totally escape tax as described in *Example 25* above. However, § 2044 requires that when the surviving spouse dies, the entire value of the qualifying terminable interest property at that time must be included in the spouse's gross estate. If the surviving spouse gives away the income interest during life, § 2519 requires that the gift will consist of the entire value of the property.

> **Example 26.** H and W, husband and wife, have been married for ten years. They have three children, A, B, and C, ages 9, 7, and 4. H wants to ensure that their children receive the couple's assets after he dies. For this reason, he does not want to leave the property outright to his spouse nor does he want to leave the property in trust to her with a general power of appointment. To this end, his will provides that upon his death, all of his assets are transferred to a trust that gives W an income interest for life and the remainder interest to A, B and C upon W's death. Note that H has provided for W but has retained control over who ultimately receives the property. From a tax perspective, this normally would be considered a nondeductible terminable interest as described above and would not qualify for the marital deduction. However, if an election is made by the executor of H's estate, this otherwise nondeductible terminable interest becomes qualifying terminable interest property, that is, a QTIP, and qualifies for the marital deduction. When W dies, the value of the property at her death is automatically included in her gross estate. In this way, the property does not escape estate tax. Any estate tax that is attributable to inclusion of the property in the W's estate can be paid by her estate. However, if this is not suitable, the law requires that the tax will be paid from the property itself (e.g., the property could be sold to pay the estate tax and the property net of the estate tax would be passed to the children of H and W).

While the examples above provide some measure of the trade-offs that must be considered when planning with the marital deduction, these issues are just part of the story. Other factors that must be considered in order to effectively design marital bequests are discussed in Chapter 26.

COMPUTATION OF THE ESTATE TAX

Once the value of the taxable estate has been determined, the first step in computing the estate tax liability is to add the taxable estate to the amount of the decedent's *adjusted taxable gifts*. Adjusted taxable gifts are defined in Code § 2001(b) as the total amount of taxable gifts (after any available exclusion or deduction) made after December 31, 1976 *other than* gifts includible in the gross estate of the decedent.

The transfer tax rates of § 2001(c) are then applied to the sum of the taxable estate plus adjusted taxable gifts. The tentative tax calculated is then reduced by any gift taxes paid or payable at current rates for gifts made after December 31, 1976. The result is the Federal estate tax liability *before* credits.

ESTATE TAX CREDITS

The major credit available to reduce the Federal estate tax is the unified credit of Code § 2010. As seen in Exhibit 24-3, the estate and gift tax credits are the same until 2004 at which time the gift tax credit is frozen at $345,800 and the estate tax credit continues to increase until the elimination of the estate tax in 2010. The mechanics of the estate tax calculation ensure that the decedent's estate benefits from the credit only to the extent that it was not used to offset any gift tax during his or her lifetime. It is important to understand that the two credits combined will shelter a maximum of $1,500,000 (in 2005) of transfers from the imposition of any Federal transfer tax.

The remaining estate tax credits are:

- Foreign death tax credit
- Credit for taxes on prior transfers
- Credit for pre-1977 gift taxes

Foreign Death Tax Credit. Section 2014 allows the estate a credit for all or part of the death taxes that must be paid to a foreign country on account of property located in that country that is included in the gross estate. The amount of the credit is limited to the lesser of (1) the foreign death tax attributable to the foreign property, or (2) the Federal estate tax attributable to the foreign property.

Credit for Tax on Prior Transfers. If two family members die within a short period of time, the same property may be included in both taxable estates and be subject to two rounds of estate taxation in rapid succession. Section 2013 provides a credit to the estate of the second decedent to mitigate this excessive taxation. The credit generally is computed as a percentage of the amount of tax attributable to the inclusion of property in the estate of the first decedent. The percentage is based on the number of years between the two deaths as follows:

0–2 years	100%
3–4 years	80%
5–6 years	60%
7–8 years	40%
9–10 years	20%

If the second decedent outlived the first by more than 10 years, no § 2013 credit is allowed.

Example 27. Individual A died in March 2003. Under the terms of his will, A left $1,000,000 in assets to his younger sister, B. B died unexpectedly in December 2005 and the assets inherited from A were included in B's taxable estate. The amount of tax paid by A's estate that is attributable to the assets is calculated at $100,000. The § 2013 credit available to B's estate is $80,000 (80% × $100,000).

Gift Taxes Paid on Pre-1977 gifts. If a taxable gift was made prior to 1977 (i.e., prior to unification) and the gifted property is included in the transferor's gross estate (e.g., under the rules of §§ 2036, 2037, or 2038), § 2012 allows a credit for any gift tax paid. The amount of the credit is limited to the lesser of the gift tax paid or the estate tax attributable to inclusion of the gifted property in the taxpayer's gross estate.

A COMPREHENSIVE EXAMPLE

The following example illustrates the complete computation of the Federal estate tax. In 1997, taxpayer M makes his first taxable gift to his son S. The fair market value of the property transferred is $200,000. The gift tax is computed as follows:

Value of gift	$ 200,000
Less: Annual exclusion (1997)	−10,000
Taxable gift	$ 190,000
Gift tax before credits.	$ 51,600
Less: Unified credit	−51,600
Gift tax liability for 1997	$ 0

In 1998, M makes gifts to son S and daughter D. The value of each transfer is $250,000.

Value of gifts	$ 500,000
Less: Annual exclusions	−20,000
Taxable gifts for 1998	$ 480,000
Plus: 1997 taxable gift.	+190,000
Taxable transfers to date	$ 670,000
Tentative tax on total transfers to date.	$ 218,700
Less: Tax on 1997 gift	−51,600
Less: 1998 unified credit	
($202,050 − $51,600)	−150,450
1998 gift tax liability	$ 16,650

M dies in 2005, leaving a taxable estate valued at $1.6 million. The estate tax is computed as follows:

Taxable estate		$1,600,000
Plus: Taxable gifts made in prior years		+670,000
Total taxable transfers		$2,270,000
Tentative tax on total transfers.		$ 906,900
Less the sum of		
Gift taxes paid on post-1976		
taxable gifts (on 1998 gift)	$ 16,650	
Unified credit.	555,800	−572,450
Estate tax liability		$ 334,450

PAYMENT OF THE ESTATE TAX

The Federal estate tax return, Form 706, is due nine months after the date of the decedent's death, and any tax liability shown is payable with the return. However, Congress appreciates the fact that the payment of the estate tax is often unforeseen, and has provided for a variety of relief measures for the estate with a substantial tax liability and insufficient liquidity to pay the tax nine months after death.

Section 6161 authorizes the Secretary of the Treasury to extend the time of payment of the estate tax for up to 10 years past the normal due date. To obtain an extension, the executor must show reasonable cause for the delay in payment. For example, the fact that the executor of an estate requires additional time to sell a particularly illiquid asset to generate the cash with which to pay the estate tax might be accepted as reasonable cause for an extension of the payment date for the estate tax.

Section 6166 allows an estate to pay a portion of its estate tax liability in installments if a substantial portion of the estate consists of the decedent's interest in a closely held business.[40] To be considered "closely-held" at least 20 percent of the total capital of the partnership or 20 percent of the total value of the corporation's voting stock must be included in the gross estate or the decedent is a partner in the partnership or a shareholder in the corporation and such partnership or corporation has 45 or fewer partners or shareholders (as increased by the 2001 legislation). An estate is eligible if more than 35 percent of the *adjusted gross estate* (gross estate less §§ 2053 and 2054 deductions for debts of the decedent, funeral and administrative expenses, and losses) consists of the value of such an interest. The percentage of the estate tax liability that can be deferred is based on the ratio of the value of the closely held business to the value of the adjusted gross estate.

If a decedent owned an interest in more than one closely held business, the values of the interests can be combined to meet the 35 percent test *if* the decedent's interest represents 20 percent or more of the total value of the business.

Example 28. The taxable estate of decedent X is composed of the following:

		Value
Sole proprietorship		$ 300,000
40% interest in closely held corporation		1,500,000
Other assets		2,500,000
Gross estate		$4,300,000
Less sum of		
Code §§ 2053 and 2054 deductions	$300,000	
Code § 2055 charitable deduction	500,000	− 800,000
Taxable estate		$3,500,000

The decedent owned 100% of the value of the sole proprietorship and 40% of the value of the closely held corporation. The combined values of these interests, $1,800,000, represents 45% of the adjusted gross estate of $4,000,000 ($4,300,000 −$300,000). Therefore, the executor may elect to defer payment on 45% of the estate tax liability.

The tax deferred under § 6166 is payable in 10 equal annual installments. The first installment is payable five years and nine months after death. The IRS does charge the estate interest on the unpaid balance for the entire 15-year period.[41] Historically the

---

[40] § 6166(b) provides specific definition of the phrase "interest in a closely held business."

[41] See § 6601(j) for applicable interest rate.

interest rate charged on the deferred tax has been substantially less than the current market rate. Legislation in 1997 cut the rate even more. Currently, the interest rate is only two-percent of the deferred tax on the so-called *two-percent portion*. The tax on the two-percent portion is limited to the tax on the sum of $1,170,000 (as adjusted for inflation in 2005) and the exemption equivalent for the year of death less the applicable unified credit. For example, in 2005, the maximum two percent portion would be $539,900 computed as follows:

Base amount	$1,170,000
Exemption equivalent (2005)	1,500,000
Two percent portion	$2,670,000
Gross tax on two percent portion	
[$780,800 + (47% × ($2,670,000 − $2,000,000))]	$1,095,700
Unified credit (2005)	(555,800)
Tax on two-percent portion	$ 539,900

In addition, the interest rate imposed on the amount of the deferred estate tax attributable to the taxable value of the business in excess of this amount ($1,170,000 + the exemption of $1,500,000 or $2,670,000 in 2005) is reduced to 45 percent of the rate applicable to underpayments of estimated taxes. No estate tax deduction is allowed for the interest paid. If the estate disposes of 50 percent or more of the value of the qualifying closely held interest, any outstanding amount of deferred estate tax must be paid immediately.

THE GENERATION-SKIPPING TRANSFER TAX

As part of the Tax Reform Act of 1976, Congress added a third type of transfer tax to the Internal Revenue Code. The *generation-skipping transfer tax* (GSTT) was designed to "plug a loophole" in the coverage of the gift and estate taxes. The original version of the GSTT was intimidatingly complex, and was criticized by tax practitioners from the moment of enactment.

The Tax Reform Act of 1986 retroactively repealed the 1976 version of the GSTT and replaced it with a new tax applicable to testamentary transfers occurring after the date of enactment and to inter vivos transfers made after September 25, 1985. Any tax actually paid under the 1976 GSTT is fully refundable.

A traditional generation-skipping transfer involves at least three generations of taxpayers. In its simplest form, a generation-skipping transfer occurs whenever there is a so-called *direct skip*, an outright transfer of wealth for the sole benefit of persons at least two generations younger than the transferor.[42]

> **Example 29.** This year Grandpa made a gift to his grandchild. Although a gift tax may be imposed on Grandpa, no gift or estate tax is imposed on the intervening generation, that is, the child's father. Therefore there is a direct skip of the estate and gift tax.

A more complicated yet equally important example involves a so-called *taxable termination* as illustrated below.

---

[42]   § 2612.

Example 30. Several years ago, Mother, M, died. Her will created a trust with income to Daughter, D, for life, remainder to the grandchildren. In this case, M would pay an estate tax at the time of her death on the value of the property used to create the trust. More important, however, is the result when D dies and her interest terminates. Even though D is able to enjoy the income from the trust property for life, there is no estate tax imposed on her when she dies because her interest terminates at death. As a result, there is no estate or gift tax imposed on the second generation.

Generally, the value of property transferred in a taxable generation-skipping transaction is subject to a flat-rate tax of 47 percent (2005).[43] However, each transferor is allowed a lifetime exemption of $1,500,000 (as adjusted for inflation in 2005) for generation-skipping transfers of any type.[44] In addition, the tax is not imposed to the extent that the transfer is not subject to gift taxes (e.g., due to the annual exclusion or the exemption on transfers for medical or educational purposes). For example, small gifts from grandparents to grandchildren which fall within the annual exclusion would not be subject to the tax.

TAX PLANNING CONSIDERATIONS

The statutory rules of Federal gift, estate, and generation-skipping taxes have been examined in this chapter. Any individual taxpayer who desires to maximize the accumulated wealth available to family members will want to minimize the burden of these three transfer taxes. Tax planning for transfer taxes would be incomplete, however, without consideration of any interrelated Federal income taxes. Many gifts are made by transfers to a trust, and the income taxation of the trust entity and its beneficiaries may have a significant impact upon the original tax minimization plan. For this reason, the Federal income taxation of trusts, estates, and beneficiaries is discussed in the next chapter (Chapter 25). The tax planning considerations for transfer taxes and any attendant income taxes are incorporated in Chapter 26, *Family Tax Planning*.

PROBLEM MATERIALS

DISCUSSION QUESTIONS

24-1 *Interrelation of Federal Estate and Gift Taxes.* Discuss the various reasons why the Federal gift and estate taxes can be considered as a single, unified transfer tax.

24-2 *Entity for Transfer Tax Purposes.* Why can the married couple rather than each individual spouse be considered the taxable entity for transfer tax purposes?

24-3 *What Constitutes a Gift?* Businessperson B offers X $40,000 for an asset owned by X. Although X knows the asset is worth $60,000, he is in desperate need of cash and agrees to sell. Has X made a $20,000 taxable gift to B? Explain.

24-4 *Adequate Consideration.* During the current year, K offered to pay $50,000 to his only son, S, if S would agree to live in the same town as K for the rest of K's life. K is very elderly and frail and desires to have a relative close at hand in case of emergency. Does the $50,000 payment constitute a taxable gift made by K?

---

[43] § 2641.

[44] § 2631.

24-5   *When Is a Gift Complete?* Wealthy Grandmother G wants to provide financial support for her Grandson GS. She opens a joint checking account with $20,000 of cash. At any time, G or GS may withdraw funds from this account. Has G made a completed gift to GS by opening this account? At what point is the gift complete?

24-6   *Cumulative Nature of Transfer Taxes.* The Federal income tax is computed on an annual basis. How does this contrast to the computation of the Federal gift tax?

24-7   *Purpose of Unified Transfer Tax Rates.* A decedent's taxable estate can be considered the last taxable gift the decedent makes. Why?

24-8   *Incomplete Transfers.* The Federal gift tax and estate tax are not mutually exclusive. Give examples of transfers that may be treated as taxable gifts but that do not remove the transferred assets from the donor's gross estate.

24-9   *Computation of Taxable Estate.* What are the three steps involved in computing the taxable estate of a decedent?

24-10   *Probate Estate vs. Gross Estate.* How can the value of a decedent's probate estate differ from the value of his or her gross estate for tax purposes?

24-11   *Deduction for Closely Held Businesses.* Individuals H, W, and S own the stock of X Corporation. This year H died. Indicate whether his estate can deduct the value of his X stock. Assume that the stock qualifies for the deduction unless the facts imply otherwise.
  a.   Assume W is H's wife and each own 25 percent of the stock.
  b.   Assume H, W, and S are unrelated and they own the stock equally.
  c.   The stock represents 35 percent of H's adjusted gross estate.
  d.   X operates a small strip center consisting of a sandwich shop, liquor store, copying business, and bike shop.
  e.   The business is worth $2,000,000 on his date of death.
  f.   Due to his illness, H did not work in the business the two years before he died.
  g.   H owned 60 percent of the stock and left it all to his daughter who quit working in the business three years after her dad died.

24-12   *Special Use Valuation of § 2032A.* The gross estate of decedent F consists of a very successful farming operation located 80 miles east of an expanding metropolitan area. The estate includes 2,000 acres of real estate worth $400,000 as agricultural land. However, a real estate developer is willing to pay $1.5 million for the property because of its potential for suburban development. Discuss the utility of § 2032A to F's estate.

24-13   *Powers of Appointment.* What are some *nontax* reasons for the creation of a power of appointment? What is the difference between a specific and a general power?

24-14   *Gifts in Contemplation of Death.* Discuss the scope of § 2035 concerning gifts made within three years of death after the enactment of ERTA 1981.

24-15   *Estate Tax Credits.* With the exception of the unified credit of § 2010, what is the basic purpose of the various estate tax credits?

24-16   *Due Date of Estate Tax Return and Payment.* Why is the tax law particularly lenient in authorizing extensions for payment of the Federal estate tax?

24-17   *Unified Transfer Tax Credit.* Section 2010 appears to allow a second $192,800 credit against the Federal estate tax (in addition to the credit allowed for gift tax purposes under § 2505). Is this the case?

24-18 *Generation-Skipping Transfers.* Decedent T's will created a trust, the income from which is payable to T's invalid daughter D for her life. Upon D's death, the trust assets will be paid to T's two sons (D's brothers) in equal shares. Has T made a generation-skipping transfer? Explain.

PROBLEMS

24-19 *Gift Splitting.* During 2005, Mr. and Mrs. Z make the following cash gifts to their adult children:

Mr. Z:

to son M	$30,000
to daughter N	8,000
Total.	$38,000

Mrs. Z:

to son M	$ 2,000
to daughter N	12,000
to daughter O	18,000
Total.	$32,000

   a. Assume Mr. and Mrs. Z do *not* elect to split their gifts per § 2513. Compute the total taxable gifts after exclusions for each.

   b. How does the amount of taxable gifts change if Mr. and Mrs. Z *elect* to split their gifts?

24-20 *Computing Gift Tax Liability.* B, a single individual, made a cash gift of $200,000 his niece C in 1996. In 2005, B gives C an additional $700,000 and nephew D $900,000. Compute B's gift tax liability for the current year.

24-21 *Computing Taxable Gifts.* C, a single individual, makes the following transfers during current year.

	Fair Market Value
Cash to sister D	$13,000
Real estate:	
Life estate to brother B	28,000
Remainder to nephew N	21,000
Cash to First Baptist Church	25,000

What is the total amount of taxable gifts C must report?

24-22 *Amount of the Gift and the Annual Exclusion.* In 2005, Mr. C decided he wanted to set up trusts for his adult daughter and his grandson. To this end, he transferred $50,000 cash to a trust. The income of the trust was payable annually to his daughter, D, for 20 years with the remainder to D's son, R. For your computations, assume 120% of the applicable Federal midterm rate is 4.8 percent.

   a. What is (are) the amount(s) of the taxable gift(s)?

   b. Same as (a) except D is to receive the income for the rest of her life (she is age 40).

24-23   *Computing Taxable Gifts.* During 2004, L, a widower, makes the following transfers:

	Fair Market Value
Tuition payment to State College for nephew N, age 32	$ 6,000
New automobile to nephew N	9,000
Cash to a local qualified political committee. . . .	15,000

What is the total amount of taxable gifts L must report?

24-24   *Computing Taxable Gifts.* During 2005, Z, a widow, makes the following transfers:

	Fair Market Value
Real estate located in France to son J.	$500,000
City of Philadelphia municipal bonds to daughter K	120,000
Payment to local hospital for medical expenses of brother-in-law M	18,000

What is the total amount of taxable gifts Z must report?

24-25   *Basis of Gifted Assets.* During the current year, L received a gift of land from his grandmother. The land had a basis to the grandmother of $100,000 and a fair market value of $250,000 on the date of the gift. A gift tax of $30,000 was paid on the transfer.

   a.   If L subsequently sells the land for $300,000, how much gain or loss will he recognize?

   b.   What would be the amount of L's recognized gain or loss on the sale if the land had a tax basis of $325,000 (rather than $100,000) to the grandmother?

24-26   *Marital Deduction.* F died during the current year, leaving a gross estate valued at $5 million. F's will specifically provided that no amount of her wealth was to be left to her estranged husband, G. However, under applicable state law, G is legally entitled to $1 million of his deceased wife's assets. How does the payment of $1 million affect the value of

   a.   F's *gross* estate,

   b.   F's *taxable* estate?

24-27   *Gross Estate Inclusions.* Q was a cash basis taxpayer who died in the current year. On the date of Q's death, he owned corporate bonds, principal amount of $50,000, with accrued interest of $3,950. On the date of death, the bonds were selling on the open market for $54,000. Six months later the market price of the bonds had dropped to $51,500; there was $3,200 of accrued interest on the bonds as of this date. Neither market price includes any payment for accrued interest.

   a.   Assuming the executor of Q's estate does not elect the alternate valuation date, what amounts should be included in Q's gross estate because of his ownership of the bonds?

   b.   Assuming the executor does elect the alternate valuation date, what amounts should be included in Q's gross estate?

24-28   *Interests in Trusts Included in Gross Estate.* M's mother left property in trust (Trust A), with the income payable to M for M's lifetime and the remainder to M's daughter. At M's death, Trust A was worth $6.5 million. M's grandfather created a trust (Trust B), with the income payable to M's father for his lifetime. Upon the father's death, the remainder in Trust B was payable to M or M's estate. At M's death, his 82-year-old father was still living and Trust B was worth $2.1 million. Assuming a 9.8 percent interest rate, what are the values of the inclusions in M's gross estate attributable to M's interests in Trust A and Trust B? (See Table S, contained in Appendix A-1.)

24-29 *Computing Gross Estate.* Upon A's death, certain assets were valued as follows:

	Fair Market Value
Probate estate	$ 750,000
Insurance proceeds on a policy on A's life. The policy has always been owned by A's niece, the beneficiary	150,000
Corpus of Trust A. A possessed the right to give the ownership of the corpus to herself or any of her family. In her will she left the corpus to cousin K	15,000,000

Based on these facts, what is the value of A's gross estate?

24-30 *Computing Gross Estate.* Upon G's death, the following assets were valued:

	Fair Market Value
Probate estate	$ 350,000
Social security benefits payable to G's widow.	38,000
Annuity payable to G's widow out of G's employer's pension plan	20,000
Corpus of revocable trust created by G for the benefit of his children 10 years prior to death. Upon G's death, the trust becomes irrevocable	1,000,000

What is the value of G's gross estate?

24-31 *Gifts Included in Gross Estate.* Donor D, age 66, makes a gift in trust for his grandchildren K and L. Under the terms of the trust instrument, D will receive the income from the trust for the rest of his life. Upon his death, the trust assets will be distributed equally between K and L. Upon the date of D's death, at age 77, the value of the trust assets is $2.5 million. What amount, if any, is included in D's gross estate?

24-32 *Gifts in Contemplation of Death.* In 2003 S made a taxable gift of marketable securities to his nephew and paid a gift tax of $14,250. In 2004 S gave an income interest in trust property to the same nephew and paid a gift tax of $5,000. S originally created the trust in 1990, retaining the income interest for life and giving the remainder to another family member. S died in 2005, when the marketable securities were worth $300,000 and the trust property was worth $972,000. Based on these facts, what amounts, if any, are included in S's gross estate?

24-33 *Gifts Included in Gross Estate.* In 1995 F transferred real estate into a trust, the income from which was payable to M during her lifetime. Upon M's death, the trust property will be distributed in equal portions among M's children. However, the trust instrument gives F the right to change the remainder beneficiaries at any time. F dies in the current year without ever having changed the original trust provisions. At date of death, the trust property is worth $3.9 million and M is 60 years old. Assuming a five percent interest rate, determine the amount, if any, to be included in F's gross estate. (See Table S, contained in Appendix A-1.)

24-34 *Gifts Included in Gross Estate.* In 1991 P transferred $500,000 of assets into an irrevocable trust for the exclusive benefit of his children. Under the terms of the trust agreement, annual income must be distributed among the children according to P's direction. When the youngest child attains the age of 25 years, the trust corpus will be distributed equally among the living children. P dies in the current year while the trust is still in existence and the corpus has a fair market value of $3,200,000. How much, if any, of the corpus must be included in P's gross estate?

24-35 *Powers of Appointment.* In 1997 donor D transferred $100,000 of assets into an irrevocable trust for the exclusive benefit of her minor grandchildren. Under the terms of the trust agreement, the grandchildren will receive the annual income from the trust, and when the youngest grandchild attains the age of 21, the trust corpus will be divided among the living grandchildren as S, D's only child, so directs. S dies in the current year while the trust is still in existence and the corpus has a fair market value of $400,000. S's valid will directs that the corpus of the trust will go entirely to grandchild Q. How much, if any, of the corpus must be included in S's gross estate?

24-36 *Including Insurance in Gross Estate.* Decedent R left a probate estate of $3,000,000. Two years prior to his death, R gave all incidents of ownership in an insurance policy on his own life to his daughter S, the policy beneficiary. Because the policy had a substantial cash surrender value, R paid a gift tax of $77,000 on the transfer. Upon death, the insurance policy paid $5,000,000 to S. What is the value of R's gross estate?

24-37 *Joint Tenancy.* In 2000 individual Q pays $500,000 for an asset and takes title with his brother R as joint tenants with right of survivorship. R makes no contribution toward the purchase price. In the current year, when the asset is worth $1.2 million, Q dies and ownership of the asset vests solely in R.
  a. What are the gift tax consequences of the creation of the joint tenancy?
  b. How much of the date of death value of the asset must be included in Q's gross estate?
  c. How much would be included in the gross estate of R if R, rather than Q, died in the current year?

24-38 *Computing Taxable Estate.* Decedent T left a gross estate for tax purposes of $1.1 million. T had personal debts of $60,000 and his estate incurred funeral expenses of $12,000 and legal and accounting fees of $35,000. T's will provided for $100,000 bequest to the American Cancer Society, with all other assets passing to his grandchildren. Compute T's taxable estate.

24-39 *Sections 2053 and 2054 Expenses.* Decedent D died on July 1 of the current year. D owned a sailboat valued at $85,000 as of the date of death. However, on December 1 of the current year, the boat was destroyed in a storm, and the estate was unable to collect any insurance to compensate for the loss. In December, the executor of D's estate received a $2,200 bill from the company that had stored the sailboat from January 1 through December 1 of the current year.
  a. If the executor does not elect the alternate valuation date, will the $85,000 value of the boat be included in D's gross estate? D's taxable estate?
  b. May any portion of the $2,200 storage fee be deducted on D's Federal estate tax return? On the first income tax return filed by the estate?

24-40 *Marital Deduction Assets.* J, who was employed by Gamma Inc. at the date of his death, had been an active participant in Gamma's qualified retirement plan. Under the terms of the plan, J's widow will receive an annuity of $1,500 per month for the next 20 years. The replacement value of the annuity is $145,000. In his will, J left his interest in a patent worth $50,000 to his widow; the patent will expire in eight years. To what extent will these transfers qualify for a marital deduction from J's gross estate?

24-41 *Qualified Terminable Interest Trust.* Under the will of decedent H, all his assets (fair market value of $10 million) are to be put into trust. His widow, W, age 64, will be paid all the income from the trust every quarter for the rest of her life. Upon W's death, all the assets in the trust will be distributed to the couple's children and grandchildren. During W's life, no part of the trust corpus can be distributed to anyone but W.

   a. What amount of marital deduction is available on H's estate tax return?

   b. W dies eight years after H and under the terms of H's will the trust assets are distributed. What percentage, if any, of the value of these assets must be included in W's gross estate?

24-42 *Deferring Estate Tax Payments.* Decedent X has the following taxable estate:

Sole proprietorship.		$ 1,800,000
Ten percent interest in a closely held corporation		200,000
Other assets		1,200,000
Gross estate		$ 3,200,000
Less sum of		
§§ 2053 and 2054 deductions.	$800,000	
§ 2056 marital deduction.	400,000	−1,200,000
Taxable estate.		$ 2,000,000

Assume the estate tax liability on this estate is $300,000.

   a. How much of the liability may be deferred under § 6166?

   b. If X died in November 2005, when is the first installment payment of tax due?

24-43 *Computing Estate Tax Liability.* Decedent Z dies in 2005 and leaves a taxable estate of $2.4 million. During his life, Z made the following unrestricted gifts and did not elect gift splitting with his wife:

	Fair Market Value
1995: Gift of 2,000 shares of Acme stock to son S	$900,000
1997: Gift of cash to daughter D	600,000
1999: Gift of cash to wife W.	700,000

Compute Z's estate tax liability after utilization of the available unified credit.

RESEARCH PROBLEMS

24-44 In 1998, JW gifted 30 percent of her stock in W Corporation to her favorite nephew, N. Although she retained a 50 percent interest in W Corporation and her husband owned the remaining 20 percent of the outstanding stock, JW was concerned that the family might eventually lose control of the firm. To reassure JW, the three stockholders agreed to restrict transferability of their stock by signing an agreement that any shareholder wishing to dispose of W Corporation stock must offer the stock to the corporation for a formula price based on the average net earnings per share for the three previous years. The corporation would then be obligated to purchase the stock at the formula price. At the time the buy-sell agreement was entered into, this formula resulted in a price very close to the stock's actual fair market value.

   JW died in the current year at a time when the value of her W Corporation stock was substantially depreciated because of certain unfavorable local economic conditions. Several independent appraisals of the stock valued JW's 50 percent interest at $650,000. However, the formula under the 1998 buy-sell agreement resulted in a value of only $150,000 for the decedent's 50 percent interest. What is the correct value of the 50 percent interest in the corporation for estate tax purposes?

Some suggested research materials:

Rev. Rul. 59-60, 1959-1 C.B. 237.

Estate of Littick, 31 T.C. 181 (1958), acq. 1959-2 C.B. 5.

Code § 2703.

24-45   In 2001, Mr. and Mrs. B (residents of a common law state) created two trusts for the benefit of their children. Mr. B transferred $600,000 of his own property into trust, giving the income interest to his wife for her life, and the remainder interest to the children. Mrs. B transferred $640,000 of her own property into trust, giving the income interest to her husband for his life, and the remainder interest to the children. In the current year, Mrs. B dies. How much, if any, of the current value of the corpus of the 2001 trust created by Mrs. B will be included in her gross estate?

Some suggested research materials:

United States v. Estate of Grace, 69-1 USTC ¶12,609.
23 AFTR 2d 69-1954, 395 U.S. 316 (USSC, 1969).

Chapter 25

INCOME TAXATION OF ESTATES AND TRUSTS

LEARNING OBJECTIVES

Upon completion of this chapter you will be able to:

- Compute fiduciary accounting income and determine the required allocation of such income among the various beneficiaries of the fiduciary
- Identify the special rules that apply to the computation of fiduciary taxable income
- Explain the concept of income and deductions in respect of a decedent
- Compute both the taxable and nontaxable components of a fiduciary's distributable net income

- Describe the defining characteristics of a simple and a complex trust, including
  - The computation of the deduction for distributions to beneficiaries for both types of trusts
  - The distinction between tier one and tier two distributions from a complex trust
- Determine the tax consequences of fiduciary distributions to the recipient beneficiaries

CHAPTER OUTLINE

INTRODUCTION

Trusts and estates are taxable entities subject to a specialized set of tax rules contained in Subchapter J of the Internal Revenue Code (§§ 641 through 692). The income taxation of trusts and estates (commonly referred to as fiduciary taxpayers) and their beneficiaries is the subject of this chapter. Grantor trusts, a type of trust not recognized as a taxable entity and therefore not subject to the rules of Subchapter J, are discussed in Chapter 26.

THE FUNCTION OF ESTATES AND TRUSTS

ESTATES

An estate as a legal entity comes into existence upon the death of an individual. During the period of time in which the decedent's legal affairs are being settled, assets owned by the decedent are managed by an executor or administrator of the estate. Once all legal requirements have been satisfied, the estate terminates and ownership of all estate assets passes to the decedent's beneficiaries or heirs.

During its existence, the decedent's estate is a taxable entity that files a tax return and pays Federal income taxes on any income earned.[1] Normally an estate is a transitional entity that bridges the brief gap in time between the death of an individual taxpayer and the distribution of that individual's wealth to other taxpayers. However, estates as taxpayers may continue in existence for many years if the correct distribution of a decedent's wealth is in question. If the administration of a decedent's estate is unreasonably prolonged, the IRS may treat the estate as terminated for tax purposes after a reasonable amount of time for settlement of the decedent's affairs has elapsed.[2]

---

[1] § 641(a)(3).

[2] Reg. § 1.641(b)-3(a).

TRUSTS

A trust is a legal arrangement in which an individual, the *grantor*, transfers legal ownership of assets to one party, the *trustee*, and the legal right to enjoy and benefit from those assets to a second party, the *beneficiary* (or beneficiaries). Such an arrangement is usually designed for the protection of the beneficiary. Often trust beneficiaries are minor children or family members incapable of competently managing the assets themselves.

The terms of the trust, the duties of the trustee, and the rights of the various beneficiaries are specified in a legal document, the *trust instrument*. The assets put into trust are referred to as the trust *corpus*, or *principal*.

The role of the trustee is that of a fiduciary; he or she is required to act in the best interests of the trust beneficiaries rather than for his or her own interests. The position of trustee is usually filled by the professional trust department of a bank or a competent friend or family member. Professional trustees receive an annual fee to compensate them for services rendered.

The purpose of a trust is to protect and conserve trust assets for the sole benefit of the trust beneficiaries, not to operate a trade or business. A trust that becomes involved in an active, profit-making business activity runs the risk of being classified as an *association* for Federal tax purposes, with the unfavorable result that it will be taxed as a corporation rather than under the rules of Subchapter J.[3]

TRUST BENEFICIARIES

An individual who desires to establish a trust has virtually unlimited discretion as to the identity of the trust beneficiaries and the nature of the interest in the trust given to each beneficiary. For example, assume grantor G creates a trust consisting of $1 million of assets. G could specify in the trust instrument that individual I is to receive all the income of the trust for I's life, and upon I's death the assets in the trust are to be distributed to individual R. In this example, both I and R are trust beneficiaries. I owns an *income interest* in the trust, while R owns a *remainder interest* (the right to the trust principal at some future date).

A grantor can give trust beneficiaries any mix of rights to trust income or principal (trust assets) that will best accomplish the goals of the trust. In the previous example, if grantor G decided that the trust income might be insufficient to provide for I, the trust document could specify that I also will receive a certain amount of trust principal every year. Alternatively, if G believed that I might not need all the trust income annually, the trust document could provide that the trustee could accumulate income to distribute to I at some later point. As may be apparent, a trust can be a very flexible arrangement for providing for the needs of specific beneficiaries.

FIDUCIARY ACCOUNTING INCOME

There is no standard accounting system that applies to fiduciaries. The accounting income of an estate or trust is determined by reference to the decedent's valid will or the trust instrument. These documents can specify how fiduciary receipts, disbursements, and other transactions affect income, principal, or both. In other words, every fiduciary may have its own unique set of rules for the computation of accounting income, and the executor or trustee must refer exclusively to this income number in carrying out his or her duties. If a will or trust instrument is silent concerning the impact of a particular transaction on accounting income, such impact must be determined by reference to controlling state law. Most states have enacted a version of the Revised Uniform

---

[3]   See *Morrissey v. Comm.*, 36-1 USTC ¶9020, 16 AFTR 1274, 296 U.S. 344 (USSC, 1936), for this result.

Principal and Income Act, a model set of fiduciary accounting rules proposed by the Uniform Commission on State Laws.

One common difference between fiduciary accounting income and taxable income is the classification of fiduciary capital gains. Typically, capital gains represent an increase in the value of the principal of the fiduciary and normally are not available for distribution to income beneficiaries. Of course, for Federal tax purposes capital gains represent taxable income. Similarly, stock dividends are often regarded as an increase in principal rather than trust income, even though the dividend may be taxable income under the Internal Revenue Code.

Trustee fees are generally deductible for tax purposes. However, for fiduciary accounting purposes such fees may be charged *either* to trust income or to trust principal.

Depreciation may or may not have an effect on fiduciary accounting income. If local law or the trust instrument requires the fiduciary to establish a reserve for depreciation, depreciation is computed in accordance with the local law or the trust instrument and subtracted in computing trust accounting income. In effect, the fiduciary transfers cash out of income (reducing the amount that can be distributed to the income beneficiary) and sets this amount aside for future replacement of the depreciable property. Note that the amount of depreciation computed for tax purposes can be quite different than the amount of depreciation for fiduciary accounting income purposes. For this reason, tax depreciation requires special treatment as described below.

Exhibit 25-1 identifies various items of income and expense and shows how they are normally allocated between income and corpus.

EXHIBIT 25-1
Fiduciary Accounting Income

Typical income items

> Interest
> Dividends
> Royalties
> Net rental income (income less expenses) from real or personal property
> Net profits from operation of a trade or business; losses are usually charged to corpus
> All or a portion of trustee commissions
> Depreciation to the extent of any required reserve

Typical corpus items

> Gain or loss on the sale or exchange of trust property (capital gains)
> Casualty losses
> Stock dividends
> All or a portion of trustee commissions

Example 1. During the year, the records of a trust revealed the following information.

Receipts:

Dividends	$10,000
Interest from municipal bonds	12,000
Long-term capital gain allocable to principal under state law	6,500
Stock dividend allocable to principal under the trust instrument	4,000
Total receipts	$32,500

Disbursements:

Trustee fee (half allocable to trust income; half allocable to principal under the trust instrument)	$ 3,000

Based on the above, the accounting income of the trust would be $20,500, computed as follows:

Dividends.	$10,000
Interest from municipal bonds	12,000
	$22,000
Less: One-half of the trustee fee ($3,000 ÷ 2).	(1,500)
Trust accounting income	$20,500

If the trustee of this particular trust was required to distribute the entire amount of trust income to a particular group of beneficiaries, the trustee would make a payment of $20,500. Note that this amount bears little relationship to the *taxable income* generated by the trust's activities.

INCOME TAXATION OF FIDUCIARIES

For Federal tax purposes, fiduciaries are taxable entities.[4] Every estate that has annual gross income of $600 or more, and every trust that has either annual gross income of $600 or more *or* any taxable trust income, must file an income tax return. Furthermore, if a fiduciary has a beneficiary who is a nonresident alien, that fiduciary must file a return regardless of the amount of its gross or taxable income for the year.[5]

Form 1041, the U.S. Fiduciary Income Tax Return, must be filed by the 15th day of the fourth month following the close of the fiduciary's taxable year (see Appendix for sample Form 1041). An estate may adopt a calendar or any fiscal taxable year. However, the taxable year of a trust must be a calendar year.[6] In the case of an estate, the first taxable year begins on the day following the date of death of the decedent.[7] In the case of a trust, the date of creation as specified in the controlling trust instrument marks the beginning of the first taxable year.

Fiduciaries generally must make quarterly estimated tax payments in the same manner as individuals. However, no estimated taxes must be paid by an estate or a grantor trust to which the residual of the grantor's estate is distributed for any taxable year ending within the two years following the decedent's death.[8] A trustee may *elect* to treat any portion of an excess estimated tax payment made by a trust as a payment of estimated tax made by a beneficiary. If the election is made, the payment is considered as having been distributed to the beneficiary on the last day of the trust's taxable year and then remitted to the government as estimated tax paid by the beneficiary on January 15th of the following year.[9]

> **Example 2.** On April 15, 2005 Trust T made an estimated tax payment of $14,000. However, later in the year, the trustee decided to distribute all 2005 trust income to beneficiary B. Because Trust T will have no 2005 tax liability, the trustee may elect to treat the $14,000 payment as a cash distribution made to beneficiary B on December 31, 2005. Beneficiary B will report the $14,000 as part of his 2005 estimated tax payment made on January 15, 2006.

---

[4]   See §§ 7701(a)(6) and 641(a).

[5]   § 6012(a)(3), (4), and (5).

[6]   § 645. This requirement does not apply to tax-exempt and charitable trusts.

[7]   See Reg. §§ 1.443-1(a)(2), and 1.461-1(b).

[8]   § 6654(l).

[9]   § 643(g).

Section 641 (b) provides that "the taxable income of an estate or trust shall be computed in the same manner as in the case of an individual, except as otherwise provided in this part." Thus, many of the rules governing the taxation of individuals apply to fiduciaries. Before examining the specific rules unique to fiduciary income taxation, it will be useful to look at the basic approach for computing fiduciary taxable income.

Step One: Compute fiduciary accounting income and identify any receipts and disbursements allocated to principal (under either the trust instrument or state law).

Step Two: Compute fiduciary taxable income *before* the deduction for distributions to beneficiaries authorized by Code §§ 651 and 661.

Step Three: Compute the deduction for distributions to beneficiaries. This step will require a computation of fiduciary "distributable net income" (DNI).

Step Four: Subtract the deduction for distributions to arrive at *fiduciary taxable income.*

Step One, the computation of fiduciary accounting income, was discussed earlier. Detailed discussions of Steps Two and Three constitute most of the remainder of this chapter.

FIDUCIARY TAXABLE INCOME

Unless otherwise modified, the fiduciary computes its taxable income in a manner identical to that of an individual taxpayer. The major difference is the deduction granted for distributions made to beneficiaries, explained later in this chapter. In addition, § 642 contains a number of special provisions that must be followed in computing fiduciary taxable income and the final tax. These unique aspects of estate and trust taxation are considered below.

FIDUCIARY TAX RATES

The tax rates for estates and trusts for 2005 are shown in Exhibit 25-2. Note that the 10 percent rate that applies to individuals does not apply to trusts or estates. Also note that there is very little progressivity in the fiduciary rate schedule; taxable income in excess of $9,750 is taxed at the highest 35 percent rate. However, under § 1(j), any component of fiduciary taxable income consisting of net long-term capital gain or dividend income is taxed at a maximum 15 percent rate.

EXHIBIT 25-2
Income Tax Rates for Estates and Trusts

For Taxable Years Beginning in 2005

If taxable income is		The tax is		Of the amount over—
Over—	But not over—			
$ 0	$2,000		15%	$ 0
2,000	4,700	$ 300 +	25%	2,000
4,700	7,150	975 +	28%	4,700
7,150	9,750	1,661 +	33%	7,150
9,750	–	2,519 +	35%	9,750

In determining their final tax liability, fiduciaries are subject to the alternative minimum tax provisions.[10]

STANDARD DEDUCTION AND PERSONAL EXEMPTION

Unlike individual taxpayers, fiduciaries are not entitled to a standard deduction.[11] However, a fiduciary, like an individual taxpayer, is entitled to a personal exemption. The amount of the exemption depends on the type of fiduciary. The personal exemption for an estate is $600. The exemption for a trust that is required by the trust instrument to distribute all trust income currently is $300. The exemption for any trust not subject to this requirement is $100.[12]

LIMITATIONS ON DEDUCTIBILITY OF FIDUCIARY EXPENSES

Because fiduciaries generally do not engage in the conduct of a business, the gross income of a fiduciary usually consists of investment income items such as dividends, interest, rents, and royalties. Fiduciary expenses are normally deductible under the authority of § 212, which provides for the deduction of ordinary and necessary expenses paid for the management, conservation, or maintenance of property held for the production of income. However, there are several limitations on the deduction of expenses that apply to individuals that also apply to fiduciaries.

Limitations on Deductions Related to Tax-Exempt Income. As a general rule, § 265 denies the deduction for any expenses related to tax-exempt income. In contrast, any expense that is *directly related* to taxable fiduciary income is fully deductible. For example, rent expenses are directly related to rental income and would not be subject to this limitation. Expenses that are not directly related to a particular type of income— sometimes referred to as *indirect* expenses—must be allocated proportionately between taxable and tax-exempt income.[13] For example, consider a common expenditure of trusts such as trustee commissions. These fees are viewed as relating to both taxable and tax-exempt income and, therefore, an allocation is required. Assuming 20 percent of the trust's income is tax-exempt, then 20 percent of the trustee commission would be nondeductible. On the other hand, most practitioners take the position that tax

---

[10] See § 59(c). A special computation is used that is beyond the scope of this text.

[11] § 63(c)(6)(D).

[12] § 642(b).

[13] Reg. § 1.642(g)-2.

preparation fees need not be allocated to tax-exempt income since they are only related to taxable income.

The portion of an indirect expense that is not deductible can be determined using the following formula.

$$\frac{\text{Tax exempt income}}{\text{Total trust income}} \times \frac{\text{Expenses not directly related to}}{\text{a particular type of income}} = \frac{\text{Nondeductible}}{\text{expenses}}$$

In computing the denominator of the above formula, trust accounting income does not include capital gains unless capital gains are actually included in trust accounting income.[14] In addition, the denominator is computed using gross receipts.

Example 3. This year Trust T paid trustee fees of $7,000, $5,000 allocable to income and $2,000 allocable to corpus. Its records reveal the following additional information.

	Amounts
Rental income	$ 70,000
Rental expenses	(30,000)
Net rental income	$ 40,000
Long-term capital gains allocable to corpus	$ 25,000
Long-term capital losses allocable to corpus	(5,000)
Net capital gain	$ 20,000
Sales	$ 20,000
Costs of goods sold	(15,000)
Gross income	$ 5,000
Interest on State of New York bonds	$ 10,000

To determine the amount of commissions that are not deductible, the denominator does not include the net capital gain allocable to corpus of $20,000. However, the denominator does include the gross amounts of income received and is not reduced by expenses. Thus the denominator includes the rent of $70,000, sales of $20,000, and tax-exempt interest of $10,000 for a total of $100,000. Therefore 10% ($10,000/ $100,000) of the $7,000 of trustee's commissions or $700 is not deductible, and the remaining $6,300 is deductible. Note that in computing the amount of the deductible commissions, the fact that they are allocable to income or corpus for trust accounting purposes is irrelevant.

Limitation on Double Deduction of Administrative Expenses. Section 642(g) provides a second major limitation on the deductibility of fiduciary expenses. If an administrative expense is claimed as a deduction on the estate tax return of a decedent, it may not also be claimed as a deduction on an income tax return of the decedent's estate or subsequent trust. However, Regulation § 1.642(g)-2 provides that administrative expenses that could be deducted for either estate tax or income tax purposes can be divided between the two returns in whatever portions achieve maximum tax benefit.

Limitation on Miscellaneous Itemized Deductions. Section 67(a) limits certain miscellaneous itemized deductions, including the § 212 deduction for investment

---

[14]   Rev. Rul. 77-365.

expenses. Such itemized deductions are allowed only to the extent they exceed 2 percent of adjusted gross income. Section 67(e) provides that the deduction for expenses paid or incurred in connection with the administration of a fiduciary that would have been avoided if the property were not held by the fiduciary shall be allowable in computing the adjusted gross income of the fiduciary. In other words, fiduciary expenses such as trustee fees which are incurred only because of the choice of the trust form are not considered itemized deductions subject to the 2 percent floor. The treatment of fees paid by a fiduciary for general investment advice is unclear.[15]

The computation of the limitation on miscellaneous itemized deductions can be quite cumbersome. Since adjusted gross income of the trust depends on the amount of the distribution deduction and the distribution deduction in turn depends on taxable income after taking into account the deduction for miscellaneous itemized deductions (taxable DNI as explained below), the calculation of allowable miscellaneous itemized deductions may require the use of simultaneous algebraic equations.

Three-Percent Cutback. Section 68 requires that the total of an individual's itemized deductions for the year be reduced by 3 percent of any amount of adjusted gross income in excess of an inflation adjusted threshold. This requirement is expressly inapplicable to any estate or trust.[16]

Medical Expenses. Medical expenses paid by an estate or trust require special consideration. Medical expenses paid for the care of a *decedent* prior to his death that are paid by an estate within one year after death can be deducted either on the income tax return of the decedent (final Form 1040) or the estate tax return (Form 706), but not both. Medical expenses paid after the one-year period are deductible only as liabilities on the estate tax return (Form 706) if such return is actually filed. Medical expenses of *beneficiaries* that are paid by the trust or estate are treated as distributions of income to the beneficiaries and are not deductible per se on the fiduciary income tax return.

CHARITABLE CONTRIBUTIONS

Section 642(c) authorizes an unlimited charitable deduction for any amount of gross income paid by a fiduciary to a qualified charitable organization. Fiduciaries are given a great deal of flexibility as to the timing of charitable contributions; if a contribution is paid after the close of one taxable year but before the close of the next taxable year, the fiduciary may elect to deduct the payment in the earlier year.[17]

If a fiduciary receives tax-exempt income that is available for charitable distribution, its deduction for any charitable contribution made normally must be reduced by that portion of the contribution attributable to tax-exempt income.[18]

Example 4. During the current year, Trust T receives $30,000 of tax-exempt interest, $25,000 of taxable interest, and $45,000 of taxable dividends. The trust makes a charitable contribution of $20,000 during the year. Because 30% of the trust's income available for distribution is nontaxable, 30% of the charitable distribution is nondeductible and the trust's deduction for charitable contributions is limited to $14,000.

---

[15] Compare *William J. O'Neill, Jr., Irrevocable Trust*, 93-1 USTC ¶50,332, 71 AFTR2d 2052, 994 F.2d 302 (CA-6, 1993) and *Mellonbank, N.A., et.al. v. U.S.*, 86 AFTR2d 2000-5321.

[16] § 68(e).

[17] § 642(c)(1). See Reg. § 1.642(c)-1(b) for the time and manner in which such an election is to be made.

[18] Reg. § 1.642(c)-3(b).

DEPRECIATION, DEPLETION, AND AMORTIZATION

The total allowable amount of depreciation, depletion, and amortization that may be deducted by the fiduciary (or passed through to the beneficiaries) is determined in the normal manner. A fiduciary is entitled to bonus depreciation but not allowed to expense any portion of the cost of eligible property under § 179.

Deductions for depreciation and depletion available to a fiduciary depend upon the terms of the controlling will or trust instrument. If the controlling instrument authorizes a reserve for depreciation or depletion, any *allowable* (deductible) tax depreciation or depletion will be deductible by the fiduciary to the extent of the specified reserve. If the allowable tax depreciation or depletion exceeds the reserve, the excess deduction is allocated between the fiduciary and beneficiaries based upon the amount of fiduciary income allocable to each.[19]

> **Example 5.** Trust R owns rental property with a basis of $300,000. The trust instrument authorizes the trustee to maintain an annual depreciation reserve of $15,000 (5% of the cost of the property). For tax purposes, however, the current year's depreciation deduction is $22,000. The trust instrument provides that one-half of annual trust income including rents will be distributed to the trust beneficiaries. For the current year, the trust is entitled to a depreciation deduction of $18,500 [5% of $300,000 + one-half the tax depreciation in excess of $15,000 (½ × $7,000 = $3,500)].

Note that if the controlling instrument is silent, depreciation and depletion deductions are simply allocated between fiduciary and beneficiaries on the basis of fiduciary income allocable to each. If a fiduciary is entitled to statutory amortization, the amortization deduction also will be apportioned among fiduciary and beneficiaries on the basis of income allocable to each.[20]

FIDUCIARY LOSSES

Because the function of a trust generally is to conserve and protect existing wealth rather than to engage in potentially risky business activities, it is unusual for a trust to incur a net operating loss. It is not unusual, however, for an estate or trust that owns a business interest (e.g., an interest in a partnership or an S corporation) to incur this type of loss. In any case, if a net operating loss does occur, a fiduciary may carry the loss back two years and forward for 20.[21] Capital losses incurred by a fiduciary are deductible against capital gains; a maximum of $3,000 of net capital loss may be deducted against other sources of income.[22] Nondeductible net capital losses are carried forward to subsequent taxable years of the fiduciary.[23]

Fiduciaries are also subject to the limitations imposed on passive activity losses and credits by § 469.[24] Therefore, a fiduciary may only deduct current losses from passive activities against current income from passive activities. Any nondeductible loss is suspended and carried forward to subsequent taxable years. If an interest in a passive activity is distributed by a fiduciary to a beneficiary, any suspended loss of the activity is added to the tax basis of the distributed interest.[25]

---

[19] Reg. § 1.167(h)-1; Reg. § 1.611-1(c)(4).

[20] Reg. § 1.642(f)-1.

[21] §§ 172(b)(1) and 642(d).

[22] § 1211(b).

[23] § 1212(b).

[24] § 469(a)(2)(A).

[25] § 469(j)(12).

Section 469(I) normally provides for a $25,000 *de minimis* offset for losses attributable to rental real estate. However, this allowance is extended only to "natural persons" and, therefore, normally does not apply to trusts or estates. This rule prevents taxpayers from circumventing the $25,000 limitation by transferring multiple properties to multiple trusts with each claiming a $25,000 allowance. However, the provision is extended to estates for losses occurring for tax years ending less than two years after the decedent's date of death.

NOLs, Capital Losses, and Excess Deductions. Unlike the net losses of a partnership or an S corporation, fiduciary losses do not flow through to beneficiaries. An exception to this rule applies for the year in which a trust or estate terminates. If the terminating fiduciary has net operating losses, capital loss carryforwards, or current year deductions in excess of current gross income, § 642(h) provides that such unused losses and excess deductions become available to the beneficiaries succeeding to the property of the fiduciary.

> **Example 6.** D died in 2005. In 2006, the year of termination, the estate had gross income of $5,000 and legal fees of $15,000. The excess deductions of $10,000 do not create an NOL (that would carryover to the beneficiaries) since legal fees are considered a nonbusiness expense and are not deductible in computing an NOL. However, because the excess deductions occur in the year of termination, they pass through to the beneficiary who can claim the $10,000 as an itemized deduction subject to the 3% cutback rule. It should be emphasized that had this not been the year of termination, the $10,000 excess would be wasted. Due to this treatment, the fiduciary should take steps to ensure that excess deductions occur only in the year of termination. For example, a cash basis estate could postpone paying the legal fees until the final year.

Casualty losses of a fiduciary are subject to the rules pertaining to individual taxpayers. For casualty losses, the limitation of the deduction to that amount in excess of 10 percent of adjusted gross income applies, although the concept of adjusted gross income is normally not associated with trusts or estates.[26] In addition, § 642(g) prohibits the deduction by a fiduciary of any loss that has already been claimed as a deduction on an estate tax return.

INCOME AND DEDUCTIONS IN RESPECT OF A DECEDENT

The death of an individual taxpayer can create a peculiar timing problem involving the reporting of income items earned or deductible expenses incurred by the taxpayer prior to death. For example, if a cash basis individual had performed all the services required to earn a $5,000 consulting fee but had not collected the fee before death, by whom shall the $5,000 of *income in respect of a decedent* (IRD) be reported? The individual taxpayer who earned the income never received payment, but the recipient of the money, the individual's estate, is not the taxpayer who earned it. Section 691(a) gives a statutory solution to this puzzling question by providing that any income of an individual not properly includible in the taxable period prior to the individual's death will be included in the gross income of the recipient of the income, typically the estate of the decedent or a beneficiary of the estate. Common IRD items include unpaid salary or commissions, retirement income (e.g., IRA), rent income, or interest accrued but unpaid at death, and the amount of a § 453 installment obligation that would have been recognized as income if payment had been received by the decedent prior to death.

---

[26]   See Form 4684 and its instructions for this computation.

Certain expenses incurred by a decedent but not properly deductible on the decedent's final return because of nonpayment are afforded similar statutory treatment. Under § 691(b), these *deductions in respect of a decedent* (DRD) are deducted by the taxpayer who is legally required to make payment. Allowable DRD items include business and income-producing expenses, interest, taxes, and depletion.

ESTATE TAX TREATMENT AND THE § 691(C) DEDUCTION

Items of IRD and DRD represent assets and liabilities of the deceased taxpayer. As such, these items will be included on the decedent's estate tax return. Because IRD and DRD also have future income tax consequences, special provisions in the tax law apply to these items. First, even though the right to IRD is an asset acquired from a decedent, the basis of an IRD item does not become the item's fair market value at date of death. Instead, under § 1014(c), the basis of the item to the decedent carries over to the new owner. This special rule preserves the potential income that must be recognized when the IRD item is eventually collected. The character of IRD also is determined by reference to the decedent taxpayer.

Secondly, items of DRD that are deducted as administrative expenses on an estate tax return are *not* subject to the rule prohibiting a deduction on a subsequent income tax return.[27] Therefore, unlike administrative expenses of an estate that cannot be deducted on both the fiduciary income tax return (Form 1041) and the estate tax return (Form 706), DRD can be deducted on both.

Perhaps the most important reason for identifying items of IRD is the allowance of a special deduction for the recipient. To appreciate this deduction, consider the normal estate tax treatment given to a decedent's income. Such income is included *net* of any income tax that the decedent has paid. In contrast, items of IRD are included without reduction for the related income tax since the income tax on IRD is not a liability of the decedent but a liability of the recipient. Consequently, the amount of IRD income that is included in the gross estate is overstated and, therefore, the related estate tax is overstated. An heir who is the recipient of the income ends up with less than he would have had if the income had been taxed to the decedent and passed on to the heir net of the estate tax.

Example 7. D died on March 7, 2002. He was in the 40% income tax bracket and the 50% estate tax bracket. At the time of his death, D's employer owed him $10,000 of income. The following analysis shows the tax consequences that result if D had collected the $10,000 before he died as compared to those which would occur if his son, his heir, collects the $10,000 (assuming he is in the 40% tax bracket).

	D Collects Before Death	Total Tax	Heir Collects After Death	Total Tax
Income......................	$10,000		$10,000	
Income tax to decedent	(4,000)	$4,000	0	$ 0
Aftertax income in estate	$ 6,000		$10,000	
Estate tax at 50%..............	$ 3,000	3,000	$ 5,000	5,000
Income to heir	$ 0		$10,000	
Income tax to heir			$ 4,000	4,000
Total income and estate tax......		$7,000		$9,000

---

[27] § 642(g).

In this case, the total income and estate tax imposed on the $10,000 if D collected the $10,000 is $7,000. In contrast, if the heir collects the $10,000 from the employer the total income and estate tax is $9,000. The $2,000 difference is attributable to the fact that the entire $10,000 is subject to estate tax in the latter case while only $6,000 ($10,000 net of the income tax of $4,000) is subject to estate tax in the first case (50% × $4,000 = $2,000).

Perhaps the best way to treat this problem is to estimate the amount of income tax that the decedent would have paid had he or she received the income and give the estate a deduction for this amount. However, because this amount would presumably be difficult to estimate, the authors of § 691 opted for an alternative that produces about the same result. Section 691(c) allows the recipient of IRD a deduction for any estate tax attributable to the income.

The deduction is a percentage of the estate tax attributable to the total *net* IRD included in an estate based on the ratio of the recognized IRD item to all IRD items. Estate tax attributable to net IRD is the excess of the actual tax over the tax computed without including the IRD in the taxable estate.

The § 691(c) deduction can be computed using the following two steps.

1. Determine the estate tax attributable to net IRD:

$$
\begin{array}{l}
\ \text{Estate tax actually incurred (including net IRD)} \\
-\ \underline{\text{Estate tax without NIRD}} \\
=\ \underline{\underline{\text{Total estate tax attributable to IRD}}}
\end{array}
$$

2. Recipient's deduction is based on the proportionate amount of IRD (not net IRD) that is received.

$$
\frac{\text{IRD received}}{\text{Total IRD}} \times \frac{\text{Total estate tax}}{\text{attributable to IRD}} = \frac{\text{Section 691(c)}}{\text{deduction}}
$$

Note that if an estate or trust is the recipient of the IRD, it is not subject to the 3 percent cutback for itemized deductions. In contrast, if an individual taxpayer receives the IRD, the amount is considered an itemized deduction subject to the 3 percent cutback.

> **Example 8.** Taxpayer T's estate tax return included total IRD items valued at $145,000. DRD items totaled $20,000. If the *net* IRD of $125,000 had not been included in T's estate, the Federal estate tax liability would have decreased by $22,000. During the current year, the estate of T collected half ($72,500) of all IRD items and included this amount in estate gross income. T's estate is entitled to a § 691(c) deduction of $11,000. The $11,000 is not subject to the three percent cutback since such rule does not apply to estates or trusts.

THE DISTRIBUTION DEDUCTION AND THE TAXATION OF BENEFICIARIES

The central concept of Subchapter J is that income recognized by a fiduciary will be taxed *either* to the fiduciary itself or to the beneficiaries of the fiduciary. The determination of the amount of income taxable to each depends upon the amount of annual distributions from the fiduciary to the beneficiary. Conceptually, distributions to beneficiaries represent a flow-through of trust income that will be taxed to the beneficiary. Under §§ 651 and 661, the amount of the distribution will then be available as a *deduction* to the fiduciary, reducing the taxable income the fiduciary must report.

Income that flows through the fiduciary to a beneficiary retains its original character; therefore, the fiduciary acts as a *conduit*, similar to a partnership in this respect.[28]

In computing the deduction for distributions, the law generally presumes that *every distribution consists of a pro rata portion of current taxable and nontaxable income that is in fact distributable.* Sections 651 and 661 refer to this quantity as *a distributable net income* (DNI) and allow the fiduciary a deduction for amounts distributed but limit the deduction to taxable DNI. It should be emphasized that whatever amount is deductible by the fiduciary is the same amount that is taxable to the beneficiaries. This follows from the fact that the deduction merely serves to allocate taxable income from the fiduciary to the beneficiary. Distributions exceeding DNI represent accumulated income of the fiduciary that has been previously taxed, or corpus. Such amounts are neither deductible by the fiduciary nor taxable to the beneficiary.

Before further examining the computation of the deduction concept and DNI, it is important to understand that a trust or estate can make distributions of either cash or property, both of which may or may not carry out DNI (i.e., taxable and nontaxable income). However, § 663(a)(1) provides that *specific* gifts or bequests properly distributed from a fiduciary to a beneficiary under the terms of the governing instrument are distributions of principal rather than of income. Correspondingly, the fiduciary does not recognize gain or loss upon the distribution of a specific property bequest.

> **Example 9.** During the current year, the Estate of Z recognized $30,000 of income, all of which is taxable. During the year, the executor of the estate distributed a pearl necklace to beneficiary B. The necklace had a fair market value of $6,000. If the will of decedent Z specifically provided for the distribution of the necklace to B, no estate income will be taxed to her. Alternatively, if there were no such specific bequest and B received the necklace as part of her general interest in estate assets, she will have received an income distribution.

The amount of income associated with a property distribution from a fiduciary depends upon the tax treatment of the distribution *elected* by the fiduciary. Section 643(e)(3) provides an election under which the fiduciary recognizes gain on the distribution of appreciated property as if the property had been sold at its fair market value. In this case, the amount of fiduciary income carried by the property distribution and the basis of the property in the hands of the beneficiary equals the property's fair market value. If the election is not made, the distribution of property produces no gain or loss to the fiduciary, and the amount of fiduciary income carried by the distribution is the lesser of the basis of such property in the hands of the fiduciary or the property's fair market value.[29] In the case where the election is not made, the basis of the property in the hands of the fiduciary will carry over as the basis of the property in the hands of the beneficiary.[30]

> **Example 10.** During the current year, Trust T distributes property to beneficiary B. The distribution is not a specific gift of property. On the date of distribution, the property has a basis to the trust of $10,000 and a fair market value of $17,000. If the trust so elects, it will recognize a $7,000 gain on the distribution, and B will be considered to have received a $17,000 income distribution and will have a $17,000 basis in the property. If the trustee does not make the election, it will not recognize any gain upon distribution of the property. B will be considered to have received only a $10,000 income distribution and will have only a $10,000 basis in the property.

---

[28]   §§ 652(b) and 662(b).

[29]   § 643(e)(2).

[30]   § 643(e)(1).

When a beneficiary is entitled to a specific gift or bequest of a sum of money (a pecuniary gift or bequest), and the fiduciary distributes property in satisfaction of such gift or bequest, any appreciation or depreciation in the property is recognized as a gain or loss to the fiduciary.[31]

> **Example 11.** Under the terms of E's will, beneficiary M is to receive the sum of $60,000. E's executor distributes 600 shares of corporate stock to M to satisfy this pecuniary bequest. At the time of distribution, the stock has a fair market value of $100 a share and a basis to E's estate of $75 a share. Upon distribution, the estate must recognize a capital gain of $15,000 (600 shares × $25 per share appreciation). Note that because this distribution represents a specific bequest, it is not an income distribution to M and the § 643(e)(3) election is inapplicable. The basis of the stock to M will be its fair market value.

In any case in which the distribution of depreciated property by a trust or an estate to a beneficiary results in the recognition of loss, § 267 disallows any deduction of the loss by the trust.

COMPUTATION OF DISTRIBUTION DEDUCTION AND DNI

To calculate the distribution deduction available to a fiduciary and the amount of fiduciary income taxable to beneficiaries, it is first necessary to calculate the *distributable net income* (DNI) of the fiduciary. DNI represents the net income of a fiduciary available for distribution to income beneficiaries.

DNI has several important characteristics. First, it does not include taxable income that is unavailable for distribution to income beneficiaries. For example, in most states capital gains realized upon the sale of fiduciary assets are considered to represent a part of *trust principal* and are not considered *fiduciary income*. Such capital gains, while taxable, are not included in DNI. Secondly, DNI may include nontaxable income that is available for distribution to income beneficiaries.

At this point, it would appear that the amount of DNI is the same amount as fiduciary accounting income. However, there is an important difference between the two concepts. All expenses that are deductible *for tax purposes* by the fiduciary enter into the DNI calculation, even if some of these expenses are chargeable to principal and not deducted in computing fiduciary accounting income.

A beneficiary who receives a distribution from a fiduciary with both taxable and nontaxable DNI is considered to have received a proportionate share of each.[32]

> **Example 12.** Trust A has DNI of $80,000, $30,000 of which is nontaxable. During the year, beneficiary X receives a distribution of $16,000. This distribution consists of $10,000 of taxable DNI [$16,000 distribution × ($50,000 taxable DNI ÷ $80,000 total DNI)] and $6,000 of nontaxable DNI.

The amount of a fiduciary's *taxable* DNI represents *both* the maximum income that may be taxed to beneficiaries and the maximum deduction for distributions available to the fiduciary in computing its own taxable income.[33] Therefore, computing DNI is crucial to the correct computation of the taxable incomes of both beneficiary and fiduciary. Note that in *Example 12* Trust A is entitled to a deduction for distributions to beneficiaries of $10,000.

---

[31]   Reg. § 1.661(a)-2(f)(1).

[32]   Reg. § 1.662(b)-1.

[33]   §§ 651(b) and 661(c).

THE COMPUTATION OF DNI

Section 643 defines DNI as fiduciary taxable income before any deduction for distributions to beneficiaries, adjusted as follows:

1. No deduction for a personal exemption is allowed.

2. No deduction against ordinary income for net capital losses is allowed.

3. Taxable income allocable to principal and not available for distribution to income beneficiaries is excluded.

4. Tax-exempt interest reduced by expenses allocable thereto is included.

Example 13. A trust that is not required to distribute all income currently has the following items of income and expense during the current year:

Tax-exempt interest	$10,000
Dividends	5,000
Rents	20,000
Long-term capital gains allocable to principal	8,000
Rent expense	6,700
Trustee fee allocable to income	3,500

The trust's taxable income before any deduction for distributions to beneficiaries is $23,700, computed as follows:

Dividends		$ 5,000
Rents		20,000
Capital gain		8,000
		$33,000
Less: Rent expense	$6,700	
Trust fee allocable to *taxable* trust income*	2,500	
Exemption	100	(9,300)
Taxable income before distribution deduction		$23,700

$$*\$3{,}500 \text{ fee} \times \frac{\$25{,}000 \text{ taxable trust income}}{\$35{,}000 \text{ total trust income}}$$

The trust's DNI is $24,800, computed as follows:

Trust taxable income before distribution deduction	$23,700
Add back exemption	100
	$23,800
Exclude: Nondistributable capital gain	(8,000)
Include: *Net* tax-exempt interest ($10,000 total − $1,000 allocable to trustee fee)**	9,000
Distributable net income (DNI)	$24,800

$$**\$3{,}500 \text{ fee} \times \frac{\$10{,}000 \text{ tax-exempt income}}{\$35{,}000 \text{ total trust income}}$$

SIMPLE TRUSTS

Section 651 defines a *simple trust* as one that satisfies these conditions:

1. Distributes all trust income currently

2. Does not take a deduction for a charitable contribution for the current year

3. Does not make any current distributions out of trust principal

Because of the requirement that a simple trust distribute all trust income to its beneficiaries, all taxable DNI of a simple trust is taxed to the beneficiaries, based upon the relative income distributable to each.

> **Example 14.** Trust S is required to distribute 40% of trust income to beneficiary A and 60% of trust income to B. The trust's DNI for the current year is $100,000, of which $20,000 is nontaxable. For the current year, beneficiary A must report $32,000 of trust income (40% of *taxable* DNI) and B must report $48,000 of trust income (60% of *taxable* DNI). Trust S's deduction for distributions to beneficiaries is $80,000 (i.e., taxable DNI).

In *Example 14*, the tax results would not change if the trustee had failed to make actual distributions to the beneficiaries. In the case of a simple trust, the taxability of income to beneficiaries is not dependent upon cash flow from the trust.[34]

COMPLEX TRUSTS AND ESTATES

Any trust that does not meet all three requirements of a simple trust is categorized as a *complex trust*. The categorization of a trust may vary from year to year. For example, if a trustee is required to distribute all trust income currently but also has the discretion to make distributions out of trust principal, the trust will be *simple* in any year in which principal is not distributed, but *complex* in any year in which principal is distributed.

Computing the taxable income of complex trusts and estates generally is more difficult than computing the taxable income of a simple trust. Complex trusts and estates potentially may distribute amounts of cash and property that are less than or in excess of DNI.

If distributions to beneficiaries are less than or equal to DNI, each beneficiary is required to report the amount of the distribution representing *taxable* DNI in his or her gross income. Taxable DNI remaining in the fiduciary is taxed to the fiduciary.

> **Example 15.** In the current year, Trust C has DNI of $50,000, of which $20,000 or 40% is nontaxable. During the year, the trustee makes a $5,000 distribution to both beneficiary M and beneficiary N. M and N will each report $3,000 of income from Trust C [$5,000 distribution × ($30,000 taxable DNI ÷ $50,000 total DNI)]. Trust C is allowed a $6,000 deduction for distributions to beneficiaries.[35] As a result, $24,000 of taxable DNI will be reported by (and taxed to) Trust C.

> **Example 16.** Using the same facts as in *Example 13*, assume the trust distributes $10,000. The trust is generally entitled to a deduction for amounts distributed. However, this amount is further limited to the portion of taxable DNI contained in

---

[34] § 652(a).

[35] § 661(c).

the distribution. In this case, the amount of the distribution deduction and the amount taxable to the beneficiaries is $6,371 computed as follows.

Distributable net income	$24,800
Net tax-exempt income	
($10,000 − $1,000)	(9,000)
Taxable DNI.	$15,800

$$\frac{\text{Taxable DNI}}{\text{Total DNI}} \times \frac{\text{Amount}}{\text{distributed}} = \frac{\text{Distribution}}{\text{deduction}}$$

$$\frac{\$15,800}{\$24,800} \times \$10,000 = \underline{6,371}$$

In this case, the trust did not distribute all of its DNI, $24,800, but only a portion, $10,000. Consequently, the calculation effectively treats a portion of the amount distributed as taxable (63.71% or $6,371) and a portion as nontaxable (36.29% or $3,629). Taxable income of the trust would be $17,329 as computed below.

Taxable income before distribution deduction	$23,700
Deduction for distributions	(6,371)
Trust taxable income	$17,329

When distributions to beneficiaries exceed DNI, the entire taxable portion of DNI will be reported as income by the beneficiaries. Amounts distributed in excess of DNI are nontaxable, representing either accumulated income that has been previously taxed or corpus.

Allocation of DNI. In those cases when distributions exceed DNI and there are multiple beneficiaries, DNI must be allocated among the beneficiaries. In determining the amount of DNI allocated to each beneficiary (and, therefore, the amount of taxable income and nontaxable income that is allocable to each), the distribution rules acknowledge that some beneficiaries' rights to income may be superior to those of others. For example, the trust agreement may provide that distributions of income must be made to certain beneficiaries each year while other beneficiaries receive distributions solely at the discretion of the trustee. In recognition of this possibility, the Code establishes a so-called tier system to allocate DNI.[36]

Under the tier system, DNI (increased for charitable contributions) is first allocated proportionately to the distributions that are *required* to be made. These mandatory distributions are commonly referred to as *first-tier* or *tier-one* distributions. After allocating DNI to first-tier distributions, *any* DNI remaining (as reduced by first-tier distributions and charitable contributions) is allocated proportionately to *second tier* or *tier-two* distributions (i.e., discretionary distributions).

Example 17. This year Trust T reported taxable DNI of $60,000. During the year, the trust made required distributions of $40,000 to beneficiary R. In addition, the trustee made discretionary distributions of $40,000 to R and $20,000 to S. DNI would be allocated as follows:

---

[36] §§ 662(a)(1) and (2).

	Total	R	S
Required distributions	$ 40,000	$40,000	—
Discretionary distributions	60,000	40,000	$20,000
Total distributions received	$100,000	$80,000	$20,000

	Total	R	S
DNI before contributions	$ 60,000		
First-tier distributions	(40,000)	$40,000	—
DNI available for charity................	20,000		
Charitable distributions	(0)		
DNI for second tier....................	$ 20,000		
Second-tier distributions	(20,000)	13,333*	$ 6,667*
DNI received		$53,333	$ 6,667

$$*\text{DNI for second tier} \ \times \ \frac{\text{Beneficiary's second-tier distribution}}{\text{Total second-tier distribution}}$$

$$\$20,000 \times \$40,000/\$60,000 = \$13,333 \text{ to R}$$
$$\$20,000 \times \$20,000/\$60,000 = \$ 6,667 \text{ to S}$$

Observe that the first $40,000 of DNI must be allocated to R because this distribution was mandatory thus making it a first-tier distribution. The remaining $20,000 of DNI is allocated proportionally to the discretionary or second-tier distributions received by R and S. Note that all of the trust's DNI is allocated and taxed to the beneficiaries and none is taxed to the trust. In this case, R received $80,000 from the trust of which $53,333 is taxable while S received $20,000 of which $6,667 is taxable. The balance of each distribution represents either accumulated income or corpus. Although the trust distributed $100,000, its deduction for distributions is limited to its taxable DNI for the year, $60,000.

In determining the treatment of a beneficiary's distributions, the treatment of charitable contributions can be a bit confusing. On the one hand, a contribution is treated as an expense that reduces the trust's taxable income (i.e., it is reported on Line 13 of Form 1041 and not on a Schedule K-1). On the other hand, the charity itself is treated like a beneficiary in the sense that it absorbs taxable and nontaxable DNI just like any other beneficiary. It should be emphasized that the charity is not considered a beneficiary when computing the deduction for distributions to beneficiaries. Instead, the distribution is accounted for as an expense.[37]

Example 18. This year the F Trust reported $80,000 of dividend income. Pursuant to the trust instrument the trustee distributed $90,000 as follows: (1) a required distribution to beneficiary J of $50,000; (2) a charitable contribution of $30,000; and (3) a discretionary distribution to K of $10,000. Taxable DNI would be $50,000 ($80,000 − $30,000) all of which would be allocated to J as computed below:

---

[37] § 662(a)(2). For purposes of determining DNI available for first-tier distribution only, no charitable contribution deduction is allowed.

DNI before contributions ($50,000 + $ 30,000)............	$ 80,000
First-tier distribution to J......................	(50,000)
DNI available for charity.......................	$ 30,000
Charitable distribution	(30,000)
DNI for second tier........................	$ 0

Note that J would report $50,000 of DNI, all of which would be taxable. In contrast, K receives no taxable DNI since there is none available after taking into account the charitable contribution. Although the trust distributed $60,000 to J and K, its distribution deduction is limited to taxable DNI of $50,000. Trust taxable income would be $0 as calculated below.

Dividends...........................	$ 80,000
Contribution...........................	(30,000)
Distribution deduction (limited to taxable DNI)...............	(50,000)
Trust taxable income......................	$ 0

CHARACTER OF BENEFICIARY'S INCOME

Not only must a beneficiary determine the amount of taxable income received from a trust or estate, but he or she must determine its character as well. As stated at the outset, estates and trusts generally serve as conduits to the extent they make distributions. Consequently, each distribution is deemed to contain a pro rata portion of each type of distributable income received by the trust or estate. For example, if a portion of a trust's income consisted of dividends, a portion of the distribution received by the beneficiary is considered dividend income.

To determine the composition of a distribution, the gross amount of each item of distributable income must be reduced by any deduction directly related to that item of income. Any other expenses may be allocated against whatever class of distributable income the fiduciary selects. However, charitable contributions are treated as consisting of a proportionate share of each type of distributable income.

Example 19. This year the records of the T Trust revealed the following information, resulting in DNI of $60,000.

	Income and Expenses	DNI
Rental income	$70,000	$ 70,000
Dividends...........................	30,000	30,000
Long-term capital gain...................	50,000	
Charitable contribution..................	10,000	(10,000)
Rent expense........................	23,000	(23,000)
Trustee commission allocable between income and corpus.................	7,000	(7,000)
DNI		$ 60,000

During the year, the trust distributed $6,000 to its only beneficiary, X. The character of the distribution is determined below:

Elements of DNI	Rents	Dividends	Total
Income..........................	$ 70,000	$30,000	$100,000
Expenses:			
Rental expenses...............	(23,000)		(23,000)
Trustee fees		(7,000)	(7,000)
Contribution..................	(7,000)*	(3,000)*	(10,000)
Total DNI	$ 40,000	$20,000	$ 60,000
Percentage of DNI.................	67%	33%	100%

*$10,000 × $70,000/$100,000 = $7,000
$10,000 × $30,000/$100,000 = $3,000

Since X received 10% of the DNI ($6,000/$60,000) she is deemed to receive 10% of each item of DNI. Thus she will report rental income of $4,000 (10% × $40,000) and dividend income of $2,000 (10% × $20,000). In other words, of the $6,000 of DNI received, $4,000 or 67% is rents while $2,000 or 33% is dividends. Note how the expenses were allocated in determining the composition of DNI. The rental expenses are charged against the rental income since they are directly related. In contrast, the charitable contribution is charged proportionately against each type of distributable income. On the other hand, the trustee fees may be allocated however the trustee wishes. In this case, he elects to charge the trustee fees against the dividend income. In light of the 15% tax rate that applies to dividends, the trustee should consider allocating the fees to the rental income.

A special problem arises when the trust receives qualified dividends that are taxed at a maximum rate of 15 percent (5% if in the 15% tax bracket). A calculation must be made to determine the amount of qualified dividends *retained* by the trust to be taxed at the favorable rate. The amount deemed to be retained by the trust is equal to the proportion of distributable net income (DNI) retained by the trust.

Example 20. Same facts as in *Example 19*. The total DNI was $60,000 and the trust distributed 10% of the DNI ($6,000/$60,000) to the beneficiary and retained 90% ($54,000/$60,000). Thus the qualified dividends retained by the trust are $27,000 (90% × $30,000). Alternatively, the amount could be computed by using the amount of DNI allocated to the beneficiary as follows.

Qualified dividends..................	$30,000	$30,000
Allocation to beneficiary:		
$\dfrac{\text{DNI distributed to beneficiary } \$6,000}{\text{Total DNI } \$60,000}$	× 10%	(3,000)
Allocation to trust....................		$27,000

Note that this method of allocating the amount of qualified dividends between the beneficiary and the trust is used solely for calculating the tax liability of the trust. The actual amount of qualified dividends to be reported on the Schedule K-1 which the beneficiary must report is not $3,000 but is $2,000 (10% × $20,000) as shown above.

REPORTING REQUIREMENTS FOR BENEFICIARIES

A beneficiary who receives a distribution from a fiduciary will receive a summary of the tax consequences of the distribution in the form of a Schedule K-1 from the executor or trustee. The K-1 will tell the beneficiary the amounts and character of the various items of income that constitute the taxable portion of the distribution.

A beneficiary also may be entitled to depreciation or depletion deductions and various tax credits because of distributions of fiduciary income. Such items are also reflected on the Schedule K-1.

If the taxable year of a beneficiary is different from that of the fiduciary, the amount of fiduciary income taxable to the beneficiary is included in the beneficiary's tax year within which the fiduciary's year ends.[38]

> **Example 21.** Estate E is on a fiscal year ending January 31. During its fiscal year ending January 31, 2005, but prior to December 31, 2004, the estate made cash distributions to beneficiary Z, a calendar year taxpayer. Because of these distributions, Z must report income of $8,000. However, this income will be reported on Z's 2005 individual tax return.

THE SEPARATE SHARE RULE

In certain circumstances, the rules governing the taxation of beneficiaries of a complex trust can lead to an inequitable result. Assume a grantor created a single trust with two beneficiaries, A and B. The grantor intended that each beneficiary have an equal interest in trust income and principal. The trustee has considerable discretion as to the timing of distributions of income and principal. Consider a year in which beneficiary A was in exceptional need of funds and, as a result, the trustee distributed $15,000 to A as A's half of trust income for the year *plus* $10,000 out of A's half of trust principal. Because B had no need of current funds, the trustee distributed neither income nor principal to B.

If the trust's DNI was $30,000 for the year, the normal rules of Subchapter J would dictate that A would have to report and pay tax on $25,000 of trust income. However, the clear intent of the grantor is that A only be responsible for half of trust income and no more. To reflect such intent, § 663(c) provides the following rule: if a single trust contains substantially separate and independent shares for different beneficiaries, the trust shall be treated as separate trusts for purposes of determining DNI. Therefore, using this separate share rule, beneficiary A's *separate trust* would have DNI of only $15,000, the maximum amount taxable to A in the year of distribution. This rule is inapplicable to estates.

A COMPREHENSIVE EXAMPLE

The AB Trust is a calendar year taxpayer. In the current year, the trust books show the following:

Gross rental income.	$25,000
Taxable interest income.	10,000
Tax-exempt interest income.	15,000
Long-term capital gain	8,000
Trustee fee.	6,000
Rent expenses.	3,000
Contribution to charity	1,500
Distributions to	
Beneficiary A.	20,000
Beneficiary B.	20,000

---

[38] §§ 652(c) and 662(c).

Under the terms of the trust instrument the capital gain and one-third of the trustee fee are allocable to principal. The trustee is required to maintain a reserve for depreciation on the rental property equal to one-tenth of annual gross rental income. (For tax purposes, assume actual tax depreciation is $1,300.) The trustee is required to make an annual distribution to beneficiary A of $12,000 and has the discretion to make additional distributions to A or beneficiary B.

Based on these facts, the computation of the income taxable to the trust and the beneficiaries is as follows:

Step One: Compute fiduciary accounting income.

Gross rental income.	$25,000
Taxable interest income.	10,000
Tax-exempt interest income.	15,000
	$50,000
Trustee fee charged against income	(4,000)
Rent expenses.	(3,000)
Depreciation ($\frac{1}{10} \times$ $25,000).	(2,500)
Fiduciary accounting income	$40,500

Step Two: Compute fiduciary taxable income before the § 661 deduction for distributions to beneficiaries.

Gross rental income.	$25,000
Taxable interest income.	10,000
Long-term capital gain	8,000
	$43,000
Deductible trustee fee	(4,200)*
Deductible rent expense	(3,000)
Deductible depreciation allocable to fiduciary	(1,300)
Deductible charitable contribution	(1,050)*
Exemption	(100)
Taxable income before § 661 deduction	$33,350

*$35,000 ÷ $50,000 of gross fiduciary accounting income is taxable; thus, only 70% of both the $6,000 trustee fee and $1,500 charitable contribution is deductible.

Step Three: Compute DNI and the § 661 deduction for distributions to beneficiaries.

Taxable income from Step Two	$33,350
Add back:	
Exemption.	100
Net tax-exempt income.	12,750*
Subtract:	
Capital gain allocable to principal	(8,000)
Distributable net income (DNI).	$38,200

*$15,000 tax-exempt interest less 30% of the $6,000 trustee fee and $1,500 charitable contribution.

Step Four: Subtract the § 661 deduction for distributions to beneficiaries

Taxable income before deduction	$ 33,350
Section 661 deduction for distributions	(25,450)*
Trust taxable income	$ 7,900

Because distributions to beneficiaries exceeded DNI, the trust will deduct the entire amount of taxable DNI. $25,450 ($38,200 − $12,750).

Tax Consequences to Beneficiaries. The $40,000 cash distribution to beneficiaries exceeds the total DNI of $38,200; thus, the entire amount of DNI must be allocated to the beneficiaries.

	Total	A	B
DNI	$ 38,200		
Add-back charitable contribution	1,500		
DNI before charitable contribution	$ 39,700		
First-tier distributions	(12,000)	$12,000	—
DNI available for charity.	$ 27,700		
Charitable distributions	(1,500)		
DNI for second tier.	$ 26,200		
Second-tier distributions	(26,200)	7,483*	$18,717**
DNI received	(26,200)	$19,483	$18,717
Percentage of DNI received.		51%	49%

$$\text{*DNI for second tier} \times \frac{\text{Beneficiary's second-tier distribution}}{\text{Total second-tier distributions}}$$

*$26,200 × $8,000/$28,000 = $7,483 to A
**$26,200 × $20,000/$28,000 = $18,717 to B

The composition of DNI is as follows:

	Rent	Taxable Interest	Tax-Exempt Interest	Total
Gross receipts	$25,000	$10,000	$15,000	$50,000
Rent expense.	(3,000)			(3,000)
Depreciation.	(1,300)			(1,300)
Trustee fee*		(4,200)	(1,800)	(6,000)
Charitable contribution**	(750)	(300)	(450)	(1,500)
Total.	$19,950	$ 5,500	$12,750	$38,200

*The trustee fee allocable to taxable income may be arbitrarily allocated to **any** item of taxable income. Reg. 1.652(b)-3(b).

**In the absence of a specific provision in the trust instrument, the charitable contribution is allocated proportionally to each class of income. Reg. § 1.642(c)-3(b)(2).

Each beneficiary should report the following:

	Rent	Taxable Interest	Tax-Exempt Interest	Total DNI Allocated
Beneficiary A (51%)...............	$10,175*	$2,805	$ 6,503	$19,483
Beneficiary B (49%)...............	9,775	2,695	6,247	18,717
Total.........................	$19,950	$5,500	$12,750	$38,200

*Beneficiary A's proportionate share of DNI 51% multiplied by $19,950 total rent income included in DNI equals beneficiary A's share of rent income. This same procedure is used to determine each beneficiary's share of all other items.

A completed Form 1041 for the AB Trust and Schedule K-1 for Beneficiary A are shown on the following pages.

Form 1041

Form 1041 Department of the Treasury—Internal Revenue Service

U.S. Income Tax Return for Estates and Trusts 2004 OMB No. 1545-0092

A Type of entity (see instr.):

- [ ] Decedent's estate
- [ ] Simple trust
- [ ] Complex trust
- [ ] Qualified disability trust
- [ ] ESBT (S portion only)
- [ ] Grantor type trust
- [ ] Bankruptcy estate–Ch. 7
- [ ] Bankruptcy estate–Ch. 11
- [ ] Pooled income fund

For calendar year 2004 or fiscal year beginning , 2004, and ending , 20

Name of estate or trust (If a grantor type trust, see page 12 of the instructions.)

A B TRUST

Name and title of fiduciary

Number, street, and room or suite no. (If a P.O. box, see page 12 of the instructions.)

City or town, state, and ZIP code

C Employer identification number

D Date entity created

E Nonexempt charitable and split-interest trusts, check applicable boxes (see page 13 of the instr.):
- [ ] Described in section 4947(a)(1)
- [ ] Not a private foundation
- [ ] Described in section 4947(a)(2)

B Number of Schedules K-1 attached (see instructions) ▶

F Check applicable boxes:
- [ ] Initial return
- [ ] Final return
- [ ] Amended return
- [ ] Change in fiduciary
- [ ] Change in fiduciary's name
- [ ] Change in trust's name
- [ ] Change in fiduciary's address

G Pooled mortgage account (see page 14 of the instructions): [ ] Bought [ ] Sold Date:

Income

1	Interest income	1	10,000
2a	Total ordinary dividends	2a	
b	Qualified dividends allocable to: (1) Beneficiaries .... (2) Estate or trust		
3	Business income or (loss) (attach Schedule C or C-EZ (Form 1040))	3	
4	Capital gain or (loss) (attach Schedule D (Form 1041))	4	8,000
5	Rents, royalties, partnerships, other estates and trusts, etc. (attach Schedule E (Form 1040))	5	20,700
6	Farm income or (loss) (attach Schedule F (Form 1040))	6	
7	Ordinary gain or (loss) (attach Form 4797)	7	
8	Other income. List type and amount	8	
9	**Total income.** Combine lines 1, 2a, and 3 through 8 ▶	9	38,700

Deductions

10	Interest. Check if Form 4952 is attached ▶ [ ]	10	
11	Taxes	11	
12	Fiduciary fees	12	4,200
13	Charitable deduction (from Schedule A, line 7)	13	1,050
14	Attorney, accountant, and return preparer fees	14	
15a	Other deductions **not** subject to the 2% floor (attach schedule)	15a	
b	Allowable miscellaneous itemized deductions subject to the 2% floor	15b	
16	**Total.** Add lines 10 through 15b	16	5,250
17	Adjusted total income or (loss). Subtract line 16 from line 9. Enter here and on Schedule B, line 1 ▶	17	33,450
18	Income distribution deduction (from Schedule B, line 15) (attach Schedules K-1 (Form 1041))	18	25,450
19	Estate tax deduction (including certain generation-skipping taxes) (attach computation)	19	
20	Exemption	20	100
21	**Total deductions.** Add lines 18 through 20 ▶	21	25,550

Tax and Payments

22	Taxable income. Subtract line 21 from line 17. If a loss, see page 19 of the instructions	22	7,900
23	**Total tax** (from Schedule G, line 7)	23	991
24	Payments: **a** 2004 estimated tax payments and amount applied from 2003 return	24a	
b	Estimated tax payments allocated to beneficiaries (from Form 1041-T)	24b	
c	Subtract line 24b from line 24a	24c	
d	Tax paid with extension of time to file: [ ] Form 2758 [ ] Form 8736 [ ] Form 8800	24d	
e	Federal income tax withheld. If any is from Form(s) 1099, check ▶ [ ]	24e	
	Other payments: **f** Form 2439 .... ; **g** Form 4136 .... ; Total ▶	24h	
25	**Total payments.** Add lines 24c through 24e, and 24h ▶	25	
26	Estimated tax penalty (see page 20 of the instructions)	26	
27	**Tax due.** If line 25 is smaller than the total of lines 23 and 26, enter amount owed	27	991
28	**Overpayment.** If line 25 is larger than the total of lines 23 and 26, enter amount overpaid	28	
29	Amount of line 28 to be: **a** Credited to 2005 estimated tax ▶ ; **b** Refunded ▶	29	

Sign Here ▶

Under penalties of perjury, I declare that I have examined this return, including accompanying schedules and statements, and to the best of my knowledge and belief, it is true, correct, and complete. Declaration of preparer (other than taxpayer) is based on all information of which preparer has any knowledge.

Signature of fiduciary or officer representing fiduciary | Date | ▶ EIN of fiduciary if a financial institution

May the IRS discuss this return with the preparer shown below (see instr.)? [ ] Yes [ ] No

Paid Preparer's Use Only

| Preparer's signature | ▶ | Date | Check if self-employed [ ] | Preparer's SSN or PTIN |

Firm's name (or yours if self-employed), address, and ZIP code ▶

EIN

Phone no. ( )

For Privacy Act and Paperwork Reduction Act Notice, see the separate instructions.

Cat. No. 11370H

Form **1041** (2004)

Form 1041

Form 1041 (2004) | | | Page **2**

Schedule A   Charitable Deduction. Do not complete for a simple trust or a pooled income fund.

1	Amounts paid or permanently set aside for charitable purposes from gross income (see page 20)	1	1,500
2	Tax-exempt income allocable to charitable contributions (see page 20 of the instructions) . .	2	450
3	Subtract line 2 from line 1	3	1,050
4	Capital gains for the tax year allocated to corpus and paid or permanently set aside for charitable purposes	4	
5	Add lines 3 and 4	5	1,050
6	Section 1202 exclusion allocable to capital gains paid or permanently set aside for charitable purposes (see page 20 of the instructions) . .	6	
7	**Charitable deduction.** Subtract line 6 from line 5. Enter here and on page 1, line 13	7	1,050

Schedule B   Income Distribution Deduction

1	Adjusted total income (see page 21 of the instructions)	1	33,450
2	Adjusted tax-exempt interest	2	12,750
3	Total net gain from Schedule D (Form 1041), line 15, column (1) (see page 21 of the instructions)	3	
4	Enter amount from Schedule A, line 4 (reduced by any allocable section 1202 exclusion) . .	4	
5	Capital gains for the tax year included on Schedule A, line 1 (see page 21 of the instructions)	5	
6	Enter any gain from page 1, line 4, as a negative number. If page 1, line 4, is a loss, enter the loss as a positive number . < GAIN.>	6	<8000>
7	**Distributable net income (DNI).** Combine lines 1 through 6. If zero or less, enter -0- . . .	7	38,200
8	If a complex trust, enter accounting income for the tax year as determined under the governing instrument and applicable local law **8** 40,500		
9	Income required to be distributed currently	9	12,000
10	Other amounts paid, credited, or otherwise required to be distributed	10	28,000
11	Total distributions. Add lines 9 and 10. If greater than line 8, see page 22 of the instructions	11	40,000
12	Enter the amount of tax-exempt income included on line 11	12	12,750
13	Tentative income distribution deduction. Subtract line 12 from line 11	13	27,250
14	Tentative income distribution deduction. Subtract line 2 from line 7. If zero or less, enter -0-	14	25,450
15	**Income distribution deduction.** Enter the smaller of line 13 or line 14 here and on page 1, line 18	15	25,450

Schedule G   Tax Computation (see page 22 of the instructions)

1 Tax: a	Tax on taxable income (see page 22 of the instructions) . .	1a	991
b	Tax on lump-sum distributions (attach Form 4972)	1b	
c	Alternative minimum tax (from Schedule I, line 56)	1c	
d	**Total.** Add lines 1a through 1c . . . . ▶	1d	991
2a	Foreign tax credit (attach Form 1116)	2a	
b	Other nonbusiness credits (attach schedule)	2b	
c	General business credit. Enter here and check which forms are attached: ☐ Form 3800 ☐ Forms (specify) ▶	2c	
d	Credit for prior year minimum tax (attach Form 8801)	2d	
3	**Total credits.** Add lines 2a through 2d . . . . ▶	3	0
4	Subtract line 3 from line 1d. If zero or less, enter -0-	4	991
5	Recapture taxes. Check if from: ☐ Form 4255 ☐ Form 8611	5	
6	Household employment taxes. Attach Schedule H (Form 1040)	6	
7	**Total tax.** Add lines 4 through 6. Enter here and on page 1, line 23 . . . . ▶	7	991

Other Information

		Yes	No
1	Did the estate or trust receive tax-exempt income? If "Yes," attach a computation of the allocation of expenses Enter the amount of tax-exempt interest income and exempt-interest dividends ▶ $ _15,000_	✓	
2	Did the estate or trust receive all or any part of the earnings (salary, wages, and other compensation) of any individual by reason of a contract assignment or similar arrangement?		✓
3	At any time during calendar year 2004, did the estate or trust have an interest in or a signature or other authority over a bank, securities, or other financial account in a foreign country? . . . . See page 24 of the instructions for exceptions and filing requirements for Form TD F 90-22.1. If "Yes," enter the name of the foreign country ▶		✓
4	During the tax year, did the estate or trust receive a distribution from, or was it the grantor of, or transferor to, a foreign trust? If "Yes," the estate or trust may have to file Form 3520. See page 24 of the instructions .		✓
5	Did the estate or trust receive, or pay, any qualified residence interest on seller-provided financing? If "Yes," see page 24 for required attachment		✓
6	If this is an estate or a complex trust making the section 663(b) election, check here (see page 24) . . ▶ ☐		
7	To make a section 643(e)(3) election, attach Schedule D (Form 1041), and check here (see page 24) . ▶ ☐		
8	If the decedent's estate has been open for more than 2 years, attach an explanation for the delay in closing the estate, and check here ▶ ☐		
9	Are any present or future trust beneficiaries skip persons? See page 24 of the instructions		✓

Form **1041** (2004)

Schedule D (Forms 1041)

SCHEDULE D (Form 1041) Department of the Treasury Internal Revenue Service	**Capital Gains and Losses** ▶ Attach to Form 1041, Form 5227, or Form 990-T. See the separate instructions for Form 1041 (also for Form 5227 or Form 990-T, if applicable).	OMB No. 1545-0092 2004

Name of estate or trust _A B TRUST_	Employer identification number

Note: *Form 5227 filers need to complete **only** Parts I and II.*

Part I — Short-Term Capital Gains and Losses—Assets Held One Year or Less

(a) Description of property (Example, 100 shares 7% preferred of "Z" Co.)	(b) Date acquired (mo., day, yr.)	(c) Date sold (mo., day, yr.)	(d) Sales price	(e) Cost or other basis (see page 33)	(f) Gain or (Loss) for the entire year (col. (d) less col. (e))
1					

2 Short-term capital gain or (loss) from Forms 4684, 6252, 6781, and 8824	**2**	
3 Net short-term gain or (loss) from partnerships, S corporations, and other estates or trusts .	**3**	
4 Short-term capital loss carryover. Enter the amount, if any, from line 9 of the 2003 Capital Loss Carryover Worksheet	**4** ( )
5 **Net short-term gain or (loss).** Combine lines 1 through 4 in column (f). Enter here and on line 13, column (3) below . . . . ▶	**5**	

Part II — Long-Term Capital Gains and Losses—Assets Held More Than One Year

(a) Description of property (Example, 100 shares 7% preferred of "Z" Co.)	(b) Date acquired (mo., day, yr.)	(c) Date sold (mo., day, yr.)	(d) Sales price	(e) Cost or other basis (see page 33)	(f) Gain or (Loss) for the entire year (col. (d) less col. (e))
6					8,000

7 Long-term capital gain or (loss) from Forms 2439, 4684, 6252, 6781, and 8824	**7**	
8 Net long-term gain or (loss) from partnerships, S corporations, and other estates or trusts . .	**8**	
9 Capital gain distributions	**9**	
10 Gain from Form 4797, Part I	**10**	
11 Long-term capital loss carryover. Enter the amount, if any, from line 14 of the 2003 Capital Loss Carryover Worksheet	**11** ( )
12 **Net long-term gain or (loss).** Combine lines 6 through 11 in column (f). Enter here and on line 14a, column (3) below . . . . ▶	**12**	8,000

Part III — Summary of Parts I and II

Caution: *Read the instructions before completing this part.*

		(1) Beneficiaries' (see page 34)	(2) Estate's or trust's	(3) Total
13	**Net short-term gain or (loss)**			
14	**Net long-term gain or (loss):**			
a	Total for year **14a**		8,000	8,000
b	Unrecaptured section 1250 gain (see line 18 of the worksheet on page 34). **14b**			
c	28% rate gain or (loss) **14c**			
15	**Total net gain or (loss).** Combine lines 13 and 14a . ▶ **15**		8,000	8,000

Note: *If line 15, column (3), is a net gain, enter the gain on Form 1041, line 4. If lines 14a and 15, column (2), are net gains, go to Part V, and **do not** complete Part IV. If line 15, column (3), is a net loss, complete Part IV and the **Capital Loss Carryover Worksheet,** as necessary.*

For Paperwork Reduction Act Notice, see the Instructions for Form 1041.　　Cat. No. 11376V　　Schedule D (Form 1041) 2004

Schedule D (Forms 1041)

Schedule D (Form 1041) 2004   *SCHEDULE D – A B TRUST*   Page **2**

Part IV   **Capital Loss Limitation**

16   Enter here and enter as a (loss) on Form 1041, line 4, the **smaller** of:
   a   The loss on line 15, column (3) **or**
   b $3,000   . . . .   **16** (   )

*If the loss on line 15, column (3), is more than $3,000, **or** if Form 1041, page 1, line 22, is a loss, complete the **Capital Loss Carryover Worksheet** on page 36 of the instructions to determine your capital loss carryover.*

Part V   **Tax Computation Using Maximum Capital Gains Rates** (Complete this part **only** if both lines 14a and 15 in column (2) are gains, or an amount is entered in Part I or Part II and there is an entry on Form 1041, line 2b(2), **and** Form 1041, line 22 is more than zero.)

   Note: *If line 14b, column (2) or line 14c, column (2) is more than zero, complete the worksheet on page 37 of the instructions and skip Part V. Otherwise, go to line 17.*

17 Enter taxable income from Form 1041, line 22	**17**	*7,900*
18 Enter the **smaller** of line 14a or 15 in column (2) but not less than zero . *LTCG*	**18** *8,000*	
19 Enter the estate's or trust's qualified dividends from Form 1041, line 2b(2)	**19**	
20 Add lines 18 and 19 . *LTCG*	**20** *8,000*	
21 If the estate or trust is filing Form 4952, enter the amount from line 4g; otherwise, enter -0- ▶	**21** *– 0 –*	
22 Subtract line 21 from line 20. If zero or less, enter -0- . *LTCG* . . .	**22** *8,000*	
23 Subtract line 22 from line 17. If zero or less, enter -0-	**23** *0*	
24 Enter the **smaller** of the amount on line 17 or $1,950	**24** *1,950*	
25 Is the amount on line 23 equal to or more than the amount on line 24? ☐ **Yes.** Skip lines 25 through 27; go to line 28 and check the "No" box. ☐ **No.** Enter the amount from line 23	**25** *0*	
26 Subtract line 25 from line 24	**26** *1,950*	
27 Multiply line 26 by 5% (.05) . *TO EXTENT IN 15% BRACKET, USE 15%*	**27**	*98*
28 Are the amounts on lines 22 and 26 the same? ☐ **Yes.** Skip lines 28 through 31; go to line 32. ☐ **No.** Enter the **smaller** of line 17 or line 22	**28** *7,900*	
29 Enter the amount from line 26 (If line 26 is blank, enter -0-).	**29** *1,950*	
30 Subtract line 29 from line 28	**30** *5,950*	
31 Multiply line 30 by 15% (.15) . *BALANCE OF LTCG AT 15%*	**31**	*893*
32 Figure the tax on the amount on line 23. Use the 2004 Tax Rate Schedule on page 22 of the instructions	**32**	*–*
33 Add lines 27, 31, and 32 . *2005 TAX YEAR*	**33**	*991*
34 Figure the tax on the amount on line 17. Use the 2004 Tax Rate Schedule on page 22 of the instructions . *2005 TAX YEAR*	**34**	*1,989*
35 **Tax on all taxable income.** Enter the **smaller** of line 33 or line 34 here and on line 1a of Schedule G, Form 1041	**35**	*991*

Schedule D (Form 1041) 2004

Schedule K-1 (Forms 1041)

SCHEDULE K-1 (Form 1041) Department of the Treasury Internal Revenue Service	**Beneficiary's Share of Income, Deductions, Credits, etc.** for the calendar year 2004, or fiscal year beginning .... , 2004, ending .... , 20 .... ▶ Complete a separate Schedule K-1 for each beneficiary.	OMB No. 1545-0092 **2004**

Name of trust or decedent's estate   *A B TRUST*   ☐ Amended K-1 ☐ Final K-1

Beneficiary's identifying number ▶   Estate's or trust's EIN ▶

Beneficiary's name, address, and ZIP code   Fiduciary's name, address, and ZIP code

BENEFICIARY A   *A B TRUST*

	(a) Allocable share item		**(b)** Amount	**(c)** Calendar year 2004 Form 1040 filers enter the amounts in column (b) on:
1	Interest	1	2,805	Form 1040, line 8a
2a	Qualified dividends	2a		Form 1040, line 9b
b	Total ordinary dividends	2b		Form 1040, line 9a
3	Net short-term capital gain	3		Schedule D, line 5, column (f)
4a	Net long-term capital gain	4a		Schedule D, line 12, column (f)
b	Unrecaptured section 1250 gain	4b		Line 11 of the worksheet for Schedule D, line 19
c	28% rate gain	4c		Line 4 of the worksheet for Schedule D, line 18
5a	Annuities, royalties, and other nonpassive income before directly apportioned deductions	5a		Schedule E, Part III, column (f)
b	Depreciation	5b		⎫
c	Depletion	5c		Include on the applicable line of the
d	Amortization	5d		appropriate tax form ⎭
6a	Trade or business, rental real estate, and other rental income before directly apportioned deductions (see instructions)	6a	10,175	Schedule E, Part III
b	Depreciation	6b		⎫
c	Depletion	6c		Include on the applicable line of the
d	Amortization	6d		appropriate tax form ⎭
7	Income for minimum tax purposes	7	12,980	
8	Income for regular tax purposes (add lines 1, 2b, 3, 4a, 5a, and 6a)	8	12,980	
9	Adjustment for minimum tax purposes (subtract line 8 from line 7)	9		Form 6251, line 14
10	Estate tax deduction (including certain generation-skipping transfer taxes)	10		Schedule A, line 27
11	Foreign taxes	11		Form 1040, line 46 or Schedule A, line 8
12	Adjustments and tax preference items (itemize):			
a	Accelerated depreciation	12a		⎫
b	Depletion	12b		Include on the applicable line of Form 6251
c	Amortization	12c		⎭
d	Exclusion items	12d		2005 Form 8801
13	Deductions in the final year of trust or decedent's estate:			
a	Excess deductions on termination (see instructions)	13a		Schedule A, line 22
b	Short-term capital loss carryover	13b ( )		Schedule D, line 5, column (f)
c	Long-term capital loss carryover	13c ( )		Sch. D, line 12, col. (f); line 5 of the wksht. for Sch. D, line 18; and line 16 of the wksht. for Sch. D, line 19
d	Net operating loss (NOL) carryover for regular tax purposes	13d ( )		Form 1040, line 21
e	NOL carryover for minimum tax purposes	13e		See the instructions for Form 6251, line 27
f		13f		⎫ Include on the applicable line
g		13g		⎭ of the appropriate tax form
14	Other (itemize):			
a	Payments of estimated taxes credited to you	14a		Form 1040, line 64
b	Tax-exempt interest	14b	6,503	Form 1040, line 8b
c		14c		⎫
d		14d		
e		14e		Include on the applicable line
f		14f		of the appropriate tax form
g		14g		
h		14h		⎭

For Paperwork Reduction Act Notice, see the Instructions for Form 1041.   Cat. No. 11380D   **Schedule K-1 (Form 1041) 2004**

THE SIXTY-FIVE DAY RULE

Fiduciaries may want to avoid accumulating income since such income may be taxed at very high rates. Because DNI is often not calculated until after the close of the trust's taxable year, the amount of current distributions necessary to avoid accumulation may be unknown. To alleviate this timing problem, § 663(b) provides that a trust or an estate *may elect* that any distribution made within the first 65 days of a taxable year will be considered paid to the beneficiary on the last day of the preceding taxable year.[39] This rule allows a trustee to make distributions after the close of a year to eliminate any accumulations of DNI for that year.

TAX PLANNING CONSIDERATIONS

The tax planning considerations for the use of trusts are discussed in Chapter 26, *Family Tax Planning*.

PROBLEM MATERIALS

DISCUSSION QUESTIONS

25-1 *Trusts and Estates as Conduits.* What does it mean to describe a fiduciary as *a conduit* of income? To what extent does a fiduciary operate as a conduit?

25-2 *Purpose of Trusts.* Trusts are usually created for nonbusiness purposes. Give some examples of situations in which a trust could be useful.

25-3 *Trust as a Separate Legal Entity.* A trust cannot exist if the only trustee is also sole beneficiary. Why not?

25-4 *Trust Expenses Allocable to Principal.* For what reason might the grantor of a trust stipulate that some amount of trust expenses be paid out of trust principal rather than trust income?

25-5 *Use of Fiduciaries to Defer Income Taxation.* Although a trust must adopt a calendar year for tax purposes, an estate may adopt any fiscal year, as well as a calendar year, for reporting taxable income. Why is Congress willing to allow an estate more flexibility in the choice of taxable year?

25-6 *Trust Accounting Income vs. Taxable Income.* Even though a trustee may be required to distribute all trust income currently, the trust may still have to report taxable income. Explain.

25-7 *Deductibility of Administrative Expenses.* Explain any options available to the executor of an estate with regard to the deductibility of administrative expenses incurred by the estate.

25-8 *Capital Loss Deductions.* To what extent may a fiduciary deduct any excess of capital losses over capital gains for a taxable year?

25-9 *Operating Losses of a Fiduciary.* How does the tax treatment of operating losses incurred by a fiduciary differ from the treatment of such losses by a partnership or an S corporation?

---

[39] See Reg. § 1.663(b)-2 for the manner and time for making such an election.

25-10 *Purpose of DNI.* Discuss the function of DNI from the point of view of the fiduciary and the point of view of beneficiaries who receive distributions from the fiduciary.

25-11 *Taxable vs. Nontaxable DNI.* Why is it important to correctly identify any nontaxable component of DNI?

25-12 *Charitable Deductions.* Enumerate the differences in the charitable deduction allowable to a fiduciary and the charitable deduction allowable to an individual.

25-13 *Timing Distributions from an Estate.* Why might a beneficiary of an estate prefer *not* to receive an early distribution of property from the estate?

25-14 *Simple vs. Complex Trusts.* All trusts are complex in the year of termination. Why?

25-15 *Trust Reserves for Depreciation.* Discuss the reason why a grantor of a trust would require the trustee to maintain a certain reserve for depreciation of trust assets.

25-16 *Distributions Exceeding DNI.* How are distributions in excess of distributable net income treated?

25-17 *Sixty-five Day Rule.* Explain the sixty-five day rule and what purpose it serves.

PROBLEMS

25-18 *Computation of Fiduciary Accounting Income.* Under the terms of the trust instrument, the annual fiduciary accounting income of Trust MNO must be distributed in equal amounts to individual beneficiaries M, N, and O. The trust instrument also provides that capital gains or losses realized on the sale of trust assets are allocated to principal, and that 40 percent of the annual trustee fee is to be allocated to principal. For the current year, the records of the trust show the following:

Dividend income	$38,000
Tax-exempt interest income	18,900
Taxable interest income	12,400
Capital loss on sale of securities	(2,500)
Trustee fee	5,000

Based on these facts, determine the required distribution to each of the three trust beneficiaries.

25-19 *Tax Consequences of Property Distributions.* During the taxable year, beneficiary M receives 100 shares of Acme common stock from Trust T. The basis of the stock is $70 per share to the trust, and its fair market value at date of distribution is $110 per share. The trust's DNI for the year is $60,000, all of which is taxable. There were no other distributions made or required to be made by the trust.

   a. Assume the stock distribution was in satisfaction of an $11,000 pecuniary bequest to M. What is the tax result to M? To Trust T? What basis will M have in the Acme shares?

   b. Assume the distribution did not represent a specific bequest to M, and that Trust T did not make a § 643(e)(3) election. What is the tax result to M? To Trust T? What basis will M have in the Acme shares?

   c. Assume now that Trust T did make a § 643(e)(3) election with regard to the distribution of the Acme shares. What is the tax result to M? To Trust T? What basis will M have in the Acme shares?

25-20 *Trust's Depreciation Deduction.* Under the terms of the trust instrument, Trustee K is required to maintain a reserve for depreciation equal to $3,000 per year. All trust income, including rents from depreciable trust property, must be distributed currently to trust beneficiaries.

a. Assume allowable depreciation for tax purposes is $2,000. What is the amount of the depreciation deduction available to the trust? To the trust beneficiaries?

b. Assume allowable depreciation for tax purposes is $7,000. What is the amount of the depreciation deduction available to the trust? To the trust beneficiaries?

25-21 *Trust Losses.* Complex Trust Z has the following receipts and disbursements for the current year:

Receipts:	
Rents	$ 62,000
Proceeds from sale of securities	
(basis of securities = $55,000)	48,000
Dividends	12,000
Total receipts	$122,000

Disbursements:	
Rent expenses	$ 70,000
Trustee fee (100% allocable to income)	4,000
Total disbursements	$ 74,000

The trustee made no distributions to any beneficiaries during the current year. Based on these facts, compute trust taxable income for the current year.

25-22 *Deductibility of Funeral and Administrative Expenses.* Decedent L died on May 12 of the current year, and her executor elected a calendar taxable year for L's estate. Prior to December 31, L's estate paid $4,800 of funeral expenses, $19,900 of legal and accounting fees attributable to the administration of the estate, and a $6,100 executor's fee. Before consideration of any of these expenses, L's estate has taxable income of $60,000 for the period May 13 to December 31. Decedent L's taxable estate for Federal estate tax purposes is estimated at $1,700,000.

a. To what extent are the above expenses deductible on L's estate tax return (Form 706) or on the estate's income tax return (Form 1041) for the current year? On which return would the deductions yield the greater tax benefit?

b. Assume that L was married at the time of her death and that all the property included in her gross estate was left to her surviving spouse. Does this fact change your answer to (a)?

25-23 *Amount of Distribution Taxable to Beneficiary.* During the current year, Trust H has DNI of $50,000, of which $30,000 is nontaxable. The trustee made a $10,000 cash distribution to beneficiary P during the year; no other distributions were made.

a. How much taxable income must P report?

b. What deduction for distributions to beneficiaries may Trust H claim?

25-24 *Deductibility of Trust Expenses.* Trust A has the following receipts and disbursements for the current year:

Receipts:

Nontaxable interest	$ 40,000
Taxable interest	30,000
Rents	30,000
Total receipts	$100,000

Disbursements:

Charitable donation	$ 10,000
Rent expense	6,500
Trustee fee	5,000
Total disbursements	$ 21,500

a. What is Trust A's deduction for charitable contributions for the current year?
b. How much of the trustee fee is deductible?
c. How much of the rent expense is deductible?

25-25 *Computation of DNI and Trust's Tax Liability.* Trust M has the following receipts disbursements for the current year:

Receipts:

Nontaxable interest	$ 4,000
Taxable interest	25,000
Rents	11,000
Long-term capital gain allocable to principal	9,000
Total receipts	$49,000

Disbursements:

Rent expense	$ 2,400
Trustee fee	1,000
Total disbursements	$ 3,400

The trustee is required to distribute all trust income to beneficiary N on a quarterly basis.
a. Compute Trust M's DNI for the current year.
b. Compute Trust M's taxable income for the current year.
c. Compute Trust M's tax liability for the current year.

25-26 *Taxation of Trust and Beneficiaries.* Trust B has the following receipts and disbursements for the current year:

Receipts:

Nontaxable interest	$10,000
Dividends	10,000
Rents	30,000
Long-term capital gain allocable to principal	15,000
Total receipts	$65,000

Disbursements:

Rent expense	$ 7,500
Trustee fee	5,000
Total disbursements	$12,500

During the year, the trustee distributes $20,000 to beneficiary C and $10,000 to beneficiary D. None of these distributions is subject to the throwback rule. The trust and both beneficiaries are calendar year taxpayers.

a. Compute Trust B's DNI for the current year.

b. Compute Trust B's taxable income for the current year.

c. How much taxable income must each beneficiary report for the current year?

25-27 *Distributions from Complex Trusts.* Under the terms of the trust instrument, the trustee of Trust EFG is required to make an annual distribution of 50 percent of trust accounting income to beneficiary E. The trustee can make additional discretionary distributions out of trust income or principal to beneficiaries E, F, or G. During the current year, the trust accounting income of $85,000 equaled taxable DNI.

a. Assume that the trustee made current distributions of $60,000 to E and $10,000 to G. How much taxable income must each beneficiary report for the current year? What is the amount of the trust's deduction for distributions to beneficiaries?

b. Assume that the trustee made current distributions of $80,000 to E and $40,000 to G. How much taxable income must each beneficiary report for the current year? What is the amount of the trust's deduction for distributions to beneficiaries?

25-28 *First- and Second-Tier Distributions.* For the current year, Trust R has DNI of $100,000, of which $25,000 is nontaxable. The trustee is required to make an annual distribution of $60,000 to beneficiary S. Also during the year, the trustee made discretionary distributions of $40,000 to beneficiary T and $30,000 to beneficiary U. None of these distributions is subject to the throwback rules. How much taxable income must each beneficiary report?

25-29 *Distribution Exceeding DNI.* In 2003 and 2004, complex Trust C had taxable DNI of $18,000 and $28,500, respectively. No distributions were made to beneficiaries in either year and the trust paid income taxes totaling $13,041 for the two years. In 2005 trust DNI was $33,000 and the trustee distributed $100,000 to beneficiary W. Explain how such distribution is taxed.

25-30 *Income in Respect of a Decedent.* Individual K is a self-employed business consultant. In the current year, K performed services for a client and billed the client for $14,500. Unfortunately, K died on October 10 of the current year, before he received payment for his services. A check for $14,500 was received by K's executor on November 18. At the date of K's death, he owed a local attorney $1,600 for legal advice concerning a child custody suit in which K was involved. K's executor paid this bill on December 15.

a. Assuming that K was a cash basis taxpayer, describe the tax consequences of the $14,500 receipt and the $1,600 payment by K's executor.

b. How would your answer change if K had been an accrual basis taxpayer?

25-31 *Income in Respect of a Decedent.* Early in 2004 Z (an unmarried cash basis taxpayer) sold investment land with a basis of $50,000 for $200,000. In payment, Z received an installment note for $200,000, payable over the next ten years. Z died on December 1, 2004. As of the date of death, Z had received no principal payments on the note. Accrued interest on the note as of December 1, 2004 was $18,000, although the first interest payment was not due until early in 2005.

a. Assuming that no election is made to avoid installment sale treatment, how much of the $150,000 gain realized by Z will be included on her final income tax return? How much of the accrued interest income will be included?

b. In 2005 the estate of Z collects the first annual interest payment on the note of $19,700, and the first principal payment of $20,000. What are the income tax consequences to the estate of these collections?

c. Assume that the amount of estate tax attributable to the inclusion of the IRD represented by the installment note and the accrued interest in Z's taxable estate is $10,000, and that there are no other IRD or DRD items on the estate tax return. Compute the § 691(c) deduction available on the estate's 2005 income tax return.

TAX RETURN PROBLEMS

25-32 The MKJ trust is a calendar year, cash basis taxpayer. The trust was created pursuant to the will of Murray Kyle Jacobs, who died on November 11, 1998. For 2005 the trust's book and records reflect these transactions:

Receipts:

Dividends (qualified)		$30,000
Gross rents		25,000
Interest:		
Bonds of the City of New York		25,000
U.S. government bonds		20,000

Capital gains:

General Motors stock received from estate of MKJ:		
Sales price—December 2, 2005	$ 48,000	
Less: Basis (FMV on date of death)	(30,000)	18,000

Disbursements:

Trustee commissions (50% paid out of income, 50% paid out of principal)	5,300
Legal fee	28,800
Contribution—American Cancer Society (paid out of principal)	12,000
Depreciation—rental property	2,000
Real estate tax—rental property	4,000
Repairs and maintenance—rental property	4,200
Federal quarterly estimated tax payments	9,000

The legal fee was a legitimate trust expense and was incurred because of the choice of trust form. The fee was allocated by the trustee to the various income classes as follows:

Dividends	$ 0
Taxable interest	16,000
Tax-exempt interest	6,000
Rents	6,800
Total legal fee	$28,800

The propriety of this allocation is *not* in question. Under the terms of the trust instrument (i.e., Mr. Jacobs' will), the $2,000 depreciation reserve equals the available tax depreciation deduction for the year. The trust instrument also specifies that all capital gains are allocable to principal and that the trustee has discretion as to the amount of trust income distributed to Brenda Jacobs, the sole individual beneficiary, and several charities specified in Mr. Jacobs' will. During 2005 the trustee distributes $24,000 of income to Brenda and $12,000 of income to the American Cancer Society.

Required: Complete Form 1041 and Schedule D for the MKJ trust. If the 2005 forms are not available, use the 2004 forms. **Note:** If the student is required to complete a Schedule K-l for Brenda Jacobs, he or she should refer to Reg. §§ 1.661(b)-1, 1.661(c)-2, and 1.661(c)-4, and the comprehensive example in this chapter in order to determine the character of any income distributed to the beneficiary.

RESEARCH PROBLEM

25-33   In 1999 N transferred $600,000 of assets into an irrevocable trust for the benefit of her mother, M. The independent trustee, T, is required to distribute annually all income to M. The trust instrument also provides that any capital gains or losses realized upon the sale of trust assets are to be allocated to trust principal. In 2001 and 2003, the trustee sold trust assets and distributed an amount equal to the capital gain realized to M, in addition to the required distribution of trust income. During the current year, T sold certain trust securities and realized a net gain of $25,000. The trust also earned $10,000 of other income. During the year, $35,000 was distributed to M. Should the DNI of the trust for the current year include the $25,000 capital gain?

Chapter 26

FAMILY TAX PLANNING

LEARNING OBJECTIVES

Upon completion of this chapter you will be able to:

▶ Explain the concept of income shifting and the judicial constraints on this tax planning technique

▶ Describe the marriage penalty and the singles penalty and identify the taxpayer situations in which either might occur

▶ Identify different planning techniques that achieve tax savings by the shifting of income among family members

▶ Characterize a regular corporation, an S corporation, and a partnership in terms of their viability as intrafamily income-shifting devices

▶ Explain how the "kiddie tax" is computed on the unearned income of a minor child

▶ Understand the role of a trust as a vehicle for intrafamily income shifting

▶ Distinguish between a grantor trust and a taxable trust

▶ Specify the tax advantages of inter vivos gifts as compared to testamentary transfers of wealth

▶ Explain the potential tax advantages and disadvantages of the estate tax marital deduction

CHAPTER OUTLINE

INTRODUCTION

Under the United States system of taxation, individuals are viewed as the basic unit of taxation. However, most individuals who are members of a nuclear family tend to regard the family as the economic and financial unit. For example, the individual wage earner with a spouse and three children must budget his or her income according to the needs of five people rather than one individual. Similarly, the family that includes a teenager who has received a college scholarship may perceive the scholarship as a financial benefit to all its members.

The concept of family tax planning is a product of this family-oriented economic perspective. Such planning has as its goal the minimization of taxes paid by the family unit as opposed to the separate taxes paid by individual members. Minimization of the total annual income tax bill of a family results in greater consumable income to the family unit. Minimization of transfer taxes on shifts of wealth among family members increases the total wealth that can be enjoyed by the family as a whole.

Before beginning a study of family tax planning, it is important to remember that such planning is only one aspect of the larger issue of family financial planning. Nontax considerations may often be more important to a family than the tax consequences of a course of action. For example, a family that faces the possibility of large medical expenses might be more concerned with their short-term liquidity needs than minimization of their current tax bill. A competent tax adviser must always be sensitive to the family's nontax goals and desires before he or she can design a tax plan that is truly in the family's best interests.

FAMILY INCOME SHIFTING

A general premise in tax planning holds that, given a single amount of income, two taxpayers are always better than one. This premise results from the progressive structure of the United States income tax. As one taxpayer earns an increasing amount of income, the income is taxed at an increasing marginal rate. If the income can be diverted to a second taxpayer with less income of his or her own, the diverted amount will be taxed at a lower marginal rate. In 2005, the tax rates applicable to individuals range from 10 percent on the first dollar of taxable income to 35 percent on taxable income in excess of $326,450. This 25-percentage-point spread between the lowest and highest marginal rates is a powerful incentive for individuals to adopt tax plans that incorporate some type of income-shifting technique.

A family unit composed of several individuals theoretically represents a single economic unit, which nonetheless is composed of separate taxpayers. A shift of income from one of these taxpayers to another has no effect economically. However, if the shift moves the income from a high tax bracket to a low tax bracket, the family has enjoyed a tax savings. A simple example can illustrate this basic point.

> **Example 1.** Family F is composed of a father and his 15-year-old daughter. The father earns taxable income of $90,000 a year, an amount that represents total family income. During the summer, the daughter needs $10,000 for various personal expenses. To earn the money, she agrees to work for her father for a $10,000 salary, payment of which represents a deductible expense to him.
>
> Based on this arrangement, the family saves $2,000 [$14,573 − ($12,073 + $500 = $12,573)] as computed below.

	Father Split	Daughter Split	Father No Split
Gross income.	$80,000	$10,000	$90,000
Standard deduction	(7,300)	(5,000)	(7,300)
Exemptions	(6,400)	0	(6,400)
Taxable income	$66,300	$ 5,000	$76,300
Tax (head of household rates)	$12,073		$14,573
Tax (single rates)		$ 500	

Note that the father's income tax, standard deduction and exemptions are based on the fact that he would be considered a head of household and can claim an exemption for his daughter. Observe also that the fact that the daughter is a taxpayer does not prevent the father from qualifying as a head of household for filing purposes. However, because the daughter is eligible to be claimed as a dependent on her father's return she is not entitled to a personal exemption.[1]

The tax savings in the above example is attributable to two factors. First, the daughter as a taxpayer with earned income is entitled to a $5,000 standard deduction,

---

[1]   § 151(d)(2).

which shelters $5,000 of the income shifted to her from any taxation at all.[2] Second, the income taxable to the daughter is subject to a 10 percent tax rate; if this income had been taxed on the father's return, it would have been subject to a 25 percent tax rate.

JUDICIAL CONSTRAINTS ON INCOME SHIFTING

The Federal courts have consistently recognized that the United States system of taxation cannot tolerate arbitrary shifting of income from one family member to another. The decisions in a number of historic cases have established clear judicial doctrine that limits the assignment of income from one taxpayer to another.

The 1930 Supreme Court case of *Lucas v. Earl*[3] involved a husband and wife who entered into a contract providing that the earnings of either spouse should be considered as owned equally by each. The contract was signed in 1901, twelve years before the first Federal income tax law was written, and was legally binding upon the spouses under California law.

The taxpayers contended that because of the contract certain attorney fees earned by Mr. Earl should be taxed in equal portions to Mr. and Mrs. Earl. However, the Supreme Court agreed with the government's argument that the intent of the Federal income tax law was to tax income to the individual who earns it, an intent that cannot be avoided by anticipatory arrangements to assign the income to a different taxpayer. The decision of the Court ended with the memorable statement that the tax law must disregard arrangements "by which the fruits are attributed to a different tree from that on which they grew."[4]

The Supreme Court followed the same logic in its 1940 decision in *Helvering v. Horst*.[5] This case involved a father who owned corporate coupon bonds and who detached the negotiable interest coupons from the bonds shortly before their due date. The father then gifted the coupons to his son, who collected the interest upon maturity and reported the income on his tax return for the year.

The Court's decision focused on the fact that ownership of the corporate bonds themselves created the right to the interest payments. Because the father owned the bonds, he alone had the right to and control over the interest income. In exercising his control by gifting the interest coupons to his child, the father realized the economic benefit of the income represented by the coupons and therefore was the individual taxable on the income.

These two cases illustrate the two basic premises of the *assignment of income doctrine*. Earned income must be taxed to the individual who performs the service for which the income is paid. Investment income must be taxed to the owner of the investment capital that generated the income. All legitimate efforts to shift income from one individual to another must take into account these judicial constraints.

JOINT FILING AND THE SINGLES PENALTY

The most obvious candidates for intrafamily income shifting are a husband and wife, one of whom has a much larger income than the other. However, since 1948 married couples have been allowed to file a joint income tax return, which reports the total income earned by the couple and taxes the income on the basis of one progressive rate schedule.[6]

---

2   § 63(c)(5).

3   2 USTC ¶496, 8 AFTR 10287, 281 U.S. 111 (USSC, 1930).

4   *Ibid.* 281 U.S. 115.

5   40-2 USTC ¶9787, 24 AFTR 1058, 311 U.S. 112 (USSC, 1940).

6   § 6013. Married individuals may choose to file separate returns, but they must use the rate schedule of § 1(d), which simply halves the tax brackets of the married filing jointly rate schedule of § 1(a). As a general rule, separate filing results in a greater tax than joint filing and such filing status is elected only for nontax reasons.

Joint filing originally was intended as a benefit to married couples. Prior to 1969, the joint filing tax rates were designed to tax one-half of total marital income at the tax rates applicable to single individuals. The resultant tax was then doubled to produce the married couple's tax liability. This perfect split and the corresponding tax savings were perceived as inequitable by unmarried taxpayers, who felt they were paying an unjustifiable "singles penalty."

To illustrate, consider the situation of a single taxpayer with taxable income of $24,000. In 1965 this taxpayer owed $8,030 of income tax, with the last dollar of income taxed at a 50 percent marginal tax rate. A married couple with the same 1965 taxable income owed only $5,660 and faced a marginal tax rate of only 32 percent.

THE MARRIAGE PENALTY

In 1969 Congress attempted to alleviate the singles penalty by enacting a new (and lower) rate schedule for single taxpayers.[7] While this action did reduce (but not eliminate) the singles penalty, it also created a marriage penalty for certain individuals. In 2001, Congress addressed the marriage tax penalty by modifying the standard deduction and the tax rates. For 2005, the standard deduction for joint returns is exactly double that of single taxpayers. Similarly, the 10 percent and 15 percent rate brackets for joint filers are exactly twice the size of the corresponding bracket for an unmarried individual ($7,300 vs. $14,600 and $29,700 vs. $59,400). The brackets for the higher rates are *not* expanded to twice the corresponding single filer tax brackets. As a practical matter, these changes will eliminate the marriage tax penalty for most individuals. Nevertheless, a penalty may still result for higher income taxpayers as shown below.

> **Example 2.** J and S are thinking about getting married and starting a family. The calculations below demonstrate what may happen if (1) J and S do not marry and J earns $80,000; (2) J and S do marry and J earns $80,000; and (3) J and S marry and both earned $80,000.

	J Single	J & S Married	J & S Married
Gross income of J	$80,000	$ 80,000	$ 80,000
Gross income of S	–	–	80,000
Standard deduction	(5,000)	(10,000)	(10,000)
Exemption	(3,200)	(6,400)	(6,400)
Taxable income	$71,800	$ 63,600	$143,600
Tax	$14,615	$ 9,230	$ 29,329
Tax for two singles ($14,615 × 2)			(29,230)
Singles penalty ($14,615 − $9,230)		$ 5,385	
Marriage penalty			$ 709

Interpretations of these results differ depending on the point of view. If J is single, he may not like the fact that his married friends who make the same income pay $5,301 less tax than he does. Obviously, he needs to find a wife! If J and S are considering getting married and S does not work, they should marry immediately since they would save $5,385 or avoid the singles penalty that J currently pays. But what happens if both individuals earn income? If each had about the same income and the amounts did not exceed about $65,000, there would be no penalty. However, if they both earn $80,000, as seen above, getting married produces an additional tax of $709—some may say a

---

[7]   Act. § 803(a), P.L. 91-172, Dec. 30, 1969.

small price for marital bliss. Most individuals contemplating marriage need not worry about the cost of marriage since the penalty normally occurs only at higher income levels. For example, if J and S both earned $68,175 for a total of $136,350, there would be no marriage tax penalty (calculations not shown).

Generally, a singles penalty may occur when *one* income can be taxed at married, rather than single, rates. A marriage penalty may occur when *two* incomes are combined and taxed at married, rather than single, rates. Today, two-income families have become the rule rather than the exception, and the marriage penalty has received considerable publicity. The recent changes by Congress will go a long way to putting an end to the controversy. Nevertheless there will be married couples who want to avoid the penalty. For these people who might entertain the notion of divorce, they should be wary. Because marital status is determined as of the last day of the taxable year,[8] couples have attempted to avoid the marriage penalty by obtaining a technically legal divorce shortly before year end. When a couple has immediately remarried and the only purpose of the divorce was to enable the husband and wife to file as single taxpayers, the IRS and the courts have had little trouble in concluding that the divorce was a sham transaction and therefore ineffective for tax purposes.[9]

Before leaving this topic, one last observation is worth noting. While the recent changes should eliminate most objections to the marriage tax penalty, this does not mean the system is neutral on marriage. Inequities between married and single taxpayers have not necessarily been resolved. No doubt singles who pay more taxes that their married counterparts who earn the same income will complain—much as their ancestors did in 1969. Only time will tell if Congress will once again provide relief and start the cycle once again.

INCOME SHIFTING TO CHILDREN AND OTHER FAMILY MEMBERS

Because a married couple is considered one rather than two taxpayers for Federal tax purposes, intrafamily income shifting usually involves a transfer of income from parents to children (or, less commonly, other family members) who are considered taxpayers in their own right.

The fact that children are taxpayers separate and distinct from their parents is recognized by § 73, which states "amounts received in respect of the services of a child shall be included in his gross income and not in the gross income of the parent, even though such amounts are not received by the child." The regulations elaborate by stating that the statutory rule applies even if state law entitles the parent to the earnings of a minor child.[10]

Because children typically will have little or no income of their own, a shift of family income to such children can cause the income to be taxed at a lower marginal rate. The income shifted from parent to child also represents wealth that is owned by the child rather than the parent. Thus, the future taxable estate of the parent will not include the accumulated income that is already in the hands of younger-generation family members.

INCOME-SHIFTING TECHNIQUES

The next section of this chapter explores a variety of techniques whereby income can be successfully shifted to family members in a lower marginal tax bracket. The circumstances of each particular family situation will dictate the specific technique to be used.

---

[8]   § 7703(a).

[9]   Rev. Rul. 76-255, 1976-2 C.B. 40; and *Boyter v. Comm.*, 82-1 USTC ¶9117, 49 AFTR2d 451, 668 F.2d 1382 (CA-4, 1981).

[10]   Reg. § 1.73-1(a).

FAMILY MEMBERS AS EMPLOYEES

The first technique for intrafamily income shifting is for a low-bracket family member to become an employee of a family business. This technique does not involve the transfer of a capital interest in the business, so the family member who owns the business does not dilute his or her ownership by this technique.

In the simplest case in which the family business is a sole proprietorship, any family members who become employees must actually perform services the value of which equates to the amount of compensation received. This requirement implies that the employee is both capable and qualified for his or her job and devotes an appropriate amount of time to the performance of services.

> **Example 3.** F owns a plumbing contracting business as a sole proprietorship. During the current year, F employs his son S as an apprentice plumber for an hourly wage of $10. The total amount paid to S for the year is $9,000.

If the father can prove to the satisfaction of the IRS that his son performed services worth $10 per hour and that the son actually worked 900 hours during the year, the father may deduct the $9,000 as wage expense on his tax return and the son will report $9,000 of compensation income on his own return.

If, on the other hand, the IRS concludes that the son was not a legitimate employee of his father's business, the transfer of $9,000 to the son would be recharacterized as a gift. As a result, the father would lose the business deduction, and no income shift from father to son would occur.

Obviously, the legitimacy of the employment relationship between father and son can only be determined by an examination of all relevant facts and circumstances. Facts to be considered would include the age of the son, his prior work experience and technical training, and his actual participation on contracted jobs requiring an apprentice plumber.

When a family member is an employee of a family business, any required payroll taxes on his or her compensation must be paid. However, compensation paid to an employer's children under the age of 18 is not subject to Federal payroll tax.[11]

FAMILY EMPLOYEES OF PARTNERSHIPS AND CORPORATIONS

If a family member wants to work as an employee of a family business operated in partnership or corporate form, the requirement that the value of his or her services equate to the amount of compensation received does not change. If the employment relationship is valid, the partnership or corporation may deduct the compensation paid to the family member. If the family member is not performing services that justify the salary he or she is drawing from the business, the IRS may recharacterize the payment.

In the case of a partnership, the payment may be recharacterized as a constructive cash withdrawal by one or more partners followed by a constructive gift of the cash to the pseudo employee.

> **Example 4.** Brothers X, Y, and Z are equal partners in Partnership XYZ. The partnership hires S, the sister of the partners, to act as secretary-treasurer for the business. S's salary is $20,000 per year. Assume that S has no business or clerical training and performs only minimal services for the business on a very sporadic basis. As a result, the IRS disallows a deduction to the partnership for all but $5,000

---

11   §§ 3121(b)(3)(A) and 3306(c)(5).

of the payment to the sister. The nondeductible $15,000 will be treated as a withdrawal by the partners that was transferred as a gift to the sister.

Constructive cash withdrawals from a partnership could have adverse tax consequences to the partners. If the withdrawal exceeds a partner's basis in his or her partnership interest, the excess constitutes capital gain to the partner.[12] Similarly, a constructive gift to a family member could result in an unexpected gift tax liability.

When the employer is a family corporation and a salary or wage paid to a nonshareholder family member is disallowed, the tax results can be extremely detrimental. Not only does the corporation lose a deduction, but the payment could be recharacterized as a constructive dividend to the family members who are shareholders, followed by a constructive gift to the family member who actually received the funds.[13] Thus, the corporate shareholders would have dividend income without any corresponding cash, and a potential gift tax liability.

The lesson to be learned from the preceding discussion should be clear. If an intrafamily income shift is to be accomplished by hiring a family member as an employee of a family business, the family member must perform as a legitimate employee. If the employment relationship has no substance, the unintended tax consequences to the family could be costly indeed.

FAMILY MEMBERS AS OWNERS OF THE FAMILY BUSINESS

A second technique for intrafamily income shifting is to make a low-bracket family taxpayer a part owner of the family business. By virtue of his or her equity or capital interest, the family member is then entitled to a portion of the income generated by the business. This is a more extreme technique in that it involves an actual transfer of a valuable asset. Moreover, the disposition of a partial ownership interest may cause dilution of the original owner's control of the business. These and other negative aspects of this technique will be discussed in greater detail later in the chapter.

The gratuitous transfer of an equity interest in a business will constitute a taxable gift to the original owner.

> **Example 5.** M runs a very successful business as a sole proprietorship. She wants to bring her son S into the business as an equal general partner. Under the terms of a legally binding partnership agreement, she contributes her business, valued at $1 million, to the partnership. Although the son will have a 50% capital interest in the partnership, he contributes nothing. As a result, M has made a $500,000 taxable gift to S.

Of course, if the transfer of the equity interest is accomplished by sale rather than gift, no initial gift tax liability will result. But in a typical family situation, the equity interest is being transferred to a family member without significant income or wealth, so that family member lacks the funds to purchase the interest. Also, the income tax consequences of a sale could be more expensive than gift tax consequences, depending upon the facts and circumstances. The prudent tax adviser should explore both possible methods of transfer when designing a particular plan.

---

[12] § 731(a).

[13] *Duffey v. Lethert*, 63-1 USTC ¶9442, 11 AFTR2d 1317 (D.Ct. Minn., 1963).

FAMILY PARTNERSHIPS

A family partnership can be used as a vehicle for the co-ownership of a single business by a number of family members. As a partner, each family member will report his or her allocable share of partnership income (or loss) on his or her individual tax return.[14] Therefore, through use of a partnership, business income can be shifted to family members with relatively low marginal tax brackets.

If the family partnership is primarily a service business, only a family member who performs services can receive an allocation of partnership income. In such service partnerships, the physical assets of the business (the capital of the partnership) are not a major factor of income production. Rather, it is the individual efforts and talents of the partners that produce partnership income. An attempt to allow a family member who cannot perform the appropriate services to participate in partnership income is an unwarranted assignment of earned income.

If the family partnership is one in which capital is a major income-producing factor, the mere ownership of a capital interest will entitle a family member to participate in partnership income. The determination of whether or not capital is a material income-producing factor is made by reference to the facts of each situation. However, capital is ordinarily a material income-producing factor if the operation of the business requires substantial inventories or investment in plant, machinery, or equipment.[15]

Section 704(e)(1) specifies that a family member will be recognized as a legitimate partner if he or she owns a capital interest in a partnership in which capital is a material income-producing factor. This is true even if the family member received his or her interest as a gift. However, § 704(e)(2) limits the amount of partnership income that can be shifted to such a donee partner. Under this statute, the income allocated to the partner cannot be proportionally greater than his or her interest in partnership capital.

> **Example 6.** Grandfather F is a 50% partner in Magnum Partnership. At the beginning of the current year, F gives his grandson G a 20% capital interest in Magnum (leaving F with a 30% interest). For the current year Magnum has taxable income of $120,000. The *maximum* amount allocable to G is $24,000 (20% × $120,000). If F wanted to increase the dollar amount of partnership income shifted to G, he must give G a greater equity interest in the partnership.

Section 704(e)(2) contains a second restriction on income allocation. A donor partner who *gifts* a capital interest must receive reasonable compensation for any services he or she renders to the partnership before any income can be allocated to the donee partner.

> **Example 7.** Refer to the facts in *Example 6*. During the current year, F performs services for Magnum worth $15,000 but for which he receives no compensation. Half of the $120,000 partnership income is still allocable to F and G with respect to their combined 50% capital interests; however, the maximum amount allocable to G decreases to $18,000 [($60,000 − $15,000 allocated to F as compensation for services) × 40%].

Note that in the above example, Grandfather F might be willing to forgo any compensation for the services performed for Magnum in order to increase the amount of partnership income shifted to his grandson. Unfortunately, § 704(e)(2) effectively curtails this type of indirect assignment of earned income.

---

[14] § 702(a).

[15] Reg. § 1.704-1(e)(1)(iv).

Family members are not able to avoid the dual limitations of § 704(e) by arranging a transfer of a capital interest to a lower-bracket family member by sale rather than by gift. Under § 704(e)(3), a capital interest in a partnership purchased by one member of a family from another is considered to be created by gift from the seller. In this context the term *family* includes an individual's spouse, ancestors, lineal descendants, and certain family trusts.

REGULAR CORPORATIONS

Family businesses are frequently owned as closely held corporations. There are a number of business reasons why the corporate form is popular. For example, shareholders in a corporation have limited liability so that creditors of the corporation cannot force the shareholders to pay the debts of the corporation out of the shareholders' personal assets. There are also tax benefits to the corporate form of business. The owners of the business can function as employees of the corporate entity. As employees, they may participate in a wide variety of tax-favored employee benefit plans, such as employer-sponsored medical reimbursement plans. If the family business were in sole proprietorship or partnership form, the owners of the business would be self-employed and ineligible to participate in such employee benefit plans.

The corporate form of business must be regarded as a mixed blessing from a tax point of view. The incorporation of a family business does result in the creation of a new taxable entity, separate and distinct from its owners. Business income has been shifted to the corporate taxpayer, and because corporate tax rates are progressive, a net tax savings to the business can be the result.[16]

> **Example 8.** Individual T, married, owns a sole proprietorship that produces $100,000 of net income before taxes. Ignoring the availability of any deductions or exemptions, T's 2005 tax on this income is $18,330 (married filing jointly rates). If T incorporates the business and draws a salary of $50,000, he will pay an individual tax of only $6,770. The corporation will also have income of $50,000 ($100,000 net income − $50,000 salary to T). The corporate tax on $50,000 is $7,500. Therefore, the *total* tax on the business income has decreased by $4,060 to $14,270 ($6,770 + $7,500).

The tax savings to T's business ($4,060) achieved by incorporation is certainly dramatic. However, the potential problem created by the incorporation of T's business is that the after-tax earnings of the business are now in the corporation rather than in T's pocket. If T needs or wants more than $43,230 ($50,000 salary − $6,770 tax liability) of after-tax personal income, he may certainly have his corporation pay out some of its after-tax earnings to him as a dividend. But any dividends paid must be included in T's gross income and taxed at the individual level.

This double taxation of corporate earnings paid to shareholders as dividends can quickly offset the tax savings resulting from using a corporation as a separate entity. Therefore, shareholders in closely held corporations usually become very adept in drawing business income out of their corporations as deductible business expenses rather than nondeductible dividends.

Shareholders who are also employees will usually try to maximize the amount of compensation they receive from the corporation. Section 162(a)(1) authorizes the corporation to deduct a *reasonable* allowance for salaries or other compensation paid. If the IRS determines that the compensation paid to an owner employee is unjustifiably high

---

[16]   Because of the 5 percent surtax on taxable income between $100,000 and $335,000, corporations with taxable income between $335,000 and $10 million face a flat 34 percent tax rate rather than a progressive rate. Qualified personal service corporations pay a flat 35 percent of their total taxable income. § 11(b)(2).

and therefore *unreasonable*, the excessive compensation can be reclassified as a dividend. As a result, the corporation loses the deduction for the excessive compensation, and to a corresponding extent, business earnings are taxed twice.

Other types of deductible payments from corporations to shareholders include rents paid for corporate use of shareholder assets and interest on loans made to the corporation by shareholders. The arrangements between corporation and shareholder that give rise to such rent or interest payments will be subject to careful scrutiny by the IRS. If an arrangement lacks substance and is deemed to be a device to camouflage the payments of dividends to shareholders, the corporate deduction for the payments will be disallowed.

Because it is a taxpayer in its own right, a regular corporation cannot be effectively used to shift business income to low-bracket family members. If such family members are made shareholders in the corporation and have no other relationship to the corporate business (employee, creditor, etc.), the only way to allocate business earnings to them is by paying dividends on their stock. As previously discussed, dividend payments are usually considered prohibitively costly from a tax standpoint.

Closely held regular corporations do have tremendous utility in other areas of tax planning. However, for purposes of intrafamily income shifting, the S corporation is a highly preferable alternative to a regular corporation.

S CORPORATIONS

The complex set of statutory provisions that govern the tax treatment of S corporations is explained in Chapter 23. For family tax planning purposes, the most important characteristic of an S corporation is that the corporate income escapes taxation at the corporate level and is taxed to the corporation's shareholders. This characteristic makes an S corporation a very useful mechanism for intrafamily income shifting.

Section 1366(a) provides that the taxable income of an S corporation is allocated to the shareholders on a pro rata basis. Thus, any individual who is a shareholder will report a proportionate share of the corporate business income on his or her personal tax return for the year with or within which the S corporation's taxable year ends.

> **Example 9.** Individual M, married, owns a sole proprietorship with an annual net income before taxes of $200,000. Ignoring the availability of any itemized deductions or exemptions, M's personal tax on this income is $46,592 (joint return schedule). If at the beginning of 2005 M incorporates the business, gives each of his four unmarried children 20% of the stock, and has the shareholders elect S status for the corporation, the corporate income of $200,000 will be taxed in equal $40,000 amounts to the five shareholders. Ignoring other deductions or exemptions, the 2005 tax bill on the business income will be $31,930 [$5,270 on a joint return + (4 × $6,665 = $26,660 on a single return)]. By splitting the income, M saves $14,661 ($46,951 − $31,930).

A shareholder who is also an employee of a family-owned S corporation will not be able to divert corporate income to other shareholders by forgoing any compensation for services rendered to the corporation. Code § 1366(e) provides that if such a shareholder employee does not receive reasonable compensation from the S corporation, the IRS may reallocate corporate income to the shareholder employee so as to accurately reflect the value of his or her services.

Because shareholders of an S corporation are taxed on all the taxable income earned by the corporation, subsequent cash withdrawals of this income by shareholders are tax free.[17] However, the technical requirements for cash withdrawals from an S corporation

---

[17]   § 1368(b).

are dangerously complicated. Because of the complexity of these requirements and many other tax aspects of S corporations, family tax plans involving their use should be carefully designed and monitored by the family tax adviser.

NEGATIVE ASPECTS OF OWNERSHIP TRANSFERS

A high-bracket taxpayer who desires to shift income to low-bracket family members by making such members co-owners of the taxpayer's business must reconcile himself or herself to several facts. First, the transfer of the equity interest in the business must be complete and legally binding so that the recipient of the interest has "dominion and control" over his or her new asset. A *paper* transfer by which the transferor creates only the illusion that a family member has been given an equity interest in a business will be treated as a sham transaction, ineffective for income-shifting purposes.[18]

As a general rule, the recipient of an ownership interest in a family business is free to dispose of the interest, just as he or she is free to dispose of any asset he or she owns. If the recipient is a responsible individual and supportive of the family tax planning goals, his or her legal right to assign the interest may not be a problem. But if the recipient is a spendthrift in constant need of ready cash, he or she may sell the interest to a third party, thereby completely subverting the family tax plan.

One popular technique that can prevent an unexpected and undesired disposition of an interest in a family business is a buy-sell agreement. A taxpayer can transfer an equity interest to a low-bracket family member on the condition that should the family member desire to sell the interest he or she must first offer the interest to its original owner at an independently determined market value. Such an agreement is in no way economically detrimental to the family member, yet affords a measure of protection for both the original owner and the family tax plan.

A related aspect of the requirement that the taxpayer must legally surrender the ownership of the business interest transferred is that the transfer is irrevocable. Ownership of the interest cannot be regained if future events cause the original tax plan to become undesirable. For example, an estrangement between family members could convert a highly satisfactory intrafamily income-shifting plan into a bitterly resented trap. A father who has an ill-favored son as an employee can always fire him. It is another matter entirely if the son is a 40 percent shareholder in the father's corporation.

A change in economic circumstances could also cause a taxpayer to regret a transfer of a business interest. Consider a situation in which a formerly high-income taxpayer suffers a severe financial downturn. A tax plan that is shifting income *away* from such a taxpayer could suddenly become an economic disaster.

PRESERVATION OF CONTROL OF THE BUSINESS

A taxpayer who is contemplating transferring an ownership interest in a business to one or more family members should also consider any resultant dilution of his or her control of the business. The taxpayer may be willing to part with an equity interest in order to shift business income to low-bracket family members, but may be very reluctant to allow such family members to participate in the management of the business.

A limited partnership can be used to bring family members into a business without allowing them a voice in management. A family member who owns a capital interest as a limited partner in a partnership may be allocated a share of business income, subject to the family partnership rules, and yet be precluded from participating in management of the business.

---

[18] For example, see Reg. § 1.704-1(e)(2).

If the family business is in corporate form, various classes of stock with differing characteristics can be issued. For example, nonvoting stock can be given to family members without any dilution of the original owner's voting power, and hence control, over the business. If the original owner does not want to draw any dividends out of the corporate business but is willing to have dividends paid to low-bracket family members, nonvoting preferred stock can be issued to such family members.

Unfortunately, this flexibility in designing a corporate capital structure that maximizes income-shifting potential while minimizing loss of control is not available to S corporations. To qualify for S status a corporation may have only one class of stock outstanding.[19] Thus, all outstanding shares of stock in an S corporation must be identical with respect to the rights they convey in the profits and assets of the corporation. However, shares of stock in S corporations may have different *voting rights* without violating the single class of stock requirement.[20]

SHIFTS OF INVESTMENT INCOME

In many ways the shifting of investment income to family members is simpler than the shifting of business income. Questions of forms of co-ownership and control are not as difficult to resolve if the income-producing asset to be transferred is in the form of an investment security rather than a business interest.

The simplest means to shift investment income from one taxpayer to another is an outright gift of the investment asset. Even gifts to minors who are under legal disabilities with regard to property ownership can be accomplished under state Uniform Gifts to Minors Acts. By using a custodian to hold the property for the benefit of a minor, the donor has shifted the investment income to the minor's tax return.[21]

Although gifting of investment property is a relatively simple technique, the donor must be aware that the transfer must be complete. The asset (and the wealth it represents) is irrevocably out of the donor's hands. If the donor attempts to retain an interest in or control over the asset, the gift may be deemed incomplete and the attempted income shift ineffectual.

If a donee receives an unrestricted right to a valuable investment asset, there is always the worry that he or she will mismanage it, or worse, assign it to a third party against the wishes of the donor. Because of these negative aspects of outright gifts, the private trust has become a very popular vehicle for the transfer of investment assets, especially when minor children are involved. A subsequent section of the chapter explores the use of trusts in family tax planning.

TAXATION OF UNEARNED INCOME OF MINOR CHILDREN

Tax law significantly limits the ability of parents to shift investment income to their children. Section 1(g) provides that any *net unearned income* of a minor child in excess of a $800 (2005) base is taxed at the marginal rate applicable to the income of the child's parents.[22] A minor child is one who has not obtained the age of 14 by the close of the taxable year and who has at least one living parent on that date.

Net unearned income is generally defined as passive investment income such as interest and dividends, reduced by the $800 standard deduction available against

---

[19]   § 1361(b)(1)(D).

[20]   § 1361(c)(4).

[21]   Rev. Rul. 56-484, 1956-2 C.B. 23. However, income earned by the custodian account used for the support of the minor will be taxed to the person legally responsible for such support (i.e., the parent).

[22]   In the case of parents who are not married, the child's tax is computed with reference to the tax rate of the custodial parent. If the parents file separate tax returns, the tax rate of the parent with the *greater* taxable income is used. § 1(g)(5).

unearned income of a dependent.[23] The amount of net unearned income for any taxable year may not exceed the child's taxable income for the year. The *source* of the unearned income is irrelevant for purposes of this so-called "kiddie tax."

> **Example 10.** Several years ago grandchild G, age 10, received a gift of corporate bonds from her grandparents. G's 2005 interest income from the securities totaled $8,000. G had no other income or deductions for the year. G's parents claimed G as a dependent and reported taxable income of $500,000 on their joint return. G's taxable income is $7,200 ($8,000 gross income − an $800 standard deduction) and her net unearned income to be taxed at her parents' rate is $6,400 ($8,000 − the $800 base − an $800 standard deduction). Thus $6,400 is taxed at her parents' rates and the balance, $800, is taxed at her rates, resulting in a tax liability of $2,320 computed as follows:

Tax on unearned income at parents' rates:	
($8,000 − $1,600 = $6,400 × 35%)	$2,240
Tax on remaining taxable income at child's rates:	
($800 × 10%)	80
Tax liability	$2,320

In this example, it is important to note that the income was interest and, therefore, subject to tax at the parents' highest tax rate. In contrast, dividend income or long-term capital gains that are shifted to a child are taxed at 15% (or 5%).

In certain cases parents may elect to include a dependent's unearned income on their return, rather than filing a separate return and making the "kiddie tax" calculation.

THE TRUST AS A TAX PLANNING VEHICLE

As discussed in Chapter 25, a private trust is a legal arrangement whereby the ownership and control of property are vested in a trustee while the beneficial interest in the property is given to one or more beneficiaries. The trustee has a fiduciary responsibility to manage the property for the sole benefit of the beneficiaries.

ADVANTAGES OF THE TRUST FORM

The use of a trust has many nontax advantages. If an individual desires to make a gift of property to a donee who is not capable of owning or managing the property, the gift can be made in trust so that a competent trustee can be selected to manage the property free from interference from the donee-beneficiary.

The trust form of property ownership is very convenient in that it allows the legal title to property to be held by a single person (the trustee) while allowing the beneficial enjoyment of the property to be shared by a number of beneficiaries. If legal ownership of the property were fragmented among the various beneficiaries, they would all have to jointly participate in management decisions regarding the property. This cumbersome and oftentimes impractical co-ownership situation is avoided when a trustee is given sole management authority over the property.

If a donor would like to give property to several donees so that the donees have sequential rather than concurrent rights in the property, the trust form for the gift is commonly the solution.

---

[23] § 63(c)(5).

Example 11. Individual K owns a valuable tract of income-producing real estate. She would like ownership of the real estate to ultimately pass to her three minor grandchildren. She also would like to give her invalid brother an interest in the real estate so as to provide him with a future source of income. K can transfer the real estate into trust, giving her brother an income interest for a designated time period. Upon termination of the time period, ownership of the real estate will go to K's grandchildren.

TAX CONSEQUENCES OF TRANSFERS INTO TRUST

The use of the trust form can have distinct income tax advantages to a family because both the trust itself and any beneficiaries who receive income from the trust are taxpayers in their own right.

Example 12. F, a high-bracket taxpayer, transfers income-producing assets into a trust of which his four grandchildren are discretionary income beneficiaries. In the current year, the trust assets generate $100,000 of income, of which the trustee distributes $24,000 to each child. The $100,000 of investment income will be taxed to five taxpayers, the four grandchildren and the trust itself.

In determining the benefit of splitting income in *Example 12*, it is important to remember that unearned income *distributed* from a trust to a beneficiary who is under the age of 14 is subject to the rule of § 1(g). The income will be taxed at the marginal rate applicable to the beneficiary's parents, even if the parents did not create the trust. However, once the beneficiaries reach age 14, substantial savings can be obtained.

GIFT-LEASEBACKS

A popular and controversial method for family income shifting through use of a trust involves a technique known as a gift-leaseback. Typically, a taxpayer who owns assets that he or she uses in a trade or business transfers the assets as a gift in trust for the benefit of the taxpayer's children (or other low-bracket family members). The independent trustee then leases the assets back to the taxpayer for their fair rental value. The rent paid by the taxpayer to the trust is deducted as a § 162 ordinary and necessary business expense and becomes income to the taxpayer's children because of their status as trust beneficiaries.

The IRS has refused to recognize the validity of gift-leaseback arrangements and has consistently disallowed the rent deduction to the transferor of the business assets under the theory that the entire transaction has no business purpose. However, if the trust owning the leased assets has an independent trustee and the leaseback arrangement is in written form and requires payment to the trust of a reasonable rent, the Tax Court and the Second, Third, Seventh, Eighth, and Ninth Circuits have allowed the transferor to deduct the rent paid.[24] To date, only the Fourth and Fifth Circuits have supported the government's position that gift-leaseback transactions are shams to be disregarded for tax purposes.[25]

GIFT TAX CONSIDERATIONS

The obvious income tax advantage of a family trust, such as the one described in *Example 12* above, can be offset if the original gift of property into the trust is subject

---

[24]   See *May v. Comm.*, 76 T.C. 7(1981), *aff'd.* 84-1 USTC ¶9166, 53 AFTR2d 84-626 (CA-9. 1984).

[25]   See *Mathews v. Comm.*, 75-2 USTC ¶9734, 36 AFTR2d 75-5965, 520 F.2d 323 (CA-5, 1975), *cert. denied*, 424 U.S. 967 (1976).

to a substantial gift tax. Thus, the first step in designing a family trust is the minimization of any front-end gift tax. If the fair market value of the transferred property is less than the taxable amount sheltered by the unified credit of § 2505, no gift tax will be paid. However, the reader should bear in mind that the use of the credit against inter vivos gifts reduces the future shelter available on the donor's estate tax return.

An essential element in the minimization of any gift tax for transfers into trust is securing the $11,000 annual exclusion (§ 2503) for the amount transferred to each beneficiary-donee. This can be difficult when certain of the donees are given only a prospective or future interest in the trust property.

> **Example 13.** Donor Z transfers $100,000 into trust. The independent trustee has the discretion to distribute income currently among Z's five children, or she may accumulate it for future distribution. Upon trust termination, the trust assets will be divided equally among the children. Because the five donees have only future interests in the $100,000, Z may not claim any exclusions in computing the amount of the taxable gift.[26]

SECTION 2503(c) AND CRUMMEY TRUSTS

One method of securing the exclusion for transfers into trust is to rely on the *safe harbor* rules of § 2503(c). Under this subsection a transfer into trust will not be considered a gift of a future interest if:

1. The property and income therefrom may be expended for the benefit of the donee-beneficiary before he or she reaches age 21; and

2. If any property or income is not so expended, it will pass to the donee-beneficiary at age 21 or be payable to his or her estate if he or she dies before that age.

One drawback to the "§ 2503(c) trust" is that the trust assets generally must go to the beneficiaries at age 21. Many parent-donors would prefer to postpone trust termination until their children-donees attain a more mature age. This goal can be accomplished through the use of a *Crummey trust*.[27]

A Crummey trust is one in which the beneficiaries are directly given only a future right to trust income or corpus. The term of the trust may extend well beyond the time when the beneficiaries reach age 21. However, the trust instrument contains a clause (the Crummey clause) that authorizes any beneficiary or his or her legal representative to make a current withdrawal of any current addition to the trust of up to $11,000. The withdrawal right is made noncumulative from year to year. As long as the beneficiary is given notification of this right within a reasonable period before it lapses for the year, the donor will be entitled to an exclusion for the current transfers into trust.[28] It should be noted that most donors anticipate that their donees will never exercise their withdrawal right; the Crummey clause is included in the trust instrument for the *sole purpose* of securing the $11,000 exclusion for gift tax purposes.

---

[26]   Reg. § 25.2503-3(c), Ex. 3.

[27]   The amusing designation comes from the court case which established the validity of the technique— *Crummey v. Comm.*, 68-2 USTC ¶12,541, 22 AFTR2d 6023, 397 F.2d 82 (CA-9, 1968). The IRS *acquiesced* to this decision in Rev. Rul. 73-405, 1973-2 C.B. 321.

[28]   Rev. Rul. 81-7, 1981-1 C.B. 27.

GRANTOR TRUSTS

In certain cases a taxpayer may desire to transfer property into trust but does not want to surrender complete control over the property. Alternatively, the taxpayer may want to dispose of the property (and the right to income from the property) for only a limited period of time. Prior to the enactment of the 1954 Internal Revenue Code there was no statutory guidance as to when the retention of powers over a trust by the grantor (transferor) would prevent the trust from being recognized as a separate taxable entity. Nor was there statutory guidance as to the tax status of a reversionary trust, the corpus of which reverted to the grantor after a specified length of time.

The judicial attitude toward these *grantor* trusts was reflected in the Supreme Court decision of *Helvering v. Clifford*.[29] This case involved a taxpayer who transferred securities into trust for the exclusive benefit of his wife. The trust was to last for five years, during which time the taxpayer as trustee would manage the trust corpus as well as decide how much, if any, of the trust income was to be paid to his wife. Upon trust termination, corpus was to return to the taxpayer while any accumulated income was to go to the wife.

In reaching its decision, the Court noted the lack of a precise standard or guide supplied by statute or regulations. As a result, the Court turned to a subjective evaluation of all the facts and circumstances of this particular short-term trust arrangement and held that "the short duration of the trust, the fact that the wife was the beneficiary, and the retention of control over the corpus by respondent all lead irresistibly to the conclusion that the respondent continued to be the owner."[30] As a result, the trust income was held to be taxable to the grantor rather than the trust or its beneficiary.

The authors of the 1954 Internal Revenue Code recognized that the uncertainty regarding the tax treatment of grantor trusts was undesirable and supplanted the subjective *Clifford* approach with a series of code sections (§§ 671 through 679) containing more objective rules as to the taxability of such trusts. The basic operative rule is contained in § 671. If §§ 673 through 679 specify that the grantor (or another person) shall be treated as the owner of any portion of a trust, the income, deductions, or credits attributable to that portion of the trust shall be reported on the grantor's (or other person's) tax return. If §§ 673 through 679 are inapplicable, the trust shall be treated as a separate taxable entity under the normal rules of Subchapter J (see Chapter 25).

REVERSIONARY TRUSTS

Section 673 provides that the grantor shall be treated as the owner of any portion of a trust in which he or she has a reversionary interest, if upon creation of the trust the value of the reversion exceeds 5 percent of the value of the assets subject to reversion.

Example 14. In the current year grantor G transfers assets worth $500,000 into trust. Niece N, age 20, will receive the income from the trust for 15 years, after which the trust will terminate and the assets returned to G. On the date the trust is created, the reversion is properly valued at $121,000. Because the reversion is worth more than 5% of $500,000, the income will be taxed to G, even though it will be distributed to N.

---

[29] 40-1 USTC ¶9265, 23 AFTR 1077, 309 U.S. 331 (1940).

[30] *Ibid.*, 309 U.S. 332.

Example 15. If in the previous example, N had been given the income from the trust for her life, the proper value of G's reversion would only be $13,000. Because this reversionary interest is worth only 2.6% of the value of the trust assets, the trust is not a grantor trust and the income will be taxed to N.

In the case of a trust in which a lineal descendant of the grantor (child, grandchild, etc.) is the income beneficiary, and the grantor owns a reversionary interest that takes effect only upon the death of the beneficiary prior to the age of 21, the trust *will not* be considered a grantor trust.[31]

INTEREST-FREE LOANS

Through use of a reversionary trust, a taxpayer may divert income to low-bracket family members only if he or she is willing to part with control of the trust corpus for a significant period of time. For many years the use of an interest-free demand loan between family members provided an alternative to a reversionary trust. A taxpayer could loan a sum of money to a family member on a demand basis and the money could be invested to earn income for that family member. Because the loan was interest-free, the creditor-taxpayer had no income from the temporary shift of wealth and could call the loan (demand payment) at any time.

The IRS was understandably hostile to such loans and argued that the creditor was making a gift of the use of the money to the borrower and that the amount of the gift equaled the interest that the creditor would have charged an unrelated borrower. In 1984, Congress codified the IRS position by enacting Code § 7872, concerning below-market-rate-interest and no-interest loans. The thrust of this provision is to impute interest income to the creditor donor and correspondingly allow an interest deduction for the borrower-donee. Therefore, the creditor-donor is effectively treated as having received interest income and then gifting such income to the borrower. The deemed transfer is subject to the gift tax to the extent the interest exceeds the annual exclusion. As a result, interest-free loans are no longer an effective device for shifting income.

Example 16. On January 1 of the current year, father F loaned $175,000 to his daughter, S. The loan was interest free and F may demand repayment at any time. The current interest rate as determined by the IRS is 10% per annum. On December 31 of the current year, S is considered to have paid $17,500 of deductible interest to F, and F is considered to have received $17,500 of taxable interest income from S. On the same date, F is considered to have made a $17,500 gift to S which is eligible for the $11,000 annual gift tax exclusion.

POWER TO CONTROL BENEFICIAL ENJOYMENT

Section 674(a) contains the general rule that a grantor shall be treated as the owner of any portion of a trust of which the grantor, a nonadverse party, or both, controls the beneficial enjoyment. However, if the exercise of such control requires the approval or consent of an *adverse party*, the general rule shall not apply. An adverse party is defined in § 672(a) as any person who has a substantial beneficial interest in the trust that would be adversely affected by the exercise of the control held by the grantor.

Example 17. F transfers income-producing property into trust with City Bank as independent trustee. F's two children are named as trust beneficiaries. However, F retains the unrestricted right to designate which of the children is to receive annual

---

[31] § 673(b).

distributions of trust income. This is a grantor trust with the result that all trust income is taxed to F.

Example 18. Refer to the facts in *Example 17*. Assume that the trust instrument provides that the trust income will be paid out on an annual basis in equal portions to F's two children. However, F retains the right to adjust the amount of the income distributions at any time with the consent of the older child C. Because C is an adverse party with respect to the one-half of the income to which he is entitled, only the other half of the income is considered subject to F's control. As a result, only half the trust property is deemed owned by F and only half the trust income is taxable directly to him.[32]

The general rule of § 674(a) is subject to numerous exceptions contained in §§ 674(b), (c), and (d). Any tax adviser attempting to avoid the grantor trust rules should be aware of these exceptions. For example, § 674(c) provides that the power to distribute income within a class of beneficiaries will not cause the grantor trust rules to apply if the power is solely exercisable by an *independent* trustee.

Example 19. M transfers income-producing property into trust and names Midtown Bank as independent trustee. The trustee has the right to *sprinkle* (distribute) the annual income of the trust among M's three children in any proportion the trustee deems appropriate. Even though the power to control the enjoyment of the income is held by a nonadverse party, such party is independent of the grantor and the trust is not a grantor trust.

OTHER GRANTOR TRUSTS

Section 675 provides that the grantor shall be treated as the owner of any portion of a trust in respect of which he or she holds certain administrative or management powers.

Example 20. T transfers 60% of the common stock in his closely held corporation into trust with City National Bank as independent trustee. All income of the trust must be paid to T's only grandchild. However, T retains the right to vote the transferred shares. Because T has retained an administrative power specified in § 675(4), he will be taxed on the income generated by the corporate stock.

If a grantor, a nonadverse party, or both have the right to revest in the grantor the ownership of any portion of trust property, § 676 provides that such portion of the trust is considered to be owned by the grantor. Therefore, revocable trusts are grantor trusts for income tax purposes.

Under § 677, a grantor also is treated as owner of any portion of a trust the income of which *may be* distributed to the grantor or spouse without the approval of any adverse party. This rule also applies if trust income may be used to pay premiums for insurance on the life of the grantor and spouse. This provision is inapplicable if the beneficiary of the policy is a charitable organization.

Example 21. Individual J transfers income-producing assets into trust and designates Second National Bank as independent trustee. Under the terms of the trust instrument, the trustee may distribute trust income to either J's spouse or J's brother. In the current year the trustee distributes all trust income to J's brother.

---

[32] Reg. § 1.672(a)-1(b).

Because a nonadverse party (the trustee) could have distributed the trust income to J's spouse, this is a grantor trust and all income is taxed to J.

If trust income may be expended to discharge a legal obligation of the grantor, § 677 applies,[33] subject to two important exceptions. Section 682 creates an exception for *alimony trusts*. In certain divorce situations an individual who is required to pay alimony may fund a reversionary trust, the income from which will be paid to the grantor's former spouse in satisfaction of the alimony obligation. Under § 682, the recipient of the trust income rather than the grantor will be taxed on the income regardless of the applicability of any other of the grantor trust rules.

As a second exception, § 677(b) specifies that if trust income may be distributed for the support or maintenance of a beneficiary (other than the grantor's spouse) whom the grantor is legally obligated to support, such a provision by itself will not cause the trust to be a grantor trust. However, to the extent trust income is actually distributed for such purposes, it will be taxed to the grantor.

The final type of trust that is not recognized as a separate taxable entity is described in § 678. Under this provision, a person *other than* the grantor may be treated as the owner of a portion of a trust if such person has an unrestricted right to vest trust corpus or income in himself or herself. Section 678 shall not apply to the situation in which a person, in the capacity of trustee, has the right to distribute trust income to a beneficiary whom the person is legally obligated to support. Only to the extent that trust income is actually so expended will the income be taxed to the person.

> **Example 22.** Grantor G creates a trust with an independent corporate trustee and names his children and grandchildren as beneficiaries. The trust instrument also provides that G's sister S has the unrestricted right to withdraw up to one-third of trust corpus at anytime. S is considered the owner of one-third of the trust and will be taxed on one-third of the income, regardless of the fact that such income is not distributable to her.

GRANTOR TRUSTS AND THE TRANSFER TAX RULES

As a general rule, a transfer of assets into trust that is incomplete for income tax purposes, so that the grantor is taxed on trust income, is also incomplete for gift and estate tax purposes.

> **Example 23.** M transfers income-producing properties into a trust but retains the right to designate which of the specified trust beneficiaries will receive a distribution of trust income. The arrangement is a grantor trust per § 674. Under the gift tax Regulations, M has not made a completed gift of the income interest in the trust, and per § 2036 the value of the trust corpus will be included in M's gross estate upon his death.

However, it should be emphasized that the general rule does not always hold.

> **Example 24.** Grantor G transfers assets into a reversionary trust that will last only eight years. During the existence of the trust, all income must be paid to G's cousin, C. For income tax purposes, this is a grantor trust and all trust income is taxable to G. However, for gift tax purposes G has made a completed gift of the income interest to C.

---

[33] Reg. § 1.677(a)-1(d).

TRANSFER TAX PLANNING

The first part of this chapter dealt with a variety of techniques to shift income within a family group and thereby minimize the family's income tax burden. The second part of the chapter focuses on family tax planning techniques designed to reduce any transfer tax liability on intrafamily shifts of wealth. At this point, the student should be cautioned against thinking of income tax planning and transfer tax planning as two separate areas; both types of planning should be considered as highly interrelated aspects of a single integrated family tax plan.

A second aspect of transfer tax planning of which any tax adviser should be aware is that a client's nontax estate planning goals may conflict with an optimal tax-oriented estate plan. From a client's point of view, an orderly disposition of wealth that benefits the heirs in the precise manner that the client desires may be the primary planning objective, regardless of the tax cost. A client planning for his or her own death may be most concerned with his or her own emotional and psychological needs as well as those of other family members. Minimization of the Federal estate tax levied on the estate simply may not be a central concern. A tax adviser who fails to appreciate the client's priorities and who designs an estate plan that fails to reflect the client's nontax needs is not acting in the best interest of that client.

TAX PLANNING WITH INTRAFAMILY GIFTS

Before enactment of the Tax Reform Act of 1976, the Federal transfer tax savings associated with gifting assets to family members during the donor's life rather than transferring the assets at death were obvious. The gift tax rates were only 75 percent of the estate tax rates, and because of the progressive nature of both rate schedules, inter vivos gifts could shift an individual's wealth out of a high marginal estate tax bracket into a lower marginal gift tax bracket.

The Tax Reform Act of 1976 integrated the gift and estate taxes by providing a single rate schedule for both taxes and by including in the estate tax base the amount of post-1976 gifts made by a decedent.[34] Thus, any inter vivos gift made by a decedent after 1976 has the effect of boosting his or her taxable estate into a higher tax bracket.

> **Example 25.** In 1998, D made a taxable gift of $400,000, her only taxable inter vivos transfer. D dies in the current year, leaving a taxable estate of $1,500,000. The base for computing D's estate tax is $1.9 million, her taxable estate plus the $400,000 taxable gift.

Because of the integration of the gift and estate taxes, the tax benefit of inter vivos giving has been reduced but certainly not eliminated. The following advantages of making gifts have survived the integration process.

1. All appreciation in value of the transferred property that occurs after the date of gift escapes taxation in the donor's gross estate. Refer to *Example 25*. If the value of the gifted asset increased from $400,000 in 1998 to $700,000 in the current year, the $300,000 appreciation is not taxed in D's estate. It should be noted that inter vivos transfers of appreciating assets do have a potentially serious negative income tax consequence. The basis of such assets to the donee will be a carryover basis from the donor, increased by the amount of any gift tax paid attributable to the difference between the value of the gift and the

---

[34]   § 2001(b).

donor's tax basis.[35] If the donor retained the property until death, the basis of the property would be stepped up to its fair market to value at date of death.[36] Thus, a transfer of the asset during life rather than at death preserves rather than eliminates pre-death appreciation in the value of the asset that will be subject to income taxation on subsequent sale.

2. Future income generated by property that the donor has transferred will be accumulated by younger generation family members rather than in the estate of the donor.

3. The availability of the annual $11,000 exclusion allows a donor to give away a substantial amount of wealth completely tax free.

4. All other factors being equal, it is cheaper to pay a gift tax rather than an estate tax. This is true because the dollars used to pay a gift tax are never themselves subject to a Federal transfer tax. However, dollars used to pay an estate tax have been included in the taxable estate and are subject to the estate tax.

For this reason, the estate tax is said to be *tax inclusive* (since the estate tax is itself taxed) while the gift tax is sometimes said to be *tax exclusive* (the gift tax itself is not taxed).

Example 26. D has $10,000,000 in assets and wants to transfer $4,500,000 to a beneficiary. Ignore the annual exclusion, the unified credit and assume a flat rate of 55%. If D dies with an estate of $10,000,000, the estate will pay a tax of $5,500,000 out of the estate's assets and $4,500,000 will be left to pass to the heirs. In contrast, if the individual had made a $4,500,000 gift before he died, he would have had to pay only a $2,475,000 tax for the privilege of transferring $4,500,000. In other words, it would cost $3,025,000 less ($5,500,000 − $2,475,000) to give $4,500,000 than to *will* such amount. In effect, if he gave $4,500,000 while he was living, he would have had $3,025,000 left to do with as he pleases. By making the gift and paying the gift tax, he is removing the gift tax amount ($2,475,000) from his estate, never to be taxed!

Example 27. W has only $1,000,000 of assets. Assume a 47% (2005) rate and ignore the unified credit and annual exclusion. If W dies and leaves the $1,000,000 to her child, W pays a tax of $470,000 and the child receives $530,000. If W had used the same $1,000,000 to make a gift and pay the tax, she could have given her child $680,272, determined as follows:

$$
\begin{aligned}
x &= \text{Amount of the gift} \\
.47x &= \text{Gift tax} \\
\\
x + .47x &= \$1,000,000 \\
1.47x &= \$1,000,000 \\
x &= \$680,272 \\
.47x &= \$319,728
\end{aligned}
$$

Thus if W makes a gift of $680,272, she will pay a gift tax of $319,728, exhausting the $1,000,000. Note that by giving, the child receives $680,272 rather than $530,000 or $150,272 more!

---

[35] § 1015.

[36] § 1014.

"FREEZING" THE VALUE OF ASSETS IN THE GROSS ESTATE

A long-range plan of inter vivos giving from older generation to younger generation family members is a basic component of most family tax plans. However, elderly individuals can be very reluctant about making substantial gifts of their wealth, even when they fully understand the tax advantages in doing so. Psychologically it is difficult to part with wealth that is the result of a lifetime of endeavor. Elderly individuals often fear that gifts of property might leave them without sufficient income or capital to provide for their future comfort and security. They may even worry that their children and grandchildren might "desert" them if the offspring were given the family wealth too soon.

For these and many other reasons it may be difficult for the tax adviser to persuade an older client to transfer existing wealth during his or her lifetime. However, the same client may be much more amenable to simply "freezing" the value of his or her current estate, so that future accumulations of wealth are somehow transferred to younger members of the family and therefore not subject to estate tax upon the client's death.

Gifts of Property. The simplest type of estate freeze is a gift. A gift of appreciating property is taxed at its current value for gift tax purposes and any future appreciation is forever removed from the estate tax base. Note, however, that this technique is not without problems. Taxpayers who want to maximize the amount of wealth that their heirs ultimately receive must balance the trade-offs between giving the property during their lifetime or willing the property at death.

If a taxpayer gives appreciating property during life, the gift removes any appreciation from the estate. However, the basis of the property to the donee will normally be the same as the donor's basis. In such case, the donee would be required to pay an income tax on a subsequent sale of the property. Note that this income tax would not have resulted had the property been retained till death due to the step-up in basis for inherited property. Moreover, if the taxpayer must pay gift tax on the transfer, the time value of any gift tax paid would be lost. In short, a gift of appreciating property normally saves transfer taxes at a rate up to 48 percent but results in an income tax of up to 15 percent (assuming the property is a capital asset) and loss of the time value of gift tax (net of estate tax). Conversely, retaining the property normally saves on income taxes but at the cost of an estate tax on the appreciation.

Example 28. In 1989, T purchased 300 acres of land on the far west side of Dallas for $100,000. While the land was truly in a remote area, T expected that it would one day be prime property since it is near an interstate highway. By 1998, it was clear that an increase in the value of the property was imminent. Assume the property will triple in value to $300,000 by the time T dies in 10 years. Also assume that the transfer tax rate is 47%, the applicable income tax rate is 15%, and the aftertax interest rate is 8%. The following is a simple comparison (ignoring present values) of what happens if (1) T gives the property now, or (2) holds it until death.

1.	Give property now before it appreciates		Tax cost
	Gift tax now ($100,000 × 47%)		$ 47,000
	Income tax to beneficiaries later due to carryover basis		
	Gift: [($300,000 − $100,000 = $200,000) × 15%]		30,000
	Value of gift tax paid today lost:		
	Gift tax ($47,000 × 8% × 10 years)	$ 37,600	
	Estate tax [$37,600 − (47% × $37,600)] . . .	(19,928)	17,672
	Tax cost		$ 94,672

2.	Retain property until death	Tax cost
	Estate tax later ($300,000 × 47%)	$141,000
	No income tax later	
	Bequest ($300,000 − $300,000 = $0 × 15%)	0
	Tax cost	$141,000

In this case, it would appear that giving the property away during T's life would produce a smaller overall tax cost than retaining it till death. However, this result is based on many assumptions and fails to consider many others. Nevertheless, the example illustrates some of the basic considerations that should be taken into account when doing estate planning.

Interests in Closely Held Businesses. For individuals who have a stake in a business, such as stock in a family-held C or S corporation or an interest in a partnership or LLC, the interest in the company is not only their lifeblood but in most cases represents a substantial portion of their estate. Indeed, the business often represents the bulk of the assets that they wish to leave to their heirs. Unfortunately, without proper planning, the costs associated with transferring such business (e.g., illiquidity, the estate, gift and generation-skipping transfer taxes, probate) can decimate the business, leaving the heirs with little or no inheritance. Over the years, practitioners have addressed these problems in a number of ways. Most of these plans are directed at valuation of the assets and how that value can be reduced and frozen. In this regard, it should not be forgotten that for estate and gift tax purposes, the minimum marginal tax rate is 45 percent, meaning that every $1,000 of reduced valuation produces $450 of savings!

Closely held businesses normally present valuation problems of monumental proportions. The difficulty lies in the fact that, unlike their publicly traded cousins, there is no market where closely held businesses are actively traded.

For its part, the government's primary contribution concerning the valuation problem is contained in the often cited Revenue Ruling 59-60. In this ruling, the IRS has identified a list of factors to be considered in valuing such businesses. These are

1. Book value and financial condition of the corporation.

2. Earning capacity of the company.

3. Dividend paying capacity.

4. Whether the enterprise has goodwill or other intangible value.

5. The economic outlook in general and the condition and outlook of the specific industry in particular.

6. The nature of the business and the history of the enterprise from its inception.

7. Sales of stock and the size of the block of stock to be valued.

8. The market price of stocks of corporations engaged in the same or a similar line of business that are actively traded in a free and open market.

Unfortunately, the ruling provides little guidance regarding how these factors are to be used. The ruling simply states that the weight to be accorded each factor depends upon the facts of each case. While experts in business valuation (a niche industry in and of itself) utilize these and other widely accepted methods, there is no certainty that the value obtained is objective and unbiased. As a practical matter, the estate is left to its own devices to determine the value of the company and convince the IRS and/or judge that its method and value are correct.

Valuation: Premiums and Discounts. In establishing the value of an interest in a closely held company, additional value is generally attributed to the interest if it represents control. A so-called *control premium* is warranted since it enables the holder to extract more value from the firm through his or her ability to dominate management. For example, an individual with control can elect the entire board of directors, remove a director, control the business and affairs of the company, elect and remove all of the officers, fix their salaries, and control the declaration of dividends. The major valuation issue when control is present is determining how much value, if any should be assigned to the control element. This has often been the source of a great deal of controversy.

> **Example 29.** The uncertainties of valuation are made abundantly clear in *Estate of Joseph E. Salsbury*[37]. In this case, the value of the company, particularly the amount of premium, was the primary issue. Salsbury died holding 51.8% of the stock of Salsbury Laboratories, a manufacturer of drug and health products for the poultry industry. At the time of his death, all of the stock of the corporation was owned by the decedent, members of his family, trusts for their benefit and a private charitable foundation. The IRS asserted an estate tax deficiency of $6,007,503 primarily attributable to the difference in values placed on the stock held by the decedent. The date of death values placed on the decedent's shares by the parties and the expert witnesses for the taxpayer and the IRS were worlds apart as shown below:
>
> | | |
> |---|---:|
> | Value claimed on estate tax return. . . . . | $ 372,152 |
> | Value asserted by the IRS in deficiency notice . . . . | 11,655,000 |
> | Expert witness for the taxpayer . . . . | 558,228 |
> | Expert witness for the IRS . . . . | 8,748,152 |
> | Expert witness for the IRS . . . . | 1,400,000 |
>
> The sole issue of contention regarding the valuation was the amount that should be assigned to the control element held by the decedent. Note the difference in valuation even though these are valuation experts. Interestingly, the court ultimately held that the stock was worth $514,000.

Discounts. In contrast to a control premium, a *discount* may be available. Over the years, taxpayers have identified a number of reasons why a discount should be allowed.

It is well accepted that a discount may be appropriate when valuing large blocks of stock. When a taxpayer owns such a large block of stock that the price at which the stock would be traded in the market would *not* be representative of the value, a *blockage discount* may be claimed. Blockage discounts are available if the executor can show that the block of stock to be valued is so large in relation to the actual sales on the existing market that the stock could not be liquidated in a reasonable time without depressing the market.

---

[37]   T.C. Memo 1975-33.

Discounts have also been granted for the tax consequences that could result upon a disposition of the business. For example, if a taxpayer owns stock in a C corporation, the ultimate value that the owner can extract from the company can be substantially reduced because of the double taxation problems that can occur on liquidation of the corporation.

By far the most important types of discount are those available if the taxpayer's ownership represents a minority interest or where there is lack of marketability or both. In reviewing the court decisions addressing this issue, it is not uncommon to see discounts of between 25 and 50 percent and sometimes more! With proper planning, taxpayers can successfully secure these discounts to obtain literally huge savings. For this reason, understanding the justification for these discounts and the techniques used to achieve them is extremely important.

The lack of marketability discount is based on the fact that an interest in a closely held business is generally less attractive because it is illiquid—hard to convert to cash—and more difficult to sell than an interest for which there is an active trading market. This is a particularly acute problem when the majority of interests are owned by family members. Stock that if publicly traded would be worth $1,000,000 would be worth far less because it would be unlikely to find an outside buyer to purchase the stock. Adding to the discount is the fact there would be substantial costs incurred such as underwriting expenses involved if a company were to go public.

The rationale for *minority interest discounts* is founded upon the owner's limited power to influence business decisions (e.g., control day-to-day or long-range managerial decisions, affect future earnings, control efforts for growth potential, establish executive compensation or dividend policy, or compel a sale of assets or a liquidation). As a practical matter, a discount is warranted due to the fact that an unrelated party interested in purchasing an interest in a family-owned business would not pay full value for such an interest.

> **Example 30.** D owns all of the stock of Close Corporation, which has a value of $9,000,000. If D were to die, the entire value of the stock would be included in his estate. D might be able to reduce the transfer cost substantially if he were to give one-third of the stock to his son, one-third to his daughter and die holding one-third. At first thought, it might appear that the value of the gifts would be one-third of the total or aggregate value or $3,000,000 each. However, by arguing that the each gift constitutes a minority interest, he may be able to claim a substantial discount when he makes the gifts or at death.

The IRS has not always accepted the minority discount theory, particularly when the person acquiring the interest is related. Historically, the government consistently argued that for purposes of valuing gifts and bequests of stock or partnership interests to family members, the ownership interests of the family members should be aggregated and valued as a whole.[38] Applying this approach to the example above, the IRS may take the position that no discount is allowed and the value of each gift is $3,000,000. In fact, when the IRS took this approach, using an aggregate value, it often included a control premium, and then used the increased value as the basis for assigning a value to the fraction of shares transferred.

After years of denying taxpayers minority discounts in the family setting, the IRS finally abandoned its position. In Revenue Ruling 93-12, the IRS stated that it would no longer challenge a discount solely because the transferred interest, when aggregated with interests held by family members, would be considered part of a controlling

---

[38] See Revenue Ruling 81-253 1981-2 C.B. 187 which held that no minority interest discount would be allowed for intrafamily transfers of stock in a corporation controlled by the family absent discord among the family members.

interest.[39] For example, when the taxpayer transferred all of his stock in equal gifts to each of his 11 children, the IRS ruled that the value of the gift to each is computed by considering each gift separately and not by aggregating all of the donor's holdings.[40]

Since the government's surrender in 1993, fractionalizing an owner's interest to obtain minority discounts has become virtually an indispensable part of estate planning. As explained below, corporate and partnership freezes, particularly the use of family limited partnerships, has become a staple of the estate planning industry.

Freezing the Value of the Estate: C Corporations. To freeze the transfer tax value of an interest in a C corporation, the corporation engages in a type "E" reorganization referred to as a recapitalization. The following steps are taken:

1. The owner exchanges common stock for both new voting preferred and new nonvoting common which together has a value equal to his original shares of common.

2. Pursuant to the reorganization provisions of § 368(a)(1)(E), this exchange of stock is nontaxable.

3. At the time of the exchange, the preferred stock is structured to represent the majority of the value of the corporation while the common stock has little value. The preferred stock typically carried a fixed-rate, non-cumulative dividend and preferential treatment for dividends and assets upon liquidation. Other rights and privileges may be attached.

4. The owner gives the nonvoting common stock to the heirs at little or no gift tax cost since all of the value of the corporation is in the preferred stock which is held by the owner.

5. The result is that all of the future appreciation of the corporation is attributable to the common stock and shifted to the donees since the preferred stock's value is locked in at time of exchange (i.e., its value is attributable to its preferred claim on assets in the event of liquidation and its yield). Moreover, the owner has retained income security.

Example 31. F owns all of the voting common stock of C corporation with a value of $1,500,000 (basis $100,000). Approaching retirement, F wants to transfer the ownership of the business to his daughter and do so at the least possible tax cost. In addition, he wants to maintain control of the business and retain a steady stream of income for life. To this end, he exchanged his voting common stock for nonvoting common stock worth $1,000,000 and voting preferred stock with a par value set such that it is equal to $500,000. F has a non-cumulative "put" with the corporation that enables him to sell the preferred stock back to the corporation at its par value of $500,000. The preferred stock pays a non-cumulative dividend of 15 percent. The put and the dividend enable F to claim the stock is at least worth $500,000 since at any time the stock could be sold to the corporation for $500,000. F realizes a gain of $1,400,000 ($500,000 + $1,000,000 − $100,000) but under the reorganization provisions this gain is not recognized. F subsequently gives the common worth $1,000,000 ($1,500,000 total value − $500,000 value of preferred) to his daughter and pays no gift tax due to the unified credit which shelters the $1,000,000 taxable gift. If the value of the preferred is respected, F has (1) retained control of the corporation since he owns all of the voting stock, (2) ensured a steady stream of income for retirement since he can vote himself a dividend at any time, (3) frozen

---

[39] 1993-1 C.B. 202.

[40] TAM 9449001.

the value of his estate at $500,000 and (4) shifted all of the appreciation to his daughter who holds the common stock. As might be expected, in these situations, the Service was reluctant to accept the value placed on the preferred since it was unlikely that F would ever exercise his put nor would he ever vote himself a dividend.

While this plan can be used successfully, there are certain restrictions that limit its value as discussed below.

Freezing the Value of the Estate: Partnerships. Steps similar to that used in freezing the value of an interest in a family-held C corporation can be taken to freeze the value of an interest in a partnership (or LLC). In addition, a partnership could be used to freeze the value of appreciating property such as farms, ranches, timberland, and other unimproved or improved real estate. The partnership form provides an almost perfect vehicle to fractionalize interests in the property to create minority discounts. A partnership freeze normally involves recapitalizing an existing partnership or the formation of a new partnership. Family limited partnerships are the vehicle commonly used. The following steps are taken:

1. The owners of property (e.g., the senior members of the family such as parents or grandparents) normally transfer the property to a limited partnership in exchange for (1) a general partnership interest which represents growth interest and (2) a limited partnership interest which represents the frozen interest.

2. The exchange normally is nontaxable under § 721.

3. The transferors retain a small general partnership interest and transfer a large limited partnership interest.

Example 32. H and W transfer 1,000 acres of land worth $10,000,000 to a family limited partnership. In exchange H and W each receive one percent general partnership interests and 49% limited partnership interests. H and W then transfer the limited partnership interests to their children. Significant discounts are normally available for transfers of limited partnership interests. Normally there is a minority interest discount since limited partners have no control over the partnership (e.g., no voice in management and no right to force a liquidation) as well as a lack of marketability discount since such interests are usually illiquid.

Valuation Issues in Corporate and Partnership Freezes. The approach normally used to value the interest transferred in a corporate or partnership freeze is a residual one. The entire business is valued and then the value of the retained interest is identified. Any residual value is the value of the transferred interest. This method is show in the formula below.

FMV of business
− FMV of retained interest
= FMV of transferred interest and gift to heirs

For many years, planners kept the value of the transferred interest (e.g., the common stock) low by assigning valuable rights to the retained interest (e.g., the preferred stock) in order to increase the value of the retained interest. For example, in a preferred stock freeze, these included an above market-rate cumulative (and often noncumulative) dividend, conversion rights, call rights, liquidation preferences and voting rights. Even if it was clear that it was unlikely that those rights would be exercised, the courts usually took them into account in valuing the preferred stock.[41]

Congress became concerned about assigning value to these "discretionary" rights given to the owner in that such rights probably would not be exercised. To address this problem, in 1987 Congress enacted the now infamous anti-freeze rules of §2036(c) that were so controversial that they were subsequently repealed in 1990. In their place, Congress substituted § 2701, which contains the rules currently in operation today. Section 2701 attempts to more accurately value the property that is transferred among family members when the transferor retains some interest in the business. The approach is to value certain retained discretionary rights (e.g., rights to dividends or distributions, liquidation rights, put, call, and conversion rights) at *zero* unless they meet tests that virtually guarantee their exercise. Note that if these retained rights are valued at zero, a transfer of the common stock or limited partnership interests would be treated as a gift of the full fair market value of the business.

Section 2701 generally operates only if the following conditions exist (note this is the normal pattern of a corporate or partnership freeze discussed above):

1. The taxpayer makes a transfer of an interest in a corporation or partnership.

2. The transferor controls the entity. Control is defined as ownership of at least 50 percent of the entity either directly or indirectly.

3. The transfer is made to a family member (i.e., spouse, lineal descendant of the transferor or spouse, or a spouse of such descendant).

4. The transferor retains an applicable retained right (distribution rights).

In general, the retained interests must provide for a periodic *qualified payment* (e.g., a dividend or distribution). If there is no provision for qualified payments, no value may be assigned to the retained interest, resulting in a gift of the full value of the business.

Qualified payments. A qualified payment depends on the type of entity. For corporations, a qualified payment is any dividend payable at a fixed rate on a periodic basis on cumulative preferred stock. For partnerships, a qualified payment is a comparable payment at a fixed rate made with respect to any partnership interest. The value of the retained interest must be determined by calculating the present value of the future cash flows from the retained interest or more precisely discounting the qualified payment. No value is assigned to any other rights (put, call, conversion) attached to the stock or partnership interest. Note that if a very low payout rate is selected, there will be a lower annual cash payout required but there will also be a lower value placed on the preferred stock or retained partnership interest. In contrast, if there is a high payout rate, the value of the retained interest is greater, yielding a smaller gift. However, selecting a high payout rate in order to increase the value of the retained interest and reduce the value of the gifted interest has the effect of returning more value (e.g., dividends) to the taxpayer's estate. In any event, a minimum value is placed on the common stock or partnership interest that is transferred. At least 10 percent of the value of the business must be assigned to the gifted stock or partnership interest. This ensures that there is a gift of at least 10 percent of the value of the corporation.

> **Example 33.** This year D decided to transfer her business, a C corporation, to her children. To this end, she exchanged all of her common stock in the corporation for nonvoting common and voting preferred in a transaction qualifying as a tax-free recapitalization. After the transfer, D owned 3,000 shares of $1,000 par value voting preferred stock, each share paying a cumulative annual dividend of seven percent. In

---

[41] Rev. Rul. 83-120, 1983-2 C.B. 170.

addition, there are 10,000 shares of nonvoting common stock outstanding. D gave all of the common stock to her daughter. Pursuant to an appraisal, the corporation's value was estimated to be $3,100,000. The value of the preferred stock must be determined by discounting the future dividends. Here the annual dividends are $210,000 ($1,000 par value × 7% = $70 per share × 3,000 shares). According to the regulations, the value is determined by assuming that the dividend is paid in perpetuity. Assuming the applicable federal rate is ten percent, the present value of a $210,000 annuity discounted at ten percent is $2,100,000 (1/.1 × $210,000). Thus the value of the preferred is $2,100,000 and the value of the common is $1,000,000 ($3,100,000 − $2,100,000). Consequently, D is treated as making a $1,000,000 gift. If D has not made any other taxable gifts during her lifetime, the entire transfer is tax-free. More important, if the corporation's value increases at a rate greater than the dividend rate of seven percent, all of the excess appreciation is attributable to the common and, therefore, out of her estate.

Family Limited Partnerships. Although the corporate or partnership freeze can be useful, the qualified payment requirement can be a difficult hurdle when trying to accomplish the taxpayer's goals. For this reason, some plans do not meet or do not attempt to meet the qualified payment rule. In such case, the gift is the full value of the interest. However, to minimize this problem, a family limited partnership (FLP) is often formed to create minority and marketability discounts that reduce the value of the transferred interests.

Example 34. H and W, husband and wife, together own all of the stock of a corporation worth $4,000,000. As part of a plan to transfer the stock to their children, they transfer all of the stock to a limited partnership in exchange for a one percent general partnership interest and a 99 percent limited partnership interest. The couple then transfers the limited partnership interest to their children, claiming minority and marketability discounts totaling 50 percent. As a result, the partnership interests transferred by each are about $1,000,000 each and totally tax free because of the unified credit.

Due to the power of the FLP, they have become extremely popular and, at the same time, frequently abused. The most flagrant situations involve transfers of publicly traded securities to FLPs and taking substantial discounts. Although the IRS retreated in their challenge of such arrangements in Revenue Ruling 93-12, it is now pursuing these with some recent successes. Only time will tell the final outcome.[42]

Sales of Property. Another technique for freezing the value of an asset in a taxpayer's estate is for the taxpayer to sell the asset to a younger generation family member.

Example 35. Grandfather G owns several acres of undeveloped real estate with a current value of $1 million. The land is located near a rapidly growing metropolitan area and its value is expected to triple over the next decade. If G sells the real estate to his granddaughter D for $1 million cash, the value of his current estate is unchanged. However, the future increase in the value of the land has been removed from G's estate and will belong to D. In addition, D's basis is at least equal to the value of the property at the time of the transfer rather than G's basis had it been gifted.

An attractive variation of the selling technique illustrated in *Example 35* is an installment sale to the granddaughter. If D does not have $1 million of cash readily available (a most realistic assumption), G could simply accept his granddaughter's bona fide installment note as payment for the land. If the note is to be paid off over 20 years, G could use the installment sale method of reporting any taxable gain on the sale. If G

---

[42] For example, see *Estate of Charles Reichardt v. Comm.*, 114 T.C. 144 (2000)

had no need for cash during the term of the note, he could forgive his granddaughter's note payments and interest as they become due. Such forgiveness of indebtedness would not change the income tax consequences of the installment sale to G and would represent a gift to D eligible for the annual $11,000 exclusion.[43]

GRITs, GRATs, and GRUTs. Another freezing technique that gained popularity over the years is the so-called *GRIT*, the acronym for *grantor retained income trust*. Under this arrangement, the grantor transfers property to a trust, retains the income for a period of years, and gifts the remainder. Under the right circumstances, substantial benefits can be obtained. If the grantor survives the term, nothing is pulled back into the grantor's estate under § 2036 since the grantor did not retain an interest until death. As a result, the taxpayer has transferred the property at the cost of a gift tax on the remainder which normally represents only a fraction of the value of the entire property. In addition, all of the appreciation in the property is out of the estate. Note, however, that if the grantor does not survive the term, the property is included in the estate at its date of death value and nothing has been accomplished.

> **Example 36.** R owns rapidly appreciating real estate. Its current value is $1,500,000. In 2004 he transferred the property to a trust, retaining the income from the property for 10 years and giving the remainder to his son. Assume the income interest is worth $500,000. As a result, the remainder interest is $1,000,000 and due to the unified credit there is no gift tax on the transfer. Eleven years after the transfer R died when the property was worth $6,000,000. Under prior law, nothing would be included in R's gross estate under § 2036 since he did not have an interest in the property at the time of his death. Moreover, if the property did not in reality produce any income, the $500,000 assigned to the retained interest is a fiction and is never subject to income or estate taxes. Thus, if R survives the transfer by more than 10 years, he was able to transfer property worth $6,000,000 and avoid all transfer tax.

> **Example 37.** Same facts as above except R died five years after the trust was created. In such case, all of the property is included in R's gross estate at its date of death value and nothing will have been accomplished.

Historically, the value of the retained income interest in a GRIT was determined using IRS tables that often placed a higher value on the retained income interest than was justified by the actual income generated on the property. The effect of this was to deflate the value of the gift of the remainder which could be sheltered by the donor's unified credit. As might be expected, the IRS attacked this technique primarily on the grounds that the retained income interest was undervalued. Consequently, legislation was enacted to ensure that the value of the income interest was indeed real.

Under § 2702, the value of the retained income interest is *zero* and the gifted value of the remainder is the entire value of the property unless the transfer is to a *grantor retained annuity trust (GRAT)* or a grantor retained unit trust (GRUT). When either of these is used, the value of the gift of the remainder is the value of the property less the value of the annuity or unitrust interest as shown below.

Fair market value of property
Value of income interest
_____
FMV of remainder and gift to heirs (no exclusion since future interest)

When the transfer is made, the grantor specifies how much income will be retained [e.g., either a fixed dollar amount (i.e., an annuity trust) or a percentage of the annual

---

[43] See Rev. Rul. 77-299, 1977-2 C.B. 343 for the IRS's negative reaction to this tax plan.

asset value (i.e., a unitrust)] as well as the period for which the annuity will last. If the grantor retains an annuity interest, the arrangement is referred to as a GRAT. If the grantor retains a unitrust interest, the arrangement is called a GRUT. Note that in either case the income interest-retained annuity effectively replaces the transferred property. One of the biggest differences between a GRIT and GRATs and GRUTs is that annual payments under GRATs and GRUTs *must be made* even if the trust assets do not generate sufficient income to make the payments. Trust principal may have to be invaded to meet the distribution requirement (however, a debt obligation may suffice).

Example 38. In 1997 R transferred land worth $1,000,000 to a GRAT. He wanted the amount of the gift of the remainder interest to be $600,000 in order to use his unified credit (exemption equivalent of $600,000 in 1997), but no more. R is 55 and he decides to use a term of 15 years to compute the required annuity. The present value of an annuity of $1 for 15 years using the IRS tables and a discount rate of 10% is $7.6061. Thus the present value of an annuity of $52,589 ($400,000/7.6061) at 10% for 15 years is $400,000. Therefore to achieve the desired result, the annuity rate is set at 5.26% and payments of $52,589 must be paid annually, even if the property does not generate sufficient income. This departs drastically from the GRIT where no payment was required if there was in fact no income. Note that if R lives the entire term, he will receive $788,835 ($52,589 × 15) which is the original $400,000 retained income interest plus the growth on the $400,000 at 10% for 15 years. Although R's estate may contain $788,835, he will have removed any appreciation from his estate. In short, if the property appreciates (or produces income at a rate exceeding the annuity rate) all of the excess appreciation or income is removed from his estate. In addition, R could remove part of this $788,835 by embarking on a gift-giving program.

MARITAL DEDUCTION PLANNING

At first glance, it would appear that all of a decedent's property should be left to his or her spouse to avoid estate taxes. However, using the marital deduction to reduce a decedent's taxable estate to zero could result in a waste of the decedent's unified credit under § 2010. Moreover, all of the property would be taxed as part of the surviving spouse's estate to the extent it is not consumed or given away. For these reasons, an effective estate plan usually attempts to leave a *taxable estate* exactly equal to the tax shelter provided by this credit.

Example 39. H and W are happily married. The couple currently has simple wills, providing that upon either's death, all of the assets of one will be left to the other. Upon the death of the survivor, all of the assets are to be passed to the children. They both had assets worth $1,500,000 for a total of $3,000,000. In 2005, H died with an estate of $1,500,000 and left it all to W who dies shortly thereafter. In this case, the estate passing to the kids shrinks by a tax liability of $695,000 as computed below.

	1st to Die	Surviving Spouse
Gross estate	$ 1,500,000	$3,000,000
Marital deduction	(1,500,000)	—
Taxable estate	$ 0	$3,000,000
Tax	$ 0	$1,250,800
Unified credit	—	(555,800)
Tax due	$ 0	$ 695,000

Note that with this simple, but common, arrangement H has wasted his unified credit. In contrast, had H left his estate of $1,500,000 to his children and W had done the same, both would have utilized their unified credits and neither would have paid any estate tax as shown below. As a result, the children would be better off by the taxes saved of $695,000! In short, with just a small amount of planning, a married couple in 2005 can pass $3,000,000 to their heirs tax-free. Note that due to the gradually increasing exemption amount, a will must be carefully drawn to ensure that the exemption is fully utilized.

	1st to Die	Surviving Spouse
Gross estate	$1,500,000	$1,500,000
Marital deduction	—	—
Taxable estate	$1,500,000	$1,500,000
Tax.	$ 555,800	$ 555,800
Unified credit	(555,800)	(555,800)
Tax due	$ 0	$ 0

The unlimited marital deduction permits a deferral of any estate tax on the wealth accumulated by a married couple until the death of the second spouse. This deferral can be highly advantageous even if the bequest to the surviving spouse causes the wealth to be subsequently taxed at a higher marginal tax rate.

To illustrate, assume that W has a net estate of $1,400,000. W's will provides that all her wealth in excess of the amount sheltered by the available unified credit shall pass to her husband, H. W dies in 2000, when the credit shelters a taxable estate of $625,000; therefore, $775,000 of her estate is transferred to her husband and becomes a marital deduction against W's gross estate. No estate tax is due upon W's death. If H has $2 million of wealth in addition to his $775,000 inheritance from W, and if he outlives his wife by five years, the estate tax upon his death in 2005 is $589,250 [($780,800 + .47 × ($2,775,000 − $2,000,000) = $1,145,050) − $555,800 credit].[44]

If W had not left any of her estate to H, the estate tax payable on her death would have been $310,750 ($512,800 tax − $202,050 unified credit), computed at a marginal rate of 43 percent. However, because of the marital bequest, her estate was "stacked" on that of her surviving spouse. As a result, the actual tax on her estate was $364,250 computed at a marginal rate of 47 percent.[45] But the actual tax payment was deferred for five years. Using a conservative discount rate of 8 percent, the present value of a $364,250 tax paid at the end of five years is only $285,399 ($364,250 × 0.7835). Thus, the use of the unlimited marital deduction saved the family of H and W approximately $78,851 ($364,250 − $285,399) in estate taxes.

In addition to the deferral of tax available through use of the unlimited marital deduction; the postponement of tax until the death of the second spouse increases the length of time during which estate planning objectives can be accomplished. The surviving spouse can continue or even accelerate a program of inter vivos giving to younger generation family members. Deferral also provides the surviving spouse with the opportunity to seek advice about areas of estate planning neglected before the death of the first spouse.

---

[44]   For simplicity's sake, this example assumes no appreciation in assets between the two deaths.

[45] $364,250 is the difference between $589,250 (the tax on H's estate of $2,775,000 including his inheritance from W) and $225,000 (the tax on H's estate of $2,000,000 without an inheritance from W).

QUALIFYING TERMINAL INTEREST PROPERTY

Section 2056(b) denies a marital deduction for an interest in property that passes to a surviving spouse if the interest will terminate at some future date and if after termination someone other than the surviving spouse will receive an interest in the property. This restriction was designed to ensure that assets escaping taxation in the estate of the first spouse by virtue of a marital deduction do, in fact, become the property of the surviving spouse includible in that spouse's taxable estate.

Prior to the enactment of the Economic Recovery Tax Act of 1981 (ERTA 1981), a wealthy taxpayer desiring to secure the tax savings offered by the use of the marital deduction had to be willing to entrust to his or her surviving spouse the ultimate disposition of the assets passing to that spouse. Because of § 2056(b), the surviving spouse had to receive control over the transferred assets sufficient to pull the assets into that spouse's gross estate. This generally required an outright transfer of the property to the surviving spouse, or transfer in trust giving the spouse a general power of appointment. In certain situations wealthy taxpayers were reluctant to accept this condition. For example, a taxpayer with children from a previous marriage might be concerned that his surviving second wife might not leave the marital deduction assets to these children upon her death. As a result, the taxpayer might not take advantage of the marital deduction in order to leave his wealth directly to his children.

To increase the utility of the marital deduction, Congress added § 2056(b)(7) to the law as part of ERTA 1981. This paragraph allows a marital deduction equal to the value of *qualifying terminable interest property*. Such property is defined as property in which the surviving spouse is entitled to all the income, payable at least annually for life. During the life of the spouse, no one may have a power to appoint any part of the property to anyone other than the spouse.

> **Example 40.** Under the will of X, $1 million worth of assets are transferred into trust. X's surviving spouse, S, must be paid the entire trust income on a quarterly basis. During S's life, no person has any power of appointment over trust corpus, and upon S's death, trust corpus will be divided equally among X's living grandchildren. Because the assets are qualifying terminable interest property, X's estate may claim a marital deduction of $1 million.

Upon the death of the surviving spouse, the entire date of death value of the qualifying terminable interest property must be included in the surviving spouse's gross estate per § 2044. Thus, even though the property is passing to a recipient chosen by the first spouse to die, it is taxed in the estate of the second spouse.[46]

CHARITABLE GIVING

Another important tool that estate planners often use to reduce a family's tax burden is the charitable transfer. Obviously, an individual can reduce or even eliminate any estate taxes by simply leaving part or all of his or her property to a qualified charity. As explained in Chapter 24, bequests to qualified charitable organizations may be deducted from the gross estate without limitation. However, from a tax planning perspective it is usually preferable for the taxpayer to make a charitable donation during life rather than at death.

---

[46] If the surviving spouse gives away the income interest in the qualifying terminable interest property during life, § 2519 requires that the entire value of the property constitute a taxable gift. When either § 2044 or § 2519 applies, § 2207(A) allows the estate or donor to recover an appropriate amount of transfer tax from the party receiving the actual property.

While many individuals would like to make large contributions of property to a charity during their lifetime, they often delay the contribution to their deaths believing they may need the income and the property before that time. Unfortunately, these kindhearted donors, while securing the contribution deduction for estate tax purposes, lose the income tax deduction. On the other hand, some individuals may be willing to give the property and its income to a charity temporarily but ultimately want to pass the property to their heirs. Long ago charitable organizations recognized these problems and designed a solution, the so-called split interest gift.

A split-interest gift is simply a transfer of property—typically to a trust—where part of the property is given to a charity and the other part is retained by the donor. There are two common types of charitable trusts: charitable remainder trusts, and charitable lead trusts.

Charitable Remainder Trusts. With a charitable remainder trust, an individual transfers property to a trust, leaving the income from the property to a noncharitable beneficiary (e.g., a spouse or child) typically for life, and upon the beneficiary's death, the property passes to the charitable beneficiary. The beauty of a charitable remainder trust is that the donor retains the security of a steady income stream yet is entitled to an income tax deduction for the present value of the remainder interest—a deduction that would be lost had the gift been postponed until death. In order to secure the deduction for the remainder interest, a number of special requirements must be met to ensure that the charity in fact receives something once the income interest terminates.

Charitable Lead Trusts. Charities also have an answer for individuals who wish to transfer property and its income to a charity for a period of years yet want the property returned after the term has run. The solution is referred to as a charitable lead trust. In this case, the donor receives both an income and gift-tax deduction for the present value of the income interest given to the charity. However, the income tax deduction is limited to 20 percent of A.G.I., since it is for the "use of the charity" rather than "to the" charity. No carryover is allowed.

For many years, the grantor of a charitable lead trust was not charged with the income of the trust but simply got a deduction for income given to the trust that he was never taxed on! In 1969, Congress believed that this was an "unwarranted tax advantage"—a duplication of benefits—and eliminated such favorable treatment. Currently, the trust must be a grantor trust to qualify. The effect in such case is to accelerate the deduction to the current year, yet defer the income to the year it is actually received.

Using a charitable lead trust is particularly beneficial when taxpayers want to bunch all of their charitable deductions in one year. Bunching or accelerating deductions to a particular year may be advantageous in situations when taxpayers have a particularly good year with high income and need the deduction or they simply expect to be in a lower bracket in the future. As with charitable remainder trusts, a number of requirements must be met in order to secure the deduction for the income interest.

> **Example 41.** This year J sold his business, recognizing a large amount of income. To offset some of this income, J gave $100,000 to a charitable lead trust for his alma mater, the University of Nebraska. According to the terms of the gift, the university receives the income for the next five years after which the property is returned to J. Assuming the present value of the income over the next five years is $60,000, J receives a $60,000 deduction this year. Assume that next year, the trust earns $12,000. Because J has retained a reversionary interest that reverts too quickly, the trust is a grantor trust and J is taxed on the income of $12,000.

LIQUIDITY PLANNING

The Federal estate tax is literally a once-in-a-lifetime event. Because taxpayers do not have to pay the tax on a regular recurring basis, many individuals give little thought to the eventual need for cash to pay the tax.

When an individual dies leaving a large estate but little cash with which to pay death taxes and other expenses, serious problems can result. The family may be forced to sell assets at distress prices just to obtain cash. In a severe situation, a decedent's carefully designed dispositive plan may be shattered because of the failure to anticipate the liquidity needs of the estate.

One of the functions of a competent tax adviser is to foresee any liquidity problem of his or her client's potential estate and to suggest appropriate remedies. The remainder of this chapter covers some of the common solutions to the problem of a cash-poor estate.

SOURCE OF FUNDS

An excellent source of funds with which to pay an estate tax is insurance on the life of the potential decedent. For a relatively small cash outlay, a taxpayer can purchase enough insurance coverage to meet all the liquidity needs of his or her estate. It is absolutely vital that the insured individual does not possess any incidents of ownership in the policies and that his or her estate is not the beneficiary of the policies. If these two rules are observed the policy proceeds will not be included in the insured's estate and needlessly subjected to the estate tax.[47]

A second source of funds is any family business in which the decedent owned an interest. Under the terms of a binding buy-sell agreement, the business could use its cash to liquidate the decedent's interest. If the business is in corporate form, a redemption of the decedent's interest under § 303 can be a highly beneficial method of securing funds. If the fairly straightforward requirements of § 303 are met, the corporation can purchase its own stock from the decedent's estate without danger of the payment being taxed as a dividend. Because the estate's basis in the stock has been stepped up to its fair market value at date of death, the estate normally will realize little or no taxable gain on sale. The amount of the corporate distribution protected by § 303 cannot exceed the amount of death taxes and funeral and administrative expenses payable by the estate.[48]

In order for a redemption of stock to qualify under § 303, the value of the stock must exceed 35 percent of the value of the gross estate less § 2053 and § 2054 expenses.[49] Careful pre-death planning may be necessary to meet this requirement.

> **Example 42.** C owns a 100% interest in F Corporation, a highly profitable business with substantial cash flow. However, the value of the F stock is only 29% of the value of C's projected estate. As C's tax adviser, you could recommend that C (1) gift away other assets to reduce the estate, or (2) transfer assets into F Corporation as a contribution to capital in order to increase the stock's value.

---

[47] § 2042.

[48] § 303(a).

[49] § 303(b)(2)(A).

FLOWER BONDS

Certain issues of Treasury bonds known as *flower bonds* may be used to pay the Federal estate tax at their par value plus accrued interest.[50] Because these bonds have very low interest rates, they are obtainable on the open market at a price well below their par value. Thus, an estate can satisfy its Federal tax liability with bonds that cost much less than the amount of that liability. The bonds must be included in the decedent's estate at their par, rather than market value.[51]

PLANNING FOR DEFERRED PAYMENT OF THE ESTATE TAX

Under § 6166, an estate may be entitled to pay its Federal estate tax liability on an installment basis over a 15-year period. This provision can be a blessing for an illiquid estate. However, only estates that meet the requirements of § 6166 may use the installment method of payment. As a result, pre-death planning should be undertaken to ensure qualification.

Basically, only an amount of estate tax attributable to a decedent's interest in a closely held business may be deferred.[52] In addition, the value of the closely held business must exceed 35 percent of the gross estate minus Code § 2053 and § 2054 deductions. If a deferral of estate tax is desirable in a specific situation, the tax adviser should make certain that such requirements are met on a prospective basis.

CONCLUSION

This chapter has introduced the reader to one of the most fascinating and satisfying areas of tax practice—family tax planning. Such planning involves arrangements whereby family income can be shifted to low-bracket members so as to reduce the income taxes paid by the family unit. The use of trusts also has been discussed, and grantor trusts whose income is taxed not to the trust or its beneficiaries but to the grantor have been described.

Transfer tax planning techniques for reducing the family transfer tax burden have been introduced. Such techniques include long-range programs of inter vivos giving, asset freezes, selective use of the marital deduction, and liquidity planning. The family tax planner should never lose sight of the basic premise of family tax planning: only a plan that meets the subjective nontax goals and desires of a family as well as the objective goal of tax minimization is a truly well-designed plan.

PROBLEM MATERIALS

DISCUSSION QUESTIONS

26-1 *Assignment of Income Doctrine.* Explain the assignment of income doctrine as it relates to earned income. How does the doctrine apply to investment income?

26-2 *Income Shifting.* Assignment of income from one taxpayer to another can result in a tax savings only in a tax system with a progressive rate structure. Discuss.

---

[50] § 6312 provided the authorization for such usage. However, the section was repealed with respect to bonds issued after March 3, 1971. Bonds issued before this date and still outstanding continue to be eligible for payment of the estate tax.

[51] Rev. Rul. 69-489, 1969-2 C.B. 172.

[52] § 6166(a)(2).

26-3 *Family Employees.* List some of the factors the IRS might consider in determining whether a particular family member is a bona fide employee of a family business.

26-4 *Shareholder/Employee.* Discuss the tax consequences if the IRS determines that a family member is receiving an amount of unreasonable compensation from a family-owned corporation if that family member is a shareholder. What if the family member is not a shareholder?

26-5 *Gift of Business Interest.* An individual who transfers an equity interest in his or her business to a family member may be accomplishing an income shift to that family member. What are some nontax risks associated with such an equity transfer?

26-6 *Buy-Sell Arrangements.* How may a buy-sell agreement be utilized when an intrafamily transfer of an equity interest in a business is contemplated?

26-7 *Regular Corporation vs. S Corporation.* As a general rule, a regular corporation is an inappropriate vehicle by which to shift business income to low-bracket family members. Discuss.

26-8 *Limitation on Using S Corporations.* An S corporation may have only a single class of common stock outstanding. How does this fact limit the utility of the S corporation in many family tax plans?

26-9 *Use of Grantor Trusts.* Grantor trusts are ineffective as devices for shifting income to trust beneficiaries. However, such trusts may be very useful in achieving nontax family planning goals. Explain.

26-10 *Crummey Trusts.* What is a Crummey trust and why might a grantor prefer a Crummey trust to a § 2503(c) trust?

26-11 *Reversionary Trusts and Interest-Free Loans.* Can a trust in which the grantor has the right to receive his or her property back after a specified period of time be considered a valid trust for tax purposes so that the income is taxed to the beneficiaries rather than the grantor? Can an interest-free demand loan achieve an income shift from the lender to the debtor?

26-12 *Inter Vivos Gifts.* Why are inter vivos gifts beneficial from a transfer tax planning viewpoint?

26-13 *Limitations of Inter Vivos Gifts.* For what reasons might an elderly taxpayer be reluctant to make inter vivos gifts?

26-14 *Estate Freezes.* Define an "asset freeze" as the term relates to estate planning.

26-15 *Current vs. Testamentary Contributions.* Is it preferable to make a charitable contribution during a taxpayer's life or at his or her death under the terms of his or her will?

26-16 *Marital Deduction.* Discuss the tax benefits associated with the unlimited marital deduction of § 2056.

26-17 *Limiting Estate Taxes.* Why is it generally inadvisable for a taxpayer to plan to reduce his or her taxable estate to zero? What can be considered an "optimal" size for a decedent's taxable estate?

26-18 *Qualifying Terminable Interests.* In what circumstances would a taxpayer desire to make a bequest to a surviving spouse in the form of qualifying terminable interest property? What are the tax consequences of such a bequest?

PROBLEMS

26-19 *Using Family Employees.* F runs a carpet installation and cleaning business as a sole proprietorship. In the current year, the business generates $83,000 of net income.

    a. Assume F is married, has three children (all under the age of 19), does not have any other source of taxable income, and does not itemize deductions. What is his current year tax liability?

    b. Assume F can use all three children in his business as legitimate part-time employees. He pays each child $6,000 per year, but continues to provide more than one-half of their support. Compute the family's total tax bill for the current year.

26-20 *Sole Proprietorship vs. Corporation.* Single individual K owns a sole proprietorship that is K's only source of income. In the current year, the business has net income of $130,000.

    a. If K does not itemize deductions, what is her current year tax liability?

    b. If K incorporates the business on January 1 and pays herself a $40,000 salary (and no dividends), by how much will she have reduced the tax bill on her business income? (Assume the corporation will not be a personal service corporation.)

26-21 *Sole Proprietorship vs. Corporation.* Mr. and Mrs. C own their own business, which they currently operate as a sole proprietorship. Annual income from the business averages $400,000. Mr. and Mrs. C are considering incorporating the business. They estimate that each of them could draw a reasonable annual salary of $75,000. In order to maintain their current standard of living, they would also have to draw an additional $50,000 cash out of the business annually in the form of dividends. Based on these facts, compute the income tax savings or cost that would result from the incorporation. In making your calculation, ignore any deductions or exemptions available on the C's joint return.

26-22 *Singles Penalty.* Single taxpayer S has current year taxable income of $35,000 (after all available deductions and exemptions). His fiancé F has a taxable income of $6,000. Assuming they both itemize deductions, and that no deductions are affected by their combined adjusted gross income, should F and S marry before or after December 31? Support your conclusion with calculations.

26-23 *Marriage Penalty.* Taxpayers H and W are married and file a joint return. Both are professionals and earn salaries of $28,000 and $39,000, respectively. Assuming H and W have no other income and do not itemize deductions, compute any *marriage penalty* they will pay.

26-24 *Married vs. Head-of-Household.* Refer to the facts in *Problem 26-23*. Assume H and W are not married and H has a child by a previous marriage that entitles him to file as a head-of-household. If H and W marry, will the marriage penalty they incur be more or less than in *Problem 26-23*?

26-25 *Unearned Income of a Minor Child.* In the current year, taxpayer M receives $12,000 of interest income and earns a salary of $2,500 from a summer job. M has no other income or deductions. M is 13 years old and is claimed as a dependent on his parents' jointly filed tax return. His parents report taxable income of $200,000. Based on these facts, compute M's income tax liability.

26-26 *Sheltering Unearned Income of a Minor Child.* Taxpayer P made a gift of investment securities to his 13-year-old dependent daughter, D, under the Uniform Gift to Minors Act. The securities generate annual dividend income of $4,000. P is considering a second gift to D that would generate an additional $3,000 of investment income annually. Calculate the amount of tax savings to the family if P could employ D in his business and pay her an annual salary of $3,000, rather than making the second gift. In making your calculation, assume P is in a 40 percent tax bracket.

26-27 *Family Partnerships.* F owns a 70 percent interest in Mako Partnership, in which capital is a material income-producing factor. On January 1 of the current year, F gives his son S a 35 percent interest in Mako (leaving F with a 35% interest). For the current year, Mako has taxable income of $200,000.

    a. Assume F does not perform any services for Mako. What is the maximum amount of partnership income allocable to S?

    b. Assume F performs services for Mako for which he normally would receive $30,000. However, F has not charged the partnership for his services. Based on these facts, what is the maximum amount of partnership income allocable to S in the current year?

26-28 *Gift of S Corporation Stock.* Grandfather G owns all 100 shares of the outstanding stock of Sigma, Inc., a calendar year S corporation. On January 1 of the current year, G gives 10 shares of Sigma stock to each of his four minor grandchildren under the Uniform Gift to Minors Act. For the current year, Sigma reports taxable income of $70,000. To whom is this income taxed?

26-29 *Gift-Leaseback.* Taxpayer B owns land used in his sole proprietorship with a tax basis of $75,000 and a fair market value of $100,000. B gives this land to an irrevocable simple trust for the equal benefit of his three children (ages 14, 16, and 19) and leases back the land from the trust for a fair market rental of $9,000 per year.

    a. Assuming that all three children are B's dependents and have no other source of income, calculate the tax savings to the family of this gift-leaseback arrangement. In making your calculation, assume B is in a 40 percent tax bracket.

    b. What are the gift and estate tax consequences of this transaction to B and his family? Assume that B has made no prior taxable gifts and that he is married.

26-30 *Use of Trusts.* Grandfather Z is in the habit of giving his 15-year-old grandchild, A, $10,000 annually as a gift. Z's taxable income is consistently over $500,000 per year, and A has no income. If Z creates a valid trust with investment assets just sufficient to yield $12,000 of income a year and specifies in the trust instrument that A is to receive the trust income annually, what will be the net tax savings to the family? (For purposes of this problem, *ignore* the fact that A may be claimed as a dependent on the return of another taxpayer.)

26-31 *Reversionary Trusts.* Grantor G transfers $100,000 of assets into a trust that will last for 10 years, after which time the assets will revert to G or his estate. During the trust's existence all income must be paid to beneficiary M on a current basis. For the current year, ordinary trust income is $18,000. To whom is this income taxed?

26-32 *Reversionary Trusts.* Refer to the facts in *Problem 26-31*. Assume that under the terms of the trust agreement the trust will last for M's lifetime. Upon M's death, the trust corpus will revert to G or his estate. On the date the trust is created, M is 18 years old. For the current year, ordinary trust income is $40,000. To whom is this income taxed?

26-33 *Irrevocable Trusts.* F transfers assets into an irrevocable trust and designates First City Bank as independent trustee. F retains no control over the trust assets. The trustee may distribute income to either of F's two adult brothers or to S, F's minor son whom F is legally obligated to support. During the year, the trustee distributed all of the trust income to one of F's brothers. To whom will the income be taxed?

26-34 *Irrevocable Trusts.* M transfers assets into an irrevocable trust and appoints National Bank independent trustee. M retains no control over trust assets. Under the terms of the trust agreement, M's sister N is given the right to determine which of M's three minor children will receive trust income for the year. N herself is not a trust beneficiary. During the year, N directs that trust income be divided equally among M's three children. To whom will the income be taxed?

26-35 *Irrevocable Trusts.* Grantor B transfers assets into an irrevocable trust and designates Union State Bank independent trustee. B retains no control over trust assets. Under the terms of the trust instrument the trustee must use trust income to pay the annual insurance premium on a policy on B's life. Any remaining income must be distributed to B's grandson, GS. For the current year, trust income totals $60,000, of which $9,000 is used to pay the required insurance premium. To whom will the income be taxed?

26-36 *Grantor Trusts.* Although T is not a beneficiary of the ABC Trust, T does have the right under the terms of the trust instrument to appoint up to 10 percent of the trust assets to himself or any member of his family. T has never exercised this right. For the current year, the trust income of $80,000 is distributed to the income beneficiaries of the trust.
   a. To whom will the income be taxed?
   b. If T dies before exercising his right to appoint trust corpus, will the possession of the right have any estate tax consequences?

26-37 *Gift Splitting.* Every year D gives each of her nine grandchildren $15,000 in cash to be used toward their education.
   a. If D is unmarried, what is the amount of her annual taxable gift?
   b. If D is married and she and her husband elect to "gift split," what is the amount of her annual taxable gift?

26-38 *Terminable Interest Trusts.* Taxpayer Q dies in 2006 and leaves a net estate of $4 million. Under the terms of his will, $3 million of the estate will be put into trust. Q's widow, W, will be paid trust income annually and during W's life no person has the right to appoint any of the trust corpus. Upon W's death, the trust corpus will be divided among Q's offspring from a previous marriage. The remaining $1,000,000 of Q's estate is to be paid to unrelated friends named in Q's will.
   a. What is the amount of Q's taxable estate?
   b. What is the estate tax liability on Q's taxable estate? (Q made no taxable gifts during his lifetime.)
   c. W outlives Q by only eight years. If the value of the corpus of the trust created for W's benefit by Q is $6.3 million at the date of W's death, what amount must be included in W's gross estate?

26-39 *Inter Vivos Gifts.* Decedent T died in the current year and left the following taxable estate:

	Fair Market Value
Investment real estate	$1,000,000
Cash and securities	3,500,000
Gross estate	$4,500,000
Less: § 2053 and § 2054 expenses	(500,000)
Taxable estate	$4,000,000

After payment of all death taxes, the estate will be divided equally among T's five surviving married children.
   a. If T has never made any inter vivos gifts, compute the estate's Federal estate tax liability (before credit for any state death tax paid).
   b. How much tax could have been saved if T had made cash gifts equal to the maximum annual exclusion under § 2503 to each of his children and their spouses in each of the 10 years preceding his death?

26-40 *Power of Giving.* W is thinking about the possibility of dying in the next ten years. She currently has an estate of $5,000,000. Assuming W is in the 48% transfer tax bracket, how much more could she give to her child if she made a gift to her child rather than dying with the entire $5,000,000? Ignore the annual exclusion and the unified credit.

26-41 *Liquidity Planning.* Decedent D left the following taxable estate:

	Fair Market Value
Life insurance proceeds from policy on D's life (D owned the policy at his death)	$ 500,000
Real estate	1,300,000
Stock in Acme Corporation (100% owned by D)	650,000
Gross estate	$2,450,000
Less: § 2053 and § 2054 expenses	(450,000)
Taxable estate	$2,000,000

    a. If D has never made any inter vivos gifts and dies in 2005, what is the estate's Federal estate tax liability (before credit for any state death tax paid)?

    b. How much tax could have been avoided if D had not been the owner of the life insurance policy?

    c. Can the Acme stock qualify for a § 303 redemption? What if the life insurance proceeds were not included in the gross estate?

RESEARCH PROBLEMS

26-42 In 1994, P, a resident of St. Louis, Missouri, created an irrevocable trust for the benefit of his teenage son, S, and his brother, B. The independent trustee, T, has discretionary power to use the trust income for the "payment of tuition, books, and room and board at any institution of higher learning that S chooses to attend." After an 11-year period, the trust will terminate with any accumulated income payable to S and the trust corpus payable to B. In the current year, S received an income distribution of $7,000 from the trust, which he used to attend a state-supported school, the University of Missouri. To whom will the $7,000 of trust income be taxed?

Some suggested research aids:

§ 677 and accompanying regulations

Morrill, Jr. v. United States, 64-1 USTC ¶9463, 13 AFTR2d 1334, 228 F.Supp. 734 (D.Ct. Maine, 1964).

Braun, Jr., 48 TCM 210, T.C. Memo 1984-285.

26-43 Decedent D died on January 19, 2000. Under the terms of D's will, D's sister S, age 57, is to receive $500,000 as a specific bequest. The remainder of D's estate will be distributed to D's various grandchildren. On June 8, 2002, S decides to join a religious community and take a vow of poverty. She makes written notification to the executor of D's estate that she will not accept her bequest from her late sister, and that the $500,000 should be added to the amount to be distributed to the grandchildren. What are the transfer tax consequences of S's action?

Suggested research aid:

§ 2518

APPENDICES

❖ **Contents** ❖

Appendix A
Tax Rate Schedules and Tables

Appendix B
Tax Forms

Appendix C
Modified ACRS and Original ACRS Tables

Appendix D
Two Individual Comprehensive Tax
Return Problems for 2004

Appendix E
Glossary of Tax Terms

Appendix A

TAX RATE SCHEDULES AND TABLES

2004 Tax Rate Schedules

The Tax Rate Schedules are shown so you can see the tax rate that applies to all levels of taxable income. Do not use them to figure your tax. Instead, see the instructions for line 43 that begin on page 33.

Schedule X—If your filing status is Single

If your taxable income is:		The tax is:	of the amount over—
Over—	But not over—		
$0	$7,150	———— 10%	$0
7,150	29,050	$715.00 + 15%	7,150
29,050	70,350	4,000.00 + 25%	29,050
70,350	146,750	14,325.00 + 28%	70,350
146,750	319,100	35,717.00 + 33%	146,750
319,100	————	92,592.50 + 35%	319,100

Schedule Y-1—If your filing status is Married filing jointly or Qualifying widow(er)

If your taxable income is:		The tax is:	of the amount over—
Over—	But not over—		
$0	$14,300	———— 10%	$0
14,300	58,100	$1,430.00 + 15%	14,300
58,100	117,250	8,000.00 + 25%	58,100
117,250	178,650	22,787.50 + 28%	117,250
178,650	319,100	39,979.50 + 33%	178,650
319,100	————	86,328.00 + 35%	319,100

Schedule Y-2—If your filing status is Married filing separately

If your taxable income is:		The tax is:	of the amount over—
Over—	But not over—		
$0	$7,150	———— 10%	$0
7,150	29,050	$715.00 + 15%	7,150
29,050	58,625	4,000.00 + 25%	29,050
58,625	89,325	11,393.75 + 28%	58,625
89,325	159,550	19,989.75 + 33%	89,325
159,550	————	43,164.00 + 35%	159,550

Schedule Z—If your filing status is Head of household

If your taxable income is:		The tax is:	of the amount over—
Over—	But not over—		
$0	$10,200	———— 10%	$0
10,200	38,900	$1,020.00 + 15%	10,200
38,900	100,500	5,325.00 + 25%	38,900
100,500	162,700	20,725.00 + 28%	100,500
162,700	319,100	38,141.00 + 33%	162,700
319,100	————	89,753.00 + 35%	319,100

A-2   2004 Income Tax Tables

2004 Tax Table

See the instructions for line 43 that begin on page 33 to see if you must use the Tax Table below to figure your tax.

Example. Mr. and Mrs. Brown are filing a joint return. Their taxable income on Form 1040, line 42, is $25,300. First, they find the $25,300–25,350 taxable income line. Next, they find the column for married filing jointly and read down the column. The amount shown where the taxable income line and filing status column meet is $3,084. This is the tax amount they should enter on Form 1040, line 43.

Sample Table

At least	But less than	Single	Married filing jointly *	Married filing separately	Head of a household
			Your tax is—		
25,200	25,250	3,426	3,069	3,426	3,274
25,250	25,300	3,434	3,076	3,434	3,281
25,300	25,350	3,441	(3,084)	3,441	3,289
25,350	25,400	3,449	3,091	3,449	3,296

If line 42 (taxable income) is—		And you are—			
At least	But less than	Single	Married filing jointly *	Married filing separately	Head of a household
			Your tax is—		
0	5	0	0	0	0
5	15	1	1	1	1
15	25	2	2	2	2
25	50	4	4	4	4
50	75	6	6	6	6
75	100	9	9	9	9
100	125	11	11	11	11
125	150	14	14	14	14
150	175	16	16	16	16
175	200	19	19	19	19
200	225	21	21	21	21
225	250	24	24	24	24
250	275	26	26	26	26
275	300	29	29	29	29
300	325	31	31	31	31
325	350	34	34	34	34
350	375	36	36	36	36
375	400	39	39	39	39
400	425	41	41	41	41
425	450	44	44	44	44
450	475	46	46	46	46
475	500	49	49	49	49
500	525	51	51	51	51
525	550	54	54	54	54
550	575	56	56	56	56
575	600	59	59	59	59
600	625	61	61	61	61
625	650	64	64	64	64
650	675	66	66	66	66
675	700	69	69	69	69
700	725	71	71	71	71
725	750	74	74	74	74
750	775	76	76	76	76
775	800	79	79	79	79
800	825	81	81	81	81
825	850	84	84	84	84
850	875	86	86	86	86
875	900	89	89	89	89
900	925	91	91	91	91
925	950	94	94	94	94
950	975	96	96	96	96
975	1,000	99	99	99	99

1,000

At least	But less than	Single	Married filing jointly *	Married filing separately	Head of a household
1,000	1,025	101	101	101	101
1,025	1,050	104	104	104	104
1,050	1,075	106	106	106	106
1,075	1,100	109	109	109	109
1,100	1,125	111	111	111	111
1,125	1,150	114	114	114	114
1,150	1,175	116	116	116	116
1,175	1,200	119	119	119	119
1,200	1,225	121	121	121	121
1,225	1,250	124	124	124	124
1,250	1,275	126	126	126	126
1,275	1,300	129	129	129	129

If line 42 (taxable income) is—		And you are—			
At least	But less than	Single	Married filing jointly *	Married filing separately	Head of a household
			Your tax is—		
1,300	1,325	131	131	131	131
1,325	1,350	134	134	134	134
1,350	1,375	136	136	136	136
1,375	1,400	139	139	139	139
1,400	1,425	141	141	141	141
1,425	1,450	144	144	144	144
1,450	1,475	146	146	146	146
1,475	1,500	149	149	149	149
1,500	1,525	151	151	151	151
1,525	1,550	154	154	154	154
1,550	1,575	156	156	156	156
1,575	1,600	159	159	159	159
1,600	1,625	161	161	161	161
1,625	1,650	164	164	164	164
1,650	1,675	166	166	166	166
1,675	1,700	169	169	169	169
1,700	1,725	171	171	171	171
1,725	1,750	174	174	174	174
1,750	1,775	176	176	176	176
1,775	1,800	179	179	179	179
1,800	1,825	181	181	181	181
1,825	1,850	184	184	184	184
1,850	1,875	186	186	186	186
1,875	1,900	189	189	189	189
1,900	1,925	191	191	191	191
1,925	1,950	194	194	194	194
1,950	1,975	196	196	196	196
1,975	2,000	199	199	199	199

2,000

At least	But less than	Single	Married filing jointly *	Married filing separately	Head of a household
2,000	2,025	201	201	201	201
2,025	2,050	204	204	204	204
2,050	2,075	206	206	206	206
2,075	2,100	209	209	209	209
2,100	2,125	211	211	211	211
2,125	2,150	214	214	214	214
2,150	2,175	216	216	216	216
2,175	2,200	219	219	219	219
2,200	2,225	221	221	221	221
2,225	2,250	224	224	224	224
2,250	2,275	226	226	226	226
2,275	2,300	229	229	229	229
2,300	2,325	231	231	231	231
2,325	2,350	234	234	234	234
2,350	2,375	236	236	236	236
2,375	2,400	239	239	239	239
2,400	2,425	241	241	241	241
2,425	2,450	244	244	244	244
2,450	2,475	246	246	246	246
2,475	2,500	249	249	249	249
2,500	2,525	251	251	251	251
2,525	2,550	254	254	254	254
2,550	2,575	256	256	256	256
2,575	2,600	259	259	259	259
2,600	2,625	261	261	261	261
2,625	2,650	264	264	264	264
2,650	2,675	266	266	266	266
2,675	2,700	269	269	269	269

If line 42 (taxable income) is—		And you are—			
At least	But less than	Single	Married filing jointly *	Married filing separately	Head of a household
			Your tax is—		
2,700	2,725	271	271	271	271
2,725	2,750	274	274	274	274
2,750	2,775	276	276	276	276
2,775	2,800	279	279	279	279
2,800	2,825	281	281	281	281
2,825	2,850	284	284	284	284
2,850	2,875	286	286	286	286
2,875	2,900	289	289	289	289
2,900	2,925	291	291	291	291
2,925	2,950	294	294	294	294
2,950	2,975	296	296	296	296
2,975	3,000	299	299	299	299

3,000

At least	But less than	Single	Married filing jointly *	Married filing separately	Head of a household
3,000	3,050	303	303	303	303
3,050	3,100	308	308	308	308
3,100	3,150	313	313	313	313
3,150	3,200	318	318	318	318
3,200	3,250	323	323	323	323
3,250	3,300	328	328	328	328
3,300	3,350	333	333	333	333
3,350	3,400	338	338	338	338
3,400	3,450	343	343	343	343
3,450	3,500	348	348	348	348
3,500	3,550	353	353	353	353
3,550	3,600	358	358	358	358
3,600	3,650	363	363	363	363
3,650	3,700	368	368	368	368
3,700	3,750	373	373	373	373
3,750	3,800	378	378	378	378
3,800	3,850	383	383	383	383
3,850	3,900	388	388	388	388
3,900	3,950	393	393	393	393
3,950	4,000	398	398	398	398

4,000

At least	But less than	Single	Married filing jointly *	Married filing separately	Head of a household
4,000	4,050	403	403	403	403
4,050	4,100	408	408	408	408
4,100	4,150	413	413	413	413
4,150	4,200	418	418	418	418
4,200	4,250	423	423	423	423
4,250	4,300	428	428	428	428
4,300	4,350	433	433	433	433
4,350	4,400	438	438	438	438
4,400	4,450	443	443	443	443
4,450	4,500	448	448	448	448
4,500	4,550	453	453	453	453
4,550	4,600	458	458	458	458
4,600	4,650	463	463	463	463
4,650	4,700	468	468	468	468
4,700	4,750	473	473	473	473
4,750	4,800	478	478	478	478
4,800	4,850	483	483	483	483
4,850	4,900	488	488	488	488
4,900	4,950	493	493	493	493
4,950	5,000	498	498	498	498

(Continued on page 61)

* This column must also be used by a qualifying widow(er).

2004 Tax Table—*Continued*

If line 42 (taxable income) is—		Single	Married filing jointly *	Married filing separately	Head of a household
At least	But less than				
		Your tax is—			
5,000					
5,000	5,050	503	503	503	503
5,050	5,100	508	508	508	508
5,100	5,150	513	513	513	513
5,150	5,200	518	518	518	518
5,200	5,250	523	523	523	523
5,250	5,300	528	528	528	528
5,300	5,350	533	533	533	533
5,350	5,400	538	538	538	538
5,400	5,450	543	543	543	543
5,450	5,500	548	548	548	548
5,500	5,550	553	553	553	553
5,550	5,600	558	558	558	558
5,600	5,650	563	563	563	563
5,650	5,700	568	568	568	568
5,700	5,750	573	573	573	573
5,750	5,800	578	578	578	578
5,800	5,850	583	583	583	583
5,850	5,900	588	588	588	588
5,900	5,950	593	593	593	593
5,950	6,000	598	598	598	598
6,000					
6,000	6,050	603	603	603	603
6,050	6,100	608	608	608	608
6,100	6,150	613	613	613	613
6,150	6,200	618	618	618	618
6,200	6,250	623	623	623	623
6,250	6,300	628	628	628	628
6,300	6,350	633	633	633	633
6,350	6,400	638	638	638	638
6,400	6,450	643	643	643	643
6,450	6,500	648	648	648	648
6,500	6,550	653	653	653	653
6,550	6,600	658	658	658	658
6,600	6,650	663	663	663	663
6,650	6,700	668	668	668	668
6,700	6,750	673	673	673	673
6,750	6,800	678	678	678	678
6,800	6,850	683	683	683	683
6,850	6,900	688	688	688	688
6,900	6,950	693	693	693	693
6,950	7,000	698	698	698	698
7,000					
7,000	7,050	703	703	703	703
7,050	7,100	708	708	708	708
7,100	7,150	713	713	713	713
7,150	7,200	719	718	719	718
7,200	7,250	726	723	726	723
7,250	7,300	734	728	734	728
7,300	7,350	741	733	741	733
7,350	7,400	749	738	749	738
7,400	7,450	756	743	756	743
7,450	7,500	764	748	764	748
7,500	7,550	771	753	771	753
7,550	7,600	779	758	779	758
7,600	7,650	786	763	786	763
7,650	7,700	794	768	794	768
7,700	7,750	801	773	801	773
7,750	7,800	809	778	809	778
7,800	7,850	816	783	816	783
7,850	7,900	824	788	824	788
7,900	7,950	831	793	831	793
7,950	8,000	839	798	839	798

If line 42 (taxable income) is—		Single	Married filing jointly *	Married filing separately	Head of a household
At least	But less than				
		Your tax is—			
8,000					
8,000	8,050	846	803	846	803
8,050	8,100	854	808	854	808
8,100	8,150	861	813	861	813
8,150	8,200	869	818	869	818
8,200	8,250	876	823	876	823
8,250	8,300	884	828	884	828
8,300	8,350	891	833	891	833
8,350	8,400	899	838	899	838
8,400	8,450	906	843	906	843
8,450	8,500	914	848	914	848
8,500	8,550	921	853	921	853
8,550	8,600	929	858	929	858
8,600	8,650	936	863	936	863
8,650	8,700	944	868	944	868
8,700	8,750	951	873	951	873
8,750	8,800	959	878	959	878
8,800	8,850	966	883	966	883
8,850	8,900	974	888	974	888
8,900	8,950	981	893	981	893
8,950	9,000	989	898	989	898
9,000					
9,000	9,050	996	903	996	903
9,050	9,100	1,004	908	1,004	908
9,100	9,150	1,011	913	1,011	913
9,150	9,200	1,019	918	1,019	918
9,200	9,250	1,026	923	1,026	923
9,250	9,300	1,034	928	1,034	928
9,300	9,350	1,041	933	1,041	933
9,350	9,400	1,049	938	1,049	938
9,400	9,450	1,056	943	1,056	943
9,450	9,500	1,064	948	1,064	948
9,500	9,550	1,071	953	1,071	953
9,550	9,600	1,079	958	1,079	958
9,600	9,650	1,086	963	1,086	963
9,650	9,700	1,094	968	1,094	968
9,700	9,750	1,101	973	1,101	973
9,750	9,800	1,109	978	1,109	978
9,800	9,850	1,116	983	1,116	983
9,850	9,900	1,124	988	1,124	988
9,900	9,950	1,131	993	1,131	993
9,950	10,000	1,139	998	1,139	998
10,000					
10,000	10,050	1,146	1,003	1,146	1,003
10,050	10,100	1,154	1,008	1,154	1,008
10,100	10,150	1,161	1,013	1,161	1,013
10,150	10,200	1,169	1,018	1,169	1,018
10,200	10,250	1,176	1,023	1,176	1,024
10,250	10,300	1,184	1,028	1,184	1,031
10,300	10,350	1,191	1,033	1,191	1,039
10,350	10,400	1,199	1,038	1,199	1,046
10,400	10,450	1,206	1,043	1,206	1,054
10,450	10,500	1,214	1,048	1,214	1,061
10,500	10,550	1,221	1,053	1,221	1,069
10,550	10,600	1,229	1,058	1,229	1,076
10,600	10,650	1,236	1,063	1,236	1,084
10,650	10,700	1,244	1,068	1,244	1,091
10,700	10,750	1,251	1,073	1,251	1,099
10,750	10,800	1,259	1,078	1,259	1,106
10,800	10,850	1,266	1,083	1,266	1,114
10,850	10,900	1,274	1,088	1,274	1,121
10,900	10,950	1,281	1,093	1,281	1,129
10,950	11,000	1,289	1,098	1,289	1,136

If line 42 (taxable income) is—		Single	Married filing jointly *	Married filing separately	Head of a household
At least	But less than				
		Your tax is—			
11,000					
11,000	11,050	1,296	1,103	1,296	1,144
11,050	11,100	1,304	1,108	1,304	1,151
11,100	11,150	1,311	1,113	1,311	1,159
11,150	11,200	1,319	1,118	1,319	1,166
11,200	11,250	1,326	1,123	1,326	1,174
11,250	11,300	1,334	1,128	1,334	1,181
11,300	11,350	1,341	1,133	1,341	1,189
11,350	11,400	1,349	1,138	1,349	1,196
11,400	11,450	1,356	1,143	1,356	1,204
11,450	11,500	1,364	1,148	1,364	1,211
11,500	11,550	1,371	1,153	1,371	1,219
11,550	11,600	1,379	1,158	1,379	1,226
11,600	11,650	1,386	1,163	1,386	1,234
11,650	11,700	1,394	1,168	1,394	1,241
11,700	11,750	1,401	1,173	1,401	1,249
11,750	11,800	1,409	1,178	1,409	1,256
11,800	11,850	1,416	1,183	1,416	1,264
11,850	11,900	1,424	1,188	1,424	1,271
11,900	11,950	1,431	1,193	1,431	1,279
11,950	12,000	1,439	1,198	1,439	1,286
12,000					
12,000	12,050	1,446	1,203	1,446	1,294
12,050	12,100	1,454	1,208	1,454	1,301
12,100	12,150	1,461	1,213	1,461	1,309
12,150	12,200	1,469	1,218	1,469	1,316
12,200	12,250	1,476	1,223	1,476	1,324
12,250	12,300	1,484	1,228	1,484	1,331
12,300	12,350	1,491	1,233	1,491	1,339
12,350	12,400	1,499	1,238	1,499	1,346
12,400	12,450	1,506	1,243	1,506	1,354
12,450	12,500	1,514	1,248	1,514	1,361
12,500	12,550	1,521	1,253	1,521	1,369
12,550	12,600	1,529	1,258	1,529	1,376
12,600	12,650	1,536	1,263	1,536	1,384
12,650	12,700	1,544	1,268	1,544	1,391
12,700	12,750	1,551	1,273	1,551	1,399
12,750	12,800	1,559	1,278	1,559	1,406
12,800	12,850	1,566	1,283	1,566	1,414
12,850	12,900	1,574	1,288	1,574	1,421
12,900	12,950	1,581	1,293	1,581	1,429
12,950	13,000	1,589	1,298	1,589	1,436
13,000					
13,000	13,050	1,596	1,303	1,596	1,444
13,050	13,100	1,604	1,308	1,604	1,451
13,100	13,150	1,611	1,313	1,611	1,459
13,150	13,200	1,619	1,318	1,619	1,466
13,200	13,250	1,626	1,323	1,626	1,474
13,250	13,300	1,634	1,328	1,634	1,481
13,300	13,350	1,641	1,333	1,641	1,489
13,350	13,400	1,649	1,338	1,649	1,496
13,400	13,450	1,656	1,343	1,656	1,504
13,450	13,500	1,664	1,348	1,664	1,511
13,500	13,550	1,671	1,353	1,671	1,519
13,550	13,600	1,679	1,358	1,679	1,526
13,600	13,650	1,686	1,363	1,686	1,534
13,650	13,700	1,694	1,368	1,694	1,541
13,700	13,750	1,701	1,373	1,701	1,549
13,750	13,800	1,709	1,378	1,709	1,556
13,800	13,850	1,716	1,383	1,716	1,564
13,850	13,900	1,724	1,388	1,724	1,571
13,900	13,950	1,731	1,393	1,731	1,579
13,950	14,000	1,739	1,398	1,739	1,586

* This column must also be used by a qualifying widow(er).

(Continued on page 62)

2004 Tax Table—Continued

(Continued on page 63)

If line 42 (taxable income) is— At least	But less than	Single	Married filing jointly *	Married filing separately	Head of a household
14,000					
14,000	14,050	1,746	1,403	1,746	1,594
14,050	14,100	1,754	1,408	1,754	1,601
14,100	14,150	1,761	1,413	1,761	1,609
14,150	14,200	1,769	1,418	1,769	1,616
14,200	14,250	1,776	1,423	1,776	1,624
14,250	14,300	1,784	1,428	1,784	1,631
14,300	14,350	1,791	1,434	1,791	1,639
14,350	14,400	1,799	1,441	1,799	1,646
14,400	14,450	1,806	1,449	1,806	1,654
14,450	14,500	1,814	1,456	1,814	1,661
14,500	14,550	1,821	1,464	1,821	1,669
14,550	14,600	1,829	1,471	1,829	1,676
14,600	14,650	1,836	1,479	1,836	1,684
14,650	14,700	1,844	1,486	1,844	1,691
14,700	14,750	1,851	1,494	1,851	1,699
14,750	14,800	1,859	1,501	1,859	1,706
14,800	14,850	1,866	1,509	1,866	1,714
14,850	14,900	1,874	1,516	1,874	1,721
14,900	14,950	1,881	1,524	1,881	1,729
14,950	15,000	1,889	1,531	1,889	1,736
15,000					
15,000	15,050	1,896	1,539	1,896	1,744
15,050	15,100	1,904	1,546	1,904	1,751
15,100	15,150	1,911	1,554	1,911	1,759
15,150	15,200	1,919	1,561	1,919	1,766
15,200	15,250	1,926	1,569	1,926	1,774
15,250	15,300	1,934	1,576	1,934	1,781
15,300	15,350	1,941	1,584	1,941	1,789
15,350	15,400	1,949	1,591	1,949	1,796
15,400	15,450	1,956	1,599	1,956	1,804
15,450	15,500	1,964	1,606	1,964	1,811
15,500	15,550	1,971	1,614	1,971	1,819
15,550	15,600	1,979	1,621	1,979	1,826
15,600	15,650	1,986	1,629	1,986	1,834
15,650	15,700	1,994	1,636	1,994	1,841
15,700	15,750	2,001	1,644	2,001	1,849
15,750	15,800	2,009	1,651	2,009	1,856
15,800	15,850	2,016	1,659	2,016	1,864
15,850	15,900	2,024	1,666	2,024	1,871
15,900	15,950	2,031	1,674	2,031	1,879
15,950	16,000	2,039	1,681	2,039	1,886
16,000					
16,000	16,050	2,046	1,689	2,046	1,894
16,050	16,100	2,054	1,696	2,054	1,901
16,100	16,150	2,061	1,704	2,061	1,909
16,150	16,200	2,069	1,711	2,069	1,916
16,200	16,250	2,076	1,719	2,076	1,924
16,250	16,300	2,084	1,726	2,084	1,931
16,300	16,350	2,091	1,734	2,091	1,939
16,350	16,400	2,099	1,741	2,099	1,946
16,400	16,450	2,106	1,749	2,106	1,954
16,450	16,500	2,114	1,756	2,114	1,961
16,500	16,550	2,121	1,764	2,121	1,969
16,550	16,600	2,129	1,771	2,129	1,976
16,600	16,650	2,136	1,779	2,136	1,984
16,650	16,700	2,144	1,786	2,144	1,991
16,700	16,750	2,151	1,794	2,151	1,999
16,750	16,800	2,159	1,801	2,159	2,006
16,800	16,850	2,166	1,809	2,166	2,014
16,850	16,900	2,174	1,816	2,174	2,021
16,900	16,950	2,181	1,824	2,181	2,029
16,950	17,000	2,189	1,831	2,189	2,036

If line 42 (taxable income) is— At least	But less than	Single	Married filing jointly *	Married filing separately	Head of a household
17,000					
17,000	17,050	2,196	1,839	2,196	2,044
17,050	17,100	2,204	1,846	2,204	2,051
17,100	17,150	2,211	1,854	2,211	2,059
17,150	17,200	2,219	1,861	2,219	2,066
17,200	17,250	2,226	1,869	2,226	2,074
17,250	17,300	2,234	1,876	2,234	2,081
17,300	17,350	2,241	1,884	2,241	2,089
17,350	17,400	2,249	1,891	2,249	2,096
17,400	17,450	2,256	1,899	2,256	2,104
17,450	17,500	2,264	1,906	2,264	2,111
17,500	17,550	2,271	1,914	2,271	2,119
17,550	17,600	2,279	1,921	2,279	2,126
17,600	17,650	2,286	1,929	2,286	2,134
17,650	17,700	2,294	1,936	2,294	2,141
17,700	17,750	2,301	1,944	2,301	2,149
17,750	17,800	2,309	1,951	2,309	2,156
17,800	17,850	2,316	1,959	2,316	2,164
17,850	17,900	2,324	1,966	2,324	2,171
17,900	17,950	2,331	1,974	2,331	2,179
17,950	18,000	2,339	1,981	2,339	2,186
18,000					
18,000	18,050	2,346	1,989	2,346	2,194
18,050	18,100	2,354	1,996	2,354	2,201
18,100	18,150	2,361	2,004	2,361	2,209
18,150	18,200	2,369	2,011	2,369	2,216
18,200	18,250	2,376	2,019	2,376	2,224
18,250	18,300	2,384	2,026	2,384	2,231
18,300	18,350	2,391	2,034	2,391	2,239
18,350	18,400	2,399	2,041	2,399	2,246
18,400	18,450	2,406	2,049	2,406	2,254
18,450	18,500	2,414	2,056	2,414	2,261
18,500	18,550	2,421	2,064	2,421	2,269
18,550	18,600	2,429	2,071	2,429	2,276
18,600	18,650	2,436	2,079	2,436	2,284
18,650	18,700	2,444	2,086	2,444	2,291
18,700	18,750	2,451	2,094	2,451	2,299
18,750	18,800	2,459	2,101	2,459	2,306
18,800	18,850	2,466	2,109	2,466	2,314
18,850	18,900	2,474	2,116	2,474	2,321
18,900	18,950	2,481	2,124	2,481	2,329
18,950	19,000	2,489	2,131	2,489	2,336
19,000					
19,000	19,050	2,496	2,139	2,496	2,344
19,050	19,100	2,504	2,146	2,504	2,351
19,100	19,150	2,511	2,154	2,511	2,359
19,150	19,200	2,519	2,161	2,519	2,366
19,200	19,250	2,526	2,169	2,526	2,374
19,250	19,300	2,534	2,176	2,534	2,381
19,300	19,350	2,541	2,184	2,541	2,389
19,350	19,400	2,549	2,191	2,549	2,396
19,400	19,450	2,556	2,199	2,556	2,404
19,450	19,500	2,564	2,206	2,564	2,411
19,500	19,550	2,571	2,214	2,571	2,419
19,550	19,600	2,579	2,221	2,579	2,426
19,600	19,650	2,586	2,229	2,586	2,434
19,650	19,700	2,594	2,236	2,594	2,441
19,700	19,750	2,601	2,244	2,601	2,449
19,750	19,800	2,609	2,251	2,609	2,456
19,800	19,850	2,616	2,259	2,616	2,464
19,850	19,900	2,624	2,266	2,624	2,471
19,900	19,950	2,631	2,274	2,631	2,479
19,950	20,000	2,639	2,281	2,639	2,486

If line 42 (taxable income) is— At least	But less than	Single	Married filing jointly *	Married filing separately	Head of a household
20,000					
20,000	20,050	2,646	2,289	2,646	2,494
20,050	20,100	2,654	2,296	2,654	2,501
20,100	20,150	2,661	2,304	2,661	2,509
20,150	20,200	2,669	2,311	2,669	2,516
20,200	20,250	2,676	2,319	2,676	2,524
20,250	20,300	2,684	2,326	2,684	2,531
20,300	20,350	2,691	2,334	2,691	2,539
20,350	20,400	2,699	2,341	2,699	2,546
20,400	20,450	2,706	2,349	2,706	2,554
20,450	20,500	2,714	2,356	2,714	2,561
20,500	20,550	2,721	2,364	2,721	2,569
20,550	20,600	2,729	2,371	2,729	2,576
20,600	20,650	2,736	2,379	2,736	2,584
20,650	20,700	2,744	2,386	2,744	2,591
20,700	20,750	2,751	2,394	2,751	2,599
20,750	20,800	2,759	2,401	2,759	2,606
20,800	20,850	2,766	2,409	2,766	2,614
20,850	20,900	2,774	2,416	2,774	2,621
20,900	20,950	2,781	2,424	2,781	2,629
20,950	21,000	2,789	2,431	2,789	2,636
21,000					
21,000	21,050	2,796	2,439	2,796	2,644
21,050	21,100	2,804	2,446	2,804	2,651
21,100	21,150	2,811	2,454	2,811	2,659
21,150	21,200	2,819	2,461	2,819	2,666
21,200	21,250	2,826	2,469	2,826	2,674
21,250	21,300	2,834	2,476	2,834	2,681
21,300	21,350	2,841	2,484	2,841	2,689
21,350	21,400	2,849	2,491	2,849	2,696
21,400	21,450	2,856	2,499	2,856	2,704
21,450	21,500	2,864	2,506	2,864	2,711
21,500	21,550	2,871	2,514	2,871	2,719
21,550	21,600	2,879	2,521	2,879	2,726
21,600	21,650	2,886	2,529	2,886	2,734
21,650	21,700	2,894	2,536	2,894	2,741
21,700	21,750	2,901	2,544	2,901	2,749
21,750	21,800	2,909	2,551	2,909	2,756
21,800	21,850	2,916	2,559	2,916	2,764
21,850	21,900	2,924	2,566	2,924	2,771
21,900	21,950	2,931	2,574	2,931	2,779
21,950	22,000	2,939	2,581	2,939	2,786
22,000					
22,000	22,050	2,946	2,589	2,946	2,794
22,050	22,100	2,954	2,596	2,954	2,801
22,100	22,150	2,961	2,604	2,961	2,809
22,150	22,200	2,969	2,611	2,969	2,816
22,200	22,250	2,976	2,619	2,976	2,824
22,250	22,300	2,984	2,626	2,984	2,831
22,300	22,350	2,991	2,634	2,991	2,839
22,350	22,400	2,999	2,641	2,999	2,846
22,400	22,450	3,006	2,649	3,006	2,854
22,450	22,500	3,014	2,656	3,014	2,861
22,500	22,550	3,021	2,664	3,021	2,869
22,550	22,600	3,029	2,671	3,029	2,876
22,600	22,650	3,036	2,679	3,036	2,884
22,650	22,700	3,044	2,686	3,044	2,891
22,700	22,750	3,051	2,694	3,051	2,899
22,750	22,800	3,059	2,701	3,059	2,906
22,800	22,850	3,066	2,709	3,066	2,914
22,850	22,900	3,074	2,716	3,074	2,921
22,900	22,950	3,081	2,724	3,081	2,929
22,950	23,000	3,089	2,731	3,089	2,936

* This column must also be used by a qualifying widow(er).

2004 Tax Table—Continued

If line 42 (taxable income) is—		And you are—				If line 42 (taxable income) is—		And you are—				If line 42 (taxable income) is—		And you are—			
At least	But less than	Single	Married filing jointly *	Married filing separately	Head of a household	At least	But less than	Single	Married filing jointly *	Married filing separately	Head of a household	At least	But less than	Single	Married filing jointly *	Married filing separately	Head of a household
		Your tax is—						Your tax is—						Your tax is—			
23,000						**26,000**						**29,000**					
23,000	23,050	3,096	2,739	3,096	2,944	26,000	26,050	3,546	3,189	3,546	3,394	29,000	29,050	3,996	3,639	3,996	3,844
23,050	23,100	3,104	2,746	3,104	2,951	26,050	26,100	3,554	3,196	3,554	3,401	29,050	29,100	4,006	3,646	4,006	3,851
23,100	23,150	3,111	2,754	3,111	2,959	26,100	26,150	3,561	3,204	3,561	3,409	29,100	29,150	4,019	3,654	4,019	3,859
23,150	23,200	3,119	2,761	3,119	2,966	26,150	26,200	3,569	3,211	3,569	3,416	29,150	29,200	4,031	3,661	4,031	3,866
23,200	23,250	3,126	2,769	3,126	2,974	26,200	26,250	3,576	3,219	3,576	3,424	29,200	29,250	4,044	3,669	4,044	3,874
23,250	23,300	3,134	2,776	3,134	2,981	26,250	26,300	3,584	3,226	3,584	3,431	29,250	29,300	4,056	3,676	4,056	3,881
23,300	23,350	3,141	2,784	3,141	2,989	26,300	26,350	3,591	3,234	3,591	3,439	29,300	29,350	4,069	3,684	4,069	3,889
23,350	23,400	3,149	2,791	3,149	2,996	26,350	26,400	3,599	3,241	3,599	3,446	29,350	29,400	4,081	3,691	4,081	3,896
23,400	23,450	3,156	2,799	3,156	3,004	26,400	26,450	3,606	3,249	3,606	3,454	29,400	29,450	4,094	3,699	4,094	3,904
23,450	23,500	3,164	2,806	3,164	3,011	26,450	26,500	3,614	3,256	3,614	3,461	29,450	29,500	4,106	3,706	4,106	3,911
23,500	23,550	3,171	2,814	3,171	3,019	26,500	26,550	3,621	3,264	3,621	3,469	29,500	29,550	4,119	3,714	4,119	3,919
23,550	23,600	3,179	2,821	3,179	3,026	26,550	26,600	3,629	3,271	3,629	3,476	29,550	29,600	4,131	3,721	4,131	3,926
23,600	23,650	3,186	2,829	3,186	3,034	26,600	26,650	3,636	3,279	3,636	3,484	29,600	29,650	4,144	3,729	4,144	3,934
23,650	23,700	3,194	2,836	3,194	3,041	26,650	26,700	3,644	3,286	3,644	3,491	29,650	29,700	4,156	3,736	4,156	3,941
23,700	23,750	3,201	2,844	3,201	3,049	26,700	26,750	3,651	3,294	3,651	3,499	29,700	29,750	4,169	3,744	4,169	3,949
23,750	23,800	3,209	2,851	3,209	3,056	26,750	26,800	3,659	3,301	3,659	3,506	29,750	29,800	4,181	3,751	4,181	3,956
23,800	23,850	3,216	2,859	3,216	3,064	26,800	26,850	3,666	3,309	3,666	3,514	29,800	29,850	4,194	3,759	4,194	3,964
23,850	23,900	3,224	2,866	3,224	3,071	26,850	26,900	3,674	3,316	3,674	3,521	29,850	29,900	4,206	3,766	4,206	3,971
23,900	23,950	3,231	2,874	3,231	3,079	26,900	26,950	3,681	3,324	3,681	3,529	29,900	29,950	4,219	3,774	4,219	3,979
23,950	24,000	3,239	2,881	3,239	3,086	26,950	27,000	3,689	3,331	3,689	3,536	29,950	30,000	4,231	3,781	4,231	3,986
24,000						**27,000**						**30,000**					
24,000	24,050	3,246	2,889	3,246	3,094	27,000	27,050	3,696	3,339	3,696	3,544	30,000	30,050	4,244	3,789	4,244	3,994
24,050	24,100	3,254	2,896	3,254	3,101	27,050	27,100	3,704	3,346	3,704	3,551	30,050	30,100	4,256	3,796	4,256	4,001
24,100	24,150	3,261	2,904	3,261	3,109	27,100	27,150	3,711	3,354	3,711	3,559	30,100	30,150	4,269	3,804	4,269	4,009
24,150	24,200	3,269	2,911	3,269	3,116	27,150	27,200	3,719	3,361	3,719	3,566	30,150	30,200	4,281	3,811	4,281	4,016
24,200	24,250	3,276	2,919	3,276	3,124	27,200	27,250	3,726	3,369	3,726	3,574	30,200	30,250	4,294	3,819	4,294	4,024
24,250	24,300	3,284	2,926	3,284	3,131	27,250	27,300	3,734	3,376	3,734	3,581	30,250	30,300	4,306	3,826	4,306	4,031
24,300	24,350	3,291	2,934	3,291	3,139	27,300	27,350	3,741	3,384	3,741	3,589	30,300	30,350	4,319	3,834	4,319	4,039
24,350	24,400	3,299	2,941	3,299	3,146	27,350	27,400	3,749	3,391	3,749	3,596	30,350	30,400	4,331	3,841	4,331	4,046
24,400	24,450	3,306	2,949	3,306	3,154	27,400	27,450	3,756	3,399	3,756	3,604	30,400	30,450	4,344	3,849	4,344	4,054
24,450	24,500	3,314	2,956	3,314	3,161	27,450	27,500	3,764	3,406	3,764	3,611	30,450	30,500	4,356	3,856	4,356	4,061
24,500	24,550	3,321	2,964	3,321	3,169	27,500	27,550	3,771	3,414	3,771	3,619	30,500	30,550	4,369	3,864	4,369	4,069
24,550	24,600	3,329	2,971	3,329	3,176	27,550	27,600	3,779	3,421	3,779	3,626	30,550	30,600	4,381	3,871	4,381	4,076
24,600	24,650	3,336	2,979	3,336	3,184	27,600	27,650	3,786	3,429	3,786	3,634	30,600	30,650	4,394	3,879	4,394	4,084
24,650	24,700	3,344	2,986	3,344	3,191	27,650	27,700	3,794	3,436	3,794	3,641	30,650	30,700	4,406	3,886	4,406	4,091
24,700	24,750	3,351	2,994	3,351	3,199	27,700	27,750	3,801	3,444	3,801	3,649	30,700	30,750	4,419	3,894	4,419	4,099
24,750	24,800	3,359	3,001	3,359	3,206	27,750	27,800	3,809	3,451	3,809	3,656	30,750	30,800	4,431	3,901	4,431	4,106
24,800	24,850	3,366	3,009	3,366	3,214	27,800	27,850	3,816	3,459	3,816	3,664	30,800	30,850	4,444	3,909	4,444	4,114
24,850	24,900	3,374	3,016	3,374	3,221	27,850	27,900	3,824	3,466	3,824	3,671	30,850	30,900	4,456	3,916	4,456	4,121
24,900	24,950	3,381	3,024	3,381	3,229	27,900	27,950	3,831	3,474	3,831	3,679	30,900	30,950	4,469	3,924	4,469	4,129
24,950	25,000	3,389	3,031	3,389	3,236	27,950	28,000	3,839	3,481	3,839	3,686	30,950	31,000	4,481	3,931	4,481	4,136
25,000						**28,000**						**31,000**					
25,000	25,050	3,396	3,039	3,396	3,244	28,000	28,050	3,846	3,489	3,846	3,694	31,000	31,050	4,494	3,939	4,494	4,144
25,050	25,100	3,404	3,046	3,404	3,251	28,050	28,100	3,854	3,496	3,854	3,701	31,050	31,100	4,506	3,946	4,506	4,151
25,100	25,150	3,411	3,054	3,411	3,259	28,100	28,150	3,861	3,504	3,861	3,709	31,100	31,150	4,519	3,954	4,519	4,159
25,150	25,200	3,419	3,061	3,419	3,266	28,150	28,200	3,869	3,511	3,869	3,716	31,150	31,200	4,531	3,961	4,531	4,166
25,200	25,250	3,426	3,069	3,426	3,274	28,200	28,250	3,876	3,519	3,876	3,724	31,200	31,250	4,544	3,969	4,544	4,174
25,250	25,300	3,434	3,076	3,434	3,281	28,250	28,300	3,884	3,526	3,884	3,731	31,250	31,300	4,556	3,976	4,556	4,181
25,300	25,350	3,441	3,084	3,441	3,289	28,300	28,350	3,891	3,534	3,891	3,739	31,300	31,350	4,569	3,984	4,569	4,189
25,350	25,400	3,449	3,091	3,449	3,296	28,350	28,400	3,899	3,541	3,899	3,746	31,350	31,400	4,581	3,991	4,581	4,196
25,400	25,450	3,456	3,099	3,456	3,304	28,400	28,450	3,906	3,549	3,906	3,754	31,400	31,450	4,594	3,999	4,594	4,204
25,450	25,500	3,464	3,106	3,464	3,311	28,450	28,500	3,914	3,556	3,914	3,761	31,450	31,500	4,606	4,006	4,606	4,211
25,500	25,550	3,471	3,114	3,471	3,319	28,500	28,550	3,921	3,564	3,921	3,769	31,500	31,550	4,619	4,014	4,619	4,219
25,550	25,600	3,479	3,121	3,479	3,326	28,550	28,600	3,929	3,571	3,929	3,776	31,550	31,600	4,631	4,021	4,631	4,226
25,600	25,650	3,486	3,129	3,486	3,334	28,600	28,650	3,936	3,579	3,936	3,784	31,600	31,650	4,644	4,029	4,644	4,234
25,650	25,700	3,494	3,136	3,494	3,341	28,650	28,700	3,944	3,586	3,944	3,791	31,650	31,700	4,656	4,036	4,656	4,241
25,700	25,750	3,501	3,144	3,501	3,349	28,700	28,750	3,951	3,594	3,951	3,799	31,700	31,750	4,669	4,044	4,669	4,249
25,750	25,800	3,509	3,151	3,509	3,356	28,750	28,800	3,959	3,601	3,959	3,806	31,750	31,800	4,681	4,051	4,681	4,256
25,800	25,850	3,516	3,159	3,516	3,364	28,800	28,850	3,966	3,609	3,966	3,814	31,800	31,850	4,694	4,059	4,694	4,264
25,850	25,900	3,524	3,166	3,524	3,371	28,850	28,900	3,974	3,616	3,974	3,821	31,850	31,900	4,706	4,066	4,706	4,271
25,900	25,950	3,531	3,174	3,531	3,379	28,900	28,950	3,981	3,624	3,981	3,829	31,900	31,950	4,719	4,074	4,719	4,279
25,950	26,000	3,539	3,181	3,539	3,386	28,950	29,000	3,989	3,631	3,989	3,836	31,950	32,000	4,731	4,081	4,731	4,286

* This column must also be used by a qualifying widow(er).

(Continued on page 64)

2004 Tax Table—Continued

If line 42 (taxable income) is— At least	But less than	And you are— Single	Married filing jointly*	Married filing separately	Head of a household
					Your tax is—

32,000

At least	But less than	Single	Married filing jointly*	Married filing separately	Head of a household
32,000	32,050	4,744	4,089	4,744	4,294
32,050	32,100	4,756	4,096	4,756	4,301
32,100	32,150	4,769	4,104	4,769	4,309
32,150	32,200	4,781	4,111	4,781	4,316
32,200	32,250	4,794	4,119	4,794	4,324
32,250	32,300	4,806	4,126	4,806	4,331
32,300	32,350	4,819	4,134	4,819	4,339
32,350	32,400	4,831	4,141	4,831	4,346
32,400	32,450	4,844	4,149	4,844	4,354
32,450	32,500	4,856	4,156	4,856	4,361
32,500	32,550	4,869	4,164	4,869	4,369
32,550	32,600	4,881	4,171	4,881	4,376
32,600	32,650	4,894	4,179	4,894	4,384
32,650	32,700	4,906	4,186	4,906	4,391
32,700	32,750	4,919	4,194	4,919	4,399
32,750	32,800	4,931	4,201	4,931	4,406
32,800	32,850	4,944	4,209	4,944	4,414
32,850	32,900	4,956	4,216	4,956	4,421
32,900	32,950	4,969	4,224	4,969	4,429
32,950	33,000	4,981	4,231	4,981	4,436

33,000

At least	But less than	Single	Married filing jointly*	Married filing separately	Head of a household
33,000	33,050	4,994	4,239	4,994	4,444
33,050	33,100	5,006	4,246	5,006	4,451
33,100	33,150	5,019	4,254	5,019	4,459
33,150	33,200	5,031	4,261	5,031	4,466
33,200	33,250	5,044	4,269	5,044	4,474
33,250	33,300	5,056	4,276	5,056	4,481
33,300	33,350	5,069	4,284	5,069	4,489
33,350	33,400	5,081	4,291	5,081	4,496
33,400	33,450	5,094	4,299	5,094	4,504
33,450	33,500	5,106	4,306	5,106	4,511
33,500	33,550	5,119	4,314	5,119	4,519
33,550	33,600	5,131	4,321	5,131	4,526
33,600	33,650	5,144	4,329	5,144	4,534
33,650	33,700	5,156	4,336	5,156	4,541
33,700	33,750	5,169	4,344	5,169	4,549
33,750	33,800	5,181	4,351	5,181	4,556
33,800	33,850	5,194	4,359	5,194	4,564
33,850	33,900	5,206	4,366	5,206	4,571
33,900	33,950	5,219	4,374	5,219	4,579
33,950	34,000	5,231	4,381	5,231	4,586

34,000

At least	But less than	Single	Married filing jointly*	Married filing separately	Head of a household
34,000	34,050	5,244	4,389	5,244	4,594
34,050	34,100	5,256	4,396	5,256	4,601
34,100	34,150	5,269	4,404	5,269	4,609
34,150	34,200	5,281	4,411	5,281	4,616
34,200	34,250	5,294	4,419	5,294	4,624
34,250	34,300	5,306	4,426	5,306	4,631
34,300	34,350	5,319	4,434	5,319	4,639
34,350	34,400	5,331	4,441	5,331	4,646
34,400	34,450	5,344	4,449	5,344	4,654
34,450	34,500	5,356	4,456	5,356	4,661
34,500	34,550	5,369	4,464	5,369	4,669
34,550	34,600	5,381	4,471	5,381	4,676
34,600	34,650	5,394	4,479	5,394	4,684
34,650	34,700	5,406	4,486	5,406	4,691
34,700	34,750	5,419	4,494	5,419	4,699
34,750	34,800	5,431	4,501	5,431	4,706
34,800	34,850	5,444	4,509	5,444	4,714
34,850	34,900	5,456	4,516	5,456	4,721
34,900	34,950	5,469	4,524	5,469	4,729
34,950	35,000	5,481	4,531	5,481	4,736

35,000

At least	But less than	Single	Married filing jointly*	Married filing separately	Head of a household
35,000	35,050	5,494	4,539	5,494	4,744
35,050	35,100	5,506	4,546	5,506	4,751
35,100	35,150	5,519	4,554	5,519	4,759
35,150	35,200	5,531	4,561	5,531	4,766
35,200	35,250	5,544	4,569	5,544	4,774
35,250	35,300	5,556	4,576	5,556	4,781
35,300	35,350	5,569	4,584	5,569	4,789
35,350	35,400	5,581	4,591	5,581	4,796
35,400	35,450	5,594	4,599	5,594	4,804
35,450	35,500	5,606	4,606	5,606	4,811
35,500	35,550	5,619	4,614	5,619	4,819
35,550	35,600	5,631	4,621	5,631	4,826
35,600	35,650	5,644	4,629	5,644	4,834
35,650	35,700	5,656	4,636	5,656	4,841
35,700	35,750	5,669	4,644	5,669	4,849
35,750	35,800	5,681	4,651	5,681	4,856
35,800	35,850	5,694	4,659	5,694	4,864
35,850	35,900	5,706	4,666	5,706	4,871
35,900	35,950	5,719	4,674	5,719	4,879
35,950	36,000	5,731	4,681	5,731	4,886

36,000

At least	But less than	Single	Married filing jointly*	Married filing separately	Head of a household
36,000	36,050	5,744	4,689	5,744	4,894
36,050	36,100	5,756	4,696	5,756	4,901
36,100	36,150	5,769	4,704	5,769	4,909
36,150	36,200	5,781	4,711	5,781	4,916
36,200	36,250	5,794	4,719	5,794	4,924
36,250	36,300	5,806	4,726	5,806	4,931
36,300	36,350	5,819	4,734	5,819	4,939
36,350	36,400	5,831	4,741	5,831	4,946
36,400	36,450	5,844	4,749	5,844	4,954
36,450	36,500	5,856	4,756	5,856	4,961
36,500	36,550	5,869	4,764	5,869	4,969
36,550	36,600	5,881	4,771	5,881	4,976
36,600	36,650	5,894	4,779	5,894	4,984
36,650	36,700	5,906	4,786	5,906	4,991
36,700	36,750	5,919	4,794	5,919	4,999
36,750	36,800	5,931	4,801	5,931	5,006
36,800	36,850	5,944	4,809	5,944	5,014
36,850	36,900	5,956	4,816	5,956	5,021
36,900	36,950	5,969	4,824	5,969	5,029
36,950	37,000	5,981	4,831	5,981	5,036

37,000

At least	But less than	Single	Married filing jointly*	Married filing separately	Head of a household
37,000	37,050	5,994	4,839	5,994	5,044
37,050	37,100	6,006	4,846	6,006	5,051
37,100	37,150	6,019	4,854	6,019	5,059
37,150	37,200	6,031	4,861	6,031	5,066
37,200	37,250	6,044	4,869	6,044	5,074
37,250	37,300	6,056	4,876	6,056	5,081
37,300	37,350	6,069	4,884	6,069	5,089
37,350	37,400	6,081	4,891	6,081	5,096
37,400	37,450	6,094	4,899	6,094	5,104
37,450	37,500	6,106	4,906	6,106	5,111
37,500	37,550	6,119	4,914	6,119	5,119
37,550	37,600	6,131	4,921	6,131	5,126
37,600	37,650	6,144	4,929	6,144	5,134
37,650	37,700	6,156	4,936	6,156	5,141
37,700	37,750	6,169	4,944	6,169	5,149
37,750	37,800	6,181	4,951	6,181	5,156
37,800	37,850	6,194	4,959	6,194	5,164
37,850	37,900	6,206	4,966	6,206	5,171
37,900	37,950	6,219	4,974	6,219	5,179
37,950	38,000	6,231	4,981	6,231	5,186

38,000

At least	But less than	Single	Married filing jointly*	Married filing separately	Head of a household
38,000	38,050	6,244	4,989	6,244	5,194
38,050	38,100	6,256	4,996	6,256	5,201
38,100	38,150	6,269	5,004	6,269	5,209
38,150	38,200	6,281	5,011	6,281	5,216
38,200	38,250	6,294	5,019	6,294	5,224
38,250	38,300	6,306	5,026	6,306	5,231
38,300	38,350	6,319	5,034	6,319	5,239
38,350	38,400	6,331	5,041	6,331	5,246
38,400	38,450	6,344	5,049	6,344	5,254
38,450	38,500	6,356	5,056	6,356	5,261
38,500	38,550	6,369	5,064	6,369	5,269
38,550	38,600	6,381	5,071	6,381	5,276
38,600	38,650	6,394	5,079	6,394	5,284
38,650	38,700	6,406	5,086	6,406	5,291
38,700	38,750	6,419	5,094	6,419	5,299
38,750	38,800	6,431	5,101	6,431	5,306
38,800	38,850	6,444	5,109	6,444	5,314
38,850	38,900	6,456	5,116	6,456	5,321
38,900	38,950	6,469	5,124	6,469	5,331
38,950	39,000	6,481	5,131	6,481	5,344

39,000

At least	But less than	Single	Married filing jointly*	Married filing separately	Head of a household
39,000	39,050	6,494	5,139	6,494	5,356
39,050	39,100	6,506	5,146	6,506	5,369
39,100	39,150	6,519	5,154	6,519	5,381
39,150	39,200	6,531	5,161	6,531	5,394
39,200	39,250	6,544	5,169	6,544	5,406
39,250	39,300	6,556	5,176	6,556	5,419
39,300	39,350	6,569	5,184	6,569	5,431
39,350	39,400	6,581	5,191	6,581	5,444
39,400	39,450	6,594	5,199	6,594	5,456
39,450	39,500	6,606	5,206	6,606	5,469
39,500	39,550	6,619	5,214	6,619	5,481
39,550	39,600	6,631	5,221	6,631	5,494
39,600	39,650	6,644	5,229	6,644	5,506
39,650	39,700	6,656	5,236	6,656	5,519
39,700	39,750	6,669	5,244	6,669	5,531
39,750	39,800	6,681	5,251	6,681	5,544
39,800	39,850	6,694	5,259	6,694	5,556
39,850	39,900	6,706	5,266	6,706	5,569
39,900	39,950	6,719	5,274	6,719	5,581
39,950	40,000	6,731	5,281	6,731	5,594

40,000

At least	But less than	Single	Married filing jointly*	Married filing separately	Head of a household
40,000	40,050	6,744	5,289	6,744	5,606
40,050	40,100	6,756	5,296	6,756	5,619
40,100	40,150	6,769	5,304	6,769	5,631
40,150	40,200	6,781	5,311	6,781	5,644
40,200	40,250	6,794	5,319	6,794	5,656
40,250	40,300	6,806	5,326	6,806	5,669
40,300	40,350	6,819	5,334	6,819	5,681
40,350	40,400	6,831	5,341	6,831	5,694
40,400	40,450	6,844	5,349	6,844	5,706
40,450	40,500	6,856	5,356	6,856	5,719
40,500	40,550	6,869	5,364	6,869	5,731
40,550	40,600	6,881	5,371	6,881	5,744
40,600	40,650	6,894	5,379	6,894	5,756
40,650	40,700	6,906	5,386	6,906	5,769
40,700	40,750	6,919	5,394	6,919	5,781
40,750	40,800	6,931	5,401	6,931	5,794
40,800	40,850	6,944	5,409	6,944	5,806
40,850	40,900	6,956	5,416	6,956	5,819
40,900	40,950	6,969	5,424	6,969	5,831
40,950	41,000	6,981	5,431	6,981	5,844

* This column must also be used by a qualifying widow(er).

(Continued on page 65)

2004 Tax Table—*Continued*

If line 42 (taxable income) is—		And you are—			
At least	But less than	Single	Married filing jointly *	Married filing separately	Head of a household
		Your tax is—			
41,000					
41,000	41,050	6,994	5,439	6,994	5,856
41,050	41,100	7,006	5,446	7,006	5,869
41,100	41,150	7,019	5,454	7,019	5,881
41,150	41,200	7,031	5,461	7,031	5,894
41,200	41,250	7,044	5,469	7,044	5,906
41,250	41,300	7,056	5,476	7,056	5,919
41,300	41,350	7,069	5,484	7,069	5,931
41,350	41,400	7,081	5,491	7,081	5,944
41,400	41,450	7,094	5,499	7,094	5,956
41,450	41,500	7,106	5,506	7,106	5,969
41,500	41,550	7,119	5,514	7,119	5,981
41,550	41,600	7,131	5,521	7,131	5,994
41,600	41,650	7,144	5,529	7,144	6,006
41,650	41,700	7,156	5,536	7,156	6,019
41,700	41,750	7,169	5,544	7,169	6,031
41,750	41,800	7,181	5,551	7,181	6,044
41,800	41,850	7,194	5,559	7,194	6,056
41,850	41,900	7,206	5,566	7,206	6,069
41,900	41,950	7,219	5,574	7,219	6,081
41,950	42,000	7,231	5,581	7,231	6,094
42,000					
42,000	42,050	7,244	5,589	7,244	6,106
42,050	42,100	7,256	5,596	7,256	6,119
42,100	42,150	7,269	5,604	7,269	6,131
42,150	42,200	7,281	5,611	7,281	6,144
42,200	42,250	7,294	5,619	7,294	6,156
42,250	42,300	7,306	5,626	7,306	6,169
42,300	42,350	7,319	5,634	7,319	6,181
42,350	42,400	7,331	5,641	7,331	6,194
42,400	42,450	7,344	5,649	7,344	6,206
42,450	42,500	7,356	5,656	7,356	6,219
42,500	42,550	7,369	5,664	7,369	6,231
42,550	42,600	7,381	5,671	7,381	6,244
42,600	42,650	7,394	5,679	7,394	6,256
42,650	42,700	7,406	5,686	7,406	6,269
42,700	42,750	7,419	5,694	7,419	6,281
42,750	42,800	7,431	5,701	7,431	6,294
42,800	42,850	7,444	5,709	7,444	6,306
42,850	42,900	7,456	5,716	7,456	6,319
42,900	42,950	7,469	5,724	7,469	6,331
42,950	43,000	7,481	5,731	7,481	6,344
43,000					
43,000	43,050	7,494	5,739	7,494	6,356
43,050	43,100	7,506	5,746	7,506	6,369
43,100	43,150	7,519	5,754	7,519	6,381
43,150	43,200	7,531	5,761	7,531	6,394
43,200	43,250	7,544	5,769	7,544	6,406
43,250	43,300	7,556	5,776	7,556	6,419
43,300	43,350	7,569	5,784	7,569	6,431
43,350	43,400	7,581	5,791	7,581	6,444
43,400	43,450	7,594	5,799	7,594	6,456
43,450	43,500	7,606	5,806	7,606	6,469
43,500	43,550	7,619	5,814	7,619	6,481
43,550	43,600	7,631	5,821	7,631	6,494
43,600	43,650	7,644	5,829	7,644	6,506
43,650	43,700	7,656	5,836	7,656	6,519
43,700	43,750	7,669	5,844	7,669	6,531
43,750	43,800	7,681	5,851	7,681	6,544
43,800	43,850	7,694	5,859	7,694	6,556
43,850	43,900	7,706	5,866	7,706	6,569
43,900	43,950	7,719	5,874	7,719	6,581
43,950	44,000	7,731	5,881	7,731	6,594

If line 42 (taxable income) is—		And you are—			
At least	But less than	Single	Married filing jointly *	Married filing separately	Head of a household
		Your tax is—			
44,000					
44,000	44,050	7,744	5,889	7,744	6,606
44,050	44,100	7,756	5,896	7,756	6,619
44,100	44,150	7,769	5,904	7,769	6,631
44,150	44,200	7,781	5,911	7,781	6,644
44,200	44,250	7,794	5,919	7,794	6,656
44,250	44,300	7,806	5,926	7,806	6,669
44,300	44,350	7,819	5,934	7,819	6,681
44,350	44,400	7,831	5,941	7,831	6,694
44,400	44,450	7,844	5,949	7,844	6,706
44,450	44,500	7,856	5,956	7,856	6,719
44,500	44,550	7,869	5,964	7,869	6,731
44,550	44,600	7,881	5,971	7,881	6,744
44,600	44,650	7,894	5,979	7,894	6,756
44,650	44,700	7,906	5,986	7,906	6,769
44,700	44,750	7,919	5,994	7,919	6,781
44,750	44,800	7,931	6,001	7,931	6,794
44,800	44,850	7,944	6,009	7,944	6,806
44,850	44,900	7,956	6,016	7,956	6,819
44,900	44,950	7,969	6,024	7,969	6,831
44,950	45,000	7,981	6,031	7,981	6,844
45,000					
45,000	45,050	7,994	6,039	7,994	6,856
45,050	45,100	8,006	6,046	8,006	6,869
45,100	45,150	8,019	6,054	8,019	6,881
45,150	45,200	8,031	6,061	8,031	6,894
45,200	45,250	8,044	6,069	8,044	6,906
45,250	45,300	8,056	6,076	8,056	6,919
45,300	45,350	8,069	6,084	8,069	6,931
45,350	45,400	8,081	6,091	8,081	6,944
45,400	45,450	8,094	6,099	8,094	6,956
45,450	45,500	8,106	6,106	8,106	6,969
45,500	45,550	8,119	6,114	8,119	6,981
45,550	45,600	8,131	6,121	8,131	6,994
45,600	45,650	8,144	6,129	8,144	7,006
45,650	45,700	8,156	6,136	8,156	7,019
45,700	45,750	8,169	6,144	8,169	7,031
45,750	45,800	8,181	6,151	8,181	7,044
45,800	45,850	8,194	6,159	8,194	7,056
45,850	45,900	8,206	6,166	8,206	7,069
45,900	45,950	8,219	6,174	8,219	7,081
45,950	46,000	8,231	6,181	8,231	7,094
46,000					
46,000	46,050	8,244	6,189	8,244	7,106
46,050	46,100	8,256	6,196	8,256	7,119
46,100	46,150	8,269	6,204	8,269	7,131
46,150	46,200	8,281	6,211	8,281	7,144
46,200	46,250	8,294	6,219	8,294	7,156
46,250	46,300	8,306	6,226	8,306	7,169
46,300	46,350	8,319	6,234	8,319	7,181
46,350	46,400	8,331	6,241	8,331	7,194
46,400	46,450	8,344	6,249	8,344	7,206
46,450	46,500	8,356	6,256	8,356	7,219
46,500	46,550	8,369	6,264	8,369	7,231
46,550	46,600	8,381	6,271	8,381	7,244
46,600	46,650	8,394	6,279	8,394	7,256
46,650	46,700	8,406	6,286	8,406	7,269
46,700	46,750	8,419	6,294	8,419	7,281
46,750	46,800	8,431	6,301	8,431	7,294
46,800	46,850	8,444	6,309	8,444	7,306
46,850	46,900	8,456	6,316	8,456	7,319
46,900	46,950	8,469	6,324	8,469	7,331
46,950	47,000	8,481	6,331	8,481	7,344

If line 42 (taxable income) is—		And you are—			
At least	But less than	Single	Married filing jointly *	Married filing separately	Head of a household
		Your tax is—			
47,000					
47,000	47,050	8,494	6,339	8,494	7,356
47,050	47,100	8,506	6,346	8,506	7,369
47,100	47,150	8,519	6,354	8,519	7,381
47,150	47,200	8,531	6,361	8,531	7,394
47,200	47,250	8,544	6,369	8,544	7,406
47,250	47,300	8,556	6,376	8,556	7,419
47,300	47,350	8,569	6,384	8,569	7,431
47,350	47,400	8,581	6,391	8,581	7,444
47,400	47,450	8,594	6,399	8,594	7,456
47,450	47,500	8,606	6,406	8,606	7,469
47,500	47,550	8,619	6,414	8,619	7,481
47,550	47,600	8,631	6,421	8,631	7,494
47,600	47,650	8,644	6,429	8,644	7,506
47,650	47,700	8,656	6,436	8,656	7,519
47,700	47,750	8,669	6,444	8,669	7,531
47,750	47,800	8,681	6,451	8,681	7,544
47,800	47,850	8,694	6,459	8,694	7,556
47,850	47,900	8,706	6,466	8,706	7,569
47,900	47,950	8,719	6,474	8,719	7,581
47,950	48,000	8,731	6,481	8,731	7,594
48,000					
48,000	48,050	8,744	6,489	8,744	7,606
48,050	48,100	8,756	6,496	8,756	7,619
48,100	48,150	8,769	6,504	8,769	7,631
48,150	48,200	8,781	6,511	8,781	7,644
48,200	48,250	8,794	6,519	8,794	7,656
48,250	48,300	8,806	6,526	8,806	7,669
48,300	48,350	8,819	6,534	8,819	7,681
48,350	48,400	8,831	6,541	8,831	7,694
48,400	48,450	8,844	6,549	8,844	7,706
48,450	48,500	8,856	6,556	8,856	7,719
48,500	48,550	8,869	6,564	8,869	7,731
48,550	48,600	8,881	6,571	8,881	7,744
48,600	48,650	8,894	6,579	8,894	7,756
48,650	48,700	8,906	6,586	8,906	7,769
48,700	48,750	8,919	6,594	8,919	7,781
48,750	48,800	8,931	6,601	8,931	7,794
48,800	48,850	8,944	6,609	8,944	7,806
48,850	48,900	8,956	6,616	8,956	7,819
48,900	48,950	8,969	6,624	8,969	7,831
48,950	49,000	8,981	6,631	8,981	7,844
49,000					
49,000	49,050	8,994	6,639	8,994	7,856
49,050	49,100	9,006	6,646	9,006	7,869
49,100	49,150	9,019	6,654	9,019	7,881
49,150	49,200	9,031	6,661	9,031	7,894
49,200	49,250	9,044	6,669	9,044	7,906
49,250	49,300	9,056	6,676	9,056	7,919
49,300	49,350	9,069	6,684	9,069	7,931
49,350	49,400	9,081	6,691	9,081	7,944
49,400	49,450	9,094	6,699	9,094	7,956
49,450	49,500	9,106	6,706	9,106	7,969
49,500	49,550	9,119	6,714	9,119	7,981
49,550	49,600	9,131	6,721	9,131	7,994
49,600	49,650	9,144	6,729	9,144	8,006
49,650	49,700	9,156	6,736	9,156	8,019
49,700	49,750	9,169	6,744	9,169	8,031
49,750	49,800	9,181	6,751	9,181	8,044
49,800	49,850	9,194	6,759	9,194	8,056
49,850	49,900	9,206	6,766	9,206	8,069
49,900	49,950	9,219	6,774	9,219	8,081
49,950	50,000	9,231	6,781	9,231	8,094

* This column must also be used by a qualifying widow(er).

(Continued on page 66)

2004 Tax Table—Continued

50,000

At least	But less than	Single	Married filing jointly*	Married filing separately	Head of a household
50,000	50,050	9,244	6,789	9,244	8,106
50,050	50,100	9,256	6,796	9,256	8,119
50,100	50,150	9,269	6,804	9,269	8,131
50,150	50,200	9,281	6,811	9,281	8,144
50,200	50,250	9,294	6,819	9,294	8,156
50,250	50,300	9,306	6,826	9,306	8,169
50,300	50,350	9,319	6,834	9,319	8,181
50,350	50,400	9,331	6,841	9,331	8,194
50,400	50,450	9,344	6,849	9,344	8,206
50,450	50,500	9,356	6,856	9,356	8,219
50,500	50,550	9,369	6,864	9,369	8,231
50,550	50,600	9,381	6,871	9,381	8,244
50,600	50,650	9,394	6,879	9,394	8,256
50,650	50,700	9,406	6,886	9,406	8,269
50,700	50,750	9,419	6,894	9,419	8,281
50,750	50,800	9,431	6,901	9,431	8,294
50,800	50,850	9,444	6,909	9,444	8,306
50,850	50,900	9,456	6,916	9,456	8,319
50,900	50,950	9,469	6,924	9,469	8,331
50,950	51,000	9,481	6,931	9,481	8,344

51,000

At least	But less than	Single	Married filing jointly*	Married filing separately	Head of a household
51,000	51,050	9,494	6,939	9,494	8,356
51,050	51,100	9,506	6,946	9,506	8,369
51,100	51,150	9,519	6,954	9,519	8,381
51,150	51,200	9,531	6,961	9,531	8,394
51,200	51,250	9,544	6,969	9,544	8,406
51,250	51,300	9,556	6,976	9,556	8,419
51,300	51,350	9,569	6,984	9,569	8,431
51,350	51,400	9,581	6,991	9,581	8,444
51,400	51,450	9,594	6,999	9,594	8,456
51,450	51,500	9,606	7,006	9,606	8,469
51,500	51,550	9,619	7,014	9,619	8,481
51,550	51,600	9,631	7,021	9,631	8,494
51,600	51,650	9,644	7,029	9,644	8,506
51,650	51,700	9,656	7,036	9,656	8,519
51,700	51,750	9,669	7,044	9,669	8,531
51,750	51,800	9,681	7,051	9,681	8,544
51,800	51,850	9,694	7,059	9,694	8,556
51,850	51,900	9,706	7,066	9,706	8,569
51,900	51,950	9,719	7,074	9,719	8,581
51,950	52,000	9,731	7,081	9,731	8,594

52,000

At least	But less than	Single	Married filing jointly*	Married filing separately	Head of a household
52,000	52,050	9,744	7,089	9,744	8,606
52,050	52,100	9,756	7,096	9,756	8,619
52,100	52,150	9,769	7,104	9,769	8,631
52,150	52,200	9,781	7,111	9,781	8,644
52,200	52,250	9,794	7,119	9,794	8,656
52,250	52,300	9,806	7,126	9,806	8,669
52,300	52,350	9,819	7,134	9,819	8,681
52,350	52,400	9,831	7,141	9,831	8,694
52,400	52,450	9,844	7,149	9,844	8,706
52,450	52,500	9,856	7,156	9,856	8,719
52,500	52,550	9,869	7,164	9,869	8,731
52,550	52,600	9,881	7,171	9,881	8,744
52,600	52,650	9,894	7,179	9,894	8,756
52,650	52,700	9,906	7,186	9,906	8,769
52,700	52,750	9,919	7,194	9,919	8,781
52,750	52,800	9,931	7,201	9,931	8,794
52,800	52,850	9,944	7,209	9,944	8,806
52,850	52,900	9,956	7,216	9,956	8,819
52,900	52,950	9,969	7,224	9,969	8,831
52,950	53,000	9,981	7,231	9,981	8,844

53,000

At least	But less than	Single	Married filing jointly*	Married filing separately	Head of a household
53,000	53,050	9,994	7,239	9,994	8,856
53,050	53,100	10,006	7,246	10,006	8,869
53,100	53,150	10,019	7,254	10,019	8,881
53,150	53,200	10,031	7,261	10,031	8,894
53,200	53,250	10,044	7,269	10,044	8,906
53,250	53,300	10,056	7,276	10,056	8,919
53,300	53,350	10,069	7,284	10,069	8,931
53,350	53,400	10,081	7,291	10,081	8,944
53,400	53,450	10,094	7,299	10,094	8,956
53,450	53,500	10,106	7,306	10,106	8,969
53,500	53,550	10,119	7,314	10,119	8,981
53,550	53,600	10,131	7,321	10,131	8,994
53,600	53,650	10,144	7,329	10,144	9,006
53,650	53,700	10,156	7,336	10,156	9,019
53,700	53,750	10,169	7,344	10,169	9,031
53,750	53,800	10,181	7,351	10,181	9,044
53,800	53,850	10,194	7,359	10,194	9,056
53,850	53,900	10,206	7,366	10,206	9,069
53,900	53,950	10,219	7,374	10,219	9,081
53,950	54,000	10,231	7,381	10,231	9,094

54,000

At least	But less than	Single	Married filing jointly*	Married filing separately	Head of a household
54,000	54,050	10,244	7,389	10,244	9,106
54,050	54,100	10,256	7,396	10,256	9,119
54,100	54,150	10,269	7,404	10,269	9,131
54,150	54,200	10,281	7,411	10,281	9,144
54,200	54,250	10,294	7,419	10,294	9,156
54,250	54,300	10,306	7,426	10,306	9,169
54,300	54,350	10,319	7,434	10,319	9,181
54,350	54,400	10,331	7,441	10,331	9,194
54,400	54,450	10,344	7,449	10,344	9,206
54,450	54,500	10,356	7,456	10,356	9,219
54,500	54,550	10,369	7,464	10,369	9,231
54,550	54,600	10,381	7,471	10,381	9,244
54,600	54,650	10,394	7,479	10,394	9,256
54,650	54,700	10,406	7,486	10,406	9,269
54,700	54,750	10,419	7,494	10,419	9,281
54,750	54,800	10,431	7,501	10,431	9,294
54,800	54,850	10,444	7,509	10,444	9,306
54,850	54,900	10,456	7,516	10,456	9,319
54,900	54,950	10,469	7,524	10,469	9,331
54,950	55,000	10,481	7,531	10,481	9,344

55,000

At least	But less than	Single	Married filing jointly*	Married filing separately	Head of a household
55,000	55,050	10,494	7,539	10,494	9,356
55,050	55,100	10,506	7,546	10,506	9,369
55,100	55,150	10,519	7,554	10,519	9,381
55,150	55,200	10,531	7,561	10,531	9,394
55,200	55,250	10,544	7,569	10,544	9,406
55,250	55,300	10,556	7,576	10,556	9,419
55,300	55,350	10,569	7,584	10,569	9,431
55,350	55,400	10,581	7,591	10,581	9,444
55,400	55,450	10,594	7,599	10,594	9,456
55,450	55,500	10,606	7,606	10,606	9,469
55,500	55,550	10,619	7,614	10,619	9,481
55,550	55,600	10,631	7,621	10,631	9,494
55,600	55,650	10,644	7,629	10,644	9,506
55,650	55,700	10,656	7,636	10,656	9,519
55,700	55,750	10,669	7,644	10,669	9,531
55,750	55,800	10,681	7,651	10,681	9,544
55,800	55,850	10,694	7,659	10,694	9,556
55,850	55,900	10,706	7,666	10,706	9,569
55,900	55,950	10,719	7,674	10,719	9,581
55,950	56,000	10,731	7,681	10,731	9,594

56,000

At least	But less than	Single	Married filing jointly*	Married filing separately	Head of a household
56,000	56,050	10,744	7,689	10,744	9,606
56,050	56,100	10,756	7,696	10,756	9,619
56,100	56,150	10,769	7,704	10,769	9,631
56,150	56,200	10,781	7,711	10,781	9,644
56,200	56,250	10,794	7,719	10,794	9,656
56,250	56,300	10,806	7,726	10,806	9,669
56,300	56,350	10,819	7,734	10,819	9,681
56,350	56,400	10,831	7,741	10,831	9,694
56,400	56,450	10,844	7,749	10,844	9,706
56,450	56,500	10,856	7,756	10,856	9,719
56,500	56,550	10,869	7,764	10,869	9,731
56,550	56,600	10,881	7,771	10,881	9,744
56,600	56,650	10,894	7,779	10,894	9,756
56,650	56,700	10,906	7,786	10,906	9,769
56,700	56,750	10,919	7,794	10,919	9,781
56,750	56,800	10,931	7,801	10,931	9,794
56,800	56,850	10,944	7,809	10,944	9,806
56,850	56,900	10,956	7,816	10,956	9,819
56,900	56,950	10,969	7,824	10,969	9,831
56,950	57,000	10,981	7,831	10,981	9,844

57,000

At least	But less than	Single	Married filing jointly*	Married filing separately	Head of a household
57,000	57,050	10,994	7,839	10,994	9,856
57,050	57,100	11,006	7,846	11,006	9,869
57,100	57,150	11,019	7,854	11,019	9,881
57,150	57,200	11,031	7,861	11,031	9,894
57,200	57,250	11,044	7,869	11,044	9,906
57,250	57,300	11,056	7,876	11,056	9,919
57,300	57,350	11,069	7,884	11,069	9,931
57,350	57,400	11,081	7,891	11,081	9,944
57,400	57,450	11,094	7,899	11,094	9,956
57,450	57,500	11,106	7,906	11,106	9,969
57,500	57,550	11,119	7,914	11,119	9,981
57,550	57,600	11,131	7,921	11,131	9,994
57,600	57,650	11,144	7,929	11,144	10,006
57,650	57,700	11,156	7,936	11,156	10,019
57,700	57,750	11,169	7,944	11,169	10,031
57,750	57,800	11,181	7,951	11,181	10,044
57,800	57,850	11,194	7,959	11,194	10,056
57,850	57,900	11,206	7,966	11,206	10,069
57,900	57,950	11,219	7,974	11,219	10,081
57,950	58,000	11,231	7,981	11,231	10,094

58,000

At least	But less than	Single	Married filing jointly*	Married filing separately	Head of a household
58,000	58,050	11,244	7,989	11,244	10,106
58,050	58,100	11,256	7,996	11,256	10,119
58,100	58,150	11,269	8,006	11,269	10,131
58,150	58,200	11,281	8,019	11,281	10,144
58,200	58,250	11,294	8,031	11,294	10,156
58,250	58,300	11,306	8,044	11,306	10,169
58,300	58,350	11,319	8,056	11,319	10,181
58,350	58,400	11,331	8,069	11,331	10,194
58,400	58,450	11,344	8,081	11,344	10,206
58,450	58,500	11,356	8,094	11,356	10,219
58,500	58,550	11,369	8,106	11,369	10,231
58,550	58,600	11,381	8,119	11,381	10,244
58,600	58,650	11,394	8,131	11,394	10,256
58,650	58,700	11,406	8,144	11,408	10,269
58,700	58,750	11,419	8,156	11,422	10,281
58,750	58,800	11,431	8,169	11,436	10,294
58,800	58,850	11,444	8,181	11,450	10,306
58,850	58,900	11,456	8,194	11,464	10,319
58,900	58,950	11,469	8,206	11,478	10,331
58,950	59,000	11,481	8,219	11,492	10,344

* This column must also be used by a qualifying widow(er).

(Continued on page 67)

2004 Tax Table—*Continued*

* This column must also be used by a qualifying widow(er).

(Continued on page 68)

If line 42 (taxable income) is— At least	But less than	Single	Married filing jointly *	Married filing separately	Head of a household
59,000					
59,000	59,050	11,494	8,231	11,506	10,356
59,050	59,100	11,506	8,244	11,520	10,369
59,100	59,150	11,519	8,256	11,534	10,381
59,150	59,200	11,531	8,269	11,548	10,394
59,200	59,250	11,544	8,281	11,562	10,406
59,250	59,300	11,556	8,294	11,576	10,419
59,300	59,350	11,569	8,306	11,590	10,431
59,350	59,400	11,581	8,319	11,604	10,444
59,400	59,450	11,594	8,331	11,618	10,456
59,450	59,500	11,606	8,344	11,632	10,469
59,500	59,550	11,619	8,356	11,646	10,481
59,550	59,600	11,631	8,369	11,660	10,494
59,600	59,650	11,644	8,381	11,674	10,506
59,650	59,700	11,656	8,394	11,688	10,519
59,700	59,750	11,669	8,406	11,702	10,531
59,750	59,800	11,681	8,419	11,716	10,544
59,800	59,850	11,694	8,431	11,730	10,556
59,850	59,900	11,706	8,444	11,744	10,569
59,900	59,950	11,719	8,456	11,758	10,581
59,950	60,000	11,731	8,469	11,772	10,594
60,000					
60,000	60,050	11,744	8,481	11,786	10,606
60,050	60,100	11,756	8,494	11,800	10,619
60,100	60,150	11,769	8,506	11,814	10,631
60,150	60,200	11,781	8,519	11,828	10,644
60,200	60,250	11,794	8,531	11,842	10,656
60,250	60,300	11,806	8,544	11,856	10,669
60,300	60,350	11,819	8,556	11,870	10,681
60,350	60,400	11,831	8,569	11,884	10,694
60,400	60,450	11,844	8,581	11,898	10,706
60,450	60,500	11,856	8,594	11,912	10,719
60,500	60,550	11,869	8,606	11,926	10,731
60,550	60,600	11,881	8,619	11,940	10,744
60,600	60,650	11,894	8,631	11,954	10,756
60,650	60,700	11,906	8,644	11,968	10,769
60,700	60,750	11,919	8,656	11,982	10,781
60,750	60,800	11,931	8,669	11,996	10,794
60,800	60,850	11,944	8,681	12,010	10,806
60,850	60,900	11,956	8,694	12,024	10,819
60,900	60,950	11,969	8,706	12,038	10,831
60,950	61,000	11,981	8,719	12,052	10,844
61,000					
61,000	61,050	11,994	8,731	12,066	10,856
61,050	61,100	12,006	8,744	12,080	10,869
61,100	61,150	12,019	8,756	12,094	10,881
61,150	61,200	12,031	8,769	12,108	10,894
61,200	61,250	12,044	8,781	12,122	10,906
61,250	61,300	12,056	8,794	12,136	10,919
61,300	61,350	12,069	8,806	12,150	10,931
61,350	61,400	12,081	8,819	12,164	10,944
61,400	61,450	12,094	8,831	12,178	10,956
61,450	61,500	12,106	8,844	12,192	10,969
61,500	61,550	12,119	8,856	12,206	10,981
61,550	61,600	12,131	8,869	12,220	10,994
61,600	61,650	12,144	8,881	12,234	11,006
61,650	61,700	12,156	8,894	12,248	11,019
61,700	61,750	12,169	8,906	12,262	11,031
61,750	61,800	12,181	8,919	12,276	11,044
61,800	61,850	12,194	8,931	12,290	11,056
61,850	61,900	12,206	8,944	12,304	11,069
61,900	61,950	12,219	8,956	12,318	11,081
61,950	62,000	12,231	8,969	12,332	11,094

If line 42 (taxable income) is— At least	But less than	Single	Married filing jointly *	Married filing separately	Head of a household
62,000					
62,000	62,050	12,244	8,981	12,346	11,106
62,050	62,100	12,256	8,994	12,360	11,119
62,100	62,150	12,269	9,006	12,374	11,131
62,150	62,200	12,281	9,019	12,388	11,144
62,200	62,250	12,294	9,031	12,402	11,156
62,250	62,300	12,306	9,044	12,416	11,169
62,300	62,350	12,319	9,056	12,430	11,181
62,350	62,400	12,331	9,069	12,444	11,194
62,400	62,450	12,344	9,081	12,458	11,206
62,450	62,500	12,356	9,094	12,472	11,219
62,500	62,550	12,369	9,106	12,486	11,231
62,550	62,600	12,381	9,119	12,500	11,244
62,600	62,650	12,394	9,131	12,514	11,256
62,650	62,700	12,406	9,144	12,528	11,269
62,700	62,750	12,419	9,156	12,542	11,281
62,750	62,800	12,431	9,169	12,556	11,294
62,800	62,850	12,444	9,181	12,570	11,306
62,850	62,900	12,456	9,194	12,584	11,319
62,900	62,950	12,469	9,206	12,598	11,331
62,950	63,000	12,481	9,219	12,612	11,344
63,000					
63,000	63,050	12,494	9,231	12,626	11,356
63,050	63,100	12,506	9,244	12,640	11,369
63,100	63,150	12,519	9,256	12,654	11,381
63,150	63,200	12,531	9,269	12,668	11,394
63,200	63,250	12,544	9,281	12,682	11,406
63,250	63,300	12,556	9,294	12,696	11,419
63,300	63,350	12,569	9,306	12,710	11,431
63,350	63,400	12,581	9,319	12,724	11,444
63,400	63,450	12,594	9,331	12,738	11,456
63,450	63,500	12,606	9,344	12,752	11,469
63,500	63,550	12,619	9,356	12,766	11,481
63,550	63,600	12,631	9,369	12,780	11,494
63,600	63,650	12,644	9,381	12,794	11,506
63,650	63,700	12,656	9,394	12,808	11,519
63,700	63,750	12,669	9,406	12,822	11,531
63,750	63,800	12,681	9,419	12,836	11,544
63,800	63,850	12,694	9,431	12,850	11,556
63,850	63,900	12,706	9,444	12,864	11,569
63,900	63,950	12,719	9,456	12,878	11,581
63,950	64,000	12,731	9,469	12,892	11,594
64,000					
64,000	64,050	12,744	9,481	12,906	11,606
64,050	64,100	12,756	9,494	12,920	11,619
64,100	64,150	12,769	9,506	12,934	11,631
64,150	64,200	12,781	9,519	12,948	11,644
64,200	64,250	12,794	9,531	12,962	11,656
64,250	64,300	12,806	9,544	12,976	11,669
64,300	64,350	12,819	9,556	12,990	11,681
64,350	64,400	12,831	9,569	13,004	11,694
64,400	64,450	12,844	9,581	13,018	11,706
64,450	64,500	12,856	9,594	13,032	11,719
64,500	64,550	12,869	9,606	13,046	11,731
64,550	64,600	12,881	9,619	13,060	11,744
64,600	64,650	12,894	9,631	13,074	11,756
64,650	64,700	12,906	9,644	13,088	11,769
64,700	64,750	12,919	9,656	13,102	11,781
64,750	64,800	12,931	9,669	13,116	11,794
64,800	64,850	12,944	9,681	13,130	11,806
64,850	64,900	12,956	9,694	13,144	11,819
64,900	64,950	12,969	9,706	13,158	11,831
64,950	65,000	12,981	9,719	13,172	11,844

If line 42 (taxable income) is— At least	But less than	Single	Married filing jointly *	Married filing separately	Head of a household
65,000					
65,000	65,050	12,994	9,731	13,186	11,856
65,050	65,100	13,006	9,744	13,200	11,869
65,100	65,150	13,019	9,756	13,214	11,881
65,150	65,200	13,031	9,769	13,228	11,894
65,200	65,250	13,044	9,781	13,242	11,906
65,250	65,300	13,056	9,794	13,256	11,919
65,300	65,350	13,069	9,806	13,270	11,931
65,350	65,400	13,081	9,819	13,284	11,944
65,400	65,450	13,094	9,831	13,298	11,956
65,450	65,500	13,106	9,844	13,312	11,969
65,500	65,550	13,119	9,856	13,326	11,981
65,550	65,600	13,131	9,869	13,340	11,994
65,600	65,650	13,144	9,881	13,354	12,006
65,650	65,700	13,156	9,894	13,368	12,019
65,700	65,750	13,169	9,906	13,382	12,031
65,750	65,800	13,181	9,919	13,396	12,044
65,800	65,850	13,194	9,931	13,410	12,056
65,850	65,900	13,206	9,944	13,424	12,069
65,900	65,950	13,219	9,956	13,438	12,081
65,950	66,000	13,231	9,969	13,452	12,094
66,000					
66,000	66,050	13,244	9,981	13,466	12,106
66,050	66,100	13,256	9,994	13,480	12,119
66,100	66,150	13,269	10,006	13,494	12,131
66,150	66,200	13,281	10,019	13,508	12,144
66,200	66,250	13,294	10,031	13,522	12,156
66,250	66,300	13,306	10,044	13,536	12,169
66,300	66,350	13,319	10,056	13,550	12,181
66,350	66,400	13,331	10,069	13,564	12,194
66,400	66,450	13,344	10,081	13,578	12,206
66,450	66,500	13,356	10,094	13,592	12,219
66,500	66,550	13,369	10,106	13,606	12,231
66,550	66,600	13,381	10,119	13,620	12,244
66,600	66,650	13,394	10,131	13,634	12,256
66,650	66,700	13,406	10,144	13,648	12,269
66,700	66,750	13,419	10,156	13,662	12,281
66,750	66,800	13,431	10,169	13,676	12,294
66,800	66,850	13,444	10,181	13,690	12,306
66,850	66,900	13,456	10,194	13,704	12,319
66,900	66,950	13,469	10,206	13,718	12,331
66,950	67,000	13,481	10,219	13,732	12,344
67,000					
67,000	67,050	13,494	10,231	13,746	12,356
67,050	67,100	13,506	10,244	13,760	12,369
67,100	67,150	13,519	10,256	13,774	12,381
67,150	67,200	13,531	10,269	13,788	12,394
67,200	67,250	13,544	10,281	13,802	12,406
67,250	67,300	13,556	10,294	13,816	12,419
67,300	67,350	13,569	10,306	13,830	12,431
67,350	67,400	13,581	10,319	13,844	12,444
67,400	67,450	13,594	10,331	13,858	12,456
67,450	67,500	13,606	10,344	13,872	12,469
67,500	67,550	13,619	10,356	13,886	12,481
67,550	67,600	13,631	10,369	13,900	12,494
67,600	67,650	13,644	10,381	13,914	12,506
67,650	67,700	13,656	10,394	13,928	12,519
67,700	67,750	13,669	10,406	13,942	12,531
67,750	67,800	13,681	10,419	13,956	12,544
67,800	67,850	13,694	10,431	13,970	12,556
67,850	67,900	13,706	10,444	13,984	12,569
67,900	67,950	13,719	10,456	13,998	12,581
67,950	68,000	13,731	10,469	14,012	12,594

2004 Tax Table—Continued

68,000 / 71,000 / 74,000

If line 42 (taxable income) is—		And you are—				If line 42 (taxable income) is—		And you are—				If line 42 (taxable income) is—		And you are—			
At least	But less than	Single	Married filing jointly *	Married filing separately	Head of a house-hold	At least	But less than	Single	Married filing jointly *	Married filing separately	Head of a house-hold	At least	But less than	Single	Married filing jointly *	Married filing separately	Head of a house-hold
		Your tax is—						Your tax is—						Your tax is—			
68,000	68,050	13,744	10,481	14,026	12,606	71,000	71,050	14,514	11,231	14,866	13,356	74,000	74,050	15,354	11,981	15,706	14,106
68,050	68,100	13,756	10,494	14,040	12,619	71,050	71,100	14,528	11,244	14,880	13,369	74,050	74,100	15,368	11,994	15,720	14,119
68,100	68,150	13,769	10,506	14,054	12,631	71,100	71,150	14,542	11,256	14,894	13,381	74,100	74,150	15,382	12,006	15,734	14,131
68,150	68,200	13,781	10,519	14,068	12,644	71,150	71,200	14,556	11,269	14,908	13,394	74,150	74,200	15,396	12,019	15,748	14,144
68,200	68,250	13,794	10,531	14,082	12,656	71,200	71,250	14,570	11,281	14,922	13,406	74,200	74,250	15,410	12,031	15,762	14,156
68,250	68,300	13,806	10,544	14,096	12,669	71,250	71,300	14,584	11,294	14,936	13,419	74,250	74,300	15,424	12,044	15,776	14,169
68,300	68,350	13,819	10,556	14,110	12,681	71,300	71,350	14,598	11,306	14,950	13,431	74,300	74,350	15,438	12,056	15,790	14,181
68,350	68,400	13,831	10,569	14,124	12,694	71,350	71,400	14,612	11,319	14,964	13,444	74,350	74,400	15,452	12,069	15,804	14,194
68,400	68,450	13,844	10,581	14,138	12,706	71,400	71,450	14,626	11,331	14,978	13,456	74,400	74,450	15,466	12,081	15,818	14,206
68,450	68,500	13,856	10,594	14,152	12,719	71,450	71,500	14,640	11,344	14,992	13,469	74,450	74,500	15,480	12,094	15,832	14,219
68,500	68,550	13,869	10,606	14,166	12,731	71,500	71,550	14,654	11,356	15,006	13,481	74,500	74,550	15,494	12,106	15,846	14,231
68,550	68,600	13,881	10,619	14,180	12,744	71,550	71,600	14,668	11,369	15,020	13,494	74,550	74,600	15,508	12,119	15,860	14,244
68,600	68,650	13,894	10,631	14,194	12,756	71,600	71,650	14,682	11,381	15,034	13,506	74,600	74,650	15,522	12,131	15,874	14,256
68,650	68,700	13,906	10,644	14,208	12,769	71,650	71,700	14,696	11,394	15,048	13,519	74,650	74,700	15,536	12,144	15,888	14,269
68,700	68,750	13,919	10,656	14,222	12,781	71,700	71,750	14,710	11,406	15,062	13,531	74,700	74,750	15,550	12,156	15,902	14,281
68,750	68,800	13,931	10,669	14,236	12,794	71,750	71,800	14,724	11,419	15,076	13,544	74,750	74,800	15,564	12,169	15,916	14,294
68,800	68,850	13,944	10,681	14,250	12,806	71,800	71,850	14,738	11,431	15,090	13,556	74,800	74,850	15,578	12,181	15,930	14,306
68,850	68,900	13,956	10,694	14,264	12,819	71,850	71,900	14,752	11,444	15,104	13,569	74,850	74,900	15,592	12,194	15,944	14,319
68,900	68,950	13,969	10,706	14,278	12,831	71,900	71,950	14,766	11,456	15,118	13,581	74,900	74,950	15,606	12,206	15,958	14,331
68,950	69,000	13,981	10,719	14,292	12,844	71,950	72,000	14,780	11,469	15,132	13,594	74,950	75,000	15,620	12,219	15,972	14,344

69,000 / 72,000 / 75,000

At least	But less than	Single	Married filing jointly *	Married filing separately	Head of a house-hold	At least	But less than	Single	Married filing jointly *	Married filing separately	Head of a house-hold	At least	But less than	Single	Married filing jointly *	Married filing separately	Head of a house-hold
69,000	69,050	13,994	10,731	14,306	12,856	72,000	72,050	14,794	11,481	15,146	13,606	75,000	75,050	15,634	12,231	15,986	14,356
69,050	69,100	14,006	10,744	14,320	12,869	72,050	72,100	14,808	11,494	15,160	13,619	75,050	75,100	15,648	12,244	16,000	14,369
69,100	69,150	14,019	10,756	14,334	12,881	72,100	72,150	14,822	11,506	15,174	13,631	75,100	75,150	15,662	12,256	16,014	14,381
69,150	69,200	14,031	10,769	14,348	12,894	72,150	72,200	14,836	11,519	15,188	13,644	75,150	75,200	15,676	12,269	16,028	14,394
69,200	69,250	14,044	10,781	14,362	12,906	72,200	72,250	14,850	11,531	15,202	13,656	75,200	75,250	15,690	12,281	16,042	14,406
69,250	69,300	14,056	10,794	14,376	12,919	72,250	72,300	14,864	11,544	15,216	13,669	75,250	75,300	15,704	12,294	16,056	14,419
69,300	69,350	14,069	10,806	14,390	12,931	72,300	72,350	14,878	11,556	15,230	13,681	75,300	75,350	15,718	12,306	16,070	14,431
69,350	69,400	14,081	10,819	14,404	12,944	72,350	72,400	14,892	11,569	15,244	13,694	75,350	75,400	15,732	12,319	16,084	14,444
69,400	69,450	14,094	10,831	14,418	12,956	72,400	72,450	14,906	11,581	15,258	13,706	75,400	75,450	15,746	12,331	16,098	14,456
69,450	69,500	14,106	10,844	14,432	12,969	72,450	72,500	14,920	11,594	15,272	13,719	75,450	75,500	15,760	12,344	16,112	14,469
69,500	69,550	14,119	10,856	14,446	12,981	72,500	72,550	14,934	11,606	15,286	13,731	75,500	75,550	15,774	12,356	16,126	14,481
69,550	69,600	14,131	10,869	14,460	12,994	72,550	72,600	14,948	11,619	15,300	13,744	75,550	75,600	15,788	12,369	16,140	14,494
69,600	69,650	14,144	10,881	14,474	13,006	72,600	72,650	14,962	11,631	15,314	13,756	75,600	75,650	15,802	12,381	16,154	14,506
69,650	69,700	14,156	10,894	14,488	13,019	72,650	72,700	14,976	11,644	15,328	13,769	75,650	75,700	15,816	12,394	16,168	14,519
69,700	69,750	14,169	10,906	14,502	13,031	72,700	72,750	14,990	11,656	15,342	13,781	75,700	75,750	15,830	12,406	16,182	14,531
69,750	69,800	14,181	10,919	14,516	13,044	72,750	72,800	15,004	11,669	15,356	13,794	75,750	75,800	15,844	12,419	16,196	14,544
69,800	69,850	14,194	10,931	14,530	13,056	72,800	72,850	15,018	11,681	15,370	13,806	75,800	75,850	15,858	12,431	16,210	14,556
69,850	69,900	14,206	10,944	14,544	13,069	72,850	72,900	15,032	11,694	15,384	13,819	75,850	75,900	15,872	12,444	16,224	14,569
69,900	69,950	14,219	10,956	14,558	13,081	72,900	72,950	15,046	11,706	15,398	13,831	75,900	75,950	15,886	12,456	16,238	14,581
69,950	70,000	14,231	10,969	14,572	13,094	72,950	73,000	15,060	11,719	15,412	13,844	75,950	76,000	15,900	12,469	16,252	14,594

70,000 / 73,000 / 76,000

At least	But less than	Single	Married filing jointly *	Married filing separately	Head of a house-hold	At least	But less than	Single	Married filing jointly *	Married filing separately	Head of a house-hold	At least	But less than	Single	Married filing jointly *	Married filing separately	Head of a house-hold
70,000	70,050	14,244	10,981	14,586	13,106	73,000	73,050	15,074	11,731	15,426	13,856	76,000	76,050	15,914	12,481	16,266	14,606
70,050	70,100	14,256	10,994	14,600	13,119	73,050	73,100	15,088	11,744	15,440	13,869	76,050	76,100	15,928	12,494	16,280	14,619
70,100	70,150	14,269	11,006	14,614	13,131	73,100	73,150	15,102	11,756	15,454	13,881	76,100	76,150	15,942	12,506	16,294	14,631
70,150	70,200	14,281	11,019	14,628	13,144	73,150	73,200	15,116	11,769	15,468	13,894	76,150	76,200	15,956	12,519	16,308	14,644
70,200	70,250	14,294	11,031	14,642	13,156	73,200	73,250	15,130	11,781	15,482	13,906	76,200	76,250	15,970	12,531	16,322	14,656
70,250	70,300	14,306	11,044	14,656	13,169	73,250	73,300	15,144	11,794	15,496	13,919	76,250	76,300	15,984	12,544	16,336	14,669
70,300	70,350	14,319	11,056	14,670	13,181	73,300	73,350	15,158	11,806	15,510	13,931	76,300	76,350	15,998	12,556	16,350	14,681
70,350	70,400	14,332	11,069	14,684	13,194	73,350	73,400	15,172	11,819	15,524	13,944	76,350	76,400	16,012	12,569	16,364	14,694
70,400	70,450	14,346	11,081	14,698	13,206	73,400	73,450	15,186	11,831	15,538	13,956	76,400	76,450	16,026	12,581	16,378	14,706
70,450	70,500	14,360	11,094	14,712	13,219	73,450	73,500	15,200	11,844	15,552	13,969	76,450	76,500	16,040	12,594	16,392	14,719
70,500	70,550	14,374	11,106	14,726	13,231	73,500	73,550	15,214	11,856	15,566	13,981	76,500	76,550	16,054	12,606	16,406	14,731
70,550	70,600	14,388	11,119	14,740	13,244	73,550	73,600	15,228	11,869	15,580	13,994	76,550	76,600	16,068	12,619	16,420	14,744
70,600	70,650	14,402	11,131	14,754	13,256	73,600	73,650	15,242	11,881	15,594	14,006	76,600	76,650	16,082	12,631	16,434	14,756
70,650	70,700	14,416	11,144	14,768	13,269	73,650	73,700	15,256	11,894	15,608	14,019	76,650	76,700	16,096	12,644	16,448	14,769
70,700	70,750	14,430	11,156	14,782	13,281	73,700	73,750	15,270	11,906	15,622	14,031	76,700	76,750	16,110	12,656	16,462	14,781
70,750	70,800	14,444	11,169	14,796	13,294	73,750	73,800	15,284	11,919	15,636	14,044	76,750	76,800	16,124	12,669	16,476	14,794
70,800	70,850	14,458	11,181	14,810	13,306	73,800	73,850	15,298	11,931	15,650	14,056	76,800	76,850	16,138	12,681	16,490	14,806
70,850	70,900	14,472	11,194	14,824	13,319	73,850	73,900	15,312	11,944	15,664	14,069	76,850	76,900	16,152	12,694	16,504	14,819
70,900	70,950	14,486	11,206	14,838	13,331	73,900	73,950	15,326	11,956	15,678	14,081	76,900	76,950	16,166	12,706	16,518	14,831
70,950	71,000	14,500	11,219	14,852	13,344	73,950	74,000	15,340	11,969	15,692	14,094	76,950	77,000	16,180	12,719	16,532	14,844

* This column must also be used by a qualifying widow(er).

(Continued on page 69)

2004 Tax Table—Continued

If line 42 (taxable income) is—		And you are—				If line 42 (taxable income) is—		And you are—				If line 42 (taxable income) is—		And you are—			
At least	But less than	Single	Married filing jointly *	Married filing separately *	Head of a household	At least	But less than	Single	Married filing jointly *	Married filing separately *	Head of a household	At least	But less than	Single	Married filing jointly *	Married filing separately *	Head of a household
		Your tax is—						Your tax is—						Your tax is—			
77,000						**80,000**						**83,000**					
77,000	77,050	16,194	12,731	16,546	14,856	80,000	80,050	17,034	13,481	17,386	15,606	83,000	83,050	17,874	14,231	18,226	16,356
77,050	77,100	16,208	12,744	16,560	14,869	80,050	80,100	17,048	13,494	17,400	15,619	83,050	83,100	17,888	14,244	18,240	16,369
77,100	77,150	16,222	12,756	16,574	14,881	80,100	80,150	17,062	13,506	17,414	15,631	83,100	83,150	17,902	14,256	18,254	16,381
77,150	77,200	16,236	12,769	16,588	14,894	80,150	80,200	17,076	13,519	17,428	15,644	83,150	83,200	17,916	14,269	18,268	16,394
77,200	77,250	16,250	12,781	16,602	14,906	80,200	80,250	17,090	13,531	17,442	15,656	83,200	83,250	17,930	14,281	18,282	16,406
77,250	77,300	16,264	12,794	16,616	14,919	80,250	80,300	17,104	13,544	17,456	15,669	83,250	83,300	17,944	14,294	18,296	16,419
77,300	77,350	16,278	12,806	16,630	14,931	80,300	80,350	17,118	13,556	17,470	15,681	83,300	83,350	17,958	14,306	18,310	16,431
77,350	77,400	16,292	12,819	16,644	14,944	80,350	80,400	17,132	13,569	17,484	15,694	83,350	83,400	17,972	14,319	18,324	16,444
77,400	77,450	16,306	12,831	16,658	14,956	80,400	80,450	17,146	13,581	17,498	15,706	83,400	83,450	17,986	14,331	18,338	16,456
77,450	77,500	16,320	12,844	16,672	14,969	80,450	80,500	17,160	13,594	17,512	15,719	83,450	83,500	18,000	14,344	18,352	16,469
77,500	77,550	16,334	12,856	16,686	14,981	80,500	80,550	17,174	13,606	17,526	15,731	83,500	83,550	18,014	14,356	18,366	16,481
77,550	77,600	16,348	12,869	16,700	14,994	80,550	80,600	17,188	13,619	17,540	15,744	83,550	83,600	18,028	14,369	18,380	16,494
77,600	77,650	16,362	12,881	16,714	15,006	80,600	80,650	17,202	13,631	17,554	15,756	83,600	83,650	18,042	14,381	18,394	16,506
77,650	77,700	16,376	12,894	16,728	15,019	80,650	80,700	17,216	13,644	17,568	15,769	83,650	83,700	18,056	14,394	18,408	16,519
77,700	77,750	16,390	12,906	16,742	15,031	80,700	80,750	17,230	13,656	17,582	15,781	83,700	83,750	18,070	14,406	18,422	16,531
77,750	77,800	16,404	12,919	16,756	15,044	80,750	80,800	17,244	13,669	17,596	15,794	83,750	83,800	18,084	14,419	18,436	16,544
77,800	77,850	16,418	12,931	16,770	15,056	80,800	80,850	17,258	13,681	17,610	15,806	83,800	83,850	18,098	14,431	18,450	16,556
77,850	77,900	16,432	12,944	16,784	15,069	80,850	80,900	17,272	13,694	17,624	15,819	83,850	83,900	18,112	14,444	18,464	16,569
77,900	77,950	16,446	12,956	16,798	15,081	80,900	80,950	17,286	13,706	17,638	15,831	83,900	83,950	18,126	14,456	18,478	16,581
77,950	78,000	16,460	12,969	16,812	15,094	80,950	81,000	17,300	13,719	17,652	15,844	83,950	84,000	18,140	14,469	18,492	16,594
78,000						**81,000**						**84,000**					
78,000	78,050	16,474	12,981	16,826	15,106	81,000	81,050	17,314	13,731	17,666	15,856	84,000	84,050	18,154	14,481	18,506	16,606
78,050	78,100	16,488	12,994	16,840	15,119	81,050	81,100	17,328	13,744	17,680	15,869	84,050	84,100	18,168	14,494	18,520	16,619
78,100	78,150	16,502	13,006	16,854	15,131	81,100	81,150	17,342	13,756	17,694	15,881	84,100	84,150	18,182	14,506	18,534	16,631
78,150	78,200	16,516	13,019	16,868	15,144	81,150	81,200	17,356	13,769	17,708	15,894	84,150	84,200	18,196	14,519	18,548	16,644
78,200	78,250	16,530	13,031	16,882	15,156	81,200	81,250	17,370	13,781	17,722	15,906	84,200	84,250	18,210	14,531	18,562	16,656
78,250	78,300	16,544	13,044	16,896	15,169	81,250	81,300	17,384	13,794	17,736	15,919	84,250	84,300	18,224	14,544	18,576	16,669
78,300	78,350	16,558	13,056	16,910	15,181	81,300	81,350	17,398	13,806	17,750	15,931	84,300	84,350	18,238	14,556	18,590	16,681
78,350	78,400	16,572	13,069	16,924	15,194	81,350	81,400	17,412	13,819	17,764	15,944	84,350	84,400	18,252	14,569	18,604	16,694
78,400	78,450	16,586	13,081	16,938	15,206	81,400	81,450	17,426	13,831	17,778	15,956	84,400	84,450	18,266	14,581	18,618	16,706
78,450	78,500	16,600	13,094	16,952	15,219	81,450	81,500	17,440	13,844	17,792	15,969	84,450	84,500	18,280	14,594	18,632	16,719
78,500	78,550	16,614	13,106	16,966	15,231	81,500	81,550	17,454	13,856	17,806	15,981	84,500	84,550	18,294	14,606	18,646	16,731
78,550	78,600	16,628	13,119	16,980	15,244	81,550	81,600	17,468	13,869	17,820	15,994	84,550	84,600	18,308	14,619	18,660	16,744
78,600	78,650	16,642	13,131	16,994	15,256	81,600	81,650	17,482	13,881	17,834	16,006	84,600	84,650	18,322	14,631	18,674	16,756
78,650	78,700	16,656	13,144	17,008	15,269	81,650	81,700	17,496	13,894	17,848	16,019	84,650	84,700	18,336	14,644	18,688	16,769
78,700	78,750	16,670	13,156	17,022	15,281	81,700	81,750	17,510	13,906	17,862	16,031	84,700	84,750	18,350	14,656	18,702	16,781
78,750	78,800	16,684	13,169	17,036	15,294	81,750	81,800	17,524	13,919	17,876	16,044	84,750	84,800	18,364	14,669	18,716	16,794
78,800	78,850	16,698	13,181	17,050	15,306	81,800	81,850	17,538	13,931	17,890	16,056	84,800	84,850	18,378	14,681	18,730	16,806
78,850	78,900	16,712	13,194	17,064	15,319	81,850	81,900	17,552	13,944	17,904	16,069	84,850	84,900	18,392	14,694	18,744	16,819
78,900	78,950	16,726	13,206	17,078	15,331	81,900	81,950	17,566	13,956	17,918	16,081	84,900	84,950	18,406	14,706	18,758	16,831
78,950	79,000	16,740	13,219	17,092	15,344	81,950	82,000	17,580	13,969	17,932	16,094	84,950	85,000	18,420	14,719	18,772	16,844
79,000						**82,000**						**85,000**					
79,000	79,050	16,754	13,231	17,106	15,356	82,000	82,050	17,594	13,981	17,946	16,106	85,000	85,050	18,434	14,731	18,786	16,856
79,050	79,100	16,768	13,244	17,120	15,369	82,050	82,100	17,608	13,994	17,960	16,119	85,050	85,100	18,448	14,744	18,800	16,869
79,100	79,150	16,782	13,256	17,134	15,381	82,100	82,150	17,622	14,006	17,974	16,131	85,100	85,150	18,462	14,756	18,814	16,881
79,150	79,200	16,796	13,269	17,148	15,394	82,150	82,200	17,636	14,019	17,988	16,144	85,150	85,200	18,476	14,769	18,828	16,894
79,200	79,250	16,810	13,281	17,162	15,406	82,200	82,250	17,650	14,031	18,002	16,156	85,200	85,250	18,490	14,781	18,842	16,906
79,250	79,300	16,824	13,294	17,176	15,419	82,250	82,300	17,664	14,044	18,016	16,169	85,250	85,300	18,504	14,794	18,856	16,919
79,300	79,350	16,838	13,306	17,190	15,431	82,300	82,350	17,678	14,056	18,030	16,181	85,300	85,350	18,518	14,806	18,870	16,931
79,350	79,400	16,852	13,319	17,204	15,444	82,350	82,400	17,692	14,069	18,044	16,194	85,350	85,400	18,532	14,819	18,884	16,944
79,400	79,450	16,866	13,331	17,218	15,456	82,400	82,450	17,706	14,081	18,058	16,206	85,400	85,450	18,546	14,831	18,898	16,956
79,450	79,500	16,880	13,344	17,232	15,469	82,450	82,500	17,720	14,094	18,072	16,219	85,450	85,500	18,560	14,844	18,912	16,969
79,500	79,550	16,894	13,356	17,246	15,481	82,500	82,550	17,734	14,106	18,086	16,231	85,500	85,550	18,574	14,856	18,926	16,981
79,550	79,600	16,908	13,369	17,260	15,494	82,550	82,600	17,748	14,119	18,100	16,244	85,550	85,600	18,588	14,869	18,940	16,994
79,600	79,650	16,922	13,381	17,274	15,506	82,600	82,650	17,762	14,131	18,114	16,256	85,600	85,650	18,602	14,881	18,954	17,006
79,650	79,700	16,936	13,394	17,288	15,519	82,650	82,700	17,776	14,144	18,128	16,269	85,650	85,700	18,616	14,894	18,968	17,019
79,700	79,750	16,950	13,406	17,302	15,531	82,700	82,750	17,790	14,156	18,142	16,281	85,700	85,750	18,630	14,906	18,982	17,031
79,750	79,800	16,964	13,419	17,316	15,544	82,750	82,800	17,804	14,169	18,156	16,294	85,750	85,800	18,644	14,919	18,996	17,044
79,800	79,850	16,978	13,431	17,330	15,556	82,800	82,850	17,818	14,181	18,170	16,306	85,800	85,850	18,658	14,931	19,010	17,056
79,850	79,900	16,992	13,444	17,344	15,569	82,850	82,900	17,832	14,194	18,184	16,319	85,850	85,900	18,672	14,944	19,024	17,069
79,900	79,950	17,006	13,456	17,358	15,581	82,900	82,950	17,846	14,206	18,198	16,331	85,900	85,950	18,686	14,956	19,038	17,081
79,950	80,000	17,020	13,469	17,372	15,594	82,950	83,000	17,860	14,219	18,212	16,344	85,950	86,000	18,700	14,969	19,052	17,094

* This column must also be used by a qualifying widow(er).

(Continued on page 70)

2004 Tax Table—Continued

86,000 / 89,000 / 92,000

If line 42 (taxable income) is— At least	But less than	Single	Married filing jointly *	Married filing separately	Head of a household
86,000					
86,000	86,050	18,714	14,981	19,066	17,106
86,050	86,100	18,728	14,994	19,080	17,119
86,100	86,150	18,742	15,006	19,094	17,131
86,150	86,200	18,756	15,019	19,108	17,144
86,200	86,250	18,770	15,031	19,122	17,156
86,250	86,300	18,784	15,044	19,136	17,169
86,300	86,350	18,798	15,056	19,150	17,181
86,350	86,400	18,812	15,069	19,164	17,194
86,400	86,450	18,826	15,081	19,178	17,206
86,450	86,500	18,840	15,094	19,192	17,219
86,500	86,550	18,854	15,106	19,206	17,231
86,550	86,600	18,868	15,119	19,220	17,244
86,600	86,650	18,882	15,131	19,234	17,256
86,650	86,700	18,896	15,144	19,248	17,269
86,700	86,750	18,910	15,156	19,262	17,281
86,750	86,800	18,924	15,169	19,276	17,294
86,800	86,850	18,938	15,181	19,290	17,306
86,850	86,900	18,952	15,194	19,304	17,319
86,900	86,950	18,966	15,206	19,318	17,331
86,950	87,000	18,980	15,219	19,332	17,344
87,000					
87,000	87,050	18,994	15,231	19,346	17,356
87,050	87,100	19,008	15,244	19,360	17,369
87,100	87,150	19,022	15,256	19,374	17,381
87,150	87,200	19,036	15,269	19,388	17,394
87,200	87,250	19,050	15,281	19,402	17,406
87,250	87,300	19,064	15,294	19,416	17,419
87,300	87,350	19,078	15,306	19,430	17,431
87,350	87,400	19,092	15,319	19,444	17,444
87,400	87,450	19,106	15,331	19,458	17,456
87,450	87,500	19,120	15,344	19,472	17,469
87,500	87,550	19,134	15,356	19,486	17,481
87,550	87,600	19,148	15,369	19,500	17,494
87,600	87,650	19,162	15,381	19,514	17,506
87,650	87,700	19,176	15,394	19,528	17,519
87,700	87,750	19,190	15,406	19,542	17,531
87,750	87,800	19,204	15,419	19,556	17,544
87,800	87,850	19,218	15,431	19,570	17,556
87,850	87,900	19,232	15,444	19,584	17,569
87,900	87,950	19,246	15,456	19,598	17,581
87,950	88,000	19,260	15,469	19,612	17,594
88,000					
88,000	88,050	19,274	15,481	19,626	17,606
88,050	88,100	19,288	15,494	19,640	17,619
88,100	88,150	19,302	15,506	19,654	17,631
88,150	88,200	19,316	15,519	19,668	17,644
88,200	88,250	19,330	15,531	19,682	17,656
88,250	88,300	19,344	15,544	19,696	17,669
88,300	88,350	19,358	15,556	19,710	17,681
88,350	88,400	19,372	15,569	19,724	17,694
88,400	88,450	19,386	15,581	19,738	17,706
88,450	88,500	19,400	15,594	19,752	17,719
88,500	88,550	19,414	15,606	19,766	17,731
88,550	88,600	19,428	15,619	19,780	17,744
88,600	88,650	19,442	15,631	19,794	17,756
88,650	88,700	19,456	15,644	19,808	17,769
88,700	88,750	19,470	15,656	19,822	17,781
88,750	88,800	19,484	15,669	19,836	17,794
88,800	88,850	19,498	15,681	19,850	17,806
88,850	88,900	19,512	15,694	19,864	17,819
88,900	88,950	19,526	15,706	19,878	17,831
88,950	89,000	19,540	15,719	19,892	17,844

89,000 / 90,000 / 91,000

If line 42 (taxable income) is— At least	But less than	Single	Married filing jointly *	Married filing separately	Head of a household
89,000					
89,000	89,050	19,554	15,731	19,906	17,856
89,050	89,100	19,568	15,744	19,920	17,869
89,100	89,150	19,582	15,756	19,934	17,881
89,150	89,200	19,596	15,769	19,948	17,894
89,200	89,250	19,610	15,781	19,962	17,906
89,250	89,300	19,624	15,794	19,976	17,919
89,300	89,350	19,638	15,806	19,990	17,931
89,350	89,400	19,652	15,819	20,006	17,944
89,400	89,450	19,666	15,831	20,023	17,956
89,450	89,500	19,680	15,844	20,039	17,969
89,500	89,550	19,694	15,856	20,056	17,981
89,550	89,600	19,708	15,869	20,072	17,994
89,600	89,650	19,722	15,881	20,089	18,006
89,650	89,700	19,736	15,894	20,105	18,019
89,700	89,750	19,750	15,906	20,122	18,031
89,750	89,800	19,764	15,919	20,138	18,044
89,800	89,850	19,778	15,931	20,155	18,056
89,850	89,900	19,792	15,944	20,171	18,069
89,900	89,950	19,806	15,956	20,188	18,081
89,950	90,000	19,820	15,969	20,204	18,094
90,000					
90,000	90,050	19,834	15,981	20,221	18,106
90,050	90,100	19,848	15,994	20,237	18,119
90,100	90,150	19,862	16,006	20,254	18,131
90,150	90,200	19,876	16,019	20,270	18,144
90,200	90,250	19,890	16,031	20,287	18,156
90,250	90,300	19,904	16,044	20,303	18,169
90,300	90,350	19,918	16,056	20,320	18,181
90,350	90,400	19,932	16,069	20,336	18,194
90,400	90,450	19,946	16,081	20,353	18,206
90,450	90,500	19,960	16,094	20,369	18,219
90,500	90,550	19,974	16,106	20,386	18,231
90,550	90,600	19,988	16,119	20,402	18,244
90,600	90,650	20,002	16,131	20,419	18,256
90,650	90,700	20,016	16,144	20,435	18,269
90,700	90,750	20,030	16,156	20,452	18,281
90,750	90,800	20,044	16,169	20,468	18,294
90,800	90,850	20,058	16,181	20,485	18,306
90,850	90,900	20,072	16,194	20,501	18,319
90,900	90,950	20,086	16,206	20,518	18,331
90,950	91,000	20,100	16,219	20,534	18,344
91,000					
91,000	91,050	20,114	16,231	20,551	18,356
91,050	91,100	20,128	16,244	20,567	18,369
91,100	91,150	20,142	16,256	20,584	18,381
91,150	91,200	20,156	16,269	20,600	18,394
91,200	91,250	20,170	16,281	20,617	18,406
91,250	91,300	20,184	16,294	20,633	18,419
91,300	91,350	20,198	16,306	20,650	18,431
91,350	91,400	20,212	16,319	20,666	18,444
91,400	91,450	20,226	16,331	20,683	18,456
91,450	91,500	20,240	16,344	20,699	18,469
91,500	91,550	20,254	16,356	20,716	18,481
91,550	91,600	20,268	16,369	20,732	18,494
91,600	91,650	20,282	16,381	20,749	18,506
91,650	91,700	20,296	16,394	20,765	18,519
91,700	91,750	20,310	16,406	20,782	18,531
91,750	91,800	20,324	16,419	20,798	18,544
91,800	91,850	20,338	16,431	20,815	18,556
91,850	91,900	20,352	16,444	20,831	18,569
91,900	91,950	20,366	16,456	20,848	18,581
91,950	92,000	20,380	16,469	20,864	18,594

92,000 / 93,000 / 94,000

If line 42 (taxable income) is— At least	But less than	Single	Married filing jointly *	Married filing separately	Head of a household
92,000					
92,000	92,050	20,394	16,481	20,881	18,606
92,050	92,100	20,408	16,494	20,897	18,619
92,100	92,150	20,422	16,506	20,914	18,631
92,150	92,200	20,436	16,519	20,930	18,644
92,200	92,250	20,450	16,531	20,947	18,656
92,250	92,300	20,464	16,544	20,963	18,669
92,300	92,350	20,478	16,556	20,980	18,681
92,350	92,400	20,492	16,569	20,996	18,694
92,400	92,450	20,506	16,581	21,013	18,706
92,450	92,500	20,520	16,594	21,029	18,719
92,500	92,550	20,534	16,606	21,046	18,731
92,550	92,600	20,548	16,619	21,062	18,744
92,600	92,650	20,562	16,631	21,079	18,756
92,650	92,700	20,576	16,644	21,095	18,769
92,700	92,750	20,590	16,656	21,112	18,781
92,750	92,800	20,604	16,669	21,128	18,794
92,800	92,850	20,618	16,681	21,145	18,806
92,850	92,900	20,632	16,694	21,161	18,819
92,900	92,950	20,646	16,706	21,178	18,831
92,950	93,000	20,660	16,719	21,194	18,844
93,000					
93,000	93,050	20,674	16,731	21,211	18,856
93,050	93,100	20,688	16,744	21,227	18,869
93,100	93,150	20,702	16,756	21,244	18,881
93,150	93,200	20,716	16,769	21,260	18,894
93,200	93,250	20,730	16,781	21,277	18,906
93,250	93,300	20,744	16,794	21,293	18,919
93,300	93,350	20,758	16,806	21,310	18,931
93,350	93,400	20,772	16,819	21,326	18,944
93,400	93,450	20,786	16,831	21,343	18,956
93,450	93,500	20,800	16,844	21,359	18,969
93,500	93,550	20,814	16,856	21,376	18,981
93,550	93,600	20,828	16,869	21,392	18,994
93,600	93,650	20,842	16,881	21,409	19,006
93,650	93,700	20,856	16,894	21,425	19,019
93,700	93,750	20,870	16,906	21,442	19,031
93,750	93,800	20,884	16,919	21,458	19,044
93,800	93,850	20,898	16,931	21,475	19,056
93,850	93,900	20,912	16,944	21,491	19,069
93,900	93,950	20,926	16,956	21,508	19,081
93,950	94,000	20,940	16,969	21,524	19,094
94,000					
94,000	94,050	20,954	16,981	21,541	19,106
94,050	94,100	20,968	16,994	21,557	19,119
94,100	94,150	20,982	17,006	21,574	19,131
94,150	94,200	20,996	17,019	21,590	19,144
94,200	94,250	21,010	17,031	21,607	19,156
94,250	94,300	21,024	17,044	21,623	19,169
94,300	94,350	21,038	17,056	21,640	19,181
94,350	94,400	21,052	17,069	21,656	19,194
94,400	94,450	21,066	17,081	21,673	19,206
94,450	94,500	21,080	17,094	21,689	19,219
94,500	94,550	21,094	17,106	21,706	19,231
94,550	94,600	21,108	17,119	21,722	19,244
94,600	94,650	21,122	17,131	21,739	19,256
94,650	94,700	21,136	17,144	21,755	19,269
94,700	94,750	21,150	17,156	21,772	19,281
94,750	94,800	21,164	17,169	21,788	19,294
94,800	94,850	21,178	17,181	21,805	19,306
94,850	94,900	21,192	17,194	21,821	19,319
94,900	94,950	21,206	17,206	21,838	19,331
94,950	95,000	21,220	17,219	21,854	19,344

* This column must also be used by a qualifying widow(er).

(Continued on page 71)

2004 Tax Table—*Continued*

If line 42 (taxable income) is—		And you are—				If line 42 (taxable income) is—		And you are—			
At least	But less than	Single	Married filing jointly *	Married filing separately	Head of a household	At least	But less than	Single	Married filing jointly *	Married filing separately	Head of a household
		Your tax is—						Your tax is—			

95,000 / 98,000

At least	But less than	Single	MFJ	MFS	HoH	At least	But less than	Single	MFJ	MFS	HoH
95,000	95,050	21,234	17,231	21,871	19,356	98,000	98,050	22,074	17,981	22,861	20,106
95,050	95,100	21,248	17,244	21,887	19,369	98,050	98,100	22,088	17,994	22,877	20,119
95,100	95,150	21,262	17,256	21,904	19,381	98,100	98,150	22,102	18,006	22,894	20,131
95,150	95,200	21,276	17,269	21,920	19,394	98,150	98,200	22,116	18,019	22,910	20,144
95,200	95,250	21,290	17,281	21,937	19,406	98,200	98,250	22,130	18,031	22,927	20,156
95,250	95,300	21,304	17,294	21,953	19,419	98,250	98,300	22,144	18,044	22,943	20,169
95,300	95,350	21,318	17,306	21,970	19,431	98,300	98,350	22,158	18,056	22,960	20,181
95,350	95,400	21,332	17,319	21,986	19,444	98,350	98,400	22,172	18,069	22,976	20,194
95,400	95,450	21,346	17,331	22,003	19,456	98,400	98,450	22,186	18,081	22,993	20,206
95,450	95,500	21,360	17,344	22,019	19,469	98,450	98,500	22,200	18,094	23,009	20,219
95,500	95,550	21,374	17,356	22,036	19,481	98,500	98,550	22,214	18,106	23,026	20,231
95,550	95,600	21,388	17,369	22,052	19,494	98,550	98,600	22,228	18,119	23,042	20,244
95,600	95,650	21,402	17,381	22,069	19,506	98,600	98,650	22,242	18,131	23,059	20,256
95,650	95,700	21,416	17,394	22,085	19,519	98,650	98,700	22,256	18,144	23,075	20,269
95,700	95,750	21,430	17,406	22,102	19,531	98,700	98,750	22,270	18,156	23,092	20,281
95,750	95,800	21,444	17,419	22,118	19,544	98,750	98,800	22,284	18,169	23,108	20,294
95,800	95,850	21,458	17,431	22,135	19,556	98,800	98,850	22,298	18,181	23,125	20,306
95,850	95,900	21,472	17,444	22,151	19,569	98,850	98,900	22,312	18,194	23,141	20,319
95,900	95,950	21,486	17,456	22,168	19,581	98,900	98,950	22,326	18,206	23,158	20,331
95,950	96,000	21,500	17,469	22,184	19,594	98,950	99,000	22,340	18,219	23,174	20,344

96,000 / 99,000

At least	But less than	Single	MFJ	MFS	HoH	At least	But less than	Single	MFJ	MFS	HoH
96,000	96,050	21,514	17,481	22,201	19,606	99,000	99,050	22,354	18,231	23,191	20,356
96,050	96,100	21,528	17,494	22,217	19,619	99,050	99,100	22,368	18,244	23,207	20,369
96,100	96,150	21,542	17,506	22,234	19,631	99,100	99,150	22,382	18,256	23,224	20,381
96,150	96,200	21,556	17,519	22,250	19,644	99,150	99,200	22,396	18,269	23,240	20,394
96,200	96,250	21,570	17,531	22,267	19,656	99,200	99,250	22,410	18,281	23,257	20,406
96,250	96,300	21,584	17,544	22,283	19,669	99,250	99,300	22,424	18,294	23,273	20,419
96,300	96,350	21,598	17,556	22,300	19,681	99,300	99,350	22,438	18,306	23,290	20,431
96,350	96,400	21,612	17,569	22,316	19,694	99,350	99,400	22,452	18,319	23,306	20,444
96,400	96,450	21,626	17,581	22,333	19,706	99,400	99,450	22,466	18,331	23,323	20,456
96,450	96,500	21,640	17,594	22,349	19,719	99,450	99,500	22,480	18,344	23,339	20,469
96,500	96,550	21,654	17,606	22,366	19,731	99,500	99,550	22,494	18,356	23,356	20,481
96,550	96,600	21,668	17,619	22,382	19,744	99,550	99,600	22,508	18,369	23,372	20,494
96,600	96,650	21,682	17,631	22,399	19,756	99,600	99,650	22,522	18,381	23,389	20,506
96,650	96,700	21,696	17,644	22,415	19,769	99,650	99,700	22,536	18,394	23,405	20,519
96,700	96,750	21,710	17,656	22,432	19,781	99,700	99,750	22,550	18,406	23,422	20,531
96,750	96,800	21,724	17,669	22,448	19,794	99,750	99,800	22,564	18,419	23,438	20,544
96,800	96,850	21,738	17,681	22,465	19,806	99,800	99,850	22,578	18,431	23,455	20,556
96,850	96,900	21,752	17,694	22,481	19,819	99,850	99,900	22,592	18,444	23,471	20,569
96,900	96,950	21,766	17,706	22,498	19,831	99,900	99,950	22,606	18,456	23,488	20,581
96,950	97,000	21,780	17,719	22,514	19,844	99,950	100,000	22,620	18,469	23,504	20,594

97,000

At least	But less than	Single	MFJ	MFS	HoH
97,000	97,050	21,794	17,731	22,531	19,856
97,050	97,100	21,808	17,744	22,547	19,869
97,100	97,150	21,822	17,756	22,564	19,881
97,150	97,200	21,836	17,769	22,580	19,894
97,200	97,250	21,850	17,781	22,597	19,906
97,250	97,300	21,864	17,794	22,613	19,919
97,300	97,350	21,878	17,806	22,630	19,931
97,350	97,400	21,892	17,819	22,646	19,944
97,400	97,450	21,906	17,831	22,663	19,956
97,450	97,500	21,920	17,844	22,679	19,969
97,500	97,550	21,934	17,856	22,696	19,981
97,550	97,600	21,948	17,869	22,712	19,994
97,600	97,650	21,962	17,881	22,729	20,006
97,650	97,700	21,976	17,894	22,745	20,019
97,700	97,750	21,990	17,906	22,762	20,031
97,750	97,800	22,004	17,919	22,778	20,044
97,800	97,850	22,018	17,931	22,795	20,056
97,850	97,900	22,032	17,944	22,811	20,069
97,900	97,950	22,046	17,956	22,828	20,081
97,950	98,000	22,060	17,969	22,844	20,094

$100,000 or over — use the Tax Computation Worksheet on page 72

* This column must also be used by a qualifying widow(er).

A-3   Unified Transfer Tax Rate Schedule

2004 Estate and Gift Tax Rates

If taxable transfer is Over	But not over	Tax liability	Of the Amount over
$ 0	$ 10,000	18%	$ 0
10,000	20,000	$ 1,800 + 20%	10,000
20,000	40,000	3,800 + 22%	20,000
40,000	60,000	8,200 + 24%	40,000
60,000	80,000	13,000 + 26%	60,000
80,000	100,000	18,200 + 28%	80,000
100,000	150,000	23,800 + 30%	100,000
150,000	250,000	38,800 + 32%	150,000
250,000	500,000	70,800 + 34%	250,000
500,000	750,000	155,800 + 37%	500,000
750,000	1,000,000	248,300 + 39%	750,000
1,000,000	1,250,000	345,800 + 41%	1,000,000
1,250,000	1,500,000	448,300 + 43%	1,250,000
1,500,000	2,000,000	555,800 + 45%	1,500,000
2,000,000	2,500,000	780,800 + 49%	2,000,000
	Over 2,500,000	1,025,800 + 50%	

Appendix A-4
Table S (4.4)
Single Life Factors Based on Life Table 90CM
Interest at 4.4 Percent

Age	Annuity	Life Estate	Remainder	Age	Annuity	Life Estate	Remainder
0	21.3340	.93870	.06130	55	13.9945	.61576	.38424
1	21.4784	.94505	.05495	56	13.7202	.60369	.39631
2	21.4394	.94333	.05667	57	13.4415	.59143	.40857
3	21.3934	.94131	.05869	58	13.1595	.57902	.42098
4	21.3428	.93908	.06092	59	12.8748	.56649	.43351
5	21.2885	.93669	.06331	60	12.5879	.55387	.44613
6	21.2312	.93417	.06583	61	12.2985	.54113	.45887
7	21.1706	.93151	.06849	62	12.0057	.52825	.47175
8	21.1071	.92871	.07129	63	11.7095	.51522	.48478
9	21.0402	.92577	.07423	64	11.4106	.50207	.49793
10	20.9697	.92266	.07734	65	11.1090	.48879	.51121
11	20.8958	.91941	.08059	66	10.8043	.47539	.52461
12	20.8187	.91602	.08398	67	10.4959	.46182	.53818
13	20.7392	.91252	.08748	68	10.1845	.44812	.55188
14	20.6586	.90898	.09102	69	9.8709	.43432	.56568
15	20.5774	.90540	.09460	70	9.5565	.42049	.57951
16	20.4960	.90182	.09818	71	9.2427	.40668	.59332
17	20.4139	.89821	.10179	72	8.9302	.39293	.60707
18	20.3308	.89455	.10545	73	8.6197	.37927	.62073
19	20.2453	.89079	.10921	74	8.3102	.36565	.63435
20	20.1569	.88690	.11310	75	8.0009	.35204	.64796
21	20.0652	.88287	.11713	76	7.6909	.33840	.66160
22	19.9704	.87870	.12130	77	7.3803	.32474	.67526
23	19.8719	.87437	.12563	78	7.0700	.31108	.68892
24	19.7695	.86986	.13014	79	6.7614	.29750	.70250
25	19.6627	.86516	.13484	80	6.4572	.28412	.71588
26	19.5514	.86026	.13974	81	6.1593	.27101	.72899
27	19.4352	.85515	.14485	82	5.8687	.25822	.74178
28	19.3145	.84984	.15016	83	5.5856	.24577	.75423
29	19.1893	.84433	.15567	84	5.3080	.23355	.76645
30	19.0595	.83862	.16138	85	5.0344	.22152	.77848
31	18.9254	.83272	.16728	86	4.7671	.20975	.79025
32	18.7865	.82661	.17339	87	4.5092	.19841	.80159
33	18.6426	.82028	.17972	88	4.2610	.18749	.81251
34	18.4938	.81373	.18627	89	4.0224	.17698	.82302
35	18.3393	.80693	.19307	90	3.7933	.16691	.83309
36	18.1796	.79990	.20010	91	3.5774	.15740	.84260
37	18.0143	.79263	.20737	92	3.3782	.14864	.85136
38	17.8431	.78510	.21490	93	3.1950	.14058	.85942
39	17.6659	.77730	.22270	94	3.0250	.13310	.86690
40	17.4824	.76922	.23078	95	2.8643	.12603	.87397
41	17.2921	.76085	.23915	96	2.7137	.11940	.88060
42	17.0951	.75218	.24782	97	2.5746	.11328	.88672
43	16.8914	.74322	.25678	98	2.4443	.10755	.89245
44	16.6811	.73397	.26603	99	2.3175	.10197	.89803
45	16.4648	.72445	.27555	100	2.1946	.09656	.90344
46	16.2425	.71467	.28533	101	2.0737	.09124	.90876
47	16.0147	.70465	.29535	102	1.9554	.08604	.91396
48	15.7811	.69437	.30563	103	1.8382	.08088	.91912
49	15.5419	.68385	.31615	104	1.7135	.07540	.92460
50	15.2968	.67306	.32694	105	1.5917	.07004	.92996
51	15.0459	.66202	.33798	106	1.4363	.06320	.93680
52	14.7901	.65076	.34924	107	1.2491	.05496	.94504
53	14.5295	.63930	.36070	108	.9620	.04233	.95767
54	14.2643	.62763	.37237	109	.4789	.02107	.97893

Appendix A-4
Table S (4.6)   Section 1
Single Life Factors Based on Life Table 90CM
Interest at 4.6 Percent

Age	Annuity	Life Estate	Remainder	Age	Annuity	Life Estate	Remainder
0	20.5247	.94414	.05586	55	13.6915	.62981	.37019
1	20.6670	.95068	.04932	56	13.4290	.61773	.38227
2	20.6330	.94912	.05088	57	13.1621	.60545	.39455
3	20.5923	.94725	.05275	58	12.8915	.59301	.40699
4	20.5475	.94518	.05482	59	12.6183	.58044	.41956
5	20.4990	.94295	.05705	60	12.3426	.56776	.43224
6	20.4477	.94059	.05941	61	12.0641	.55495	.44505
7	20.3934	.93809	.06191	62	11.7822	.54198	.45802
8	20.3363	.93547	.06453	63	11.4967	.52885	.47115
9	20.2760	.93269	.06731	64	11.2082	.51558	.48442
10	20.2122	.92976	.07024	65	10.9169	.50218	.49782
11	20.1453	.92669	.07331	66	10.6223	.48863	.51137
12	20.0754	.92347	.07653	67	10.3238	.47489	.52511
13	20.0032	.92015	.07985	68	10.0219	.46101	.53899
14	19.9300	.91678	.08322	69	9.7177	.44701	.55299
15	19.8562	.91339	.08661	70	9.4124	.43297	.56703
16	19.7824	.90999	.09001	71	9.1074	.41894	.58106
17	19.7079	.90656	.09344	72	8.8034	.40496	.59504
18	19.6325	.90309	.09691	73	8.5011	.39105	.60895
19	19.5549	.89953	.10047	74	8.1995	.37718	.62282
20	19.4746	.89583	.10417	75	7.8977	.36329	.63671
21	19.3911	.89199	.10801	76	7.5950	.34937	.65063
22	19.3046	.88601	.11199	77	7.2915	.33541	.66459
23	19.2148	.88388	.11612	78	6.9878	.32144	.67856
24	19.1211	.87957	.12043	79	6.6857	.30754	.69246
25	19.0232	.87507	.12493	80	6.3875	.29382	.70618
26	18.9212	.87037	.12963	81	6.0952	.28038	.71962
27	18.8143	.86546	.13454	82	5.8100	.26726	.73274
28	18.7032	.86035	.13965	83	5.5319	.25447	.74553
29	18.5877	.85503	.14497	84	5.2590	.24191	.75809
30	18.4679	.84952	.15048	85	4.9898	.22953	.77047
31	18.3438	.84382	.15618	86	4.7265	.21742	.78258
32	18.2153	.83790	.16210	87	4.4725	.20573	.79427
33	18.0818	.83176	.16824	88	4.2277	.19448	.80552
34	17.9435	.82540	.17460	89	3.9922	.18364	.81636
35	17.7998	.81879	.18121	90	3.7661	.17324	.82676
36	17.6510	.81195	.18805	91	3.5527	.16342	.83658
37	17.4968	.80486	.19514	92	3.3558	.15437	.84563
38	17.3368	.79749	.20251	93	3.1747	.14604	.85396
39	17.1710	.78987	.21013	94	3.0065	.13830	.86170
40	16.9990	.78195	.21805	95	2.8475	.13098	.86902
41	16.8204	.77374	.22626	96	2.6984	.12413	.87587
42	16.6351	.76522	.23478	97	2.5606	.11779	.88221
43	16.4434	.75640	.24360	98	2.4315	.11185	.88815
44	16.2450	.74727	.25273	99	2.3059	.10607	.89393
45	16.0408	.73788	.26212	100	2.1841	.10047	.89953
46	15.8306	.72821	.27179	101	2.0642	.09496	.90504
47	15.6149	.71829	.28171	102	1.9463	.08955	.91045
48	15.3935	.70810	.29190	103	1.8306	.08421	.91579
49	15.1665	.69766	.30234	104	1.7069	.07852	.92148
50	14.9336	.68694	.31306	105	1.5860	.07296	.92704
51	14.6949	.67596	.32404	106	1.4316	.06585	.93415
52	14.4512	.66475	.33525	107	1.2455	.05729	.94271
53	14.2026	.65332	.34668	108	.9597	.04415	.95585
54	13.9494	.64167	.35833	109	.4780	.02199	.97801

Section 1

Appendix A-4
Table S (4.8)
Single Life Factors Based on Life Table 90CM
Interest at 4.8 Percent

Age	Annuity	Life Estate	Remainder	Age	Annuity	Life Estate	Remainder
0	19.7689	.94891	.05109	55	13.3993	.64317	.35683
1	19.9088	.95562	.04436	56	13.1480	.63110	.36890
2	19.8792	.95420	.04580	57	12.8921	.61882	.38118
3	19.8433	.95248	.04752	58	12.6326	.60636	.39364
4	19.8034	.95056	.04944	59	12.3701	.59377	.40623
5	19.7601	.94848	.05152	60	12.1051	.58104	.41896
6	19.7141	.94628	.05372	61	11.8371	.56818	.43182
7	19.6653	.94393	.05607	62	11.5655	.55515	.44485
8	19.6139	.94147	.05853	63	11.2903	.54193	.45807
9	19.5594	.93885	.06115	64	11.0118	.52857	.47143
10	19.5017	.93608	.06392	65	10.7303	.51505	.48495
11	19.4410	.93317	.06683	66	10.4454	.50138	.49862
12	19.3774	.93011	.06989	67	10.1563	.48750	.51250
13	19.3117	.92696	.07304	68	9.8637	.47346	.52654
14	19.2451	.92376	.07624	69	9.5685	.45929	.54071
15	19.1780	.92054	.07946	70	9.2720	.44505	.55495
16	19.1109	.91732	.08268	71	8.9754	.43082	.56918
17	19.0433	.91408	.08592	72	8.6796	.41662	.58338
18	18.9748	.91079	.08921	73	8.3852	.40249	.59751
19	18.9043	.90741	.09259	74	8.0912	.38838	.61162
20	18.8312	.90390	.09610	75	7.7968	.37425	.62575
21	18.7550	.90024	.09976	76	7.5011	.36005	.63995
22	18.6762	.89646	.10354	77	7.2044	.34581	.65419
23	18.5941	.89252	.10748	78	6.9073	.33155	.66845
24	18 5083	.88840	.11160	79	6.6114	.31735	.68265
25	18.4186	.88409	.11591	80	6.3191	.30332	.69668
26	18.3249	.87959	.12041	81	6.0324	.28955	.71045
27	18.2265	.87487	.12513	82	5.7524	.27611	.72389
28	18.1242	.86996	.13004	83	5.4791	.26300	.73700
29	18.0175	.86484	.13516	84	5.2108	.25012	.74988
30	17.9068	.85953	.14047	85	4.9459	.23740	.76260
31	17.7919	.85401	.14599	86	4.6866	.22496	.77504
32	17.6728	.84829	.15171	87	4.4362	.21294	.78706
33	17.5488	.84234	.15766	88	4.1949	.20135	.79865
34	17.4203	.83617	.16383	89	3.9624	.19020	.80980
35	17.2865	.82975	.17025	90	3.7391	.17948	.82052
36	171478	.82309	.17691	91	3.5283	.16936	.83064
37	17 0038	.81618	.18382	92	3.3337	.16002	.83993
38	16.8542	.80900	.19100	93	3.1546	.15142	.84858
39	16.6989	.80155	.19845	94	2.9882	.14343	.85657
40	16.5376	.79380	.20620	95	2.8308	.13588	.86412
41	16.3697	.78575	.21425	96	2.6832	.12879	.87121
42	16.1955	.77738	.22262	97	2.5468	.12225	.87775
43	16.0148	.76871	.23129	98	2.4189	.11611	.88389
44	15.8277	.75973	.24027	99	2.2945	.11013	.88987
45	15.6347	.75047	.24953	100	2.1736	.10433	.89567
46	15.4358	.74092	.25908	101	2.0548	.09863	.90137
47	15.2315	.73111	.26889	102	1.9384	.09304	.90696
48	15.0215	.72103	.27897	103	1.8230	.08751	.91249
49	14.8060	.71069	.28931	104	1.7003	.08161	.91839
50	14.5845	.70005	.29995	105	1.5803	.07585	.92415
51	14.3572	.68915	.31085	106	1.4269	.06849	.93151
52	14.1250	.67800	.32200	107	1.2420	.05961	.94039
53	13.8878	.66661	.33339	108	.9574	.04596	.95404
54	13.6459	.65500	.34500	109	.4771	.02290	.97710

Appendix A-4
Table S (5.0)   Section 1
Single Life Factors Based on Life Table 90CM
Interest at 5.0 Percent

Age	Annuity	Life Estate	Remainder	Age	Annuity	Life Estate	Remainder
0	19.0619	.95309	.04691	55	13.1173	.65587	.34413
1	19.1994	.95997	.04003	56	12.8766	.64383	.35617
2	19.1736	.95868	.04132	57	12.6313	.63156	.36844
3	19.1418	.95709	.04291	58	12.3821	.61911	.38089
4	19.1063	.95531	.04469	59	12.1300	.60650	.39350
5	19.0675	.95338	.04662	60	11.8751	.59376	.40624
6	19.0262	.95131	.04869	61	11.6172	.58086	.41914
7	18.9823	.94911	.05089	62	11.3555	.56777	.43223
8	18.9359	.94679	.05321	63	11.0899	.55450	.44550
9	18 8866	.94433	.05567	64	10.8211	.54105	.45895
10	18.8343	.94171	.05829	65	10.5490	.52745	.47255
11	18.7791	.93896	.06104	66	10.2733	.51366	.48634
12	18.7212	.93606	.06394	67	9.9933	.49966	.50034
13	18.6613	.93307	.06693	68	9.7096	.48548	.51452
14	18.6006	.93003	.06997	69	9.4231	.47115	.52885
15	18.5395	.92697	.07303	70	9.1350	.45675	.54325
16	18.4784	.92392	.07608	71	8.8466	.44233	.55767
17	18.4169	.92084	.07916	72	8.5587	.42794	.57206
18	18.3546	.91773	.08227	73	8.2719	.41360	.58640
19	18.2904	.91452	.08548	74	7.9853	.39927	.60073
20	18.2238	.91119	.08881	75	7.6980	.38490	.61510
21	18.1544	.90772	.09228	76	7.4093	.37046	.62954
22	18.0824	.90412	.09588	77	7.1192	.35596	.64404
23	18.0072	.90036	.09964	78	6.8284	.34142	.65858
24	17.9287	.89643	.10357	79	6.5385	.32692	.67308
25	17.8463	.89232	.10768	80	6.2519	.31260	.68740
26	17.7601	.88801	.11199	81	5.9706	.29853	.70147
27	17.6696	.88348	.11652	82	5.6957	.28478	.71522
28	17.5751	.87876	.12124	83	5.4272	.27136	.72864
29	17.4766	.87383	.12617	84	5.1633	.25817	.74183
30	17.3741	.86871	.13129	85	4.9027	.24513	.75487
31	17.2678	.86339	.13661	86	4.6473	.23236	.76764
32	17.1572	.85786	.14214	87	4.4005	.22002	.77998
33	17.0421	.85210	.14790	88	4.1625	.20812	.79188
34	16.9225	.84612	.15388	89	3.9331	.19665	.80335
35	16.7978	.83989	.16011	90	3.7125	.18563	.81437
36	16.6683	.83342	.16658	91	3.5042	.17521	.82479
37	16.5338	.82669	.17331	92	3.3119	.16559	.83441
38	16.3938	.81969	.18031	93	3.1347	.15674	.84326
39	16.2483	.81241	.18759	94	2.9701	.14851	.85149
40	16.0968	.80484	.19516	95	2.8144	.14072	.85928
41	15.9391	.79695	.20305	96	2.6682	.13341	.86659
42	15.7750	.78875	.21125	97	2.5331	.12665	.87335
43	15.6046	.78023	.21977	98	2.4064	.12032	.87968
44	15.4279	.77140	.22860	99	2.3631	.11415	.88585
45	15.2455	.76228	.23772	100	2.1633	.10817	.89183
46	15.0572	.75286	.24714	101	2.0455	.10228	.89772
47	14.8636	.74318	.25682	102	1.9300	.09650	.90350
48	14.6643	.73322	.26678	103	1.8156	.09078	.90922
49	14.4595	.72298	.27702	104	1.6937	.08468	.91532
50	14.2488	.71244	.28756	105	1.5746	.07873	.92127
51	14.0323	.70162	.29838	106	1.4223	.07111	.92889
52	13.8109	.69054	.30946	107	1.2384	.06192	.93808
53	13.5844	.67922	.32078	108	.9551	.04776	.95224
54	13.3533	.66766	.33234	109	.4762	.02381	.97619

Appendix A-4

Section 3

Table B
Annuity, Income, and Remainder Interests For a Term Certain

	5.0%			Interest Rates		5.2%	
Years	Annuity	Income Interest	Remainder	Years	Annuity	Income Interest	Remainder
1	0.9524	.047619	.952381	1	0.9506	.045430	.950570
2	1.8594	.092971	.907029	2	1.8542	.096416	.903584
3	2.7232	.136162	.863838	3	2.7131	.141080	.858920
4	3.5460	.177298	.822702	4	3.5295	.183536	.816464
5	4.3295	.216474	.783526	5	4.3056	.223894	.776106
6	5.0757	.253785	.746215	6	5.0434	.262256	.737744
7	5.7864	.289319	.710681	7	5.7447	.298723	.701277
8	6.4632	.323161	.676839	8	6.4113	.333387	.666613
9	7.1078	.355391	.644609	9	7.0449	.366337	.633663
10	7.7217	.386087	.613913	10	7.6473	.397659	.602341
11	8.3064	.415321	.584679	11	8.2199	.427432	.572568
12	8.8633	.443163	.556837	12	8.7641	.455734	.544266
13	9.3936	.469679	.530321	13	9.2815	.482637	.517363
14	9.8986	.494932	.505068	14	9.7733	.508210	.491790
15	10.3797	.518983	.481017	15	10.2408	.532519	.467481
16	10.8378	.541888	.458112	16	10.6851	.555628	.444374
17	11.2741	.563703	.436297	17	11.1075	.577592	.422408
18	11.6896	.584479	.415521	18	11.5091	.598471	.401529
19	12.0853	.604266	.395734	19	11.8907	.618319	.381681
20	12.4622	.623111	.376889	20	12.2536	.637185	.362815
21	12.8212	.641058	.358942	21	12.5984	.655119	.344881
22	13.1630	.658150	.341850	22	12.9263	.672166	.327834
23	13.4886	.674429	.325571	23	13.2379	.688371	.311629
24	13.7986	.689932	.310068	24	13.5341	.703775	.296225
25	14.0939	.704697	.295303	25	13.8157	.718417	.281583
26	14.3752	.716759	.281241	26	14.0834	.732336	.267664
27	14.6430	.732152	.267848	27	14.3378	.745566	.254434
28	14.8981	.744906	.255094	28	14.5797	.758143	.241357
29	15.1411	.757054	.242946	29	14.8096	.770098	.229902
30	15.3725	.768623	.231377	30	15.0281	.781462	.218538
31	15.5928	.779641	.220359	31	15.2358	.792264	.207736
32	15.8027	.790134	.209666	32	15.4333	.802532	.197468
33	16.0025	.800127	.199873	33	15.6210	.812293	.187707
34	16.1929	.809645	.190355	34	15.7994	.821571	.178429
35	16.3742	.818710	.181290	35	15.9691	.830391	.169609
36	16.5469	.827343	.172657	36	16.1303	.838775	.161225
37	16.7113	.835564	.164436	37	16.2835	.846744	.153256
38	16.8679	.843395	.156605	38	16.4292	.854319	.145681
39	17.0170	.850852	.149148	39	16.5677	.861520	.138480
40	17.1591	.857954	.142046	40	16.6993	.868365	.131635
41	17.2944	.864718	.135282	41	16.6245	.874872	.125128
42	17.4232	.871160	.128840	42	16.9434	.881057	.118943
43	17.5459	.877296	.122704	43	17.0565	.886936	.113064
44	17.6628	.883139	.116861	44	17.1639	.892525	.107475
45	17.7741	.888703	.111297	45	17.2661	.897837	.102163
46	17.8801	.894003	.105997	46	17.3632	.902887	.097113
47	17.9810	.899051	.100949	47	17.4555	.907688	.092312
48	18.0772	.903858	.096142	48	17.5433	.912251	.087749
49	18.1687	.908436	.091564	49	17.6267	.916588	.083412
50	18.2559	.912796	.087204	50	17.7060	.920711	.079289
51	18.3390	.916949	.083051	51	17.7814	.924630	.075370
52	18.4181	.920904	.079096	52	17.8530	.928356	.071644
53	18.4934	.924670	.075330	53	17.9211	.931897	.068103
54	18.5651	.928257	.071743	54	17.9858	.935263	.064737
55	18.6335	.931674	.068326	55	18.0474	.938463	.061537
56	18.6985	.934927	.065073	56	18.1059	.941505	.058495
57	18.7605	.938026	.061974	57	18.1615	.944396	.055604
58	18.8195	.940977	.059023	58	18.2143	.947145	.052855
59	18.8758	.943788	.056212	59	18.2646	.949757	.050243
60	18.9293	.946464	.053536	60	18.3123	.952241	.047759

A-5 Optional State Sales Tax Tables

Department of the Treasury
Internal Revenue Service

Publication 600
Cat. No. 46600Y

Optional State Sales Tax Tables

For use in preparing
2004 Returns

Get forms and other information faster and easier by:

Internet • www.irs.gov

FAX • 703–368–9694 (from your fax machine)

Purpose

We are providing this publication so you can figure your deduction for state and local general sales taxes using the Optional State Sales Tax Tables. A general sales tax is a sales tax imposed at one rate with respect to the retail sale of a broad range of classes of items. In addition, certain selective sales taxes (sales taxes imposed at a different rate on certain selected items) are deductible as general sales taxes, as explained below.

Introduction

New for 2004, you can elect to deduct state and local general sales taxes instead of state and local income taxes as an itemized deduction on Schedule A (Form 1040). You cannot deduct both. Generally, to figure your state and local general sales tax deduction, you can use either your actual expenses or the Optional State Sales Tax Tables contained in this publication.

Actual expenses. Generally, you can deduct the actual state and local general sales taxes (including compensating use taxes) you paid in 2004 only if the tax rate was the same as the general sales tax rate. Do not include sales taxes paid on items used in your trade or business.

Rate less than general rate. Sales taxes on food, clothing, medical supplies, and motor vehicles are deductible as a general sales tax even if the tax rate was less than the general sales tax rate.

Rate more than general rate. Sales taxes on motor vehicles also are deductible as a general sales tax if the tax rate was more than the general sales tax rate, but the tax is deductible only up to the amount of tax that would have been imposed at the general sales tax rate. Motor vehicles include:

- Cars,
- Motorcycles,
- Motor homes,
- Recreational vehicles,
- Sport utility vehicles,
- Trucks,
- Vans, and
- Off-road vehicles.

Also include any state and local general sales taxes paid for a leased motor vehicle.

 You must keep your actual receipts showing general sales taxes paid to use this method.

2004 Optional State Sales Tax Tables *(Continued)*

Optional State Sales Tax Tables. Instead of using your actual expenses, you can use the Optional State Sales Tax Tables on pages 3 through 5 to figure your state and local general sales tax deduction. You may also be able to add the following items to the table amount.

- Local general sales taxes if your locality imposes a general sales tax.
- State and local general sales taxes paid on certain specified items.

How To Use the Optional State Sales Tax Tables

To figure your state and local general sales tax deduction using the Optional State Sales Tax Tables, follow Steps 1 through 5 and complete the worksheet below.

 If your filing status is married filing separately, both you and your spouse elect to deduct sales taxes, and your spouse elects to use the Optional State Sales Tax Tables, you also must use the tables to figure your state and local general sales tax deduction.

Step 1. Find the state where you lived in 2004 in the Optional State Sales Tax Tables shown on pages 3 through 5. But see *What If You Lived in More Than One Place*, on page 3, if applicable.

Step 2. Read down the "At least – But less than" columns for your state and find the line that includes your 2004 total available income. Total available income is the amount shown on your Form 1040, line 37, plus any nontaxable items, such as the following.

- Tax-exempt interest.
- Veterans' benefits.
- Nontaxable combat pay.
- Workers' compensation.
- Nontaxable part of social security and railroad retirement benefits.
- Nontaxable part of IRA, pension, or annuity distributions. Do not include rollovers.

- Public assistance payments.

Note. If your filing status is married filing separately, use your own total available income. Follow the above instructions, beginning with the amount shown on your Form 1040, line 37.

Step 3. Go to the column that includes the total number of exemptions you claimed on your Form 1040, line 6d. Enter the amount from that column on line 1 of the worksheet below.

Step 4. If your locality imposes a general sales tax, complete lines 2a through 2d of the worksheet below. Otherwise, skip lines 2a through 2c of the worksheet, enter -0- on line 2d, and go to line 3. If your local general sales tax rate changed during 2004, use a prorated amount, based on the number of days each rate was in effect, to figure the amount to enter on line 2a.

 During 2004, the general sales tax rate for Arkansas, California, and Virginia increased. If you were a resident of one of these states, enter the applicable general sales tax rate as a decimal on line 2b of the worksheet below: Arkansas, 5.9% (.059); California, 6.1% (.061); Virginia, 3.7% (.037).

Example. State A imposes a 6.5% (.065) general sales tax. City B in State A imposes an additional 0.5% (.005) general sales tax. To figure your local general sales taxes, enter .005 (the local general sales tax rate) on line 2a of the worksheet below. Enter .065 (the state general sales tax rate) on line 2b. Divide the amount on line 2a (.005) by the amount on line 2b (.065) and enter the result (.077) on line 2c. If the amount on line 1 of the worksheet is $1,000, multiply this amount by the amount on line 2c (.077) and enter the result, $77, on line 2d.

Step 5. Enter on line 3 of the worksheet below any state and local general sales taxes paid on the following specified items.

- A motor vehicle (including a car, motorcycle, motor home, recreational vehicle, sport utility vehicle, truck, van, and off-road vehicle). Also include any state and local general sales taxes paid for a leased motor vehicle. If the state sales tax rate on these items is higher than the general sales tax rate, only include

State and Local General Sales Tax Deduction Worksheet
(Using the Optional State Sales Tax Tables)

(Keep for Your Records)

1. State general sales taxes. See *Step 1* through *Step 3* above	**1.** _____
2a. Local general sales tax rate. If zero, skip lines 2a through 2c, enter -0- on line 2d, and go to line 3	**2a.** . _____
2b. State general sales tax rate	**2b.** . _____
2c. Divide line 2a by line 2b. Enter the result as a decimal (rounded to at least three places)	**2c.** . _____
2d. Local general sales taxes. Multiply line 1 by line 2c	**2d.** _____
3. General sales taxes paid on specified items, if any. See *Step 5* above	**3.** _____
4. **Deduction for general sales taxes.** Add lines 1, 2d, and 3. Enter the result here and on Schedule A (Form 1040), line 5, and be sure to check box b on that line	**4.** _____

Note. If you elect to deduct general sales taxes, you cannot deduct your state and local income taxes.

2004 Optional State Sales Tax Tables (Continued)

the amount of tax you would have paid at the general sales tax rate.

- An aircraft, boat, home (including mobile and prefabricated), or home building materials, if the tax rate was the same as the general sales tax rate.

Do not include sales taxes paid on items used in your trade or business.

What If You Lived in More Than One Place?

If you lived in more than one state during 2004, multiply the table amount for each state you lived in by a fraction. The numerator of the fraction is the number of days you lived in the state and the denominator is the total number of days in the year (366).

Also prorate any local general sales taxes based on the number of days you resided in the locality for which you are determining the local sales tax deduction.

Example. You lived in State A from January 1 through August 31, 2004 (244 days), and in State B from September 1 through December 31, 2004 (122 days). The table amount for State A is $500. The table amount for State B is $400. You would figure your state general sales tax (line 1 of the worksheet on page 2) as follows:

State A: $500 × 244/366 = $333
State B: $400 × 122/366 = 133

Total $466

2004 Optional State Sales Tax Tables

Alaska residents only. If you paid any local sales taxes, you must use your actual expenses to figure your deduction.

Income		Exemptions						Exemptions						Exemptions						Exemptions					
At least	But less than	1	2	3	4	5	Over 5	1	2	3	4	5	Over 5	1	2	3	4	5	Over 5	1	2	3	4	5	Over 5
		Alabama						**Arizona**						**Arkansas**						**California**					
$0	$20,000	288	344	381	410	434	468	332	374	402	422	439	463	430	510	564	605	640	688	363	416	451	477	499	529
20,000	30,000	366	434	481	517	547	590	430	485	520	547	568	598	542	641	708	760	803	863	469	537	581	615	643	681
30,000	40,000	416	494	547	587	621	669	496	558	599	629	654	688	616	727	802	860	908	976	540	617	668	706	738	782
40,000	50,000	460	545	602	647	684	736	552	621	666	699	727	765	678	800	882	945	998	1072	600	685	741	784	819	867
50,000	60,000	498	590	652	700	740	796	603	678	726	763	792	833	734	864	952	1021	1077	1157	654	747	807	854	892	944
60,000	70,000	532	630	695	747	789	849	648	728	780	819	851	895	783	922	1015	1088	1148	1232	702	801	866	916	956	1012
70,000	80,000	565	667	737	791	835	898	690	776	831	872	906	952	829	976	1074	1150	1214	1302	748	853	922	974	1017	1077
80,000	90,000	593	701	773	830	877	942	728	818	876	920	955	1004	871	1023	1126	1206	1272	1365	789	899	971	1027	1072	1134
90,000	100,000	621	733	809	868	916	985	765	859	920	965	1003	1054	910	1070	1177	1260	1328	1425	828	944	1019	1077	1124	1189
100,000	120,000	657	775	855	917	968	1040	814	913	977	1026	1065	1119	962	1130	1242	1330	1402	1503	880	1002	1082	1143	1193	1262
120,000	140,000	706	832	916	982	1037	1114	878	985	1054	1106	1148	1206	1031	1210	1330	1422	1499	1607	949	1080	1166	1232	1285	1359
140,000	160,000	749	881	971	1040	1098	1179	935	1048	1122	1177	1222	1283	1093	1280	1407	1504	1585	1699	1010	1149	1240	1310	1366	1445
160,000	180,000	789	928	1022	1095	1155	1240	990	1109	1186	1244	1292	1357	1151	1347	1479	1582	1667	1785	1069	1215	1310	1384	1444	1526
180,000	200,000	827	972	1070	1146	1209	1298	1041	1166	1247	1308	1357	1425	1205	1410	1548	1654	1743	1866	1123	1277	1377	1454	1516	1602
200,000 or more		995	1166	1281	1371	1445	1549	1267	1417	1514	1587	1647	1728	1443	1684	1846	1971	2074	2220	1365	1549	1669	1761	1835	1939
Income		**Colorado**						**Connecticut**						**District of Columbia**						**Florida**					
$0	$20,000	160	183	197	208	217	230	338	387	419	444	464	492	327	375	407	431	451	478	394	450	487	515	537	569
20,000	30,000	209	238	257	271	283	299	440	503	545	577	603	639	428	490	531	563	588	624	509	580	627	662	691	731
30,000	40,000	242	275	297	313	327	345	509	581	629	665	695	736	496	568	615	651	680	721	585	666	720	760	793	838
40,000	50,000	271	307	331	349	364	384	567	647	700	740	773	819	555	635	687	727	759	805	650	740	799	843	880	930
50,000	60,000	296	336	362	382	398	420	620	707	764	808	844	894	608	695	752	795	831	880	709	806	870	918	957	1012
60,000	70,000	319	362	390	411	428	452	667	760	822	869	907	960	655	748	810	856	894	947	761	865	933	984	1027	1085
70,000	80,000	341	386	416	438	457	482	712	811	876	926	966	1023	700	799	864	914	954	1011	810	920	992	1047	1092	1153
80,000	90,000	360	408	439	463	482	509	751	856	924	976	1019	1079	740	845	913	966	1008	1067	854	970	1045	1103	1150	1215
90,000	100,000	379	429	462	487	507	535	790	899	971	1026	1071	1133	779	889	961	1016	1060	1122	896	1018	1097	1157	1206	1274
100,000	120,000	404	457	492	518	539	569	840	956	1032	1090	1138	1204	831	947	1023	1082	1129	1195	952	1080	1164	1228	1280	1351
120,000	140,000	437	494	531	560	583	614	908	1032	1114	1177	1228	1298	900	1025	1107	1170	1221	1292	1026	1164	1254	1322	1378	1455
140,000	160,000	466	527	567	597	621	655	968	1100	1187	1253	1307	1382	961	1094	1181	1248	1302	1377	1092	1238	1333	1406	1465	1546
160,000	180,000	494	559	600	632	658	694	1025	1164	1256	1325	1383	1462	1019	1160	1252	1322	1380	1459	1155	1309	1409	1485	1547	1633
180,000	200,000	521	588	632	665	693	730	1079	1225	1320	1394	1454	1536	1074	1222	1319	1393	1453	1536	1214	1375	1480	1560	1625	1714
200,000 or more		638	720	773	813	846	891	1315	1491	1606	1694	1766	1866	1319	1498	1615	1704	1777	1877	1474	1667	1792	1888	1965	2073
Income		**Georgia**						**Hawaii**						**Idaho**						**Illinois**					
$0	$20,000	247	285	310	330	345	367	325	386	428	460	487	525	405	482	535	575	609	657	480	578	644	696	740	801
20,000	30,000	328	377	410	435	455	484	416	493	545	586	620	667	519	615	681	732	775	835	603	723	806	870	924	999
30,000	40,000	382	439	477	506	529	562	476	564	623	669	707	761	594	703	777	835	883	951	683	819	911	983	1043	1128
40,000	50,000	429	493	535	567	593	630	527	624	689	739	781	840	658	778	859	923	976	1050	751	899	999	1078	1144	1236
50,000	60,000	471	541	587	622	651	691	573	677	747	802	847	911	715	845	933	1001	1058	1138	812	970	1078	1163	1233	1332
60,000	70,000	509	584	634	672	703	746	614	725	800	858	906	974	767	904	998	1071	1131	1216	866	1034	1148	1237	1312	1417
70,000	80,000	545	625	678	719	752	798	652	770	849	910	961	1033	815	960	1059	1136	1200	1290	916	1093	1213	1308	1387	1496
80,000	90,000	578	662	718	761	796	844	687	809	892	957	1010	1085	858	1010	1114	1194	1261	1355	961	1146	1272	1370	1452	1567
90,000	100,000	609	698	757	802	838	889	720	848	935	1002	1058	1136	900	1059	1166	1250	1320	1418	1005	1197	1327	1430	1515	1635
100,000	120,000	651	746	808	855	894	949	763	899	990	1061	1120	1202	954	1122	1236	1324	1398	1501	1061	1263	1401	1508	1597	1723
120,000	140,000	707	809	876	927	969	1028	821	966	1063	1139	1202	1290	1027	1206	1327	1422	1500	1611	1137	1351	1497	1611	1706	1840
140,000	160,000	757	865	937	991	1036	1099	873	1025	1129	1209	1275	1368	1092	1281	1409	1508	1591	1708	1203	1429	1583	1703	1803	1943
160,000	180,000	804	919	995	1053	1100	1166	921	1082	1190	1274	1344	1442	1153	1352	1486	1591	1677	1800	1266	1503	1664	1789	1893	2041
180,000	200,000	849	970	1050	1110	1160	1230	967	1135	1248	1336	1409	1511	1211	1418	1558	1668	1758	1886	1326	1572	1739	1870	1979	2132
200,000 or more		1049	1196	1293	1367	1428	1512	1169	1368	1502	1607	1693	1814	1467	1711	1877	2006	2113	2264	1585	1874	2069	2222	2349	2529

(Continued on page 4)

2004 Optional State Sales Tax Tables *(Continued)*

Income At least	Income But less than	Indiana 1	2	3	4	5	Over 5	Iowa 1	2	3	4	5	Over 5	Kansas 1	2	3	4	5	Over 5	Kentucky 1	2	3	4	5	Over 5
$0	$20,000	375	431	467	495	518	550	304	348	377	399	417	442	390	464	514	553	585	631	337	388	421	446	467	496
20,000	30,000	489	561	608	644	673	714	400	457	494	523	546	578	496	589	652	700	741	798	441	507	549	582	609	646
30,000	40,000	566	648	702	743	776	823	465	530	573	606	632	669	566	671	742	797	843	907	511	586	635	673	704	747
40,000	50,000	631	722	782	828	865	917	520	593	641	677	707	748	626	741	819	879	929	999	572	655	709	751	785	833
50,000	60,000	691	789	854	904	944	1001	570	650	702	741	774	819	679	803	887	952	1006	1082	626	716	776	821	858	910
60,000	70,000	744	849	919	972	1015	1076	616	701	757	799	834	882	727	858	948	1017	1074	1155	675	772	835	884	924	979
70,000	80,000	794	906	980	1036	1082	1146	658	749	808	854	891	942	771	910	1004	1078	1138	1223	721	824	892	943	986	1045
80,000	90,000	839	957	1035	1094	1142	1210	696	792	855	902	941	995	811	957	1055	1132	1195	1284	762	871	942	997	1041	1103
90,000	100,000	882	1006	1088	1150	1200	1271	734	834	900	950	991	1047	849	1001	1104	1184	1250	1343	802	916	991	1048	1095	1160
100,000	120,000	940	1071	1157	1223	1277	1351	783	889	959	1012	1056	1116	900	1060	1168	1252	1322	1420	855	976	1055	1116	1166	1234
120,000	140,000	1016	1157	1250	1321	1379	1459	848	963	1038	1095	1142	1207	966	1138	1253	1343	1417	1521	925	1056	1141	1206	1260	1334
140,000	160,000	1085	1234	1333	1408	1469	1554	906	1029	1109	1169	1219	1288	1026	1206	1328	1423	1501	1611	988	1127	1217	1287	1343	1422
160,000	180,000	1150	1308	1411	1490	1555	1645	962	1091	1176	1240	1293	1365	1082	1272	1399	1499	1581	1696	1048	1194	1290	1363	1423	1506
180,000	200,000	1211	1377	1485	1568	1636	1730	1015	1150	1239	1307	1362	1438	1135	1333	1466	1570	1656	1776	1104	1258	1359	1436	1498	1585
200,000 or more		1483	1682	1813	1913	1994	2107	1249	1413	1520	1602	1669	1761	1367	1601	1759	1881	1983	2125	1355	1541	1662	1755	1831	1936

Income At least	Income But less than	Louisiana 1	2	3	4	5	Over 5	Maine 1	2	3	4	5	Over 5	Maryland 1	2	3	4	5	Over 5	Massachusetts 1	2	3	4	5	Over 5
$0	$20,000	216	247	268	283	296	313	264	301	325	344	359	379	241	280	306	326	343	366	279	315	339	357	372	392
20,000	30,000	282	322	349	369	385	408	352	400	432	456	475	502	326	378	413	440	462	493	370	418	449	473	492	519
30,000	40,000	327	373	403	426	445	470	411	467	504	532	554	586	384	445	486	517	543	579	432	487	524	551	573	604
40,000	50,000	365	416	449	475	496	524	463	525	566	597	623	658	435	504	549	585	614	654	485	547	588	618	643	677
50,000	60,000	399	455	491	519	541	573	509	578	622	656	684	723	481	557	607	646	678	722	534	602	646	679	706	744
60,000	70,000	430	489	528	558	582	616	551	625	673	710	740	781	523	605	659	701	736	784	578	651	698	734	763	804
70,000	80,000	459	522	564	595	621	657	591	670	721	760	792	836	563	650	709	754	791	842	619	697	748	786	817	860
80,000	90,000	485	551	595	628	656	693	627	710	765	806	840	886	599	692	753	801	840	895	656	739	792	832	865	911
90,000	100,000	510	580	626	661	689	728	662	749	806	850	885	934	634	732	797	847	888	946	692	779	835	878	912	960
100,000	120,000	543	617	666	703	733	775	708	801	862	908	946	998	680	785	854	908	952	1014	740	832	892	937	974	1025
120,000	140,000	587	667	719	759	792	837	770	870	936	986	1027	1083	743	856	932	990	1038	1105	804	904	968	1017	1057	1112
140,000	160,000	626	711	767	809	844	892	825	932	1002	1056	1099	1159	799	920	1001	1063	1114	1186	861	967	1036	1088	1131	1189
160,000	180,000	664	754	812	857	893	944	878	992	1066	1122	1168	1232	852	981	1067	1133	1188	1264	916	1028	1101	1156	1201	1263
180,000	200,000	699	793	855	902	940	993	928	1047	1126	1185	1233	1300	903	1039	1130	1200	1257	1337	967	1086	1162	1221	1268	1333
200,000 or more		855	969	1043	1100	1146	1209	1151	1297	1392	1465	1524	1605	1131	1299	1411	1497	1568	1667	1198	1342	1436	1506	1564	1643

Income At least	Income But less than	Michigan 1	2	3	4	5	Over 5	Minnesota 1	2	3	4	5	Over 5	Mississippi 1	2	3	4	5	Over 5	Missouri 1	2	3	4	5	Over 5
$0	$20,000	349	396	426	450	469	495	379	429	462	487	508	536	510	607	673	724	766	826	323	385	427	460	488	527
20,000	30,000	448	507	545	575	599	632	495	561	603	636	662	698	643	762	844	907	959	1033	409	487	539	580	614	662
30,000	40,000	514	580	624	657	684	722	573	649	698	735	765	806	729	864	955	1026	1085	1167	466	553	612	658	697	751
40,000	50,000	570	643	691	727	757	798	640	724	778	820	853	899	802	949	1049	1126	1191	1281	514	609	674	724	766	825
50,000	60,000	621	699	751	790	822	867	701	792	851	896	933	983	868	1026	1133	1216	1285	1381	557	660	729	783	828	892
60,000	70,000	666	749	804	846	880	927	755	853	916	964	1003	1057	926	1093	1207	1295	1368	1470	595	704	778	836	883	951
70,000	80,000	708	796	854	898	934	984	806	910	978	1029	1071	1128	980	1157	1276	1369	1446	1554	631	746	824	885	935	1006
80,000	90,000	746	838	899	945	983	1035	852	962	1033	1087	1130	1191	1029	1213	1338	1434	1515	1628	663	783	865	928	981	1055
90,000	100,000	783	879	942	990	1030	1084	896	1011	1086	1142	1188	1252	1075	1267	1397	1498	1581	1699	694	819	904	970	1025	1102
100,000	120,000	831	933	999	1050	1091	1148	955	1077	1156	1216	1265	1332	1137	1338	1475	1580	1668	1792	735	866	955	1025	1083	1164
120,000	140,000	896	1004	1074	1128	1173	1234	1033	1164	1250	1314	1367	1439	1218	1432	1577	1690	1783	1914	789	929	1024	1098	1159	1246
140,000	160,000	953	1067	1141	1198	1245	1309	1102	1242	1333	1401	1457	1534	1290	1515	1668	1786	1885	2023	837	984	1084	1162	1227	1318
160,000	180,000	1007	1127	1205	1265	1313	1381	1168	1316	1412	1484	1543	1624	1358	1594	1754	1878	1981	2125	882	1037	1141	1223	1290	1386
180,000	200,000	1059	1183	1264	1327	1378	1448	1231	1386	1486	1562	1624	1710	1421	1668	1834	1963	2070	2221	925	1086	1195	1280	1350	1450
200,000 or more		1285	1431	1527	1600	1660	1744	1507	1695	1816	1908	1983	2085	1701	1990	2185	2336	2461	2637	1112	1301	1429	1529	1612	1728

Income At least	Income But less than	Nebraska 1	2	3	4	5	Over 5	Nevada 1	2	3	4	5	Over 5	New Jersey 1	2	3	4	5	Over 5	New Mexico 1	2	3	4	5	Over 5
$0	$20,000	318	363	392	414	432	457	304	355	389	415	437	467	317	367	400	425	446	475	371	439	484	519	548	589
20,000	30,000	417	475	513	541	565	597	406	472	517	551	579	619	418	482	525	558	585	623	471	555	611	655	691	742
30,000	40,000	484	550	594	627	654	691	474	551	603	643	675	721	485	560	610	647	679	722	536	631	695	744	785	842
40,000	50,000	541	615	663	700	730	771	534	620	677	722	758	810	544	627	682	724	759	807	592	696	766	820	864	927
50,000	60,000	593	674	726	766	799	844	588	682	745	794	834	890	597	688	748	794	831	884	641	753	829	887	935	1003
60,000	70,000	639	726	782	825	860	908	636	738	806	858	901	961	644	742	806	856	896	953	686	805	885	947	998	1069
70,000	80,000	683	775	835	881	918	970	682	791	863	919	965	1029	689	793	862	914	957	1017	727	853	937	1002	1056	1132
80,000	90,000	723	820	883	931	970	1024	724	838	915	974	1022	1090	730	839	911	967	1012	1076	764	896	984	1052	1109	1188
90,000	100,000	761	863	929	980	1021	1078	764	884	965	1027	1078	1149	769	884	960	1018	1066	1132	800	937	1029	1100	1159	1241
100,000	120,000	811	920	990	1044	1087	1147	817	945	1031	1097	1151	1228	821	943	1023	1085	1136	1206	847	991	1088	1163	1225	1312
120,000	140,000	879	995	1071	1129	1176	1241	888	1027	1120	1191	1250	1332	890	1021	1108	1175	1229	1305	909	1063	1166	1246	1312	1405
140,000	160,000	939	1063	1143	1205	1255	1324	952	1100	1198	1275	1337	1425	951	1091	1184	1255	1313	1394	964	1126	1235	1320	1389	1487
160,000	180,000	996	1127	1212	1277	1330	1403	1012	1169	1274	1355	1421	1514	1010	1158	1256	1331	1392	1478	1016	1187	1301	1389	1462	1564
180,000	200,000	1050	1187	1277	1345	1400	1477	1070	1235	1345	1430	1500	1597	1066	1222	1324	1403	1467	1557	1065	1243	1362	1454	1531	1637
200,000 or more		1289	1456	1564	1647	1714	1806	1326	1528	1662	1765	1851	1970	1313	1502	1626	1722	1800	1908	1281	1491	1631	1740	1830	1955

Income At least	Income But less than	New York 1	2	3	4	5	Over 5	North Carolina 1	2	3	4	5	Over 5	North Dakota 1	2	3	4	5	Over 5	Ohio 1	2	3	4	5	Over 5
$0	$20,000	224	262	287	306	322	344	269	304	327	344	358	377	291	331	357	377	393	415	364	412	443	467	486	512
20,000	30,000	296	345	378	403	424	453	350	395	424	445	463	488	383	434	468	494	514	543	475	536	576	606	631	665
30,000	40,000	345	401	439	468	492	526	403	455	488	513	533	561	444	503	542	572	596	629	549	619	665	699	727	766
40,000	50,000	387	450	492	524	551	588	449	506	543	571	593	624	497	563	606	639	665	702	612	690	741	779	810	853
50,000	60,000	425	494	540	575	604	645	491	552	592	622	647	681	544	617	664	699	728	768	670	754	809	851	885	932
60,000	70,000	459	533	582	620	652	696	528	594	636	669	695	731	587	665	715	753	784	828	721	812	871	915	951	1001
70,000	80,000	491	570	623	663	697	743	563	633	678	712	740	778	627	710	764	804	838	883	769	866	928	976	1014	1067
80,000	90,000	520	604	659	702	737	786	594	668	715	751	781	821	664	751	807	850	885	934	813	914	980	1030	1071	1126
90,000	100,000	549	636	694	739	776	828	624	701	751	789	820	862	699	790	850	895	931	982	855	961	1030	1083	1125	1184
100,000	120,000	586	679	741	788	828	883	664	746	799	839	871	916	745	842	905	953	992	1046	911	1023	1096	1152	1197	1259
120,000	140,000	635	736	802	854	896	956	717	805	862	905	940	988	807	912	980	1031	1073	1131	985	1106	1185	1244	1292	1359
140,000	160,000	680	786	858	912	958	1021	764	857	918	963	1000	1051	862	973	1046	1101	1145	1207	1051	1180	1263	1326	1377	1448
160,000	180,000	722	835	910	968	1016	1083	809	907	971	1019	1058	1112	915	1032	1109	1167	1214	1279	1114	1250	1338	1404	1458	1533
180,000	200,000	762	881	960	1021	1071	1141	851	954	1021	1072	1112	1169	964	1088	1168	1229	1279	1347	1173	1316	1408	1478	1534	1612
200,000 or more		940	1084	1180	1254	1315	1399	1038	1162	1242	1303	1352	1420	1185	1335	1432	1505	1566	1648	1437	1608	1719	1803	1871	1965

(Continued on page 5)

2004 Optional State Sales Tax Tables *(Continued)*

Oklahoma

Income At least	Income But less than	Exemptions 1	2	3	4	5	Over 5
$0	$20,000	327	388	430	462	489	527
20,000	30,000	412	487	539	578	612	658
30,000	40,000	468	552	609	654	691	744
40,000	50,000	515	607	669	718	759	816
50,000	60,000	557	656	723	775	818	879
60,000	70,000	595	699	770	825	871	936
70,000	80,000	630	739	814	872	920	988
80,000	90,000	661	775	853	913	964	1035
90,000	100,000	691	810	891	954	1006	1080
100,000	120,000	731	855	940	1006	1061	1139
120,000	140,000	784	915	1005	1075	1134	1216
140,000	160,000	830	968	1063	1136	1198	1284
160,000	180,000	874	1019	1117	1194	1258	1348
180,000	200,000	916	1066	1168	1248	1315	1409
200,000 or more		1098	1272	1391	1484	1561	1670

Pennsylvania

Income At least	Income But less than	Exemptions 1	2	3	4	5	Over 5
$0	$20,000	284	328	357	380	398	424
20,000	30,000	382	440	478	508	532	566
30,000	40,000	448	516	561	595	623	663
40,000	50,000	506	582	632	671	702	746
50,000	60,000	558	642	697	739	774	822
60,000	70,000	605	696	755	801	838	890
70,000	80,000	650	747	811	859	899	955
80,000	90,000	691	793	860	912	954	1013
90,000	100,000	730	838	909	963	1008	1070
100,000	120,000	782	897	973	1031	1079	1145
120,000	140,000	852	977	1059	1122	1173	1245
140,000	160,000	915	1048	1135	1203	1258	1335
160,000	180,000	975	1116	1209	1280	1339	1420
180,000	200,000	1031	1180	1278	1354	1415	1501
200,000 or more		1285	1468	1588	1681	1756	1862

Rhode Island

Income At least	Income But less than	Exemptions 1	2	3	4	5	Over 5
$0	$20,000	302	342	368	387	403	425
20,000	30,000	403	455	489	515	536	565
30,000	40,000	472	532	571	601	625	659
40,000	50,000	531	598	642	676	703	740
50,000	60,000	585	658	706	743	773	814
60,000	70,000	633	712	764	803	835	880
70,000	80,000	678	763	819	861	895	942
80,000	90,000	719	809	868	912	948	998
90,000	100,000	759	854	915	962	1000	1053
100,000	120,000	812	913	978	1028	1068	1124
120,000	140,000	882	991	1062	1116	1160	1220
140,000	160,000	945	1061	1137	1194	1241	1306
160,000	180,000	1005	1128	1208	1269	1319	1387
180,000	200,000	1062	1191	1276	1340	1392	1464
200,000 or more		1314	1472	1575	1653	1717	1805

South Carolina

Income At least	Income But less than	Exemptions 1	2	3	4	5	Over 5
$0	$20,000	379	449	496	533	563	606
20,000	30,000	481	568	627	672	710	763
30,000	40,000	547	646	712	764	806	866
40,000	50,000	604	712	785	841	888	953
50,000	60,000	655	771	849	910	960	1031
60,000	70,000	700	823	906	971	1024	1099
70,000	80,000	742	872	960	1028	1085	1164
80,000	90,000	780	916	1008	1079	1138	1221
90,000	100,000	816	958	1054	1128	1190	1276
100,000	120,000	864	1014	1114	1193	1257	1348
120,000	140,000	927	1087	1194	1278	1347	1443
140,000	160,000	983	1152	1265	1353	1426	1527
160,000	180,000	1036	1213	1332	1424	1500	1607
180,000	200,000	1086	1271	1395	1491	1570	1682
200,000 or more		1306	1523	1670	1783	1876	2008

South Dakota

Income At least	Income But less than	Exemptions 1	2	3	4	5	Over 5
$0	$20,000	263	319	358	388	414	450
20,000	30,000	344	417	466	505	538	585
30,000	40,000	399	482	539	584	621	674
40,000	50,000	446	537	601	650	692	751
50,000	60,000	488	588	656	711	756	820
60,000	70,000	526	633	706	764	813	882
70,000	80,000	562	675	753	815	867	940
80,000	90,000	594	713	796	860	915	991
90,000	100,000	625	750	836	904	961	1042
100,000	120,000	666	799	890	962	1022	1108
120,000	140,000	721	864	962	1039	1104	1195
140,000	160,000	770	921	1025	1107	1176	1273
160,000	180,000	816	976	1086	1172	1245	1347
180,000	200,000	860	1028	1143	1234	1310	1417
200,000 or more		1055	1257	1395	1504	1596	1725

Tennessee

Income At least	Income But less than	Exemptions 1	2	3	4	5	Over 5
$0	$20,000	506	601	666	717	758	817
20,000	30,000	628	745	824	886	937	1008
30,000	40,000	708	838	926	995	1052	1132
40,000	50,000	775	916	1012	1086	1148	1235
50,000	60,000	835	986	1088	1168	1233	1326
60,000	70,000	887	1047	1155	1239	1309	1407
70,000	80,000	937	1105	1218	1306	1379	1482
80,000	90,000	981	1155	1273	1365	1441	1548
90,000	100,000	1023	1204	1327	1422	1501	1612
100,000	120,000	1078	1268	1397	1496	1579	1695
120,000	140,000	1151	1353	1489	1594	1682	1805
140,000	160,000	1216	1427	1570	1681	1773	1902
160,000	180,000	1277	1498	1647	1762	1858	1993
180,000	200,000	1334	1563	1718	1838	1938	2078
200,000 or more		1583	1850	2030	2169	2284	2446

Texas

Income At least	Income But less than	Exemptions 1	2	3	4	5	Over 5
$0	$20,000	375	427	461	487	509	538
20,000	30,000	488	555	599	633	660	697
30,000	40,000	564	641	691	730	761	804
40,000	50,000	629	714	770	812	847	895
50,000	60,000	687	780	841	887	925	976
60,000	70,000	740	840	904	954	994	1049
70,000	80,000	789	895	964	1017	1059	1118
80,000	90,000	834	945	1018	1073	1118	1180
90,000	100,000	877	994	1070	1127	1174	1239
100,000	120,000	933	1057	1138	1199	1249	1318
120,000	140,000	1009	1142	1229	1294	1348	1422
140,000	160,000	1076	1217	1309	1379	1436	1515
160,000	180,000	1140	1289	1386	1460	1520	1603
180,000	200,000	1200	1357	1459	1536	1599	1686
200,000 or more		1467	1656	1779	1872	1948	2052

Utah

Income At least	Income But less than	Exemptions 1	2	3	4	5	Over 5
$0	$20,000	345	411	456	491	521	562
20,000	30,000	437	520	576	620	657	708
30,000	40,000	498	592	655	705	746	804
40,000	50,000	550	652	722	776	821	884
50,000	60,000	596	707	781	840	888	956
60,000	70,000	637	755	834	896	947	1020
70,000	80,000	676	800	884	949	1003	1079
80,000	90,000	711	840	928	996	1053	1132
90,000	100,000	744	879	970	1041	1100	1183
100,000	120,000	787	929	1026	1100	1163	1250
120,000	140,000	845	997	1099	1179	1245	1339
140,000	160,000	897	1056	1164	1248	1318	1416
160,000	180,000	945	1113	1226	1314	1387	1490
180,000	200,000	991	1166	1284	1376	1452	1559
200,000 or more		1192	1398	1537	1645	1735	1861

Vermont

Income At least	Income But less than	Exemptions 1	2	3	4	5	Over 5
$0	$20,000	259	300	327	348	365	389
20,000	30,000	352	406	442	470	493	525
30,000	40,000	416	479	521	554	581	618
40,000	50,000	471	543	590	627	657	699
50,000	60,000	522	601	653	693	726	772
60,000	70,000	568	653	710	753	789	839
70,000	80,000	612	703	764	810	849	902
80,000	90,000	651	748	812	862	902	959
90,000	100,000	690	792	859	912	955	1014
100,000	120,000	741	850	922	978	1024	1088
120,000	140,000	809	928	1006	1067	1117	1186
140,000	160,000	871	998	1082	1147	1200	1274
160,000	180,000	930	1065	1154	1223	1280	1359
180,000	200,000	986	1128	1223	1296	1355	1439
200,000 or more		1238	1414	1531	1620	1694	1797

Virginia

Income At least	Income But less than	Exemptions 1	2	3	4	5	Over 5
$0	$20,000	270	322	357	385	408	440
20,000	30,000	345	411	455	490	519	559
30,000	40,000	395	470	520	559	592	638
40,000	50,000	438	520	575	618	654	704
50,000	60,000	476	564	624	670	709	763
60,000	70,000	510	604	667	717	758	816
70,000	80,000	542	641	708	761	804	865
80,000	90,000	571	675	745	800	845	909
90,000	100,000	598	707	780	837	885	952
100,000	120,000	635	749	827	887	937	1007
120,000	140,000	683	805	888	952	1006	1081
140,000	160,000	726	855	942	1010	1067	1146
160,000	180,000	767	902	994	1065	1125	1208
180,000	200,000	805	947	1043	1117	1179	1266
200,000 or more		974	1142	1256	1344	1417	1520

Washington

Income At least	Income But less than	Exemptions 1	2	3	4	5	Over 5
$0	$20,000	389	439	471	496	516	543
20,000	30,000	500	564	605	636	662	696
30,000	40,000	574	647	694	729	758	797
40,000	50,000	637	717	769	808	840	883
50,000	60,000	694	780	836	879	913	960
60,000	70,000	744	837	896	942	978	1029
70,000	80,000	791	890	953	1001	1040	1093
80,000	90,000	834	937	1004	1054	1095	1151
90,000	100,000	875	983	1052	1105	1148	1206
100,000	120,000	929	1043	1116	1172	1217	1279
120,000	140,000	1000	1123	1201	1261	1309	1376
140,000	160,000	1064	1193	1277	1340	1391	1462
160,000	180,000	1124	1261	1349	1415	1469	1543
180,000	200,000	1181	1324	1416	1485	1542	1619
200,000 or more		1431	1602	1712	1795	1862	1955

West Virginia

Income At least	Income But less than	Exemptions 1	2	3	4	5	Over 5
$0	$20,000	493	585	646	694	734	789
20,000	30,000	622	736	812	872	921	990
30,000	40,000	706	835	921	988	1043	1121
40,000	50,000	778	918	1013	1086	1146	1231
50,000	60,000	842	993	1094	1173	1238	1329
60,000	70,000	899	1059	1166	1250	1319	1416
70,000	80,000	952	1121	1234	1322	1395	1497
80,000	90,000	999	1176	1294	1386	1462	1569
90,000	100,000	1045	1229	1352	1448	1527	1639
100,000	120,000	1105	1298	1428	1529	1612	1729
120,000	140,000	1184	1390	1528	1636	1725	1849
140,000	160,000	1254	1471	1617	1730	1824	1955
160,000	180,000	1320	1548	1701	1819	1917	2055
180,000	200,000	1383	1620	1779	1903	2005	2148
200,000 or more		1656	1935	2123	2268	2388	2556

Wisconsin

Income At least	Income But less than	Exemptions 1	2	3	4	5	Over 5
$0	$20,000	293	334	360	380	396	419
20,000	30,000	388	440	475	501	522	551
30,000	40,000	452	513	552	582	607	641
40,000	50,000	507	575	619	652	680	718
50,000	60,000	557	631	679	716	746	787
60,000	70,000	602	681	733	773	805	849
70,000	80,000	644	729	785	827	861	908
80,000	90,000	683	772	831	875	911	961
90,000	100,000	720	814	875	922	960	1012
100,000	120,000	769	869	934	983	1024	1080
120,000	140,000	834	942	1013	1066	1110	1170
140,000	160,000	893	1008	1083	1140	1186	1250
160,000	180,000	949	1071	1150	1210	1259	1327
180,000	200,000	1001	1130	1213	1276	1328	1399
200,000 or more		1237	1392	1494	1571	1633	1720

Wyoming

Income At least	Income But less than	Exemptions 1	2	3	4	5	Over 5
$0	$20,000	337	401	445	479	507	547
20,000	30,000	428	508	563	605	640	689
30,000	40,000	487	578	640	687	727	783
40,000	50,000	538	637	705	757	800	861
50,000	60,000	583	690	763	819	866	932
60,000	70,000	623	737	814	874	924	994
70,000	80,000	661	781	863	926	978	1052
80,000	90,000	695	821	906	972	1026	1104
90,000	100,000	727	858	947	1016	1073	1153
100,000	120,000	770	908	1001	1074	1134	1219
120,000	140,000	826	974	1073	1150	1215	1305
140,000	160,000	876	1032	1137	1218	1286	1381
160,000	180,000	924	1087	1197	1282	1353	1453
180,000	200,000	969	1138	1253	1342	1416	1520
200,000 or more		1164	1365	1500	1605	1692	1814

By double-clicking on the icon to the left, you may access
the Microsoft Excel (.xls) version of the sales tax tables

Appendix B

TAX FORMS

B-1   Form 1040A   U.S. Individual Income Tax Return

Form
1040A

Department of the Treasury—Internal Revenue Service

U.S. Individual Income Tax Return   (99) **2004**   IRS Use Only—Do not write or staple in this space.

OMB No. 1545-0085

Label
(See page 18.)

L
A
B
E
L

H
E
R
E

Your first name and initial | Last name

Your social security number

If a joint return, spouse's first name and initial | Last name

Spouse's social security number

Use the IRS label.
Otherwise, please print or type.

Home address (number and street). If you have a P.O. box, see page 18. | Apt. no.

City, town or post office, state, and ZIP code. If you have a foreign address, see page 18.

▲ **Important!** ▲
You **must** enter your SSN(s) above.

Presidential Election Campaign
(See page 18.)

► Note. Checking "Yes" will not change your tax or reduce your refund.
Do you, or your spouse if filing a joint return, want $3 to go to this fund?. . . ►

You ☐ Yes ☐ No   Spouse ☐ Yes ☐ No

Filing status
Check only one box.

1 ☐ Single
2 ☐ Married filing jointly (even if only one had income)
3 ☐ Married filing separately. Enter spouse's SSN above and full name here. ►
4 ☐ Head of household (with qualifying person). (See page 19.) If the qualifying person is a child but not your dependent, enter this child's name here. ►
5 ☐ Qualifying widow(er) with dependent child (see page 19)

Exemptions

6a ☐ **Yourself.** If someone can claim you as a dependent, **do not** check box 6a.
b ☐ **Spouse**

c **Dependents:**

(1) First name Last name	(2) Dependent's social security number	(3) Dependent's relationship to you	(4) ✓if qualifying child for child tax credit (see page 21)
			☐
			☐
			☐
			☐
			☐
			☐

If more than six dependents, see page 20.

Boxes checked on 6a and 6b ____

No. of children on 6c who:
• lived with you ____
• did not live with you due to divorce or separation (see page 21) ____

Dependents on 6c not entered above ____

Add numbers on lines above ► ☐

d Total number of exemptions claimed.

Income

Attach Form(s) W-2 here. Also attach Form(s) 1099-R if tax was withheld.

If you did not get a W-2, see page 22.

Enclose, but do not attach, any payment.

7 Wages, salaries, tips, etc. Attach Form(s) W-2. 7

8a **Taxable** interest. Attach Schedule 1 if required. 8a
 b **Tax-exempt** interest. **Do not** include on line 8a. 8b

9a Ordinary dividends. Attach Schedule 1 if required. 9a
 b Qualified dividends (see page 23). 9b

10 Capital gain distributions (see page 23). 10

11a IRA distributions. 11a | 11b Taxable amount (see page 23). 11b

12a Pensions and annuities. 12a | 12b Taxable amount (see page 24). 12b

13 Unemployment compensation and Alaska Permanent Fund dividends. 13

14a Social security benefits. 14a | 14b Taxable amount (see page 26). 14b

15 Add lines 7 through 14b (far right column). This is your **total income.** ► 15

Adjusted gross income

16 Educator expenses (see page 26). 16
17 IRA deduction (see page 26). 17
18 Student loan interest deduction (see page 29). 18
19 Tuition and fees deduction (see page 29). 19
20 Add lines 16 through 19. These are your **total adjustments.** 20

21 Subtract line 20 from line 15. This is your **adjusted gross income.** ► 21

For Disclosure, Privacy Act, and Paperwork Reduction Act Notice, see page 57.   Cat. No. 11327A   Form **1040A** (2004)

Form 1040A (2004) Page **2**

Tax, credits, and payments	**22** Enter the amount from line 21 (adjusted gross income).	22

23a Check if: □ **You** were born before January 2, 1940, □ Blind ⎱ **Total boxes**
□ **Spouse** was born before January 2, 1940, □ Blind ⎰ checked ▶ 23a

b If you are married filing separately and your spouse itemizes deductions, see page 30 and check here ▶ 23b □

Standard Deduction for—

- People who checked any box on line 23a or 23b **or** who can be claimed as a dependent, see page 31.
- All others:

Single or Married filing separately, $4,850

Married filing jointly or Qualifying widow(er), $9,700

Head of household, $7,150

24 Enter your **standard deduction** (see left margin). | 24

25 Subtract line 24 from line 22. If line 24 is more than line 22, enter -0-. | 25

26 If line 22 is $107,025 or less, multiply $3,100 by the total number of exemptions claimed on line 6d. If line 22 is over $107,025, see the worksheet on page 32. | 26

27 Subtract line 26 from line 25. If line 26 is more than line 25, enter -0-. This is your **taxable income.** ▶ 27

28 **Tax,** including any alternative minimum tax (see page 31). | 28

29 Credit for child and dependent care expenses. Attach Schedule 2. | 29

30 Credit for the elderly or the disabled. Attach Schedule 3. | 30

31 Education credits. Attach Form 8863. | 31

32 Retirement savings contributions credit. Attach Form 8880. | 32

33 Child tax credit (see page 36). | 33

34 Adoption credit. Attach Form 8839. | 34

35 Add lines 29 through 34. These are your **total credits.** | 35

36 Subtract line 35 from line 28. If line 35 is more than line 28, enter -0-. | 36

37 Advance earned income credit payments from Form(s) W-2. | 37

38 Add lines 36 and 37. This is your **total tax.** ▶ 38

39 Federal income tax withheld from Forms W-2 and 1099. | 39

40 2004 estimated tax payments and amount applied from 2003 return. | 40

If you have a qualifying child, attach Schedule EIC.

41a **Earned income credit (EIC).** | 41a

b Nontaxable combat pay election. 41b

42 Additional child tax credit. Attach Form 8812. | 42

43 Add lines 39, 40, 41a, and 42. These are your **total payments.** ▶ 43

Refund

Direct deposit? See page 50 and fill in 45b, 45c, and 45d.

44 If line 43 is more than line 38, subtract line 38 from line 43. This is the amount you **overpaid.** | 44

45a Amount of line 44 you want **refunded to you.** ▶ 45a

▶ **b** Routing number | ▶ **c** Type: □ Checking □ Savings

▶ **d** Account number

46 Amount of line 44 you want **applied to your 2005 estimated tax.** | 46

Amount you owe

47 **Amount you owe.** Subtract line 43 from line 38. For details on how to pay, see page 51. ▶ 47

48 Estimated tax penalty (see page 51). | 48

Third party designee

Do you want to allow another person to discuss this return with the IRS (see page 52)? □ **Yes.** Complete the following. □ **No**

Designee's name ▶ | Phone no. ▶ ( ) | Personal identification number (PIN) ▶

Sign here

Under penalties of perjury, I declare that I have examined this return and accompanying schedules and statements, and to the best of my knowledge and belief, they are true, correct, and accurately list all amounts and sources of income I received during the tax year. Declaration of preparer (other than the taxpayer) is based on all information of which the preparer has any knowledge.

Joint return? See page 18.

Keep a copy for your records.

Your signature | Date | Your occupation | Daytime phone number ( )

Spouse's signature. If a joint return, **both** must sign. | Date | Spouse's occupation

Paid preparer's use only

Preparer's signature ▶ | Date | Check if self-employed □ | Preparer's SSN or PTIN

Firm's name (or yours if self-employed), address, and ZIP code ▶ | EIN | Phone no. ( )

Form **1040A** (2004)

Schedule 1
(Form 1040A)

Department of the Treasury—Internal Revenue Service

Interest and Ordinary Dividends
for Form 1040A Filers   (99)   **2004**

OMB No. 1545-0085

Name(s) shown on Form 1040A

Your social security number

Part I

Interest

(See back
of schedule
and the
instructions
for Form
1040A,
line 8a.)

Note. If you received a Form 1099-INT, Form 1099-OID, or substitute statement from a brokerage firm, enter the firm's name and the total interest shown on that form.

1 List name of payer. If any interest is from a seller-financed mortgage and the buyer used the property as a personal residence, see back of schedule and list this interest first. Also, show that buyer's social security number and address.

Amount

| | 1 | |

2 Add the amounts on line 1. | 2 |

3 Excludable interest on series EE and I U.S. savings bonds issued after 1989. Attach Form 8815. | 3 |

4 Subtract line 3 from line 2. Enter the result here and on Form 1040A, line 8a. | 4 |

Part II

Ordinary dividends

(See back
of schedule
and the
instructions
for Form
1040A,
line 9a.)

Note. If you received a Form 1099-DIV or substitute statement from a brokerage firm, enter the firm's name and the ordinary dividends shown on that form.

5 List name of payer.

Amount

| | 5 | |

6 Add the amounts on line 5. Enter the total here and on Form 1040A, line 9a. | 6 |

For Paperwork Reduction Act Notice, see Form 1040A instructions.   Cat. No. 12075R   **Schedule 1 (Form 1040A) 2004**

B-2   Form 1040EZ   Income Tax Return for Single Filers with No Dependents

Department of the Treasury—Internal Revenue Service

Form **1040EZ**

Income Tax Return for Single and Joint Filers With No Dependents (99) **2004**

OMB No. 1545-0675

Label (See page 11.) **Use the IRS label.** Otherwise, please print or type.

L A B E L   H E R E

Your first name and initial   Last name

If a joint return, spouse's first name and initial   Last name

Home address (number and street). If you have a P.O. box, see page 11.   Apt. no.

City, town or post office, state, and ZIP code. If you have a foreign address, see page 11.

Your social security number

Spouse's social security number

▲ **Important!** ▲

You **must** enter your SSN(s) above.

Presidential Election Campaign (page 11) ▶

Note. Checking "Yes" will not change your tax or reduce your refund.

Do you, or your spouse if a joint return, want $3 to go to this fund? . . . . . . ▶

You   Spouse

☐ Yes ☐ No   ☐ Yes ☐ No

Income

Attach Form(s) W-2 here. Enclose, but do not attach, any payment.

1 Wages, salaries, and tips. This should be shown in box 1 of your Form(s) W-2. Attach your Form(s) W-2.   **1**

2 Taxable interest. If the total is over $1,500, you cannot use Form 1040EZ.   **2**

3 Unemployment compensation and Alaska Permanent Fund dividends (see page 13).   **3**

4 Add lines 1, 2, and 3. This is your **adjusted gross income.**   **4**

Note. You **must** check Yes or No.

5 Can your parents (or someone else) claim you on their return?

☐ **Yes.** Enter amount from worksheet on back.

☐ **No.** If **single,** enter $7,950. If **married filing jointly,** enter $15,900. See back for explanation.   **5**

6 Subtract line 5 from line 4. If line 5 is larger than line 4, enter -0-. This is your **taxable income.**   ▶   **6**

Payments and tax

7 Federal income tax withheld from box 2 of your Form(s) W-2.   **7**

8a **Earned income credit (EIC).**   **8a**

b Nontaxable combat pay election.   **8b**

9 Add lines 7 and 8a. These are your **total payments.**   ▶   **9**

10 **Tax.** Use the amount on **line 6 above** to find your tax in the tax table on pages 24–32 of the booklet. Then, enter the tax from the table on this line.   **10**

Refund

Have it directly deposited! See page 18 and fill in 11b, 11c, and 11d.

11a If line 9 is larger than line 10, subtract line 10 from line 9. This is your **refund.**   ▶   **11a**

▶ **b** Routing number   ▶ **c** Type: ☐ Checking ☐ Savings

▶ **d** Account number

Amount you owe

12 If line 10 is larger than line 9, subtract line 9 from line 10. This is the **amount you owe.** For details on how to pay, see page 19.   ▶   **12**

Third party designee

Do you want to allow another person to discuss this return with the IRS (see page 19)? ☐ **Yes.** Complete the following. ☐ **No**

Designee's name ▶   Phone no. ▶ (   )   Personal identification number (PIN) ▶

Sign here

Joint return? See page 11.

Keep a copy for your records.

Under penalties of perjury, I declare that I have examined this return, and to the best of my knowledge and belief, it is true, correct, and accurately lists all amounts and sources of income I received during the tax year. Declaration of preparer (other than the taxpayer) is based on all information of which the preparer has any knowledge.

Your signature   Date   Your occupation   Daytime phone number ( )

Spouse's signature. If a joint return, **both** must sign.   Date   Spouse's occupation

Paid preparer's use only

Preparer's signature ▶   Date   Check if self-employed ☐   Preparer's SSN or PTIN

Firm's name (or yours if self-employed), address, and ZIP code ▶   EIN   Phone no. (   )

For Disclosure, Privacy Act, and Paperwork Reduction Act Notice, see page 23.   Cat. No. 11329W   Form **1040EZ** (2004)

Form 1040EZ (2004)

Use this form if

- Your filing status is single or married filing jointly. If you are not sure about your filing status, see page 11.
- You (and your spouse if married filing jointly) were under age 65 and not blind at the end of 2004. If you were born on January 1, 1940, you are considered to be age 65 at the end of 2004.
- You do not claim any dependents. For information on dependents, use TeleTax topic 354 (see page 6).
- Your taxable income (line 6) is less than $100,000.
- You do not claim any adjustments to income. For information on adjustments to income, use TeleTax topics 451-458 (see page 6).
- The only tax credit you can claim is the earned income credit. For information on credits, use TeleTax topics 601-608 and 610 (see page 6).
- You had only wages, salaries, tips, taxable scholarship or fellowship grants, unemployment compensation, or Alaska Permanent Fund dividends, and your taxable interest was not over $1,500. But if you earned tips, including allocated tips, that are not included in box 5 and box 7 of your Form W-2, you may not be able to use Form 1040EZ (see page 12). If you are planning to use Form 1040EZ for a child who received Alaska Permanent Fund dividends, see page 13.
- You did not receive any advance earned income credit payments. If you cannot use this form, use TeleTax topic 352 (see page 6).

Filling in your return

For tips on how to avoid common mistakes, see page 20.

If you received a scholarship or fellowship grant or tax-exempt interest income, such as on municipal bonds, see the booklet before filling in the form. Also, see the booklet if you received a Form 1099-INT showing federal income tax withheld or if federal income tax was withheld from your unemployment compensation or Alaska Permanent Fund dividends.

Remember, you must report all wages, salaries, and tips even if you do not get a Form W-2 from your employer. You must also report all your taxable interest, including interest from banks, savings and loans, credit unions, etc., even if you do not get a Form 1099-INT.

Worksheet for dependents who checked "Yes" on line 5

(keep a copy for your records)

Use this worksheet to figure the amount to enter on line 5 if someone can claim you (or your spouse if married filing jointly) as a dependent, even if that person chooses not to do so. To find out if someone can claim you as a dependent, use TeleTax topic 354 (see page 6).

A. Amount, if any, from line 1 on front _____

+ 250.00 Enter total ▶ **A.** _____

B. Minimum standard deduction . . . . **B.** _____ 800.00

C. Enter the **larger** of line A or line B here . . . . **C.** _____

D. Maximum standard deduction. If **single,** enter $4,850; if **married filing jointly,** enter $9,700 . . . . **D.** _____

E. Enter the **smaller** of line C or line D here. This is your standard deduction . . . . **E.** _____

F. Exemption amount.

- If single, enter -0-.
- If married filing jointly and—

    —both you and your spouse can be claimed as dependents, enter -0-.

    —only one of you can be claimed as a dependent, enter $3,100.

F. _____

G. Add lines E and F. Enter the total here and on line 5 on the front . . **G.** _____

If you checked "No" on line 5 because no one can claim you (or your spouse if married filing jointly) as a dependent, enter on line 5 the amount shown below that applies to you.

- Single, enter $7,950. This is the total of your standard deduction ($4,850) and your exemption ($3,100).
- Married filing jointly, enter $15,900. This is the total of your standard deduction ($9,700), your exemption ($3,100), and your spouse's exemption ($3,100).

Mailing return

Mail your return by **April 15, 2005.** Use the envelope that came with your booklet. If you do not have that envelope or if you moved during the year, see the back cover for the address to use.

Form **1040EZ** (2004)

B-3   Form 1040   U.S. Individual Income Tax Return and Schedules

Form **1040**

Department of the Treasury—Internal Revenue Service

U.S. Individual Income Tax Return 2004   (99)   IRS Use Only—Do not write or staple in this space.

For the year Jan. 1–Dec. 31, 2004, or other tax year beginning _____, 2004, ending _____, 20 ____

OMB No. 1545-0074

Label

(See instructions on page 16.)

Use the IRS label. Otherwise, please print or type.

L A B E L   H E R E

Your first name and initial | Last name | Your social security number

If a joint return, spouse's first name and initial | Last name | Spouse's social security number

Home address (number and street). If you have a P.O. box, see page 16. | Apt. no.

▲ **Important!** ▲
You **must** enter your SSN(s) above.

City, town or post office, state, and ZIP code. If you have a foreign address, see page 16.

Presidential Election Campaign
(See page 16.)

► **Note.** Checking "Yes" will not change your tax or reduce your refund.
Do you, or your spouse if filing a joint return, want $3 to go to this fund? . . . ►

You | Spouse
☐ Yes ☐ No | ☐ Yes ☐ No

Filing Status

Check only one box.

1 ☐ Single
2 ☐ Married filing jointly (even if only one had income)
3 ☐ Married filing separately. Enter spouse's SSN above and full name here. ►
4 ☐ Head of household (with qualifying person). (See page 17.) If the qualifying person is a child but not your dependent, enter this child's name here. ► _____
5 ☐ Qualifying widow(er) with dependent child (see page 17)

Exemptions

If more than four dependents, see page 18.

6a ☐ **Yourself.** If someone can claim you as a dependent, **do not** check box 6a . . . . .
b ☐ **Spouse** . . . .

c **Dependents:**

(1) First name Last name	(2) Dependent's social security number	(3) Dependent's relationship to you	(4) ✓ if qualifying child for child tax credit (see page 18)
			☐
			☐
			☐
			☐

Boxes checked on 6a and 6b ____
No. of children on 6c who:
• lived with you ____
• did not live with you due to divorce or separation (see page 18) ____
Dependents on 6c not entered above ____

d Total number of exemptions claimed . . . .

Add numbers on lines above ► ☐

Income

Attach Form(s) W-2 here. Also attach Forms W-2G and 1099-R if tax was withheld.

If you did not get a W-2, see page 19.

Enclose, but do not attach, any payment. Also, please use Form 1040-V.

7 Wages, salaries, tips, etc. Attach Form(s) W-2 . . . . | 7 |
8a **Taxable** interest. Attach Schedule B if required . . . . | 8a |
b **Tax-exempt** interest. **Do not** include on line 8a . . . | 8b |
9a Ordinary dividends. Attach Schedule B if required . . . . . . | 9a |
b Qualified dividends (see page 20) . . . . . . | 9b |
10 Taxable refunds, credits, or offsets of state and local income taxes (see page 20) . . | 10 |
11 Alimony received . . . . | 11 |
12 Business income or (loss). Attach Schedule C or C-EZ . . . . | 12 |
13 Capital gain or (loss). Attach Schedule D if required. If not required, check here ► ☐ | 13 |
14 Other gains or (losses). Attach Form 4797 . . . . | 14 |
15a IRA distributions . . | 15a | b Taxable amount (see page 22) | 15b |
16a Pensions and annuities | 16a | b Taxable amount (see page 22) | 16b |
17 Rental real estate, royalties, partnerships, S corporations, trusts, etc. Attach Schedule E | 17 |
18 Farm income or (loss). Attach Schedule F . . . . | 18 |
19 Unemployment compensation . . . . | 19 |
20a Social security benefits . | 20a | b Taxable amount (see page 24) | 20b |
21 Other income. List type and amount (see page 24) _____ | 21 |
22 Add the amounts in the far right column for lines 7 through 21. This is your **total income** ► | 22 |

Adjusted Gross Income

23 Educator expenses (see page 26) . . . . . . | 23 |
24 Certain business expenses of reservists, performing artists, and fee-basis government officials. Attach Form 2106 or 2106-EZ | 24 |
25 IRA deduction (see page 26) . . . . | 25 |
26 Student loan interest deduction (see page 28) . . . . | 26 |
27 Tuition and fees deduction (see page 29) . . . . | 27 |
28 Health savings account deduction. Attach Form 8889 . . | 28 |
29 Moving expenses. Attach Form 3903 . . . . . . | 29 |
30 One-half of self-employment tax. Attach Schedule SE . . | 30 |
31 Self-employed health insurance deduction (see page 30) . . | 31 |
32 Self-employed SEP, SIMPLE, and qualified plans . . . | 32 |
33 Penalty on early withdrawal of savings . . . . . | 33 |
34a Alimony paid b Recipient's SSN ► _____ | 34a |
35 Add lines 23 through 34a . . . . | 35 |
36 Subtract line 35 from line 22. This is your **adjusted gross income** . . . . . ► | 36 |

For Disclosure, Privacy Act, and Paperwork Reduction Act Notice, see page 75.   Cat. No. 11320B   Form **1040** (2004)

Form 1040 (2004)   Page **2**

Tax and Credits	37	Amount from line 36 (adjusted gross income)	37	
	38a	Check if: ☐ **You** were born before January 2, 1940, ☐ Blind. ☐ **Spouse** was born before January 2, 1940, ☐ Blind. } Total boxes checked ▶ **38a**		
Standard Deduction for—	b	If your spouse itemizes on a separate return or you were a dual-status alien, see page 31 and check here ▶ 38b ☐		
	39	**Itemized deductions** (from Schedule A) **or** your **standard deduction** (see left margin) .	39	
	40	Subtract line 39 from line 37	40	
• People who checked any box on line 38a or 38b **or** who can be claimed as a dependent, see page 31.	41	If line 37 is $107,025 or less, multiply $3,100 by the total number of exemptions claimed on line 6d. If line 37 is over $107,025, see the worksheet on page 33	41	
	42	**Taxable income.** Subtract line 41 from line 40. If line 41 is more than line 40, enter -0-	42	
	43	**Tax** (see page 33). Check if any tax is from: **a** ☐ Form(s) 8814 **b** ☐ Form 4972 . . .	43	
• All others:	44	**Alternative minimum tax** (see page 35). Attach Form 6251	44	
Single or Married filing separately, $4,850	45	Add lines 43 and 44 . . . . ▶	45	

Married filing jointly or Qualifying widow(er), $9,700	46	Foreign tax credit. Attach Form 1116 if required . . .	46	
	47	Credit for child and dependent care expenses. Attach Form 2441	47	
	48	Credit for the elderly or the disabled. Attach Schedule R .	48	
	49	Education credits. Attach Form 8863	49	
Head of household, $7,150	50	Retirement savings contributions credit. Attach Form 8880 . .	50	
	51	Child tax credit (see page 37)	51	
	52	Adoption credit. Attach Form 8839	52	
	53	Credits from: **a** ☐ Form 8396 **b** ☐ Form 8859 . .	53	
	54	Other credits. Check applicable box(es): **a** ☐ Form 3800 **b** ☐ Form 8801 **c** ☐ Specify _____	54	

	55	Add lines 46 through 54. These are your **total credits**	55	
	56	Subtract line 55 from line 45. If line 55 is more than line 45, enter -0- . . . . . ▶	56	
Other Taxes	57	Self-employment tax. Attach Schedule SE	57	
	58	Social security and Medicare tax on tip income not reported to employer. Attach Form 4137 . .	58	
	59	Additional tax on IRAs, other qualified retirement plans, etc. Attach Form 5329 if required .	59	
	60	Advance earned income credit payments from Form(s) W-2	60	
	61	Household employment taxes. Attach Schedule H	61	
	62	Add lines 56 through 61. This is your **total tax** . . . . ▶	62	

Payments	63	Federal income tax withheld from Forms W-2 and 1099 . .	63	
	64	2004 estimated tax payments and amount applied from 2003 return	64	
If you have a qualifying child, attach Schedule EIC.	65a	**Earned income credit (EIC)**	65a	
	b	Nontaxable combat pay election ▶ 65b		
	66	Excess social security and tier 1 RRTA tax withheld (see page 54)	66	
	67	Additional child tax credit. Attach Form 8812	67	
	68	Amount paid with request for extension to file (see page 54)	68	
	69	Other payments from: **a** ☐ Form 2439 **b** ☐ Form 4136 **c** ☐ Form 8885	69	
	70	Add lines 63, 64, 65a, and 66 through 69. These are your **total payments** . . . . ▶	70	

Refund	71	If line 70 is more than line 62, subtract line 62 from line 70. This is the amount you **overpaid**	71	
Direct deposit? See page 54 and fill in 72b, 72c, and 72d.	72a	Amount of line 71 you want **refunded to you** . . . . ▶	72a	
	▶ b	Routing number ⬚⬚⬚⬚⬚⬚⬚⬚⬚ ▶ **c** Type: ☐ Checking ☐ Savings		
	▶ d	Account number ⬚⬚⬚⬚⬚⬚⬚⬚⬚⬚⬚⬚⬚⬚⬚⬚⬚		
	73	Amount of line 71 you want **applied to your 2005 estimated tax** ▶ 73		
Amount You Owe	74	**Amount you owe.** Subtract line 70 from line 62. For details on how to pay, see page 55 ▶	74	
	75	Estimated tax penalty (see page 55) 75		

Third Party Designee

Do you want to allow another person to discuss this return with the IRS (see page 56)? ☐ **Yes.** Complete the following. ☐ **No**

Designee's name ▶	Phone no. ▶ ( )	Personal identification number (PIN) ▶ ⬚⬚⬚⬚⬚

Sign Here

Under penalties of perjury, I declare that I have examined this return and accompanying schedules and statements, and to the best of my knowledge and belief, they are true, correct, and complete. Declaration of preparer (other than taxpayer) is based on all information of which preparer has any knowledge.

Joint return? See page 17.
Keep a copy for your records.

Your signature	Date	Your occupation	Daytime phone number
			( )
Spouse's signature. If a joint return, **both** must sign.	Date	Spouse's occupation	

Paid Preparer's Use Only

Preparer's signature ▶	Date	Check if self-employed ☐	Preparer's SSN or PTIN
Firm's name (or yours if self-employed), address, and ZIP code ▶		EIN	
		Phone no. ( )	

Form **1040** (2004)

SCHEDULES A&B (Form 1040) Department of the Treasury Internal Revenue Service (99)	Schedule A—Itemized Deductions (Schedule B is on back) ▶ Attach to Form 1040. ▶ See Instructions for Schedules A and B (Form 1040).	OMB No. 1545-0074 2004 Attachment Sequence No. 07

Name(s) shown on Form 1040 | Your social security number

Medical and Dental Expenses

Caution. Do not include expenses reimbursed or paid by others.

1. Medical and dental expenses (see page A-2) . . . **1**
2. Enter amount from Form 1040, line 37 | **2** |
3. Multiply line 2 by 7.5% (.075). **3**
4. Subtract line 3 from line 1. If line 3 is more than line 1, enter -0- **4**

Taxes You Paid

(See page A-2.)

5. State and local (**check only one box**):
   a ☐ Income taxes, **or**
   b ☐ General sales taxes (see page A-2) } . . . **5**
6. Real estate taxes (see page A-3). **6**
7. Personal property taxes **7**
8. Other taxes. List type and amount ▶ **8**
9. Add lines 5 through 8 . . . . **9**

Interest You Paid

(See page A-3.)

Note.
Personal interest is not deductible.

10. Home mortgage interest and points reported to you on Form 1098 **10**
11. Home mortgage interest not reported to you on Form 1098. If paid to the person from whom you bought the home, see page A-4 and show that person's name, identifying no., and address ▶

    .... **11**
12. Points not reported to you on Form 1098. See page A-4 for special rules . . . **12**
13. Investment interest. Attach Form 4952 if required. (See page A-4.) **13**
14. Add lines 10 through 13 . . . . **14**

Gifts to Charity

If you made a gift and got a benefit for it, see page A-4.

15. Gifts by cash or check. If you made any gift of $250 or more, see page A-4 . . . . **15**
16. Other than by cash or check. If any gift of $250 or more, see page A-4. You **must** attach Form 8283 if over $500 **16**
17. Carryover from prior year **17**
18. Add lines 15 through 17 . . . . **18**

Casualty and Theft Losses

19. Casualty or theft loss(es). Attach Form 4684. (See page A-5.) **19**

Job Expenses and Most Other Miscellaneous Deductions

(See page A-5.)

20. Unreimbursed employee expenses—job travel, union dues, job education, etc. Attach Form 2106 or 2106-EZ if required. (See page A-6.) ▶ ....
    ....
    .... **20**
21. Tax preparation fees. **21**
22. Other expenses—investment, safe deposit box, etc. List type and amount ▶ ....
    .... **22**
23. Add lines 20 through 22 . . . . **23**
24. Enter amount from Form 1040, line 37 | **24** |
25. Multiply line 24 by 2% (.02) **25**
26. Subtract line 25 from line 23. If line 25 is more than line 23, enter -0- **26**

Other Miscellaneous Deductions

27. Other—from list on page A-6. List type and amount ▶ ....
    .... **27**

Total Itemized Deductions

28. Is Form 1040, line 37, over $142,700 (over $71,350 if married filing separately)?
   ☐ **No.** Your deduction is not limited. Add the amounts in the far right column for lines 4 through 27. Also, enter this amount on Form 1040, line 39. } ▶ **28**
   ☐ **Yes.** Your deduction may be limited. See page A-6 for the amount to enter.

For Paperwork Reduction Act Notice, see Form 1040 instructions.   Cat. No. 11330X   Schedule A (Form 1040) 2004

Schedules A&B (Form 1040) 2004   OMB No. 1545-0074   Page **2**

Name(s) shown on Form 1040. Do not enter name and social security number if shown on other side. | **Your social security number**

Schedule B—Interest and Ordinary Dividends

Attachment
Sequence No. **08**

			Amount
Part I **Interest** (See page B-1 and the instructions for Form 1040, line 8a.)	**1**	List name of payer. If any interest is from a seller-financed mortgage and the buyer used the property as a personal residence, see page B-1 and list this interest first. Also, show that buyer's social security number and address ▶	
			1
Note. If you received a Form 1099-INT, Form 1099-OID, or substitute statement from a brokerage firm, list the firm's name as the payer and enter the total interest shown on that form.			
	2	Add the amounts on line 1	**2**
	3	Excludable interest on series EE and I U.S. savings bonds issued after 1989. Attach Form 8815	**3**
	4	Subtract line 3 from line 2. Enter the result here and on Form 1040, line 8a ▶	**4**

Note. If line 4 is over $1,500, you must complete Part III.

			Amount
Part II **Ordinary** **Dividends** (See page B-2 and the instructions for Form 1040, line 9a.)	**5**	List name of payer ▶	
			5
Note. If you received a Form 1099-DIV or substitute statement from a brokerage firm, list the firm's name as the payer and enter the ordinary dividends shown on that form.			
	6	Add the amounts on line 5. Enter the total here and on Form 1040, line 9a . ▶	**6**

Note. If line 6 is over $1,500, you must complete Part III.

			Yes	No
Part III **Foreign** **Accounts** **and Trusts** (See page B-2.)	You must complete this part if you **(a)** had over $1,500 of taxable interest or ordinary dividends; or **(b)** had a foreign account; or **(c)** received a distribution from, or were a grantor of, or a transferor to, a foreign trust.			
	7a	At any time during 2004, did you have an interest in or a signature or other authority over a financial account in a foreign country, such as a bank account, securities account, or other financial account? See page B-2 for exceptions and filing requirements for Form TD F 90-22.1.		
	b	If "Yes," enter the name of the foreign country ▶		
	8	During 2004, did you receive a distribution from, or were you the grantor of, or transferor to, a foreign trust? If "Yes," you may have to file Form 3520. See page B-2		

For Paperwork Reduction Act Notice, see Form 1040 instructions.   Schedule B (Form 1040) 2004

SCHEDULE C (Form 1040)	Profit or Loss From Business	OMB No. 1545-0074

SCHEDULE C
(Form 1040)

Department of the Treasury
Internal Revenue Service

Profit or Loss From Business
(Sole Proprietorship)

▶ **Partnerships, joint ventures, etc., must file Form 1065 or 1065-B.**

▶ **Attach to Form 1040 or 1041.**   ▶ **See Instructions for Schedule C (Form 1040).**

OMB No. 1545-0074

2004

Attachment
Sequence No. **09**

Name of proprietor

Social security number (SSN)

A Principal business or profession, including product or service (see page C-2 of the instructions)

B Enter code from pages C-7, 8, & 9
▶

C Business name. If no separate business name, leave blank.

D Employer ID number (EIN), if any

E Business address (including suite or room no.) ▶ ....
City, town or post office, state, and ZIP code

F Accounting method: **(1)** ☐ Cash   **(2)** ☐ Accrual   **(3)** ☐ Other (specify) ▶ ....

G Did you "materially participate" in the operation of this business during 2004? If "No," see page C-3 for limit on losses   ☐ Yes ☐ No

H If you started or acquired this business during 2004, check here . . . . ▶ ☐

Part I Income

1	Gross receipts or sales. **Caution.** If this income was reported to you on Form W-2 and the "Statutory employee" box on that form was checked, see page C-3 and check here . . . . . . ▶ ☐	**1**	
2	Returns and allowances	**2**	
3	Subtract line 2 from line 1	**3**	
4	Cost of goods sold (from line 42 on page 2)	**4**	
5	**Gross profit.** Subtract line 4 from line 3.	**5**	
6	Other income, including Federal and state gasoline or fuel tax credit or refund (see page C-3) . . .	**6**	
7	**Gross income.** Add lines 5 and 6 . . . . ▶	**7**	

Part II Expenses. Enter expenses for business use of your home **only** on line 30.

8	Advertising	**8**	**19** Pension and profit-sharing plans	**19**	
9	Car and truck expenses (see page C-3).	**9**	**20** Rent or lease (see page C-5):		
10	Commissions and fees . .	**10**	**a** Vehicles, machinery, and equipment .	**20a**	
11	Contract labor (see page C-4)	**11**	**b** Other business property . . .	**20b**	
12	Depletion	**12**	**21** Repairs and maintenance . .	**21**	
13	Depreciation and section 179 expense deduction (not included in Part III) (see page C-4)	**13**	**22** Supplies (not included in Part III) .	**22**	
			23 Taxes and licenses	**23**	
			24 Travel, meals, and entertainment:		
			a Travel	**24a**	
14	Employee benefit programs (other than on line 19).	**14**	**b** Meals and entertainment		
15	Insurance (other than health) .	**15**	**c** Enter nondeductible amount included on line 24b (see page C-5) .		
16	Interest:				
a	Mortgage (paid to banks, etc.) .	**16a**	**d** Subtract line 24c from line 24b .	**24d**	
b	Other	**16b**	**25** Utilities	**25**	
17	Legal and professional services	**17**	**26** Wages (less employment credits) .	**26**	
18	Office expense	**18**	**27** Other expenses (from line 48 on page 2)	**27**	

28	**Total expenses** before expenses for business use of home. Add lines 8 through 27 in columns . . ▶	**28**	
29	Tentative profit (loss). Subtract line 28 from line 7	**29**	
30	Expenses for business use of your home. Attach **Form 8829**	**30**	
31	**Net profit or (loss).** Subtract line 30 from line 29.		
	• If a profit, enter on **Form 1040, line 12,** and **also** on **Schedule SE, line 2** (statutory employees, see page C-6). Estates and trusts, enter on Form 1041, line 3.	**31**	
	• If a loss, you **must** go to line 32.		
32	If you have a loss, check the box that describes your investment in this activity (see page C-6).		
	• If you checked 32a, enter the loss on **Form 1040, line 12,** and **also** on **Schedule SE, line 2** (statutory employees, see page C-6). Estates and trusts, enter on Form 1041, line 3.	**32a** ☐ All investment is at risk.	
	• If you checked 32b, you **must** attach **Form 6198.**	**32b** ☐ Some investment is not at risk.	

For Paperwork Reduction Act Notice, see Form 1040 instructions.   Cat. No. 11334P   **Schedule C (Form 1040) 2004**

| **Part III** | **Cost of Goods Sold** (see page C-6) |

33   Method(s) used to value closing inventory: **a** ☐ Cost   **b** ☐ Lower of cost or market   **c** ☐ Other (attach explanation)

34   Was there any change in determining quantities, costs, or valuations between opening and closing inventory? If "Yes," attach explanation . . . . ☐ **Yes**   ☐ **No**

35	Inventory at beginning of year. If different from last year's closing inventory, attach explanation . .	**35**	
36	Purchases less cost of items withdrawn for personal use	**36**	
37	Cost of labor. Do not include any amounts paid to yourself	**37**	
38	Materials and supplies	**38**	
39	Other costs	**39**	
40	Add lines 35 through 39	**40**	
41	Inventory at end of year	**41**	
42	**Cost of goods sold.** Subtract line 41 from line 40. Enter the result here and on page 1, line 4 . .	**42**	

| **Part IV** | **Information on Your Vehicle.** Complete this part **only** if you are claiming car or truck expenses on line 9 and are not required to file Form 4562 for this business. See the instructions for line 13 on page C-4 to find out if you must file Form 4562. |

43   When did you place your vehicle in service for business purposes? (month, day, year) ▶ ..../......../........ .

44   Of the total number of miles you drove your vehicle during 2004, enter the number of miles you used your vehicle for:

a   Business ....   **b** Commuting ....   **c** Other ....

45   Do you (or your spouse) have another vehicle available for personal use? . . . . ☐ **Yes**   ☐ **No**

46   Was your vehicle available for personal use during off-duty hours? . . . . ☐ **Yes**   ☐ **No**

47a   Do you have evidence to support your deduction? . . . . ☐ **Yes**   ☐ **No**

   b   If "Yes," is the evidence written? . . . . ☐ **Yes**   ☐ **No**

| **Part V** | **Other Expenses.** List below business expenses not included on lines 8–26 or line 30. |

....	
....	
....	
....	
....	
....	
....	
....	
....	
48 **Total other expenses.** Enter here and on page 1, line 27	**48**

Schedule C (Form 1040) 2004

SCHEDULE D
(Form 1040)

Department of the Treasury
Internal Revenue Service   (99)

Capital Gains and Losses

▶ **Attach to Form 1040.**   ▶ **See Instructions for Schedule D (Form 1040).**

▶ **Use Schedule D-1 to list additional transactions for lines 1 and 8.**

OMB No. 1545-0074

2004

Attachment
Sequence No. **12**

Name(s) shown on Form 1040

Your social security number

Part I   Short-Term Capital Gains and Losses—Assets Held One Year or Less

	(a) Description of property (Example: 100 sh. XYZ Co.)	(b) Date acquired (Mo., day, yr.)	(c) Date sold (Mo., day, yr.)	(d) Sales price (see page D-6 of the instructions)	(e) Cost or other basis (see page D-6 of the instructions)	(f) Gain or (loss) Subtract (e) from (d)
1						

2	Enter your short-term totals, if any, from Schedule D-1, line 2	**2**	
3	**Total short-term sales price amounts.** Add lines 1 and 2 in column (d)	**3**	
4	Short-term gain from Form 6252 and short-term gain or (loss) from Forms 4684, 6781, and 8824	**4**	
5	Net short-term gain or (loss) from partnerships, S corporations, estates, and trusts from Schedule(s) K-1	**5**	
6	Short-term capital loss carryover. Enter the amount, if any, from line 8 of your **Capital Loss Carryover Worksheet** on page D-6 of the instructions	**6**	( )
7	**Net short-term capital gain or (loss).** Combine lines 1 through 6 in column (f)	**7**	

Part II   Long-Term Capital Gains and Losses—Assets Held More Than One Year

	(a) Description of property (Example: 100 sh. XYZ Co.)	(b) Date acquired (Mo., day, yr.)	(c) Date sold (Mo., day, yr.)	(d) Sales price (see page D-6 of the instructions)	(e) Cost or other basis (see page D-6 of the instructions)	(f) Gain or (loss) Subtract (e) from (d)
8						

9	Enter your long-term totals, if any, from Schedule D-1, line 9	**9**	
10	**Total long-term sales price amounts.** Add lines 8 and 9 in column (d)	**10**	
11	Gain from Form 4797, Part I; long-term gain from Forms 2439 and 6252; and long-term gain or (loss) from Forms 4684, 6781, and 8824	**11**	
12	Net long-term gain or (loss) from partnerships, S corporations, estates, and trusts from Schedule(s) K-1	**12**	
13	Capital gain distributions. See page D-1 of the instructions	**13**	
14	Long-term capital loss carryover. Enter the amount, if any, from line 13 of your **Capital Loss Carryover Worksheet** on page D-6 of the instructions	**14**	( )
15	**Net long-term capital gain or (loss).** Combine lines 8 through 14 in column (f). Then go to Part III on the back	**15**	

For Paperwork Reduction Act Notice, see Form 1040 instructions.   Cat. No. 11338H   Schedule D (Form 1040) 2004

Schedule D (Form 1040) 2004   Page **2**

| **Part III** | **Summary** |

16 Combine lines 7 and 15 and enter the result. If line 16 is a loss, skip lines 17 through 20, and go to line 21. If a gain, enter the gain on Form 1040, line 13, and then go to line 17 below . . **16**

17 Are lines 15 and 16 **both** gains?
☐ **Yes.** Go to line 18.
☐ **No.** Skip lines 18 through 21, and go to line 22.

18 Enter the amount, if any, from line 7 of the **28% Rate Gain Worksheet** on page D-7 of the instructions . . . . ▶ **18**

19 Enter the amount, if any, from line 18 of the **Unrecaptured Section 1250 Gain Worksheet** on page D-8 of the instructions . . . . ▶ **19**

20 Are lines 18 and 19 **both** zero or blank?
☐ **Yes.** Complete Form 1040 through line 42, and then complete the **Qualified Dividends and Capital Gain Tax Worksheet** on page 34 of the Instructions for Form 1040. **Do not** complete lines 21 and 22 below.

☐ **No.** Complete Form 1040 through line 42, and then complete the **Schedule D Tax Worksheet** on page D-9 of the instructions. **Do not** complete lines 21 and 22 below.

21 If line 16 is a loss, enter here and on Form 1040, line 13, the **smaller** of:

● The loss on line 16 or
● ($3,000), or if married filing separately, ($1,500) } . . . . **21** (   )

Note. When figuring which amount is smaller, treat both amounts as positive numbers.

22 Do you have qualified dividends on Form 1040, line 9b?
☐ **Yes.** Complete Form 1040 through line 42, and then complete the **Qualified Dividends and Capital Gain Tax Worksheet** on page 34 of the Instructions for Form 1040.
☐ **No.** Complete the rest of Form 1040.

Schedule D (Form 1040) 2004

SCHEDULE E
(Form 1040)

Department of the Treasury
Internal Revenue Service   (99)

Supplemental Income and Loss

(From rental real estate, royalties, partnerships,
S corporations, estates, trusts, REMICs, etc.)

▶ **Attach to Form 1040 or Form 1041.**   ▶ **See Instructions for Schedule E (Form 1040).**

OMB No. 1545-0074

2004

Attachment
Sequence No. **13**

Name(s) shown on return | Your social security number

Part I   **Income or Loss From Rental Real Estate and Royalties**   **Note.** If you are in the business of renting personal property, use **Schedule C** or **C-EZ** (see page E-3). Report farm rental income or loss from **Form 4835** on page 2, line 40.

1 List the type and location of each **rental real estate property:**

A ....

B ....

C ....

2 For each rental real estate property listed on line 1, did you or your family use it during the tax year for personal purposes for more than the greater of:
● 14 days **or**
● 10% of the total days rented at fair rental value?
(See page E-3.)

	Yes	No
A		
B		
C		

Income:

		Properties			Totals (Add columns A, B, and C.)
		A	B	C	
3 Rents received	3				3
4 Royalties received	4				4

Expenses:

5 Advertising	5				
6 Auto and travel (see page E-4)	6				
7 Cleaning and maintenance	7				
8 Commissions	8				
9 Insurance	9				
10 Legal and other professional fees	10				
11 Management fees	11				
12 Mortgage interest paid to banks, etc. (see page E-4)	12				12
13 Other interest	13				
14 Repairs	14				
15 Supplies	15				
16 Taxes	16				
17 Utilities	17				
18 Other (list) ▶	18				
19 Add lines 5 through 18	19				19
20 Depreciation expense or depletion (see page E-4)	20				20
21 Total expenses. Add lines 19 and 20	21				
22 Income or (loss) from rental real estate or royalty properties. Subtract line 21 from line 3 (rents) or line 4 (royalties). If the result is a (loss), see page E-4 to find out if you must file **Form 6198**	22				
23 Deductible rental real estate loss. **Caution.** Your rental real estate loss on line 22 may be limited. See page E-4 to find out if you must file **Form 8582.** Real estate professionals must complete line 43 on page 2	23	( )(	)(	)	

24 Income. Add positive amounts shown on line 22. **Do not** include any losses | **24** |

25 Losses. Add royalty losses from line 22 and rental real estate losses from line 23. Enter total losses here | **25** | ( )

26 **Total rental real estate and royalty income or (loss).** Combine lines 24 and 25. Enter the result here. If Parts II, III, IV, and line 40 on page 2 do not apply to you, also enter this amount on Form 1040, line 17. Otherwise, include this amount in the total on line 41 on page 2 | **26** |

For Paperwork Reduction Act Notice, see Form 1040 instructions.   Cat. No. 11344L   Schedule E (Form 1040) 2004

Schedule E (Form 1040) 2004   Attachment Sequence No. **13**   Page **2**

Name(s) shown on return. Do not enter name and social security number if shown on other side. | Your social security number

Caution. The IRS compares amounts reported on your tax return with amounts shown on Schedule(s) K-1.

| **Part II** | **Income or Loss From Partnerships and S Corporations**   **Note.** If you report a loss from an at-risk activity for which **any** amount is **not** at risk, you **must** check column **(e)** on line 28 and attach **Form 6198**. See page E-1. |

27 Are you reporting any loss not allowed in a prior year due to the at-risk or basis limitations, a prior year unallowed loss from a passive activity (if that loss was not reported on Form 8582), or unreimbursed partnership expenses?   ☐ **Yes**   ☐ **No**
If you answered "Yes," see page E-6 before completing this section.

28	(a) Name	(b) Enter P for partnership; S for S corporation	(c) Check if foreign partnership	(d) Employer identification number	(e) Check if any amount is not at risk
A					
B					
C					
D					

	Passive Income and Loss		Nonpassive Income and Loss		
	(f) Passive loss allowed (attach **Form 8582** if required)	(g) Passive income from **Schedule K-1**	(h) Nonpassive loss from **Schedule K-1**	(i) Section 179 expense deduction from **Form 4562**	(j) Nonpassive income from **Schedule K-1**
A					
B					
C					
D					
29a Totals					
b Totals					

30 Add columns (g) and (j) of line 29a . . . . | **30** |
31 Add columns (f), (h), and (i) of line 29b . . . . . . | **31** ( )
32 **Total partnership and S corporation income or (loss).** Combine lines 30 and 31. Enter the result here and include in the total on line 41 below. . . . . | **32** |

| **Part III** | **Income or Loss From Estates and Trusts** |

33	(a) Name	(b) Employer identification number
A		
B		

	Passive Income and Loss		Nonpassive Income and Loss	
	(c) Passive deduction or loss allowed (attach **Form 8582** if required)	(d) Passive income from **Schedule K-1**	(e) Deduction or loss from **Schedule K-1**	(f) Other income from **Schedule K-1**
A				
B				
34a Totals				
b Totals				

35 Add columns (d) and (f) of line 34a . . . . | **35** |
36 Add columns (c) and (e) of line 34b . . . . | **36** ( )
37 **Total estate and trust income or (loss).** Combine lines 35 and 36. Enter the result here and include in the total on line 41 below | **37** |

| **Part IV** | **Income or Loss From Real Estate Mortgage Investment Conduits (REMICs)—Residual Holder** |

38	(a) Name	(b) Employer identification number	(c) Excess inclusion from **Schedules Q**, line 2c (see page E-6)	(d) Taxable income (net loss) from **Schedules Q**, line 1b	(e) Income from **Schedules Q**, line 3b

39 Combine columns (d) and (e) only. Enter the result here and include in the total on line 41 below | **39** |

| **Part V** | **Summary** |

40 Net farm rental income or (loss) from **Form 4835.** Also, complete line 42 below . . . . . . | **40** |
41 **Total income or (loss).** Combine lines 26, 32, 37, 39, and 40. Enter the result here and on Form 1040, line 17 ▶ | **41** |

42 **Reconciliation of farming and fishing income.** Enter your **gross** farming and fishing income reported on Form 4835, line 7; Schedule K-1 (Form 1065), box 14, code B; Schedule K-1 (Form 1120S), box 17, code N; and Schedule K-1 (Form 1041), line 14 (see page E-6) | **42** |

43 **Reconciliation for real estate professionals.** If you were a real estate professional (see page E-1), enter the net income or (loss) you reported anywhere on Form 1040 from all rental real estate activities in which you materially participated under the passive activity loss rules . . . | **43** |

✱   **Schedule E (Form 1040) 2004**

SCHEDULE F
(Form 1040)

Department of the Treasury
Internal Revenue Service (99)

Profit or Loss From Farming

▶ Attach to Form 1040, Form 1041, Form 1065, or Form 1065-B.

▶ See Instructions for Schedule F (Form 1040).

OMB No. 1545-0074

2004

Attachment
Sequence No. **14**

Name of proprietor

Social security number (SSN)

A Principal product. Describe in one or two words your principal crop or activity for the current tax year.

B Enter code from Part IV
▶

D Employer ID number (EIN), if any

C Accounting method: **(1)** ☐ Cash   **(2)** ☐ Accrual

E Did you "materially participate" in the operation of this business during 2004? If "No," see page F-2 for limit on passive losses.   ☐ Yes   ☐ No

Part I   **Farm Income—Cash Method. Complete Parts I and II** (Accrual method taxpayers complete Parts II and III, and line 11 of Part I.)
Do not include sales of livestock held for draft, breeding, sport, or dairy purposes; report these sales on Form 4797.

1	Sales of livestock and other items you bought for resale	**1**	
2	Cost or other basis of livestock and other items reported on line 1 . . .	**2**	
3	Subtract line 2 from line 1	**3**	
4	Sales of livestock, produce, grains, and other products you raised	**4**	
5a	Total cooperative distributions (Form(s) 1099-PATR) **5a**	**5b** Taxable amount **5b**	
6a	Agricultural program payments (see page F-2) **6a**	**6b** Taxable amount **6b**	
7	Commodity Credit Corporation (CCC) loans (see page F-3):		
a	CCC loans reported under election	**7a**	
b	CCC loans forfeited **7b**	**7c** Taxable amount **7c**	
8	Crop insurance proceeds and certain disaster payments (see page F-3):		
a	Amount received in 2004 . . . . . . **8a**	**8b** Taxable amount **8b**	
c	If election to defer to 2005 is attached, check here ▶ ☐ **8d** Amount deferred from 2003	**8d**	
9	Custom hire (machine work) income	**9**	
10	Other income, including Federal and state gasoline or fuel tax credit or refund (see page F-3)	**10**	
11	**Gross income.** Add amounts in the right column for lines 3 through 10. If accrual method taxpayer, enter the amount from page 2, line 51 . . . . ▶	**11**	

Part II   **Farm Expenses—Cash and Accrual Method. Do not** include personal or living expenses such as taxes, insurance, repairs, etc., on your home.

12	Car and truck expenses (see page F-4—also attach **Form 4562**)	**12**	**25**	Pension and profit-sharing plans	**25**	
13	Chemicals	**13**	**26**	Rent or lease (see page F-5):		
14	Conservation expenses (see page F-4)	**14**	**a**	Vehicles, machinery, and equipment	**26a**	
15	Custom hire (machine work) .	**15**	**b**	Other (land, animals, etc.) . .	**26b**	
16	Depreciation and section 179 expense deduction not claimed elsewhere (see page F-4) .	**16**	**27**	Repairs and maintenance . .	**27**	
			28	Seeds and plants purchased .	**28**	
			29	Storage and warehousing . .	**29**	
17	Employee benefit programs other than on line 25	**17**	**30**	Supplies purchased	**30**	
18	Feed purchased	**18**	**31**	Taxes	**31**	
19	Fertilizers and lime	**19**	**32**	Utilities	**32**	
20	Freight and trucking. . . .	**20**	**33**	Veterinary, breeding, and medicine	**33**	
21	Gasoline, fuel, and oil . . .	**21**	**34**	Other expenses (specify):		
22	Insurance (other than health) .	**22**	**a**	_____	**34a**	
23	Interest:		**b**	_____	**34b**	
a	Mortgage (paid to banks, etc.).	**23a**	**c**	_____	**34c**	
b	Other	**23b**	**d**	_____	**34d**	
24	Labor hired (less employment credits)	**24**	**e**	_____	**34e**	
			f	_____	**34f**	

35	**Total expenses.** Add lines 12 through 34f . . . . ▶	**35**	
36	**Net farm profit or (loss).** Subtract line 35 from line 11. If a profit, enter on **Form 1040, line 18,** and **also** on **Schedule SE, line 1.** If a loss, you **must** go on to line 37 (estates, trusts, and partnerships, see page F-6) . .	**36**	
37	If you have a loss, you **must** check the box that describes your investment in this activity (see page F-6).	**37a** ☐ All investment is at risk.	
	● If you checked 37a, enter the loss on **Form 1040, line 18,** and **also** on **Schedule SE, line 1.**	**37b** ☐ Some investment is not at risk.	
	● If you checked 37b, you **must** attach **Form 6198.**		

For Paperwork Reduction Act Notice, see Form 1040 instructions.   Cat. No. 11346H   **Schedule F (Form 1040) 2004**

Schedule F (Form 1040) 2004   Page **2**

Part III Farm Income—Accrual Method (see page F-6)

Do not include sales of livestock held for draft, breeding, sport, or dairy purposes; report these sales on Form 4797 and do not include this livestock on line 46 below.

38	Sales of livestock, produce, grains, and other products during the year	**38**
39a	Total cooperative distributions (Form(s) 1099-PATR) [**39a** _____] [**39b** Taxable amount]	**39b**
40a	Agricultural program payments . . . . . [**40a** _____] [**40b** Taxable amount]	**40b**
41	Commodity Credit Corporation (CCC) loans:	
a	CCC loans reported under election	**41a**
b	CCC loans forfeited . . . . [**41b** _____] [**41c** Taxable amount]	**41c**
42	Crop insurance proceeds	**42**
43	Custom hire (machine work) income	**43**
44	Other income, including Federal and state gasoline or fuel tax credit or refund	**44**
45	Add amounts in the right column for lines 38 through 44	**45**

46	Inventory of livestock, produce, grains, and other products at beginning of the year	**46**
47	Cost of livestock, produce, grains, and other products purchased during the year	**47**
48	Add lines 46 and 47	**48**
49	Inventory of livestock, produce, grains, and other products at end of year	**49**

50	Cost of livestock, produce, grains, and other products sold. Subtract line 49 from line 48*	**50**
51	**Gross income.** Subtract line 50 from line 45. Enter the result here and on page 1, line 11 . . . . . ▶	**51**

*If you use the unit-livestock-price method or the farm-price method of valuing inventory and the amount on line 49 is larger than the amount on line 48, subtract line 48 from line 49. Enter the result on line 50. Add lines 45 and 50. Enter the total on line 51.

Part IV Principal Agricultural Activity Codes

⚠ CAUTION File **Schedule C** (Form 1040), Profit or Loss From Business, or **Schedule C-EZ** (Form 1040), Net Profit From Business, instead of Schedule F if:

● Your principal source of income is from providing agricultural services such as soil preparation, veterinary, farm labor, horticultural, or management for a fee or on a contract basis or

● You are engaged in the business of breeding, raising, and caring for dogs, cats, or other pet animals.

These codes for the Principal Agricultural Activity classify farms by the type of activity they are engaged in to facilitate the administration of the Internal Revenue Code. These six-digit codes are based on the North American Industry Classification System (NAICS).

Select one of the following codes and enter the six-digit number on page 1, line B.

Crop Production

111100	Oilseed and grain farming
111210	Vegetable and melon farming
111300	Fruit and tree nut farming
111400	Greenhouse, nursery, and floriculture production
111900	Other crop farming

Animal Production

112111	Beef cattle ranching and farming
112112	Cattle feedlots
112120	Dairy cattle and milk production
112210	Hog and pig farming
112300	Poultry and egg production
112400	Sheep and goat farming
112510	Animal aquaculture
112900	Other animal production

Forestry and Logging

113000	Forestry and logging (including forest nurseries and timber tracts)

Schedule F (Form 1040) 2004

Schedule R (Form 1040) Department of the Treasury Internal Revenue Service (99)	**Credit for the Elderly or the Disabled** ▶ **Attach to Form 1040.** ▶ **See Instructions for Schedule R (Form 1040).**	OMB No. 1545-0074 20**04** Attachment Sequence No. **16**
Name(s) shown on Form 1040		Your social security number

You may be able to take this credit and reduce your tax if by the end of 2004:

● You were age 65 or older **or**   ● You were under age 65, you retired on **permanent and total** disability, and you received taxable disability income.

But you must also meet other tests. See page R-1.

TIP   In most cases, the IRS can figure the credit for you. See page R-1.

Part I   Check the Box for Your Filing Status and Age

If your filing status is:	And by the end of 2004:	Check only one box:	
Single, Head of household, or Qualifying widow(er)	**1** You were 65 or older	**1**	☐
	2 You were under 65 and you retired on permanent and total disability	**2**	☐
	3 Both spouses were 65 or older	**3**	☐
	4 Both spouses were under 65, but only one spouse retired on permanent and total disability	**4**	☐
Married filing jointly	**5** Both spouses were under 65, and both retired on permanent and total disability	**5**	☐
	6 One spouse was 65 or older, and the other spouse was under 65 and retired on permanent and total disability	**6**	☐
	7 One spouse was 65 or older, and the other spouse was under 65 and **not** retired on permanent and total disability	**7**	☐
Married filing separately	**8** You were 65 or older and you lived apart from your spouse for all of 2004	**8**	☐
	9 You were under 65, you retired on permanent and total disability, and you lived apart from your spouse for all of 2004	**9**	☐

Did you check box 1, 3, 7, or 8?	—— **Yes** ——▶ Skip Part II and complete Part III on back.
	—— **No** ——▶ Complete Parts II and III.

Part II   Statement of Permanent and Total Disability (Complete **only** if you checked box 2, 4, 5, 6, or 9 above.)

If: 1 You filed a physician's statement for this disability for 1983 or an earlier year, or you filed or got a statement for tax years after 1983 and your physician signed line B on the statement, **and**

  2 Due to your continued disabled condition, you were unable to engage in any substantial gainful activity in 2004, check this box   . . . . ▶ ☐

    ● If you checked this box, you do not have to get another statement for 2004.

    ● If you **did not** check this box, have your physician complete the statement on page R-4. You **must** keep the statement for your records.

For Paperwork Reduction Act Notice, see Form 1040 instructions.   Cat. No. 11359K   **Schedule R (Form 1040) 2004**

Schedule R (Form 1040) 2004   Page **2**

Part III **Figure Your Credit**

10 **If you checked (in Part I):**   **Enter:**
   Box 1, 2, 4, or 7 . . . . $5,000 ⎫
   Box 3, 5, or 6 . . . . $7,500 ⎬ **10**
   Box 8 or 9 . . . . $3,750 ⎭

   ┌─────────────────────┐
   │ **Did you check**   │──── Yes ────▶ You **must** complete line 11.
   │ **box 2, 4, 5, 6,** │
   │ **or 9 in Part I?** │──── No ─────▶ Enter the amount from line 10
   └─────────────────────┘   on line 12 and go to line 13.

11 **If you checked (in Part I):**
   ● Box 6, add $5,000 to the taxable disability income of the   ⎫
     spouse who was under age 65. Enter the total.   ⎪
   ● Box 2, 4, or 9, enter your taxable disability income.   ⎬ . . . **11**
   ● Box 5, add your taxable disability income to your spouse's ⎪
     taxable disability income. Enter the total.   ⎭

   (TIP) For more details on what to include on line 11, see page R-3.

12 If you completed line 11, enter the **smaller** of line 10 or line 11; **all others,** enter the
   amount from line 10 . . . . **12**

13 Enter the following pensions, annuities, or disability income that
   you (and your spouse if filing a joint return) received in 2004.

   a Nontaxable part of social security benefits and   ⎫
       Nontaxable part of railroad retirement benefits   ⎬ . . . **13a**
       treated as social security (see page R-3).   ⎭

   b Nontaxable veterans' pensions and   ⎫
       Any other pension, annuity, or disability benefit that   ⎪ . . . **13b**
       is excluded from income under any other provision   ⎬
       of law (see page R-3).   ⎭

   c Add lines 13a and 13b. (Even though these income items are
       not taxable, they **must** be included here to figure your credit.)
       If you did not receive any of the types of nontaxable income
       listed on line 13a or 13b, enter -0- on line 13c **13c**

14 Enter the amount from Form 1040,
   line 37 . . . . **14**

15 **If you checked (in Part I):** **Enter:**
   Box 1 or 2 . . . . . . $7,500 ⎫
   Box 3, 4, 5, 6, or 7 . . . $10,000 ⎬ **15**
   Box 8 or 9 . . . . . . $5,000 ⎭

16 Subtract line 15 from line 14. If zero or
   less, enter -0- **16**

17 Enter one-half of line 16 . . . . **17**

18 Add lines 13c and 17 . . . . **18**

19 Subtract line 18 from line 12. If zero or less, **stop;** you **cannot** take the credit. Otherwise,
   go to line 20 . . . . **19**

20 Multiply line 19 by 15% (.15) **20**

21 Enter the amount from Form 1040, line 45 . . . . **21**

22 Add the amounts from Form 1040, lines 46 and 47, and enter
   the total **22**

23 Subtract line 22 from line 21 . . . . **23**

24 **Credit for the elderly or the disabled.** Enter the **smaller** of line 20 or line 23 here and
   on Form 1040, line 48 . . . . **24**

                                    ✳

                                                    Schedule R (Form 1040) 2004

SCHEDULE SE	Self-Employment Tax	OMB No. 1545-0074
(Form 1040)		**20 04**
Department of the Treasury Internal Revenue Service	▶ **Attach to Form 1040.** ▶ **See Instructions for Schedule SE (Form 1040).**	Attachment Sequence No. **17**

Name of person with **self-employment** income (as shown on Form 1040)	Social security number of person with **self-employment** income ▶	

Who Must File Schedule SE

You must file Schedule SE if:

● You had net earnings from self-employment from **other than** church employee income (line 4 of Short Schedule SE or line 4c of Long Schedule SE) of $400 or more **or**

● You had church employee income of $108.28 or more. Income from services you performed as a minister or a member of a religious order **is not** church employee income (see page SE-1).

Note. Even if you had a loss or a small amount of income from self-employment, it may be to your benefit to file Schedule SE and use either "optional method" in Part II of Long Schedule SE (see page SE-3).

Exception. If your only self-employment income was from earnings as a minister, member of a religious order, or Christian Science practitioner **and** you filed Form 4361 and received IRS approval not to be taxed on those earnings, **do not** file Schedule SE. Instead, write "Exempt–Form 4361" on Form 1040, line 57.

May I Use Short Schedule SE or Must I Use Long Schedule SE?

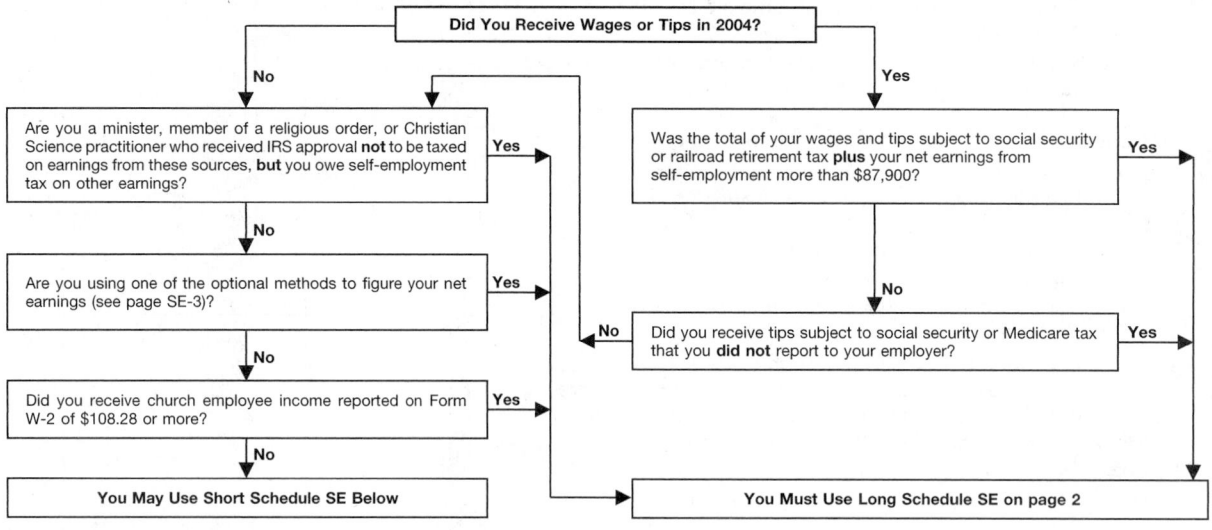

Section A—Short Schedule SE. Caution. Read above to see if you can use Short Schedule SE.

1	Net farm profit or (loss) from Schedule F, line 36, and farm partnerships, Schedule K-1 (Form 1065), box 14, code A	**1**	
2	Net profit or (loss) from Schedule C, line 31; Schedule C-EZ, line 3; Schedule K-1 (Form 1065), box 14, code A (other than farming); and Schedule K-1 (Form 1065-B), box 9. Ministers and members of religious orders, see page SE-1 for amounts to report on this line. See page SE-2 for other income to report	**2**	
3	Combine lines 1 and 2	**3**	
4	**Net earnings from self-employment.** Multiply line 3 by 92.35% (.9235). If less than $400, **do not** file this schedule; you do not owe self-employment tax . . . . ▶	**4**	
5	**Self-employment tax.** If the amount on line 4 is: ● $87,900 or less, multiply line 4 by 15.3% (.153). Enter the result here and on **Form 1040, line 57.** ● More than $87,900, multiply line 4 by 2.9% (.029). Then, add $10,899.60 to the result. Enter the total here and on **Form 1040, line 57.**	**5**	
6	**Deduction for one-half of self-employment tax.** Multiply line 5 by 50% (.5). Enter the result here and on **Form 1040, line 30**	**6**	

For Paperwork Reduction Act Notice, see Form 1040 instructions.	Cat. No. 11358Z	Schedule SE (Form 1040) 2004

Name of person with **self-employment** income (as shown on Form 1040)	Social security number of person with **self-employment** income ▶	

Section B—Long Schedule SE

Part I Self-Employment Tax

Note. If your only income subject to self-employment tax is **church employee income,** skip lines 1 through 4b. Enter -0- on line 4c and go to line 5a. Income from services you performed as a minister or a member of a religious order **is not** church employee income. See page SE-1.

A If you are a minister, member of a religious order, or Christian Science practitioner **and** you filed Form 4361, but you had $400 or more of **other** net earnings from self-employment, check here and continue with Part I . . . . . . ▶ ☐

1	Net farm profit or (loss) from Schedule F, line 36, and farm partnerships, Schedule K-1 (Form 1065), box 14, code A. **Note.** Skip this line if you use the farm optional method (see page SE-4)	**1**	
2	Net profit or (loss) from Schedule C, line 31; Schedule C-EZ, line 3; Schedule K-1 (Form 1065), box 14, code A (other than farming); and Schedule K-1 (Form 1065-B), box 9. Ministers and members of religious orders, see page SE-1 for amounts to report on this line. See page SE-2 for other income to report. **Note.** Skip this line if you use the nonfarm optional method (see page SE-4)	**2**	
3	Combine lines 1 and 2	**3**	
4a	If line 3 is more than zero, multiply line 3 by 92.35% (.9235). Otherwise, enter amount from line 3	**4a**	
b	If you elect one or both of the optional methods, enter the total of lines 15 and 17 here . . .	**4b**	
c	Combine lines 4a and 4b. If less than $400, **stop;** you do not owe self-employment tax. **Exception.** If less than $400 and you had **church employee income,** enter -0- and continue. . . . . . ▶	**4c**	
5a	Enter your **church employee income** from Form W-2. See page SE-1 for definition of church employee income **5a**		
b	Multiply line 5a by 92.35% (.9235). If less than $100, enter -0-	**5b**	
6	**Net earnings from self-employment.** Add lines 4c and 5b	**6**	
7	Maximum amount of combined wages and self-employment earnings subject to social security tax or the 6.2% portion of the 7.65% railroad retirement (tier 1) tax for 2004	**7**	87,900 00
8a	Total social security wages and tips (total of boxes 3 and 7 on Form(s) W-2) and railroad retirement (tier 1) compensation. If $87,900 or more, skip lines 8b through 10, and go to line 11 . . . . **8a**		
b	Unreported tips subject to social security tax (from Form 4137, line 9) **8b**		
c	Add lines 8a and 8b	**8c**	
9	Subtract line 8c from line 7. If zero or less, enter -0- here and on line 10 and go to line 11 . ▶	**9**	
10	Multiply the **smaller** of line 6 or line 9 by 12.4% (.124)	**10**	
11	Multiply line 6 by 2.9% (.029)	**11**	
12	**Self-employment tax.** Add lines 10 and 11. Enter here and on **Form 1040, line 57**	**12**	
13	**Deduction for one-half of self-employment tax.** Multiply line 12 by 50% (.5). Enter the result here and on **Form 1040, line 30** **13**		

Part II Optional Methods To Figure Net Earnings (see page SE-3)

Farm Optional Method. You may use this method **only** if **(a)** your gross farm income[1] was not more than $2,400 **or (b)** your net farm profits[2] were less than $1,733.

14	Maximum income for optional methods	**14**	1,600 00
15	Enter the **smaller** of: two-thirds (⅔) of gross farm income[1] (not less than zero) **or** $1,600. Also include this amount on line 4b above	**15**	

Nonfarm Optional Method. You may use this method **only** if **(a)** your net nonfarm profits[3] were less than $1,733 and also less than 72.189% of your gross nonfarm income[4] **and (b)** you had net earnings from self-employment of at least $400 in 2 of the prior 3 years.

Caution. You may use this method no more than five times.

16	Subtract line 15 from line 14	**16**	
17	Enter the **smaller** of: two-thirds (⅔) of gross nonfarm income[4] (not less than zero) **or** the amount on line 16. Also include this amount on line 4b above	**17**	

[1] From Sch. F, line 11, and Sch. K-1 (Form 1065), box 14, code B.

[2] From Sch. F, line 36, and Sch. K-1 (Form 1065), box 14, code A.

[3] From Sch. C, line 31; Sch. C-EZ, line 3; Sch. K-1 (Form 1065), box 14, code A; and Sch. K-1 (Form 1065-B), box 9.

[4] From Sch. C, line 7; Sch. C-EZ, line 1; Sch. K-1 (Form 1065), box 14, code C; and Sch. K-1 (Form 1065-B), box 9.

SCHEDULE EIC
(Form 1040A or 1040)

Department of the Treasury
Internal Revenue Service

Earned Income Credit

Qualifying Child Information

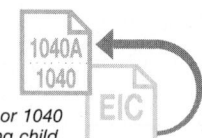

*Complete and attach to Form 1040A or 1040
only if you have a qualifying child.*

OMB No. 1545-0074

2004

Attachment
Sequence No. **43**

Name(s) shown on return | Your social security number

Before you begin: See the instructions for Form 1040A, lines 41a and 41b, or Form 1040, lines 65a and 65b, to make sure that **(a)** you can take the EIC and **(b)** you have a qualifying child.

- If you take the EIC even though you are not eligible, you may not be allowed to take the credit for up to 10 years. See back of schedule for details.

- It will take us longer to process your return and issue your refund if you do not fill in all lines that apply for each qualifying child.

- Be sure the child's name on line 1 and social security number (SSN) on line 2 agree with the child's social security card. Otherwise, at the time we process your return, we may reduce or disallow your EIC. If the name or SSN on the child's social security card is not correct, call the Social Security Administration at 1-800-772-1213.

Qualifying Child Information

	Child 1		Child 2	
1 Child's name If you have more than two qualifying children, you only have to list two to get the maximum credit.	First name	Last name	First name	Last name
2 Child's SSN The child must have an SSN as defined on page 42 of the Form 1040A instructions or page 44 of the Form 1040 instructions unless the child was born and died in 2004. If your child was born and died in 2004 and did not have an SSN, enter "Died" on this line and attach a copy of the child's birth certificate.				
3 Child's year of birth	Year _ _ _ _ *If born after 1985, skip lines 4a and 4b; go to line 5.*		Year _ _ _ _ *If born after 1985, skip lines 4a and 4b; go to line 5.*	
4 If the child was born before 1986— **a** Was the child under age 24 at the end of 2004 and a student?	☐ **Yes.** *Go to line 5.*	☐ **No.** *Continue*	☐ **Yes.** *Go to line 5.*	☐ **No.** *Continue*
b Was the child permanently and totally disabled during any part of 2004?	☐ **Yes.** *Continue*	☐ **No.** The child is not a qualifying child.	☐ **Yes.** *Continue*	☐ **No.** The child is not a qualifying child.
5 Child's relationship to you (for example, son, daughter, grandchild, niece, nephew, foster child, etc.)				
6 Number of months child lived with you in the United States during 2004 • If the child lived with you for more than half of 2004 but less than 7 months, enter "7." • If the child was born or died in 2004 and your home was the child's home for the entire time he or she was alive during 2004, enter "12."	_____ months *Do not enter more than 12 months.*		_____ months *Do not enter more than 12 months.*	

You may also be able to take the additional child tax credit if your child **(a)** was under age 17 at the end of 2004, **(b)** is claimed as your dependent on line 6c of Form 1040A or Form 1040, **and (c)** is a U.S. citizen or resident alien. For more details, see the instructions for line 42 of Form 1040A or line 67 of Form 1040.

For Paperwork Reduction Act Notice, see Form 1040A or 1040 instructions.

Cat. No. 13339M

Schedule EIC (Form 1040A or 1040) 2004

Purpose of Schedule

The purpose of this schedule is to give the IRS information about your qualifying child after you have figured your earned income credit (EIC).

To figure the amount of your credit or to have the IRS figure it for you, see the instructions for Form 1040A, lines 41a and 41b, or Form 1040, lines 65a and 65b.

Taking the EIC when not eligible. If you take the EIC even though you are not eligible and it is determined that your error is due to reckless or intentional disregard of the EIC rules, you will not be allowed to take the credit for 2 years even if you are otherwise eligible to do so. If you fraudulently take the EIC, you will not be allowed to take the credit for 10 years. You may also have to pay penalties.

Qualifying Child

A qualifying child is a child who is your . . .

Son, daughter, adopted child, stepchild, or a descendant of any of them (for example, your grandchild)

or

Brother, sister, stepbrother, stepsister, or a descendant of any of them (for example, your niece or nephew), whom you cared for as you would your own child

or

Foster child (any child placed with you by an authorized placement agency whom you cared for as you would your own child)

was at the end of 2004 . . .

Under age 19

or

Under age 24 and a student

or

Any age and permanently and totally disabled

who . . .

Lived with you in the United States for more than half of 2004. If the child did not live with you for the required time, see *Exception to "time lived with you" condition* on page 41 of the Form 1040A instructions or page 44 of the Form 1040 instructions.

 If the child was married or meets the conditions to be a qualifying child of another person (other than your spouse if filing a joint return), special rules apply. For details, see page 42 of the Form 1040A instructions or page 44 of the Form 1040 instructions.

 Do you want part of the EIC added to your take-home pay in 2005? To see if you qualify, get Form W-5 from your employer, call the IRS at 1-800-TAX-FORM (1-800-829-3676), or go to *www.irs.gov.*

B-4   U.S. Income Tax Return for Estates and Trusts

Form **1041** Department of the Treasury—Internal Revenue Service
U.S. Income Tax Return for Estates and Trusts   **2004**   OMB No. 1545-0092

A Type of entity (see instr.):	For calendar year 2004 or fiscal year beginning , 2004, and ending , 20	
☐ Decedent's estate	Name of estate or trust (If a grantor type trust, see page 12 of the instructions.)	C Employer identification number
☐ Simple trust		
☐ Complex trust	Name and title of fiduciary	D Date entity created
☐ Qualified disability trust		
☐ ESBT (S portion only)	Number, street, and room or suite no. (If a P.O. box, see page 12 of the instructions.)	E Nonexempt charitable and split-interest trusts, check applicable boxes (see page 13 of the instr.):
☐ Grantor type trust		
☐ Bankruptcy estate–Ch. 7		☐ Described in section 4947(a)(1)
☐ Bankruptcy estate–Ch. 11	City or town, state, and ZIP code	☐ Not a private foundation
☐ Pooled income fund		☐ Described in section 4947(a)(2)

B Number of Schedules K-1 attached (see instructions) ▶ _____

F Check applicable boxes: ☐ Initial return ☐ Final return ☐ Amended return   ☐ Change in trust's name
☐ Change in fiduciary   ☐ Change in fiduciary's name   ☐ Change in fiduciary's address

G Pooled mortgage account (see page 14 of the instructions): ☐ Bought ☐ Sold Date:

Income

1	Interest income	**1**	
2a	Total ordinary dividends	**2a**	
b	Qualified dividends allocable to: **(1)** Beneficiaries _____ **(2)** Estate or trust _____		
3	Business income or (loss) (attach Schedule C or C-EZ (Form 1040))	**3**	
4	Capital gain or (loss) (attach Schedule D (Form 1041))	**4**	
5	Rents, royalties, partnerships, other estates and trusts, etc. (attach Schedule E (Form 1040))	**5**	
6	Farm income or (loss) (attach Schedule F (Form 1040))	**6**	
7	Ordinary gain or (loss) (attach Form 4797)	**7**	
8	Other income. List type and amount _____	**8**	
9	**Total income.** Combine lines 1, 2a, and 3 through 8 ▶	**9**	

Deductions

10	Interest. Check if Form 4952 is attached ▶ ☐	**10**	
11	Taxes	**11**	
12	Fiduciary fees	**12**	
13	Charitable deduction (from Schedule A, line 7)	**13**	
14	Attorney, accountant, and return preparer fees	**14**	
15a	Other deductions **not** subject to the 2% floor (attach schedule)	**15a**	
b	Allowable miscellaneous itemized deductions subject to the 2% floor	**15b**	
16	**Total.** Add lines 10 through 15b	**16**	
17	Adjusted total income or (loss). Subtract line 16 from line 9. Enter here and on Schedule B, line 1 ▶	**17**	
18	Income distribution deduction (from Schedule B, line 15) (attach Schedules K-1 (Form 1041))	**18**	
19	Estate tax deduction (including certain generation-skipping taxes) (attach computation)	**19**	
20	Exemption	**20**	
21	**Total deductions.** Add lines 18 through 20 ▶	**21**	

Tax and Payments

22	Taxable income. Subtract line 21 from line 17. If a loss, see page 19 of the instructions	**22**	
23	**Total tax** (from Schedule G, line 7)	**23**	
24	**Payments: a** 2004 estimated tax payments and amount applied from 2003 return	**24a**	
b	Estimated tax payments allocated to beneficiaries (from Form 1041-T)	**24b**	
c	Subtract line 24b from line 24a	**24c**	
d	Tax paid with extension of time to file: ☐ Form 2758 ☐ Form 8736 ☐ Form 8800	**24d**	
e	Federal income tax withheld. If any is from Form(s) 1099, check ▶ ☐	**24e**	
	Other payments: **f** Form 2439 _____ ; **g** Form 4136 _____ ; Total ▶	**24h**	
25	**Total payments.** Add lines 24c through 24e, and 24h ▶	**25**	
26	Estimated tax penalty (see page 20 of the instructions)	**26**	
27	**Tax due.** If line 25 is smaller than the total of lines 23 and 26, enter amount owed	**27**	
28	**Overpayment.** If line 25 is larger than the total of lines 23 and 26, enter amount overpaid	**28**	
29	Amount of line 28 to be: **a** Credited to 2005 estimated tax ▶ ; **b** Refunded ▶	**29**	

Sign Here ▶

Under penalties of perjury, I declare that I have examined this return, including accompanying schedules and statements, and to the best of my knowledge and belief, it is true, correct, and complete. Declaration of preparer (other than taxpayer) is based on all information of which preparer has any knowledge.

Signature of fiduciary or officer representing fiduciary	Date	▶ EIN of fiduciary if a financial institution	May the IRS discuss this return with the preparer shown below (see instr.)? ☐ Yes ☐ No

Paid Preparer's Use Only

Preparer's signature ▶	Date	Check if self-employed ☐	Preparer's SSN or PTIN
Firm's name (or yours if self-employed), address, and ZIP code ▶		EIN	
		Phone no. ( )	

For Privacy Act and Paperwork Reduction Act Notice, see the separate instructions.   Cat. No. 11370H   Form **1041** (2004)

Form 1041 (2004)   Page **2**

Schedule A	**Charitable Deduction.** Do not complete for a simple trust or a pooled income fund.	
1	Amounts paid or permanently set aside for charitable purposes from gross income (see page 20)	**1**	
2	Tax-exempt income allocable to charitable contributions (see page 20 of the instructions) . .	**2**	
3	Subtract line 2 from line 1	**3**	
4	Capital gains for the tax year allocated to corpus and paid or permanently set aside for charitable purposes	**4**	
5	Add lines 3 and 4	**5**	
6	Section 1202 exclusion allocable to capital gains paid or permanently set aside for charitable purposes (see page 20 of the instructions)	**6**	
7	**Charitable deduction.** Subtract line 6 from line 5. Enter here and on page 1, line 13	**7**	

Schedule B	**Income Distribution Deduction**	
1	Adjusted total income (see page 21 of the instructions)	**1**	
2	Adjusted tax-exempt interest	**2**	
3	Total net gain from Schedule D (Form 1041), line 15, column (1) (see page 21 of the instructions)	**3**	
4	Enter amount from Schedule A, line 4 (reduced by any allocable section 1202 exclusion) . .	**4**	
5	Capital gains for the tax year included on Schedule A, line 1 (see page 21 of the instructions)	**5**	
6	Enter any gain from page 1, line 4, as a negative number. If page 1, line 4, is a loss, enter the loss as a positive number . . .	**6**	
7	**Distributable net income (DNI).** Combine lines 1 through 6. If zero or less, enter -0- . . .	**7**	
8	If a complex trust, enter accounting income for the tax year as determined under the governing instrument and applicable local law	**8**	
9	Income required to be distributed currently	**9**	
10	Other amounts paid, credited, or otherwise required to be distributed	**10**	
11	Total distributions. Add lines 9 and 10. If greater than line 8, see page 22 of the instructions	**11**	
12	Enter the amount of tax-exempt income included on line 11	**12**	
13	Tentative income distribution deduction. Subtract line 12 from line 11	**13**	
14	Tentative income distribution deduction. Subtract line 2 from line 7. If zero or less, enter -0-	**14**	
15	**Income distribution deduction.** Enter the smaller of line 13 or line 14 here and on page 1, line 18	**15**	

Schedule G	**Tax Computation** (see page 22 of the instructions)	
1 **Tax:** a	Tax on taxable income (see page 22 of the instructions) . .	**1a**	
b	Tax on lump-sum distributions (attach Form 4972)	**1b**	
c	Alternative minimum tax (from Schedule I, line 56)	**1c**	
d	**Total.** Add lines 1a through 1c . . . . ▶	**1d**	
2a	Foreign tax credit (attach Form 1116)	**2a**	
b	Other nonbusiness credits (attach schedule)	**2b**	
c	General business credit. Enter here and check which forms are attached: ☐ Form 3800 ☐ Forms (specify) ▶	**2c**	
d	Credit for prior year minimum tax (attach Form 8801)	**2d**	
3	**Total credits.** Add lines 2a through 2d . . . . . . ▶	**3**	
4	Subtract line 3 from line 1d. If zero or less, enter -0-	**4**	
5	Recapture taxes. Check if from: ☐ Form 4255 ☐ Form 8611	**5**	
6	Household employment taxes. Attach Schedule H (Form 1040)	**6**	
7	**Total tax.** Add lines 4 through 6. Enter here and on page 1, line 23 . . . . . . ▶	**7**	

	Other Information	Yes	No
1	Did the estate or trust receive tax-exempt income? If "Yes," attach a computation of the allocation of expenses Enter the amount of tax-exempt interest income and exempt-interest dividends ▶ $		
2	Did the estate or trust receive all or any part of the earnings (salary, wages, and other compensation) of any individual by reason of a contract assignment or similar arrangement?		
3	At any time during calendar year 2004, did the estate or trust have an interest in or a signature or other authority over a bank, securities, or other financial account in a foreign country? . . . . See page 24 of the instructions for exceptions and filing requirements for Form TD F 90-22.1. If "Yes," enter the name of the foreign country ▶		
4	During the tax year, did the estate or trust receive a distribution from, or was it the grantor of, or transferor to, a foreign trust? If "Yes," the estate or trust may have to file Form 3520. See page 24 of the instructions .		
5	Did the estate or trust receive, or pay, any qualified residence interest on seller-provided financing? If "Yes," see page 24 for required attachment		
6	If this is an estate or a complex trust making the section 663(b) election, check here (see page 24) . ▶ ☐		
7	To make a section 643(e)(3) election, attach Schedule D (Form 1041), and check here (see page 24) . ▶ ☐		
8	If the decedent's estate has been open for more than 2 years, attach an explanation for the delay in closing the estate, and check here ▶ ☐		
9	Are any present or future trust beneficiaries skip persons? See page 24 of the instructions		

Form **1041** (2004)

Form 1041 (2004)   Page **3**

Schedule I   Alternative Minimum Tax (see pages 25 through 31 of the instructions)

Part I—Estate's or Trust's Share of Alternative Minimum Taxable Income

1	Adjusted total income or (loss) (from page 1, line 17)	**1**	
2	Interest	**2**	
3	Taxes	**3**	
4	Miscellaneous itemized deductions (from page 1, line 15b)	**4**	
5	Refund of taxes	**5**	( )
6	Depletion (difference between regular tax and AMT)	**6**	
7	Net operating loss deduction. Enter as a positive amount	**7**	
8	Interest from specified private activity bonds exempt from the regular tax	**8**	
9	Qualified small business stock (see page 26 of the instructions)	**9**	
10	Exercise of incentive stock options (excess of AMT income over regular tax income)	**10**	
11	Other estates and trusts (amount from Schedule K-1 (Form 1041), line 9)	**11**	
12	Electing large partnerships (amount from Schedule K-1 (Form 1065-B), box 6)	**12**	
13	Disposition of property (difference between AMT and regular tax gain or loss)	**13**	
14	Depreciation on assets placed in service after 1986 (difference between regular tax and AMT)	**14**	
15	Passive activities (difference between AMT and regular tax income or loss)	**15**	
16	Loss limitations (difference between AMT and regular tax income or loss)	**16**	
17	Circulation costs (difference between regular tax and AMT)	**17**	
18	Long-term contracts (difference between AMT and regular tax income)	**18**	
19	Mining costs (difference between regular tax and AMT)	**19**	
20	Research and experimental costs (difference between regular tax and AMT)	**20**	
21	Income from certain installment sales before January 1, 1987	**21**	( )
22	Intangible drilling costs preference	**22**	
23	Other adjustments, including income-based related adjustments	**23**	
24	Alternative tax net operating loss deduction (See the instructions for the limitation that applies.)	**24**	( )
25	Adjusted alternative minimum taxable income. Combine lines 1 through 24	**25**	

Note: *Complete Part II below before going to line 26.*

26	Income distribution deduction from Part II, line 44 . . . . . . **26**		
27	Estate tax deduction (from page 1, line 19) **27**		
28	Add lines 26 and 27	**28**	
29	Estate's or trust's share of alternative minimum taxable income. Subtract line 28 from line 25	**29**	

If line 29 is:

- $22,500 or less, stop here and enter -0- on Schedule G, line 1c. The estate or trust is not liable for the alternative minimum tax.
- Over $22,500, but less than $165,000, go to line 45.
- $165,000 or more, enter the amount from line 29 on line 51 and go to line 52.

Part II—Income Distribution Deduction on a Minimum Tax Basis

30	Adjusted alternative minimum taxable income (see page 29 of the instructions)	**30**	
31	Adjusted tax-exempt interest (other than amounts included on line 8)	**31**	
32	Total net gain from Schedule D (Form 1041), line 15, column (1). If a loss, enter -0-	**32**	
33	Capital gains for the tax year allocated to corpus and paid or permanently set aside for charitable purposes (from Schedule A, line 4)	**33**	
34	Capital gains paid or permanently set aside for charitable purposes from gross income (see page 29 of the instructions)	**34**	
35	Capital gains computed on a minimum tax basis included on line 25	**35**	( )
36	Capital losses computed on a minimum tax basis included on line 25. Enter as a positive amount	**36**	
37	Distributable net alternative minimum taxable income (DNAMTI). Combine lines 30 through 36. If zero or less, enter -0-	**37**	
38	Income required to be distributed currently (from Schedule B, line 9)	**38**	
39	Other amounts paid, credited, or otherwise required to be distributed (from Schedule B, line 10)	**39**	
40	Total distributions. Add lines 38 and 39	**40**	
41	Tax-exempt income included on line 40 (other than amounts included on line 8)	**41**	
42	Tentative income distribution deduction on a minimum tax basis. Subtract line 41 from line 40	**42**	
43	Tentative income distribution deduction on a minimum tax basis. Subtract line 31 from line 37. If zero or less, enter -0-	**43**	
44	**Income distribution deduction on a minimum tax basis.** Enter the smaller of line 42 or line 43. Enter here and on line 26	**44**	

Form **1041** (2004)

Form 1041 (2004)

Part III—Alternative Minimum Tax

45	Exemption amount	**45**	$22,500	00
46	Enter the amount from line 29	**46**		
47	Phase-out of exemption amount	**47** $75,000 00		
48	Subtract line 47 from line 46. If zero or less, enter -0-	**48**		
49	Multiply line 48 by 25% (.25)	**49**		
50	Subtract line 49 from line 45. If zero or less, enter -0-	**50**		
51	Subtract line 50 from line 46	**51**		

52 Go to Part IV of Schedule I to figure line 52 if the estate or trust has qualified dividends or has a gain on lines 14a and 15 of column (2) of Schedule D (Form 1041) (as refigured for the AMT, if necessary). Otherwise, if line 51 is—

- $175,000 or less, multiply line 51 by 26% (.26).
- Over $175,000, multiply line 51 by 28% (.28) and subtract $3,500 from the result . . . . | **52** |

53	Alternative minimum foreign tax credit (see page 29 of the instructions)	**53**
54	Tentative minimum tax. Subtract line 53 from line 52	**54**
55	Enter the tax from Schedule G, line 1a (minus any foreign tax credit from Schedule G, line 2a)	**55**
56	**Alternative minimum tax.** Subtract line 55 from line 54. If zero or less, enter -0-. Enter here and on Schedule G, line 1c	**56**

Part IV—Line 52 Computation Using Maximum Capital Gains Rates

Caution: *If you did not complete Part V of Schedule D (Form 1041), the Schedule D Tax Worksheet, or the Qualified Dividends Tax Worksheet, see page 31 of the instructions before completing this part.*

57 Enter the amount from line 51 . . . . | **57** |

58 Enter the amount from Schedule D (Form 1041), line 22, line 13 of the Schedule D Tax Worksheet, or line 4 of the Qualified Dividends Tax Worksheet, whichever applies (as refigured for the AMT, if necessary) | **58** |

59 Enter the amount from Schedule D (Form 1041), line 14b, column (2) (as refigured for the AMT, if necessary). If you did not complete Schedule D for the regular tax or the AMT, enter -0- . . . . . . | **59** |

60 If you did not complete a Schedule D Tax Worksheet for the regular tax or the AMT, enter the amount from line 58. Otherwise, add lines 58 and 59 and enter the **smaller** of that result or the amount from line 10 of the Schedule D Tax Worksheet (as refigured for the AMT, if necessary) | **60** |

61	Enter the **smaller** of line 57 or line 60	**61**
62	Subtract line 61 from line 57	**62**

63 If line 62 is $175,000 or less, multiply line 62 by 26% (.26). Otherwise, multiply line 62 by 28% (.28) and subtract $3,500 from the result . . . . ▶ | **63** |

64 Maximum amount subject to the 5% rate . . . . | **64** $1,950 00 |

65 Enter the amount from line 23 of Schedule D (Form 1041), line 14 of the Schedule D Tax Worksheet, or line 5 of the Qualified Dividends Tax Worksheet, whichever applies (as figured for the regular tax). If you did not complete Schedule D or either worksheet for the regular tax, enter -0- . . . . | **65** |

66	Subtract line 65 from line 64. If zero or less, enter -0-	**66**
67	Enter the **smaller** of line 57 or line 58	**67**
68	Enter the **smaller** of line 66 or line 67	**68**
69	Multiply line 68 by 5% (.05) . . . . ▶	**69**
70	Subtract line 68 from line 67	**70**
71	Multiply line 70 by 15% (.15) . . . . ▶	**71**

If line 59 is zero or blank, skip lines 72 and 73 and go to line 74. Otherwise, go to line 72.

72	Subtract line 67 from line 61	**72**
73	Multiply line 72 by 25% (.25) . . . . ▶	**73**
74	Add lines 63, 69, 71, and 73	**74**

75 If line 57 is $175,000 or less, multiply line 57 by 26% (.26). Otherwise, multiply line 57 by 28% (.28) and subtract $3,500 from the result . . . . | **75** |

76 Enter the **smaller** of line 74 or line 75 here and on line 52 . . . . | **76** |

Form **1041** (2004)

Printed on recycled paper

| SCHEDULE K-1
(Form 1041)

Department of the Treasury
Internal Revenue Service | Beneficiary's Share of Income, Deductions, Credits, etc.
for the calendar year 2004, or fiscal year
beginning .... , 2004, ending .... , 20 ....
► Complete a separate Schedule K-1 for each beneficiary. | OMB No. 1545-0092

2004 |

Name of trust or decedent's estate

☐ Amended K-1
☐ Final K-1

Beneficiary's identifying number ►   Estate's or trust's EIN ►

| Beneficiary's name, address, and ZIP code | Fiduciary's name, address, and ZIP code |

(a) Allocable share item		(b) Amount	(c) Calendar year 2004 Form 1040 filers enter the amounts in column (b) on:
1	Interest	**1**		Form 1040, line 8a
2a	Qualified dividends	**2a**		Form 1040, line 9b
b	Total ordinary dividends	**2b**		Form 1040, line 9a
3	Net short-term capital gain	**3**		Schedule D, line 5, column (f)
4a	Net long-term capital gain	**4a**		Schedule D, line 12, column (f)
b	Unrecaptured section 1250 gain	**4b**		Line 11 of the worksheet for Schedule D, line 19
c	28% rate gain	**4c**		Line 4 of the worksheet for Schedule D, line 18
5a	Annuities, royalties, and other nonpassive income before directly apportioned deductions	**5a**		Schedule E, Part III, column (f)
b	Depreciation	**5b**		⎫ Include on the applicable line of the appropriate tax form
c	Depletion	**5c**		
d	Amortization	**5d**		⎭
6a	Trade or business, rental real estate, and other rental income before directly apportioned deductions (see instructions) . .	**6a**		Schedule E, Part III
b	Depreciation	**6b**		⎫ Include on the applicable line of the appropriate tax form
c	Depletion	**6c**		
d	Amortization	**6d**		⎭
7	Income for minimum tax purposes	**7**		
8	Income for regular tax purposes (add lines 1, 2b, 3, 4a, 5a, and 6a)	**8**		
9	Adjustment for minimum tax purposes (subtract line 8 from line 7)	**9**		Form 6251, line 14
10	Estate tax deduction (including certain generation-skipping transfer taxes)	**10**		Schedule A, line 27
11	Foreign taxes	**11**		Form 1040, line 46 or Schedule A, line 8
12	Adjustments and tax preference items (itemize):			
a	Accelerated depreciation	**12a**		⎫ Include on the applicable line of Form 6251
b	Depletion	**12b**		
c	Amortization	**12c**		⎭
d	Exclusion items	**12d**		2005 Form 8801
13	Deductions in the final year of trust or decedent's estate:			
a	Excess deductions on termination (see instructions)	**13a**		Schedule A, line 22
b	Short-term capital loss carryover	**13b**	( )	Schedule D, line 5, column (f)
c	Long-term capital loss carryover	**13c**	( )	Sch. D, line 12, col. (f); line 5 of the wksht. for Sch. D, line 18; and line 16 of the wksht. for Sch. D, line 19
d	Net operating loss (NOL) carryover for regular tax purposes .	**13d**	( )	Form 1040, line 21
e	NOL carryover for minimum tax purposes	**13e**		See the instructions for Form 6251, line 27
f	....	**13f**		⎫ Include on the applicable line
g	....	**13g**		⎭ of the appropriate tax form
14	Other (itemize):			
a	Payments of estimated taxes credited to you . . .	**14a**		Form 1040, line 64
b	Tax-exempt interest	**14b**		Form 1040, line 8b
c	....	**14c**		
d	....	**14d**		
e	....	**14e**		⎫ Include on the applicable line
f	....	**14f**		of the appropriate tax form
g	....	**14g**		
h	....	**14h**		⎭

For Paperwork Reduction Act Notice, see the Instructions for Form 1041.   Cat. No. 11380D   **Schedule K-1 (Form 1041) 2004**

Instructions for Beneficiary Filing Form 1040

Note: *The fiduciary's instructions for completing*
Schedule K-1 are in the Instructions for Form 1041.

General Instructions

Purpose of Form

The fiduciary of a trust or decedent's estate uses Schedule K-1 to report your share of the trust's or estate's income, credits, deductions, etc. Keep it for your records. Do not file it with your tax return. A copy has been filed with the IRS.

Inconsistent Treatment of Items

Generally, you must report items shown on your Schedule K-1 (and any attached schedules) the same way that the estate or trust treated the items on its return.

If the treatment on your original or amended return is inconsistent with the estate's or trust's treatment, or if the estate or trust was required to but has not filed a return, you must file Form 8082, Notice of Inconsistent Treatment or Administrative Adjustment Request (AAR), with your original or amended return to identify and explain any inconsistency (or to note that an estate or trust return has not been filed).

If you are required to file Form 8082 but fail to do so, you may be subject to the accuracy-related penalty. This penalty is in addition to any tax that results from making your amount or treatment of the item consistent with that shown on the estate's or trust's return. Any deficiency that results from making the amounts consistent may be assessed immediately.

Errors

If you believe the fiduciary has made an error on your Schedule K-1, notify the fiduciary and ask for an amended or a corrected Schedule K-1. Do not change any items on your copy. Be sure that the fiduciary sends a copy of the amended Schedule K-1 to the IRS. If you are unable to reach an agreement with the fiduciary regarding the inconsistency, you must file Form 8082.

Tax Shelters

If you receive a copy of Form 8271, Investor Reporting of Tax Shelter Registration Number, see the Instructions for Form 8271 to determine your reporting requirements.

Beneficiaries of Generation-Skipping Trusts

If you received Form 706-GS(D-1), Notification of Distribution From a Generation-Skipping Trust, and paid a generation-skipping transfer (GST) tax on Form 706-GS(D), Generation-Skipping Transfer Tax Return for Distributions, you can deduct the GST tax paid on income distributions on Schedule A (Form 1040), line 8. To figure the deduction, see the Instructions for Form 706-GS(D).

Specific Instructions

Lines 3 and 4a

If there is an attachment to this Schedule K-1 reporting a disposition of a passive activity, see the Instructions for Form 8582, Passive Activity Loss Limitations, for information on the treatment of dispositions of interests in a passive activity.

Lines 6b through 6d

The deductions on lines 6b through 6d may be subject to the passive loss limitations of Internal Revenue Code section 469, which generally limits deductions from passive activities to the income from those activities. The rules for applying these limitations to beneficiaries have not yet been issued. For more details, see Pub. 925, Passive Activity and At-Risk Rules.

Line 12d

If you pay alternative minimum tax in 2004, the amount on line 12d will help you figure any minimum tax credit for 2005. See the 2005 Form 8801, Credit for Prior Year Minimum Tax—Individuals, Estates, and Trusts, for more information.

Line 14a

To figure any underpayment and penalty on Form 2210, Underpayment of Estimated Tax by Individuals, Estates, and Trusts, treat the amount entered on line 14a as an estimated tax payment made on January 15, 2005.

Lines 14c through 14h

The amount of gross farming and fishing income is included on line 6a. This income is also separately stated on line 14 to help you determine if you are subject to a penalty for underpayment of estimated tax. Report the amount of gross farming and fishing income on Schedule E (Form 1040), line 42.

SCHEDULE J (Form 1041) Department of the Treasury Internal Revenue Service	**Accumulation Distribution for Certain Complex Trusts** ▶ Attach to Form 1041. ▶ See the Instructions for Form 1041.	OMB No. 1545-0092 20**04**

Name of trust | Employer identification number

Part I   **Accumulation Distribution in 2004**

Note: *See the Form 4970 instructions for certain income that minors may exclude and special rules for multiple trusts.*

1 Other amounts paid, credited, or otherwise required to be distributed for 2004 (from Schedule B of Form 1041, line 10)	**1**	
2 Distributable net income for 2004 (from Schedule B of Form 1041, line 7) . . .	**2**	
3 Income required to be distributed currently for 2004 (from Schedule B of Form 1041, line 9)	**3**	
4 Subtract line 3 from line 2. If zero or less, enter -0-	**4**	
5 Accumulation distribution for 2004. Subtract line 4 from line 1	**5**	

Part II   **Ordinary Income Accumulation Distribution** (Enter the applicable throwback years below.)

Note: *If the distribution is thrown back to more than five years (starting with the earliest applicable tax year beginning after 1968), attach additional schedules. (If the trust was a simple trust, see Regulations section 1.665(e)-1A(b).)*		**Throwback year ending** -----------	**Throwback year ending** -----------	**Throwback year ending** -----------	**Throwback year ending** -----------	**Throwback year ending** -----------
6 Distributable net income (see page 38 of the instructions).	**6**					
7 Distributions (see page 38 of the instructions).	**7**					
8 Subtract line 7 from line 6 .	**8**					
9 Enter amount from page 2, line 25 or line 31, as applicable.	**9**					
10 Undistributed net income Subtract line 9 from line 8 .	**10**					
11 Enter amount of prior accumulation distributions thrown back to any of these years	**11**					
12 Subtract line 11 from line 10	**12**					
13 Allocate the amount on line 5 to the earliest applicable year first. Do not allocate an amount greater than line 12 for the same year (see page 38 of the instructions). . .	**13**					
14 Divide line 13 by line 10 and multiply result by amount on line 9	**14**					
15 Add lines 13 and 14 . . .	**15**					
16 Tax-exempt interest included on line 13 (see page 38 of the instructions)	**16**					
17 Subtract line 16 from line 15	**17**					

For Paperwork Reduction Act Notice, see the Instructions for Form 1041.   Cat. No. 11382Z   **Schedule J (Form 1041) 2004**

Schedule J (Form 1041) 2004

Page **2**

Part III   Taxes Imposed on Undistributed Net Income   (Enter the applicable throwback years below.) (See page 38 of the instructions.)

Note: *If more than five throwback years are involved, attach additional schedules. If the trust received an accumulation distribution from another trust, see Regulations section 1.665(d)-1A.*

If the trust elected the alternative tax on capital gains (repealed for tax years beginning after 1978), **skip** lines 18 through 25 and **complete** lines 26 through 31.		Throwback year ending ------------	Throwback year ending ------------	Throwback year ending ------------	Throwback year ending ------------	Throwback year ending ------------
18	Regular tax	18				
19	Trust's share of net short-term gain	19				
20	Trust's share of net long-term gain	20				
21	Add lines 19 and 20	21				
22	Taxable income	22				
23	Enter percent. Divide line 21 by line 22, but do not enter more than 100%	23	%	%	%	%	%
24	Multiply line 18 by the percentage on line 23	24				
25	Tax on undistributed net income. Subtract line 24 from line 18. Enter here and on page 1, line 9	25				
Do not complete lines 26 through 31 unless the trust elected the alternative tax on long-term capital gain.						
26	Tax on income other than long-term capital gain	26				
27	Trust's share of net short-term gain	27				
28	Trust's share of taxable income less section 1202 deduction	28				
29	Enter percent. Divide line 27 by line 28, but do not enter more than 100%	29	%	%	%	%	%
30	Multiply line 26 by the percentage on line 29	30				
31	Tax on undistributed net income. Subtract line 30 from line 26. Enter here and on page 1, line 9	31				

Part IV   Allocation to Beneficiary

Note: *Be sure to complete **Form 4970,** Tax on Accumulation Distribution of Trusts.*

Beneficiary's name

Identifying number

Beneficiary's address (number and street including apartment number or P.O. box)

City, state, and ZIP code

			(a) This beneficiary's share of line 13	(b) This beneficiary's share of line 14	(c) This beneficiary's share of line 16
32	Throwback year	32			
33	Throwback year	33			
34	Throwback year	34			
35	Throwback year	35			
36	Throwback year	36			
37	Total. Add lines 32 through 36. Enter here and on the appropriate lines of Form 4970	37			

Schedule J (Form 1041) 2004

B-5   U.S. Partnership Return of Income

Form **1065**	**U.S. Return of Partnership Income**	OMB No. 1545-0099
Department of the Treasury Internal Revenue Service	For calendar year 2004, or tax year beginning ...., 2004, and ending ...., 20..... ▶ See separate instructions.	2004

A Principal business activity	Use the IRS label. Other-wise, print or type.	Name of partnership	D Employer identification number
B Principal product or service		Number, street, and room or suite no. If a P.O. box, see page 14 of the instructions.	E Date business started
C Business code number		City or town, state, and ZIP code	F Total assets (see page 14 of the instructions) $

G Check applicable boxes: **(1)** ☐ Initial return **(2)** ☐ Final return **(3)** ☐ Name change **(4)** ☐ Address change **(5)** ☐ Amended return
H Check accounting method: **(1)** ☐ Cash **(2)** ☐ Accrual **(3)** ☐ Other (specify) ▶ ---------------------------------
I Number of Schedules K-1. Attach one for each person who was a partner at any time during the tax year ▶ ---------------------

Caution: *Include **only** trade or business income and expenses on lines 1a through 22 below. See the instructions for more information.*

Income

1a Gross receipts or sales	**1a**		
b Less returns and allowances	**1b**	**1c**	
2 Cost of goods sold (Schedule A, line 8)		**2**	
3 Gross profit. Subtract line 2 from line 1c		**3**	
4 Ordinary income (loss) from other partnerships, estates, and trusts *(attach schedule)* . . .		**4**	
5 Net farm profit (loss) *(attach Schedule F (Form 1040))* . .		**5**	
6 Net gain (loss) from Form 4797, Part II, line 17		**6**	
7 Other income (loss) *(attach statement)*		**7**	
8 **Total income (loss).** Combine lines 3 through 7		**8**	

Deductions (see page 16 of the instructions for limitations)

9 Salaries and wages (other than to partners) (less employment credits)		**9**	
10 Guaranteed payments to partners		**10**	
11 Repairs and maintenance		**11**	
12 Bad debts		**12**	
13 Rent		**13**	
14 Taxes and licenses		**14**	
15 Interest		**15**	
16a Depreciation *(if required, attach Form 4562)*	**16a**		
b Less depreciation reported on Schedule A and elsewhere on return	**16b**	**16c**	
17 Depletion **(Do not deduct oil and gas depletion.)**		**17**	
18 Retirement plans, etc.		**18**	
19 Employee benefit programs		**19**	
20 Other deductions *(attach statement)*		**20**	
21 **Total deductions.** Add the amounts shown in the far right column for lines 9 through 20 .		**21**	

| **22** **Ordinary business income (loss).** Subtract line 21 from line 8 . . . . | | **22** | |

Sign Here
Under penalties of perjury, I declare that I have examined this return, including accompanying schedules and statements, and to the best of my knowledge and belief, it is true, correct, and complete. Declaration of preparer (other than general partner or limited liability company member) is based on all information of which preparer has any knowledge.

▶ _____
Signature of general partner or limited liability company member manager   Date

May the IRS discuss this return with the preparer shown below (see instructions)? ☐ Yes ☐ No

Paid Preparer's Use Only	Preparer's signature		Date	Check if self-employed ▶ ☐	Preparer's SSN or PTIN
	Firm's name (or yours if self-employed), address, and ZIP code			EIN ▶	
				Phone no. ( )	

For Privacy Act and Paperwork Reduction Act Notice, see separate instructions.   Cat. No. 11390Z   Form **1065** (2004)

Form 1065 (2004)   Page **2**

Schedule A **Cost of Goods Sold** (see page 19 of the instructions)

1	Inventory at beginning of year.	**1**
2	Purchases less cost of items withdrawn for personal use	**2**
3	Cost of labor	**3**
4	Additional section 263A costs *(attach statement)*	**4**
5	Other costs *(attach statement)*.	**5**
6	**Total.** Add lines 1 through 5	**6**
7	Inventory at end of year	**7**
8	**Cost of goods sold.** Subtract line 7 from line 6. Enter here and on page 1, line 2	**8**

9a Check all methods used for valuing closing inventory:

(i) ☐ Cost as described in Regulations section 1.471-3

(ii) ☐ Lower of cost or market as described in Regulations section 1.471-4

(iii) ☐ Other (specify method used and attach explanation) ▶ ....

b Check this box if there was a writedown of "subnormal" goods as described in Regulations section 1.471-2(c) . . . ▶ ☐

c Check this box if the LIFO inventory method was adopted this tax year for any goods *(if checked, attach Form 970).* . ▶ ☐

d Do the rules of section 263A (for property produced or acquired for resale) apply to the partnership?. . . ☐ **Yes** ☐ **No**

e Was there any change in determining quantities, cost, or valuations between opening and closing inventory? ☐ **Yes** ☐ **No**
If "Yes," attach explanation.

Schedule B **Other Information**

		Yes	No
1	What type of entity is filing this return? Check the applicable box:		

a ☐ Domestic general partnership   b ☐ Domestic limited partnership

c ☐ Domestic limited liability company   d ☐ Domestic limited liability partnership

e ☐ Foreign partnership   f ☐ Other ▶ ....

2 Are any partners in this partnership also partnerships? . . . .

3 During the partnership's tax year, did the partnership own any interest in another partnership or in any foreign entity that was disregarded as an entity separate from its owner under Regulations sections 301.7701-2 and 301.7701-3? If yes, see instructions for required attachment . . . .

4 Did the partnership file Form 8893, Election of Partnership Level Tax Treatment, or an election statement under section 6231(a)(1)(B)(ii) for partnership-level tax treatment, that is in effect for this tax year? See Form 8893 for more details . . . .

5 Does this partnership meet all three of the following requirements?

a The partnership's total receipts for the tax year were less than $250,000;

b The partnership's total assets at the end of the tax year were less than $600,000; and

c Schedules K-1 are filed with the return and furnished to the partners on or before the due date (including extensions) for the partnership return.

If "Yes," the partnership is not required to complete Schedules L, M-1, and M-2; Item F on page 1 of Form 1065; or Item N on Schedule K-1.

6 Does this partnership have any foreign partners? If "Yes," the partnership may have to file Forms 8804, 8805 and 8813. See page 20 of the instructions . . . .

7 Is this partnership a publicly traded partnership as defined in section 469(k)(2)? . . . .

8 Has this partnership filed, or is it required to file, Form 8264, Application for Registration of a Tax Shelter? . . .

9 At any time during calendar year 2004, did the partnership have an interest in or a signature or other authority over a financial account in a foreign country (such as a bank account, securities account, or other financial account)? See page 20 of the instructions for exceptions and filing requirements for Form TD F 90-22.1. If "Yes," enter the name of the foreign country. ▶ ....

10 During the tax year, did the partnership receive a distribution from, or was it the grantor of, or transferor to, a foreign trust? If "Yes," the partnership may have to file Form 3520. See page 21 of the instructions . . . .

11 Was there a distribution of property or a transfer (e.g., by sale or death) of a partnership interest during the tax year? If "Yes," you may elect to adjust the basis of the partnership's assets under section 754 by attaching the statement described under *Elections Made By the Partnership* on page 9 of the instructions . . . .

12 Enter the number of Forms 8865, Return of U.S. Persons With Respect to Certain Foreign Partnerships, attached to this return . . . . ▶

Designation of Tax Matters Partner (see page 21 of the instructions)

Enter below the general partner designated as the tax matters partner (TMP) for the tax year of this return:

Name of
designated TMP ▶ _____   Identifying
number of TMP ▶ _____

Address of
designated TMP ▶ _____

Form **1065** (2004)

Form 1065 (2004)   Page **3**

Schedule K	Partners' Distributive Share Items		Total amount	

Income (Loss)

1	Ordinary business income (loss) (page 1, line 22)		**1**		
2	Net rental real estate income (loss) *(attach Form 8825)*		**2**		
3a	Other gross rental income (loss)	**3a**			
b	Expenses from other rental activities *(attach statement)*.	**3b**			
c	Other net rental income (loss). Subtract line 3b from line 3a		**3c**		
4	Guaranteed payments		**4**		
5	Interest income		**5**		
6	Dividends: **a** Ordinary dividends		**6a**		
	b Qualified dividends	**6b**			
7	Royalties		**7**		
8	Net short-term capital gain (loss) *(attach Schedule D (Form 1065))* . . .		**8**		
9a	Net long-term capital gain (loss) *(attach Schedule D (Form 1065))* . . .		**9a**		
b	Collectibles (28%) gain (loss)	**9b**			
c	Unrecaptured section 1250 gain *(attach statement)*	**9c**			
10	Net section 1231 gain (loss) *(attach Form 4797)*		**10**		
11	Other income (loss) *(attach statement)*		**11**		

Deductions

12	Section 179 deduction *(attach Form 4562)*	**12**	
13a	Contributions	**13a**	
b	Deductions related to portfolio income *(attach statement)*	**13b**	
c	Investment interest expense	**13c**	
d	Section 59(e)(2) expenditures: **(1)** Type ▶ _____ **(2)** Amount ▶	**13d(2)**	
e	Other deductions *(attach statement)*	**13e**	

Self-Employment

14a	Net earnings (loss) from self-employment	**14a**	
b	Gross farming or fishing income	**14b**	
c	Gross nonfarm income	**14c**	

Credits & Credit Recapture

15a	Low-income housing credit (section 42(j)(5))	**15a**	
b	Low-income housing credit (other)	**15b**	
c	Qualified rehabilitation expenditures (rental real estate) *(attach Form 3468)*. . .	**15c**	
d	Other rental real estate credits	**15d**	
e	Other rental credits	**15e**	
f	Other credits and credit recapture *(attach statement)*	**15f**	

Foreign Transactions

16a	Name of country or U.S. possession ▶ _____		
b	Gross income from all sources	**16b**	
c	Gross income sourced at partner level	**16c**	
	Foreign gross income sourced at partnership level		
d	Passive ▶ _____ **e** Listed categories *(attach statement)* ▶ _____ **f** General limitation ▶	**16f**	
	Deductions allocated and apportioned at partner level		
g	Interest expense ▶ _____ **h** Other . . . . ▶	**16h**	
	Deductions allocated and apportioned at partnership level to foreign source income		
i	Passive ▶ _____ **j** Listed categories *(attach statement)* ▶ _____ **k** General limitation ▶	**16k**	
l	Foreign taxes: **(1)** Paid ▶ _____ **(2)** Accrued . . . . ▶	**16l(2)**	
m	Reduction in taxes available for credit *(attach statement)*	**16m**	

Alternative Minimum Tax (AMT) Items

17a	Post-1986 depreciation adjustment	**17a**	
b	Adjusted gain or loss	**17b**	
c	Depletion (other than oil and gas)	**17c**	
d	Oil, gas, and geothermal properties—gross income	**17d**	
e	Oil, gas, and geothermal properties—deductions	**17e**	
f	Other AMT items *(attach statement)*	**17f**	

Other Information

18a	Tax-exempt interest income	**18a**	
b	Other tax-exempt income	**18b**	
c	Nondeductible expenses	**18c**	
19a	Distributions of cash and marketable securities	**19a**	
b	Distributions of other property	**19b**	
20a	Investment income	**20a**	
b	Investment expenses	**20b**	
c	Other items and amounts *(attach statement)*		

Form **1065** (2004)

Form 1065 (2004)   Page **4**

Analysis of Net Income (Loss)

1	Net income (loss). Combine Schedule K, lines 1 through 11. From the result, subtract the sum of Schedule K, lines 12 through 13e, 16l(1), and 16l(2)		**1**			

2 Analysis by partner type:	**(i)** Corporate	**(ii)** Individual (active)	**(iii)** Individual (passive)	**(iv)** Partnership	**(v)** Exempt organization	**(vi)** Nominee/Other
a General partners						
b Limited partners						

Note: Schedules L, M-1, and M-2 are not required if Question 5 of Schedule B is answered "Yes."

Schedule L **Balance Sheets per Books**	Beginning of tax year		End of tax year	
Assets	**(a)**	**(b)**	**(c)**	**(d)**
1 Cash				
2a Trade notes and accounts receivable				
b Less allowance for bad debts				
3 Inventories				
4 U.S. government obligations				
5 Tax-exempt securities				
6 Other current assets (attach statement) . . .				
7 Mortgage and real estate loans				
8 Other investments (attach statement)				
9a Buildings and other depreciable assets. . . .				
b Less accumulated depreciation				
10a Depletable assets				
b Less accumulated depletion				
11 Land (net of any amortization).				
12a Intangible assets (amortizable only)				
b Less accumulated amortization				
13 Other assets (attach statement)				
14 Total assets				
Liabilities and Capital				
15 Accounts payable				
16 Mortgages, notes, bonds payable in less than 1 year .				
17 Other current liabilities (attach statement) . . .				
18 All nonrecourse loans				
19 Mortgages, notes, bonds payable in 1 year or more .				
20 Other liabilities (attach statement)				
21 Partners' capital accounts				
22 Total liabilities and capital				

Schedule M-1   Reconciliation of Income (Loss) per Books With Income (Loss) per Return

1 Net income (loss) per books		**6** Income recorded on books this year not included on Schedule K, lines 1 through 11 (itemize):	
2 Income included on Schedule K, lines 1, 2, 3c, 5, 6a, 7, 8, 9a, 10, and 11, not recorded on books this year (itemize):		**a** Tax-exempt interest $	
3 Guaranteed payments (other than health insurance)		**7** Deductions included on Schedule K, lines 1 through 13e, 16l(1), and 16l(2), not charged against book income this year (itemize):	
4 Expenses recorded on books this year not included on Schedule K, lines 1 through 13e, 16l(1), and 16l(2) (itemize):		**a** Depreciation $	
a Depreciation $			
b Travel and entertainment $		**8** Add lines 6 and 7	
		9 Income (loss) (Analysis of Net Income (Loss), line 1). Subtract line 8 from line 5	
5 Add lines 1 through 4			

Schedule M-2   Analysis of Partners' Capital Accounts

1 Balance at beginning of year		**6** Distributions: **a** Cash	
2 Capital contributed: **a** Cash		**b** Property	
b Property . . .		**7** Other decreases (itemize):	
3 Net income (loss) per books			
4 Other increases (itemize):		**8** Add lines 6 and 7	
5 Add lines 1 through 4		**9** Balance at end of year. Subtract line 8 from line 5	

Form **1065** (2004)

Schedule K-1
(Form 1065)

Department of the Treasury
Internal Revenue Service

2004

Tax year beginning _____ , 2004

and ending _____ , 20__

Partner's Share of Income, Deductions, Credits, etc.
► See back of form and separate instructions.

☐ Final K-1   ☐ Amended K-1   OMB No. 1545-0099

Part III	**Partner's Share of Current Year Income, Deductions, Credits, and Other Items**

1	Ordinary business income (loss)	15 Credits & credit recapture
2	Net rental real estate income (loss)	
3	Other net rental income (loss)	16 Foreign transactions
4	Guaranteed payments	
5	Interest income	
6a	Ordinary dividends	
6b	Qualified dividends	
7	Royalties	
8	Net short-term capital gain (loss)	
9a	Net long-term capital gain (loss)	17 Alternative minimum tax (AMT) items
9b	Collectibles (28%) gain (loss)	
9c	Unrecaptured section 1250 gain	
10	Net section 1231 gain (loss)	18 Tax-exempt income and nondeductible expenses
11	Other income (loss)	
12	Section 179 deduction	19 Distributions
13	Other deductions	
14	Self-employment earnings (loss)	20 Other information

Part I   Information About the Partnership

A Partnership's employer identification number

B Partnership's name, address, city, state, and ZIP code

C IRS Center where partnership filed return

D ☐ Check if this is a publicly traded partnership (PTP)

E ☐ Tax shelter registration number, if any _____

F ☐ Check if Form 8271 is attached

Part II   Information About the Partner

G Partner's identifying number

H Partner's name, address, city, state, and ZIP code

I ☐ General partner or LLC member-manager   ☐ Limited partner or other LLC member

J ☐ Domestic partner   ☐ Foreign partner

K What type of entity is this partner? _____

L Partner's share of profit, loss, and capital:

	Beginning		Ending	
Profit		%		%
Loss		%		%
Capital		%		%

M Partner's share of liabilities at year end:

Nonrecourse . . . . $_____

Qualified nonrecourse financing . $_____

Recourse . . . . $_____

N Partner's capital account analysis:

Beginning capital account . . . $_____

Capital contributed during the year . $_____

Current year increase (decrease) . $_____

Withdrawals & distributions . . . $(_____)

Ending capital account . . . . $_____

☐ Tax basis ☐ GAAP ☐ Section 704(b) book
☐ Other (explain)

*See attached statement for additional information.

For IRS Use Only

For Privacy Act and Paperwork Reduction Act Notice, see Instructions for Form 1065.   Cat. No. 11394R   **Schedule K-1 (Form 1065) 2004**

B-6 U.S. Corporation Income Tax Return

Form 1120
Department of the Treasury
Internal Revenue Service

U.S. Corporation Income Tax Return

For calendar year 2004 or tax year beginning .... , 2004, ending .... , 20 ....
► See separate instructions.

OMB No. 1545-0123

2004

A Check if:
1 Consolidated return (attach Form 851) . ☐
2 Personal holding co. (attach Sch. PH) . ☐
3 Personal service corp. (see instructions) . ☐
4 Schedule M-3 required (attach Sch. M-3) ☐

Use IRS label. Otherwise, print or type.

Name

Number, street, and room or suite no. If a P.O. box, see page 9 of instructions.

City or town, state, and ZIP code

B Employer identification number

C Date incorporated

D Total assets (see page 8 of instructions)
$

E Check if: (1) ☐ Initial return (2) ☐ Final return (3) ☐ Name change (4) ☐ Address change

Income

1a	Gross receipts or sales _____ **b** Less returns and allowances _____ **c** Bal ►	1c
2	Cost of goods sold (Schedule A, line 8)	2
3	Gross profit. Subtract line 2 from line 1c	3
4	Dividends (Schedule C, line 19)	4
5	Interest	5
6	Gross rents	6
7	Gross royalties	7
8	Capital gain net income (attach Schedule D (Form 1120))	8
9	Net gain or (loss) from Form 4797, Part II, line 17 (attach Form 4797)	9
10	Other income (see page 11 of instructions—attach schedule)	10
11	**Total income.** Add lines 3 through 10 ►	11

Deductions (See instructions for limitations on deductions.)

12	Compensation of officers (Schedule E, line 4)	12
13	Salaries and wages (less employment credits)	13
14	Repairs and maintenance	14
15	Bad debts	15
16	Rents	16
17	Taxes and licenses	17
18	Interest	18
19	Charitable contributions (see page 14 of instructions for 10% limitation)	19
20	Depreciation (attach Form 4562) . . . 20	
21	Less depreciation claimed on Schedule A and elsewhere on return . . 21a	21b
22	Depletion	22
23	Advertising	23
24	Pension, profit-sharing, etc., plans	24
25	Employee benefit programs	25
26	Other deductions (attach schedule)	26
27	**Total deductions.** Add lines 12 through 26 ►	27
28	Taxable income before net operating loss deduction and special deductions. Subtract line 27 from line 11	28
29	**Less:** **a** Net operating loss deduction (see page 16 of instructions) . . 29a	
	b Special deductions (Schedule C, line 20) 29b	29c

Tax and Payments

30	**Taxable income.** Subtract line 29c from line 28 (see instructions if Schedule C, line 12, was completed)	30
31	**Total tax** (Schedule J, line 11)	31
32	Payments: **a** 2003 overpayment credited to 2004 . 32a	
b	2004 estimated tax payments . . . 32b	
c	Less 2004 refund applied for on Form 4466 32c ( ) **d** Bal ► 32d	
e	Tax deposited with Form 7004 . . . . . . 32e	
f	Credit for tax paid on undistributed capital gains (attach Form 2439) . . 32f	
g	Credit for Federal tax on fuels (attach Form 4136). See instructions. . . 32g	32h
33	Estimated tax penalty (see page 17 of instructions). Check if Form 2220 is attached . . ► ☐	33
34	**Tax due.** If line 32h is smaller than the total of lines 31 and 33, enter amount owed	34
35	**Overpayment.** If line 32h is larger than the total of lines 31 and 33, enter amount overpaid . . .	35
36	Enter amount of line 35 you want: **Credited to 2005 estimated tax** ► **Refunded** ►	36

Sign Here ►

Under penalties of perjury, I declare that I have examined this return, including accompanying schedules and statements, and to the best of my knowledge and belief, it is true, correct, and complete. Declaration of preparer (other than taxpayer) is based on all information of which preparer has any knowledge.

► _____ ► _____
Signature of officer   Date   Title

May the IRS discuss this return with the preparer shown below (see instructions)? ☐ **Yes** ☐ **No**

Paid Preparer's Use Only

Preparer's signature ►		Date		Check if self-employed ☐	Preparer's SSN or PTIN
Firm's name (or yours if self-employed), address, and ZIP code ►				EIN	
				Phone no. ( )	

For Privacy Act and Paperwork Reduction Act Notice, see separate instructions. Cat. No. 11450Q Form **1120** (2004)

Form 1120 (2004)   Page **2**

Schedule A	**Cost of Goods Sold** (see page 17 of instructions)		
1	Inventory at beginning of year	**1**	
2	Purchases	**2**	
3	Cost of labor	**3**	
4	Additional section 263A costs (attach schedule)	**4**	
5	Other costs (attach schedule)	**5**	
6	**Total.** Add lines 1 through 5	**6**	
7	Inventory at end of year	**7**	
8	**Cost of goods sold.** Subtract line 7 from line 6. Enter here and on page 1, line 2	**8**	

9a Check all methods used for valuing closing inventory:

   (i) ☐ Cost as described in Regulations section 1.471-3

   (ii) ☐ Lower of cost or market as described in Regulations section 1.471-4

   (iii) ☐ Other (Specify method used and attach explanation.) ▶ --

   b Check if there was a writedown of subnormal goods as described in Regulations section 1.471-2(c) . . . . ▶ ☐

   c Check if the LIFO inventory method was adopted this tax year for any goods (if checked, attach Form 970) . . . . ▶ ☐

   d If the LIFO inventory method was used for this tax year, enter percentage (or amounts) of closing inventory computed under LIFO **9d**

   e If property is produced or acquired for resale, do the rules of section 263A apply to the corporation? . . . . . ☐ Yes ☐ No

   f Was there any change in determining quantities, cost, or valuations between opening and closing inventory? If "Yes," attach explanation . . . . ☐ Yes ☐ No

Schedule C	**Dividends and Special Deductions** (see page 18 of instructions)	**(a)** Dividends received	**(b)** %	**(c)** Special deductions (a) × (b)
1	Dividends from less-than-20%-owned domestic corporations that are subject to the 70% deduction (other than debt-financed stock)		70	
2	Dividends from 20%-or-more-owned domestic corporations that are subject to the 80% deduction (other than debt-financed stock)		80	
3	Dividends on debt-financed stock of domestic and foreign corporations (section 246A)		see instructions	
4	Dividends on certain preferred stock of less-than-20%-owned public utilities		42	
5	Dividends on certain preferred stock of 20%-or-more-owned public utilities		48	
6	Dividends from less-than-20%-owned foreign corporations and certain FSCs that are subject to the 70% deduction		70	
7	Dividends from 20%-or-more-owned foreign corporations and certain FSCs that are subject to the 80% deduction		80	
8	Dividends from wholly owned foreign subsidiaries subject to the 100% deduction (section 245(b))		100	
9	**Total.** Add lines 1 through 8. See page 19 of instructions for limitation			
10	Dividends from domestic corporations received by a small business investment company operating under the Small Business Investment Act of 1958		100	
11	Dividends from affiliated group members and certain FSCs that are subject to the 100% deduction		100	
12	Dividends from controlled foreign corporations subject to the 85% deduction (attach Form 8895)		85	
13	Other dividends from foreign corporations not included on lines 3, 6, 7, 8, 11, or 12			
14	Income from controlled foreign corporations under subpart F (attach Form(s) 5471)			
15	Foreign dividend gross-up (section 78)			
16	IC-DISC and former DISC dividends not included on lines 1, 2, or 3 (section 246(d))			
17	Other dividends			
18	Deduction for dividends paid on certain preferred stock of public utilities	▶		
19	**Total dividends.** Add lines 1 through 17. Enter here and on page 1, line 4	▶		
20	**Total special deductions.** Add lines 9, 10, 11, 12, and 18. Enter here and on page 1, line 29b		▶	

Schedule E	**Compensation of Officers** (see instructions for page 1, line 12, on page 13 of instructions)					

Note: *Complete Schedule E only if total receipts (line 1a plus lines 4 through 10 on page 1) are $500,000 or more.*

(a) Name of officer	**(b)** Social security number	**(c)** Percent of time devoted to business	Percent of corporation stock owned		**(f)** Amount of compensation
			(d) Common	**(e)** Preferred	
1		%	%	%	
		%	%	%	
		%	%	%	
		%	%	%	
		%	%	%	

2	Total compensation of officers	
3	Compensation of officers claimed on Schedule A and elsewhere on return	
4	Subtract line 3 from line 2. Enter the result here and on page 1, line 12	

Form **1120** (2004)

Form 1120 (2004)   Page **3**

Schedule J   Tax Computation (see page 20 of instructions)

1   Check if the corporation is a member of a controlled group (see sections 1561 and 1563). . . . . ▶ ☐

Important: Members of a controlled group, see page 20 of instructions.

2a If the box on line 1 is checked, enter the corporation's share of the $50,000, $25,000, and $9,925,000 taxable income brackets (in that order):

(1) $ _____   (2) $ _____   (3) $ _____

b   Enter the corporation's share of: **(1)** Additional 5% tax (not more than $11,750) $ _____

(2) Additional 3% tax (not more than $100,000) $ _____

3	Income tax. Check if a qualified personal service corporation under section 448(d)(2) (see page 21) . . ▶ ☐	**3**
4	Alternative minimum tax (attach Form 4626)	**4**
5	Add lines 3 and 4	**5**

6a	Foreign tax credit (attach Form 1118)	**6a**	
b	Possessions tax credit (attach Form 5735)	**6b**	
c	Check: ☐ Nonconventional source fuel credit ☐ QEV credit (attach Form 8834)	**6c**	
d	General business credit. Check box(es) and indicate which forms are attached: ☐ Form 3800 ☐ Form(s) (specify) ▶	**6d**	
e	Credit for prior year minimum tax (attach Form 8827)	**6e**	
f	Qualified zone academy bond credit (attach Form 8860)	**6f**	

7	**Total credits.** Add lines 6a through 6f	**7**
8	Subtract line 7 from line 5	**8**
9	Personal holding company tax (attach Schedule PH (Form 1120))	**9**
10	Other taxes. Check if from: ☐ Form 4255 ☐ Form 8611 ☐ Form 8697 ☐ Form 8866 ☐ Other (attach schedule)	**10**
11	**Total tax.** Add lines 8 through 10. Enter here and on page 1, line 31	**11**

Schedule K   Other Information (see page 23 of instructions)

		Yes	No
1	Check accounting method: **a** ☐ Cash **b** ☐ Accrual **c** ☐ Other (specify) ▶		
2	See page 25 of the instructions and enter the:		
a	Business activity code no. ▶		
b	Business activity ▶		
c	Product or service ▶		
3	At the end of the tax year, did the corporation own, directly or indirectly, 50% or more of the voting stock of a domestic corporation? (For rules of attribution, see section 267(c).)		

If "Yes," attach a schedule showing: **(a)** name and employer identification number (EIN), **(b)** percentage owned, and **(c)** taxable income or (loss) before NOL and special deductions of such corporation for the tax year ending with or within your tax year.

4   Is the corporation a subsidiary in an affiliated group or a parent-subsidiary controlled group? . . . . . .

If "Yes," enter name and EIN of the parent corporation ▶ ....

5   At the end of the tax year, did any individual, partnership, corporation, estate, or trust own, directly or indirectly, 50% or more of the corporation's voting stock? (For rules of attribution, see section 267(c).)

If "Yes," attach a schedule showing name and identifying number. (Do not include any information already entered in **4** above.) Enter percentage owned ▶ ....

6   During this tax year, did the corporation pay dividends (other than stock dividends and distributions in exchange for stock) in excess of the corporation's current and accumulated earnings and profits? (See sections 301 and 316.) . .

If "Yes," file **Form 5452,** Corporate Report of Nondividend Distributions.

If this is a consolidated return, answer here for the parent corporation and on **Form 851,** Affiliations Schedule, for each subsidiary.

		Yes	No
7	At any time during the tax year, did one foreign person own, directly or indirectly, at least 25% of **(a)** the total voting power of all classes of stock of the corporation entitled to vote or **(b)** the total value of all classes of stock of the corporation?		

If "Yes," enter: **(a)** Percentage owned ▶ ....

and **(b)** Owner's country ▶ ....

c   The corporation may have to file **Form 5472,** Information Return of a 25% Foreign-Owned U.S. Corporation or a Foreign Corporation Engaged in a U.S. Trade or Business. Enter number of Forms 5472 attached ▶ ....

8   Check this box if the corporation issued publicly offered debt instruments with original issue discount . ▶ ☐

If checked, the corporation may have to file **Form 8281,** Information Return for Publicly Offered Original Issue Discount Instruments.

9   Enter the amount of tax-exempt interest received or accrued during the tax year ▶ $ ....

10 Enter the number of shareholders at the end of the tax year (if 75 or fewer) ▶ ....

11 If the corporation has an NOL for the tax year and is electing to forego the carryback period, check here ▶ ☐

If the corporation is filing a consolidated return, the statement required by Temporary Regulations section 1.1502-21T(b)(3)(i) or (ii) must be attached or the election will not be valid.

12 Enter the available NOL carryover from prior tax years (Do not reduce it by any deduction on line 29a.) ▶ $ ....

13 Are the corporation's total receipts (line 1a plus lines 4 through 10 on page 1) for the tax year **and** its total assets at the end of the tax year less than $250,000? . . .

If "Yes," the corporation is not required to complete Schedules L, M-1, and M-2 on page 4. Instead, enter the total amount of cash distributions and the book value of property distributions (other than cash) made during the tax year. ▶ $...........................

Note: *If the corporation, at any time during the tax year, had assets or operated a business in a foreign country or U.S. possession, it may be required to attach Schedule N (Form 1120), Foreign Operations of U.S. Corporations, to this return. See Schedule N for details.*

Form **1120** (2004)

Form 1120 (2004)   Page **4**

Note: *The corporation is not required to complete Schedules L, M-1, and M-2 if Question 13 on Schedule K is answered "Yes."*

Schedule L — Balance Sheets per Books

	Assets	Beginning of tax year (a)	(b)	End of tax year (c)	(d)
1	Cash				
2a	Trade notes and accounts receivable				
b	Less allowance for bad debts	( )		( )	
3	Inventories				
4	U.S. government obligations				
5	Tax-exempt securities (see instructions)				
6	Other current assets (attach schedule)				
7	Loans to shareholders				
8	Mortgage and real estate loans				
9	Other investments (attach schedule)				
10a	Buildings and other depreciable assets				
b	Less accumulated depreciation	( )		( )	
11a	Depletable assets				
b	Less accumulated depletion	( )		( )	
12	Land (net of any amortization)				
13a	Intangible assets (amortizable only)				
b	Less accumulated amortization	( )		( )	
14	Other assets (attach schedule)				
15	Total assets				

	Liabilities and Shareholders' Equity				
16	Accounts payable				
17	Mortgages, notes, bonds payable in less than 1 year				
18	Other current liabilities (attach schedule)				
19	Loans from shareholders				
20	Mortgages, notes, bonds payable in 1 year or more				
21	Other liabilities (attach schedule)				
22	Capital stock: a Preferred stock				
	b Common stock				
23	Additional paid-in capital				
24	Retained earnings—Appropriated (attach schedule)				
25	Retained earnings—Unappropriated				
26	Adjustments to shareholders' equity (attach schedule)				
27	Less cost of treasury stock		( )		( )
28	Total liabilities and shareholders' equity				

Schedule M-1 — Reconciliation of Income (Loss) per Books With Income per Return (see page 24 of instructions)

1	Net income (loss) per books		7	Income recorded on books this year not included on this return (itemize):	
2	Federal income tax per books			Tax-exempt interest $	
3	Excess of capital losses over capital gains			....	
4	Income subject to tax not recorded on books this year (itemize):		8	Deductions on this return not charged against book income this year (itemize):	
	....		a	Depreciation . . . . $..........	
5	Expenses recorded on books this year not deducted on this return (itemize):		b	Charitable contributions $..........	
a	Depreciation . . . . $..........			....	
b	Charitable contributions $..........		9	Add lines 7 and 8	
c	Travel and entertainment $..........		10	Income (page 1, line 28)—line 6 less line 9	
6	Add lines 1 through 5				

Schedule M-2 — Analysis of Unappropriated Retained Earnings per Books (Line 25, Schedule L)

1	Balance at beginning of year		5	Distributions: a Cash	
2	Net income (loss) per books			b Stock	
3	Other increases (itemize):			c Property	
	....		6	Other decreases (itemize):	
			7	Add lines 5 and 6	
4	Add lines 1, 2, and 3		8	Balance at end of year (line 4 less line 7)	

Form **1120** (2004)

B-7   U.S. Income Tax Return for an S Corporation

Form **1120S**	**U.S. Income Tax Return for an S Corporation**	OMB No. 1545-0130
Department of the Treasury Internal Revenue Service	▶ Do not file this form unless the corporation has timely filed Form 2553 to elect to be an S corporation. ▶ See separate instructions.	20**04**

For calendar year 2004, or tax year beginning _____ , 2004, and ending _____ , 20 ___

A Effective date of S election	**Use the IRS label. Otherwise, print or type.** Name	**C** Employer identification number
	Number, street, and room or suite no. (If a P.O. box, see page 12 of the instructions.)	**D** Date incorporated
B Business code number (see pages 36–38 of the Insts.)	City or town, state, and ZIP code	**E** Total assets (see page 12 of instructions) $

F Check applicable boxes: (1) ☐ Initial return (2) ☐ Final return (3) ☐ Name change (4) ☐ Address change (5) ☐ Amended return
G Enter number of shareholders in the corporation at end of the tax year . . . . ▶

Caution: Include **only** trade or business income and expenses on lines 1a through 21. See page 13 of the instructions for more information.

Income

1a Gross receipts or sales [_____] **b** Less returns and allowances [_____] **c** Bal ▶	**1c**	
2 Cost of goods sold (Schedule A, line 8)	**2**	
3 Gross profit. Subtract line 2 from line 1c	**3**	
4 Net gain (loss) from Form 4797, Part II, line 17 (attach Form 4797)	**4**	
5 Other income (loss) (attach schedule)	**5**	
6 **Total income (loss).** Add lines 3 through 5. . . . . ▶	**6**	

Deductions (see page 14 of the instructions for limitations)

7 Compensation of officers	**7**	
8 Salaries and wages (less employment credits) . . .	**8**	
9 Repairs and maintenance	**9**	
10 Bad debts	**10**	
11 Rents.	**11**	
12 Taxes and licenses	**12**	
13 Interest	**13**	
14a Depreciation (attach Form 4562)	14a	
b Depreciation claimed on Schedule A and elsewhere on return .	14b	
c Subtract line 14b from line 14a	**14c**	
15 Depletion **(Do not deduct oil and gas depletion.)**	**15**	
16 Advertising	**16**	
17 Pension, profit-sharing, etc., plans	**17**	
18 Employee benefit programs.	**18**	
19 Other deductions (attach schedule)	**19**	
20 **Total deductions.** Add the amounts shown in the far right column for lines 7 through 19 ▶	**20**	
21 Ordinary business income (loss). Subtract line 20 from line 6	**21**	

Tax and Payments

22 Tax: a Excess net passive income tax (attach schedule) . . .	22a	
b Tax from Schedule D (Form 1120S)	22b	
c Add lines 22a and 22b (see page 18 of the instructions for additional taxes) .	**22c**	
23 Payments: a 2004 estimated tax payments and amount applied from 2003 return	23a	
b Tax deposited with Form 7004.	23b	
c Credit for Federal tax paid on fuels (attach Form 4136) . . .	23c	
d Add lines 23a through 23c	**23d**	
24 Estimated tax penalty (see page 18 of instructions). Check if Form 2220 is attached. . ▶ ☐	**24**	
25 **Tax due.** If line 23d is smaller than the total of lines 22c and 24, enter amount owed. . . .	**25**	
26 **Overpayment.** If line 23d is larger than the total of lines 22c and 24, enter amount overpaid .	**26**	
27 Enter amount of line 26 you want: **Credited to 2005 estimated tax** ▶ _____	**Refunded** ▶	**27**	

Sign Here

Under penalties of perjury, I declare that I have examined this return, including accompanying schedules and statements, and to the best of my knowledge and belief, it is true, correct, and complete. Declaration of preparer (other than taxpayer) is based on all information of which preparer has any knowledge.

▶ _____   _____   ▶ _____
Signature of officer   Date   Title

May the IRS discuss this return with the preparer shown below (see instructions)? ☐ Yes ☐ No

Paid Preparer's Use Only	Preparer's signature ▶	Date	Check if self-employed ☐	Preparer's SSN or PTIN
	Firm's name (or yours if self-employed), address, and ZIP code ▶		EIN	
			Phone no. ( )	

For Privacy Act and Paperwork Reduction Act Notice, see the separate instructions.   Cat. No. 11510H   Form **1120S** (2004)

Form 1120S (2004)   Page **2**

Schedule A   Cost of Goods Sold (see page 18 of the instructions)

1	Inventory at beginning of year	**1**	
2	Purchases	**2**	
3	Cost of labor	**3**	
4	Additional section 263A costs (attach schedule)	**4**	
5	Other costs (attach schedule)	**5**	
6	**Total.** Add lines 1 through 5	**6**	
7	Inventory at end of year	**7**	
8	**Cost of goods sold.** Subtract line 7 from line 6. Enter here and on page 1, line 2	**8**	

9a Check all methods used for valuing closing inventory: *(i)* ☐ Cost as described in Regulations section 1.471-3

   (ii) ☐ Lower of cost or market as described in Regulations section 1.471-4

   (iii) ☐ Other (specify method used and attach explanation) ▶ ....

b Check if there was a writedown of subnormal goods as described in Regulations section 1.471-2(c) . . . . ▶ ☐

c Check if the LIFO inventory method was adopted this tax year for any goods (if checked, attach Form 970) . . . . . ▶ ☐

d If the LIFO inventory method was used for this tax year, enter percentage (or amounts) of closing inventory computed under LIFO | **9d** | |

e If property is produced or acquired for resale, do the rules of Section 263A apply to the corporation? . . . . ☐ Yes ☐ No

f Was there any change in determining quantities, cost, or valuations between opening and closing inventory? . . ☐ Yes ☐ No
   If "Yes," attach explanation.

Schedule B   Other Information (see page 19 of instructions) | Yes | No |

1 Check method of accounting: **(a)** ☐ Cash   **(b)** ☐ Accrual   **(c)** ☐ Other (specify) ▶....................

2 See pages 36 through 38 of the instructions and enter the:

   (a) Business activity ▶.................................   **(b)** Product or service ▶.................................

3 At the end of the tax year, did the corporation own, directly or indirectly, 50% or more of the voting stock of a domestic corporation? (For rules of attribution, see section 267(c).) If "Yes," attach a schedule showing: **(a)** name, address, and employer identification number and **(b)** percentage owned . . . .

4 Was the corporation a member of a controlled group subject to the provisions of section 1561? . . . .

5 Check this box if the corporation has filed or is required to file **Form 8264,** Application for Registration of a Tax Shelter ▶ ☐

6 Check this box if the corporation issued publicly offered debt instruments with original issue discount . . ▶ ☐

   If checked, the corporation may have to file **Form 8281,** Information Return for Publicly Offered Original Issue Discount Instruments.

7 If the corporation: **(a)** was a C corporation before it elected to be an S corporation **or** the corporation acquired an asset with a basis determined by reference to its basis (or the basis of any other property) in the hands of a C corporation **and (b)** has net unrealized built-in gain (defined in section 1374(d)(1)) in excess of the net recognized built-in gain from prior years, enter the net unrealized built-in gain reduced by net recognized built-in gain from prior years . . . . ▶ $ ....

8 Check this box if the corporation had accumulated earnings and profits at the close of the tax year . . ▶ ☐

9 Are the corporation's total receipts (see page 19 of the instructions) for the tax year **and** its total assets at the end of the tax year less than $250,000? If "Yes," the corporation is not required to complete Schedules L and M-1.

Note: *If the corporation had assets or operated a business in a foreign country or U.S. possession, it may be required to attach* **Schedule N (Form 1120),** *Foreign Operations of U.S. Corporations, to this return. See Schedule N for details.*

Schedule K   Shareholders' Shares of Income, Deductions, Credits, etc.

	Shareholders' Pro Rata Share Items			Total amount	
1	Ordinary business income (loss) (page 1, line 21)			**1**	
2	Net rental real estate income (loss) (attach Form 8825)			**2**	
3a	Other gross rental income (loss)	**3a**			
b	Expenses from other rental activities (attach schedule) . .	**3b**			
c	Other net rental income (loss). Subtract line 3b from line 3a			**3c**	
4	Interest income			**4**	
5	Dividends: **a** Ordinary dividends			**5a**	
	b Qualified dividends	**5b**			
6	Royalties			**6**	
7	Net short-term capital gain (loss)			**7**	
8a	Net long-term capital gain (loss)			**8a**	
b	Collectibles (28%) gain (loss)	**8b**			
c	Unrecaptured section 1250 gain (attach schedule) . .	**8c**			
9	Net section 1231 gain (loss) (attach Form 4797)			**9**	
10	Other income (loss) (attach schedule)			**10**	

Income (Loss) (vertical label)

Form **1120S** (2004)

Form 1120S (2004)   Page **3**

	Shareholders' Pro Rata Share Items (continued)		Total amount	
Deductions	**11** Section 179 deduction *(attach Form 4562)*	**11**		
	12a Contributions	**12a**		
	b Deductions related to portfolio income *(attach schedule)*	**12b**		
	c Investment interest expense	**12c**		
	d Section 59(e)(2) expenditures **(1)** Type ▶................................ **(2)** Amount ▶	**12d(2)**		
	e Other deductions *(attach schedule)*	**12e**		
Credits & Credit Recapture	**13a** Low-income housing credit (section 42(j)(5))	**13a**		
	b Low-income housing credit (other)	**13b**		
	c Qualified rehabilitation expenditures (rental real estate) *(attach Form 3468)*	**13c**		
	d Other rental real estate credits	**13d**		
	e Other rental credits	**13e**		
	f Credit for alcohol used as fuel *(attach Form 6478)*	**13f**		
	g Other credits and credit recapture *(attach schedule)*.	**13g**		
Foreign Transactions	**14a** Name of country or U.S. possession ▶................................			
	b Gross income from all sources	**14b**		
	c Gross income sourced at shareholder level	**14c**		
	Foreign gross income sourced at corporate level:			
	d Passive	**14d**		
	e Listed categories *(attach schedule)*	**14e**		
	f General limitation	**14f**		
	Deductions allocated and apportioned at shareholder level:			
	g Interest expense	**14g**		
	h Other	**14h**		
	Deductions allocated and apportioned at corporate level to foreign source income:			
	i Passive	**14i**		
	j Listed categories *(attach schedule)*	**14j**		
	k General limitation	**14k**		
	Other information:			
	l Foreign taxes paid	**14l**		
	m Foreign taxes accrued	**14m**		
	n Reduction in taxes available for credit *(attach schedule)*.	**14n**		
Alternative Minimum Tax (AMT) Items	**15a** Post-1986 depreciation adjustment	**15a**		
	b Adjusted gain or loss	**15b**		
	c Depletion (other than oil and gas)	**15c**		
	d Oil, gas, and geothermal properties—gross income	**15d**		
	e Oil, gas, and geothermal properties—deductions.	**15e**		
	f Other AMT items *(attach schedule)*	**15f**		
Items Affecting Shareholder Basis	**16a** Tax-exempt interest income	**16a**		
	b Other tax-exempt income	**16b**		
	c Nondeductible expenses	**16c**		
	d Property distributions	**16d**		
	e Repayment of loans from shareholders.	**16e**		
Other Information	**17a** Investment income	**17a**		
	b Investment expenses	**17b**		
	c Dividend distributions paid from accumulated earnings and profits	**17c**		
	d Other items and amounts *(attach schedule)*			
	e **Income/loss reconciliation.** (Required only if Schedule M-1 must be completed.) Combine the amounts on lines 1 through 10 in the far right column. From the result, subtract the sum of the amounts on lines 11 through 12e and lines 14l or 14m, whichever applies	**17e**		

Form **1120S** (2004)

Form 1120S (2004)   Page **4**

Note: The corporation is not required to complete Schedules L and M-1 if question 9 of Schedule B is answered "Yes."

Schedule L   **Balance Sheets per Books**

		Beginning of tax year		End of tax year	
Assets		**(a)**	**(b)**	**(c)**	**(d)**
1	Cash				
2a	Trade notes and accounts receivable . . .				
b	Less allowance for bad debts				
3	Inventories				
4	U.S. government obligations.				
5	Tax-exempt securities				
6	Other current assets *(attach schedule)* .				
7	Loans to shareholders				
8	Mortgage and real estate loans . . .				
9	Other investments *(attach schedule)* . .				
10a	Buildings and other depreciable assets .				
b	Less accumulated depreciation				
11a	Depletable assets				
b	Less accumulated depletion.				
12	Land (net of any amortization)				
13a	Intangible assets (amortizable only) . . .				
b	Less accumulated amortization.				
14	Other assets *(attach schedule)*				
15	Total assets				
	Liabilities and Shareholders' Equity				
16	Accounts payable				
17	Mortgages, notes, bonds payable in less than 1 year .				
18	Other current liabilities *(attach schedule)* . .				
19	Loans from shareholders.				
20	Mortgages, notes, bonds payable in 1 year or more				
21	Other liabilities *(attach schedule)*				
22	Capital stock				
23	Additional paid-in capital.				
24	Retained earnings				
25	Adjustments to shareholders' equity *(attach schedule)*.				
26	Less cost of treasury stock		( )		( )
27	Total liabilities and shareholders' equity .				

Schedule M-1   **Reconciliation of Income (Loss) per Books With Income (Loss) per Return**

1	Net income (loss) per books.		5	Income recorded on books this year not included on Schedule K, lines 1 through 10 (itemize):	
2	Income included on Schedule K, lines 1, 2, 3c, 4, 5a, 6, 7, 8a, 9, and 10, not recorded on books this year (itemize): -------------------------		a	Tax-exempt interest $ -----------------	
3	Expenses recorded on books this year not included on Schedule K, lines 1 through 12, and 14l or (14m) (itemize):		6	Deductions included on Schedule K, lines 1 through 12, and 14l or (14m), not charged against book income this year (itemize):	
a	Depreciation $ -----------------		a	Depreciation $ -----------------	
b	Travel and entertainment $ -----------------		7	Add lines 5 and 6.	
4	Add lines 1 through 3.		8	Income (loss) (Schedule K, line 17e). Line 4 less line 7	

Schedule M-2   **Analysis of Accumulated Adjustments Account, Other Adjustments Account, and Shareholders' Undistributed Taxable Income Previously Taxed** (see page 32 of the instructions)

		(a) Accumulated adjustments account	**(b)** Other adjustments account	**(c)** Shareholders' undistributed taxable income previously taxed
1	Balance at beginning of tax year			
2	Ordinary income from page 1, line 21. . .			
3	Other additions.			
4	Loss from page 1, line 21	( )		
5	Other reductions	( )	( )	
6	Combine lines 1 through 5			
7	Distributions other than dividend distributions			
8	Balance at end of tax year. Subtract line 7 from line 6			

Form **1120S** (2004)

☐ Final K-1   ☐ Amended K-1   OMB No. 1545-0130

Schedule K-1
(Form 1120S)
Department of the Treasury
Internal Revenue Service

20**04**

Tax year beginning _____ , 2004

and ending _____ , 20__

Shareholder's Share of Income, Deductions, Credits, etc.

► See back of form and separate instructions.

Part I	**Information About the Corporation**

A Corporation's employer identification number

B Corporation's name, address, city, state, and ZIP code

C IRS Center where corporation filed return

D ☐ Tax shelter registration number, if any _____

E ☐ Check if Form 8271 is attached

Part II	**Information About the Shareholder**

F Shareholder's identifying number

G Shareholder's name, address, city, state and ZIP code

H Shareholder's percentage of stock ownership for tax year . . . . _____ %

For IRS Use Only

Part III	**Shareholder's Share of Current Year Income, Deductions, Credits, and Other Items**

1	Ordinary business income (loss)	**13**	Credits & credit recapture
2	Net rental real estate income (loss)		
3	Other net rental income (loss)		
4	Interest income		
5a	Ordinary dividends		
5b	Qualified dividends	**14**	Foreign transactions
6	Royalties		
7	Net short-term capital gain (loss)		
8a	Net long-term capital gain (loss)		
8b	Collectibles (28%) gain (loss)		
8c	Unrecaptured section 1250 gain		
9	Net section 1231 gain (loss)		
10	Other income (loss)	**15**	Alternative minimum tax (AMT) items
11	Section 179 deduction	**16**	Items affecting shareholder basis
12	Other deductions		
		17	Other information

* See attached statement for additional information.

For Privacy Act and Paperwork Reduction Act Notice, see Instructions for Form 1120S.   Cat. No. 11520D   **Schedule K-1 (Form 1120S) 2004**

B-8   Amended Tax Return Forms

Form 1040X
(Rev. November 2004)

Department of the Treasury—Internal Revenue Service

Amended U.S. Individual Income Tax Return

▶ See separate instructions.

OMB No. 1545-0091

This return is for calendar year ▶ _____, or fiscal year ended ▶ _____, _____.

Your first name and initial	Last name

Your social security number

If a joint return, spouse's first name and initial	Last name

Spouse's social security number

Home address (no. and street) or P.O. box if mail is not delivered to your home	Apt. no.

Phone number ( )

City, town or post office, state, and ZIP code. If you have a foreign address, see page 2 of the instructions.

For Paperwork Reduction Act Notice, see page 6.

A If the name or address shown above is different from that shown on the original return, check here . . . . . . ▶ ☐

B Has the original return been changed or audited by the IRS or have you been notified that it will be? . . ☐ **Yes** ☐ **No**

C Filing status. Be sure to complete this line. **Note.** You cannot change from joint to separate returns after the due date.

On original return ▶ ☐ Single ☐ Married filing jointly ☐ Married filing separately ☐ Head of household ☐ Qualifying widow(er)

On this return ▶ ☐ Single ☐ Married filing jointly ☐ Married filing separately ☐ Head of household* ☐ Qualifying widow(er)

* If the qualifying person is a child but not your dependent, see page 2.

Use Part II on the back to explain any changes

			A. Original amount or as previously adjusted (see page 3)	B. Net change— amount of increase or (decrease)— explain in Part II	C. Correct amount
Income and Deductions (see pages 2–6)					
1 Adjusted gross income (see page 3)	**1**				
2 Itemized deductions or standard deduction (see page 3). .	**2**				
3 Subtract line 2 from line 1	**3**				
4 Exemptions. If changing, fill in Parts I and II on the back .	**4**				
5 Taxable income. Subtract line 4 from line 3	**5**				
6 Tax (see page 4). Method used in col. C _____	**6**				
7 Credits (see page 4)	**7**				
8 Subtract line 7 from line 6. Enter the result but not less than zero .	**8**				
9 Other taxes (see page 4)	**9**				
10 Total tax. Add lines 8 and 9	**10**				
11 Federal income tax withheld and excess social security and tier 1 RRTA tax withheld. If changing, see page 4	**11**				
12 Estimated tax payments, including amount applied from prior year's return	**12**				
13 Earned income credit (EIC)	**13**				
14 Additional child tax credit from Form 8812	**14**				
15 Credits from Form 2439, Form 4136, or Form 8885 . . .	**15**				
16 Amount paid with request for extension of time to file (see page 5)	**16**				
17 Amount of tax paid with original return plus additional tax paid after it was filed	**17**				
18 Total payments. Add lines 11 through 17 in column C	**18**				
Refund or Amount You Owe					
19 Overpayment, if any, as shown on original return or as previously adjusted by the IRS	**19**				
20 Subtract line 19 from line 18 (see page 5)	**20**				
21 **Amount you owe.** If line 10, column C, is more than line 20, enter the difference and see page 5 .	**21**				
22 If line 10, column C, is less than line 20, enter the difference	**22**				
23 Amount of line 22 you want **refunded to you**	**23**				
24 Amount of line 22 you want **applied to your** estimated tax	**24**				

Sign Here
Joint return? See page 2.
Keep a copy for your records.

Under penalties of perjury, I declare that I have filed an original return and that I have examined this amended return, including accompanying schedules and statements, and to the best of my knowledge and belief, this amended return is true, correct, and complete. Declaration of preparer (other than taxpayer) is based on all information of which the preparer has any knowledge.

▶ Your signature _____ Date _____

▶ Spouse's signature. If a joint return, **both** must sign. _____ Date _____

Paid Preparer's Use Only

Preparer's signature ▶	Date	Check if self-employed ☐	Preparer's SSN or PTIN
Firm's name (or yours if self-employed), address, and ZIP code ▶		EIN	
		Phone no. ( )	

Cat. No. 11360L

Form **1040X** (Rev. 11-2004)

Form 1040X (Rev. 11-2004) Page **2**

Part I — Exemptions. See Form 1040 or 1040A instructions.

If you are **not changing your exemptions,** do not complete this part.
If claiming **more exemptions,** complete lines 25–31.
If claiming **fewer exemptions,** complete lines 25–30.

		A. Original **number** of exemptions reported or as previously adjusted	B. Net change	C. Correct **number** of exemptions
25	Yourself and spouse **25**			
	Caution. If someone can claim you as a dependent, you cannot claim an exemption for yourself.			
26	Your dependent children who lived with you **26**			
27	Your dependent children who did not live with you due to divorce or separation **27**			
28	Other dependents. **28**			
29	Total number of exemptions. Add lines 25 through 28 . . . . **29**			
30	Multiply the number of exemptions claimed on line 29 by the amount listed below for the tax year you are amending. Enter the result here and on line 4. **30**			

Tax year	Exemption amount	But see the instructions for line 4 on page 3 if the amount on line 1 is over:
2004	$3,100	$107,025
2003	3,050	104,625
2002	3,000	103,000
2001	2,900	99,725

31 Dependents (children and other) not claimed on original (or adjusted) return:

(a) First name Last name	(b) Dependent's social security number	(c) Dependent's relationship to you	(d) ✔ if qualifying child for child tax credit (see page 5)
			☐
			☐
			☐
			☐
			☐

No. of children on 31 who:
● **lived with** you . . . ▶ ☐
● **did not** live with you due to divorce or separation (see page 5) . . ▶ ☐
Dependents on 31 not entered above ▶ ☐

Part II — Explanation of Changes to Income, Deductions, and Credits

Enter the line number from the front of the form for each item you are changing and give the reason for each change. **Attach only the supporting forms and schedules for the items changed. If you do not attach the required information, your Form 1040X may be returned. Be sure to include your name and social security number on any attachments.**

If the change relates to a net operating loss carryback or a general business credit carryback, attach the schedule or form that shows the year in which the loss or credit occurred. See page 2 of the instructions. Also, check here. . . . . ▶ ☐

_____

_____

_____

_____

_____

_____

Part III — Presidential Election Campaign Fund. Checking below will not increase your tax or reduce your refund.

If you did not previously want $3 to go to the fund but now want to, check here . . . . ▶ ☐
If a joint return and your spouse did not previously want $3 to go to the fund but now wants to, check here . . . . ▶ ☐

Form **1040X** (Rev. 11-2004)

Form **1120X** (Rev. December 2004) Department of the Treasury Internal Revenue Service	**Amended U.S. Corporation Income Tax Return**	OMB No. 1545-0132

For tax year ending
▶ ------------------------------
(Enter month and year.)

Please Type or Print	Name	Employer identification number
	Number, street, and room or suite no. (If a P.O. box, see instructions.)	
	City or town, state, and ZIP code	Telephone number (optional) ( )

Enter name and address used on original return (If same as above, write "Same.")

Internal Revenue Service Center
where original return was filed ▶

Fill in applicable items and use Part II on the back to explain any changes

Part I Income and Deductions (see instructions)		**(a)** As originally reported or as previously adjusted	**(b)** Net change — increase or (decrease) — explain in Part II	**(c)** Correct amount
1	Total income (Form 1120 or 1120-A, line 11) . . .	**1**			
2	Total deductions (total of lines 27 and 29c, Form 1120, or lines 23 and 25c, Form 1120-A)	**2**			
3	Taxable income. Subtract line 2 from line 1	**3**			
4	Tax (Form 1120, line 31, or Form 1120-A, line 27) . .	**4**			

Payments and Credits (see instructions)

5a	Overpayment in prior year allowed as a credit . . .	**5a**	
b	Estimated tax payments	**5b**	
c	Refund applied for on Form 4466	**5c**	
d	Subtract line 5c from the sum of lines 5a and 5b . .	**5d**	
e	Tax deposited with Form 7004	**5e**	
f	Credit from Form 2439	**5f**	
g	Credit for Federal tax on fuels	**5g**	
6	Tax deposited or paid with (or after) the filing of the original return	**6**	
7	Add lines 5d through 6, column (c)	**7**	
8	Overpayment, if any, as shown on original return or as later adjusted	**8**	
9	Subtract line 8 from line 7	**9**	

Tax Due or Overpayment (see instructions)

10	**Tax due.** Subtract line 9 from line 4, column (c). If paying by check, make it payable to the "**United States Treasury**". . . . . ▶	**10**	
11	**Overpayment.** Subtract line 4, column (c), from line 9 . . . . ▶	**11**	
12	Enter the amount of line 11 you want: **Credited to 20__ estimated tax** ▶ Refunded ▶	**12**	

Sign Here

Under penalties of perjury, I declare that I have filed an original return and that I have examined this amended return, including accompanying schedules and statements, and to the best of my knowledge and belief, this amended return is true, correct, and complete. Declaration of preparer (other than taxpayer) is based on all information of which preparer has any knowledge.

▶ _____   _____   ▶ _____
Signature of officer   Date   Title

Paid Preparer's Use Only	Preparer's signature ▶	Date	Check if self-employed ☐	Preparer's SSN or PTIN
	Firm's name (or yours if self-employed), address, and ZIP code ▶		EIN	
			Phone no. ( )	

For Privacy Act and Paperwork Reduction Act Notice, see page 4.   Cat. No. 11530Z   Form **1120X** (Rev. 12-2004)

Form 1120X (Rev. 12-2004)   Page **2**

Part II   **Explanation of Changes to Items in Part I** (Enter the line number from page 1 for the items you are changing, and give the reason for each change. Show any computation in detail. Also, see **What To Attach** on page 3 of the instructions.)

If the change is due to a net operating loss carryback, a capital loss carryback, or a general business credit carryback, see **Carryback Claims** on page 3, and check here .   .   .   . ▶ ☐

Form **1120X** (Rev. 12-2004)

B-9 Application for Extension of Time to File Income Tax Returns

Form 4868
Department of the Treasury
Internal Revenue Service (99)

Application for Automatic Extension of Time To File U.S. Individual Income Tax Return

OMB No. 1545-0188

2004

It's Convenient, Safe, and Secure

IRS *e-file* is the IRS's electronic filing program. You can get an automatic extension of time to file your tax return by filing Form 4868 electronically. You will receive an electronic acknowledgment or confirmation number once you complete the transaction. Keep it with your records. Do not send in Form 4868 if you file electronically.

Complete Form 4868 to use as a worksheet. If you think you may owe tax when you file your return, you will need to estimate your total tax liability and subtract how much you have already paid (lines 4, 5, and 6 below).

If you think you may owe tax and wish to make a payment, you may pay by electronic funds withdrawal using option 1 or 2 below or you may pay by credit card using option 3.

1 ☎ *E-file* by Phone—February 7–April 15
Call toll free **1-888-796-1074**

Anyone who filed a tax return for 2003 can file Form 4868 by phone. The telephone system will accept extensions any time from February 7 through April 15, 2005, and your extension will be good through August 15, 2005. Filing by telephone is advantageous because it is free and you get a confirmation number.

If you wish to make a payment by electronic funds withdrawal, you will be asked for the adjusted gross income (AGI) from your 2003 tax return. The AGI for your 2003 tax return is located on your Form 1040, line 34; Form 1040A, line 21; Form 1040EZ, line 4; Form 1040NR, line 33; Form 1040NR-EZ, line 10; or your TeleFile Tax Record, line I. If you choose, you may also file your extension by phone and mail a payment to the address shown in the middle column on page 4.

2 🖥 *E-file* Using Your Personal Computer or Through a Tax Professional

Refer to your tax software package or tax preparer for ways to file electronically. Be sure to have a copy of your 2003 tax return

— you will be asked to provide information from the return for taxpayer verification. If you wish to make a payment, you can pay by electronic funds withdrawal (see page 4) or send your payment to the address shown in the middle column on page 4.

3  *E-file* and Pay by Credit Card

You can get an extension if you pay part or all of your estimate of income tax due by using a credit card (American Express® Card, Discover® Card, MasterCard® card, or Visa® card). Your payment must be at least $1. You may pay by phone or over the Internet through one of the service providers listed below.

Each service provider will charge a convenience fee based on the amount of the tax payment you are making. Fees may vary between service providers. You will be told what the fee is during the transaction and will have the option to continue or cancel the transaction. You may also obtain the convenience fee by calling the providers' toll-free automated customer service numbers or visiting their websites. Do not add the convenience fee to your tax payment.

Official Payments Corporation
1-800-2PAY-TAX℠
(1-800-272-9829)
1-877-754-4413 (Customer Service)
www.officialpayments.com

Link2Gov Corporation
1-888-PAY-1040℠
(1-888-729-1040)
1-888-658-5465 (Customer Service)
www.PAY1040.com

 File a Paper Form 4868

If you wish to file on paper instead of electronically, fill in the Form 4868 below and mail it to the address shown on page 4.

▼ DETACH HERE ▼

Form 4868
Department of the Treasury
Internal Revenue Service

Application for Automatic Extension of Time To File U.S. Individual Income Tax Return

For calendar year 2004, or other tax year beginning   , 2004, ending   ,   .

OMB No. 1545-0188

2004

Part I Identification	**Part II Individual Income Tax**
1 Your name(s) (see instructions)	**4** Estimate of total tax liability for 2004 . $_____
	5 Total 2004 payments . . . . . . _____
Address (see instructions)	**6** **Balance due.** Subtract 5 from 4 . . _____
	7 Amount you are paying . . . . . ▶ _____
City, town or post office, state, and ZIP code	**Confirmation Number**
	If you file electronically, you will receive a confirmation number telling you that your Form 4868 has been accepted. Enter the confirmation number here and keep it for your records . . . . ▶
2 Your social security number **3** Spouse's social security number	

For Privacy Act and Paperwork Reduction Act Notice, see page 4.   Cat. No. 13141W   Form **4868** (2004)

Form 2688

Department of the Treasury
Internal Revenue Service

Application for Additional Extension of Time To File
U.S. Individual Income Tax Return

▶ See instructions on back.
▶ You must complete all items that apply to you.

OMB No. 1545-0066

2004

Please type or print.	Your first name and initial	Last name	Your social security number
	If a joint return, spouse's first name and initial	Last name	Spouse's social security number

File by the due date for filing your return.

Home address (number and street)

City, town or post office, state, and ZIP code

Please fill in the Return Label at the bottom of this page.

1 I request an extension of time until.. , to file Form 1040EZ, Form 1040A, Form 1040, Form 1040NR-EZ, or Form 1040NR for the calendar year 2004, or other tax year ending ....

2 Explain why you need an extension. You must give an adequate explanation ▶ ....

....

....

....

....

3 Have you filed Form 4868 to request an automatic extension of time to file for this tax year? . . . . ☐ **Yes** ☐ **No**
If you checked "No," we will grant your extension only for undue hardship. Fully explain the hardship in item 2. Attach any information you have that helps explain the hardship.

Signature and Verification

Under penalties of perjury, I declare that I have examined this form, including accompanying schedules and statements, and to the best of my knowledge and belief, it is true, correct, and complete; and, if prepared by someone other than the taxpayer, that I am authorized to prepare this form.

Signature of taxpayer ▶ _____ Date ▶ _____

Signature of spouse ▶ _____ Date ▶ _____
                     (If filing jointly, **both** must sign even if only one had income.)

Signature of preparer
other than taxpayer ▶ _____ Date ▶ _____

Please fill in the **Return Label** below with your name, address, and social security number. The IRS will complete the **Notice to Applicant** and return it to you. If you want it sent to another address or to an agent acting for you, enter the other address and add the agent's name.

(Do not detach)

Notice to Applicant

To Be Completed by the IRS

☐ We **have** approved your application.
☐ We **have not** approved your application.
However, we have granted a 10-day grace period to .... This grace period is considered a valid extension of time for elections otherwise required to be made on a timely return.

☐ We **have not** approved your application. After considering the information you provided in item 2 above, we cannot grant your request for an extension of time to file. We are not granting a 10-day grace period.

☐ We cannot consider your application because it was filed after the due date of your return.

☐ Other...

_____ _____
Director   Date

Return Label (Please type or print)

Taxpayer's name (and agent's name, if applicable). If a joint return, also give spouse's name.

Taxpayer's social security number

Number and street (include suite, room, or apt. no.) or P.O. box number

Spouse's social security number

City, town or post office, state, and ZIP code

Agents:
Always include taxpayer's name on Return Label.

For Privacy Act and Paperwork Reduction Act Notice, see back of form.

Cat. No. 11958F

Form **2688** (2004)

| Form **7004** (Rev. September 2003) Department of the Treasury Internal Revenue Service | **Application for Automatic Extension of Time To File Corporation Income Tax Return** | OMB No. 1545-0233 |

| Name of corporation | Employer identification number |

Number, street, and room or suite no. (If a P.O. box or outside the United States, see instructions.)

City or town, state, and ZIP code

Check type of return to be filed:

☐ Form 990-C	☐ Form 1120-FSC	☐ Form 1120-PC	☐ Form 1120S
☐ Form 1120	☐ Form 1120-H	☐ Form 1120-POL	☐ Form 1120-SF
☐ Form 1120-A	☐ Form 1120-L	☐ Form 1120-REIT	
☐ Form 1120-F	☐ Form 1120-ND	☐ Form 1120-RIC	

● Form 1120-F filers: Check here if the foreign corporation does not maintain an office or place of business in the United States . . . . ▶ ☐

1   Request for Automatic Extension (see instructions)

a   Extension date. I request an automatic 6-month (or, for certain corporations, 3-month) extension of time until ...., 20......., to file the income tax return of the corporation named above for ▶ ☐ calendar year 20 .... or ▶ ☐ tax year beginning ...., 20........., and ending ...., 20......

b   Short tax year. If this tax year is for less than 12 months, check reason:
☐ Initial return   ☐ Final return   ☐ Change in accounting period   ☐ Consolidated return to be filed

2   Members of an affiliated group of corporations filing a consolidated return (consolidated group) (see instructions).

Name and address of each member of the affiliated group	Employer identification number

3 Tentative tax (see instructions).	**3**	
4 **Payments and refundable credits:** (see instructions)		
a Overpayment credited from prior year.	**4a**	
b Estimated tax payments for the tax year	**4b**	
c Less refund for the tax year applied for on Form 4466	**4c** ( ) **Bal ▶** **4d**	
e Credit for tax paid on undistributed capital gains (Form 2439) . .	**4e**	
f Credit for Federal tax on fuels (Form 4136)	**4f**	
5 Total. Add lines 4d through 4f (see instructions)	**5**	
6 **Balance due.** Subtract line 5 from line 3. **Deposit this amount using the Electronic Federal Tax Payment System (EFTPS) or with a Federal Tax Deposit (FTD) Coupon** (see instructions)	**6**	

Signature. Under penalties of perjury, I declare that I have been authorized by the above-named corporation to make this application, and to the best of my knowledge and belief, the statements made are true, correct, and complete.

_____   _____   _____
(Signature of officer or agent)   (Title)   (Date)

For Paperwork Reduction Act Notice, see instructions.   Cat. No. 13804A   Form **7004** (Rev. 9-2003)

B-10   Underpayment of Estimated Tax

Form **2210**

Department of the Treasury
Internal Revenue Service

Underpayment of
Estimated Tax by Individuals, Estates, and Trusts
▶ See separate instructions.
▶ **Attach to Form 1040, 1040A, 1040NR, 1040NR-EZ, or 1041.**

OMB No. 1545-0140

2004

Attachment
Sequence No. **06**

Name(s) shown on tax return

Identifying number

Do You Have To File Form 2210?

Complete lines 1 through 7 below. Is line 7 less than $1,000? → **Yes** → **Do not file Form 2210.** You do not owe a penalty.

↓ **No**

Complete lines 8 and 9 below. Is line 6 equal to or more than line 9? → **Yes** → You do not owe a penalty. **Do not file Form 2210** (but if box **E** below applies, you must file page 1 of Form 2210 below).

↓ **No**

You may owe a penalty. Does any box in Part II below apply? → **Yes** → You **must** file Form 2210. Does box **B, C,** or **D** apply?

No   **Yes**

→ You must figure your penalty.

↓ **No**

Do not file Form 2210. You are not required to figure your penalty because the IRS will figure it and send you a bill for any unpaid amount. If you want to figure it, you may use Part III or Part IV as a worksheet and enter your penalty amount on your tax return (see page 2 of the instructions), but **do not file Form 2210.**

You are **not** required to figure your penalty because the IRS will figure it and send you a bill for any unpaid amount. If you want to figure it, you may use Part III or Part IV as a worksheet and enter your penalty amount on your tax return (see page 2 of the instructions), but **file only page 1 of Form 2210.**

Part I	**Required Annual Payment**	(see page 2 of the instructions)

1   Enter your 2004 tax after credits from Form 1040, line 56 (or comparable line of your return) · · | **1** |
2   Other taxes, including self-employment tax (see page 2 of the instructions) . . . . | **2** |
3   Refundable credits. Enter the total of your earned income credit, additional child tax credit, credit for federal tax paid on fuels, and health coverage tax credit for eligible individuals . . . . | **3** ( )
4   Current year tax. Combine lines 1, 2, and 3 . . . . | **4** |
5   Multiply line 4 by 90% (.90) . . . . **5** | | **6** |
6   Withholding taxes. **Do not** include estimated tax payments. See page 2 of the instructions . . | **6** |
7   Subtract line 6 from line 4. If less than $1,000, you do not owe a penalty; **do not file Form 2210** | **7** |
8   Maximum required annual payment based on prior year's tax (see page 2 of the instructions) | **8** |
9   **Required annual payment.** Enter the **smaller** of line 5 or line 8 . . . . | **9** |

Next: Is line 9 more than line 6?

☐ **No. You do not** owe a penalty. **Do not file Form 2210** unless box **E** below applies.

☐ **Yes.** You may owe a penalty, but **do not file Form 2210** unless one or more boxes in Part II below applies.
- If box **B, C,** or **D** applies, you must figure your penalty and file Form 2210.
- If only box **A** or **E** (or both) applies, file only page 1 of Form 2210. You are **not** required to figure your penalty; the IRS will figure it and send you a bill for any unpaid amount. If you want to figure your penalty, you may use Part III or IV as a worksheet and enter your penalty on your tax return (see page 2 of the instructions), but **file only page 1 of Form 2210.**

Part II	**Reasons for Filing.** Check applicable boxes. If none apply, **do not file Form 2210.**

A ☐ You request a **waiver** (see page 1 of the instructions) of your entire penalty. You must check this box and file page 1 of Form 2210, but you are not required to figure your penalty.

B ☐ You request a waiver (see page 1 of the instructions) of part of your penalty. You must figure your penalty and waiver amount and file Form 2210.

C ☐ Your income varied during the year and your penalty is reduced or eliminated when figured using the **annualized income installment method.** You must figure the penalty using Schedule AI and file Form 2210.

D ☐ Your penalty is lower when figured by treating the federal income tax withheld from your wages as paid on the dates it was actually withheld, instead of in equal amounts on the payment due dates. You must figure your penalty and file Form 2210.

E ☐ You filed or are filing a joint return for either 2003 or 2004, but not for both years, and line 8 above is smaller than line 5 above. You must file page 1 of Form 2210, but you are **not** required to figure your penalty (unless box **B, C,** or **D** applies).

For Paperwork Reduction Act Notice, see page 6 of separate instructions.   Cat. No. 11744P   Form **2210** (2004)

Form 2210 (2004)   Page **2**

Part III	**Short Method**

You may use the short method if:

- You made no estimated tax payments (or your only payments were withheld federal income tax) **or**
- You paid estimated tax in **equal** amounts on your due dates.

You must use the regular method (Part IV) instead of the short method if:

- You made any estimated tax payments late,
- You checked box **C** or **D** in Part II, **or**
- You are filing Form 1040NR or 1040NR-EZ and you did not receive wages as an employee subject to U.S. income tax withholding.

Note: *If any payment was made earlier than the due date, you may use the short method, but using it may cause you to pay a larger penalty than the regular method. If the payment was only a few days early, the difference is likely to be small.*

10	Enter the amount from line 9, Form 2210	**10**	
11	Enter the amount, if any, from line 6, Form 2210 . . . . **11**		
12	Enter the total amount, if any, of estimated tax payments you made **12**		
13	Add lines 11 and 12	**13**	
14	**Total underpayment for year.** Subtract line 13 from line 10. If zero or less, stop here; you do not owe the penalty. **Do not file Form 2210 unless you checked box E on page 1**	**14**	
15	Multiply line 14 by .03184	**15**	
16	• If the amount on line 14 was paid **on or after** 4/15/05, enter -0-. • If the amount on line 14 was paid **before** 4/15/05, make the following computation to find the amount to enter on line 16. Amount on line 14 ✕ Number of days paid before 4/15/05 ✕ .00014	**16**	
17	**Penalty.** Subtract line 16 from line 15. Enter the result here and on Form 1040, line 75; Form 1040A, line 48; Form 1040NR, line 73; Form 1040NR-EZ, line 26; or Form 1041, line 26, **but do not file Form 2210 unless you checked a box in Part II on page 1** . . . . ▶	**17**	

Form **2210** (2004)

Form 2210 (2004)   Page **3**

Part IV	**Regular Method** (See page 2 of the instructions if you are filing Form 1040NR or 1040NR-EZ.)					

Section A—Figure Your Underpayment

			Payment Due Dates			
			(a) 4/15/04	**(b)** 6/15/04	**(c)** 9/15/04	**(d)** 1/15/05
18	**Required installments.** If box C in Part II applies, enter the amounts from Schedule AI, line 25. Otherwise, enter 25% (.25) of line 9, Form 2210, in each column .	**18**				
19	Estimated tax paid and tax withheld (see page 2 of the instructions). For column (a) only, also enter the amount from line 19 on line 23. If line 19 is equal to or more than line 18 for all payment periods, stop here; you do not owe a penalty. **Do not file Form 2210 unless you checked a box in Part II** .	**19**				
	Complete lines 20 through 26 of one column before going to the next column.					
20	Enter the amount, if any, from line 26 in previous column	**20**				
21	Add lines 19 and 20	**21**				
22	Add the amounts on lines 24 and 25 in previous column	**22**				
23	Subtract line 22 from line 21. If zero or less, enter -0-. For column (a) only, enter the amount from line 19	**23**				
24	If line 23 is zero, subtract line 21 from line 22. Otherwise, enter -0-	**24**				
25	**Underpayment.** If line 18 is equal to or more than line 23, subtract line 23 from line 18. Then go to line 20 of the next column. Otherwise, go to line 26. ▶	**25**				
26	**Overpayment.** If line 23 is more than line 18, subtract line 18 from line 23. Then go to line 20 of the next column .	**26**				

Section B—Figure the Penalty (Complete lines 27 through 34 of one column before going to the next column.)

Rate Period 1			4/15/04	6/15/04		
		April 16, 2004—June 30, 2004	*Days:*	*Days:*		
	27	Number of days **from** the date shown above line 27 **to** the date the amount on line 25 was paid **or** 6/30/04, whichever is earlier	**27**			
	28	Underpayment on line 25 (see page 4 of the instructions) $\times \dfrac{\text{Number of days on line 27}}{366} \times .05$ ▶	**28**	$	$		

Rate Period 2			6/30/04	6/30/04	9/15/04	
		July 1, 2004—September 30, 2004	*Days:*	*Days:*	*Days:*	
	29	Number of days **from** the date shown above line 29 **to** the date the amount on line 25 was paid **or** 9/30/04, whichever is earlier	**29**			
	30	Underpayment on line 25 (see page 4 of the instructions) $\times \dfrac{\text{Number of days on line 29}}{366} \times .04$ ▶	**30**	$	$	$

Rate Period 3			9/30/04	9/30/04	9/30/04	
		October 1, 2004—December 31, 2004	*Days:*	*Days:*	*Days:*	
	31	Number of days **from** the date shown above line 31 **to** the date the amount on line 25 was paid **or** 12/31/04, whichever is earlier . . .	**31**			
	32	Underpayment on line 25 (see page 4 of the instructions) $\times \dfrac{\text{Number of days on line 31}}{366} \times .05$ ▶	**32**	$	$	$

Rate Period 4			12/31/04	12/31/04	12/31/04	1/15/05
		January 1, 2005—April 15, 2005	*Days:*	*Days:*	*Days:*	*Days:*
	33	Number of days **from** the date shown above line 33 **to** the date the amount on line 25 was paid **or** 4/15/05, whichever is earlier	**33**			
	34	Underpayment on line 25 (see page 5 of the instructions) $\times \dfrac{\text{Number of days on line 33}}{365} \times .05$ ▶	**34**	$	$	$	$

35	**Penalty.** Add all amounts on lines 28, 30, 32, and 34 in all columns. Enter the total here and on Form 1040, line 75; Form 1040A, line 48; Form 1040NR, line 73; Form 1040NR-EZ, line 26; or Form 1041, line 26, **but do not file Form 2210 unless you checked a box in Part II** . . . . ▶	**35**	$

Form **2210** (2004)

Form 2220

Underpayment of Estimated Tax by Corporations

Department of the Treasury
Internal Revenue Service

▶ See separate instructions.

▶ Attach to the corporation's tax return.

OMB No. 1545-0142

2004

Name	Employer identification number

Note: *In most cases, the corporation is not required to file Form 2220 (see Part I below for exceptions) because the IRS will figure any penalty owed and bill the corporation. Even if Form 2220 is not required, the corporation may still use it to figure the penalty. In such a case, enter the amount from page 2, line 38 on the estimated tax penalty line of the corporation's income tax return, but **do not** attach Form 2220.*

Part I   Reasons for Filing—Check the boxes below that apply. If any boxes are checked, and line 6, below, is $500 or more, the corporation **must** file Form 2220 even if it does not owe a penalty.

1 ☐ The corporation is using the adjusted seasonal installment method.
2 ☐ The corporation is using the annualized income installment method.
3 ☐ The corporation is a "large corporation" figuring its first required installment based on the prior year's tax.

Part II   Figuring the Underpayment

4	Total tax (see instructions)	4
5a	Personal holding company tax (Schedule PH (Form 1120), line 26) included on line 4	5a
b	Look-back interest included on line 4 under section 460(b)(2) for completed long-term contracts or section 167(g) for depreciation under the income forecast method . .	5b
c	Credit for Federal tax paid on fuels (see instructions)	5c
d	**Total.** Add lines 5a through 5c	5d
6	Subtract line 5d from line 4. If the result is less than $500, **do not** complete or file this form. The corporation does not owe the penalty	6
7	Enter the tax shown on the corporation's 2003 income tax return (see instructions). **Caution:** *If the tax is zero or the tax year was for less than 12 months, skip this line and enter the amount from line 6 on line 8* .	7
8	Enter the **smaller** of line 6 or line 7. If the corporation is required to skip line 7, enter the amount from line 6	8

		(a)	(b)	(c)	(d)	(e)
9	**Installment due dates.** Enter in columns (a) through (d) the 15th day of the 4th (**Form 990-PF filers:** Use 5th month), 6th, 9th, and 12th months of the corporation's tax year . . .	9					
	Exception. If one of your installment due dates is September 15, 2004, see the instructions.						
10	**Required installments.** If the box on line 1 and/or line 2 above is checked, enter the amounts from Schedule A, line 38. If the box on line 3 (but not 1 or 2) is checked, see instructions for the amounts to enter. If none of these boxes are checked, enter 25% of line 8 above in each column	10					
11	Estimated tax paid or credited for each period (see instructions). For column (a) only, enter the amount from line 11 on line 15	11					
	Complete lines 12 through 18 of one column before going to the next column.						
12	Enter amount, if any, from line 18 of the preceding column .	12					
13	Add lines 11 and 12	13					
14	Add amounts on lines 16 and 17 of the preceding column .	14					
15	Subtract line 14 from line 13. If zero or less, enter -0- . . .	15					
16	If the amount on line 15 is zero, subtract line 13 from line 14. Otherwise, enter -0-	16					
17	**Underpayment.** If line 15 is less than or equal to line 10, subtract line 15 from line 10. Then go to line 12 of the next column. Otherwise, go to line 18	17					
18	**Overpayment.** If line 10 is less than line 15, subtract line 10 from line 15. Then go to line 12 of the next column	18					

Go to Part III on page 2 to figure the penalty. Do not go to Part III if there are no entries on line 17—no penalty is owed.

For Paperwork Reduction Act Notice, see separate instructions.   Cat. No. 11746L   Form **2220** (2004)

Form 2220 (2004)

Page **2**

Part III Figuring the Penalty

		(a)	(b)	(c)	(d)	(e)
19	Enter the date of payment or the 15th day of the 3rd month after the close of the tax year, whichever is earlier (see instructions). *(Form 990-PF and Form 990-T filers: Use 5th month instead of 3rd month.)* **19**					
20	Number of days from due date of installment on line 9 to the date shown on line 19. **20**					
21	Number of days on line 20 after 4/15/2004 and before 7/1/2004 **21**					
22	Underpayment on line 17 $\times \dfrac{\text{Number of days on line 21}}{366} \times 5\%$. **22**	$	$	$	$	$
23	Number of days on line 20 after 6/30/2004 and before 10/1/2004 **23**					
24	Underpayment on line 17 $\times \dfrac{\text{Number of days on line 23}}{366} \times 4\%$. **24**	$	$	$	$	$
25	Number of days on line 20 after 9/30/2004 and before 1/1/2005 **25**					
26	Underpayment on line 17 $\times \dfrac{\text{Number of days on line 25}}{366} \times 5\%$. **26**	$	$	$	$	$
27	Number of days on line 20 after 12/31/2004 and before 4/1/2005 **27**					
28	Underpayment on line 17 $\times \dfrac{\text{Number of days on line 27}}{365} \times 5\%$. **28**	$	$	$	$	$
29	Number of days on line 20 after 3/31/2005 and before 7/1/2005. **29**					
30	Underpayment on line 17 $\times \dfrac{\text{Number of days on line 29}}{365} \times {}^*\%$. **30**	$	$	$	$	$
31	Number of days on line 20 after 6/30/2005 and before 10/1/2005. **31**					
32	Underpayment on line 17 $\times \dfrac{\text{Number of days on line 31}}{365} \times {}^*\%$. **32**	$	$	$	$	$
33	Number of days on line 20 after 9/30/2005 and before 1/1/2006. **33**					
34	Underpayment on line 17 $\times \dfrac{\text{Number of days on line 33}}{365} \times {}^*\%$. **34**	$	$	$	$	$
35	Number of days on line 20 after 12/31/2005 and before 2/16/2006 **35**					
36	Underpayment on line 17 $\times \dfrac{\text{Number of days on line 35}}{365} \times {}^*\%$. **36**	$	$	$	$	$
37	Add lines 22, 24, 26, 28, 30, 32, 34, and 36 **37**	$	$	$	$	$

38 **Penalty.** Add columns (a) through (e) of line 37. Enter the total here and on Form 1120, line 33; Form 1120-A, line 29; or the comparable line for other income tax returns . . . . **38** $

*For underpayments paid after March 31, 2005: For lines 30, 32, 34, and 36, use the penalty interest rate for each calendar quarter, which the IRS will determine during the first month in the preceding quarter. These rates are published quarterly in an IRS News Release and in a revenue ruling in the Internal Revenue Bulletin. To obtain this information on the Internet, access the IRS website at **www.irs.gov.** You can also call 1-800-829-1040 to get interest rate information.

Form **2220** (2004)

B-11   Forms for Computation of Minimum Tax

Form **4626**	**Alternative Minimum Tax—Corporations**	OMB No. 1545-0175
Department of the Treasury Internal Revenue Service	▶ See separate instructions. ▶ Attach to the corporation's tax return.	20**04**

Name		Employer identification number

Note: *See page 1 of the instructions to find out if the corporation is a small corporation exempt from the alternative minimum tax (AMT) under section 55(e).*

1	Taxable income or (loss) before net operating loss deduction	**1**	
2	**Adjustments and preferences:**		
a	Depreciation of post-1986 property	**2a**	
b	Amortization of certified pollution control facilities	**2b**	
c	Amortization of mining exploration and development costs	**2c**	
d	Amortization of circulation expenditures (personal holding companies only)	**2d**	
e	Adjusted gain or loss	**2e**	
f	Long-term contracts	**2f**	
g	Merchant marine capital construction funds	**2g**	
h	Section 833(b) deduction (Blue Cross, Blue Shield, and similar type organizations only) . .	**2h**	
i	Tax shelter farm activities (personal service corporations only).	**2i**	
j	Passive activities (closely held corporations and personal service corporations only) . .	**2j**	
k	Loss limitations	**2k**	
l	Depletion	**2l**	
m	Tax-exempt interest income from specified private activity bonds.	**2m**	
n	Intangible drilling costs	**2n**	
o	Other adjustments and preferences	**2o**	
3	Pre-adjustment alternative minimum taxable income (AMTI). Combine lines 1 through 2o . . .	**3**	
4	**Adjusted current earnings (ACE) adjustment:**		
a	ACE from line 10 of the worksheet on page 11 of the instructions	**4a**	
b	Subtract line 3 from line 4a. If line 3 exceeds line 4a, enter the difference as a negative amount. See examples on page 6 of the instructions	**4b**	
c	Multiply line 4b by 75% (.75). Enter the result as a positive amount	**4c**	
d	Enter the excess, if any, of the corporation's total increases in AMTI from prior year ACE adjustments over its total reductions in AMTI from prior year ACE adjustments (see page 6 of the instructions). **Note:** *You **must** enter an amount on line 4d (even if line 4b is positive)*	**4d**	
e	ACE adjustment. • If line 4b is zero or more, enter the amount from line 4c • If line 4b is less than zero, enter the **smaller** of line 4c or line 4d as a negative amount } . . .	**4e**	
5	Combine lines 3 and 4e. If zero or less, stop here; the corporation does not owe any AMT . . .	**5**	
6	Alternative tax net operating loss deduction (see page 7 of the instructions)	**6**	
7	**Alternative minimum taxable income.** Subtract line 6 from line 5. If the corporation held a residual interest in a REMIC, see page 7 of the instructions	**7**	
8	**Exemption phase-out** (if line 7 is $310,000 or more, skip lines 8a and 8b and enter -0- on line 8c):		
a	Subtract $150,000 from line 7 (if completing this line for a member of a controlled group, see page 7 of the instructions). If zero or less, enter -0- **8a**		
b	Multiply line 8a by 25% (.25) **8b**		
c	Exemption. Subtract line 8b from $40,000 (if completing this line for a member of a controlled group, see page 7 of the instructions). If zero or less, enter -0-.	**8c**	
9	Subtract line 8c from line 7. If zero or less, enter -0-	**9**	
10	Multiply line 9 by 20% (.20)	**10**	
11	Alternative minimum tax foreign tax credit (AMTFTC) (see page 7 of the instructions)	**11**	
12	Tentative minimum tax. Subtract line 11 from line 10	**12**	
13	Regular tax liability before all credits except the foreign tax credit and possessions tax credit . .	**13**	
14	**Alternative minimum tax.** Subtract line 13 from line 12. If zero or less, enter -0-. Enter here and on Form 1120, Schedule J, line 4, or the appropriate line of the corporation's income tax return . . .	**14**	

For Paperwork Reduction Act Notice, see page 10 of the instructions.   Cat. No. 12955I   Form **4626** (2004)

Form 6251

Department of the Treasury
Internal Revenue Service (99)

Alternative Minimum Tax—Individuals

▶ See separate instructions.

▶ Attach to Form 1040 or Form 1040NR.

OMB No. 1545-0227

2004

Attachment Sequence No. **32**

Name(s) shown on Form 1040

Your social security number

Part I   Alternative Minimum Taxable Income (See instructions for how to complete each line.)

1	If filing Schedule A (Form 1040), enter the amount from Form 1040, line 40, and go to line 2. Otherwise, enter the amount from Form 1040, line 37, and go to line 7. (If less than zero, enter as a negative amount.)	**1**
2	Medical and dental. Enter the **smaller** of Schedule A (Form 1040), line 4, **or** 2½% of Form 1040, line 37 .	**2**
3	Taxes from Schedule A (Form 1040), line 9	**3**
4	Enter the home mortgage interest adjustment, if any, from line 6 of the worksheet on page 2 of the instructions	**4**
5	Miscellaneous deductions from Schedule A (Form 1040), line 26	**5**
6	If Form 1040, line 37, is over $142,700 (over $71,350 if married filing separately), enter the amount from line 9 of the **Itemized Deductions Worksheet** on page B-1 of the Instructions for Schedules A & B (Form 1040)	**6** ( )
7	Tax refund from Form 1040, line 10 or line 21	**7** ( )
8	Investment interest expense (difference between regular tax and AMT)	**8**
9	Depletion (difference between regular tax and AMT)	**9**
10	Net operating loss deduction from Form 1040, line 21. Enter as a positive amount . . .	**10**
11	Interest from specified private activity bonds exempt from the regular tax	**11**
12	Qualified small business stock (7% of gain excluded under section 1202)	**12**
13	Exercise of incentive stock options (excess of AMT income over regular tax income)	**13**
14	Estates and trusts (amount from Schedule K-1 (Form 1041), line 9)	**14**
15	Electing large partnerships (amount from Schedule K-1 (Form 1065-B), box 6) . . .	**15**
16	Disposition of property (difference between AMT and regular tax gain or loss)	**16**
17	Depreciation on assets placed in service after 1986 (difference between regular tax and AMT) . . .	**17**
18	Passive activities (difference between AMT and regular tax income or loss)	**18**
19	Loss limitations (difference between AMT and regular tax income or loss)	**19**
20	Circulation costs (difference between regular tax and AMT)	**20**
21	Long-term contracts (difference between AMT and regular tax income)	**21**
22	Mining costs (difference between regular tax and AMT)	**22**
23	Research and experimental costs (difference between regular tax and AMT) . . .	**23**
24	Income from certain installment sales before January 1, 1987	**24** ( )
25	Intangible drilling costs preference	**25**
26	Other adjustments, including income-based related adjustments	**26**
27	Alternative tax net operating loss deduction	**27** ( )
28	**Alternative minimum taxable income.** Combine lines 1 through 27. (If married filing separately and line 28 is more than $191,000, see page 6 of the instructions.)	**28**

Part II   Alternative Minimum Tax

29	Exemption. (If this form is for a child under age 14, see page 6 of the instructions.)	

IF your filing status is . . .	AND line 28 is not over . . .	THEN enter on line 29 . . .	
Single or head of household	$112,500	$40,250	
Married filing jointly or qualifying widow(er) . .	150,000	58,000	**29**
Married filing separately	75,000	29,000	

If line 28 is **over** the amount shown above for your filing status, see page 6 of the instructions.

30	Subtract line 29 from line 28. If zero or less, enter -0- here and on lines 33 and 35 and stop here . .	**30**
31	● If you reported capital gain distributions directly on Form 1040, line 13; **or** you reported qualified dividends on Form 1040, line 9b; **or** you had a gain on both lines 15 and 16 of Schedule D (Form 1040) (as refigured for the AMT, if necessary), complete Part III on the back and enter the amount from line 55 here. ● **All others:** If line 30 is $175,000 or less ($87,500 or less if married filing separately), multiply line 30 by 26% (.26). Otherwise, multiply line 30 by 28% (.28) and subtract $3,500 ($1,750 if married filing separately) from the result.	**31**
32	Alternative minimum tax foreign tax credit (see page 7 of the instructions)	**32**
33	Tentative minimum tax. Subtract line 32 from line 31	**33**
34	Tax from Form 1040, line 43 (minus any tax from Form 4972 and any foreign tax credit from Form 1040, line 46). If you used Schedule J to figure your tax, the amounts for lines 43 and 46 of Form 1040 must be refigured without using Schedule J (see page 8 of the instructions)	**34**
35	**Alternative minimum tax.** Subtract line 34 from line 33. If zero or less, enter -0-. Enter here and on Form 1040, line 44	**35**

For Paperwork Reduction Act Notice, see page 8 of the instructions.   Cat. No. 13600G   Form **6251** (2004)

B-12   Other Tax Forms

Form **1116**	**Foreign Tax Credit**	OMB No. 1545-0121
	(Individual, Estate, or Trust)	**20 04**
Department of the Treasury Internal Revenue Service (99)	▶ Attach to Form 1040, 1040NR, 1041, or 990-T. ▶ See separate instructions.	Attachment Sequence No. **19**

Name	Identifying number as shown on page 1 of your tax return

Use a separate Form 1116 for each category of income listed below. See **Categories of Income** on page 3 of the instructions. Check only one box on each Form 1116. Report all amounts in U.S. dollars except where specified in Part II below.

a ☐ Passive income
b ☐ High withholding tax interest
c ☐ Financial services income
d ☐ Shipping income
e ☐ Dividends from a DISC or former DISC
f ☐ Certain distributions from a foreign sales corporation (FSC) or former FSC
g ☐ Lump-sum distributions
h ☐ Section 901(j) income
i ☐ Certain income re-sourced by treaty
j ☐ General limitation income

k Resident of (name of country) ▶

Note: *If you paid taxes to only one foreign country or U.S. possession, use column A in Part I and line A in Part II. If you paid taxes to* **more than one** *foreign country or U.S. possession, use a separate column and line for each country or possession.*

Part I   Taxable Income or Loss From Sources Outside the United States (for Category Checked Above)

		Foreign Country or U.S. Possession			Total
		A	**B**	**C**	(Add cols. A, B, and C.)
l	Enter the name of the foreign country or U.S. possession ▶				
1	Gross income from sources within country shown above and of the type checked above (see page 13 of the instructions):				**1**
	Deductions and losses (*Caution: See pages 13 and 14 of the instructions*):				
2	Expenses **definitely related** to the income on line 1 (attach statement)				
3	Pro rata share of other deductions **not definitely related:**				
a	Certain itemized deductions or standard deduction (see instructions)				
b	Other deductions (attach statement)				
c	Add lines 3a and 3b				
d	Gross foreign source income (see instructions) .				
e	Gross income from all sources (see instructions)				
f	Divide line 3d by line 3e (see instructions) . .				
g	Multiply line 3c by line 3f				
4	Pro rata share of interest expense (see instructions):				
a	Home mortgage interest (use worksheet on page 13 of the instructions)				
b	Other interest expense				
5	Losses from foreign sources				
6	Add lines 2, 3g, 4a, 4b, and 5				**6**
7	Subtract line 6 from line 1. Enter the result here and on line 14, page 2 . . . . ▶			**7**	

Part II   Foreign Taxes Paid or Accrued (see page 14 of the instructions)

Country	Credit is claimed for taxes (you must check one)		Foreign taxes paid or accrued							
			In foreign currency				In U.S. dollars			
	(m) ☐ Paid **(n)** ☐ Accrued		Taxes withheld at source on:			**(s)** Other foreign taxes paid or accrued	Taxes withheld at source on:			**(w)** Other foreign taxes paid or accrued
	(o) Date paid or accrued	**(p)** Dividends	**(q)** Rents and royalties	**(r)** Interest		**(t)** Dividends	**(u)** Rents and royalties	**(v)** Interest		**(x)** Total foreign taxes paid or accrued (add cols. (t) through (w))
A										
B										
C										

8	Add lines A through C, column (x). Enter the total here and on line 9, page 2 . . . . ▶	**8**	

For Paperwork Reduction Act Notice, see page 18 of the instructions.   Cat. No. 11440U   Form **1116** (2004)

Form 1116 (2004)   Page **2**

Part III   Figuring the Credit

9 Enter the amount from line 8. These are your total foreign taxes paid or accrued for the category of income checked above Part I . . | **9** |

10 Carryback or carryover (attach detailed computation). . . . . | **10** |

11 Add lines 9 and 10. . . . . | **11** |

12 Reduction in foreign taxes (see page 15 of the instructions). . . | **12** |

13 Subtract line 12 from line 11. This is the total amount of foreign taxes available for credit . . . | **13** |

14 Enter the amount from line 7. This is your taxable income or (loss) from sources outside the United States (before adjustments) for the category of income checked above Part I (see page 15 of the instructions) . | **14** |

15 Adjustments to line 14 (see page 16 of the instructions) . . . | **15** |

16 Combine the amounts on lines 14 and 15. This is your net foreign source taxable income. (If the result is zero or less, you have no foreign tax credit for the category of income you checked above Part I. Skip lines 17 through 21. However, if you are filing more than one Form 1116, you must complete line 19.) . . . . | **16** |

17 **Individuals:** Enter the amount from Form 1040, line 40. If you are a nonresident alien, enter the amount from Form 1040NR, line 37. **Estates and trusts:** Enter your taxable income without the deduction for your exemption. . . . . | **17** |

Caution: *If you figured your tax using the lower rates on qualified dividends or capital gains, see page 17 of the instructions.*

18 Divide line 16 by line 17. If line 16 is more than line 17, enter "1" . . . . | **18** |

19 **Individuals:** Enter the amount from Form 1040, line 43. If you are a nonresident alien, enter the amount from Form 1040NR, line 40.

Estates and trusts: Enter the amount from Form 1041, Schedule G, line 1a, or the total of Form 990-T, lines 36 and 37 . | **19** |

Caution: *If you are completing line 19 for separate category **g** (lump-sum distributions), see page 18 of the instructions.*

20 Multiply line 19 by line 18 (maximum amount of credit) . . . | **20** |

21 Enter the **smaller** of line 13 or line 20. If this is the only Form 1116 you are filing, skip lines 22 through 30 and enter this amount on line 31. Otherwise, complete the appropriate line in Part IV (see page 18 of the instructions) . . . . ▶ | **21** |

Part IV   Summary of Credits From Separate Parts III (see page 18 of the instructions)

22 Credit for taxes on passive income . . . . | **22** |

23 Credit for taxes on high withholding tax interest . . . . . | **23** |

24 Credit for taxes on financial services income . . . . . . | **24** |

25 Credit for taxes on shipping income . . . . | **25** |

26 Credit for taxes on dividends from a DISC or former DISC and certain distributions from a FSC or former FSC . . . . | **26** |

27 Credit for taxes on lump-sum distributions . . . . | **27** |

28 Credit for taxes on certain income re-sourced by treaty . . . . | **28** |

29 Credit for taxes on general limitation income . . . . | **29** |

30 Add lines 22 through 29 . . . . | **30** |

31 Enter the **smaller** of line 19 or line 30 . . . . | **31** |

32 Reduction of credit for international boycott operations. See instructions for line 12 on page 15 . | **32** |

33 Subtract line 32 from line 31. This is your **foreign tax credit.** Enter here and on Form 1040, line 46; Form 1040NR, line 43; Form 1041, Schedule G, line 2a; or Form 990-T, line 40a . . . . . ▶ | **33** |

Form **1116** (2004)

Form **2441**

Department of the Treasury
Internal Revenue Service (99)

Child and Dependent Care Expenses

▶ Attach to Form 1040.

▶ See separate instructions.

OMB No. 1545-0068

2004

Attachment
Sequence No. **21**

Name(s) shown on Form 1040

Your social security number

Before you begin: You need to understand the following terms. See **Definitions** on page 1 of the instructions.

● **Dependent Care Benefits** ● **Qualifying Person(s)** ● **Qualified Expenses**

Part I **Persons or Organizations Who Provided the Care**—You **must** complete this part.
(If you need more space, use the bottom of page 2.)

1	**(a)** Care provider's name	**(b)** Address (number, street, apt. no., city, state, and ZIP code)	**(c)** Identifying number (SSN or EIN)	**(d)** Amount paid (see instructions)

Did you receive **dependent care benefits?**	No ──▶ Complete only Part II below.
	Yes ──▶ Complete Part III on the back next.

Caution. If the care was provided in your home, you may owe employment taxes. See the instructions for Form 1040, line 61.

Part II **Credit for Child and Dependent Care Expenses**

2 Information about your **qualifying person(s).** If you have more than two qualifying persons, see the instructions.

(a) Qualifying person's name		**(b)** Qualifying person's social security number	**(c) Qualified expenses** you incurred and paid in 2004 for the person listed in column (a)
First	Last		

3	Add the amounts in column (c) of line 2. **Do not** enter more than $3,000 for one qualifying person or $6,000 for two or more persons. If you completed Part III, enter the amount from line 32	**3**	
4	Enter your **earned income.** See instructions	**4**	
5	If married filing jointly, enter your spouse's earned income (if your spouse was a student or was disabled, see the instructions); **all others,** enter the amount from line 4 . . .	**5**	
6	Enter the **smallest** of line 3, 4, or 5	**6**	
7	Enter the amount from Form 1040, line 37 . . . . . **7**		
8	Enter on line 8 the decimal amount shown below that applies to the amount on line 7		

If line 7 is:			If line 7 is:		
Over	But not over	Decimal amount is	Over	But not over	Decimal amount is
$0—15,000		.35	$29,000—31,000		.27
15,000—17,000		.34	31,000—33,000		.26
17,000—19,000		.33	33,000—35,000		.25
19,000—21,000		.32	35,000—37,000		.24
21,000—23,000		.31	37,000—39,000		.23
23,000—25,000		.30	39,000—41,000		.22
25,000—27,000		.29	41,000—43,000		.21
27,000—29,000		.28	43,000—No limit		.20

		8	X .
9	Multiply line 6 by the decimal amount on line 8. If you paid 2003 expenses in 2004, see the instructions	**9**	
10	Enter the amount from Form 1040, line 45, minus any amount on Form 1040, line 46 .	**10**	
11	**Credit for child and dependent care expenses.** Enter the **smaller** of line 9 or line 10 here and on Form 1040, line 47	**11**	

For Paperwork Reduction Act Notice, see page 4 of the instructions. Cat. No. 11862M Form **2441** (2004)

Part III   Dependent Care Benefits

12	Enter the total amount of **dependent care benefits** you received in 2004. Amounts you received as an employee should be shown in box 10 of your Form(s) W-2. **Do not** include amounts reported as wages in box 1 of Form(s) W-2. If you were self-employed or a partner, include amounts you received under a dependent care assistance program from your sole proprietorship or partnership	12	
13	Enter the amount forfeited, if any (see the instructions)	13	
14	Subtract line 13 from line 12	14	

15	Enter the total amount of **qualified expenses** incurred in 2004 for the care of the **qualifying person(s)** . .	15	
16	Enter the **smaller** of line 14 or 15	16	
17	Enter your **earned income.** See instructions . . .	17	
18	Enter the amount shown below that applies to you.	18	

- If married filing jointly, enter your spouse's earned income (if your spouse was a student or was disabled, see the instructions for line 5).
- If married filing separately, see the instructions for the amount to enter.
- All others, enter the amount from line 17.

19	Enter the **smallest** of line 16, 17, or 18	19	
20	Enter the amount from line 12 that you received from your sole proprietorship or partnership. If you did not receive any such amounts, enter -0-	20	
21	Subtract line 20 from line 14	21	
22	Enter $5,000 ($2,500 if married filing separately **and** you were required to enter your spouse's earned income on line 18)	22	
23	**Deductible benefits.** Enter the **smallest** of line 19, 20, or 22. Also, include this amount on the appropriate line(s) of your return (see the instructions)	23	
24	Enter the **smaller** of line 19 or 22	24	
25	Enter the amount from line 23	25	
26	**Excluded benefits.** Subtract line 25 from line 24. If zero or less, enter -0-	26	
27	**Taxable benefits.** Subtract line 26 from line 21. If zero or less, enter -0-. Also, include this amount on Form 1040, line 7. On the dotted line next to line 7, enter "DCB" . . .	27	

To claim the child and dependent care
credit, complete lines 28–32 below.

28	Enter $3,000 ($6,000 if two or more qualifying persons)	28	
29	Add lines 23 and 26	29	
30	Subtract line 29 from line 28. If zero or less, **stop.** You cannot take the credit. **Exception.** If you paid 2003 expenses in 2004, see the instructions for line 9	30	
31	Complete line 2 on the front of this form. **Do not** include in column (c) any benefits shown on line 29 above. Then, add the amounts in column (c) and enter the total here	31	
32	Enter the **smaller** of line 30 or 31. Also, enter this amount on line 3 on the front of this form and complete lines 4–11	32	

Form **3468**

Department of the Treasury
Internal Revenue Service

Investment Credit

▶ **Attach to your tax return.**

OMB No. 1545-0155

2004

Attachment
Sequence No. **52**

Name(s) shown on return

Identifying number

Part I **Current Year Credit**

1 Rehabilitation credit (see instructions for requirements that must be met):

a Check this box if you are electing under section 47(d)(5) to take your qualified rehabilitation expenditures into account for the tax year in which paid (or, for self-rehabilitated property, when capitalized). See instructions. **Note:** *This election applies to the current tax year and to all later tax years. You may not revoke this election without IRS consent* . . . . ▶ ☐

Enter the amount of qualified rehabilitation expenditures and multiply by the percentage shown:

b Pre-1936 buildings . . . . $_____ × 10% (.10) | **1b**

c Certified historic structures . . . . $_____ × 20% (.20) | **1c**

    (1) Enter the assigned NPS project number or the pass-through entity's employer identification number (see instructions) . . . . . _____

    (2) Enter the date that the NPS approved the Request for Certification of Completed Work (see instructions). . . . . ___/___/___

d **(1)** Enter the date on which the 24- or 60-month measuring period begins ___/___/___ and ends ___/___/___

    (2) Enter the adjusted basis of the building as of the beginning date above (or the first day of your holding period, if later). . . . . . $_____

    (3) Enter the amount of the qualified rehabilitation expenditures incurred, or treated as incurred, during the period on line 1d(1) above . . . $_____

e Rehabilitation credit from an electing large partnership (Schedule K-1 (Form 1065-B), box 9) . | **1e**

2 Energy credit. Enter the basis of energy property placed in service during the tax year (see instructions) . . . . $_____ × 10% (.10) | **2**

3 Reforestation credit. Enter the amortizable basis of qualified timber property acquired before 10/23/04 (see instructions) $_____ × 10% (.10) | **3**

4 Credit from cooperatives. Enter the unused investment credit from cooperatives . . . . . . | **4**

5 **Current year credit.** Add lines 1b through 4 . . . . | **5**

Part II **Allowable Credit** (See **Who must file Form 3800** to find out if you complete Part II or file Form 3800.)

6 Regular tax before credits:

    ● Individuals. Enter the amount from Form 1040, line 43 . . . . . .

    ● Corporations. Enter the amount from Form 1120, Schedule J, line 3; Form 1120-A, Part I, line 1; or the applicable line of your return . . . .

    ● Estates and trusts. Enter the sum of the amounts from Form 1041, Schedule G, lines 1a and 1b, or the amount from the applicable line of your return . . . . | **6**

7 Alternative minimum tax: Enter the alternative minimum tax (AMT) from the following line of the appropriate form or schedule. | **7**

    ● Individuals: Form 6251, line 35 . . . .

    ● Corporations: Form 4626, line 14 . . . .

    ● Estates and trusts: Form 1041, Schedule I, line 56 . . . .

8 Add lines 6 and 7 . . . . | **8**

9a Foreign tax credit . . . . | **9a**

b Credits from Form 1040, lines 47 through 53. . . . . . . | **9b**

c Possessions tax credit (Form 5735, line 17 or 27) . . . . . | **9c**

d Credit for fuel from a nonconventional source . . . . . . | **9d**

e Qualified electric vehicle credit (Form 8834, line 20) . . . . | **9e**

f Add lines 9a through 9e . . . . | **9f**

10 Net income tax. Subtract line 9f from line 8. If zero, skip lines 11 through 14 and enter -0- on line 15 . . | **10**

11 Net regular tax. Subtract line 9f from line 6. If zero or less, enter -0- | **11**

12 Enter 25% (.25) of the excess, if any, of line 11 over $25,000 (see instructions) | **12**

13 Tentative minimum tax (see instructions) . . . . | **13**

14 Enter the greater of line 12 or line 13 . . . . | **14**

15 Subtract line 14 from line 10. If zero or less, enter -0- . . . . | **15**

16 **Credit allowed for the current year.** Enter the **smaller** of line 5 or line 15 here and on Form 1040, line 54; Form 1120, Schedule J, line 6d; Form 1120-A, Part I, line 2; Form 1041, Schedule G, line 2c; or the applicable line of your return. If line 15 is smaller than line 5, see instructions. | **16**

For Paperwork Reduction Act Notice, see page 4.   Cat. No. 12276E   Form **3468** (2004)

Form **3800**	**General Business Credit**	OMB No. 1545–0895
Department of the Treasury Internal Revenue Service (99)	▶ See instructions on pages 3 and 4. ▶ Attach to your tax return.	20**04** Attachment Sequence No. **22**

Name(s) shown on return | Identifying number

Part I   Current Year Credit

1a	Current year investment credit (Form 3468)	**1a**
b	Current year work opportunity credit (Form 5884)	**1b**
c	Current year welfare-to-work credit (Form 8861)	**1c**
d	Current year credit for alcohol used as fuel (Form 6478)	**1d**
e	Current year credit for increasing research activities (Form 6765)	**1e**
f	Current year low-income housing credit (Form 8586)	**1f**
g	Current year enhanced oil recovery credit (Form 8830)	**1g**
h	Current year disabled access credit (Form 8826)	**1h**
i	Current year renewable electricity production credit (Form 8835, Section A only)	**1i**
j	Current year Indian employment credit (Form 8845)	**1j**
k	Current year credit for employer social security and Medicare taxes paid on certain employee tips (Form 8846)	**1k**
l	Current year orphan drug credit (Form 8820)	**1l**
m	Current year new markets credit (Form 8874)	**1m**
n	Current year credit for small employer pension plan startup costs (Form 8881)	**1n**
o	Current year credit for employer-provided child care facilities and services (Form 8882) . . .	**1o**
p	Current year biodiesel fuels credit (Form 8864)	**1p**
q	Current year low sulfur diesel fuel production credit (Form 8896)	**1q**
r	Current year credit for contributions to selected community development corporations (Form 8847)	**1r**
s	Current year trans-Alaska pipeline liability fund credit (see instructions)	**1s**
t	Current year general credits from an electing large partnership (Schedule K-1 (Form 1065-B))	**1t**
2	**Current year credit.** Add lines 1a through 1t	**2**
3	Passive activity credits included on line 2 (see instructions)	**3**
4	Subtract line 3 from line 2	**4**
5	Passive activity credits allowed for 2004 (see instructions)	**5**
6	Carryforward of general business credit to 2004. See instructions for the schedule to attach	**6**
7	Carryback of general business credit from 2005 (see instructions)	**7**
8	**Current year credit.** Add lines 4 through 7	**8**

Part II   Allowable Credit

9	Regular tax before credits (see instructions)		**9**
10	Alternative minimum tax (see instructions)		**10**
11	Add lines 9 and 10		**11**
12a	Foreign tax credit	**12a**	
b	Credits from Form 1040, lines 47 through 53	**12b**	
c	Possessions tax credit (Form 5735, line 17 or 27)	**12c**	
d	Credit for fuel from a nonconventional source	**12d**	
e	Qualified electric vehicle credit (Form 8834, line 20)	**12e**	
f	Add lines 12a through 12e		**12f**
13	Net income tax. Subtract line 12f from line 11. If zero, skip lines 14 through 17 and enter -0- on line 18		**13**
14	Net regular tax. Subtract line 12f from line 9. If zero or less, enter -0-	**14**	
15	Enter 25% (.25) of the excess, if any, of line 14 over $25,000 (see instructions)	**15**	
16	Tentative minimum tax (see instructions)	**16**	
17	Enter the greater of line 15 or line 16		**17**
18	Subtract line 17 from line 13. If zero or less, enter -0-		**18**
19	**Credit allowed for the current year.** Enter the **smaller** of line 8 or line 18 here and on Form 1040, line 54; Form 1120, Schedule J, line 6d; Form 1120-A, Part I, line 2; Form 1041, Schedule G, line 2c; or the applicable line of your return. If line 19 is smaller than line 8, see instructions. **Individuals, estates, and trusts:** See instructions if claiming the research credit. **C corporations:** See Schedule A if claiming any regular investment credit carryforward and the line 19 instructions if there has been an ownership change, acquisition, or reorganization		**19**

For Paperwork Reduction Act Notice, see page 2.   Cat. No. 12392F   Form **3800** (2004)

Form 3800 (2004)   Page **2**

Schedule A— Additional General Business Credit Allowed by Internal Revenue Code Section 38(c)(2) (Before Repeal by the Revenue Reconciliation Act of 1990)—Only Applicable to C Corporations

A corporation (other than an S corporation) may be entitled to a larger general business credit or additional credit against the AMT if: **(a)** it is claiming a regular investment credit carryforward on line 6 attributable, in whole or in part, to the regular investment credit under section 46 (before amendment by the Revenue Reconciliation Act of 1990), **(b)** some of that investment credit cannot be used because line 18 is smaller than line 8, **and (c)** it is required to file **Form 4626,** Alternative Minimum Tax—Corporations. Complete Schedule A to see if the corporation is entitled to an additional credit.

20	Enter the portion of the credit shown on line 6 that is attributable to the regular investment credit under section 46 (before amendment by the Revenue Reconciliation Act of 1990)	**20**	
21	Tentative minimum tax (from line 16)	**21**	
22	Multiply line 21 by 25% (.25)	**22**	
23	Enter the amount from line 18	**23**	
24	Enter the portion of the credit shown on line 8 that is **not** attributable to the regular investment credit under section 46 (before amendment by the Revenue Reconciliation Act of 1990)	**24**	
25	Subtract line 24 from line 23. If zero or less, enter -0-	**25**	
26	Subtract line 25 from line 20. If zero or less, enter -0-	**26**	
27	For purposes of this line only, refigure the amount on Form 4626, line 10, by using zero on Form 4626, line 6, and enter the result here	**27**	
28	Multiply line 27 by 10% (.10)	**28**	
29	Net income tax (from line 13)	**29**	
30	Enter the amount from line 19	**30**	
31	Subtract line 30 from line 29	**31**	
32	Subtract line 28 from line 31	**32**	
33	Enter the smallest of line 22, line 26, or line 32	**33**	
34	Subtract line 33 from line 21	**34**	
35	Enter the greater of line 15 or line 34	**35**	
36	Subtract line 35 from line 29. Also enter this amount on line 19 instead of the amount previously figured on that line. Write "Sec. 38(c)(2)" next to your entry on line 19	**36**	

Form **3800** (2004)

Form **2106** Department of the Treasury Internal Revenue Service (99)	**Employee Business Expenses** ▶ **See separate instructions.** ▶ **Attach to Form 1040.**	OMB No. 1545-0139 20**04** Attachment Sequence No. **54**
Your name	Occupation in which you incurred expenses	Social security number

Part I   Employee Business Expenses and Reimbursements

Step 1 Enter Your Expenses		Column A Other Than Meals and Entertainment		Column B Meals and Entertainment
1	Vehicle expense from line 22 or line 29. (Rural mail carriers: See instructions.)	**1**		
2	Parking fees, tolls, and transportation, including train, bus, etc., that **did not** involve overnight travel or commuting to and from work . .	**2**		
3	Travel expense while away from home overnight, including lodging, airplane, car rental, etc. **Do not** include meals and entertainment.	**3**		
4	Business expenses not included on lines 1 through 3. **Do not** include meals and entertainment.	**4**		
5	Meals and entertainment expenses (see instructions)	**5**		
6	**Total expenses.** In Column A, add lines 1 through 4 and enter the result. In Column B, enter the amount from line 5	**6**		

Note: *If you were not reimbursed for any expenses in Step 1, skip line 7 and enter the amount from line 6 on line 8.*

Step 2   Enter Reimbursements Received From Your Employer for Expenses Listed in Step 1

7	Enter reimbursements received from your employer that were **not** reported to you in box 1 of Form W-2. Include any reimbursements reported under code "L" in box 12 of your Form W-2 (see instructions)	**7**		

Step 3   Figure Expenses To Deduct on Schedule A (Form 1040)

8	Subtract line 7 from line 6. If zero or less, enter -0-. However, if line 7 is greater than line 6 in Column A, report the excess as income on Form 1040, line 7	**8**		
	Note: *If **both columns** of line 8 are zero, you cannot deduct employee business expenses. Stop here and attach Form 2106 to your return.*			
9	In Column A, enter the amount from line 8. In Column B, multiply line 8 by 50% (.50). (Employees subject to Department of Transportation (DOT) hours of service limits: Multiply meal expenses incurred while away from home on business by 70% (.70) instead of 50%. For details, see instructions.)	**9**		
10	Add the amounts on line 9 of both columns and enter the total here. **Also, enter the total on Schedule A (Form 1040), line 20.** (Reservists, qualified performing artists, fee-basis state or local government officials, and individuals with disabilities: See the instructions for special rules on where to enter the total.) . . . . ▶	**10**		

For Paperwork Reduction Act Notice, see instructions.   Cat. No. 11700N   Form **2106** (2004)

Form 2106 (2004)   Page **2**

Part II   Vehicle Expenses

Section A—General Information (You must complete this section if you are claiming vehicle expenses.)

		(a) Vehicle 1	(b) Vehicle 2
11	Enter the date the vehicle was placed in service	11 / /	/ /
12	Total miles the vehicle was driven during 2004	12 miles	miles
13	Business miles included on line 12	13 miles	miles
14	Percent of business use. Divide line 13 by line 12	14 %	%
15	Average daily roundtrip commuting distance	15 miles	miles
16	Commuting miles included on line 12	16 miles	miles
17	Other miles. Add lines 13 and 16 and subtract the total from line 12	17 miles	miles

18	Do you (or your spouse) have another vehicle available for personal use?	☐ Yes	☐ No
19	Was your vehicle available for personal use during off-duty hours?	☐ Yes	☐ No
20	Do you have evidence to support your deduction?	☐ Yes	☐ No
21	If "Yes," is the evidence written?	☐ Yes	☐ No

Section B—Standard Mileage Rate (See the instructions for Part II to find out whether to complete this section or Section C.)

22	Multiply line 13 by 37.5¢ (.375)	22	

Section C—Actual Expenses

			(a) Vehicle 1		(b) Vehicle 2	
23	Gasoline, oil, repairs, vehicle insurance, etc.	23				
24a	Vehicle rentals	24a				
b	Inclusion amount (see instructions)	24b				
c	Subtract line 24b from line 24a	24c				
25	Value of employer-provided vehicle (applies only if 100% of annual lease value was included on Form W-2—see instructions)	25				
26	Add lines 23, 24c, and 25	26				
27	Multiply line 26 by the percentage on line 14	27				
28	Depreciation (see instructions)	28				
29	Add lines 27 and 28. Enter total here and on line 1	29				

Section D—Depreciation of Vehicles (Use this section only if you owned the vehicle and are completing Section C for the vehicle.)

			(a) Vehicle 1		(b) Vehicle 2	
30	Enter cost or other basis (see instructions)	30				
31	Enter section 179 deduction and special allowance (see instructions)	31				
32	Multiply line 30 by line 14 (see instructions if you claimed the section 179 deduction or special allowance)	32				
33	Enter depreciation method and percentage (see instructions)	33				
34	Multiply line 32 by the percentage on line 33 (see instructions)	34				
35	Add lines 31 and 34	35				
36	Enter the applicable limit explained in the line 36 instructions	36				
37	Multiply line 36 by the percentage on line 14	37				
38	Enter the **smaller** of line 35 or line 37. Also enter this amount on line 28 above	38				

Form **2106** (2004)

Form **2120**
(Rev. December 2002)

Department of the Treasury
Internal Revenue Service

Multiple Support Declaration

▶ **Attach to Form 1040 or Form 1040A.**

OMB No. 1545-0071

Attachment
Sequence No. **114**

Name(s) shown on return

Your social security number

During the calendar year _____ , the eligible persons listed below **each** paid over 10% of the support of:

_____
Name of person supported

I have a signed statement from each eligible person waiving his or her right to claim this person as a dependent for any tax year that began in the above calendar year.

Eligible person's name

Social security number

Address (number, street, apt. no., city, state, and ZIP code)

Eligible person's name

Social security number

Address (number, street, apt. no., city, state, and ZIP code)

Eligible person's name

Social security number

Address (number, street, apt. no., city, state, and ZIP code)

Eligible person's name

Social security number

Address (number, street, apt. no., city, state, and ZIP code)

Instructions

A Change to Note

The signature of another eligible person is no longer required on Form 2120. However, you still must obtain a signed statement from each other eligible person. For details, see **Signed Statement** on this page.

Purpose of Form

Use Form 2120 to:

● Identify each other eligible person (see below) who paid over 10% of the support of another person whom you are claiming as a dependent and

● Indicate that you have a signed statement from each other eligible person waiving his or her right to claim that person as a dependent.

An **eligible person** is someone who could have claimed another person as a dependent except that he or she did not pay over half of that person's support.

If there are more than four other eligible persons, attach a statement to your return with the required information.

Who Can Claim the Dependent

Generally, to claim someone as a dependent, you must pay over half of that person's support. However, even if you did not meet this support test, you may be able to claim him or her as a dependent if **all five** of the following apply.

1. You and one or more other eligible person(s) (see above) together paid over half of that person's support.

2. You paid over 10% of the support.

3. No one alone paid over half of that person's support.

4. The other four dependency tests are met. See **Dependents** in the Form 1040 or Form 1040A instructions.

5. Each other eligible person who paid over 10% of the support agrees not to claim that person as a dependent by giving you a signed statement. See **Signed Statement** on this page.

Note: *To find out what is included in support, see **Pub. 501**, Exemptions, Standard Deduction, and Filing Information.*

Signed Statement

You must have received, from each other eligible person listed above, a signed statement waiving his or her right to claim the person as a dependent for the calendar year indicated on this form. The statement must include:

● The calendar year the waiver applies to,

● The name of the person the eligible person helped to support, and

● The eligible person's name, address, and social security number.

Do not file the signed statement with your return. **But** you **must** keep it for your records and be prepared to furnish it and any other information necessary to show that you qualify to claim the person as your dependent.

Additional Information

See Pub. 501 for details.

Cat. No. 11712F

Form **2120** (Rev. 12-2002)

Form **3903**

Department of the Treasury
Internal Revenue Service   (99)

Moving Expenses

▶ Attach to Form 1040.

OMB No. 1545-0062

20**04**

Attachment
Sequence No. **62**

Name(s) shown on Form 1040

Your social security number

Before you begin: √ See the **Distance Test** and **Time Test** in the instructions to find out if you can deduct your moving expenses.

√ If you are a member of the Armed Forces, see the instructions to find out how to complete this form.

1   Enter the amount you paid for transportation and storage of household goods and personal effects (see instructions) **1**

2   Enter the amount you paid for travel and lodging in moving from your old home to your new home (see instructions). **Do not** include the cost of meals **2**

3   Add lines 1 and 2 . . . .   **3**

4   Enter the total amount your employer paid you for the expenses listed on lines 1 and 2 that is **not** included in the wages box (box 1) of your Form W-2. This amount should be shown in box 12 of your Form W-2 with code **P** **4**

5   Is line 3 **more than** line 4?

☐ **No.**   You **cannot** deduct your moving expenses. If line 3 is less than line 4, subtract line 3 from line 4 and include the result on Form 1040, line 7.

☐ **Yes.**   **Moving expense deduction.** Subtract line 4 from line 3. Enter the result here and on Form 1040, line 29 . . . .   **5**

General Instructions

What's New

For 2004, the standard mileage rate for using your vehicle to move to a new home is 14 cents a mile.

Purpose of Form

Use Form 3903 to figure your moving expense deduction for a move related to the start of work at a new principal place of work (workplace). If the new workplace is outside the United States or its possessions, you must be a U.S. citizen or resident alien to deduct your expenses.

If you qualify to deduct expenses for more than one move, use a separate Form 3903 for each move.

For more details, see Pub. 521, Moving Expenses.

Who May Deduct Moving Expenses

If you move to a new home because of a new principal workplace, you may be able to deduct your moving expenses whether you are self-employed or an employee. But you must meet both the distance test and time test that follow.

Distance Test

Your new principal workplace must be at least 50 miles farther from your old home than your old workplace was. For example, if your old workplace was 3 miles from your old home, your new workplace must be at least 53 miles from that home. If you did not have an old workplace, your new workplace must be at least 50 miles from your old home. The distance between the two points is the shortest of the more commonly traveled routes between them.

   To see if you meet the distance test, you can use the worksheet below.

Distance Test Worksheet

Keep a Copy for Your Records

TIP   Members of the Armed Forces may not have to meet this test. For details, see the instructions on the back of this form.

1.   Enter the number of miles from your **old home** to your **new workplace** . . . . **1.** _____ miles

2.   Enter the number of miles from your **old home** to your **old workplace** . . . . **2.** _____ miles

3.   Subtract line 2 from line 1. If zero or less, enter -0-. . . . . **3.** _____ miles

Is line 3 at least 50 miles?

☐ **Yes.** You meet this test.

☐ **No.** You do not meet this test. You **cannot** deduct your moving expenses. **Do not** complete Form 3903.

For Paperwork Reduction Act Notice, see back of form.   Cat. No. 12490K   Form **3903** (2004)

Form **4562**

Department of the Treasury
Internal Revenue Service

Depreciation and Amortization
(Including Information on Listed Property)

▶ See separate instructions.   ▶ Attach to your tax return.

OMB No. 1545-0172

20**04**

Attachment
Sequence No. **67**

Name(s) shown on return	Business or activity to which this form relates	Identifying number

Part I **Election To Expense Certain Property Under Section 179**
Note: *If you have any listed property, complete Part V before you complete Part I.*

1	Maximum amount. See page 2 of the instructions for a higher limit for certain businesses . . .	**1**	$102,000
2	Total cost of section 179 property placed in service (see page 3 of the instructions)	**2**	
3	Threshold cost of section 179 property before reduction in limitation	**3**	$410,000
4	Reduction in limitation. Subtract line 3 from line 2. If zero or less, enter -0-	**4**	
5	Dollar limitation for tax year. Subtract line 4 from line 1. If zero or less, enter -0-. If married filing separately, see page 3 of the instructions.	**5**	

(a) Description of property	(b) Cost (business use only)	(c) Elected cost
6		

7	Listed property. Enter the amount from line 29	**7**	
8	Total elected cost of section 179 property. Add amounts in column (c), lines 6 and 7	**8**	
9	Tentative deduction. Enter the **smaller** of line 5 or line 8.	**9**	
10	Carryover of disallowed deduction from line 13 of your 2003 Form 4562	**10**	
11	Business income limitation. Enter the smaller of business income (not less than zero) or line 5 (see instructions)	**11**	
12	Section 179 expense deduction. Add lines 9 and 10, but do not enter more than line 11 . . .	**12**	
13	Carryover of disallowed deduction to 2005. Add lines 9 and 10, less line 12 ▶	**13**	

Note: *Do not use Part II or Part III below for listed property. Instead, use Part V.*

Part II **Special Depreciation Allowance and Other Depreciation (Do not** include listed property.**)**

14	Special depreciation allowance for qualified property (other than listed property) placed in service during the tax year (see page 3 of the instructions)	**14**	
15	Property subject to section 168(f)(1) election (see page 4 of the instructions)	**15**	
16	Other depreciation (including ACRS) (see page 4 of the instructions)	**16**	

Part III **MACRS Depreciation (Do not** include listed property.**) (See page 5 of the instructions.)**

Section A

17	MACRS deductions for assets placed in service in tax years beginning before 2004	**17**	
18	If you are electing under section 168(i)(4) to group any assets placed in service during the tax year into one or more general asset accounts, check here . . . . ▶ ☐		

Section B—Assets Placed in Service During 2004 Tax Year Using the General Depreciation System

(a) Classification of property	(b) Month and year placed in service	(c) Basis for depreciation (business/investment use only—see instructions)	(d) Recovery period	(e) Convention	(f) Method	(g) Depreciation deduction
19a 3-year property						
b 5-year property						
c 7-year property						
d 10-year property						
e 15-year property						
f 20-year property						
g 25-year property			25 yrs.		S/L	
h Residential rental property			27.5 yrs.	MM	S/L	
			27.5 yrs.	MM	S/L	
i Nonresidential real property			39 yrs.	MM	S/L	
				MM	S/L	

Section C—Assets Placed in Service During 2004 Tax Year Using the Alternative Depreciation System

20a Class life					S/L	
b 12-year			12 yrs.		S/L	
c 40-year			40 yrs.	MM	S/L	

Part IV **Summary (see page 8 of the instructions)**

21	Listed property. Enter amount from line 28	**21**	
22	**Total.** Add amounts from line 12, lines 14 through 17, lines 19 and 20 in column (g), and line 21. Enter here and on the appropriate lines of your return. Partnerships and S corporations—see instr.	**22**	
23	For assets shown above and placed in service during the current year, enter the portion of the basis attributable to section 263A costs . .	**23**	

For Paperwork Reduction Act Notice, see separate instructions.   Cat. No. 12906N   Form **4562** (2004)

Form 4562 (2004)   Page **2**

Part V   **Listed Property** (Include automobiles, certain other vehicles, cellular telephones, certain computers, and property used for entertainment, recreation, or amusement.)

Note: *For any vehicle for which you are using the standard mileage rate or deducting lease expense, complete **only** 24a, 24b, columns (a) through (c) of Section A, all of Section B, and Section C if applicable.*

Section A—Depreciation and Other Information (Caution: *See page 9 of the instructions for limits for passenger automobiles.***)**

24a Do you have evidence to support the business/investment use claimed? ☐ **Yes** ☐ **No**   **24b** If "Yes," is the evidence written? ☐ **Yes** ☐ **No**

(a) Type of property (list vehicles first)	(b) Date placed in service	(c) Business/ investment use percentage	(d) Cost or other basis	(e) Basis for depreciation (business/investment use only)	(f) Recovery period	(g) Method/ Convention	(h) Depreciation deduction	(i) Elected section 179 cost
25 Special depreciation allowance for qualified listed property placed in service during the tax year and used more than 50% in a qualified business use (see page 8 of the instructions) **25**								
26 Property used more than 50% in a qualified business use (see page 8 of the instructions):								
		%						
		%						
		%						
27 Property used 50% or less in a qualified business use (see page 8 of the instructions):								
		%				S/L –		
		%				S/L –		
		%				S/L –		

28 Add amounts in column (h), lines 25 through 27. Enter here and on line 21, page 1. . | **28** |
29 Add amounts in column (i), line 26. Enter here and on line 7, page 1. . . . . | **29** |

Section B—Information on Use of Vehicles

Complete this section for vehicles used by a sole proprietor, partner, or other "more than 5% owner," or related person.
If you provided vehicles to your employees, first answer the questions in Section C to see if you meet an exception to completing this section for those vehicles.

		(a) Vehicle 1		(b) Vehicle 2		(c) Vehicle 3		(d) Vehicle 4		(e) Vehicle 5		(f) Vehicle 6	
30	Total business/investment miles driven during the year (**do not** include commuting miles—See page 2 of the instructions) .												
31	Total commuting miles driven during the year												
32	Total other personal (noncommuting) miles driven												
33	Total miles driven during the year. Add lines 30 through 32												
34	Was the vehicle available for personal use during off-duty hours?.	Yes	No	Yes	No	Yes	No	Yes	No	Yes	No	Yes	No
35	Was the vehicle used primarily by a more than 5% owner or related person?												
36	Is another vehicle available for personal use?												

Section C—Questions for Employers Who Provide Vehicles for Use by Their Employees

Answer these questions to determine if you meet an exception to completing Section B for vehicles used by employees who **are not** more than 5% owners or related persons (see page 10 of the instructions).

		Yes	No
37	Do you maintain a written policy statement that prohibits all personal use of vehicles, including commuting, by your employees?		
38	Do you maintain a written policy statement that prohibits personal use of vehicles, except commuting, by your employees? See page 10 of the instructions for vehicles used by corporate officers, directors, or 1% or more owners		
39	Do you treat all use of vehicles by employees as personal use?		
40	Do you provide more than five vehicles to your employees, obtain information from your employees about the use of the vehicles, and retain the information received?		
41	Do you meet the requirements concerning qualified automobile demonstration use? (See page 10 of the instructions.) .		

Note: *If your answer to 37, 38, 39, 40, or 41 is "Yes," do not complete Section B for the covered vehicles.*

Part VI   **Amortization**

(a) Description of costs	(b) Date amortization begins	(c) Amortizable amount	(d) Code section	(e) Amortization period or percentage	(f) Amortization for this year
42 Amortization of costs that begins during your 2004 tax year (see page 11 of the instructions):					

43 Amortization of costs that began before your 2004 tax year. . . . . | **43** |
44 **Total.** Add amounts in column (f). See page 12 of the instructions for where to report. . . | **44** |

Form **4562** (2004)

Form **4684**

Department of the Treasury
Internal Revenue Service

Casualties and Thefts

▶ See separate instructions.
▶ Attach to your tax return.
▶ **Use a separate Form 4684 for each casualty or theft.**

OMB No. 1545-0177

2004

Attachment
Sequence No. **26**

Name(s) shown on tax return

Identifying number

SECTION A—Personal Use Property (Use this section to report casualties and thefts of property **not** used in a trade or business or for income-producing purposes.)

1 Description of properties (show type, location, and date acquired for each property). Use a separate line for each property lost or damaged from the same casualty or theft.

Property **A** _____

Property **B** _____

Property **C** _____

Property **D** _____

		Properties			
		A	**B**	**C**	**D**
2	Cost or other basis of each property				
3	Insurance or other reimbursement (whether or not you filed a claim) (see instructions) . . . . . **Note:** *If line 2 is more than line 3, skip line 4.*				
4	Gain from casualty or theft. If line 3 is **more** than line 2, enter the difference here and skip lines 5 through 9 for that column. See instructions if line 3 includes insurance or other reimbursement you did not claim, or you received payment for your loss in a later tax year				
5	Fair market value **before** casualty or theft . . .				
6	Fair market value **after** casualty or theft				
7	Subtract line 6 from line 5				
8	Enter the **smaller** of line 2 or line 7				
9	Subtract line 3 from line 8. If zero or less, enter -0-				

10	Casualty or theft loss. Add the amounts on line 9 in columns A through D	**10**	
11	Enter the **smaller** of line 10 or $100	**11**	
12	Subtract line 11 from line 10	**12**	
	Caution: *Use only one Form 4684 for lines 13 through 18.*		
13	Add the amounts on line 12 of all Forms 4684	**13**	
14	Add the amounts on line 4 of all Forms 4684	**14**	
15	• If line 14 is **more** than line 13, enter the difference here and on Schedule D. **Do not** complete the rest of this section (see instructions). • If line 14 is **less** than line 13, enter -0- here and go to line 16. • If line 14 is **equal** to line 13, enter -0- here. **Do not** complete the rest of this section.	**15**	
16	If line 14 is **less** than line 13, enter the difference	**16**	
17	Enter 10% of your adjusted gross income from Form 1040, line 37. Estates and trusts, see instructions . .	**17**	
18	Subtract line 17 from line 16. If zero or less, enter -0-. Also enter the result on Schedule A (Form 1040), line 19. Estates and trusts, enter the result on the "Other deductions" line of your tax return	**18**	

For Paperwork Reduction Act Notice, see page 4 of the instructions.   Cat. No. 12997O   Form **4684** (2004)

Form 4684 (2004)   Attachment Sequence No. **26**   Page **2**

Name(s) shown on tax return. Do not enter name and identifying number if shown on other side. | Identifying number

SECTION B—Business and Income-Producing Property

Part I   Casualty or Theft Gain or Loss (Use a separate Part I for each casualty or theft.)

19 Description of properties (show type, location, and date acquired for each property). Use a separate line for each property lost or damaged from the same casualty or theft.

Property **A** _____

Property **B** _____

Property **C** _____

Property **D** _____

		Properties			
		A	**B**	**C**	**D**
20	Cost or adjusted basis of each property.	20			
21	Insurance or other reimbursement (whether or not you filed a claim). See the instructions for line 3. **Note:** *If line 20 is **more** than line 21, skip line 22*.	21			
22	Gain from casualty or theft. If line 21 is **more** than line 20, enter the difference here and on line 29 or line 34, column (c), except as provided in the instructions for line 33. Also, skip lines 23 through 27 for that column. See the instructions for line 4 if line 21 includes insurance or other reimbursement you did not claim, or you received payment for your loss in a later tax year.	22			
23	Fair market value **before** casualty or theft	23			
24	Fair market value **after** casualty or theft.	24			
25	Subtract line 24 from line 23	25			
26	Enter the **smaller** of line 20 or line 25. **Note:** *If the property was totally destroyed by casualty or lost from theft, enter on line 26 the amount from line 20.*	26			
27	Subtract line 21 from line 26. If zero or less, enter -0-	27			
28	Casualty or theft loss. Add the amounts on line 27. Enter the total here and on line 29 **or** line 34 (see instructions)		28		

Part II   Summary of Gains and Losses (from separate Parts I)

(a) Identify casualty or theft	(b) Losses from casualties or thefts		(c) Gains from casualties or thefts includible in income
	(i) Trade, business, rental or royalty property	*(ii)* Income-producing and employee property	

Casualty or Theft of Property Held One Year or Less

29	_____	( )	( )	
		( )	( )	
30	Totals. Add the amounts on line 29	30	( )	( )	

31 Combine line 30, columns (b)(i) and (c). Enter the net gain or (loss) here and on Form 4797, line 14. If Form 4797 is not otherwise required, see instructions | 31

32 Enter the amount from line 30, column (b)(ii) here. Individuals, enter the amount from income-producing property on Schedule A (Form 1040), line 27, and enter the amount from property used as an employee on Schedule A (Form 1040), line 22. Estates and trusts, partnerships, and S corporations, see instructions | 32

Casualty or Theft of Property Held More Than One Year

33	Casualty or theft gains from Form 4797, line 32		33	
34	_____	( )	( )	
		( )	( )	
35	Total losses. Add amounts on line 34, columns (b)(i) and (b)(ii)	35 ( )	( )	
36	Total gains. Add lines 33 and 34, column (c)		36	
37	Add amounts on line 35, columns (b)(i) and (b)(ii)		37	

38 If the loss on line 37 is **more** than the gain on line 36:

   a Combine line 35, column (b)(i) and line 36, and enter the net gain or (loss) here. Partnerships (except electing large partnerships) and S corporations, see the note below. All others, enter this amount on Form 4797, line 14. If Form 4797 is not otherwise required, see instructions | 38a

   b Enter the amount from line 35, column (b)(ii) here. Individuals, enter the amount from income-producing property on Schedule A (Form 1040), line 27, and enter the amount from property used as an employee on Schedule A (Form 1040), line 22. Estates and trusts, enter on the "Other deductions" line of your tax return. Partnerships (except electing large partnerships) and S corporations, see the note below. Electing large partnerships, enter on Form 1065-B, Part II, line 11. | 38b

39 If the loss on line 37 is **less** than or **equal** to the gain on line 36, combine lines 36 and 37 and enter here. Partnerships (except electing large partnerships), see the note below. All others, enter this amount on Form 4797, line 3 | 39

   Note: *Partnerships, enter the amount from line 38a, 38b, or line 39 on Form 1065, Schedule K, line 11.*
   S corporations, enter the amount from line 38a or 38b on Form 1120S, Schedule K, line 10.

Printed on recycled paper   Form **4684** (2004)

Form **4797**

Department of the Treasury
Internal Revenue Service (99)

Sales of Business Property
(Also Involuntary Conversions and Recapture Amounts
Under Sections 179 and 280F(b)(2))
▶**Attach to your tax return.** ▶**See separate instructions.**

OMB No. 1545-0184

2004

Attachment
Sequence No. **27**

Name(s) shown on return | Identifying number

---

1 Enter the gross proceeds from sales or exchanges reported to you for 2004 on Form(s) 1099-B or 1099-S (or substitute statement) that you are including on line 2, 10, or 20 (see instructions). **1**

Part I **Sales or Exchanges of Property Used in a Trade or Business and Involuntary Conversions From Other Than Casualty or Theft—Most Property Held More Than 1 Year** (see instructions)

(a) Description of property	**(b)** Date acquired (mo., day, yr.)	**(c)** Date sold (mo., day, yr.)	**(d)** Gross sales price	**(e)** Depreciation allowed or allowable since acquisition	**(f)** Cost or other basis, plus improvements and expense of sale	**(g)** Gain or (loss) Subtract (f) from the sum of (d) and (e)
2						

3 Gain, if any, from Form 4684, line 39 . . . . **3**

4 Section 1231 gain from installment sales from Form 6252, line 26 or 37 . . . . **4**

5 Section 1231 gain or (loss) from like-kind exchanges from Form 8824 . . . . **5**

6 Gain, if any, from line 32, from other than casualty or theft **6**

7 Combine lines 2 through 6. Enter the gain or (loss) here and on the appropriate line as follows: **7**

   Partnerships (except electing large partnerships) and S corporations. Report the gain or (loss) following the instructions for Form 1065, Schedule K, line 10, or Form 1120S, Schedule K, line 9. Skip lines 8, 9, 11, and 12 below.

   All others. If line 7 is zero or a loss, enter the amount from line 7 on line 11 below and skip lines 8 and 9. If line 7 is a gain and you did not have any prior year section 1231 losses, or they were recaptured in an earlier year, enter the gain from line 7 as a long-term capital gain on Schedule D and skip lines 8, 9, 11, and 12 below.

8 Nonrecaptured net section 1231 losses from prior years (see instructions) **8**

9 Subtract line 8 from line 7. If zero or less, enter -0-. If line 9 is zero, enter the gain from line 7 on line 12 below. If line 9 is more than zero, enter the amount from line 8 on line 12 below and enter the gain from line 9 as a long-term capital gain on Schedule D (see instructions) **9**

Part II **Ordinary Gains and Losses**

10 Ordinary gains and losses not included on lines 11 through 16 (include property held 1 year or less):

11 Loss, if any, from line 7. . . . . **11** ( )

12 Gain, if any, from line 7 or amount from line 8, if applicable **12**

13 Gain, if any, from line 31 . . . . **13**

14 Net gain or (loss) from Form 4684, lines 31 and 38a **14**

15 Ordinary gain from installment sales from Form 6252, line 25 or 36 . . . . **15**

16 Ordinary gain or (loss) from like-kind exchanges from Form 8824 . . . . **16**

17 Combine lines 10 through 16 . . . . **17**

18 For all except individual returns, enter the amount from line 17 on the appropriate line of your return and skip lines a and b below. For individual returns, complete lines a and b below:

   a If the loss on line 11 includes a loss from Form 4684, line 35, column (b)(ii), enter that part of the loss here. Enter the part of the loss from income-producing property on Schedule A (Form 1040), line 27, and the part of the loss from property used as an employee on Schedule A (Form 1040), line 22. Identify as from "Form 4797, line 18a." See instructions **18a**

   b Redetermine the gain or (loss) on line 17 excluding the loss, if any, on line 18a. Enter here and on Form 1040, line 14 . . . . **18b**

For Paperwork Reduction Act Notice, see page 8 of the instructions.   Cat. No. 13086I   Form **4797** (2004)

Form 4797 (2004)   Page **2**

Part III   Gain From Disposition of Property Under Sections 1245, 1250, 1252, 1254, and 1255

19	(a) Description of section 1245, 1250, 1252, 1254, or 1255 property:	(b) Date acquired (mo., day, yr.)	(c) Date sold (mo., day, yr.)
A			
B			
C			
D			

	These columns relate to the properties on lines 19A through 19D. ▶		Property A	Property B	Property C	Property D
20	Gross sales price (**Note:** See line 1 before completing.)	20				
21	Cost or other basis plus expense of sale	21				
22	Depreciation (or depletion) allowed or allowable	22				
23	Adjusted basis. Subtract line 22 from line 21	23				
24	Total gain. Subtract line 23 from line 20	24				
25	**If section 1245 property:**					
a	Depreciation allowed or allowable from line 22	25a				
b	Enter the **smaller** of line 24 or 25a	25b				
26	**If section 1250 property:** If straight line depreciation was used, enter -0- on line 26g, except for a corporation subject to section 291.					
a	Additional depreciation after 1975 (see instructions)	26a				
b	Applicable percentage multiplied by the **smaller** of line 24 or line 26a (see instructions)	26b				
c	Subtract line 26a from line 24. If residential rental property **or** line 24 is not more than line 26a, skip lines 26d and 26e	26c				
d	Additional depreciation after 1969 and before 1976	26d				
e	Enter the **smaller** of line 26c or 26d	26e				
f	Section 291 amount (corporations only)	26f				
g	Add lines 26b, 26e, and 26f	26g				
27	**If section 1252 property:** Skip this section if you did not dispose of farmland or if this form is being completed for a partnership (other than an electing large partnership).					
a	Soil, water, and land clearing expenses	27a				
b	Line 27a multiplied by applicable percentage (see instructions)	27b				
c	Enter the **smaller** of line 24 or 27b	27c				
28	**If section 1254 property:**					
a	Intangible drilling and development costs, expenditures for development of mines and other natural deposits, and mining exploration costs (see instructions)	28a				
b	Enter the **smaller** of line 24 or 28a	28b				
29	**If section 1255 property:**					
a	Applicable percentage of payments excluded from income under section 126 (see instructions)	29a				
b	Enter the **smaller** of line 24 or 29a (see instructions)	29b				

Summary of Part III Gains. Complete property columns A through D through line 29b before going to line 30.

30	Total gains for all properties. Add property columns A through D, line 24	30	
31	Add property columns A through D, lines 25b, 26g, 27c, 28b, and 29b. Enter here and on line 13	31	
32	Subtract line 31 from line 30. Enter the portion from casualty or theft on Form 4684, line 33. Enter the portion from other than casualty or theft on Form 4797, line 6	32	

Part IV   Recapture Amounts Under Sections 179 and 280F(b)(2) When Business Use Drops to 50% or Less (see instructions)

			(a) Section 179	(b) Section 280F(b)(2)
33	Section 179 expense deduction or depreciation allowable in prior years	33		
34	Recomputed depreciation. See instructions	34		
35	Recapture amount. Subtract line 34 from line 33. See the instructions for where to report	35		

Form **4797** (2004)

Form 4952

Department of the Treasury
Internal Revenue Service   (99)

Investment Interest Expense Deduction

▶ Attach to your tax return.

OMB No. 1545-0191

2004

Attachment
Sequence No. **51**

Name(s) shown on return

Identifying number

Part I	Total Investment Interest Expense		
1	Investment interest expense paid or accrued in 2004 (see instructions)	**1**	
2	Disallowed investment interest expense from 2003 Form 4952, line 7	**2**	
3	**Total investment interest expense.** Add lines 1 and 2	**3**	

Part II	Net Investment Income				
4a	Gross income from property held for investment (excluding any net gain from the disposition of property held for investment)	**4a**			
b	Qualified dividends included on line 4a	**4b**			
c	Subtract line 4b from line 4a			**4c**	
d	Net gain from the disposition of property held for investment	**4d**			
e	Enter the **smaller** of line 4d or your net capital gain from the disposition of property held for investment (see instructions)	**4e**			
f	Subtract line 4e from line 4d			**4f**	
g	Enter the amount from lines 4b and 4e that you elect to include in investment income (see instructions)			**4g**	
h	Investment income. Add lines 4c, 4f, and 4g			**4h**	
5	Investment expenses (see instructions)			**5**	
6	**Net investment income.** Subtract line 5 from line 4h. If zero or less, enter -0-			**6**	

Part III	Investment Interest Expense Deduction		
7	Disallowed investment interest expense to be carried forward to 2005. Subtract line 6 from line 3. If zero or less, enter -0-	**7**	
8	**Investment interest expense deduction.** Enter the **smaller** of line 3 or 6. See instructions.	**8**	

Section references are to the Internal Revenue Code unless otherwise noted.

General Instructions

Purpose of Form

Use Form 4952 to figure the amount of investment interest expense you can deduct for 2004 and the amount you can carry forward to future years. Your investment interest expense deduction is limited to your net investment income.

For more information, see Pub. 550, Investment Income and Expenses.

Who Must File

If you are an individual, estate, or a trust, you must file Form 4952 to claim a deduction for your investment interest expense.

Exception. You do not have to file Form 4952 if all of the following apply.

● Your investment interest expense is not more than your investment income from interest and ordinary dividends minus any qualified dividends.

● You have no other deductible investment expenses.

● You have no disallowed investment interest expense from 2003.

Allocation of Interest Expense

If you paid or accrued interest on a loan and used the loan proceeds for more than one purpose, you may have to allocate the interest. This is necessary because different rules apply to investment interest, personal interest, trade or business interest, home mortgage interest, and passive activity interest. See Pub. 535, Business Expenses.

Specific Instructions

Part I—Total Investment Interest Expense

Line 1

Enter the investment interest expense paid or accrued during the tax year, regardless of when you incurred the indebtedness. Investment interest expense is interest paid or accrued on a loan or part of a loan that is allocable to property held for investment (as defined on this page).

Include investment interest expense reported to you on Schedule K-1 from a partnership or an S corporation. Include amortization of bond premium on taxable bonds purchased after October 22, 1986, but before January 1, 1988, unless you elected to offset amortizable bond premium against the interest payments on the bond. A taxable bond is a bond on which the interest is includible in gross income.

Investment interest expense does not include any of the following:

● Home mortgage interest.

● Interest expense that is properly allocable to a passive activity. Generally, a passive activity is any business activity in which you do not materially participate and any rental activity. See the Instructions for Form 8582, Passive Activity Loss Limitations, for details.

● Any interest expense that is capitalized, such as construction interest subject to section 263A.

● Interest expense related to tax-exempt interest income under section 265.

● Interest expense, disallowed under section 264, on indebtedness with respect to life insurance, endowment, or annuity contracts issued after June 8, 1997, even if the proceeds were used to purchase any property held for investment.

Property held for investment. Property held for investment includes property that produces income, not derived in the ordinary course of a trade or business, from interest, dividends, annuities, or royalties. It also includes property that produces gain or loss, not derived in the ordinary course of a trade or business, from the disposition of property that produces these types of income or is held for investment. However, it does not include an interest in a passive activity.

Exception. A working interest in an oil or gas property that you held directly or through an entity that did not limit your liability is property held for investment, but only if you did not materially participate in the activity.

Part II—Net Investment Income

Line 4a

Gross income from property held for investment includes income, unless derived in the ordinary course of a trade or business, from interest, ordinary dividends (except Alaska Permanent Fund dividends), annuities, and royalties.

For Paperwork Reduction Act Notice, see back of form.   Cat. No. 13177Y   Form **4952** (2004)

Form **6252**	**Installment Sale Income**	OMB No. 1545-0228
Department of the Treasury Internal Revenue Service	▶ **Attach to your tax return.** ▶ **Use a separate form for each sale or other disposition of property on the installment method.**	**20**○**04** Attachment Sequence No. **79**

Name(s) shown on return	Identifying number

1 Description of property ▶ ....

2a Date acquired (month, day, year) ▶ ____/____/____ **b** Date sold (month, day, year) ▶ ____/____/____

3 Was the property sold to a related party (see instructions) after May 14, 1980? If "No," skip line 4 . . . ☐ Yes ☐ No

4 Was the property you sold to a related party a marketable security? If "Yes," complete Part III. If "No," complete Part III for the year of sale and the 2 years after the year of sale . . . . ☐ Yes ☐ No

Part I **Gross Profit and Contract Price.** Complete this part for the year of sale only.

5	Selling price including mortgages and other debts. **Do not** include interest whether stated or unstated	**5**	
6	Mortgages, debts, and other liabilities the buyer assumed or took the property subject to (see instructions)	**6**	
7	Subtract line 6 from line 5 .	**7**	
8	Cost or other basis of property sold	**8**	
9	Depreciation allowed or allowable	**9**	
10	Adjusted basis. Subtract line 9 from line 8	**10**	
11	Commissions and other expenses of sale	**11**	
12	Income recapture from Form 4797, Part III (see instructions) . .	**12**	
13	Add lines 10, 11, and 12	**13**	
14	Subtract line 13 from line 5. If zero or less, **do not** complete the rest of this form (see instructions)	**14**	
15	If the property described on line 1 above was your main home, enter the amount of your excluded gain (see instructions). Otherwise, enter -0-	**15**	
16	**Gross profit.** Subtract line 15 from line 14	**16**	
17	Subtract line 13 from line 6. If zero or less, enter -0-	**17**	
18	**Contract price.** Add line 7 and line 17	**18**	

Part II **Installment Sale Income.** Complete this part for the year of sale **and** any year you receive a payment or have certain debts you must treat as a payment on installment obligations.

19	Gross profit percentage. Divide line 16 by line 18. For years after the year of sale, see instructions	**19**	
20	If this is the year of sale, enter the amount from line 17. Otherwise, enter -0-	**20**	
21	Payments received during year (see instructions). **Do not** include interest, whether stated or unstated	**21**	
22	Add lines 20 and 21	**22**	
23	Payments received in prior years (see instructions). **Do not** include interest, whether stated or unstated **23**		
24	**Installment sale income.** Multiply line 22 by line 19	**24**	
25	Enter the part of line 24 that is ordinary income under the recapture rules (see instructions) . .	**25**	
26	Subtract line 25 from line 24. Enter here and on Schedule D or Form 4797 (see instructions)	**26**	

Part III **Related Party Installment Sale Income. Do not** complete if you received the final payment this tax year.

27 Name, address, and taxpayer identifying number of related party ....

28 Did the related party resell or dispose of the property ("second disposition") during this tax year? . . . . ☐ Yes ☐ No

29 **If the answer to question 28 is "Yes," complete lines 30 through 37 below unless one of the following conditions is met. Check the box that applies.**

a ☐ The second disposition was more than 2 years after the first disposition (other than dispositions of marketable securities). If this box is checked, enter the date of disposition (month, day, year) ▶ ____/____/____

b ☐ The first disposition was a sale or exchange of stock to the issuing corporation.

c ☐ The second disposition was an involuntary conversion and the threat of conversion occurred after the first disposition.

d ☐ The second disposition occurred after the death of the original seller or buyer.

e ☐ It can be established to the satisfaction of the Internal Revenue Service that tax avoidance was not a principal purpose for either of the dispositions. If this box is checked, attach an explanation (see instructions).

30	Selling price of property sold by related party (see instructions)	**30**	
31	Enter contract price from line 18 for year of first sale	**31**	
32	Enter the **smaller** of line 30 or line 31	**32**	
33	Total payments received by the end of your 2004 tax year (see instructions)	**33**	
34	Subtract line 33 from line 32. If zero or less, enter -0-	**34**	
35	Multiply line 34 by the gross profit percentage on line 19 for year of first sale	**35**	
36	Enter the part of line 35 that is ordinary income under the recapture rules (see instructions) . .	**36**	
37	Subtract line 36 from line 35. Enter here and on Schedule D or Form 4797 (see instructions)	**37**	

For Paperwork Reduction Act Notice, see page 4. Cat. No. 13601R Form **6252** (2004)

Form **8283**
(Rev. October 1998)

Department of the Treasury
Internal Revenue Service

Noncash Charitable Contributions

▶ Attach to your tax return if you claimed a total deduction
of over $500 for all contributed property.

▶ See separate instructions.

OMB No. 1545-0908

Attachment
Sequence No. **55**

Name(s) shown on your income tax return	Identifying number

Note: *Figure the amount of your contribution deduction before completing this form. See your tax return instructions.*

Section A—List in this section **only** items (or groups of similar items) for which you claimed a deduction of $5,000 or less. Also, list certain publicly traded securities even if the deduction is over $5,000 (see instructions).

Part I Information on Donated Property—If you need more space, attach a statement.

1	**(a)** Name and address of the donee organization	**(b)** Description of donated property
A		
B		
C		
D		
E		

Note: *If the amount you claimed as a deduction for an item is $500 or less, you do not have to complete columns (d), (e), and (f).*

	(c) Date of the contribution	**(d)** Date acquired by donor (mo., yr.)	**(e)** How acquired by donor	**(f)** Donor's cost or adjusted basis	**(g)** Fair market value	**(h)** Method used to determine the fair market value
A						
B						
C						
D						
E						

Part II Other Information—Complete line 2 if you gave less than an entire interest in property listed in Part I. Complete line 3 if conditions were attached to a contribution listed in Part I.

2 If, during the year, you contributed less than the entire interest in the property, complete lines a–e.

a Enter the letter from Part I that identifies the property ▶ _____. If Part II applies to more than one property, attach a separate statement.

b Total amount claimed as a deduction for the property listed in Part I: **(1)** For this tax year ▶ _____ .
(2) For any prior tax years ▶ _____ .

c Name and address of each organization to which any such contribution was made in a prior year (complete only if different from the donee organization above):

Name of charitable organization (donee)

Address (number, street, and room or suite no.)

City or town, state, and ZIP code

d For tangible property, enter the place where the property is located or kept ▶ _____

e Name of any person, other than the donee organization, having actual possession of the property ▶ _____

3 If conditions were attached to any contribution listed in Part I, answer questions a – c and attach the required statement (see instructions).

		Yes	No
a	Is there a restriction, either temporary or permanent, on the donee's right to use or dispose of the donated property?		
b	Did you give to anyone (other than the donee organization or another organization participating with the donee organization in cooperative fundraising) the right to the income from the donated property or to the possession of the property, including the right to vote donated securities, to acquire the property by purchase or otherwise, or to designate the person having such income, possession, or right to acquire?		
c	Is there a restriction limiting the donated property for a particular use?		

For Paperwork Reduction Act Notice, see page 4 of separate instructions.   Cat. No. 62299J   Form **8283** (Rev. 10-98)

Form 8283 (Rev. 10-98)   Page **2**

Name(s) shown on your income tax return	Identifying number

Section B—Appraisal Summary—List in this section only items (or groups of similar items) for which you claimed a deduction of more than $5,000 per item or group. **Exception.** Report contributions of certain publicly traded securities only in Section A.

If you donated art, you may have to attach the complete appraisal. See the **Note** in Part I below.

Part I	**Information on Donated Property**—To be completed by the taxpayer and/or appraiser.

4 Check type of property:

☐ Art* (contribution of $20,000 or more)   ☐ Real Estate   ☐ Gems/Jewelry   ☐ Stamp Collections
☐ Art* (contribution of less than $20,000)   ☐ Coin Collections   ☐ Books   ☐ Other

*Art includes paintings, sculptures, watercolors, prints, drawings, ceramics, antique furniture, decorative arts, textiles, carpets, silver, rare manuscripts, historical memorabilia, and other similar objects.

Note: *If your total art contribution deduction was $20,000 or more, you must attach a complete copy of the signed appraisal. See instructions.*

5	**(a)** Description of donated property (if you need more space, attach a separate statement)	**(b)** If tangible property was donated, give a brief summary of the overall physical condition at the time of the gift	**(c)** Appraised fair market value
A			
B			
C			
D			

	(d) Date acquired by donor (mo., yr.)	**(e)** How acquired by donor	**(f)** Donor's cost or adjusted basis	**(g)** For bargain sales, enter amount received	**(h)** Amount claimed as a deduction	**(i)** Average trading price of securities
					See instructions	
A						
B						
C						
D						

Part II	**Taxpayer (Donor) Statement**—List each item included in Part I above that the appraisal identifies as having a value of $500 or less. See instructions.

I declare that the following item(s) included in Part I above has to the best of my knowledge and belief an appraised value of not more than $500 (per item). Enter identifying letter from Part I and describe the specific item. See instructions. ▶ _____

Signature of taxpayer (donor) ▶   Date ▶

Part III	**Declaration of Appraiser**

I declare that I am not the donor, the donee, a party to the transaction in which the donor acquired the property, employed by, or related to any of the foregoing persons, or married to any person who is related to any of the foregoing persons. And, if regularly used by the donor, donee, or party to the transaction, I performed the majority of my appraisals during my tax year for other persons.

Also, I declare that I hold myself out to the public as an appraiser or perform appraisals on a regular basis; and that because of my qualifications as described in the appraisal, I am qualified to make appraisals of the type of property being valued. I certify that the appraisal fees were not based on a percentage of the appraised property value. Furthermore, I understand that a false or fraudulent overstatement of the property value as described in the qualified appraisal or this appraisal summary may subject me to the penalty under section 6701(a) (aiding and abetting the understatement of tax liability). I affirm that I have not been barred from presenting evidence or testimony by the Director of Practice.

Sign Here

Signature ▶	Title ▶	Date of appraisal ▶

Business address (including room or suite no.)	Identifying number

City or town, state, and ZIP code

Part IV	**Donee Acknowledgment**—To be completed by the charitable organization.

This charitable organization acknowledges that it is a qualified organization under section 170(c) and that it received the donated property as described in Section B, Part I, above on ▶ _____
(Date)

Furthermore, this organization affirms that in the event it sells, exchanges, or otherwise disposes of the property described in Section B, Part I (or any portion thereof) within 2 years after the date of receipt, it will file **Form 8282,** Donee Information Return, with the IRS and give the donor a copy of that form. This acknowledgment does not represent agreement with the claimed fair market value.

Does the organization intend to use the property for an unrelated use? . . . . ▶ ☐ Yes   ☐ No

Name of charitable organization (donee)	Employer identification number
Address (number, street, and room or suite no.)	City or town, state, and ZIP code
Authorized signature	Title	Date

Form **8582**

Department of the Treasury
Internal Revenue Service (99)

Passive Activity Loss Limitations

▶ See separate instructions.

▶ Attach to Form 1040 or Form 1041.

OMB No. 1545-1008

2004

Attachment
Sequence No. **88**

Name(s) shown on return

Identifying number

Part I **2004 Passive Activity Loss**

Caution: *See the instructions for Worksheets 1, 2, and 3 on pages 7 and 8 before completing Part I.*

Rental Real Estate Activities With Active Participation (For the definition of active participation see **Special Allowance for Rental Real Estate Activities** on page 3 of the instructions.)

1a Activities with net income (enter the amount from Worksheet 1, column (a)) **1a**

b Activities with net loss (enter the amount from Worksheet 1, column (b)) . . . . **1b** ( )

c Prior years unallowed losses (enter the amount from Worksheet 1, column (c)) . . . . **1c** ( )

d Combine lines 1a, 1b, and 1c. **1d**

Commercial Revitalization Deductions From Rental Real Estate Activities

2a Commercial revitalization deductions from Worksheet 2, column (a) **2a** ( )

b Prior year unallowed commercial revitalization deductions from Worksheet 2, column (b) . . . . **2b** ( )

c Add lines 2a and 2b. . . . . **2c** ( )

All Other Passive Activities

3a Activities with net income (enter the amount from Worksheet 3, column (a)) **3a**

b Activities with net loss (enter the amount from Worksheet 3, column (b)) . . . . **3b** ( )

c Prior years unallowed losses (enter the amount from Worksheet 3, column (c)) . . . . **3c** ( )

d Combine lines 3a, 3b, and 3c. **3d**

4 Combine lines 1d, 2c, and 3d. If the result is net income or zero, all losses are allowed, including any prior year unallowed losses entered on line 1c, 2b, or 3c. **Do not** complete Form 8582. Report the losses on the forms and schedules normally used **4**

If line 4 is a loss and: • Line 1d is a loss, go to Part II.
• Line 2c is a loss (and line 1d is zero or more), skip Part II and go to Part III.
• Line 3d is a loss (and lines 1d and 2c are zero or more), skip Parts II and III and go to line 15.

Caution: *If your filing status is married filing separately and you lived with your spouse at any time during the year, **do not** complete Part II or Part III. Instead, go to line 15.*

Part II **Special Allowance for Rental Real Estate With Active Participation**

Note: *Enter all numbers in Part II as positive amounts. See page 8 for an example.*

5 Enter the **smaller** of the loss on line 1d or the loss on line 4 . . . . **5**

6 Enter $150,000. If married filing separately, see page 8 . . . **6**

7 Enter modified adjusted gross income, but not less than zero (see page 8) **7**

Note: *If line 7 is greater than or equal to line 6, skip lines 8 and 9, enter -0- on line 10. Otherwise, go to line 8.*

8 Subtract line 7 from line 6 . . . . **8**

9 Multiply line 8 by 50% (.5). **Do not** enter more than $25,000. If married filing separately, see page 8 **9**

10 Enter the **smaller** of line 5 or line 9. . . . . **10**

If line 2c is a loss, go to Part III. Otherwise, go to line 15.

Part III **Special Allowance for Commercial Revitalization Deductions From Rental Real Estate Activities**

Note: *Enter all numbers in Part III as positive amounts. See the example for Part II on page 8.*

11 Enter $25,000 reduced by the amount, if any, on line 10. If married filing separately, see instructions **11**

12 Enter the loss from line 4 . . . . **12**

13 Reduce line 12 by the amount on line 10 . . . . **13**

14 Enter the **smallest** of line 2c (treated as a positive amount), line 11, or line 13 . . . . . **14**

Part IV **Total Losses Allowed**

15 Add the income, if any, on lines 1a and 3a and enter the total. **15**

16 **Total losses allowed from all passive activities for 2004.** Add lines 10, 14, and 15. See pages 10 and 11 of the instructions to find out how to report the losses on your tax return . **16**

For Paperwork Reduction Act Notice, see page 12 of the instructions.

Cat. No. 63704F

Form **8582** (2004)

Form 8582 (2004)

Page **2**

Caution: *The worksheets must be filed with your tax return. Keep a copy for your records.*

Worksheet 1—For Form 8582, Lines 1a, 1b, and 1c (See page 7 of the instructions.)

Name of activity	Current year		Prior years	Overall gain or loss	
	(a) Net income (line 1a)	(b) Net loss (line 1b)	(c) Unallowed loss (line 1c)	(d) Gain	(e) Loss
Total. Enter on Form 8582, lines 1a, 1b, and 1c . . . . ▶					

Worksheet 2—For Form 8582, Lines 2a and 2b (See pages 7 and 8 of the instructions.)

Name of activity	(a) Current year deductions (line 2a)	(b) Prior year unallowed deductions (line 2b)	(c) Overall loss
Total. Enter on Form 8582, lines 2a and 2b . . . . ▶			

Worksheet 3—For Form 8582, Lines 3a, 3b, and 3c (See page 8 of the instructions.)

Name of activity	Current year		Prior years	Overall gain or loss	
	(a) Net income (line 3a)	(b) Net loss (line 3b)	(c) Unallowed loss (line 3c)	(d) Gain	(e) Loss
Total. Enter on Form 8582, lines 3a, 3b, and 3c . . . . ▶					

Worksheet 4—Use this worksheet if an amount is shown on Form 8582, line 10 or 14 (See page 9.)

Name of activity	Form or schedule and line number to be reported on (see instructions)	(a) Loss	(b) Ratio	(c) Special allowance	(d) Subtract column (c) from column (a)
Total . . . . ▶			1.00		

Worksheet 5—Allocation of Unallowed Losses (See page 9 of the instructions.)

Name of activity	Form or schedule and line number to be reported on (see instructions)	(a) Loss	(b) Ratio	(c) Unallowed loss
Total . . . . ▶			1.00	

Form **8582** (2004)

Form 8582 (2004)

Worksheet 6—Allowed Losses (See pages 9 and 10 of the instructions.)

Name of activity	Form or schedule and line number to be reported on (see instructions)	(a) Loss	(b) Unallowed loss	(c) Allowed loss
Total . . . . ▶				

Worksheet 7—Activities With Losses Reported on Two or More Different Forms or Schedules (See page 10.)

Name of Activity:	(a)	(b)	(c) Ratio	(d) Unallowed loss	(e) Allowed loss
Form or schedule and line number to be reported on (see instructions):					
1a Net loss plus prior year unallowed loss from form or schedule. ▶					
b Net income from form or schedule . . . . . . ▶					
c Subtract line 1b from line 1a. If zero or less, enter -0- ▶					
Form or schedule and line number to be reported on (see instructions):					
1a Net loss plus prior year unallowed loss from form or schedule. ▶					
b Net income from form or schedule . . . . . . ▶					
c Subtract line 1b from line 1a. If zero or less, enter -0- ▶					
Form or schedule and line number to be reported on (see instructions):					
1a Net loss plus prior year unallowed loss from form or schedule. ▶					
b Net income from form or schedule . . . . . . ▶					
c Subtract line 1b from line 1a. If zero or less, enter -0- ▶					
Total . . . . ▶			1.00		

Printed on recycled paper

Form **8582** (2004)

| Form **8615** | | **Tax for Children Under Age 14 With Investment Income of More Than $1,600** ▶ Attach only to the child's Form 1040, Form 1040A, or Form 1040NR. ▶ See separate instructions. | | OMB No. 1545-0998 **2004** Attachment Sequence No. **33** |

Department of the Treasury
Internal Revenue Service (99)

| Child's name shown on return | Child's social security number |

Before you begin: If the child, the parent, or any of the parent's other children under age 14 must use the Schedule D Tax Worksheet or has income from farming or fishing, see **Pub. 929,** Tax Rules for Children and Dependents. It explains how to figure the child's tax using the **Schedule D Tax Worksheet** or **Schedule J** (Form 1040).

A Parent's name (first, initial, and last). **Caution:** *See instructions before completing.*

B Parent's social security number

C Parent's filing status (check one):

☐ Single ☐ Married filing jointly ☐ Married filing separately ☐ Head of household ☐ Qualifying widow(er)

Part I   Child's Net Investment Income

1	Enter the child's investment income (see instructions)	**1**	
2	If the child **did not** itemize deductions on **Schedule A** (Form 1040 or Form 1040NR), enter $1,600. Otherwise, see instructions	**2**	
3	Subtract line 2 from line 1. If zero or less, **stop;** do not complete the rest of this form but **do** attach it to the child's return	**3**	
4	Enter the child's **taxable income** from Form 1040, line 42; Form 1040A, line 27; or Form 1040NR, line 39	**4**	
5	Enter the **smaller** of line 3 or line 4. If zero, **stop;** do not complete the rest of this form but **do** attach it to the child's return	**5**	

Part II   Tentative Tax Based on the Tax Rate of the Parent

6	Enter the parent's **taxable income** from Form 1040, line 42; Form 1040A, line 27; Form 1040EZ, line 6; TeleFile Tax Record, line K(1); Form 1040NR, line 39; or Form 1040NR-EZ, line 14. If zero or less, enter -0-	**6**	
7	Enter the total, if any, from Forms 8615, line 5, of **all other** children of the parent named above. **Do not** include the amount from line 5 above	**7**	
8	Add lines 5, 6, and 7 (see instructions).	**8**	
9	Enter the tax on the amount on line 8 based on the **parent's** filing status above (see instructions). If the Qualified Dividends and Capital Gain Tax Worksheet, Schedule D Tax Worksheet, or Schedule J (Form 1040) is used to figure the tax, check here ▶ ☐	**9**	
10	Enter the parent's tax from Form 1040, line 43; Form 1040A, line 28, minus any alternative minimum tax; Form 1040EZ, line 10; TeleFile Tax Record, line K(2); Form 1040NR, line 40; or Form 1040NR-EZ, line 15. **Do not** include any tax from **Form 4972** or **8814.** If the Qualified Dividends and Capital Gain Tax Worksheet, Schedule D Tax Worksheet, or Schedule J (Form 1040) was used to figure the tax, check here ▶ ☐	**10**	
11	Subtract line 10 from line 9 and enter the result. If line 7 is blank, also enter this amount on line 13 and go to **Part III**	**11**	
12a	Add lines 5 and 7	**12a**	
b	Divide line 5 by line 12a. Enter the result as a decimal (rounded to at least three places)	**12b**	× .
13	Multiply line 11 by line 12b	**13**	

Part III   Child's Tax—If lines 4 and 5 above are the same, enter -0- on line 15 and go to line 16.

14	Subtract line 5 from line 4	**14**	
15	Enter the tax on the amount on line 14 based on the **child's** filing status (see instructions). If the Qualified Dividends and Capital Gain Tax Worksheet, Schedule D Tax Worksheet, or Schedule J (Form 1040) is used to figure the tax, check here ▶ ☐	**15**	
16	Add lines 13 and 15	**16**	
17	Enter the tax on the amount on line 4 based on the **child's** filing status (see instructions). If the Qualified Dividends and Capital Gain Tax Worksheet, Schedule D Tax Worksheet, or Schedule J (Form 1040) is used to figure the tax, check here ▶ ☐	**17**	
18	Enter the **larger** of line 16 or line 17 here and on the **child's** Form 1040, line 43; Form 1040A, line 28; or Form 1040NR, line 40	**18**	

For Paperwork Reduction Act Notice, see the instructions.   Cat. No. 64113U   Form **8615** (2004)

Form **8814**

Department of the Treasury
Internal Revenue Service

Parents' Election To Report
Child's Interest and Dividends

▶ See instructions on back.
▶ **Attach to parents' Form 1040 or Form 1040NR.**

OMB No. 1545-1128

2004

Attachment
Sequence No. **40**

Name(s) shown on your return

Your social security number

Caution: *The Federal income tax on your child's income, including qualified dividends and capital gain distributions, may be less if you file a separate tax return for the child instead of making this election. This is because you cannot take certain tax benefits that your child could take on his or her own return. For details, see* **Tax benefits you may not take** *on page 2.*

A   Child's name (first, initial, and last)

B Child's social security number

C   If more than one Form 8814 is attached, check here . . . . ▶ ☐

Part I   Child's Interest and Dividends To Report on Your Return

1a   Enter your child's **taxable** interest. If this amount is different from the amounts shown on the
child's Forms 1099-INT and 1099-OID, see the instructions **1a**

b   Enter your child's **tax-exempt** interest. **Do not** include this
amount on line 1a   .   .   .   . | **1b** |

2   Enter your child's ordinary dividends, including any Alaska Permanent Fund dividends. If your
child received any ordinary dividends as a nominee, see the instructions **2**

3   Enter your child's capital gain distributions. If your child received any capital gain distributions
as a nominee, see the instructions **3**

4   Add lines 1a, 2, and 3. If the total is $1,600 or less, skip lines 5 and 6 and go to line 7. If the
total is $8,000 or more, **do not** file this form. Your child **must** file his or her own return to report
the income **4**

5   Base amount   .   .   .   .   **5** | 1,600 | 00

6   Subtract line 5 from line 4. See the instructions for where to report this amount. Go to line 7
below   .   .   .   .   ▶   **6**

Part II   Tax on the First $1,600 of Child's Interest and Dividends

7   Amount not taxed   .   .   .   .   **7** | 800 | 00

8   Subtract line 7 from line 4. If the result is zero or less, enter -0- **8**

9   **Tax.** Is the amount on line 8 less than $800?
  ☐ **No.**   Enter $80 here and see the **Note** below.
  ☐ **Yes.**   Multiply line 8 by 10% (.10). Enter the result here and see the **Note** below.   ⎫   ⎬   .   .   **9**

Note: *If you checked the box on line C above, see the instructions. Otherwise, include the amount from line 9 in the tax you enter on Form 1040, line 43, or Form 1040NR, line 40. Be sure to check box* **a** *on Form 1040, line 43, or Form 1040NR, line 40.*

For Paperwork Reduction Act Notice, see page 3.   Cat. No. 10750J   Form **8814** (2004)

General Instructions

Purpose of form. Use this form if you elect to report your child's income on your return. If you do, your child will not have to file a return. You can make this election if your child meets all of the following conditions.

- The child was under age 14 at the end of 2004. A child born on January 1, 1991, is considered to be age 14 at the end of 2004.
- The child's only income was from interest and dividends, including capital gain distributions and Alaska Permanent Fund dividends.
- The child's gross income for 2004 was less than $8,000.
- The child is required to file a 2004 return.
- There were no estimated tax payments for the child for 2004 (including any overpayment of tax from his or her 2003 return applied to 2004 estimated tax).
- There was no federal income tax withheld from the child's income.

You must also qualify. See *Parents who qualify to make the election* below.

How to make the election. To make the election, complete and attach Form(s) 8814 to your tax return and file your return by the due date (including extensions). A separate Form 8814 must be filed for each child whose income you choose to report.

Parents who qualify to make the election. You qualify to make this election if you file Form 1040 or Form 1040NR and any of the following apply.

- You are filing a joint return for 2004 with the child's other parent.
- You and the child's other parent were married to each other but file separate returns for 2004 and you had the higher taxable income.
- You were unmarried, treated as unmarried for federal income tax purposes, or separated from the child's other parent by a divorce or separate maintenance decree. You must have had custody of your child for most of the year (you were the custodial parent). If you were the custodial parent and you remarried, you may make the election on a joint return with your new spouse. But if you and your new spouse do not file a joint return, you qualify to make the election only if you had higher taxable income than your new spouse.

Note. If you and the child's other parent were not married but lived together during the year with the child, you qualify to make the election only if you are the parent with the higher taxable income.

Tax benefits you may not take. If you elect to report your child's income on your return, you may not take any of the following deductions that your child could take on his or her own return.

- Standard deduction of $2,000 for a blind child.
- Penalty on early withdrawal of child's savings.
- Itemized deductions such as child's investment expenses or charitable contributions.

If your child received qualified dividends or capital gain distributions, you may pay up to $40.00 more tax if you make this election instead of filing a separate tax return for the child. This is because the tax rate on the child's income between $800 and $1,600 is 10% if you make this election. However, if you file a separate return for the child, the tax rate may be as low as 5% because of the preferential tax rates for qualified dividends and capital gain distributions.

If any of the above apply to your child, first figure the tax on your child's income as if he or she is filing a return. Next, figure the tax as if you are electing to report your child's income on your return. Then, compare the methods to determine which results in the lower tax.

Alternative minimum tax. If your child received tax-exempt interest (or exempt-interest dividends paid by a regulated investment company) from certain private activity bonds, you must take this into account in determining if you owe the alternative minimum tax. See Form 6251, Alternative Minimum Tax—Individuals, and its instructions for details.

Investment interest expense. Your child's income (other than qualified dividends, Alaska Permanent Fund dividends, and capital gain distributions) that you report on your return is considered to be your investment income for purposes of figuring your investment interest expense deduction. If your child received qualified dividends, Alaska Permanent Fund dividends, or capital gain distributions, see Pub. 550, Investment Income and Expenses, to figure the amount you may treat as your investment income.

Foreign accounts and trusts. Complete Schedule B (Form 1040), Part III, for your child if he or she (a) had a foreign financial account or (b) received a distribution from, or was the grantor of, or transferor to, a foreign trust. If you answer "Yes" to either question, you must file this Schedule B with your return. Enter "Form 8814" next to line 7a or line 8, whichever applies. Also, complete line 7b if applicable.

Change of address. If your child filed a return for a previous year and the address shown on the last return filed is not your child's current address, be sure to notify the IRS, in writing, of the new address. To do this, you may use Form 8822, Change of Address.

Additional information. See Pub. 929, Tax Rules for Children and Dependents, for more details.

Line Instructions

Name and social security number. If filing a joint return, include your spouse's name but enter the social security number of the person whose name is shown first on the return.

Line 1a. Enter all taxable interest income received by your child in 2004. If your child received a Form 1099-INT for tax-exempt interest, such as from municipal bonds, enter the amount and "Tax-exempt interest" on the dotted line next to line 1a. Do not include this interest in the total for line 1a but be sure to include it on line 1b.

If your child received, as a nominee, interest that actually belongs to another person, enter the amount and "ND" (for nominee distribution) on the dotted line next to line 1a. Do not include amounts received as a nominee in the total for line 1a.

If your child had accrued interest that was paid to the seller of a bond, amortizable bond premium (ABP) allowed as a reduction to interest income, or if any original issue discount (OID) is less than the amount shown on your child's Form 1099-OID, enter the nontaxable amount on the dotted line next to line 1a and "Accrued interest," "ABP adjustment," or "OID adjustment," whichever applies. Do not include any nontaxable amounts in the total for line 1a.

Line 1b. If your child received any tax-exempt interest income, such as from certain state and municipal bonds, report it on line 1b. Also, include any exempt-interest dividends your child received as a shareholder in a mutual fund or other regulated investment company.

Note. If line 1b includes tax-exempt interest or exempt-interest dividends paid by a regulated investment company from private activity bonds, see *Alternative minimum tax* on this page.

Line 2. Enter the ordinary dividends received by your child in 2004. Ordinary dividends should be shown in box 1a of Form 1099-DIV. Also, include ordinary dividends your child received through a partnership, an S corporation, or an estate or trust.

If your child received, as a nominee, ordinary dividends that actually belong to another person, enter the amount and "ND" on the dotted line next to line 2. Do not include amounts received as a nominee in the total for line 2.

(continued)

Form 8829

Department of the Treasury
Internal Revenue Service (99)

Expenses for Business Use of Your Home

▶ File only with Schedule C (Form 1040). Use a separate Form 8829 for each home you used for business during the year.

▶ See separate instructions.

OMB No. 1545-1266

2004

Attachment
Sequence No. **66**

Name(s) of proprietor(s)

Your social security number

Part I Part of Your Home Used for Business

1	Area used regularly and exclusively for business, regularly for day care, or for storage of inventory or product samples (see instructions)	1	
2	Total area of home	2	
3	Divide line 1 by line 2. Enter the result as a percentage	3	%

- For day-care facilities not used exclusively for business, also complete lines 4–6.
- All others, skip lines 4–6 and enter the amount from line 3 on line 7.

4	Multiply days used for day care during year by hours used per day	4		h r .
5	Total hours available for use during the year (366 days × 24 hours) (see instructions)	5	8,784	h r .
6	Divide line 4 by line 5. Enter the result as a decimal amount	6	.	
7	Business percentage. For day-care facilities not used exclusively for business, multiply line 6 by line 3 (enter the result as a percentage). All others, enter the amount from line 3 ▶	7		%

Part II Figure Your Allowable Deduction

		(a) Direct expenses	(b) Indirect expenses	
8	Enter the amount from Schedule C, line 29, **plus** any net gain or (loss) derived from the business use of your home and shown on Schedule D or Form 4797. If more than one place of business, see instructions			8
	See instructions for columns (a) and (b) before completing lines 9–20.			
9	Casualty losses (see instructions)			
10	Deductible mortgage interest (see instructions)			
11	Real estate taxes (see instructions)			
12	Add lines 9, 10, and 11			
13	Multiply line 12, column (b) by line 7		13	
14	Add line 12, column (a) and line 13			14
15	Subtract line 14 from line 8. If zero or less, enter -0-			15
16	Excess mortgage interest (see instructions)			
17	Insurance			
18	Repairs and maintenance			
19	Utilities			
20	Other expenses (see instructions)			
21	Add lines 16 through 20			
22	Multiply line 21, column (b) by line 7		22	
23	Carryover of operating expenses from 2003 Form 8829, line 41		23	
24	Add line 21 in column (a), line 22, and line 23			24
25	Allowable operating expenses. Enter the **smaller** of line 15 or line 24			25
26	Limit on excess casualty losses and depreciation. Subtract line 25 from line 15			26
27	Excess casualty losses (see instructions)	27		
28	Depreciation of your home from Part III below	28		
29	Carryover of excess casualty losses and depreciation from 2003 Form 8829, line 42	29		
30	Add lines 27 through 29			30
31	Allowable excess casualty losses and depreciation. Enter the **smaller** of line 26 or line 30			31
32	Add lines 14, 25, and 31			32
33	Casualty loss portion, if any, from lines 14 and 31. Carry amount to **Form 4684,** Section B			33
34	Allowable expenses for business use of your home. Subtract line 33 from line 32. Enter here and on Schedule C, line 30. If your home was used for more than one business, see instructions ▶			34

Part III Depreciation of Your Home

35	Enter the **smaller** of your home's adjusted basis or its fair market value (see instructions)	35	
36	Value of land included on line 35	36	
37	Basis of building. Subtract line 36 from line 35	37	
38	Business basis of building. Multiply line 37 by line 7	38	
39	Depreciation percentage (see instructions)	39	%
40	Depreciation allowable (see instructions). Multiply line 38 by line 39. Enter here and on line 28 above	40	

Part IV Carryover of Unallowed Expenses to 2005

41	Operating expenses. Subtract line 25 from line 24. If less than zero, enter -0-	41	
42	Excess casualty losses and depreciation. Subtract line 31 from line 30. If less than zero, enter -0-	42	

For Paperwork Reduction Act Notice, see page 4 of separate instructions.   Cat. No. 13232M   Form **8829** (2004)

Form **8863**

Department of the Treasury
Internal Revenue Service   (99)

Education Credits
(Hope and Lifetime Learning Credits)
▶ See instructions.
▶ Attach to Form 1040 or Form 1040A.

OMB No. 1545-1618

20**04**

Attachment
Sequence No. **50**

Name(s) shown on return

Your social security number

Caution: *You **cannot** take both an education credit and the tuition and fees deduction (Form 1040, line 27, or Form 1040A, line 19) for the **same student** in the same year.*

Part I   Hope Credit. Caution: *You **cannot** take the Hope credit for more than **2** tax years for the **same student**.*

1	**(a)** Student's name (as shown on page 1 of your tax return) First name Last name	**(b)** Student's social security number (as shown on page 1 of your tax return)	**(c)** Qualified expenses (see instructions). **Do not** enter more than $2,000 for each student.	**(d)** Enter the **smaller** of the amount in column (c) or $1,000	**(e)** Subtract column (d) from column (c)	**(f)** Enter one-half of the amount in column (e)

2	Add the amounts in columns (d) and (f)	**2**		
3	Tentative Hope credit. Add the amounts on line 2, columns (d) and (f). If you are taking the lifetime learning credit for another student, go to Part II; otherwise, go to Part III ▶		**3**	

Part II   **Lifetime Learning Credit**

4	**Caution:** *You **cannot** take the Hope credit and the lifetime learning credit for the **same student** in the same year.*	**(a)** Student's name (as shown on page 1 of your tax return) First name Last name	**(b)** Student's social security number (as shown on page 1 of your tax return)	**(c)** Qualified expenses (see instructions)

5	Add the amounts on line 4, column (c), and enter the total	**5**	
6	Enter the **smaller** of line 5 or $10,000	**6**	
7	Tentative lifetime learning credit. Multiply line 6 by 20% (.20) and go to Part III . . ▶	**7**	

Part III   **Allowable Education Credits**

8	Tentative education credits. Add lines 3 and 7		**8**	
9	Enter: $105,000 if married filing jointly; $52,000 if single, head of household, or qualifying widow(er)	**9**		
10	Enter the amount from Form 1040, line 37*, or Form 1040A, line 22	**10**		
11	Subtract line 10 from line 9. If zero or less, **stop;** you cannot take any education credits	**11**		
12	Enter: $20,000 if married filing jointly; $10,000 if single, head of household, or qualifying widow(er)	**12**		
13	If line 11 is equal to or more than line 12, enter the amount from line 8 on line 14 and go to line 15. If line 11 is less than line 12, divide line 11 by line 12. Enter the result as a decimal (rounded to at least three places)		**13**	× .
14	Multiply line 8 by line 13 . . . . ▶		**14**	
15	Enter the amount from Form 1040, line 45, or Form 1040A, line 28		**15**	
16	Enter the total, if any, of your credits from Form 1040, lines 46 through 48, or Form 1040A, lines 29 and 30		**16**	
17	Subtract line 16 from line 15. If zero or less, **stop;** you cannot take any education credits . . . . ▶		**17**	
18	**Education credits.** Enter the **smaller** of line 14 or line 17 here and on Form 1040, line 49, or Form 1040A, line 31 . . . . ▶		**18**	

* If you are filing Form 2555, 2555-EZ, or 4563 or you are excluding income from Puerto Rico, see Pub. 970 for the amount to enter.

For Paperwork Reduction Act Notice, see page 3.   Cat. No. 25379M   Form **8863** (2004)

General Instructions

Purpose of Form

Use Form 8863 to figure and claim your education credits. The education credits are:

- The Hope credit and
- The lifetime learning credit.

Who Can Take the Credits

You may be able to take the credits if you, your spouse, or a dependent you claim on your tax return was a student enrolled at or attending an eligible educational institution. The credits are based on the amount of qualified expenses paid for the student in 2004 for academic periods beginning in 2004 and the first 3 months of 2005.

 Qualified expenses must be reduced by any expenses paid directly or indirectly using tax-free educational assistance. See Tax-Free Educational Assistance and Refunds of Qualified Expenses on this page.

Note. If a student is claimed as a dependent on another person's tax return, only the person who claims the student as a dependent can claim the credits for the student's qualified expenses. If a student is not claimed as a dependent on another person's tax return, only the student can claim the credits.

Generally, qualified expenses paid on behalf of the student by someone other than the student (such as a relative) are treated as paid by the student. Also, qualified expenses paid (or treated as paid) by a student who is claimed as a dependent on your tax return are treated as paid by you. Therefore, you are treated as having paid expenses that were paid from your dependent student's earnings, gifts, inheritances, savings, etc.

You cannot take the education credits if any of the following apply.

- You are claimed as a dependent on another person's tax return, such as your parent's return (but see the *Note* above).
- Your filing status is married filing separately.
- Your adjusted gross income on Form 1040, line 37, or Form 1040A, line 22, is (a) $105,000 or more if married filing jointly, or (b) $52,000 or more if single, head of household, or qualifying widow(er).
- You are taking a deduction for tuition and fees on Form 1040, line 27, or Form 1040A, line 19, for the same student.
- You (or your spouse) were a nonresident alien for any part of 2004 and the nonresident alien did not elect to be treated as a resident alien.

Additional Information

See Pub. 970, Tax Benefits for Education, for more information about these credits.

Rules That Apply to Both Credits

What Expenses Qualify?

Generally, qualified expenses are amounts paid in 2004 for tuition and fees required for the student's enrollment or attendance at an eligible educational institution. It does not matter whether the expenses were paid in cash, by check, by credit card, or with borrowed funds.

Qualified expenses do not include amounts paid for:

- Room and board, insurance, medical expenses (including student health fees), transportation, or other similar personal, living, or family expenses.

- Course-related books, supplies, equipment, and nonacademic activities, except for fees required to be paid to the institution as a condition of enrollment or attendance.
- Any course or other education involving sports, games, or hobbies, unless such course or other education is part of the student's degree program or (for the lifetime learning credit only) helps the student to acquire or improve job skills.

If you or the student take a deduction for higher education expenses, such as on Schedule A or Schedule C (Form 1040), you cannot use those expenses when figuring your education credits.

 Any qualified expenses used to figure the education credits cannot be taken into account in determining the amount of a distribution from a Coverdell ESA or a qualified tuition program that is excluded from gross income.

Tax-Free Educational Assistance and Refunds of Qualified Expenses

Tax-free educational assistance includes a tax-free scholarship or Pell grant or tax-free employer-provided educational assistance.

You must reduce the total of your qualified expenses by any tax-free educational assistance and by any refunds of qualified expenses. If the refund or tax-free assistance is received in the same year in which the expenses were paid or in the following year before you file your tax return, reduce your qualified expenses by the amount received and figure your education credits using the reduced amount of qualified expenses. If the refund or tax-free assistance is received after you file your return for the year in which the expenses were paid, you must figure the amount by which your education credits would have been reduced if the refund or tax-free assistance had been received in the year for which you claimed the education credits. Include that amount as an additional tax for the year the refund or tax-free assistance was received on the tax line of your 2004 tax return (Form 1040, line 43, or Form 1040A, line 28). Enter the amount and "ECR" next to that line.

Example. You paid $2,250 tuition on December 26, 2003, and your child began college on January 27, 2004. You filed your 2003 tax return on February 2, 2004, and claimed a Hope credit of $1,500. After you filed your return, your child dropped two courses (but maintained one-half of a full-time workload), and you received a refund of $750. You must refigure your 2003 Hope credit using $1,500 of qualified expenses instead of $2,250. The refigured credit is $1,250. You must include the difference of $250 on your 2004 Form 1040, line 43, or Form 1040A, line 28.

Prepaid Expenses

Qualified expenses paid in 2004 for an academic period that begins in the first 3 months of 2005 can be used in figuring your 2004 education credits. For example, if you pay $2,000 in December 2004 for qualified tuition for the 2005 winter quarter that begins in January 2005, you can use that $2,000 in figuring your 2004 education credits (if you meet all the other requirements).

 You cannot use any amount paid in 2003 or 2005 to figure your 2004 education credits.

What Is an Eligible Educational Institution?

An eligible educational institution is generally any accredited public, nonprofit, or proprietary (private) college, university, vocational school, or other postsecondary institution. Also, the institution must be eligible to participate in a student aid program administered by the Department of Education. Virtually all accredited postsecondary institutions meet this definition.

Specific Instructions

Part I
Hope Credit

You may be able to take a credit of up to $1,500 for qualified expenses (defined earlier) paid for each student who qualifies for the Hope credit. You can take the Hope credit for a student if all of the following apply.

● As of the beginning of 2004, the student had not completed the first 2 years of postsecondary education (generally, the freshman and sophomore years of college), as determined by the eligible educational institution. For this purpose, do not include academic credit awarded solely because of the student's performance on proficiency examinations.

● The student was enrolled in 2004 in a program that leads to a degree, certificate, or other recognized educational credential.

● The student was taking at least one-half the normal full-time workload for his or her course of study for at least one academic period beginning in 2004.

● The Hope credit was not claimed for that student's expenses in more than one prior tax year.

● The student has not been convicted of a felony for possessing or distributing a controlled substance.

If a student does not meet all of the above conditions, you may be able to take the lifetime learning credit for part or all of that student's qualified expenses instead.

Line 1

Complete columns (a) through (f) on line 1 for each student who qualifies for and for whom you elect to take the Hope credit.

Column (c)

Enter only qualified expenses paid for the student in 2004 for academic periods beginning after 2003 but before April 1, 2005, as explained earlier. If the student's expenses are more than $2,000, enter $2,000.

Note. If you have more than three students who qualify for the Hope credit, enter "See attached" next to line 1 and attach a statement with the required information for each additional student. Include the totals from line 1, columns (d) and (f), for all students in the amount you enter on line 2, columns (d) and (f).

Part II
Lifetime Learning Credit

The maximum lifetime learning credit for 2004 is $2,000, regardless of the number of students.

You cannot take the lifetime learning credit for any student for whom you are taking the Hope credit.

Line 4

Complete columns (a) through (c) for each student for whom you are taking the lifetime learning credit.

Column (c)

Enter only qualified expenses paid for the student in 2004 for academic periods beginning after 2003 but before April 1, 2005, as explained earlier.

Note. If you are taking the lifetime learning credit for more than three students, enter "See attached" next to line 4 and attach a statement with the required information for each additional student. Include the totals from line 4, column (c), for all students in the amount you enter on line 5.

Paperwork Reduction Act Notice. We ask for the information on this form to carry out the Internal Revenue laws of the United States. You are required to give us the information. We need it to ensure that you are complying with these laws and to allow us to figure and collect the right amount of tax.

You are not required to provide the information requested on a form that is subject to the Paperwork Reduction Act unless the form displays a valid OMB control number. Books or records relating to a form or its instructions must be retained as long as their contents may become material in the administration of any Internal Revenue law. Generally, tax returns and return information are confidential, as required by Internal Revenue Code section 6103.

The time needed to complete and file this form will vary depending on individual circumstances. The estimated average time is: **Recordkeeping,** 12 min.; **Learning about the law or the form,** 8 min.; **Preparing the form,** 32 min.; **Copying, assembling, and sending the form to the IRS,** 33 min.

If you have comments concerning the accuracy of these time estimates or suggestions for making this form simpler, we would be happy to hear from you. See the Instructions for Form 1040 or Form 1040A.

Appendix C

MODIFIED ACRS AND
ORIGINAL ACRS TABLES

ORIGINAL ACRS TABLES

Modified ACRS Accelerated Depreciation Percentages
Using the Half Year Convention
for 3-, 5-, 7-, 10-, 15-, and 20-Year Property
Placed in Service after December 31, 1986

Recovery Year	Property Class					
	3-Year	5-Year	7-Year	10-Year	15-Year	20-Year
1	33.33	20.00	14.29	10.00	5.00	3.750
2	44.45	32.00	24.49	18.00	9.50	7.219
3	14.81	19.20	17.49	14.40	8.55	6.677
4	7.41	11.52	12.49	11.52	7.70	6.177
5		11.52	8.93	9.22	6.93	5.713
6		5.76	8.92	7.37	6.23	5.285
7			8.93	6.55	5.90	4.888
8			4.46	6.55	5.90	4.522
9				6.56	5.91	4.462
10				6.55	5.90	4.461
11				3.28	5.91	4.462
12					5.90	4.461
13					5.91	4.462
14					5.90	4.461
15					5.91	4.462
16					2.95	4.461
17						4.462
18						4.461
19						4.462
20						4.461
21						2.231

Modified ACRS Depreciation Rates
for Residential Rental Property
Placed in Service after December 31, 1986

Recovery Year	Month Placed in Service					
	1	2	3	4	5	6
1	3.485	3.182	2.879	2.576	2.273	1.970
2	3.636	3.636	3.636	3.636	3.636	3.636
3	3.636	3.636	3.636	3.636	3.636	3.636
4	3.636	3.636	3.636	3.636	3.636	3.636
5	3.636	3.636	3.636	3.636	3.636	3.636
6	3.636	3.636	3.636	3.636	3.636	3.636
7	3.636	3.636	3.636	3.636	3.636	3.636
8	3.636	3.636	3.636	3.636	3.636	3.636
9	3.636	3.636	3.636	3.636	3.636	3.636
10	3.637	3.637	3.637	3.637	3.637	3.637
11	3.636	3.636	3.636	3.636	3.636	3.636
12	3.637	3.637	3.637	3.637	3.637	3.637
13	3.636	3.636	3.636	3.636	3.636	3.636
14	3.637	3.637	3.637	3.637	3.637	3.637
15	3.636	3.636	3.636	3.636	3.636	3.636
16	3.637	3.637	3.637	3.637	3.637	3.637
17	3.636	3.636	3.636	3.636	3.636	3.636
18	3.637	3.637	3.637	3.637	3.637	3.637
19	3.636	3.636	3.636	3.636	3.636	3.636
20	3.637	3.637	3.637	3.637	3.637	3.636
21	3.636	3.636	3.636	3.636	3.636	3.636
22	3.637	3.637	3.637	3.637	3.637	3.637
23	3.636	3.636	3.636	3.636	3.636	3.636
24	3.637	3.637	3.637	3.637	3.637	3.637
25	3.636	3.636	3.636	3.636	3.636	3.636
26	3.637	3.637	3.637	3.637	3.637	3.637
27	3.636	3.636	3.636	3.636	3.636	3.636
28	1.970	2.273	2.576	2.879	3.182	3.485
29	0.000	0.000	0.000	0.000	0.000	0.000

Recovery Year	Month Placed in Service					
	7	8	9	10	11	12
1	1.667	1.364	1.061	0.758	0.455	0.152
2	3.636	3.636	3.636	3.636	3.636	3.636
3	3.636	3.636	3.636	3.636	3.636	3.636
4	3.636	3.636	3.636	3.636	3.636	3.636
5	3.636	3.636	3.636	3.636	3.636	3.636
6	3.636	3.636	3.636	3.636	3.636	3.636
7	3.636	3.636	3.636	3.636	3.636	3.636
8	3.636	3.636	3.636	3.636	3.636	3.636
9	3.636	3.636	3.636	3.636	3.636	3.636
10	3.636	3.636	3.636	3.636	3.636	3.636
11	3.637	3.637	3.637	3.637	3.637	3.637
12	3.636	3.636	3.636	3.636	3.636	3.636
13	3.637	3.637	3.637	3.637	3.637	3.637
14	3.636	3.636	3.636	3.636	3.636	3.636
15	3.637	3.637	3.637	3.637	3.637	3.637
16	3.636	3.636	3.636	3.636	3.636	3.636
17	3.637	3.637	3.637	3.637	3.637	3.637
18	3.636	3.636	3.636	3.636	3.636	3.636
19	3.637	3.637	3.637	3.637	3.637	3.637
20	3.636	3.636	3.636	3.636	3.636	3.636
21	3.637	3.637	3.637	3.637	3.637	3.637
22	3.636	3.636	3.636	3.636	3.636	3.636
23	3.637	3.637	3.637	3.637	3.637	3.637
24	3.636	3.636	3.636	3.636	3.636	3.636
25	3.637	3.637	3.637	3.637	3.637	3.637
26	3.636	3.636	3.636	3.636	3.636	3.636
27	3.637	3.637	3.637	3.637	3.637	3.637
28	3.636	3.636	3.636	3.636	3.636	3.636
29	0.152	0.455	0.758	1.061	1.364	1.667

Modified A CRS Depreciation Percentages
for Nonresidential Real Property
Placed in Service after December 31, 1986
and before May 13, 1993

Recovery Year	Month Placed in Service					
	1	2	3	4	5	6
1	3.042	2.778	2.513	2.249	1.984	1.720
2	3.175	3.175	3.175	3.175	3.175	3.175
3	3.175	3.175	3.175	3.175	3.175	3.175
4	3.175	3.175	3.175	3.175	3.175	3.175
5	3.175	3.175	3.175	3.175	3.175	3.175
6	3.175	3.175	3.175	3.175	3.175	3.175
7	3.175	3.175	3.175	3.175	3.175	3.175
8	3.175	3.174	3.175	3.174	3.175	3.174
9	3.174	3.175	3.174	3.175	3.174	3.175
10	3.175	3.174	3.175	3.174	3.175	3.174
11	3.174	3.175	3.174	3.175	3.174	3.175
12	3.175	3.174	3.175	3.174	3.175	3.174
13	3.174	3.175	3.174	3.175	3.174	3.175
14	3.175	3.174	3.175	3.174	3.175	3.174
15	3.174	3.175	3.174	3.175	3.174	3.175
16	3.175	3.174	3.175	3.174	3.175	3.174
17	3.174	3.175	3.174	3.175	3.174	3.175
18	3.175	3.174	3.175	3.174	3.175	3.174
19	3.174	3.175	3.174	3.175	3.174	3.175
20	3.175	3.174	3.175	3.174	3.175	3.174
21	3.174	3.175	3.174	3.175	3.174	3.175
22	3.175	3.174	3.175	3.174	3.175	3.174
23	3.174	3.175	3.174	3.175	3.174	3.175
24	3.175	3.174	3.175	3.174	3.175	3.174
25	3.174	3.175	3.174	3.175	3.174	3.175
26	3.175	3.174	3.175	3.174	3.175	3.174
27	3.174	3.175	3.174	3.175	3.174	3.175
28	3.175	3.174	3.175	3.174	3.175	3.174
29	3.174	3.175	3.174	3.175	3.174	3.175
30	3.175	3.174	3.175	3.174	3.175	3.174
31	3.174	3.175	3.174	3.175	3.174	3.175
32	1.720	1.984	2.249	2.513	2.778	3.042
33	0.000	0.000	0.000	0.000	0.000	0.000

Recovery Year	Month Placed in Service					
	7	8	9	10	11	12
1	1.455	1.190	0.926	0.661	0.397	0.132
2	3.175	3.175	3.175	3.175	3.175	3.175
3	3.175	3.175	3.175	3.175	3.175	3.175
4	3.175	3.175	3.175	3.175	3.175	3.175
5	3.175	3.175	3.175	3.175	3.175	3.175
6	3.175	3.175	3.175	3.175	3.175	3.175
7	3.175	3.175	3.175	3.175	3.175	3.175
8	3.175	3.175	3.175	3.175	3.175	3.175
9	3.174	3.175	3.175	3.175	3.174	3.175
10	3.175	3.174	3.175	3.174	3.175	3.174
11	3.174	3.175	3.174	3.175	3.174	3.175
12	3.175	3.174	3.175	3.174	3.175	3.174
13	3.174	3.175	3.174	3.175	3.174	3.175
14	3.175	3.174	3.175	3.174	3.175	3.174
15	3.174	3.175	3.174	3.175	3.174	3.175
16	3.175	3.174	3.175	3.174	3.175	3.174
17	3.174	3.175	3.174	3.175	3.174	3.175
18	3.175	3.174	3.175	3.174	3.175	3.174
19	3.174	3.175	3.174	3.175	3.174	3.175
20	3.175	3.174	3.175	3.174	3.175	3.174
21	3.174	3.175	3.174	3.175	3.174	3.175
22	3.175	3.174	3.175	3.174	3.175	3.174
23	3.174	3.175	3.174	3.175	3.174	3.175
24	3.175	3.174	3.175	3.174	3.175	3.174
25	3.174	3.175	3.174	3.175	3.174	3.175
26	3.175	3.174	3.175	3.174	3.175	3.174
27	3.174	3.175	3.174	3.175	3.174	3.175
28	3.175	3.174	3.175	3.174	3.175	3.174
29	3.174	3.175	3.174	3.175	3.174	3.175
30	3.175	3.174	3.175	3.174	3.175	3.174
31	3.174	3.175	3.174	3.175	3.174	3.175
32	3.175	3.174	3.175	3.174	3.175	3.174
33	0.132	0.397	0.661	0.926	1.190	1.455

Modified A CRS Depreciation Percentages
for Nonresidential Real Property
Placed in Service after May 13, 1993

Month Placed in Service	Recovery Year				
	1	2	· · · ·	39	40
1	2.461%	2.564%		2.564%	0.107%
2	2.247	2.564		2.564	0.321
3	2.033	2.564		2.564	0.535
4	1.819	2.564		2.564	0.749
5	1.605	2.564		2.564	0.963
6	1.391	2.564		2.564	1.177
7	1.177	2.564		2.564	1.391
8	0.963	2.564		2.564	1.605
9	0.749	2.564		2.564	1.819
10	0.535	2.564		2.564	2.033
11	0.321	2.564		2.564	2.247
12	0.107	2.564		2.564	2.461

Modified ACRS Accelerated Depreciation Percentages

Using the Mid-Quarter Convention

for 3-, 5-, 7-, 10-, 15-, and 20-Year Property

Placed in Service after December 31, 1986

3-Year Property:

Recovery Year	Quarter Placed in Service			
	1	2	3	4
1	58.33	41.67	25.00	8.33
2	27.78	38.89	50.00	61.11
3	12.35	14.14	16.67	20.37
4	1.54	5.30	8.33	10.19

5-Year Property:

	1	2	3	4
1	35.00	25.00	15.00	5.00
2	26.00	30.00	34.00	38.00
3	15.60	18.00	20.40	22.80
4	11.01	11.37	12.24	13.68
5	11.01	11.37	11.30	10.94
6	1.38	4.26	7.06	9.58

7-Year Property:

	1	2	3	4
1	25.00	17.85	10.71	3.57
2	21.43	23.47	25.51	27.55
3	15.31	16.76	18.22	19.68
4	10.93	11.37	13.02	14.06
5	8.75	8.87	9.30	10.04
6	8.74	8.87	8.85	8.73
7	8.75	8.87	8.86	8.73
8	1.09	3.33	5.53	7.64

10-Year Property:

	1	2	3	4
1	17.50	12.50	7.50	2.50
2	16.50	17.50	18.50	19.50
3	13.20	14.00	14.80	15.60
4	10.56	11.20	11.84	12.48
5	8.45	8.96	9.47	9.98
6	6.76	7.17	7.58	7.99
7	6.55	6.55	6.55	6.55
8	6.55	6.55	6.55	6.55
9	6.56	6.56	6.56	6.56
10	0.82	6.55	6.55	6.55
11		2.46	4.10	5.74

Recovery Year	Quarter Placed in Service			
	1	2	3	4
15-Year Property:				
1	8.75	6.25	3.75	1.25
2	9.13	9.38	9.63	9.88
3	8.21	8.44	8.66	8.89
4	7.39	7.59	7.80	8.00
5	6.65	6.83	7.02	7.20
6	5.99	6.15	6.31	6.48
7	5.90	5.91	5.90	5.90
8	5.91	5.90	5.90	5.90
9	5.90	5.91	5.91	5.90
10	5.91	5.90	5.90	5.91
11	5.90	5.91	5.91	5.90
12	5.91	5.90	5.90	5.91
13	5.90	5.91	5.91	5.90
14	5.91	5.90	5.90	5.91
15	5.90	5.91	5.91	5.90
16	0.74	2.21	3.69	5.17
20-Year Property:				
1	6.563	4.688	2.813	0.938
2	7.000	7.148	7.289	7.430
3	6.482	6.612	6.742	6.872
4	5.996	6.116	6.237	6.357
5	5.546	5.658	5.769	5.880
6	5.130	5.233	5.336	5.439
7	4.746	4.841	4.936	5.031
8	4.459	4.478	4.566	4.654
9	4.459	4.463	4.460	4.458
10	4.459	4.463	4.460	4.458
11	4.459	4.463	4.460	4.458
12	4.460	4.463	4.460	4.458
13	4.459	4.463	4.461	4.458
14	4.460	4.463	4.460	4.458
15	4.459	4.462	4.461	4.458
16	4.460	4.463	4.460	4.458
17	4.459	4.462	4.461	4.458
18	4.460	4.463	4.460	4.459
19	4.459	4.462	4.461	4.458
20	4.460	4.463	4.460	4.459
21	0.557	1.673	2.788	3.901

Alternative Depreciation System
Recovery Periods

General Rule: Recovery period is the property's class life unless:
1. There is no class life (see below), or
2. A special class life has been designated (see below).

Type of Property	Recovery Period
Personal property with no class life	12 years
Nonresidential real property with no class life	40 years
Residential rental property with no class life	40 years
Cars, light general purpose trucks, certain technological equipment, and semiconductor manufacturing equipment	5 years
Computer-based telephone central office switching equipment	9.5 years
Railroad track	10 years
Single purpose agricultural or horticultural structures	15 years
Municipal waste water treatment plants, telephone distribution plants	24 years
Low-income housing financed by tax-exempt bonds	27.5 years
Municipal sewers	50 years

Modified ACRS and ADS Straight-Line Depreciation Percentages
Using the Half-Year Convention
for 3-, 5-, 7-, 10-, 15-, and 20-Year Property
Placed in Service after December 31, 1986

Recovery Year	Property Class					
	3-Year	*5-Year*	*7-Year*	*10-Year*	*15-Year*	*20-Year*
1	16.67	10.00	7.14	5.00	3.33	2.50
2	33.33	20.00	14.29	10.00	6.67	5.00
3	33.33	20.00	14.29	10.00	6.67	5.00
4	16.67	20.00	14.28	10.00	6.67	5.00
5		20.00	14.29	10.00	6.67	5.00
6		10.00	14.28	10.00	6.67	5.00
7			14.29	10.00	6.67	5.00
8			7.14	10.00	6.66	5.00
9				10.00	6.67	5.00
10				10.00	6.66	5.00
11				5.00	6.67	5.00
12					6.66	5.00
13					6.67	5.00
14					6.66	5.00
15					6.67	5.00
16					3.33	5.00
17						5.00
18						5.00
19						5.00
20						5.00
21						2.50

ADS Straight-Line Depreciation Percentages
Real Property
Using the Mid-Month Convention
for Property Placed in Service after December 31, 1986

Month Placed In Service	Recovery Year		
	1	2-40	41
1	2.396	2.500	0.104
2	2.188	2.500	0.312
3	1.979	2.500	0.521
4	1.771	2.500	0.729
5	1.563	2.500	0.937
6	1.354	2.500	1.146
7	1.146	2.500	1.354
8	0.938	2.500	1.562
9	0.729	2.500	1.771
10	0.521	2.500	1.979
11	0.313	2.500	2.187
12	0.104	2.500	2.396

Original ACRS
Accelerated Recovery Percentages
for 3-, 5-, 10-, and 15-Year Public Utility Property

Personalty Placed in Service after 1980 and before 1987

Recovery Year	Property Class			
	3-Year	*5-Year*	*10-Year*	*15-Year Public Utility*
1	25 %	15 %	8 %	5 %
2	38	22	14	10
3	37	21	12	9
4		21	10	8
5		21	10	7
6			10	7
7			9	6
8			9	6
9			9	6
10			9	6
11				6
12				6
13				6
14				6
15				6

Original ACRS
Accelerated Recovery Percentages
for 15-Year Realty

Placed in Service after 1980 and before March 16, 1984

Recovery Year	Month Placed in Service											
	1	2	3	4	5	6	7	8	9	10	11	12
1	12	11	10	9	8	7	6	5	4	3	2	1
2	10	10	11	11	11	11	11	11	11	11	11	12
3	9	9	9	9	10	10	10	10	10	10	10	10
4	8	8	8	8	8	8	9	9	9	9	C	9
5	7	7	7	7	7	7	8	8	8	8	8	8
6	6	6	6	6	7	7	7	7	7	7	7	7
7	6	6	6	6	6	6	6	6	6	6	6	6
8	6	6	6	6	6	6	5	6	6	6	6	6
9	6	6	6	6	5	6	5	5	5	6	6	6
10	5	6	6	6	5	5	5	5	5	5	6	5
11	5	5	5	5	5	5	5	5	5	5	5	5
12	5	5	5	5	5	5	5	5	5	5	5	5
13	5	5	5	5	5	5	5	5	5	5	5	5
14	5	5	5	5	5	5	5	5	5	5	5	5
15	5	5	5	5	5	5	5	5	5	5	5	5
16			1	1	2	2	3	3	4	4	4	5

Original ACRS
Accelerated Recovery Percentages
for Low-Income Housing

Placed in Service after 1980 and before March 16, 1984

Recovery Year	Month Placed in Service											
	1	2	3	4	5	6	7	8	9	10	11	12
1	13	12	11	10	9	8	7	6	4	3	2	1
2	12	12	12	12	12	12	12	13	13	13	13	13
3	10	10	10	10	11	11	11	11	11	11	11	11
4	9	9	9	9	9	9	9	9	10	10	10	10
5	8	8	8	8	8	8	8	8	8	8	8	9
6	7	7	7	7	7	7	7	7	7	7	7	7
7	6	6	6	6	6	6	6	6	6	6	6	6
8	5	5	5	5	5	5	5	5	5	5	6	6
9	5	5	5	5	5	5	5	5	5	5	5	5
10	5	5	5	5	5	5	5	5	5	5	5	5
11	4	5	5	5	5	5	5	5	5	5	5	5
12	4	4	4	5	4	5	5	5	5	5	5	5
13	4	4	4	4	4	4	5	4	5	5	5	5
14	4	4	4	4	4	4	4	4	4	5	4	4
15	4	4	4	4	4	4	4	4	4	4	4	4
16			1	1	2	2	2	3	3	3	4	4

Original ACRS
Accelerated Recovery Percentages
for 18-Year Realty

Realty Placed in Service after March 15, 1984 and before May 9, 1985

Recovery Year	Month Placed in Service											
	1	2	3	4	5	6	7	8	9	10	11	12

The applicable percentage is:

Recovery Year	1	2	3	4	5	6	7	8	9	10	11	12
1	9	9	8	7	6	5	4	4	3	2	1	0.4
2	9	9	9	9	9	9	9	9	9	10	10	10.0
3	8	8	8	8	8	8	8	8	9	9	9	9.0
4	7	7	7	7	7	8	8	8	8	8	8	8.0
5	7	7	7	7	7	7	7	7	7	7	7	7.0
6	6	6	6	6	6	6	6	6	6	6	6	6.0
7	5	5	5	5	6	6	6	6	6	6	6	6.0
8	5	5	5	5	5	5	5	5	5	5	5	5.0
9	5	5	5	5	5	5	5	5	5	5	5	5.0
10	5	5	5	5	5	5	5	5	5	5	5	5.0
11	5	5	5	5	5	5	5	5	5	5	5	5.0
12	5	5	5	5	5	5	5	5	5	5	5	5.0
13	4	4	4	5	4	4	5	4	4	4	5	5.0
14	4	4	4	4	4	4	4	4	4	4	4	4.0
15	4	4	4	4	4	4	4	4	4	4	4	4.0
16	4	4	4	4	4	4	4	4	4	4	4	4.0
17	4	4	4	4	4	4	4	4	4	4	4	4.0
18	4	3	4	4	4	4	4	4	4	4	4	4.0
19		1	1	1	2	2	2	3	3	3	3	3.6

Original ACRS
Accelerated Cost Recovery Percentages
for 19-Year Realty

Realty Placed in Service after May 8, 1985 and before 1987

Recovery Year	Month Placed in Service											
	1	2	3	4	5	6	7	8	9	10	11	12

The applicable percentage is:

Recovery Year	1	2	3	4	5	6	7	8	9	10	11	12
1	8.8	8.1	7.3	6.5	5.8	5.0	4.2	3.5	2.7	1.9	1.1	0.4
2	8.4	8.5	8.5	8.6	8.7	8.8	8.8	8.9	9.0	9.0	9.1	9.2
3	7.6	7.7	7.7	7.8	7.9	7.9	8.0	8.1	8.1	8.2	8.3	8.3
4	6.9	7.0	7.0	7.1	7.1	7.2	7.3	7.3	7.4	7.4	7.5	7.6
5	6.3	6.3	6.4	6.4	6.5	6.5	6.6	6.6	6.7	6.8	6.8	6.9
6	5.7	5.7	5.8	5.9	5.9	5.9	6.0	6.0	6.1	6.1	6.2	6.2
7	5.2	5.2	5.3	5.3	5.3	5.4	5.4	5.5	5.5	5.6	5.6	5.6
8	4.7	4.7	4.8	4.8	4.8	4.9	4.9	5.0	5.0	5.1	5.1	5.1
9	4.2	4.3	4.3	4.4	4.4	4.5	4.5	4.5	4.5	4.6	4.6	4.7
10	4.2	4.2	4.2	4.2	4.2	4.2	4.2	4.2	4.2	4.2	4.2	4.2
11	4.2	4.2	4.2	4.2	4.2	4.2	4.2	4.2	4.2	4.2	4.2	4.2
12	4.2	4.2	4.2	4.2	4.2	4.2	4.2	4.2	4.2	4.2	4.2	4.2
13	4.2	4.2	4.2	4.2	4.2	4.2	4.2	4.2	4.2	4.2	4.2	4.2
14	4.2	4.2	4.2	4.2	4.2	4.2	4.2	4.2	4.2	4.2	4.2	4.2
15	4.2	4.2	4.2	4.2	4.2	4.2	4.2	4.2	4.2	4.2	4.2	4.2
16	4.2	4.2	4.2	4.2	4.2	4.2	4.2	4.2	4.2	4.2	4.2	4.2
17	4.2	4.2	4.2	4.2	4.2	4.2	4.2	4.2	4.2	4.2	4.2	4.2
18	4.2	4.2	4.2	4.2	4.2	4.2	4.2	4.2	4.2	4.2	4.2	4.2
19	4.2	4.2	4.2	4.2	4.2	4.2	4.2	4.2	4.2	4.2	4.2	4.2
20	0.2	0.5	0.9	1.2	1.6	1.9	2.3	2.6	3.0	3.3	3.7	4.0

Original ACRS
Straight-Line Recovery Percentages
for 3-, 5-, 10-, and 15-Year Public Utility Property
Personally Placed in Service Before 1987

Recovery Year	Optional Recovery Period in Years							
	3	5	10	12	15	25	35	45
The applicable percentage is:								
1	17	10	5	4	3	2	1	1.1
2	33	20	10	9	7	4	3	2.3
3	33	20	10	9	7	4	3	2.3
4	17	20	10	9	7	4	3	2.3
5		20	10	9	7	4	3	2.3
6		10	10	8	7	4	3	2.3
7			10	8	7	4	3	2.3
8			10	8	7	4	3	2.3
9			10	8	7	4	3	2.3
10			10	8	7	4	3	2.3
11			5	8	7	4	3	2.3
12				8	6	4	3	2.2
13				4	6	4	3	2.2
14					6	4	3	2.2
15					6	4	3	2.2
16					3	4	3	2.2
17						4	3	2.2
18						4	3	2.2
19						4	3	2.2
20						4	3	2.2
21						4	3	2.2
22						4	3	2.2
23						4	3	2.2
24						4	3	2.2
25						4	3	2.2
26						2	3	2.2
27							3	2.2
28							3	2.2
29							3	2.2
30							3	2.2
31							3	2.2
32							2	2.2
33							2	2.2
34							2	2.2
35							2	2.2
36							1	2.2
37								2.2
38								2.2
39								2.2
40								2.2
41								2.2
42								2.2
43								2.2
44								2.2
45								2.2
46								1.1

Original ACRS
Straight-Line Recovery Percentages
for 18-Year Realty

Realty Placed in Service after March 15, 1984 and before May 9, 1985

Month Placed in Service

Recovery Year	1-2	3-4	5-7	8-9	10-11	12
	The applicable percentage is:					
1	5	4	3	2	1	0.2
2	6	6	6	6	6	6.0
3	6	6	6	6	6	6.0
4	6	6	6	6	6	6.0
5	6	6	6	6	6	6.0
6	6	6	6	6	6	6.0
7	6	6	6	6	6	6.0
8	6	6	6	6	6	6.0
9	6	6	6	6	6	6.0
10	6	6	6	6	6	6.0
11	5	5	5	5	5	5.8
12	5	5	5	5	5	5.0
13	5	5	5	5	5	5.0
14	5	5	5	5	5	5.0
15	5	5	5	5	5	5.0
16	5	5	5	5	5	5.0
17	5	5	5	5	5	5.0
18	5	5	5	5	5	5.0
19	1	2	3	4	5	5.0

Original ACRS
Straight-Line Recovery Percentages
for 19-Year Realty

Realty Placed in Service after May 8, 1985 and before 1987

Recovery Year	Month Placed in Service											
	1	2	3	4	5	6	7	8	9	10	11	12

The applicable percentage is:

Recovery Year	1	2	3	4	5	6	7	8	9	10	11	12
1	5.0	4.6	4.2	3.7	3.3	2.9	2.4	2.0	1.5	1.1	.7	.2
2	5.3	5.3	5.3	5.3	5.3	5.3	5.3	5.3	5.3	5.3	5.3	5.3
3	5.3	5.3	5.3	5.3	5.3	5.3	5.3	5.3	5.3	5.3	5.3	5.3
4	5.3	5.3	5.3	5.3	5.3	5.3	5.3	5.3	5.3	5.3	5.3	5.3
5	5.3	5.3	5.3	5.3	5.3	5.3	5.3	5.3	5.3	5.3	5.3	5.3
6	5.3	5.3	5.3	5.3	5.3	5.3	5.3	5.3	5.3	5.3	5.3	5.3
7	5.3	5.3	5.3	5.3	5.3	5.3	5.3	5.3	5.3	5.3	5.3	5.3
8	5.3	5.3	5.3	5.3	5.3	5.3	5.3	5.3	5.3	5.3	5.3	5.3
9	5.3	5.3	5.3	5.3	5.3	5.3	5.3	5.3	5.3	5.3	5.3	5.3
10	5.3	5.3	5.3	5.3	5.3	5.3	5.3	5.3	5.3	5.3	5.3	5.3
11	5.3	5.3	5.3	5.3	5.3	5.3	5.3	5.3	5.3	5.3	5.3	5.3
12	5.3	5.3	5.3	5.3	5.3	5.3	5.3	5.3	5.3	5.3	5.3	5.3
13	5.3	5.3	5.3	5.3	5.3	5.3	5.3	5.3	5.3	5.3	5.3	5.3
14	5.2	5.2	5.2	5.2	5.2	5.2	5.2	5.2	5.2	5.2	5.2	5.2
15	5.2	5.2	5.2	5.2	5.2	5.2	5.2	5.2	5.2	5.2	5.2	5.2
16	5.2	5.2	5.2	5.2	5.2	5.2	5.2	5.2	5.2	5.2	5.2	5.2
17	5.2	5.2	5.2	5.2	5.2	5.2	5.2	5.2	5.2	5.2	5.2	5.2
18	5.2	5.2	5.2	5.2	5.2	5.2	5.2	5.2	5.2	5.2	5.2	5.2
19	5.2	5.2	5.2	5.2	5.2	5.2	5.2	5.2	5.2	5.2	5.2	5.2
20	.2	.6	1.0	1.5	1.9	2.3	2.8	3.2	3.7	4.1	4.5	5.0

Appendix D

TWO INDIVIDUAL COMPREHENSIVE TAX RETURN PROBLEMS FOR 2004

1. **David R. and Susan L. Holman**

   a. David and Susan Holman are married and file a joint return. David is 38 years of age and Susan is 36. David is a self-employed certified real estate appraiser (C.R.E.), and Susan is employed by Wells Fargo Bank as a trust officer. They have two children: Richard Lawrence, age 7, and Karen Ann, age 4. The Holmans currently live at 5901 W. 75th Street, Los Angeles, California 90034, in a home they purchased and occupied on September 6, 2004.

   Until August 12, 2004 the Holman family lived at 3085 Windmill Lane in Dallas, Texas, where David was employed by Vestpar Company, a real estate appraisal company and Susan was a bank officer for First National Bank. They sold their home in Dallas and moved to Los Angeles so that Susan could assume her new job as a trust officer and David could become self-employed.

   b. David and Susan sold their home in Dallas for $315,000 and incurred the following expenses:

Sales commission	$18,900
Attorney's fee	1,800
Title insurance	2,650
Document preparation fee	90
Recording fee	30
Pest inspection fee	190
Prepayment penalty for early retirement of home mortgage (3 points)	1,500

   The Holmans had purchased the Dallas home on August 4, 1996 and never held it for rent or used it for business purposes. The home originally cost $177,500, and they had paid $6,200 for a cedar fence and $7,900 for landscaping. Within seven weeks of receiving a contract of sale on their house, the Holmans paid $8,500 for interior and exterior painting and $600 for steam-cleaning of the carpets. The sale was closed on August 1, 2004 and the Holmans were required to move out of the home by August 15, 2004.

   c. In moving from Dallas to Los Angeles, the Holmans incurred the following expenses, none of which were reimbursed:

Cost of moving household goods	$9,250
Meals	295
Lodging	350
House-hunting expenses (including $150 for meals)	1,000
Temporary living expenses (20 days; including meals costing $400)	1,700

   Not included in any of the above expenses are the costs for driving two automobiles from Dallas to Los Angeles. David and Susan each drove a car, taking turns driving with the children. Although neither one of them kept receipts, Susan noted that her auto mileage was 1,500 miles. In addition, David noted that the number of miles from their old home to their old workplace was 24 miles, and the number of miles from their old home to their new workplace is 1,514 miles.

d. The Holmans purchased their new home for $525,000 by making a $125,000 down payment and financing the remaining balance with a 30-year, 6% conventional mortgage loan from California Federal Savings and Loan. They were required to prepay 2 points ($8,000) in return for the favorable mortgage terms. New furniture and drapes cost an additional $27,500.

e. The Holmans received the following Forms W-2, reporting their salaries for 2004:

1) David R. Holman, Social Security No. 452-64-5837:

Gross salary.	$75,000
Federal income taxes withheld.	9,050
F.I.C.A. taxes withheld:	
Social security.	4,650
Medicare.	1,088

2) Susan L. Holman, Social Security No. 467-32-5452:

	First Nat'l Bank	Wells Fargo Bank	Total
Gross salary.	$17,500	$34,000	$51,500
Federal income taxes withheld.	1,100	4,150	5,250
F.I.C.A. taxes withheld:			
Social security.	1,085	2,108	3,193
Medicare.	254	493	747
California income taxes withheld.	—	2,950	2,950

f. On October 1, 2004 David rented office space at 5510 Wacker Drive, Los Angeles, California 90025. The terms of the one-year lease agreement called for a monthly rent of $800, with the first and last month's rent paid in advance.

David decided to operate his business in the name of "David R. Holman, Certified Real Estate Appraiser," and he elected to use the cash method of accounting for his revenues and expenses. Thze following items relate to his business for 2004:

Gross receipts	$85,000
Expenses:	
Advertising	250
Bank service charges	50
Dues and publications.	450
Insurance	600*
Interest	275
Professional services	525
Office rent.	3,200**
Office supplies	700
Meals and entertainment.	500
Miscellaneous expenses.	75

*Three months of coverage
**Includes prepayment of rent for September, 2005

David drove hisf personal automobile, a 2003 Buick LeSabre, 5,000 miles for business purposes from October 1 through December 31. Rather than keeping receipts, he elected to use the automatic mileage method (37.5 cents per mile for 2004) for determining his auto expenses. David's total auto mileage for the year was 20,000 miles.

On October 3, 2004 David purchased the following furniture and equipment for use in his business:

Office furniture	$17,000
Copying machine	5,800
Computers	6,500
Laser printers	2,500
Telephone system	3,100

David elects to expense the maximum amount allowed under the optional expensing rules of § 179. He also elects to compute the maximum depreciation allowance using the appropriate MACRS percentages.

g. The Holmans received interest income during 2004 from the following:

U.S. Treasury bills	$1,475
First National Bank, Dallas	625
Wells Fargo Bank	400
Tarrant County municipal bonds	800

h. David and Susan received the following dividends during 2004:

Ford Motor Company	$ 300
Eastman Kodak Company	575
IBM Corporation	125
General Motors stock dividend (20 new shares of stock valued at $60 per share, received March 9, 2004)	1,200

i. The Holmans have never maintained foreign bank accounts or created foreign trusts.

j. The Holmans report the following stock transactions for 2004:

1) Sold 100 shares of IBM stock for $120 per share on August 1, 2004. David had inherited 500 shares of IBM stock from his uncle on July 18, 2000, and the stock was valued at $170 per share on the date of his uncle's death (the value used for estate tax purposes).

2) Sold 400 shares of General Motors stock for $78 per share on September 20, 2004. Susan had received 1,000 shares of General Motors stock as a wedding present from her grandfather on June 3, 1992. Her grandfather had purchased the stock for $35 per share on May 7, 1989, and the stock was valued at $50 per share on the date of the gift. Susan's grandfather paid gift taxes of $10,000 as a result of the gift.

3) Sold 300 shares of Eastman Kodak stock for $40 per share on December 28, 2004, but did not receive the sales proceeds until January 3, 2005. The Holmans had paid $25 per share for the stock on October 21, 2002.

k. Susan has summarized the following cash expenditures for 2004 from canceled checks, mortgage company statements, and other documents:

Prescription medicines and drugs	$ 982
Medical insurance premiums (paid by Susan)	2,830
Doctors' and hospital bills (net of reimbursements)	1,535
Contact lenses for David	218
Real estate taxes paid on	
Dallas residence	3,400
Los Angeles residence	5,600
Sales taxes paid on Susan's new auto.	1,485
Ad valorem taxes paid on both autos.	350
Interest paid for	
Dallas home mortgage	5,250*
Los Angeles home mortgage	10,200**
Credit card interest	480
Personal car loan	1,720
Cash contributions to	
United Methodist Church	5,000
American Heart Fund	200
United Way Campaign	1,500
George W. Bush Campaign Fund.	250
Susan's unreimbursed employee expenses.	470***
David's unreimbursed employee expenses	360***
Tax return preparation fee	375

*Does not include the mortgage prepayment penalty identified in item (b) above.
**Does not include the interest points charged for the new mortgage identified in item (d) above.
***Does not include any costs for meals or entertainment.

Susan also noted that she and David had driven their personal automobiles 500 miles to receive medical treatment for themselves and their children. She also has a receipt for 100 shares of General Motors stock that she gave to her alma mater, Southern Methodist University, on November 12, 2004. The stock was valued at $70 per share on the date of the gift and was from the block of General Motors stock Susan had received as a wedding present from her grandfather [see item (j)(2) above for details].

l.   The Holmans paid the following child care expenses during 2004:

    1)   Kindergarten Day Care School $2,800
          1177 Valley View
          Dallas, Texas 75210
          EIN: 74-0186254

    2)   Happy Trails Day Center   2,200
          3692 Airport Blvd.
          Los Angeles, California 90034
          EIN: 78-0593676

m.   Social security numbers for the Holman children are provided below:

    Richard L. Holman, Social Security No. 582-60-4732
    Karen A. Holman, Social Security No. 582-60-5840

n.   David and Susan made estimated Federal income tax payments of $1,750 each quarter, on 4/15/04, 6/15/04, 9/15/04, and 1/15/05.

o.   The Holmans have always directed that $6 go to the Presidential Election Campaign by checking the "yes" boxes on their Form 1040.

Required:

Complete the Holmans' Federal income tax return for 2004. If they have a refund due, they would prefer having it credited against their 2005 taxes.

2.   Richard M. and Anna K. Wilson

a.   Richard and Anna Wilson are married and file a joint return. Richard is 47 years of age and Anna is 46. Richard is employed by Telstar Corporation as its controller and Anna is self-employed as a travel agent. They have three children: Michael, age 22; Lisa, age 17; and Laura, age 14. Michael is a full-time student at Rutgers University. Lisa and Laura both live at home and attend school full-time. The Wilsons currently live at 3721 Chestnut Ridge Road, Montvale, New Jersey 07645, in a home they have owned since July 1987.

Richard and Anna provided over half of the support of Anna's mother, who currently lives in a nursing home in Mahwah, New Jersey. They also provided over half of the support of their son, Michael, who earned $4,750 during the summer as an accounting student intern for a national accounting firm.

b. Richard received a Form W-2 from his employer reporting the following information for 2004:

Richard M. Wilson, Social Security No. 294-38-6249:

Gross wages and taxable benefits.	$63,000
Federal income taxes withheld.	11,400
F.I.C.A. taxes withheld:	
Social security.	3,571
Medicare.	914
State income taxes withheld	1,850

The taxable benefits reported on his W-2 Form include $2,700 (37.5 cents per mile) for Richard's personal use of the company car provided by his employer.

c. Anna operates her business under the name "Wilson's Travel Agency," located at 7200 Treeline Drive, Montvale, NJ 07645. Anna has one full-time employee, and her Federal employer identification number is 74-2638596

Anna uses the cash method of accounting for her business, and her records for 2004 show the following:

Fees and commissions	$134,000
Expenses:	
Advertising	1,425
Bank service charges	75
Dues and subscriptions.	560
Insurance	1,100
Interest on furniture loan.	960
Professional services	700
Office rent.	6,000
Office supplies	470
Meals and entertainment	1,000
Payroll taxes.	2,170
Utilities and telephone.	3,480
Wages paid to full-time employee.	22,800
Miscellaneous expenses.	20

Automobile expenses and amounts paid to her children are not included in the above expenses. Anna paid her daughters Lisa and Laura $750 and $450, respectively, for working part-time during the summer. Since she did not withhold or pay any Federal income or employment taxes on these amounts, Anna is not certain that she is allowed a deduction. She does feel that the amounts paid to her children were reasonable, however.

Anna purchased a new 2003 Oldsmobile on November 20 of last year, and her tax accountant used the actual cost method in determining the deductible business expenses for her 2003 Federal tax return. Because the deductible amount seemed so small, she is not certain whether she should claim actual expenses (including depreciation), or simply use the automatic mileage method. She has the following records relating to the business auto:

Original cost (including sales tax and auto title)...................... $18,000
Depreciation claimed in 2003
    ($18,000 × 5% = $900 × 80% business use)................. 720

Gas, oil, and repairs in 2004 1,790
Parking and tolls paid in 2004 410
Insurance for 2004.. 650
Interest on car loan for 2004 750

Anna drove the auto 20,000 miles for business purposes and 5,000 miles for personal purposes during the year. The above expenses for 2004 have not been reduced to reflect her personal use of the vehicle.

On January 7, 2004 Anna purchased the following items for use in her business:

Office furniture................................ $8,900
Copying machine.............................. 5,700
Dell notebook computer........................ 1,500
Printer 1,600
Fax machine 300

Anna wishes to claim the maximum amount of depreciation deductions or other cost recovery allowed on the office furniture and equipment.

d. Richard attended an accounting convention in Washington, D.C. for three days in October. He incurred the following unreimbursed expenses related to the trip:

Air fare (round-trip) $470
Registration fee for meeting.................... 225
Hotel cost.................................... 375
Meals.. 130
Taxis 20
Airport parking............................... 18
Road tolls.................................... 2

e. Richard and Anna received Forms 1099-INT reporting interest income earned during 2004 from the following:

Citibank of Mahwah......................... $845
Montvale National Bank...................... 900
Telstar Employees' Credit Union 755

f. The Wilsons received the following dividends during 2004:

Telstar Corporation $300
Exxon Corporation............................ 200

g. The Wilsons have never had a foreign bank account or created a foreign trust.

h. The Wilsons had the following property transactions for 2003:

1) Anna sold 300 shares of Exxon Corporation stock on September 9, 2004 in order to pay for Michael's fall semester of college. She received a check in the amount of $14,950 from Shearson Lehman on September 16, 2004. The stock was from a block of 1,000 shares that Richard and Anna had purchased for $35 per share on February 1, 1981.

2) They gave each of the children 100 shares of Exxon stock on December 30, 2004, when the stock was valued at $62.50 per share. The stock was from the same block of stock purchased for $35 per share in February, 1981. No gift taxes were paid on these gifts.

3) They gave 100 shares of Exxon stock to Richard's alma mater, Rider College, on December 29, 2004. The average trading price of Exxon stock on that day was $61.25. This stock was also from the original block of 1,000 shares the Wilsons had purchased for $35 per share in 1981. Rider College is located in Lawrenceville, New Jersey.

4) On May 17, 2004, Richard and Anna were notified by the bankruptcy judge handling the affairs of Bubbling Crude Oil Company in Houston, Texas that the company's shareholders would not receive anything for their stock ownership because all of the assets were used to satisfy claims of creditors. Richard had purchased 2,000 shares of the stock for $6 per share on April 1, 1987. Unfortunately, the stock did not meet the requirements of § 1244.

i. Richard and Anna own a rental condominium located at 7777 Boardwalk in Atlantic City, New Jersey. The unit was purchased on July 29, 2003 for $25,000 cash and a $125,000 mortgage. The following items relate to the rental unit for 2004:

Gross rents	$16,400
Expenses:	
Management fee	2,460
Cleaning and maintenance	1,200
Insurance	840
Property taxes	2,750
Interest paid on mortgage	13,675
Utilities	850

Although the unfurnished unit was vacant for 11 weeks during the year, the Wilsons never used the property for personal purposes. When the property is rented, the tenant is required to pay for all utilities, and the Wilsons are charged a management fee equal to 15 percent of the rents collected.

j. The Wilsons have prepared the following summary of their other expenditures for 2004:

Prescription medicines and drugs	$ 425
Medical insurance premiums (paid by Richard)	1,595
Doctors' and hospital bills (net of reimbursements)	805*
Dentist	2,750**
Real estate taxes paid on home	1,625
State income taxes paid during 2004	2,100***
Interest paid for	
Original home mortgage	2,690
Home equity loan	6,410****
Credit card interest	275
Personal car loan	725
Cash contributions to First Presbyterian Church	1,200
Fee for preparation of 2003 tax return	450

*Does not include $1,485 of doctor bills paid by Richard and Anna for medical treatment provided to Anna's mother at the nursing home. Also not included is $115 that Anna paid for a new pair of eyeglasses for her mother.

**$2,350 of this amount represents a prepayment of Laura's braces. The dentist required the prepayment before he would begin the two-year dental program involved.

***Does not include amounts withheld from Richard's wages.

****Represents interest paid on a $75,000 home equity loan made by the Wilsons in 2004.

k. Anna made an $11,500 deductible contribution to her Keogh plan on December 15, 2004.

l. Richard paid the following unreimbursed employee business expenses:

Professional dues	$450
Professional journals	385
Office gifts to subordinates (none over $25)	115

m. During the year, the Wilsons paid tuition of $9,350 and spent $1,875 on books and supplies for Michael's senior year of college.

n. The Wilsons received a state income tax refund of $130 in 2004. They had $18,750 of itemized deductions for 2003, and their 2003 taxable income was $52,825.

o. Richard and Anna made timely estimated Federal income tax payments of $2,250 each quarter on 4/15/04, 6/15/04, 9/15/04, and 1/15/05.

p. Social security numbers for Anna, the children, and Anna's mother are provided below:

	Number
Anna K. Wilson	296-48-2385
Michael D. Wilson	256-83-4421
Lisa M. Wilson	257-64-7573
Laura D. Wilson	258-34-2894
Ruth Knapp	451-38-3790

q. The Wilsons have always checked the "no" boxes on their Form 1040 regarding the Presidential Election Campaign fund contribution.

Required:

Complete the Wilsons' Federal income tax return for 2004. If they have a refund due, they would prefer having it credited against their 2005 taxes.

Appendix E

GLOSSARY OF TAX TERMS

—A—

A. (*see* Acquiescence).

Accelerated Cost Recovery System (ACRS). An alternate form of depreciation enacted by the Economic Recovery Tax Act of 1981 and significantly modified by the Tax Reform Act of 1986. The modified cost recovery system applies to assets placed into service after 1986 and is referred to as MACRS. Under both systems, the cost of a qualifying asset is recovered over a set period of time. Salvage value is ignored. § 168.

Accelerated Depreciation. Various depreciation methods that produce larger depreciation deductions in the earlier years of an asset's life than straight-line depreciation. Examples: double-declining balance method (200% declining balance) and sum-of-the-years'-digits method. § 167 (*see* Depreciation).

Accounting Method. A method by which an entity's income and expenses are determined. The primary accounting methods used are the accrual method and the cash method. Other accounting methods include the installment method, the percentage-of-completion method (for construction), and various methods for valuing inventories, such as FIFO and LIFO. §§ 446 and 447 (*see also specific accounting methods*).

Accounting Period. A period of time used by a taxpayer in determining his or her income, expenses, and tax liability. An accounting period is generally a year for tax purposes, either a calendar year, a fiscal year, or a 52-53 week year. §§ 441 and 443.

Accrual Method of Accounting. The method of accounting that reflects the income earned and the expenses incurred during a given tax period. However, unearned income of an accrual basis taxpayer must generally be included in an entity's income in the year in which it is received, even if it is not actually earned by the entity until a later tax Period. § 446.

Accumulated Adjustment Account (AAA). A summary of all includible income and gains, expenses, and losses of an S Corporation for taxable years after 1982, except those that relate to excludable income, distributions, and redemptions of an S Corporation. Distributions from the AAA are not taxable to the shareholders. §§1368(c)(1) and (3)(1).

Accumulated Earnings Credit. A reduction in arriving at a corporation's accumulated taxable income (in computing the Accumulated Earnings Tax). Its purpose is to avoid penalizing a corporation for retaining sufficient earnings and profits to meet the reasonable needs of the business. § 535(c).

Accumulated Earnings Tax. A penalty tax on the unreasonable accumulation of earnings and profits by a corporation. It is intended to encourage the distribution of earnings and profits of a corporation to its shareholders. §§ 531-537.

Accumulated Taxable Income. The amount on which the accumulated earnings tax is imposed. §§ 531 and 535.

Accuracy-Related Penalty. Any of the group of penalties that includes negligence or disregard of rules or regulations, substantial understatement of income tax, substantial valuation misstatement for income tax purposes, substantial overstatement of pension liabilities, and substantial estate or gift valuation understatement. § 6662.

Acquiescence. The public endorsement of a regular Tax Court decision by the Commissioner of the Internal Revenue Service. When the Commissioner acquiesces to a regular Tax Court decision, the IRS generally will not dispute the result in cases involving substantially similar facts (*see* Nonacquiescence).

Ad Valorem Tax. A tax based on the value of property.

Adjusted Basis. The basis (i.e., cost or other basis) of property plus capital improvements minus depreciation allowed or allowable. See § 1016 for other adjustments to basis. § 1016 (*see* Basis).

Adjusted Gross Income. A term used with reference to individual taxpayers. Adjusted gross income consists of an individual's gross income less certain deductions and business expenses. § 62.

Adjusted Ordinary Gross Income (AOGI). A term used in relation to personal holding companies. Adjusted ordinary gross income is determined by subtracting certain expenses related to rents and mineral, oil, and gas royalties, and certain interest expense from ordinary gross income § 543(b)(2).

Administrator. A person appointed by the court to administrate the estate of a deceased person. If named to perform these duties by the decedent's will, this person is called an executor (executrix).

AFTR (American Federal Tax Reports). These volumes contain the Federal tax decisions issued by the U.S. District Courts, U.S. Court of Federal Claims, U.S. Circuit Courts of Appeals, and the U.S. Supreme Court (*see* AFTR2d).

AFTR2d (American Federal Tax Reports, Second Series). The second series of the American Federal Tax Reports. These volumes contain the Federal tax decisions issued by the U.S. District Courts, U.S. Court of Federal Claims. U.S. Circuit Courts of Appeals, and the U.S. Supreme Court (see AFTR).

Alternate Valuation Date. The property contained in a decedent's gross estate must be valued at either the decedent's date of death or the alternate valuation date. The alternate valuation date is six months after the decedent's date of death, or, if the property is disposed of prior to that date. the Particular property disposed of is valued as of the date of its disposition. § 2032.

Alternative Minimum Tax. A tax imposed on taxpayers only if it exceeds the "regular" tax of the taxpayer. Regular taxable income is adjusted by certain timing differences, then increased by tax preferences to arrive at alternative minimum taxable income.

Amortization. The systematic write-off (deduction) of the cost or other basis of an intangible asset over its estimated useful life. The concept is similar to depreciation (used for tangible assets) and depletion (used for natural resources) (*see* Goodwill; Intangible Asset).

Amount Realized. Any money received, plus the fair market value of any other property or services received, plus any liabilities discharged on the sale or other disposition of property. The determination of the amount realized is the first step in determining realized gain or loss. § 1001(b).

Annual Exclusion. The amount each year that a donor may exclude from Federal gift tax for each donee. Currently, the annual exclusion is $11,000 per donee (2005). The annual exclusion does not generally apply to gifts of future interests. § 2503(b).

Annuity. A fixed amount of money payable to a person at specific intervals for either a specific period of time or for life.

Appellate Court. A court to which other court decisions are appealed. The appellate courts for Federal tax purposes include the Courts of Appeals and the Supreme Court.

Arm's-Length Transaction. A transaction entered into by unrelated parties, all acting in their own best interests. It is presumed that in an arm's length transaction the prices used are the fair market values of the properties or services being transferred in the transaction.

Articles of Incorporation. The basic instrument filed with the appropriate state agency when a business is incorporated.

Assessment of Tax. The imposition of an additional tax liability by the Internal Revenue Service (i.e.. as the result of an audit).

Assignment of Income. A situation in which a taxpayer assigns income or income-producing property to another person or entity in an attempt to avoid paying taxes on that income. An assignment of income or income-producing property is generally not recognized for tax purposes, and the income is taxable to the assignor.

Association. An entity that possesses a majority of the following characteristics: associates; profit motive; continuity of life; centralized management; limited liability; free transferability of interests. Associations are taxed as corporations. §§ 7701(a)(3). Reg. § 301.7701-2.

At-Risk Limitation. A provision that limits a deduction for losses to the amounts "at risk." A taxpayer is generally not "at risk" in situations where nonrecourse debt is used. § 465.

Attribution. (*see* Constructive Ownership).

Audit. The examination of a taxpayer's return or other taxable transactions by the Internal Revenue Service in order to determine the correct tax liability. Types of audits include correspondence audits, office audits, and field audits(*see also* Correspondence Audit; Office Audit; Field Audit).

—B—

Bad Debt. An uncollectible debt. A bad debt may be classified either as a business bad debt or a nonbusiness bad debt. A business bad debt is one that has arisen in the course of the taxpayer's business (with a business purpose). Nonbusiness bad debts are treated as short-term capital losses rather than as ordinary losses. § 166.

Bargain Sale, Rental, or Purchase. A sale, rental, or purchase of property for less than its fair market value. The difference between the sale, rental, or purchase price and the property's fair market value may have its own tax consequences, such as consideration as a constructive dividend or a gift.

Bartering. The exchange of goods and services without using money.

Basis. The starting point in determining the gain or loss from the sale or other disposition of an asset, or the depreciation (or depletion or amortization) on an asset. For example, if an asset is purchased for cash, the basis of that as set is the cash paid. §§ 1012, 1014, 1015, 334, 359, 362.

Beneficiary. Someone who will benefit from an act of another, such as the beneficiary of a life insurance contract, the beneficiary of a trust (i.e., income beneficiary), or the beneficiary of an estate.

Bequest. A testamentary transfer (by will) of personal property (personalty).

Board of Tax Appeals (B.T.A.). The predecessor of the United States Tax Court, in existence from 1924 to 1942.

Bona Fide. Real; in good faith.

Boot. Cash or property that is not included in the definition of a particular type of nontaxable exchange [see §§ 351(b) and 1031(b)]. In these nontaxable exchanges, a taxpayer who receives boot must recognize gain to the extent of the boot received or the realized gain, whichever is less.

Brother-Sister Corporations. A controlled group of two or more corporations owned (in certain amounts) by five or fewer individuals, estates, or trusts. § 1563(a)(2).

Burden of Proof. The weight of evidence in a legal case or in a tax proceeding. Generally, the burden of proof is on the taxpayer in a tax case. However, the burden of proof is on the government in fraud cases. § 7454.

Business Purpose. An actual business reason for following a course of action. Tax avoidance alone is not considered to be a business purpose. In areas such as corporate formation and corporate reorganizations, business purpose is especially important.

—C—

Capital Asset. All proper by held by a taxpayer (e.g., house, car, clothing) except for certain assets that are specifically excluded from the definition of a capital asset, such as inventory and depreciable and real property used in a trade or business.

Capital Contribution. Cash, services, or property contributed by a partner to a partnership or by a shareholder to a corporation. Capital contributions are not income to the recipient partnership or corporation. §§ 721 and 118.

Capital Expenditure. Any amount paid for new buildings or for permanent improvements; any expendi-tures that add to the value or prolong the life of property or adapt the property to a new or different use. Capital expenditures should be added to the basis of the property improved. § 263.

Capital Gain. A gain from the sale or other disposition of a capital asset. § 1222.

Capital Loss. A loss from the sale or other disposition of a capital asset. § 1222.

Cash Method of Accounting. The method of accounting that reflects the income received (or constructively received) and the expenses paid during a given period. However, prepaid expenses of a cash basis taxpayer that benefit more than one year may be required to be deducted only in the periods benefited (e.g., a premium for a three-year insurance policy may have to be spread over three years).

CCH. (*see* Commerce Clearing House).

C Corporation. A so-called regular corporation that is a separate tax-paying entity and is subject to the tax rules contained in Subchapter C of the Internal Revenue Code (as opposed to an S corporation, which is subject to the tax rules of Subchapter S of the Code).

Certiorari. A Writ of Certiorari is the form used to appeal a lower court (U.S. Court of Appeals) decision to the Supreme Court. The Supreme Court then decides, by reviewing the Writ of Certiorari, whether it will accept the appeal or not. The Supreme Court generally does not accept the appeal unless a constitutional issue is involved or the lower courts are in conflict. If the Supreme Court refuses to accept the appeal, then the certiorari is denied (cert. den.).

Claim of Right Doctrine. If a taxpayer has an unrestricted claim to income, the income is included in that taxpayer's income when it is received or constructively received, even if there is a possibility that all or part of the income may have to be returned to another party.

Closely Held Corporation. A corporation whose voting stock is owned by one or a few shareholders and is operated by this person or closely knit group.

Collapsible Corporation. A corporation that liquidates before it has realized a substantial portion of its income. Shareholders treat the gain on these liquidating distributions as ordinary income (rather than dividend income or capital gains). § 341.

Commerce Clearing House. A publisher of tax materials, including a multivolume tax service, volumes that contain the Federal courts' decisions on tax matters (USTC) and the Tax Court regular (T.C.) and memorandum (TCM) decisions.

Community Property. Property that is owned together by husband and wife, where each has an undivided one-half interest in the property due to their marital status. The ten community property states are Alaska, Arizona, California, Idaho, Louisiana, Nevada, New Mexico, Texas, Washington, and Wisconsin.

Complex Trust. Any trust that does not meet the requirements of a simple trust. For example, a trust will be considered to be a complex trust if it does not distribute the trust income currently, if it takes a deduction for a charitable contribution for the current year, or if it distributes any of the trust corpus currently. § 661.

Condemnation. The taking of private property for a public use by a public authority, an exercise of the power of eminent domain. The public authority compensates the owner of the property taken in a condemnation (see also Involuntary Conversion).

Conduit Principle. The provisions in the tax law that allow specific tax characteristics to be passed through certain entities to the owners of the entity without losing their identity. For example, the short-term capital gains of a partnership would be passed through to the partners and retain their character as short-term capital gains on the tax returns of the partners. This principle applies in varying degrees to partnerships, S corporations, estates, and trusts

Consent Dividend. A term used in relation to the accumulated earnings tax and the personal holding company tax. A consent dividend occurs when the shareholders consent to treat a certain amount as a taxable dividend on their tax returns even though there is no distribution of cash or property. The purpose of this is to obtain a dividends-paid deduction. § 565.

Consolidated Return. A method used to determine the tax liability of a group of affiliated corporations. The aggregate income (with certain adjustments) of a group is viewed as the income of a single enterprise. § 1501.

Consolidation. The statutory combination of two or more corporations in a new corporation. § 368(a)(1)(A).

Constructive Dividends. The constructive receipt of a dividend. Even though a taxable benefit was not designated as a dividend by the distributing corporation, a shareholder may be designated by the IRS as having received a dividend if the benefit has the appearance of a dividend. For example, if a shareholder uses corporate property for personal purposes rent-free, he or she will have a constructive dividend equal to the fair rental value of the corporate property.

Constructive Ownership. In certain situations the tax law attributes the ownership of stock to persons "related" to the person or entity that actually owns the stock. The related party is said to constructively own the stock of that person. For example, under § 267(c) a father is considered to constructively own all stock actually owned by his son. §§ 267, 318, and 544(a).

Constructive Receipt. When income is available to a taxpayer, even though it is not actually received by the taxpayer, the amount is considered to be constructively received by the taxpayer and should be included in income (e.g., accrued interest on a savings account). However, if there are restrictions on the availability of the income, it is generally not considered to be constructively received until the restrictions are removed (e.g., interest on a 6-month certificate of deposit is not constructively received until the end of the 6-month period if early withdrawal would result in loss of interest or principal).

Contributions to the Capital of a Corporation. (*see* Capital Contributions).

Corpus. The principal of a trust, as opposed to the income of the trust. Also called the *res* of the trust.

Correspondence Audit. An IRS audit conducted through the mail. Generally, verification or sub-stantiation for specified items is requested by the IRS, and the taxpayer mails the requested information to the IRS (*see* Field Audit; Office Audit).

Cost Depletion. (*see* Depletion).

Court of Appeals. The U.S. Federal court system has 13 circuit Courts of Appeals, which consider cases appealed from the U.S. Court of Federal Claims, the U.S. Tax Court, and the U.S. District Courts. A writ of certiorari is used to appeal a case from a Court of Appeals to the U.S. Supreme Court (see Appellate Court).

Creditor. A person or entity to whom money is owed. The person or entity who owes the money is called the debtor.

—D—

Death Tax. A tax imposed on property upon the death of the owner, such as an estate tax or inheritance tax.

Debtor. A person or entity who owes money to another. The person or entity to whom the money is owed is called the creditor.

Decedent. A deceased person.

Deductions in Respect of a Decedent (DRD). Certain expenses that are incurred by a decedent but are not properly deductible on the decedent's first return because of nonpayment. Deductions in respect of a decedent are deducted by the taxpayer who is legally required to make payment. § 691(b).

Deficiency. An additional tax liability owed to the IRS by a taxpayer. A deficiency is generally proposed by the IRS through the use of a Revenue Agent's Report.

Deficit. A negative balance in retained earnings or in earnings and profits.

Dependent. A person who derives his or her primary support from another. In order for a taxpayer to claim a dependency exemption for a person, there are five tests that must be met: support test, gross income test, citizenship or residency test, relationship or member of household test, and joint return test. § 152.

Depletion. As natural resources are extracted and sold, the cost or other basis of the resource is recovered by the use of depletion. Depletion may be either cost or percentage (statutory) depletion. Cost depletion has to do with the recovery of the cost of natural resources based on the units of the resource sold. Percentage depletion uses percentages given in the Internal Revenue Code multiplied by the gross income from the interest. subject to limitations. §§ 613 and 613A.

Depreciation. The systematic write-off of the basis of a tangible asset over the asset's estimated useful life. Depreciation is intended to reflect the wear, tear, and obsolescence of the asset(*see* Amortization; Depletion).

Depreciation Recapture. The situation in which all or part of the realized gain from the sale or other disposition of depreciable business property could be treated as ordinary income. See text for discussion of §§ 291, 1245, and 1250.

Determination Letter. A written statement regarding the tax consequences of a transaction issued by an IRS District Director in response to a written inquiry by a taxpayer that applies to a particular set of facts. Determination letters are frequently used to state whether a pension or profit-sharing plan is qualified or not, to determine the tax-exempt status of nonprofit organizations, and to clarify employee status.

Discretionary Trust. A trust in which the trustee or another party has the right to determine whether to accumulate or distribute the trust income currently, and/or which beneficiary is to receive the trust income.

Discriminant Function System (DIF). The computerized system used by the Internal Revenue Service in identifying and selecting returns for examination. This system uses secret mathematical formulas to select those returns that have a probability of tax errors.

Dissent. A disagreement with the majority opinion. The term is generally used to mean the explicit disagreement of one or more judges in a court with the majority decision on a particular case.

Distributable Net Income (DNI). The net income of a fiduciary that is available for distribution to income beneficiaries. DNI is computed by adjusting an estate's or trust's taxable income by certain modifications. § 643(a).

Distribution in Kind. A distribution of property as it is. For example, rather than selling property and distributing the proceeds to the shareholders, the property itself is distributed to the shareholders.

District Court. A trial court in which Federal tax matters can be litigated; the only trial court in which a jury trial can be obtained.

Dividend. A payment by a corporation to its shareholders authorized by the corporation's board of directors to be distributed pro rata among the outstanding shares. However, a constructive dividend does not need to be authorized by the shareholders(*see also* Constructive Dividend).

Dividends-Paid Deduction. A deduction allowed in determining the amount that is subject to the accumulated earnings tax and the personal holding company tax. §§ 561-565.

Dividends-Received Deduction. A deduction available to corporations on dividends received from a domestic corporation. The dividends-received deduction is generally 70 percent of the dividends received. If the recipient corporation owns 20 percent or more of the stock of the paying corporation, an 80 percent deduction is allowed. The dividends-received deduction is 100 percent of the dividends received from another member of an affiliated group, if an election is made §§ 243-246.

Domestic Corporation. A corporation which is created or organized in the United States or under the law of the United States or of any state. § 7701(a)(4).

Donee. The person or entity to whom a gift is made.

Donor. The person or entity who makes a gift.

Double Taxation. A situation in which income is taxed twice. For example, a regular corporation pays tax on its taxable income, and when this income is distributed to the corporation's shareholders, the shareholders are taxed on the dividend income.

—E—

Earned Income. Income from personal services. § 911(d)(2).

Earnings and Profits (E&P). The measure of a corporation's ability to pay dividends to its shareholders. Distributions made by a corporation to its shareholders are dividends to the extent of the corporation's earnings and profits. §§ 312 and 316.

Eminent Domain. (see Condemnation).

Employee. A person in the service of another, where the employer has the power to specify how the work is to be performed (see Independent Contractor).

Employee Achievement Award. An award of tangible personalty that is made for length of service achievement or safety achievement. § 274(j).

Encumbrance. A liability.

Entity. For tax purposes, an organization that is considered to have a separate existence, such as a partnership, corporation, estate, or trust.

Escrow. Cash or other property that is held by a third party as security for an obligation.

Estate. All of the property owned by a decedent at the time of his or her death

Estate Tax. A tax imposed on the transfer of a decedent's taxable estate. The estate, not the heirs, is liable for the estate tax. §§ 2001-2209 (see Inheritance Tax).

Estoppel. A bar or impediment preventing a party from asserting a fact or a claim in court that is inconsistent with a position he or she had previously taken.

Excise Tax. A tax imposed on the sale, manufacture, or use of a commodity or on the conduct of an occupation or activity; considered to include every Internal Revenue Tax except the income tax.

Executor. A person appointed in a will to carry out the provisions in the will and to administer the estate of the decedent. (Feminine of *executor* is *executrix*.)

Exempt Organization. An organization (such as a charitable organization) that is exempt from Federal income taxes. §§ 501-528.

Exemption. A deduction allowed in computing taxable income. Personal exemptions are available for the taxpayer and his or her spouse. Dependency exemptions are available for the taxpayer's dependents. §§ 151-154 (*see* Dependent).

Expatriate (U.S.). U.S. citizen working in a foreign country.

—F—

F.2d (Federal Reporter, Second Series). Volumes in which the decisions of the U.S. Court of Federal Claims and the U.S. Courts of Appeals are published.

F. Supp. (Federal Supplement). Volumes in which the decisions of the U.S. District Courts are published.

Fair Market Value. The amount that a willing buyer would pay a willing seller in an arm's-length transaction.

Fed. (Federal Reporter). Volumes in which the decisions of the U.S. Court of Federal Claims and the U.S. Courts of Appeals are published.

FICA (Federal Insurance Contributions Act). The law dealing with social security taxes and benefits. §§ 3101-3126.

Fiduciary. A person or institution who holds and manages property for another, such as a guardian, trustee, executor, or administrator. § 7701 (a)(6).

Field Audit. An audit conducted by the IRS at the taxpayer's place of business or at the place of business of the taxpayer's representative. Field audits are generally conducted by Revenue Agents(*see* Correspondence Audit: Office Audit).

FIFO (First-in, First-out). A method of determining the cost of an inventory. The first inventory units acquired are considered to be the first sold. Therefore, the cost of the inventory would consist of the most recently acquired inventory.

Filing Status. The filing status of an individual taxpayer determines the tax rates that are applicable to that taxpayer. The filing statuses include Single, Head of Household, Married Filing Jointly, Married Filing Separately, and Surviving Spouse (Qualifying Widow or Widower).

Fiscal Year. A period of 12 consecutive months, other than a calendar year, used as the accounting period of a business. § 7701(a)(24).

Foreign Corporation. A corporation that is not organized under U.S. laws. other than a domestic corporation. § 7701(a)(5).

Foreign Tax Credit. A credit available against taxes for foreign income taxes paid or deemed paid. A deduction may be taken for these foreign taxes as an alternative to the foreign tax credit. §§ 27 and 901-905.

Fraud. A willful intent to evade tax. For tax purposes, fraud is divided into civil fraud and criminal fraud. The IRS has the burden of proof of proving fraud. Civil fraud has a penalty of 75 percent of the underpayment [§ 6653(b)]. Criminal fraud requires a greater degree of willful intent to evade tax (§§ 7201-7207).

Freedom of Information Act. The means by which the public may obtain information held by Federal agencies.

Fringe Benefits. Benefits received by an employee in addition to his or her salary or wages, such as insurance and recreational facilities.

FUTA (Federal Unemployment Tax Act). A tax imposed on the employer on the wages of the employees. A credit is generally given for amounts contributed to state unemployment tax funds. §§ 3301-3311.

Future Interest. An interest, the possession or enjoyment of which will come into being at some point in the future. The annual exclusion for gifts applies only to gifts of present interests, as opposed to future interests.

—G—

General Partner. A partner who is jointly and severally liable for the debts of the partnership. A general partner has no limited liability(see Limited Partner).

Generation-Skipping Tax. A transfer tax imposed on a certain type of transfer involving a trust and at least three generations of taxpayers. The transfer generally skips a generation younger than the original transferor. The transfer therefore results in the avoidance of one generation's estate tax on the transferred property. §§ 2601-2622.

Gift. A transfer of property or money given for less than adequate consideration in money or money's worth.

Gift-Splitting. A tax provision that allows a married person who makes a gift of his or her property to elect, with the consent of his or her spouse, to treat the gift as being made one-half by each the taxpayer and his or her spouse. The effect of gift-splitting is to take advantage of the annual gift tax exclusions for both the taxpayer and his or her spouse. § 2513.

Gift Tax. A tax imposed on the donor of a gift. The tax applies to transfers in trust or otherwise, whether the gift is direct or indirect, real or personal, tangible or intangible. §§ 2501-2524.

Goodwill. An intangible that has an indefinite useful life, arising from the difference between the purchase price and the value of the assets of an acquired business. Goodwill is amortizable over a 15-year period. § 263(b).

Grantor. The person who creates a trust.

Gross Estate. The value of all property, real or personal, tangible or intangible, owned by a decedent at the time of his or her death. §§ 2031-2046.

Gross Income. Income that is subject to Federal income tax. All income from whatever source derived, unless it is specifically excluded from income (e.g., interest on state and local bonds). § 61.

Guaranteed Payment. A payment made by a partnership to a partner for services or the use of capital, without regard to the income of the partnership. The payment generally is deductible by the partnership and taxable to the partner. § 707(c).

—H—

Half-Year Convention. When using ACRS or MACRS, personalty placed in service at any time during the year is treated as placed in service in the middle of the year, and personalty disposed of or retired at any time during the year is treated as disposed of in the middle of the year. However, if more than 40 percent of all personalty placed in service during the year is placed in service during the last three months of the year, the mid-quarter convention applies. § 168(d)(4)(A).

Heir. One who inherits property from a decedent.

Hobby. An activity not engaged in for profit. § 183.

Holding Period. The period of time that property is held. Holding period is used to determine whether a gain or loss is short-term or long-term. §§ 1222 and 1223.

H.R. 10 Plans. (*see* Keogh Plans).

—I—

Incident of Ownership. Any economic interest in a life insurance policy, such as the power to change the policy's beneficiary, the right to cancel or assign the policy, and the right to borrow against the policy. § 2042(2).

Income Beneficiary. The person or entity entitled to receive the income from property. Generally used in reference to trusts.

Income in Respect of a Decedent (IRD). Income that had been earned by a decedent at the time of his or her death, but is not included on the final tax return because of the decedent's method of accounting. Income in respect of a decedent is included in the decedent's gross estate and also on the tax return of the person who receives the income. § 691.

Independent Contractor. One who contracts to do a job according to his or her own methods and skills. The employer has control over the independent contractor only as to the final result of his or her work (*see* Employee).

Indirect Method. A method used by the IRS in order to determine whether a taxpayer's income is correctly reported when adequate records do not exist. Indirect methods include the Source and Applications of Funds Method and the Net Worth Method.

Information Return. A return that must be filed with the Internal Revenue Service even though no tax is imposed, such as a partnership return (Form 1065), Form W-2, and Form 1099.

Inheritance Tax. A tax imposed on the privilege of receiving property of a decedent. The tax is imposed on the heir.

Installment Method. A method of accounting under which a taxpayer spreads the recognition of his or her gain ratably over time as the payments are received. §§ 453, 453A, and 453B.

Intangible Asset. A nonphysical asset, such as goodwill, copyrights, franchises, or trademarks.

Inter Vivos Transfer. A property transfer during the life of the owner.

Intercompany Transaction. A transaction that occurs during a consolidated return year between two or more members of the same affiliated group.

Internal Revenue Service. Part of the Treasury Department, it is responsible for administering and enforcing the Federal tax laws.

Intestate. No will existing at the time of death.

Investment Tax Credit. A credit against tax that was allowed for investing in depreciable tangible personalty before 1986. The credit was equal to 10 percent of the qualified investment. §§ 38 and 46-48.

Investment Credit Recapture. When property on which an investment credit has been taken is disposed of prior to the full time period required under the law to earn the credit, then the amount of unearned credit must be added back to the taxpayer's tax liability-this is called recapture of the investment credit. § 47.

Involuntary Conversion. The complete or partial destruction, theft, seizure, requisition, or condemnation of property. § 1033.

Itemized Deductions. Certain expenditures of a personal nature that are specifically allowed to be deductible from an individual taxpayer's adjusted gross income. Itemized deductions (e.g., medical expenses, charitable contributions, interest, taxes, and miscellaneous itemized deductions) are deductible if they exceed the taxpayer's standard deduction.

—J—

Jeopardy Assessment. If the IRS has reason to believe that the collection or assessment of a tax would be jeopardized by delay, the IRS may assess and collect the tax immediately. §§ 6861-6864.

Joint and Several Liability. The creditor has the ability to sue one or more of the parties who have a liability, or all of the liable persons together. General partners are jointly and severally liable for the debts of the partnership. Also, if a husband and wife file a joint return, they are jointly and severally liable to the IRS for the taxes due.

Joint Tenancy. Property held by two or more owners, where each has an undivided interest in the property. Joint tenancy includes the right of survivorship, which means that upon the death of an owner, his or her share passes to the surviving owner(s).

Joint Venture. A joining together of two or more persons in order to undertake a specific business project. A joint venture is not a continuing relationship like a partnership, but may be treated as a partnership for Federal income tax purposes. § 761(a).

—K—

Keogh Plans. A retirement plan available for self-employed taxpayers. § 401.

Kiddie Tax. Unearned income of a child under age 14 is taxed at the child's parents' marginal tax rate. § 1(i).

—L—

Leaseback. A transaction in which a taxpayer sells property and then leases back the property.

Lessee. A person or entity who rents or leases property from another.

Lessor. A person or entity who rents or leases property to another. Life Insurance. A form of insurance that will pay the beneficiary of the policy a fixed amount upon the death of the insured person.

Life Estate. A trust or legal arrangement by which a certain person (life tenant) is entitled to receive the income from designated property for his or her life.

Life Insurance. A form of insurance that will pay the beneficiary of the policy a fixed amount upon the death of the insured person.

LIFO (Last-in, First-out). A method of determining the cost of an inventory. The last inventory units acquired are considered to be the first sold. Therefore, the cost of the inventory would consist of the earliest acquired inventory.

Like-Kind Exchange. The exchange of property held for productive use in a trade or business or for investment (but not inventory, stock, bonds, or notes) for property that is also held for productive use or for investment (i.e., realty for realty; personalty for personalty). No gain or loss is generally recognized by either party unless boot (other than qualifying property) is involved in the transaction. § 1031.

Limited Liability. The situation in which the liability of an owner of an organization for the organization's debts is limited to the owner's investment in the organization. Examples of taxpayers with limited liability are corporate shareholders and the limited partners in a limited partnership.

Limited Liability Company (LLC). A form of business entity permitted by all states in the U.S. under which the owners are treated as partners and the company is subject to the rules of partnership taxation for Federal tax purposes.

Limited Partner. A partner whose liability for partnership debts is limited to his or her investment in the partnership. A limited partner may take no active part in the management of the partnership according to the Uniform Limited Partnership Act (see General Partner).

Limited Partnership. A partnership with *one* or more general partners *and* one or more limited partners. The limited partners are liable only up to the amount of their contribution plus any personally guaranteed debt. Limited partners cannot participate in the management or control of the partnership.

Liquidation. The cessation of all or part of a corporation's operations or the corporate form of business and the distribution of the corporate assets to the shareholders. §§ 331-337.

Lump Sum Distribution. Payment at one time of an entire amount due, or the entire proceeds of a pension or profit-sharing plan, rather than installment payments.

—M—

Majority. Of legal age (see Minor).

Marital Deduction. Upon the transfer of property from one spouse to another, either by gift or at death. the Internal Revenue Code allows a transfer tax deduction for the amount transferred.

Market Value. (*see* Fair Market Value).

Material Participation. Occurs when a taxpayer is involved in the operations of an activity on a regular, continuous, and substantial basis. § 469(h).

Merger. The absorption of one corporation (target corporation) by another corporation (acquiring corporation). The target corporation transfers its assets to the acquiring corporation in return for stock or securities of the acquiring corporation. Then the target corporation dissolves by exchanging the acquiring corporation's stock for its own stock held by its shareholders.

Mid-Month Convention. When a taxpayer is using ACRS or MACRS, realty placed in service at any time during a month is treated as placed in service in the middle of the month, and realty disposed of or retired at any time during a month is treated as disposed of in the middle of the month. § 168(d)(4)(B).

Mid-Quarter Convention. Used for all personalty placed in service during the year if more than 40 percent of all personalty placed in service during the year is placed in service during the last three months of the year. § 168(d)(4)(C).

Minimum Tax. (*see* Alternative Minimum Tax).

Minor. A person who has not yet reached the age of legal majority. In most states, a minor is a person under 18 years of age.

Mortgagee. The person or entity that holds the mortgage; the lender; the creditor.

Mortgagor. The person or entity that is mortgaging the property; the debtor.

—N—

NA. (*see* Nonacquiescence).

Negligence Penalty. A penalty imposed by the IRS on taxpayers who are negligent or intentionally disregard the rules or regulations (but are not fraudulent), in the determination of their tax liability. § 6662.

Net Operating Loss (NOL). The amount by which deductions exceed a taxpayer's gross income. § 172.

Net Worth Method. An indirect method of determining a taxpayer's income used by the IRS when adequate records do not exist. The net worth of the taxpayer is determined for the end of each year in question, and adjustments are made to the increase in net worth from year to year for nontaxable sources of income and nondeductible expenditures. This method is often used when a possibility of fraud exists.

Ninety-Day Letter. (*see* Statutory Notice of Deficiency).

Nonacquiescence. The public announcement that the Commissioner of the Internal Revenue Service disagrees with a regular Tax Court decision. When the Commissioner nonacquiesces to a regular Tax Court decision, the IRS generally will litigate cases involving similar facts (see Acquiescence).

Nonresident Alien. A person who is not a resident or citizen of the United States.

—O—

Office Audit. An audit conducted by the Internal Revenue Service on IRS premises. The person conducting the audit is generally referred to as an Office Auditor(*see* Correspondence Audit; Field Audit).

Office Auditor. An IRS employee who conducts primarily office audits, as opposed to a Revenue Agent, who conducts primarily field audits (*see also* Revenue Agent).

Ordinary Gross Income. A term used in relation to personal holding companies. Ordinary gross income is determined by subtracting capital gains and § 1231 gains from gross income. § 1231 gains from gross income. § 543(b)(1).

—P—

Partial Liquidation. A distribution that is not essentially equivalent to a dividend, or a distribution that is attributable to the termination one of two or more businesses (that have been active businesses for at least five years). § 302(e).

Partner. (*see* General Partner; Limited Partner).

Partnership. A syndicate, group, pool, joint venture, or other unincorporated organization, through or by means of which any business, financial operation, or venture is carried on, and which is not a trust, estate, or corporation. §§ 761(a) and 7701(a)(2).

Passive Activity. Any activity that involves the conduct of any trade or business in which the taxpayer does not materially participate. Losses from passive activities generally are deductible only to the extent of passive activity income. § 469.

Passive Investment Income. A term used in relation to S corporations. Passive investment income is generally defined as gross receipts derived from royalties, rents, dividends, interest, annuities, and gains on sales or exchanges of stock or securities. § 1362(d)(3)(D).

Pecuniary Bequest. Monetary bequest (*see* Bequest).

Percentage Depletion. (*see* Depletion).

Percentage of Completion Method of Accounting. A method of accounting that may be used on certain long-term contracts in which the income is reported as the contract reaches various stages of completion.

Percentage of Completion Method of Accounting. A method of accounting that may be used on certain long-term contracts in which the income is reported as the contract reaches various stages of completion.

Personal Holding Company. A corporation in which five or fewer individuals owned more than 50 percent of the value of its stock at any a time during the last half of the taxable year and at least 60 percent of the corporation's adjusted ordinary gross income consists of personal holding company income. § 542.

Personal Property. All property that is not realty; personalty. This term is also often used to mean personal use property (*see* Personal Use Property; Personalty).

Personal Use Property. Any property used for personal, rather than business, purposes. Distinguished from "personal property."

Personalty. All property that is not realty (e.g., automobiles, trucks, machinery, and equipment).

Portfolio Income. Interest and dividends. Portfolio income, annuities, and royalties are not considered to be income from a passive activity for purposes of the passive activity loss limitations. § 469(e).

Power of Appointment. A right to dispose of property that the holder of the power does not legally own.

Preferred Stock Bailout. A scheme by which shareholders receive a nontaxable preferred stock dividend, sell this preferred stock to a third party, and report the gain as a long-term capital gain. This scheme, therefore, converts what would be ordinary dividend income to capital gain. Section 306 was created to prohibit use of this scheme.

Present Interest. An interest in which the donee has the present right to use, possess, or enjoy the donated property. The annual exclusion is available for gifts of present interests, but not for gifts of future interests (*see* Future Interest).

Previously Taxed Income (PTI). A term used to refer to the accumulated earnings and profits for the period that a Subchapter S election was in effect prior to 1983. Distributions from PTI are not taxable to the shareholders.

Private Letter Ruling. A written statement from the IRS to a taxpayer in response to a request by the taxpayer for the tax consequences of a specific set of facts. The taxpayer who receives the Private Letter Ruling is the only taxpayer that may rely on that specific ruling in case of litigation.

Probate. The court-directed administration of a decedent's estate.

Prop. Reg. (Proposed Regulation). Treasury (IRS) Regulations are generally issued first in a proposed form in order to obtain input from various sources before the regulations are changed (if necessary) and issued in final form.

Pro Rata. Proportionately.

—Q—

Qualified Pension or Profit-Sharing Plan. A pension or profit-sharing plan sponsored by an employer that meets the requirements set forth by Congress in § 401. §§ 401-404.

Qualified Residence Interest. Interest on indebtedness that is secured by the principal residence or one other residence of a taxpayer. §§ 162(h)(3) and (5)(A).

Qualified Terminable Interest Property (QTIP). Property that passes from the decedent in which the surviving spouse has a qualifying income interest for life. An election to treat the property as qualified terminable interest property has been made. § 2056(b).

—R—

RAR. (*see* Revenue Agent's Report).

Real Property. (*see* Realty).

Realized Gain or Loss. The difference between the amount realized from the sale or other disposition of an asset and the adjusted basis of the asset. § 1001.

Realty. Real estate; land, including any objects attached thereto that are not readily movable (e.g., buildings, sidewalks, trees, and fences).

Reasonable Needs of the Business. In relation to the accumulated earnings tax, a corporation may accumulate sufficient earnings and profits to meet its reasonable business needs. Examples of reasonable needs of the business include working capital needs, amounts needed for bona fide business expansion, and amounts needed for redemptions for death taxes § 537.

Recapture. The recovery of the tax benefit from a previously taken deduction or credit. The recapture of a deduction results in its inclusion in income, and the recapture of a credit results in its inclusion in tax(*see* Depreciation Recapture; Investment Credit Recapture).

Recognized Gain or Loss. The amount of the realized gain or loss that is subject to income tax. § 1001.

Redemption. The acquisition by a corporation of its own stock from a shareholder in exchange for property. § 317(b).

Reg. (*see* Regulations).

Regulations (Treasury Department Regulations). Interpretations of the Internal Revenue Code by the Internal Revenue Service.

Related Party. A person or entity that is related to another under the various code provisions for constructive ownership. §§ 267, 318, and 544(a).

Remainder Interest. Property that passes to a remainderman after the life estate or other income interest expires on the property.

Remainderman. The person entitled to the remainder interest.

Remand. The sending back of a case by an appellate court to a lower court for further action by the lower court. The abbreviation for "remanding" is "rem'g."

Reorganization. The combination, division, or restructuring of a corporation or corporations.

Research Institute of America (RIA). A publisher of tax materials, including a multi-volume tax service and volumes that contain the Federal courts' decisions on tax matters (AFTR, AFTR2d).

Resident Alien. A person who is not a citizen of the United States, and who is a resident of the United States or meets the substantial presence test. § 7701(b).

Revenue Agent. An employee of the Internal Revenue Service who performs primarily field audits.

Revenue Agent's Report (RAR). The report issued by a Revenue Agent in which adjustments to a taxpayer's tax liability are proposed. (IRS Form 4549; Form 1902 is used for office audits.)

Revenue Officer. An employee of the Internal Revenue Service whose primary duty is the collection of tax. (As opposed to a Revenue Agent, who audits returns.)

Revenue Procedure. A procedure published by the Internal Revenue Service outlining various processes and methods of handling various matters of tax practice and administration. Revenue Procedures are published first in the Internal Revenue Bulletin and then compiled annually in the Cumulative Bulletin.

Revenue Ruling. A published interpretation by the Internal Revenue Service of the tax law as applied to specific situations. Revenue Rulings are published first in the Internal Revenue Bulletin and then compiled annually in the Cumulative Bulletin.

Reversed (Rev'd). The reverse of a lower court's decision by a higher court.

Reversing (Rev'g). The reversing of a lower court's decision by a higher court. Rev. Proc. (*see* Revenue Procedure).

Revocable Transfer. A transfer that may be revoked by the transferor. In other words, the transferor keeps the right to recover the transferred property.

Rev. Proc. (*see* Revenue Procedure).

Rev. Rul. (*see* Revenue Ruling).

Right of Survivorship. (*see* Joint Tenancy).

Royalty. Compensation for the use of property, such as natural resources or copyrighted material.

—S—

S Corporation. A corporation that qualifies as a small business corporation and elects to have §§ 1361-1379 apply. Once a Subchapter S election is made, the corporation is treated similarly to a partnership for tax purposes. An S corporation uses Form 1120S to report its income and expenses.(*see* C Corporation).

Section 751 Assets. Unrealized receivables and appreciated inventory items of a partnership. A disproportionate distribution of § 751 assets generally results in taxable income to the partners.

Section 1231 Property. Depreciable property and real estate used in a trade or business held for more than one year. Section 1231 property may also include timber, coal, domestic iron ore, livestock, and unharvested crops.

Section 1244 Stock. Stock of a small business corporation issued pursuant to § 1244. A loss on § 1244 stock is treated as an ordinary loss (rather than a capital loss) within limitations. § 1244.

Section 1245 Property. Property that is subject to depreciation recapture under § 1245.

Section 1250 Property. Property that is subject to depreciation recapture under § 1250.

Securities. Evidences of debt or of property, such as stock, bonds, and notes.

Separate Property. Property that belongs separately to only one spouse (as contrasted with com-munity property in a community property state). In a community property state, a spouse's separate property generally includes property acquired by the spouse prior to marriage, or property acquired after marriage by gift or inheritance.

Severance Tax. At the time they are severed or removed from the earth. a tax on minerals or timber.

Sham Transaction. A transaction with no substance or bona fide business purpose that may be ignored for tax purposes.

Simple Trust. A trust that is required to distribute all of its income currently and does not pay, set aside, or use any funds for charitable purposes. § 651 (a).

Small Business Corporation. There are two separate definitions of a small business corporation, one relating to S corporations and one relating to § 1244. If small business corporation status is met under § 1361(b), a corporation may elect Subchapter S. If small business corporation status is met under § 1244(c)(3), losses on § 1244 stock may be deducted as ordinary (rather than capital) losses, within limitations.

Small Business Corporation. There are two separate definitions of a small business corporation, one relating to S corporations, and one relating to § 1244. If small business corporation status is met under § 1361(b), then a corporation may elect Subchapter S. If small business corporation status is met under § 1244(c)(3), then losses on § 1244 stock may be deducted as ordinary (rather than capital) losses, within limitations.

Special Use Valuation. A special method of valuing real estate for estate tax purposes. The special use valuation allows that qualifying real estate used in a closely held business may be valued based on its business usage rather than market value. § 2032A.

Specific Bequest. A bequest made by a testator in his or her will giving an heir a particular piece of property or money.

Spin-off. A type of divisive corporate reorganization in which the original corporation transfers some of its assets to a newly formed subsidiary in exchange for all of the subsidiary's stock which it then distributes to its shareholders. The shareholders of the original corporation do not surrender any of their ownership in the original corporation for the subsidiary's stock.

Split-off. A type of divisive corporate reorganization in which the original corporation transfers some of its assets to a newly formed subsidiary in exchange for all of the subsidiary's stock which it then distributes to some or all of its shareholders in exchange for some portion of their stock.

Split-up. A type of divisive corporate reorganization in which the original corporation transfers some of its assets to one newly created subsidiary and the remainder of the assets to another newly created subsidiary. The original corporation then liquidates, distributing the stock of both subsidiaries in exchange for its own stock.

Standard Deduction. A deduction that is available to most individual taxpayers. The standard deduction or total itemized deductions, whichever is larger, is subtracted in computing taxable income. §§ 63(c) and (f).

Statute of Limitations. Law provisions that limit the period of time in which action may be taken after an event occurs. The limitations on the IRS for assessments and collections are included in §§ 6501-6504, and the limitations on taxpayers for credits or refunds are included in §§ 6511-6515.

Statutory Depletion. (*see* Depletion).

Stock Option. A right to purchase a specified amount of stock for a specified price at a given time or times.

Subchapter S. Sections 1361-1379 of the Internal Revenue Code(*see also* S Corporation).

Substance vs. Form. The essence of a transaction as opposed to the structure or form that the transaction takes. For example, a transaction may formally meet the requirements for a specific type of tax treatment, but if what the transaction is actually accomplishing is different from the form of the transaction, the form may be ignored.

Surtax. An additional tax imposed on corporations with taxable income in excess of $100,000. The surtax is 5 percent of the corporation's taxable income in excess of $100,000 up to a maximum surtax of $11,750. § 11(b).

—T—

Tangible Property. Property that can be touched (e.g., machinery, automobile, desk) as opposed to intangibles, which cannot (e.g., goodwill, copyrights, patents).

Tax Avoidance. Using the tax laws to avoid paying taxes or to reduce one's tax liability(*see* Tax Evasion).

Tax Benefit Rule. The doctrine by which the amount of income that a taxpayer must include in income when the taxpayer has recovered an amount previously deducted is limited to the amount of the previous deduction that produced a tax benefit.

Tax Court (United States Tax Court). One of the three trial courts that hears cases dealing with Federal tax matters. A taxpayer need not pay his or her tax deficiency in advance if he or she decides to litigate the case in Tax Court (as opposed to the District Court or Claims Court).

Tax Credits. An amount that is deducted directly from a taxpayer's tax liability, as opposed to a deduction, which reduces taxable income.

Tax Evasion. The illegal evasion of the tax laws. § 7201 (*see* Tax Avoidance).

Tax Preference Items. Those items specifically designated in § 57 that may be subject to a special tax (*see also* Alternative Minimum Tax).

Tax Shelter. A device or scheme used by taxpayers either to reduce taxes or defer the payment of taxes.

Taxable Estate. Gross estate reduced by the expenses, indebtedness, taxes, losses, and charitable contributions of the estate, and by the marital deduction. § 2051.

Taxable Gifts. The total amount of gifts made during the calendar year, reduced by charitable gifts and the marital deduction. § 2503.

T.C. (Tax Court: United States Tax Court). This abbreviation is also used to cite the Tax Court's Regular Decisions (*see also* Tax Court; T.C. Memo).

T.C. Memo. The term used to cite the Tax Court's Memorandum Decisions (*see also* Tax Court; T.C.).

Tenancy by the Entirety. A form of ownership between a husband and wife wherein each has an undivided interest in the property, with the right of survivorship.

Tenancy in Common. A form of joint ownership wherein each owner has an undivided interest in the property, with no right of survivorship.

Testator. A person who makes or has made a will; one who dies and has left a will.

Thin Corporation. A corporation in which the amount of debt owed by the corporation is high in relationship to the amount of equity in the corporation. § 385.

Treasury Regulations. (*see* Regulations).

Trial Court. The first court to consider a case, as opposed to an appellate court.

Trust. A right in property that is held by one person or entity for the benefit of another. §§ 641-683.

—U—

Unearned Income. Income that is not earned or is not yet earned. The term is used to refer to both prepaid (not vet earned) income and to passive (not earned) income.

Unearned Income of a Minor Child. (*see* "Kiddie" tax).

Uniform Gift to Minors Act. An Act that provides a way to transfer property to minors. A custodian manages the property on behalf of the minor, and the custodianship terminates when the minor achieves majority.

USSC (U.S. Supreme Court). This abbreviation is used to cite U.S. Supreme Court cases.

U.S. Tax Court. (*see* Tax Court).

USTC (U.S. Tax Cases). Published by Commerce Clearing House. These volumes contain all the Federal tax-related decisions of the U.S. District Courts, the U.S. Court of Federal Claims, the U.S. Courts of Appeals, and the U.S. Supreme Court.

—V—

Valuation.(*see* Fair Market Value).

Vested. Fixed or settled; having the right to absolute ownership, even if ownership will not come into being until sometime in the future.

INDEX

—C—

—E—

—H—

—I—

—Q—

—R—

—T—